W9-BMZ-324
360-405-6105

ART

THROUGH THE AGES

NINTH EDITION

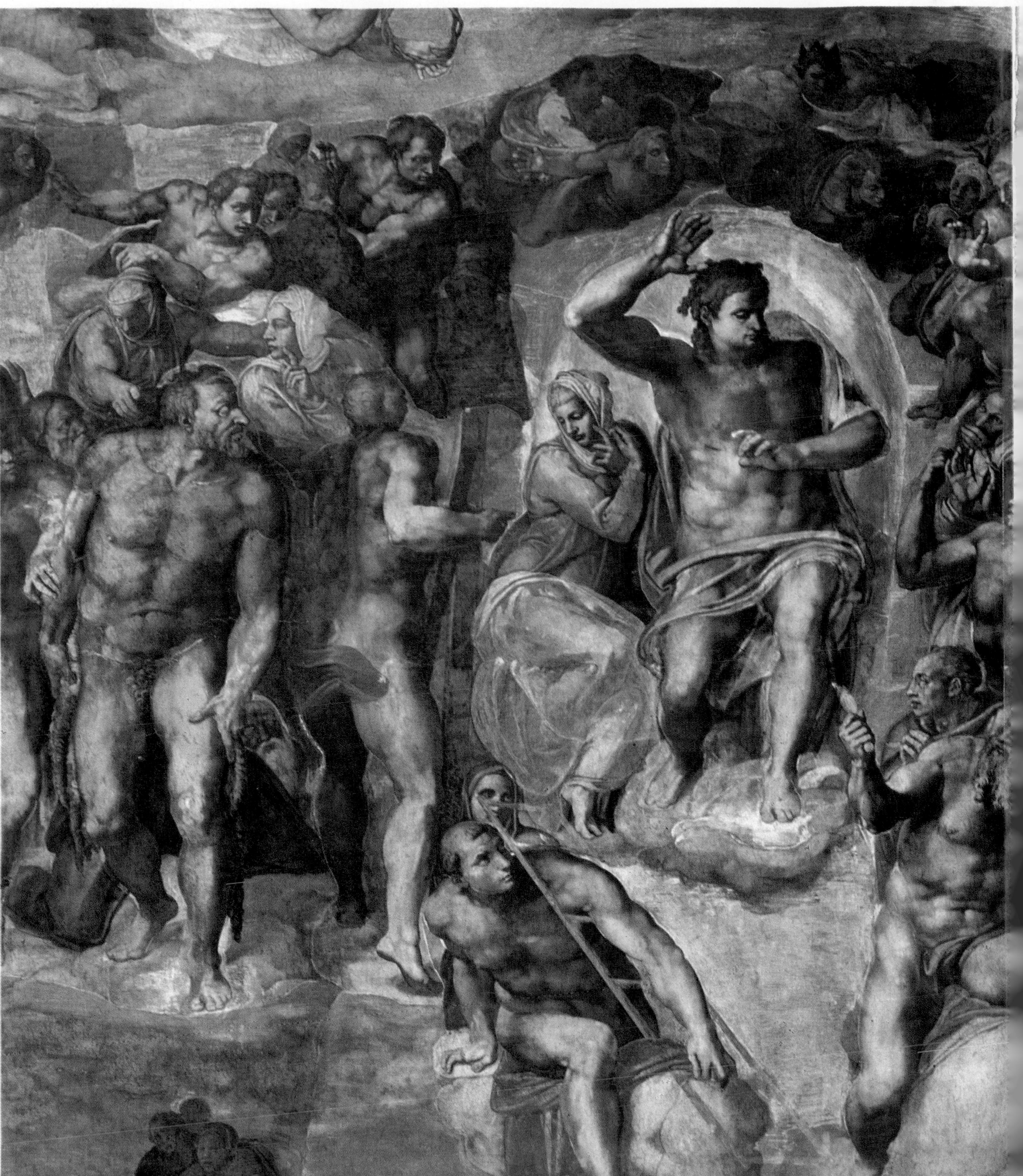

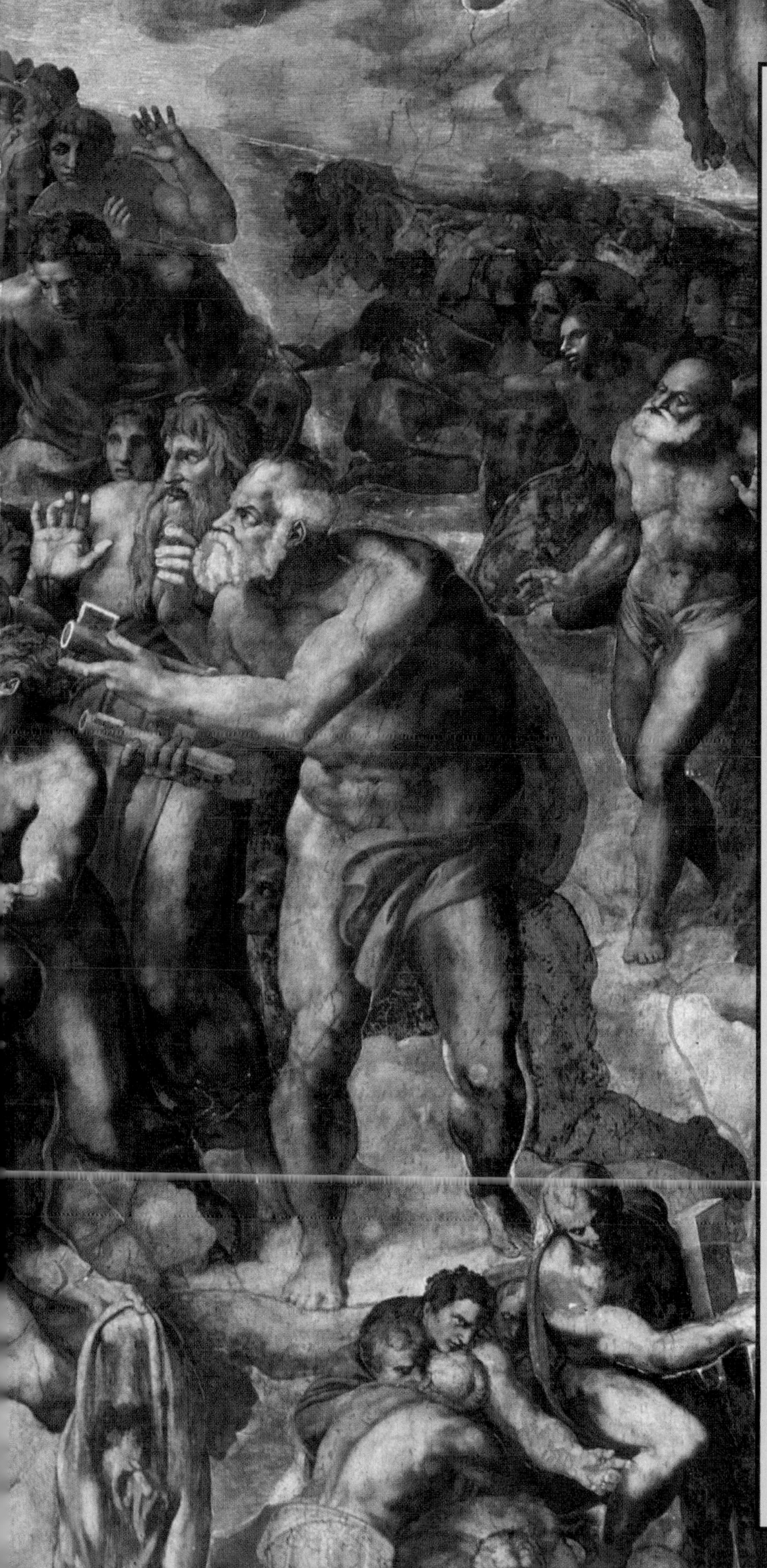

GARDNER'S

ART THROUGH THE AGES

NINTH EDITION

HORST DE LA CROIX

RICHARD G. TANSEY

DIANE KIRKPATRICK
University of Michigan, Ann Arbor

HARCOURT BRACE COLLEGE PUBLISHERS
Fort Worth Philadelphia San Diego New York
Orlando Austin San Antonio Toronto
Montreal London Sydney Tokyo

ISBN: 0-15-503769-2 (hardbound)
0-15-503770-6 (paperbound, Vol. I)
0-15-503771-4 (paperbound, Vol. II)

Library of Congress Catalog Card Number: 90-83735 (hardbound)
90-83737 (paperbound)

Printed in the United States of America

Picture credits appear on page 1118, which constitutes a continuation of the copyright page.

PREFACE

Since publication of the first edition in 1926, Helen Gardner's *Art through the Ages* has been a favorite with generations of students and general readers who have found it an exciting and informative survey of world art. Helen Gardner's enthusiasm, knowledge, and humanity have made it possible for the beginner to learn how to see and thereby to penetrate the seeming mysteries of even the most complex artistic achievements. In this volume, we have made every effort to preserve her freshness of style and, above all, her sympathetic approach to individual works of art and the styles of which they are a part.

Helen Gardner completed the third edition shortly before her death in 1946. The fourth edition was prepared in 1959 by Professor Sumner Crosby and his colleagues at Yale University. Professors Horst de la Croix and Richard Tansey assumed editorial responsibility for the project with the fifth edition in 1970, and prepared the sixth edition in 1975, the seventh in 1980, and the eighth in 1986. For this, the ninth edition, Professor Diane Kirkpatrick joins as a third coauthor. She is responsible for the revision of the final four chapters, which deal with the art of the modern world. The authors were led to prepare this edition not only by the steady appearance of new works of art and new interpretations and re-interpretations but also by suggestions received from readers. We hope that the ninth edition of *Art through the Ages* will continue its long tradition as a standard and popular survey of the history of world art.

In this edition, in addition to emendations made throughout the book, the text and the number of pictures have been expanded to include works of art recently discovered, restudied, or considered by the authors to be particularly characteristic of their periods and illustrative of developmental trends. Fuller treatment has been given to periods and monuments when warranted. Many new pictures are in color, and a large number of pictures that were black and white in previous editions have been converted to color in this one. Every effort has been made to accommodate the results of recent research in as comprehensive and detailed a survey of the material as the physical limits of a textbook of this scope permit.

In presenting a balanced historical introduction to the art of the whole world, the hardest task is selection—in effect, limitation—of the monuments to be discussed and illustrated. Though a corpus of monuments essential to the art history survey course has long been forming, and though considerable agreement exists as to its makeup, differences of choice, deriving from differences of emphasis, will naturally occur. A radical departure from the corpus might well obliterate the outlines of the study. To avoid the random, systemless distribution of material that might result, we have generally adhered to the corpus and have only occasionally introduced movements less well known, newly discovered, or not customarily treated in a survey. The latter classifications are especially applicable to the works selected for the modern period, which have yet to be subjected to the judgment of history. In the modern section of the book, more than in any other, the selection of monuments is designed to attempt to present significant representatives of the major approaches. Our aim throughout has been to present and interpret works as reflections of an intelligible development rather than merely as items of a catalogue. We have tried to give coherence to the assortment of materials by stressing the ways in which art, in many historical variations, has expressed and participated in the crucial transformations of human beings' views of themselves and of their world.

In recent years, in what has been called a "crisis of art history," new art-historical methods have been changing the perspectives and concerns of many scholars. Theories of interpretation, built upon anthropological, sociological, psychological, semiotic, and feminist conceptual foundations, have been transforming—sometimes in competition, sometimes in concert—the writing of art history as well as the way it looks at its objects. In the process, the role of the traditional method of stylistic analysis and periodicity is being minimized; there is the wish in some quarters to modify the customary apparatus of categories—style-period, master, school, influence, development, and the like. We feel that our method of presentation, rooted as it is in the recognition, differentiation, and classification of styles in art and architecture, and the firm binding of them to the times and places of their origin, is best for introducing art history. Confronted with any new domain of knowledge, beginners want to know first how to discriminate among its multitude of data. For the history of art, this means learning how to distinguish one work of art from another by style, culture, and time. The classification and chronological mapping of the world of art as an intelligible continuum is the business of the survey, and the survey has long proved its pedagogical value.

Various teaching aids accompany the ninth edition of Gardner's *Art through the Ages.* For the first time, a pronunciation guide to artists' names, compiled by Cara-lin Getty of the University of South Carolina at Sumter and Mikle Ledgerwood of Rhodes College is included at the end of the book. The *Study Guide* by Kathleen Cohen contains chapter-by-chapter drills on the identification of geographical locations, time periods, styles, terms, iconography, major art movements, and specific philosophical, religious, and historical movements as they relate to particular works of art examined in the textbook. Self-quizzes and discussion questions enable students to evaluate their grasp of the material. Kathleen Cohen is also the author of the *Instructor's Manual,* which includes sample lecture topics for each chapter, a testbank of questions in formats ranging from matching to essay, studio projects, and lists of resources. A computerized testbank consisting of questions from the *Instructor's Manual* has been put on disk for textbook users. A manual for new teachers and teaching assistants, *Opening the Doors: A Practical Guide for Teachers of Art History Survey* by Mary Sweeney Ellett of Randolph-Macon Woman's College, is also available.

A work as extensive as a history of world art could not be undertaken or completed without the counsel and active participation of experts in fields other than our own. In some cases, this took the form of preparation of portions of chapters; in others, of reviews of work in progress or already prepared. For such contributions to this edition and to previous ones, we offer our sincere thanks to James Ackerman, Harvard University; Majorie P. Balge, Mount Holyoke College; Colleen Bercsi, California State University, Northridge; Barbara W. Blackmun, San Diego Mesa College; Jacques Bordaz, University of Pennsylvania; Louise Alpers Bordaz, Columbia University; James Cahill, University of California, Berkeley; Miles L. Chappell, College of William and Mary; Herbert M. Cole, University of California, Santa Barbara; George Corbin, Lehman College, City University of New York; Gerald Eknoian, DeAnza College; Mary S. Ellett, Randolph-Macon Woman's College; Roger K. Elliott, Central Virginia Community College; Mary F. Francey, University of Utah; Ian Fraser, Herron School of Art, Indiana University; Stockton Garver, Wichita State University; Judith Paetow George, Miami University; Oleg Grabar, Harvard University; Sandra C. Haynes, Pasadena City College; Hamilton Hazelhurst, Vanderbilt University; M. F. Hearn, University of Pittsburgh; Howard Hibbard, late of Columbia University; Philancy N. Holder, Austin Peay State University; John Howett, Emory University; Joseph M. Hutchinson, Texas A & M University; Joel Isaacson, University of Michigan; R. Steven Janke, State University of New York at Buffalo; M. Barry Katz, Virginia Commonwealth University; Herbert L. Kessler, Johns Hopkins University; Fred S. Kleiner, Boston University; Robert A. Koch, Princeton University; Avra Liakos, Northern Illinois University; Elizabeth Lipsmeyer, Old Dominion University; William L. MacDonald, formerly of Smith College; A. Dean McKenzie, University of Oregon; Mary Jo McNamara, Wayne State University; Kathleen Maxwell, Santa Clara University; Milan Mihal, Vanderbilt University; Diane Degasis Moran, Sweet Briar College; Harry Murutes, University of Akron; Kristi Nelson, University of Cincinnati; Jane S. Peters, University of Kentucky;

Edith Porada, Columbia University; Bruce Radde, San Jose State University; Gervais Reed, University of Washington; Raphael X. Reichert, California State University at Fresno; Richard Rubenfeld, Eastern Michigan University; Grace Seiberling, University of Rochester; Peter Selz, University of California, Berkeley; David Simon, Colby College; Pamela H. Simpson, Washington and Lee University; David M. Sokol, University of Illinois at Chicago; Lilla Sweatt, San Diego State University; Marcia E. Vetrocq, University of New Orleans; Richard Vinograd, University of Southern California; Joanna Williams, University of California, Berkeley; and the Art History Department, Herron School of Art, Indiana University–Purdue University at Indianapolis.

We would also like to thank the following instructors, who sent helpful reactions and suggestions for the ninth edition of *Art through the Ages:* James Allen-Toth, Skyline College; Eric C. Apfelstadt, Santa Clara University; Peter G. Arnovick, Menlo College; Vicki Artimovich, Bellevue Community College; Helen C. Austin, John C. Calhoun State Community College; Larry Bakke, Syracuse University; C. Roy Blackwood, Southeastern Louisiana University; Art Bond, John C. Calhoun State Community College; George A. Civey III, Eastern Kentucky University; Patricia Coronel, Colorado State University; Kenneth M. Davis, Ball State University; George F. Deremo, Cerritos College; William R. Derrevere, Tulsa Junior College; Ruth Deshaies, Tallahassee Community College; Richard P. Dewitt, Merced College; Suzette J. Doyon-Bernard, University of West Florida; Peter W. Guenther, University of Houston; Janet Higgins, Middle Tennessee State University; Donald R. Johnson, Emporia State University; Klaus Kallenberger, Middle Tennessee State University; W. Eugene Kleinbauer, Middle Tennessee State University; Carolyn Kolb, University of New Orleans; Kristine Koozin, University of North Dakota; Harry D. Korn, Ventura College; Lynne Lokensgard, Lamar University; Richard A. Luehrman, Central Missouri State University; Jane C. Maller, San Francisco State University; Nina A. Mallory, State University of New York at Stony Brook; Peggy Pulliam McDowell, University of New Orleans; Robert O. Mellown, University of Alabama; Bob Owens, North Georgia College; Angelika Pagel, Weber State College; Stephen Polcari; Kenneth J. Proctor, University of Montevallo; Marceil V. Pultorak, Carroll College; Wayne L. Roosa, Bethel College; Margaret Rothman, William Patterson College; Patricia Sanders, San Jose State University; Gregory P. Senn, Eastern New Mexico University; Anthony Stansfeld, Mercer University; Thomas Sternal, Morehead State University; Duncan Stewart, University of West Florida; Grant Throp, East Central University; Mary Jane Timmerman, Murray State University; Jeanne L. Trabold, California State University at Northridge; Patricia Trutty-Coohill, Western Kentucky University; Richard J. Tuttle, Tulane University; Elizabeth M. Walter, University of North Alabama; Marilyn Wyman, San Jose State University; Jay J. Zumeta, Art Academy of Cincinnati. We owe a special debt of gratitude to Joel G. Tansey, who compiled the bibliography for the first nineteen chapters of the text and made valuable suggestions on its content, and to Cara-lin Getty and Mikle Ledgerwood, who compiled the pronunciation guide.

Among those at Harcourt Brace Jovanovich who have contributed their efforts to the management of an enormously detailed manuscript are our acquisitions editor, Julia Berrisford; our manuscript editor, Helen Triller; our production editors, Joan Harlan and Mary Allen, and their assistant Michael Ferreira; our art editor, Susan Holtz, and her assistants on this project, Cindy Robinson and Louise Sandy-Karkoutli; our designer, Cathy Reynolds; and our production manager, Lynne Bush. We would like to thank all those, named and unnamed, who have helped immeasurably in the production of this book, and hope that, as with the previous editions, it will prove a pleasurable first guide through the immense landscape of its subject, art through the ages.

Horst de la Croix
Richard G. Tansey
Diane Kirkpatrick

CONTENTS

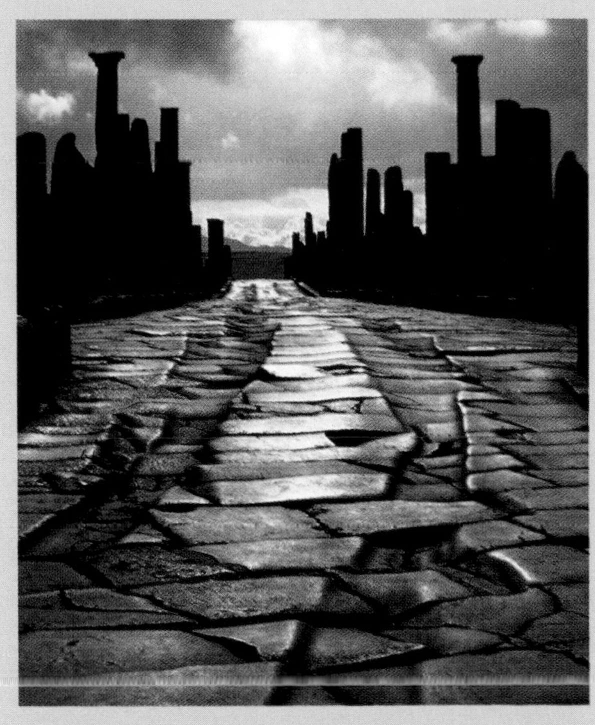

2 THE ANCIENT NEAR EAST 40

3 THE ART OF EGYPT 72

4 THE AEGEAN: CYCLADIC, MINOAN, AND MYCENAEAN ART 104

5 THE ART OF GREECE 124

6 ETRUSCAN AND ROMAN ART 186

7 EARLY CHRISTIAN, BYZANTINE, AND ISLAMIC ART 252

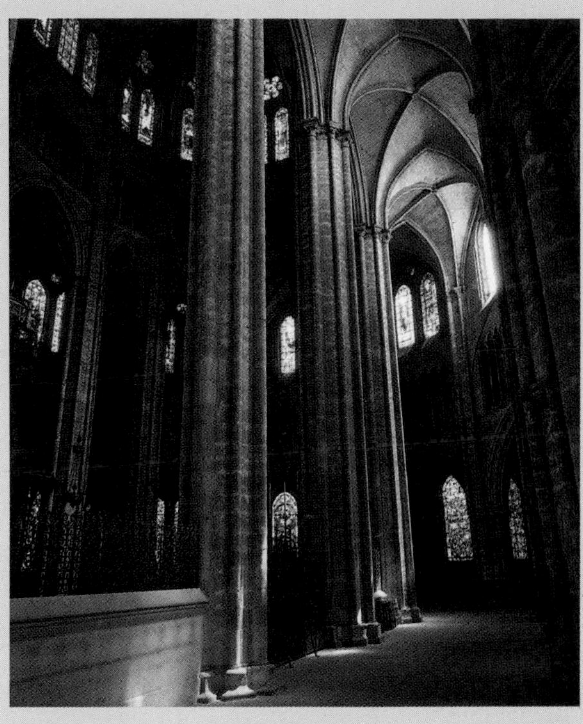

II THE MIDDLE AGES 314

8 EARLY MEDIEVAL ART 318

9 ROMANESQUE ART 346

10 GOTHIC ART 378

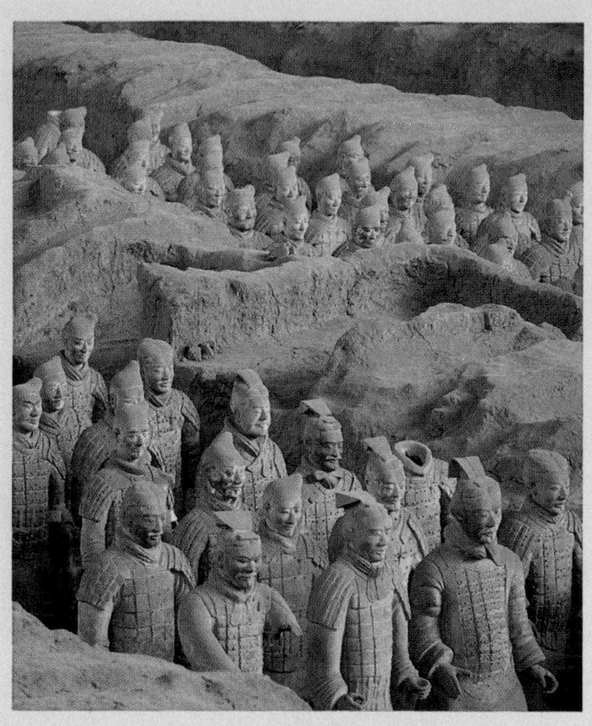

III THE NON-EUROPEAN WORLD 420

11 THE ART OF INDIA 424

12 THE ART OF CHINA 448

13 THE ART OF JAPAN 474

14 THE NATIVE ARTS OF THE AMERICAS, AFRICA, AND THE SOUTH PACIFIC 498

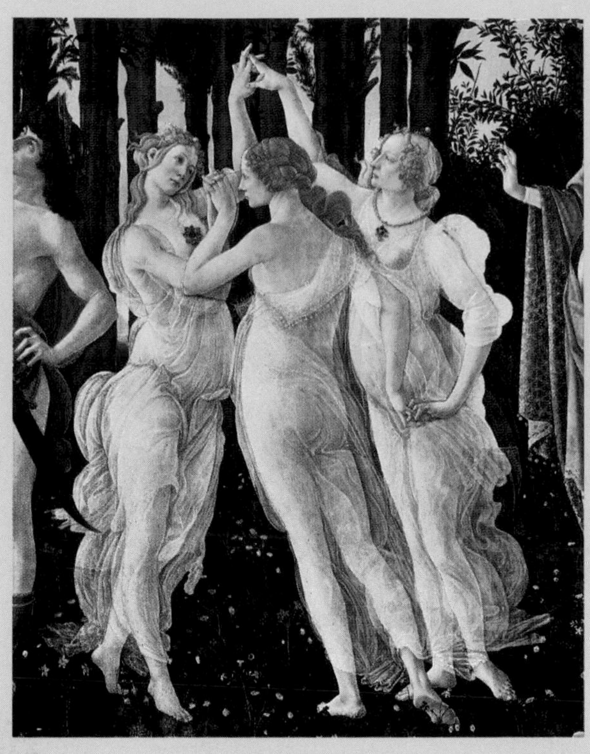

19 BAROQUE ART 748

20 THE EIGHTEENTH CENTURY: ROCOCO AND THE BIRTH OF THE MODERN WORLD 816

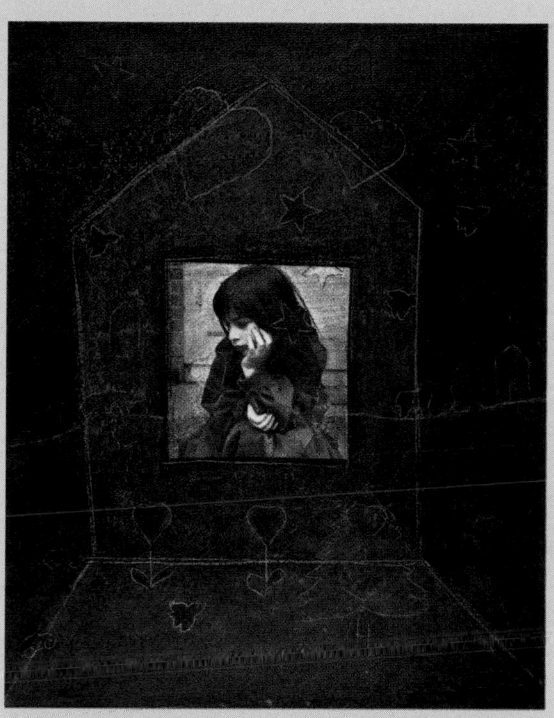

V THE MODERN WORLD 858

21 THE NINETEENTH CENTURY: PLURALISM OF STYLE 862

ART

THROUGH THE AGES

NINTH EDITION

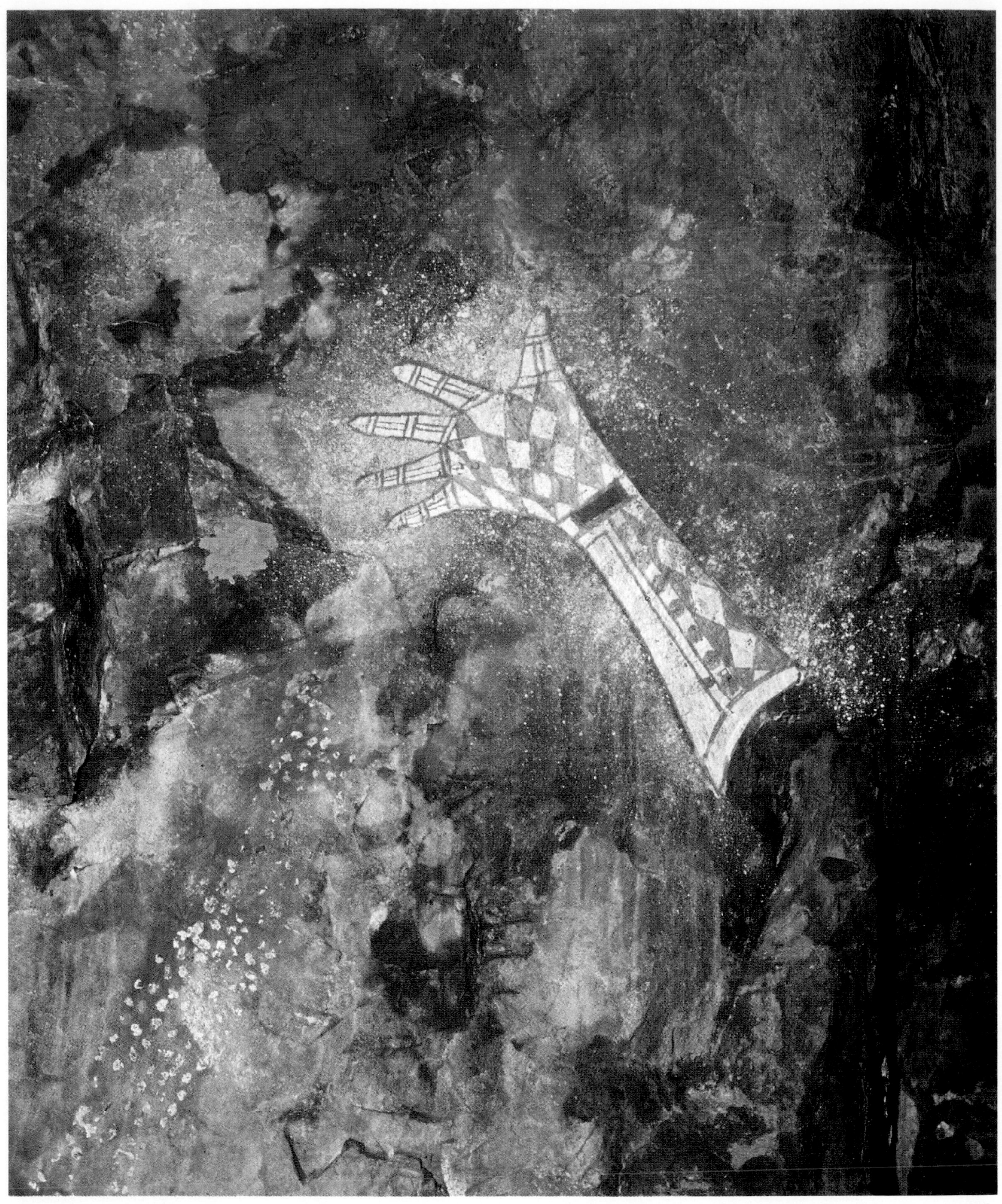

Nineteenth-century native Australians painted this hand at Inagurdurwil, West Arnhem Land. Similar motifs are found as far away in time and place as Upper Paleolithic Europe.

INTRODUCTION

The goal of art history is the discerning appreciation and enjoyment of art, from whatever time and place it may have come, by whatever hands it may have been made. Outside the academic world, the terms *art* and *history* are not often juxtaposed. People tend to think of history as the record and interpretation of past human actions, particularly social and political actions. Most think of art—quite correctly—as something *present* to the eye and touch, which, of course, the vanished human events that make up history are not. The fact is that a visible and tangible work of art is a kind of *persisting event*. It was made at a particular time and place by particular persons, even if we do not always know just when, where, and by whom. Although it is the creation of the past, art continues to exist in the present, long surviving its times; Charlemagne has been dead for a thousand years, but his chapel still stands at Aachen.

THE BASES OF ART HISTORY

Style

The time in which a work of art was made has everything to do with the way it looks—with, in one key term, its *style*. In other words, the style of a work of art is a function of its historical *period*. The historiography of art proceeds by sorting works of architecture, sculpture, and painting into stylistic classes on the bases of their similarities and the times or periods in which they were produced. It is a fundamental hypothesis of art history that works of art produced at the same time and in the same place will generally have common stylistic traits. Of course, all historiography assumes that events derive their character from the time in which they happen (and perhaps from their "great men," also products of their time). Thus, we can speak of the Periclean Age, the Age of Reason, or even the Age of Roosevelt. We also must know the time of a work if we are to know its meaning—to know it for what it is. Yet if the work of art still stands before us, persisting from the past, is not this sufficient? By virtue of its survival, is not the work in a sense *independent* of time? May not a work of art speak to people of all times as long as it survives? The key to this last question is the word *speak.* Indeed, it may speak, but what is its language? What does it say to us? Art may be more than a form of communication, but it is certainly that, and it is the business of art history to learn the "languages" of the art of many different periods as they are embodied in the monuments from their respective times. We can assume that artists in every age express in their works some sort of meaning that is intelligible both to themselves and to others. We can discover that meaning only by comparing a particular work to other works like it that were made about the same time. By grouping works in this way, we can infer a community of meaning as well as of *form;* a style will then be outlined. In a chronological series of works having common stylistic features, we may find also stylistic *differences* between the later and the earlier works. The art historian tends to think of this phenomenon as reflecting an evolution, a *development.*

It is important to stress, however, that "development" does not mean an orderly progression of styles toward some ideal type or formal perfection, such as, for example, absolute truth to natural appearances. Although at times in the development of Western art the "imitation of nature" has been an expressed goal of the artist, photographic realism—the mechanical reporting of what the eye supposedly perceives in the visual field—has been rarely either the purpose or the result of that development. Moreover, stylistic development does not lead to ever increasing esthetic value; later phases cannot be appraised as "better" than earlier ones simply because they are presumed closer to some imagined goal of competence and achievement. Instead, we should understand stylistic development as an irregular series of steps of varying duration, in which the possibilities of a given style are worked out by artists, both independently and in collaboration with others, until those possibilities are fully realized, and new stylistic traits and tendencies appear and are distinguishable as such. Thus, when we talk of stylistic development in art, we do not mean artistic *progress*—certainly not in the sense of scientific or technological progress, whereby our knowledge appears to increase in a sequence of necessary and interdependent steps toward ever greater scope and certainty.

Chronology

It is obvious that before stylistic development can be inferred, it is necessary to be sure that each monument is correctly dated; without this certainty, art-historical order and intelligibility are impossible. Thus, an indispensable tool of the historian is *chronology,* the measuring scale of historical time. Without chronology, there could be no history of style—only a confusion of unclassifiable monuments, impossible to describe in any sequence of change.

The table of contents of this book reflects what is essentially a series of periods and subperiods arranged in chronological order—the historical sequence that embraces the sequence of art styles. Until the later eighteenth century, the history of art was really a disconnected account of the lives and the works of individual artists. We now regard art history as a record of the dynamic change of styles in time, and the art of individual masters as substyles of the overall period styles. Although one speaks of "change" in the history of art, the objects themselves obviously do not change; as we have said, they persist, although each naturally suffers some material wear and tear with time. But the fact that works of art from one period look different from those of other periods leads us to infer that *something* changes. This something can only be the points of view of the artists with respect to the meaning of life and of art. Modern historiography is heavily influenced by modern philosophies of change and evolution, and, from the terms and data of biological science, our modern history of art was bound to borrow a sense of continuous process to help explain art-historical change.

In art history, as in the sciences and in other historical disciplines, we have made considerable progress in knowing a thing once we have classified it. Art historians, having done this, resemble experienced travelers who learn to discriminate the different "styles" peculiar to different places. Such travelers know that one must not expect the same style of life in the Maine woods as on the Riviera, and when they have seen a great many places and peoples, they are not only at ease with them, but can be said to know and appreciate them for what they are. As their experience broadens, so does their discrimination or perception of distinctive differences. As world travelers come to see that the location contributes to the unique quality and charm of a town, so students of art, viewing it in the historical dimension, become convinced that a work's peculiar significance, quality, and charm are a function of the time of its making.

Purpose

Is the historical "placing" of a work of art, then, irrelevant to the *appreciation* of it? Is art-historical knowledge *about* a work of art in some way different from the direct experience of it? The answers lie in the fact that uninstructed appreciators, no matter how well intentioned, still approach a work of art with the esthetic presuppositions of their own time, rather than of the time of the work itself. Their presuppositions can be tantamount to prejudices, so that their appreciation, even if genuine, may well be for the wrong reasons. It will, in fact, be undiscerning and indiscriminate, so that they may view dozens of works of art in the same way, without savoring the individual significance and quality of each. Thus, as a work of art is intended for a particular audience at a particular time and place, its *purpose* also may be quite particular, and its purpose necessarily enters into its meaning. For example, the famous *Vladimir Madonna* (FIG. 7-59, p. 296) is a Byzantine-Russian icon, a species of art produced not as a work of "fine art" but as a sacred object endowed with religio-magical power. It was considered, moreover, the especially holy picture of Russia that miraculously saved the city of Vladimir from the hosts of Tamerlane, the city of Kazan from the later Tartar invasions, and all of Russia from the Poles in the seventeenth century. We may admire it for its innate beauty of line, shape, and color, its expressiveness, and its craftsmanship, but unless we are aware of its special historical function as a wonder-working image, we miss the point. We can admire many works of art for their form, content, and quality, but we need a further characterizing experience; otherwise, we are admiring very different works without discriminating their decisive differences. We will be confused, and our judgment will be faulty.

Place of Origin

Although our most fundamental way of classifying works of art is by the time of their making, classification by *place of origin* is also crucial. In many periods, a general style (Gothic, for example) will have a great many regional variations: French Gothic architecture is strikingly different from both English and Italian Gothic. Differences of climate helped to make French Gothic an architecture with no bearing walls and with great spaces for stained-glass windows and Italian Gothic an architecture with large expanses of wall wonderfully suited to mural painting. Art history, then, is also concerned with the spread of a style from its place of origin. Supplementing time of origin with place of origin therefore adds another dimension to our understanding of the overall stylistic development of art monuments.

The Artist

The *artist* provides still another dimension in the history of art. As we have noted, early "histories" of art, written before the advent of modern concepts of style and stylistic development, were simply biographies of artists. Biography as one dimension is still important, for through it we can trace stylistic development within the career of the artist. We can learn much from contemporaneous historical accounts, from documents such as commission contracts, and from the artist's own theoretical writings and literary remains. All of this is useful in "explaining" an artist's works, although no complete "explanation" exhausts the meaning of them. Relationships to predecessors, contemporaries, and followers can be described in terms of the concepts *influence* and *school*. It is likely that artists are influenced by their masters and then influence or are influenced by fellow artists working somewhat in the same style at the same time and place. We designate a group of such artists as a *school*. By this, we do not mean an academy, but a classification of time, place, and style. We speak of the Dutch school of the seventeenth century and, within it, of subschools such as those of Haarlem, Utrecht, and Leyden.

The art-historical record often has tended to exclude the contributions of women to art. Evidence from many times and places (some of it collected quite recently), however, indicates that women clearly have produced art and craftwork of extremely high quality. Women artists were known in classical antiquity and have been recognized in China, Japan, India, and many other cultures. In the Western Middle Ages, women were renowned as skilled illuminators of manuscripts and workers of textiles. With the Renaissance, women painters began to come into prominence, along with women printmakers and sculptors. Artistic talent, skill, competence, inventiveness, and refinement clearly are not functions of gender.

Iconography

The categories of time and place, the record of the artist, influences, and schools are all used in the composition of the picture of stylistic development. Another kind of classification, another key to works of art, is *iconography*—the study of the subject matter and symbolism of works of art. Iconography groups paintings and sculptures in terms of their themes rather than their styles, and the development of subject matter becomes a major focus of critical study. Iconographic studies have an ancillary function in stylistic analysis; they often are valuable in tracing influences and in assigning dates and places of origin.

Recently, a new method of analysis has been used to supplement the information acquired as a result of iconographic studies. *Semiotics* is not the study of images per se, but of images "read" as *signs* by which human beings communicate. In semiotics, pictorial images are taken to signify the conscious or unconscious attitudes, inclinations, wishes, intentions, convictions, and values of peoples in different cultures and periods. Born of the science of linguistics (the study of the common structure of all languages), semiotic analysis draws art into relation with literature, psychology, sociology, and anthropology, finding structures and meanings common to the data in all of these fields. In the semiotic analysis of art, the intentions of the artist are reconstructed from an examination of the images made, within the context of the conventional meanings they have for a particular society. Often the analysis attempts to recover the artist's own psychological set to explain the image choices.

Historical Context

Another very broad source of knowledge about a work of art lies outside the realm of artistic concerns, yet encloses them and interacts with them. This is the *general historical context*—the political, social, economic, scientific, technological, and intellectual background that accompanies and influences specifically art-historical events. The fall of Rome, the coming of Christianity, and the barbarian invasions all had much to do with stylistic changes in architecture, sculpture, and painting in the early centuries of our era. The triumph of science and technology had everything to do with the great transformation of the Renaissance tradition that took place in what we call "modern art"—the art of our own time. The work of art, the persisting event, is, after all, a historical document.

THE WORK OF ART

This book is concerned primarily with the plastic arts, which differ from the temporal arts in several very basic ways. The temporal arts—music, dance, and poetry, for example—require time for their performance or presentation. They are transitory or ephemeral in the sense that, once performed, they cease to exist to the observer, except in memory. On the other hand, the plastic arts—painting, sculpture, and architecture, for instance—have physical bulk and a tangible, enduring existence in space. To describe and analyze a plastic work of art, we use categories and vocabularies that have become standard and that are indispensable to an understanding of this book.

General Concepts

Form, for the purposes of art history, refers to the shape of the "object" of art; in the made object, form is the shape that the expression of content takes. To create forms, to make a work of art, artists must shape materials with tools. Each of the many materials, tools, and processes available has its own potentialities and limitations; it is part of all artists' creative activity to select the tools most suitable to their purpose. The technical processes that the artists employ, as well as the distinctive, personal ways in which they handle them, we call their *technique*. If the material that artists use is the substance of their art, then their technique is their individual manner of giving that substance form. Form, technique, and material are interrelated, as we can readily see in a comparison of the marble statue of *Apollo* from Olympia (FIG. 5-40, p. 152) with the bronze *Charioteer of Delphi* (FIG. 5-37, p. 150). The Apollo is firmly modeled in broad, generalized planes, reflecting the ways of shaping stone that are more or less dictated by the character of that material and by the tool used—the chisel. On the other hand, the Charioteer's fineness of detail, seen in the crisp, sharp folds of the drapery, reflects the qualities inherent in cast metal. However, a given medium can lend itself to more than

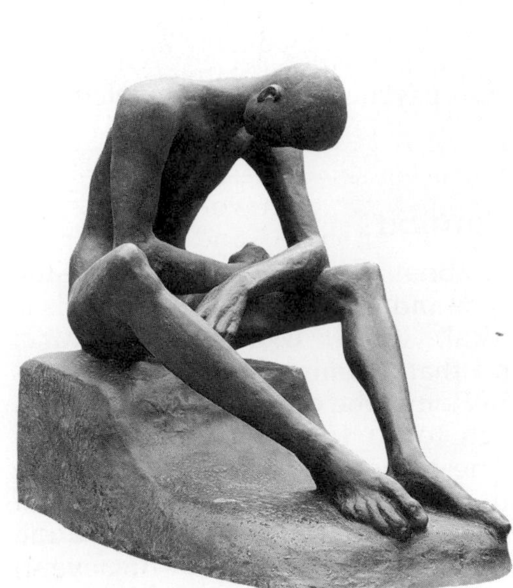

1 Wilhelm Lehmbruck, *Seated Youth*, 1918. Bronze. Wilhelm-Lehmbruck-Museum, Duisburg.

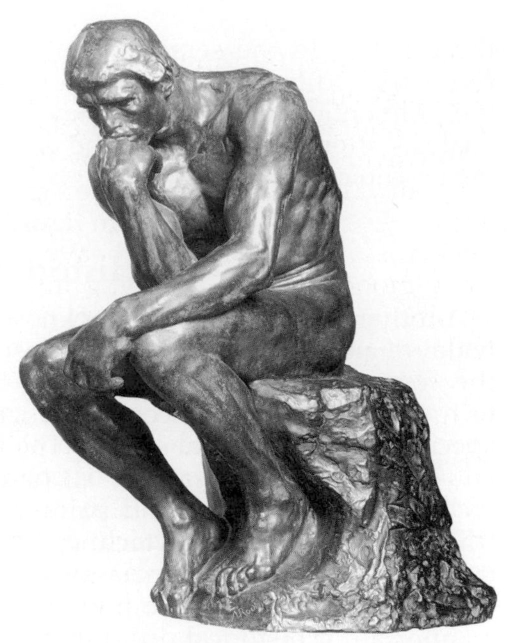

2 Auguste Rodin, *The Thinker*, 1880. Bronze. Metropolitan Museum of Art, New York (gift of Thomas F. Ryan, 1910).

one kind of manipulation. The technique of Lehmbruck's bronze *Seated Youth* (FIG. **1**), for example, contrasts strikingly with Rodin's *The Thinker* (FIG. **2**), also in bronze. The surfaces of Lehmbruck's figure are smooth, flowing, quiet; those of Rodin's figure are rough, broken, and tortuous. Here, it is not so much the bronze that determines the form as it is the sculptor's difference of purpose and of personal technique.

Space, in our commonsense experience, is the bounded or boundless "container" of collections of objects. For the analysis of works of art, we regard space as bounded by and susceptible to esthetic and expressive organization. Architecture provides us with our most common experience of the actual manipulation of space; the art of painting frequently projects an image (or illusion) of our three-dimensional spatial world onto a two-dimensional surface.

Area and *plane* describe a limited, two-dimensional space and generally refer to surface. A plane is flat and two-dimensional—like this page and like elements dealt with in plane geometry (a circle, square, or triangle). An area, which also can be described in terms of plane geometry, is often a plane or a flat surface that is enclosed or bounded. Bernini created an oval area when he defined the essentially plane surface in front of St. Peter's by means of his curving colonnades (FIG. 19-3, p. 753).

Mass and *volume,* in contradistinction to plane and area, describe three-dimensional space. In both architecture and sculpture, mass is the bulk, density, and weight of matter in space. Yet the mass need not be solid; it can be the exterior form of enclosed space. For example, "mass" can apply to a pyramid (FIG. 3-10, p. 81), which is essentially solid, or to the exterior of Hagia Sophia (FIG. 7-40, p. 284), which is essentially a shell enclosing vast spaces. Volume is the space that is organized, divided, or enclosed by mass. It may be the spaces of the interior of a building, the intervals between the masses of a building, or the amount of space occupied by three-dimensional objects like sculpture, ceramics, or furniture. Volume and mass describe the exterior as well as the interior forms of a work of art—the forms of the matter of which it is composed *and* the forms of the spaces that exist immediately around that matter and interact with it. For example, in the Lehmbruck statue (FIG. 1), the expressive volumes enclosed by the attenuated masses of the torso and legs play an important part in the open design of the piece. The absence of enclosed volumes in the Rodin figure (FIG. 2) is equally expressive, closing the design, making it compact, heavy, and confined. Yet both works convey the same mood—one of brooding introversion. These closed and open forms, manifest throughout the history of art, demonstrate the intimate connection between mass and the space that surrounds and penetrates it.

Line is one of the most important, but most difficult, terms to comprehend fully. In both science and art, line can be understood as the path of a point moving in space, the track of a motion. Because the directions of motions can be almost infinite, the quality of line can be incredibly various and subtle. It is well known that psychological responses are attached to the direction of a line: a vertical line is active; a horizontal line, passive; a diagonal line, suggestive of movement, energy, or unbalance; and so on. Hogarth regarded the serpentine or S-curve line as the "line of beauty." Our psychological response to line is also bound up with our esthetic sense of its quality. A line may be very thin, wirelike, and delicate, conveying a sense of fragility, as in Klee's *Twittering Machine* (FIG. 22-42, p. 989). Or it may alternate quickly from thick to thin, the strokes jagged, the outline broken, as in a 600-year-old Chinese painting (FIG. 12-19, p. 465) in which the effect is of vigorous action and angry agitation. A gentle, undulating, but firm line, like that in Picasso's *Bathers* (FIG. **3**), defines a *contour* that is restful and quietly sensuous. A contour continuously and subtly contains and suggests mass and volume. In the Picasso drawing, the line is distinct, dark against the white of the paper. But line can be felt as a controlling presence in a hard edge, profile, or boundary created by a contrasting area, even when its tone differs only

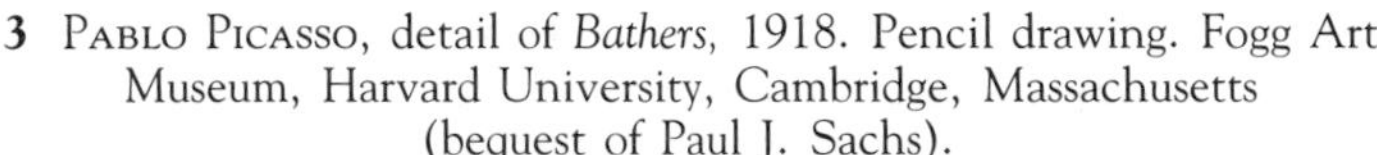
3 PABLO PICASSO, detail of *Bathers*, 1918. Pencil drawing. Fogg Art Museum, Harvard University, Cambridge, Massachusetts (bequest of Paul J. Sachs).

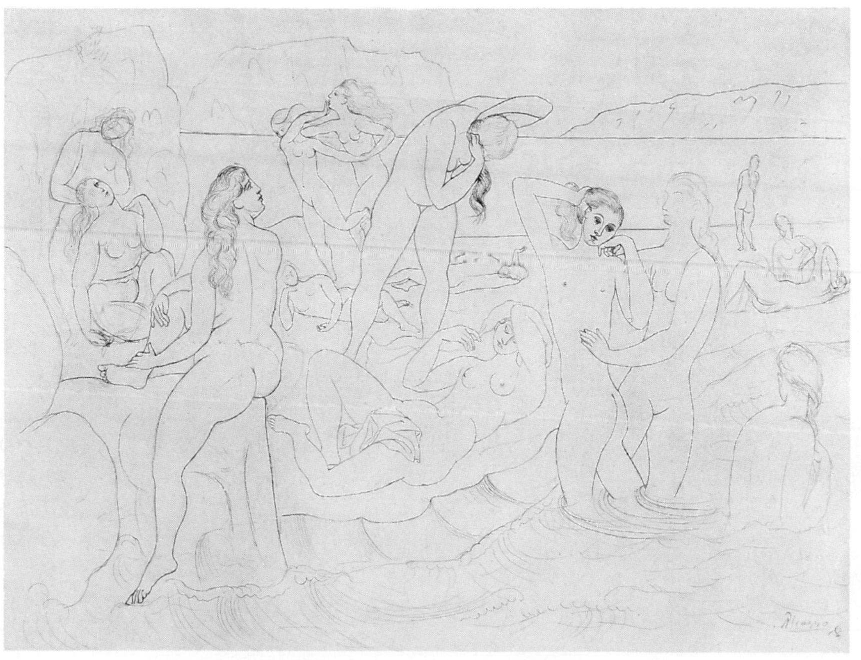

slightly from the tone of the area it bounds. A good example of this can be seen in the central figure of the goddess in Botticelli's *The Birth of Venus* (FIG. 16-60, p. 624).

An *axis* is a line along which forms are organized. The axis line itself may not be evident; several axis lines may converge (usually with one dominant), as in the layout of a city. Although we are most familiar with directional axes in urban complexes, they occur in all the arts. A fine example of the use of axis in large-scale architecture is the plan of the Palace of Versailles and its magnificent gardens (FIG. 19-66, p. 807). Axis, whether vertical, horizontal, or diagonal, is also an important compositional element in painting.

Perspective, like axis, is a method of organizing forms in space, but perspective is used primarily to create an illusion of depth or space on a two-dimensional surface. Because we are conditioned by exposure to Western, single-point perspective, an invention of the Italian Renaissance (see pages 634–67), we tend to see perspective as a systematic ordering of pictorial space in terms of a single point—a point at which lines converge to mark the diminishing size of forms as they recede into the distance (FIG. 17-16, p. 647). Renaissance and Baroque artists created masterpieces of perspective illusionism. In Leonardo's *The Last Supper* (FIG. **4**), for example, the lines of perspective (dashed lines) converge on Christ and, in the foreground, project the picture space into the room on the wall of which the painting appears, creating the illusion that the space of the picture and the space of the room are continuous. Yet we must remember that Renaissance perspective is only one of several systems for depicting depth. Other systems were used in ancient Greece and Rome and still others in the East. Some of these other systems, as well as the Italian Renaissance perspective, continue to be used. There is no final or absolutely correct projection of what we "in fact" see.

Proportion deals with the relationships (in terms of size) of the parts of a work. The experience of proportion is common to all of us. We seem to recognize at once when the features of the human face or body are "out of proportion." If the nose or ears are too large for the face or the legs are too short for the body, an instinctive or conventional sense of proportion leads us to regard the disproportionate elements as ludicrous or ugly. Formalized

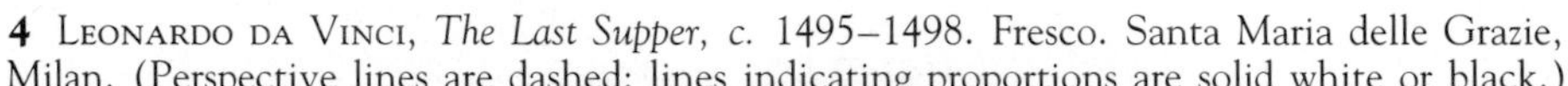

4 LEONARDO DA VINCI, *The Last Supper,* c. 1495–1498. Fresco. Santa Maria delle Grazie, Milan. (Perspective lines are dashed; lines indicating proportions are solid white or black.)

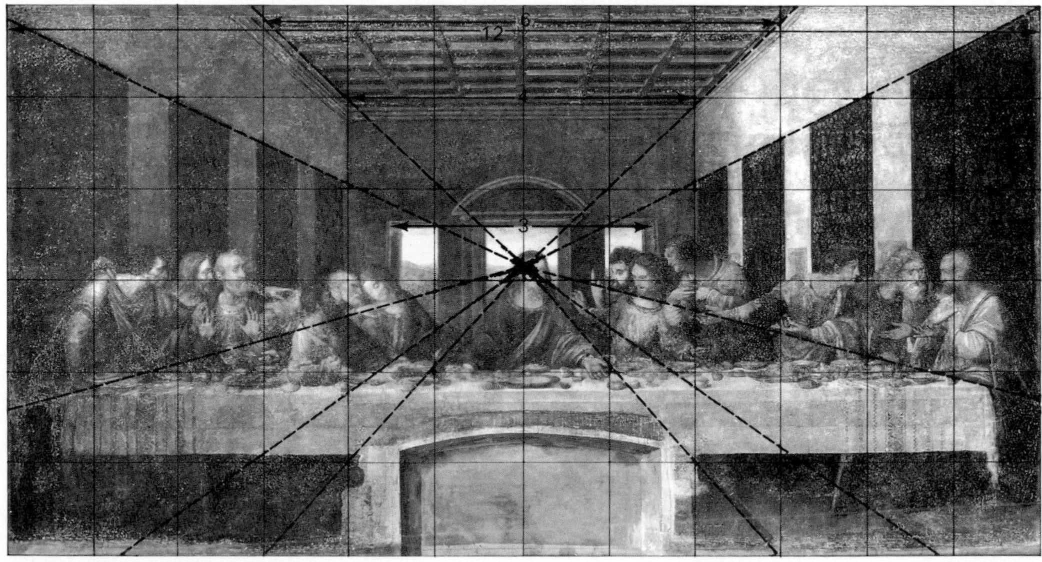

proportion is the mathematical relationship in size of one part of a work of art to the other parts within the work, as well as to the totality of the parts; it implies the use of a denominator that is common to the various parts. One researcher has shown that the major elements of Leonardo's *Last Supper* exhibit proportions found in harmonic ratios in music—12:6:4:3 (FIG. 4). These figures (with the greatest width of a ceiling panel taken as one unit) are the horizontal widths, respectively, of the painting, the ceiling (at the front), the rear wall, and the three windows (taken together and including interstices); they apply to the vertical organization of the painting as well. Leonardo found proportion everywhere: "not only in numbers and measures, but also in sounds, weights, intervals of time, and in every active force in existence."* The ancient Greeks, who considered beauty to be "correct" proportion, sought a canon (rule) of proportion, not only in music, but also for the human figure. The famous Canon of Polykleitos (page 163), expressed in his statue of the *Doryphoros* (FIG. 5-58, p. 163), long served as an exemplar of correct proportion. But it should be noted that canons of proportion differ from time to time and culture to culture and that, occasionally, artists have used disproportion deliberately. Part of the task facing students of art history is to perceive and adjust to these differences in an effort to understand the wide universe of art forms. Proportional relationships are often based on a *module,* a dimension of which the various parts of a building or other work are fractions or multiples. A module might be the diameter of a column, the height of the human body, or an abstract unit of measurement. For example, the famous "ideal" plan of the ninth-century monastery of St. Gall (FIG. 8-22, p. 337) has a modular base of $2\frac{1}{2}$ feet, so that all parts of the structure are multiples or fractions of this dimension.

Scale also refers to the dimensional relationships of the parts of a work to its totality (or of a work to its setting), usually in terms of appropriateness to use or function. We do not think that a private home should be as high as an office building or that an elephant's house at the zoo should be the size of a hen coop, or vice versa. This sense of scale is necessary to the construction of form in all the arts. Most often, but not necessarily, it is the human figure that gives the scale to form.

Light in the world of nature is so pervasive that we often take its function for granted. Few of us realize the extraordinary variations wrought by light, either natural or artificial, on our most familiar surroundings. Daylight, for example, changes with the hour or season. Few of us realize the full extent to which light affects and reveals form. One who did—the French artist Monet (pages 923–24)—painted the reflections in a water-lily pond according to their seasonal variations and, in a series of more than forty canvases of the façade of Rouen Cathedral, revealed its changing appearance from dawn until twilight in different seasons (FIG. 5). Light is as important for the perception of form as is the matter of which form is made.

Value is one function of light. In painting, and in the graphic arts generally, value refers to lightness, or the amount of light that is (or appears to be) reflected from a surface. Value is a subjective experience, as FIG. 6 shows. In absolute terms (if measured, for example, by a photoelectric device), the center bar in this diagram is uniform in value. Yet where the bar is adjacent to a dark area, it *looks* lighter, and where the bar is adjacent to a lighter area, it *looks* darker. Value is the basis of the quality called, in Italian, *chiaroscuro* (*chiaro,* or light; *scuro,* or dark), which refers to the gradations between light

*Thomas Brachert, "A Musical Canon of Proportion in Leonardo da Vinci's *Last Supper,*" *Art Bulletin,* Vol. 53, No. 4 (December 1971), pp. 461–66.

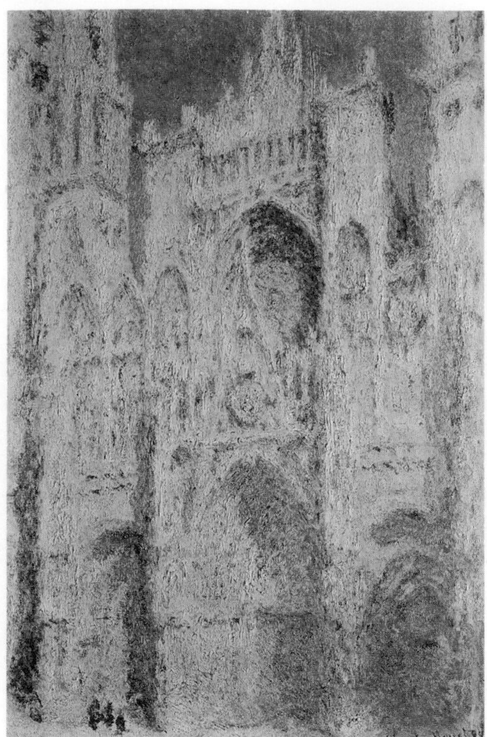
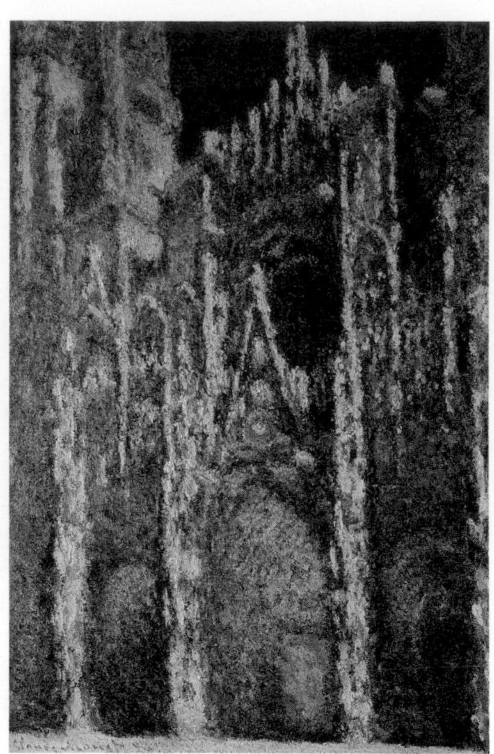

5 CLAUDE MONET, façade of Rouen Cathedral, early 1890s. (*Right*) Museum of Fine Arts, Boston (bequest of Hanna Marcy Edwards); (*left*) National Gallery of Art, Washington, D.C. (Chester Dale Collection).

and dark that produce the effect of *modeling*, or of light reflected from three-dimensional surfaces, as exemplified in Leonardo's superb rendering of *The Virgin and Child with St. Anne and the Infant St. John* (FIG. 17-2, p. 636).

In the analysis of light, an important distinction must be made for the realm of art. Natural light, or sunlight, is whole or additive light, whereas the painter's light in art—the light reflected from pigments and objects—is subtractive light. Natural light is the sum of all the wavelengths composing the visible spectrum, which may be disassembled or fragmented into the individual colors of the spectral band. (Recent experiments with lasers—*l*ight *a*mplification by *s*timulated *e*mission of *r*adiation—have produced color of incredible brilliance and intensity, opening possibilities of color composition that, until now, were unsuspected. The range and strength of color produced in this way approach, although at considerable distance, those of the sun.) Although the esthetics of color is largely the province of the artist and can usually be genuinely experienced and understood only through intense practice and experimentation, some aspects can be analyzed and systematized. Paint pigments produce their individual colors by reflecting a segment of the spectrum while absorbing all the rest. "Green" pigment, for example, subtracts or absorbs all the light in the spectrum except that seen by us as green, which it reflects to the eye. (In the case of transmitted, rather than reflected, light, the coloring matter blocks or screens out all wavelengths of the spectrum except those of the color we see.) Thus, theoretically, a mixture of pigments that embraced all the colors of the spectrum would subtract all light—that is, it would be black; actually, such a mixture of pigments never produces more than a dark gray.

Hue is the property that gives a color its name—red, blue, yellow. Although the colors of the spectrum merge into each other, artists usually conceive of

6 Effect of adjacent value on apparent value. Actual value of center bar is constant.

their hues as distinct from each other, giving rise to many different devices for representing color relationships. There are basically two variables in color—the apparent amount of light reflected and the apparent purity; a change in one must produce a change in the other. Some terms for these variables are *value* and *tonality* (for lightness) and *chroma, saturation,* and *intensity* (for purity).

One of the more noteworthy diagrams of the relationships of colors is the triangle (FIG. 7), once attributed to Goethe, in which red, yellow, and blue (the *primary colors*) are the vertexes of the triangle and orange, green, and purple (the *secondary colors,* which result from mixing pairs of primaries) lie between them. Colors that lie opposite each other, such as red and green, are called *complementary* colors, because they complement, or complete, one another, each absorbing those colors that the other reflects. The result is a neutral tone or gray (theoretically, black), which is produced when complementaries are mixed in the right proportions. The inner triangles in FIG. 7 are the products of such mixing.

7 Color triangle. Developed by Josef Albers and Sewell Sillman, Yale University, New Haven, Connecticut.

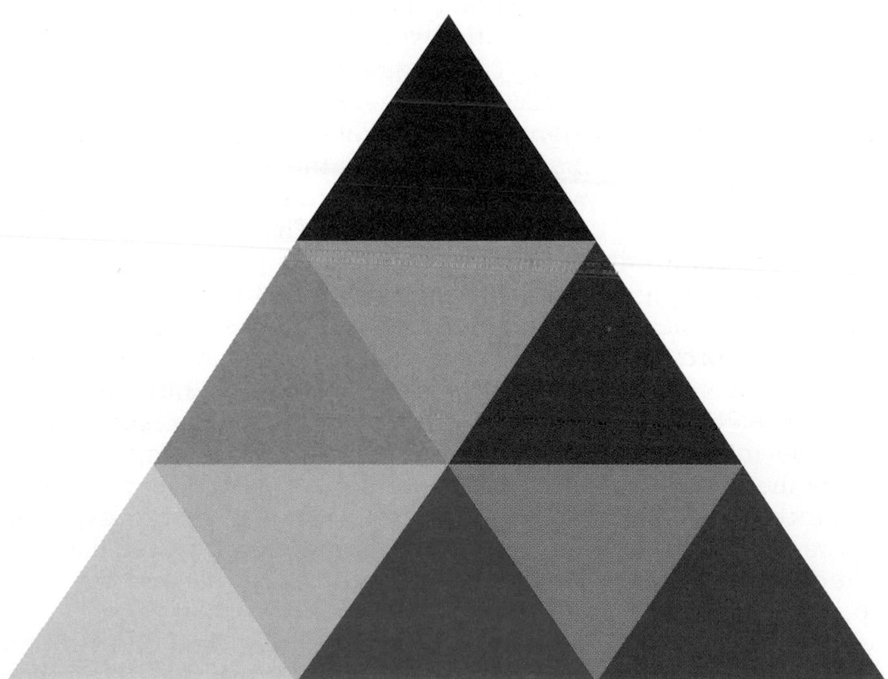

Color also has a psychological dimension: red and yellow, quite naturally, connote warmth; blue and green, coolness. Generally, *warm* colors seem to *advance* and *cool* colors seem to *recede*.

Texture is the quality of a surface (rough, smooth, hard, soft, shiny, dull) as revealed by light. The many painting media and techniques permit the creation of a variety of textures. The artist may simulate the texture of the materials represented, as in Kalf's *Still Life* (FIG. 19-55, p. 797), or create arbitrary surface differences, even using materials other than canvas, as in Picasso's *Still Life with Chair-Caning* (FIG. 22-9, p. 926).

Specialized Concepts

The terms we have been discussing have connotations for all the visual arts. Certain observations, however, are relevant to only one category of artistic endeavor—either to architecture, or to sculpture, or to painting.

IN ARCHITECTURE

Works of architecture are so much a part of our environment that we accept them as fixed and scarcely notice them until our attention is summoned. People have long known how to enclose space for the many purposes of life. The spatial aspect of the arts is most obvious in architecture. The architect makes groupings of enclosed spaces and enclosing masses, always keeping in mind the function of the structure, its construction and materials, and, of course, its design—the correlative of the other two. We experience architecture both visually and by moving through and around it, so that we perceive architectural space and mass together. The articulation of space and mass in building is expressed graphically in several ways; the principal ones include plans, sections, and elevations.

A *plan* is essentially a map of a floor, showing the placement of the masses of a structure and, therefore, the spaces they bound and enclose (FIG. 7-42, p. 286). A *section*, like a vertical plan, shows placement of the masses as if the building were cut through along a plane, often along a plane that is a major axis of the building (FIG. 3-11, p. 82). An *elevation* is a head-on view of an external or internal wall, showing its features and often other elements that would be visible beyond or before the wall (FIG. 5-54, p. 161).

Our response to a building can range from simple contentment to astonishment and awe. Such reactions are products of our experience of a building's function, construction, and design; we react differently to a church, a gymnasium, and an office building. The very movements we must make to experience one building will differ widely and profoundly from the movements required to experience another. These movements will be controlled by the continuity (or discontinuity) of the plan or by the placement of its axes. For example, in a central plan—one that radiates from a central point, as in the Pantheon in Rome (FIG. 6-58, p. 228)—we perceive the whole spatial entity at once. In the long axial plan of a Christian basilica (FIG. 7-26, p. 273) or a Gothic cathedral (FIG. 10-18, p. 392), however, our attention tends to focus on a given point—the altar at the eastern end of the nave. Mass and space can be interrelated to produce effects of great complexity, as, for example, in the Byzantine Church of the Katholikon (FIG. 7-46, p. 288) or in Le Corbusier's church at Ronchamp (FIG. 23-9, p. 1038). Thus, our experience of architecture will be the consequence of a great number of material and formal factors, including training, knowledge, and our perceptual and psychological makeup, which function in our experience of any work of art.

The architect must have the sensibilities of a sculptor and of a painter and, in establishing the plan of a building, must be able to use the instruments of a

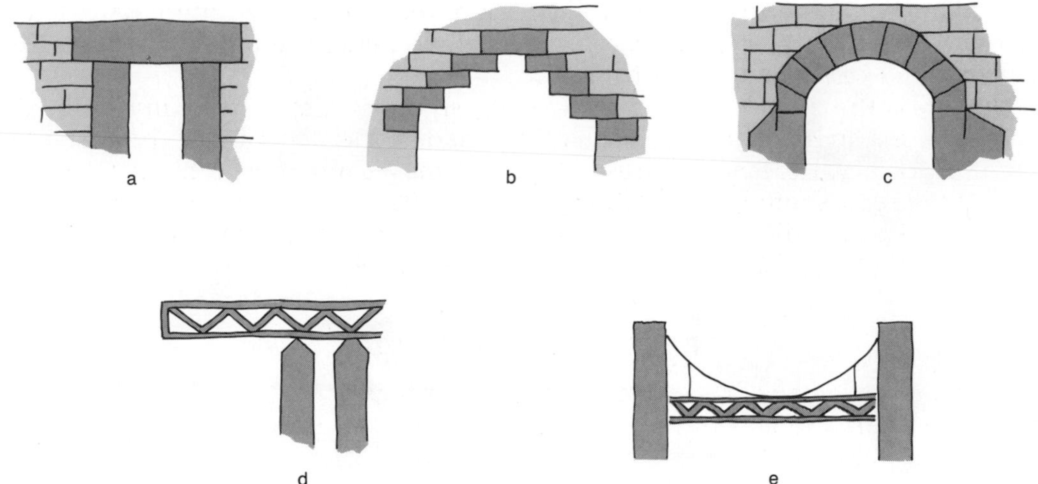

8 Basic structural devices: (a) post and lintel; (b) corbeled arch; (c) arch; (d) cantilever; (e) suspension.

mathematician. As architects resolve structural problems, they act as (or with) engineers who are cognizant of the structural principles underlying all architecture (FIG. **8**). Their major responsibilities, however, lie in the manner in which they interpret the *program* of the building. We are not talking in architectural terms when we describe a structure simply as a church, a hospital, an airport concourse, or a house. Any proposed building presents an architect with problems peculiar to it alone—problems related to the site and its surroundings, the requirements of the client, and the materials available, as well as the function of the building. A program, then, deals with more than function; it addresses all of the problems embodied in a specific building.

IN SCULPTURE

Like architecture, sculpture exists in the three-dimensional space of our physical world. But sculpture as image is closer to painting than is architecture. Until recently, sculpture has been concerned primarily with the representation of human and natural forms in tangible materials, which exist in the same space as the forms they represent. However, sculpture also may embody visions and ideals and consistently has presented images of deities and people in their most heroic as well as their most human aspects (FIGS. 17-19, p. 652 and 5-76, p. 174). Today, sculpture often dispenses with the figure as image, and even with the image itself, producing new forms in new materials and with new techniques (FIGS. 23-6, p. 1036; 23-39, p. 1060; 23-44, p. 1064; 23-79, p. 1092).

Sculpture may be associated intimately with architecture, often to such a degree that it is impossible to disassociate the two (FIG. 10-15, p. 390). Sculpture is called *relief* sculpture when it is attached to a back slab or back plate (FIG. 3-44, p. 102); *high relief,* if the figures or design project boldly (FIG. 5-78, p. 175); and *low relief,* or *bas-relief,* if the figures or design project slightly (FIG. 3-44, p. 102).

Sculpture that exists in its own right, independent of any particular architectural frame or setting (FIG. 17-46, p. 673), is usually referred to as *freestanding* sculpture, or "sculpture in the round," although, in the art of Greece and of the Renaissance, freestanding sculpture has been allied closely to architecture on many occasions. Indeed, sculpture is such a powerful agent in creating a spatial as well as an intellectual environment that its presence in

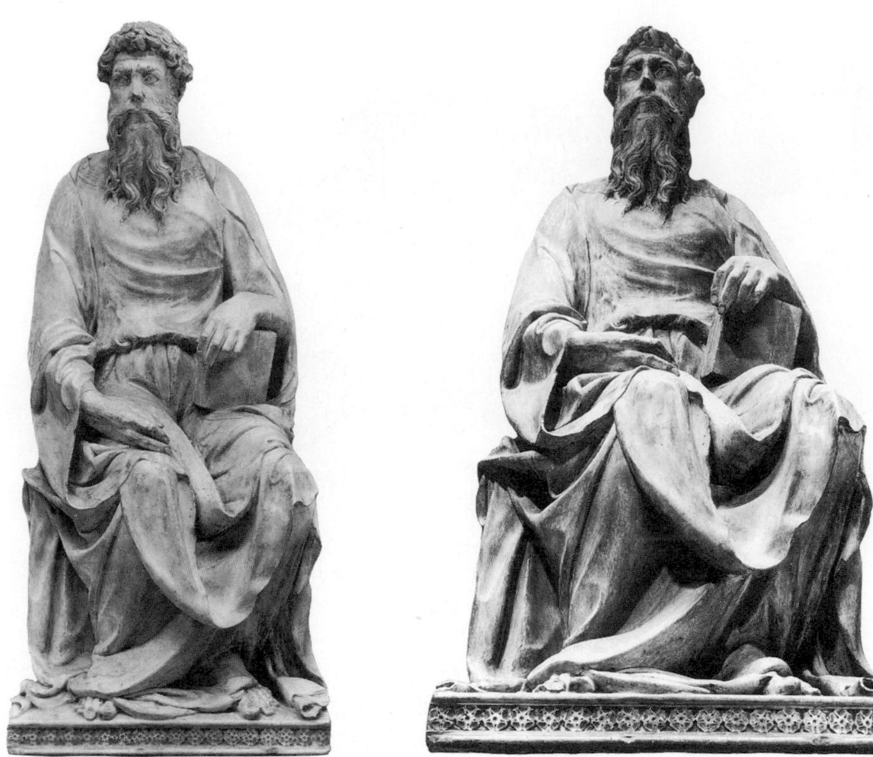

9 DONATELLO, *St. John the Evangelist,* 1412–1415. Marble. Museo del Duomo, Florence. (*Left*) as seen in museum; (*right*) as intended to be seen on façade of Florence Cathedral.

city squares or in parks and gardens is usually the controlling factor in creating their "atmosphere" or general effect (FIG. 19-73, p. 812).

Some statues are meant to be seen as a whole—to be walked around (FIG. 17-46, p. 673). Others have been created to be viewed only from a restricted angle. How a sculpture is meant to be seen must be taken into account by the sculptor and by those who exhibit the work. The effect of ignoring this is illustrated in FIG. **9**. The left photograph is taken directly from the front, as the piece is now seen in the museum; the right photograph is taken from below, at approximately the same angle from which the statue was originally meant to be seen in its niche on the façade of the cathedral of Florence.

In sculpture, perhaps more than in any other medium, textures, or tactile values, are important. One's first impulse is almost always to handle a piece of sculpture, to run one's finger over its surfaces. The sculptor plans for this, using surfaces that vary in texture from rugged coarseness to polished smoothness (FIGS. 10-56, p. 414, and 16-50, p. 615). Textures, of course, are often intrinsic to a material, and this influences the type of stone, wood, plastic, clay, or metal that the sculptor selects. There are two basic categories of sculptural technique: *subtractive* and *additive*. Carving, for instance, is a subtractive technique; the final form is a reduction of the original mass (FIG. **10**). Additive sculpture is built up, usually in clay around a framework, or armature; the piece is fired and used to make a mold in which the final work is cast in a material such as bronze (FIG. 16-52, p. 617). Casting is a popular technique today. Another common additive technique is the direct construction of forms accomplished by welding shaped metals together (FIG. 23-6, p. 1036).

Within the sculptural family, we must include ceramics and metalwork, and numerous smaller, related arts, all of which employ highly specialized

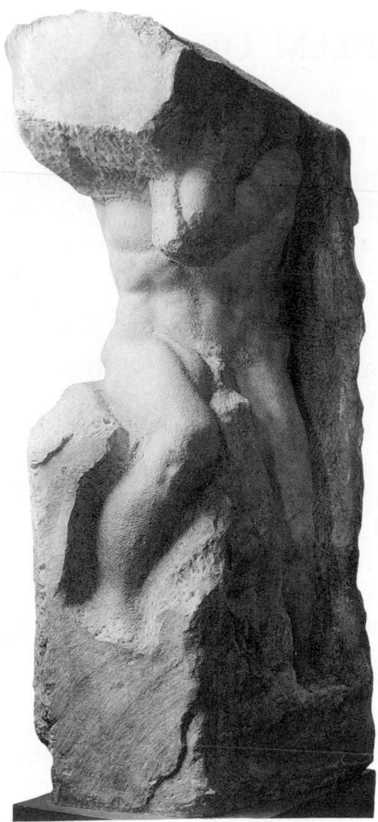

10 MICHELANGELO, *Unfinished Bound Slave,* 1519. Marble. Accademia, Florence.

techniques described in distinct vocabularies. These will be considered as they arise in the text.

IN THE PICTORIAL ARTS

The forms of architecture and sculpture exist in actual, three-dimensional space. The forms of painting (and of its relatives, drawing, engraving, and the like) exist almost wholly on a two-dimensional surface on which the artist creates an illusion, something that replicates what we see around us or something that is unique to the artist's imagination and corresponds only vaguely or slightly to anything we can see in the optical world. Human discovery of the power to project illusions of the three-dimensional world onto two-dimensional surfaces goes back thousands of years and marks an enormous step in the control and manipulation of the things we perceive. To achieve this illusion, the artist configures images or representations drawn from the world of common visual experience. Throughout the history of art, this world has been interpreted in an almost infinite variety of ways. Undoubtedly, there is much that all people *see* in common and can agree on: the moon at night, a flying bird, an obstacle in one's path. Many people may differ, though, in their *interpretation* of the seen. Seeing and then representing what is seen are very different matters. The difference between *seeing* and *representing* determines the variability of artistic styles, both cultural and personal. What we *actually* see (the optical "fact") is not necessarily reported in what we represent. In other words, in art, there is and need be little agreement between the *likeness* of a thing and the *representation* of it. This lack of agreement makes for a persisting problem in the history of art. How are we to interpret or "read" images or replicas of the seen? Is there a "correct" vision of the "real" world?

THE PROBLEM OF REPRESENTATION

The conundrum of seeing something and making a representation of it is artfully illustrated in FIG. **11**, a cartoon of a life-drawing class in ancient Egypt that Gombrich uses to introduce his invaluable *Art and Illusion*. The cartoon and the actual representation of an Egyptian queen (FIG. **12**) raise many questions: Did Egyptian artists copy models exactly as they saw them? (Did Egyptians actually *see* each other in this way?) Or did they translate what they saw according to some formula dictated by conventions of representation peculiar to their culture? Would we have to say—if what was seen and what was recorded were optically the same—that this is the way Egyptians must have looked? or wished to look? Beginning students usually have questions somewhat like these in mind when they perceive deviations in historical styles from the recent Western realism to which they are conditioned. They ask whether the Egyptians, or other artists, were simply unskilled at matching eye and hand, so to speak, and could not draw from what they saw. But such a question presupposes that the objective of the artist has always been to match appearances with cameralike exactitude. This is not the case, nor is it the case that artists of one period "see" more "correctly" and render more "skillfully" than those of another. Rather, it seems that artists represent what they *conceive* to be real, not what they *perceive*. They bring to the making of images conceptions that have been instilled in them by their cultures. They understand the visible world in certain unconscious, culturally agreed on ways and thus bring to the artistic process ideas and meanings out of a common stock. They record not so much what they *see* as what they *know* or

11 ALAIN. Drawing. Copyright © 1955, 1983, The New Yorker Magazine, Inc.

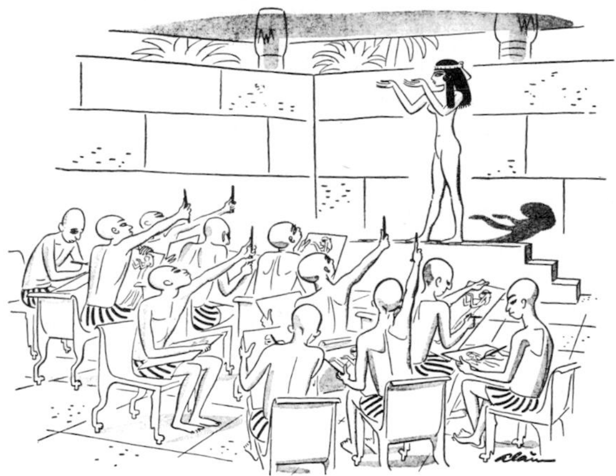

12 *Queen Nofretari,* from her tomb at Thebes, c. 1250 B.C. Detail of a painted bas-relief.

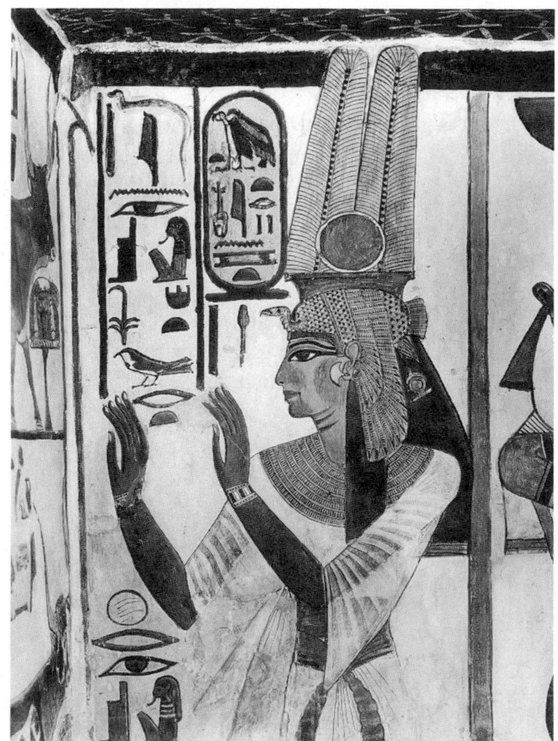

mean. Even in the period of dominant realism in recent western European art, great deviations from camera realism have set in. Moreover, in our everyday life there are images familiar to all of us that distort optical "reality" quite radically; consider, for example, the images of the ubiquitous comic strip.

Solutions to the problem of representation constitute the history of artistic style. It is useful to examine some specimens of sharp divergence in representational approach. Compare, for example, the lion drawn by the Medieval artist Villard de Honnecourt (FIG. **13**) with those done by the Renaissance artist Albrecht Dürer (FIG. **14**). In the de Honnecourt lion—which, it is important to notice, the artist asserts was drawn from life—the figure is entirely adequate for identification but preconceived and constructed according to the formulas of its time. Dürer's lions, drawn some three centuries later, obviously are a much different report of what the artist saw. So are the Assyrian lions of the hunting reliefs (FIG. 2-33, p. 63), the *Lion from the Processional Way* of the Ishtar Gate (FIG. 2-35, p. 64), the lion in Henri Rousseau's *The Sleeping Gypsy* (FIG. 21-90, p. 943), or (in slight shift of species) Barye's sculpture of a jaguar in his *Jaguar Devouring a Hare* (FIG. 21-7, p. 870). In each case, *personal vision* joins with the *artistic conventions* of time and place to decide the manner and effect of the representation. Yet, even at the same time and place (for example, nineteenth-century Paris), we can find sharp differences in representation when the opposing personal styles of Ingres and Delacroix record the same subject (FIGS. 21-16 and 21-17, pp. 876–77).

A final example will underscore the relativity of vision and representation that differences in human cultures produce. We recognize, moreover, that close matching of appearances has mattered only in a few times and places.

13 VILLARD DE HONNECOURT, *Lion Portrayed from Life*, *c.* 1230–1235. Drawing. Cabinet des Manuscripts, Bibliothèque Nationale, Paris.

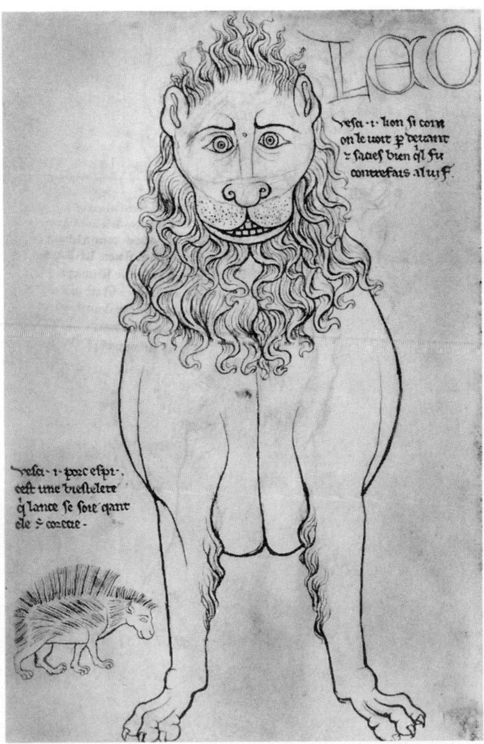

14 ALBRECHT DÜRER, *Two Lions*, *c.* 1521. Drawing. Staatliche Museen Preussischer Kulturbesitz, Kupferstichkabinet, Berlin.

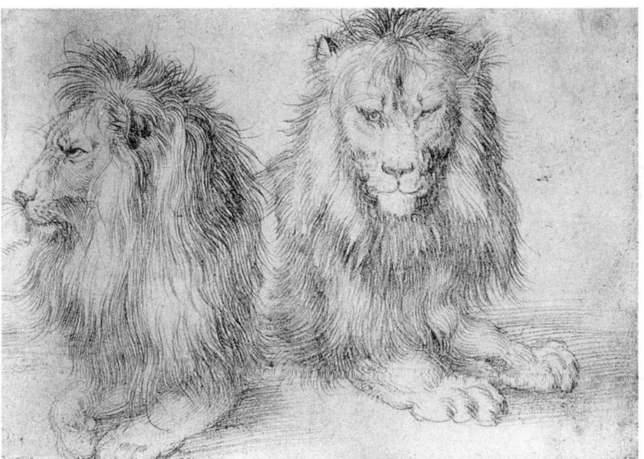

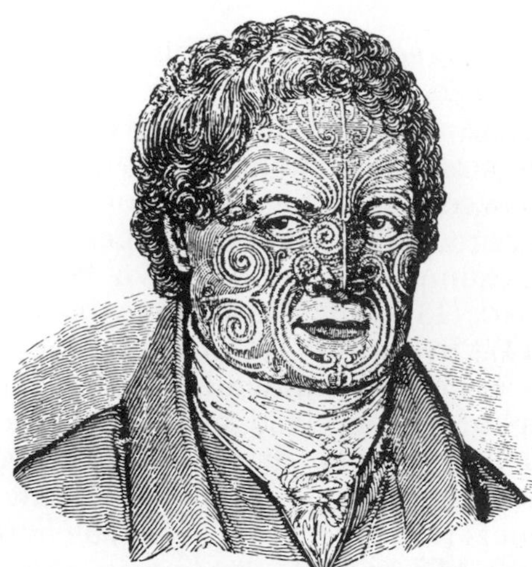

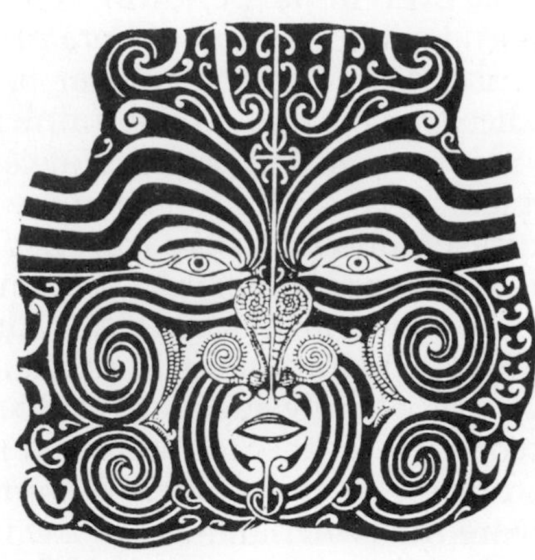

15 *The Maori Chief Tupai Kupa,* c. 1800. (*Left*) after a drawing by John Sylvester; (*right*) a self-portrait. From *The Childhood of Man* by Leo Frobenius, 1909. Reproduced by permission of J. B. Lippincott Company.

Although both portraits of a Maori chieftain from New Zealand (FIG. **15**)—one by a European, the other by the chieftain himself—reproduce his facial tatooing, the first portrait is a simple, commonplace likeness that underplays the tatooing. The self-portrait is a statement by the chieftain of the supreme importance of the design that symbolizes his rank among his people. It is the splendidly composed insignia that is his image of himself, the European likeness being superficial and irrelevant to him.

Students of the history of art, then, learn to distinguish works by scrutinizing them closely within the context of their time and place of origin. But this is only the beginning. The causes of stylistic change over time are mysterious and innumerable, and it is only through the continuing process of art-historical research that we can hope to make the picture even fragmentarily recognizable. Incomplete though the picture is and will remain, the panorama of art, changing in time, lies before students, and as their art-historical perspective gains depth and focus, they will come to perceive the continuity of the art of the past with that of the present. It will become clear that one cannot be understood without the other and that our understanding of the one will constantly change with changes in our understanding of the other. The great American poet and critic T. S. Eliot has cogently expressed this truth for all art in a passage that suggests the philosophy and method of this book:

> What happens when a new work of art is created is something that happens simultaneously to all the works of art which preceded it. The existing monuments form an ideal order among themselves, which is modified by the introduction of the new (the really new) work of art among them. . . . Whoever has approved this idea of order . . . will not find it preposterous that the past should be altered by the present as much as the present is directed by the past.*

As new works of art continue to be created, old ones, buried by time, are recovered and others, known to have existed, disappear. Many come to light by chance, and many are destroyed by catastrophe or neglect. Restoration and reconstruction either damage or rescue them. The whole domain of art

*T. S. Eliot, "Tradition and the Individual Talent," in *Selected Essays 1917–1932* (New York: Harcourt, Brace, 1932), p. 5.

constantly shifts in outline and population, as does our knowledge of it. Identification of a work of art may be accepted at one time, rejected at another. Attribution of certain works to certain artists may be challenged; the chronology of stylistic change may be readjusted; and the dating of particular works may be debated and revised. Critics may disagree as to the number of works to be ascribed to a single artist. (Some credit Rembrandt with as many as 600 paintings; others credit him with as few as 350.) Reinterpretation of the meanings and functions of works of art is an ongoing process, as is the reassessment of their artistic value and stylistic importance. Our knowledge of art history is as much in flux as artistic creation itself; what seems to be certain at one time proves to be inconclusive or erroneous at another. Evidence for our conclusions is never all in; more of it is always turning up, and much of it cannot be found.

Students are therefore cautioned not to expect this book to contain an outlay of facts that are incontestable beyond all alteration. The facts are the works of art themselves, as made palpable to our senses; our descriptions of these works—our dating, attributions, classifications, interpretations—are forever provisional and open to doubt. What is not open to doubt is the presence in our world of a small universe of objects of art that expresses, in myriad, arresting forms, the highest values and ideals of the human race. It is essential to the quality of our own experience to encounter, comprehend, appreciate, and preserve these precious works.

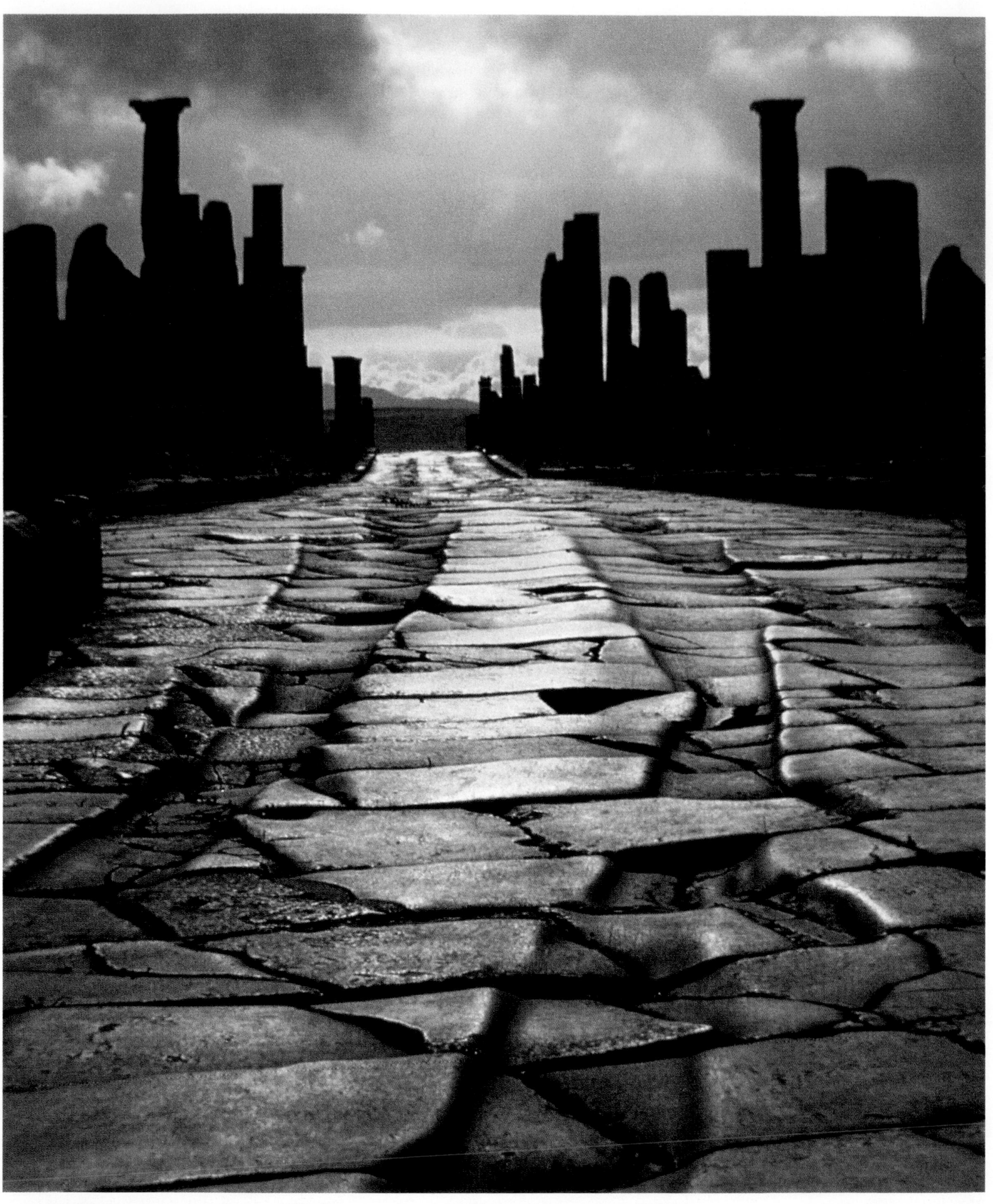

The Roman road to Timgad in North Africa stands as a legacy
of the greatest empire of the ancient world.

I
THE ANCIENT WORLD

The Christian civilizations of the Western world early distinguished an ancient past from a new age—the times, respectively, before (B.C.) and after (A.D.) Christ. For them the ancient world, the world of the Old Testament, had the character of a preparation; it was related to the new era as promise is related to fulfillment. This slightly condescending view toward antiquity changed during the Renaissance, when scholars and artists deeply admired the Greek and Roman past and often debated the question of which was superior, the "ancient" or the "modern." Interest in Greco-Roman antiquity was later broadened to encompass the great civilizations that preceded it: the pre-Greek Mediterranean, the Egyptian, the Near Eastern, and the very remote, prehistoric cave cultures of western Europe.

From the end of the eighteenth century to the present, archeologists and art historians, utilizing ever-improving methods of investigation, have recovered great tracts of forgotten history to fill out our picture of the distant past with increasing accuracy. Within the past few decades, evidence of the existence of civilizations that flourished as early as 7500 B.C. has been uncovered.

Historical perspective is likely to produce a distortion of view similar to that of the early Christian depreciation of the pre-Christian world. Until we have become familiar with the ancient world, it seems to us to be simply *that* (ancient, exceedingly old), and we imagine it in terms and images of faded inscriptions, dusty ruins, fallen idols, and long-outdated institutions. More properly, we should see *ourselves* as ancient—as living in the later eras of a great epoch at the beginning of which, thousands of years ago, some of our most fundamental beliefs, institutions, folkways, and art and science had their inception.

Following the development of agriculture and the widespread domestication of animals, the precarious, furtive life of the cave-dwelling hunter and the later nomadic herdsman was succeeded by the more sedentary, predictable, and ordered life of the village farmer. Aside from the technological revolutions of our times, this leap from food gathering to food production brought perhaps the most significant transformation of the human condition and made possible all that has followed. In Mesopotamia, Asia Minor, and Egypt, more complex forms of human community were created—

cities, city-states, and kingdoms. Formal religion and codes of law were developed to regulate the relationships among human beings and between gods and human beings. Writing was invented, as well as numbers and the art of calculation. The courses of the stars were plotted in order to predict the seasons and the times for planting and harvesting. Architecture, sculpture, and painting flourished in the service of kingly magnificence. The sacred books of Judaism and Christianity were produced in the shadow of mighty and hostile empires, and the legacy of Israel, which has contributed so much to the formation of the Western spirit, was preserved through all the vicissitudes of a remarkably tenacious people.

With the Greeks, there emerged what might be called the specifically "Western intelligence," with its respect for reason, scientific inquiry, the physical concept of nature, and the humanistic view of humankind. The city-states of Greece were more than seats of commerce and government; the loyalties of the citizens of each city-state had social, educative, and local religious bases as well. It was in some of these city-states—Athens in particular—that democracy first evolved in a limited form. About twenty-five hundred years ago, the government of Athens was largely run by a council of citizens, who were chosen by lot, and a kind of legislative assembly made up of all citizens—although citizenship did not extend to women or to the slaves who made up nearly half the population. With the repulsion of the Persian invaders in the fifth century B.C., the Greeks inaugurated the first authentic phase of European culture, the content and spirit of which, commingled with Hebraism, are still largely with us in our patterns of life and thought today.

Rome, although never matching Greek achievements in intellectual and artistic culture, produced the greatest empire of the ancient world. During a period of about eight hundred years, Rome progressed from its beginnings as a trading center under Etruscan kings to the zenith of its empire, which extended from what are now the borders of Scotland to Jordan and to the far

British archeologist Howard Carter spent six years searching for the tomb of the Eighteenth Dynasty pharaoh, Tutankhamen, and another eight years removing, cataloguing, and restoring the more than two thousand objects found in the tomb. Examining one of the three coffins of the young pharaoh, Carter brushes dust off the gilt wood.

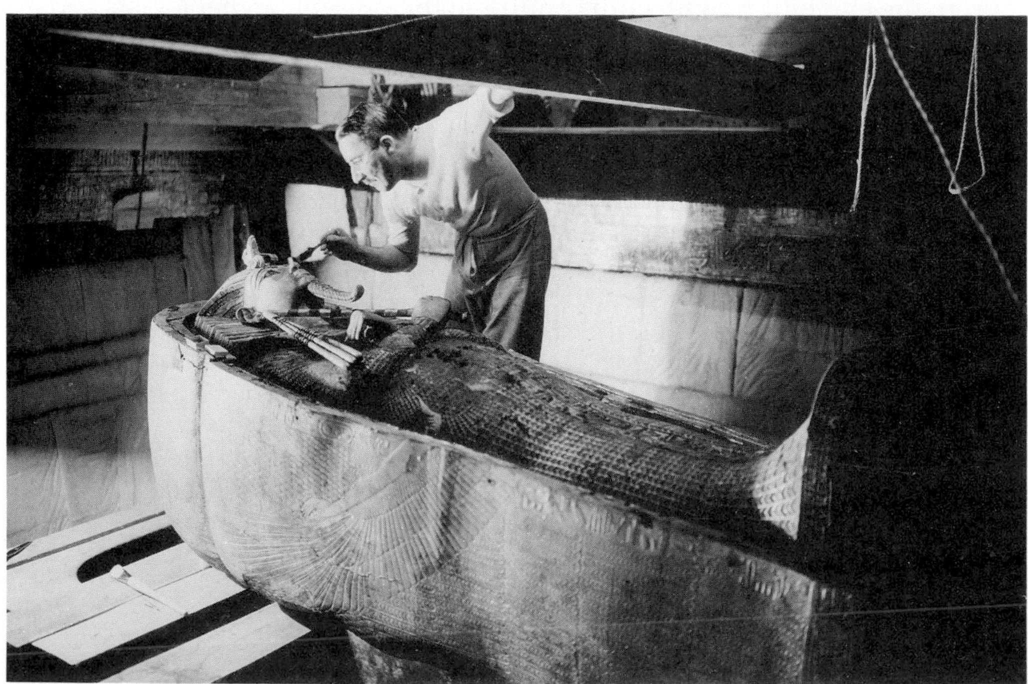

shores of the Black Sea, asserting its dominance over a multitude of peoples and lands. The dynamic and aggressive Roman spirit was reflected in and supported by an astonishing military machine and technology, although Roman control over diverse peoples was exercised as much by the encouragement of their participation in the empire as by the naked assertion of Roman power. The Romanization of western Europe—through the Roman genius for government and the "Roman Peace"—still has much to do with the character of Europe, and the Roman ideal of a single, peaceful community of all humankind is very much in our view today as at least an ideal and a hope.

NOTE: Most of the time spans shown on the chronologies involving early dates have been determined by the method of *radiocarbon dating* invented in 1955. This is such an effective dating method that archeologists have called it "the radiocarbon revolution." Radiocarbon dating is based on the fact that living organisms constantly absorb carbon isotopes, including the radioactive carbon-14, which continually disintegrates into nonradioactive nitrogen-14. On the death of the organism, absorption ceases but disintegration continues. Because the rate of disintegration is known, the age of organic matter—such as charcoal or carbonized bone—can be calculated on the basis of the amount of carbon-14 remaining in it.

In recent years, the chemical "clock" provided by the disintegration of carbon-14 has sometimes been out of phase with known dates before about 1000 B.C., making them later than they should be; it may be that other energy phenomena interfere with the regularity of this chemical "clock." Radiocarbon dating has therefore been supplemented and corrected by another dating technique called *dendrochronology*, which determines the age of timber. By counting the annual rings of trees, visible in the cross sections of their trunks (notably, the very ancient bristlecone pines of California), accurate dates as far back as about the year 4000 B.C. can be obtained.

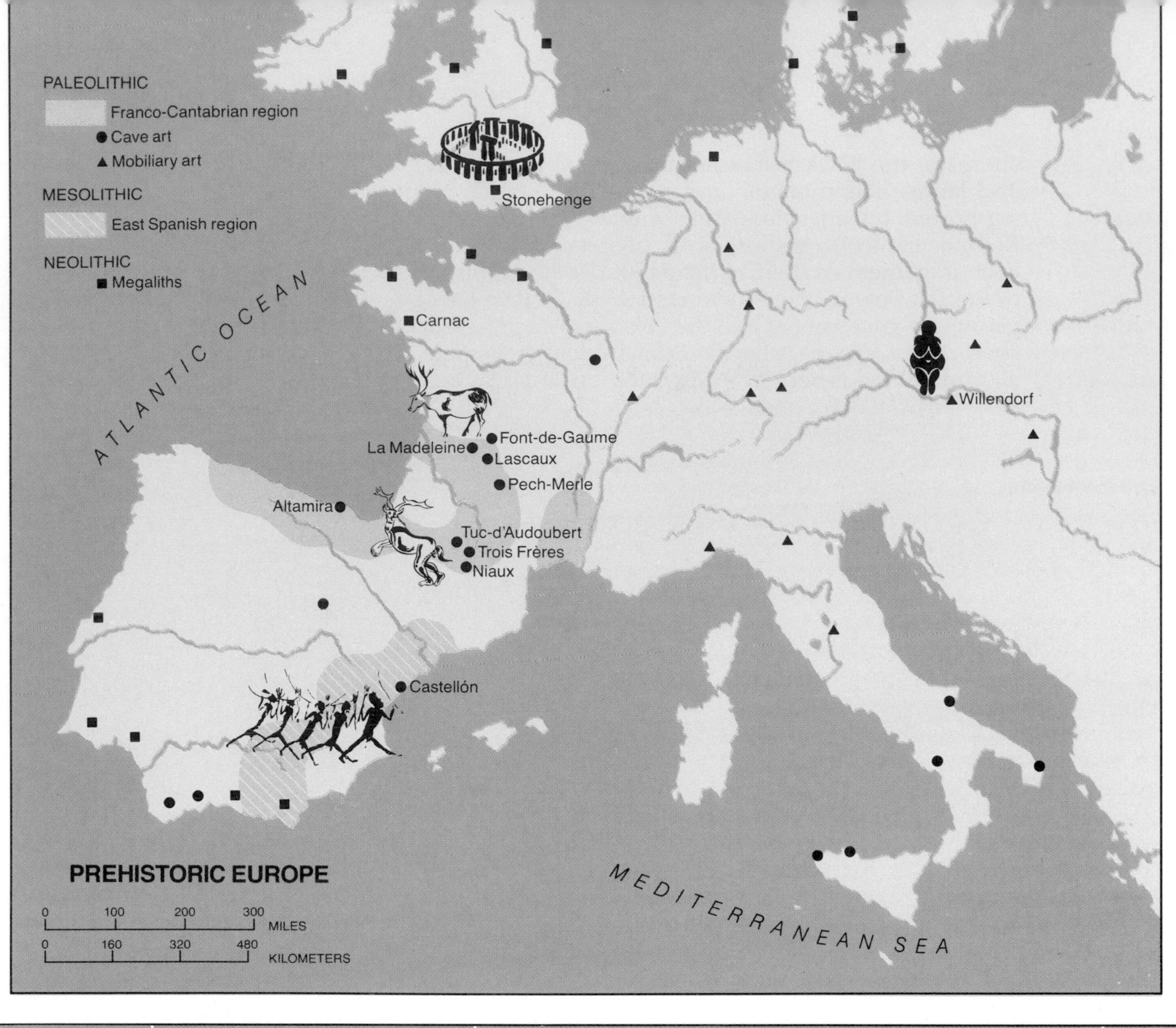

35,000 B.C.	32,000	28,000	20,000
UPPER PALEOLITHIC PERIOD			
	AURIGNACIAN	GRAVETTIAN	SOLUTREAN
		Venus of Willendorf *c.* 28,000–25,000 B.C.	
Neanderthal Era	Emergence of Cro-Magnons		

1
THE BIRTH OF ART

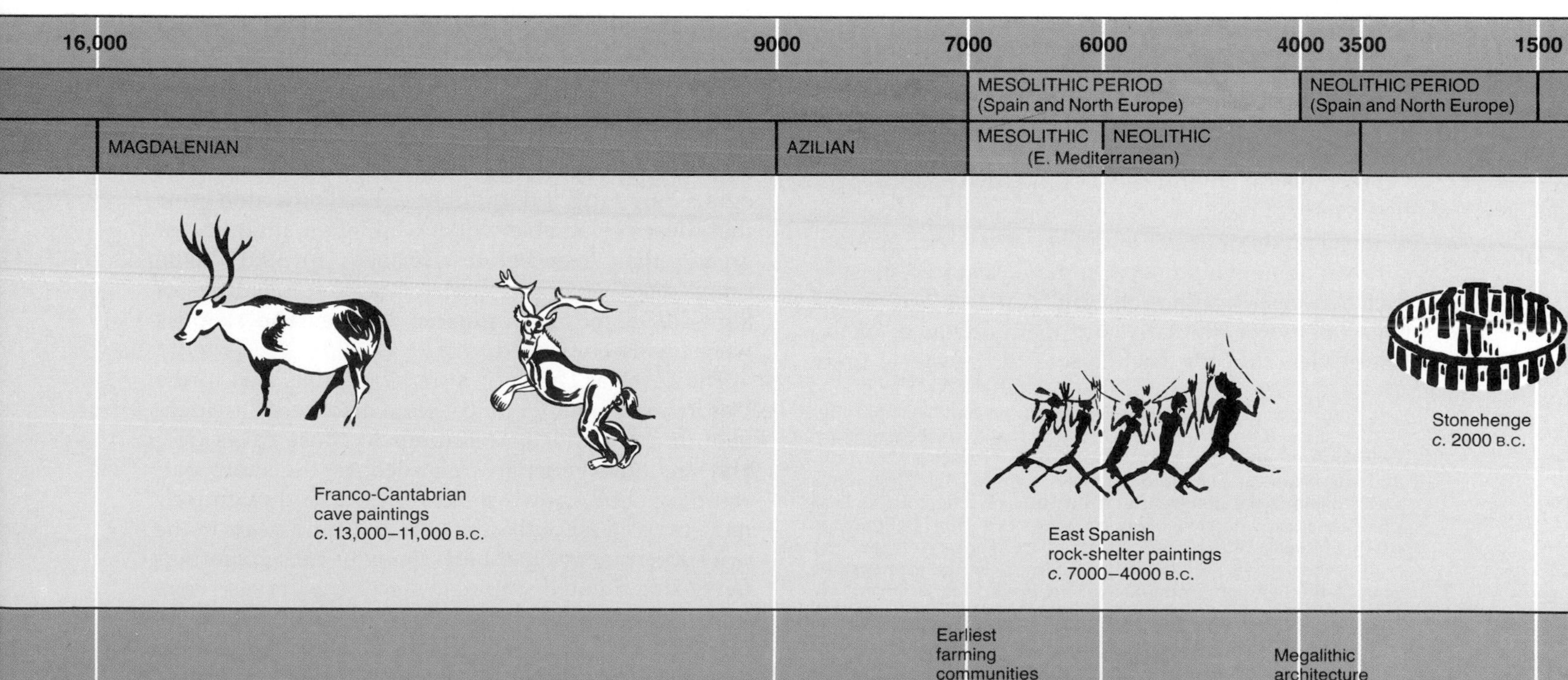

WHAT GENESIS is to the biblical account of the fall and redemption of humankind, early cave art is to the history of human intelligence, imagination, and creative power. In the caves of southern France and of northern Spain, which were discovered only about a century ago and are still being explored (as well as in central Europe, North Africa, and Asia), we may witness the birth of that characteristically human capability that has made us masters of our environment—the making of images and symbols. By this original and tremendous feat of abstraction, Upper Paleolithic cave dwellers were able to fix in place the world of their experience, rendering the continuous processes of life in discrete and unmoving shapes that had the identity and meaning of the living animals that were their prey. Like Adam, Paleolithic peoples gathered and named the animals, and the faculty of imagination came into being along with the concepts of identity and meaning.

In that remote time during the last advance and retreat of the great glaciers, Stone Age people made the critical breakthrough and became wholly human. Our intellectual and imaginative processes function through the recognition and construction of images and symbols. We see and understand the world around us much as we are taught to, according to representations of that world that are familiar to our particular time and place. The immense achievement of Stone Age people, the invention of *representation,* cannot be exaggerated.

THE LATER OLD STONE AGE (UPPER PALEOLITHIC)*

The physical environment of the cave peoples over thousands of years would not appear to be favorable to the creation of an art of quality and sophistication; survival alone would seem to have required most of their energies. Although the Aurignacian period began between the early and main advances of the last glaciers and for a while was temperate, it grew cold toward its end. The great ice sheet advanced south from Scandinavia over the plains of north central Europe, and glaciers spread down from the Alps and other mountain ranges to produce a tundra and forest-tundra climate. With the end of the Magdalenian period about 9000 B.C., the final recession of the ice and the onset of temperate weather began. In the cold periods, human hunters and food gatherers took refuge in caves. It was here that Cro-Magnon peoples, who first appeared during the Aurignacian period, replacing Neanderthals, took the remarkable steps that made them not simply fabricators of stone tools, but artists.

*The prehistoric periods Paleolithic, Mesolithic, and Neolithic refer to the stone (Greek: *lithos*) technology that prevailed through thousands of years of early human life; the prefixes *paleo-*, *meso-*, and *neo-* mean early, middle, and late, respectively. These terms were coined in the nineteenth century and no longer fit the facts precisely as modern archeology now classifies them, but they are used habitually and are difficult to replace. For convenience, we will use them here. Subdivisions within these three prehistoric periods (Perigordian, Aurignacian, Solutrean, Magdalenian) are named for the sites (mostly in France) at which characteristic artifacts, such as tools and weapons, have been found. The terms *lower* and *upper,* placed before these names, signify the earlier and later phases of a period.

Cave Painting

The first example of cave painting was discovered accidentally by amateurs in 1879 near Santander in northern Spain. Marcelino de Sautuola, a local resident interested in the antiquity of the human race, was exploring the Altamira caves on his estate, in which he had already found specimens of flint and carved bone. His little daughter was with him. Because the ceiling of the debris-filled cavern was only a few inches above the father's head, it was the child who was first able to discern, from her lower vantage point, the shadowy forms of painted beasts on the cave roof. De Sautuola was the first modern man to explore this cave, and he was certain that these paintings dated back to prehistoric times. Archeologists, however, were highly dubious of the authenticity of these works, and at the Lisbon Congress on Prehistoric Archeology in 1880, the Altamira paintings were officially dismissed as forgeries. But in 1896, at Pair-non-Pair in the Gironde district of France, paintings were discovered partially covered by calcareous deposits that would have taken thousands of years to accumulate. These paintings were the first to be recognized by experts as authentic. The conviction grew that these remarkable works were of an antiquity far greater than ever before dreamed. In 1901, Abbé Breuil discovered and verified the cave paintings of Font-de-Gaume in Dordogne, France. The skeptics were finally convinced.

The caves at Lascaux, near Montignac, also in the Dordogne region of France, were discovered accidentally in 1940, and the paintings in those caves (FIG. **1-1**) are now generally regarded as the most outstanding of all known prehistoric art. Although they had survived more than fifteen thousand years in the dry subterranean chambers, many of these paintings have deteriorated rapidly since the caves were opened to the public in recent decades. At Lascaux, for example, it was found that moisture and carbon dioxide exhaled by hordes of visitors settled on the

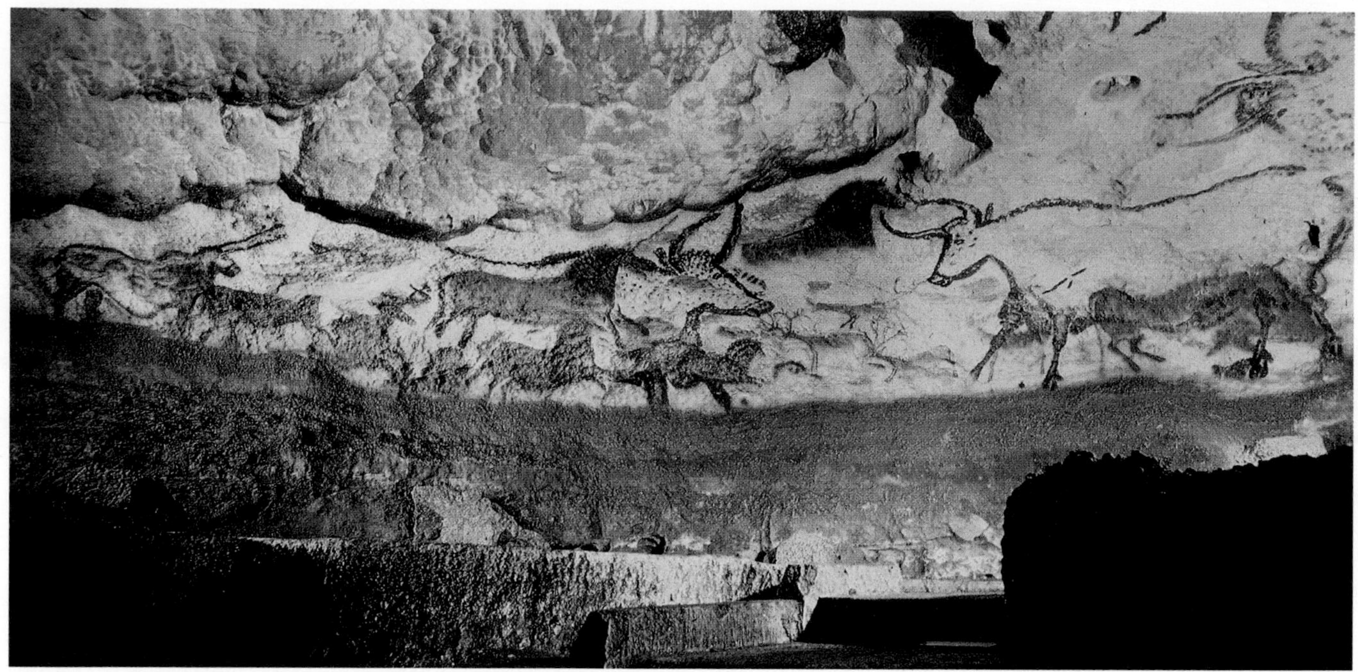

1-1 *Hall of Bulls* (left wall), Lascaux, *c.* 13,000 B.C. Dordogne, France.

walls and encouraged the growth of fungi destructive to the paintings. For this reason, and to prevent further damage, the caves have been closed to the general public since 1963.

The Lascaux caverns (FIG. **1-2**), like the others, had served as subterranean water channels, a few hundred to some 4,000 feet long. They are often choked, sometimes almost impassably, by faults or by deposits, such as stalactites and stalagmites. Far inside these caverns, well removed from the cave mouths that they often chose for habitation, the hunter-artists engraved and painted on the walls pictures of animals—mammoth, bison, reindeer, horse, boar, wolf. For light, they used tiny stone lamps filled with marrow or fat, with a wick, perhaps, of moss. For drawing, they used chunks of red and yellow ocher; for painting, they ground these same ochers into powders that they blew onto the walls or mixed with some medium, such as animal fat, before applying. A large flat bone served as a palette; they could make brushes from reeds or bristles; they could use a blowpipe of reeds to trace outlines of figures and to put pigments on out-of-reach surfaces; and they had stone scrapers for smoothing the wall and sharp flint points for engraving. Along with the more famous paintings, more than a thousand engravings (FIG. **1-3**) have recently been found on the walls and ceilings at Lascaux, indicating that engraving was as much a practiced technique as painting—and quite as important for our appreciation of the art of the caves.

During the years that the caves of Lascaux have been closed to tourism, archeologists, such as the late

1-2 Diagram of the caves of Lascaux. Dordogne, France. (After Arlette Leroi-Gourhan.)

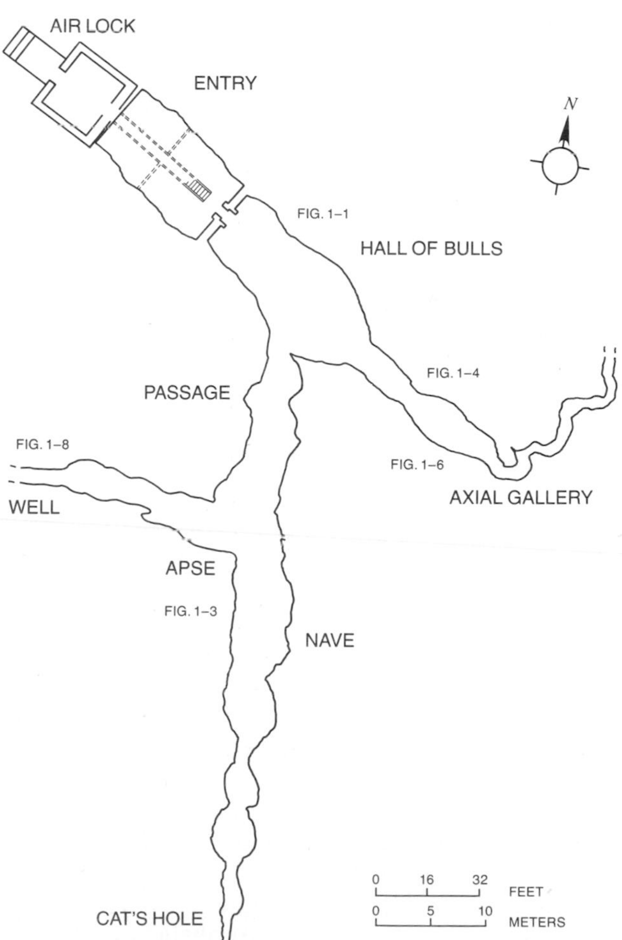

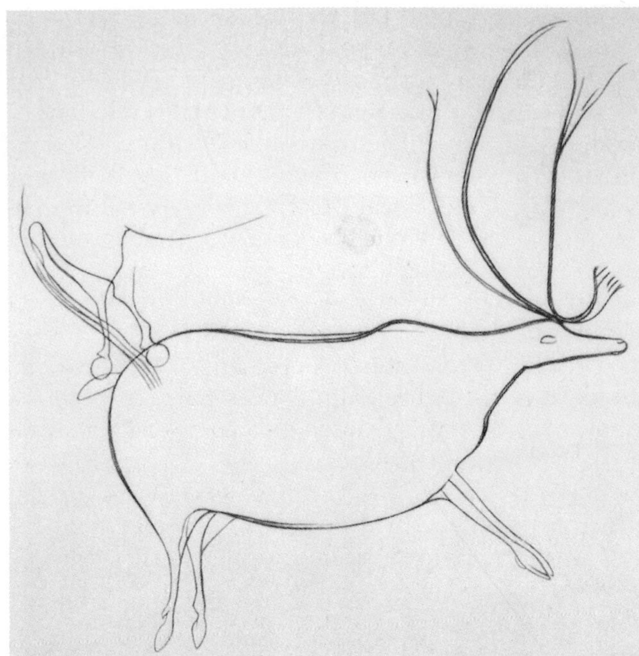

1-3 Engraved reindeer, Lascaux, c. 13,000 B.C. Engraving on rock, 28″ long. Dordogne, France. (Simplified copy of a tracing by Abbé André Glory.)

Abbé André Glory, who made careful tracings of all the engravings, have worked indefatigably, recovering artifacts that provide firm evidence of the Magdalenian artists' methods and materials. Some 130 stone lamps have been found, and from the remains of their burnt tallow and wicks, it has been shown that their light must have been as strong and steady as candlelight and must have lasted for an hour at a time. Numerous flat stones have been found that served as palettes for mixing colors. The colors themselves have been found, lumps of pigment have been chemically analyzed, and the different mineral powders that composed them have been ascertained. Recesses cut into the rock wall some seven feet or more above the floor must have held joists for a scaffolding that could support a platform made of saplings lashed together. This permitted the painters access to the upper surfaces of the caves, where they could occupy themselves for hours if necessary; remains of meals indicate that they could take them without having to descend. Carbon-14 analysis of the charcoal in the lamps and of bone artifacts associated with the various strata of the paintings confirms a date for the art of Lascaux of around 13,000 B.C. Researchers think it likely that thc period of artistic activity may have extended over a relatively short span of time, coinciding with only several centuries of human occupation of the caves.

The artist's approach to the figures, as seen at Lascaux and at other sites, is "naturalistic"; each artist attempts to represent as convincing a pose and action as possible. Each painting reflects the keen observation and extraordinary memory of the hunter-artist, whose accuracy in capturing fleeting poses (FIGS. 1-1 and 1-6) is hardly surpassed by today's camera. Yet this observation was selective; the artist saw and recorded only those aspects that were essential to interpret the appearance and the character of the animal—its grace or awkwardness, its cunning, dignity, or ferocity. It is almost as if the artist were constructing a pictorial definition of the animal, capturing its very essence.

PURPOSE AND FUNCTION

Any modern interpretation of this cave art must, of course, remain speculative. Properties common to all these paintings, however, provide some fairly definite clues as to what they may have meant to their creators. For instance, the fact that the paintings are never found in those parts of the caves that were inhabited or near daylight rules out any purely decorative purpose. The first paintings at Font-de-Gaume were encountered about 70 yards behind the cave mouth, and the painted animals in the "Salon Noir" in the cave at Niaux were found some 850 tortuous yards from the entrance. The remoteness and difficulty of access of many of these sites and the fact that they appear to have been used for centuries suggest that the prehistoric hunter attributed magical properties to them. Therefore, the paintings themselves could have had magical meaning for their creators. As Abbé Breuil has suggested, "by confining the animal within the limits of a painting, one subjected it to one's power in the hunting grounds." Within this context, the artist's aim to be realistic may be explained by the probable conviction that the painting's magical power was directly related to its lifelike characteristics.

The naturalistic pictures of animals in the caves are often accompanied by geometric signs, some of which seem to represent man-made structures, or *tectiforms* (FIG. **1-4**); others consist of checkers, dots, squares, or other arrangements of lines. Several observers have seen a primitive form of writing in these representations of nonliving things, but they, too, may have had magical significance. The ones that look like traps or snares, for example, may have been drawn to ensure success in hunting with these devices. In many places, representations of human hands, most of them "negative," appear where the artist placed one hand against the wall and then painted or blew pigment around it (FIG. **1-5**). Occasionally, the artist would dip a hand in paint and then press it against the wall, leaving a "positive" imprint. These handprints, too, may have had magical signifi-

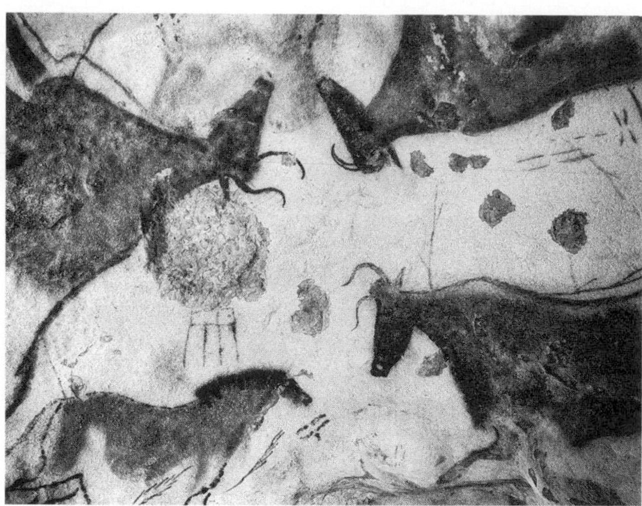

1-4 *Three Cows and One Horse,* ceiling of the Axial Gallery, Lascaux, c. 13,000 B.C. Approx. life size. Dordogne, France.

cance or may simply have been the "signatures" left by whole generations of visitors to these sacred places, much as modern tourists leave some memento of their presence.

The figures are in themselves striking approximations of optical fact, but their arrangement on the cave walls shows little concern for any consistency of placement in relationship to each other or to the wall space, although this has been claimed. Certainly, we find no compositional adjustment to suggest the perspective effect and no notion of separation and enframement. Figures, far from being proportionally related, are often superimposed at random and are of quite different sizes (FIGS. 1-1 and 1-3). Generations of artists, working in the same sanctuaries, covered and recovered the crowded walls, although pains often seem to have been taken not to break through the outlines of an earlier figure. It seems that attention to a single figure—the rendering of a single image—in itself fulfilled the purpose of the artist.

The hunter-artists made frequent and skillful use of the naturally irregular surfaces of the walls, utilizing projections, recessions, fissures, and ridges to help give the illusion of real presence to their forms. An outward swelling of the wall could be used within the outline of a charging bison to suggest the bulging volume of the beast's body. The spotted horse at Pech-Merle (FIG. 1-5) may have been inspired by a rock formation that resembles a horse's head and neck (on the right of the figure), although the artist's eventual version of the head is much smaller than the formation and is highly abstract. Natural forms, like those of foliage or clouds, the profile of a mountain, or the shapes of eroded earth and rock, can represent for any of us—sometimes quite startlingly—the features of people, animals, or objects. Thus, the first artistic representations may have followed some primal experience of resemblance between the chance configuration of a cave wall and the animal the artist had just been hunting. This resemblance might have had for the artist the effect of an awesome apparition of the very animal—a miraculous and magical reappearance of its vanished life. With the impulse to give the apparition even more presence, the artist could have "finished" the form by cutting an outline around the relief and continuing it until a more or less complete and familiar silhouette emerged. The addition of color would enhance the reality of the image.

Researchers have evidence that the hunters in the caves, perhaps in a frenzy stimulated by magical rites and dances, treated the painted animals as if they were alive. Not only was the quarry often painted as pierced by arrows (FIG. **1-6**), but hunters actually may

1-5 *Spotted Horses and Negative Hand Imprints,* Pech-Merle, c. 13,000 B.C. 11′ 2″ long. Lot, France.

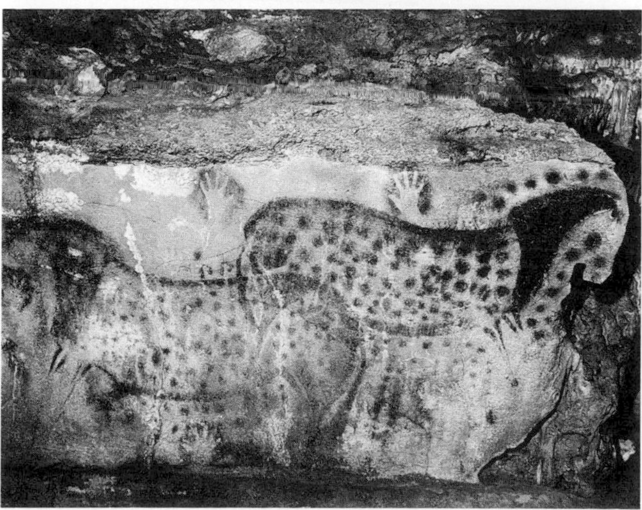

1-6 *Chinese Horse* (detail of FIG. 1-4), Axial Gallery, Lascaux, c. 13,000 B.C. Approx. 56″ long. Dordogne, France.

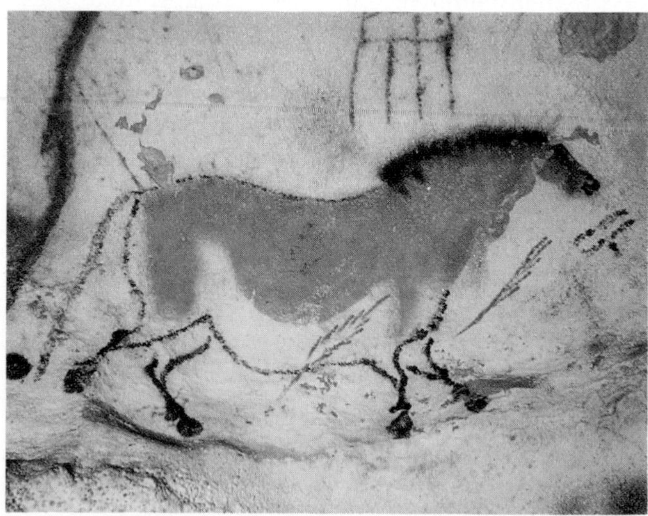

have thrown spears at the images, as sharp gouges in the side of the bison at Niaux (FIG. **1-7**) suggest. This practice, intended to predestinate and magically command the death of the animals, would be analogous to the kind of magic, still cultivated in parts of the world today, that is based on the belief that harm can be done to an enemy by abusing an image of that person.

This art produced in caverns deep in the earth must have had some profound magical functions. Familiar in religious architecture, which had its beginning thousands of years after the era of the caves, are the cavelike spaces of the sanctuary where the most sacred and hidden mysteries are kept and where the god dwells in silence. The sacred often has meant the mysterious—a place of darkness, lit only by fitful light, where at the culmination of rituals, absolute silence reigns. These features of the sacred environment were already present in the "architecture" of the caves, and the central theme has never been lost despite its myriad variations.*

It is significant that the miracle of abstraction—the creation of image and symbol—should take place in such secret and magical caverns. Abstraction is representation, a human device of fundamental power, by which not only art but ultimately science comes into existence. Both art and science are methods for the control of human experience and the mastery of the environment. And that was also the end purpose of the hunter-magicians—to control the world of the beasts they hunted. The making of the image was, by itself, a form of magic. By painting an animal, the hunter fixed and controlled its soul within the prison of an outline; from this initial magic, all the rest would follow. Rites before the paintings may have served to improve the hunter's luck. At the same time, prehistoric peoples must have been anxious to preserve their food supply, and the representations of pregnant animals (FIG. 1-6) suggest that these cavalcades of painted beasts may also have served magically to assure the survival of the actual herds.

But magic must not be considered the sole function of cave art; other functions also have been suggested. The processions and groupings of the animals are not

*In the later Paleolithic, magic may have been developing into religious ritual and communal belief. At the El Juyo cave site near Santander in northern Spain (the neighborhood of the Altamira caves), a sanctuary was uncovered containing an altarlike stone slab that weighs nearly a ton and is supported by other vertical slabs of stone. It appears to be the shrine of the sanctuary, the focus of a group religion. The shrine area, covering 118 square feet, contains clay-faced mounds that cover trenches in the floor. The trenches hold a variety of deliberately arranged objects that may have been used as sacred accessories in ceremonies of some sort. Structured cave, sanctuary, shrine, and repositories—the rudimentary elements of religious architecture—are already here in primitive form. The site dates from about 12,000 B.C.

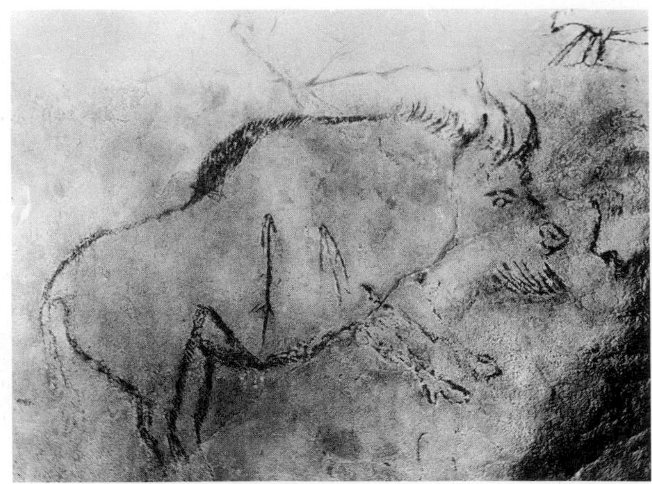

1-7 *Bison with Superposed Arrows,* Niaux, c. 13,000 B.C. 50″ long. Ariège, France.

entirely haphazard and seem to express an order in terms of the preferences and concerns of the hunter. Cattle and horses, for example, regularly appear together. The *palimpsest effect* of superimposing images one on top of another may be a spatial representation of time (one hunting season taking the place of another—a sort of mark-off calendar). The animals may be a kind of heraldic-totemistic image, representative of their blood relationship to different tribes, or they may be objects of worship, as was the buffalo for the peoples of the North American plains.

Abbé Breuil's "hunting-magic" theory had wide currency during the first half of this century. It is appealingly simple and has parallels in modern hunter-gatherer societies. In the late 1960s, Abbé Breuil's views were challenged and partly superseded by other, more complex interpretations. Two French anthropologists, André Leroi-Gourhan and Annette Laming-Emperaire, recognized a certain order in the arrangement of cave paintings, which formerly had been felt to be chaotically arranged. Leroi-Gourhan and Laming-Emperaire found that animals that represent maleness predominate in the peripheral areas of caves, while those that represent femaleness are concentrated in central areas. From such a seeming division between male and female, they extrapolated a social organization that was much more complex than any that formerly had been attributed to a foraging society.

Leroi-Gourhan's interpretation of cave painting, which does not explain the great diversity in image production, nor the effects that these images may have produced on their prehistoric viewers, is today dismissed as "monolithic" by a majority of scholars. In a partial return to Abbé Breuil's theory, Henri Delporte, of the Musée des Antiquités Nationales near

Paris, says: "I think it is possible that sometimes images were made for hunting magic in the way that Abbé Henri Breuil imagined. But I think there were probably many different reasons why people produced art of different kinds, and we should not just think of single explanations." Today the emphasis is on "context and a diversity of explanations." Anthropologists are searching for the social context of Paleolithic art and for those elements inherent in it that made it meaningful to the people who produced it. But so far, no one has found a completely satisfactory answer to the enigma of the caves.

THE REPRESENTATION OF THE HUMAN FIGURE

Human figures almost never appear among the vivid troops of animals portrayed in the cave paintings. At least two notable exceptions, however, are known to exist. A very puzzling picture at Lascaux (FIG. **1-8**) shows a stick-figure man, falling or fallen, before a huge bison that has been disemboweled, probably by the rhinoceros at the left, which slouches away from the scene. The two animals are rendered with all the skilled attention to animal detail we are accustomed to in cave art: the rhinoceros heavy and lumbering; the buffalo tense and bristling with rage, its bowels hanging from it in a heavy coil. But the bird-faced (masked?) man is rendered with the crude and clumsy touch of the unskilled at any time or place. His position is ambiguous. Is he dead or in an ecstatic trance? The meaning of the bird on the staff and of the spear and throw stick is no more obvious. We will not add to the already abundant speculation as to the meaning of this picture. A more important question deals with why the human and the animal figures are treated differently. Did early peoples distinguish themselves so much from the beasts that they could find no images suitable to self-depiction? Or were they afraid to cast a spell on themselves, as they cast it on the animals, by rendering their images visible?

Another (equally problematical) representation is found at Trois Frères in the Pyrenees. This depiction of a very strange humanoid creature—the so-called *Sorcerer*—is masked and wears the antlers of a reindeer (FIG. **1-9**). Is this the memory sketch of a shaman or witch doctor? The chamber in which the figure appears is crowded with beasts, and Abbé Breuil has suggested that the figure may be their god, who has descended into the witch doctor and filled him with his bestial power. It has also been suggested that this

1-8 *Well Scene,* Lascaux, *c.* 13,000 B.C. Bison 55″ high. Dordogne, France.

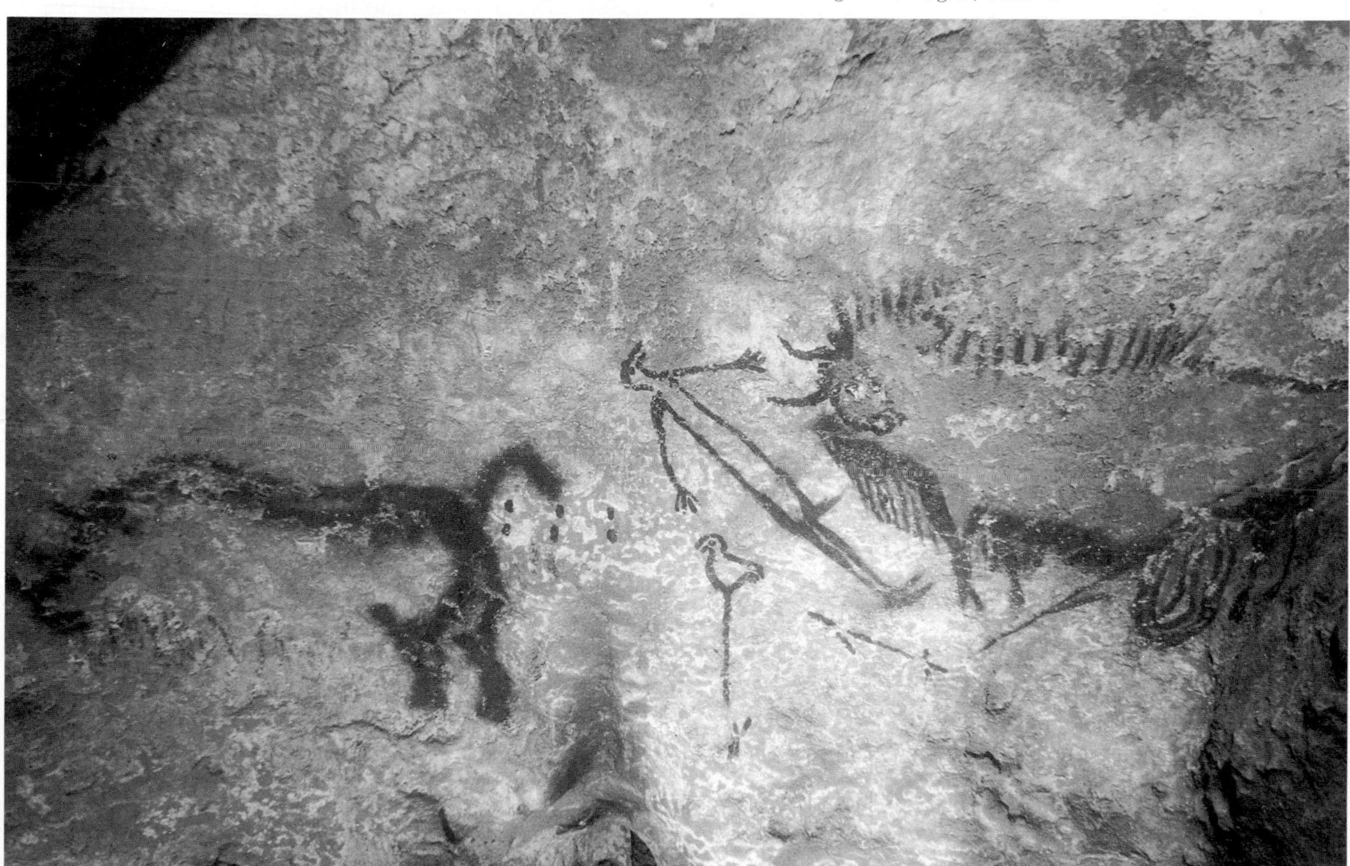

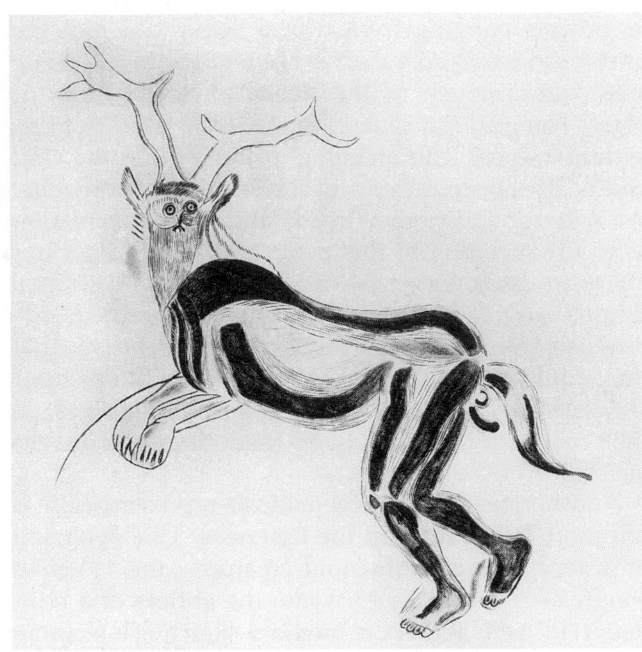

1-9 *Sorcerer,* Trois Frères, c. 13,000–11,000 B.C. 24″ high. Ariège, France.

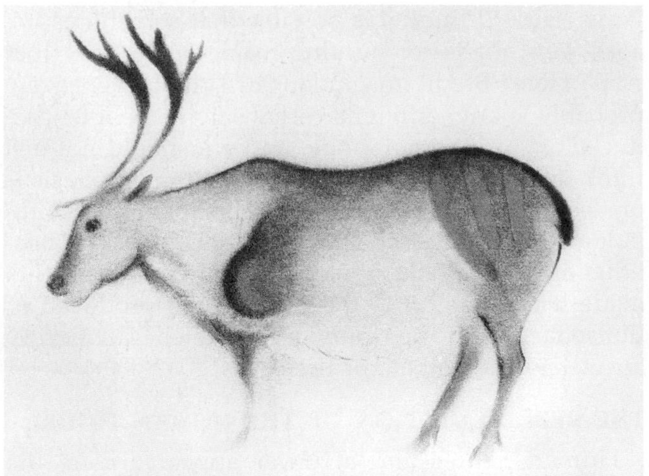

1-10 *Reindeer,* Font-de-Gaume, c. 13,000–11,000 B.C. Dordogne, France. (After a copy by Abbé Breuil.)

is only a hunter camouflaged to stalk deer, but again it would appear that, for Paleolithic peoples, human beings simply were not to be counted among the animals. At least their figures must be so disguised—perhaps to avoid magical self-involvement—as to be unrecognizable as human beings.

QUALITY

In trying to explain the great accomplishment of Stone Age peoples, we must not forget that their art is *art*. It is not simply that they made images, but that they made them skillfully and beautifully. Ancient and modern art have produced, along with masterpieces, images that are dull, prosaic, and of indifferent quality. The art of the caves is of extraordinary caliber. The splendid horse in the Axial Gallery at Lascaux (FIG. 1-6) has been called the *Chinese Horse* because its style strangely resembles Chinese painting of the highest quality. Not only do the outlines have the elastic strength and fluency that we find in Chinese calligraphy and brushwork, but the tone is so managed as to suggest both the turning under of the belly of the pregnant animal and the change in the color of the coat. At Font-de-Gaume, a painted reindeer (FIG. **1-10**) was executed with deft elegance in the contours and remarkable subtlety in the modeling tones. The grace of the antlers is effortlessly translated into an upward-sweeping line that renders the natural shapes with both strength and delicacy. Abbé Breuil, while copying the originals, discerned some highly sophisticated pictorial devices that one expects to find only in the art of far later times; for example, note the darkening of the forward contour of the left hind leg, which serves to bring it nearer to the observer than the right leg.

The pictures of cattle at Lascaux and elsewhere (FIG. 1-4) show a convention of representation of the horns that has been called *twisted perspective,* because we see the heads in profile but the horns from a different angle. Thus, the approach of the artist is not strictly or consistently *optical* (organized from the perspective of a fixed viewpoint). Rather, the approach is *descriptive* of the fact that cattle have two horns. Two horns would be part of the concepts "cow" and "bull." In strict optical-perspective profile, only one horn would be visible, but to paint the animal in that way would, as it were, amount to an incomplete definition of it. Twisted perspective was not used universally, however, and there is a style, thought to be a later development, that dispenses with it in favor of a very convincing illusionism.

Sculpture

The principal bequests of the hunter-artists are their paintings and engravings; we have seen that both abound at Lascaux. They also have left us sculpture in stone, ivory, bone, and antler. In the *Bison with Turned Head* (FIG. **1-11**), we are impressed by the striking vitality and simplicity with which the formal beauty is expressed. This piece, executed on reindeer horn, exhibits a simplicity and economy of means that distinguishes the great paintings. The head is turned so that it is entirely framed by the massive bulk of the body. The artist has achieved a vivid play of curve and countercurve and a surface contrast obtained by the use of decorative hatching to indicate

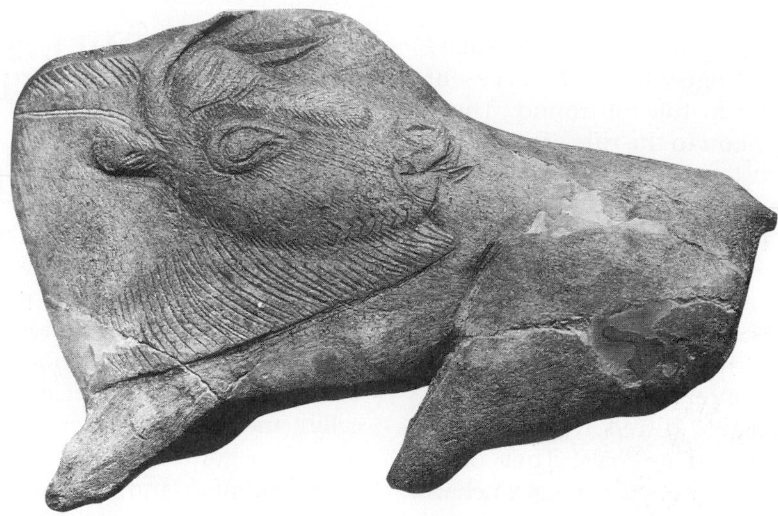

1-11 *Bison with Turned Head,* La Madeleine, *c.* 11,000–9,000 B.C. Reindeer horn, $4\frac{1}{8}''$ high. From Dordogne, France. Musée des Antiquités Nationales, St. Germain-en-Laye.

the mane. The artist would have been perfectly familiar with incising techniques; incising the outlines of a figure before the tones were introduced was the usual procedure for painting. But the artists of the caves went beyond incision and produced sculpture in *deep relief* and in the *full round.* An especially fine example of deep relief has been found in a rotundalike space that terminates a succession of chambers in the caves at Tuc d'Audoubert. Independent of the rock wall against which they are propped, a pair of lifelike bison has been modeled in clay (FIG. **1-12**). The distinguishing features are delineated as carefully as those of the reindeer-horn bison, and their placement produces sharp shadows that create an illusion of three-dimensionality, an effect doubtless intended by the sculptor. These Tuc d'Audoubert bison are related stylistically to painted examples (FIG. 1-7) and provide striking evidence of an already mature sense of three-dimensional form.

The Magdalenian culture and the cultures that went before were not uniquely French-Spanish. A distinct culture, Gravettian (28,000–20,000 B.C.), produced artifacts that are found from the Rhine to Russia, most abundantly in central Europe. Best known

1-12 *Bison,* Tuc d'Audoubert, *c.* 13,000–8000 B.C. Unbaked clay, each about 2′ long. Ariège, France.

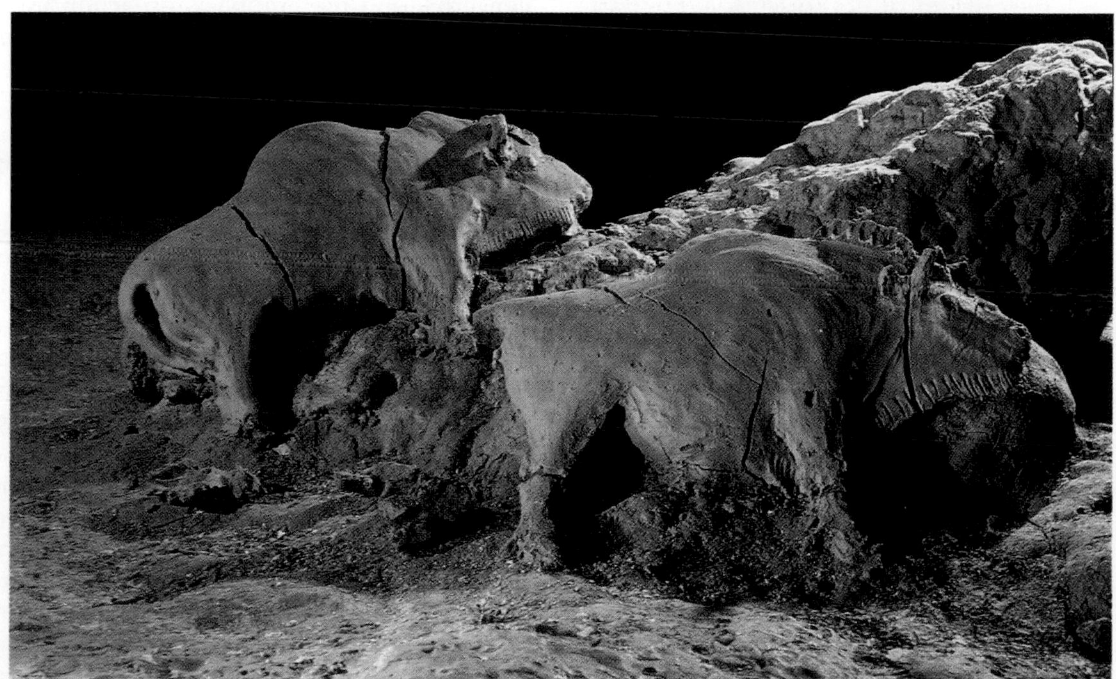

among these are small sculptures (formerly called "Venus figures" by archeologists), which represent the female figure executed in the full round. These figures constitute an exception to the rule of exclusion of the human figure from the cave artist's inventory of forms. Perhaps the most famous of them is the *Venus of Willendorf* (FIG. **1-13**), a figurine of a woman that is composed of a cluster of almost ball-like shapes. The anatomical exaggeration suggests that this and similar statuettes served as fertility fetishes; the needs for game and human offspring were one in the dangerous life of the hunter. But again the artistic approach to the human figure differs from the way these early artists represented animals. They obviously do not aim for that heightened realism so characteristic of their animal representations; facial features, for instance, are seldom indicated in these statuettes, and not even the heads are shown in some specimens. Evidently, the aim was not to show the female of the species, but rather the idea of female fecundity; the artist depicted not woman, but fertility.

1-13 *Venus of Willendorf*, c. 28,000–25,000 B.C. Limestone, $4\frac{1}{8}''$ high. Naturhistorisches Museum, Vienna. (Cast of original.)

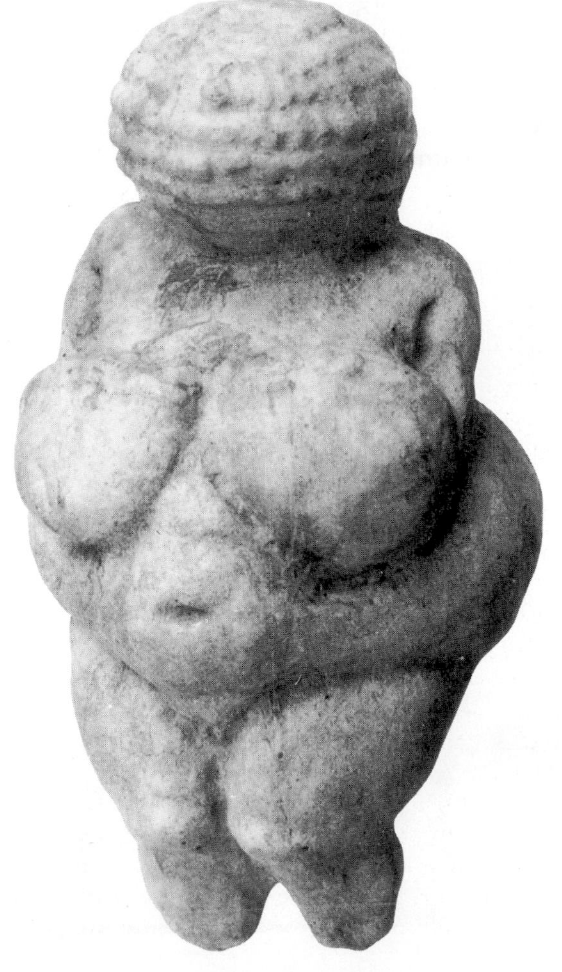

THE MIDDLE STONE AGE (MESOLITHIC)

Rock-shelter Paintings

Around 7000 B.C., the ice of the Paleolithic period melted as the climate grew warmer. The reindeer migrated north, the woolly mammoth and rhinoceros disappeared, and the hunters left their caves. The Ice Age gave way to a transitional period, the Mesolithic, during which Europe became climatically, geographically, and biologically much as it is today. In this period, a culture flourished and produced art that complements—and, indeed, may have partially originated from—cave art. Since 1903, diminutive, extraordinarily lively paintings of animals and men in scenes of the hunt, battle, ritual dance, and harvest have been discovered on the stone walls of shallow rock shelters among the barren hills along the east coast of Spain (the Spanish Levant). The artists show the same masterful skill in depicting animal figures as that demonstrated by their predecessors in the caves, and it may be that we have here specimens of a lingering tradition or long-persisting habit of vision and representation of animals. But what is strikingly new is the appearance of the human figure—not only singly, but in large, coherent groups with a wide variety of poses, subjects, and settings. We have seen that the human figure almost never appears in cave art; the falling or fallen man of the *Well Scene* (FIG. 1-8) at Lascaux is quite exceptional. In the rock-shelter paintings, the new sentiment for human themes and concerns, and the emphasis on action in which humans dominate animals are central. The new inventory of forms may have migrated across the Mediterranean from North Africa, where many paintings similar to those in the Spanish Levant have been found. Scholars have debated the dating of Spanish rock-shelter art and some now agree that its beginnings were around 7000 B.C. and that the style may have lasted (with many variations) until about 4000 B.C.

Some characteristic features of the rock paintings appear in an energetic group of five warriors found in the Gasulla gorge (FIG. **1-14**). The group, only about nine inches in width, shows a customary tense exaggeration of movement, a rhythmic repetition of basic shape, and a general sacrifice of naturalistic appearance to narrative and to unity of action. Even so, we can distinguish details that are economically descriptive—bows, arrows, and the feathered headdress of the leader. The widely splayed legs communicate a leaping stride, perhaps a march to battle or a ritual dance.

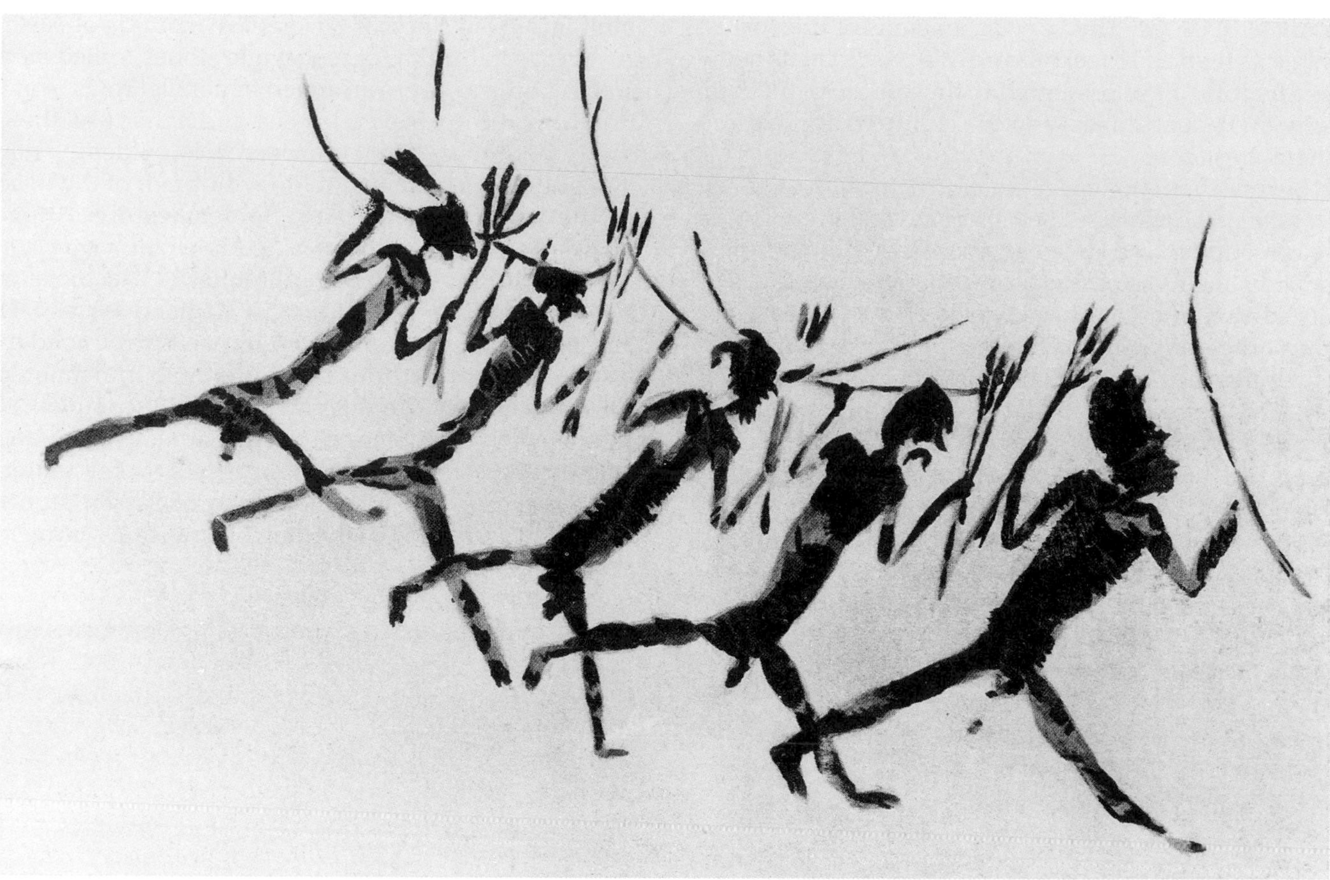

1-14 *Marching Warriors* (ritual dance?), Gasulla gorge, *c.* 7000–4000 B.C. Approx. 9″ wide. Castellón, Spain.

Other such paintings show an even greater uniformity of basic shape and a nervous, sharp angularity, which suggest the *pictograph* or even the *phonetic hieroglyph*. And over the millennia, rock-painting styles did become more abstract and schematic, more symbol than picture; it is likely that they recorded a step in the evolution of the *symbolic* from the *pictorial*—an evolution that in the Near East culminated in the invention of writing. Later on, the liveliness and spontaneity of the rock paintings were lost in the rigid uniformities of almost letterlike shapes repeated as if from a limited stock of signs.

Like the cave paintings, the rock paintings are probably of magical-religious significance, although some observers believe them to be no more than pictorial records of memorable events. The rock paintings are concentrated at particular sites that were used for long periods; nearby places, better suited for painting, were not used. This fact suggests that the sites were held sacred, not only by the Mesolithic painters, but also by artists working well into the historical period. Iberian and Latin inscriptions indicate that supernatural powers were ascribed to some of these holy places as late as the Roman era.

THE NEW STONE AGE (NEOLITHIC)

In a supreme feat of intellection, Paleolithic peoples learned to abstract their world by making a picture of it. They sought to control the world by capturing and holding its image. In the Neolithic period, human beings took a giant stride toward the actual, concrete control of their environment by settling in fixed abodes and domesticating plants and animals. Their food supply assured, they changed from hunters to herdsmen, to farmers, and, perhaps as early as 7000 B.C. in the Near East, to townsmen. The wandering hunter settled down to organized community living in villages surrounded by cultivated fields. Then began the long evolution toward the incredible technological command of the physical environment that exists today.

Recent research seems to indicate that local Neolithic populations in several areas of western Europe developed a monumental architecture consisting of graves and of rows or circles of massive, rough-hewn stones. These constructions have been dated to as early as 4000 B.C. The very dimensions of the stones, some as high as 17 feet tall and at a weight of as many as fifty tons, have prompted the historian to call them *megaliths* (great stones) and the culture that produced them *megalithic*.

Several types of megalithic structures have been classified. The *dolmen* consists of several great stones set on end, with a large covering slab. Dolmens may be the remains of passage graves from which a covering earth mound has been washed away. The *passage grave*, the dominant megalithic tomb type (with literally thousands having been found in France and England), has a corridor lined with large stone slabs leading to a circular chamber in which each of numerous rings of stones projects inward beyond the underlying course, until the rings close at the top (a *corbeled* vault construction). These graves were frequently built into a hill slope or covered by mounds of earth. At Carnac in Brittany, great single stones, called *menhirs*, set on end, were arranged in parallel rows, some of which run for several miles and consist of thousands of stones. Their purpose was evidently religious and may have had to do with a cult of the dead or the worship of the sun. Sometimes these huge stones were arranged in a circle known as a *cromlech*. Among the most imposing cromlechs are those at Avebury and at Stonehenge in England (FIGS. **1-15** and **1-16**). The structure at Avebury is surrounded by a stone bank about four-fifths of a mile in diameter. The remains at Stonehenge are of a complex of rough-cut sarsen (a form of sandstone) stones and smaller "bluestones" (various igneous rocks). Outermost is a ring of large monoliths of sarsen stones capped by lintels. Next is a ring of bluestones, which,

1-15 Stonehenge, *c.* 2000 B.C. 97′ in diameter. Salisbury Plain, Wiltshire, England.

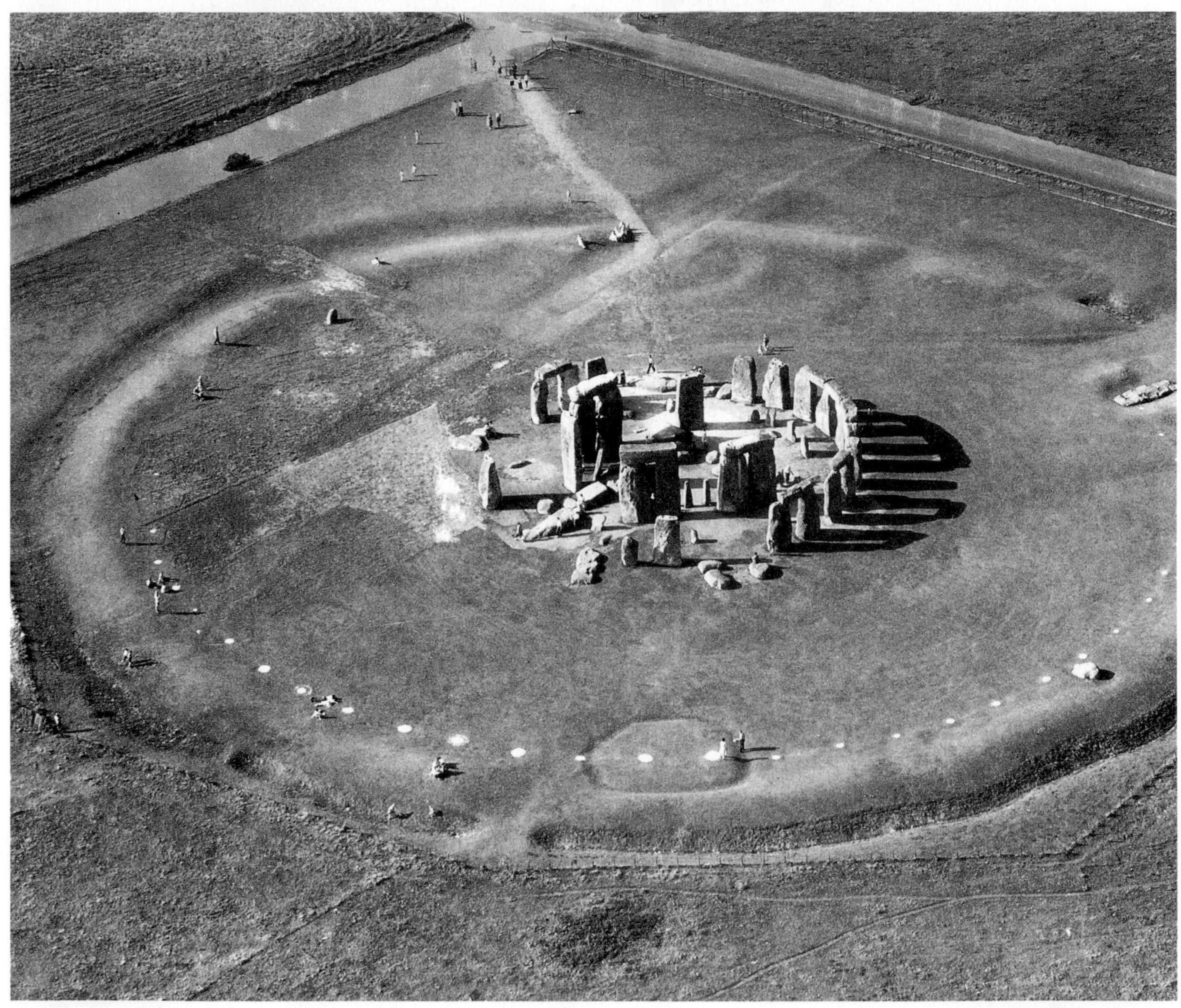

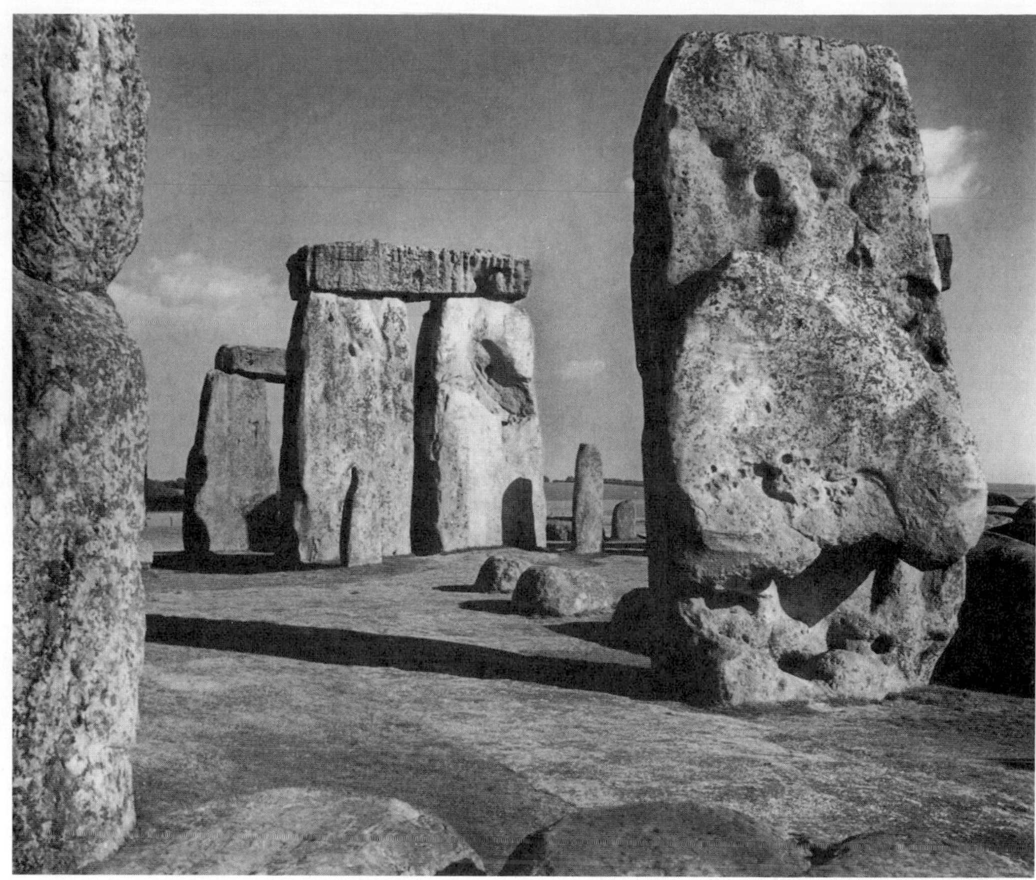

1-16 Stonehenge, trilithons (lintel-topped pairs of stones at center). Approx. 24′ high (including lintel). Salisbury Plain, Wiltshire, England.

in turn, encircled a horseshoe (open end facing east) of *trilithons*—five lintel-topped pairs of the largest sarsens, each weighing forty-five to fifty tons. Standing apart and to the east is the "heel-stone," which, for a person looking outward from the center of the complex, would have marked the point at which the sun rose at the midsummer solstice.

Stonehenge seems to have been built in several phases around 2000 B.C., according to recently corrected radiocarbon dates. Computer-based calculations have raised something of a controversy, not so much over the date as over the purpose of Stonehenge, which seems to have been a kind of astronomical observatory. These mysterious structures, believed in the Middle Ages to have been the work of the magician Merlin, who spirited them from Ireland, or the work of a race of giants, have come in our own time to be thought of as a remarkably accurate calendar—a testimony to the rapidly developing intellectual powers of humans. Even in their ruined condition, the monoliths of Stonehenge, created by heroic physical and intellectual human effort, possess a solemn majesty. At Avebury, as at Stonehenge, the series of concentric circles with connecting curvilinear pathways or avenues conveys a feeling for order, symmetry, and rhythm that is evidence not only of well-developed and systematized ceremonial rituals, but perhaps also of a maturing geometrical sense born of the observation of the apparent movements of the sun and moon.

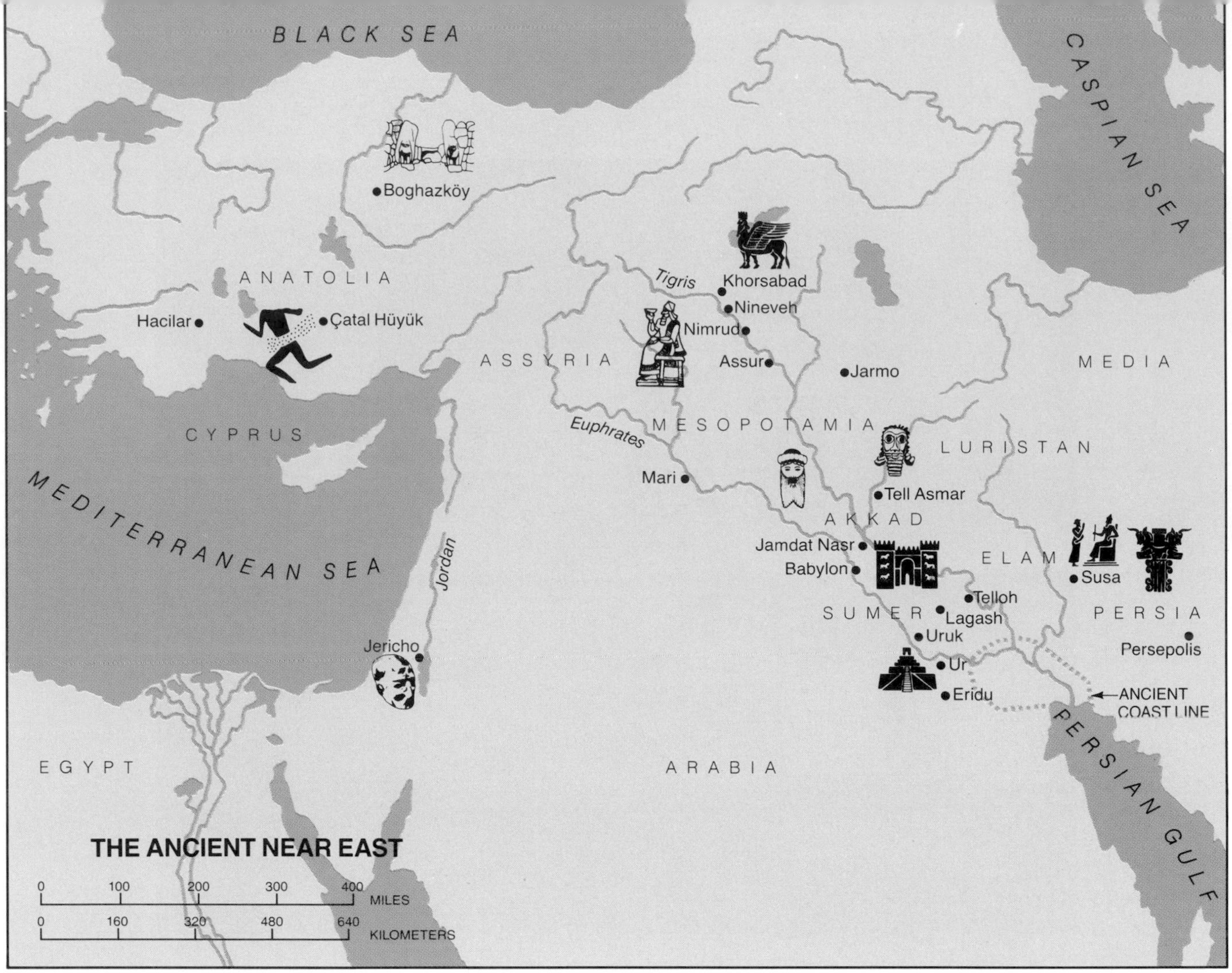

THE ANCIENT NEAR EAST

BLACK SEA
CASPIAN SEA
MEDITERRANEAN SEA
PERSIAN GULF
Boghazköy
ANATOLIA
Hacilar
Çatal Hüyük
CYPRUS
Tigris
Khorsabad
Nineveh
Nimrud
Assur
Jarmo
ASSYRIA
MEDIA
Euphrates
MESOPOTAMIA
LURISTAN
Mari
Tell Asmar
AKKAD
Jamdat Nasr
Babylon
ELAM
Susa
Telloh
SUMER
Lagash
PERSIA
Uruk
Persepolis
Ur
Eridu
ANCIENT COAST LINE
Jordan
Jericho
EGYPT
ARABIA

0 100 200 300 400 MILES
0 160 320 480 640 KILOMETERS

7000 B.C.	6000	3500	3000	2500	2300	c. 2150	2000
MESOLITHIC PERIOD	NEOLITHIC PERIOD	PROTOLITERATE PERIOD	EARLY DYNASTIC PERIOD (SUMERIAN)	FIRST DYNASTY OF UR (SUMERIAN)	AKKADIAN DYNASTY	THIRD DYNASTY OF UR (NEO-SUMERIAN)	

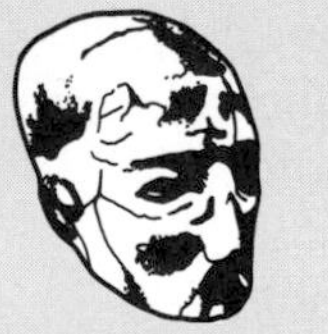

Human Skull, Jericho
c. 7000–6000 B.C.

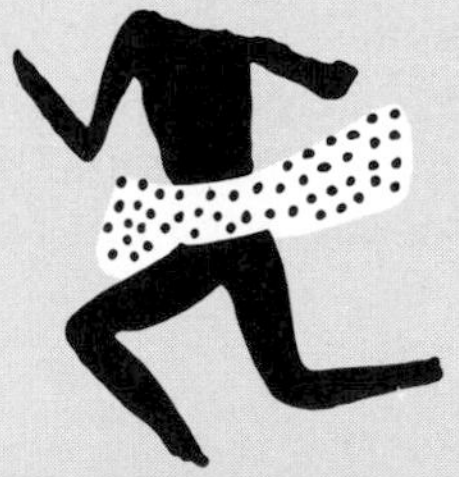

Dancing Hunter
c. 5750 B.C.

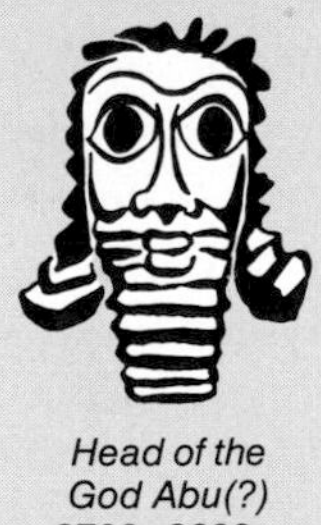

Head of the God Abu(?)
c. 2700–2600 B.C.

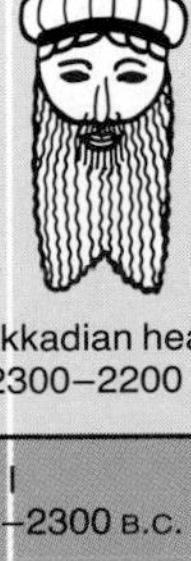

Akkadian head
c. 2300–2200 B.C.

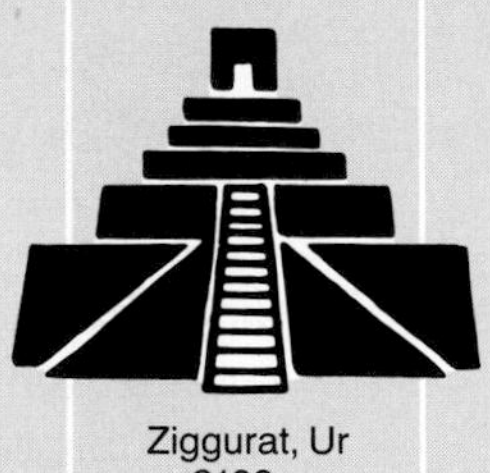

Ziggurat, Ur
c. 2100 B.C.

Jericho settled

Çatal Hüyük settled

Irrigation methods developed

Invention of the wheel

Beginnings of formal religion

Development of writing and beginnings of recorded history

Flowering of independent city-states

Sargon I
c. 2350–2300 B.C.

Guti invasions

2

THE ANCIENT NEAR EAST

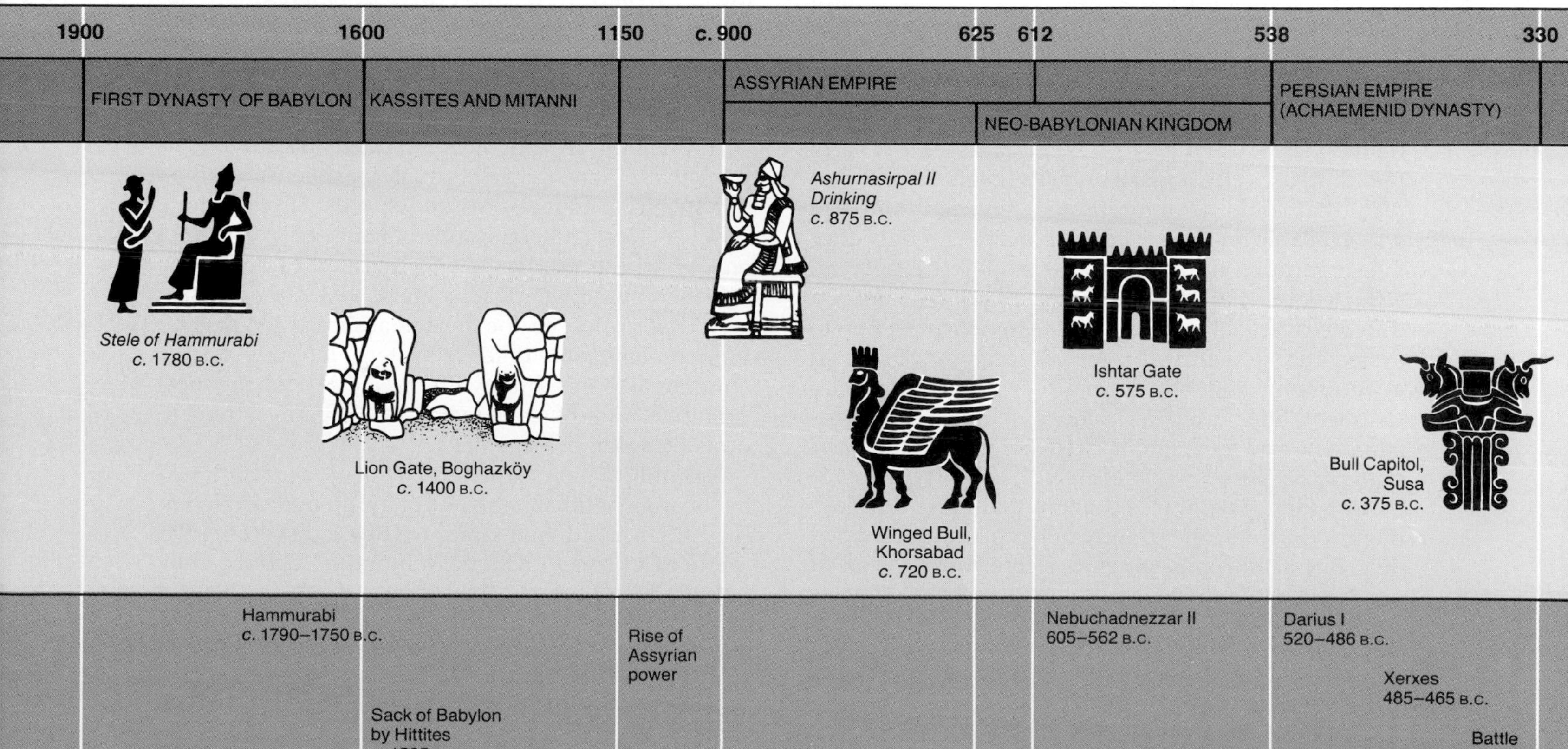

JUST HOW AND WHY the state of human society that we call civilization began, we are not certain; we are more certain where and when it began. Since World War II, archeologists have been uncovering sites in the Near East that give clear evidence of a definite transformation beginning as early as 8000 B.C. The onset of civilized life is marked off from all that went before by the development of agriculture. The conventional division of prehistory into the Paleolithic, Mesolithic, and Neolithic periods is based on the development of stone implements. That distinction, however, is not as basic and decisive as the simpler distinction between an age of food gathering and an age of food production. In this scheme, the Paleolithic period corresponds roughly to the age of food gathering, and the Mesolithic period, the last phase of that age, is marked by intensified food gathering and the domestication of the dog. The proto-Neolithic period of incipient food production and greater domestication of animals precedes the Neolithic period, when agriculture and stock-raising became man's major food sources.

At one time, researchers proposed that the area we know today as the Near East (Egypt, Israel, Syria, Iraq, Iran, Lebanon, Jordan, and Turkey) dried out into desert and semidesert after the last retreat of the glaciers, compelling the inhabitants to move to the fertile alluvial valleys of the Nile in Egypt and the Tigris and Euphrates in Mesopotamia (parts of modern Syria and Iraq). This view is no longer tenable in light of archeological and paleoenvironmental findings. The oldest settled communities are found not in the river valleys but in the grassy uplands bordering them. These regions provided the necessary preconditions for the development of agriculture. Species of native plants, such as wild wheat and barley, were plentiful, as were herds of animals (goats, sheep, and pigs) that could be domesticated; sufficient rain also was available for the raising of crops. It was only after village farming life was well developed that settlers, attracted by the greater fertility of the soil, moved into the river valleys and deltas. There, in addition to systematic agriculture, civilized societies originated government, law, and formal religion, and such instrumentalities and techniques as writing, measurement and calculation, weaving, metalcraft, and pottery.

For a long time, it was thought that these developments occurred concurrently in Egypt and Mesopotamia. But again, archeology has forced a revision of our views. It is now clear that Mesopotamia and its neighbors were far ahead of Egypt temporally. Village farming communities like Jarmo in Iraq and Çatal Hüyük in southern Anatolia (Turkey) date back to the mid-seventh millennium B.C., and the remarkable fortified town of Jericho, before whose walls Joshua appeared thousands of years later, is even older. The oldest villages in Egypt, in the Faiyûm district near the Nile Delta, do not seem to have been founded before 4500 B.C., and an urban society like that of Mesopotamia seems never to have developed there. The invention of writing in Mesopotamia preceded writing in Egypt by several hundred years, and it may be that the whole development of Egyptian civilization was the result of Mesopotamian influence.

THE BEGINNINGS

Jericho

By 7000 B.C., agriculture was well established in at least three Near Eastern regions: Jordan, Iran, and Anatolia (Turkey). Although no remains of domestic cereal grains have been found that can be dated before 7000 B.C., the advanced state of agriculture at that time presupposes a long development; indeed, the very existence of a town like Jericho gives strong support to this assumption. The site of Jericho—a plateau in the Jordan River valley with an unfailing spring—was occupied by a small village as early as the ninth millennium B.C. This proto-Neolithic village underwent spectacular development around 8000 B.C., when a new town was built with houses of mud brick on round or oval stone foundations. As the town's wealth grew and powerful neighbors established themselves, the need for protection resulted in the first known permanent stone fortifications. By approximately 7500 B.C., the town, estimated to have had a population of over two thousand people, was surrounded by a wide, rock-cut ditch and a five-foot-thick wall. Into this wall, which has been preserved to a height of 12 feet, was built a great circular stone tower, 30 feet in height and diameter (FIG. **2-1**). Not enough of the site has been excavated to determine whether this tower was solitary, like the keeps in medieval castles, or one of several similar towers that formed a complete defense system. In either case, a structure like this, built with the aid of only the most primitive kinds of stone tools, was certainly a tremendous technical achievement.

Around 7000 B.C., the Jericho site was abandoned by its original inhabitants, but new settlers arrived in the early seventh millennium. They built rectangular mud-brick houses on stone foundations and carefully plastered and painted their floors and walls. Several of the excavated buildings seem to have served as shrines, the plan of one of them being remarkably similar to that of the later Greek *megaron* (see FIG.

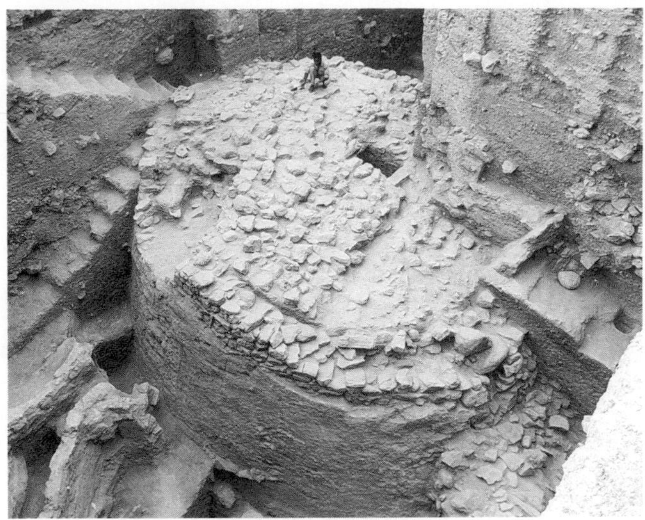

2-1 Great stone tower built into the settlement wall, Jericho, *c.* 8000–7000 B.C.

5-20a). These settlers fashioned statuettes of a mother goddess and of animals associated with a fertility cult. Most striking is a group of human skulls on which the features have been "reconstructed" in plaster (FIG. **2-2**). Subtly modeled, with inlaid seashells for eyes and painted hair (including a painted mustache that has been preserved on one specimen), their appearance is strikingly lifelike. Because the skulls were detached from the bodies before burial and displayed above ground, they may have been regarded as "spirit traps," implying a well-developed belief in survival after the death of the body.

2-2 Human skull, Jericho, *c.* 7000–6000 B.C. Features molded in plaster, painted and inlaid with shell.

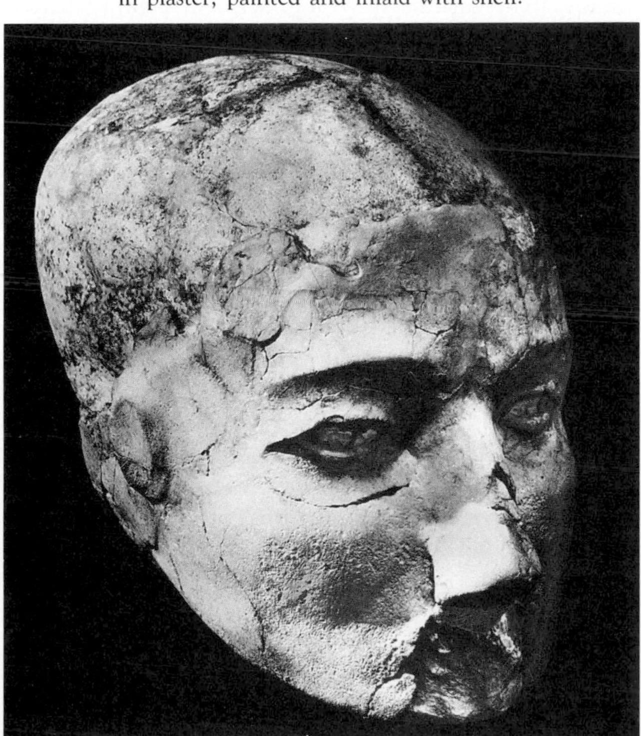

Çatal Hüyük

Perhaps even more remarkable than the Jericho finds are discoveries in Anatolia. Excavations at Hacilar and Çatal Hüyük have shown not only that the central Anatolian plateau was the site of a flourishing Neolithic culture between 7000 and 5000 B.C., but also that it may well have been culturally the most advanced region of its time. Twelve successive building levels excavated at Çatal Hüyük between 1961 and 1965 have been dated between 6500 and 5700 B.C. On a single 32-acre site (of which only one acre has been explored), it is possible to retrace, in an unbroken sequence, the evolution of a Neolithic culture over a period of eight hundred years.

Along with Jericho, Çatal Hüyük has been called "one of man's first essays in the development of town life." The regularity of the town plan suggests that it was built according to some a priori scheme. A peculiarity of the town is its complete lack of streets; the houses adjoin each other, and access is provided over their roofs (FIG. **2-3**). Impractical as such an arrangement may appear today (although it survives in parts of central Turkey and western Iran), it did offer some advantages. The buildings, being attached, were more stable than freestanding structures and, at the limits of the town site, formed a perimeter wall well suited to defense against human or natural forces. Thus, if an enemy managed to breach the exterior wall, he would find himself not inside the town, but inside a single room with the defenders waiting for him on the roof—a dismal prospect at best.

2-3 Schematic reconstruction of a section of Level VI, Çatal Hüyük, *c.* 6000–5900 B.C. (After J. Mellaart.)

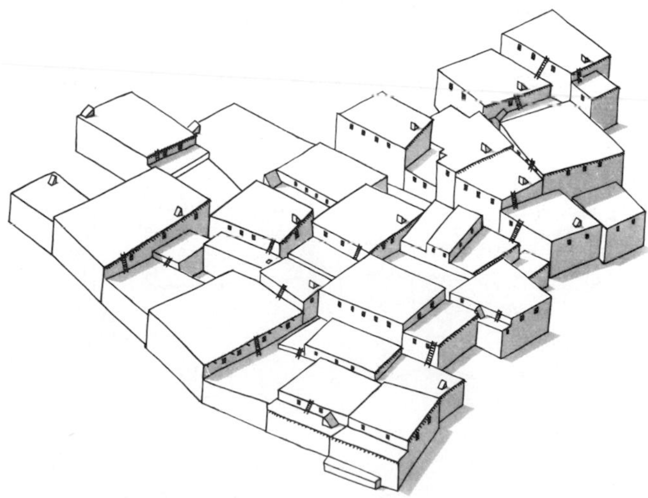

Here and there, the dense building mass at Çatal Hüyük is interrupted by an open court, which served as a garbage dump. Liberal amounts of ashes mixed in with the refuse acted as sterilizers, although probably not as deodorants. The houses, constructed of mud brick strengthened by sturdy timber frames, varied in size but were of a standard plan. Walls and floors were plastered and painted, and platforms along walls served for sleep, work, and eating. A great number of shrines have been found intermingled with standard houses. Varying with the different levels, the average ratio is about one shrine to every four houses. This figure may not hold true for the entire town; only about one-thirtieth of the settlement area has been excavated.

The shrines (FIG. **2-4**) are distinguished from the house structures by the greater richness of their interior decoration, which consisted of wall paintings, plaster reliefs, animal heads, bucrania (bovine skulls), and cult statuettes. Bulls' horns, which adorn most shrines, sometimes in considerable numbers, were set into stylized, remodeled heads of bulls or into benches and pillars and may have been thought to protect the inhabitants and ward off evil. Nothing, however, suggests that the bull, or any other animal, was regarded as a deity. Cult statuettes found at Çatal Hüyük indicate that the people believed their gods to have human form, either male or female. When represented in association with animals (the female deity usually with leopards; the male, with a bull), the animals are always shown as subservient.

The statuettes are of stone or baked clay. Most are quite small (2–8 inches high); only a few reach 12 inches. All the female figures, which predominate, seem to represent a mother goddess, but in a great variety of aspects: young, old, in ritual marriage, in pregnancy, giving birth, and as ruler of wild animals. These figures are described explicitly, and although the bulbous forms of the headless *Seated Goddess* (FIG. **2-5**) may remind us of the *Venus of Willendorf* (FIG. 1-13), the artist's approach to the subject is quite realistic. Unlike the Paleolithic artist, who tried to represent the abstract concept of fertility, the Neolithic sculptor converts an abstract being (a goddess) into a human figure. The breasts are sensitively modeled, the small hands carefully rendered, and, judging from other examples, it may be safely assumed that the lost head had fairly well described facial features. The figure is painted with crosslike floral patterns that are known also from wall paintings and may endow the goddess with the specific function of an agrarian deity.

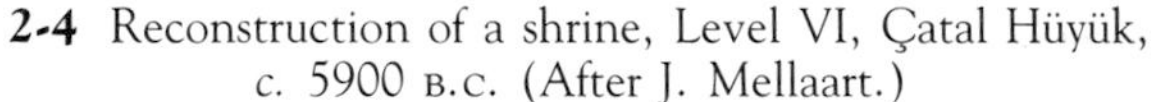
2-4 Reconstruction of a shrine, Level VI, Çatal Hüyük, c. 5900 B.C. (After J. Mellaart.)

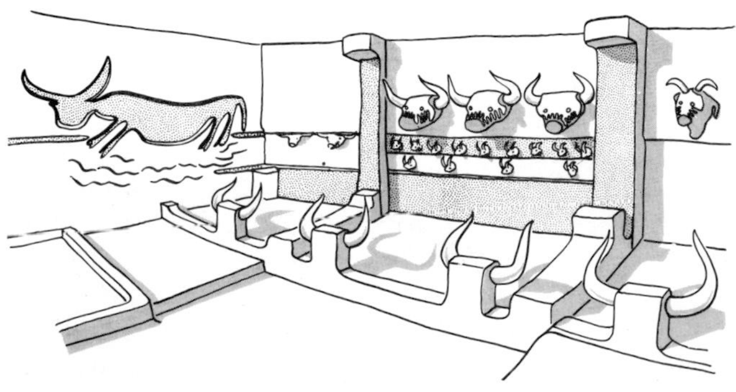

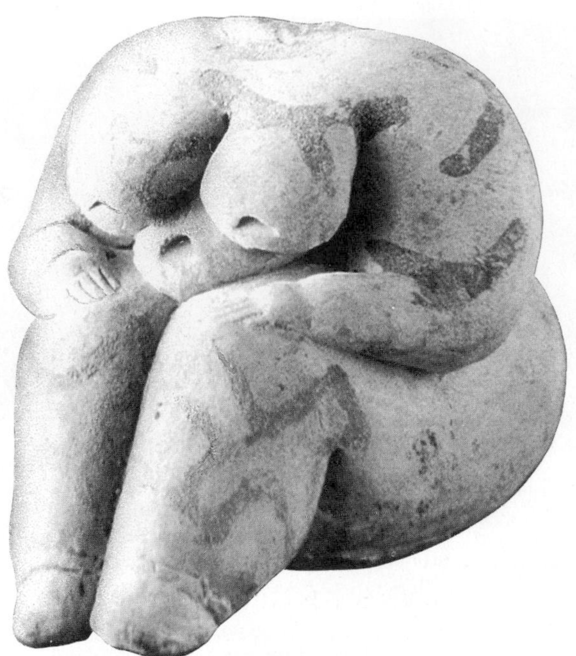
2-5 *Seated Goddess*, Çatal Hüyük, c. 5900 B.C. Fired clay, approx. 2″ high.

Fertility and agricultural symbolism dominate the art of the upper (later) levels of Çatal Hüyük, but hunting also played an important part in the early Neolithic economy; Paleolithic hunting rituals survived far into the Neolithic period. Numerous crude animal figurines, broken and damaged, have been found at Çatal Hüyük. They may have served as animal surrogates during hunting rites and then have been buried in pits. The importance of hunting as a food source (until about 5700 B.C.) is reflected also in wall paintings, in which, in the older shrines, hunting scenes predominate. In style and concept, the *Deer Hunt* (FIG. **2-6**) recalls the rock-shelter paintings of the Spanish Levant, but the figures at Çatal Hüyük are more full-bodied and are rendered with greater realism. The artist used a full range of pigments, primarily derived from minerals, which were applied with a brush to the white background of dry plaster.

Paris, says: "I think it is possible that sometimes images were made for hunting magic in the way that Abbé Henri Breuil imagined. But I think there were probably many different reasons why people produced art of different kinds, and we should not just think of single explanations." Today the emphasis is on "context and a diversity of explanations." Anthropologists are searching for the social context of Paleolithic art and for those elements inherent in it that made it meaningful to the people who produced it. But so far, no one has found a completely satisfactory answer to the enigma of the caves.

THE REPRESENTATION OF THE HUMAN FIGURE

Human figures almost never appear among the vivid troops of animals portrayed in the cave paintings. At least two notable exceptions, however, are known to exist. A very puzzling picture at Lascaux (FIG. **1-8**) shows a stick-figure man, falling or fallen, before a huge bison that has been disemboweled, probably by the rhinoceros at the left, which slouches away from the scene. The two animals are rendered with all the skilled attention to animal detail we are accustomed to in cave art: the rhinoceros heavy and lumbering; the buffalo tense and bristling with rage, its bowels hanging from it in a heavy coil. But the bird-faced (masked?) man is rendered with the crude and clumsy touch of the unskilled at any time or place. His position is ambiguous. Is he dead or in an ecstatic trance? The meaning of the bird on the staff and of the spear and throw stick is no more obvious. We will not add to the already abundant speculation as to the meaning of this picture. A more important question deals with why the human and the animal figures are treated differently. Did early peoples distinguish themselves so much from the beasts that they could find no images suitable to self-depiction? Or were they afraid to cast a spell on themselves, as they cast it on the animals, by rendering their images visible?

Another (equally problematical) representation is found at Trois Frères in the Pyrenees. This depiction of a very strange humanoid creature—the so-called *Sorcerer*—is masked and wears the antlers of a reindeer (FIG. **1-9**). Is this the memory sketch of a shaman or witch doctor? The chamber in which the figure appears is crowded with beasts, and Abbé Breuil has suggested that the figure may be their god, who has descended into the witch doctor and filled him with his bestial power. It has also been suggested that this

1-8 *Well Scene,* Lascaux, *c.* 13,000 B.C. Bison 55″ high. Dordogne, France.

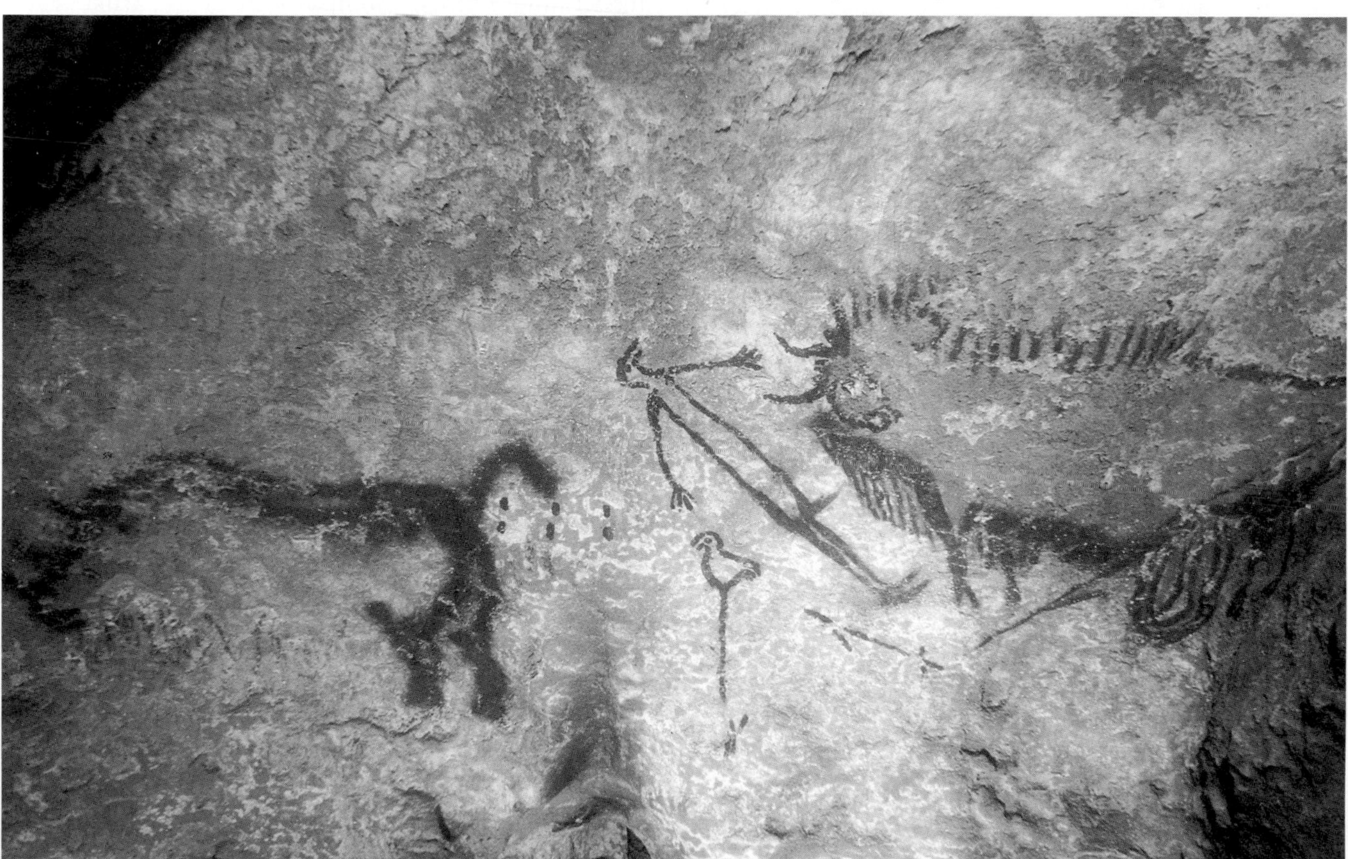

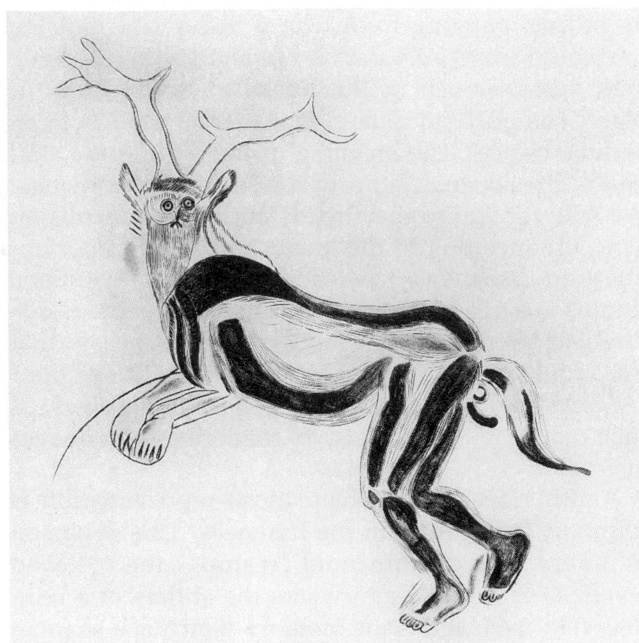

1-9 *Sorcerer*, Trois Frères, c. 13,000–11,000 B.C. 24″ high. Ariège, France.

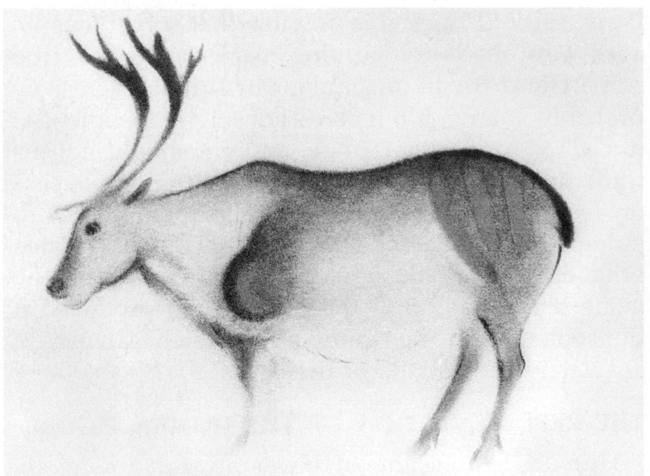

1-10 *Reindeer*, Font-de-Gaume, c. 13,000–11,000 B.C. Dordogne, France. (After a copy by Abbé Breuil.)

is only a hunter camouflaged to stalk deer, but again it would appear that, for Paleolithic peoples, human beings simply were not to be counted among the animals. At least their figures must be so disguised—perhaps to avoid magical self-involvement—as to be unrecognizable as human beings.

QUALITY

In trying to explain the great accomplishment of Stone Age peoples, we must not forget that their art is *art*. It is not simply that they made images, but that they made them skillfully and beautifully. Ancient and modern art have produced, along with masterpieces, images that are dull, prosaic, and of indifferent quality. The art of the caves is of extraordinary caliber. The splendid horse in the Axial Gallery at Lascaux (FIG. 1-6) has been called the *Chinese Horse* because its style strangely resembles Chinese painting of the highest quality. Not only do the outlines have the elastic strength and fluency that we find in Chinese calligraphy and brushwork, but the tone is so managed as to suggest both the turning under of the belly of the pregnant animal and the change in the color of the coat. At Font-de-Gaume, a painted reindeer (FIG. **1-10**) was executed with deft elegance in the contours and remarkable subtlety in the modeling tones. The grace of the antlers is effortlessly translated into an upward-sweeping line that renders the natural shapes with both strength and delicacy. Abbé Breuil, while copying the originals, discerned some highly sophisticated pictorial devices that one expects to find only in the art of far later times; for example, note the darkening of the forward contour of the left hind leg, which serves to bring it nearer to the observer than the right leg.

The pictures of cattle at Lascaux and elsewhere (FIG. 1-4) show a convention of representation of the horns that has been called *twisted perspective*, because we see the heads in profile but the horns from a different angle. Thus, the approach of the artist is not strictly or consistently *optical* (organized from the perspective of a fixed viewpoint). Rather, the approach is *descriptive* of the fact that cattle have two horns. Two horns would be part of the concepts "cow" and "bull." In strict optical-perspective profile, only one horn would be visible, but to paint the animal in that way would, as it were, amount to an incomplete definition of it. Twisted perspective was not used universally, however, and there is a style, thought to be a later development, that dispenses with it in favor of a very convincing illusionism.

Sculpture

The principal bequests of the hunter-artists are their paintings and engravings; we have seen that both abound at Lascaux. They also have left us sculpture in stone, ivory, bone, and antler. In the *Bison with Turned Head* (FIG. **1-11**), we are impressed by the striking vitality and simplicity with which the formal beauty is expressed. This piece, executed on reindeer horn, exhibits a simplicity and economy of means that distinguishes the great paintings. The head is turned so that it is entirely framed by the massive bulk of the body. The artist has achieved a vivid play of curve and countercurve and a surface contrast obtained by the use of decorative hatching to indicate

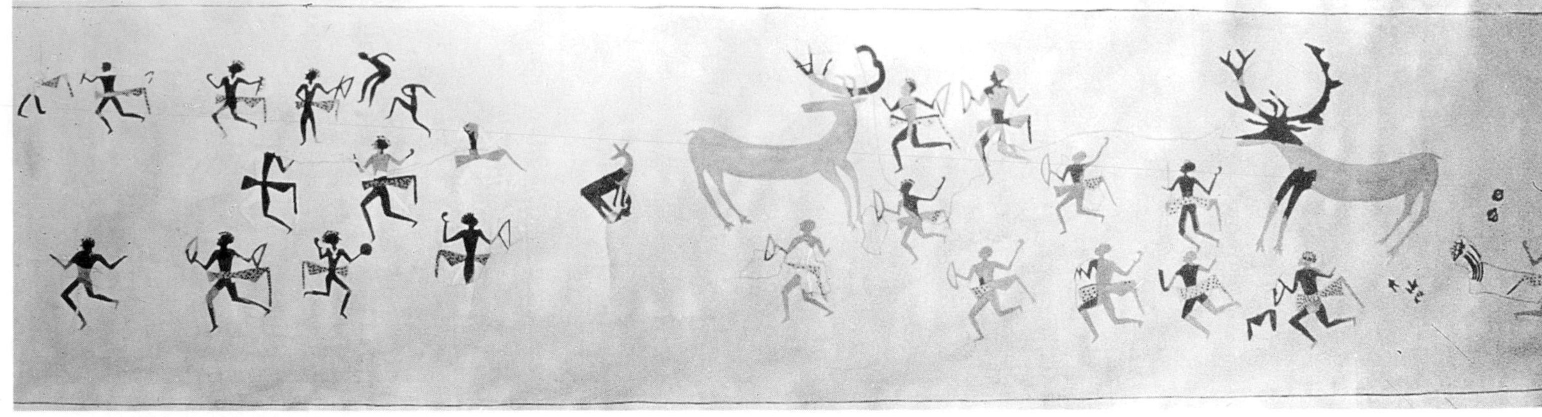

2-6 *Deer Hunt,* detail of a copy of a wall painting from Level III, Çatal Hüyük, *c.* 5750 B.C.

A fragment from the *Deer Hunt* (FIG. **2-7**) shows a dancing hunter, dressed in a white loincloth and a leopard skin, holding a bow in one hand. The speed of his movement is emphasized by the manner in which the leopard skin whirls around his waist. Once the apparently ritual function of these paintings had been fulfilled, they were covered with a layer of white plaster and later replaced with a new painting of a similar or a different subject.

In one of the older shrines at Çatal Hüyük, a painting was uncovered that has been interpreted as a pure landscape (FIG. **2-8**). As such, it would be unique for thousands of years into the future. According to carbon-14 dating, the painting was executed soon after 6200 B.C. In the foreground is what may be a town, with rectangular houses neatly laid out side by side, perhaps representing Çatal Hüyük itself. Behind the town, on a smaller scale, as though far away, appears a mountain with two peaks; dots and lines issuing from the higher of the two cones may represent a volcanic eruption. The mountain has been tentatively identified as the 10,600-foot Hasan Dag, which was located within view of Çatal Hüyük and was the only twin-peaked volcano in central Anatolia. Because the painting appears on the walls of a shrine, the conjectured volcanic eruption would have had some religious meaning. Although the artist may have linked the event with the underworld and witnessed it with fearful awe, this dread may have been mingled with gratitude to a bountiful Mother Earth; it is believed that Çatal Hüyük derived much of its wealth from trade in obsidian, a vitreous volcanic stone easily chipped into fine cutting edges and highly valued by Neolithic tool- and weapon-makers.

2-7 *Dancing Hunter,* fragment of a wall painting, a part of which is shown in copy in FIG. 2-6.

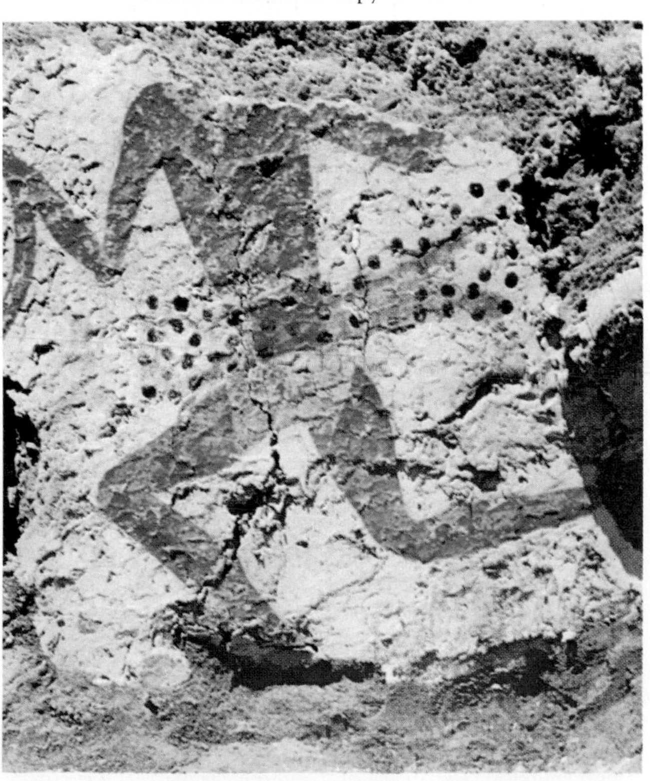

The rich finds at Çatal Hüyük give the impression of a prosperous and well-ordered society that practiced a great variety of arts and crafts. In addition to painting and sculpture, weaving and pottery were well established, and even the art of smelting copper and lead in small quantities was known before 6000 B.C. The society seems to have been conservative in its long retention of Paleolithic traditions and practices, but it also was progressive in its slow but relentless achievement of a complex, fully food-producing economy. In the arts, this development is perhaps mirrored in a de-emphasis of realism in favor of a more abstract symbolism, in a gradual decline in the production of statuettes representing male deities,

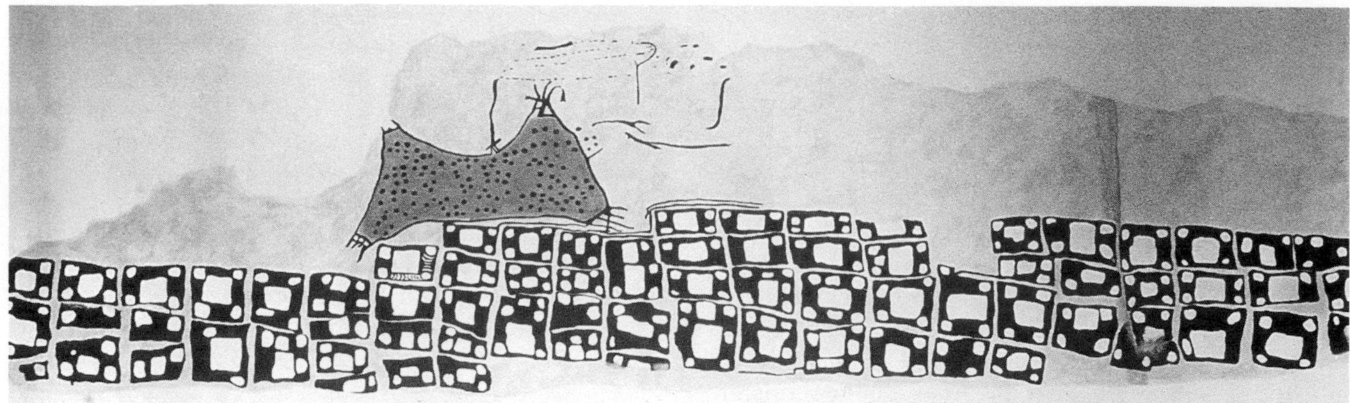

2-8 *Landscape with Volcanic Eruption* (?), detail of a copy of a wall painting from Level VII, Çatal Hüyük, c. 6150 B.C.

and in the disappearance of hunting scenes. At the same time, representations of the mother goddess increased in number, perhaps reflecting a corresponding change in the importance, if not the social position, of women. As agriculture took precedence over hunting, female occupations, like the milling of grain, baking, weaving, and the care and feeding of domestic animals, became ever more important. At Çatal Hüyük, the conversion to a fully agrarian economy appears to have been completed by about 5700 B.C. Less than a century later, the site was abandoned. A probably related culture at Hacilar, two hundred miles to the west, provided an afterglow, but by about 5000 B.C., the limelight shifted eastward to Mesopotamia and Iran, and southward to Syria.

SUMER

Some time in the early fourth millennium B.C., a critical event—the settlement of the great river valleys—took place in Mesopotamia. Writing, art, monumental architecture, and new political forms were introduced in Mesopotamia and Egypt shortly thereafter, but with striking differences in function. As Henri Frankfort describes it:

> The earliest written documents of Mesopotamia . . . facilitated the administration of large economic units, the temple communities. The earliest Egyptian inscriptions were legends on royal monuments or seal engravings identifying the king's officials. The earliest representations in Mesopotamian art are preponderantly religious; in Egyptian art, they celebrate royal achievements and consist of historical subjects. Monumental architecture consists, in Mesopotamia, of temples; in Egypt, of royal tombs. The earliest civilized society of Mesopotamia crystallized, in separate nuclei, a number of distinct, autonomous cities—clear-cut, self-assertive polities—with the surrounding lands to sustain each one. Egyptian society assumed the form of the single, united, but rural domain of an absolute monarch.*

Thus, not one, but *two* civilizations emerged, each with its own special character. From this time forward, world history was to be the record of the birth, development, and disappearance of civilizations and the rise and decline within them of peoples, states, and nations. It is with these two mighty, contrasting civilizations bordering the eastern Mediterranean region that the drama of Western man truly begins. One must not think, however, that these two distinct societies were geographically or culturally isolated from one another. Ancient Palestine (land of the Phoenicians) and Syria connected them on the west. On the east, Mesopotamia adjoined the vast territory of Iran and the north Indian civilization of the Indus River valley, with its important city of Mohenjo-Daro. Thus, a continuous range of more or less contemporaneous city civilizations existed from Egypt to India, linked by trade, cultural diffusion, and conquest, and ringed about by nomadic peoples or sedentary farmer villages in Arabia, North Africa, and northern Eurasia.

In the fertile lower valley of the Tigris and Euphrates, humans may have found the equivalent of the Garden of Eden, which was celebrated in Genesis and was long a part of Mesopotamian tradition. Once the art of irrigation and, to a degree, the control of floods had been learned, human beings saw the possibility of creating a great oasis. The turbulence of its history strongly suggests that this land, with its promise of a hitherto unknown life of abundance, was enormously attractive.

At the dawn of recorded history, southern Mesopotamia was occupied by the Sumerians, a group whose origin is still one of the great puzzles of an-

*Henri Frankfort, *The Art and Architecture of the Ancient Orient* (Baltimore: Penguin, 1971).

cient history. Researchers have suggested that the Sumerians came from the east in the Preliterate period, from the area bordering the Persian Gulf that is now western Iran. Their migration to southern Mesopotamia was preceded by that of a people whose culture is given the name Jamdat Nasr, after its cultural type site in Iraq.

A handsome *minotaur* (man-bull) figure in soldered silver (FIG. **2-9**) is assigned to the Jamdat Nasr period. Seated and making an offering of a vessel, which it holds between the hooves of its extended forelegs, the statuette is an early example of a universal theme in Ancient Near Eastern art: the man-animal monster. We shall see it often, in both miniature and monumental form (consider the Egyptian Sphinx). In the Jamdat Nasr figure, the sculptor shows a grasp of the essential form of the bodies of beast and man, the natural sweep of planes and contours. With an astonishing sureness of touch, a gesture is portrayed that is both solemn and graceful. Such mastery could only be the result of a long tradition of observation of natural form and of the craft of metalwork. The religious import of this figure (it is performing a ritual act of some sort) must also express a long tradition of religious art that goes back millennia. Through its long development, this tradition came to align the figures of the great beasts with the figure of man. It is a tradition received and shared by the Sumerians and their successors in Mesopotamia.

2-9 *Kneeling Man-Bull,* from Jamdat Nasr, *c.* 3000 B.C. Silver, $6\frac{1}{2}''$ high. Metropolitan Museum of Art, New York (Joseph Pulitzer Bequest).

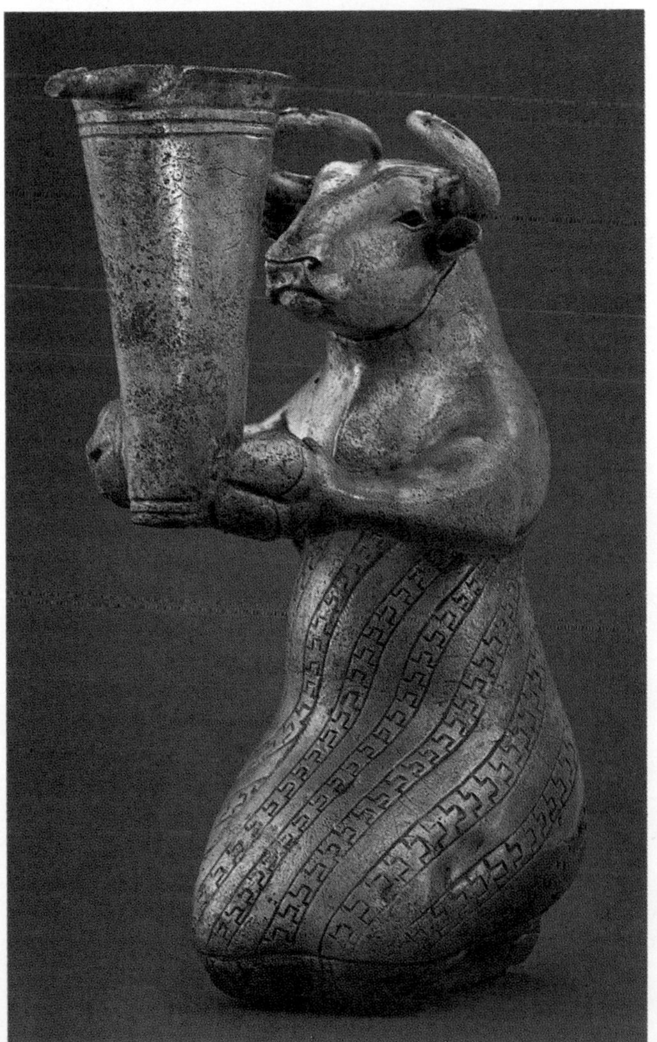

The Sumerians were an agricultural people who learned to control floods and built strong-walled towns, such as Warka (the biblical Erech and the ancient Uruk) and Al-Hiba (the ancient Lagash). Sumerian influence extended widely from its base in southern Mesopotamia, eastward to Susa in Iran, northward to Assur, and westward to Syria, where recently discovered archives, consisting of thousands of clay tablets in the Sumerian language, testify to the far-flung network of contacts Sumer made throughout the ancient Near East as it engaged in a kind of cultural colonialism. After several centuries, Semitic nomad shepherds came from the western desert; they adopted agriculture, absorbed much from Sumerian culture, and built their own cities—Kish, Akkad, Mari, and Babylon—farther north. Over the centuries, dominion oscillated between the two peoples, but the Semites produced two of the mightiest kings, Sargon and Hammurabi.

From as early a time as the Paleolithic caves, we have evidence of people's efforts to control their environment by picture magic. With the appearance of the Sumerians and the beginning of recorded history, the older magic was replaced by a religion of gods, benevolent or malevolent, who personified the forces of nature that often contended destructively with human hopes and designs. In the fertile valleys of the Tigris and Euphrates, the fiery heat of summer and the catastrophic floods, droughts, blights, and locusts might easily have persuaded people that powers above and beyond their control must somehow be placated and won over. Formal religion, a kind of system of transactions between gods and human beings, may have begun with the Sumerians; no matter how it has been systematized and diversified since then, religion has retained its original propitiatory devices—prayer, sacrifice, and ritual—as well as a view of humans as imperfect by nature and dependent on and obligated to some higher being. The religion of the Sumerians and of those who followed them centered about nature gods: Anu, god of the sky; En-lil (Bel), a creator and ruler of earth and "lord of the storm"; Ea (or Enki), lord of the waters (a healing, benevolent god); Nannar (Sin), the moon god;

Utu (Shamash), the sun god; and Inanna (associated with the planet Venus), goddess of love and fertility, who, as Ishtar, is later also endowed with the functions of battle goddess.*

Architecture

Religion, which dominated life and invested it with meaning, determined the form of society as well as architectural and artistic expression. The Mesopotamian city-state was under the protection of the god of the city; the king was his representative on earth and the steward of his earthly treasure. The relationship of the king to the gods and to his subjects may be read in the prayer of an early Sumerian king to the god En-lil of the city of Nippur:

> O En-lil, the king of the lands, may Anu to his beloved father speak my prayer; to my life may he add life, and cause the lands to dwell in security; may he give me warriors as many as the grass; the herds of heaven may he watch over; the land with prosperity endow; the good fortune which the gods have given me, may he not change; and may I ever remain the shepherd, who standeth at the head.

The plan of the city reflected the central role of the god in city life, his temple being the city's monumental nucleus. The temple was the focus not only of local religious practice but also served as an administrative and economic center. It was indeed the domain of the god, who was regarded as a great and rich holder of lands and herds as well as the protector of the city. The whole function of the city was to serve the god as a master, as the function of all people in general was to serve the gods. The vast temple complex, a kind of city within a city, had multiple functions. A temple staff of priests and scribes carried on city business, looking after the possessions of the god and of the king. It must have been in such a setting that writing developed into an instrument of precision; the very earliest examples have to do with the keeping of accounts and the description of simple transactions, stores, and supplies.

Bel and *Shamash* are Akkadian names; *Sin* is Babylonian.

Two types of temples can be distinguished, both dating from the fourth millennium B.C. One type stands at ground level, the other on a raised platform. They have been classified as "low" and "high" temples, and it has been surmised that the latter form eventually evolved into a chapel that stood on top of a stepped pyramid, or *ziggurat*. With rare exceptions, only the bases of early Mesopotamian temples can still be recognized; their mud-brick superstructures usually have eroded. The typical low temple, its corners oriented to the cardinal points, centered around a rectangular or T-shaped inner courtyard that contained an offering table and the statue of a god, housed in a niche. This core was surrounded by rooms that served as storage areas, offices, and lodgings for the priests. The basic components of the high temple were the same, albeit with a somewhat changed interior arrangement.

An early example of a high temple is the White Temple of Warka (FIG. **2-10**), which dates from about 3200 to 3000 B.C. Its preservation is exceptional. Enough of the structure remains to permit a fairly reliable reconstruction (FIG. **2-11**). The temple stands on a platform 40 feet above street level in the center of the city. Like most of the older platforms, this one is composed of the ruins of earlier temples filled in with

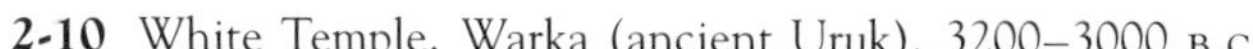

2-10 White Temple, Warka (ancient Uruk), 3200–3000 B.C.

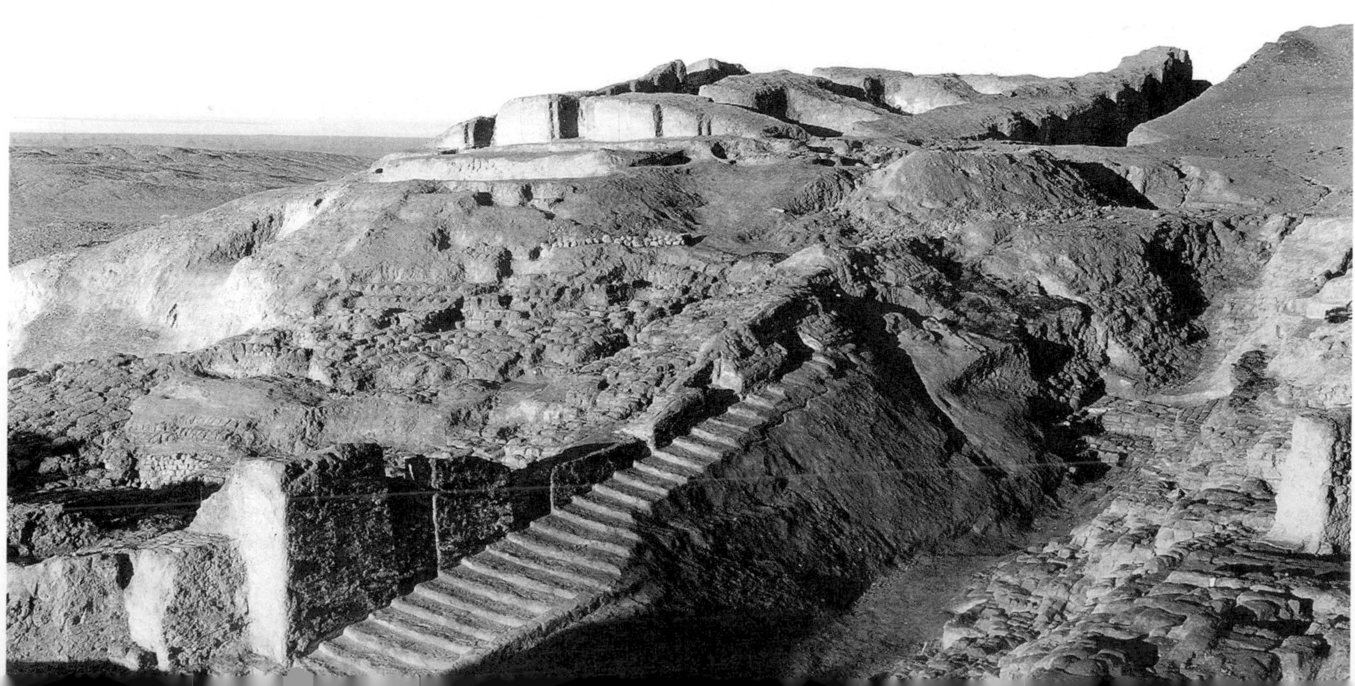

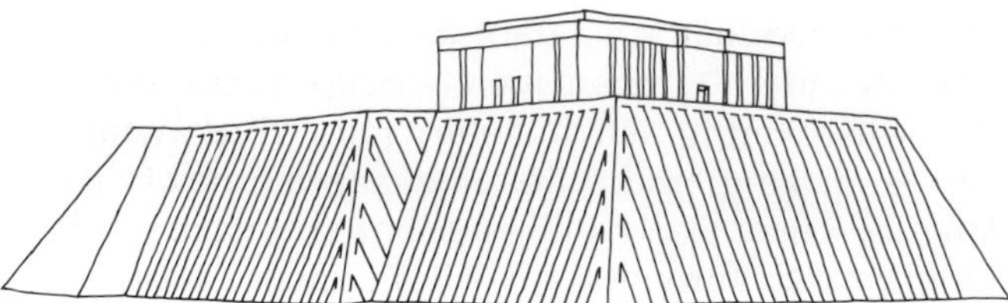

2-11 Reconstruction of the White Temple, Warka. (After E. S. Piggott.)

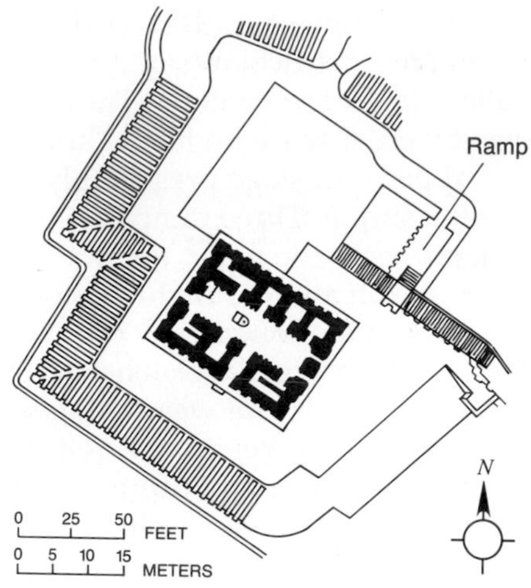

2-12 Plan of the White Temple, Warka. (After Frankfort.)

brickwork, a fact that hints at the possible origin of the custom of raising temples above the level of their surroundings. This feature, of course, is not only pregnant with symbolism but also most practical in a flood-prone river valley; gradually the practical form must have taken on religious meaning and was sanctified.

The platform of the White Temple has sloping sides of paneled brickwork, and the walls of the temple show traces of the whitewash that gave it its name. Unusual, and unlike the layout of the low temples, is the fact that worshipers entered the sanctuary from one of its sides (FIG. **2-12**), despite the presence of imposing gateways at either end, one of which displaced the altar from its axial position. This arrangement has been explained by identifying the high temple as a portal through which the god could pass on his visits to earth. In the low temples, his presence was symbolized by a cult statue.

While its evolution from the platform supporting high temples remains uncertain, the ziggurat is undoubtedly the most characteristic structure found in Mesopotamia. Its function as a stairway by which the gods of the country mounted to heaven every night likewise remains speculative. No shrines have been preserved, although researchers believe that such structures must have stood on the top of the ziggurats and that they were the setting in which the priests prayed to the "gods of the night" (the planets and constellations), prepared meals for the gods, or sacrificed lambs for an omen. An old Babylonian text (*c.* 1900–1600 B.C.) reads

> The gods and goddesses of the country—
> Shamash, Sin, Adad, and Ishtar—
> have gone home to heaven to sleep.
> They will not give decisions or verdicts [tonight].

Most of the ruined cities of Sumer—Ur, Warka, Nippur, Larsa, Eridu—are still dominated by their eroded ziggurats. The ziggurat at Ur dates from the period called Neo-Sumerian (2100–2000 B.C.), when builders were attempting to attain the greatest heights possible. The base structure is a solid mass of mud brick 50 feet high (FIG. **2-13**), which is truncated

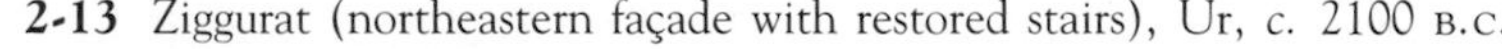

2-13 Ziggurat (northeastern façade with restored stairs), Ur, *c.* 2100 B.C.

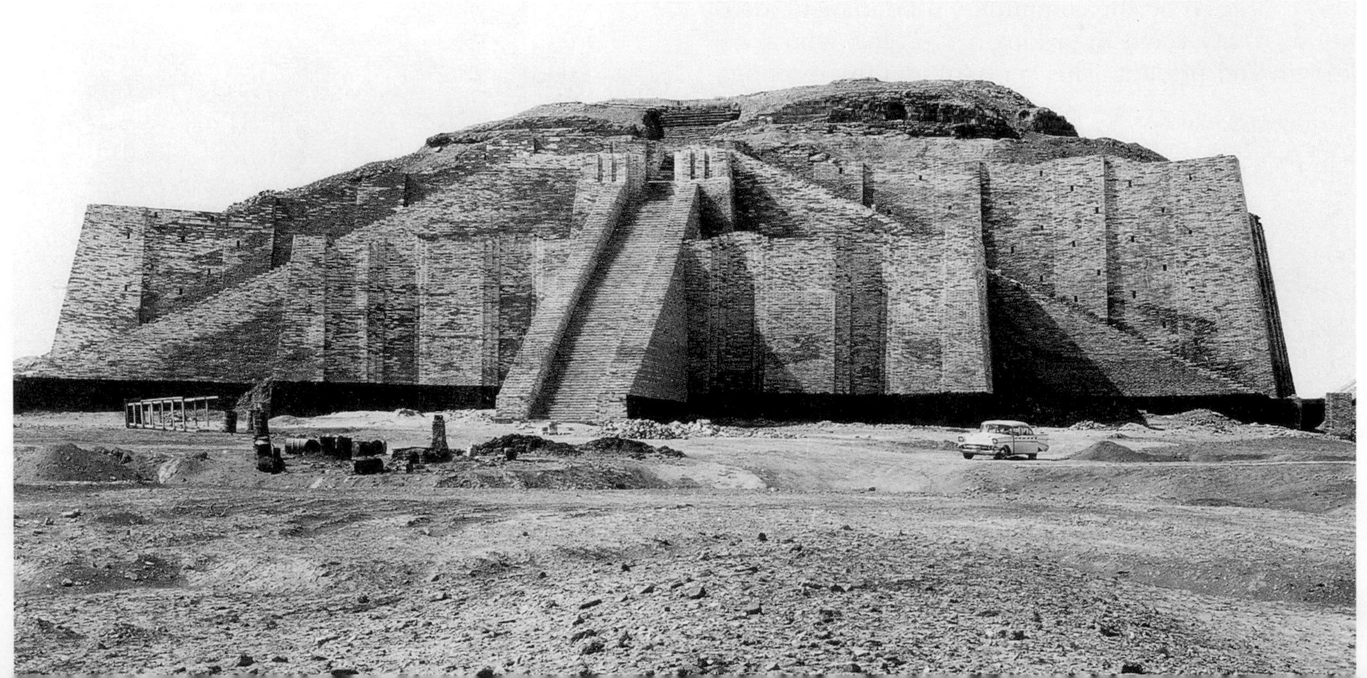

and edge-worn by time, weather, and depredation. In a conjectural reconstruction (FIG. **2-14**), two successively smaller stages are evident. The base and the stage above it were faced with baked brick laid in bitumen. The uppermost stage presumably served as a pedestal for the shrine. Three ramplike stairways of a hundred steps each converge on a tower-flanked gateway from which another flight of steps probably led to the shrine. Only officiating priests were permitted access to the shrine level. The structure's facing has withstood floods and weathering so well that the ziggurat at Ur is the best preserved in southern Mesopotamia. The loftiness of the great ziggurats—especially of the one at Babylon, which was about 270 feet high and intended by its pious builders to reach into Heaven—made a profound impression on the ancient Hebrews, who memorialized the Babylon ziggurat as the Tower of Babel, a monument to the insolent pride of man.

The three great inventions of the Sumerians—a system of gods and god-man relationships, the city-state itself, and the art of writing—provided the basis for a new order of human society. In the city-state, consecrated by the presence of the civic deity, human beings experienced new interrelationships with their god and with each other, and formalized and gave permanence to these interrelationships by recording them in writing. Life became regularized, and the community assumed functions, such as defense against others and the caprices of nature, that formerly had been left to the individual. This integration and the division of labor (specialization), which is encouraged where large numbers of people are concentrated in a coherent community, emancipated the inhabitants from the consuming necessities of daily life, so that they could develop and apply skills and talents unthinkable in fluid and unintegrated societies. The relatively fixed character of the city-state also conferred on the community a permanent identity as a city ruled by a king and a god who were known and present. This sense of identity extended to the individual inhabitant as well, who received a personal identity from membership in the community, discovering self in interrelationships with the city, god, king, and other citizens. The new written language may also have contributed to this growing identification through which individuals came to perceive themselves as names among the names for other things and actions. Thus, from the Sumerian creation of stable life patterns begins that sense of identity—that self-awareness—that will mature and reach its highest development in the civilization of Greece.

2-14 Reconstruction of the ziggurat at Ur. (Adapted from a drawing at the British Museum, London.)

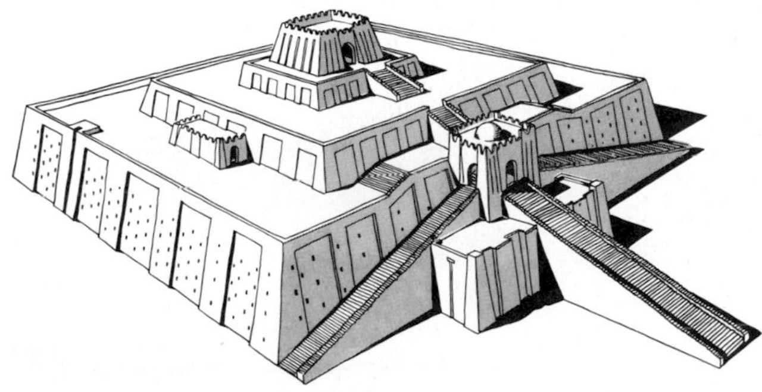

Sculpture

In the animal paintings of the caves, human figures almost never appear; humans have not yet entered the area of self-awareness. Although the rock paintings of the Spanish Levant do indeed represent the human figure, they do so only schematically and almost in the form of picture-writing. Thus, we are not prepared for the beautiful female head from Warka (FIG. **2-15**). Its ancestry is unknown. Dating from the so-called Protoliterate period, when writing first appeared, it is not a complete head but a marble face meant to be attached to a wood backing and wigged, perhaps, in gold. The deep recesses for the eyebrows were filled with colored shell or stone, as were the

2-15 *Female Head*, from Warka, c. 3500–3000 B.C. Alabaster, approx. 8″ high. The Iraq Museum, Baghdad.

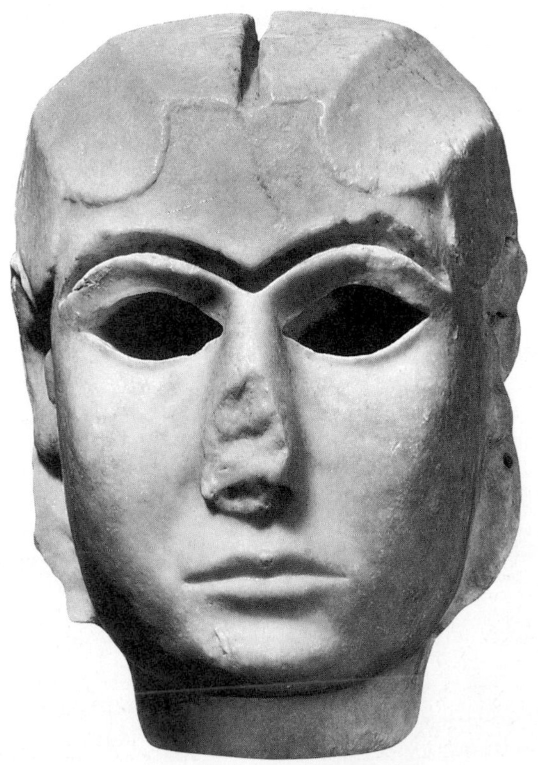

large eyes. The subject is unknown (goddess, priestess, queen?), but our ignorance of her and of the history of the head does not diminish our appreciation of its exquisite refinement of feature and expression, despite the mutilations of time and accident. The soft modeling of the cheeks, the sensitivity of the mouth, and the hesitancy of the expression between sweet and somber not only present us with a person in herself beguiling and mysterious but also suggest a sophistication in the artist beyond our expectation of the time in which the work was produced.

One notices at once in the Warka head the disproportionately large eyes. This trait is characteristic of a whole group of figures from Tell Asmar (FIGS. **2-16** and **2-17**). The reason for this convention, which is not only Sumerian but appears throughout ancient art, can only be guessed. Long before Aristotle asserted that people are distinguished from the animals by being rational and that sight is the most "rational" of all of the senses, humans must have perceived and feared the power of the eye to hold, charm, and hypnotize for ends good or ill. The "evil eye" was feared in the ancient world, as it is feared still. It is a popular belief and a part of folklore that one can learn much about another's intentions and character by "looking him straight in the eye," and the modern affectation of dark glasses (curiously Sumerian when oversized!) may be both a defense and a badge of attractive mystery. To the ancient artist, the eyes, the "windows of the soul," could have had several associations. Large eyes fixed in unflagging gaze see all, and frontal, binocular vision, distinguishing human from mere animal sight, represents the all-seeing vigilance and omniscience of the gods and the guarantee of justice. In the conventionalization of the human image, vision understandably becomes a peculiarly human trait—in its lesser physical sense as well as in its greater intellectual, spiritual, and theistic sense.

2-16 Statuettes from the Abu Temple, Tell Asmar, *c.* 2700–2600 B.C. Marble with shell and black limestone inlay, tallest figure approx. 30" high. The Iraq Museum, Baghdad, and The Oriental Institute, University of Chicago.

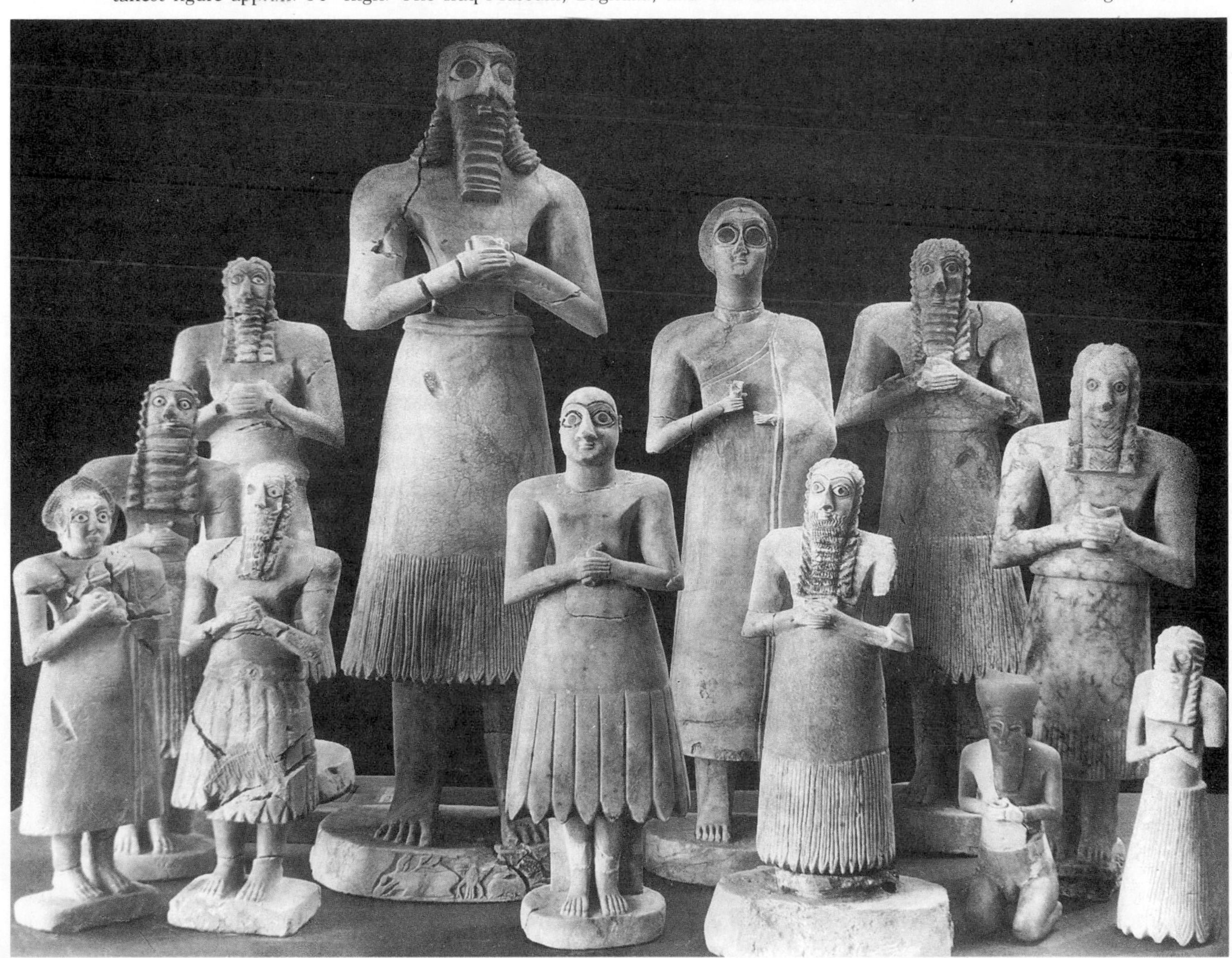

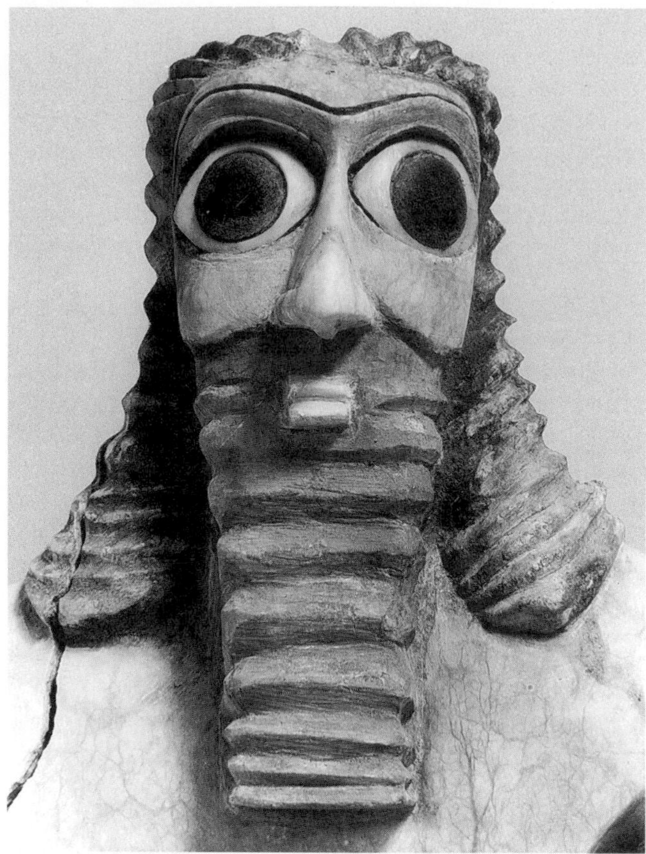

2-17 Head formerly believed to be of the god Abu (detail of FIG. 2-16), Tell Asmar, c. 2700–2600 B.C. Marble with shell and black limestone inlay. The Iraq Museum, Baghdad.

Godlike vision as the foundation of law and justice is evident in the stories of the great lawgivers of the ancient world, including Hammurabi of Babylon, Moses, Lycurgus of Sparta, and Solon of Athens.

Although it may be that none of our speculations entered the mind of the artist of the Tell Asmar figures, some association of vision with supernatural powers seems to be indicated by the fact that the two largest figures, formerly identified as deities, also have the largest eyes in relationship to their heads (FIG. 2-17). The other statuettes represent worshipers (the larger ones, priests; the smaller ones, laymen). With their hands tightly clasped across their chests in the attitude of prayer, their large eyes seem to express reverent awe in the presence of their gods. The purpose of these votive figures was to offer constant prayers to the gods on behalf of their donors; thus, their open-eyed stares may symbolize the eternal wakefulness necessary to fulfill their duty.

CONVENTIONALIZATION

Just as the Sumerians created a new kind of human experience through formal religion and civic life, they found a new way to represent that experience through writing and figurative art. Writing had been invented by simplifying pictures into signs, or wedge-shaped *(cuneiform)* strokes in numerous combinations, pressed by a stylus into wet clay tablets. An analogous simplification in figurative art employed a few telling traits to present the human figure and human action. This process of simplification is variously named schematization, stylization, conventionalization, generalization, or formalization. *Conventional* simplifications of the human figure are universal and are not characteristic only of ancient art. Indeed, all artistic styles are conventional in that, in the societies in which they prevail, they are tacitly accepted as a comprehensible means of representation. The conventions may be broad or narrow, slow to change or under continual revision, as in our times. In any case, such criteria as fidelity to optical "fact" should not be used in evaluating a style. Although the main trends in modern art since the 1800s have been away from optical fact, and today's artists often deliberately disregard photographic "truth," the images they make, such as those seen in comic strips and in commercial art and advertising, are perfectly recognizable to us.

The Sumerians, working out patterns and conventions that regulated the new life that they had in effect devised, also established conventions for the construction of the human image. The large eyes of the Warka and Tell Asmar figures are not the only conventionalized details. In the small figures of a shell-inlaid box, the so-called *Standard of Ur* (FIG. **2-18**), several devices of representation simplify the narrative, explain the action, and even convey the impression of motion. The panel shown here depicts a Sumerian military victory—the advance of the foot soldiers, the charge of the chariots. A second panel (not shown) represents the aftermath of the victorious battle, with lines of prisoners and servants bringing in booty and the king relaxing, drinking with his nobles, listening to harp and song. The figures are all carefully arranged in superimposed strips, each strikingly suggestive of a film or comic strip; doubtless, the purpose is the same—to achieve a continuous narrative effect. Each individual figure is carefully spaced, with little overlapping. (Compare this regularized, formal presentation with the casual, haphazard placement of the figures in Paleolithic and Mesolithic art.) Poses are repeated, as in the line of foot soldiers, to suggest large numbers. The horses of the war chariots (with the lines of the legs repeated to suggest the other horses of the team and their alignment in space) change from a walk to a gallop as they attack. The figures are essentially in profile, but it is an almost universal convention in the ancient Near East that the eyes—again, very large—are in front

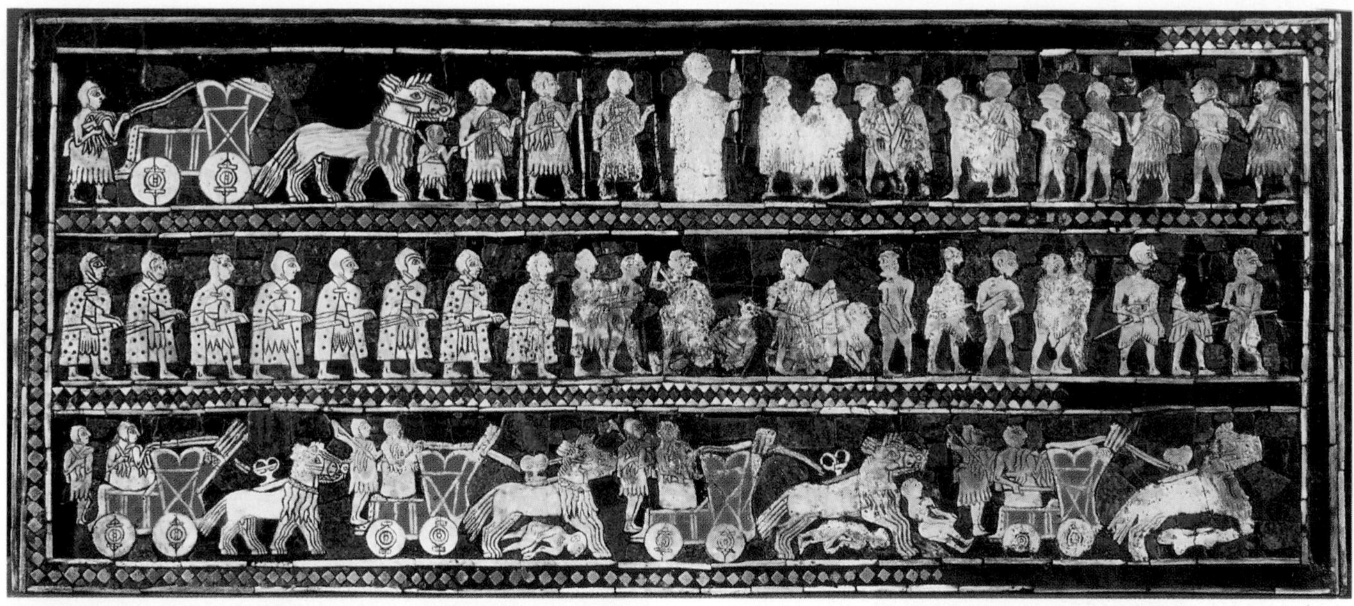

2-18 *Scenes of War*, panel from the *Standard of Ur*, c. 2700 B.C. Panel inlaid with shell, lapis lazuli, and red limestone, approx. 8″ × 19″. British Museum, London.

view, as are the torsos. The artist indicates the parts of the human body that enter into our concept of what the human form looks like and avoids positions, attitudes, or views that would conceal or obscure the characterizing parts. For example, if the figures were in strict profile, an arm and perhaps a leg would be concealed; the body would appear to have only half its breadth; and the eye would not "read" as an eye at all, because it would not have its distinctive flat oval shape and the pupil, so important in the Tell Asmar figures, would not appear.

We could call this approach "conceptual" rather than "optical," because the artist records not the immediate, fleeting aspect of things but rather a concept of the distinguishing and abiding properties of the human body. It is the fundamental forms of things and the artist's knowledge of them, not their accidental appearance, that direct the artist's hand. But this approach is simply a reflection of the general *formalism* that was imposed at the beginning of the historical period in an effort to create an enduring order. This formalism continued to rule human conduct throughout history in thousands of customs, conventions, and ceremonies regarded as sacred and above change. In Greece, many centuries later, Plato conceived the famous philosophy of forms, claiming that the world of pure form, in which the ultimate and unchanging truths of mathematical figures and relationships exist, is the real world, whereas the world we see, the world of mere appearance, is the realm of the unreal, of illusion, of change, and of death.

THE UNION OF THE FORMAL AND THE NATURAL

On the inlaid sound box of a lyre from Ur (FIG. **2-19**), figures in the top register represent a Sumerian hero wrestling with two man-headed bulls. In the lower registers, real and fantastic animals prepare a banquet. The topmost register of the panel presents the figures in heraldic symmetry, and, except that the heads are in front view, they exhibit the conventional formalized pose of the *Standard of Ur*. On the other hand, the animal figures in the other registers exhibit a markedly relaxed formalism. The dog wearing a dagger and carrying a laden table, the lion bringing in the wine service, the ass playing the lyre, the jackal playing the zither, the bear steadying the lyre (or perhaps dancing), and the gazelle offering goblets of wine to the scorpion-man are all seen in more or less true profile. Torsos naturally cut off the view of the far arms, and the near legs obstruct the far legs. Shoulders are properly placed, and features are carefully noted and designated. The heroic human figures have the formality we find in the stylized animals on a coat of arms, but the banquet animals are at ease and seem almost to be burlesquing a stately parade of servants and musicians. Long before the human figure appeared in art, naturalistic animal figures were painted in the Paleolithic caves. Then for a long time, as if by rule, humans were represented with rigid formality, but animal figures looked and moved much as they would appear to the eye. The sound-box panel shows a delightful Aesop-like scene (the comedy of which may not have been intended)

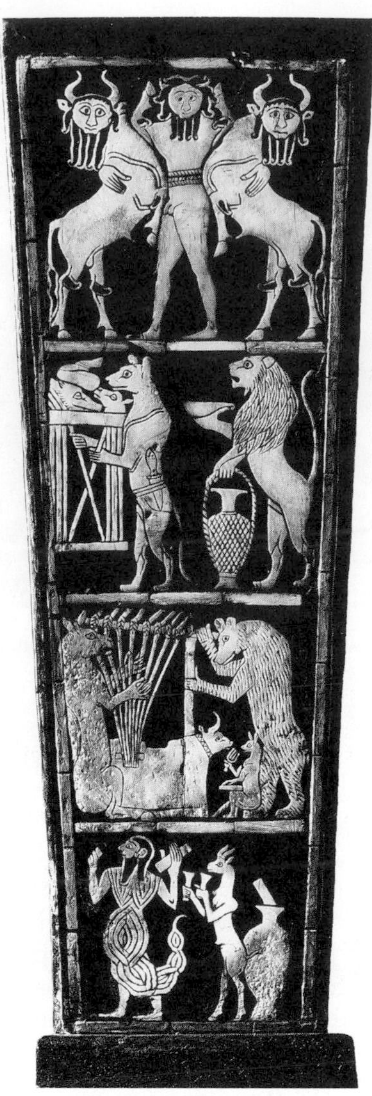

2-19 Sound box of a royal lyre from the tomb of Queen Puabi, Ur, *c.* 2600 B.C. Wood with inlaid gold, lapis lazuli, and shell, approx. 12″ high. University Museum, Philadelphia.

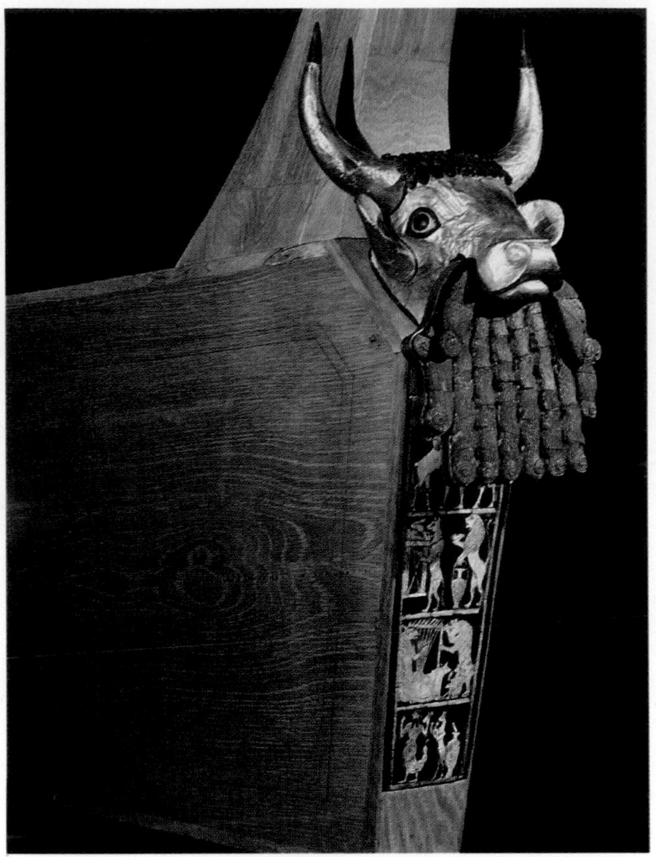

2-20 Bull's head from the lyre sound box shown in FIG. 2-19. Gold leaf and lapis lazuli with inlaid eyes over a wooden core, approx. 18″ high. University Museum, Philadelphia.

in what is probably a representation of ancient myths. Surely it is a very early specimen of the theme in both literature and art in which animals act as people; thus, we pass from the artist of this panel to Aesop's fables, to the medieval bestiaries, and to the zoological creations of Walt Disney.

Archaic artists share with their prehistoric predecessors the genius for rendering with sharp perception the features, almost the personality, of animals. The bull was revered throughout the ancient Near East and the Mediterranean. A splendid bull's head (FIG. **2-20**), finished in gold leaf with beard and details in lapis lazuli, is part of the Ur lyre. (Note where the head is attached to the lyre, as it is shown on the third register from the top in FIG. 2-19.) The bull, an exemplification of fertility and strength, naturally would have been worshiped by early herdsmen, who might have invoked its power against the natural enemies of cattle—drought and predatory beasts. In this example, the beard may represent some supernatural amplification of the bull's power. The beard and such humanizing features as the man-heads added to the bulls in the top register of the sound-box panel foreshadow the man-headed bulls and lions that appeared much later in Assyria.

The contest between natural and supernatural forces in the Mesopotamian world is expressed as a struggle between animals and monsters. Such a struggle is represented in miniature with exquisite refinement on a cylinder seal only $1\frac{1}{2}$ inches high (FIG. **2-21**), dating perhaps from the Akkadian period. A seal consisted of a cylindrical piece of stone, usually about an inch or so in height, pierced for the attachment of a cord. Made of various colored stones, both hard and soft, such as rock crystal, agate, carnelian and jasper, lapis lazuli, marble, and alabaster, seals were decorated with a design in *intaglio* (incised), so that a raised pattern was left when the seal was rolled over soft clay. With this device, the Sumerians sealed, signed, and identified their letters and documents, which were written on clay tablets. Our illus-

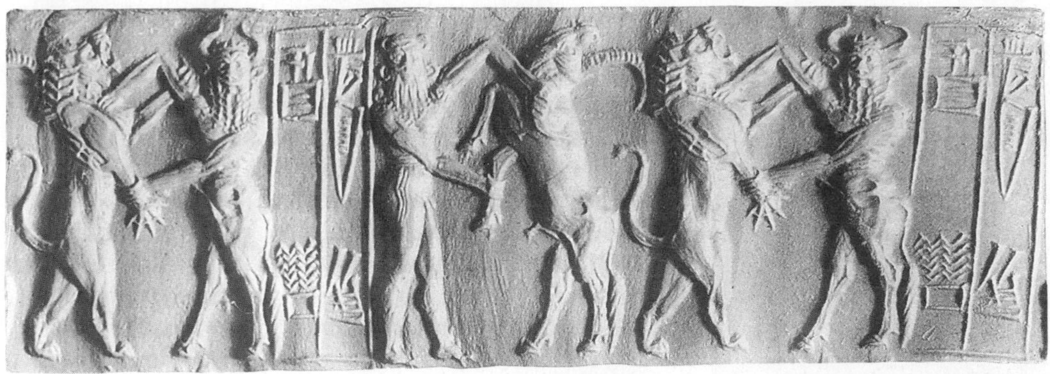

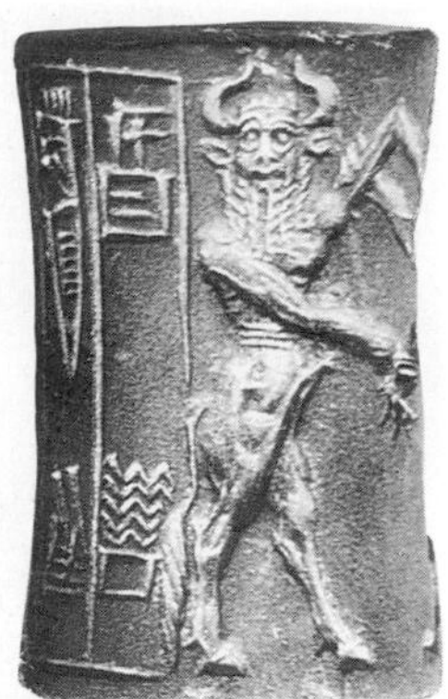

2-21 Cylinder seal (detail) and its impression, from Ur, *c.* 2300 B.C. Stone, approx. 1½" high. The Oriental Institute, University of Chicago.

tration shows both a detail of the seal and the more complete relief design made from it. A hero fights a bull, and a being that is half-man and half-bull fights a lion. The heraldic attitudes and groupings reflect the formal method of representation, but even in the small area of the seal, the skillful artist shows such mastery of animal form that we can almost hear the roaring and bellowing of the struggle.

AKKAD

At about 2300 B.C., the loose group of cities known as Sumer, where the tremendous change from prehistory to civilization had begun, came under the domination of a great ruler, Sargon of Akkad. The Akkadians, although they were Semitic in origin and spoke a language entirely different from that of Sumer, had assimilated Sumerian culture. Under Sargon and his followers, they introduced a new concept of royal power; its basis was unswerving loyalty to the king rather than to the city-state. During the rule of Sargon's grandson, Naram-Sin, governors of cities were called "slaves" of the king, who, in turn, called himself "King of the Four Quarters"—in effect, ruler of the earth.

A magnificent bronze head of a king from Nineveh (FIG. **2-22**), perhaps a portrait of Naram-Sin, embodies this new concept of absolute monarchy. The elaborate coiffure, Sumerian in style, attests to the persistence of the tradition of Sumer and serves as crown to the remarkable face with its expression of majestic serenity. The sensitive mouth, the large eyes, made even larger by the absence of the precious stones once embedded in the sockets, and the emphatic ridgelike brows seem to echo a long tradition that extends back even to the Warka head (FIG. 2-15). This Akkadian bronze shows to particular advantage the union of the formal and the natural that is so common in Mesopotamian art. The symmetry of the head and the stylized motifs of the curly locks of hair manage to be consistent with the projection of personality—a strong-minded and commanding one, but in a pensive and composed mood, with perhaps just a trace of irony. The age of metals has come, and the piece demonstrates the craftsman's sophisticated skill in casting and in the engraving of details.

Roughly contemporary with the Akkadian portrait is the copper-cast head of a ruler whose name we do not know (FIG. **2-23**); the provenance and date are also uncertain. This head rivals that of the Akkadian king in its masterful blending of formal simplicity and firmness, with carefully observed particularity of detail. The features are those of a specific individual—

2-22 *Head of an Akkadian Ruler,* from Nineveh, *c.* 2200 B.C. Bronze, approx. 12" high. The Iraq Museum, Baghdad.

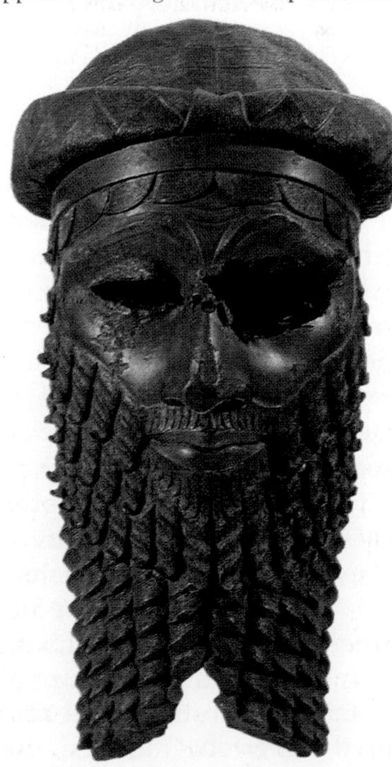

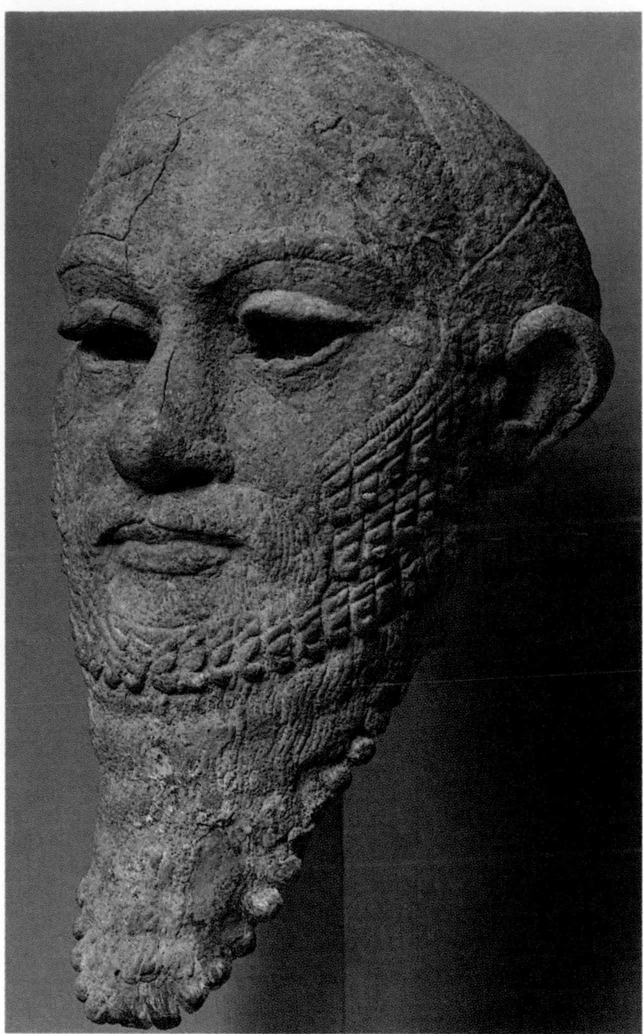

2-23 *Portrait Head of a Ruler,* from ancient Iran (Elam?), c. 2100–2000 B.C. Copper, 13½″ high. Metropolitan Museum of Art, New York (Rogers Fund).

large eyes, prominent nose, the compressed lips of a wide mouth, a beard that adds strength to the jaw—the speaking likeness of a grave, thoughtful, and wise man. The sculptor sets the features within spare, firm contours, composing a mask of dignity and authority. A sensitive reading of personality is thus disciplined by a convention that imposes a certain immobility of expression; this treatment is characteristic of the formality of portraiture in the ancient Near East, especially of persons of high rank. We will presently see it in the portraits of Egyptian pharaohs.

The godlike sovereignty claimed by the kings of Akkad is also evident in another masterpiece of Akkadian art, the *Victory Stele of Naram-Sin* (FIG. **2-24**). On the stele, the warlike grandson of Sargon is represented leading his victorious armies up the slopes of a wooded mountain and through the routed enemy, who are crushed underfoot, fall, flee, die, or beg for mercy. The king stands alone, far taller than his men, treading on the bodies of two of the fallen enemy. He wears the horned helmet that signifies his deification, and two auspicious astral bodies, representing Shamash and Ishtar, shine on his triumph. The artist shows an almost startling originality, not only in his ingenious management of the theme but also in the variety of poses and in the setting. The king's troops, a whole army suggested by eight figures marching in two orderly files, carry spears and flying banners as they encounter the shattered enemy (seven figures), one of whom falls headlong down the mountainside. In comparison with the stele figures, those of the *Standard of Ur* seem rather static and formal. The *Naram-Sin* artist is a daring inventor, and although he adheres to older conventions, especially in portraying the king and his soldiers in simultaneous profile and front view, he nevertheless relies on his own perception to create the first landscape in Near Eastern art since Çatal Hüyük (FIG. 2-8).

2-24 *Victory Stele of Naram-Sin,* from Susa, c. 2300–2200 B.C. Pink sandstone, approx. 6′ 6″ high. Louvre, Paris.

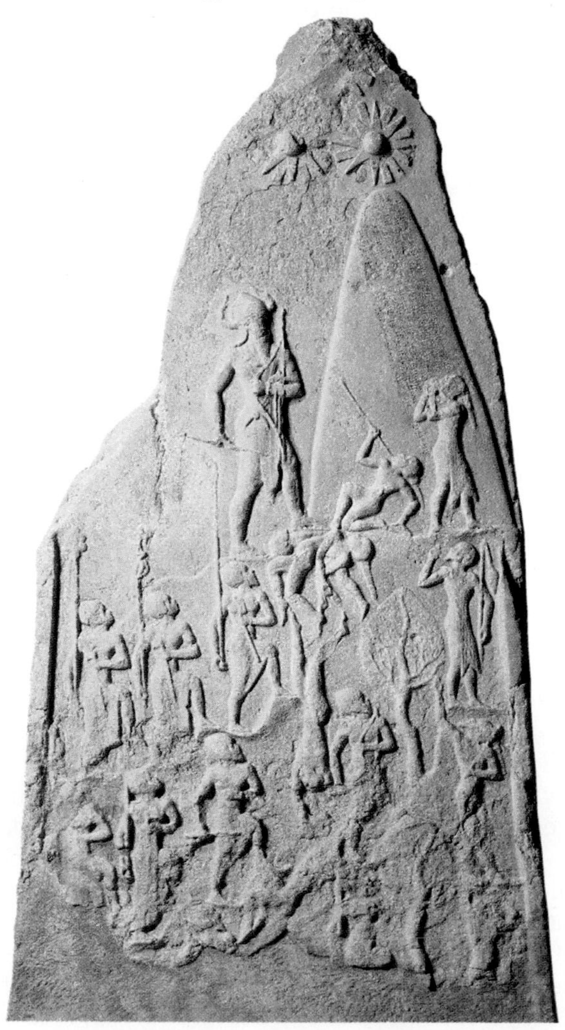

The achievements of Akkad were brought to an end by an incursion of barbarous mountaineers, the Guti, who dominated life in central and lower Mesopotamia for sixty years, until the cities of Sumer, responding to the alien presence, reasserted themselves and established a Neo-Sumerian polity under the kings of Ur. During this age, the most conspicuous contribution came from the city of Lagash, under its ruler, Gudea. There are about twenty statues of Gudea, showing him seated or standing, hands tightly clasped, and sometimes wearing a woolen cap; the statue illustrated here (FIG. **2-25**) is typical. Gudea attributed his good fortune and that of his city to the favor of the gods, and he was a zealous overseer of the performance of rites in their honor. His statues were numerous so that he could take his symbolic place in the temples and there render perpetual service to the benevolent deities. Like the others, the standing Gudea shown here is of dolerite, an extremely hard stone that the sculptor worked with consummate skill. The difficulty of working such hard stone was compounded by the fact that stone, almost nonexistent in southern Mesopotamia, was rare and costly, and had to be imported. Blocks and boulders of irregular size and shape were usually not large enough to permit the sculptor to execute the whole length of the standing figure without sacrificing its natural proportions; hence, a certain stumpiness often resulted. The sculptor emphasized the portrait head at the expense of the rest of the body, often preferring the seated to the standing figure. The capped figure of Gudea stands in the formal frontal pose that descends from the age of Tell Asmar; the great eyes and eyebrow ridges are in the Mesopotamian tradition. One shoulder and arm are bare; the drapery pulls about the torso and under the arm and falls almost vertically from the other arm. The overall contour is simple in the extreme, with no irregular or complex relief. The singular unity and compactness of the figure arise from the artist's conception of it as a cylindrical or conical form that resides in the mass of the finely textured stone. The smooth sweep of its contours, the elegance of the profile, and the richness of the polished dolerite all complement each other.

2-25 *Gudea Worshiping*, from Telloh, c. 2100 B.C. Dolerite, approx. 42″ high. Louvre, Paris.

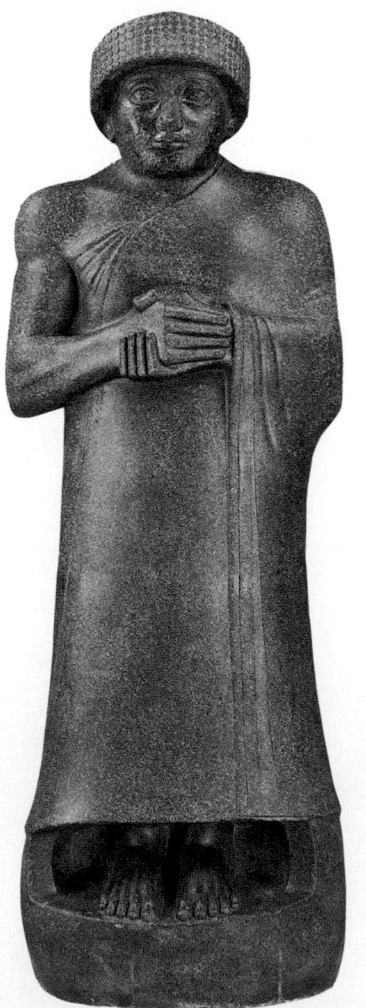

BABYLONIA

Lagash, which had retained its independence during the Guti invasion, became a dependency of Ur during that city's brief resurgence late in the third millennium B.C. For a little over a century, the Third Dynasty of Ur ruled a once-more united realm. Its last king fell before the attacks of foreign invaders, and the following two centuries witnessed the reemergence of the traditional Mesopotamian political pattern in which several independent city-states existed side by side. Until its most powerful king, Hammurabi, was able to reestablish a centralized government that ruled the whole country, Babylon was one of these city-states. Perhaps the most renowned king in Mesopotamian history, Hammurabi was famous for his codification of the confused, conflicting, and often unwritten laws of the Mesopotamian towns. Although not the first to try to bring order out of the chaos, Hammurabi was the first to succeed; echoes of his code are found in the Law of Moses.

The code, beautifully inscribed on a tall, irregularly surfaced black basalt stele, is capped by a relief sculpture of Hammurabi receiving the inspiration for the laws from the flame-shouldered sun god, Shamash (FIG. **2-26**). The god is seated on a mountain, indicated by a scale pattern beneath his feet. He holds the symbols of divine power, ring and staff, in a hand stretched toward Hammurabi, who is represented in

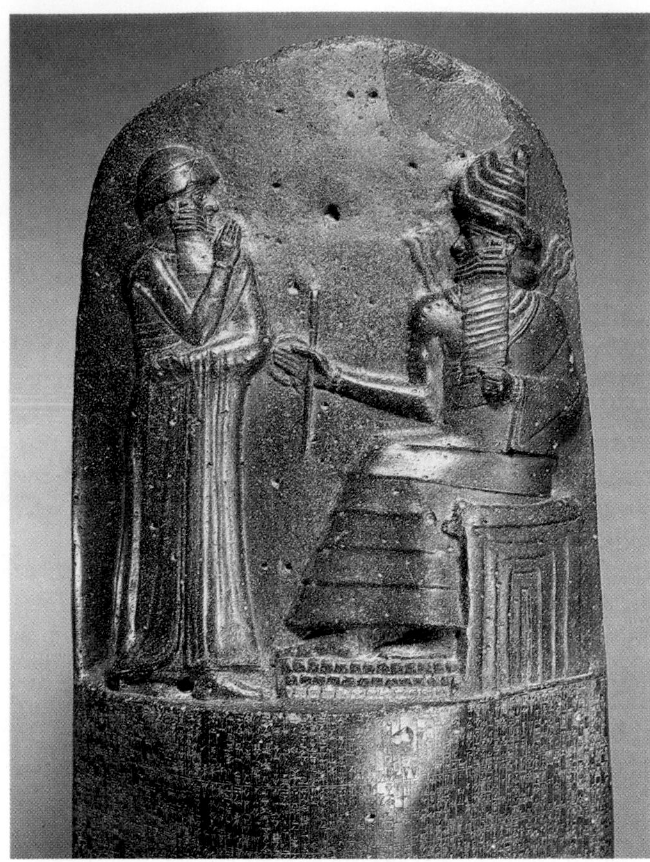

2-26 *Stele of Hammurabi* (upper part), from Susa, *c.* 1780 B.C. Basalt, entire stele approx. 7′ 4″ high. Louvre, Paris.

a gesture of reverent attention, his hand raised in prayer. The Mesopotamian artist's instinct for cylindrical volume is again evident. Shamash is represented in the familiar convention of combined front and side views, which gives his figure great breadth; Hammurabi, his servant, is shown in a position closer to profile, so that he occupies far less space. This confrontation between god and man expresses the increasing humanization of natural and supernatural forces, as man, increasingly self-aware, began (in Babylon) to attribute human form to the gods.

Hammurabi's Babylonian empire was brought down by the Hittites, who, after sacking Babylon around 1595 B.C., retired to Anatolia, the seat of Hittite power. Babylonia was left in the hands of marauding mountaineers, the Kassites. The Hittites, who spoke an Indo-European tongue, developed an art of great power and originality. Their strongly fortified capital, near the modern Turkish village of Boghazköy, was fronted with massive stone gates set between towers (FIG. **2-27**). Projecting from the Cyclopean stones, a building material very different from the brick of Mesopotamian architecture, are rugged figures of lions, blunt and brutal in aspect. Whatever the source for this concept of guardian beasts, be it Mesopotamia, Syria, or Egypt, the Hittite realization of it is original, the figures being strongly bound to and dominated by the architecture, rather than freestanding and in the round.

2-27 Lion Gate, Boghazköy, Anatolia (Turkey), *c.* 1400 B.C. Lions approx. 7′ high.

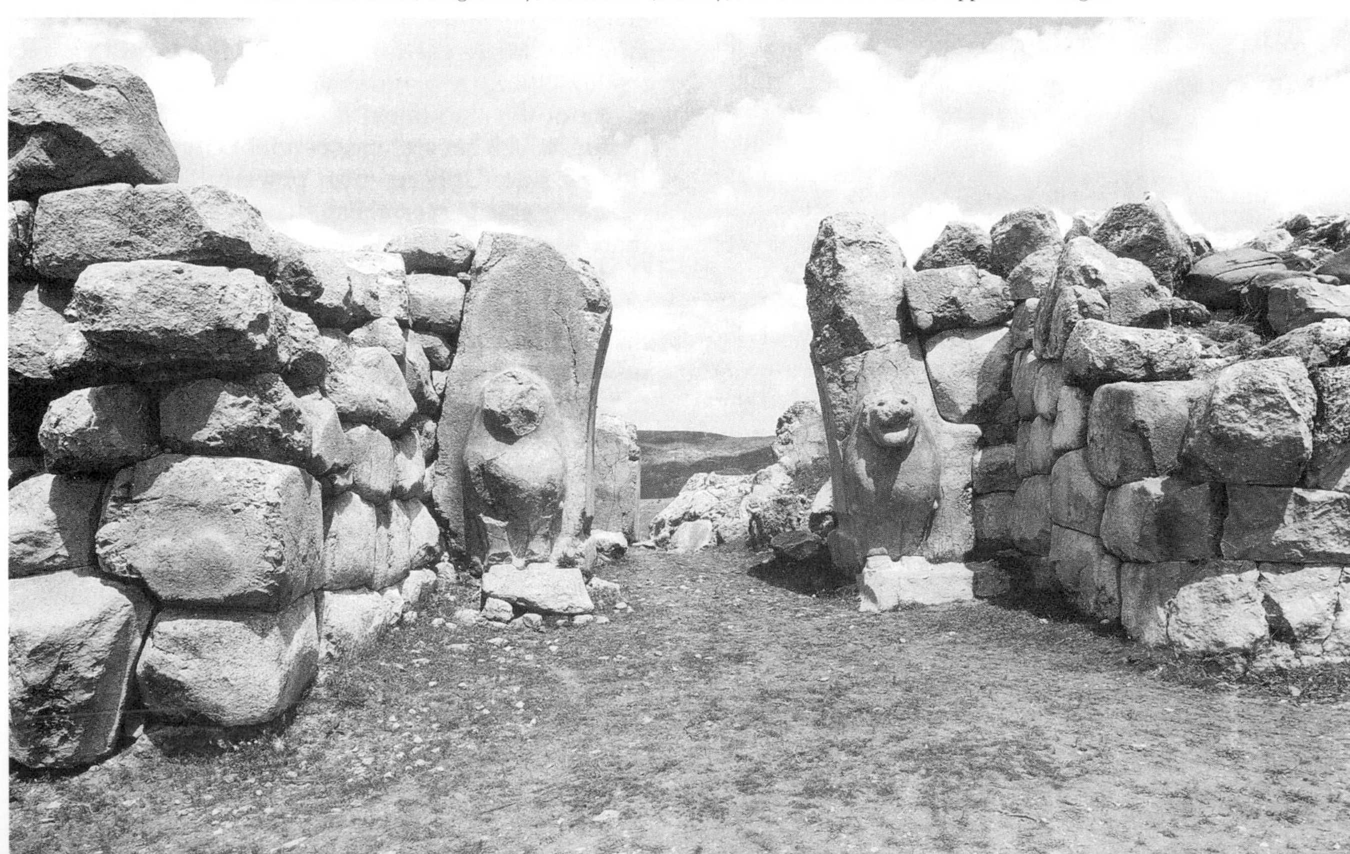

ASSYRIA

While Sumer, Akkad, and Babylon flourished in southern Mesopotamia, what was happening in the northern sector of the great river valleys? For a long time, archeologists thought of it as a kind of empty region—a staging area for nomadic migrations southward or an unstable territory without significant settlement. In the last few years, however, archeological exploration has uncovered evidence for the existence of powerful northern communities that rival the centers of southern Mesopotamia (until now the focus of archeological investigation) in historic importance and influence. We now know that many centuries before the later Assyrian empire extended its sway over all of the ancient Near East, a king named Shamshi Adad, a contemporary of Hammurabi, dominated the north and built his palaces at a site in northeastern Syria near the later Assur, which gives Assyria its name. Shamshi Adad called his city Shubat Enlil (Shagar Bazar) and built it on the ruins of a great city more ancient than his own by two millennia. The immense walls of that city, which measure 50 feet high and about 60 feet thick, have been uncovered beneath the two palaces of Shamshi Adad. The walls form a two-mile perimeter around what must have been the capital of a northern empire as powerful and perhaps older than Sumer. Its origins are still a mystery; its language was neither Semitic nor Sumerian, and it has been suggested that its people may have been Indo-Aryans from the east. Below this level are still earlier remains of human habitation that date to the sixth millennium B.C.

The later Assyrians, familiar to us from the Old Testament and from their inscriptions and monuments, were frustrated in their impulse to power by the kingdoms of the south—Sumer, Akkad, and Babylon—and, on the northwest, by the Mitanni, to whom they were subject for a while. Their opportunity came when their Mitannian overlords were broken by the Hittites and when the weak Kassite kingdom that had succeeded the Babylonian dynasty proved incapable of effective resistance. By about 900 B.C., Assyrian destiny was already becoming an actuality, and for the next three centuries, Assyria was the dominant power in the Near East. Assyrian kings became military commanders, and Assyria itself, with its center successively at Nimrud (ancient Calah), Khorsabad (ancient Dur Sharrukin), and Nineveh, became a garrison state with an imperial structure that extended from the Tigris to the Nile and from the Persian Gulf to Asia Minor. Centuries of unremitting warfare against their neighbors and often rebellious subjects hardened the Assyrians into a cruel and merciless people whose atrocities in warfare were bitterly decried throughout the ancient world. Although they held the restless Babylonian south in thrall, the Assyrians respected the religion and the culture of Sumer-Babylon and were, in fact, dependent on its advanced civilization.

Architecture

The unfinished royal citadel of Sargon II of Assyria, built at Khorsabad reveals in its ambitious layout (FIG. **2-28**) the confidence of the "great kings" in their all-conquering might. The palace covered some 25 acres and had over two hundred courtyards and rooms. The city itself, above which the citadel-palace stood on a mound 50 feet high, measures about a square mile in area. The palace may have been elevated solely to raise it above flood level, but its elevation also served to put the king's residence above those of his subjects and midway between his subjects and the gods. Although the builders probably aimed at symmetry, the plan is rambling, embracing an aggregation of rectangular rooms and halls grouped around square and rectangular courts (FIG. **2-29**). The shape of the long, narrow rooms and the massiveness of the side walls suggest that the rooms were covered by brick *barrel vaults* (see FIG. 6-53), the most practical roofing method in a region that lacks both timber and good building stone. Behind the main courtyard, each side of which measures 300 feet in length, were the residential quarters of the king, who received foreign emissaries in the long, high, brilliantly painted throne room. All visitors entered from another large courtyard, passing through the central entrance between huge guardian demons, over 13 feet tall. The walls of the court were lined with giant figures of the king and his courtiers.

Sargon II regarded his city and palace as an expression of his grandeur, which he viewed as founded on

2-28 Reconstruction drawing of the citadel of Sargon II, Khorsabad, c. 720 B.C. (After Charles Altman.)

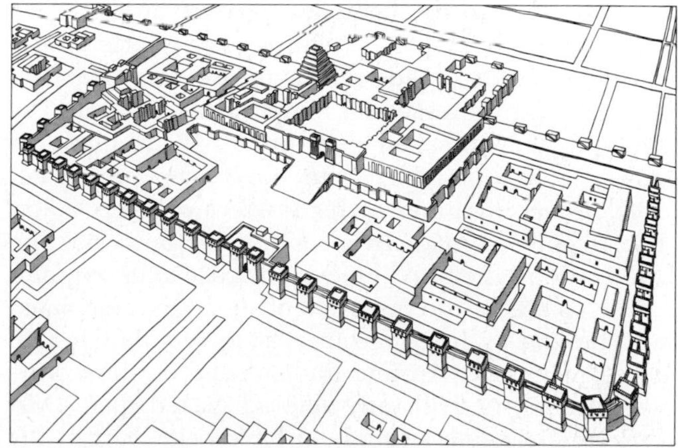

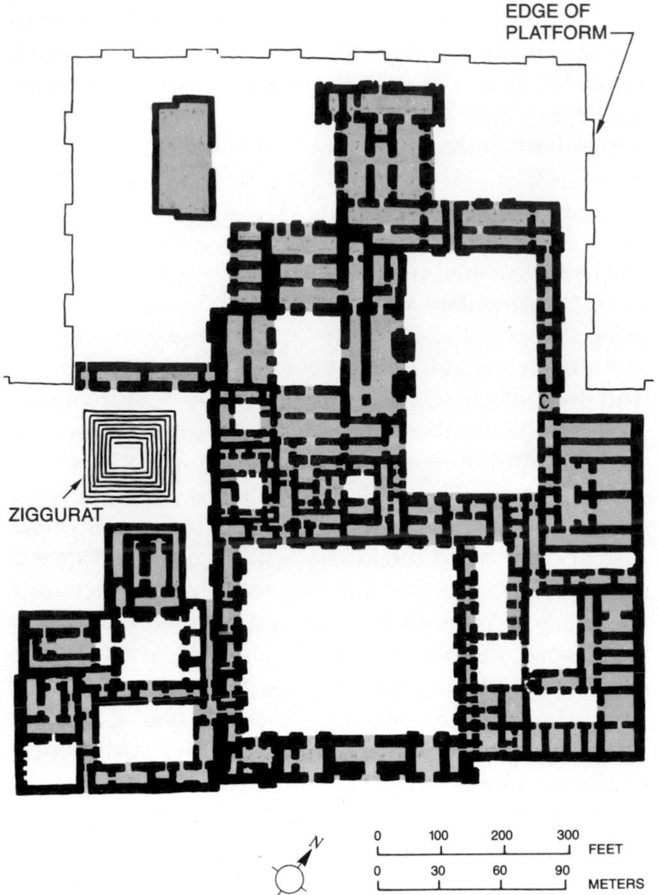

2-29 Plan of the inner precincts of the citadel of Sargon II, Khorsabad.

the submission and enslavement of his enemies. He writes in an inscription: "I built a city with [the labors of] the peoples subdued by my hand, whom Assur, Nabu, and Marduk had caused to lay themselves at my feet and bear my yoke at the foot of Mount Musri, above Nineveh." And in another text, he proclaims: "Sargon, King of the World, has built a city. Dur Sharrukin he has named it. A peerless palace he has built within it."

In addition to the complex of courtyards, throne room, state chambers, harem, service quarters, and guard rooms that made up the palace, the royal citadel included the essential temple and ziggurat. The ziggurat at Khorsabad may have had as many as seven stages, of which four have been preserved, each 18 feet high and each painted a different color. The ascent was made by a continuous ramp that spiraled around the building from its base to its summit.

The palace façade consisted of a massive crenelated wall broken by huge rectangular towers flanking an arched doorway. Around the arch and on the towers were friezes of brilliantly colored glazed tiles. Dazzling brilliance also seems to have been part of the royal Assyrian plan to overwhelm the visitor. The doorway was guarded by colossal winged bulls called *lamassu* (FIG. **2-30**). These man-headed bulls, derived from age-old composite creatures of Mesopotamian art, served to ward off enemies, visible and invisible, and to guard the kings whose features their faces probably reflect. Carved partly in the round and partly in high relief, these figures combine the front view at rest with the side view in motion, contriving this combination by the addition of a fifth leg. The gigantic size, the bold, vigorous carving, the fine sweep of the wings, and the patterning of the surface by the conventional treatment of details together produce a splendor and strength that are awesome even today. We may think of the lamassu in all their majesty not so much as guardians of the king but as augmentations of his regality. They wear the horned crowns of the god-kings of Akkad and the large-eyed, bearded masks familiar ever since Sumer. The bull and lion bodies and eagle wings of the Khorsabad gate figures suggest the superhuman strength and fierceness of the king and his swiftness to bring justice or vengeance. The virtues of Assyrian kingship are written large in these hybrid beasts. Ancient art repeatedly testifies to people's persisting fear and

2-30 *Winged Human-Headed Bull (lamassu)*, from Khorsabad, c. 720 B.C. Limestone, approx. 13′ 10″ high. Louvre, Paris.

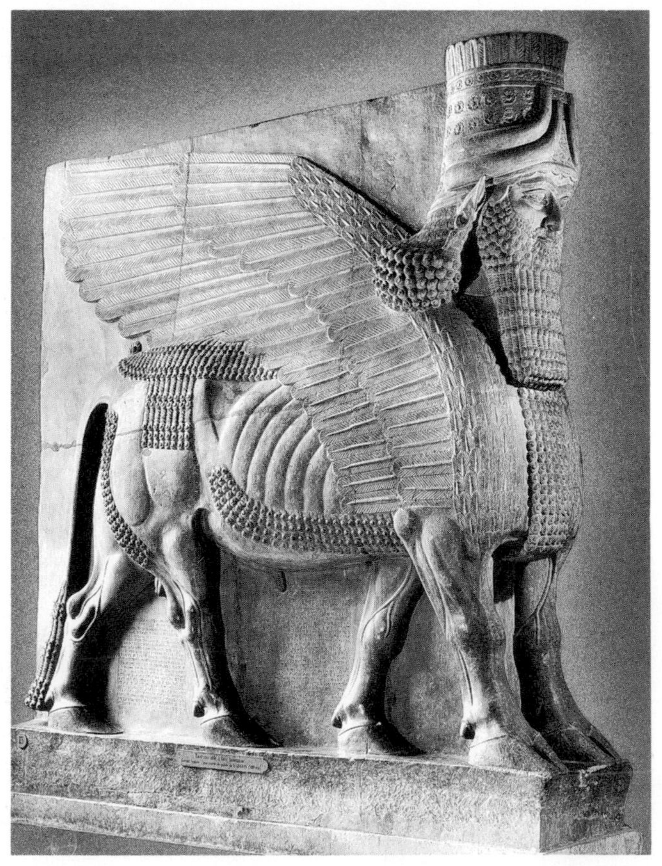

admiration of the great beasts that serve as their metaphors for the powers of nature and for the gods themselves.

Relief Sculpture

Although the kings of Assyria had their power depicted in nonhuman forms, they considered themselves very much a part of the world and expected their greatness to be recorded in unmistakably exact and concrete terms. In conformity with his position between his subjects and his gods, every action of the king had importance. His conquests in battle had the significance of auspicious events, and the same appears to have been true of his successes in hunting. These two royal activities were recorded in the throne rooms of the earlier palaces; later, they also were carved on the walls of what may have been less official rooms. The style of the reliefs, different in the reign of each king who left them, reflects the Assyrian desire for factual reporting, which also is found in the accounts of the campaigns given in bands of inscriptions that accompany the reliefs.

The history of Assyrian art is mainly the history of relief carving; very little sculpture in the round survives. Even the great winged beasts are thought of as relief sculpture and are locked into their stone slabs, presenting three relief surfaces. To narrate the royal feats pictorially, Assyrian carvers used flat, continuous surfaces on which numerous campaigns, sieges, conquests, slaughters, hunts, and scenes of ritual significance could be repeated. For the narrative scenes, the artists devised a vocabulary of forms that, although conventional, was sharply descriptive. At first, continuity was broken by the edges of the fitted block; in their most developed stage, the reliefs extended over the entire wall or walls of a room or corridor.

The astonishing multiplicity of a relief of Ashurnasirpal II at war (FIG. **2-31**) compels careful study of the composition in order to discriminate its details. The king stands in his chariot drawing his bow. He is accompanied by officers, and, in the sky above him, the winged god of Assyria, Ashur, leads him on. The king's team, the reins tight, is passing an enemy chariot that is already breaking up; its driver has been thrown down and one horse has fallen. Assyrian foot soldiers cut the throats of the wounded enemies. At the upper center, an Assyrian soldier slays a foe while another enemy warrior tries to save his comrade. Behind them a soldier is lying dead; in the upper right, enemy bowmen desperately defend the towers of their city. The ease with which we read these incidents is quite remarkable, especially since they are not depicted in perspective or in logical sequence. The artist uses the space of the limestone block as a field to be divided as narrative convenience and a sense of both the factual and the dramatic dictate. The liveliness of individual poses and movements is exceptionally fine and convincing, and despite the formality that exists in Mesopotamian art side by side with naturalistic details, sophisticated spatial devices appear throughout. One is the overlapping of figures to suggest greater or lesser distance from the observer; the king overlapping his officers is a good example.

The formality of Assyrian art at its most rigid can be seen in another relief of Ashurnasirpal II (FIG. **2-32**),

2-31 *Ashurnasirpal II at War,* from Nimrud, *c.* 875 B.C. Limestone, approx. 39″ high. British Museum, London.

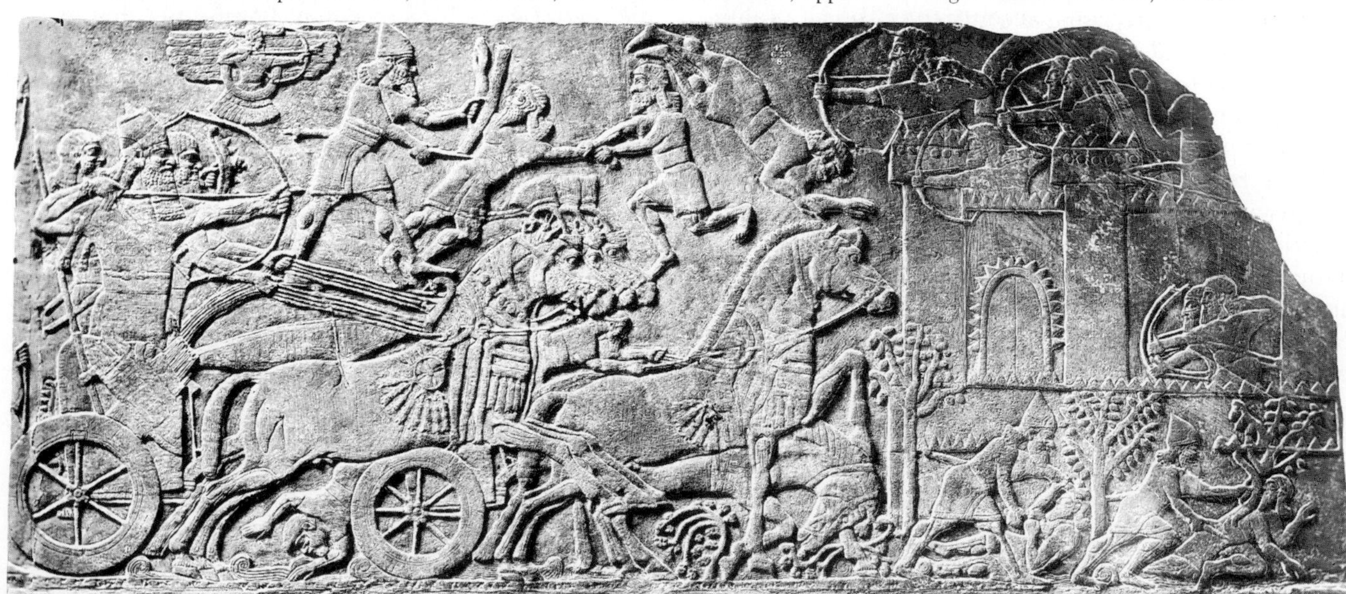

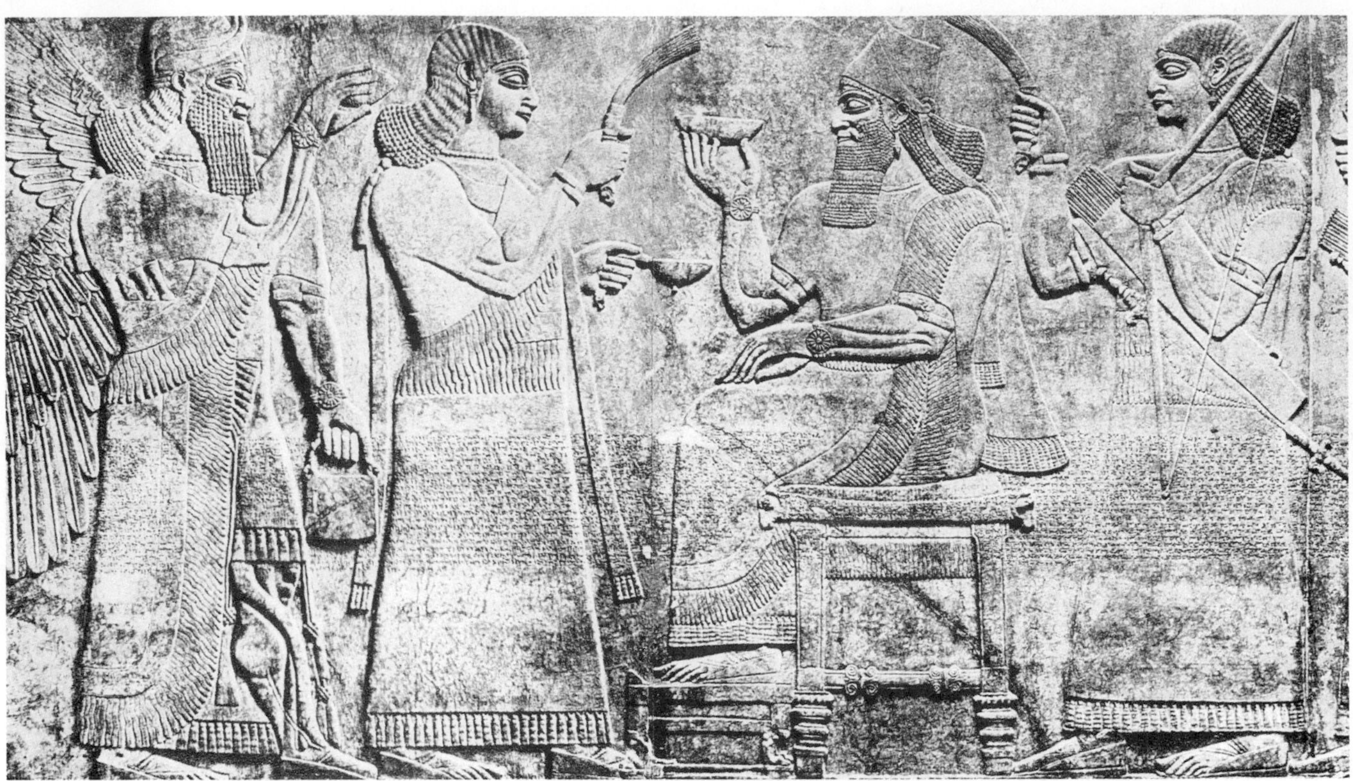

2-32 *Ashurnasirpal II Drinking*, from Nimrud, *c.* 875 B.C. Limestone, approx. 7′ 8″ high. British Museum, London.

in which the king, seated right of center, solemnly raises a ceremonial cup, while the presence of an august personage at the far left, a winged genius who sprinkles holy water, makes it clear that the king's act is part of a sacred ritual. The slow gestures and stately mien are what we would expect of some grave liturgy; we recognize these characteristics in religious services today. The cuneiform inscriptions on the flat, thin slabs of relief continue across the shallow recesses between the slabs, accentuating the neutrality of the planes and suggesting that the carving is meant to be not so much a three-dimensional form as a report of an event in pictures and in writing. An interesting Assyrian convention nevertheless makes itself felt: the human body is represented as thickset and weighty and the limbs are portrayed bulging with muscle. This second characteristic is especially evident in the advanced left leg of the genius and the arms of the king. The calf and forearm muscles are exaggerated, and the veins are like cables—an example of realistic observation converted to a kind of symbol of brute human strength. Also noteworthy is the way in which the profile view of the arms comprises, with the front-view torso, a kind of three-quarter view. The artist, although subject to the conventions of the time, is experimenting here with the problems of representing what the eyes see.

Two centuries later, in a relief from Nineveh showing Ashurbanipal hunting lions (FIG. **2-33**), the conventions of the time of Ashurnasirpal II persist, although more realistic elements are introduced. In this relief, lions released from cages in a large, enclosed arena charge the king, who, in his chariot and with his servants protecting his blind sides, shoots down the enraged animals. The king, menaced by the savage spring of a lion at his back, is saved by the quick action of two of his spearmen. Behind his chariot lies a pathetic trail of dead and dying animals, pierced by what would appear to be far more arrows than are needed to kill them. A wounded lioness (FIG. **2-34**) drags her hindquarters, paralyzed by arrows that pierce her spine. Blood streams from her wounds, a detail that recurs often in Assyrian art and reveals the savage character of its patrons. The artist gives a ruthless reading of the straining muscles, the swelling veins, the corrugations of the muzzle, and the flattened ears—hard realism under the control of the formality of a silhouette in low relief. Modern sympathies make this scene of carnage a kind of heroic tragedy, with the lions as protagonists, but it is unlikely that the artists of the king had any intention other than to aggrandize his image by piling up his kills, by showing the king of men pitting himself against the king of beasts and conquering him.

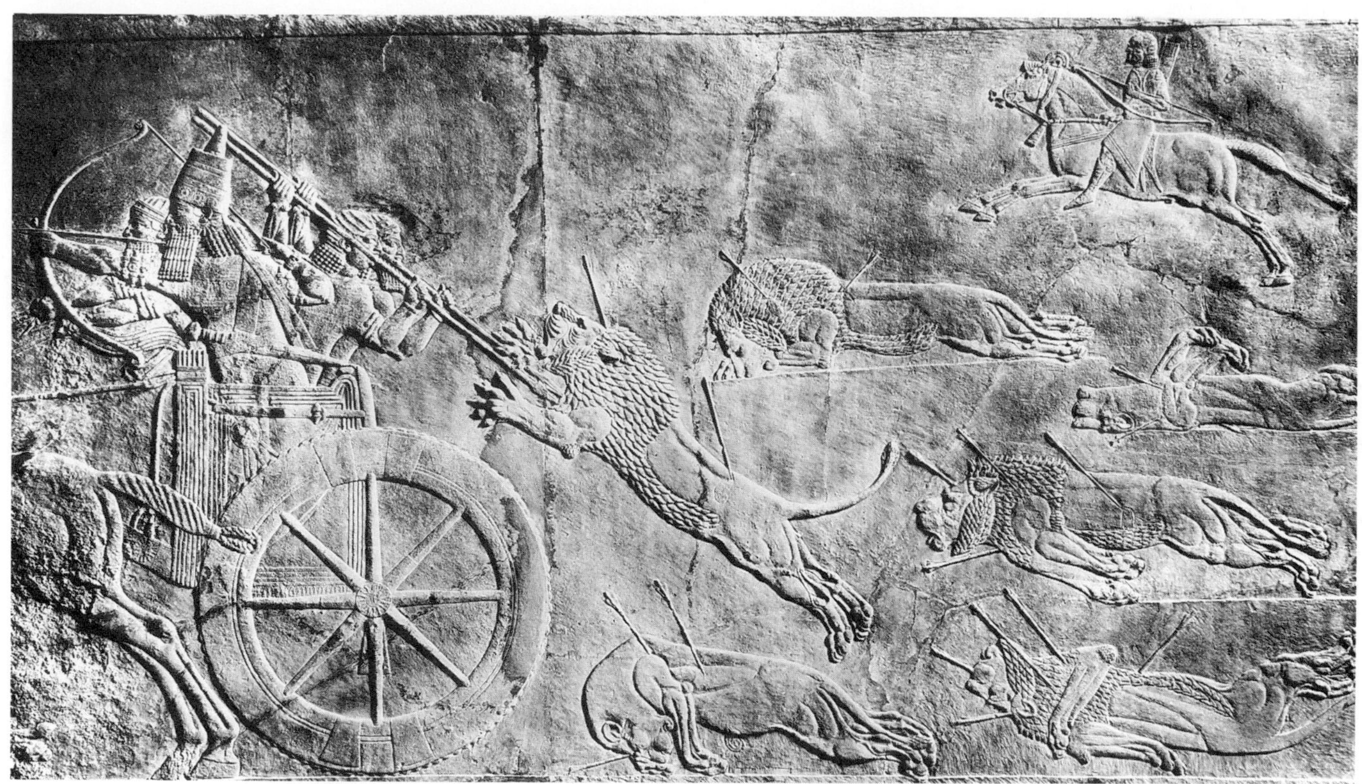

2-33 *Ashurbanipal Hunting Lions,* from Nineveh, *c.* 650 B.C. Alabaster, approx. 60″ high. British Museum, London.

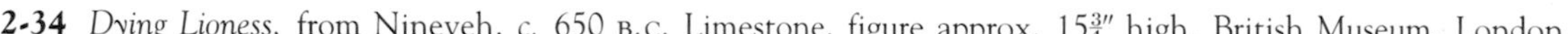

2-34 *Dying Lioness,* from Nineveh, *c.* 650 B.C. Limestone, figure approx. 15¾″ high. British Museum, London.

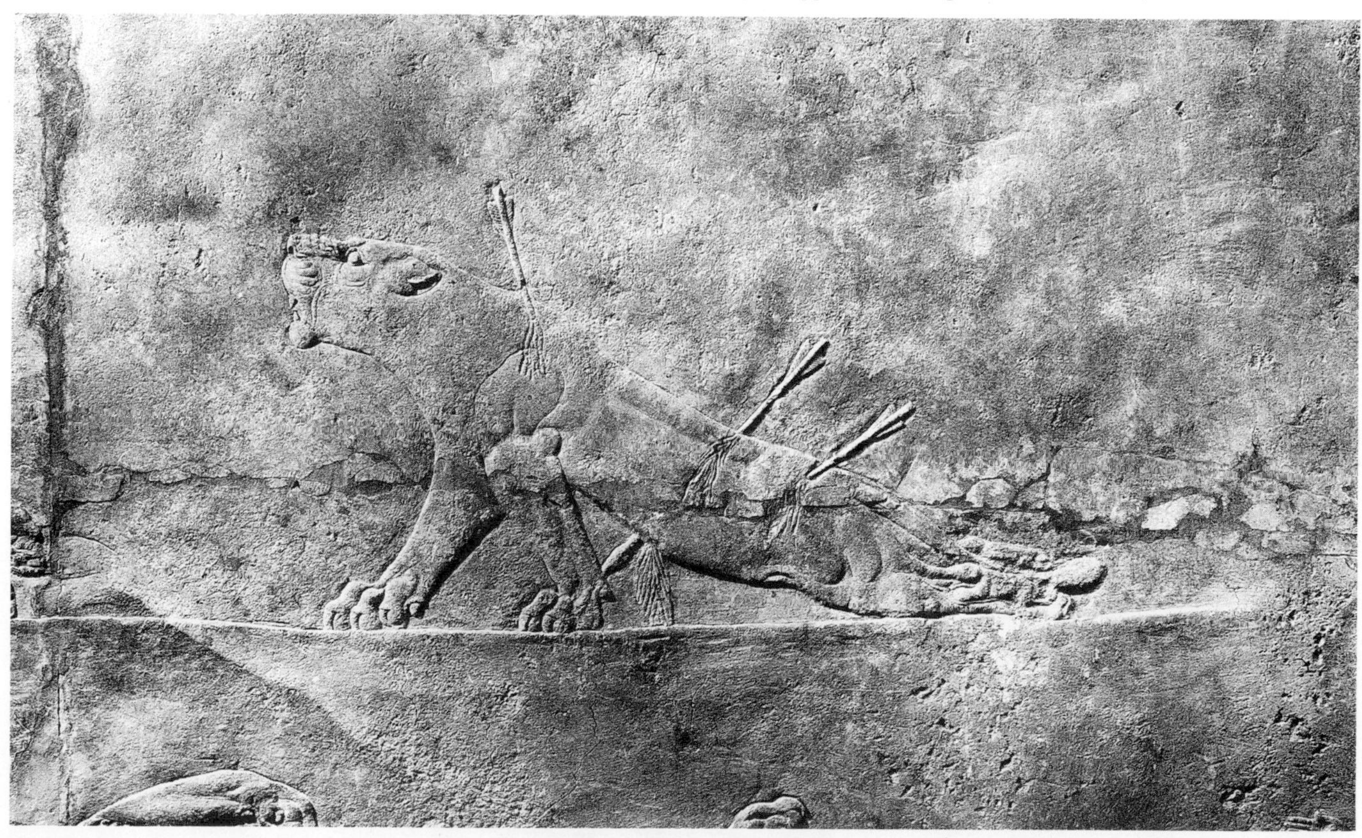

NEO-BABYLONIA

The Assyrian empire was never very secure, and most of its kings had to fight revolts in large sections of the Near East. Opposition to Assyrian rule increased steadily throughout the seventh century B.C., and during the last years of Ashurbanipal's reign, the empire began to disintegrate. Under his son and successor, it collapsed before the simultaneous onslaught of the Medes from the east and the resurgent Babylonians from the south. Babylon rose once again, and in a brief renewal (612–538 B.C.), the old southern Mesopotamian culture flourished. King Nebuchadnezzar, whose exploits we read of in the Book of Daniel, made Babylon a fabulous city once again and its famous "hanging gardens" one of the seven wonders of the ancient world. Only a little of the great ziggurat of Babylon's temple to Bel (the Hebrews' Tower of Babel) remains, but Herodotus, the ancient Greek traveler and "father of history," has left us the following description in a brief account of his visit to the temple complex during the fifth century B.C.:

> In the one [division of the city] stood the palace of the kings, surrounded by a wall of great strength and size; in the other was the sacred precinct of Zeus-Bel, an enclosure a quarter of a mile square, with gates of solid brass, which was also remaining in my time. In the middle of the precinct, there was a tower of solid masonry, a furlong in length and breadth, on which was raised a second tower, and on that a third, and so on up to eight. The ascent to the top is on the outside, by a path which winds round all the towers. When one is about halfway up, one finds a resting place and seats, where persons are wont to sit some time on their way to the summit. On the top-most tower, there is a spacious temple, and inside the temple, stands a couch of unusual size, richly adorned, with a golden table by its side. . . . They also declare that the god comes down in person into this chamber, and sleeps on the couch, but I do not believe it.

A grand approach to the temple complex led down a walled processional way lined with sixty stately figures of lions molded in relief on brightly colored glazed bricks (FIG. **2-35**). These remarkable beasts, sacred to the goddess Ishtar, are glazed in yellow-brown and red against a ground of turquoise or dark blue. The Babylonian glazes are opaque and hard; possibly, each brick was molded and enameled separately. It may be that, as a result of this technique, these animals, whose vigor is suggested by snarling muzzles, long, nervous tails, and carefully depicted muscles, are more stylized than those of the Assyrian hunting reliefs.

The processional way passed through the monumental, brilliantly glazed Ishtar Gate (FIG. **2-36**), the design of which, with its flanking crenelated towers, conforms to the type of gate found in earlier Babylonian and Assyrian architecture. Glazed tiles had been used much earlier, but the surface of the bricks, even of those on which figures appeared, was flat. On the surfaces of the Ishtar Gate, laboriously reassembled, are superposed tiers of the alternating profile figures of the dragon of Marduk and the bull of Adad. This gate is characteristic Mesopotamian formality at its best. The figures compose a stately heraldry proclaiming the gods of the temples toward which the Sacred Way leads. The lessons of architectural sculp-

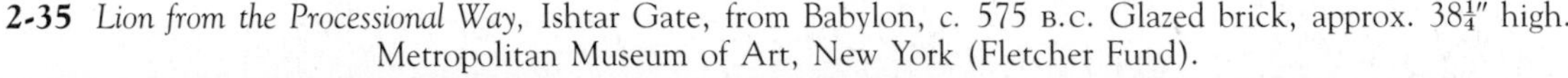
2-35 *Lion from the Processional Way*, Ishtar Gate, from Babylon, c. 575 B.C. Glazed brick, approx. 38¼" high. Metropolitan Museum of Art, New York (Fletcher Fund).

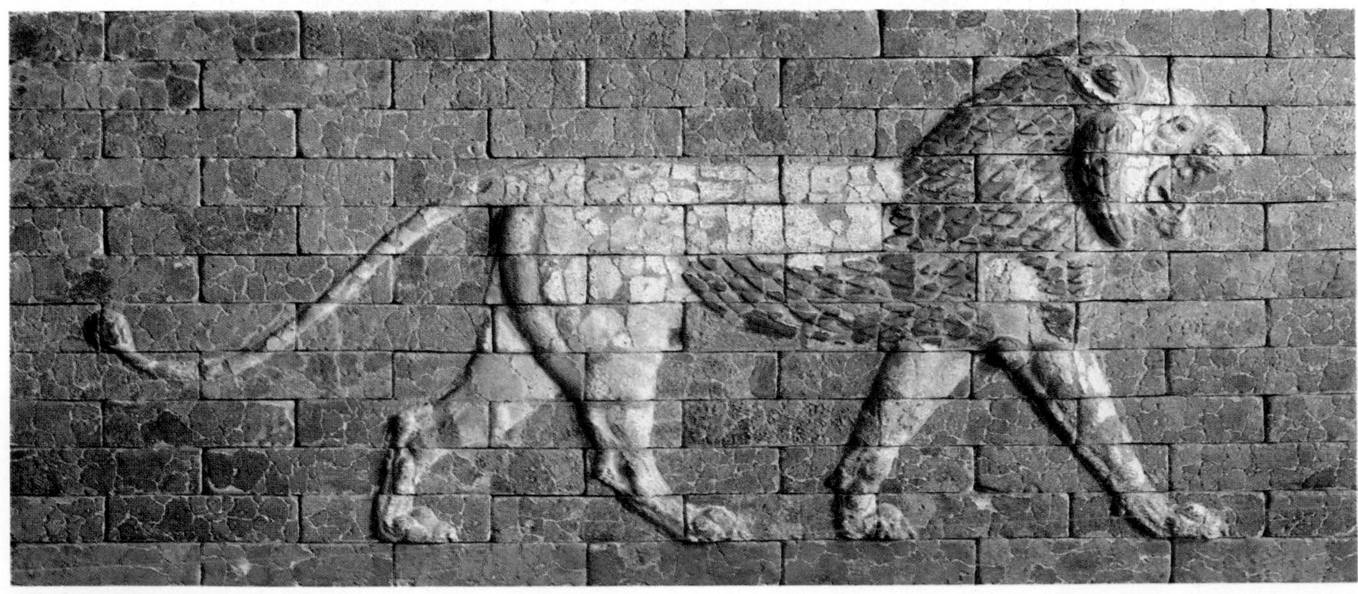

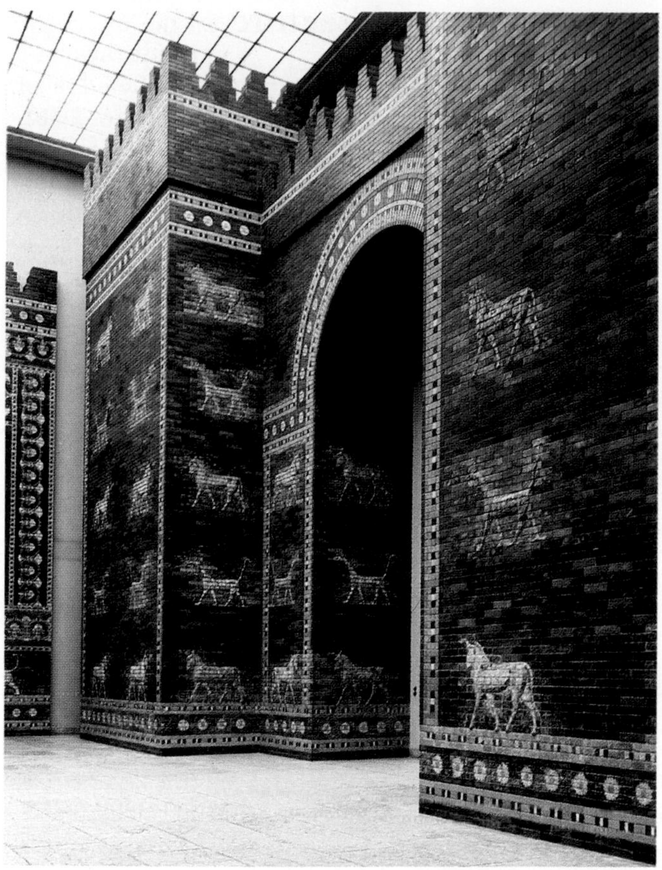

2-36 The Ishtar Gate (restored), from Babylon, *c.* 575 B.C. Glazed brick. Pergamon Museum, East Berlin.

ture from Boghazköy and Khorsabad have been well learned, and the perfect adjustment of figure to wall found in the Ishtar animals rarely has been surpassed; certainly, in the history of architecture, few more colorful and durable surface ornaments are known.

ANCIENT IRAN: ELAM AND ACHAEMENID PERSIA

The later Persian Empire that came into conflict with the Greeks was preceded at a considerable distance in time by a civilization contemporary with the civilizations of Akkad and Old Babylon and regularly in cultural and political transaction with them. Situated in western Iran, this civilization was known by the biblical name Elam.* The empire of Elam corresponded roughly to the Iranian province of Khuzistan. Although most often dominated by Mesopotamia, Elam was strong enough on one occasion to plunder Babylon and to carry off the stele of Naram-Sin and the stele of Hammurabi (FIGS. 2-24 and 2-26). The empire of Elam was destroyed by the Assyrian king, Ashurbanipal, who, in 641 B.C., sacked its capital, Susa (a city that would rise again to great importance under the Achaemenid Persian Empire).

During a relatively brief flowering of Elamite culture in about 1300 B.C., a sculptor cast a freestanding bronze portrait statue of Niparasu, a queen of Elam (FIG. **2-37**). Although sadly mutilated, enough remains of the work to show how obedient the sculptor was to the conventions of Mesopotamian art: the tight silhouette, strict frontality, firmly clasped hands held close to the body—characteristics we have seen in the Tell Asmar and Gudea figures. Yet within these rigid conventions of form and pose, the artist manages to create refinements that could only be the result of close observation: the feminine softness of arm and bust, the grace and elegance of the long-fingered hands, the supple and quiet bend of the wrist, the ring and bracelets, the brocaded gown and the wave pattern of its hem. The figure presents the ideal in queenly deportment, with just a touch of demureness to mitigate the severity of the conventional pose. As

2-37 *Statue of Queen Niparasu,* from Susa, Elam (ancient Iran), *c.* 1300 B.C. Bronze, solid cast, 56″ high. Louvre, Paris.

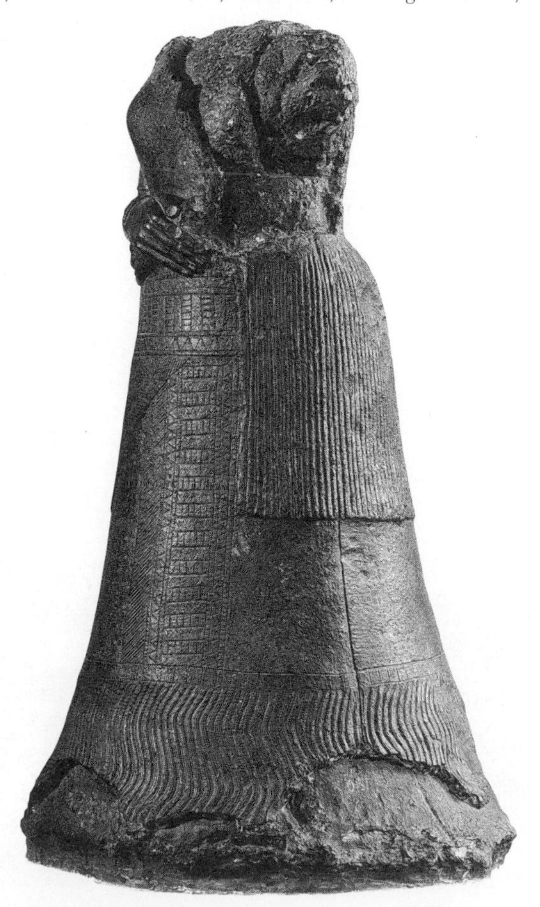

*Some critics have suggested that the fine portrait head of a ruler seen earlier in this chapter (FIG. 2-23) may have originated in Elam at the time when Sumer was at its peak of influence.

we have seen in Assyrian sculpture, it is possible to wed convention with observed details, as the Elamite artist does so successfully here.

The Assyrians succumbed to the Babylonians, who were to fall, in their turn, once and for all. The later Babylonian King Nebuchadnezzar, Daniel's "King of Kings," boasted: "I caused a mighty wall to circumscribe Babylon . . . so that the enemy who would do evil would not threaten . . . [and] of the city of Babylon [I] made a fortress." Nevertheless, the handwriting on the wall appeared, and the city was taken in the sixth century by Cyrus of Persia (559–529 B.C.), founder of the Achaemenid dynasty, who traced his ancestry back to a mythical King Achaemenes and who may have been descended from an Elamite line. The impetus of the Persians' expansion carried them far beyond Babylon. Egypt fell to them in 525 B.C. By 480 B.C., the Persian Empire extended from the Indus to the Danube, and only the successful resistance of the Greeks in the fifth century prevented it from embracing southeastern Europe as well. The Achaemenid line came to an end with the death of Darius III in 330 B.C., after his defeat in the Battle of Issus and the fall of his empire to Alexander the Great.

Architecture

The most important source of our knowledge of Persian building is the palace at Persepolis (FIG. **2-38**), built between 520 and 460 B.C. by Darius I and Xerxes I, successors of Cyrus. Situated on the high plateau, the heavily fortified palace stood on a wide platform overlooking the plain. Although destroyed by Alexander the Great in a gesture symbolizing the destruction of Persian imperial power, the still impressive ruins of the palace complex permit a fairly complete reconstruction of its original appearance, ambitious scale, and spatial intricacy.

Unlike the Assyrian palace, with its tightly enclosed courts (FIG. 2-29), the Persepolis buildings, although axially aligned, were loosely grouped and separated from each other by streets and irregular open spaces (FIG. **2-39**). The dominant structure was a vast columned hall, 60 feet high and over 200 feet square. Standing on its own rock-cut podium, which is about 10 feet high, this huge royal audience hall *(apadana)* has been called "one of the noblest structures of the ancient world." It contained thirty-six columns (each 40 feet high) with fluted shafts and

2-38 Royal audience hall and stairway, Palace of Darius in the background, Persepolis, Persia, *c.* 500 B.C.

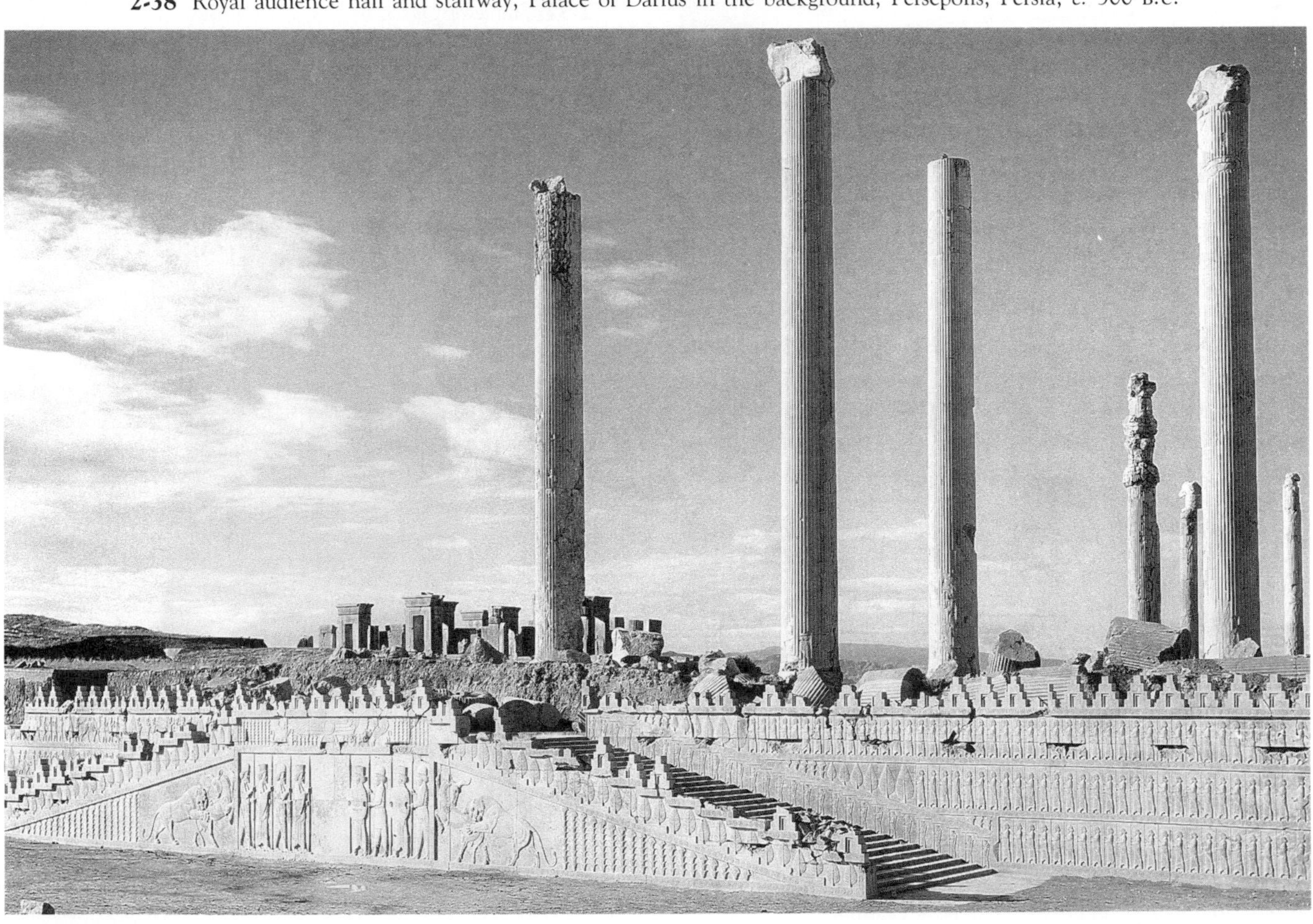

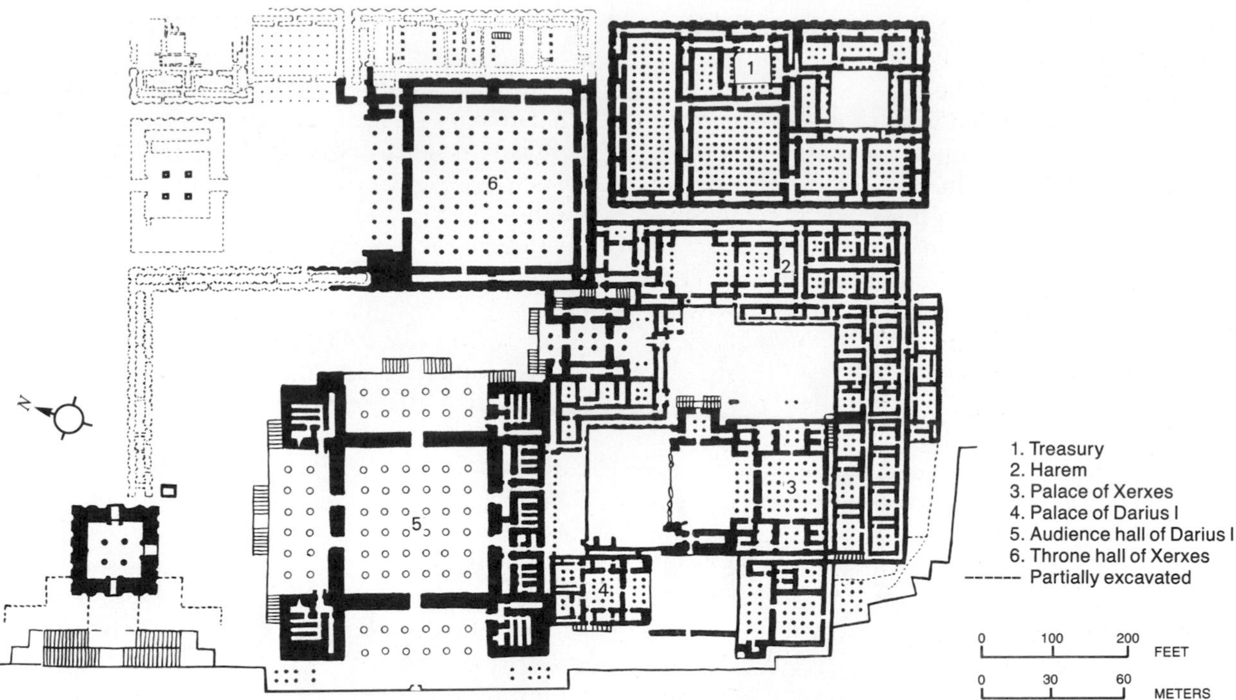

2-39 Plan of the palace complex at Persepolis.

capitals composed of the foreparts of bulls or lions, arranged to provide a firm cradle for the roof timbers. A well-preserved example from the somewhat later palace of Artaxerxes II at Susa is shown in FIG. **2-40**. These unique capitals are an impressive and decorative Persian invention with no known antecedents or descendants. The genesis of the square, many-columned hall so characteristic of the Persepolis palace is also unknown. It has been suggested that it may have been derived from Median architecture, which has remained a blank page in archeologists' books. The Medes were the northern allies and later subjects of the Persians and are believed to have been the intermediaries through whom Persian art received a variety of Iranian stylistic elements that became permanent constituents of it.

Stone, easily available at the site, was used liberally at Persepolis for platforms, gateways, stairs, and columns; brick was used for the walls, however, while the smaller columns and the roofs were made of wood. The ruins of the palace at Persepolis (FIG. **2-41**) show that stone also was used for door and window frames. The forms are derived from Egyptian architecture, which had impressed Darius, but here the frames are not composed structurally of posts, lintels, and sills but are cut in an arbitrary manner and used as sculptural ornaments. In fact, the entire complex of buildings, and particularly the apadana, seems to have been designed primarily for visual effect; it is a gigantic stage setting for magnificent ceremonials celebrating not only traditional festivals but also the

2-40 Bull capital from the royal audience hall of the palace of Artaxerxes II, from Susa, Persia, *c.* 375 B.C. Gray marble, 7′ 7″ high, 12′ 3″ wide. Louvre, Paris.

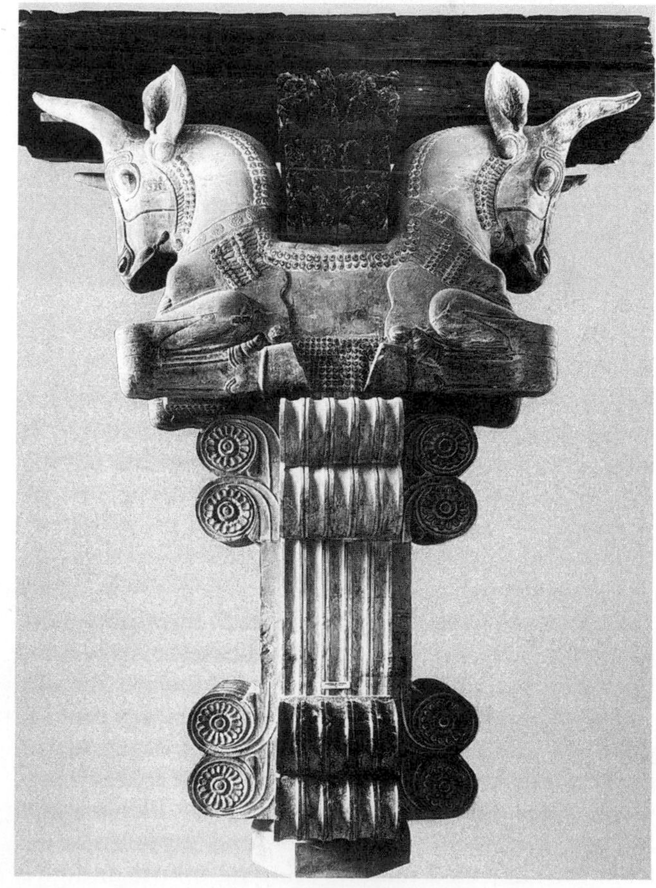

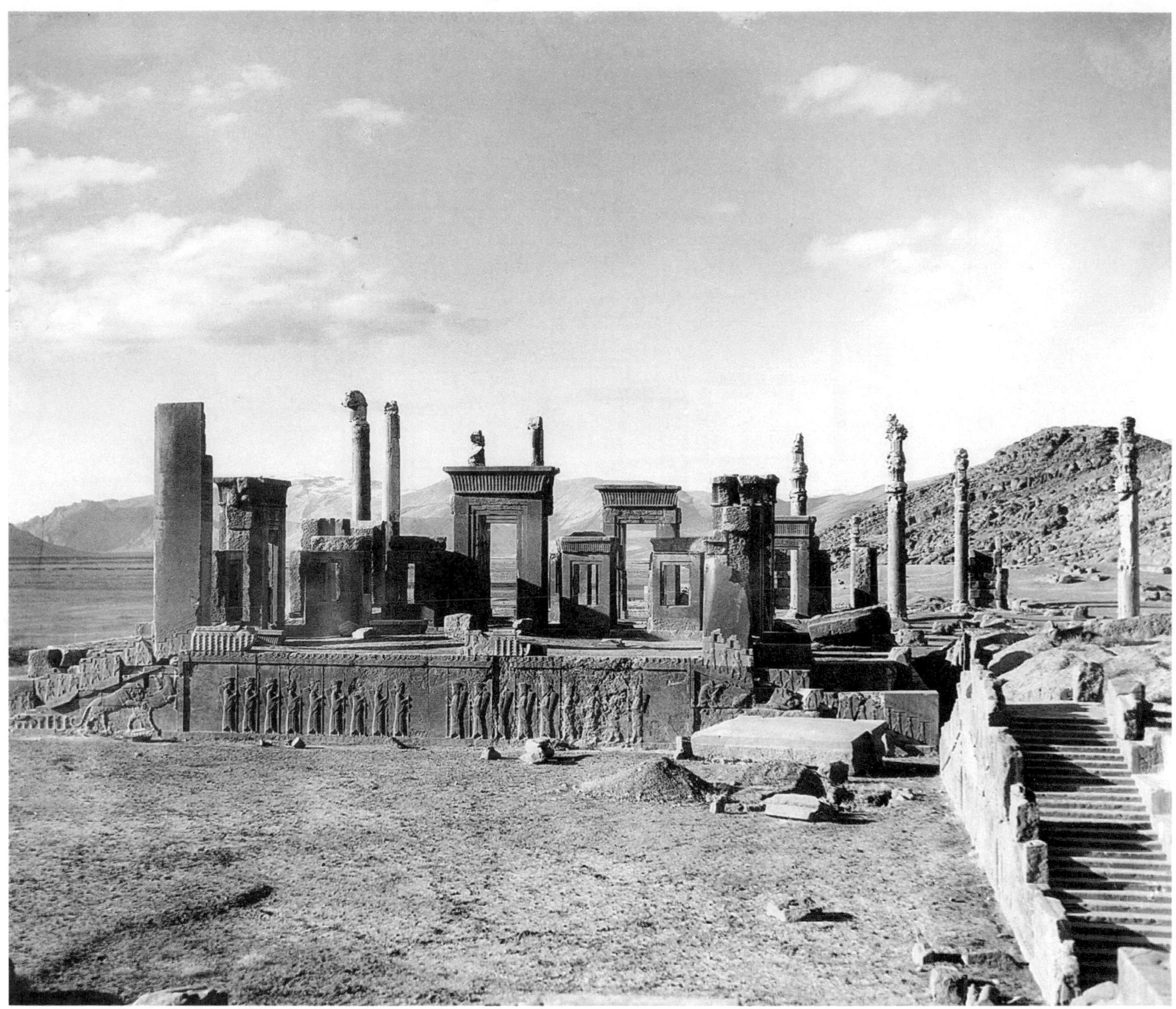

2-41 Palace of Darius, Persepolis, c. 500 B.C.

greatness of the Persian Empire, the power of its king, and the weight of his authority on his numerous tributaries.

Sculpture

The approach to the apadana leads through a monumental gateway flanked by colossal man-headed bulls and then turns at right angles toward the elevated great hall. Broad, ceremonial stairways provide access to the royal audience hall. The walls of the terrace and staircases are decorated with reliefs representing processions of royal guards, Persian and Median nobles and dignitaries, and representatives from the subjected nations bringing tribute and gifts to the king (FIG. **2-42**). These reliefs are thought to represent, in a shorthand version, the actual ceremonies that took place at Persepolis during the great New Year festivals. Traces of color found on similar monuments at other Persian sites suggest that these reliefs were colored, at least in part. Their original effect must have been even greater than it is today, as the rows of figures sparkled in a blaze of colors rivaling that presented by the court during the festivals. On the other hand, the present denuded state of the reliefs makes it easier for us to appreciate their highly refined sculptural style. The cutting of the stone, both in the subtly modeled surfaces and the crisply chiseled details, is technically superb. Although they may have been inspired by Assyrian reliefs (FIGS. 2-31,

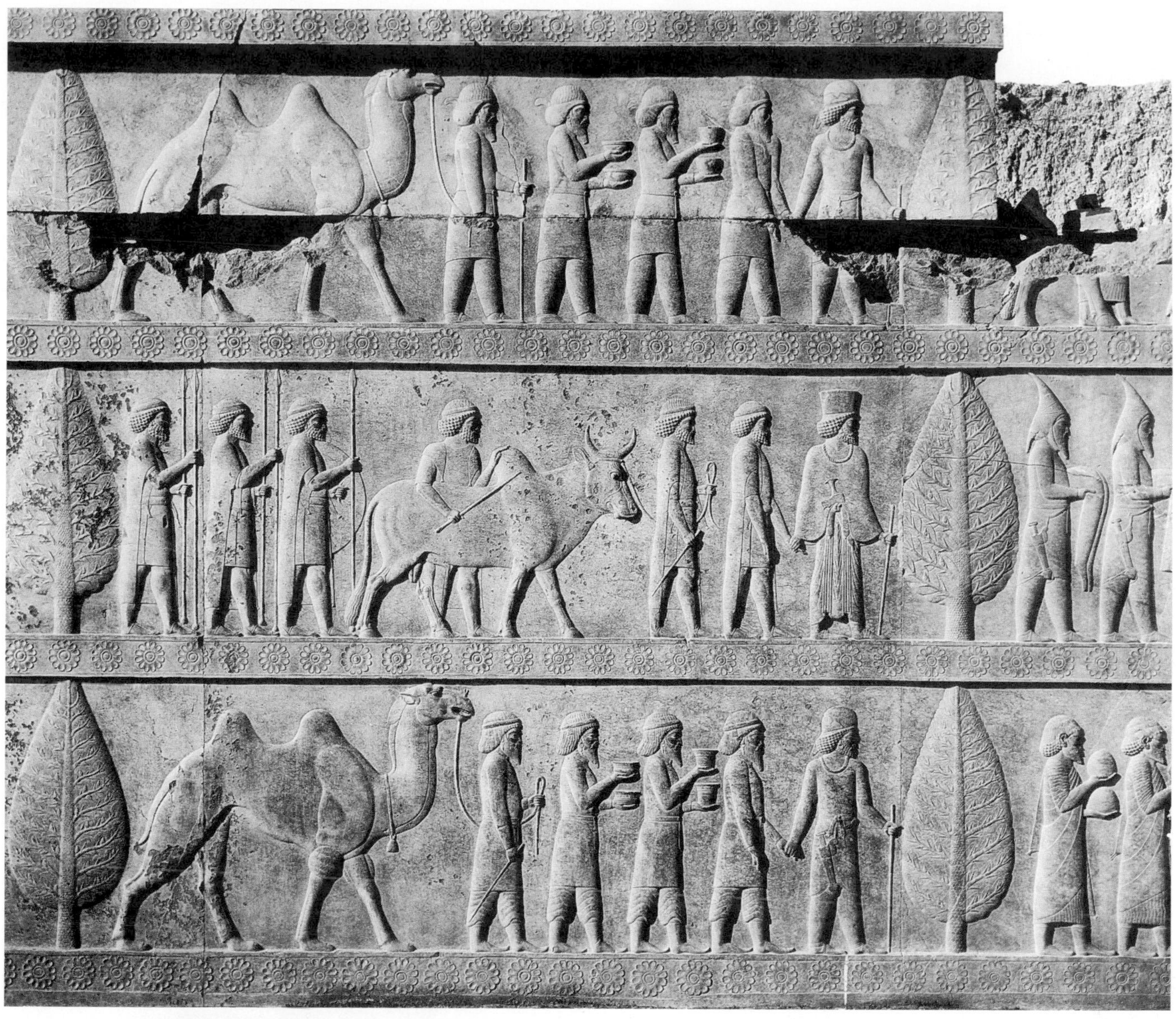

2-42 *Subjects Bringing Gifts to the King* (detail), from the stairway to the royal audience hall, Persepolis, Persia, c. 500 B.C. Limestone.

2-32, and 2-33), these Persian reliefs are strikingly different in style. The forms are more rounded, and they project more from the background; such details as straining sinews and bulging muscles are emphasized less; and, most important perhaps, the figures seem organically more unified, as the torsos are now shown in natural side view and are thus more convincingly related to heads and legs. The supposition that most of these modifications of traditional formal elements are the result of Greek (Ionian) influence becomes almost a certainty when we note how the garments worn by the figures have been stylized in accordance with Greek Archaic practice (see FIGS. 5-14, 5-18, 5-28). Despite the modifications, the Persepolis reliefs represent a triumph of Near Eastern formality in art. Their purpose and function—to glorify the king in a manner both decorative and monumental—is fulfilled most successfully.

Craft Art

Love for well-ordered forms enabled Persian designers to create, on a vast scale, a rich and unified setting for official ceremonials. But the Persians also could work successfully on a much smaller scale. They were excellent goldsmiths and silversmiths; a jar handle in the form of a winged ibex (FIG. **2-43**) typifies their exquisite and enduring art. The ibex, of silver inlaid with gold, rears up on a palmette growing from the head of a satyr. The leaping, lithe body

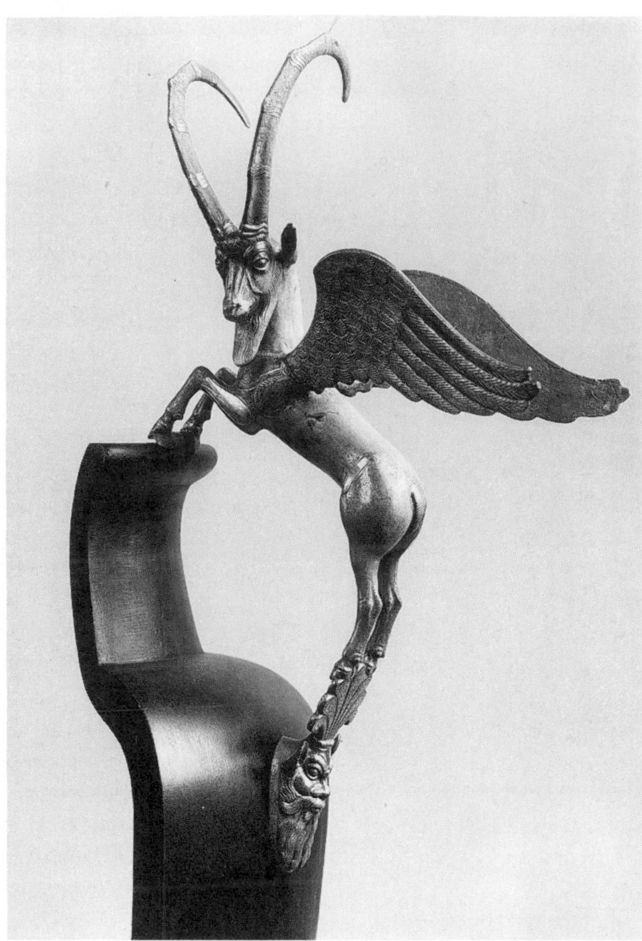

2-43 Jar handle in the form of a winged ibex, from Persia, 400–300 B.C. Silver inlaid with gold, approx. $10\frac{1}{2}''$ high, Louvre, Paris.

rises into the higher curve of the horns, and the suave curves of the wings smooth the motion. All that is needed of truth to nature is here, and none of it intrudes on the effortless play of fancy.

As with most elements of Persian art, it is not difficult to trace the genesis of this winged ibex. Although the animal's body has regained its organic unity, probably through Mesopotamian influence, its original source of inspiration is to be found among the Luristan bronzes. Luristan, a mountainous region to the east of the Mesopotamian river valleys, inhabited at different times by Kassites, Medes, and other seminomadic tribes, was the home of a flourishing bronze industry that reached its peak during the eighth and seventh centuries B.C. Luristan craftsmen produced a variety of portable objects, such as cups, bowls, weapons, bridles, and articles of personal adornment that, collectively, are referred to as "nomad's gear." Although we do not know by and for whom these objects were made, they form a homogeneous group that is rooted in an old and widespread tradition whose exponents delighted in working with animal forms. This so-called animal style may have originated in the Luristan region; at any rate, it spread over much of the ancient world, from the Asiatic steppes to central and western Europe. The Luristan bronzes are characterized by a high degree of abstraction that converts the representations of animals into purely decorative devices. In the handle of the ceremonial cauldron illustrated in FIG. **2-44**, the two rearing ibexes make interlocking arcs that echo in linear

2-44 Ceremonial cauldron, from Luristan, eighth century B.C. Bronze, approx. 12″ high. Cincinnati Art Museum (The Mary Hanna Fund).

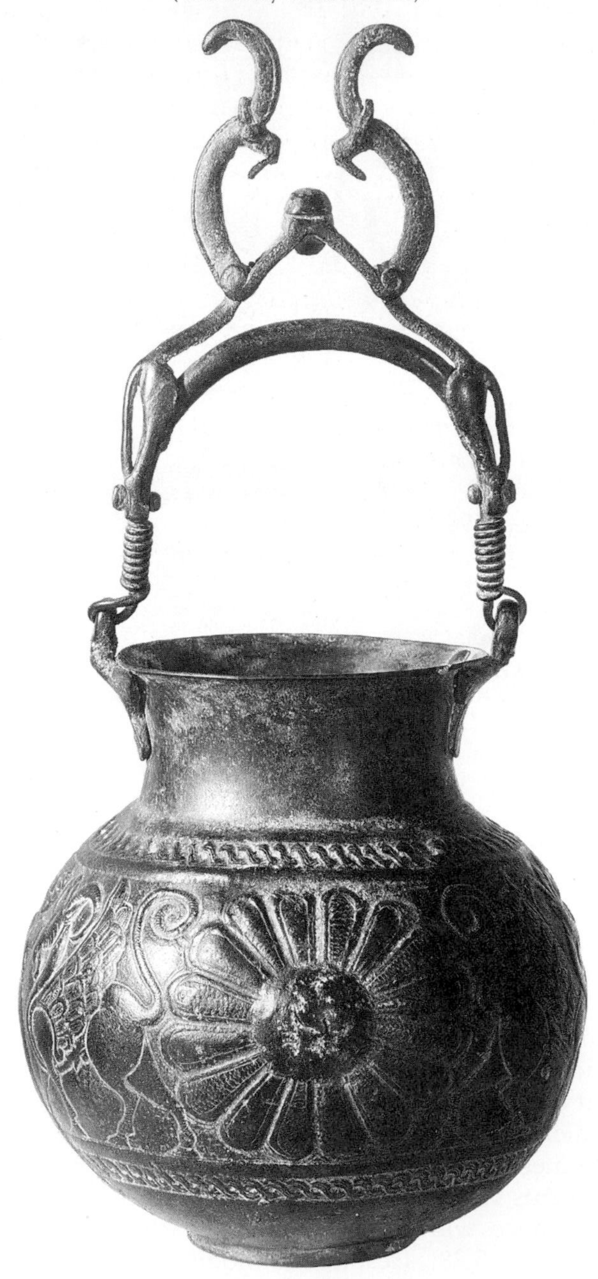

form the three-dimensional shape of the vessel to which they are attached. Although wingless, their pose, attitude, and purpose leave little room for doubt that they are the forerunners of the Persian ibex. The source of inspiration for the Persian animal's wings seems to appear in the embossed decoration of the bowl, where the Luristan artist has boldly copied Assyrian winged bulls and sacred emblems in Assyrian style and technique.

Eclecticism of Achaemenid Art

Thirty years ago, Achaemenid art was called eclectic—that is, derivative and lacking in originality. Today, as more knowledge has been accumulated about the earlier periods of art in Iran, much art that seemed to have been brought in from the outside also can be shown to have had roots in earlier Iranian periods and to have been accepted in a new form from that source. Thus, the platforms of the palaces at Persepolis are similar to those found in Mesopotamia, but the fact that Persepolis was built on the terrace of a mountain spur may reflect ancient Persian custom. The inhabitants of southwest Iran carved rock reliefs with lines of marching figures, the monotony of which has been compared with some of the reliefs adorning the stairway façades at Persepolis. On the other hand, the guardian figures are of Assyrian origin, the machinelike precision in the carving of details is reminiscent of Assyrian relief sculpture, the columned halls may have been influenced by Egyptian or Median models, and the fluting of columns is derived from Greek (Ionian) practice. Yet the manner in which these various elements have been combined produces an ensemble that is quite new and different from the art of those nations from which they may derive. A Persian column cannot be mistaken for an Egyptian or a Greek one, and nothing like the Persian apadana has been found in earlier architecture. Even with all their derivative elements, the architecture and sculpture of Persepolis produce a coherent and majestic impression.

Prior to the Persian conquest of the Near East, Persian art had consisted mainly of small-scale nomad's gear. Their monumental art was not created until they found themselves masters of the Near East and heirs to its rich culture. To glorify and eternalize their military and political achievements, the Persians not only adopted those features of foreign and conquered cultures that seemed to serve this purpose but also brought into the country the artisans who could best realize their ambitious projects. A building inscription at Susa names Ionians, Sardians, Medes, Egyptians, and Babylonians among the workmen who built and decorated the palace. Under the single-minded direction of its Persian masters, this mixed crowd, with a widely varied cultural and artistic background, created a new and coherent style that was perfectly suited to the expression of Persian imperial ambitions. A court style, like that of Louis XIV over two millennia later, the new style compelled its contributors into an artistic synthesis that was to remain remarkably uniform during the two-hundred-year reign of the Achaemenid dynasty.

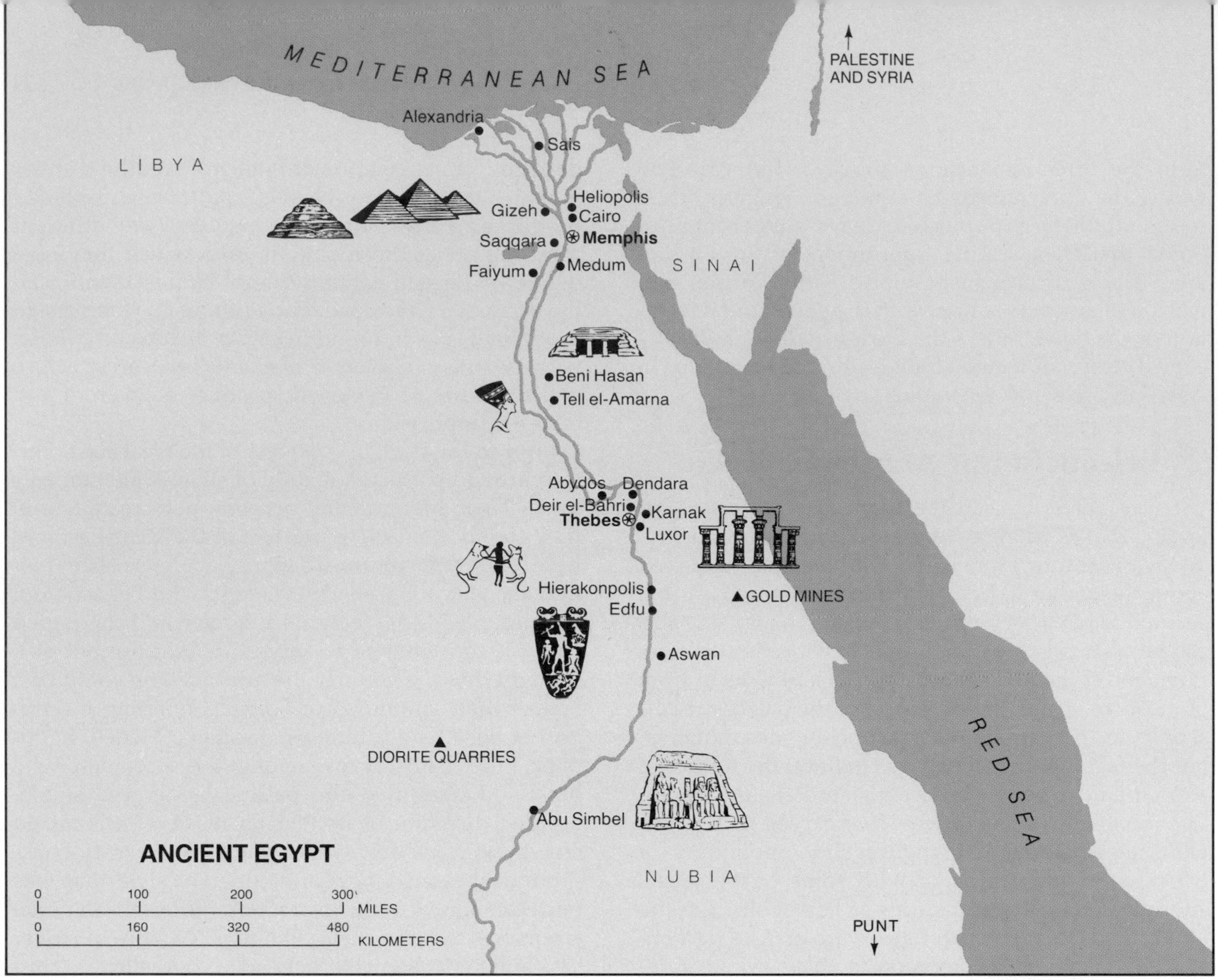

MEDITERRANEAN SEA

PALESTINE AND SYRIA

LIBYA

Alexandria

Sais

Heliopolis

Gizeh

Cairo

Saqqara

Memphis

Faiyum

Medum

SINAI

Beni Hasan

Tell el-Amarna

Abydos

Dendara

Deir el-Bahri

Karnak

Thebes

Luxor

Hierakonpolis

Edfu

GOLD MINES

Aswan

RED SEA

DIORITE QUARRIES

Abu Simbel

ANCIENT EGYPT

NUBIA

0 100 200 300 MILES

0 160 320 480 KILOMETERS

PUNT

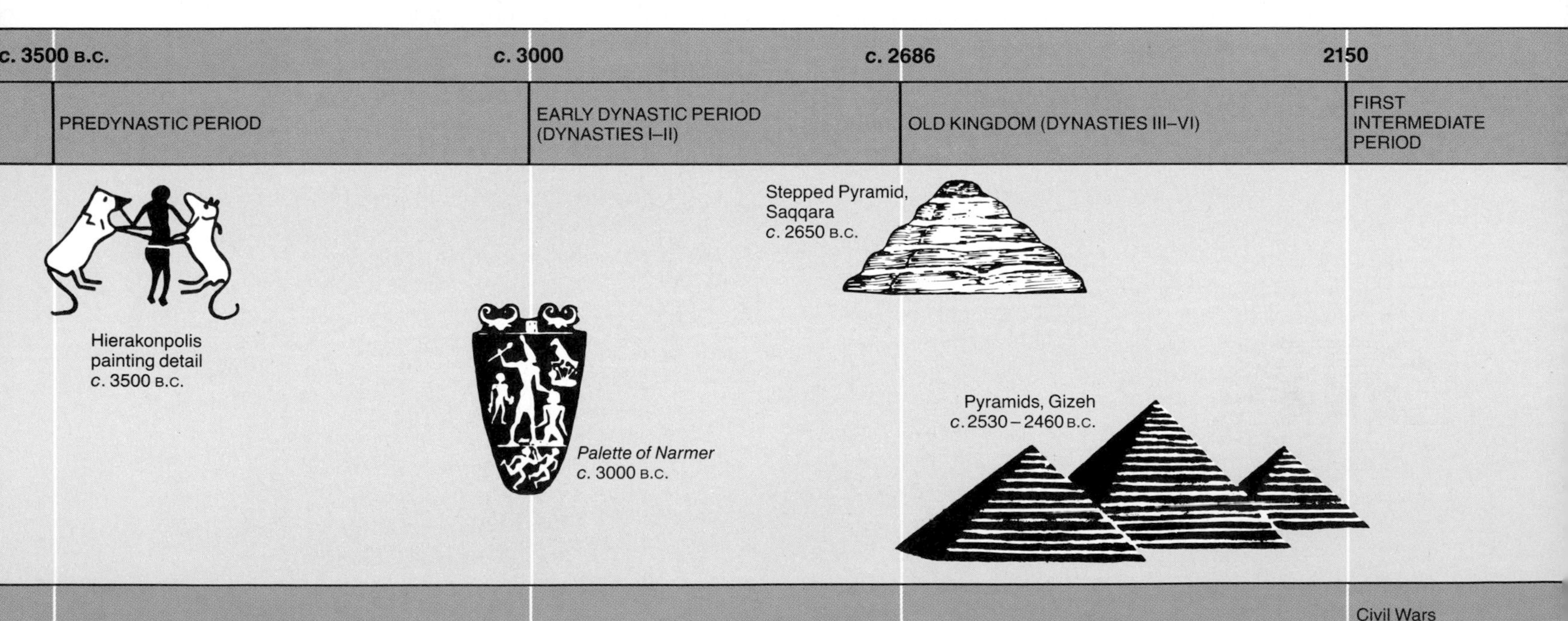

3

THE ART OF EGYPT

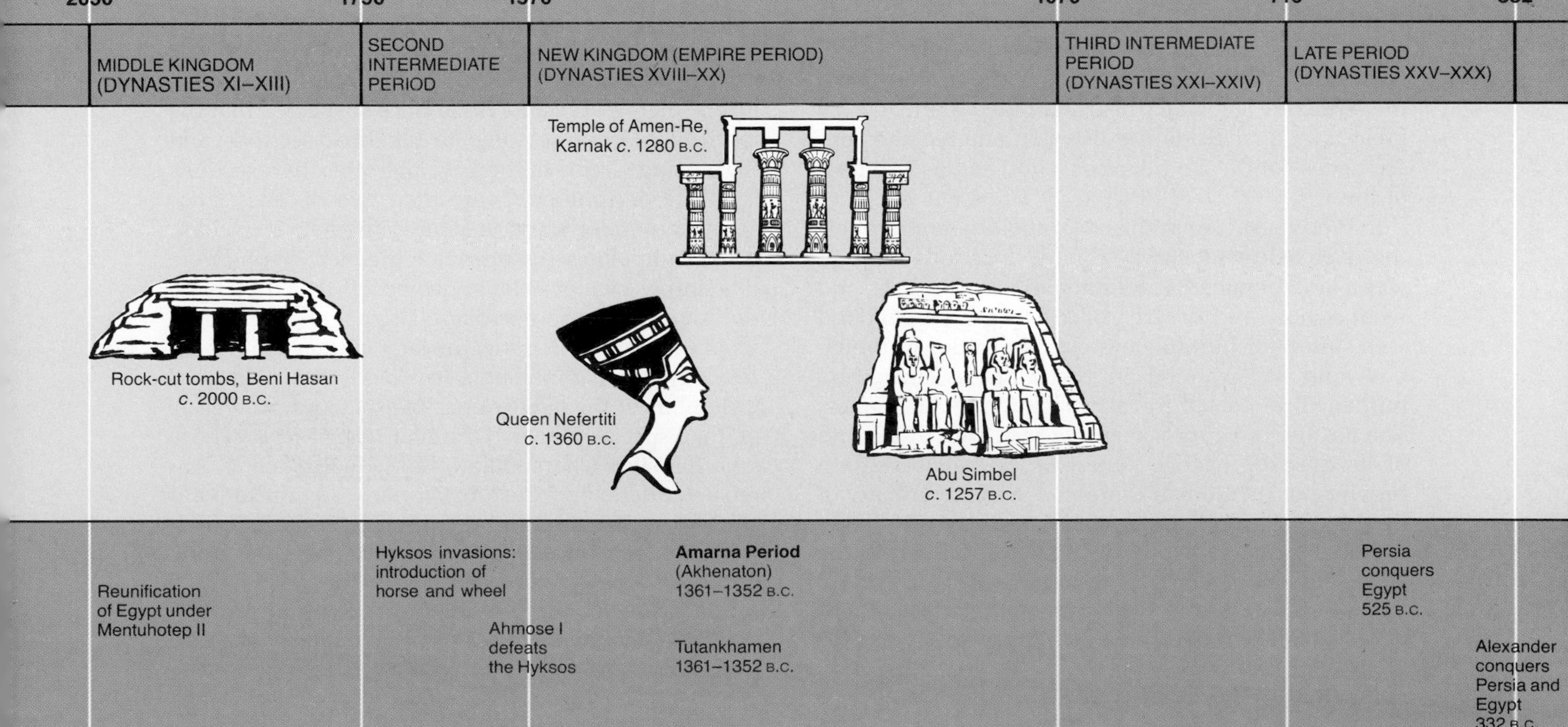

OVER TWO THOUSAND years ago, Herodotus wrote: "Concerning Egypt itself I shall extend my remarks to a great length, because there is no country that possesses so many wonders, nor any that has such a number of works which defy description." A little later, he added: "They [the Egyptians] are religious to excess, far beyond any other race of men." People of discernment, aware of the profusion of monuments left to the world by the ancient Egyptians, have long been in agreement with these observations. Although the Egyptians built their dwellings of impermanent materials, they constructed their tombs (which they believed would preserve their bodies forever), their temples to the immortal gods, and the statues of their equally immortal god-king of imperishable stone. The stone cliffs of the Libyan and Arabian deserts, from which the building materials were hewn, and the Nile flowing between them could represent, respectively, the timelessness of the Egyptian world and the endless cycles of natural process. Religion and permanence are the elements that characterize the solemn and ageless art of Egypt and express the unchanging order that, for the ancient Egyptians, was divinely ordained.

Even more than the Tigris and the Euphrates, the Nile, by virtue of its presence, defined the cultures that developed along its banks. Originating deep in Africa, the world's longest river descended through many cataracts to sea level in Egypt, where, in annual flood, it deposited rich soil brought thousands of miles from the African hills. Hemmed in by the narrow valley, which reaches a width of only about twelve miles in its widest parts, the Nile flows through regions that may not have a single drop of rainfall in a decade. Yet, crops grew luxuriantly from the fertilizing silt. Game also abounded then, and the great river that made life possible entered the consciousness of the Egyptians as a god and as a symbol of life.

In Predynastic, or prehistoric, and Pharaonic times, the river held wider sway than it does today. Egypt was a land of marshes dotted with island ridges, and what is now arid desert valley was grassy parkland well suited for hunting and grazing cattle. Amphibious animals swarmed in the marshes and were hunted through tall forests of papyrus and rushes. The fertility of Egypt was proverbial, and, at the end of its dynastic history, when Egypt had become a province of the Roman Empire, it was the granary of the Mediterranean world.

Before settled communities could be built along the Nile's banks, however, it was necessary to control the annual floods. The Egyptians built dams to divert flood waters into fields instead of attempting to control the flow of the river; the communal effort put forth to construct these dams provided the basis for the growth of an Egyptian civilization, just as the irrigation projects in the Mesopotamian valley had furnished the civilizing impetus for that region a few centuries earlier.

In the Middle Ages, when the history of Egypt was thought of as part of the history of Islam, Egypt's reputation as an ancient land of wonders and mystery lived on in more or less fabulous report. Until the later eighteenth century, its undeciphered writing and exotic monuments were regarded as treasures of occult wisdom, locked away from any but those initiated in the mystic arts. Scholars knew something of the history of Egypt from references in the Old Testament, from the unreliable reports of ancient and modern travelers, and from a history of Egypt written in Greek by an Egyptian named Manetho in the second century B.C. Manetho described the succession of pharaohs, dividing them into the still-useful groups we call *dynasties*, but his chronology is inaccurate and his account untrustworthy.

Scientific history—or, at least, scientific archeology—had its start at the end of the eighteenth century, when modern Europe rediscovered Egypt. Egypt became the first subject of archeological exploration, followed by the uncovering of the ancient civilizations of the Tigris and the Euphrates. In 1799, Napoleon Bonaparte, on a military expedition to Egypt, took with him a small troop of scholars, linguists, antiquarians, and artists. The chance discovery of the famed *Rosetta Stone*, now in the British Museum, gave the eager scholars a key to deciphering Egyptian hieroglyphic writing. The stone bears an inscription in three sections: one in Greek, which was easily read; one in *demotic* (Late Egyptian); and one in formal hieroglyphic. It was at once suspected that the inscription was the same in all three sections and that, using Greek as the key, the other two sections could be deciphered. More than two decades later, after many false starts, a young linguist, Jean François Champollion, deduced that the hieroglyphs were not simply pictographs; he proposed that they were the signs of a once-spoken language, vestiges of which survived in Coptic, the later language of Christian Egypt. Champollion's feat made him a kind of Columbus of the new science of *archeology*, as well as of that special branch within it, *Egyptology*. Those who followed Champollion, individuals such as Auguste Mariette and Gaston Maspero, sought to build classified collections and to protect Egyptian art from unscrupulous plundering. Men like Flinders Petrie introduced new excavating techniques, laying the groundwork for the development of sounder methods for validating knowledge of Egyptian civilization.

Ideally, the foundation of archeological knowledge is a reliable chronology. Yet, as the body of archeological evidence grows and new scientific methods of dating are developed, the chronology must change to accommodate them. Sometimes, what was thought to be close to certain becomes problematical; sometimes, what was guesswork or speculation suddenly becomes probable. Because this is more often the case the further back we travel in time, the Predynastic beginnings of Egyptian civilization are chronologically vague, as are those of Mesopotamia. Some time around 3500 B.C., a people of native African stock may have been exposed to influences from Mesopotamia, or it is possible that, as in Sumer, the sudden cultural development may have been due to an actual incursion of a new people.

A wall painting from the Late Predynastic period (FIG. **3-1**), found in a shrine at Hierakonpolis in Upper Egypt, represents men, animals, and boats in a lively, helter-skelter fashion. The boats, symbolic of the journey down the river of life and death, are painted white and seem to carry a cargo of tombs mourned over by women. Other depictions include a heraldic grouping of two animals (perhaps lions) shown flanking a human figure, many figures of gazelles, and men fighting. The heraldic group, a compositional type usually associated with Mesopotamian art, suggests that influences from Mesopotamia not only had reached Egypt by this time but had already made the thousand-mile journey upstream. The stick figures and their apparently random arrangement remind us of the Mesolithic rock paintings from the Spanish Levant and North Africa, the style of which flourished also in the central Sahara and may have been another impetus to the development of Egyptian art.

The Hierakonpolis mural is the earliest known representative of that millennia-long tradition of painting that reveals to us the *funerary customs* of Egypt, so much at the center of Egyptian life. Most paintings are found in tombs and provide the principal archeological evidence for the historical reconstruction of Egyptian civilization. Religion pervaded that civilization. In Herodotus' words, the Egyptians were "religious to excess," and their concern for immortality amounted to near obsession; the overall preoccupation in this life was to ensure safety and happiness in the next life. The majority of the monuments the Egyptians left behind them were dedicated to this preoccupation.

The sharp distinction between body and soul, long familiar to Christians and to adherents of other later

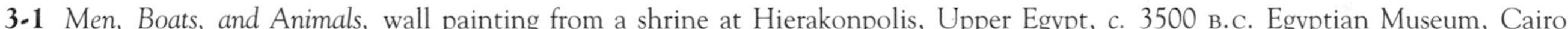

3-1 *Men, Boats, and Animals,* wall painting from a shrine at Hierakonpolis, Upper Egypt, *c.* 3500 B.C. Egyptian Museum, Cairo.

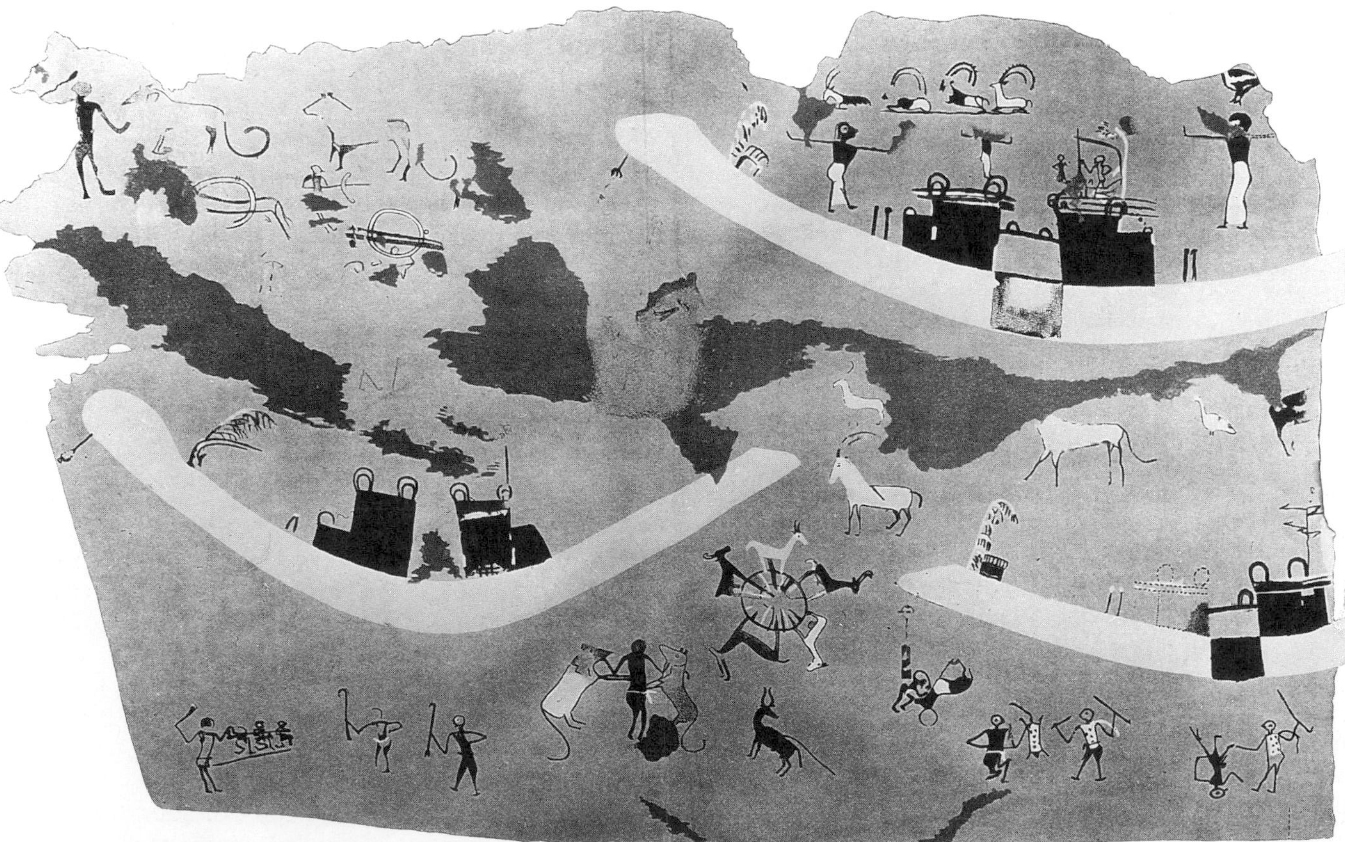

religions, was not made by the Egyptians. Rather, they believed that, from birth, one was accompanied by a kind of other self, the *ka*, which, on the death of the fleshly body, could inhabit the corpse and live on. For the ka to live securely, however, the dead body had to remain as nearly intact as possible. To ensure that it did, the Egyptians developed the technique of embalming to a high art; their success is evident in numerous well-preserved mummies of kings, princes and others of noble birth, as well as those of some common persons. *Mummification* was only the first requirement for immortality. Food and drink also had to be provided, as did clothing, utensils, and all the apparatus of living, so that nothing would be lacking that had been enjoyed on earth. Images of the deceased, sculptured in the round and placed in shallow recesses, guaranteed the permanence of one's identity by providing substitute dwelling places for the ka in case the mummy disintegrated. Wall paintings (for the use and delectation of the ka) recorded, with great animation and detail, the recurring round of human activities—a cycle of "works and days" that changed with the calendar and the seasons. The Egyptians hoped and expected that the images and inventory of life, collected and set up within the protective stone walls of the tomb, would ensure immortality, but almost from the beginning of the elaborate interments, the thorough plundering of tombs became a profitable occupation. Only one royal burial place escaped nearly intact. At the time of its discovery in 1924, the tomb of the Eighteenth Dynasty ruler Tutankhamen revealed to a fascinated world the full splendor of a pharaoh's funerary assemblage.

THE EARLY DYNASTIC PERIOD AND THE OLD KINGDOM

Egypt has been known as the "Kingdom of the Two Lands," a reference to its very early physical and political division into Upper Egypt and Lower Egypt. The upper land was dry, rocky, and culturally rustic; the lower land was opulent, urban, and populous. Even in Predynastic times, conflict must have erupted between the two, for the ancient Egyptians began the history of Egypt, as we do, with the forcible unification of the two lands by a ruler named Menes.

The *Palette of Narmer*

Menes is thought to be King Narmer, whose image and name appear on a slate slab, or *palette*, from Hierakonpolis (FIG. **3-2**). The *Palette of Narmer* is an elaborate, formalized version of a utilitarian object commonly used in the Predynastic period as a tablet on which eye makeup was prepared to protect the eyes against irritation and the glare of the sun. It is important, not only as a historical document that records the unification of the two Egypts and the beginning of the Dynastic period, but also as a kind of early blueprint of the formula of figure representation that was to rule Egyptian art for three thousand years. On the back of the palette, the king, wearing the high, bowling-pin-shaped crown of Upper Egypt, is about to slay an enemy as a sacrifice. A hawk, symbol of the sky god, Horus, and protector of the king, faces Narmer and takes captive a man-headed hieroglyph for land from which papyrus grows (a symbol for Lower Egypt). Below the king are two fallen enemies. Two heads of Hathor, a goddess favorably disposed to Narmer, are depicted at the top. The front of the

3-2 *Palette of Narmer* (back and front), from Hierakonpolis, Upper Egypt, *c.* 3000 B.C. Slate, 25" high. Egyptian Museum, Cairo.

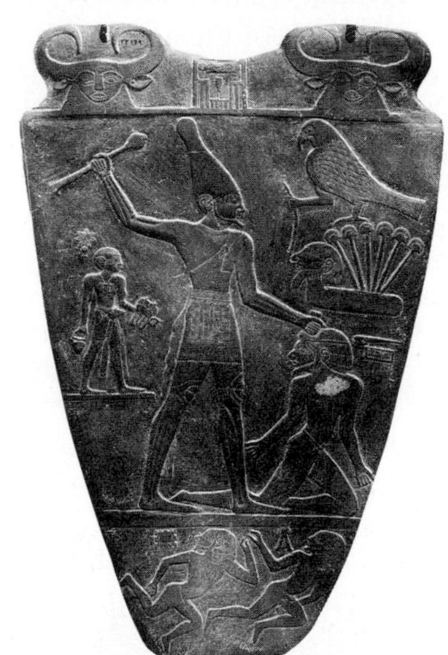

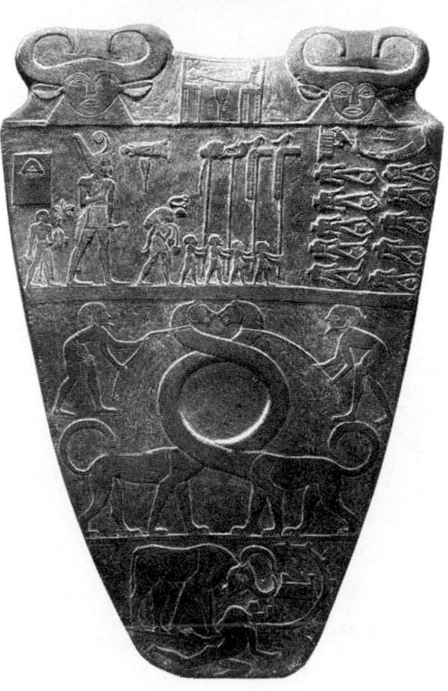

palette shows Narmer wearing the cobra crown of Lower Egypt and reviewing the beheaded bodies of the enemy. By virtue of his superior rank, the king in both cases performs his ritual task alone and towers over his own men and the enemy. The superhuman strength of the king is symbolized by a great bull knocking down a rebellious city, perhaps Hierakonpolis. Historical narrative, as we find it in Mesopotamian reliefs (see the *Victory Stele of Naram-Sin,* FIG. 2-24), is not of primary importance in this work. What is important is the concentration on the king as a deified figure, isolated from all ordinary men and solely responsible for his triumph. As early as the Narmer palette (about 3000 B.C.), we see evidence of the Egyptian convention of thought, of art, and of state policy that establishes the kingship as divine and proclaims that its prestige is one with the prestige of the gods.

If what belongs to the gods and to nature is unchanging and if the king is divine, then his attributes must be eternal. We have already seen in Mesopotamian art that natural shapes are formalized into simple poses, attitudes, and actions. The same thing happens in Egypt, even though the instinct for convention leads to a somewhat different style. In the figure of Narmer, we find the stereotype of kingly transcendence that, with several slight variations, will be repeated in subsequent representations of all Egyptian dynasts except the fourteenth-century pharaoh, Akhenaton (see FIG. 3-38). The king is seen in a perspective that combines the profile views of head, legs, and arms with the front views of eye and shoulders. Although the proportions of the figure would change, the method of its representation becomes a standard for all later Egyptian art. Like a set of primordial commandments, the *Palette of Narmer* sets forth the basic laws that would govern art along the Nile for thousands of years. In the Hierakonpolis painting (FIG. 3-1), figures are scattered across the wall more or less haphazardly; on the palette, the surface is subdivided into a number of bands, and the pictorial elements are inserted into their organized setting in a neat and orderly way. The horizontal lines that separate the bands also define the ground that supports the figures, a mode of representation that would persist in hundreds of acres of Egyptian wall paintings and reliefs.

In addition to recording an important historical event and to laying down ground rules for the pictorial arts, the *Palette of Narmer* also illustrates several stages in the development of Egyptian writing. The story of Narmer's victories is represented in the different registers, with varying degrees of symbolism. Straight pictorial narrative is used to show the king following his standard-bearers in triumphal procession and inspecting the bodies of his slain enemies. This simple picture writing becomes symbolic when, in a bottom register, the king is shown as a bull breaking down the walls of an enemy fortress. The symbolism becomes more abstract in the pile of decapitated foes; here, each body, its severed head neatly placed between its legs, is probably a numerical symbol representing a specific number of fallen enemies. Finally, in the signs appearing near the heads of the more important figures, pictographs take on phonetic values, as the names of the respective individuals, including that of the all-victorious king, have been written in true hieroglyphs, making this palette the earliest labeled work of historical art extant.

Nearly three centuries after the *Palette of Narmer,* we find the basic conventions of Egyptian figure representation that were set up in the palette refined and systematized on a carved wooden panel (FIG. **3-3**) representing Hesire, a high official from the court of King Zoser. The figure's swelling forms have been modeled with greater subtlety, and its proportions

3-3 *Panel of Hesire,* from Saqqara, c. 2650 B.C. Wood, 45″ high. Egyptian Museum, Cairo.

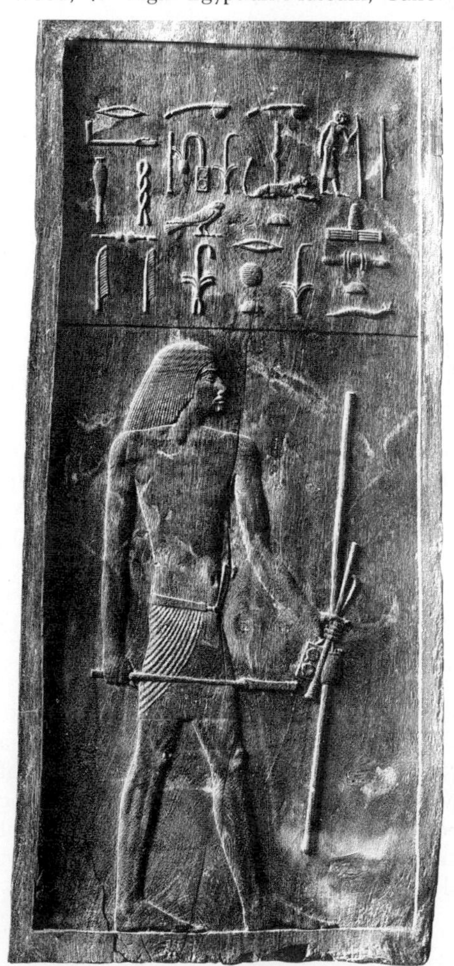

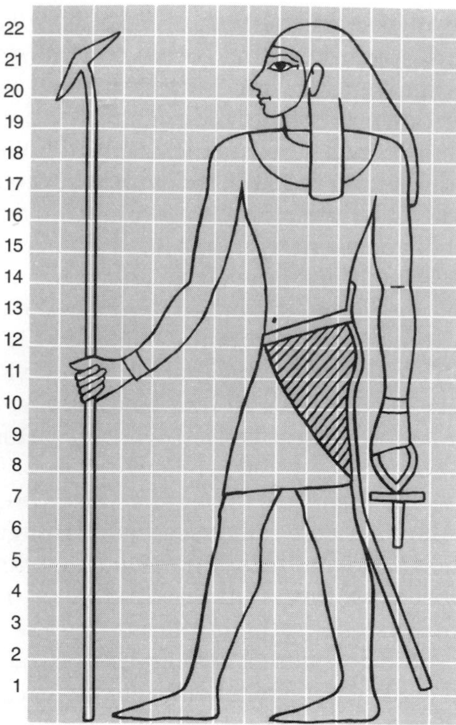

3-4 The *Later Canon* (rule of proportion) of Egyptian art. (After Panofsky.)

have been changed to a broad-shouldered, narrow-hipped ideal. The artist uses the conceptual approach (see page 53), rather than the optical, representing what is known to be true of the object, instead of some random view of it, and showing its most characteristic parts at right angles to the line of vision. This conceptual approach expresses a feeling for the constant and changeless aspect of things and lends itself to systematic methods of figure construction (FIG. **3-4**). Although perhaps not quite as simple as his description of it might imply, the system is explained by Erwin Panofsky as follows:

> With its more significant lines permanently fixed on specific points of the human body, the Egyptian network [of equal squares] immediately indicates to the painter or sculptor how to organize his figure: he will know from the outset that he must place the ankle on the first horizontal line, the knee on the sixth, . . . and so on. . . . It was, for instance, agreed that in a [lunging] figure, . . . the length of pace . . . should amount to $10\frac{1}{2}$ units, while this distance in a figure quietly standing was set at $4\frac{1}{2}$ or $5\frac{1}{2}$ units. Without too much exaggeration, one could maintain that, when an Egyptian artist familiar with this system of proportion was set the task of representing a standing, sitting, or striding figure, the result was a foregone conclusion once the figure's absolute size was determined.*

*Erwin Panofsky, *Meaning in the Visual Arts* (Garden City, NY: Doubleday, 1955), pp. 58–61.

Architecture

Similar principles of permanence and regularity appear in the design of the Egyptian tomb, the symbol of the timeless and the silent house of the dead. The standard tomb shape during the Old Kingdom was the *mastaba* (FIG. **3-5**). The mastaba (Arabic for "bench") was a rectangular brick or stone structure with battered (sloping) sides erected over a subterranean tomb chamber that was connected with the outside by a shaft, which provided the ka with access to the tomb. The form probably was developed from mounds of earth or stone that had covered earlier tombs. Although mastabas originally housed single burials, during the latter part of the Old Kingdom, they were used for multiple family burials and became increasingly complex. The central, underground chamber was surrounded by storage rooms and compartments, whose number and size increased with time, until the area covered far surpassed that of the tomb chamber proper. Built into the superstructure, or sometimes attached to the outside of its eastern face, was the funerary chapel, which contained a statue of the deceased in a small,

3-5 Mastabas *(bottom)*, with plan *(middle)* and schematic section *(top)*.

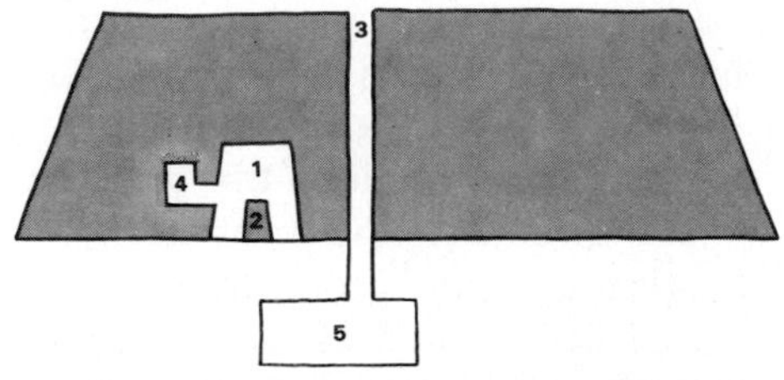

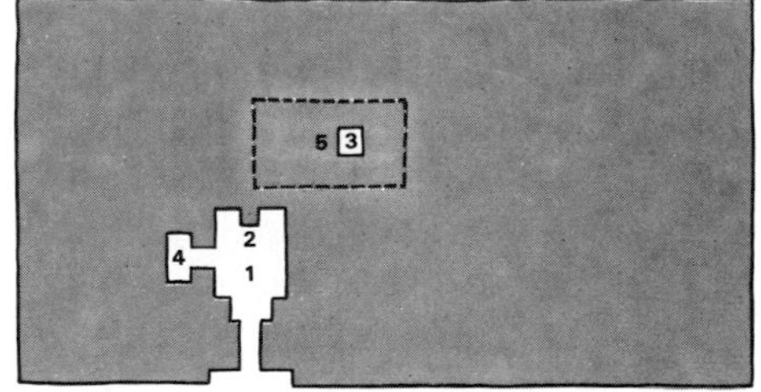

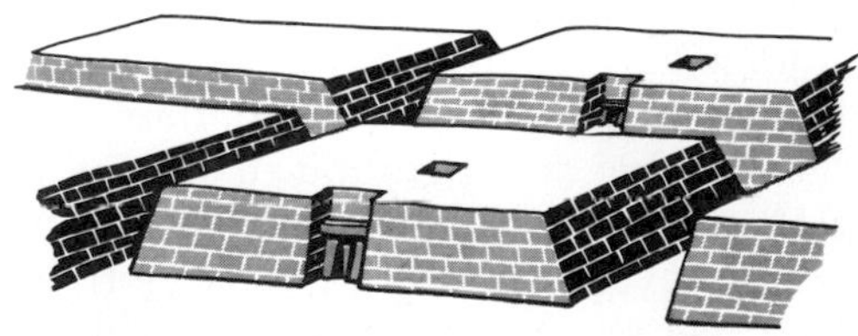

1. Chapel
2. False door
3. Shaft into burial chamber
4. Serdab (chamber for statue of deceased)
5. Burial chamber

concealed chamber called the *serdab*. The interior walls of the chapel and the ancillary rooms were decorated with colored relief carvings and with paintings of scenes from daily life intended magically to provide the deceased with food and entertainment.

About 2650 B.C., the Stepped Pyramid of King Zoser (or Djeser) of the Third Dynasty was raised at Saqqara, the ancient *necropolis* (city of the dead) of Memphis (FIG. **3-6**). It is one of the oldest stone structures in Egypt and the first monumental royal tomb. Begun as a large mastaba, the structure was enlarged twice before taking on its final shape, which appears to be a sort of compromise between a mastaba and the later "true" pyramids at Gizeh. About 200 feet high, it seems to be composed of a series of mastabas of diminishing size, piled one on top of another to form a structure that resembles the great ziggurats of Mesopotamia. Unlike the ziggurats, however, Zoser's pyramid is a tomb, not a temple platform, and its dual function was to protect the mummified king and his possessions and to symbolize, by its gigantic presence, his absolute and godlike power.

The pyramid stands near the center of a rectangular enclosure that measures about 1,800 feet by 900 feet and is surrounded by a monumental, 35-foot high, niched wall of white limestone (FIG. **3-7**). Against the pyramid's northern face stands the funerary temple where daily rituals for the deceased were performed. Numerous buildings in the temple complex are arranged around several courts. With the exception of the funerary temple and a royal pavilion, all are dummy structures with stone walls enclosing fills of rubble, sand, or gravel. The buildings imitate in stone masonry various types of temporary structures made of plant stems and mats that were erected in Upper and Lower Egypt for the celebration of the Jubilee Festival, the rituals of which perpetually renewed the affirmation of the royal existence in the hereafter. The

3-6 IMHOTEP, Stepped Pyramid of King Zoser, Saqqara, *c.* 2650 B.C.

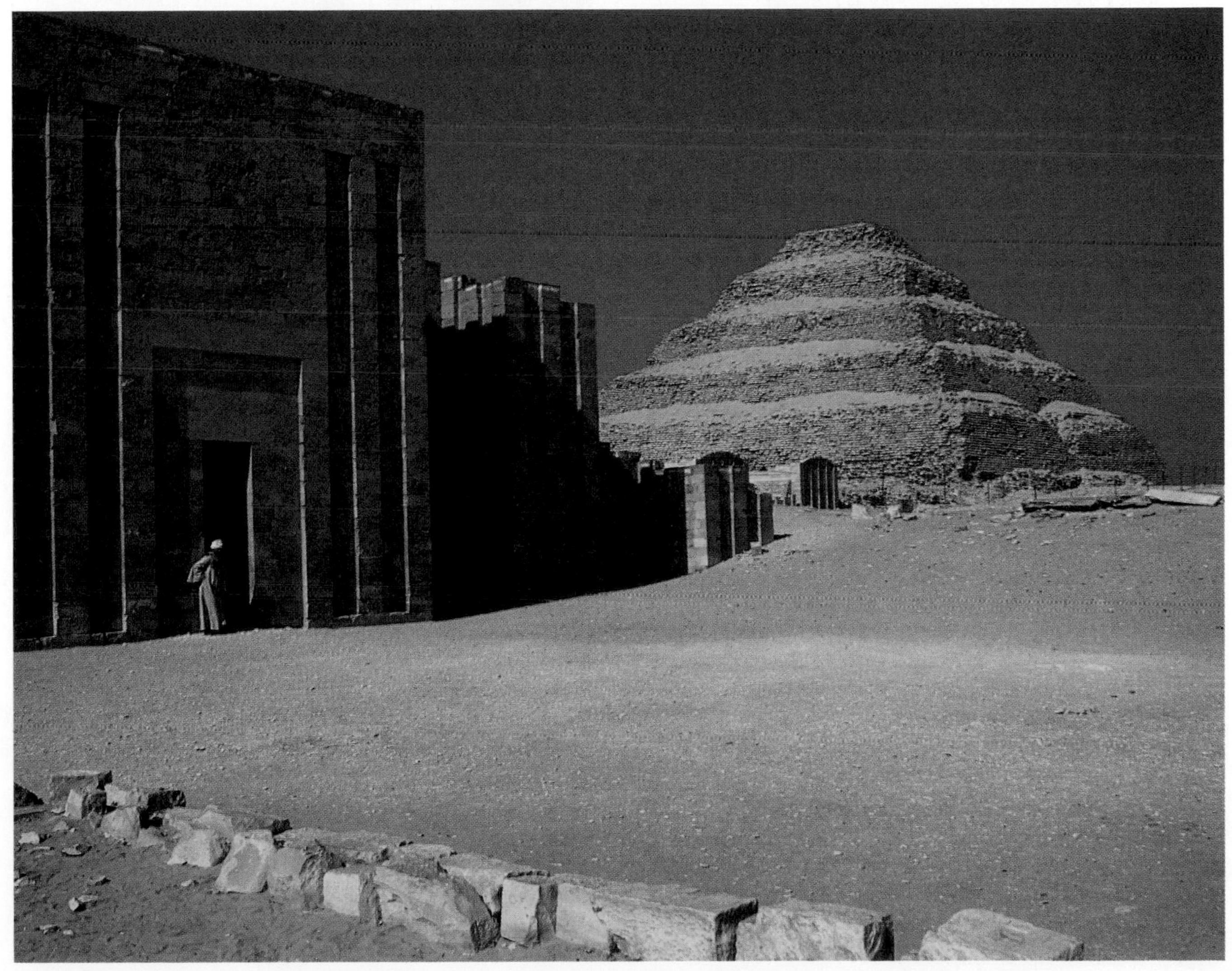

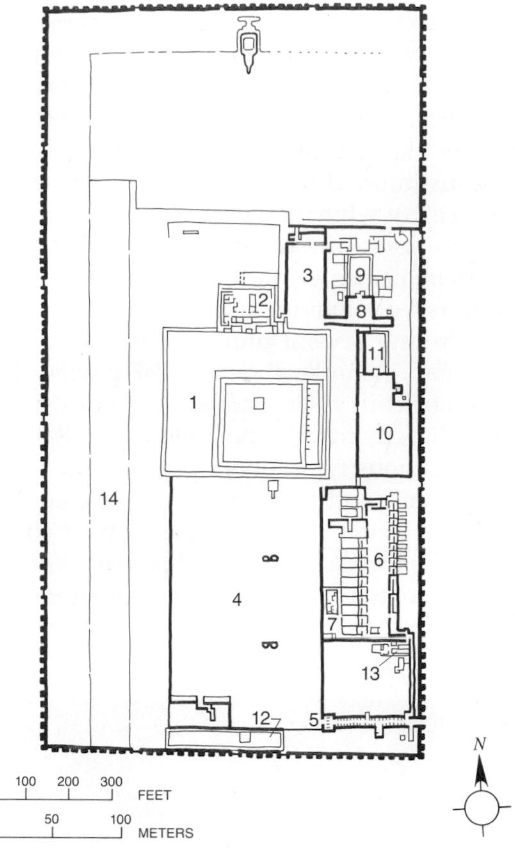

1. Stepped pyramid derived from square-plan mastaba
2. Funerary temple of Zoser
3. Court with serdab
4. Large court with altar and two B-shaped stones
5. Entrance portico
6. Heb-Sed court flanked by sham chapels
7. Small temple
8. Court before North Palace
9. North Palace
10. Court before South Palace
11. South Palace
12. South tomb
13. Royal Pavilion
14. Magazines

3-7 Plan of the mortuary precinct of King Zoser, Saqqara. (After Lange and Hirmer.)

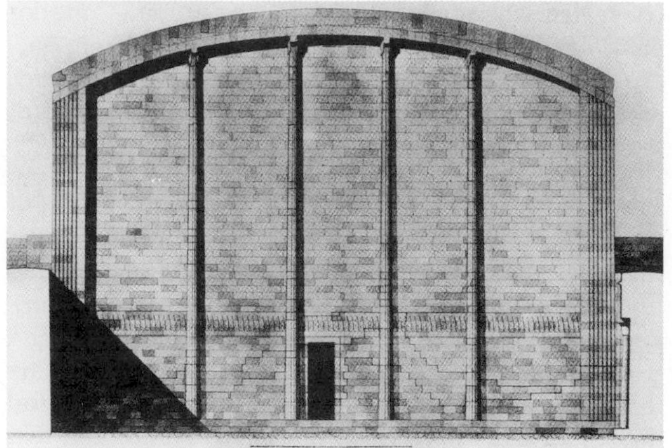

3-8 Reconstruction of an Upper Egyptian tent building, mortuary precinct of King Zoser, Saqqara. (After J. P. Lauer.)

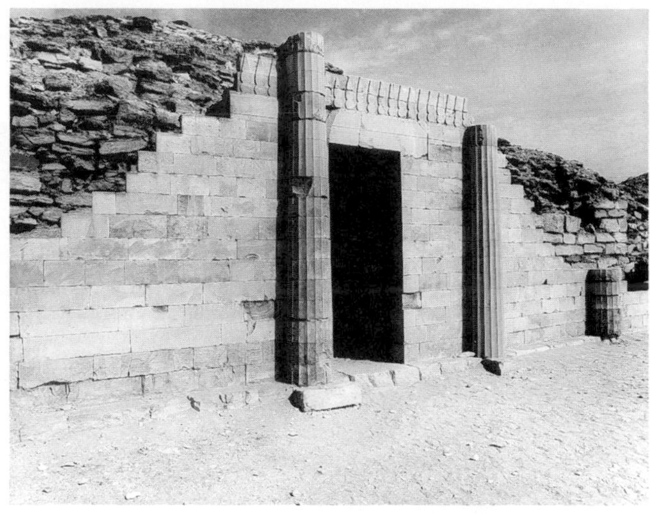

3-9 Remains of an Upper Egyptian tent building.

reconstructed façade of one of these rubble-filled dummy buildings (FIG. **3-8**) imitates an Upper Egyptian tent building in which tall poles support a mat roof that billows in a desert breeze. A striking feature of the preserved lower parts of these supporting "poles" (FIG. **3-9**) is their fluting, which is of the type that was to become characteristic of Greek Doric columns many centuries later. Egyptian columns, if they did not imitate reed or papyrus bundles, generally were smooth-shafted or beveled to polygonal shapes. Here, the "proto-Doric" fluting is believed to be derived from the dressing of softwood trunks with the rounded cutting edge of the Egyptian adze. While these tall and slender shafts hardly qualify as columns, more "properly" proportioned stone columns appear in considerable numbers elsewhere in the compound. Their design is inspired by natural plant forms, and they imitate bundled reeds or papyrus stalks whose blossoms serve as capitals. Not freestanding, they are attached to walls and wall projections, as though the builders had not realized yet the full structural potential of stone columns. Still, this is their first appearance in the history of architecture and thus epoch-making for its subsequent development in later periods.

The architect of Zoser's mortuary complex and the first known artist of recorded history was IMHOTEP, the king's grandvizier and a man of legendary powers. Priest, scribe, physician, and architect, Imhotep came to be known as the "father of medicine," and in Greek times was associated with Aesculapius, the patron god of physicians. As an architect, his greatest achievement was to translate the impermanent building types of both Upper and Lower Egypt into stone and combine them with two funerary traditions in a single compound, thereby consolidating and giving visual permanence to the idea of a unified Egyptian kingdom.

At Gizeh, near modern Cairo but on the west side of the Nile (the dead were always buried on the side where the sun sets), stand the three pyramids (FIG. **3-10**) of the Fourth Dynasty pharaohs Khufu (the Greek Cheops), Khafre (Chephren), and Menkure (Mycerinus). Built around 2500 B.C., the pyramids of Gizeh represent the culmination of an architectural evolution that began with the mastaba. The pyramid form did not evolve out of necessity; kings could have gone on indefinitely piling mastabas, one on top of another, to make their weighty tombs. Rather, it has been suggested that when the kings of the Third Dynasty moved their permanent residence to Memphis, they came under the influence of nearby Heliopolis. This city was the seat of the powerful cult of Re, the sun god, whose fetish was a pyramidal stone, the *ben-ben*. By the Fourth Dynasty, the pharaohs considered themselves the sons of Re and his incarnation on earth. It would have been only a small step for the pharaohs from the belief that the spirit and power of Re resided in the pyramidal ben-ben to the belief that their divine spirits and bodies would be similarly preserved within pyramidal tombs.

Is the pyramid form, then, an invention inspired by a religious demand, rather than the result of a formal evolution? We need not resolve this question here. Our concern is with the remarkable features of the Fourth Dynasty pyramid. Of the three pyramids at Gizeh, that of Khufu is the oldest and largest. Except for the galleries and burial chamber, it is an almost solid mass of limestone masonry—a stone mountain built on the same principle as the Stepped Pyramid of King Zoser, the interior spaces in plan and elevation being relatively tiny, as if crushed out of the scheme by the sheer weight of stone (FIG. **3-11**). The limestone was quarried in the eastern Nile cliffs and floated across the river during the seasonal floods. After the masons finished cutting the stones, they marked them with red ink to indicate the place of each stone in the structure. Then great gangs of laborers dragged them up temporary ramps (the wheel was not yet known) and laid them course on course. Finally the pyramid was surfaced with a casing of pearly white limestone, cut so precisely that the eye

3-10 Great Pyramids of Gizeh. *From left:* Menkure, *c.* 2460 B.C.; Khafre, *c.* 2500 B.C.; Khufu, *c.* 2530 B.C.

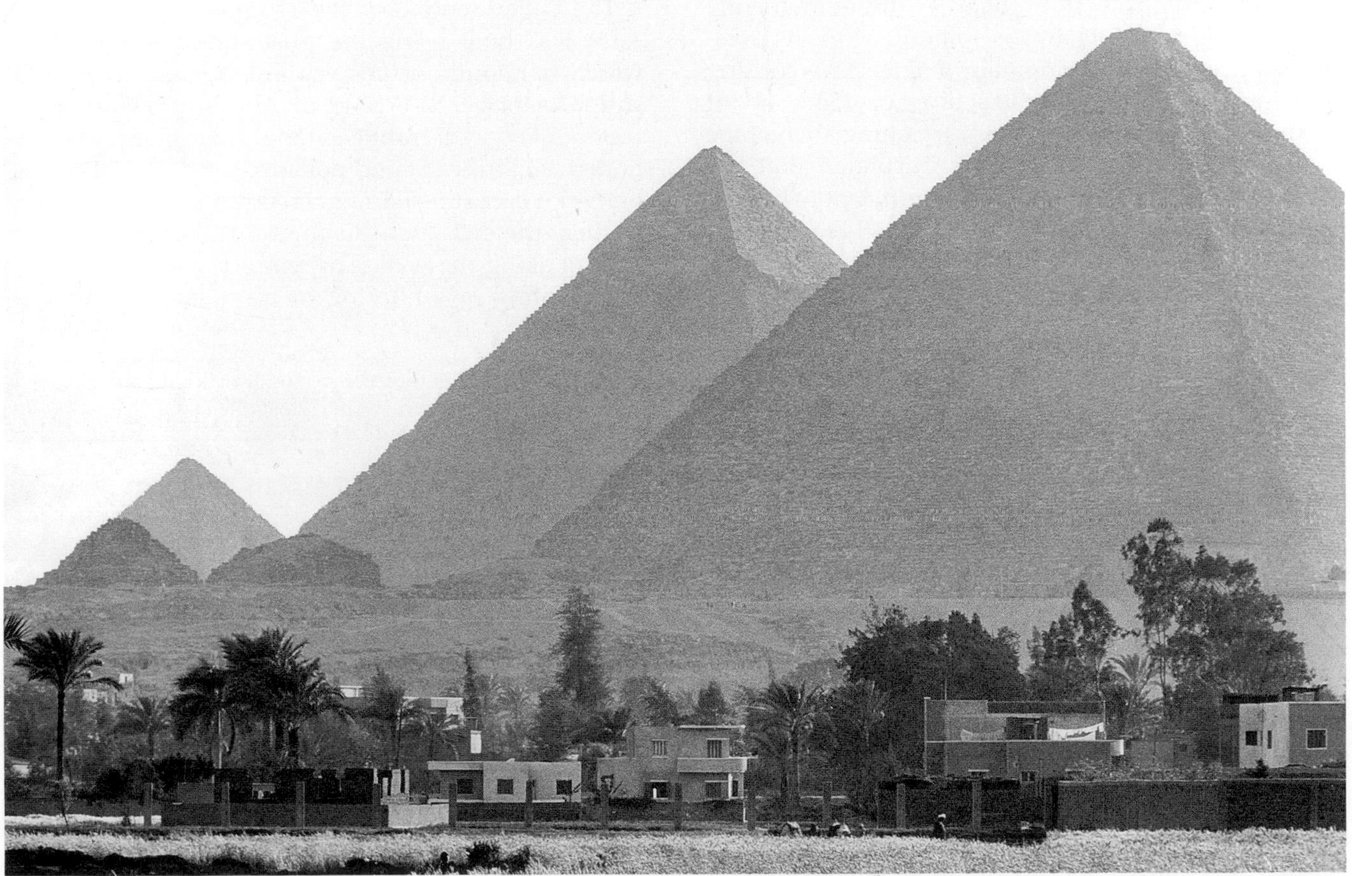

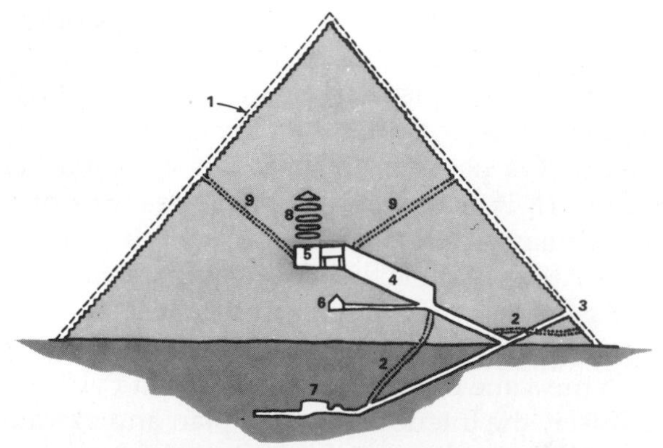

1. Silhouette with original facing stone
2. Thieves' tunnels
3. Entrance
4. Grand gallery
5. King's chamber
6. So-called queen's chamber
7. False tomb chamber
8. Relieving blocks
9. Airshafts?

3-11 Section of the Pyramid of Khufu, Gizeh. (After Hoelscher.)

could scarcely detect the joints. A few casing stones can still be seen in the cap that covers the Pyramid of Khafre, all that remain after many centuries during which the pyramids were stripped to supply limestone for the Islamic builders of Cairo. The immensity of the Pyramid of Khufu is indicated by some dimensions in round numbers: at the base, the length of one side is 775 feet and its area is some 13 acres; its present height is 450 feet (originally 480 feet). According to Flinders Petrie, the structure contains about 2.3 million blocks of stone, each weighing an average of $2\frac{1}{2}$ tons. Napoleon's scholars calculated that the blocks in the three pyramids were sufficient to build a wall 1 foot wide and 10 feet high around France. The art of this structure is inherent not only in its huge size and successful engineering but also in its formal design. The proportions and immense dignity are consistent with its funerary and religious functions and well adapted to its geographical setting. The four sides are oriented to the cardinal points of the compass, and the simple mass dominates the flat landscape to the horizon. The ironic outcome of this stupendous effort may be read from the cross section shown in FIG. 3-11. The dotted lines at the base of the structure (2) indicate the path cut into the pyramid by ancient grave robbers. Unable to locate the carefully sealed and hidden entrance, they started some 40 feet above the base and tunneled into the structure until they intercepted the ascending corridor. Many royal tombs were plundered almost as soon as the funeral ceremonies had ended; the very conspicuousness of the pyramid was an invitation to despoilment. The successors of the Old Kingdom pyramid-builders had learned this hard lesson; they built few pyramids, and those were relatively small and inconspicuous.

From the remains surrounding the pyramid of Khafre at Gizeh, we can reconstruct an entire pyramid complex (FIG. **3-12**) consisting of the pyramid itself, within or below which was the burial chamber; the chapel, adjoining the pyramid on the east side, where offerings were made, ceremonies were performed, and cloth, food, and ceremonial vessels were stored; the covered causeway leading down to the valley; and the valley temple, or vestibule, of the causeway. Beside the causeway and dominating the temple of Khafre rose the Great Sphinx (FIG. **3-13**), carved from a spur of rock to commemorate the pharaoh and to serve as a silent guardian of his tomb. The rock was cut so that the immense figure, adjacent to the temple's west front, gives visitors coming from the east the illusion that it rests on a great pedestal. The lion figure with a human head, possibly a portrait of Khafre, again shows us the conjunction of a powerful beast with the attributes of absolute kingship, as we have seen in the hawk and the bull of the *Palette of Narmer* (FIG. 3-2). For centuries, the huge head of the Great Sphinx stood up above the drifting tides of desert sand that covered the body, providing generations of ancient and modern travelers with an awe-inspiring and unforgettable image of mysterious power.

The valley temple of the Pyramid of Khafre (FIG. **3-14**) was built using the post-and-lintel system in which horizontal beams, or lintels, rest on upright supports, or posts. Both posts and lintels were huge, rectangular, red-granite monoliths, finely proportioned, skillfully cut and polished, and devoid of decoration. Alabaster slabs covered the floor, and seated statues, the only embellishment of the temple, were ranged along the wall. The interior was lighted by a few slanting rays filtering in from above. Although

3-12 Reconstruction of the pyramids of Khufu and Khafre, Gizeh. (After Hoelscher.)

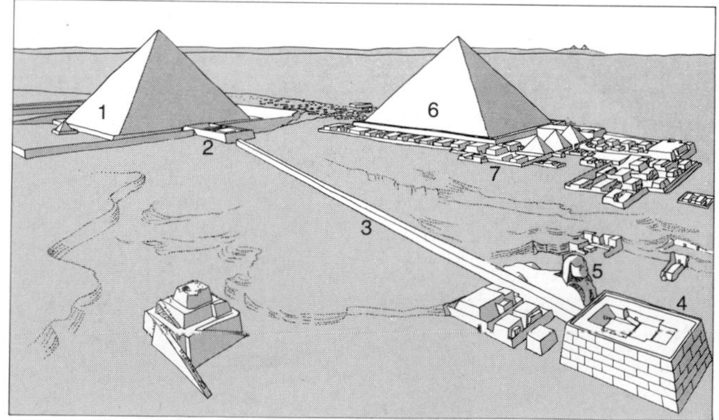

1. Pyramid of Khafre
2. Mortuary temple
3. Covered causeway
4. Valley temple
5. Great Sphinx
6. Pyramid of Khufu
7. Pyramids of the royal family and mastabas of nobles

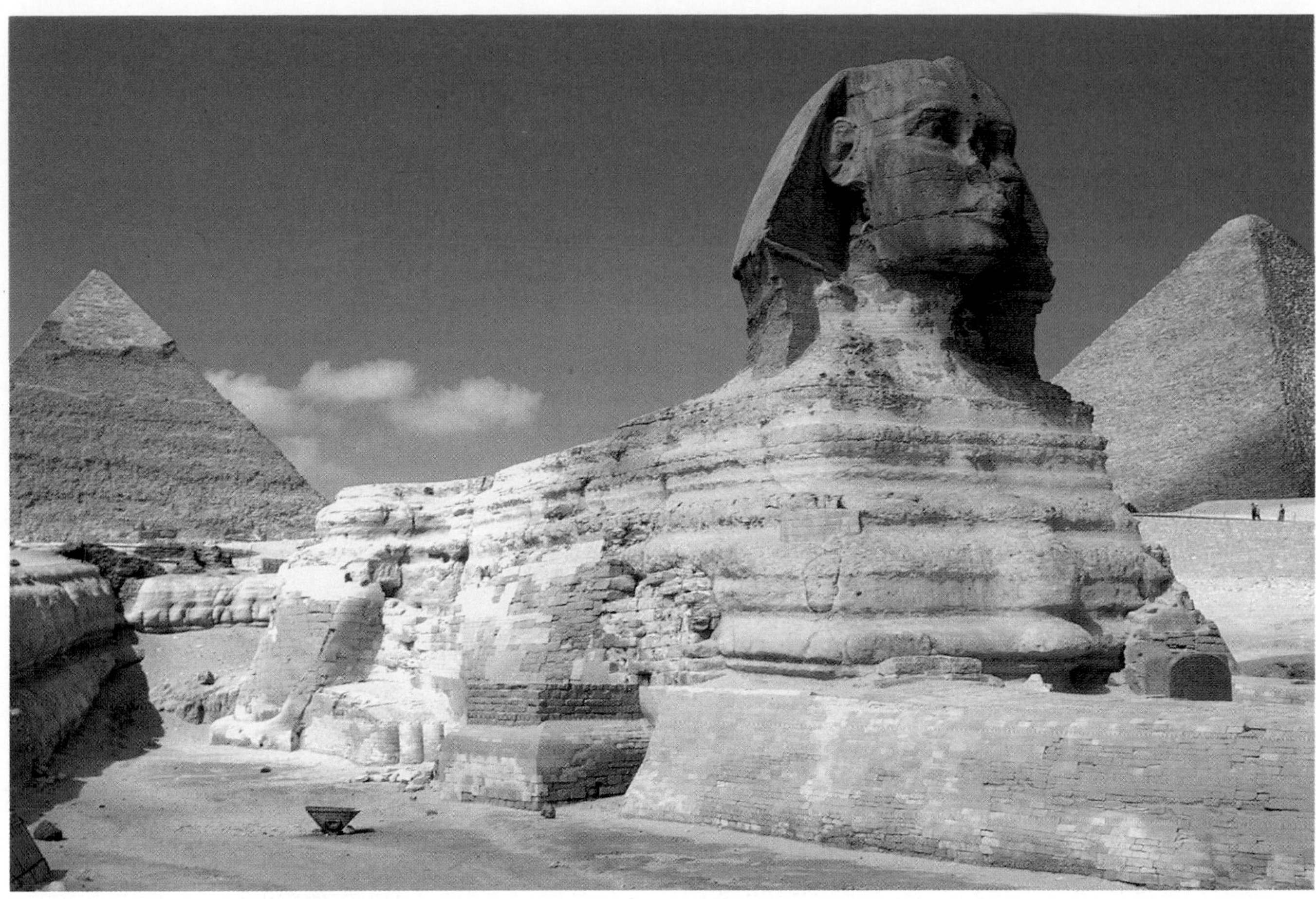

3-13 The Great Sphinx (with Pyramid of Khafre in left background), Gizeh, *c.* 2530 B.C. Sandstone, 65′ high, 240′ long.

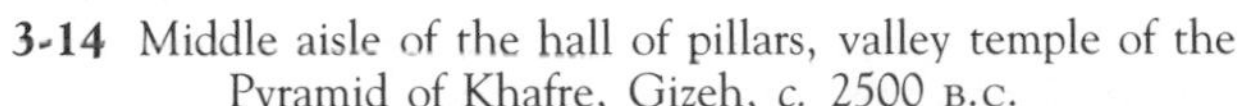

3-14 Middle aisle of the hall of pillars, valley temple of the Pyramid of Khafre, Gizeh, *c.* 2500 B.C.

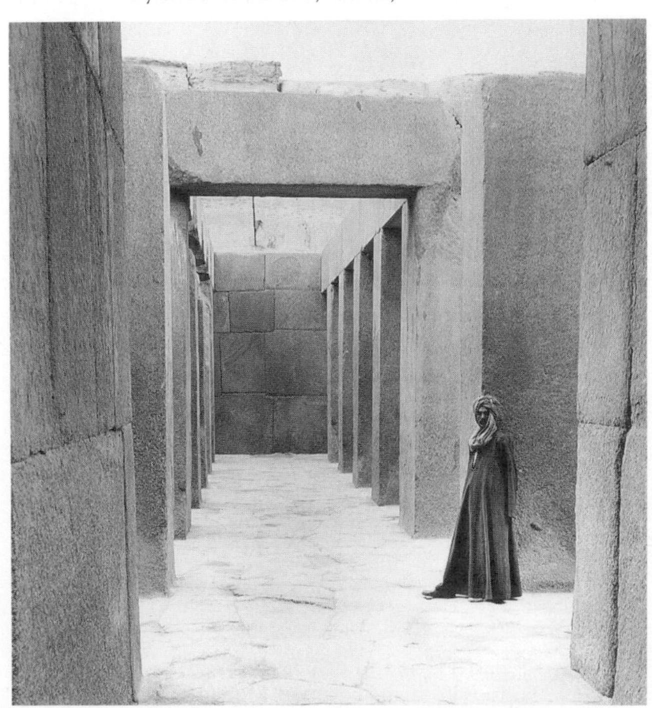

the Egyptians knew of the arch and the vault and had used them occasionally in Predynastic tombs, they rarely used them after about 3000 B.C., the beginning of the Dynastic period. Egyptian architects preferred the static forms of the post-and-lintel system, which, if cast into the heavy, massive shapes of the Khafre temple, expressed, perhaps better than any other architectural style, the changeless and the eternal.

Sculpture

In Egyptian tombs, we have already noted that sculpture in the round served the important function of creating an image of the deceased that could serve as an abode for the ka (the other self), should the mummy be destroyed. For this reason, an interest in portraiture developed early in Egypt. Thus, too, permanence of style and material were essential. Although wood, clay, and bronze were used, mostly for images of those not of the royal or noble classes, stone was the primary material. Limestone and sandstone were brought from the Nile cliffs, granite from the cataracts of the upper Nile, and diorite from the desert.

A seated statue of Khafre (FIG. **3-15**), who ruled from 2558–2533 B.C., was one of a series of similar statues carved for Khafre's valley temple near the Great Sphinx. These statues, the only organic forms in the geometric severity of the temple structure, with its flat-planed posts and lintels, help create a striking atmosphere of solemn majesty. Khafre is seated on a throne at the base of which is carved a symbol of the united Egypt, an intertwined lotus and papyrus. Sheltering his head are the protecting wings of the hawk, symbol of the sun, indicating Khafre's divine status as son of Re. He wears the simple kilt of the Old Kingdom and a linen headdress that covers his forehead and falls in pleated folds over his shoulders. The representation of the king is permeated with an imperturbable calm, reflecting the enduring power of the pharaoh and of kingship in general. This effect, common to royal statues of the ka, is achieved by devices of form and technique that we can still admire. The figure has great compactness and solidity, with few projecting, breakable parts; the form manifests the purpose—to last for eternity. The body is attached to a back slab, the arms are held close to the torso and thighs, the legs are close together and attached to the throne by stone webs. Like Mesopotamian statues, the pose is frontal, rigid, and bisymmetrical. This repeatable scheme arranges the parts of the body so that they are presented in a totally frontal projection or entirely in profile. As Erwin Panofsky observed:

> We can recognize from many unfinished pieces that even in sculpture the final form is always determined by an underlying geometrical plan originally sketched on the surfaces of the block. It is evident that the artist drew four separate designs on the vertical surfaces of the block . . . that he then evolved the figure by working away the surplus mass of stone, so that the form was bounded by a system of planes meeting at right angles and connected by slopes. . . . There is a sculptor's working drawing . . . that illustrates the mason-like method of these sculptors even more clearly: as if he were constructing a house, the sculptor drew up plans for his sphinx in frontal elevation, ground plan, and profile elevation . . . so that even today the figure could be executed according to plan.*

This *subtractive* method of "working away the surplus . . . stone" accounts for the blocklike look of the standard Egyptian statue, which differs strongly from the cylindrical or conical shape seen, for example, in the Mesopotamian statues of Gudea (FIG. 2-25). The hardest stone was used to ensure the permanence of the image, and Egypt (unlike Mesopotamia) was rich

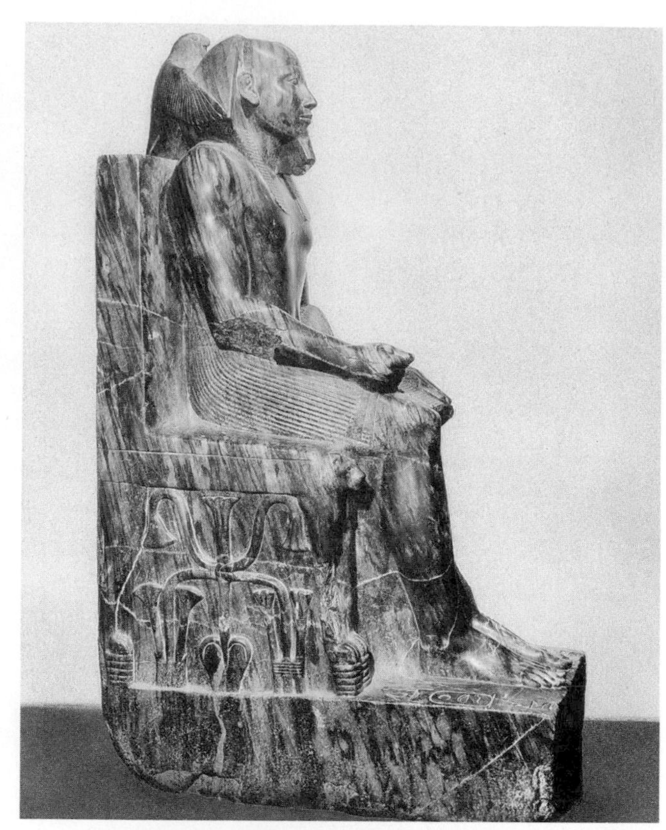

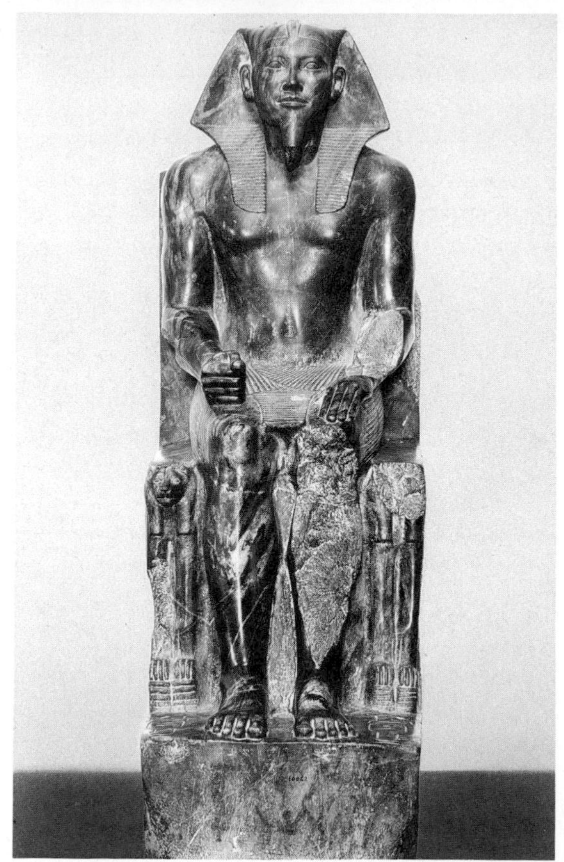

3-15 *Khafre* (side and front), from Gizeh, c. 2500 B.C. Diorite, 66″ high. Egyptian Museum, Cairo.

*Erwin Panofsky, *Meaning in the Visual Arts* (Garden City, NY: Doubleday, 1955), pp. 58–59.

in stone. Even so, the difficulty of working granite and diorite with bronze tools made production too expensive for all but the wealthiest. Much of the finishing had to be done by abrasion.

Since the figure was cut to plan, its proportions were determined beforehand. A canon of ideal proportions, designated as appropriate for the representation of imposing majesty, was accepted and applied quite independently of optical fact. The generalized anatomy persisted in Egyptian statuary even into the Ptolemaic period, when Greek influence might have been expected to shift it toward realism. The Egyptian sculptor seems to have been indifferent to realistic representation of the body, preferring to strive for fidelity to nature in the art of portraiture, at which the Egyptians excelled.

An example of their skill is a so-called reserve (duplicate, or spare) head of a prince of the family of Khufu (FIG. **3-16**). Attention is given only to the execution of the face, which shows the union of the formal and the realistic that gives distinction to so many portrait busts of its type. Reserve heads were placed outside the burial chamber, and their purpose is not understood. This head displays the extraordinary sensitivity of Old Kingdom portraiture. The personality, that of a sharply intelligent, vivacious, and alert individual, is read by the sculptor with a penetration and sympathy seldom achieved in sculptural representation.

3-16 *"Reserve" Head of a Prince,* Gizeh, c. 2500 B.C. Limestone, life size. Egyptian Museum, Cairo.

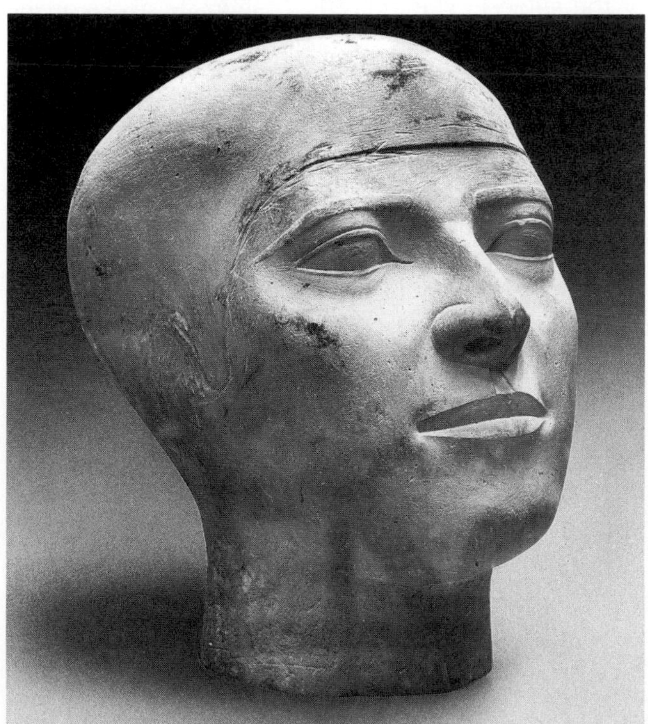

In the history of art, especially portraiture, it is almost a rule that formality is relaxed and realism is increased when the subject is a person of lesser importance. The famous wood statue of Ka-Aper (Sheikh el Beled) is a case in point (FIG. **3-17**). The work is a lively representation of a man whose function was to serve the king in the spirit world as he had in life. The face is startlingly alive, an effect that is heightened by eyes of rock crystal. The figure stands erect in conventional frontal pose, left leg advanced. His paunchy physique lacks the idealized proportions found in representations of royalty and nobility; he was, after all, only a minor official. The wood medium permitted the artist to omit the back slab and try a freer pose. Actually, what we see is the wood core that was covered originally with painted plaster, a common procedure when soft or unattractive woods were used.

3-17 *Ka-Aper (Sheikh el Beled),* from his tomb at Saqqara, c. 2400 B.C. Wood, approx. 43" high. Egyptian Museum, Cairo. (Partially restored.)

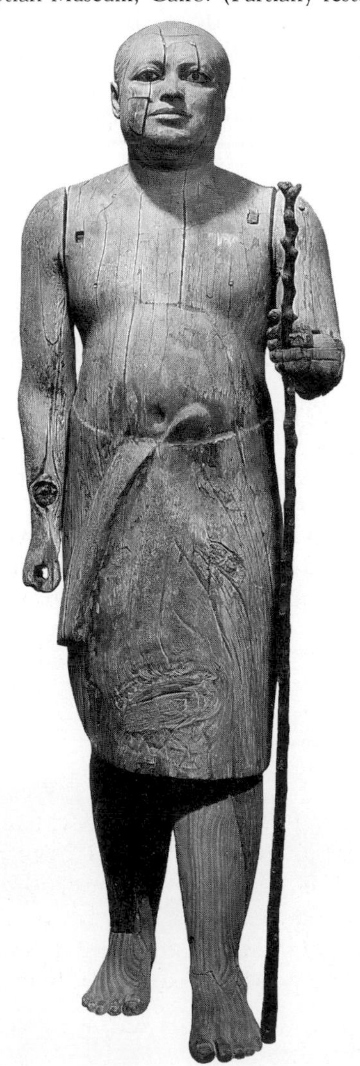

Painting and Relief

The scenes in painted limestone relief that decorate the walls of the tomb of an Old Kingdom official, Ti, typify the subjects favored by patrons adorning their tombs. Most often they are of agriculture and hunting (FIG. **3-18**), activities that represent the fundamental human concern with nature and that are associated with the provisioning of the ka in the hereafter. Ti, his men, and his boats move slowly through the marshes, hunting birds and hippopotamuses in a dense growth of towering papyrus. The slender, reedy stems of the plants are delineated with repeated fine grooves that fan out gracefully at the top into a commotion of frightened birds and stalking beasts. Beneath the boats, the water, signified by a pattern of wavy lines, is crowded with hippopotamuses and other aquatic fauna. Ti's men seem frantically busy with their spears, while Ti himself, who is portrayed twice their size, stands impassive and aloof in the formal stance seen earlier in the figure of Hesire (FIG. 3-3). The outsize and ideal proportions bespeak Ti's rank, as does the conventional pose, which contrasts with the realistically rendered activity of his diminutive servants and with the precisely observed figures of the birds and animals among the papyrus buds.

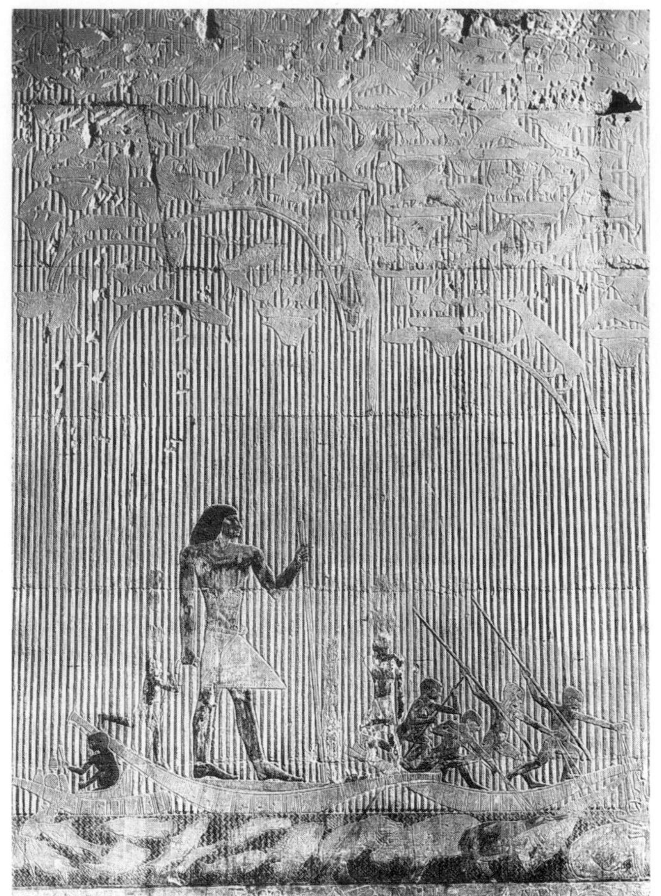

3-18 *Ti Watching a Hippopotamus Hunt,* tomb of Ti, Saqqara, c. 2400 B.C. Painted limestone relief, approx. 48″ high.

A rare and fine example of Old Kingdom painting is the frieze called the *Geese of Medum* (FIG. **3-19**). In the prehistoric art of the caves, the rock paintings, and the art of Mesopotamia, we have admired the peculiar sensitivity of early artists to the animal figure. They seem to have empathized with the nonhuman creature, to have possessed what Keats called "negative capability"—the power almost to share the being of the animal and to feel as it feels.

The dry-fresco *(fresco secco)* technique used, in which the artist lets the plaster dry before painting on it, lends itself to slow and meticulous work, encouraging the trained professional to take pains in rendering the image and in expressing an exact knowledge of the subject. The delicate, prehensile necks of the geese, the beaks, the suppleness of the bodies, and the animals' characteristic step and carriage are rendered with an exactitude and discernment that would elicit the admiration of an Audubon. The firm, strong execution of the figures is the work of an expert with a superbly trained eye and hand. It is probable, too, that religious motives mingled here with esthetic ones, for, after all, once a tomb was sealed, no mortal

3-19 *Geese of Medum* (detail of a fresco), c. 2530 B.C. Tempera on plaster, approx. 18″ × 68″. Egyptian Museum, Cairo.

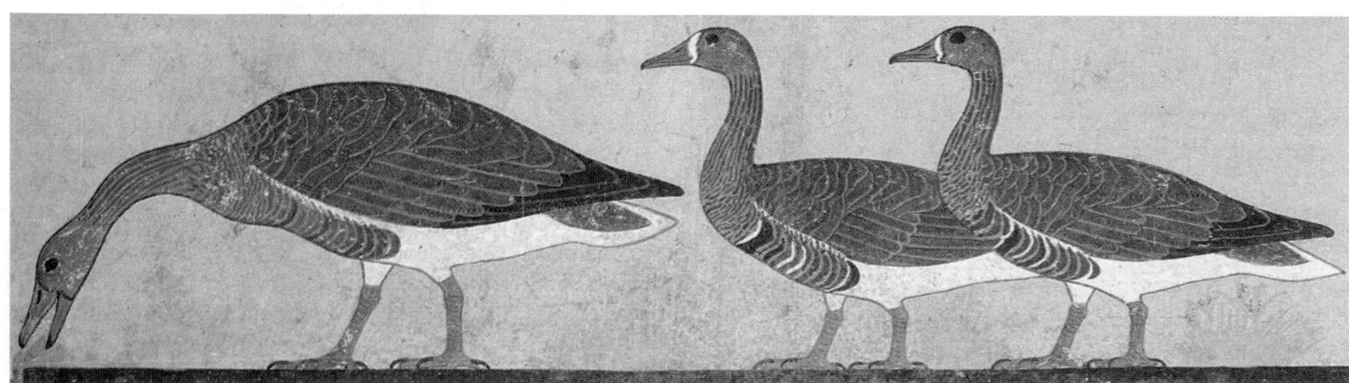

eyes were ever expected to see the paintings again. It must have been thought that, in the darkness and silence, the pictures worked their own spell, creating a force that would serve the ka eternally; some of the magical intent of the Stone Age cave paintings seems to persist here.

The art of the Old Kingdom is the classic art of Egypt in that its conventions, definitively established, remained the basis of subsequent styles of Egyptian art through three millennia.

THE MIDDLE KINGDOM

About 2150 B.C., the power of the pharaohs was challenged by ambitious feudal lords; for about a century, the land was in a state of civil unrest and near anarchy. Eventually, a Theban ruler, Mentuhotep II, managed to unite Egypt again under the rule of a single king. In the Eleventh, Twelfth, and Thirteenth Dynasties (the Middle Kingdom) that followed, art was revived and a rich and varied literature appeared.

The Egyptians continued to build pyramids but on a much smaller scale than in the Old Kingdom. Since it had become apparent that size was no defense against tomb robbers, builders now attempted to thwart thieves with intricate and ingenious interior layouts. Entrances were not placed in the center of the north side, as was traditional, but were hidden and screened from the secret tomb chamber by various types of sliding portcullises and by a series of passages that turned and doubled back on themselves at various levels in labyrinthine fashion. Less massive than their Old Kingdom predecessors, Middle Kingdom pyramids were built either entirely of brick or as stone frameworks filled with brick or rubble. What the pyramids lost in size and mass during the Middle Kingdom, however, was partly recompensed by the increased size of the sarcophagi, which became extremely large and heavy. Designed like small tomb chambers and weighing up to 150 tons, these granite coffins were intended to foil potential robbers by their very bulk and mass.

Rock-cut Tombs

Among the most characteristic remains of the Middle Kingdom are the rock-cut tombs at Beni Hasan (FIG. **3-20**), south of Memphis. One of the best preserved is the tomb of Khnumhotep, who boasted in an inscription of its elaborateness, saying that its doors were of cedar, seven cubits (about 20 feet) high. Expressing the characteristic Egyptian attitude toward the last resting place, he added:

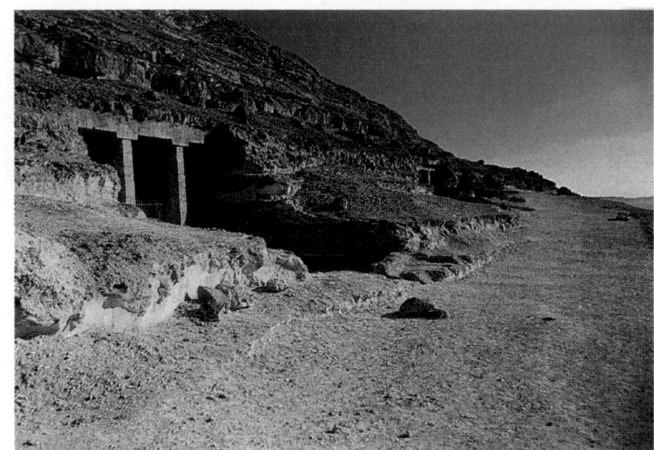

3-20 Rock-cut tombs, Beni Hasan, *c.* 2000 B.C.

> My chief nobility was: I executed a cliff-tomb, for a man should imitate that which his father does. My father made for himself a house of the *ka* in the town of Menofret, of good stone of Ayan, in order to perpetuate his name forever and establish it eternally.

The rock-cut tombs of the Middle Kingdom largely replaced the Old Kingdom mastabas. Hollowed out of the living rock at remote sites, these tombs, fronted by a shallow, columned portico, contained the fundamental units of Egyptian architecture: a portico or vestibule, a columned hall, and a sacred chamber (FIG. **3-21**). In the hall of the rock-cut tomb of

3-21 Plan *(bottom)* and section *(top)* of a rock-cut tomb. (After Sir Banister Fletcher.)

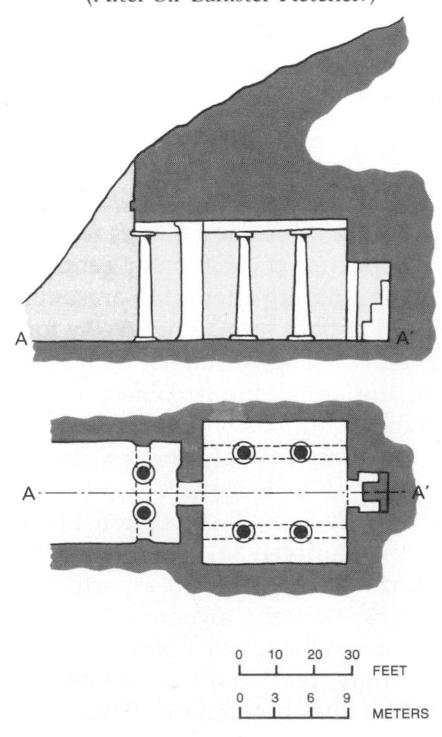

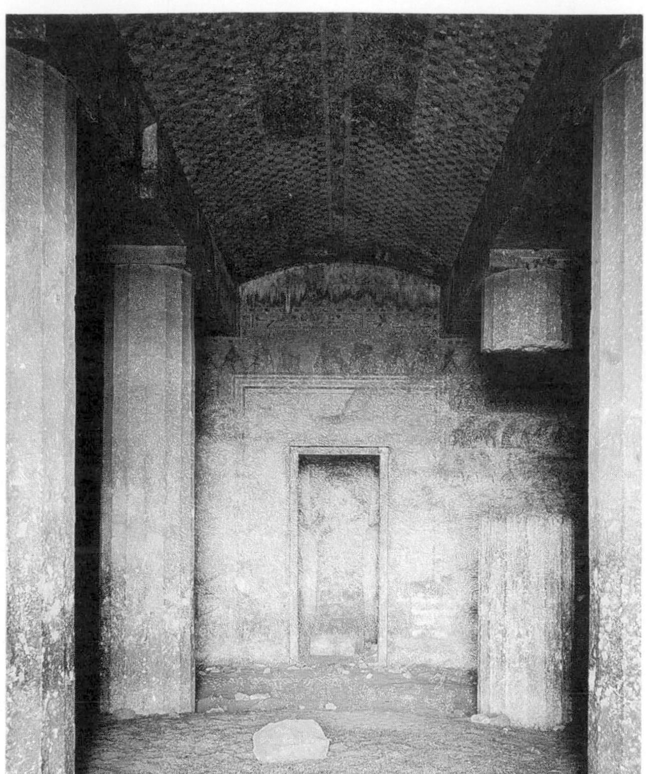

3-22 Hall interior of the tomb of Amenemhet, Beni Hasan, *c.* 1930 B.C.

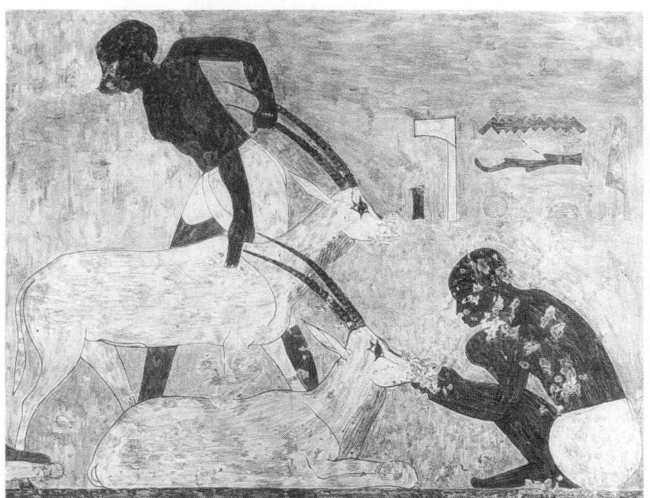

3-23 *Feeding of Oryxes,* fresco from the tomb of Khnumhotep, Beni Hasan, *c.* 1900 B.C. Tempera facsimile.

Amenemhet (FIG. **3-22**), the *reserve* columns serve no supporting function, being, like the portico columns, continuous parts of the rock fabric. (Note the broken column in the rear, suspended from the ceiling like a stalactite.) Tomb walls were decorated with paintings and painted reliefs, as in former times, and the subjects were much the same.

Painting and Sculpture

A painting from the tomb of Khnumhotep (FIG. **3-23**) shows servants feeding oryxes (antelopes), the domesticated pets of the Egyptian gentry. Here the artist has made a daring attempt to present the shoulders and backs of both human figures by foreshortening. However, working within the rigid framework of convention, the artist simply joined their front and side views in an unusual combination. As a result, the action reads convincingly enough, but the figures fall short of optical consistency.

A somewhat deepened perception of personality and mood can be noted in portrait sculpture of the Middle Kingdom, as shown in a partially damaged head (FIG. **3-24**) thought to be of Sesostris III. The head, detail of a sphinx, has a pessimistic expression that, interestingly, reflects the dominant mood of the literature of the Middle Kingdom. The strong mouth, the drooping lines about the nose and eyes, and the shadowy brows show a determined ruler, who had also shared in the cares of the world, sunk in brooding meditation. The portrait is strangely different from the typically realistic and "public" Old Kingdom faces; it is personal, almost intimate, in its revelation of the mark of anxiety that a troubled age might leave on the soul of a king.

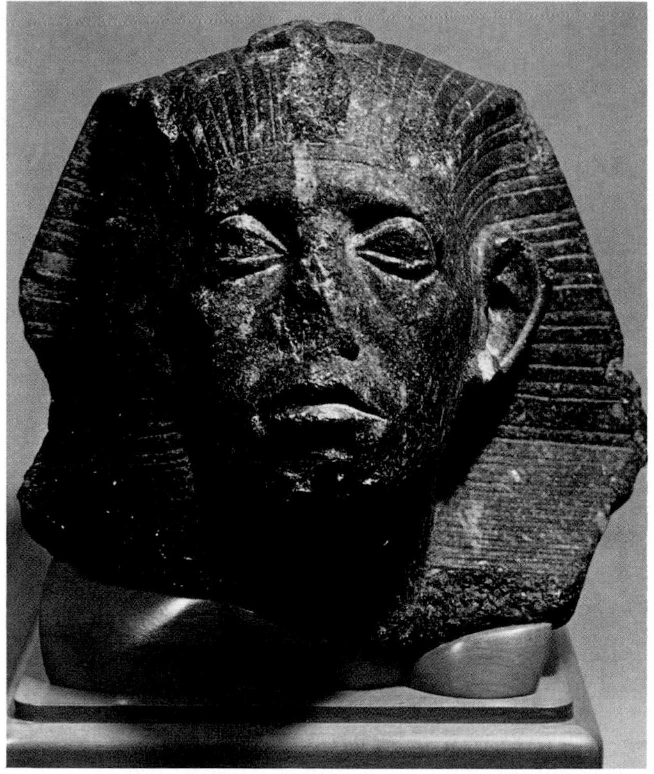

3-24 *Sesostris III* (ruled 1878–1843 B.C.), from the Temple of Medamud. Granite, 11" high. Egyptian Museum, Cairo.

THE NEW KINGDOM

This anxiety may have reflected premonitions of disaster. Like the one that preceded it, the Middle Kingdom disintegrated, and power passed to a line of migrant Semitic Asiatics from the Syrian and Mesopotamian uplands. The Hyksos, or Shepherd Kings, brought with them a new and influential culture and that practical instrument, the horse. The invasion and domination of the Hyksos, traditionally thought to have been disastrous, were later reassessed and judged seminal influences that kept Egypt in the mainstream of Bronze Age culture in the eastern Mediterranean. In any event, the innovations introduced by the Hyksos, especially in weaponry and the techniques of war, contributed to their own overthrow by native Egyptian kings of the Seventeenth Dynasty. Ahmose I, final conqueror of the Hyksos and first king of the Eighteenth Dynasty, ushered in the New Kingdom (the Empire)—the most brilliant period in Egypt's long history. At this time, Egypt extended her borders by conquest from the Euphrates in the east deep into Nubia (the Sudan) to the south. Wider foreign contact was afforded by visiting embassies and by new and profitable trade with Asia and the Aegean islands. The booty taken in wars and the tribute exacted from subjected peoples made possible the development of a new capital, Thebes, which became a great and luxurious metropolis with magnificent palaces, tombs, and temples along both banks of the Nile. Thutmose III, who died in the fifty-first year of his reign in the second half of the fifteenth century B.C., was the greatest pharaoh of the New Kingdom, if not of all Egyptian history, and his successors continued the grand traditions he established. The optimistic mood of the new era is recorded in an inscription above the heads of revelers in a painting now in the British Museum:

> The Earth-god has implanted his beauty in every body.
> The Creator has done this with his two hands as balm to his heart.
> The channels are filled with waters anew
> And the land is flooded with his love.

Architecture

If the most impressive monuments of the Old Kingdom are its pyramids, those of the New Kingdom are its grandiose temples. Burial still demanded the elaborate care shown earlier, and, partly in keeping with the tradition of the Middle Kingdom, nobles and kings hollowed their burial chambers deep in the cliffs west of the Nile. In the Valley of the Kings, the rock-cut tombs are approached by long corridors that extend as far as 500 feet into the hillside. The entrances to these burial chambers were concealed carefully, and the mortuary temples were built along the banks of the Nile at some distance from the tombs. The temple, which provided the king with a place for worshiping his patron god and then served as a mortuary chapel after his death, became elaborate and sumptuous, befitting both the king and the god.

The most majestic of these royal mortuary temples, at Deir el-Bahri, was the Temple of Queen Hatshepsut (FIG. **3-25**), who preceded the conquering

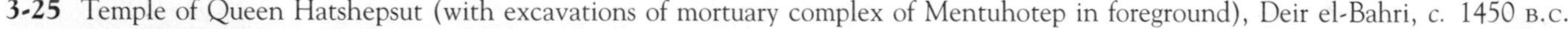

3-25 Temple of Queen Hatshepsut (with excavations of mortuary complex of Mentuhotep in foreground), Deir el-Bahri, c. 1450 B.C.

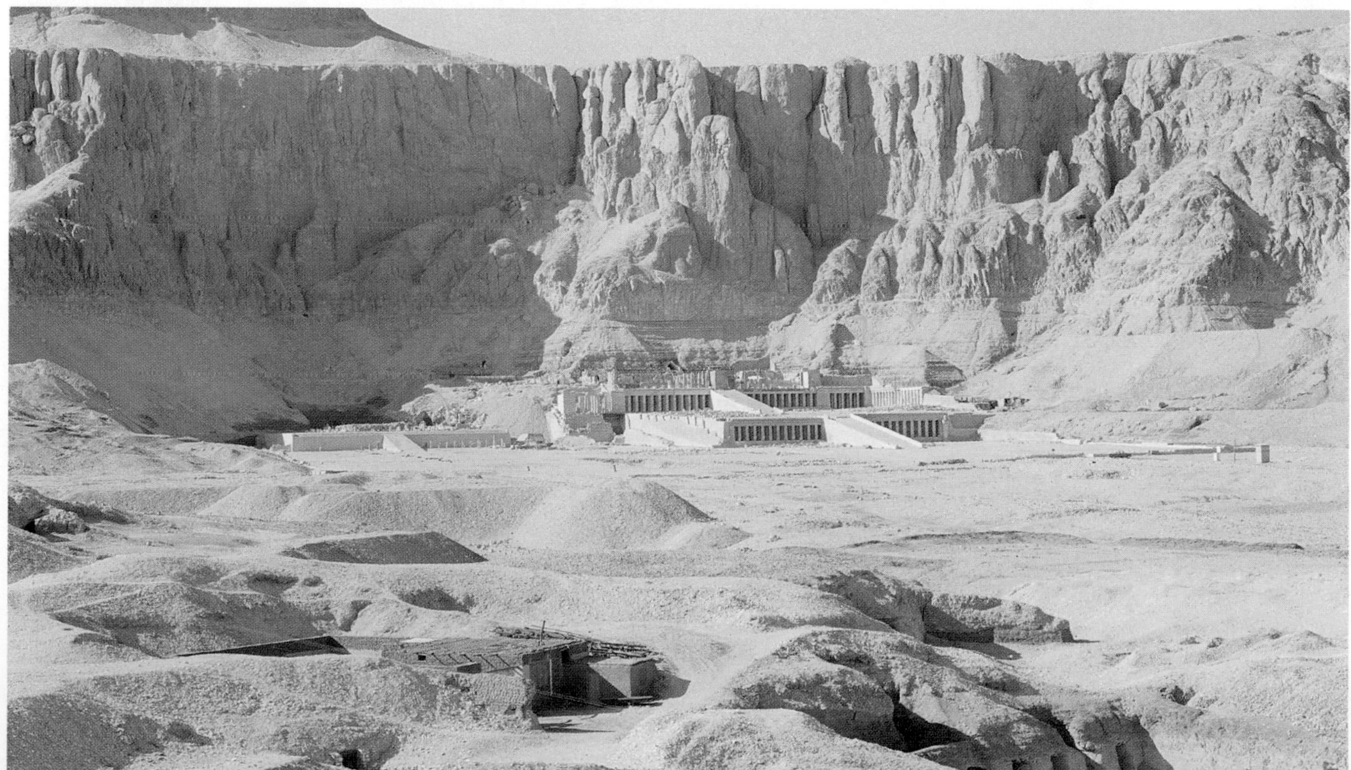

pharaoh Thutmose III. A princess who became queen when there were no legitimate male heirs old enough to rule, she boasted of having made the "Two Lands to labour with bowed back for her." Built about 1450 B.C. along the lines of the neighboring Middle Kingdom temple of Mentuhotep I, her mortuary temple rises from the valley floor in three colonnaded terraces connected by ramps. It is remarkable how visually well suited the structure is to its natural setting. The long horizontals and verticals of the colonnades and their rhythm of light and dark repeat, in manmade symmetry, the pattern of the rocky cliffs above. The pillars of the colonnades, which are either simply rectangular or *chamfered* (beveled, or flattened at the edges) into sixteen sides, are esthetically proportioned and spaced. Statues in the round, perhaps as many as two hundred, were intimately associated with the temple architecture. The brightly painted low relief (whose remnants may still be seen) that covered the walls also was carefully integrated into the structure's design. The relief represented Hatshepsut's birth, coronation, and great deeds. In her day, the terraces were not the barren places they are now but gardens with frankincense trees and rare plants brought by the queen from an expedition to the faraway "land of Punt" on the Red Sea, an event that figures prominently in the temple's relief decorations.

The immense rock-cut temple of Ramses II, Egypt's last great warrior-pharaoh, who lived a little before the Exodus from Egypt under Moses, was built far up the Nile at Abu Simbel. (The whole monument was moved in 1968 to save it from submersion in the Aswân High Dam reservoir.) Ramses, proud of his many campaigns to restore the empire, augmented his greatness by placing four colossal images of himself in the temple façade (FIG. **3-26**). In later times, the glories of kings and emperors in periods of conquest and imperial grandeur were also celebrated in huge monuments; gigantism seems characteristic of much of the art of empires that have reached their peaks. At Abu Simbel, Ramses' artists use the principle of augmentation both by size and by repetition. The massive statues lack the refinement of earlier periods, because much is sacrificed to overwhelming size. The grand scale is carried out in the interior also (FIG. **3-27**), where giant figures of the king, formed as col-

3-26 Temple of Ramses II, Abu Simbel, Nubia (now relocated), 1257 B.C. Colossi approx. 60′ high.

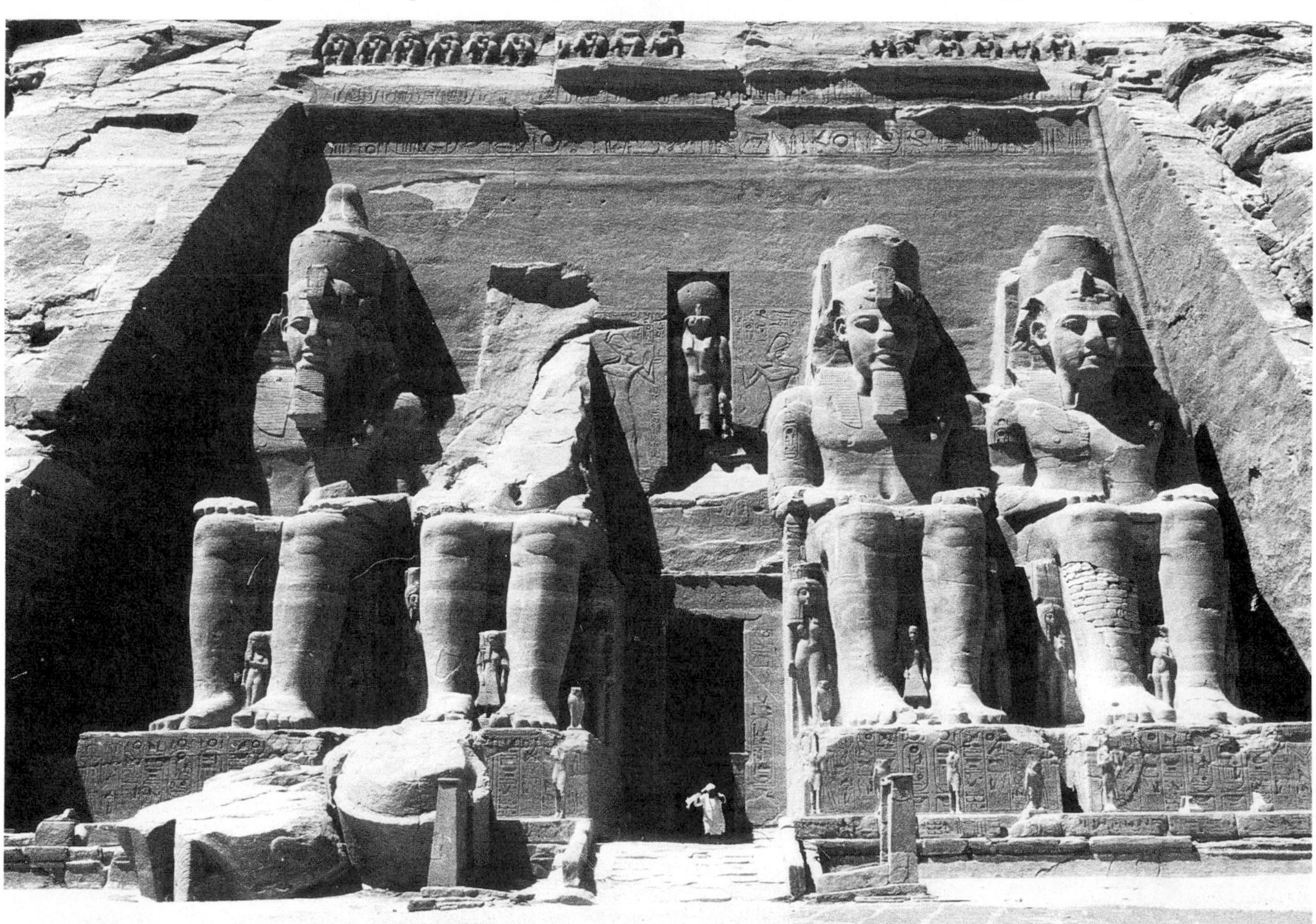

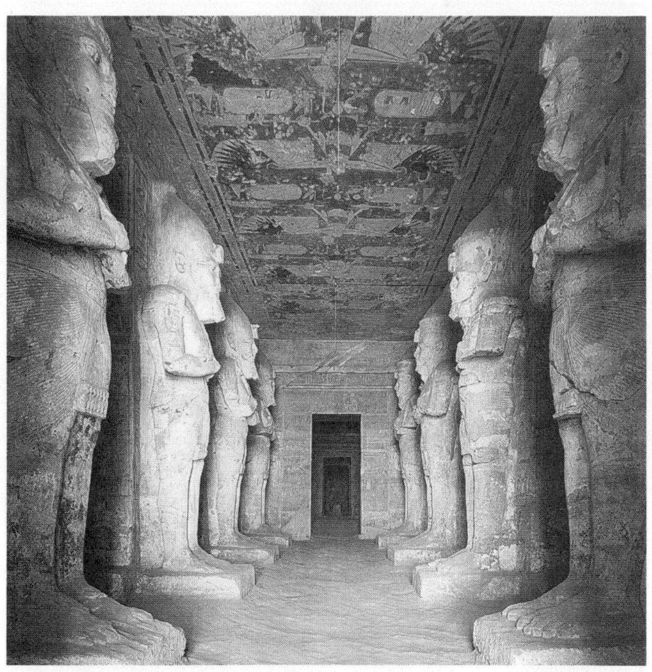

3-27 Interior of the Temple of Ramses II, Abu Simbel.

umns, face each other across the narrow corridor; their exaggerated mass appears to appropriate the architectural space. The columns are reserved (hewn from the living rock) and have no bearing function; in this respect, they resemble the columns in the tombs at Beni Hasan. The figure-as-column, the *atlantid* (male) or *caryatid* (female) form, will appear later in Greek architecture, and its presence at Abu Simbel may be its earliest use.

Distinct from the mortuary temples were the edifices built to honor one or more of the gods and often added to by successive kings until they reached gigantic size (as seen in the temples at Karnak and Luxor, FIGS. 3-32 and 3-33). These temples all had similar plans. A typical *pylon temple* plan (FIG. **3-28**) is bilaterally symmetrical along a single axis that runs from an approaching avenue through a colonnaded court and hall into a dimly lighted sanctuary. The dominating feature of the statuary-lined approach is the façade of the pylon, simple and massive, with sloping walls. The pylon shown in FIG. **3-29** is from the Temple of Horus at Edfu, which was constructed

3-28 Plan of a typical pylon temple.

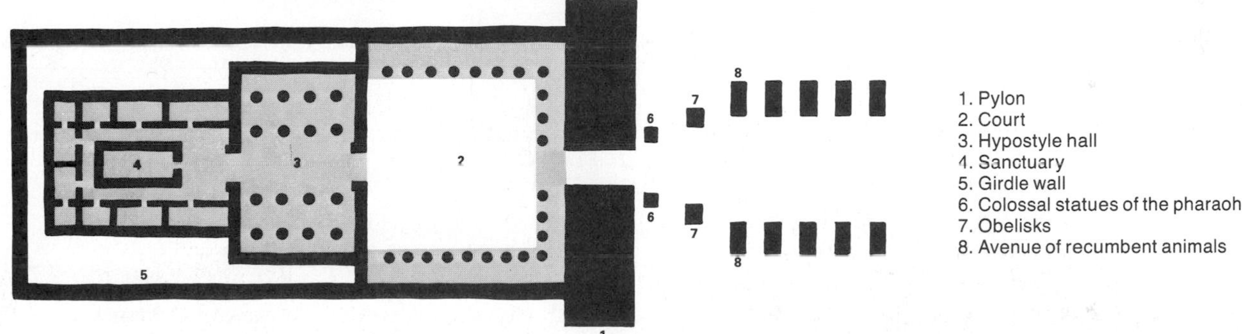

3-29 Pylon Temple of Horus, Edfu, *c.* 237–212 B.C.

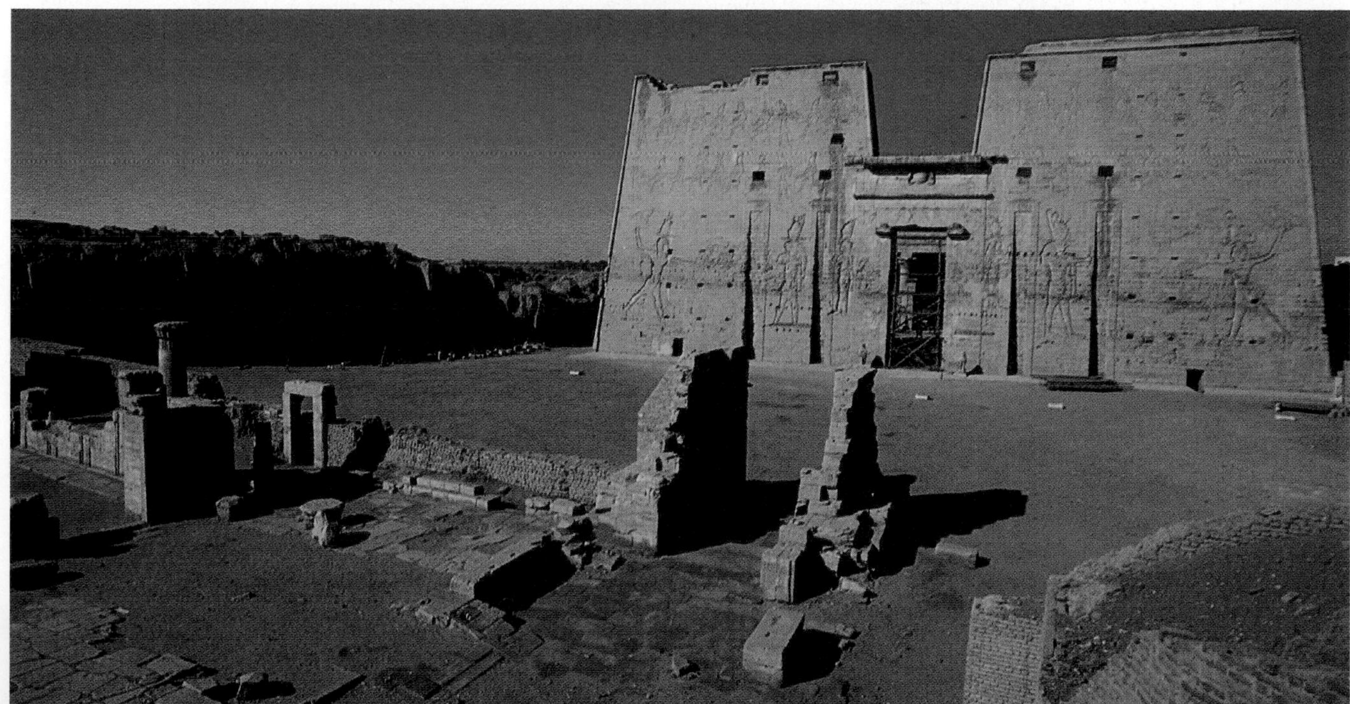

during the Ptolemaic period and is a striking monument to the persistence of Egyptian artistic traditions. Its broad surface is broken by the doorway with its overshadowing cornice, by deep channels to hold great flagstaffs, and by sunken reliefs. Moldings finish its top and sides. Inside is an open court colonnaded on three sides, followed by a hall between court and sanctuary, its long axis placed at right angles to that of the entire building complex. This "broad" or *hypostyle* hall (one having a roof supported by columns) is crowded with massive columns and roofed by stone slabs carried on lintels that rest on impost blocks supported by the great capitals. In the hypostyle hall of the Temple of Amen-Re (a variant reading is Imen-Re) at Karnak (FIGS. **3-30** and **3-31**), the columns are 66 feet high, and the capitals are 22 feet in diameter at the top, large enough to hold one hundred people. The Egyptians, who used no cement, depended on the weight of the huge stones to hold the columns in place. In many hypostyle halls, the central rows of columns were higher than those at the sides, raising the roof of the central section and creating a *clerestory*. Openings in the clerestory permitted light to filter into the interior. This method of construction appears in primitive form as early as the Old Kingdom in the valley temple of the Pyramid of Khafre. Evidently an Egyptian invention, it has remained an important architectural feature down to our times and was particularly important in the design of medieval cathedrals.

The Egyptian temple plan evolved from ritualistic requirements. Only the pharaoh and the priest could enter the sanctuary; a chosen few were admitted to the hypostyle hall; the mass of the people was allowed only as far as the open court, and a high mud-

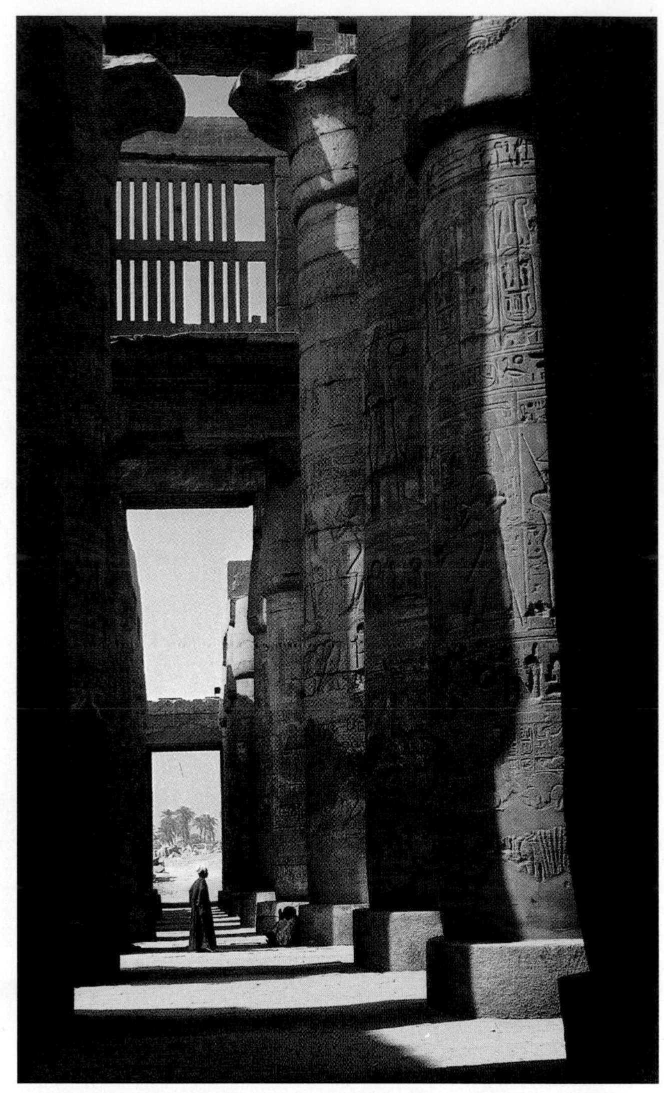

3-30 Hypostyle hall, Temple of Amen-Re, Karnak, *c.* 1280 B.C.

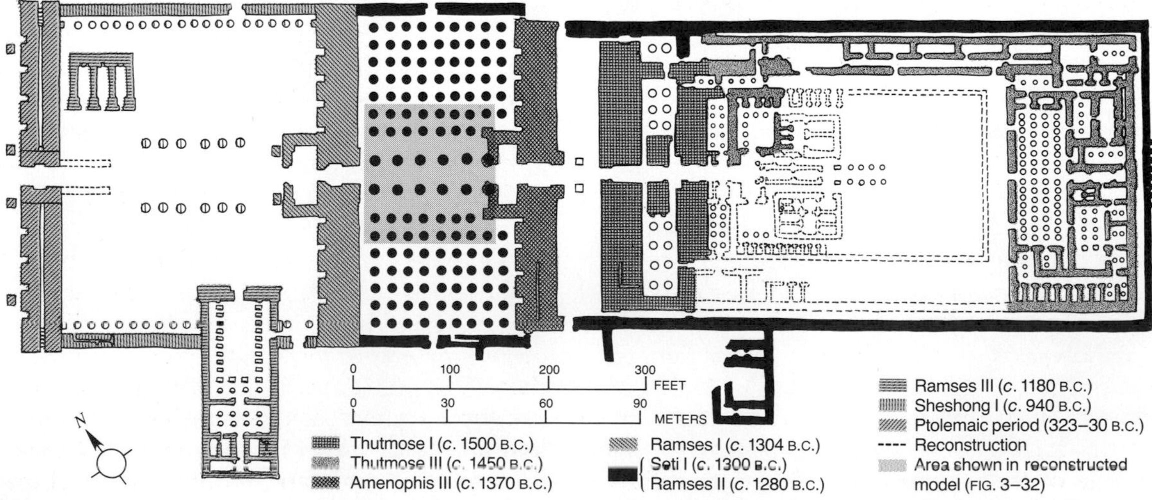

3-31 Plan of the Temple of Amen-Re, Karnak. (After Sir Banister Fletcher.) Dates in parentheses indicate time of construction.

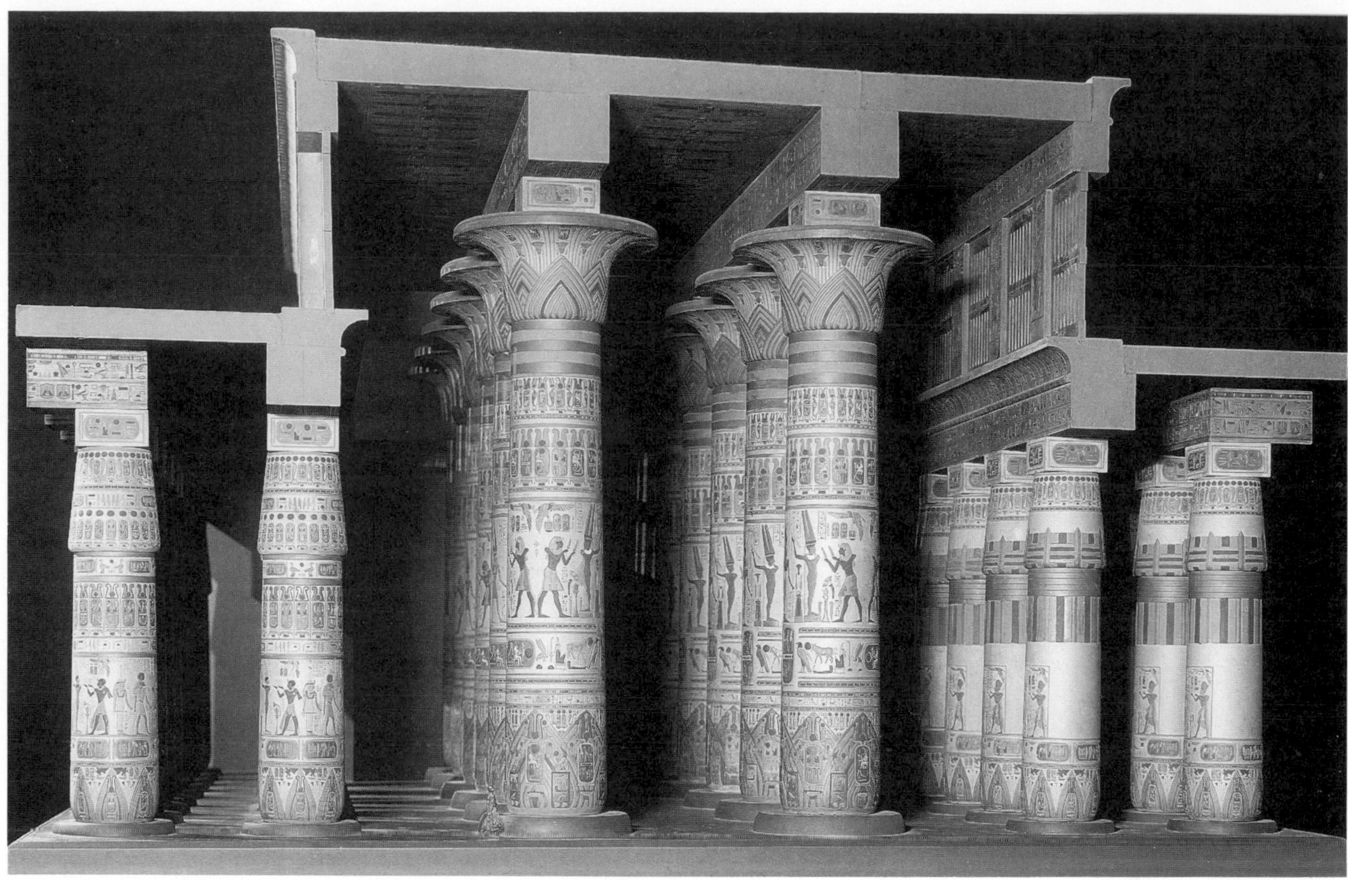

3-32 Model of hypostyle hall, Temple of Amen-Re, Karnak, *c.* 1280 B.C. Metropolitan Museum of Art, New York (bequest of Levi Hale Willard, 1890).

brick wall shut off the site from the outside world. The conservative Egyptians did not deviate from this basic plan for hundreds of years. The *corridor axis,* which dominates the plan, makes the temple not so much a building as, in Oswald Spengler's phrase, "a path enclosed by mighty masonry." Like the Nile, the corridor may have symbolized the Egyptian concept of life. Spengler suggests that the Egyptians saw themselves moving down a narrow, predestined life-path that ended before the judges of the dead. The whole of Egyptian culture can be regarded as illustrating this theme.

A model of the hypostyle hall at Karnak (FIG. **3-32**) shows the smooth-shafted (as opposed to fluted) Egyptian columns with the two basic types of capitals: bud shaped and bell shaped, or campaniform. Although the columns are structural members, unlike the reserve "columns" of the Middle Kingdom tombs at Beni Hasan and the figure-columns at Abu Simbel (see FIGS. 3-22 and 3-27), their function as carriers of vertical stress is almost hidden by horizontal bands of relief sculpture and painting, suggesting that the intention of the architects was not to emphasize the functional role of the columns so much as to utilize them as surfaces for decoration. This contrasts sharply with later Greek practice, which emphasizes the vertical lines of the column and its structural function by freeing the surfaces of the shaft from all ornament.

The courts and colonnades of the Temple of Amen-Mut-Khonsu at Luxor (FIG. **3-33**) exhibit the columnar style especially well. The post-and-lintel structure of the temples appears to have had its origin in an early building technique that used firmly bound sheaves of reeds and swamp plants as roof supports in adobe structures. We have seen how Imhotep, some fourteen centuries earlier, first translated such early and relatively impermanent building methods into stone at Saqqara (see page 79). Evidence of their swamp-plant origin is still seen in these columns at Karnak and Luxor, which are carved to resemble lotus or papyrus, with bud-cluster or bell-shaped capitals. Painted decorations, traces of which still can be seen on the surfaces of the shafts and capitals, emphasized these natural details. In fact, the flora of the Nile valley supplied the basic decorative motifs in all Egyptian art. With respect to possible Mesopotamian influence, it is important to note that, until the time of

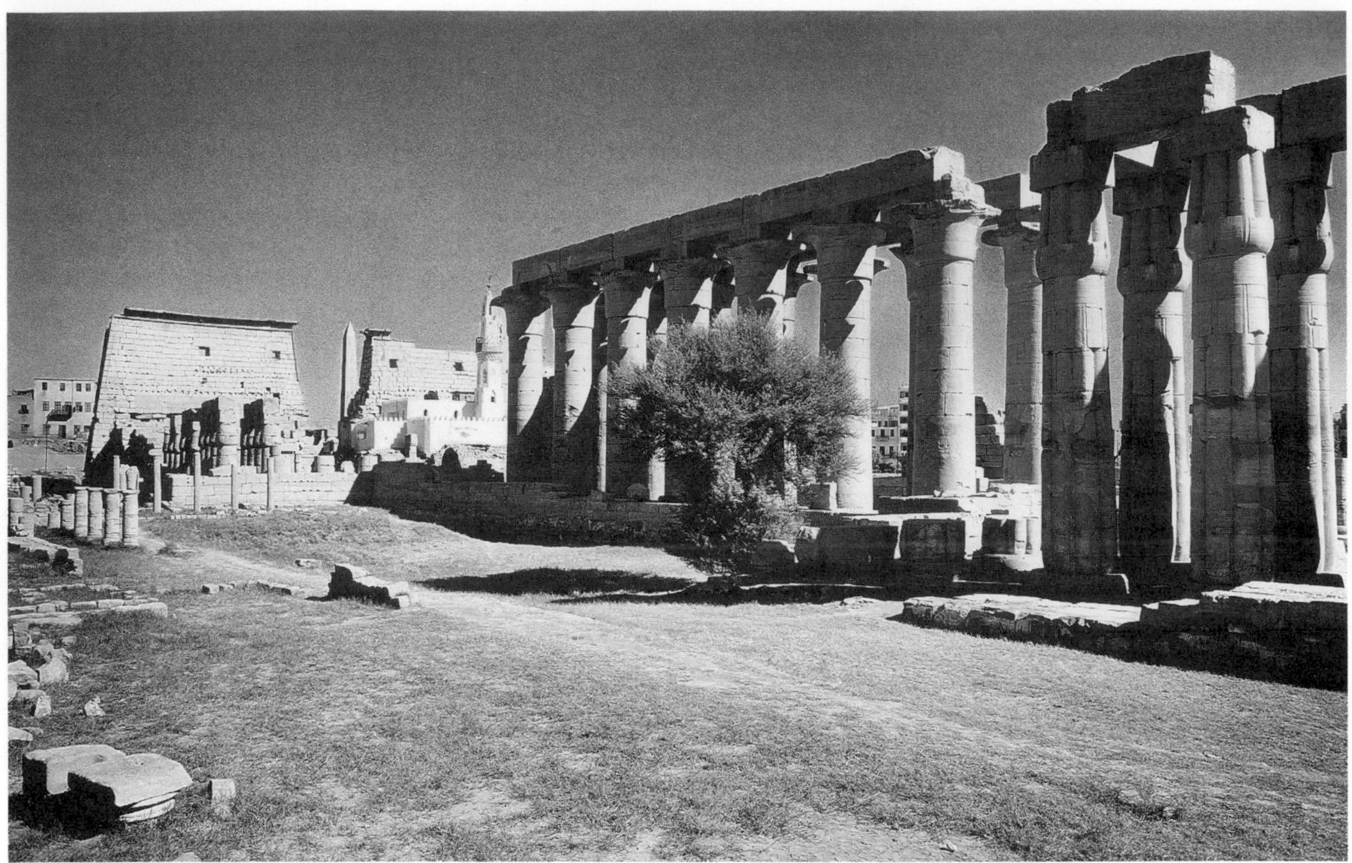

3-33 *Left:* court and pylon of Ramses II, *c.* 1280 B.C.; *right:* court and colonnade of Amenhotep III, *c.* 1370 B.C. Temple of Amen-Mut-Khonsu, Luxor.

Persia, Mesopotamian architecture seldom employed the post-and-lintel system; the column was rarely seen. Moreover, the formalization of plant forms into the rigid profiles of architecture is precisely the same thing as the formalization of human bodies and action that the Egyptians achieved so skillfully in tomb painting and sculpture.

Sculpture and Painting

This radical simplification of form, which preserves in the ka figures the cubic essence of the block, can be seen to advantage in the statue showing Senmut (Queen Hatshepsut's chancellor and architect of her temple at Deir el-Bahri) with Princess Nefrua (FIG. **3-34**). This curious design, evidently popular in the New Kingdom, concentrates attention on the portrait head and leaves the "body" a cubic block, given over to inscriptions. With surfaces turning subtly about smoothly rounded corners, it seems another expression of the Egyptian fondness for volume enclosed by flat, unambiguous planes. The polished stone shape has its own simple beauty.

The persistence of the formulas for projection of an image onto a flat surface can be seen in wall paintings

3-34 *Senmut with Princess Nefrua,* from Thebes, *c.* 1450 B.C. Black stone, block statue approx. 40″ high. Staatliche Museen, Berlin.

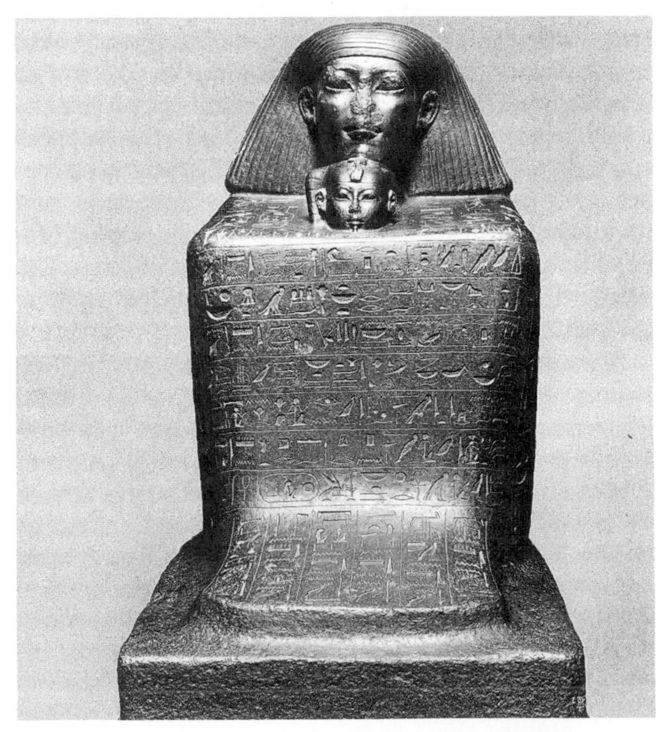

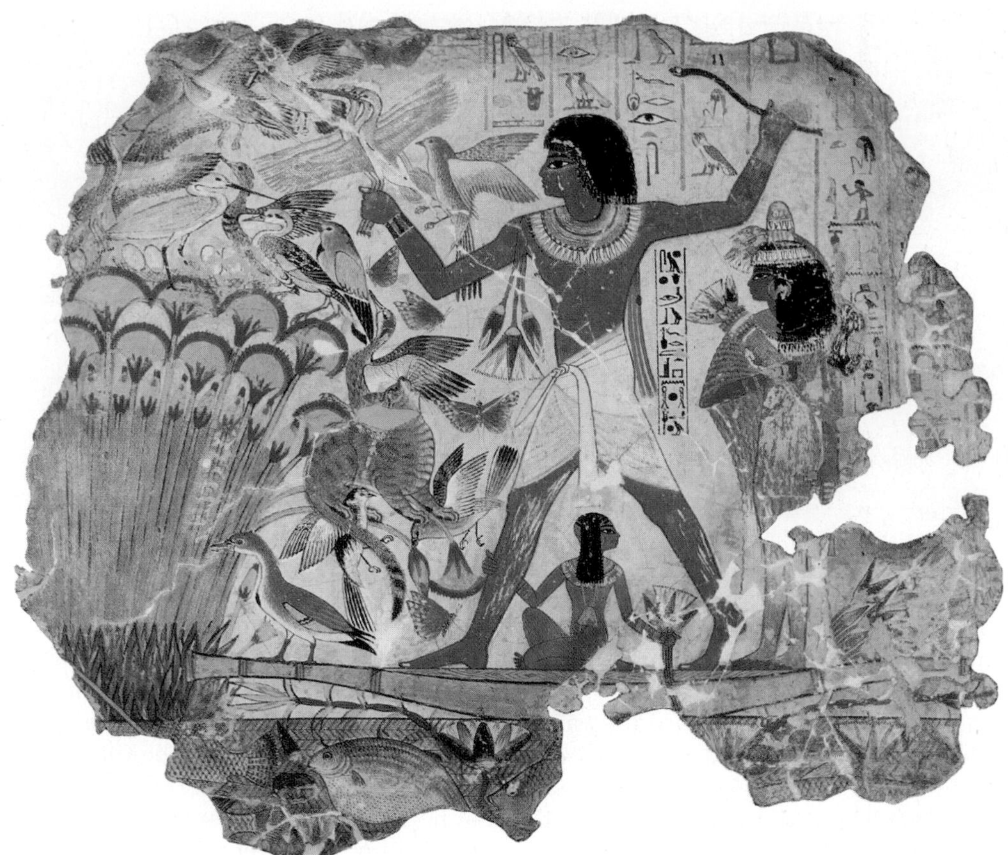

3-35 *Fowling Scene,* wall painting from the tomb of Nebamun (?), Thebes, *c.* 1400 B.C. Painting on dry plaster. British Museum, London.

in the tomb of Nebamun (?) at Thebes (FIG. **3-35**), which dates from the Eighteenth Dynasty. The deceased nobleman is standing in his boat, flushing the birds from a papyrus swamp. In contrast to the static pose of the hippopotamus-hunting Ti (FIG. 3-18), Nebamun is shown striding forward and swinging his throwstick vigorously. In his right hand, he holds three birds he has caught; a wild cat, on a papyrus stem just in front of him, has caught two more in her claws and is holding the wings of a third in her teeth. His two companions, perhaps his wife and daughter, their figures scaled down in proportion to their rank, are holding the lotuses they have gathered. Although the water and the figures are represented by the usual conventions, cat, fish, and birds show a naturalism based on visual perception similar to what we see in the *Geese of Medum* (FIG. 3-19).

The tomb chamber, as we see it in the well-preserved New Kingdom tomb of Nakht at Thebes (FIG. **3-36**), is similar to the tomb chambers of the Old Kingdom. In the mural, the system of registers still preserves the rigid separation of the zones of action, but some innovations of detail appear here, such as a new liveliness and a closer inspection of life. Another fresco fragment, probably from the tomb of Nebamun

3-36 Tomb of Nakht, Thebes, *c.* 1450 B.C. Fresco on rear wall 60″ × 55″.

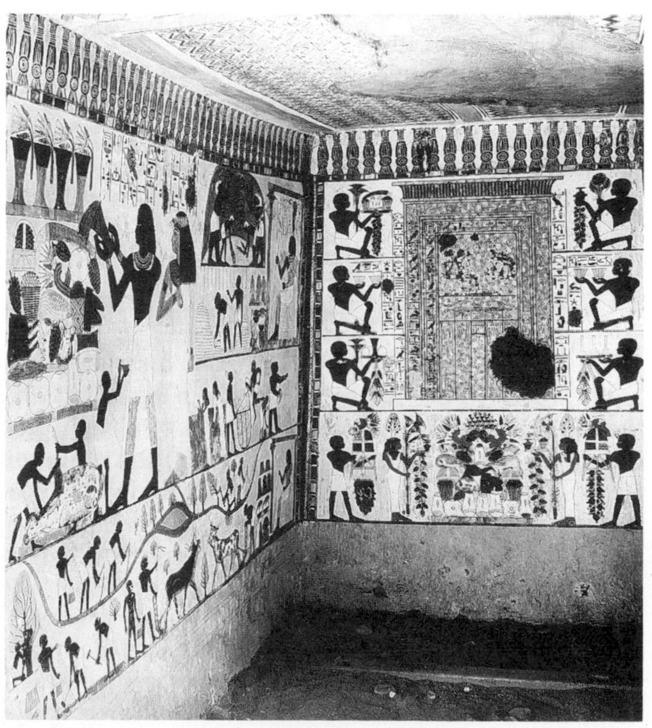

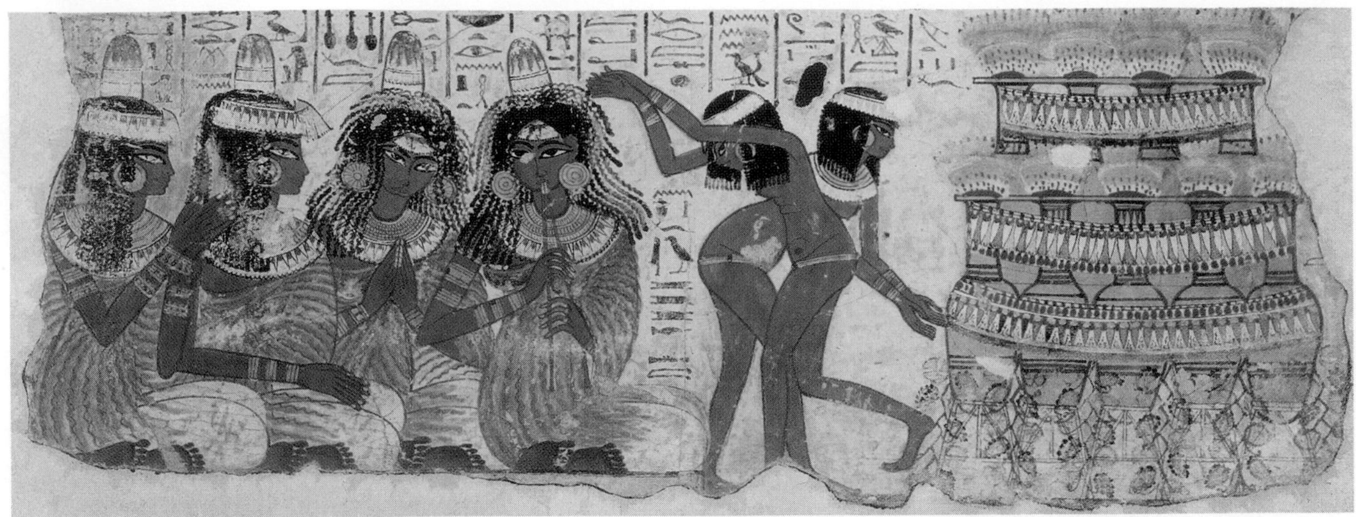

3-37 *Musicians and Dancers,* detail of a wall painting from the tomb of Nebamun (?), Thebes, c. 1400 B.C. Fragment $11\frac{3}{4}'' \times 27\frac{1}{4}''$. British Museum, London.

(FIG. **3-37**), shows four ladies watching and apparently participating in a musicale and dance in which two nimble little nude dancing girls perform. The overlapping of the girls' figures, facing in opposite directions, and the rather complicated gyrations of the dance are carefully and accurately observed and executed. Of the four ladies of the audience, two at the left are represented conventionally, but the other two face the observer in what is a most unusual and very rarely attempted frontal pose. They seem to beat time to the dance; one of them plays the reeds. The artist takes careful note of the soles of their feet as they sit cross-legged. This informality constitutes a relaxation not only of the stiff rules of representation but also of the set themes once thought appropriate for tomb painting. In addition, we may have here the reflection of a more luxurious mode of life in the New Kingdom; at this point, the ka may have required not only necessities and comforts in the hereafter but formal entertainment as well.

Akhenaton and the Amarna Period

These small variations on age-old formulas heralded a short but violent upheaval in Egyptian art, the only major break in the continuity of its long tradition. In the fourteenth century B.C., the emperor Amenophis IV (Amenhotep IV), later known as Akhenaton (or Ikhnaton), proclaimed the religion of Aton, the universal and only god of the sun. He thus contested and abolished the native cult of Amen, sacred to Thebes and professed by the mighty priests of such temples as Karnak and Luxor, as well as by the people of Egypt. He blotted out the name of Amen from all inscriptions, and even from his own name and that of his father, Amenophis III. He emptied the great temples, embittered the priests and people, and moved his capital downriver from Thebes to a site now called Tell el-Amarna, where he built his own city and shrines to the religion of Aton.

These actions by Amenophis IV—now Akhenaton—although they might savor of the psychotic or of the fanaticism of sudden conversion, were portended by events in the formation and expansion of the power of the great Eighteenth Dynasty. Egyptian might had formed the first world empire. The conquering imperialist pharaohs—ruling over an empire that included Syria in the north and Nubia in the south—had gradually enlarged the powers of their old sun god, Amen, to make him not simply god of the Egyptians, but god of all men. Even before Egypt had become the main force in the Mediterranean world, Thutmose I, a founder of the fortunes of the dynasty, could say of the sun god that his kingdom extended as far as "the circuit of the sun." The military pharaoh, Thutmose III, said of this aggrandized god: "He seeth the whole earth hourly." Thus, Akhenaton was exploiting already-gathering forces when he raised the imperialized god of the sun to be the only god of all the earth and proscribed any rival as blasphemous. He appropriated to himself the new and universal god, making himself both the son and prophet, even the sole experient, of Aton. To him alone could the god make revelation. Akhenaton's hymn to Aton survives:

> Thou art in my heart.
> There is no other that knoweth thee
> Save thy son Ikhnaton.
> Thou hast made him wise
> In thy designs and might.
> The world is in thy hand,

Even as thou hast made them . . .
Thou didst establish the world,
And raise them up for thy son,
Who came forth from thy limbs,
The king of Upper and Lower Egypt,
Living in Truth, Lord of Two Lands . . .

Egypt has left us the ingredients, as it were, of the later monotheisms so influential in the world. Akhenaton's brief theocracy seems to have embodied the seeds of later concepts of one god, of an eternal son who is also a king, of a world created by that one god, and of the intimate revelation of that god's spirit to a chosen one.

One effect of the new religious philosophy seems to have been a temporary relaxation of the Egyptian preoccupation with death and the hereafter and a correspondingly greater concern with life on earth. In art, this change is reflected in a different attitude toward the representation of the human figure. Artists aimed for a new sense of life and movement, expressed in swelling, curvilinear forms; their long-fostered naturalistic tendencies, thus far confined largely to the representation of animals, were extended not only to the lowly human figure but, significantly, to royalty as well. A colossal statue of Akhenaton from Karnak (FIG. **3-38**) retains the standard frontal pose, but the strange, epicene body, with its curving contours, and the long, full-lipped face, heavy-lidded eyes, and dreaming expression, show that the artist has studied the subject with care and rendered him with all the physiognomical and physical irregularities that were part of the king's actual appearance. The predilection for curved lines stresses the softness of the slack, big-hipped body, a far cry indeed from the heroically proportioned figures of Akhenaton's predecessors. In a daring mixture of naturalism and stylization, the artist has given us an informal and uncompromising portrayal of the king, charged with both vitality and a psychological complexity that has been called expressionistic.

The famous painted limestone bust of Akhenaton's queen, Nefertiti (FIG. **3-39**), exhibits a similar expression of entranced musing and an almost mannered sensitivity and delicacy of curving contour. The sculptor may have been deliberately alluding to a heavy flower on its slender stalk by exaggerating the weight of the crowned head and the length of the almost serpentine neck. One thinks of those modern descendants of Queen Nefertiti—the models in the

3-38 *Akhenaton,* from a pillar statue in the Temple of Amen-Re, Karnak, *c.* 1375 B.C. Sandstone, approx. 13′ high. Egyptian Museum, Cairo.

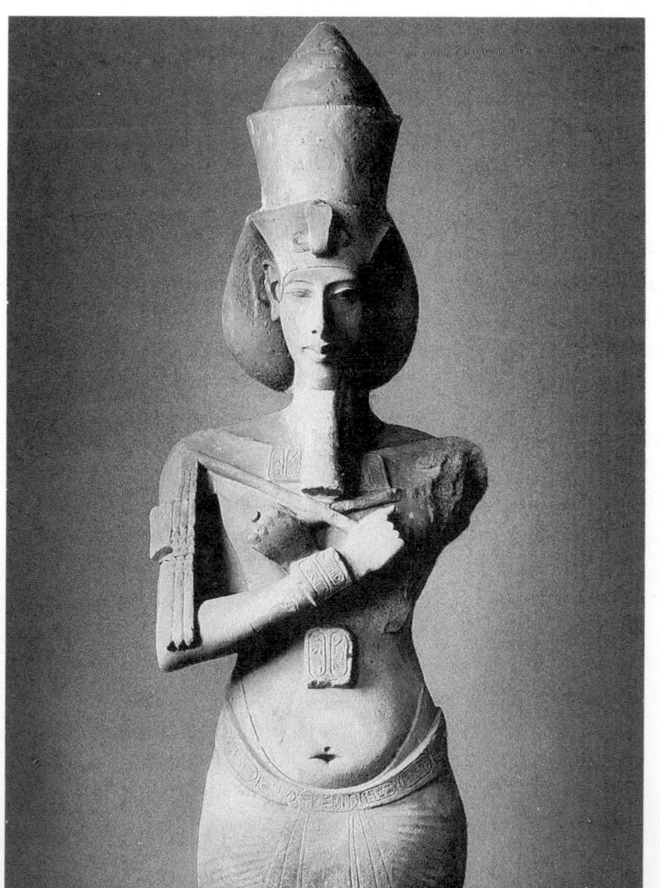

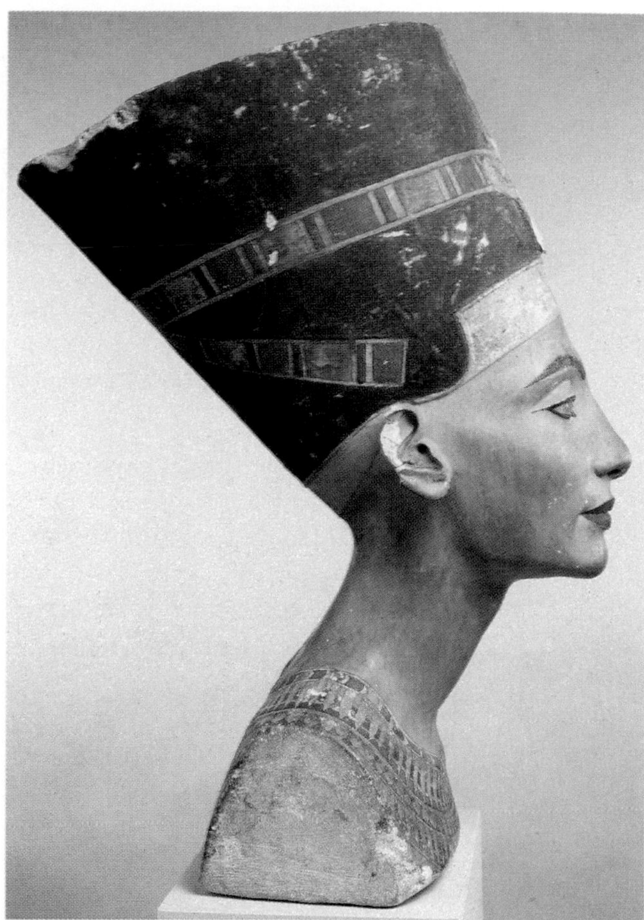

3-39 *Queen Nefertiti,* from Tell el-Amarna, *c.* 1360 B.C. Limestone, approx. 20″ high. Ägyptisches Museum, Berlin.

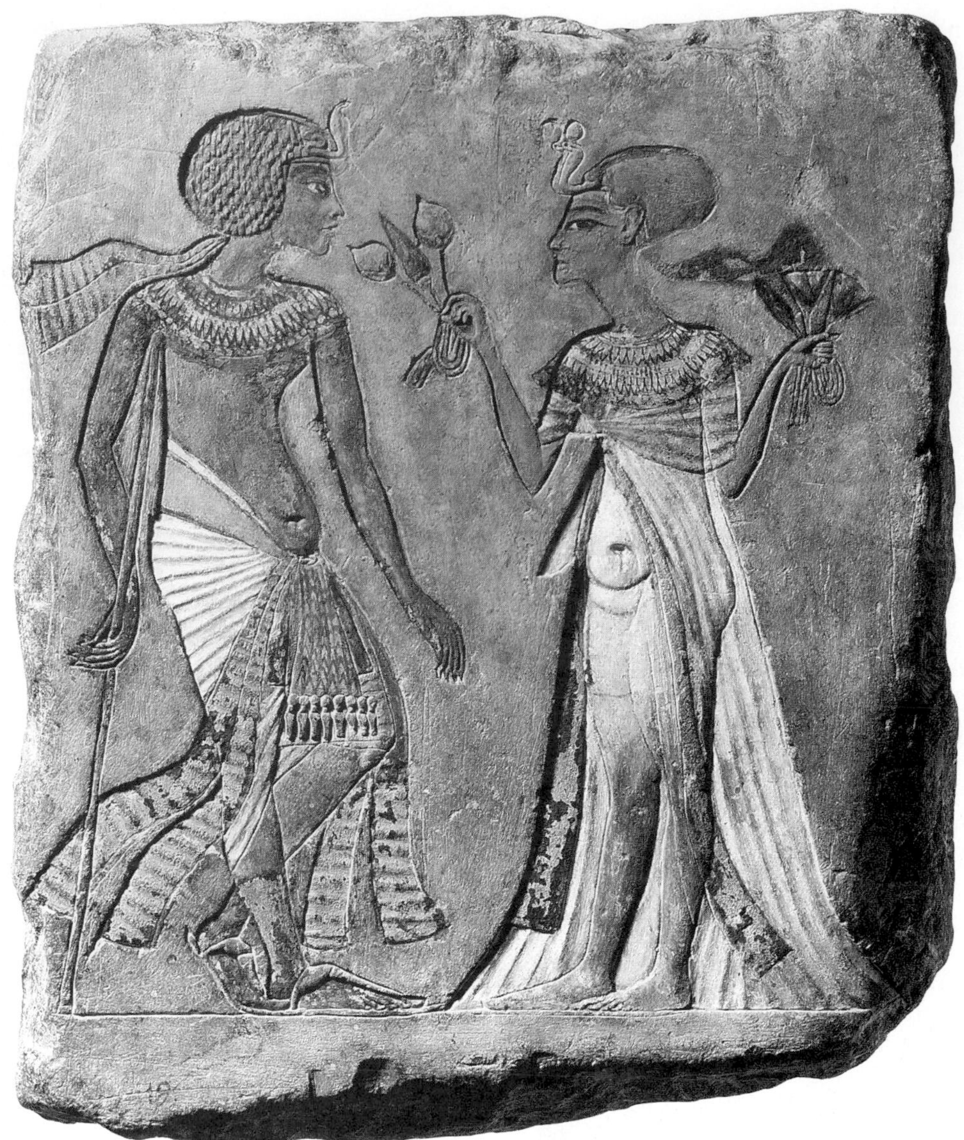

3-40 *King Smenkhkare and Meritaten (?),* from Tell el-Amarna, *c.* 1360 B.C. Painted limestone relief, approx. 9½″ high. Staatliche Museen, Berlin.

fashion magazines, with their gaunt, swaying frames, masklike, pallid faces, and enormous, shadowed eyes. As the modern mannerism shapes the living model to its dictates, so the sculptors of Tell el-Amarna may have had some standard of spiritual beauty to which they adjusted the actual likenesses of their subjects. Even so, one is made very much aware of the reality of the queen through her contrived mask of beauty, a masterpiece of cosmetic art. The Nefertiti bust is one more example of that elegant blending of the real and the formal that we have noticed so often in the art of the ancient Near East.

During the last three years of his reign, Akhenaton's coregent was his half-brother, Smenkhkare. A relief from Tell el-Amarna may show Smenkhkare and his wife Meritaten (FIG. **3-40**) in an informal, even intimate, pose that contrasts strongly with the traditional formality in the representation of exalted persons. Once-rigid lines have become undulating curves, and the pose of Smenkhkare has no known precedent. The prince leans casually on his staff, one leg at ease, in an attitude that presumes knowledge on the sculptor's part of the flexible shift of body masses, a principle not really grasped until the Classical period in Greece. This quite realistic detail accompanies others that are the result of a freer expression of what is observed: details of costume and the departures from the traditional formality, such as the elongated and bulging head of Meritaten and the prominent bellies that characterize figures of the Amarna school. Proportions of figures no longer depend on rank; the princess is depicted in the same scale as her husband on the basis of their natural proportions.

We have seen some slight loosening of the conventions of sculpture and painting even before Akhenaton, but the Amarna style (and a subsequent return to the earlier tradition) marks a break too abrupt and emphatic to permit us to conclude that the style was simply a local, native flowering. It is possible that there was some influence from the Mediterranean world. We know that Egypt dealt commercially with Crete, beginning in the Predynastic period, and the livelier, less convention-bound art of the Minoans could have proved suggestive and stimulating to the Amarna artists. Although the Cretan palace culture came to an end around 1400 B.C. (see Chapter 4), and Akhenaton did not ascend the Egyptian throne until 1378 B.C. (first as co-ruler with his father), the time lag does not seem too great to preclude such an influence. It may be that some Cretan artists, finding refuge in Egypt and a sympathetic artistic climate under Akhenaton's rule, fertilized the Amarna style.

The Tomb of Tutankhamen and the Late Period

The survival of the Amarna style is seen in the fabulously rich art and artifacts found in the unplundered tomb of the young pharaoh Tutankhamen (1361–1352 B.C.), who is known in modern folklore as "King Tut." The treasures of the tomb, which include sculpture, furniture, jewelry, and accessories of all sorts, were uncovered in 1922. The adventure of their discovery gained world renown. Installed in the Egyptian Museum in Cairo, a selection of these treasures was made available to a larger public in the late 1970s, when they were sent on a tour of museums throughout the world. It has been estimated that the collection attracted the greatest number of visitors recorded for any single tour of works of art. It reawakened public interest in the legend of "King Tut" and undoubtedly stimulated appreciation of ancient Egyptian art.

The principal monument in the collection is, of course, the tomb of the king himself. The royal mummy reposed in the innermost of three coffins, nested one within the other and shaped in the form of Osiris, god of death (FIG. **3-41**). The innermost coffin was the most sumptuously wrought of the three. Made of beaten gold (about a quarter ton of it) and inlaid with such semiprecious stones as lapis lazuli, turquoise, and carnelian, it is a supreme monument to the sculptor's and goldsmith's craft. The stylized

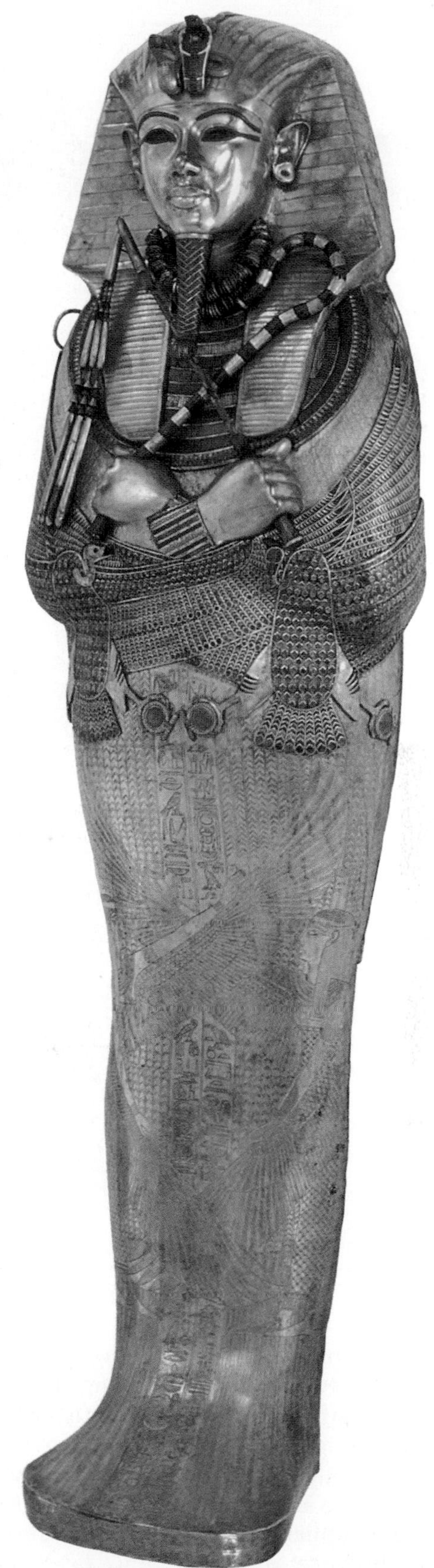

3-41 The innermost coffin of Tutankhamen (ruled 1361–1352 B.C.). Gold with inlay of enamel and semiprecious stones, 6′ $\frac{7}{8}$″ long. Egyptian Museum, Cairo.

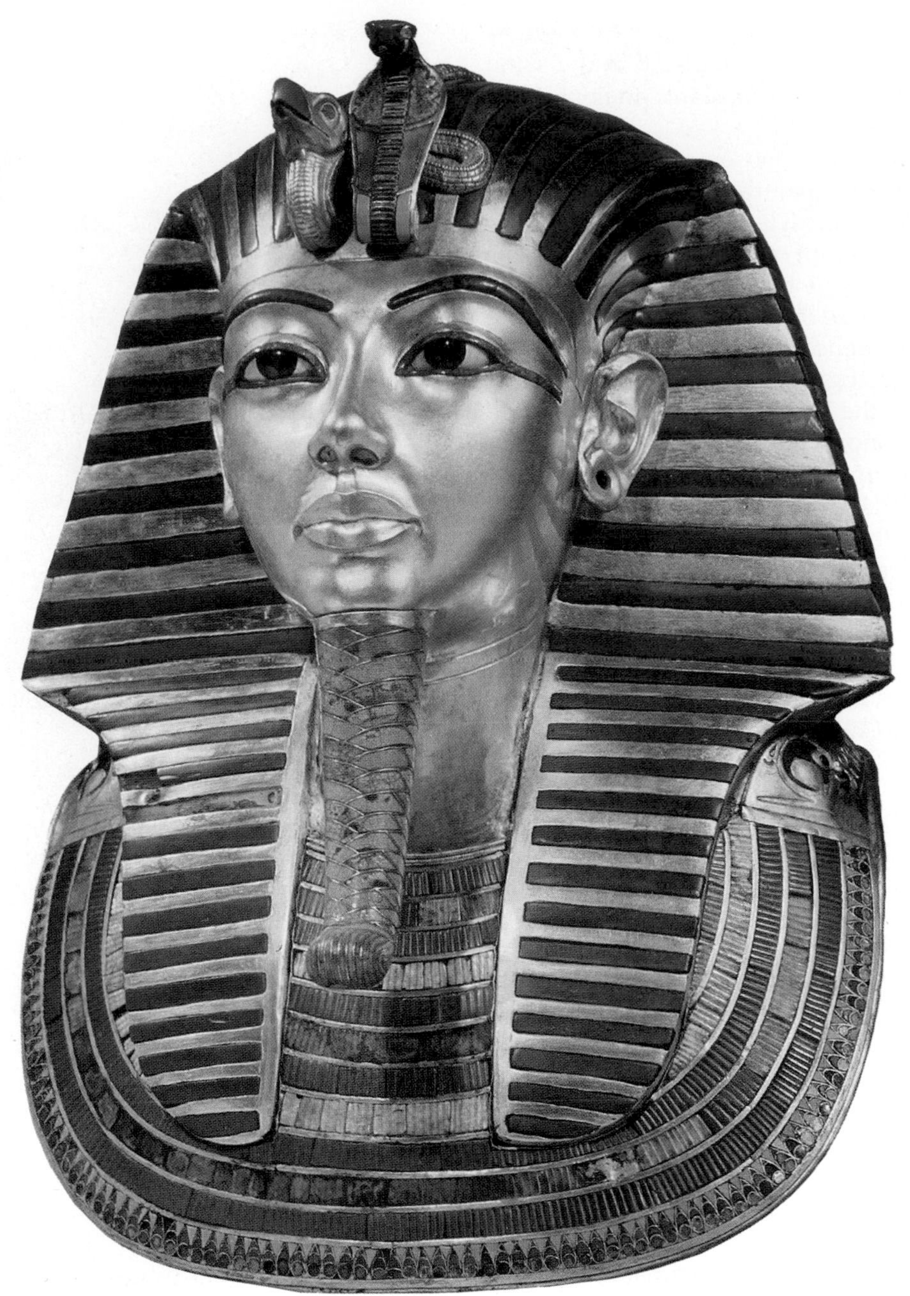

3-42 Death mask of Tutankhamen, found in innermost coffin. Gold with inlay of semiprecious stones. Egyptian Museum, Cairo.

portrait mask, which covered the king's face, shows his features relaxed in a kind of musing serenity that betokens his confidence in eternal life (FIG. **3-42**). Despite a lingering Amarnan sensitivity, softness of contour, and subtlety in the reading of personality, the general effect is one of grandeur and richness expressive of Egyptian power, pride, and affluence at the time of the onset of empire.

That the king must have defined his mission as imperial conqueror, and would have himself so represented, is shown in the panels of a painted chest from the treasures of the young pharaoh's tomb (FIG. **3-43**). The lid panel shows the king as a great hunter, pursuing droves of fleeing animals in the desert, and the side panel shows him as a great warrior. Together, the two panels are a double advertisement of royal power familiar in Assyrian art. From a war chariot drawn by spirited, plumed horses, Tutankhamen, shown larger than all other figures on the chest, draws his bow against a cluster of bearded, Asian enemies, who fall in confusion before him. He slays the enemy, like game, in great numbers. Above him,

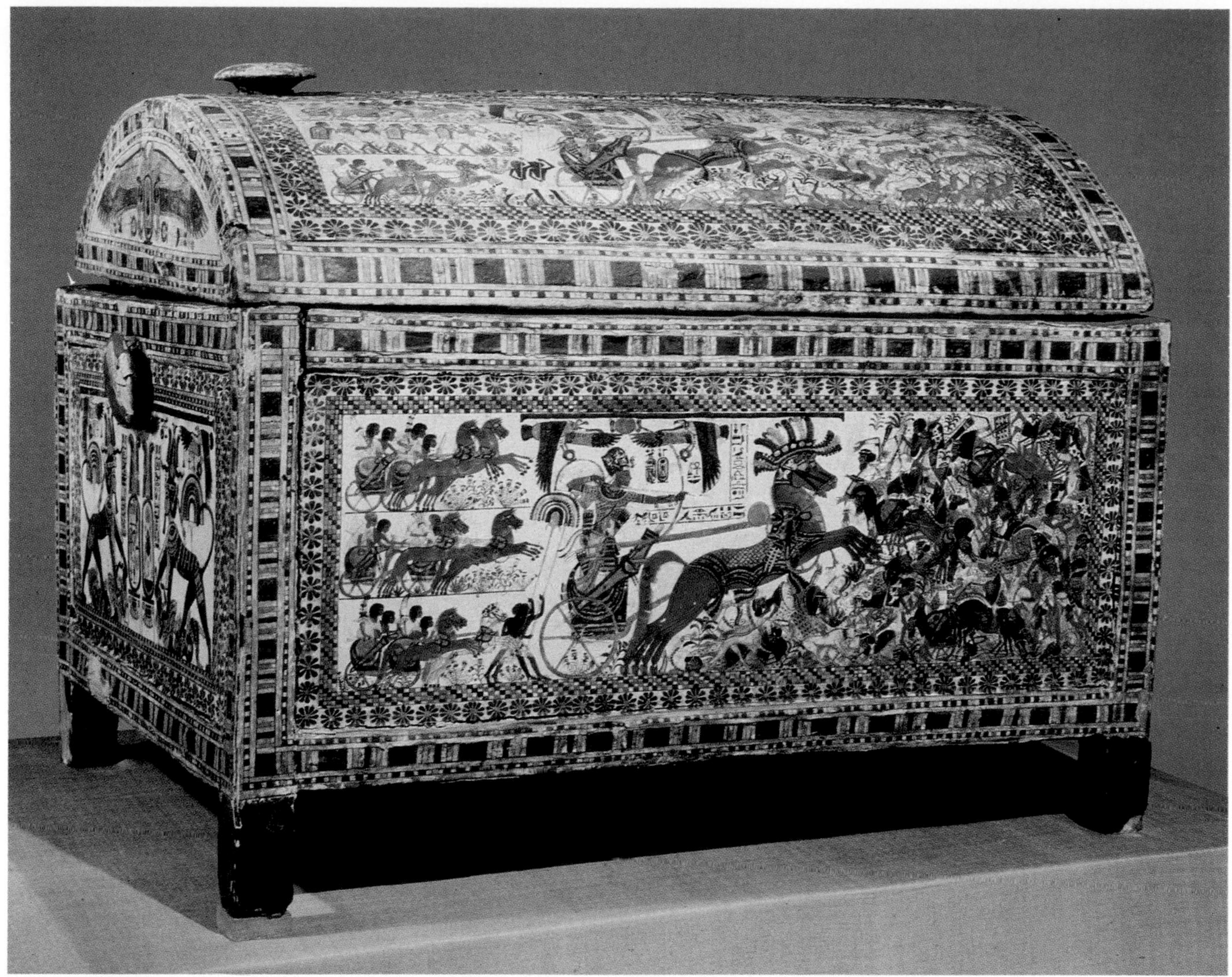

3-43 Painted chest, from the tomb of Tutankhamen, Thebes, *c.* 1350 B.C. Approx. 20″ long. Egyptian Museum, Cairo.

the sun disc shines on his victory and the vulture goddess Nekh-bet, his special protectress, shelters him with her wings. Behind him are three tiers of war chariots in diminutive scale, which serve to magnify the figure of the king and to increase the count of his warriors. The themes are traditional, but the fluid, curvilinear forms, the dynamic compositions with their emphasis on movement and action, and the disposition of the hunted, overthrown animals and enemy—who, freed of conventional ground lines, race wildly across the panels—are features reminiscent not only of the Amarna style but, as we shall see, of the lively naturalism of Cretan art as well.

The pharaohs who followed Akhenaton reestablished the cult and priesthood of Amen, restored the temples and the inscriptions, and returned to the old manner in art. Akhenaton's monuments were wiped out, his heresy anathematized, and his city abandoned. The conservative reaction can be seen in a relief of the pharaoh Seti I (FIG. **3-44**). The rigid, flattened shapes repeat the formula of the *Palette of Narmer* (FIG. 3-2) and the static formality of Old Kingdom art.

Seti I and his successor, Ramses II, were builders both of the Egyptian Empire and the titanic colonnades of Karnak at Thebes, where their victories are celebrated in thousands of feet of relief sculpture and hieroglyphic inscription. Karnak was a monument to the Theban god Amen, restored to favor after the heresy of Akhenaton. Sixteen miles northwest of Karnak at Abydos, Seti I also constructed a great temple to the death god Osiris, whose religion he expanded from a local to a national one. The gods of Thebes were official, belonging to the state religion; their temples were in the care of an elite, privileged priesthood isolated from the people. But Osiris, god of the

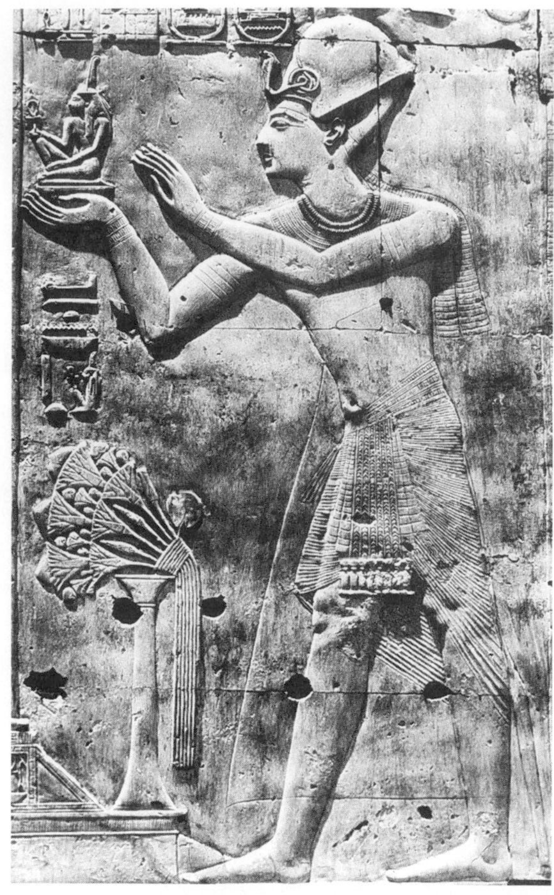

3-44 *Seti I Offering,* from the Temple of Seti I, Abydos, c. 1300 B.C. Painted limestone. Louvre, Paris.

dead and king of the underworld as well as giver of eternal life, became the object of devotion for all Egyptians, including the humblest among them. According to the myth of Osiris, he is slain and dismembered but rises again and, by his resurrection, conquers death; thus, he becomes the source of immortality for all humanity.

The ritual of the cult of Osiris is recorded in collections of spells, prayers, formulas, and counsels that compose the so-called Book of the Dead. Illuminated papyrus scrolls, some as long as 70 feet, were the essential equipment of the tombs of well-to-do persons. The papyrus scroll of Hu-Nefer, found in his tomb in the Theban necropolis, represents the final judgment of the deceased (FIG. **3-45**). At the left, he is led into the hall of judgment by Anubis, the jackal-headed god of embalming. Anubis then adjusts the scales to weigh the heart of the dead man against the feather of the goddess Maat, protectress of truth and right. A hybrid monster, half hippopotamus and half lion, the devourer of souls awaits the decision of the scales; if it is unfavorable to the deceased, the monster will destroy his soul on the spot. The ibis-headed god Thoth records the proceedings. Above, the gods of the Egyptian pantheon are arranged as witnesses. Having been justified by the scales, Hu-Nefer is brought by Osiris' son, the falcon-headed Horus, into the presence of the green-faced Osiris, the goddess Isis (wife of Osiris and mother of Horus), and the

3-45 *Psychostasis* (soul-raising) *of Hu-Nefer,* from Thebes. Painted papyrus scroll, $2\frac{3}{4}''$ high. British Museum, London.

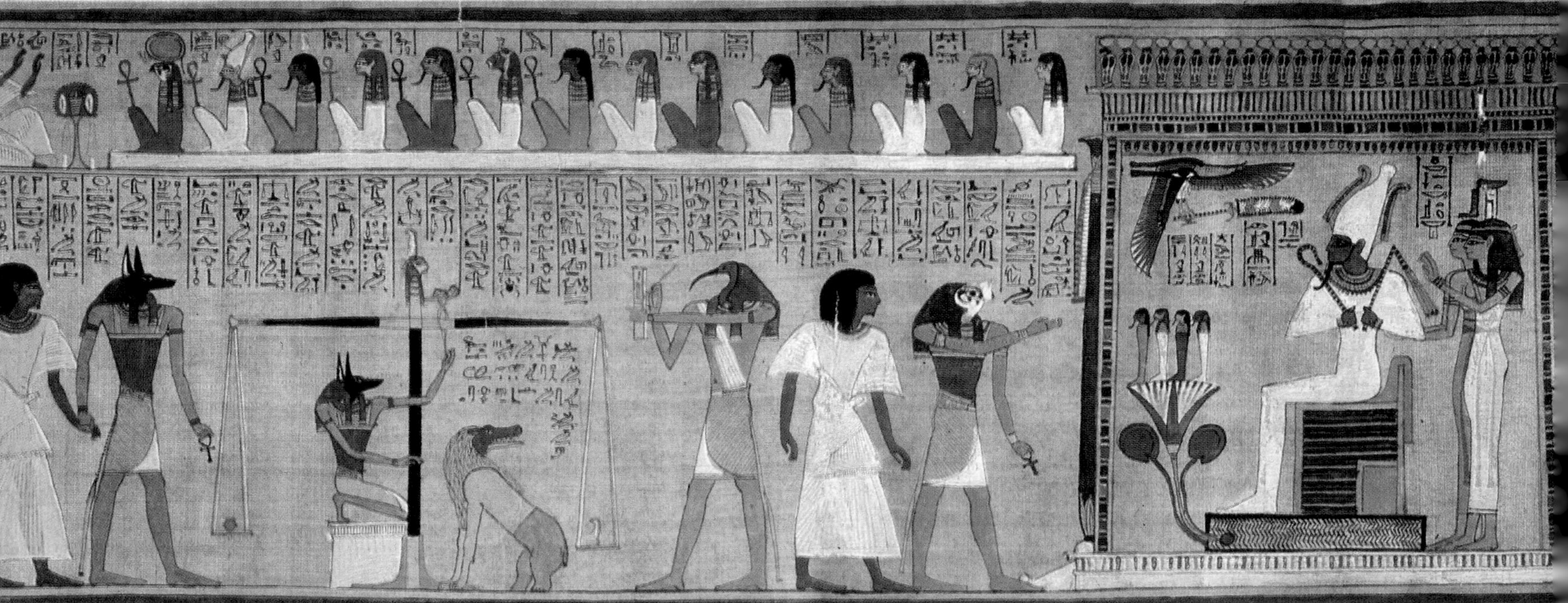

goddess Nephtys (the sister of Isis and Osiris) to receive the award of eternal life.

The figures have all the formality of stance, shape, and attitude—all the flat linearity—that we find in the art of the Old Kingdom. Abstract figures and hieroglyphs alike are aligned rigidly along the same planar surface. There is nothing here of the flexible, curvilinear style suggestive of movement that is evident in the art of Amarna and Tutankhamen. The conservatism is complete, as it is in the Seti I relief.

And so, in essence, it remained through the last centuries of Egyptian figural art. During this time, Egypt lost the commanding role it once had played in the Near East. The empire dwindled away, and the land was invaded, occupied, and ruled by foreign powers, Assyria and Persia, and peoples from the west (Libya) and south (Nubia-Ethiopia). From the period of the last-mentioned reign in Egypt, a portrait statue, *Mentemhet the Governor* (FIG. **3-46**), survives that easily could be mistaken for a Memphite work of the Old Kingdom (FIGS. 3-15 and 3-17). Yet this statue dates from the Twenty-fifth Dynasty in the seventh century B.C. The Old Kingdom formulas, conventions, and details of representation are all here in summary: the rigidity of stance, frontality, spareness of silhouette, arms at the side and one leg advanced, the kilt, the headdress, even the material (granite) and the carving technique recall the Old Kingdom. Only the realism of the head, with its rough, almost brutal, characterization, differentiates the work from that of the earlier age. The pharaohs of the late period deliberately referred back to the art of Egypt's classical phase to give authority to their royal image; religious and political motives only partly explain this deliberate archaism, however. As we noted at the beginning of this chapter, conservatism is a trait of the Egyptian character, perhaps the principal trait. The Egyptians' resistance to significant change over a period of almost three millennia may stem from a profound religiosity inspired by the steady sun, the eternal desert, the slow pulse of the Nilotic seasons, and the enduring conviction that life is not really interrupted by death.

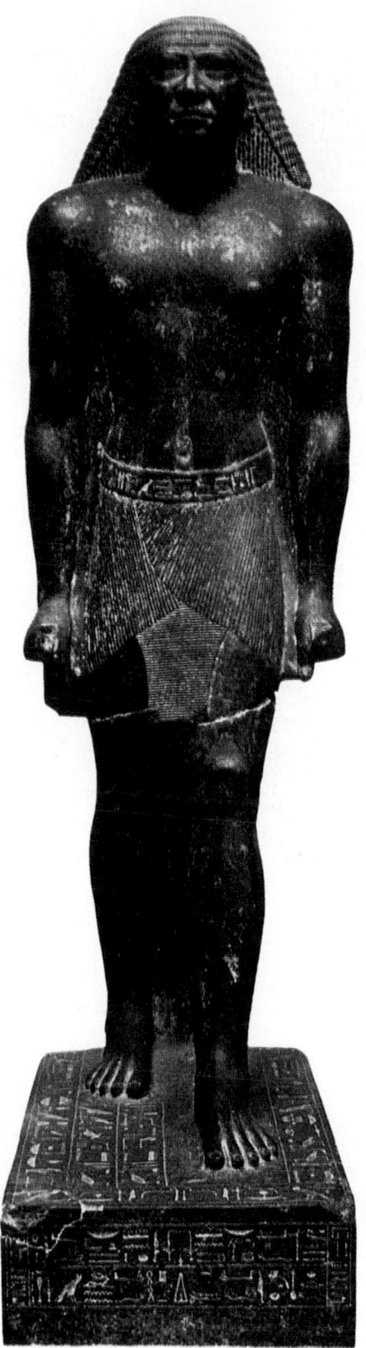

3-46 *Mentemhet the Governor,* c. 650 B.C. Granite, 53″ high. Egyptian Museum, Cairo.

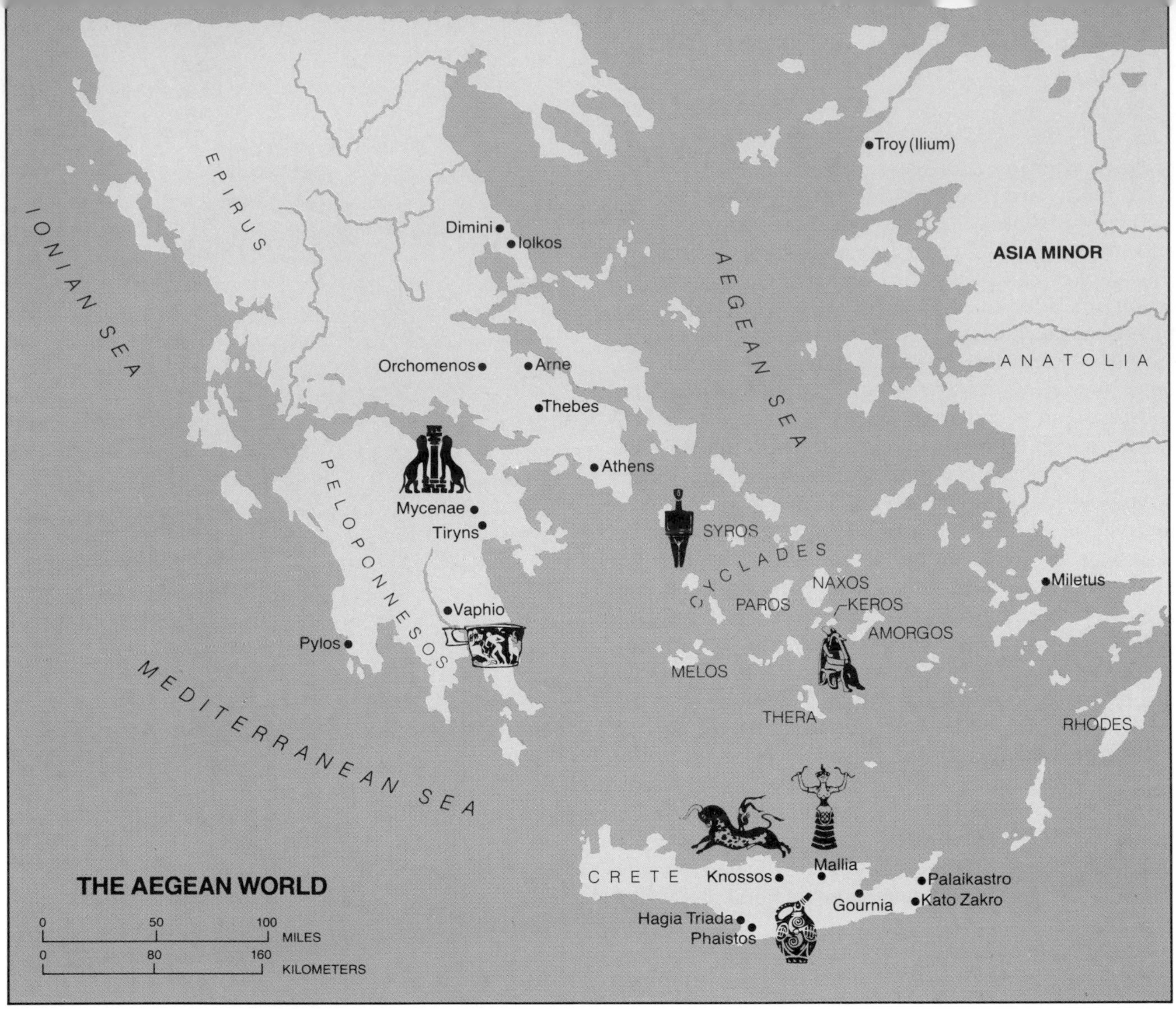

THE AEGEAN WORLD

IONIAN SEA
EPIRUS
Dimini
Iolkos
Troy (Ilium)
AEGEAN SEA
ASIA MINOR
ANATOLIA
Orchomenos
Arne
Thebes
Athens
PELOPONNESOS
Mycenae
Tiryns
SYROS
CYCLADES
NAXOS
PAROS
KEROS
AMORGOS
Miletus
Vaphio
Pylos
MELOS
THERA
RHODES
MEDITERRANEAN SEA
CRETE
Knossos
Mallia
Palaikastro
Kato Zakro
Gournia
Hagia Triada
Phaistos
0 50 100 MILES
0 80 160 KILOMETERS

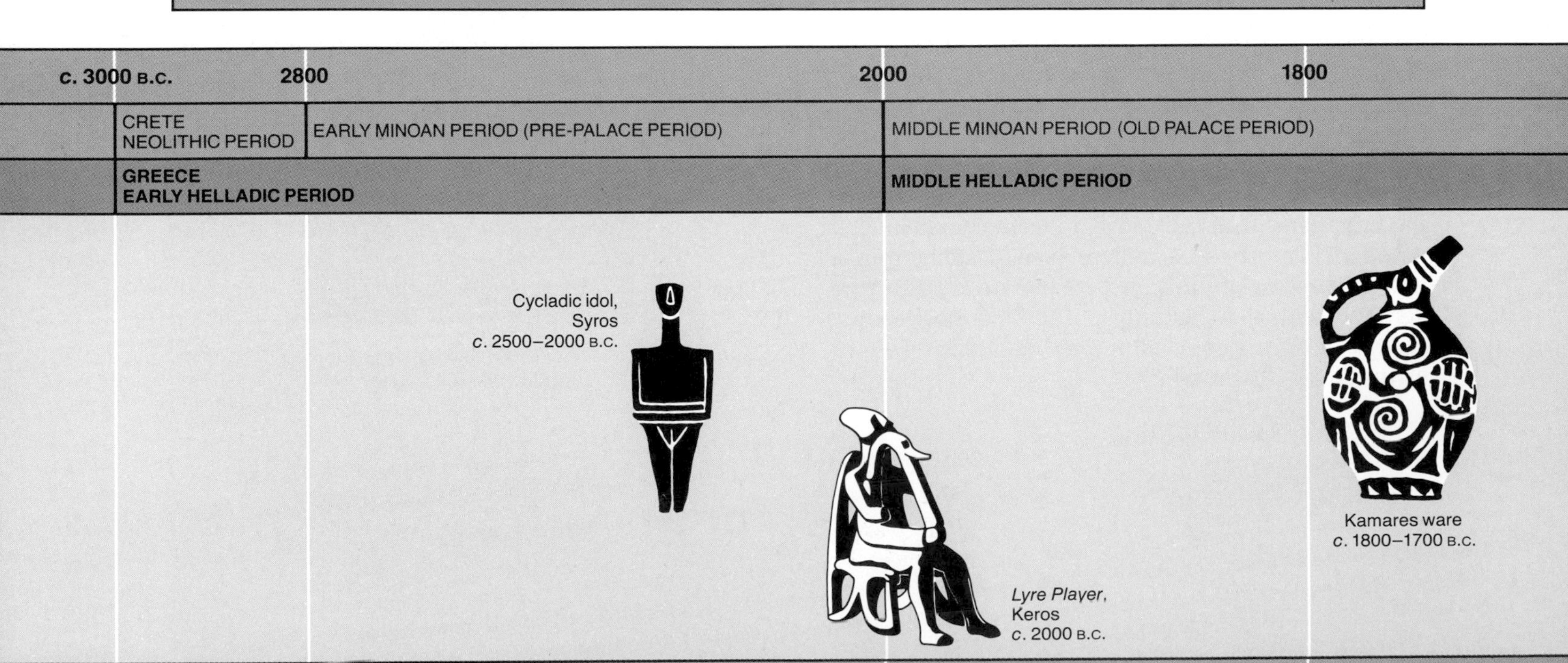

*Bold type indicates Helladic and Mycenaean chronology.

4

THE AEGEAN: CYCLADIC, MINOAN, AND MYCENAEAN ART

1700	1600	1500	1400	1200	1000
		LATE MINOAN PERIOD (NEW PALACE PERIOD)		SUB-MINOAN PERIOD	
		LATE HELLADIC (MYCENAEAN) PERIOD		**SUB-MYCENAEAN PERIOD**	

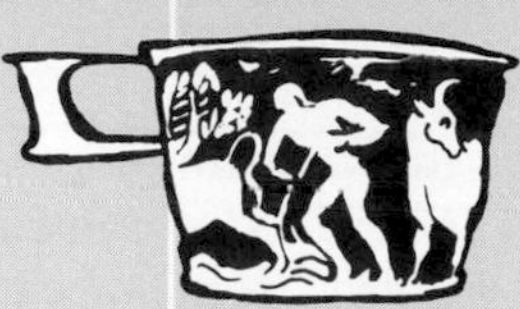

The Vaphio Cups
c. 1500 B.C.

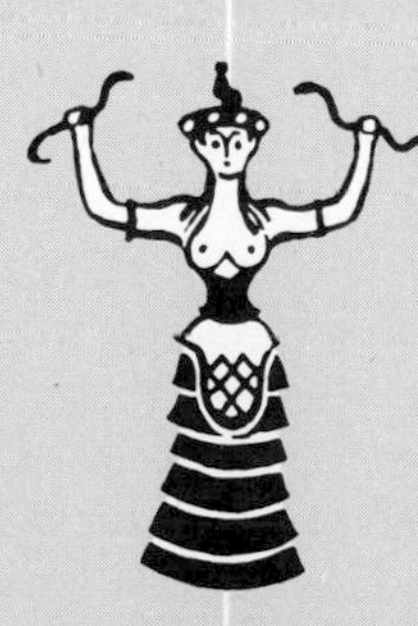

Snake Goddess, Knossos
c. 1600 B.C.

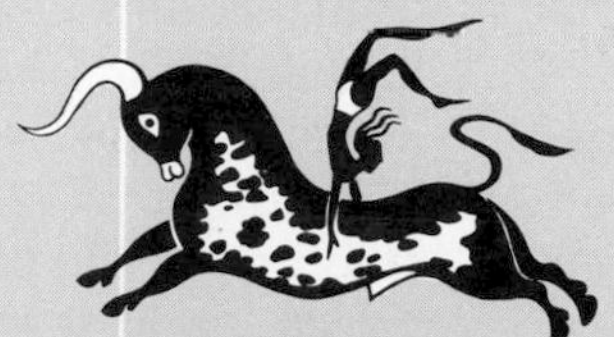

The Toreador Fresco, Knossos *c.* 1500 B.C.

Lion Gate, Mycenae
c. 1300 B.C.

Destruction of old palaces *c.* 1700

Decline of new palaces *c.* 1400–1200

Dorian invasion of Greece *c.* 1200

HOMER, IN THE *ILIAD*, wrote of the might and splendor of the Achaean host deployed for war against Troy:

> So clan after clan poured out from the ships and huts onto the plain of Scamander, and . . . found their places in the flowery meadows by the river, innumerable as the leaves and blossoms in their season . . . the Locrians . . . the Athenians . . . the citizens of Argos and Tiryns of the Great Walls . . . troops from the great stronghold of Mycenae, from wealthy Corinth . . . from Lacedaemon . . . from Pylos . . . Knossos in Crete, Phaistos . . . and the other troops that had their homes in Crete of the Hundred Towns.

The list goes on and on, outlining the peoples and the geography of the Aegean world in intimate detail. Until about 1870, historians of ancient Greece, although they acknowledged Homer's superb art, discounted him as a historian, attributing the profusion of names and places in his writings to the rich abundance of his imagination. The prehistory of Classical Greece remained shadowy and lost, historians believed, in an impenetrable world of myth. That they had done less than justice to the truth of Homer's account, or for that matter, to ancient Greek literary sources in general, was proved by a German amateur archeologist. Between 1870 and his death twenty years later, Heinrich Schliemann uncovered some of the very cities of the Trojan and Achaean heroes Homer celebrates: Troy, Mycenae, Orchomenos, and Tiryns. In 1870, at Hissarlik in the northwest corner of Asia Minor, which Schliemann's knowledge of the *Iliad* had led him to believe was the site of Homer's Troy, he dug into a vast *tell,* or mound, and found there a number of fortified cities built on the remains of one another, together with the evidence of the destruction of one of them by fire. Schliemann continued his excavations at Mycenae on the Greek mainland, from which, he believed, Agamemnon and Achilles had sailed to avenge the capture of Helen, and here his finds were even more startling. Massive fortress-palaces, elaborate tombs, quantities of gold jewelry and ornaments, cups, and inlaid weapons revealed a magnificent pre-Classical civilization.

But further discoveries were to prove that Mycenae had not been the center of this fabulous civilization. Nor had the lesson of Schliemann's success in pursuing hunches based on the careful reading of ancient legends been lost on his successors. An important Greek legend told of Minos, king of Crete, who had exacted from Athens a tribute of youths and maidens to be fed to the Minotaur, a creature half bull and half man that was housed in a vast labyrinth. Might this legend too be based on historical fact? An Englishman, Arthur Evans, had long considered Crete a potentially fertile field for investigation, and Schliemann himself, shortly before his death, had wanted to explore the site of Knossos. In 1900, Evans began work on Crete, and a short time later he uncovered extensive palaces, built by the old sea-kings of Crete, which indeed did resemble labyrinths (FIG. 4-6). His findings, primarily at Knossos, were augmented by additional excavations there and at Phaistos, Hagia Triada, and other important sites along the southern coast of the island. In 1962, excavation of another palace was begun on the eastern tip of Crete at Kato Zakro; more recently, a queen's burial chamber judged to be thirty-four hundred years old was found near Knossos.

The civilization of the coasts and islands of the Aegean emerged about the same time as the river valley civilizations of Egypt and Mesopotamia. Although close contact existed at various times and an active exchange of influences took place, each civilization manifested an originality of its own. The Aegean civilization has a special significance as the forerunner of the first truly European civilization—that of Greece. The sea-dominated geography of the Aegean contrasts sharply with that of the Near East, as does its temperate climate. In ancient times, these conditions produced a busy, commercial, seafaring culture with decentralized authority and a vigorous, vivacious, and pleasure-loving way of life. This description is especially true of Crete, the ancient center of Aegean civilization and the source from which its creative forces radiated. As a commercial crossroads for the ancient world, Crete was placed strategically in the eastern Mediterranean, and her agricultural products and manufactured goods were exported widely. The sea provided a natural defense against the frequent and often disruptive invasions that checker the histories of land-bound civilizations like those of Mesopotamia, and the navies of the sea-kings maintained a prosperous maritime empire that served for the transmission of ideas and influences as well as goods. The controlled accessibility to Crete of impulses from abroad, especially from Egypt and Mesopotamia, may account for the emergence and influence of its culture, which was felt in all of the Aegean area. Modifications of it on the Greek mainland and in the islands of the Cyclades north of Crete have been identified. Thus, the art of the islands is called Cycladic; that of Crete, Minoan, after King Minos; and that of the mainland, Helladic. The culture associated with Mycenae on the mainland, the Mycenaean culture, is classed under Late Helladic (about 1550–1100 B.C.).

The archeological problems confronting investigators of Near Eastern civilizations were much less difficult than those that confronted archeologists working in the Aegean area. Very few documents survived in

Aegean sites with which to correlate the archeological findings and no "absolute" dates were agreed upon that could be expressed numerically. Chronicles and inscriptions such as those discovered for Egypt and Mesopotamia did not exist for the Aegean. Evans had to construct a "relative" dating system based on different ceramics and different decorative styles from various sites on Crete, in the Cyclades, and at Mycenae. His tripartite division of Minoan art into Early, Middle, and Late Minoan and the further division of each large period into three subperiods are a classic example of a relative chronology used by archeologist-historians who lack absolute dates. The Minoan chronology received some corroboration when points of contact with the chronology of Egyptian art were established. Imported objects of a certain style from one country were uncovered in datable contexts in the other, and in this way, for example, the Middle Minoan period was found to be roughly contemporary with the Middle Kingdom in Egypt.

The two earliest of several scripts found on Crete seem to have been inspired by Egyptian hieroglyphs. Of the later scripts, Linear A and Linear B, only the latter has been deciphered (as late as 1953); it is a pre-Homeric form of Greek, but the tablets inscribed with it almost exclusively represent inventories and tallies of objects and are of little aid in delineating the Minoan culture. For Minoan history, pottery remains have provided by far the greatest evidence, since figurative art is relatively scarce and often so fragmentary and diminutive as to preclude building a stylistic continuity on it. Potsherds are one of the mainstays of archeology when documentary and monumental evidence is sparse or missing. Broken kitchenware, for example, was often thrown on a garbage heap, where the perishable materials decayed over the years, leaving only the pottery sherds, which settled into firmly stratified mounds. The careful excavation of these mounds can produce relative chronologies. Although the sequence of Cretan pottery styles was well established by Evans, some archeologists now feel that his method of dating is inadequate in view of increased knowledge of the Minoan civilization. A new chronology has been suggested that is based on the construction of the great Cretan palaces. Its relationship to the traditional chronology is shown on page 104.

Overall, absolute dates for Minoan civilization are few, and our knowledge of Minoan history remains vague and provisional. Even the origin of the Cretans is problematical. Some believe that they may have come from Anatolia as early as 6000 B.C., bringing with them a well-developed Neolithic culture, complete with pottery. The Bronze Age then may have been ushered in by a new wave of immigrants (also possibly from Anatolia) around the year 2800 B.C.

THE EARLY MINOAN PERIOD

The Early Minoan (pre-Palace) period is known to us primarily through pottery and a few scattered pieces of minor sculpture. Mochlos stoneware, dated to this period, is named after the site at which it was found and apparently was copied from Egyptian pieces of the First to Fourth Dynasties. Other representative pieces include handmade clay pots decorated with incised geometric patterns.

The most striking and perhaps the most appealing Aegean products of the Early Bronze Age are the numerous marble statuettes from the Cyclades. Most of them are representations of nude females with their arms folded across their abdomens. Varying in height from a few inches to life size, these flat "plank idols" are highly schematized descendants of the Neolithic mother goddess (see FIG. 2-5). They differ in style as much as in size and range from figures of almost normal proportions to shapes that resemble violins rather than human figures. The example shown (FIG. **4-1**) occupies a middle ground: the organic forms have been converted into geometric shapes (triangles, rectangles, ovals, and cylinders),

4-1 Cycladic idol, Syros, c. 2500–2000 B.C. Marble, 8½" high.

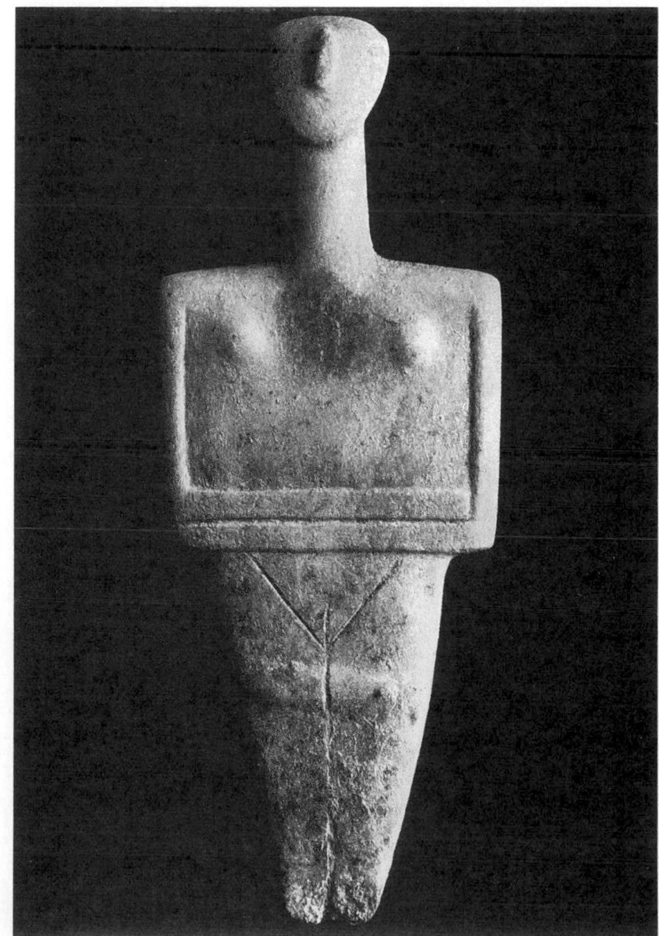

but the reference to the female figure remains clear, and the manner in which the various stylized parts have been combined has considerable esthetic appeal. Traces of paint found on some specimens show that at least parts of these figures were colored. The eyes were usually painted, and additional color touches were provided by painted necklaces and bracelets.

Male figures also occur occasionally in the Cycladic repertoire. They usually take the form of musicians, like the *Lyre Player* (FIG. **4-2**), who, wedged between the echoing shapes of chair and lyre, performs a task that seems to have been a part of funerary rituals. In the rendering of the figure, the disk-shaped head and the long, tubular neck are in the same style as the plank figures, but the body has gained mass and volume, and the composition has a three-dimensional quality lacking in the plank idols. Although it has not been possible to establish a chronological sequence for these Cycladic figurines, most seem to date from the second half of the third millennium B.C.; the *Lyre Player* is believed to belong to the end of this period and may have been contemporary with the Cretan palaces.

4-2 *Lyre Player,* from Keros, *c.* 2000 B.C. Marble, 9″ high. National Archeological Museum, Athens.

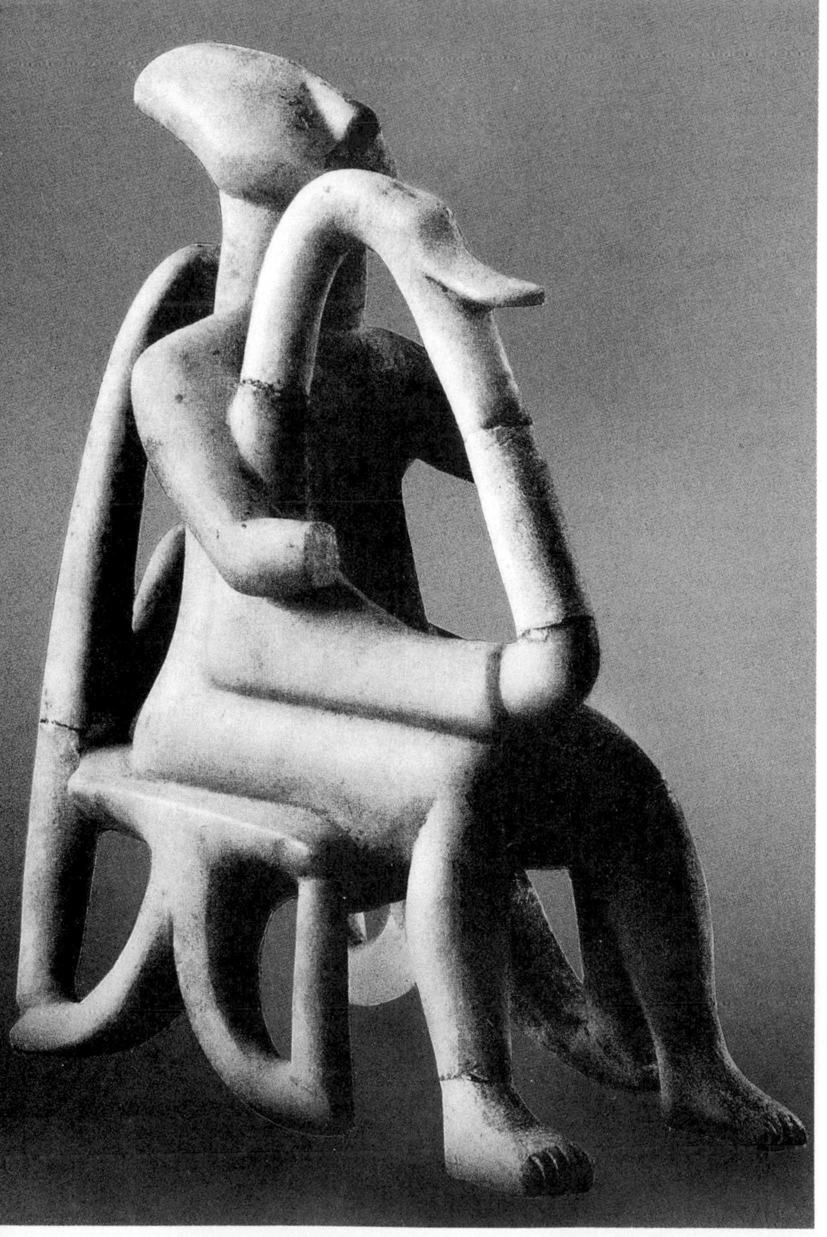

THE MIDDLE MINOAN PERIOD

The Middle Minoan period is marked by the founding of the old palaces around the year 2000 B.C. Building in Crete did not emphasize tombs, temples, or fortresses. Palaces for the king and his retainers were the most permanent architectural form, and royal towns grew up around them. The absence of fortification on Crete is conspicuous in the Aegean world; fortified sites appear everywhere in the Helladic and Cycladic areas. This fact attests either to the power of the Cretan navies, or to a long-enduring insular peace, or to both. But after only about three centuries, around 1700 B.C., these old palaces were destroyed, by what cause is still a matter of archeological conjecture.

An important technological advance that took place at the beginning of the Old Palace period was the introduction of the potter's wheel, which permitted the throwing of vessels with thinner walls and subtler shapes and led to the development of a thriving industry. In this so-called eggshell ware, the Minoan potter's art reached a degree of excellence that deserves our highest admiration, if for the delicacy of the ceramic technique alone. But Cretan artists also developed a style of decoration that complemented the delicate fabric and sophisticated shapes of their pottery. Beginning with relatively simple, curvilinear patterns painted dark on light (FIG. **4-3**), Cretan potters moved toward a fully polychrome style of decoration that found its culmination in the splendid pottery discovered in the cave at Kamares on the slope of Mount Ida (FIG. **4-4**). On a surface swelling robustly with the peculiarly Minoan feel for the vigor and buoyancy of active life, we find a lustrous black ground on which a quasi-geometric pattern of creamy white is interspersed with yellow and red to form a colorful and harmonious decoration. As in Egypt, the motifs derive from natural forms; on the Kamares pitcher, they are simplified into a play of spirals, beautifully adjusted to and integrated with the shape of the vessel.

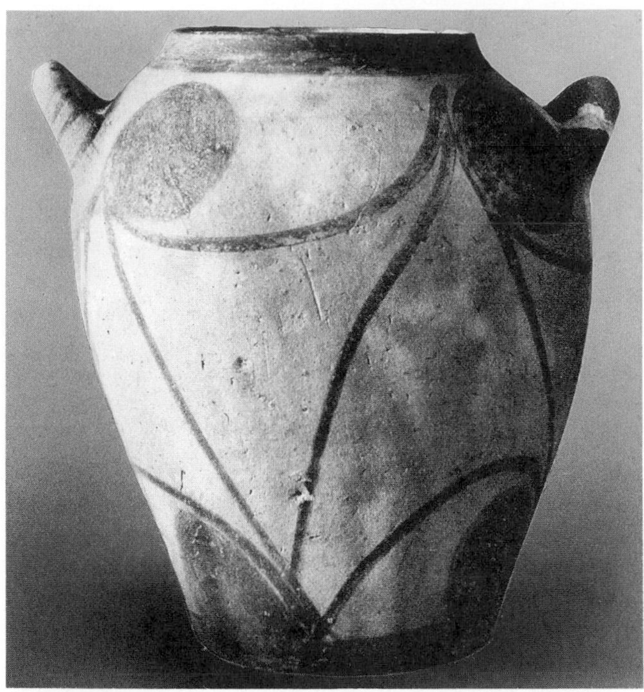

4-3 Small storage jar, from Psyra, c. 2000–1850 B.C. 11" high.

4-4 Kamares pitcher, from Phaistos, c. 1800–1700 B.C. Approx. 10⅝" high. Archeological Museum, Herakleion.

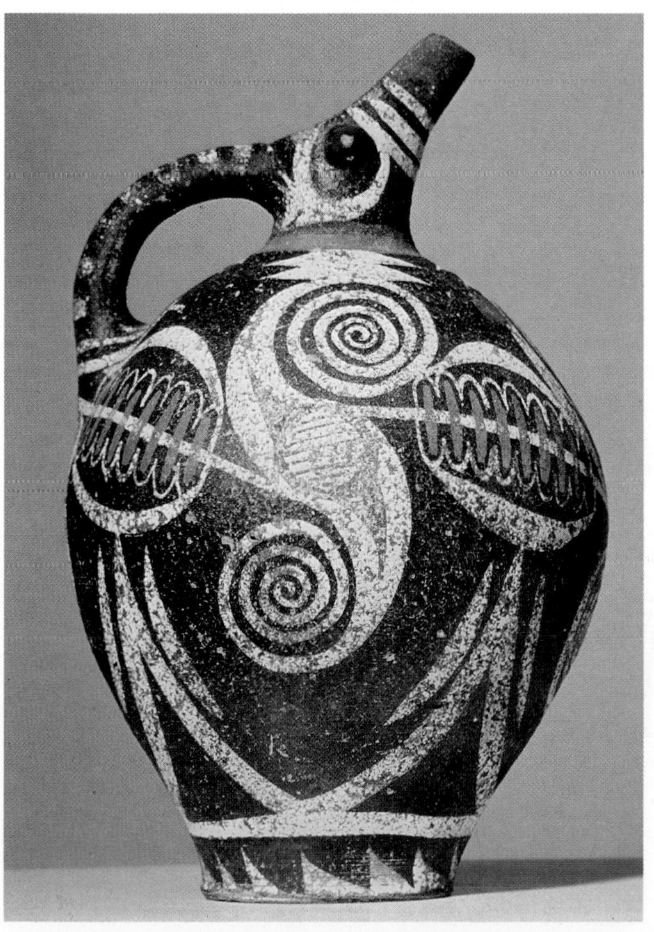

THE LATE MINOAN PERIOD

The New Palace period began somewhere between 1600 and 1500 B.C., when the destroyed palaces were rebuilt and the golden age of Crete produced the first great Western civilization. The bulk of the surviving archeological material—the evidence of an age of unsurpassed creative energy and precocious artistic achievement—dates from this era, which ended about 1400 B.C.

Architecture

The palaces rebuilt for the kings and their retainers were large, comfortable, and handsome, with ample staircases and courtyards for pageants, ceremonies, and games. Archeologists have recovered their ruins, along with rich treasures of art and artifacts that document the power and prosperity of Minoan civilization. The principal palace sites on Crete are at Knossos, Phaistos, Mallia, and Kato Zakro, situated at the eastern tip of the island. All of these are laid out along similar lines. The largest of the palaces, that at Knossos (FIGS. **4-5** and **4-6**), is a rambling structure built against the upper slopes and across the top of a low hill that rises from a fertile plain. The great rectangular court, around which the units of the palace are grouped, had been leveled in the time of the old palace; the manner of the grouping of buildings suggests that the palace was not preplanned but that several building nuclei grew together, with the court as the major organizing element. A secondary organization of the palace plan is provided by two long corridors. On the west side of the court, a north–south corridor separates official and ceremonial rooms from the magazines, where wine, grain, oil, and honey were stored in large jars *(pithoi)*. On the east side of the court, an east–west corridor separates the king's and queen's quarters and reception rooms (to the south) from the workmen's and servant's quarters (on the north). At the northwest corner of the entire building complex is the "arena," a theaterlike area with steps on two sides that may have served as seats. This form is a possible forerunner of the later Greek theater. Its purpose is unknown, but it is a feature that, like the central court, appears in other Cretan palaces. For the Greeks, the complexity of the palace's plan came to be associated with the cult of the double axe *(labrys)*, perhaps giving rise to the Greek myth of the Cretan *labyrinth*. Certainly, the palace's layout was the product of wealth and luxurious tastes and of a love for the convenient. Beneath the palace is a remarkably efficient drainage system of terra-cotta pipes that must have made Knossos one of the most sanitary cities in the world before the twentieth century.

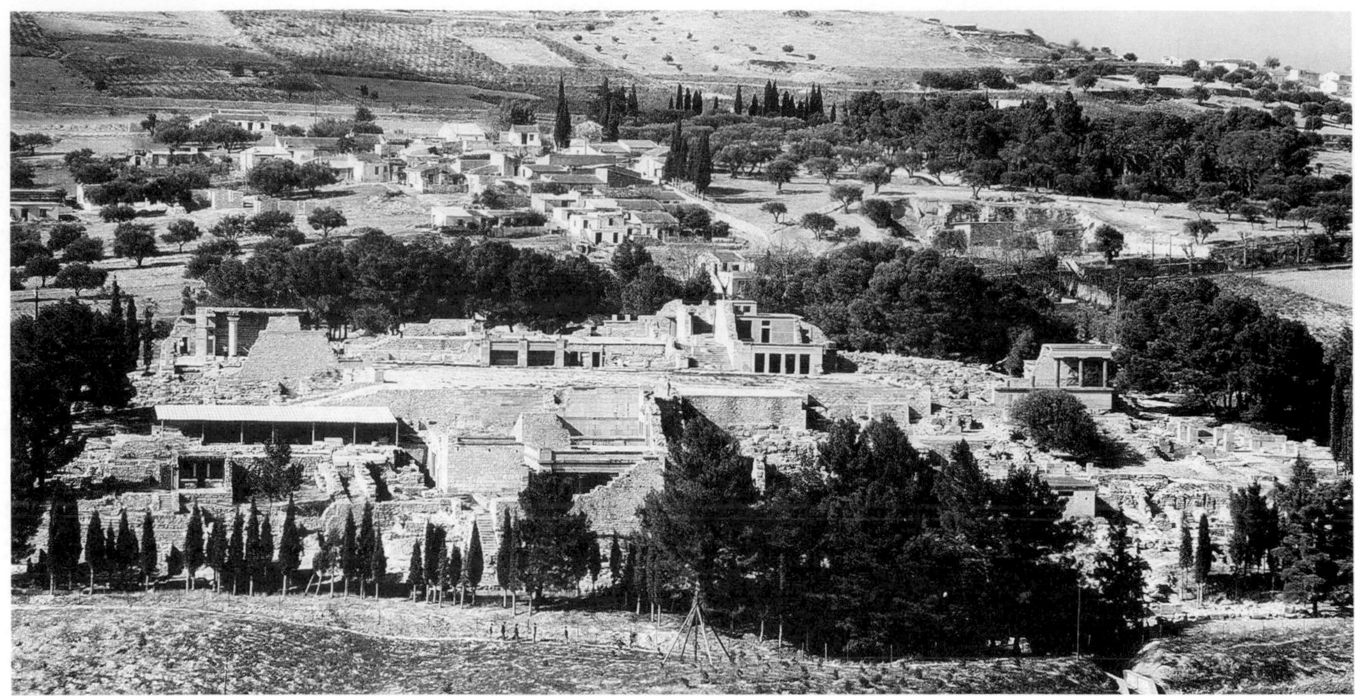

4-5 Palace at Knossos, c. 1600–1400 B.C. (view from the east).

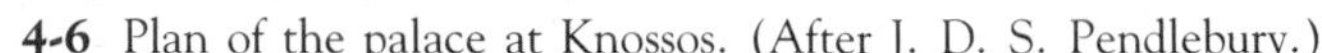

4-6 Plan of the palace at Knossos. (After J. D. S. Pendlebury.)

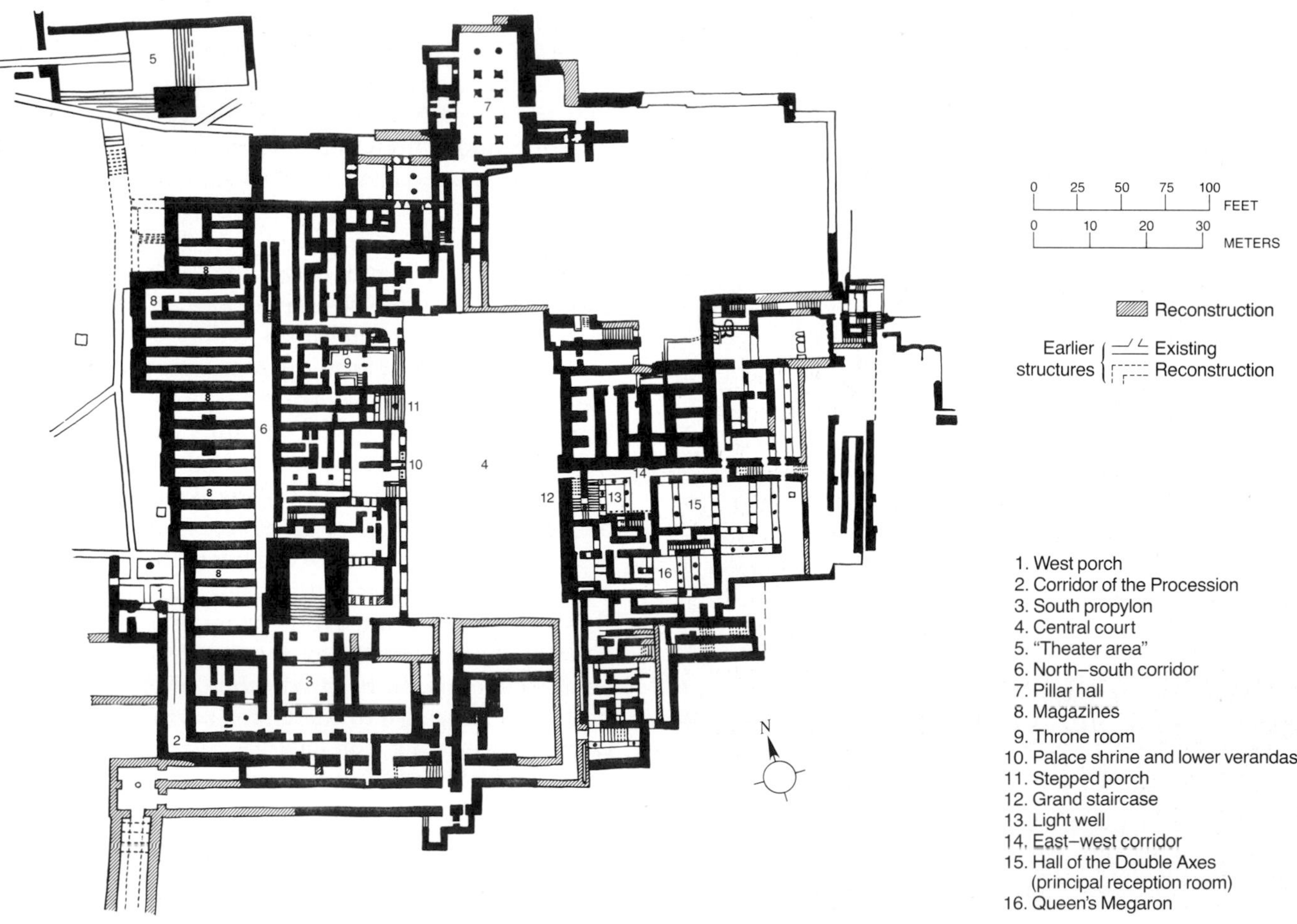

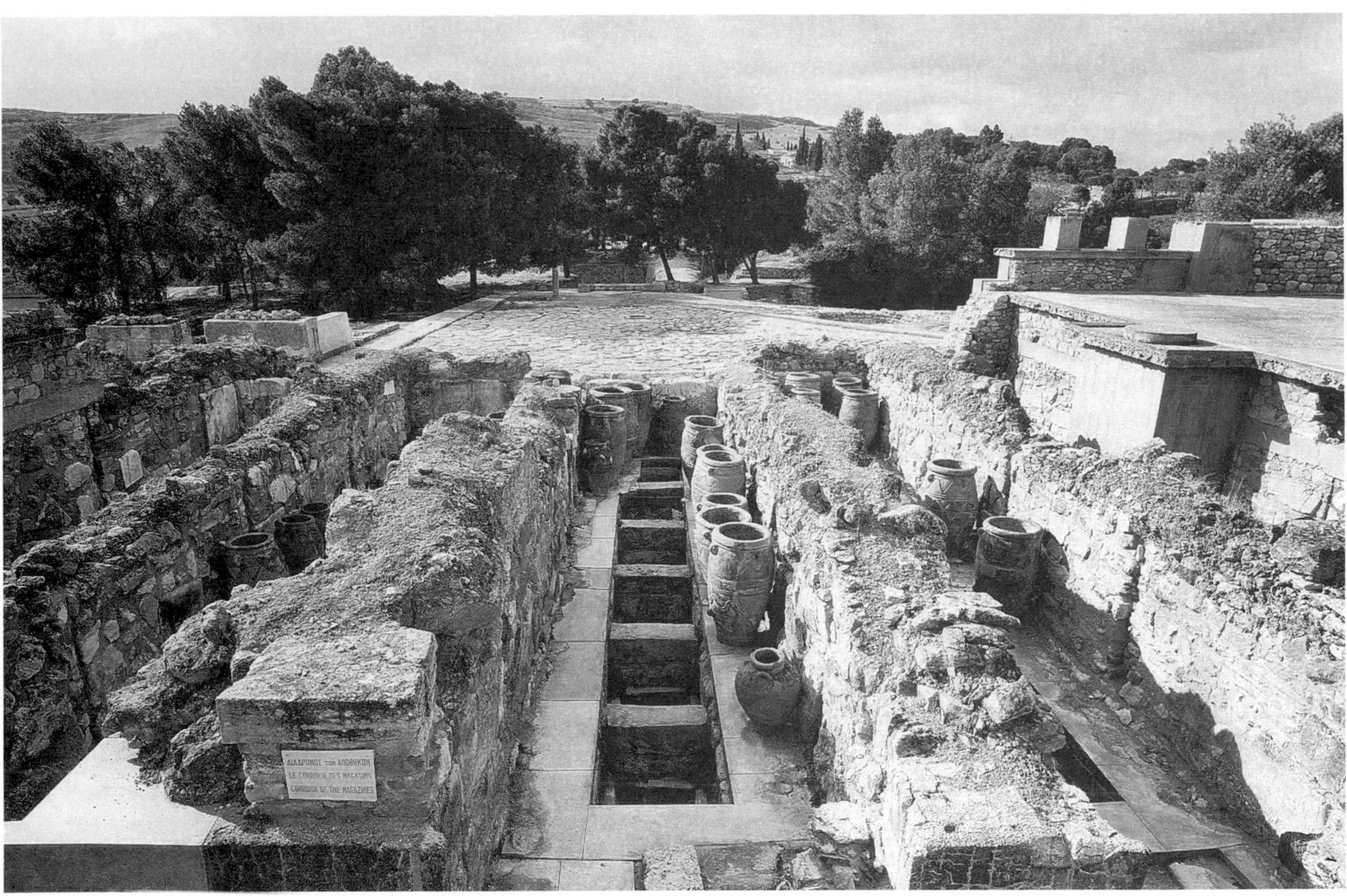

4-7 View of the magazine, west wing of the palace at Knossos, with large pithoi in situ.

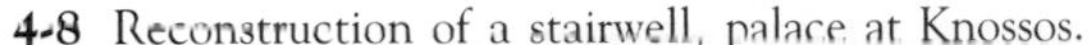

4-8 Reconstruction of a stairwell, palace at Knossos.

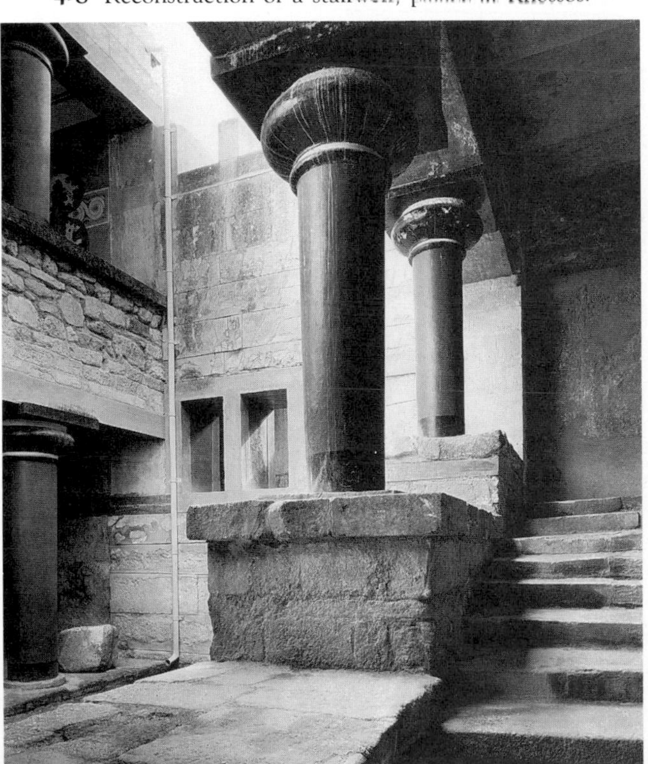

The practical storage system is exhibited in the magazines of the west wing (FIG. **4-7**), where some of the pithoi are still in place. Some of the rooms had flat floors; others (like those shown here) had stone-lined pits. The walls were quite thick, as must have been the roofing over these magazines; the masonry may have been covered with earth to keep the interior cool. In most parts of the palace, the masonry walls were rough, consisting of unshaped field stones imbedded in mortar. Ashlar masonry, made of shaped blocks of stone, was used at building corners and around door and window openings.

The palace had as many as three stories, with interior staircases built around light and air wells (FIG. **4-8**), which provided necessary illumination and ventilation. Distinguishing features of the Minoan columns, which were originally fashioned of wood but were restored in stone (with, it is now thought, mistakenly bulky proportions), are their bulbous, cushionlike capitals and the manner in which the column shafts taper toward the base. Strong evidence that the column had religious significance for the Cretans is found in the fact that the base of a column in one of the lower stories of the palace at Knossos is surrounded by a trough that was used for libations.

Painting

A view into the Queen's Megaron, with its pillared hall and light well (FIG. **4-9**), shows the typically elaborate wall decoration of the more important rooms at Knossos. Here, plastered walls were painted with frescoes, which, together with the red- or blue-shafted columns, must have provided an extraordinarily rich effect. The frescoes depicted many aspects of Cretan life (bullfights, processions, and ceremonies) and of nature (birds, animals, flowers, and—as here—marine life, with dolphins frolicking among other fauna of the sea).*

One of the most memorable figures from the art of Crete is from a procession of cupbearers in a fresco in the south propylon at Knossos. *The Cupbearer*† (FIG. **4-10**) is the only one preserved from a sequence, shown in two registers, that may have contained over five-hundred figures, if those from the Corridor of the Procession (FIG. 4-6) are included. The figure itself is unmistakably Minoan. The youth has long curly hair, wears an elaborately embroidered loincloth with a silver-mounted girdle, and has ornaments on his arms, neck, ankles, and wrist. Although the profile pose with the full-view eye was a familiar convention in Egypt and Mesopotamia, the elegance of the Cretan figure, with its pinched waist, proud, self-confident bearing, and free movement, distinguishes it from all other early figure styles. The angularity of the older styles is modified in the curving line that suggests the elasticity of the living and moving being. The ceremonial *rhyton* (vessel for pouring ritual libations) carried by the youth has a typically Minoan shape, found nowhere else except as a Minoan import.

Vivacity and spontaneity also characterize *The Toreador Fresco* (FIG. **4-11**). Although only fragments of it have been recovered, they are extraordinary in their depiction of the vigorous movements of the girls and the young man who is shown in the air, having, perhaps, grasped the bull's horns and somersaulted over its back. We have seen how important the bull is in the Near East, especially in Mesopotamian art. The difference in the Minoan paintings is in the relationship of the bull to human beings. In this fresco, man and beast contest with each other in a dangerous game that takes place in the here and now, the human beings as conspicuous in the action as the

*The Dolphin Fresco in the Queen's Megaron has recently been shown to be misrestored; it originally may have decorated the floor of another room in the palace.

†The scarred, patchy, and broken surface that makes the figure of *The Cupbearer* hard to discern is a good illustration of the fact that Minoan painting, like so much painting throughout the world, has survived only in fragments. To make sense of the fragments, the archeologist has had to reconstruct or restore the ruined painting to some semblance of its original appearance. Using exact, painstaking methods, experts have replaced fallen fragments in agreement with those remaining on the wall, and by careful deduction or even by conjecture and guesswork, they have achieved the complete picture. The task is like putting together an enormously complex jigsaw puzzle when many parts are missing and many completions are possible. A key to reading *The Cupbearer* and other fragmentary pictures will help: the smooth, lighter tonal areas show what is missing; the streaked and mottled, darker tonal areas are surviving fragments that have remained attached or that have been picked up and replaced.

4-9 Reconstruction of the Queen's Megaron, palace at Knossos.

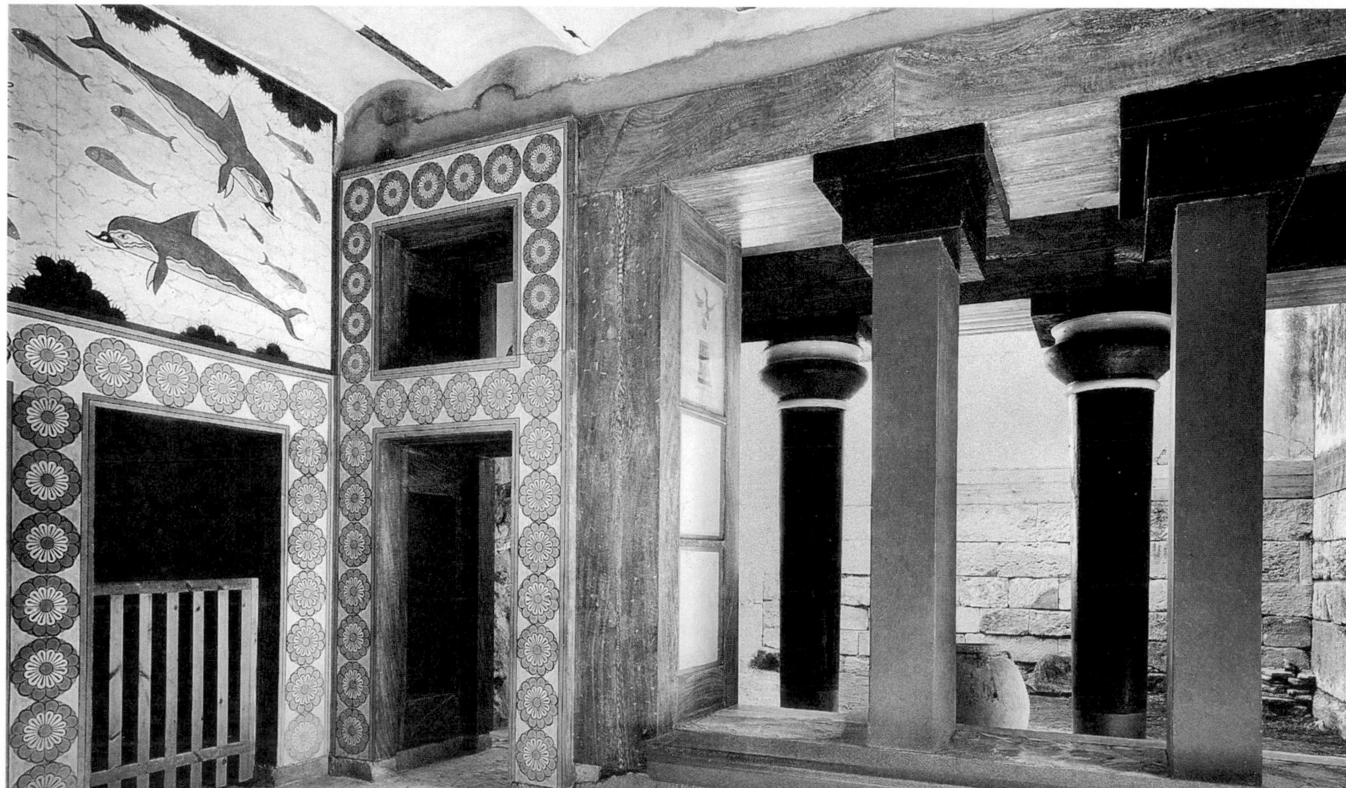

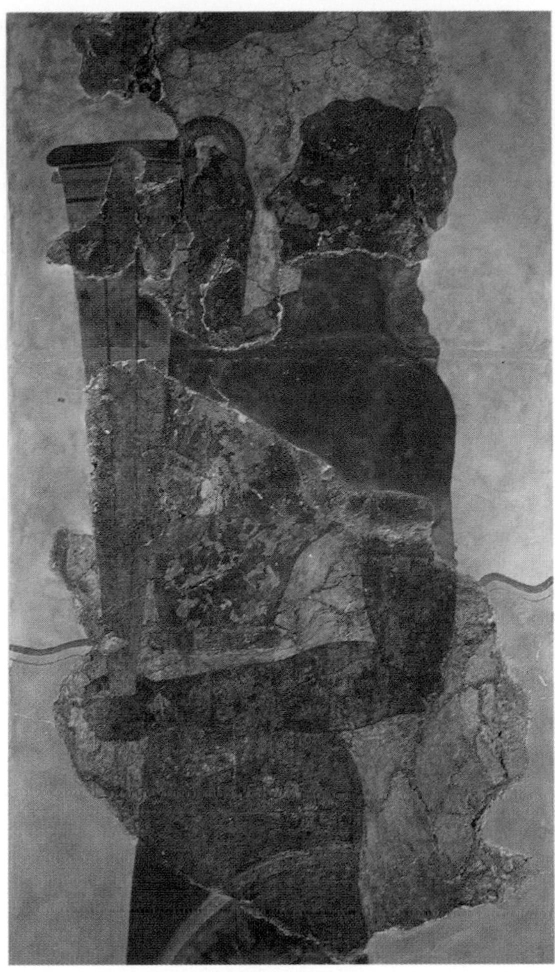

4-10 *The Cupbearer,* from the palace at Knossos, c. 1500 B.C. Fresco, approx. 60″ high. Archeological Museum, Herakleion.

bull. In a powerful characterization of the natures of both man and beast, the poise and agility of the toreadors play off against the exploding energy of the bull. (We are reminded of the charging bulls of the Paleolithic caves; see FIG. 1-1.) Everywhere within the frame are curving lines, the directional lines of action, and nowhere are they more conspicuous and vital than in the electric energy of the line that sweeps from the head of the bull to the whip of his tail.

Because of her cosmetic prettiness, which resembles that of a sophisticated, modern woman, a girl represented in a fragment of another fresco has been labeled *La Parisienne* (FIG. **4-12**). With her conventionally enlarged and front-view eye, her turned-up nose, full red lips, and elaborate coiffure, she is almost disturbingly of our own times, especially as we conventionalize her type in popular art. Surely, nothing quite like this sprightly charm, freshness, and joie de vivre appears in the art of the ancient Near East. The painting method used is appropriate to the lively spirit of the Minoans. Unlike the Egyptians, who painted in the dry-fresco *(fresco secco)* technique, the Minoans used a *true,* or *wet,* fresco method, which required rapid execution and a skill in achieving quick, almost impressionistic effects. If one is to catch an interesting but fugitive aspect of an object or a scene, one must work quickly, even spontaneously, allowing for happy accidents. Thus, because the wet-fresco technique compelled the artist to work rapidly, the spirit of *La Parisienne* is also a product of the resultant verve of the artist's hand, and the simple, light delicacy of the technique exactly matches the vivacity

4-11 *The Toreador Fresco,* from the palace at Knossos, c. 1500 B.C. Approx. 32″ high, including border. Archeological Museum, Herakleion.

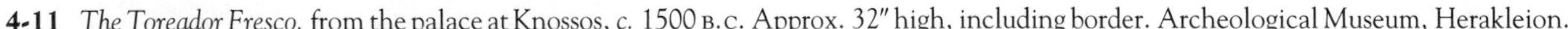

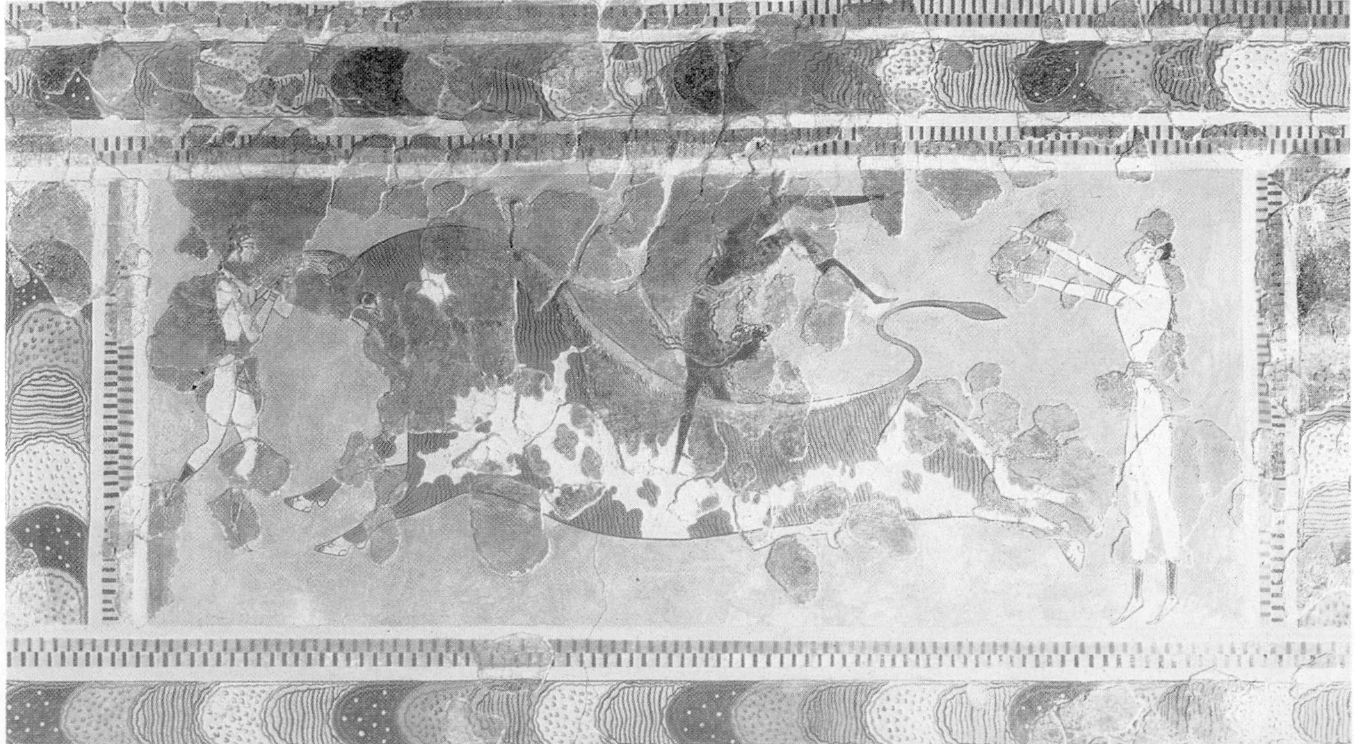

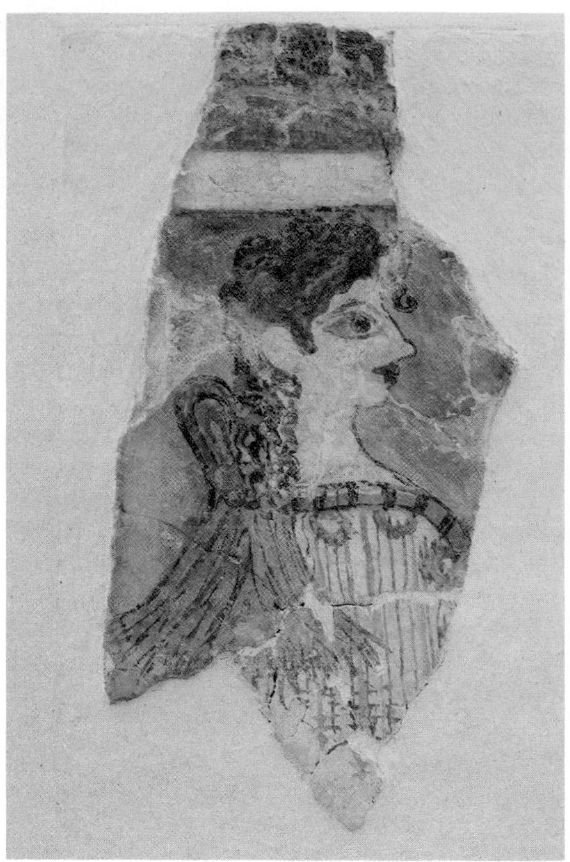

4-12 *La Parisienne,* from the palace at Knossos, c. 1500 B.C. Fragment of a fresco, approx. 10″ high. Archeological Museum, Herakleion.

of the subject. It is the Minoan sense of immediate life and the skill in catching it that strike us as novel in the ancient world and prophetic of great changes in people's outlook on nature.

This sense and skill are vividly present in wall paintings recently found in ruins on the volcanic island of Santorini (ancient Thera), sixty miles north of Crete. Thera was the site of an enormous seismic explosion that left a huge crater in the center of the island. Archeologists formerly dated the event at 1500 B.C. and speculated that it must have had disastrous effects on the palaces of Crete to the south of Thera. But recent radiocarbon investigation of the algae beds in the sea-filled crater have pushed the date of its marine life, and, hence that of the catastrophe, back as far as 1800 B.C.

Today, Santorini is regarded as a kind of early Pompeii, so well preserved are the remains of its streets, buildings, and especially its painted walls. We can feel the freshness and vitality of the Minoan vision of nature in the lovely mural *The Springtime Fresco* (FIG. **4-13**). The undulating earth, the graceful lillies, and the darting swallows express vernal qualities—the vigor of growth, the delicacy of flowering, and the lightness of bird song and flight. In the lyrical language of curving line, the artist celebrates the breezy rhythms of spring. Landscape painting of this naturalistic sort is a Minoan innovation in the art of the ancient world, as far as we have yet discovered, and the forerunner of Greek and Roman landscape.

4-13 *The Springtime Fresco,* from Room Delta 2, Akrotiri, Santorini (ancient Thera), c. 1500 B.C. Approx. 7′ 6″ high. National Archeological Museum, Athens.

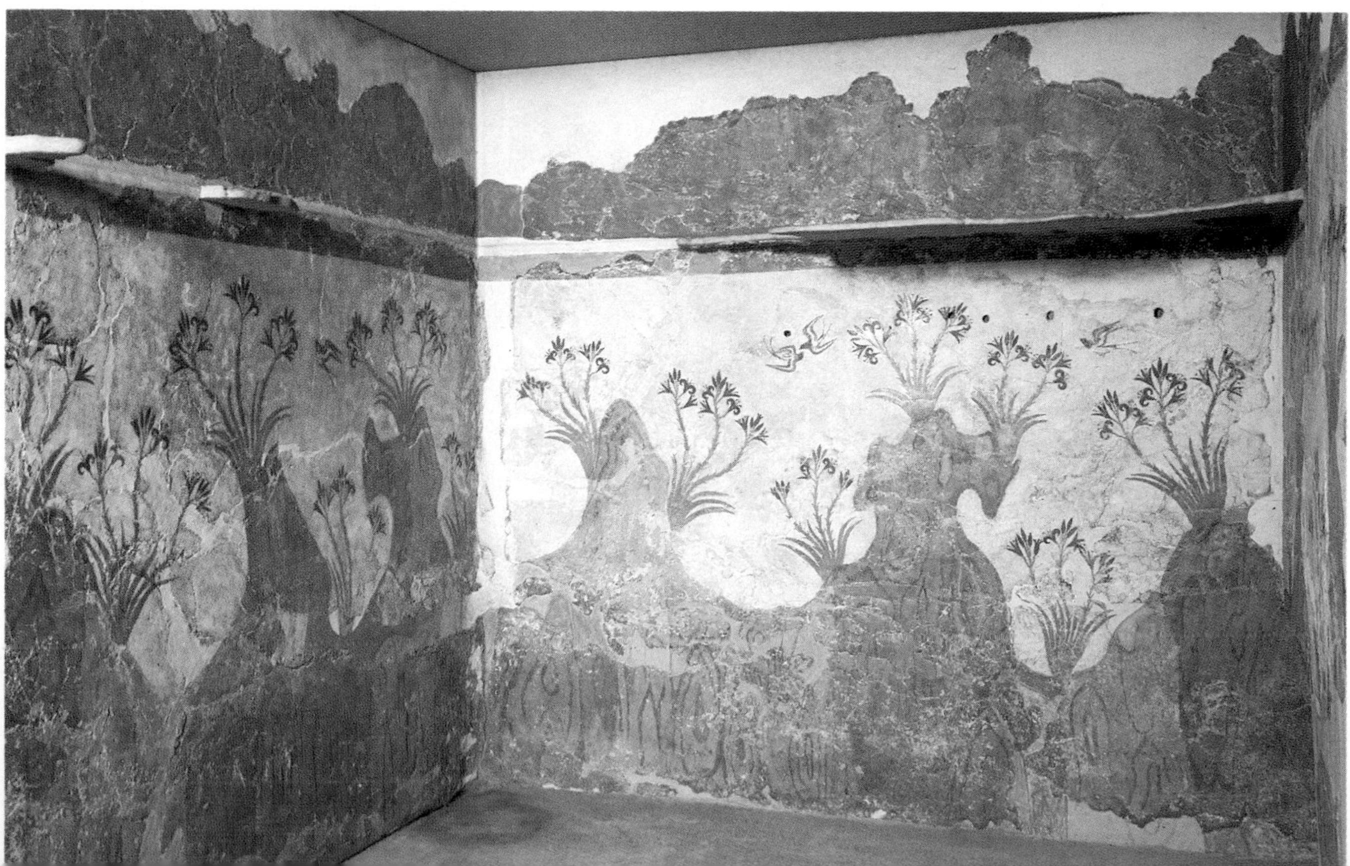

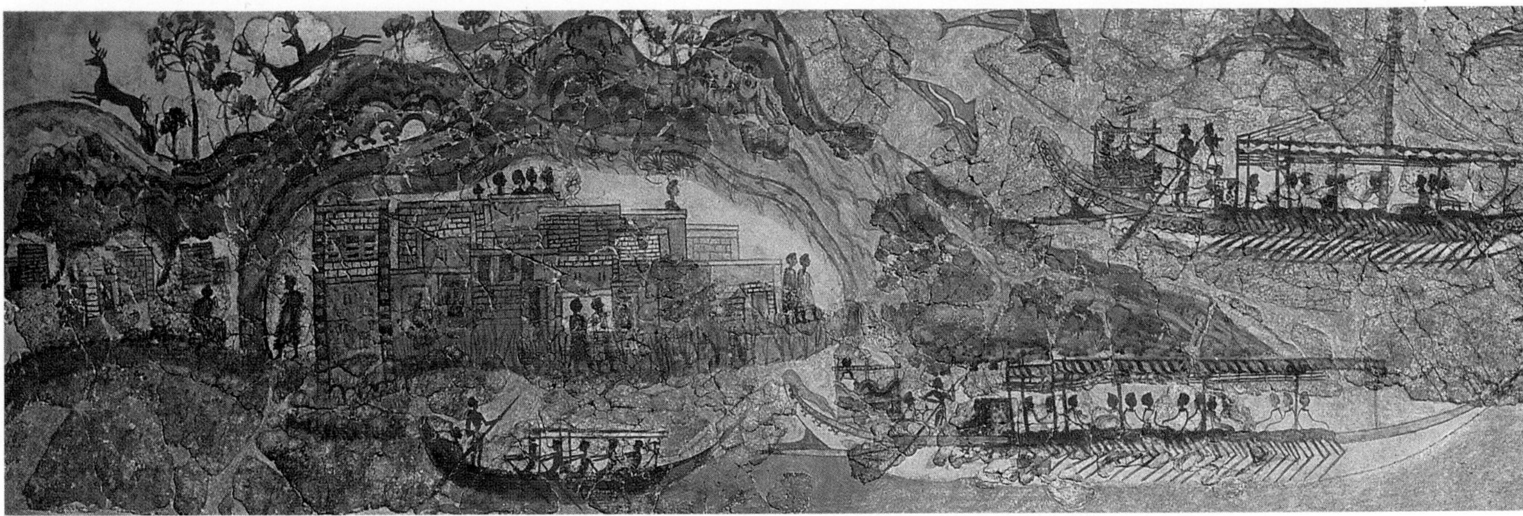

4-14 *The Flotilla Fresco,* from Room 5, West House, Akrotiri, Santorini, *c.* 1500 B.C. 17″ high. National Archeological Museum, Athens.

Another painting of high quality from Santorini gives us a detailed picture of scenes from Minoan life. Seascape and landscape combined, *The Flotilla Fresco* (FIG. **4-14**) shows a fleet of ships plying between two ports. The details of ship design and of sailing are carefully observed, as if by one who knew ships well. Just as carefully observed are the placements and poses of steersmen, supercargoes, sailors, rowers, and passengers. Little of the conventional stereotyping and repetition that we find, for example, in much of Ancient Near Eastern art (FIG. 2-18) is evident here; instead, we find an almost casual arrangement of figures and variation of pose according to the role being played—steering, tending to the sail, rowing, or simply sitting and conversing. Dolphins resembling those in the Queen's Megaron at Knossos (FIG. 4-9) frolic about the ships, and on the shore (at the upper left), a lion pursues fleeing deer. The ports—the one at the left encircled by a river represented as arching above it—show quays, houses, and streets occupied by a variety of people attentive to the coming of the ships, waiting to unload them, or simply going about their business. The whole composition has the openness and lightness of the seagirt lands of Crete and the Greek islands, suggesting the freedom of movement of a people for whom seafaring is second nature, and nature—with all its flora and fauna—is, in itself, delightful and worthy of representation.

A painting of a young fisherman holding his abundant catch in both hands is yet another indication of the keen attention the Minoan artist paid to natural appearances (FIG. **4-15**). What at first appears to be the Egyptian convention of pose, frontal and profile views combined, can be read as an adjustment of the figure to allow both clusters of fish to be seen at the

4-15 *Young Fisherman Fresco,* from Room 5, West House, Akrotiri, Santorini, *c.* 1500 B.C. 53″ high. National Archeological Museum, Athens.

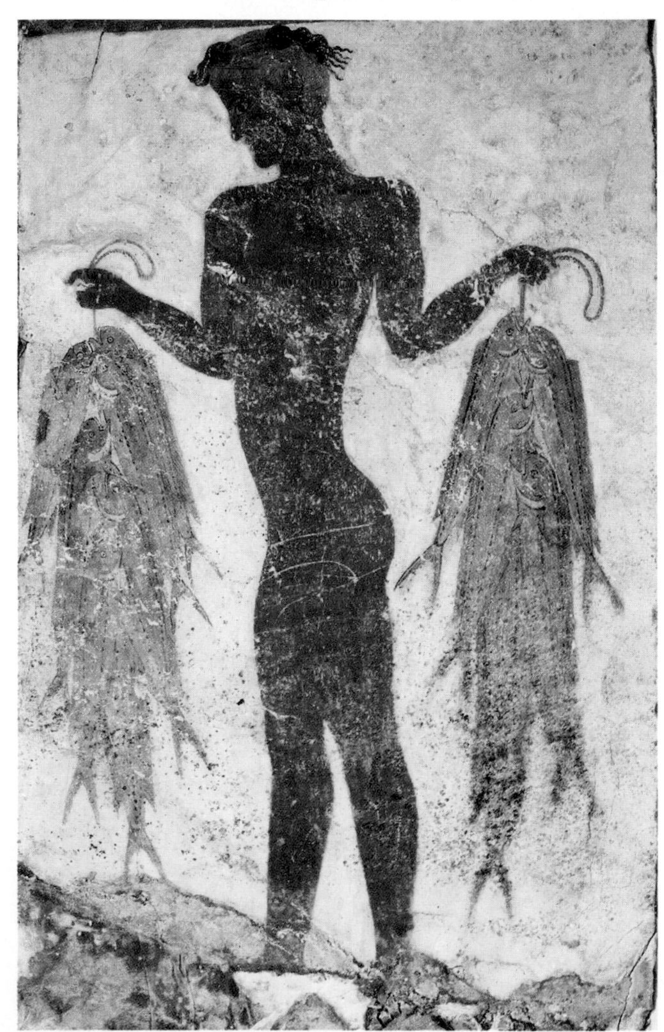

same time, much as a modern sport fisherman, proud of his catch, might turn slowly to display it as his picture is being taken. The informality of the young fisherman might be compared with the strict formality of profile found in the cupbearer at Knossos (FIG. 4-10), the contrast reflecting differences of rank and occupation, with the lesser rank and humble occupation of the fisherman calling for, or permitting, a more realistic representation. We have found elsewhere in ancient art that persons of lower rank and scenes from common life are treated with less formality and greater realism than are kings and nobles, or scenes of royal and religious ritual.

Pottery and Sculpture

The Minoan feeling for the dynamics of nature, revealed in their figurative and landscape art, is no less visible in their pottery, which is among the finest in history. In the Kamares ware (FIG. 4-4), this interest in animate nature did not appear at once; the taste was for abstract spiral forms, scrolls, whorls, and the like. As time went on, however, the tendency toward naturalism in decoration increased. Motifs such as dolphins, seaweed, and octopuses were derived from sea life. The tentacles reaching out over the curving surfaces of *The Octopus Jar* (FIG. **4-16**) embrace the piece and emphasize its elastic volume. This is a masterful realization of the relationship between the decoration of the vessel and its shape, always a problem for the ceramist. From the Kamares silhouetting of light, abstract forms on a dark ground, we proceed, in *The Octopus Jar,* to a silhouetting of dark, naturalistic forms on a light ground. This manner of presentation lasted from about 1600 to 1500 B.C., when the fluid, open, and lively naturalistic style became increasingly stiff and abstract. This late style can be seen in a three-handled jar from Knossos (FIG. **4-17**), dated about 1425 B.C. The stalks of its papyrus decoration grow symmetrically, and the flowers turn into stylized scrolls and fans, symmetrically balanced. Wavy bands, simple concentric circles with crosses, and other rudimentary space-fillers occupy the surface rather than adjust to it and embrace it. Such devolution from naturalism to formalism and abstraction can be observed frequently in the history of world art.

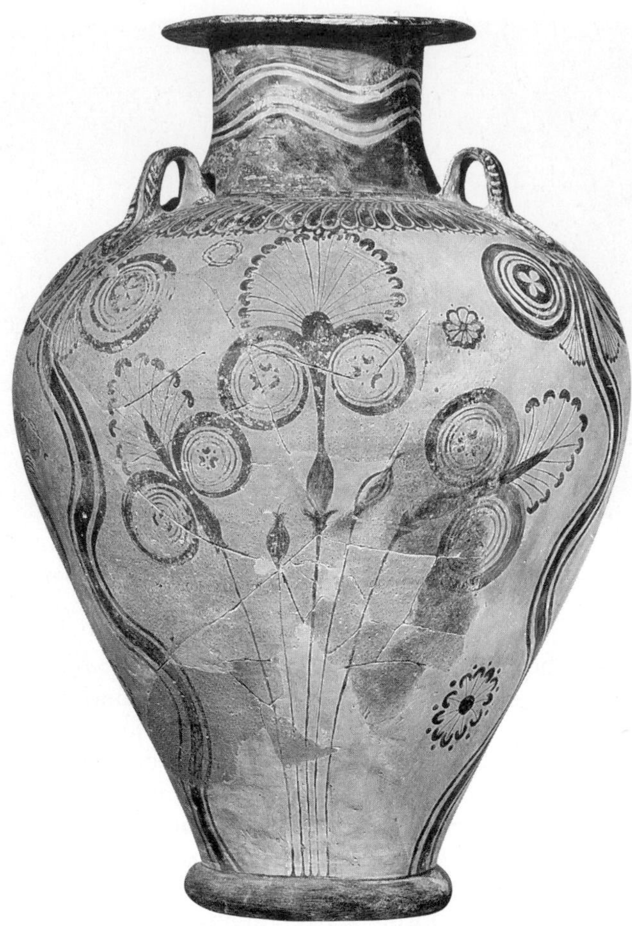

4-17 Three-handled jar with papyrus decoration, from the palace at Knossos, *c.* 1425 B.C. Approx. 53″ high. Archeological Museum, Herakleion.

4-16 *The Octopus Jar,* from Palaikastro, *c.* 1500 B.C. Amphora approx. 11″ high. Archeological Museum, Herakleion.

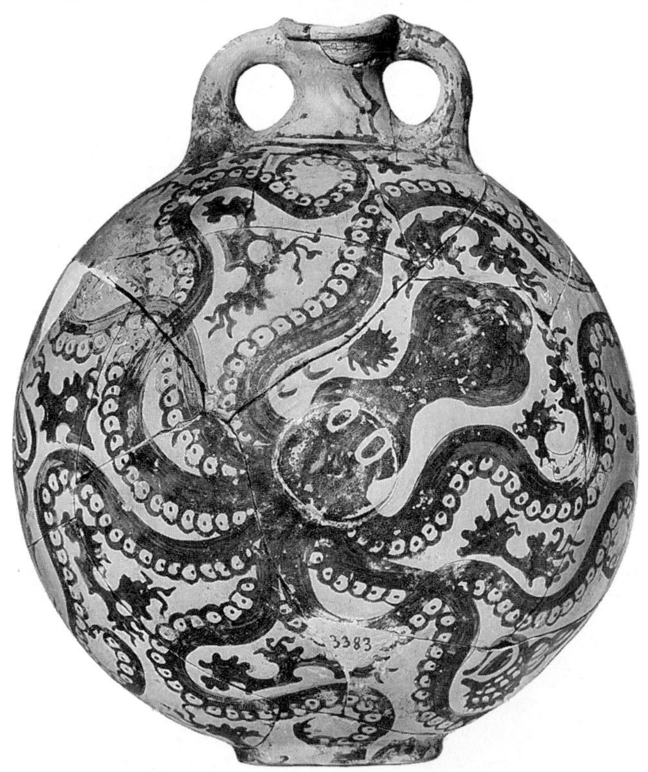

An increasing self-awareness, which we have watched evolve slowly in ancient art, requires that humans represent themselves ever more as they are, in more conditions and situations, with fewer restric-

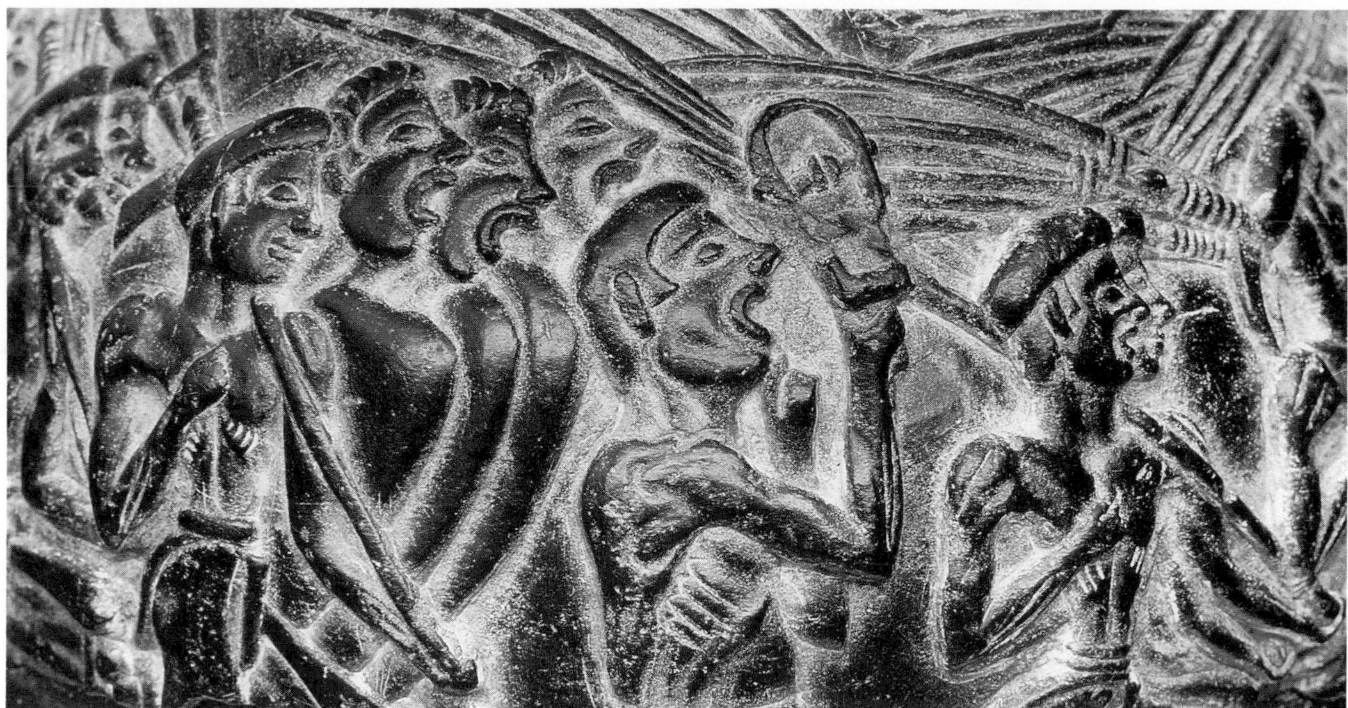

4-18 Detail of *The Harvester Vase* (FIG. 4-19). Archeological Museum, Herakleion.

tions imposed by tradition. *The Harvester Vase* (FIGS. **4-18** and **4-19**), made of steatite (soapstone), gives a sharp new glimpse of man as he is in his usual physical context. This egg-shaped rhyton, its lower half missing, shows a riotous crowd of olive harvesters, singing and shouting. Their forward movement and lusty exuberance are vividly expressed. The pattern of pitchforks fills the upper part of the band; the figures below, in higher relief, create a variation in surface. The entire design, like the octopus of the Palaikastro jar (FIG. 4-16), hugs the shape so tightly that it seems to be an integral part of the wall of the vase. But the figures themselves are depicted with a gusto that matches their mood. They are led by a man who carries a *sistrum,* or rattle, and beats time, while his lungs are so inflated with air that his ribs show. The harvesters' facial expressions are rendered with astonishing exactitude; degrees of hilarity and vocal effort are clearly visible, all marked in the tension or relaxation of facial muscles. This reading of the human face as a vehicle of emotional states is without precedent in ancient art before the Minoans.

Minoan art includes little sculpture in the round, and what there is generally is small. Monumental sculpture of gods, kings, and monsters, such as we find in Mesopotamia and Egypt, has not been found. This absence of large-scale sculpture may reflect an absence of systematic and formal religion, although this assumption is entirely speculative due to our ignorance of Minoan religion. The small figures of

4-19 *The Harvester Vase,* from Hagia Triada, *c.* 1500 B.C. Steatite, approx. 5″ wide. Archeological Museum, Herakleion. (Lower part is lost.)

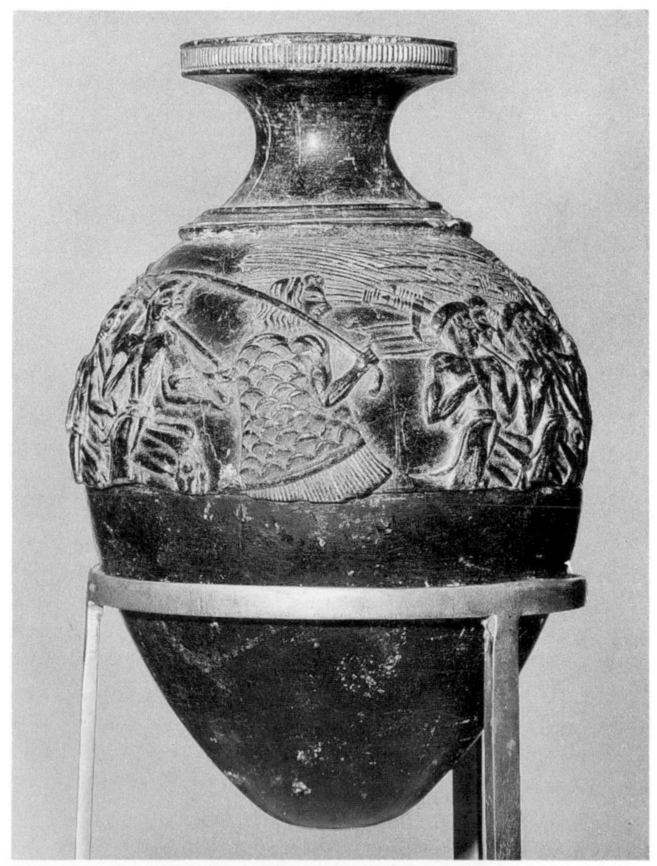

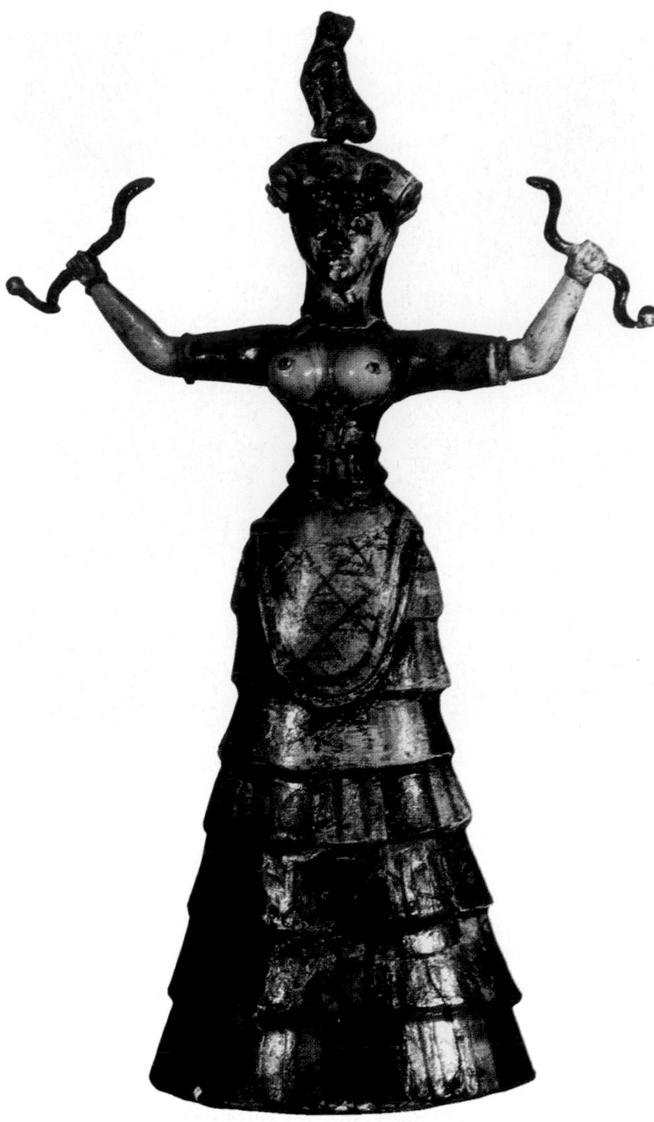

4-20 *Snake Goddess,* from the palace at Knossos, *c.* 1600 B.C. Faïence, approx. 13½″ high. Archeological Museum, Herakleion.

"snake goddesses" like the one shown from Knossos (FIG. **4-20**) are hardly more than of talisman or fetish size. They exhibit most of the rigid conventions, including the frontal pose, found in Egypt and Mesopotamia, but the arms have been released from the core of the block and are held forward or aloft. Thus, they are shown to be active and, somehow, appear more alive than their Near Eastern or Egyptian cousins. The Cretans seem to have worshiped a mother goddess sacred to many places and manifest in many forms. Whether these miniature figures brandishing snakes are images of her is not certain, but they are identified clearly as Minoan by their costume. We find the open bodice and flounced skirt worn by Minoan women depicted many times over. This touch of the real may be another example of human beings fashioning their gods in their own images.

The circumstances under which the Minoan civilization came to an end are still disputed, although it is now widely believed that Mycenaeans moved onto the island and established themselves at Knossos without meeting major resistance. From the repaired palace at Knossos, these intruders appear to have ruled the island for at least half a century, perhaps much longer. Parts of the palace continued to be occupied until its final destruction around 1200 B.C., this time by the Dorians, but its importance as a cultural center faded soon after 1400 B.C., as the focus of Aegean civilization shifted to the Greek mainland.

MYCENAEAN ART

The origins of the Mycenaean culture also are still being debated. The primitive Greeks may have moved onto the mainland about the time that the old palaces were being built in Crete—that is, about the beginning of the second millennium B.C. Doubtless these people were influenced by Crete even then, and some believe that the mainland was a Minoan colony for a long time, although the mainlanders developed and held to many cultural features of their own. At any rate, Mycenaean power developed on the mainland in the palmy days of the new palaces on Crete, and by 1500 B.C., a new and splendid culture was flourishing in Greece—a culture to which, some seven hundred years later, Homer was to give the epithet "rich in gold."

It is possible that the Mycenaeans made close contact in this new era not only with Crete but also with Egypt, with which they may have been allied against the Hittites during the early part of the New Kingdom. The Mycenaeans' taste for gold, as well as their actual treasure, may have been acquired in the mercenary service of Egypt, which was known in the ancient world for its lavish use of the metal. Thus, the awakening of the Mycenaean world may have been the consequence of a kind of three-way route of influence connecting the mainland, Crete, and Egypt. The destruction of the Cretan palaces left the Mycenaean (mainland) culture supreme, but new waves of migrating proto-Greek peoples, the so-called Peoples of the Sea, finally submerged the Mycenaean civilization. The steady infiltration of these peoples had already led to the development of a fortress architecture (unnecessary in Crete), and by about 1200 B.C., the fortified citadels of the mainland were overwhelmed by the invaders. The heroes and battles of these last centuries of Aegean civilization must have provided the tradition that, hundreds of years later, Homer would immortalize in the first great European epics, the *Iliad* and the *Odyssey.*

Although Mycenae appears to have been the cultural center of the mainland development, the remains of other large citadels have been found at Vaphio, Pylos, Orchomenos, Arne, and Iolkos. The best preserved and most impressive Mycenaean remains are those of the fortified palaces at Tiryns and Mycenae, both built at the beginning of the Late Mycenaean period, about 1400 B.C., and razed (along with the others) between 1250 and 1200 B.C.

The Citadel of Tiryns (FIG. **4-21**)—located only ten miles from Mycenae, so that at times they may have been under the same lord—was known by Homer as Tiryns of the Great Walls and by the ancient world as the birthplace of Herakles (Hercules). The ancient sightseer and guidebook writer, Pausanias, considered the walls of Tiryns to be as spectacular as the pyramids of Egypt. The heavy walls contrast sharply with the open Cretan palaces and clearly reveal their defensive character. The buildings within the 20-foot-thick walls are aligned axially and seem to have been laid out according to a predetermined plan. Unlike the rambling and often confusing layout of the Cretan palaces, the Mycenaean plan is an example of a clear and simple arrangement of the units. The *megaron,* a three-chambered structure at the heart of the design and the center of life in the citadel, embodies the germ of the Classical temples of Greece. This fundamental building type does not appear in the palaces of Crete, but does appear, surprisingly, at Troy as early as 2000 B.C. A hall of state, the megaron was rectangular, with a central hearth and four columns supporting the roof.

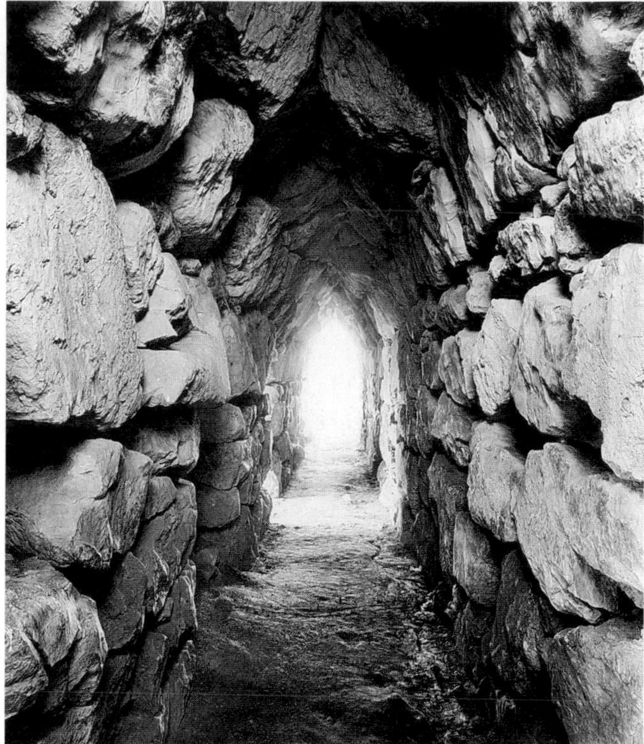

4-22 Corbeled gallery, Tiryns.

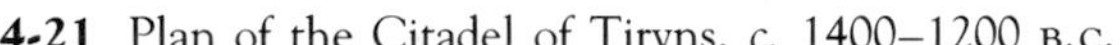

4-21 Plan of the Citadel of Tiryns, *c.* 1400–1200 B.C.

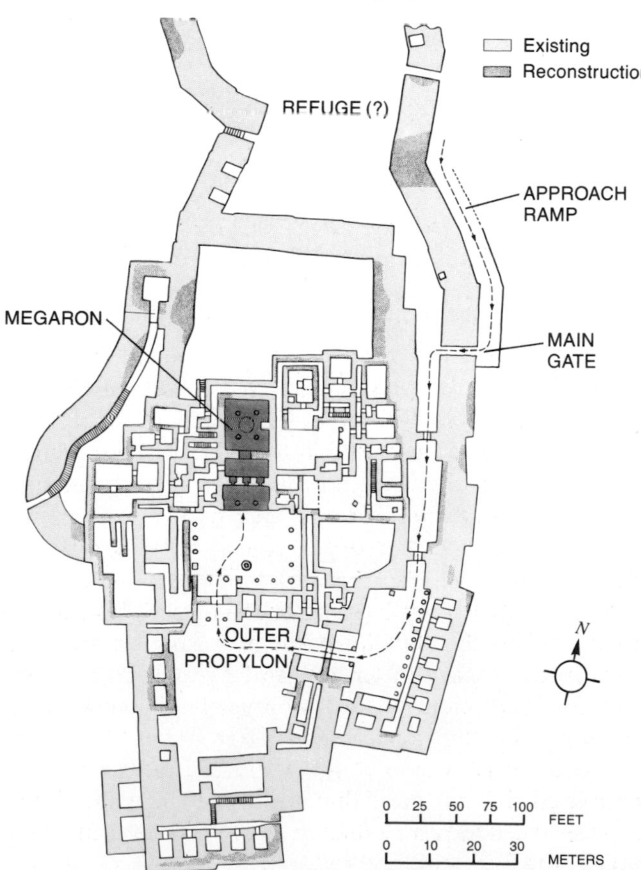

The massive fortification walls at Tiryns and other Mycenaean sites, built of unhewn or roughly dressed stone, were called Cyclopean by later Greeks, who imagined them to have been built by that mythical race of giants, the Cyclopes. Through the walls at intervals run corbeled galleries (FIG. **4-22**), which may have been part of the defensive structure or part of a complicated and dramatic ceremonial path leading, through a porch and vestibule, to the megaron. The corbeled gallery pictured makes use, as its name indicates, of the primitive corbeled arch. The rough appearance of these Cyclopean structures is most impressive in its crude monumentality; it possesses an earthy dynamism not found in other, more sophisticated, ancient architectural styles.

The technique of building in large, unhewn stones *(megaliths)* did not originate in Mycenaean Greece but has a long tradition going back within the Neolithic period to well before 3000 B.C. The huge megalithic construction at Stonehenge belongs to an extensive family of megalithic structures found throughout the Mediterranean world and many areas of Europe. The

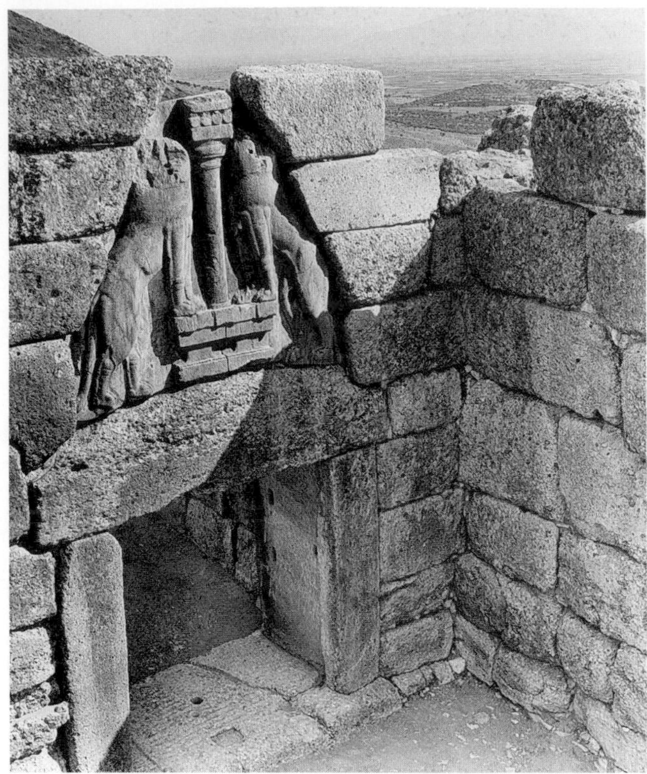

4-23 The Lion Gate, Mycenae, *c.* 1300 B.C. Limestone, relief panel approx. 9½′ high.

island of Malta has well-preserved megalithic monuments, "temples," and tombs, constructed of great stones, which were dressed and fitted. Perhaps the most ancient of masonry edifices in Europe, these enclose variously shaped spaces. The monumental fortress walls, palace gates, and vaulted tombs at Tiryns and Mycenae represent high points in the development of megalithic structural composition.

The sternness of these fortress-palaces was relieved by frescoes, by carvings, and, at Mycenae at least, by monumental architectural sculpture. The Lion Gate at Mycenae (FIG. **4-23**) is the outer gateway of the stronghold. It is protected on the left by a wall and on the right by a projecting bastion and is formed of two great monoliths capped with a huge lintel. Above the lintel, the layers of stone form a corbeled arch, leaving a triangular opening that serves to lighten the weight to be carried by the lintel itself. The triangular space is filled with a slab on which two lions, carved in high relief, confront each other on either side of a column of the probably sacred Minoan type, resting their forepaws on its base. (This column of the Lion Gate supplies evidence of what the vanished wooden Minoan columns looked like.) Holes near the top of the animals indicate that the heads, now lost, were made of separate pieces of stone or metal. The lions are carved with breadth and vigor, and the whole design admirably fills its triangular space, harmonizing in dignity, strength, and scale with the massive stones that form the walls and gate. We find similar groups in miniature on Cretan seals, and one senses that these lions are not too distant from Mesopotamian heraldic composition.

Within the gate and to the right lies the *grave circle*, an enclosure containing a number of simple shaft graves, covered and marked by a stele. These stone-lined pits served as tombs for kings and their families. Another similar grave circle was recently discovered outside the walls of Mycenae. Both grave circles date from about 1600–1500 B.C. But, at this time, shaft graves were gradually being replaced by the so-called beehive tombs, of which the best preserved is the remarkable "Treasury of Atreus" (FIGS. **4-24** and **4-25**).

4-24 Plan and sections of the "Treasury of Atreus," Mycenae, *c.* 1400 B.C. (After A. W. Lawrence.)

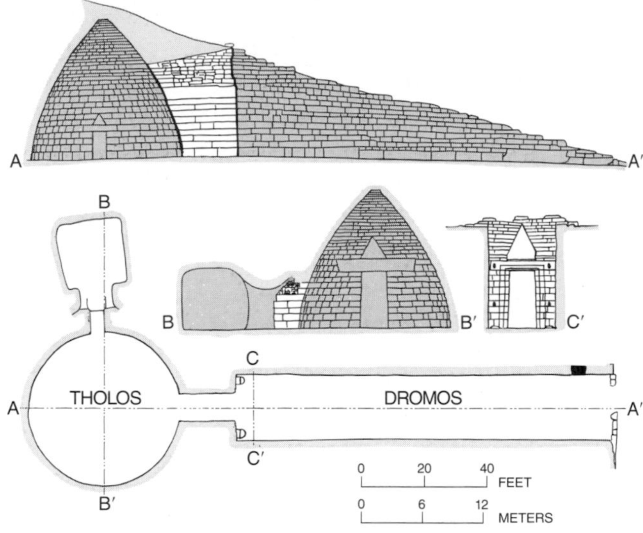

4-25 Interior of the tholos, "Treasury of Atreus," Mycenae. Vault approx. 40′ high.

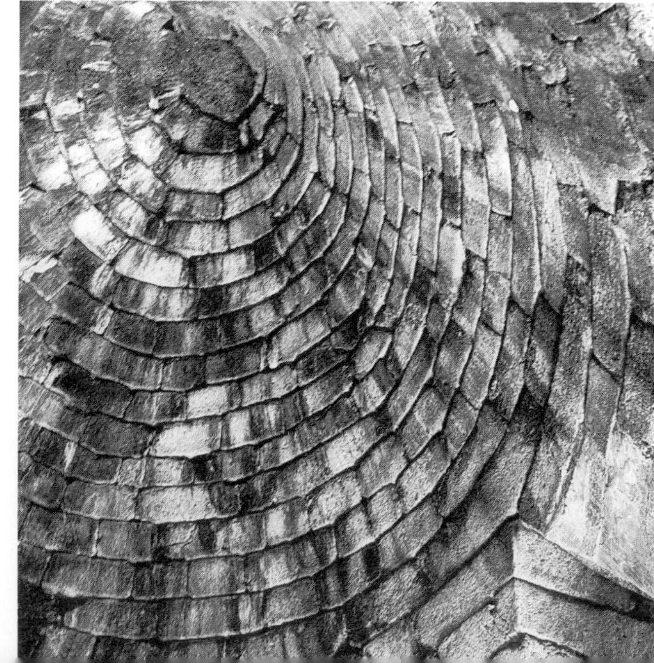

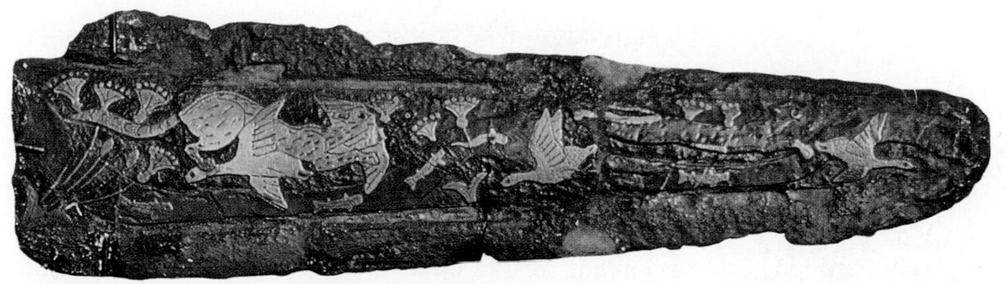

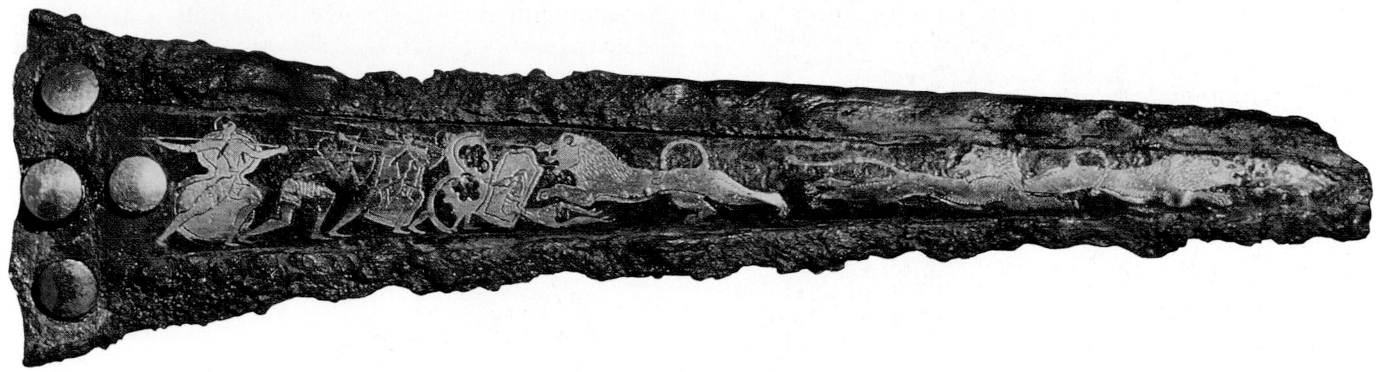

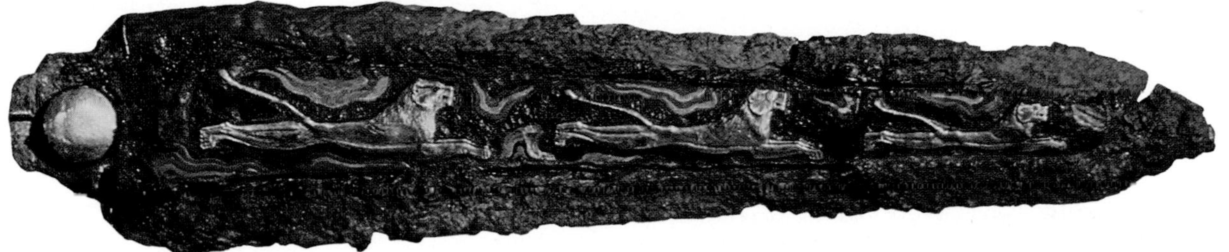

4-26 Inlaid dagger blades from the royal tombs at Mycenae, *c.* 1600–1500 B.C. Bronze inlaid with gold and electrum, longest blade approx. 9″ long. National Archeological Museum, Athens.

This structure was misnamed by Heinrich Schliemann, who thought it to be the storehouse for the treasure of Atreus, father of Agamemnon and Menelaus. Approached by a long passage, or *dromos,* the beehive shape of the round tomb chamber, or *tholos,* was achieved by use of corbeled courses of stone laid on a circular base, splendidly cut to the curve of the wall and ending in a lofty dome, which, after completion, was covered with earth. About 40 feet high, this vaulted structure, without interior supports, was the largest unified space in all antiquity until the Roman Pantheon was built fifteen hundred years later.

Most of the beehive tombs had been thoroughly looted long before their modern rediscovery, but rich finds were made in shaft graves at Mycenae. Inlaid with gold and electrum (an alloy of gold and silver), some bronze daggers found in these graves reveal the influence of the Minoan figure style (FIG. **4-26**). On the longest of the three blades illustrated, three hunters with spears, bows, and shields attack a lion that has struck down a fourth hunter, while two other lions flee. The subject is of Mesopotamian derivation, but the costumes are Cretan and the vigorous, spirited movements of the hunters, the lithe strength and spring of the lions, are Minoan.

Beaten gold *(repoussé)* masks were found in the shaft graves, attached to the faces of the mummified Mycenaean princes (FIG. **4-27**). Recording fairly closely the features of the deceased, they also testify to the influx of gold from Egypt. This and the elaboration of funeral practices lend strong support to the supposition that the impulse that started this high phase of Mycenaean civilization originated partly in Egypt and partly in Crete.

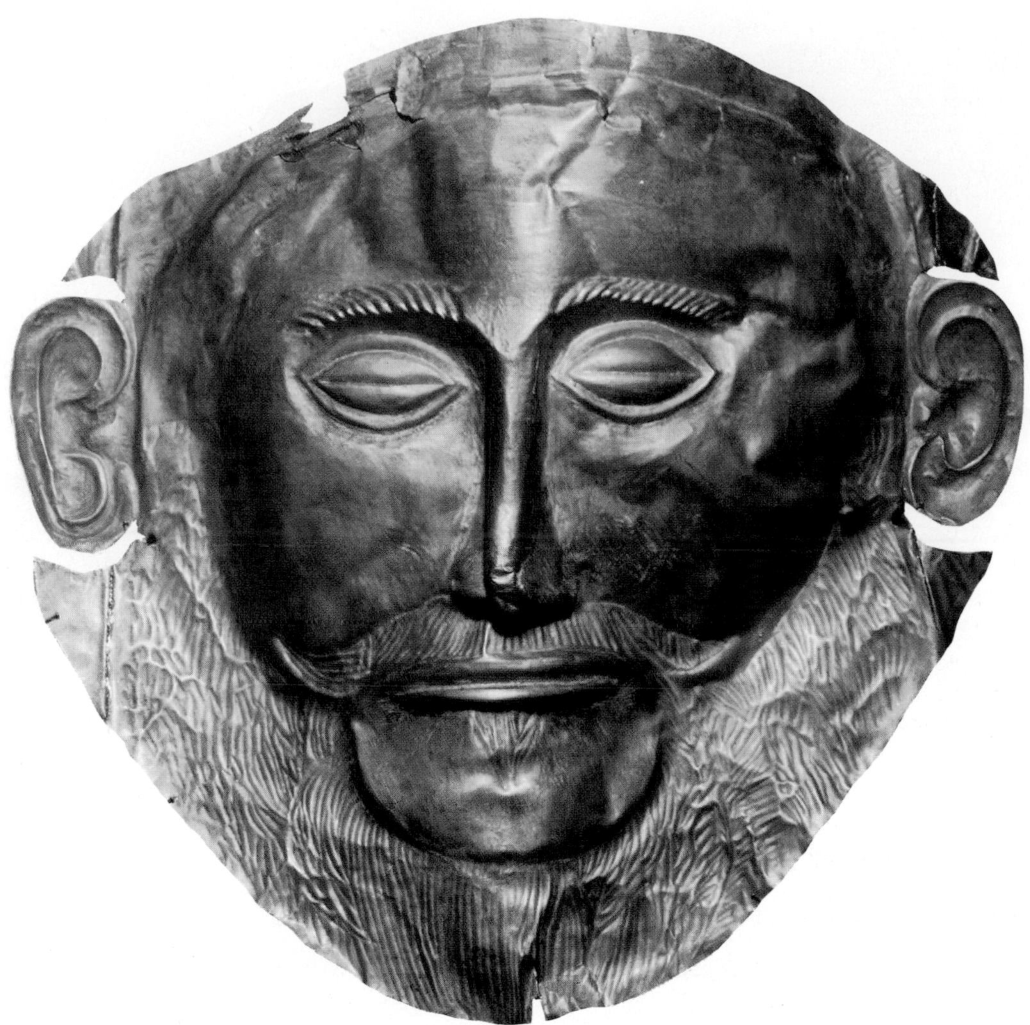

4-27 Funeral mask from the royal tombs of Mycenae, *c.* 1500 B.C. Beaten gold, approx. 12″ high. National Archeological Museum, Athens.

The golden culture of Mycenae produced such masterpieces as the famous cups from Vaphio (FIG. **4-28**). Found in a beehive tomb, these beautiful vessels are still the subject of much debate among experts who see them as originating in Crete and those who insist that, despite their undoubted resemblance to Minoan figure style, they are Mycenaean. The cups are a pair, each made of two plates of gold. One plate was worked in *repoussé* for the outside of the cup, the other left plain to make a smooth surface for the inside. The plates were fastened together, the handles riveted on, and some of the details then engraved. The subject seems to be Minoan (the men are costumed in the Minoan manner) and related to the bull-leaping ritual; bulls are being trapped and snared, with a cow used as a lure in one case. Continuing around each cup, the scenes together compose a complete narrative. On the cup at the right, a bull, charging furiously, impales a man, while another bull (on the side not visible) dashes madly from the fracas. The scene visible on the cup on the left shows a bull moving slowly toward a decoy cow. The climax of the episode is shown on the opposite side of this cup; the bellowing bull is captured and hobbled. The scenes are pulled together compositionally by the trees and, on the cup on the right, by the figure of the falling man. The whole design is admirably composed to fit its space. In both cups, areas not filled by the animal and human figures contain landscape motifs of trees, rocks, and clouds similar to those in contemporary painting. The shallowness of the relief and the conventional treatment of the trees produce a rich play of light and shade and a variety of textures.

The Warrior Vase (FIG. **4-29**) represents a file of Mycenaean soldiers strikingly different in costume and physiognomy from the Cretan figure types we have seen in Minoan art. This fact would seem to strengthen the argument that the Mycenaeans were of different racial stock from the Minoans and the indigenous builders of their own civilization. It may

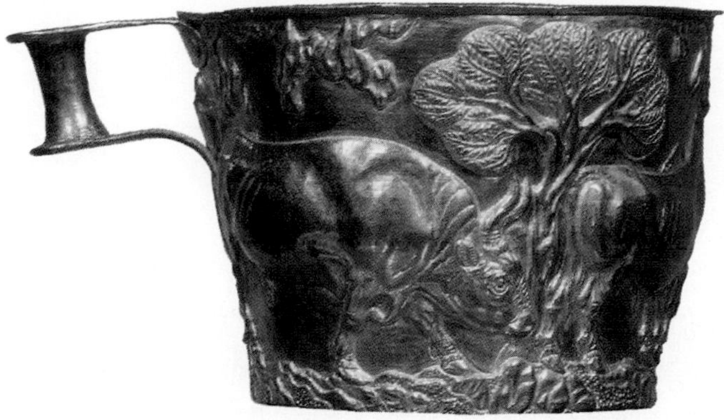

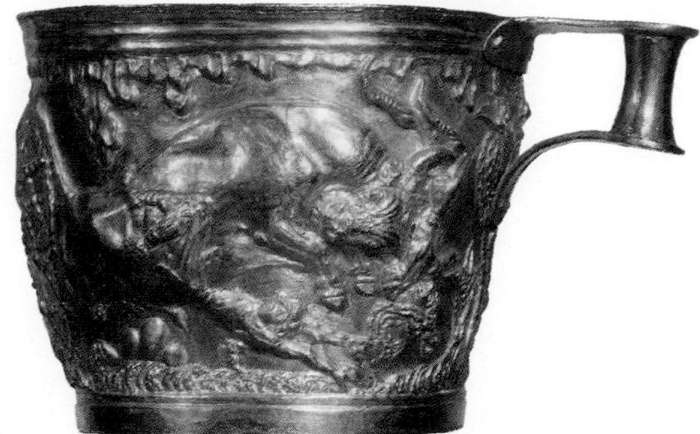

4-28 *The Vaphio Cups,* Laconia, c. 1500 B.C. Gold with *repoussé* decoration, approx. 3½″ high. National Archeological Museum, Athens.

be, too, that we are looking here at the last Mycenaean warriors who marched forth to meet the invaders, or perhaps internal enemies, under whose onslaught the Mycenaean civilization collapsed after 1200 B.C. The victors carried iron weapons, superior to the softer bronze of the Mycenaeans, and their success illustrates the historical commonplace that a superior technology can overcome an otherwise more highly developed civilization.

The centuries-long period that followed the obliteration of Aegean culture, although little survives from it, cannot be considered merely a historical void. The proto-Greek language of Linear B must have evolved toward Archaic and Classical Greek; the rites of the gods of the Olympian cult were already celebrated and no doubt transmitted, as were common types and motifs in the craft arts, metalwork, pottery, gems, and ornaments in gold. Though much has disappeared that would make the continuity exactly and fully traceable, enough remains and continues to be uncovered that would suggest the direct descent of Classical Greek art from Mycenaean. Through the "dark age," new energies were gathering that would form one of the greatest civilizations the world has ever known—a civilization new, bold, self-confident, and modern.

4-29 *The Warrior Vase,* from Mycenae, c. 1200 B.C. Approx. 14″ high. National Archeological Museum, Athens.

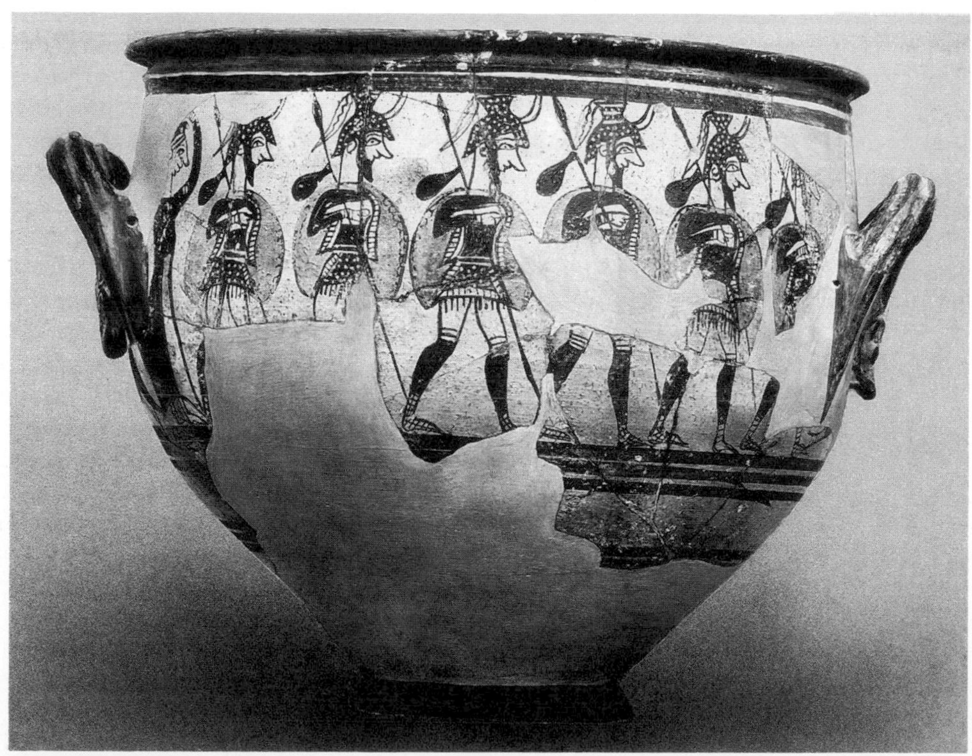

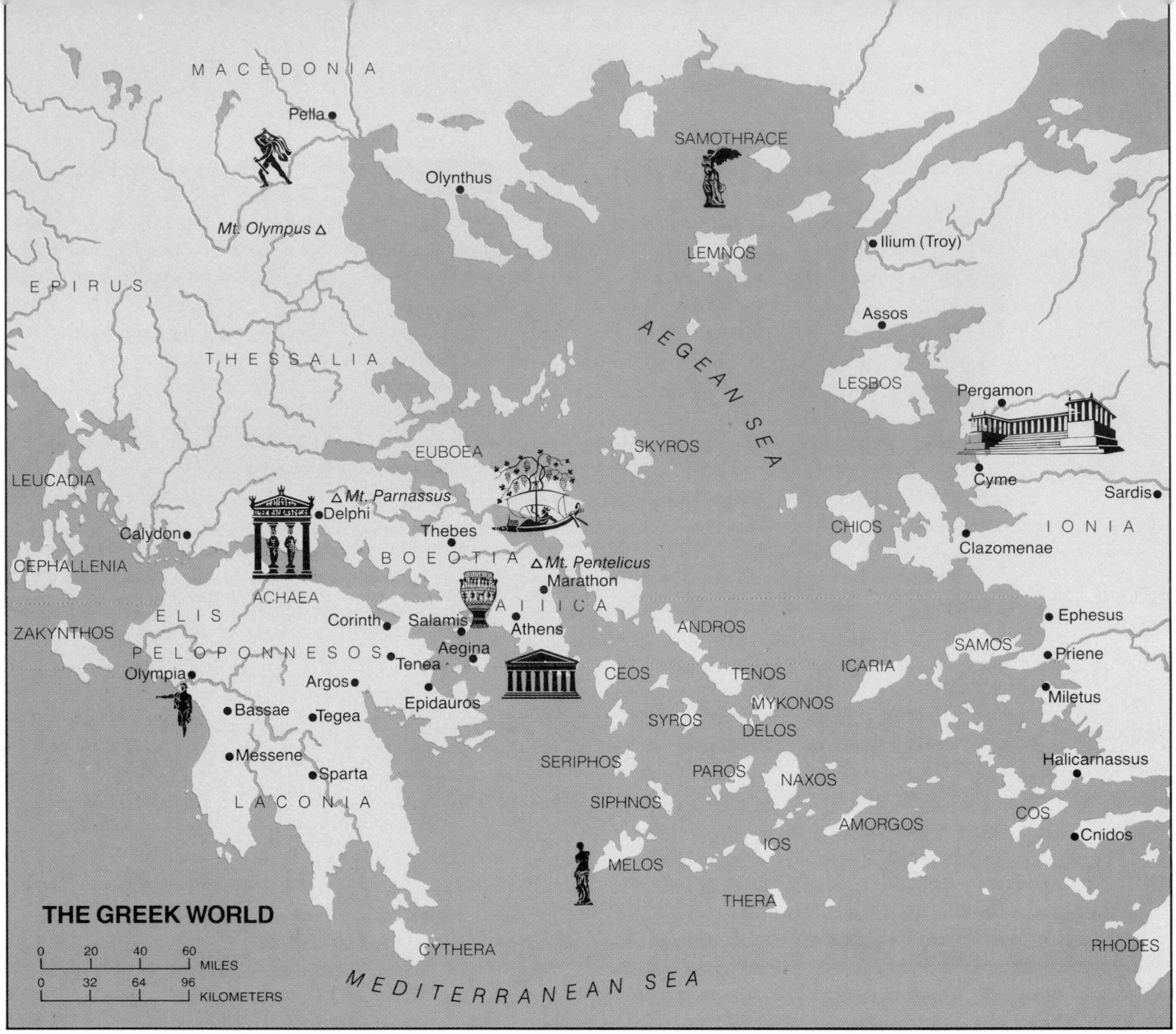

THE GREEK WORLD

0 20 40 60 MILES
0 32 64 96 KILOMETERS

MACEDONIA
Pella
Olynthus
Mt. Olympus
SAMOTHRACE
LEMNOS
Ilium (Troy)
Assos
EPIRUS
THESSALIA
AEGEAN SEA
LESBOS
Pergamon
EUBOEA
SKYROS
Cyme
Sardis
LEUCADIA
Mt. Parnassus
Delphi
Calydon
Thebes
CHIOS
Clazomenae
IONIA
CEPHALLENIA
BOEOTIA
Mt. Pentelicus
Marathon
ACHAEA
ATTICA
ELIS
Corinth
Salamis
Athens
ANDROS
Ephesus
ZAKYNTHOS
PELOPONNESOS
Tenea
Aegina
SAMOS
Olympia
Argos
CEOS
TENOS
ICARIA
Priene
Bassae
Tegea
Epidauros
SYROS
MYKONOS
DELOS
Miletus
Messene
SERIPHOS
PAROS
NAXOS
Halicarnassus
Sparta
LACONIA
SIPHNOS
AMORGOS
COS
Cnidos
IOS
MELOS
THERA
CYTHERA
RHODES
MEDITERRANEAN SEA

1200 B.C.	1000	900	735	700	650

SUB-MYCENAEAN PERIOD (1200–1000) · PROTO-GEOMETRIC PERIOD (1000–900) · GEOMETRIC PERIOD (900–700) · ARCHAIC PERIOD (700–)

ORIENTALIZING PERIOD (735–650)

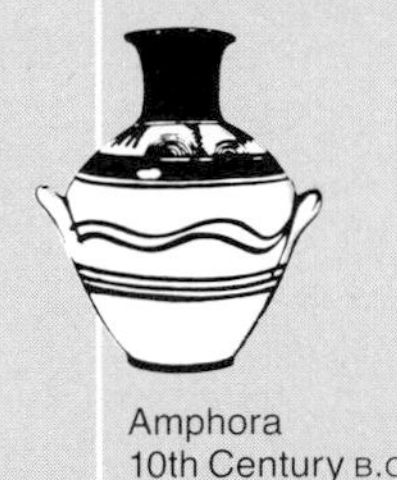
Amphora
10th Century B.C.

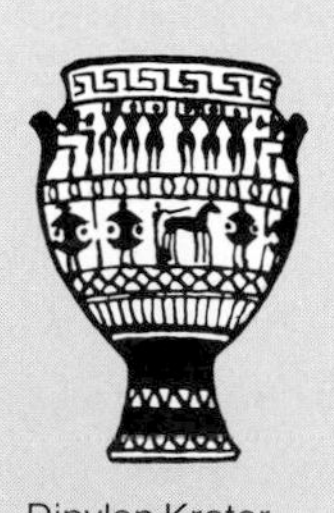
Dipylon Krater
8th Century B.C.

EXEKIAS
Dionysos in a Sailboat
c. 550–525 B.C.

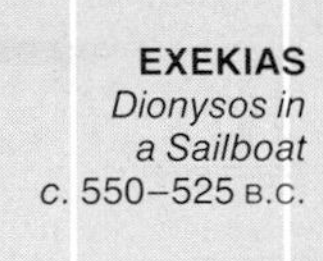

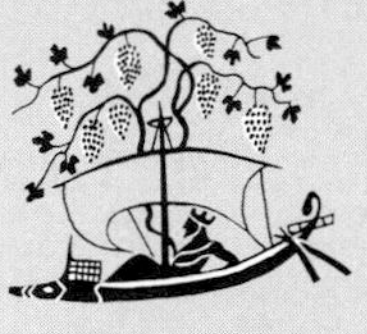

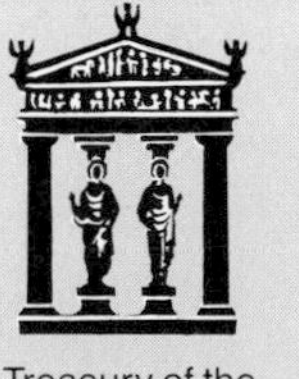
Treasury of the Siphnians, Delphi
c. 530 B.C.

Doric Invasions

Beginnings of democracy

Vases signed for first time

Foundation of Italian colonies from *c.* 730 B.C.

Origin of red-figure technique *c.* 530 B.C.

Homer
c. 850–800 B.C.

First Olympiad
776 B.C.

5
THE ART OF GREECE

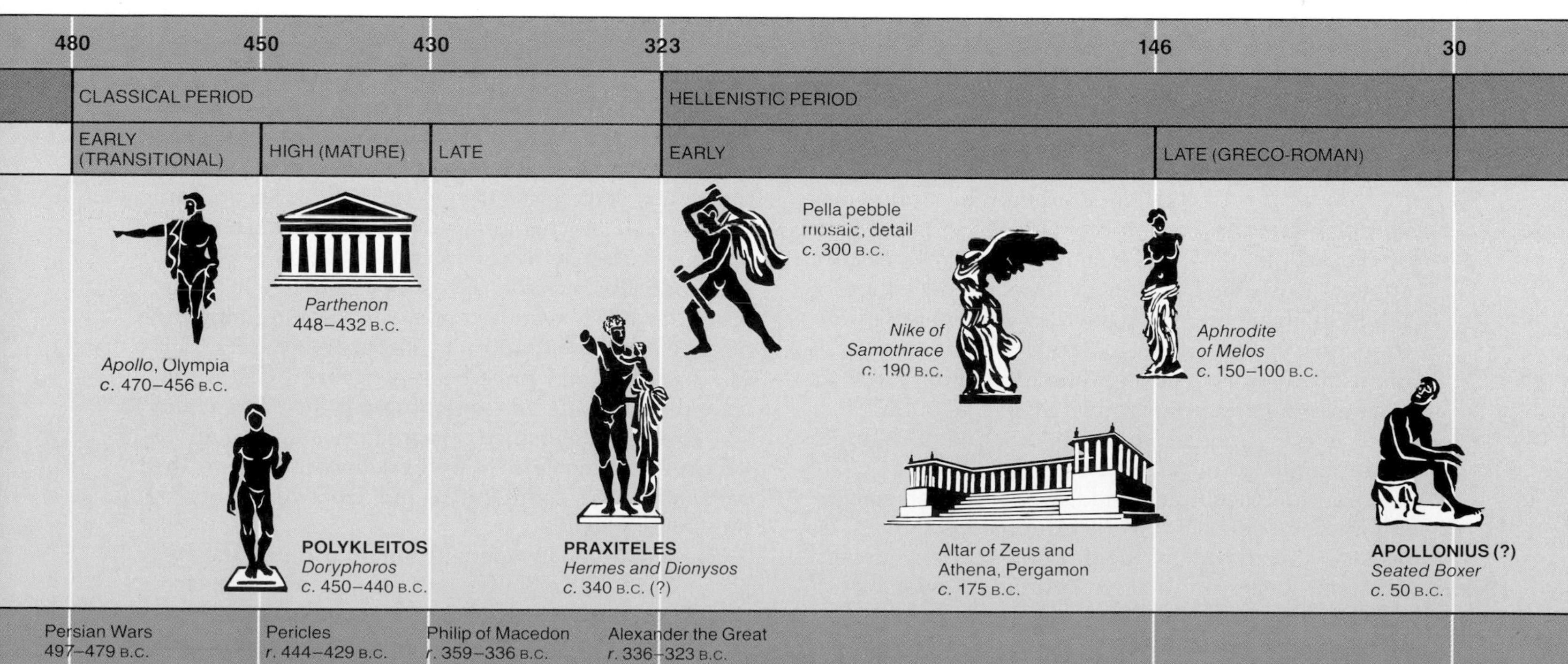

"FOR WE ARE LOVERS of the beautiful, yet with simplicity, and we cultivate the mind without loss of manliness. . . . We are the school of Greece." In the fifth century B.C., the golden age of Athens, Thucydides had Pericles make this assertion in praise of the Athenians, comparing their open, democratic society with the closed, barracks-state of their rivals, the Spartans. But Pericles might have been speaking in general of Greek culture, as we have received it, and of the ideal of humanistic education and life created by that culture. In the humanistic view, man is what matters, and he is, in the words of Protagoras, the "measure of all things."

For the Greeks, what set human beings apart was their intelligence, and human intelligence, trained in reasoning, was the highest function nature had created. Moreover, Aristotle assured us that "all men by nature desire to know." And what we know is the order of nature, which is one with the order of human reason.

The order of both nature and reason, said the Greeks, is beautiful and simple, and the beauty of things is one with our knowledge of them; thus, the good life, the achievement of the "beautiful soul," follows on compliance with that typically Greek command, "Know thyself!" One achieves the good life, then, through an intellectual process; one lives "according to nature," according to the natural laws of life discoverable by reason. The self now becomes of first importance, and as human beings come to full self-awareness, they necessarily become aware of nature as well.

Humanity is regarded as the highest creation of and value in nature, and it was the Greeks who created democracy as well as the natural human image in art. A late, great scholar of Classical Greece, Werner Jaeger, wrote of the Greeks' exaltation of humanity: "As against the Oriental exaltation of one God-king . . . and the . . . suppression of the great mass of the people . . . , the beginning of Greek history appears to be the beginning of a new conception of the individual. . . . the history of personality in Europe must start with [the Greeks]."* This honoring of the individual, and through the individual, the laws of human nature, is so completely part of our habit of mind that we are scarcely aware of it and of its origin in the minds of the Greeks.

From the Paleolithic period, we have been surveying human beings in a world dominated by the great beasts—threatened by them, fighting them, dependent on them (or their embodiment), worshiping them, conceding their might and our own weakness. Now, in Greece, humans assert that their own peculiar power—the power of intelligence—puts them far above the beasts. But the Greek mind was not dryly or pallidly rationalistic; it knew well the forces of the irrational against which reason must struggle constantly. In fact, Greek art constitutes with Greek culture a compact synthesis of opposites, a harmony between profound passion and rational order. Its clarity and symmetry are not cold, but vital; its forms can be rigorous and mathematical, yet full of life.

In marked contrast to Egypt, with its long horizontals of alluvial plain between desert plateaus and seemingly invariable sunshine, Greece is a country of diversified geography and climate. The bays of its deeply indented, rugged coastline make the country half land and half sea; mountain ridges divide it into many small units. The climate is vigorous—cold in winter, dry and hot in summer. A breeze almost always blows from the sea. The unusually clear, almost crystalline atmosphere is often softened by a haze. Both sky and sea are brilliant in color. It is little wonder that the Greeks, attuned to nature, should people their mountains, woods, streams, sky, and sea with divinities—that they should picture Zeus, the king of this realm of gods, as reigning from their loftiest peak, Olympus; the Muses as dwelling in the deep, cool groves on the long slopes of Parnassus and Cithaeron; and Apollo as speaking from the awe-inspiring rocky clefts of Delphi.

Nature worship evolved into personification. The Greek gods assumed human forms whose grandeur and nobility were not free from human frailty; indeed, unlike the gods of Egypt and Mesopotamia, the Greek gods differed from human beings only in that they were immortal. It has been said that the Greeks made their gods into men and their men into gods. Man, becoming the measure of all things, in turn must represent, if all things in their perfection are beautiful, the unchanging standard of the best; to create the perfect individual became the Greek ideal.

The Greeks, or Hellenes, as they called themselves, appear to have been the product of an intermingling of Aegean peoples and Indo-European invaders. This intermingling may have been a vitalizing factor that should be considered, together with the climate and the strongly diversified mountain-valley terrain of the Greek peninsula, in hypothesizing the causes of the peculiarly high competitive and creative energy of the Greek peoples.

The first of the invaders began to drift into the area about 2000 B.C., and after 1600 B.C., as we have seen, they formed the Mycenaean civilization on the Greek peninsula. After about 1200 B.C., the Mycenaeans were apparently overwhelmed in turn by new invad-

*Werner Jaeger, *Paideia: The Ideals of Greek Culture* (New York: Oxford University Press, 1939), Vol. 1, p. xix.

ers from the north—the Dorians and perhaps the Ionians. The Dorians made the Peloponnesos the center of their power and may have forced the Ionians eastward across the Aegean to the coast of Asia Minor. The origin of the Ionians is still a matter of dispute. Some scholars feel that proto-Ionians lived at Athens during Mycenaean times and were displaced during the Doric invasions. Others hold that the Ionians developed on the coast of Asia Minor between the eleventh and eighth centuries B.C. out of a mixed stock of settlers. In either case, the Ionians seem to have been more individualistic than the tribally ordered Dorians, whose most characteristic city became conservative Sparta.

In Ionia, on the east coast of Asia Minor, epics of individual greatness had come to be celebrated by the eighth century B.C., and by the seventh century, the rational philosophers of Miletus had begun to interpret the world in terms of reason rather than religion, beginning the immense transformation of the worship of nature into the science of nature. Between Ionia and the Peloponnesos lay Attica, and there, in Athens, a conservative tribal order and individualistic striving combined to produce the most fruitful of all the *poleis*, or city-states, of Greece—the one that Thucydides could boast was the "school of Greece."

By the eighth century B.C., the separate Greek-speaking states had held their first ceremonial games in common, the Olympiad of 776 B.C., from which time the historical Greeks calculated their chronology. From then on, despite their chronic rivalries and wars, they regarded themselves as Hellenes, distinct from the surrounding "barbarians" who did not speak Greek. The enterprising Hellenes, greatly aided by their indented coasts and island stepping-stones, became a trading and colonizing people who enlarged the geographic and cultural boundaries of Hellas. Tribal organizations had evolved into city-states, with each an individual unit. Political development differed from state to state, but a pattern emerged in which rule was first by kings, then by nobles, and then by tyrants who seized personal power. At last, in Athens, appeared the dynamic balance called *democracy*.

Athens has in many ways become the symbol of Greek culture; many of the finest products of Greek civilization were created by Athenians or by others closely associated with Athens and its traditions. But Athens must not be considered the sole focus and center of Greek civilization, though it is convenient for us to use it as a distinctive type and standard. Increasingly, art-historical and archeological investigation find that the creative energy of Greek civilization was widely and fairly evenly distributed throughout the Mediterranean world, bound by Phoenician territories to the west and the Persian Empire to the east. From the mother cities of Greece on the Ionian coast of Asia Minor—long under the sway of Persia—Greek influence extended westward through Cyprus and the opulent cities of southern Italy (Magna Graecia) and Sicily to the coasts of France and Spain; it reached from the shores of the Black Sea to the Libyan coast, where it met the culture of Egypt. The language, industry, art, and political institutions of the Greeks were diffused through this broad area by maritime commercial traffic and political expansion. Thus we can place Athens and her achievements within the context of an extensive Hellenic cultural empire, whose far-flung city-states could often rival her in power and magnificence, as well as in artistic invention and influence.

Athens, at the time of its brief flowering after the Persian Wars, was an active city of one hundred thousand people. Above its olive groves and rooftops towered the Acropolis, or higher city, formerly a Mycenaean fortress but, in this age, crowned with temples rising in bright colors against an intensely blue sky. Under the covered colonnades *(stoas)* that surrounded the city's central marketplace *(agora)*, the citizens congregated to discuss the latest political development or philosophical idea. Among the Athenians, argument was both a public and a private exercise that went on wherever a few disputants could be assembled. This love of intellectual contest, the vigorous forerunner of science itself, was astonishingly popular; whether in the house of a rich man or in the marketplace, in the gymnasium, or on the street corner, such discussion was the key to the intense political and intellectual life that developed in the Greek city-state. Physical exercise also played a large part in education and daily life; the Athenian aim of achieving a balance of intellectual and physical discipline, an ideal of humanistic education, is expressed in the Latin, *mens sana in corpore sano* (a sound mind in a sound body).

The tragedies of Aeschylus and Sophocles, played before the eager citizens, presented the individual as having an obligation to the gods and the rise and fall of his fortunes as reflecting the contest between blind fate and the new-found power of reason.

The constants of Greek culture were humanity, nature, and reason, and the Greeks understood goodness to be the harmony of all three. On this elementary conviction, they built their grand achievements in art, poetry, mathematics, philosophy, logic, history, and science—the heritage on which the modern Western world in turn was constructed. In discovering man, the Greeks discovered and confronted the problem of persistence and change: individuals pass away, but humanity remains. And although they aspired toward the timeless ideal, the Greeks realized the changes that produce growth and development.

To modern eyes, the realities of Greek life and society may seem to fall well short of what we would call "ideal," although the word has a different meaning in Greek philosophy than it does in modern usage. Slavery was regarded as natural, even beneficial, and was a universal institution among the Greeks. Aristotle declared at the beginning of his *Politics:* "It is clear that some are free by nature, and others are slaves." Women were secluded in their homes and played no part in public or political life. Aristotle may have been expressing the general view when he described woman as "more dispirited, more despondent, and more given to falsehood than the male. . . . she is more envious, more querulous, more slanderous, and more contentious." Womanly virtues were beauty, temperance, and industriousness. In the man's world of Greece, love between men was not considered illicit; in Plato's *Symposium,* Socrates is praised by the lascivious Alcibiades for his almost superhuman imperviousness to seduction. Although the Greeks invented and passed on to us the concept and practice of democracy, most Greek states, even those constituted as democracies, were ruled by the wellborn and affluent, in effect by aristocrats, and the most admired virtues were not wisdom and justice, but statecraft and military valor. Greek men were educated in the values of the heroes of Homer and the athletic exercises of the *palestrae.* War among the city-states was chronic and often atrocious. Fighting among themselves and incapable of unifying, the Greeks eventually fell prey to the autocracy of Macedon and the imperialism of Rome.

In our own time, the uncritical admiration of Greek art and culture that characterized the eighteenth and nineteenth centuries has undergone sharp revision; Greek art is no longer regarded as perfect and worthy of imitation. What we call "modern art" turns its back on the ancient Greek example (Gauguin called Greek art "a lie!"). Greek language and literature are rarely studied in schools, and Greek ideals and values, even the best of them, are clearly not to the modern taste. Yet insofar as the Greeks sought and revered ideal beauty, found it in the order of nature—above all, in the human body—and revealed it in their art, we may still enjoy the art of Greece if we approach it with a sympathetic comprehension of its contexts, intentions, and archetypal forms.

The remains of Greek civilization enable us to reconstruct the development of the Greek style in art. That the Greek style should in fact have *developed* is in itself significant. Development in the art of Egypt, for example, was minimal; the pattern of ritual and of form was not to be broken. Change in Egypt occurred, when it did, *despite* the pattern of the culture as a whole. Of course, we must remember that an important factor in the sudden historical eminence of Greece was the base from which Greek civilization rose—the civilizations of Egypt and the Near East. The Greeks quite honestly acknowledged borrowing ideas, motifs, conventions, and skills from these older civilizations. But from the beginning, the Greeks embraced experiment, even while adopting and holding to the older forms. Development and change were inherent in Greek culture (as conservatism was in Egyptian culture), and change has recognizable forms. Greek art displays much more readily discernible stages than the relatively unchanging art of the ancient Near East.

THE GEOMETRIC AND ARCHAIC PERIODS: 900–480 B.C.

Pottery serves, as no other artistic medium can, to link the very late Mycenaean (sub-Mycenaean) period with that of historical Greece. For one thing, it has survived. We can trace a continuity from the sub-Mycenaean period into the Classical fifth century B.C. entirely in terms of the figurative decoration of Greek ceramic ware, which shows the artist's confrontation with radically new ideas and problems and some equally radical interpretations and solutions. It is appropriate, then, given this continuity and the Greek concept of the development of forms, to begin the study of Greek art with vase paintings, for these illuminate changes that were profoundly influential in human history and that take place in a curiously logical order.

Already, we have seen numerous examples of how artists represent the human form, from the strange, falling stick figure in the *Well Scene* at Lascaux (FIG. 1-8) to the agile Minoans of *The Vaphio Cups* (FIG. 4-28). Now we can review changes in the representation of the human body that are the result not of accidental differences of convention but of carefully accumulated increments of knowledge. In Greece, these changes were firmed into a tradition of technical procedure that did not backslide, as was the case in the Egyptian return to old forms after the death of the innovative Akhenaton (see Chapter 3). In the Archaic Greek vases, the human figure became the subject of intense analytical study for the first time. As the Greek philosopher questioned human nature and purpose, the Greek artist began to inquire how human beings look to others of their kind in the world of optical experience. The conceptual way of placing the figure and enumerating its features, which we have seen in the art of older civilizations, gradually was given up and replaced by a method of painstaking observation of the pose and motion of the body in life. This did not happen all at once; centuries were involved in the great transformation, and the dated sequence of vases reveals the ordered phases of the change. It is useful to describe these changes at the outset, for, from its earliest appearances on vases, the human figure remained the principal motif of Greek art, as the human being was central to its thought and interest.

Vase Painting

A proto-Geometric *amphora* (FIG. **5-1**), a two-handled jar for wine or oil, from the tenth century B.C. shows us the formative phase of what is called the *Geometric style.* Although it borrows the decorative devices of the earlier sub-Mycenaean style, its execution is neater and more painstaking. The artist now uses compasses to form careful, regular concentric circles, a new motif that contrasts sharply with the casual brush strokes used elsewhere on the shoulder of the vessel. As the Geometric style developed, the Minoan stock of curvilinear forms was gradually replaced by rectilinear shapes arranged in tight bands to cover more of the vessel's surface.

5-1 Proto-Geometric amphora, from the Dipylon cemetery, tenth century B.C. Approx. 16½″ high. Keramikos Museum, Athens.

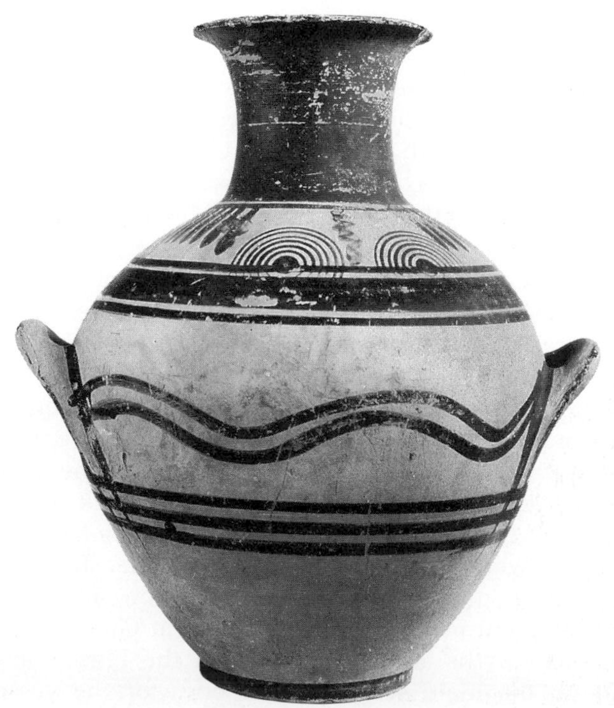

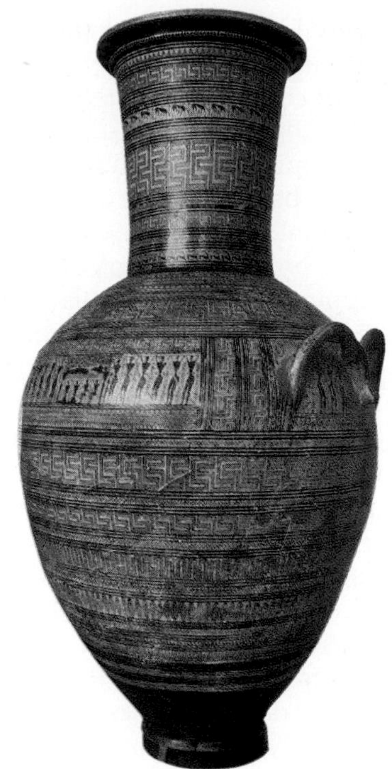

5-2 *Dipylon Vase* (Geometric amphora), from the Dipylon cemetery, eighth century B.C. Approx. 61″ high. National Archeological Museum, Athens.

The human figure reappeared in the decorative scheme during the period of the culminating Geometric style, specifically in the so-called *Dipylon Vase* (FIG. **5-2**), from the eighth century B.C., named after the Dipylon cemetery in Athens, where it was found. The figures are hardly more than symbols, fashioned of diamond and wedge shapes that fit the severe, regular, geometric characteristics of the banded decoration. Carefully arranged on a panel that has been placed prominently on the shoulder of the vessel, the figures represent a funeral scene with mourners attending the deceased, who is laid out on a bier—an appropriate subject for this funerary vase, which was set up over a grave. This vase represents a key moment in the development of Greek art; it marks the reintroduction of the human figure and the figure's use as a vehicle for pictorial narrative. But its historical importance should not blind us to the vase's high artistic quality. In a subtle crescendo, the sophisticated design builds up from below to the climactic figured panel, decreasing again above it in a sequence that is repeated with variations on the tall neck of the vase. If a major problem of the painter is to adjust the design to the shape of the vase, then this geometric amphora surely must represent a high point in the history of vase painting. It is difficult to imagine a design that is more closely bound to its carrier than these encircling bands, which seemingly contain and compress the flexing volume of the vase's form.

Another type of Greek vase, the *krater,* had a larger body and wider mouth than the amphora. A krater from the Dipylon cemetery (FIG. **5-3**), possibly of the same date as the *Dipylon Vase* (FIG. 5-2) or somewhat later, shows a certain loss of refinement as the geometric ornament becomes secondary. The figures represent a funeral procession, with horse-drawn chariots occupied by warriors carrying shields. In the old conceptual manner, both wheels of each chariot are represented, and the horses are carefully distinguished, each with the correct number of legs. The warriors are standing behind their shields, which are shown in front view. The number of figures represented is markedly greater than the number shown in FIG. 5-2, suggesting that the artist was intrigued with the rediscovery of the human figure, which had been absent from mainland pottery decoration for over four hundred years. Even if the fascination with figured representation overwhelms the abstract geometric pattern on this vase, however, a sense of order and restraint still dominates its design. The regimented figures as yet seem incapable of escaping from the two bands into which they have been placed. Soon they will no longer be constrained in this manner.

5-3 Geometric krater, from the Dipylon cemetery, eighth century B.C. Approx. 40½″ high. Metropolitan Museum of Art, New York (Rogers Fund).

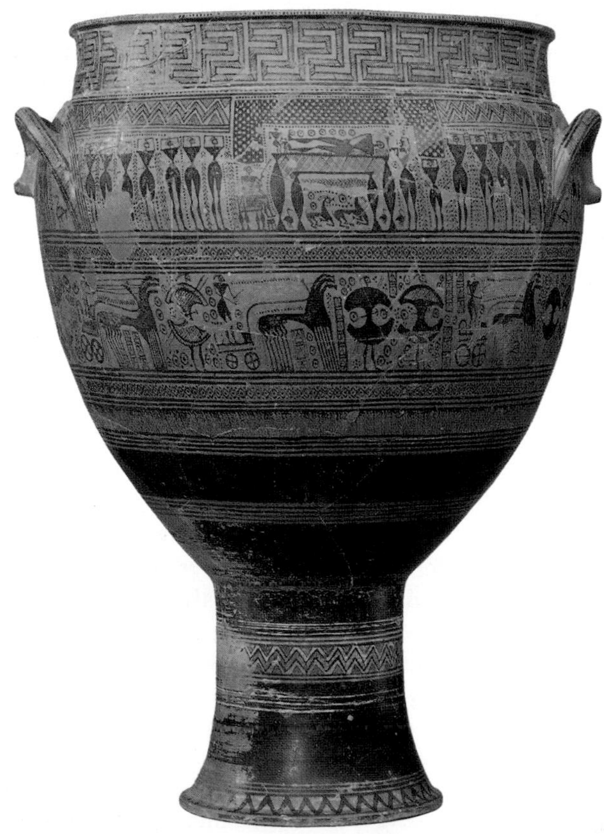

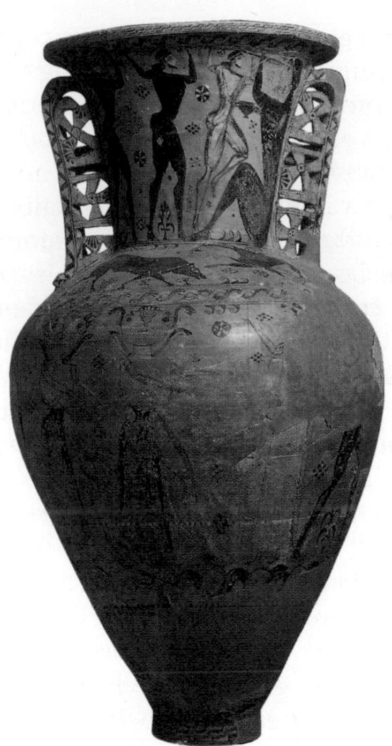

5-4 *The Blinding of Polyphemus* and *Gorgons* (proto-Attic amphora), from Eleusis, *c.* 675–650 B.C. Approx. 56″ high. Archeological Museum, Eleusis.

The Geometric period was succeeded by the Orientalizing phase of the Archaic period, a time of marked commercial and colonial expansion that brought the Greeks into closer contact with ancient Near Eastern civilizations. A consequence of these new relationships was the frequent appearance of Oriental animals and composite monsters on Greek vases. Motifs familiar to us from Mesopotamian and Egyptian art include lions, sphinxes, griffins, and centaurs.

Stylistically, a vase from Eleusis (FIG. **5-4**), typical of the Orientalizing period, represents a complete and radical break with the orderly Geometric manner. The figurative decor occupies most of the vessel; the arrangement of the motifs is loose, almost casual, and the shapes are mostly curvilinear. It is as if the artist were intentionally throwing off the Geometric straitjacket as an awkward restraint on a new interest—the representation of narrative scenes, some from Homeric legend. On the amphora in FIG. 5-4, human figures, resembling those of the Geometric period, but much more filled out, rounded, and active, now occupy the largest areas of the vessel, and the ornament retreats to the smaller areas in the neck, shoulder, and base. In the Geometric period, the Homeric themes were collected in the great epics. The Orientalizing period marks their diffusion and their achievement of universal popularity in Greece. Two popular myths are represented on the Eleusis amphora: the main scene on the body of the vessel shows the Gorgons pursuing Perseus after he had beheaded Medusa; on the neck of the vase, Ulysses is blinding the one-eyed giant, Polyphemus. The illustration of the epics was to occupy the surfaces of vases for centuries to come; it might almost seem that this first great reflection of human action, in Greek epic, launched the enterprise of representing it in art.

During the Geometric and Archaic periods, numerous pottery centers developed throughout the Aegean world. They have been divided into two main groups: those of the mainland and those of eastern Greece (the regions east of the mainland). On the mainland, the most important centers were Athens in Attica and Corinth in the Peloponnesos; after 550 B.C., Athens became the principal ceramic center and the largest exporter of vases in the Mediterranean basin. In this brief survey, we shall confine ourselves to Athenian wares.

The number of basic Attic (Athenian) vase shapes was limited to six or seven, each subject to four or five variations. The shapes developed out of specific usages and were entirely functional (FIG. **5-5**).

The François Vase (FIG. **5-6**), which was named after its discoverer and is perhaps the finest extant example of an Archaic krater, with its volute handles and extraordinarily vigorous shape, was found in an Etruscan necropolis. (We are indebted to the Etruscans for their avid collecting of Greek vases; many of the best preserved have been found in Etruscan tombs.) It is especially important, not only for its high quality but also for the fact that it is signed by both ERGOTIMOS, the potter ("Ergotimos made it"), and KLEITIAS, the painter ("Kleitias drew it"). Signed vases appear for the first time in the early sixth century B.C. and suggest that their makers had pride in their profession and that their art was becoming increasingly popular and prestigious.

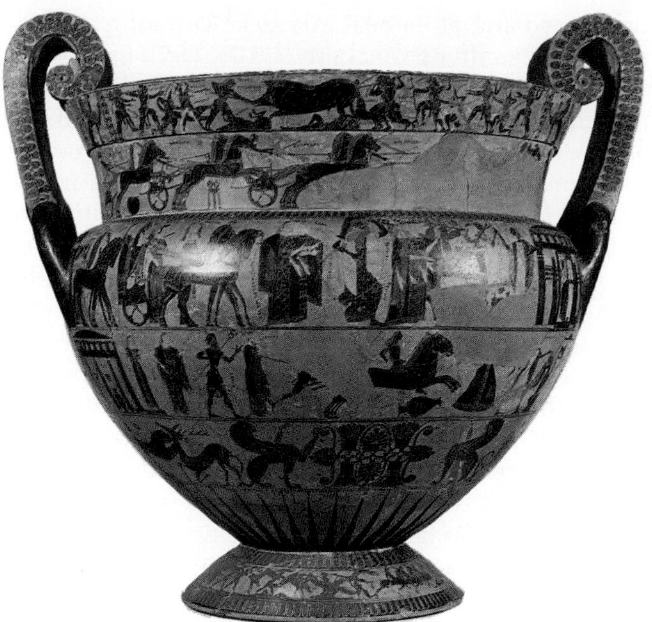

5-6 ERGOTIMOS and KLEITIAS, *The François Vase* (Attic black-figure krater), from Chiusi, c. 575 B.C. Approx. 26" high. Museo Archeologico, Florence.

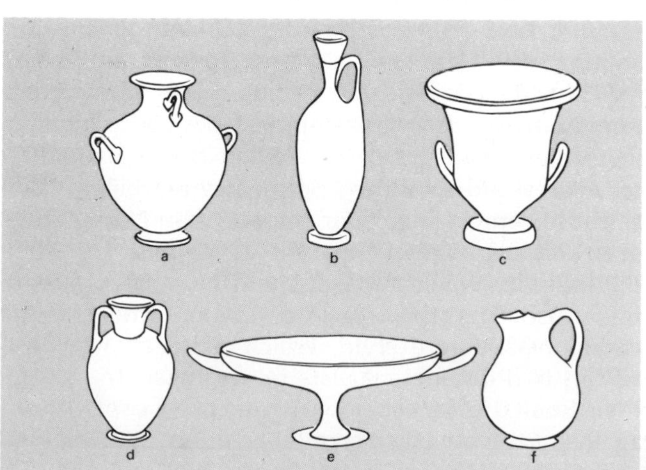

5-5 Greek vase shapes: **(a)** the *hydria* (from the Greek for "water"), a water jar with three handles, two for lifting and one for carrying; **(b)** the *lekythos*, an oil flask with a long, narrow neck adapted for pouring oil slowly, used chiefly in funeral rites; **(c)** the *krater* (from the Greek "to mix"), a bowl for mixing wine and water, the usual beverage of the Greeks; **(d)** the *amphora* (meaning "to carry on both sides," referring to the two handles), a vessel for storing provisions (wine, corn, oil, honey), with an opening large enough to admit a ladle and usually fitted with a cover; **(e)** the *kylix* (from the Greek "to roll," referring to the vase being turned on the potter's wheel), chief form of the drinking cup; **(f)** the *oenochoe* (from the Greek "to pour out wine"), a wine jug, the lip pinched into a trefoil shape to facilitate pouring.

The François Vase is ornamented with over two hundred figures distributed in bands around the vessel. Representing almost the entire Greek pantheon, the figures provide one of our first pictorial glimpses of the forms and personages of Greek religion. The subject is the wedding of Peleus, with the gods in attendance; pictured in addition to the scene of the gods and Peleus, father of Achilles, are depictions of the Calydonian boar hunt, the ambush of Troilus, and the funeral games for Patroclus. Several more scenes are shown on the other side of the vase, and on its foot is an account of an animated battle between cranes and pygmies, above which rays felicitously augment the swelling surface of the krater. The lively scenes are rigidly organized in six bands of varying widths, the widest placed on the vessel's shoulders, a return to the discipline and formality of the Geometric style after the casual and permissive Orientalizing style of the vase from Eleusis (FIG. 5-4).

The François Vase is decorated in an early form of the so-called *black-figure* technique, which is shown fully developed and at its best in a *kylix* (drinking cup) by the potter-painter EXEKIAS (FIG. **5-7**). Dark figures are silhouetted against the light background of the natural reddish clay. Details are incised into the silhouettes with a sharp, pointed instrument to expose the red beneath; touches of white and purple, particularly on the earlier wares, add color to the dominantly monochrome decoration. Although the black areas are customarily referred to as "glazes," it should be pointed out that the black on these Greek pots is neither a pigment nor a glaze but *engobe,* a slip of finely sifted clay that originally is of the same color as the clay of the pot. In the three-phase firing process used by Greek potters, the first (oxidizing) phase turns both pot and slip red; during the second (reducing) phase, the oxygen supply into the kiln is shut off and both pot and slip turn black; in the final (reoxidizing) phase, the coarser material of the pot reabsorbs oxygen and becomes red again, while the smoother, silica-laden slip does not and remains black. After long experiment, Greek potters developed a velvety, jet-black "glaze" of this kind. The touches of white and purple were used more sparingly, with the result that the figures stood in even stronger contrast against their reddish backgrounds. This superb formal control provides the framework for a wealth of naturalistic detail, some of it strikingly novel.

On the inside of Exekias' cup, we see Dionysos, the god of wine and a popular subject for drinking cups such as this one, sailing over the sea carrying his gifts to mankind. He is accompanied by sporting dolphins, and his boat's mast is entwined by a grapevine. The representation introduces a spectacular innovation that heralds the beginning of a revolution in Western art. In his drawing, Exekias does not show a traditional and conventional symbol that "reads" as a sail; instead, he shows a sail as it would actually look, bellying out and filled with wind. It is an image of the action of wind itself, the wind made palpable as a force, and it must have come from a new awareness of the physical presence of nature. This awareness was abroad; it is in the Ionian speculations about the physical constitution of the world and in the reality-charged poetry of Homer: "But soon an offshore breeze blew to our liking—a canvas-bellying breeze. . . . The bows went plunging . . . sails cracked and lashed out."

5-7 EXEKIAS, *Dionysos in a Sailboat* (interior of an Attic black-figure kylix), from Vulci, *c.* 550–525 B.C. 12″ in diameter. Staatliche Antikensammlungen und Glyptothek, Munich.

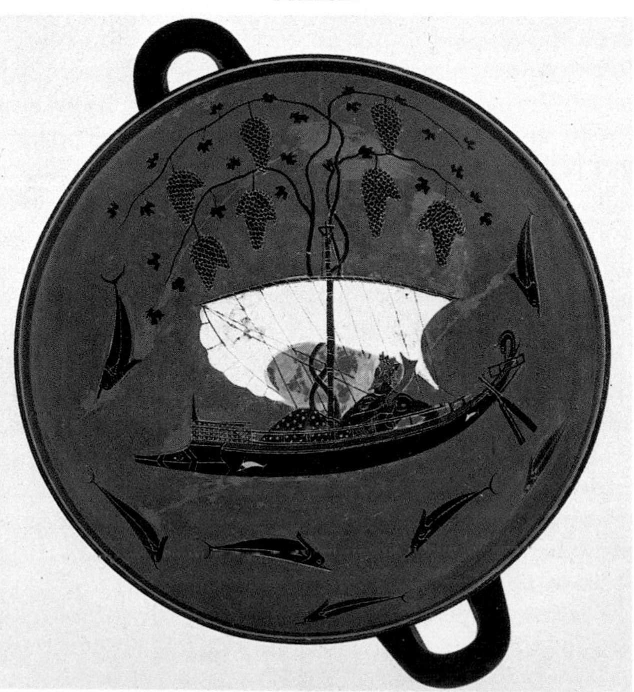

Although in Homer the gods are still the manipulators of the elements, it is men who feel their effects, who hear the howl of the great winds, smell the brine, and feel the harsh ropes and drenching rain. Man's experience of the world, as well as the world itself, begins to be understood by him in physical terms. Such a profound change in man's awareness of his relationship to nature and, in consequence, of his own nature is one that is bound to make itself felt in art. From Exekias' sail on, Greek art manifests an increasing comprehension of physical nature as it is apprehended by vision.

Exekias' skill and subtlety also solve to perfection a difficult compositional problem: how to fix the ship within its circular frame. Part of his solution lies in the down-branching weight of the loaded vines; part lies in the reverse hooklike dolphins, which seem to stitch the composition to its frame.

Around 530 B.C., a new painting technique was invented that reversed the black-figure style by making the background black and leaving the figures reserved in red. Human and animal figures are no longer dark and earthy, massive against a light ground; now they are luminous, like light and air, shining forth from the black background. In this new *red-figure* technique, the major interior markings were rendered with relief lines applied with a syringelike instrument that squeezed out the black "glaze" matter evenly and smoothly. Secondary markings, such as those representing hair, muscles, and sometimes even shading, were painted in "dilute glaze" (engobe diluted with water), which could be applied with a fine brush. The style is freer and more facile than the earlier black-figure style, which it largely replaced within two decades. Artists felt no need to enlarge their limited color scheme; the polished coppery red against a velvety black created an effect that was rich and elegant. The artist usually credited with the invention of the red-figure technique is the ANDOKIDES

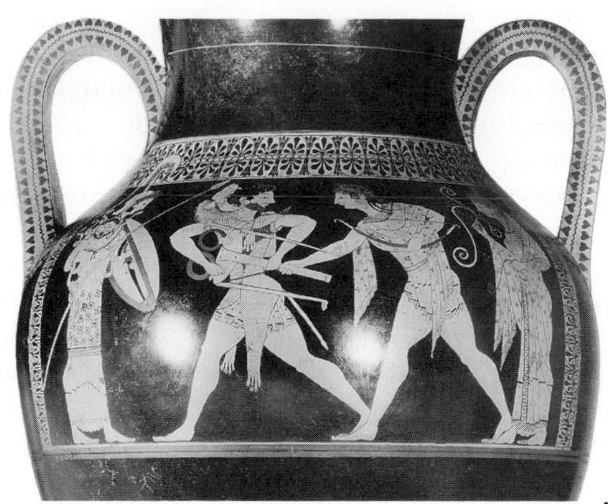

5-8 ANDOKIDES PAINTER, *Herakles and Apollo Struggling for the Tripod* (detail from amphora), c. 530 B.C. Outline drawing at right indicates relation to whole vessel. Portion shown approx. 11″ high, whole vessel approx. 23″ high. Staatliche Museen, Berlin.

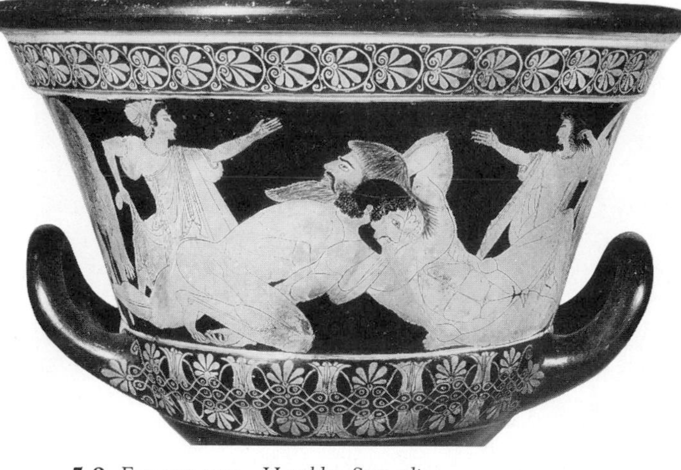

5-9 EUPHRONIOS, *Herakles Strangling Antaios* (detail from krater), from Cerveteri, c. 510–500 B.C. Outline drawing at right indicates relation to whole vessel. Portion shown approx. 12″ high, whole vessel approx. 19″ high. Louvre, Paris.

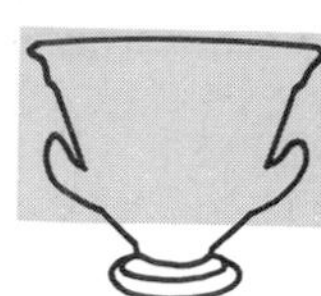

PAINTER, who is named for the potter Andokides, several of whose signed vases he decorated. Sometimes considered to be a student of Exekias, the Andokides Painter uses pictorial devices that are rooted in the style of the older master. On an amphora that depicts *Herakles and Apollo Struggling for the Tripod* (FIG. **5-8**), he shows an interest in rich drapery ornaments and textural effects such as those found in the work of his presumed master. His work lacks some of the warmth and sympathy of Exekias', because he is more concerned with exploiting the possibilities of his newly discovered technique. And there he breaks new ground, experimenting with novel and varied effects of color (he liked to use both purple and white) and, in a technique that dispenses with the laborious process of incision, creating new decorative schemes of great elegance.

A krater painted by EUPHRONIOS, one of the most forceful red-figure painters working near the end of the sixth century B.C., shows *Herakles Strangling Antaios* (FIG. **5-9**). Euphronios was among the first to devote himself seriously to the study of anatomy, and he was famous for this even in his own time. Here, he shows two male figures in a complicated wrestling pose. One figure is shown from the side, the other from the front. Euphronios attempts such radical experiments as the doubled-under leg of Antaios and the rendering of Antaios' face in white to suggest the pallor of impending death. He makes an effort to describe Herakles' and Antaios' straining, powerful bodies with painstaking attention to the musculature, and although he does not entirely succeed in producing a correct representation, his attempt to apply knowledge gained through observation of bodily action is significant.

EUTHYMIDES was a contemporary and competitor of Euphronios and, like him, an experimenter. As we can see from his picture of *Revelers*, done on an amphora (FIG. **5-10**), Euthymides is less concerned with anatomical description than with the problems of foreshortening and of showing the figures from different viewpoints. The fairly tipsy dancers, mightily

5-10 EUTHYMIDES, *Revelers*, from Vulci, c. 510–500 B.C. Approx. 24″ high. Staatliche Antikensammlungen und Glyptothek, Munich.

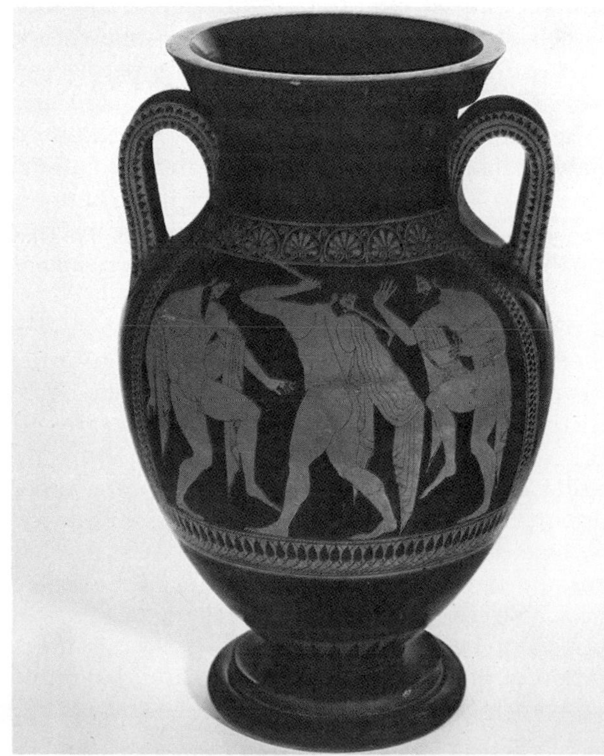

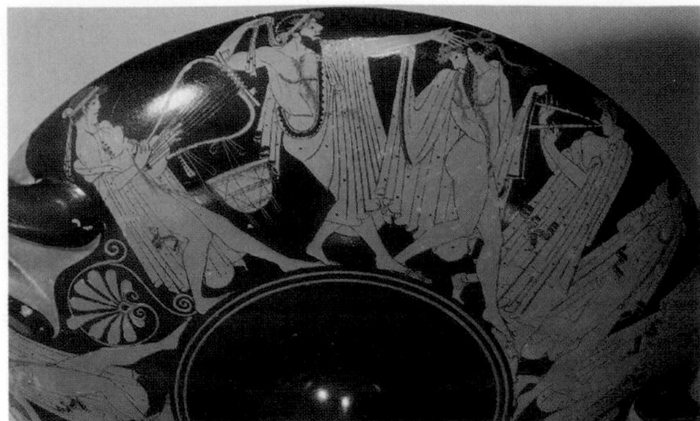

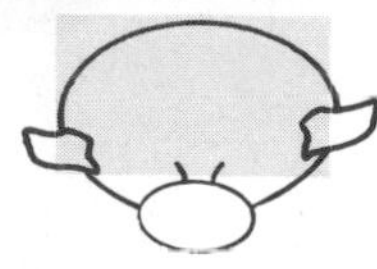

5-11 BRYGOS PAINTER, *Revelers* (detail from kylix), from Vulci, *c.* 490 B.C. Outline drawing at right indicates relation to whole vessel. Portion shown approx. 10″ wide, whole vessel approx. 13″ wide. Martin V. Wagner Museen der Universität, Würzburg.

enjoying themselves, are a rather popular subject on Late Archaic and Early Classical vases and celebrate the Hellenic sense of the comic that served as counterpoint to the Greek genius for tragic art in the drama. In this case, the drunken dancers theme gave Euthymides an opportunity to present the figures in informal motion and in fairly successful three-quarter back and front views. The turning and twisting of the figures indicate that the artist is beginning to conceive of them as three-dimensional volumes that have free mobility in a space deeper than the flat, two-dimensional surface of the picture plane—a significant departure from pre-Greek tradition. The maturing self-consciousness of the Greeks is shown not only in their concern for the human figure, but also, of course, in their consciousness of themselves as artists. They signed their names to their work and they were aware that they were doing new and revolutionary things as collaborators and rivals in a common professional enterprise. Euthymides, in an inscription on this amphora (FIG. 5-10), proclaimed with naïve pride: "Euphronios never did anything like it."

As revolutionary as Euphronios and Euthymides had been, the BRYGOS PAINTER (an anonymous artist who is named after the potter whose vases he decorated) took a significant step beyond them, around 490 B.C. Again the *Revelers* theme, with its gaily swinging movement, gave the experimenting artist his opportunity (FIG. **5-11**). For twenty-five hundred years, since the *Palette of Narmer* (FIG. 3-2), painted figures and figures in relief had advanced the *far* leg to show a stride—which, after all, is the best way if the torso is to be shown in front view with minimum distortion of the figure. Euthymides had broken this rule, advancing the *near* leg of a figure to show it in a three-quarter rear view (FIG. 5-10). But the Brygos Painter, for the first time, presents a striding figure with the near leg advanced and its shoulder turned diagonally toward the observer (see the two central figures in FIG. 5-11). The result is the first true *contrapposto* stance that we have. The figure is now understood as an acting unit, not merely an assemblage of parts; the problem of its engineering has been solved to the extent that it can be represented in convincing movement. At first, this matter may seem unimportant, but this apparently superficial detail may be the manifestation of an epoch-making change in the concept of what human beings perceive.

Sculpture

Trends in the development of sculpture in Greece are just as evident as those we have traced in vase painting, although much less sculpture survives. The earliest pieces go back to the beginning of the ninth century B.C. and consist of small-scale representations of animals (horses, oxen, deer, birds) and of human figures in various materials: copper, bronze, lead, ivory, and terra-cotta. Some of these figures were ornaments on larger objects, like vases and bronze tripods; others, found near ancient sanctuaries, were separate votive offerings. At Olympia, these figures seem to have been manufactured on the spot for sale to visitors to the shrines.

A bronze warrior from the Acropolis of Athens, dated to the late eighth century B.C. (FIG. **5-12**), shows all the clear simplifications of the Geometric period. The figure, a favorite type in Geometric art, is solid cast. Given its diminutive size, this would be the reasonable casting method; hollow casting, which was understood at this time, would not have saved much bronze. The warrior originally held a spear in one raised arm and a shield in the other, although both shield and spear are missing in most surviving examples of such figures. The rather carefully rendered head and face, with the large eyes and broad grimace attest to the fact that this figure is a late specimen of a type whose earlier examples had heads and faces that were little more than shapeless lumps. Moreover, the later body forms have become smoother, losing some of their former angularity, as if the artist were trying to rid himself of centuries-old conventions of Geometric figure representation before trying the new visual approach. The inspiration for these warrior statuettes may have come from Syria, but an important difference in the evolution of Greek sculpture should be noted: the Greek figures are represented nude, while the Syrian prototypes wear loincloths. As early as the eighth century B.C., the Greek instinct for the natural beauty of the human figure, which

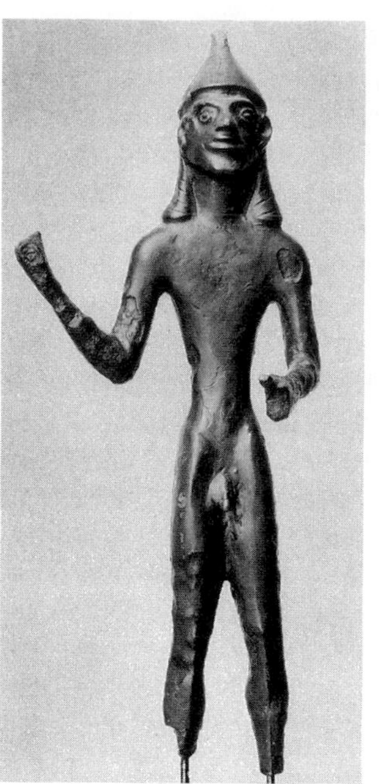

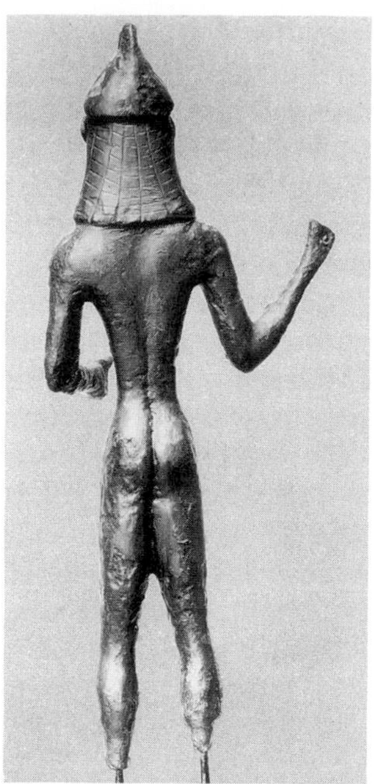

5-12 Geometric bronze warrior (front and back views), from the Acropolis, Athens, late eighth century B.C. Bronze, approx. 8″ high. National Archeological Museum, Athens.

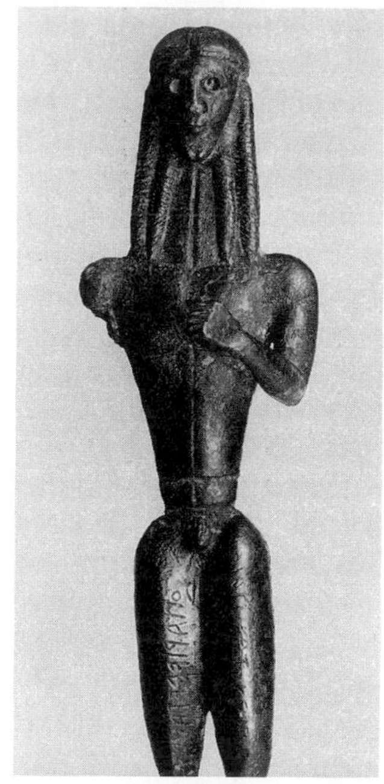

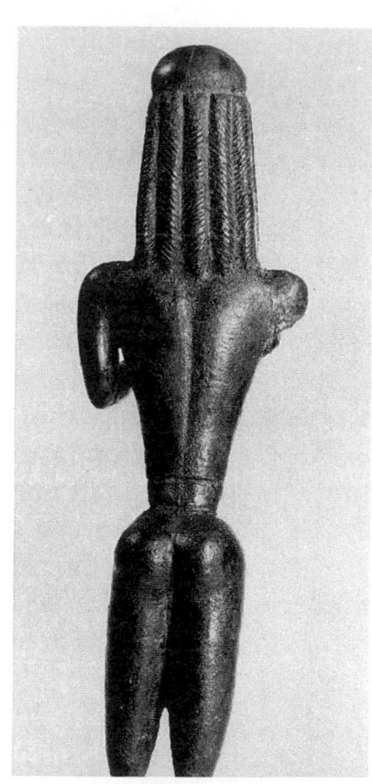

5-13 *Mantiklos "Apollo"* (front and back views), from Thebes, *c.* 680 B.C. Bronze, approx. 8″ high. Museum of Fine Arts, Boston (Francis Bartlett Fund).

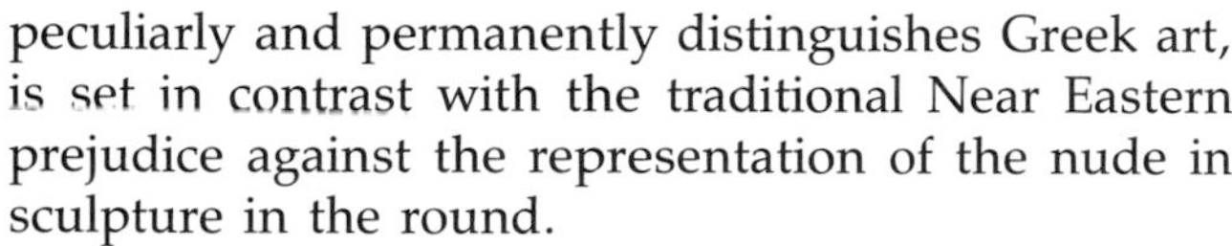

peculiarly and permanently distinguishes Greek art, is set in contrast with the traditional Near Eastern prejudice against the representation of the nude in sculpture in the round.

KOUROS AND KORE

A bronze figure of a youth from around 680 B.C. (FIG. **5-13**) can be dated to the beginning of the Archaic period; it is a small forerunner of the later *kouros* figures (see FIGS. 5-15 and 5-16). The silhouette remains essentially geometric, with a triangular torso, a narrow waist, and bulging thighs, but the forms have gained volume. The modeling of the pectoral muscles and the description of other anatomical details by means of incised lines show an incipient interest in the structure of the body.

Monumental, freestanding sculpture (life-size or larger) first appeared about 600 B.C., in the earlier stages of the Archaic period. Its rise was contemporary with the Orientalizing period in vase painting and was probably inspired by foreign sources, most likely Egypt and Mesopotamia, which were the only areas at that time that could show monumental sculpture in abundance. An early Greek example of this monumental, freestanding sculpture is the *Hera* from Samos (FIG. **5-14**), which is over six feet tall and has a cylindrical shape that could have been derived only from Mesopotamia (compare FIGS. 2-25 and 2-26). The goddess stands in a frontal pose, feet together, the right arm held tightly to the side, the left bent to the

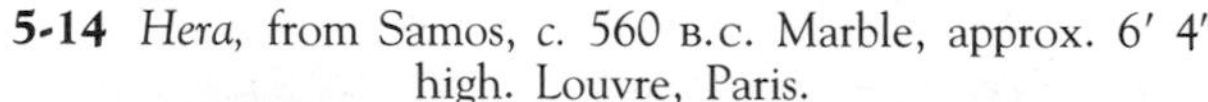

5-14 *Hera,* from Samos, *c.* 560 B.C. Marble, approx. 6′ 4″ high. Louvre, Paris.

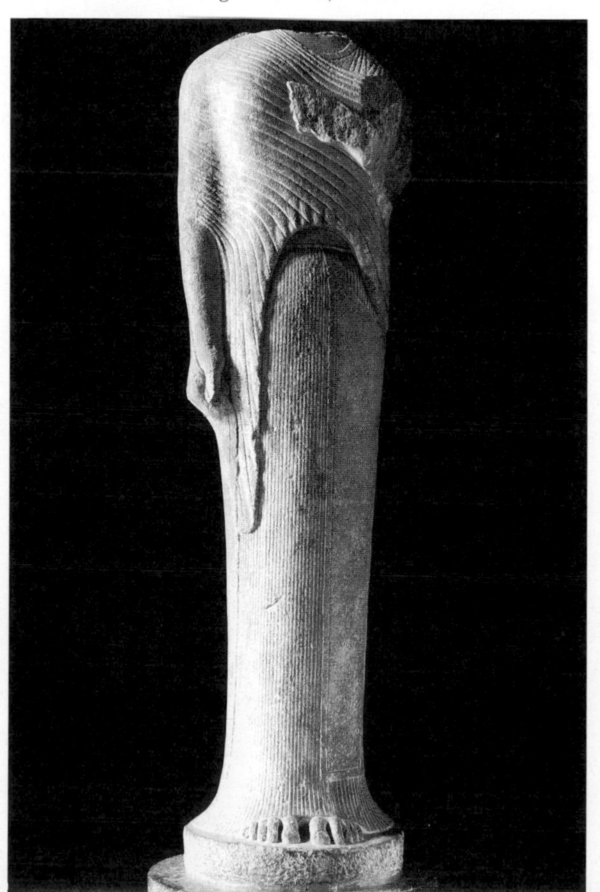

breast and probably originally holding some attribute, or symbol, of authority. Her form is that of a sheathed column as were those of the deities of Crete and Mycenae, but here the Greek artist displays an extraordinary sensitivity for surface ornamentation. The stability of the lower portions, where the striations of the *chiton* (or tunic) are placed against the plain surface of the *himation* (a kind of cape) contrasts with the movement in the upper portions, where the himation is drawn in gracefully curving folds around the delicate modeling of the swelling bosom.

The early kouros figures (FIGS. **5-15** and **5-16**) remind us of Egyptian statues. Some of these figures are of youths who are dedicated to a god and are apparently advancing into his presence; others are memorial statues that stand over the graves of noblemen. Thus, they are figures of men, not gods (not, as once thought, "Apollos"), and this glorification of men in monumental statues that commemorate their triumph and give them a godlike scale and presence is significant. The kouroi recall Egyptian statues in the pose (the left foot advanced), in the broad, square shoulders, and in the rigidly frontal and symmetrical design. Egyptian and Mesopotamian artists thought of the sculptured human body as a smooth envelope of stone, but Greek sculptors were interested in the structural parts and how they fit together.

The kouros from Tenea (FIG. 5-15) shows us characteristic traits of the figure type, although the kouroi differ markedly from each other. Because the figures were freestanding, without the Egyptian stone slab for support, most kouroi have been found broken at

5-15 Kouros from Tenea, c. 570 B.C. Marble, approx. 60″ high. Staatliche Antikensammlungen und Glyptothek, Munich.

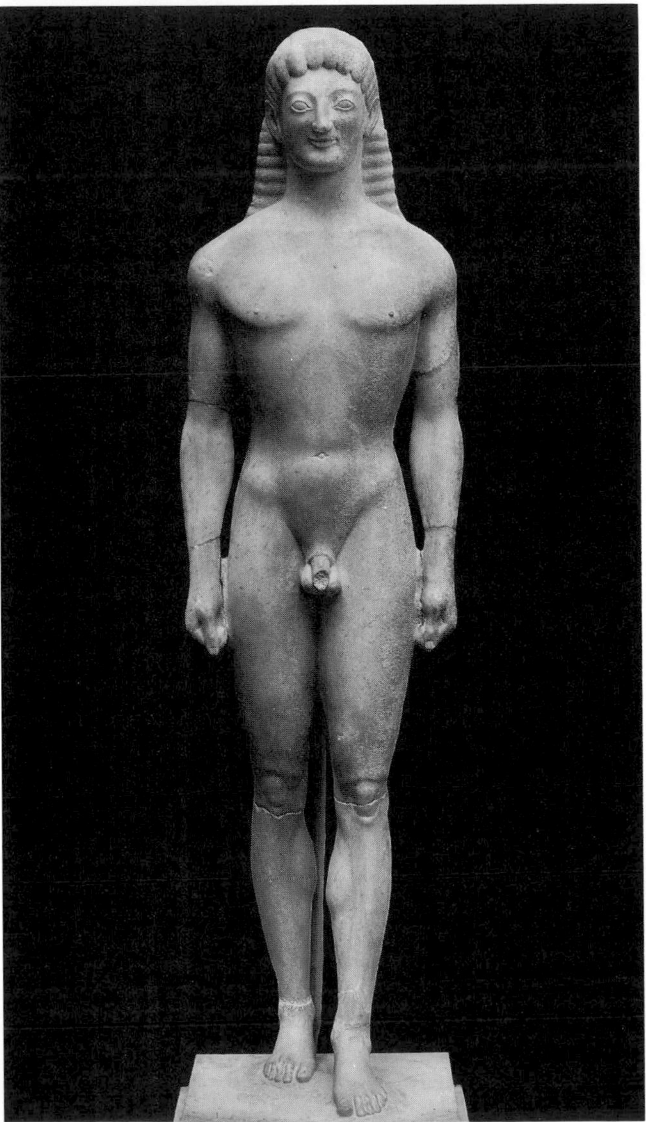

5-16 *Kroisos* (kouros), from Anavysos, c. 540–515 B.C. Marble, approx. 6′ 4″ high. National Archeological Museum, Athens.

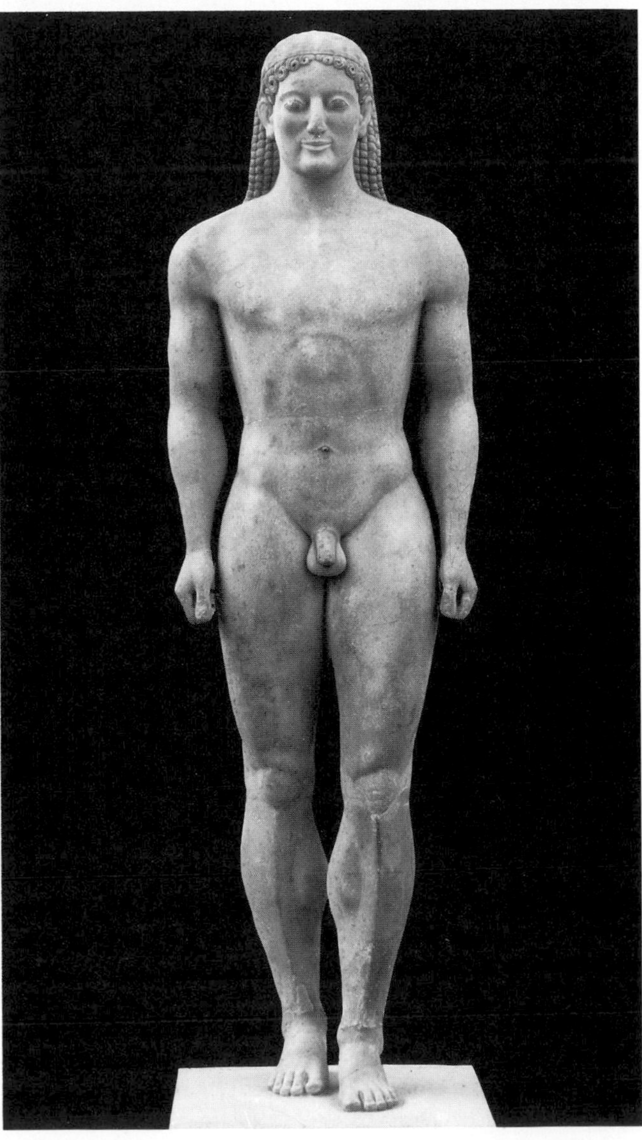

the ankles. Obviously, the Greek sculptor was not aiming for Egyptian permanence as much as for fidelity to appearance, and one of the first steps toward that goal was the liberation of the figure from the original block of stone. On the broad planes of the figure, anatomical details are carefully modeled, as we see in the chest and the knee joints. The head is geometrically simplified into flat planes: the eyes are large and protruding, and the nose, mouth, ears, and headdress are all highly stylized attributes of the almost cubic mass of the head. Although still almost provincial Egyptian, the Tenea kouros is quite un-Egyptian in its nudity and in its more dynamic, half-striding stance. Moreover, this figure is slender and elegant, with the alert, elastic physique of a sprinter. Description of the anatomy by incised line, typical of the earlier models, has been given up, and the torso, thighs, and calves are modeled in the full round with ever-closer approximation of anatomical truth.

With the *Kroisos* from Anavysos (FIG. 5-16), we come to the verge of a breakthrough similar to the one we have seen in vase painting. According to an inscription on its base, the statue is a funerary monument of a youth, Kroisos, who died a hero's death in battle. Where the anatomy of the Tenea figure is still somewhat generalized, here it becomes specific and accurate. The artist not only understands the structural parts of the figure and their natural relationship and how to represent their surfaces by modeling the stone, but he is able to give us what amounts to a *portrait* of the body, a likeness of a particular physique—in this case, that of a muscular wrestler, heavier and more massive than the taut, spare Tenea figure. It is noteworthy that the Greeks began their monumental sculpture with portraits not of the head but of the body. This "bodiliness" of Greek sculpture persisted for centuries until it became lost in a realism that compelled the sculptor to use illusional devices more appropriate to painting.

What we might think of as companion figures to the *kouroi* (youths) are the draped *korai* (maidens), contemporaneous with the former and manifesting in their own style similar features of concept and design. The *Peplos Kore* (FIG. **5-17**), contemporary with the *Kroisos*, is one of numerous figures found on the Acropolis of Athens, thrown down by the Persians during their sack of the city in 480 B.C. The purpose of the korai is obscure, but they may have been votive figures attending the deities in a kind of permanent and perpetual ritual. In contrast with earlier types, the face of this kore is more expressively modeled; the chin, cheeks, and corners of the mouth are subtly planed. The great eyes, originally with painted lids, may have been intended to have hypnotic power: we think back to the ancient head from Warka (FIG. 2-15).

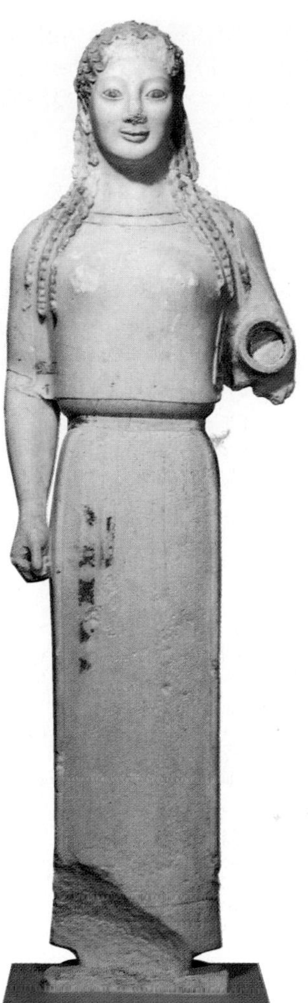

5-17 *Peplos Kore,* from the Acropolis, Athens, c. 530 B.C. Marble, approx. 48" high. Acropolis Museum, Athens.

The missing left arm was extended, a break from the frontal compression of the arms at the sides in Egyptian statues. The body itself is modeled with a soft smoothness that takes account of the figure beneath the drapery, much like the earlier *Hera* from Samos (FIG. 5-14) but anatomically more realistic. Traces of paint may be seen on parts of the figure; all Greek stone statues were painted, the powder-white of Classical statues being an error of modern interpretation. But the Greeks did not smear their statues garishly with bright colors, indifferent to their place and effect; only the decisive parts, such as the eyes, lips, hair, edges of drapery, and other decorative details were painted to provide accents and contrast with the soft color of the marble itself, which was waxed and polished. The whole purpose of coloring was to make the statue more lifelike, more convincing as a kind of person confronting visitors to the shrines of the Acropolis. The painting was done in the very durable technique of *encaustic,* in which pigment is mixed with wax and applied to the surface while hot. This

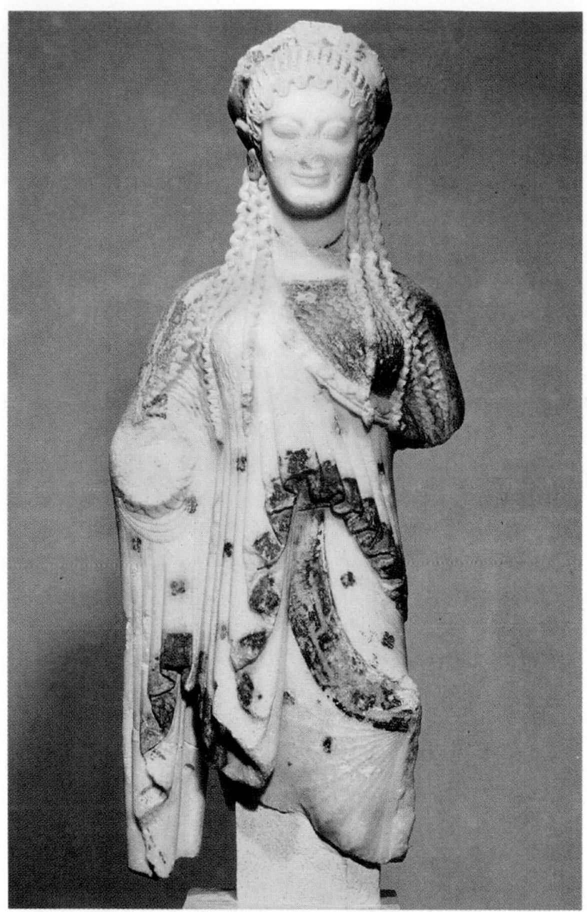

5-18 Kore from Chios (?), c. 510 B.C. Marble, approx. 21½″ high. Acropolis Museum, Athens.

method was widely used in ancient wall painting and on wooden panels, as well as in the embellishment of statues.

The preservation of the color of many of the kore statues is a result of the Athenians' use of fragments of broken statues and temples as rubble fill in rebuilding the temples and retaining walls of the Acropolis after the Persian destruction. In this fill, modern archeologists have found works such as the kore from Chios (?) (FIG. **5-18**), which had been buried there since 480 B.C. The luxurious gowns of the korai figures may be evidence that they were made in Ionia, where the wealthy Greek states cultivated the Oriental taste for rich ornamentation in both life and art. Ionian influence was strong in Athens during the Archaic period, and Ionian fashions, featuring the intricately folded, chic chiton, interested not only women but sculptors, who found in the representation of delicate texture and fold a peculiarly difficult challenge. For some time, sculptors seemed to delight in working out the complexities of the pleats and folds made by the thin, soft material and were content to let the matter remain one of decoration rather than structure. At this point, although sculptors must have learned much about the movement of a surface independent of the body beneath it, the kore figures remained frontal and basically unchanged for a considerable period. Although there were slight changes, the scheme of this example was repeated over and over until the end of the Archaic period. The attractive problem of surface texture appears to have deflected the sculptors of the kore figures from larger issues.

The larger issues involve not the draped female figure but the nude kouros figure type that we have been describing; at least, the break with age-old sculptural traditions takes place in connection with the kouroi. The female nude does not appear in ancient sculpture, with some minor exceptions, until the fourth century B.C. We will see that its appearance in Greek art accompanies changes of a fundamental kind in Greek culture and morals. The Greek artist found early, as any student of the living model in art has found, that the male figure is much more revealing of human anatomical structure. Nude male models could be observed in exercises and at the games; we know that in the Dorian world, of which Sparta was the capital, the Greek artist would also have been able to observe female models, yet the male figure was given priority. By the time of Plato, nudity in the context of athletics was commonplace in the Greek world, and the prejudice against it could be regarded as barbarous—that is, merely a prejudice of the non-Hellenic Near East. In Plato's *Republic,* Socrates remarked:

> Not long ago . . . the Hellenes were of the opinion, which is still generally received among the barbarians, that the sight of a naked man was ridiculous and improper. . . . But experience showed that to let all things be uncovered was far better than to cover them up.

Certainly by about 520 B.C., the male nude must have been familiar enough for the artist to construct a convincingly real image from the observation of it. The establishment of this new convention, the propriety of the nude, implied the setting aside of the three-thousand-year-old convention of the pre-Greek world that inhibited the study of the structure of the human body as given to the eye, probably because nudity was the badge of slavery.

In the *Kroisos* figure (FIG. 5-16), the independent elements of the body are sufficiently described. The question now becomes one of how the elements work together. From the time of King Narmer, sculptors had attempted more or less successful approximations of the human figure with enumerated parts, the attitudes universally stiff and immobile. What can put these parts into motion? The answer appears in a Late Archaic or Early Transitional figure found in the Acropolis rubble that dates from just before the Persian destruction. The statue, which must have been the consequence of a mind deliberating on what had already been done, is called the *Kritios Boy* (FIG. **5-19**), after its presumed sculptor. It is not in action, but stands at rest; that is to say, it *really* stands at rest, not merely in a stiff-legged pose or a pose bound to a block. The secret of this new and radical naturalness lies in the artist's knowledge of the principle of *weight shift*, the shifting of position of the main parts of the body around the vertical, but flexible, axis of the spine. The shifting of the human body in life never takes place in a rigid stiff-legged manner; indeed, we laugh at or are in terror of the science-fiction monster that moves in this ponderous, mechanical way. Rather, when we change place and move, the elastic musculoskeletal structure of our bodies dictates a harmonious, smooth motion of all the elements of the body. Greek artists were the first to grasp this fact, and the artist of the *Kritios Boy* was the first to represent it. The youth turns his head only very slightly away from the central axis. The slight dip to the shoulders and the hips indicates the shifting of weight onto the left leg; the right leg is at ease. (One can easily assume this pose and the contrasting flat-footed poses of the earlier kouros statues.) Once the principle of weight shift has been realized, all motion of the human figure is possible in the world of representation—not simply in terms of the signs of motion evident in simple gesture, but also in terms of the motion of the whole body as we see *and* experience it. After the *Kritios Boy*, Greek sculpture rapidly passes through the possibilities of the figure understood as having its own physical principle of motion, a principle revealed to the eye in ordinary optical experience and confirmed by the observer's own physical sense of motion.

5-19 *Kritios Boy* (front and side views), from the Acropolis, Athens, *c.* 480 B.C. Marble, approx. 34" high. Acropolis Museum, Athens.

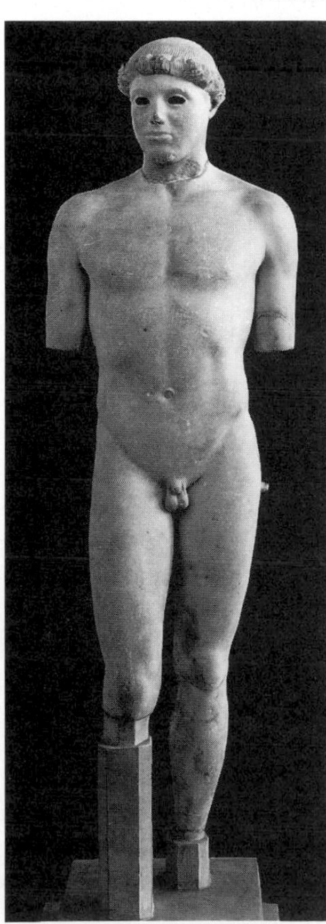

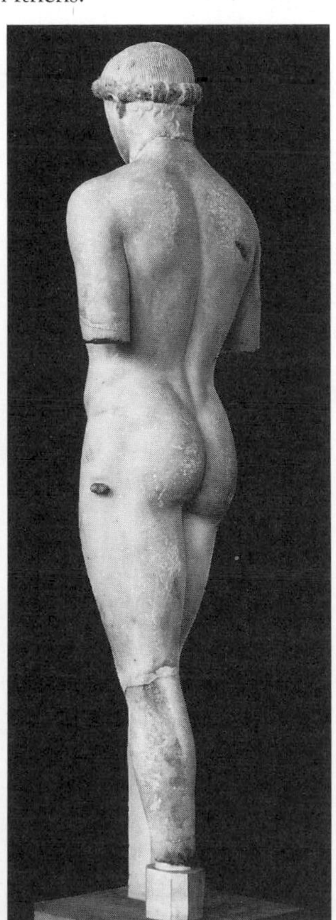

So far, we have been considering sculpture apart from architecture. But the decoration of buildings, especially temples, with sculpture, both in relief and in the round, offered the Greek sculptor a major opportunity. Because sculpture was applied only to very specific and limited areas of temples, it is necessary first to become acquainted with the basic structure of the various buildings that it adorned.

Architecture

Greek architecture and its Roman and Renaissance descendants and hybrids are almost as familiar to us as modern architecture. The so-called Greek revival instituted by European architects in the late eighteenth century brought about a wide diffusion of the Greek architectural style; official public buildings (court houses, banks, city halls, legislative chambers), designed for impressive formality, especially imitated the architecture of Classicism, which was fundamentally Greek in inspiration. The ancient Greeks were industrious builders, even though their homes were unpretentious places, they had no monarchs to house royally until Hellenistic times, and they performed state religious rites in the open. Their significant buildings began primarily as simple shrines to protect the statues of their gods. More and more attention was lavished on these structures over time. Eventually, the belief may have arisen that the qualities of the god were embodied in the buildings themselves. Figure sculpture played its part in this construction program, partly to embellish the protective building, partly to tell something about the deity symbolized within, and partly as a votive offering. But the building itself also was conceived as sculpture, abstract in form and possessing the power of sculpture to evoke human responses. The commanding importance of the sculptured temple, its inspiring function in public life, was emphasized in its elevated site, often on a hill above the city (the *acropolis*). As

Aristotle stipulated: "The site should be a spot seen far and wide, which gives due elevation to virtue and towers over the neighborhood." And the reverent awe that must have been attached to the temple and to the genius of its founders later was echoed by Plato: "Gods and temples are not easily instituted, and to establish them rightly is the work of a mighty intellect."

Although still a matter of ardent debate, one theory holds that the earliest temples were made of wood, and that these wooden forms were in time translated into the more permanent materials of limestone and sometimes marble. Marble was expensive, but mountains of it were available: bluish-white stone came from Hymettus, just east of Athens; glittering white stone, particularly adapted for carving, was brought from Pentelicus, northeast of the city; and from the islands of the Aegean, Paros in particular, marble of varying quantities and qualities was supplied.

In its plan, the Greek temple discloses a close affinity with the Mycenaean megaron and, even in its most elaborate form, it retains the latter structure's basic simplicity (FIG. **5-20**): a single or double room (the *naos*) with no windows and one door (two for a double naos) and with (**a**) a portico with two columns between the extended walls (columns *in antis*), or (**b**) a colonnade across the front *(prostyle),* or (**c**) a colonnade across both front and back *(amphiprostyle),* or any of these plans surrounded by (**d** and **e**) a single *(peripteral)* or (**f**) a double *(dipteral)* colonnade. What strikes the eye first in the Greek scheme, after what has been seen of the architecture of the ancient Near East, is its remarkable order, compactness, and symmetry, in contrast, say, to the relative irregularity of the Egyptian temple. The difference lies in the Greeks' sense of proportion and in their effort to achieve ideal forms in terms of regular numerical relationships and the rules of geometry.

We can discern in the plans a kind of development from quite simple to more complex units, without, however, any fundamental change in the nature of the units or of their grouping. Classical Greek architecture, like classical music, has a simple core theme from which a series of complex, but always quite in-

5-20 Six representative plans of the Greek temple: (**a**) a temple *in antis,* in which the portico is formed by the projecting side walls of the naos with two columns set between their ends *(antae)*; (**b**) Temple B at Selinus, Sicily, a *prostyle* temple, in which the columns stand in front of the naos and extend to its width; (**c**) Temple of Athena Nike on the Acropolis at Athens, an *amphiprostyle* temple, in which the prostyle plan has a porch added at the rear; (**d**) Temple of Hera at Olympia and (**e**) Temple of Aphaia at Aegina, *peripteral* temples, in which a single colonnade surrounds the naos; and (**f**) Temple of Apollo at Didyma, near Miletus, a *dipteral* temple, in which two colonnades surround the naos. *(Drawings are not to scale.)*

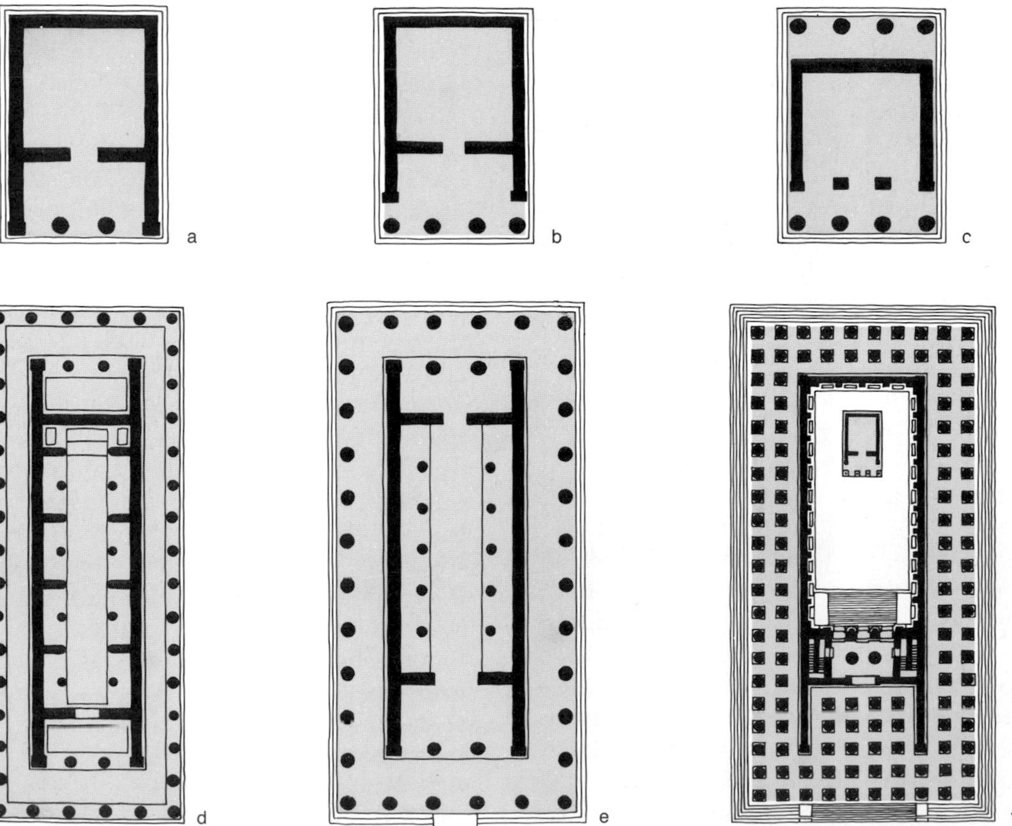

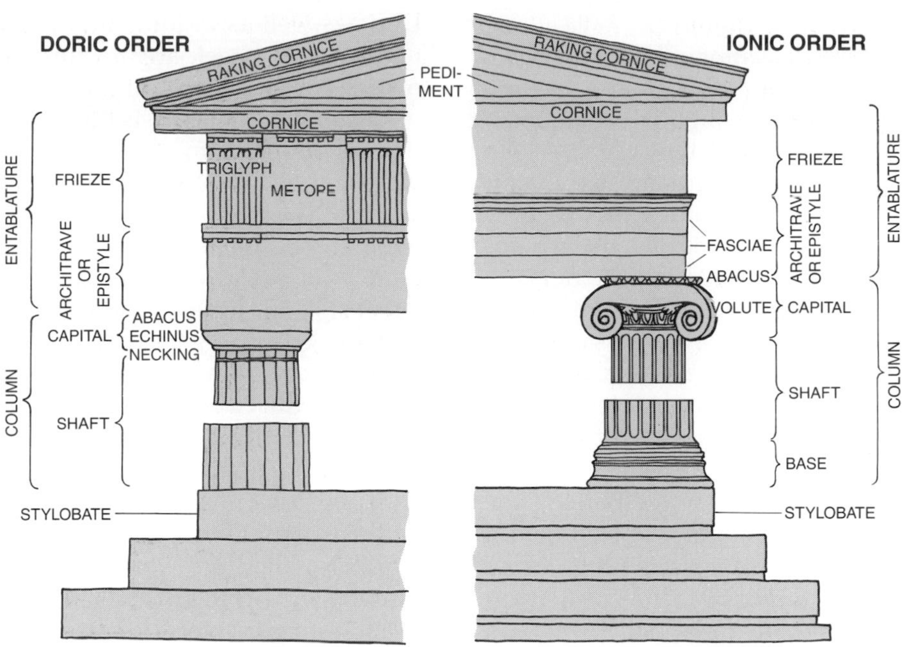

5-21 Doric and Ionic orders. (After I. H. Grinnell.)

telligible, variations is developed. And, to change the analogy, the development of the temple scheme is like that other great invention of the Greeks, geometry, in which theorems, propositions, and their corollaries are deduced from a simple original set of axioms. The Greeks' insistence on proportional order guided the experiments with the proportions of temple plans. The earlier, Archaic temples tended to be long and narrow (FIG. 5-20d), with the proportion of the ends to the sides roughly expressible as 1:3. Late Classical and Hellenistic plans approached but rarely had a proportion of exactly 1:2, with Classical temples tending to be a little longer than twice their width (FIG. 5-20e) and Hellenistic temples tending to be a little shorter (FIG. 5-20f). Proportion in architecture and sculpture, and harmony in music, were much the same to the Greek mind and reflected and embodied the cosmic order, just as did the rationally pursued "good life."

The elevation of a Greek building is described in terms of the platform, column, and *entablature* (FIG. **5-21**); this combination and relationship of three units is called an *order*. The three orders developed by Greek builders are differentiated partly by details but chiefly by the relative proportions of the parts. Each order served different purposes and embodied different meanings. The earliest of the Greek architectural orders to be formulated were the *Doric*, of mainland Greece, and the *Ionic*, of Asia Minor and the Aegeans (FIG. 5-21). The *Corinthian* order followed much later.

The columns, which rest on a platform *(stylobate)*, have two or three parts, depending on the order: the *shaft*, which is marked with vertical channels *(fluting)*; the *capital*; and (in the Ionic and Corinthian orders) the *base*. As the shaft rises, its diameter decreases gradually, giving the profile a subtle curve *(entasis)*; the top (in the Doric) is marked with one or several horizontal lines *(necking)* that furnish the transition to the capital. The capital has two elements, the lower of which (the *echinus*) varies with the order: in the Doric, it is convex and cushionlike; in the Ionic, it is small and supports a bolster ending in scroll-like spirals (the *volutes*); and in the Corinthian, it is shaped like an inverted bell and is decorated with a design of stylized acanthus leaves. The upper element, present in all orders, is a flat, square block (the *abacus*) that provides the immediate support for the entablature. The entablature has three parts: the *architrave* or *epistyle*, the main weight-bearing and weight-distributing element; the *frieze*; and the *cornice*, a molded horizontal projection. In some buildings, the third part, with two sloping *(raking)* cornices, forms a triangle that enframes the *pediment*. The architrave is usually subdivided into three horizontal bands *(fasciae)* in the Ionic and Corinthian orders. The frieze is subdivided into *triglyphs* and *metopes* in the Doric order and is left open in the Ionic to provide a continuous field for reliefs.

The Doric order is massive in appearance, its sturdy columns firmly planted on the stylobate. Compared with the weighty and severe Doric, the Ionic order seems light, airy, and much more decorative. Its columns are more slender and rise from molded bases. The Doric flutings meet in sharp ridges *(arrises),* but the Ionic ridges are flat (*fillets*). The most obvious differences among the three orders are, of course, in the capitals: the Doric, severely plain; the Ionic and Corinthian, highly ornamental.

In ancient times, the Doric and Ionic orders were contrasted as masculine and feminine. The Corinthian order was not developed until the fifth century B.C., when it appeared inside the temple, like a natural form growing in the darkness of the interior. On the exteriors of buildings, however, it was not widely used until Roman times. Since the Renaissance and until about two generations ago, much of the architecture in the Western world was considered to be in essence the display of the refined beauty of these architectural orders.

According to one theory, many of the parts of the Doric order seem to be translations into stone of an earlier timber architecture. Pausanias, writing in the second century A.D., noted that in the even-then ancient Temple of Hera at Olympia (FIG. 5-20d), a wooden column was still in place; the others had been replaced by stone columns. It has been inferred, from the varying proportions of these columns, that the wooden columns were replaced at different times, probably as the wood of the original columns rotted. One feature of the Doric order, the organization of the frieze into triglyphs and metopes, can be explained best as a translation from the wooden original into stone. The triglyphs most likely derived from the ends of crossbeams that rested on the main horizontal support, the architrave. The metopes would then correspond to the voids between the beam ends in the original wooden structure.

Sculptural ornament, which played an important part in the design of the temple, was concentrated on the upper part of the building, in the frieze and pediments. The sculpture was gaily painted in red and blue, with touches of green, yellow, black, and perhaps a little gold, and was usually applied only to those parts of the building that had no structural function or that suggested a former structural function. This is true particularly of the Doric style, in which decorative sculpture was applied only to the "voids" of the metopes and of the pediment. Ionic builders, less severe in this respect, were willing to decorate the entire frieze and sometimes even the lower drums of columns. Occasionally, they replaced their columns with female figures *(caryatids),* something the Doric builder probably would not have done. Using color, the designer could bring out more clearly the relationships of the structural parts, soften the glitter of the stone at specific points, and provide a background to set off the figures.

Although color was used for emphasis and to mitigate what might have seemed too bare a simplicity (in Doric as well as in Ionic buildings), the primary dependence in Greek architecture, as in Greek mathematics, science, and philosophy, was on the setting of clear limits. This thesis had to begin with the axiom that the limits themselves must never be encroached on, must always define, and must never be vague. The three Greek architectural orders just described were embodiments of codified limits that appeared plainly to the eye as functioning realities. To the Greeks, it was unthinkable to use surfaces in the way that the Egyptians used their gigantic columns—as fields for complicated ornamentation. The very building itself, the Greek temple as given to the eye, must have the clarity of a Euclidean demonstration. This principle is borne out not only by its plan, elevation, and function-enhancing ornamentation, but also by its "dry-jointed" construction (construction without mortar), which provides evidence that Greek architects looked on their temples not as "buildings" but as monumental pieces of sculpture.

The placement of the building strengthened its sculptural aspect. Unlike Egyptian temples, Greek temples faced outward. Rites were performed at altars in front of the temple, and the building itself served to house the cult statue and perhaps trophies and treasure. Private cults were frowned on, and public ritual prevailed. Thus, it was on the exterior of the building and its surfaces that the architect generally concentrated all efforts at making the temple a suitable monument to the deity. The studied visual relationships of solids and voids, of light and shade in the colonnades, and the lighter accents of the entablature made a sculptural form out of the rectangular mass of the temple. The history of Greek architecture is the history of Greek artists' unflagging efforts to express the form of the temple in its most satisfactory (that is to say, what they believed to be perfect) proportions.

The experiment in proportions can be followed rather easily if we begin with the Archaic Doric architecture of the Greek colonies, especially in Sicily and southern Italy, for it is here that the best-preserved examples of Archaic temples are found. (In examining Greek architecture, it is useful to keep in mind the development of the human figure in Greek painting and in sculpture; the architectural events are not only contemporaneous, but reflect a similar concern with proportions.)

The "Basilica" at Paestum, south of Naples, dates from about 550 B.C., and is a typical example of Archaic Doric style (FIG. **5-22**). Called the "Basilica" after a Roman building type that early investigators felt it resembled, we now know that this structure was dedicated to Hera. It is referred to as Hera I in current literature, to distinguish it from the later Temple of

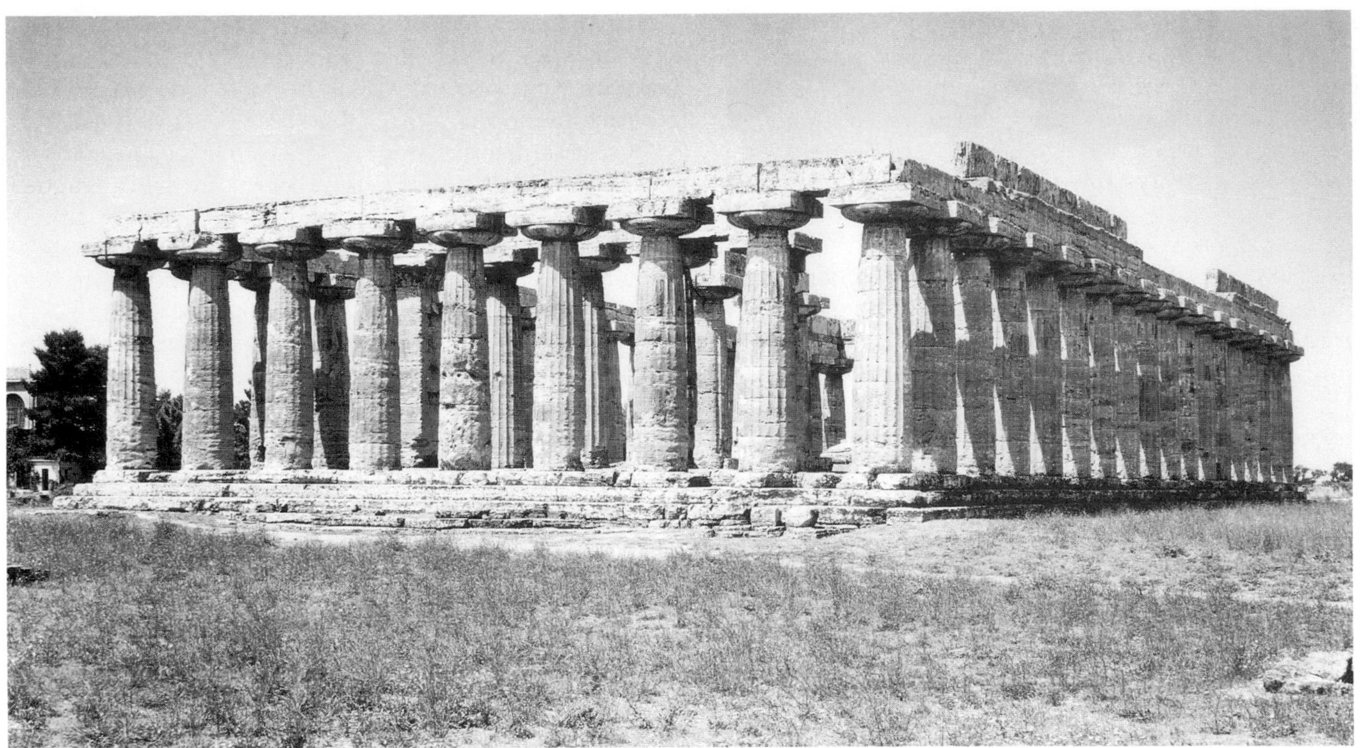

5-22 The "Basilica," Paestum, Italy, *c.* 550 B.C.

Hera II, which stands nearby. The misnomer is partly due to the building's plan (FIG. **5-23**), which differs from that of most other Greek temples. The unusual feature, which is found in only a few very early Archaic temples, but which here has survived well into the sixth century B.C., is the central row of columns that divides the naos into two aisles. Placing columns underneath the ridgepole might seem to be the logical way to provide interior support for the roof structure, but it resulted in several disadvantages. Among these was the fact that this interior arrangement allowed no place for a central cult statue. Also, the peripteral colonnade, in order to correspond with the interior, had to have an odd number of columns across the building's façade. This, in turn, ruled out a central doorway through which the cult statue could be viewed.

5-23 Plan of the "Basilica."

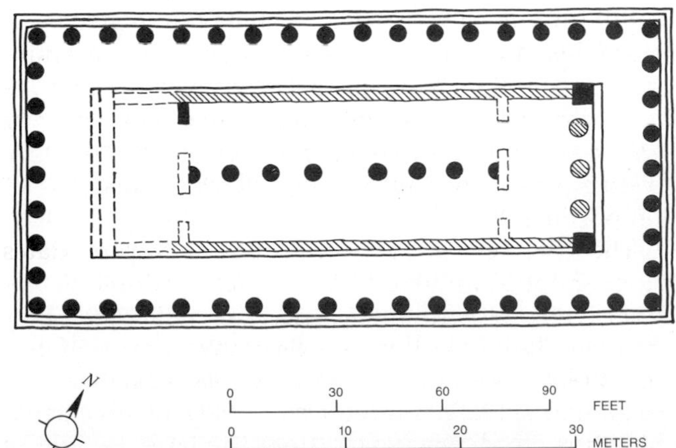

The elevation of the temple is characterized by heavy, closely spaced columns with pronounced entasis and large, bulky, pillowlike capitals. These columns carry a high and massive entablature that makes them seem proportionately squat. In later Doric structures, these parts of the order gradually will be adjusted until a lighter and taller combination is achieved. One structural reason, perhaps, for the heaviness of the design and the narrowness of the spans between the columns might be that the Archaic builders, uncertain of the strength of their materials, were trying to provide a broad margin of safety. A detail of the "Basilica" colonnade (FIG. **5-24**) shows the extreme spread of the cushion capitals and exaggeration of the supporting surface in relation to the spans bridged by the architrave. The columns are built up of separate, dry-jointed "drums," fitted with square metal plugs to prevent turning as well as shifting. The whole temple was of this typically Greek construction, the blocks of stone in a horizontal course being held together by metal cramps, while those of different courses, one above the other, were joined vertically by metal dowels. Through the "Basilica" colonnade can be seen the nearby Temple of

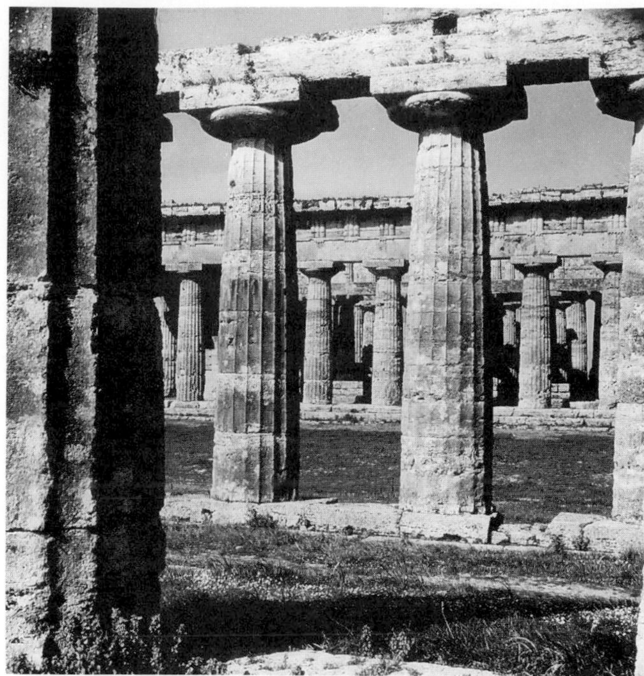

5-24 "Basilica" colonnade, with view of the Temple of Hera II beyond.

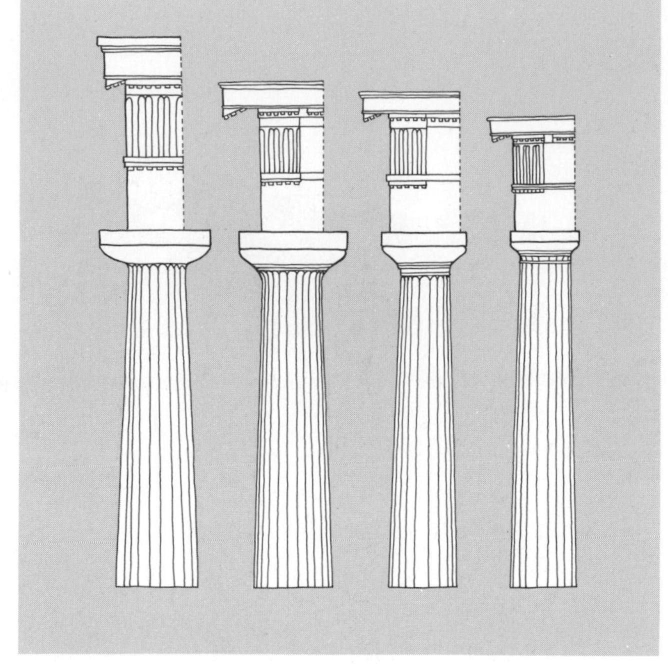

5-25 Evolution of Doric order proportions, Archaic to Classical. *(Examples are not drawn to same scale.)*

Hera II, which was built eighty to ninety years later with columns of strikingly different proportions from those of the "Basilica."

The diagram showing the evolution in the proportions of the Doric order from Archaic to Classical (FIG. **5-25**) emphasizes the thesis that Greek art evolved in conjunction with a certain logic, whether in its figurative or its architectural forms, that moved toward a conclusion that was as satisfactory as it was true. Plato, in speaking of the imitative arts, declared the degree of their truth or rightness to be determined by the proportionality of their elements. If they were to be judged at all, they must be judged by the "standard of truth, and by no other whatever." In this diagram, we see the architects working toward proportions that could be thought of as "true" and final. Some of the earliest columns (not shown) were extremely slender, under massive capitals. The shafts soon thickened to the shape of the "Basilica" type, as the builders searched for a better relationship between the shaft and the capital. From then on, the forms were constantly refined, the shafts becoming more slender, the entasis subtler, the capitals smaller, and the entablature lighter. The final Classical proportions were considered to be ideal ones, beyond which further refinement was impossible.

The Temple of Hera II at Paestum (FIG. **5-26**) dates from about 460 B.C. Although the forms have been refined, the columns are still massive and closely spaced. This temple was erected at a time when, on the Greek mainland, the Doric order had already achieved its Classical proportions (as early as 490 B.C.) in the Temple of Aphaia at Aegina. There was a considerable time lag between developments on the mainland and their adoption by the colonies in Italy and Sicily, so that the colonial architecture exhibits the usual provincial conservatism characteristic of styles distant from their source of inspiration in the cultural capital. The plan and section of the Temple of Hera II (FIG. **5-27**) show an improvement on the earlier Paestum temple. The even number of façade columns, the single central doorway and the open middle aisle of the now three-aisled naos combined to permit the placement of the cult statue on the central axis of the temple, where it could be seen from the outside. These changes in plan were made possible by a different interior roof-support system, which here consists of two rows of small Doric columns flanking the middle aisle. Each of the two double-tiered rows is made up of two sets of columns, a small one standing on a stone course supported by a larger set of columns below. This arrangement was standard where Doric columns were used to support the roof. The reason for this may have been that a single row of large columns, as in the "Basilica," would produce a distortion of scale and look oppressively out of

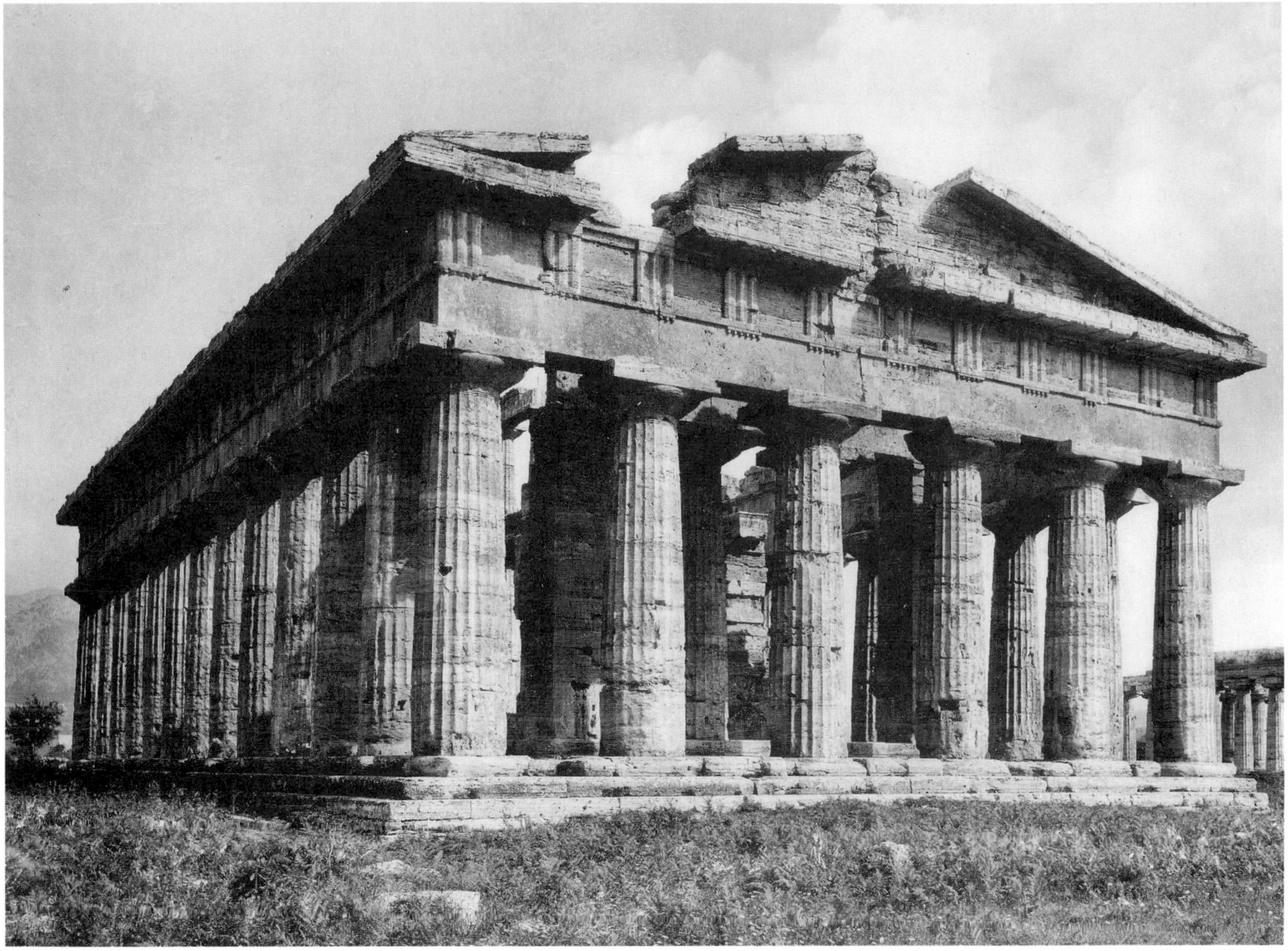

5-26 Temple of Hera II at Paestum, Italy, *c.* 460 B.C.

5-27 Plan *(left)* and section *(right)* of the Temple of Hera II at Paestum. (After Sir Banister Fletcher.)

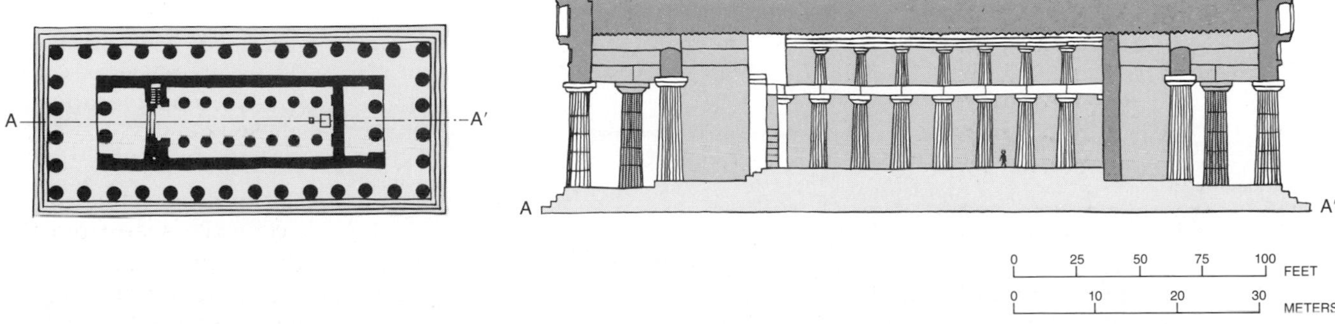

proportion inside the relatively small naos. Later, the support problem was solved by using Ionic or Corinthian columns in the interior; they were taller than the Doric ones in relation to their diameters.

One of the earliest Ionic buildings in Greece is the Treasury of the Siphnians at Delphi, constructed about 530 B.C. (FIG. **5-28**). Although it has no Ionic columns (the supporting function is assumed by luxuriously carved caryatids, whose style and drapery match those of the Ionian kore of the Athenian Acropolis shown in FIG. 5-18), the Treasury has the identifying Ionic feature—the continuous frieze—that appears here as part of a heavy Archaic entablature. The caryatids, with their elaborate costume and

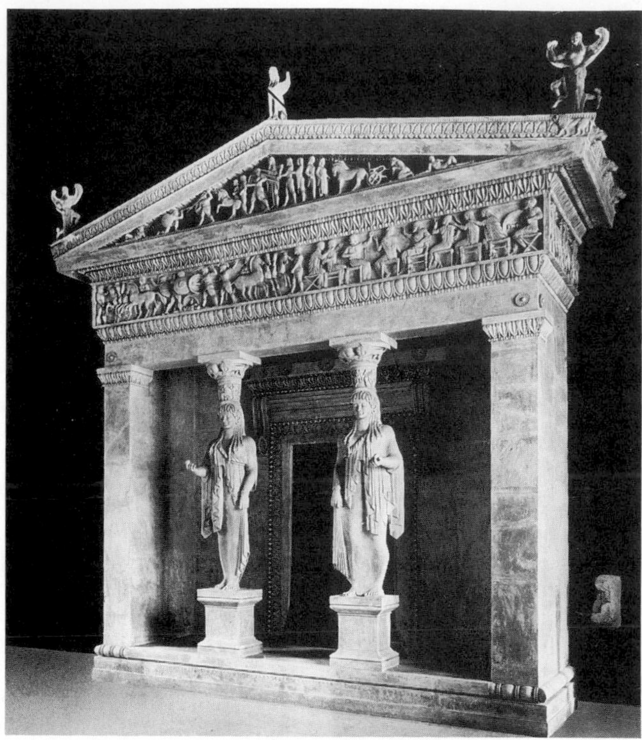

5-28 Treasury of the Siphnians from the Sanctuary of Apollo at Delphi, *c.* 530 B.C. Archeological Museum, Delphi. (Façade reconstructed.)

very irregular silhouettes, would never have fitted into a context of Doric architecture, with its severity of line and disdain of ornament.

ARCHITECTURAL SCULPTURE

We have noted already that decorative sculpture was applied only to those parts of a temple that had no evident structural function—the frieze and the pediment. The caryatids are exceptional, but their use is fairly rare. Ordinarily, the weight-carrying columns and the weight-distributing architraves were not decorated, although war trophies may have been hung on the blank Doric architrave. In the Doric order, only the metopes bore relief sculpture. Some may argue that the fluting of columns is a form of decoration, but, in fact, the fluting simply explains and emphasizes the form and function of the column, stressing its verticality. It also exhibits the column's rotundity, for when the sunlight strikes sharply on the shaft (FIG. 5-24), the fluting throws numerous shadows of graduated width and darkness that lead the eye around the shaft in a series of graded steps, making the effect of roundness more evident. In the nonfluted column, the sunlight creates a single, indistinct line separating the light and dark sides.

The Greek architectural sculptor faced a problem similar to that of the Greek vase painter: how to adjust the image to the surface on which it is placed. This is not apparent in the frieze from the Treasury of the Siphnians (FIG. **5-29**), for here the sculptor has a continuous blank zone to manage and can arrange the figures in a simple file, their heads on the same level, each filling a unit of space of approximately the same dimension. This is a good example of the formalizing effect of architectural line on figurative composition, just as the surface of the ceramic vessel imposed its necessities on the vase painter, encouraging simplicity and elegance of style. In fact, a stylistic resemblance exists between the Siphnian figures and such contemporary painting as that of the Andokides Painter (FIG. 5-8). But an awkward space like that of the triangular pediment of the Archaic Temple of Artemis (early sixth century B.C.) on the island of Corfu

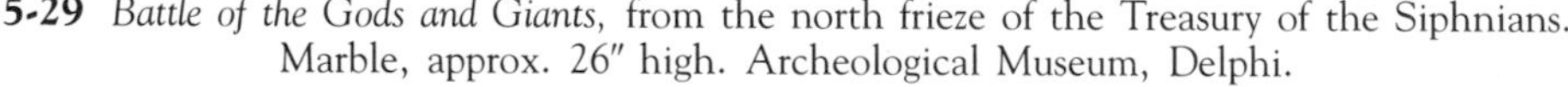

5-29 *Battle of the Gods and Giants,* from the north frieze of the Treasury of the Siphnians. Marble, approx. 26″ high. Archeological Museum, Delphi.

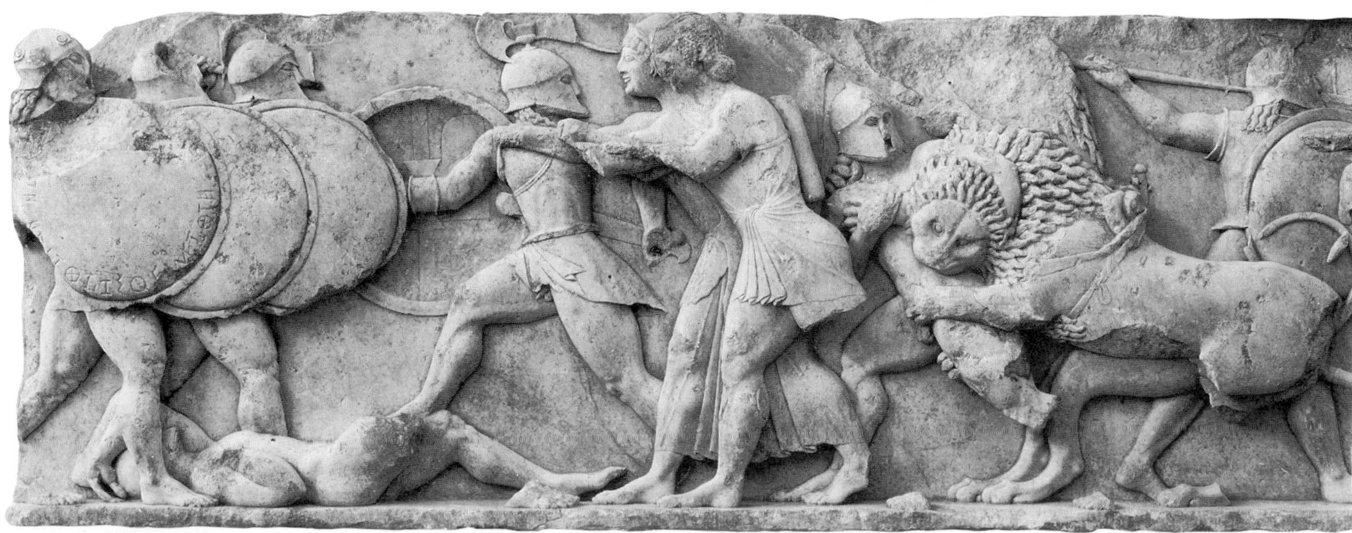

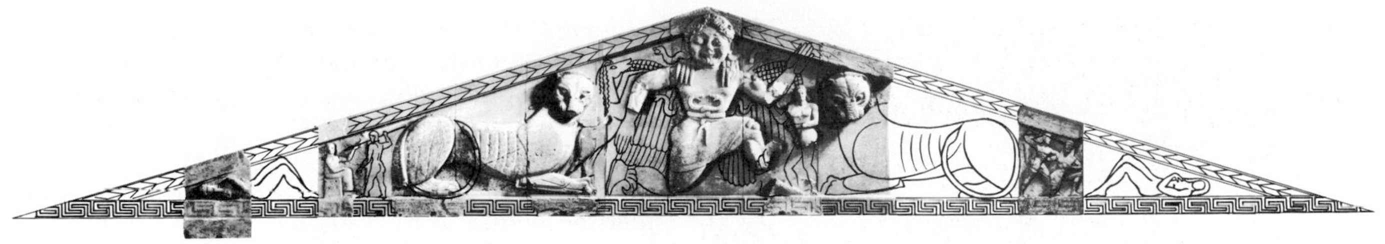

5-30 Reconstruction drawing superimposed on a photograph of the remaining fragments of the west pediment of the Temple of Artemis at Corfu, *c.* 600–580 B.C. Limestone fragments. Archeological Museum, Cairo.

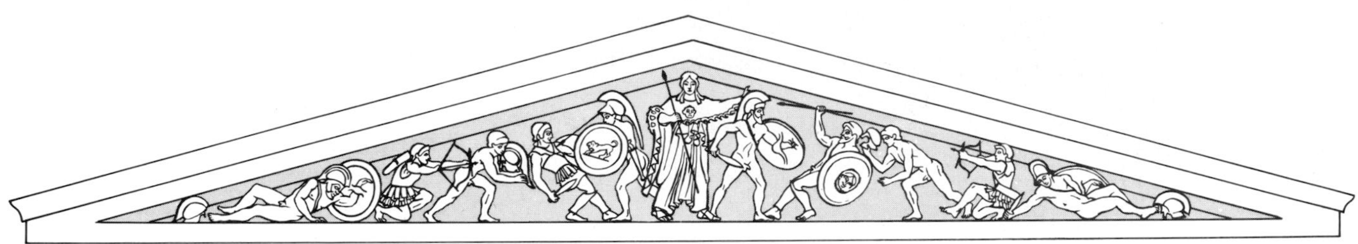

5-31 Reconstruction drawing of the east pediment of the Temple of Aphaia at Aegina, *c.* 490 B.C.

(FIG. **5-30**) is more troublesome to manage. Here, the figures are arranged heraldically and bring to mind compositions that go back beyond the Lion Gate at Mycenae (FIG. 4-23) to the symmetrical man-beast compositions of Mesopotamia (FIG. 2-9). On the thin panel of stone that fills the space between the cornices of the pediment, the sculptor presents the Gorgon, Medusa, flanked by spotted panthers. The Gorgon, a guardian monster whose glance could turn men to stone, grimaces hideously, exposing her boar's teeth and fulfilling her function as a winged demon to repulse all enemies from the sanctuary of the goddess. To the left and right of the Medusa figure appear her children, Chrysaor and Pegasus, who, according to legend, sprang from the Gorgon's head when she was struck by the sword of Perseus. They are both represented on a smaller scale. Still smaller are two groups of figures beyond the panthers: Zeus slaying a giant (on the observer's right) and one of the climactic events of the Trojan War, Neoptolemus killing Priam. In the outer ends of the pediment, recumbent figures represent a fallen Trojan and a dead giant. As pieced together from the surviving fragments, the artist's narrative intention is clear enough, but the odd shape of the surface on which he worked compelled him to distribute his figures somewhat haphazardly around the central ones and to show them on different scales. As time progressed, the Greek artist attempted to fill the space more organically, with figures grouped so that they appeared to be of the same size, participating in a unified way in a single event.

Toward the end of the Archaic period, Greek sculptors were arriving at a solution to the problem of pedimental composition. In the pedimental sculptures of the Temple of Aphaia at Aegina (FIGS. **5-31** to **5-33**), we find that the figures, in different poses but of the same scale, have been fitted into the difficult triangular space. Only the goddess Athena is shown on a slightly larger scale than the human combatants around her. The figures, which were heavily cleaned and over-restored in the nineteenth century, but recently restored anew to their original condition, probably represent some episode of the Trojan War. The exact original arrangement is still a matter of dispute, and art historians have suggested various solutions. Athena, with aegis and spear, stands in the center, with fighting groups on either side. We notice most the freedom of movement and the variety of pose. The figures are modeled with great vigor and an understanding of the human physique that, as we have seen in the contemporary vase paintings, reflect a careful observation of nature. The figure of the *Fallen Warrior* from the left angle of the pediment (FIG. 5-32) exhibits the daring with which the sculptor tackles the challenging problem of a difficult twisted pose. The bold composition of the turning masses of the body manifests the artist's new confidence in having mastered the science of representation. The dynamics of muscular tension and relaxation are appreciated and are close to life in their rendering. Mistakes are still made, and the transition from chest to pelvis has not been fully solved in this complex pose (note the misplaced navel). However, these rather technical considerations should not blind us to the marvelously expressive power of this figure. The *Fallen Warrior* brings to mind the spare and monumental nobility of Homer's heroes and particularly the Homeric simile,

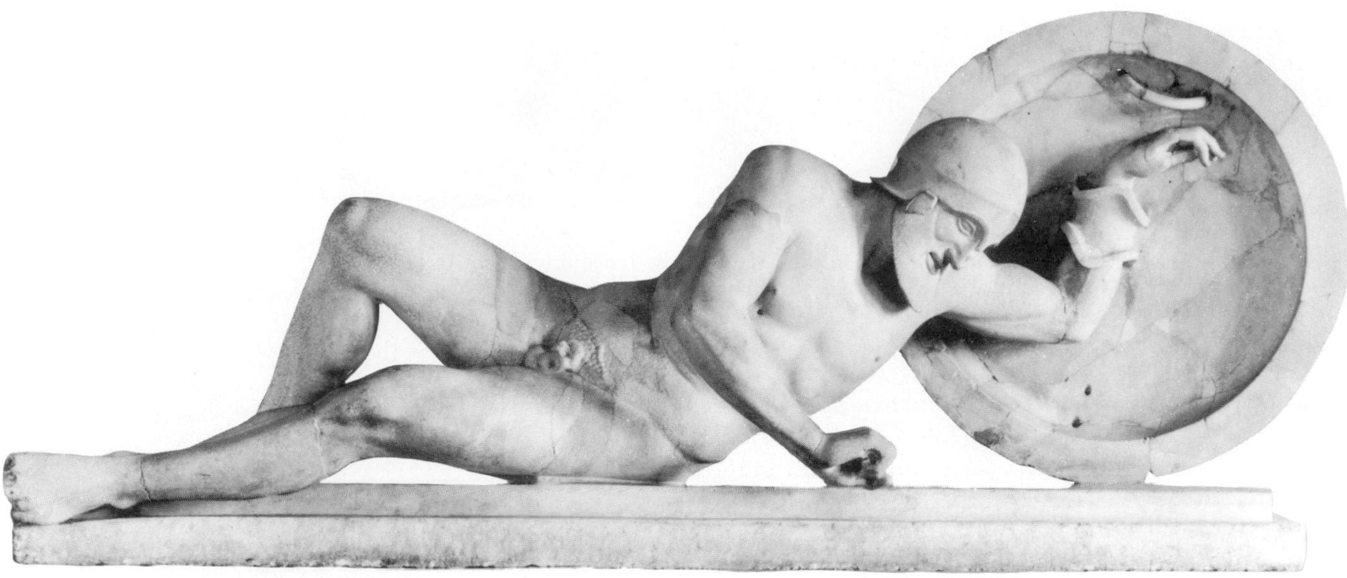

5-32 *Fallen Warrior,* from the east pediment of the Temple of Aphaia at Aegina. Marble, 6′ long. Staatliche Antikensammlungen und Glyptothek, Munich.

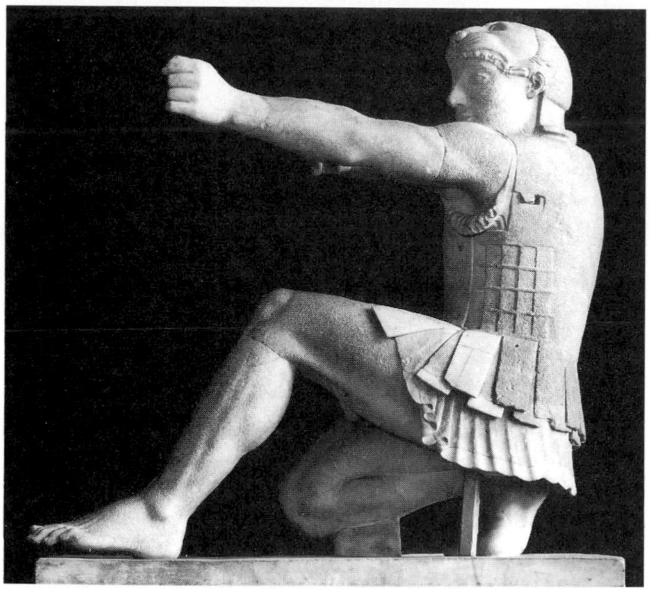

5-33 *Herakles,* from the east pediment of the Temple of Aphaia at Aegina. Marble, approx. 31″ high. Staatliche Antikensammlungen und Glyptothek, Munich.

"darkness came down upon his eyes, and he crashed in the battle like a falling tower."

The figure of the archer *Herakles* (FIG. 5-33), from the same pediment, is another instance of the Greek sculptor's triumph over age-old taboos and difficulties of representation. It is thought that this nimble archer is executing a maneuver hard to perform without long practice but required in the Greek war games and in actual combat. Running forward, he has dropped suddenly almost to one knee, and, from this tense position, takes aim and rapidly fires a flight of arrows. Soon he will spring to his feet to run forward again. The practiced strength and poise demanded by such a feat are beautifully caught in the elastic, though momentarily rigid, pose. One might read here the expression of a new spirit in Greek life and art—a spirit buoyant and optimistic as it meets the great challenge of the Persians at Marathon and looks to a future that the ancient Near Eastern world could never envision and never encompass.

THE EARLY CLASSICAL (TRANSITIONAL) PERIOD: 480–450 B.C.

The thirty or so years of the Early Classical period constitute the heroic age of the Athenians and of all the Hellenes who joined forces against the invasion of Greece by the Persians. Just as we look back to the age of the American Revolution and to the founding fathers of the republic for our models of heroism and civic wisdom and virtue, so the Greeks of the later fifth century revered the men of Marathon, Thermopylae, and Salamis—the battles that daunted and finally turned back the mighty hosts of Asia led by Xerxes. The new world of the Greeks, which they attributed to the Homeric feats of their heroes, turned away from Asia, barbarism, tyranny, and ignorance (it was all the same to the Greeks) to build a Hellenic civilization productive of a new species of mankind. Typical of the time were the views of the great dramatist Aeschylus, who celebrated, in his *Oresteia*, the triumph of reason and law over barbarous crime, blood feud, and mad vengeance. Himself a veteran of Marathon, Aeschylus repudiated in majestic verse all the slavish and inhuman traits of nature that the Greeks at that time of crisis associated with the Persians.

The Severe Style

Shortly after Athens was occupied and sacked in 480 B.C., the Greeks won a great naval victory over the Persians at Salamis. This resilient toughness of the Athenians signified a new pride that was to mature into a sense of Hellenic identity so strong that thenceforth the history of European civilization would be distinct from the civilization of Asia, even though in interaction with it. The period of struggle with the Persians, calling repeatedly for courage and endurance, produced in the Hellenes a kind of austere grandeur that manifested itself in the art of that period in what usually is referred to as the *severe style.* Stern simplification of outline and surface, fixed pose, firm stance, and immobility of expression characterize the severe style as we find it in two superb, life-size bronze statues of warriors recovered from the sea in 1972 and restored to their original appearance, although without their original attributes, such as shields and weapons (FIGS. **5-34** to **5-36**). *The Riace Bronzes* take their name from Riace Marina, a shore resort in Reggio Calabria, the site of an ancient Greek colony at the toe of the Italian boot. These priceless additions to the history of world art were found by an underwater swimmer just offshore, buried in the sand some 25 feet beneath the surface of the sea. Painstakingly cleaned—the cleaning itself a masterpiece of the modern restorer's art—the statues are now generally regarded as original Greek bronzes of the Transitional period of the so-called severe style, which preceded the Classical period. Weight, cost, and the tendency of large masses of bronze to distort when cooling would have made life-size castings in solid bronze impractical, if not impossible. Larger sculptures in bronze were (and are) hollow-cast in the *cire perdue* (lost-wax) method (see Glossary). This art of bronze casting, used since Sumerian times and probably learned by the Greeks from the Egyptians in the sixth century B.C., is found here in all perfection, as is the craft of working the metal surfaces to produce the greatest subtlety of detail. The mastery of material and technique is matched by the sculptor's sure knowledge of the structure and dynamics of the human body. Although one leg of the *Warrior* is advanced (FIG. 5-34) in the tradition of the Archaic kouroi (FIGS. 5-15 and 5-16), the weight shift, which we noted in the *Kritios Boy* (FIG. 5-19), is more pronounced, and the articulation of the body masses is at once more defined and fluent (FIG. 5-35). The slight

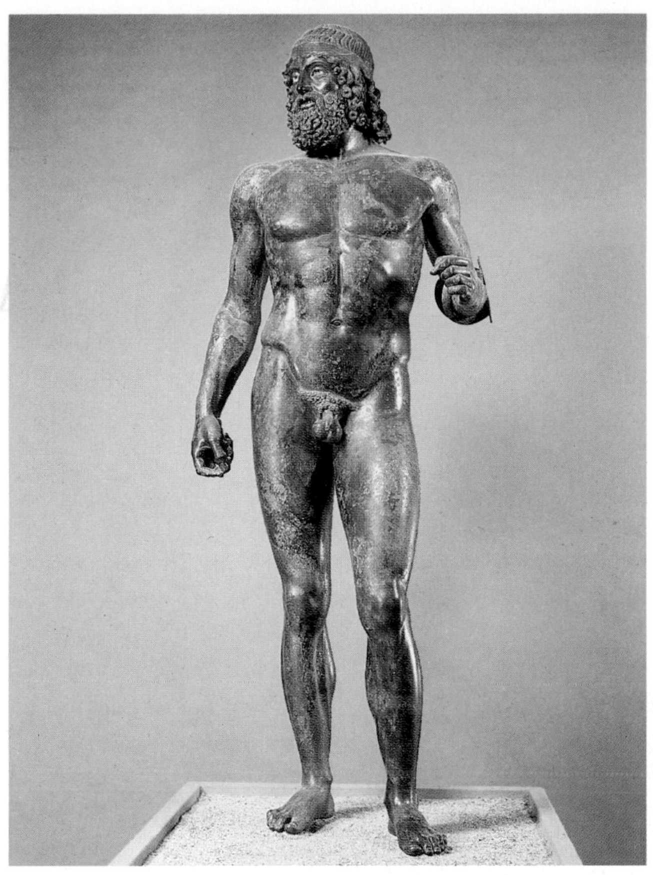

5-34 *The Riace Bronzes, Warrior Figure,* 460–450 B.C. Bronze, silver teeth and eyelashes, copper lips and nipples; each figure 6′ 1″ high. Archeological Museum, Reggio Calabria, Italy.

5-35 *Warrior,* rear view (restored).

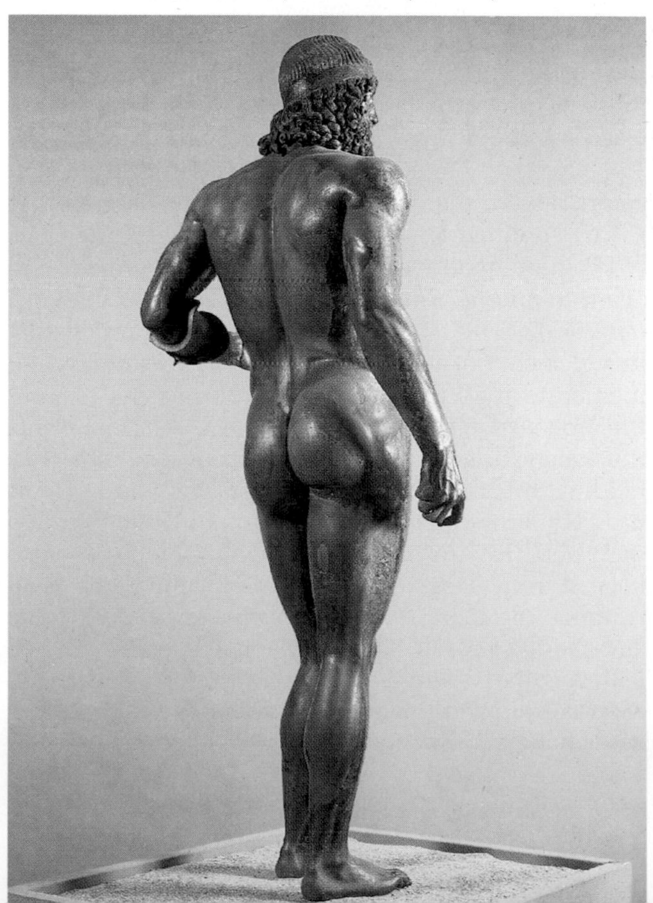

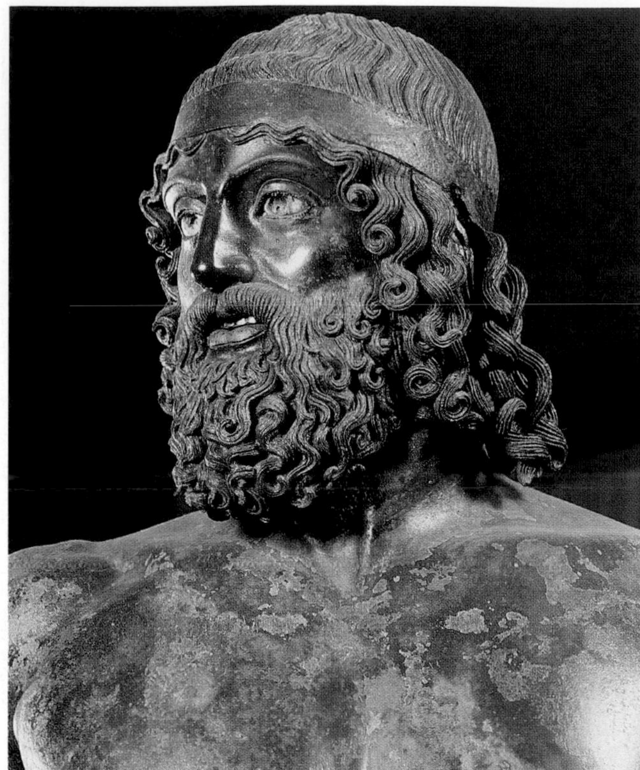

5-36 Detail of FIG. 5-34.

turning of the head and tilting of the shoulders, the unlocking of the arms from the body, and the lifting and crooking of the left arm (which perhaps held a shield) are all features that break through the rigid "slab" of space confining the Archaic kouros and suggest the beginning of natural movement and the shift of viewpoint from the strictly frontal aspect. The massive physique and the alert, menacing stance express extraordinary strength and a brutal ferocity. The face (FIG. 5-36), its silver teeth bared in a snarl, could be imagined as the very mask of merciless "War," defined by Homer as "the bane of men."

The high quality of *The Riace Bronzes* can be found again in another fine bronze, *The Charioteer of Delphi* (FIG. **5-37**). This statue belonged to a grouping that included chariot and horses, probably erected to commemorate the victory of King Polyzalos of Gela at the races in 478 B.C. *The Charioteer of Delphi* represents the king's driver, who stands firmly on both feet, holding the reins in his outstretched hand. He is dressed in the customary garment of a driver, girdled high and held in at the shoulders and the back to keep it from flapping. A band tied behind the head confines the hair. The eyes are made of glass paste and shaded by lashes of hairlike pieces of bronze. We feel the sharp clarity of Archaic work in the figure, especially in the lower part (where the folds of the dress have almost the quality of a fluted column), in

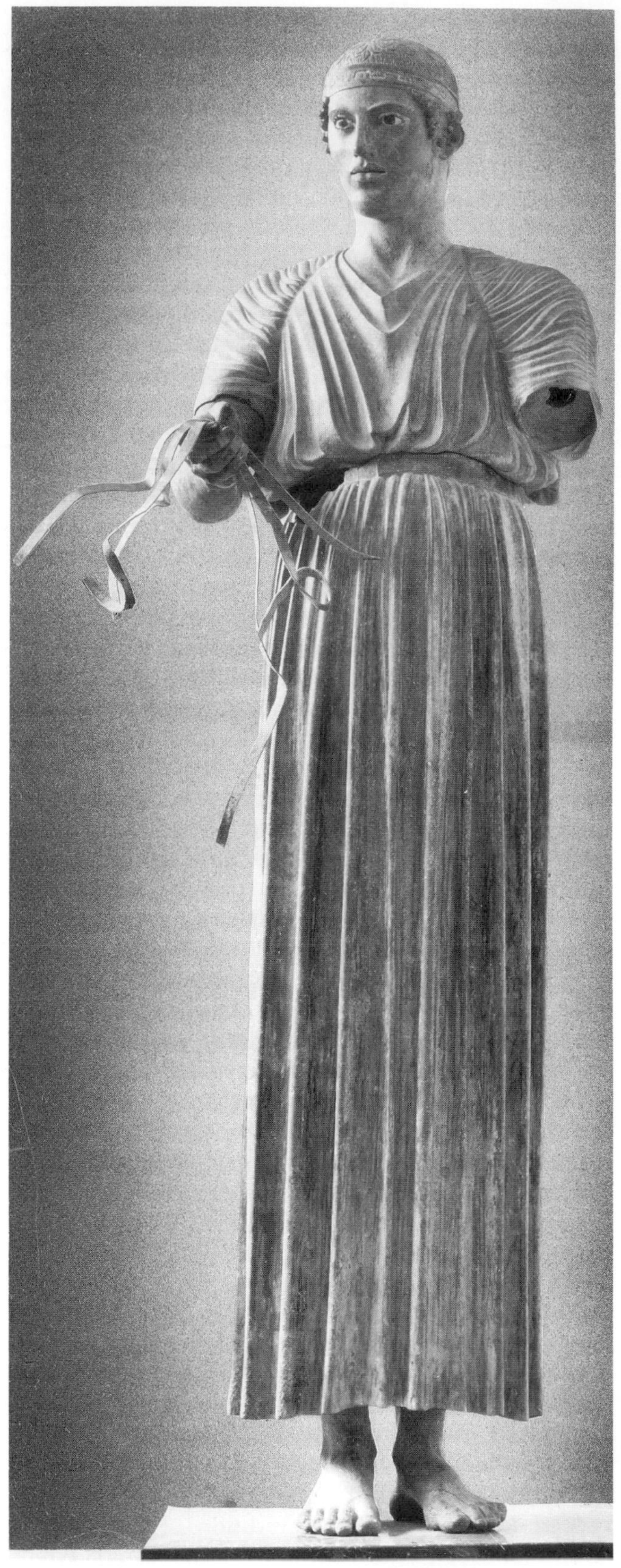

5-37 *The Charioteer of Delphi,* from the Sanctuary of Apollo at Delphi, *c.* 470 B.C. Bronze, approx. 5′ 11″ high. Archeological Museum, Delphi.

the sharp lines of the brow, and in the conventional way in which the hair is worked. But we notice also the skillful modeling of the hand and the feet, and the slight twist of the torso, which gives the feeling of an organic structure beneath the drapery. These subtleties are not seen at first, and we might mistake the statue for another example of the Archaic formula of rigid frontality. But it is only the formality of the pose, not ignorance of the principle of weight distribution, that determines the tight composure of the figure; it is as "alive" as the pose of a soldier at parade rest. The statue may be a portrait, yet few individualized traits are shown. This lack of individualized traits typified most works of the Greek Classical period and distinguished Greek from Egyptian portrait statues, which had a religious function (the preservation of the deceased's likeness to preserve the ka). Although, with the Greeks, man comes to complete self-consciousness ("Know thyself!"), and although the *human figure* is idealized, no individual is regarded as being true or perfect or, consequently, an appropriate subject for representation. In the words of Bruno Snell:

> If we want to describe the statues of the fifth century in the words of their age, we should say that they represent beautiful or perfect men, or, to use a phrase employed in the early lyrics for purposes of eulogy, "godlike" men. Even for Plato, the norm of judgment still rests with the gods, and not with men.*

Thus, our observations at the beginning of this chapter must be modified. Although, according to the philosopher Protagoras, "man is the measure of all things," for art, the gods are the measure of man, and to achieve the ideal is to achieve the "godlike."

The rapid process of liberation from Archaic limits continues in the renowned *Discobolos* of the sculptor MYRON (FIG. **5-38**), which dates from about 450 B.C. Like most freestanding statues by the "Great Masters" of Greek sculpture, the *Discobolos* has survived only in Roman marble copies of the bronze original (see page 163). Myron's representation of an athlete engaged in the discus throw was revolutionary as a result of its vigorous and convincing movement. It has been widely reproduced in both the ancient and modern worlds. However, the motion of the *Discobolos* has clearly been restricted to one plane, which means that only two distinct views are possible. The figure is represented at the point between the backward swing and the forward thrust of the arm and by means of certain formal devices becomes an expression of concentrated force. The composition is in terms of two intersecting arcs, creating the impression of a tightly stretched bow a moment before the string is released.

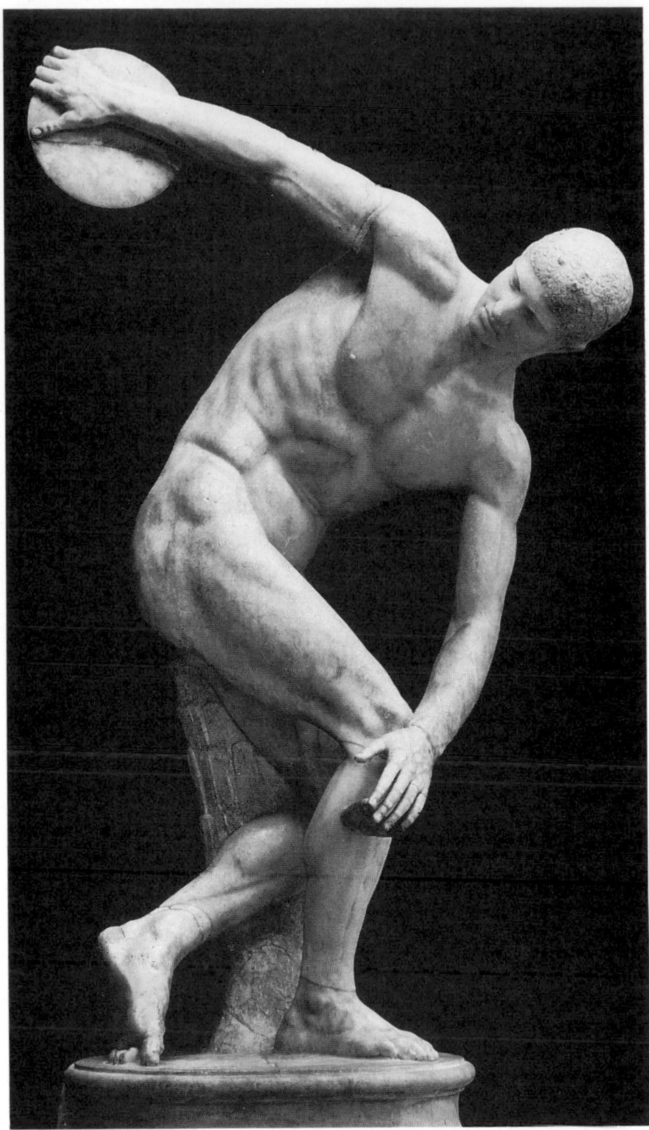

5-38 MYRON, *Discobolos*. Roman marble copy after a bronze original of c. 450 B.C., life size. Museo Nazionale Romano, Rome.

The severe early style of the Transitional period finds its clearest and most representative expression in the pedimental sculptures of the Temple of Zeus at Olympia (FIG. **5-39**). On the west pediment, the combat of centaurs and Lapiths at the wedding feast of Peirithous is represented. The centaurs (half man, half beast) had been invited to the celebration, but they became drunk and attempted to abduct the bride and her maidens. They were prevented from doing so by Peirithous and Theseus; Apollo, appearing above the combat, approves the heroes' chastisement of this breach of hospitality. The scene symbolizes three things: the Greek victories over the Persians; the sacred truce of Olympia (which outlawed strife

*Bruno Snell, *The Discovery of the Mind: The Greek Origins of European Thought* (New York: Harper & Row, 1960), p. 247.

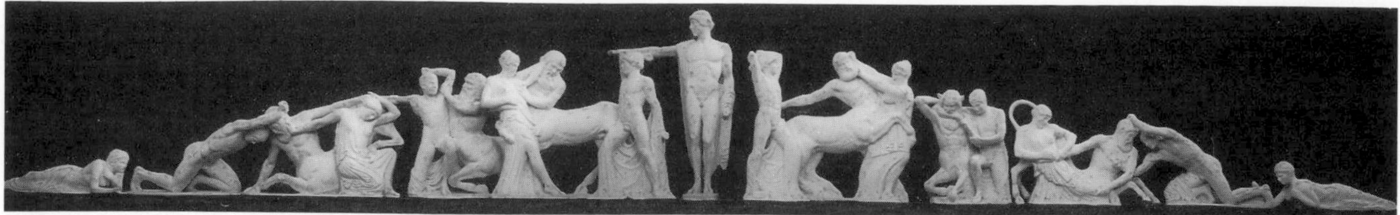

5-39 Reconstruction of the west pediment of the Temple of Zeus at Olympia, 468–460 B.C. Approx. 91′ wide.

within or on the approaches to the consecrated precincts of the temple); and the responsibility of men, who, unlike animals, acknowledge the rule of law.

The grouping of the figures in the Olympia pediments shows considerable improvement over the older Aegina grouping (FIG. 5-31) in the adjustment of the poses to fit the triangular pediment. In the center, Apollo thrusts out his arm amid the tumult (FIG. **5-40**). The figure should be compared with the Archaic kouroi (FIGS. 5-15 and 5-16). From its formality and such lingering archaisms as the tight, decorative treatment of the hair, it seems the last of that great line, although the new understanding of bodily structure shows in the splendid and exact modeling of the athletic physique. The musculature is no longer schematic, but swelling with life and power. The transitions from one group of muscles to another are made smoothly and subtly, and this soft flow of planes and contours belies the formal rigidity of the pose.

The face of the *Apollo,* like those of *The Charioteer of Delphi* and the *Discobolos,* is composed in the expressionless mask of regular beauty deemed appropriate to gods and godlike men, despite their action or potential for action. This ideal mask, expressing the conviction of Greek philosophy that reason must be above and in control of the passions, precludes the distortion of the face by any strain of emotion, even in scenes of the most violent action. In the twisted complication of the group of *Hippodameia and the Centaur* (FIG. **5-41**), where the bride of Peirithous tries to wrench the centaur's clutching hand from her breast, the girl's face remains serenely neutral. Her predicament is dire, as the artful sculptor dramatically describes it; yet, and significantly, it is only the cen-

5-40 *Apollo,* from the west pediment of the Temple of Zeus at Olympia, *c.* 470–456 B.C. Marble, height of Apollo 10′ 2″. Archeological Museum, Olympia.

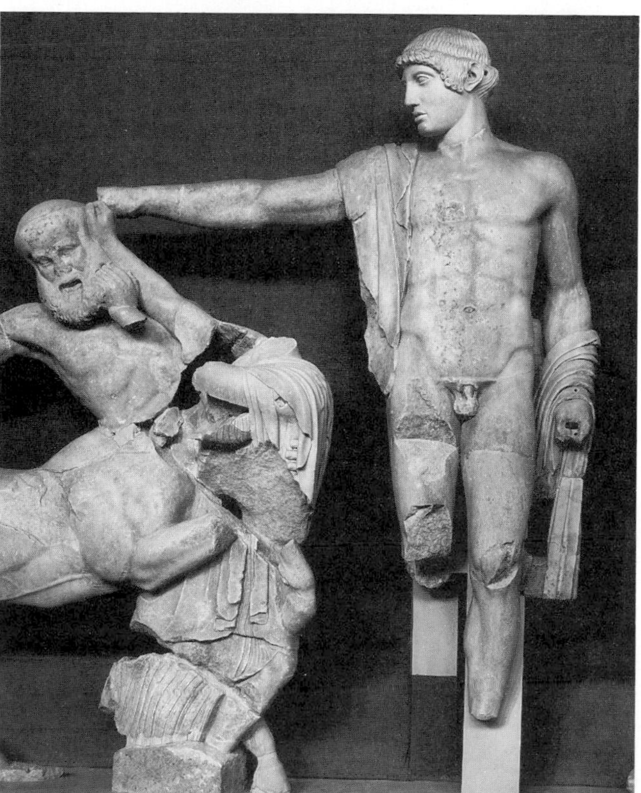

5-41 *Hippodameia and the Centaur,* from the west pediment of the Temple of Zeus at Olympia. Marble, slightly over life size. Archeological Museum, Olympia.

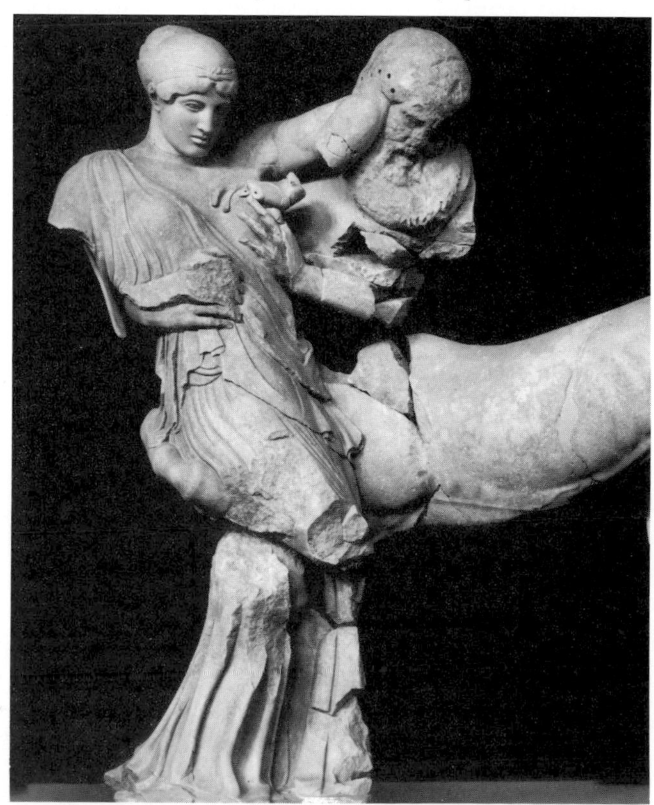

taur's face that is distorted, as befits such a low creature, surrendering to drunkenness and lust. This distinction between the calm of noble men and women and the frenzy of the creature abandoned to impulse prevailed for centuries in Greek art. The Greeks were convinced that overwhelming disaster awaited those who yielded to the spell cast by Dionysos, the dark god of intoxication and madness; this conviction is reflected in their drama and in their persistent appeal to reason and order, both in art and in life. Against Dionysos they attempted to raise the shining figure of Apollo, god of light, beauty, and wisdom. Thus, it was with the pediments of Olympia that the visual arts moved into the realm of philosophy and drama, and it was in the presence of these sculptures that the Greek athletes took their oath at the altar of Zeus before the Olympic Games.

THE HIGH (MATURE) CLASSICAL PERIOD: 450–430 B.C.

The prestige that the Athenians won by their leading role in the repulse of the Persians, and by virtue of the powerful fleet they built in the process, made them the dominant political force in the Greek world. They acquired a sea empire disguised as a religious and more or less democratic alliance of city- and island-states throughout the Aegean. Members of the alliance, which was called the Delian League, had cause enough to complain bitterly that they were more the subjects of Athens than her allies and that she siphoned off a large part of the common treasury (raised as a fund for defense against Persia) for her own uses. Despite chronic warfare within the alliance (and between it and the rival league led by Sparta), Athens, under the leadership of its adroit statesman, Pericles, became an immensely prosperous and proud community. The brief period of Athenian glory under Pericles saw a concentration of human creative energy and a triumph of drama, philosophy, and art that has been known in no other place or time in all of Western history.

Architecture

Disdaining to reassemble the desecrated stones of the Athenian Acropolis after the sack of the city in 480 B.C., the Athenians, led by Pericles, signalized their new power and independence by completely rebuilding the Acropolis, undertaking one of the greatest building projects of antiquity before Roman times. Their success stands as a rare human achievement against the larger history of human failure. The beauty of the buildings, set on a towering platform of rock with difficult access (FIGS. **5-42** and **5-43**), was

5-42 Plan of the Acropolis of Athens, restored as of 400 B.C.

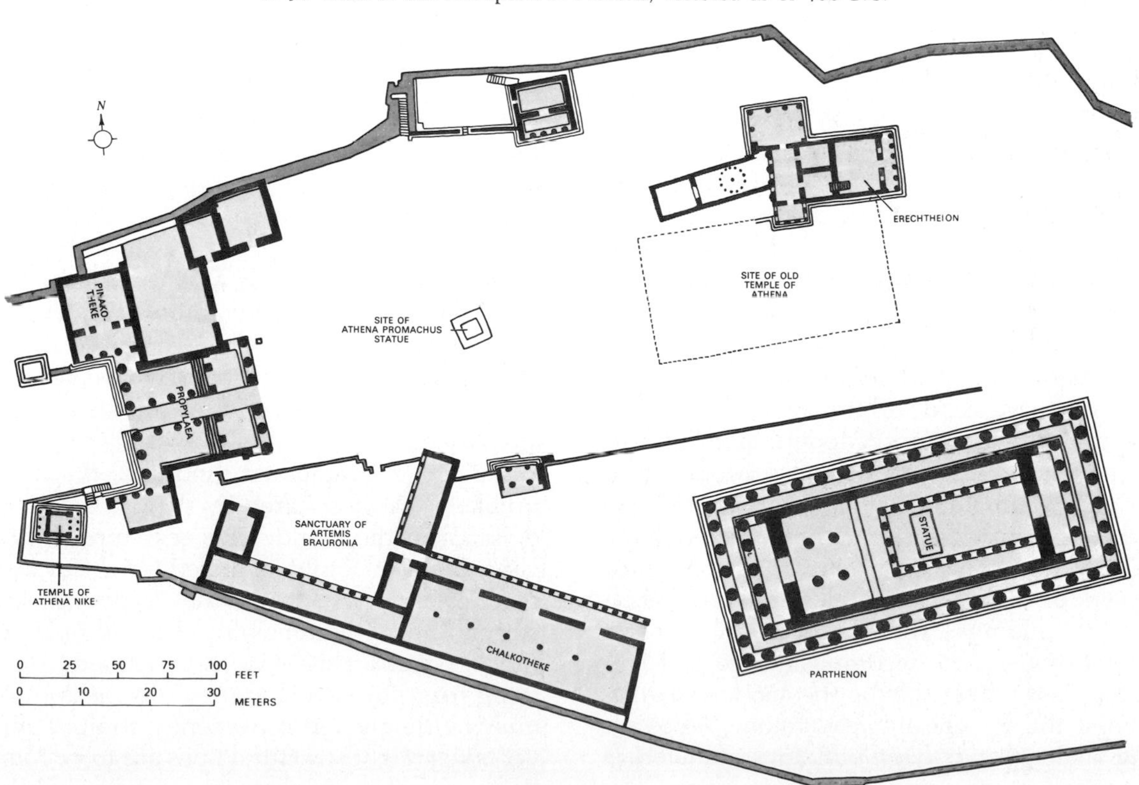

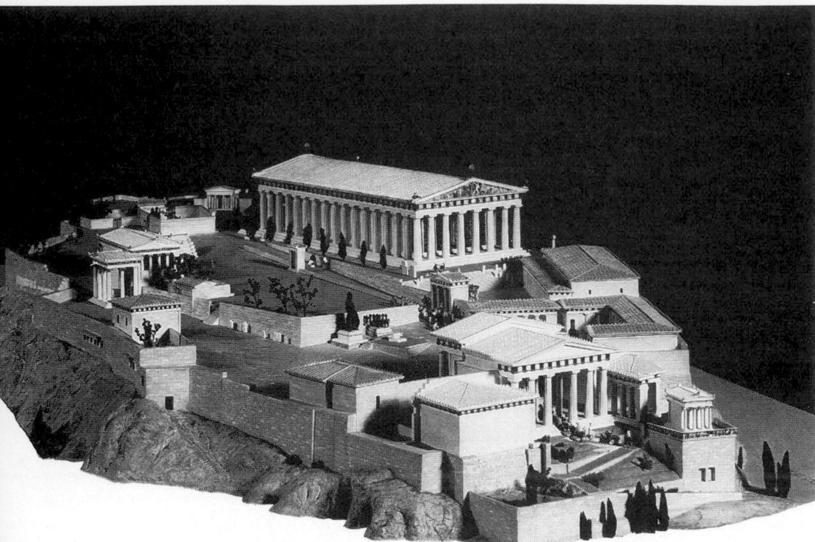

5-43 Restoration (model) of the Acropolis of Athens toward the end of the fifth century B.C.: the Parthenon *(upper center)*, the Erechtheion *(left center)*, and the Propylaia and the Temple of Athena Nike *(right foreground)*. Royal Ontario Museum, Toronto.

recognized and celebrated in ancient times as it is today. Plutarch, writing some five hundred years after the rebuilding of the Acropolis, commented:

> Pericles' works are especially admired, as having been made quickly, to last long. For every particular piece of his work was immediately, even at that time when it was new, recognized as ancient, because of its beauty and elegance; and yet in its vigor and freshness it looks to this day as if it has just been done. There is a sort of bloom and newness upon those works of his, preserving them from the touch of time.

Architect Eric Mendelssohn (1887–1953) made almost the same observation when he first visited Athens. Expecting to be depressed by viewing the original source of that academic Classicism from which his generation was fighting to free itself, he found himself exclaiming that the Parthenon is "modern," meaning that good architecture is always good, and so, always "modern."

Time, vandalism, accident, and neglect had, by the nineteenth century, reduced the buildings of the Acropolis to a clutter of ruins. Modern archeologists have cleared away centuries of encumbering, later structures and accumulated rubble that obscured and defaced the original design and have restored the Periclean works to some broken semblance of their former splendor. Today, a uniquely modern blight threatens the buildings. The corrosive emissions of automobile exhaust are decomposing the ancient marbles; the smog-laden air of the modern traffic-clogged city is the solvent of ancient stone. Steps are now being taken to encase the buildings in materials that will resist further damage from corrosion. The restoration and preservation of a priceless heritage has become a modern obligation and task.

THE PARTHENON

Of the Periclean buildings on the Acropolis, the Parthenon (the temple sacred to Athena Parthenos) was the first and the largest to be constructed (FIG. 5-44). Its architects were IKTINOS and KALLIKRATES, and its sculptures were produced under the direction of PHIDIAS, friend of Pericles and one of the great sculptors of all time. In plan (FIG. 5-42), the Parthenon is a peripteral temple, its short side slightly less than half the length of its long side. Its naos is subdivided into two parts: the larger contained the ivory and gold cult statue of Athena Parthenos, a figure some 40 feet in height, the work of Phidias; the smaller had been designed to serve as the treasury of the Delian League, but most of the revenues contributed by the Aegean members were expended on Pericles' ambitious building projects. The interiors of the two rooms are organized differently. The naos proper had two double rows of small columns for roof support; although long disputed, the purpose of the rows may have been to provide a second-story gallery from which visitors could view the statue, the foundation of which is still visible. The treasury had four single Ionic columns, one of several Ionic features in the otherwise Doric building, another being the continuous frieze of sculpture that runs around the top of the naos wall on the exterior. Except for these Ionic elements, the Parthenon epitomizes the Classical Doric temple, exhibiting that order at the peak of its refinement.

Seen today, the building is a partial restoration. Through the centuries, the Parthenon has undergone many transformations, having been both a Greek temple and a Christian church; after the Ottoman conquest of Greece, a Turkish mosque was built inside its naos. In 1687, the Turks used the naos as an ammunition dump while at war with the Venetians. A Venetian rocket scored a direct hit, and the resultant explosion blew out the center of the building. During the past century the colonnades have been reassembled, but the core of the structure remains a ruin.

Despite its dilapidated condition, the Parthenon is probably the most carefully surveyed and measured building in the world. This searching study has revealed that the builders aimed for unsurpassable excellence in every detail; the "refinements" of the structure have become almost a subtopic in the history of Greek architecture. If we are led to expect anything from the severe Doric order, it is that its lines must be rigidly and consistently straight and plumb; yet few straight structural lines are to be found in the Parthenon. The stylobate is convex, so subtly as to be

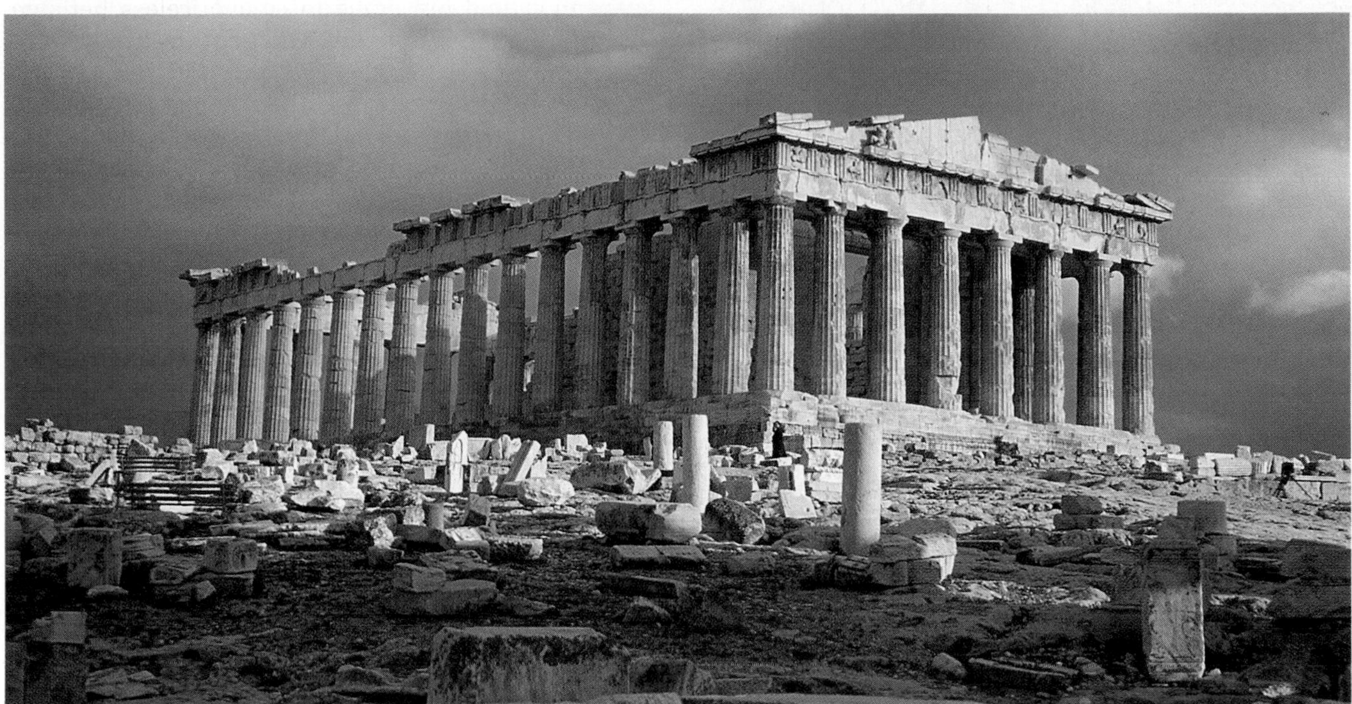

5-44 IKTINOS and KALLIKRATES, the Parthenon, Acropolis, Athens, 448–432 B.C. (view from the northwest).

almost imperceptible as a curve; only if one sights along it from one end does the curvature, which is repeated in the entablature, become visible. The columns tilt slightly inward and are not uniformly spaced, standing closer to each other at the corners of the building. Moreover, not all the columns are of the same diameter; those at the corners have a somewhat greater girth than the rest. The entasis, which gives a kind of muscle-tense elasticity and buoyancy to the profile of the column, has the same subtlety seen in the curvature of the stylobate and the entablature.

These deviations from the mechanical, plumb-line, straight-edged norm are plainly intentional; most have been found in other temples. But interpretations of these refinements do not agree. Some feel that they are purely functional; the curvature of the stylobate, for example, may have been designed to facilitate drainage, or perhaps in anticipation of the settling of the central part of the building. Others believe that the deviations were intended to offset marginal distortions in the human visual field—optical illusions that might make columns with exactly vertical profiles look pinched and weak. Still other speculation is that the Greek instinct for completeness in the look of the building and for integrity with its surroundings required such refinements; the downward-tending curve of the stylobate would find its limit in the earth, for example, making a visually stable and strong base for the building's aspect. A reasonable conjecture would be that the builders intended the Parthenon to be more than a product of engineering logic—that it was to be viewed and appreciated as a great work of sculpture, having the elasticity, resilience, and life of the human figure in statuary. Thus, the particulars would be designed to work in smooth relationship to each other and to the whole structure in an organic way in which, of course, the curved line predominates over the straight. The Parthenon columns especially display this principle in their entasis, appearing to respond to the burden they bear by the seeming swell of their compressed contours—expressing their function not mechanically, but organically.

Parts of the building were painted. This painting provided background against which sculpture could be seen clearly and, perhaps more important, delineated the upper parts of the building against the bright sky, so that the temple's basic proportions were shown crisply and could not be misread. Color also ensured that the visible parts of the building would be defined clearly and distinguished from one another.

The insistence on clarity in argument, which led the Greeks to invent *logic,* operates just as strongly in the "arguments" of their architectural design. Unfortunately, the *syllogism,* that early triumph of Greek thought, with its three propositions ending in a logically correct conclusion, cannot quite be matched in the Doric order. As examination of a corner of the Parthenon (FIG. **5-45**) will show, Greek architecture was not as "rational" as Greek logic. The Doric frieze was organized according to three inflexible rules: (1) a triglyph must be exactly over the center of each column; (2) a triglyph must be over the center of each intercolumniation; and (3) triglyphs at the corners of the frieze must meet, so that no space is left over. But the architectural "syllogism" is faulty, for the conclusion cannot be harmonized with proposition (1): if the corner triglyphs must meet, then they cannot be placed over the center of the corner column. Although irremediable, this might seem to us a minor flaw, even in a building that aimed at perfection in all details. The Greeks wanted to be sure, and they worked out, in logic, a method for making series of statements conform to a rule for validity. But in Doric architecture, something was left over; something did not fit. To the Greeks, it must have appeared to be like one of the incommensurable "irrational" numbers (such as the square root of two)—a disturbing thing with no limit or definition. (According to a singular and significant Greek legend, the man who first revealed the mystery of the irrationals perished by shipwreck, "for the unspeakable and the formless must be left hidden forever!") In much the same manner as mathematicians and logicians faced with some disturbing contradiction in their results, the architects and artists who aimed at perfection must have found this problem of the corner triglyph a constant irritation and embarrassment. Indeed, it may have contributed to the eventual decline of the Doric order, which began in the fourth century B.C., and to the rise of the Ionic and Corinthian orders, the continuous friezes of which eliminate the problem.

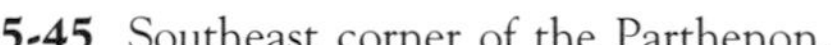
5-45 Southeast corner of the Parthenon.

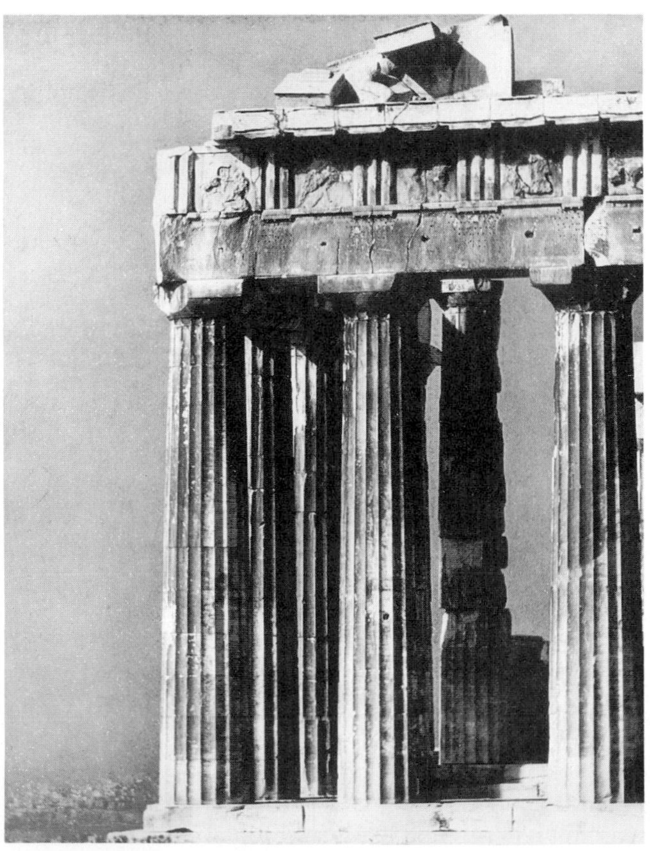

As already noted, the main purpose of the Parthenon was to house the cult statue of Athena Parthenos. Because the image of Athena, for whom the city of Athens was named, was made of ivory and gold, it did not survive centuries of depredation, although it seems to have been in existence as late as the second century A.D. We know the look of it only from accounts by Pausanias and others and from a few small replicas that differ in detail. Plutarch, in his *Life of Pericles,* tells us that its artist, Phidias, probably the scapegoat in an anti-Pericles plot, was convicted of stealing some of the gold intended for the statue and died in prison (although we know from other sources and recent excavations that Phidias was working on a statue of Zeus at Olympia after he left Athens and that he died in exile).

Because work on the colossal cult statue for the naos of the Parthenon must have taken up most of Phidias' time, it is quite likely that he planned and designed the pedimental groups and friezes but left the carving of these architectural sculptures to his students and assistants. Nevertheless, they undoubtedly reflect his style, and they are among the most marvelous of all surviving Greek works of sculpture and among the supreme masterworks of all time. The sculptures of the pediments, the metopes, and the great frieze compose the most elaborate sculptural program in the history of Greek art. As in the cases of Aegina and Olympia, scholars still debate the arrangement of the pedimental statues. While they differ in their interpretations and reconstructions, they seem to agree that the east pedimental group depicted the birth of Athena, the tutelary goddess of Athens; the west group is conceded to depict her contest with Poseidon for possession of the city. The import is clear: the immortal glory of Athens is manifested in its divine genealogy and patronage.

Most of these sculptures are now in the British Museum in London, where they are known popularly as the "Elgin marbles." Between 1801 and 1803, while Greece was still under Turkish rule, Lord Elgin, the British ambassador to the Ottoman court at Constantinople, was permitted to dismantle some of the Parthenon sculptures and to ship the best-preserved ones to England. He eventually sold them to the British government at a great financial loss to himself. Although he was criticized severely for having "stolen" the treasures of Athens (the Greek government is attempting to retrieve them), Lord Elgin's quite civilized motives in saving the statues from almost certain ruin are no longer in doubt. During his time, it was an unlikely prospect that the statues, surrounded by rubble and neglected for centuries, might one day be salvaged and protected against further damage and decay.

The figure of *Dionysos* (identified by some as *Herakles*) from the Parthenon (FIG. **5-46**) shows the final relaxation of all the limitations of Archaic figurative art. Phidias and his assistants are in full possession of the knowledge of the organic, coordinated human body and render it effortlessly and with entirely convincing consistency in all its parts. This fidelity to nature was a revelation, even in the nineteenth century, an age that was at the end of a long tradition of respect for nature in art. Artist Benjamin Robert Haydon, writing at that time, described his reaction to the reclining figure of *Dionysos (Herakles?)*, which he called Theseus:

> But when I turned to the Theseus, and saw that every form was altered by action or repose—when I saw that the two sides of his back varied, one side stretched from the shoulder blade being pulled forward, and the other being compressed from the shoulder blade being pushed close to the spine, as he rested on his elbow, with the belly flat because the bowels fell into the pelvis as he sat—when I saw in fact the most heroic style of art, combined with all the essential detail of actual life, the thing was done at once and forever. . . . Here were principles which the great Greeks in their finest time established.*

These principles seem indeed to be the monumental or heroic style "combined," as Haydon wrote, "with all the essential detail of actual life," the calm grandeur and simplicity of the one being in no way weakened by the precise, dynamic, anatomical logic of the other.

*In F. H. Taylor, *The Taste of Angels* (Boston: Little, Brown, 1948), p. 502.

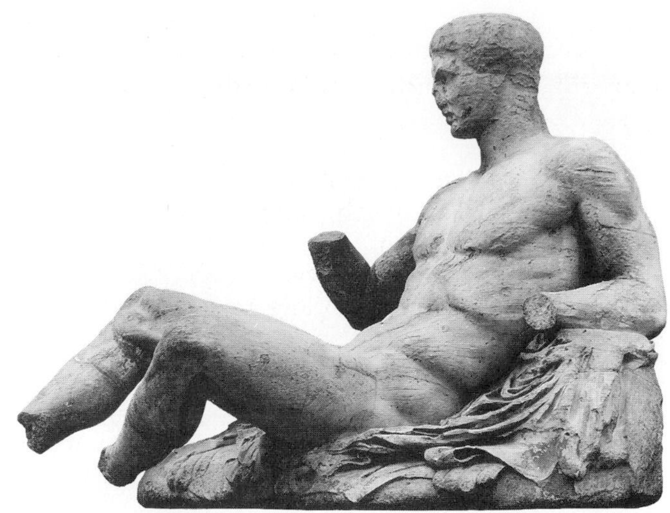

5-46 *Dionysos (Herakles?)*, from the east pediment of the Parthenon. Marble, over life size. British Museum, London.

The *Three Goddesses* from the east pediment of the Parthenon (FIG. **5-47**) shows even more than the *Dionysos (Herakles?)* the reinforcing and complementary actions of the principles of monumentality of scale and simplicity of pose with the "essential detail of actual life." The statues are typically Phidian in style, at once majestic and utterly "real" in the reading of the relaxed forms. In thin and heavy folds, the drapery alternately reveals and conceals the main and lesser masses of the bodies, at the same time swirling in a compositional tide that subtly unifies the group; the articulation and integration of the bodies produce a wonderful variation of surface and play of light and shade. Not only are the bodies fluidly related to each other, but they are related to the draperies as well, although the latter remain distinct from the bodies materially. The treatment of body and drapery as obviously different but in functional relationship to one another illustrates the thoroughly reasoned laws

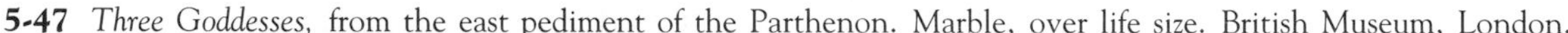

5-47 *Three Goddesses*, from the east pediment of the Parthenon. Marble, over life size. British Museum, London.

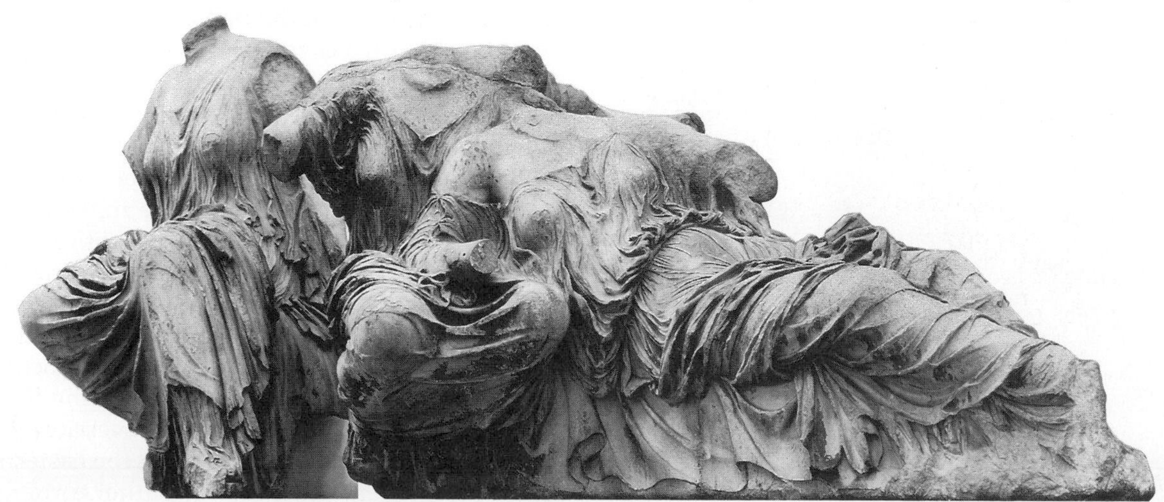

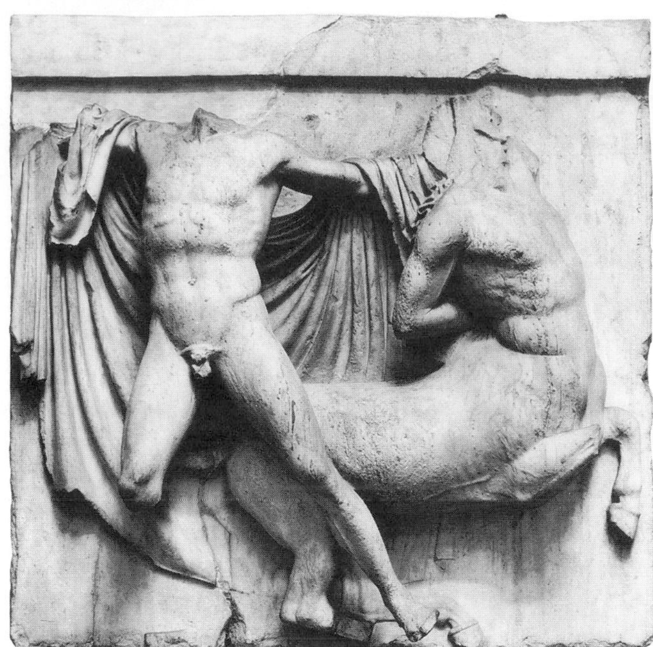

5-48 *Lapith and Centaur,* metope from the Parthenon. Marble, 56" high. British Museum, London.

of appearance that Phidias and his generation had come to know and respect.

In addition to the statuary of the pediments, sculptured metopes were set between the triglyphs in the outer face of the Doric colonnade (FIG. 5-45). Within the colonnade, at the top of the external naos wall, a continuous Ionic frieze ran around the four sides of the building, forming an unbroken band of bas-relief sculpture some 524 feet long. The metope sculptures provide an accent of movement, notably by the use of diagonal forms in successive compositions of pairs of struggling, interlocking figures in high relief—centaurs and Lapiths, gods and giants, Greeks and Amazons. The metope illustrated (FIG. **5-48**) shows a battle between a Lapith and a centaur, the theme of the Apollo pediment at Olympia (FIG. 5-39). Although

5-49 *Horsemen,* from the west frieze of the Parthenon. Marble, approx. 43" high. British Museum, London.

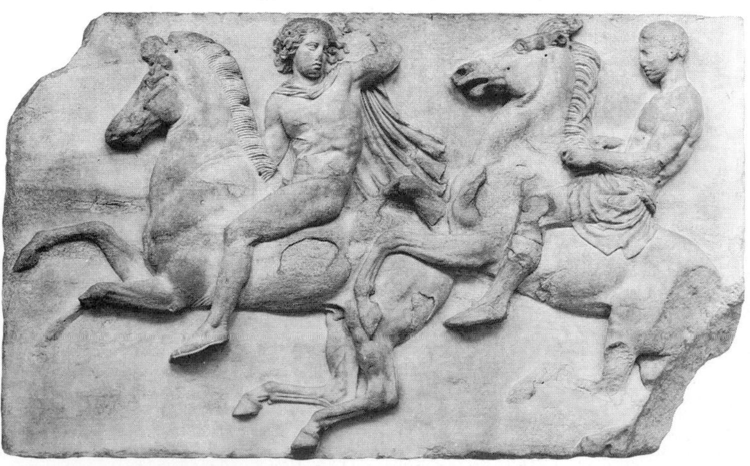

some of the metope designs are more successful than others, the figures generally are accommodated to the square spaces with great adroitness, and the whole series displays the ingenuity of the Phidian school in varying the poses and attitudes of the figures and avoiding the monotony that a regularly repeated space could impose. It is interesting also that the fortunes of the contestants are about equally balanced, the Greeks seeming to win or lose as often as their opponents.

The inner Ionic frieze of figures (FIGS. **5-49** and **5-50**) was seen from below in reflected light against a colored ground. It enriched the plain wall and directed attention toward the entrance to the temple. Though its subject is still a matter of scholarly dispute ("the riddle of the Parthenon frieze"), it probably represents the Panathenaic procession that took place every four years when the citizens of Athens gathered in the marketplace and carried the *peplos,* or robe, for the statue of Athena to the Parthenon. The robe was not for Phidias' ivory and gold statue, but for an older, Archaic one, kept, ultimately, in the Erechtheion of the Acropolis. This is the first known representation of a nonmythological subject in Greek temple reliefs.

The Panathenaic frieze is unique in the ancient world for its careful creation of the impression of the passage of time, albeit a brief fragment of time. The effect is achieved by the use of a sequence of figures posed to present a gradation of motion—a rudimentary picture of time as an acceleration or deceleration. In order to experience the illusion, the observer must also be in motion, following the frieze around the colonnade of the temple. In the part of the frieze that decorated the western side of the naos, the viewer can see the procession forming: youths are lacing their sandals and holding or mounting their horses; they are guided by marshals who stand at intervals, and particularly at the corners, to slow movement and guide the horsemen at the turn. In the friezes of the two long sides of the naos, the procession moves in parallel lines, a cavalcade of spirited youths, chariots, elders, jar carriers, and animals for sacrifice. Seen throughout the procession is that balance of the monumentally simple and the actual, of the tactile and the optical, of the "ideal" and the "real," of the permanent and the momentary that, again, is characteristically Greek and the perfect exemplification of the "inner concord of opposites" that Heraclitus, the philosopher, wrote of in the sixth century B.C. The eye follows the movement of light and shade in the drapery, pausing at any point by shifting focus to the broad areas of planes, with their sharply linear outlines. The movement of the procession becomes slower and more solemn as it nears the eastern side of the naos, when, after turning the corner, it ap-

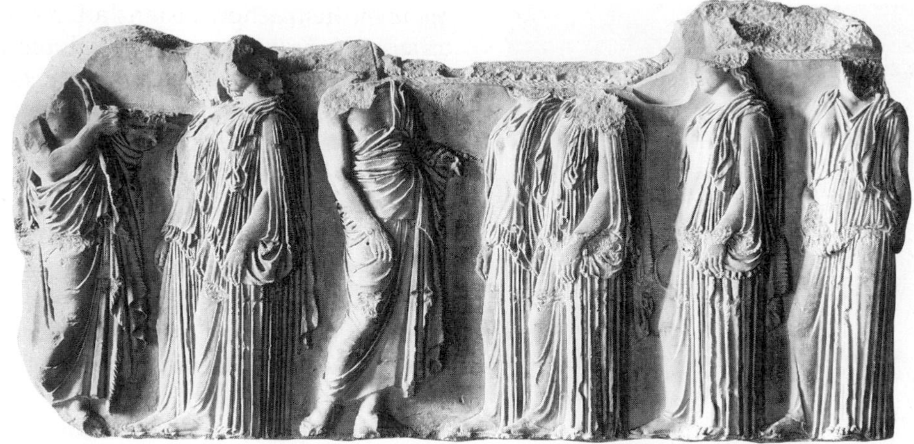

5-50 *Head of the Procession,* from the east frieze of the Parthenon. Marble, approx. 43″ high. Louvre, Paris.

proaches the seated divinities, who appear to be guests of Athena at her great festival. Standing figures—to note one device of the artists—face against the general movement at ever-closer intervals, slowing the forward motion of the procession (FIG. 5-50).

OTHER BUILDINGS OF THE ACROPOLIS

To reach the Parthenon, the Panathenaic procession would have wound its way from the lower level of the city of Athens, up the steep slope of the Acropolis, and through the gate called the Propylaia (FIGS. 5-42 and **5-51**), another structure of the Periclean project. Built by MNESIKLES between 437 and 432 B.C., the Propylaia was begun immediately following the completion of the Parthenon but was never finished, partly because of the financial drain of the Peloponnesian War and partly, it is believed, because one of its wings would have trespassed on the sanctuary of Artemis Brauronia. The design is a monumental and subtle elaboration of a gate unit leading through a city wall, the gate hall itself being flanked by buildings containing a library and perhaps the first picture gallery *(pinakotheke)* in history. Here, members of the procession could rest in beautiful surroundings after the steep climb, before passing on to the sacred buildings on the summit. The Propylaia shows modifications of Doric regularity in the broadening of the space between the central columns to make the passageway wide enough for wheeled traffic, and (like the Parthenon) the gateway includes Ionic elements, such as the columns that line the corridor for the purpose of giving greater height where necessary to

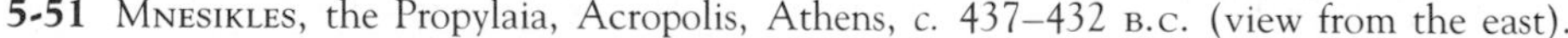

5-51 MNESIKLES, the Propylaia, Acropolis, Athens, *c.* 437–432 B.C. (view from the east).

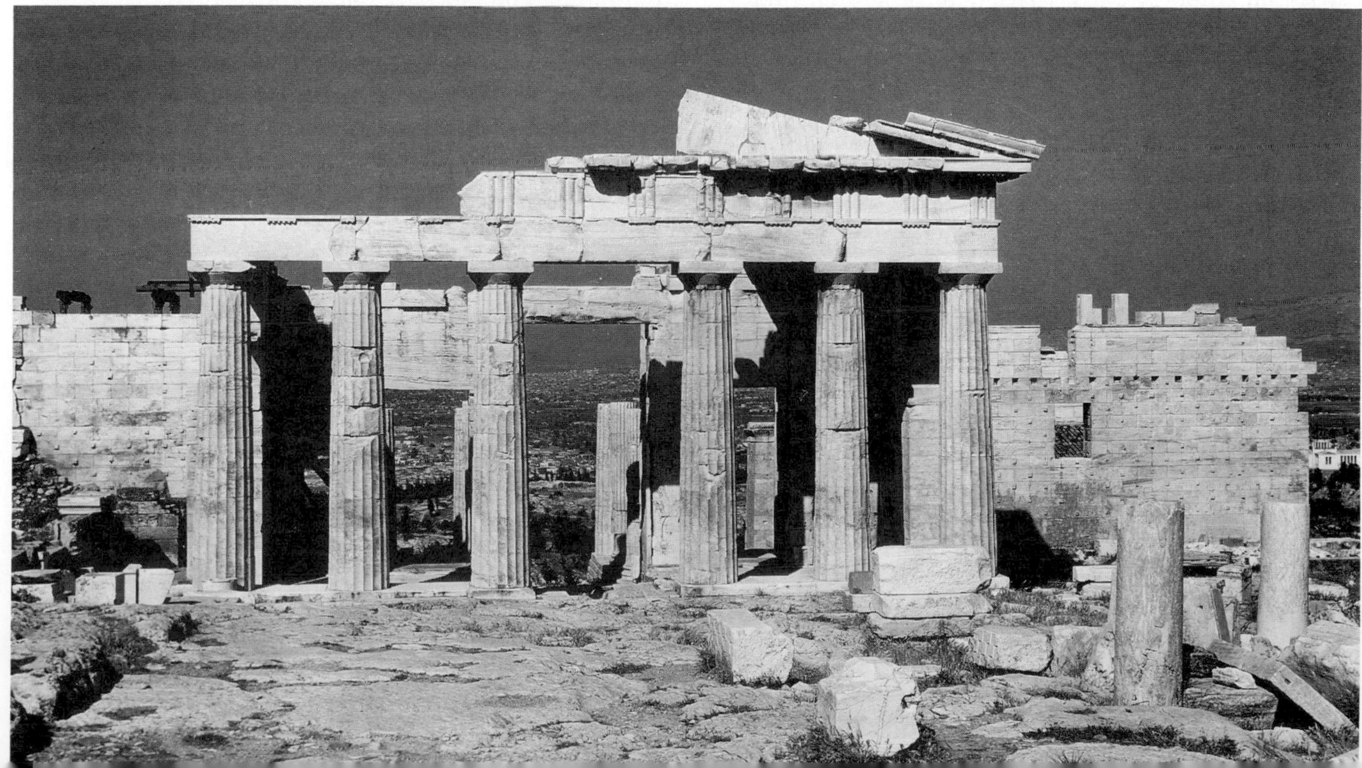

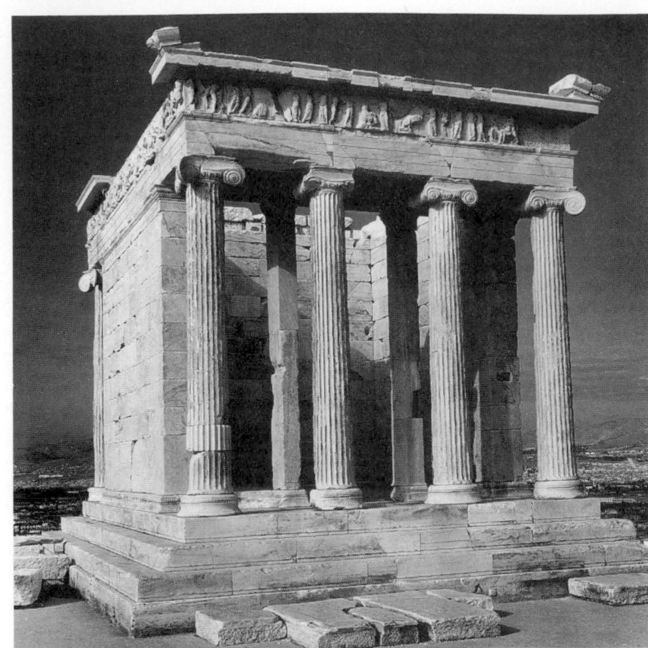

5-52 KALLIKRATES, the Temple of Athena Nike, Acropolis, Athens, 427–424 B.C. (view from the east).

support the central roof structure. Mnesikles innovated here in another respect. Greek buildings, whether religious or secular, ordinarily existed in isolation, self-sufficient and relatively independent of their surroundings. Here, for the first time, buildings of different types and functions (propylon and halls) were combined into an axially aligned grouping that looks ahead to later Hellenistic designs and the axial compositions of the Roman Imperial forums (FIG. 6-45).

The beautiful, little Ionic Temple of Athena Nike, built under the direction of Kallikrates between 427 and 424 B.C. (FIGS. 5-20c, 5-42, and **5-52**), is the earliest completely Ionic building extant on the Acropolis. Before this time, the Ionic order had been employed in the construction of a whole building only in the cases of a few treasuries at Olympia and Delphi on the Greek mainland (for example, the Treasury of the Siphnians, FIG. 5-28), and these buildings had been constructed by Aegean islanders, not by Greeks of the mainland. It was through Athens' rule of the islands that the city became open to eastern Greek and Ionian influences. The little amphiprostyle Ionic temple stands on what used to be a Mycenaean bastion near the Propylaia. The slender, exquisite proportions of the temple offer a striking contrast to the Doric severity of the gate unit, heightening the effects of both.

Another Ionic building situated on the Acropolis is the Erechtheion (FIGS. 5-42, **5-53,** and **5-54**), the last of the Periclean program. Constructed between 421 and 405 B.C., the Erechtheion is most unusual in plan and quite unlike any other Greek temple. It was named after a mythical Athenian hero, Erechtheus, to whom, in part, it was dedicated. Its many unusual features are due partly to the irregularity of its site and partly to the number of shrines included within it. According to Pausanias, the Greek geographer and historian of the second century A.D., the Erechtheion stood on the traditional site of the contest between Poseidon and Athena for dominion over Athens, the theme of the sculpture group in the west pediment of the Parthenon. Also located at the site were a rock supposed to be positioned at the imprint of Poseidon's trident, the spring of saltwater that the stroke of the trident produced, Athena's olive tree, and the tomb of the legendary King Kekrops, who judged the Athena-Poseidon contest. The asymmetrical plan of the building resulted from the need to bring these traditionally revered sites together and from the fact that pious reluctance to disturb the sacred places precluded terracing of the uneven ground. Hence, this

5-53 The Erechtheion, Acropolis, Athens, 421–405 B.C. (view from the south).

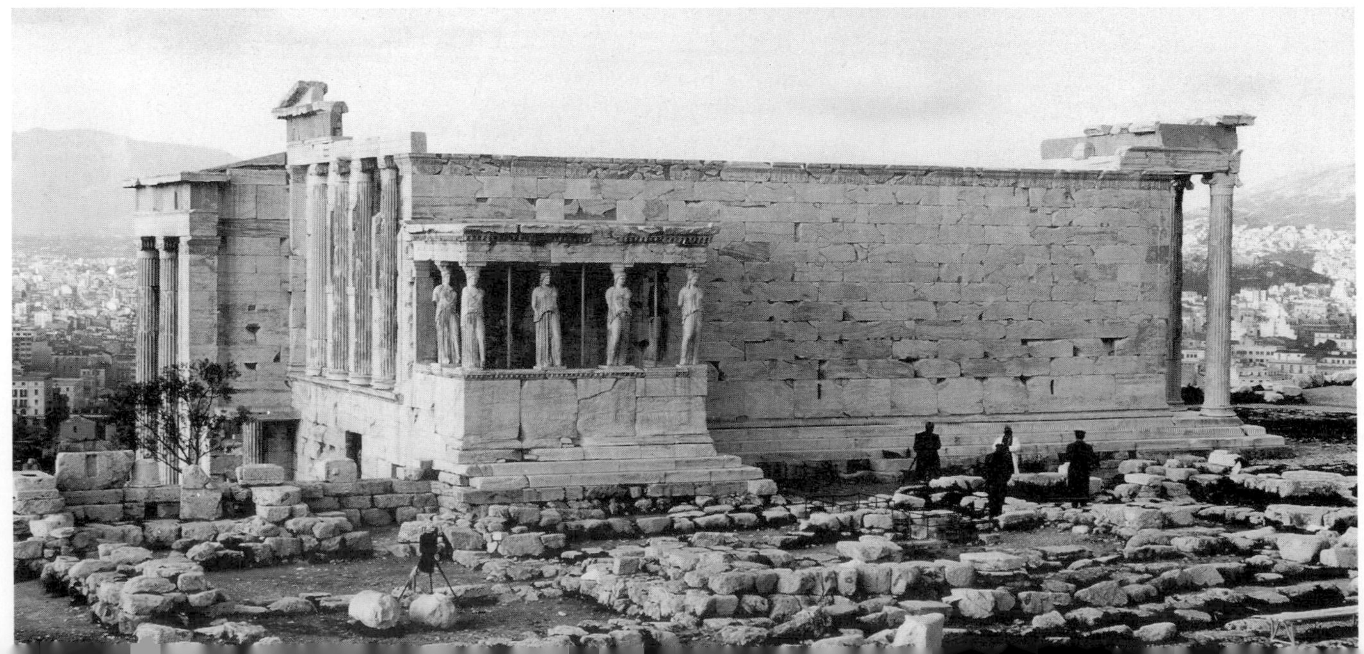

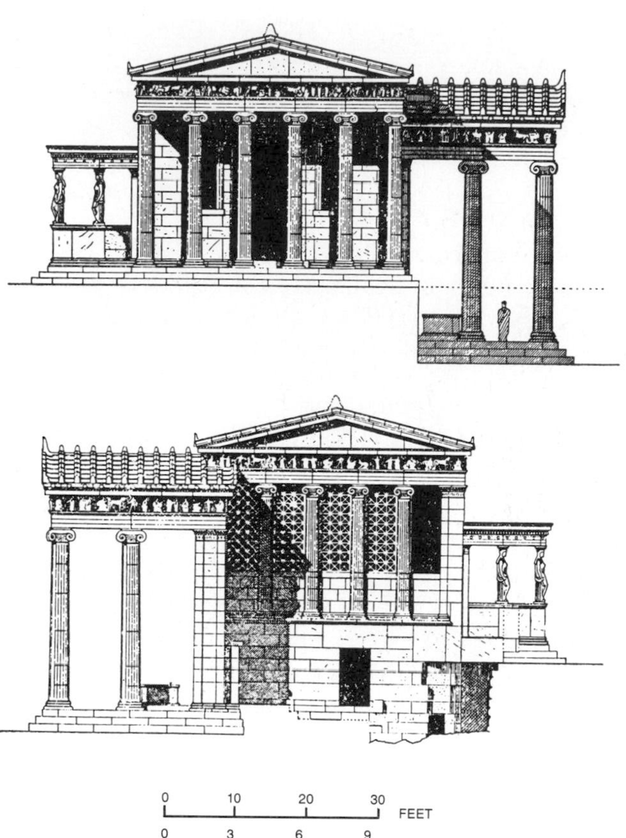

5-54 Reconstructed elevations of the east and west façades of the Erechtheion, Acropolis, Athens.

5-55 Porch of the Maidens, the Erechtheion.

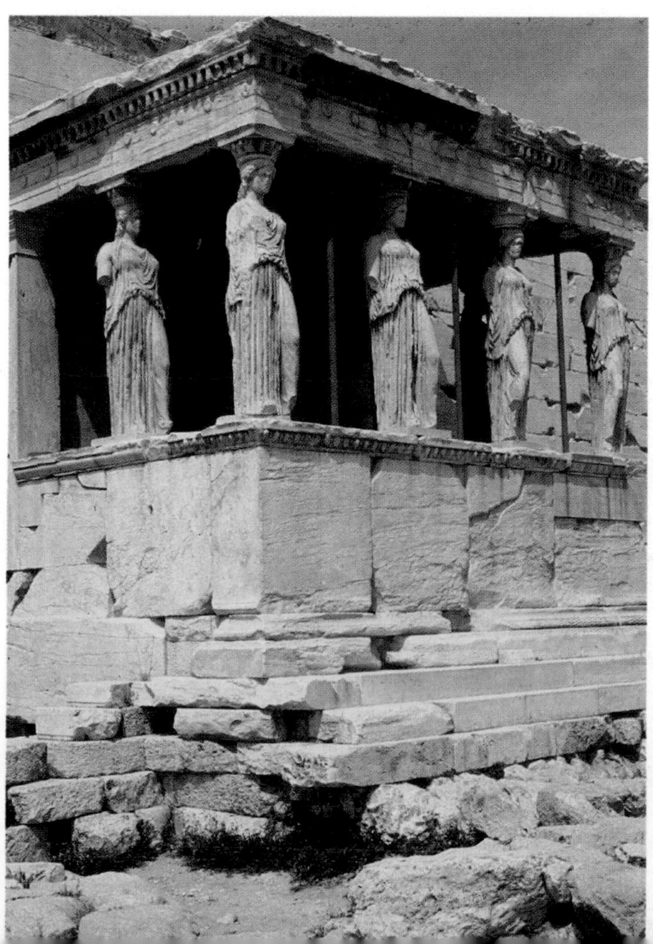

unique building stands on several levels, with different porches projecting from three sides and an unusual screen wall closing off the fourth. The irregularity of the structure, a feature so uncommon in Greek architecture, was formerly explained as the result of a kind of hurried, *ad hoc* completion necessitated by political and financial problems brought on by the duress of the Peloponnesian War; we now believe that the Erechtheion was finished according to plan and that the architect adjusted the design with great ingenuity to the difficult demands of ritual and site. In no way an esthetic failure, the asymmetrical form of the structure offers an effective counterpoint to the symmetrical unity of the nearby Parthenon; the graceful caryatids of the Porch of the Maidens (FIG. 5-55) strikingly complement the severity of the Parthenon's Doric columns, and the building's carved details are among the most refined and subtle in all of Greek art. The Erechtheion beautifully balances its larger neighbor, the Parthenon, setting Ionic complexity and elaboration against Doric simplicity and monumentality, repeating on a major scale the juxtaposition of the Propylaia and the Nike temple at the entrance of the *temenos* (sacred precinct).

Sculpture

The Porch of the Maidens, the south porch of the Erechtheion, takes its name from the caryatids that are its dominating feature (FIG. 5-55). It brings to mind that earlier Ionic caryatid design, the Treasury of the Siphnians (FIG. 5-28), and comparison of the two is useful. Unlike the Siphnian caryatids, those of the south porch of the Erechtheion do not carry a full entablature; they support instead one that consists of architrave and cornice only, the topmost *fascia* (flat, horizontal band) that makes up the architrave being decorated with medallions to simulate the missing frieze. This arrangement seems to be a deliberate, proportional adjustment undertaken by the sculptors of the Erechtheion figures to avoid the effect seen in the Siphnian caryatids, which look overloaded by the entablature; the sculptors must have been aware that figures graceful in attitude and dimension could scarcely harmonize with a massive architectural superstructure they would be presumed to be supporting. Technical and esthetic reasons may be given for the Erechtheion adjustment. Although the weight of a full entablature was borne by the Siphnian caryatids, in this case the load could have been too great for the necks of the figures, their weakest point; however, esthetic considerations were probably the more persuasive. Thus, again, we find the Classical architect-sculptor balancing the realities of structure with the necessities of ideal beauty. The figures have enough rigidity to suggest the structural column and just the degree of flexibility necessary to suggest the living body. The compromise is superbly executed. The corner figures determine the stance by representing the weight as falling on the outer leg. The inner figures repeat this pose, so that the legs not carrying the weight, and bent at the knee, do not determine the architectural verticals or disturb their natural plumb-line straightness. These figures have all the monumental majesty of the Phidian figures on the Parthenon pediments; the pleats and folds of their draperies reveal the quiet power of their bodies, and the very obligation imposed on them by the architecture serves only to strengthen their noble poise.

The Phidian style dominated Athenian sculpture until the end of the fifth century B.C. Due to the Peloponnesian War, fewer large-scale sculptural enterprises were launched, although the style lingered on in smaller works, such as the popular grave stelae produced in considerable numbers for both local use and export. One of the most harmoniously designed of these is the *Grave Stele of Hegeso* (FIG. **5-56**), which was found in the Dipylon cemetery. As is often the case in grave reliefs of the Classical period, the figures are placed in an architectural framework. The

5-56 *Grave Stele of Hegeso,* from the Dipylon cemetery, c. 410–400 B.C. Marble, 59″ high. National Archeological Museum, Athens.

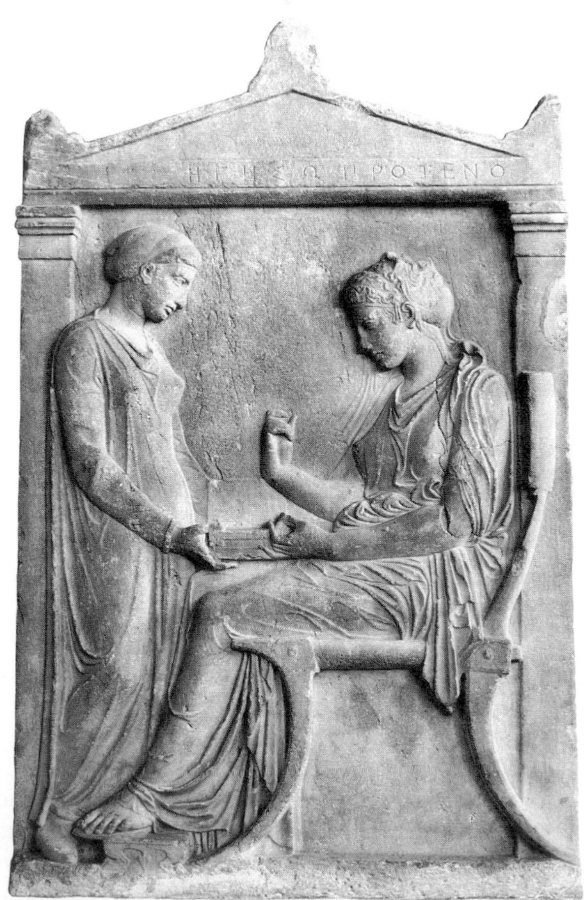

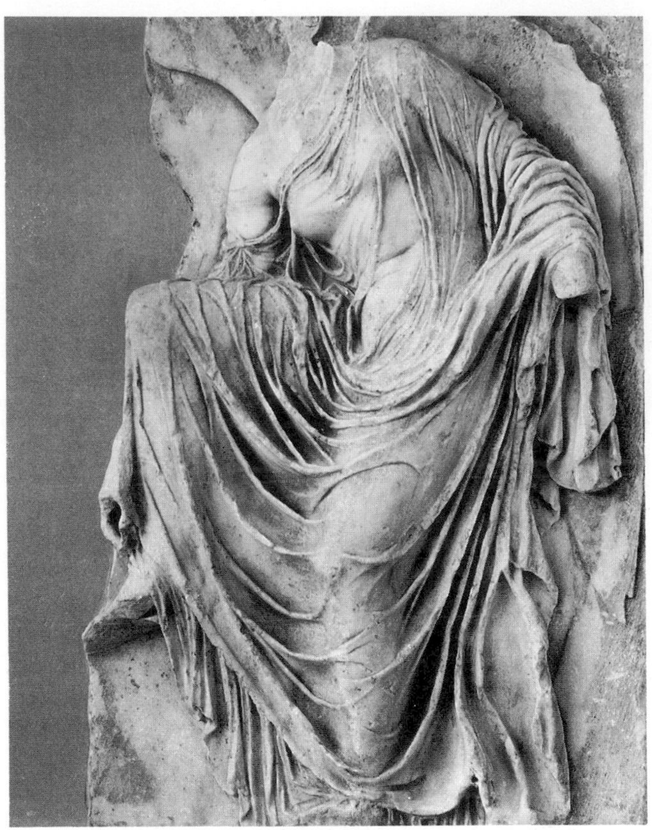

5-57 *Nike Fastening Her Sandal,* from the parapet of the Temple of Athena Nike, Acropolis, Athens, c. 410 B.C. Marble, approx. 42″ high. Acropolis Museum, Athens.

deceased is seated on a chair with sweepingly curved back and legs that provide an effective transition from the frozen forms of the architecture to the organic forms of the figures. Hegeso is contemplating a necklace (originally rendered in paint) that she has taken from the box held by her girl servant. The quiet glances of mistress and servant are directed at Hegeso's right hand, which, placed exactly in the center of the panel, is the compositional focal point. Although the stele was carved toward the end of the fifth century B.C., it is devoid of the sentimentality found in many other works of its day; the solemn pathos of the scene links the stele with the grandiose conception of the Parthenon sculptures.

The relief of *Nike Fastening Her Sandal* (FIG. **5-57**), from a parapet constructed around the Temple of Athena Nike about 410 B.C., shows how sculptors, having achieved the Classical perfection of the human form, now exhibited their virtuosity. The function of the concentrically arranged draperies, heavy and clinging to the form as if drenched with water, is to reveal the supple beauty of the young body. The interplay of the intricately moving drapery and the smooth volumes of the body seen in the *Three Goddesses* of the Parthenon (FIG. 5-47) is here refined to make a deliberately transparent veil for the female

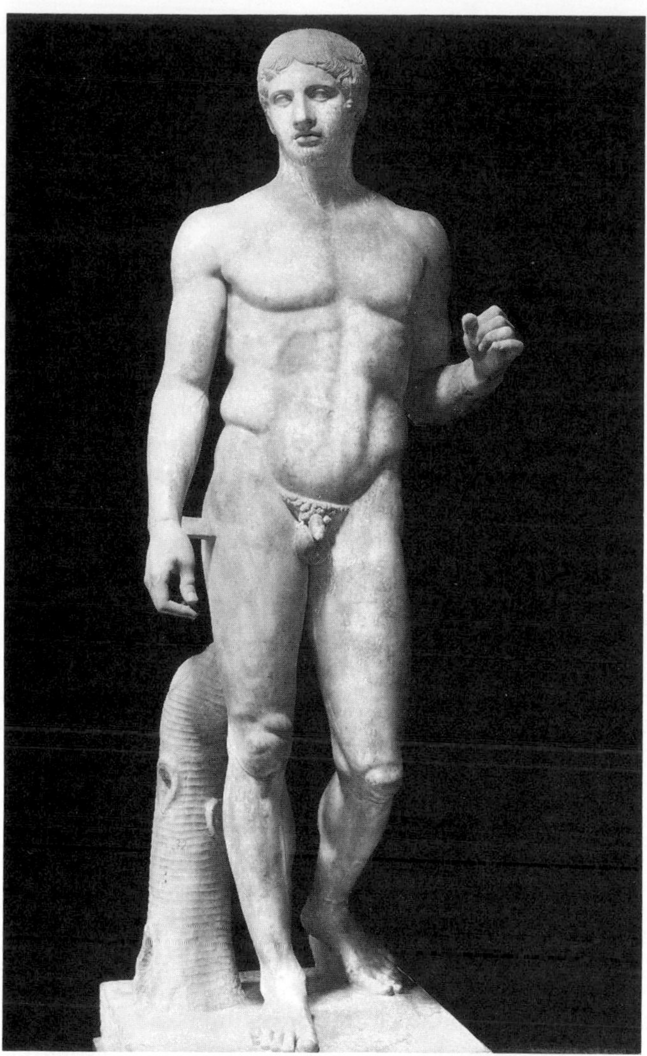

5-58 POLYKLEITOS, *Doryphoros.* Roman marble copy after a bronze original of c. 450–440 B.C. 6′ 6″ high. Museo Nazionale, Naples.

figure, which now emerges fully from the elaborate costume of the kore tradition.

In contrast with the Ionian sumptuousness of the Phidian style is a work of the Argive school of southern Greece, the *Doryphoros* (FIG. **5-58**) of POLYKLEITOS, a sculptor whose fame rivaled that of Phidias in the ancient world. The work shown here, the original of which is dated 450–440 B.C., is a Roman copy made much later.

Almost all extant works of the so-called Great Masters of Greek sculpture are replicas, the originals having disappeared. Originals of Roman copies can be identified through descriptions by ancient authors, especially Pausanias and Pliny the Elder, and occasionally through representations on ancient coins. A number of factors account for the disappearance of the originals. In war, statues made of precious materials were often pillaged, and bronze statues were melted to make weapons or utensils; during the barbarian invasions, in the time of the fall of the Roman Empire, marble statues were used to make lime for mortar. After the Romans conquered Greece in the second century B.C., they took Greek works of art to Rome to adorn the imperial palaces and the villas of the rich. Numerous copies were made of some statues, reflecting their popularity and fame. Many of the copyists took liberties with the originals; changes were made to conform with popular taste, and very few of the copies even approach the quality and refinement that the originals must have had. When the Romans were copying bronze in marble, they used awkward devices, such as a tree trunk placed next to a statue's leg or braces and struts attached to the arms (as can be seen in the *Doryphoros*), to strengthen weak points. Nevertheless, the copy of the *Doryphoros* does provide evidence of the appearance of the original, and we can compare its blocky solidity and strength with the subtle grace of the Phidian style. Although the unity and equilibrium that pervade the works of Phidias also are apparent in the Polykleitan statue, the origins differ; the artists at work on the Parthenon seem to have achieved their results with a deft, spontaneous translation of natural appearances, but Polykleitos worked according to a canon of proportions in which he formulated the principles that gave rise to unity. Although Polykleitos' own treatise enunciating his canon has been lost, a physician, Galen, who lived during the second century A.D., interpreted it as follows in his *Placita Hippocratis et Platonis:*

> [beauty consists] in the proportions, not of the elements, but of the parts, that is to say, of finger to finger, and of all the fingers to the palm and the wrist, and of these to the forearm, and of the forearm to the upper arm, and of all the other parts to each other, as they are set forth in the Canon of Polykleitos.

It has been said that in the *Doryphoros* Polykleitos had made not simply a statue but had manifested sculpture itself, and Aristotle used "sculptor" and "Polykleitos" interchangeably. The Greeks saw proportion as the central problem in architecture and in sculpture, and they viewed Polykleitos' canon as the embodiment of proportional rationality for sculpture.

Movement, which began to be expressed successfully in the early fifth century B.C., is disciplined in the *Doryphoros* through the use of an imposed system of proportions. The mighty body, with its broad shoulders, thick torso, and muscular limbs, strikes us as the embodiment of the Spartan ideal of the warrior physique, the human equivalent of the Doric order. And, like the Doric order, the figure appeals to the intellect and must be studied carefully for a long period before it reveals itself fully to the observer. The slow forward walk, the standard Polykleitan pose, stresses the principle of weight shift, the maneuver that must be made before we can move at all and with which the whole development of the representation of the moving human figure begins. What appears to be a casually natural pose is, in fact, the result of an extremely complex and subtle organization of the various parts of the figure. Note, for instance, how the function of the supporting leg is echoed by the straight-hanging arm to provide the right side of the figure with the columnar stability needed to anchor the dynamically flexed limbs of the left side. If read anatomically, on the other hand, the tensed and relaxed limbs may be seen to oppose each other diagonally (that is, the right arm and the left leg are relaxed, and the tensed supporting leg is opposed by the flexed left arm, which held a spear). Thus, all parts of the figure have been carefully composed to achieve the utmost variety within a compact and stable whole. A most circumspect and subtle artist has combined realism, monumentality, and diversity in a unified design that seems to be beyond the cavil of even the most discriminating critic.

Painting

Of Greek wall (mural) painting, little remains. Most of our knowledge of what it looked like must be drawn from vase painting and from the later Roman painting derived from it. We do have a specimen of Greek mural painting, however, that dates from the early fifth century B.C. On a wall of the so-called Tomb of the Diver at Paestum in southern Italy (the site of the well-preserved Doric temples examined earlier in FIGS. 5-22, 5-23, and 5-25), a banquet or symposium (Greek: *sympósion*, a drinking party) is represented. This subject appears often on Greek vase painting. In the detail of the fresco shown here (FIG. **5-59**), reclining guests at the left play a game that originated in Sicily and was widely popular throughout Greece. One individual holds out his wine cup, while another attempts to flick the remainder of his wine into it. A third guest looks over with curious interest at the affectionate pair to the right. The figures are silhouetted as dark shapes against a flat, light ground. Modeling is not used; details of facial and bodily features are indicated by line. The composition is friezelike, as in sculpture, all of the heads at one level. Each figure is sharply delineated in profile, with only sparing detail. Enough information is given to present the amusing situation clearly, and though the actions of each of the figures are discerned easily by pose and gesture, they are all bound into a group by the rhythmically curving directional lines of the carefully planned design.

We know from ancient accounts that great painters lived and worked in all periods of Greek art. The mural painter POLYGNOTOS enjoyed almost as much fame in antiquity as his contemporaries, Phidias and Polykleitos. Unfortunately, none of his works survive. On the basis of ancient literary sources, it is believed that his compositional style is reflected in the vase decoration of the NIOBID PAINTER, whose *Argonaut Krater* (FIG. **5-60**) illustrates a radical break with the traditional decorative style. For over two centuries, figures had been arranged *isocephalically* (with all the heads at one level) in horizontal bands, not only in Greek vase decoration but also in monumental painting. Evidence to support an isocephalic arrange-

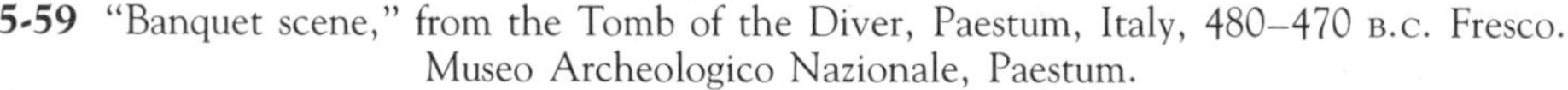

5-59 "Banquet scene," from the Tomb of the Diver, Paestum, Italy, 480–470 B.C. Fresco. Museo Archeologico Nazionale, Paestum.

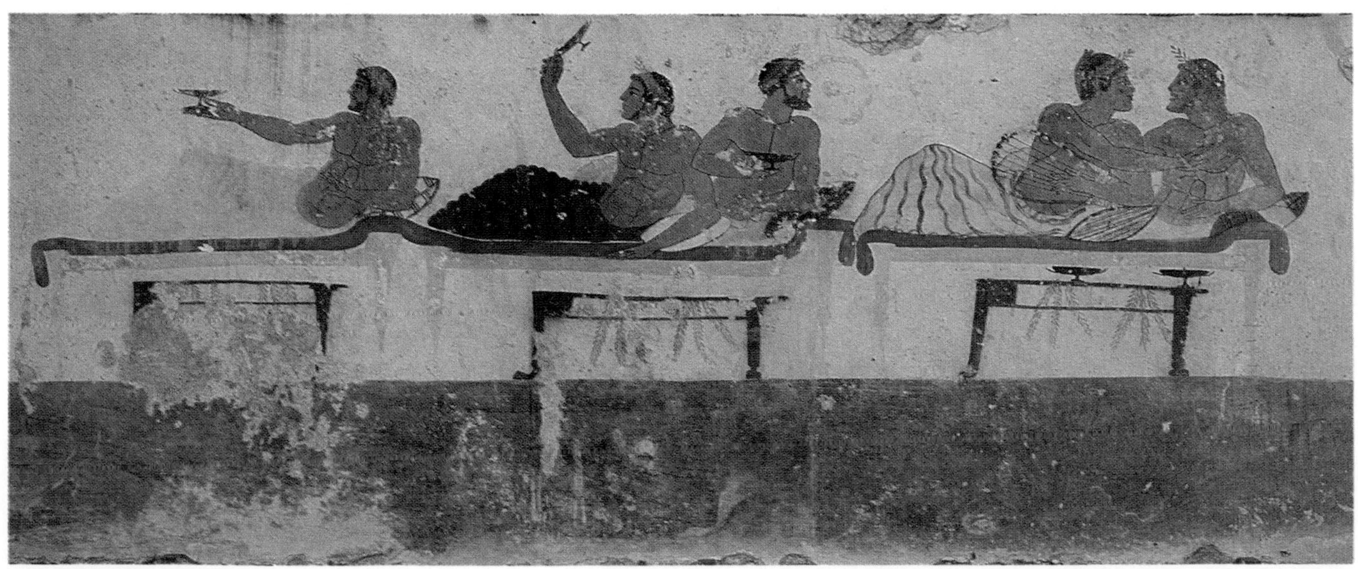

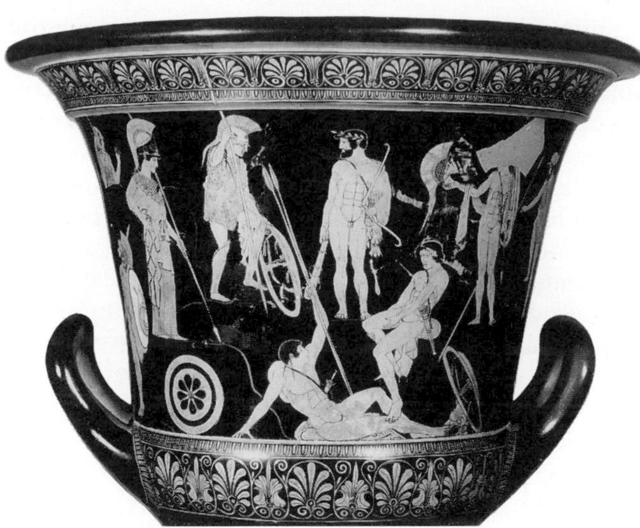

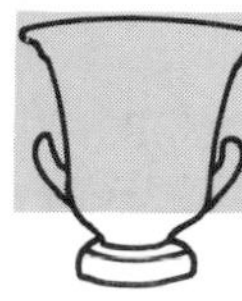

5-60 NIOBID PAINTER, *Argonaut Krater,* from Orvieto, *c.* 455–450 B.C. Outline drawing at right indicates relation to whole vessel. Portion shown approx. 15″ high, whole vessel approx. 21″ high. Louvre, Paris.

ment in Greek monumental painting seems to be provided by surviving Etruscan frescoes, which presumably reflect contemporary, or slightly earlier, Greek mural styles (see Chapter 6). On the *Argonaut Krater,* the figures have been placed on different levels, and the ground lines on which they stand or recline attempt to introduce into painting the illusion of depth, an effect that is thwarted here by the uniform size of the figures. Ancient reports state that Polygnotos modeled his figures in dark and light, aiming for three-dimensional and sculptural effects. This last feature was not adopted by the Niobid Painter, whose style remains linear and does not reveal what must have been an impressive statuesque quality of Polygnotan figures. The Niobid Painter's works are important as dim reflections of the monumental manner of Polygnotos, but they also represent the decline of vase painting; as the figurative decoration loses contact with the body of the vessel, the earlier cohesion of figure and surface becomes mere adhesion.

Although the work of the Niobid Painter may provide us with some idea of the general compositional schemes of Polygnotos, it tells nothing of his use of color. A pale reflection of his color usage may be found in the so-called *white-ground* vases of the fifth century B.C. Experiments with the white-ground technique date back to the Andokides Painter, but the method became popular only toward the middle of the fifth century B.C. The white-ground technique is essentially a variation of the red-figure technique; the pot was first covered with a slip of very fine white clay that, when burnished, provided a glossy or *matte* white surface on which to draw in black glaze or dilute brown wash. The range of colors remained limited to purple, brown, and several kinds of red; few colors known to the Greeks could survive the heat of the kiln. Another shortcoming was the fact that the white slip, although highly effective as background for drawing and coloring, was not durable and tended to flake off. This impermanence was crucial for wares that saw daily use, such as cups and kraters, but was less important in vessels that had a more limited use, such as funerary *lekythoi* (oil flasks), which were not handled after they had been deposited in the tomb. After mid-century, the white-ground technique was reserved almost exclusively for funerary vases of this type, some of which were even painted in full polychrome *after* the vase had been fired (and at an even greater cost in durability).

The krater by the PHIALE PAINTER, illustrated in FIG. **5-61**, shows Hermes handing the infant Dionysos to Papposilenos ("granddad-satyr"). The other figures represent the nymphs in the shady glens of Nysa, where Zeus had sent Dionysos, one of his numerous natural sons, to be raised, safe from the possible wrath of his wife, Hera. The artist has used the conservative colors that could withstand firing—reds, brown, purple, and a special snowy white. The white was used for the flesh of the nymphs and for such details as the hair, beard, and shaggy body of Papposilenos. Despite this rather limited color scheme, the painting's effect is warm and rich; in

5-61 PHIALE PAINTER, *Hermes Bringing the Infant Dionysos to Papposilenos* (krater), from Vulci, c. 440–435 B.C. Approx. 14″ high. Vatican Museums, Rome.

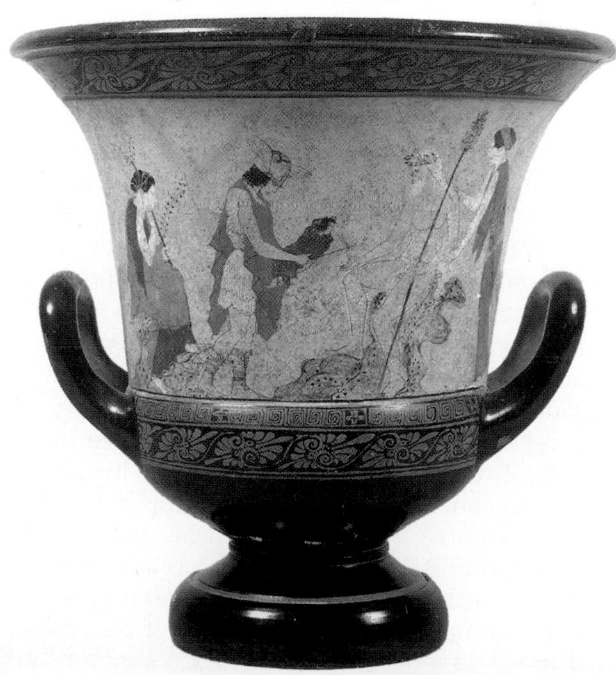

combination with the compositional devices of the Niobid Painter, it may provide a shadowy idea of the appearance of the famed Polygnotan murals, which so impressed ancient viewers.

The grandeur of the age of Phidias and Polykleitos, when their styles briefly dominated Greek art, passed with them. What followed, although exquisite and virtuoso, constituted a descent from the heights, as Greek art became more elegant, slight, naturalistic, and less concerned with lofty themes and majestic forms. The statues of "godlike" men became statues of men of this world.

THE LATE CLASSICAL PERIOD: 430–323 B.C.

The Peloponnesian War, which began in 431 B.C., ended in 404 B.C. with the complete defeat of Athens and left Greece drained of its strength. Sparta and then Thebes took the leadership of Greece, both unsuccessfully. In the latter half of the fourth century B.C., the Greek states lost their liberty to Philip of Macedon. Athens lost its precedence, and the whole structure of life changed; the traditional balance between the city-state and the individual was lost. The serene idealism of the fifth century, born of a simple, robust concept of mind and matter, of man and the state, gave way to chronic civil wars, social and political unrest, skepticism, and cynicism.

The Apollonian command, "Know thyself," which Socrates had taught the people as he spoke with them in their daily gathering places, inevitably changed the Greek point of view to a more individualistic one. Euripides, too, seems to have regarded the individual as paramount, and his dramas depict a whole spectrum of human passions and crises. Aristophanes, however, ridiculed both Socrates and Euripides for their apparent departures from the good old classical ways and customs, and especially for their emphasis on the role and value of the individual. During the fourth century B.C., intellectual independence was firmly established by Plato (however much he himself regretted the passing of the old ways), whose doctrine of such eternal forms as "virtue," "justice," and "courage" served as the rational model on which the individual could construct his life. Aristotle, perhaps the most versatile of all thinkers, formulated the operations of reason in the science we call "logic," converting reason into an instrument applicable to all human discourse. Aristotle turned his attention systematically to just about everything that could be of interest to the questing intellect, and among his fundamental contributions is the outline of the sciences of nature.

Thus, gradually separating themselves from the old assurances—the gods, their oracles, and time-honored custom—as prime interpreters of the meaning of life, the Greeks carried on their search to know themselves and to achieve knowledge of the world and life through observant experience. Their dependence on the city-state lessened, until they boasted with Diogenes of being citizens "of the world." Knowing the real, for whatever purpose, became the conspicuously Greek faculty and value. In the midst of political disaster, Greece, in the fourth century, enacted a daring drama of human discovery.

Sculpture

The humanizing tendency that had been gathering force throughout the fifth century B.C. achieved characteristic expression in the sculpture of the fourth century B.C.; themes lost something of the earlier, solemn grandeur and representations of the greater gods gave way to those of lesser gods. At the same time, the naturalistic view of the human figure became fully focused.

Hermes and Dionysos (FIG. **5-62**), once attributed to PRAXITELES himself, is a work of such high quality that it may be taken as a later superb example of that

5-62 Once attributed to PRAXITELES, *Hermes and Dionysos,* from Olympia, *c.* 340 B.C. (?). Marble, approx. 7′ high. Archeological Museum, Olympia.

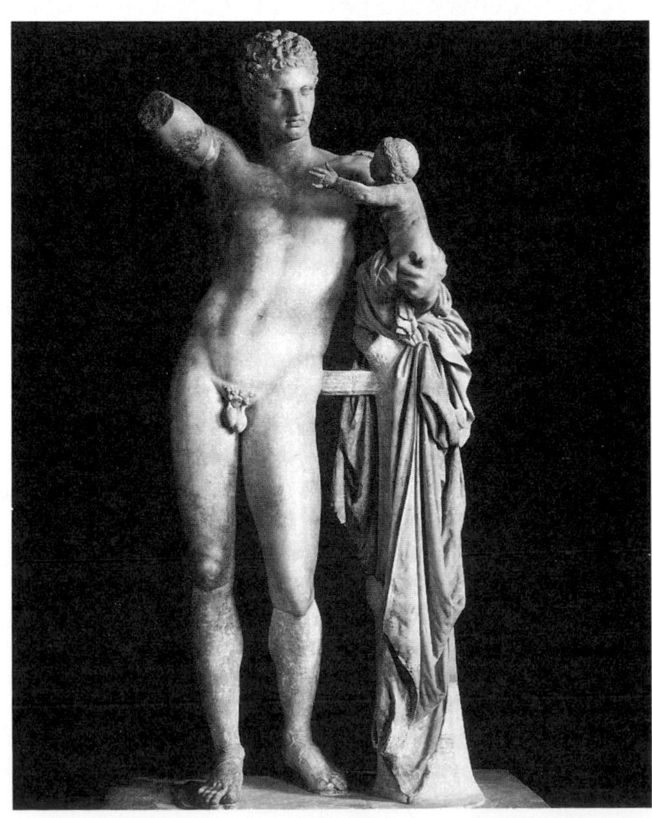

sculptor's style. (Some scholars would even date it as late as the second century B.C., long after Praxiteles' time.) The god is represented standing, with a shift in weight from the left arm (supporting the upper body) to the right leg, so that the double distribution of the weight gives the pose, with its fluid axis, the form of a sinuous, shallow S-curve that becomes a manner with Praxiteles. On his arm, Hermes holds the infant Dionysos, who reaches for something (probably a bunch of grapes) that Hermes held in his right hand. Hermes is looking off into space with a dreamy expression, half smiling. The whole figure, particularly the head, seems in deep reverie, the god withdrawn in self-admiration. The modeling is deliberately smooth and subtle, producing soft shadows that follow the planes as they flow almost imperceptibly one into another. The delicacy of the features is enhanced by the rough, impressionistic way in which the hair is indicated, and the deep folds of the realistic drapery are sharply contrasted with the flow and gloss of the languidly graceful figure. We need but a comparative glance at Polykleitos' *Doryphoros* (FIG. 5-58) to see how broad a change in artistic attitude and intent took place from the mid-fifth to the mid-fourth century. Majestic strength and rationalizing design are replaced by sensuous languor and an order of beauty that appeals more to the eye than to the mind.

Praxiteles' esthetic of the human nude, slenderer in its proportions, with its emphasis on the exquisitely smooth modeling that reproduces the tones of resilient flesh, naturally led him to popularize the nude female statue. His *Aphrodite of Cnidos* was regarded widely in antiquity as the most beautiful of all statues and was the pride of Cnidos, the city that owned it. Its presumed fidelity to natural appearance, a quality much prized by its ancient admirers, is reflected in an old story. The goddess Aphrodite herself, viewing the statue, cried out, "Oh! ye Gods! where could Praxiteles have seen me naked?" The charm of the work can be understood, not from the inferior Roman copy of it, but from a much later, Hellenistic work, the *Aphrodite of Cyrene* (FIG. **5-63**), which, two centuries removed, conveys a Praxitelean poetry of sensual beauty. For both the male and female nude, Praxiteles set a new, more personal and naturalistic ideal of physical beauty.

Although his style was greatly admired and his theme of the bathing Aphrodite was represented again and again long after his time, Praxiteles was not the only influential sculptor of the Late Classical period. A fellow Athenian, SCOPAS, is known for a robust and vigorous style more suited to the representation of action and perhaps derived from Polykleitos. A head fragment from Tegea in Greece (FIG. **5-64**) illustrates Scopas' style and shows a hitherto

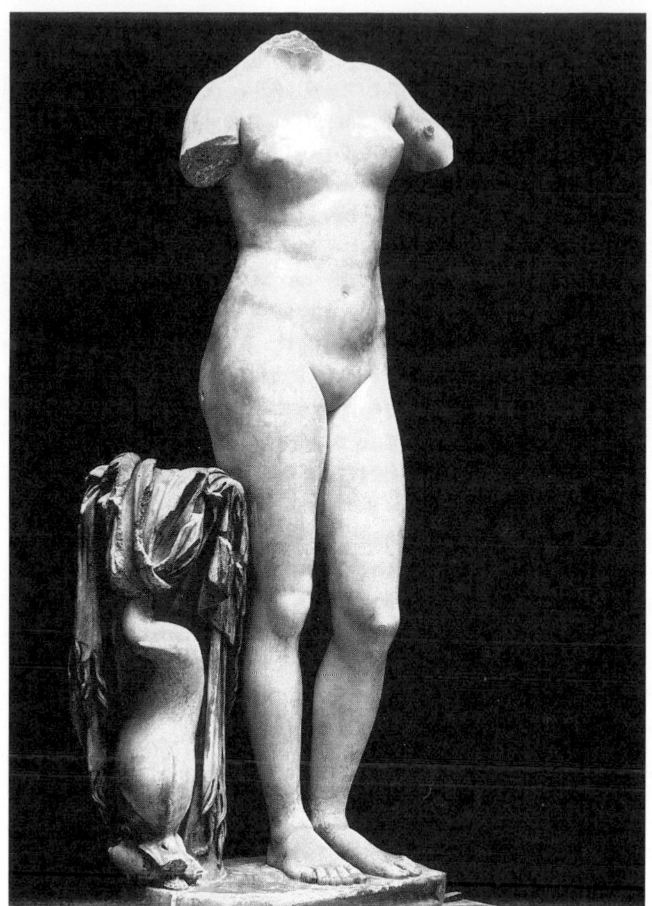

5-63 *Aphrodite of Cyrene,* from North Africa, *c.* 100 B.C. (?). Marble, approx. 56″ high. Museo Nazionale Romano, Rome.

5-64 Attributed to SCOPAS, *Warrior's Head,* from the Temple of Athena Alea at Tegea, Greece, *c.* 350 B.C. Marble, approx. $11\frac{3}{4}$″ high. National Archeological Museum, Athens.

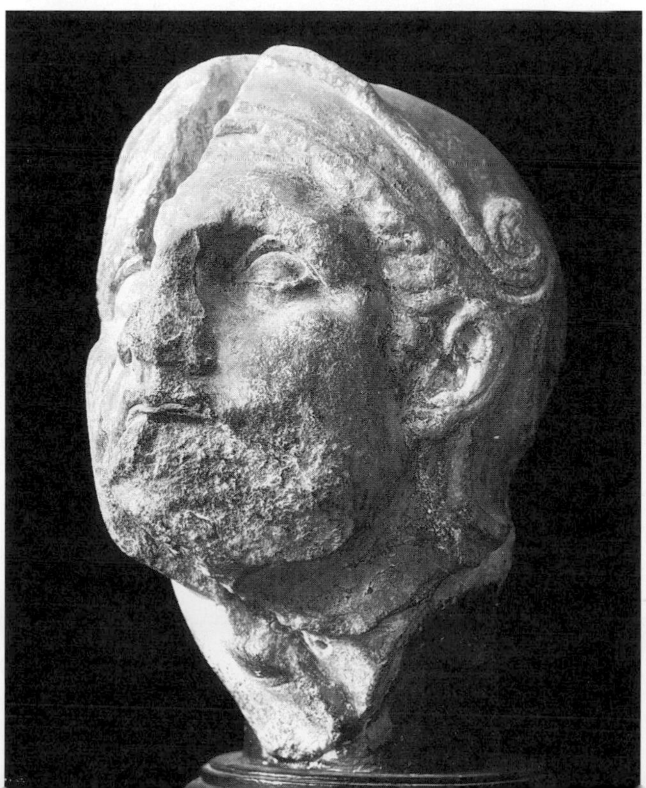

undepicted tension of facial expression. The features are broad and strong, the eyes large, round, and set deeply under knitted brows. As a reflection of inner states through varied facial expressions, this work breaks with the Classical tradition of benign, serene features and prefigures later Hellenistic art, when the depiction of emotion became more important to sculpture.

The monumental Tomb of Mausolus, another of the seven wonders of the ancient world, was built for King Mausolus and his queen, Artemisia. Mausolus was king of Caria, a non-Greek state in southwest Asia Minor, and was in the service of the king of Persia. The colossal portrait-statue of the king (FIG. **5-65**) and another of his queen, which is not shown here, date from about 355 B.C. Presumably, they are intended to be likenesses; the sculptor, who is unknown, is particular about the hair and the dynamics of the drapery. He continues that study of the drapery masses begun in the previous century and is at pains to read them so closely and realistically that folds and pleats are differentiated from the minute creases thin drapery would acquire in use. The colossal tomb monument and the large figures reflect an Eastern influence, and already we sense that mingling of East and West that is to compose the Hellenistic styles of the last centuries before Christ.

The most renowned sculptor of the second half of the fourth century B.C. was LYSIPPOS, court sculptor to Alexander the Great. Although Lysippos was very prolific, his work is extant in copies only, including, notably, the *Apoxyomenos* (FIG. **5-66**), which represents a young athlete scraping oil and mud from his body before taking his bath. The figure embodies two important innovations of the time, which may be credited to Lysippos. One was a new canon of proportions, replacing the Polykleitan canon and reflecting a change in taste noticeable in all the arts. The new canon required a more slender, supple, and tall figure, a conception toward which we have already seen Praxiteles moving. This innovation may indeed have been influenced by the second (also foreshad-

5-65 *Mausolus,* from the mausoleum at Halicarnassus (modern Bodrum, Turkey), *c.* 355 B.C. Marble, approx. 9′ 10″ high. British Museum, London.

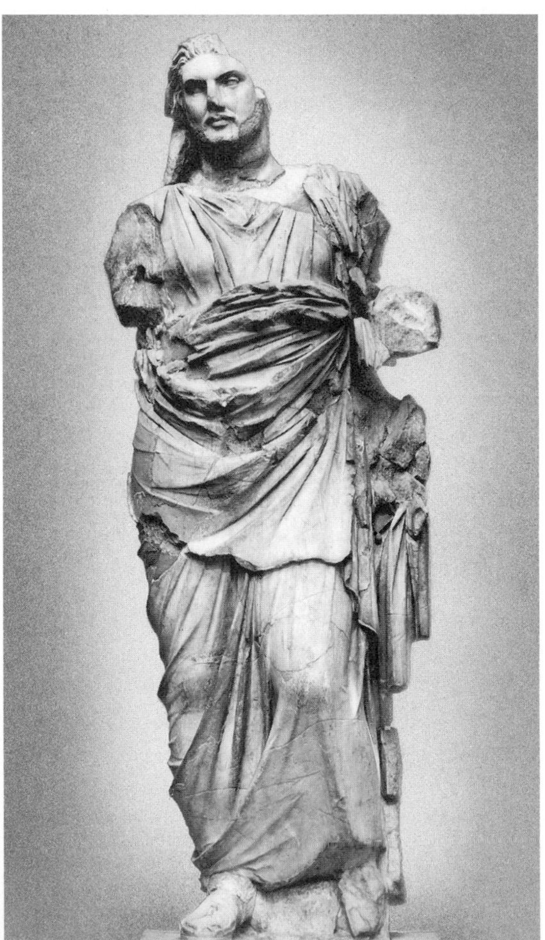

5-66 LYSIPPOS, *Apoxyomenos.* Roman marble copy after a bronze original of *c.* 330 B.C., approx. 6′ 9″ high. Vatican Museums, Rome.

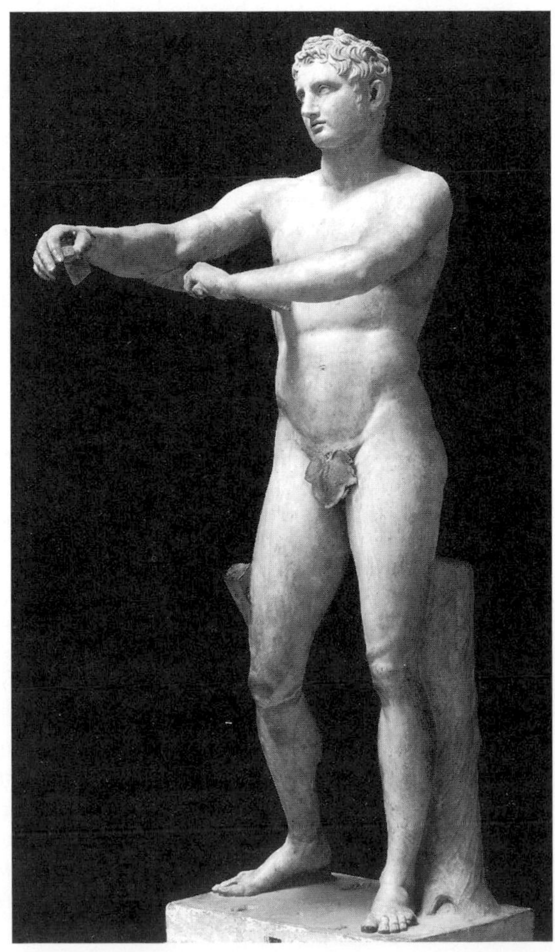

owed in earlier works)—the full realization of the figure as if moving in space, not in the two dimensions of the figures hitherto examined (whether Phidian, Polykleitan, or Praxitelean), but in *three* dimensions. Thus, the figure now seems to move in a kind of free spiral through the space around it; it is made to be seen from a variety of angles and is related to things in its environment other than itself. The earliest Greek figures had been shown in a stiff frontal position, with the planes closely related to the stone block from which they had been carved; they were best seen from only one or two positions. Even when the figure was treated less rigidly, so that the torso as well as the arms and legs moved in a curve, it was still seen satisfactorily only from one or two points of view. In this respect, the Archaic kouros (FIG. 5-16) and the *Hermes and Dionysos* of Praxiteles (FIG. 5-62) are more nearly alike than are the *Hermes* and the *Apoxyomenos* of Lysippos. In the last, the arms curve forward, the figure enclosing space in its reach and twisting in it; the small head is thrown into stronger perspective by the large hand interposed between it and the viewer. Lysippos said that he wished to make men the way the eye sees them, allowing for accidents of perspective.

A bronze figure of a youth (FIG. **5-67**), recovered from the Adriatic Sea near Fano, so clearly expresses the Lysippic intention to show the human body in natural movement through space, that, given its recognizably Lysippic traits, some scholars believe it may be an original from that sculptor's own hand. The tall, slender, elegant young man, whose proportions are certainly Lysippic and whose individualized physique is more that of a runner than a wrestler, appears to be gliding past the observer. His gesture, it has been suggested, is that of an athlete at the games, placing on his head the wreath of victory. The facial features are like those we find in the Roman copies of the statues of Lysippos that record his style, and the naturalness of physique and pose in this masterful work clearly shows the artist's wish to render an image of nature given momentarily to the eye.

Although Lysippos' art tends toward the visually real, something of the older Polykleitan ideal persists in the sculpture of the fourth century, suppressing some features of the real in the interest of ideal form. Indeed, at this time, two stylistic tendencies, *idealizing* and *naturalizing*, prevailed—sometimes moving separately, sometimes merging. In the *Antikythera Youth* (FIG. **5-68**), we find them merging. The head is Polykleitan, as are the massive physique and the forward-walking stance; the unengaged left arm and hand resemble, in attitude and flexure, the right arm and hand of the *Doryphoros* (FIG. 5-58). But in the free

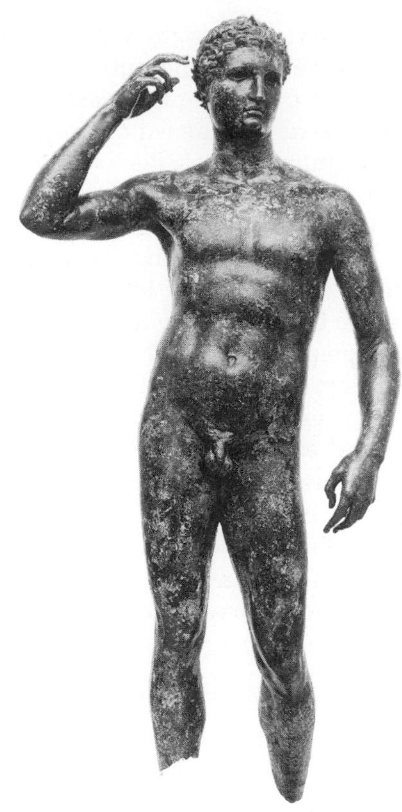

5-67 LYSIPPOS (?), *Athlete (The Getty Bronze)*, late fourth century B.C. Bronze, 6′ high. J. Paul Getty Museum, Malibu, California.

5-68 *Antikythera Youth*, late fourth century B.C., found in the sea off Antikythera, Greece. Bronze, 6′ 4½″ high. National Archeological Museum, Athens.

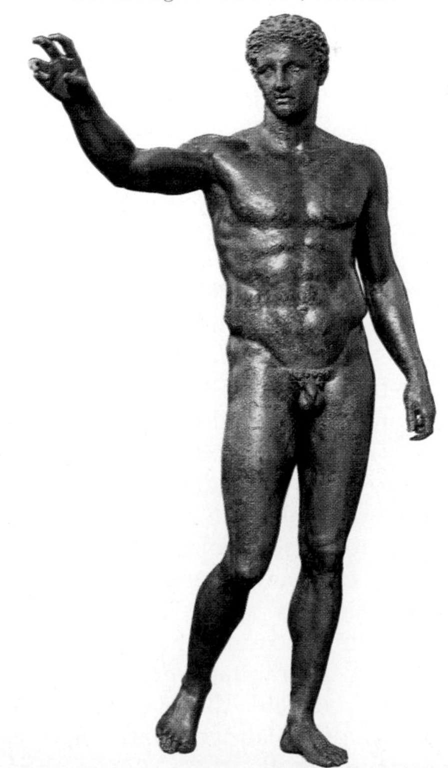

sweep of the far-extended right arm and in the slenderer proportions and flowing outline, we sense the influence of Lysippic style. The gesture the youth makes suggests a subject; he is not simply an athlete throwing a ball, but perhaps a Perseus holding up the severed head of Medusa, or a Herakles reaching for the golden apple he has sought in the Garden of the Hesperides. The meaning of the statue is uncertain, but its exquisite refinement of form and its technical perfection make this one of the finest examples of the Greek art of representing the human figure in bronze.

As Praxiteles prepared the way for developing optical realism in his subtle surface effects, so Scopas and Lysippos foreshadowed Hellenistic themes, demanding force, action, and dramatic emotion. Before the new drama could develop in sculpture, however, space had to be understood in a new way—not merely as the limit of the body, but as an environment in which the body could act freely, as in nature.

Architecture

It is noteworthy that, in its full development of the Corinthian order, the architecture of the fourth century also produced a "body" that offered a complete aspect from any angle. The first Corinthian capital (remember that the order differs from the Ionic only in its capital) appeared on the inside of the naos of the Temple of Apollo at Bassae, in the second half of the fifth century B.C. It crowned a column that, because it stood as a divider between two parts of the naos, could be seen from all sides. Presumably designed for this purpose, the Corinthian capital provided a much more satisfactory solution than the Ionic capital, which was designed to be seen effectively from two sides only. When Ionic colonnades were required to turn corners, as on peripteral structures, special "corner capitals" had to be designed that looked the same on the two sides that faced outward. The sharply projecting edge formed by the two meeting volutes never quite satisfied Classical architects, who also may have felt that this solution was achieved only at the expense of the structural logic of the Ionic capital and by a distortion of its functional parts. The problem was solved by the Corinthian capital, which can be seen to equal advantage from all sides.

The original design of the capital has been associated with the relief sculptor and metalworker Callimachos, who may have been at Bassae when the Temple of Apollo was built. The sentimental story was told of Callimachos in antiquity that he was inspired to design the capital when he saw acanthus leaves—which decorate the Corinthian capital—growing up around a slab-weighted votive basket on the grave of a maiden. Be that as it may, although the Corinthian order appeared in the fifth century B.C., it was used only on the inside of Greek temples for almost a century. Whether this interior use is to be attributed to religious conservatism, which would tend to preserve a feature that had taken on a certain sanctity from its function at the temple's center, or whether Ionic experiments were continuing and a Doric tradition persisting is uncertain. In any event, full emergence of the Corinthian order on a public exterior takes place about the same time as Lysippos' freeing of the sculptured figure from its two-aspect limits.

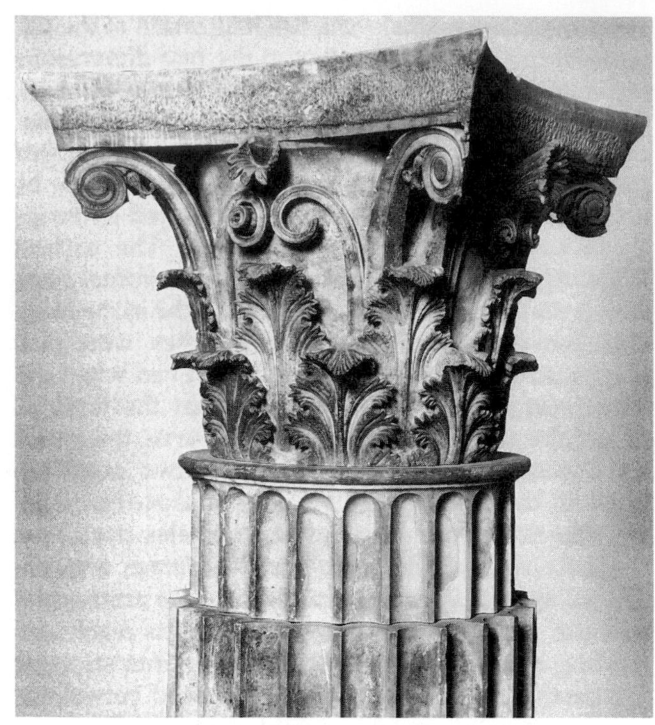

5-69 Corinthian capital from the tholos at Epidauros, c. 350 B.C. Museum, Epidauros.

A mid-fourth century capital from Epidauros (FIG. **5-69**) illustrates a step along the elaborative route of the Corinthian order, which culminates in the characteristic Hellenistic and Roman luxuriance. Here, the bell of the capital is clothed with carved acanthus leaves and manifests that same increasing attention to the deep and detailed sculpturing of stone surfaces noted in sculptured figures.

The Monument of Lysikrates (FIG. **5-70**), constructed in Athens in 334 B.C., shows the first known use of the Corinthian order on the outside of a building. Significantly, the innovation appears not on a religious but on a commemorative monument. The graceful cylinder to which the Corinthian columns are engaged memorializes the victory of a choric group, patronized by Lysikrates, which had won the prized trophy of the tripod in the wild, dithyrambic

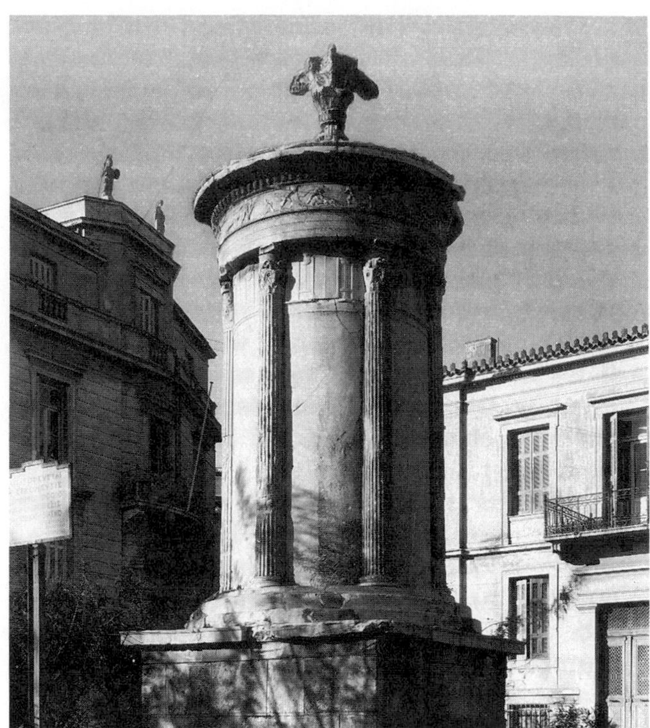

5-70 The Monument of Lysikrates, Athens, 334 B.C.

contest of song in honor of Dionysos. The little tholos serves as a base for the monumentalized tripod. Henceforth, the Corinthian order was used more and more on the exterior of public buildings, enjoying particular favor among Roman builders. In addition to having solved the vexing problems of the Doric and Ionic orders (the corner-triglyph and the corner-volute dilemmas), the Corinthian order, with its ornateness, was bound to suit the developing taste for sumptuous elaboration of form and realistic representation that guided artistic effort in the Hellenistic world.

The capital from Epidauros predates the Monument of Lysikrates by some fifteen years and, significantly, was designed for the interior colonnade of a Doric round temple, or *tholos*. The temple was part of an extensive building program that converted the town of Epidauros into one of the greatest spas of the ancient world. The influx of ever more visitors to the sanctuary of Asklepios, the god of healing, required the construction of ancillary buildings to provide not only for the spiritual and physical health of the numerous patients, but also for their accommodation and entertainment. One of the chief architects at the site was Polykleitos the Younger, who, in addition to the tholos, also designed a theater that Pausanias declared was the finest in Greece.

Almost all major Greek towns had a theater. The precursor of the formal Greek theater was a place where ancient rites, songs, and dances were performed. This circular piece of earth with a hard and level surface later became the *orchestra* of the theater. The rituals were a spectacle and Greek architects provided a convenient place (a *theatron* or "place for seeing") from which nonparticipants could watch. The most practical location was a slope rising above the orchestra; such siting, both logical and efficient, persisted and almost all later Greek theaters were built against or into the natural slopes of hills. If a suitable place could be found at the base of the town's acropolis, as was the case in Athens, the commingling of practical and symbolic elements rendered the site ideal.

At Epidauros, the theater (FIGS. **5-71** and **5-72**) is sited some 500 yards southeast of the sanctuary of

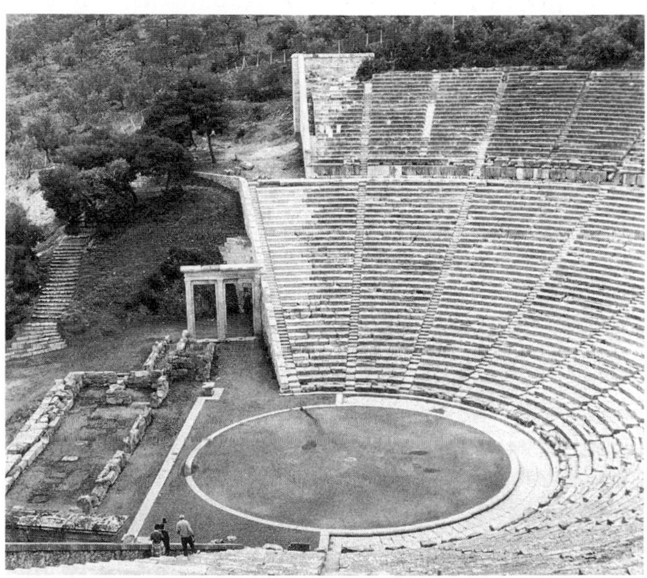

5-71 POLYKLEITOS THE YOUNGER, theater at Epidauros, Greece, *c.* 350 B.C.

5-72 Plan of the theater at Epidauros. (After F. Krischen.)

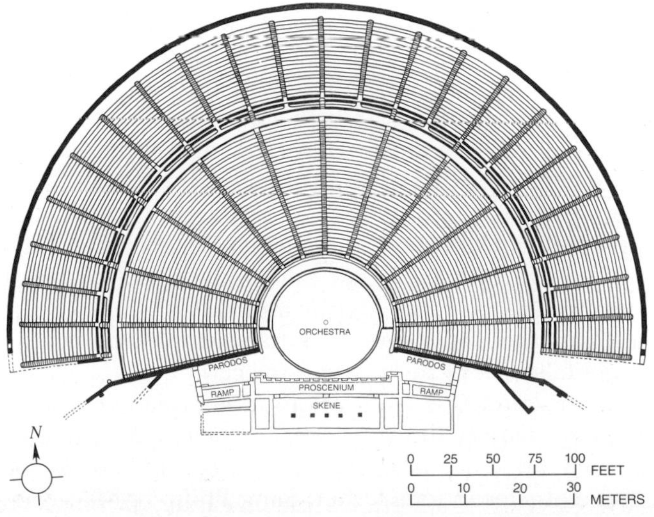

Asklepios. The slightly more than semicircular auditorium, with a diameter of 387 feet and a capacity of about fourteen thousand spectators, is built into the side of a hill. Staircase aisles, laid out on radii projecting from the center of the circular orchestra (where the chorus of Greek dramas performed), separate blocks of stone benches that are divided into two tiers by a broad corridor. The *proscenium* and the *skene* were arranged for maximum viewing convenience of the performance. The *parados,* a passageway between stage and seats, is wide enough to permit rapid exit. Unfortunately, the superstructure of the stage has not survived, but the acoustics are still excellent and the theater is used even today for summer productions of ancient Greek drama. When the acoustic excellence is added to the superb layout of the theater, the result is a harmonious structure that is admirably efficient and perfectly suited to its purpose. Such careful planning for the convenience of an audience represents a shift away from the ritualistic origins of the theater and marks, as did the New Comedy plays performed at the time the theater was built, increasing concern for individual views and responses.

THE HELLENISTIC PERIOD: 323–30 B.C.

Philip of Macedon brought the once-free Greek city-states into subjection. His son, Alexander the Great, educated in Hellenism, the culture of Greece, by none other than Aristotle, returned the visit the Persians had made to Greece a century and a half before, overthrew their empire, and conquered all the Near East, including Egypt. Greek conquest of this vast area produced a culture and period called Hellenistic—a curious mingling of Western and Eastern ideas, religions, and arts—and a long period of Greek cultural and partly political dominance that made her the cosmopolitan heir of Sumer, Babylon, Egypt, Assyria, and Persia. Greedy for the lands their young leader had conquered, his generals asked Alexander on his death bed, "To which one of us do you leave your empire?" In the skeptical manner of the age, but also with more than a tinge of an older irony, he supposedly answered, "To the strongest." Although probably apocryphal, this exchange points up the near inevitability of what followed—the division of Alexander's far-flung empire among his Greek generals and their subsequent naturalization among the Orientals whom they held subject.

In the late 1970s, excavations at Vergina in northern Greece, within the territory of ancient Macedonia, turned up what is now widely regarded to be the grave of Alexander's father, King Philip of Macedon. Among the rich finds, which only a royal tomb might be thought to yield, were five tiny portrait heads in ivory, presumably representing Philip, Alexander, and other members of the family. The portrait thought to be that of King Philip (FIG. **5-73**) shows in miniature those tendencies toward realism, already appearing in the earlier fourth century B.C., that ripened to maturity in the Hellenistic period. The king's features are highly personalized, vividly mobile, and expressive—broadly and surely modeled in the details. Undoubtedly, the sculptor was closely familiar with his king and patron's face, so confident is he in the representation of it. In the Hellenistic world, the relationship of royal patron and artist was to draw ever closer.

The centers of culture in the Hellenistic period were the court cities of Greek kings—Antioch in Syria, Alexandria in Egypt, Pergamon in Asia Minor, and others. An international culture united the Hellenistic world, and its language was Greek. Hellenistic princes became enormously rich on the spoils of the East, priding themselves on their libraries, art collections, scientific enterprises, and skills as critics and connoisseurs, as well as on the learned men they could assemble at their courts. The world of the small, austere, and heroic city-state passed away, as had the power and prestige of its center, Athens; a "world" civilization, much like today's, replaced it.

5-73 *Philip of Macedon* (?), from Vergina, c. 350 B.C. Ivory, $1\frac{1}{4}$" high. Archeological Museum, Salonika.

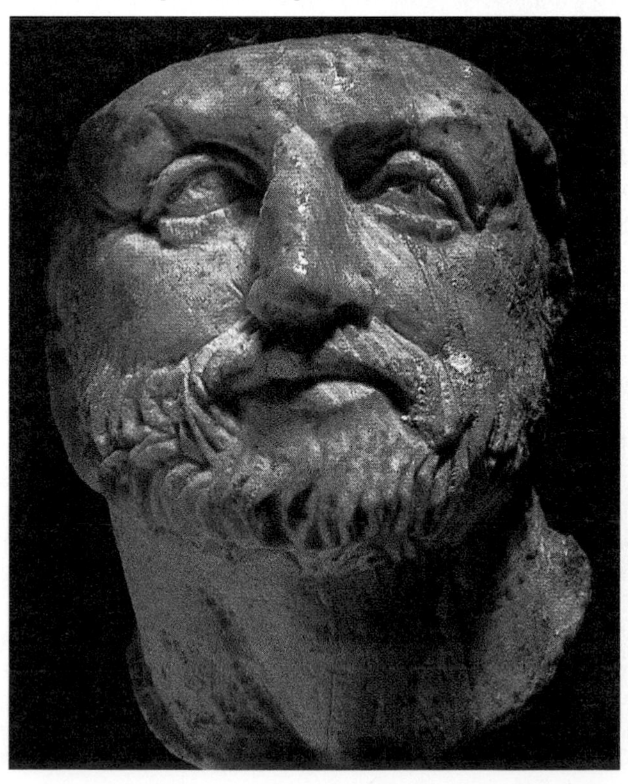

Sculpture

The tendencies traced thus far from the Archaic period were not interrupted by this complex change in political fortunes and cultural affiliations but simply proceeded to anticipated completions. The Hellenistic artists' technical command of the medium and virtuosity in manipulation of form mutually reinforce one another in a masterpiece of the second century B.C., the *Dherveni Krater* (FIG. **5-74**). Composed of hammered gilt-bronze with encrustations of silver, this sumptuous vessel is an incomparable specimen of the metalworker's craft, perfected by a long tradition that may reach back to Mycenaean times. The material, perfectly malleable in the artist's hands, embodies effortlessly wrought representations of the human figure, gracefully disposed upon and around the body of the piece. Hard metal is transfigured into a glowing vision of the erotic; ecstatic Maenads, almost nude, dance exuberantly in celebration of the rites of their god Dionysos. The god himself, tall, slender, and supple, reclines in sensual indolence, his right leg across the lap of Ariadne, who demurely removes her veil. Yet, despite the theme of voluptuous pleasure that dominates the vessel, the purpose of the krater is funerary; it was intended as part of the burial treasure of a doubtless

5-74 *Dherveni Krater,* second century B.C. Bronze with silver incrustations, 27½" high. Archeological Museum, Salonika.

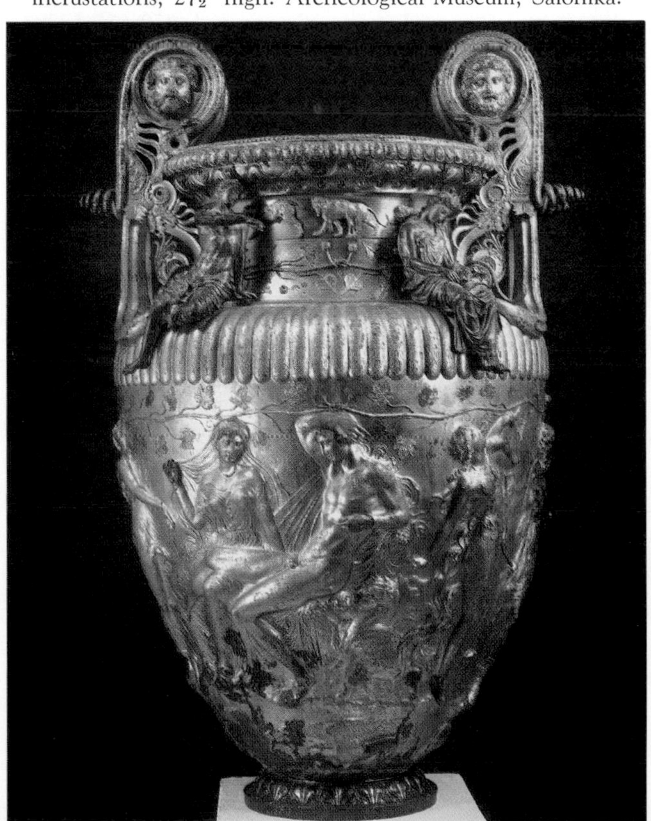

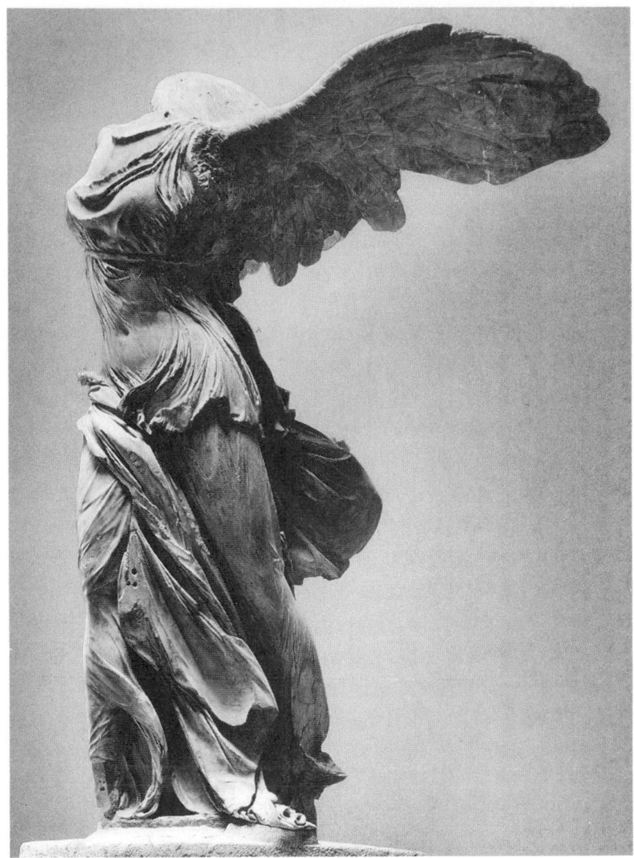

5-75 *Nike of Samothrace,* c. 190 B.C. Marble, approx. 8′ high. Louvre, Paris.

wealthy and sybaritic patron. The four solid-cast female figures around the neck of the krater may, by their pensive mien, provide the note of mourning we would think appropriate to the vessel's mortuary purpose; yet, as we have seen so often in ancient art, themes of life can be associated with those of death in tomb paintings and furnishings. In any event, the *Dherveni Krater* exemplifies the high degree of sophistication achieved by the cosmopolitan culture of the Hellenistic world, its artists' superb technical mastery, their expert rendering of the human figure in its natural aspects, and the scope and refinement of their knowledge of the great themes of Greek myth, lyric, and drama. Here, the themes of Eros (love) and Thanatos (death) meet in perfect harmony.

The "environment" that opened up around the *Apoxyomenos* of Lysippos (FIG. 5-66) opened up still more around the *Nike of Samothrace* (FIG. **5-75**). The goddess of victory is represented as alighting on the prow of a war galley, triumphant in some conflict among the successors of Alexander in the Greek world around 190 B.C. One of the masterpieces of the Hellenistic age, the *Nike of Samothrace,* windswept, her wings still beating, her missing right arm (a fragment of the hand survives) once raised high in an imperious gesture of victory, brings strength, weight, and airy grace into an equipoise one would not expect to see achieved in the hard mass of sculptured marble. Here, the sculptors have worked their stone with a freedom emulative of painters, achieving shadows and gradations of shadows by variations of surface carving, almost as if they were using heavy instead of light brush strokes. The gauzelike stretch of material across the stomach and the waves of drapery around the striding thighs and legs amount not only to an exercise in virtuosity of stonecraft but a successful effort to make stone do what poetry and painting do—render at the same time the visual nuances of the moment and the ongoing essence of action. In the end, the sculptor wants us to sense, from the figure itself, an atmosphere of wind and sea.

The statue was found on the island of Samothrace in the ruins of a monumental fountain situated on a lofty rise overlooking the harbor and the sea. Reconstruction of the site shows that the Nike and the war galley were part of a larger composition. The group was set into a rock-walled grotto and dominated a great, two-tiered fountain, its reflection caught in the rippling pool of the lower basin. The effect was an illusion of the victorious galley in full sail, breasting the brisk sea breeze and the surge of the waves. The wind that whips the drapery about the body of the Nike and the moving waters that buoy the ship are thus replicated in a composition that binds together artificial and natural elements, integrating the sculptured group with its environment of shaped rock and flowing water. Much visited in ancient times, the Nike ship-fountain at Samothrace is perhaps the finest example of the victorious ship motif familiar on the coins and sculptural reliefs of the Greco-Roman world; the motif appears again in the Baroque period of later European art.

The extension of the spatial environment of the figure, so as to suggest a stage on which it may and does act, appears in sculptures associated with the Hellenistic kingdom of Pergamon and the island republic of Rhodes, in the third, second, and first centuries B.C. From a group dedicated by Attalus I of Pergamon (241–197 B.C.), a figure, in Roman copy, survives of a *Dying Gaul* (FIG. **5-76**). The figure is on stage, realistic, and also historical, representing a Gallic casualty in the wars Attalus had just fought with barbarian invaders. Comparison of the *Dying Gaul* and the *Fallen Warrior* from Aegina (FIG. 5-32) shows that, in a little more than two centuries, the principle of uniformity of movement had been learned well. The Gaul, dying from a chest wound that bleeds heavily, slowly loses strength, his weight falling rapidly on his last support, the trembling right arm; its collapse will be his own. The observer reads this at once from the lines and planes of the body—visually, with no need to interpret or expand the meaning. The statue is a triumph of realism. It also may mark the surrender of the interests of sculpture to the stage, where, we know, spectacles of human suffering painted with all realism of detail were sapping the great tradition of drama and diminishing human life in bloody scenes that could only present it as worthless. With the *Dying Gaul,* the sculpture of action degenerates into brutal stagecraft. Realism can go no further, even while it triumphs.

A later school of Pergamon exhibits a realism not quite so explicit, yet nonetheless related to the Hel-

5-76 *Dying Gaul.* Roman marble copy after a bronze original from Pergamon of *c.* 240 B.C., life size. Museo Capitolino, Rome.

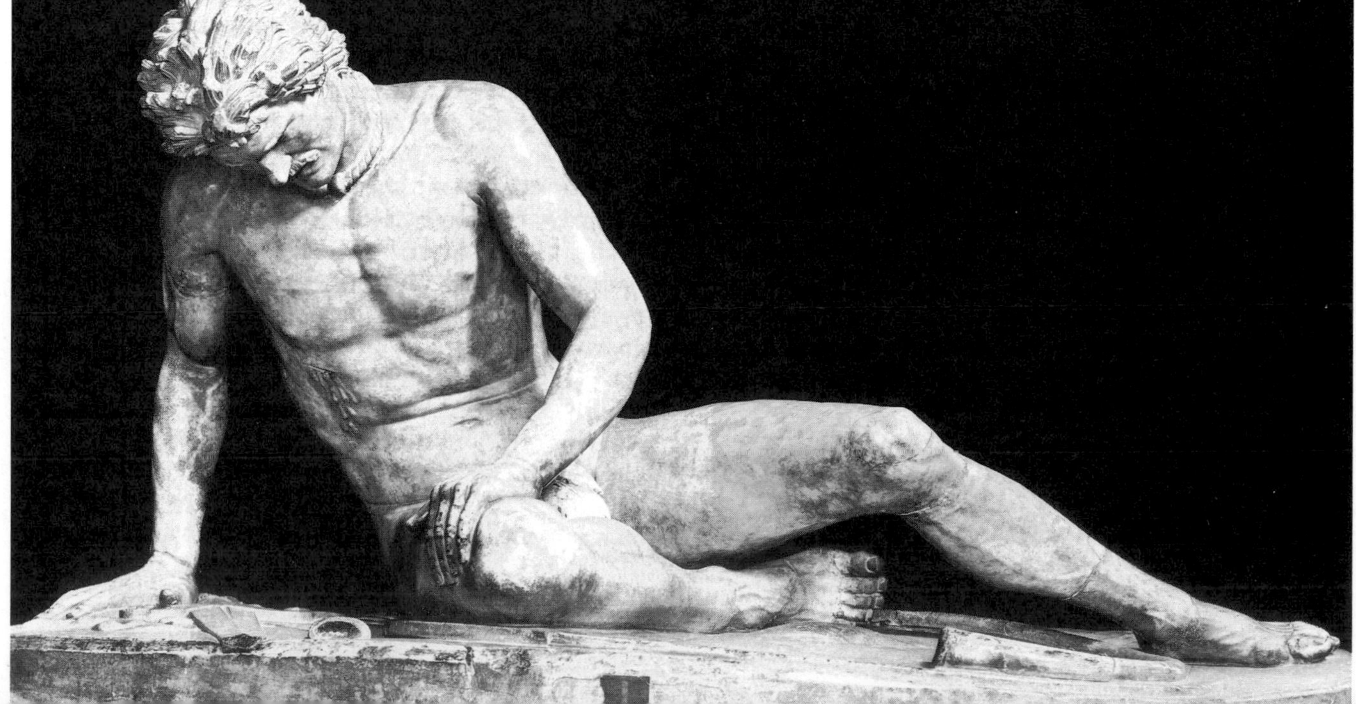

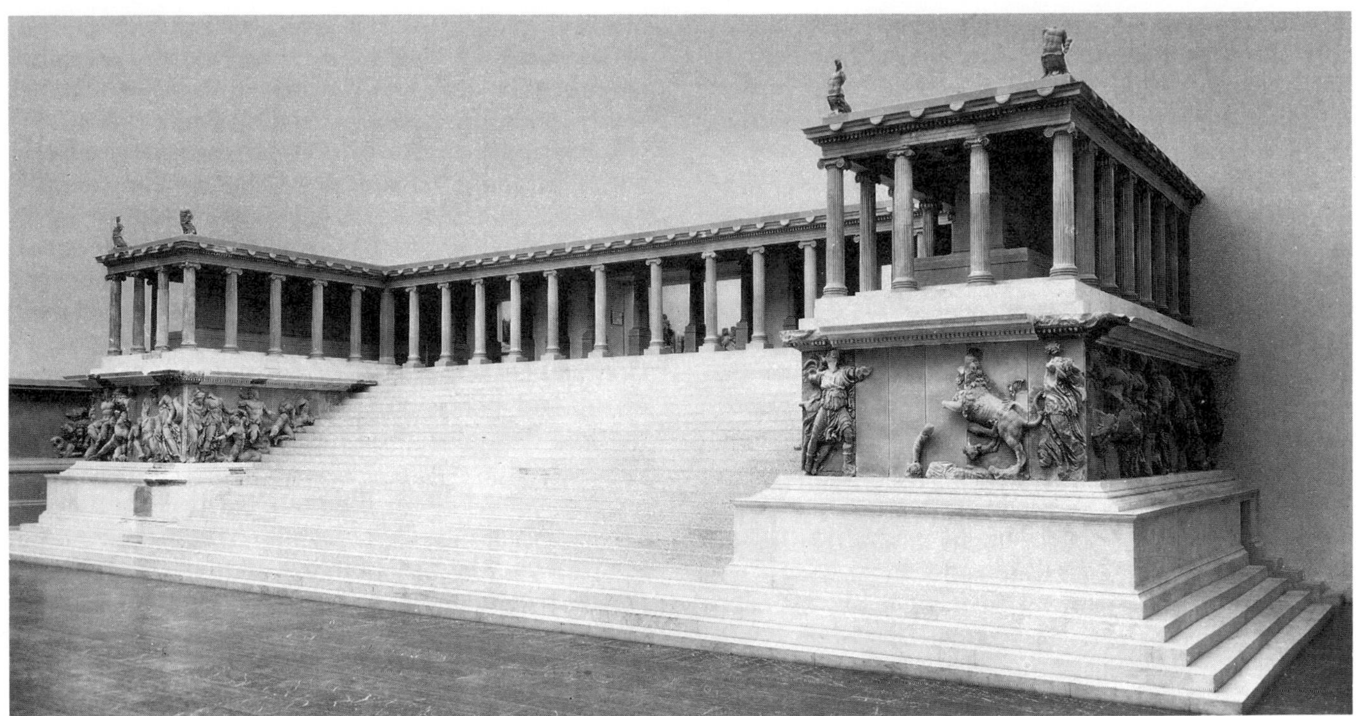

5-77 Altar of Zeus and Athena, Pergamon, *c.* 175 B.C. Staatliche Museen, Antiken-Sammlung, East Berlin. (West front restored.)

lenistic taste for tableaux of monumental suffering. A section of the great frieze of the *Battle of the Gods and Giants* from the Pergamon Altar of Zeus and Athena (FIGS. **5-77** and **5-78**) illustrates the highly dramatic kind of figurative sculpture that descended from Scopas and Lysippos. The altar was erected about 175 B.C. by the son and successor of Attalus I to glorify his father's victories. In a representation less factual than the group of dying Gauls, the artists here revert to the traditional Greek approach of presenting historical events in mythological disguise. The suffering and death, the writhing gesticulation, are somewhat formalized and we do not feel so much that we are in the presence of pain that ordinary men might feel. In the figure of Alcyoneos, the young giant whom Athena takes by the hair (FIG. 5-78), the anguish of the face is based on Scopas and the twisting of the figure on the athleticism of both Scopas and Lysippos. The tragic content is read through the increasingly dramatic style of stonecraft. The Greek revision of the climactic instant is still seen against a neutral background. Now, however, shadows almost obscure the background, from which the figures project like bursts of light. All these devices are "baroque" and closely related to those developed in seventeenth-century Europe. The unity of the design is achieved by a fluid, yet binding organization of parts, not unlike that of the figures of the *Three Goddesses* of the Parthenon (FIG. 5-47). Indeed, the two major figures of the frieze, Zeus and Athena, are inspired directly by the figures of Poseidon and Athena from the Parthenon pediments; yet this dynamic integration of the whole composition is unlike the carefully studied relationships of *separate* parts seen in the Early Classical period. In such pictorial unity, produced by the movement of light and the contrast of shade, we again recognize the strong influence of painting.

5-78 *Athena Taking Young Alcyoneos by the Hair,* from the frieze of the Altar of Zeus and Athena, Pergamon. Marble, 7′ 6″ high. Staatliche Museen, Antiken-Sammlung, East Berlin.

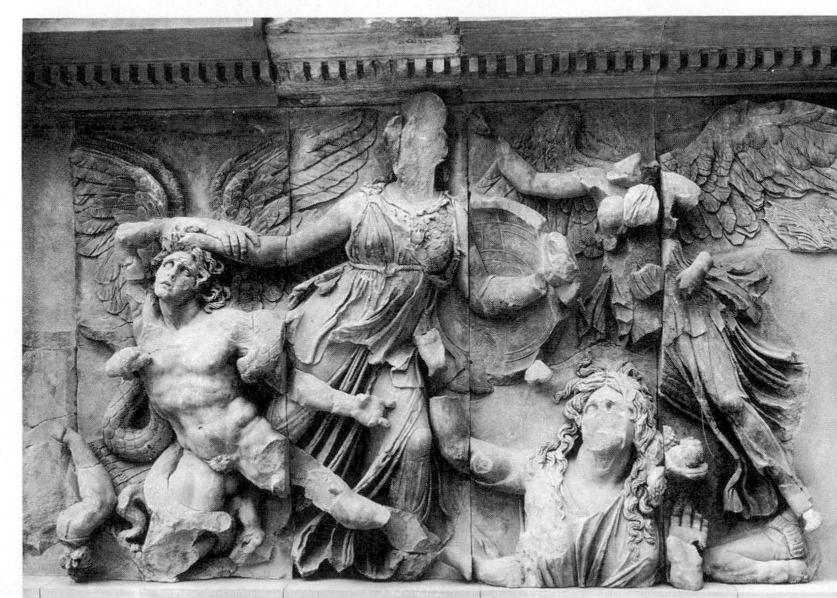

The theme of suffering is so pervasive in the Hellenistic world and its art that it could almost be understood as *the* interpretation of life by those who felt the hopelessness attendant on the decline of an older, more reasonable system. A late work of Hellenistic sculpture, the *Laocoön* group (now thought to date from the first century A.D.), was the product of a still quite active school at Rhodes (FIG. **5-79**). It shows the Trojan priest, Laocoön, and his sons being strangled by sea serpents, some say because of his defiance of Apollo, others, because he offended Poseidon (who sided with the Greeks) by warning his Trojan compatriots about the Trojan Horse. Whatever his offense, Vergil described his plight with unsparing realism:

> Laocoön . . . they [the sea serpents] seize and bind in mighty folds; and now, twice encircling his waist, twice winding their scaly backs around his throat, they tower above with head and lofty necks. He the while strains his hands to burst the knots, his fillets steeped in blood and black venom; the while he lifts to heaven hideous cries, like the bellowings of a wounded bull that has fled from the altar and shaken from its neck the ill-aimed axe. (*Aeneid*, II, 40–56, 199–231)

5-79 *Laocoön* group, first century B.C. to first century A.D. Marble, 8′ high. Vatican Museums, Rome. (Partially restored.)

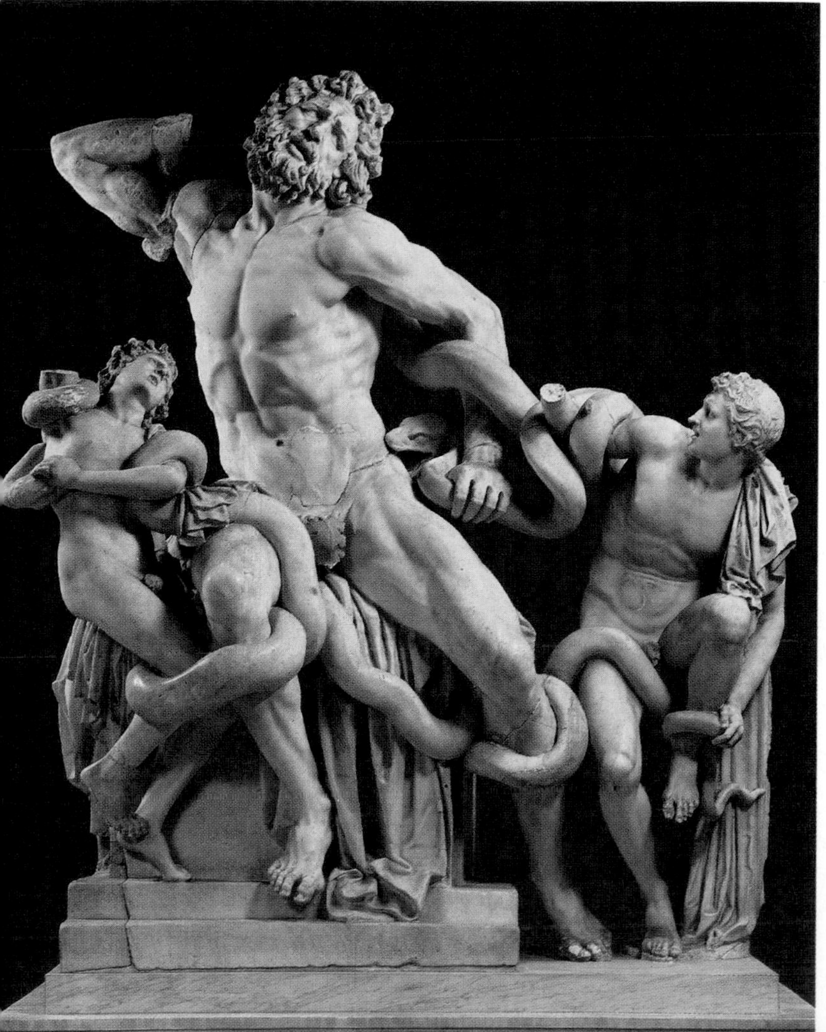

The spectacular torment of Laocoön and his sons is presented with all the devices of rhetorical realism available to artists as well as poets—the tortuous poses, straining muscles, and swelling veins. Yet, curiously, the figures exhibit lapses from consistent visual fact, as in the perhaps deliberate disproportion of the size of the sons in relationship to the size of the father, indicating them as *sons*, although they appear simply as small men.* The exceedingly popular group was reproduced frequently, sometimes on a colossal scale; in the eighteenth century, the analysis of it by Gotthold Lessing in his *Laocoön* led to his designation of art and poetry as opposed in function and to the foundation of the branch of philosophy called *esthetics*.

Pliny named three Rhodians as the sculptors of the *Laocoön* group: AGESANDER, ATHENODOROS, and POLYDOROS. The same three names are inscribed on the stern of a marble ship (FIG. **5-80**) that formed part of one of several sculptured groups, fragments of which have been found in a large grotto near the sea at Sperlonga, some eighty miles south of Rome. The cave, adjacent to a large imperial Roman villa built early in the first century A.D., had been used as a kind of dining room. Multifigured, sculptured groups appear to have been displayed in two niches and in a round central pool within the grotto. At least some of the sculptures must have been brought from Rhodes and were installed in the grotto around A.D. 29, when the cave was refashioned after a partial collapse.

A definitive interpretation of the scenes is difficult because the groups were found only in fragments, the figures evidently having been smashed to make lime or out of religious fanaticism. Three scenes from the *Odyssey* seem to have been represented: the blinding of Polyphemos (among the finds are the legs of a colossus that must have stood nearly 20 feet high), Scylla attacking Odysseus' ship, and a sinking ship. Our illustration shows the terrified helmsman falling from the stern of the sinking vessel (FIG. 5-80). The dramatic group may have been placed, quite strikingly, against the dark, stalactite-covered walls of the cave. Probably the finest of the fragments is the *Head of Odysseus* (FIG. **5-81**) from another group. Less convulsed and emotional than Laocoön's head, it nevertheless reflects strikingly the horrifying situation and the fear of impending death. The effect is produced not by the use of grimaces or the exaggerated eyes and anguished mouth of Laocoön but by the wind-tossed, whirling hair and beard that frame the face of the Homeric hero. The dating of the Sperlonga sculptures has been a matter of ardent debate

*The second son, on the viewer's right, may have been added by the sculptors when working from an earlier group that had only two figures. The greater compositional integration of the two left figures is obvious.

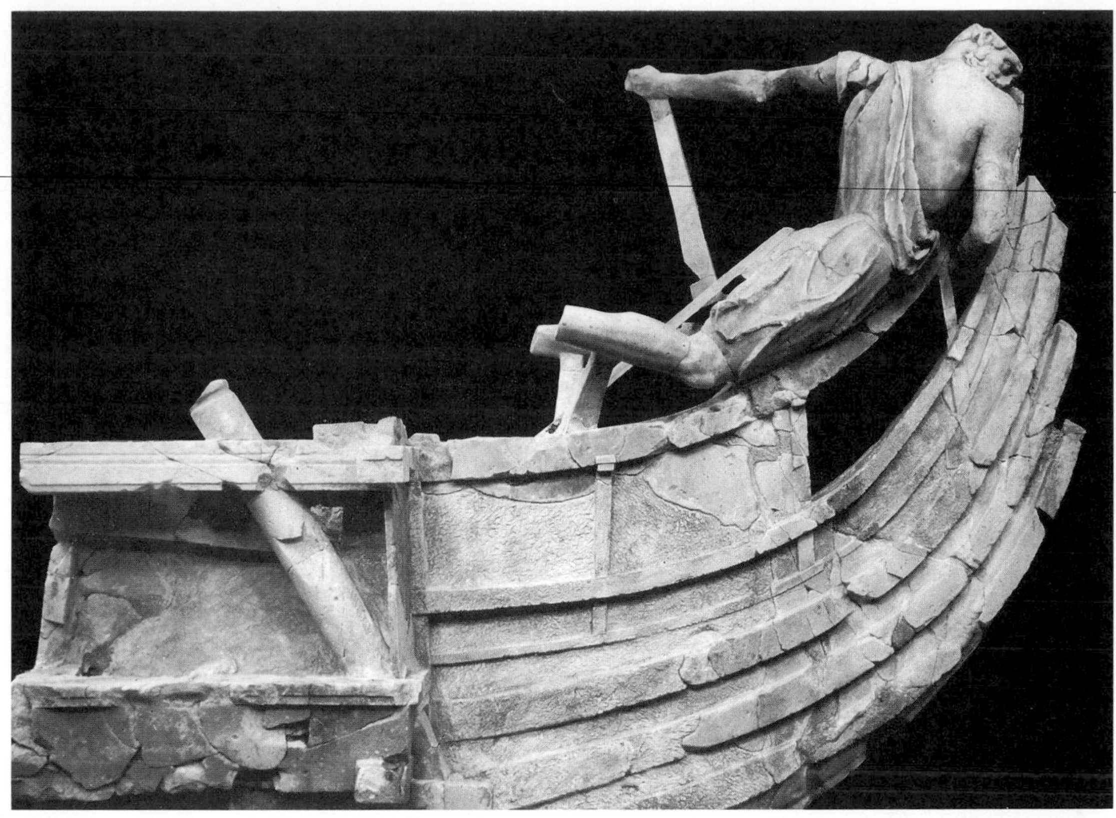

5-80 AGESANDER, ATHENODOROS, and POLYDOROS, *Odysseus' Helmsman Falling*, first century B.C. to first century A.D. Marble, approx. life size. Museo Archeologico Nazionale, Sperlonga, Italy.

5-81 AGESANDER, ATHENODOROS, and POLYDOROS, *Head of Odysseus*, first century B.C. to first century A.D. Marble, life size. Museo Archeologico Nazionale, Sperlonga, Italy.

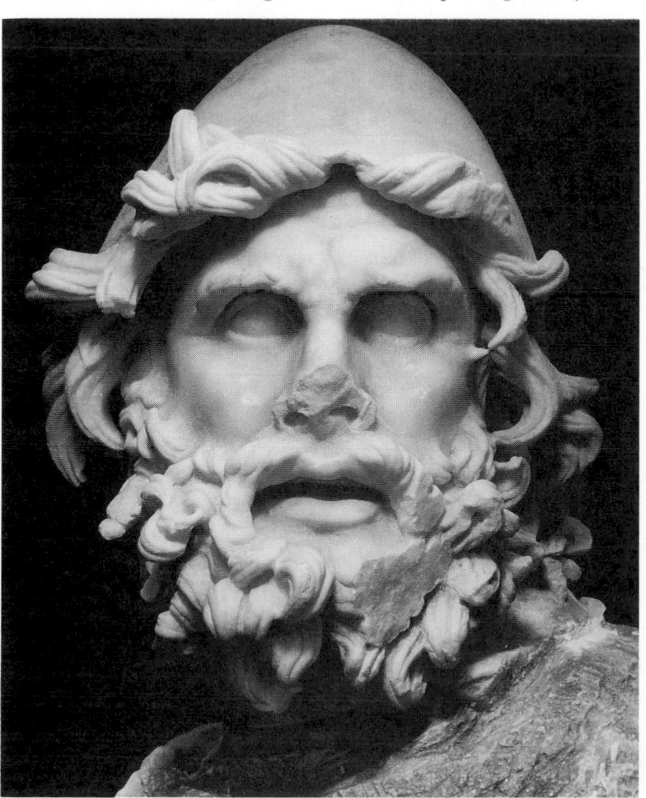

since their discovery in 1957. Dates from the second century B.C. to the first century A.D. have been advanced, shifting the *Laocoön* dates accordingly. If the same masters produced the two groups, scholars suggest that the Sperlonga figures must be earlier than the *Laocoön* group, because they show the expressive power of the Rhodian sculptors at its height, before it succumbed to the theatrical exhibitionism that marks the *Laocoön* sculpture.

Side by side with the drama of suffering, Hellenistic sculpture continued the tradition of ideal, Praxitelean beauty seen in the *Aphrodite of Cyrene* (FIG. 5-63). Another Hellenistic descendant of this Praxitelean line is the *Aphrodite of Melos* (FIG. **5-82**), the famed *Venus de Milo.* Here, again the ideal is taken out of the hypersensible world of reasoned proportions and made into an apparition of living flesh, like the coming alive of Pygmalion's statue of Galatea. The feeling for stone as stone has quite surrendered to the ambition of making stone look as though it were the soft, warm substance of the human body. Such effects as these can be obtained only by an artist with brilliant technical facility working in the conviction that the business of the artist is to produce from stone a vision of beauty, faithful to optical reality but modified to make the keenest appeal to the senses as a flawless manifestation of the human form. In some cases, faithfulness to optical fact also can lead the

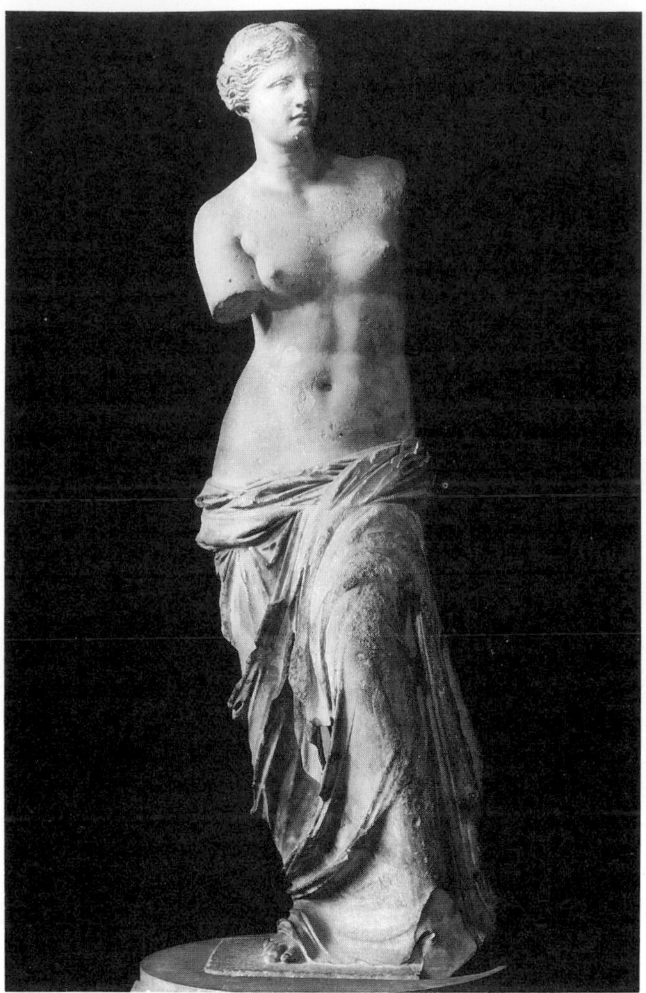

5-82 *Aphrodite of Melos,* c. 150–100 B.C. Marble, approx. 6′ 10″ high. Louvre, Paris.

sculptor to represent, with unflattering explicitness, the opposite of beauty, as seen in the *Old Market Woman* (FIG. **5-83**). This bent, hobbling creature is offered to the viewer as an object of contempt, pity, or disgust, depending on one's temperament.

The disparity in subject of these two works reflects the wide scope of theme and the visual curiosity of Hellenistic sculptors. They aim to move the observer in terms of the themes of their work. They wish, moreover, for recognition by the observer of those traits in the statue that the observer knows in life, so that a large part of the response to the statue comes from the observer's familiarity with its model or type in the context of personal experience. Thus, while the Classical sculptor generally showed young adults at the height of their physical development, the Hellenistic artist expanded the subject matter to include not only the very old but also the very young. A group of two figures, *Eros and Psyche* (FIG. **5-84**), who symbolize love and the human soul, represent adolescents in fond embrace, oblivious to all but themselves. The story of Eros and Psyche was popular in the Hellenistic and Roman worlds and was often retold; the reader can find a late and beautiful retelling of it in Apuleius' *The Golden Ass.* The repertory of worldly and profane (that is, not religious in any formal sense) subjects was opened wide in Hellenistic art, and a principal theme, erotic art, was not overlooked. Plumply sensual, the nude and half-nude figures turn together in an artfully managed contrary motion, not unlike that of a slow, insinuating dance. The rhythmic flow of contour and plane enhances the softly amorous effect, although the artist's intent seems to be to convey prettiness and charm rather than blunt sexuality. In any event, Hellenistic sculptors are now in complete possession of the formal and technical means to render whatever subjects they might choose or might be chosen for them.

It seems unlikely that a fifth-century B.C. sculptor would have imagined that a *Boy Strangling a Goose*

5-83 *Old Market Woman,* second century B.C. Marble, 49½″ high. Metropolitan Museum of Art, New York (Rogers Fund).

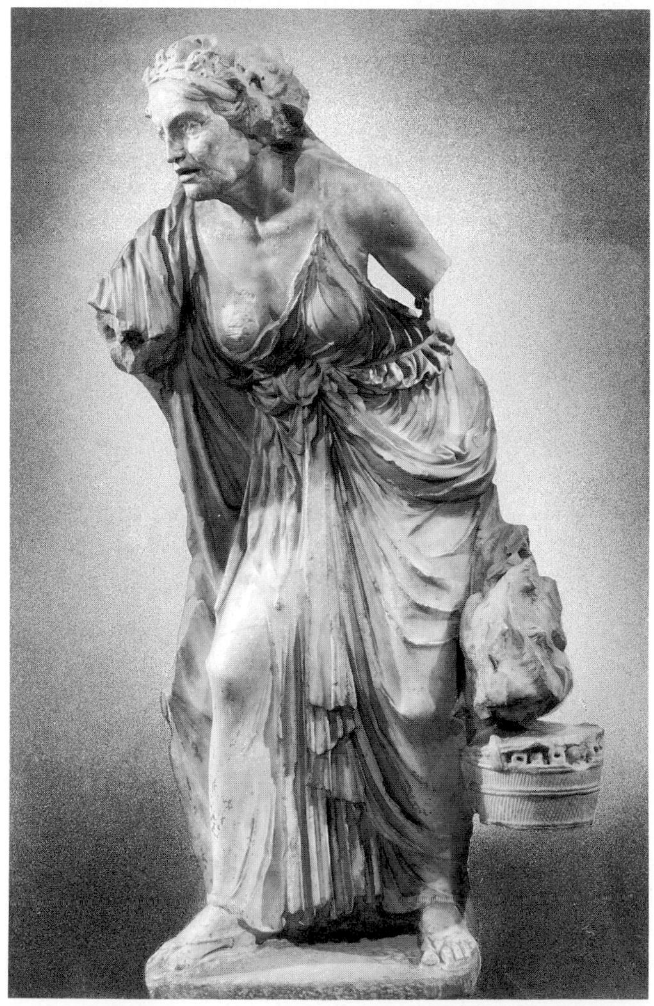

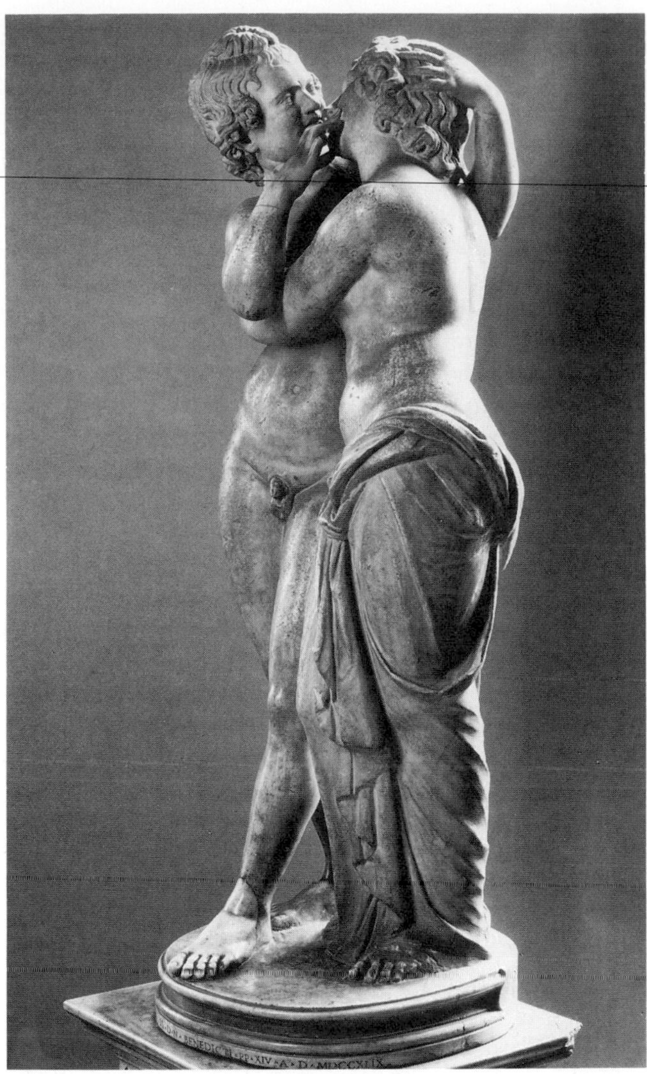

5-84 *Eros and Psyche,* c. 150 B.C. Marble, 49″ high. Museo Capitolino, Rome.

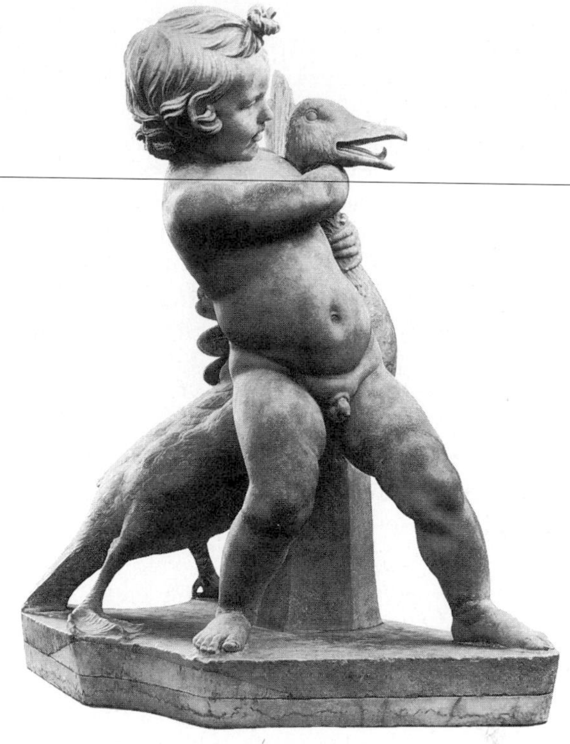

5-85 BOETHOS, *Boy Strangling a Goose,* second century B.C. Marble, approx. 33″ high. Staatliche Antikensammlungen und Glyptothek, Munich.

5-86 Attributed to APOLLONIUS, *Seated Boxer,* c. 50 B.C. Bronze, approx. 50″ high. Museo Nazionale Romano, Rome.

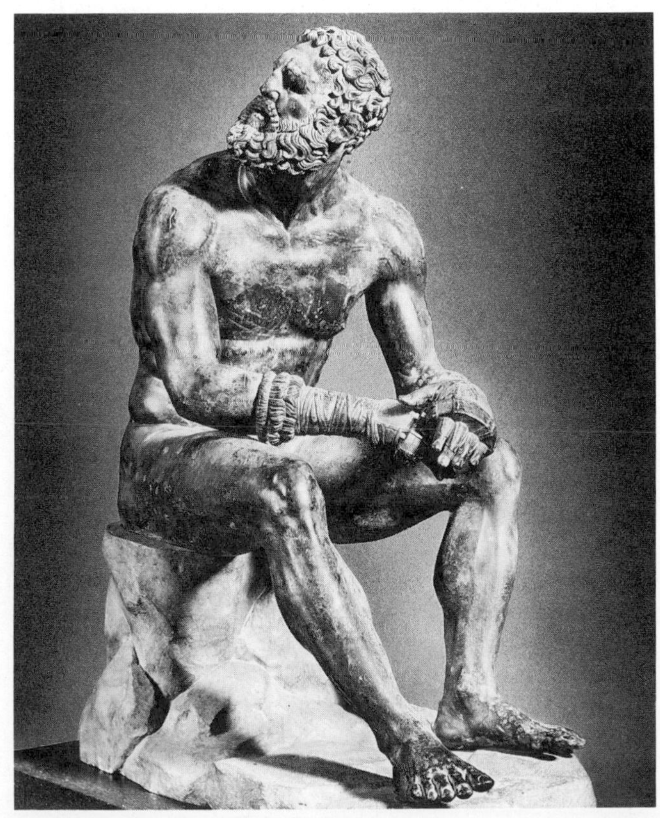

(FIG. **5-85**) could be a subject worthy of representation. The sculpture may strike us as somewhat unpleasant, with its sadistic overtones, but doubtless it was intended to be "cute" and to elicit fond smiles as well as praise for the artist, BOETHOS, for his ingenuity in inventing a curious subject. And it must be admitted that Boethos has succeeded, from the formal point of view, in converting a trivial subject into a remarkably effective work of art. The swirling forms have been contained in a compact, pyramidal composition, at once complex and unified, in which the voids, like the solids, have been studied carefully and used as functioning parts of the whole.

Attributed to APOLLONIUS, the *Seated Boxer* (FIG. **5-86**), a very late Hellenistic work (perhaps more properly referred to as Greco-Roman, since it dates about a century after the absorption of Greece into the Roman Empire), shows a heavily battered veteran of the arena resting. He has perhaps been beaten and is listening to the berating of his manager. The boxer is a man of huge physique, but his smashed face, broken nose, and deep scars tell the gist of his story. The sculptor appeals not to our intellect but to our emotions in striving to evoke compassion for the battered hulk of a once-mighty fighter. Story, realism, and human interest became the Hellenistic artist's focus at the end of the development of Greek sculpture, which ran, in a few centuries, a spectrum of possibilities and realizations ranging from the *Apollo* of Olympia (FIG. 5-40) to a brutish boxer past his prime. This should in no sense be construed as a decline of artistic quality or a failure of spiritual force. Hellenistic art is to be appreciated within the whole history of art for its thematic variety, its virtuosity of technique, and its power and passion in expressing the drama of human life. Its strength is felt throughout the development of Roman art, which, in many ways, is the extension of it.

Architecture

The greater variety, complexity, and sophistication of Hellenistic culture called for an architecture on an imperial scale and of wide diversity, something far beyond the requirements of the Classical city-state. Building activity shifted from the old centers on the Greek mainland to the opulent cities of the Hellenistic monarchs in Asia Minor—sites more central to the Hellenistic world. Great scale and ingenious development of interior space, the latter peculiarly a feature of Hellenistic architecture, are shown in the oracular Temple of Apollo at Didyma (the Didymaion) near Miletus, the old Ionian city on the west coast of Asia Minor (FIGS. 5-20f and **5-87**). This dipteral Ionic temple, begun in 313 B.C., is raised on a seven-stepped base some 13 feet above the level of the large naos, which was intentionally left open to the sky *(hypaethral)*. The temple is 167 feet by 358 feet, and the great columns are over 64 feet high. The deep and column-filled pronaos precedes an antechamber from which oracles may have been delivered. Entrance to the temple's interior was not through this room, which has a threshold some five feet high, but through two lateral, barrel-vaulted tunnels that sloped down toward the inner court, which was planted with bay trees in honor of Apollo. In the back of this court stood a small prostyle shrine that protected the cult statue, the foundations of which may be seen in the illustration. On the opposite end of the court, a stairway some 50 feet wide rose majestically toward three portals leading into the oracular room, which, approachable from both front and back, was the focal point of the entire design. This complex spatial planning of large interiors leads directly into later

5-87 Interior of the Temple of Apollo at Didyma (the Didymaion), near Miletus, Anatolia (Turkey), begun 313 B.C.

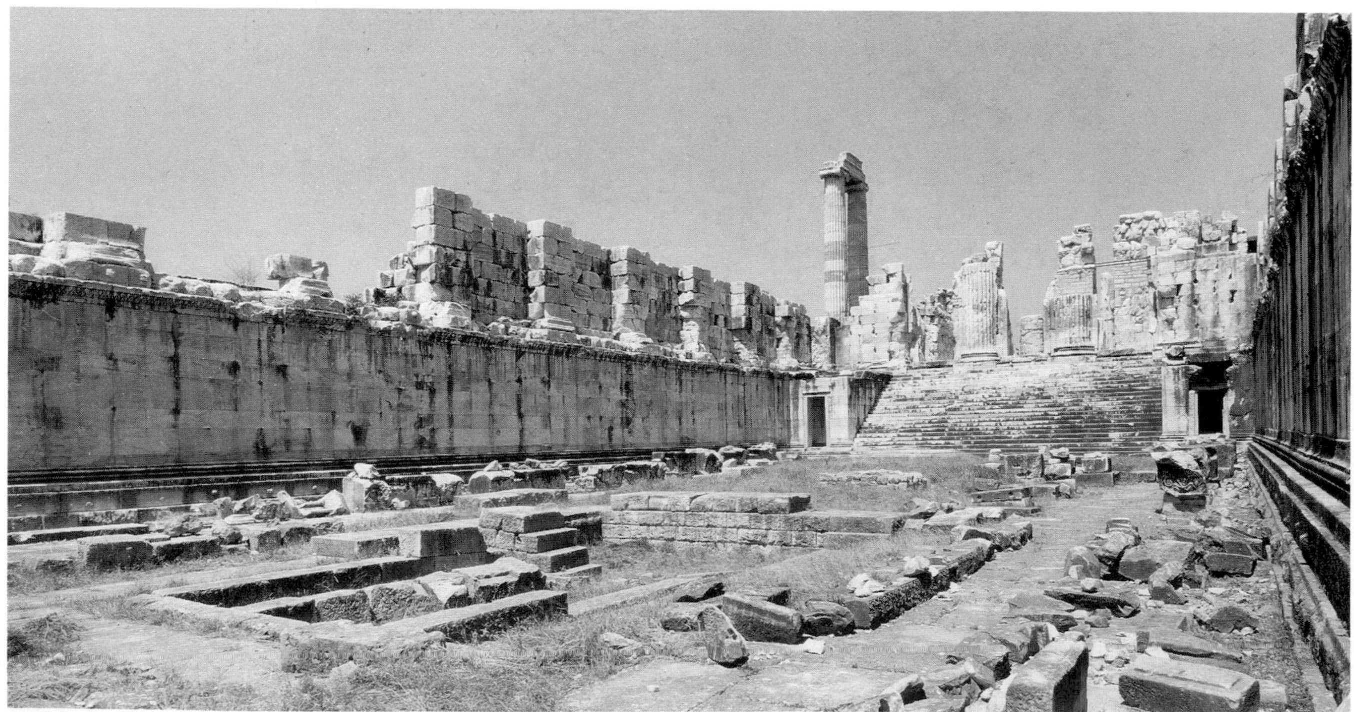

Roman practice and marks a sharp departure from Classical Greek architecture, which stressed the exterior of the building almost as a work of sculpture and left the interior relatively undeveloped.

The thoughtful adaptation of space to serve human uses, rather than, as in ancient times, to honor gods and to satisfy the whims of kings, is part of Greek humanism's contribution to history. The Hellenistic Greeks also broadened their conception of architectural design to take in whole cities. The regular street patterns of the gridiron type, which date from the Archaic period in Greece, were systematized during the fifth century B.C. by HIPPODAMOS, a Milesian architect, whose name has been linked with the rectangular plans of urban Hellenistic building foundations.* The *Hippodamian plan,* as illustrated by the city of Priene (FIG. **5-88**), consists of a close-meshed network of streets that intersect at right angles, without any particular axial emphasis that might suggest dominant traffic patterns. At Priene, the plan has been superimposed on an irregular, sloping site, without regard to the nature of the terrain. Only the defensive walls on the city's perimeter closely follow the topographical contours, with the result that walls and street plan are unrelated. On the other hand, the system is neat and orderly and, because it makes few distinctions of either a social or an economic nature, it is essentially democratic.

The major ordering principles of so-called Hippodamian plans were the rectangle and rectangular relationships. The *agora* was centrally located and easily accessible to all citizens. It was partially surrounded by long, roofed, colonnaded *stoas,* which housed shops and offices and were the architectural expression of the public life of the city. In these structures, the city's business and politics, its administration, and its gossip went on, and it is from the fact that they taught their rational, moral discipline in a stoa that the philosophy of the Stoics takes its name.

The *bouleuterion* (part of the agora) was as important as the stoa to the life of the civic organism. It served as a meeting place for the city council, a function that required a large, roofed, and enclosed space within which lines of sight were uninterrupted and acoustics were good. Efforts to fulfill these requirements came to fruition in the late third century B.C. in a new building type, an impressive example of which is the bouleuterion of Miletus (FIGS. **5-89** and **5-90**). Here, the architectural problems were solved by incorporating a curved, theaterlike auditorium of steeply rising tiers of seats into a rectilinear masonry shell with a timber roof supported by four columns,

*Knowledge of ancient urbanism is rather scanty, since archeologists generally prefer to investigate limited sites, and it is rarely economically feasible for them to uncover and trace miles of city streets. The fragmentary evidence shows, however, that cities with regular, usually rectangular street plans existed in both ancient Egypt and Mesopotamia.

5-88 City of Priene, fourth century B.C. *Right:* Simplified ground plan. Shaded rectangle indicates area shown in detail at *left.*

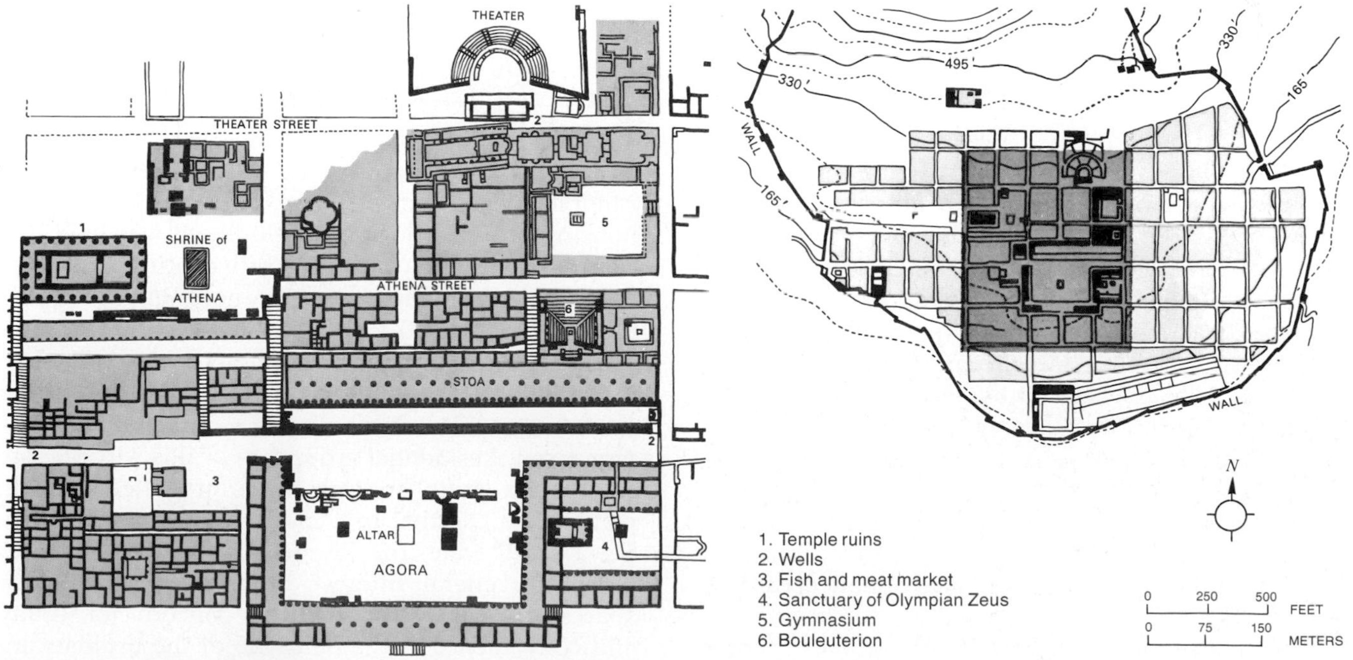

1. Temple ruins
2. Wells
3. Fish and meat market
4. Sanctuary of Olympian Zeus
5. Gymnasium
6. Bouleuterion

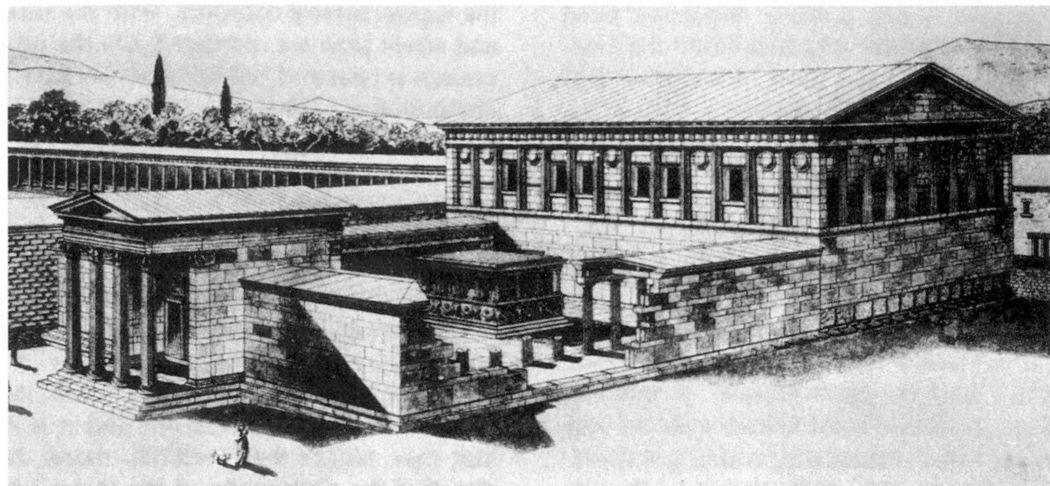

5-89 Bouleuterion at Miletus, late third century B.C.

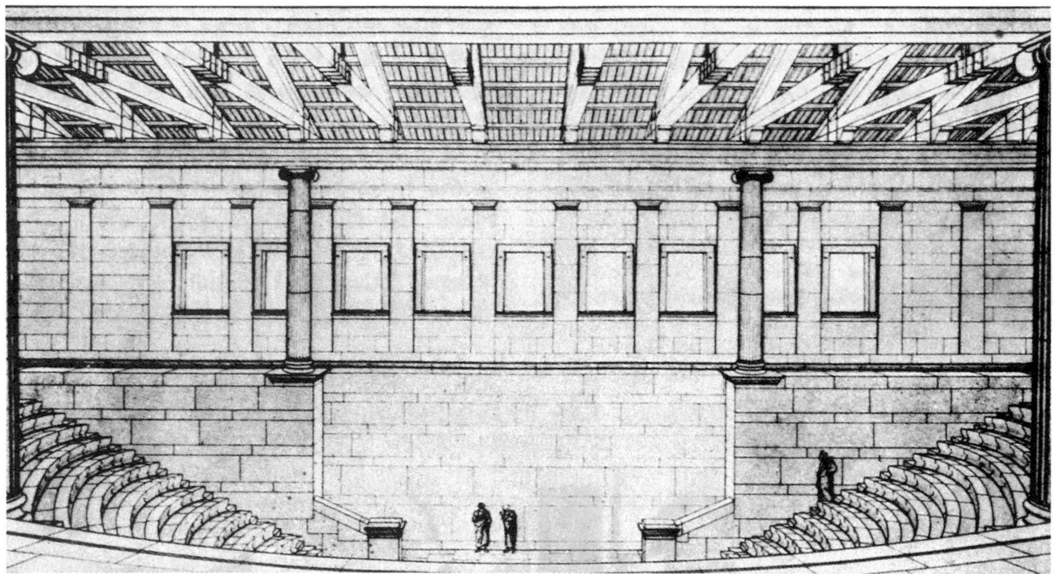

5-90 Reconstruction of council chamber, bouleuterion at Miletus.

ingeniously placed so as not to obstruct the audience's view of the rostrum.

It is at this point in the history of architecture that we can speak of domestic building and examine a human dwelling capable of being called a "house" (FIG. **5-91**). Typically, the lot on which the Hellenistic house stood was enclosed by a wall to shut out the dirt and noise of the narrow street. A single door opened into an office, or service quarters, from which a covered passage led to the main unit through a courtyard, into which roofed chambers opened. Wealthier residents had, in addition to a forecourt (similar to the Roman *atrium*), a colonnaded garden, the *peristyle*.

The residential requirements of ordinary people without means were recognized and occasionally satisfied in Classical and Hellenistic Greece by planned housing projects. Such a development was built in a suburb of Olynthus in the late fifth century B.C. Here, groups of ten houses were arranged in rectangular blocks of about 300 feet × 120 feet, neatly fitted together in a Hippodamian grid pattern (FIG. **5-92**). The individual houses varied in plan, but one feature, a spacious central courtyard with verandas, was common to all. Residential groupings of this sort predate the Roman *insula,* an even more integrated housing plan not unlike that of a modern apartment house. On a small scale, the Priene and Olynthus houses reflect a general interest in convenient, interior spaces, as well as a growing concern for utility and convenience in the daily life of the ordinary individual.

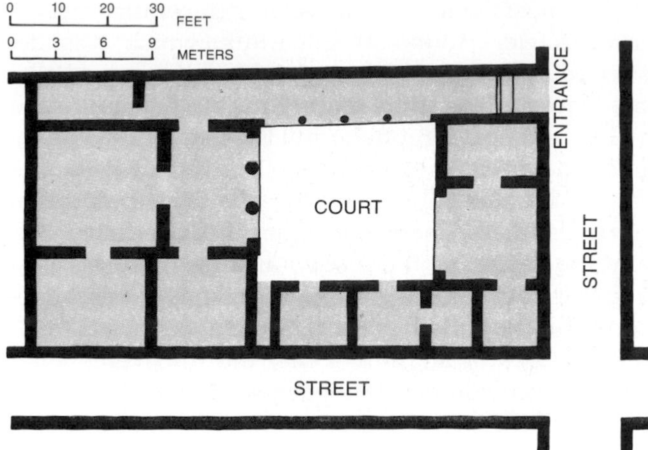

5-91 Plan of House XXXIII, Priene, fourth century B.C.

Priene was a provincial town, and its houses were relatively unpretentious. In the capitals of the Hellenistic kingdoms—at Alexandria in Egypt, Pergamon in Asia Minor, and Pella in Macedonia—life unfolded its richest and most sumptuous aspects. The kings and their retainers surrounded themselves with luxury that became proverbial, and their way of life set a standard that was to be surpassed only by the Roman emperors in later antiquity.

The great, urbanized citadel of the Attalid kings at Pergamon was a wonder of the ancient world and, even in its present, ruined state, still commands our admiration. Beautifully accommodated to its dramatic, mountainous site, the city proper was linked with the acropolis, some 800 feet above it, by an agora, a gymnasium, and the Sanctuary of Demeter, which were sited on intermediate levels. On the acropolis stood the fortress-palace of the rulers and, grouped around a theater, temples and sanctuaries like the Altar of Zeus and Athena (FIGS. 5-77 and 5-78). It was here on the acropolis that Pergamon achieved its greatest splendor in a sophisticated and dynamic grouping of architectural masses (FIGS. **5-93** and **5-94**). The deployment of the structures along flexible axes for maximum visibility is a free departure from the symmetric regularity of the Hippodamian plan and must have produced, at a distance, the faceted effect of a great gem, reflecting in its brilliance the wealth and power of the Pergamene dynasty. We have seen the sculptural celebration of Pergamon's

5-92 Plan of residential blocks, Olynthus, late fifth century B.C.

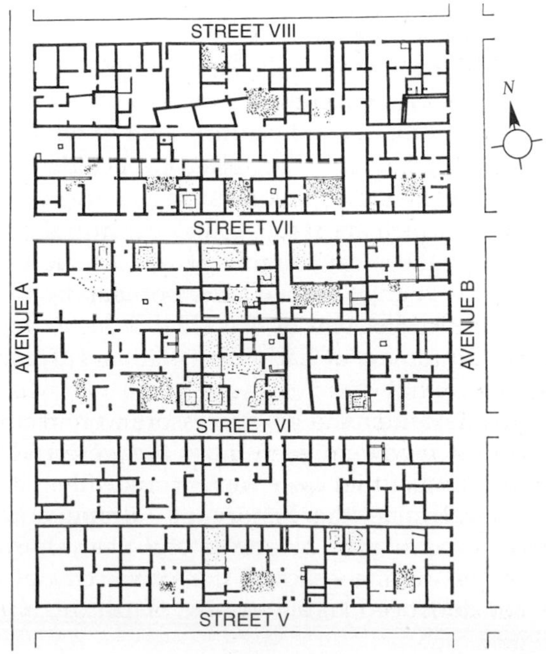

5-93 Plan of the acropolis, Pergamon, third to second century B.C.

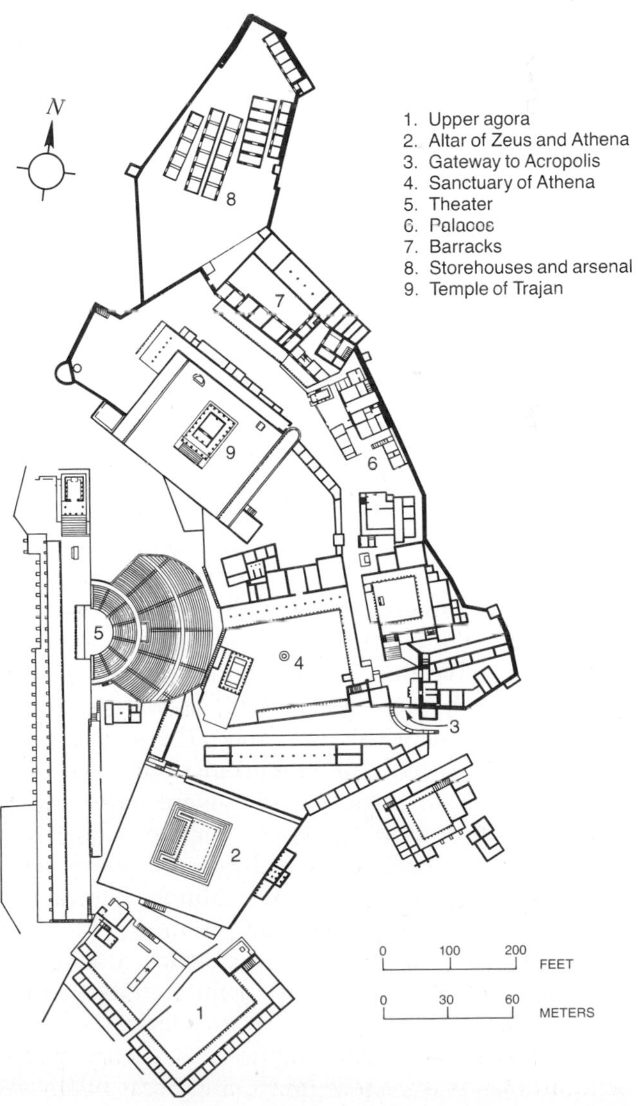

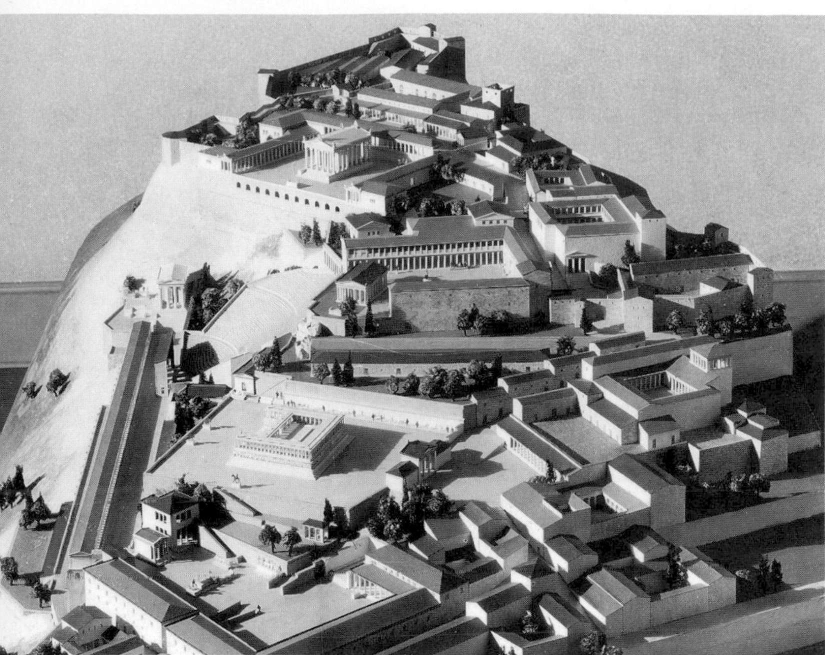

5-94 Model of the acropolis, Pergamon. Staatliche Museen, Antiken-Sammlung, East Berlin.

victories over the Gauls, and it is noteworthy that the Attalid kings were known in Hellenistic times as patrons of culture and art just as much as for their statecraft and their prowess in war.

Mosaics

Among the most lasting symbols of Hellenistic luxury were the floor mosaics with which the wealthy residents of the court cities embellished their houses. As an art form, mosaic had a rather prosaic and utilitarian beginning. (The Sumerian custom of covering walls with baked-clay cones and the technique of shell inlay, as found in the *Standard of Ur,* FIG. 2-18, were not long-lived.) In the Mediterranean region, the mosaic technique seems to have been invented primarily for the purpose of developing an inexpensive and durable flooring. Originally, small pebbles collected from beaches and riverbanks were set into a thick coat of cement. Artisans soon discovered, however, that the stones could be arranged in decorative patterns. At first, these patterns were quite simple and were confined to geometric shapes; examples of this type, dating back to the eighth century B.C., have been found at Gordium in Asia Minor. Eventually, the stones were arranged to form more complex pictorial designs, and, by the fourth century B.C., the technique had developed to the point that mythological subjects could be represented on a large scale with a rich variety of colors.

The most famous of these fourth-century pebble mosaics were found at Olynthus, which was destroyed by Philip of Macedon in 348 B.C., and at Pella, the Macedonian capital under King Archelaus around 400 B.C. Almost forgotten until the late 1950s (excavations there were begun in 1957), it was at Pella that Alexander was born, that Aristotle taught, and that Euripides died. Under Alexander, Pella became virtually the capital of the world, and he ruled his vast empire from there. Although little has been preserved of the buildings' superstructures, furniture, or other works of art from Pella, the uncovered floor mosaics provide ample evidence of the luxury and beauty of the city's houses. A detail from one of several well-preserved pebble mosaics (FIG. **5-95**) shows an almost life-sized figure from a scene representing a lion hunt. The stones that have been arranged to form the picture are neither hewn nor shaped, but natural pebbles. A variety of colors has been used to produce a polychrome effect, but the chief pictorial impact is derived from a strong dark and light contrast. Some outlines and interior markings are defined with thin strips of terra cotta, a refinement that increases the clarity of the design but that was to enjoy no lasting favor.

Because they were cheap and durable, pebble mosaics remained popular through Roman times; in fact, they are still used for decorative pavements in Mediterranean countries. However, the desire for ever-greater pictorial realism led to the simple, but revolutionary, practice of cutting stones to desired shapes, so that they could be fitted together more closely. At first, these shaped stones, or *tesserae,* which permitted more precise description of detail, were used together with pebbles in limited areas that were felt to require greater definition. "True" mosaics, composed entirely of cut stones, may have originated in Hellenistic Sicily. They were being designed at Pergamon and Delos by the second century B.C., at which time the technique had been perfected to include colored glass *(smalto)* for strong colors, such as pure blue, red, and green, which are rarely found in natural materials. One of the most durable of the artistic media, mosaic was highly refined and popular in Roman times and became one of the chief vehicles for the pictorial expression of Early Christian and Byzantine artists.

While Alexander and his successors were Hellenizing the East, a power was rising in the western Mediterranean that, in its own way, would, like Greece, greatly determine the history of Europe and the Europeanized world. In one fateful year, 146 B.C., that power—Rome—sacked the Greek city of Corinth and destroyed an old enemy, Carthage, absorbing the small Greek states into the Roman province of Achaea and constructing around the ruins of Carthage the province of Africa. Thus, in a double stroke, Rome took under its aegis the culture of Greece and brought to an end in the Mediterranean West the ancient Near Eastern civilization that had continued to flourish in the old Phoenician (eastern contemporary of the Minoan) sea-empire. Although this constituted another step in the westernizing of the ancient world, it did not mean a blocking of the channels of commercial and intellectual intercourse with the East. For what Rome adopted from Greece it passed on to the medieval and modern worlds in a form much transformed by the Oriental message of Christianity. If Greece was peculiarly the inventor of the European spirit, Rome was its propagator and amplifier.

5-95 *Hunter*, detail of the *Lion Hunt* mosaic, Pella, *c.* 300 B.C. Pebble mosaic, approx. 66″ high. Archeological Museum, Pella.

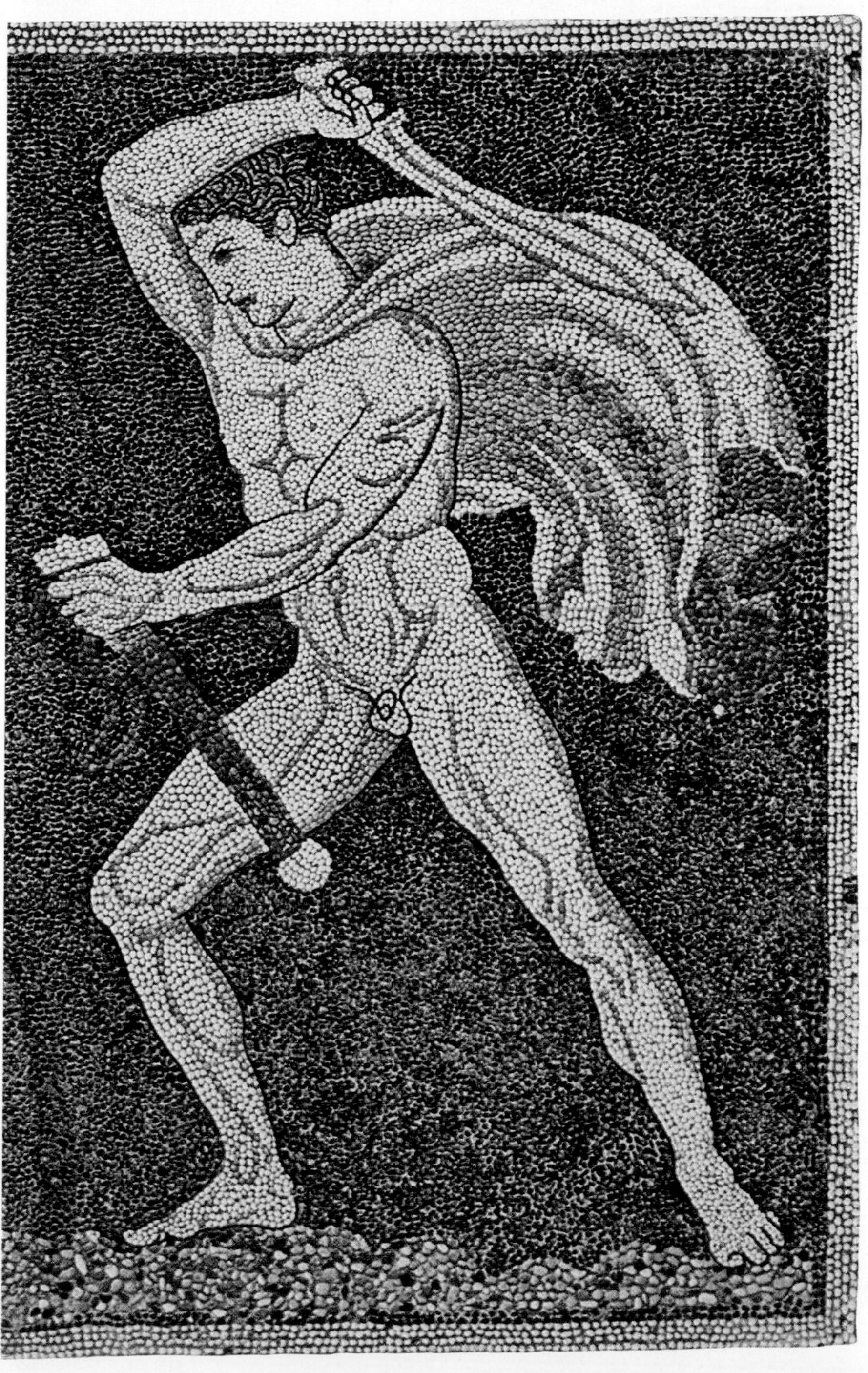

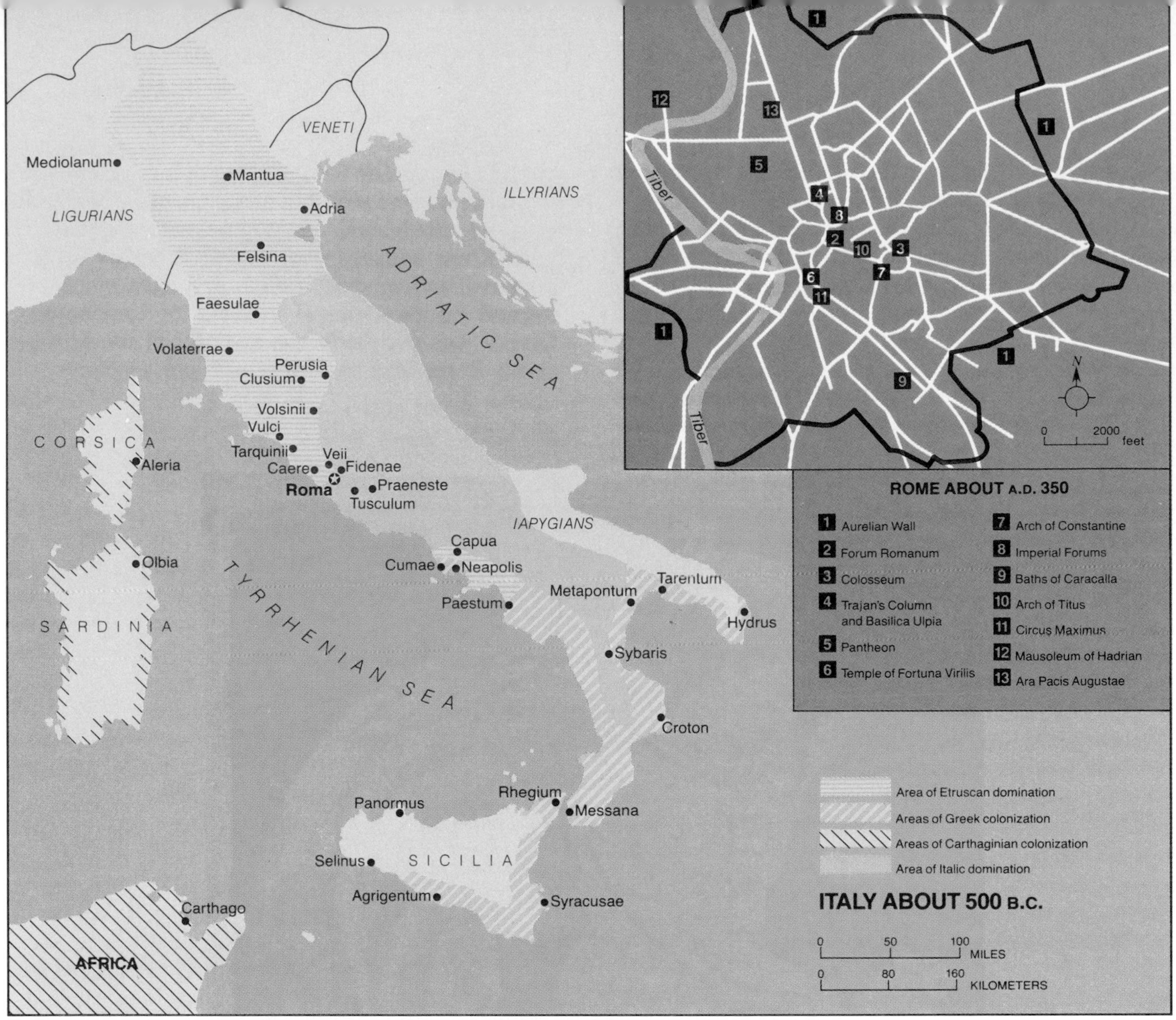

ITALY ABOUT 500 B.C.

Area of Etruscan domination
Areas of Greek colonization
Areas of Carthaginian colonization
Area of Italic domination

0 50 100 MILES
0 80 160 KILOMETERS

Mediolanum, Mantua, Adria, Felsina, Faesulae, Volaterrae, Perusia, Clusium, Volsinii, Vulci, Tarquinii, Veii, Caere, Fidenae, Roma, Praeneste, Tusculum, Capua, Cumae, Neapolis, Paestum, Metapontum, Tarentum, Hydrus, Sybaris, Croton, Rhegium, Messana, Panormus, Selinus, Agrigentum, Syracusae, Carthago, Aleria, Olbia

VENETI, LIGURIANS, ILLYRIANS, IAPYGIANS, CORSICA, SARDINIA, SICILIA, AFRICA, ADRIATIC SEA, TYRRHENIAN SEA

ROME ABOUT A.D. 350

1	Aurelian Wall	7	Arch of Constantine
2	Forum Romanum	8	Imperial Forums
3	Colosseum	9	Baths of Caracalla
4	Trajan's Column and Basilica Ulpia	10	Arch of Titus
5	Pantheon	11	Circus Maximus
6	Temple of Fortuna Virilis	12	Mausoleum of Hadrian
		13	Ara Pacis Augustae

Tiber

0 2000 feet

800 B.C. | 700 | c. 510 | 300 | 100

ETRUSCAN DOMINATION | ROMAN REPUBLICAN PERIOD

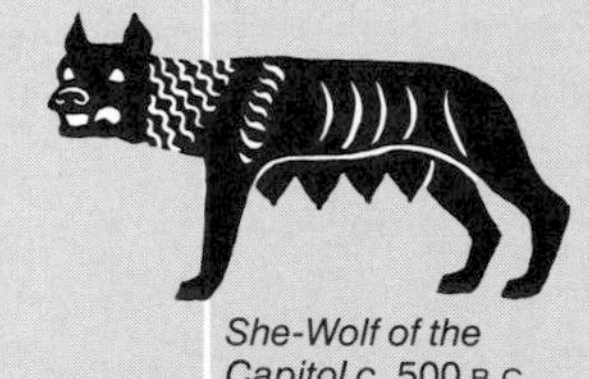

She-Wolf of the Capitol c. 500 B.C.

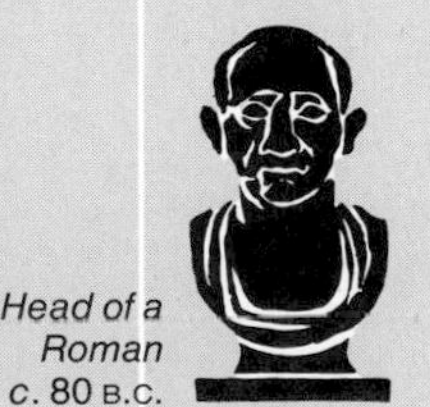

Head of a Roman c. 80 B.C.

Foundation of Rome (traditional) 753 B.C.

Unification of Italy c. 350–275 B.C.

Roman conquest of Greece 146 B.C.

Assumed arrival of Etruscans in Italy 1200–700 B.C.

Greek colonization of South Italy 900–600 B.C.

Expulsion of Kings 509 B.C.

Peace between Rome and Tarquinii 351 B.C.

Punic Wars 264–201 B.C.

Vergil 70–19 B.C.

6
ETRUSCAN AND ROMAN ART

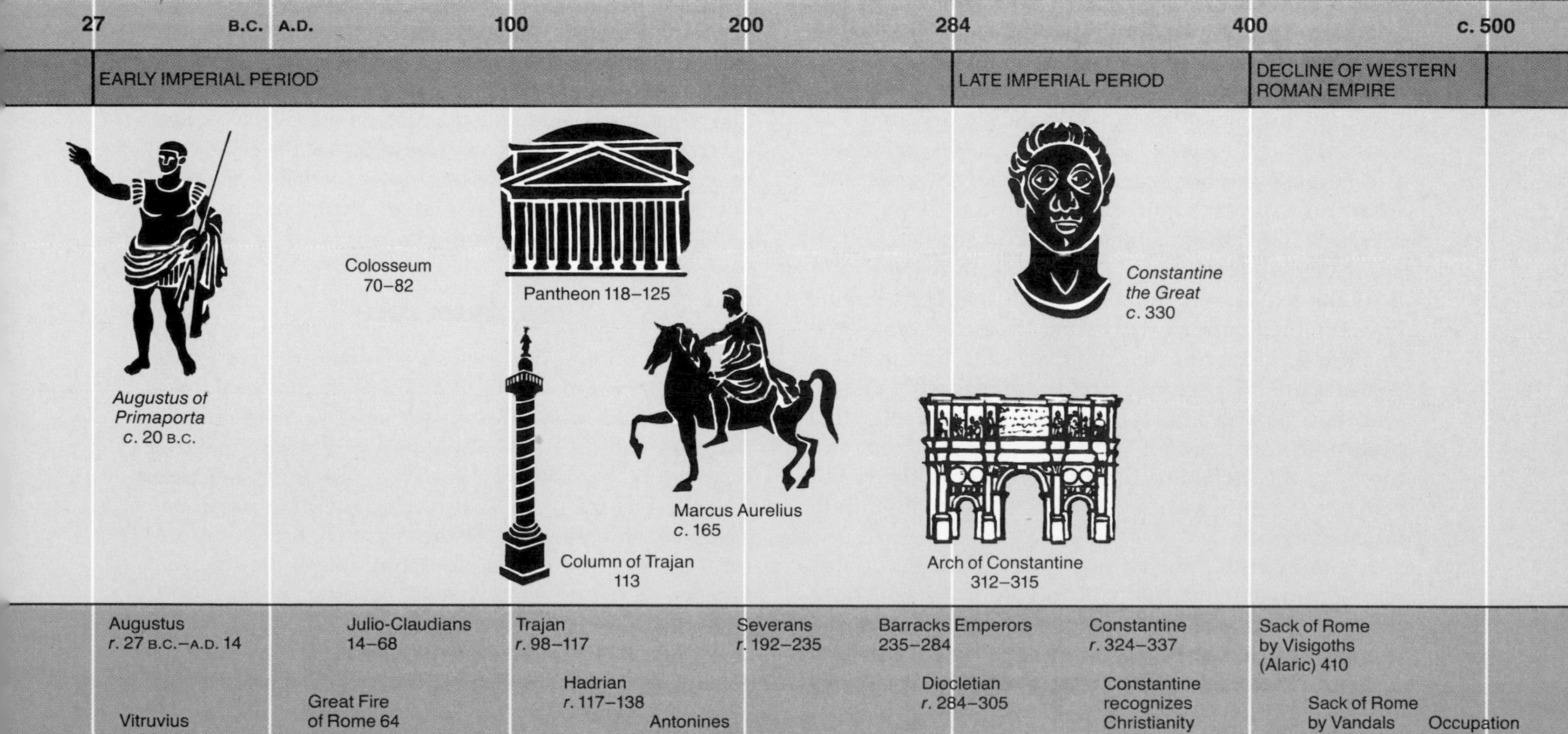

THE PEOPLE of Italy, while touched at an early date by the radiance of Greece, had deep and tenacious qualities of their own. Both Etruscan (or Etrurian) and Roman art, like the art of any other culture or area, must be recognized as a synthesis of influences from outside sources and of elements indigenous to the country. Roman art, the immediate heir of all earlier Mediterranean cultures, was in many ways a synthesis of the arts of antiquity, as was Greek art, although in quite a different way. Rome was also deeply involved in bringing civilization to western Europe and to North Africa. The art of Rome was, therefore, in later times often regarded as the symbol of the art of antiquity.

In terms of political development, the early histories of Greece and Italy are roughly parallel, but the vigorous advances in Greece after the Persian Wars of the fifth century B.C., culminating in the Age of Pericles, found no counterpart in Italy, where culture was retarded by the bitter struggles among competing Italic peoples and between Italic groups and the Etruscans.

THE ETRUSCANS

The origin of the Etruscans, like that of the Mycenaeans, has long been one of the mysteries of the ancient world. Their language, although written in a Greek-derived script and extant in inscriptions that are still obscure, is unrelated to the Indo-European linguistic family. Ancient historians, as fascinated by the puzzle as modern scholars, generally felt that the Etruscans emigrated from Asia Minor; Herodotus, the "father of history," specifically declared that they came from Lydia. This tradition has persisted, and because the Etruscan culture emerges as distinct from those of other Italic peoples around 700 B.C., its arrival in Italy has long been put at the eighth century B.C. Such a view seems too simple, however, and does not explain adequately the evident connections between the Etruscan and earlier Italic cultures. Some modern scholars feel that the Etruscans are the direct descendants of very old pre–Indo-European people who had moved into Italy from the north. But this theory, in turn, cannot fully account for certain elements of the Etruscan culture, particularly the elaborate burial cult, which seems to be linked with Oriental customs.

A compromise theory points out that Herodotus gives no dates and that the migration to which he referred could well have occurred during the period of the great Mediterranean shifting of peoples around 1200 B.C. that caused the collapse of the Mycenaean civilization. At that time, immigrants from Asia Minor could have settled in Italy, mingled with the native population, and produced the culture of the so-called Villanovans, who, in turn, may have been the direct predecessors of the Etruscans. The changes that produced the Etruscan culture proper then would have to be explained in terms of increasing exposure to Oriental and then Greek influences, brought about by expanding commerce and trade. The Etruscans enjoyed high repute as skilled seafarers (or disrepute as pirates) in antiquity and emerged into the light of history during the so-called Orientalizing period.

Historians now generally concede that Etruscan art developed largely as a consequence of the Greek colonization of southern Italy during the eighth and seventh centuries B.C. Although they were responsible for halting further Greek expansion northward along the Tyrrhenian coast, and despite deep-rooted distrust and antagonism toward their southern neighbors, the Etruscans eagerly absorbed Greek influences, without relinquishing any of their native characteristics. Using the Greek colonial cities as a model, the Etruscans shifted from village life to an urban civilization and established themselves in strongly fortified hilltop cities. By the sixth century B.C., they controlled most of northern and central Italy from such strongholds as Tarquinia (ancient Tarquinii), Cerveteri (ancient Caere), Veii, Perugia (ancient Perusia), and Orvieto (ancient Volsinii). But these cities never united to form a state, and so it is improper to speak of an Etruscan "nation" or "kingdom." The cities coexisted, flourishing or fading independently, and any semblance of unity among them was based primarily on common linguistic ties and religious beliefs and practices. This lack of political cohesion eventually made the Etruscans relatively easy prey for the Roman aggressors. During the ten-year siege of Veii, for instance, no Etruscan city came to the aid of its beleaguered cousin.

Architecture

Little is known of Etruscan architecture. The cities were either razed or rebuilt by the Romans, and those that survived were located on sites so well chosen that they continue to be inhabited to this day, making excavation impossible. Scattered remnants suggest that the Etruscans, at least during their later history, made considerable use of the masonry arch, a structural device used occasionally but not favored by the Greeks, and one that was to become of profound importance in later Roman building.

We know about early Etruscan houses chiefly from clay models that served as cinerary urns and from tomb chambers in which domestic interiors were emulated. To judge from the interior of the Tomb of the Reliefs (FIG. 6-3), an originally simple, rectangular structure with a sloping roof grew progressively more elaborate, reaching its climactic development in the *atrium* houses of Pompeii and Herculaneum. Inventiveness showed itself in the development of the atrium, a high, square or rectangular central hall that was lighted through a large opening in the roof and around which the other rooms were arranged symmetrically. The atrium was the focus of family life and the shrine for the *lares* and *penates,* the household gods. The ancient sacred hearth of Mediterranean family religion found an appropriate architectural expression in the noble atrium, which gave to Italic domestic architecture an importance and dignity beyond that developed by the Greeks.

Our knowledge of the Etruscan temple (FIG. **6-1**) is based on a few preserved foundations and on a description given by the ancient Roman authority on architecture, Vitruvius (see page 220). The temple form very possibly may have had its origins in Greece. Its plan, for example, closely resembles the Greek prostyle plan (FIG. 5-20b). Yet the Etruscan adaptation, in typical fashion, developed its own characteristics. Resting on a high base *(podium),* with steps at one end only, the temple was constructed mostly of wood and sun-dried brick in a post-and-lintel system and had a heavy wooden superstructure richly decorated with brightly painted terra-cotta reliefs. The Etruscan emphasis on a highly ornate façade, with relatively spare treatment of the sides and rear, concentrated attention on the entrance porch. The axial organization was quite different from that of the Greek temple. Behind the sunlit pavilion of the porch, the shrine, which was divided into three *cellae* of equal size, formed dark cavelike spaces. The temple was not meant to be seen as a sculptural mass from the outside and from all directions, as the Greek temple was, but was intended to function instead primarily as a confined interior space for the cult god. It was a place of shelter, protected by the wide overhang of its roof.

6-1 Plan *(left)* and elevations *(right)* of an Etruscan temple. (After Vitruvius.)

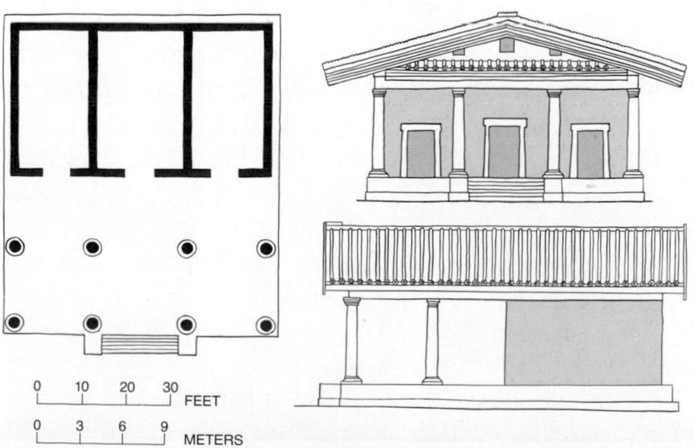

The Etruscans have revealed themselves to us with the greatest clarity, however, in the remains of their elaborate burial grounds. In the rich array of wall paintings and painted reliefs with which they decorated the interiors of their tombs, they recount their zestful lives, their banquets, and their dances (which, in their suppleness and verve, seem partly Ionian and partly barbarian). They tell us of both their athletic contests and of their wars. Their rise and fall from power is reflected in a gradual change from optimism to pessimism and in the choice of ever-more morbid and bloodthirsty subjects as their political fortunes declined. Although the Etruscans' reputation for cruel and unrestrained behavior is based largely on the testimony of the ancient Greeks and Romans, who were their enemies, elements in their tomb paintings indicate that many aspects of their society were in fact violent and extravagant. Indeed, these qualities may have played a decisive role in the formation of an energetic and creative culture that was to contribute to the rise to world rulership of their Roman successors.

The Etruscans built their cemeteries at some distance from their cities. Hundreds of tombs arranged in an orderly manner along a network of streets produce the effect of veritable cities of the dead. The tombs varied according to region and local custom. In the northern part of Etruria, they were usually constructed above ground; in the south, they were often excavated from the live rock, particularly in areas where tufa soil facilitated digging. Tufa, primarily strongly compressed volcanic ash, is excavated easily and hardens to a concretelike consistency on exposure to the atmosphere; it also can be cut into durable building blocks that require no firing. Tufa was used extensively by the Etruscans and Romans, and a minor tufa-brick industry still flourishes in Italy today.

A characteristic Etruscan tomb type is the *tumulus,* a round structure containing one or more subterranean tomb chambers and covered by a large mound of earth (FIG. **6-2**). This form was favored in Cerveteri (ancient Caere) and, in view of its domical shape, seems to carry on an ancient Mediterranean tradition. The majority of Etruscan tomb interiors, however, including those of the tumuli, are rectangular and imitate the rooms of domestic architecture. A striking example is the Tomb of the Reliefs (FIG. **6-3**), a large underground chamber in Cerveteri, in which massive piers with pseudo-Ionic (Aeolic) capitals support a

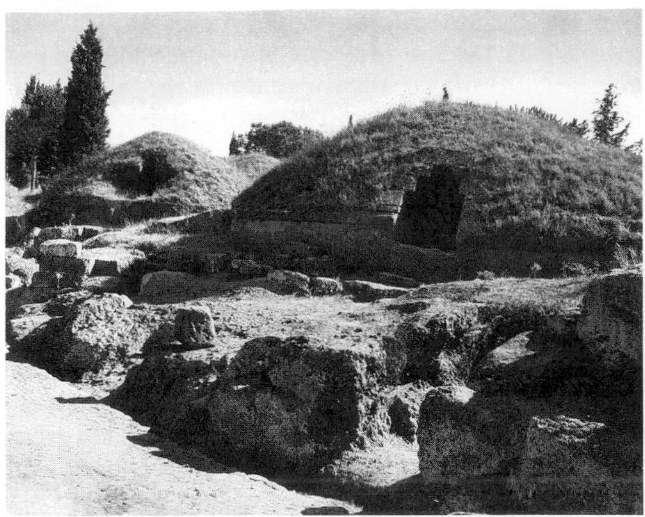

6-2 Necropolis at Cerveteri (ancient Caere), Italy, fifth to fourth century B.C.

slanting, beamed ceiling. The piers are *reserved,* having been formed by cutting away the live tufa until the remaining rock assumes the shape of a pier or column, as in the Egyptian rock-cut tombs at Beni Hasan (FIG. 3-20). The Tomb of the Reliefs, like most Etruscan tombs, was designed for multiple burials, the final resting place of an entire family and its servants. Sarcophagi, cinerary urns, and other tomb furnishings were placed in niches and on the benchlike projection at the base of the walls. Decoration in the Tomb of the Reliefs consists of painted plaster representations of weapons, tools, and kitchen utensils and displays a generous inventory of Etruscan objects of daily use. Occasionally, tombs at Cerveteri also were decorated with mural paintings.

Painting

The Tarquinians adorned the walls of most of their subterranean tomb chambers with colorful and lively murals. Although the subjects of tomb painting in Etruria are sometimes drawn from Greek legend, more often they are concerned with scenes of banquet and revel, as in the Tomb of the Leopards of Tarquinia (FIG. **6-4**). This small chamber tomb is decorated in the manner favored in Tarquinia during the fifth century B.C.; a banquet scene appears on the wall opposite the entrance, and groups of dancers and musicians enliven the side walls. In contrast to the all-male festivities shown in the Greek tomb at Paestum (FIG. 5-59), women share in this banquet. Their light skin color distinguishes them from their dark-skinned male partners, a pictorial convention in ancient art that goes back to early Egyptian times. The men are bare chested, while the ladies wear chi-

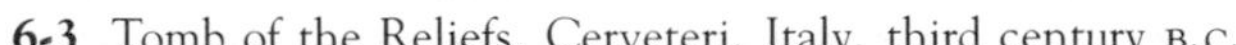

6-3 Tomb of the Reliefs, Cerveteri, Italy, third century B.C.

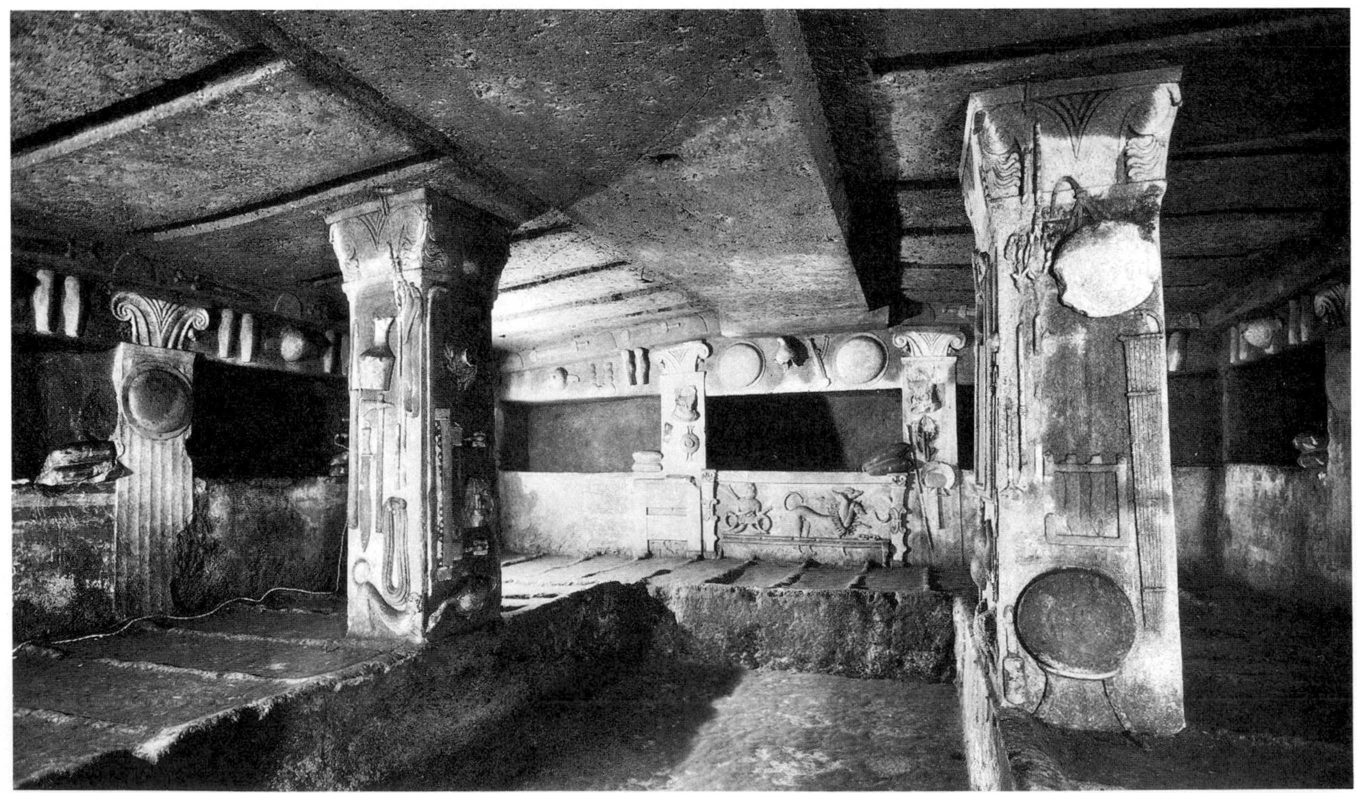

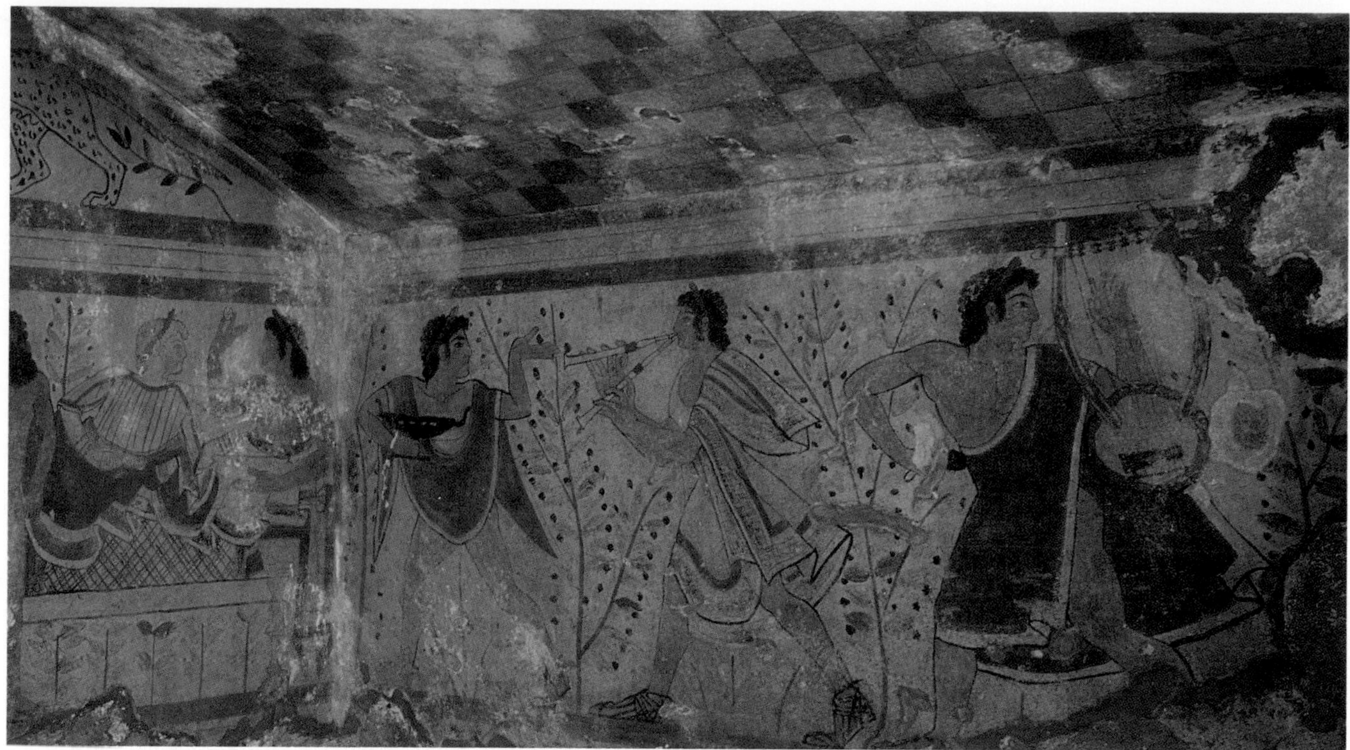

6-4 *Revelers*, detail of a wall painting from the Tomb of the Leopards, Tarquinia (ancient Tarquinii), c. 470 B.C.

tons. The ladies also share the men's interest in an egg, which the reclining celebrant second from left ritually holds up. This gesture identifies the event as a funeral banquet; the egg was the symbol of young life and regeneration and thus an object of reverent contemplation and consolation on this somber occasion.

The contemplative mood of the banqueting scene changes into life-affirming exuberance on the adjoining wall. Three young men, one clad only in a light scarf, the other two in the elegant *chlamys* (cloak), seem to be hurrying through a grove of graceful little laurel trees, the leader carrying a cup of wine and beckoning the others, who play the double flute and the seven-stringed lyre. They already seem to be dancing, facing rhythmically in opposite directions, as if performing some circling step. The gestures have a kind of choreographic exaggeration, especially those of the enlarged hands and fingers of the flutist, which hold and touch the instrument with such sureness and delicacy. Spirited movement rarely is portrayed so convincingly in the painting of the ancient world, and it would be difficult to find from that time a more fitting monument to the beauty of youth, springtime, music, and the dance. The picture is a kind of fresco painting on a thin slip applied to the living tufa wall or on a stucco paste made from tufa. The colors (blacks, blues, blue-greens, and ocher-reds) still retain much of their original freshness and harmonize easily and naturally with the creamy yellow ground.

The later Etruscans seem to have surrendered their native, joyous vigor for a quiet, classicizing formalism like that seen in the *Woman of the Velcha Family* (FIG. 6-5), from a chamber in the Tomb of Orcus (Hades) in Tarquinia. The composed, even reflective, expression

6-5 Detail of the *Woman of the Velcha Family*, wall painting from the Tomb of Orcus (Hades), Tarquinia, fourth century B.C.

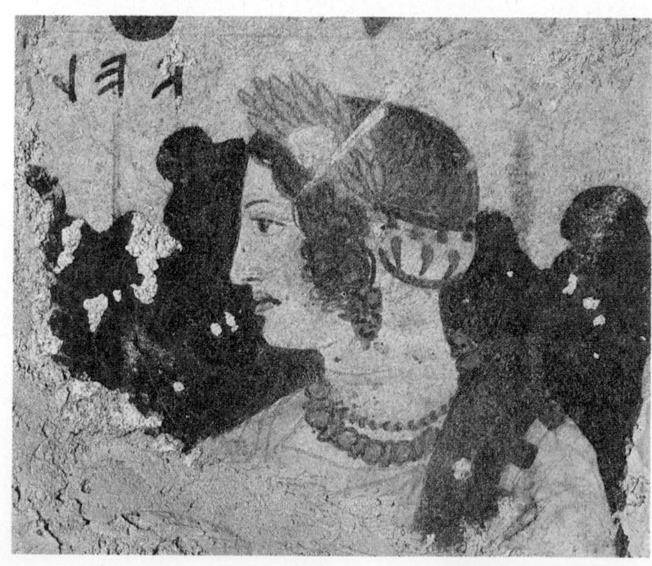

of this splendidly painted head (note the advanced draftsmanship of the foreshortened eye) suits the somber theme that is its context—the sufferings of the dead in Hades in the midst of the menacing demons of the underworld. The earlier Etruscan euphoria has disappeared, extinguished by the more cosmopolitan religions of the Hellenistic world, which stressed not the last happiness of the funeral revels, but the sadness of humanity's fate.

Sculpture

The Etruscan tombs yield a notable furniture of sculptured objects in both clay and bronze, materials that the Etruscans apparently preferred, although numerous stone sarcophagi also survive. The forms are modeled rather than carved, modeling being a technique congenial to the impetuous temperament and fluid style characteristic of the Etruscans. Funerary urns and sarcophagi with recumbent portrait figures present some of the best examples of Etruscan sculpture. A canopic (cinerary) urn (FIG. **6-6**) from Chiusi (ancient Clusium) has a terra-cotta head for a lid and is set in a bronze model of a chair; the head is obviously intended to be a portrait likeness of the deceased whose ashes the urn contained. The strongly rounded form of the urn has a crude vitality that is carried into the head, with its blunt, aggressive features and massive neck.

In the reclining effigies of a man and his wife on the lid of a sarcophagus from Cerveteri (FIG. **6-7**), we read

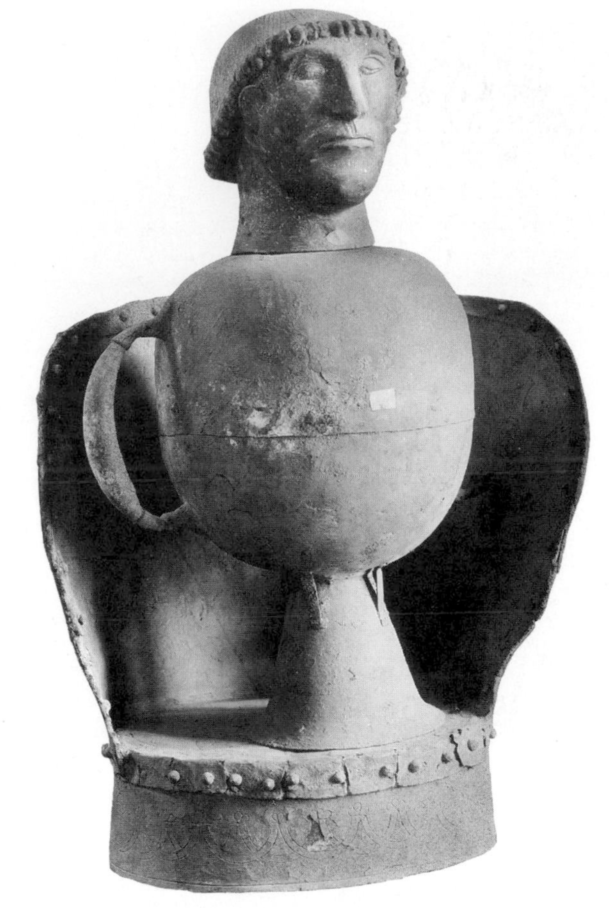

6-6 Canopic urn, from Chiusi (ancient Clusium), second half of the seventh century B.C. Hammered bronze with terra-cotta head, approx. 33″ high. Museo Etrusco, Chiusi.

6-7 Sarcophagus from Cerveteri, *c.* 520 B.C. Painted terra-cotta, approx. 6′7″ long. Museo Nazionale di Villa Giulia, Rome.

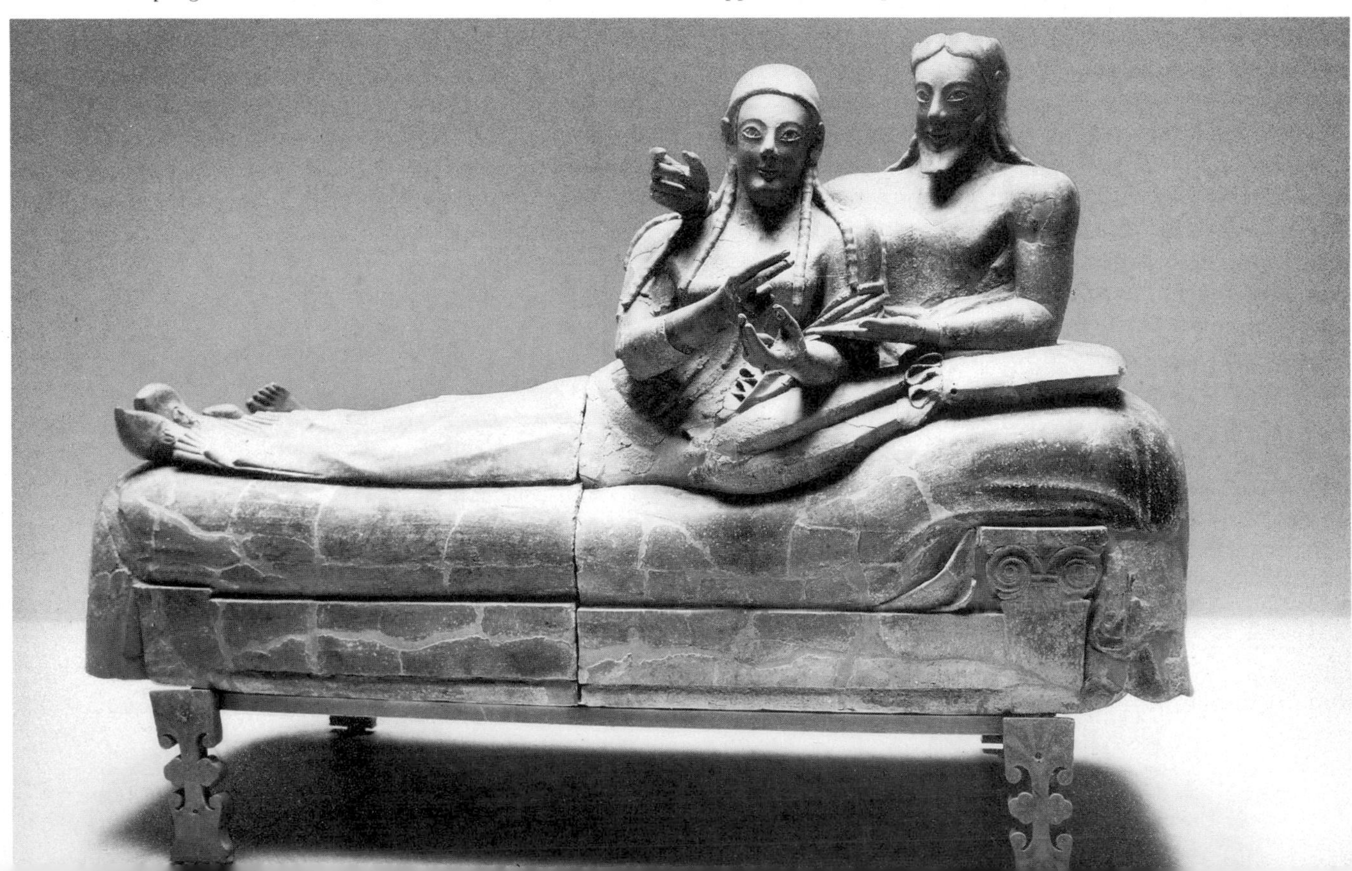

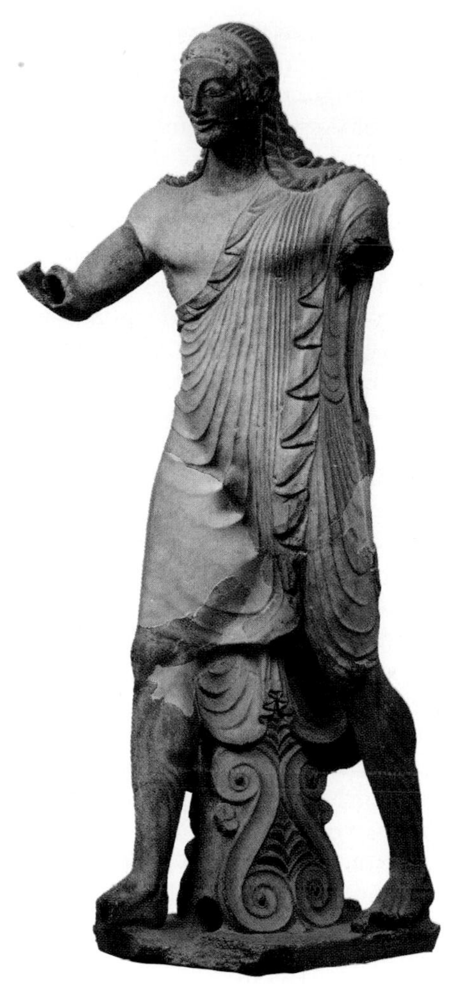

6-8 *Apollo,* from Veii, *c.* 510 B.C. Painted terra-cotta, approx. 70" high. Museo Nazionale di Villa Giulia, Rome.

the traits of Archaism as we have found them in early Greek art. The work is a kind of three-dimensional formalization of the animated banquet scenes painted on Etruscan tomb walls to satisfy the demands of some cult ritual of the dead, the details of which are unknown. But there is nothing here of the solemn or the macabre, and the Etruscan instinct for the lifelike is preserved. The figures are relaxed and genial, much in contrast with the funerary formality of Egyptian statues, and the Archaic features of style, although present, produce neither stiffness nor awkwardness.

The *Apollo* from Veii (FIG. **6-8**), an *acroterium* figure from the ridgepole of an Etruscan temple, is evidence that, like the Greeks, the Etruscans made use of architectural sculpture. But the Greek Archaic elements—the closed contour, the grimacing mask, the frontality—although immediately evident here, are superficial; the awkward, lurching vigor of the powerful figure is a forceful example of Etruscan clay-modeling techniques and the use to which the confident, quick-conceiving, and quick-executing sculptor could put them. In contrast with, say, the serene majesty of the *Apollo* at Olympia (FIG. 5-40), this Apollo moves like a dangerous giant. His overpowering physical presence reflects small concern for the Greek preoccupation with harmonious proportions or idealized humanity. The Ionian elaboration of the drapery lines bespeaks the Eastern component in Etruscan art, but the animal force, the huge, swelling contours, and the plunging motion are certainly not Ionian and show little mainland Greek influence. The *Apollo* from Veii, given its architectural function, naturally differs from the painted Etruscan forms we have seen; yet it has in common with them the peculiarly Etruscan strength, energy, and excitement.

Greek influences on Etruscan art continued even when the Etruscans were at the height of their power—sending their own art commodities throughout the Mediterranean area, including Greece—and through the centuries of their decline. The so-called *Mars from Todi* (FIG. **6-9**) exemplifies the Etruscan interpretation of the Greek Classical style in the beginning of the fourth century B.C. The figure, dressed in

6-9 *Mars from Todi,* early fourth century B.C. Bronze, approx. 56" high. Vatican Museums, Rome.

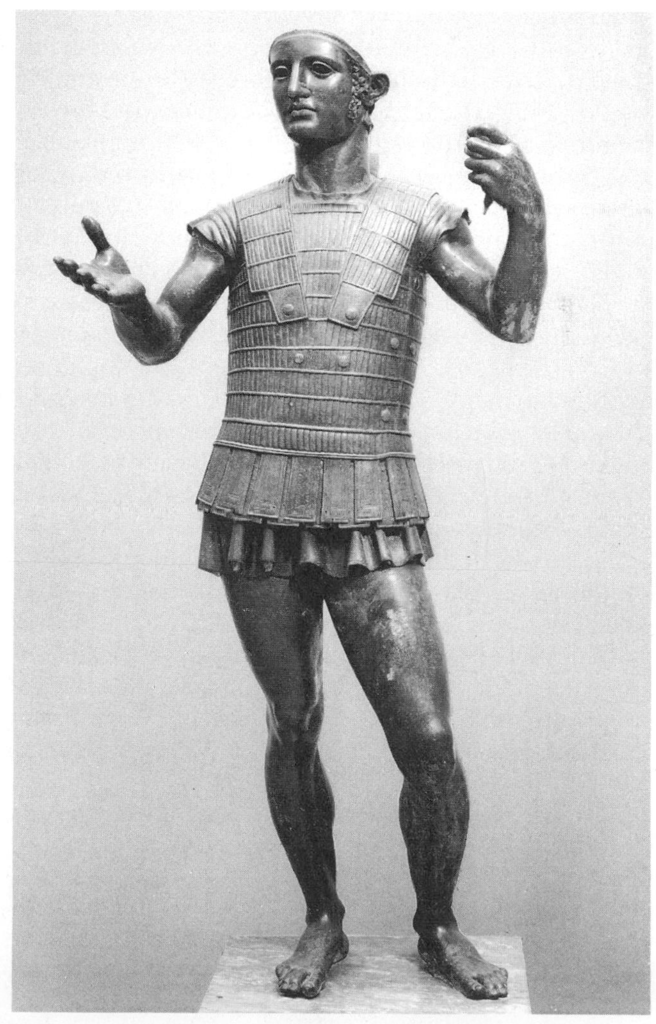

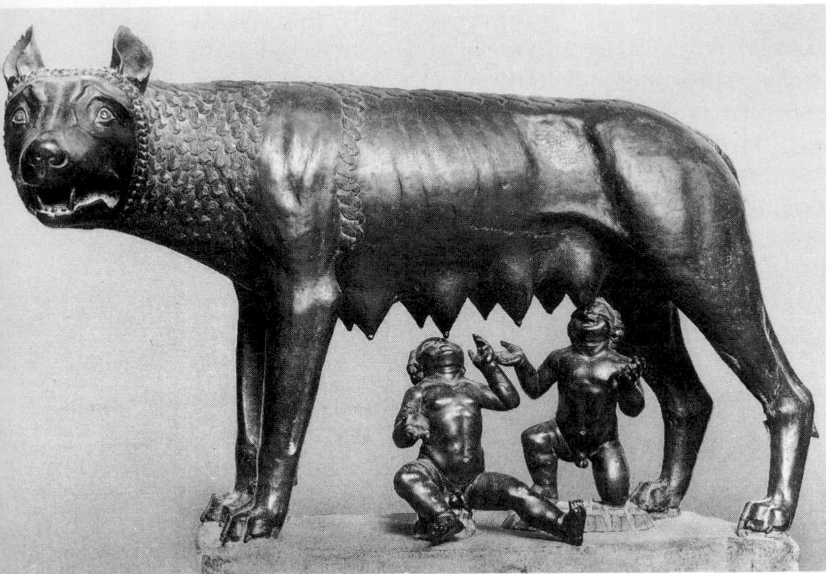

6-10 *She-Wolf of the Capitol,* c. 500 B.C. Bronze, approx. 33½" high. Museo Capitolino, Rome.

more or less contemporary military garb, executes a peculiar movement of the whole body, involving sideways and contrary directions of head, torso, arms, and legs, without seeming to move from his position. The sculptor may have been exaggerating the Polykleitan weight-shift stance but renders it with a kind of agility quite unlike the Polykleitan balance of weight and poise. We find again, as in the much earlier *Apollo* from Veii, that an Etruscan interpretation of prevailing Greek style brings out the native quality of energy, whether in the blunt drive of the *Apollo* or in the almost sprightly stance of the *Mars.*

One of the most famous animals in the history of world art, the *She-Wolf of the Capitol* (FIG. **6-10**), owes her fame not simply to her antiquity and her magnificence as a work of art, but also to the fact that, for centuries, she has been the totem of the city of Rome. Ancient legend tells us that the founding heroes of Rome, Romulus and Remus, were abandoned as infants and suckled by a she-wolf. The cult of Romulus and Remus was as old as the fourth century B.C., and we know that a statue of a she-wolf was dedicated on the Capitoline Hill in Rome in 296 B.C. We do *not* know whether the present statue of the she-wolf on the Capitoline Hill is the original (the suckling infants were cast during the Renaissance); its dating has been hotly debated, but its Etruscan origin now is accepted widely. Here, the vitality we have noted in the human figure in Etruscan art is concentrated in the tense, watchful animal body, with its spare flanks, gaunt ribs, and taut, powerful legs. The lowering of the neck and head, alert ears, glaring eyes, and ferocious muzzle render the psychic vibrations of the fierce and, at the same time, protective beast; the incised lines along the neck describe its rising hackles as it watches danger approach. Not even the great animal reliefs of Assyria can match, much less surpass, this profound reading of animal temper.

A somewhat later bronze figure is the splendid *Chimera* (FIG. **6-11**) from Arezzo (ancient Arretium), a monster with a rough-maned lion's head, a serpent's tail (restored in the Renaissance by Benvenuto Cellini), and a second head—that of a goat—whose right horn is seized by the serpent. Although the *Chimera* bears the wounds inflicted by the hero Bellerophon, who hunted and slew it, the figure does not merely illustrate that event but almost certainly has some further demonic significance. The Etruscans, much of whose art is associated with mortuary ritual, had a well-developed *demonology* (an aggregation of demonic types that plague the dead in the underworld). Unlike the Greeks, who preferred to humanize their demons, the Etruscans, perhaps as a result of their Asiatic origins, employed their customary expressive force in representing *their* demons as dreadful animal hybrids. The precedents for the monster types go back to the sphinxes of Egypt, the winged, man-headed bulls of Mesopotamia, the ornamental animal bronzes of Luristan, and the associated animal-heraldic style of much of the metalwork of central Asia. It may be that these traditions lingered in the Etruscan spirit, and the manifestation of them in such powerful form as the *Chimera*—a highly anti-Greek and forcefully Asiatic figure—attests most firmly to the Eastern component in Etruscan culture. By the time of the Middle Ages, a whole population of monsters swarmed through Western art.

6-11 *Chimera,* from Arezzo (ancient Arretium), fifth to fourth century B.C. Bronze, approx. 31½" high. Museo Archeologico Nazionale, Florence.

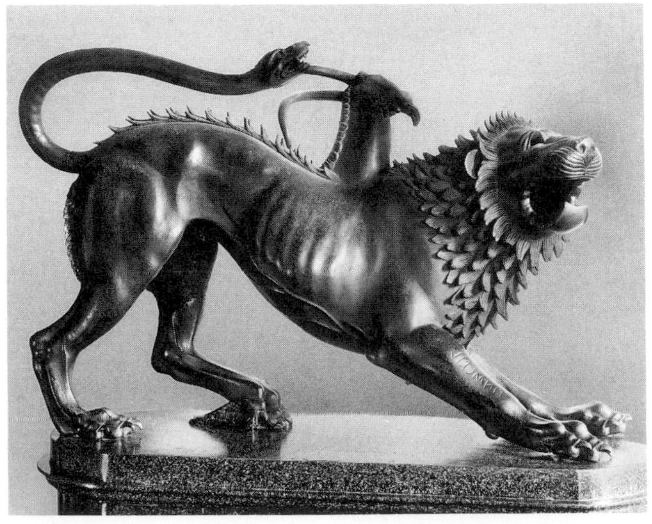

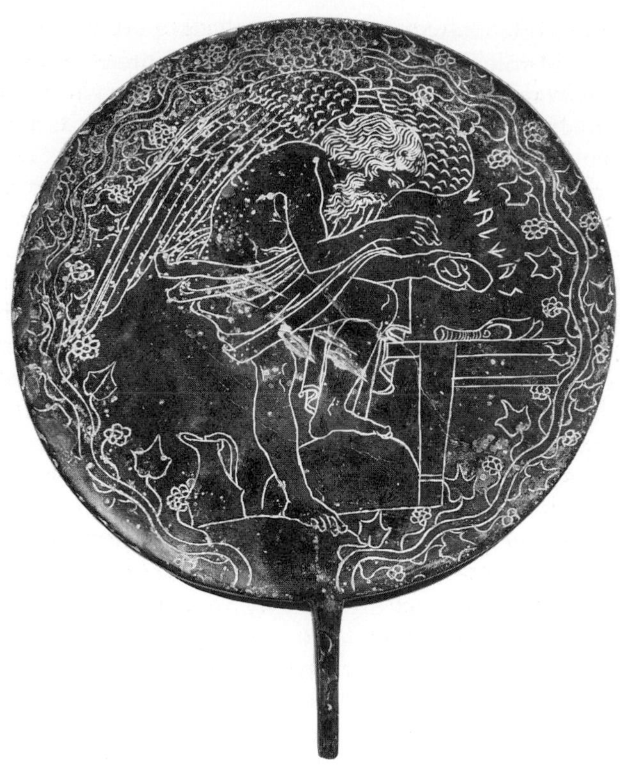

6-12 Engraved back of a mirror, *c.* 400 B.C. Bronze, approx. 6″ in diameter. Vatican Museums, Rome.

The Etruscans also assimilated the practice of *divination* from Eastern cultures and passed it on to the Romans. Diviners (priests) sought to predict the future, which was viewed as a product of arcane forces personified as gods or demons. On the assumption that all nature constituted a universe of affinities, prediction was based on the state of the viscera (especially the liver) of sacrificed animals, the flights of flocks of birds, and unseasonable and unusual events. The engraved back of an exquisitely wrought bronze mirror (FIG. **6-12**) displays all the refinement for which the Etruscan craft arts were celebrated. The engraving represents a winged figure labeled Calchas, a priest in Homer's *Iliad*, divining from a liver that he holds in his hand and on which he muses. The figure is a kind of miniature emblem for that world of benign and malign forces that surrounded human beings in antiquity and that they tried to approach or fend off by prophecy, sacrifice, oracle, omen, spell, and incantation. Greek rationalism made very little headway against the ancient world's overwhelming faith in the magical manipulation of nature.

Closely related to the delicately incised, Classical mirrors of the fourth century B.C., like the Calchas mirror, are the bronze cists of Palestrina (ancient Praeneste), which undoubtedly echo the styles of the great Greek masters of mural painting—Polygnotos, Euphranor, and others. Etruscan bronze vessels and mirrors with incised mythological scenes were famous and highly prized objects in Greece. Perhaps the outstanding example of this type is the *Ficoroni Cist* (FIG. **6-13**). Most significantly, the artist, NOVIUS PLAUTIUS, is not Etruscan; he signed his work in Latin and made it in Rome. Here, Plautius has skillfully adapted a frieze of Greek figures, faithfully taking over the idealized naturalism of the Late Classical period. Many think that the composition may have been copied directly from a lost Greek panel painting. Naturalistic innovations include figures seen entirely from behind or in three-quarter rear view, complicated seated poses, figures on several levels rather than rigidly attached to a single ground line, details of landscape, and a kind of approximate perspective space. In his work, the artist represents the passing of the Etruscan genius and the acceptance of the irresistible influence of Greece. Yet something of the Etruscan sense for the real was to persist through the formal Classicism of Greece and, in turn, partly direct the course of the art of Rome; this earlier Etruscan sense would sharpen into the characteristic Roman taste for the factual in art, as in human affairs.

6-13 NOVIUS PLAUTIUS, *The Ficoroni Cist*, from Palestrina (ancient Praeneste), late fourth century B.C. Bronze, approx. 21″ high. Museo Nazionale di Villa Giulia, Rome.

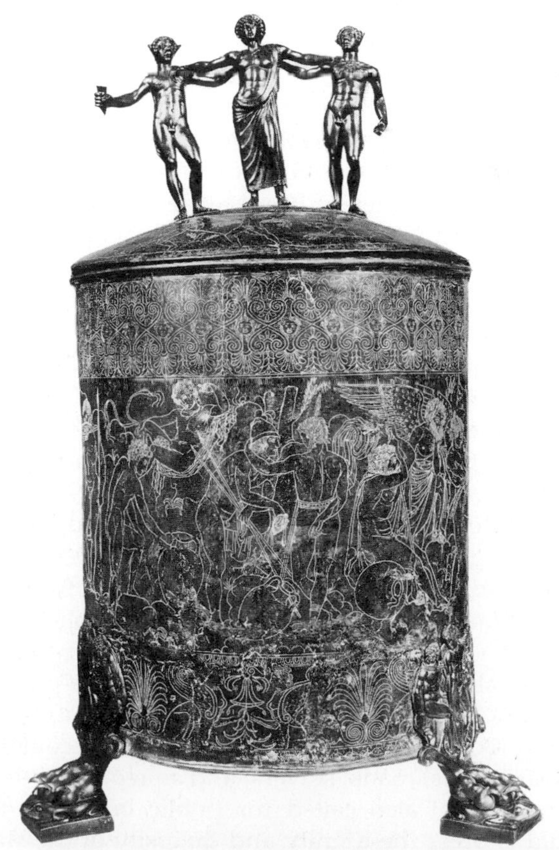

THE ROMANS

The Roman power that succeeded and replaced the Etruscan and Greek colonial powers on the Apennine peninsula compelled the contesting peoples of Italy into a Roman state and, eventually, the peoples of western Europe, the Mediterranean shores, North Africa, and the Near East into the Roman Empire. The rise and triumph of Rome, and the awesome spectacles of its decline and fall, make, in the stately words of its great historian, Edward Gibbon, "a revolution which will ever be remembered, and is still felt, by the nations of the earth." A single government stretched from the Tigris and Euphrates to the borders of Scotland. Under its energetic and efficient—if sometimes ruthless and brutal—rule lived people of innumerable races, creeds, tongues, traditions, and cultures: Britons, Gauls, Spaniards, Germans, Greeks, Africans, Egyptians, Syrians, and Arabs, to name only a very few. If the Greek genius, as we review it, shone most brightly in art, science, philosophy, history, and, in general, creations of the intellect and imagination, the Roman genius shone in the realm of worldly action—in law and in government. Roman monuments of art and architecture are distributed throughout the world that the Romans governed and are the most conspicuous and numerous of all the remains of the ancient civilizations we have studied thus far. But Roman monuments of a kind also survive in our concepts of law and government; in our calendar; in our festivals, rituals, languages, and religions; in the nomenclature of many of the sciences; and, for our special interest here, in the concept of art as worthy of historical study and criticism.

The main energies of Rome were devoted to conquest and administration, with conquest opening the way for the spread of Roman civilization. Roman cities sprang up not only all around the Mediterranean basin but also as far north as the Danube, the Rhine, and the Thames. Each city was a center for the propagation of Roman government, language, and customs and was closely connected with the city of Rome itself by a well-planned system of roads and harbors. By about A.D. 200, Rome was the capital of the greatest empire the world had ever known, an empire efficiently organized with fifty thousand miles of sea routes and expertly engineered highways for travel and commerce. Rome itself was cosmopolitan and splendid. The size, power, and complexity of the empire called for an impressive capital. The practical demands arising from the administration of a great empire required engineering skills for the construction of bridges, roads, sewers, and aqueducts, but the imperial ideal also called for public buildings that would express the dignity and diversity of the state. Roman art takes its character in large part from the imperial role the Roman state was required to play.

Roman art came to have its own quite distinctive characteristics, although both Etruscan and Greek influences played a role in its early development. The Romans, almost from the beginning of their rise to power, had been fully aware of Greek art, but it was only in the later Republican and Augustan ages that Hellenism became a conscious fashion. "Conquered Greece," wrote Horace, "led her proud conqueror captive." Shiploads of Greek marbles and bronzes were brought to Rome by generals and provincial governors to adorn their mansions, and when the supply was exhausted, copies were made or Greek artists were employed to create new works. Fashionable art for a time became, to a large extent, the mere copying of Greek works. Finally, a deeper assimilation took place, and the art of imperial Rome emerged, a product of its richly varied heritage and its own unique genius.

This art-historical view of Roman art is comparatively new. Until about 1900, scholars saw Roman art merely as decadent Greek art, unoriginal and inferior. It is true that, drawing as it necessarily does on what went before, Roman art does not have the degree of originality that distinguishes the great styles of Egypt, Mesopotamia, Greece, or even Etruria. Yet it is more than a mere "propagator and preserver of the classical heritage"; it is the "first comprehensive stage of western European art." Roman art makes use of Classical forms, but expresses non-Classical concepts. It combines an interest in individual personality with an interest in such abstract concepts as "law," "state," and "civilization." The vast body of the material of Roman art—found on three continents, with much still not evaluated and with much more still underground—almost suggests methods of mass production, in which anonymous artists (virtually no names survive, in contrast with Roman writers and poets) became the servants of their patrons: private or public, wealthy connoisseur or the Roman state. Nevertheless, in the collective as well as in the individual case, Roman art has survived as an imposing style that took its own course in the days of the late republic.

THE REPUBLICAN PERIOD

The Roman republic was founded after the last of the (possibly Etruscan) kings had been driven out of Italy. From the fifth century B.C. to the collapse of the republic and the assassination of Julius Caesar in 44 B.C., the external business of Rome was expansion abroad and the consolidation of imperial power in the

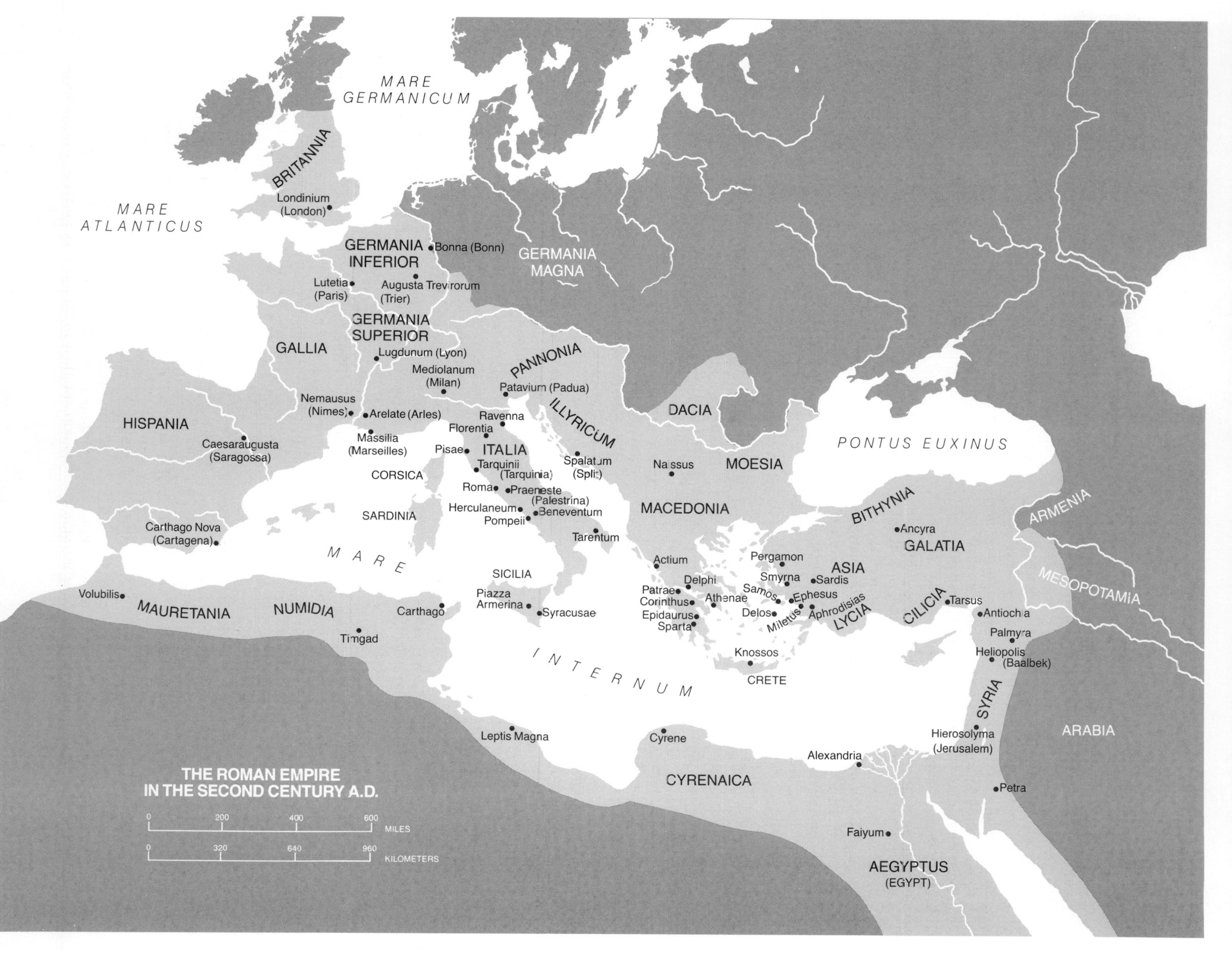
THE ROMAN EMPIRE
IN THE SECOND CENTURY A.D.
0 200 400 600 MILES
0 320 640 960 KILOMETERS
MARE GERMANICUM
MARE ATLANTICUS
BRITANNIA
Londinium (London)
GERMANIA INFERIOR
Bonna (Bonn)
GERMANIA MAGNA
Lutetia (Paris)
Augusta Treverorum (Trier)
GERMANIA SUPERIOR
GALLIA
Lugdunum (Lyon)
Mediolanum (Milan)
PANNONIA
Patavium (Padua)
Nemausus (Nimes)
Arelate (Arles)
Massilia (Marseilles)
HISPANIA
Caesaraugusta (Saragossa)
Carthago Nova (Cartagena)
CORSICA
SARDINIA
Ravenna
Florentia
Pisae
ITALIA
Tarquinii (Tarquinia)
Roma
Praeneste (Palestrina)
Herculaneum
Beneventum
Pompeii
ILLYRICUM
Spalatum (Split)
DACIA
Naissus
MOESIA
PONTUS EUXINUS
MACEDONIA
Tarentum
SICILIA
Piazza Armerina
Syracusae
MARE
INTERNUM
Volubilis
MAURETANIA
NUMIDIA
Carthago
Timgad
Leptis Magna
Cyrene
CYRENAICA
Actium
Delphi
Patrae
Corinthus
Athenae
Epidaurus
Sparta
Pergamon
Smyrna
Samos
Ephesus
Delos
Miletus
Aphrodisias
ASIA
Sardis
LYCIA
Knossos
CRETE
BITHYNIA
Ancyra
GALATIA
ARMENIA
CILICIA
Tarsus
MESOPOTAMIA
Antiochia
Palmyra
Heliopolis (Baalbek)
SYRIA
Hierosolyma (Jerusalem)
ARABIA
Alexandria
Petra
Faiyum
AEGYPTUS (EGYPT)

Western world. In a succession of wars, the most harrowing and dangerous of which were the wars with Carthage, the Romans developed their peculiar qualities of character: disciplined valor, tenacity, practicality, obedience to authority, and a pitiless realism in recognizing the facts of power. Yet the constitutional structure of the republic, adequate to a limited city-state, could not begin to meet the requirements of an empire. Internal quarrels between the *patrician* and the *plebeian* classes were inflamed by disputes over disposition of the enormous wealth won abroad. When successful armies led by popular generals intervened in the politics of the republic, civil war began. The war, which lasted almost a hundred years, exhausted the state and destroyed its constitution; dictators like Marius, Sulla, Caesar, and Pompey ruled. When the great-nephew of Julius Caesar, Octavian (who called himself Augustus), finally found himself alone at the head of the Roman polity, the republic was little more than a pious, ritualized memory.

It is in this period of the crisis of the republic, even while Greek influence became increasingly strong, that Roman art began to emerge as an entity distinguishable from the Late Hellenistic style. In 146 B.C., when Greece was absorbed into the Roman Empire as the province of Achaea, a sculptural style came into being that we call *Greco-Roman*. The coining of this term is an admission that the two styles cannot be readily separated. Much of the original sculpture of the period was produced by immigrant Greek artists, like the sculptor (perhaps Apollonius) of the *Seated Boxer* (FIG. 5-86). But the growing Roman fascination with individual traits of personality is apparent in portrait sculpture, a field in which the Romans made one of their most original contributions (the others being architecture and landscape painting) and one in which they achieved a quite typical, uncompromising, and often unflattering realism. However, the Hellenizing idealism that is found balancing this hard Roman realism in the last days of the republic bears witness to the peculiar dualism in the Roman attitude toward the defeated Greeks: admiration for their art and grace was mixed with contempt for their "unmanly" cleverness and for their lack of skill in managing their own affairs as a people. Cicero described this Roman ambiguity of sentiment and scored the Greeks on their un-Roman insincerity in terms a little like those of nineteenth-century American travelers commenting on the French:

> I grant them literature, I grant them a knowledge of many arts, I do not deny the charm of their speech, the keenness of their intellects, the richness of their diction; finally, if they make other claims, I do not deny them. But truth and honor in giving testimony that nation has never cherished. . . . Greeks never trouble to prove what they say, but only make a display of themselves by talking.

Still, somehow it was the idealism of Greek art that again and again captivated the Romans. Greek statues in great profusion stood in the Roman forums and in both public and private buildings; villas and baths were museums of Greek sculpture, filled with originals, copies, or adaptations suited to Roman taste. We read of 285 bronze and 30 marble statues brought from Corinth in 146 B.C., after the barbarous sack of that city, and of 500 bronzes brought from Delphi by Nero; when the stockpile of originals ran low, the demand for Greek sculpture was satisfied by copies of Greek works.

Portrait Sculpture

Even while under the spell of Hellenism, Roman portraitists produced works that have no parallel in Greek art. During the Hellenistic period, the quality of generalization that had distinguished earlier portraits already had given way to a style that was more particularizing and descriptive. The Roman's desire for literalness, together with the custom of keeping in the house, always before one's eyes, the *imagines* (death masks, usually of wax) of one's ancestors, influenced sculptors to accentuate individual traits still further. Etruscan influence, with its expressionistic realism, also persisted in Late Republican portraiture. The *Head of a Roman* (FIG. **6-14**), for example, is striking by virtue of its "character"—at once alive and masklike. But the character may simply be accidental, the result of the artist's painstaking report of each rise and fall, each bulge and fold, of the facial surface, executed as if the sculptor were proceeding like a mapmaker, concerned not to miss the slightest detail of surface change. The artist apparently tries neither to idealize the subject—that is, to improve him in conformity with an ideal, as in Greek practice—nor to interpret his personality. The blunt and bald record of his features, the kind given by a life mask or a death mask, is quite enough. Thus, this *verism,* a kind of superrealism, is the artist's objective, and it is determined not so much by esthetic motives as by religious convention. The habit of mind that demands faithful records of this kind is similar to our curiosity about the fidelity of photographs of our forebears.

A quite different approach to the portrait subject can be seen in a head (probably from a statue) of *Pompey the Great* (FIG. **6-15**). A sculptor confronting a powerful and famous man may be conscious of the need for a method different from mere recording; the goal may be to idealize, but also to personalize—to inter-

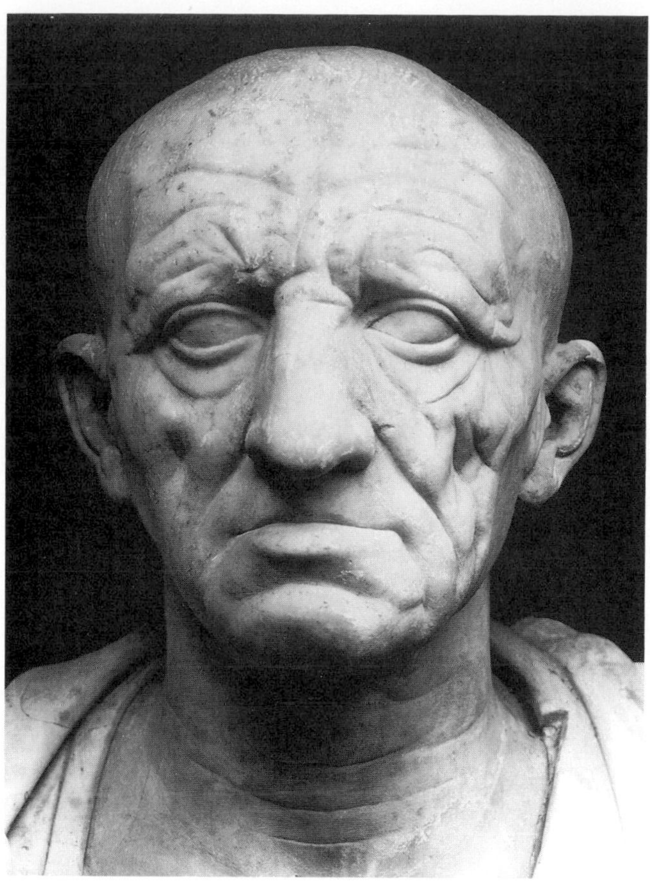

6-14 *Head of a Roman*, c. 80 B.C. Marble, life size. Palazzo Torlonia, Rome.

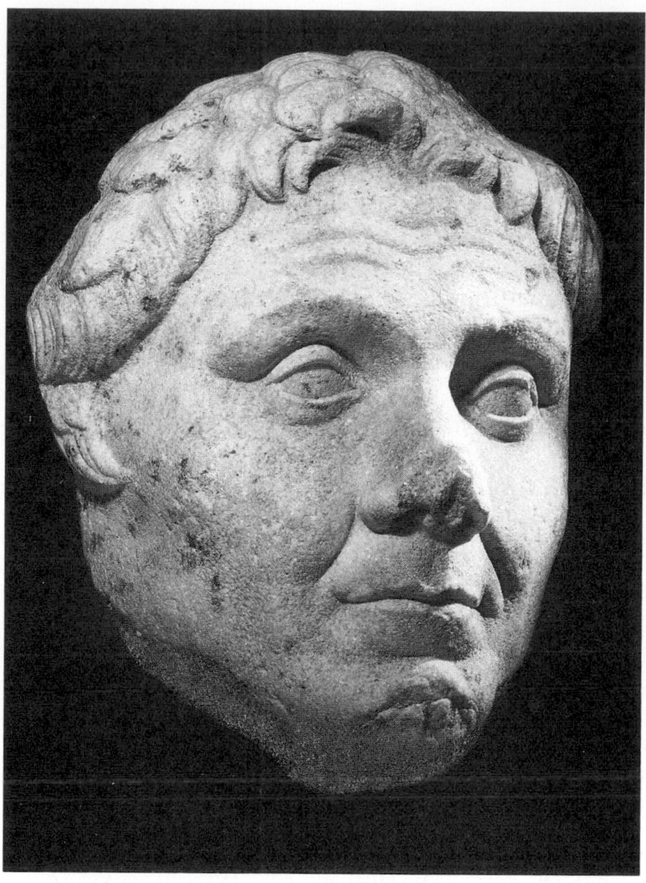

6-15 *Pompey the Great*, c. 55 B.C. Marble, life size. Frank E. Brown Collection, Rome.

pret the subject's personality. Viewing this head two thousand years after Pompey lived, we scan his face with far more knowledge of the man than we could ever bring to the contemplation of a portrait of an unknown Roman. Pompey was first the partner and then the rival of Julius Caesar in the devastating civil war that wrecked the Roman republic in the first century B.C. We know of him as a great general, successful in war and the near proprietor of all the Eastern world held by Rome. We know of him also as a political incompetent and as an ambitious man of the middle class who allowed himself to be made the dupe of the extremists of the Senatorial party. We know of him as hopelessly irresolute, a man who disappointed even his closest friends because he was unable to make up his mind. We know that he lost to Caesar in the bloody battle of Pharsalus, after which he was ignominiously assassinated by one of his own men. Yet he was a good man who refused to enrich himself by plunder of the provinces, a practice from which most of his contemporaries did not refrain. Cicero wrote of Pompey to a friend: "I knew him as a man honest, grave, and high-minded."

Thus, Pompey is a complex of traits played on by the accidents of history. Yet what kind of man of only slightly more than good talent could have bested Caesar? Knowing what we do about Pompey's main strengths and weaknesses, his triumphs and ultimate failure, we naturally approach his portrait as we might approach a bust of Washington or Lafayette—with curiosity about the individual man and his history. In the same way, it is likely that the artist of this work, although different from us in general cultural responses, would still have cared to make a likeness that would be more than a mere facial record. This desire is evident in this head, which has none of the rigidity of the death mask and possesses a subtly modeled surface, over which the light plays softly. The modeling is obviously contrived to suggest rather than to describe. The strong lines of the broad head and the somewhat flat surfaces of the face are softened by a curiously ambiguous expression. Would we be wrong to read in it self-doubt mingled with affectation or bluster under an official mask of power? At any rate, the very fact that we are tempted to such interpretation testifies to the sophisticated artist's power to make us thoughtful before this image of a great and unfortunate man.

Architecture

As striking as the manifestation of Roman originality is in naturalistic portraiture, it is even more pronounced in Roman architecture. During the Republican period, the Roman identity was first and most fully expressed in architecture and city planning. Unlike the religious architecture of the civilizations that preceded it (including that of the Greeks), the Roman temple was not particularly inventive or conspicuous. Although they built temples modeled on plans that blended Greek and Etruscan elements in unique fashion, Roman builders concentrated on imposing and utilitarian civic structures and plans. The Temple of "Fortuna Virilis" in Rome (FIG. **6-16**), dating from the late second century B.C., looks at first glance like an Ionic, peripteral temple. Now thought to have been dedicated to Portunus, god of the harbor, and standing appropriately on the banks of the Tiber River, this structure consists of a large cella located behind a deep porch. But the building stands on a high podium, which may be of Etruscan origin (see FIG. 6-1), and the cella occupies its entire width. This layout means that only the porch columns are freestanding and that the columns along the exterior walls of the cella are *engaged*, being purely decorative and having no supporting function. Seen from a distance, the engaged columns give the illusion of being freestanding; this type of construction is therefore designated *pseudoperipteral*. As a favorite with Roman builders, this temple type has survived in many examples, most of them larger than the one shown and most employing the Corinthian order.

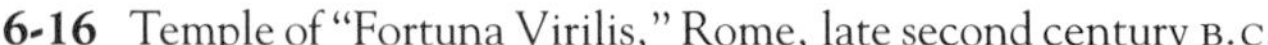

6-16 Temple of "Fortuna Virilis," Rome, late second century B.C.

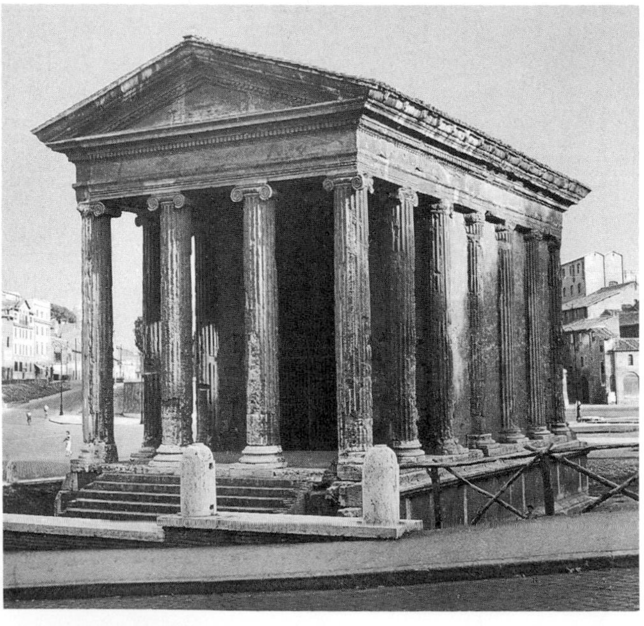

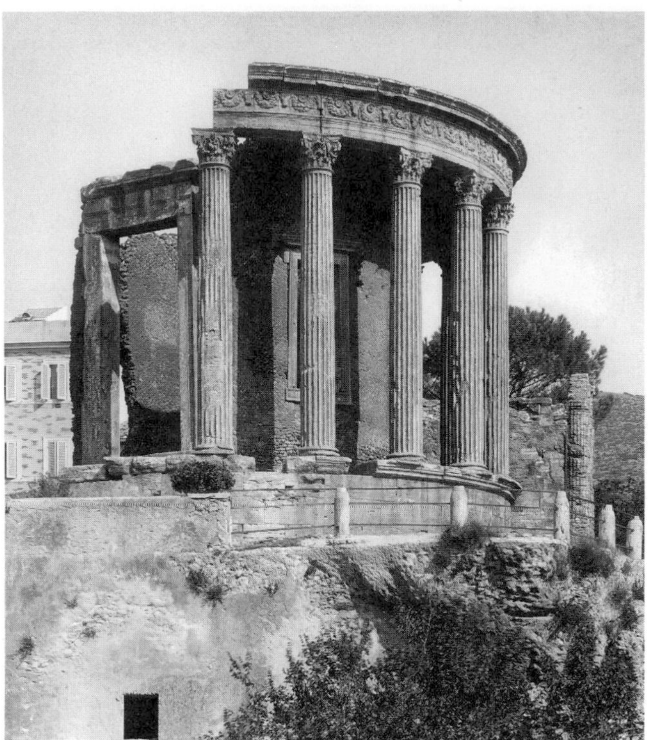

6-17 Temple of the "Sibyl" ("Vesta"?), Tivoli (ancient Tibur), Italy, early first century B.C.

The same superficial resemblance to Greek architecture appears in the Temple of the "Sibyl" (or "Vesta"?, FIG. **6-17**) at Tivoli (ancient Tibur). Built in the early first century B.C., the temple looks at first like a Corinthian tholos. However, like the "Fortuna Virilis," it stands on a podium and is accessible by means of a single flight of stairs that leads to the entrance of the cella. This arrangement introduces an axial alignment not found in Greek tholoi and serves to lessen the isolation of the building from its surroundings, diminishing somewhat the independent sculptural aspect so prized by the Greeks. A closer examination of the Temple of the "Sibyl" reveals other un-Greek features. The columns are *monolithic* (all of one piece) and not built up in the drum sections that were usual with the Greeks; the Romans preferred to use the monolithic column, often on a great scale, wherever possible. The frieze is embellished not with figure sculpture, as would be the case in Greece, but with a favorite Roman decorative motif—garlands held up by the heads of oxen—that repeats rhythmically around the whole frieze. (These are not the *bucrania*, or ox skulls, that became popular in later imperial architecture.) Finally, and also in contrast with Greek practice, the cella wall is built, not of cut stone, but of concrete, into which blocks of tufa have been set in an ornamental pattern.

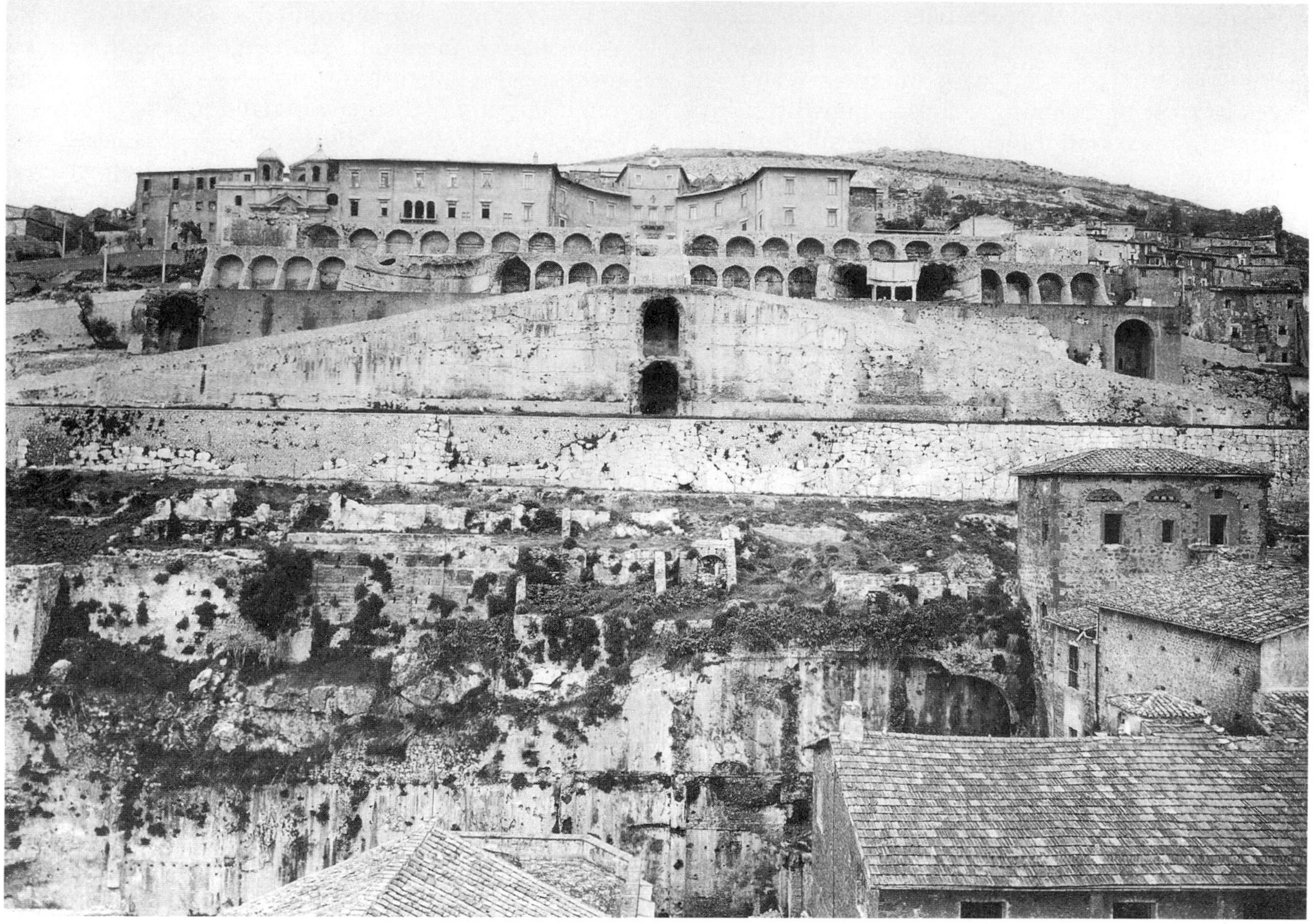

6-18 Sanctuary of Fortuna Primigenia, Palestrina, Italy, 120–80 B.C. (?)

These significant departures from the Greek model are seen even more clearly in the sanctuary at Palestrina (FIGS. **6-18** and **6-19**), which was dedicated to Fortuna Primigenia. The sanctuary was built under Sulla, the first Roman dictator of the republic, around 80 B.C., at a site where oracular lots had long been cast. (The date is disputed; some scholars move it back forty to fifty years.) The great size of the sanctuary reflects the growing taste for colossal Hellenistic designs during the Late Republican period. Seven terraces rising against the hillside were placed with rigid, axial symmetry. The top terrace carried a semicircular, double colonnade that probably enclosed a small, round temple. We have full knowledge of the great temple only by an accident of war: Palestrina, modern successor of the medieval town that had been built over Praeneste, was bombed during World War II, and clearing of the resultant ruins disclosed the impressive remains of the Roman buildings. The Roman builders had converted an entire hillside here into a man-made design in a symbolic and ostentatious display of power and dominion. This assertive

6-19 Model of the reconstructed Sanctuary of Fortuna Primigenia. Museo Archeologico Nazionale, Palestrina.

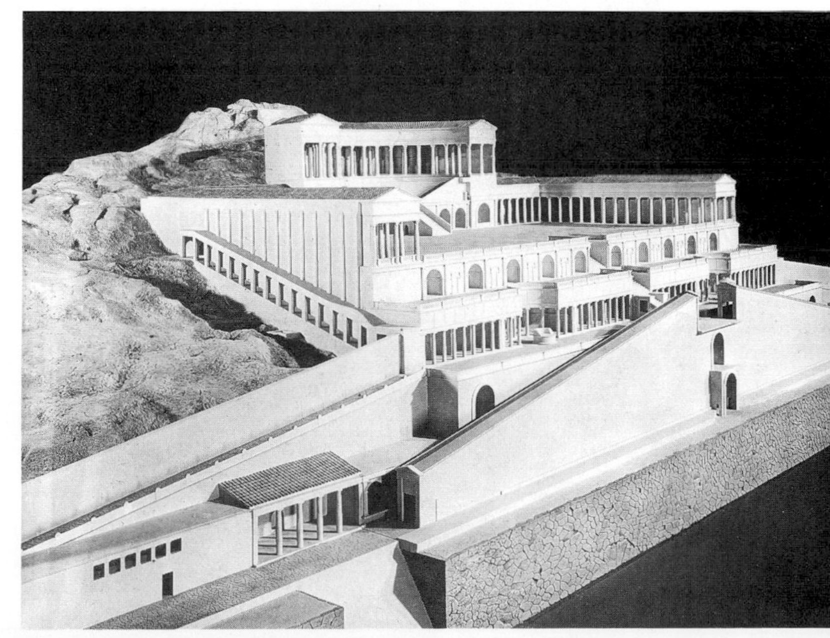

subjection of nature to man's will and rational order is the first full-blown manifestation of the Roman imperial spirit and contrasts with the more restrained Greek practice of crowning a chosen hill with sacred buildings rather than transforming the hill itself into architecture.

The substructures for the terraces (FIG. **6-20**) were built in concrete *(opus caementicium)*, a favorite Roman building material. Roman concrete was a mixture of lime mortar, water, and volcanic dust (found in limited areas, chiefly in central Italy). Developed in the second century B.C. and applied for centuries wherever the necessary ingredients were available, concrete (of generally inferior quality) had been used in the Near East, chiefly for the building of fortification walls, but its combination with the arch and the vault, as here at Praeneste, was revolutionary. As perfected during the Early Imperial period, concrete vaulting permitted Roman builders to cover spaces of unprecedented scale, without interior supports. Its use enabled the Roman architect to think of architecture in radically different terms from those of earlier builders—as an architecture of space rather than of sheer mass, as was the case with the Egyptian pyramid, or the Mesopotamian ziggurat, or even the lighter, but still space-encumbering, post-and-lintel system of the Greeks. (See the discussion of the Roman Pantheon, pages 226–28.) Roman concrete was poured over rubble that had been laid in courses between forms. Once solidified, this rubble concrete was cohesive and strong, although rough in appearance; it was Roman custom, however, to face the rough surfaces with marble slabs, plaster, or ornamental brickwork or stonework. In Praeneste, the concrete is faced with small, flat, irregularly shaped stones that produce a figuration called *opus incertum*.

In the eighteenth century, the imagination of Europe was excited by the discovery of the buried cities of Pompeii and Herculaneum, which had been overwhelmed by an eruption of Mount Vesuvius in A.D. 79. The discovery of these cities, prior to the first archeological expeditions to Egypt, fascinated Europe and provided the initial impetus for modern archeological curiosity. What made the discoveries of such poignant human interest, as well as so infinitely valuable for scientific history, was that they revealed to modern eyes, in almost perfect preservation and detail, the everyday communal life of these times and places past. Pompeii, a prosperous city of about twenty thousand inhabitants, had been preserved intact in volcanic ashes, invisible and forgotten for some sixteen hundred years. The remains of the city, which are still being excavated, permit us to reconstruct the Roman way of life during the Early Imperial period with a completeness far beyond that achieved at any other archeological site. The fullness of the archeological record, the city's appeal to our sense of the dramatic and terrible accidents of life, and its use-

6-20 Detail of the Sanctuary of Fortuna Primigenia.

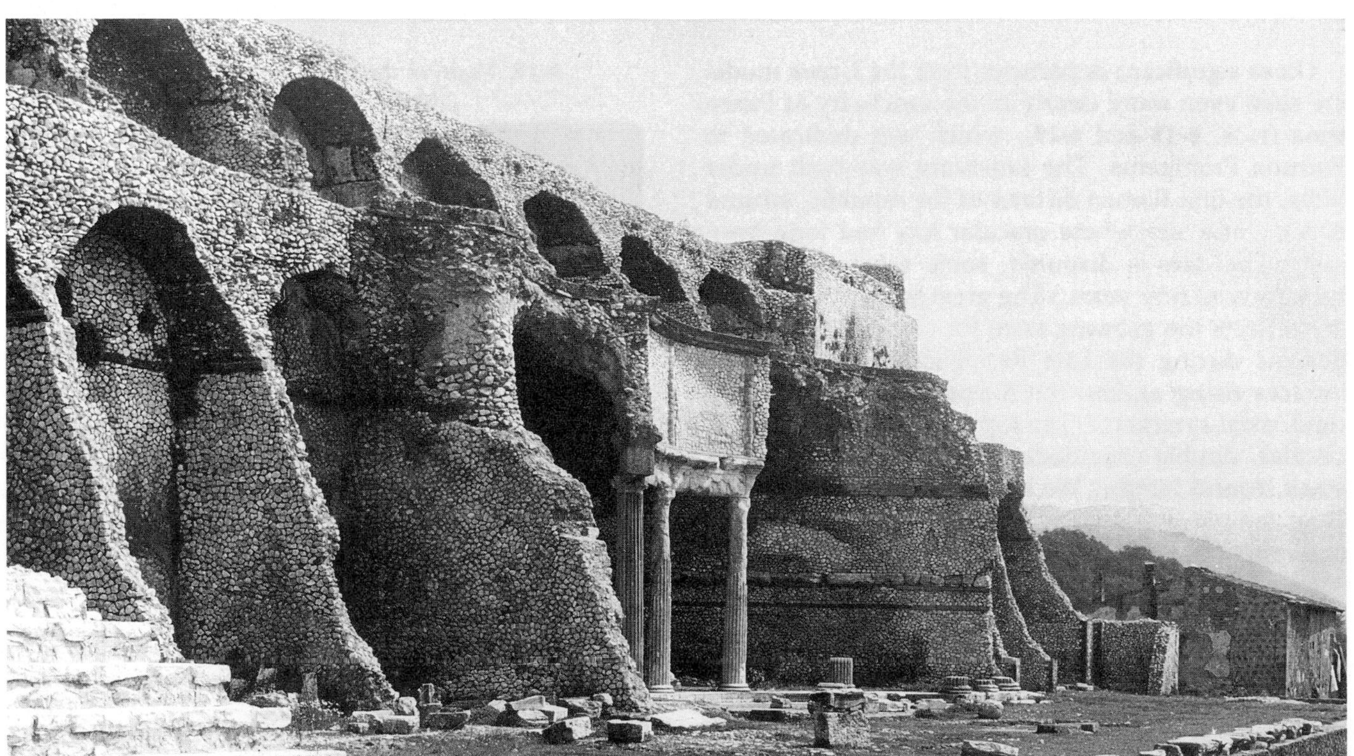

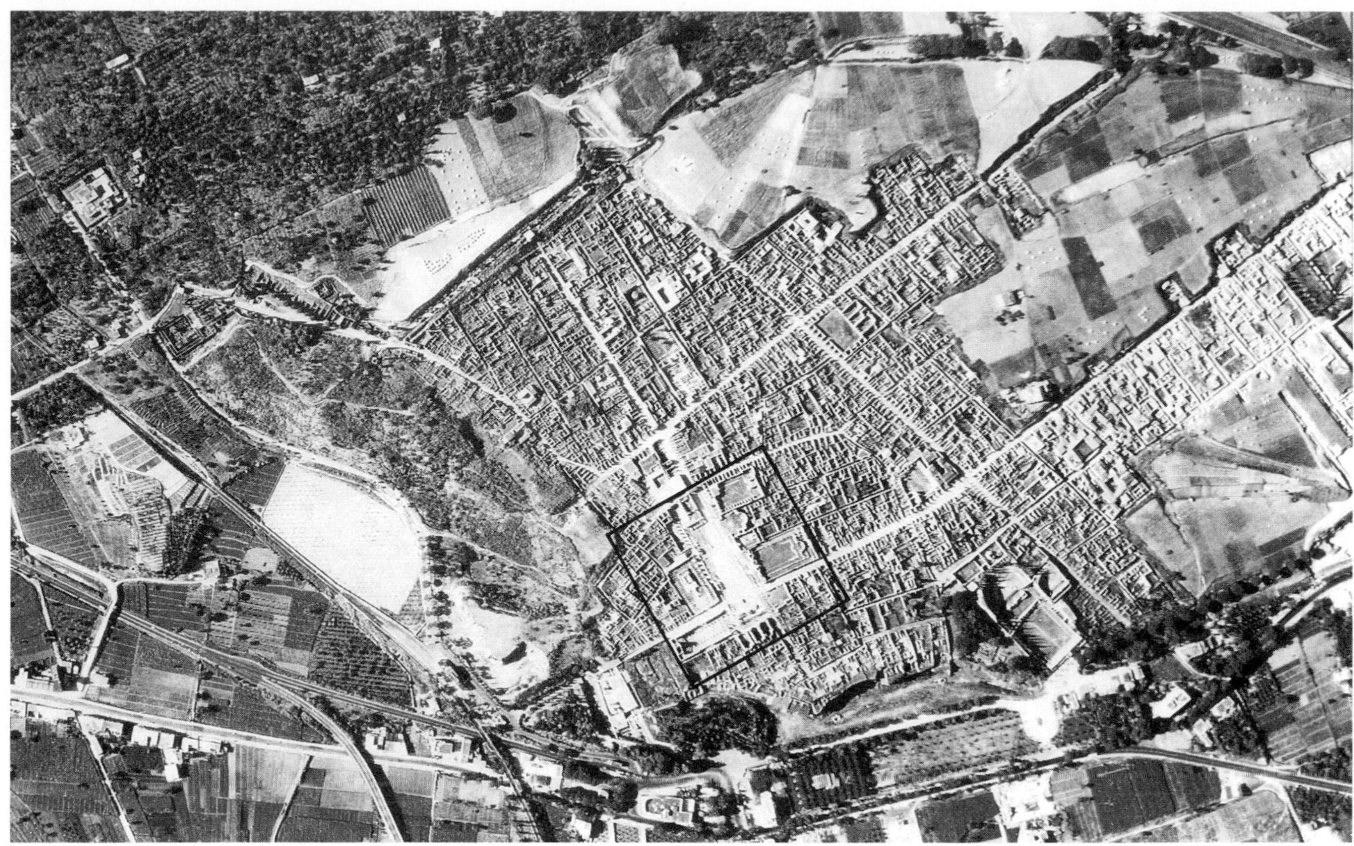

6-21 Aerial view of the excavated portion of Pompeii, Italy. Area enclosed by rectangle near center of photograph is shown in FIG. 6-22.

fulness for describing the architectural and artistic environment of quite ordinary people in an ancient city warrant considerable attention.

Although destroyed during the Early Imperial period, the city and many of its architectural monuments date from the Republican period. The plan of Pompeii, as seen in the parts excavated thus far (FIG. **6-21**), is not that of the ideal castrum type (see pages 218–19), but rather the irregular plan of a "grown" city that was subjected to revisions and regularizing at various periods. The Roman castrum type of city plan, based on the layout of a military camp, was used in the outlying, frontier, colonial regions and had its major development during the Early Imperial period (see FIG. 6-44), although an early form of it was used at Ostia in the fourth century B.C. Pompeii started as a small, unplanned settlement in the vicinity of the Greek colony of Naples (ancient Neapolis). The Oscans, early local rivals of the Romans, founded it in the sixth century B.C. It was seized in 425 B.C. by the Samnites, also rivals of the Romans, who fortified and replanned it under the influence of expanding Greek concepts of rational, urban planning. But the Greek grid system could not be applied rigidly without tearing down most of the city; as a result, the main organizing features—the north–south and east–west thoroughfares—do not intersect at right angles, and the blocks between them are irregular. The city was conquered by Sulla in the 80s and refounded as a Roman colony in 80 B.C. In A.D. 62, it was partially destroyed by an earthquake and had not yet been entirely rebuilt at the time of its final destruction seventeen years later. Pompeii has been especially valuable to the historian of Roman architecture; many building types that later were to become standard are found there, including the oldest amphitheater extant and the earliest known public baths.

Next to the Forum Romanum in Rome, from which it differs significantly in design, the forum of Pompeii (FIGS. **6-22** and **6-23**) is the most important example of an early Roman civic center. The Pompeian forum is a rectangular court in the proportion of $3\frac{1}{2}:1$, unified by continuous colonnades around three sides, which define its boundaries. The other type of plan, represented by the Forum Romanum, is bordered by more monumental, but individual and disconnected, structures. Like most Roman forums, the Pompeian forum was set apart from major traffic arteries and vehicles could not enter it. Its long, north–south axis is dominated by the Temple of Jupiter, a large temple set on a

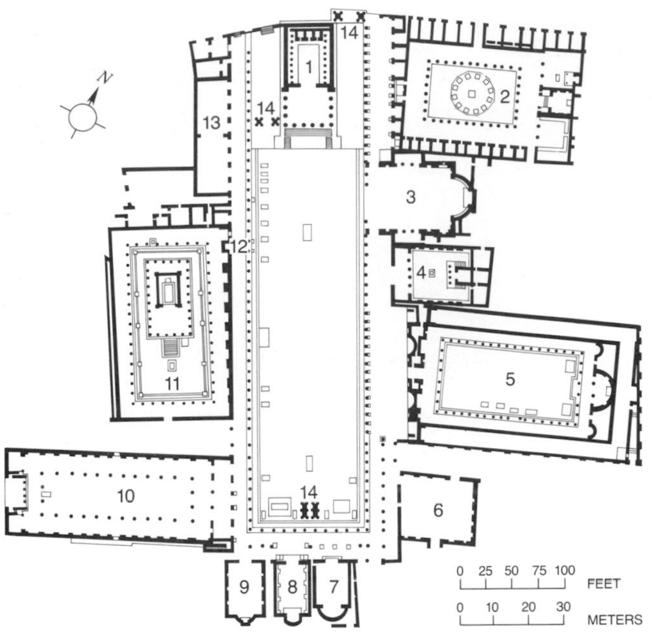

1. Temple of Jupiter
2. Macellum (provisions market)
3. Sanctuary of the City Lares
4. Temple of Vespasian
5. Building of Eumachia (fullers hall)
6. Comitium (voting hall)
7. Duovirs' (chief magistrates') office
8. Council chamber
9. Aediles' (junior magistrates') office
10. Basilica
11. Temple of Apollo
12. Control of weights and measures
13. Cereals market
14. Commemorative arches

6-22 Plan of the forum of Pompeii. Area diagrammed is indicated in FIG. 6-21 by rectangle inscribed near center of photograph.

high podium and dedicated to the three gods who protected Rome and her colonies. The Romans liked to place their temples in a dominant position at the end of an enclosure, in contrast to the Greek practice of building freestanding temples in sanctuaries where they could be seen and approached from all sides. Several smaller temples flank the long sides of the forum. At the south end stand the triple halls of the Curia (city council), representing civic authority, and the Basilica, the seat of law and business. This basilica, dating back to about 100 B.C., is an early example of one of the most important and influential classes of Roman buildings, the one from which the basic form of the Christian church building will derive. Thus, the forum combines the functions of a religious, commercial, and administrative civic center. In the same way, it is a kind of imperial center in miniature, and this combination of functions, as architecturally expressed in the Roman forum, would come to represent the central concerns and focus of the whole Roman Empire.

One would not expect the formality of a civic center also to be found in the streets that surround it. These, logically, would be less monumental and regular, their spaces less ample or perhaps even narrow and cramped. The streets had heavy flagstone pavements with flanking sidewalks. Stepping-stones for pedestrians crossing the street were spaced so that they could be straddled by the wheels of vehicles. Most

6-23 Forum of Pompeii

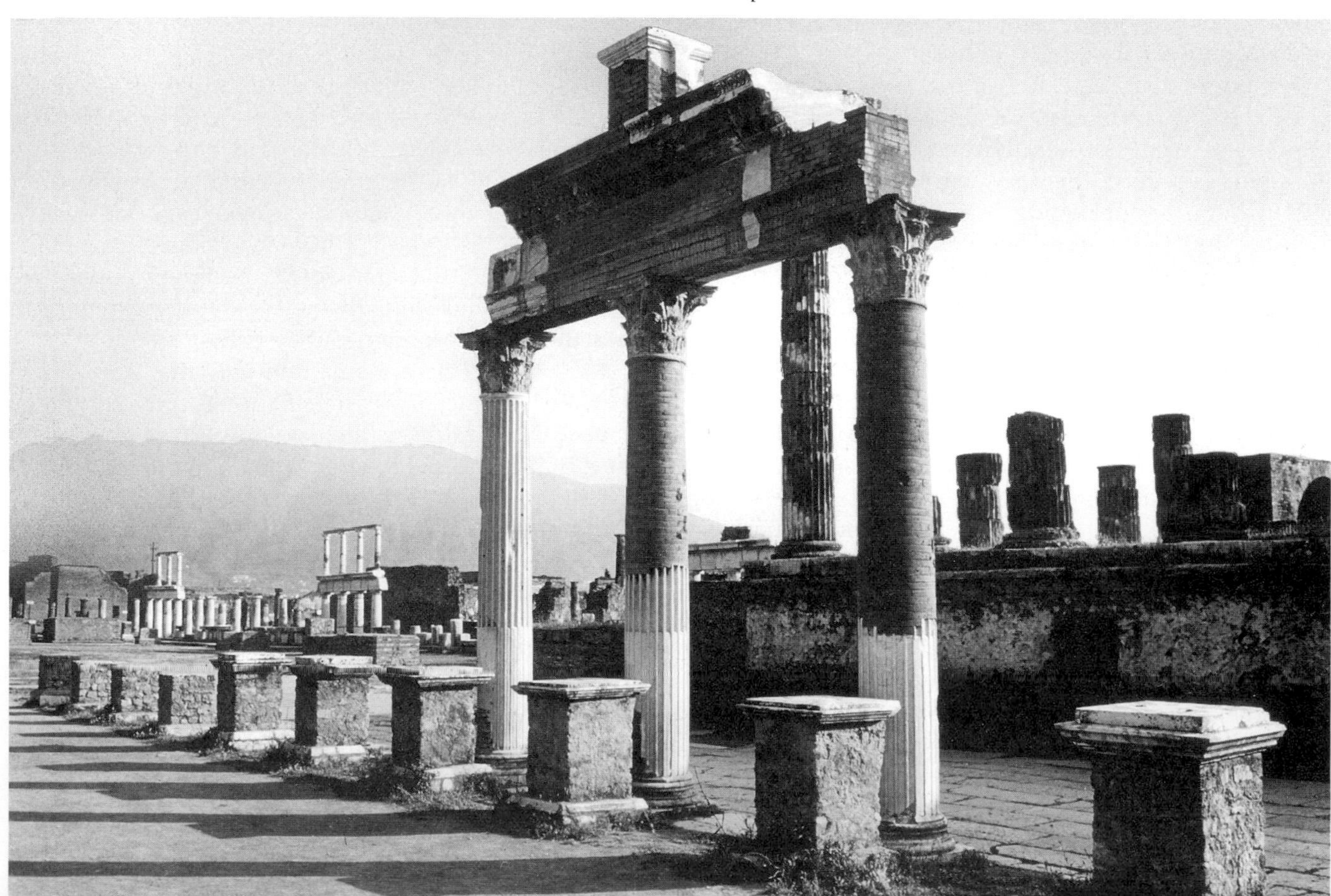

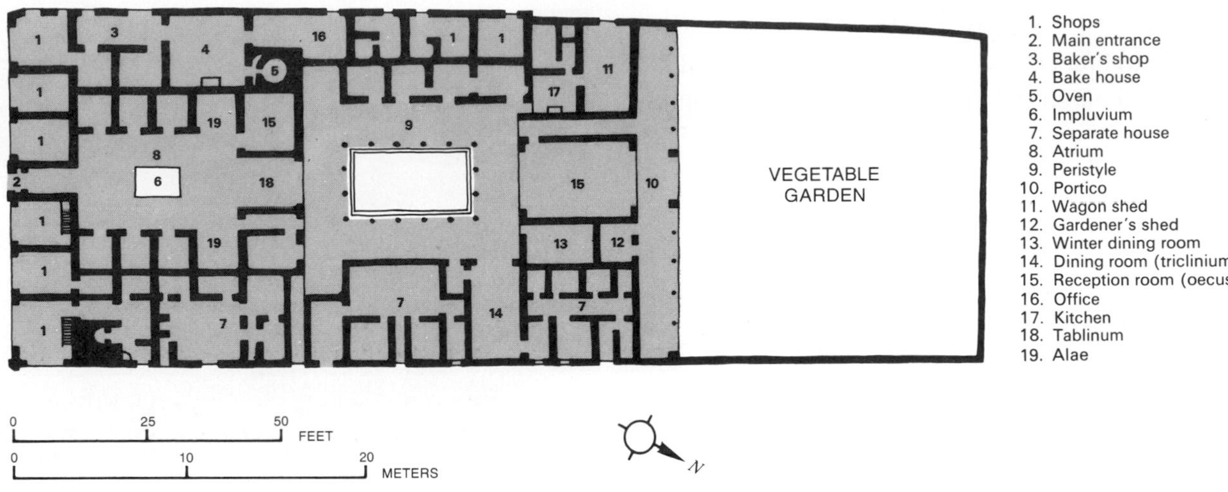

6-24 Plan of the House of Pansa, Pompeii, second century B.C. (After Sir Banister Fletcher.)

intersections had continuously flowing public fountains. The problem of human convenience in an urban society, although not dealt with on the enormous scale that it is today, was worked out in Pompeii with an efficiency we can believe suited the needs of the people. The town had its commercial sections, like that of the Via dell' Abbondanza, where rows of small shops, offices, taverns, and bakeries flanked the streets. We still can see many painted advertisements on the walls in this section. Here and there, the rows of shops were interrupted by a gateway leading into a private residence, which spread out in the back of the shops and was entirely enclosed and isolated from them and from the noise and dust of the street.

The private house is probably the most precious and best-preserved record of urban life to come from Pompeii. The town houses of the well-to-do, like the House of Pansa (FIG. **6-24**), were frequently protected in Pompeii and Herculaneum by the volcanic ash and lava in which they were buried, and are extraordinarily well preserved, with their mural decorations still fresh and some equipment and household utensils intact. Such a house, known as an atrium type, stood flush with the sidewalk. Through a narrow door, one entered a vestibule that led into the *atrium*. The latter had an opening in the center of the roof (the *compluvium*) to admit light and air and a depression in the floor below it (the *impluvium*) to collect rainwater. Along the sides were small rooms; at the end, where the atrium extended the full width of the building, were two wings, or *alae*. Behind the atrium was the *tablinum*, in which family archives and statues were kept. The tablinum could be shut off or, in later Pompeian houses, could afford a passage to the *peristyle*, a large colonnaded court of Hellenistic origin. This court contained fountains and a garden, around which the family's private apartments were arranged. At the back, a vegetable garden or an orchard was sometimes planted. Along the outer sides of the house and opening onto the street were the shops. The house faced inward, depending on its courts for light and air. Whenever space allowed it, units were symmetrically arranged on a long axis that reached back from the street. When opened through its entire length, this arrangement afforded a charming vista of open court, gardens, fountains, statues, colored marbles, mosaics, and brightly painted walls. Some of the largest of these atrium houses in Pompeii could truly be called palatial; the House of the Faun, in which *The Battle of Issus* mosaic (FIG. 6-37) served as a floor ornament, covered almost 30,000 square feet. A typical modern suburban house measures roughly 1,500 square feet. Of course, these houses, popular particularly in the region around Mount Vesuvius, were the homes of patricians and rich merchants; artisans, craftsmen, and shopkeepers lived in much more modest quarters, often in single rooms in back of or above their shops.

In their fullest development in the late Roman republic, the elaborate, skillfully planned houses of the great Romans combined an older Italic nucleus with features of the Hellenistic house and represented the highest achievements of domestic architecture in antiquity. The character of Roman domestic religion, which exhibited a traditional Italic feeling for the home, family, and hearth as sacred, helps to explain the careful elaboration of domestic architecture and the prominent role it played in Roman civilization throughout the empire.

Painting and Mosaic

The interiorizing design, with its open and independent arrangement of units, guaranteed complete privacy in Roman houses. Because of the small number of doors and windows, the design also offered considerable stretches of wall space suitable for decoration, as the atrium of the House of the Silver Wedding in Pompeii (FIG. **6-25**) clearly shows. The decorations commonly used varied between types that emphasized the wall as a barrier and others that visually opened the wall and enhanced the space of the room. The colors were sometimes delicate greens and tans, sometimes striking reds and black (to throw the panels or figures into relief), and a rich creamy white used in the borders. The Romans obtained a certain brilliance of surface by careful preparation of the wall. The plaster, specially compounded with marble dust, was laid on in several layers and beaten with a smooth trowel until it became very dense. The surface then was polished to a marblelike finish.

The progression from flat to spatial wall decoration in Pompeii and Herculaneum has been divided, somewhat arbitrarily, into four successive, but overlapping and often coexisting styles. The first style (*c.* 200–60 B.C.), called *incrustation,* divides the wall into bright, polychrome panels of solid colors with occasional, schematically rendered textural contrasts (FIG. **6-26**). This style is a continuation of Hellenistic practice, and examples of it have been found in houses at Priene and on the island of Delos.

A wall painting from the Villa Boscoreale, near Pompeii (FIG. **6-27**), shows the second, or *architectural,*

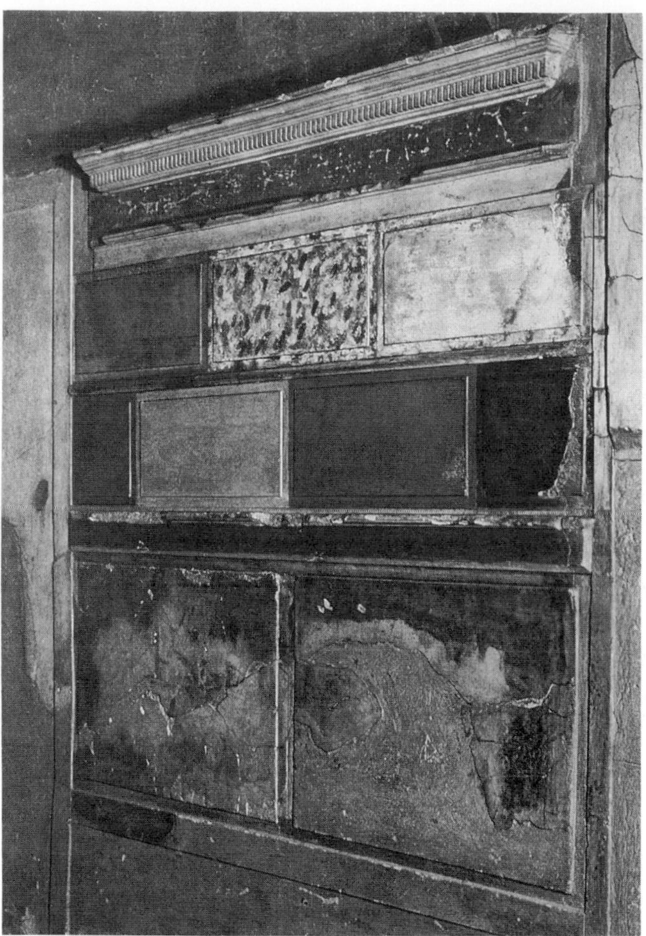

6-26 First-style *(incrustation)* wall painting from a Samnite house, Herculaneum, second century B.C.

6-25 Atrium of the House of the Silver Wedding, Pompeii, early first century B.C.

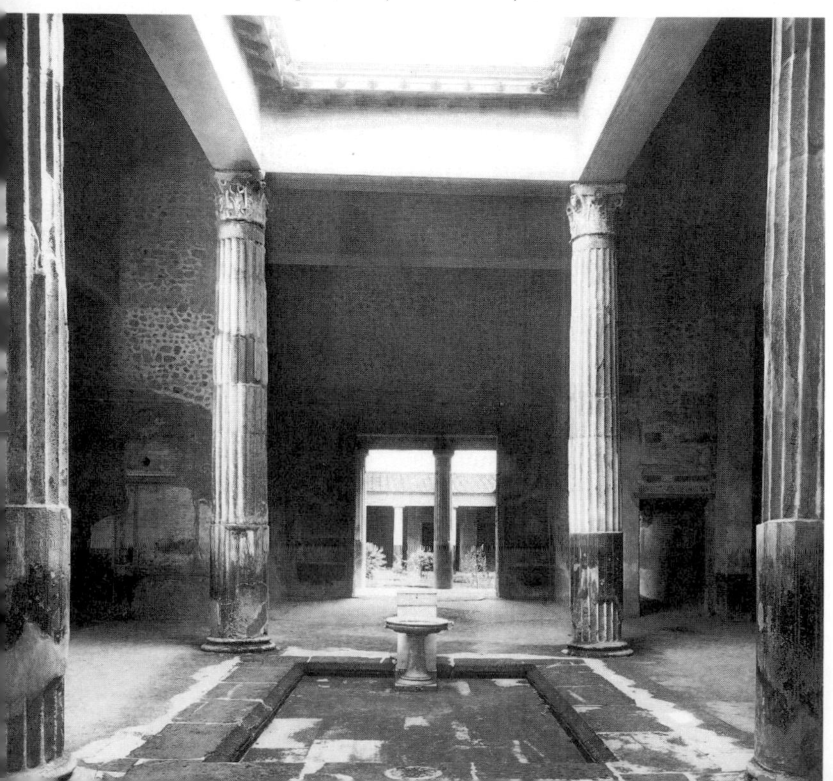

6-27 Second-style *(architectural)* wall painting from the Villa Boscoreale, near Pompeii, first century B.C. Metropolitan Museum of Art, New York (Rogers Fund, 1903).

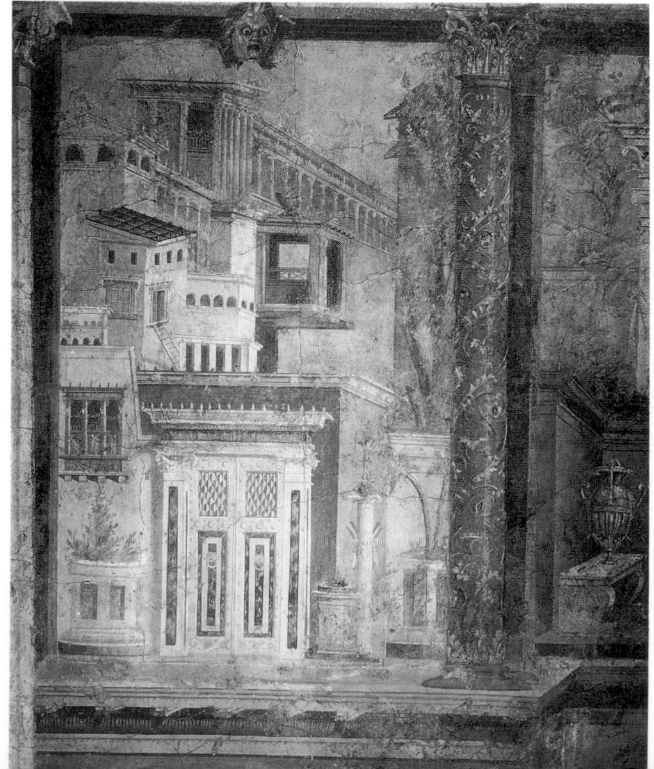

style (*c.* 60–20 B.C.), in which decoration is no longer restricted to a single visual plane. The space of the room is made to look as if it extends beyond the room itself by the representation of architectural forms in a visually convincing, but not really systematic, perspective. Columns, pilasters, and window frames painted on the wall serve to enframe distant views of cities and landscape. In the *herringbone perspective* used here, the *orthogonals*, or lines of perspective projection, do not converge on a single vanishing point on the horizon (as in Renaissance perspective); instead, several vanishing points (with associated orthogonals) tend to be distributed on an axis that runs vertically through the center of the panel. Although not consistently employed, this method does give a rather convincing illusion of objects receding in space. In halls over one story high, the architectural style is sometimes used to provide a firm, structural base for an upper register in a later style.

A second-style mural in the Villa of the Mysteries near Pompeii (*c.* 50 B.C.) displays painted figures that are among the finest to have come down to us from the ancient world (FIG. **6-28**). Although other rooms in the villa are decorated in a style very similar to the pure architectural style of the Villa Boscoreale, the second-style illusionism here is confined to a painted ledge that looks like a shallow extension of the room proper and affords the figures a kind of narrow, supporting stage. The figures, set against a red-paneled background, in the style of a relief, are part of a large composition that circles the walls of the room, which may have doubled as a banqueting room and as a place for the celebration of the rites of some mystery cult, perhaps that of Dionysos. The meaning of these scenes is in dispute. We may, however, be fairly certain that this group represents the initiation of a young novice into the cult. Whipped by a winged genius or deity, the novice crouches for solace in the lap of a solicitous older woman, while a splendidly painted nude dances in Bacchic frenzy. The mystery cults, discussed later in connection with Christianity, made their way into the Roman Empire in increasing numbers from the Hellenized East. All cults included mysteries that were never to be divulged by the initiate, and that, when understood after painful introduction into the secret rites, would afford salvation through mystical union with a deity. The pictured ceremony from the Villa of the Mysteries is not only a

6-28 Second-style wall painting, details of a frieze from the Villa of the Mysteries, near Pompeii, *c.* 50 B.C. Figures approx. 60″ high.

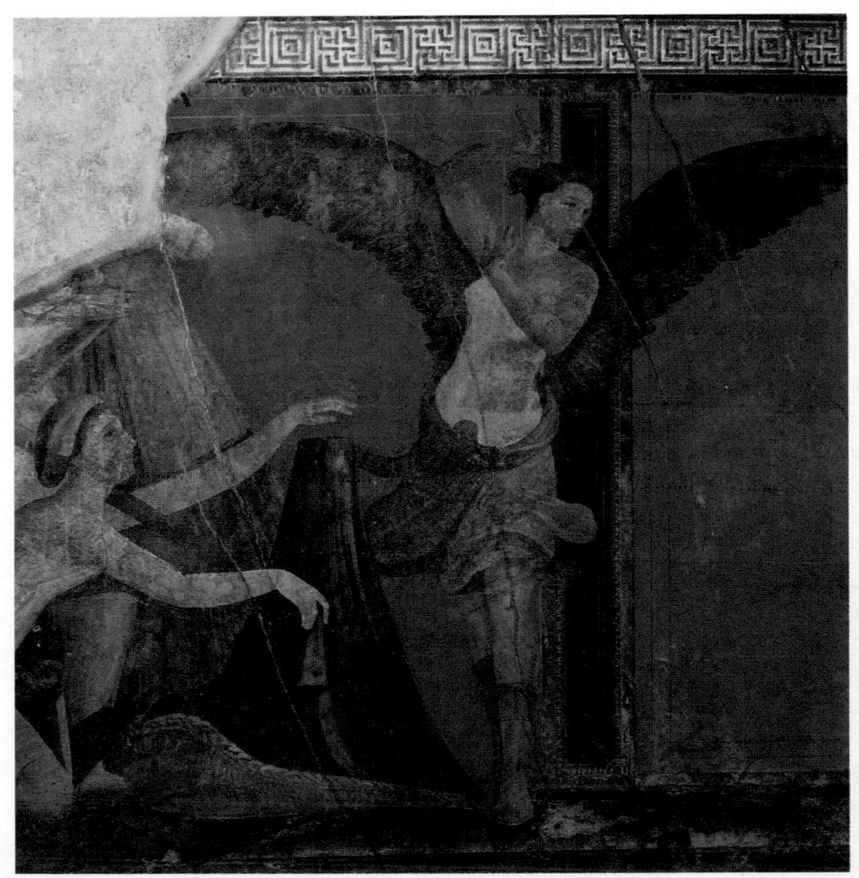

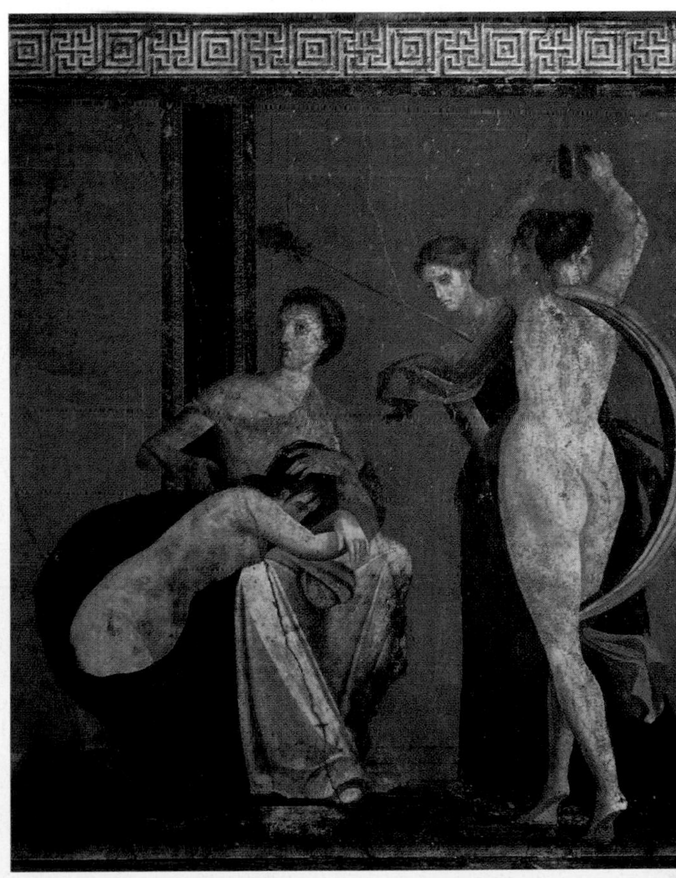

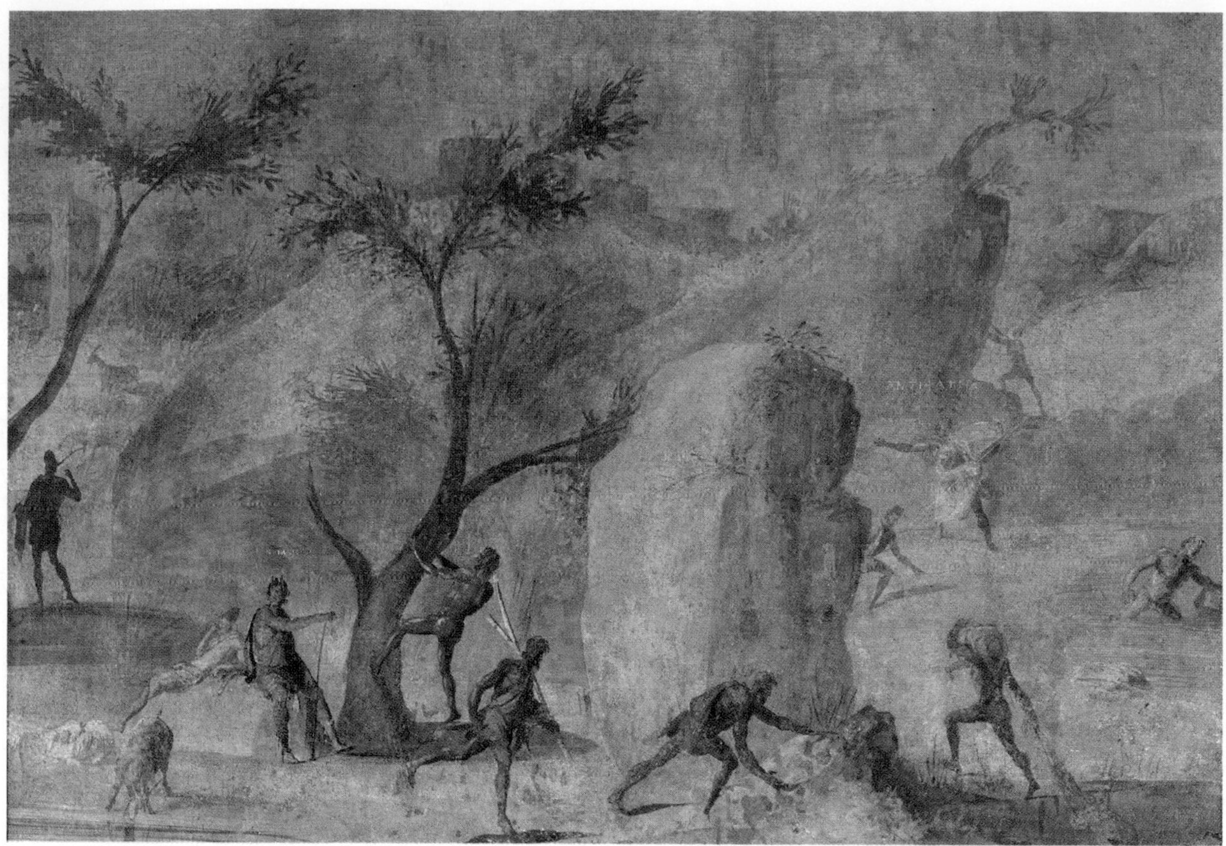

6-29 *Ulysses in the Land of the Lestrygonians* (scene from the *Odyssey Landscapes*), second-style wall painting from a house in Rome, late first century B.C. Approx. 60″ high. Vatican Library, Rome.

work of art of high order, but a most important record of one aspect of the gradual religious transformation of the Roman world by the westward migration of Oriental spiritualism. As always with Roman paintings of quality, we question whether this mural is an original Roman work or a derivative from a Hellenistic Greek original in some temple that is now lost. No decisive answer can be given.

The same question arises again, and more insistently, when we look at the second-style *Odyssey Landscapes* (FIG. **6-29**) from a house on the Esquiline Hill in Rome, which are now in the Vatican. In these landscapes, dating from the late first century B.C., painted piers divide the otherwise continuous stretch of landscape into eight compartments, in which scenes from the Homeric epic are represented. The shimmering landscapes extend the space of the room and their luminosity almost absorbs the subordinated, rapidly sketched figures. At the same time, the landscapes seem to be brought into the room almost magically—the flickering play of color and light, and especially the shaded edges of the solids, providing a stagelike presence, as of easily shifted props, that suggests distance and isolated action. The second style, although "architectural," here exhibits its versatility, for the sole purpose of the rigid frames is to create the illusion of open and unconstrained landscape. If it could be established that the conception of an all-encompassing space in works like the *Odyssey Landscapes* is original with Rome, then a solid Roman contribution to the history of art could be acknowledged.

The architectural quality of the second style faded toward the end, and the triumph of the illusionism evident in the *Odyssey Landscapes* may be seen in the detail of a wall painting (FIG. **6-30**) from the House of Livia in Primaporta, near Rome, made toward the end of the first century B.C. The extension of the space of the room and its complementary effect, the bringing of the landscape into the room, creates an image of a garden just outside the limit of the wall. (This is a curious anticipation of the widely popular "picture window" of recent modern architecture, in which one enjoys the "view" by fixing it within a frame and at the same time thinking of the landscape as continuous with the room.) Here, deep perspectives and distant views are not desired, but rather the intimacy and freshness of natural beauty easily

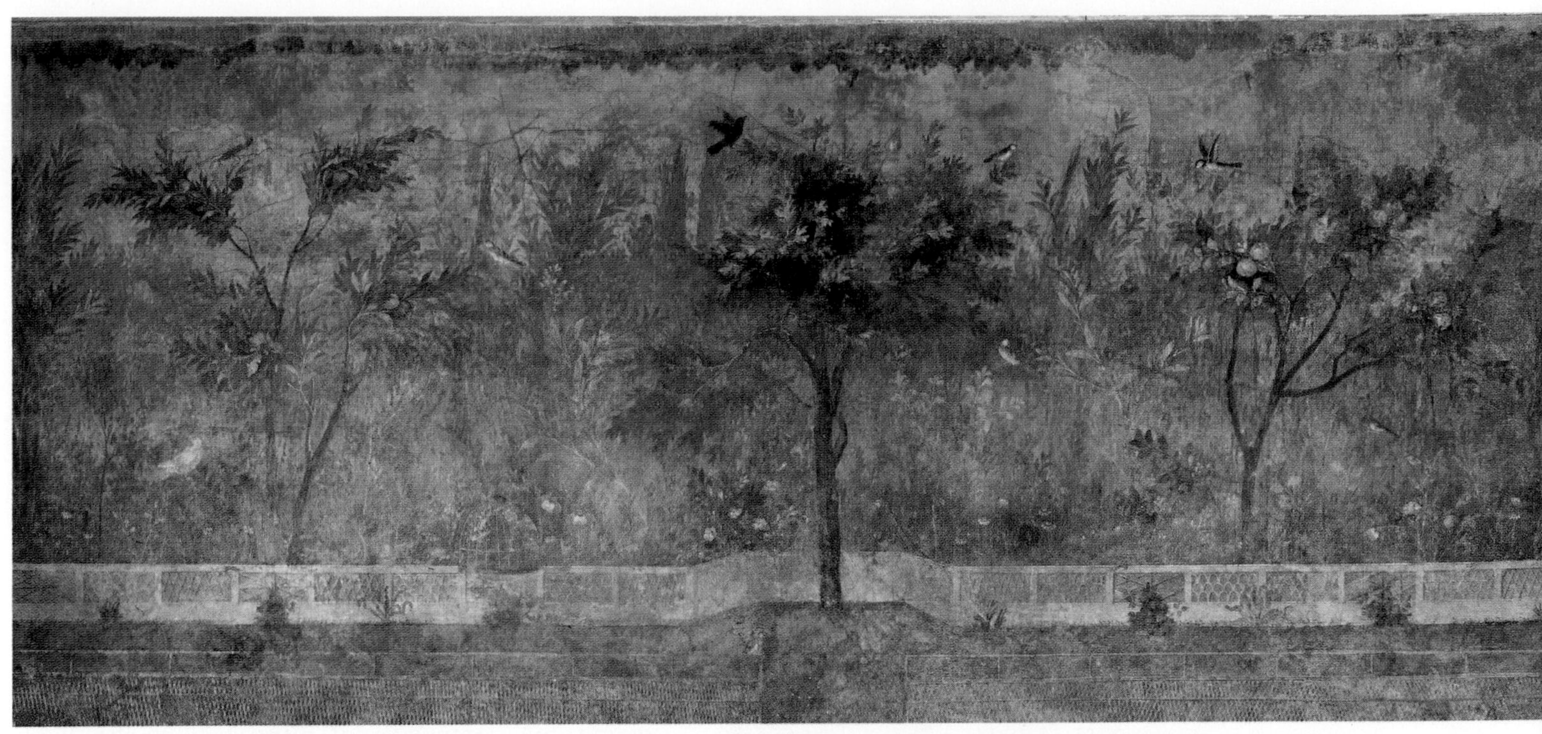

6-30 *Garden Scene,* detail of a second-style wall painting from the House of Livia, Primaporta, late first century B.C. Portion shown approx. 9′ wide. Museo Nazionale Romano, Rome.

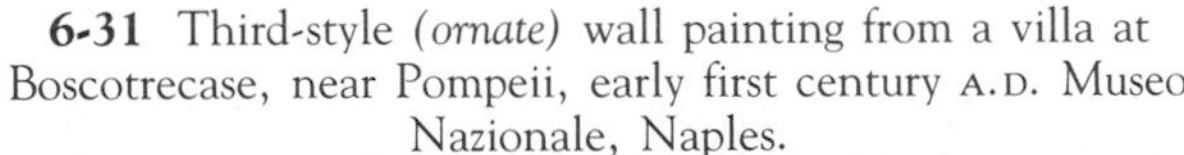

6-31 Third-style *(ornate)* wall painting from a villa at Boscotrecase, near Pompeii, early first century A.D. Museo Nazionale, Naples.

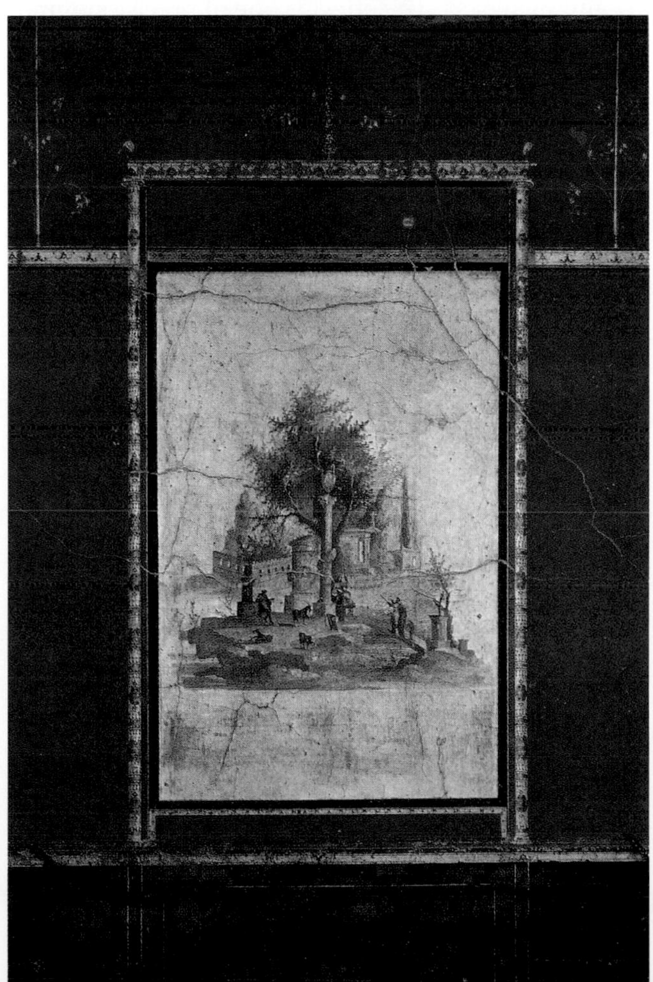

within contact. In the second style, as it developed, the view comes ever closer, until one may think that it is one's own garden, free of any human intrusion, enclosed and isolated by the painted limits of the fence and by the backstopping of the foliage itself, which occupies a plane close to the viewer and shuts out distance.

In the third, or *ornate,* style (*c.* 20 B.C.–A.D. 60), during the time of the early Roman Empire, the wall ceased to serve as a framed view into nature and became a mere support for smaller, framed views. Simulated architecture disappeared, as the wall was subdivided into a number of panels by means of vertical and horizontal bands filled with vine scrolls or other decorative designs (FIG. **6-31**). The flat nature of the wall is here reaffirmed, and illusionism is confined to the pictures set into and emphasized by the decoratively patterned framework. At times whimsical and capricious, this style is characterized by delicate forms and colors, graceful elegance, and a deliberate rejection of the monumental constructions and broad illusionism of the second style. What might have become a view through an illusionistic window in the second style has been reduced here to a flat, white panel with a floating landscape motif on it.

The fourth Pompeian wall style, the *intricate,* dates from around A.D. 60 to A.D. 79 and may be seen to good advantage in the Ixion Room from the House of

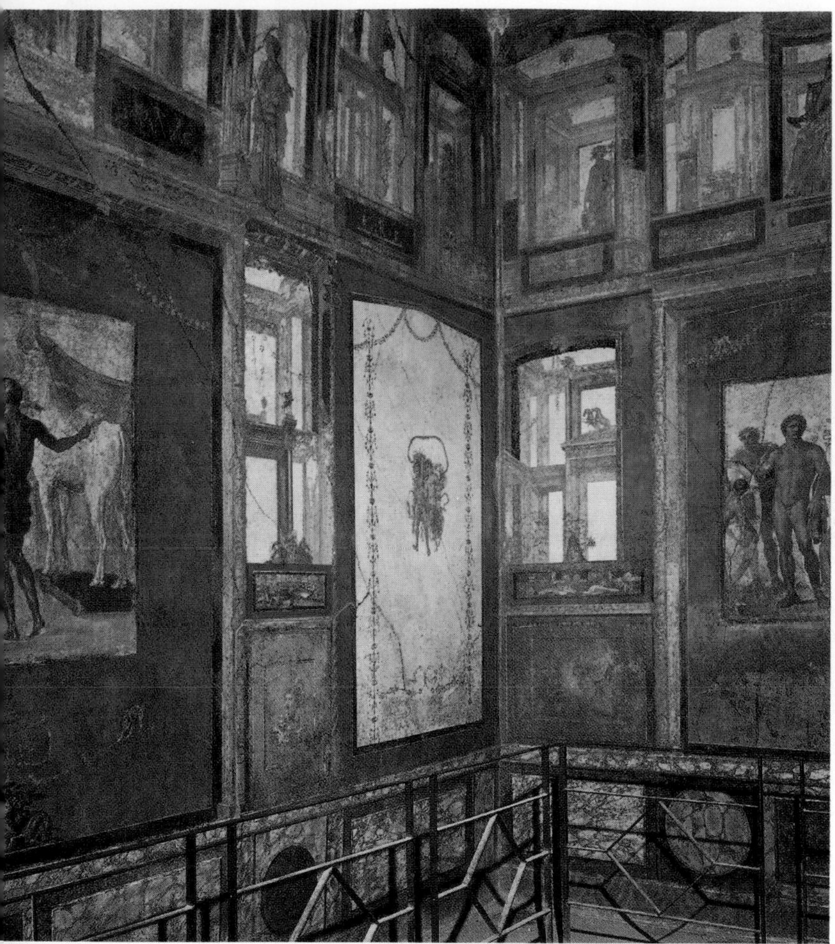

6-32 Fourth-style *(intricate)* wall painting from the Ixion Room, House of the Vetii, Pompeii, first century A.D.

the Vetii (FIG. **6-32**). Here, under the influence of contemporary Roman theatrical design, the painters returned to the use of architectural frames and open vistas. However, an aerial perspective, rather than a linear one, is created by areas of color flooded with light and atmosphere, which unite the wall in a complex way, incorporating all the lessons of previous experiments in optical illusion. In fact, the fourth style is a kind of résumé of its predecessors. The incrustation style appears along the lower walls, and architectural panels are set into the ornate, third-style wall articulation, which is also reflected in the individual picture panels. Although the aerial perspective produces a certain unifying effect, the designs cannot be taken in or related to one another from any single point of view; obviously, the artists intended that we pass the pictures as we do in a gallery, stopping at each one, aware that it need have no relationship in subject or style to its neighbor.

A masterpiece of the fourth style (FIG. **6-33**), from the Domus Aurea of the emperor Nero (A.D. 54–68) in Rome, is an earlier and more austere design preceding the compositional intricacies of the Ixion Room paintings. Here, the paintings exhibit the greatest elegance and delicacy in the placing and rendering of details and in the proportions and spacing of the panels. The artist makes a virtue of vacant space and slender enframements, avoiding all crowding and busyness. The effect is one of precise symmetry, but with subtle variations of balancing. The color scheme is a harmony of white, gold, and accents of

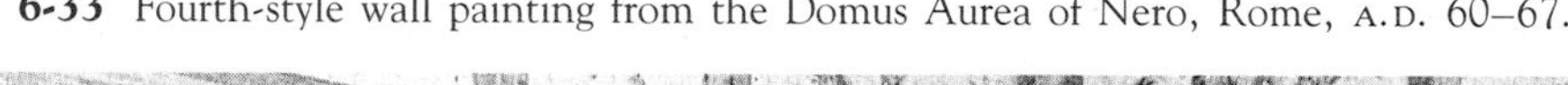

6-33 Fourth-style wall painting from the Domus Aurea of Nero, Rome, A.D. 60–67.

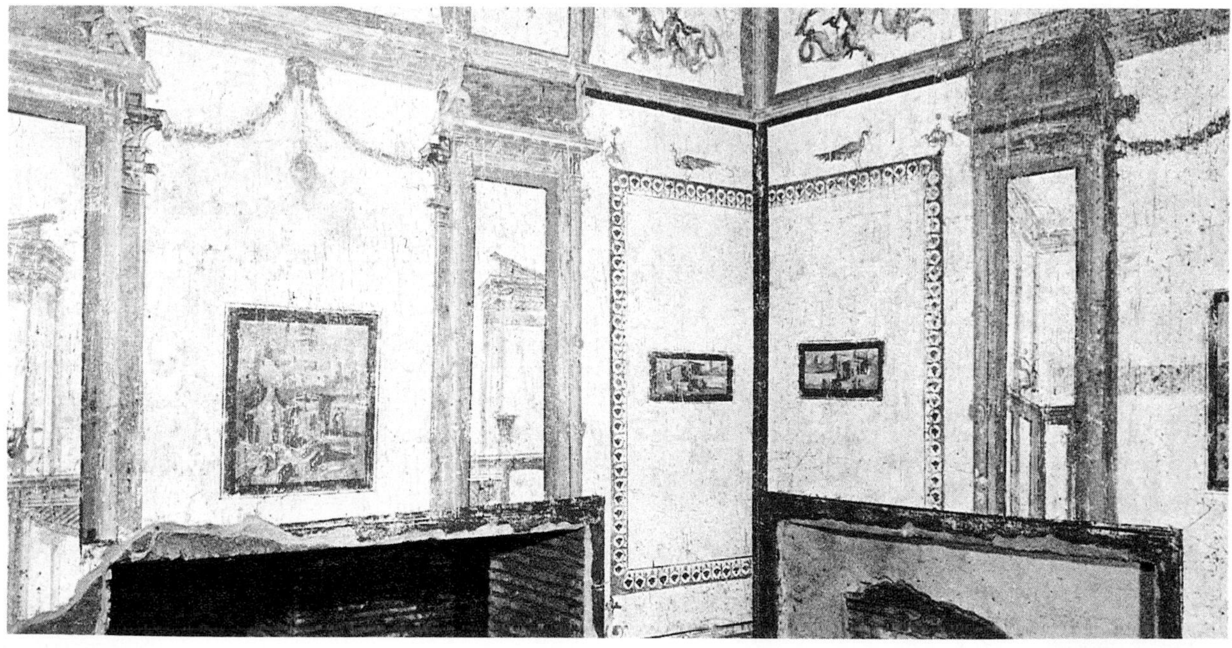

blue, deftly placed. The ornamental vocabulary is limited intentionally to a few motifs: in the transom panels, masks and sea-gods; below, birds, garlands, and architectural vistas. Centered in the main panels are framed landscapes, providing windowlike extensions of the space of the room. In the history of ancient painting and interior decoration, this work has scarcely an equal.

A still life with peaches and a carafe, a detail of a larger mural from Herculaneum (FIG. **6-34**), demonstrates that the Roman painter sought illusionistic effects in depicting small objects as much as in depicting architectural forms and landscape spaces. Here, the method used involves light and shade, with scrupulous attention to contour shadows and to highlights; undoubtedly, the artist worked directly from an arrangement made specifically for this painting. The fruit, the stem and leaves, and the translucent jar were set out on shelves to give the illusion of the casual, almost accidental, relationship of objects in a cupboard. But the picture is exact in neither drawing nor perspective, and the light and shade are approximate. Still, the illusion the painter contrives here marks the point of furthest advancement made by the ancients in the technique of representation. The artist seems to have an inkling that the look of things is a function of light. The goal is to paint light as one would strive to paint the touchable object that reflects and absorbs it. Painters like Paul Cézanne—often called the founder of modern art—in discarding the systematic, organizing devices of perspective and chiaroscuro (light and dark), produced distortions and irregularities in painted objects that resemble those of this ancient still life. It is unlikely, however, that Cézanne was familiar with Roman painting.

6-34 *Still Life with Peaches,* from Herculaneum, c. A.D. 50. Detail of a wall painting transferred to wood, approx. 14″ × 13½″. Museo Nazionale, Naples.

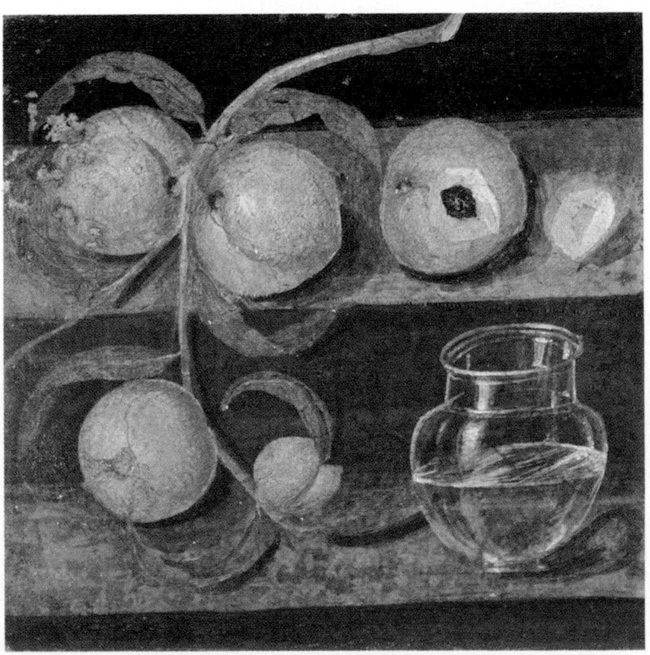

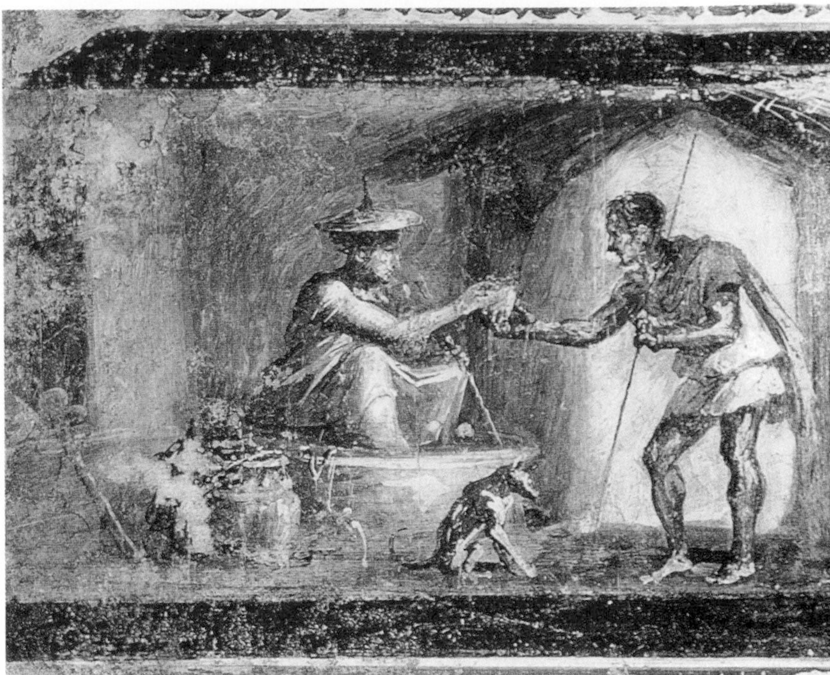

6-35 Genre scene (?) from the House of the Dioscuri, Pompeii, first century A.D. Detail of a wall painting transferred to wood, entire painting approx. 15″ × 17″. Museo Nazionale, Naples.

A painting from the House of the Dioscuri in Pompeii (FIG. **6-35**) offers evidence of the skillful illusionism achieved by the painters of the fourth style. The subject may be a scene from mythology or a genre scene. A woman seated before a stone building and a small hut receives a cup from a bowing man or perhaps extends the cup to him. It is difficult to decide. Whatever the interpretation, the brush technique is a deft impressionism, the strokes firm and practiced. The painter is entirely sure of the poses and the relationship of the figures in space. The problems of figural attitude, anatomy, movement, and proportion, which we have seen confronting the ancient artist for millennia, seem now to have their familiar solutions, so that the artist of this work proceeds easily and confidently, the paintbrush quickly expressing the painter's knowledge.

The style of the Dioscuri painting was contemporaneous with other, quite different styles. Several differences are apparent in a painting from Herculaneum that represents Herakles finding the infant Telephos being nursed by a doe in Arcadia (FIG. **6-36**).

The subject indicates that the picture was copied from one or more Hellenistic originals. One likely source of inspiration is the great Altar of Zeus and Athena at Pergamon (FIG. 5-77), where the inner frieze is devoted to the legend of Telephos and includes this theme. In the Herculaneum painting, the artist proceeds as if lifting figures from different sources and arranging them with little relationship to one another. Thus, the personification of Arcadia, the large seated figure, is not in proportion to Herakles, nor is their treatment the same. The statuesque Arcadia exhibits the pale, hard modeling we associate with sculpture, while the play of light and highlight on the supple surfaces of the Herakles figure is related to the effects we expect in pictorial illusionism, though the technique is by no means the free, "painterly" one we see in the Dioscuri work. All the figures are precisely modeled, with firm outlines. The artist is concerned chiefly with the solid volumes of the bodies, not with light or with the space the whole group occupies; each figure is contained, as it were, by its own particular space, the space it "fits." The depiction of space as an enveloping and unifying factor in

6-36 *Herakles and Telephos,* from Herculaneum, c. A.D. 70, after an original from the second century B.C. Wall painting, approx. 7′ 2″ × 6′ 2″. Museo Archeological Nazionale, Naples.

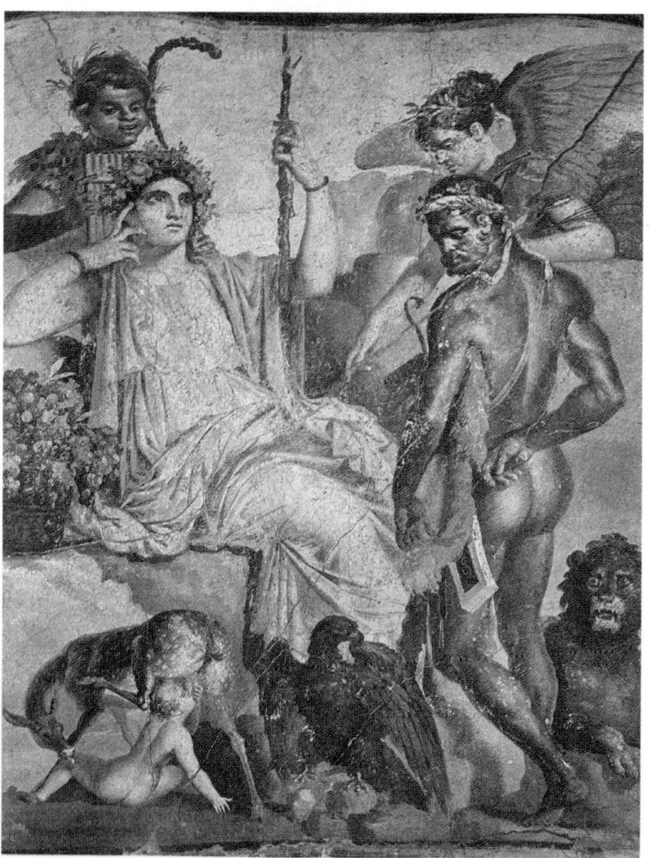

pictorial design may not be characteristic in Greek art, and this picture, as we have said, copies a Greek model. On the other hand, the special Roman contribution to painting may be precisely the representation of space as surrounding the whole group of objects and figures in any given composition, rather than merely coming between them.

It still seems to be a general tendency to deny any originality in Roman paintings and to insist that they are direct copies of, or closely inspired by, Hellenistic originals. Many Roman paintings do appear to be direct copies, among them the *Herakles and Telephos* just discussed and *The Battle of Issus* mosaic shown in FIG. 6-37. In fact, many paintings were probably done by transplanted Greek artists, and we might even grant that the Greek-derived style was the dominant one. But the Roman *landscape* seems to represent a radically different approach, particularly in its expression of a concept of space that simply is not evident in Greek art, and all attempts to derive Roman landscape painting from Hellenistic Greece lead us into extremely tenuous speculation based on unknown (or nonexistent) Greek prototypes. All extant Greek works show the Greek artist thinking in terms of solid volumes, like those of human figures (as in the *Herakles and Telephos* painting), and confining the role of space to a mere separating function, rather than an all-containing one. Thus, it might be much simpler to credit the Romans with the development of a new concept in painting: the projection of an enveloping, unifying volume of space on a flat surface. This refinement of abstraction, in which space, filled with air and light, is actually represented as being just as real as the objects it surrounds and contains, would complete the long development of representation that began with the silhouettes of early Egypt and Mesopotamia, or even earlier. At any rate, many now accept the view that the architectural illusionism of the second style was a Roman development and that this illusionism was a step in the transition to the spaces depicted in the smaller landscape panels (FIG. 6-31). For an artist thinking of the wall surface as a kind of extension of the space of the room (as in architectural illusionism), the next step would be to take a segment of the wall and convert it, windowlike, into a small block of framed space that extends "through" the wall and contains its own little universe of depicted objects.

In any case, the artist of the fourth style, chiefly interested in representing space, made the objects as small as possible and unified the whole composition, as we have seen, with light and atmosphere. Of course, recession in depth is suggested, not accurately projected. The Romans had no system of mathematical perspective. Instead, they employed (effectively, if unsystematically) the diminution of figures and objects and, particularly, atmospheric perspective, with its hazed and sketchy outlines, the shift from local color toward blue, and the blurring of distant contours (compare FIG. 6-29).

The love of country life and the idealizing of nature—what we may call the Arcadian spirit—prevails in these landscapes. Characteristically, they contain shepherds, goats, fauns, little temples, garlanded columns, copses of trees, and other accessories, which from their part religious, part idyllic mood have been called *sacral-idyllic* scenes (FIG. 6-31). The Arcadian spirit of the time speaks in the formal, pastoral poetry of Vergil, and in one of his odes, Horace, proclaiming the satisfactions afforded the city man by his villa in the countryside, where life is beautiful, simple, and natural in contrast with the urban greed for gold and power, asks, "Why should I change my Sabine dale for splendor full of trouble?"

The attitude that celebrates the virtues of rustic life must be associated very closely with an original Roman development in architecture. Many Arcadian landscapes have been found in *villas*—country residences developed by the Romans when congestion in the cities became severe, as it did in Pompeii during the first century B.C. The villas were located close to town (one might call them "suburban"), so that their wealthy owners could enjoy the advantages of city life and the quiet of the countryside. The very spaciousness of the landscape around the villa came to be the subject matter of the wall paintings we have been examining. The modern desire to escape the tensions of the city and to return to nature is ancient in its architectural and pictorial expression, not to mention its appearance in literature. We will encounter this Arcadianism again and again in the history of the West, in the Renaissance and in the nineteenth and twentieth centuries, as urban pressures begin to strain human nerves.

The floors as well as the walls of Roman buildings were ornamented, usually in mosaics. *Mosaic* had its beginnings in the ancient Near East (see pages 184–85). It was used by the Greeks, often in geometric patterns, in place of carpets. The Romans continued the practice and, from the first century A.D. on, even applied mosaic to walls.* A striking aspect of Roman mosaics is the frequent attempt to copy not only the subject matter of painting but also the painter's technique in modeling, shading, and the like. Use of this technique was possible only if extremely small *tesserae* (the bits of glass or stone composing the mosaic) were used, as, for example, in the famous mosaic from the House of the Faun in Pompeii (FIG. **6-37**), which, according to a widely accepted theory, is a copy of a

*The Romans used the words *tesselatum* (hence, *tesserae*) for floor mosaics and *musivum* (source of *mosaic*) for wall mosaics.

6-37 *The Battle of Issus,* from the House of the Faun, Pompeii, c. 80 B.C. Mosaic, approx. 8′ 10″ × 16′ 9″. Museo Nazionale, Naples.

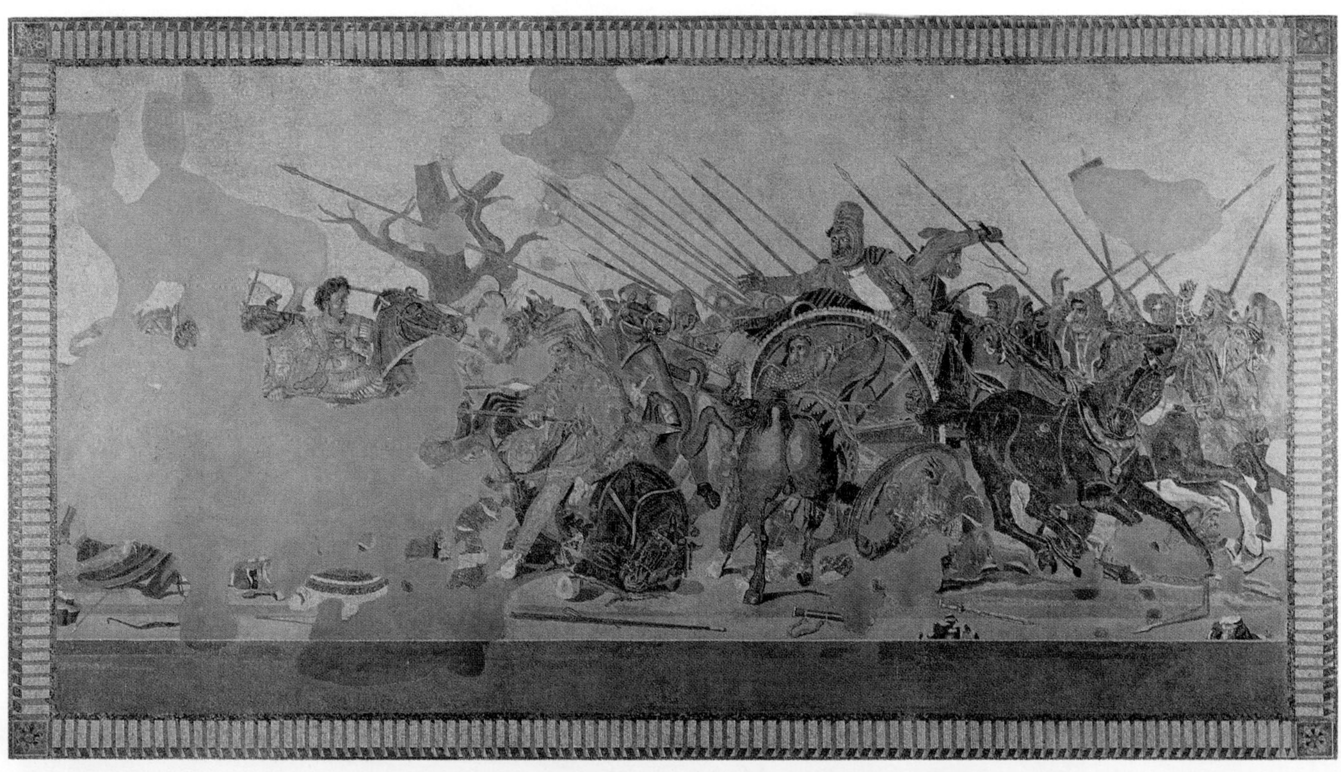

painting by the Hellenistic painter Philoxenos of Eretria. The mosaic, which represents the rout of Darius and his army by Alexander the Great at the battle of Issus, has those qualities of Greek style we have noted: the essentially sculpturesque emphasis on the solid forms, space defined by the forms themselves, and no attempt to show an enveloping space. Nevertheless, a remarkable taste for fidelity to appearance is shown in the details of action. The horses plunge into and out of the picture at the most daring angles, and the human figures are posed in such a variety of descriptive attitudes as to convince us that the artist was pursuing an ultimate realism. In keeping with this pursuit is the high degree of tonal smoothness achieved by the setting-in of tesserae so small that some fifty separate bits were used to model a single eye perhaps 1½ inches wide. The Romans appear to have developed a taste for this kind of minute workmanship, and the technical quality of mosaics must have been judged by the size of the tesserae used—the smaller, the better. Since, after all, the mosaics were seen at a distance of only five or six feet (one walked on them), such a criterion seems natural enough. The standard changed during the Early Christian period, when mosaics were placed high on church walls and apse vaults, making such minute differences scarcely noticeable and such painstaking technique meaningless.

The vast range of subjects represented in mosaics is comparable to that found in Roman painting. Themes from classical mythology vied in popularity with historical subjects or with topical ones, such as genre aspects of rural existence and scenes from the popular theater, gladiatorial battles, chariot races, and hunting.

Stylistically, the development was toward simplification of the extremely complex and detailed work exemplified in *The Battle of Issus* mosaic (FIG. 6-37). Tesserae tended to become larger, the designs, flatter and less illusionistic. From the middle of the first century A.D. on, human figures and animal forms appeared in black silhouette on white ground, prefacing the black and white mosaics that were to become the favorite floor decorations in Italy during the second and third centuries A.D. These floor mosaics were especially popular in bathing establishments, and a masterpiece of this type was found in the Baths of Neptune at Ostia (FIG. **6-38**). Here, appropriately enough, marine divinities, accompanied by Nereids and Tritons, are carried across the waters by dolphins

6-38 Floor mosaic from the Baths of Neptune, Ostia, second century A.D.

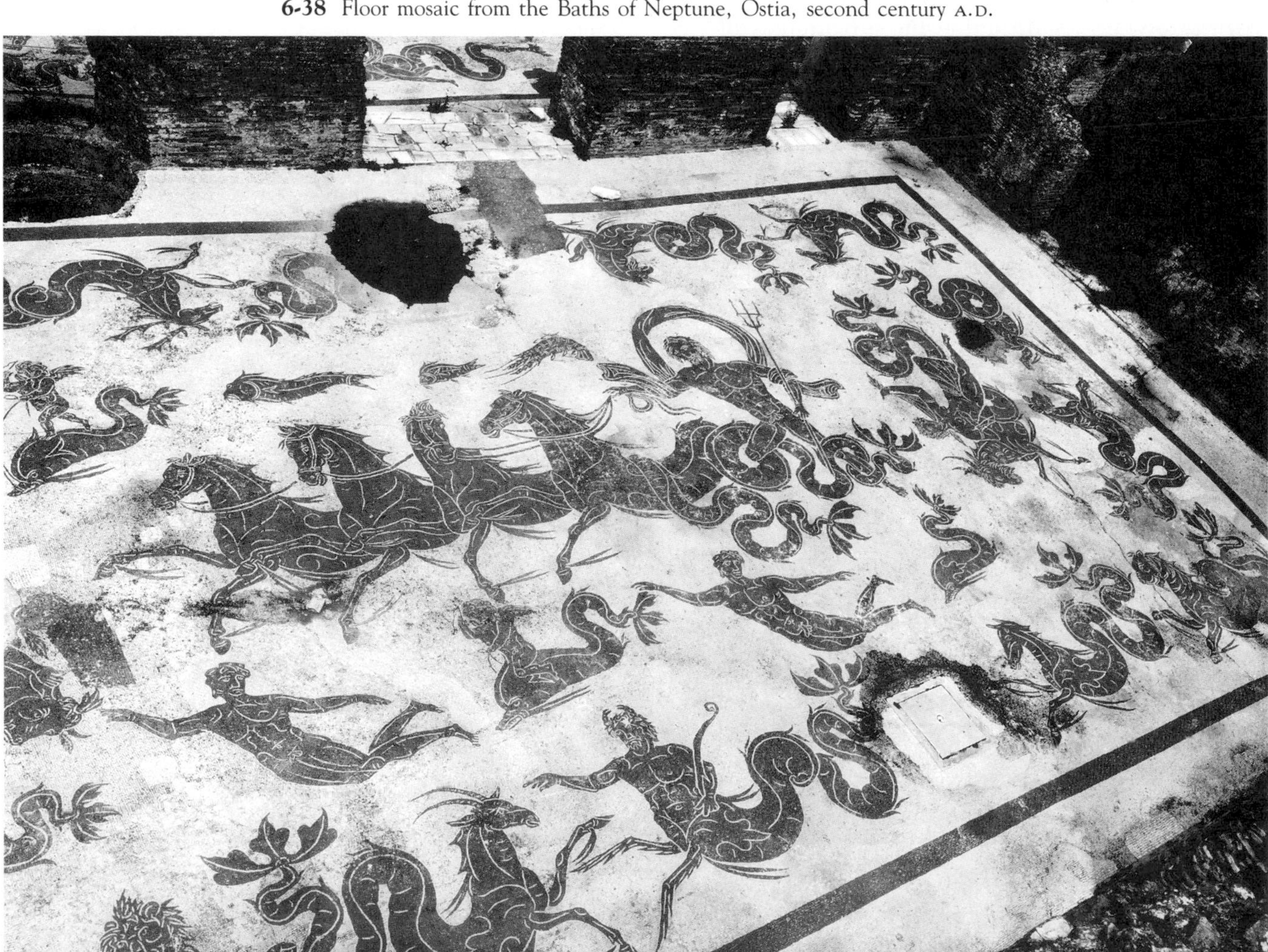

and horses with fish-tail bodies. The fluid, dynamic design is based on a repetition of curvilinear forms that evokes the movement of the sea.

During the second and third centuries A.D., polychrome mosaics also moved up from the floors—at first, to decorate grottoes and fountains, but eventually to cover walls. Less exposed to wear from sandaled feet, wall mosaics permitted the use of relatively fragile materials, such as glass paste *(smalto)* and enamel, and the achievement of stronger coloristic effects than were possible with colored stone or marble tesserae. The brilliant blue of the wall mosaic in the House of Neptune and Amphitrite in Herculaneum (FIG. **6-39**), achieved largely through the liberal use of smalto, also contributes to the rich tonality in the modeling of the figures, recalling the glassy surfaces in the Herakles figure from *Herakles and Telephos* (FIG. 6-36).

Painting, with all its advanced illusionistic devices, remains the standard for mosaic representation. What was achieved by way of subtle, pictorial effect can be seen equally in mural painting and, on a smaller scale, in the painted panel. We may judge the quality of panel painting by a portrait from Faiyum in Egypt, some sixty miles south of modern Cairo (FIG. **6-40**). In Greek and Roman times, Faiyum was a busy, populous province, and its cemeteries have yielded some six hundred portraits painted on wood panels attached to the mummy cases of the deceased. The making of such portraits must have been a regional custom, as very few have been found elsewhere; they provide for us our largest gallery of ordinary people from the vast Roman imperial world when it was at the height of its power. Some Pompeian wall frescoes hint at what Greek murals may have looked like, but the Faiyum portraits give us the best idea we have of Hellenistic Greek painting techniques. Most of the portraits were done using the *encaustic* technique (pigments in hot wax; see pages 137–38), but *tempera* (pigments in egg yolk) also was used occasionally. Easel painting, on small, portable panels, had been highly esteemed in Greece, where the encaustic technique had a long tradition. Polygnotos had worked in encaustic in Classical times, and, as mentioned earlier, it had been used for the architectural decoration of buildings like the Parthenon. The example here (FIG. **6-40**) shows the very highest level of craftsmanship: refined brushwork, soft and delicate modeling, and the subtlest possible reading of a sensitive subject. The Faiyum portraits

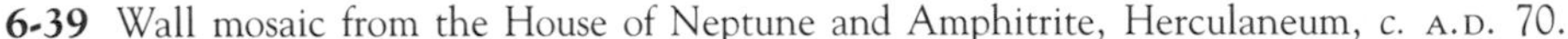

6-39 Wall mosaic from the House of Neptune and Amphitrite, Herculaneum, c. A.D. 70.

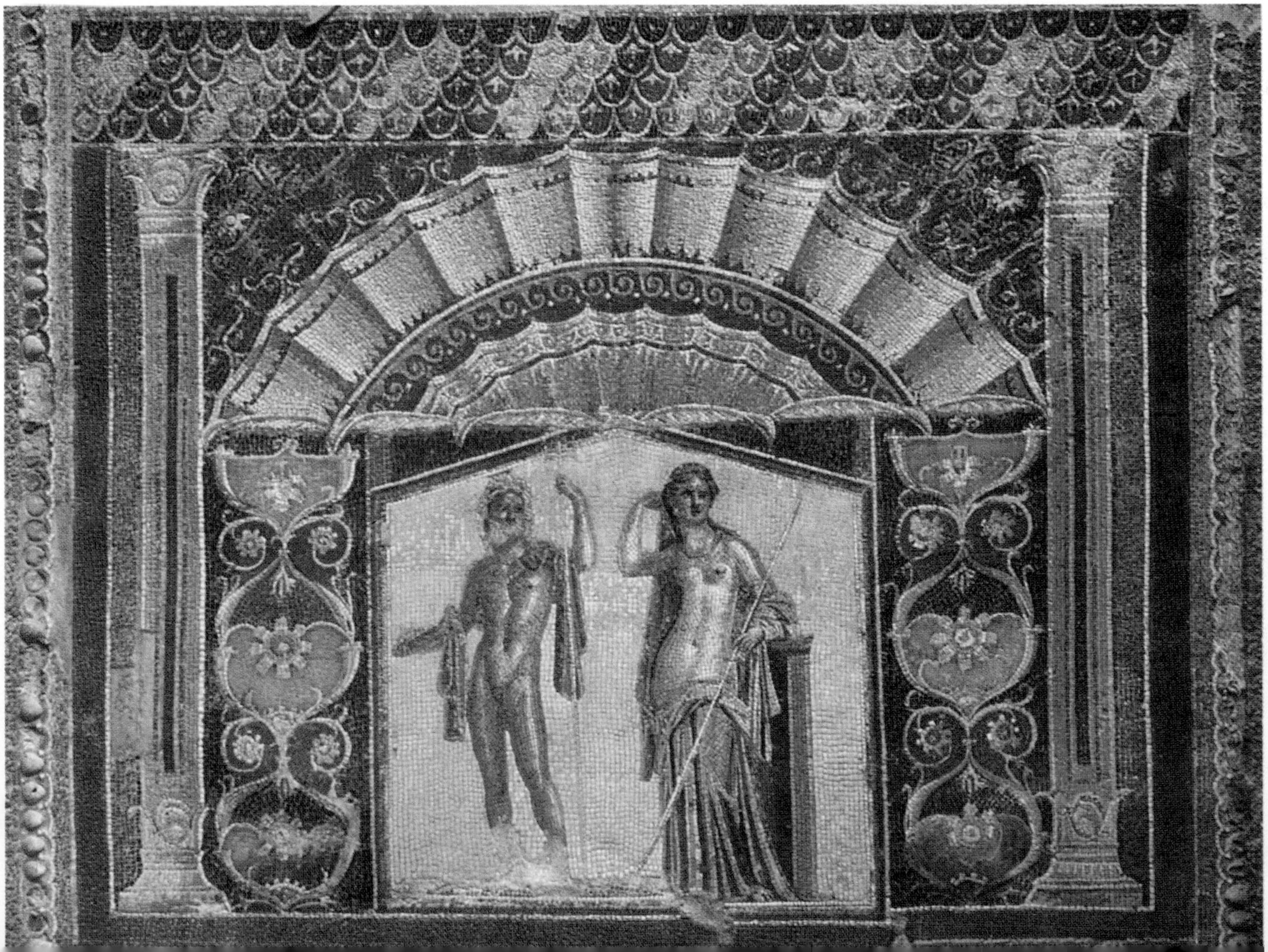

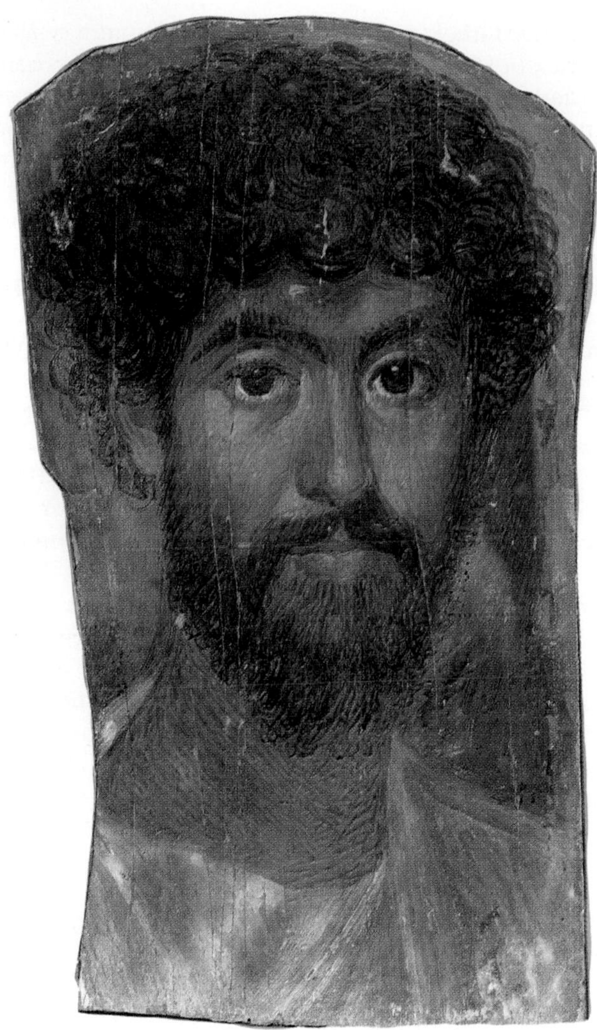

6-40 *Mummy Portrait of a Man,* from Faiyum, Egypt, c. A.D. 160–170. Encaustic painting on wooden mummy case, approx. 13¾" × 8". Albright-Knox Art Gallery, Buffalo (Charles Clifton Fund, 1938).

probably were painted from living persons, and, in this instance, we have the meeting of an unusually perceptive artist with a subject whose personality would require all of the artist's skill to render. The composure, the emphasized, thoughtful eyes, and the Hellenizing hairstyle are familiar in portraits made during the time of the Stoic emperor Marcus Aurelius (*c.* A.D. 160) and in the portraits of the emperor himself. The calm demeanor of the subject, the gaze that "sees the world steadily and sees it whole," evokes the philosophy of the emperor as set forth in his *Meditations.* As earlier we confronted the head of Pompey, familiar with his history, so may it aid us in meeting this image from the age of the Antonines to read the philosophic emperor as we read the painted features of our subject:

> Every moment think steadily as a Roman and a man to do what you have in hand with perfect and simple dignity. . . . do every act of your life as if it were the last, laying aside all carelessness and passionate aversion from the commands of reason, and all hypocrisy, and self-love, and discontent with the destiny which has been given to you.

Our history has taken us beyond the period of the republic into that of the empire to show how Rome carried the ancient world's representation of landscape and of human individuality, which started in Mesopotamia and Egypt, to its fullest expression.

THE EARLY EMPIRE

When Octavian Caesar, the grand-nephew and heir of Julius Caesar, routed the forces of Antony and Cleopatra at Actium in 31 B.C., he brought to an end some ninety long years of destructive civil war that had shattered the Roman republic. Although Octavian proclaimed himself to be the restorer of the republic and the protector of its constitution and traditions, he became, in fact, the first emperor of Rome and, to all intents and purposes, ruled as emperor, taking the venerable name "Augustus," which was bestowed on him by a grateful Senate. The peace that began with Augustus has been called the "Pax Romana"; under the auspices of a long line of emperors, peace prevailed within the Roman world for 150 years, a record in world history.

Augustus (27 B.C.–A.D. 14), determined to establish his authority unshakably, kept command of the military and financial resources of the empire in his own hands and deliberately set out to build a new and magnificent Rome in order to give a splendid image to the imperial reality. As they carried the boundaries of the empire further in all directions, the Julio-Claudian emperors, Augustus's successors in the first century A.D., continued his policy of glorifying the visible aspect of empire (sometimes to an extravagant degree) in architecture, art, and a vast variety of public works. In the second century, under Trajan, Hadrian, and the Antonines, the empire reached its greatest geographical extent and the summit of its power (see map, page 197). Rome's might and influence were unchallenged in the Western world, although pressure was constantly being applied by the Germanic peoples in the north, the Berbers in the south, and the Parthians and resurgent Persians in the east. These pressures increased in the third century and, in combination with the decline of imperial authority within the empire, disintegration of the economic and administrative structure, and military anarchy, almost brought the empire to collapse. In A.D. 285, imperial authority was restored by one of the last pagan emperors, the capable Diocletian, who became the overseer of the savage persecution of a sect called the Christians. Within a generation, the triumph of this sect would mark a major turning point in the history of the world.

Architecture and Public Works

The grandiose imperial designs of the early Roman Empire are reflected, perhaps most conspicuously, in its architecture. The relatively stable conditions produced by the Pax Romana facilitated the Romanization of the provinces, and *urbanism*—the planning and building of cities—played a principal role in this process. The rapid growth of population, especially city population, already has been cited as a reason for the escape to the suburban villa. The pressure of population in the city itself made the sprawling atrium house, which was wasteful of space, obsolete.

In Rome, a population of close to one million had to be housed in multistory apartment blocks *(insulae)*, built primarily of brick-faced concrete. Some forty-five thousand of these, constructed to the maximum legal height of five stories (60–70 feet), accommodated nearly 90 percent of Rome's population. Most of the almost fifty thousand inhabitants of Ostia, Rome's port city, also were housed in such apartments, some of which have been preserved to the level of the third story. The ground floors were occupied by shops; above were the apartments, which were accessible by individual staircases. Many of the apartments were substantially more spacious than are most of ours today, the suites sometimes containing as many as twelve rooms arranged on two levels. A reconstruction of an Ostian insula (FIG. **6-41**) shows the apartment blocks built around a central court; some of the larger courts may have been landscaped to contain a small shrine. Apparently, many apartments had balconies, still a standard feature of modern Italian apartment houses. Only deluxe apartments had private toilets; others were served by community latrines, usually on the ground floor. The insulae had no private baths, but public baths were located conveniently throughout various quarters of the city and were equipped with highly developed heating systems, which private houses and apartments lacked. The crowded conditions encouraged rent gouging and jerry-building. Deficiency in materials was often compounded by bad design, such as a foundation area too small in relationship to the height of a building—a means of maximal exploitation of the limited space available. The poet Juvenal wryly complained about the poorly constructed city buildings:

> We inhabit a city propped up for the most part by slats: for that is how the landlord patches up the crack in the old wall, bidding the inmates sleep at ease under the ruin that hangs above their heads.

The convenience of the ancient Roman of ordinary and less-than-ordinary means depended to a great

6-41 Reconstruction of an insula, Ostia, Italy.

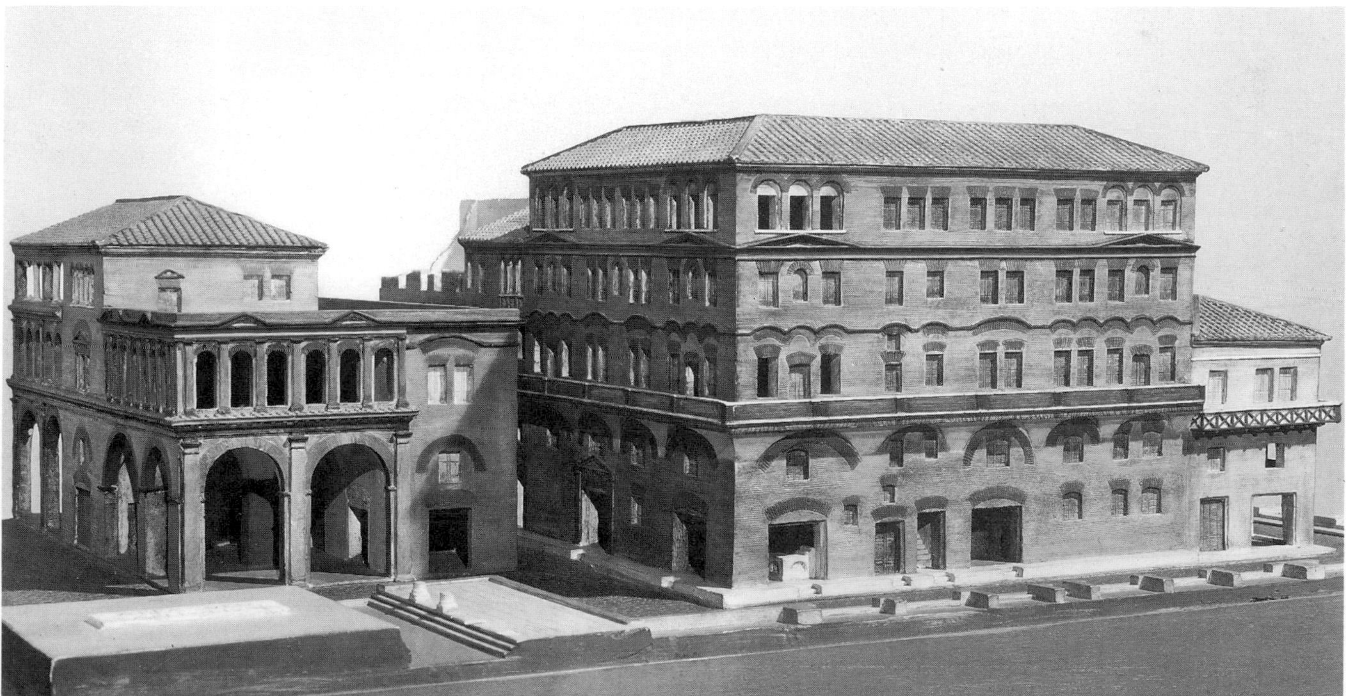

extent on facilities provided by imperial, provincial, or municipal authority. Millions of individuals depended on the government for food distribution, water supply and sanitation, recreation and entertainment, and roads and bridges, not to mention the protection afforded by police and firefighters. The administration of these services in the days of the empire was efficient even by our standards, given, of course, the limitations we would expect from a less highly developed technology and communications system. Second only to food distribution, an adequate water supply for the population of the overcrowded cities was the most imperative need. The Romans methodically developed water-supply systems as part of urban planning. The city of Rome began to build *aqueducts* for itself as early as the fourth century B.C., and Roman aqueducts or their ruins still stand in many former Roman cities, both in Italy and in the provinces. Water was carried from the source to the city by gravity flow, which required the building of channels with a continuous gradual decline over distances often exceeding fifty miles; we can appreciate, even in modern terms, what an important achievement of engineering this represents. The Pont du Gard (FIG. **6-42**) near Nîmes (ancient Nemausus) in France is one of the most impressive specimens of Roman engineering skill. It carried the water channel across the valley of the river Gard. Each large arch spans some 82 feet and is constructed of uncemented blocks weighing up to two tons each. The quickening rhythm of the small top arches (which carry the channel), placed in groups of threes over the larger arches, manifests the Roman engineer's sense for the esthetic as well as the practical. The finished aqueduct carried water to Nîmes over a distance of some thirty miles and provided each inhabitant with about one hundred gallons of water a day. Services like this, and the awesome structures that provided them, could not help but impress on the diverse peoples who had come under the rule of Rome the advantages to be gained by complying with such practical power and the benefits that could accrue to them as the result of Romanization.

If the construction of aqueducts showed the value of homage to Rome, imagine how much more impressive the erection of a whole city would be. At Timgad (ancient Thamugadis) in North Africa (FIGS. **6-43** and **6-44**), the Romans built a city, around A.D. 100, that lasted until the sixth century A.D. Built along a major military road one hundred miles from the sea, Timgad was probably planned to house a military garrison charged with keeping order locally. But this primary function was soon expanded, and no costs were spared in making this little provincial town into an attractive focal point for the local inhabitants. Here, the empire was a physical presence to the Africans; the city represented the authority of the emperor and the civilization of Rome. Like many other colonial settlements, Timgad served as a key to the process of Romanization. The town was planned with great precision, its design probably based on the layout of the Roman military encampment, the

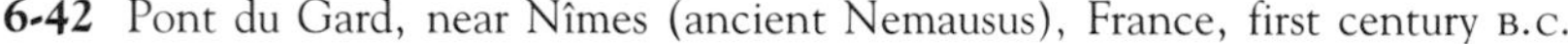

6-42 Pont du Gard, near Nîmes (ancient Nemausus), France, first century B.C.

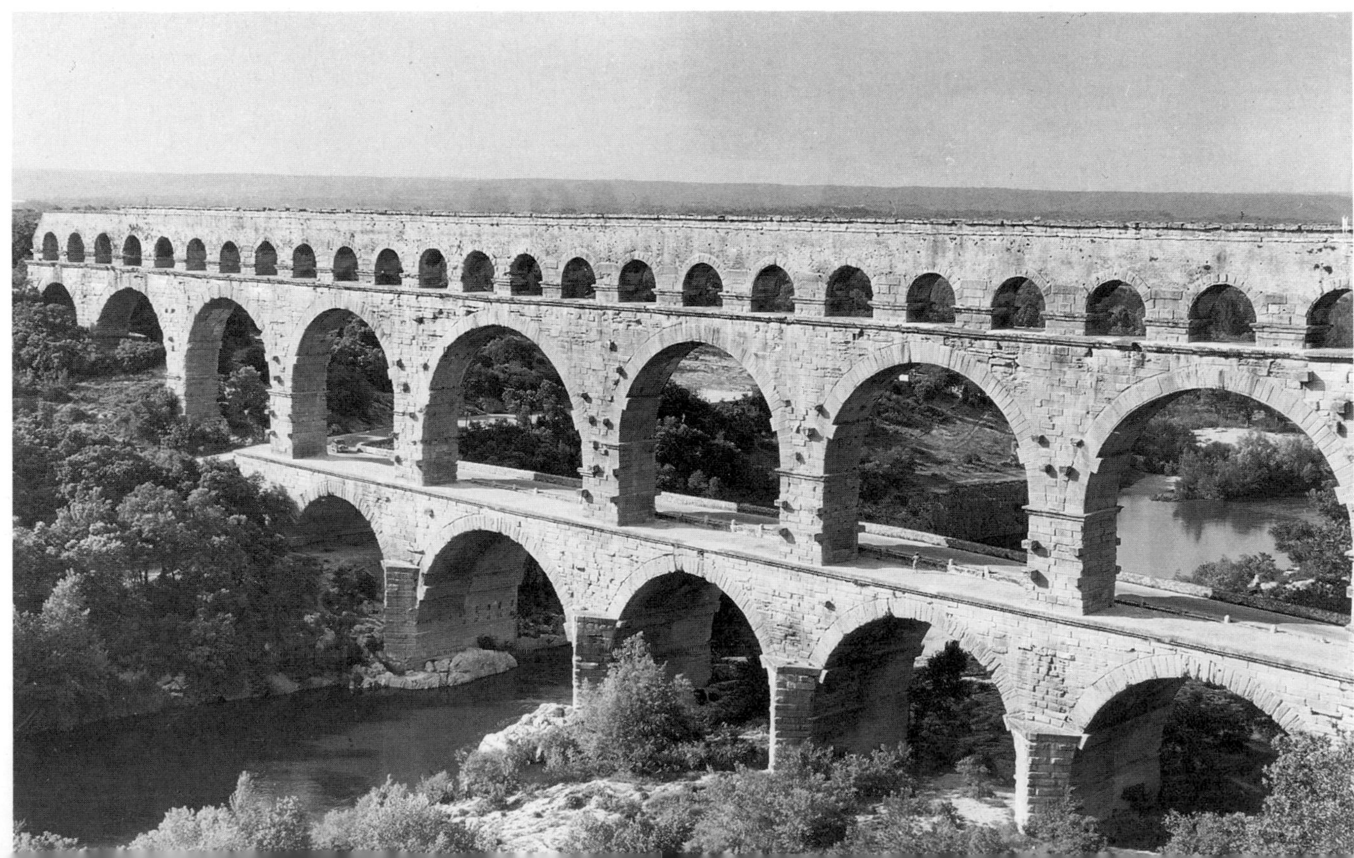

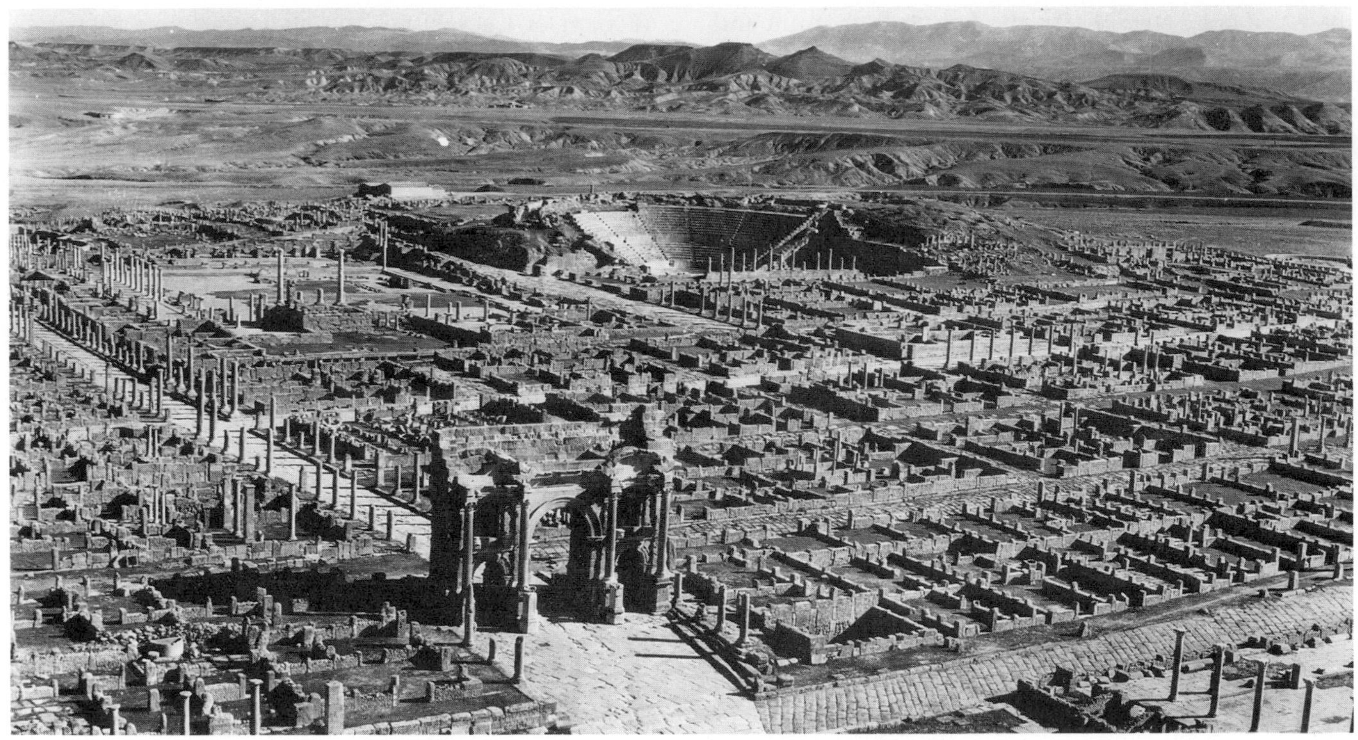

6-43 View of the ruins, Timgad (ancient Thamugadis), Algeria, founded c. A.D. 100.

6-44 Plan of Timgad, Algeria.

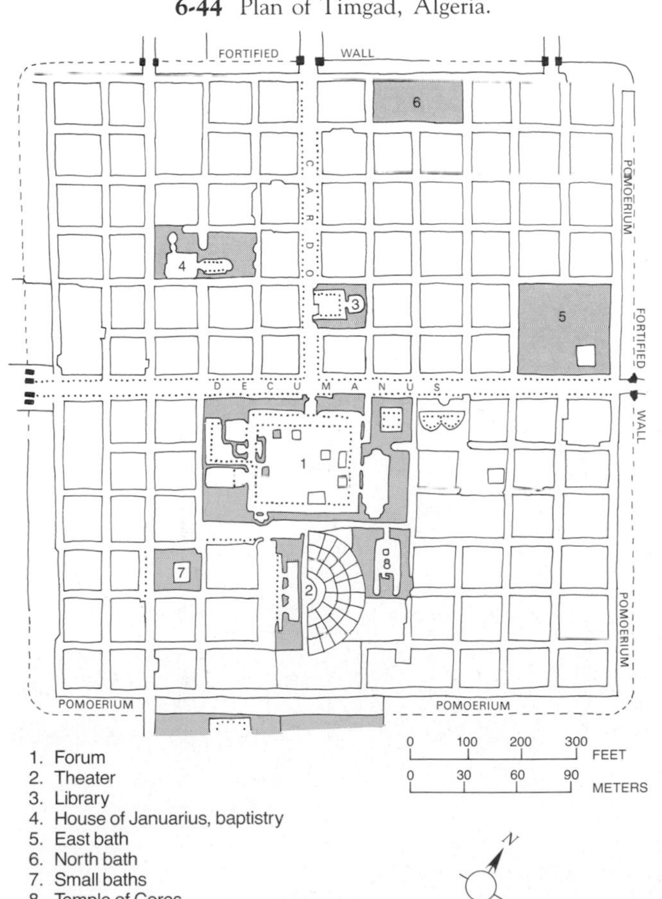

castrum. (The question of precedence remains unresolved: the castrum may have been based on the layout of the Roman colonial city.) The typical provincial Roman city takes the form of a square that is divided into equal quarters by two main arteries—the *cardo* (the north–south axis) and the *decumanus* (the east–west axis)—that cross at right angles. The *forum* is located near this crossing. The quarters are subdivided into square blocks, and the forum and public buildings, like the theater, baths, and library, occupy areas that are multiples of these blocks. At Timgad, monumental gates led into the colonnaded streets of the city. The city itself covered some thirty acres, and its original population of two thousand soon grew to fifteen thousand. The whole plan was essentially a modification of the Hippodamian plan (see FIG. 5-88), but more rigidly ordered and systematized, with the forum set off from the main traffic pattern. The fact that most of these colonial settlements were laid out in the same manner, regardless of whether they were located in North Africa, the Near East, or England, expresses more concretely than any building type or other construction project the unity and centralized power characteristic of the Roman Empire at its height (see also photo on page 22).

The architectural images of Rome set up in the outlying reaches of the empire had their even more monumental equivalents in the capital city itself. When all roads did indeed lead to Rome, they found their symbolic terminus in the Forum Romanum and its imperial extensions. Even before the end of the Republican period, Rome's population had outgrown the old forum, and several new forums, beginning with that of Julius Caesar, were added to the original to provide space for larger crowds and for the growing ceremonial pomp of state functions. Beyond their practical purposes, these new imperial forums (FIG. **6-45**) created a monumental architectural setting for the exaltation of their sponsors' achievements and the glorification of Roman imperial power. They stood witness to the "piety, might, good fortune, magnanimity, and happiness"—as their triumphal inscriptions proclaimed—of the successive emperors who built them. These new forums were not planned as a unit but were added one to another and their unity achieved by strict, axial alignment. They generally consisted of a large colonnaded court, designed to set off a temple dedicated to the god who was the special protector of the emperor under whose aegis the forum was constructed. The Forum Julium (Forum of Caesar) set the style that was repeated, with modifications and on a larger scale, by the Forum Augustum. Both were dwarfed by the Forum of Trajan a century later.

6-45 Plan of the imperial forums in Rome, c. 46 B.C.–A.D. 117.

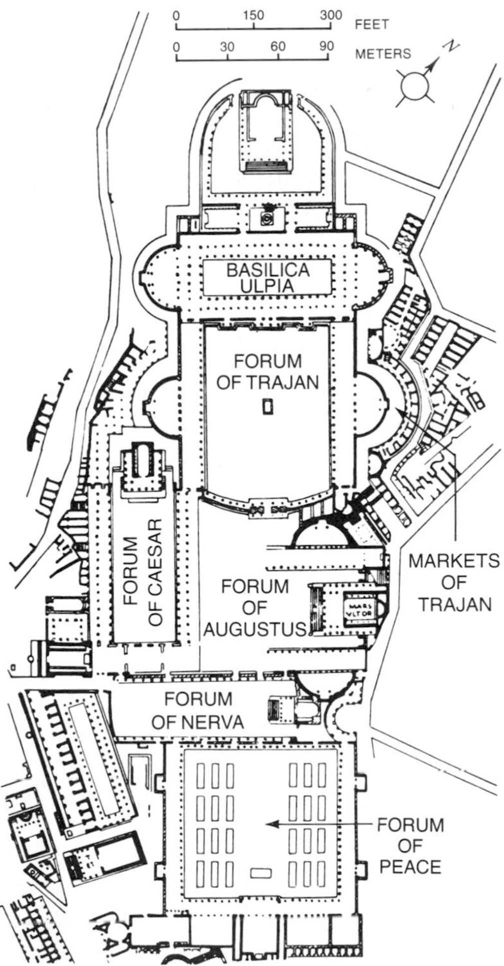

OFFICIAL CONSERVATISM

The artistic taste of Augustus tended to be conservative (see Sculpture also). In architecture, he favored the trabeated style and a sumptuous display of the Greek orders, an attitude that seems to be reflected by VITRUVIUS, whose treatise, *The Ten Books of Architecture,* became the oracle of Renaissance architects. Vitruvius (c. 90–20 B.C.) was one of Caesar's military engineers during the latter's campaigns in Gaul and North Africa. After Caesar's death, Vitruvius entered the service of Octavian (Augustus), to whom the treatise is dedicated. Unquestionably, Vitruvius was a competent architect-engineer, and the description of the technology of his day shows him to be fully aware of all contemporary developments. On the other hand, his writings also reveal that he was conservative by nature; while he described brick and concrete construction, he emphasized more traditional approaches and quite obviously preferred trabeated Hellenistic buildings to the vaulted ones of Sulla's period. His admiration for Greek architecture paralleled Augustus's taste and must have made him a most compatible servant.

The Augustan style, however, was far from uniform. Classicizing tendencies occurred side by side with native Italic trends, and pseudoperipteral temples, like the Maison Carrée in Nîmes (FIG. **6-46**) perpetuated a type that originated in the Republican period. Larger than the Temple of "Fortuna Virilis" in Rome (FIG. 6-16) and better preserved, the Maison

6-46 Maison Carrée, Nîmes, France, c. 20 B.C.

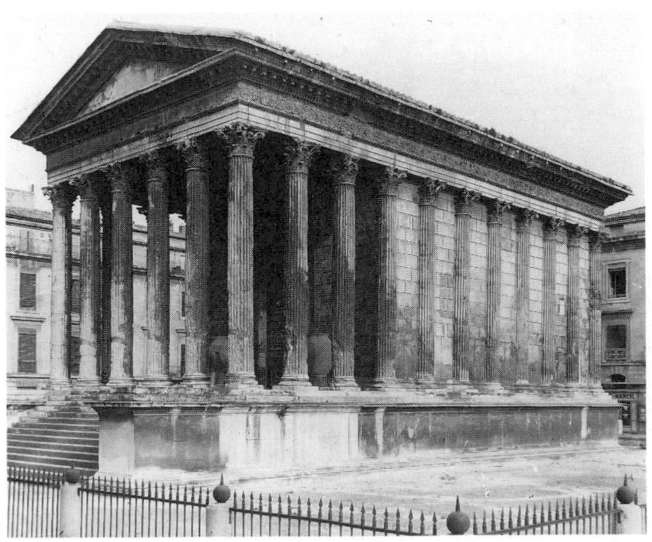

Carrée employs a Corinthian order that emphasizes height; its podium is higher and its monolithic columns are proportioned to look taller and more slender than those of its Classical Greek predecessors. Today, the structure serves as a museum.

A high podium and tall Corinthian columns also characterize the Temple of Mars Ultor (Mars the Avenger), the focal point of the Forum Augustum in Rome. Backed up against a high retaining wall, the temple faced forward into a large, colonnaded court and was the finial of a strictly symmetrical, axial composition. A significant innovation of the Forum Augustum was the widespread use of marble. By about the middle of the first century B.C., the newly opened quarries at Carrara began to produce marble, and this stone, formerly an exotic luxury imported from Greece and the Aegean, soon became commonplace. By the end of the century, marble had become the favored material for official buildings, and the claim of Augustus that he had converted Rome from a city of brick into one of marble became more than an idle boast.

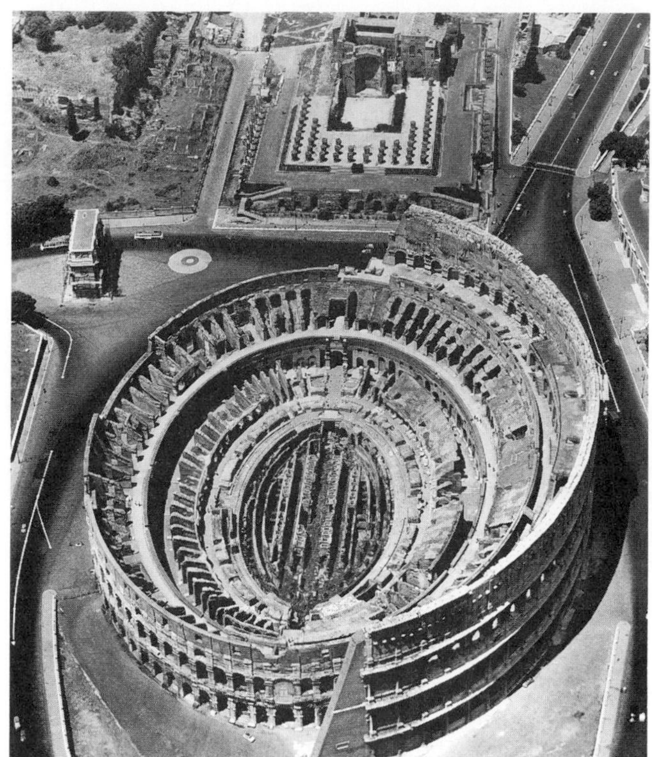

6-47 Aerial view of the Colosseum, Rome, A.D. 70–82.

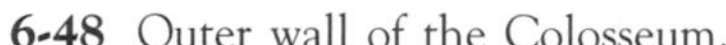

6-48 Outer wall of the Colosseum.

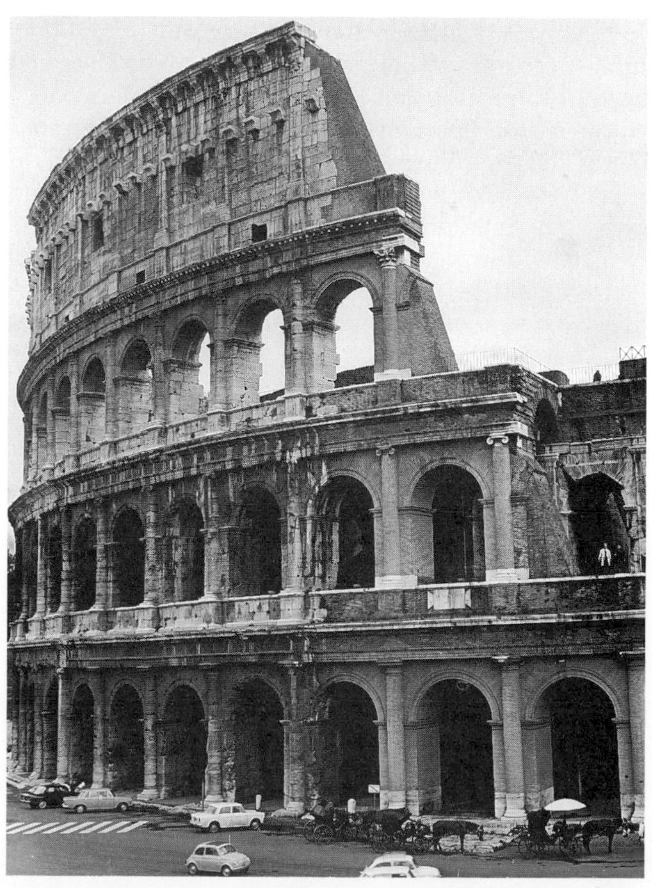

THE COLOSSEUM

At the same time, of course, builders continued to use concrete, especially for utilitarian structures and in places where vaulting seemed to call for it. For instance, the Romans built theaters on level ground, unlike the Greeks, who backed them up against hillsides. The ascending seat rows of the auditorium demanded a massive substructure composed of a complex, multileveled system of vaults that could be constructed best in concrete. Concrete vaulting was used on a huge scale in the Colosseum (FIGS. **6-47** and **6-48**), which, for most people, still represents Rome as does no other building. So closely was it identified in the past with the city and the empire that an aphorism out of the early Middle Ages stated: "While the Colosseum stands, Rome stands; when the Colosseum falls, Rome falls; and when Rome, the world!"

The Flavian Amphitheater (popularly renamed the Colosseum after a now-lost colossal statue of Nero that stood nearby) was begun by Vespasian (A.D. 69–79), first in the Flavian line of emperors. The structure was dedicated in A.D. 80 by Vespasian's successor, Titus (A.D. 79–81), who employed prisoners from the Jewish Wars as builders. The building type is a Roman invention, designed by architects who expanded the *theater* into an *amphitheater*, which is essentially two facing theaters enclosing an oval space (the *arena*). The Roman Colosseum is the largest of its type, but most major cities in the empire had an amphitheater. Some, like the one at Verona, are still being used today for games or theatrical performances. The Colosseum was originally designed for the staging of lavish spectacles—battles between animals and gladiators in various combinations. The mythical beast-men struggles represented in Mesopotamian art here came to bloody reality. The extravagantly inhuman shows cost thousands of lives, among them those of many Christians, and the Colosseum never quite has outlived its infamy. The emperors competed with each other to see who could produce the most elaborate spectacles. For the opening performance in A.D. 80, the arena was flooded and a complete naval battle, with over three thousand participants, was duplicated.

The oval arena of the Colosseum (FIG. 6-47) is surrounded by steeply rising rows of seats, which could hold over fifty thousand spectators. Its substructure consists of a complex system of radial and concentric corridors, covered by concrete vaults that rise to support the upper rows of seats. Originally, tall poles around the top of the structure supported ropes on which awnings could be spread to provide shade for the spectators. The basements below the arena proper contained animal cages, barracks for gladiators, and machinery for raising and lowering stage settings as well as the animal and human combatants. A great deal of technical ingenuity involving lifting tackle was employed to hurl hungry beasts suddenly from their dark dens into the violent light of the arena.

Roman ingenuity in the management of architectural space to fit a complex function may be observed even in the exterior of the Colosseum. The arcuated entrance-exit openings must have permitted rapid filling and emptying of the vast interior; no less than seventy-six numbered entrances led into the seating areas. The relationship of these openings to the tiers of seats within was very carefully thought out and, in essence, may be observed in the modern football stadium. The Colosseum exemplifies the Roman talent for coordinating public and private convenience within large-scale service structures.

The exterior of the building (FIG. 6-48), with its numerous functional openings, consists of *ashlar masonry,* in which dry-jointed blocks are held together by metal cramps and dowels, as in Greek architecture. Its present pockmarked appearance (as if it had been blasted by large shrapnel) is due to the fact that the metal fittings were pried from the joints during the Middle Ages, when metal was very hard to obtain. Indeed, for centuries the structure served as a convenient quarry for ready-made building materials, including marble and precut travertine blocks. The aerial view (FIG. 6-47) shows how much of the building has been dismantled, although what remains is impressive enough.

The exterior shell is 161 feet high, the height of a modern sixteen-story building. It is divided into four horizontal bands, with large, arched openings piercing the lower three. The arches are framed by ornamental Greek orders whose arrangement follows the standard Roman sequence for multistoried buildings: Doric-Ionic-Corinthian, from the ground up. This sequence is based on the inherent proportions of the orders, with the Doric, which appears to be the strongest, viewed as capable of supporting the heaviest load. The smooth wall of the top level is articulated with flat, Corinthian pilasters.

The arrangement in which an arch is framed by engaged columns that carry a lintel is a characteristic Roman combination that appears in triumphal arches and other Roman buildings. Revived in the Italian Renaissance, it has a long, illustrious history in Classical architecture. The framed arch has no structural purpose but fulfills the esthetic function of introducing variety into a monotonous surface, while unifying a multistoried façade by casting a net of verticals and horizontals over it that ties everything together.

THE FORUM AND MARKETS OF TRAJAN

The Forum of Trajan (FIG. 6-45) was the last and greatest of the imperial forums and, to the ancient visitor, must have been just as impressive as the Colosseum. The forum glorified Trajan's victories (he ruled from A.D. 98 to 117) in his two wars against the Dacians and was the work of his chief architect, APOLLODORUS of Damascus, who had served the emperor as military engineer during his Dacian campaigns. The plan incorporated many of the features of earlier forums, including that of Augustus, but deviated from them in one important respect: a huge basilica, not a temple, dominated the colonnaded open square. Visitors gained access to the forum through a monumental gate surmounted by a six-horse chariot; a colossal statue of Trajan stood in the center of the square, and in obvious symbolism, the attic story above the colonnades was decorated with now-lost atlantids representing Dacian prisoners.

The huge Basilica Ulpia (Trajan's family name was Ulpius), built in about A.D. 112, dominated the Forum of Trajan (FIG. **6-49**). A larger version of the basilica in Pompeii, this structure was of a type that was perhaps the most characteristic of those developed by the Romans. The *basilica* was a public hall designed to accommodate large numbers of various kinds of business people. It was the locale of stock exchanges, law courts, business offices, and administrative bureaus and must have provided a center for civic services analogous to those of multiple-building municipal centers today. Years later, the Christians

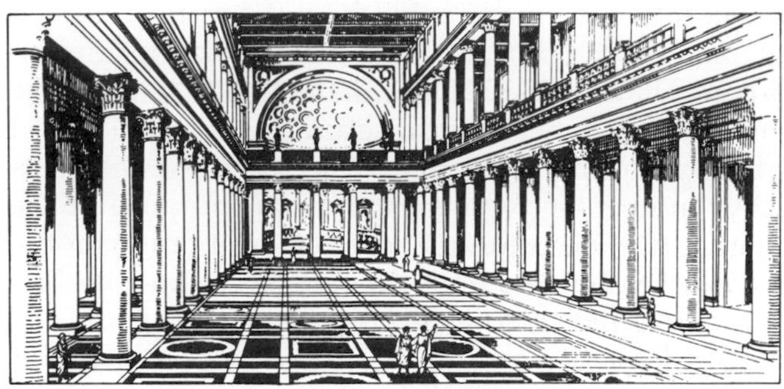

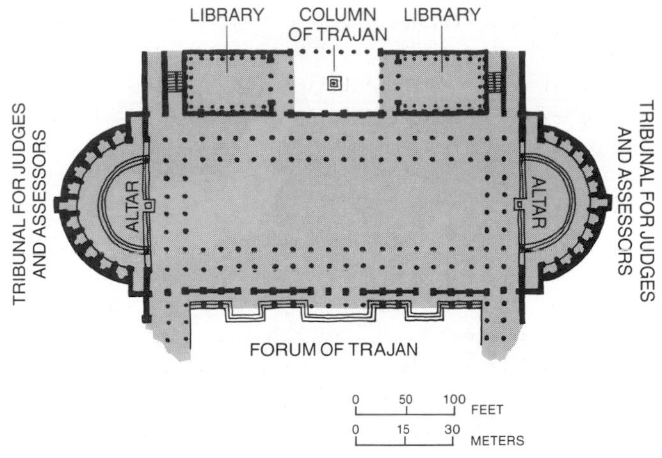

6-49 Reconstruction *(left)* and plan *(right)* of the Basilica Ulpia, Rome, c. A.D. 112. (After Sir Banister Fletcher.)

adapted the basilica (but more especially its subtype, the *palace audience hall*) to religious purposes, modifying it into the typical Christian church building. In plan, the basilica was rectangular, with two or more semicircular *apses*. In the Basilica Ulpia, one of the apses contained the Shrine of Liberty, where slaves were set free; the other may have served in ceremonies of the emperor's cult. The entrance was on one of the long sides of the basilica, an orientation that was changed by the Christians. The building was vast—400 feet long (without the apses) and 200 feet wide. Illumination for this great interior space was afforded by clerestory windows, provided by elevation of the timber-roofed nave above the colonnaded aisles. In the Basilica Ulpia, we once again encounter the Romans' instinctive feeling for broad, uninterrupted, architectural spaces, enclosed for the convenience of human transaction. Despite an imposing exterior, the interior space is what counts here, and although it is a colonnaded space, its effect is not like that of the externally perceived Greek temple, but rather like a dipteral Greek temple inverted: it is to be experienced from within, not from without.

Two simple rectangular, brick-faced concrete buildings that served as libraries were attached to the back of the basilica. Between the buildings, placed on the forum's central axis, stood Trajan's column (see page 234), the cubical base of which served as the emperor's mausoleum. What stood beyond it, on the north end of the forum complex, is unknown. Whatever it was, it was replaced a few years after Trajan's death by a temple that Hadrian built to honor his deified predecessor.

To provide a level space for the forum, the lower slopes of the Quirinal Hill had to be cut back a considerable distance and cut down to a depth of 125 feet. To replace the shops and businesses destroyed by these excavations, Trajan ordered that a new commercial quarter be built to the east of his forum. The Markets of Trajan (FIGS. 6-45, and **6-50** to **6-52**), an urban development of considerable size, were built up in a series of terraces against the steep slope of the Quirinal Hill. The original extent of the development is unknown; what remains are some 170 rooms and a large, groin-vaulted market hall, arranged on six different levels and interconnected by a carefully

6-50 Interior of the "aula," Markets of Trajan, Rome. c. A.D. 100–112.

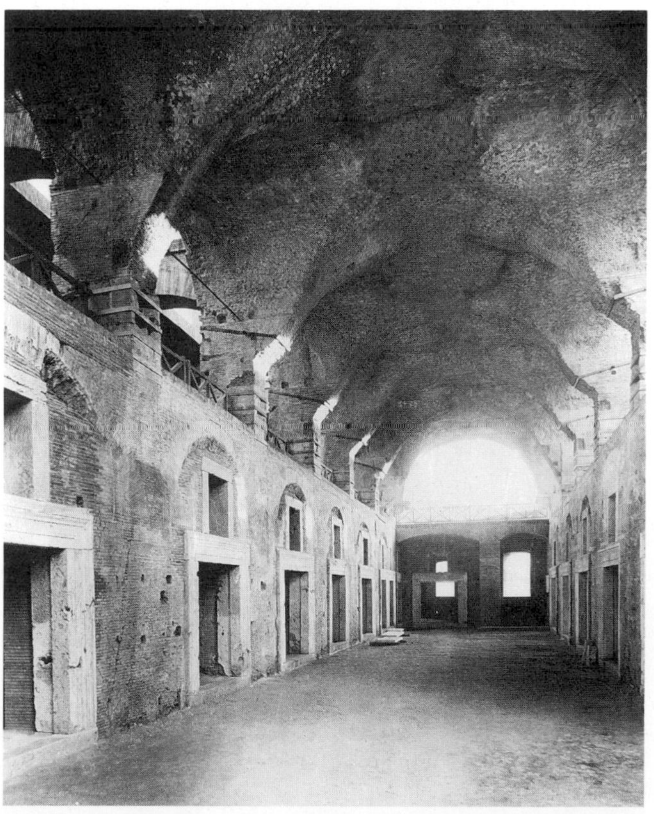

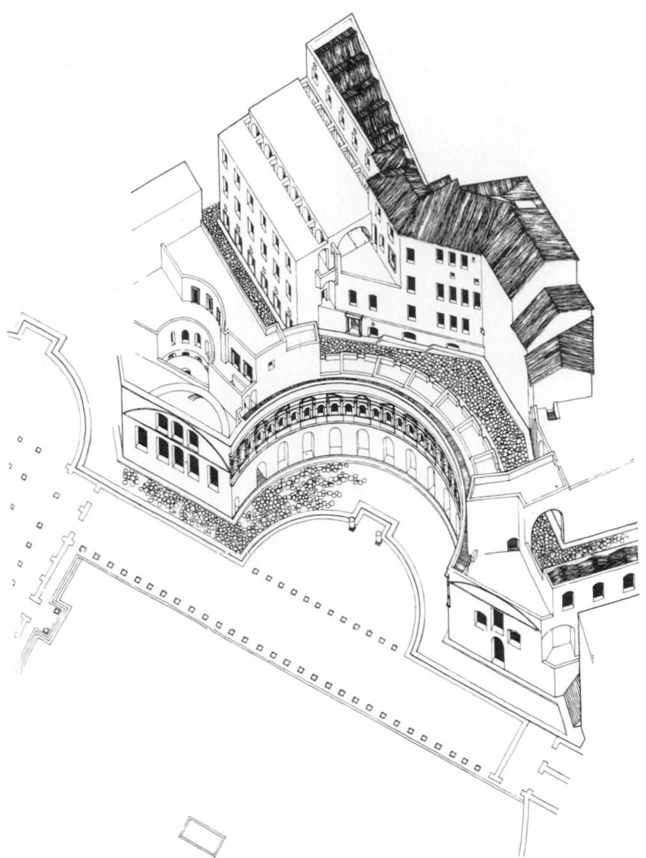

6-51 Markets of Trajan, Rome. (Axonometric view after A. Boethius and Ward-Perkins.)

6-52 Markets of Trajan, Rome.

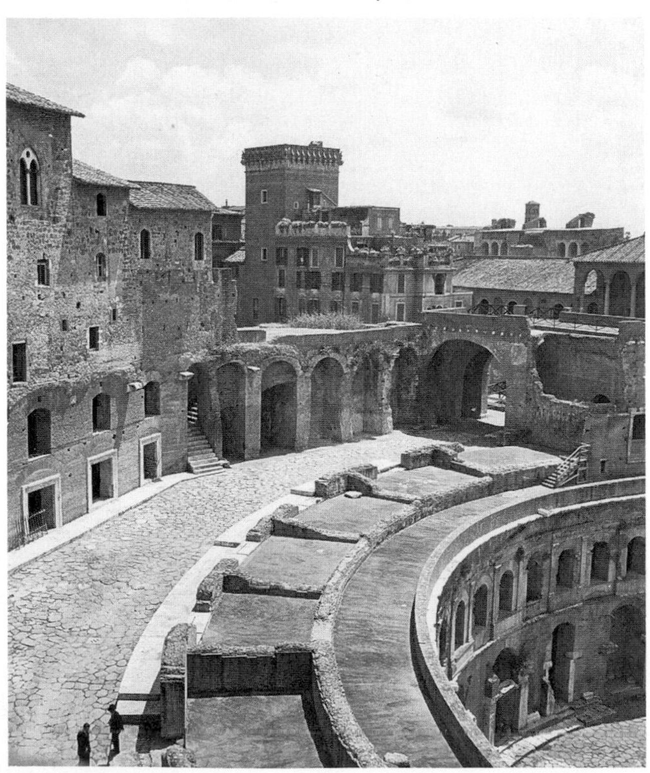

planned system of stairs, ramps, and corridors. The basic unit was the single shop (*taberna*), a barrel-vaulted room with a wide doorway facing a street, passageway, or the vaulted market hall. Some of the shops seem to have had a second interior level built on wooden supports, with a window above the doorway. In keeping with the utilitarian purpose of the buildings, their exteriors were left plain; only on the second level of the front facing the forum (the first level was masked by a curving precinct wall and not visible from the forum) were the arched openings framed with brick pilasters to provide some sort of visual transition from the Sunday magnificence of the imperial forum to the weekday simplicity of the markets. Otherwise, the brick-faced concrete walls of the market buildings were unadorned, except for the simple travertine framing of doorways and some windows. Without marble veneer, engaged orders, or screens of columns, the utilitarian structures could display their architectonic form without disguise. They revealed that their architect, Apollodorus, was a brilliant designer who, despite the orthodoxy he displayed in Trajan's Forum, was fully aware of contemporary structural and stylistic developments.

THE ARCHITECTURAL REVOLUTION

The official style of public buildings during Trajan's administration was conservative and Hellenizing, and, like the deliberately classicizing style during the time of Augustus, expressed prosperous stability. At the same time, however, the native Roman school continued to investigate and to exploit the properties of concrete, mainly in connection with private, commercial, and utilitarian structures. Apollodorus evidently could work with equal facility in the traditional, trabeated style and in the "modern" style of concrete vaulting; it is in this latter field that Rome made its great, original contribution to the history of architecture. The arch, the vault, and the dome were structural devices that the Romans adopted from earlier builders. By combining these forms with steadily refined concrete and an engineering knowledge of the properties of solids and the statics of inert masses, Roman builders acquired a flexibility unknown to their predecessors. Basically, the problem for the Roman builder was this: how does one enclose, roof over, and illuminate the largest possible space while keeping it open and free of interior roof supports?

The simplest vault used by the Romans was the *barrel* or *tunnel* vault (FIG. **6-53c**), a deep arch that forms a half-cylindrical roof over an oblong space; the edges of the half-cylinder rest directly on the side walls, which must be either thick enough to support the weight or reinforced by *buttresses*. Such a vault

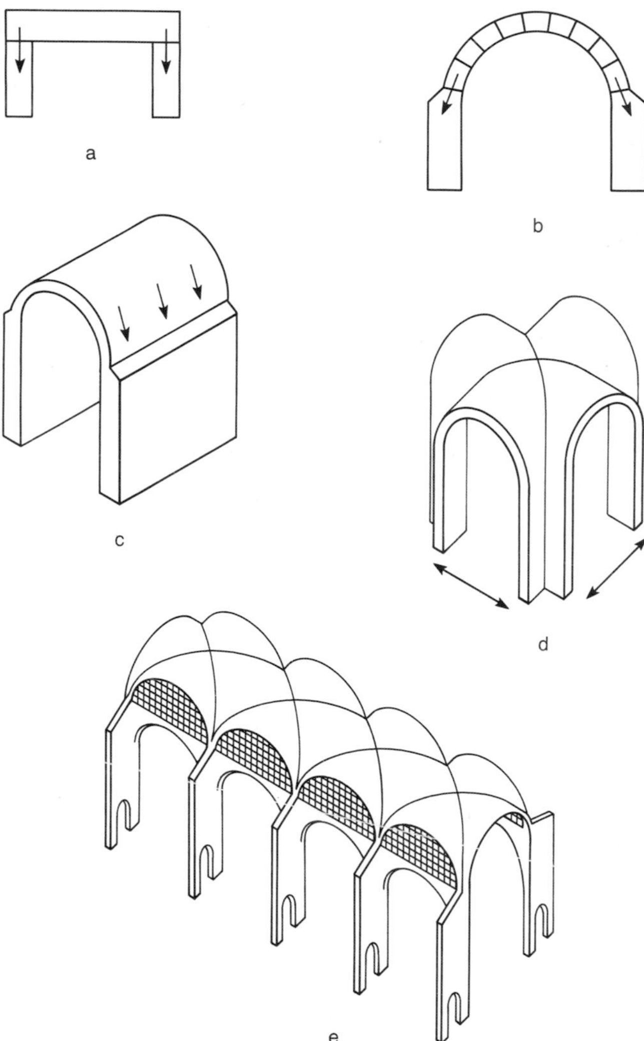

6-53 Roman vaulting systems: (**a**) post-and-lintel construction, (**b**) round arch, (**c**) barrel vault, (**d**) cross-barrel or groin vault, (**e**) fenestrated sequence of groin vaults. (Arrows indicate direction of thrust.)

can be made of brick or stone, as was done by earlier cultures, or of concrete, as preferred by the Romans. Both methods require the use of a temporary form (*centering*) that is the size and shape of the finished vault and that, in the case of concrete, holds the fluid mass until it hardens. If a barrel vault is intersected at right angles by another barrel vault of equal size, the result is a *groin vault;* the line of intersection is called the groin (FIG. **6-53d**). Besides being lighter in appearance than the barrel vault, the groin vault requires less buttressing. In the barrel vault, the thrust is concentrated along the entire length of the supporting wall and requires corresponding buttressing. In the groin vault, the thrust is concentrated along the groins, and buttressing is needed only at those points where the groins meet the vault's vertical supports (piers, walls, or columns). The system leaves the covered area open and free of load-carrying members. Moreover, more light can be admitted through clerestory windows set into the open ends of the cross vaults (FIG. **6-53e;** compare also FIGS. 6-52 and 6-61).

Some of the most significant experiments with concrete vaulting were made in the second half of the first century A.D., during the design and construction of the large, semiprivate, imperial palaces of Nero and Domitian. Augustus, who led an unobtrusively simple life, had been content to live in the house of a well-to-do citizen. His successors were neither as politically astute nor as frugal. Both Nero (A.D. 54–68) and Domitian (A.D. 81–96) built huge palaces for themselves. Nero's, never quite completed, was largely built over in later periods; Domitian's, which continued to be in use until the sixth century A.D., became the prototype for later imperial and vice-imperial residences throughout the Roman Empire.

The great fire of A.D. 64 destroyed large sections of Rome, including Nero's old palace, the Domus Transitoria. The city was rebuilt in accordance with a new code that required greater fireproofing, resulting in the increased use of concrete, which was both cheap and fire-resistant. This increased use gave rise to an entirely new attitude toward a still relatively new material—an attitude that found one of its first full expressions when Nero's architect, SEVERUS, was given the opportunity to use concrete inventively in the building of Nero's new palace, the Domus Aurea, or Golden House (FIGS. **6-54** and **6-55**).

As described by the Roman historians Tacitus and Suetonius, Nero's new palace was a huge and luxurious country villa in the heart of Rome, extending from the Palatine Hill to the Esquiline Hill. With a mile-long portico, it faced an artificial lake (later drained to become the site of the Colosseum) that was surrounded by a landscaped park in which tilled fields and vineyards alternated with pastures and woods filled with great numbers of wild and domestic animals. Probably, the palace was never completed. Vespasian, in a shrewd move to ingratiate himself with his subjects, turned most of the park over to the people in the 70s. Domitian preferred the Palatine Hill and had a new palace built there. What remained of the Domus Aurea was largely built over by later emperors, who, like Domitian, preferred to live on the Palatine.

The so-called Esquiline Wing of the Domus Aurea is the largest fragment of the Neronian palace known today; most of it was found imbedded in the basements of the Baths of Trajan. The excavated area measures about 660 feet long and 200 feet wide and contains a great number of rooms of uncertain purpose. Their walls and piers are of brick-faced concrete, most of them covered by vaults. The more important

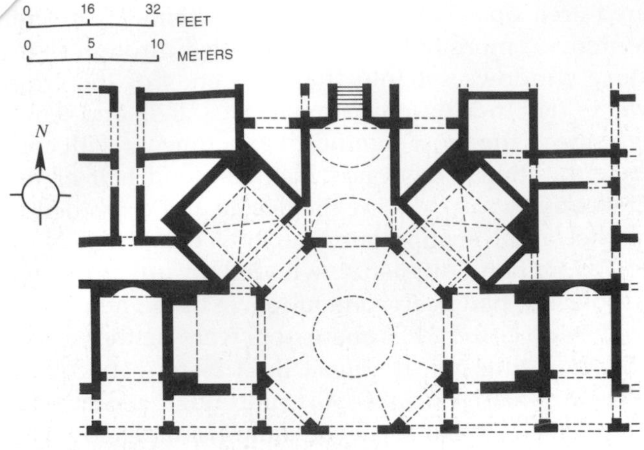

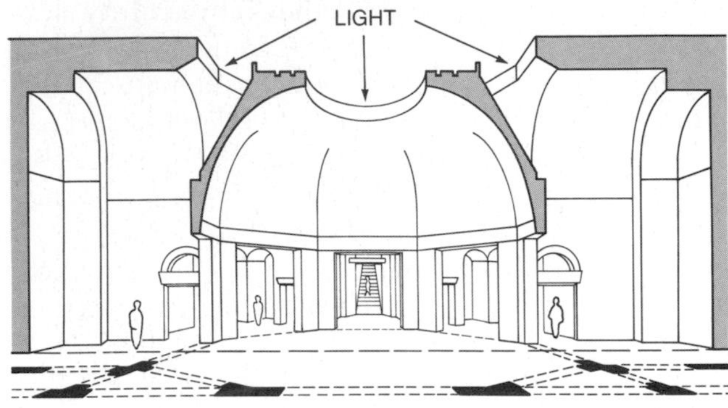

6-54 SEVERUS, plan *(above)* and section *(below)* of the Octagonal Hall, the Domus Aurea of Nero, Rome, A.D. 60–67.

6-55 Octagonal Hall, the Domus Aurea of Nero.

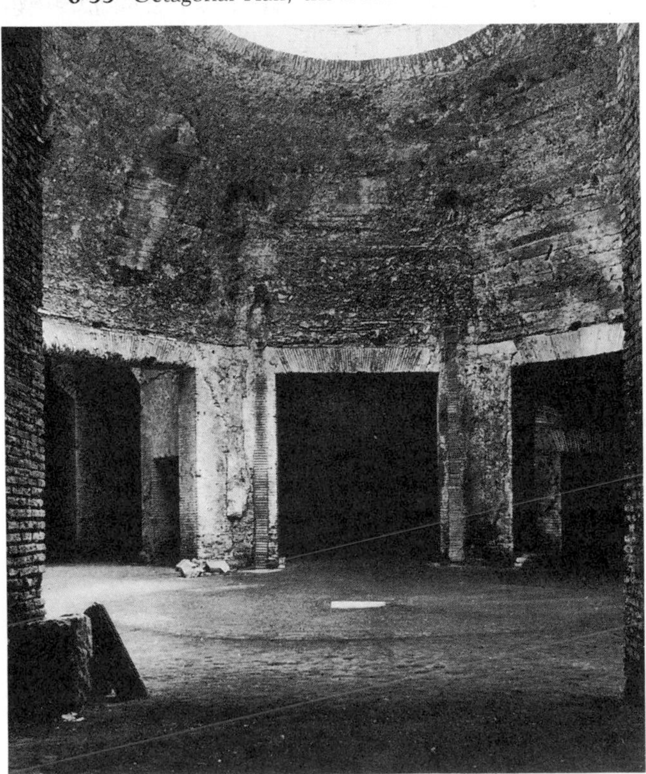

rooms of the wing seem to have been located on its southern side, where they faced the artificial lake. Traces of rich decorations, with marble paneling and painted and gilded stucco, have been found in them. The wing's general plan was fairly conventional, derived from the seaside villas, represented on Pompeian frescoes, that faced the ocean with porticoed façades. But, in what may have been the wing's central axis, a group of rooms expresses an entirely new approach to concrete architecture. An octagonal room is covered by a dome that modulates from an eight-sided to a hemispherical form as it rises toward a round central opening, the *oculus* (eye). Radiating outward from the pavilion's five inside sides (the other three, directly or indirectly, face the outside) are smaller, rectangular rooms, alternately covered by barrel and groin vaults (FIG. 6-54). These satellite rooms were enlivened by decorative recesses and, in the middle one, by a cascade. Their lighting was achieved in a most ingenious manner through what may be described as an inversion of a modified clerestory system. But most significant in the design of this group of rooms is the fact that here, for the first time, the architect appears to have been thinking of the architectural solids—the walls and vaults—not as space-limiting but as *space-molding* agents.

Today, deprived of its marble and stucco incrustation, the concrete shell stands without disguise and may appear crude to the casual observer (FIG. 6-55). Indeed, neither camera nor drawing board can capture the spatial complexity of this design, which only reveals itself fully to the visitor who actually walks through the rooms. Then the central, domed octagon is found to be defined not by walls, but by eight angled piers—the wide, square openings between them so large that the rooms beyond appear to be mere extensions of the central pavilion. The grouping of spatial units of different sizes and proportions under a variety of vaults constitutes a dynamic, three-dimensional composition that is both complex and unified. It reveals Severus as an original and inventive architect, whose design is not only unique, but also progressive in its recognition of the malleable nature of concrete, a material no longer bound by the rectilinear forms of traditional post-and-lintel construction.

THE PANTHEON

In the following century, the Pantheon (FIGS. **6-56** to **6-58**), one of the best preserved and most influential buildings in the history of architecture, revealed the full potential of concrete both as a building material and as a means for the shaping of architectural space. In this structure, the builder has created a single, unencumbered, interior space of overwhelming

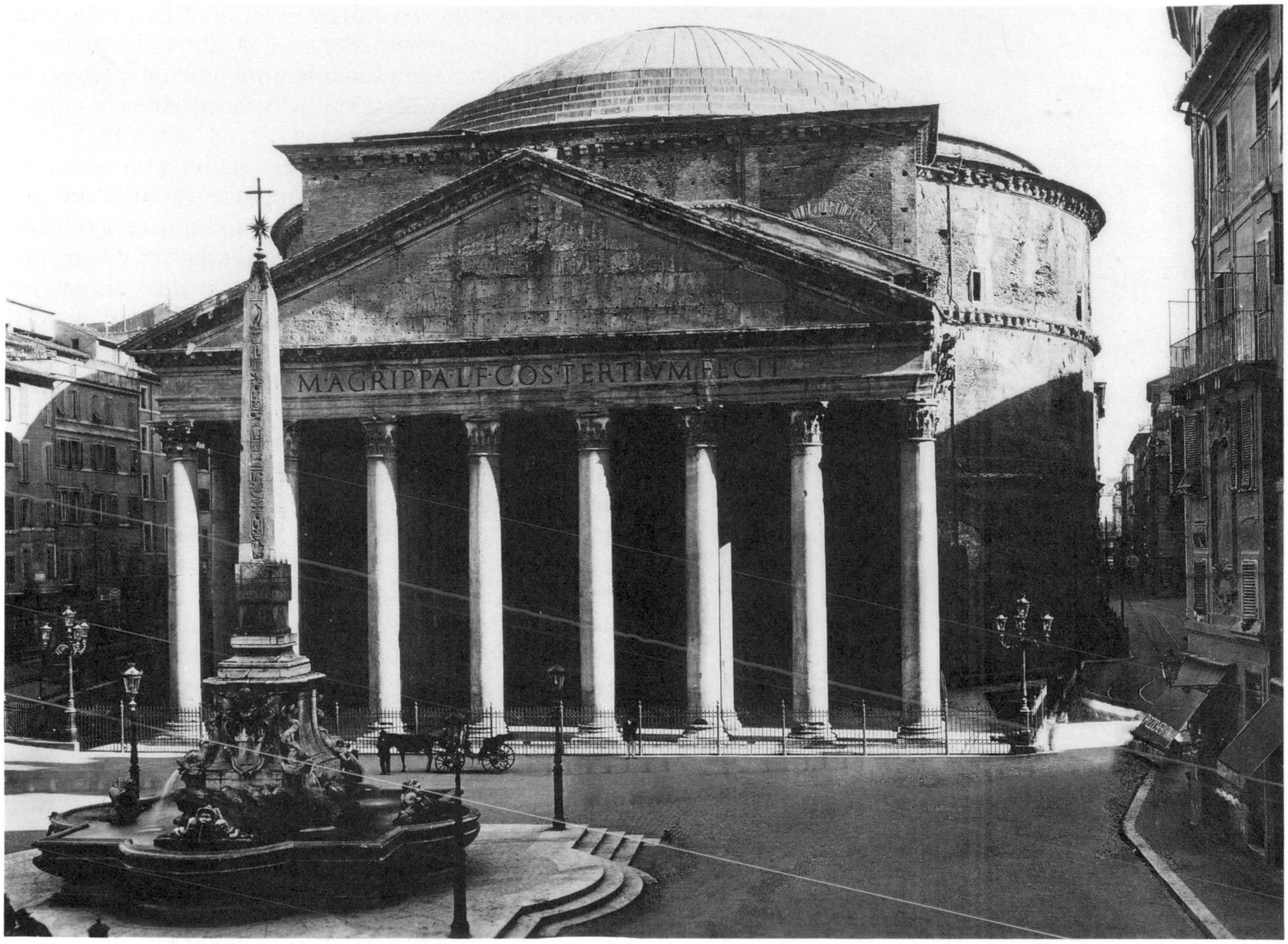

6-56 The Pantheon, Rome, A.D. 118–125.

6-57 Half-plan *(above)* and section *(below)* of the Pantheon. (Plan is symmetrical.)

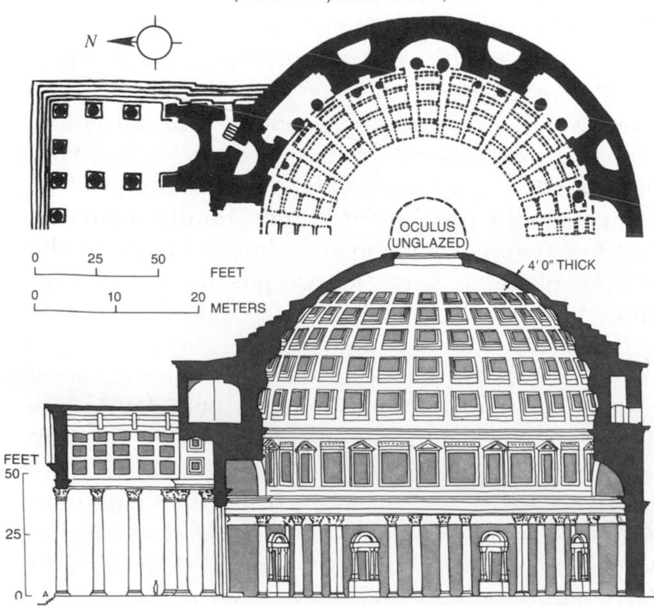

scale, a monumental space scarcely suggested by the exterior. The Pantheon is a domed rotunda fronted with a rectangular portico. The original effect must have been different, for the building was only partly freestanding, its back and one of its sides hidden by older structures. Moreover, the portico stood at one end of a no-longer-extant colonnaded court, its siting similar to that of temples in the imperial forums and the Temple of Jupiter at Pompeii. Built during the rule of Hadrian (A.D. 117–138), the temple may have been conceived by that versatile emperor.

The Pantheon is of monumental simplicity and great scale. A hemispheric dome 144 feet in diameter covers the circular interior. The summit of the dome is the same distance from the floor. The design is thus based on the intersection of two circles (one horizontal, the other vertical), imaginable as sections of a globe of space inscribed within the building. The dome is a shell of concrete that gradually thickens toward the base to augment structural strength where it is most needed. The center of the dome is

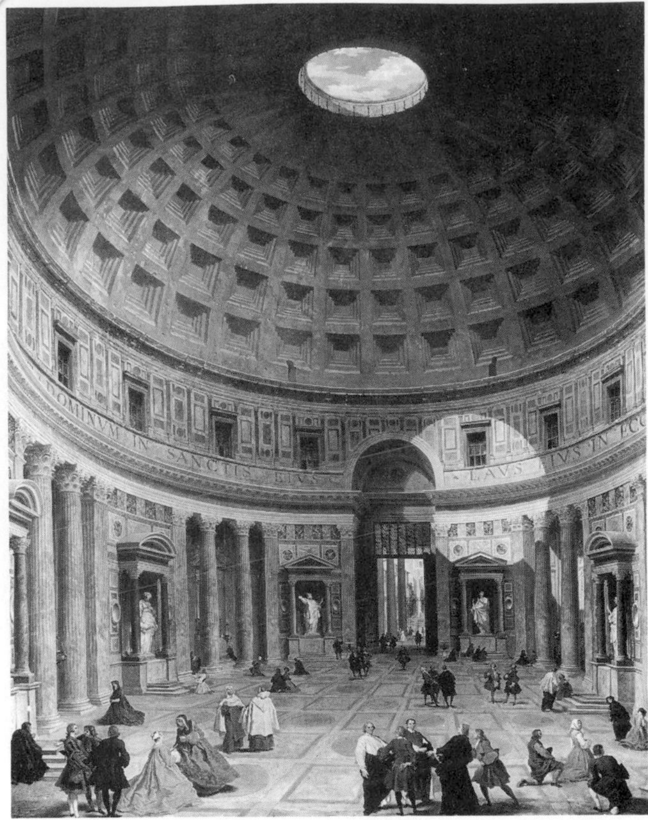

6-58 GIOVANNI PANNINI, *Interior of the Pantheon*, c. 1740. National Gallery of Art, Washington, D.C. (Samuel H. Kress Collection).

pierced dramatically by the oculus, a round opening 30 feet in diameter, which, left unglazed and open to the sky, is the only source of light for the interior. Supporting the dome are piers of immense thickness, formed by alternating rectangular and rounded niches, each covered by a vault that channels pressures exerted by the weight of the dome into solid masonry. The dome is *coffered* (furnished with decorative, sunken panels called coffers) for the multiple purposes of making a handsome geometric foil of squares within the vast circle, reducing the weight and mass of the dome without weakening its structure, and symbolizing the starry heavens, each coffer having a gilded, bronze rosette at its center. The floor of the building is slightly convex, and drains are cut into the shallow depression in the center (directly under the oculus) to carry off any rain that falls through the opening far above.

Giovanni Pannini's painting of the interior of the Pantheon (FIG. 6-58) exhibits, better than any photograph, the unity and scale of the design, the simplicity of its relationships, and its breathtaking grandeur. Pannini's work almost records the experience one has on first entering this tremendous, shaped space—a feeling not of the weight of the enclosing masses, but of the palpable presence of space itself, for the architecture here displayed is first of all an *architecture of space*. In the architectures studied thus far, the form of the enclosed space is determined by the placement of the solids, which do not so much shape as interrupt the space. The solids are so prominent in Egyptian and Mesopotamian architecture that it is the solids we *see*; space is only "negative," simply happening between the solids. We think of this as an *architecture of mass*. Greek architecture, also primarily concerned with masses and their relationships and with the shaping of solid units, is designated as *skeletal* or *sculptural architecture*. It is the Roman architects who initially conceived of architecture in terms of units of space that could be shaped by enclosures. The interior of the Pantheon, in keeping with this interest, is a single, unified, self-sufficient whole, uninterrupted by supporting solids; it is a whole that encloses visitors without imprisoning them, a small cosmos that opens through the oculus to the drifting clouds, the blue sky, the sun, universal nature, and the gods. To escape from the noise and torrid heat of a Roman summer day into the sudden cool and calm immensity of the Pantheon is an experience almost impossible to describe and one that should not be missed. Above all, it is an *architectural* experience.

THE BATHS OF CARACALLA

The gigantic Baths of Caracalla (FIGS. **6-59** to **6-61**) date from about A.D. 215. The enclosure of great spaces by vaulting was common practice at this time. Although nothing of the covering is left, the baths reveal traces of the vaults that sprang up from the thick walls to heights of up to 140 feet; under them, spread out in unending variety, were spaces designed for the intellectual as well as physical recreation of thousands of leisured Romans, all at the expense of the state. The central buildings of the huge complex, in which the emperors hoped to keep an unruly and indigent populace preoccupied with pleasure, covered a large area (roughly 240 yards long and 120 yards wide); the baths, which were the center of interest, as well as the architectural center of the design, had a capacity of sixteen hundred bathers. The functions of various parts of the complex are still matters of controversy. The design was symmetrical along a central axis occupied by pools filled with water of different temperatures: the *frigidarium*, the cold-water pool; the *tepidarium*, the central room containing smaller, warm-water pools; and the *calidarium*, a circular, hot-water pool in a domed rotunda. The central buildings also contained steam baths, dressing rooms, lounges, lecture halls, and *palestrae* (exercise rooms). This whole core complex was surrounded by landscaped gardens bordered by secondary buildings that housed shops, restaurants, libraries, gymnasiums, and perhaps a stadium. The

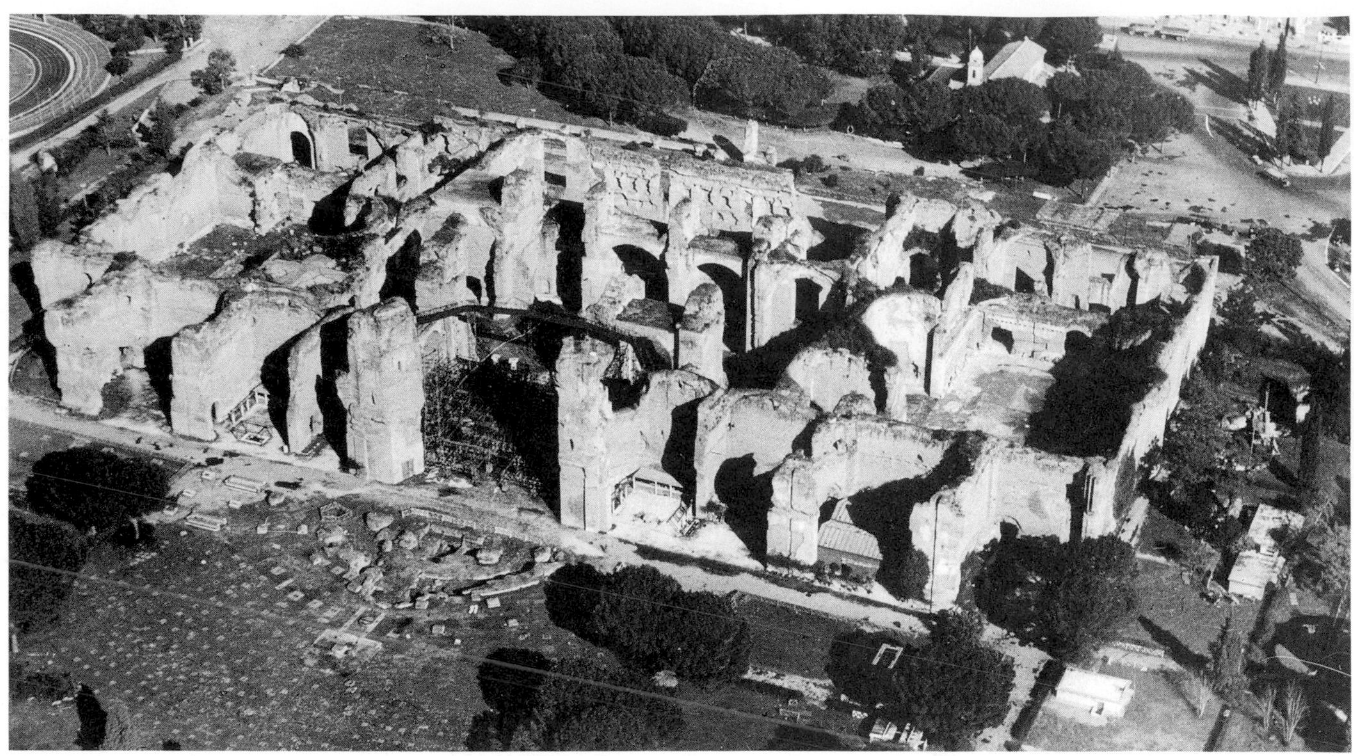

6-59 Aerial view of the Baths *(thermae)* of Caracalla, Rome, c. A.D. 215.

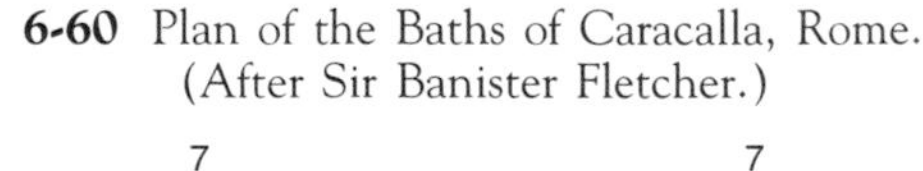

6-60 Plan of the Baths of Caracalla, Rome. (After Sir Banister Fletcher.)

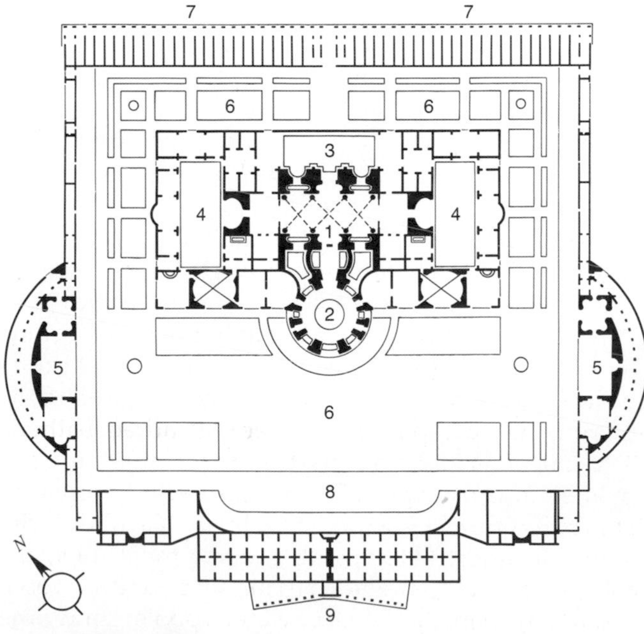

1. Central hall (tepidarium)
2. Calidarium
3. Natatio (frigidarium)
4. Palaestra
5. Lecture halls and libraries
6. Gardens
7. Shops
8. Stadium (?)
9. Aqueduct and reservoirs

0 160 320 FEET
0 50 100 METERS

long side of the entire complex measured almost one-quarter of a mile. Beneath it all was a subterranean world of corridors (some wide enough to accommodate vehicles), storerooms, and heating chambers populated by slaves and stokers. The halls and the water were heated by a system in which hot air was circulated through tubes and hollow bricks beneath the floors, in the walls, and sometimes in the vaults. The water was plentifully supplied by an individual aqueduct.

This enormous dedication of human ingenuity was directed toward the service of human ease. For a negligible admission fee, Romans could lounge for a whole day at the baths, in surroundings of the greatest magnificence. In fact, the baths were so lavish, ornate, and luxurious that moralists of the time complained of their wasteful ostentation. In his "Epistula Morales," the Roman philosopher-statesman Seneca, comparing his degenerate times with those of the heroic general Scipio, who bathed in austerely simple surroundings, complained:

> But who in these days could bear to bathe in such a fashion? We think ourselves poor and mean if our walls are not resplendent with large and costly mirrors; if our marbles from Alexandria are not set off by mosaics of Numidian stone; if their borders are not faced over on all sides with difficult patterns, arranged in many colours like paintings; if our vaulted ceilings are not buried in glass; if our swimming

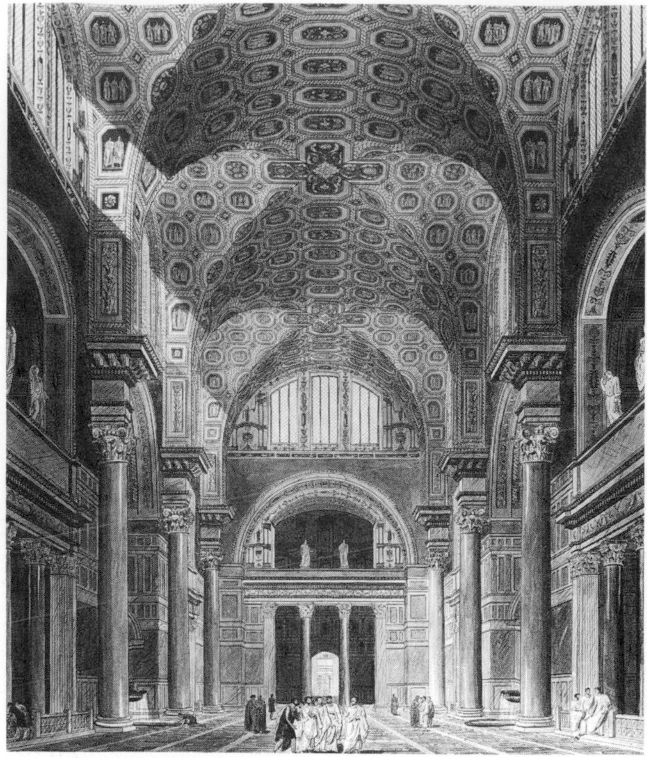

6-61 Central Hall *(tepidarium)* of the Baths of Caracalla, Rome. (Restoration drawing by G. ABEL BLONET.)

pools are not lined with Thasian marble, once a rare and wonderful sight in any temple. . . . What a vast number of statues, of columns that support nothing, but are built for decoration, merely in order to spend money! And what masses of water that fall crashing from level to level! We have become so luxurious that we will have nothing but precious stones to walk upon.

The baths were, of course, social centers in which the whole day could be spent "sweetly doing nothing." And the baths were cultural centers as well, with their libraries and their profusion of magnificent statues. A large number of Roman copies after Greek originals were found in public baths, a few of the most important in the Baths of Caracalla. To the Romans, baths of this type were a natural and indispensable part of "civilization."

Sculpture and Monumental Relief

Sculpture in the Roman Empire began under the influence of Augustan Rome's admiration of Hellenic culture and of the emperor's apparent determination to base a cultural renewal of Rome on it. That the Hellenized glorification of the empire was politically motivated is undoubtedly true; we already have seen how Roman architecture was molded to the end of manifesting the imperial authority. But the imperial motivation produced the esthetic consequence that work of the highest quality in all the arts bore the seal, as it were, of the Hellenic spirit. The *Augustus of Primaporta* (FIG. **6-62**), about 20 B.C., is an example of the sedate, idealizing manner we have come to recognize as "Augustan" (the same statement can be made concerning Vergil's *Aeneid*). The statue, which once stood in front of the imperial villa in Primaporta, about ten miles north of Rome, represents Augustus addressing his troops in the field. Though only a copy, the work is of the highest quality. At first glance, it might appear to be in the realistic mode of Republican statues, but on second glance, we find it strongly idealized, made according to Polykleitan proportions and even reminiscent of the *Doryphoros* (FIG. 5-58), especially in the walking pose. The reliefs on the emperor's breastplate are Roman in subject and refer to contemporaneous events, at least in the central theme: a Parthian returning a Roman standard to a Roman soldier. But these historical references are framed by mythological and allegorical figures representing the sky god, the earth goddess, and the pacified provinces of Spain and Gaul. Together, the figures symbolize the blessings of the new golden age that were expected to come with the Augustan peace. They also place, side by side, the idealizing and realistic tendencies in Roman art that would alternate and intermingle throughout imperial times.

6-62 *Augustus of Primaporta,* c. 20 B.C. Marble, 6′ 8″ high. Vatican Museums, Rome.

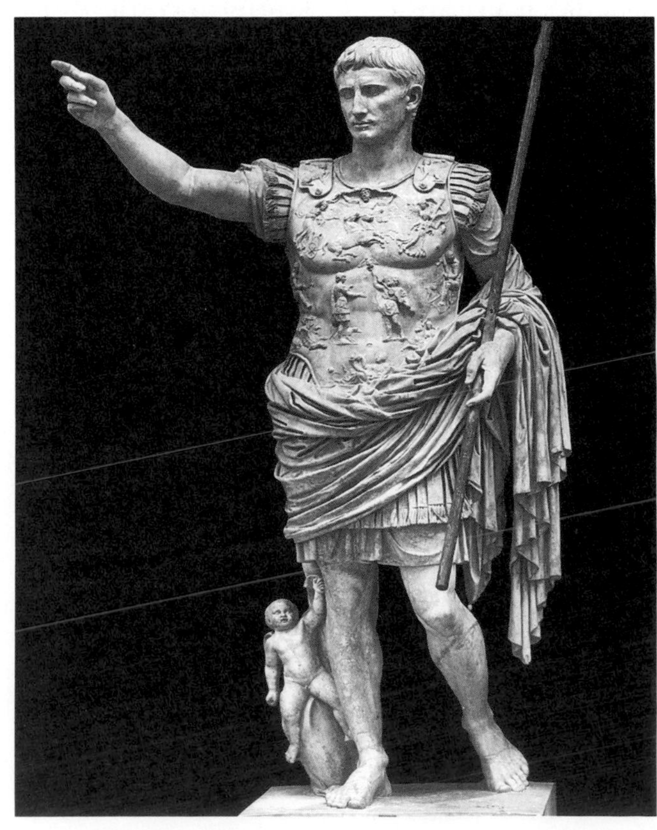

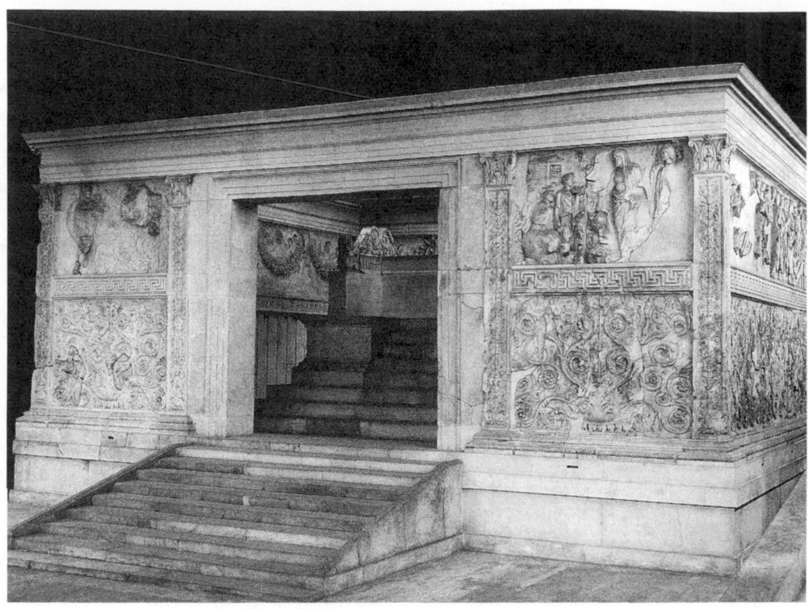

6-63 Ara Pacis Augustae, Rome, 13–9 B.C. Marble, approx. 35′ wide. Museum of the Ara Pacis Augustae. (Cornice restored.)

The idealistic and realistic mingle, yet remain distinguishable, in the sculptured figures of the Ara Pacis Augustae, or Altar of the Augustan Peace (FIG. **6-63**). Completed and dedicated in January, 9 B.C., to commemorate pacification of Spain and Gaul in 13 B.C., the altar can stand as a monument to the pacification of the whole Roman Empire in the Augustan years following the establishment of the new government in 27 B.C. Scholars disagree regarding the meaning of the altar's theme and figures. The actual altar is raised on an interior platform that is surrounded by a nearly square enclosure ($35\frac{1}{2}$ feet long and 39 feet wide). The exterior and interior surfaces of the enclosing walls are decorated with reliefs. Garlands are suspended from bucrania on the interior walls. On the exterior walls, a lower zone displays a delicately carved, decorative, acanthus-leaf pattern, arranged in spiral designs. An upper zone depicts a procession of men, women, and children and, on separate panels, allegorical subjects. The wall surfaces are framed by florid, Corinthian pilasters in a composition reminiscent of the second style of Pompeian wall painting.

The *"Tellus" Relief* panel from the Ara Pacis Augustae (FIG. **6-64**) may represent the ancient Roman earth mother, Tellus, flanked by personifications of the elements, their draperies blowing about them. The figures are seated in a fertile landscape against clouds simulated in low relief. Although we have come to think of the interest in the illusion of landscape as a Roman trait, the poses here, the style of the draperies, and the lateral placement of the figures in a single plane attest to the Greek influence. The whole tableau celebrates the Augustan peace as the source of a new bounty of nature and the new richness and fertility of earth as the foundation of Roman wealth and power.

The *Procession* (FIG. **6-65**) carved on the Ara Pacis Augustae, led by the emperor himself, almost certainly was intended to represent the actual solemnities when the altar was dedicated. The historical particularity of the frieze is characteristic of the Roman feeling for the factual, especially as we have seen it expressed in the portrait bust, in a pragmatic architecture, and, to a degree, in landscape painting. This contrasts with the Greek practice of disguising historical events in the mythological, as in the great frieze of Pergamon (FIG. 5-78), on which a historical war between Greeks and Gauls becomes a struggle between gods and giants. In some respects, the Roman feeling for narrative bound to actual events resembles more the Assyrian than the Greek approach. Yet the style of the figures of the *Procession* is Hellenizing and

6-64 *"Tellus" Relief,* marble panel from the Ara Pacis Augustae, approx. 63″ high.

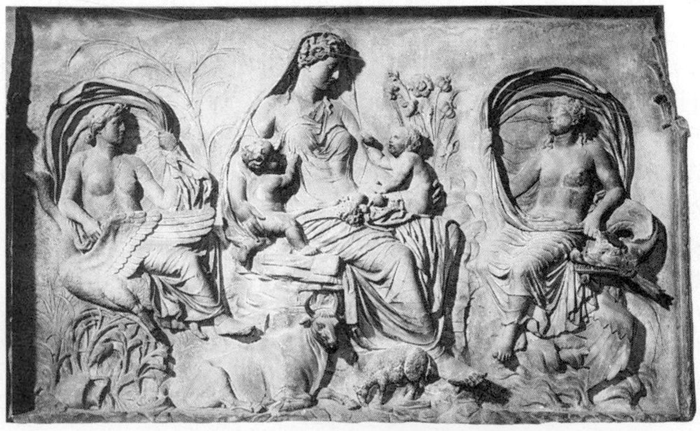

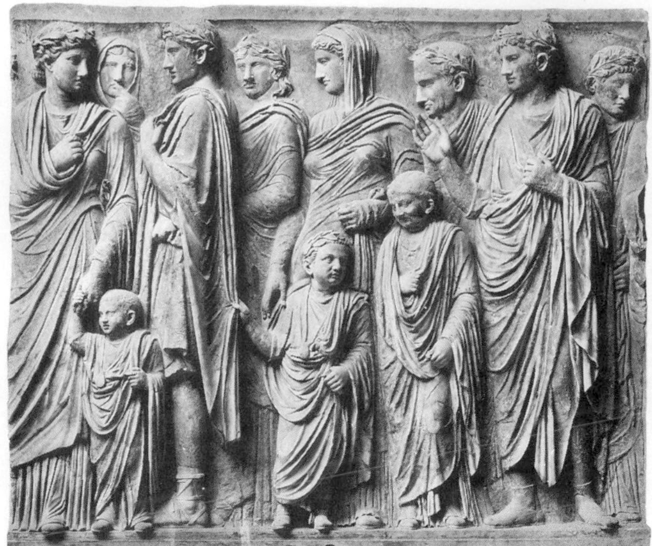

6-65 *Procession,* portion of the frieze of the Ara Pacis Augustae. Marble relief, approx. 63″ high.

may be directly inspired by the Panathenaic frieze of the Parthenon (FIG. 5-50). In the Ara Pacis Augustae, the *Procession* moves in several files. Differences in distance are signified by differences in degree of relief—the nearer the figure, the higher the relief. Individuals are differentiated carefully; the heads are moderately idealized portraits, and the artists added "human interest" touches—for example, clinging, restless children quieted by adults. The overall demeanor is solemn, as would have befitted the occasion, and the impression is of a quiet concourse of participants behaving in a manner they believe to be appropriate to a quasi-religious ceremony. The draperies, the quiet dignity, the ordered deployment within a shallow plane of space echo the older, Classical style, and the Ara Pacis Augustae, with its blend of the real and the ideal, signifies the Augustan style and the style of the empire in general.

The memorializing of actual events in monumental form finds striking expression in the imperial *triumphal arch,* one of the most popular types of commemorative monument. Essentially, the triumphal arch is an ornamental version of a city gate, often moved to the center of the city, but also located in other places, such as on bridges or on roads leading out of cities. The Arch of Titus (FIG. **6-66**), dated A.D. 81, is located at a point at which the Via Sacra enters the Forum Romanum. These arches commemorated a wide variety of persons and events. As a building type, the triumphal arch exerted considerable influence on the architecture of the Renaissance. Closely related to the Colosseum-arch order, it consists of a single arch flanked by massive piers, to which the *Composite* order (a combination of Ionic and Corinthian) has been attached decoratively. Its typical superstructure, the *attic,* bears the commemorative inscription. Occasionally, the flanking piers also are pierced by arches, producing a triple arch like the Arch of Constantine (FIG. 6-95). The walls of the passageway of the Arch of Titus are decorated with relief panels representing the triumphal return of Titus from the conquest of Jerusalem at the end of the Jewish Wars (A.D. 66–70). In later arches, the sculptural decor moved to the outside surfaces of the structure, as seen in the Arch of Constantine.

One of the archway reliefs shows soldiers of the Roman army carrying *Spoils from the Temple in Jerusalem,* including the seven-branched candelabrum from the Holy of Holies (FIG. **6-67**). The panel is severely damaged. Beam holes in the upper part date from the Middle Ages, when the family of the Frangipani converted the arch into a private fortress and built a second story into the vault, only one of many examples of later indifference to the esthetic and historic value discovered in recent times in the ruins of Rome. But enough of the relief remains to show that spatial effects aimed at in the Ara Pacis Augustae reach full development here. The illusion of movement is complete and convincing. The marching files press forward from the left background into the center foreground and disappear through the obliquely placed arch in the right background. The energy and swing of the column of soldiers suggest a rapid marching cadence and the chant of triumph. The carving is extremely deep. The heads of the forward figures have been broken off, probably because they stood vulnerably free from the block, emphasizing their different placement in space from the heads in low relief, which are intact. The deep relief produces strong shadows and the light and shade quicken the move-

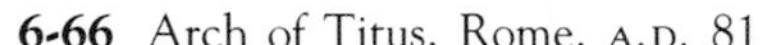

6-66 Arch of Titus, Rome, A.D. 81.

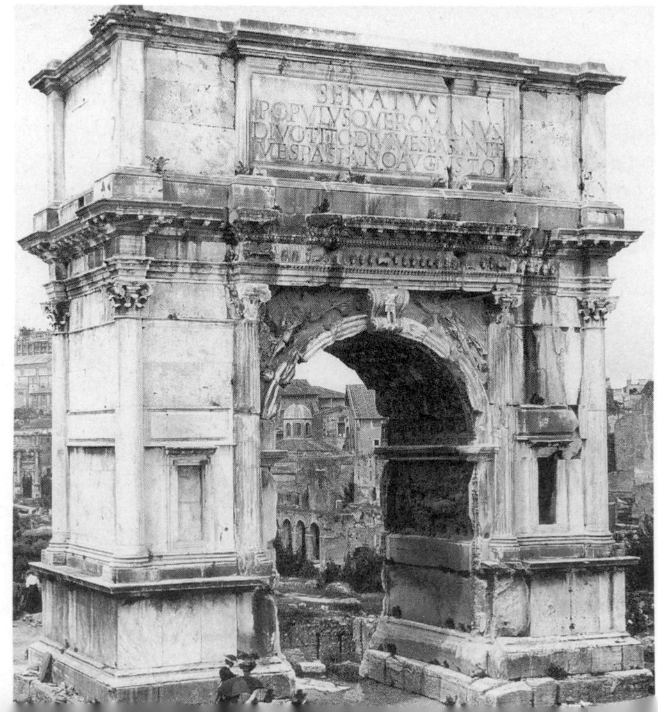

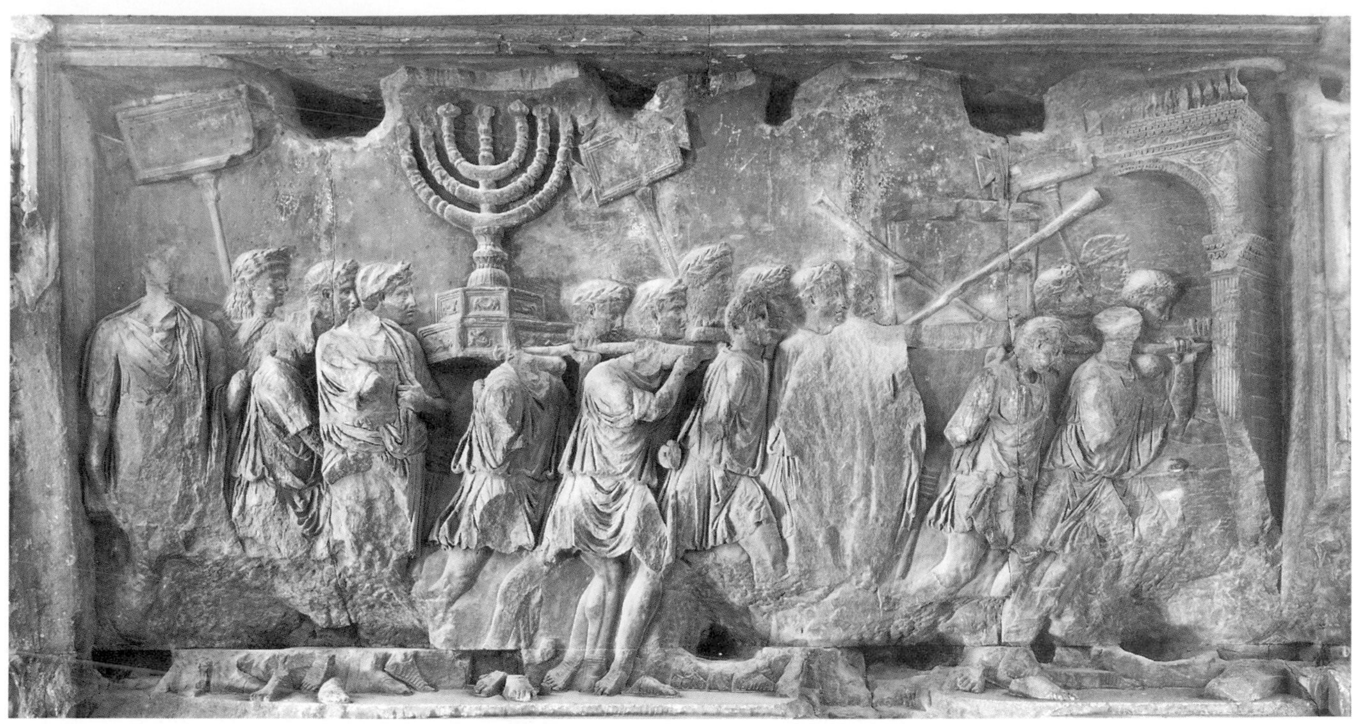

6-67 *Spoils from the Temple in Jerusalem,* from the Arch of Titus. Marble relief, approx. 7′ 10″ high.

ment and strikingly suggest the "momentary flash of a passing parade." The work brings to mind the experiments with light and space in imperial painting and architecture.

The *Triumph of Titus* (FIG. **6-68**), represented across the archway, is more slowly paced, without the thrusting movement of the marching soldiers carrying the spoils from the temple and without the spatial experiments found there. The numerous layers of figures do create an illusion of depth, and a bold attempt at representing the overlapping horses turning into the roadway, drawing the chariot of Titus, persuades us that the sculptor's intentions are alike in both panels. Close correspondence exists between the event as shown in the panels and as described by Josephus (contemporaneous Jewish soldier, statesman, and historian):

> Most of the spoils that were carried were heaped up indiscriminately, but more prominent than all the rest were those captured in the Temple of Jerusalem—a golden table weighing several hundredweight, and a lampstand similarly made of gold. . . . The central shaft was fixed to a base, and from it extended slender branches placed like the prongs of a trident, and

6-68 *Triumph of Titus,* from the Arch of Titus. Marble relief, approx. 7′ 10″ high.

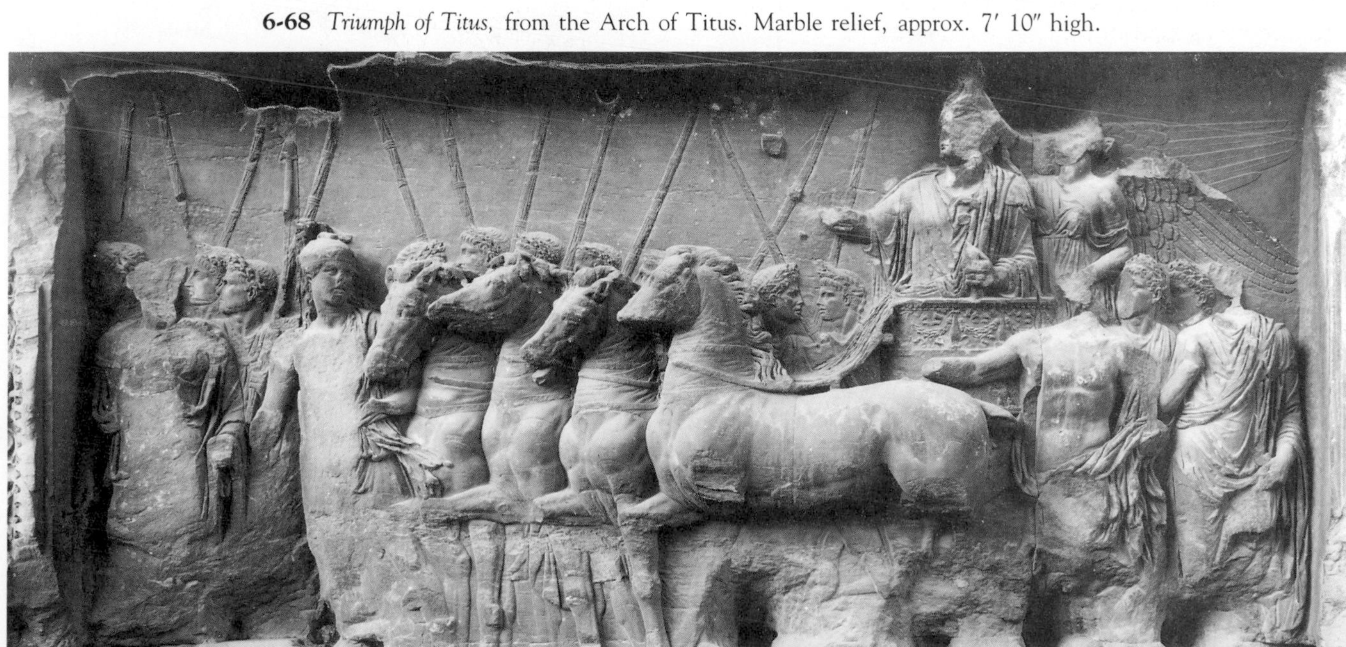

with the end of each one forged into a lamp: these numbered seven, signifying the honour paid to that number by the Jews. After these was carried the Jewish Law, the last of the spoils. Next came a large group carrying images of Victory, all fashioned of ivory and gold. Behind them drove Vespasian first with Titus behind him: Domitian rode alongside, magnificently adorned himself, and with his horse a splendid sight.

The Column of Trajan, another kind of commemorative monument, dating from A.D. 113, stood in his forum before the unexcavated temple of Trajan (FIGS. **6-69** and **6-70**). The column, perhaps the work of Trajan's favorite architect and military engineer, Apollodorus of Damascus, was often copied. As late as the nineteenth century, a column inspired by the Column of Trajan was erected in the Place Vendôme in Paris, in commemoration of the victories of Napoleon. The original column is 128 feet high. It was once crowned by a statue of Trajan, which was lost in the Middle Ages and replaced by a statue of St. Peter in the sixteenth century. The square base served as Trajan's mausoleum, and his ashes were deposited there in a golden urn in A.D. 117. The column records Trajan's two successful campaigns against the Dacians, which resulted in the extension of Roman dominion across the Danube into what is now Hungary and Rumania. Under Trajan, the limits of the Roman Empire reached their greatest extent. The marble reliefs, in a 625-foot band that winds the

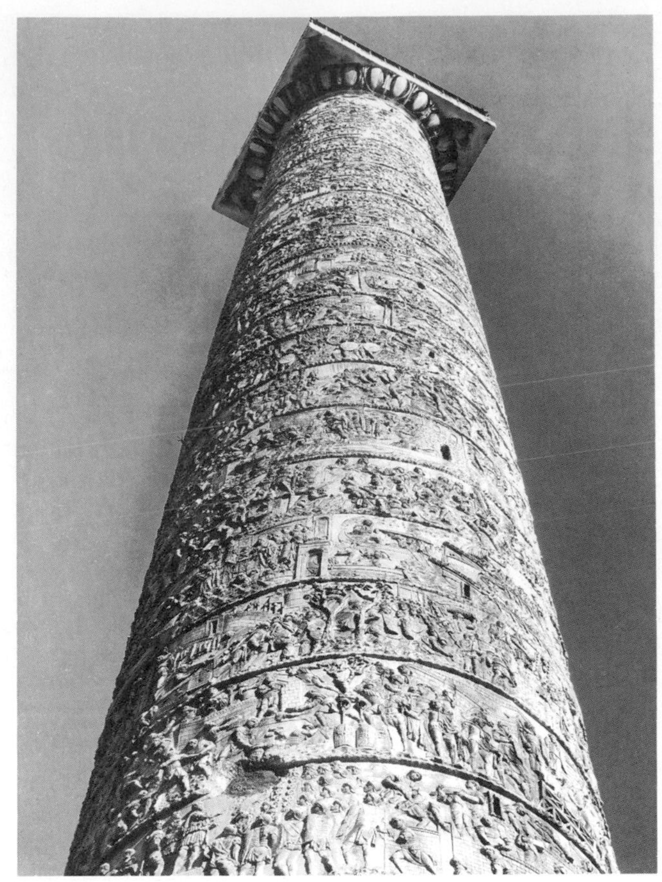

6-69 Attributed to APOLLODORUS, Column of Trajan, Rome, A.D. 113. Marble, 128′ high.

6-70 Detail of the two lowest bands of the Column of Trajan. Marble relief, each band approx. 36″ high.

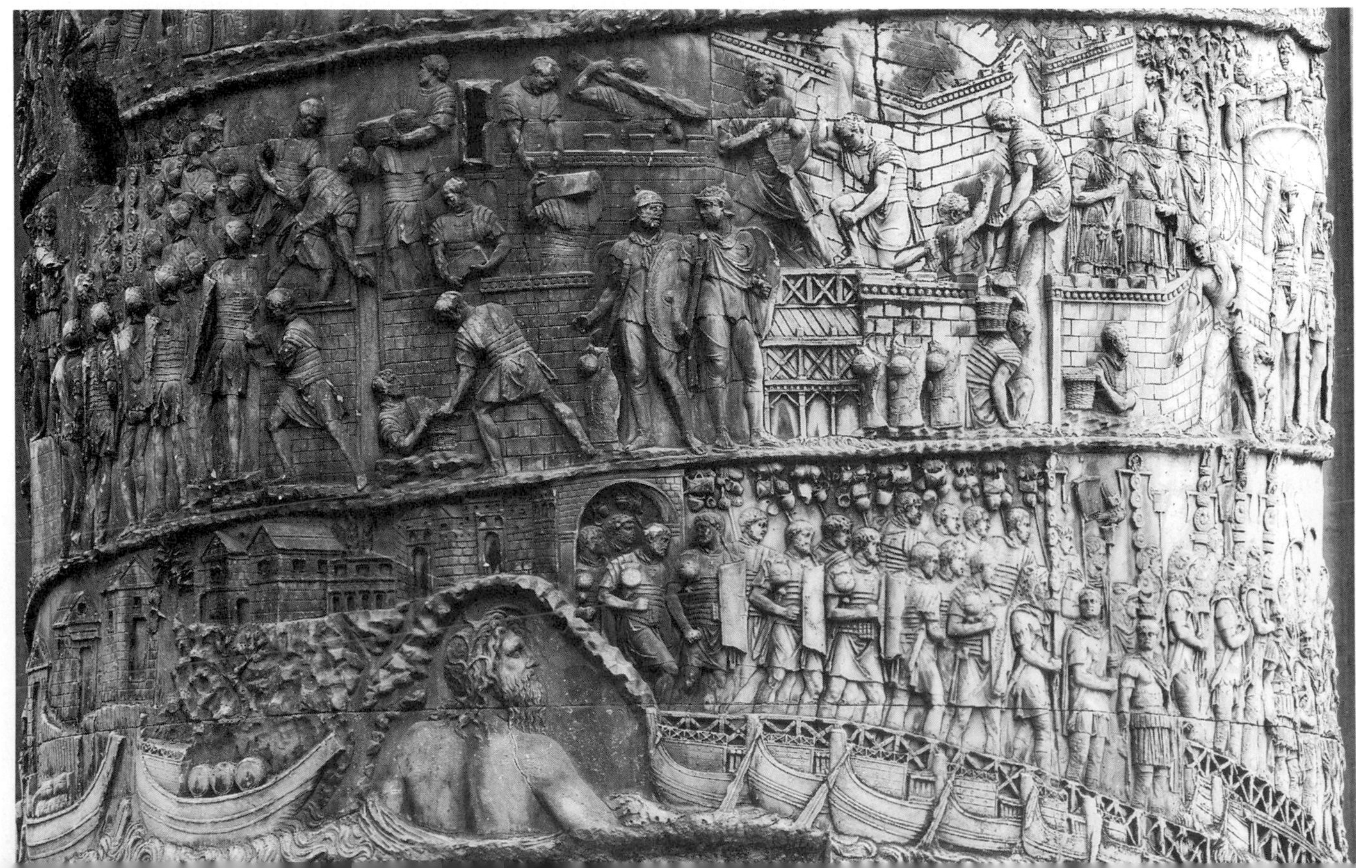

height of the column, represent a continuous record of the campaigns, told in 150 separate episodes with literally thousands of figures. The band increases in width as it winds to the top of the column (from approximately 36 inches to 50 inches) for better visibility from the ground. Recognition of the upper subjects must have been a problem, even though the column originally stood in a small courtyard surrounded by two-story buildings, from the upper story or roofs of which the topmost reliefs may have been recognizable.

The carving is executed in relatively low relief to reduce shadows to a minimum, as they would have tended to impair the legibility of the work. This low relief constitutes a significant reduction in illusionistic depth. The sculptured narrative places much emphasis on military architecture, fortifications, bridges, and the like, to demonstrate Roman technical superiority over the barbarian foe. At the bottom of the column a pontoon bridge is built across the Danube, while the river-god looks on in amazement at this achievement (FIG. 6-70); on the fourth circuit of the column, Trajan is shown speaking to his troops. The emperor's figure is seen many times throughout the narrative, appearing as a major motif. The story of the campaigns is told with objectivity; the enemy is not belittled, and the Roman victories are hard won. But only about a quarter of the reliefs show battle scenes. Much of the balance represents the Roman mission of bringing civilization to the benighted. Towns are built, crops harvested, rituals performed, and imperial speeches given. In short, the reliefs of the column are not only an exaltation of Trajan, but a hymn to *Romanitas*.

The Column of Trajan reliefs embody some features of great importance for the art of the Middle Ages. We already have indicated one of them—a *flattening of relief*—and the functional reason for it (better visibility). But the sacrifice of the strong illusionism seen in the Arch of Titus reliefs, or even in the Ara Pacis Augustae reliefs, may have another explanation: a desire for completeness of narrative description that required that a great number of actions be shown in a limited space. Thus, *narrative* fact, rather than *visual* fact, is required, and truth to appearance ("illusionism," "realism"), to a greater or lesser degree, can be sacrificed. A very singular and important sacrifice is made in the Column of Trajan compositions, and that is in the representation of space. In the Ara Pacis Augustae and the Arch of Titus reliefs, the figures are represented as standing and moving on the same ground line, at the eye level of a presumed observer who occupies an imagined place on the same line; thus, all the heads are approximately on the same level. But the figures of the Column of Trajan are superposed (placed in rows one above the other), a device altogether different from the approximate perspective of illusionism. From a perspective viewpoint, the figures and architecture of the Column of Trajan are entirely haphazard in their arrangement; from a narrative viewpoint, they occur where the story demands. Relative proportions often are sacrificed: soldiers are represented as large as the walls they attack, or (although not visible in our illustrations here) cavalrymen are as large as, or larger than, their horses. We can say that conventions of Medieval art already appear in the sculptures of the Column of Trajan.

The new conventions were not adopted immediately. They appear in the somewhat later Column of Marcus Aurelius, but in a relief of *Marcus Aurelius Sacrificing* (FIG. **6-71**), the older illusionism persists, although not to the degree we find it in the Arch of Titus. In this relief, one of three panels surviving from a triumphal arch dedicated to the emperor and carved about A.D. 180, the procession was cut up into panels (each a part of a larger whole to be imagined by the viewer), because the narrative requirements were not so demanding. The poses of the figures and their draperies echo Hellenic Classicism. Hadrian, Antoninus Pius, and Marcus Aurelius were all Hellenophiles, and it is in their reigns that perhaps the last powerful influence of Classical Greece was felt in Roman art. The figures in the *Sacrificing* relief are cut to ideal proportions, but a considerable Roman realism appears in the details and in such illusionistic

6-71 *Marcus Aurelius Sacrificing*, panel from a triumphal arch dedicated to Marcus Aurelius, late second century A.D. Marble relief, approx. 10′ 6″ high. Palazzo dei Conservatori, Rome.

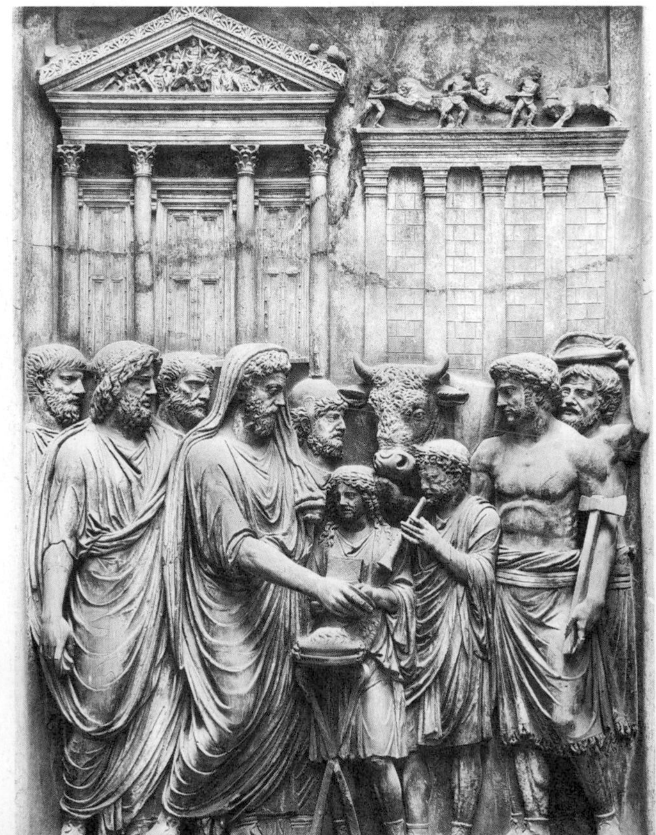

devices as the perspective of the background architecture and the varying depth of relief to show distance. The bland composure of the faces of the Ara Pacis Augustae does not appear; the times have changed and the end of the golden age has come. A kind of brooding solemnity prevails as the grave philosopher-emperor (the sculptor gives us a portrait likeness) prepares the sacrifice that may produce omens of a troubled future for the empire.

PORTRAIT SCULPTURE

Two portraits from Republican times (FIGS. 6-14 and 6-15) already have shown us the Roman aptitude for and skill in the art of portrait sculpture—an expression of the now-familiar Roman instinct for the factual. It is scarcely an accident that the historical reliefs just discussed contain portrait figures. Literally thousands of portrait busts have been found from the times of the republic and the empire, and the best are evidence of the important contributions the Romans made to portrait art. Two tendencies of style determine the production of portrait sculpture: the *verism* of the republic, and the Hellenizing *idealism* of the empire. In the later period, the tendencies alternate and sometimes converge. Significantly, members of the lower social classes generally are portrayed realistically in all periods, but official portraits of the ruling class tend to shift between realism and idealism, depending in part on the general style of the period, the preference of the sitters, or the artist's own interest in the psychological probing of personality.

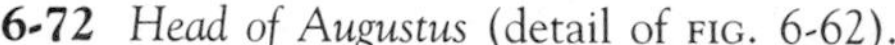

6-72 *Head of Augustus* (detail of FIG. 6-62).

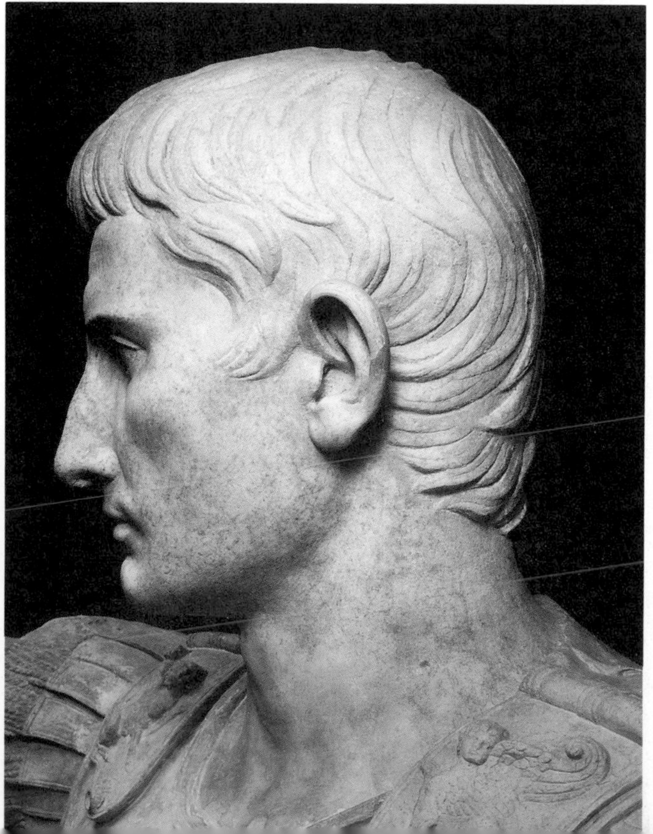

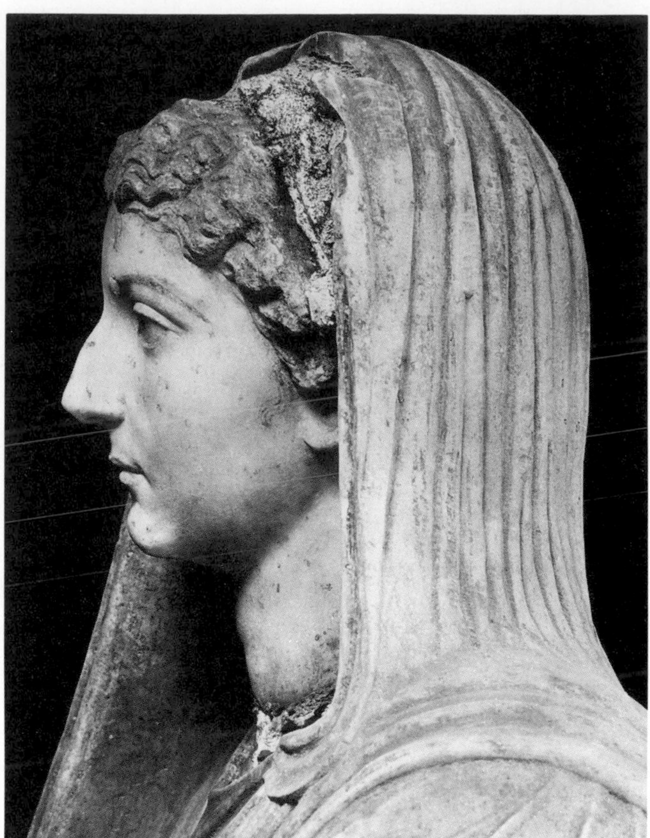

6-73 *Livia* (second wife of Augustus), c. A.D. 20. Marble, head approx. 15″ high. Antiquarium, Pompeii.

A portrait of the emperor Augustus (FIG. **6-72**), a detail of the Primaporta figure (FIG. 6-62), which can be profitably compared with earlier portraits from the republic, is very subtly idealized without any apparent loss of likeness. The hair, adhering closely to the skull, is reminiscent of the fifth-century B.C. Greek style and reflects Augustus's Classical taste prevailing over Hellenistic realism. We have met the Classicism of the Augustan Age in the Ara Pacis Augustae and have pointed out that Vergil's *Aeneid,* deliberately imitating Homer and commissioned by Augustus himself, reveals the same Classical spirit in its form. Livia, the second wife of Augustus and mother of the emperor Tiberius, is shown in a portrait bust as the tactful and elegant woman she is believed to have been (FIG. **6-73**). The same Augustan idealization and the same retention of the likeness are evident here. The lifelike quality is enhanced by effective use of color, much of which is preserved in the hair, eyes, and lips.

The emperor Vespasian, successor to Nero, reigned from A.D. 69 to 79. The portrait bust of this first emperor of the Flavian line (FIG. **6-74**) forcefully reveals the veteran general who had fought successfully in all parts of the empire. Vespasian was a man of simple origin and simple tastes, who desired to return to

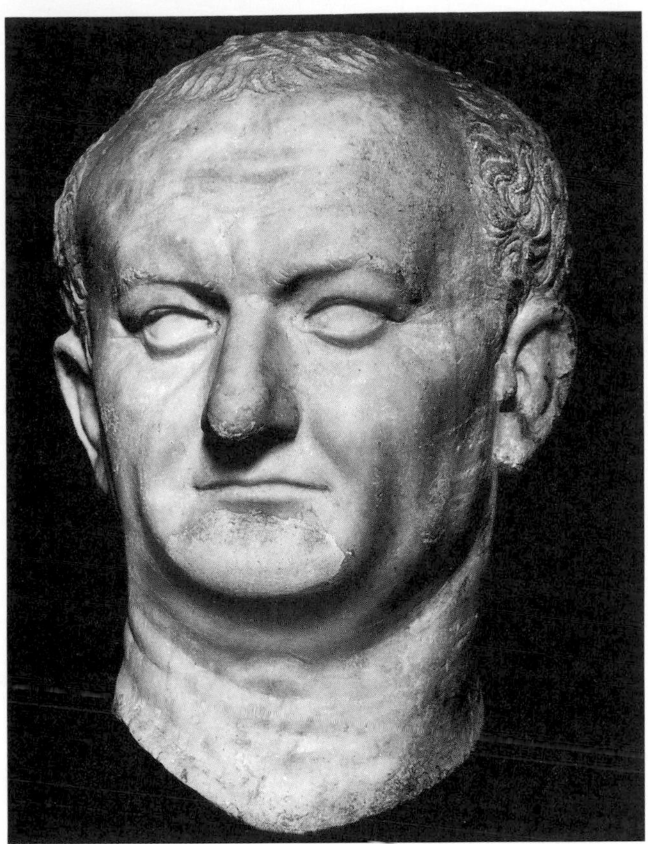

6-74 *Vespasian*, c. A.D. 75. Marble, life size. Museo Nazionale Romano, Rome.

Republican simplicity after Nero's extravagant misrule. He was a good administrator—honest, shrewd, and earthily humorous. These qualities speak from his portrait. The artist has attempted no flattery. Quite possibly, Vespasian himself discouraged the sculptor from idealizing too much; he preferred the blunt, rugged aspect of the soldier. From the portrait, we can understand the active man whose care was restoration of the empire and who is reported to have said on his deathbed, "An emperor should die standing." The portrait, although a little subtler in characterization, is almost Republican in its directness.

The *Portrait of a Lady* (FIG. **6-75**) from the reign of Domitian (A.D. 81–96) is a departure from the usually rather stern portraits of Roman women. This portrait is a rare masterpiece in its inimitable union of sensitive beauty, noble elegance, and lucid intelligence. The elaborate coiffure, its corkscrew curls punched out by the adroit use of a drill, stands in striking textural contrast to the delicate, softly modeled features; the technique and effort needed to reproduce the luminosity and glow of actual flesh recall the art of Praxiteles. This truly regal work, exemplar of Roman portrait art at its height, can be instructively compared with the head of *Queen Nefertiti* (FIG. 3-39), done in the subtle Amarna style of Egypt.

Portraits of great persons who exhibit ambivalent qualities, such as that of Pompey (FIG. 6-15), are perhaps more interesting to us than portraits of persons of more uniform character. This quality of ambivalence was especially true of the emperor Hadrian (FIG. **6-76**). We approach his portrait informed by the account of his personality given by an ancient biographer. Hadrian, beyond all other Roman emperors a lover of Greek art and culture and himself a skillful artist and architect, poet, scholar, and writer, is thus described:

> He was grave and gay, affable and dignified, cruel and gentle, mean and generous, eager for fame yet not vain, impulsive and cautious, secretive and open. He hated eminent qualities in others, but gathered round him the most distinguished men of the state; at one time affectionate towards his friends, at another he mistrusted and put them to death. In fact he was only consistent in his inconsistency [*semper in omnibus varius*]. Although he endeavored to win the popular favor, he was more feared than loved. A man of unnatural passions and grossly superstitious, he was an ardent lover of nature. But, with all his faults, he devoted himself so indefatigably to the service of the state, that the period of his reign could be characterized as a "golden age."*

*Aelius Spartianus, in *Scriptores Historiae Augustae* (Cambridge, MA: Harvard University Press, Loeb Classical Library, rev. 1985).

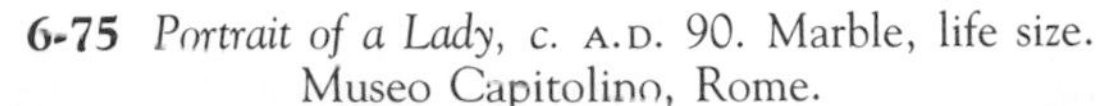

6-75 *Portrait of a Lady*, c. A.D. 90. Marble, life size. Museo Capitolino, Rome.

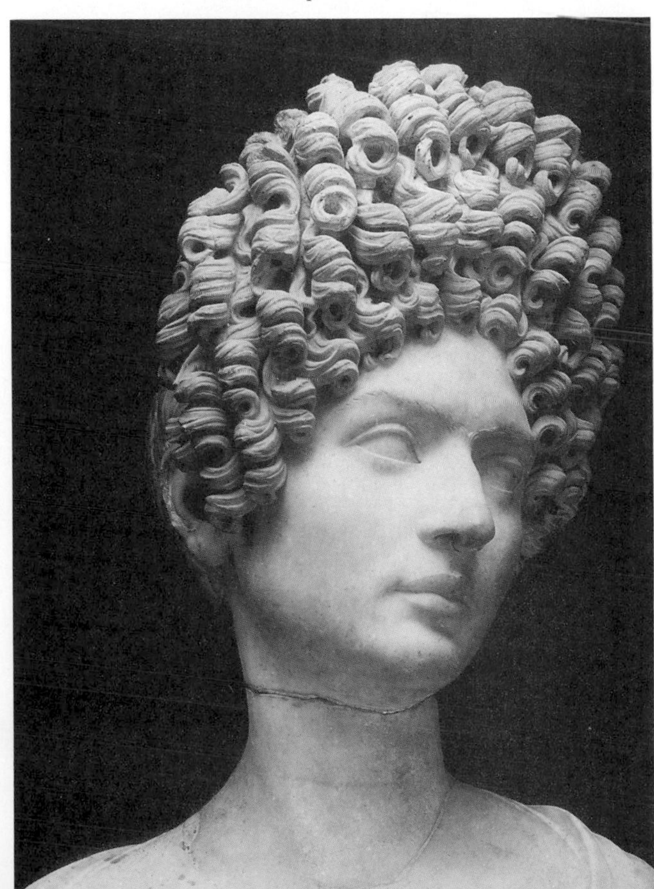

We might bring also to the contemplation of his portrait the poem, long famous, that Hadrian wrote at the end of his life:

> Charming, fleeting, little soul,
> My body's guest and comrade,
> Where now will you go
> Naked, pallid, unmoving
> Never again to play?

In this portrait (FIG. 6-76), *Hadrian* affects the Greek coiffure, in form much like the Early Classical ringlets of the *Apollo* from the Temple of Zeus at Olympia (FIG. 5-40). Perhaps inspired by portraits of Pericles, the artist also has adopted the Greek beard, abandoning the age-old tradition of the clean-shaven face. From this point on, most Roman emperors would be presented bearded. The head is idealized, but with restraint; the features are a little regularized and retouched, perhaps, but not so as to interfere with the likeness. A certain ambiguity and inscrutability shadows the face, but when we know a little about Hadrian, we are prepared for this.

6-76 *Hadrian,* c. A.D. 120. Marble, approx. 16" high. Museo Ostiense, Ostia.

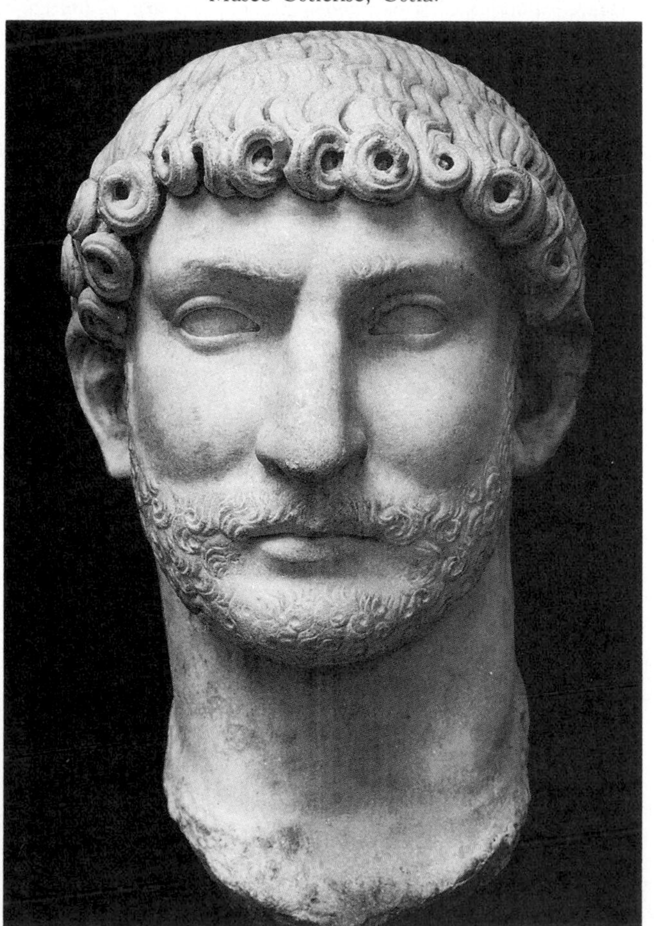

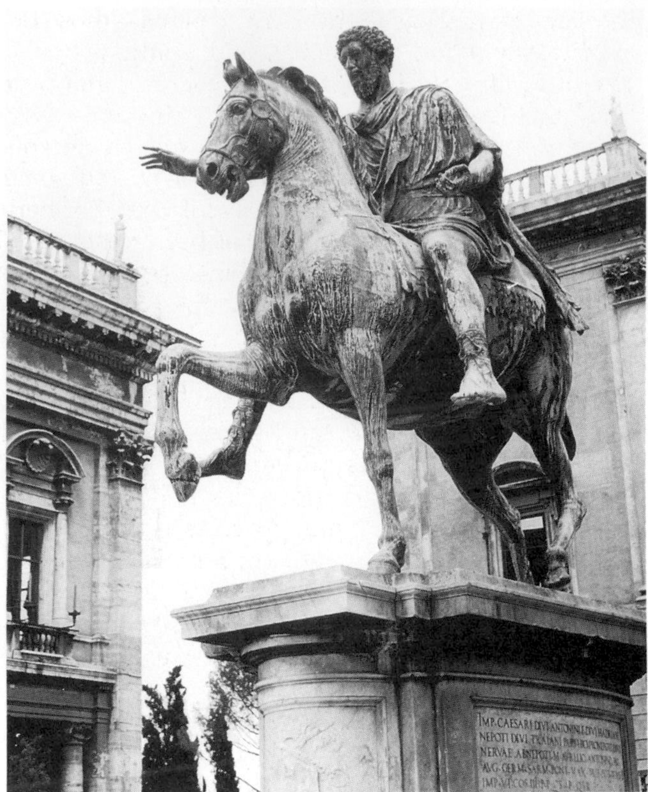

6-77 Equestrian statue of Marcus Aurelius, Capitoline Hill, Rome, c. A.D. 165. Bronze, over life size.

The last emperor of the great imperial line that included Trajan and Hadrian was the Stoic Marcus Aurelius. We have touched on his philosophy in looking at the Faiyum portrait (FIG. 6-40) of a man whose serenely gentle and reflective face manifests the emperor's philosophy. A great equestrian, bronze, portrait statue of Marcus Aurelius (FIG. **6-77**) has survived from the ancient world, unique in that it *did* survive, for there are no other examples of what must have been a statue type popular with the Roman emperors. (Medieval Christians probably melted the statues down for their bronze, because they were impious images from the pagan, demonic world of the Caesars. Some believe that the Christians mistook the statue of Marcus Aurelius for that of the first pro-Christian emperor, Constantine, and that is why it escaped destruction.) The emperor, whom we have seen earlier in his role as head priest, with his toga drawn over his head (FIG. 6-71), is portrayed in the equestrian statue exercising his office as commander of the legions, perhaps passing before the people. His gesture here is magisterial, benignly authoritative, and much like a later papal blessing. It conveys at once the awesome and universal significance of the Roman *imperium,* the almost godlike emperor presiding over the whole world. Yet, at closer view, we see the same features as in the sacrifice panel—those of a man calmly aloof, meditative, and a little resigned. The magnificent, high-stepping charger, the warhorse mettlesome and impatient with the tameness of the parade, breathes hotly through dilated nostrils. This superb bronze was the inspiration, and sometimes the despair, of Renaissance sculptors. Formerly placed on the Capitoline Hill (it has been removed for restoration), this authentic, ancient centerpiece of Michelangelo's great architectural design (see Chapter 17), represents, as does no other single object, the lost authority of the Roman Empire.

After the rule of Marcus Aurelius, the downward course of the empire became precipitous, although not at once; Septimius Severus held it level for a while. His son Caracalla (FIG. **6-78**), under whom the great baths named after him progressed toward completion, was a brutal man, murderer of his own brother. He reigned briefly (A.D. 211–217), and his murder grieved no one. Edward Gibbon writes of him: "Caracalla was the common enemy of mankind." To render his violent traits, the sculptor had to return to realism. We find a burly, suspicious, almost snarling man, more a cutthroat than an emperor, a man who could scarcely be more the opposite of Marcus Aurelius. Significantly for what was to follow—the military anarchy of the third century, when the "barracks emperors" were set up (and pulled down) by the army—Caracalla pursued the tyrant's rule that if one has the loyalty of the army, one need not consider the people. His soldiers, however, were not wary enough to protect him from the dagger of an assassin, and his death was the model death of the tyrant, a form repeated again and again throughout the terrible third century. "Such," writes Gibbon, "was the end of a monster who disgraced human nature." Yet Michelangelo was later to base his noble bust of Brutus on this bust of Caracalla.

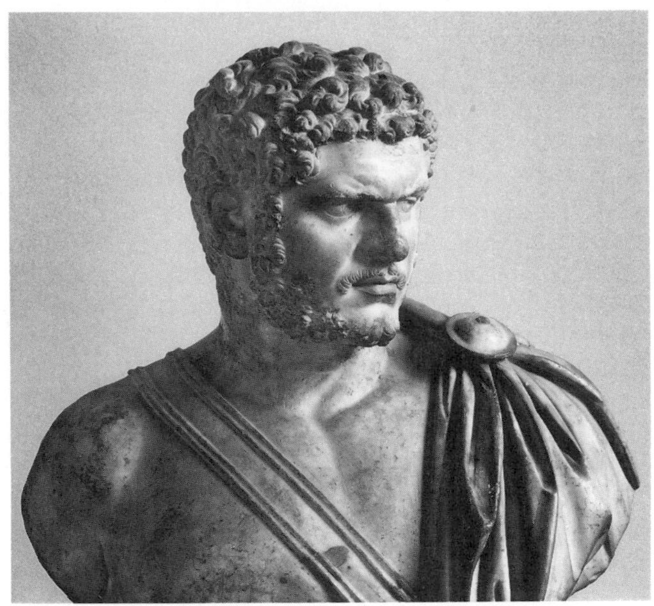

6-78 *Caracalla,* c. A.D. 215. Marble, life size. Vatican Museums, Rome.

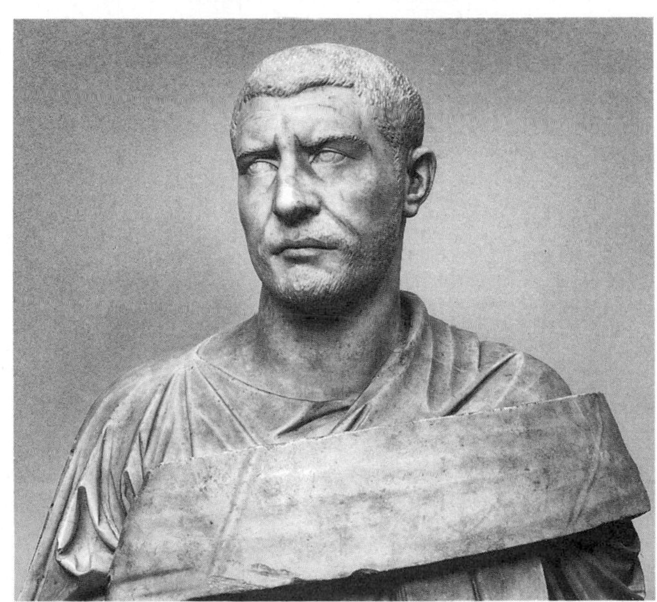

6-79 *Philip the Arab,* A.D. 244–249. Marble, life size, Vatican Museums, Rome.

Internal unrest, combined with attacks on frontiers by the new Sassanian line of Persian kings in the east and German tribes in the north, brought the empire to the verge of collapse. In the space of fifty years, some twenty barracks emperors were exalted and then assassinated by factions of the army. This created anguish and foreboding throughout the empire, which were curiously reflected in numerous portraits, including that of a barracks emperor himself, *Philip the Arab* (FIG. **6-79**). Philip became emperor after having his predecessor, Gordianus, executed. In considering his portrait, it is useful to know something about the close of his career. An adventurer himself, he knew that he was surrounded by adventurers (especially in the army), who were ready to follow his example. Faced with a revolt, Philip appointed a brave and intelligent aristocrat, Decius, to put it down and to calm the army. The army accepted Decius as its leader on condition that he agree to depose Philip or be put to death himself. Decius then led the best of the army against Philip, who was slain, and Decius became emperor. The portrait of Philip shows the face of a man who knows he is utterly without security. Fear, distrust, and suspicion work the face into a mask of guilt and anxiety. The brow is furrowed; the deep-set eyes shift sideways. The eye pupils are carved, an innovation that focuses on the psychic state. The hair is cropped short; the beard is stubbly. The short, nervous chisel strokes adapt to the nervous mood. (In the works of later sculptors, these strokes would become increasingly abrupt and schematic, leading to the geometric patterning of the fourth century.) But it is the face, with its terrible tensions, that rarely had been seen before in the history of art. From the Archaic masks, we come at last, in the third century A.D., to a face so "modern" in what it reflects of trouble that we experience a shock of recognition. Both the ideal and the real in Roman sculpture have been replaced with something new, *expression,* wherein the sculptor is concerned first of all with expressing an emotional state—either the subject's or the artist's, or perhaps both.

THE LATE EMPIRE

The anarchy of the third century A.D., when at one time as many as eighteen claimants struggled for the throne and it seemed as if the empire would be divided into a number of small states, was brought to an end by a vigorous leader, Diocletian, in A.D. 285. Diocletian (A.D. 284–305) saw the impossibility of ruling a vast empire alone, given the continual German and Persian attacks in the north and east and countless revolts in the provinces. He restored political order by dividing authority among four officials, the *tetrarchs,* appointing himself as one of them. Diocletian appointed a coruler called, like himself, "augustus," and each of the two "augusti" then adopted an assistant of slightly lower rank, the "caesar." One augustus and one caesar ruled in the east; the other pair ruled in the west. Although political control was restored, a fatal precedent was set for the division of authority within the Roman Empire.

Constantine (A.D. 324–337) did away with Diocletian's system and ruled alone. He also instituted the practice of dividing the empire, like personal property, among the emperor's sons—a crippling, divisive custom that was to last into the Middle Ages. Even more divisive was Constantine's founding of a city he named after himself (Constantinople, now Istanbul, on the site of the ancient Greek city of Byzantium), which led inevitably to the decline of the city of Rome and the shift of imperial emphasis to the east. Byzantium gives its name to the later civilization of the eastern Roman Empire.

After the reign of Theodosius, at the end of the fourth century, the empire was irreparably divided, although the emperors of the east, at Constantinople, continued for centuries to claim the west. These claims were made in vain; in the fifth century, the barbarians took power in the west—the Ostrogoths in Italy, the Vandals in Africa, the Visigoths in Spain, the Franks and Burgundians in Gaul, and the Angles and Saxons in Britain. These Romano-Germanic petty kingdoms succeeded to the once centralized and almost universal power of Rome and became the predecessors of the nations of modern Europe. The eastern half of the empire lived on as the Byzantine Empire for a thousand years, until the conquest of Constantinople by the Turks in 1453.

Architecture

Developments in architecture powerfully express the ebbing authority of the Roman Empire. In the days of Augustus and Trajan, the "walls" of the empire had been the might of the legions on its remotest borders; behind the bulwark of the legions, a great empire could rest secure. But late in the third century, the emperor Aurelian was forced to girdle the city of Rome itself with walls, turning it into a fortress; Rome became what it had been at the start, a walled city, now dwindling into the ghost of an empire. Aurelian's insecurity was shared by Diocletian, who, unlike Tiberius in the first century A.D., could not afford to retire to the undefended paradise of Capri (ancient Capreae). Instead, about A.D. 300, he built, for his retirement, a well-fortified palace (FIGS. **6-80** and **6-81**) on the Dalmatian coast at Split (ancient Spalatum) in Yugoslavia. The complex, which covers about ten acres, is laid out like a Roman colonial city. The plan is almost identical to the plan of Timgad (FIG. 6-44), although its military aspects, such as the fortified walls and tower-flanked gates, appear to be even more prominent in comparison with the relatively small scale of a palace. Such a fusion of military and imperial palace architecture strikingly reflects the changed life-style of the Late Imperial period, when increased centralization and standardization infused all levels of Roman society, private citizens and public officials alike, with militaristic thinking. In architecture, such standards of military behavior as obedience and subordination are reflected in symmetry, axiality, and unity of direction, all apparent in the plan of the Split palace.

The broad, columned street leading toward the palace constitutes a ceremonial axis that dominates the architectural layout. All other architectural features are arranged symmetrically around this wide avenue, which leads into a large columned (peristyle) court (FIG. **6-82**) fronting the entrance of the palace proper. Designed as a three-bay Classical portico, the façade is marked by an unusual and quite un-Classical feature: over the central bay, the entablature arches

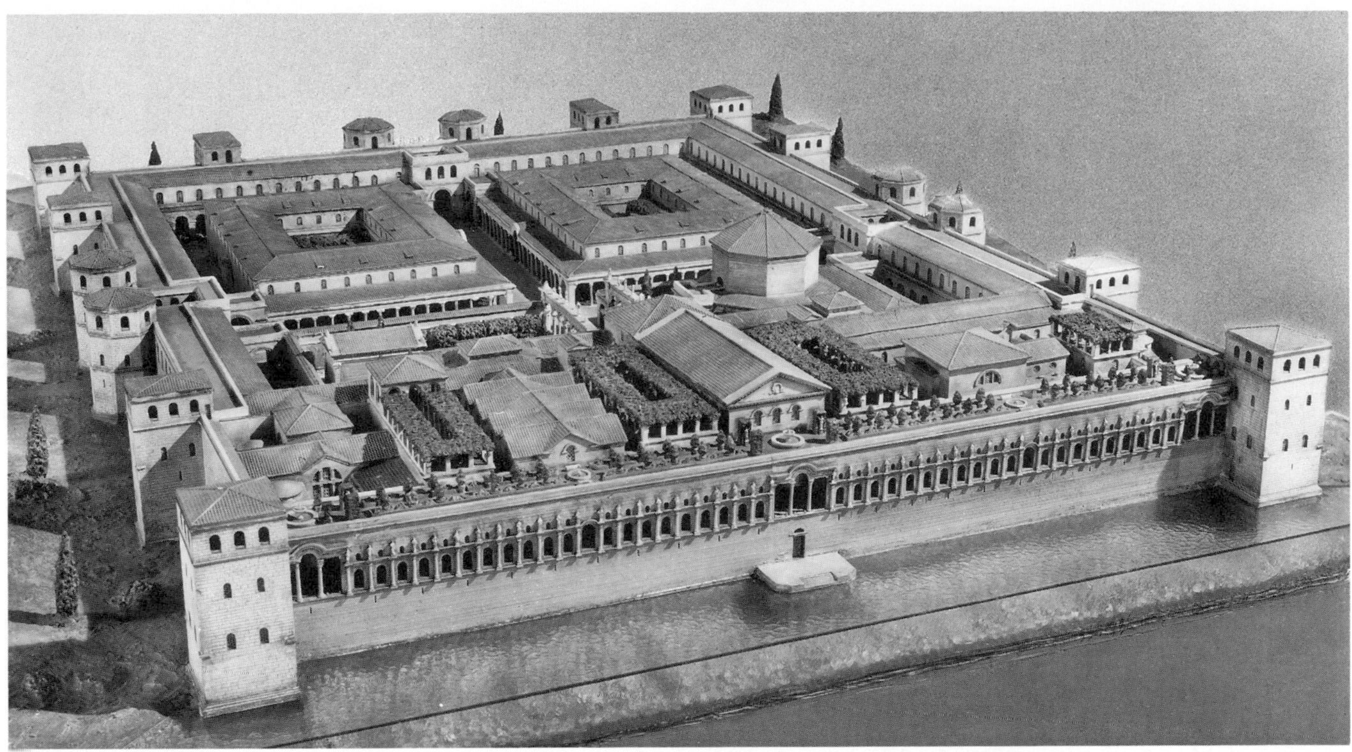

6-80 Palace of Diocletian, Split (ancient Spalatum), Yugoslavia, A.D. 300–305. Museo della Civilta Romana, Rome. (Reconstruction by E. HEBRARD.)

6-81 Plan of the palace of Diocletian, Split. Original Roman masonry is shown in solid black.

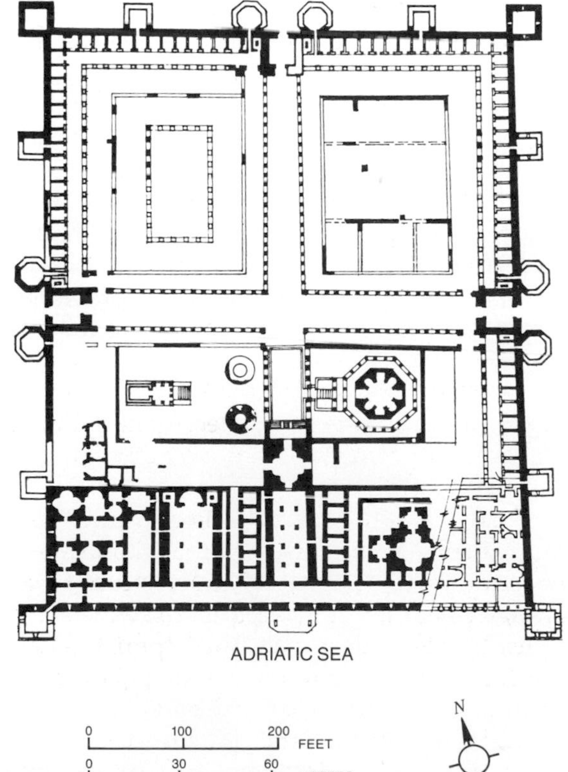

upward into the triangular face of the pediment. Formally, the purpose of this "broken pediment" undoubtedly was to emphasize the central axis of the design. Symbolically, it became the "gable of glorification," under which the emperor appeared before those who gathered in the peristyle court.

The feature of the broken pediment had appeared earlier, mostly in the eastern provinces of the Roman Empire. It was found, for example, in the façade of the propylon to the Sanctuary of Jupiter and in the Temple of Venus at Baalbek (ancient Heliopolis) in Syria. It is, to repeat, an un-Classical device that represents a transitional stage between the Classical, column-supported, horizontal entablature and the springing of arches directly from column capitals, as is the case in the flanking colonnades of this same peristyle at Split. (Examples of this direct springing of the arch occur in Pompeian painting of the first century B.C., as well as in the architecture of Hadrian's villa at Tivoli [ancient Tibur].) The process of change from the *trabeated* (post-and-lintel) architecture of Greco-Roman antiquity (and earlier) to the *arcuated* (arch-column) architecture of the Middle Ages began in the first century A.D., and we see it here, in the arcade of the Split palace, in its perfected form and on a grand scale. It is interesting to observe the gradual emergence of arcuated architecture from the Roman

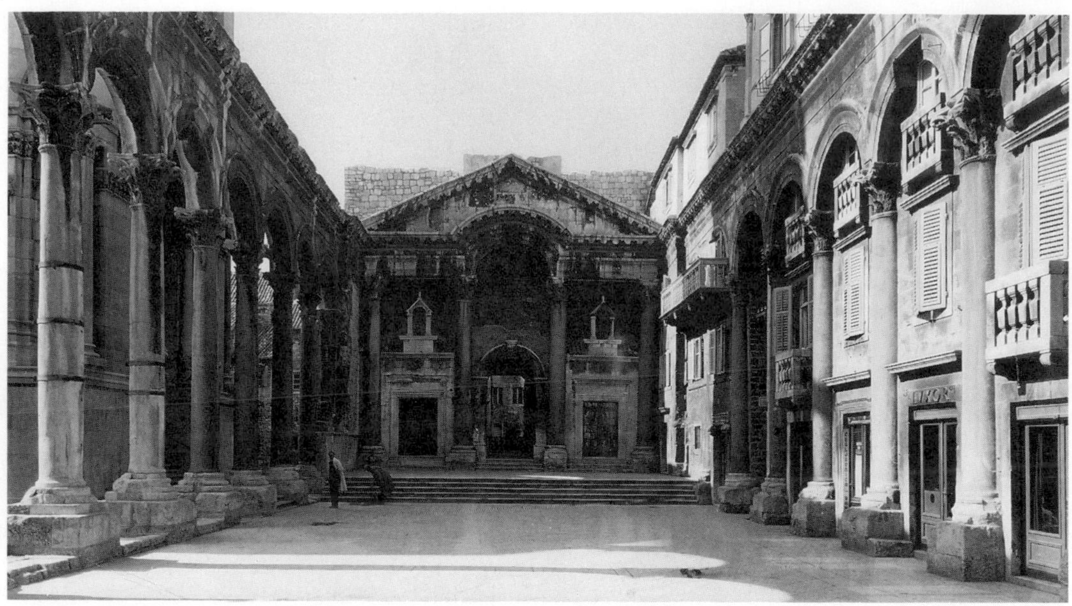

6-82 Peristyle court, palace of Diocletian.

arch order (FIG. **6-83**) and the Roman architect's reluctance to give up the conventional three-part division of the entablature, even once it had become only a blocklike fragment, as in the capital from the Baths of Caracalla (FIG. 6-61). Later, Byzantine architects would retain the entablature block but rid it of the old Classical features, geometrizing it into a flat-sided, trapezoidal, "impost" block (FIG. 7-35).

From early in imperial times, structural changes in Roman architecture continued to be based on Hellenistic developments but were accompanied by experiments in nonstructural design. Throughout the empire, purely ornamental combinations of the elements of Classical architecture could be found. These compositions were often so dramatically elaborate that they have been called "baroque" (see Chapter 19). A striking example is Al-Khazneh, the so-called Treasury, at Petra (FIG. **6-84**), in modern Jordan. This rock-cut structure of imposing scale (over 130 feet in height) has a decorative façade in two stories. The lower story contains a six-columned portico, the columns irregularly spaced, with niches for statuary between the outer pairs. The upper level splits the façade and the pediment to make way for a cylindrically shaped, tholos-like element, which contrasts sharply with the rectangles and triangles of the design. (Exactly this same feature appeared on a painted wall of the second style in one room of the House of the Labyrinth at Pompeii as early as 50 B.C.) The rhythmic alternation of deep projection and indentation creates dynamic patterns of light and shade, an effect of restless oppositions of form. The façade of the Treasury deliberately seems to contradict the ordered regularity we expect of Classical architecture. Its theatricality reflects, and perhaps was derived from, the scene buildings that backed the stages of Greek and Roman theaters, providing an elaborate backdrop for action and spectacle.

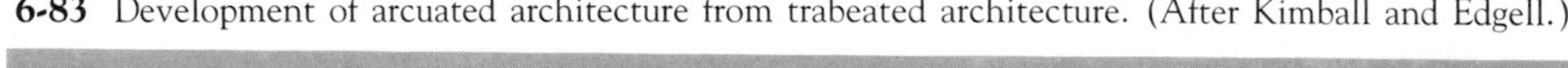

6-83 Development of arcuated architecture from trabeated architecture. (After Kimball and Edgell.)

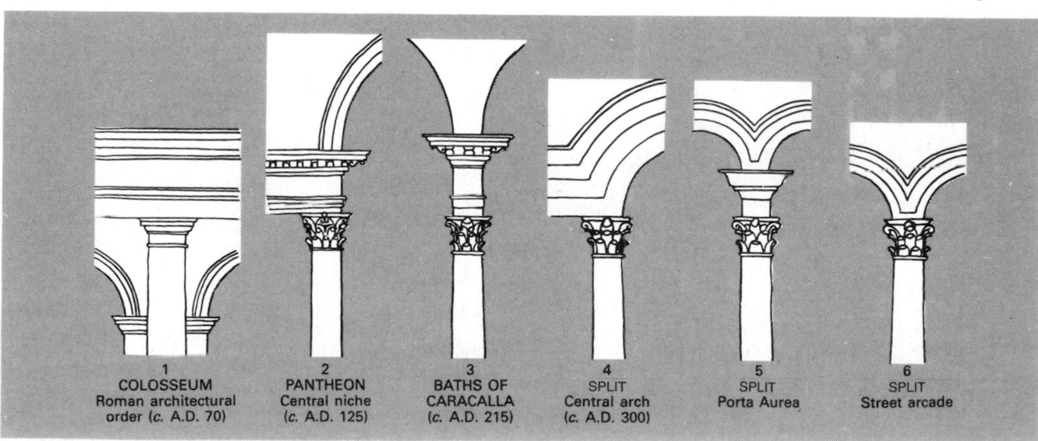

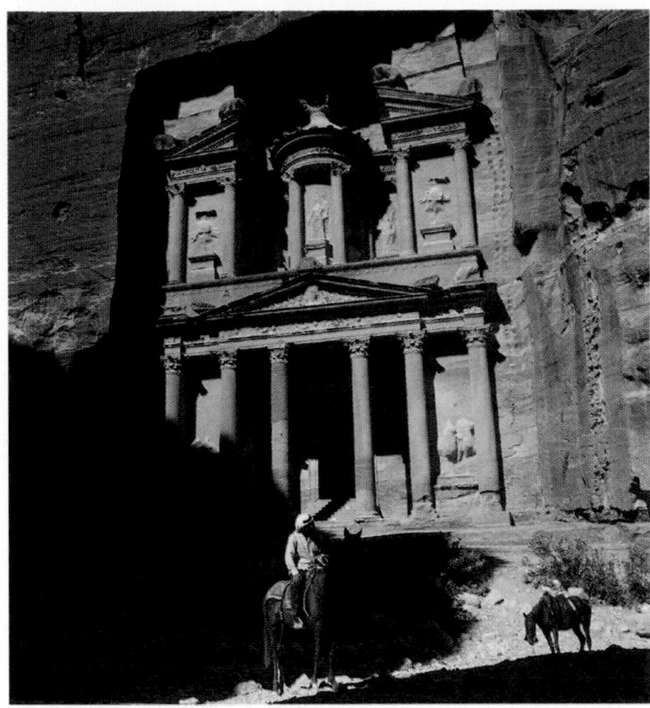

6-84 Al-Khazneh (the Treasury), rock-cut mausoleum, Petra, Jordan, second century A.D.

Symptomatic of the decline of Rome's central power and authority, major building efforts began to shift toward the provinces. After the division of the Roman Empire under Diocletian, who realized that the far-flung imperial holdings could no longer be ruled effectively from Rome, Constantius Chlorus, father of Constantine the Great, became caesar of the western empire and established his residence at Trier (ancient Augusta Trevirorum), West Germany, on the Moselle river. Trier became the largest city in the northwestern sector of the empire.

After being sacked by the Franks and Alemanni in A.D. 275–276, Trier was rebuilt and ringed with defensive walls. The Porta Nigra, or "Black Gate" (FIG. **6-85**), which probably dates between this period and about A.D. 310, was never quite completed. Large enough to be converted into a Christian church later on, it is an outstanding example of a Roman city gate, built not only for defensive purposes, but also for the impression it would make on a visitor, manifesting the might of imperial Rome. The rough, blunt exterior gives it an unintended effect of *rustication,* partly due to the building's unfinished state. Its defensive function, moreover, scarcely would have permitted refined details, and the structure expresses Roman features like the Colosseum-arch order with a heavy, provincial accent.

The Porta Nigra is the north gate of a vast palace complex of some seven hundred acres. At the center of the palace complex stands the audience hall of the palace proper (FIG. **6-86**), which dates from about A.D. 310. Its basic design is quite simple: a rectangular hall measuring about 190 feet long and 95 feet wide, covered by a flat, wooden, coffered ceiling some 95 feet above the floor. Added to the short,

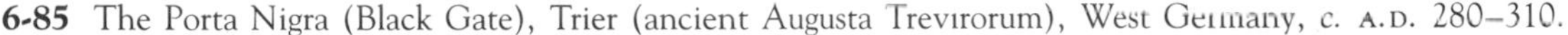

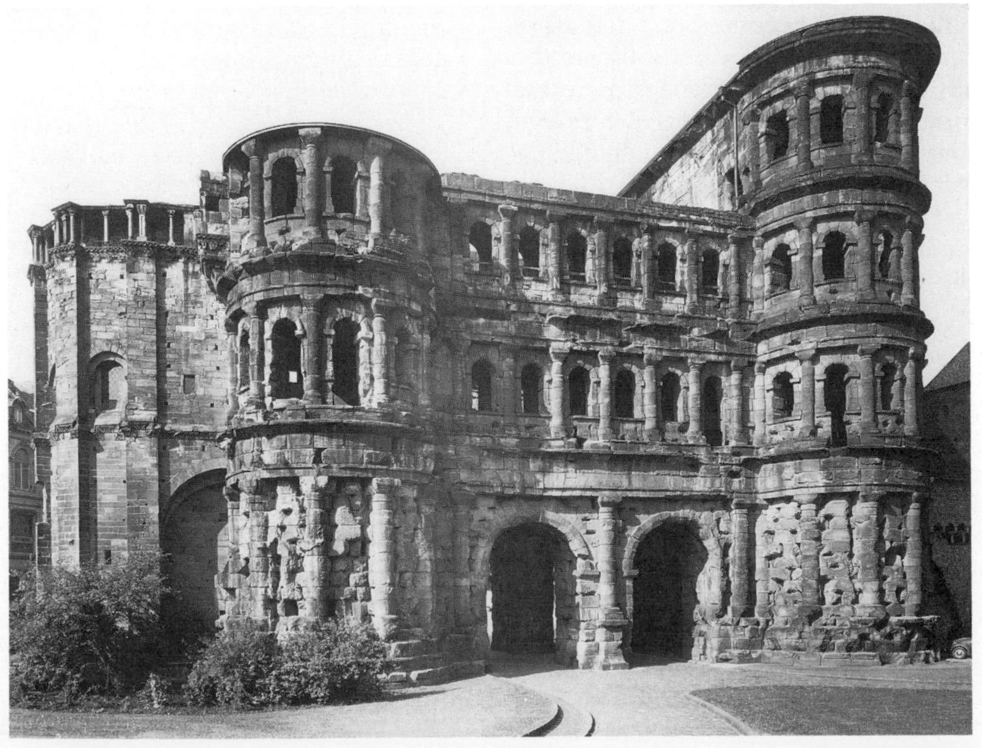

6-85 The Porta Nigra (Black Gate), Trier (ancient Augusta Trevirorum), West Germany, c. A.D. 280–310.

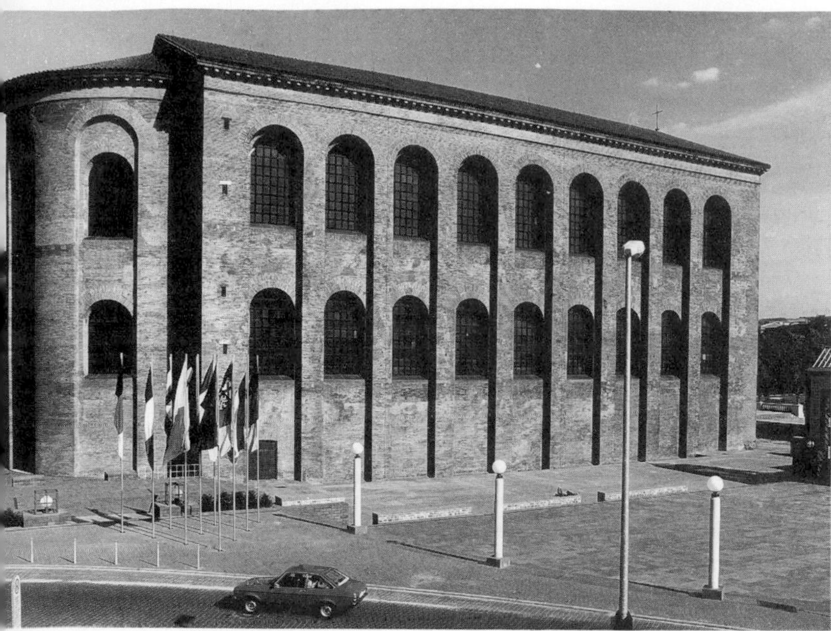

6-86 The Aula Palatina (audience hall of the palace), Trier, West Germany, *c.* A.D. 310.

north side is a semicircular apse, also with a flat ceiling, separated from the main hall by a triumphal arch. Arch and apse originally were decorated with marble incrustation and mosaics to provide a magnificent environment for the enthroned caesar. The interior was brightly lighted through double rows of large, arched windows.

The articulation of the building's exterior with boldly projecting vertical buttresses to create a pattern of alternating voids and solids is a significant feature and one that would become characteristic of much later Roman architecture. The verticality of the building originally was lessened by horizontal timber galleries, which permitted the servicing of the windows. The exterior was stuccoed in gray-white, with windows framed in color. The interior could be heated through a *hypocaust* system (hot air circulating through tubes built into the walls to a height of 24 feet). The growing taste for large windows was due to the development and increasing use of lead-framed panes of window glass, which offered late Roman builders the possibility of giving life and movement to blank exterior surfaces.

The villa at Piazza Armerina in Sicily (FIG. **6-87**) is a fascinating monument of the late Roman Empire and recalls, on a much smaller scale, the intricate planning of Nero's villa-palace, the Domus Aurea. The villa shows that patrons of great wealth still could live the opulent life of the caesars of the golden age. Excavated and studied in very recent times, the villa is still the subject of scholarly debate regarding its date of construction and its ownership; we place it in time between A.D. 310 and A.D. 350 and leave to further study the question of whether its owner was Maxentius, the defeated rival of Constantine, or a multimillionaire with sufficient resources to live in imperial style. The rambling plan displays almost every spatial arrangement and building type in the Roman architectural repertory—porticoes, peristyles, tri-lobed and poly-lobed halls, thermae, a basilica, aqueducts—all arranged along a variety of axes. Although a contrapuntal play of square, round, and elliptical spaces is evident, the effect is quite casual. Many of the elements constitutive of the ecclesiastical architecture of early Christianity are present here in this pagan villa of the late Roman Empire.

Perhaps the most exciting feature of the villa is its 7,000 square feet of floor mosaic. The mosaics, which may be the work of craftsmen from North Africa, provide a compendium of late Roman themes: the hunt, the games, wild and domestic animals, river and forest life, genre scenes, scenes from mythology, allegorical subjects, and the like. A seated female figure, an *Allegory of Africa* (FIG. **6-88**), holds a horn of plenty as she embraces a sacred tree. She is flanked by animals symbolic of the tropical orient—an elephant, a tiger, and the mythical phoenix. Another frieze (FIG. **6-89**) shows briefly attired young women, who often are referred to as the "bikini girls," performing vigorous exercise and displaying trophies. The style of the Piazza Armerina mosaics is not distinguished; it represents a kind of commonplace vernacular familiar throughout the empire. But these mosaics do present an encyclopedia of pagan images drawn from real life or imagination. Many of them will survive, in some transformed state, through the Christian period.

6-87 Plan of the Roman villa at Piazza Armerina, Sicily, *c.* A.D. 310–350.

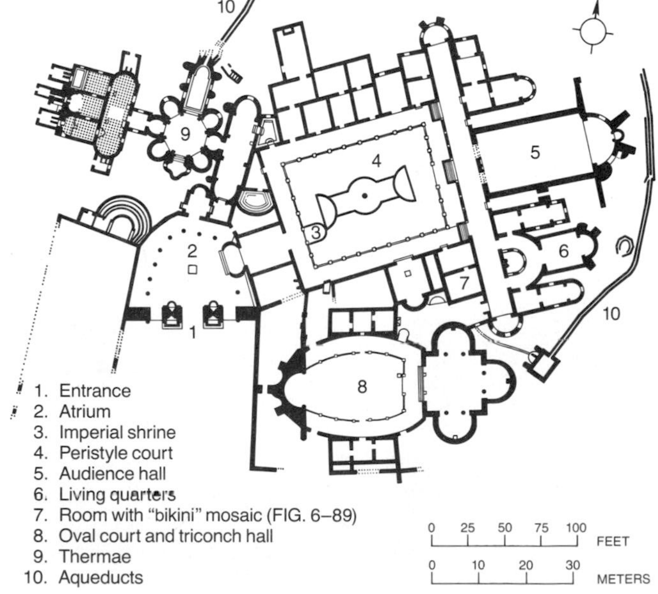

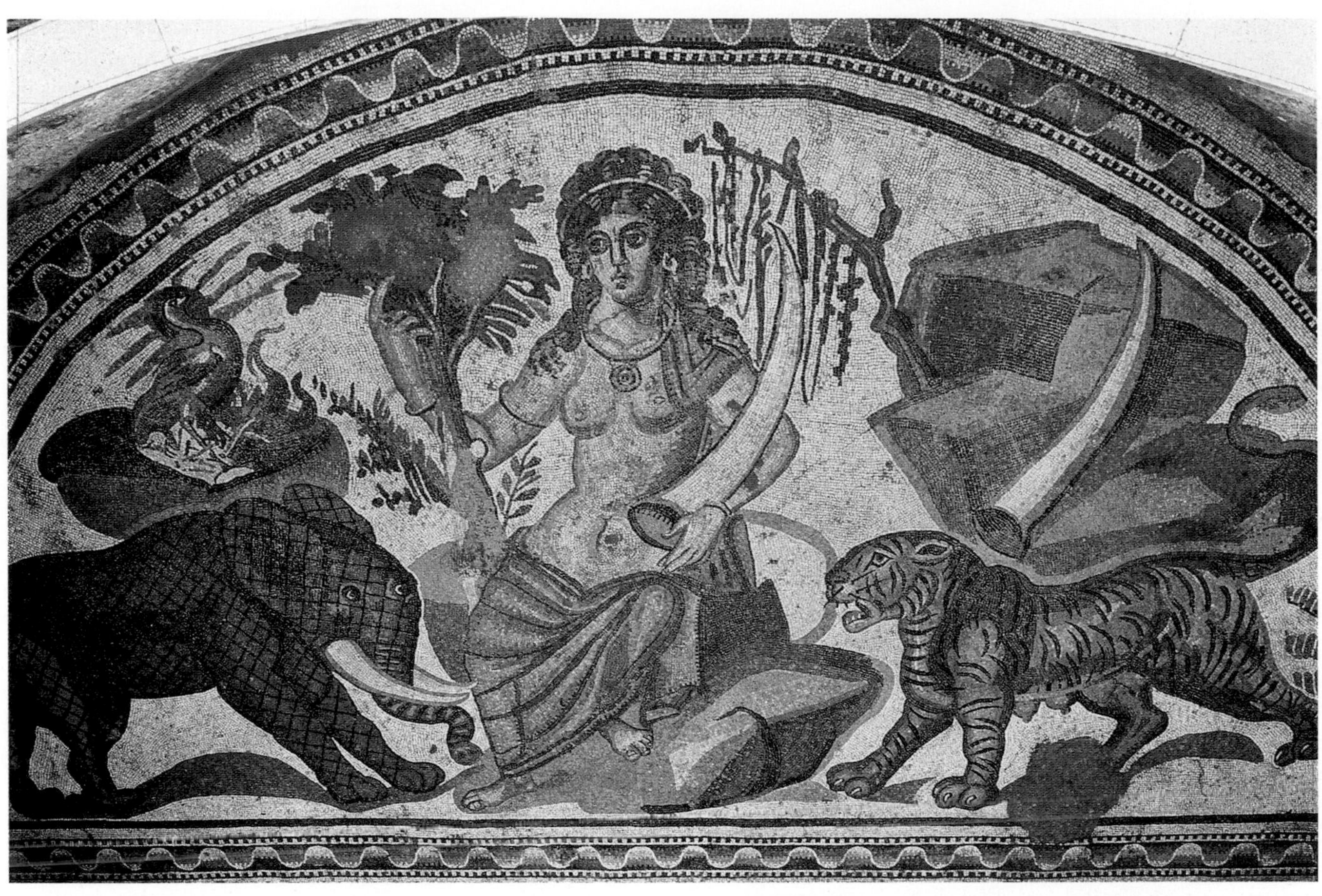

6-88 *Allegory of Africa,* from the Roman villa at Piazza Armerina, Sicily, early fourth century A.D. Mosaic.

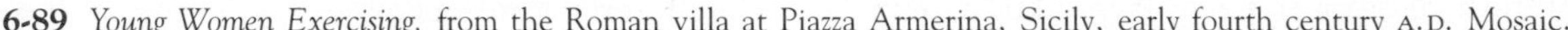

6-89 *Young Women Exercising,* from the Roman villa at Piazza Armerina, Sicily, early fourth century A.D. Mosaic.

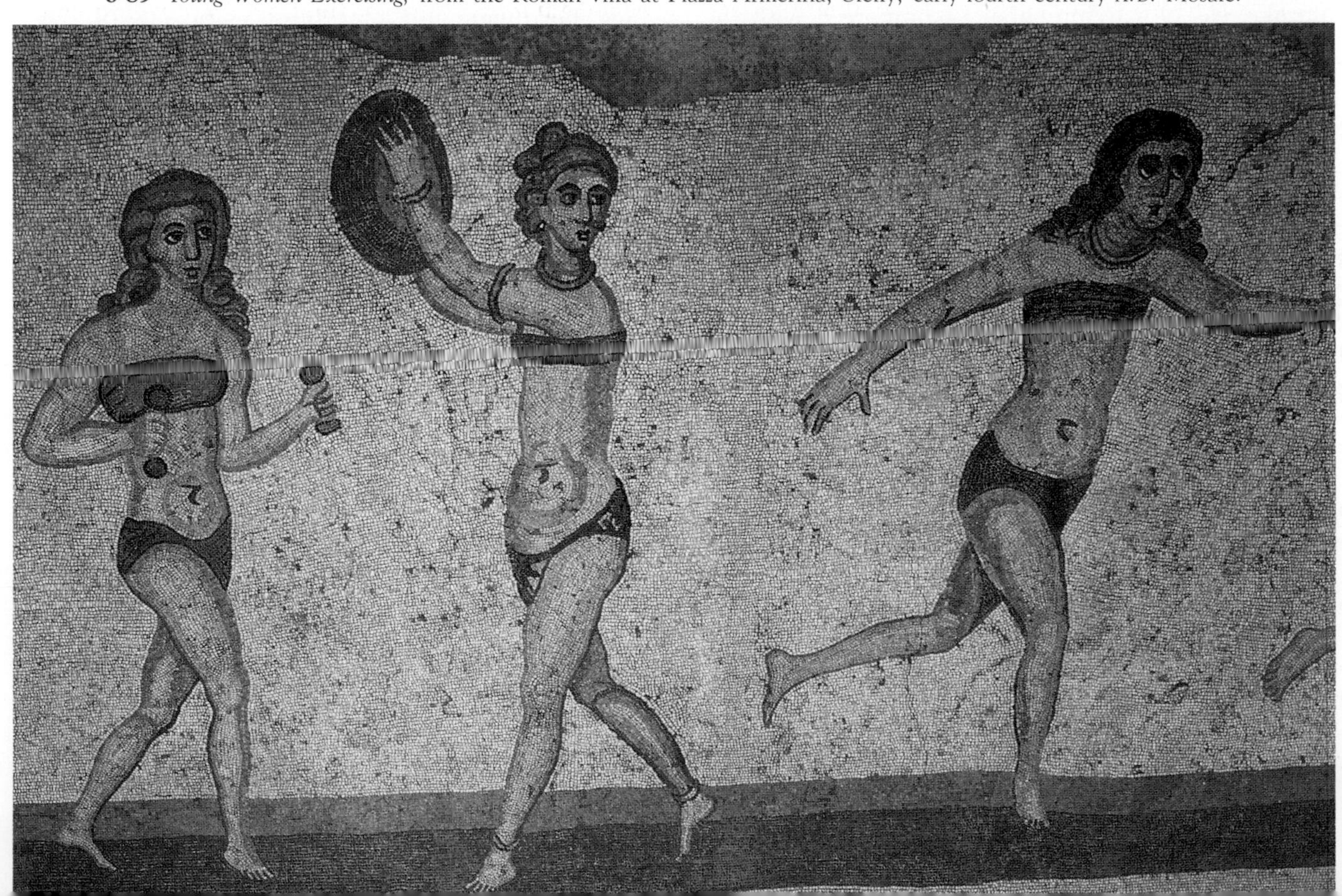

The style of the Piazza Armerina mosaics, in its reduction of modeling tonality to inner line and closed outline, is a denaturalization of Classical naturalism, foreshadowing the more abstract and schematized art of the earlier Middle Ages. But Classical art does not terminate in the fourth century; indeed, we can trace it through more or less authentic survivals and revivals for a thousand years until its commanding reappearance in the Italian Renaissance (Chapters 15–17). Classical themes and images, as well as Classical modes of representation, even though modified in the development of Medieval art by anti-Classical forms and tendencies, recognizably persist. Often, Classical and anti-Classical features, iconographic and stylistic, will exist side by side.

This opposition is strikingly evident as early as the fourth century, when we compare the de-classicizing style of the mosaics of Piazza Armerina with the mature, sophisticated Classicism of a work of art contemporary with them (FIG. **6-90**). A vast Roman floor mosaic recently discovered in Zippori, Israel (1988), and doubtless belonging to another luxurious, Late Imperial villa of the Piazza Armerina sort, yields a detail representing the head of a woman, as yet unidentified. The floor itself is decorated with theatrical masks and emblems of the rites of Dionysos, the ritual source of Classical drama. The fact that the site of the floor is adjacent to a theatrical building suggests that the lovely person represented may have been an actress, rather than a deity or allegorical figure. The beauty of the face is not stylized. It could be a deliberate likeness of a living subject (compare it with the head of the *Allegory of Africa*, FIG. 6-88). The lifelike, sensuous coloration, the slight, graceful tilt of the head, the individualized features, and the intimate glance aimed directly at the viewer, are what we might expect of a personal, quite private portrait made to record a beloved countenance. This portrait is not at all the conventionally idealized mask common in Roman pictorial and decorative design. All the resources of representational technique noted in the figurative art of the Greco-Roman world are brought into play here in the rendering of the head and facial features by subtle, illusionistic modeling. The gradations of light and shade (chiaroscuro) move so lightly across the woman's features as to create a vagueness of expression, an ambiguous and mysterious effect that has prompted the romantic, yet suggestive, comparison of this fascinating face with that of the *Mona Lisa* (FIG. 17-4). In any event, we have before us an unforgettable example of the vitality of Classical naturalism in the very period of its apparent decline, an apparition of its authentic spirit at a time when we would not expect it. Other works of this period yet may be unearthed that might cause us to alter our determination of the time limits that separate the Classical world from the Medieval.

We shall see presently that Classical forms, especially from the art of the Early Empire, will be appropriated by Constantine to give ideological weight and the endorsement of tradition to his own designs. He never lost sight of the political-historical significance of imperial Rome as expressed in the art of its golden age, borrowing and adapting it as he saw fit.

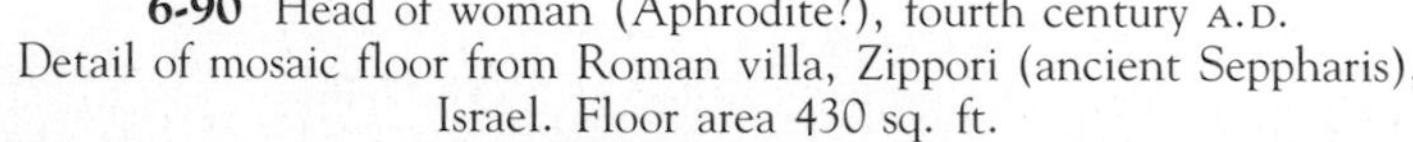
6-90 Head of woman (Aphrodite?), fourth century A.D. Detail of mosaic floor from Roman villa, Zippori (ancient Seppharis), Israel. Floor area 430 sq. ft.

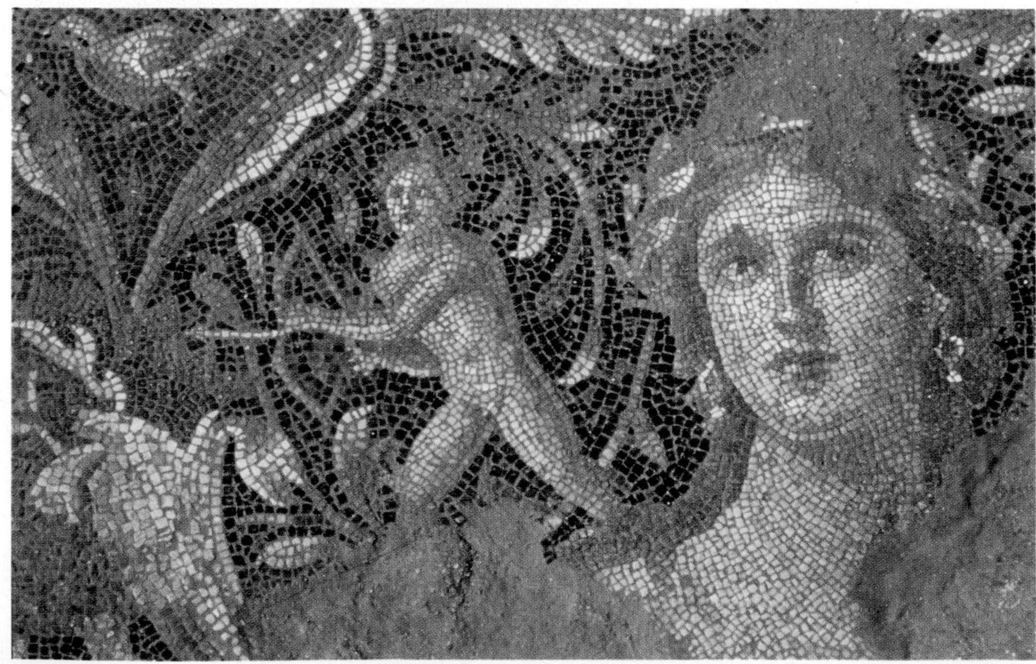

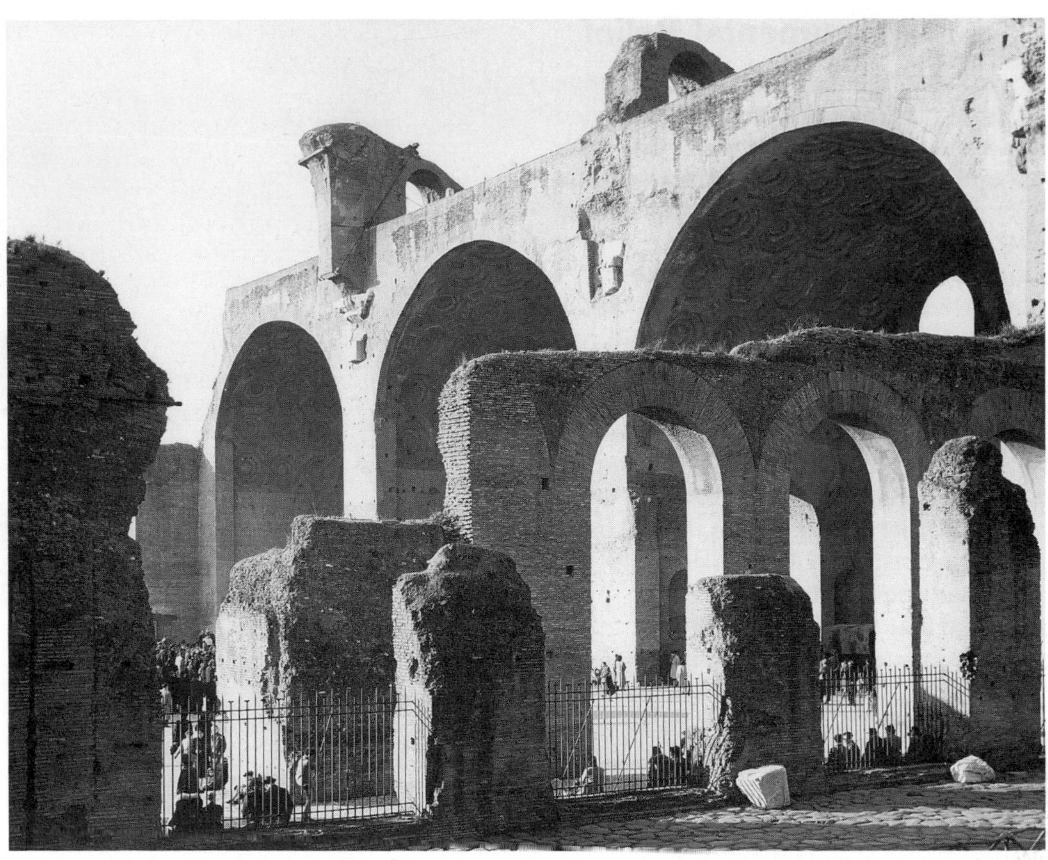

6-91 Basilica of Constantine, Rome, c. A.D. 310–320.

Although he moved the center of the Roman Empire to his new city on the site of ancient Byzantium, Constantine completed some important building projects prior to leaving Rome. One of these was the vast basilica begun between A.D. 306 and A.D. 310 by Maxentius, a rival of Constantine, and finished by Constantine after A.D. 313 (FIGS. **6-91** and **6-92**). All that remains of the building are three barrel-vaulted bays of the north aisle, with brick-faced concrete walls 20 feet thick supporting the coffered vaults. The interior, like that of the Baths of Caracalla (FIG. 6-61), was richly marbled and stuccoed. The ruins, most impressive by virtue of their size and mass, represent only a small part of the original structure, which measured 300 feet long and 215 feet wide and had a groin-vaulted central nave 114 feet high. The reconstruction (FIG. 6-92) shows groin vaults (over the central nave) that permitted lighting of the interior through the ends of the cross vaults, which were left open in a manner similar to clerestory construction. Buttresses reinforced the vault (where the groins join vertical supports) and channeled part of the pressures exerted by the weight of the vault across the aisles and into the outside walls. Remains of the springing of the central vault and of the buttresses can be seen in FIG. 6-91. This late, great building of the ancient world is a monument to the ingenuity of Roman architects. Exemplar of an architecture of space, it is designed on a grand, imperial scale—spacious, fully illuminated, uninterrupted by rows of vertical supports, and constructed of a highly malleable, versatile, fireproof material. In this respect, the Basilica of Constantine fulfills the requirements of architecture in periods of high civilization; not until Hagia Sophia would they be represented so artfully again.

6-92 Reconstruction of the Basilica of Constantine, Rome.

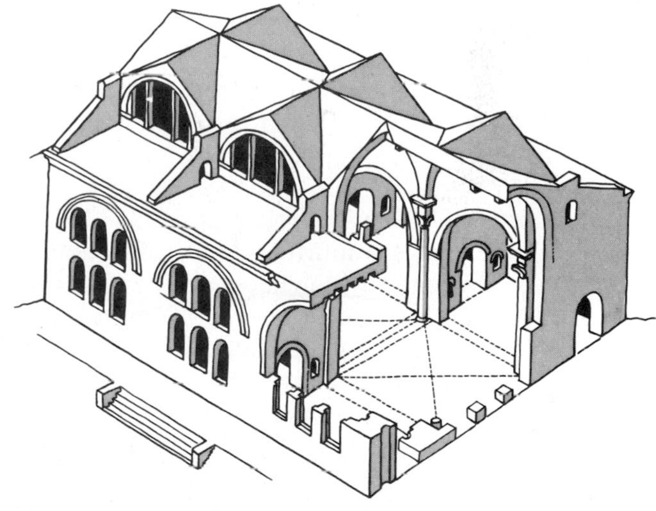

Sculpture and Monumental Relief

The western apse of the Basilica of Constantine contained a colossal statue of the emperor, a seated figure some 30 feet high, the head of which has been preserved (FIG. **6-93**). The figure was composed of a brick core, a wooden torso covered with bronze, and head and limbs of marble. The head alone is 8½ feet high and weighs over eight tons. The characteristics of the earlier busts we have described, in which the real and the ideal alternate or blend, are no longer dominant here. Rather, we note the onset of traits familiar in the earlier, Archaic period: simplification of detail, with a regularizing and a flattening of the features that make the face a rigid mask, uncompromisingly frontal in aspect.* The eyes become enormously large in proportion to the rest of the features, although they still turn slightly to the side and upward in the Constantine head, as in certain third-century portraits like that of *Philip the Arab* (FIG. 6-79). Those unchanging qualities of the permanent form (first seen in Egypt and Mesopotamia, particularly in the representation of kings) once more make their appearance. The personality of the emperor is lost in the immense image of eternal authority. It is his authority, not his personality or his psychic state, that the sculptor exhibits. The colossal size, the Archaic rigidities, the eyes directed at no thing or person of this world—all combine to produce the formula of overwhelming power appropriate to the exalted position of Constantine as absolute despot, which he had certainly become by the early fourth century. It is not surprising that the first of the Christian emperors—in authority, the European equivalent of Ramses II—should be embodied in colossal form like the giant statues of the Egyptian king at Luxor and (formerly) Abu Simbel (FIG. 3-26).

The profound changes in style that occurred at an accelerated pace in the fourth century, introducing the epoch of Medieval art, can be seen in the group of two pairs of figures called *The Tetrarchs*, dating from about A.D. 305 (FIG. **6-94**). Although it is an earlier work than the portrait of Constantine, this piece is a much stronger reflection of the trend toward Archaism. Carved from porphyry (purple marble) in

*The living emperor himself, on formal occasions may have approximated a statue in appearance. H. P. L'Orange quotes the ancient writer Ammianus Marcellinus describing Constantius II, a successor to Constantine, on his entry into Rome: "He looked so stiffly ahead as if he had an iron band around his neck and he turned his face neither to the right nor the left; he was not as a living person, but as an image." L'Orange adds: "This hieratic emperor style, which as divine majesty *(divina maiestas)* in the same way leaves its mark upon palace, image and living reality, can furthermore be traced through Byzantium all the way down to the Holy Russian Empire." *Art Forms and Civic Life in the Late Roman Empire* (Princeton, NJ: Princeton University Press, 1965), pp. 124–25.

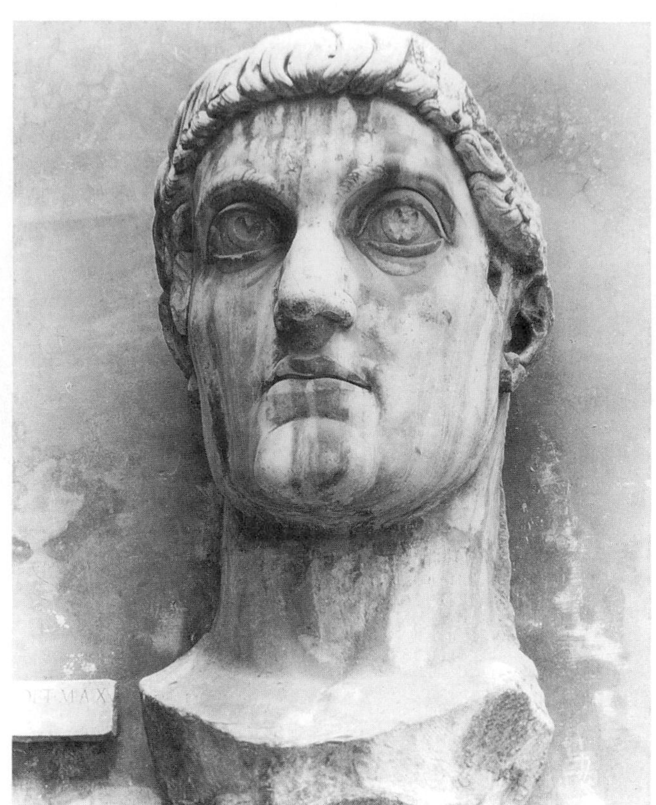

6-93 *Constantine the Great,* c. A.D. 330. Marble, approx. 8′ 6″ high. Palazzo dei Conservatori, Rome.

6-94 *The Tetrarchs,* c. A.D. 305. Porphyry, approx. 51″ high. Piazza San Marco, Venice.

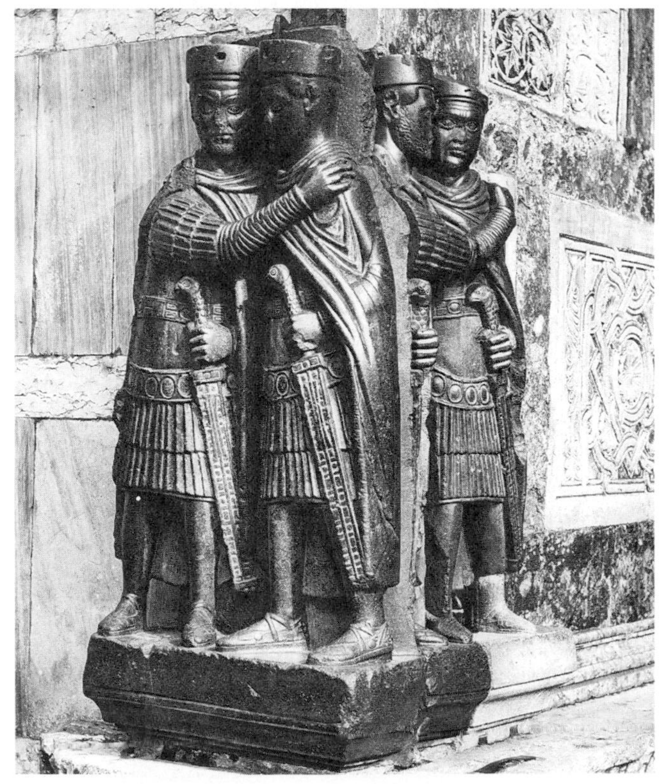

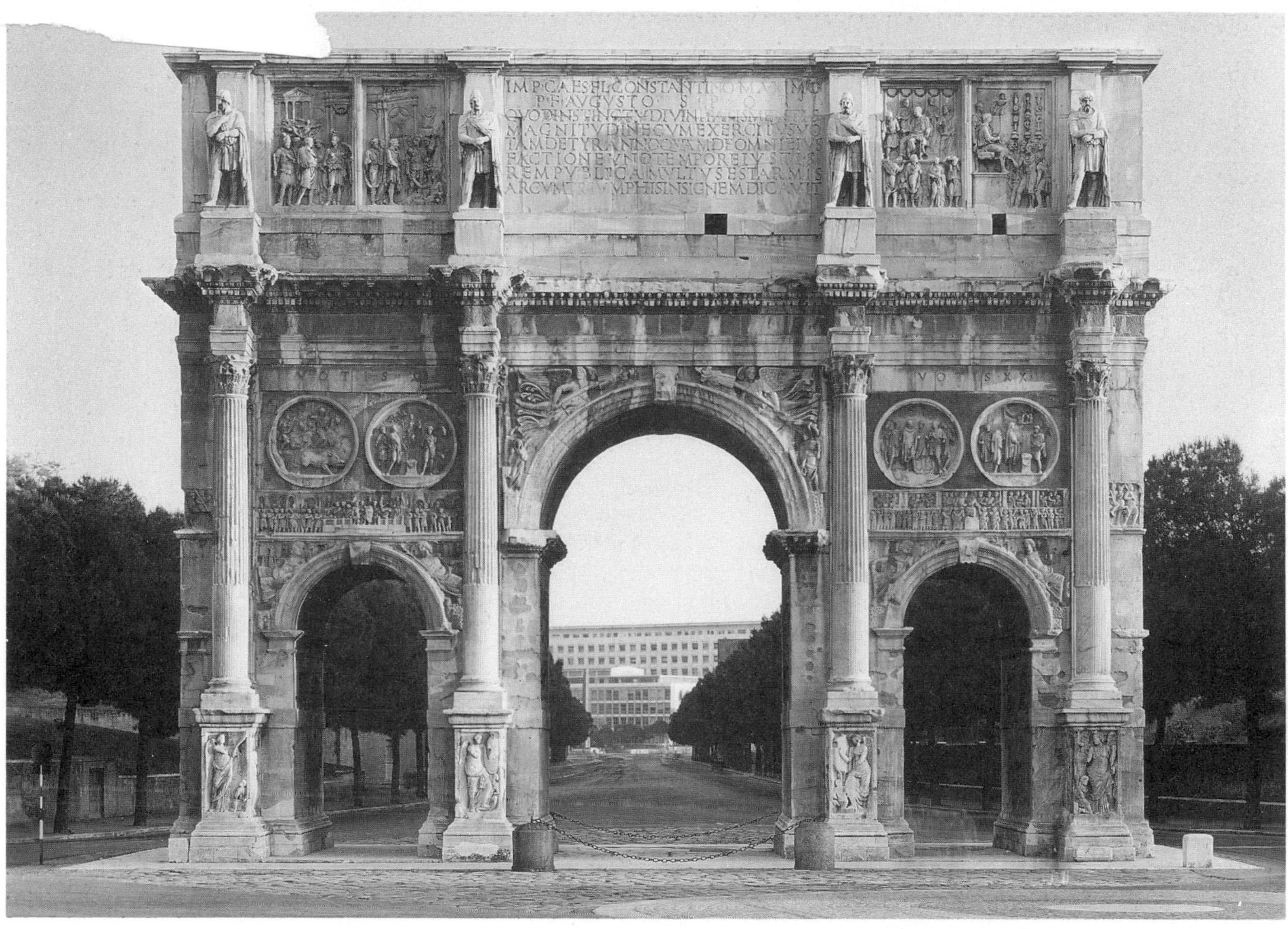

6-95 Arch of Constantine, Rome, A.D. 312–315.

one of the eastern provinces (perhaps Egypt), the group represents the four corulers of the empire: Diocletian and Maximian (the augusti) and Galerius and Constantius Chlorus (the caesars). They embrace each other to symbolize their hoped-for, but unrealized, serenity and concord. They seem, even as they embrace, to be huddled in fear and foreboding, facing some impending disaster, in an expression of the already noted prevalent anxiety of the age. Classical features have disappeared; the figures are not proportioned well, with large heads on squat bodies giving them a gnomelike appearance. The drapery is schematic and the bodies, shapeless. Here, some seven hundred years of Greek and Roman idealism and naturalism terminate. No portrait likenesses are attempted; the masklike faces are the same face in quadruplicate. Individuality and personality already belong to the past.

The waning creative power and technical skill of Rome in the west can be seen in the Arch of Constantine (A.D. 312–315) in the city of Rome (FIG. **6-95**). It is the last great triumphal arch preserved in the declining city. Dedicated to Constantine by a figurehead Senate, it commemorates the ruler's victory over his rival Maxentius, a victory that made Constantine the Great absolute monarch of the Roman Empire. But the occasion failed to stimulate the imagination of his builders. The design of the arch is similar to that of the Arch of Septimius Severus, of the early third century, and most of its decorative sculpture is taken from the monuments of rulers like Trajan, Hadrian, and Marcus Aurelius.

Beneath two Hadrianic medallions, which the emperor has refitted for his own narrative purpose, are reliefs belonging to Constantine's own period (FIGS. **6-96** and **6-97**), which give us an opportunity to estimate the degree of change from the style of the Early Imperial age to a new style that it is not inappropriate to call Medieval. Constantine, surrounded by his entourage, stands at the center of a rostrum, addressing the people. His central position corresponds to the frontality of his colossal statue and expresses a new, rigid formality of composition that increasingly would be based on the fixed positions of

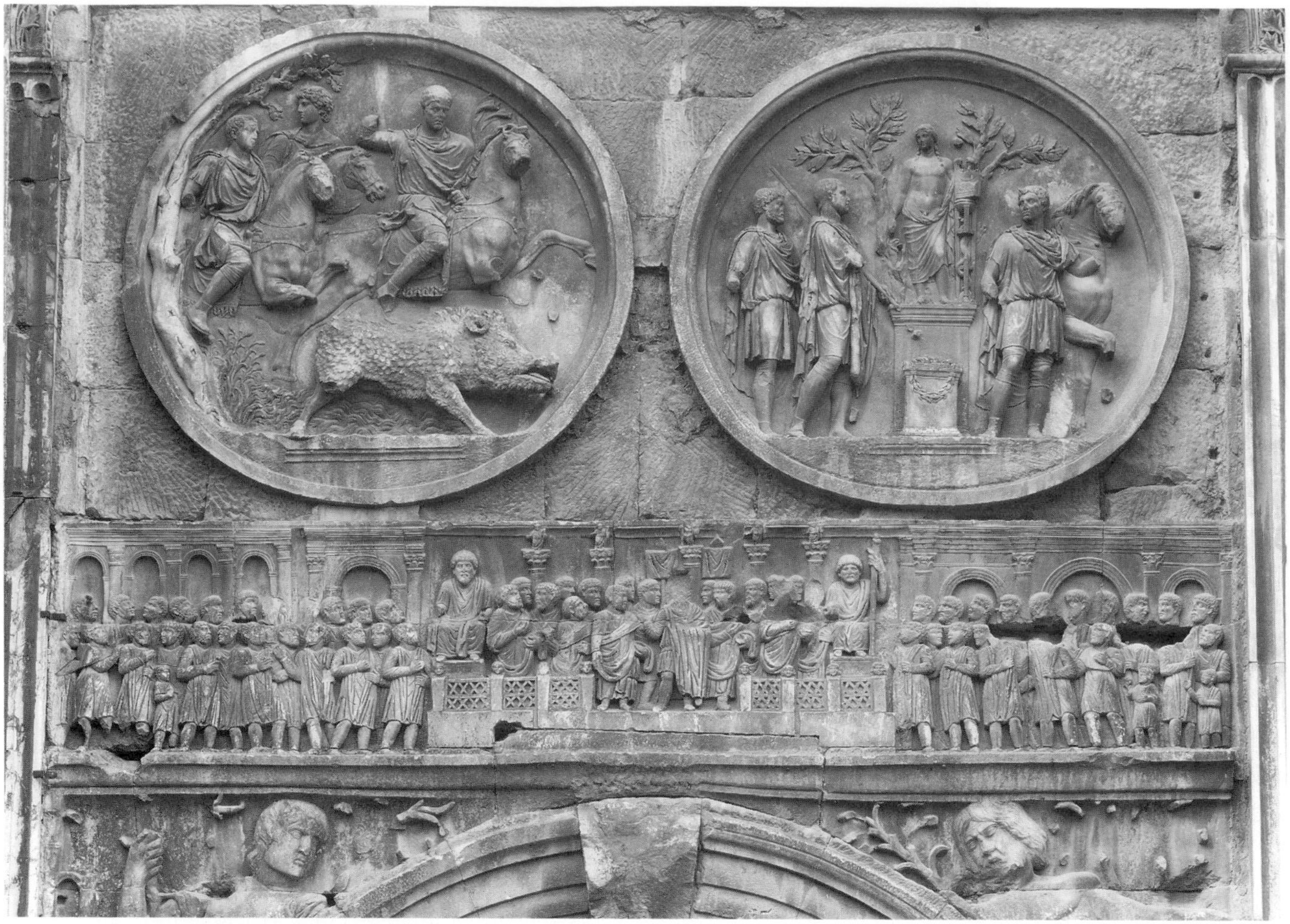

6-96 Reliefs from the Arch of Constantine: medallions, A.D. 117–138; frieze, early fourth century A.D. Marble, frieze approx. 40″ high.

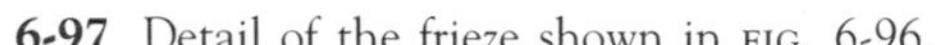

6-97 Detail of the frieze shown in FIG. 6-96.

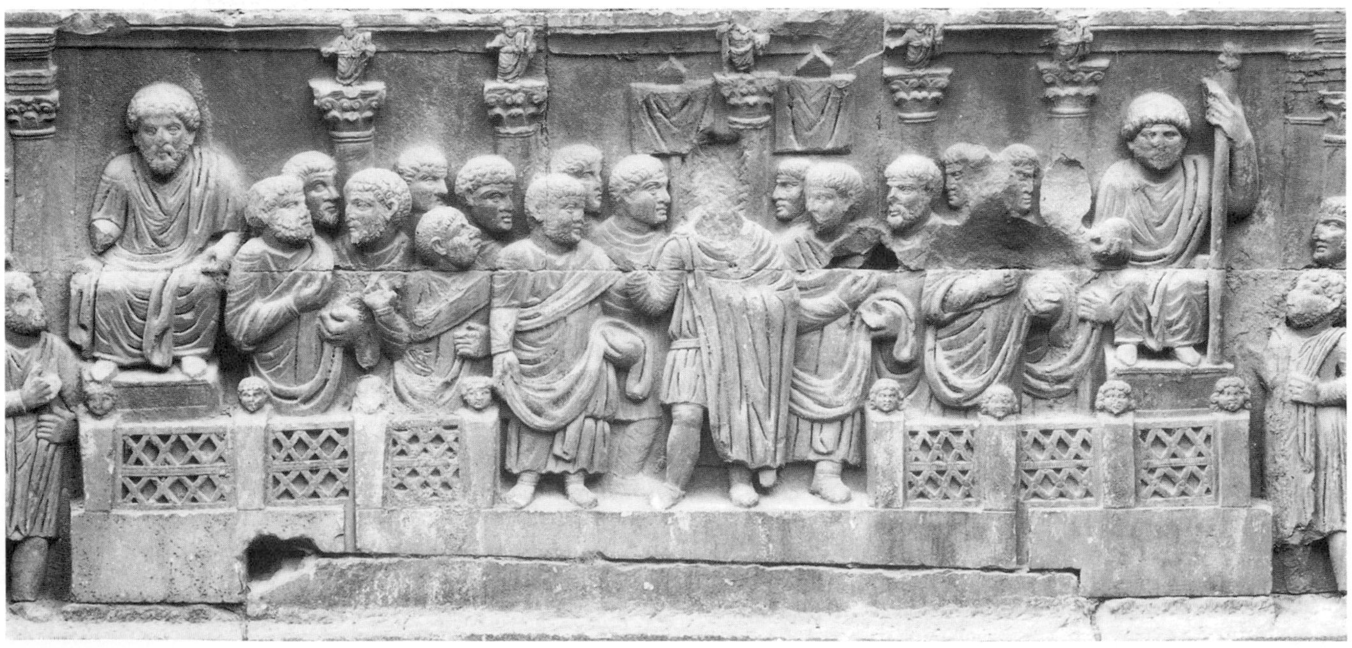

figures instead of on the representation of action. The figures are non-Classical in their lack of proportionality; in this respect, they are much like *The Tetrarchs*. Moreover, they do not move according to any principle of Classical-naturalistic movement, but rather with the mechanical and repeated stances and gestures of puppets. The relief is flattened back into the block; the forms are no longer fully modeled, and the details are incised. The lines of figures are superposed (a device used in the Column of Trajan, shown in FIG. 6-70); the spatial arrangement is, as noted, not casual, but a careful, head-counting lineup. The gestures are few and, like the uniform heads, are reproduced again and again. This presentation is not so much a historical narrative of action as the labeling of an event frozen into a tableau, so that the ordered groups can quickly be read and labeled as "crowd," "emperor," "servants of the emperor." The artist wished to include all the essential participants without the ambiguity that can accompany the description of particulars. These details have been reduced to an absolute minimum and replaced with formal placement and repetition of attitude and gesture.

We began the story of Roman art with two sculptured portraits that define, in different ways, the Roman bent for realism. We can end the story with two portraits stamped on Roman medallions (FIG. **6-98**). These are the portraits of emperors whose reigns are separated by two centuries: Hadrian (A.D. 117–138), and the emperor Maximin Daia (A.D. 308–314), tetrarch of the east, in the tetrarchy with Constantine, Licinius, and Galerius at the time of the first Edict of Toleration of the Christians. We have described the portrait and character of Hadrian and, in this bronze medallion, we have a sensitive, classicizing, naturalistic report of the emperor's features. This Classical naturalism contrasts markedly with the almost startling abstraction of the features portrayed on the gold medallion of Maximin Daia, which convey, through both sharp and blunt simplifications of form, the awesome strength of Late Imperial authority. Two centuries have transformed the image of the emperor as a particular man into an image of the emperor as the mask of power. Individual traits are suppressed in the force of the idea and the idea of force. The idea—not the thing—would henceforth dominate in art.

The archaizing of Greek and Roman figurative art in the Constantinian reliefs, *The Tetrarchs*, and the medallion portrait of Maximin Daia reflects a transformation in the way the peoples of the late Roman world interpreted the structure of appearance. Underlying this change in interpretation is a mighty spiritual change: the assimilation of Christianity into Greco-Roman civilization—a phenomenon so far-reaching in its influence as to separate the psychologies of two millennia, that of Greece-Rome and that of medieval Christianity.

6-98 *Left:* medallion of Hadrian (A.D. 117–138). Bronze, 1 3/5" diameter. *Right:* gold coin with portrait of Maximin Daia (A.D. 308–314). Gold, 4/5" in diameter. Both Museo Nazionale, Rome.

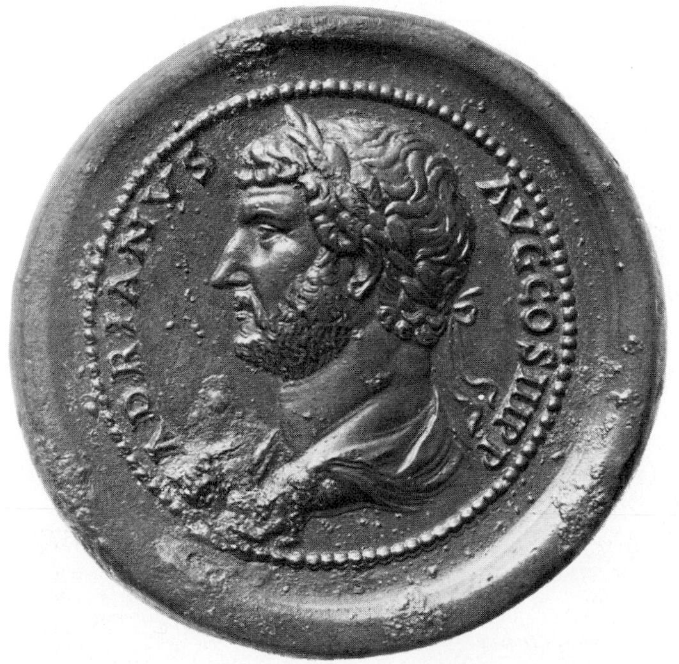

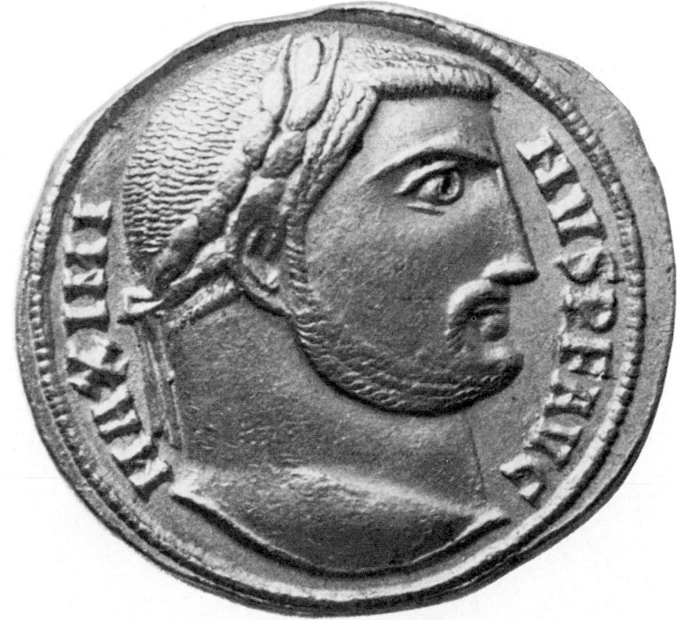

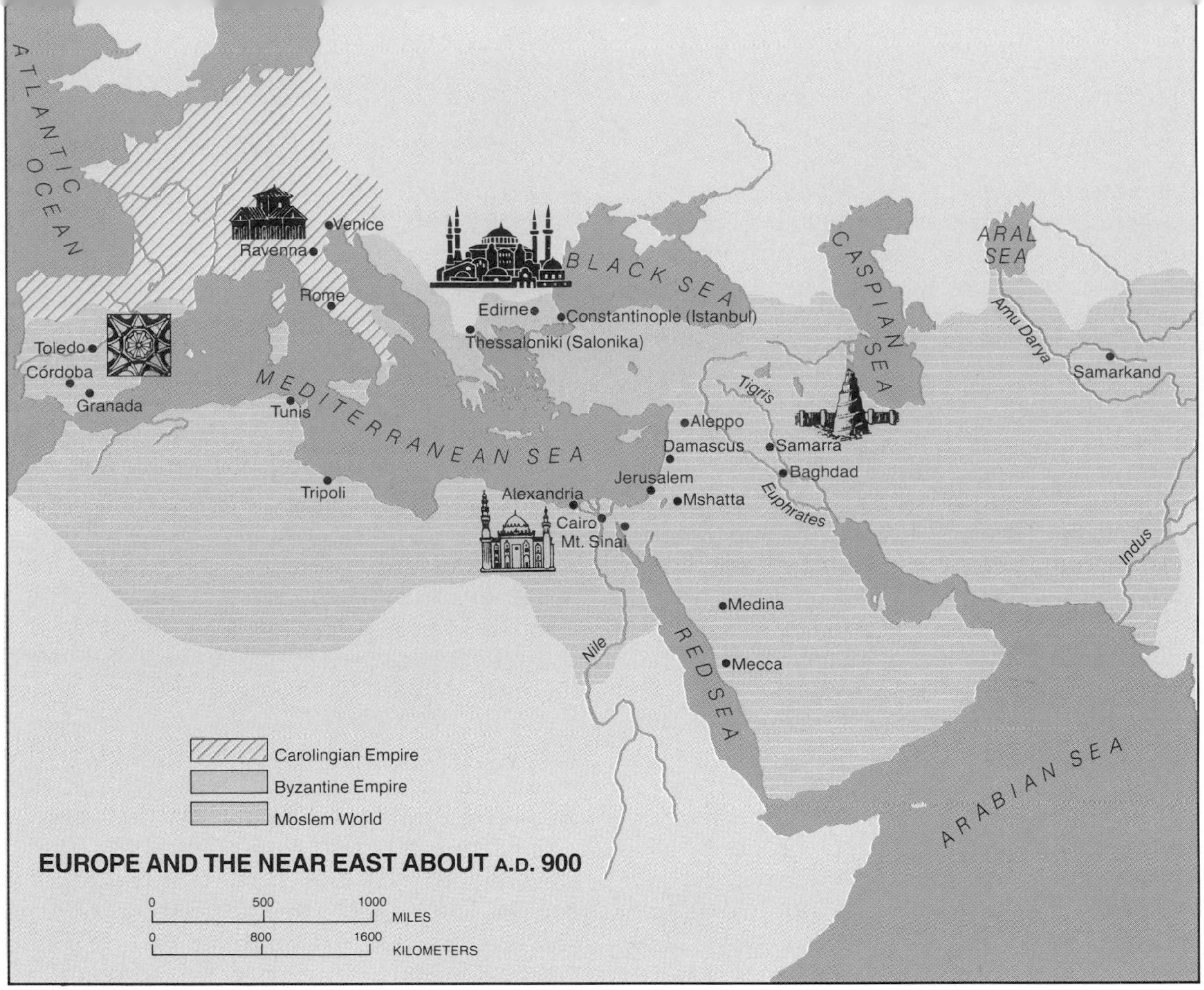

EUROPE AND THE NEAR EAST ABOUT A.D. 900

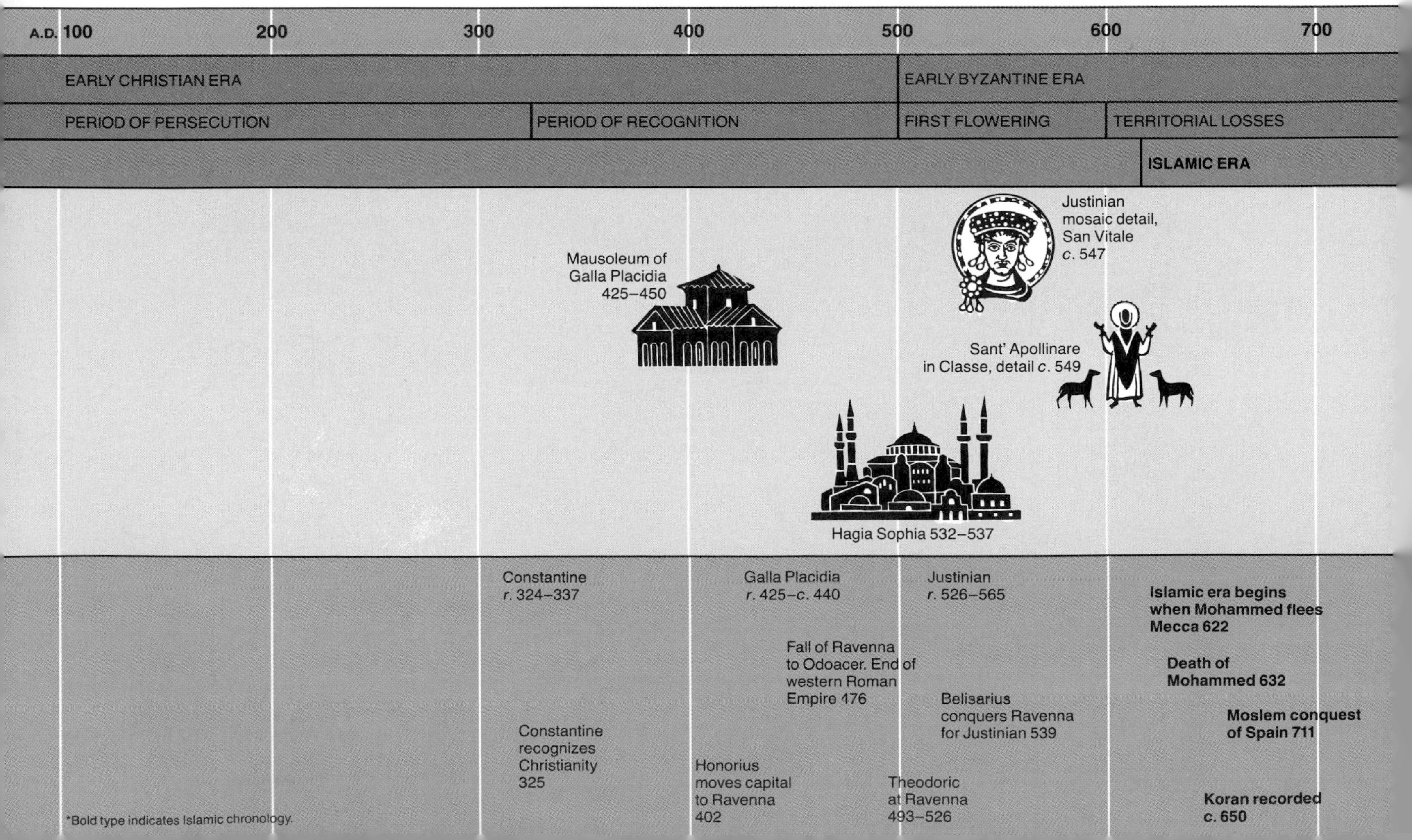

Carolingian Empire
Byzantine Empire
Moslem World

0 500 1000 MILES
0 800 1600 KILOMETERS

ATLANTIC OCEAN
MEDITERRANEAN SEA
BLACK SEA
CASPIAN SEA
ARAL SEA
RED SEA
ARABIAN SEA
Venice
Ravenna
Rome
Toledo
Córdoba
Granada
Tunis
Tripoli
Edirne
Constantinople (Istanbul)
Thessaloniki (Salonika)
Aleppo
Damascus
Samarra
Baghdad
Jerusalem
Mshatta
Alexandria
Cairo
Mt. Sinai
Medina
Mecca
Samarkand
Tigris
Euphrates
Nile
Amu Darya
Indus

A.D. 100 | 200 | 300 | 400 | 500 | 600 | 700

EARLY CHRISTIAN ERA | EARLY BYZANTINE ERA

PERIOD OF PERSECUTION | PERIOD OF RECOGNITION | FIRST FLOWERING | TERRITORIAL LOSSES

ISLAMIC ERA

Mausoleum of Galla Placidia 425–450

Justinian mosaic detail, San Vitale *c.* 547

Sant' Apollinare in Classe, detail *c.* 549

Hagia Sophia 532–537

Constantine *r.* 324–337

Constantine recognizes Christianity 325

Honorius moves capital to Ravenna 402

Galla Placidia *r.* 425–*c.* 440

Fall of Ravenna to Odoacer. End of western Roman Empire 476

Theodoric at Ravenna 493–526

Justinian *r.* 526–565

Belisarius conquers Ravenna for Justinian 539

Islamic era begins when Mohammed flees Mecca 622

Death of Mohammed 632

Koran recorded c. 650

Moslem conquest of Spain 711

*Bold type indicates Islamic chronology.

7

EARLY CHRISTIAN, BYZANTINE, AND ISLAMIC ART

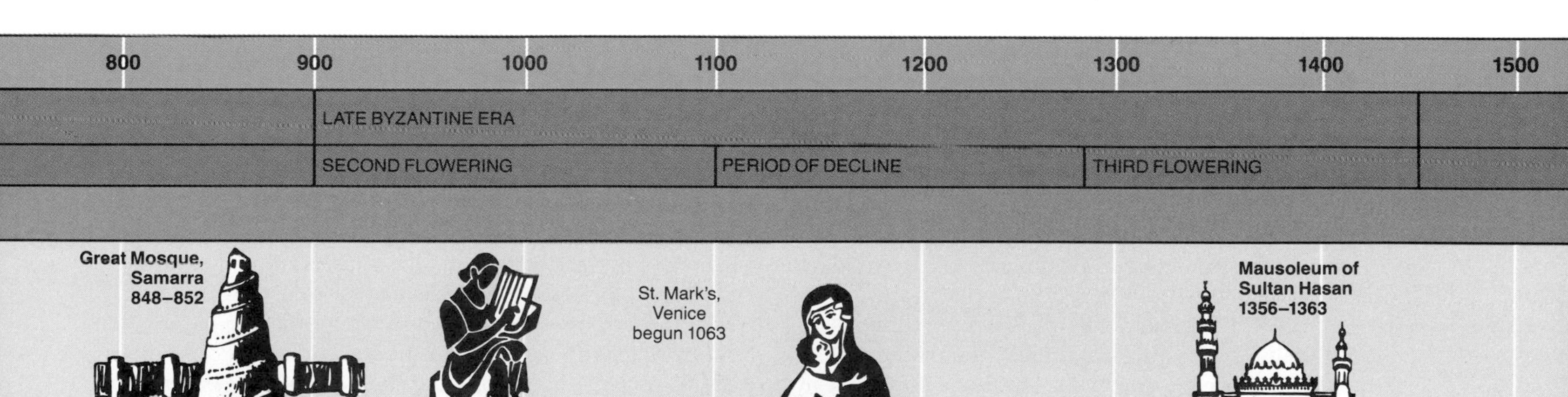

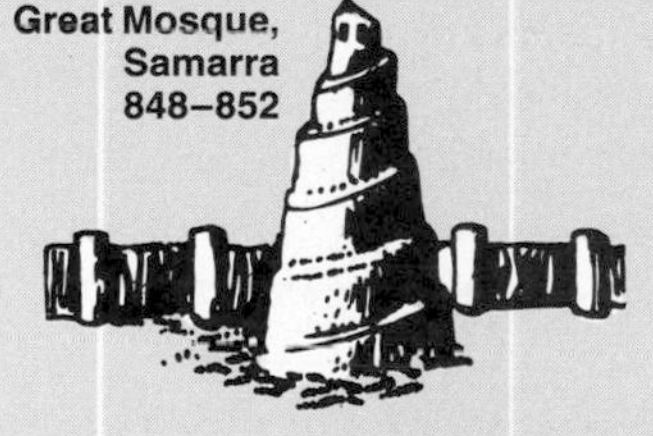

Great Mosque, Samarra 848–852

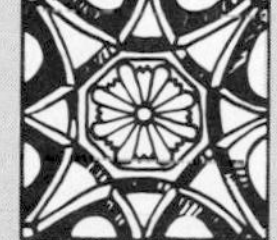

Mosque, Córdoba 8th–10th centuries

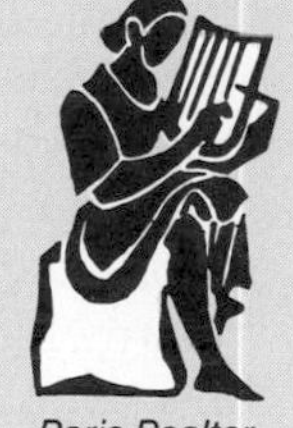

Paris Psalter c. 960

Church of the Katholikon c. 1020

St. Mark's, Venice begun 1063

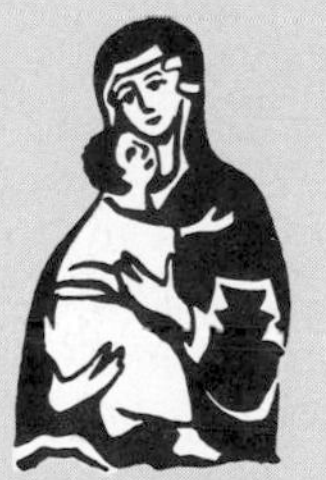

The Vladimir Madonna 12th century

The Harrowing of Hell c. 1310–1320

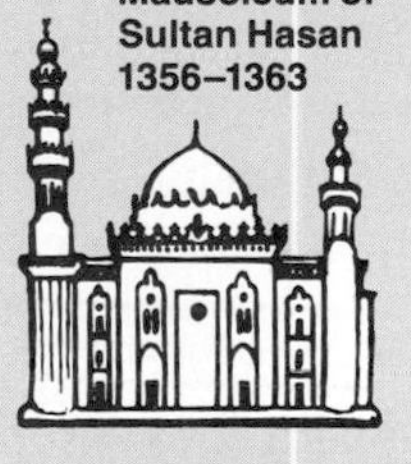

Mausoleum of Sultan Hasan 1356–1363

Battle of Poitiers 732

Iconoclastic Controversy 730–843

Turks convert to Islam 9th–10th century

End of Caliphate of Córdoba 1031

First Crusade 1095–1099

Fourth Crusade 1202–1204

Osman I, founder of Ottoman Empire ***r.*** **1290–1326**

Ottoman conquest of Constantinople 1453

CHRISTIANITY, like many Eastern cults, was a peculiarly persuasive religion of salvation. Its immense success in making converts among the teeming populations within the great imperial cities brought it to the attention of the Roman authorities. Because Christians refused to acknowledge the state religion, which was the cult of the emperor, and because they refused to participate in its rather perfunctory rites, they were regarded as politically subversive and were bitterly persecuted. Tacitus, reflecting the attitudes of his time, regarded the Christians as believers in a degenerate doctrine and practitioners of obscene and perverse rites that, he felt, were typical of Eastern cults; he referred to the Christians as "a class hated for its abominations." Pliny the Younger, reporting to the emperor Trajan on his investigation of Christian beliefs, wrote that he found merely a "depraved and extravagant superstition," although Christian ritual was innocent enough.

The pagan Romans believed in many gods; the Christians believed only in one. To the educated pagan, the Christian doctrines—the incarnation of a god in the body of a man, and the salvation or redemption of all mankind through the death and resurrection of the god-man Christ—must have seemed absurd to the point of insanity. The Christians exulted in this imputation of absurdity to their faith: *Credo quia absurdum* ("I believe *because* it is absurd") became their slogan. Pagan and Christian had opposed orientations: the pagan looked to this world; the Christian looked to the next. The religion of the empire, *Romanitas,* based its ritual and practice on imperial dominion, but Christ declared "My kingdom is not of this world." (John 18:36).

The differences between pagan and Christian were profound, as were the differences between the Judaic world and the Christian church. Further differences would divide the cultures of the Greek-speaking eastern Mediterranean and the Latin-speaking west. These divisions would cut deeply several ways. The fundamental opposition between the eastern and western spirit proclaimed in Zechariah, "when I have raised up thy sons, O Zion, against thy sons, O Greece . . ." (9:13), rings angrily once again in the words of the early Christian Tertullian: *"Quid Athenae Hierosolymis!"* ("What is there in common between Athens and Jerusalem? what between the Academy [of Plato] and the Church!"). Although the unmitigated hostility of Tertullian was by no means shared by all Christians, an antagonism between the ancient Semitic east and the Hellenic world that had, for a while, conquered it was inevitable and could not be suppressed.

Greek naturalism and rationalism had become integral to the western Roman world; yet, at the same time, they had been changed through contact with the old civilizations of the Middle East. Although the mystery cults, with their suspiciously secret rites, their redemptive messages and occult sciences, their solar and fertility myths and their savior gods, drew heavily on Egypt, Babylon, Persia, and even India, they also borrowed a good deal of the intellectual apparatus of Hellenic philosophy, mysticizing it and making of it a kind of magical formula and a *gnosis*—the privileged knowledge of only an initiated few.

Christianity, based as it was on Jewish teaching and tradition, differed radically from many of the crude cults with which Romans, like Tacitus, confused it. But Christianity also joined with those cults in the long, vast, historical reaction against the Hellenized West—against both its world view and that material manifestation of it, the increasingly oppressive Roman Empire. To Christians, the empire, with its exactions, cruelties, materialism, wars, and false gods, became *regnum Caesaris, regnum Diaboli* (the kingdom of Caesar, the kingdom of the Devil). Yet this same empire would be inherited by the Christians in 325,* when Constantine recognized Christianity; by the end of the century, Theodosius, his successor, had made it the official religion of the state.

In the eighteenth century, Edward Gibbon, in his monumental history, *The Decline and Fall of the Roman Empire,* accused Christianity of being the principal cause of that (in his time) calamity. We now do not believe that Christianity had that effect, but, as early as the fifth century, Augustine wrote his *City of God* to defend the Church against the pagan accusation that the sack of the city of Rome (in 410 by the Goths) was a punishment sent by the ancient gods because the city had become Christian. The disintegration of the Roman Empire, beginning with its nominal separation into the western and eastern empires toward the end of the third century, was a phenomenon of considerable complexity that cannot be laid at the door of the Christians, nor entirely at the door of the "barbarians," those Celtic, Germanic, Slavic, and other peoples who had been pressing slowly into the Mediterranean world for thousands of years. (We have met their predecessors in the great migrations that disturbed Egypt, Mesopotamia, Asia Minor, Crete, and Greece.)

At any rate, from the end of the third century, a slow, sometimes hardly perceptible, takeover was occurring—a takeover not of the unified empire, but of its already fragmented remains. The spiritual and ideological conquest made by the Christians in the politically consequential form of mass conversion paralleled the gradual infiltration and settlement by

*The epoch time designation A.D. will be dropped from now on.

the "barbarians," who, in actuality, had been present in the administrative and military structure as well as in recognized possession of imperial territories for a long time. The subsequent actions of these "barbarians," who were Christianized and in control of the western empire by the end of the fifth century, make up the history of the Middle Ages in the west. The eastern empire, which was actually but not officially severed from the western empire by the beginning of the fifth century, was to go its own continuous way as the Byzantine Empire, reverting to its Greek language and traditions, which, to be sure, had become much "Orientalized." The Byzantine world was a kind of protraction of the life of the late Roman Empire and the Early Christian culture that filled it. With a quite Oriental conservatism, which reminds us somewhat of the ancient Near Eastern civilizations, the Byzantine Empire remained Greek, orthodox, and unchanging for a thousand years, preserving the forms of its origin, oblivious to and isolated from the new.

In the seventh century, Islam, a new spiritual force, erupted from Arabia and swept across the Near East and the southern Mediterranean with astonishing speed. Islam created a new civilization that rivaled Christianity and that would have far-ranging influence in medieval Europe: Arabic translations of Aristotle and other Greek writers of antiquity were studied eagerly by Christian scholars of the twelfth and thirteenth centuries; Arabic love lyrics and poetic descriptions of nature inspired the early French troubadours; Arab scholars laid the foundations of arithmetic and algebra, as they are still taught in our schools, and their contributions to astronomy, medicine, and the natural sciences have made a lasting impression in the Western world. Although Islamic art may not fall within the scope of Western art in the more limited sense, it deserves attention at this point in our survey, particularly because its early monuments, like the Early Christian and Byzantine monuments, derive from earlier Near Eastern and Mediterranean artistic traditions. Most early monuments of Islamic art belong to the succession of Late Roman, Early Byzantine, and Iranian (Sassanian) art, although different social and religious needs soon would transform similar prototypes into quite different forms in the Islamic world than they would take in the Christian world.

EARLY CHRISTIAN ART

The style that we call Early Christian could as accurately be called Late Roman, or, in art-historical usage, Late Antique. Christian works are distinguished from pagan works only by subject, not by style. After all, the Christians of the time were as "Roman" as the pagans; they were trained in the same crafts, were brought up in the same environment, and spoke the same language. The Christian church itself, both in its organization and its philosophy, owed much to the Greco-Roman structure of life. Early Christian art shows the simple transformation of pagan into Christian themes and the freest kind of borrowing of pagan motifs and manners. Hybrid forms are produced throughout the Christianized late empire in the greatest profusion and with the greatest intermingling of regional styles, making it almost impossible to recognize any one style, or even half a dozen, that could definitely be called Early Christian or that could serve as an exclusive exemplar of what we mean by Early Christian.

In sculpture and painting, Greco-Roman naturalism underwent a kind of "denaturing," something that began as early as the Column of Trajan (FIG. 6-69) and was well advanced in the reliefs from the Arch of Constantine (FIG. 6-96), the sculpture group *The Tetrarchs* (FIG. 6-94), and the coin portrait of Maximin Daia (FIG. 6-98). Archaizing modes supervene on the old naturalism, and things come to look less and less like the Greco-Roman prototypes from which, ultimately, they derive. This "denaturing" process, variously influenced by barbarian styles, continues well into the western Medieval period. It should by no means be viewed as merely the negation of the Greco-Roman style, or as a clumsy botching of it by artists who had lost the sense of it and the necessary manual skill. Rather, it is the product of an entirely new world view—one that inevitably was to bring about the transformation of the naturalistic Classical tradition. Early Christian art shows that transformation in progress, already well under way in the late third century, while the Roman Empire was still intact.

The Early Christian era can be divided conveniently into the Period of Persecution (when the earliest communities were established in the first century) and the Period of Recognition (from 325, when Constantine recognized Christianity, along with other religions of the Roman Empire, until about 500, when the western provinces of the empire came under the sway of barbarian princes). Some authorities would extend the period of Early Christian art to the eighth century, when it was terminated in the east by the Iconoclastic Controversy. In the Period of Persecution, the Christians were, in the Roman view, a troublesome, even dangerous, sect that needed to be curbed. During this time, it is likely that the Christians, shrinking from the kind of attention public shrines might attract, worshiped in the private houses of their wealthier communicants, perhaps in the elaborate atrium houses of the type seen in Pompeii (FIG. 6-25). It is quite possible that the atrium forecourt of the later public churches, the basilicas, derived from their liturgical relationship to the earlier atrium of the private house, as well as to the public forum.

THE CATACOMBS

The most significant monuments of the Period of Persecution are the least conspicuous in Rome; they are entirely underground. The catacombs are vast subterranean networks of galleries and chambers in Rome and other cities that were designed as cemeteries for the burial of the Christian dead, many of them sainted martyrs. From the second through the fourth centuries, the catacombs were in constant use; as many as four million bodies may have been accommodated in the Roman catacombs alone. In times of persecution, they also could have served as places of concealment for fugitives; evidence of this function survives in blocked and cut-off staircases, secret embrasures (openings) and passages, and concealed entrances and exits. Undoubtedly, the Christian mysteries must have been enacted here, although the principal function of the catacombs was mortuary.

In Rome, the catacombs were tunneled out of a stratum of granular tufa, the convenient properties of which had been exploited earlier by the Etruscan necropolis builders (FIG. 6-2). After a plot of ground had been selected for the cemetery (Christians were not prevented by Roman law from owning property), a gallery 3–4 feet wide was dug around its perimeter at a convenient level below the surface (FIG. **7-1**). In the walls of these galleries, embrasures were opened parallel to the gallery axis to receive the bodies of the dead; these openings, called *loculi,* were placed one above another, like shelves (FIG. **7-2**). Often, small rooms, called *cubicula,* were constructed in the walls to serve as mortuary chapels, and these were variously vaulted. Once the original perimeter galleries were full of *loculi* and *cubicula,* other galleries were cut at right angles to them; this process continued as long as lateral space permitted. Lower levels would then be dug and connected by staircases, some systems extending as deep as five levels. When adjacent burial areas belonged to members of the same Christian confraternity, or by gift or purchase fell into the same hands, communications were opened between the respective cemeteries, so that they spread laterally and gradually acquired a vast extent. After Christianity received official sanction, the catacombs fell into disuse, except as holy places—monuments to the great martyrs—which were visited by the pious.

Many cubicula were decorated with frescoes that were Late Antique (pagan) in manner and even in subject, as interpreted by the Christians to conform with their own beliefs. The geometric patterning of a ceiling in the catacomb of Saints Pietro and Marcellino in Rome (FIG. **7-3**) becomes akin to the Dome of Heaven (the large circle), which has been inscribed with the basic symbol of the Christian faith, the cross. The arms of the cross terminate in four *lunettes* (semicircular fields) in which are represented the key episodes from the Old Testament story of Jonah, who is thrown from his ship on the left, emerges from the whale on the right, and, safe on land at the bottom, contemplates the miracle of his salvation and the mercy of God. (Jonah, an often-painted figure in

7-1 Plan *(top)* of the catacomb of Callixtus, Rome, second century, and section *(bottom)* through main gallery of oldest region.

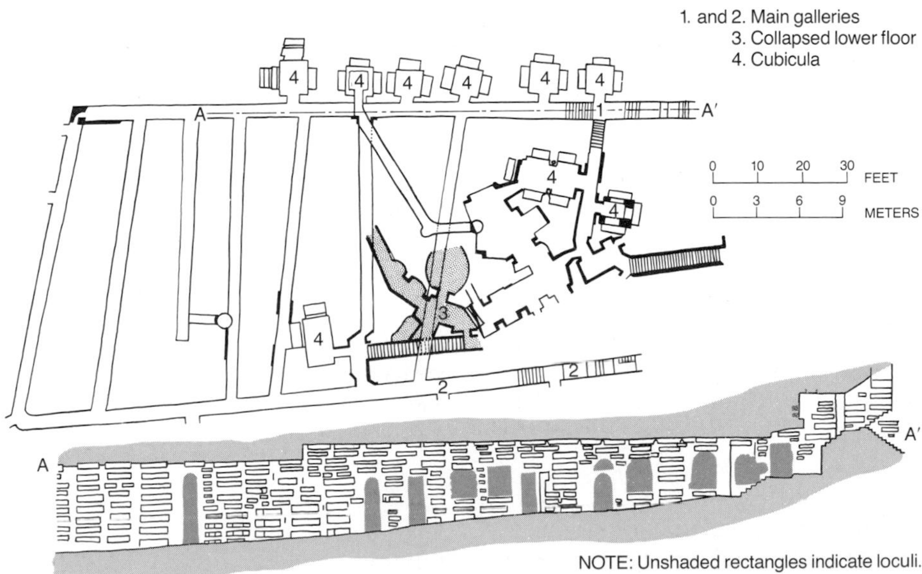

Early Christian art, was honored as a prefiguration of Christ, who rose from death as Jonah had been delivered from the belly of the whale.) The compartments between these lunettes are occupied by *orans* figures, their arms raised in the attitude of prayer; in the pagan world, from which they derive, they are symbols of piety.

The central medallion shows Christ as the Good Shepherd, whose powers of salvation are underscored by his juxtaposition with the story of Jonah. As a theme, the Good Shepherd can be traced back through Greek Archaic art to Egyptian art. In Classical art, the Good Shepherd signified the virtue of philanthropy, but here in the catacombs, it becomes the symbol for the loyal protector of the Christian flock, who said to his disciples, "Feed my lambs; feed my sheep." During the Period of Persecution, Christ almost invariably was represented in the catacombs either as the Good Shepherd or as a teacher. Only later, when Christianity became the official state religion of the Roman Empire, did Christ take on such imperial attributes as the halo, the purple robe, and the throne, which denoted rulership.

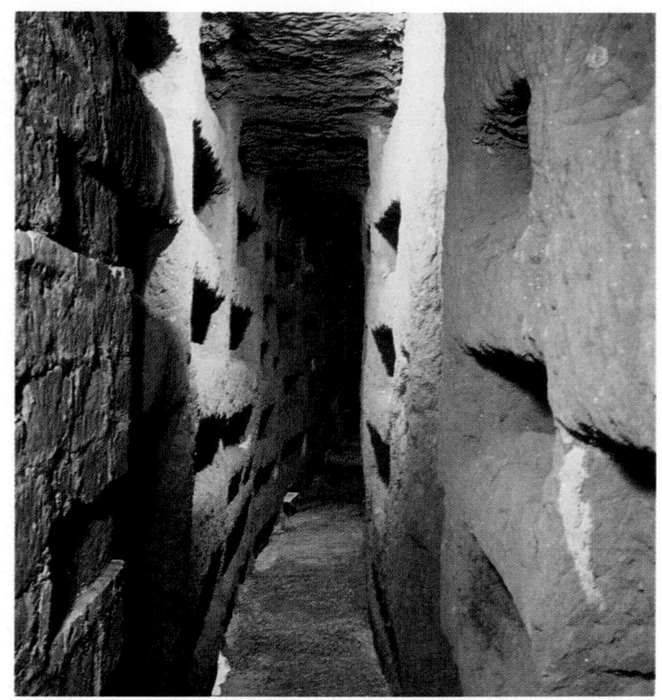

7-2 Gallery and loculi of the catacomb.

7-3 Painted ceiling from the catacomb of Saints Pietro and Marcellino, Rome, fourth century.

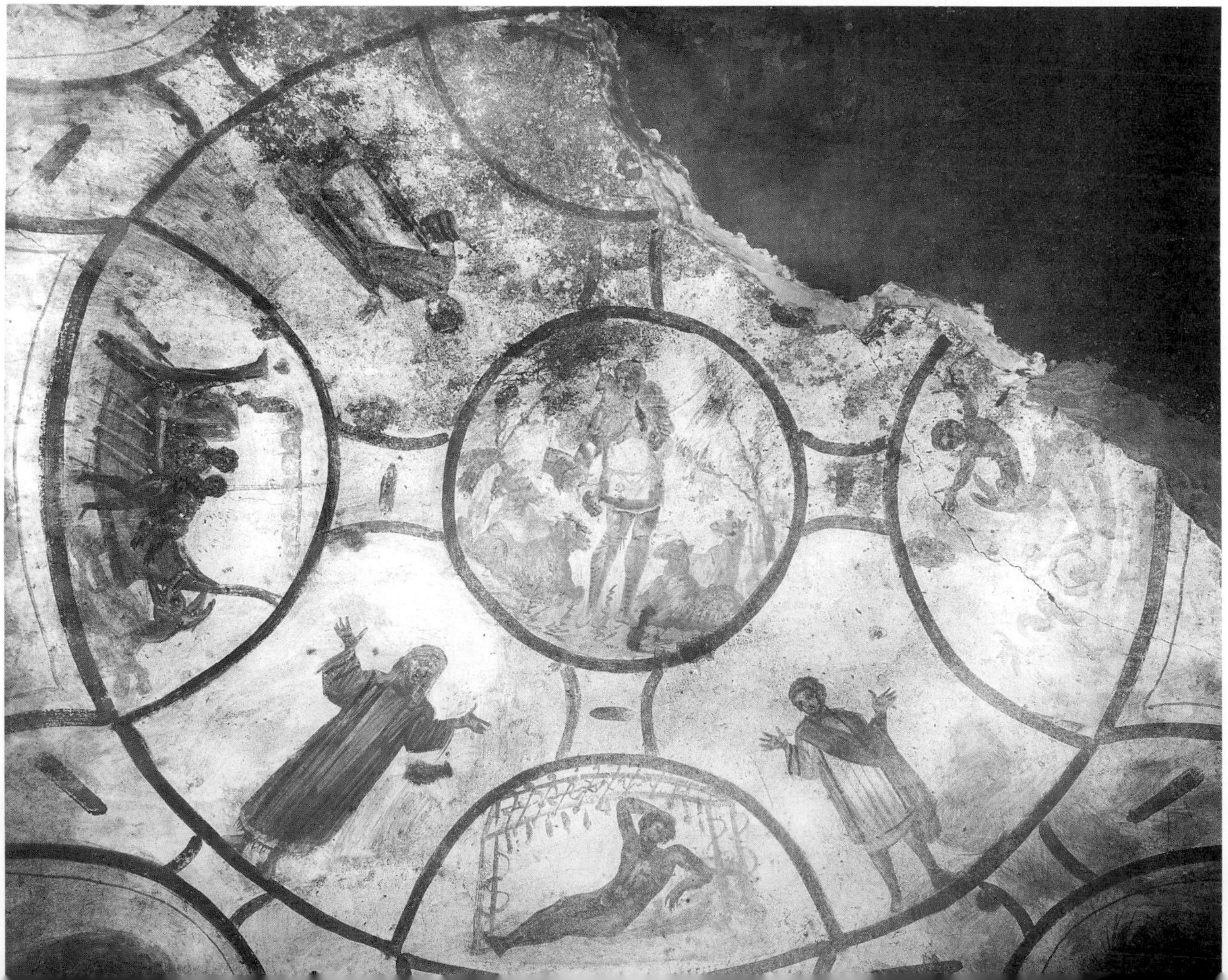

The style of the catacomb painters is most often the quick, sketchy impressionism we have seen in earlier Roman painting of the last Pompeian period, and the execution ranges from good to inferior—most often, the latter. We must take into account that the catacombs were very unpromising places for the art of the mural decorator. The air was spoiled by decomposing corpses, the humidity was excessive, and the lighting (provided largely by oil lamps) was entirely unfit for elaborate compositions or painstaking execution. For designs on ceilings, arches, and lunettes, the painter was required to assume awkward and tiring poses, and it is no wonder that the frescoes often were completed hastily and that the results frequently were of poor quality.

Architecture

Although some Christian ceremonies were held in the catacombs, regular services likely took place in private houses that were rearranged and partitioned off to make "community" houses, or in simple, columned halls. The latter were destroyed in the last great persecutions under Diocletian; the remains of one, a kind of rudimentary basilica, dating from 311, have been found beneath the cathedral of Aquileia. Dura-Europos preserves another. Once Christianity achieved imperial sanction under Constantine, an urgent need suddenly arose to set up buildings that would meet the requirements of the Christian liturgy and would aggrandize the Christian cult. Constantine was convinced that in 313 the God of the Christians had guided him to victory over Maxentius, his rival for the imperial throne. In lifelong gratitude, though he never actually became a Christian, Constantine protected and advanced the faith throughout the empire as well as in the obstinately pagan capital city of Rome. As emperor, he was, of course, obliged to safeguard the ancient Roman religion, traditions, and monuments; as we have seen, he placed works of his own, like the vast basilica and the triumphal arch (FIGS. 6-91 and 6-95) at the very center of the city. But eager to provide buildings to house the rituals of the Christians, their venerated burial places, and especially the memorials of their founding saints, Constantine discreetly drew upon his own imperial patrimony to endow an extraordinary architectural enterprise, constructing elaborate basilicas, memorials, and mausoleums not only in Rome but at other sites sacred to Christianity, notably in Bethlehem and Jerusalem. His dual role as both Roman emperor and private champion of the Christian faith is reflected in the fact that he located the new churches of Rome not within its walls, but on the outskirts of the city, so as to avoid any confrontation of Christian and pagan ideologies as expressed in their distinctive temples. The city, dominated by its proud, senatorial families, remained conservatively pagan throughout the fourth century, and the stubborn resistance of the Roman populace to Constantine's pro-Christian policies may have prompted him to establish a new Christian city—Constantinople, built on the site of ancient Byzantium.

The design of Constantine's Christian buildings incorporated familiar architectural elements: the atrium house, the catacomb chapel, the Roman basilica, and the imperial audience hall. How these elements were combined into the masterful composition that was to become one of the first Christian church buildings of the new age—Old St. Peter's in Rome (FIGS. **7-4** and 7-6)—we do not know; discussion about the origins of the Christian basilica has not ended. Begun in 333, Old St. Peter's is probably the most important design in the history of church architecture. Its wide influence was augmented by the belief that it stood where Peter, the first Apostle, had

7-4 Reconstruction of Old St. Peter's, Rome, *c.* 333.

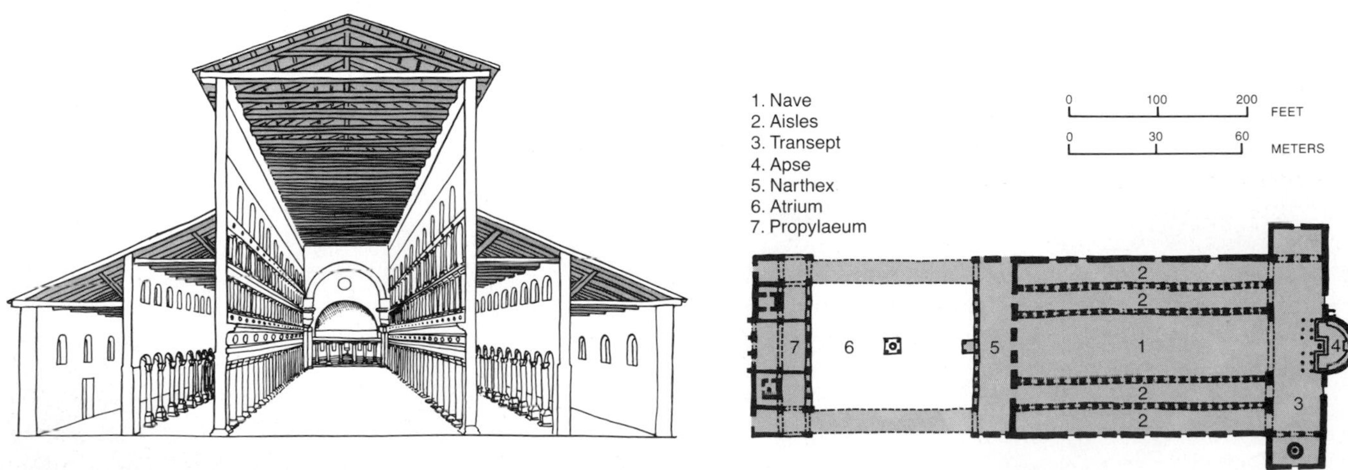

been buried. In the 1940s and 1950s, excavations some 22 feet beneath the high altar of the present basilica revealed the second-century *tropaion* (martyr's memorial) of St. Peter, set up over a grave site in a pagan Roman cemetery. Constantine and Pope Sylvester were both convinced that this was the veritable burial place of the Prince of the Apostles; thus, the great church was raised, at immense cost and labor, upon the irregular slope of the Vatican hill to enshrine beneath the crossing of transept and apse the most hallowed site in western Christendom.

The extraordinary dimensions of the Constantinian basilica are difficult to realize from the old drawings; the nave was as long, as high, and twice as wide as the nave of a great Gothic cathedral. Its interior was "one of the most spacious, most imposing, and most harmonious . . . ever built, imperially rich in its marbles and mosaics, grandiose yet forthright and large in the best Roman sense of the word."*

The plan of Old St. Peter's (FIG. 7-4) shows a rectangular building entered from the street through the *propylaeum,* a gateway building that leads into the *atrium,* an open, colonnaded court; the *narthex,* that part of the colonnade that is joined to the façade, functions as an entrance hall. The body of the church consists of the *nave,* low side *aisles,* the *apse,* and the transverse aisle, or *transept,* which is placed between the nave and the apse and projects slightly beyond the walls of the nave and aisles. This fundamental arrangement was used in subsequent Christian architecture, although it would be wrong to think that a rigid, standardized plan exists for basilican design; for instance, the transept, an occasional feature of churches in the city of Rome, is often lacking in other churches, especially in the smaller ones.

The cross section (FIG. 7-4) shows a great columned hall that obviously is related to such Roman secular basilicas as the Basilica Ulpia in the Forum of Trajan (FIG. 6-49). Unlike the slightly earlier Basilica of Constantine (FIGS. 6-91 and 6-92), Old St. Peter's was not vaulted, but timber-roofed, as were, traditionally, most Roman basilicas. (The vaulted Basilica of Constantine was an exception.) The pagan basilica's lateral entrance is moved to the short side of the Christian church. Only one of the multiple apses is retained, and that is placed opposite, and at a dramatic distance from, the entrance. Evenly spaced columns no longer surround the central nave, but flank it. All these modifications of the pagan basilica create a sweeping perspective that converges on the shrine as the focus of the whole design and the place of the principal mystery of the Christian faith.

*Kenneth Conant, *Early Medieval Church Architecture* (Baltimore: Johns Hopkins University Press, 1942), p.6.

From the time of its dedication in 354, Old St. Peter's was a focal point of reverend Christian attention. For centuries, it was the destination of multitudes of devout pilgrims from every corner of Christendom, a holy site second only to Jerusalem's Holy Sepulchre as a fountain of grace. The best-known church of the medieval West, and the fabled marvel of medieval Rome, Old St. Peter's is estimated to have accommodated over fourteen thousand worshipers at a time, congregated to witness the gorgeous ceremonies that celebrated the great festivals of the Church, especially those honoring St. Peter. For the throngs of pious visitors, standing on the marble pavement of the vast hall of the nave, or overflowing into the narthex and atrium, the basilica was monumental testimony to the legitimacy of the ordained successors of Peter, first bishop of Rome, and to the divine authority passed from Christ through Peter to all who would follow him in the episcopal chair. To the pilgrim worshipers, expecting as a result of their visit to the shrine to be absolved from their sins by the saint's God-given power to "bind or to loose," the church must have been overpowering evidence that Christ had indeed entrusted the keys of the kingdom to Peter and his successors. It must have been the palpable fulfillment of the words of the Lord: "Thou art Peter, and upon this rock (Greek: *petre*) I will build my church; and the gates of hell shall not prevail against it" (Matthew 16:18).

The old church of St. Peter no longer stands, and it is from an eighteenth-century print by Piranesi of its slightly later stylistic associate, St. Paul's (FIG. **7-5**), that we can get some idea of its grandiose space, scale, and majesty. The "spiritualizing" of the secular

7-5 Interior of St. Paul's Outside the Walls, Rome, late fourth century. (Etching by GIOVANNI BATTISTA PIRANESI.)

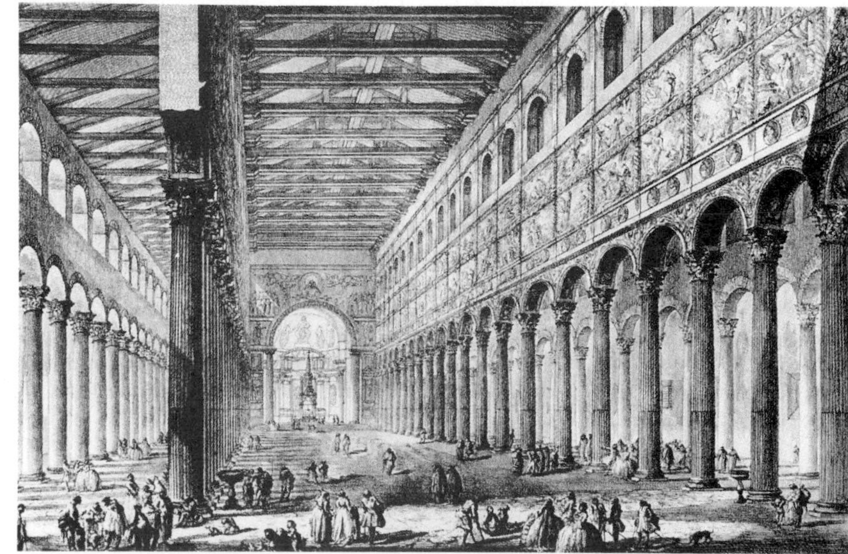

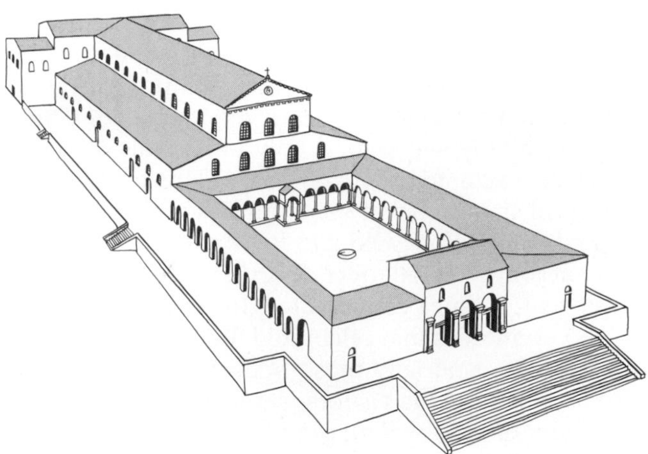

7-6 Conjectural reconstruction of Old St. Peter's, Rome. (After K. J. Conant.)

Roman design is evident not only in the realignment of the building's axis (to focus the viewer's whole experience on the ritual climax of the design), but also in its extreme simplicity of structure and the lightness of its bearing walls and columns. Roman mass—huge walls and ponderous weight, sculptured surfaces in relief and recess, and whole populations of statuary—has been lightened, rarefied, smoothed; we could say that it has been "dematerialized" to suit the new orientation toward a spiritual rather than a physical world.

The bird's-eye view of Old St. Peter's in reconstruction (FIG. **7-6**), although partly conjectural, shows the stepped podium that we have seen before in Roman temples such as the Temple of "Fortuna Virilis" (FIG. 6-16) and the Maison Carrée (FIG. 6-46), which, in turn, had Etruscan predecessors; a propylaeum and a forum converted to an atrium are other elements with not only Roman but ancient antecedents. We believe that the exterior of Old St. Peter's was, like Christian basilicas in general, unadorned, reserving the whole decorative enterprise for the interior. It is as if the building imitated the ideal Christian, with a grave and plain exterior and a glowing and beautiful soul within.

The interior splendor of Old St. Peter's may have concealed from the unschooled worshiper the spiritual organization of its physical elements, the thorough-going symbolism of its design—in a word, its iconography. The architects, drawn by Constantine from the imperial building staff, were skilled practitioners, who had worked on the great municipal structures of Rome as well as on the church of St. John Lateran, which had preceded St. Peter's as the first of Constantine's Christian basilicas. In the design and construction of St. Peter's, a Christian building of unprecedented scale and magnificence, the architects undoubtedly were directed by learned ecclesiastics, who must have prescribed the thoroughly scriptural program of the design. Architectural historians have analyzed the basic scheme and proportions of the plan and elevation; the spacing of the parts; the enumeration of elements like windows, columns, and arches; and the placement of structural units and details. We can say with some certainty that the original model for the grouping of the compositional masses and spaces was drawn from the biblical description of Solomon's temple in Jerusalem (principally 1 Kings 6), as were the simple ratios of their dimensions. This venerable source of symbolic reference was augmented by numerological and metrological correspondences, pagan as well as Christian, that had long been thought to have hidden and sacred meaning. The great church was, thus, a fabric of interwoven symbolism mystically relating the shrine of the first of the apostles to those mysteries, revelations, prophesies, and miracles, both in the Old and the New Testaments, which shaped the dogma and ritual of Christianity and gave witness to its divine origin and authority. In this respect, Old St. Peter's, at the very beginning of the history of the architecture of the Middle Ages, was the ancestor of the great medieval churches, east and west, whose "sacred geometry" was intended, for those who could construe it, to exhibit the symbolic patterns and correspondences that composed the spiritualized Christian cosmos.

The rectangular, basilican church design was long the favorite of the western Christian world, but the Early Christian architects also adopted another Classical building type: the central plan—a round or polygonal domed structure that later was favored in the east. Byzantine architects developed this form to monumental proportions and amplified its theme in numerous, ingenious variations. In the west, the central-plan building was used generally for structures adjacent to the main basilicas, like mausoleums, baptistries, and private chapels.

A highly refined example of the central-plan design is Santa Costanza in Rome (FIGS. **7-7** to **7-9**), built in the mid-fourth century as the mausoleum of Constantia, daughter of the emperor Constantine. Its antecedents can be traced to the beehive tombs of the Mycenaeans (FIG. 4-24), although its direct inspiration may have been the Pantheon (FIG. 6-56) or the pool-enclosing rotunda of some public baths, like those of Caracalla (FIG. 6-60). The Pantheon's mass, however, has been metamorphosed, as with the mutation of the pagan into the Early Christian basilica. In Santa Costanza, the circle of paired columns that carries the domed cylinder stands sufficiently free from the external walls to leave space for a barrel-vaulted corridor, or *ambulatory*. In fact, it is as if the basilican wall-arcade has been bent around a circle, the ambulatory

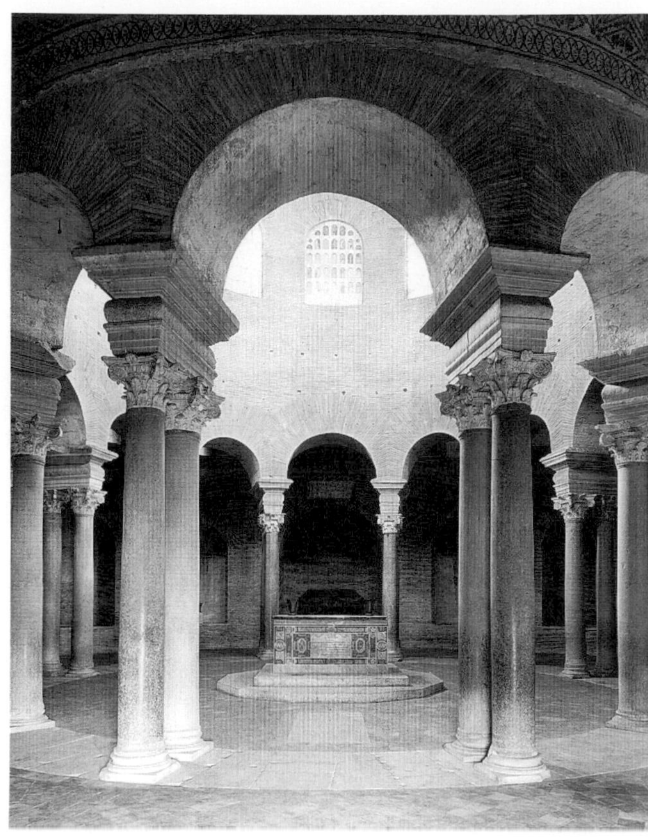

7-7 Interior of Santa Costanza, Rome, *c.* 350.

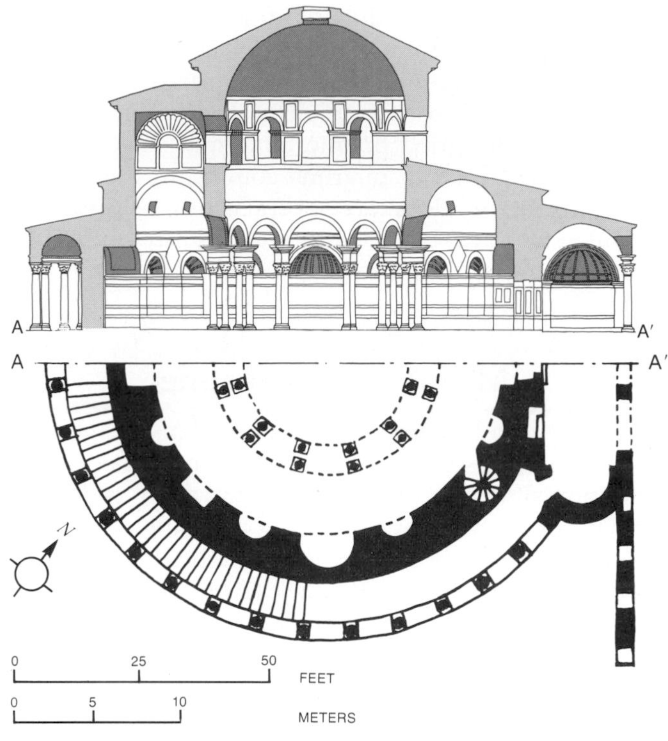

7-8 Section *(top)* and plan *(bottom)* of Santa Costanza.

corresponding to the basilican aisles and, like them, equipped with a high, ample clerestory. The exuberant naturalism of the luxurious mosaics in the vault of the ambulatory at Santa Costanza (FIG. 7-9) suggests a lingering influence of the pagan spirit.

All the important buildings of the fourth century, including Santa Costanza and the great, longitudinal basilicas, are associated closely with Constantine and his immediate relatives; it was through their patronage and supervision, as an expression of the new ideal of the Christian *imperium,* that these buildings were constructed. This close relationship between the Constantinians and Early Christian architecture may explain a certain consistency of design in the apparently diverse basilicas of the fourth and early fifth centuries. It also might explain partly how such apparently contradictory designs as the long church and the central church could be imagined as working together in meeting the requirements of Christian belief and ritual. Given centuries of tradition, it would have been perfectly natural for Constantine to memorialize

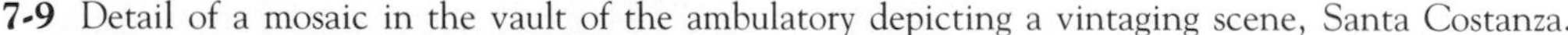

7-9 Detail of a mosaic in the vault of the ambulatory depicting a vintaging scene, Santa Costanza.

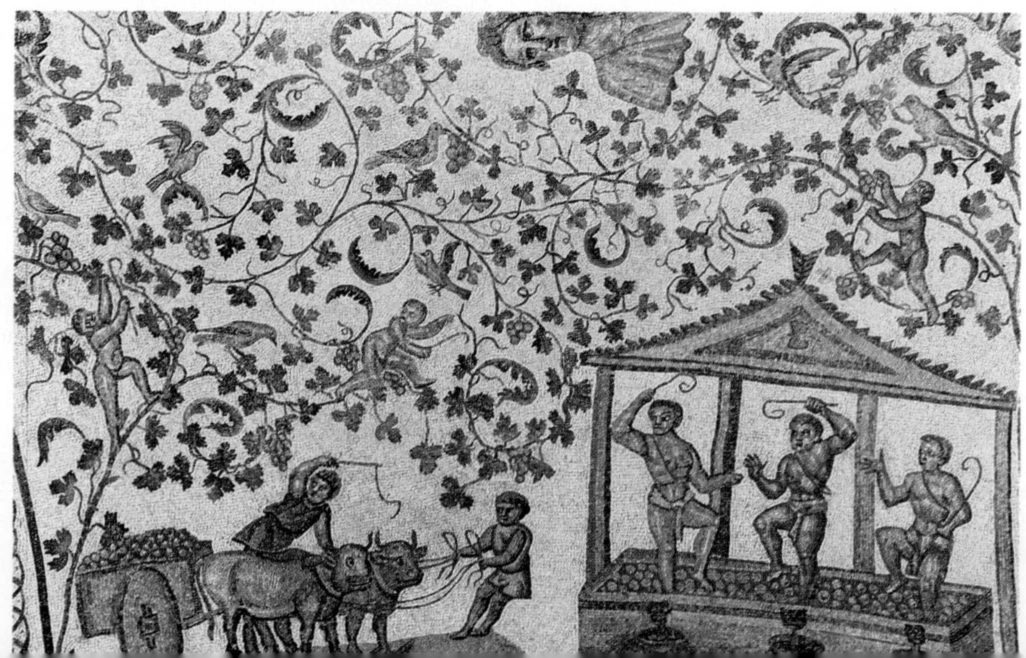

the place of Jesus' death and burial with a traditional monument, the domed rotunda, as he did in the Church of the Holy Sepulchre in Jerusalem. At the same time, the existing plan of the basilica might have been designed to offer the space needed for the congregations of pilgrims coming to the holiest place in Christendom. For several centuries then, the architectural problem, although never explicitly stated, was how to integrate the long plan and the central plan.

Mosaic and Painting

The church-building enterprise under Constantine and his successors was designed to meet the urgent ceremonial needs of Christianity, which suddenly had become official and public. As a result, wholesale programs of decoration for the churches also became necessary. To advertise the new faith in all its diverse aspects—its dogma, scriptural narrative, and symbolism—and to instruct and edify the believer, acres of walls in dozens of new churches had to be filled in the style and medium that would carry the message most effectively.

Brilliantly ornamental mosaics, with sparkling tesserae of reflective glass, rather than the opaque, marble tesserae preferred by the Romans, became the standard vehicle of expression almost at once. Mosaics were particularly suited to the flat, thin-walled surfaces of the new basilicas, becoming a durable, tangible part of the wall—a kind of architectural tapestry. The light flooding through the clerestories was caught in vibrant reflection by the mosaics, which produced abrupt effects and contrasts and sharp concentrations of color that could focus attention on the central, most relevant features of a composition. Mosaic, worked in the Early Christian manner, is not intended for the subtle changes of tone that a naturalistic painter's approach would require, although (as we have seen in the Roman mosaics) tonality is well within the mosaicist's reach. But in mosaic, color is *placed,* not blended; bright, hard, glittering texture, set within a rigorously simplified pattern, becomes the rule. For mosaics placed high on the wall, far above the observer's head, the painstaking use of tiny tesserae, seen in Roman floor mosaics, became meaningless. Early Christian mosaics, designed to be seen from a distance, employed larger stones; the surfaces were left uneven, so that the tesserae's projecting edges could catch and reflect the light, and the designs were kept simple, for optimum legibility. For several centuries, mosaic, in the service of Christian theology, was the medium of some of the supreme masterpieces of world art.

Content and style find their medium; the content of Christian doctrine took centuries to fashion, and, for a long time, even the proper manner of representing the founder of Christianity was in question. Once Christianity became the official religion of the Roman state, Jesus' status changed. In early works, he is shown as teacher and philosopher; in later works, he is imperialized as the ruler of Heaven and earth. In the fourth and fifth centuries, artists were hesitant about how to represent Jesus, and variant types of images were produced. After some crucial theological questions on Jesus' nature were resolved, a more or less standard formula for his depiction emerged.

In the minds of simple Christians who were only recently converted, Jesus easily could be identified with the familiar deities of the Mediterranean world, especially Helios (Apollo), the sun god, or his Romanized eastern aspect, Sol Invictus (the Unconquered Sun). The late third-century vault mosaic of a small Christian mausoleum in a pagan cemetery (FIG. **7-10**), excavated underneath Old St. Peter's in Rome in the 1940s, shows Jesus as Apollo, driving the horses of the sun chariot through the heavens—a conception far more grandiose than that of the Good Shepherd.

7-10 Detail of a vault mosaic from the mausoleum of the Julii, Rome, 250–275.

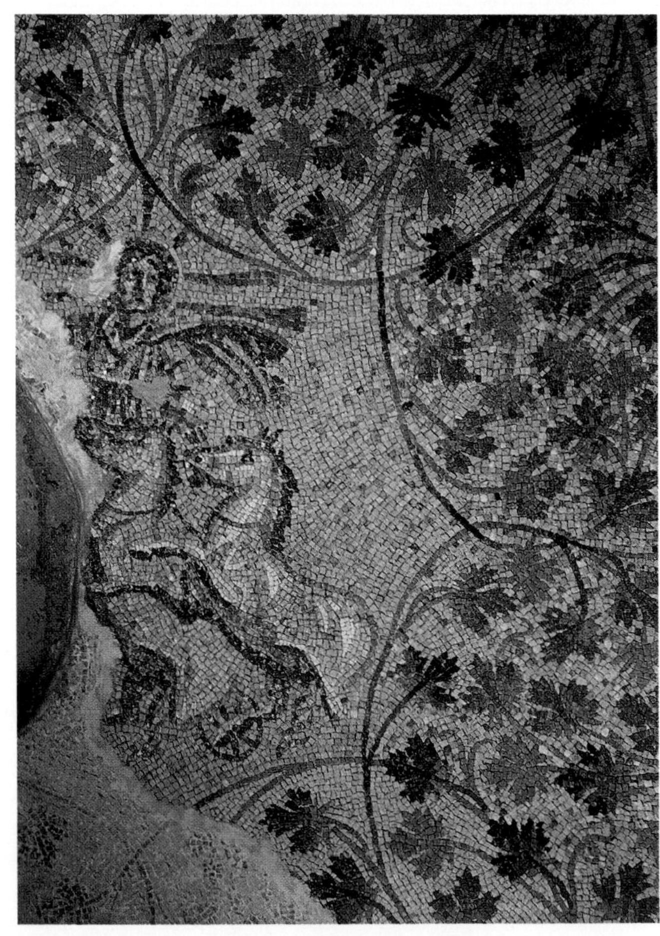

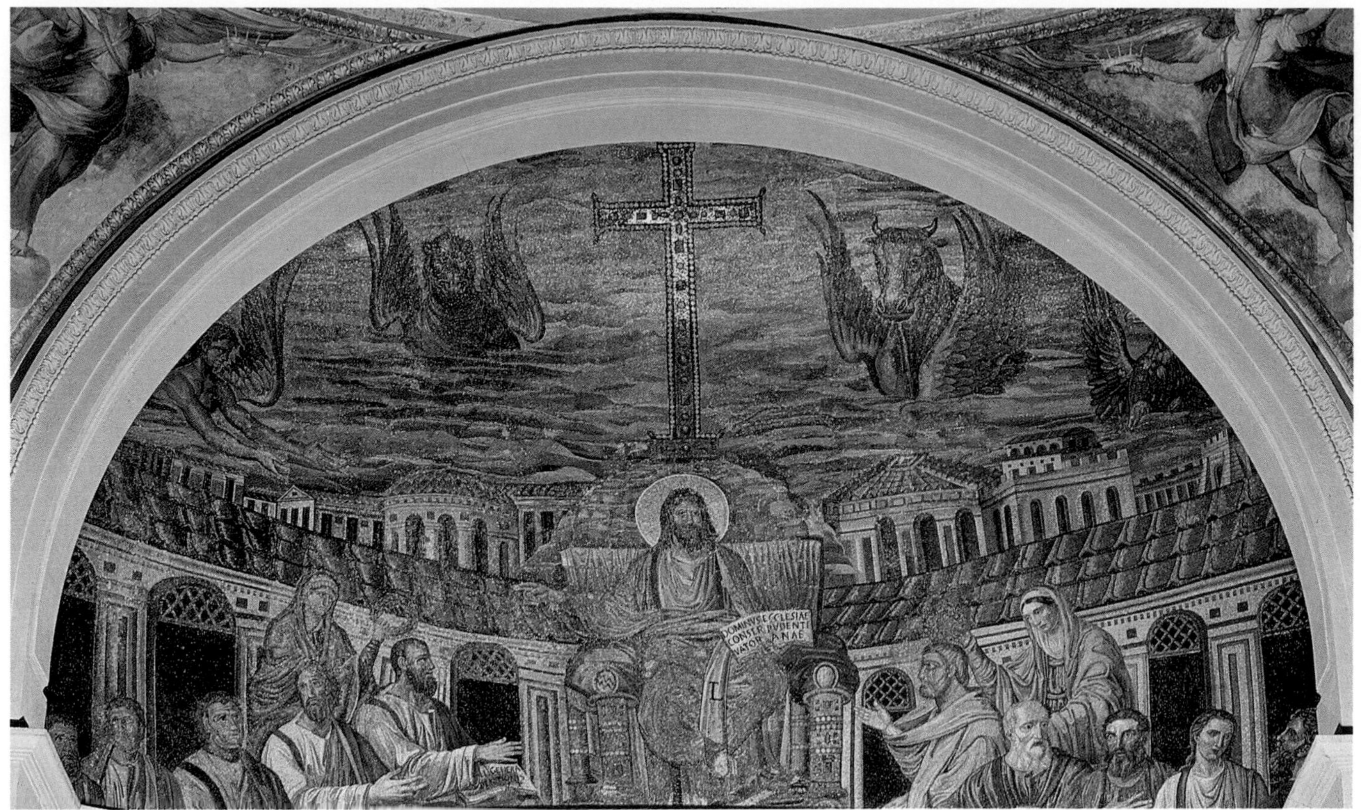

7-11 *Christ Enthroned in Majesty, with Saints,* apse mosaic, Santa Pudenziana, Rome, 402–417.

The style, or styles, of Christian art emerged as a transmutation of Greco-Roman art; for the mosaicists, the point of departure was Roman illusionism. We can see this readily in the apse mosaic of the church of Santa Pudenziana in Rome (FIG. **7-11**), dated about 410, which is the earliest surviving example in a succession of monumental apse mosaics that extend throughout the history of Christian art. Although the mosaic was drastically restored in the nineteenth century (almost the whole right half was damaged), enough remains to show the persistence of Roman forms and the assimilation of Roman imperial attributes to the image of Christ. On an emperor's throne, Christ, clad in imperial purple and gold, sits within the Heavenly Jerusalem and presides over the Church Triumphant. He is flanked on either side by ascending ranks of apostles, deployed like a Roman emperor's entourage of senators. Behind them, on either side of the throne, stand two women, the personifications of the Church of the Gentiles (New Testament) and the Church of the Synagogue (Old Testament). Above and behind the head of Christ is a representation of the jeweled cross that Constantine raised on the site of Christ's crucifixion. Within the gold-streaked, blue sky hover the four symbolic creatures of the visions of Ezekiel and the Book of Revelation, representing the Four Evangelists: the winged Man of St. Matthew (partly obscured here by the arch), the Lion of St. Mark, the Ox of St. Luke, and (also partly obscured) the Eagle of St. John. (This is an early appearance of these symbols, which we will find commonly represented throughout Medieval art; see, for example, the top of FIG. 7-30.) The background recalls the kind of perspective illusionism and naturalistic depiction of architectural forms found in Pompeian wall paintings, and the buildings may reflect, to some degree, those actually in Jerusalem at the time the mosaic was installed.

We also can note the union of the old naturalism and the new symbolism in the great mosaic cycle in Santa Maria Maggiore in Rome, which dates from about 430. The panel representing *The Parting of Lot and Abraham* (FIG. **7-12**) tells its story (Genesis 13:5–13) succinctly. Agreeing to disagree, Lot leads his family and followers to the right, toward the city of Sodom, while Abraham moves toward a building (perhaps the Church?) on the left. Lot's is the evil choice, and the instrumentalities of the evil (his two daughters) are represented in front of him; the figure of the yet unborn Isaac, the instrument of good, stands before his father, Abraham. The cleavage of the two groups is emphatic, and each is represented by a shorthand device that could be called a "head cluster," which will have a long history in Christian art. The figures turn from each other in a kind of sharp dialogue of glance and gesture, and we recognize a moving away

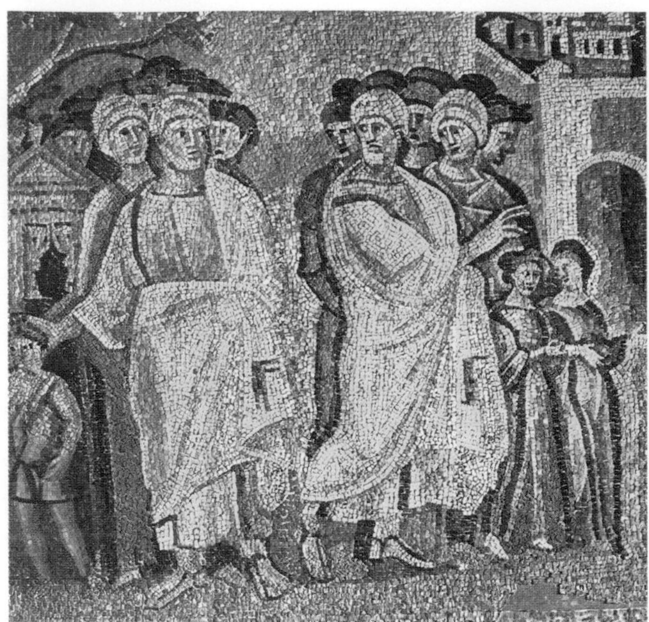

7-12 *The Parting of Lot and Abraham,* mosaic from Santa Maria Maggiore, Rome, c. 430.

from the flexibility of naturalism toward the significant gesture and that primary method of Medieval representation, *pantomime,* which simplifies all significance into body attitude and gesture. The wide eyes, turned in their sockets; the broad gestures of enlarged hands; the opposed movements of the groups all remind us of some silent, expressive chorus that comments only by gesture on the action of the drama. Thus, the complex action of Roman art stiffens into the art of simplified motion or dumb show, which has great power to communicate without ambiguity and which, in the whole course of Medieval art, will produce the richest kind of variety. The fact that the figures of the panel have been moved to the foreground and that the artist takes no great pains to describe either space or landscape setting also foreshadows the character of later Christian art; the background town and building are symbolic, rather than descriptive. But within this relatively abstract setting, the figures themselves loom with massive solidity. They cast shadows and are modeled in dark and light to give them the three-dimensional appearance that testifies to the artist's heritage of Roman pictorial illusionism. Another century and much modification under non-Hellenized Eastern influence will be required before artists will be able to think of figures entirely as flat images, rather than as plastic bodies.

The vivid narrative style of the Santa Maria Maggiore mosaic can be contrasted with the monumental stillness of the *orans* figures of martyrs in the great dome of the Church of St. George at Thessaloniki (Salonika) in northern Greece (FIG. **7-13**). These figures, with their architectural backgrounds and enframements, are the only survivors of a magnificent mosaic composition in concentric rings of golden tesserae, which climaxed at the summit of the dome in an apparition of Christ supported by flying angels. A middle zone may have contained figures in adoration before the Second Coming, to which the whole composition may have alluded. The formality of pose and the solemn, priestly demeanor of the figures—unvarying features of Byzantine art throughout its centuries of life—will coexist with the narrative approach that is brought into play when events of Scripture are illustrated. The formal style, intended to eternalize a vision of the transcendent mysteries of the faith, was confined principally to the upper levels of the church: the central dome, the apsidal dome, and the immediately lower levels that they command (FIG. 7-13). The elaborate architecture surrounding the St. George figures recalls the paintings on Pompeian walls and the actual "stage-set" architecture of buildings like the "Treasury" at Petra (FIG. 6-84). The Classical tradition persists even while the ethereal, golden splendor of the whole composition dissolves material form into spiritual phantasm. One could say that the dome mosaic of St. George completes the change from the images of the pagan floor mosaic, which are literally under the feet and of this world, to the floating images of a celestial world high above the Christian's wondering gaze. Yet the pagan substance is never entirely transformed.

7-13 *St. Onesiphorus and St. Porphyrius,* detail of dome mosaic, Church of St. George, Thessaloniki, Greece, late fifth century.

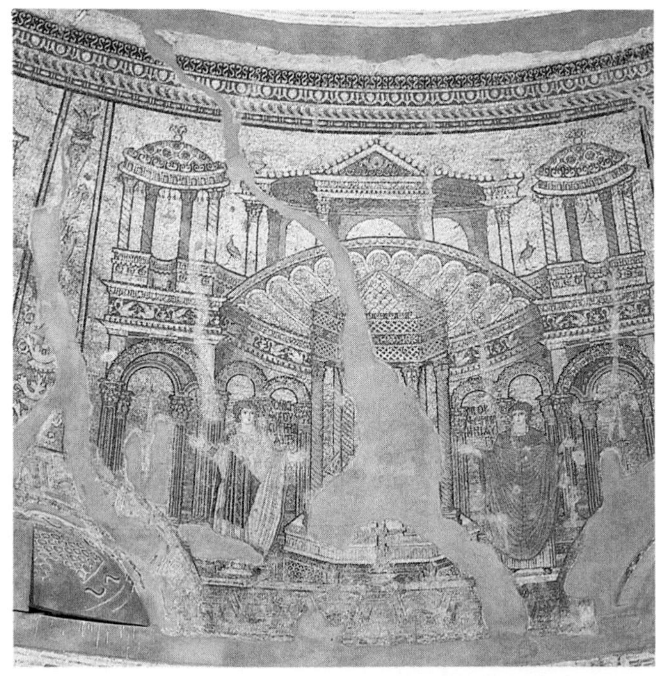

THE ILLUMINATED MANUSCRIPT

Santa Maria Maggiore is an early and outstanding example of the complementarity of the new basilican architecture and the detailed mosaics and paintings designed for it. But the earlier art of the catacombs could not have provided the resources for narratives as elaborate as those found at Santa Maria Maggiore; catacomb painting was much too narrow in scope of subject and much too rudimentary in style and technique. Rather, the church decorators must have drawn on a long tradition of pictures in manuscripts that began in pharaonic Egypt and was developed to a high degree by the Hellenistic Greeks of Alexandria. Thousands of texts must have been available to the Constantinian artists, richly illustrated with Hebrew, Greek, and Christian themes, or with combinations of all three.

Although both Jews and Christians were bound by the Second Commandment against images, the ban was somehow evaded and both sects made use of them. (Mural pictures found in the third-century Jewish synagogue at Dura-Europos in Mesopotamia illustrate themes from the Old Testament.) No Jewish illustrated manuscript has survived from ancient times; yet, it has been suggested that Jewish figural art, and certainly Jewish oral tradition, had considerable thematic influence on Christian art. We know that Constantine summoned numerous savants and literati from Alexandria, an intellectual center for both Jews and pagans since Hellenistic times and one of the great episcopal sees of the Christian church. He established a library where they gave instruction. We know also that he was a generous donor of manuscripts to the Church. Hence, it is no wonder that Constantinople became a center of traditional and Christian learning, which was transmitted by the copying and recopying of manuscripts through the centuries. The dissemination of manuscripts, as well as their preservation, was aided greatly by an important invention in the Early Imperial period. The long manuscript scroll (*rotulus*), used by Egyptians, Greeks, and Romans and made of the fragile papyrus, was superseded by the *codex*, which was made, much like the modern book, of separate pages enclosed within a cover and bound together at one side. Papyrus was replaced by the much more durable *vellum* (calfskin) and *parchment* (lambskin), which provided better surfaces for painting. These changes in the durability, reproduction, and format of texts greatly improved the possibility that the records of ancient civilizations could survive long centuries of neglect, even if not in great number.

The sacred texts were copied as faithfully as possible, as were the pictures in them. After the great fathers of the Eastern church recommended the didactic use of pictures in churches and books, the picture became only slightly less significant than the text from which it drew its authority. We can see the transition from the scroll to the codex (from continuous narrative to a series of individual pictures) in two manuscripts of different dates (the later manuscript still reflects the scroll procedure). The *Vatican Vergil* (FIG. **7-14**) dates from the early fifth century and is the oldest painted manuscript known. Its content is pagan, representing a scene from Vergil's *Georgics,* in which a seated farmer (at the left) instructs two of his slaves in the art of husbandry, while Vergil (at the right) listens and records the instructions. (We are reminded of the Roman idealization of country life and nature.) The style is Late Antique and reminiscent of Pompeian landscapes. The quick, impressionistic touches that suggest space and atmosphere, the foreshortened villa in the background, and the small, active figures in their wide, spacious setting are all familiar features of Roman illusionistic painting. The heavy, black frame that isolates a single episode was also a feature of the late Pompeian styles.

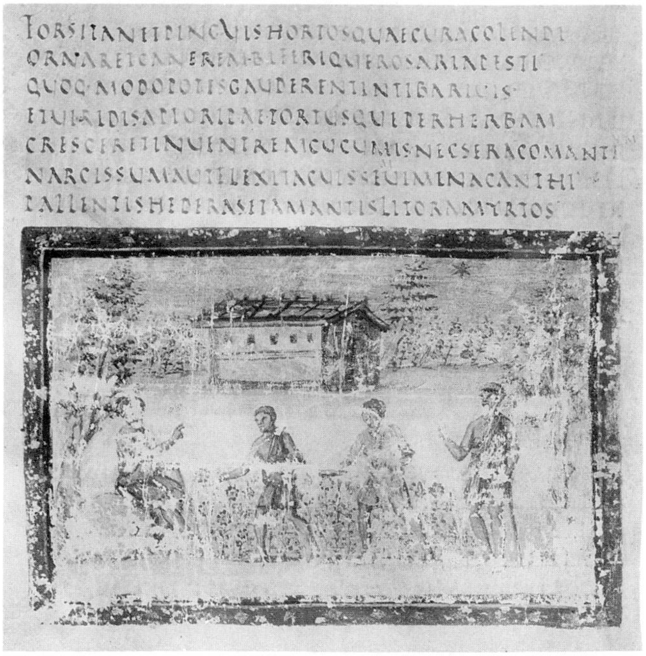

7-14 Miniature from the *Vatican Vergil,* early fifth century. Approx. 12½″ × 12″. Vatican Library, Rome.

The *Vatican Vergil* can be contrasted in form with the *Vienna Genesis* (FIG. **7-15**), the earliest, well-preserved, painted manuscript we know of that contains biblical scenes. The *Vienna Genesis* employs the continuity of a frieze in a scroll. In a continuous narrative like this, two or more scenes of a story are represented within a single frame; this will become the common form of narrative in Medieval art. In this

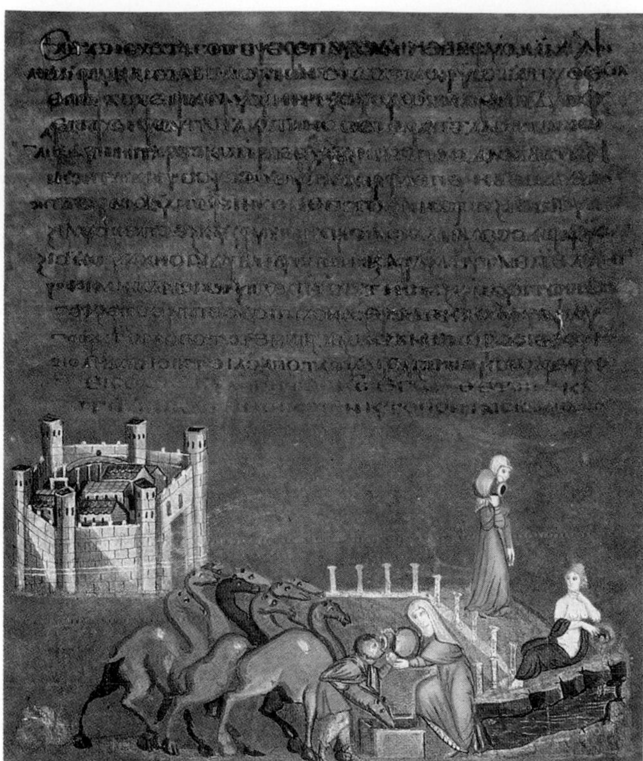

7-15 *Rebecca and Eliezer at the Well,* from the *Vienna Genesis,* early sixth century. Book illumination painted on purple vellum, $9\frac{3}{4}'' \times 12\frac{1}{4}''$. Österreichische Nationalbibliothek, Vienna.

scene from the Book of Genesis (24:15–61), Rebecca leaves the city of Nahor to fetch water from the well in the first episode. In the second, she gives water to Eliezer and his camels. Her way is marked by a colonnaded avenue; her destination is indicated by a seminude, naïvely pert, little personification of the well—a lingering reminder of a pagan river-goddess, as well as a reminder of the persistence of Classical motifs and stylistic modes in Medieval art. The action is presented with all possible simplicity in an expressive pantomime that includes convincing touches; for example, Rebecca braces herself with her raised right foot on the rim of the well as she tips up her jug for Eliezer. The figures are silhouetted against a landscape that is blank except for the toylike city. Everything necessary to bare narrative is present, and nothing else. Although the figures have only narrative significance, the page itself is sumptuous: a rich, purple ground of vellum is lettered in silver. The luxuriousness of ornament that will become more and more typical of sacred books absorbs the human figure or confines it exclusively to iconic or narrative functions. The spiritual beauty of the text and the material beauty of the vehicle that serves and intensifies it will come to count above all else. The luster of holy objects becomes the intent and the effect of Byzantine art.

Closely related to the *Vienna Genesis* is another manuscript of about the same time, the early sixth century, and perhaps of the same provenance. *The Rossano Gospels* (known also as the *Codex Rossanensis*) is the earliest illuminated book we have that contains illustrations of the New Testament (FIG. **7-16**). We can infer from them that, by this time, a canon of New Testament iconography has been fairly well established. Like the *Vienna Genesis,* the text of *The Rossano Gospels* is inscribed in silver on purple vellum. The Rossano artist, however, has attempted, with considerable success, to harmonize the colors with the purple ground. The subject of our illustration, presented in vigorous pantomime, is the judgment of Jesus by Pilate or, more particularly, the people's choice of Barabbas over Jesus (Matthew 27:2–26). In the fashion of continuous narrative, several different episodes are included. The figures are arranged on two levels separated by a simple ground line. In the upper level, Pilate presides over the tribunal, at which the people demand the death of Jesus as Judas returns the thirty pieces of silver—an inaccuracy in the time and place of the episode as it occurs in the text. Jesus and the bound thief Barabbas appear in the lower level. Jesus, at the left, is now distinguished by the cross-inscribed *nimbus* (halo) that signifies his divinity; Barabbas, at the far right, is bending low in the

7-16 *Pilate Demanding That the People Choose Between Jesus and Barabbas,* from *The Rossano Gospels,* early sixth century. Book illumination on purple vellum, $11'' \times 10\frac{1}{4}''$. The Diocesan Museum, Archepiscopal Palace, Rossano, Italy.

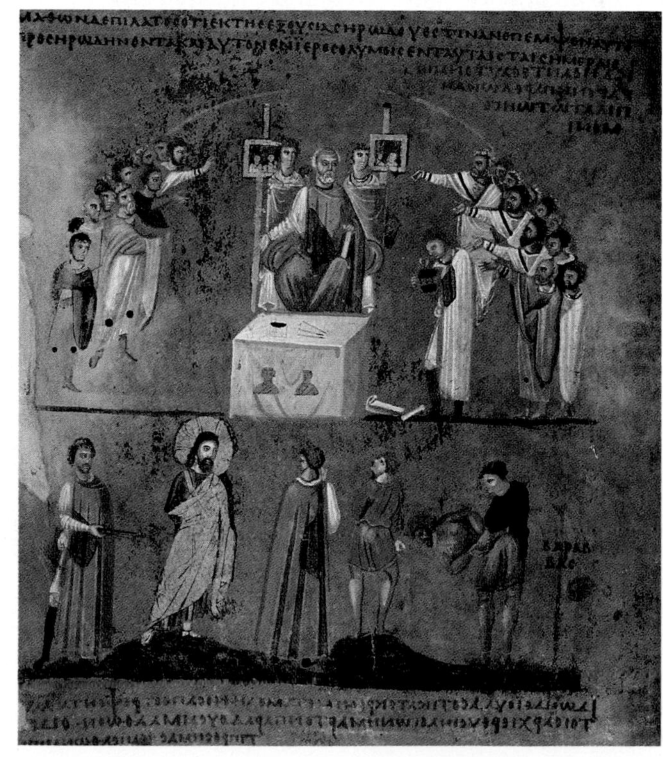

direction of Judas, who hangs himself. The illuminator has assumed that the reader is perfectly familiar with the text being illustrated and has tried to make the composition as inclusive of all relevant episodes as possible, adding labels when they were needed. Here, the artist wants the picture to be as readable as the text; the story is all that counts.

By the sixth century, the canon of Christian sacred texts, as well as the cycles of illustration appropriate to them, had been agreed on. The denaturing of Classical form is well advanced, and a new art is originating. We are now a considerable distance in time from the painting of the Roman Imperial period, with its worldly themes, naturalism, perspective illusionism, modeling in light and shade, graded tonality, and proportionality. Very little regard will be given to the pagan ideals of beauty in the centuries to come.

Sculpture and Craft Art

The transformations that occurred in architecture in the period of early Christianity—the adaption of the multipurpose pagan basilica to the single purpose of Christian ritual and the "dematerialization" of the heavy materiality of Roman buildings into the screenlike thinness and lightness of Christian structure—are paralleled in the sculpture of the time. We have seen anticipations of the change as early as the second century in the Column of Trajan (FIG. 6-70), and we have seen the change almost completed in early fourth-century reliefs on the Arch of Constantine (FIGS. 6-96 and 6-97).

A third-century relief on the so-called *Ludovisi Battle Sarcophagus* (FIG. **7-17**) should be interpolated between these two other works. This work, still quite pagan in theme and spirit, representing a struggle between Romans and barbarians, is most instructive as an illustration of the "flattened relief" and the "piled-up" perspective so characteristic of the denaturing of Greco-Roman naturalism and the emerging Medieval style. Although a strong descriptive realism persists in the details of physiognomy, dress, action, gesture, and accessories, *pattern* has taken over from figure composition. The writhing figures are all within the same plane; at the same time, the "foreground" figures (at the base of the pattern) are relatively small, while the "background" figures (at the top of the pattern) are the largest. This *reverse perspective* strengthens the surface into a dense mass with no illusion of space beyond (behind) it. Carving plays a lesser and lesser role, and quick effects of light and dark are achieved by gouging, punching, and drilling the surface. As yet, the formal placement of the figures that we find in the Arch of Constantine has not

7-17 *Battle Between Romans and Barbarians,* front panel of the so-called *Ludovisi Battle Sarcophagus,* third century. Marble, approx. 56″ high. Museo Nazionale, Rome.

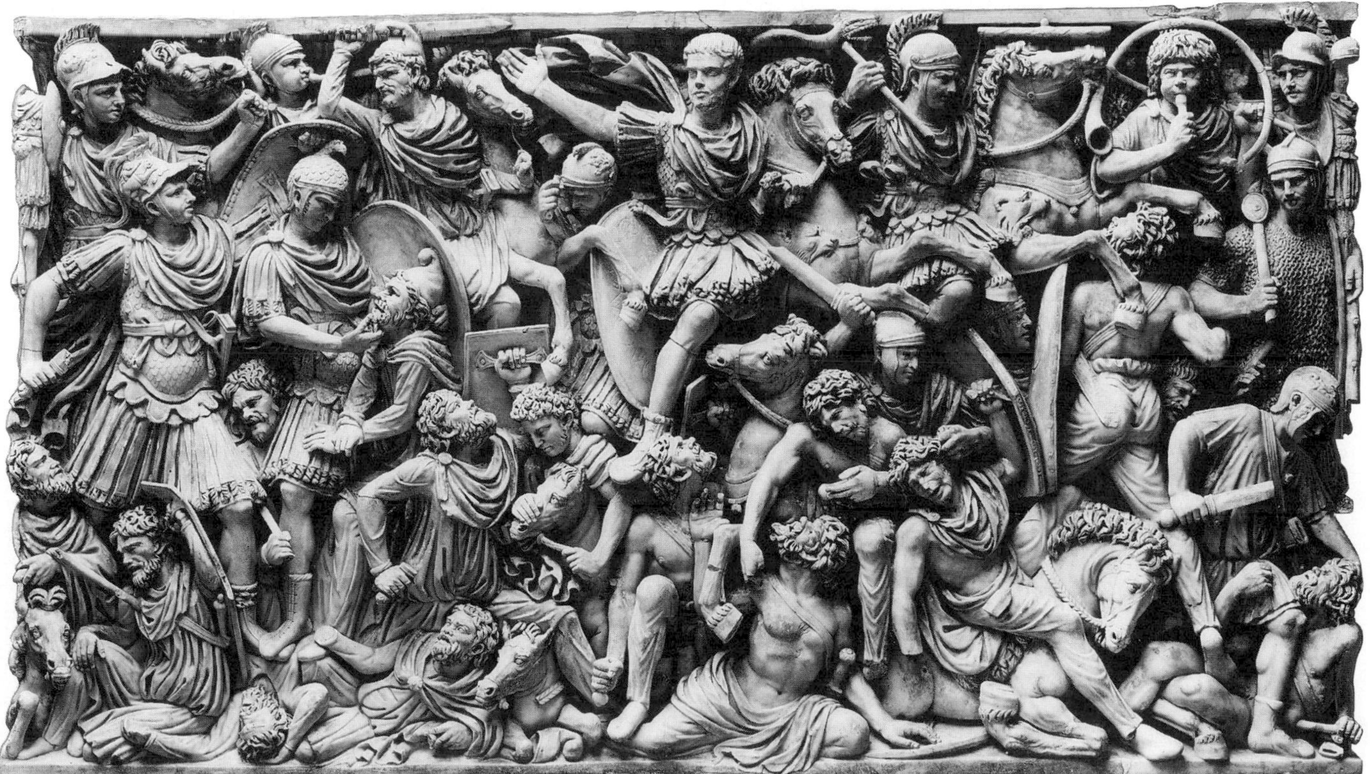

appeared; of course, the subject does not call for that, and the sarcophagus composition is more a representation of the dissolution of the style of the Trajanic reliefs than of the advent of Constantinian formalism. But the patterning and constriction of surface, the sacrifice of realism of space and proportion, are all present and characteristic of Early Christian art.

Toward the end of the fourth century, we find the flattening and patterning process well advanced. *The Good Shepherd Sarcophagus* (FIG. **7-18**) has a thick, spaceless surface that is perforated rather than carved, producing a kind of hard lacing of flat darks and lights. This sarcophagus is interesting, too, for what it reveals of the Christian adaptation of pagan material. We have seen that the Good Shepherd theme appears in pre-Christian times and that the Christians chose it to signify Christ. Here, the motif appears three times, possibly in an allusion to the Trinity. Around the Good Shepherd twines a grapevine heavy with grapes, through which busy cupids climb, bringing in the harvest. Three cupids crush the grapes in a wine press; their wine, once sacred to Bacchus, now has become symbolic of the blood of Christ. The cupids themselves, once associated with love and erotic passion (Cupid is the son of Venus), are forerunners of the Christian cherubs. Thus, a purely pagan theme with orgiastic overtones is transmuted, by Christian intention, into a symbol of redemption through the blood of Christ. The figure style, with its stumpy proportions, frontalizing pose, and stereotyping of action, had its predecessor in the reliefs of the Arch of Constantine and is common (with many variations) to a great number of sarcophagi from the fourth, fifth, and sixth centuries.

Despite the great changes in sculpture during the second half of the third century, the Classical tradition was by no means extinguished, even though many artists almost deliberately seemed to be turning away from Greco-Roman art to something Archaic, abstract, and bluntly expressive, as seen in *The Tetrarchs*, the reliefs from the Arch of Constantine, and the medallion portrait of Maximin Daia. The Classical tradition lived on through the Middle Ages, if not with entirely discernible continuity, in intermittent revivals, renovations, and restorations, commingled with—or side by side and in contrast with—the opposing, nonclassicizing Medieval styles. The end of the medieval world will be signalized by the rise of Classical art to dominance in the Renaissance. One observer recently commented that the greatest accomplishment of Early Christian art from the third to the seventh century is that it "preserved, in the face of vast and cataclysmic changes, basic and essential elements of the Greco-Roman heritage."* As we follow the course of stylistic change throughout the history of Western art, especially in the Middle Ages, the strength of the Classical tradition in its dialogue with competing strains and tendencies of style should always be kept in mind.

Monumental sculpture began to decline in the fourth century and did not recover its place in the history of art until the twelfth century. The Christian tended to be suspicious of the freestanding statue, linking it with the false gods of the pagans. In his *Apologia,* Justin Martyr, a second-century ecclesiast

*Ernst Kitzinger, *Byzantine Art in the Making* (Cambridge, MA: Harvard University Press, 1977), p. 126.

7-18 *The Good Shepherd Sarcophagus,* from the catacomb of Praetextatus, late fourth century. Museo del Laterano, Rome.

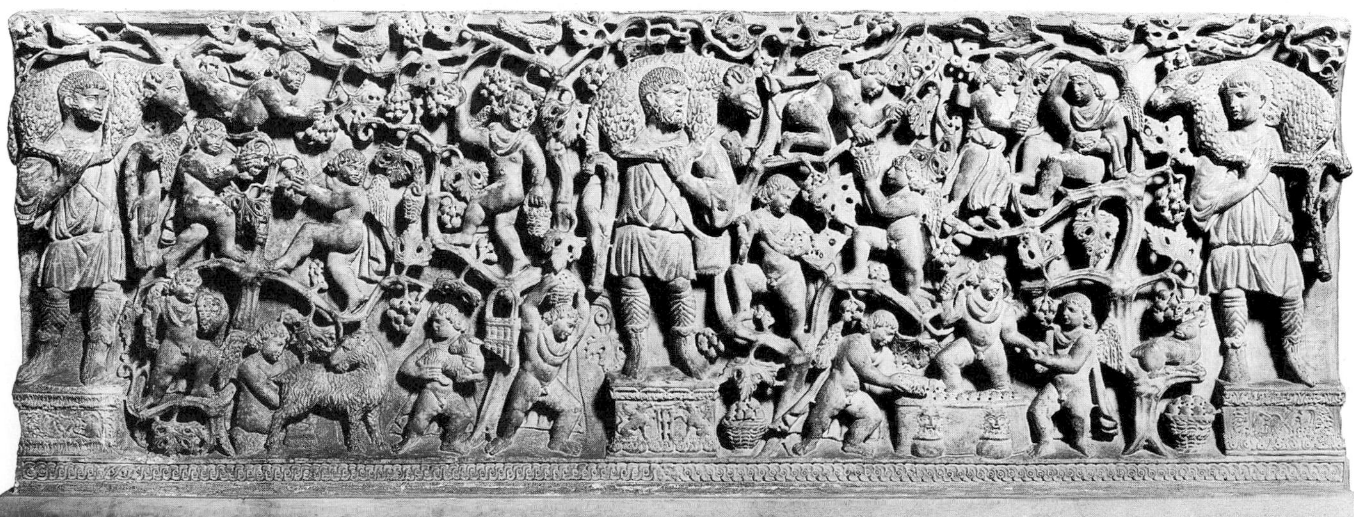

mindful of the admonition of the Second Commandment to shun graven images, accused the pagans of worshiping statues as gods. But the Greco-Roman experience was still a living part of the Mediterranean mentality, and, at least in the west, the Semitic ban on images in sacred places was not likely to be adopted. The reasoning of the fathers of the early Church, that the use of pictures and statues could be justified on the grounds that they instructed the illiterate in the mysteries and stories of the faith, was later supplemented by the theological argument that since Jesus was "made flesh and dwelt among us," he had a human nature and human likeness that could be represented in art.

In any event, during the Early Christian and Byzantine periods, sculpture dwindled to craft art and small work: sarcophagus reliefs, commemorative ivory panels, metalwork, church furniture and accessories, book covers, and the like. Yet, in this great reduction of the scope of the medium, works of exquisite craftsmanship still were produced that reflected, even in Christian times, the persistence of pagan, Classical ideals of beauty. An ivory plaque (FIG. **7-19**), probably produced in Rome toward the end of the fourth century, strikingly exhibits the endurance of Classical form. The ivory, one of a pair of leaves of a *diptych* (two carved, hinged panels), commemorates the marriage of members of two powerful Roman families of the senatorial class, the Nicomachi and the Symmachi, who remained pagan during this first triumphal period when the emperor Theodosius decreed Christianity to be the only legally recognized religion of the empire. Here, the families consciously seem to reaffirm their faith in the old pagan gods; certainly, they favor the esthetic ideals of the Classical past, much as we find these ideals realized in such works as the Parthenon frieze (FIG. 5-50) and the Ara Pacis Augustae (FIG. 6-64). The illustration represents a pagan priestess celebrating the rites of Bacchus and Jupiter; its companion piece shows a priestess honoring Ceres and Cybele. The priestess (FIG. 7-19) prepares a libation at an altar where the sacred fire burns. The precise yet fluent and graceful line, the easy, gliding pose, and the mood of spiritual serenity bespeak an artist practicing within a still vital Classical tradition, to which idealized human beauty is central. That tradition probably was sustained deliberately by the great senatorial magnates of Rome, who resisted the empirewide imposition of the Christian faith in the later fourth century.

A later work, carved in the eastern empire, perhaps in Constantinople, offers still further evidence of the persistence of Classical form, although subtle deviations from Classical rules are apparent here. The item

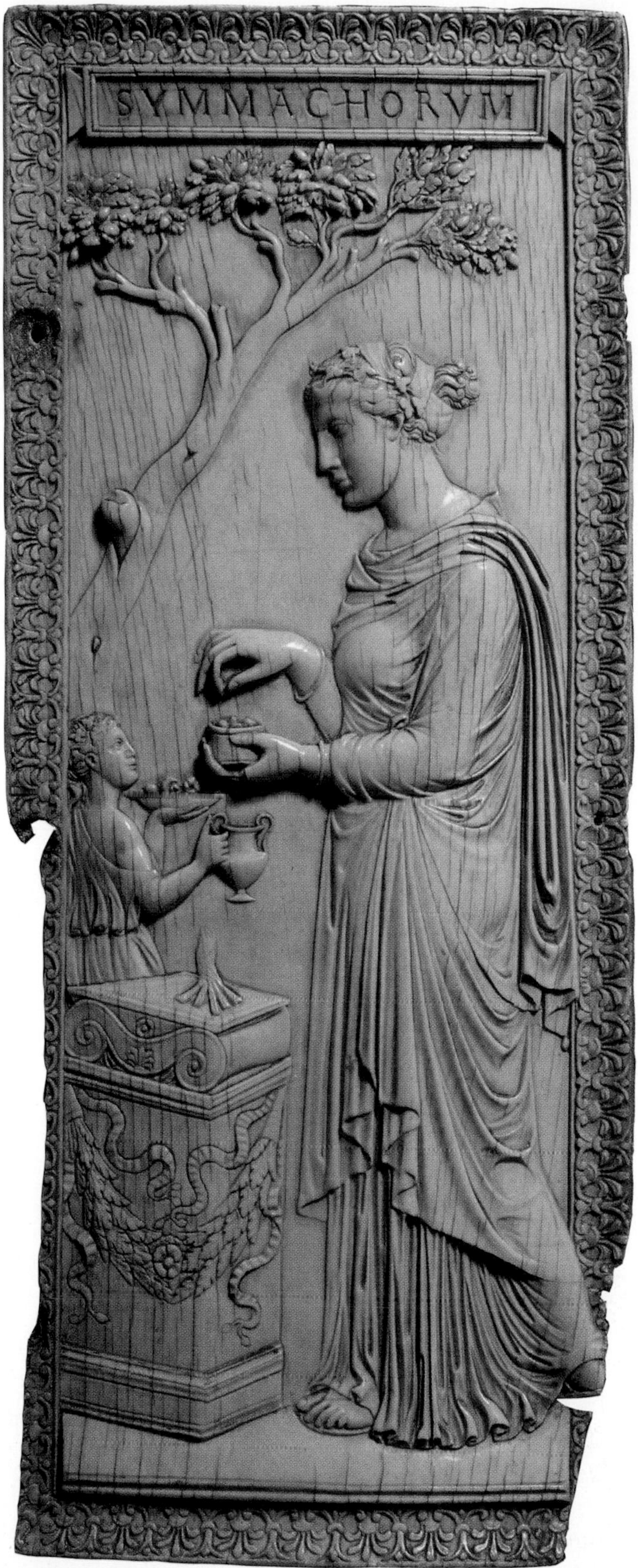

7-19 *Priestess Celebrating the Rites of Bacchus,* c. 380–400. Leaf of an ivory diptych of the Nicomachi and the Symmachi, $11\frac{3}{4}'' \times 5\frac{1}{2}''$. Victoria and Albert Museum, London.

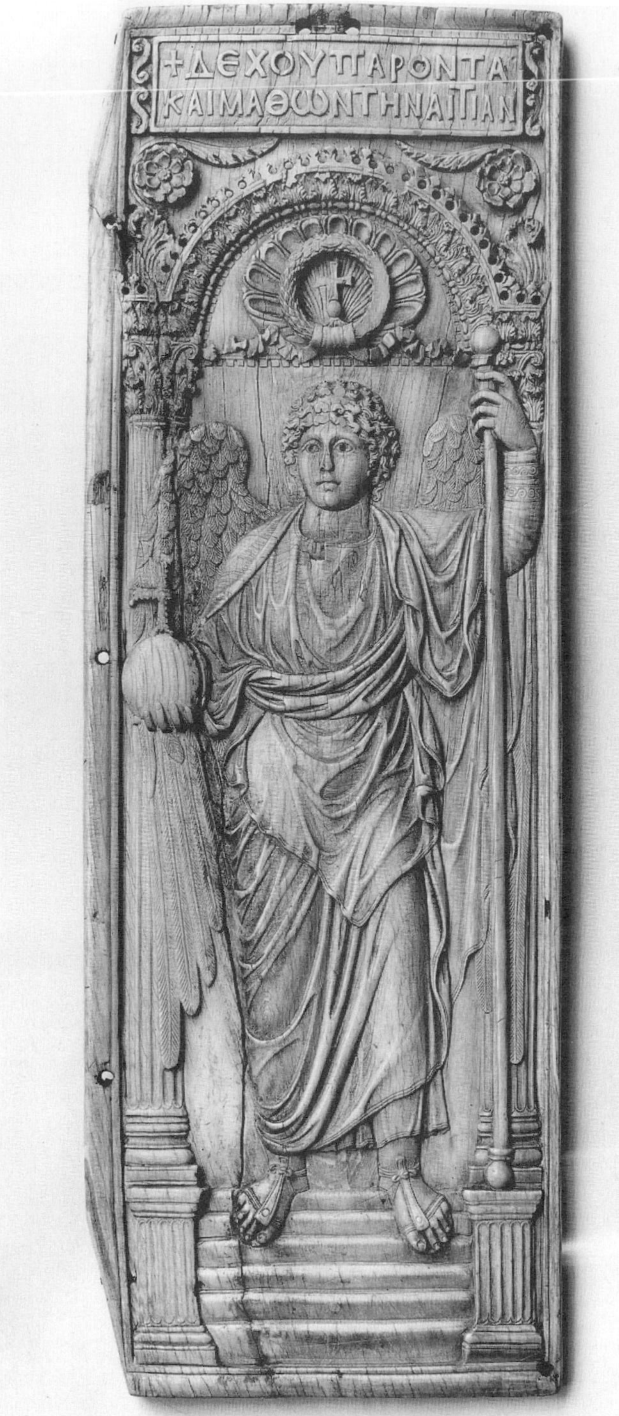

7-20 *St. Michael the Archangel,* early sixth century. Leaf of an ivory diptych, approx. 17″ × $5\frac{1}{2}$″. British Museum, London.

is an ivory leaf from a diptych dating from the early sixth century, depicting *St. Michael the Archangel* (FIG. **7-20**). The prototype of St. Michael must have been a pagan Victory; the flowing Classical yet naturalistic drapery, the delicately incised wings, and the facial type and coiffure are of the pre-Christian tradition. But even so, significant divergences—misinterpretations or misreadings of the rules of naturalistic representation—occur here. Subtle ambiguities in the relationship of the figure to its architectural setting appear in such details as the feet hovering above the stair without any real relationship to it and the placement of the scepter. These matters, of course, have little to do with the striking beauty of the form; they simply indicate the course of stylistic change, as the Greco-Roman world faded into history and the Medieval era began.

We find that change almost completed in the *Diptych of Anastasius* (FIG. **7-21**), which represents the emperor Anastasius I, as consul, about to throw down the *mappa* (handkerchief), the signal for the games shown in the arena below him to start. Although the diptych, dated 517, is almost contemporary with the St. Michael ivory, the mutation of Classical naturalism is much further advanced (a reminder that the process does not proceed evenly along the same historical front or at the same tempo). The figure of the emperor in both panels is elevated above the lively scenes taking place in the arena. He is enthroned in rigid frontality, making a static, suspended gesture—entirely symbolic, the abstraction of his consular authority. His features are masklike,

7-21 *Diptych of Anastasius,* 517. Ivory, each leaf 14″ × 5″. Bibliothèque Nationale, Paris.

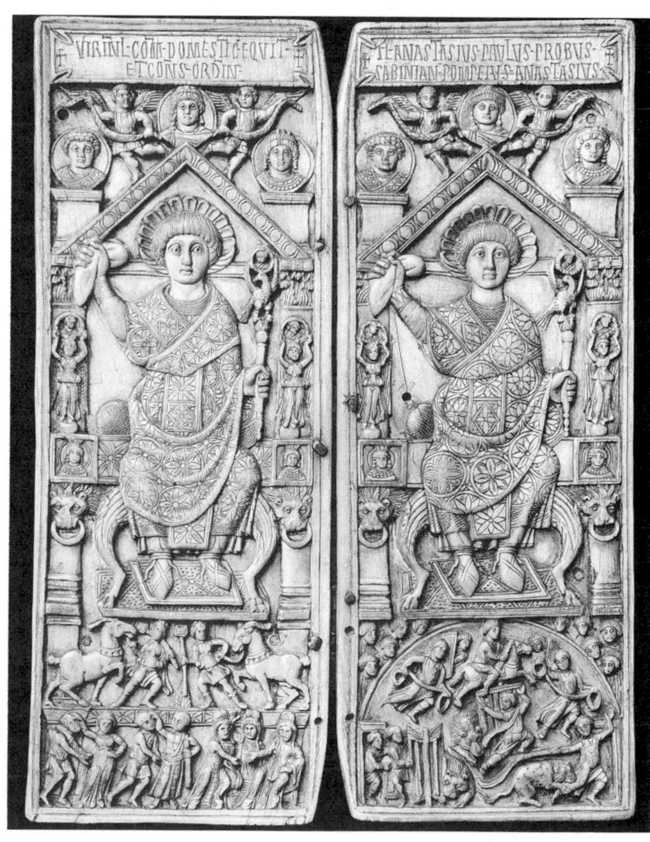

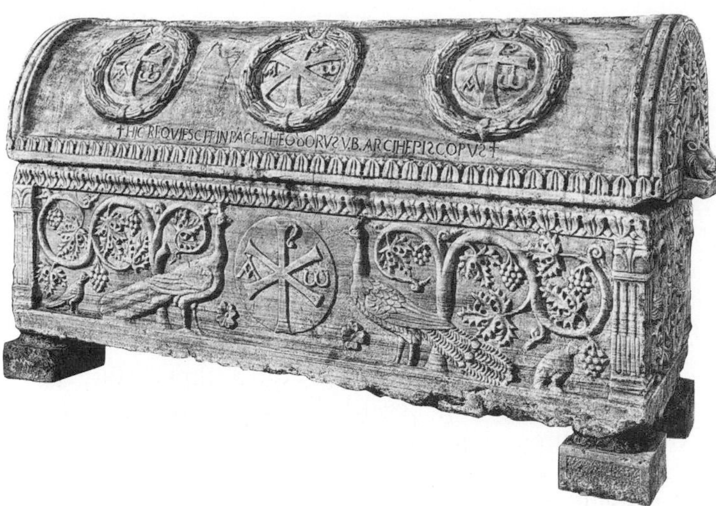

7-22 Sarcophagus of Archbishop Theodore, seventh century. Marble. Sant' Apollinare in Classe, Ravenna, Italy.

and his quasi-divine status is announced by a halo. The halo, a shell form, originally would have been an architectural feature, part of the pediment of the niche; here, in an excellent example of a misreading of a prototype, it has migrated to its place behind the emperor's head. The details of the architecture are confused and have lost their original significance. The flattening and patterning of the surface is as we have seen it developing earlier. The work is entirely ornamental and symbolic; the living man is lost in the concept—in this case, the concept of supreme and suprahuman authority.

One hundred years after the *Diptych of Anastasius,* the sarcophagus of Archbishop Theodore (FIG. 7-22) is not only ornamented with entirely symbolic forms, but the human figure is dismissed altogether. Peacocks, symbolic of eternity, flank a *chi-rho* monogram (chi [X] and rho [P] are the first two letters of "Christ" in Greek). The XP is supplemented in the monogram with the alpha (A) and the omega (Ω), the first and last letters of the Greek alphabet, representing the words of Christ, "I am the Beginning and the End." The fruiting vines behind the peacocks represent, as we have seen, the source of the redeeming blood of Christ. Set within wreaths on the lid of the tomb, the *chi-rho* monogram appears three times; it already had served as the *labarum* carried on the standards of the imperial Christian army. Thus, the hope of the deceased archbishop and the guarantee of his salvation are expressed entirely in symbol: eternity; redemption through the blood of Christ, who stands at the beginning and the end of time; and the triumph of Christianity. The accidents and irregularities of figural representation, and the busyness of narrative, are replaced by timeless signs of salvation and immortality.

BYZANTINE ART

The transition from Early Christian to Byzantine art is neither abrupt nor definite and, in fact, defies accurate definition. The almost contemporary diptychs of St. Michael (FIG. 7-20) and of Anastasius (FIG. 7-21) are both products of eastern carvers and might well be classified as Byzantine works. Yet *St. Michael the Archangel* is still firmly rooted in the Greco-Roman tradition, and the *Diptych of Anastasius* panels show the Medieval stress on the event rather than on its appearance. In the latter approach, which was essentially Near Eastern or Semitic, forms evolved into decorative symbols placed before a shallow, often neutral background that made little, if any, allusion to optical space.

One point of departure for the abstract, symbolic, Eastern Christian art may be a mural painting (FIG. 7-23) from Dura-Europos, a small garrison town on the west bank of the Euphrates in the heart of ancient Mesopotamia and on the very edge of the Roman Empire, already noted as the site of the Jewish synagogue with figural mural paintings (page 265). The mural dates from the second to third century, the time of the Roman occupation. The detail shown here may depict an attendant and priests of a forgotten

7-23 *Priests with Attendant,* detail of a mural from the Temple of the Palmyrene Gods, Dura-Europos, Syria, second to third century.

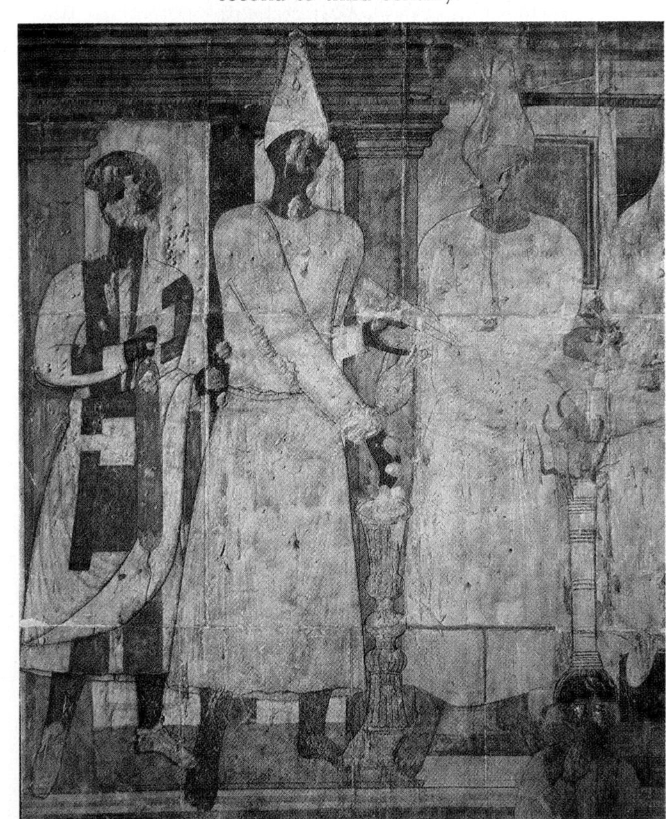

pagan cult of Parthia or Palmyra (biblical Tadmor). The figures stand with formal frontality in front of, or perhaps within, an architectural background. Their drapery is rendered by line, not tone, and their gestures are slow, ceremonial, and grave. Each figure is, in itself, a vertical design entity, isolated from its neighbor. The bodies hover weightlessly, their feet in ambiguous relationship to the ground and to the architectural setting, reminding us of the St. Michael ivory (FIG. 7-20) carved centuries later. Although the meaning of the enacted ceremony is lost to us, it must have been represented with utmost clarity to initiates, who could read the depicted symbols and gestures like a pictorial script—a script that moved laterally across the surface of the painted wall, unobstructed by perspective and other illusionistic devices.

As Christian dogma developed, this form of symbolic interpretation of reality became more favored, and a flat, decorative, abstract, "Byzantine" style, rooted in such Near Eastern works as the Dura-Europos murals, began to dominate Christian art. Although Western illusionism was tenacious and enjoyed repeated revivals, the transition was more or less complete by the middle of the sixth century.

Ravenna and Mount Sinai

Early in the fifth century, when the Visigoths, under their king, Alaric, threatened to overrun Italy, Emperor Honorius moved the capital of his crumbling empire to Ravenna, an ancient Roman city near Italy's Adriatic coast, some eighty miles south of Venice. There, in a city surrounded by swamps and thus easily defended, his imperial authority survived the fall of Rome to Alaric in 410. Honorius died in 423, and the reins of government were taken over by his half sister, Galla Placidia, whose biography reads like an outrageously exaggerated adventure story. Galla Placidia died in 450, some twenty-five years before the last of her weak successors was deposed. In 476, Ravenna fell to Odoacer. Eventually, in 493, the city was chosen by Theodoric, the Goths' greatest king, to be the capital of his Ostrogothic kingdom, which encompassed much of the Balkans and all of Italy. During the short history of Theodoric's unfortunate successors, the importance of the city declined. But in 539, the Byzantine general Belisarius conquered Ravenna for his emperor, Justinian, and led the city into the third and most important stage of its history. Reunited with the eastern "empire," Ravenna remained the "sacred fortress" of Byzantium, a Byzantine foothold in Italy for two hundred years, until its conquest first by the Lombards and then by the Franks. Ravenna enjoyed its greatest cultural and economic prosperity during the reign of Justinian, at a time when the "eternal city" of Rome was threatened with complete extinction by repeated sieges, conquests, and sackings. As the seat of Byzantine dominion in Italy, ruled by Byzantine governors, or *exarchs,* Ravenna and its culture became an extension of Constantinople, and its art, more than that of the Byzantine capital (where relatively little outside of architecture has survived), clearly reveals the transition from the Early Christian to the Byzantine style.

7-24 Mausoleum of Galla Placidia, Ravenna, Italy, 425–450.

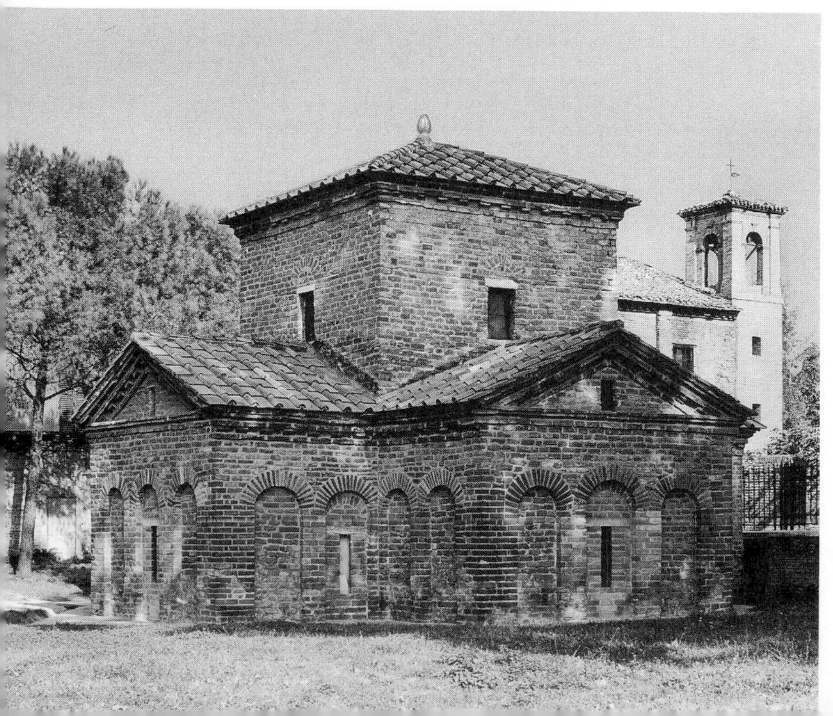

The climactic points of Ravenna's history are linked closely with the personages of Galla Placidia, Theodoric, and Justinian. All left their stamp on the city in monuments that have survived to our day (one might say "miraculously," as the city was heavily bombed in World War II) and that make Ravenna one of the richest repositories of fifth- and sixth-century mosaics in Italy. The monuments of Ravenna, particularly the Justinianic ones, represent ideas that ultimately determined the forms of the culture, and certainly of the art, of the Middle Ages.

Galla Placidia's own mausoleum (the identity of which has recently been questioned) is a rather small, cruciform structure with a dome-covered crossing (FIGS. **7-24** and **7-25**). Built shortly after 425, it was originally attached to the narthex of the now greatly altered basilican palace-church of Santa Croce. Although the mausoleum's plan is that of a Latin cross, the cross arms are very short and appear to be little more than apsidal extensions of a square. All emphasis is placed on the tall, dome-covered crossing, and the building becomes, in effect, a central-plan structure. On the other hand, this small, unassuming building also represents one of the earliest successful fusions of the two basic early church plans, the longi-

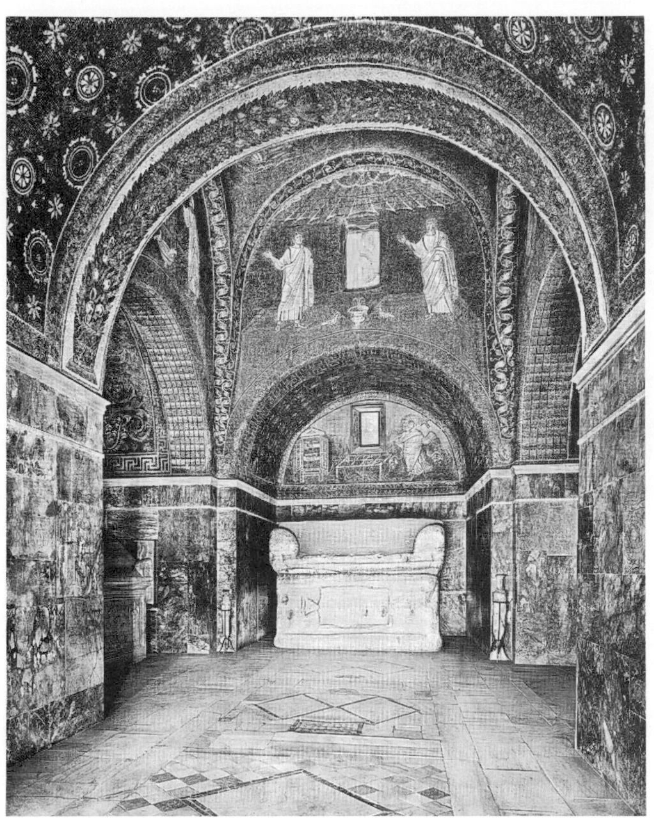

7-25 Interior of the mausoleum of Galla Placidia.

tudinal and the central, and it introduces us, on a small scale, to a building type that would have a long history in Christian architecture—the basilican plan with a domed crossing.

The mausoleum's plain, unadorned, brick shell encloses one of the richest mosaic ensembles in Early Christian art. Every square inch of the interior surfaces above the marble-faced walls is covered with mosaic decor: the barrel vaults of nave and cross arms, with garlands and decorative medallions reminiscent of snowflakes on a dark blue ground; the dome, with a large, golden cross set against a star-studded sky; other surfaces, with representations of saints and apostles; and the lunette above the entrance, with a representation of *Christ as the Good Shepherd* (FIG. **7-26**). We have seen earlier versions of the Good Shepherd, but none so regal as this. Jesus no longer carries a lamb on his shoulders but is seated among his flock in splendid isolation, haloed and robed in gold and purple. To his left and right, the sheep are distributed evenly in groups of three. But their arrangement is rather loose and informal (compare FIG. 7-28), and they have been placed in a carefully described landscape that extends from foreground to background and is covered by a blue sky. All forms are tonally rendered; they have three-dimensional bulk, cast shadows, and are disposed in

7-26 *Christ as the Good Shepherd,* mosaic from the entrance wall of the mausoleum of Galla Placidia, 425–450.

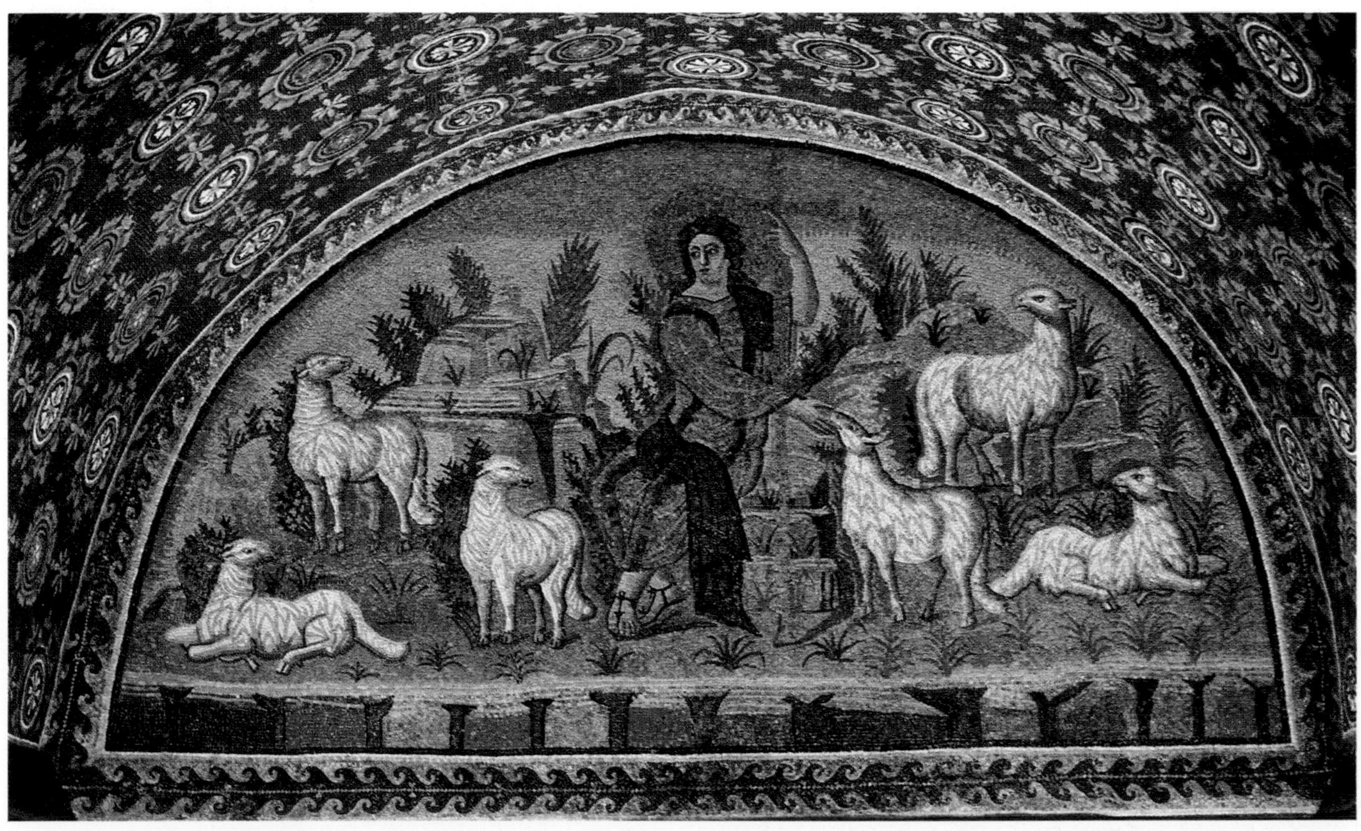

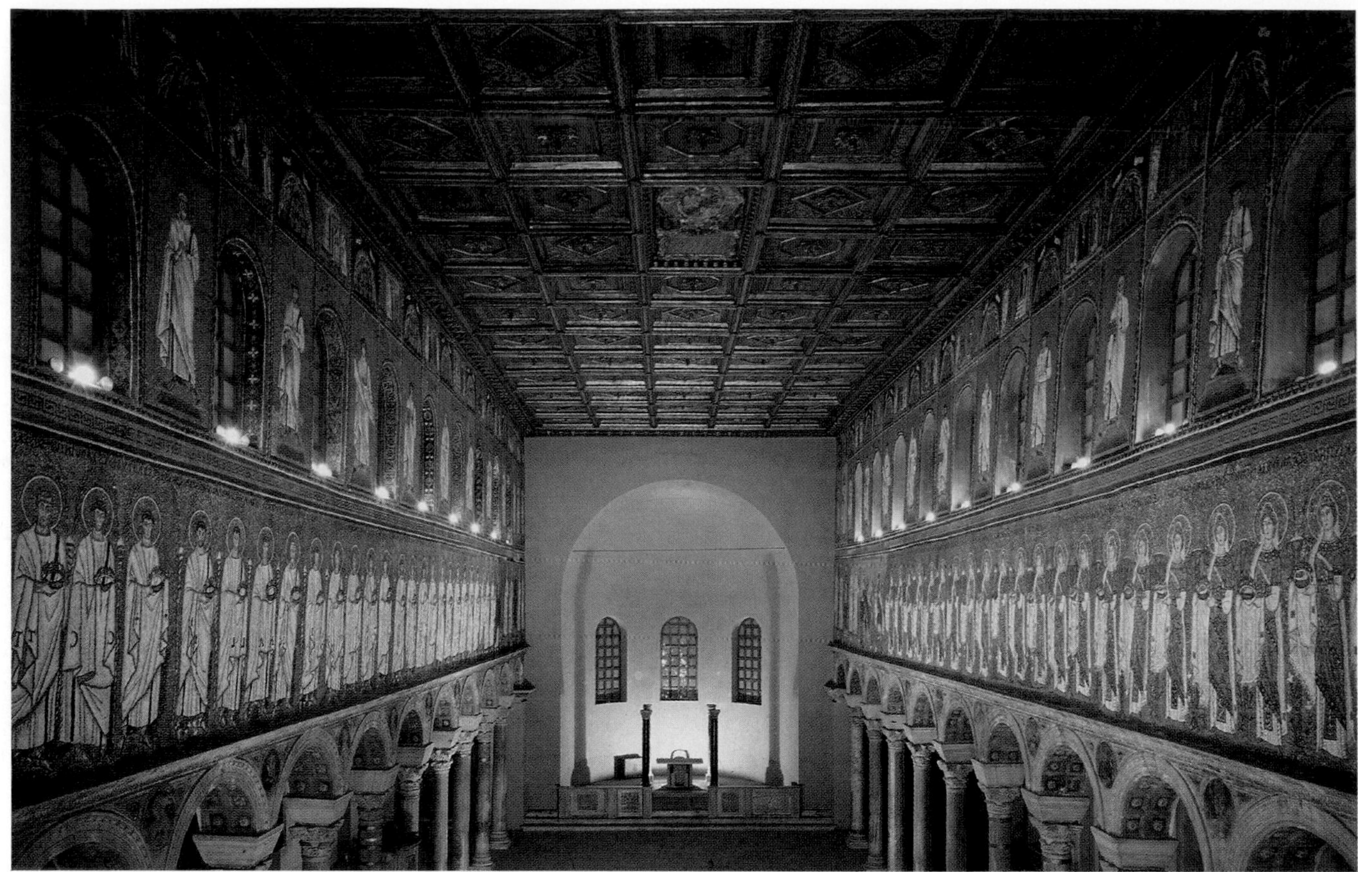

7-27 The nave of Sant' Apollinare Nuovo, Ravenna, Italy, c. 504.

depth. In short, the panel is replete with devices of Roman illusionism; its creator was still deeply rooted in the Hellenic tradition. Some fifty years later, this artist's successors would work in a much more abstract and formal manner.

Around 504, very soon after he settled in Ravenna, Theodoric ordered the construction of his own palace-church, a three-aisled basilica dedicated to the Savior. In the ninth century, the relics of Apollinaris were transferred to this church, which was rededicated and has been known since that time as Sant' Apollinare Nuovo. The rich mosaic decorations of the interior nave walls (FIG. **7-27**) are arranged in three zones, of which the upper two date from the time of Theodoric. Old Testament patriarchs and prophets are represented between the clerestory windows; above them, scenes from the life of Christ alternate with decorative panels. The lowest zone originally bore subjects of either Arian or political character. Although Christians, Theodoric and his Goths were Arians (followers of the teachings of Bishop Arius), a sect declared heretical by the Orthodox church. After the Byzantine conquest of Ravenna, Bishop Agnellus ordered all mosaics that bore reference to Theodoric or to Arianism removed and replaced with the present procession of orthodox saints (male on one side, female on the other). Agnellus had no quarrel with the subjects on the upper two levels, and they were left intact. Our example, *The Miracle of the Loaves and the Fishes* (FIG. **7-28**), must date from about 500. It illustrates well the stylistic change that has occurred since the decoration of Galla Placidia's mausoleum. Jesus, beardless and in the imperial dress of gold and purple, faces directly toward us as he directs his disciples to distribute the miraculously augmented supply of bread and fish to the great crowd to which he has preached. The artist has made no attempt to supply details to the event. The emphasis is instead on the sacramental character of it, the spiritual fact that Jesus, outstanding in the group, is performing a miracle by the power of God. The fact of the miracle takes it out of the world of time and of incident, for what is important in this scene is the presence of almighty power, which requires nothing but an unchanging presentation in terms of formal, unchanging aspect. The story is told with the bare minimum of figures necessary to make its meaning explicit; these figures have been aligned laterally, moved close to the foreground, and placed in a shallow picture box that is cut off by a golden screen close behind the

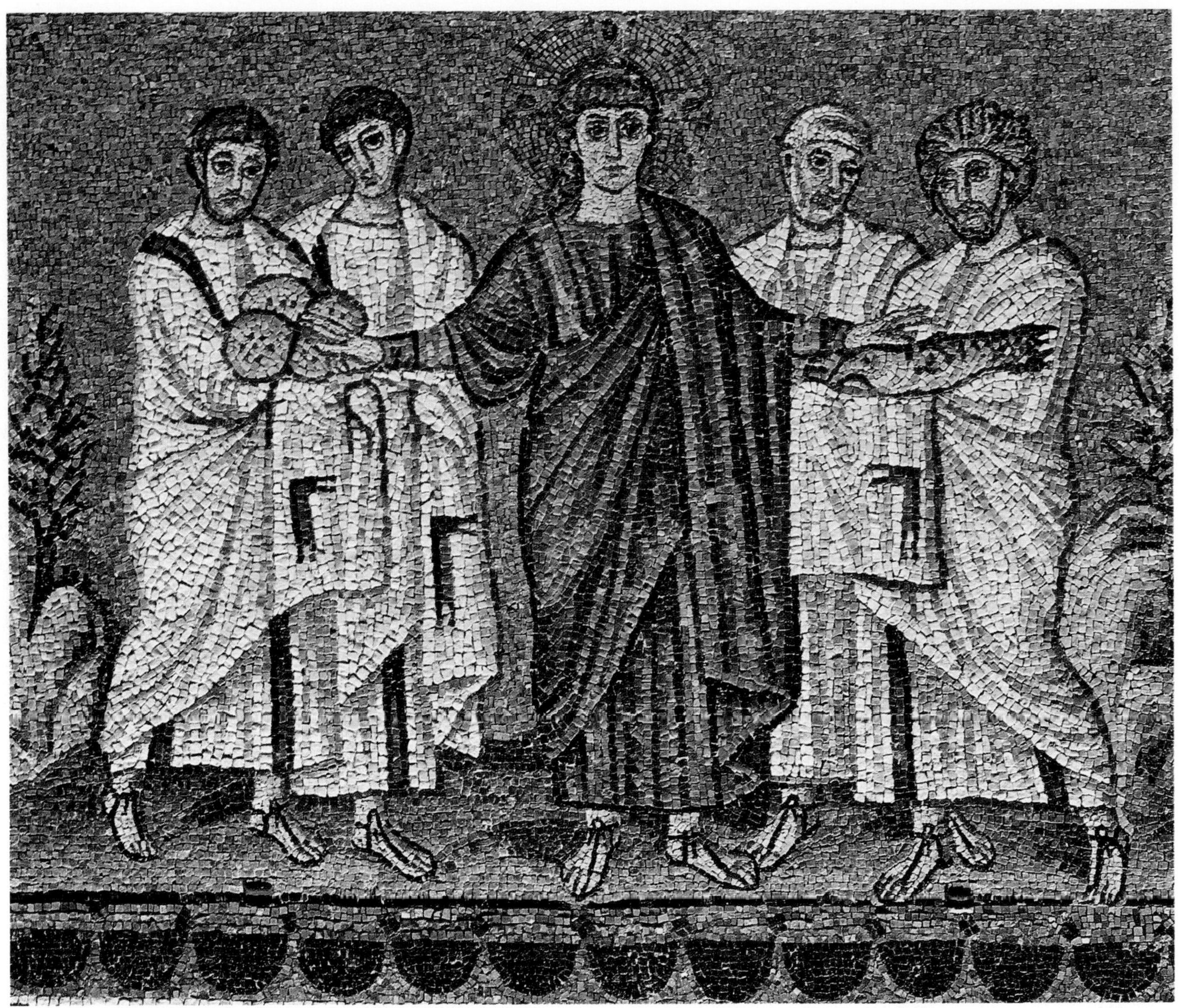

7-28 *The Miracle of the Loaves and the Fishes,* mosaic from the top register of the nave wall (above the clerestory windows) of Sant' Apollinare Nuovo, c. 504.

backs of the figures. The landscape setting, which was so explicitly described by the artist who worked for Galla Placidia, here merely is suggested by a few rocks and bushes that enclose the figure group like parentheses. That former reference to the physical world, the blue sky, is now replaced by a neutral gold, which would be the standard background color from now on. Remnants of Roman illusionism are found only in the handling of the individual figures, which still cast shadows and retain some of their former volume. But the shadows of the drapery folds have already narrowed into bars and will soon disappear completely.

The period of Justinianic Ravenna closes with the church of Sant' Apollinare in Classe, where, in the great apse mosaic, the Byzantine style reaches full maturity. Here, until the ninth century (when it was transferred to Ravenna), rested the body of St. Apollinaris, who suffered his martyrdom in Classe, Ravenna's port city. The building itself (FIG. **7-29**) is Early Christian in type, a three-aisled basilica with a plan quite similar to that of Theodoric's palace-church in Ravenna. The peculiar design of the apse, which combines a semicircular interior with a polygonal exterior, is typical of Ravenna churches and is probably of Byzantine origin. As usual for the period, the outside of the building is plain and unadorned. (The cylindrical bell tower, or *campanile,* is of a later date.)

The interior decoration in this case is confined to mosaics in the triumphal arch and the apse behind it.

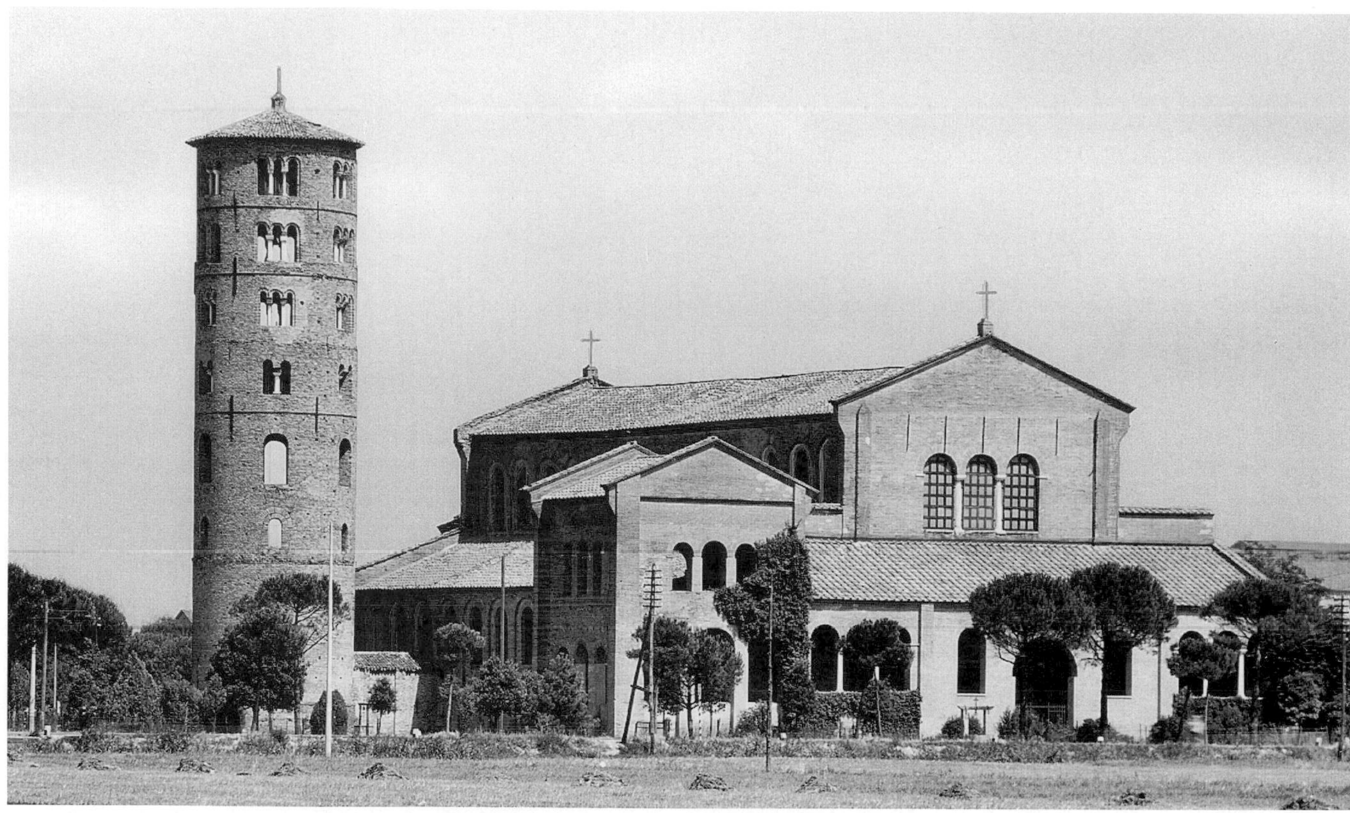

7-29 Sant' Apollinare in Classe, Ravenna, Italy, *c.* 533–549.

Of these, the mosaic decorating the semivault above the apse (FIG. **7-30**) was probably completed by 549, when the church was dedicated. It shows, against a gold ground, a large, blue medallion with a jeweled cross (symbol of the transfigured Jesus); this may be another representation of the cross Constantine had erected on the hill of Calvary to commemorate the martyrdom of Christ—the cross that we also saw represented at Santa Pudenziana in Rome (FIG. 7-11). Visible just above the cross is the hand of God. On either side of the medallion, in the clouds, appear the figures of Moses and Elijah, who appeared before Christ during his transfiguration. Below these two figures are three sheep, the three disciples who accompanied Christ to the foot of the Mount of the Transfiguration. Beneath, in the midst of green fields with trees, flowers, and birds, stands the patron saint of the church, Apollinaris. He is portrayed with uplifted arms, accompanied by twelve sheep, perhaps representing the Christian congregation under the protection of St. Apollinaris and forming, as they march in regular file across the apse, a wonderfully decorative base. On the face of the triumphal arch above, the image of Christ in a medallion and the Signs of the Evangelists are represented in the rainbow-streaked heavens. The twelve lambs, issuing from the cities of Bethlehem and Jerusalem, are the Twelve Apostles. The iconographical program is completed by the two palms of Paradise in the narrow spandrels of the arch and by the two archangels below them.

Comparison with the Galla Placidia mosaic (FIG. 7-26) shows how the style and the artist's approach to the subject have changed during the course of a century. In both cases, we are looking at a human figure and some sheep in a landscape. But in Classe, in the mid-sixth century, the artist no longer tries to recreate a segment of the physical world, but tells the story in terms of flat symbols, lined up side by side. All overlapping is carefully avoided in what must have been an intentional effort to omit all reference to the three-dimensional space of the material world and physical reality. Shapes have lost their volume and become flat silhouettes, into which details have been inscribed with lines. The effect is that of an extremely rich, flat, tapestry design that tells its story directly and explicitly without illusionistic devices. The Byzantine style has become the ideal vehicle for the conveyance of the extremely complex symbolism of the fully developed Christian dogma.

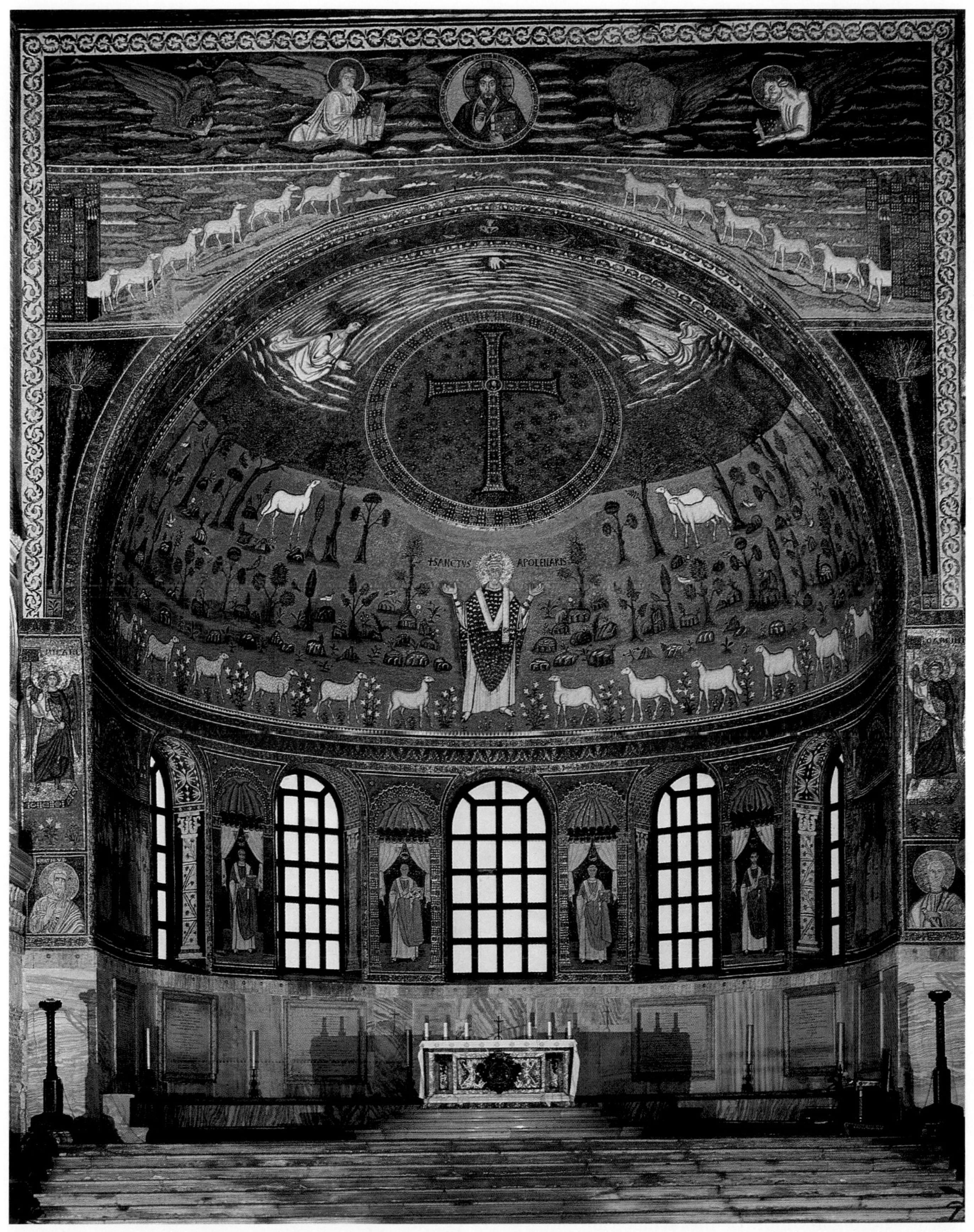

7-30 Apse mosaic from Sant' Apollinare in Classe, *c.* 549.

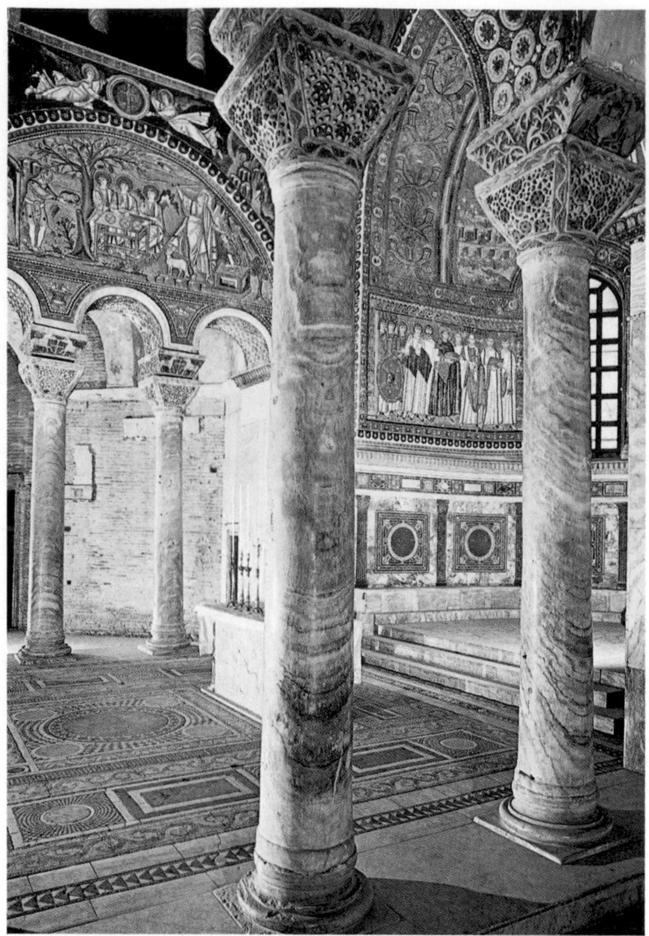

7-31 Sanctuary of San Vitale, Ravenna, Italy. Mosaics show in the forechoir *(left)*: *Abraham and the Three Angels* and *The Sacrifice of Isaac*; and in the apse *(right)*: *Justinian and Attendants*.

Our apse mosaic, for example, has much more meaning than first meets the eye. The transfiguration of Christ—here, into the image of the cross—symbolizes his own death, with its redeeming consequences, but also the death of his martyrs (in this case, St. Apollinaris). The lamb, also a symbol of martyrdom, is used appropriately to represent the martyred apostles. The whole scene expands above the altar, where the sacrament of the Eucharist—the miraculous recurrence of the supreme redemptive and transfigurative act—is celebrated. The very altars of Christian churches were, from early times, sanctified by the bones and relics of martyrs. Thus, the mystery and the martyrdom were joined in one concept: the death of the martyr, in imitation of Christ, is a triumph over death that leads to eternal life. The images above the altar present a kind of inspiring vision to the eyes of believers; the way of the martyr is open to them, and the reward of eternal life is within their reach. The organization of the symbolism and the images is hieratic, and the graphic message must have been delivered to the faithful with overwhelming force. Looming above their eyes is the apparition of a great mystery, ordered in such a way as to make perfectly simple and clear the "whole duty of man" seeking salvation. That the anonymous artists, working under the direction of the priests, expended every device of their craft to render the idea explicit is plain enough; the devout could read it as easily as an inscription. The martyr's glorification beneath the cross, inscribed in the starry heavens, presented in one great tableau the eternal meaning of Christian life in terms of its deepest mystery.

The Byzantine style, born of the Orientalizing of Hellenistic naturalism, appears in monumental grandeur and ornamental splendor in the mosaics of San Vitale (FIG. **7-31**), which, in the high quality they share with the beautiful building itself, symbolize the achievements of the age of the emperor Justinian and are worthy representatives of the First Golden Age of Byzantine art. Begun shortly after Theodoric's death and dedicated by Bishop Maximianus in 547, San Vitale (FIG. **7-32**) shares, with the other Ravenna churches, its plain exterior (slightly marred by a Renaissance portal) and the polygonal apse. But beyond these features, it is an entirely different building (FIG. **7-33**). The structure is centrally planned and consists of two concentric octagons; the dome-covered inner octagon rises above the surrounding octagon to provide the interior with clerestory lighting. The central

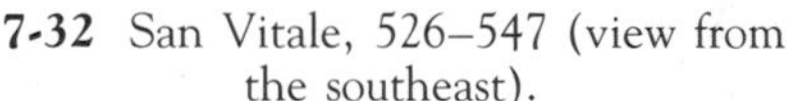

7-32 San Vitale, 526–547 (view from the southeast).

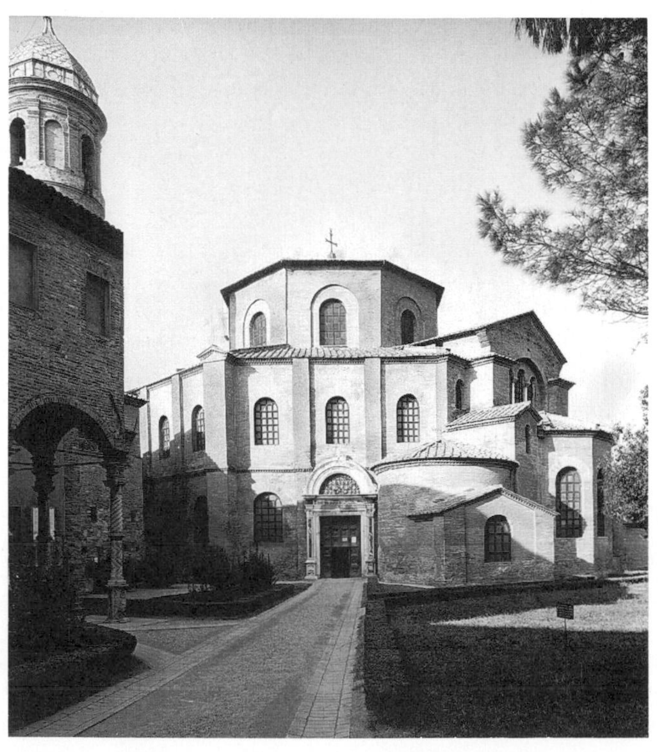

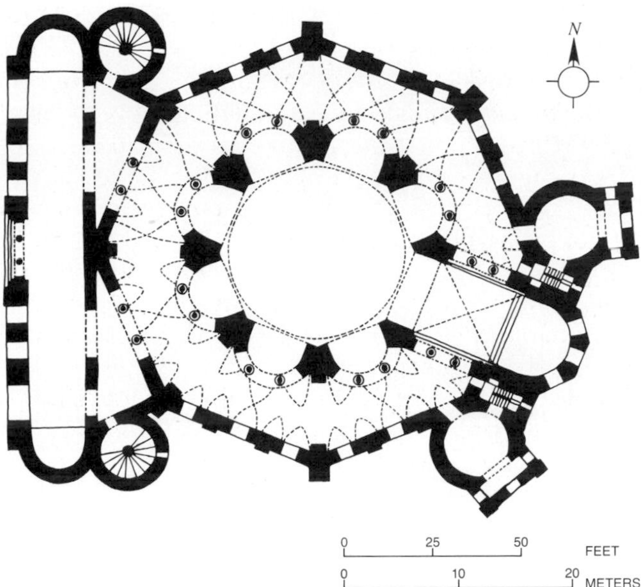

7-33 Plan of San Vitale.

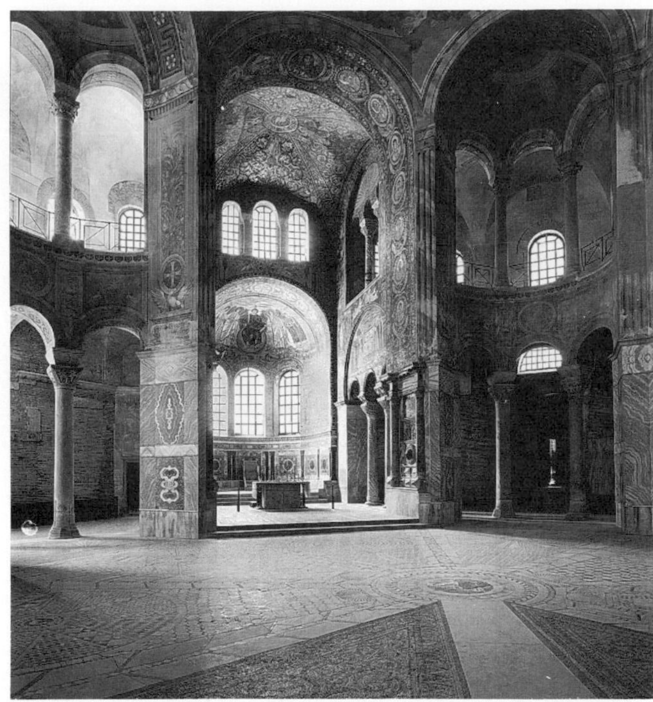

7-34 Interior of San Vitale (view facing forechoir and apse).

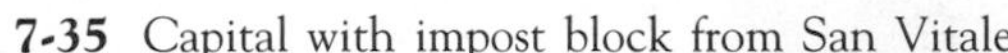

7-35 Capital with impost block from San Vitale.

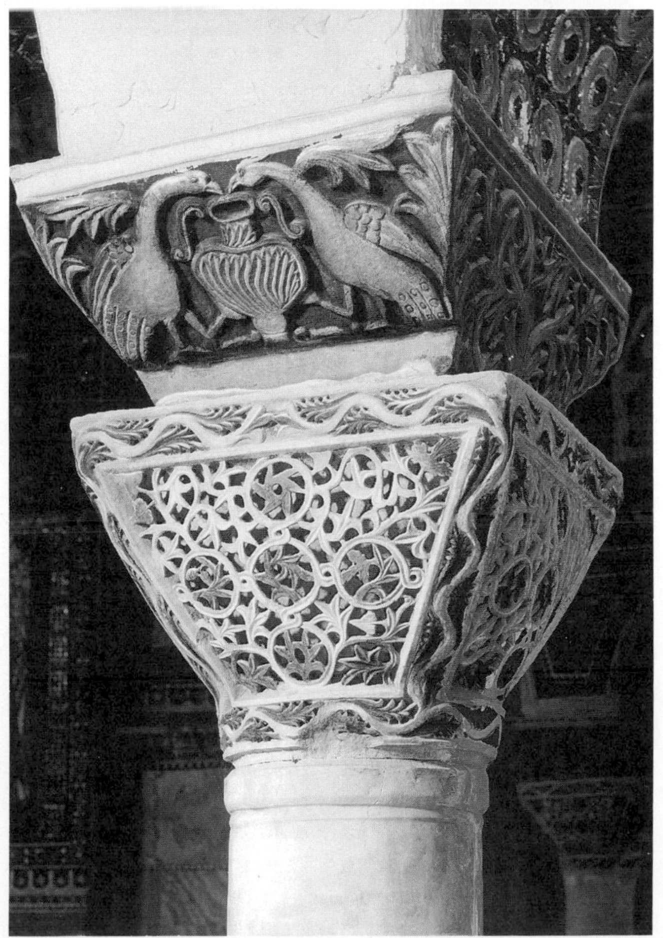

space is defined by eight large piers that alternate with curved, columned niches, pushing outward into the surrounding ambulatory and creating, on the plan, an intricate, octafoliate design. These niches effect a close integration between inner and outer spaces that, otherwise, would simply have existed side by side as independent units. A cross-vaulted sanctuary preceding the apse interrupts the ambulatory and provides the plan with some axial stability. This effect is weakened, however, by the unsymmetrical placement of the narthex, the odd angle of which never has been explained fully. (The atrium, which no longer exists, may have paralleled a street that ran in the same direction as the angle at which the narthex is placed; it also has been suggested that the angle of the narthex might have been intended to force visitors to reorient themselves as they entered the complex arrangement of the main space and, thereby, to experience the transition from the material world outside into the spiritual world of the church.) The ambulatory (FIG. **7-34**) has been provided with a second story, the gallery, which was reserved for women and is a typical feature of Byzantine churches. Probably also of Byzantine origin are the so-called *impost blocks,* which have been inserted between the simply profiled, but richly patterned, column capitals and the springing of the arches (FIG. **7-35**). Resembling an inverted, truncated pyramid, these impost blocks appear in nearly all Ravenna churches (compare FIG. 7-27) and may be highly abstracted reflections of the entablature segments inserted between column and arch by Late Roman architects (compare FIG. 6-83).

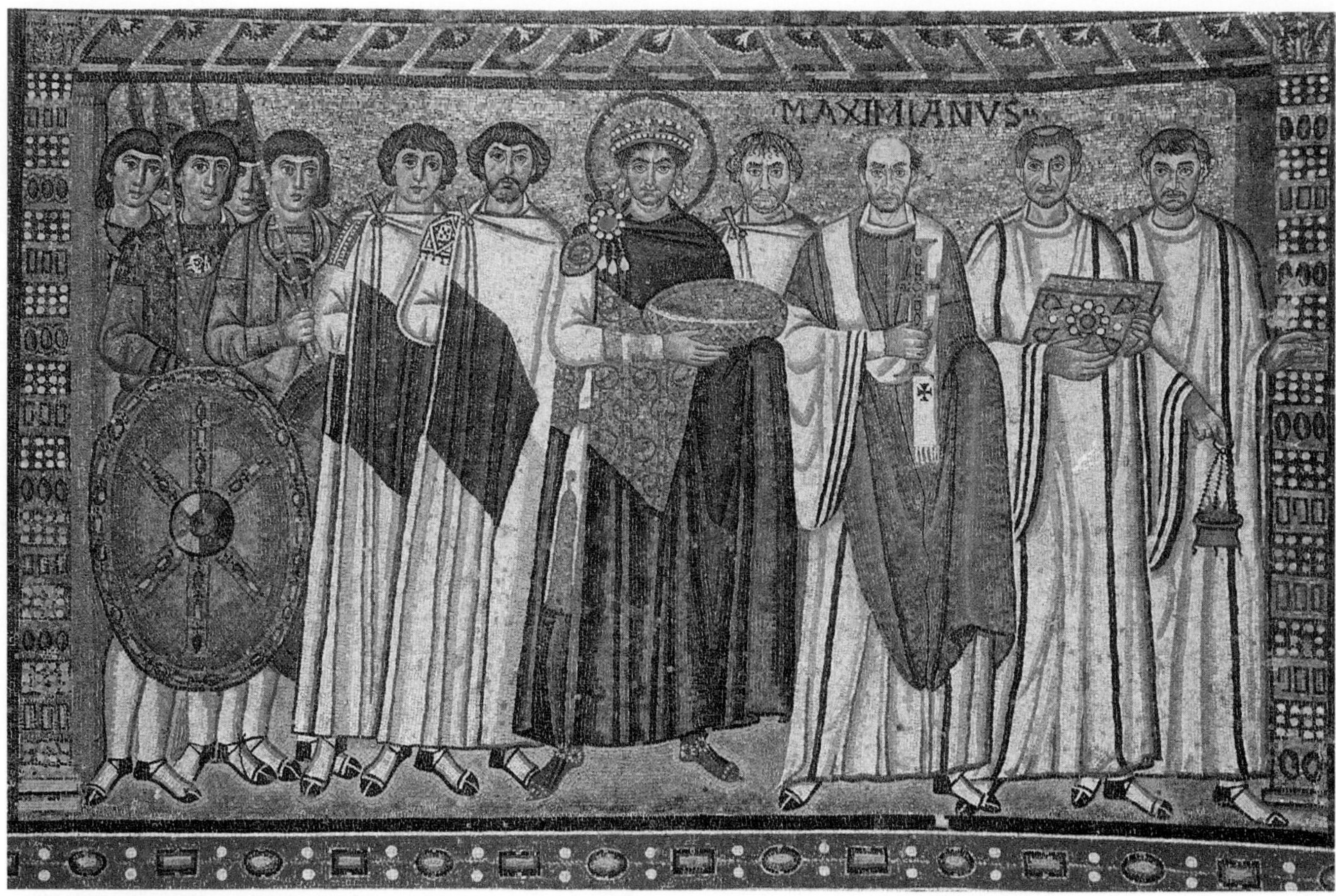

7-36 *Justinian and Attendants,* mosaic from the north wall of the apse, San Vitale, *c.* 547.

7-37 *Theodora and Attendants,* mosaic from the south wall of the apse, San Vitale.

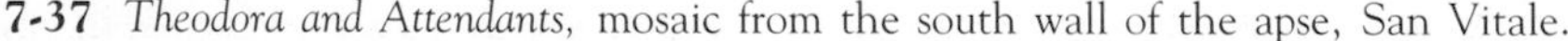

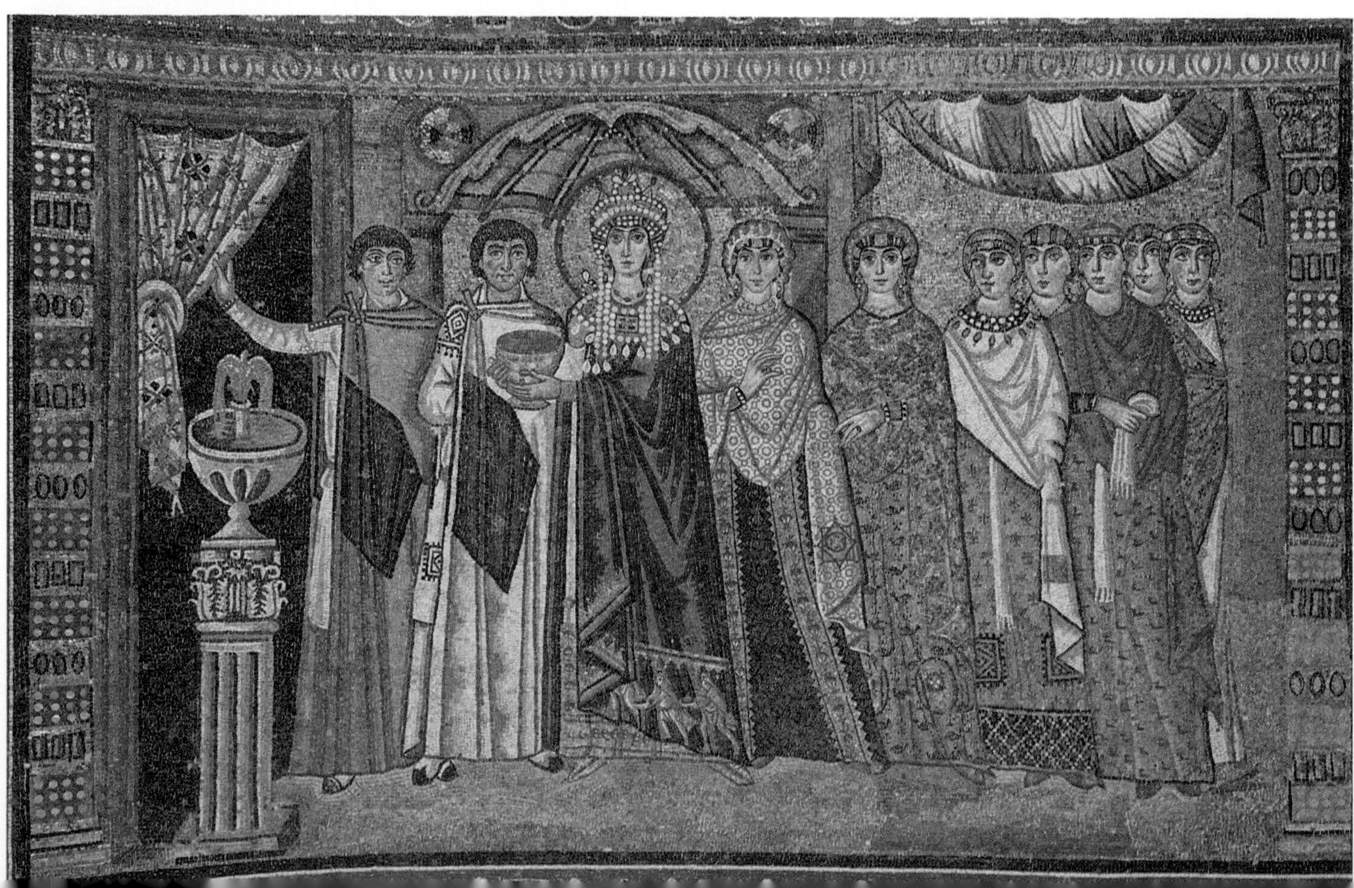

San Vitale's intricate plan and elevation combine to produce an effect of great complexity. Walking through the building, one is struck by the rich diversity of ever-changing perspectives. Arches looping over arches, curving and flattened spaces, and shapes of wall and vault seem to change constantly with the viewer's position. Light filtered through alabaster-paned windows plays over the glittering mosaics and glowing marbles that cover the building's complex surfaces, producing an effect of sumptuousness that is not Western but Oriental. And, indeed, the inspiration for this design is to be found in Byzantium, rather than Rome. In Constantinople, some ten years before the completion of San Vitale at Ravenna, a church dedicated to the saints Sergius and Bacchus appears to be a rough preparatory sketch for the later church, in which the suggestions of the earlier plan may be seen developed to their full potential.

Slightly earlier than those of Sant' Apollinare in Classe, but of higher quality, the mosaics that decorate the sanctuary of San Vitale, like the building itself, must be regarded as one of the climactic achievements of Byzantine art. Completed less than a decade after the surrender of Ravenna by the Goths, the decorations of apse and forechoir proclaim the triumph of Justinian and of the Orthodox faith. The multiple panels of the sanctuary form a unified composition, a theme of which is the holy ratification of the emperor's right to the whole western empire, of which Ravenna was now the principal city. The apse mosaics are portrait groups representing Justinian on one wall (FIG. **7-36**) and his empress, Theodora, on the other (FIG. **7-37**). The monarchs are accompanied by their retinues in a depiction of the offertory procession (the part of the liturgy when the bread and wine of the Eucharist are brought forward and presented). Justinian, represented as a priest-king, carries a vessel containing the bread, and Theodora carries the golden cup with the wine. Images and symbols covering the entire sanctuary express the single idea of man's redemption by Christ and the reenactment of it in the Eucharist. Moses, Melchizedek, Abraham, and Abel are represented as prefigurations of Christ and also as priestly leaders of the faithful, whose offerings to God were declared acceptable to heaven.

In the apse vault, the Second Coming is represented (FIG. **7-38**). Christ, seated on the orb of the world, with the four rivers of Paradise beneath him and rainbow-hued clouds above, extends a golden wreath of victory to Vitalis, the patron saint of the church, who is introduced by an angel. At Christ's left, another angel introduces Bishop Ecclesius, in whose time the foundations of the church were laid and who carries a model of it. The arrangement recalls Christ's prophecy of the last days of the world: "And then shall they see the Son of man coming in the clouds with great power and glory. And then shall he send his angels, and shall gather together his elect from the four winds, from the uttermost part of heaven" (Mark 13:26–27).

7-38 *Christ Between Angels and Saints (The Second Coming)*, mosaic from the apse vault, San Vitale.

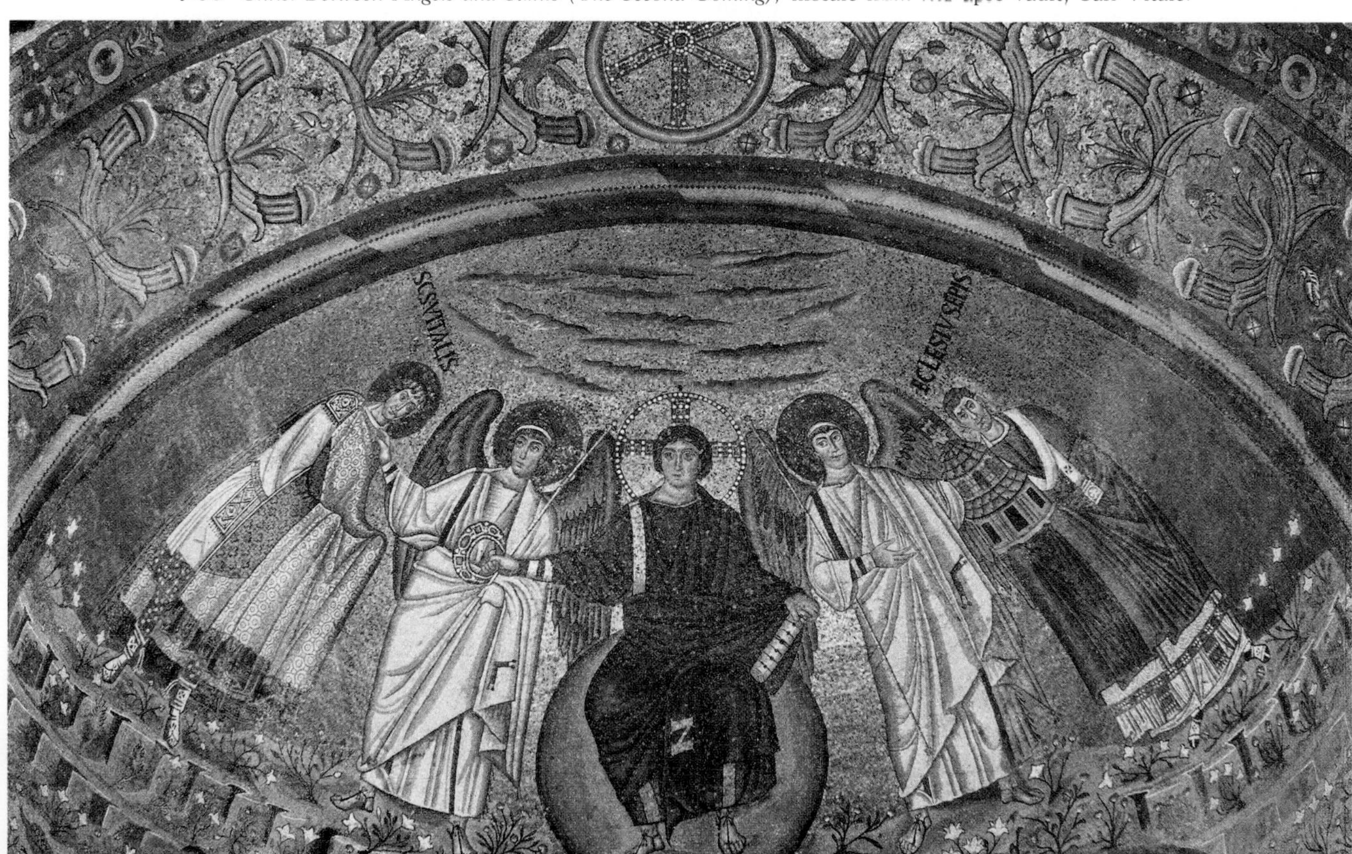

It appears that Justinian's offering is acceptable, for the wreath extended to St. Vitalis also is extended to him where he stands in a dependent mosaic on the wall below and to the right of the vault mosaic (FIGS. 7-31 and 7-36). Thus, his rule is confirmed and sanctified by these rites, in which (as is so typical of such expressions of the Byzantine imperial ideal) the political and the religious are one:

> In the atmosphere of Byzantium, the Christian emperor appeared as a Christ-like high priest and . . . the principles of his administration seemed to be symbolized in the liturgical rite. In the offertory procession, he appeared like the priest-king Melchizedek, "bringing forth bread and wine" on behalf of his people, to propitiate God.*

The laws of the Church and the laws of the state, united in the laws of God, are manifest in the person of the emperor and in his God-given right. The pagan emperors had been deified; it could not have been difficult, given that tradition, to accept the deification of the Christian emperor. Justinian is distinguished from his dignitaries not only by his wearing of the imperial purple but also by his halo, a device emanating from ancient Persia and originally signifying the descent of the honored one from the sun and, hence, his godlike origin and status.

The etiquette and protocol of the imperial court fuse here with the ritual of the liturgy of the Church (see FIG. 7-36). The positions of the figures are all-important; they express the formula of precedence and the orders of rank. Justinian is exactly at the center. At his left is Bishop Maximianus, the architect of his ecclesiastical-political policy and the man responsible for the completion of San Vitale and its consecration in 547. The bishop's importance is stressed by the label bearing his name, the only identifying inscription in the composition. Between Justinian and Maximianus is Julius Argentarius, the principal benefactor of the church. The figures are in three groups: the emperor and his staff (standing for the imperial administration); the clergy; and the army, who bear a shield with the *chi-rho* monogram seen on the sarcophagus of Archbishop Theodore (FIG. 7-22). Each group has a leader, one of whose feet precedes (by overlapping) the feet of those who follow. A curious ambiguity is observable in the positions of Justinian and Maximianus: although the emperor appears to be slightly behind the bishop, the sacred vessel he carries overlaps the bishop's arm. Thus, symbolized by place and gesture, the imperial and churchly powers are in balance. The paten (the plate holding the bread of the Eucharist) carried by Justinian, the cross carried by Maximianus, and the book and censer carried by his attendant clerics produce a movement that strikingly modifies the rigid formality of the scene. No background is indicated; the observer is expected to understand the procession as taking place in this very sanctuary, where the emperor will appear forever as a participant in the sacred rites and as the proprietor of this royal church, the very symbol of his rule of the western empire.

The portraits of the empress Theodora and her entourage (FIG. 7-37), on the other hand, are represented within a definite architecture, perhaps the narthex of San Vitale. The empress stands in state beneath an imperial canopy, waiting to follow the emperor's procession and to pass through the curtained doorway into which she is beckoned by an attendant. The fact that she is outside the sanctuary and only about to proceed attests that, in the ceremonial protocol, her rank is not quite equal to that of her consort, even though the representation of the Three Magi on the border of her robe recalls their offerings to the infant Christ and makes an allusive connection between Theodora and the Virgin Mary.

The figure style shows the maturing of conventions of representation that date back to Dura-Europos and earlier. Tall, spare, angular, and elegant, the figures have lost the rather squat proportions characteristic of much Early Christian work. The gorgeous draperies fall straight, stiff, and thin from the narrow shoulders; the organic body has dematerialized, and, except for the heads, we see a procession of solemn spirits, gliding noiselessly in the presence of the sacrament. Byzantine style will preserve this hieratic mood for centuries, no matter how many individual variations occur within its conventions.

We can hardly talk of Byzantine art without using the term "hieratic." Christianity, originating as a mystery cult, kept mystery as its center (one might say that the priest became a specialist in mystery). The priestly supernaturalism that disparages matter and material values prevails throughout the Christian Middle Ages, especially in Orthodox Byzantium. It is that hieratic supernaturalism that determines the look of Byzantine figurative art—an art without solid bodies or cast shadows, with blank, golden spaces, with the perspective of Paradise, which is nowhere and everywhere.

The portraits in San Vitale are individualized, despite the prevailing formality. However, this is true only of the principals; the lesser personages on the outskirts of the groups are treated more uniformly. In these portrait groups memorializing the dedicatory ceremony, the artists undoubtedly intended to create close likenesses of the central characters—the emperor and empress and the high officials of Church

*Otto von Simson, *Sacred Fortress: Byzantine Art and Statecraft in Ravenna* (Chicago: University of Chicago Press, 1948), p. 35.

and state. Since pagan times, the image of the deified emperor in public and sacred places has been tantamount to his actual presence, for the image and the reality were taken to be essentially one. The setting up of the image of the emperor was "an act which furnished the occasion for the declaration of submission on the part of the people";* those who gazed on the images must have known that they owed them absolute reverence: "In these awe-inspiring images, the sovereigns, though far away in Byzantium, had actually set foot on the soil of Italy."†

Thus, the symbol, the image, and what they represent are most often one and the same. Just as the image of Justinian or Theodora or a saint is venerated as if it were the person, so are a cross, relics, and mementos. Even vessels associated with holy rites came to be venerated as real presences of sacred powers that could cure not only spiritually but also physically. To the believer, this communion of reality between objects and what they represent is logical enough; if the body of Christ is reproducible through the ritual of the Eucharist, then representations of all holy things ought to be just as real as what they represent. Symbols, images, narratives, sacramental objects—the furniture and accessories of ritual—all can be venerable and spiritually potent in themselves; this is like the magic of the Paleolithic caves, in which the hunter-artists believed they summoned and controlled their animal quarry by the miracle of representation.

In Ravenna, a powerful statecraft under the management of Justinian and Maximianus had been able to combine, in a group of monuments, the full force of Christian belief and political authority. In the process, a model of religious art, sacramental and magical in its power, was created that could work in the service of both the Church and the sanctified imperial state. This model, image, or ideal unity of the spiritual and temporal would influence the Middle Ages strongly in both the east and the west. The hieratic style of Byzantium, matured and exemplified in Ravenna, will remain both the standard and the point of departure for the content and form of the art of the Middle Ages.

Only slightly later than the Ravenna mosaics, the great apse mosaic in the church of the monastery of St. Catherine on Mt. Sinai (on the Sinai peninsula, now under Egyptian control) shows striking divergences from the Ravenna style, although both are likely to have emanated from Justinian's city, Constantinople. Justinian built the fortress monastery of St. Catherine between 548 and 565; it is unlikely that the apse mosaic could have been done much later than the year of the completion of the church building. In FIG. 7-39, *The Transfiguration of Jesus* (Mark 9:2–8), Jesus appears in a deep blue mandorla, or

*Otto von Simson, *Sacred Fortress: Byzantine Art and Statecraft in Ravenna* (Chicago: University of Chicago Press, 1948), p. 28.

†Ibid., p. 39.

7-39 *The Transfiguration of Jesus,* apse mosaic from the church of the monastery of St. Catherine, Mount Sinai, Egypt, c. 560.

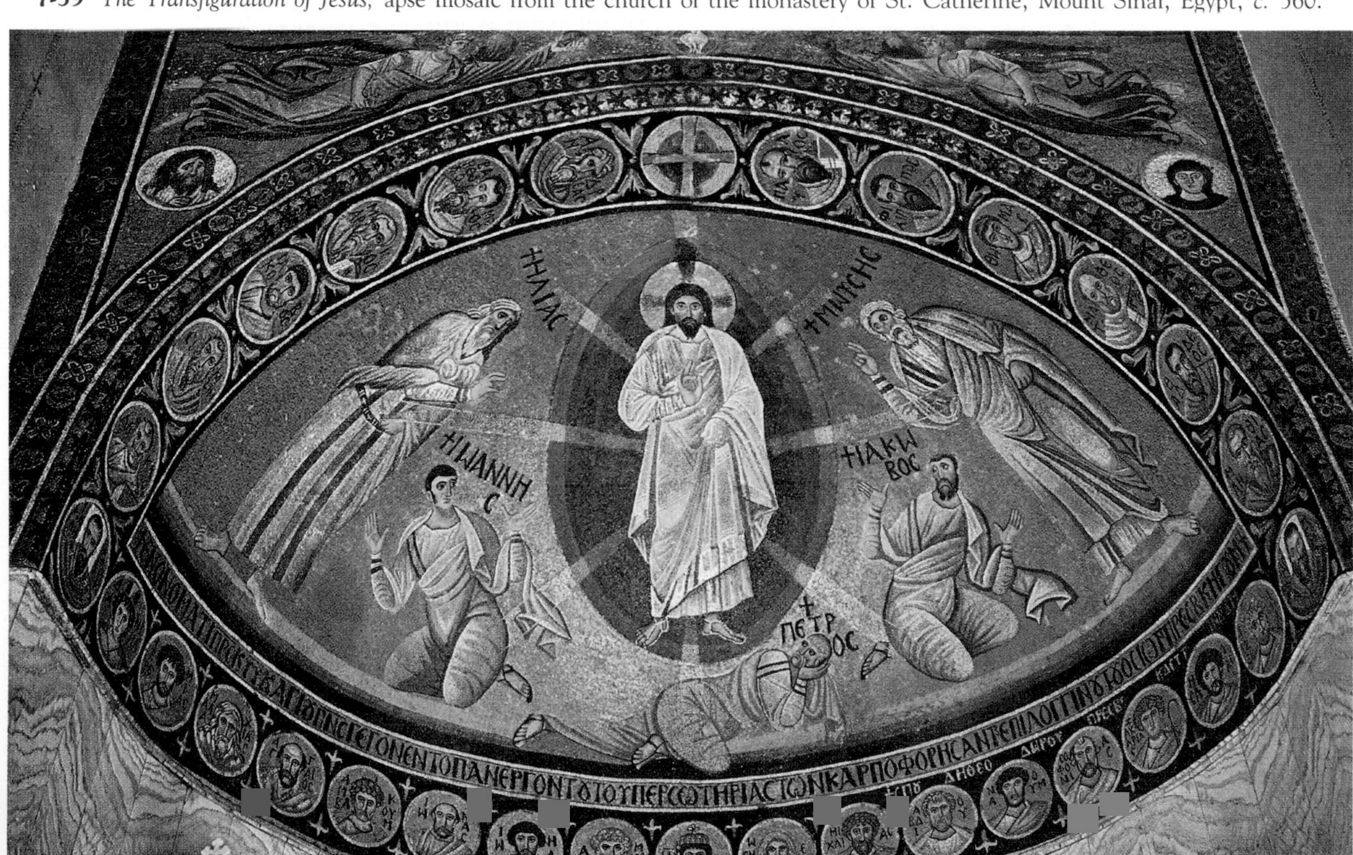

"glory," flanked by Elijah and Moses, with the disciples John, Peter, and James at his feet; the whole scene is framed by portraits of saints in medallions. The artist has stressed the intense whiteness of Jesus' transfigured, spiritualized form, from which rays stream down on the disciples. The stately figures of Elijah and Moses and the static frontality of Jesus set off the frantic terror and astonishment of the gesticulating disciples in a contrast of the eternal composure of heavenly beings with the distraught responses of the earthbound. All traces of landscape or architectural setting have been swept away and replaced by a depthless field of gold, on which the figures and their labels are fixed in isolation from one another. The gold field is bounded at its base by a rainbow band of colors graduating from yellow to blue, a ground line to which the figures are ambiguously related: sometimes they are placed behind it; sometimes they overlap it. The bodies cast no shadows, even though supernatural light streams over them. We are in the world of mystical vision, where all substance that might suggest the passage of time or motion through physical space is subtracted, so that the eternal and motionless world of religious truth can be contemplated by the devout.

The formal, hieratic style of Ravenna, appropriate to a court church, and the cultic, visionary style of Mt. Sinai, appropriate to a monastery church, although standing in obvious contrast, mark two main kinds of expression in Byzantine art and reflect their common source—Justinian's Constantinople.

Constantinople

Ravenna, the successor to Rome as imperial capital in Italy and then, as the so-called exarchate, the beachhead of Byzantium in the Germanized west, finally passed from Byzantine control. The images of Justinian and Theodora in San Vitale, proclaiming that the empire was still whole, were powerless to make it so. But the east remained firmly in the hands of successions of emperors for a thousand years; Constantinople became the magnificent citadel of Byzantine civilization, and its influence streamed to all points of the compass. At the time that the imperial presence in Ravenna was being symbolized in architecture and art, the vast church of Santa Sophia, or more properly Hagia Sophia, Church of the Holy Wisdom (FIGS. **7-40** to **7-42**), was being built for Justinian in Constantinople by the architects ANTHEMIUS OF TRALLES and ISIDORUS OF MILETUS. Even today, this church, which was built between 532 and 537, remains one of the supreme achievements in the history of world architecture. Its dimensions alone are formidable for any structure not made of steel. In plan, it is about 270 feet long and 240 feet wide; the dome is 108 feet in diameter, and its crown rises some 180 feet above the pavement. In scale, Hagia Sophia rivals the great buildings we have seen in pagan and Christian Rome: the Pantheon, the Baths of Caracalla, or the Basilica of Constantine. In exterior view, the great dome dominates the structure, but the external aspects of the building are much changed from their original appearance. Huge buttresses were added to the original design, and four towering Turkish minarets were constructed after the Ottoman conquest of 1453, when Hagia Sophia became an Islamic mosque. The building has been secularized in the twentieth century and is now a museum.

The characteristic Byzantine plainness and unpretentiousness of exterior (which, in this case, also disguise the great scale) scarcely prepare us for the inte-

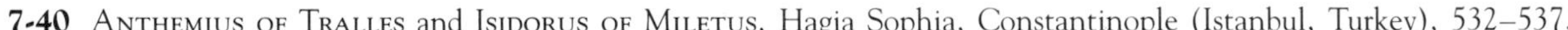

7-40 ANTHEMIUS OF TRALLES and ISIDORUS OF MILETUS, Hagia Sophia, Constantinople (Istanbul, Turkey), 532–537.

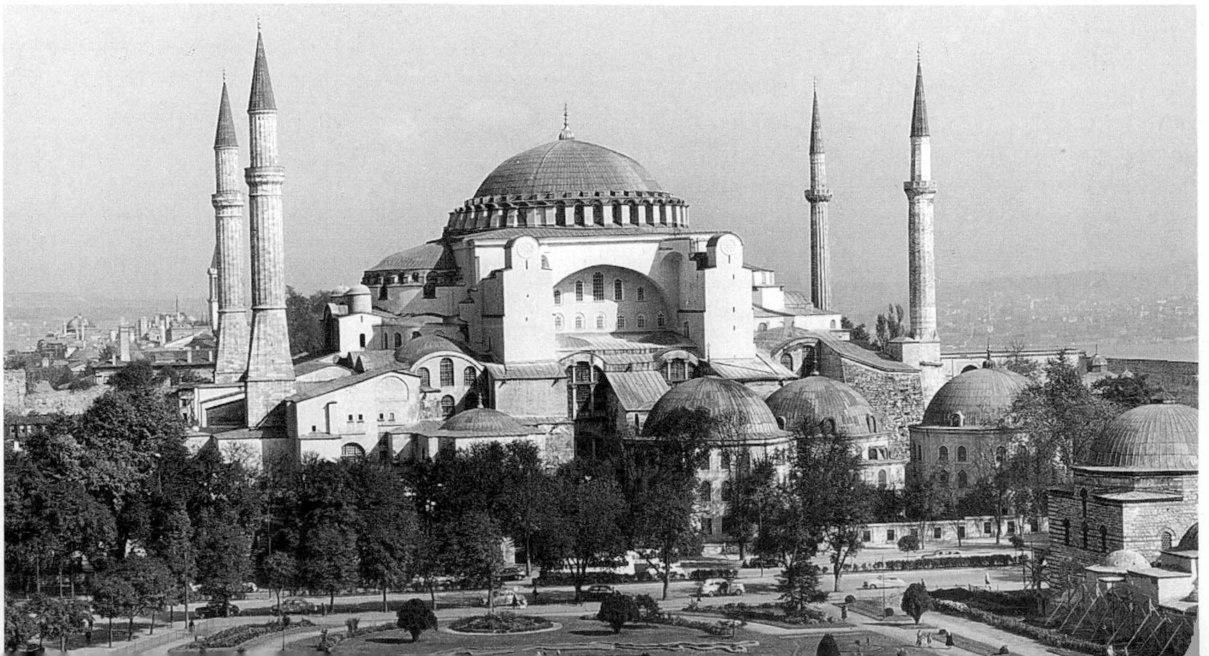

rior of the building (FIG. 7-41). The huge narthex, with its many entrances, leads into the center of the structure, over which the soaring, canopylike dome rides on a halo of light provided by windows in the dome's base. The impression made on the people of the time, an impression not lost on us, is carried in the words of the poet Paulus, an usher at the court of Justinian:

> About the center of the church, by the eastern and western half-circles, stand four mighty piers of stone, and from them spring great arches like the bow of Iris, four in all; and, as they rise slowly in the air, each separates from the other . . . and the spaces between them are filled with wondrous skill, for curved walls touch the arches on either side and spread over until they all unite above them. . . . The base of the dome is strongly fixed upon the great arches . . . while above, the dome covers the church like the radiant heavens. . . . Who shall describe the fields of marble gathered on the pavement and lofty walls of the church? Fresh green from Carystus, and many-colored Phrygian stone of rose and white, or deep red and silver; porphyry powdered with bright spots; emerald-green from Sparta, and Iassian marble with waving veins of blood-red and white; streaked red stone from Lydia, and crocus-colored marble from the hills of the Moors, and Celtic stone, like milk poured out on glittering black; the precious onyx like as if gold were shining through it, and the fresh green from the land of Atrax, in mingled contrast of shining surfaces.*

The dome rests on four *pendentives*. In pendentive construction (see FIG. 7-45), which apparently was developed after many years of experiment by builders in the Near East and constitutes *the* contribution of Byzantium to architectural engineering, a dome rests on what is, in effect, a second, larger dome. The top portion and four segments around the rim of the larger dome have been omitted and the four segments form four arches, the planes of which bound a square. By transferring the weight to piers, rather than to the wall itself, pendentive construction makes possible a lofty, unobstructed interior space, as is particularly evident in Hagia Sophia. In our view of the interior (FIG. 7-41), the arches that bound two of the great pendentives supporting the central dome can be seen converging on their massive piers. The domes of earlier, central-plan buildings, like the Pantheon, Santa Costanza, or even San Vitale, spring from the circular or polygonal bases of a continuous wall or arcade. The pendentive system is a dynamic solution to the problem of setting a round dome over a square or rectangular space, making a union of centralized and longitudinal or basilican structures possible. Hagia Sophia, in its successful fusion of these two architectural types, becomes a domed basilica—a uniquely successful conclusion to several centuries of experiment in Christian church architecture. However, the thrusts of the pendentive construction at Hagia Sophia make other elements necessary: huge wall piers to the north and south, and, to the east and west, half-domes, whose thrusts descend, in turn, into still smaller domes (FIG. 7-42), covering columned niches that give a curving flow to the design, reminiscent of San Vitale (see FIG. 7-34). And, as in San Vitale, the wandering space, the diverse vistas, and the screenlike, ornamented surfaces all mask the lines of structure. The arcades of the nave and galleries have no real structural function; like the walls they pierce, they are only part of a fragile "fill" between the great piers. Structurally, although Hagia Sophia may seem Roman in its great scale and majesty, it does not have Roman organization of its masses. The very fact that what appears to be wall in Hagia Sophia is actually a concealed (and barely adequate) pier indicates that Roman monumentality was sought as an

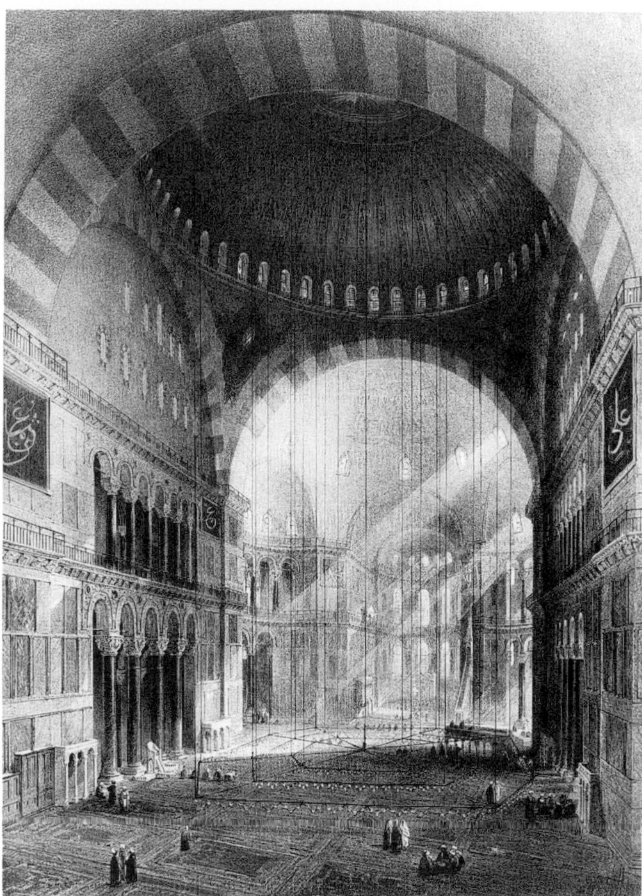

7-41 Interior of Hagia Sophia. (Engraving from *Aya Sophia* by CHEVALIER FOSSATI, London, 1852.)

*In W. R. Lethaby, "Santa Sophia, Constantinople," *Architectural Review* (April 1905), p. 12.

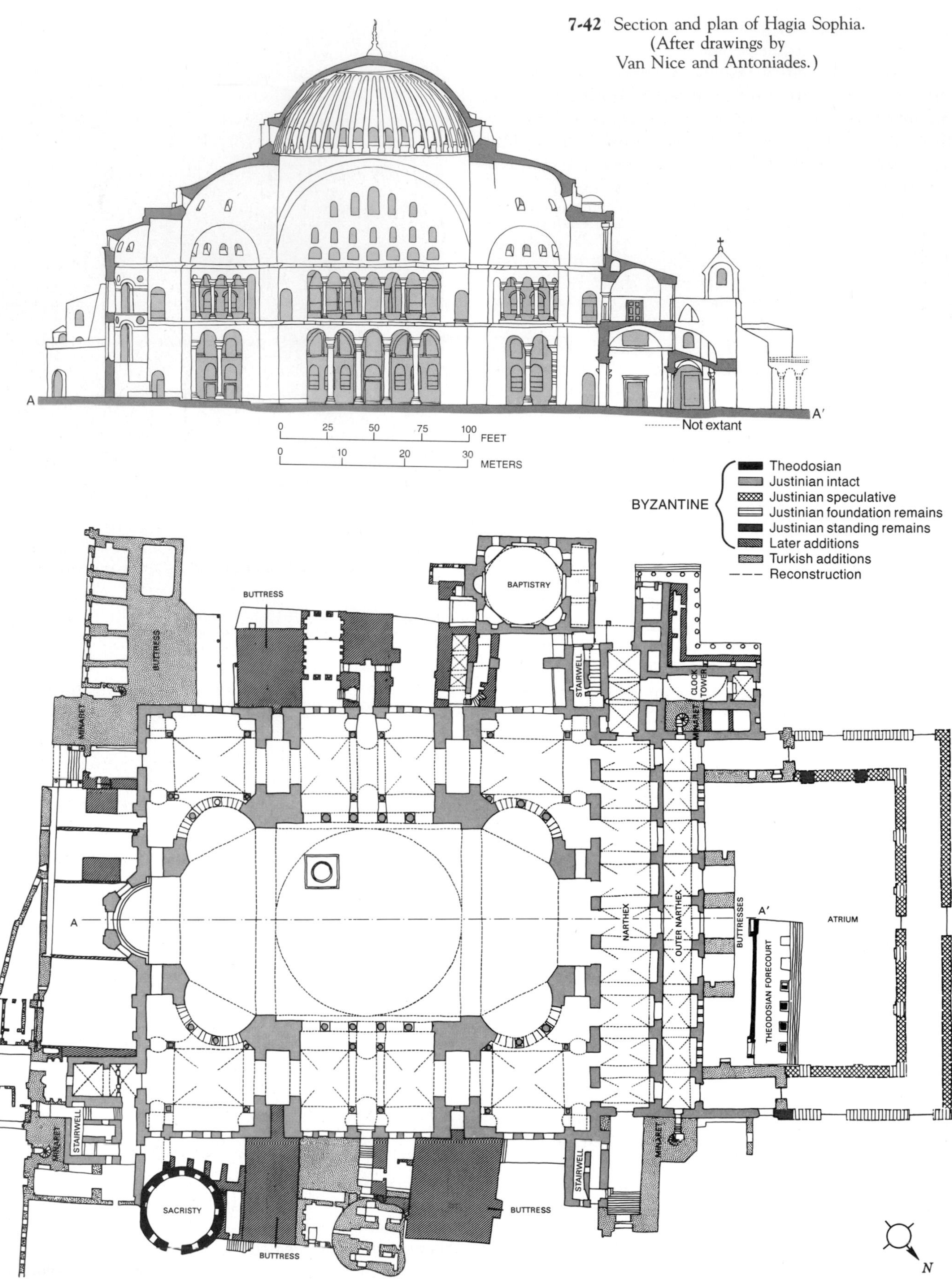

7-42 Section and plan of Hagia Sophia. (After drawings by Van Nice and Antoniades.)

effect and not derived directly from Roman building principles.

Visitors to Hagia Sophia have been struck by the quality of light within the church and the effect it has on the human spirit. The forty windows at the base of the dome create the peculiar illusion that the dome is resting on the light that floods through them; an observer of the time thought that it looked as if the dome were suspended by a "gold chain from Heaven." Procopius, the historian of the age of Justinian, wrote: "One would declare that the place were not illuminated from the outside by the sun, but that the radiance originated from within, such is the abundance of light which is shed about this shrine." Paulus observed: "The vaulting is covered over with many little squares of gold, from which the rays stream down and strike the eyes so that men can scarcely bear to look." Thus, we have a vastness of space shot through with light and a central dome that *appears* to be supported by the light it admits. Light is the mystic element—light that glitters in the mosaics, that shines forth from the marbles, and that pervades and defines spaces that, in themselves, seem to escape definition. Light becomes the agent that seems to dissolve material substance and transform it into an abstract, spiritual vision. At Hagia Sophia, the intricate logic of Greek theology, the ambitious scale of Rome, the vaulting tradition of the Near East, and the mysticism of Eastern Christianity combine to create a monument that is at once a summation of antiquity and a positive assertion of the triumph of Christian faith.

Hagia Sophia was a unique hybrid, uniting the Western basilican and the Eastern central plans into a design without successors. After it, the East forsook the long church for a thousand years or more to develop the central plan, while the basilican plan was consciously being revived in the West in Carolingian times.

LATER BYZANTINE ART

Between the tenth and the twelfth centuries, there occurred, under the auspices of the Macedonian dynasty, what has been called the Second Flowering or Second Byzantine Golden Age, during which Byzantine culture reencountered its Hellenistic sources and accommodated them to the styles inherited from the Age of Justinian, the time of the First Flowering.

Architecture

In architecture, a brilliant series of variations on the domed central theme began to appear. From the exterior, the typical later Byzantine church building is a domed cube, with the dome rising above the square on a kind of cylinder or drum. (Less often, some other rectangular form, with something other than a square as its base, was used.) The churches are small, vertical, high-shouldered, and, unlike earlier Byzantine buildings, have exterior wall surfaces with ornament in relief. In the Church of the Theotokos (FIGS. **7-43** and **7-44**), built about 1040 at Hosios Loukas in Greece, one can see the form of a domed cross with

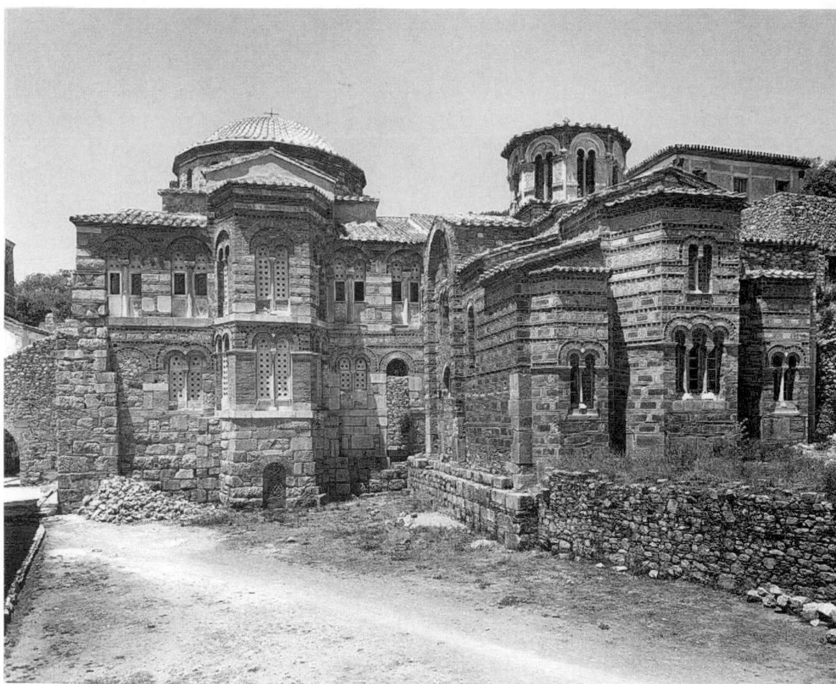

7-43 Monastery churches at Hosios Loukas, Phocis, Greece: Church of the Katholikon, *c.* 1020 *(left)*, and Church of the Theotokos, *c.* 1040 *(right)*. (View from the east.)

7-44 Plans of the Church of the Katholikon *(bottom)* and the Church of the Theotokos *(top)*, Hosios Loukas.

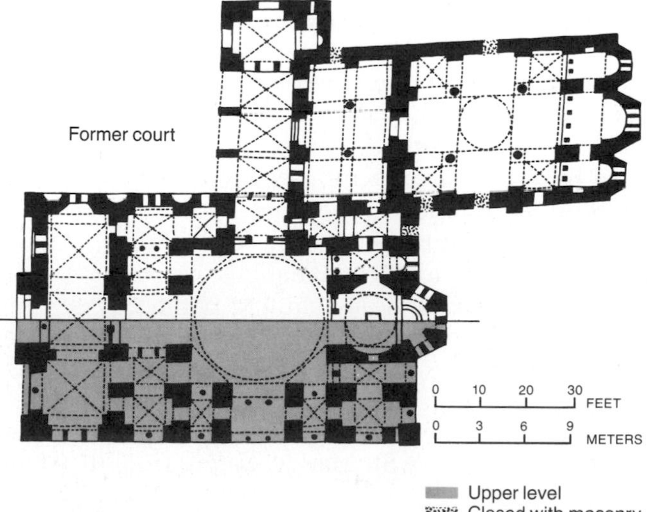

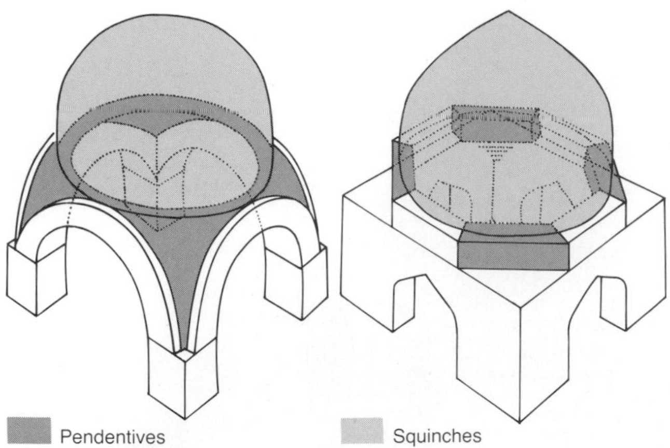

7-45 Domes on pendentives *(left)* and squinches *(right)*.

four equal-length, vaulted cross arms (the Greek cross). Around this unit, and by the duplication of it, Byzantine architects developed bewilderingly involved spaces. In the adjacent, larger Church of the Katholikon (FIGS. 7-43 and 7-44), a dome is placed over an octagon inscribed within a square; the octagon is formed by *squinches*—arches, corbeling, or lintels that bridge the corners of the square (FIG. **7-45**). This arrangement represents a subtle extension of the older designs, such as Santa Costanza's circular plan (FIG. 7-8), San Vitale's octagonal plan (FIG. 7-33), and Hagia Sophia's dome on pendentives rising from a square (FIG. 7-42). The complex core of the Church of the Katholikon lies within two rectangles, the outermost forming the exterior walls. Thus, in plan, from the center out, a circle–octagon–square–oblong series exhibits an intricate interrelationship that is at once complex and unified.

The interior elevation of the Church of the Katholikon (FIG. **7-46**) reflects its involved plan. Like earlier Byzantine buildings, the church creates a mystery out of space, surface, and light and dark. High and narrow, it forces our gaze to rise and revolve: "The overall spatial effect is overwhelmingly beautiful in its complex interplay of higher and lower elements, of core and ancillary spaces, of clear, dim, and dark zones of lighting."* Thus, the aim of Middle and Late Byzantine architecture seems to be the creation of complex interior spaces that issue into multiple domes in the upper levels; these, in exterior view, produce spectacular combinations of round forms that develop dramatically shifting perspectives.

The splendid Church of Holy Apostles, built in the time of Justinian, no longer exists. Fortunately, the great five-domed church of St. Mark's in Venice (FIGS. **7-47** to **7-49**) reflects many of its key features. The original structure of St. Mark's, dating from the elev-

*Richard Krautheimer, *Early Christian and Byzantine Architecture* (Baltimore: Penguin, 1965), p. 244.

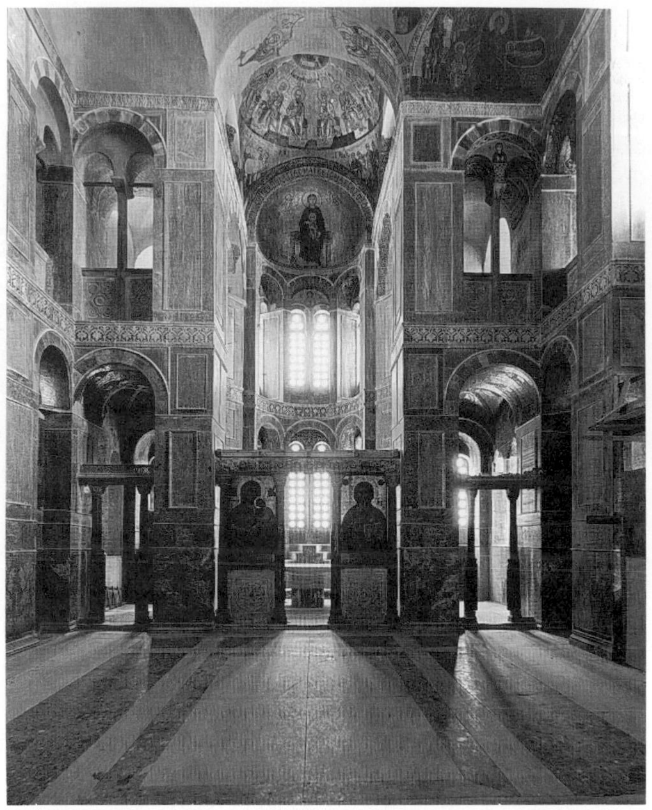

7-46 Interior of the Church of the Katholikon (view facing east).

7-47 Aerial view of St. Mark's, Venice, Italy, begun 1063.

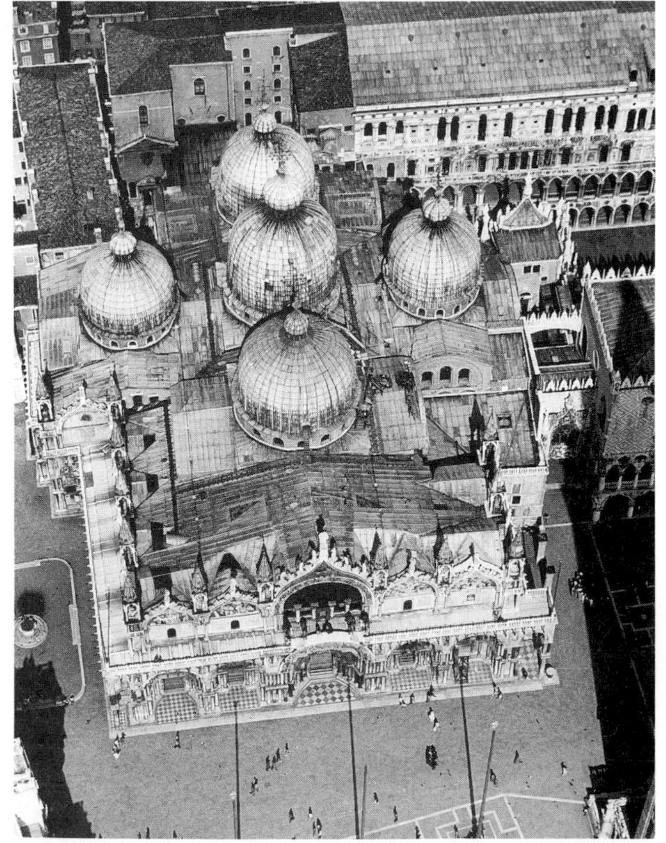

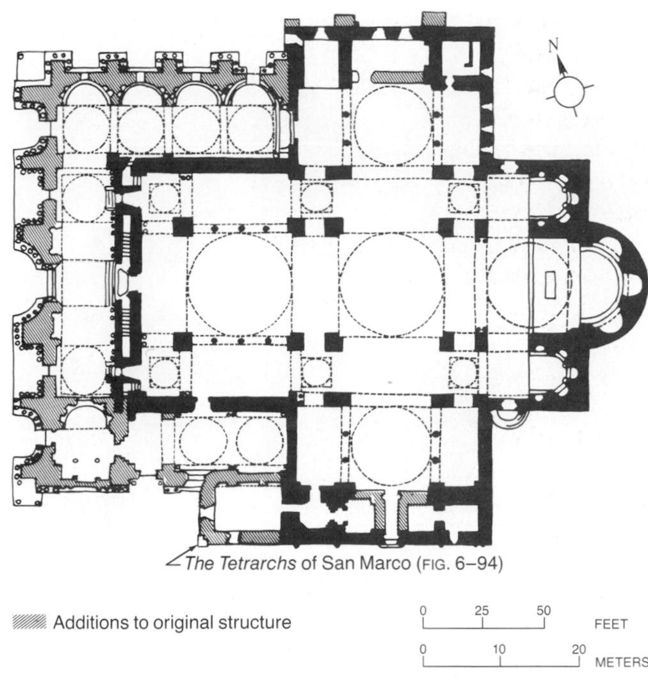

7-48 Plan of St. Mark's. (After Sir Banister Fletcher.)

enth century, is disguised on its lower levels by Romanesque and Gothic additions. But in plan, or from an aerial view, the domes, grouped along a cross of equal arms (the Greek cross again), make the Byzantine origins of St. Mark's evident at once. The inner masonry shells are covered with swelling, wooden, helmetlike forms sheathed in gilded copper; these forms protect the inner domes and contribute to the exuberant composition. Venice, like Ravenna, some eighty miles to the south, was under strong Byzantine influence, despite the independence it had won early in the Middle Ages and preserved for centuries. The interior of St. Mark's is, like its plan, Byzantine in effect, although the great Justinianic scale and intricate syncopation of domed bays here are modified slightly by western Romanesque elements. The light effects and the rich cycles of mosaics, however, are entirely Byzantine.

Byzantine influence was wide-ranging not only in Italy, but also in the Slavic lands and in the regions of the east into which Islam had expanded. Byzantium brought its script, its religion, and much of its culture to Russia. The "holy" Russia prior to the

7-49 Interior of St. Mark's (view facing east).

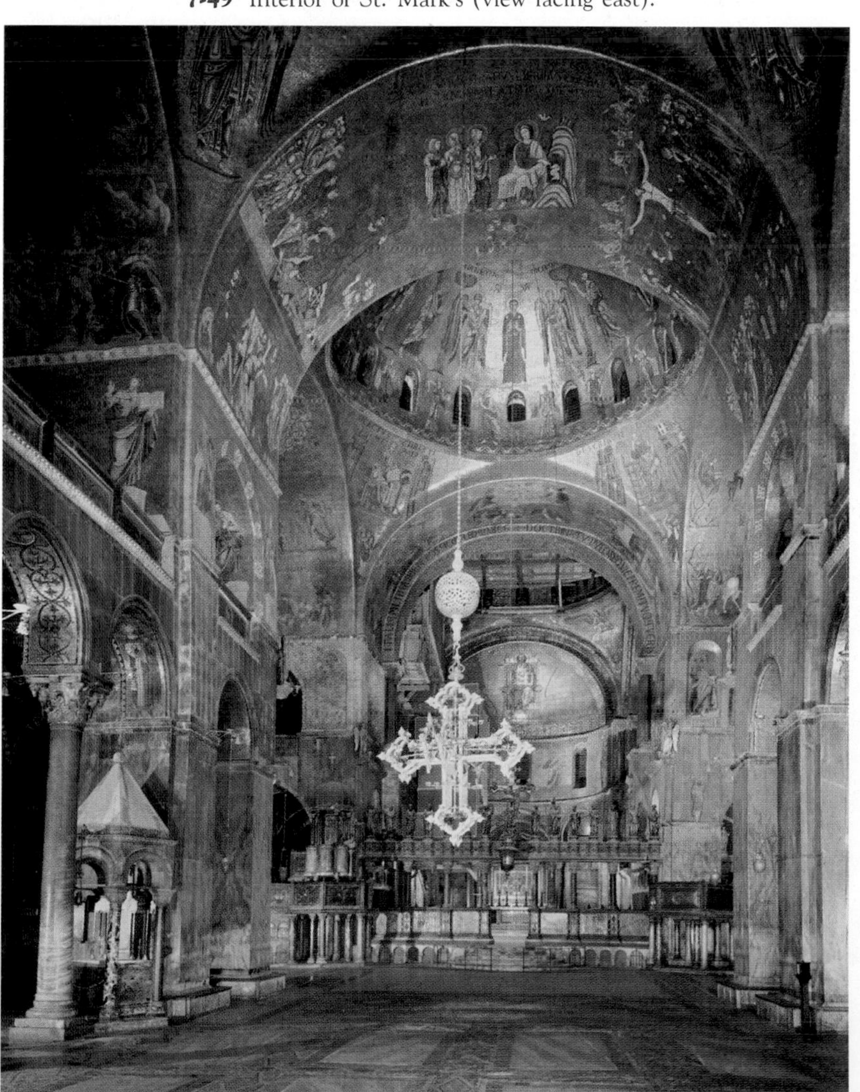

revolution of 1917 was largely Byzantine in its traditions and, one might even say, in its mood. Russian architecture, magnificently developed in the Middle Ages, is a brilliant, provincial variation on Byzantine themes.

The ecclesiastical architecture of medieval Russia was, at first, if not actually produced by Greeks, at least strongly under the influence of Constantinople. The church of St. Dmitri at Vladimir (FIG. **7-50**) is built on the typical plan of a square enclosing a Greek cross and crowned with a single dome on a high drum. The church is of stone, a rare building material in Russia, where brick, stucco, and wood are more usual. Exterior wall spaces, which have few openings, are decorated here with moldings. Some of these, rising unbroken from the ground to the roof, divide the wall into panels; others, much shorter, form blind arcadings. The surface within the arcadings is elaborately carved in low reliefs that are peculiarly well adapted to stone and are close, in subject matter and form, to Sassanian (Persian) and other western Asiatic carvings. St. Dmitri is a masterpiece of simplicity and compactness, with a classic, monumental dignity. Later structures will develop a colorful complexity of plan and elevation.

7-50 St. Dmitri at Vladimir, Soviet Union, 1194–1197.

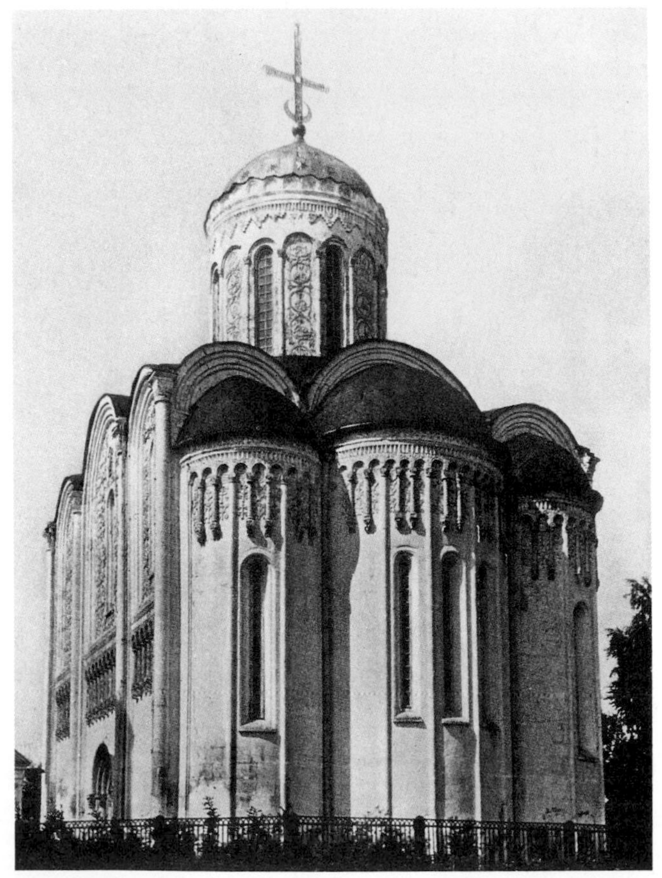

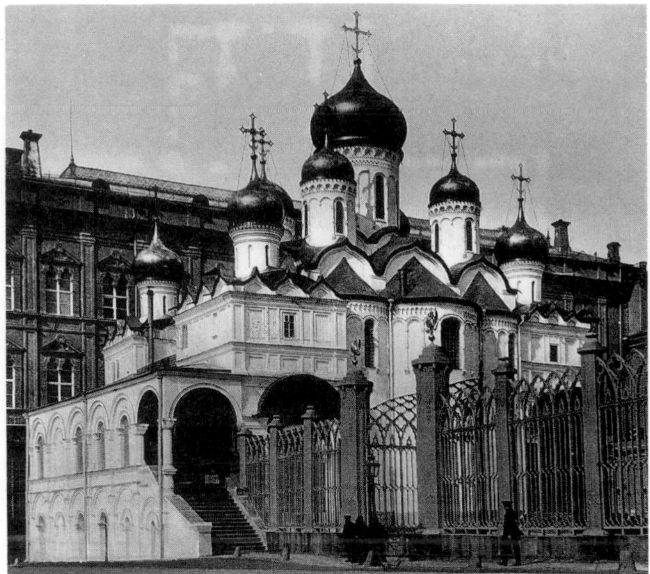

7-51 Cathedral of the Annunciation, the Kremlin, Moscow, 1482–1490.

In Moscow, within the walls of the Kremlin, stands the Cathedral of the Annunciation (FIG. **7-51**), which dates from the late fifteenth century. The domed-cross plan of Byzantium here receives a most spirited expansion. The cathedral is built on a square plan with eastern apses; its helmetlike domes, now greatly multiplied, rise in a kind of triumphant crescendo to the climax of the central unit, which is crowned with the typical Russian bulbous "onion" or "beet" dome. The bright metal caps, peaked with crosses like miniature masts, reflect the moody Russian skies and proclaim, as if in architectural polyphony, the glory of the Orthodox faith.

Painting and Sculpture

Although architecture enjoyed a fairly continuous development throughout the Byzantine period, the representational arts (painting and sculpture) suffered a severe setback during the eighth and ninth centuries, when they became the subject of a violent controversy. The Iconoclastic Controversy over the propriety of religious imagery, which raged for more than one hundred years (730–843), began with the temporary victory of the image-destroyers (*iconoclasts*), who interpreted the biblical ban against graven images literally. In 730, an imperial edict banned religious imagery throughout the Byzantine Empire, and artists either were forced to migrate to the west, where the edict could not be enforced, or, if they chose to remain in Byzantium, to turn their talents to secular subject matter, which was not affected by the ban.

Migrant Byzantine painters in Italy worked with religious subject matter in a classicizing style. Although little remains of their work, examples can be found in Rome, especially in Santa Maria Antiqua. There, in the eighth century, a succession of Greek popes provided an encouraging atmosphere for the forbidden culture and art of iconoclastic Byzantium. At Castelseprio in northern Italy, remarkable murals of uncertain date (FIG. **7-52**) are, without doubt, the work of a gifted Byzantine painter (probably from the late seventh or early eighth century) whose deft hand and fluent, sweeping style show the enduring illusionistic Classicism born in Hellenistic times and destined to recur often in the centuries after the First Golden Age of Byzantine art. This naturalistic manner could exist side by side with the austere and abstract style seen at Ravenna, or could merge with it. When the ban against religious images was lifted and religious painting was again encouraged in Byzantium, a style of painting emerged that was a subtle blend of the pictorial, classicizing Hellenistic and the later, more abstract and formalistic Byzantine style.

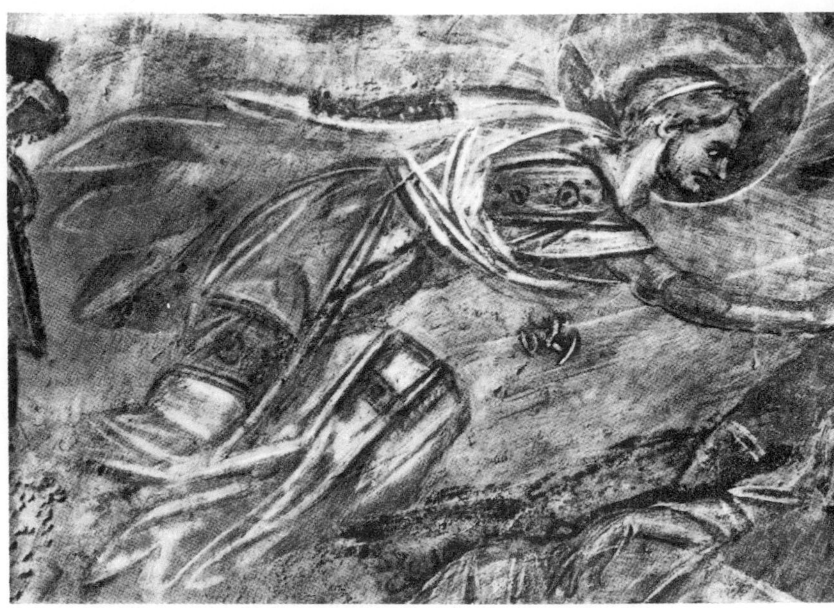

7-52 *The Angel Appearing to Joseph,* detail of wall painting, Santa Maria de Castelseprio, Castelseprio, Italy, early eighth century (?).

An eleventh-century crucifixion scene, a mosaic on the wall of the monastery church at Daphne in Greece (FIG. **7-53**) shows the simplicity, dignity, and grace of Classicism fully assimilated by the Byzantine artist into a perfect synthesis with Byzantine piety and pathos. Christ is represented on the cross, flanked by the Virgin and St. John. A skull at the foot of the cross indicates Golgotha, the "place of skulls." Nothing is needed to complete the tableau. In quiet sorrow and resignation, the Virgin and St. John point to Christ as if to indicate the meaning of the cross. Symmetry and closed space combine to produce an effect of the motionless and unchanging aspect of the deepest mystery of the Christian religion; the timeless presence is, as it were, beheld in unbroken silence. The picture is not a narrative of the historical event of the Crucifixion, but a devotional object, a thing sacramental in itself, to be viewed by the monks in silent contemplation of the mystery of the Sacrifice. Although elongated, these figures from the Second Golden Age of Byzantine art (the tenth and eleventh centuries) have regained their organic structure to a surprising degree, particularly compared to figures from the Justinian period (compare FIGS. 7-36 and 7-37). The style is a masterful adaptation of Classical, statuesque qualities to the linear Byzantine style.

7-53 *The Crucifixion,* mosaic from the monastery church in Daphne, Greece, eleventh century.

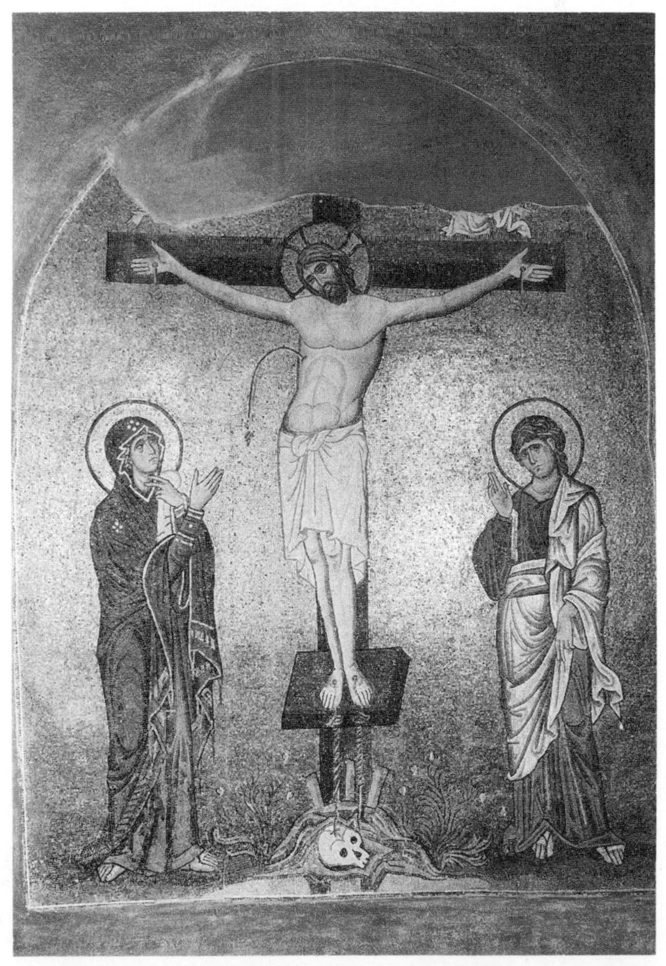

Variations of Byzantine style appeared widely in the twelfth century throughout the Balkan world (Yugoslavia, Bulgaria, Romania) and in Venice, South Italy, and Sicily, where Mediterranean powers were eager to adopt Byzantine art and culture. At Nerezi in Yugoslavia (ancient Macedonia), paintings of amazing emotional power have been found that contrast dramatically with the almost stern formalism and hieraticism of the Daphne mosaic. The *Lamentation over the Dead Christ* (FIG. **7-54**), from the second half of the twelfth century, is a tableau of passionate grief. The friends of Christ are captured in attitudes, expressions, and gestures of quite human bereavement. The artist has striven above all to make this realization of the theme utterly convincing. The stirring staging of the subject points forward to the art of thirteenth-century (Gothic) Italy, when the reception of this mode of emotional realism would carry all before it into the Italian "proto-Renaissance" and the art of Giotto (compare FIG. 15-13).

In the art of the Second Byzantine Golden Age, particularly in its later phase, a kind of dialogue takes place between the formal, symbolic, hieratic style of the Daphne mosaic and the intense, emotional, active style of the Nerezi murals. The choice of one alternative over the other depended on the site and on ecclesiastical, political, and artistic intentions. An example of the hieratic style accommodated to a monumental site is found in the apse mosaic of the royal church of Monreale in Sicily (FIG. **7-55**). This work was part of a total program of ecclesiastical-artistic aggrandizement conducted by Roger, the great Norman king of Sicily, who imported the splendor of Byzantium to glorify his reign, believing that his own sovereign power came directly from God. Christ, as Pantocrator, judge of the world, looms menacingly in the vault of the apse, a colossal image of kingly power and authority, whether spiritual or temporal. Below Christ in rank and dignity, the enthroned Virgin and saints are ranged symmetrically. Here, Byzantine formality manifests the very image of heavenly and earthly power; the former is presented explicitly, the latter, by association. From Sicily, from Venice, and from the Byzantine Balkans, the art of Byzantium found its way into the West, stimulating and influencing the art of the periods we call Romanesque and Gothic.

Recent cleaning and restoration on a grand scale have returned the mosaics of the church of St. Mark's in Venice (FIG. 7-49) to their original splendor. It is now possible to experience, in all its iconographic complexity, the awe-inspiring decorative program of a great Byzantine church and to appreciate to the fullest the radiance of mosaic (some 40,000 square feet of it!) as it covers, like a gold-brocaded and figured fabric, all architectural surfaces—walls, arches, vaults, and domes. This is the setting for the presentation of the divine personages who preside in this church as they preside in the spiritual universe; in Byzantine devotion, they are regarded not as mere representations, but as *icons* actually present and deserving of the reverence they would receive in Heaven. In the

7-54 *Lamentation over the Dead Christ,* wall painting, St. Pantaleimon, Nerezi, Yugoslavia, 1164.

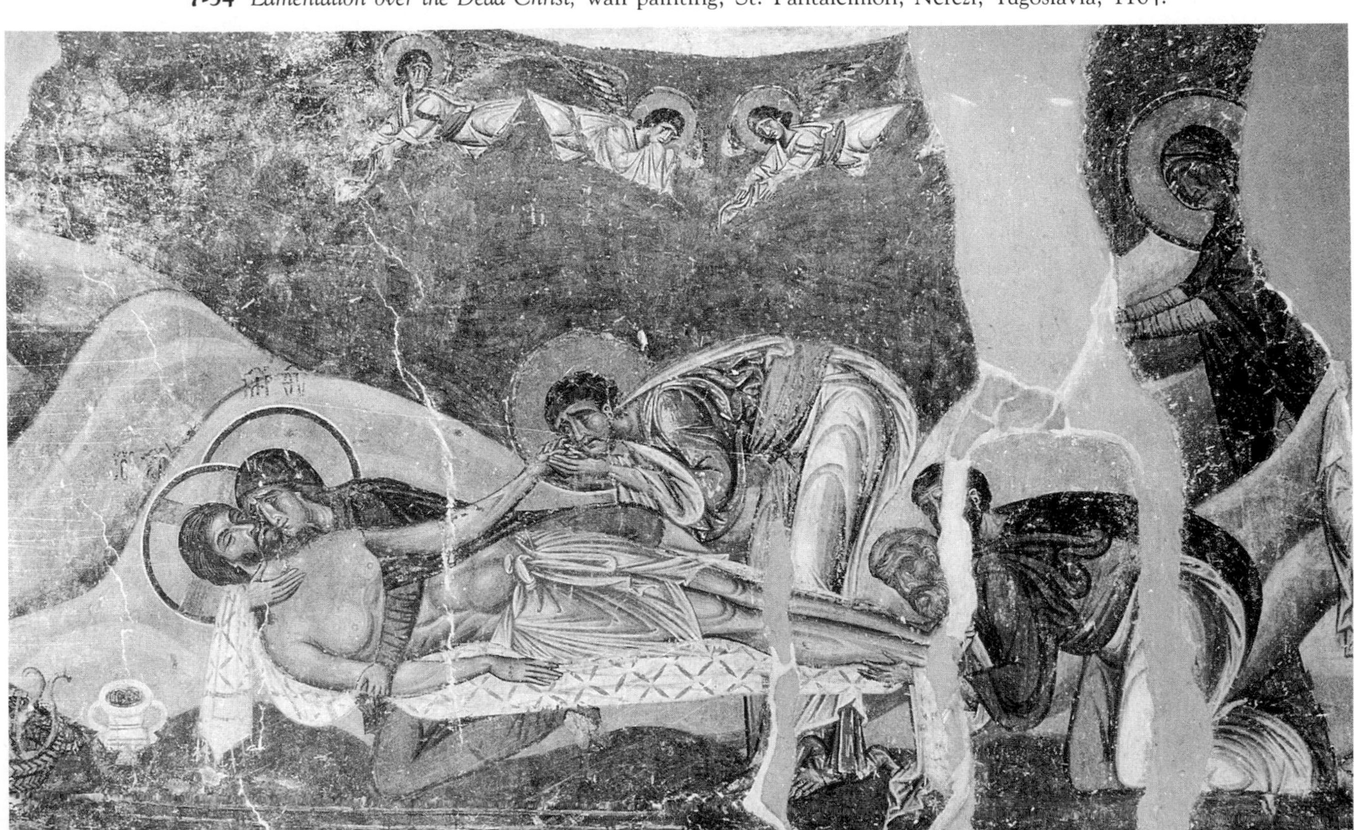

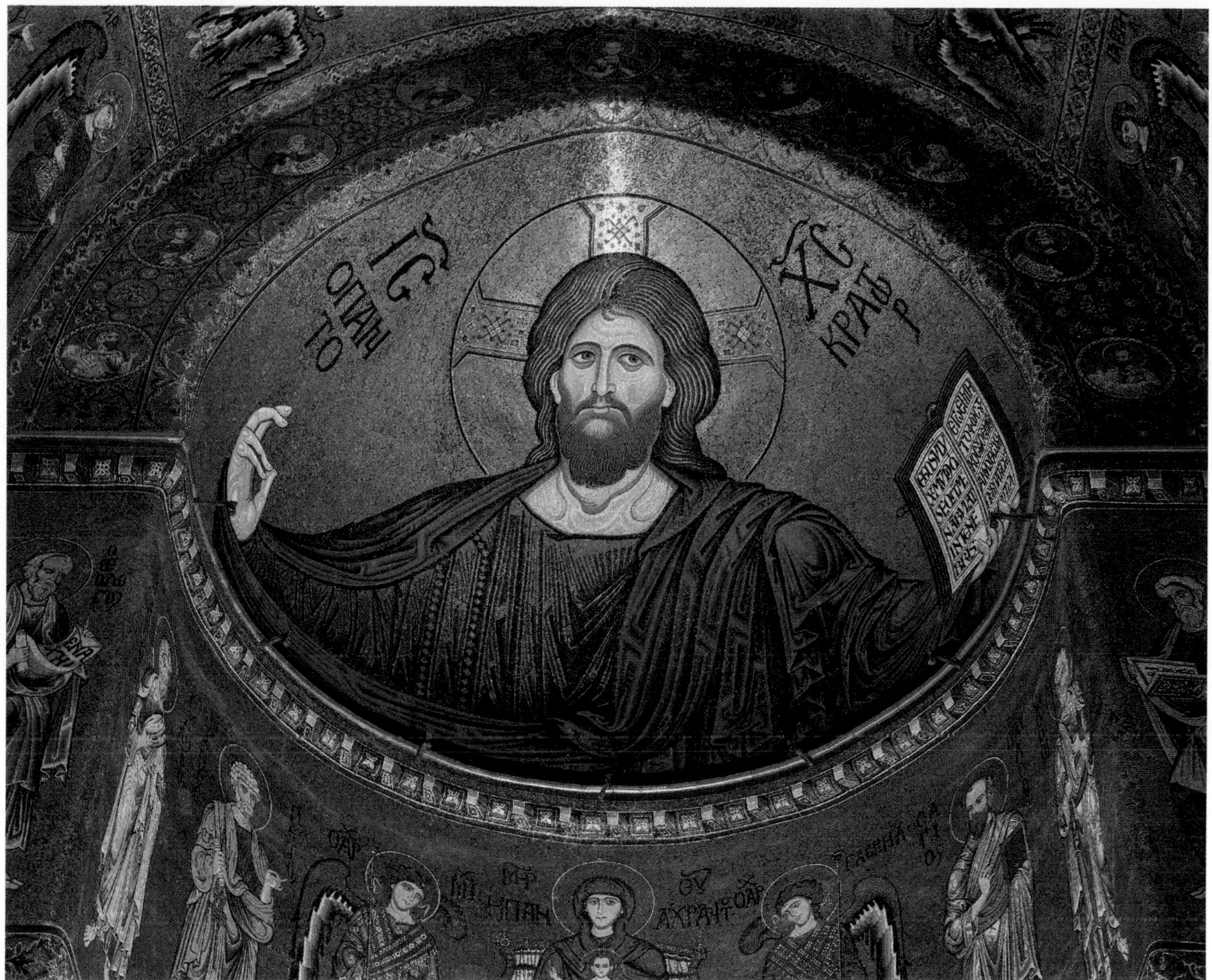

7-55 *The Pantocrator, with the Virgin, Angels, and Saints,* apse mosaic from the royal church of Monreale, Sicily, late twelfth century.

vast central dome, 80 feet above the floor and 42 feet in diameter, Christ reigns in the company of the Evangelists, the Virgin Mary, the Virtues, and the Beatitudes. The great arch, which partly interrupts our view of the dome, bears a narrative of the Crucifixion and Resurrection of Christ and of his liberation of the worthies of the Old Testament from death, the theme known as the Harrowing of Hell. On these golden surfaces, the figures ("sages standing in God's holy fire"), levitating and insubstantial, are drawn with a flowing, calligraphic line; they project from their flat field no more than the letters of the elegant Latin script that captions them. Nothing here reflects on the world of matter, of solids, of light and shade, of perspective space; the trees are ornamental standards, the furniture of Paradise. We have before us the open book of the heavenly order, its image as solemn and hieratic as the sacred text that reveals it in words. Here, in hierarchical placement, the chief mysteries and narratives of the Christian Church are arrayed to present the supernatural and eternal world to which its dogma refers.

The New Testament is set forth within the church proper. Outside, in the shallow domes of the narthex, the Old Testament is recounted, particularly the Book of Genesis, which tells the story of the creation and fall of man. One of the domes (FIG. **7-56**) depicts the sojourn of Joseph in Egypt (Genesis 39, 40, 41, 42): the affair of Potiphar's wife, Joseph imprisoned, his interpretation of the dreams of Pharaoh and the baker. The episodes, with their captions, are arranged in a circle following the curve of the dome, their radial axes converging on an exquisite, star-studded medallion vaguely resembling the great rose windows of contemporaneous cathedrals in Gothic France (see page 397). The figures, like those of the interior of the church, are rendered in sharp, precise line on a golden ground, with all the clarity and readability of the script that describes them. Again, we have the perfect harmony of architectural surface, figural image, and lettered inscription in a scintillating, rainbow-colored aureole. The mosaicists' masterly control of their medium, their consummate skill in design, their faultless geometric procedure, their subtle color harmonies, their deft, clear and economical draftsmanship make for a perfection almost without parallel in Byzantine art. The great mosaic cycles of St. Mark's would, in themselves, proclaim an artistic golden age. In them, we find the culmination and confluence of both the hieratic and narrative stylistic currents begun at Santa Maria Maggiore in Rome and at St. George in Thessaloniki (FIGS. 7-12 and 7-13) some eight centuries before.

From the last great period, the Third Golden Age of Byzantine art (thirteenth to late fourteenth century), we have a late example of vigorous, expressive action, related to the drama of the Nerezi painting but with a heightened naturalism that parallels developments in contemporaneous Italian art, and may even lead them in sophistication. A fresco completed about 1320 in the vault of a side chapel of the Mosque of the Ka'riye in Istanbul (originally the Church of the Blessed Savior of the Chora) represents, although inscribed *Anastasis* (Resurrection), *The Harrowing of Hell* (FIG. **7-57**). Christ, after his death on the cross, descends into Hell, tramples Satan, and rescues

7-56 *Joseph in Egypt*, mosaic in the dome of the narthex, St. Mark's, Venice, 1255–1260.

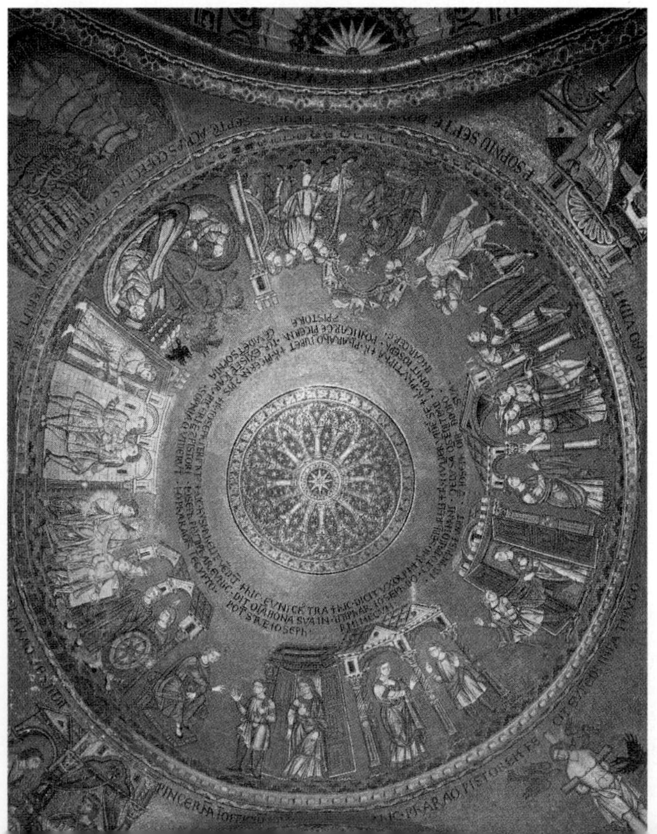

Adam and Eve, while other worthies of the Old Testament stand by awaiting their liberation. The movement of the central figures is highly dramatic. The white-robed, aureole-surrounded figure of Christ is suffused with energy as he literally tears the parents of mankind from their tombs. The dynamic postures of the figures are reinforced by swirling draperies, agitated by the winds of a supramaterial force. But we also notice that, here and there, the carefully and precisely drawn drapery folds tend to take on a life of their own, as the Late Byzantine artist often showed delight in creating linear patterns for their own sake. These abstract, decorative, linear patterns tend to obscure the fact that, in its late stages, Byzantine art became increasingly realistic.

The characteristics of Byzantine painting were developed in large-scale mural decorations, but it was through miniatures in manuscripts and small panel paintings, more popularly known as *icons*, that the elements of the style were spread abroad. A fine example of the former is a page from a book of the Psalms of David, the so-called *Paris Psalter* (FIG. **7-58**), which reasserts the artistic values of the Classical past with astonishing authority. The *Psalter* is believed to date from the early tenth century—a time of enthusiastic and careful study of the language and literature of ancient Greece as well as a time when the classics were regarded with humanistic reverence. It was only natural that, in art, inspiration should be drawn once again from the Hellenistic naturalism of the pre-Christian Mediterranean world, especially Alexandria. David, the psalmist, is seated with his harp in a flowering, Arcadian landscape recalling those of Pompeian murals. He is accompanied by an allegorical figure of Melody and is surrounded by sheep, goats, and his faithful dog. Echo (or perhaps Spring) peers from behind a trophied column, and a reclining male figure points to an inscription that identifies him as representing the mountains of Bethlehem. These allegorical figures do not appear in the Bible; they are the stock population of Alexandrian and Pompeian landscape. Apparently, the artist had seen a work from Late Antiquity or perhaps earlier and partly translated it into a Byzantine pictorial idiom. In the figure of Melody, we find some incongruity between the earlier and later styles. Her pose, head, and torso are quite Hellenistic, as is the light, impressionistic touch of the brush, but the drapery enwrapping the legs is a pattern of hard line. Byzantine illuminations like this repeatedly will exert their influence on Western painting in the Romanesque and Early Gothic periods.

The icon, a devotional panel bearing the portrait of a saint, was a characteristic type of Byzantine painting. The icon's origins derive from the mosaic portrait

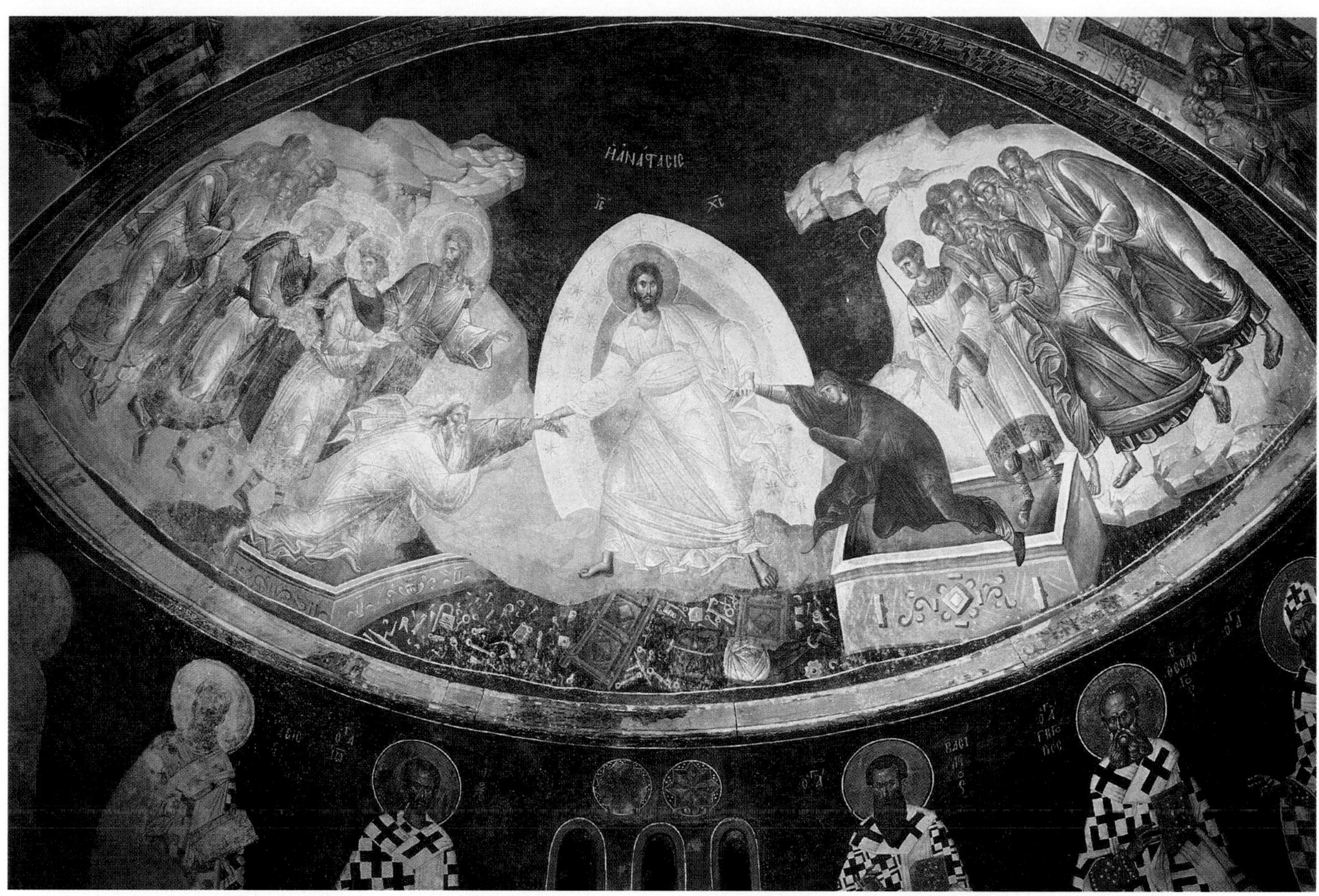

7-57 *The Harrowing of Hell,* fresco from the Mosque of the Ka'riye, Istanbul, Turkey, c. 1310–1320.

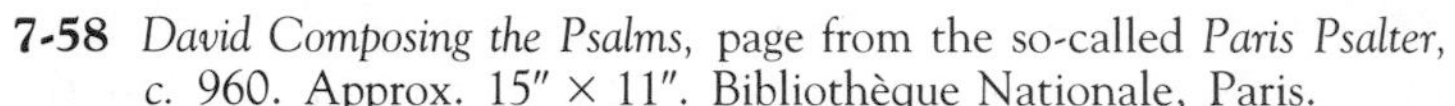

7-58 *David Composing the Psalms,* page from the so-called *Paris Psalter,* c. 960. Approx. 15″ × 11″. Bibliothèque Nationale, Paris.

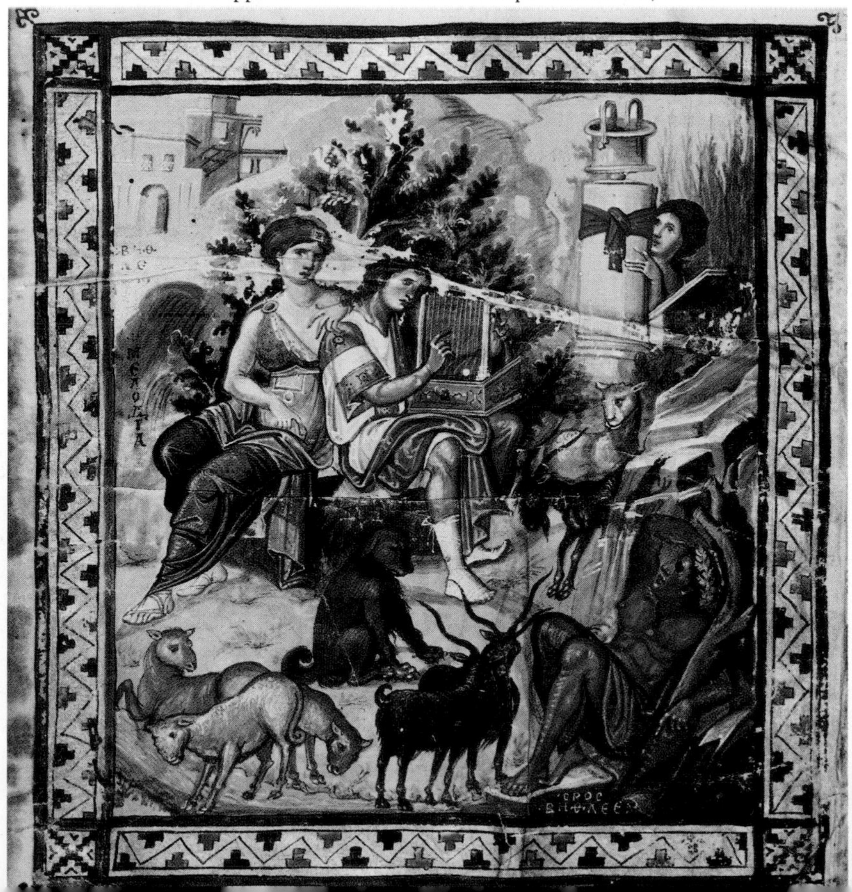

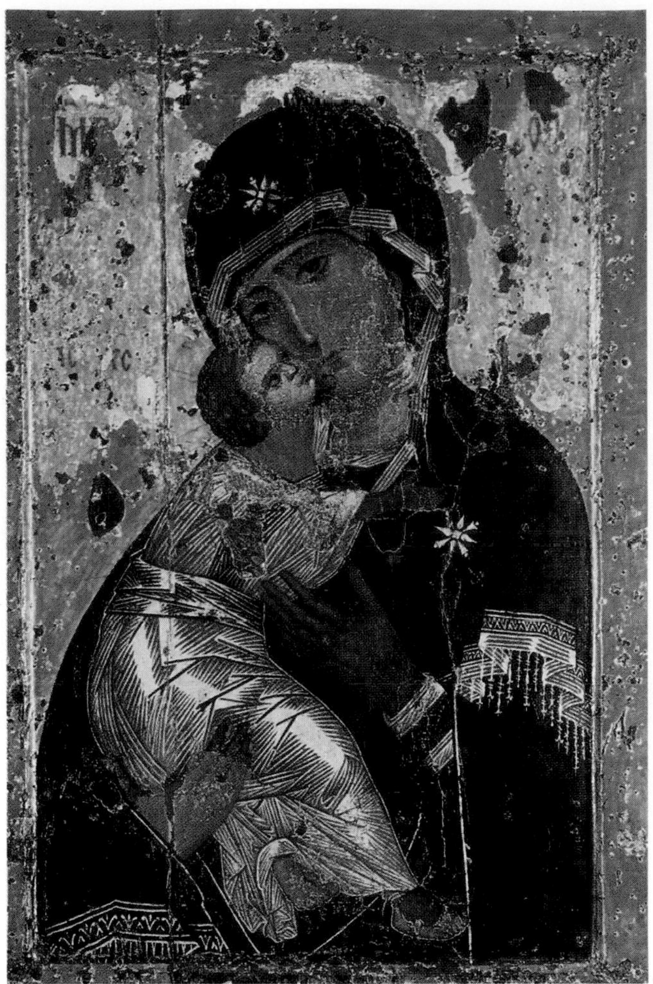

7-59 *The Vladimir Madonna,* twelfth century. Painted wood, original panel approx. 30½″ × 21″. State Historical Museum, Moscow.

medallions, like that of Christ in the triumphal arch of Sant' Apollinare in Classe (FIG. 7-30), conspicuous in Byzantine churches. A famous example of the icon is *The Vladimir Madonna* (FIG. **7-59**), which was probably painted by an artist in Byzantium in the twelfth century, exported to Vladimir, and then taken to Moscow in 1395 to protect that city from the Mongols. Because these icons were quickly blackened by incense and smoke from the devotional candles that burned before them, they frequently were repainted, often by inferior artists. In our panel, only the faces show the original surface, but the painting retains its Byzantine characteristics in the typical configuration of the Madonna's face, with its long, straight nose and tiny mouth, and in the decorative sweep of the unbroken contour that encloses the two figures and creates a flat silhouette against a golden background. The deep pathos of the Madonna's expression shows an interest in depicting emotion that would flow into the art of Russia and the West.

In Russia, icon painting flourished for centuries, extending the life of the style well beyond the collapse of the Byzantine Empire in 1453. The development of the *iconostasis*—the large, icon-bearing screen that shuts off the sanctuary from the rest of the church—into an elaborate structure with more than five tiers had an important effect on icon painting. The purpose of these paintings was to enable the worshiper to read pictorially. Clear, pictorial legibility in wavering candlelight and through clouds of incense required strong pattern, firm lines, and intense color. Hence, the relatively sober hues of the Early Byzantine paintings gave way, more characteristically, to the intense, contrasting colors used in Russia. It was under a renewed Byzantine impulse, after the waning of the Mongol domination, and through the requirements of the iconostasis (just then reaching its highest development), that Russian painting reached a climax in the work of ANDREI RUBLËV (c. 1370–1430). *The Old Testament Trinity Prefiguring the Incarnation* (FIG. **7-60**) is a work of great spiritual

7-60 ANDREI RUBLËV, *The Old Testament Trinity Prefiguring the Incarnation,* c. 1410. Painted wood, 56″ × 45″. Tretyakov Gallery, Moscow.

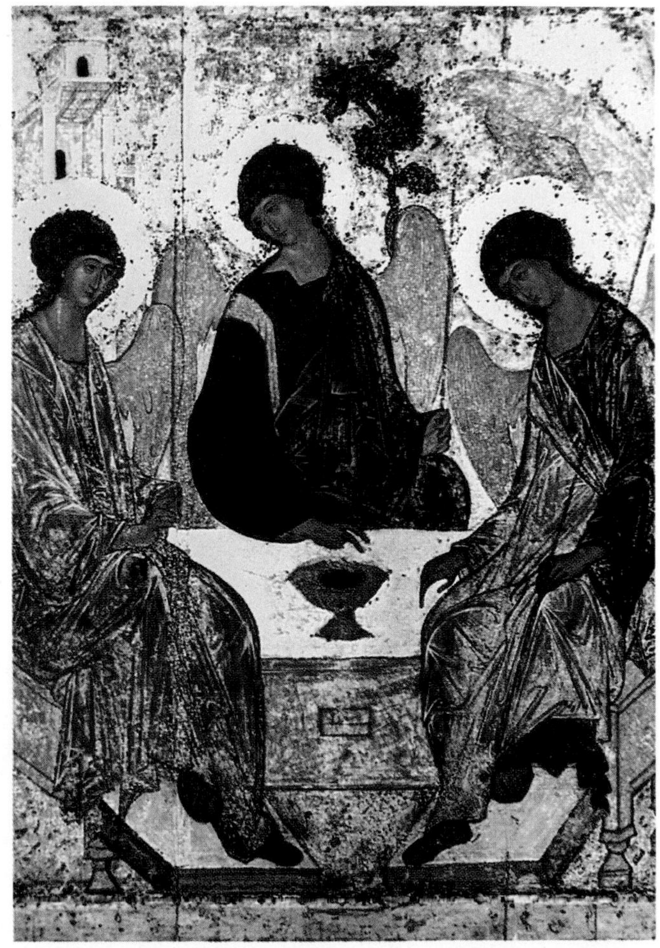

power, as well as an unsurpassed example of subtle line in union with intensely vivid color. The three angels who appeared to Abraham near the oaks of Mamre (Genesis 18:2–15) are seated about a table. (The angels are interpreted in Christian thought as a prefiguration of the Holy Trinity after the Incarnation of Christ.) The figures, each framed with a halo and sweeping wings, are suavely, languorously poised within an implicit circle, each, in its way, appearing rapt in meditation on the mystery of the Trinity. The tranquil demeanor of the figures is set off by the light, linear play of the draperies. Forms are defined by color, and areas frequently are intensified by the juxtaposition of a complementary hue. The intense blue and green folds of the cloak of the central figure, for example, stand out starkly against the deep red robe and the gilded orange of the wings. In the figure on the left, the highlights of the orange cloak are an opalescent blue-green. The color harmonies are Oriental in their unmodulated saturation, brilliance, and purity. In Russian painting, the Byzantine tradition was enlivened and enriched by a feeling and a touch that were not Byzantine or native but, rather, a fusion of the two; the same can be said of Russian architecture.

We should not forget, in considering the rich ecclesiastical art of Byzantium and Russia, the indispensable part played by other arts in the ensemble of a church interior: the carvings and rich metalwork of the iconostasis; the finely wrought, jeweled halos and other ornaments on the icons; the candlesticks and candelabra; the miters and ecclesiastical robes stiff with gold, embroidery, and jewels; the illuminated books bound in gold or ivory, inlaid with jewels and enamels; the crosses, croziers, sacred vessels, and processional banners. Each, with its great richness of texture and color, contributed to the total effect. In the life of Orthodox Byzantium, to produce this effect was to honor God and his vicar, the emperor.

Although carved ornament continued to appear in Byzantine churches, monumental stone sculpture was never encouraged to the degree that it was in western Europe. Life-size figures in the round apparently offended the Eastern Christians. Their uneasiness was underlined by the Iconoclastic Controversy; they made an early association between statues and pagan idols. Painted images, on the other hand, created forms that were less directly identified with natural figures (particularly given the stylistic conventions that were to develop). The Byzantine sculptor, however, was called on to carve small statues and reliefs, particularly in ivory, to be used primarily for devotional purposes, although secular themes also are evident. These objects were used to adorn books, caskets, portable plaques, and venerable images, in much the same manner as the painted icons.

A panel from a small work in ivory from the Second Byzantine Golden Age, the *Veroli Casket* (FIG. **7-61**), testifies to the persistence of Classical form and content in Byzantine art, and to their strong revival in the tenth century. This panel represents a scene at the end of Euripides' play, *Iphigenia in Aulis,* in which Iphigenia, at center, is about to be sacrificed. The characters are all identifiable, and the human types, poses, costumes, and accessories are all from classical antiquity, although the stunting of the proportions (perhaps partly a consequence of the diminutive space) and the bulbous modeling show the figures at a considerable distance in time and style from their prototypes in the Greco-Roman world.

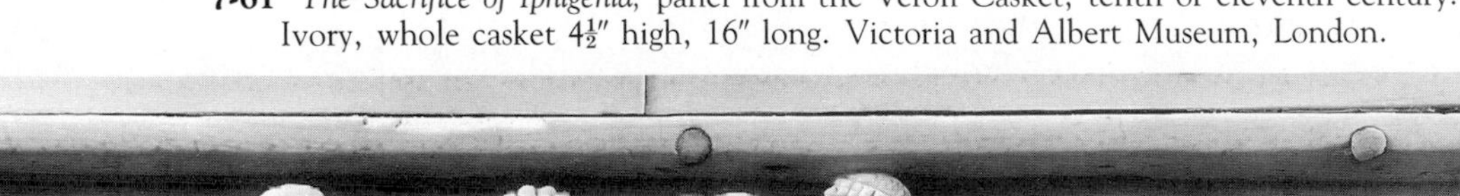

7-61 *The Sacrifice of Iphigenia,* panel from the Veroli Casket, tenth or eleventh century. Ivory, whole casket $4\frac{1}{2}$″ high, 16″ long. Victoria and Albert Museum, London.

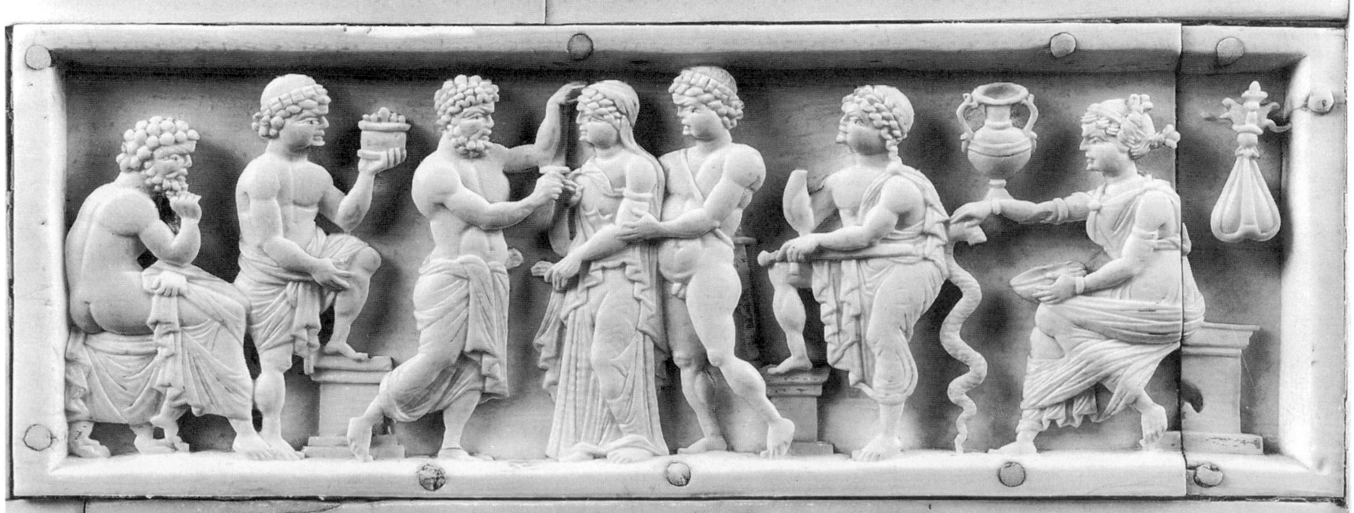

From about the same time, the *Harbaville Triptych,* a portable shrine with hinged panels (FIG. **7-62**), manifests in its figures the hieratic formality and solemnity we have learned to associate with Byzantine art and have seen as standard in the mosaics of Ravenna. A softer, more fluent technique and the looser stance of the figures mitigate the hard austerity of the customary frontal pose. This softening may also result from the influential, classicizing spirit of the Second Byzantine Golden Age. Originating in a workshop associated with the imperial palace in Constantinople, the triptych marshals Christ and the saints in such a way as to align the powers of church and state, of God and emperor. Christ is enthroned between St. John and the Virgin in the upper central zone. Beneath them are five apostles. In the wings are soldier-saints like George and Theodore and bishop-saints like Demetrius and Procopius. Between the levels are portraits of other saints. Here, we have, in effect, a miniature, sculptured iconostasis, with the sacred personages placed in their celestial ranks of authority, like officials ranked in the imperial hierarchy.

Portable works like icons and ivories found their way to distant lands as royal gifts, as items of trade, or as plunder, so that the rich and potent religious art of Byzantium became known throughout Europe. Everywhere it had directing influence and, as we have seen, nowhere more than in Russia. For the Medieval West, the art of Byzantium was to inspire, through its steady influence, a return to the principles of Classical humanism and naturalism long implicit in it.

7-62 *Christ Enthroned with Saints,* the *Harbaville Triptych,* c. 950. Ivory, central panel 9½″ × 5½″. Louvre, Paris.

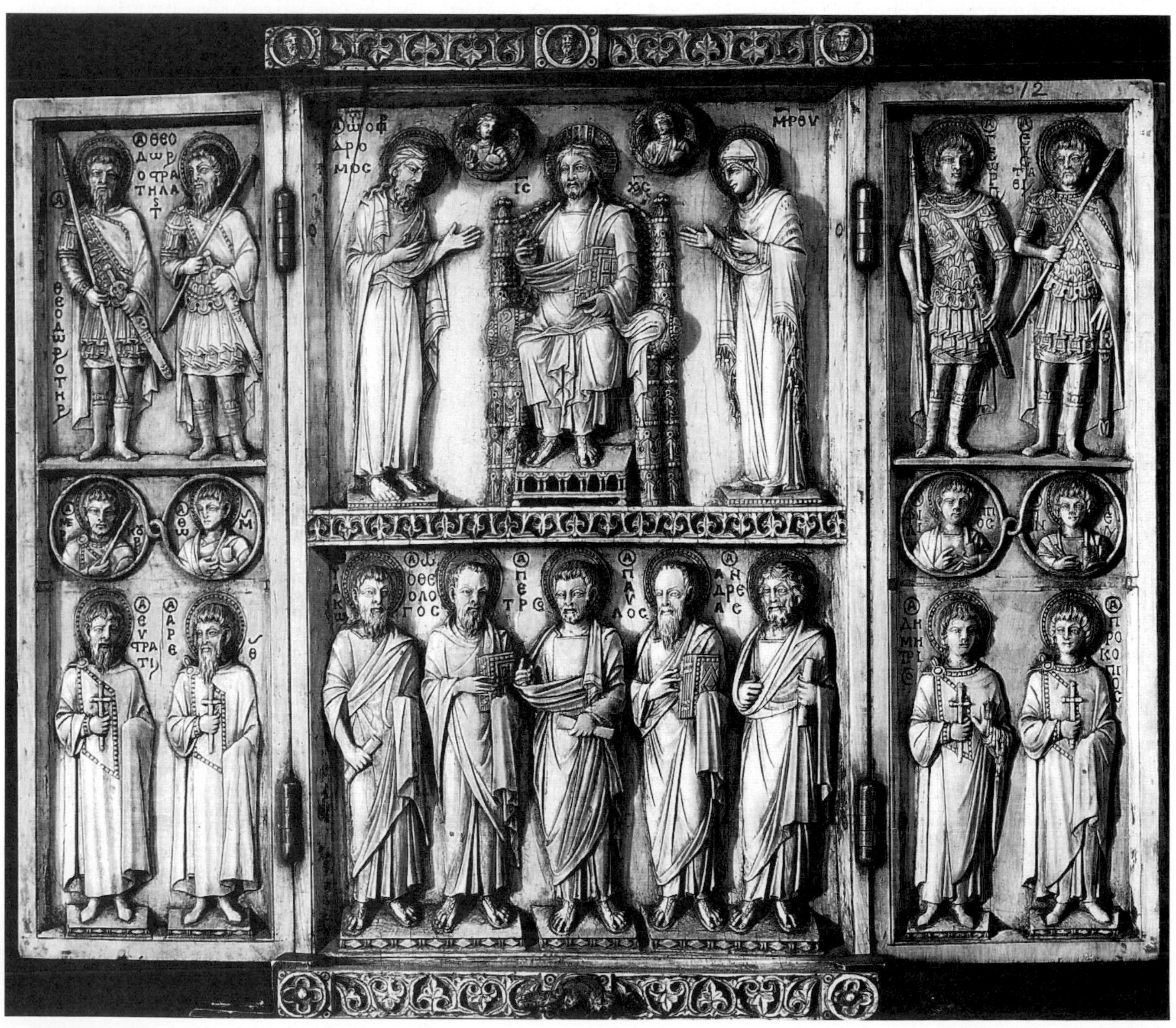

ISLAMIC ART

In 622, Mohammed fled from Mecca to Medinet-en-Nabi ("City of the Prophet," now Medina). From this flight, known as the "Hegira," Islam dates its beginnings.*

During the century that followed, the new faith spread with unprecedented speed from Arabia, where it first was espoused, through the Middle East to the Indus Valley and westward across North Africa to the Atlantic Ocean. By 640, Syria, Palestine, and Iraq had been conquered by Arab warriors in the name of Islam. In 642, the Byzantine army abandoned Alexandria, marking the Moslem conquest of Lower Egypt. In 651, Iran was conquered; by 710, all of North Africa had been overrun and a Moslem army crossed the straits of Gibraltar into Spain. A victory at Jerez de la Frontera in 711 seemed to open all of western Europe to the Mohammedans. By 732, they had advanced north to Poitiers in France, where an army of Franks under Charles Martel, the grandfather of Charlemagne, opposed them successfully. Although they continued to conduct raids in France, they were unable to extend their control beyond the Pyrenees. But in Spain, the great Caliphate of Córdoba flourished until 1031, and it was not until 1492, when Granada fell to Ferdinand and Isabella, that Islamic influence and power in the West came to a close. In the East, the Indus River had been reached by 751, and only in Anatolia was stubborn Byzantine resistance able to slow the Moslem advance. Relentless Moslem pressure against the shrinking Byzantine Empire eventually caused its collapse in 1453, when the Ottoman Turks conquered Constantinople.

The early lightning successes of Islam were due largely to the zeal and military prowess of Arab warriors who set out to conquer the earth for Allah and who burst on the Near Eastern and Mediterranean worlds when Persian and Byzantine military power were at a low ebb. But the fact that these initial conquests had effects that endured for centuries can be explained only by the nature of the Islamic faith and its appeal to millions of converts.

Many of the features of the Islamic faith are derived from the Judeo-Christian tradition. The sacred Islamic scripture is the Koran, the collection of Mohammed's revelations that was ordered gathered by the caliph Othman (644–656) and remains unchanged to the present day. The basic teachings and ethics of the Koran are similar to those of the Bible, and the Old Testament prophets, as well as Jesus, are counted among the predecessors of Mohammed. On the other hand, all Moslems believe that they have direct and equal access to God without need for complex ritual or an intervening priesthood. In addition, Mohammed established a new social order that was quite different from the Christian one; in it, he took charge of the temporal as well as the spiritual affairs of his community. This practice of uniting religious and political leadership in the hands of a single ruler was continued after Mohammed's death by his successors, the *caliphs,* who based their claims to authority on their descent from the families of the Prophet or those of his early followers.

*Islam, "exclusive worship of the one God (Allah)," was Mohammed's name for his new religion. Mohammedan, Muhammadan, Muslim, and Moslem all refer to the same faith.

Architecture and Architectural Ornament

During the early centuries of Islamic history, the political and cultural center of the Moslem world was the Fertile Crescent (Palestine, Syria, and Iraq)—that melting pot of East and West strewn with impressive ruins of earlier cultures that became one of the fountainheads of the development of Islamic art. The vast territories conquered by the Arabs were ruled by governors, originally sent out from Damascus or Baghdad, who eventually gained relative independence by setting up dynasties in various territories and provinces: the Umayyads in Syria (661–749) and in Spain (756–1031); the Abbasids in Iraq (749–1258; largely nominal after 945); the Fatimids in Tunisia and Egypt (909–1171); and so on. Despite the Koran's strictures against sumptuousness and license, the caliphs were not averse to surrounding themselves with luxuries commensurate with their enormous wealth and power. This duality is expressed by the two major architectural forms developed during the Early Islamic period: the *mosque* and the *palace.*

Moslem religious architecture is closely related to Moslem prayer, the performance of which is an obligation laid down in the Koran for all Moslems. Prayer as a private act requires neither liturgical ceremony nor a special locale; only the *qiblah*—the direction (facing Mecca) toward which the prayer is addressed—is important. But prayer also became a communal act for which a simple ritual was established by the first Moslem community. The community convened once a week, probably in the Prophet's house, the main feature of which was a large, square court with two *zullahs,* or shaded areas, along the north and south sides. These zullahs consisted of thatched roofs supported by rows of palm trunks; the southern zullah, wider and supported by a double row of trunks, indicated the qiblah. During these communal gatherings, the *imam,* or leader of collective worship, standing on a pulpit known as a *minbar,* near the qiblah wall, pronounced the *khutbah,* which is both a sermon and an act of allegiance of the community to its leader. The minbar thus represents secular authority even as it serves its function in worship.

The requirements of this ritual were satisfied by the hypostyle mosque, the origin of which is still in dispute, although one prototype may well have been the Prophet's house in Medina. Once the Moslems had firmly established themselves in their conquered territories, they began to build on a large scale, impelled perhaps by a desire to create visible symbols of their power that would surpass those of their non-Islamic predecessors in size and splendor; the great size of some of the early mosques, however, may also be explained by the fact that they were intended to contain the entire Moslem population of a given city.

The Great Mosque of Samarra on the Tigris River (FIGS. **7-63** and **7-64**), built between 848 and 852 but now ruined, was the largest mosque of the Islamic world, measuring 800 feet by 520 feet. Over half its ten-acre area was covered by a wooden roof carried by 464 supports arranged in aisles around the open central court and leading toward the qiblah wall, the importance of which was emphasized by the greater number of aisles on its side. In the center of the qiblah wall is a niche, the *mihrab,* which became a standard feature in all later mosques. Its origin, purpose, and meaning are still matters of debate; some historians

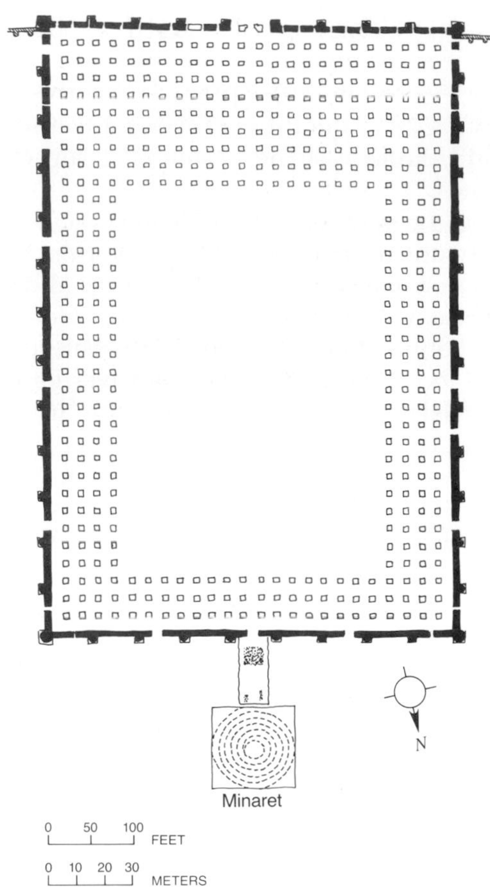

7-63 Plan of the Great Mosque, Samarra, Iraq, 848–852.

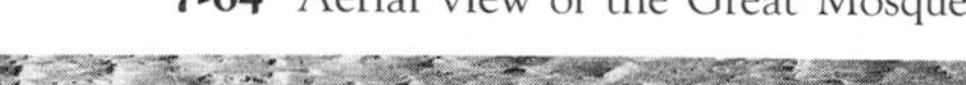

7-64 Aerial view of the Great Mosque.

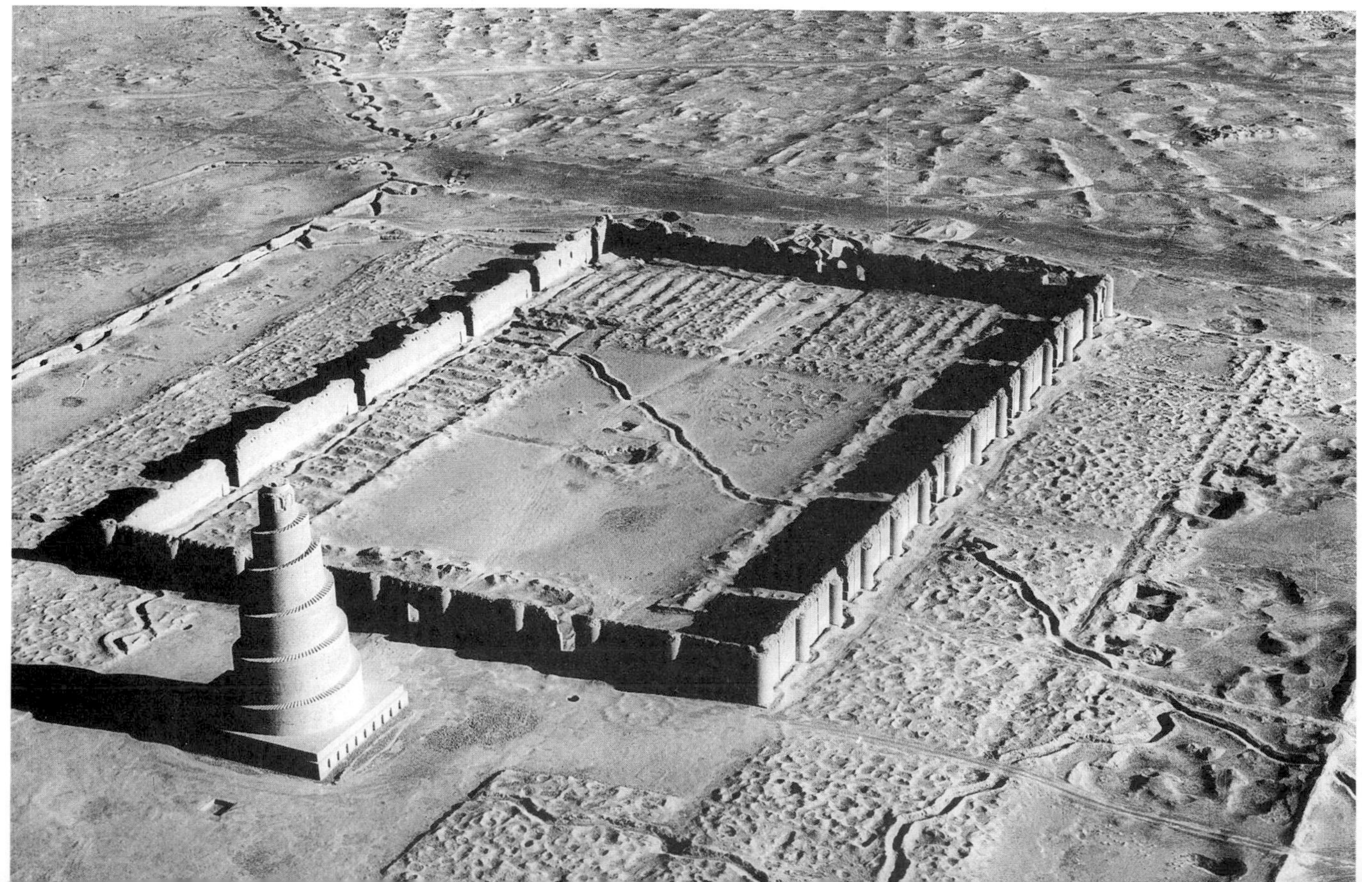

feel that the mihrab originally may have honored the place where the Prophet stood in his house at Medina when he led the communal prayers. If the mihrab has this symbolic function, it is unusual, because one of the characteristics of Early Islamic art is its concerted avoidance of symbols. In this respect, Early Islamic art offers a striking contrast to Medieval Christian art; the avoidance of religious symbolism, in fact, may reflect a conscious rejection of Christian customs and practices.

On the north side of the Great Mosque of Samarra stands a single, large minaret from which a *muezzin* called the faithful to prayer. Although its shape is reminiscent of the ancient ziggurats of Mesopotamia, it was probably inspired not by them but by a certain kind of spiral tower of unknown purpose found in Sassanian Iran. More numerous were minarets that were square in plan and derived from the towers of Early Christian churches in the Near East. Cylindrical minarets, from which the slender needles so characteristic of later mosques evolved, became popular only in the eleventh century.

The early Moslem hypostyle system, as illustrated by the Samarra mosque, was diffused and, except for the orientation of the building and the position of the qiblah wall, lacked architectural focus and direction. On the other hand, it was a flexible system that permitted enlargement and addition with minimum effort. Its main element was the single support, either a column or a pier, which could be multiplied at will and in any desired direction. A striking illustration of the flexibility of this system is the mosque of Córdoba (FIGS. **7-65** and **7-66**), which was begun in 784 and enlarged several times during the ninth and tenth centuries. The additions followed the original style

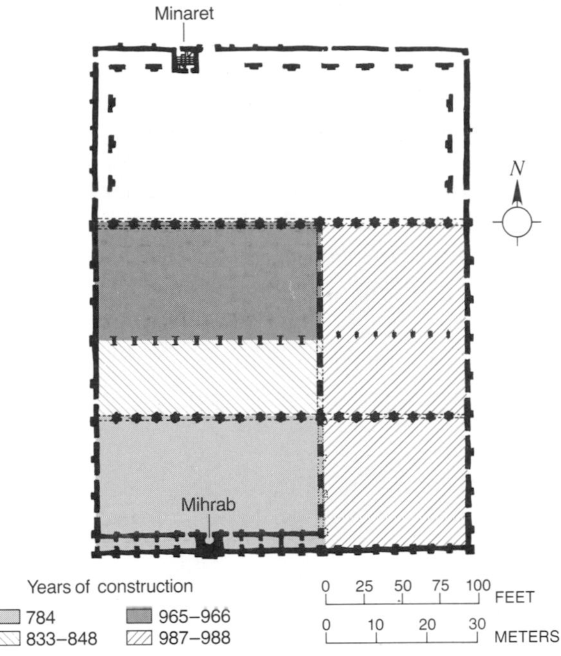

7-65 Plan of mosque at Córdoba, Spain, eighth to tenth centuries.

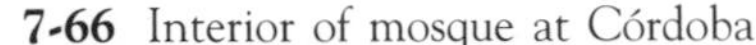

7-66 Interior of mosque at Córdoba.

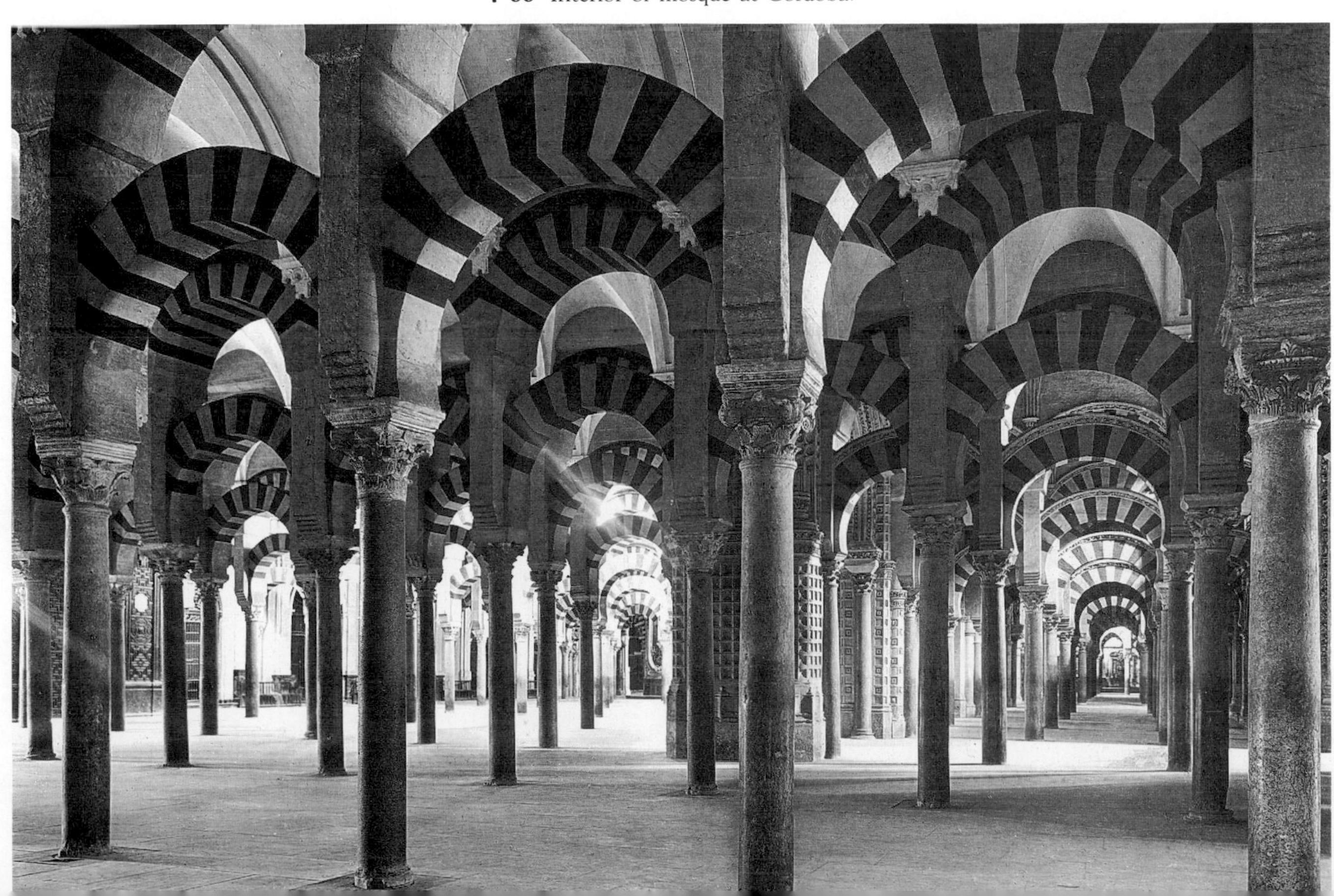

and arrangement of columns and arches, and the builders were able to maintain a striking stylistic unity for the entire building. The thirty-six piers and 514 columns are topped by a unique system of double-tiered arches that carried a wooden roof, now replaced by vaults. The lower arches are horseshoe-shaped, a form perhaps adapted from earlier Near Eastern architecture or of Visigothic origin and now closely associated with Moslem architecture. Visually, these arches seem to billow out like sails blown by the wind, and they contribute greatly to the light and airy effect of the mosque's interior.

In areas the builders wished to emphasize, like that near the mihrab (FIG. **7-67**), the arches become highly decorative, multilobed shapes. Other Early Islamic experiments with arch forms led to the pointed arch, which, however, was not used to cover variable spaces, as in Gothic buildings. Early Islamic buildings had wooden roofs, and the experiments with arch forms were motivated less by structural necessity than by a desire to create rich and varied visual effects. The same desire for decorative effect seems to have inspired the design of the dome that covers the area in front of the mihrab (FIG. **7-68**), one of four domes built during the tenth century to stress the axis leading to the mihrab. Here, the large ribs that subdivide the hemispheric surface of the dome into a number of smaller sections are primarily ornamental. Only in the hands of Gothic builders, centuries later, were ribs, in combination with the pointed arch, to become fundamental structural ingredients of a new and revolutionary architectural vocabulary.

7-67 Mihrab of mosque at Córdoba.

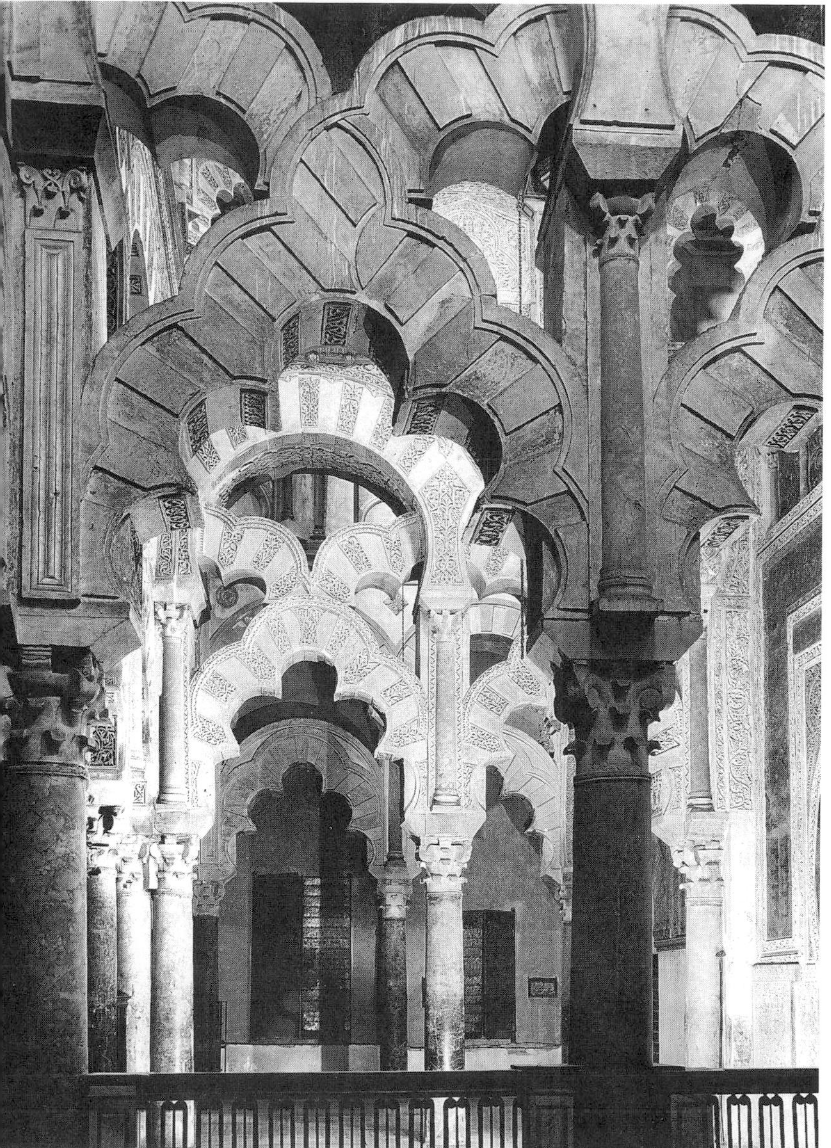

7-68 Dome before the mihrab of mosque at Córdoba.

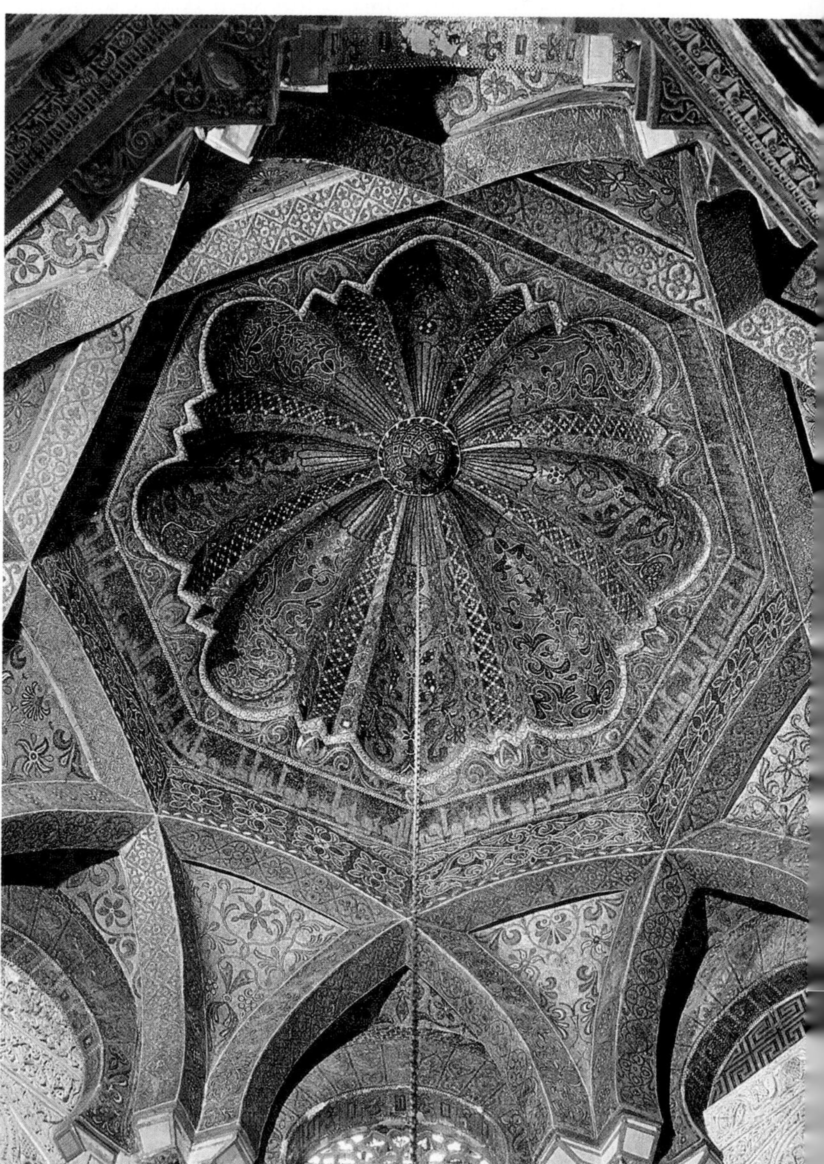

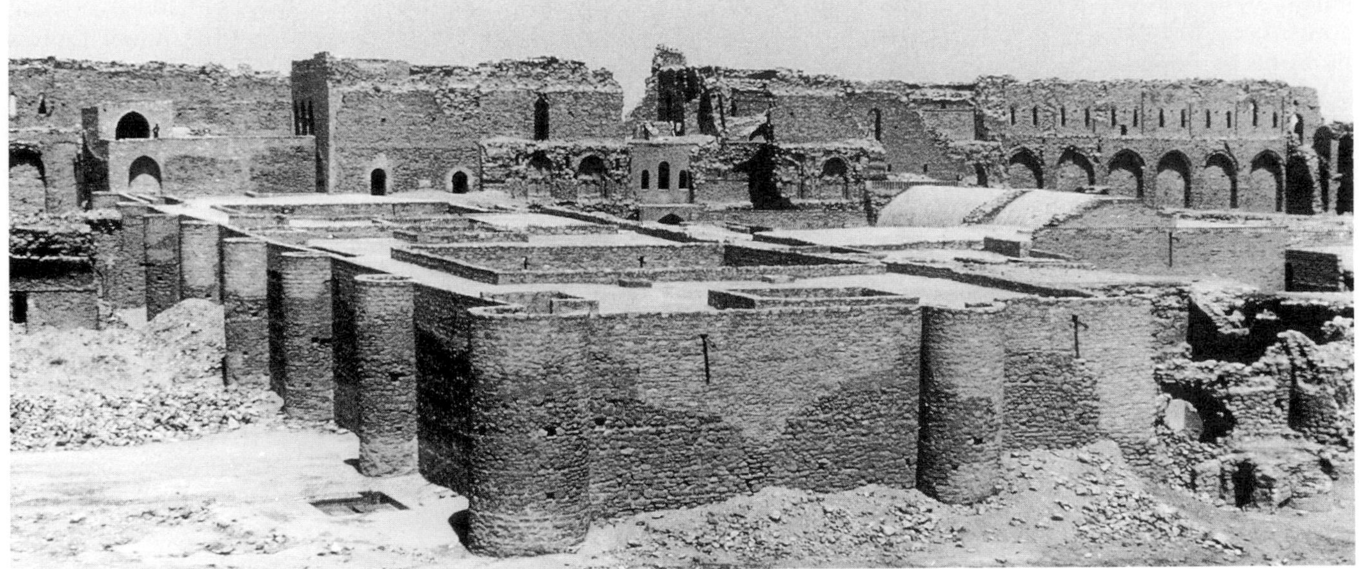

7-69 Palace at Ukhaydir, Iraq, late eighth century (view from the southeast).

Of the early palaces, only scattered remains have survived, and they are of limited historical importance, serving primarily to illustrate the way of life of Moslem aristocrats and to provide us with some notion of the decorative styles of Early Islamic art. Even the purpose of these early palaces is not quite certain. They were built both in cities and in the open country. The rural palaces, which have been better investigated, seem to have served a function similar to that of the Roman villas. That they reflect an Islamic taste for life in the desert seems too simple an explanation, although a desire to avoid plague-infested cities may well have been at least a partial motivation for their builders. But these rural palaces probably also served as nuclei for the agricultural development of conquered territories; in addition, they may have been symbols of authority over conquered and inherited lands, as well as expressions of the newly acquired wealth of their owners.

One of the better preserved of these early Moslem palaces is the palace at Ukhaydir in Iraq (FIGS. **7-69** and **7-70**), built in the second half of the eighth century. Somewhat larger than most, the palace is a separate entity within a fortified enclosure. From the outside, the high, tower-studded walls look much like those of the Great Mosque of Samarra (FIG. 7-64). This similarity illustrates a flexibility that is characteristic of Early Islamic monuments, as relatively minor changes could convert them from one purpose to another. Differences between a mosque, a palace, or a caravansary rarely were evident from the exterior; the structures tended to share a rather grim, fortified look that belied their military inefficiency. The high walls may have offered safety from marauding nomadic tribes, but they also may have fulfilled abstract considerations more important to the builders, like the promise of seclusion for a mosque or, for a palace, privacy for the prince and the symbolic assertion of his power over newly conquered territories.

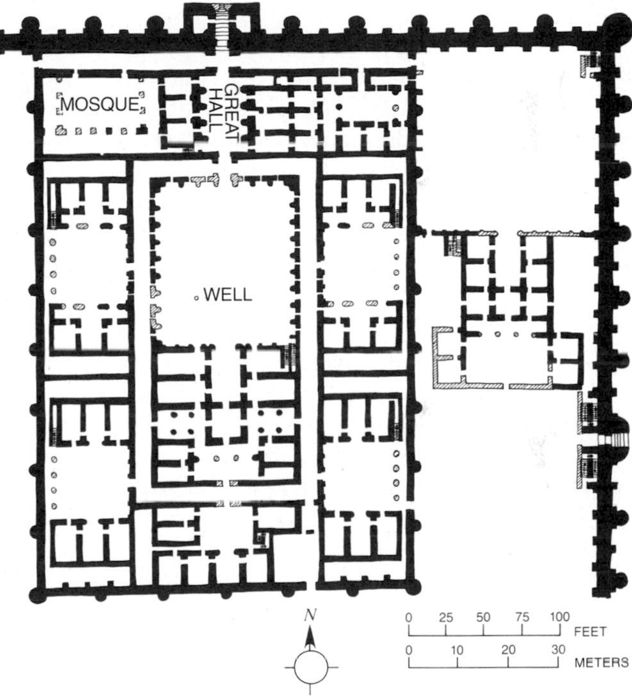

7-70 Plan of the palace at Ukhaydir.

The plan of the palace at Ukhaydir (FIG. 7-70) expresses the structure's residential and official functions. An elaborate entrance complex, consisting of a monumentalized gate and a Great Hall between two small, domed rooms, leads onto the large central court, beyond which is a reception hall surrounded by satellite rooms. Flanking this ceremonial axis are four smaller courts, all with three rooms on each of two sides. These grouped rooms appear to be self-contained and probably served as family living units or guest houses. To the right of the entrance hall is a mosque, a standard feature of these early palaces, which here is incorporated into the main building complex, although sometimes it stood by itself. Most palaces also were provided with fairly elaborate bathing facilities that displayed technical features, such as heating systems, adopted from the Roman tradition of baths. (The baths at Ukhaydir, only recently discovered near the mosque, are not shown on the plan.) Just as in classical antiquity, these baths probably served more than merely hygienic purposes. Large halls frequently attached to them seem to have been used as places of entertainment. Thus, a characteristic amenity of Classical urban culture that died out in the Christian world survived in medieval Islamic culture.

The decoration of the Ukhaydir palace seems to have been rather sparse and was confined to simply molded stucco and occasional decorative brickwork. In this respect, finds made in the western palaces in Syria and Palestine (modern Israel and Jordan) have been much richer. At Mshatta, an unfinished palace in the Jordanian desert, for instance, gate and façade are decorated by a wide, richly carved, stone frieze (FIGS. **7-71** and **7-72**). Its design, arrangement, and relation to its carrier serve well to illustrate the major characteristics of Early Islamic decoration.

A long band, almost 15 feet high, is decorated with a series of triangles of the same size framed by an elaborately carved molding. Each triangle contains a large rosette that projects from a field densely covered with curvilinear, vegetal designs; no two triangles are treated the same way, and animal figures appear in some of them (FIG. 7-71). The sources of the various design elements are easily identified as Late Classical, Early Byzantine, and Sassanian Persian, but their combination and arrangement are typically Islamic.

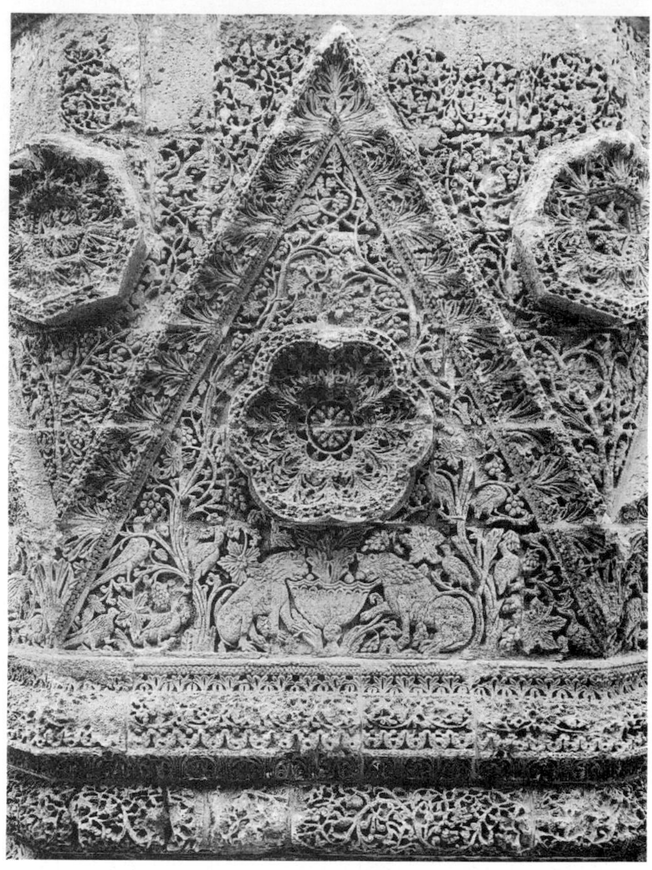

7-71 Portion of stone frieze, palace at Mshatta, Jordan, *c.* 743. Staatliche Museen, Berlin.

7-72 Reconstruction of façade of the palace at Mshatta. (After Schulz.)

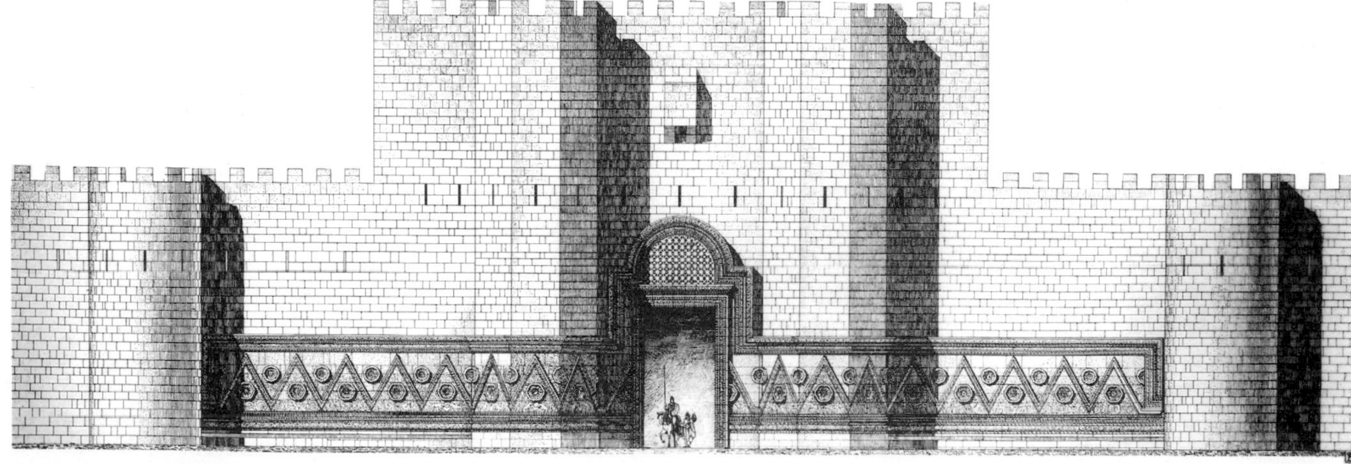

Most of the design elements of Islamic ornament are based on plant motifs, which are sometimes intermingled with symbolic geometric figures and with human and animal shapes. But the natural forms often become so stylized that they are lost in the purely decorative tracery of the tendrils, leaves, and stalks. These arabesques form a pattern that will cover an entire surface, be it that of a small utensil or the wall of a building. (This *horror vacui* is similar to tendencies in barbarian art, although other aspects of Islamic design distinguish it from the abstract, barbarian patterns.) The relationship of one form to another in Islamic art is more important than the totality of the design: the patterns have no function but to decorate. This system offers a potential for unlimited growth, as it permits extension of the designs in any desired direction. Most characteristic, perhaps, is the design's independence of its carrier; neither its size (within limits) nor its forms are dictated by anything but the design itself. This arbitrariness imparts a certain quality of impermanence to Islamic design, a quality that, it has been said, may reflect the Moslem taste for readily movable furnishings, such as rugs and hangings.

Stone carving was only one of several techniques used for architectural decoration. Floor mosaics and wall paintings continued a long Mediterranean tradition. In later periods, colored tile became increasingly important. A magnificent example of a floor mosaic was found in the bath of the palace at Khirbat al-Mafjar near Jericho in Jordan (FIG. **7-73**). Set into square and rectangular fields covered with a rich variety of floral and geometric patterns are medallions with extremely intricate abstract designs, some of them creating the illusion of a downward projection of the dome or half-dome under which they are placed.

The use of colored tile has a long history in the Middle East and Iran, reaching back into the Sumerian period. It enjoyed particular favor among the Babylonians (see FIG. 2-36). After periods of neglect, the art was revived by the Abbasids in the ninth century at Samarra, where tiles with a metallic sheen were developed. From there, the fashion spread throughout the Moslem world, reaching the height of its development during the sixteenth and seventeenth centuries in Turkey and Iran. Used as veneer over a brick core, tiles could sheathe entire buildings,

7-73 Floor mosaic, palace at Khirbat al-Mafjar, Jordan, mid-eighth century.

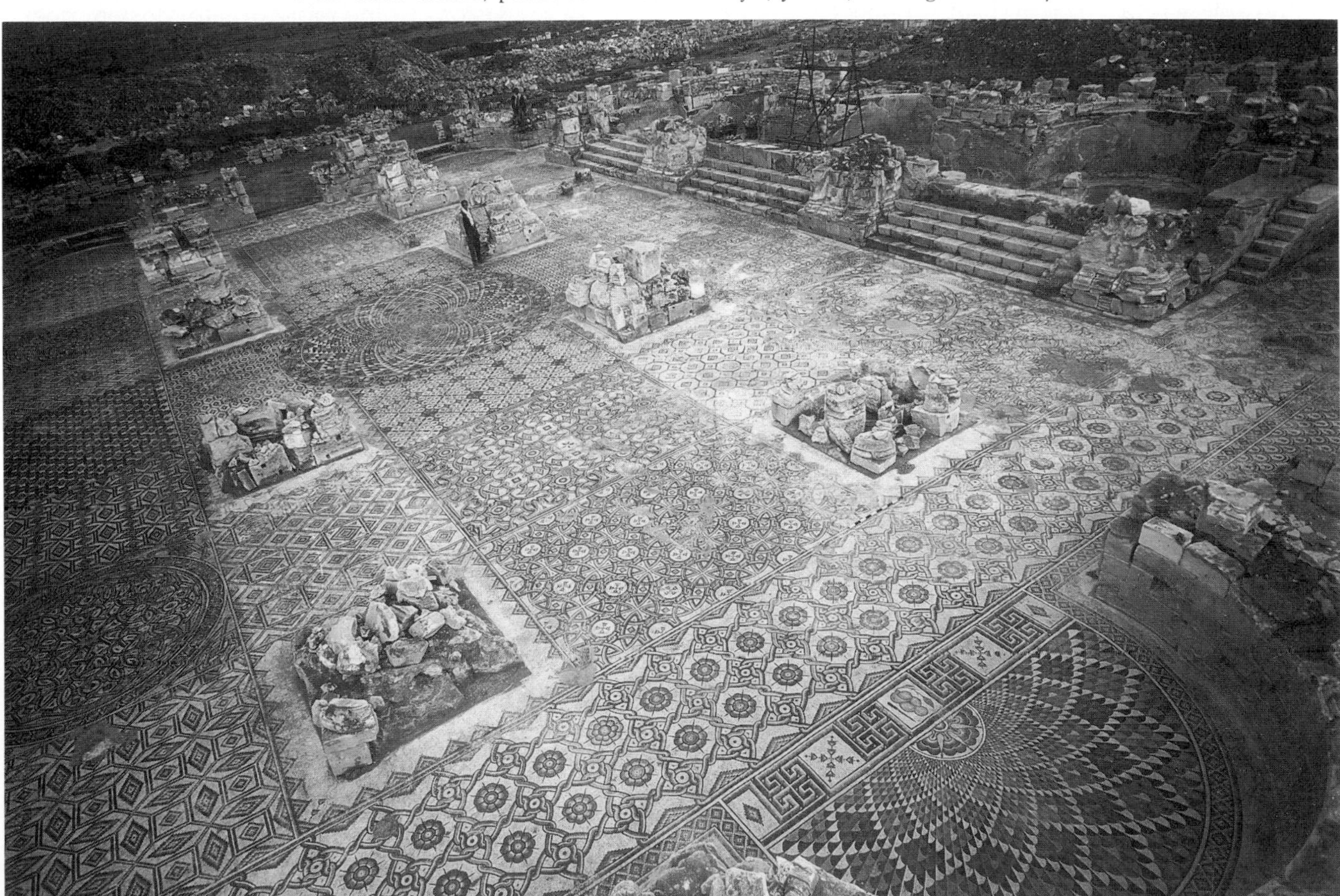

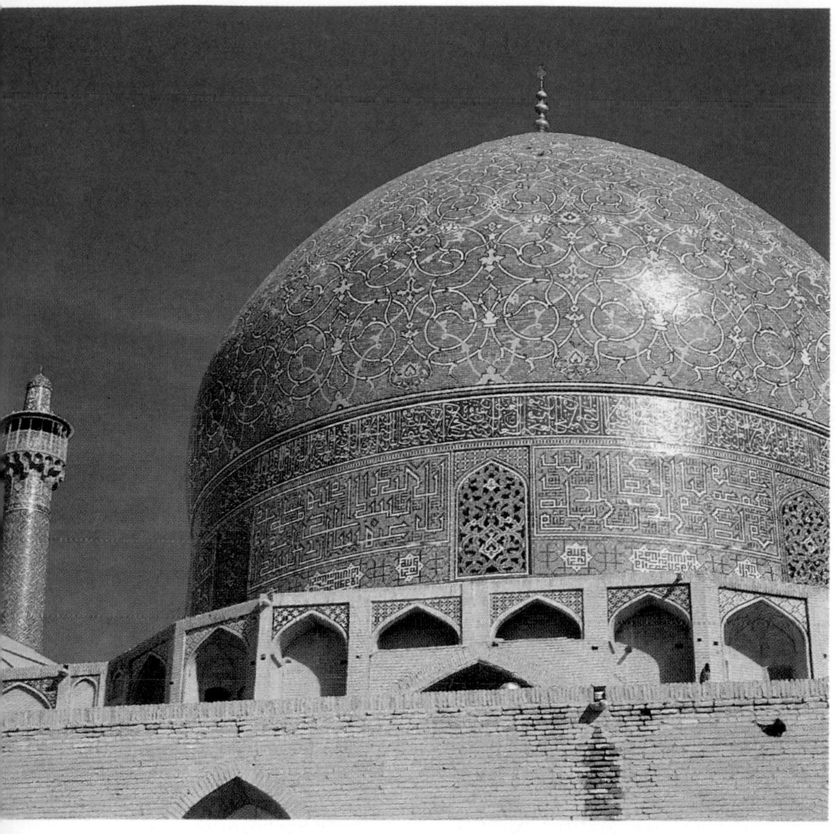

7-74 Dome of Madrasa-I-Shāh, Isfahan, Iran, 1612–1637.

including their domes and minarets. Our example, the Dome of Madrasa-I-Shāh in Isfahan (FIG. **7-74**), dates from the early seventeenth century and shows such tile work at its most brilliant. Beautifully adjusted to the shape of the dome, the design of the spiraling tendrils is at once rich and subtle, enveloping the dome without overpowering it. In contrast to the more general Islamic tendency to disguise structure, the design here enhances the dome's form without obscuring it. On parts of the dome and on the minarets, the tiles are curved to conform to the shape of the architecture.

Particularly popular were *stucco reliefs*, a method of decoration that was known, but not common, in pre-Islamic Iran and Iraq. Cheap, flexible, and effective, the basic material (wet plaster) was particularly adaptable to the execution of the freely flowing line that distinguishes Islamic ornament, and stucco decoration became a favorite technique. Some of the very richest examples are found in the Alhambra palace in Granada, Spain, the last Moslem stronghold in western Europe in the Middle Ages. In the Court of the Lions and the rooms around it (FIGS. **7-75** and **7-76**), stucco decoration runs the gamut of the medium's possibilities and creates an exuberant atmosphere of elegant fantasy that seems to be the visible counterpart of the visions of the more ornate Moslem poets.

7-75 Court of the Lions, the Alhambra, Granada, Spain, 1354–1391.

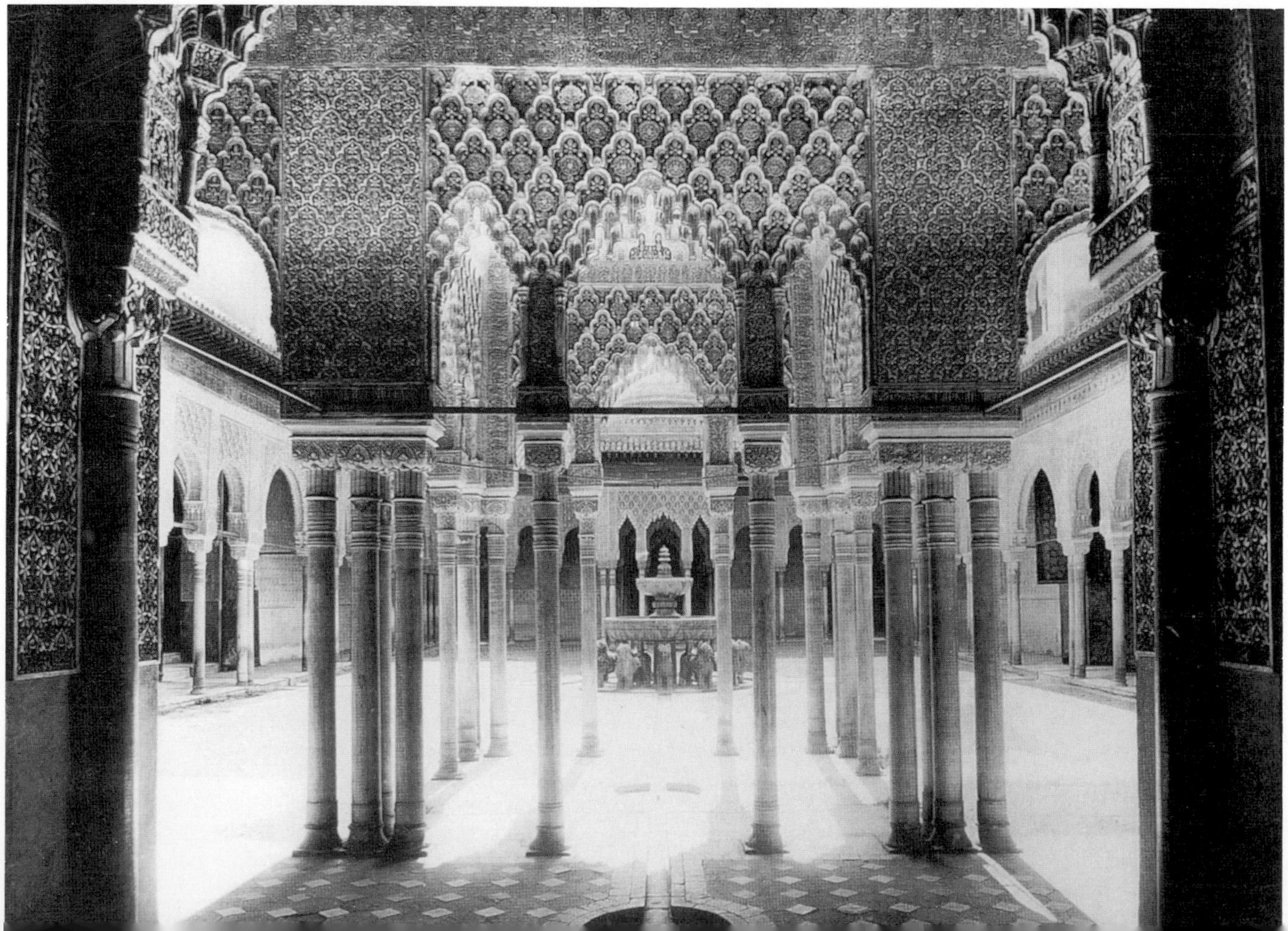

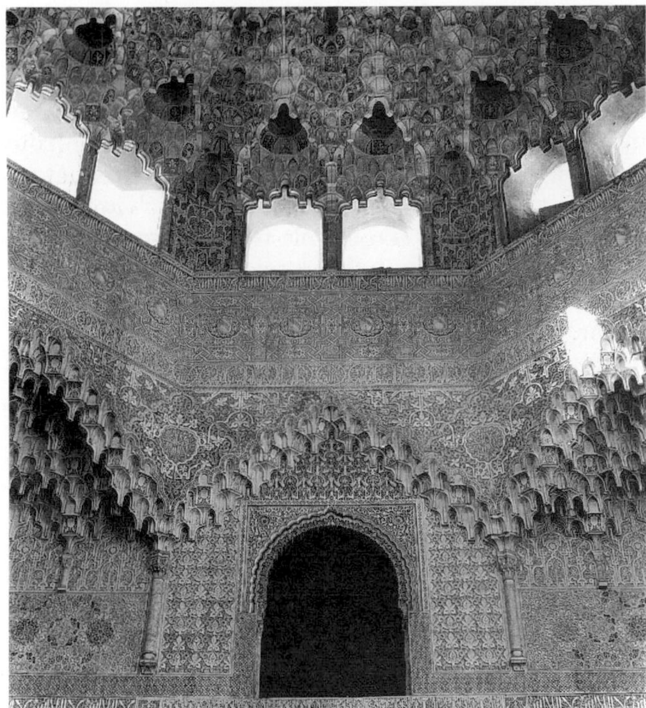

7-76 Hall of the Two Sisters, the Alhambra.

The court itself (FIG. 7-75), proportioned according to the Golden Mean, is framed by rhythmically spaced single, double, and triple columns with slender, reedlike shafts that carry richly decorated block-capitals and stilted arches of complex shape. All surfaces above the columns are covered by colored stucco moldings that seem aimed at denying the solidity of the stone structure that supports them. The resulting buoyant, airy, almost floating appearance of the building is enhanced by the "stalactite" decorations that break up the structural appearance of the arches, transforming them into near-organic forms.

This same tendency to disguise architectural forms is shown even more vividly in the Hall of the Two Sisters (FIG. 7-76), which adjoins the Court of the Lions. Here, all surfaces are covered by a polychromed lacework of stucco and tile, in which an almost limitless variety of designs is held together by symmetry and rhythmic order. The overall effect of the incredibly rich decoration is that of tapestries suspended from walls and dome, the "stalactites" resembling pendant tassels. In this hall, the Moorish (North African and Spanish) style, heralded in the mosque at Córdoba (FIG. 7-66), has reached its ultimate refinement. Its influence on Spanish art remained strong throughout the Middle Ages and well into the Renaissance, and traces of it may be observed in the art of the Hispanic colonies of America.

A very different architectural concept is expressed in the madrasah and mausoleum of Sultan Hasan in Cairo (FIGS. **7-77** and **7-78**). The *madrasah,* a combined

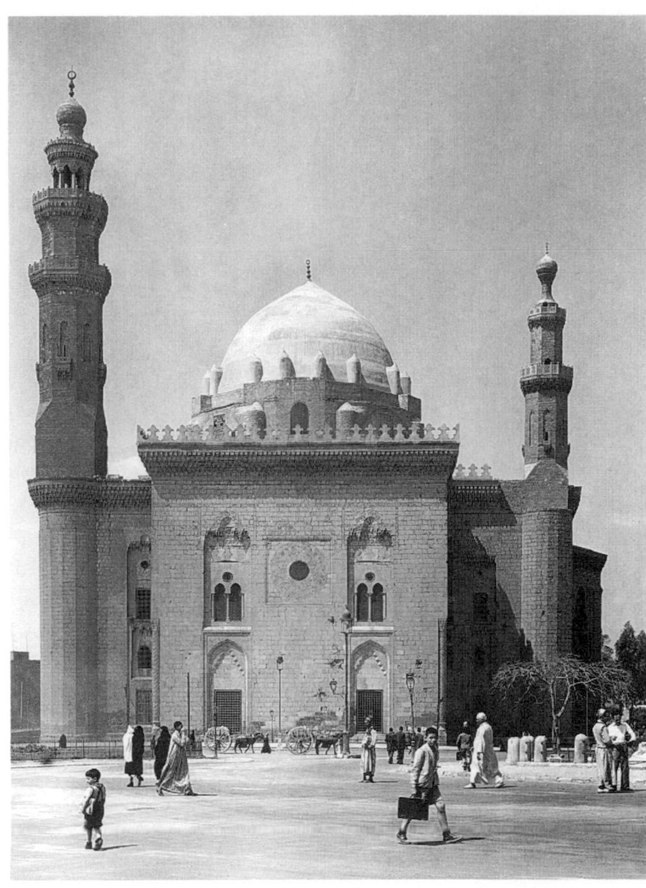

7-77 Madrasah and attached mausoleum of Sultan Hasan, Cairo, Egypt, 1356–1363 (view from the southeast).

7-78 Plan of the madrasah and mausoleum of Sultan Hasan.

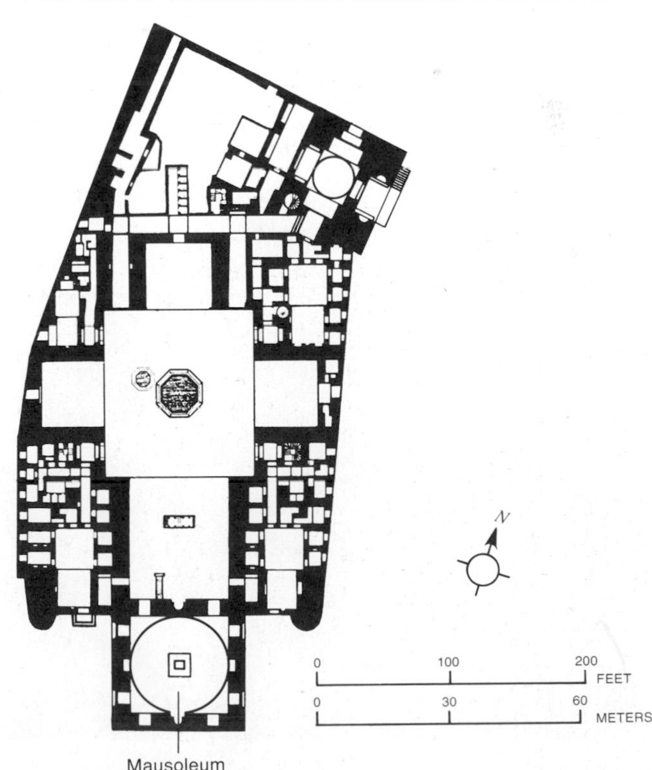

school and mosque, was a building type developed in Iran and brought westward by the advancing Seljuk Turks during the eleventh century. It shares with the hypostyle mosque the open central court but replaces the early Islamic forests of columns with austere masses of brick and stone. The court is now surrounded by four vaulted halls, the one on the qiblah side being larger than the other three. Crowded into the angles formed by these halls are the various apartments, offices, and schoolrooms of the Moslem educational institution. Decoration of the main building is confined to moldings around the wall openings and a frieze below the crenelated roofline, which serve to accentuate, rather than to disguise, the geometric clarity of the massive structure, presenting a striking contrast to the filigreed elegance of the contemporary Alhambra.

Attached to the qiblah side of the madrasah is the mausoleum, which is a simple cubical structure covered by a dome. Mausoleums (central-plan, domed structures) were adopted either from Iran or from the Antique vocabulary of the Mediterranean, as they had not been a part of the original inventory of Islamic architecture. They were built either as memorials to holy men or for the secular function of commemorating Islamic rulers. By the tenth century, the building type was well established in Iran, from which it spread both east and west; it became especially popular in Egypt, which, of course, had its own age-old tradition of large-scale funerary monuments.

The most famous of all Islamic mausoleums is the fabled Taj Mahal at Agra (FIG. **7-79**), which was built by one of the Moslem rulers in India, Shah Jahan, as a memorial to his wife, Mumtaz Mahal. The basic shape of the monument is that of the Cairo mausoleum, but modifications and refinements have converted the massive, cubical structure into an almost weightless vision of cream-colored marble that seems to float magically above the tree-lined reflecting pools. The interplay of shadowy voids with gleaming marble walls that seem paper-thin creates an impression of translucency, and elimination of the Cairo structure's heavy, projecting cornice (which separated the blocky base of the earlier building from its

7-79 Taj Mahal, Agra, India, 1632–1654.

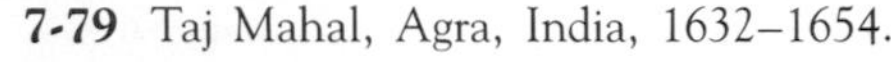

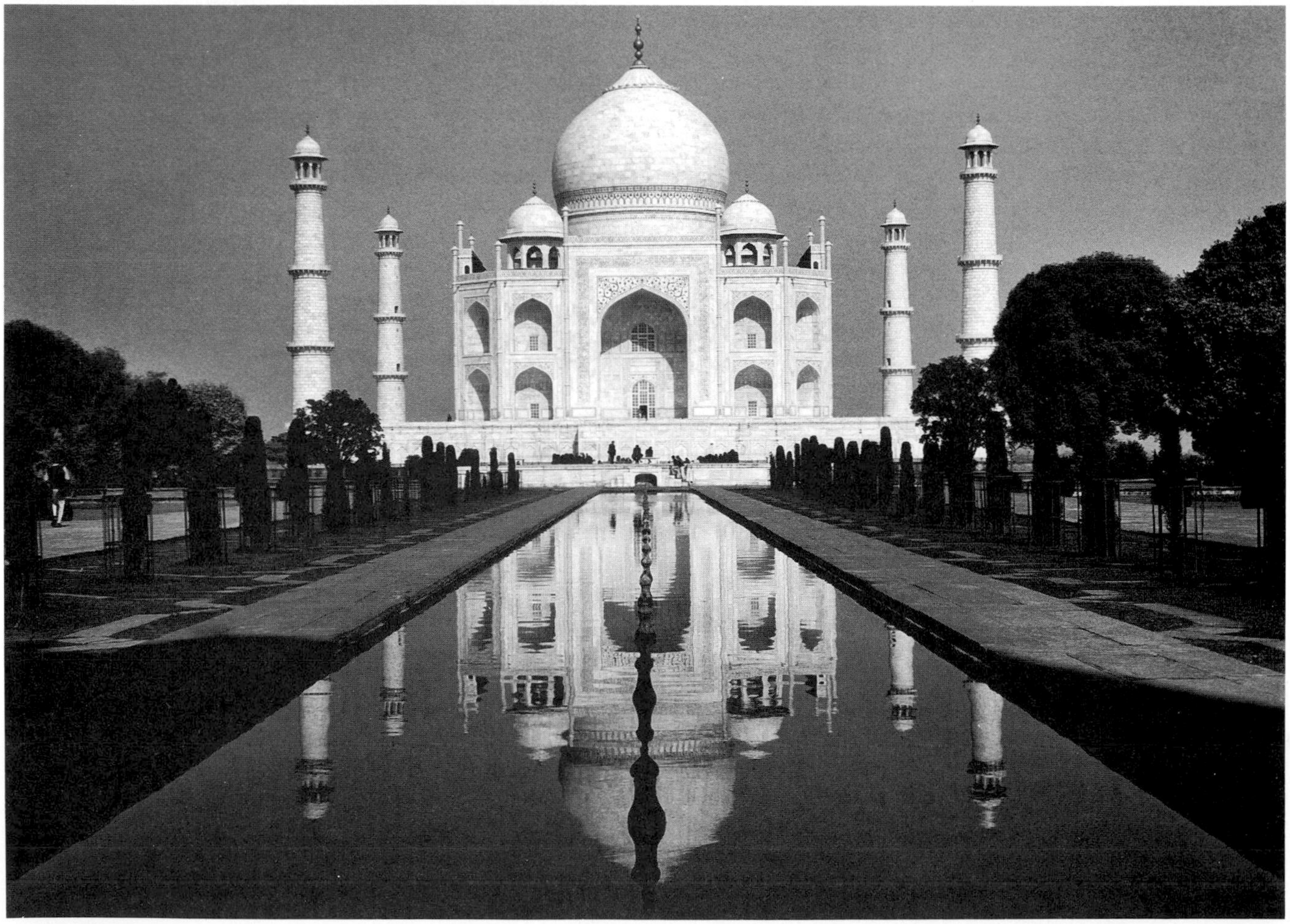

dome) ties all the elements together. The result is a sweeping, upward movement toward the climactic, balloon-shaped dome. Carefully related minarets and corner pavilions introduce, and at the same time stabilize, this soaring central theme. Although the entire monument recalls the fragile elegance of the Alhambra, it far surpasses the latter in subtle sophistication and represents one of the high-water marks of Moslem architecture.

OTTOMAN ARCHITECTURE

A related, yet different, Islamic architecture was developed by the Ottoman Turks. The Turkic people, of central Asian origin, had been converted to Islam during the ninth and tenth centuries. They moved into Iran and the Near East in the eleventh century, and, by 1055, the Seljuk Turks had built an imposing, although short-lived, empire that stretched from India to western Anatolia. It crumbled under the onslaught of the Mongols, led by Genghis Khan (about 1210–1220s). After its fall, a number of local dynasties established themselves in Anatolia, among them the Ottomans, founded by Osman I (1290–1326). Under his successors, the Ottoman state rapidly expanded over vast areas of Asia, Europe, and North Africa to become, by the middle of the fifteenth century, one of the great world powers.

Ottoman art, like Islamic art in general, expressed itself primarily in terms of architecture. But while other Moslem countries adopted the hypostyle mosque as their standard religious structure, Ottoman builders developed a new type of mosque with a square prayer hall covered by a dome as its core. In fact, the dome-covered square, which had been a dominant form in Sassanian Iran, became the nucleus of all Ottoman architecture. The combination, in addition to its appealing geometric clarity, was permeated with religious symbolism. To the Ottomans, a circle set into a square signified Heaven. (The circle, which has neither beginning nor end, symbolized eternity; the square symbolized the four corners of the universe.) At first used singly, the domed units came to be used in multiples, a turning point in Ottoman architecture, because it drew in its wake the desire to create unity of space and form out of conglomerate aggregates. The resultant Ottoman style is geometric and formalistic, rather than ornamental.

When the Ottoman Turks conquered Constantinople (which they renamed Istanbul) in 1453, their architectural code was firmly established. Although impressed by Hagia Sophia (FIG. 7-40), which, in some respects, conformed to their own ideals, Ottoman builders were not overwhelmed by it. Direct influence of Hagia Sophia was not felt until about 1500, when a second half-dome, opposite the mihrab, was used for the first time.* But the processional way of Hagia Sophia's interior never satisfied Ottoman builders, and Anatolian development moved instead toward the centralized quatrefoil mosque. The first examples of this cloverleaf plan, an ideal of Ottoman mosque design, were built in the 1520s, to be eclipsed only by the works of the most famous of Ottoman architects, SINAN THE GREAT (*c.* 1491–1588), called KOÇA ("the architect"). A contemporary of Michelangelo and with equal pretensions to immortality, Sinan carried Ottoman architecture to the height of its classical period. By his time, the use of the basic domed unit was universal. It could be enlarged or contracted as needed, and almost any number of units could be used together. Thus, the typical Ottoman building of Sinan's time was an assembly of parts, usually erected with an extravagant margin of structural safety. Measures and forms had been standardized, and design and engineering methods tended to be conservative, with little room given to experimentation. But despite such strictures, which might have been stifling to a lesser architect, Sinan constantly searched for solutions to the problems of unifying the additive elements and of creating a monumental, centralized space with ideal proportions.

In his early buildings, Sinan experimented with the cloverleaf plan, as well as with that of Hagia Sophia. In the mosque of Suleiman I in Istanbul, he flanked the central unit, in which the main dome is abutted by two half-domes, north and south, with dome-covered aisles. But where Hagia Sophia isolates the lateral aisles, Sinan, by reducing interior obstructions to a minimum, made every effort to combine them with the central area and to make central and flanking spaces flow into each other through wide and lofty arcades.

Sinan's efforts to overcome the limitations of a segmented interior found their ultimate expression in the Selimiye Cami (FIGS. **7-80** to **7-83**) at Edirne (ancient Adrianople), where he created a structure that fully expresses "the earthly squareness of the gathering place of the faithful under the canopy of eternity" and where, at the same time, the mihrab is visible from almost any spot in the building. The Selimiye Cami reputedly was built for Selim II at Edirne (which had been the capital of the Ottoman Empire from 1367 to 1472) because the Sultan could find no adequate space for it in Istanbul. Its massive dome, effectively set off by four slender, pencil-shaped minarets (each more than 200 feet high), dominates the city's

*Ottoman builders had already adopted (from Byzantine architecture) the half-dome-covered apsidal projection for the mihrab, in addition to pendentive construction, although they preferred the Seljuk method of supporting domes with squinches or series of corbels (FIG. 7-45).

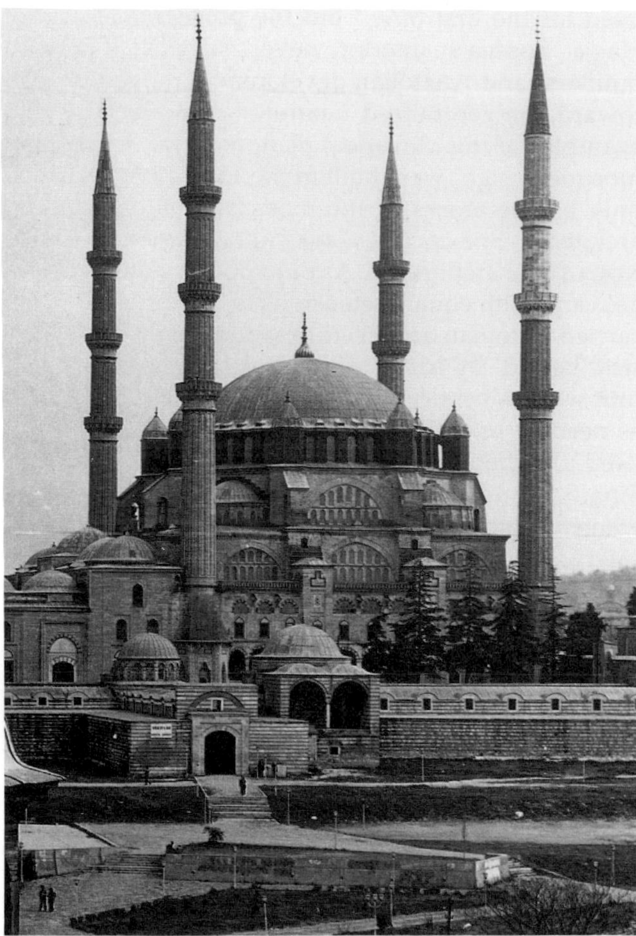

7-80 SINAN THE GREAT (KOÇA), the Selimiye Cami (Mosque of Selim II), Edirne (ancient Adrianople), Turkey, 1569–1575.

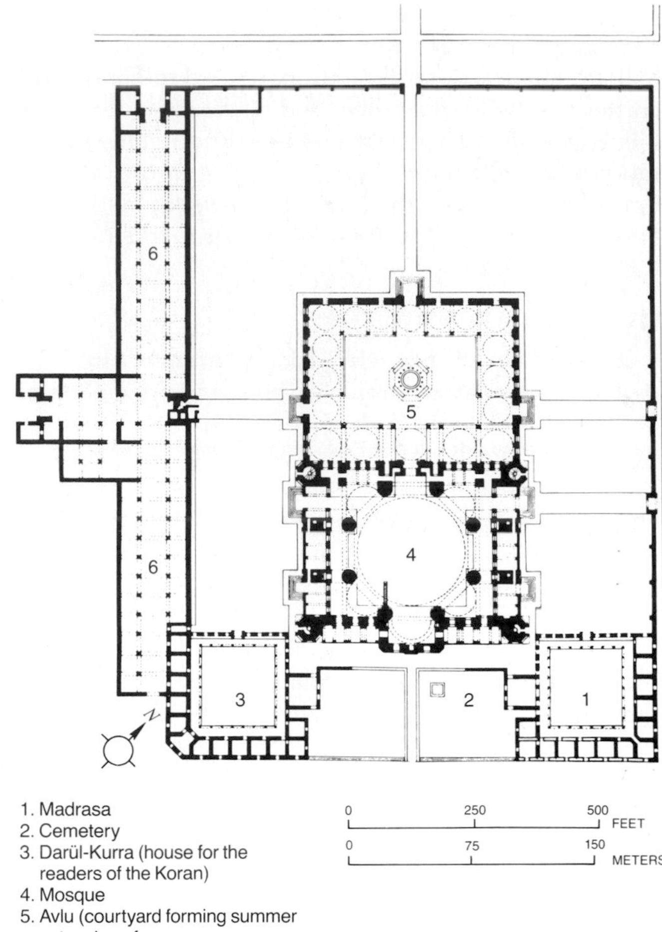

7-81 Plan of the Selimiye Cami.

skyline. Various dependencies are placed around the mosque. (Most of the important mosques had numerous annexes, including libraries and schools, hospices, baths, soup kitchens for the poor, markets, and hospitals, as well as a cemetery containing the mausoleum of the sultan responsible for the building of the mosque. These utilitarian buildings were grouped around the mosque and axially aligned with it if possible; more generally, they were adjusted to their natural site and linked with the central building by plantings of shrubs and trees.)

The mosque is preceded by a rectangular court covering an area equal to that of the building. This *avlu* (a courtyard forming a summer extension of the mosque) is surrounded by porticoes formed by domed squares. Behind it, the building rises majestically to its climactic dome, which equals that of Hagia Sophia in width. But it is the organization of the interior space of this mosque that reveals the genius of its builder. The mihrab has been recessed into an apse-like alcove deep enough to permit illumination from three sides, which makes the brilliantly colored tile panels of its lower walls sparkle as if with their own glowing light. The plan of the main hall is an ingenious fusion of an octagon with the symbolic dome-covered square. The octagon, formed by the eight massive dome supports, is pierced by the four half-dome-covered corners of the square. The result is a fluid interpenetration of several geometric volumes that represents the culminating solution to Sinan's lifelong search for a monumental, unified, interior space. The square "singing gallery" (visible in FIGS. 7-82 and 7-83), a platform for the *muezzins* (criers) that at first may seem like a distracting piece of furniture, punctuates the central space. It restates the basic squareness of the prayer hall and provides an anchoring focus to a design that might seem diffuse without it. Placed under the center of the dome, it marks "the navel of the mosque."

Sinan's building elegantly resolves complicated laws of statics. The Islamic tendency to disguise the structural function of architectural elements (as, for instance, in the Alhambra, FIG. 7-76) is minimized and confined to a "honeycomb" treatment of the

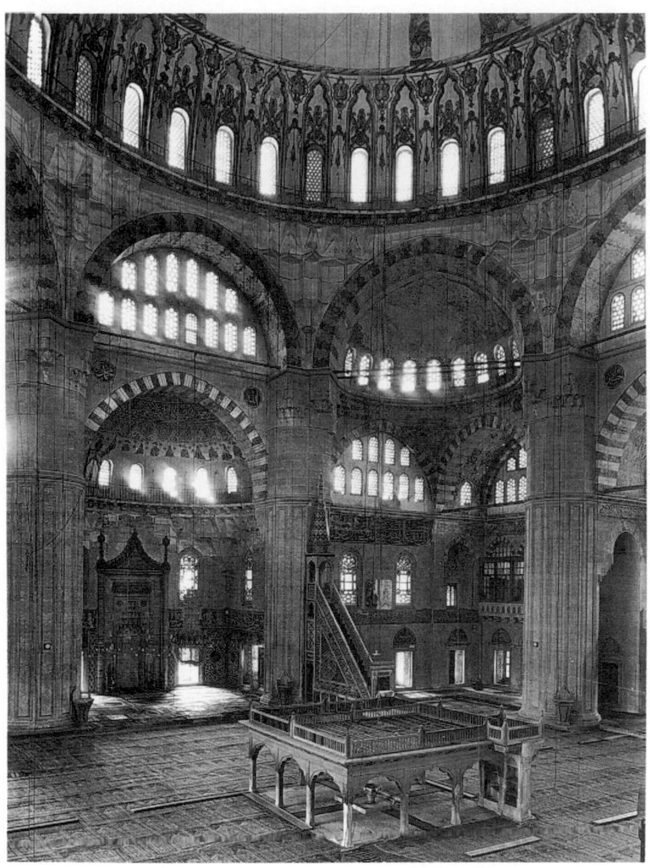

7-82 Interior of the Selimiye Cami.

7-83 Axonometric perspective of the Selimiye Cami.

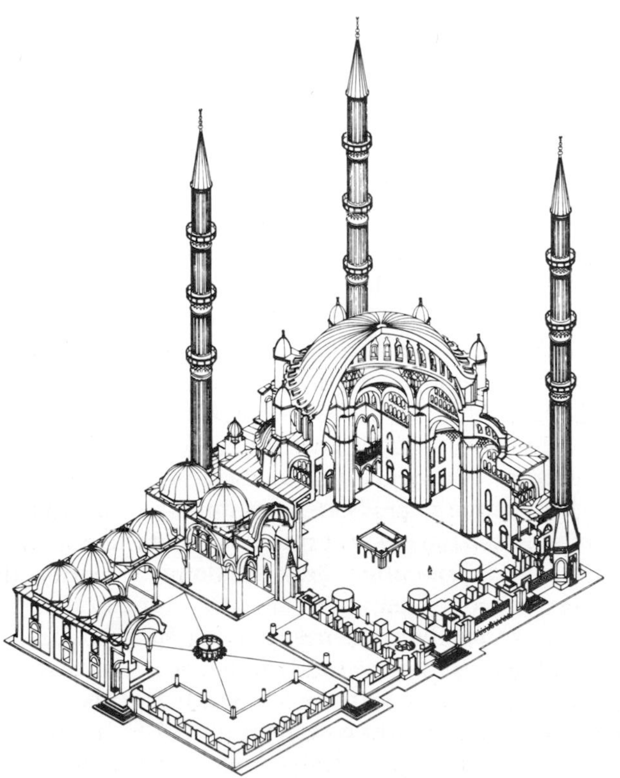

squinches and to "stalactite" capitals, a form of decoration that was popular from the twelfth century onward. Sinan's forms are clear and legible, like mathematical equations; height, width, and masses are related to each other in a simple but effective ratio of 1:2. The building is generally regarded as the climax of Ottoman architecture. Sinan himself proudly proclaimed it his masterpiece, and, indeed, it encloses one of the most impressive domed spaces ever built.

OBJECT ART AND TEXTILES

The furnishings of the palaces, as well as of the mosques, reflected a love of rich and sumptuous effects. Metal, wood, glass, and ivory were artfully worked into a great variety of objects for use in mosque or home. Basins (often huge), ewers, jewel cases, and writing boxes were made of bronze or brass, chased and inlaid with silver; enameled glass was used with striking effect in mosque lamps; richly decorated ceramics of high quality were produced in large numbers. Islamic potters, experimenting with different methods of polychrome painting, developed *luster painting,* a new and original technique that gives a metallic shine to a surface. Their designs were based on the motifs found in architectural decoration. This ready adaptability of motifs to various scales as well as to various techniques again illustrates both the flexibility of Islamic design and its relative independence from its carrier.

The most prestigious and highly valued objects of all were textiles, which, in the Islamic world, served more than purely utilitarian or decorative purposes. Produced by imperial factories, they were used not only in homes, palaces, and mosques, but also served as gifts, rewards, and signs of political favor.

The Moslem weavers adopted and developed the textile traditions of Sassanian Iran and the Mediterranean region (the latter were best known through Coptic textiles from Egypt). The art spread across the Islamic world, and by the tenth century, Moslem textiles were famous and widely exported. The art of carpet-making was developed to a particularly high degree in Iran, where the need for protection against the winter cold made carpets indispensable both in the shepherd's tent and in the prince's palace. In houses and palaces built of stone, brick, plaster, and glazed tile, carpets also provided a contrasting texture as floor and divan coverings and wall hangings.

The carpet woven for the tomb-mosque of Shah Tahmasp at Ardebil (FIG. **7-84**) is a large example of the medallion type and bears a design of effectively massed large elements surrounded and enhanced by a wealth of subordinated details. The field of rich blue is covered with leaves and flowers (chiefly peonies, a

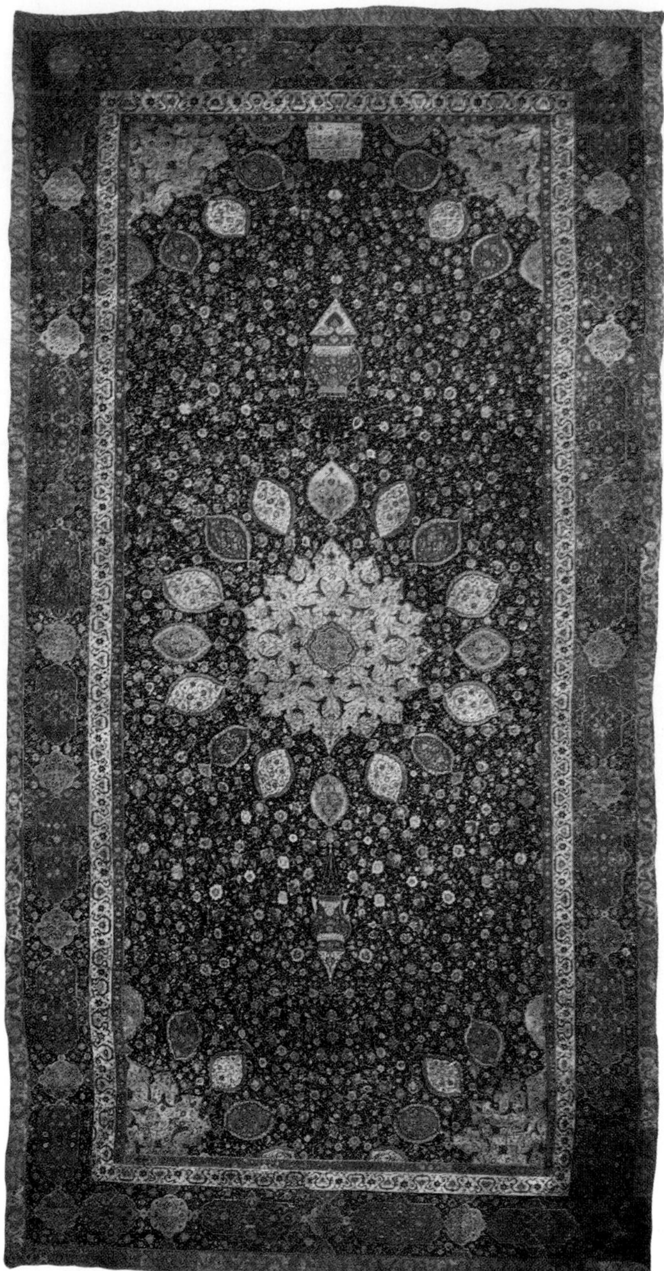

7-84 Carpet from the tomb-mosque of Shah Tahmasp at Ardebil, Iran, 1540. Approx. $34\frac{1}{2}' \times 17\frac{1}{2}'$. Victoria and Albert Museum, London.

Chinese influence) attached to a framework of delicate stems that weave a spiral design over the whole field. Great royal carpets like the one from Ardebil were products of the joint effort of a group of weavers, who probably were attached to the court. Pile weaving is a slow process at best, and because a carpet like the one from Ardebil often has more than three hundred knots to the square inch, a skilled weaver working alone would probably have needed more than twenty years to complete it.

Because the Ardebil carpet was made for a mosque, its decoration excludes human and animal figures, although other carpets from Ardebil show that the Koran's strictures against the representation of human and animal figures were not taken as seriously in secular art. The ban against the worship of idols, however, had practically eliminated the image of humans from Islamic religious art, and, even in early secular art, it appeared only occasionally in secluded parts of palaces as royal imagery. For this reason also, large sculpture in the round and mural or panel painting, as developed in Europe and in the Far East, was rather rare in Early Islamic art. Contributing to this lack of interest in monumental plastic art may have been the predilections of the people that made up the Moslem world; many of them—Arabs, Turks, Persians, Mongols—were nomads, who traditionally preferred small, movable objects (the so-called nomad's gear) to large-scale works of art. And so, perhaps, it should not be surprising that, when painting did develop in later times, it was mainly on the small scale of book illumination.

THE ART OF THE BOOK

The Arabs had no pictorial tradition of their own, and it seems possible that their interest in book illumination developed almost accidentally, as a by-product of their practice of translating and copying illustrated Greek scientific texts. In some of the earliest Islamic illuminated manuscripts (only a few dating earlier than about 1200), the illustrations seem to have been drawn by the scribes who copied the texts. Whatever its origins (often Christian and Mediterranean, but also local Iranian and Buddhist), an art of book illustration had developed, mostly in Iraq and Iran, by 1200.

The Persian rulers were lovers of fine books and maintained at their courts not only skilled calligraphers but also some of the most famous artists of their day. The secular books of the Timurids and the Safavids were illustrated by a whole galaxy of painters. Famous among them were BIHZAD (*c.* 1440–1536), AQA MIRAK, and SULTAN MUHAMMAD, court painters of Tahmasp (1524–1576), a great art patron. Although the rulers were Moslems, Orthodox Islamic restrictions regarding depiction of the human figure were interpreted rather liberally by them and did not affect their secular arts. Within the framework of illustrating specific stories, the gay scenes of their life of pleasure—the hunt, the feast, music, and romance—and battle scenes filled the pages of their books. In them, we feel the luxury, the splendor, and the fleeting happiness of Omar.

In *Laila and Majnun* (FIG. 7-85), the painter Aqa Mirak has illustrated one of Nizami's romantic poems. The scene represents a school, apparently in a mosque, and deals less with the pleasures than with some of the more earnest aspects of life. Seated on a rug is a turbaned *mullah,* or teacher, rod in hand, listening to a youth reading; around him are other youths studying, all seated on their knees and heels or with one knee raised, the customary sitting postures of the East. Here and there are cross-legged bookrests. In the foreground, one boy is pulling his companion's ear, and at the left, near the large water jar, two boys are playing ball. In the middle distance are the lovers Laila and Majnun, each obviously aware of the other's presence. Although the figures are drawn expressively with delicate, flowing lines, they are flat, with no shading and with only a hint of perspective; the tiles in the court and the rugs on the floor appear to be hanging vertically. The painting is conceived from a point of view concerned not with natural appearance but with pattern and vivid color. To this end, the tones are kept bright and clear. The decorative quality of the miniature is emphasized by the broad margins of the page, which are tinted and flecked with gold.

In its general appearance, the miniature is much more closely related to the Ardebil carpet than to any European painting or, for that matter, to Chinese painting, by which it certainly was influenced. It falls within the general framework of the Islamic decorative style, which, despite early religious restrictions and the constraints that derive from a limited formal vocabulary, became one of the richest and most harmonious decorative styles in the world.

7-85 *Laila and Majnun at School,* miniature from a manuscript of the Khamsa of Nizami, 1524–1525. Ink, colors, and gold on paper. The Metropolitan Museum of Art, New York (gift of Alexander Smith Cochran, 1913).

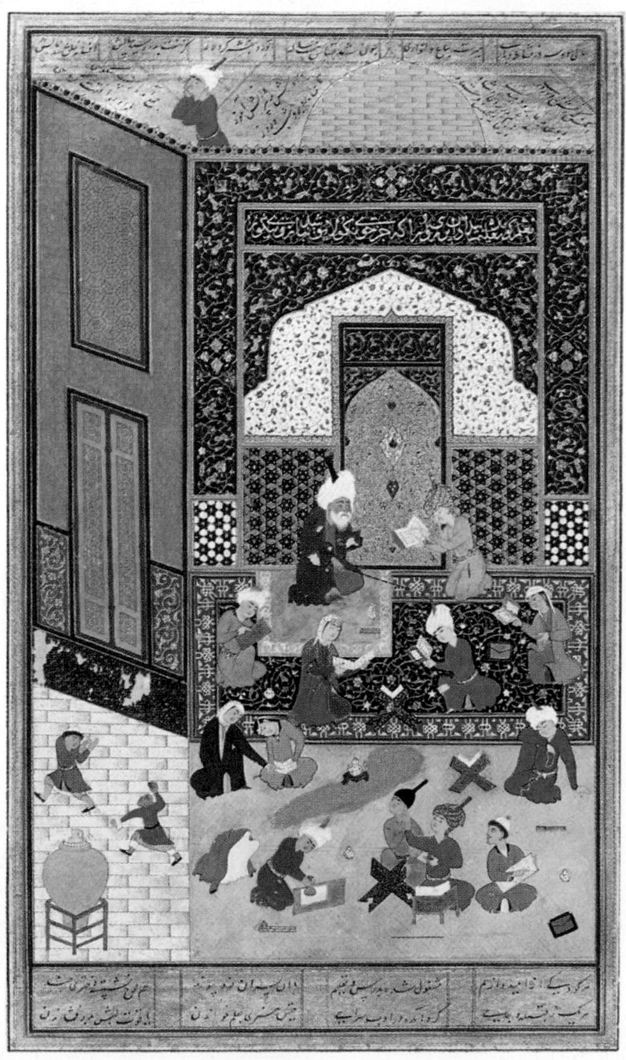

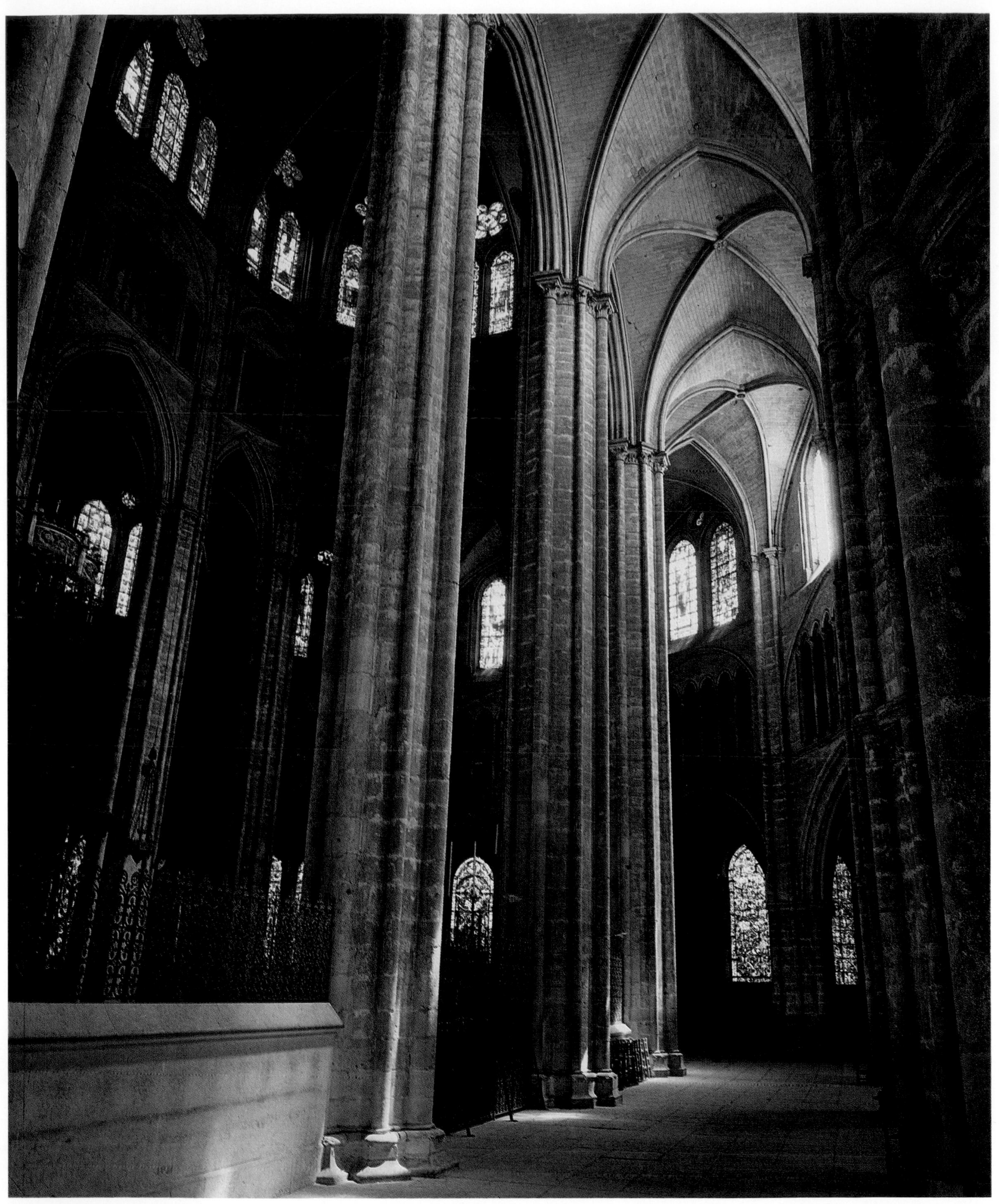

"The enchanting beauty of the House of God overwhelmed me," exclaimed Abbot Suger of his abbey church of St. Denis in Paris, the first Gothic building (see page 382). The later cathedral at Bourges (1195–1255), shown here, was designed on Gothic principles.

II
THE MIDDLE AGES

The poets of the Augustan Age were singing the glories of "eternal Rome" while Jesus of Nazareth, obscure founder of the religion that was to transform the city of man into the city of God, was born and died. Within three centuries, Christianity had become the official cult of the dying empire and the faith of the new peoples, the barbarians, who were to inherit its remains. While Byzantium, eastern remnant of the Christianized Roman Empire, maintained a continuous sovereignty, the empire in the west disintegrated. What had been the imperial provinces broke up into contesting barbarian kingdoms—those of the Franks, Burgundians, Visigoths, Anglo-Saxons, Lombards, and others. Historians have called the ensuing epoch (the thousand years from about 400 to 1400) the "Middle Ages" or the "Dark Ages." For centuries, this interval between the passing of the Roman Empire and the rebirth of its civilization in the Renaissance was thought to be rough and uncivilized (in a word, barbarous). Between the ancient and the modern world, life was viewed as empty, cruel, and "dark," simply a blank between (in the "middle" of) two great civilizations. Even today, the word *medieval* is often used disparagingly.

But since the late eighteenth century, historians have been revising this view and, with it, the long-held belief that Medieval art was crude and primitive. The same romantic enthusiasm for past civilizations that motivated the archeological revolution of Heinrich Schliemann's time, and the consequent recovery of the ancient past, sent scholars in quest of the meaning of medieval culture—the meaning of monuments that existed in great number and that, in this case, were aboveground and visible. Although we now see these centuries with very different eyes, perceiving their innovation and their greatness, the terms *Middle Ages* and *medieval* continue to be used, simply for convenience.

Medieval civilization is characterized by an interrelationship of Christianity and the Greco-Roman tradition with the new, energetic spirit of the

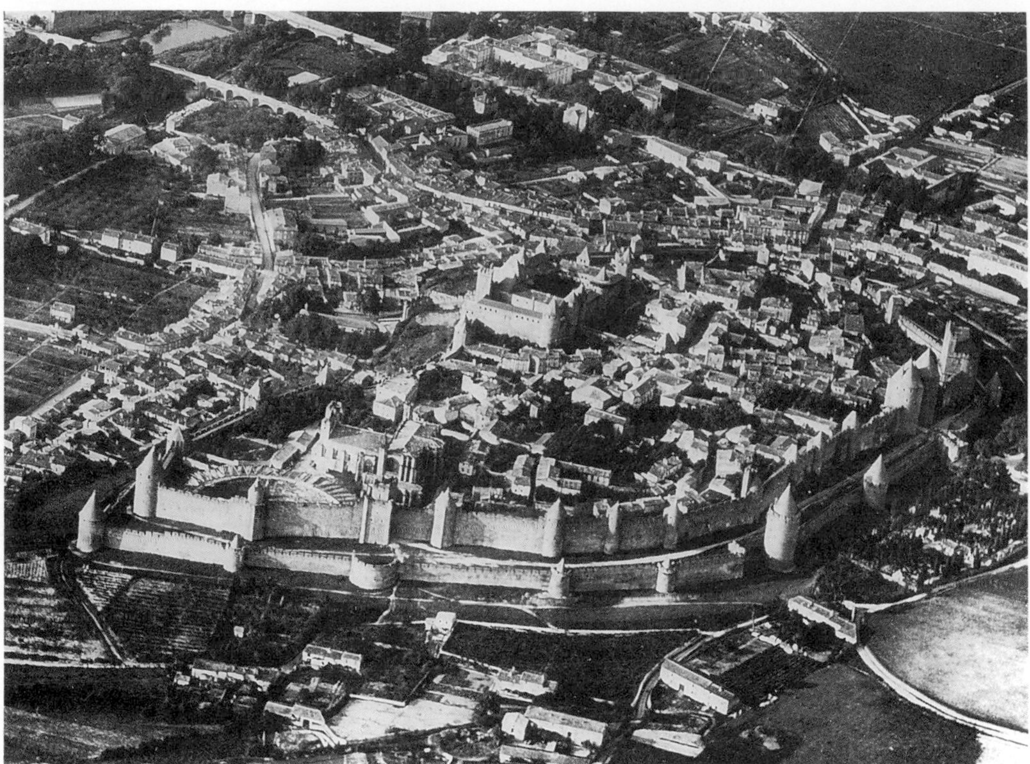

Carcassonne, in southern France, whose medieval inner walls stand on Roman foundations, illustrates the revival of an urban culture during the later Middle Ages after Latin urbanism had been temporarily eclipsed by the pastoral culture of the migrating Germanic tribes.

Celtic-Germanic peoples—the "barbarians," as the Greeks and the Romans had called them. Christianity, firmly established, constituted a unifying force, even in the midst of anarchy and chronic warfare. It mitigated the harsh passions of rough warriors. It kept alive learning and knowledge of the useful arts. Though itself often corrupted, it just as often was reformed. By the thirteenth century, when the Church was at the height of its power, western Europe had evolved into a great and original civilization, constantly stimulated by influences from the Greco-Roman past and from Byzantium and the world of Islam, but ever reworking those influences in novel ways. The Christian church, with its monopoly on education, also preserved and handed on aspects of the Roman culture not directly related to religion: the Latin language, Roman law, Roman administrative organization and practice, the idea and ideal of the Roman Empire—all elements used by the Church but, as the Renaissance would show, susceptible to entirely secular application.

Although the spirit of Christianity was oriented toward the world of the supernatural and although its learning was centered in theology, which regarded questions about the nature of the physical world as both irrelevant to salvation and irreverent in intention, by the thirteenth century, a new curiosity about the natural environment was stirring—even within the Church—that could not be stifled entirely by the prevailing religious disposition. In a thirteenth-century summation of medieval knowledge, the influential encyclopedia called the *Speculum Majus (Great Mirror),* Vincent of Beauvais, a Dominican monk, included the "Mirror of Nature," a comprehensive compilation of lore about natural things. By no means an objective or scientific analysis of nature in the modern sense, this compilation was rather a descriptive record of the appearances of things as the reflection of God's glory and beneficence. Within the medieval setting, notwithstanding its thoroughly religious view of nature, a different impulse was being felt—a secular and intellectual curiosity about the world that was to mature into modern science.

In addition, the period produced technological advances that pointed to consequences far beyond anything the ancient world had known. The invention and development of tools and mechanisms that extended humanity's powers over the environment and that facilitated manufacture were encouraged in part by the new dignity that the Church's disapproval of slavery conferred on manual labor and skills. Free craftsmen—not slaves, as in the ancient world—were the medieval agents of production; organized in guilds, they constituted the firm foundation of the medieval urban economy. Thriving towns, populated by free inhabitants, provided a stimulus for commerce and industry, and new towns were founded and flourished. Most of the prosperous European cities of today were established or underwent renovation around the twelfth century. Indeed, Florence, mother city of the modern world, had laid the foundations of its wealth early and, by the fifteenth century, had the spirit and the means to lead Europe into the bold, creative age of discovery we call the Renaissance.

NOTE: Maps at the beginning of the following (and preceding) chapters illustrate the simple fact that the boundaries of ancient civilizations do not correspond to modern political boundaries; the region where "Mesopotamian" art flourished now encompasses parts of the modern nations of Iran, Iraq, Syria, and Jordan. The same statement can be made in connection with the medieval monuments of Europe and those of the non-European civilizations that we will examine in later chapters. The medieval *artistic* regions do not correspond to the modern *political* boundaries of nations like France, Germany, or Italy. Obviously, this is because such political boundaries did not exist at the time the art was produced. Moreover, the fact that the monuments are situated or preserved within the present boundaries of the European nations does not mean that their stylistic origins or relatives were necessarily "French," "German," or "Italian." The old regional divisions that *did* exist during the Middle Ages, the boundaries within which Medieval art was produced—Northumbria, Normandy, Burgundy, Languedoc, Saxony, Tuscany—have long been absorbed within the boundaries of the nation-states we know. Thus, for example, to speak of "French," "German," or "Italian" Gothic is to refer only to the modern states where Gothic monuments are presently found and not to designate them as a uniquely national species of Gothic art produced by French, German, or Italian nationals. Actually, the boundaries of the modern states of Europe were not well in place until the seventeenth century. Germany and Italy, though long recognized as ethnic, cultural, and linguistic entities, did not become unified politically until as late as 1871. At present, the works of many of the art-producing cultures of the world, past and present, are identified by the same means—ethnic, cultural, and linguistic designations, and not political ones. Thus "Yoruba" denotes works created within the area of present-day Nigeria; "Kwakiutl," British Columbia; "Maya," Mexico, Guatemala, Belize, and Honduras; "Moche," Peru; and so forth.

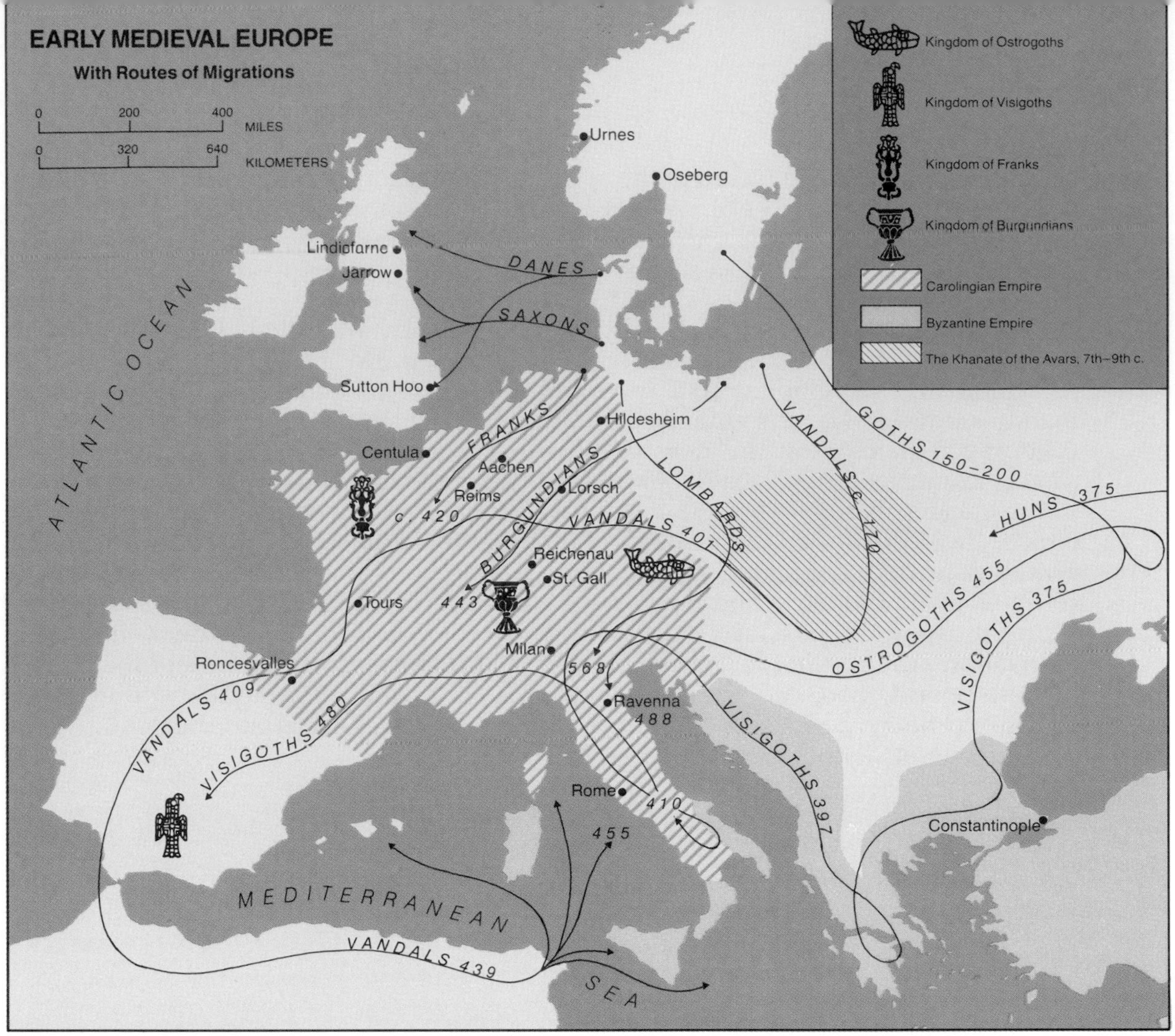

EARLY MEDIEVAL EUROPE

With Routes of Migrations

0 200 400 MILES

0 320 640 KILOMETERS

Kingdom of Ostrogoths

Kingdom of Visigoths

Kingdom of Franks

Kingdom of Burgundians

Carolingian Empire

Byzantine Empire

The Khanate of the Avars, 7th–9th c.

ATLANTIC OCEAN

Urnes

Oseberg

Lindisfarne

Jarrow

DANES

SAXONS

Sutton Hoo

FRANKS

Hildesheim

Centula

Aachen

Reims

Lorsch

c. 420

BURGUNDIANS

VANDALS 401

LOMBARDS

VANDALS c. 170

GOTHS 150–200

HUNS 375

Reichenau

St. Gall

443

Tours

Milan

568

Roncesvalles

OSTROGOTHS 455

VISIGOTHS 375

Ravenna

488

VANDALS 409

VISIGOTHS 480

VISIGOTHS

Rome

410

VISIGOTHS 397

455

Constantinople

MEDITERRANEAN

VANDALS 439

SEA

375	400	500	600	700

MIGRATION PERIOD AND FORMATION OF GERMANIC KINGDOMS

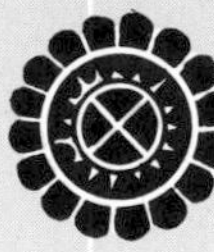

Frankish ornament 7th century

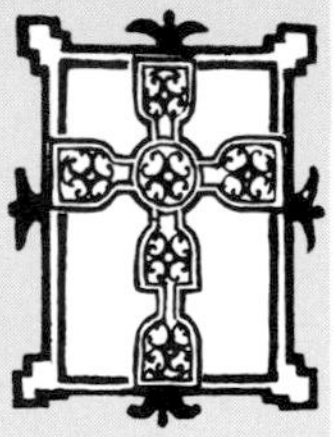

Book of Lindisfarne late 7th century

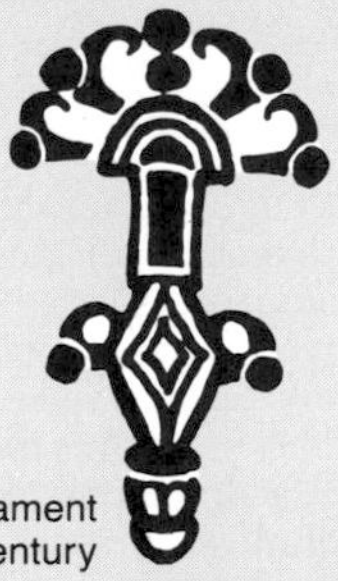

Frankish ornament 6th century

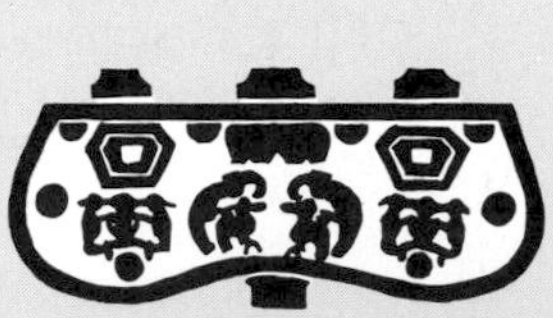

Sutton Hoo purse cover *c.* 655

Anglo-Saxons in Britain 5th century

Ostrogoths in Italy 489–540

Lombards in Italy 568 –774

Visigoths in Spain 412–672

Invasion of Huns 376

Celtic culture in Ireland *c.* 400–850

Franks in Gaul (Merovingian dynasty) 482–750

Huns reach Gaul 451

St. Basil and Eastern monasticism 4th century

St. Benedict establishes "Benedictine Rule" over Western monasticism 526

Death of Attila 453

8
EARLY MEDIEVAL ART

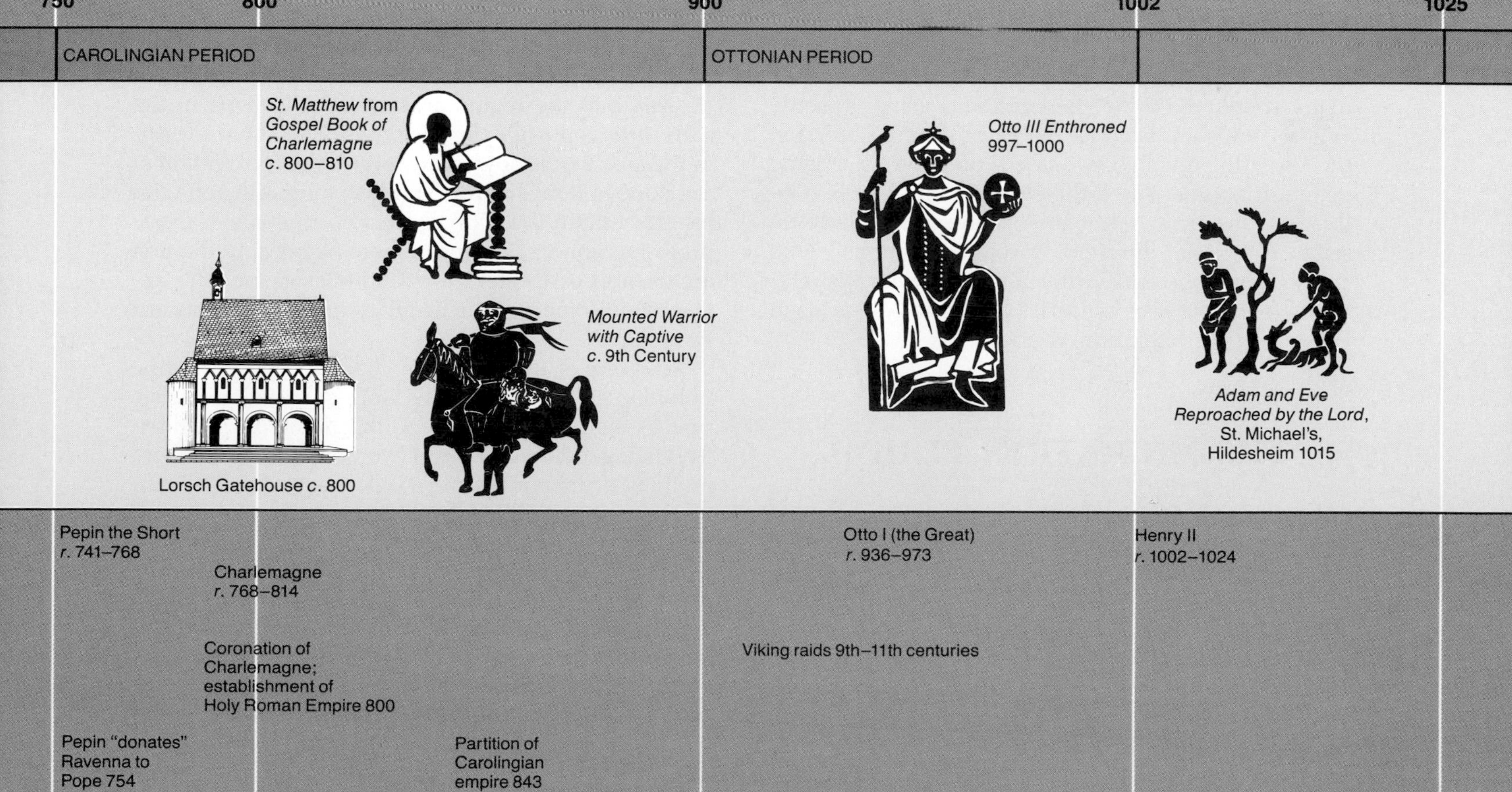

For thousands of years, waves of migrating people moved slowly across the great Eurasian steppes and down into the Mediterranean world; we have met them as the Achaeans and Dorians of Mycenaean times, and again as the Gauls, who invaded Asia Minor and were defeated by Attalus I of Pergamon in the third century B.C.

In the second century A.D., the Goths migrated southward from the Baltic region and settled on the north shore of the Black Sea, subjugating the Scythians and Sarmatians, who had inhabited the area for some eight centuries. On their march, the Goths had met and defeated the Vandals, pushing them toward central Europe and setting in motion one of the longest and most infamous migratory treks in history—one that was to end only in the fifth century with the establishment of a Vandal kingdom in North Africa. The Goths themselves split into two groups in the early fourth century: the Ostrogoths (eastern Goths), who remained in Sarmatia, and the Visigoths (western Goths), who moved on into the Danube River basin.

For centuries, these migratory movements had been checked by Roman military might along the Rhine and Danube rivers. Despite constant friction with them since the first century B.C., the Romans had been able to contain the barbarians along their northern frontiers. In the fourth century, however, the eruption of the Huns from the east pressed those tribes and nations against the Roman boundaries, which Rome found more and more difficult to defend. In 376, the Roman emperor Valens allowed the Visigoths, hard-pressed by the Huns, who had already conquered their Ostrogothic cousins, to settle west of the Danube. Maltreated by Roman officials, the Visigoths revolted two years later and, in a battle near Adrianople, killed the emperor and nearly two-thirds of his army. After this, Rome offered little resistance to the different barbarian nations, who crossed into western Europe almost at will. We refer to the following four centuries of ethnic upheavals in Europe as the Migration period.

THE MIGRATION PERIOD

As the name of the period implies, the invasions of Roman territory by barbarian tribes were, in reality, migrations of ethnic groups seeking not to overthrow the Roman Empire, for which they often had great admiration, but to find a place where they could settle peacefully. They seldom were allowed to remain in any one location, however, as other tribes and nations would press in behind them and force them to move on. The Visigoths, for example, who moved in and out of Italy and formed a kingdom in southern France, were forced southward into Spain under pressure from the Franks, who had crossed the lower Rhine and established themselves firmly in northern France. The Huns themselves, the force that triggered this chain reaction of ethnic dislocations, reached France and Italy in the mid-fifth century, and only the death of their great leader, Attila, in 453 prevented them from consolidating their vast conquests. As Hunnish power waned, the Ostrogoths shook off their yoke and moved first to Pannonia (at the junction of modern Hungary, Austria, and Yugoslavia) and then to Italy, where, under Theodoric, they established their kingdom, only to have it fall less than a century later to the Lombards.

During this time of upheaval, strife, fear, and uncertainty, the Church, benefiting from the prestige of such early leaders as Augustine and Gregory the Great, constituted the only central political and spiritual authority; the popes had, in effect, succeeded the Roman emperors. It was at this time that the foundations for the later authority of the Church were established firmly. In this connection, we should bear in mind that most of the barbarian tribes entering the Roman Empire were already Christian, although of the Arian creed, which had been condemned as heretical by the Orthodox church. In its contest with the Eastern Orthodox church for leadership in Christendom, papal Rome was strengthened when the Frankish king, Clovis, was converted to Catholicism. During his reign (481–511), the Franks gained control over the Burgundians (who had moved from the Baltic area into the region around Lake Geneva in the early fifth century), the Visigoths, and other groups in the area that is now France. With the recognition of the pope in Rome by this Frankish kingdom and with the success (in the sixth century) of the later Augustine's mission to England, where he became the first archbishop of Canterbury, Catholicism and the authority of Rome became firmly established in western Europe.

Accounts of the barbarian character vary. Tacitus, pointing up a moral for his Roman contemporaries, praises their courage, good looks, moral purity, fidelity, and good treatment of women, but finds them guilty of drunkenness and a lack of astuteness in matters of money. We get a better picture of the Germanic character from their epics, songs, and sagas, which show a somber pessimism built on a fundamental belief in fate or the inevitable. Their heroes, like Siegfried and Beowulf, struggle against a pagan world of dreadful monsters. Fierce joy in battle alternates with bragging and carousing; narratives of stoic valor alternate with expressions of despair. Interpersonal loyalty, which became the basis of feudal ties and feudal law, is glorified in their poetry, as in this fragment of an Anglo-Saxon epic describing the last stand of a band of Saxons against the Danes:

> Remember the times when we spoke over our mead, when we raised up our boasts along the benches, heroes in the hall in anticipation of a hard fight! Now let us see who is brave. . . . Byrhtivold spoke up, an old retainer . . . he taught his warriors their duty: "Mind shall be the harder, heart the keener, courage the greater as our strength grows less."

The imagination of these wandering groups teemed with fantastic creatures of all sorts. Their belief that the deep, dark forests of the north virtually swarmed with zoomorphic and demonic populations was shared widely by the nomadic hunters of all tribes. Dragons, like Siegfried's Fafnir and Beowulf's Grendel, symbolize the mysterious and threatening universe of fierce forces that the later medieval world will picture as the devils and demons of Hell. Medieval peoples, long after they ceased their wanderings and despite Christianization, remained more than half pagan; their terrors were bound up with their tribal experiences and the memories of fiend-filled forests and pagan rites. Against this background, it is not surprising to find that the Germanic tribes readily adopted an art form that, although foreign, was ideally suited to their imagination—the Eastern animal style already encountered in Mesopotamian art.

The Animal Style: Scythian Antecedents

Animal style is a generic term for the characteristic ornamentation of artifacts worn and carried by nomadic peoples, who for almost two millennia (B.C. and A.D.), moved restlessly to and fro across the vast, open grasslands that stretch from China into western Europe. Originating in prehistoric times, the decorative animal form appears in ancient Egypt and Mesopotamia; we have seen a late example in the Luristan bronzes (FIG. 2-44). Transactions between the nomads and the settled civilizations of the Near East and the Mediterranean disseminated the style and produced numerous variants of its figures and patterns. The wide and steady propagation of the animal style was made possible by the fact that it was found on small, metal objects that were portable and easily exchanged. The great revolution in metallurgy that replaced the Bronze Age with the Iron Age after 1000 B.C. put the means of fashioning metallic artifacts in abundance into the hands of numerous skilled artisans, nomadic or sedentary, and guaranteed the broadest distribution of these items through gift, exchange, plunder, or migration.

Perhaps the principal agents of the transmission of the animal style from east to west were the Scythians, an Iranian-speaking nomadic people who roamed the steppes north of the Black Sea. They were known to the ancient Assyrians, Iranians, and Greeks (Herodotus gives us a detailed account of them), with whom they were alternately in friendly and hostile contact. Though the period of Scythian predominance precedes the early medieval times we are describing, they (and their Sarmatian successors) are significant for passing on to the Germanic tribes, and to Medieval art in general, the repertory of animal ornament familiar in the art of the ancient world.

The remains of the settlements of the Scythian-Sarmatians, and especially the tombs of their kings, are scattered throughout southern Russia and the Crimea, the Caucasus, and Anatolia. From them modern archeology has recovered rich troves of metal treasure, the funeral ornaments and furnishings of elaborate royal burials. Whether of their own manufacture, or the work of Greek craftsmen, Scythian gold ornaments attest to what an ancient Roman author calls the "Scythian lust for gold." At the same time, these objects exhibit to perfection the motifs of the animal style that will be transmitted to the early medieval West.

A superb, crescent-shaped golden pectoral from about the fourth century B.C., a product of Greek craftsmanship, sums up the animal vocabulary favored by Scythian ornamental taste (FIG. **8-1**). Some

8-1 Pectoral with scenes from Scythian life (Greek craft done for the Scythians), *c.* fourth century B.C. Gold, diameter 12", weight 2½ lbs. Historical Museum, Kiev.

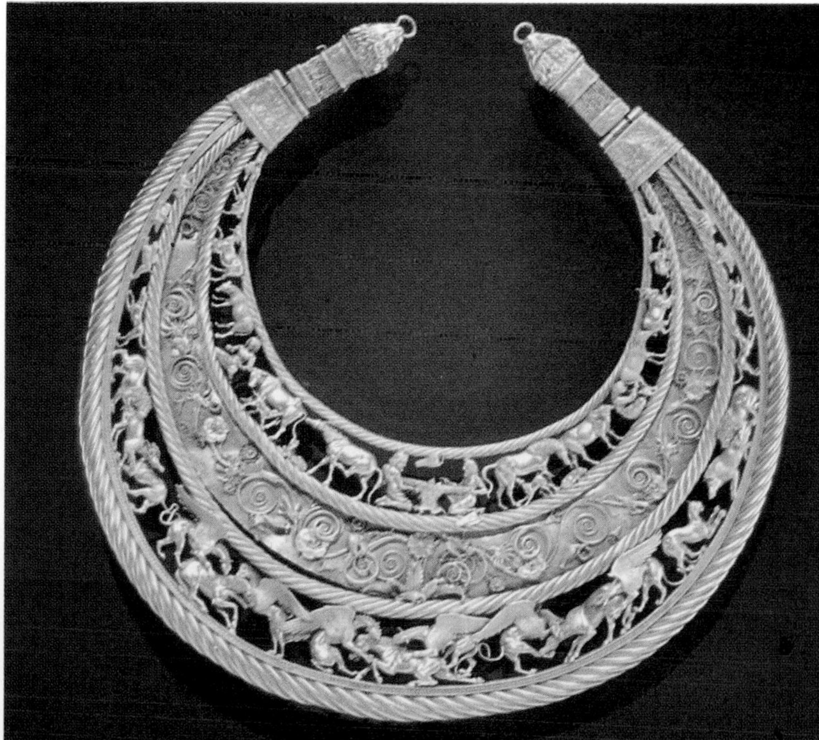

forty-eight figures, mostly of animals cast singly and soldered to the frame, are distributed friezelike on three concentric bands separated by cable moldings. The innermost band represents Scythians in an encampment accompanied by their domestic animals. Men make a shirt out of an animal skin, close an amphora, and milk sheep. Calves and foals are suckling, and a horse casually scratches itself with a hind hoof. Birds, a kid, and a goat also are depicted. The central band is Classical Greek in its ornament of rhythmical vine scrolls, acanthus, and rosettes. The figures on the outer band contrast sharply with the pastoral mood of the other two; heraldically symmetrical griffins attack horses, lions and panthers tear at a deer and a boar, hounds pursue hares, and even grasshoppers challenge each other. The animals, actual and fantastic, are rendered with crisp realism. They later will be transformed into abstract zoomorphic motifs as they are adapted to the ornamental vocabularies of the migrant German peoples, the Goths and their successors.

Art of the Germanic Peoples

The original art of the Germanic peoples was abstract, decorative, and geometric and ignored the world of organic nature. It was confined to the decoration of small, portable objects—weapons or items of personal adornment such as bracelets, pendants, and belt buckles. Most characteristic, perhaps, and produced in quantity by almost all tribes, was the *fibula,* a decorative pin usually used to fasten garments. Fibulae (FIG. **8-2**) are made of bronze, silver, or gold and are decorated profusely, often with inlaid precious or semiprecious stones. The entire surface of these objects is covered with decorative patterns, reflecting the *horror vacui* so common in the art of primitive cultures. But we also note that the decorative patterns are adjusted carefully to the basic shape of the object they adorn and that they describe and amplify its form and structure, becoming an organic part of the object itself.

This highly disciplined, abstract, and functional type of decorative design was wedded to the animal style during the early centuries of the Medieval era. The Scythians passed the animal style on to their Gothic overlords in the third century A.D. From that time on, the Goths became the main transmitters of this style, which was readily adopted by many of the other Germanic tribes. But its application was controlled severely by the native Germanic sense of order and design. Abstracted to the point of absolute integration with dominantly geometric patterns, the zoomorphic elements frequently became almost unrecognizable, and one often must examine a fibula carefully to discover that it contains a zoomorphic form (in the case of FIG. 8-2a, a fish).

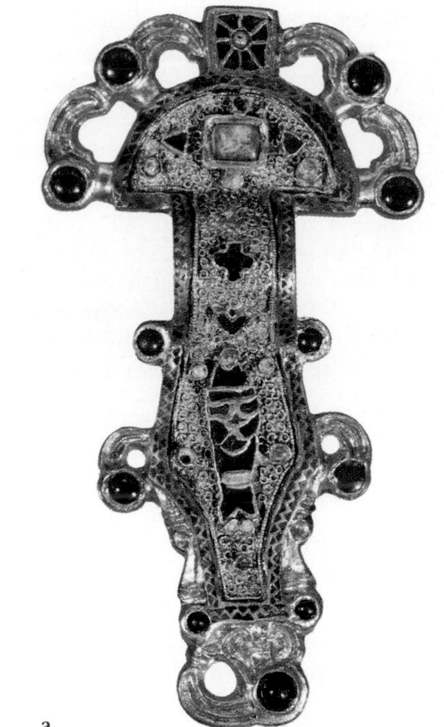

a.

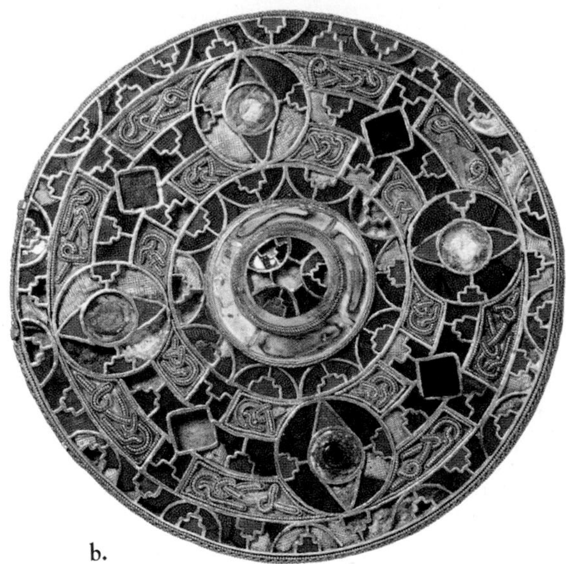

b.

8-2 Frankish ornaments, sixth and seventh centuries: (**a**) looped fibula (4″ long), silver gilt worked in filigree, with inlays of garnets and other stones, Musée des Antiquités Nationales, Saint Germain-en-Laye; (**b**) round fibula (diameter 3¼″), gold, cloisonné technique, inlay of garnets and blue stones. City of Liverpool Museums.

The art of the Germanic peoples was expressed primarily in metalcraft. One of their preferred methods of decoration was *cloisonné,* a technique that may be of Byzantine and, ultimately, of Near Eastern origin.

In this technique, used in the circular ornament shown in FIG. 8-2b, small metal strips (the *cloisons*), usually of gold, are soldered edge-up to a metal background. An enamel paste (subsequently to be fired) or semiprecious stones, such as garnets, or pieces of colored glass, are placed in the compartments thus formed. The edges of the cloisons remain visible on the surface and are an important part of the design. This cloisonné personal gear was prized highly and handed down from generation to generation. Dispersion of some of the princely hoards at an early date would account for the discoveries of identical techniques and designs in widely divergent areas. Certainly, cloisonné ware must have been given to vassals as gifts and tokens of gratitude; everywhere in barbarian poetry, the name for the prince and lord is "treasure-giver." Other collections or "treasures" must have been accumulated over time, which could explain the different forms present in the magnificent discovery made at Sutton Hoo in Suffolk, England.

Excavated in 1939, the Sutton Hoo site now is associated with the ship burial of the East Anglian king Anna, who died in 654. The purse lid shown in FIG. **8-3**, which is by no means the best of the pieces found (fine as it is), is decorated with four symmetrically arranged groups of figures. The end groups consist of a man standing between two beasts; he faces front, they appear in profile. This heraldic type of grouping goes back to ancient Mesopotamia (FIG. 2-19), though of course with variation. The two center groups represent eagles attacking ducks, again a familiar predatory motif seen in both Mesopotamian and Egyptian art. The animal figures are adjusted to each other with the cunning we associate with the whole animal style through centuries; for example, the convex beaks of the eagles fit against the concave beaks of the ducks. The two figures fit together so snugly that they seem at first to be a single, dense, abstract design; this is true also of the man-animals motif. Above these figures are three geometric designs. The outer ones are clear and linear in style. In the central design, an interlace pattern, the interlacements turn into writhing animal figures. Interlacement was known outside the barbarian world but was seldom used in combination with animal figures. The barbarian fondness for the interlace pattern may have come from the quite familiar experience of interlacing leather thongs. In any event, the interlace, with its possibilities for great complexity, had natural attraction for the adroit jeweler.

Metalcraft and its vocabulary of interlace patterns and other motifs, beautifully integrated with the animal form, is, without doubt, *the* art of the Early Middle Ages in the West. Interest in it was so great that the colorful effects of jewelry designs were imitated in the painted decorations of manuscripts, in stone sculpture, in the masonry of the early churches, and in sculpture in wood.

8-3 Purse cover from the Sutton Hoo ship burial, from Suffolk, England, *c.* 655. Gold and enamel, 7½" long. British Museum, London.

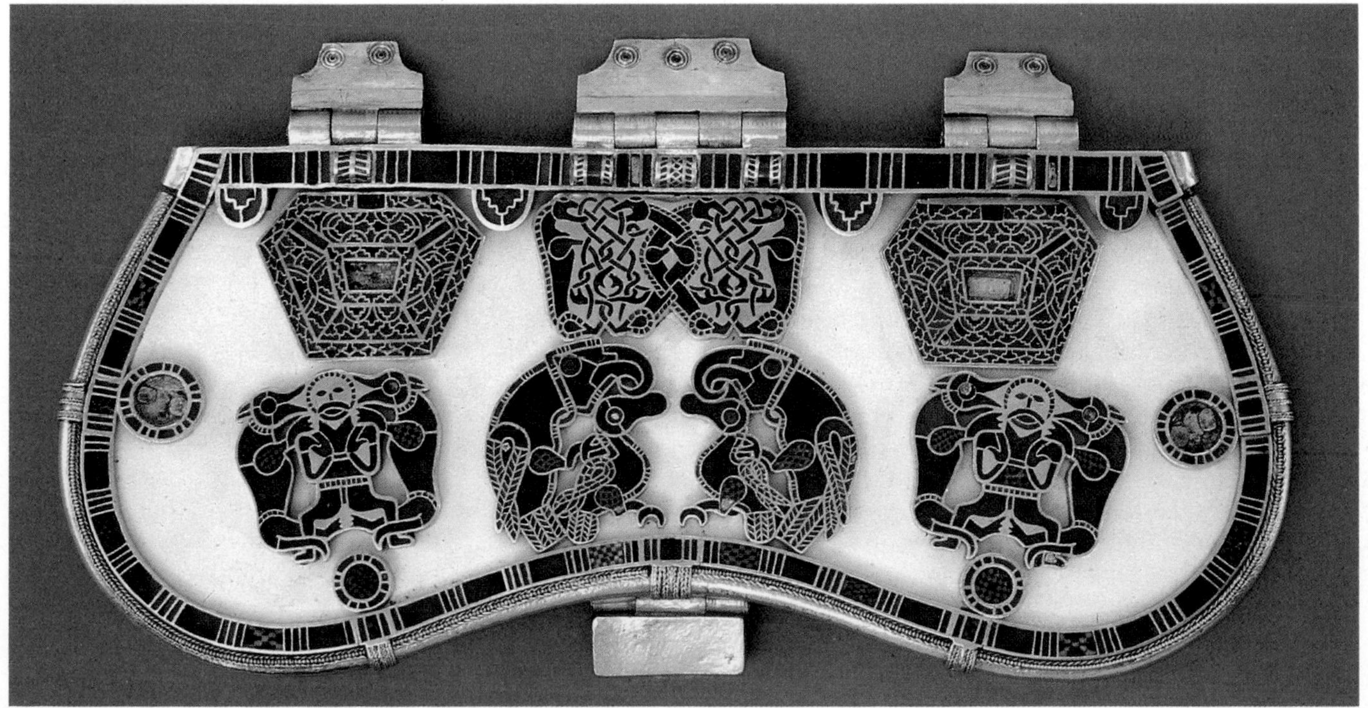

Viking Art

Wood is an especially important medium in Viking art. The Vikings (the word means "pirate" in the Norse language) were the pagan, seafaring plunderers from the Scandinavian north, who, from the ninth to the eleventh centuries, destructively raided the Celtic and Germanic settlements of Christian Europe. Once Christianized, the Vikings settled down to become the Normans (Northmen), giving their name to that part of France we call Normandy. Striking examples of Viking wood carving have been found in a royal ship buried near Oseberg, Norway. The Oseberg ship has yielded rich evidence of the quality of Early Viking art, which now has become established, along with Hiberno-Saxon art (with which it interacts), as an original and important artistic development of the Early Middle Ages. The ship has been reconstructed (FIG. **8-4**), but we can judge, from such surviving parts as the ornament of the prow, the skill of craftsmen familiar with a tradition of interlace design that was widely dispersed along the routes of the great migrations. The carved bands that follow the gracefully curving lines of the prow are embroidered with tightly interwoven animals, which writhe gripping and snapping, in serpentine and lacertine (lizardlike) interlacement. The convulsive movement is strictly controlled within the continuous margins of the composition.

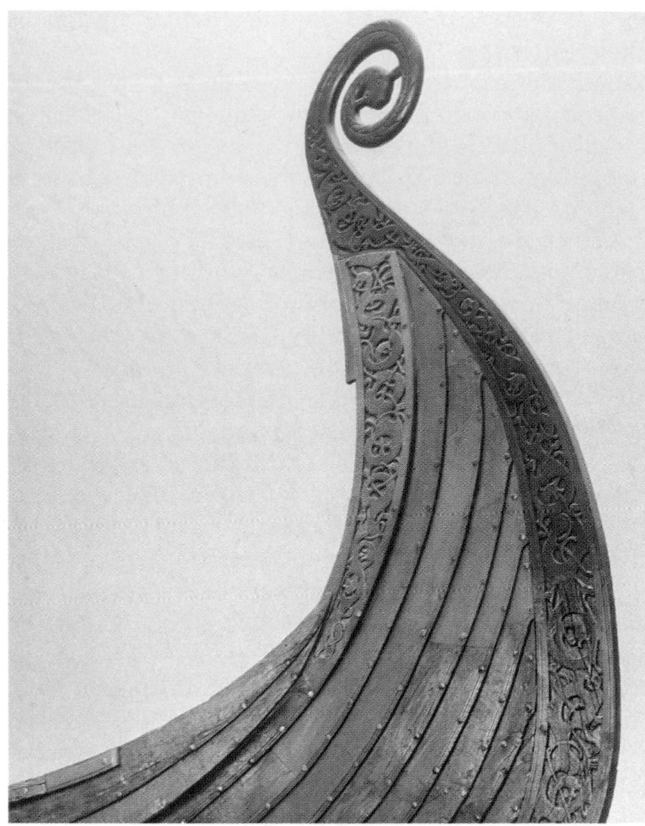

8-4 Prow of the Oseberg ship, early ninth century. Vikingskipshuset Museum, Oslo.

An animal head that caps a post (FIG. **8-5**) expresses, like other animal forms in the ship, the fierce, untamed spirit and energy of the pagan sea rovers. This head brings together in one composition the image of a roaring beast—eyes protruding, nostrils flaring in predatory excitement—and the deftly carved, controlled, and contained interlace pattern. As in the carvings of the ship's prow, firm artistic limit is put to wild vigor. The Oseberg animal head is a powerfully expressive example of the union of two fundamental motifs of barbarian art: the animal form and the interlace pattern.

8-5 Animal-head post from the Oseberg ship burial, *c.* 825. Wood, approx. 5″ high. Vikingskipshuset Museum, Oslo.

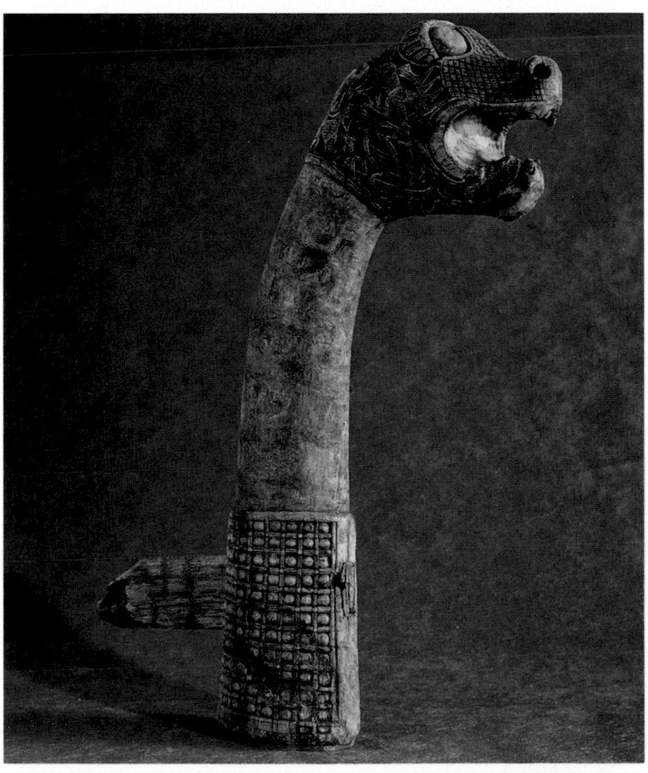

The interpatterning of these motifs culminated in the eleventh century with such elegant designs as that on the porch of the "stave" church at Urnes in Norway (FIG. **8-6**). The church itself is constructed in wood (staves are wedge-shaped timbers placed vertically), which gives the wood-carver a special opportunity to show his craft in the embellishment of the architectural features of the building (in this case, the panels of the porch walls). Here, gracefully attenuated animal forms intertwine with flexible stalks and tendrils in spiraling rhythm; the effect of natural growth is astonishing. At the same time, the elaboration of the forms is so intricate and refined that the animal-interlace art of design seems to have reached

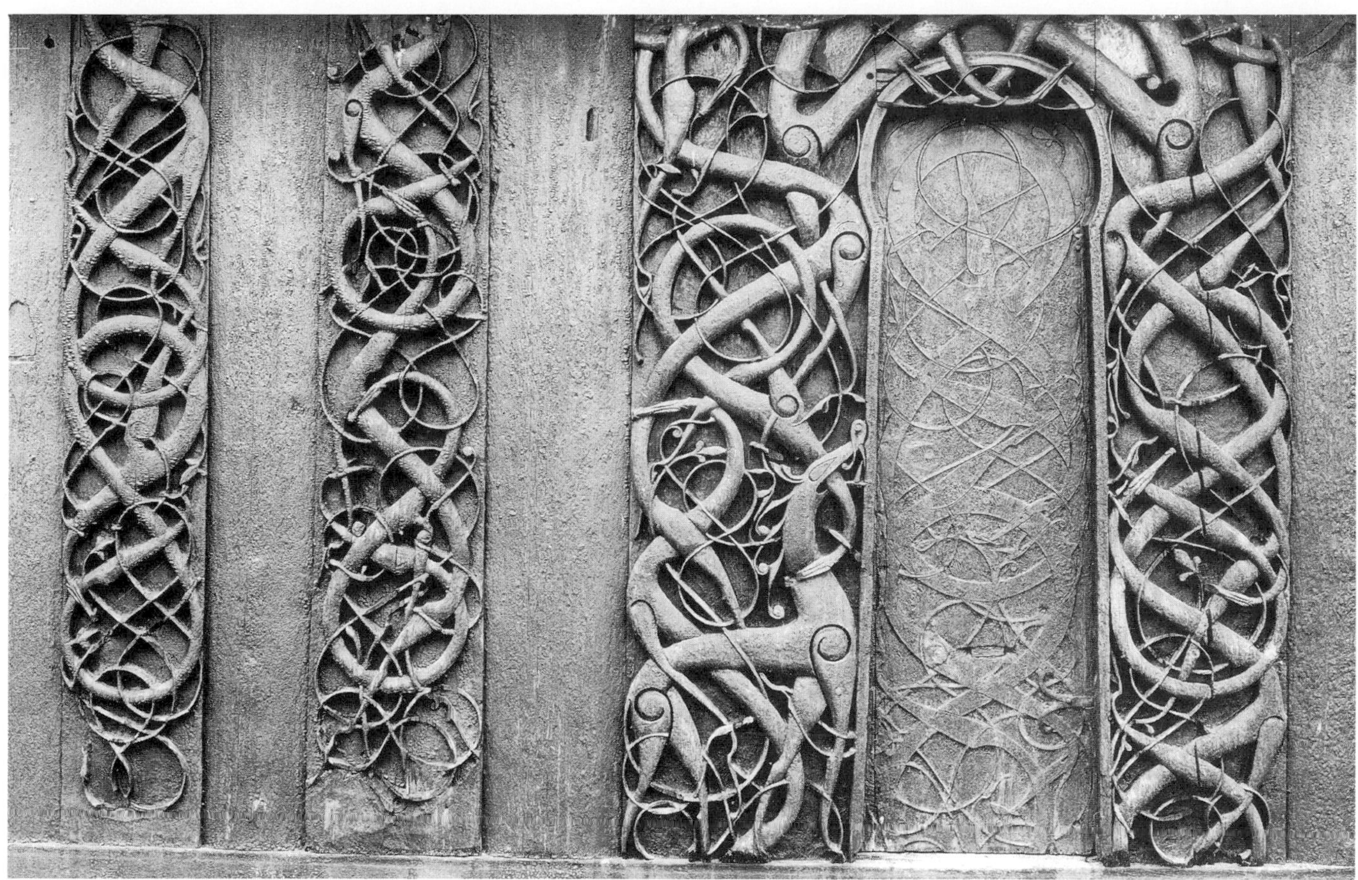

8-6 Wood-carved ornament (porch of stave church), Urnes, Norway, eleventh century.

its limit of inventiveness. The Urnes style is the culmination of three centuries of Viking art (from the eighth to the eleventh centuries), after which it merges with the Romanesque style. During the whole period that it flourished, the art of the Vikings interacted closely with Hiberno-Saxon art and the art of the continent.

Hiberno-Saxon Art

Two centuries of Viking incursions into Celtic Ireland and Anglo-Saxon England mingled artistic forms and motifs that, as we have seen, had long been elaborating into a recognizable regional style. The Christian culture of Celtic Ireland played a leading role in the civilizing of barbarian Europe. The Celts of Ireland, converted to Christianity in the fifth century, developed a form of monastic organization that preserved and cultivated literature, learning, philosophy, and the decorative and useful arts. Monasticism, a system by which communities of persons lived away from the world and dedicated themselves to the spiritual life, was instituted in the Eastern Christian world by St. Basil in the fourth century and in the West by St. Benedict in the sixth century. The Irish adopted Eastern rather than Western forms of monasticism and were not firmly connected to the Roman church or the rule of the papacy. Their independence was strengthened by their historical good luck: they were not invaded by the Germanic migrants. From about 400 to 850, while western Europe sank gradually into conflict, confusion, and ignorance, Ireland experienced a golden age. Irish monks, filled with missionary zeal, founded monastic establishments in the British islands at Iona, off the west coast of Scotland, and at Lindisfarne, on the Northumbrian (northeastern) coast of Anglo-Saxon England. From these foundations, which became great centers of learning for both Scotland and England, Irish monks, moved by a "wonderful spirit of missionary enterprise," journeyed through Europe, establishing great monasteries in Italy, Switzerland, Germany, and France, and making the names of *Scot* (the old term for *Irish*) and *Ireland* familiar in all western Christendom as synonymous with education and learning. Until the eighth century, the influence of the Irish church rivaled that of Rome.

A style of decorative art we designate "Hiberno-Saxon," (or sometimes "Insular") to denote the Irish-English islands where it was produced, flourished under the auspices of the Irish church and within its institutions. Hiberno-Saxon art brings to synthesizing focus those design elements of nomadic and Migration craft art that we have been describing. Traceable through centuries, from the Celtic Iron-Age art of western Europe, and across the Eurasian continent, they appear all together and in definitive patterns on the surfaces of the so-called *Tara Brooch,* an article of Irish costume jewelry from the eighth century (FIG. **8-7**). The art of the Migration period is summed up, as it were, in this single, exquisite piece. In an age lacking artistic expression on a monumental scale, the human instinct for design concentrates powerfully, as here, in the small utensils of life: the clasps and fasteners of clothing, for example. The functional ring and pin of the brooch are embellished with panels of delicate filigree and are punctuated with studs of amber and amethyst-glass. The panels, chip-carved, engraved, and tooled, with inlays of copper, silver, and gold, enclose fields of ornamental motifs worked with threadlike refinement of detail. All the motifs of the decorative vocabulary of Migration art appear here: interlaced birds, animals and humanoids, strap work, scrolled bands and ribbons, whorls, knots, and bosses. The patterns balance, repeat, and reflect one another in cunningly intricate play. Despite the astonishing profusion, intricacy, and density of the ornamental elements, the overall geometry of ring and pin is in strict control of their rich exuberance.

It would take pages of description and close work with a magnifying glass to do justice to the refinements of design and craftsmanship evident in the *Tara Brooch.* Though both elements are descended from long tradition and are not the consequence of unique invention, in the hands of an anonymous artisan of genius, they combine to make a world masterpiece of the jeweler's art.

8-7 *Tara Brooch,* Ireland, c. 700. Bronze with overlay of gold filigree, glass and amber settings. Front *(top),* back *(bottom).* National Museum of Ireland, Dublin.

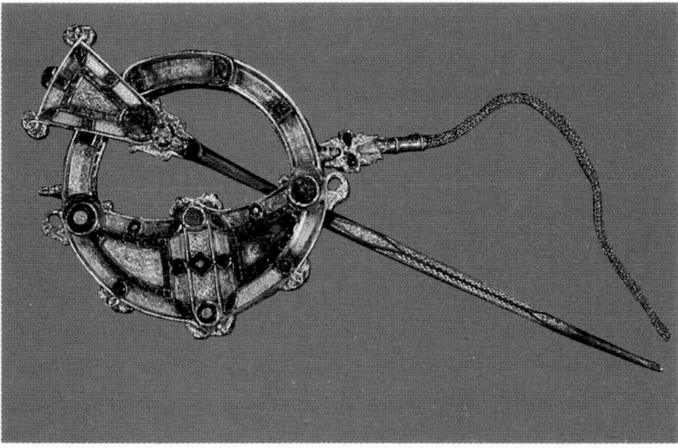

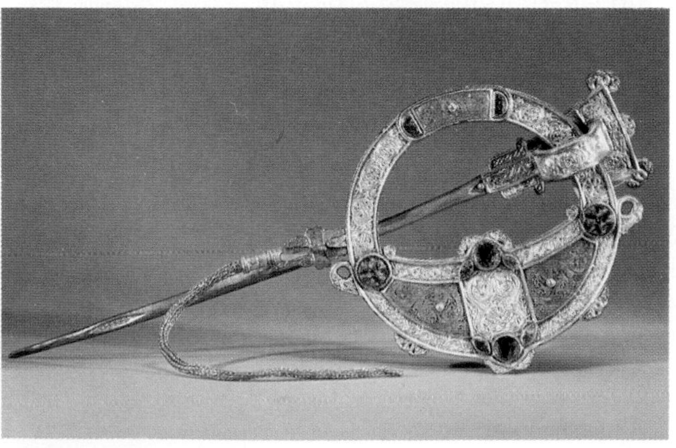

MANUSCRIPT ILLUMINATION

Remarkable as such works of secular art as the *Tara Brooch* may be, they are complemented by the illuminated manuscripts sponsored by the Church. With the Christianization of the barbarian peoples, liturgical books became an important vehicle of miniature art and a principal medium for the exchange of stylistic ideas between the northern and the Mediterranean worlds. The exchange is the result not only of restless migrations and incursions of peoples, but also of the missionary activities of the Church, Celtic or Roman, as it sought to stabilize the wandering groups and establish its authority. The encounter between Irish and Roman Christianity during the missionary enterprise is reflected in the commingling of ornamental elements on the illuminated pages of gospel books produced in Ireland and Anglo-Saxon England between the seventh and the ninth centuries. These books were easy to transport, and we can follow the movements of some of them from place to place in sequences of influence.

The Hiberno-Saxon manuscripts combine Irish and Anglo-Saxon motifs, sharing essentially, but by no means in all details, the same style. An ornamental page (FIG. **8-8**), only one of several from the *Book of Lindisfarne,* is an exquisite example of Hiberno-Saxon art at its best. Here, the craft of intricate ornamental patterning, developed through centuries and seen in Viking art, is manifested in a tightly compacted design. Serpentine interlacements of fantastic animals devour each other, curling over and returning on their writhing, elastic shapes. The rhythm of expanding and contracting forms produces a most vivid effect of motion and change—a palpable rippling, as on the surface of a rapid. The inscribed cross, a variation on the stone Celtic crosses familiar in Ireland, regularizes the rhythms of the serpentines and, perhaps by contrast with its heavy immobility, seems to heighten the effect of motion. The motifs are placed in detailed symmetries, with inversions, reversals,

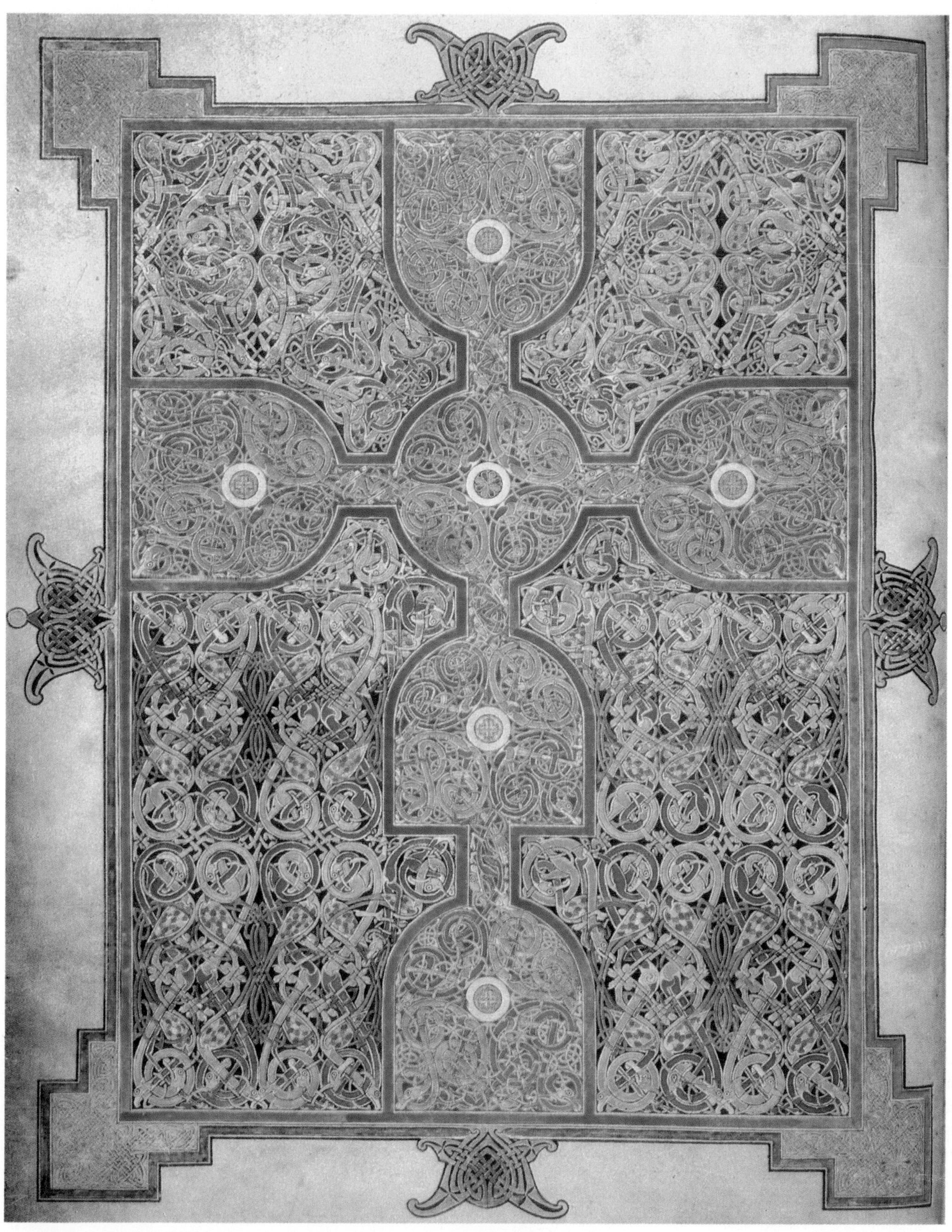

8-8 Ornamental page from the *Book of Lindisfarne,* from Northumberland, England, late seventh century. Illumination, approx. 13″ × 10″. British Library, London.

and repetitions that must be studied closely to appreciate not so much their variety as their mazelike complexity. The zoomorphic forms are intermingled with clusters and knots of line, and the whole design pulses and vibrates like an electromagnetic energy field. The color is rich yet cool; the entire spectrum is embraced, but in hues of low intensity. Shape and color are so adroitly adjusted that a smooth and perfectly even surface is achieved, a balance between an overall, steady harmony of key (color) and maximum motion of figure and line. The discipline of touch is that of a master familiar with long-established conventions; yet neither the discipline nor the convention stiffens the supple lines that tirelessly and endlessly thread and convolute their way through the design.

This joy at working on small, infinitely complex and painstaking projects—this goldsmith's, jeweler's, and weaver's craft—will endure in northern art throughout the Middle Ages in architectural detail, ivory carving, illumination, stained-glass work, and, ultimately, in panel painting. The instinct and taste for intricacy and precision, propagated in the art of the wandering Celts and Germans, will broaden beyond art into technology and the making of machines.

The barbarian craft remained, but the Hiberno-Saxon ornamental style, with its gorgeous essays in interlacements, was fated to be replaced by the Mediterranean styles that descended from Early Christian and Late Antique art. Political realities hastened its demise. Irish Christianity lost its influence in Anglo-Saxon England and on the continent; the adherents to the rule of Benedict, the Benedictine order of monks, who wholeheartedly followed the papacy and the Roman version of Christianity, gained the upper hand in power and influence, and although the Irish church held out for some time, eventually it accepted the Roman form. Even while Hiberno-Saxon art prevailed in Ireland, Scotland, and Northumbria, other monastic foundations in England were copying Mediterranean prototypes. Naturally, the ascendancy of the Roman church would be expressed in manuscripts from the Mediterranean area, and wherever the Roman orthodoxy was accepted, an orthodox style of manuscript illumination had to follow. The contrast between the two very different styles is particularly striking in juxtaposition. *The Scribe Ezra Rewriting the Sacred Records* from the *Codex Amiatinus* (FIG. **8-9**) was copied from an Italian manuscript, the *Codex Grandior of Cassiodorus,* early in the eighth century by an illuminator with Italian training acquired in some Anglo-Saxon monastery, probably Jarrow. The same original must have been seen and "translated" a few years earlier by an artist trained in the abstract Hiberno-Saxon manner; his version appears as the *St. Matthew* figure in the *Book of Lindisfarne* (FIG. **8-10**). The Ezra and the architectural environment of the *Codex Amiatinus* are closely linked with the pictorial illusionism of Late Antiquity. The style is essentially that of the brush; the color, although applied here and there in flat planes, is blended smoothly to model the figure and to provide gradual transitions from light to dark. This procedure must have been continued in the Mediterranean world throughout the Early Middle Ages, despite the formalizing into line that we have seen taking place in mosaics. But the Hiberno-Saxon artist of the *Lindisfarne Matthew,* trained in the use of hard, evenly stressed line, apparently knew nothing of the illusionistic, pictorial technique nor, for that matter, of the representation of the human figure. Although he carefully takes over the pose, he interprets the form in terms of line exclusively, "abstracting" the unfamiliar tonal scheme of his model into a patterned figure not unlike what we see in the king, queen, and jack of a deck of cards. The soft folds of drapery in the

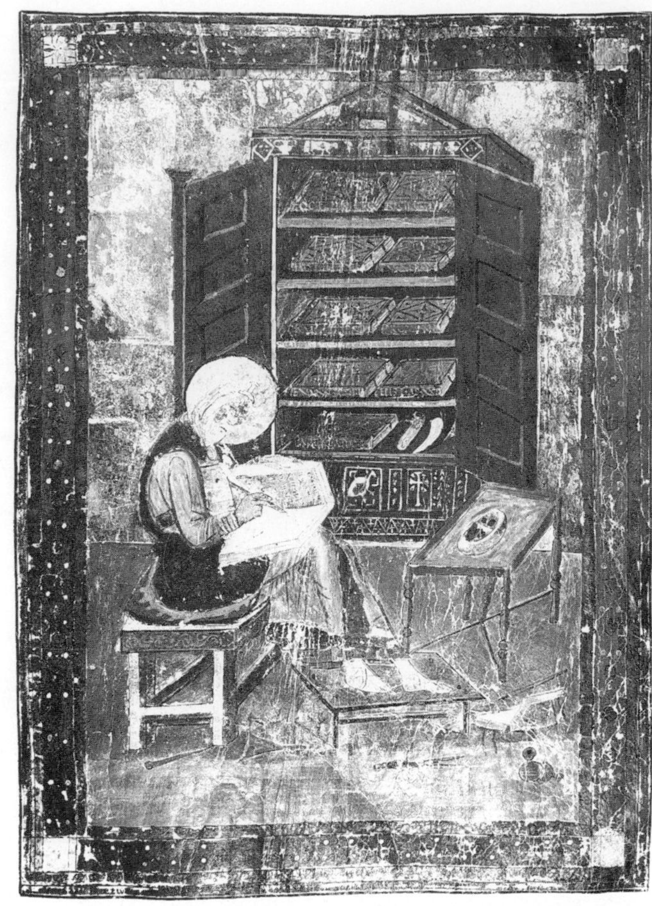

8-9 *The Scribe Ezra Rewriting the Sacred Records,* from the *Codex Amiatinus,* Jarrow, early eighth century. Approx. 14″ × 10″. Biblioteca Medicea-Laurenziana, Florence.

Ezra become, in the *St. Matthew,* a series of sharp, regularly spaced, curving lines. No modeling is used; no variations occur in light and shade. The long training in the peculiar linear style of barbarian art made it necessary for the *Lindisfarne* artist to convert the strange Mediterranean forms into the linear idiom familiar to him; he finds before him a tonal *picture* and makes of it a linear *pattern.*

The Medieval artist did not go to nature for models but to a prototype—another image, a statue, or a picture in a book. Each copy might be one in a long line of copies, and, in some cases, we can trace these copies back to a lost original, inferring its former existence. The Medieval practice of copying pictures is closely related to the copying of books, especially sacred books like the Scriptures and the books used in the liturgy. The Medieval scribe or illuminator (before the thirteenth century, most often a monk) could have reasoned that just as the text of a holy book must be copied faithfully if the copy also is to be holy, so must the pictures be rendered faithfully. Of course, in the process of copying, mistakes are made, and while scholars seek to purge the book of these textual "corruptions," "mistakes" in the copying of pictures yield new pictorial styles, or represent the confluence of different styles, as in the relationship of the *Codex Amiatinus* and the *Book of Lindisfarne.* In any event, one should realize that the style of Medieval images, whether in sculpture or in painting, was the result of copying from sources thought to have sacred authority, not from natural models. Thus, one learned what was true from authorities who declared the truth—the Scriptures and the fathers of the Church—and one painted "true" pictures or sculpted "true" statues from authoritative images. To question authority on one's own, to investigate "nature" on one's own, would be to question God's truth as revealed and interpreted. Such actions would be blasphemy and heresy. It would be wrong, however, to leave the impression that dependence on authority in art is characteristic solely of the Middle Ages. In the Renaissance and since, and certainly today, new styles gain sudden authority and win widespread reverence and imitation, even for reasons that differ from those operative in the Middle Ages.

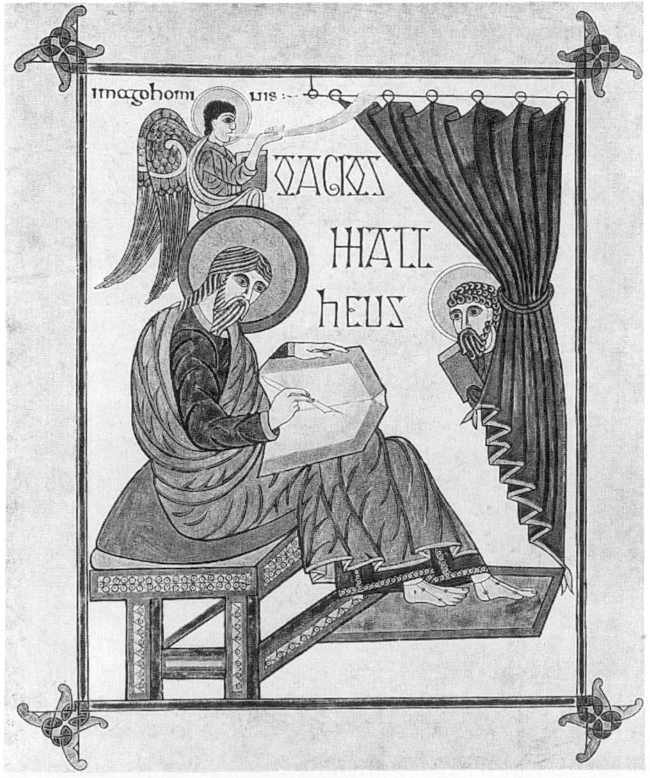

8-10 *St. Matthew,* from the *Book of Lindisfarne,* from Northumberland, England, late seventh century. Approx. 11″ × 9″. British Library, London.

Sculpture

The high crosses of Ireland, erected between the eighth and the tenth centuries, are exceptional by their mass and scale within the art of the Early Middle Ages, which, as we have seen, is confined almost exclusively to works diminutive and portable. Indeed, the crosses are unique. These majestic monuments, some 17 feet in height or taller, preside over burial grounds adjoining the ruins of monasteries at sites widely distributed throughout the Irish countryside. Though several of these crosses have been found in England, they are regarded as characteristically Irish in form and origin. The Celtic cross has become the very symbol of Christian Ireland in both religious and secular iconography. Freestanding, unattached to any architectural fabric, the high crosses have the imposing unity, weight, and presence of both building and statue, architecture and sculpture combined. The *High Cross of Muiredach* at Monasterboice (FIG. **8-11**), though a late representative of the type (dated by inscription 923), can serve as standard for the form. The cross element crowns a four-sided shaft of stone, which rises from a base with sloping sides. The concave, looping arms of the cross are joined by four arcs, which form a circle. The arms expand into squared terminals (see the initial page of the *Lindisfarne* Gospels, FIG. 8-8). The circle-intersected cross is the characteristic figure that identifies the type as Celtic. The earlier high crosses bear abstract designs, especially the familiar interlace pattern. But the later ones, such as this, have figured panels, with scenes from the life of Christ, or, occasionally, events from the life of some Celtic saint, like Columcille. In addition, fantastic animals and grotesque human figures sometimes are portrayed. Here, at the center of

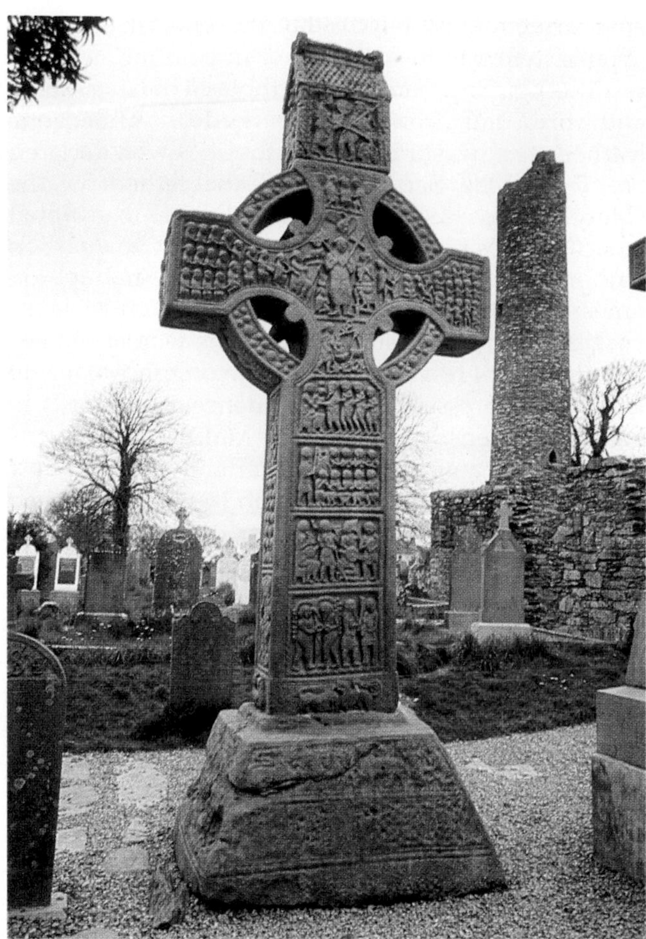

8-11 *High Cross of Muiredach,* Monasterboice, County Louth, Ireland, 923. Approx. 16′ high.

the transom of the cross, stands the risen Christ as judge of the world, the hope of the neighboring dead. The iconographic and stylistic sources of the figural carvings are far-flung: Early Christian art, the art of Coptic (Christian) Egypt, the animal motifs of the Near East and the Migration period—all evidence of the cosmopolitanism of Irish culture in the period of its great flourishing. The high crosses are the monumental, consummate expression of the religious and esthetic values of Hiberno-Saxon creativity, which, by the twelfth century, was extinct.

THE CAROLINGIAN PERIOD

The remarkable historical phenomenon now called "Charlemagne's renovation"—an energetic, brilliant emulation of the art, culture, and political ideals of Christian Rome—occurred during the late eighth and early ninth century. Out of the confusions attendant on the migrations and settlement of the barbarians, Charlemagne's immediate forerunners built, by force and political acumen, a Frankish empire that contained or controlled a large part of western Europe. Charlemagne, like Constantine, whom he often consciously imitated, wished to create a unified Christendom as a visible empire. He was crowned by the pope in Rome in 800 as head of the entity that became the Holy Roman Empire, which, waxing and waning over a thousand years and with many hiatuses, existed as a force in central Europe until its destruction by Napoleon in 1806.

Charlemagne was a sincere admirer of learning and the arts. To make his empire as splendid as that of Rome (he thought of himself as successor to the caesars), he invited to his court at Aachen the best minds and the finest craftsmen of western Europe and the Byzantine East. Although unlettered and scarcely able to write, he could speak Latin fluently and loved the discourses he frequently held with the learned men he gathered around him. Charlemagne also must have admired the splendid works created in the scriptorium of the school he established in his palace. One of his dearest projects had been the recovery of the true text of the Bible, which, through centuries of miscopying by ignorant scribes, had become almost hopelessly corrupt. Part of the great project, undertaken by the renowned scholar Alcuin of York at the new monastery at Tours, was the correction of the actual script used, which, in the hands of the scribes, had become almost unreadable. The Carolingian rehabilitation of the inherited Latin script produced a clear, precise system of letters; the letters on this page are descended from the alphabet renovated by the scribes of Tours.

Painting and Illumination

Charlemagne, his successors, and the scholars under their patronage imported whole libraries from Italy and Byzantium. The illustrations in these books must have astonished northern painters, some of whom had been trained in the Hiberno-Saxon manner of pattern making, while others were schooled in the weak and inept Frankish styles of the seventh and eighth centuries. Here, they were confronted suddenly with a sophisticated realism that somehow had survived from the Late Antique period amidst all the denaturing tendencies that followed.

The famous *Coronation Gospels* (the *Gospel Book of Charlemagne*, formerly in the Imperial Treasury in Vienna) may have been a favorite of Charlemagne himself; an old tradition records that it was found on the knees of the dead emperor when, in the year 1000, Otto III had the imperial tomb at Aachen opened. The picture of *St. Matthew* composing his gospel (FIG. **8-12**) descends from ancient depictions in sculpture

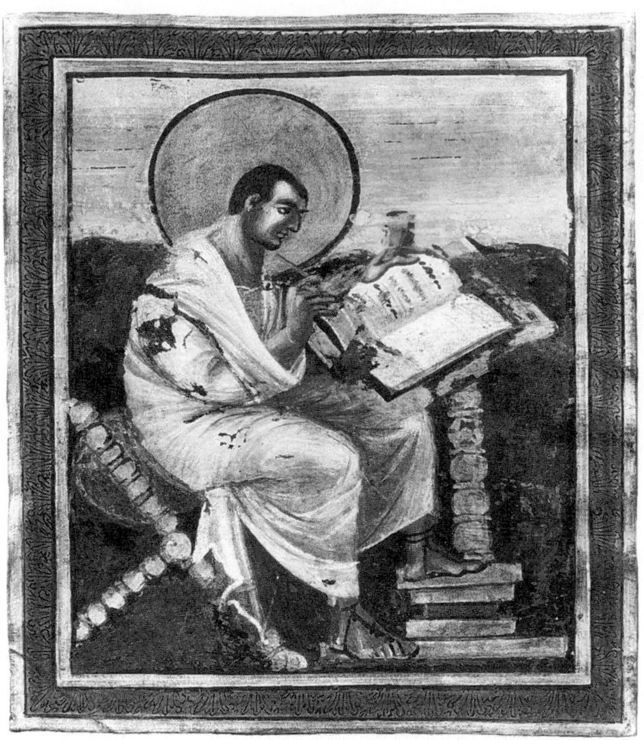

8-12 *St. Matthew,* from the *Coronation Gospels* (the *Gospel Book of Charlemagne*), c. 800–810. Approx. 9″ × 6¾″. Kunsthistorisches Museum, Vienna.

and painting of an inspired philosopher or poet seated and writing. Its technique is of the same antiquity—deft, illusionistic brushwork that easily and accurately defines the masses of the drapery as they wrap and enfold the body beneath. The acanthus of the frame of the "picture window" recalls the fourth Pompeian style (see FIG. 6-33); the landscape background is classicizing, and the whole composition seems utterly out of place in the north in the ninth century. How were the native artists to receive this new influence, so alien to what they had known and so strong as to make their own practice suddenly obsolete?

The style evident in the *Coronation Gospels* was by no means the only one that appeared suddenly in the Carolingian world. A wide variety of styles in all stages of change from Antique prototypes were distributed through the court schools and the monasteries—a bewildering array, one can believe, for the natives, who attempted to appropriate them by copying them as accurately as possible. Thus, Carolingian painting is extremely diverse and uneven, and classification becomes a difficult matter of ascertaining prototypes and the descendants of prototypes. If *St. Matthew* of the *Coronation Gospels* was painted by a Frank, rather than an Italian or a Byzantine, it is an amazing feat of approximation, since, except for the work of the Jarrow copyist, nothing is known that could have prepared the way for it in the Hiberno-Saxon or Frankish West.

Another *St. Matthew,* in a gospel book made for Archbishop Ebbo of Reims (FIG. **8-13**), may be an interpretation of a prototype very similar to the one used by the *Coronation Gospels* master, for it resembles it in pose and in brushwork technique. But there the resemblance stops. The Classical calm and solidity have been replaced by an energy that amounts to frenzy, and the frail saint almost leaps under its impulse. His hair stands on end, the folds of his drapery writhe and vibrate, the landscape behind him rears up alive. He appears in frantic haste to take down what his inspiration (the tiny angel in the upper-right-hand corner) dictates. All fidelity to bodily proportions or structure is forsaken in the artist's effort to concentrate on the act of writing; the head, hands, inkhorn, pen, and book are the focus of the composition. This presentation contrasts strongly with the settled pose of the *Matthew* of the *Coronation Gospels* with its even stress, so that no part of the composition starts out at us to seize our attention. The native power of expression is unmistakable and will become one of the important distinguishing traits of Late

8-13 *St. Matthew,* from the *Ebbo Gospels* (the *Gospel Book of Archbishop Ebbo of Reims*), Hautvilliers (near Reims), France, c. 816–835. Approx. 10″ × 8″. Bibliothèque Nationale, Paris.

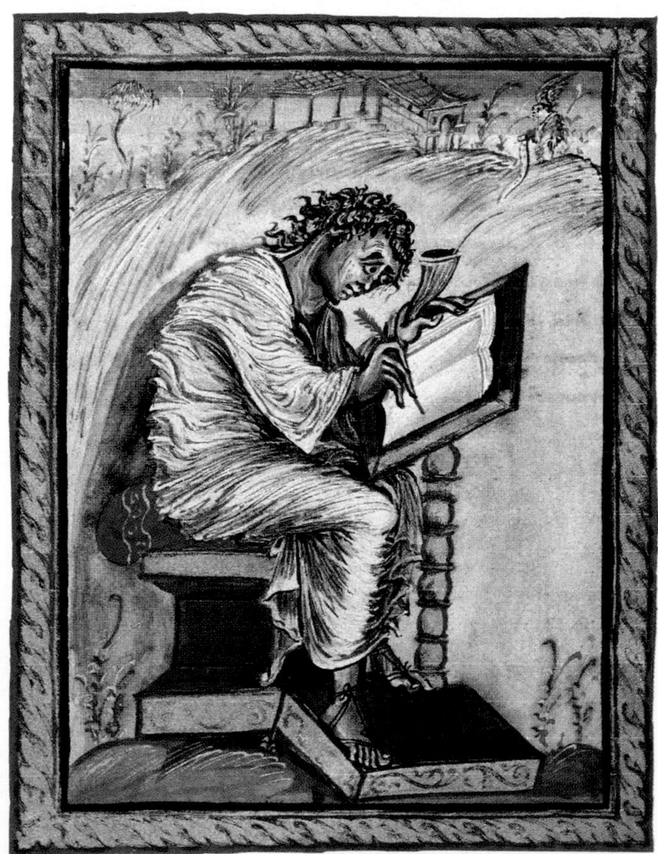

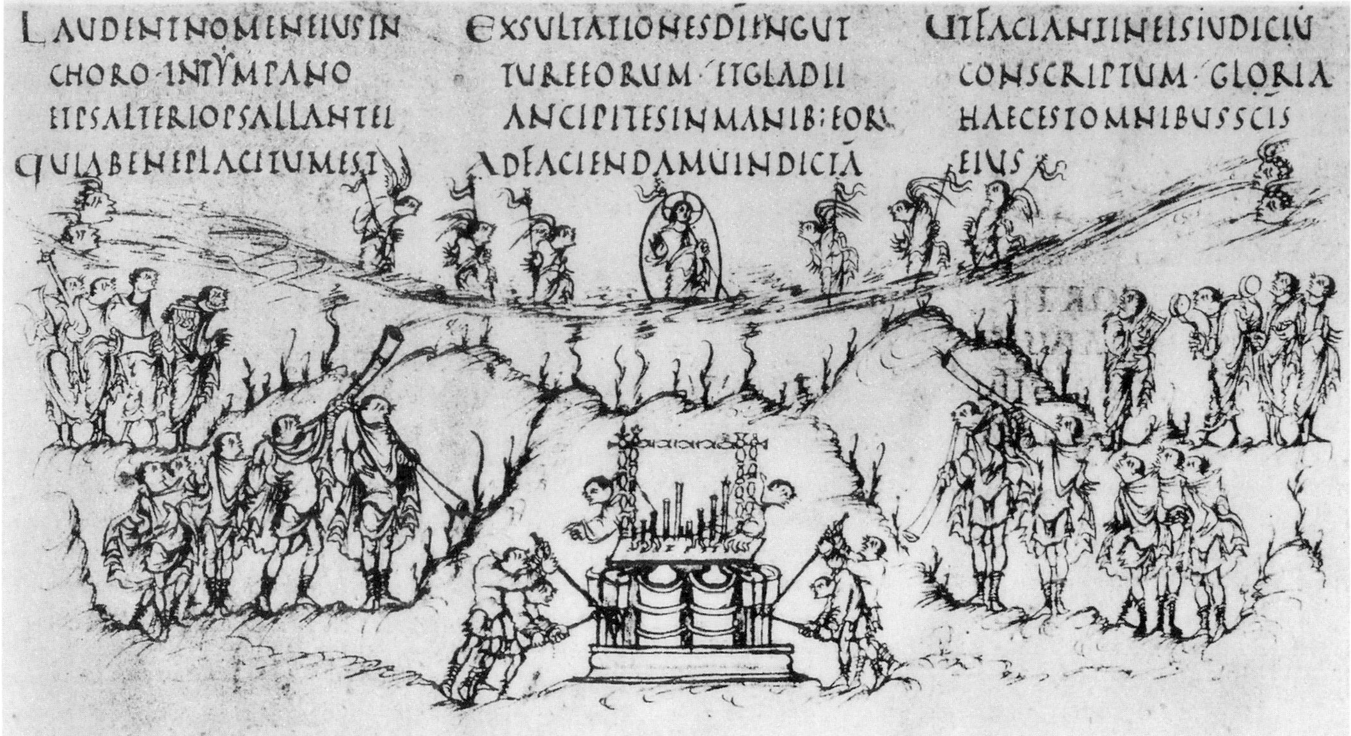

8-14 *Psalm 150,* from the *Utrecht Psalter,* from Hautvilliers, France, c. 830. $4\frac{3}{4}'' \times 9\frac{1}{2}''$. University Library, Utrecht, Netherlands.

Medieval art. Just as the painter of the *Lindisfarne Matthew* (FIG. 8-10) transformed the *Ezra* portrait in the *Codex Amiatinus* (FIG. 8-9) into something original and strong, translating its classicizing manner into his own Hiberno-Saxon idiom, so the Ebbo artist translated his Classical prototype into a Carolingian vernacular that left little Classical substance. The four pictures should be studied carefully and compared.

Narrative illustration, so richly developed in Early Christian and Byzantine art, was revived by the Carolingians, and many fully illuminated books (some, large Bibles) were produced. One of the most extraordinary and enjoyable of all Medieval manuscripts is the famous *Utrecht Psalter,* written at Hautvilliers near Reims, France, about 830. The text, in three columns, reproduces the Psalms of David and is profusely illustrated by pen-and-ink drawings in the margins. The example shown in FIG. **8-14** depicts figures acting out Psalm 150, in which the psalmist exhorts us to praise the name of God in song and with timbrel, trumpet, and organ. The style shows a vivid animation of much the same kind as the *St. Matthew* of the *Ebbo Gospels* and may have been produced in the same school. The bodies are tense, shoulders hunched, heads thrust forward. The spontaneity of their actions and the rapid, sketchy technique with which they are rendered convey the same nervous vitality as the figure in the *Ebbo Gospels.* From details of the figures, their dress, and accessories, scholars feel certain that the artist was following one or more manuscripts compiled some four hundred years earlier. His interest in simple human emotions and actions, the pantomimic skill in the variety and descriptiveness of gesture, however, are essentially Medieval characteristics, although they begin in Early Christian art. Note, for example, how the two musicians playing the pipe organ shout at their helpers to pump air more strenuously. This candid observation of human behavior, often in unguarded moments, was to lend both truth and charm to the art of the Late Middle Ages.

Craft Art

To our knowledge, little or no monumental sculpture was produced in the Carolingian period. The traditional taste for sumptuously wrought and portable metal objects, which created the barbarian works we have seen, persisted under Charlemagne and his successors and was responsible for the production of numerous precious and beautiful works, like the book cover of the *Codex Aureus of St. Emmeram* (FIG. **8-15**). Dating from the second half of the ninth century, this book cover probably originated at either the St. Denis or Reims court of Charles the Bald, a grandson of Charlemagne. Its golden surface is set with pearls and precious jewels. Within the inscribed, squared cross, Christ in Majesty appears in an attitude not far removed from that in the apse mosaic of San Vitale (FIG. 7-38)—an example of the persistence of types and attitudes from Early Christian art into subsequent periods. The Four Evangelists are seated around Christ, outside the cross, and four scenes from Christ's life are portrayed above and below the saints. In general, manuscript illumination provides the generative prototypes for ivory and metalwork. Here, the style of the figures echoes that of the *Ebbo Gospels* and the *Utrecht Psalter,* although it is modified by influences from other Carolingian schools. No trace of the intricate interlace patterns of Hiberno-Saxon art remains, although the complex and delicate floral filigree clustering about the border jewels and enamels recalls them and provides a foil for the classicizing figure style. At the core of the Carolingian renovation, the translated, classicizing style of Italy prevails, in keeping with the tastes and aspirations of the great Frankish emperor who fixed his admiring gaze on the culture of the south.

Metalcraft was extended to produce works much larger than the book cover, while maintaining the same principles in terms of materials, methods of production, design, and figure style. An example is the magnificent golden altar (the *Paliotto*) of the church of Sant' Ambrogio in Milan (FIG. **8-16**). Shaped like a kind of large tomb, the altar was designed to contain the bones of St. Ambrose, an early bishop of Milan and one of the fathers of the Latin church. Its four sides are ornamented with the jeweler's workmanship and lavish detail that we find in the *Codex Aureus* cover. Like that work, the *Paliotto* is divided into framed compartments of geometric simplicity and formality. Its gold, silver, and precious and semiprecious stones are set forth in exquisitely worked filigree to honor (in the central panels) the enthroned Christ, the Signs of the Evangelists, and the Twelve Apostles, all wrought in the classicizing figure style of the Carolingian renovation. Inscriptions on the back of the altar, where scenes from the life of Saint Ambrose are found, tell us that the donor was Archbishop Angilbert II, who governed the church in Milan between 824 and 859, which gives us a date for the monument. St. Ambrose places a crown on the bishop's head; he also places a crown on the head of the designer of the altar and its principal artist, a certain "Master Wolvinius," whose name suggests his

8-15 *Christ in Majesty, Four Evangelists, and Scenes from the Life of Christ,* cover of the *Codex Aureus of St. Emmeram,* c. 870. Gold set with pearls and precious stones, 17″ × 13″. Bayerische Staatsbibliothek, Munich.

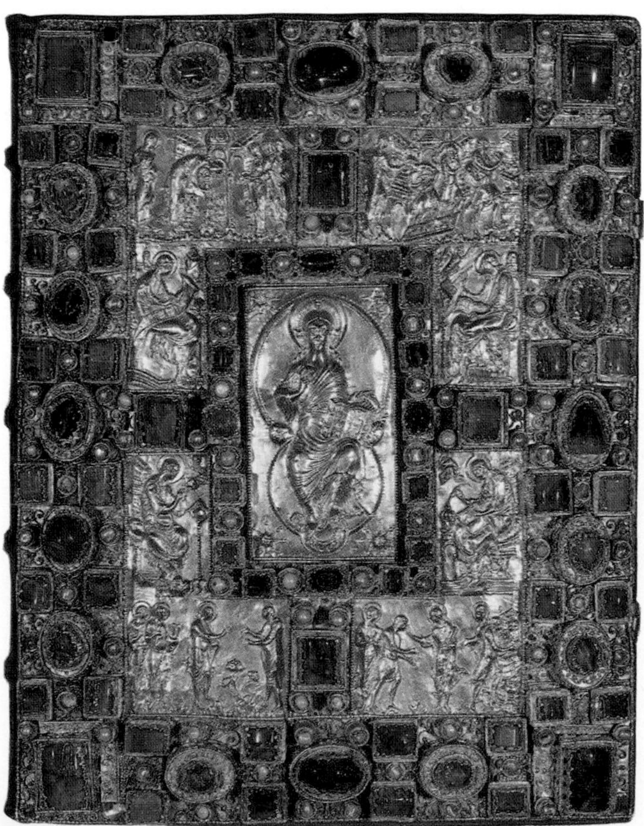

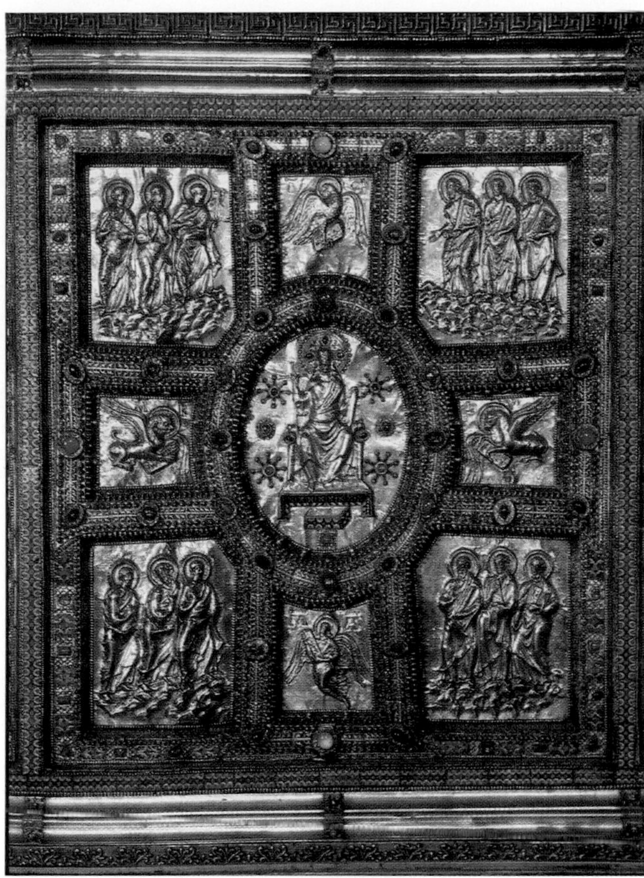

8-16 MASTER WOLVINIUS, detail of the *Paliotto* (golden altar), Sant' Ambrogio, Milan, early ninth century. Gold, silver, enamel, precious and semiprecious stones; entire altar 3′ high, 7′ long, 4′ deep.

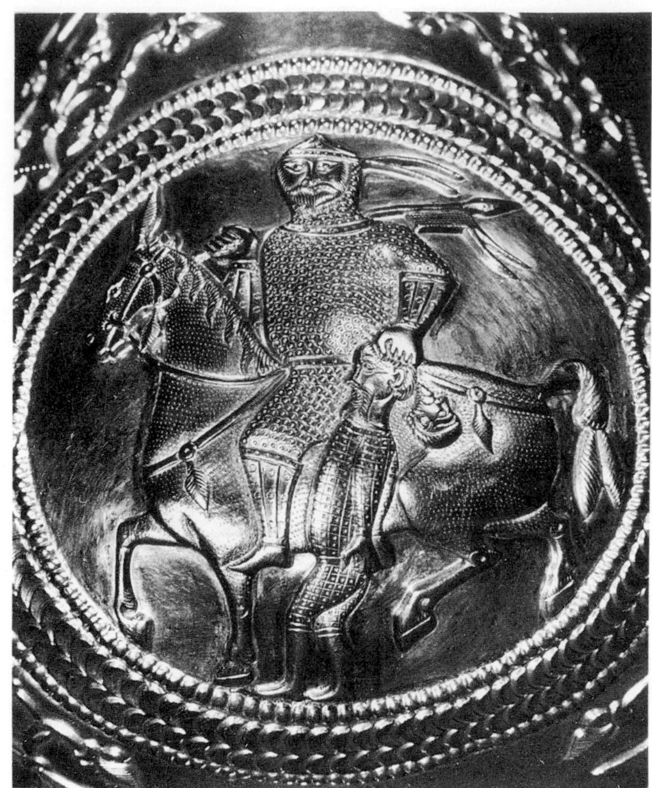

8-17 *Mounted Warrior with Captive* (detail of gold vessel; vessel $8\frac{3}{4}''$ high), from the Nagy-szent-miklós treasure hoard found at Sinicolaul, Romania, probably ninth century. Kunsthistorisches Museum, Vienna.

east Frankish origins and that he may have been trained in the main centers of Carolingian art. Whatever the questions as to its sources, this work of WOLVINIUS and his fellow craftsmen remains perhaps the supreme masterpiece of the Age of Charlemagne.

Beyond the western regions under Carolingian control, migrations of warlike peoples from the east kept eastern and central Europe in turmoil throughout the ninth century. Mounted nomads rode the great grasslands as the Vikings rode the western seas. Charlemagne managed to repulse the Avars, who had long dominated the Hungarian plain. Like the migrating peoples in general, the Avars were skilled metal-craftsmen. A detail of a vase from a hoard of golden vessels left by them (a buried treasure never reclaimed) is illustrated here (FIG. **8-17**). Made of beaten gold, it bears a medallion with the image of a mounted, armored warrior. Posed both frontally and in profile, an Archaic convention we have seen in ancient art, the warrior carries a spear over his right shoulder, and seizes a disarmed man with his left hand; the thrown-back head of another figure which appears below the horseman's left wrist, may belong to a man he already has killed. The dominating bulk of the fierce victor is made larger by the puny stature of his victims, another Archaic convention we have seen in the art of Mesopotamia (FIG. 2-24) and Egypt (FIG. 3-43). Here is the very image of the times, when armed, pagan horsemen swept all before them in endless war and depredation. Yet the art of the Avars was influenced by the art of the settled and more civilized nations they came in contact with; the bead and fish-scale molding of the medallion frame and the floral motifs of the shoulder and base of the vessel are derived from Byzantine and Sassanian (Late Persian) art. Whether inspired by the Christian God, or the god of war, the craft art of the Early Middle Ages achieves a rare distinction. The priest and the warrior are the patrons of the craftsman.

Architecture

In his eagerness to reestablish the imperial past, Charlemagne also encouraged the revival of Roman building techniques; in architecture, as in sculpture and painting, innovations made in the reinterpretation of earlier Roman-Christian sources became fundamental to Medieval designs. Perhaps *importation* is a more appropriate term here than *revival*, as the Mediterranean tradition of stonemasonry could never have been more than an admirable curiosity to northern builders. Although northern Europe was dotted with Roman colonial towns that contained many large and impressive stone structures, the Germanic tribes had always relied on the vast forests to supply them with building materials; northern architecture was a timber architecture and continued to be so well into the Middle Ages. The typical northern European dwelling was a timber-frame structure (FIG. **8-18**) that, in its essentials, has survived into our time. Its basic structural unit is the *bay*, which is constructed of four posts placed at the corners of a rectangle and interconnected and braced against each other with horizontal or oblique members. This type of unit is self-

8-18 Conjectural reconstruction of an Iron Age house on foundations excavated at Ezinge, Holland. (After W. Horn.)

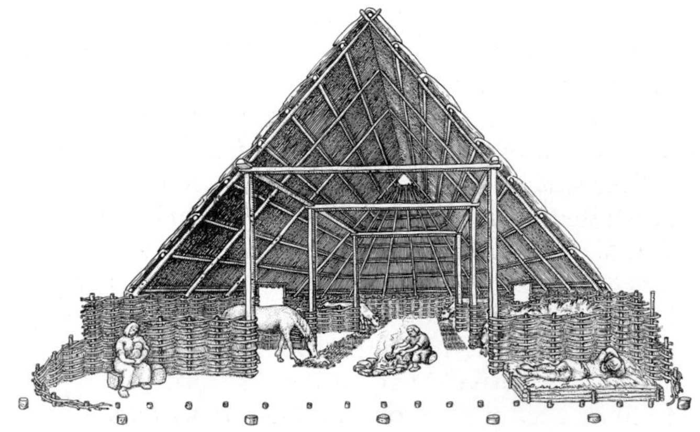

supporting; it can be roofed and, depending on the desired size of the building, multiplied at will. Thus, the interior of such a structure is characterized by a repetition of identical units that move in orderly progression down the length of the building. The plan of such a building is related to the size and proportions of one of its bays in that the bay is the *module,* or basic unit of measurement, and the structure is a multiple of that unit.

Charlemagne's adoption of southern building principles for the construction of his palaces and churches was epoch-making for the subsequent development of the architecture of northern Europe. For his models, he went to Rome and Ravenna—one, the former heart of the Roman Empire, which he wanted to revive, the other, the long-term western outpost of Byzantine might and splendor, which he wanted to emulate in his own capital at Aachen. Ravenna fell to the Lombards in 751 but was wrested from them only a few years later by the Frankish king, Pepin the Short, founder of the Carolingian dynasty and father of Charlemagne. Pepin donated the former Byzantine exarchate to the pope and thus founded the papacy's temporal power, which was to last until the late nineteenth century.

In 789, Charlemagne visited Ravenna, and historians have long thought that he chose one of its churches as the model for the Palatine Chapel of his own palace at Aachen. But although the plan of this structure (FIG. **8-19**) shows a resemblance to that of San Vitale (FIG. 7-33), recent study disproves a direct relationship between the two buildings. Nevertheless, a comparison of the two buildings is instructive. The Aachen plan is simpler; the apselike extensions reaching from the central octagon into the ambulatory have been omitted, so that the two main units stand in greater independence of one another. This solution may lack the subtle sophistication of the Byzantine building, but it gains geometric clarity. A view of the interior of the Palatine Chapel (FIG. **8-20**) shows that the "floating" quality of San Vitale has been converted into blunt massiveness and stiffened into solid geometric form. The conversion of a complex and subtle Byzantine prototype into a building that expresses robust strength and clear structural articulation foreshadows the architecture of the eleventh and twelfth centuries and the style we call Romanesque.

Charlemagne's dependence on Roman models is illustrated by a fascinating survival from his time, the Torhalle (gatehouse, FIG. **8-21**) of the Lorsch Monastery, which dates from about 800. Originally built as a freestanding structure in the atrium of the now-lost monastic church, this decorative little entrance gate is a distant relative of the Arch of Constantine (FIG. 6-95) by way of its reinterpretation in Christian terms

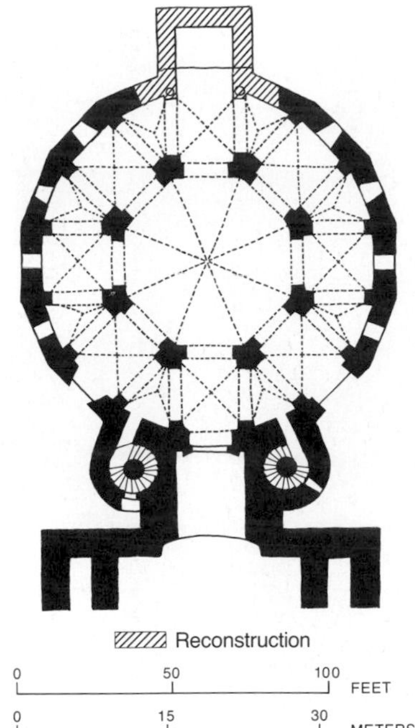

8-19 Restored plan of the Palatine Chapel of Charlemagne, Aachen, West Germany, 792–805.

8-20 Interior of the Palatine Chapel of Charlemagne.

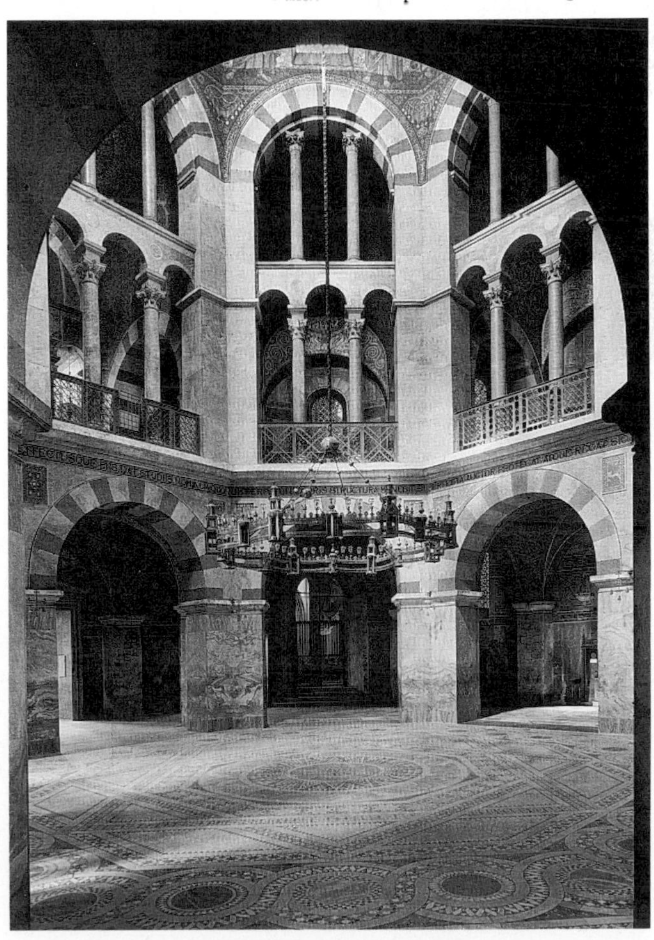

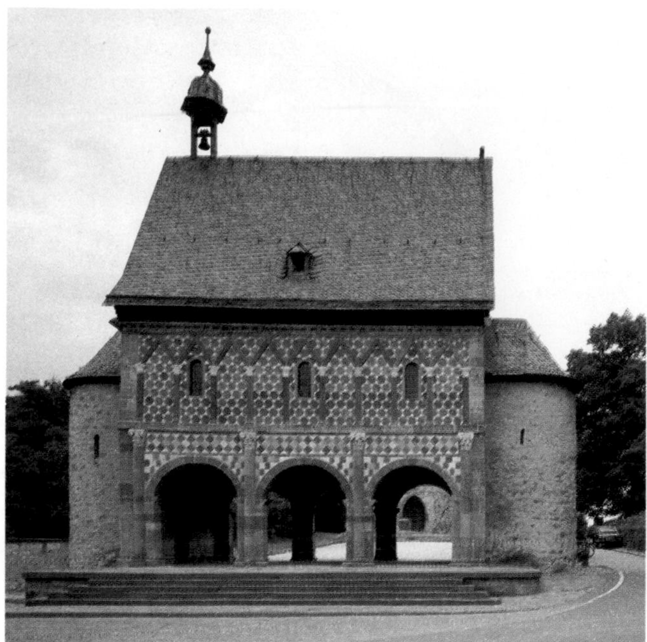

8-21 Torhalle (gatehouse), Lorsch, West Germany, *c.* 800.

of the entrance to the atrium of Old St. Peter's in Rome (if, in fact, the entrance to that structure resembled the reconstruction shown in FIG. 7-6). To Charlemagne, both the arch and the atrium entrance could have been symbols of Christian triumph over paganism. The triple-arched gateway on the lower level closely follows the design of Roman triumphal arches, with its column-arch combination, the fairly close copies of Late Roman capitals, and the decorative treatment of the flat wall surfaces with colored inlays of cream and pink stone in imitation of the Roman *opus reticulatum.* However, the columns support a decorative stringcourse instead of a full entablature, and what happens above it on the second level no longer has anything to do with triumphal arches. Instead of bearing the traditional dedicatory inscription, the second level is articulated with pseudo-Ionic pilasters that carry a zigzag of ornamental moldings, and the opus reticulatum has been converted into a decorative pattern of hexagons and triangles that form star shapes. Finally, the steeply pitched, timber roof that shelters a chapel dedicated to St. Michael unmistakably stamps this gatehouse as a northern building. Still, the source of inspiration is clear, and if the final product no longer closely resembles the original, it is due to the fact that it is not a copy but a free and fanciful interpretation of its model.

The models that carried the greatest authority for Charlemagne and his builders were those from the Christian phase of the late Roman Empire, and it was the adoption of the Early Christian basilica, rather than the domed, central plan of Byzantine churches, that was crucial to the subsequent development of Western church architecture in general and to the Romanesque style in particular. Several churches of the basilican type were built in northern Europe during the reign of Charlemagne, but none has survived. Nevertheless, it is possible to reconstruct the appearance of some of them with fair accuracy. A number of these structures appear to have followed their Early Christian models quite closely; the abbey church of Fulda (begun in 802) derives directly from Old St. Peter's and other Roman basilicas with transepts. But in other instances, Carolingian builders subjected the basilica plan to some very significant modifications, converting it into a much more complex form.

The study of a fascinating Carolingian document, the ideal plan for a monastery preserved in the library of St. Gall, Switzerland (FIG. **8-22**), may provide some insight into the motivations of the Carolingian planner. The monasteries were of central importance in the revival of learning. Monasticism held that the most perfect Christian life should be led in seclusion, removed from the temptations of ordinary life. In 526, Benedict had adapted the earlier regulations to the needs of western Europe. The Benedictine Rule, which won out over Irish monasticism and which demanded, among other things, vows of poverty, chastity, and obedience, provided the basic organization for most Western monasteries. Daily life was rigidly controlled, and each monastic community was self-sufficient. About 819, a schematic plan for one such community was copied from a lost original, probably designed by the abbot of Reichenau, and sent to the abbot of St. Gall for use as a guide in his planned rebuilding of that monastery.

Near the center, dominating everything, was the abbey church, with the cloister (not unlike the early colonnaded atrium) at one side. Around the cloister were grouped the most essential buildings: dormitory, refectory, kitchen, and storage rooms. Other buildings, including an infirmary, school, guest house, bakery, brewery, and workshops, were grouped around this central core of church and cloister. That the scheme may have been meant to be more than an ideal and actually to have been built is suggested by Walter Horn's recent discovery that the original plan must have been laid out on a modular base of $2\frac{1}{2}$ feet and by the fact that parts or multiples of this module have been used consistently throughout the plan. Therefore, the width of the nave, indicated on the plan as 40 feet, would be equal to 16 modules, the length of each monk's bed to $2\frac{1}{2}$ modules, and the width of paths in the vegetable garden to $1\frac{1}{4}$ modules.

Although the church is essentially a three-aisled basilica, it has features not found in any Early Christian churches. Perhaps most obvious is the addition of a second apse on the west end of the building. The

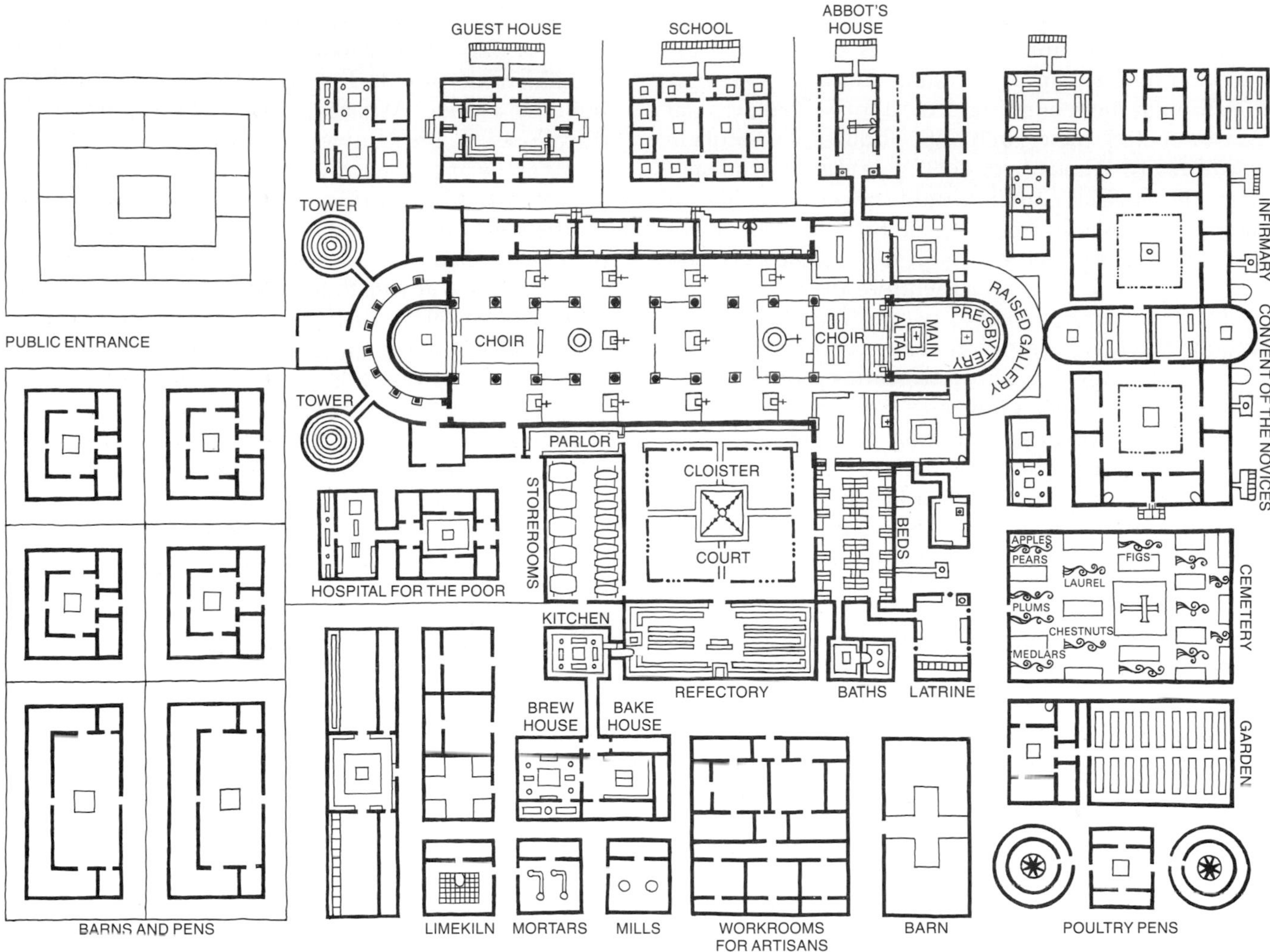

8-22 Schematic plan for a monastery at St. Gall, Switzerland, *c.* 819. (Redrawn after a ninth-century manuscript.)

origin and purpose of this feature have never been explained satisfactorily, but it remained a characteristic regional element of German churches to the eleventh century. Not quite as evident, but much more important to the subsequent development of church architecture in the north, is the fact that the transept is as wide as the nave. Early Christian builders had not been concerned with proportional relationships; they assembled the various portions of their buildings only in accordance with the dictates of liturgical needs. On the St. Gall plan, however, the various parts of the building have been related to each other by a geometric scheme that ties them together into a tight and cohesive unit. Equalizing the widths of nave and transept automatically makes the area in which they cross (the *crossing*) a square. This feature is shared by most Carolingian churches. But the St. Gall planner also took the subsequent steps that became fundamental to the development of Romanesque architecture: he used the crossing square as the unit of measurement for the remainder of the church plan. The arms of the transept are equal to 1 crossing square, the distance between transept and apse is 1 crossing square, and the nave is $4\frac{1}{2}$ crossing squares long. The fact that the aisles are half as wide as the nave integrates all parts of the church in a plan that is clear, rational, lucid, and extremely orderly.

The St. Gall plan reflects a medieval way of thinking that is important for Romanesque art and architecture. As a guide for the builder of an abbey, it expresses the authority of the Benedictine Rule and serves as a kind of prototype. In the interest of clarity and orderliness, the rule is worked out with systematic care. All units are balanced as the site is divided and subdivided. (This parallels the medieval invention of that most convenient device, the division of books into chapters and subchapters.) The neat "squaring" that characterizes the St. Gall plan and the principle of the balance of clearly defined, simple units will dominate Romanesque architectural design. The eagerness of the medieval mind to explain the Christian faith in terms of an orderly, rationalistic philosophy built on carefully distinguished propositions and well-planned arguments finds visual expression in the plan of St. Gall.

Although the rebuilding project for St. Gall was not consummated, the church of St. Riquier at Centula in northeastern France (FIG. **8-23**) gives us some idea of what the St. Gall church would have looked like. A monastery church like that of St. Gall, the now-destroyed St. Riquier was built toward the very end of the eighth century and therefore predates the St. Gall plan by approximately twenty years. Our illustration, taken from a seventeenth-century copy of a much older drawing, shows a feature not indicated on the plan of St. Gall but most likely common to all Carolingian churches—multiple, integrated towers. The St. Gall plan shows only two towers on the west side of the church, but they stand apart from it in the manner of the Italian campaniles. If we assume a tower above the crossing, the silhouette of St. Gall would have shown three towers rising above the nave. St. Riquier had six towers (not all are shown in the illustration) built directly onto or rising from the building proper. As large, vertical, cubic, and cylindrical masses, these towers rose above the horizontal roofline, balancing each other in two groups of three at each end of the basilican nave. Round stair towers on the west end provided access to the upper stories of the so-called *westwork* (entrance structure) and to the big, spired tower that balanced the spired tower above the eastern crossing. Such a grouping of three towers at the west, quite characteristic of churches built in the regions dominated by the Carolingians and their successors in German lands, probably foreshadows, in rudimentary form, the two-tower façades that were to become an almost universal standard in Late Romanesque and Gothic architecture. The St. Riquier design, particularly the silhouette with its multiple integrated towers, was highly influential, especially in Germany. On the second floor, the towered westwork contained a complete chapel flanked by aisles—a small upper church that could be used for parish services. The main floor of the building was reserved for the use of the clergy. (One must remember that this was a monastery church.) A gallery opened onto the main nave, and from it, on occasion, the emperor and his entourage could watch and participate in the service below.

8-23 Monastery church of St. Riquier, Centula, France, *c.* 800. (Engraving made in 1612 after a now-destroyed, eleventh-century miniature.)

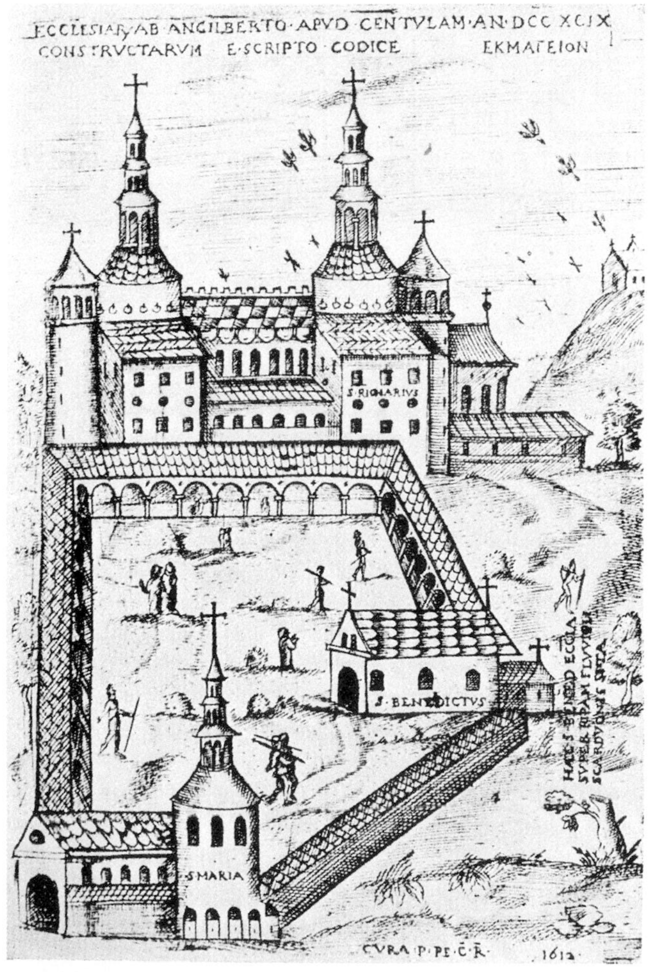

THE OTTONIAN PERIOD

Charlemagne's empire survived him by less than thirty years. Under his three grandsons, Charles the Bald, Lothair, and Louis the German, the Carolingian Empire was partitioned (by 843) into western, central, and eastern areas, very roughly foreshadowing the later sections of France, Lorraine, and the Germanies. Intensified incursions by the Vikings in the west helped bring about the collapse of the Carolingians and the suspension of their great cultural effort. The breakup of the empire into weak kingdoms, ineffectual against the invasions, brought a time of darkness and confusion that was perhaps even deeper than the seventh and eighth centuries. The scourge of the Vikings in the west was complemented by the invasions of the Magyars in the east and by the plundering and piracy of the Saracen corsairs in the Mediterranean. Only in the mid-tenth century did the eastern part of the former empire consolidate under the rule of a new Saxon line of German emperors called, after the names of the three most illustrious members of the family, the "Ottonians." The three Ottos made headway against the invaders from the east, remained free

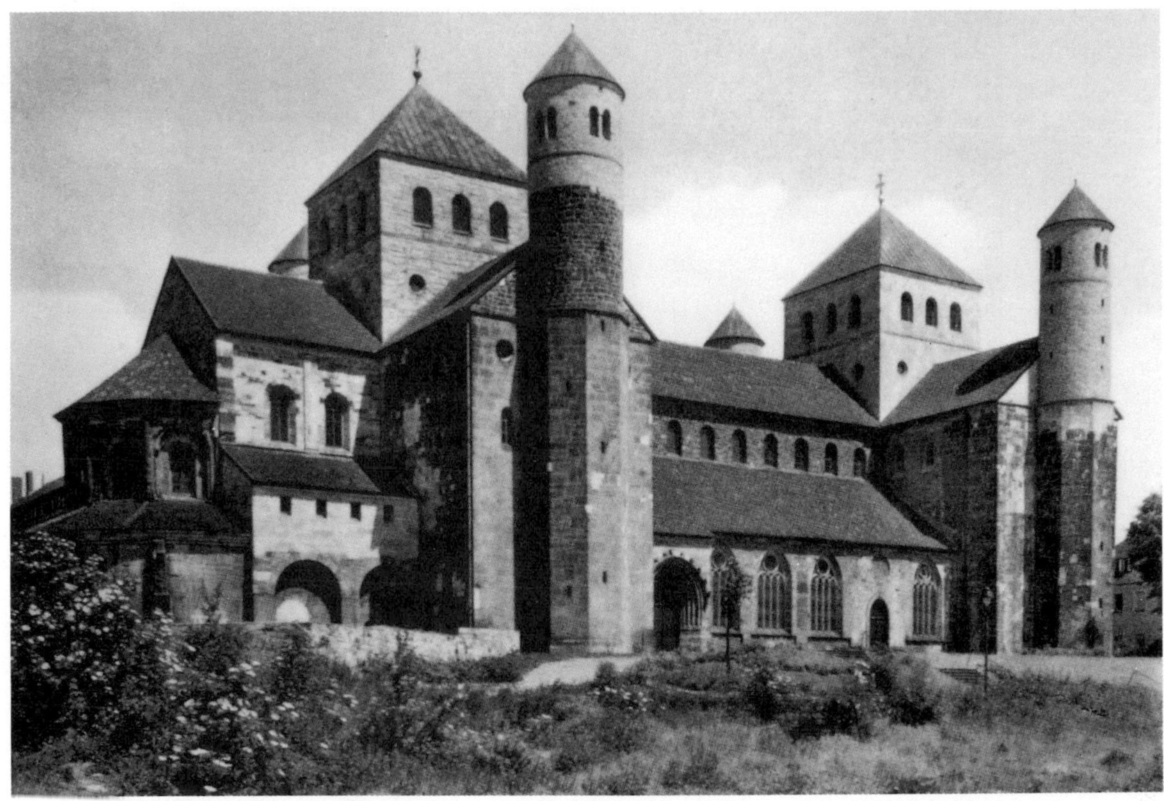

8-24 Abbey church of St. Michael, Hildesheim, West Germany, *c.* 1001–1031. (Restored.)

from Viking depredations, and were able to found an empire that, nominally at least, became the successor to Charlemagne's Holy Roman Empire. The culture and tradition of the Carolingian period not only were preserved but were advanced and enriched. The Church, which had become corrupt and disorganized, recovered in the tenth century under the influence of a great monastic reform encouraged and sanctioned by the Ottonians, who also cemented ties with Italy and the papacy. When the last of the Ottonian line, Henry II, died in the early eleventh century, the pagan marauders had become Christianized and settled, the monastic reforms had been highly successful, and several signs pointed to a cultural renewal that soon was destined to produce greater monuments than had been known since ancient Rome.

Architecture

Ottonian architects followed the direction of their Carolingian predecessors. St. Michael's, the abbey church at Hildesheim (FIG. **8-24**) built between 1001 and 1031 by Bishop Bernward, retains the tower groupings and the westwork of St. Riquier, as well as its massive, blank walls. But the addition of a second transept and apse result in a better balancing of east and west units. The plan and section of St. Michael's (FIG. **8-25**) clearly show the east and west centers of

8-25 Section *(top)* and plan *(bottom)* of St. Michael's.

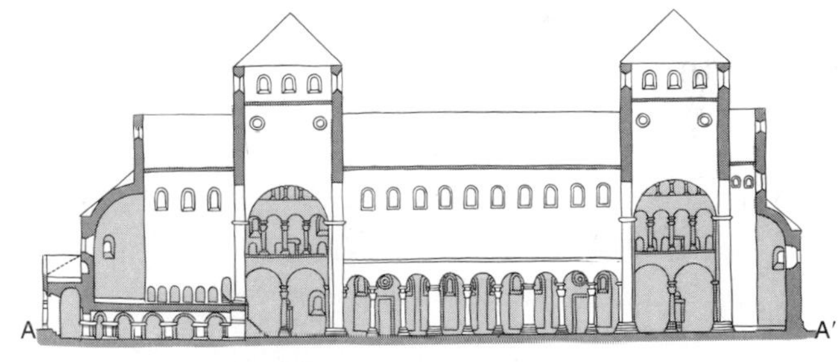

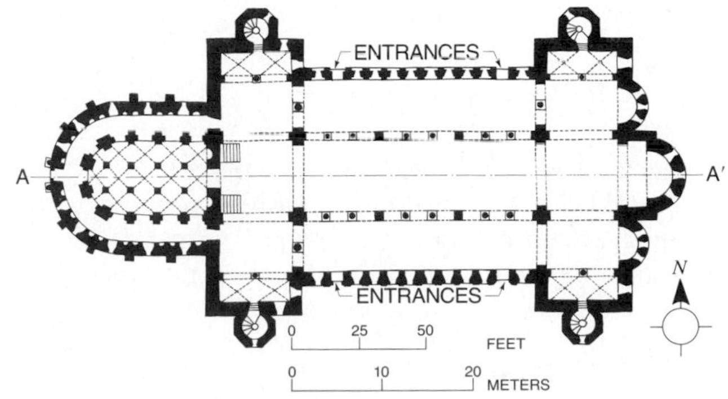

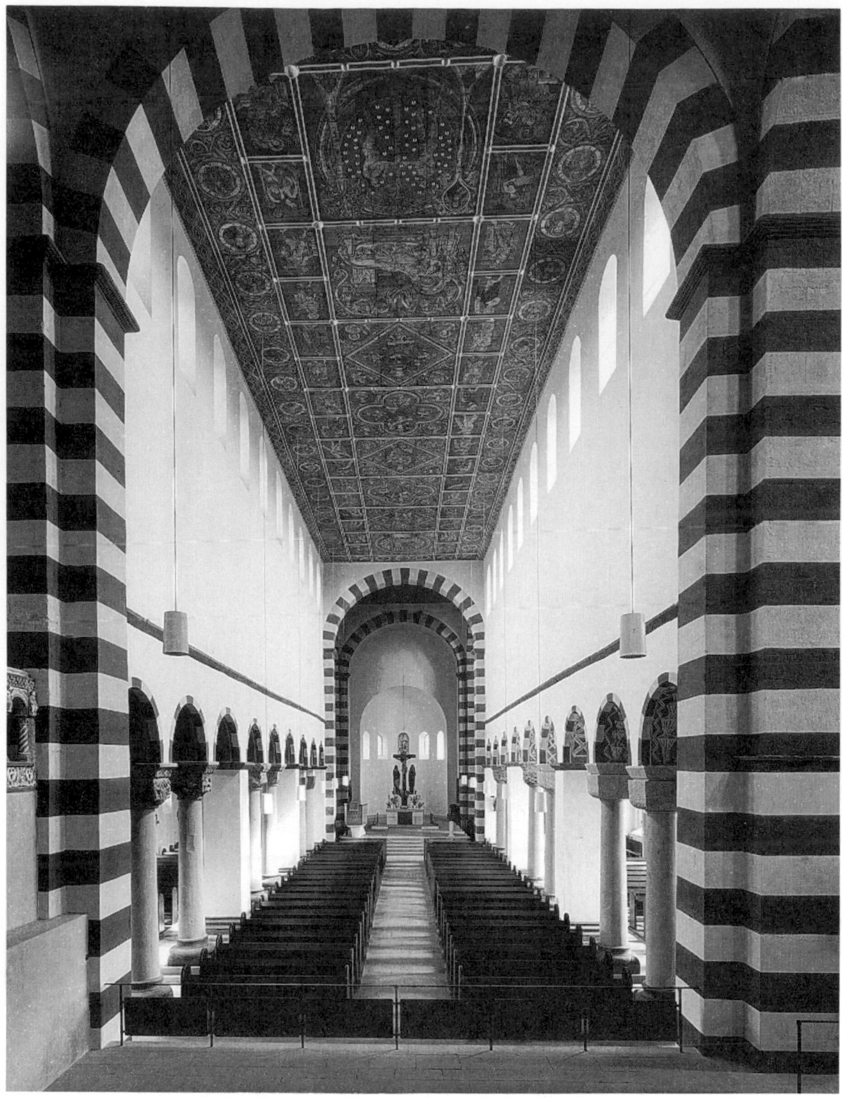

8-26 The nave of St. Michael's. (Restored.)

gravity, the nave being merely a hall that connects them. Lateral entrances leading into the aisles from the north and south are additional factors making for an almost complete loss of the traditional basilican orientation toward the east. The crossing squares have been used as a module for the dimensions of the nave, which is 3 crossing squares long and 1 square wide. This fact is emphasized visually by the placement of heavy piers at the corners of each square. These piers alternate with pairs of columns as wall supports, and the resultant "alternate-support system" will become a standard feature of many Romanesque churches in northern Europe. Contrary to one view, the alternate-support system is not related to the development of Romanesque systems of vaulting. It made its first appearance in timber-roofed structures of the tenth century (such as St. Cyriakus at Gernrode, begun in 961) and appears to be the logical outcome of the Carolingian suggestion that the length of a building could be a multiple of the crossing square. Thus, the suitability of the alternate-support system to some Romanesque vaulting systems is only incidental; it seems to have been adopted not as a structural but as an esthetic device that furnishes visual proof of the geometric organization of the building's plan. It has been suggested that the alternate-support system is an importation from the eastern empire, perhaps from Salonika (ancient Thessaloniki). If so, it seems to have been adopted enthusiastically by northern architects, who, it has been proposed lately, may have seen it as an ideal means of converting unbroken basilican interiors into the modular units to which they were accustomed in their native timber architecture (FIG. 8-18).

A view of the interior of St. Michael's (FIG. **8-26**) shows the rhythm of the alternating light and heavy wall supports. It shows as well that this rhythm is not reflected yet in the upper nave walls—that in fact it has not yet been carried further than the actual supports. Although its proportions have changed (it has become much taller in relation to its width than a Roman basilica), the nave retains the continuous and unbroken appearance of its Early Christian predecessors. We will see a fully developed Romanesque interior only when the geometric organization of the church plan is fully reflected in the elevation of the nave walls and the interior space takes on the appearance of being composed of several vertical segments.

Sculpture

St. Michael's is an important and highly refined transitional monument that fills a gap between the Carolingian and Romanesque styles. Its patron, Bishop Bernward, who made Hildesheim a center of learning, was skilled not only in affairs of state, but also was an eager scholar, a lover of the arts, and, according to his biographer, an expert craftsman and bronze caster. In 1001 he visited Rome as a guest of the emperor, Otto III, whom he had tutored and who was his friend. This stay must have acquainted him with monuments like the Column of Trajan (FIG. 6-69), which may have influenced the great, column-like, paschal candlestick he set up in St. Michael's. The wooden doors of an Early Christian church, Santa Sabina, may have inspired the remarkable bronze doors the bishop had cast for his splendid church. The doors were cast in a single piece, the first of their kind since ancient Rome. Carolingian sculpture, like most sculpture since antiquity, consisted primarily of small art executed in ivory and metal; the St. Michael's doors anticipated the coming reinstatement of large-scale sculpture in the Romanesque period. The style of the figures on the doors (FIG. **8-27**) derives from Carolingian manuscript illumination but has an expressive strength of its own—once again, a case of the form derived from a prototype becoming something new and firmly itself. God is accusing Adam and Eve after their fall from grace. As he lays on them the curse of mortality, the primal condemnation, he jabs his finger at them with the force of his whole body. The force is concentrated in the gesture, which becomes the psychic focus of the whole composition. The frightened pair crouch, not only to hide their shame but to escape the lightning bolt of the divine wrath. Each passes the blame—Adam pointing backward to Eve, Eve pointing downward to the deceitful serpent. The starkly flat setting throws the gestures and attitudes of rage, accusation, guilt, and fear into relief; once again, the story is presented with all the simplicity and impact of skilled pantomime.

We have seen how the instinct for pantomimic pose and gesture guides the representations and narratives of Medieval art from the very beginning. Such

8-27 *Adam and Eve Reproached by the Lord,* from the bronze doors commissioned by Bishop Bernward for St. Michael's, 1015. Approx. 23″ × 43″.

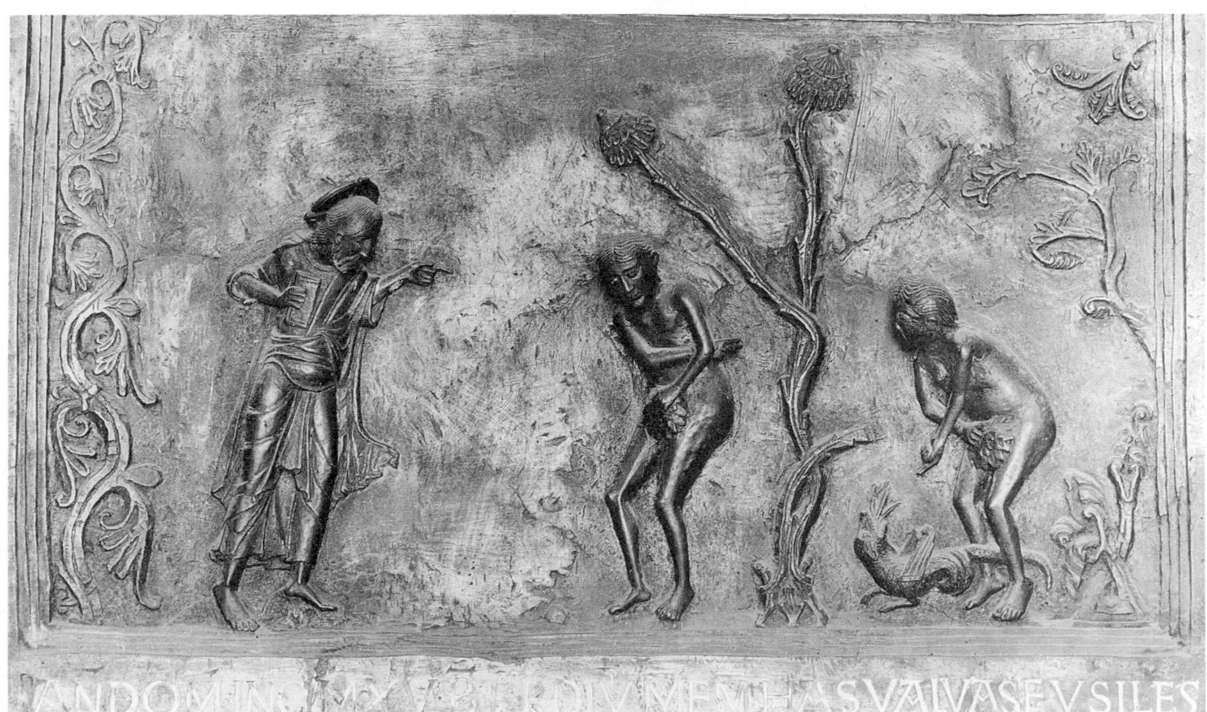

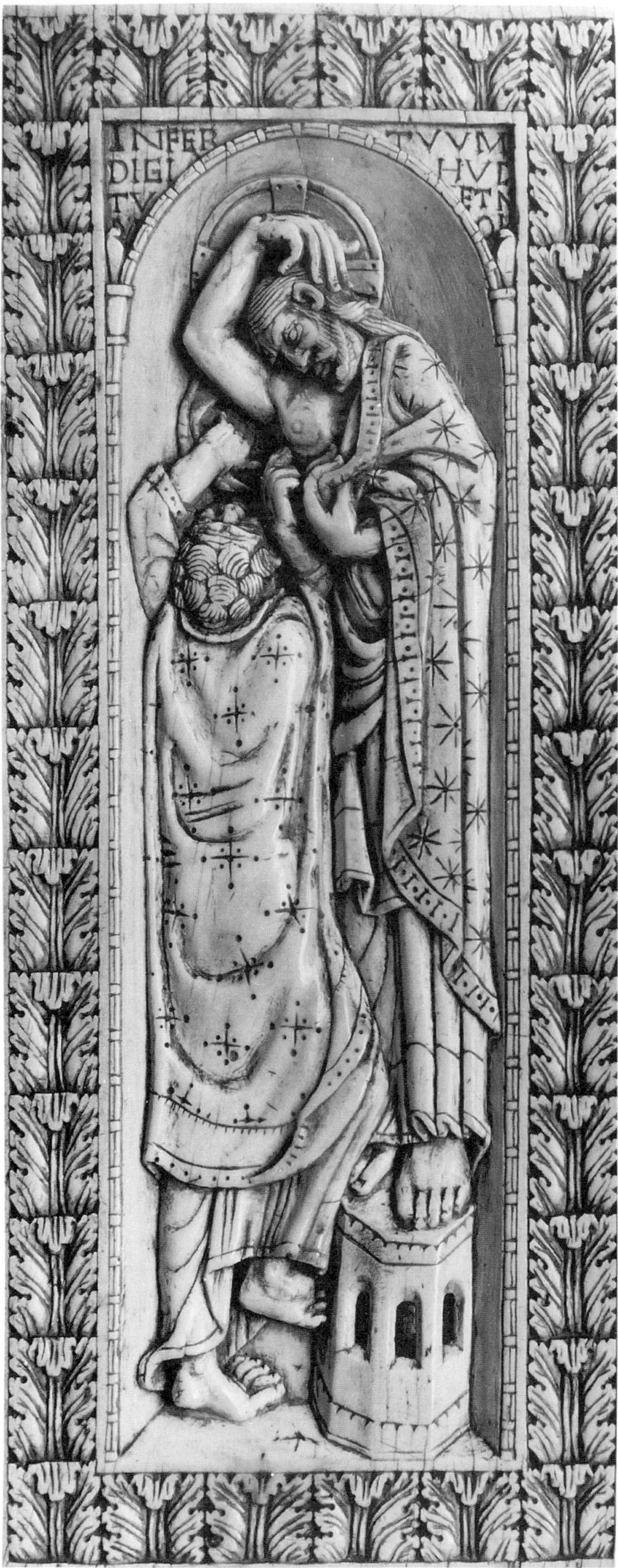

8-28 *Doubting Thomas,* c. 1000. Ivory, approx. 9″ × 4″. Staatliche Museen, Berlin.

pantomime, emphasized by telling exaggeration, appears in an ivory carving (FIG. **8-28**) that surely is among the masterpieces of the art of the Middle Ages. This small panel, only 9 inches high and 4 inches wide, carries a composition of two intertwined figures, beautifully adjusted to the space. The theme is the persuasion of Doubting Thomas. After the Resurrection, when Christ appears for the second time to his sorrowing disciples (John 20:24), all believe that he is truly Christ and truly risen except the skeptical Thomas, who demands to feel the bodily wounds of the master he has seen crucified. In the panel, Thomas explores the wound in Christ's side in a kind of climbing, aggressive curiosity. Christ, his right arm raised to reveal his side, bends over Thomas in an attitude that wonderfully combines gentleness, benign affection, protectiveness, and sorrow. The figures are represented entirely within the context of emotion; the concentration on the single act of Christ's revelation to the doubter, the emotional vibrations that accompany the doubt, and the ensuing conversion of Thomas determine every line of the rendering. We are not aware here of the influence of a prototype; we seem to have before us an original work of great power.

Painting and Illumination

We must assume that, by Ottonian times, artists had become familiar enough with the Carolingian figurative modes to work with considerable independence, developing a functional, vernacular style of their own. A supreme example of this is an illumination in the *Lectionary of Henry II* (FIG. **8-29**), in which an angel announces the birth of Christ to the shepherds. The angel has just alighted on a hill, his wings still beating, and the wind of his landing agitates his draperies. He looms immense above the startled and terrified shepherds, filling the sky, and bends on them a fierce and menacing glance as he extends his hand in the gesture of authority and instruction. Emphasized more than the message itself are the power and majesty of God's authority. The electric force of God's violent pointing in the Hildesheim doors is felt again here with the same pantomimic impact. Although the figure style may stem ultimately from the Carolingian school at Tours, the painters of the scriptorium of Reichenau (an island in Lake Constance on the German-Swiss border) who produced the *Lectionary of Henry II* have made of their received ideas something fresh and powerful; a new sureness in the touch is epitomized by the way in which the draperies are rendered in a hard, firm line

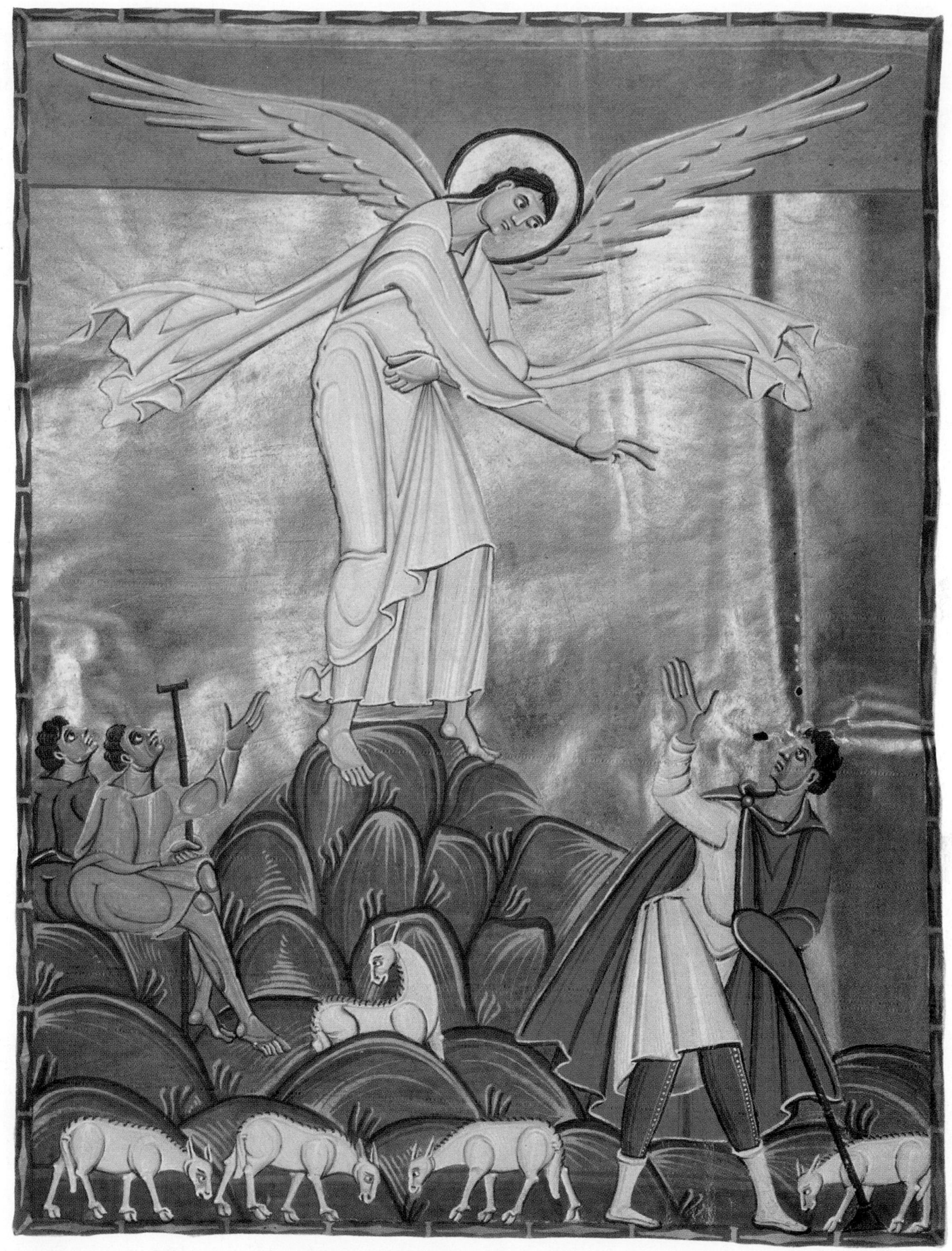

8-29 *The Annunciation to the Shepherds,* from the *Lectionary of Henry II,* 1002–1014. Approx. 17″ × 13″. Bayerische Staatsbibliothek, Munich.

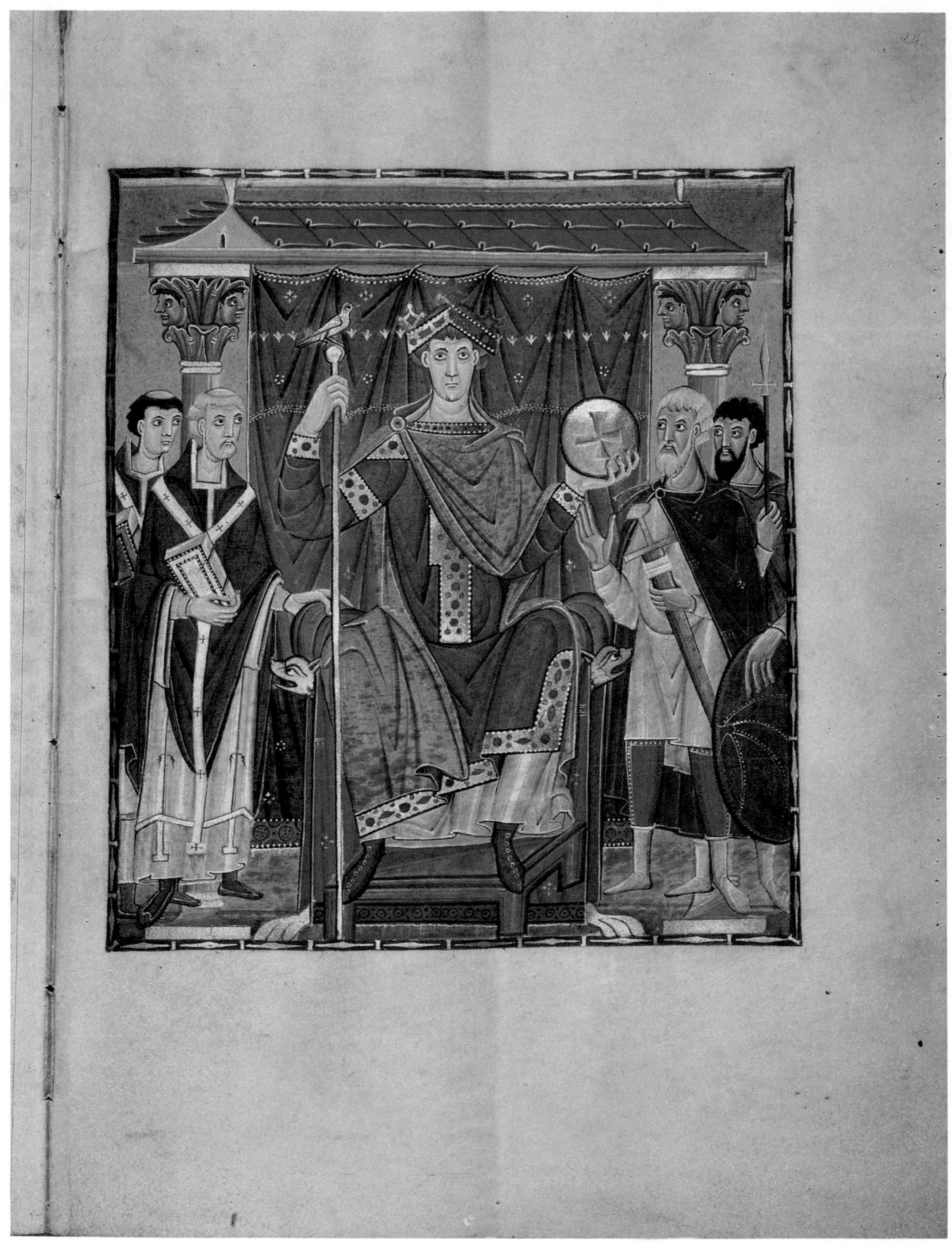

8-30 *Otto III Enthroned Receiving the Homage of Four Parts of the Empire* (with nobility and clergy), from the *Gospel Book of Otto III*, 997–1000. Approx. 14″ × 10″. Bayerische Staatsbibliothek, Munich.

and the planes are partitioned in sharp, often heavily modeled shapes. We saw these features in Middle and Late Byzantine art, and indeed a close connection existed between the Ottonian and Byzantine spheres. Yet, for the most part, the Ottonian artists went their own way; Ottonian painting was produced for the court and for the great monasteries—for learned princes, abbots, and bishops—and thus appealed to an aristocratic audience that could appreciate independent and sophisticated variations on inherited themes. Although an illumination like *The Annunciation to the Shepherds* could by no means be called Classical, it does display a certain sculpturesque clarity—a strong, relieflike projection and silhouette that suggests not a hesitating approximation of misunderstood prototypes from antiquity but a confident, if unconscious, capturing of the Antique spirit.

At the same time, the powerful means of expression of *The Annunciation to the Shepherds* miniature imply an intensification of Christian spirituality that is perhaps related to the broad monastic reforms of the tenth and eleventh centuries. With that force of expression goes a significantly new manner of fashioning the human figure in art, one that is not slavishly dependent on prototypes even when prototypes are exchanged and studied. Ottonian figurative art reveals a translation of prototypal material into a kind of ready idiom of forms and a native way of drawing. Although exceptions are known, for the most part, Ottonian figures have lost the old realism of the *Coronation Gospels* (FIG. 8-12), inherited from the Antique style, and move with an abrupt, hinged, jerky movement that is not "according to nature" but nevertheless possesses a sharp and descriptive expressiveness. This new manner would be passed on to the figurative artists of the Romanesque period. As the western European spoken and written languages emerged from the polyglot Latin-Germanic of the early centuries into the vernacular tongues we recognize today, so figurative art gradually developed out of the same kind of mixture of Latin, Germanic, and Celtic elements into a new, strong, and self-sufficient vernacular of representation.

A picture from the *Gospel Book of Otto III*, representing the emperor himself (FIG. **8-30**), sums up much of what went before and points to what is coming. The emperor is represented enthroned, holding the scepter and cross-inscribed orb that represent his universal authority. He is flanked by the clergy and the barons (the church and the state), both aligned in his support. Stylistically remote, the picture still has a clear political resemblance to the Justinianic mosaic in San Vitale (FIG. 7-36). It was the vestigial, imperial ideal—awakened in the Frankish Charlemagne and preserved for a while by his Ottonian successors in Germany—that gave partial unity to western Europe while the barbarians were settling down. This imperial ideal, salvaged from ancient Rome and bolstered by the experience of Byzantium, would survive long enough to give an example of order and law to the barbarians; to this extent, ancient Rome lived on to the millennium. But native princes in England, France, Spain, Italy, and eastern Europe would aspire to a sovereignty outside the imperial Carolingian and Ottonian hegemony; staking their claims, they make the history of the medieval power contests that led to the formation of the states of Europe as we know them. In the illumination (FIG. 8-30), Otto, sitting between the rivalrous representatives of church and state, typifies the very model of the medieval predicament that will divide Europe for centuries. The controversy of the Holy Roman Emperors with the popes will bring the German successors of the Ottonians to bitter defeat in the thirteenth century, and with that defeat, the authority of ancient Rome will come to an end. The Romanesque period that is to follow will, in fact, deny the imperial spirit that had prevailed for centuries. A new age is about to begin, one in which Rome—an august memory—will cease to be the deciding influence.

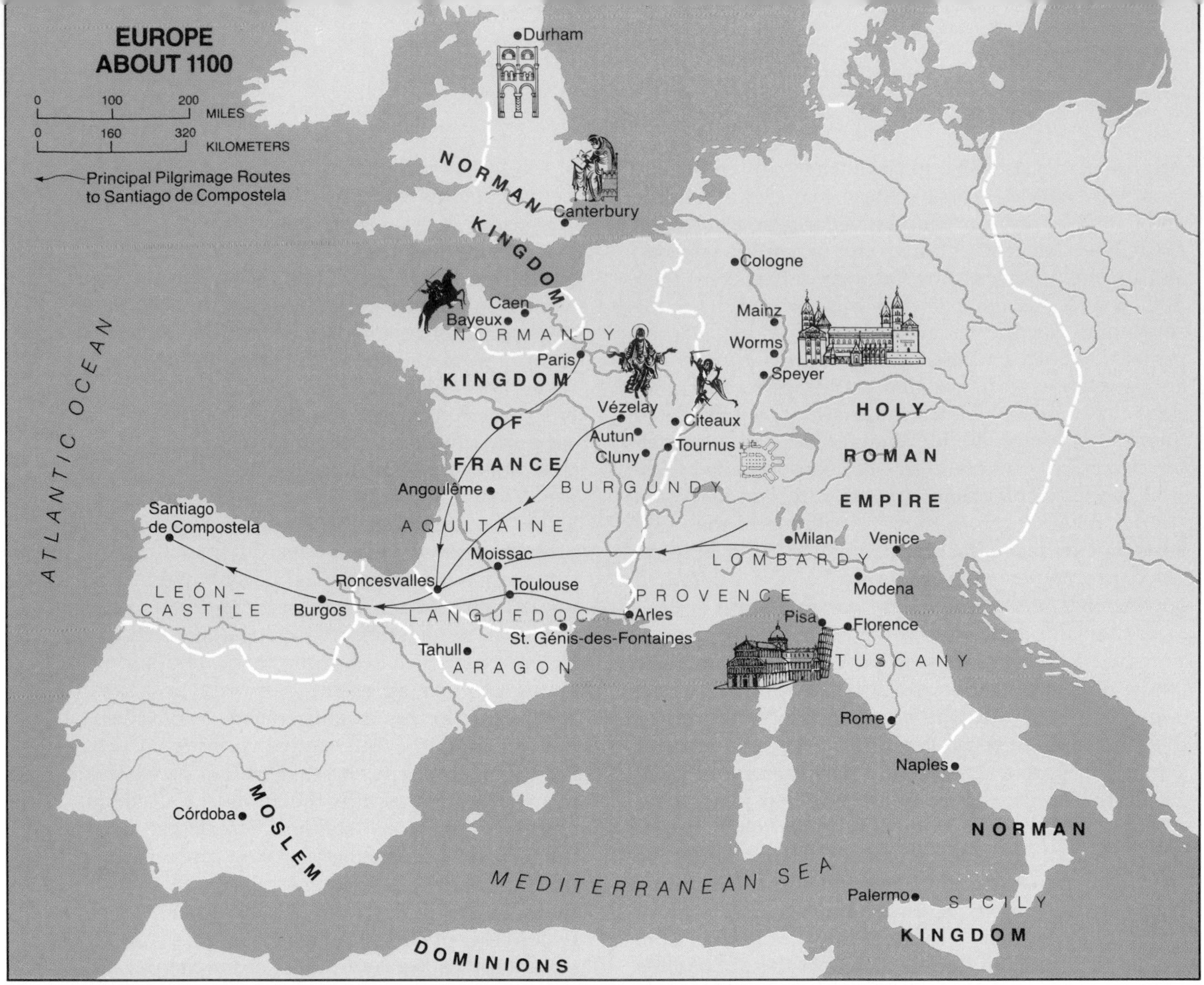

EUROPE ABOUT 1100

0 100 200 MILES
0 160 320 KILOMETERS

Principal Pilgrimage Routes to Santiago de Compostela

Durham
NORMAN KINGDOM
Canterbury
Cologne
Caen
Bayeux
NORMANDY
Mainz
Worms
Speyer
Paris
KINGDOM OF FRANCE
Vézelay
Cîteaux
Autun
Tournus
Cluny
HOLY ROMAN EMPIRE
ATLANTIC OCEAN
Angoulême
BURGUNDY
Santiago de Compostela
AQUITAINE
Milan
Venice
Moissac
LOMBARDY
Roncesvalles
Toulouse
Modena
LEÓN–CASTILE
Burgos
PROVENCE
LANGUEDOC
Arles
Pisa
Florence
St. Génis-des-Fontaines
Tahull
ARAGON
TUSCANY
Rome
Naples
Córdoba
MOSLEM DOMINIONS
NORMAN
MEDITERRANEAN SEA
Palermo
SICILY
KINGDOM

900	950	1000
FIRST ROMANESQUE		ROMANESQUE PERIOD

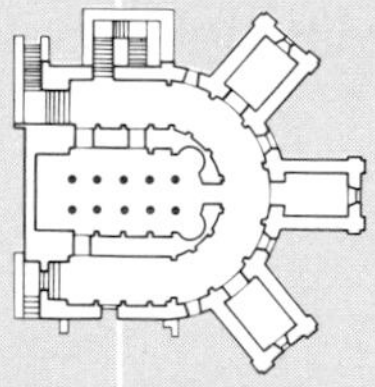

Crypt of St. Philibert, Tournus *c.* 950–1020

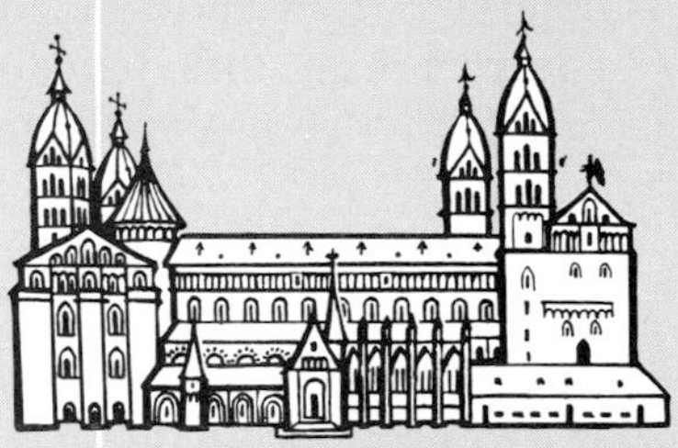

Speyer Cathedral begun 1030

Germany under Ottonian Emperors 936–1024

Germany under Salian and Franconian Emperors 1024–1138

Viking raids 9th–11th centuries

Cluniac Order founded 910

9

ROMANESQUE ART

1050	1100	1150

Pisa Cathedral
1053–1272

Bayeux Tapestry
1070–1080

Durham Cathedral
begun *c.* 1093

Moralia in Job
early 12th century

The Mission of the Apostles, Vézelay
1120–1132

The Scribe Eadwine
c. 1150

Norman conquest of England (Battle of Hastings)
1066

Norman conquest of Southern Italy and Sicily
1060–1101

First Crusade
1095

Cistercian Order founded 1098

Germany under Hohenstaufen Emperors
1138–(1268)

Second Crusade
1146

THE MID-ELEVENTH CENTURY marked a turning point in European history; Europe *as* Europe began to emerge. The past was a boiling confusion of barbarian movements, coalescing into settlements and then aggregating into empires, like the Carolingian and Ottonian, which had their spiritual and political roots in the memory of the Roman *imperium*. After about 1050, although a Latin culture and tradition persisted and still were accepted with reverence, medieval people were not as retrospective; they had new experiences and took new directions.

After the disintegration of the Carolingian state, when the successors to the imperializing Ottonians had begun to limit their concerns to Italy and the German duchies, numerous feudal political entities—petty and great, within and without the outlines of the old Frankish and Saxon "empires"—pursued their own interests and developed in their own ways. Two institutions gave them a certain coherence: the Christian church and feudalism. If the descendants of the barbarians had anything in common, it was, above all else, their Christianity. Feudalism, which had its origins both in barbarian custom and in late Roman institutions, preserved a stability, but it was a stability of a local kind and was naturally antagonistic to broad, centralized government.

Essentially, feudalism was an economic system based on land tenure that involved a complicated series of interpersonal relationships, obligations, and services. A feudal lord held a piece of land, a *fief*, and paid for it, not in money, but in service (often military service). Feudal obligation led downward from a lord to his vassal to the lower orders of society and ultimately to the serf, who was bound to the land and to the unquestioning service of the lord. The lords or nobles held fiefs in various ways from each other or from an overlord, such as a king. Inevitably, many of them became large landowners and were so powerful that they ignored their obligations and defied their king. Their time was spent in petty wars for the purpose of protecting or increasing the extent of their holdings. The *château fort*, or castle, surrounded by walls and moats, was the symbol and seat of feudal authority. The moldering ruins of these castles, found throughout the European countryside, recall the modern visitor to an age when government was always visible, singular, personal, and absolute.

The Romanesque baron or knight, still in the heroic tradition of the Germanic hero, was loyal, defiant, and proud. However, being a Christian, he was without the deep barbarian fatalism of the earlier Saxons and Norsemen and hoped not only for immortal honor in battle (won as much by the power of religious faith as by his own strength and courage) but also for life eternal in Heaven. These beliefs established the mood—the psychological set—of the aristocratic, warring magnates who led the Crusades and maintained the feudal system.

Monasticism, which reached its peak at the same time as feudalism, provided seclusion from the world, an assurance of salvation, and almost the only means of receiving an education. The history of monasticism, which, as we have seen, began in the early Middle Ages, is essentially a series of reform movements. Because gifts and bequests to them were potent means of assuring salvation, monasteries grew wealthy. With wealth came luxury and laxness and recurrent reforms to combat them. The reforms led to the formation of new monastic orders. The two great Romanesque orders were the Cluniac and the Cistercian. The former, which especially fostered the arts, was founded early in the tenth century and had its main abbey at Cluny near Mâcon in France. Encouraged by the Ottonian emperors, the Cluniac order owed allegiance only to the pope in Rome and formed, with the vast number of its priories scattered all over Europe, a centrally organized administration that contrasted sharply with the decentralizing tendencies of feudalism. The Cluniac reform, based on a liberal interpretation of St. Benedict's original rule, stressed intellectual pursuits, the study of music, and the cultivation of the other arts. The wealth and vast resources of the Cluniac order soon provoked still another reform—one that emphasized self-denial and the virtues of manual labor and gave rise to the Cistercian order, which also grew rapidly.

With feudalism and monasticism triumphant, the barons and the monastery clergy (the latter often themselves feudal lords) played a peculiarly cooperative role, and the feudal stratification of society into strictly separated classes was given religious sanction. Notwithstanding this cooperation, however, the chief conflict of the time was between the popes and the feudal principals—not over the justice or injustice of the feudal system but over the question of who should assume the position of the supreme feudal lord, that is, over the question of who is king.

The endless pilgrimages to innumerable shrines and the first two Crusades, which saw thousands of people trek from western Europe to the Holy Land during this period, involved great movements of population. The pilgrimage was a principal feature of medieval Christian life. Travel to the distant shrine of a saint, whose spiritually powerful relics there could be venerated, commonly was enjoined as a penitential act on which the salvation of the pilgrim depended. Outside of Rome itself, the most famous shrine in the West was that of St. James (Santiago) at Compostela in Spain. Travel, extremely dangerous in those turbulent times, became the duty and the hope of thousands. The Crusades were a militant expansion of the pilgrimages. Crusader and pilgrim were bound by similar vows and hoped not only to expiate sin and win salvation but to glorify God and extend the power of the Church. Most important of the immediate results of the Crusades were the establishment of the Church as a leader of the people and the reopening of commerce with the great trading centers in the Near East.

Pisan ships carried the crusading barons to the Holy Land and brought back their bones. The Pisans prospered, as did the burghers of the towns that the barons left behind them and to whom they had given charters of liberty in return for financing for their campaigns. Thus, the Crusades created subcurrents of independence; the towns obtained their charters, and a middle class of merchants and craftsmen grew up to countervail the power of feudal barons and the great monasteries. A growing city culture was quick to receive new impulses from abroad. The lines of commerce, often the arteries of ideas, conveyed new learning to Europe. The Crusades, destructive as they were, effected a new insight into Greek science and philosophy through contact with Islam, which had assimilated Greek culture much earlier and, within a century, vastly expanded the rather limited store of knowledge possessed by the Carolingians and Ottonians.

Not the least of the effects of the Crusades on the West was a new and stimulating impulse from the civilization and art of Byzantium. The disruption of the Byzantine world wrought by Crusader aggression and traffic opened to the relatively backward West new markets for ideas, new avenues of learning, and new models for art. Western European sculpture and painting came under the dominating and fertile influence of Byzantine prototypes, so much so that, despite their own integrity and quality, many western European works almost can be classified among the peripheral provinces of Byzantine art. (A style that appears at some distance from its origin, in an artistic "province" rather than at an artistic "capital," is termed *provincial*.) Classical naturalism, always latent in the figural art of Byzantium, will, in Western art, break out of Byzantine formal conventions and assume a new naturalistic form during the course of the thirteenth century.

ARCHITECTURE

As a term, *Romanesque* first was used in the nineteenth century to designate buildings with round arches and blunt, heavy walls that were supposed to bear some resemblance to ancient Roman architecture, just as the developing "Romance" languages were related to Latin. Although the Romanesque style varies widely and embraces numerous provincial differences within its almost two-century span, architectural historians now regard it as complete within itself and not as the imperfect antecedent of the Gothic style. Thus, despite its variety, Romanesque architecture readily is recognizable as such. An aerial view of the church of St. Sernin at Toulouse in the south of France (FIG. 9-3) shows certain features that appear in Romanesque buildings no matter how their arrangement differs. An overall blocky appearance is characteristic. A grouping consists of large, simple, easily definable, geometric masses—rectangles, cubes, cylinders, and half-cylinders. The main masses are subdivided by enframing buttresses or colonnettes. Exterior wall surfaces, which had been plain and unadorned through the Ottonian period, now reflect the interior organization of the structure. This enlivening of formerly blank wall surfaces foreshadows the structural translucency that would typify Gothic architecture.

The new demands of a people with religious as well as commercial reasons to travel shaped the new architecture. The building impulse, which became almost a medieval obsession, was noted by an eleventh-century monk, Raoul Glaber, who wrote:

> There occurred, throughout the world, especially in Italy and Gaul, a rebuilding of church basilicas. Notwithstanding, the greater number were already well established and not in the least in need, nevertheless each Christian people strove against the others to erect nobler ones. It was as if the whole earth, having cast off the old . . . were clothing itself everywhere in the white robe of the church.*

Glaber does not mention that a contributing cause of this eleventh-century building "obsession" may have been the widely felt relief and thanksgiving that the millennium (1000) did not bring an end to the world, as had been feared.

Great building efforts were provoked not only by the pilgrimages and the Crusades and the needs of growing cities, but also by the fact that hundreds of churches (notably in Italy and France) had been destroyed during the depredations of the Norsemen and the Magyars. Architects of the time seemed to see their fundamental problem in terms of providing a building that would have space for the circulation of its congregations and visitors and that would be solid, fireproof, well lighted, and acoustically suitable. These requirements, of course, are the necessities

*In E. G. Holt, ed., *Literary Sources of Art History* (Princeton, NJ: Princeton University Press, 1947), p. 3.

of any great civic or religious architecture, as we saw in ancient Rome, but in this case, fireproofing must have been foremost in the builders' minds, for the wooden roofs of the pre-Romanesque churches of Italy, France, and elsewhere had burned fiercely and totally when set aflame by the marauders from north, east, and south in the ninth and tenth centuries. The memory was fresh in the victims' minds; the new churches would have to be covered with cut stone, and the structural problems that arose from this need for a solid masonry were to help determine the "look" of Romanesque architecture.

Languedoc-Burgundy

A fascinating building of the so-called First Romanesque period, in which a variety of experimental solutions to the vaulting problem are illustrated, is the church of St. Philibert at Tournus on the Saône river in Burgundy (FIGS. **9-1** and **9-2**). The long and complex building history of this church explains, in part, the curious assembly of various vaulting systems found in it. Of the original building, which was begun around 950, only the crypt survived a disastrous fire in 1008. The rebuilt church was consecrated in 1019, although the nave was not vaulted until 1066 and the crossing and choir were not completed until 1120. The new choir was built according to the plan of the crypt below it, but the original westwork was replaced with a two-story narthex.

The unusual variety of vaults resulted when each successive generation of builders addressed the problem of vaulting anew and produced fresh and ingenious solutions. In the crypt, the builders used small groin vaults over square areas defined by slender, supporting columns; the corridor surrounding the central area was covered by a curving barrel vault. The vaulting of the narthex, which probably was completed by 1019, is more complex. The groin-vaulted square bays of the ground floor's central passage are flanked by aisles slightly less than half as wide as the nave; they had to be covered with shallow barrel vaults, as true groin vaults can be erected only over square areas. Above this entrance hall, on the second level, stands a three-aisled chapel dedicated to St. Michael. Here, the central nave is covered by a longitudinal barrel vault that is buttressed by *quadrant vaults* (half-barrel vaults) over the flanking aisles. Most remarkable is the main church, where groin-vaulted aisles flank a nave that rises to a series of five parallel, transverse barrel vaults that buttress each other and obviate the massive side walls that a single, longitudinal vault would have required. This solution also allowed the builders to cut generous clerestory windows into the end walls of the barrels, which serve no major supporting function. As a result, the interior is adequately illuminated and light can play with marvelous effect over the simple, curved surfaces of the ceiling and the sturdy, cylindrical columns.

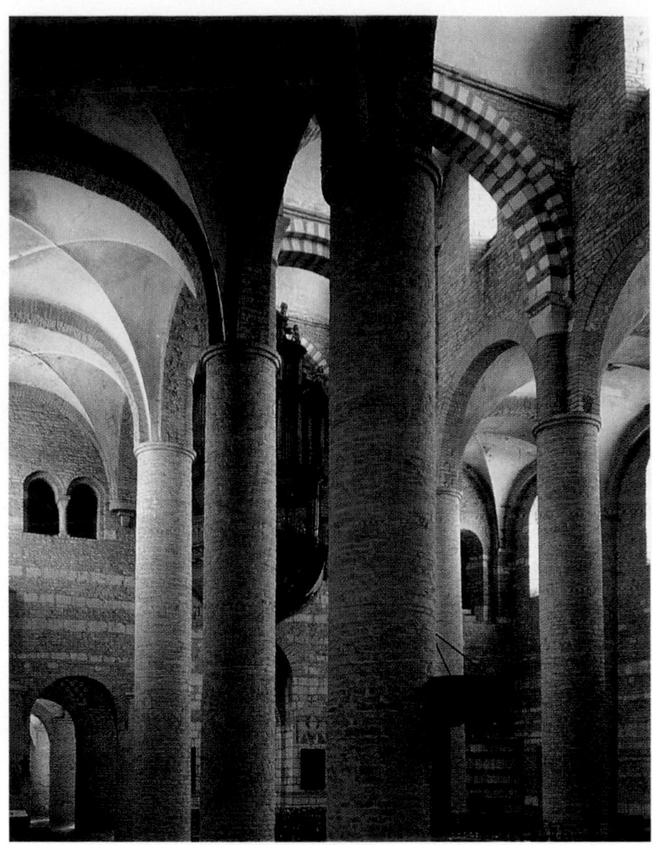

9-1 Interior of St. Philibert, Tournus, France, *c.* 950–1020 and later.

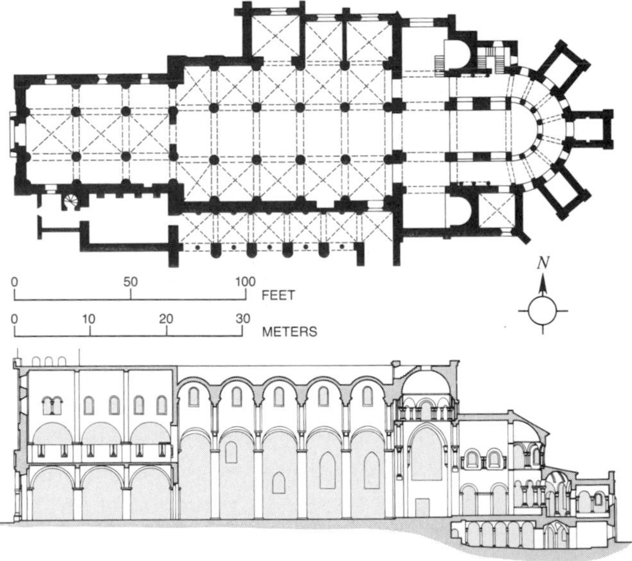

9-2 Plan and section of St. Philibert.

Just about all known vaulting methods, except the dome, were explored in this single building—a ready-to-choose-from collection of solutions for later builders. (As we will soon see, Burgundian masons opted for the longitudinal barrel vault.) But possibly an even more important and influential feature of this unique building is revealed by the plan of the choir (FIG. 9-2), which, if it does not repeat that of the one destroyed by the fire of 1008, does duplicate that of the crypt of 950. The monks' choir is surrounded by an ambulatory from which a series of chapels (and a stairwell) radiate outward. The ambulatory afforded easy circulation for the pilgrims who came to venerate the relics of St. Philibert, without interrupting the monks' obligations. This arrangement, in which subordinate chapels and ambulatories are ingeniously integrated, was to become, with due modifications, a standard feature of later pilgrimage churches.

St. Sernin at Toulouse (FIG. **9-3**) was one of the churches constructed in the Cluniac-Burgundian style that may have profited from the experiments made at Tournus; it met the requirement of a stone ceiling by using a semicircular barrel vault below a timber-roofed loft. Such churches dominated much of southern France and were related closely to those built along the pilgrimage road to Santiago de Compostela in northwest Spain. The plan of St. Sernin (FIG. **9-4**) is one of extreme regularity and geometric precision. The crossing square, flanked by massive piers and marked off by heavy arches, has been used as the module for the entire body of the church. In this *square schematism,* each nave bay measures exactly one-half and each square in the aisles exactly one-quarter of a crossing square, and so on throughout the building. The first suggestion of such a planning scheme was seen almost three centuries earlier in the St. Gall plan (FIG. 8-22). Although St. Sernin is neither the earliest nor the only (perhaps not even the ideal) solution, it does represent a crisply rational and highly refined realization of the germ of an idea first seen in Carolingian designs.

A view of the interior (FIG. **9-5**) shows that this geometric floor plan is fully reflected in the nave walls, which are articulated by half-columns that rise from the corners of each bay to the springing of the vault and are continued across the nave as transverse arches. Ever since Early Christian times, basilican interiors had been framed by long, flat walls between arcades and clerestories that enclosed a single, horizontal, unbroken volume of space. Now the aspect of the nave is changed radically, so that it seems to be composed of numerous, identical, vertical volumes of space that have been placed one behind the other, marching down the length of the building in orderly procession. This segmentation of St. Sernin's interior space corresponds with and renders visual the geometric organization of the building's plan and also is reflected in the articulation of the building's exterior walls. The result is a structure in which all parts have been integrated to a degree unknown in earlier Christian architecture.

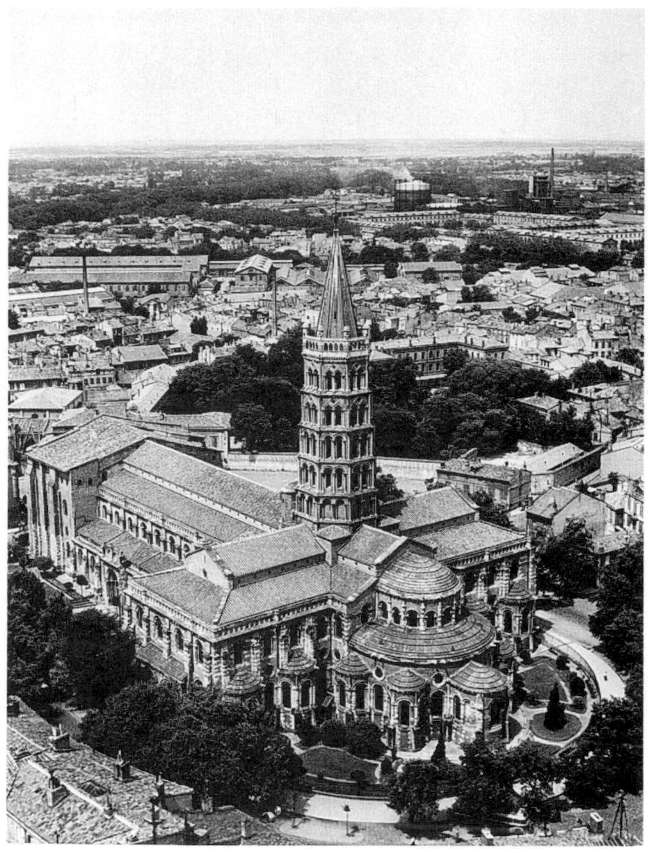

9-3 Aerial view of St. Sernin, Toulouse, France, *c.* 1080–1120 (view from the southeast).

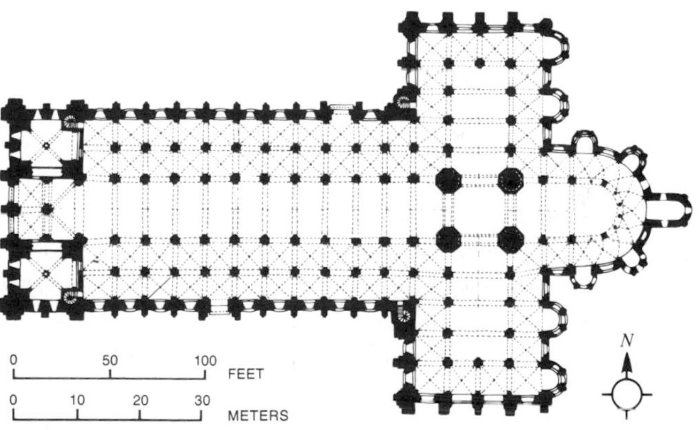

9-4 Plan of St. Sernin. (After Kenneth John Conant.)

The grand scale of St. Sernin at Toulouse is frequent in Romanesque churches. The popularity of pilgrimages and of the cult of relics brought great

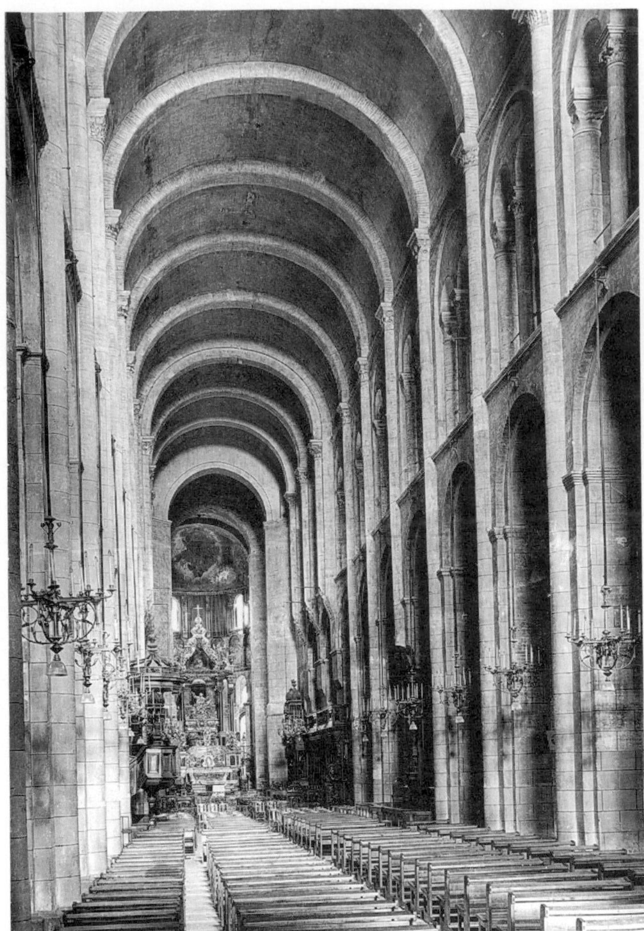

9-5 The nave of St. Sernin.

crowds even to relatively isolated places, and large congregations were common at the shrines along the great pilgrimage routes and in the reawakening cities. Additional space was provided by increasing the length of the nave; by doubling the side aisles; and by building, over the inner aisle, upper galleries, or *tribunes,* to accommodate overflow crowds on special occasions. Circulation was complicated, though, as the monks' choir often occupied a good portion of the nave. As seen in St. Philibert at Tournus, an extension of the aisles around the eastern end to make an ambulatory facilitated circulation, and the opening of the ambulatory (and often of the transepts) into separate chapels (as at St. Sernin) provided more space for worshipers and for liturgical processions. Not all Romanesque churches were as large as St. Sernin, however, nor did every one have an ambulatory with radiating chapels, but such chapels are typical Romanesque features, especially when treated as separate units projecting from the mass of the building.

The continuous, cut-stone barrel (or tunnel) vaults at St. Sernin (FIG. 9-5) put constant pressure along the entire length of the supporting masonry. If, as in most instances, including St. Sernin, the nave was flanked by side aisles, then the main vaults rested on arcades and the main thrust was transferred to the thick outer walls by the vaults over the aisles. In larger churches, the tribune galleries and their vaults (in cross section, often a quadrant, embracing a ninety-degree arc) were an integral part of the structure, buttressing the high vaults over the nave. The wall-vault system at St. Sernin is successful in its supporting function; its great scale provides ample space, and its squaring-off into cleanly marked bays, as well as the relief of wall and pier, are thoroughly Romanesque. But the system fails in one critical requirement—that of lighting. Due to the great thrust exerted by the barrel vault, a clerestory was difficult to construct, and windows cut into the haunch of the vault would make it unstable. A more complex and efficient type of vaulting was needed. One might say that, structurally, the central problem of Romanesque architecture was the development of a masonry vault system that admitted light.

In working toward this end, Romanesque architectural ingenuity produced numerous experimental consequences that appear as a rich variety of substyles. We already have mentioned that one of the apparently confusing features of Romanesque architecture is the great variety of regional and local building styles—a variety that still makes classification, coordination, and interpretation very difficult for scholars. Ten or more types may be identified in France alone, each with its distinctive system of vaulting and its varying solutions to the problems of lighting the interior.

Among the numerous experimental solutions, the groin vault turned out to be the most efficient and flexible. The groin vault had been used widely by Roman builders, who saw that its concentration of thrusts at four supporting points would allow clerestory fenestration (see FIG. 6-53). The great Roman vaults were made possible by an intricate system of brick-and-tile relieving arches, as well as by the use of concrete, which could be poured into forms, where it solidified into a homogeneous mass. The technique of mixing concrete did not survive into the Middle Ages, however, and the technical problems of building groin vaults of cut stone and heavy rubble, which had very little cohesive quality, limited their use to the covering of small areas. But during the eleventh century, Romanesque masons, using cut stone joined by mortar, developed a groin vault of monumental dimensions. Although it still employed heavy buttressing walls, this vault eventually evolved into a self-sufficient, skeletal support system.

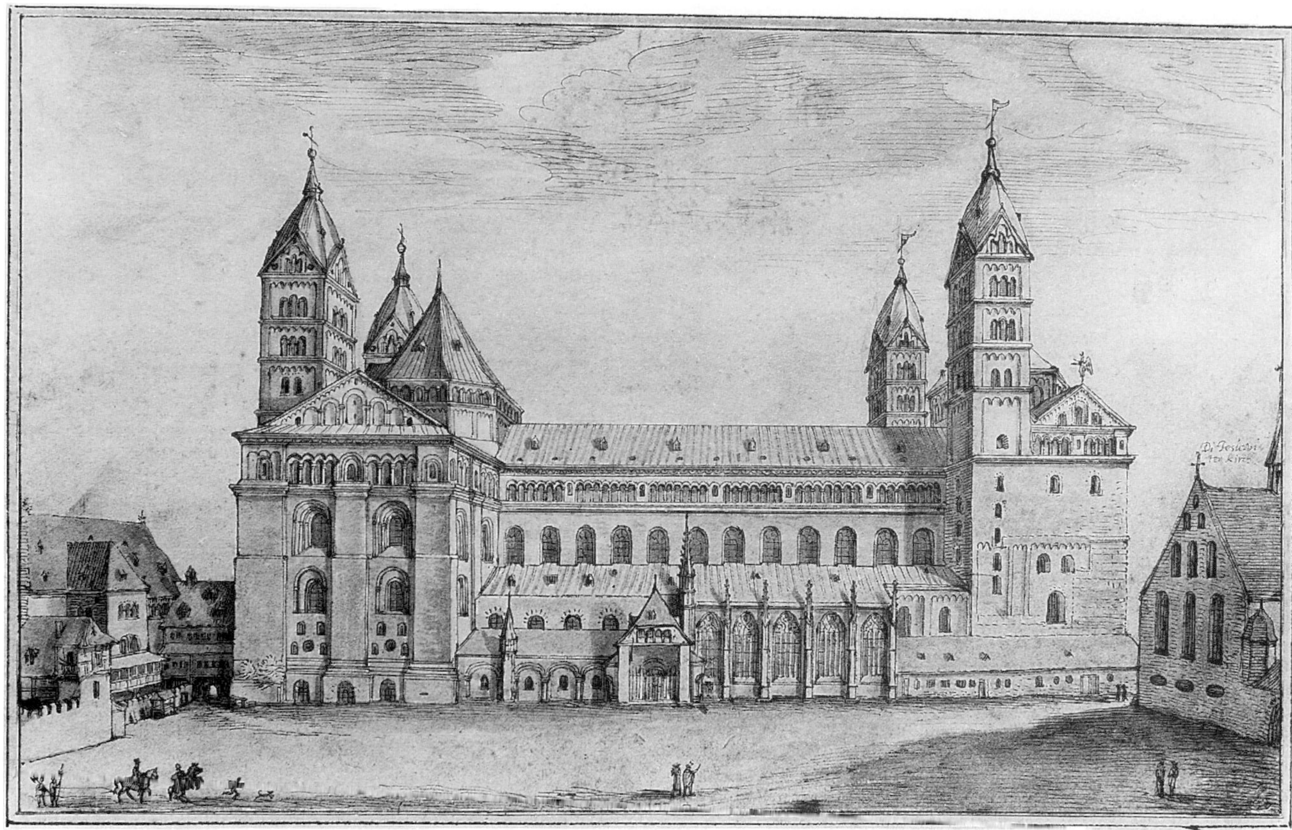

9-6 Speyer Cathedral, West Germany, begun 1030. (Pen-and-ink drawing by Wenzel Hollar, c. 1620.) Graphische Sammlung Albertina, Vienna.

Germany-Lombardy

The progress of vaulting craft can be seen best in two regions: Germany-Lombardy and Normandy-England. Speyer Cathedral in the German Rhineland (FIGS. **9-6** to **9-9**) was begun in 1030 as a timber-roofed structure. When it was rebuilt by the emperor Henry IV, between 1082 and 1106, it was covered with groin vaults. Thus, it may be one of the earliest, fully vaulted Romanesque churches in Europe. Its exterior preserves the Ottonian tradition of balanced groups of towers east and west but adds to it a rich articulation of wall surfaces. A great many of the decorative features, such as the arcades under the eaves, the stepped arcade gallery under the gable, and the moldings marking the stages of the towers, may be of Lombard origin. The inspiration for the groin vaults covering the aisles also may be Lombardic; groin-vaulting on a small scale had been used by Lombard builders throughout the early Middle Ages. The large groin vaults covering the nave (FIG. 9-8), however—probably the achievement of German masons—represent one of the most daring and successful vaulting enterprises of the time. (The nave is 45 feet wide, and the crowns of the vaults are 107 feet high.)

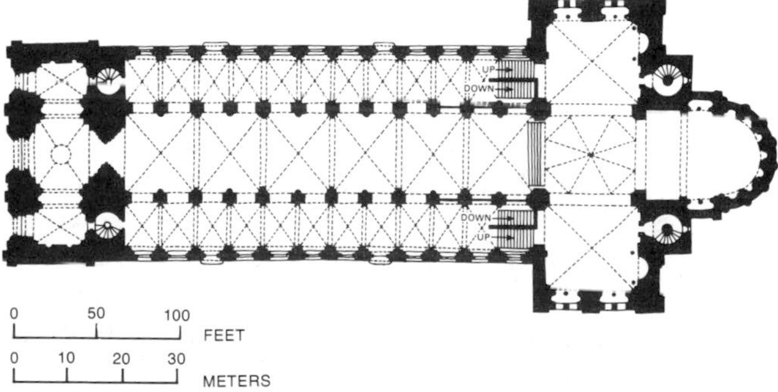

9-7 Plan of Speyer Cathedral.

The plan of the cathedral (FIG. 9-7) shows that the west apse and the lateral Ottonian entrances have been eliminated and that the entrance has been moved back to the west end, reestablishing the processional axis leading to the sanctuary. The marked-off crossing, covered by an octagonal dome, has been used as the module for the arrangement of the building's east end. Because the nave bays are not square, the use of the crossing as a unit of measurement is not as obvious. In fact, the length of the nave is almost four times the crossing square, and every third wall support marks off an area in the nave the size of

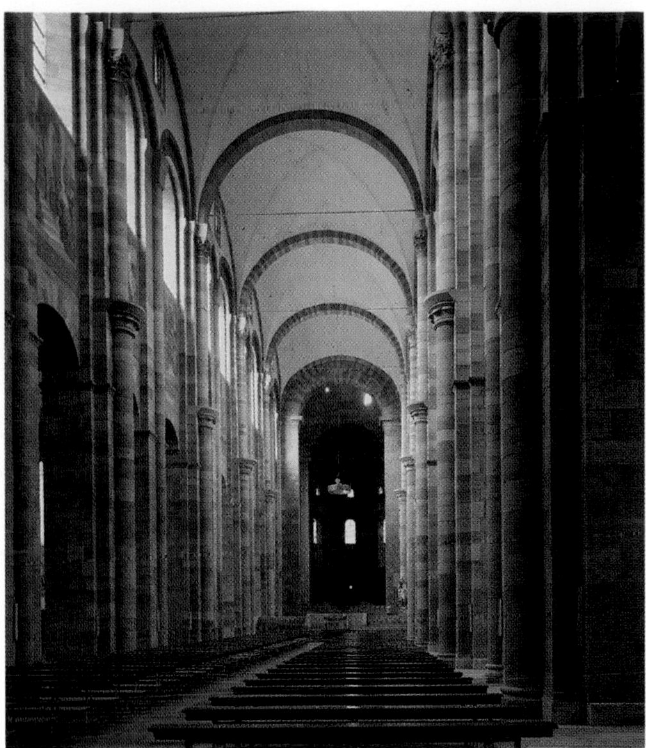

9-8 Interior of Speyer Cathedral.

the crossing; the aisles are half the width of the nave. Although the plan has some irregularities and has not been worked out as neatly and precisely as the plan of St. Sernin, the builders' intention to apply the square schematism is quite clear. Curiously, the alternate-support system, which now is carried all the way up into the vaults (FIG. 9-8), does not seem to reflect the square schematism of the building's plan. This discrepancy may be explained by the fact that the original building of 1030 was a timber-roofed structure and that the walls were articulated by a series of identical shafts that rose to enframe the clerestory windows (FIG. 9-9). The alternate-support system was introduced in the 1080s (when the building was vaulted), perhaps partially to strengthen the piers at the corners of the large vaults and to provide bases for the springing of the transverse arches across the nave. The builders may have chosen to use every other support to anchor a nave vault simply because the walls were not as stable as the massive piers that carry the crossing dome, so that it would be safer to reduce each area to be vaulted by one-third. The resultant bay arrangement, in which a large unit in the nave is flanked by two small units in each aisle, becomes almost standard in northern Romanesque architecture. Speyer's interior shows the same striving for height and the same compartmentalized effect shown in St. Sernin. By virtue of the use of the alternate-support system, the rhythm of the Speyer nave is a little more complex—a little richer, perhaps—and because each compartment is individually vaulted, the effect of a sequence of vertical blocks of space is even more convincing.

From Carolingian times, Rhineland Germany and Lombardy had been in close political and cultural contact, and it generally is agreed that the two areas cross-fertilized each other artistically. But no such agreement exists as to which source of artistic influence was dominant: the northern or the southern. The question, no doubt, will remain the subject of controversy until the construction date of the church of Sant' Ambrogio in Milan, the central monument of Lombard architecture, can be established unequivocally. Dates ranging from the tenth to the early twelfth century have been advanced for the present building, which was preceded by an earlier church that dated back to the fourth century; the late eleventh and early twelfth centuries apparently are most popular with architectural historians today.

9-9 Reconstruction of the original nave of Speyer Cathedral, c. 1030–1060.

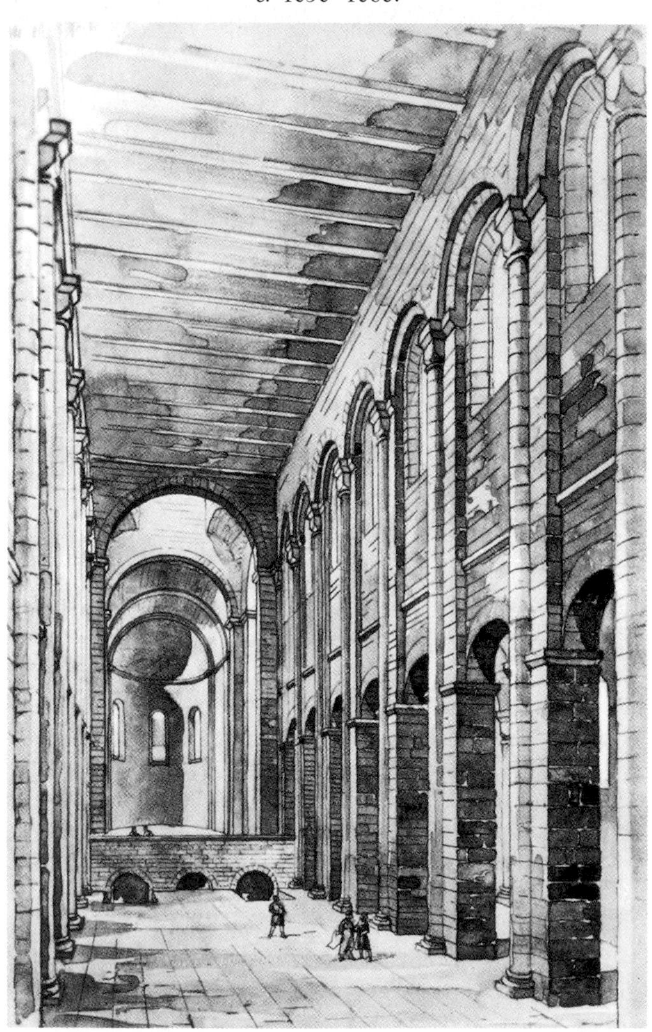

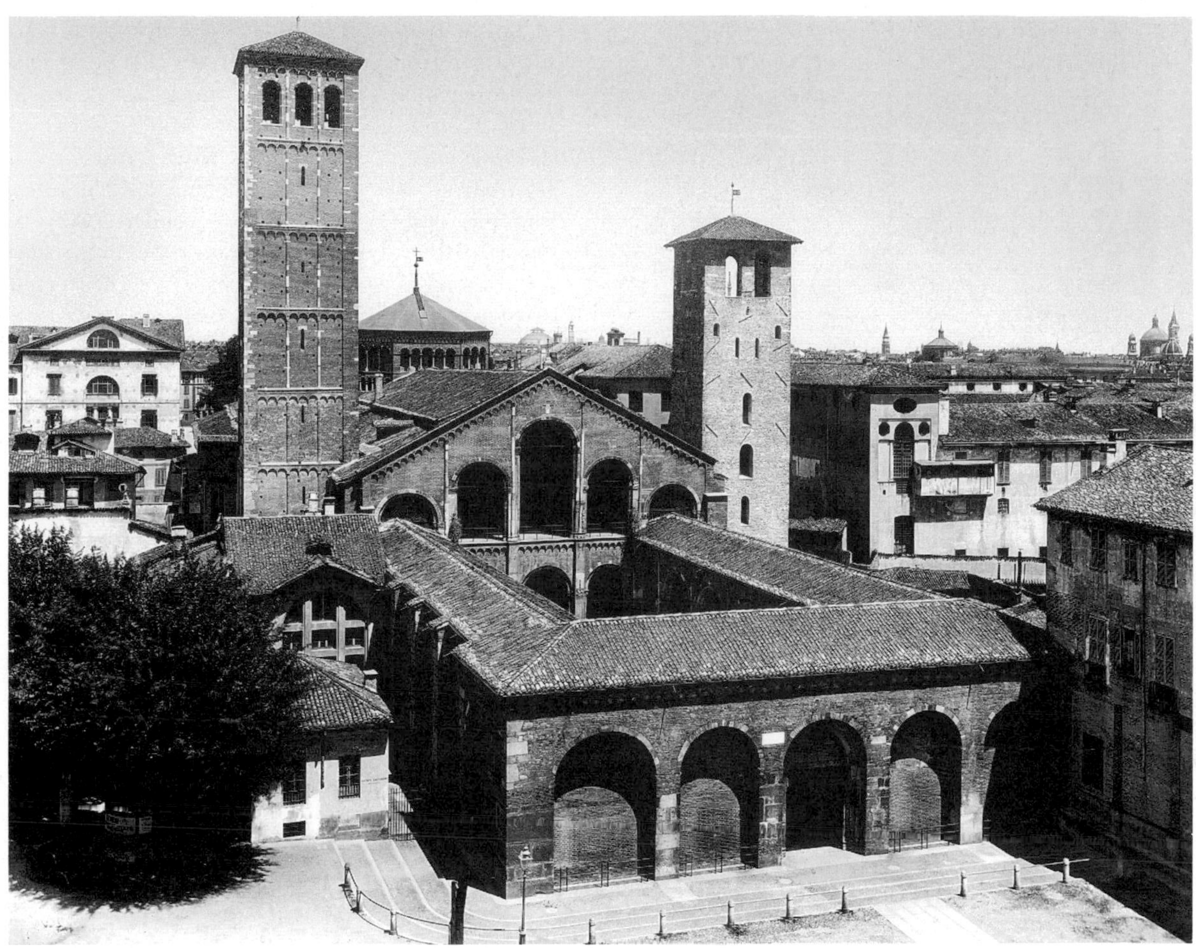

9-10 Sant' Ambrogio, Milan, Italy, late eleventh to early twelfth century (view from the northwest).

Whether or not it is a prototype, Sant' Ambrogio remains a remarkable building. As shown in FIG. **9-10,** it has an atrium (one of the last to be built), a two-story narthex pierced by arches on both levels, two towers joined to the building, and, over the east end of the nave, an octagonal tower that recalls the crossing towers of German churches. Of the façade towers, the shorter one dates back to the tenth century, while the taller north tower was built during the twelfth century. The latter is a sophisticated and typical example of Lombard tower design; it is articulated by pilasters and shafting and divided, by means of corbel tables (horizontal projections resting on corbels), into a number of levels, of which only the topmost (the bell chamber) has been opened by arches.

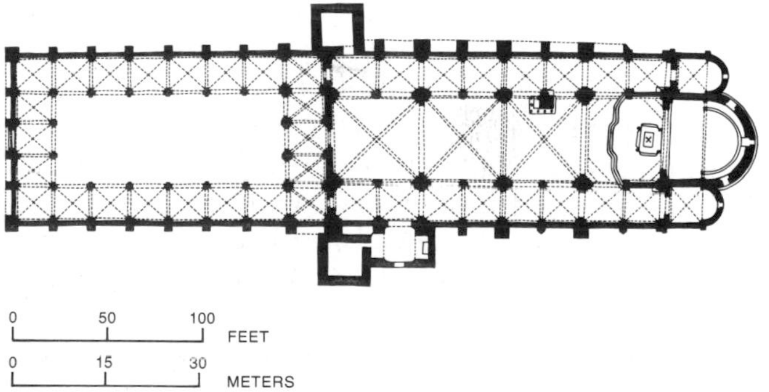

9-11 Plan of Sant' Ambrogio.

In plan (FIG. **9-11**), Sant' Ambrogio is three-aisled and without a transept. The square schematism has been applied with greater consistency and precision than at Speyer, each bay consisting of a full square in the nave flanked by two small squares in each aisle, all covered with groin vaults. The main vaults are slightly domical, rising higher than the transverse arches, and the last bay is covered by an octagonal dome that provides the major light source (the building lacks a clerestory) for the otherwise rather dark interior (FIG. **9-12**). The geometric regularity of the plan is reflected perfectly in the emphatic alternate-support system, in which the light supports are interrupted at the gallery level and the heavy ones rise to support the main vaults. These ponderous vaults, which have supporting arches along their groins, are occasionally claimed to be the first examples of

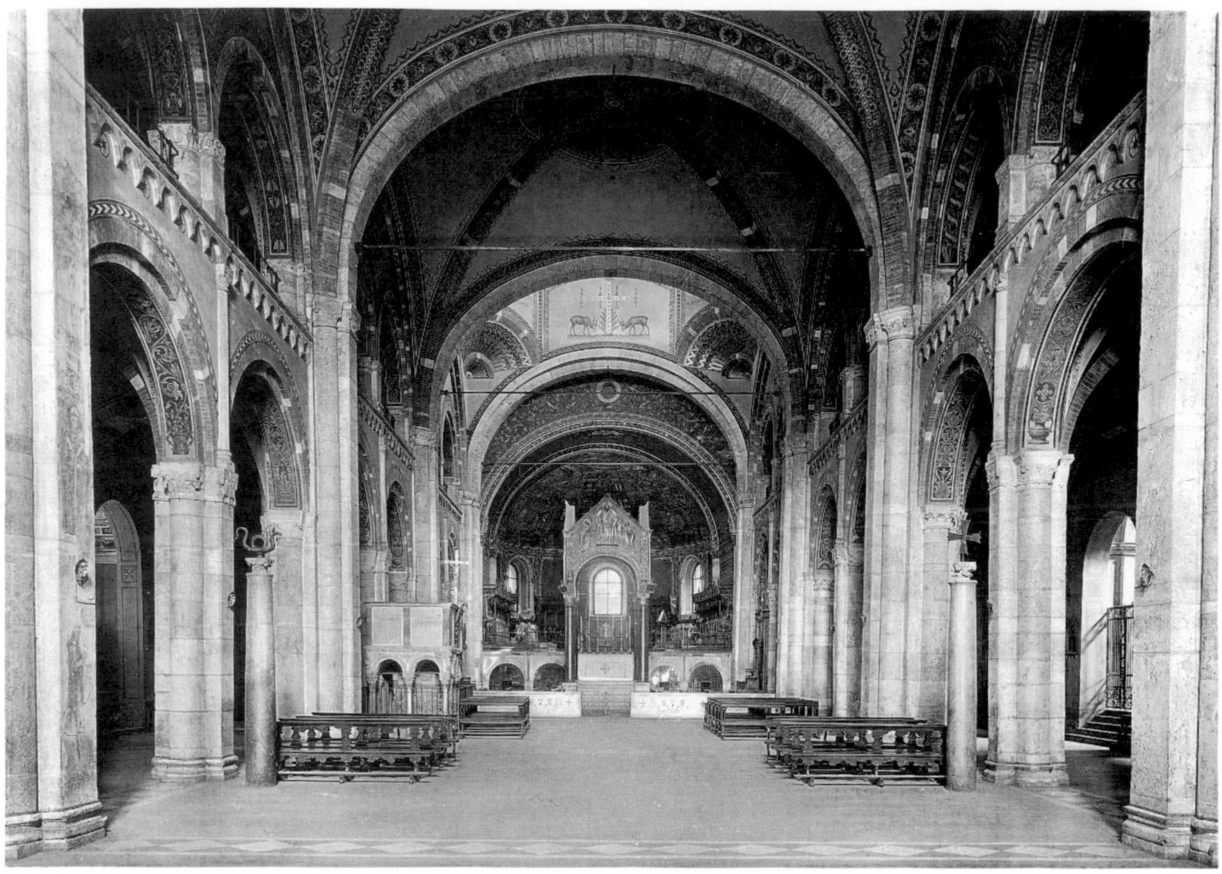

9-12 Interior of Sant' Ambrogio.

rib-vaulting; however, in fact, these vaults are solidly constructed groin vaults that have been strengthened by diagonal ribs.

The dating of the Sant' Ambrogio vaults remains controversial. Most scholars seem to feel that they were not built until after 1117, when a severe earthquake damaged the existing building. If 1117 is the correct date, the Speyer vaults would be earlier than the vaults of Sant' Ambrogio, and the inspiration and technical knowledge for the construction of groin vaults of this size would seem to have come from the north. But such possible influence did not affect the proportioning of the Milanese building, which does not aspire to the soaring height of the northern churches. Sant' Ambrogio's proportions are low and squat and remain close to those of Early Christian basilicas. As we will see, Italian architects never accepted the verticality found in northern architecture, not even during the height of the Gothic period.

The fame of German architecture rests on its achievements in the eleventh and early twelfth centuries. After the mid-twelfth century, the Germans made no major contribution to architectural design. The architectural statements at Speyer were repeated at Worms and Mainz and in other, later churches. German builders were content with refining their successful formula; beyond that, they tended to follow the lead of the more adventurous and progressive Franks and Normans.

Normandy-England

The predatory, pagan Vikings settled in northwestern France after their conversion to Christianity in the tenth century and, almost at once, proved themselves skilled administrators and builders. With astounding rapidity, they absorbed the lessons to be learned from Ottonian architecture and went on to develop the most progressive of the many Romanesque styles and the one that was to become the major source in the evolution of Gothic architecture. The church of St. Étienne at Caen in Normandy is generally considered to be the master model of Norman Romanesque architecture. It was begun by William of Normandy (William the Conqueror) in 1067 and must have advanced rapidly, as he was buried there in 1087. The west façade (FIG. **9-13**) is a striking design that looks forward to the two-tower façades of later Gothic churches. Four large buttresses divide it into three bays that correspond to the nave and aisles in the

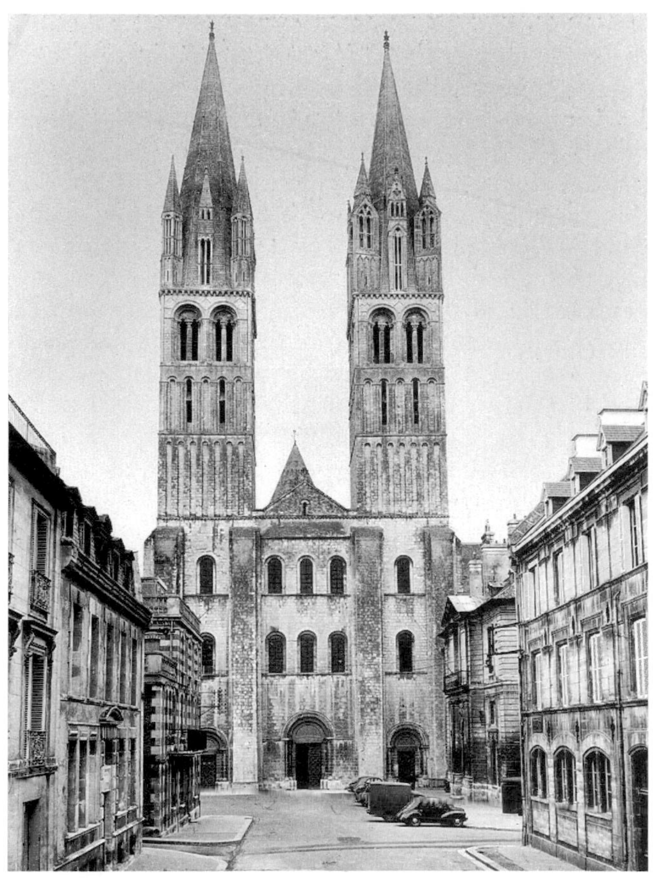

9-13 West façade of St. Étienne, Caen, France, begun 1067.

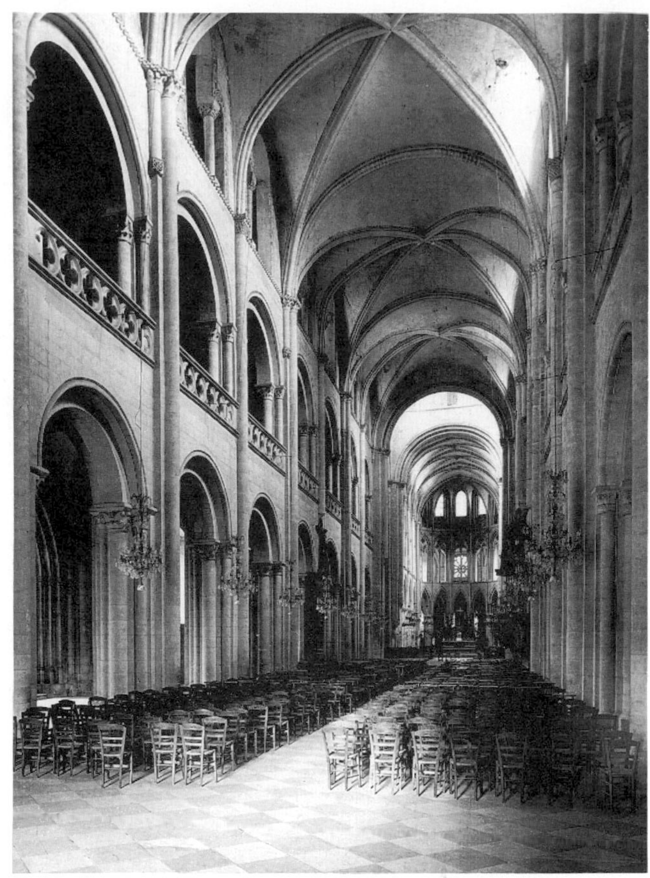

9-14 Interior of St. Étienne, vaulted c. 1115–1120.

interior. Above their buttresses, the towers also display a triple division and a progressively greater piercing of their walls from lower to upper stages. The spires are a later (Gothic) feature. The tripartite division is employed throughout the façade, both vertically and horizontally, organizing it into a close-knit, well-integrated design that reflects the careful and methodical planning of the entire structure. Like Speyer Cathedral, St. Étienne originally was planned to have a wooden roof, but, from the beginning, the walls were articulated in an alternating rhythm (simple half-columns alternating with shafts attached to pilasters) that mirrors the precise square schematism of the building's plan (FIGS. **9-14** and **9-15**). This alternate-support system was utilized effectively some time after 1110 (significantly later than it was used at Speyer), when it was decided to cover the nave with vaults. Its original installation, however, must have been motivated by esthetic rather than structural concerns. In any event, the alternating compound piers soar all the way to the springing of the vaults, and their branching ribs divide the large, square-vault compartments into six sections, making a sexpartite vault. These vaults, their crowns slightly depressed to avoid the "domed-up" effect of those at Sant'

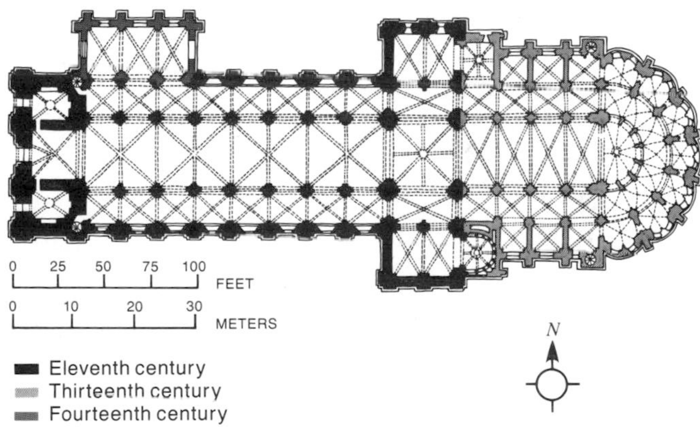

9-15 Plan of St. Étienne.

Ambrogio, rise high enough to make an efficient clerestory; they also are viewed as some of the earliest true *rib vaults,* in which the diagonal and transverse ribs compose a structural skeleton that partially supports the still fairly massive paneling between them. Rib-vaulting was to become universal practice during the Gothic period, and its development by Norman builders must be rated as one of the major structural innovations of the Middle Ages. Other elements in St. Étienne also point to the future. The complex piers, their nuclei almost concealed by attached pilasters and engaged columns, forecast the Gothic "cluster pier," and the reduction in interior wall surfaces that resulted from use of very large, arched openings anticipates the bright curtain walls of Gothic architecture. In short, St. Étienne at Caen is not only a very carefully designed structure but also a highly progressive one in which the Romanesque style begins to merge into the Early Gothic.

The conquest of Anglo-Saxon England in 1066 by William of Normandy began a new epoch in English history; in English architecture, it signaled the importation of Norman building and design methods. Durham Cathedral in northern England, begun around 1093, apparently was designed for vaulting at the outset. Like most Romanesque churches in England, it was subjected to many later alterations that, in this case, fortunately were confined largely to the exterior; the interior (FIG. **9-16**) has its original severe Romanesque appearance. Ambitious in scale—comparable to both St. Sernin at Toulouse and St. Étienne at Caen—its 400-foot length compares favorably with that of the great imperial cathedral of Speyer. With the latter, it also shares a reliance on mass for stability. But unlike Speyer, this building was conceived from the very beginning as a completely integrated skeleton in which the vaults stand in intimate and continuous relation to the vertical elements of the compound piers that support them. At Durham, the alternate-support system is interpreted with blunt power and more emphasis, perhaps, than in any other Romanesque church. Large, simple pillars ornamented with abstract designs (diamond, chevron, and cable patterns descended from the metalcraft ornamentation of the migrations) alternate with compound piers that carry the transverse arches of the vaults. The pier–vault relationship scarcely could be more visible or the structural rationale of the building better expressed. The plan (FIG. **9-17**), typically English with its long, slender proportions and strongly projecting transept, does not develop the square schematism with the same care and logic we see at Caen. But the rib vaults of the choir are the earliest in Europe (1104), and, when they were combined with slightly pointed arches in the western parts of the nave (before 1130), the two key elements that would determine the structural evolution of Gothic architecture were brought together for the first time. Only the rather massive construction and the irregular division into seven panels prevent these vaults from qualifying as Early Gothic structures.

9-16 The nave of Durham Cathedral, England, begun *c.* 1093 (view facing east).

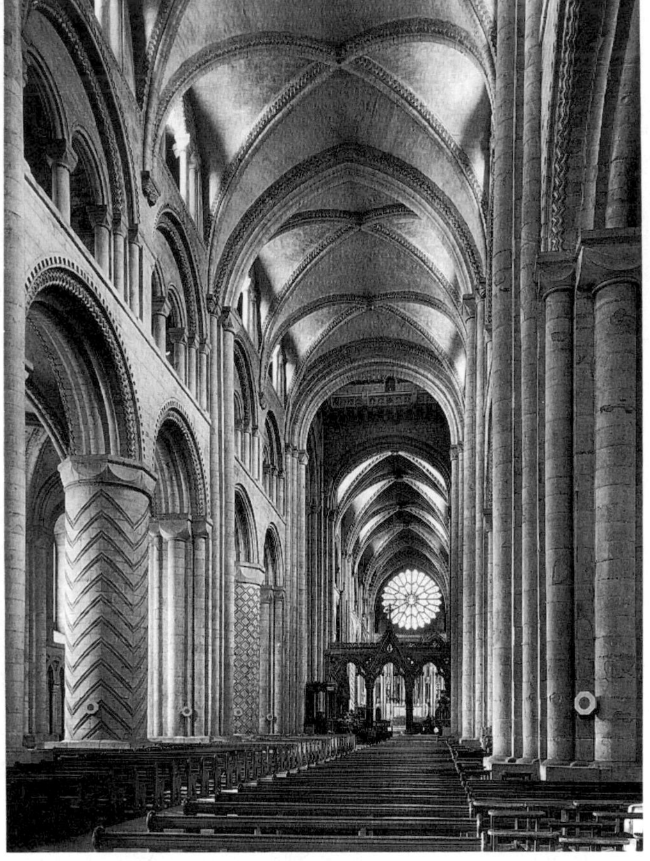

9-17 Plan of Durham Cathedral. (After Kenneth John Conant.)

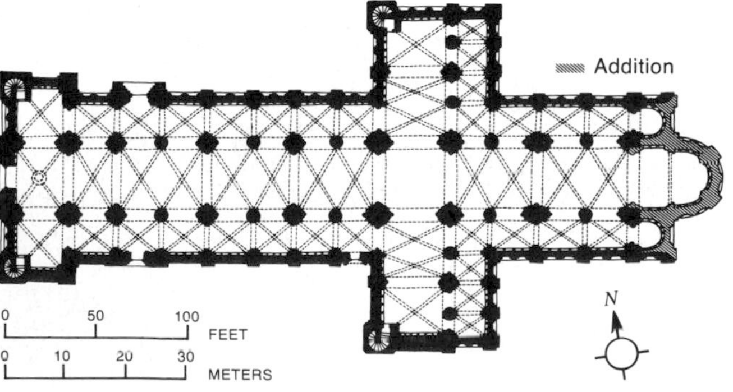

Among the numerous regional Romanesque styles of architecture, it was the northern—more specifically, the Norman—style that indirectly would influence the development of Gothic architecture; no other style had as great a potential for evolution.

Tuscany

South of the Lombard region, Italy retained its ancient traditions and, for the most part, produced Romanesque architecture that was structurally less experimental than that of Lombardy. The buildings of Tuscany seem to adhere more closely than those of any other region to the traditions of the Early Christian basilica. The cathedral group of Pisa (FIG. **9-18**)

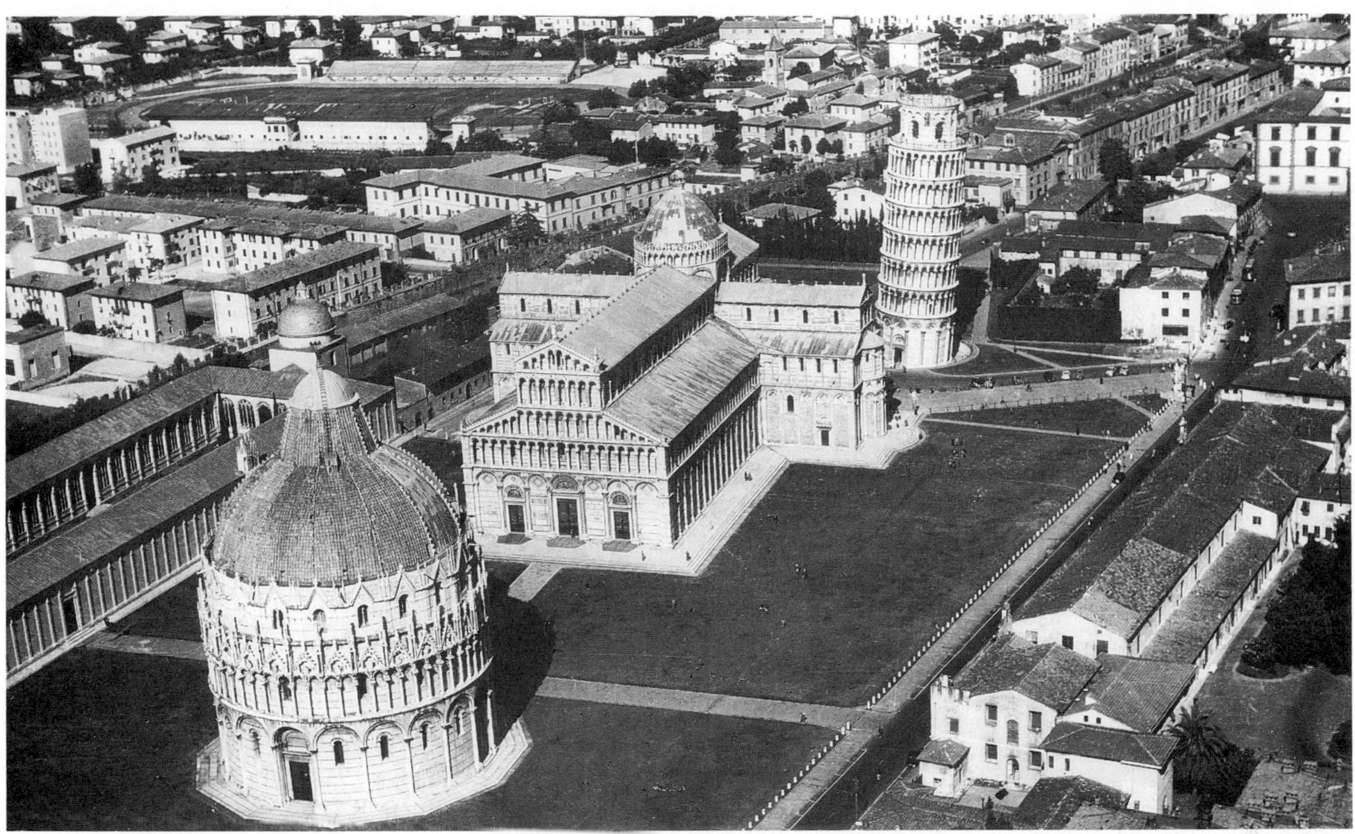

9-18 Aerial view of the cathedral group (baptistry, cathedral, and campanile) of Pisa, Italy, 1053–1272 (view from the southwest).

manifests, in addition to these conservative qualities, those of the great Classical "renaissance" of the late eleventh and twelfth centuries, when architects, craftsmen, poets, and philosophers again confronted Classical-Christian prototypes and interpreted them in an original yet familiar way. The cathedral is large, five-aisled, and one of the most impressive and majestic of all Romanesque churches. At first glance, it resembles an Early Christian basilica, but the broadly projecting transept, the crossing dome, the rich marble incrustation, and the multiple arcade galleries of the façade soon distinguish it as Romanesque.

The interior (FIG. **9-19**) also at first suggests the basilica, with its timber roof rather than vault (originally the rafters were exposed, as in Early Christian basilicas), nave arcades, and Classical (imported) columns flanking the nave in unbroken procession. Above these columns is a continuous, horizontal molding, on which rest the gallery arcades. The gallery, of course, is not a basilican feature but is of Byzantine origin. Other divergences from the basilica form include the relatively great verticality of the interior and, at the crossing, the markedly un-Classical pointed arch, which probably was inspired by Islamic architecture. The striped incrustation, produced by alternating dark green and cream-colored marble,

9-19 The nave of the cathedral of Pisa (view facing east).

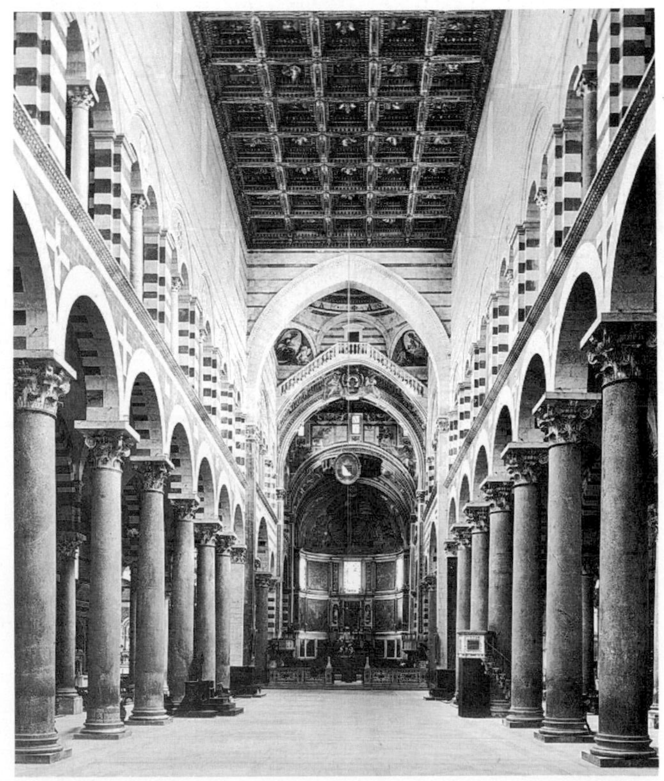

provides a luxurious polychromy that will become a hallmark of Tuscan Romanesque and Gothic buildings. The leaning campanile, the result of a settling foundation, tilted from the vertical even while it was being built and now inclines some 21 perilous feet out of plumb at the top. Round, like the Ravenna campaniles, it is much more elaborate; its stages are marked by graceful, arcaded galleries that repeat the motif of the cathedral's façade and effectively relate the tower to its mother building. Although the baptistry, with its partly remodeled Gothic exterior, may strike a slightly discordant note, the whole composition of the three buildings, with the adjacent Campo Santo (cemetery), makes one of the handsomest ensembles in the history of architecture. This grouping dramatically expresses the new building age that the prosperity enjoyed by the busy maritime cities of the Mediterranean made possible.

Another Tuscan church, San Miniato al Monte (FIG. **9-20**) in Florence, completed in 1062, recalls Early Christian architecture, although the wall arcading

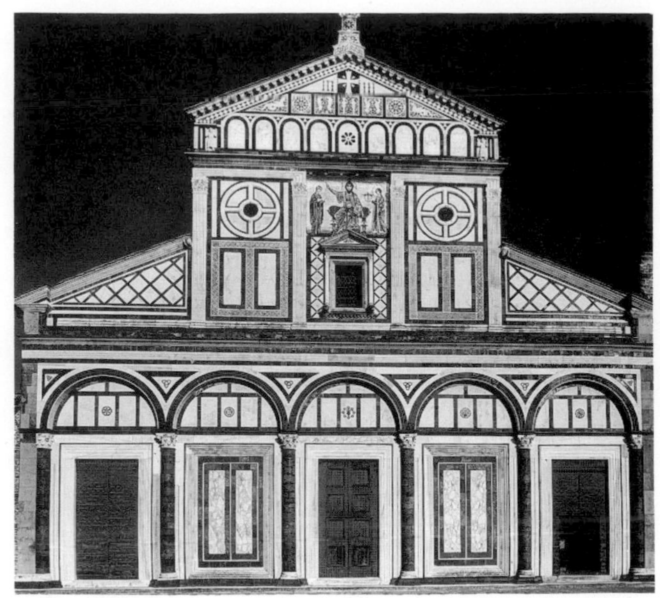

9-20 West façade of San Miniato al Monte, Florence, Italy, completed 1062.

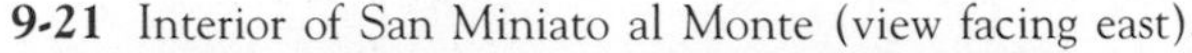

9-21 Interior of San Miniato al Monte (view facing east).

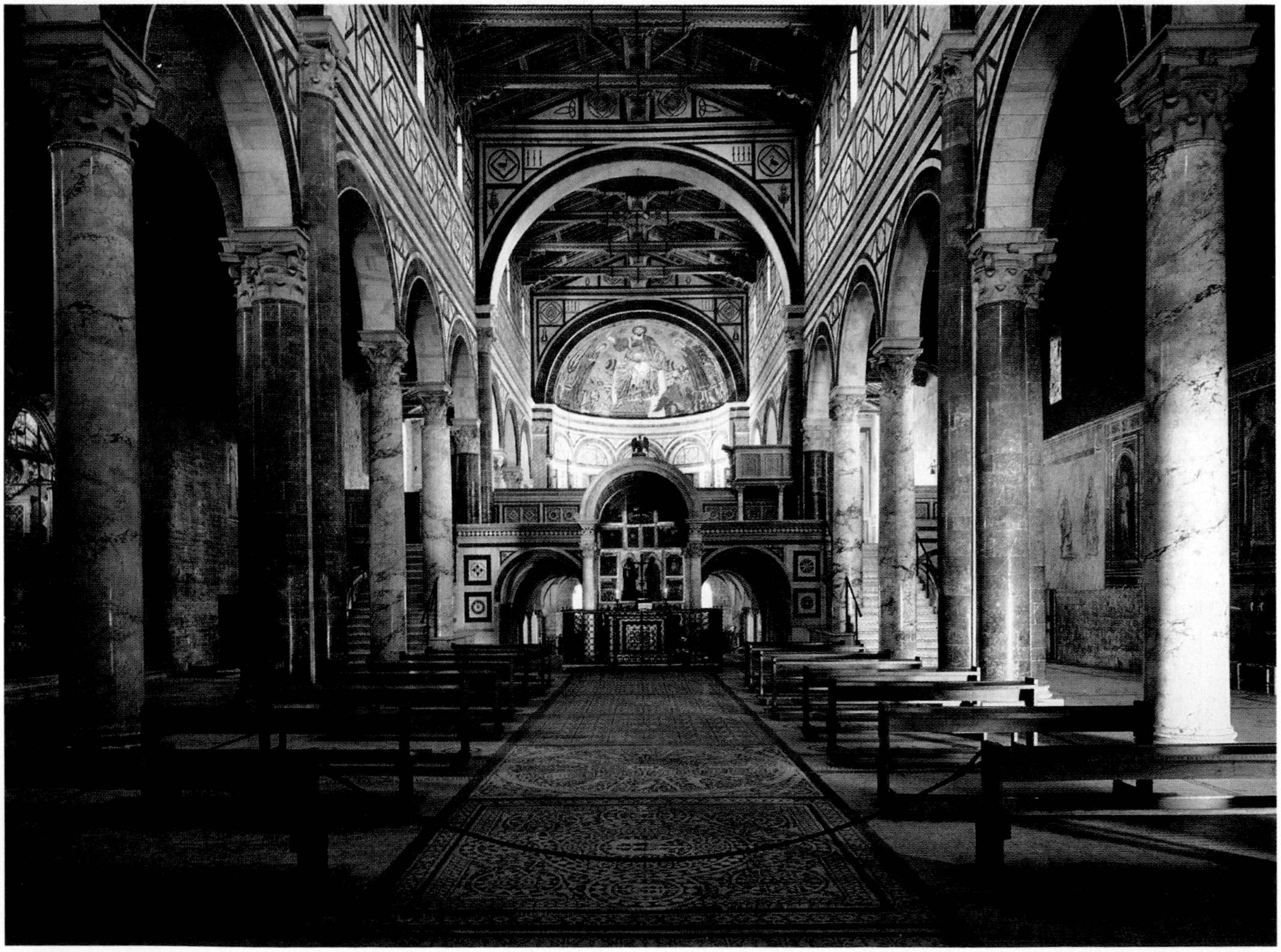

and its elaborate, geometric incrustation in colored marbles make for a rich ornamental effect foreign to the austere exteriors of the earlier buildings. Retrospective as San Miniato may appear externally, the interior (FIG. **9-21**) is another matter. Although the church is timber-roofed, as are most Tuscan Romanesque churches, the nave is divided into three equal compartments by *diaphragm arches* that rise from compound piers. The piers alternate with pairs of simple columns in a rhythm that recalls St. Michael's in Hildesheim (FIG. 8-26). The diaphragm arches, which appear here for the first time (before 1060), have multiple functional and esthetic purposes. They brace the rather high, thin walls, provide firebreaks within the wooden roof structure, and compartmentalize the basilican interior in the manner so popular with most Romanesque builders. Antique, or neo-Antique, motifs appear in the capitals as well as in the incrustation, expressing again the persistence of the Classical tradition in Tuscany.

Aquitaine

Influences crisscrossed in Romanesque architecture, creating diversity and exotic hybrids. In the region of Aquitaine in southwestern France, for instance, it became customary to roof the churches with domes, reflecting the influence of Byzantium, Armenia, and Cyprus—the Crusaders' bridge between East and West. Curiously, most of these Aquitanian churches mate the dome with a longitudinal plan to which, at first glance, it seems ill-suited. St. Pierre in Angoulême (FIGS. **9-22** and **9-23**) exhibits several characteristic features of the typical Aquitanian church. A longitudinal, aisleless nave is covered by a sequence of domes (see FIG. 7-45), which, in turn, usually are covered by pitched wooden roofs. The resulting design turns out to be highly practical, as the pendentive-supported domes require much less buttressing than, for instance, continuous barrel vaults. Also, the system automatically produces the cherished compartmentalized effect of Romanesque architecture. Although they never aimed at the soaring height of northern Romanesque structures, these Aquitanian domed churches not only represent an almost perfect fusion of geometric plan with elevation, but also are visually most effective, clearly exhibiting the functions of all their structural parts.

From about 1050 on, the old dependence of the pre-Romanesque (Carolingian and Ottonian) on Late Antique and Early Christian design concepts fades gradually, although never completely. Romanesque architecture develops a number of clear characteristics: the square schematism, the alternate-support system, and the increased relief and depth of walls and piers as they connect with the vaults above. The Romanesque architect conceives a building in terms of the geometric relation of its parts, a view basically different from that of the Early Christian architect, who never thought of large units as related geometrically and who thought of the wall not as essentially a structural element, but as a surface to receive applied decoration.

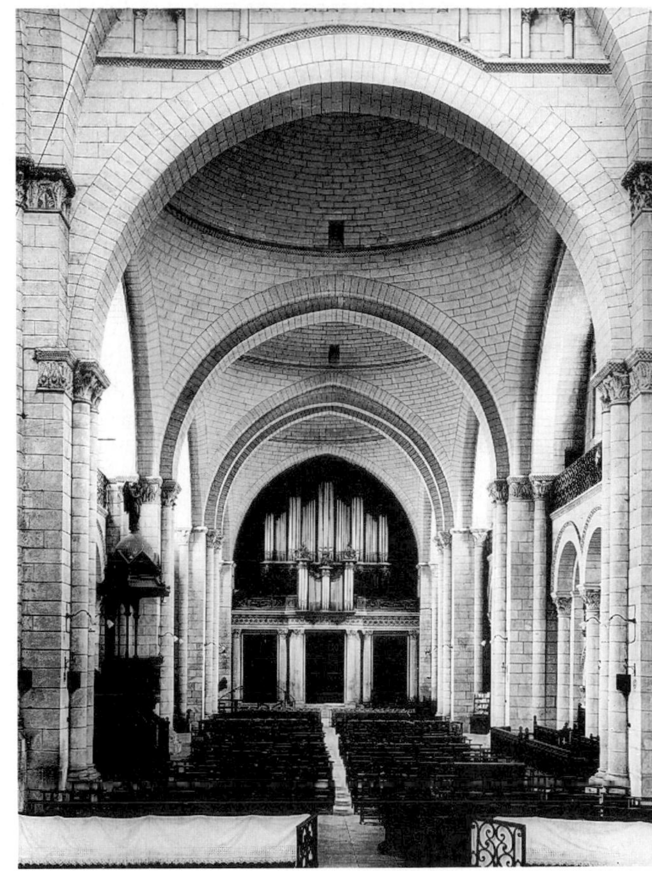

9-22 Interior of St. Pierre, Angoulême, France, twelfth century (view facing west).

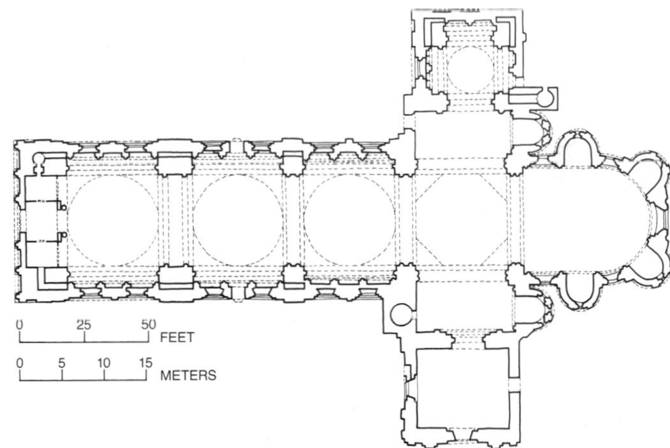

9-23 Plan of St. Pierre.

SCULPTURE

For Medieval art, the first definite relation of architecture and sculpture appears in the Romanesque style. Figurative sculpture, confined for centuries to small art, flowers again in the new Romanesque churches of the mid-eleventh century. The rich profusion of sculpture and something of its nature may be guessed from Bernard of Clairvaux's famous tirade against it, written in 1127:

> I say naught of the vast height of your churches, their immoderate length, their superfluous breadth, the costly polishings, the curious carvings and paintings. . . . [Men's] eyes are feasted with relics cased in gold, and their purse-strings are loosed. They are shown a most comely image of some saint, whom they think all the more saintly that he is the more gaudily painted. Men run to kiss him, and are invited to give; there is more admiration for his comeliness than veneration for his sanctity. Hence the church is adorned with gemmed crowns of light. . . . candelabra standing like trees of massive bronze, fashioned with marvellous subtlety of art, and glistening no less brightly with gems than with the lights they carry. . . . O vanity of vanities, yet no more vain than insane! The church is resplendent in her walls, beggarly in her poor; she clothes her stones in gold and leaves her sons naked. . . . in the cloister, under the eyes of the Brethren who read there, what profit is there in those ridiculous monsters, in that marvellous and deformed comeliness, that comely deformity? To what purpose are those unclean apes, those fierce lions, those monstrous centaurs, those half-men, those striped tigers, those fighting knights, those hunters winding their horns? Many bodies are there seen under one head, or again, many heads to a single body. . . . For God's sake, if men are not ashamed of these follies, why at least do they not shrink from the expense?*

Stone sculpture had almost disappeared from the art of western Europe during the eighth and ninth centuries. The revival of the technique is one of the most important Romanesque achievements. As stone buildings began to rise again, so did the impulse to decorate parts of the structure with relief carving in stone. One might expect that the artists should turn for inspiration to surviving Roman sculpture and to sculptural forms such as ivory carving or metalwork; it is obvious that they also relied on painted figures in manuscripts. But these Romanesque artists developed their own attitude toward ornamental design and its relation to architecture. At first, this concept was somewhat random and haphazard; the artists put the sculpture wherever there seemed to be a convenient place. A little later, the portals of the church seemed the appropriate setting, both for religious reasons and for the practical matter of display. As Romanesque sculpture turns into Gothic, the portal statuary becomes integrated with the design of the whole façade, following the lines of the architecture.

An example of the earlier, looser arrangement, in which sculpture is not yet an intrinsic part of the architecture, is the figure of *Christ in Majesty*, the center piece of a group of seven marble slabs affixed to the wall of the ambulatory of the church of St. Sernin at Toulouse (FIG. **9-24**). The sculptured figures represent angels introducing saints to Christ. An inscription on a marble altar, part of the group, indicates that these figures were all part of an ensemble, a shrine dedicated to St. Saturninus (St. Sernin), and that the artist was a certain BERNARDUS GELDUINUS. These works of Gelduinus from the year 1096 are the first indisputably datable specimens of monumental Romanesque sculpture in France. The sources of Gelduinus's style are debated; certainly, a principal one must be a Carolingian or Ottonian work in metal or ivory, perhaps a book cover. The polished marble has the gloss of both materials. Christ is seated in a mandorla, his

9-24 *Christ in Majesty*, from the ambulatory of St. Sernin, Toulouse, France, 1096.

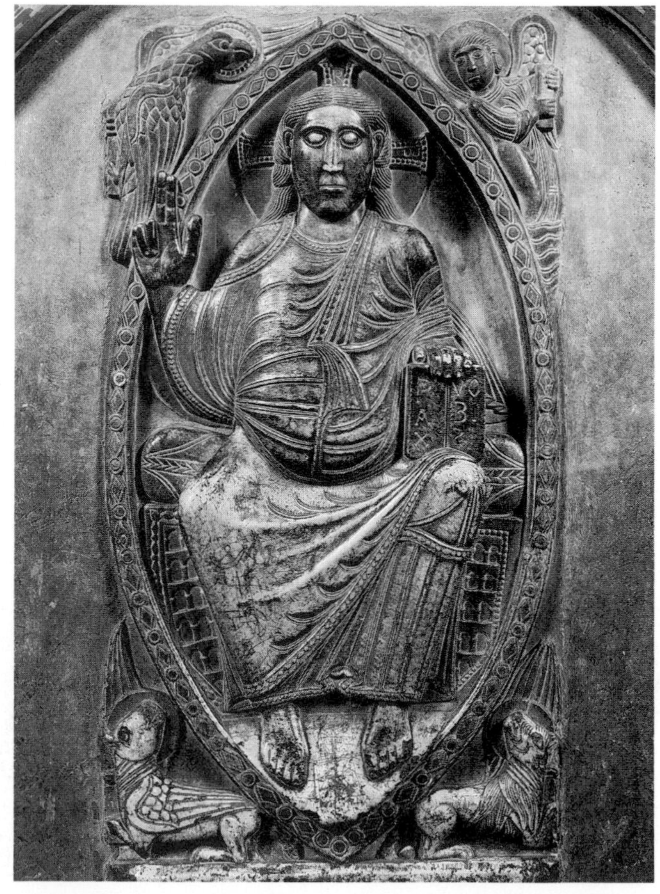

*In E. G. Holt, ed., *Literary Sources of Art History* (Princeton, NJ: Princeton University Press, 1947), pp. 17–18.

right hand raised in blessing, his left hand resting on an open book inscribed *"Pax vobis."* The Signs of the Evangelists occupy the corners of the slab: above, the Eagle of St. John and the Angel of St. Matthew, below, the Ox of St. Luke and the Lion of St. Mark. Though at this time sculpture is not structurally integrated with the architectural elements, the discrete slabs are arranged so as to make an iconographically readable group. We shall see presently that in the later mode of sculptural composition the architectural limits of the parts of a portal, or the shapes of a pier or capital, were respected as an integrating framework for sculpture. Typically, the Romanesque portal reveals this integration of sculpture in architecture. At Vézelay (FIG. 9-33) and at St. Trophime, Arles (FIG. 9-35), the standard elements are revealed: jambs, lintel, semicircular tympanum (beneath the arches [or archivolts]), the pier *(trumeau)* in the middle of the doorway (FIG. **9-25**).

Before the elements of the Romanesque portal were assembled in a unified design, they were placed in isolation inside or outside the church building, without any apparent scheme of organization. The St. Sernin figure, as we have seen, is set into the ambulatory wall. At St. Génis-des-Fontaines in the extreme south of France, sculpture appears in the lintel over a doorway (FIG. **9-26**). Dated 1020 by inscription, the quite primitive style is more or less characteristic of what we call "First Romanesque." It is representative

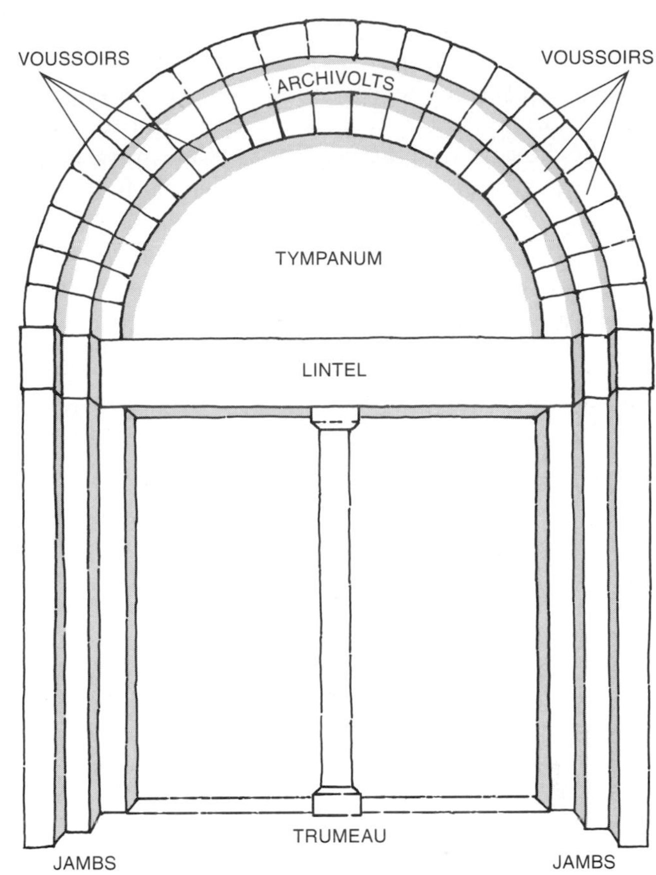

9-25 Diagram of a Romanesque portal.

9-26 *Christ in Majesty with Apostles,* lintel over doorway, St. Génis-des-Fontaines, France, *c.* 1019–1020. Marble, 24″ high.

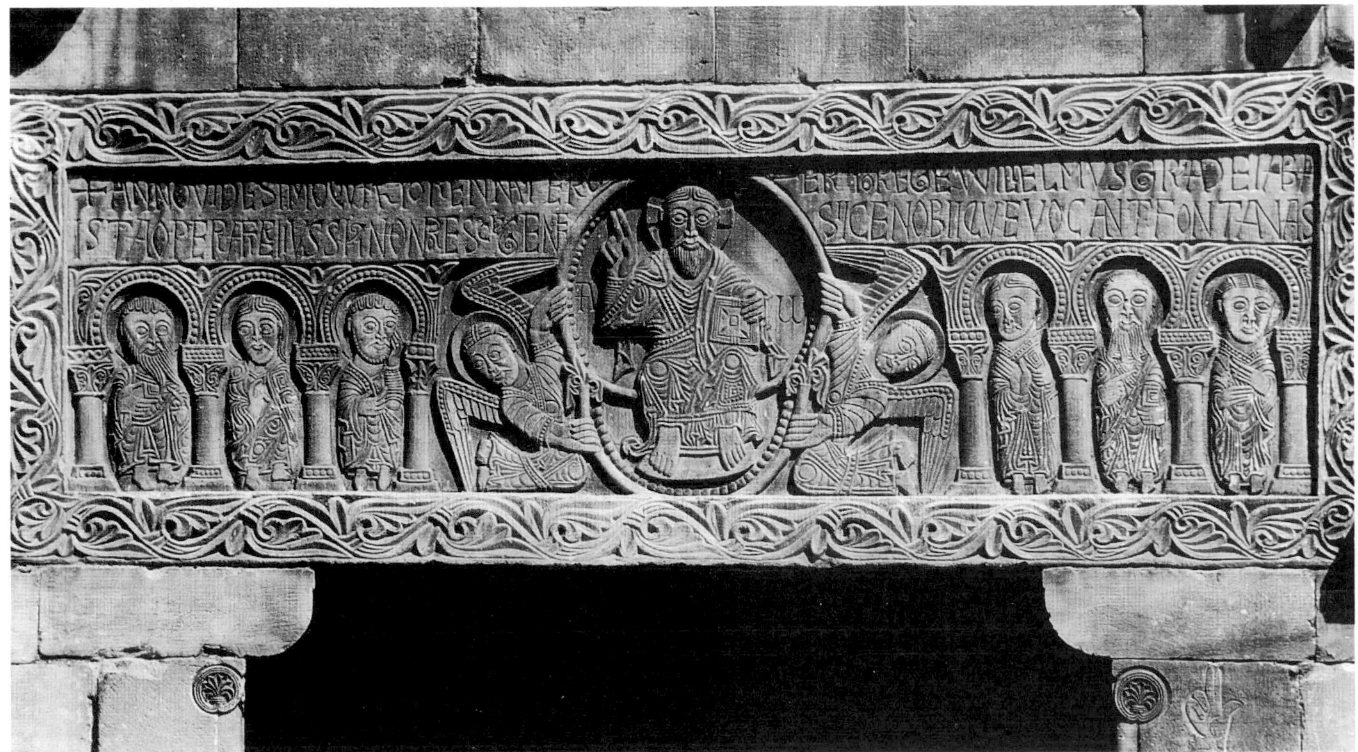

of developments in sculptural art common to northeastern Spain, southern France, and northern Italy, an artistically integrated region that can be considered as originative of Romanesque art. On the lintel at St. Génis-des-Fontaines, Christ is enthroned in a lobed mandorla supported by angels and is flanked by apostles in an arcade. The latter motif goes back centuries to Late Antiquity. Some Late Antique or Early Christian sarcophagus, or perhaps some later Carolingian or Ottonian derivative therefrom, may have been the sculptor's prototype. Whatever his source, he has translated its images into his own rudimentary idiom and similarly has adapted the original's ornament in the foliate motifs of the frame.

Almost a century later, the full Romanesque style emerges in the sculptured frieze of the façade of the Modena Cathedral in northern Italy (FIG. **9-27**). The sculpture, which extends on two levels across three bays of the façade, represents scenes from Genesis. The segment shown illustrates the *Creation and Temptation of Adam and Eve* (Genesis 2, 3:1–8) and, at the far left, Christ in a mandorla held by angels—the theme of the central section of the lintel at St. Génis-des-Fontaines. But here the style and execution are far more mature in representational sophistication. The frieze is the work of a master craftsman, whose name (Wiligelmus) is given in an inscription on another relief on the façade. The name is German, and the sculptor is believed to have been a German goldsmith. If so, the close relationship of Germany and Lombardy is indicated here in architecture as well as in sculpture. The figures have broken through the constriction of the arcade to make for a more continuous narrative. They are no longer in flat pattern but are cut in deep relief, some parts almost entirely in the round. The origins of the authoritative style of WILIGELMUS are obscure. His prototypes may have been fragments of Late Antique sarcophagi, Carolingian ivories, or the panels of doors like those at Hildesheim (FIG. 8-27). The rectilinear shape and the arrangement of the frieze suggest that it may have been inspired by sculptured altar frontals; as yet, the shape and arrangement are not logically related to the architecture of the façade, as the sculpture of the great Romanesque portals will be. Yet the Modena sculpture of Wiligelmus, whose work the inscription rightfully honors, is an outstanding and abrupt introduction to a new artistic style—"High Romanesque."

The stirring of the peoples in Romanesque Europe, the Crusades, the pilgrimages, and the commercial journeyings brought a slow realization that Europeans were of the same religion, even if of different ethnic stock. The reception of hitherto unknown documents of Greek thought and learning strongly influenced theology, bringing to it, along with new and deep challenges, a kind of order and concentration. Theologians undoubtedly dictated the subjects of the Romanesque portals; church authorities felt it

9-27 WILIGELMUS, *Creation and Temptation of Adam and Eve,* frieze on the west façade, Cathedral of Modena, Italy, c. 1110. Approx. 36" high.

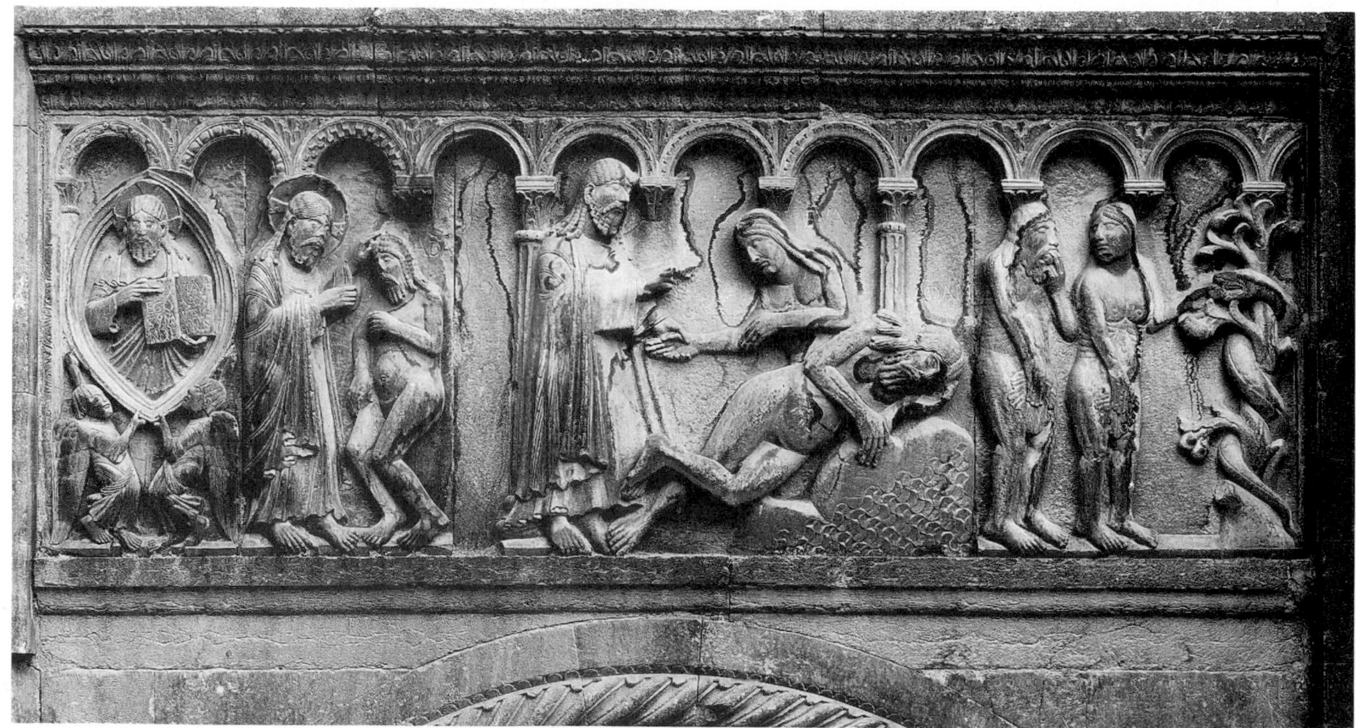

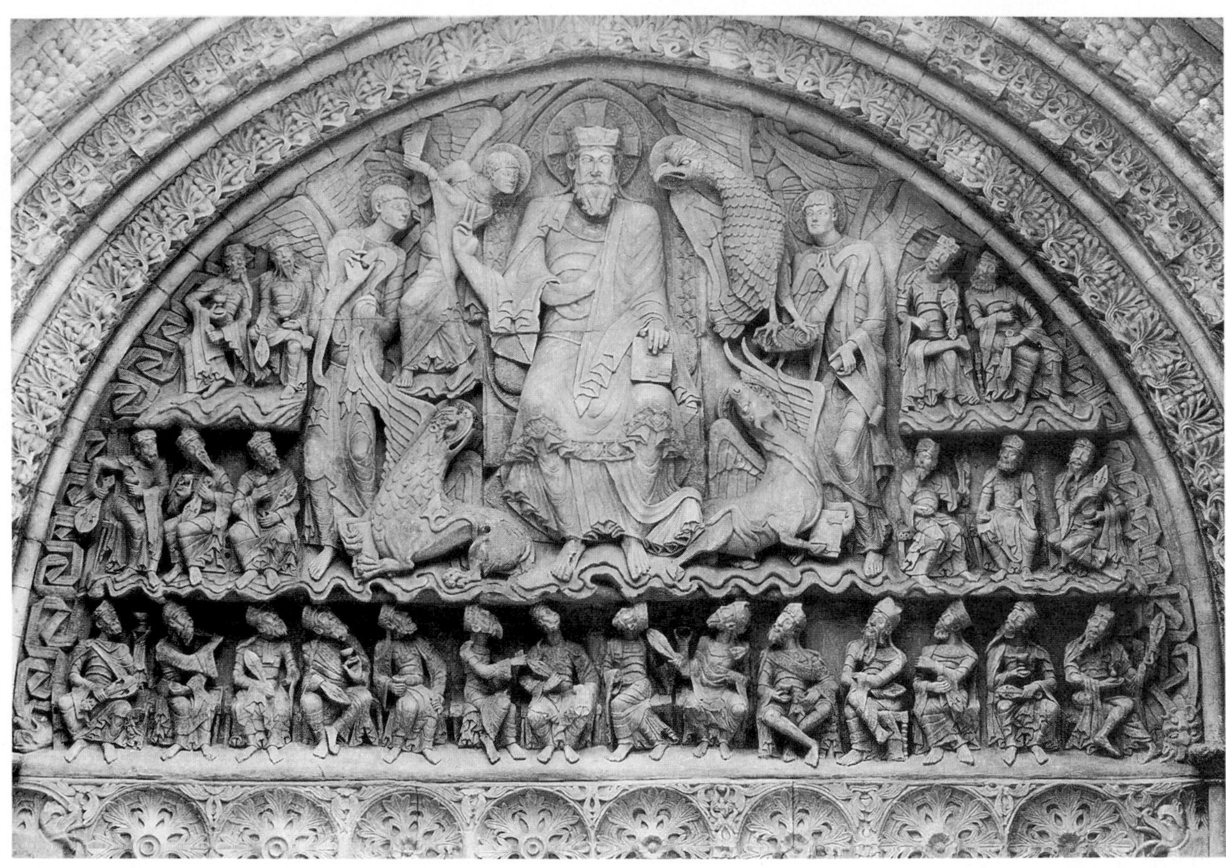

9-28 Tympanum of the south portal of St. Pierre, Moissac, France, *c.* 1115–1135. Diameter 16′ 6″.

was just as important to have the right subjects carved in the right places as to have the right arguments rightly arranged in a theological treatise. The apocalyptic vision of the Last Judgment, appalling to the imagination of twelfth-century believers, was represented conspicuously at the western entrance portal as an inescapable reminder to all who entered.

At Modena, the great frieze recounted the beginning of the human race; in a portal at Moissac, some twenty-five years later, its end was announced. With new architectural and iconographic organization giving coherence to sculptural design on a grand scale, the vast tympanum that crowns the portal of St. Pierre at Moissac depicts the Second Coming of Christ as King and Judge of the world in its last days (FIG. **9-28**). As befits his majesty, Christ is centrally enthroned, reflecting a rule of composition that we have seen followed since Early Christian times. The Signs of the Evangelists flank him: on his right side, the Angel of St. Matthew and the Lion of St. Mark, and on his left, the Eagle of St. John and the Ox of St. Luke. To one side of each pair of signs is an attendant angel holding scrolls on which to record the deeds of mankind for judgment. The figures of crowned musicians, which complete the design, are the twenty-four music-making elders who accompany Christ as the kings of all this world and make music in his praise. Each turns to face him, much as would the courtiers of a Romanesque monarch in attendance on their lord. The central group, reminiscent of the heraldic groupings of ancient Mesopotamian art, is set among the elders, who are separated into three tiers by two courses of wavy lines that symbolize the clouds of Heaven.

As many variations exist within the general style of Romanesque sculpture as within Romanesque architecture, and the figures of the Moissac tympanum constitute no exception. Yet elements familiar in painting and sculpture throughout western Europe in the eleventh and twelfth centuries also are found here. The extremely elongated figures of the recording angels, the curious, cross-legged, dancing pose of the Angel of St. Matthew, and the jerky, hinged movement are characteristic in general of the emerging vernacular style of representing the human figure. Earlier Carolingian, Ottonian, and Anglo-Saxon manners diffused and interfused to produce the now sure and unhesitating style-languages of the Romanesque. The zigzag and dovetail lines of the draperies (the linear modes of manuscript painting are everywhere apparent), the bandlike folds of the torsos, the bending back of the hands against the body, and the

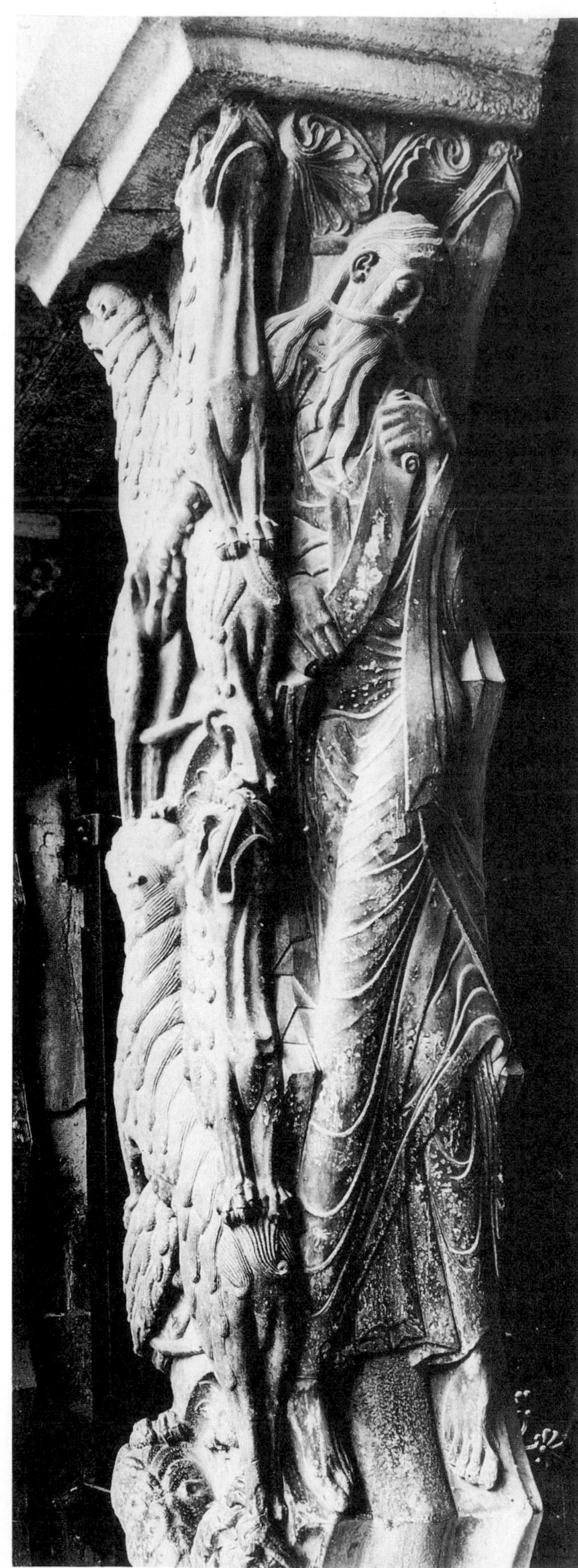

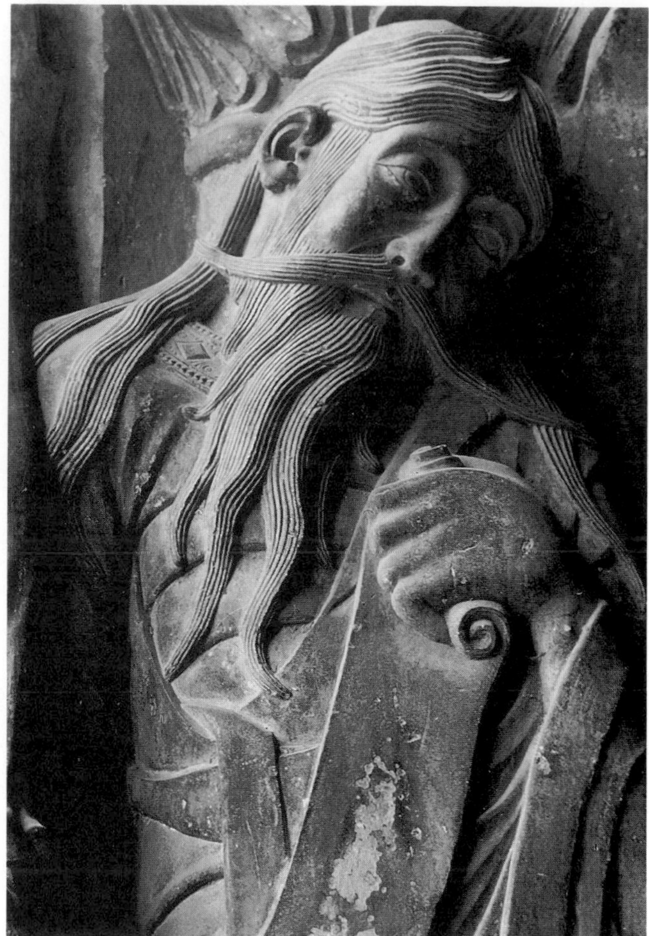

9-29 *Left: The Prophet Jeremiah (Isaiah?)* from the trumeau of the south portal of St. Pierre. Life size. *Above:* detail.

wide cheekbones are also common features of this new, cosmopolitan style.

A triumph of the style is the splendid figure of *The Prophet Jeremiah* (identified by some as Isaiah) carved in the trumeau of the Moissac portal (FIG. **9-29**). His position below the apparition of Christ as the apocalyptic judge is explained by his prophecy (recalled here by his scroll) of the end of the world, when "ruin spreads from nation to nation." He is compressed in the mass of the trumeau behind roaring, interlaced lions of the kind familiar not only in barbarian art but also in the art of ancient Mesopotamia and Persia and in Islamic Spain. The totemistic animal was never far from the instinct and imagination of the Medieval artist and was certainly not far from the medieval mind in general. Kings and barons often were named by association with animals thought to be the most fiercely courageous—for example, Richard the Lionheart, Henry the Lion, and Richard III of England, whose heraldic animal was the wild boar. It is not unthinkable that the Medieval artist, with millennia of animal lore and ornament to draw on, associated animal strength with architecture—the animal body being thought of as providing support and symbolizing the forces locked in the architectural fabric. The sphinxes and winged monsters at the palace gates in the ancient world—at Boghazköy, Khorsabad, Persepolis, and Mycenae (FIGS. 2-27, 2-30, 2-38, 4-23)—are the ancestors of the interlaced lions at Moissac.

The figure of the prophet is very tall and thin, in the manner of the angels of the tympanum, and, like the Angel of St. Matthew, he executes a cross-legged step that repeats the crisscrossing of the lions, although no representation of movement is yet apparent in terms of the actual structure of the body or its natural proportions. At this beginning of a new epoch in the history of sculpture, movement is a kind of grotesque, mechanical dance. The placing of the parts of the body depends on the architectural setting, on the sculptor's interpretation of whatever carved or painted model is being used, or on the vocabulary of the prevailing vernacular styles; the artist's originality also might play a large part, as in this case. The folds of the drapery are incised in flowing, calligraphic lines that ultimately derive from manuscript illumination and here play gracefully around the elegant figure.

A detail of the head and shoulders (FIG. 9-29) reveals the artist's striking characterization of the subject. The long, serpentine locks of hair and beard (familiar in the vocabulary of French Romanesque details) frame an arresting image of the dreaming mystic. The prophet seems entranced by his vision of what is to come, the light of ordinary day unseen by his wide eyes. His expression is slightly melancholy—at once pensive and wistful. For the Middle Ages, two alternative callings were available: one calling was to the active life *(vita activa);* the other was to the religious life of contemplation *(vita contemplativa),* the pursuit of the beatific vision of God. The sculptor of the Moissac prophet has given us the very image of the vita contemplativa. It has been said of Greek sculpture that the body becomes "alive" before the head (as in the *Fallen Warrior* from Aegina, FIG. 5-32); in the epoch that begins in the eleventh century, the head becomes humanly expressive well before the body is rendered as truly corporeal. The Moissac prophet is a remarkable instance of this.

Romanesque sculpture at Moissac is not confined to the portals; it also appears in delightful variety in the carved capitals within the church and in the cloister walk. It was sculpture such as this that Bernard of Clairvaux complained distracted the monks from their devotions. We are distracted, too—by the work's ingenuity and decorative beauty. The capitals of the Moissac cloister (FIG. **9-30**)—some of which are historiated, some purely decorative—are excellent

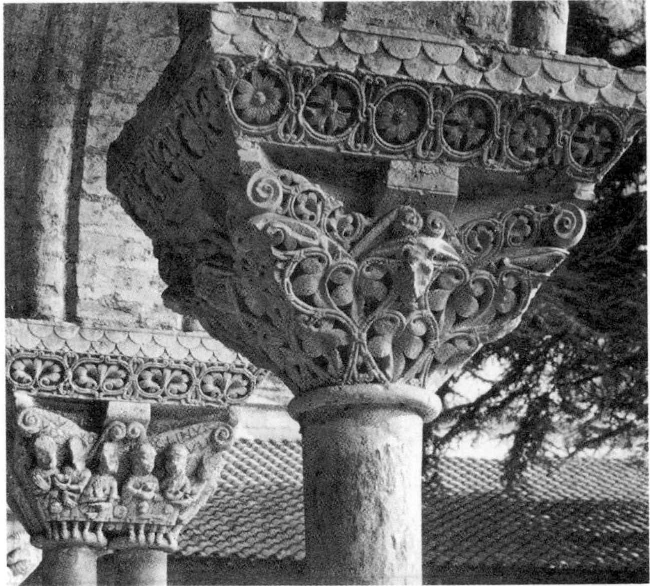

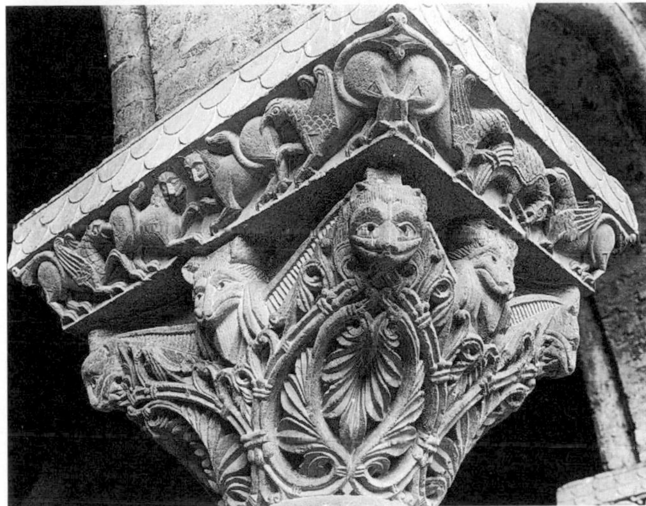

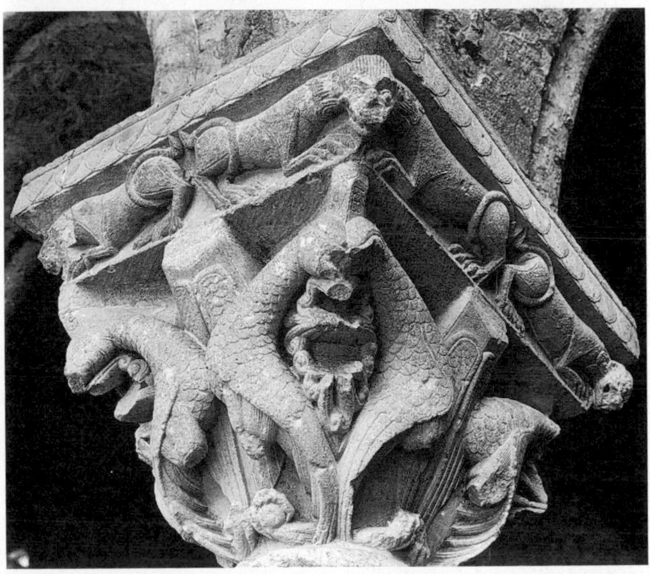

9-30 Capitals from the cloister of St. Pierre.

examples. The capital in the foreground of the view at the top has an intricate leaf-and-vine pattern with volutes, an echo of the Corinthian capital. The abacus carries rosettes, and its upper edge exhibits the fish-scale motif. The capital in the background has figures seated at a table, probably a representation of the Marriage Feast at Cana. The two other capitals shown reveal the richness and color of the Romanesque sculptor's imagination. Monsters of all sorts—basilisks, griffins, lizards, gargoyles—cluster and interlace and pass grinning before us. We have the medieval bestiary in stone.

Yet for all its distinctive stylistic characteristics and exotic appearance, Romanesque art reveals its debt to ancient Roman, Early Christian, and Byzantine art, and to their Classical heritage. For example, the beautifully carved rosettes on the lintel beneath the tympanum at Moissac (FIG. 9-28) derive from ancient Roman types. Some very late, still classicizing work, perhaps of the seventh century, probably served as model for the rosettes. Other rosettes closely resembling those of the Moissac lintel survive. At the same time, Islamic influence is unmistakable in other decorative motifs of the portal.

The relatives of the monsters of the Moissac capitals appear as the demons of Hell in the awesome tympanum of the church of St. Lazare at Autun in Burgundy (FIGS. **9-31** and **9-32**). At Moissac, we saw the apparition of the Divine Judge before he has summoned man; at Autun, the Judgment is in progress. The detail (FIG. 9-32) shows the weighing of souls (the reader may remember this theme from the Egyptian scroll in FIG. 3-45), while below, in the lintel, the dead are rising, one being plucked from the earth by giant hands. Humanity's pitiful weakness and littleness are distilled in these terror-stricken, weeping dolls, whom an angel with a trumpet summons to Judgment. Angels and devils contest at the scales where souls are being weighed, each trying to manipulate the beam for or against a soul. Hideous demons guffaw and roar. Their gaunt, lined bodies, with legs ending in sharp claws, writhe and bend like long, loathesome insects. A devil, leaning from the dragon-mouth of Hell, drags souls in, while, above him, a howling demon crams souls headfirst into a furnace. The resources of the Romanesque imagination, heated by a fearful faith, provide an appalling scene. We can appreciate the terror that the Autun tympa-

9-31 GISLEBERTUS, west tympanum of St. Lazare, Autun, France, *c.* 1130. 11′ 4″ high, 21′ wide at base.

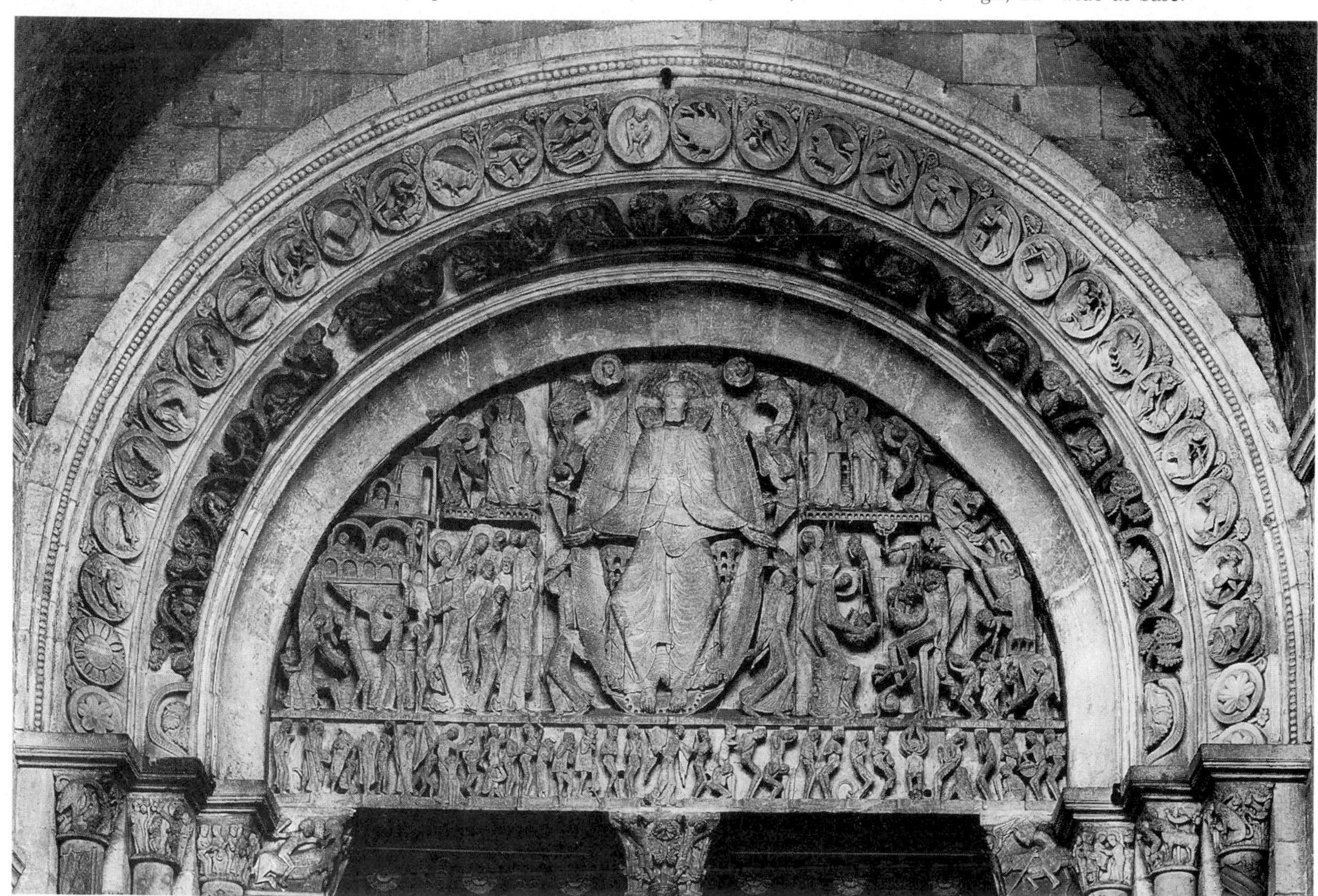

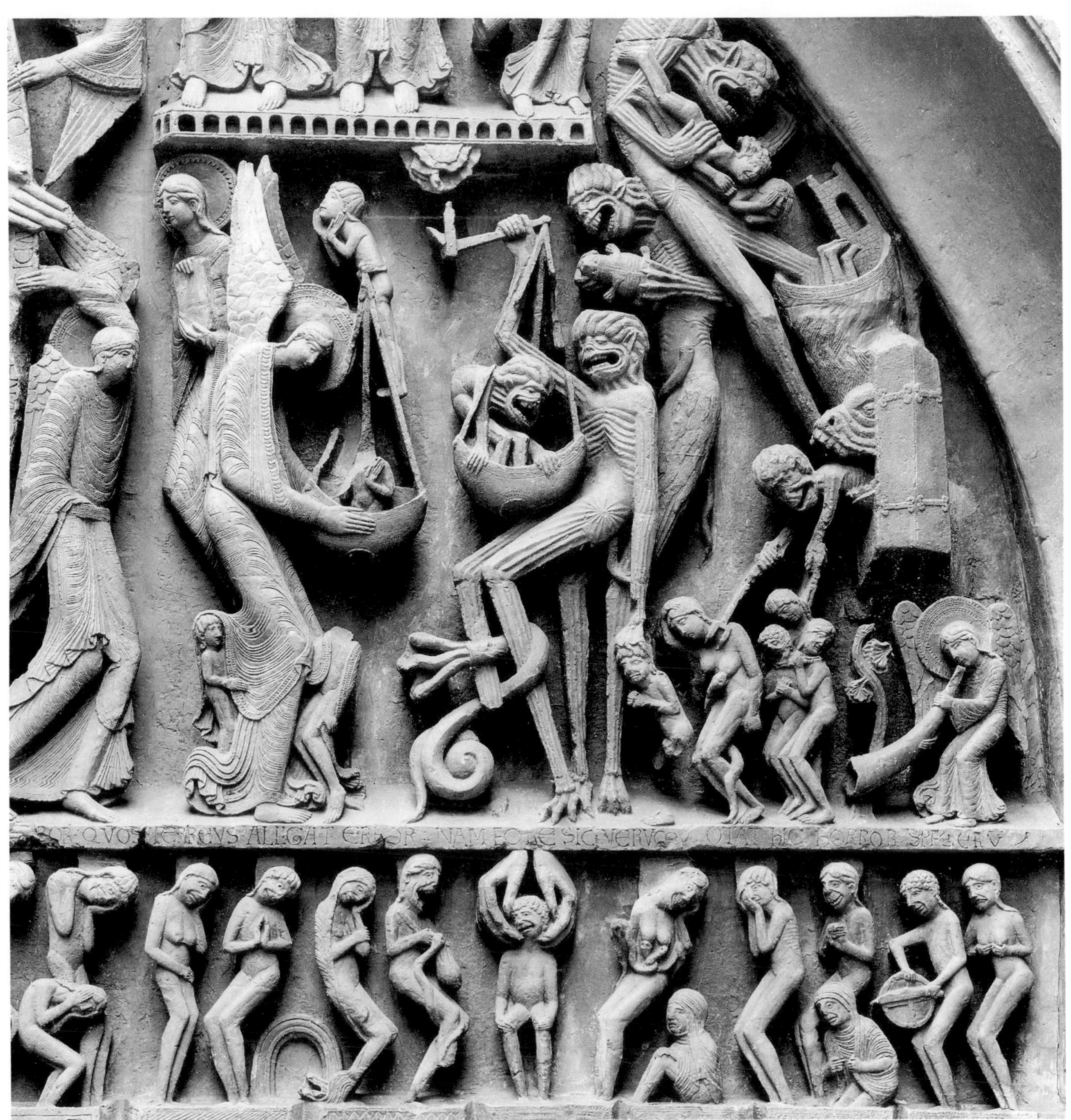

9-32 Detail of FIG. 9-31.

num must have inspired in the believers who passed beneath it as they entered the cathedral.

An inscription on the tympanum names MASTER GISLEBERTUS as the artist. This master stone-carver, whose work appears elsewhere at St. Lazare as well as on its portal, is like Wolvinius, who made the *Paliotto* in Sant' Ambrogio, Milan (FIG. 8-16), Gelduinus, who carved the St. Sernin sculptures (FIG. 9-24), and Wiligelmus, sculptor of the Modena frieze (FIG. 9-27). He wants to make sure his work is remembered in association with his name. In the twelfth century, more and more craftsmen-artists, illuminators as well as sculptors, would begin to identify themselves (we have yet to encounter MASTER HUGO [FIG. 9-40] and EADWINE THE SCRIBE [FIG. 9-41]). Although many Medieval artists remain anonymous,

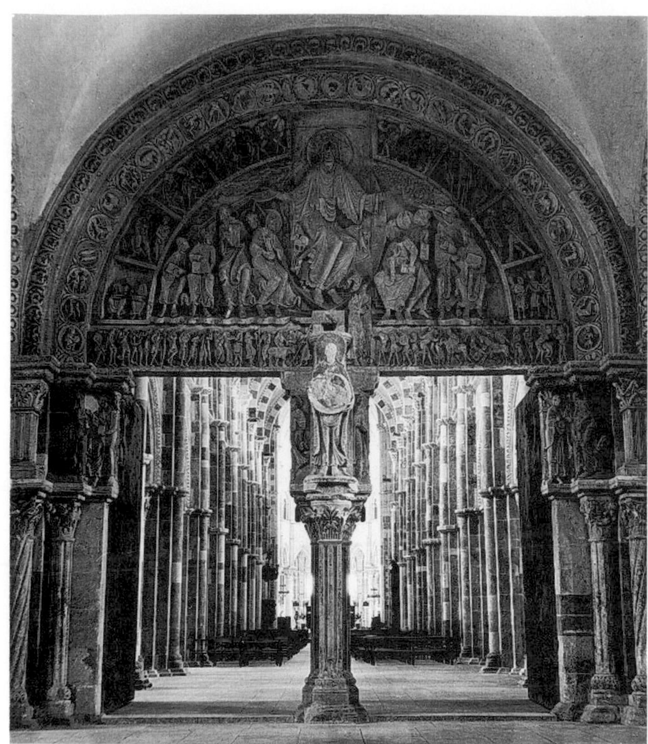

9-33 *The Ascension of Christ and the Mission of the Apostles,* center portal of the narthex of La Madeleine, Vézelay, France, 1120–1132.

the trend is now set that will culminate in the self-concerned, "fine" artist of the Renaissance, who is attentive to reputation and fame.

Another great tympanum, this one at the church of La Madeleine at Vézelay, not far from Autun, varies the theme of the apocalyptic Last Judgment, representing *The Ascension of Christ and the Mission of the Apostles* (FIGS. **9-33** and **9-34**). As related in scripture (Acts 1:4–9), Christ foretold that the apostles would receive the power of the Holy Ghost and become the witnesses of the truth of the Gospels throughout the world. The rays of light emanating from Christ's hands represent the promise of the coming of the Holy Ghost. The apostles, holding the Gospel books, receive their spiritual assignment. Christ assigns three specific tasks to the apostles and gives them the power to perform them: to save or to condemn; to preach the Gospel to all nations; to heal the sick and drive out devils. The task of saving or condemning is indicated in the central scene and in the lower four compartments adjacent to it. The task of preaching the Gospel to all nations (some at the very edge of the world) is represented on the lintel. The task of healing the sick and driving out devils is indicated in the upper four compartments. The outer archivolt has a repeated ornamental device; the inner archivolt has

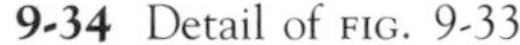

9-34 Detail of FIG. 9-33.

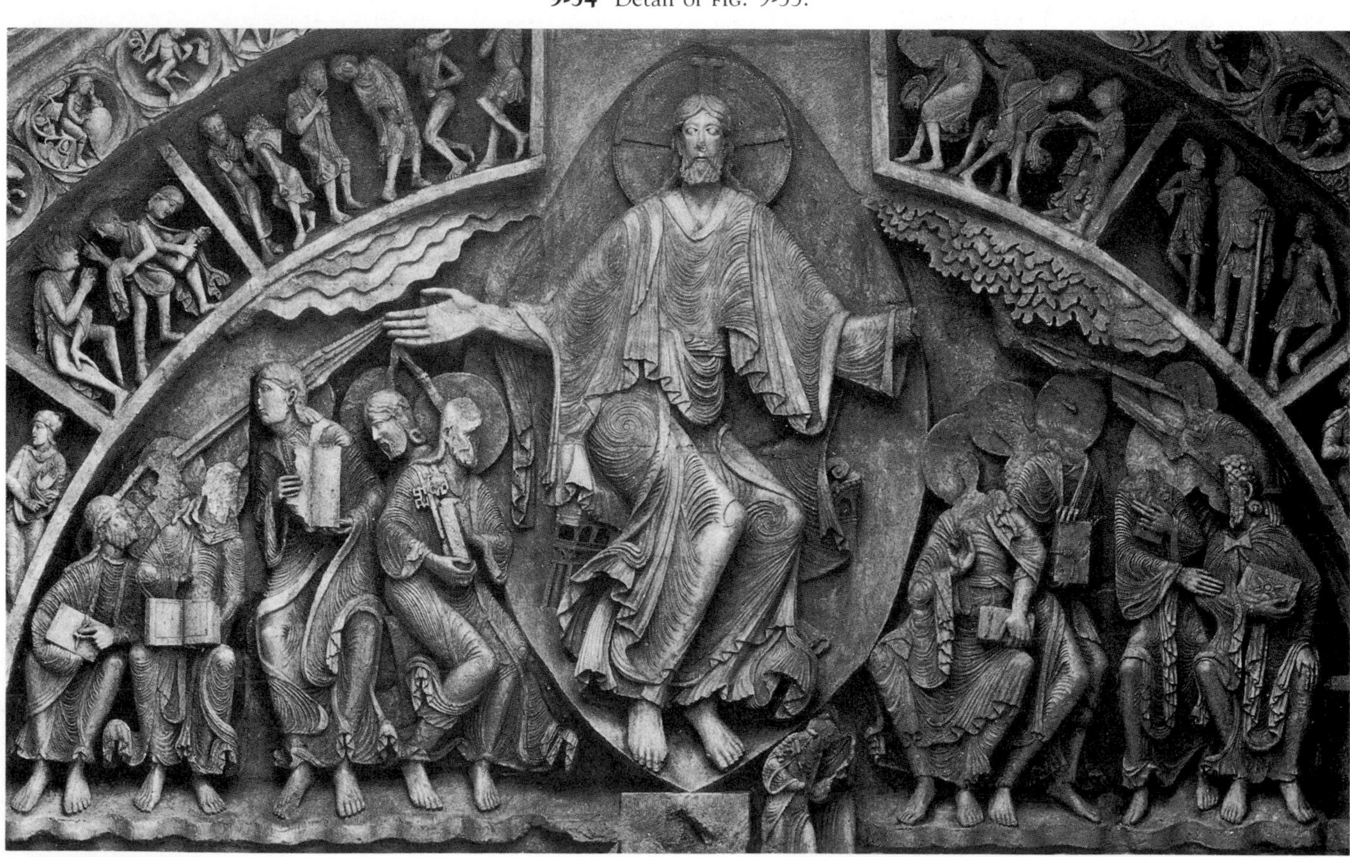

medallions with the signs of the zodiac, the seasons, and the labors characteristic of each month of a calendar year.

The Vézelay tympanum reflects, like a vast mirror, religious and secular writings and the influence of antiquity and the Byzantine East. It is a complete and encyclopedic work, in which the mission of the apostles and their power to perform it are merged in a single subject. The theme has its sources in the Acts and in the Gospels, in the prophecies of Isaiah, and in writings of antiquity and of the Middle Ages. The crowding, agitated figures reveal wild deformities. We find people with the heads of dogs, enormous ears, fiery hair, snoutlike noses; the lexicon of human defects and ailments includes hunchbacks, mutes, blind men, and lame men. Humanity, still suffering, awaits the salvation to come. The whole world is electrified by the promise of the ascended Christ, whose great figure, seeming to whirl in a vortex of spiritual energy, looms above human misery and deformity. Again, as in the Autun tympanum, we are made emphatically aware of the greatness of God and the littleness of human beings.

Vézelay is more closely associated with the Crusades than any other church in Europe. Pope Urban II had intended to preach the First Crusade at Vézelay in 1095, about thirty years before the tympanum was carved. In 1146, some fifteen years after the tympanum was in place, Bernard preached the Second Crusade, and King Louis VII of France took up the cross. In 1190, it was from Vézelay that King Richard the Lion-heart of England and King Philip Augustus of France set out on the Third Crusade. The spirit of the Crusades undoubtedly determined the iconography of the Vézelay tympanum, for it was believed that the Crusades were a kind of "second mission of the apostles" to convert the infidel.

Stylistically, the figures of the Vézelay tympanum display characteristics similar to those of the Moissac and Autun tympanums: abrupt and jerky movement (strongly exaggerated at Vézelay), rapid play of line, wind-blown drapery hems, elongation, angularity, and agitated poses, gestures, and silhouettes. The figure of the Vézelay Christ (FIG. 9-34) is a splendid essay in calligraphic theme and variation and is almost a summary of the Romanesque skill with decorative line. The lines of the drapery shoot out in rays, break into quick, zigzag rhythms, and spin into whorls, wonderfully conveying the spiritual light and energy that flow from Christ over and into the animated apostles. The technical experience of centuries of working with small art—with manuscripts, ivories, and metalcraft—is easily read from this monumental translation of such work into stone (compare the spiral whorls in FIG. 9-42 with those here).

In Provence, rich in the remains of Roman art and architecture, the vivid linear style of Languedoc (Moissac) and Burgundy (Autun and Vézelay) is considerably modified later in the twelfth century by the influence of the art of antiquity. The quieting influence of this art is seen at once in the figures on the façade of St. Trophime at Arles and in the design of the portal (FIG. **9-35**), which reflects the artist's interpretation of a Roman triumphal arch. The tympanum shows Christ surrounded by the Signs of the Evangelists. On the lintel, directly below him, the Twelve Apostles appear at the center of a continuous frieze that depicts the Last Judgment; the outermost parts of the frieze depict the saved (on Christ's right) and the damned in the flames of Hell (on his left). Below this, in the jambs and the front bays of the portals, stand grave figures of saints draped in Classical garb, their quiet stance contrasting with the spinning, twisting, dancing figures seen at Autun and Vézelay. The stiff regularity of the figures in the frieze also contrasts with the animation of the great Burgundian tympanums and reminds us of the "lining-up" seen in Early Christian sarcophagus sculpture. The draperies of these frieze figures at Arles, like those of the large statues below, are also less agitated and show

9-35 Portal on the west façade of St. Trophime, Arles, France, late twelfth century.

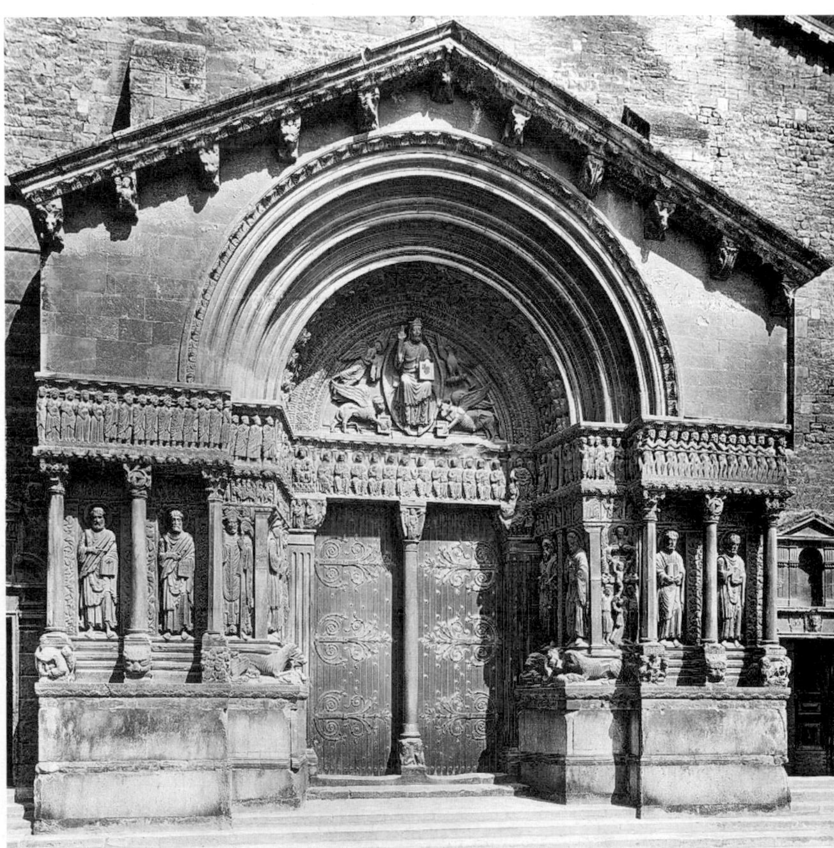

nothing of the dexterous linear play familiar at Moissac, Autun, and Vézelay. Here, the rigid lines of the architecture of the façade as a whole (rather than just an enframing element, such as a tympanum) now are determining the placement and look of the sculpture, and the freedom of execution appropriate to small art has been sacrificed to a simpler and more monumental adjustment to the architecture. In the north of France, near Paris, a new system of portal sculpture developed some thirty years earlier than that at St. Trophime. In the Royal Portals of the cathedral of Chartres (FIG. 10-14), we shall see the expansion of the whole portal design into a magnificent frontispiece, in which the architectural and sculptural elements are balanced, the sculptural style being firmly determined by the lines of the building.

PAINTING AND ILLUMINATION

We can begin an account of Romanesque painting with a work that is *not* a painting. Nor is the famous and unique *Bayeux Tapestry* (FIG. **9-36**) a woven tapestry. It is rather an embroidered (needle-worked) fabric made of wool sewn on linen. Some 20 inches high and about 230 feet long, this work is a continuous, friezelike, pictorial narrative of a crucial moment in the history of England and of the events that led up to it. The Norman defeat of the Anglo-Saxons at Hastings in 1066 brought Saxon England under the control of the Normans, uniting all of England and much of France under one rule; the dukes of Normandy (descendants of the Viking Norsemen) became the kings of England. Commissioned by Bishop Odo, the half brother of the conquering Duke William (under whose reign in Normandy St. Étienne at Caen had been begun), the "tapestry" may have been sewn by ladies at the Norman court, although some believe it was the work of English needlewomen in Kent, where Odo had been given lands and influence by Duke William.

The *Bayeux Tapestry* is unique in Romanesque art in that it depicts a contemporary event in full detail at a time shortly after it took place—a kind of distant anticipation of modern pictorial reportage. Inscriptions accompanying the pictures comment on the action. A section of the embroidered frieze shows a charge of Norman cavalry; the upper and lower margins show various fanciful beasts and birds in heraldic arrangement. Despite the schematic simplification of form, the Archaic flatness without cast shadows, and an entirely neutral background, the tapestry conveys a surprisingly exact description of arms and armor, as well as a convincing representation of action, pose, and gesture. The work is of great importance, not only as art, but also as a valuable historical document. The stylistic unity and consistency found throughout the whole length of the tapestry suggest that it is the

9-36 *Norman Cavalry Charging in the Battle of Hastings,* from the *Bayeux Tapestry,* 1070–1080. Embroidered wool on linen, 20″ high (entire length of fabric 229′ 8″). Musée de Peinture, Bayeux.

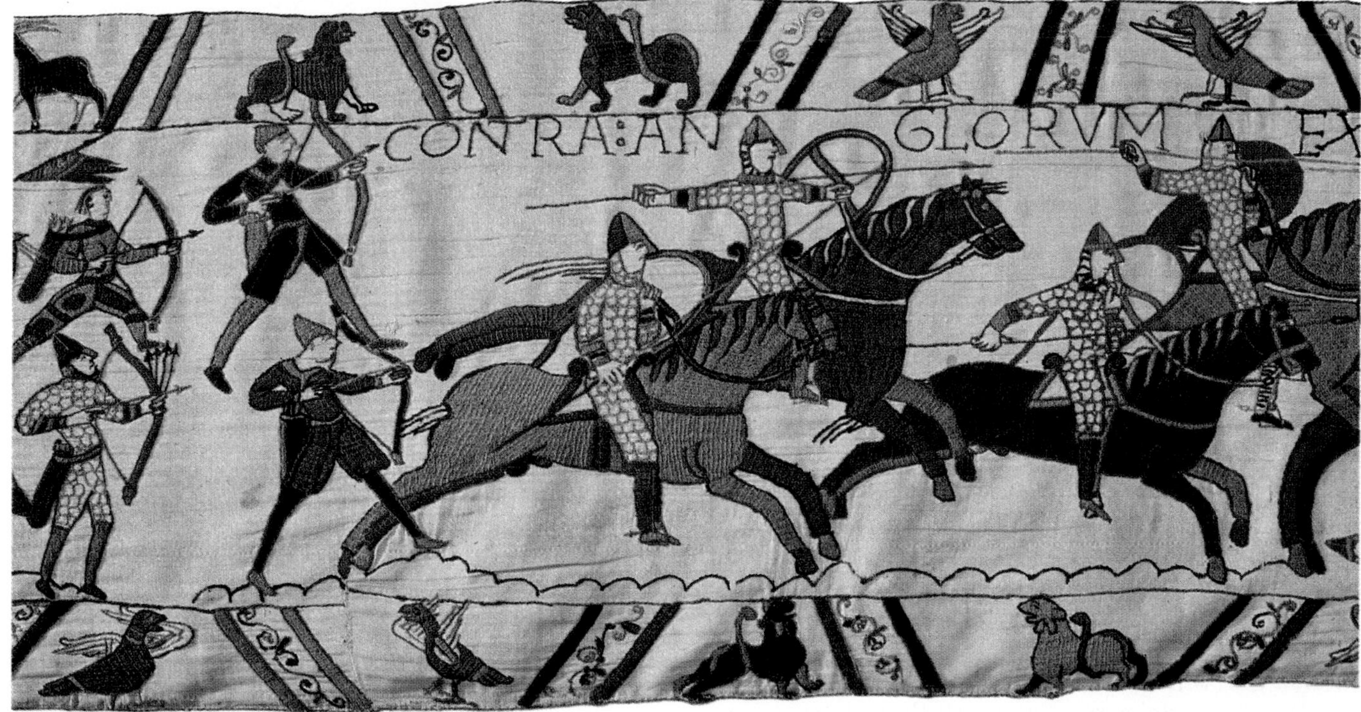

product of a single designer or a small "school" of needleworkers thoroughly trained in a distinctive idiom of representation.

Like monumental sculpture, monumental mural painting comes into its own once again in the eleventh century. Although we have several examples of it from Carolingian and Ottonian times and although an unbroken tradition of such painting existed in Italy, it blossoms in the Romanesque period. As with architecture and sculpture, mural painting exhibits many regional styles and many degrees of sophistication. Sometimes a provincial style can reveal more clearly than its sophisticated source the elements common to both. Such a case is the mural painting in the apse of the little church of Santa Maria at Tahull in Catalonia, in the extreme northeastern corner of Spain. This painting (FIG. **9-37**) could be called provincial Byzantine, as, for that matter, could much Romanesque painting. If we compare it with a Byzantine mosaic like the one at Daphne (FIG. 7-53) or the apse mosaic at Monreale (FIG. 7-55), we find that its distance from the Byzantine source—much greater than the distance from Venice or Sicily to Byzantium—results in a loss of subtlety and refinement and some misunderstanding of motifs in the original style. On the other hand, the Tahull painting has a simple and strong directness, even bluntness, that gives it a peculiarly expressive force. One emphatic feature is the partitioning of the draped figures into separate, decoratively modeled segments that almost break the figure itself into independent parts. (Note the similarity to the modulation and articulation of Romanesque architecture.) This feature is seen especially well in the pattern made by the pipelike legs and the ladderlike folds between them. The decorative banding of the surface here serves to keep the figures flat and contributes to the effect of stiff formality. The drapery, also with decorative partitioning, is scarcely distinguished from the body. Even the hands of the Madonna are subdivided, as are the heads and necks of other figures. This technique, which had begun to appear in Ottonian painting (FIG. 8-29), is almost universal in Romanesque painting; it may be seen beneath the whirling linear draperies of the sculptures at Autun and Vézelay (FIGS. 9-30 and 9-32) and in the angels of the Moissac tympanum (FIGS. 9-28 and 9-29). At Tahull, the sharp patterning of the figures is assisted by bold coloring, and the whole effect is one of rude strength, not a little of which derives from the architectural planes to which the patterned figures masterfully are adjusted.

The vernacular Romanesque style can be seen almost in exaggeration in a manuscript illumination from northern France illustrating the life of St. Audomarus (Omer) (FIG. **9-38**). Here, the figures are

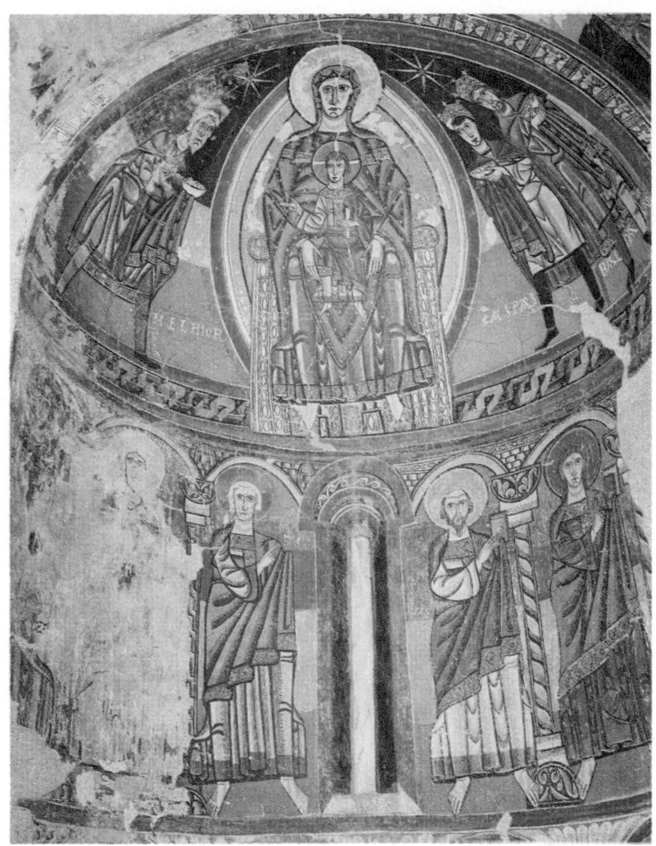

9-37 *Adoration of the Magi,* apse fresco from Santa Maria, Tahull, Spain, eleventh century.

9-38 *The Life and Miracles of St. Audomarus (Omer),* eleventh century. Illuminated manuscript. Bibliothèque Municipale, Saint-Omer.

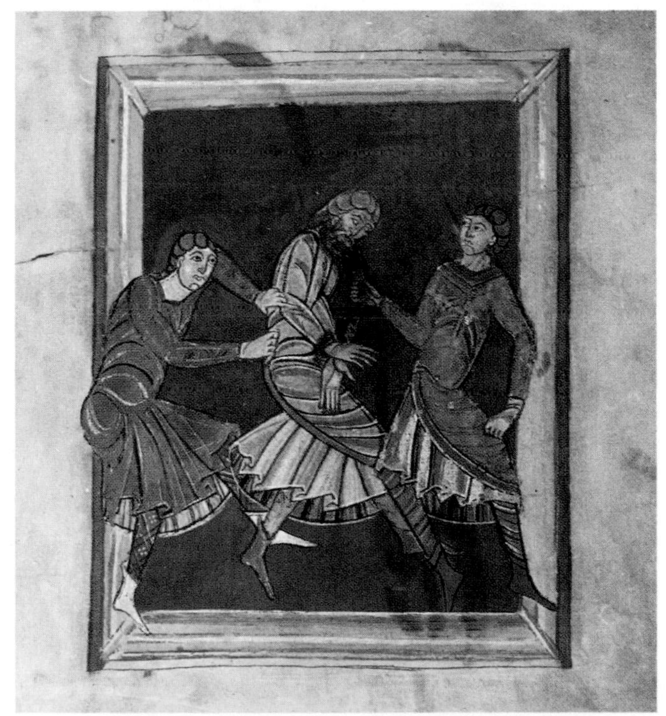

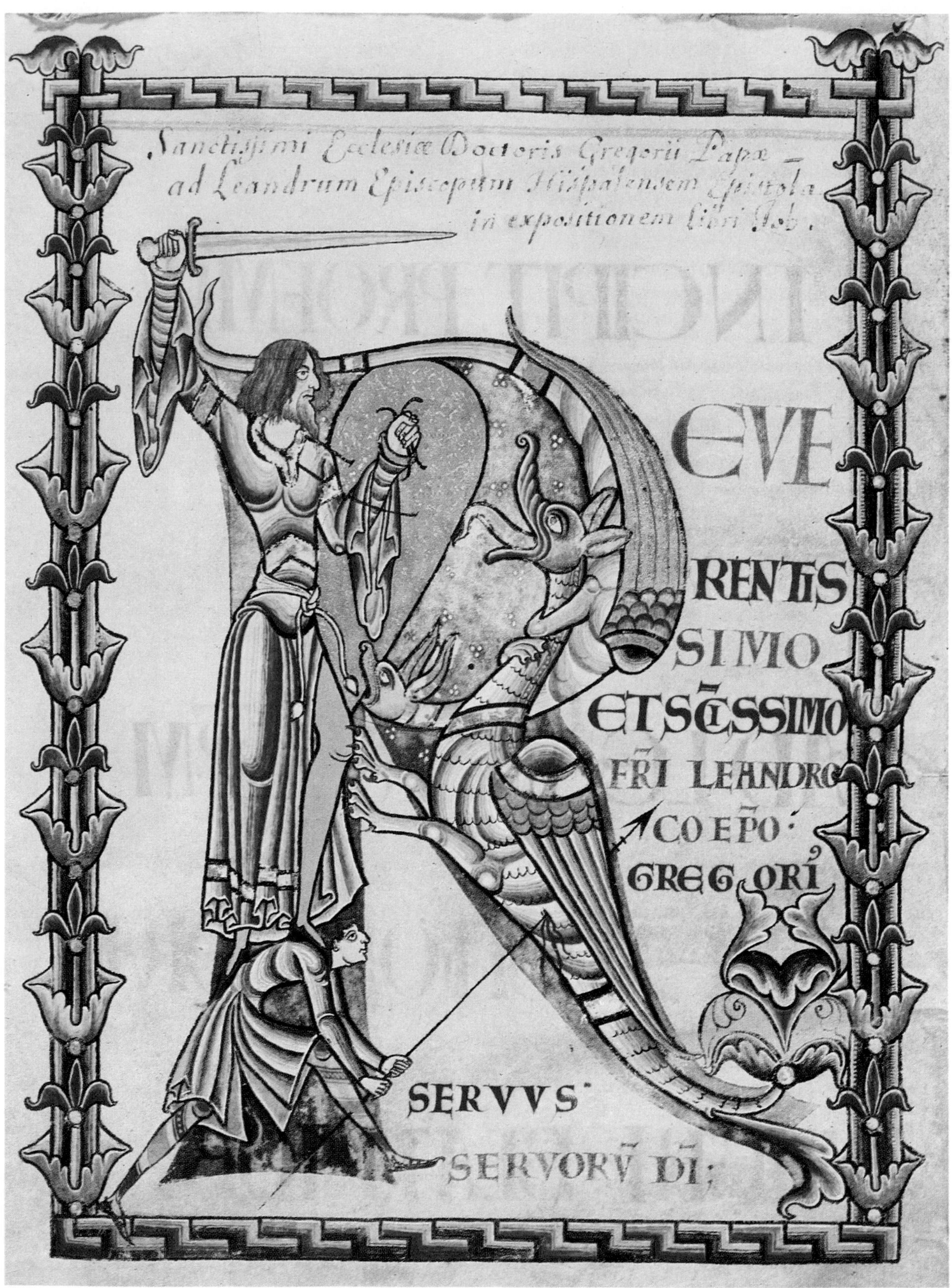

9-39 Initial *R* with *St. George and the Dragon,* from the *Moralia in Job,* Citeaux, France, early twelfth century. Illuminated manuscript, $13\frac{3}{4}'' \times 9\frac{1}{4}''$. Bibliothèque Municipale, Dijon.

cut into patterns by hard lines, and the action is remote from even an approximation of organic motion. St. Audomarus (bound and pulled by the beard) and his captors seem to be performing some bouncing ritual ballet. The frame creates no sense of containment, as it did in Anglo-Saxon and Carolingian manuscripts, and bodies and feet move arbitrarily in, out of, and across it. Although locally different from the Tahull mural, the St. Audomarus illumination shares its fundamental vocabulary.

That same vocabulary, richly applied and gracefully modulated, appears in what surely must be one of the masterpieces of Medieval art—a manuscript illuminated in Bernard's great abbey of Citeaux, the motherhouse of the Cistercian order. Citeaux, and its sister abbey, Clairvaux, where Bernard was abbot, produced magnificent illuminated manuscripts throughout the twelfth century. One of the most remarkable was Gregory's *Moralia in Job,* painted before 1111. A splendid example of Cistercian illumination, the historiated initial from this manuscript (FIG. **9-39**) represents St. George, his squire, and the roaring dragons intricately composed to make the letter *R.* St. George, a slender, regal figure, raises his shield and sword against the dragons—distinguished representations of the age-old animal style so often encountered—while the squire, crouching beneath St. George, runs a lance through one of the monsters. (An image of status, the greater and the lesser dragons correspond to the lord and his man.) The ornamented initial goes back to the Hiberno-Saxon eighth century; the inclusion of a narrative within the initial is a practice that would have an important future in Gothic illumination. The banding of the torso, the fold partitions (especially evident in the skirts of the servant), and the dovetail folds—all part of the Romanesque manner—are done here with the skill of a master who deftly avoids the stiffness and angularity that result from less skillful management of the vocabulary. Instead, this artist makes a virtue of stylistic necessity; the partitioning accentuates the verticality and elegance of the figure of St. George and the thrusting action of his servant. The flowing sleeves add a spirited flourish to St. George's gesture. The knight, handsomely garbed, cavalierly wears no armor and aims a single stroke with proud disdain. This miniature may be a reliable picture of the costume of a medieval baron and of the air of nonchalant gallantry he cultivated.

An illumination of exceedingly refined execution, exemplifying the sumptuous illustration common to the large Bibles produced in the wealthy Romanesque abbeys, is the frontispiece to the Book of Deuteronomy from the Bury Bible (FIG. **9-40**). Produced at the abbey of Bury St. Edmunds in England in the early twelfth century, this work shows two scenes from Deuteronomy enframed by symmetrical leaf motifs in softly glowing, harmonized colors. The upper register shows Moses and Aaron proclaiming the law to the Israelites; the lower portrays Moses pointing out the clean and unclean beasts. The gestures are slow and gentle and have quiet dignity. The figures of Moses and Aaron seem to glide. This presentation is quite different from the abrupt emphasis and spastic movement seen in earlier Romanesque painting; here, as the patterning softens, the movements of the figure become more integrated and smooth. Yet the patterning does remain in the multiple divisions of the draped limbs, the lightly shaded volumes being connected with sinuous lines and ladderlike folds;

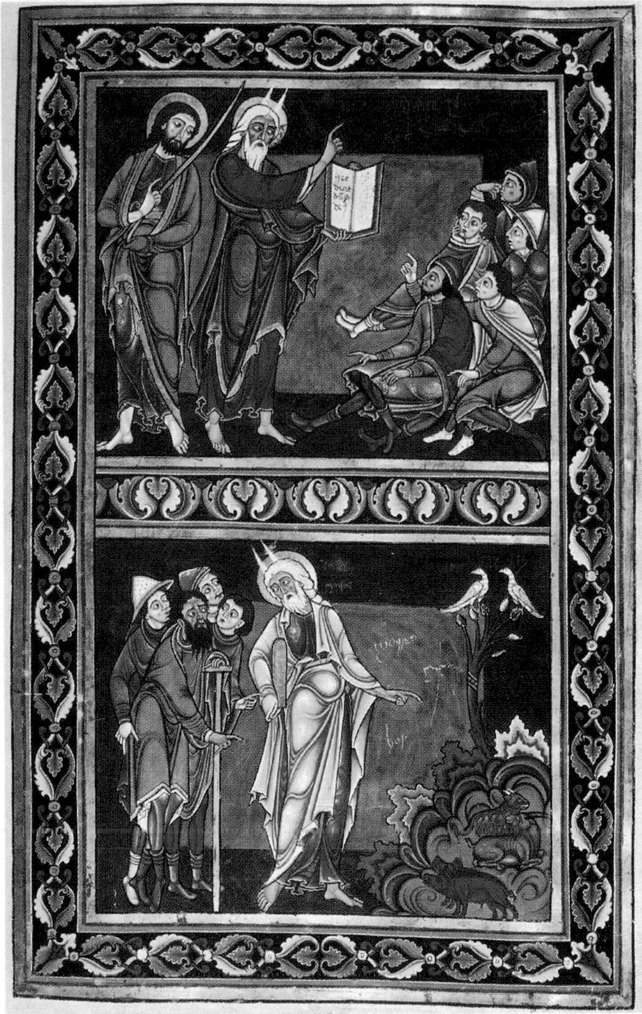

9-40 MASTER HUGO, *Moses Expounding the Law,* from the Book of Deuteronomy, Bury Bible, the abbey of Bury St. Edmunds, England, early twelfth century. Illuminated manuscript, approx. 20″ × 14″. Reproduced by permission of the Master and Fellows of Corpus Christi College, Cambridge, England.

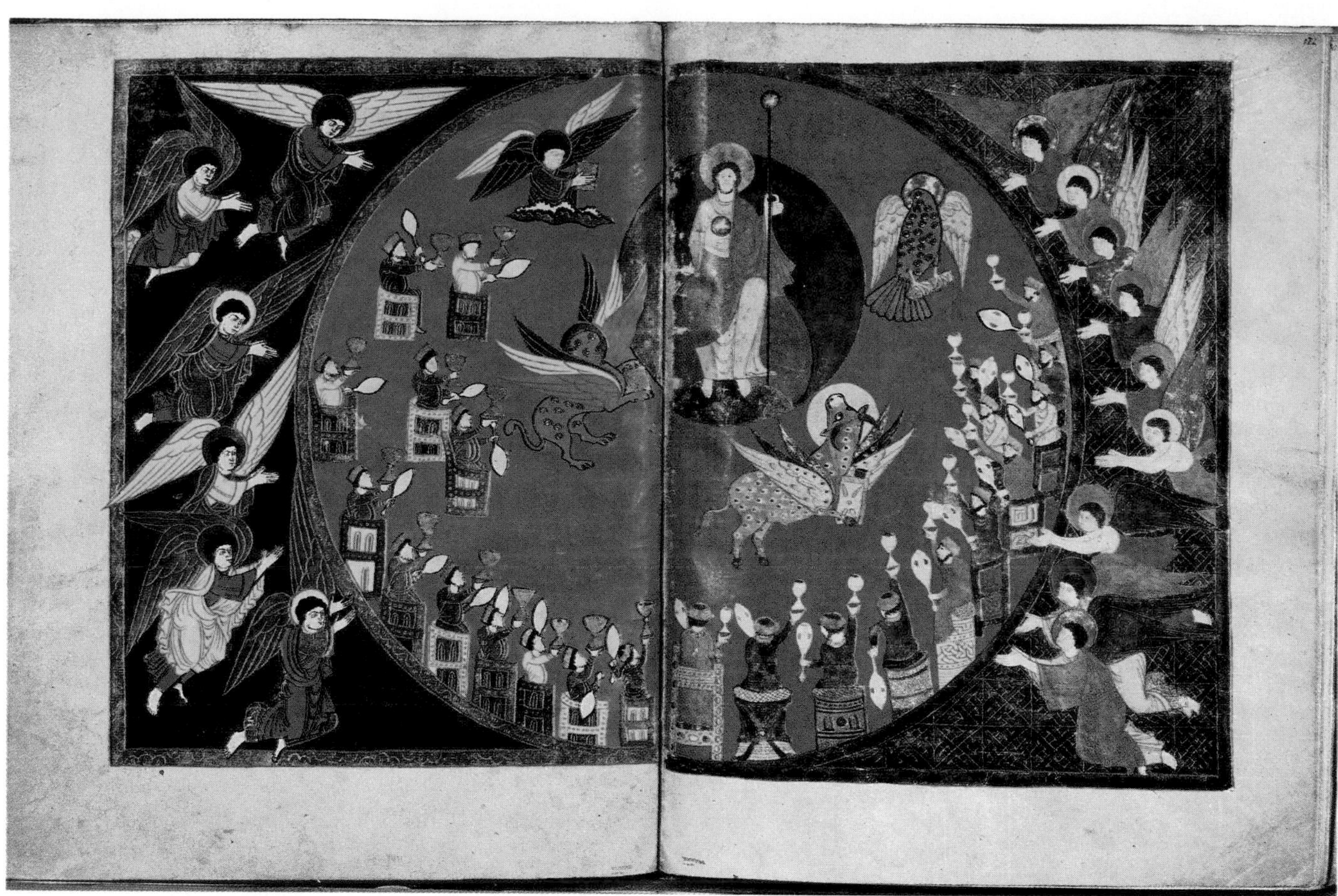

9-41 *The Revelation to St. John: Enthroned Christ with Signs of the Evangelists and the Twenty-four Elders,* from the *Apocalypse of St. Sever,* painted in the abbey of St. Sever, France, c. 1050. Bibliothèque Nationale, Paris.

the drapery and body are still thought of as somehow the same. The frame now has a quite definite limiting function, and the figures are carefully fitted within it.

The apocalyptic vision of the Second Coming of Christ, recorded in the Book of Revelation and carved on the great tympanum at Moissac (FIG. 9-27), is represented in the illuminations of the *Apocalypse of St. Sever* (FIG. **9-41**), a book of commentaries on the Apocalypse written by Beatus of Liébana, an eighth-century theologian. The theme of the Second Coming was of such interest that numerous manuscripts of Beatus's commentary were copied and illustrated; with the exception of this book, all were produced in Spain. The *Apocalypse of St. Sever,* made in the French monastery of that name, is significant not only as a masterpiece of the illuminator's art but also as a pictorial relative of the Moissac tympanum, for which it, or another book like it, may have served as a prototype. The characters in the drama are essentially the same; only the composition is different. In both cases, the artist has strictly followed the biblical account of the vision of St. John (Revelation 4:6–8, 5:8–9). Christ, enthroned in a sapphire aura, is surrounded by the Signs of the Evangelists, whose bodies are full of eyes and who are borne aloft by numerous wings. The twenty-four crowned and music-making elders offer their golden cups of incense and their stringed rebecks (viols). Flights of angels frame the great circle of the apparition. Color, intense and vivid, is harmonized with great sophistication. The agile figures are fluently drawn. The seated elders are shown in a kind of bird's-eye perspective, in which their figures overlap, and some of them are seen from behind. Within a context of visionary abstraction, these deft touches of realism still are contained by the characteristic patternings of Romanesque figural art.

The transition from the Romanesque vernacular style to something new seems to reach a midpoint in a work of great expressive power, the portrait of *The Scribe Eadwine* in the *Canterbury Psalter* (FIG. **9-42**). This portrait was made in Canterbury about the same time as the Bury Bible. Particularly noteworthy is the fact that the portrait represents a living man, a priestly scribe—not some sacred person or King David, who usually dominated the Psalter. Although it is true that Carolingian and Ottonian manuscripts included portraits of living men, those portraits were of reigning emperors, whose right to appear in sacred books was God-given, like the right of Justinian and Theodora and their court to be depicted in the sanctuary of San Vitale (FIGS. 7-36 and 7-37). Here, the inclusion of his own portrait sanctified the scribe's work, marking a change in attitude that points to the future emergence of the artist as a person and a name. Eadwine greatly has aggrandized his importance by likening his image to that of an Evangelist writing his gospel (FIGS. 8-9, 8-10, 8-12, 8-13) and by including an inscription within the inner frame that identifies him and proclaims that he is a prince among writers. He declares that, due to the excellence of his work, his fame will endure forever and that he can offer his book as an acceptable gift to God. The Medieval artist, concerned as he might be for his fame, is not yet aware of the concepts of fine art and fine artist; these will emerge in the Renaissance. As yet, his work exists not for its own sake, but for God's.

The style of the Eadwine portrait is related to that of the Bury Bible, but, although the patterning is still firm (notably in the cowl and the thigh), the drapery has begun to fall softly, to wrap about the frame, to overlap parts of it, and to follow the movements beneath. Here, the arbitrariness of the Romanesque vernacular style yields slightly, but clearly, to the requirements of a more naturalistic representation. The artist's instinct for decorative elaboration of the surface remains, as is apparent in the whorls and spirals of the gown, but significantly, these are painted in very lightly and do not conflict with the functional lines that contain them.

With the distinction of body and drapery finally achieved in the Gothic art of the thirteenth century, an epoch of increasing naturalism will begin. As did Exekias's billowing sail (FIG. 5-7), the Eadwine figure marks a turning point—in this case, in the history of Medieval representation. The Late Romanesque and Early Gothic "feel" of body and drapery as surfaces that interact forcefully implies not only a sense of their materiality but also a sense of depth. That sense will sharpen and deepen into the representational art of the Renaissance.

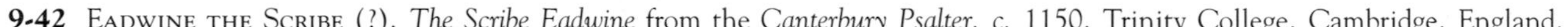

9-42 EADWINE THE SCRIBE (?), *The Scribe Eadwine* from the *Canterbury Psalter,* c. 1150, Trinity College, Cambridge, England.

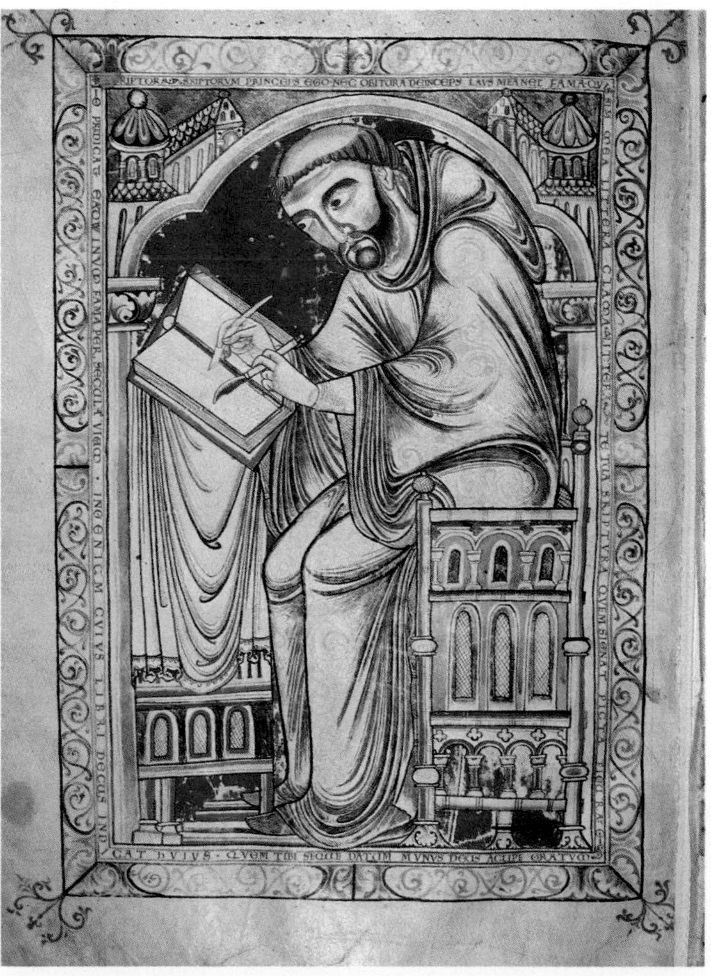

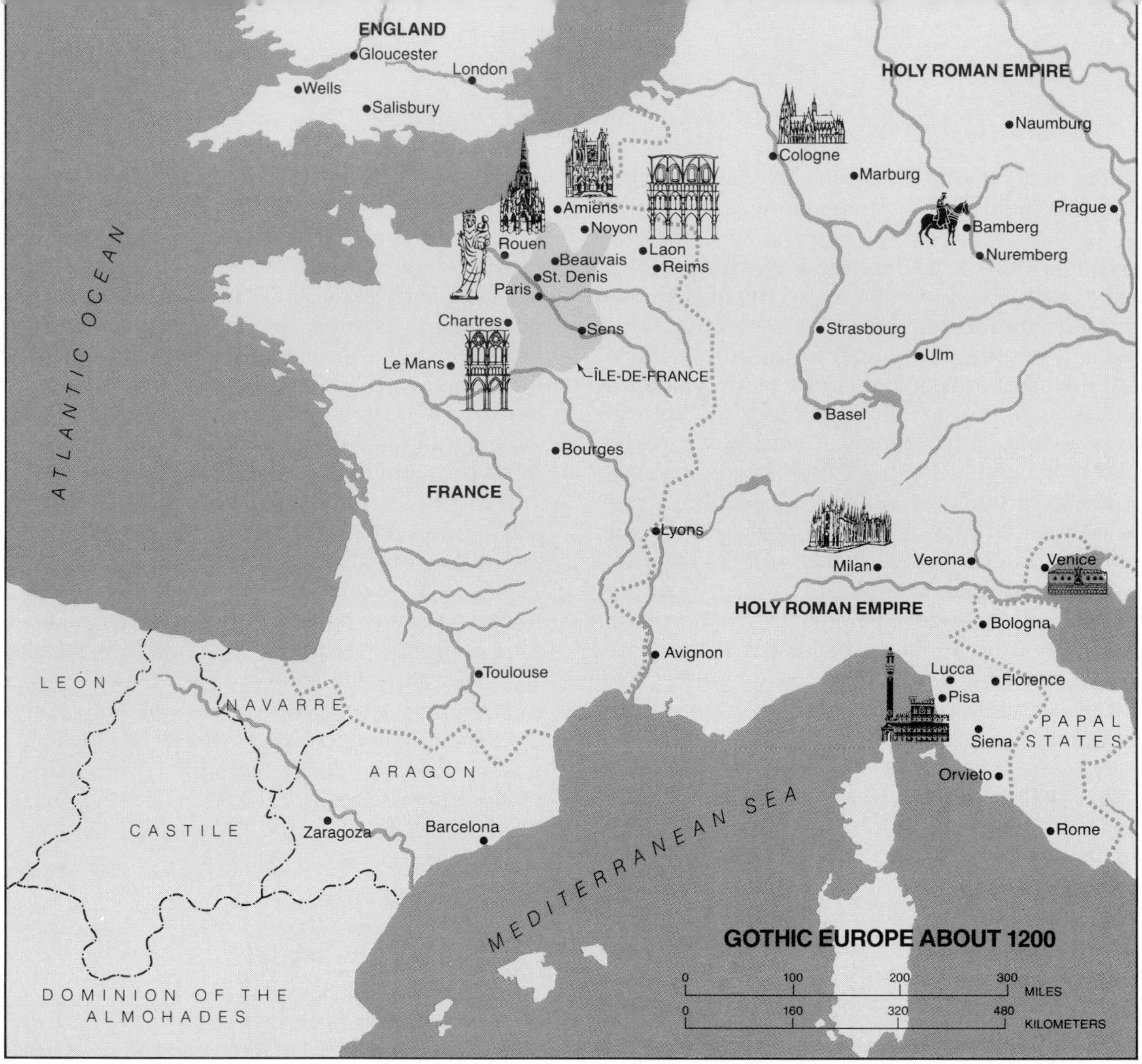

ENGLAND
Gloucester
London
Wells
Salisbury
HOLY ROMAN EMPIRE
Naumburg
Cologne
Marburg
Prague
Amiens
Noyon
Bamberg
Nuremberg
Rouen
Beauvais
Laon
Reims
St. Denis
Paris
Chartres
Sens
Strasbourg
Ulm
Le Mans
ÎLE-DE-FRANCE
Basel
Bourges
ATLANTIC OCEAN
FRANCE
Lyons
Milan
Verona
Venice
HOLY ROMAN EMPIRE
Bologna
Avignon
Toulouse
Lucca
Florence
Pisa
LEÓN
NAVARRE
PAPAL STATES
Siena
ARAGON
Orvieto
CASTILE
Zaragoza
Barcelona
MEDITERRANEAN SEA
Rome

GOTHIC EUROPE ABOUT 1200

0 100 200 300 MILES
0 160 320 480 KILOMETERS

DOMINION OF THE ALMOHADES

1140	1194	1250	1300
EARLY GOTHIC PERIOD	HIGH GOTHIC PERIOD		

Laon Cathedral
c. 1160–1205

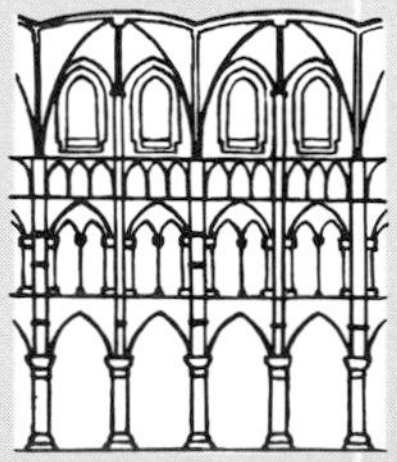

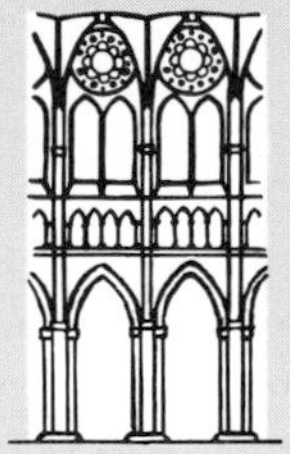

Chartres Cathedral
(rebuilt) 1194–1220

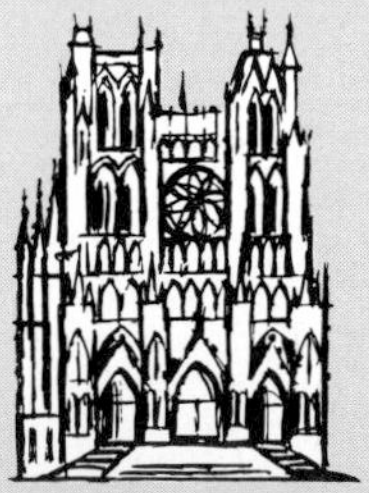

Amiens Cathedral
1220–1236

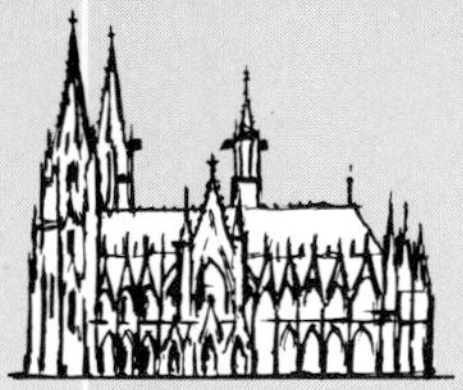

Cologne Cathedral
begun 1248

Virgin of Paris
early 14th century

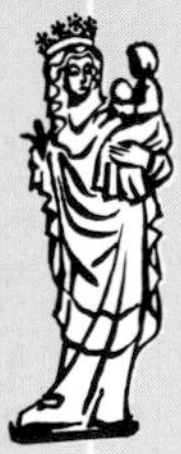

Bamberg Rider
late 13th century

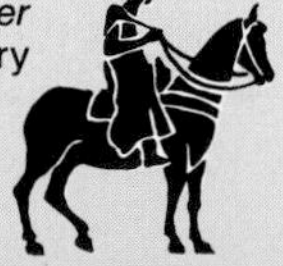

Rise of universities

Louis VII of France
r. 1137–1180

Henry II of England
r. 1154–1189

Abbot Suger
1081–1151
Abbot of St. Denis

Bernard of Clairvaux
c. 1090–1153
Abbot of Cistercian Order

Eleanor of Aquitaine

Richard the Lion-heart
r. 1189–1199

Fire destroys
Chartres Cathedral
1194

Third Crusade
1189–1192

St. Francis of Assisi
1182–1226

Franciscan Order
founded *c.* 1210

Fourth Crusade
1204

St. Thomas Aquinas
c. 1225–1274
Summa Theologica

Frederick II
1220–1250

Marco Polo in China
1271–1292

Hapsburgs of Austr
1282–(1918)

10
GOTHIC ART

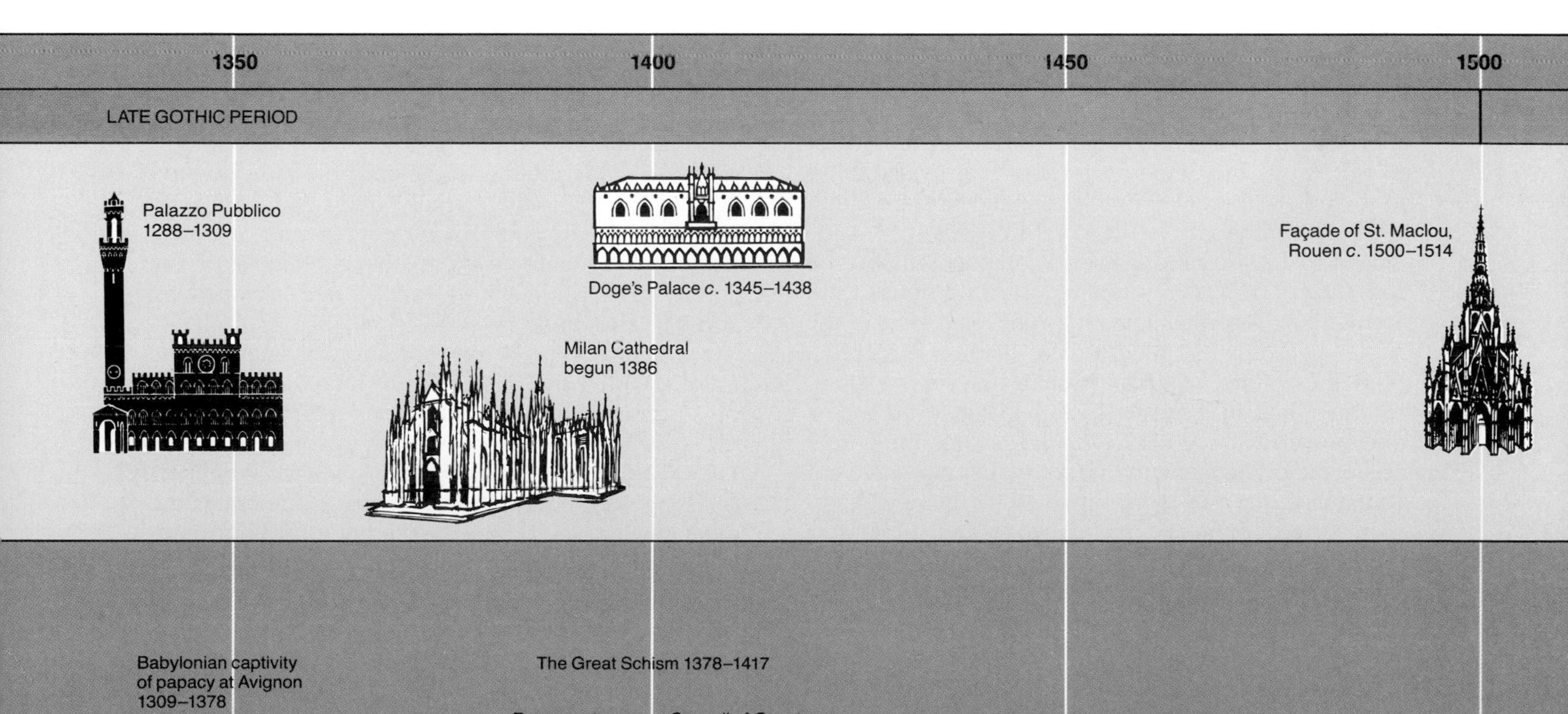

Gothic first was used as a term of derision by Renaissance critics, who condemned the lack of conformity of Gothic art to the standards of Classical Greece and Rome. "May he who invented it be cursed," wrote one of them. The style, the critics mistakenly thought, had originated with the Goths, who thus were responsible for the destruction of the good and true Classical style. People of the thirteenth and fourteenth centuries, however, referred to the Gothic cathedrals as *opus modernum* (modern work) or *opus francigenum* (Frankish work). They recognized in these structures that towered over their towns a style of building and of decoration that was original. It was with confidence in their own faith that they regarded their cathedrals as the real image of the City of God, the Heavenly Jerusalem, which they were privileged to build on earth.

The Gothic and the Romanesque environments and points of view contrast sharply. Romanesque society was dominated by the uncertainties inherent in the anarchic tendencies of feudalism. The great barons of the countryside and the great abbeys enjoyed almost total independence, and the conflict of their claims to privilege led to constant warfare. Gothic society was also feudal, but it was a comparatively ordered feudalism. Here and there, powerful barons had been able to make themselves kings, and monarchy, especially in England and France, asserted itself strongly to limit the independence of lesser lords and the Church. Centralized government was established, and law and order instilled confidence in people of all walks of life. The cities, entirely new or built on the foundations of old Roman ones, began to thrive and to become strong; allied for common defense, they very often were powerful enough to defy kings and emperors. Within their walls, those who had escaped from the land could find freedom. "The air of the city is the breath of freedom," one slogan had it. City life took on a complex but ordered form. Craft guilds, resembling strong unions, were formed to give protection and profit to artisans of the same specialties. A middle class, made up of craftsmen, merchants, and professionals (lawyers, doctors, teachers, and many others) came to constitute a new and powerful force to check and balance the feudal aristocracy. The fear and insecurity that pervaded the Romanesque world were mitigated by the new alignment of economic and social forces, and the Gothic world emerged.

Romanesque society had been dominated by men. In Gothic society, women assumed a more important role. Wandering minstrels sang less of the great deeds of heroes in war and more of love, beauty, and springtime. Eleanor of Aquitaine, wife of Louis VII of France and of Henry II Plantagenet of England and mother of King Richard the Lion-heart and John, was one of the first to rule over a "court of love," in which respect for the lady was prerequisite. The code of chivalry that so decided social relationships in the later Middle Ages was to emanate from courts such as this. The monastic prejudice against women no longer determined their representation in art. In the twelfth century, *luxuria,* sensual pleasure, is represented at Moissac as a woman with serpents at her breasts; in the thirteenth century luxuria is a pretty girl looking into a mirror. The Gothic upper classes turn almost with relief from the *chansons de geste* to the new amorous songs and romances, in which the lover adores his lady and in which such immortal lovers as Tristan and Isolde are celebrated. Marie de France, herself a noblewoman, introduced this tale, along with many other new Arthurian legends, to northern French feudal society. The poetry of the times nicely illustrates the contrast between Romanesque and Gothic taste and mood: in the Romanesque *Song of Roland,* the dying hero waxes rhapsodic over his sword, but the German minnesinger of the Gothic period, dreaming in a swooning ecstasy of his lady, is "woven round with delight."

The love of woman, celebrated in art and formalized in life, received spiritual sanction in the cult of the Virgin Mary, who, as the Mother of Heaven and of Christ and in the form of Mother Church, loved all her children. It was Mary who stood compassionately between the Judgment seat and the horrors of Hell, interceding for all her faithful. Worshipers in the later twelfth and thirteenth centuries sang hymns to her, put her image everywhere, and dedicated great cathedrals to her. Her image was carried into battle on banners, and her name sounded in the battle cry of the king of France: "Sainte Marie . . . Saint Denis . . . Mont-joie!" Mary became the spiritual lady of chivalry, and the Christian knight dedicated his life to her. The severity of Romanesque themes stressing the Last Judgment yields to the gentleness of the Gothic, in which Mary is represented crowned by Christ in Heaven.

It was not only the new position of women, the lyrical and spiritual exaltation of love, or the cult of the Virgin that softened barbarous manners. In concert with the new mood was the influence of one remarkable man, St. Francis of Assisi, who saw Christ not as the remote and terrible judge but as the loving Savior who had walked among men and himself had been one of the "rejected of men." The series of reform movements that make up the history of medieval monasticism culminates in St. Francis's founding of the religious order that bears his name—the Franciscans. St. Francis felt that the members of his order should shun the cloistered life and walk the streets of the busy cities as mendicants, preaching the original message of Christ—the love of oneself and one's neighbor. Shortly after Francis's death and against his wish that his followers never settle in monasteries, the Franciscans commenced the great basilica in his name at Assisi. The historical importance of the Franciscan movement lies in its strengthening of religious faith, its stimulating of the religious emotion among people in cities, and its weakening of the power and influence of the old, Romanesque, country abbeys. St. Francis could be said to have brought a kind of democracy to religion in Europe at the expense of its feudal establishment.

Courtly love, the development of chivalry, the cult of the Virgin Mary, and the teaching and example of St. Francis could not, of course, nullify (although they could mitigate) the cruel realities of medieval life. While St. Francis was still living, the Fourth Crusade sacked Christian Constantinople, visiting atrocities on it that would outdo those of the later conquest by the Ottoman Turks. The papacy and the king of France collaborated in the annihilation of the peoples of Languedoc and Provence in the south of France, the so-called Albigensians, who were accused of heresy but who also stood in the way of the territorial ambitions of royal France. It was this region that had fostered the new poetry of the troubadours and produced the Romanesque sculpture examined earlier. The Albigensian "crusade" also produced the Inquisition or "Holy Office," that grim and fateful instrument of heretic hunting, instituted by St. Dominic. The Dominicans, called in fearful derision *Domini Canes* (dogs of the Lord), were in many ways rivals of the Franciscans and saw themselves as rooting out unbelievers and heretics and guarding the purity of orthodox dogma. The Dominicans' concern for theology led them to be teachers, and they produced one of the great Christian theologians and philosophers, St. Thomas Aquinas, who, at mid-thirteenth century, was the leading light of the University of Paris.

The institution of the university begins to appear in the Early Gothic period in its natural setting: the city. The monastic and cathedral schools of the earlier Middle Ages had sought to keep the learning of the fathers of the Church alive and to reassess these teachings in the light of newly developing Christian thought. From these schools, the universities, communities of scholars and their pupils, evolved in the twelfth and thirteenth centuries at Bologna and Padua, Oxford and Paris. The most important study at the university was theology, but several other subjects were taught, among them mathematics, astronomy, music, grammar, logic, law, and medicine. Ancient Greek philosophy, principally that of Aristotle, was recovered from Arabic translations and had an enormously stimulating effect on theology. Here appeared a reasoned, systematic method of argument and a treasury of lore and observation of natural things. The philosophers set to work to find some way to adjust this new authoritative knowledge to Christian belief; they sought, in short, to rationalize religion. Their method was to arrive at proofs for the central dogmas of the faith by argument, or disputation. This method, taught in the schools and universities, came to be called "scholasticism," and its proponents "schoolmen." The greatest exponent of this systematic procedure was St. Thomas Aquinas. Typical of the method is his treatise, the *Summa Theologiae,* which was laid out into books, the books into questions, the questions into articles, each article into objections with contradictions and responses, and, finally, answers to the objections.

Within this framework, the shrewdest and subtlest arguments of the Middle Ages were advanced. The habit of mind it created lasted for centuries, an obstacle to the rise of empirical thought and science; yet much value still is found in it today. The Scholastic habit of disputation quite possibly is reflected in the thought processes of Gothic architects, as Erwin Panofsky suggested (see pages 396–97).

St. Thomas wrote his summary of Christian theology at a time when the great cathedrals were manifesting a kind of architectural "summation" of the Christian universe. The papacy ruled supreme in Europe, not only spiritually but temporally. At the beginning of the thirteenth century, Pope Innocent III, who, for a while took England away from King John, could claim: "Single rulers have single provinces, and single kings single kingdoms; but Peter . . . is pre-eminent over all, since he is the Vicar of Him whose is the earth and the fulness thereof, the whole wide world and all that dwell therein."

The thirteenth century represents the summit of achievement for unified Christendom: the triumph of the papacy; a successful and inspiring synthesis of religion, philosophy, and art; and the first firm formation of the states that will make modern history. The scene of this great but brief equilibrium of forces favoring religion is the Gothic city; within the city, the soaring cathedral, "flinging its passion against the sky," asserts the nature of the Gothic spirit.

EARLY GOTHIC

Architecture

On June 11, 1144, Louis VII of France, Eleanor of Aquitaine (his queen), members of the royal court, and a host of distinguished prelates, including five archbishops, as well as a vast crowd, converged on the royal abbey of St. Denis, just a few miles north of Paris, for the dedication of the new choir. This choir, with its crown of chapels radiant with stained-glass windows, set a precedent that the builders in the region surrounding Paris, the Île-de-France, were to follow for the next half century.

Two eminent persons were particularly influential in the formation of the Gothic style: Bernard of Clairvaux and Suger, abbot of St. Denis. Bernard held the belief that faith was mystical and intuitive rather than rational. In his battles with Abelard, a contemporary Scholastic philosopher whose views were a basis for the dialectical method of Aquinas, he upheld this position with all the persuasiveness of his powerful personality and eloquence and by the example of his own holiness. The Cistercian churches that were being built under Bernard's influence reflected his theology, stressing purity of outline, simplicity, and a form and lighting peculiarly conducive to meditation.

Although Bernard denounced lavish decoration and elaborate architecture, the Gothic style was initiated by a fellow abbot who, accepting Bernard's admonitions to reform his monastery, built his new church in a style that surpassed the Romanesque in splendor. The fellow churchman was the Abbot Suger, who had risen from humble parentage to become the right-hand man of both Louis VI and Louis VII, and, during the latter's absence in the Second Crusade, served as regent of France. From his youth, Suger wrote, he had dreamed of the possibility of embellishing the church that had nurtured him, the royal Church of France, within the precincts of which its kings had been buried since the ninth century. It was in fact his intention to confer authority on the claims of the kings of royal France to the territory we recognize as France today, for, in Suger's time, the power of the French king, except for scattered holdings, was confined to an area not much larger than the Île-de-France. Thus, Suger's political role and his building role were one; he sought to construct a kingdom and an architectural expression of it. In 1122, he was elected abbot of St. Denis and, within fifteen years, was at work rebuilding the old monastery, which had been in use for almost three centuries. As he made his plans for the new building, he must have recalled many of the churches seen during his travels, and the workmen and artists who labored to raise the church were summoned from many regions. St. Denis, one of the last great abbey churches to be built, became the monastic inspiration for the city cathedrals and is known as the cradle of Gothic art.

10-1 Ambulatory and radiating chapels of the abbey church of St. Denis (near Paris), 1140–1144.

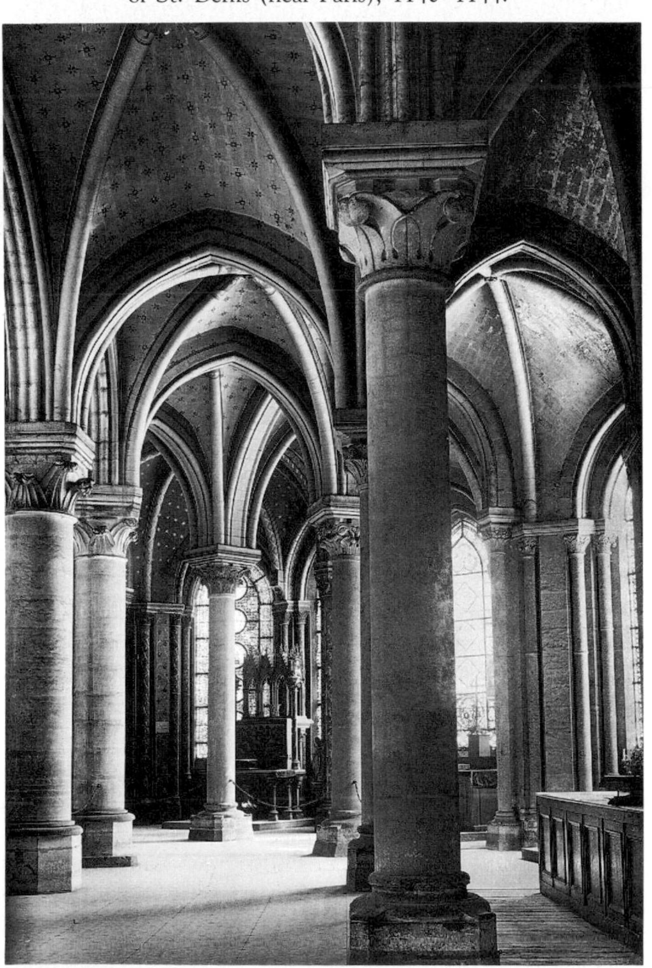

Suger described his new choir at St. Denis (FIG. **10-1**) as follows:

> Moreover, it was cunningly provided that—through the upper columns and central arches which were to be placed upon the lower ones built in the crypt—the central nave of the new addition should be made the same width, by means of geometrical and arithmetical instruments, as the central nave of the old [Carolingian] church; and, likewise, that the dimensions of the new side-aisles should be the same as the dimensions of the old side-aisles, except for that elegant and praiseworthy extension . . . a circular string of chapels, by virtue of which the whole [church] would shine with the wonderful and uninterrupted light of most luminous windows, pervading the interior beauty.*

The abbot's description is a key to the understanding of Early Gothic architecture. As he says, the major dimensions of the structure were dictated by an older church, but it was the "elegant and praiseworthy extension"—the "string of chapels" with "luminous windows"—that proclaimed the new style.

Although the crypt at St. Denis served as a foundation for the choir above it, a comparison of their respective plans and structures (FIG. **10-2**) reveals the major differences between Romanesque and Gothic

*Erwin Panofsky, trans., *Abbot Suger on the Abbey Church of St. Denis and Its Art Treasures* (Princeton, NJ: Princeton University Press, 1951), p. 101.

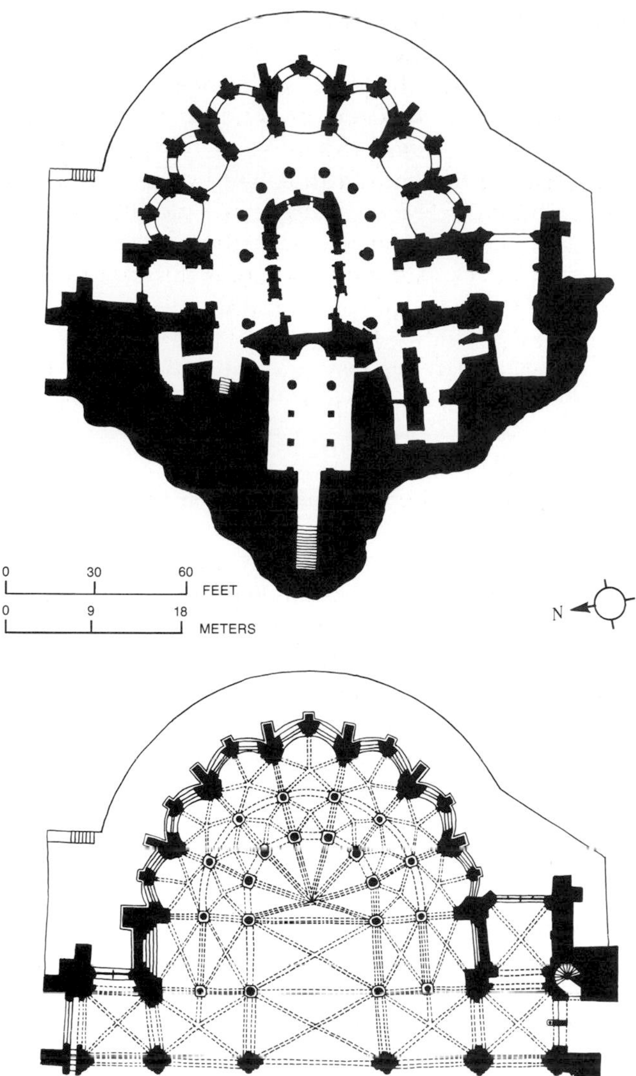

10-2 Plans of the crypt *(top)* and choir *(bottom)* of St. Denis. (After Sumner Crosby.)

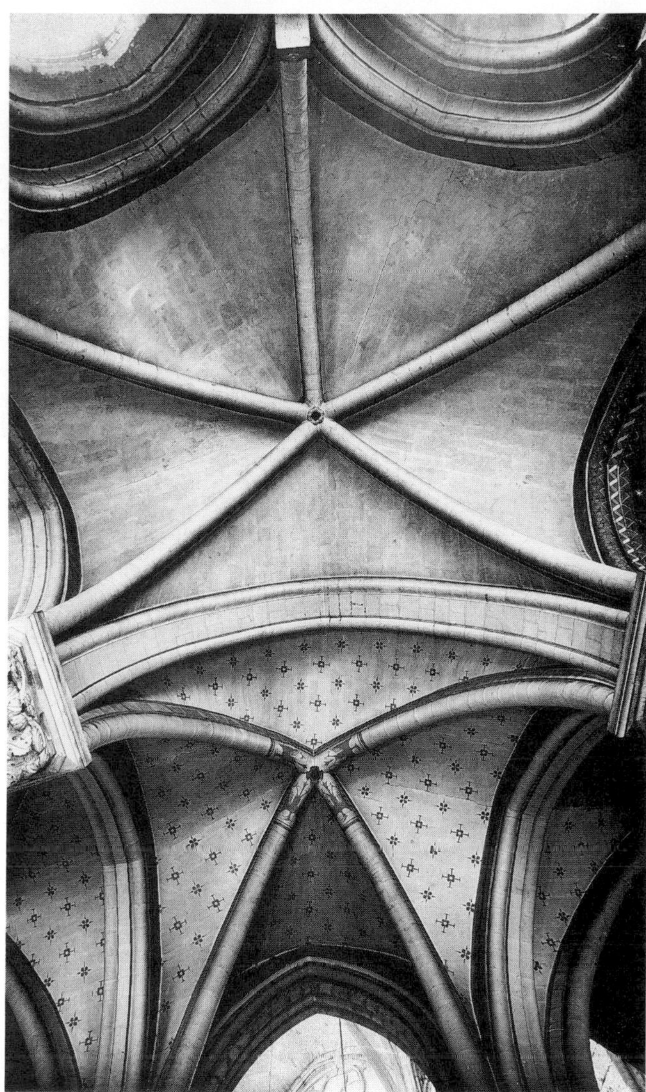

10-3 Vaults of the ambulatory and radiating chapels of the choir of St. Denis.

building. The thick walls of the crypt create a series of separate volumes (a careful Romanesque "partitioning" into units), whereas the absence of walls in the choir above produces a unified space. The crypt is essentially a wall construction, and it is covered with groin vaults; the choir, on the other hand, is a skeletal construction, and its vaults are Gothic rib vaults (FIG. **10-3**).

The ancestors of the Gothic rib vault were found at Caen and Durham. A rib vault is identified easily by the presence of crossed, or diagonal, arches under the groins of a vault. These arches form the armature, which serves as the framework for Gothic skeletal construction. The Gothic vault may be distinguished from other rib or arched vaults by its use of the pointed, or broken, arch as an integral part of the skeletal armature, by the presence of thinly vaulted webs, or severies, between the arches, and by the fact that usually, regardless of the space to be vaulted, the crowns of all the arches are at approximately the same level—something the Romanesque architects could not achieve with their semicircular arches (FIG. **10-4**). Thus, a major advantage of the Gothic vault is its flexibility, which permits the vaulting of compartments of varying shapes, as may be seen readily in the plan of the choir of St. Denis and in many other Gothic choir plans. Moreover, although it does not support the webs entirely, the Gothic armature allows the builder to predetermine the alignment and concentration of thrusts to be buttressed.

Despite the fact that the medieval mason unquestionably derived great satisfaction from his mastery of these technical problems and at times must have been preoccupied with them, he did not permit them to be

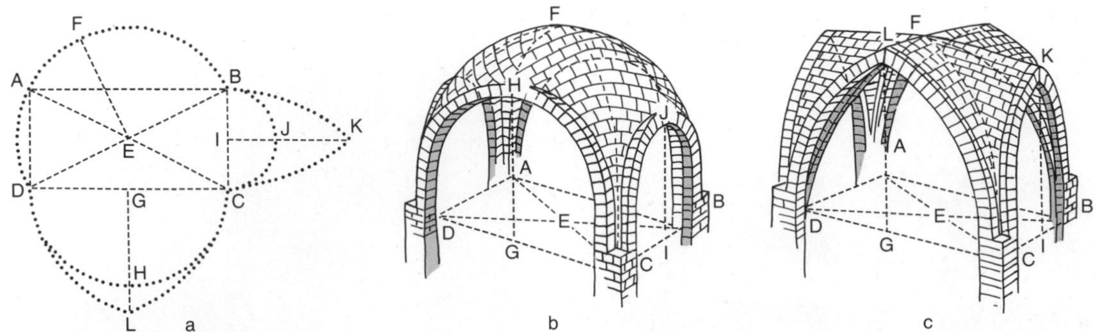

10-4 The Gothic rib vault and the domical vault differ in ways that derive from the fact that they are based on the pointed arch and the semicircular arch, respectively. Diagram **a** illustrates this: *ABCD* is an oblong bay to be vaulted; *AC* and *BD* are the diagonal ribs; *AB* and *DC*, the transverse arches; and *AD* and *BC*, the wall arches. If semicircular arches (the dotted arcs) are used, their radii, and therefore their heights (*EF, GH,* and *IJ*), will be different. The result will be a domical vault (diagram **b**), irregular in shape and difficult to light. If pointed arches are used, the points (and hence the ribs) can have the same heights (*IK* and *GL*). The result will be a Gothic rib vault (diagram **c**), a lighter, more flexible system than the domical vault, affording ample space for large clerestory windows.

an end in themselves. The ambulatories and chapels at St. Denis are proof that the rib vault was exploited, as Suger wrote, so that the whole church "would shine with . . . wonderful and uninterrupted light." This concept was, in medieval terms, the *scientia,* or the theory, that motivated the creation of the Gothic style, and it was *ars,* or technical knowledge and practical skill, that made it possible. The difference between the two was akin to the difference between modern physics and engineering; when a medieval architect spoke of the "art of geometry," he meant not the abstract nature of geometric forms, but the practical uses to which mathematical formulations might be put in designing a piece of sculpture or in erecting a building. An understanding of Gothic architecture will not be reached, however, by trying to decide whether Gothic architects predominantly were concerned with ars or with scientia, but rather by realizing that the cathedrals were the result of both. And it is in the stones themselves—in the extraordinary sensitivity of the Gothic mason for stone as a building material—that the spirit of Gothic architecture is to be discovered. The fact is that procedure was often hit or miss and rule of thumb; buildings often collapsed and were rebuilt with very large margins of safety. No one sure way was accepted and Gothic builders certainly had not reached a fundamental agreement about method. The certainties of modern engineering—themselves sometimes not so certain—were centuries beyond the Gothic reach. Even so, what still stands of Gothic architecture is a monument to the supreme skill, persistence, and vision of the Gothic architects.

It was the scientia of light that led Suger to the invention of the Gothic building. The slender, skeletal structure permitted the flooding of the interior with light. This "theory" came from the writings of a fifth-century mystic called "pseudo-Dionysius the Areopagite" because of his claim to be the true Dionysius, a first-century Athenian follower of St. Paul. This pseudo-Dionysius had become confused with the patron saint of royal France, St. Denis, making it natural for Suger to take the former's mystical identification of light with the divine as a kind of prescription for any building dedicated to St. Denis. When Suger, steeped in the theology of the Areopagite, envisioned the new St. Denis, he saw it as a mystic radiance. This example demonstrates once again the significance of religious authority in the Middle Ages. Scripture and the works of the fathers of the Church were the keys to reality, and things had to be interpreted in terms of the authority that churchmen exercised.

The evolution of Gothic architecture is a continuing adjustment of scale, proportion, buttressing, vault arrangement, and wall and façade design that, in Erwin Panofsky's image, is like the steps of a complex Scholastic argument. Only the choir and narthex of St. Denis were completed in the twelfth century; for a fairly complete view of the Early Gothic style of the second half of the century, one must turn to Laon Cathedral (FIGS. **10-5** to **10-8**). Begun about 1160 and

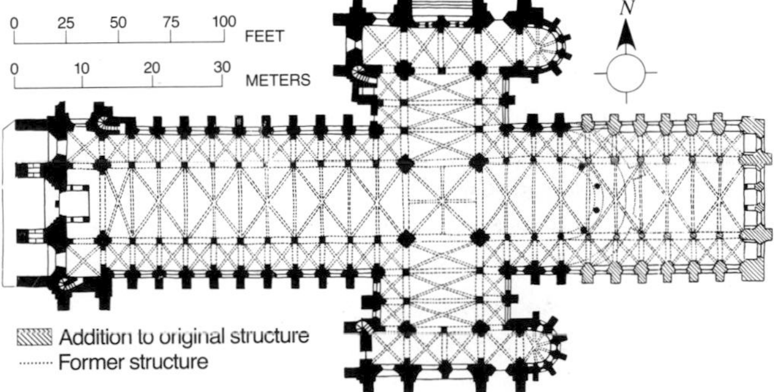

10-5 Plan of Laon Cathedral, France, c. 1160–1205. Choir extended after 1210. (After E. Gall.)

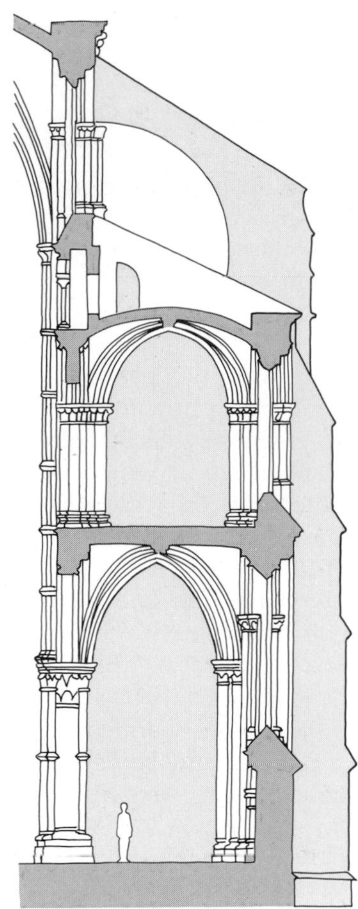

10-6 Section through the aisle, gallery, triforium, and clerestory of Laon Cathedral. (After E. Gall.)

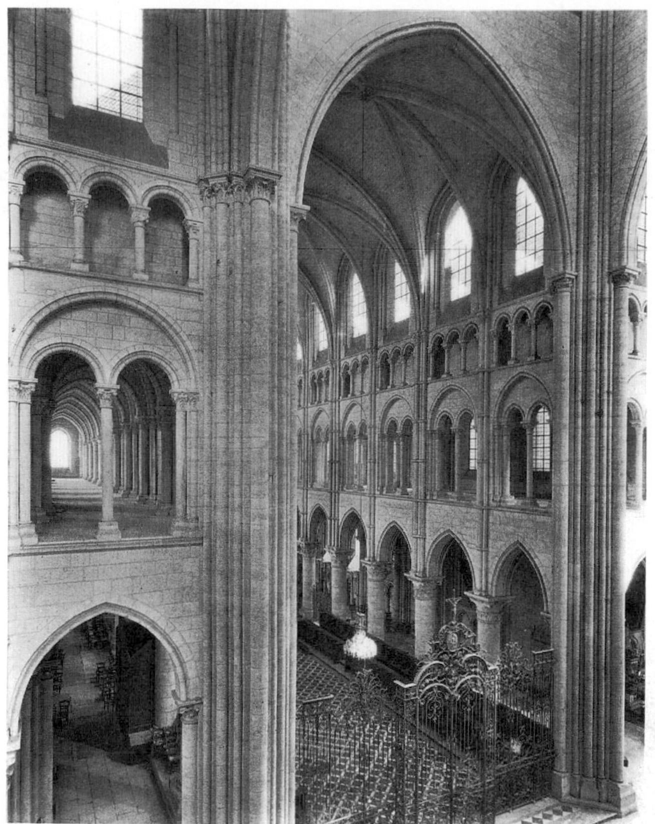

10-7 Laon Cathedral (view into the choir from the gallery of the north transept).

completed shortly after 1200, this building retains many Romanesque features but combines them with the new Gothic structural devices of the rib vault and the pointed arch. Shortly after the building's completion, the choir was enlarged, and the present plan, relatively long and narrow with a square east end, has a decidedly English flavor.

Among the plan's easily discernible Romanesque features are the strongly marked-off crossing square and the bay system, composed of a large unit in the nave flanked by two small squares in each aisle (FIG. 10-5). The nave bays are defined by sexpartite rib vaults and an alternate-support system that, in combination, continue the Romanesque tradition of subdividing the interior into a number of separate compartments. Both features, as well as the gallery above the aisles, have been derived from Norman Romanesque architecture, which enjoyed great prestige in northern France throughout the twelfth century (FIGS. 9-14 and 9-15). A new feature of the interior, however, is the *triforium,* the band of arcades below the clerestory that occupies the space corresponding to the exterior strip of wall covered by the sloping timber roof above the galleries. The triforium expresses a growing desire to break up and eliminate all continuous wall surfaces. Its insertion produces the characteristic Early Gothic nave-wall elevation of four parts: nave arcade, gallery, triforium, and clerestory (FIGS. 10-6 and 10-7).

At Laon, the alternate-support system is treated less emphatically than in other Early Gothic churches (Sens or Noyon, for example). It is not reflected in the nave arcade (although colonnettes were added to a few of the columns as an afterthought), as alternating bundles of three and five shafts have their origin above the level of the main wall supports (FIG. 10-7). It appears that the Laon architect no longer is completely happy with the compartmentalized effect of Romanesque interiors, which tends to make visitors pause as they advance from unit to unit. Gothic builders aim, as yet rather timidly at Laon, to create an integrated, unified interior space that sweeps uninterruptedly from west to east. The alternate-support system, hugging the ground in Ottonian times and rising to dominate nave walls in northern Romanesque, has lost its footing at Laon and, like the solid masonry of Romanesque walls, is about to evaporate.

Important changes in the design of the church exterior were also part of the Early Gothic experience. At Laon, the doorways (under protective porches) and

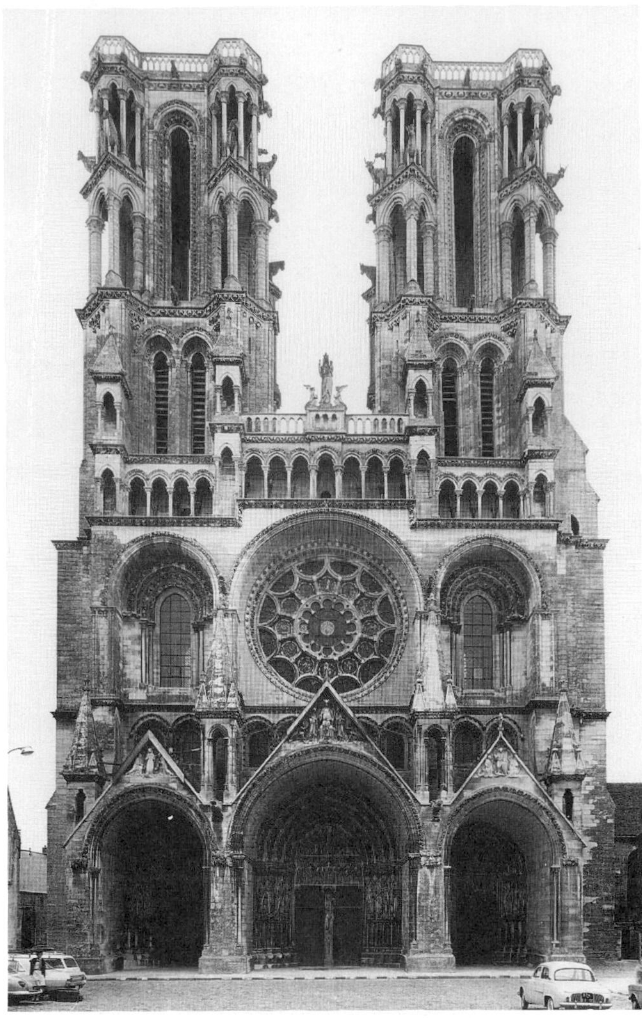

10-8 West façade of Laon Cathedral, begun c. 1190.

the towers have been treated as integral parts of the mass of the building (FIG. 10-8). The interior stories are reflected in the levels into which the façade is divided. (A noticeable discontinuity between the central and flanking portions of the façade was to be regulated in later designs.) Typically Gothic are the deep embrasures of the doorways and windows and the open structure of the towers. A comparison of the façades of Laon and St. Étienne at Caen (FIG. 9-13) reveals how deep the penetration of the mass of the wall has become. Here, as in Gothic architecture generally, the operating principle is one of the reduction of sheer mass by its replacement with intricately framed voids.

Laon has a pair of towers flanking each arm of the transept (only two were actually completed) and a lantern tower over the crossing, which, with the two western towers, gives a total of seven, the perfect mystic number. (Composed of three and four, it represents the Trinity and the Evangelists or the Gospels.) This complement of towers was the Early Gothic ideal and continued the German Romanesque tradition of multiple integrated towers. Rarely, however, did building funds suffice for the completion of all towers. Even the façade towers of French cathedrals seldom were finished; most, including those of Laon, lacked the crowning spires planned for them. Eventually, the massed towers of the east end were omitted from building plans, and the Norman two-tower façade became the French High Gothic standard.

Transept towers were not part of the plan for the cathedral of Paris, the renowned Notre Dame (FIG. **10-9**). Thus, this essentially Early Gothic building has a High Gothic silhouette in which only the slender crossing spire interrupts the long horizontal roof line that extends eastward behind the massive façade towers (FIG. **10-10**). Notre Dame of Paris, begun in 1163, only a few years after Laon, embodies a fascinating mixture of conservative and progressive ideas. Choir and transept were completed by 1182; the nave, by 1225; and the façade, by 1250. The plan (FIG. **10-11**) shows an ambitiously scaled, five-aisled structure in which a Romanesque bay system is combined with Early Gothic six-part (sexpartite) nave vaulting.

10-9 West façade of Notre Dame, Paris, begun c. 1215.

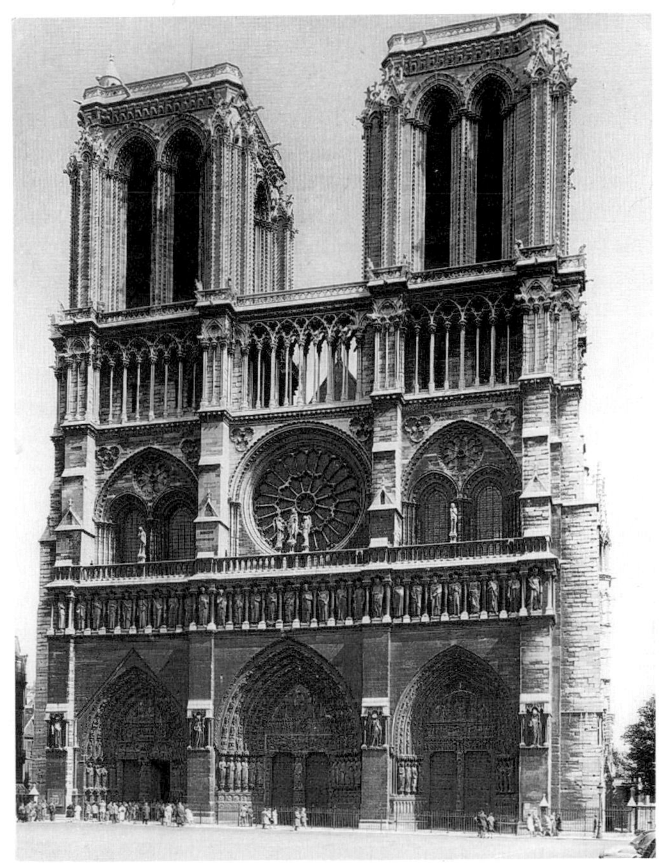

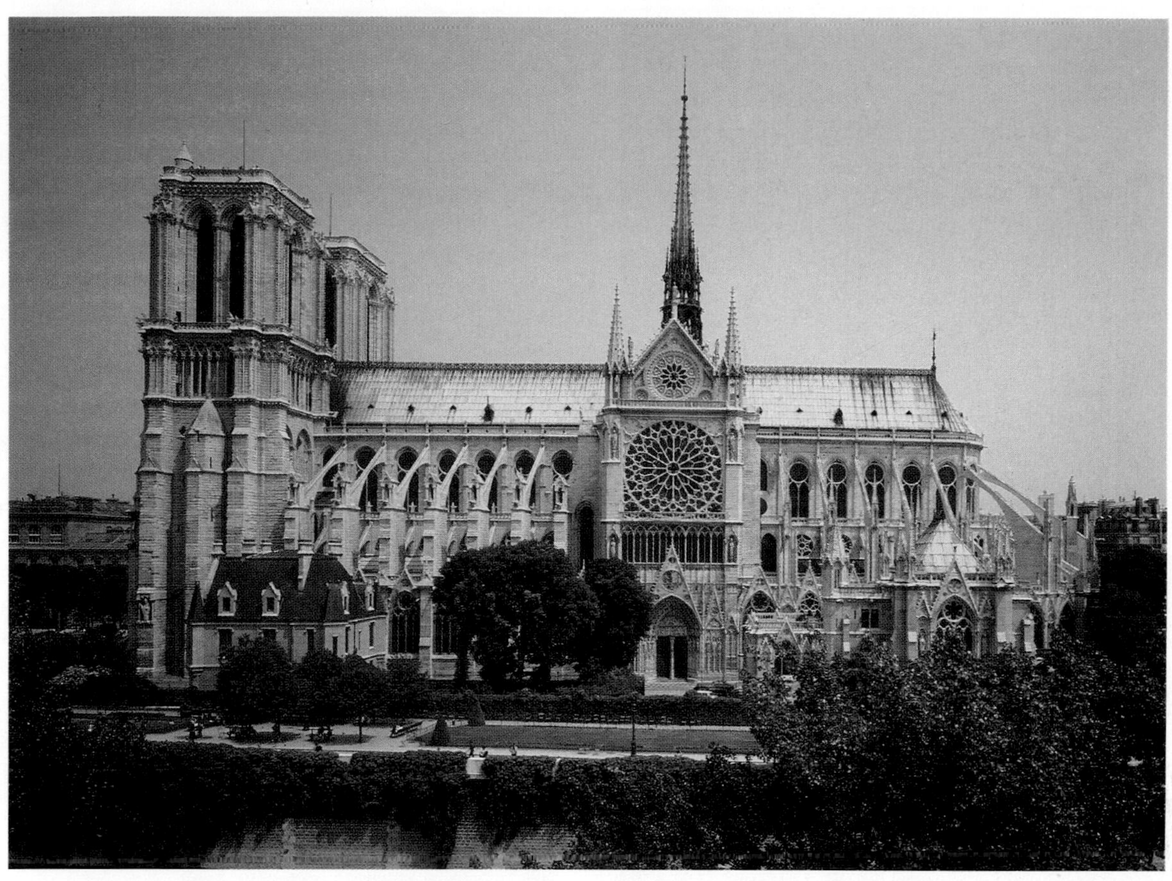

10-10 South flank of Notre Dame, Paris.

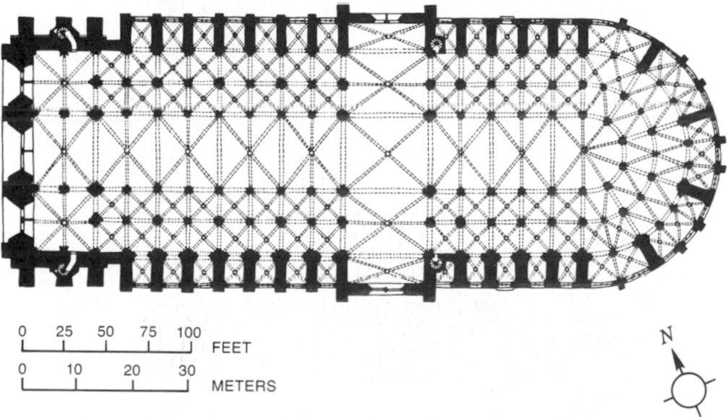

10-11 Plan of Notre Dame, Paris. (After Frankl.)

The original transept was short and did not project beyond the outer aisles. The original nave wall elevation had four parts, in the Early Gothic manner, with a triforium in the form of a series of rosettes.

The building was extensively modified shortly after it was completed. Between 1225 and 1250, chapels were built into the spaces between buttresses, and in 1250 the transept arms were lengthened. At the same time—perhaps as the result of a fire (according to Viollet-le-Duc, the cathedral's nineteenth-century restorer), but probably to admit more light into the nave—changes were made in the nave wall (the bays adjacent to the crossing were redone by Viollet-le-Duc), as shown in FIG. **10-12**. By this time, the nave of Chartres Cathedral (FIG. 10-18) had been completed and had rendered Early Gothic galleries and four-level wall elevations obsolete. As the galleries of Notre Dame already had been built, the "modernization" of the nave there had to be a compromise. The clerestory windows were lowered to the top of the gallery by suppressing the rosettes of the triforium. This alteration, in turn, required that the gallery roof be lowered and redesigned. The solution was a pitched roof with one slope inclined toward the nave wall, which created a difficult drainage problem that was solved only in the nineteenth century, when Viollet-le-Duc designed a single-slope roof to throw the water outward.

Like the interior, the façade of Notre Dame (FIG. 10-9) seems to waver between the old and the new. Begun after the Laon façade had been completed, it appears to be much more conservative and, in the preservation of its "mural presence," more closely related to Romanesque than to High Gothic façades. From the modern observer's point of view, this may be one of its great assets. Less perforated and more

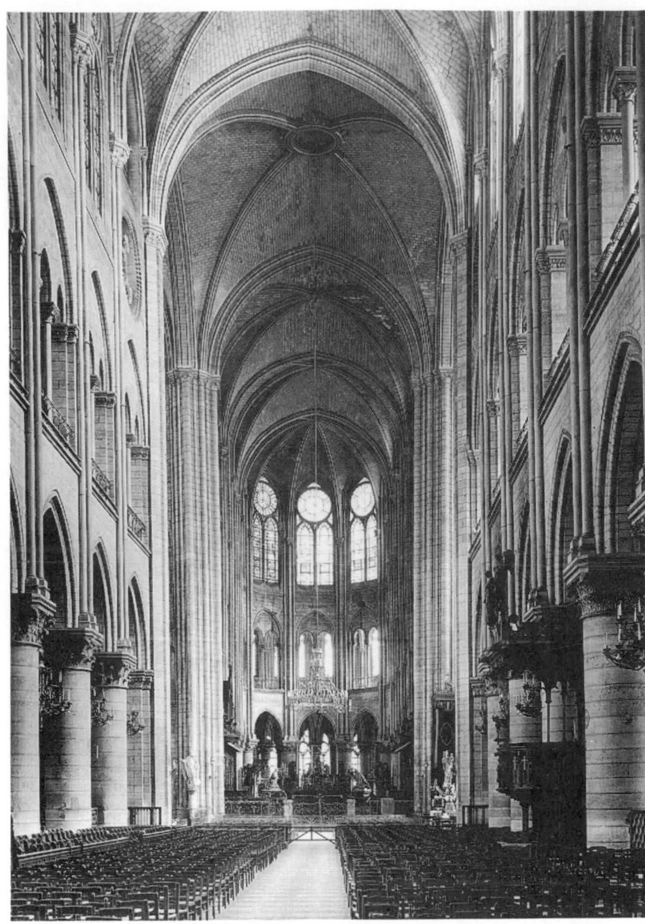

10-12 East end and part of the nave of Notre Dame, Paris, begun 1163; modified 1225–1250.

orderly than that of Laon, Notre Dame's façade exudes a sense of strength and permanence that is lacking in many contemporary and later designs. Careful balancing of vertical against horizontal elements has achieved a quality of restful stability that makes this façade one of the most satisfying and memorable in Gothic architecture.

While the new Gothic style was developing in northern France, the regional Romanesque style prevailed in the south of France and in most of Europe. We have seen the Romanesque church of St. Trophime at Arles (FIG. 9-35), which, like its neighbor St. Gilles-du-Gard, reflects ancient Roman architectural motifs, such as the gabled portico and triumphal arch. This region of the lower Rhône valley is crowded with remnants of Roman monuments, some of which, such as the Pont du Gard near Nîmes (FIG. 6-42), the Maison Carrée at Nîmes (FIG. 6-46), and the triumphal arch at Orange (not discussed in this text) are very well preserved. The classicizing Romanesque style in Italy (FIG. 9-20) almost can be regarded as an anticipation of the classicizing Renaissance style to come.

Sculpture

Gothic sculpture makes its first appearance in the Île-de-France and its environs with the same dramatic suddenness as Gothic architecture and, it is likely, in the very same place—the abbey church of St. Denis. Almost nothing of the sculpture of the west façade of St. Denis survived the French Revolution, but it was there that sculpture emerged completely from the interior of the church to dominate the western entrances, which were regarded as the "gateways to Heavenly Jerusalem" and as the "Royal Portals." These Royal Portals, so named because of the statues of kings and queens on the embrasures flanking the doorways, are typified by the west portals of Chartres Cathedral (FIGS. **10-13** to **10-15**), carved between 1145 and 1170. The lower parts of the massive west towers at Chartres and the portals between them are all that survived of an Early Gothic cathedral that was destroyed in a disastrous fire in 1194 before it had been completed. The cathedral was reconstructed immedi-

10-13 West façade of Chartres Cathedral, France, c. 1145–1170.

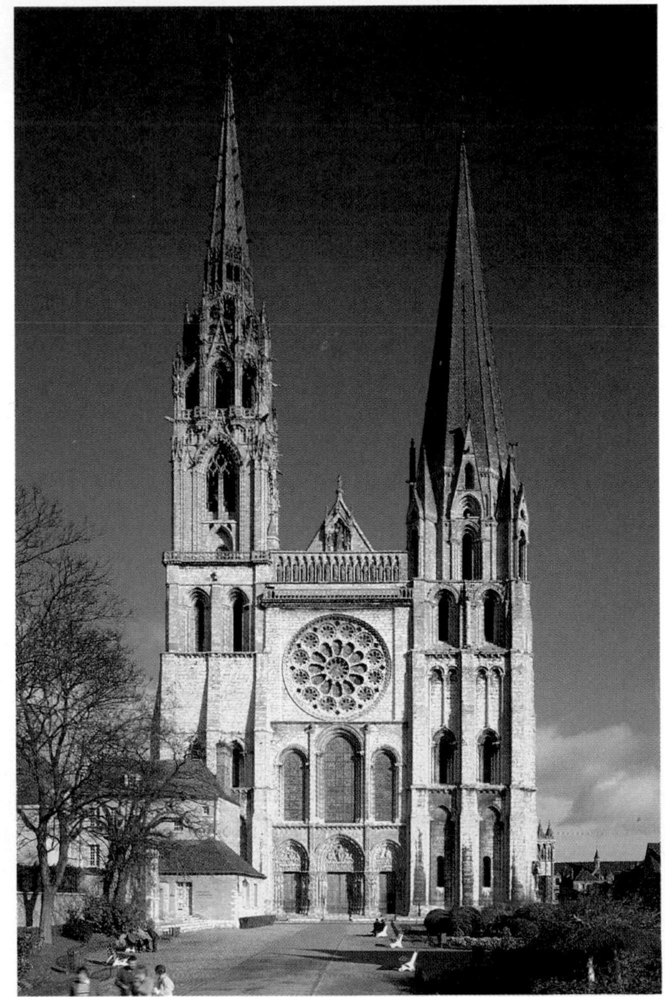

ately, but in the High Gothic style. The portals, however, constitute the most complete and impressive corpus of Early Gothic sculpture.

The three west portals of Chartres, treated as a unit, proclaim the majesty and omnipotence of Christ. His Birth, the Presentation at the Temple, and Christ in Majesty with the Virgin Mother are shown on the right portal; Christ's Ascension into Heaven is shown on the left portal. Scenes from his life and from the Passion are carved vividly on the capitals, which continue as a frieze from one portal to the next. The Second Coming is depicted on the central portal. Christ is surrounded by the Signs of the Four Evangelists, and the Twelve Apostles are shown below, seated as representing the corporate body of the Christian church. The Second Coming—in essence, the Last Judgment theme—remains centrally important, as in the Romanesque works we have seen, which are only twenty years older than the west portals of Chartres. Here, however, this theme has become a symbol of salvation rather than damnation. It is, moreover, combined with other scenes and symbolic figures as part of a larger theme rather than a symbol of the dogma itself. In the archivolts of the right portal the seven liberal arts are shown. These represent the core of medieval learning and therefore are symbolic of man's knowledge, which will lead him to the true faith. The signs of the zodiac and scenes representing the various labors of the months of the year are carved into the left-portal archivolts as symbols of the cosmic and terrestrial worlds. Around the central tympanum are the twenty-four elders of the Apocalypse, accompanying the Second Coming. Decorating the multiple jambs flanking each doorway are the most striking figures: the great statues of the kings and queens of the Old Testament, the royal ancestors of Christ. The medieval observer undoubtedly also regarded them as the figures of the kings and queens of France, symbols of secular as well as of biblical authority. The unity of the triple portal in its message and composition complements the unity of the cathedral itself, which, in its fluent, uninterrupted, vast, and soaring space, compounds earth and Heaven in a symbol of the spiritually perfected universe to come.

The jamb statues are among the few original forms of architectural sculpture to have appeared in any age. At first glance, in their disregard of normal proportions and their rigid adherence to an architectural frame, they seem to follow many of the precepts of Romanesque architectural sculpture. Yet the differences are striking and important. The statues stand out from the plane of the wall; they are not cut back into it. They are conceived and treated as three-dimensional volumes. They move into the space of the observer and participate in it with him. Most significant of all is the first trace of a new naturalism: drapery folds are no longer calligraphic exercises translated into stone; they now either fall vertically or radiate naturally from their points of suspension. Although carefully arranged in regular patterns, these folds suggest that the artist is no longer copying

10-14 Royal (west) Portals of Chartres Cathedral.

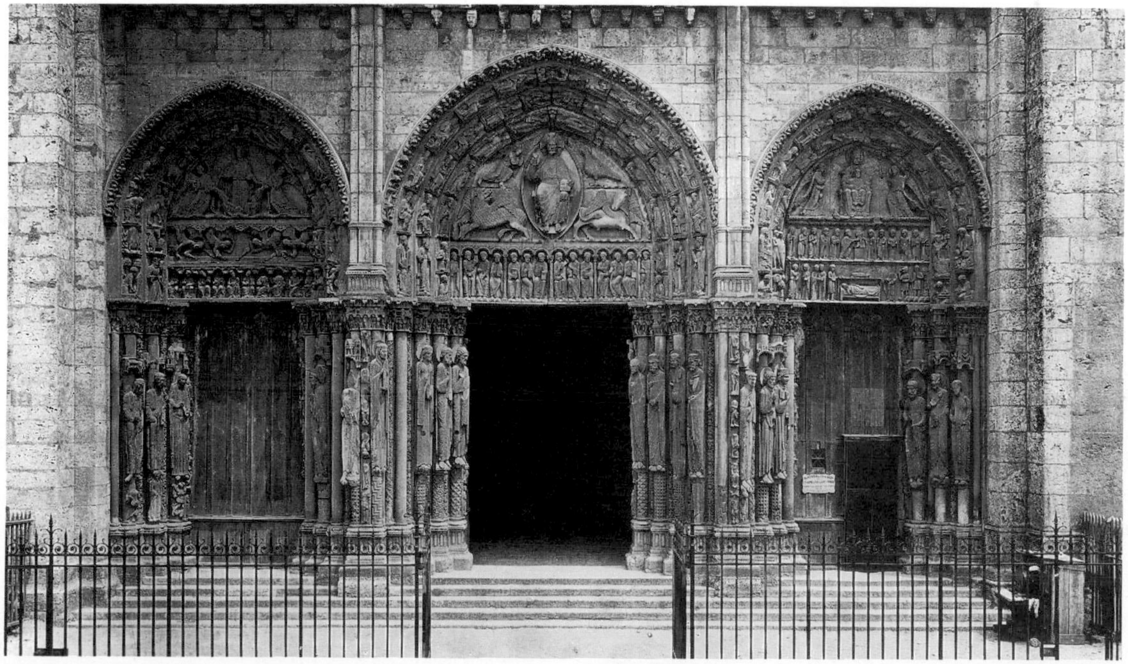

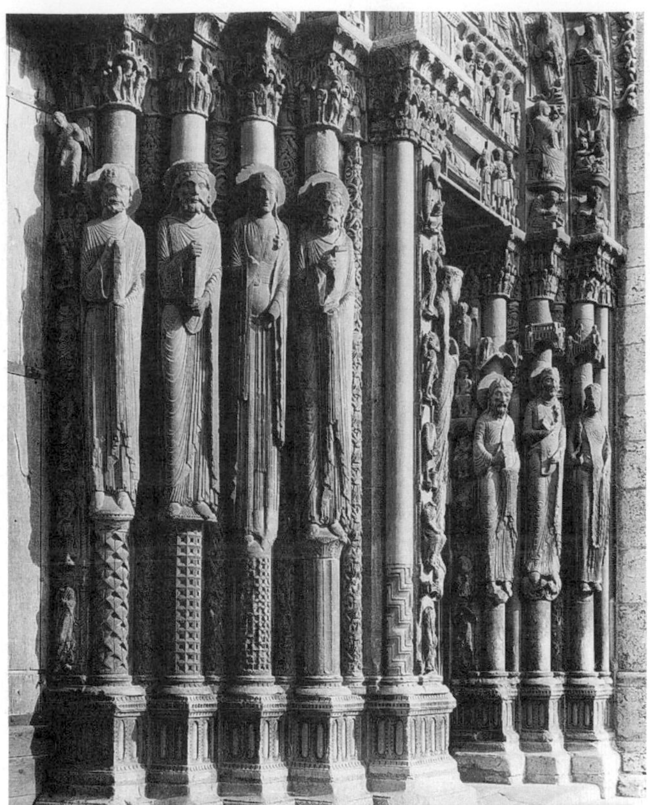

10-15 Jamb statues, Royal Portals, Chartres Cathedral.

painted images but that actual models have been used here.

This observation is true particularly of the figures flanking the central doorway (some appear in the left foreground of FIG. 10-15), which are the work of the anonymous HEADMASTER, the artist in charge of the overall design and decoration of the portals. The advanced nature of his style becomes noticeable especially when his figures are compared with those on the outside jamb of the lateral portal (right background in FIG. 10-15), which evidently were carved by a different, perhaps older, and certainly more conservative artist. The latter's approach still is rooted deeply in the Romanesque tradition. His figures seem more agitated; their silhouettes are curvilinear and broken. The drapery folds are treated decoratively and, here and there, continue to rotate in abstract swirls. Only the windblown lower garment edges, characteristic of much Romanesque sculpture, have come to rest—reluctantly, it seems, and perhaps at the Headmaster's insistence. Even so, the figures fail to adjust themselves as neatly to their architectural setting as do the Headmaster's statues, which—although they have stepped out of the wall and have become corporeal—are severely disciplined and have been rigorously subordinated to their architectural background. Seen from a distance, they appear to be little more than vertical, decorative accents within the larger designs of portals and façade (FIG. 10-14). And yet, within and despite this architectural straitjacket, the incipient naturalism has softened the appearance of the figures. This softening is noticeable particularly in their faces, in which the masklike features of the Romanesque can be seen being converted into human likenesses. A personalizing naturalism has begun that will become transformed first into idealized portraits of the perfect Christian and finally into the portraiture of specific individuals.

During the early twelfth century, great changes were taking place in Western humanity's view of itself, especially with respect to the relation of body and soul. Previously, the old Augustinian view had prevailed. The essence of the soul was completely unlike that of the body: the soul was spiritual and immortal; the body was material and subject to corruption. With the rediscovery of the main works of Aristotle, people gradually came to believe that the soul and the body were closely interrelated, that the soul was the *form* of the body, and that, therefore, the body no longer was to be despised as merely the corruptible prison of the soul from which it is released only when the body dies. One Scholastic philosopher saw the soul and the body as meeting and that union as responsible for the personality of the individual. Another saw the soul as ruling the body but also cherishing its prison. These views, in which the body is seen as coming into its own, reflected a universally changing outlook. John of Salisbury (*c.* 1110–1180), the great English Scholastic, took the perhaps radical view that the soul is stimulated and acted on by sensations from the world, rather than inspired and moved by entirely spiritual principles. He even declared that some of the principal problems of Scholastic philosophy could be solved by psychological examination of the way we think. The West was now speaking with a new voice: souls must be manifested through bodies—the individual bodies of men and women. Thus, the new, individualized heads of Chartres herald an era of artistic concern with the realization of personality and individuality that may only now, in our times, be terminating. The figures of the Royal Portals of Chartres hold a place analogous to the works of Greek artists in the late sixth century B.C.; they turn the corner into a historical avenue of tremendous possibility.

HIGH GOTHIC

Architecture

The new cathedral of Chartres, as rebuilt after the fire of 1194 and largely completed by 1220, is usually considered to be the first of the High Gothic build-

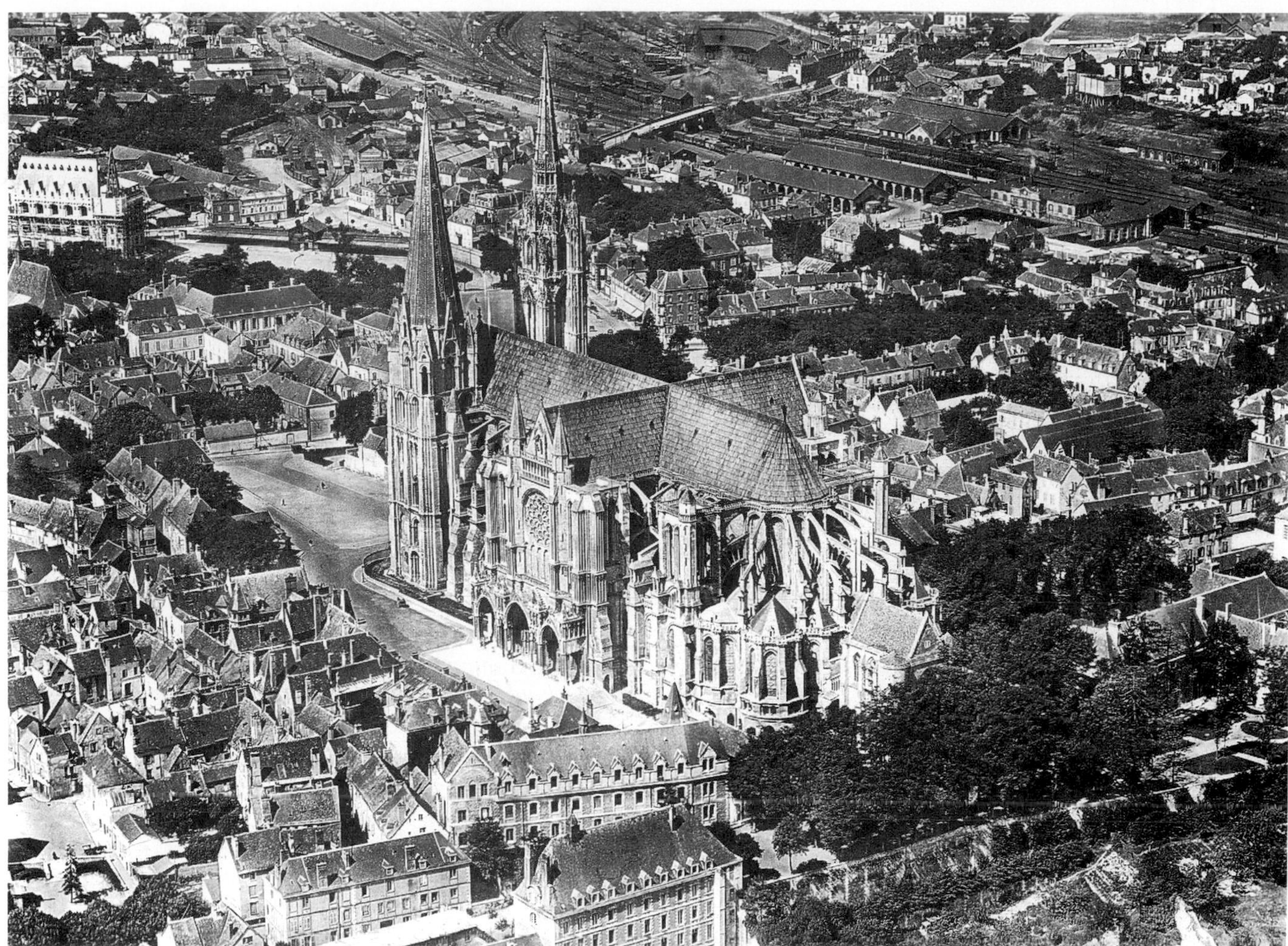

10-16 Chartres Cathedral, as rebuilt after 1194 (aerial view from the southeast).

ings—the first to have been planned from the beginning for the use of flying buttresses.

The flying buttress, that exceedingly useful and characteristic Gothic structural device, seems to have been employed by about 1180 for the bracing of the nave of Notre Dame in Paris and, shortly thereafter, at Laon. A section through Laon Cathedral (FIG. 10-6) shows how the flying buttress (lightly shaded at top right) reaches across the lower vaults of aisle and gallery and abuts the nave walls at the points at which the vaults exert their major thrusts. Similar methods for strengthening the walls of vaulted naves already had been used in Romanesque architecture, but there the buttresses were concealed under the aisle roofing. Now, they are left exposed in a manner that has been both condemned as "architectural crudity" and praised as "structural honesty."

An aerial view of Chartres Cathedral (FIG. **10-16**) shows that a series of these highly dramatic devices has been placed around the *chevet* (the east end of the church), thus supporting the vaults with permanent arms, like scaffolding left in place. With the mastery of this structural form, the technical vocabulary of Gothic architecture became complete. The buttress eliminates the need for Romanesque walls and permits the construction of a self-consistent and self-supporting skeletal structure. The Chartres architect was the first to arrive at this conclusion and to design his building accordingly.

At Chartres, after the great fire, the overall dimensions of the new structure were determined by the façade left standing to the west and by the masonry of the crypt to the east. For reasons of piety and economy, the crypt—the repository of the most precious relic of Chartres, the mantle of the Virgin—was used as the foundation for the new structure. The earlier forms did not limit the plan (FIG. **10-17**), however; it shows an unusual equilibrium between chevet, transept, and nave, which are almost equal in dimension. More important, perhaps, the plan reveals a new kind of organization. The last remnants of square schematism, still present in Early Gothic churches, have been replaced by a "rectangular-bay system" that will become the High Gothic norm. Now a rectangular unit in the nave, defined by its own vault, is flanked by a single square in each aisle. This new bay

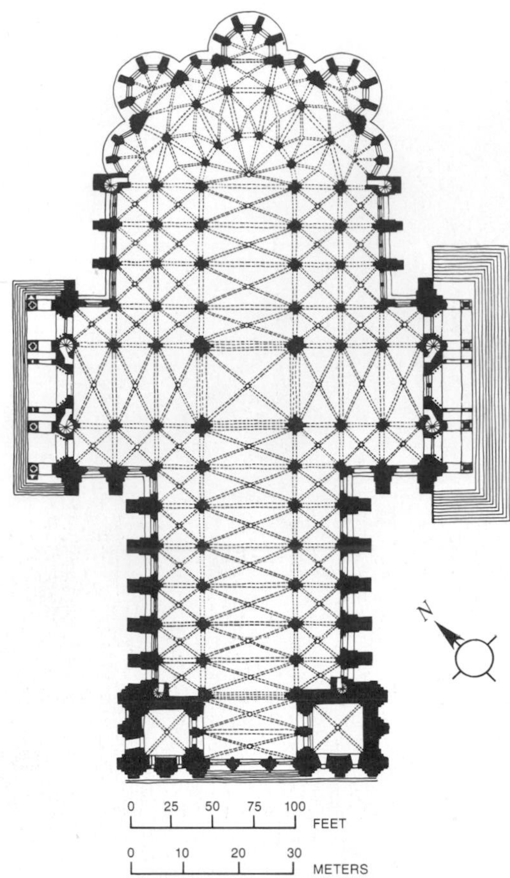

10-17 Plan of Chartres Cathedral. (After Frankl.)

arrangement was accompanied by a change in vault design. The new High Gothic vault, which covers a relatively smaller area and therefore is braced more easily than its Early Gothic predecessor, has only four panels. The visual effect of these changes is to decompartmentalize the interior (FIG. **10-18**); identical units have been aligned so that they are seen in too rapid a sequence to be discriminated as individual volumes of space. The alternate-support system, of course, is gone, and the nave, although richly articulated, has become a vast, continuous hall.

The organic, "flowing" quality of the High Gothic interior was enhanced by a new nave-wall elevation, which admits more light to the nave through greatly enlarged clerestory windows. The use of flying buttresses made it possible to eliminate the tribune gallery above the aisle, which had partially braced Romanesque and Early Gothic naves. The new, High Gothic, tripartite nave elevation, consisting of arcade, triforium, and clerestory, emphasizes the large clerestory windows; those at Chartres are almost as high as the main arcade. A comparison of the elevations of Laon and Chartres (FIG. **10-19**) illustrates the radical changes that could be achieved by logical application of the flying buttress, which had been used only tentatively at Laon.

Despite the vastly increased size of the clerestory windows, some High Gothic interiors remain relatively dark, largely due to the light-muffling effects of

10-18 Nave of Chartres Cathedral (view facing east).

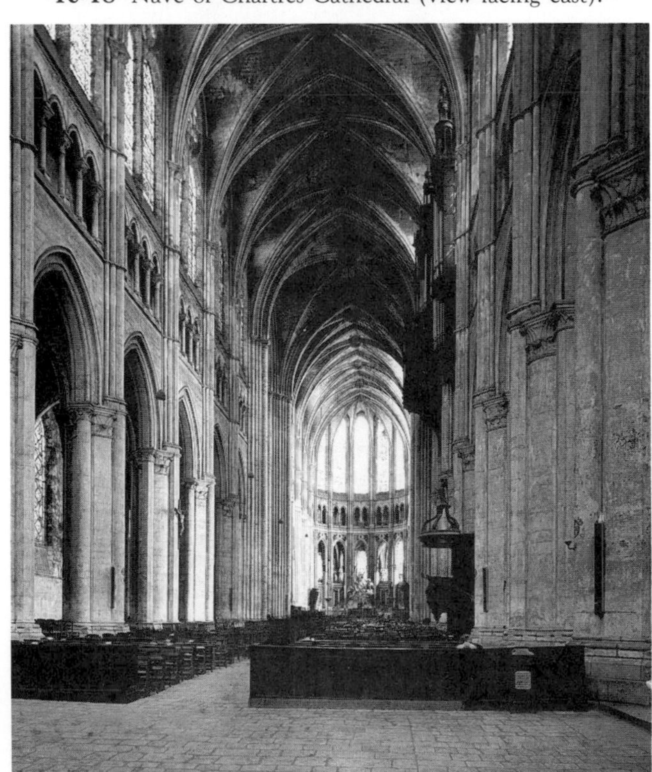

10-19 Elevations of the nave walls of the cathedrals of Laon *(left)* and Chartres *(right)*, which is drawn to a smaller scale than the Laon elevation. (Umschau-Verlag, Frankfurt/Main.)

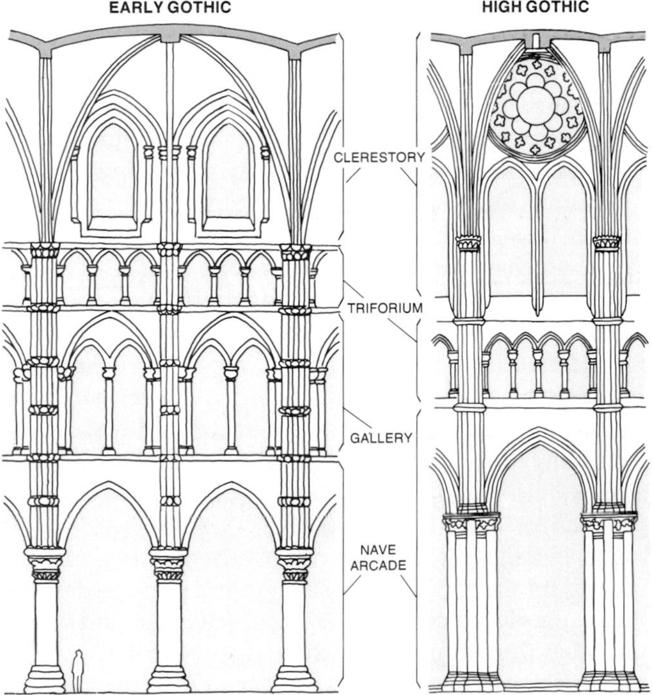

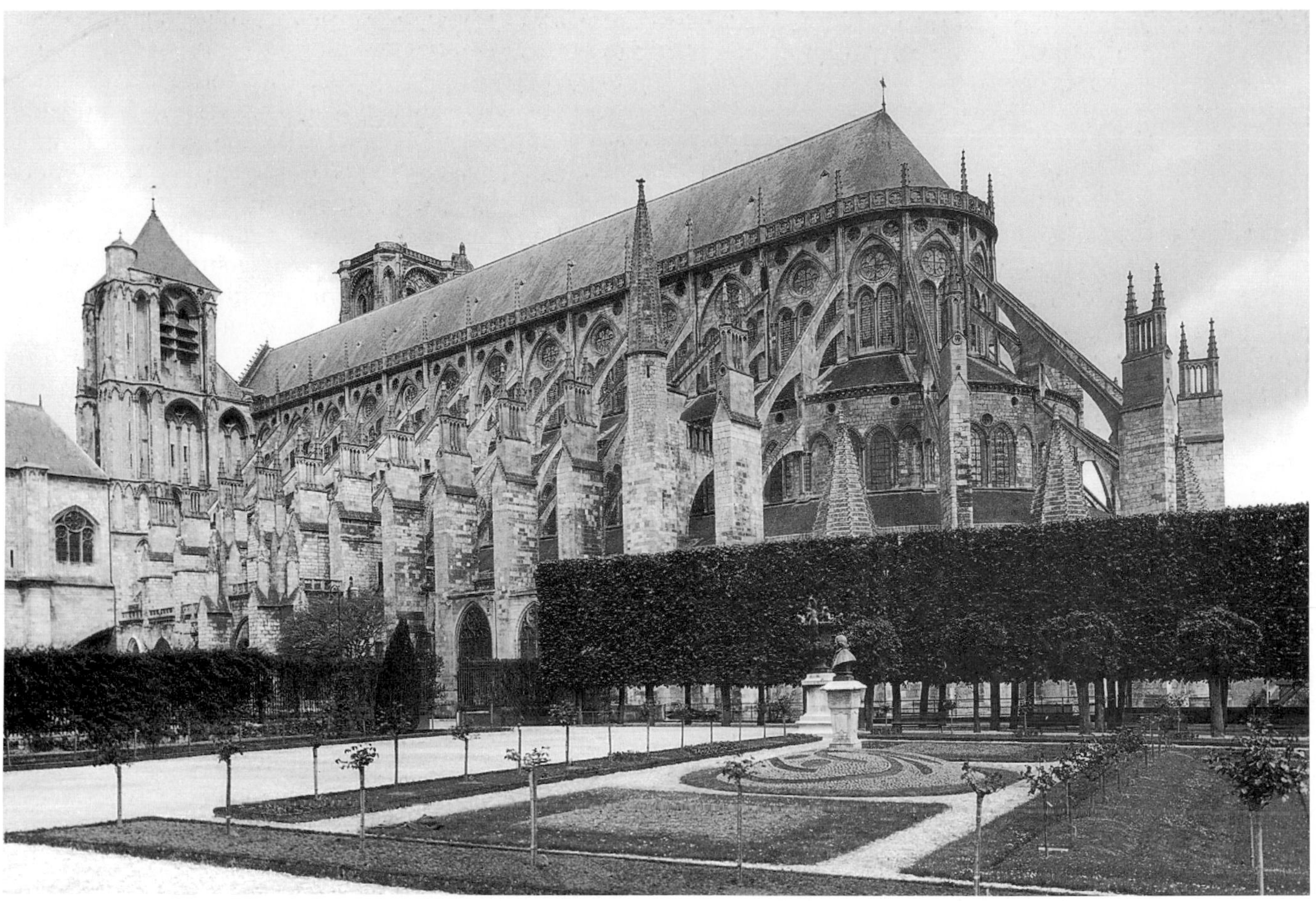

10-20 Bourges Cathedral, France, 1195–1255 (view from the southeast).

their colored glass. Chartres has retained almost the full complement of its original stained glass, which, although it dims the interior, sheds a color-shot light of great beauty that has helped to make Chartres the favorite church of lovers of Gothic architecture.

Whatever the glory of Chartres, it had a contemporary rival in Bourges Cathedral (FIG. **10-20**), which, although it may lack the esthetic power of Chartres, may have been, to a degree, its superior in structural ingenuity, stability, and economy of means. The two buildings, begun at about the same time, were completely different yet satisfactory solutions to the problems of Gothic architectural design. As such, they offered architects two alternative models. The design of Chartres later was perfected at Amiens and Reims, and at Beauvais, the first master architect conceived a kind of synthesis of Chartres and Bourges.

The plan of Bourges Cathedral (FIG. **10-21**) is strikingly different from that of Chartres Cathedral, resembling more the plan of Notre Dame in Paris (FIG. 10-11). At Chartres, the chevet, transept, and nave are of almost equal dimension. At Bourges, the plan is continuous, eliminating the transept entirely, so that the double side aisles continue without interruption from the western façade around the choir to the east. The unity and sweeping continuity of the plan is furthered by the unusual elevation (FIG. **10-22**). Instead of one aisle on each side of the nave, Bourges has two; the inner one is higher and boasts its own clerestory, triforium, and arcade, all of which are visible through the nave arcade. The stepping upward of the heights of the side aisles to a climax in the nave vaults and the restatement in the inner aisle (albeit on a smaller scale) of the three-part nave-wall elevation provide a rhythmic, vertical repetition of the distinctive High Gothic arrangement. At the same time, windows at three levels enhance the fluent opening of the space of the nave into the aisles by saturating the interior with a form-dissolving permeation of light—the goal of Gothic architecture.

The retention of older, Romanesque features at Bourges, like the sexpartite vaults, the alternate-support system (seen in the slight differentiation in the membering of alternate piers), and the small clerestory, does not reflect structural uncertainty. Modern engineering analyses of wind and dead-load

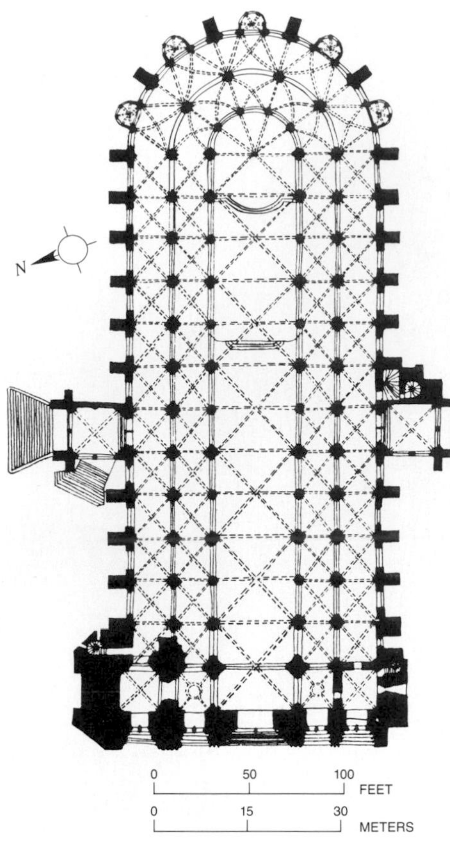

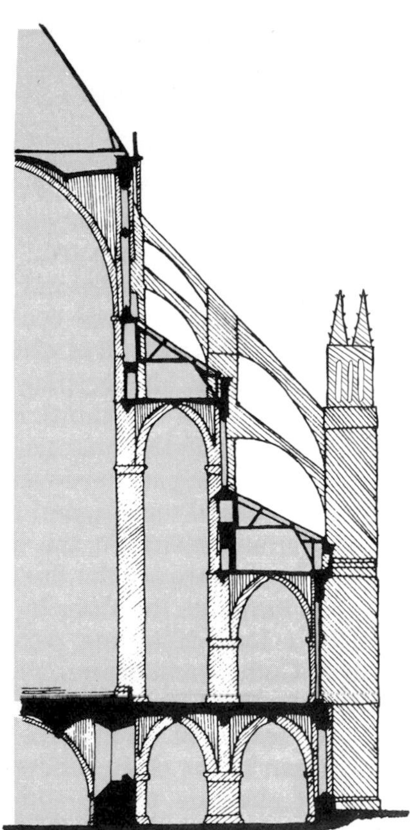

10-21 Plan *(top)* and section *(bottom)* of Bourges Cathedral.

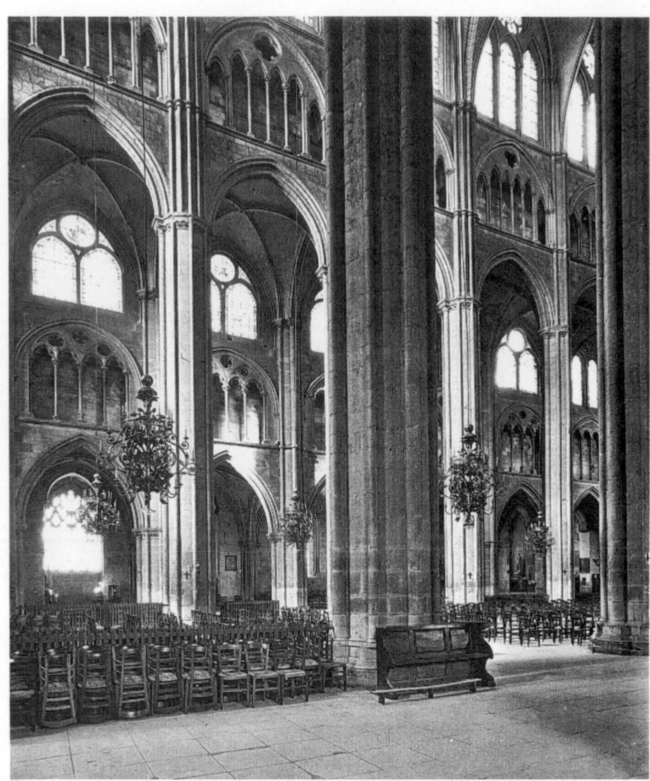

10-22 Bourges Cathedral, 1225–1250 (view across the nave from the south side).

stresses (necessary for the high-rise structures of today) show that the lighter and more open buttresses of Bourges transfer structural forces to the foundations more efficiently than the massive ones at Chartres; a pier buttress at Chartres is estimated to weigh one thousand tons, versus four hundred tons at Bourges, yet the stress levels for high winds have been shown to be equivalent. Nevertheless, the Chartres design, with its balanced, additive, and logical arrangements of plan and elevation, became the more influential of the two. At Bourges, the relationships of the parts were perhaps too elusive and individual to be grasped readily and applied widely as a standard.

The Cathedral of Amiens (FIGS. **10-23** to **10-26**) continued the Chartrian manner and gracefully refined it. Amiens was begun in 1220, according to the designs of ROBERT DE LUZARCHES. The nave was finished in 1236 and the radiating chapels were completed by 1247, but work on the choir continued until almost 1270. The façade (FIG. 10-23), slightly marred by uneven towers (the shorter dates from the fourteenth century, the taller from the fifteenth century), was begun at the same time as the nave (1220). Its lower parts seem to reflect the influence of the Laon façade in the spacing of its funnellike and gable-covered portals. However, unlike Laon's, the Amiens portals do not project from the façade but are recessed behind the building's buttress-defined frontal plane. The upper parts of the façade, on the other hand, seem to be related to Notre Dame in Paris, the rose window (with fifteenth-century tracery) being placed above the "king's gallery" and between double-arched openings in the towers. But the Amiens façade goes well beyond its apparent models in the richness and intricacy of its surface decoration. The deep piercing of walls and towers seems to have left few continuous surfaces to be decorated, but the ones that remain have been covered with a network of articulating colonnettes, arches, pinnacles, rosettes, and other decorative stonework that visually screens and nearly dissolves the structure's solid core. Despite its decorative intricacy, the façade retains its monumental grandeur and is one of the first to achieve full integration with the building behind it. The cavernous portals correspond in width and placement to the nave and aisles, and (although in slightly different proportions) the façade's three-part elevation reflects that of the nave, the rose window corresponding to the clerestory.

The plan of Amiens (FIG. 10-24), like the façade, is exemplary of the grand High Gothic style. Derived from Chartres and perhaps even more elegant in its proportions, it reflects the builder's unhesitating and confident use of the complete Gothic structural vocabulary: the rectangular-bay system, the four-paneled rib vault, and a buttressing system that permits almost complete dissolution of the heavy masses and thick weight-bearing walls of the Romanesque style. The concept of a self sustaining, skeletal architecture has reached full maturity; what remains of the walls has been stretched like a skin between the piers and seems to serve no purpose other than to provide a weather screen for the interior (FIG. 10-25). From a height of 144 feet, the tense, strong lines of the vault ribs converge to the colonnettes and speed down the shell-like walls to the compound piers; almost every part of the superstructure has its corresponding element below, the only exception being the wall rib (the rib at the junction of the vault and the wall). The overall effect is one of an effortless strength, of a buoyant lightness one would never associate with the obdurate materiality of stone. Viewed directly from below, the vaults of the choir (FIG. 10-26) seem like a canopy, tentlike and suspended from bundled masts. The light flooding in from the clerestory imparts even more "lift" and, at the same time, blurs structural outlines. The effect is visionary, and we are reminded of another great building, one utterly different from Amiens, in which light plays an analogous role—Hagia Sophia in Constantinople (FIG. 7-41). Not only is the physical mass of the building reduced by structural ingenuity and daring, but what remains visually is dematerialized further by light. As with Scholastic philosophy, the logic of the structure here is in the service of mystery. Although philosophy might prove the existence of God with reason, the experience of the beatific vision gave the believer a mystical proof, like Dante's experience in Paradise as he gazed, rapt, into the "heart of Light, the heart of Silence."

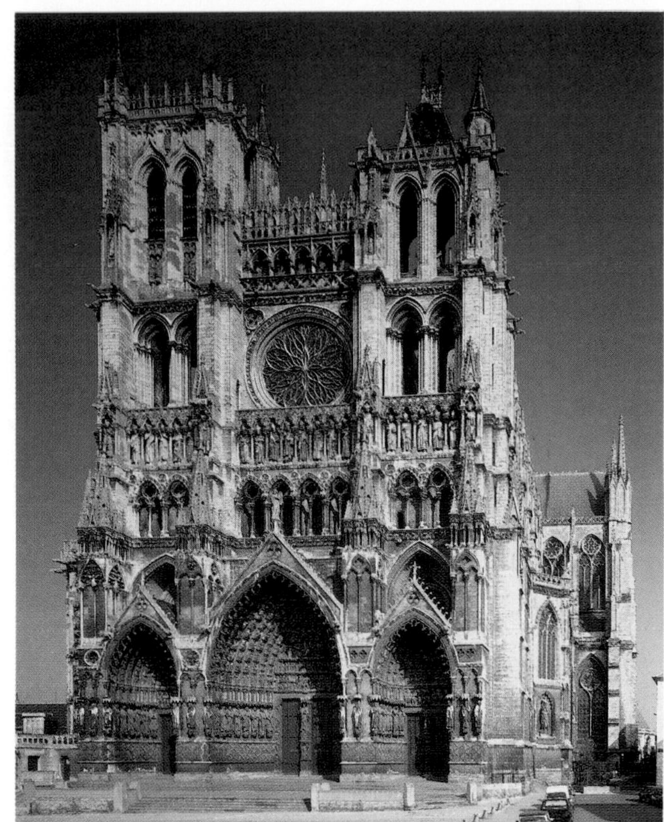

10-23 West façade of Amiens Cathedral, France, *c.* 1220–1236 (area above the rose window, early sixteenth century).

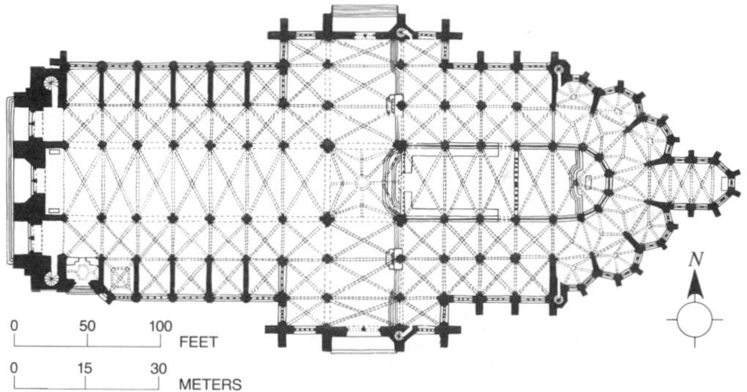

10-24 ROBERT DE LUZARCHES, plan of Amiens Cathedral. (After Frankl.)

In examining the interior of Amiens, it may be useful to reconsider Erwin Panofsky's suggestion of a

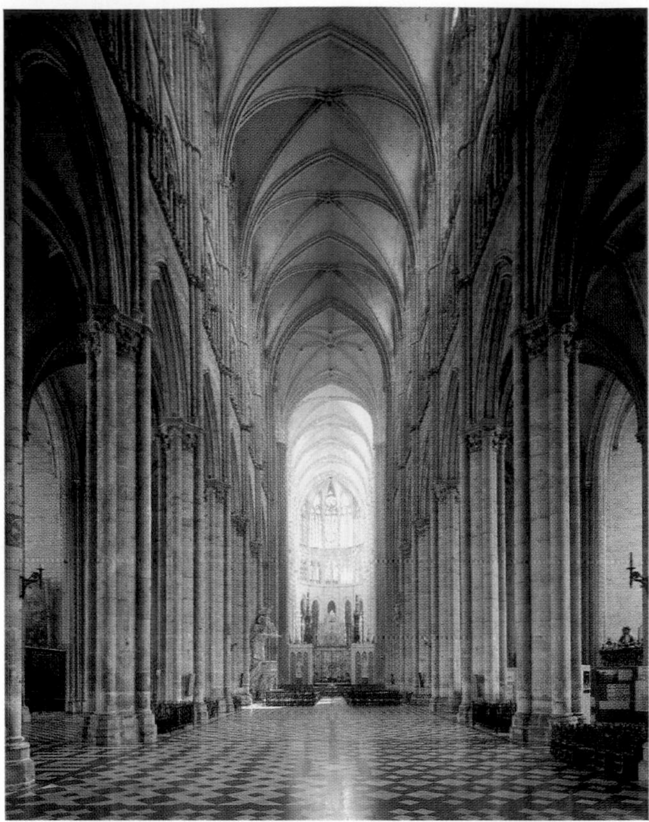

10-25 Nave of Amiens Cathedral (view facing east).

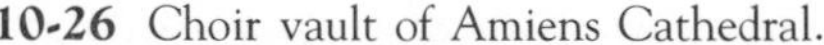

10-26 Choir vault of Amiens Cathedral.

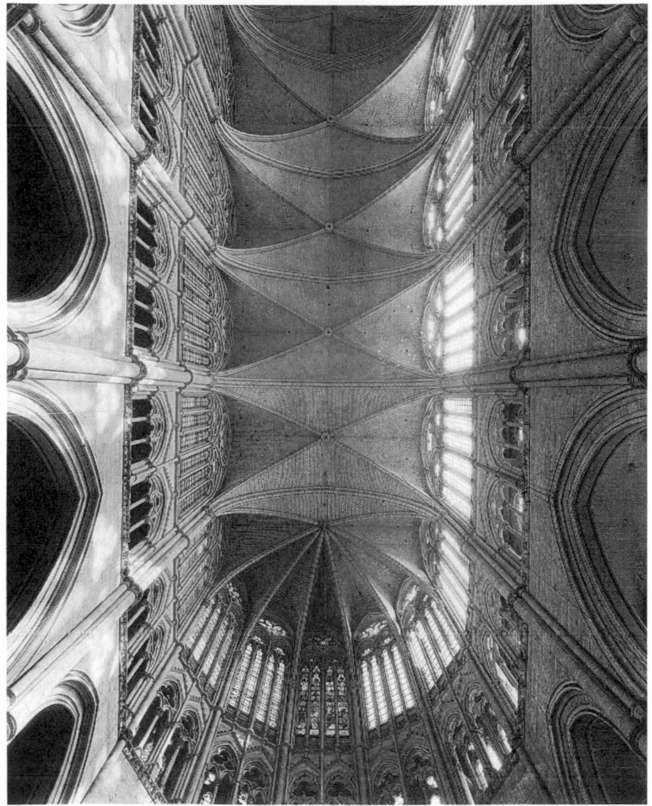

connection between Gothic architecture and Scholastic philosophy and the description of the method as typified in Aquinas's *Summa Theologiae.* Most striking in the propositions of Aquinas and in the structure of Amiens is an insistence on an order and unity made up of clearly distinguished and clearly related parts—the philosopher aiming at logical consistency, the architect striving for structural coherence. In neither is the order intended to be less than total. Aquinas's *Summa* was designed to treat *all* possible questions in which faith and reason touch; in Amiens, all individual elements are subordinated to the whole, unlike the sharply subdivided, often opposed units of Romanesque design. This principle of *manifestatio* (manifestation, transparency) determines the look of the philosophic system, as it does the look of the cathedral. As Panofsky wrote:

> A man imbued with the Scholastic habit [of thought] . . . would look upon the mode of architectural presentation, just as he looked upon the mode of literary presentation, from the point of view of *manifestatio.* He would have taken it for granted that the primary purpose of the many elements that compose a cathedral was to ensure stability, just as he took it for granted that the primary purpose of the many elements that constitute a *Summa* was to ensure validity.
>
> But he would not have been satisfied had not the membrification of the edifice permitted him to re-experience the very processes of architectural composition, just as the membrification of the *Summa* permitted him to re-experience the very processes of cogitation. To him, the panoply of shafts, ribs, buttresses, tracery, pinnacles, and crockets was a self-analysis and self-explication of . . . architecture, much as the customary apparatus of parts, distinctions, questions, and articles was, to him, a self-analysis and self-explication of reason. . . . The Scholastic mind demanded a maximum of explicitness. It accepted and insisted upon a gratuitous clarification of function through form, just as it accepted and insisted upon a gratuitous clarification of thought through language.*

The other principle Panofsky saw at work in philosophy and architecture is that of *concordantia* (harmony), whereby contradictory possibilities are accepted and ultimately reconciled. This reconciliation is achieved by careful debate, the *disputatio,* in which a possibility is stated, one authoritative view is cited, another authoritative view is cited in objection, the solution (a reconciliation of positions) is given, and finally a reply is given to each of the original arguments now rejected. Panofsky saw this process in the resolution of three "questions" in Gothic architec-

*Erwin Panofsky, *Gothic Architecture and Scholasticism* (Latrobe, PA: Archabbey Press, 1951), pp. 58–60.

ture: the placement and design of the rose window in the west façade, the design of the interior wall beneath the clerestory, and the conformation of the pier. (Very likely the development of the Gothic plan also could be seen as an evolved "solution" to a "question.") Evidence that the habit of mind reflected in the disputatio was not exclusive with the Scholastics in the universities, but was more broadly shared, is found on a page from the "album" of drawings by the thirteenth-century architect Villard de Honnecourt (Introduction, FIG. 13 and FIG. 10-37). According to the inscription, Villard and another architect, Pierre de Corbie, arrived at an ideal plan for a chevet after a disputatio.

THE RAYONNANT STYLE

From the grand style of the first half of the thirteenth century came a period of great refinement, the so-called *rayonnant* (radiant) style, which dominated the second half of the century and was associated with the royal Paris court of Louis IX (St. Louis), famed throughout Europe for his justice, chivalry, and piety, and the medieval ideal of the "saint-king." Royal France, growing increasingly wealthy, powerful, and prestigious, radiated its art and culture throughout Europe. The king was lavish in embellishing the realm, especially with religious architecture.

Preeminent examples of rayonnant design are the two great rose windows in the north and south transept façades of Notre Dame in Paris (FIGS. 10-10 and **10-27**). The tremendous north rose window, the work of the master builder JEAN DE CHELLES, is a masterpiece of architectural ingenuity. Almost the entire mass of wall opens up into stained glass, which is held in place by an intricate armature of stone tracery that practically has the tensile strength of steel. Here, the Gothic passion for light leads to a most daring and successful attempt to subtract all superfluous material bulk just short of destabilizing the structure and to transform hard substance into insubstantial, luminous color. The fact that this vast, complex fabric of stone-set glass has maintained its structural integrity and equilibrium against the disintegrative forces of nature and time for seven hundred years attests to the master builder's engineering genius.

10-27 JEAN DE CHELLES, rose window of the north transept, Notre Dame, Paris, 1240–1250. Stained glass, iron and lead stone-bar tracery, diameter 43′.

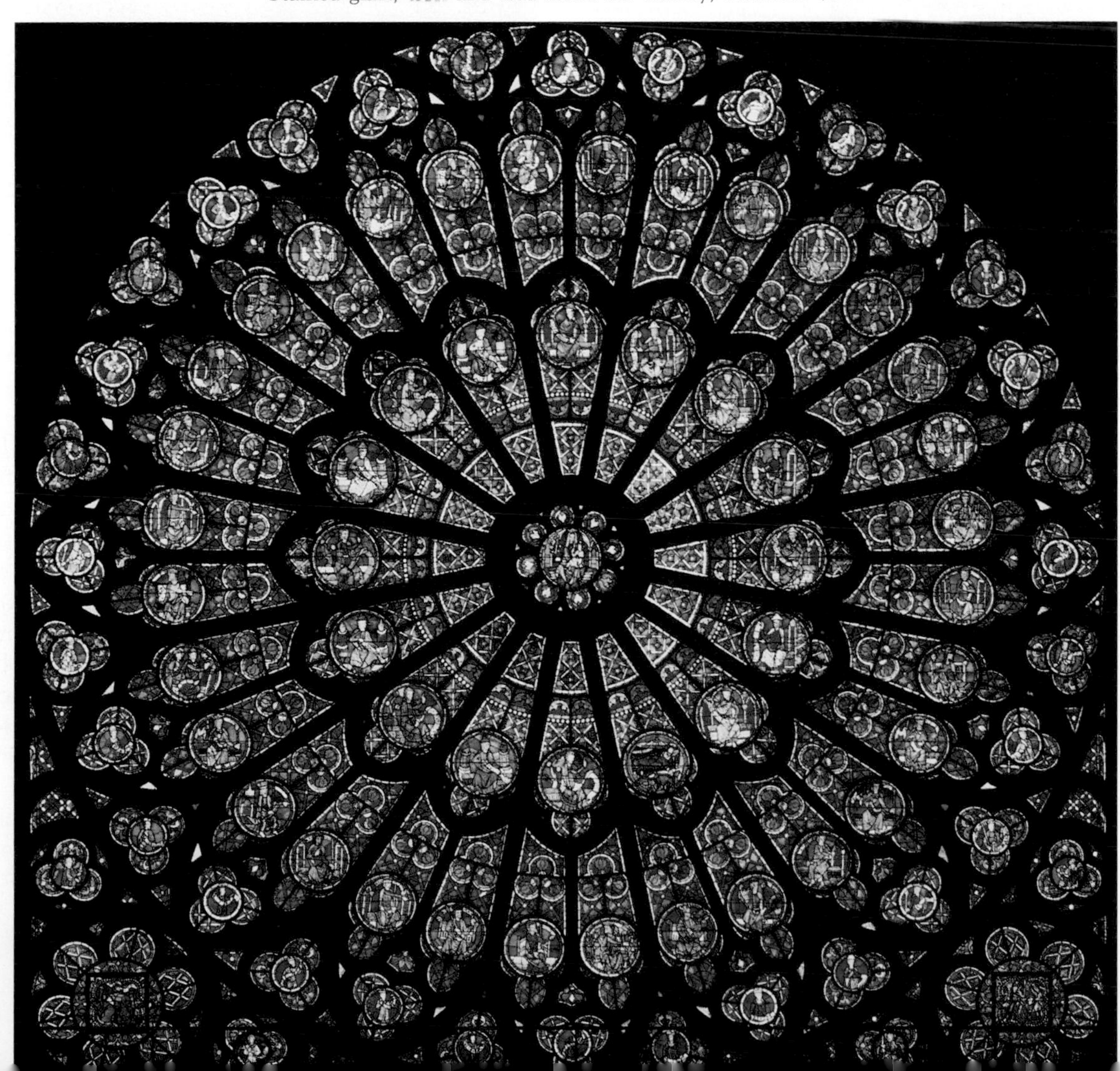

The "multifoliate rose" of light, ever-changing in hue and intensity with the hours of the day, seems to turn solid architecture into a floating vision of the celestial heavens—a constellation of radiant, jewellike stars. Expressive of the Gothic adoration of the Virgin Mary, the concentric circles exalt her as Mother of Christ; she appears at the very center of the design. Around her are figures of the prophets who foretold the Incarnation; in the second circle, are thirty-two Old Testament kings, the ancestors of Christ; in the outermost circle, are thirty-two high priests and patriarchs, who also testify to the royal lineage and divinity of Christ. The light of the north rose window is predominantly blue, the color of the northern sky, of the heavens, and of the mantle of the Virgin, which she throws protectively around all those devoted to her as the queen of Heaven.

10-28 Sainte Chapelle, Paris, 1243–1248 (view toward the tribune). The rose window was installed after 1485.

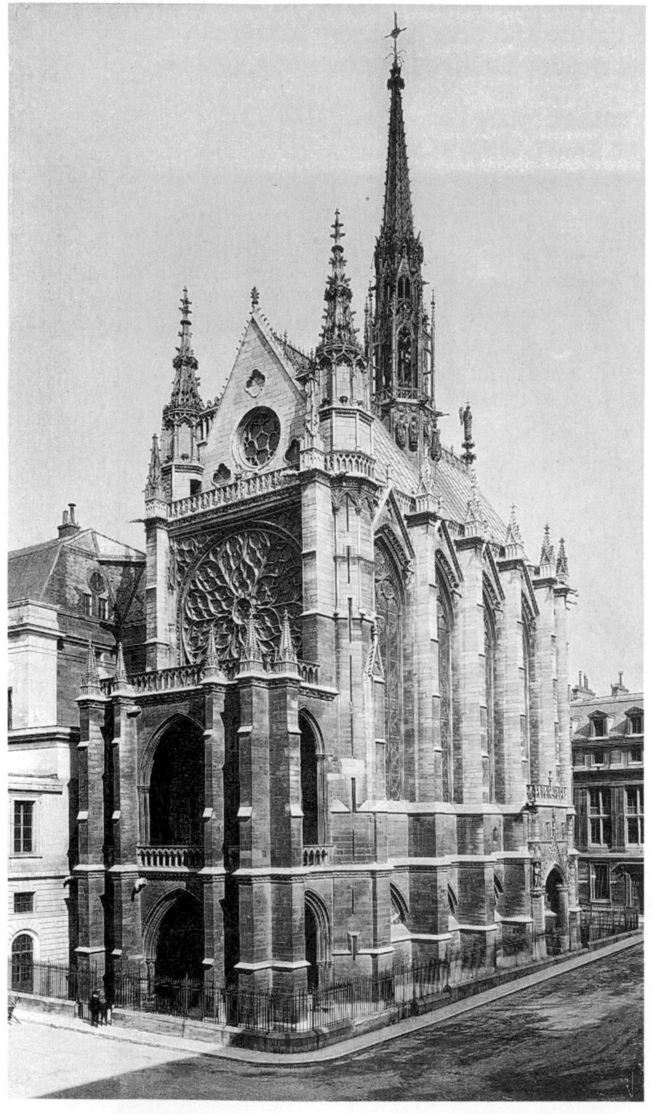

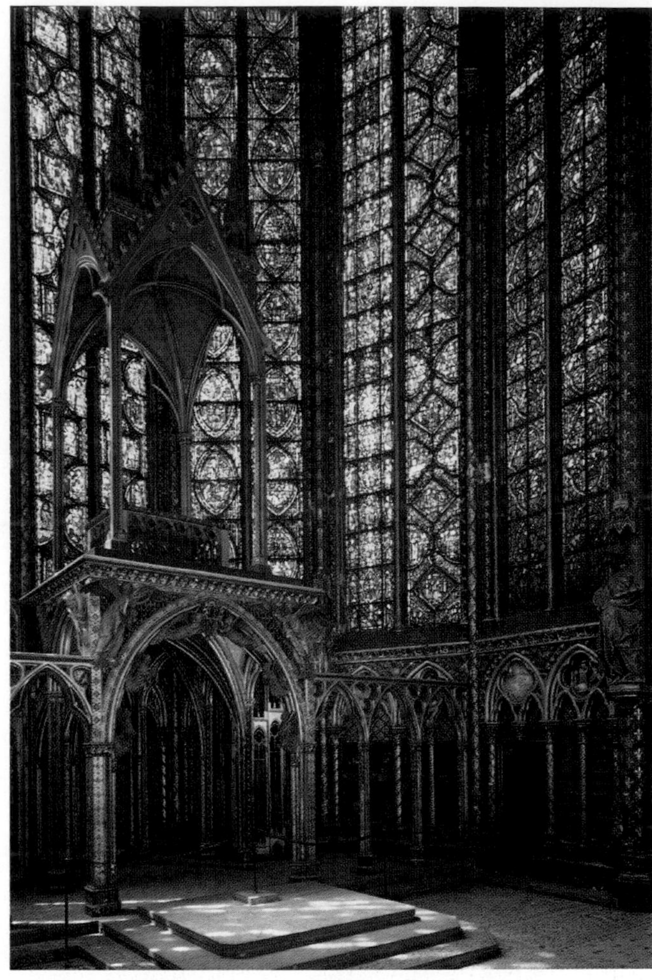

10-29 Interior of Sainte Chapelle.

The Gothic architect uses light as a medium, as does the Byzantine, but they use it in opposite ways. In Gothic architecture, light is *transmitted through* a kind of diffracting screen of stone-set glass; in Byzantine architecture, light is *reflected from* myriad glass tesserae set into the hard bed of the wall (FIGS. 7-28 and 7-38). With light, both stained glass and mosaic create an opalescent splendor that transforms solid substance into insubstantial vision—the material world into the spiritual.

If the rose windows of the transepts of Notre Dame demonstrate the wall-dissolving architecture of rayonnant design, the Sainte Chapelle in Paris shows the principle of the style applied to a whole building (FIGS. **10-28** and **10-29**). The building, joined to the royal palace, was intended to be a repository for relics of the Passion of Christ brought back by Louis IX after the ill-fated Sixth Crusade, so that its resemblance to an intricately carved reliquary is intentional. Here, the dissolution of the wall and the reduction of the bulk of the supports has been carried to the point that more than three-quarters of the structure is composed of stained glass. The supporting elements have been so reduced that they are hardly more than large *mullions* separating the enormous windows, which are approximately 49 feet high and 15 feet wide and are the largest designed up to their time. Although the chapel was heavily restored during the nineteenth century (after being damaged in the French Revolution), it has retained most of its original thirteenth-century glass, which filters the light and fills the interior with an unearthly rose-violet atmosphere. Amid richly colored stone surfaces and shimmering strips of decorative mosaic stand statues of the apostles. Multicolored also, they stand on *soffits* almost independent of the architecture, and their related poses, with multiple axes, foreshadow the graceful rhythms of later thirteenth- and fourteenth-century sculpture. The technical and esthetic refinements here would have upset the solemn harmonies and monumentality of the art of the earlier part of the century. The emphasis on the extreme slenderness of the architectural forms and on linearity in general, with exquisite color and precise carving of details, does recall the richly ornamented reliquaries of the time.

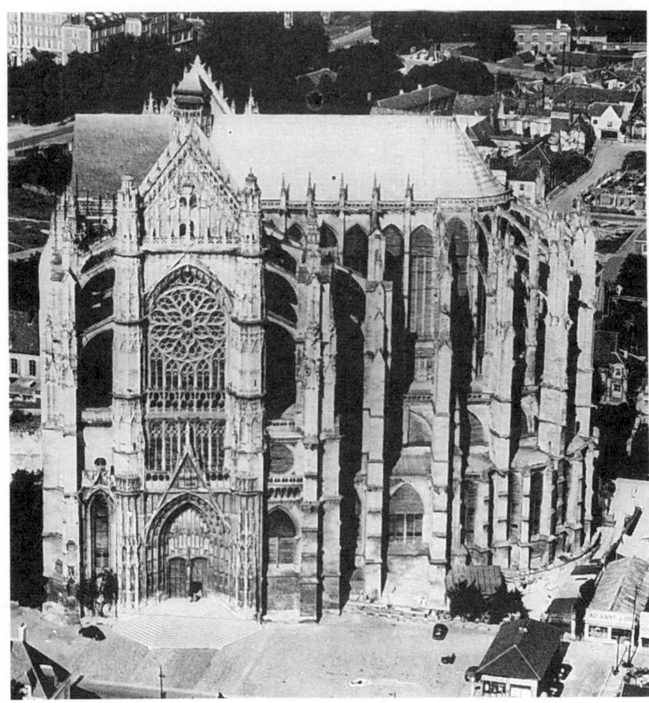

10-30 Beauvais Cathedral, France, begun 1247 (aerial view from the south).

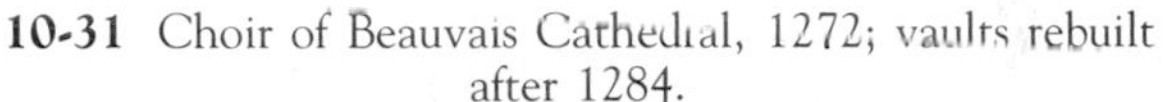

10-31 Choir of Beauvais Cathedral, 1272; vaults rebuilt after 1284.

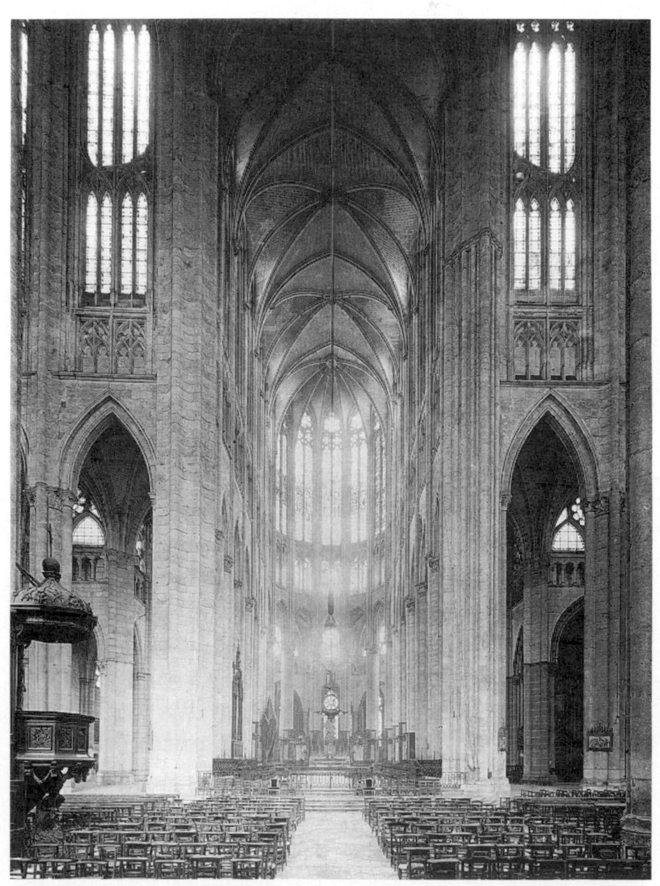

Beauvais Cathedral (FIGS. **10-30** and **10-31**) was begun in 1247, after plans that had been drawn in the 1230s. As was customary, the builders began construction at the east end, so that apse and choir would be finished and ready for use while the remainder of the building was being completed. In contrast to monastic churches, which usually were assured of funding before construction began and which were completed in fairly short order, the building histories of urban cathedrals often extended over decades, and sometimes over centuries. Their financing depended largely on collections and public contributions (not always voluntary), and building programs were often interrupted by a lack of funds. Unforeseen events, such as wars, famines, or plagues, could stop construction, which might not be resumed for years, or even decades. The rebuilding of Chartres Cathedral took a relatively short twenty-seven years; the building history of Cologne Cathedral (see FIG. 10-57) extended over six centuries, and Beauvais Cathedral never was completed.

The wisdom of starting at the east end and working westward was proven at Beauvais, where construction stopped around 1500 after a "flamboyant" Late Gothic transept had been added to the choir. Although the building is unfinished, the completed and serviceable part stands to this day as one of the most impressive examples of the Gothic "rush into the skies." That skyward impulse, seen first in the height of the nave of Notre Dame at Paris, became an obsession with French Gothic builders. With their new skeletal frames of stone, they attempted goals almost beyond limit, pushing with ever-slenderer supports to new heights, aiming always at effects of insubstantial visions floating far beyond human reach. The nave vaults at Laon had risen to a height of about 80 feet; at Paris, to 107 feet; at Chartres, to 118 feet; and at Amiens, to 144 feet. In 1272, the builders of the choir of Beauvais planned a height of 157 feet.

In 1284, the vaults collapsed; the cause of the failure is still a matter of scholarly debate. The original design of the first master architect had been brilliant, audacious, and stable; the parts of the choir hemicycle completed by him remained standing. Modern engineering analysis, of the kind we have mentioned in the discussion of Chartres and Bourges, indicates that succeeding builders seem to have miscalculated wind and dead-load stresses, particularly those on the external intermediate piers. The choir, rebuilt with a broad margin of safety, has additional piers and old-fashioned, sexpartite vaults, not unlike those at Bourges. Unfortunately, the rebuilt vaults and piers disfigure the original design, for it was exactly those former features of wide-spread piers and slender buttresses that the rayonnant architects had sought in their effort to make an architecture seemingly out of nothing but line and light. Henceforth, the great structural innovations of the High Gothic style and the vast scale in which they were worked out would be things of the past. Late Gothic architecture, born of the linear rayonnant design, would be confined to buildings of quite modest size, conservative in structure and ornamented with restless designs of intricately meshed, pointed motifs.

Sculpture

Sculpture, as it had been since the Romanesque period, was subservient to architecture during the High Gothic period, but rapid changes were taking place. The unity of idea that controls the design of the Royal Portals of Chartres (FIG. 10-14) expanded to embrace the whole cathedral (see the façade of Amiens Cathedral, FIG. 10-23). The sculptural program came to include not only the huge portals but the upper levels of the building as well. The summit of Gothic art—the cathedral-building and cathedral-adorning age—lasted from about 1210 to 1260. The range of the iconography of the sculpture is as vast and complex as the buildings themselves. Most of the carved figures are symbolic, but many, particularly the grotesque gargoyles (used as rainspouts) and other details of the upper portions, are purely decorative and show the vivacity and charm of the medieval spirit at this moment, when it was confident in its faith. The iconographic program, no longer confined almost entirely to the letter of the dogma (as in Romanesque art), is extensive enough to embrace all the categories of medieval thought. Indeed Émile Mâle showed that many iconographic schemes were based on the *Speculum Majus* (Great Mirror) of Vincent of Beauvais, a comprehensive summary of medieval knowledge in which accounts of natural phenomena, scriptural themes, and moral philosophy serve a didactic religious purpose.

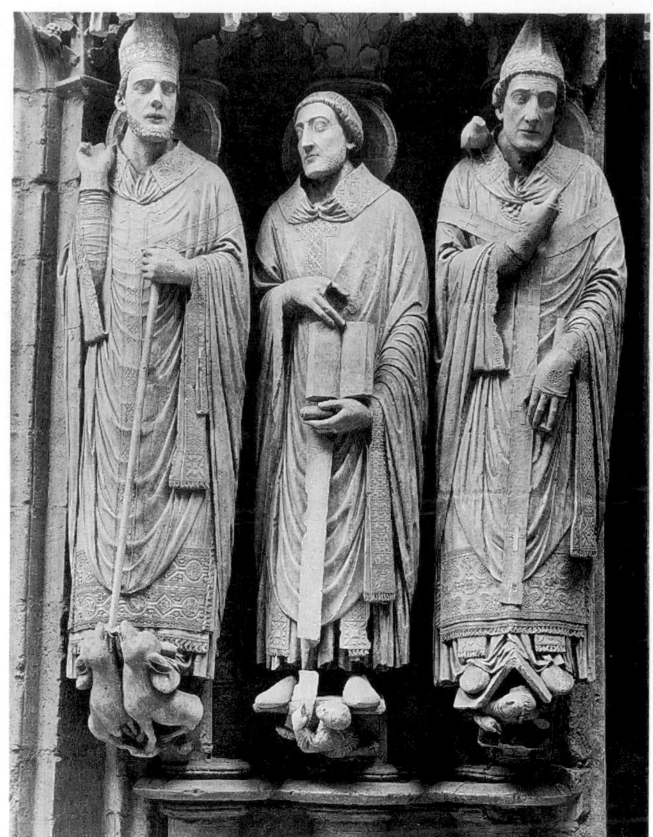

10-32 *St. Martin, St. Jerome, and St. Gregory,* c. 1220–1230, from the Porch of the Confessors, Chartres Cathedral, France.

Nature begins to come forward as important, and in art the human figure comes forward with it. Three figures from the Porch of the Confessors in the south transept of Chartres Cathedral illustrate how much the incipient realism of the Royal Portals has advanced. The figures, representing St. Martin, St. Jerome, and St. Gregory (FIG. **10-32**), date from 1220–1230. Although attached to the architectural matrix, their poses are not determined by it as much as they would have been earlier. The setting now allows the figures to communicate quietly with one another, like waiting dignitaries; they turn slightly toward and away from each other, breaking the rigid vertical lines that, on the Royal Portals, fix the figures immovably. Their draperies no longer are described by the stiff and reedy lines of the figures of the Royal Portals;

the fabric falls and laps over the bodies in soft, if still regular, folds.

The faces are most remarkable. They show, for the first time since the ancient world, the features of specifically Western men, with no admixture whatever of the denatured mask passed down over a thousand years. Moreover, they seem to have been taken from particular persons, and we have no difficulty characterizing them. St. Martin is tall and ascetic, an intense priest with gaunt features (compare the spiritually moved but not particularized face of the Moissac Jeremiah or Isaiah in FIG. 9-29). The subject may have been a saintly canon of Chartres who reluctantly became a bishop; in any event, in another realistic touch, his vestments are the liturgical costume of the time. One of his companions, St. Jerome, who appears as a humorous, kindly, practical administrator-scholar, holds his Vulgate translation of the Scriptures. Standing beside St. Jerome, the introspective St. Gregory seems lost in thought as he listens to the dove of the Holy Ghost on his shoulder. Thus, the three men are not simply contrasted in terms of their poses, gestures, and attributes but, most particularly and emphatically, as *persons,* so that personality, revealed in human faces, makes the real difference—a rarity even in Classical art. In another century or so, the identifiable portrait will emerge.

The fully ripened Gothic style can be seen in the west portals of Reims Cathedral (FIG. **10-33**), built in the mid-thirteenth century. At first glance, the jamb statues appear to be completely detached from their architectural background. The columns to which they are attached have shrunk into insignificance and in no way impede the free and easy movement of the full-bodied figures. (On the Royal Portals of Chartres, the background columns occupy a volume equal to that of the figures; see FIG. 10-15.) However, two architectural devices limit the statues' spheres of activity and tie them to the larger design of the portal and the architectural matrix—the pedestals on which they stand and the canopies above their heads. Less submissive than their predecessors from the Royal Portals of Chartres, these Reims figures create an electric tension within the portal design; they were designed for this portal, however, and would look incongruous in any other setting. Gothic portal statues placed in museums to protect them from weathering look, without exception, forlorn and out of place.

On the right jamb of the central portal, the two figures on the left in our illustration (FIG. **10-34**) represent *The Annunciation* while those on the right portray *The Visitation.* Their different styles reflect the hands of several anonymous masters. The master of the *Visitation* group, quite original in his manner, manifests a classicizing bent startlingly unlike anything seen

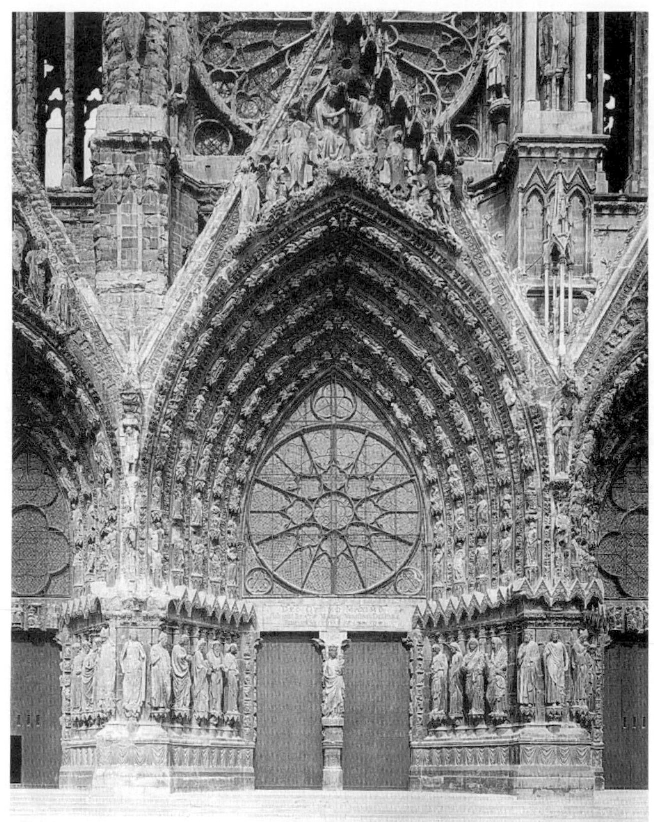

10-33 Central portal of the west façade of Reims Cathedral, France, c. 1225–1290.

10-34 *The Annunciation (left)* and *The Visitation* (detail of FIG. 10-33). Jamb statues over life size.

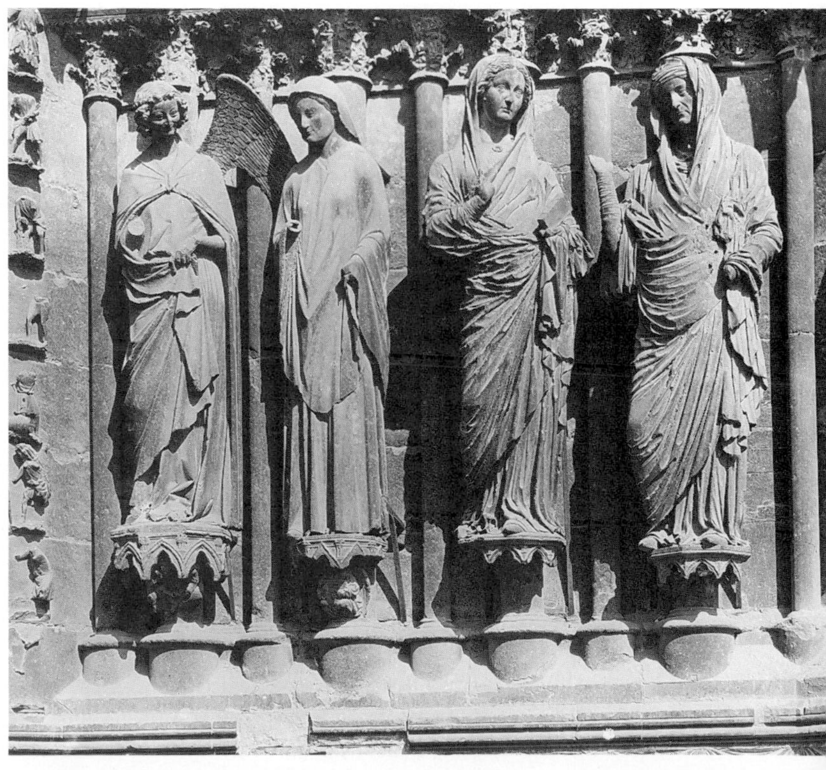

since Roman times. The group illustrates the impact on its master carver of either actual Classical statuary he had seen or of manuscripts or ivories from Late Antiquity or Byzantium. Whatever the artist's source, the facial types, costumes, and drapery treatment are astonishing approximations of the naturalistic style traits of ancient figure sculpture. The sculptor even has tried to represent the Classical contrapposto stance, although the only partially successful result betrays his ignorance of human anatomy.

The two figures of the *Annunciation* group evidently were carved by different masters. The Virgin is by a sculptor who may have worked at Amiens before he came to Reims and whose style is characterized by a weighty, massive quality. Drapery resembling a thick, flannellike material falls heavily from the figure's shoulders to her feet and, by stressing mass and verticality, imparts an aspect of grave solemnity. The angel of the *Annunciation* group differs strikingly from the Virgin. This almost dainty figure is tall and slender, animated by a kind of swaying curve, the head quite small, the face bright with a winsome smile. The angel figure, contrasting with the still and somber Virgin, represents the new, courtly style—corresponding to the rayonnant style in architecture—that was ushered in with the reign of Louis IX and the cultural dominance of the Île-de-France after mid-century.

The influence of these great cathedral statues must have been felt widely by those who contemplated them. John of Garland, writing in the thirteenth century on how university students should conduct themselves, advised, " . . . regard as models of deportment the graven images of the churches, which you should carry in your mind as living and indelible pictures." Certainly, the statues' influence on artists must have been great, as in the case of the painter of the *Psalter of St. Louis* (see FIG. 10-38). Although the degree and the progress of that influence had not yet been worked out in complete detail, it is certain that, by the fourteenth century, Gothic sculpture was widely naturalized in Italy and elsewhere outside of France. In Italy, by the beginning of the fifteenth century, the native Gothic sense for realism had fused with a new classicizing impulse—generated partly from Byzantine art and partly from the discovery of the art of ancient Rome—to form the first distinctive styles of the Renaissance.

Stained Glass and Illumination

Gothic accomplishments in architecture and sculpture are matched by the magnificent stained glass of the time, which we already have seen at Notre Dame and Sainte Chapelle in Paris. This medium almost is synonymous with the Gothic style; no other age has managed it with such craft and beauty. The mysticism of light that induced Abbot Suger to design an architecture that would allow for great windows is widespread in Gothic theology. "Stained-glass windows," wrote Hugh of St. Victor, "are the Holy Scriptures . . . and since their brilliance lets the splendor of the True Light pass into the church, they enlighten those inside." St. Bernard compared the manner in which light is tinted by a stained-glass window to the process of the Incarnation and virgin Birth of Jesus. The Gothic mood seems to take its inspiration from the Gospel of John (1:4–5): "In him was life; and the life was the light of men. And the light shineth in darkness."

The difference between these words and the sonorous verses of Revelation, which provide the program of the Romanesque "Last Judgments," reflects the

10-35 *Crucifixion*, detail of a window from St. Remi, Reims, France, c. 1190. Stained glass, approx. 12′ high.

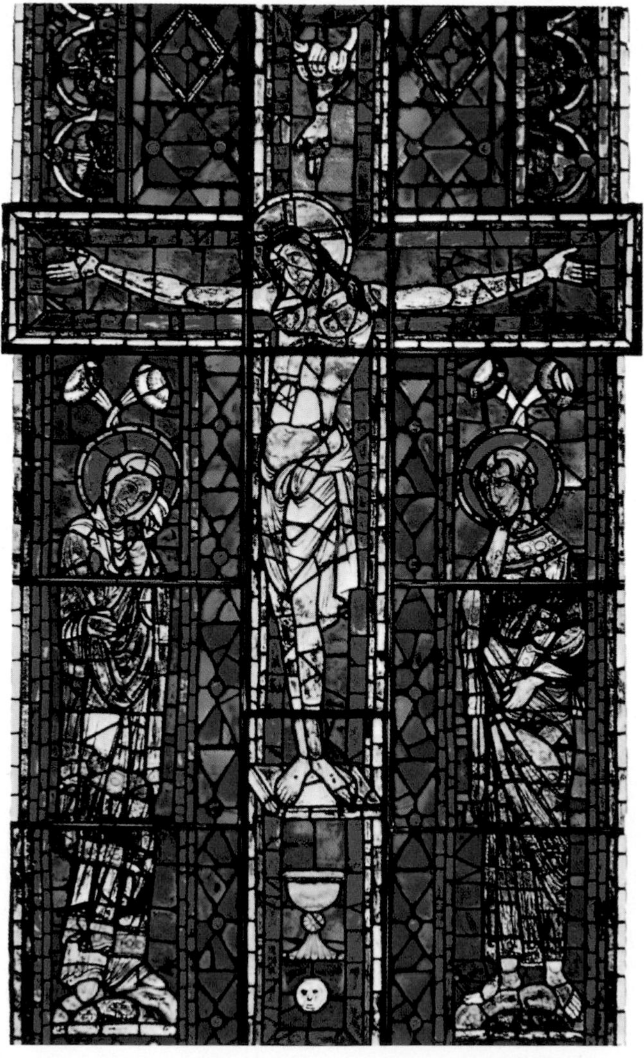

difference between the shining walls of colored light, which change with every passing hour or cloud, and the painted walls of Romanesque churches or the shimmering Byzantine mosaics.

Colored glass was used as early as the fourth century to decorate the windows of churches. Perfection of the technique must have been gradual, with the greatest advancements made during the tenth and eleventh centuries. The first accurately dated windows, those of the choir of St. Denis (1144), show a high degree of skill; according to Suger, they were "painted by the exquisite hands of many masters from different regions," proving that the art was known widely at that time. Yet the stained-glass window may be said to be the hallmark of the Gothic style, particularly in northern Europe, where the almost total dissolution of walls left few surfaces that were suitable for decoration with frescoes.

Imperfections or unexpected results in making colored glass were frequent; yet this was not an art left entirely to chance. The different properties of colors were well understood and carefully controlled. The glass was blown and either "spun" into a "crown" plate of varying thickness or shaped into a cylindrical "muff," which was cut and rolled out into square pieces. These pieces were broken or cut into smaller fragments and assembled on a flat table on which a design had been marked with chalk dust. Many of the pieces actually were "painted" with a dark pigment, so that details, such as those of a face or clothing, could be rendered. The fragments then were "leaded," or joined by strips of lead that were used to separate colors or to heighten the effect of the design as a whole (FIGS. **10-35** and **10-36**). The completed window was strengthened with an armature of iron bands, which, in the twelfth century, took the form of a grid over the whole design (FIG. 10-35); in the thirteenth century, these bands were shaped to follow the outlines of the medallions and of the surrounding areas (FIG. 10-36).

The technical difficulties of assembling a large stained-glass window and fixing it firmly within its frame were matched by compositional problems. Illuminated manuscripts, the painter's chief vehicle during the earlier Middle Ages, had little instructional value for artists who not only had to work on an unprecedented scale but who also had to adjust their designs to the larger whole of the church building and its architecture. Sculptors, of course, already had solved these problems, and it is not surprising

10-36 Detail of the *Good Samaritan* window, Chartres Cathedral, France, early thirteenth century. Stained glass.

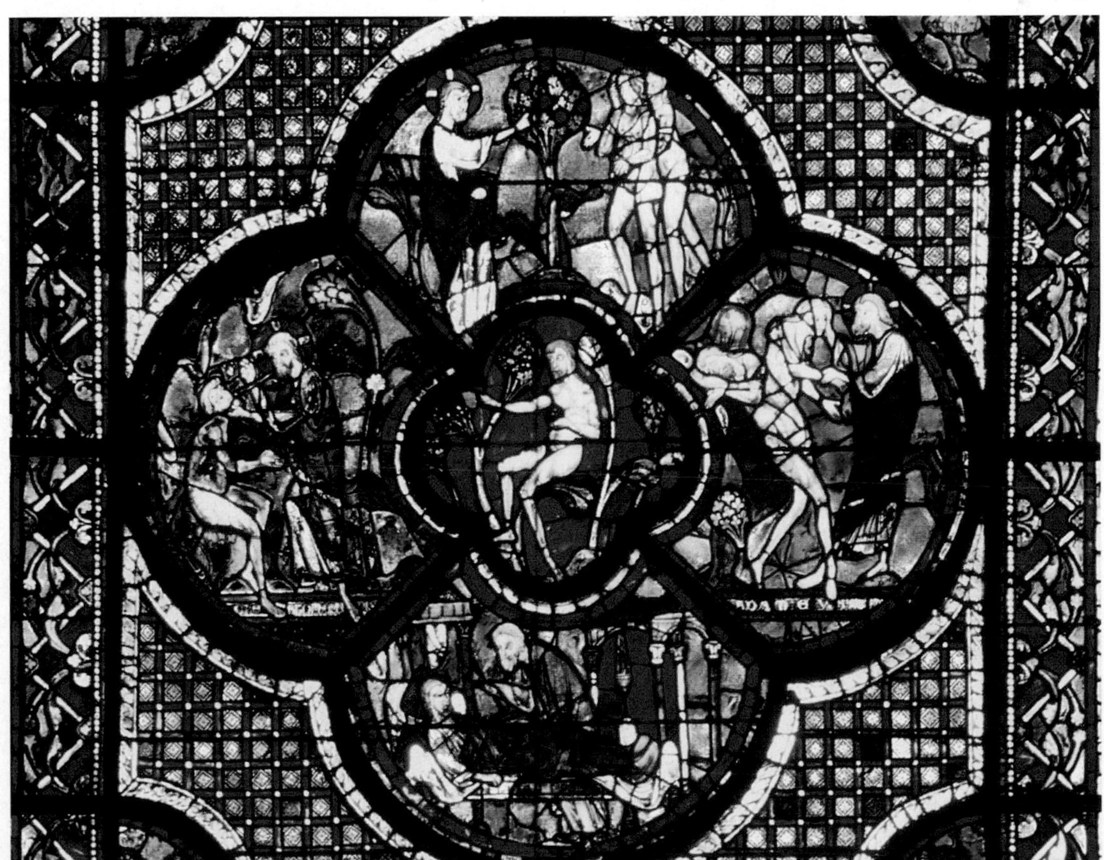

to learn that painters turned to them for instruction. Certainly, the saints flanking the cross in the St. Remi window (FIG. 10-35) seem vaguely familiar. Their erect poses, the straight, almost unbroken silhouettes, and the rather precarious manner in which they perch on their hilltop pedestals stamp them as not too distant relatives of the jamb statues from the Royal Portals at Chartres. Here, the Romanesque process has been reversed, and the sculptors—the former students who found their inspiration in paintings—now have become the teachers.

Like the architects and sculptors with whom they worked in close collaboration, the stained-glass artists relied heavily on the *ars de geometria* for their designs, layouts, and assemblies. The sketchbook compiled by VILLARD DE HONNECOURT, the mid-thirteenth-century architect, was intended as a text for his students, but in it he does not confine his instruction to architecture alone. In addition to details of buildings, plans of choirs with radiating chapels, and church towers, he also presents information on lifting devices, a saw mill, and stained-glass windows. Sprinkled liberally throughout the pages are drawings of figures, religious and worldly, and animals—some surprisingly realistic, others purely fantastic. In our illustration (FIG. **10-37**), Villard evidently is informing his students of the usefulness of the ars de geometria in designing human heads and animals. In some instances, he claimed to have drawn his animals from nature, but even these appear to have been composed around a skeleton not of bones but of abstract geometric figures. The designers of stained-glass windows probably proceeded in a similar manner. No matter how their designs and layouts were arrived at, the effect of these glowing, translucent paintings, which often seem to be suspended in space, is as spellbinding today as it must have been to the medieval churchgoer (FIG. 10-27). For the first time in centuries, the art of painting was accessible to the common man—painting in a form so compelling that the desire to have more and more of it, from pavement to vault, well may have influenced the development of Gothic architecture. By about the mid-thirteenth century, architectural techniques had advanced to the point that the space of cathedrals seems to be defined by the burning intensity of the stained-glass windows, rather than by the stone structure.

10-37 VILLARD DE HONNECOURT, page from a notebook, c. 1240. Bibliothèque Nationale, Paris.

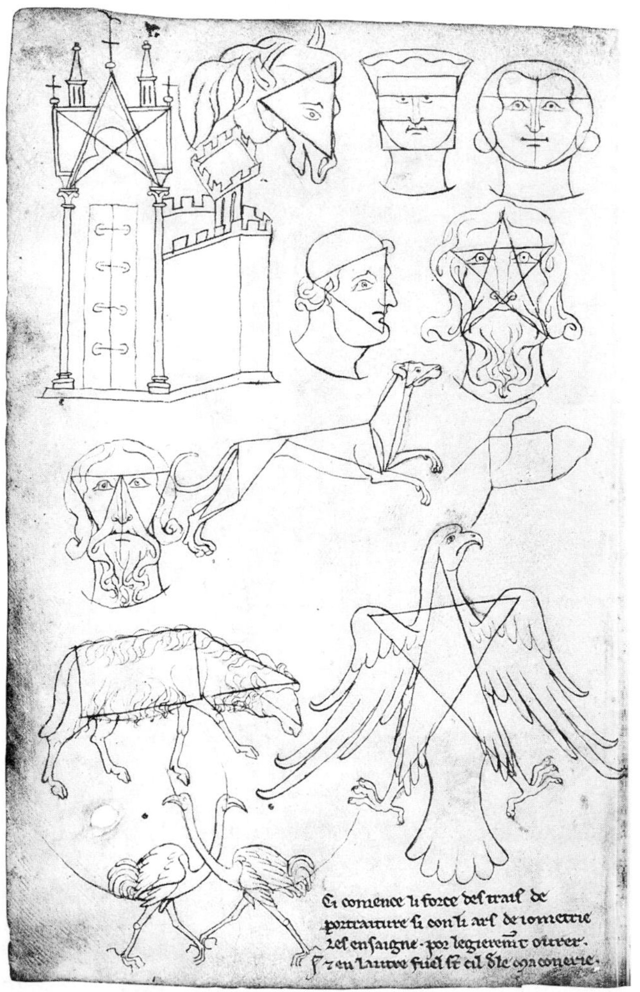

The radiance of stained glass must have inspired the glowing color of illuminated manuscripts; in some cases, glass and book must have been produced by masters in the same shop, or perhaps by one master who was expert in both arts. The *Psalter of St. Louis* (FIG. **10-38**) is believed to have been one of a number of books produced in Paris in the late thirteenth century for King Louis IX of France (St. Louis) by craftsmen associated with those who made the stained glass for Sainte Chapelle (FIGS. 10-28 and 10-29). Certainly, the figures in the illuminated *Psalter* express the same aristocratic elegance as the "court" style of architecture (the rayonnant) favored by royal Paris. The painted architectural setting in the *Psalter* reflects the pierced, screenlike lightness and transparency of royal buildings like Sainte Chapelle and the new work at St. Denis. The intense colors, especially the blues, emulate glass; the borders resemble glass partitioned by leading; and the gables, pierced by rose windows, are almost portraits of rayonnant architectural features.

The subject of the page from the *Psalter of St. Louis* shown here (FIG. 10-38) is *Abraham and the Three Angels.* (See Andrei Rublëv's version of essentially the same theme in FIG. 7-60.) Two episodes are included, separated by the Tree of Mamre. In one, Abraham greets the three angels; in the other, he entertains

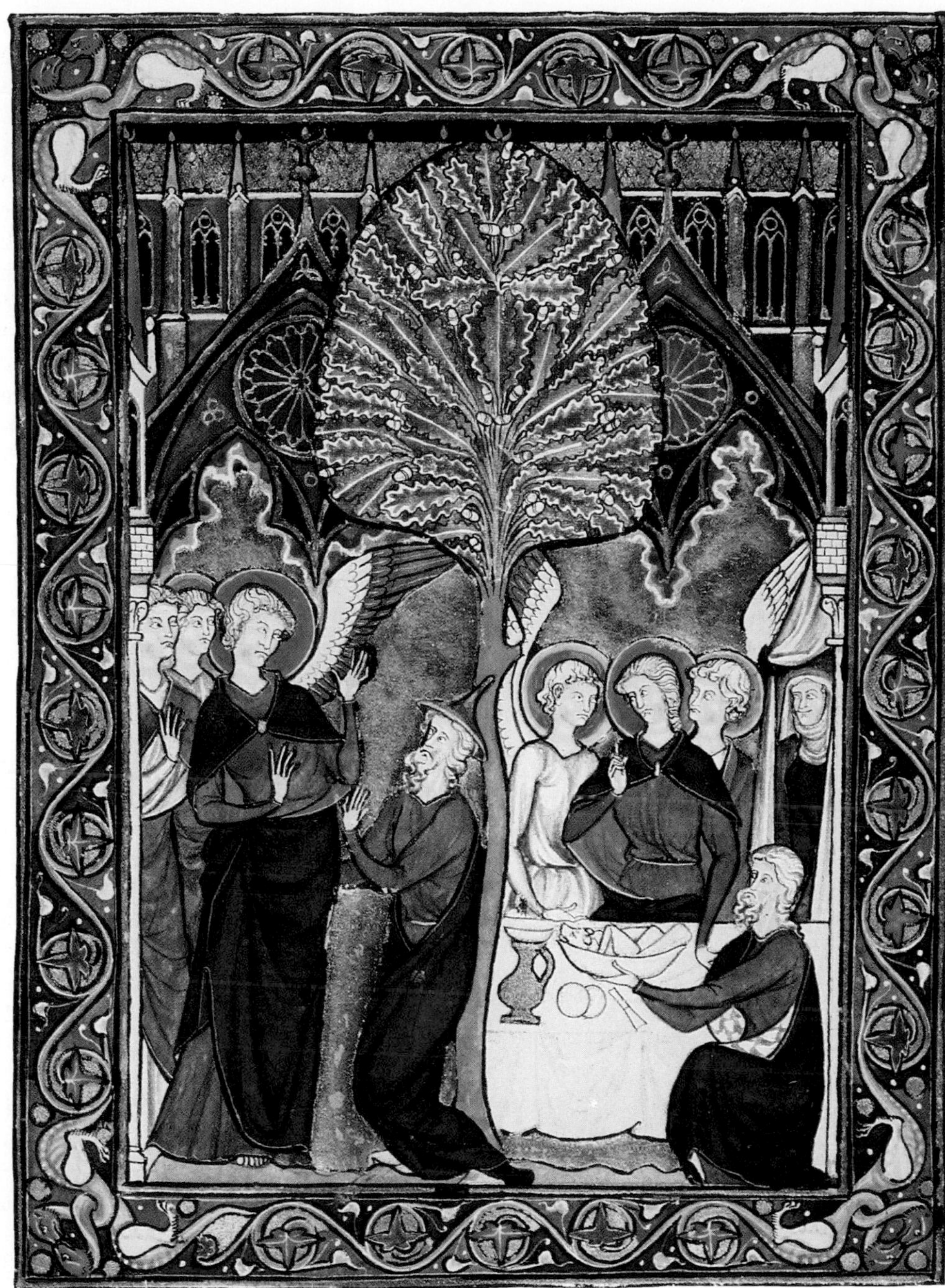

10-38 *Abraham and the Three Angels,* illuminated page from the *Psalter of St. Louis,* 1253–1270. Bibliothèque Nationale, Paris.

them while Sarah peers at them from the tent. Compared with the figures in Romanesque illumination (FIG. 9-38), these are quieter in pose and attitude and have a firmness of stance and a sense of weight suggestive of sculpture. Moreover, here the busyness of the drapery lines is subdued, making us less mindful of the flat areas that encourage decorative line-play and more aware of the modeling tones that suggest plastic form and contour.

Although these figures owe much of their color to stained-glass works, the influence of sculpture also is evident. The lead angel in the group at the left closely resembles the angel of the *Annunciation* group at Reims (FIG. 10-34), and if we look at the general arrangement of the portal (FIG. 10-33) in which the Reims group appears, we see that the *Psalter* illuminator thinks of the sacred personages in the *Abraham* episodes as framed, canopied, and backed by the architecture and their placement as determined by it—like the actual sculptures of the portal.

The artist's response to the monumental, over-life-size sculptures of the cathedral portals may have led to a new sense of the possibilities of representation—the function of light and shade, for example, and of volume, contour, and silhouette. These imposing figures could have had a new, awesome authority that was not conveyed by the traditional prototypes (ivory carvings, say, or painted pages). The impulse toward naturalism and pictorial illusionism, endemic in the Greco-Roman world, and by no means lost in Early Christian and Byzantine art, could be receiving here a new and powerful impulse from monumental sculpture. The illusionistic effect of sculpture may have caught and held the Gothic artist's attention.

Byzantine artists will go in a different direction—working within received conventions, disdaining sculpture and the pictorial form built on it, respecting the flat surface, and showing little regard for the more or less systematic pursuit of three-dimensional illusionism widely favored in the West from this time till the twentieth century. We read of a Byzantine priest in the sixteenth century rejecting some paintings by Titian, the great Venetian master of the Renaissance (FIGS. 17-60 and 17-61), because "the figures stand quite out from the canvas" and therefore look "as bad as a group of statues."* The Byzantine artist did not find monumental sculpture like that of the Gothic portals in his environment. Would Byzantine painting and mosaic have been different if he had? The Gothic painter could not help but be struck by these majestic figures of great scale. The attention paid them is clearly evident in the figures of the *Psalter of St. Louis.*

LATE GOTHIC

The collapse of the vaults of Beauvais Cathedral would seem to have brought the great thirteenth-century architectural debate to an unarguable conclusion. Analogously, the followers of Aquinas came to believe that his accommodation of faith and reason was impossible and that both must go their separate ways. This conviction was the beginning of the dissolution of the medieval synthesis, which would lead to the eventual destruction of the unity of Christendom. The resolution of opposites could not be achieved; the conflict that would reshape western Europe was about to begin.

*Edward Gibbon, *The Decline and Fall of the Roman Empire.* Quoted with citation in Ernst Kitzinger, *Byzantine Art in the Making* (Cambridge, MA: Harvard University Press, 1977), p. 107.

Villard de Honnecourt left us a record of these years in which so much was expected of art because art already had achieved so much. The search for an ideal solution for a building and the codification of artistic, as well as philosophical, procedures were essentially academic in spirit—conscious evaluations of a style that already had reached and passed its complete definition. For a long time, artistic practice and Scholastic method would retrace ground already covered, dealing with elaborations of surface forms but no longer attempting grandiose innovations in structure.

By the early fourteenth century, the monumental and solemn sculpture of the High Gothic portals had been replaced by the "court" style developed from the angel in the *Annunciation* group at Reims (FIG. 10-34), a quite rarefied example of which may be seen in the statue of *The Virgin of Paris* within Notre Dame (FIG. **10-39**). The curving sway of the figure, emphasized by the bladelike sweeps of drapery

10-39 *The Virgin of Paris,* Notre Dame, Paris, early fourteenth century.

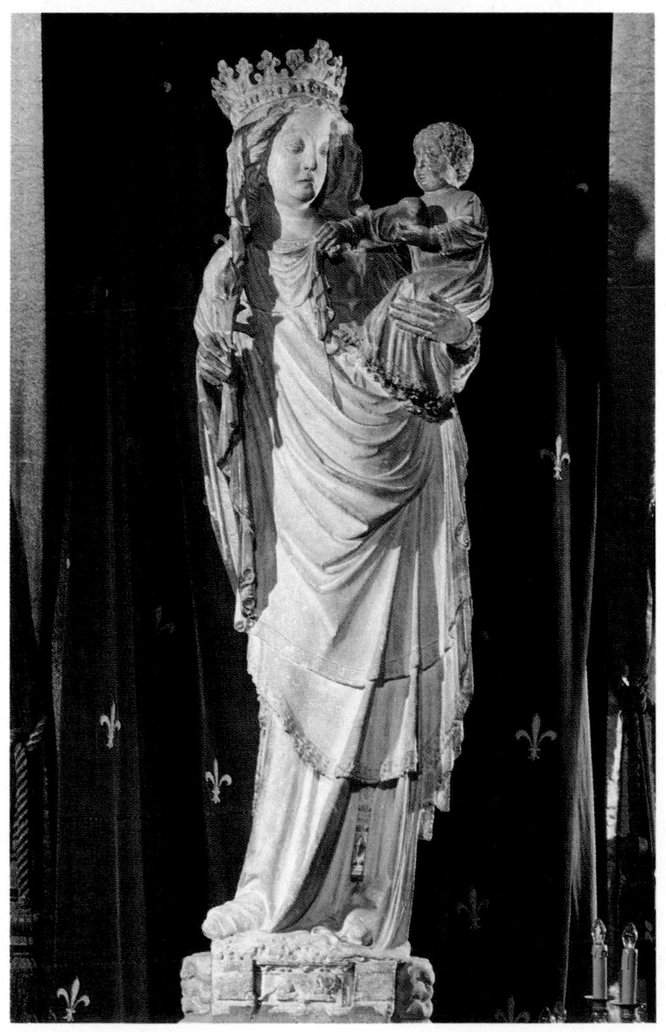

that converge to the child, has a mannered elegance that will mark Late Gothic sculpture in general. This famed Late Gothic S-curve will be encountered again and again during the fourteenth and fifteenth centuries. Superficially, it somewhat resembles the shallow S-curve adopted by Praxiteles in the fourth century B.C. (FIG. 5-62), but unlike its Classical predecessor, the Late Gothic S is not organic (deriving from within the figure), nor is it the result of a rational, if pleasing, organization of the figure's anatomical parts. Rather, it is an artificial form imposed on the figure—a decorative device that may produce the desired effect of elegance but that has nothing to do with the figure's structure. In fact, in our example, the body is quite lost behind the heavy drapery, which, deeply cut and hollowed, would almost deny the figure a solid existence. The ornamental line created by the flexible fabric is analogous to the complex, restless tracery of the "flamboyant" style in architecture, which dominated northern Europe in the fourteenth and fifteenth centuries. The emphasis on ornament for its own sake is in harmony with the artificial prettiness the artist has contrived in the Virgin's doll-like face, with its large eyes and tiny mouth under a heavy, gem-encrusted crown.

The change from rayonnant architecture to the Late Gothic or *flamboyant* style (named for the flamelike appearance of its pointed tracery) took place in the fourteenth century. The style reached its florid maturity nearly a century later. This period was a difficult one for royal France. Long wars against England and Burgundy sapped its economic and cultural strength, and building projects in the royal domain either were halted or not begun. The new style found its most enthusiastic acceptance in regions outside the Île-de-France. Normandy is particularly rich in flamboyant architecture, and its close ties with England suggest that the Anglo-Norman school of "decorated" architecture may have had much to do with the development of the flamboyant style.

The church of St. Maclou (FIG. **10-40**), in Rouen, the capital of Normandy, presents a façade that differs widely from the thirteenth-century style. St. Maclou, some 75 feet high and 180 feet long, is almost diminutive compared with the great cathedrals. The five portals, two of them blind, bend outward in an arc and are crowned by five gables, pierced through and filled with sinuous, wiry, flamboyant tracery. Spidery arcades climb steeply to the center bay, marching along behind the transparent gables. The overlapping of all features, pierced as they are, confuses the structural lines and produces a bewildering complexity of views. It is almost as if the Celtic-Germanic instinct for intricate line, expressed in works like the *Book of Lindisfarne* (FIG. 8-8), is manifesting itself once again against the form and logic newly abstracted from the traditions of the Mediterranean. Yet the Renaissance is not far off, and, within a generation or two, France will adopt a new Classical style from Italy.

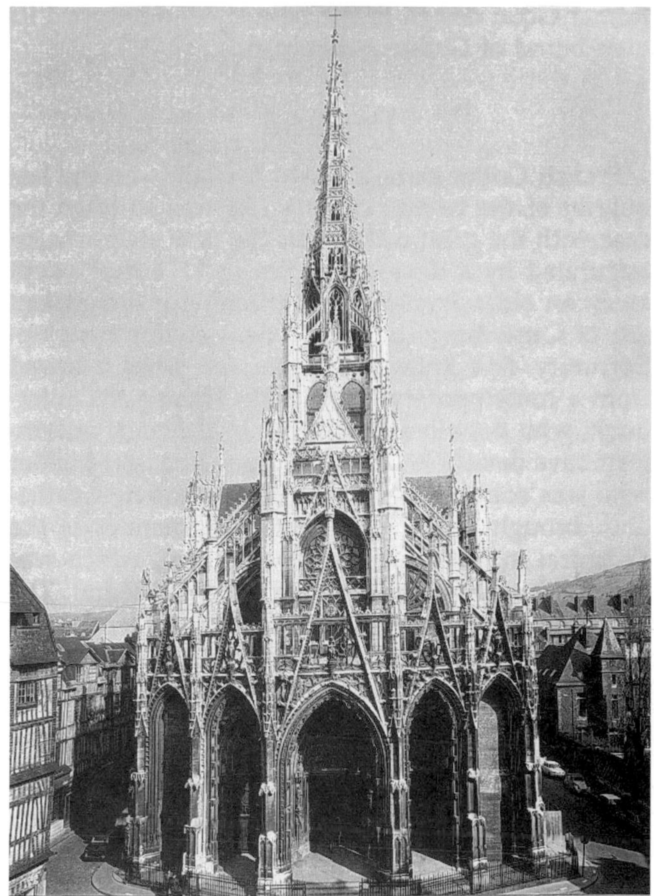

10-40 West façade of St. Maclou, Rouen, France, c. 1500–1514.

NON-FRENCH GOTHIC

Around 1269, the prior of a German monastery "hired a skilled architect who had just come from the city of Paris" to rebuild his monastery church. The architect reconstructed the church *opere francigeno* (in the Frankish manner)—that is, in the Gothic style of the Île-de-France. In 1268, Pope Clement IV, stipulating the conditions for the building of a new cathedral at Narbonne, wrote that the building was "to imitate the noble and magnificently worked churches . . . , which are built in the kingdom of France." The diffusion of the French Gothic style had begun even earlier, but it was in the second half of the thirteenth century that the new style became dominant and European architecture turned Gothic in many different ways. Because the old Romanesque traditions lingered on in many places, each area, marrying its local

Romanesque design to the new style, developed its own brand of Gothic architecture.

England

French Gothic came early to England—in the last quarter of the twelfth century. As was so often the case with the great cathedrals, the new style was inaugurated by a devastating fire in 1174 that swept away an older Romanesque structure in the ancient see of Canterbury, creating a new architectural opportunity. (We know of the fire and what followed from a contemporary chronicler, Gervase of Canterbury, who describes the events in dramatic and informative detail.) William of Sens, a master builder who was commissioned to construct the new cathedral, brought to it the Early Gothic manner of the cathedral in Sens (his home in France), which was related closely to the design of Laon Cathedral. The choir and choir chapel of Canterbury Cathedral, completed by William the Englishman (fig. **10-41**), resemble those of Sens and Laon (fig. 10-7) and are essentially French—much more so than most of the mature English Gothic churches to follow, which will retain older Norman features in balance with importations from France. In the end, these later churches will be distinctively English.

The characteristics of English Gothic architecture are embodied admirably in Salisbury Cathedral (figs. **10-42** to **10-45**), built, for the most part, between 1220

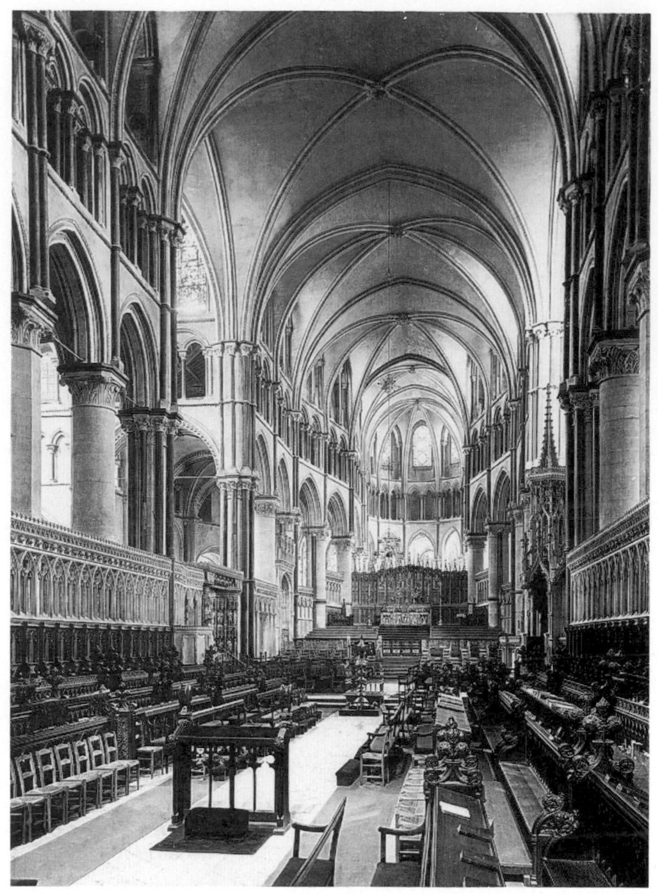

10-41 William of Sens and William the Englishman, choir and Trinity Chapel, Canterbury Cathedral, England, 1179–1184.

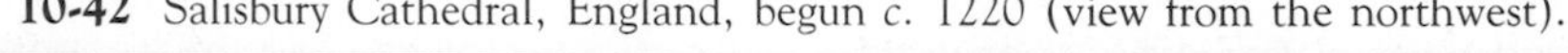

10-42 Salisbury Cathedral, England, begun *c.* 1220 (view from the northwest).

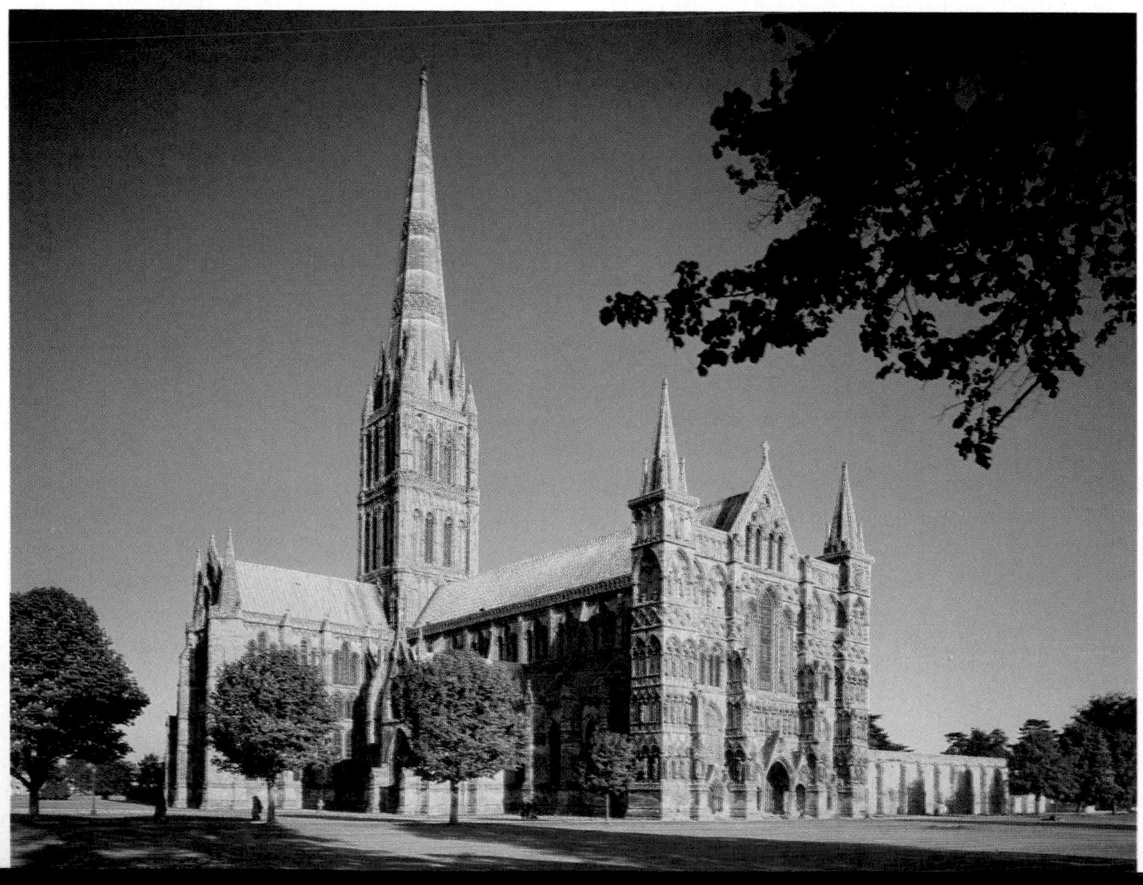

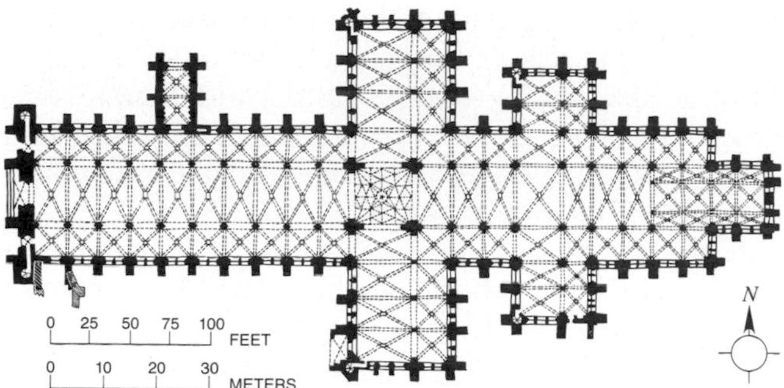

10-43 Plan of Salisbury Cathedral.

and 1260 (the tower and flying buttresses were erected in the fourteenth century). Its location in a park (or *close*), surrounded by lawns and stately trees, contrasts markedly with that of continental churches, around which city dwellings nestle closely. The screenlike façade (FIG. 10-42) reaches beyond and does not correspond to the interior. With its dwarf towers, horizontal tiers of niches, and small entrance portals, the Salisbury façade differs emphatically from the façades of either Notre Dame of Paris (FIG. 10-9) or Amiens Cathedral (FIG. 10-23). Also different is the emphasis on the great crossing tower (*c.* 1320), which dominates the silhouette. The height of Salisbury is modest compared with that of the almost contemporary cathedral of Amiens; as height in the English building is not a decisive factor, the flying buttress is used sparingly and as a rigid prop rather than as an integral part of the armature of arches. The exterior of the building at Salisbury, were it not for its pointed features, would look more like an "additive" Romanesque than a Gothic building.

Equally distinctive is the long rectilinear plan (FIG. 10-43), with its double transept and flat eastern end. The latter feature was characteristic of Cistercian churches and had been favored in England since Romanesque times. The interior (FIG. 10-44), although Gothic in its three-story elevation, pointed arches, rib vaults, and compound piers (actually a combination of columnar piers with detached monolithic shafts or colonnettes), shows conspicuous differences from the French Gothic style. The pier colonnettes do not ride up the wall to connect with the vault ribs; instead, the vault ribs rise from corbels in the triforium, producing a strong horizontal emphasis. The rich detail in the moldings of the arches and the tracery of the triforium, enhanced by the contrast of colored stone, gives a peculiarly crisp and vivid sparkle to the interior. The structural craft of the English stonemason is at its best in the Lady Chapel (dedicated to the Virgin Mary) of Salisbury Cathedral (FIG.

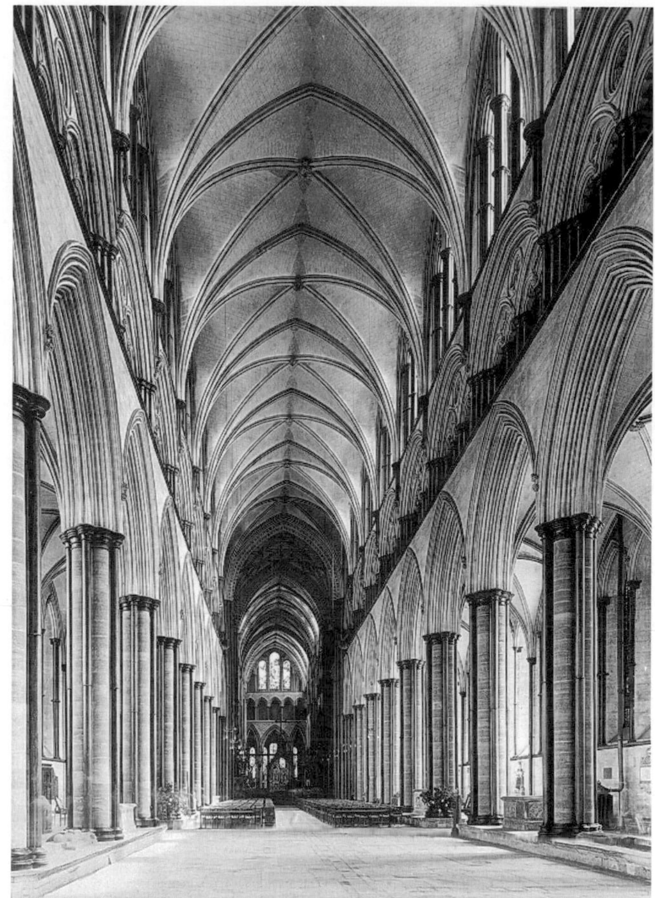

10-44 Nave of Salisbury Cathedral (view facing east).

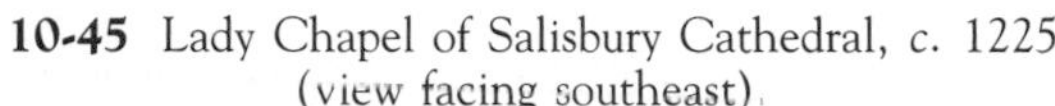

10-45 Lady Chapel of Salisbury Cathedral, *c.* 1225 (view facing southeast).

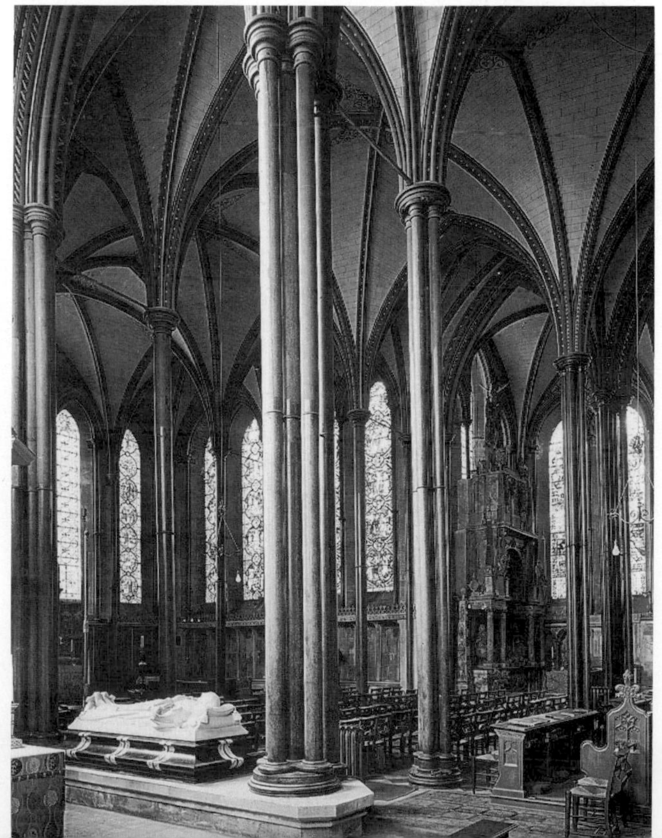

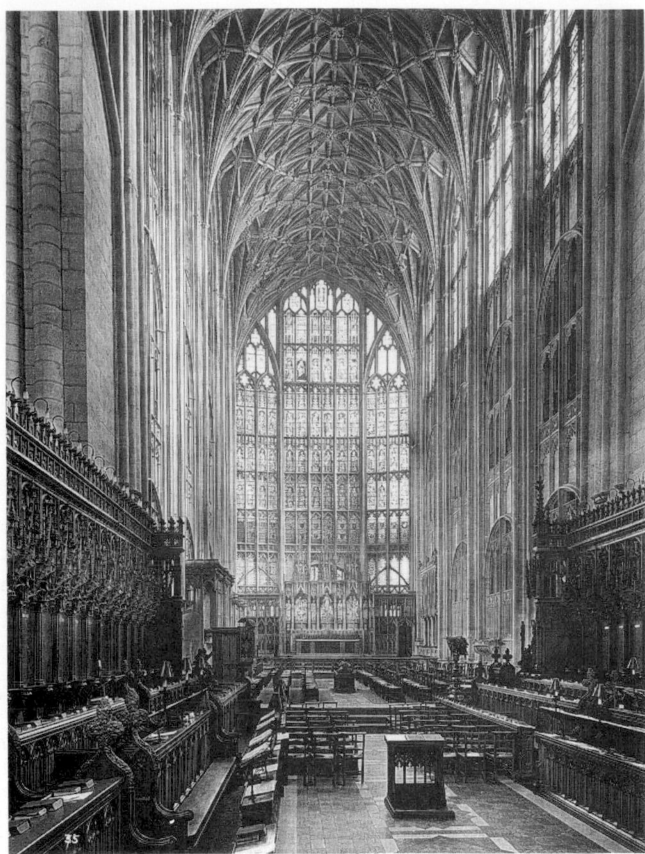

10-46 Choir of Gloucester Cathedral, England, 1332–1357 (view facing east).

10-47 Detail of the vault of the Chapel of Henry VII, 1503–1519, Westminster Abbey, London.

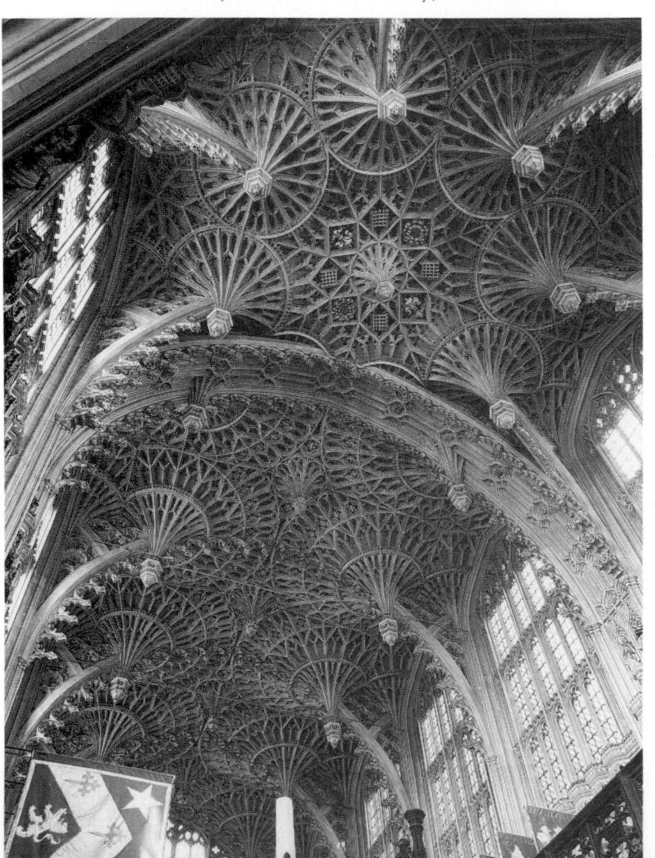

10-45). There, incredibly slender piers composed of unattached shafts of Purbeck marble seem to tether the billowing vaults to the ground rather than to support them. The linearity and slender forms of this daring construction are analogous to the rayonnant style found on the continent.

Early on, English architecture finds its native language in the elaboration of architectural pattern for its own sake; structural logic, expressed in the building fabric, is secondary. The pier, wall, and vault elements became increasingly complex and decorative in the fourteenth century, and English Gothic architecture of that period has been described as "decorated." The choir of Gloucester Cathedral (FIG. **10-46**), built about a century after Salisbury, illustrates the transition from the decorated to the last English Gothic style, the *perpendicular* or "Tudor," which was named after the line of English kings that began with Henry VII in 1485.

The characteristically flat east end of Gloucester Cathedral opens into a single, enormous window divided into horizontal tiers of "transom" windows of like shape and proportion, reminiscent of the screen façade of Salisbury. In the nave wall, however, the strong, horizontal accents of Salisbury have been erased, as the vertical wall elements (the *responds*) lift directly from the floor to the vaulting, pulling the whole elevation into a fluent unity. The vault ribs, which had begun to multiply soon after Salisbury, now have become a dense thicket of entirely ornamental strands that serve no structural purpose. This vault, in fact, is no longer a rib vault, but a continuous barrel vault with applied decorations.

We can see the culmination of the English perpendicular style and the flowering of the Tudor style (one of the late phases of the perpendicular) in the vault of the Chapel of Henry VII (FIG. **10-47**), which adjoins Westminster Abbey and was built in the first two decades of the sixteenth century. Here, the linear play of ribs has become a kind of architectural embroidery, pulled into "fan vault" shapes with pendent keystones resembling stalactites. The vault looks like something organic that has been petrified in the process of melting. The chapel represents the dissolution of structural Gothic into decorative fancy; its original lines, released from function, multiply, variegate, and flower into uninhibited architectural virtuosity and theatrics. The perpendicular style in this Tudor structure expresses peculiarly well the precious, affected, even dainty style of life codified in the dying etiquette of chivalry at the end of the Middle Ages. Life was, of course, as violent as ever—indeed, we are at the threshold of the boisterous English Renaissance—but the description and expression of it in art comes in forms that are delicate rather than robust.

Germany

The architecture of Germany remained conservatively Romanesque well into the thirteenth century. The plan and massing of German churches included the familiar Rhenish double-apse system, with towers flanking both apses. In many of these, the only Gothic feature is the rib vault, which is buttressed solely by the heavy masonry of the walls. By mid-century, though, French influence had increased, and the great 150-foot-high choir of Cologne Cathedral (FIG. **10-48**) is a skillful and energetic interpretation of Amiens (FIG. 10-26). Cologne Cathedral (page 415) has one of the longest building histories on record. Begun in 1248, it stood without a nave and with only its chevet, transept, and lower parts of the façade towers completed for some five centuries. Only in the early nineteenth century, when the original designs for the building were found, was the decision made that the structure should be completed.

The choir of Cologne Cathedral (FIG. 10-48) expresses the Gothic "rush into the skies" even more emphatically than the taller (but wider) choir of Beauvais Cathedral (FIG. 10-31). The nave walls (FIG. **10-49**) of Cologne are among the most weightless and translucent designed during the Gothic period. (Remember that the nave, although actually built in the nineteenth century, was constructed strictly in accordance with the original thirteenth-century plan, and its walls can be accepted as some of the most refined examples of High Gothic curtain-wall design.) Stretched tautly, like skins, between slender vertical supports, the walls have reached a degree of transparency unmatched in earlier architecture. Their luminous quality is enhanced by the fact that the triforium also has been fenestrated—a feature made possible by the replacement of the traditional, single-sloped shed roofs over the aisles with double-sloped tent roofs. This change created difficult drainage problems that appear to have been solved during the second half of the thirteenth century. Now, clerestory and triforium could act together to form an enormous glass wall, held together by a seemingly insubstantial framework of slender piers supported on the outside by an intricate system of vertical and flying buttresses. The impression of weightlessness—of the dematerialization of the building's very substance—is complete here. And yet the design is not weak or uncertain; all of the lines are crisp and sharply defined, describing forms that seem to have the resiliency of living organic growth.

Despite the cathedral's seeming lack of substance, the structure's stability was proven effectively during World War II, when the city of Cologne was subjected to extremely heavy aerial bombardments. The church

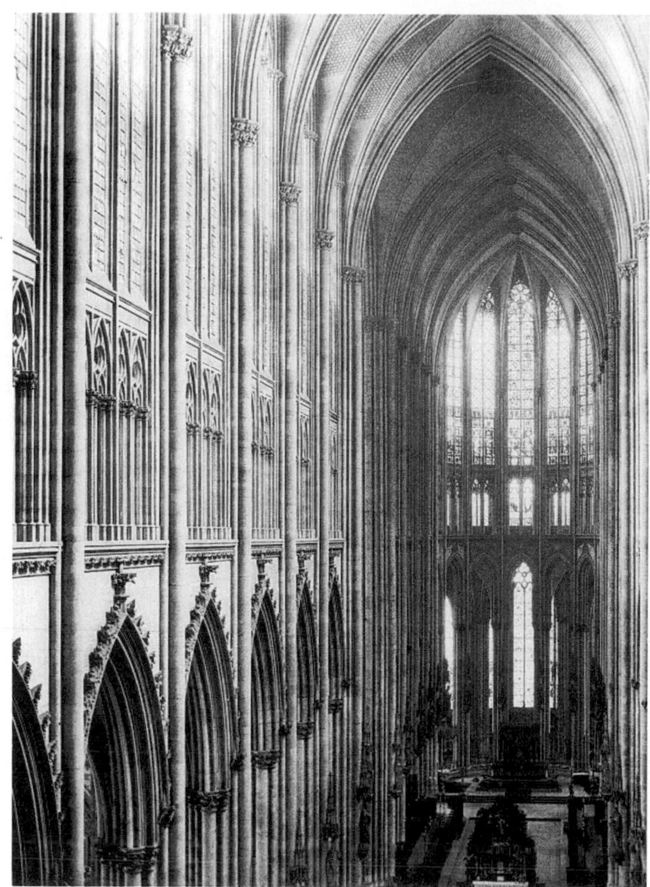

10-48 Choir of Cologne Cathedral, West Germany, thirteenth and fourteenth centuries.

10-49 Nave wall, Cologne Cathedral, nineteenth century (thirteenth-century design).

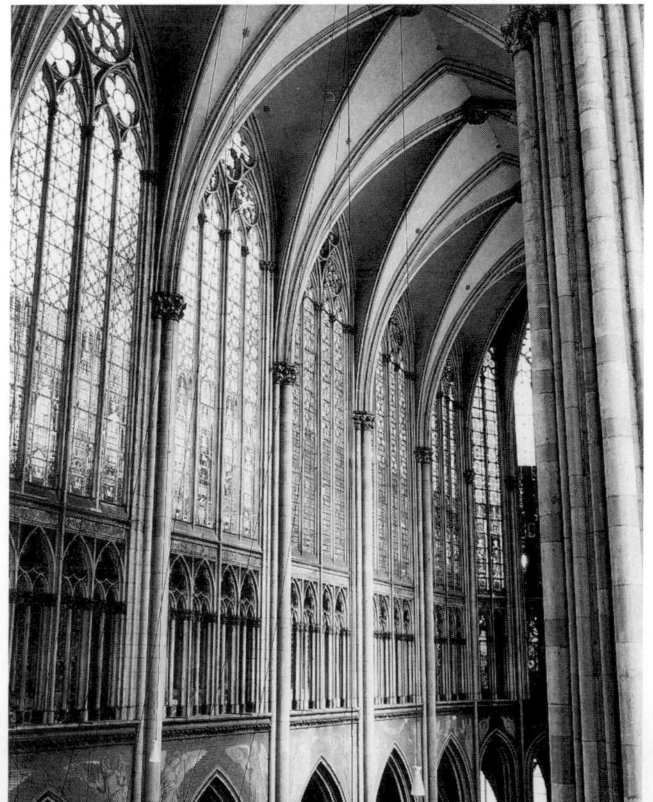

survived the war by virtue of its Gothic, skeletal design. Once the first few bomb blasts had blown out all of its windows, the structure offered no further resistance to the effects of subsequent blasts, and the skeleton remained intact and structurally sound.

A different type of design, probably of French origin, that met with great favor and was developed broadly in Germany is that of the *hallenkirche,* or hall church. The term applies to those buildings in which the aisles rise to the same height as the nave section. An early and successful example of this type is the church of St. Elizabeth at Marburg (FIGS. **10-50** to **10-52**), built between 1233 and 1283. Because the aisles provide much of the bracing for the central vault, the exterior of St. Elizabeth is without the dramatic parade of flying buttresses that circles French Gothic chevets and appears rather prosaic. But the interior, lighted by double rows of tall windows, is

10-50 Plan and section of St. Elizabeth, Marburg, West Germany.

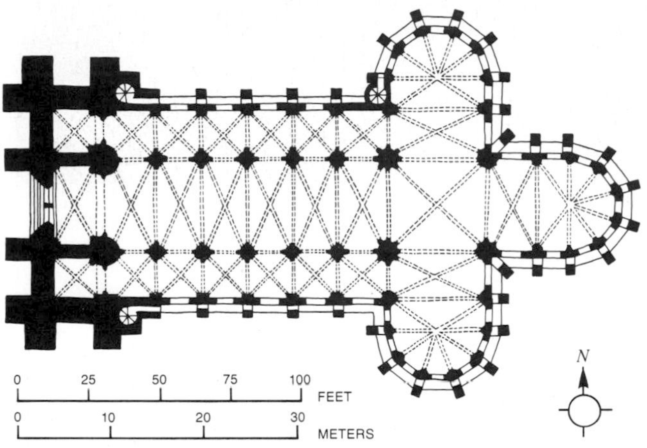

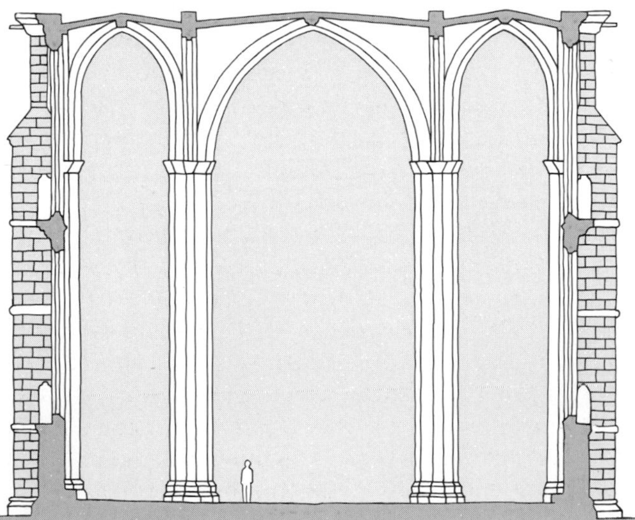

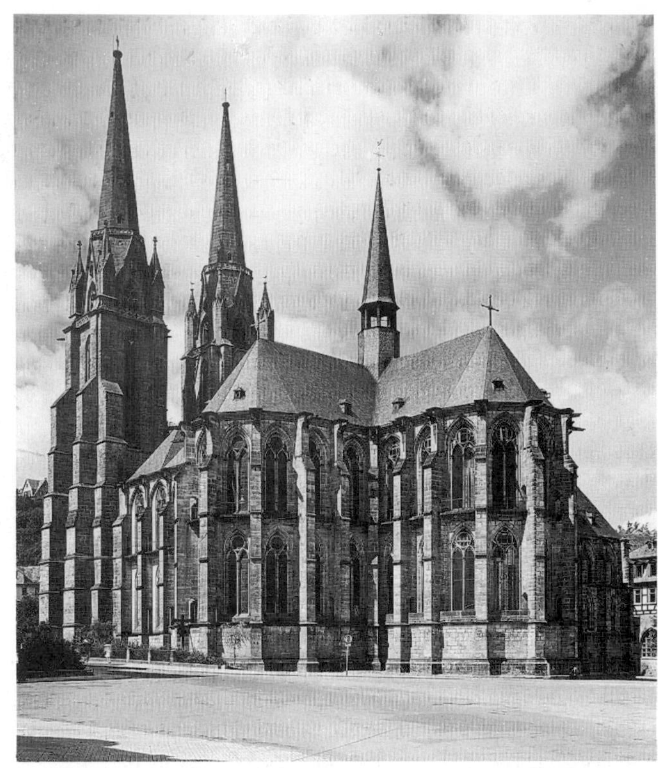

10-51 St. Elizabeth, 1233–1283 (view from the southeast).

10-52 Interior of St. Elizabeth (view facing west).

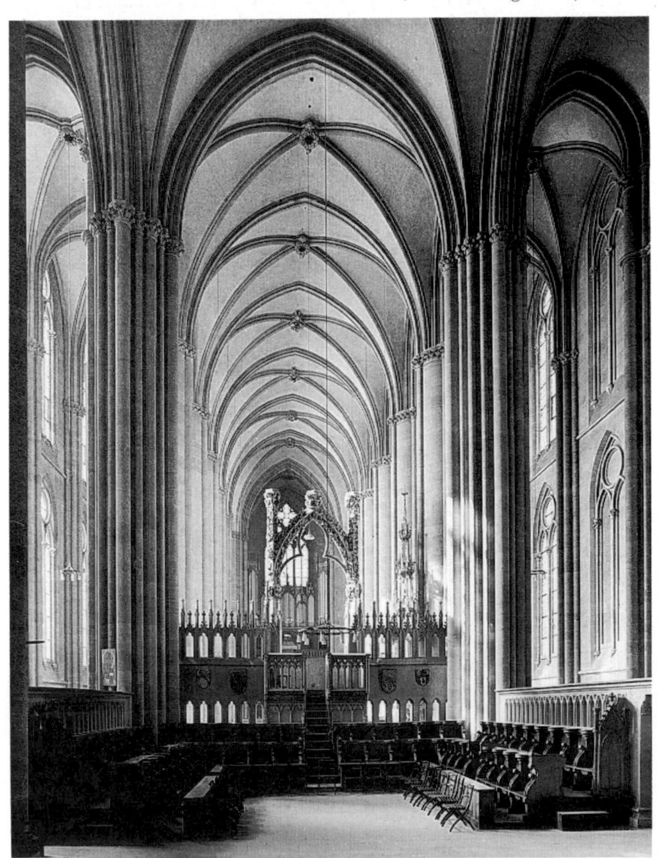

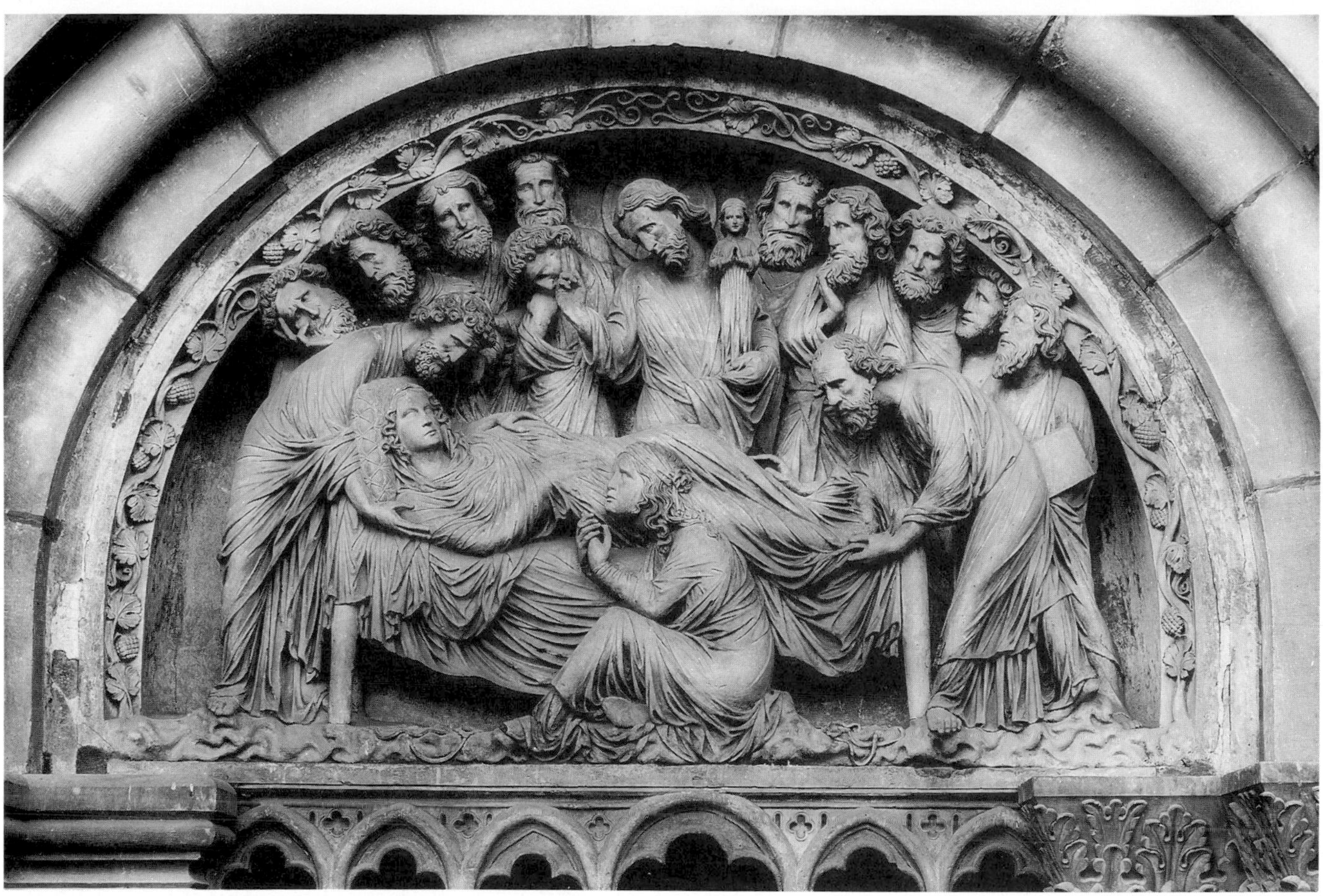

10-53 *Death of the Virgin*, tympanum, south transept portal, Strasbourg Cathedral, France, c. 1230.

more unified and free flowing, less narrow and divided, than the interiors of other Gothic churches. A form widely used by later Gothic architects, the hall church heralds the age of the Protestant Reformation in Germany, when the old ritual, which focuses on the altar, will be modified by a new emphasis on preaching, which will center attention on the pulpit.

Like French Gothic architecture, French sculpture also had its effect abroad. In Germany, the commingled influences of the statuary of the transept portals at Chartres (FIGS. 10-32 and 16-7) and the west façade at Reims (FIG. 10-34) directed the sculptors of the south transept portal at Strasbourg Cathedral (FIG. **10-53**). The sculptured tympanum represents the death of the Virgin Mary. She is surrounded by the Twelve Apostles; at their center, Christ receives her soul (the doll-like figure near his left shoulder). Mary Magdalene, wringing her hands in grief, crouches beside the deathbed. The sorrowing figures express emotion in varying degrees of intensity, from serene resignation to gesturing agitation. The group is organized not only by dramatic unification and by pose and gesture but also by the rippling flow of deeply incised drapery that passes among them like a rhythmic, electric pulse. The sculptor's objective is not to produce a timeless tableau presenting some mystery of the faith, but to depict a human event in a particular space and time—an event designed to stir an emotional response in the observer as if he or she were present. In the Gothic world, art is increasingly being humanized and made natural; in the art of the German lands, we will find an increasing and characteristic emphasis on passionate drama.

The Strasbourg style, with its feverish emotionalism, is balanced and complemented by two stately and reposeful statues from the west choir of Naumburg Cathedral (FIG. **10-54**) that depict the quiet, regal deportment of the French statuary of the High Gothic portals, but with a stronger tincture of realism. *Ekkehard and Uta* represent persons of the nobility who, in former times, had been patrons of the church; the particularity of costume and visage almost makes these figures portrait statues, although the subjects lived well before the sculptor's time. Ekkehard, blunt and Teutonic, contrasts with the charming Uta, who, with a wonderfully graceful gesture, draws the collar

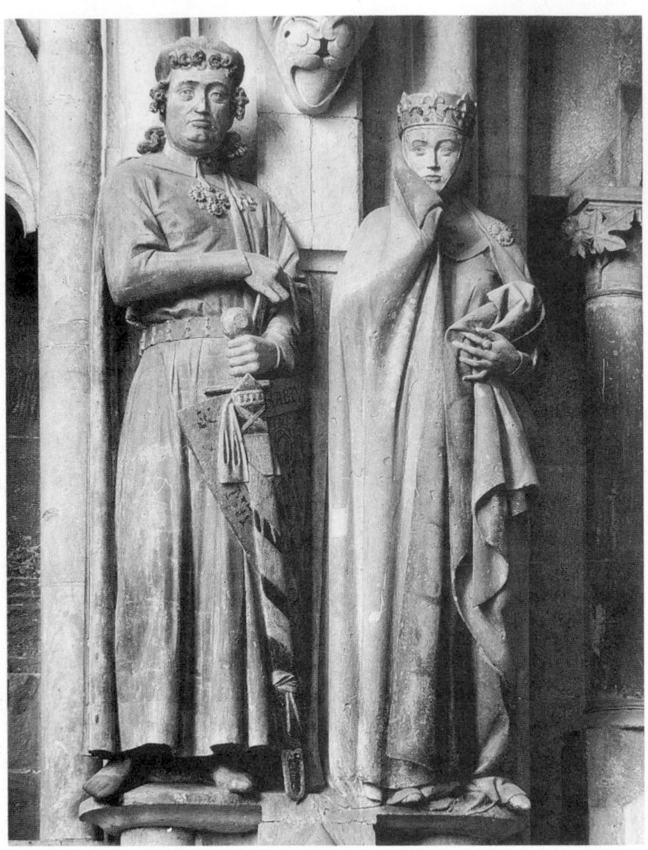

10-54 *Ekkehard and Uta,* c. 1250–1260, west choir, Naumburg Cathedral, West Germany.

10-55 *Bamberg Rider,* late thirteenth century, Bamberg Cathedral, West Germany. Sandstone, 90½" high.

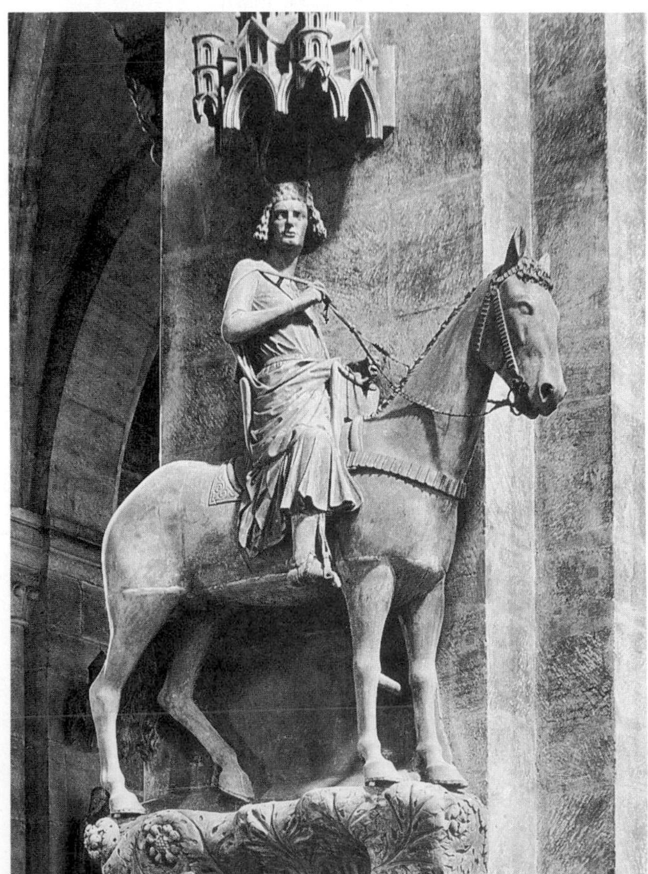

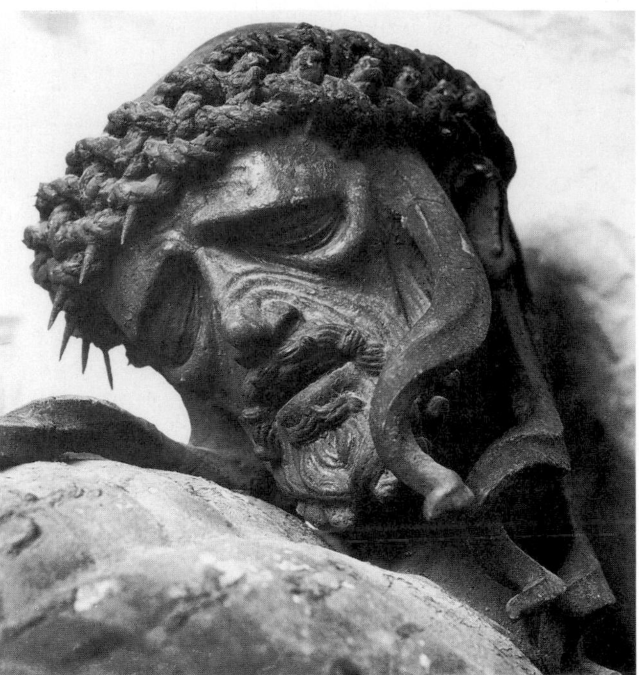

10-56 Head of a crucifix, 1301. Wood. St. Maria im Kapitol, Cologne, West Germany.

of her gown partly across her face while she gathers up a soft fold of drapery with a jeweled, delicate hand. The drapery and the body it enfolds now are understood as distinct entities. The shape of the arm that draws the collar is subtly and accurately revealed beneath the drapery, as is the full curve of the bosom. The drapery folds are rendered with an accuracy that indicates the artist's use of a model. We have before us an arresting image of medieval people—a feudal baron and his handsome wife—as they may well have appeared in life. By mid-thirteenth century, images not only of sacred but also of secular personages had found their way into the cathedral.

The equestrian figure of a Gothic nobleman mounted against a pier in the cathedral of Bamberg (FIG. **10-55**) is familiarly known as the *Bamberg Rider.* Like *Ekkehard and Uta,* this statue has the quality of portraiture; some believe it represents the German emperor Conrad III. The artist has carefully described the costume of the rider, the high saddle, and the trappings of the horse. The proportions of horse and rider are real, although the anatomy of the animal is not quite comprehended and its shape is rather stiffly schematic. An ever-present pedestal and canopy firmly establish dependence on the architectural setting and manage to hold the horse in strict profile. The rider, however, turns easily toward the observer, as if presiding at a review of troops, and is beginning to break away from the pull of the wall. The stirring and turning of this figure seem to reflect the same impatience with subordination to architecture that is found in the portal statues at Reims (FIG. 10-34).

The gradual growth of naturalism during the thirteenth century was modified during the fourteenth century by an impulse toward charmingly ornamental effects and courtly convention, as seen in *The Virgin of Paris* (FIG. 10-39). A new intensity of expression, anticipated in the *Death of the Virgin* at Strasbourg (FIG. 10-53), also was developing at this time. The Crucifixion, the Man of Sorrows, and the Sorrows of the Virgin Mary became common themes. The head of a crucifix in St. Maria im Kapitol in Cologne (FIG. **10-56**), the features wrenched with pain and sorrow, shows the new preference for interpretations of sacred story in terms of human feeling rather than of dogma and mystery. The humanizing that began in the twelfth century is accelerated. The anguish of the suffering Christ is represented with such force that it could not fail to stir the emotions powerfully and to arouse deep empathy in the observer. As motion was introduced into portal sculpture, so motion—read as emotion—here activates the human face. Increasingly, images reach out, not only into physical space but into the emotions of the observer. The artist presents more than the simple theological tenet in terms of some impersonal symbol; the mystery is brought back to earth once more, incarnate in the image of physical and psychic suffering.

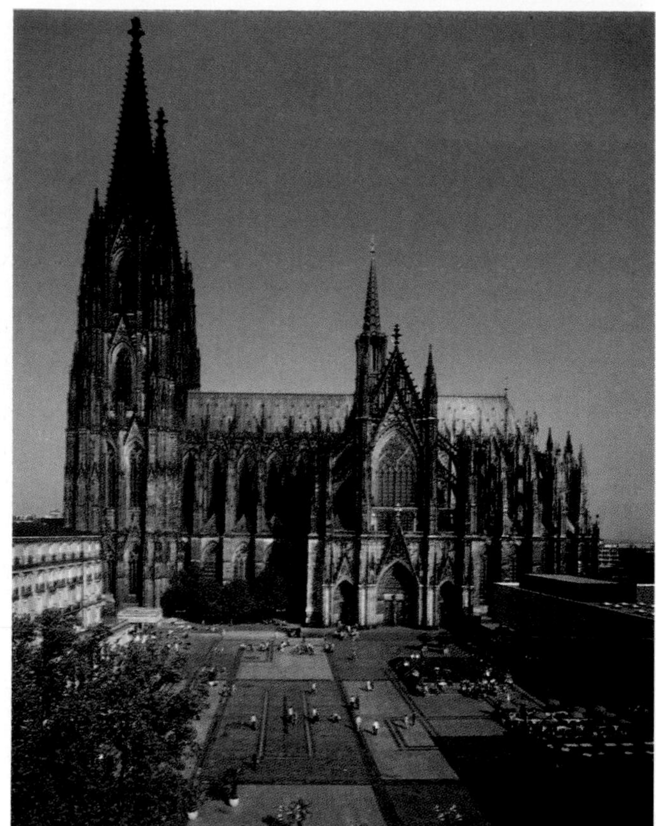

10-57 Cologne Cathedral, West Germany, 1248; nave, façade, and towers, nineteenth century (view from the south).

Italy

Few Italian architects accepted the northern Gothic style, and the question has been raised as to whether it is proper to speak of buildings like Florence Cathedral (FIGS. **10-58** to **10-60**) as Gothic structures. Begun in 1296 by ARNOLFO DI CAMBIO and so large that it seemed to the fifteenth-century architect Leon Battista Alberti to cover "all of Tuscany with its shade," the cathedral scarcely looks Gothic. Most of the familiar Gothic features are missing; the building has neither flying buttresses nor stately clerestory windows, and its walls are pierced only by a few, relatively small openings. Like the façades of San Miniato al Monte (FIG. 9-20), the building's surfaces are ornamented, in the old Tuscan fashion, with marble-incrusted geometric designs to match it to the eleventh-century Romanesque baptistry nearby. Beyond an occasional ogival window and the fact that the nave is covered by rib vaults, very little identifies this building as Gothic. The vast gulf that separates this Italian church from its northern European cousins is strikingly evident when the former is compared with a full-blown German representative of the High Gothic style, such as the cathedral of Cologne (FIG. **10-57**).

10-58 Florence Cathedral, Italy, 1296–1436 (view from the south).

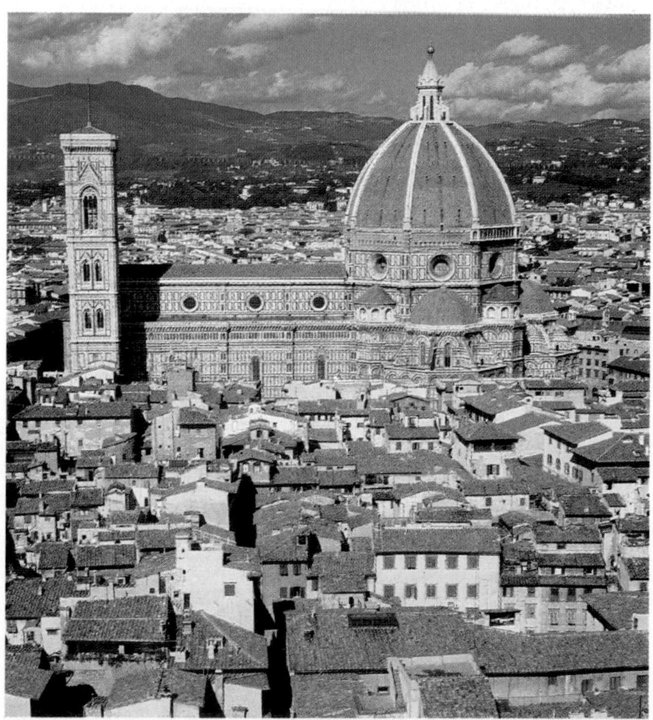

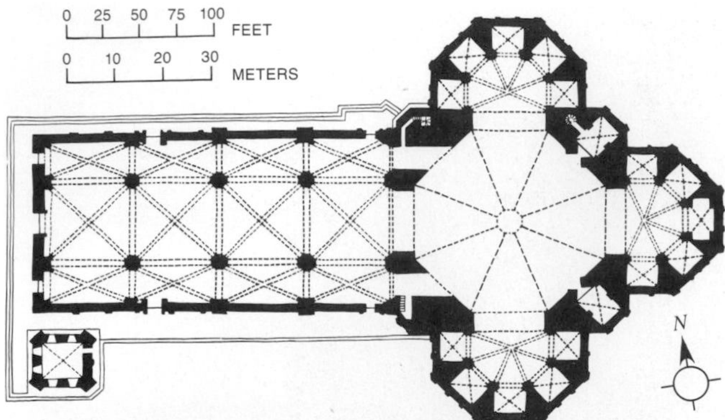

10-59 Plan of Florence Cathedral. (After Sir Banister Fletcher.)

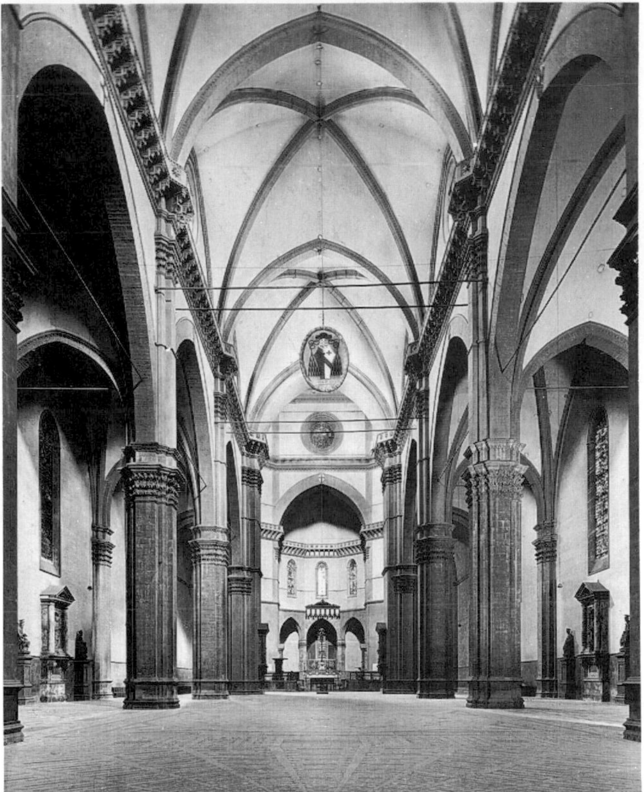

10-60 Nave of Florence Cathedral (view facing east).

In Cologne Cathedral, an emphatic stress on the vertical produces an awe-inspiring upward rush of almost unmatched vigor and intensity. The building has the character of an organic growth shooting heavenward, its toothed upper portions engaging the sky. The pierced, translucent stone tracery of the spires merges with the atmosphere. Florence Cathedral clings to the ground and has no aspirations to flight. All emphasis is on the horizontal elements of the design, and the building rests firmly and massively on the ground. Simple, geometric volumes are defined clearly and show no tendency to merge either into each other or into the sky. The dome, though it may seem to be rising because of its ogival section, has a crisp, closed silhouette that sets it off emphatically against the sky behind it. But because this dome is the monument with which architectural historians usually introduce the Renaissance (it was built by Filippo Brunelleschi between 1420 and 1436), a comparison of the campanile with the Cologne towers may be somewhat more appropriate. Designed by the painter Giotto di Bondone in 1334 (and completed with some minor modifications after his death), the Florence campanile (FIG. 10-58) stands apart from the cathedral in the Italian tradition. In fact, it could stand anywhere else in Florence without looking out of place; it is essentially self-sufficient. The same can hardly be said of the Cologne towers (FIG. 10-57); they are essential elements of the building behind them, and it would be unthinkable to detach one of them and place it somewhere else. Heinrich Wölfflin compared buildings of this kind to a flame from which no single tongue can be separated.* This comparison holds true for every part of the Cologne structure, down to its smallest details. No individual element seems to be capable of an independent existence; one form merges into the next, in an unending series of rising movements that pull the eye upward and never permit it to rest until it reaches the sky. This structure's beauty is amorphous rather than formal; it is a beauty that speaks to the heart rather than to the intellect.

The Italian tower is entirely different. Neatly subdivided into cubic stages, Giotto's tower is the sum of its clearly distinguished parts. Not only could this tower be removed from the building without adverse effects, but each of the component parts—cleanly separated from one another by continuous, unbroken moldings—seems capable of existing independently as an object of considerable esthetic appeal. This compartmentalization is reminiscent of Romanesque, but it also forecasts the ideals of Renaissance architecture: to express structure in the clear, logical relationships of its component parts and to produce self-sufficient works that could exist in complete independence. Compared to the north towers of Cologne, Giotto's campanile has a cool and rational quality that appeals more to the intellect than to the emotions.

In the plan of Florence Cathedral (FIG. 10-59), the nave almost appears to have been added to the crossing complex as an afterthought; in fact, the nave was built first, pretty much according to Arnolfo's original plans (except for the vaulting), and the crossing was redesigned midway through the fourteenth century to increase the cathedral's interior space. In its present form, the area beneath the dome is the focal point

*Heinrich Wölfflin, *Classic Art*, 2nd ed. (London: Phaidon, 1953).

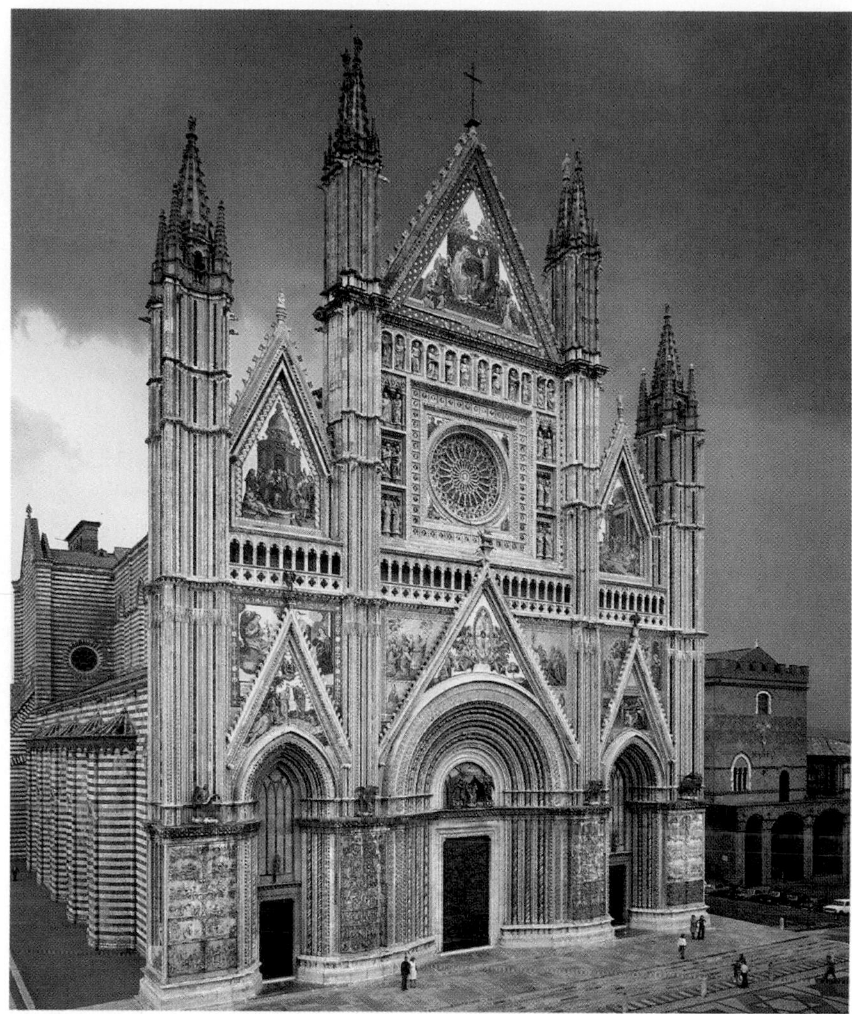

10-61 West façade of Orvieto Cathedral, Italy, begun *c.* 1310.

of the design, and the nave leads to it, as Paul Frankl says, "like an introduction of slow chords, to a goal of self-contained finality." To the visitor from the north, the nave seems as strange as the plan; neither has a northern European counterpart. The Florence nave bays (FIG. 10-60) are twice as deep as those of Amiens (FIG. 10-25), and the wide arcades permit the shallow aisles to become part of the central nave. The result is an interior that has an unmatched spaciousness. The accent here, as in the exterior, is on the horizontal elements. The substantial capitals of the piers prevent them from soaring into the vaults and emphasize their function as supports. This interior lacks the mystery of northern naves, and Nikolaus Pevsner has observed that its serene calm and clarity tell the visitor that the Tuscan architects never entirely rejected or forgot their Classical heritage and that it is indeed only here, in central Italy, that the Renaissance could have been born.

The façade of Florence Cathedral was not completed until the nineteenth century, and then in a form much altered from its beginnings. In fact, Italian builders exhibited little concern for the façades of their churches, and dozens remain unfinished to this day. One reason for this may be that the façades were not conceived as integral parts of the structures, but rather as screens that could be added to the fabric at any time. The façade of Orvieto Cathedral (FIG. **10-61**) is a typical and handsome example. Begun in the early fourteenth century, it pays the graceful compliment of imitation to some parts of the French Gothic repertory of ornament, especially in the four large pinnacles that divide the façade into three bays. But these pinnacles—the outer ones serving as miniature substitutes for the big, northern, west-front towers—grow up, as it were, from an old Tuscan façade (FIG. 9-20) and, ultimately, from the Early Christian. The rectilinearity and triangularity of the old Tuscan marble incrustation (here enframing and pointing to the precisely wrought rose window) are seen clearly behind the transparent Gothic overlay. The whole effect of the Orvieto façade is that of a great altar screen, its

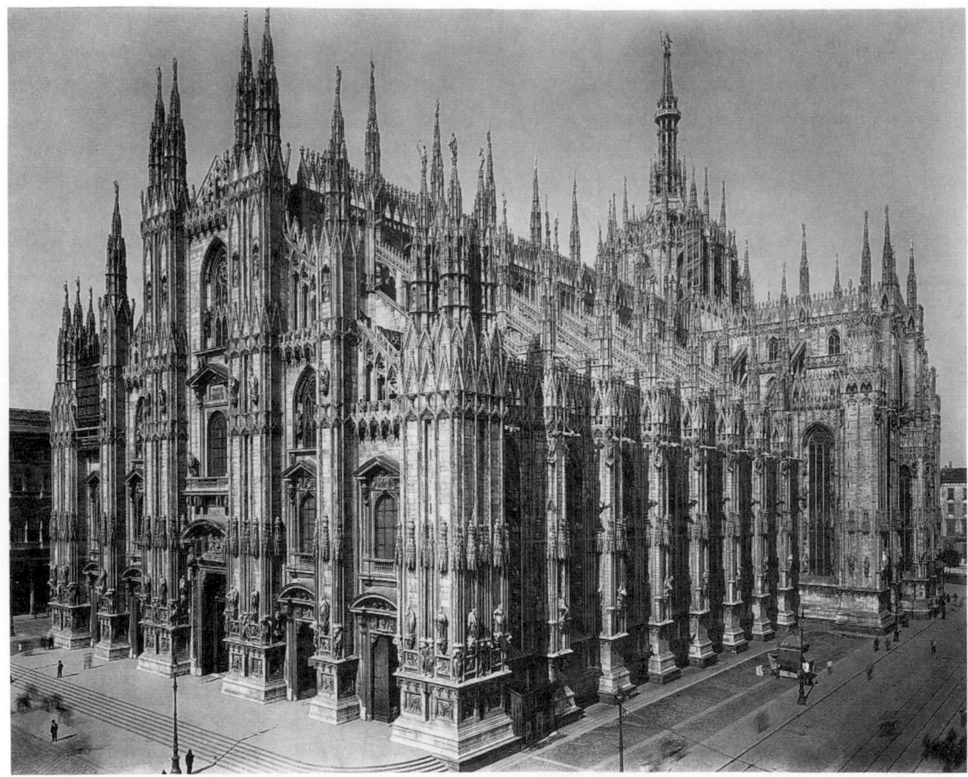

10-62 Milan Cathedral, Italy, begun 1386 (view from the southwest).

single plane covered with carefully placed carved and painted ornament. In principle, Orvieto belongs with San Miniato al Monte or the cathedral of Pisa, rather than with Amiens or Notre Dame of Paris.

Since Romanesque times, northern European influences had been felt more strongly in Lombardy than in central Italy. When the citizens of Milan decided to build their own cathedral (FIG. **10-62**) in 1386, they invited and consulted experts not only from Italy but also from France, Germany, and England. These experts must have carried on a rough disputatio about the strength of the foundations and the composition and adequacy of the piers and the vaults—the application of the true geometric scientia in working out plan and elevation. The result was a compromise; the proportions of the building, particularly those of the nave, became Italian (that is, wide in relation to height), and the surface decorations and details remained Gothic. But even before the cathedral was half finished, the new Classical style of the Renaissance had been well launched and the Milan design had become anachronistic. The elaborate façade represents a confused mixture of Late Gothic and Classical elements and stands as a symbol of the waning of the Gothic style.

The city churches of the Gothic world were just as much monuments of civic pride as they were temples or symbols of the spiritual and natural world. To undertake the construction of a great cathedral, a city had to be rich with thriving commerce. The profusion of large churches during the period attests to the affluence of those who built and maintained them, as well as to the general revival of the economy of Europe in the thirteenth century.

The secular center of the community, the town hall, was almost as much the object of civic pride as the cathedral. A building like the Palazzo Pubblico of Siena (FIG. **10-63**), the proud commercial and political rival of Florence, must have earned the admiration of Siena's citizens as well as of visiting strangers, inspiring in them respect for the city's power and success. More symmetrical in its design than most buildings of its type and period, it is flanked by a lofty tower, which (along with Giotto's campanile in Florence) is one of the finest in Italy. This tall structure served as lookout over the city and the countryside around it and as a bell tower from which signals of all sorts could be rung to the populace. The medieval city, a self-contained political unit, had to defend itself against neighboring cities and often against kings and emperors; in addition, it had to be secure against internal upheavals, which were common in the history of the Italian city-republics. Feuds between rich and powerful families, class struggle, even uprisings of the whole populace against the city fathers were constant threats to a city's internal security. The heavy

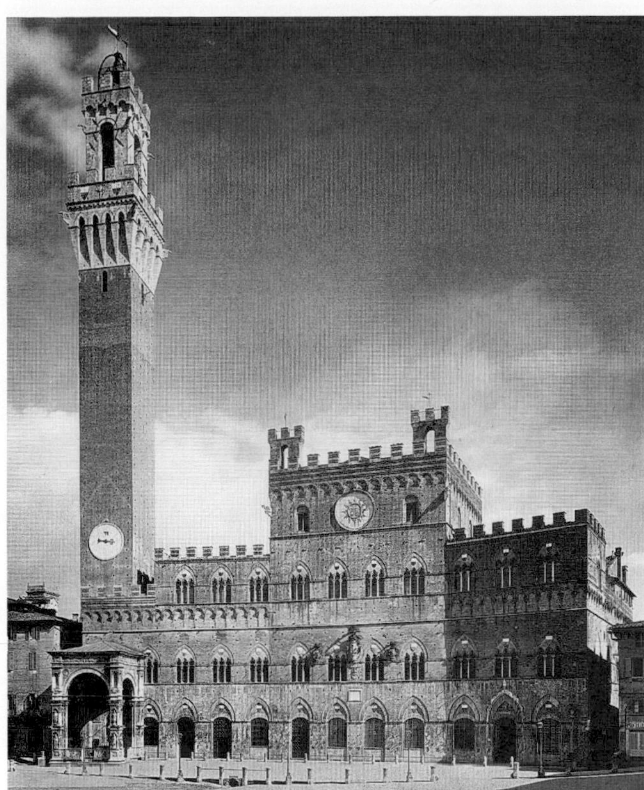

10-63 Palazzo Pubblico, Siena, Italy, 1288–1309.

walls and battlements of the Italian town hall eloquently express the frequent need of city governors to defend themselves against their own citizens. The high tower, out of reach of most missiles, is further protected by *machicolated* galleries, built out on corbels around the top of the structure to provide openings for a vertical (downward) defense of the tower's base.

The secular architecture of the Italian mainland tends to have this fortified look. But Venice, some miles out in the Venetian lagoon, was secure from land attack and could rely on a powerful navy for protection against attacks from the sea. Internally, Venice was a tight corporation of ruling families that, for centuries, provided an unshakable and efficient establishment, free from disruptive tumults within. Such a stable internal structure made possible the development of an unfortified, "open" architecture, exemplified in the Doge's Palace (FIG. **10-64**), the seat of government of the Venetian republic. This, the most splendid public building of medieval Italy, seems to invite passersby to enter rather than to ward them off. In a stately march, the short and heavy columns of the first level support low-pointed arches and look strong enough to carry the weight of the upper structure. Their rhythm is doubled in the upper arcades, where more slender columns carry ogival arches, which terminate in flamelike tips between medallions pierced with quatrefoils. Each story is taller than the one beneath it, the topmost being as high as the two lower arcades combined. Yet the building does not look top-heavy—a fact due in part to the complete absence of articulation in the top story and in part to the delicate patterning of the walls, in cream and rose-colored marbles, which somehow makes them appear paper-thin. The Doge's Palace is the monumental representative of a delightful and charming variant of Late Gothic architecture. Its slightly exotic style reminds us of Venice's strategic position at the crossroads of the West and the Orient, where it could synthesize artistic stimuli received from either direction. Colorful, decorative, light and airy in appearance, and never overloaded, the Venetian Gothic is ideally suited to the lagoon city of Venice, which floats between water and air.

10-64 The Doge's Palace, Venice, Italy, c. 1345–1438.

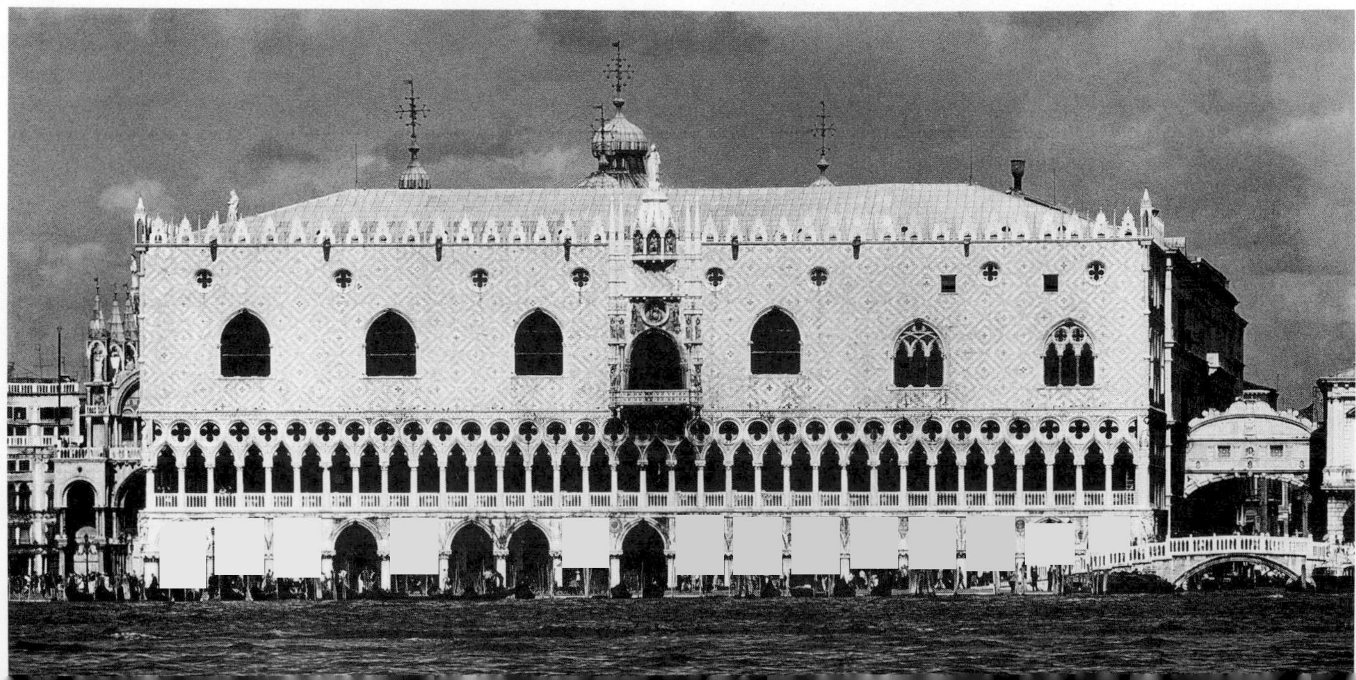

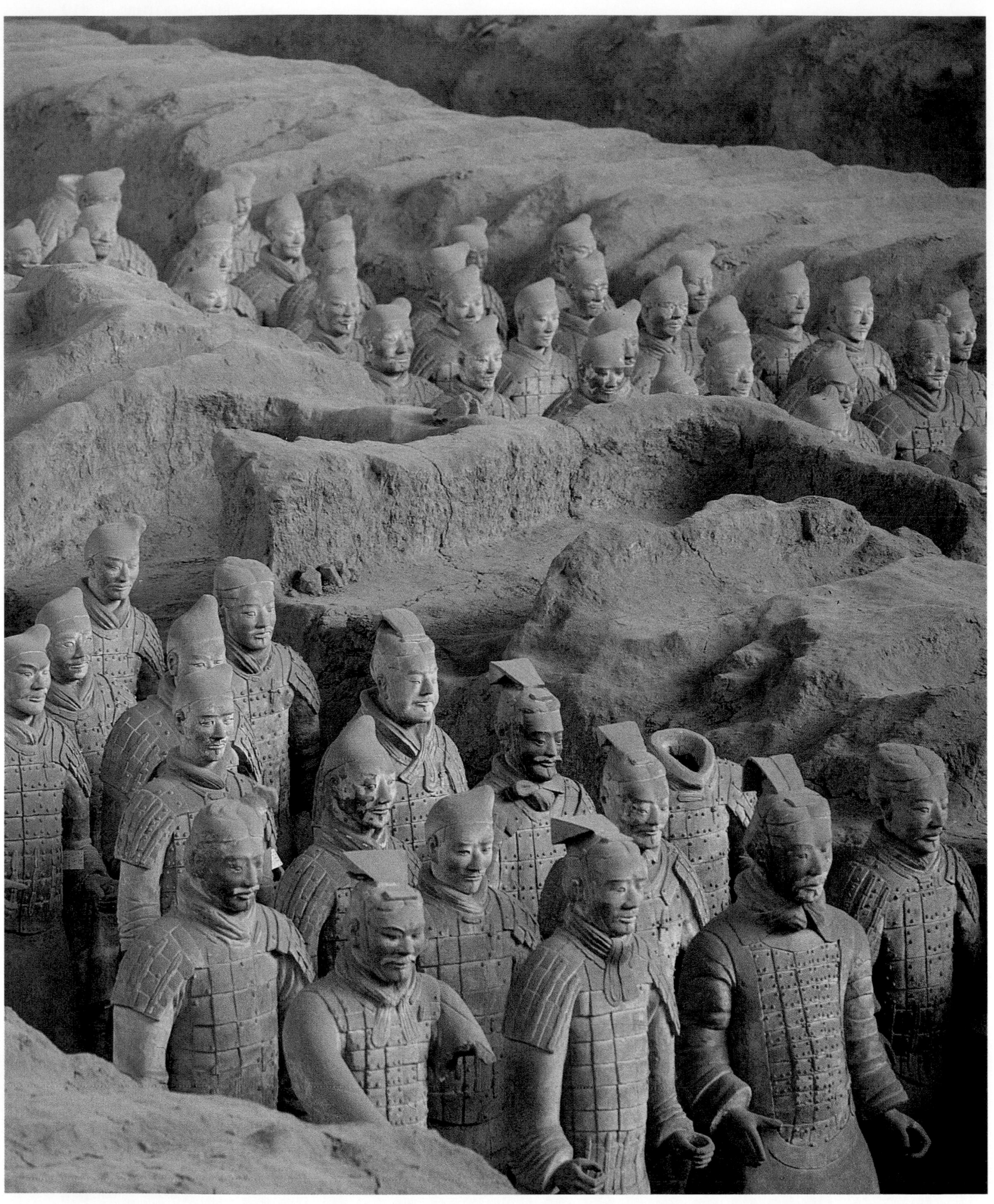

Emperor Shih Huang Ti's bodyguards march again after more than two thousand years as the result of excavations at Xi'an, Shensi, China.

III
THE NON-EUROPEAN WORLD

The art of non-European civilizations is introduced at this point in our survey because much of it is more closely related to the art of the prehistoric period and of the earlier Middle Ages than to the art of the Renaissance and of subsequent times until the twentieth century. In these latter periods, the Western artist moves from a dominantly religious and conceptual approach toward an increasingly secular and perceptual one. This drive toward optical realism and the persistent search for a rational, if not scientific, basis for the objectivization of natural appearances were not shared by the numerous cultures outside the mainstream of European history. Thus, non-European art is more akin to Byzantine and other art of the Middle Ages, although its forms, which are based on non-Western cultural and spiritual precepts, are, of course, very different.

Sporadic contacts between Africa and the Far East and the West have occurred since antiquity. The Phoenicians are said to have circumnavigated Africa as early as 600 B.C., and Alexander the Great, bent on exploration as much as conquest, took his armies beyond the Indus River into India. Nomadic peoples from central Asia made repeated incursions into the Near East and Europe; the Huns, under Attila, reached France in the fifth century. In the later Middle Ages, the search for trade routes to the East inspired the exploratory journeys of such enterprising merchants as the Polo brothers, Nicolo and Maffeo, and Nicolo's famous son, Marco, who reached Peking in the late thirteenth century.

Yet all of these contacts were transient and, even when given permanence through the establishment of sea routes during the Renaissance and Baroque periods, served commercial rather than cultural interests. Imported objects were admired as exotic curiosities, and even the eighteenth-century fascination with things Chinese was little more than a superficial and passing fashion. Only toward the end of the nineteenth century, when Western art had exhausted itself in its persistent drive toward realism and was beginning to search for alternative approaches, did non-Western art begin to have a more serious impact on the West.

Even though conquests, colonization, and missionary activity after the Middle Ages carried Christianity well beyond the boundaries of western Europe, we may identify the non-European world as the non-Christian world. This vast region, which dwarfs the area of Europe, produced a great variety of artistic styles and ideas. Of these, the art of Islam already has been surveyed (Chapter 7). The enormous remainder can be subdivided roughly into Oriental art and Third World art. The former embraces the art of Southeast Asia, China, Korea, and Japan; the latter includes the essentially tribal arts of the North and South American Indian, of Africa, and of the South Pacific.

The earliest art works from the great Eastern civilizations in India, China, Korea, and Japan date from Paleolithic and Neolithic times. Buddhism was the common denominator of the later arts of these different countries, although each developed a distinctive style—or, rather, a series of styles. Indian sculpture, from its beginnings, has been characterized by a pulsating vigor in reproducing the living body. Early Chinese bronzes display amazing technical virtuosity in the use of highly symbolic, though abstract, decorative motifs. In later dynasties, in sculpture and particularly in painting, carefully observed details are rendered lyrically and produce a haunting image of nature. Japanese art, in spite of being subject to recurring waves of foreign

An archeologist measures one of the six thousand figures that were buried near the Chinese emperor Shih Huang Ti to guard him through eternity (see page 453).

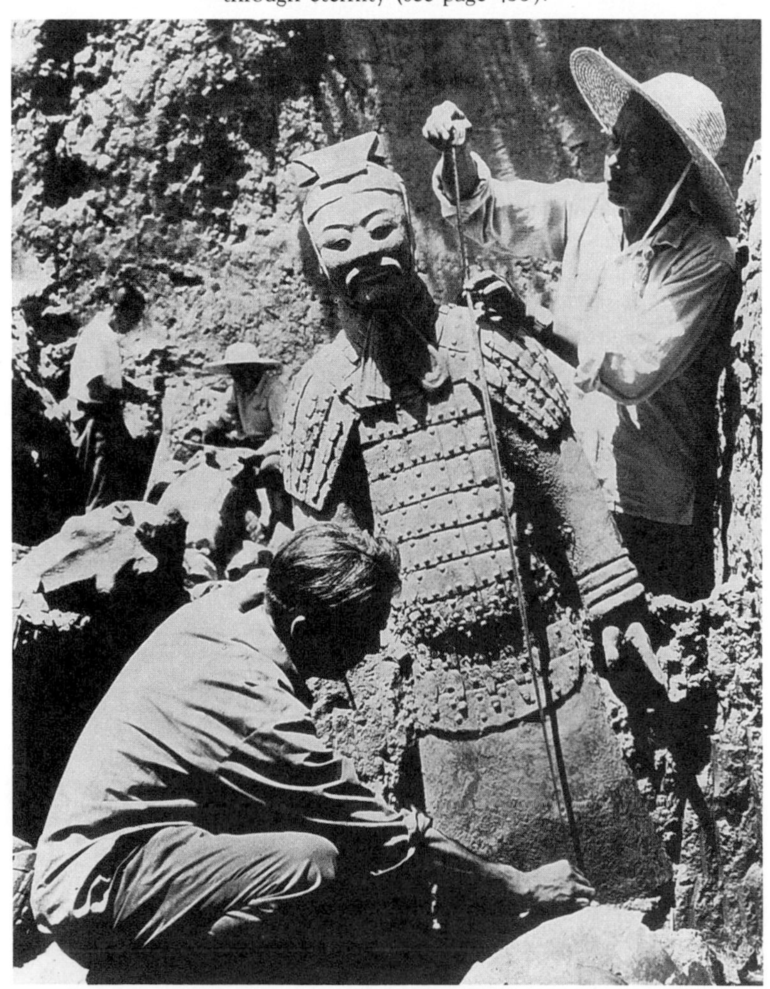

influence (especially from China), insistently returns to native traditions. Painting and, above all, architecture show a sensitivity to the relationship between decorative designs and natural forms.

In pre-Columbian Mexico, Central America, and the Andean region of South America, highly cultured peoples, using Stone Age technology, erected great temple complexes elaborately decorated with reliefs and practiced the crafts of weaving and pottery with great skill. About A.D. 500, the native North Americans began to settle in agricultural communities. Some groups, such as the Pueblo of the southwestern United States, reached a highly developed state in the eleventh, twelfth, and thirteenth centuries. Their stylized arts reflect an extraordinary understanding of the decorative qualities of abstract design.

The peoples native to Africa and the South Sea Islands produced a distinguished and individual art until contact with Europeans either modified it or brought it to a halt. This art, far from being technically or esthetically crude, is sophisticated in its presentation of conceptual rather than naturalistic images and has asserted itself in the West with ever-stronger effect and ever more respectful recognition and appreciation. As we shall see in subsequent chapters, its rhythmical, abstract forms have become a valuable resource and inspiration for many modern artists of great distinction and originality.

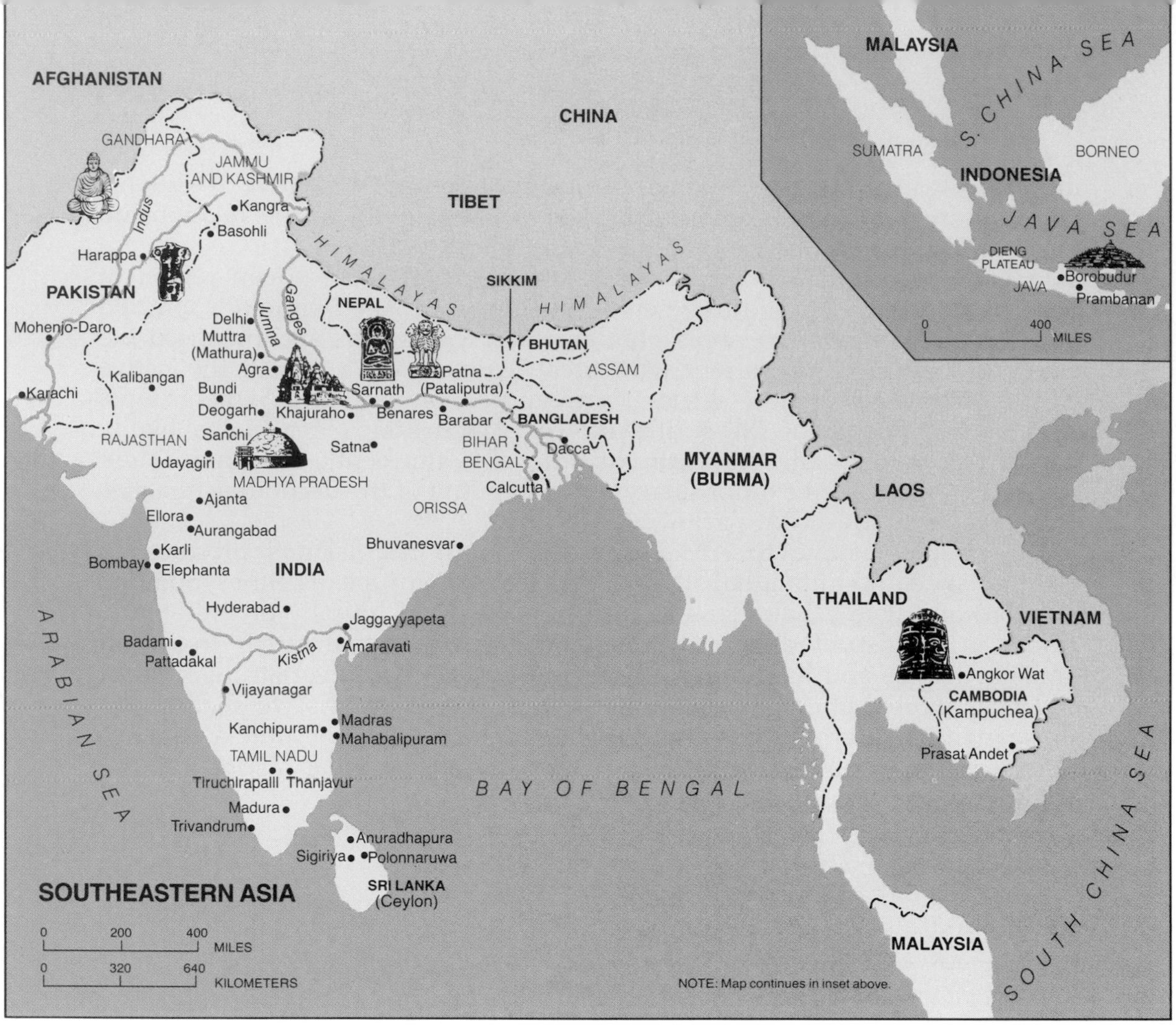

SOUTHEASTERN ASIA

NOTE: Map continues in inset above.

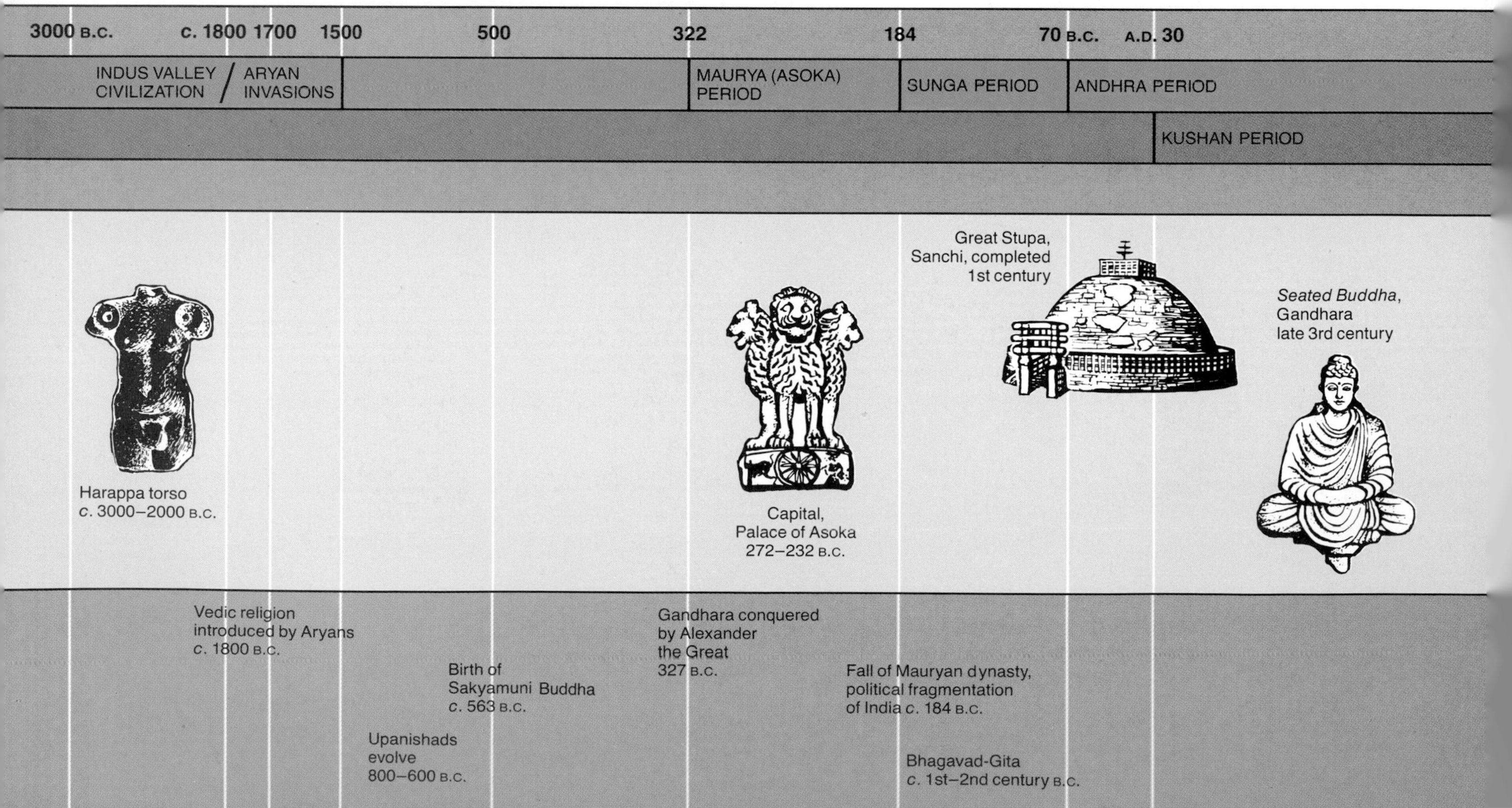

3000 B.C.	c. 1800	1700	1500	500	322	184	70 B.C.	A.D. 30

INDUS VALLEY CIVILIZATION / ARYAN INVASIONS — MAURYA (ASOKA) PERIOD — SUNGA PERIOD — ANDHRA PERIOD

KUSHAN PERIOD

Harappa torso
c. 3000–2000 B.C.

Capital,
Palace of Asoka
272–232 B.C.

Great Stupa,
Sanchi, completed
1st century

Seated Buddha,
Gandhara
late 3rd century

Vedic religion
introduced by Aryans
c. 1800 B.C.

Upanishads
evolve
800–600 B.C.

Birth of
Sakyamuni Buddha
c. 563 B.C.

Gandhara conquered
by Alexander
the Great
327 B.C.

Fall of Mauryan dynasty,
political fragmentation
of India *c.* 184 B.C.

Bhagavad-Gita
c. 1st–2nd century B.C.

11

THE ART OF INDIA

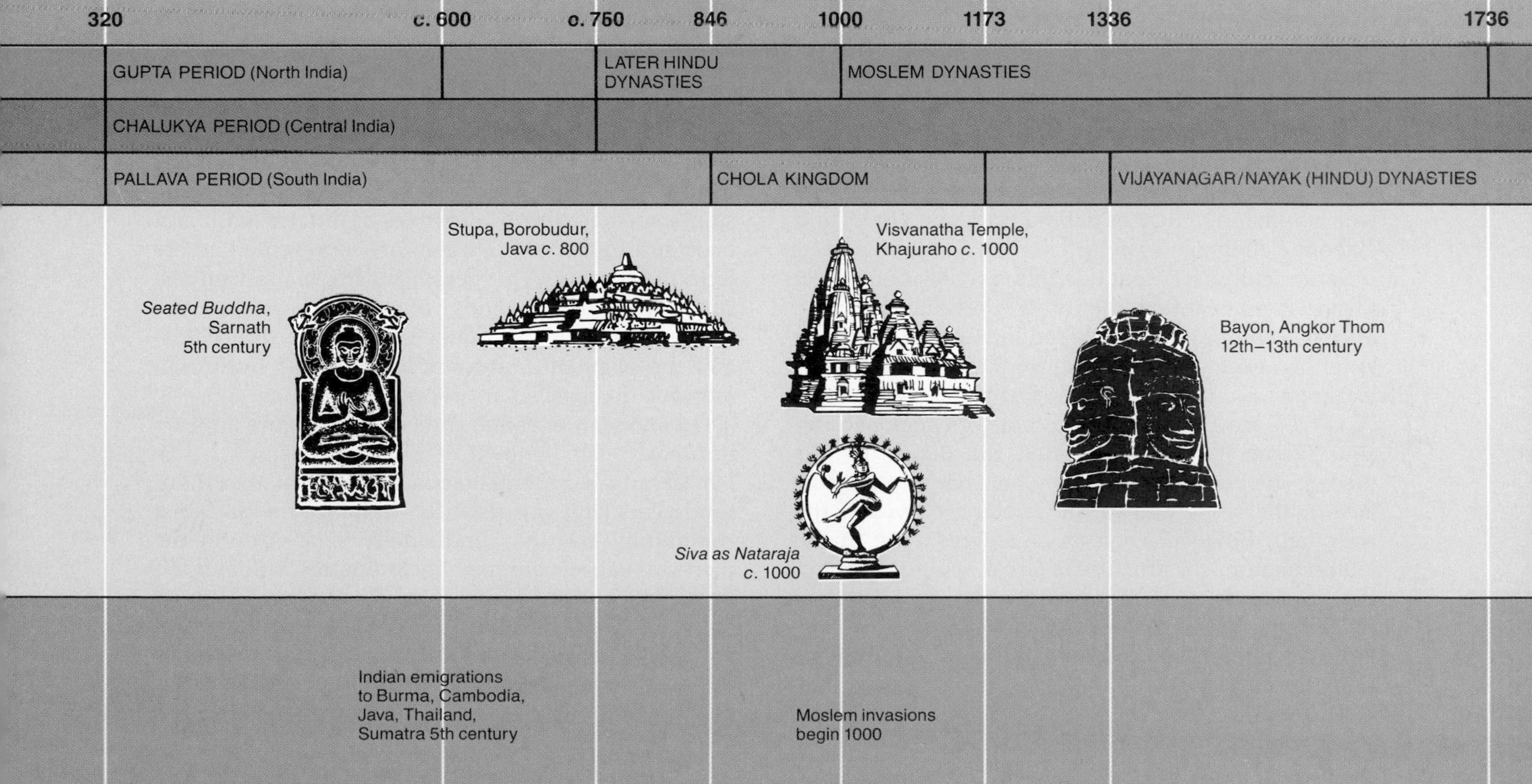

THE SUBCONTINENT OF INDIA, contiguous with the Asian mainland on its northern boundaries, has three distinct geographical areas: the northeast, where the massive Himalayas, the traditional home of the gods, rise as a barrier; the fertile, densely populated area to the northwest and to the south of the Himalayas, where the valleys of the Indus and the Ganges rivers lie; and peninsular India, composed of tropical tablelands separated from the northern rivers by mountains and forests. These areas exhibit great extremes of climate that range from tropical heat to perpetual snow and glaciers, from desert conditions to some of the heaviest rainfall in the world.

The ethnic characteristics and religions of the people vary as much as the geography. The most common language of north central India is Hindi, a Sanskrit derivative. Urdu, closely related, is spoken by most of the Moslem population. Several Dravidian languages, unrelated to Sanskrit, are spoken in the south. Hinduism is the main religion of India, as Islam is of Pakistan, but Jainism and Christianity have many adherents, and Buddhism and Judaism also have a few.

BEGINNINGS

The first major culture of India centered around the upper reaches of the Indus River valley during the late third and early second millennia B.C. Mohenjo-Daro and Harappa in Pakistan were the chief sites. Recently, other important centers of this culture have been found farther south at Kalibangan in Rajasthan, India, and near Karachi, Pakistan.

The architectural remains of Mohenjo-Daro suggest a modern commercial center, with major avenues along a north–south orientation, streets as wide as 40 feet, multistoried houses of fired brick and wood, and elaborate drainage systems.

Some sculptures from this Indus civilization reflect Mesopotamian influences; others indicate the presence of a thoroughly developed Indian tradition. The latter is exemplified by a miniature torso from Harappa (FIG. **11-1**), which, at first glance, appears to be carved according to the precepts of Greek naturalism. (Some historians question the dating of this piece.) The emphasis given (by polishing) to the surface of the stone and to the swelling curves of the abdomen, however, reveals an interest, not in the logical anatomical structure of Greek sculpture, but in the fluid movement of a living body. This sense of pulsating vigor and the emphasis on sensuous surfaces were chief characteristics of Indian sculpture for four thousand years.

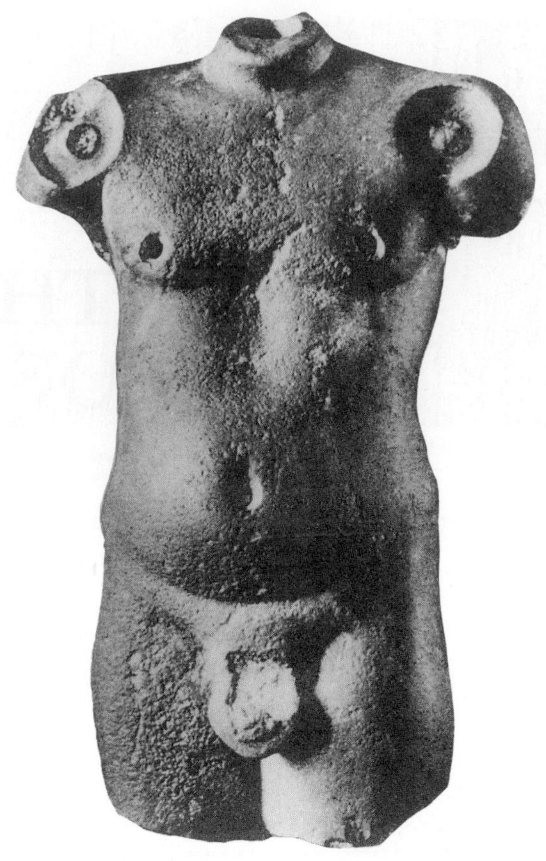

11-1 *Male Nude,* Harappa, Pakistan, late third to early second millennium B.C. Red sandstone, $3\frac{1}{2}''$ high. National Museum, New Delhi.

Great numbers of intaglio steatite seals found at Mohenjo-Daro exhibit a blend of Indian and Near Eastern elements (FIG. **11-2**). Indeed, it was the finding of a Mohenjo-Daro seal at a datable Mesopotamian site that enabled scholars to assign dates to the Indus valley cultures. The script on the seals has not been deciphered. Varied devices worked into the stone, such as trees (sometimes associated with animals and humanoid figures), are represented as objects of worship. The beasts most common on the seals are various kinds of bulls (including the humped variety), the water buffalo, the rhinoceros, and the elephant. Fantastic animals and anthropomorphic deities also are represented.

On one seal, a seated, three-headed figure appears in what is later known as a "yoga position." The heads carry a trident-shaped device that two thousand years later was used to symbolize the Buddhist community and the Hindu deity Siva. Around the deity are various animals, including the bull and the tiger, which also became symbols of Siva. Given its date, this seal probably represented a prototype of that god. Such continuity of iconography indicates the deep roots of religious tradition in India.

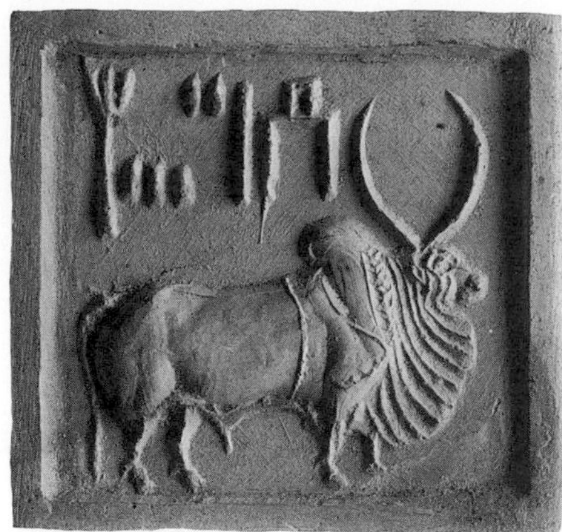
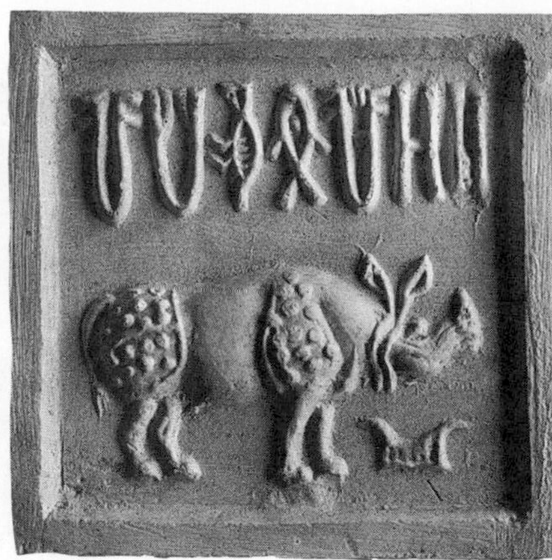
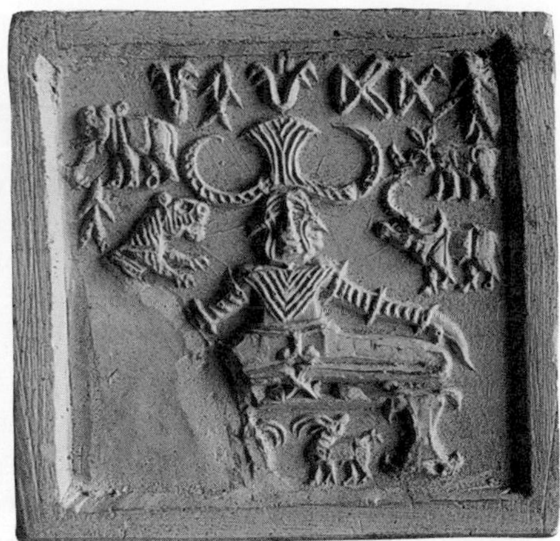

11-2 Seals, from Mohenjo-Daro, Pakistan, third millennium B.C. Steatite. National Museum, New Delhi.

Style, too, shows a continuous tradition. The animals on the Indus valley seals have the flowing contours and sensuous surfaces (also seen in the Harappa figure) that characterize sculpture throughout most of Indian history. This artistic continuity is remarkable, not only because of the time spanned, but also because of the fact that virtually no remains of the visual arts have been found for the period between the disappearance of the Indus civilization (about 1700 B.C.) and the rise of the Maurya Empire (third century B.C.). The Aryan invasions, which began about 1800 B.C., may account for the break in the sequence of Indian art. The persistence of so many indigenous traits is even more amazing in view of the Aryans' profound effect on Indian culture. Destruction by the invaders, as well as the perishability of the materials used, undoubtedly accounted for the disappearance of many of the objects by which Indian traditions were passed on during the two thousand years following the collapse of the Indus civilization.

The Aryans brought the Vedic religion with them to India. The term derives from the hymns (Vedas), which have survived to this day. These hymns are addressed to the gods, who are personified aspects of nature. The warrior god Indra is thunder; Surya, the sun; and Varuna, the sky. These are but three of many. All were worshiped by means of hymns and sacrificial offerings in conformance with strict laws of ritual. Fire altars, built according to prescribed formulas, served as the focus of devotion. So important was the act of ritual that, in time, Agni (the sacrificial fire) and Soma (the sacrificial brew) became personified as gods in their own right.

The rather simple form of religion and propitiation so beautifully expressed in the Vedic hymns was elaborated greatly in the Upanishads (800–600 B.C.), a series of treatises on the nature of man and the universe that introduced a number of concepts alien to the simple nature worship of the northern invaders. Chief among the new ideas were those of *samsara* and *karma*. Samsara meant the transformation of the soul into some other form of life on the death of the body. The type of existence into which the reborn soul entered depended on karma, the consequence of actions in all previous lifetimes. A bad karma meant a dark future—rebirth in a hell or in this world as a lower animal (a reptile, for example, or an insect). A good karma meant that the soul might go into the body of a king, a priest, or even a god, for gods also were subject to eventual death and to the endless cycle of rebirth. The goal of religion therefore became the submersion of individual life in a world soul, which was attainable only after an individual's karma had been perfected through countless rebirths. Penance, meditation, and asceticism were believed to speed the process.

During the sixth century B.C., two major religions developed in India. One, Buddhism, exerted a profound influence on the culture and art of India as a whole from the third century B.C. to the sixth or seventh century A.D. (In some parts, like Bengal and Bihar, it was influential to the eleventh century and, in the south, to an even later date.) Although Jainism, the other major religion, never achieved Buddhism's dominance, it continues to the present day as a small but distinct religion in India, while Buddhism is practically extinct there.

The arts of many Asian countries derive from Indian Buddhism, which began with the birth of the Buddha Sakyamuni about 563 B.C. The son of a king who ruled a small area on the border of Nepal and India, the child, according to legend, was miraculously conceived and sprang from his mother's side. Named Siddhartha, and also known as Gautama, the child displayed prodigious abilities. A sage predicted that he would become a Buddha, an "enlightened" holy man destined to achieve "nirvana." After a series of confrontations with old age, sickness, religious asceticism, and death, called the Four Encounters, Siddhartha renounced courtly luxury and the secular life. While meditating under a pipal tree in the city of Bodh Gaya, he obtained illumination—the complete understanding of the universe that is Buddhahood. His teachings may be summed up as follows: all existence implies sorrow; the cause of sorrow is attachment to work and the self; this attachment can be dissolved through the elimination of desires, which also bind the self to a countless succession of rebirths; the cessation of rebirth can be accomplished by following the Eightfold Path, which prescribes simple practices of right thought, right speech, and right action. This initial formulation of Buddhism, in which salvation was achieved by individual efforts, was later known as Hinayana Buddhism. The religion of Buddhism, so conceived, was not opposed to basic Hindu thought, but was rather a minor heresy deriving from certain speculations in the Upanishads. What Buddhism did was to offer a specific method for solving the ancient Indian problem of how to break the chain of existence so that the individual could find ultimate peace.

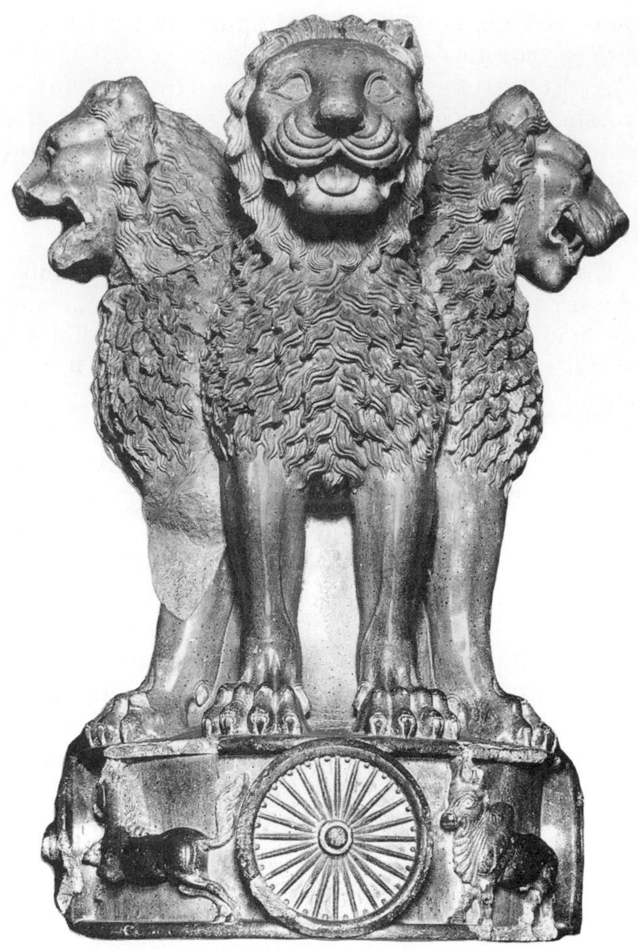

11-3 Lion capital of column erected by Emperor Asoka (272–232 B.C.), from Patna (ancient Pataliputra), India. Polished sandstone, 7′ high. Archeological Museum, Sarnath.

BUDDHIST DOMINANCE

Early Architecture and Sculpture

The earliest known examples of art in the service of Buddhism (from the middle of the third century B.C.) are both monumental and sophisticated. Emperor Asoka (272–232 B.C.), the grandson of Chandragupta, founder of the Maurya dynasty (*c.* 322–184 B.C.), was converted to Buddhism after witnessing the horrors of the brutal military campaigns by which he himself forcibly had unified most of northern India. His palace at Patna in Bihar (ancient Pataliputra) was designed after the Achaemenid palace at Persepolis (FIG. 2-38).

Megasthenes, a Greek ambassador at the court of Asoka, has left a glowing report of Pataliputra. Only parts of columns, the foundations of buildings, and remnants of a wooden palisade now remain, but we may draw some idea of the architectural details from a series of commemorative and sacred columns that Asoka raised throughout much of northern India. These monolithic pillars were of polished sandstone, some as high as 60 or 70 feet. The capital of one (FIG. **11-3**), now in the Sarnath Museum near Benares, typifies the style of the period. It consists of a *lotiform* capital (a capital in the form of a lotus petal), on which rests a horizontal disk sculptured with a frieze of four animals alternating with four wheels. Seated on the disk are four *addorsed* (back-to-back) lions that originally were surmounted by another huge wheel. All of the forms are symbolic. The lotus, traditional symbol of divinity, also connoted humanity's salvation in Buddhism. The wheel represented the cycle of life, death, and rebirth. This "wheel of life" often had other levels of meaning. In this instance, it was the teaching of Buddha—the "turning of the wheel of the law." The wheel itself (probably developed from ancient sun symbols) and the four animals (the four quarters of the compass) with which it is associated here imply a cosmological meaning in which the pillar as a whole symbolizes the world axis. The lions also had manifold meanings, but here they were specifically equated with Sakyamuni Buddha, who was known as the lion of the Sakya clan.

The pillars are noteworthy not only for their symbolism, but also because they exemplify continuity of style. Although the stiff, heraldic lions are typical of Persepolis, the low-relief animals around the disk are treated in the much earlier, fluid style of Mohenjo-

Daro. So, too, are the colossal figures of *yakshas* and *yakshis*, sculptured during Asoka's time or somewhat later. These male and female divinities, originally worshiped as local nature spirits, gods of trees and rocks, now were incorporated into the Buddhist and Hindu pantheons.

THE CAVE TEMPLE

The Mauryan period also witnessed the beginnings of a unique architectural form—sanctuaries cut into the living rock of cliffs. Parts of the exteriors (and later the interiors) of these caves were carved to imitate in accurate detail the wooden constructions of the time. The Lomas Rishi cave, hollowed out during Asoka's reign, exhibits an entrance type (FIG. **11-4**) that will be perpetuated for a thousand years. This faithful replica of a wooden façade has a doorway with a curving eave that mimics a flexible wooden roof bent over rectangular beams. A decorative frieze of elephants over the doorway carries on the indigenous sculptural traditions.

THE STUPA

The fall of the Mauryan dynasty, around the beginning of the second century B.C., led to the political fragmentation of India. Under the Sungas and the Andhras, who were the chief successors of the Mauryas, numerous *chaitya* (Buddhist assembly halls) and *viharas* (monasteries) were cut into the hills that run across central India from east to west. At the same time, the *stupa*, which originally was a small burial or reliquary mound of earth, evolved as an important architectural program. Asoka is supposed to have built thousands of stupas throughout India. By the end of the second century B.C., huge stupas were being constructed. Sculptured fragments from early stupas have been found at Muttra (ancient Mathura), near Satna (ancient Bharhut), and elsewhere in India, but the grandeur of this type of structure can be seen best at Sanchi in the state of Madhya Pradesh. There, on a hill overlooking a wide plain, several stupas containing sacred relics were built over a period of centuries. Of these, the Great Stupa (FIG. **11-5**), the tallest and finest, was originally dedicated by Asoka. Enlarged and finally completed about the middle of the first century,* it now stands as the culminating monument of an era.

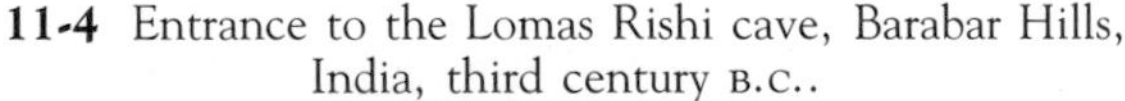

11-4 Entrance to the Lomas Rishi cave, Barabar Hills, India, third century B.C..

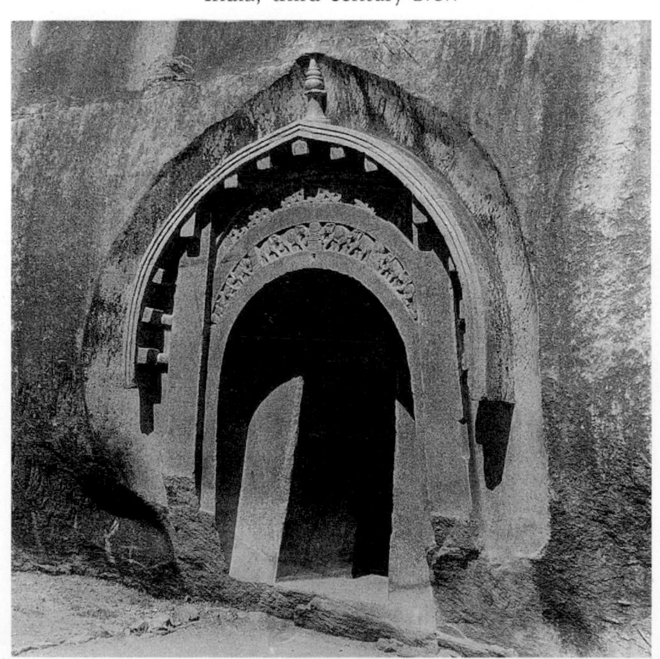

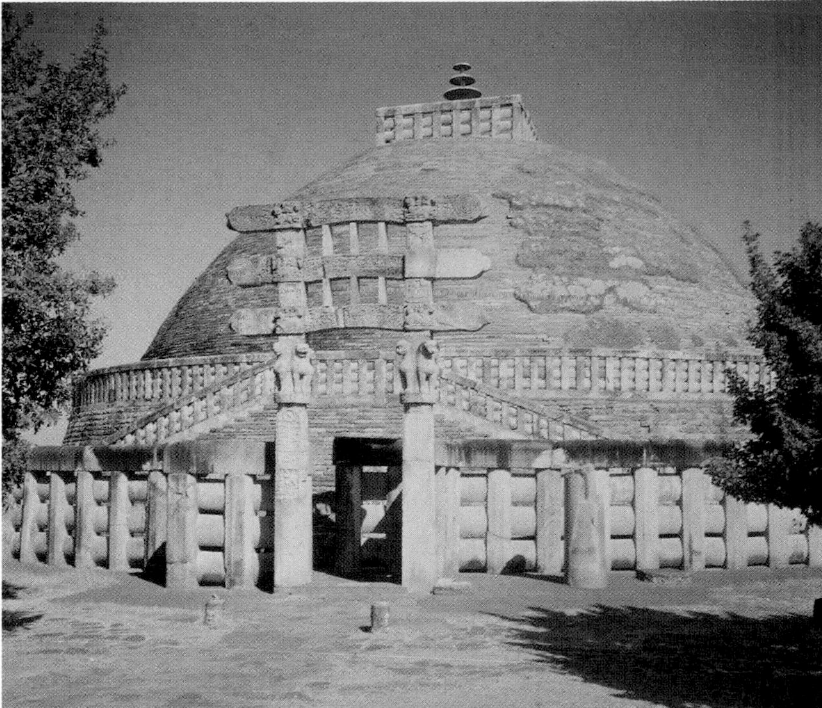

11-5 The Great Stupa, Sanchi, India, completed first century.

A double stairway at the south side leads from the base to a drum about 20 feet high and permits access to a narrow, railed walk around the solid dome, which rises 50 feet above the ground. Surmounting the dome is the *harmika*, a square enclosure from the center of which arises the *yasti*, or mast. The yasti is itself adorned with a series of *chatras* (umbrellas). Around the whole structure is a circular stone railing with ornamented *toranas* (gateways; FIG. **11-6**) on the north, east, south, and west sides.

The stupa, like most Indian structures, has more than just one function. As a receptacle for relics, it is an object of adoration, a symbol of the death of the

*As a reminder, all dates not designated by the epoch time designation B.C. refer to the period A.D. Unless required for clarification, especially in Chapters 11–14, where large ranges of time from B.C. to A.D. are being covered, A.D. will no longer be used throughout the text.

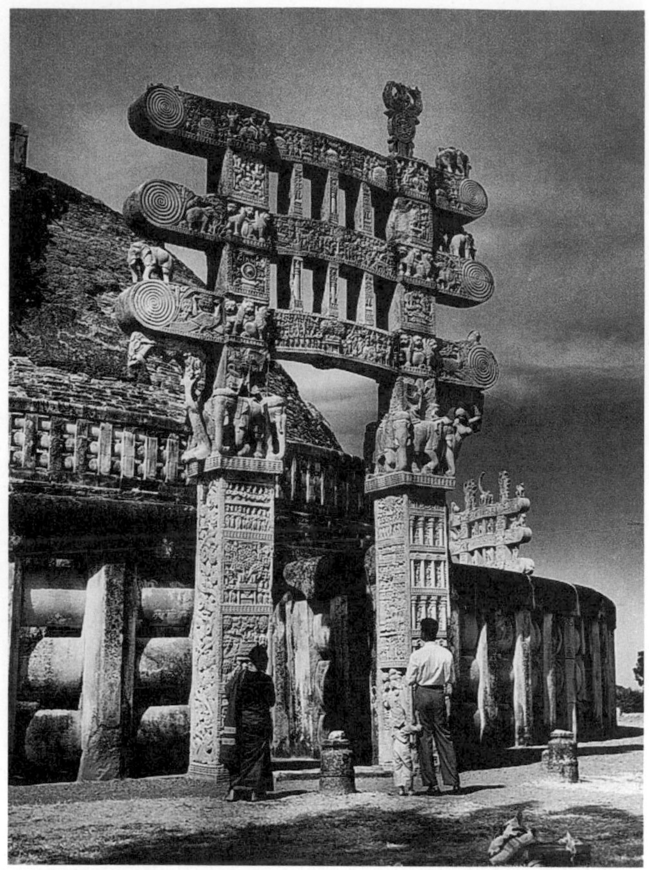

11-6 Eastern gateway, the Great Stupa, completed first century.

Buddha, or a token of Buddhism in general. Devotion is given the stupa by the believer, who circumambulates its dome. But, in another sense, the stupa is a cosmic diagram, the world mountain with the cardinal points emphasized by the toranas. The harmika symbolizes the heaven of the thirty-three gods; the yasti, as the axis of the universe, rises from the mountain-dome and through the harmika, thus uniting this world with the paradises above.

The railings and domes of some stupas were decorated with relief sculpture. The toranas at Sanchi are covered with Buddhist symbols, deities, and narrative scenes, but the figure of the Buddha never appears. Instead, he is symbolized by such devices as an empty throne, the tree under which he meditated, the wheel of the law, or his footprints.

The awe expressed in this iconographic restraint, echoed by the quiet mass of the dome itself, is contradicted strikingly and paradoxically by the sculptural luxuriance that crowds the toranas. Lush foliage mingles with the flowing forms of human bodies, and warm vitality pervades both animal and human forms. Sensuous yakshis hang like ripe fruit from tree brackets. This almost hedonistic expression is alien to the Buddhist renunciation of life. It is an assertion, rather, of a basic Indian attitude that at all times unites and dominates almost all of Buddhist, Hindu, and Jain art.

Sanchi is the greatest constructed monument of early Buddhism, much as the chaitya at Karli is the finest of the sculptured cave temples. During the second and first centuries B.C., the cave sanctuaries had developed complexities far beyond their simple beginnings in the Lomas Rishi cave. Splendid façades reproducing wooden architecture in exact detail were given permanence in stone. Around the year 100, at Karli, in the Western Ghats near Bombay, a cliff was hollowed out and carved into an apsidal temple nearly 45 feet high and 125 feet long. The nave of the hall leads to a monolithic stupa in the apse (FIG. **11-7**),

11-7 Interior of the chaitya hall at Karli, India, c. 100.

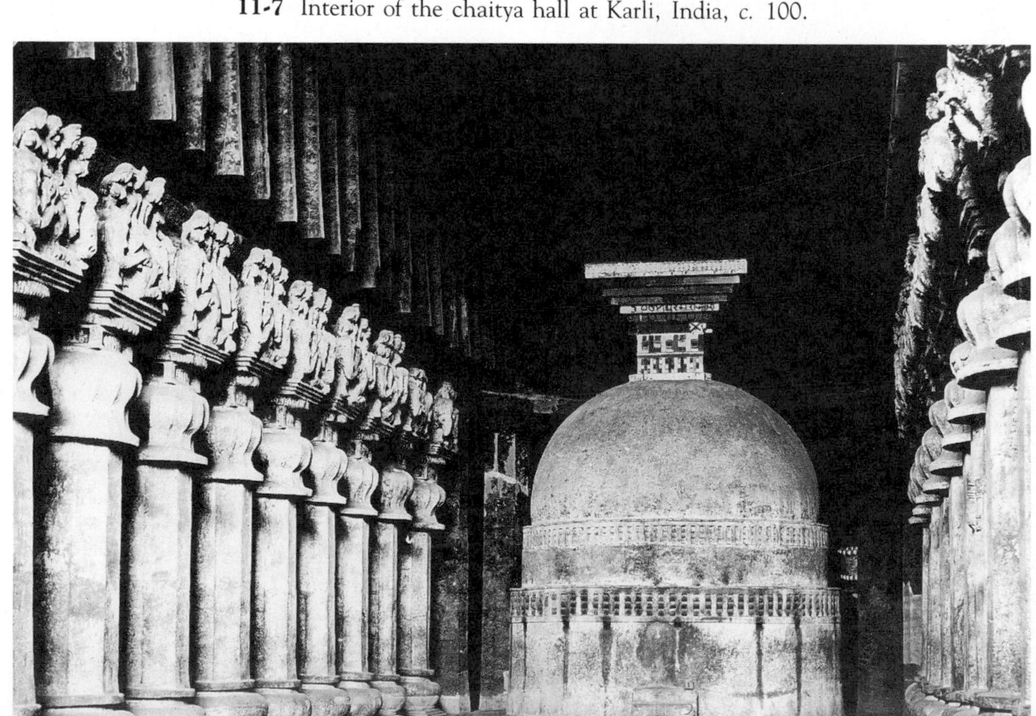

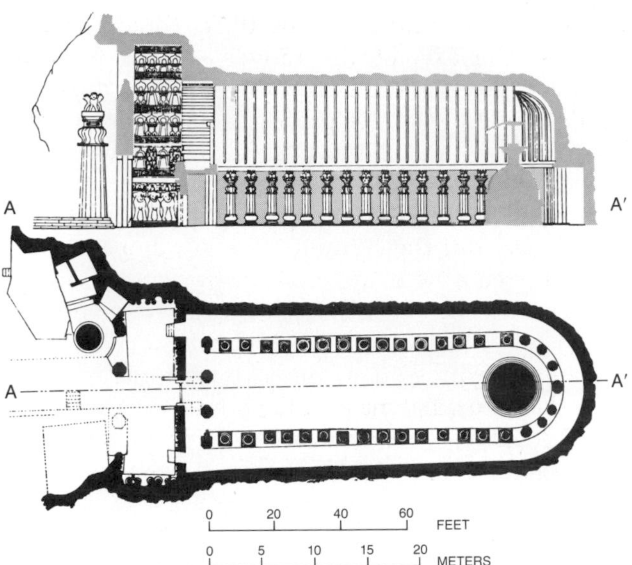

11-8 Section *(top)* and plan *(bottom)* of the chaitya hall at Karli.

and on either side of the nave is an aisle formed by a series of massive columns crowned with male and female riders on elephants. These great columns follow the curve of the apse, thus providing an ambulatory behind the stupa (FIG. **11-8**). The inner wall of the narthex, despite some later additions, is almost intact, and today it functions as a magnificent façade. On each side of the entrance, massive elephants, like atlantids, support a multistoried building, while male and female pairs (related to yakshas and yakshis) flank the central doorway, enhancing the rich surfaces with heroic and voluptuous forms. These undulant figures (FIG. **11-9**) contrast with the immobile severity of the stupa within and, like the yakshis of Sanchi, speak of life, not death.

11-9 *Amorous Couple,* from the entrance of the chaitya hall at Karli.

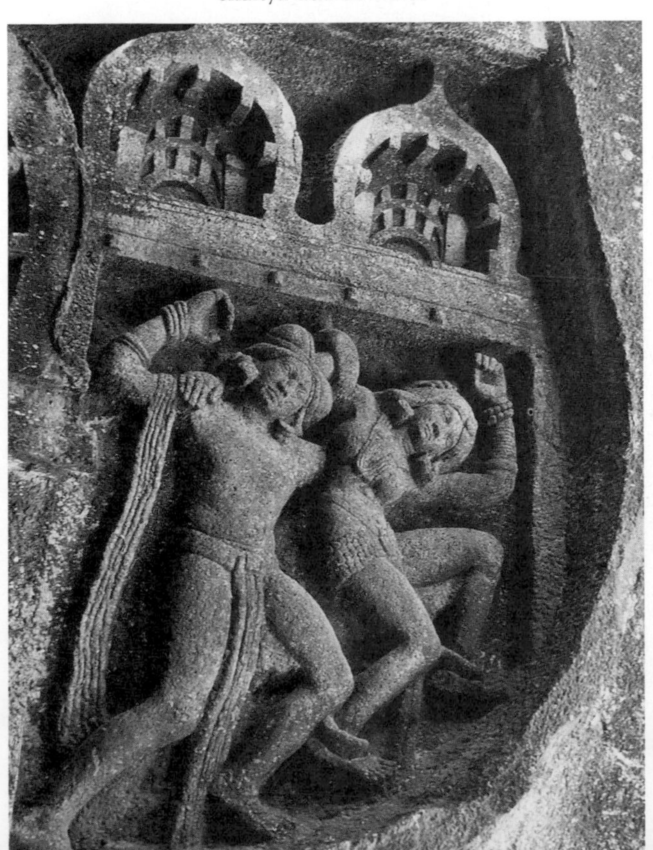

THE BUDDHA IMAGE

For some four hundred years before the second century, the Buddha was represented only in symbols. At the end of the first century, in both Gandhara and Mathura, he suddenly was depicted in anthropomorphic form. The explanation for his sudden depiction is to be found partly in the development of the Buddhist movement, which, during the first century, was divided by two conflicting philosophies. The more traditional believers regarded the Buddha as a great teacher who had taught a method by which man ultimately might attain nirvana. The newer thought, called *Mahayana* (the Great Vehicle) as opposed to the older *Hinayana* (the Lesser Vehicle), deified the Buddha and provided him with a host of divinities (*Bodhisattvas*) to aid him in saving humanity. According to the older belief, Sakyamuni was the last of seven Buddhas to exist on earth. The Mahayanists peopled the universe with thousands of Buddhas, of whom Amitabha, Lord of the Western Paradise, and Maitreya, a messiah who was to appear on this earth, soon rivaled Sakyamuni in popular favor. Symbols of the Buddha were too cold and abstract to appeal to great masses of people and were not suited to the pageantry of the new faith. In addition, Buddhism had borrowed from a reviving Hinduism the practice of *bhakti* (the adoration of a personalized deity as a means of achieving unity with it), which demanded the human figure as its focus. Thus Buddhism, out of emulation of its rival, produced its most distinct symbol, the Buddha image.

Gandhara, where one of the two versions of the anthropomorphic Buddha first appeared, may be taken loosely to include much of Afghanistan and the westernmost section of northern India, now part of modern Pakistan. In 327 B.C., Gandhara was conquered by the armies of Alexander the Great. Although the Greek occupation lasted only a short time, it led to continued contact with the Classical West. It is not surprising, then, that the Buddha image that developed at Gandhara (FIG. **11-10**) had Hellenistic and especially Roman sculpture as its model. Indeed, the features of the Master often suggest those of a marble Apollo, and many details, such as drapery patterns and coiffures, recall successive styles in contemporaneous Roman carving. Although the iconography was Indian, even the distinguishing marks of the Buddha *(lakshanas)* sometimes were translated into a

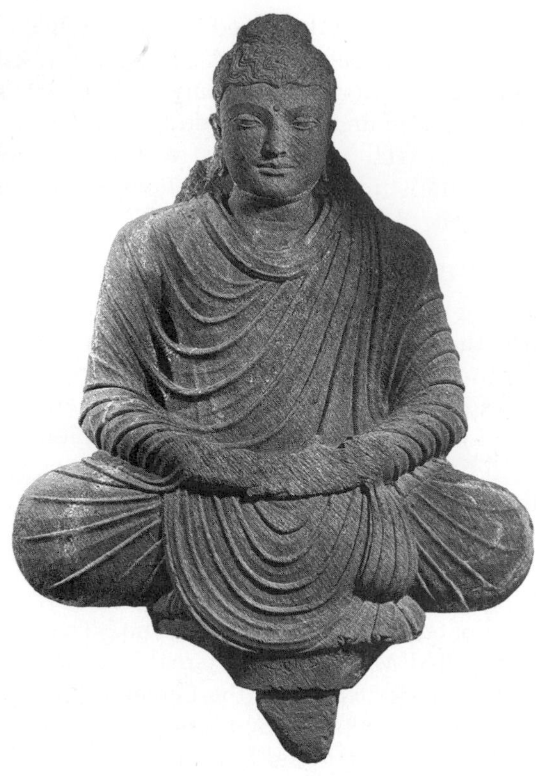

11-10 *Seated Buddha,* from Gandhara, Pakistan, late third century. Stone, 28¾″ high. Yale University Art Gallery.

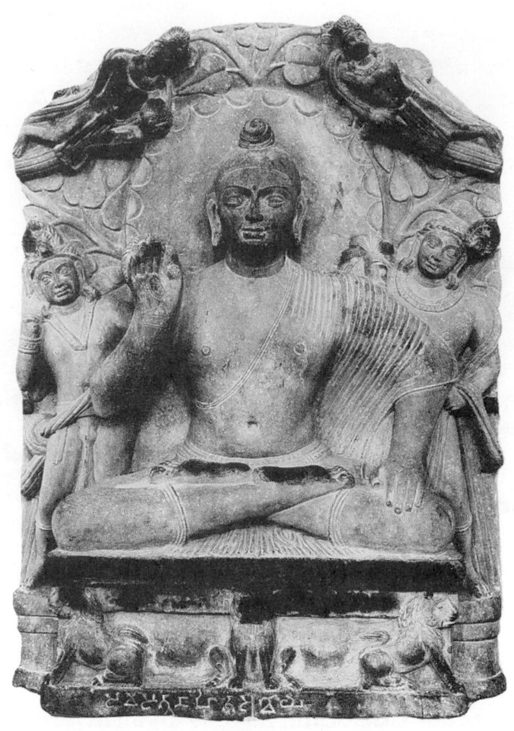

11-11 *Seated Buddha,* from Mathura, India, second to third centuries. Red sandstone, 27¼″ high. Archeological Museum, Muttra.

Western idiom. Thus, the *ushnisha,* a knot of hair on the head, took on the appearance of a Classical chignon. At times, even the robe of the Indian monk was replaced by the Roman toga, and minor divinities were transformed into Western water gods, nymphs, or atlantids.

While this intrusion of Western style was dominating the northwest, the purely Indian version of the anthropomorphic Buddha was evolving one hundred miles south of Delhi in the holy city of Mathura. This image (FIG. **11-11**) is carved in stele form, which is common to most seated Buddha images in India. Sitting on a throne, with heraldic lions at its base, and flanked by two turbaned men, the Buddha is surrounded by the leaves and branches of the Tree of Enlightenment. The image derives directly from the yaksha of popular art and, like the yaksha, is draped in a mantle so thin and clinging that, at first glance, the figure seems to be nude. The Mathura Buddha also has broad shoulders, a narrow waist, and a supple grace. Only such iconographic details as the ushnisha, the *urna* (a whorl of hair between the brows, represented as a dot), the long-lobed ears, and the *mudra* (a symbolic hand gesture) distinguish the Buddha from the earlier yaksha.

By the third century, the two anthropomorphic Buddha types began to coalesce into a form that served as a model for the earliest Chinese versions. But it is the Buddha at Sarnath (FIG. **11-12**), from the

11-12 *Seated Buddha Preaching the First Sermon,* from Sarnath, India, fifth century. Stele, sandstone, 63″ high. Archeological Museum, Sarnath.

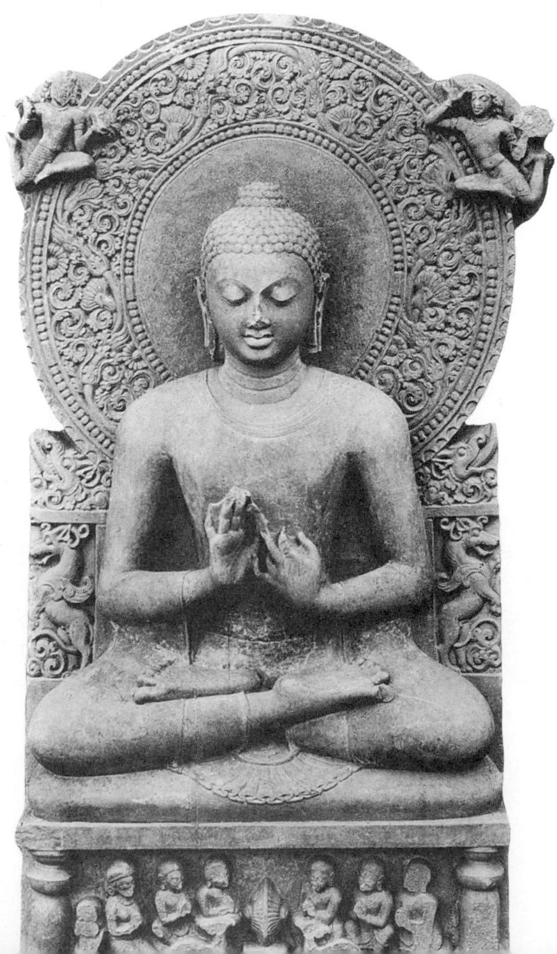

end of the fifth century, that conveys both the abstract idealism of the religion and the sensuousness of Indian art. The first element is evident in the simplified planes of the face; the second is found in the clinging drapery, which reveals the human form.

HINDU RESURGENCE

While Buddhism was at its height, Hinduism slowly was gathering the momentum that eventually was to crush its heretical offspring. Buddhism owed its original victory to the clearness of its formula for achieving salvation. About the first or second century B.C., Hinduism's answer appeared in the Bhagavad Gita, a poetic gospel that has been fundamental to Hindu doctrine ever since. According to the Gita, meditation and reason can lead to ultimate absorption in the godhead; so, too, can the selfless fulfillment of everyday duties. Because the Gita also stressed bhakti, which answered a fundamental emotional need, the Gita swept Hinduism to final supremacy in the sixth and seventh centuries A.D.

Architecture and Sculpture

Sporadic examples of Hindu art dating from the last centuries B.C. have been found, but we know of no great monuments before the fourth century A.D. At that time, the Hindus began to emulate Buddhist cave temples, first by carving out monumental icons in shallow niches. One such temple is the *Boar Avatar of Vishnu* (FIG. **11-13**)* at Udayagiri near Sanchi. Here, a 12-foot figure of Varaha, a manlike creature with a boar's head, is shown raising the earth goddess from the ocean—an act symbolic of the rescuing of the earth from destruction. The powerful form of Varaha, first formulated by the Kushans, served as a model for innumerable later sculptures of this popular theme. Within a few decades, more developed caves at the same site acquired sculptural doorways, interior columns, and central icons.

During the sixth century, in the rock hillsides at Badami to the south, the Chalukyans carved out rectangular temples that had pillars, walls, and ceilings ornamented with figures of their favorite deities. Porches and interiors were defined by the embellished columns, which were so ordered as to focus attention on the shrine in the center of the rear wall. In a temple dedicated to Siva (with Vishnu, one of the two chief divinities of the Hindu pantheon), the god is shown in his cosmic dance, with numerous arms spread fanlike around his body (FIG. **11-14**). Some of

*An *avatar* is a manifestation of a deity in which the deity performs a necessary function on earth; the number of avatars varies, with Vishnu usually having ten, or sometimes twenty-nine.

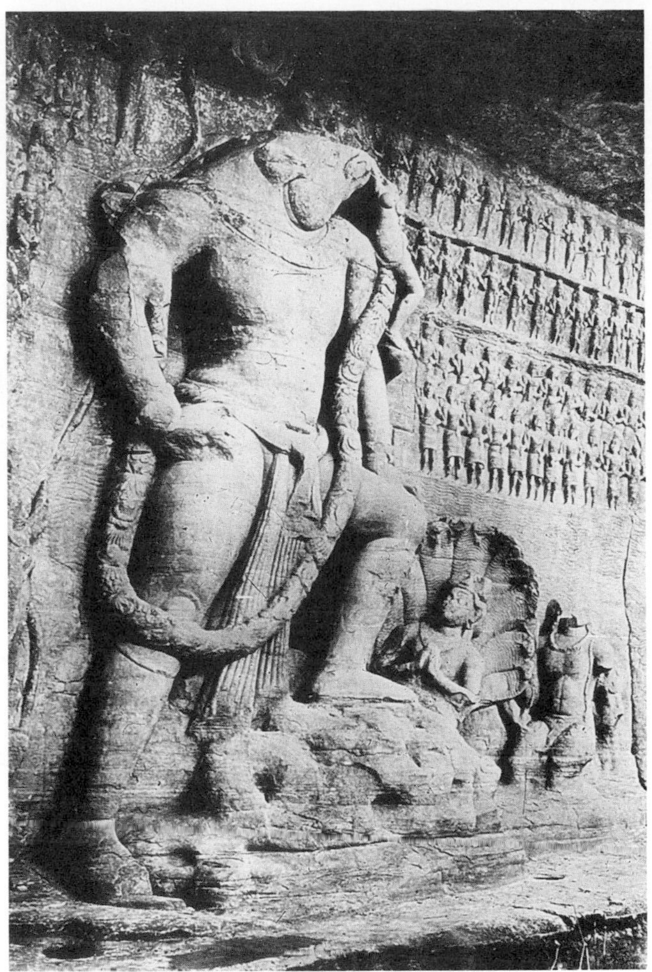

11-13 *Boar Avatar of Vishnu,* Cave V at Udayagiri, India, c. 400. Vishnu is 12′ 8″ high.

11-14 *Dancing Siva,* relief from cave temple, Badami, India, sixth century.

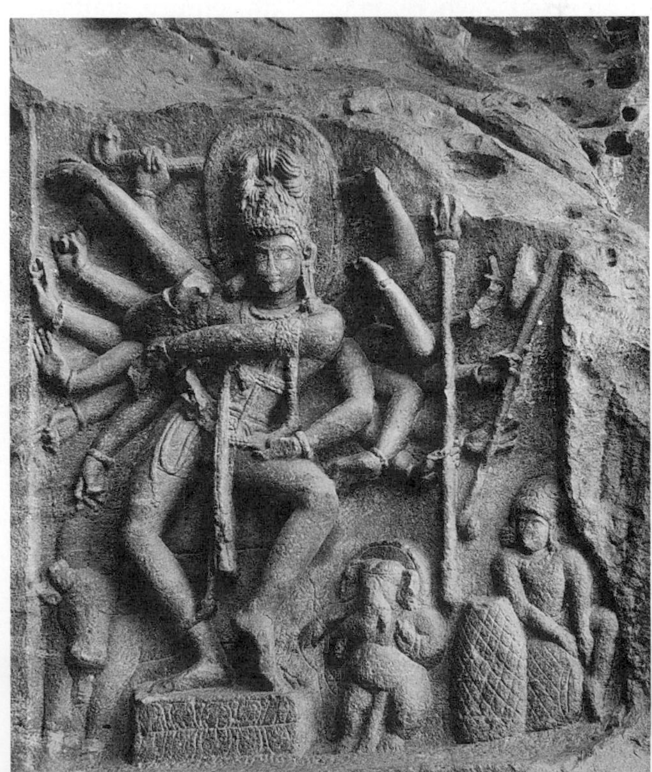

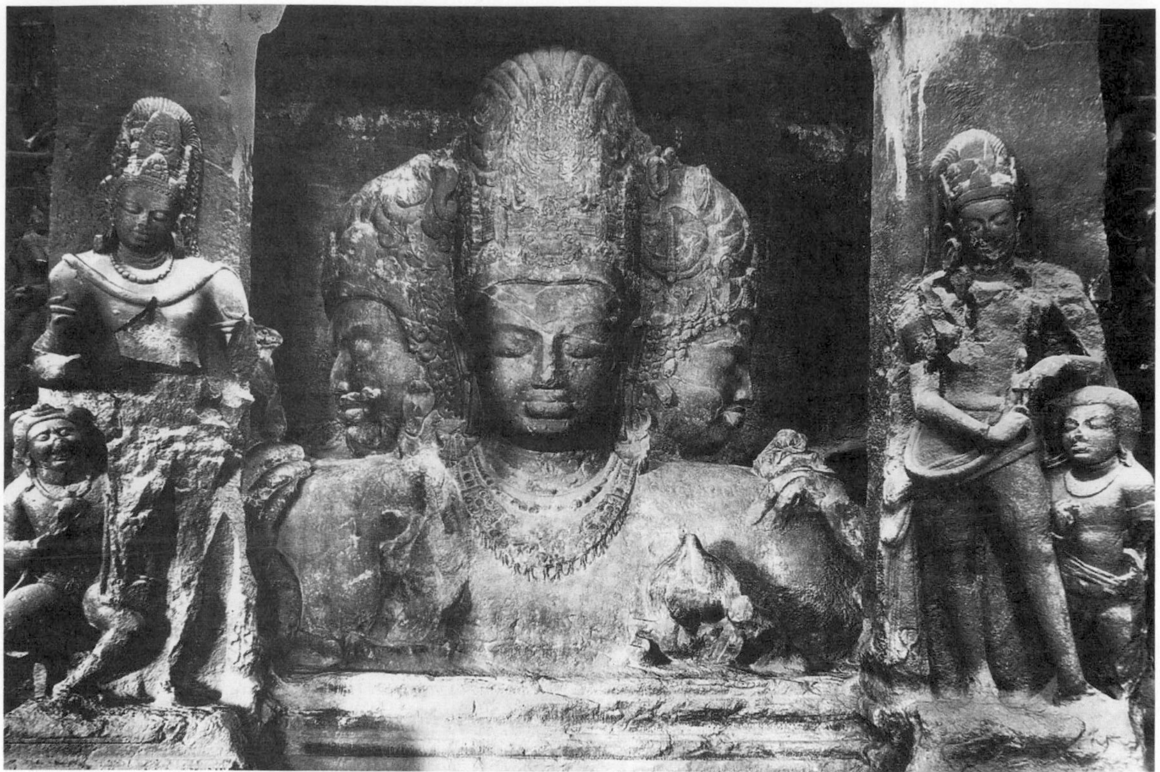

11-15 *Siva as Mahadeva* in rock-cut temple, Elephanta, India, sixth century. Siva is 17′ high.

the god's hands hold objects; others are represented in prescribed gestures (mudra). Each object and each mudra signifies a specific power of the deity. The arrangement of the limbs is so skillful and logical that it is hard to realize that the sculptor conceived of the figure as a symbol and not as an image of a many-armed being.

Perhaps the supreme achievement of Hindu art is at Elephanta, where, in the sixth century, craftsmen excavated a hilltop and carved out a pillared hall almost 100 feet square. On entering this sanctuary, the visitor peers through rows of heavy columns. As one's eyes adjust to the dark, the gigantic forms of three heads (FIG. **11-15**) begin to emerge from the end wall. The heads represent Siva as Mahadeva, Lord of Lords and incarnation of the forces of creation, preservation, and destruction. The concept of power is immediately transmitted by the sheer size of the heads, which rise nearly 17 feet from the floor, dwarfing the onlooker.

The trinity of colossal faces is placed so as to receive light from all of the different entrances of the cave, creating the awe-inspiring illusion that the forms rise mysteriously out of the shapeless darkness of the background. Each of the three faces expresses a different aspect of the eternal. The center one, neither harsh nor compassionate, looks beyond humanity in the supreme indifference of eternal meditation. The other two faces—one soft and gentle, one angry and fearsome—speak of the sequence of birth and destruction that can be ended only by union with the godhead. The assurance of the period is manifest in the guardians of the shrine, who stand tall and relaxed. On the surrounding walls, deeply cut panels illustrating the legends of Siva carry on the robust and sensuous traditions of Harappa (FIG. 11-1) and Karli (FIG. 11-9).

During the fourth, fifth, and sixth centuries, Buddhism, in turn, borrowed heavily from Hindu doctrine. Elaborate rituals and incantations, inspired by similar Hindu practices, replaced the simple activities the Buddha had prescribed. Esoteric sects sprouted, and the popular Hindu worship of Sakti, the female power of the deity, was adapted for Buddhist usage. A sixth-century relief in a Buddhist cave temple at Aurangabad (FIG. **11-16**) depicts worship of the Buddha through music and dance in a scene that might have been taken from a Hindu temple; the volatile and rapturous figures of the musicians and the dancer represent an Indian, rather than Buddhist, way of life. With little to distinguish it from Hinduism, Buddhism and its art gradually withered and, within a few centuries, virtually disappeared.

In the same burst of creativity that produced cave temples, other innovative Hindu architects were building the first structural temples with stone. One

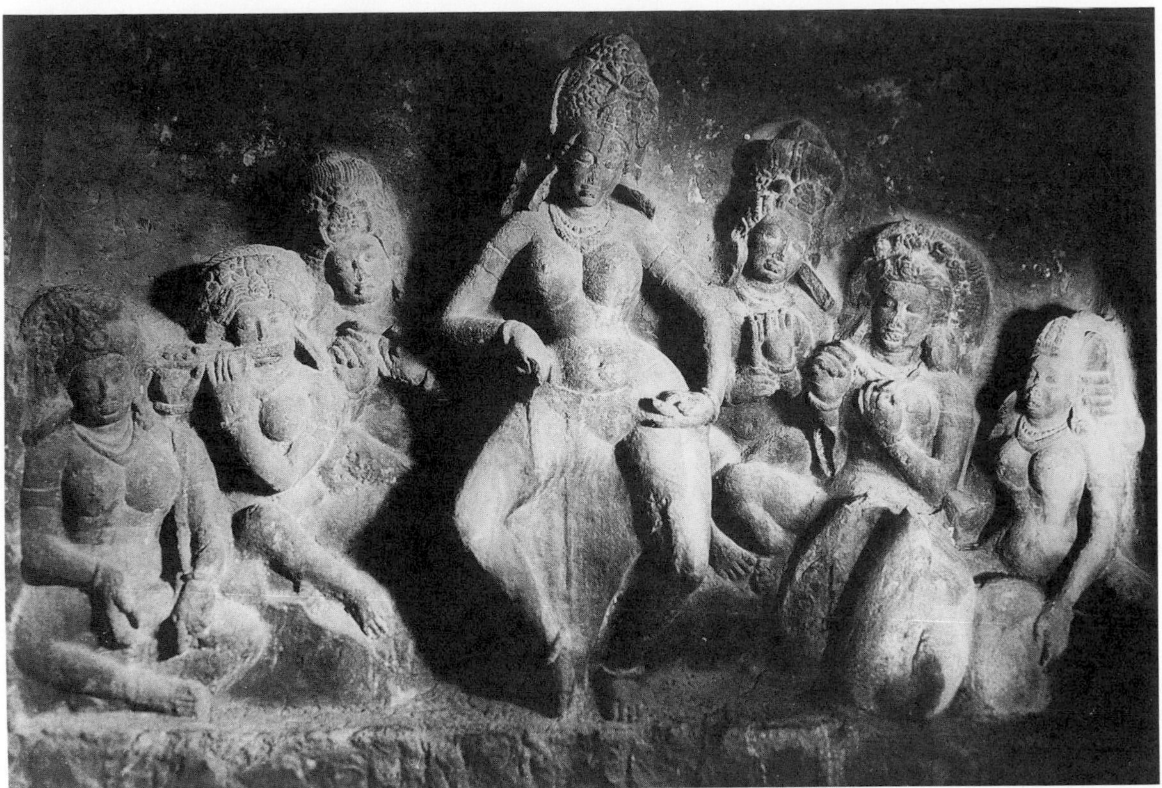

11-16 Relief with dancers and musicians, Aurangabad, India, sixth century.

of the earliest that remains is the Vishnu temple built in the early sixth century during the Gupta period (320–*c.* 600) at Deogarh in north central India (FIG. **11-17**). All later developments of the Hindu temple were in many ways elaborations on the principles embodied in Deogarh.

The Hindu temple is not a hall for congregational worship; it is the residence of the god. The basic requirement is a cubic cella for the cult image or symbol. This most holy of places, called the *garbha griha,* or womb chamber, has thick walls and a heavy ceiling to protect the deity. A doorway through which the devotee may enter is the only other architectural necessity. Like the stupa, the temple has other meanings, for it is also the symbol of the *purusha,* or primordial human being. In addition, in its plan, it is a *mandala,* or magic diagram of the cosmos, and its proportions are based on modules that have magical reference. Thus, the temple itself is a symbol to be observed from the exterior. Contemporary Western theories of architecture, defining it as the art or science that deals with the space-enclosing forms within which people carry on their activities, do not apply to the Hindu temple, which is to be appreciated as sculpture rather than as architecture.

In early temples, such as Deogarh, decoration is limited and restrained, and the form is a simple cube that originally was surmounted by a tower *(sikhara).*

11-17 Vishnu Temple (side view), Deogarh, India, early sixth century.

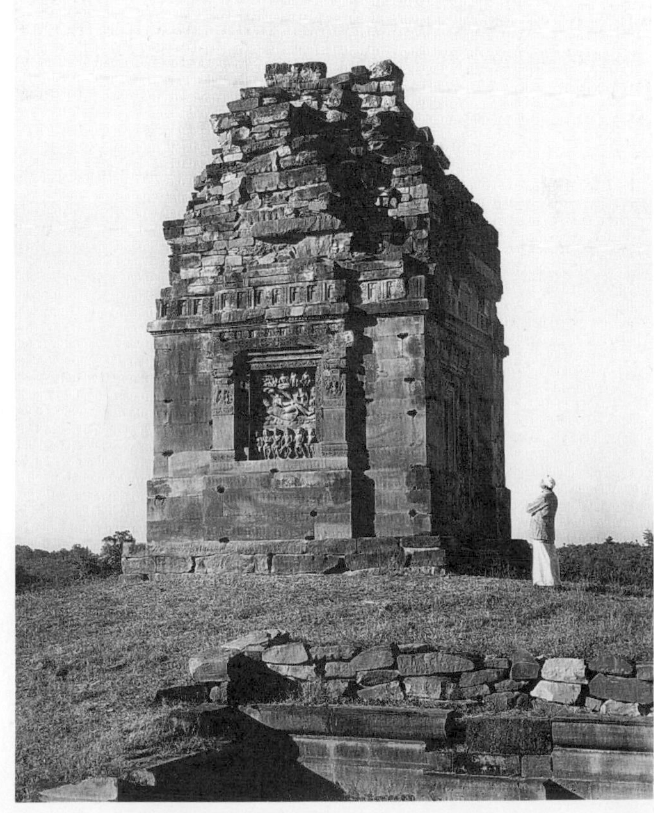

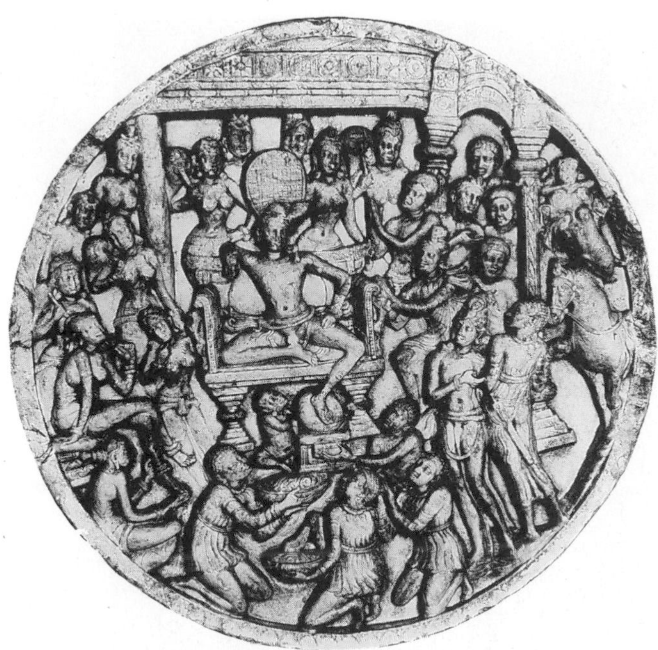

11-18 Relief from stupa, from Amaravati, India, second century. Musée Guimet, Paris.

All of the walls except the entrance wall are solid but include sculptured panels, some like false doorways, framed in the walls. On these panels, in scenes from Hindu mythology, relaxed and supple figures carry on the Indian tradition of ease and poise.

In striking contrast to the robust plasticity of northern sculpture are the carvings on the Buddhist monuments situated at the mouth of the Kistna River on the Bay of Bengal. The major sites, in chronological order (dating roughly from the second century B.C. to the third century A.D.), are Jaggayyapeta, Amaravati, and Nagarjunakonda. Little remains from the first, but many reliefs from the other two sites are extant. These are ornamented elaborately and filled with hosts of figures that, particularly in the later Amaravati scenes (FIG. **11-18**), are slender and graceful, rendered almost as if by brush.

The record of Indian art farther to the south begins with a cave temple at Mandagadippattu (early seventh century) that was commissioned by the first great ruler of the Pallavas, Mahendravarman I, and dedicated to the Hindu trinity. Mahendravarman soon was surpassed by his immediate successors at Mahabalipuram, on the coast not far from the city of Madras. Here, near a miscellany of monuments that includes cave shrines, carved cliff sides, and a masonry temple, a unique group of five, small, freestanding temples, known as *rathas* (FIG. **11-19**), were sculptured, perhaps as architectural models, from some of the huge boulders that litter the area. One of the temples is apsidal; another has a long, vaulted shape with a barrel roof, the ends of which reproduce the bentwood curves of the ancient chaitya halls. The smallest is a square shrine with a pyramidal roof that mimics in stone the thatch of primitive shrines as they appear in reliefs on the rails of early stupas. The Dharmaraja, largest of the rathas, has a simple cubic cella, as at Deogarh, but the *vimana* (composed of the garbha griha and the sikhara) ascends, in typical southern style, in pronounced tiers of cornices deco-

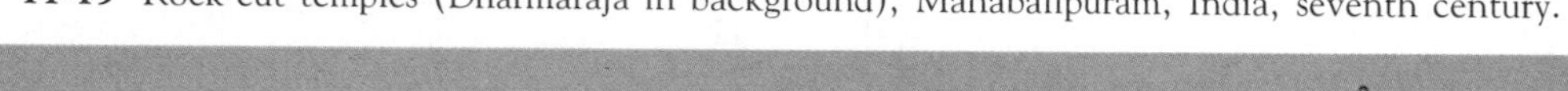

11-19 Rock-cut temples (Dharmaraja in background), Mahabalipuram, India, seventh century.

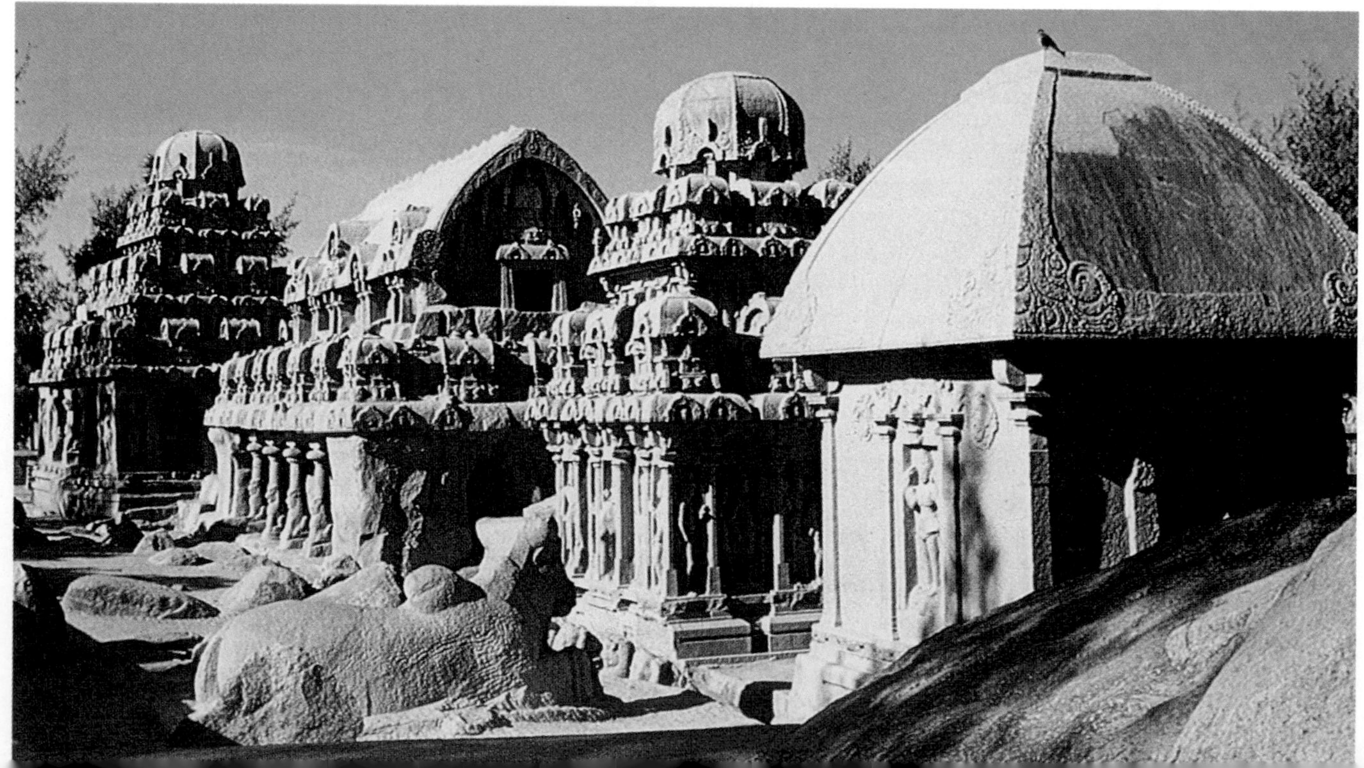

rated with miniature shrines (foreground, FIG. 11-19). Niches spaced along the walls contain figures of the major deities; these niches will become a regular feature of the southern temple.

The southern Indian temple was developed further at the beginning of the eighth century in nearby Kanchipuram and by the artists of the Chalukya dynasty in the Virupaksha Temple (*c.* 740) at Pattadakal near Badami. The vimana here is related to the Dharmaraja ratha, but porches and an assembly hall *(mandapa)* have been added in front of the garbha griha. The interior of this shrine consists of a dimly lighted ambulatory surrounding the cella, which is entered through a large, columned assembly hall, and two subsidiary shrines. Light that enters the mandapa through narrow windows and two projecting porches plays over elaborate relief carvings on the columns and walls. The devotee, who entered through an open porch, walked from the blazing light through a cool, softly lighted, and spacious area before reaching, in darkness, the enigma of the garbha griha itself. There, in the austere chamber, the worshiper came face to face with the barely visible symbol of the deity. The sense of mystery offered the worshiper was as satisfying to the Hindu as the soaring exultation of the Gothic cathedral was to the Christian.

In the following few centuries, a different architectural order evolved in northern India, characterized by a smoother integration of halls and porches with the main shrine and tower and by an increased vertical emphasis in all parts. The problem of creating a unified exterior was solved in separate stages. The first step, adding height to the mandapa to mitigate the disparity between the vertical vimana and the horizontal mandapa, is illustrated in the immense Kailasa Temple (*c.* 750), an extraordinary rock-cut monument at Ellora. A second step is exemplified by the lovely Muktesvar Temple at Bhuvanesvar, Orissa (FIG. **11-20**), where a high, pyramidal superstructure over the mandapa brought disproportionately horizontal elements into complete harmony with the tall sikhara. This evolution culminated during the tenth and eleventh centuries at Khajuraho (FIG. **11-21**) in north central India. There, the temples, numbering over twenty, became larger, more elaborate, and, by virtue of their high plinths, even more prominent. Two and sometimes three mandapa were put before the cella. The greatest esthetic advance was made in the roofs of the mandapa and their pyramidal eaves, which unite with the sikhara to create a rapid and torrential sequence of cascading forms. The lower sections of the building, bound by a series of horizontal registers, are laden with sculptured deities, legends, and erotic scenes. Elongated figures often are set in complex, twisting poses that emphasize the

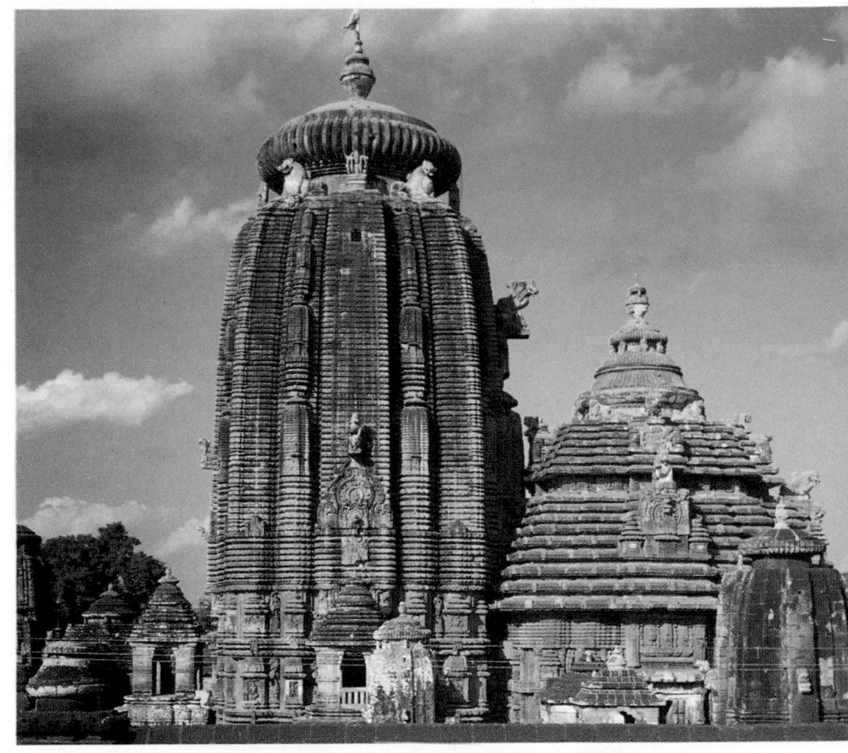

11-20 Muktesvar Temple, Bhuvanesvar, India, *c.* 950.

11-21 Visvanatha Temple, Khajuraho, India, *c.* 1000.

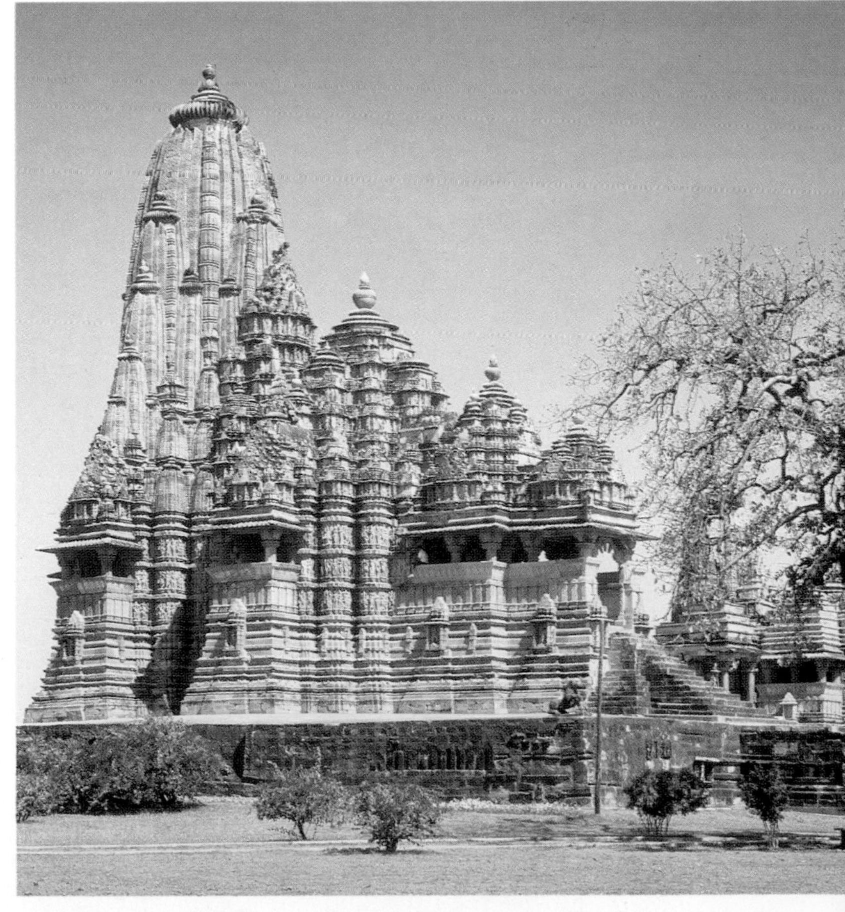

sinuously curved lines of the body. Although the rendering of living forms has become less natural and at times even disturbingly contorted, the sculptures function superbly in leading the eye around the shifting planes of the sides of the temple.

In the year 1000, the first of a series of Moslem invasions sounded the knell of Hindu architecture in northern India. But in the south—first under the Chola kingdom (846–1173) and later under the Hoysala (1022–1342), the Vijayanagar (1336–1565), and the Nayak (1420–1736) dynasties—sculpture and architecture continued to flourish.

Of particular beauty are the small, early Chola temples scattered throughout Tamil Nadu. Many are incomparable in their architectonic order, sensitive detail, and sculpture. A trend toward larger buildings, reflecting the imperial grandeur of the Chola kingdom, led to the great Brihadesvara Temple (*c.* 1000) of Thanjavur, which is 160 feet high and replete with architectural elements and figures. Many deities are represented on its walls, although fewer than at Khajuraho, and most appear in niches spaced with restraint at ordered intervals.

Bronze images were made to grace the shrines and to be carried in processions during important ceremonies. Some of the world's superb bronzes were produced in the Chola kingdom, where the figures of Siva as Nataraja, Lord of the Dance, reached a high point of quality in the tenth century. The Nataraja (*c.* 1000) at the Naltunai Isvaram Temple at Punjai, Tamil Nadu (FIG. **11-22**), shows the god, represented in an ideal human form, dancing vigorously within a flaming nimbus, one foot on the Demon of Ignorance. His flying locks terminate in rearing cobra heads and, on one side, support a tiny figure of the river goddess, Ganga. One of Siva's four hands sounds a drum, while, from another, a flame flashes. Dancing thus, the god periodically destroys the universe so that it may be reborn again. Exquisitely balanced, yet full of movement, this bronze is a triumph of three-dimensional sculpture and the art of bronze casting.

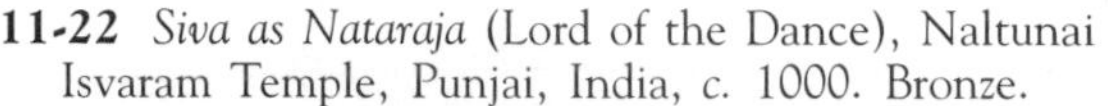

11-22 *Siva as Nataraja* (Lord of the Dance), Naltunai Isvaram Temple, Punjai, India, c. 1000. Bronze.

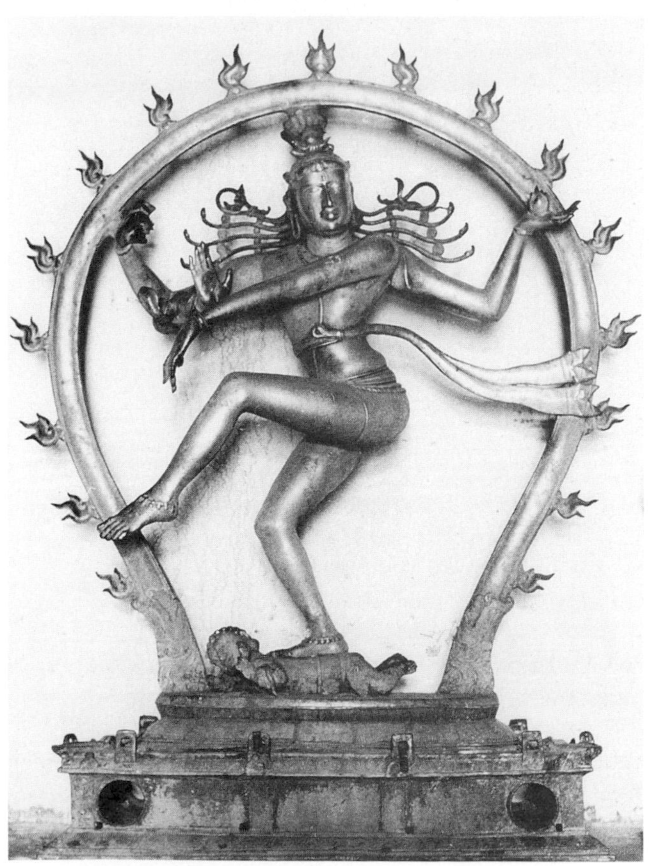

Enormous temple compounds were built around the nucleus of earlier temples. The Minakshi Temple at Madura and the Srirangam Temple at Tiruchirapalli eventually covered acres of ground. "Thousand-pillared" halls, built almost one beside the other, have the aspect of a continuous structure, interrupted only by courtyards and sacred water tanks for ritual bathing. Elaborate monolithic columns, carved with high- and low-relief figures, evoke a solemn mood, the stone sculpture having the effect of iron castings. The original walled enclosure came to be surrounded by other walls as the temple expanded, and the gateways *(gopuram)* at each of the four cardinal points grew progressively higher with each additional wall. The fully developed gopuram is multistoried and crowded with sculpture. Many gopurams are over 150 feet high, and for this reason they dominate the landscape of southern India.

The spread of Moslem domination gradually weakened the Indian tradition, even in the south. By the seventeenth century, the harmonious proportions of earlier figures had been lost, and even the metal castings had become inferior.

Painting

In India, the art of painting was probably as great as the art of sculpture but, unfortunately, less of it survives. The earliest traces are a few fragments in Cave X at Ajanta that date from approximately the first century B.C. Like the ornamentation on the toranas at Sanchi (FIG. 11-6), to which they are related in style, these fragments illustrate scenes from the past lives of the Buddha.

In Caves I and XVII at Ajanta, we find the next and most magnificent examples of Indian painting. These murals, dating from the fifth, sixth, and seventh centuries, embody all the clarity, dignity, and serenity of

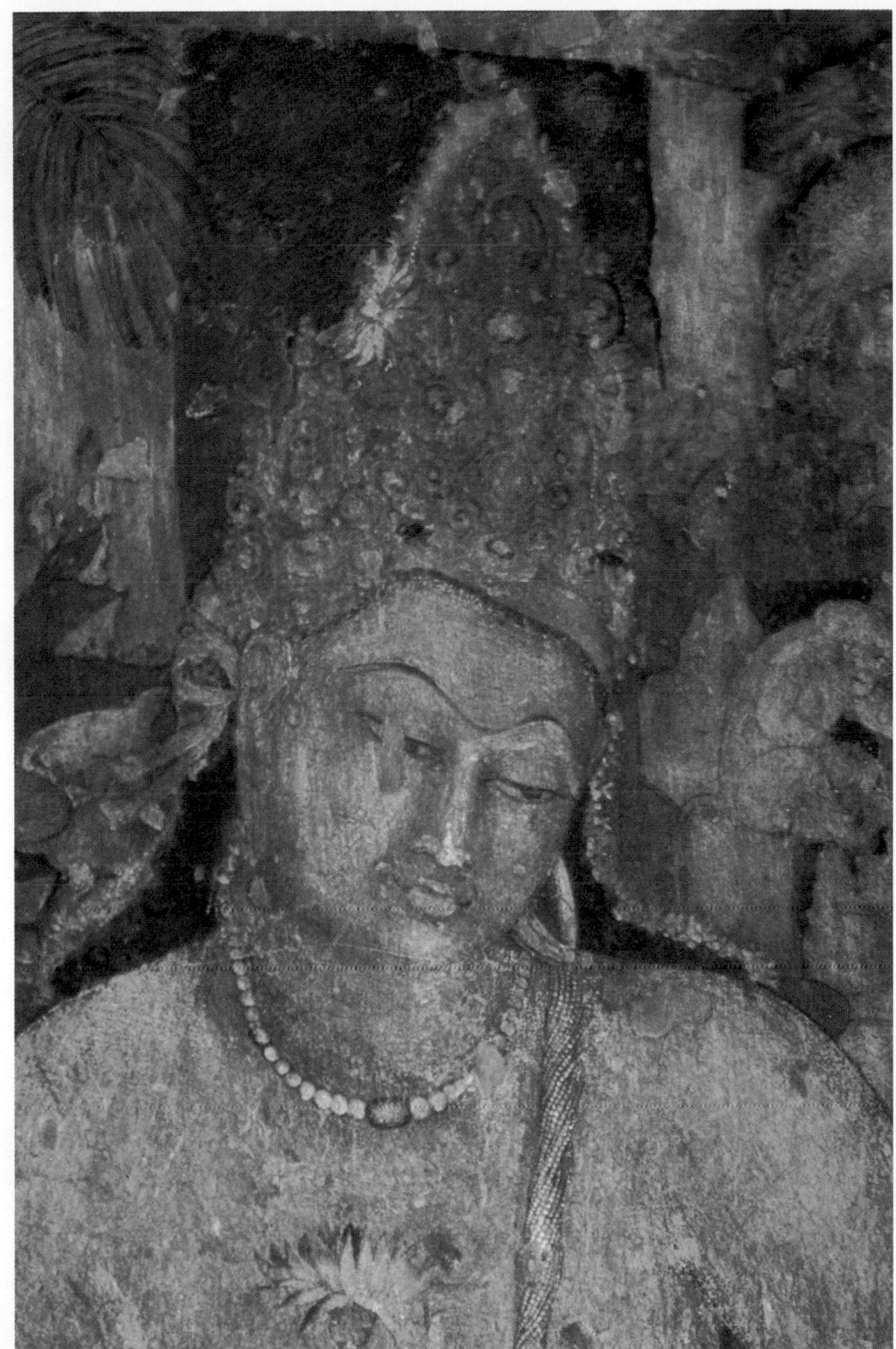

11-23 *Beautiful Bodhisattva Padmapani,* fresco from Cave I, Ajanta, India, c. 450–500.

Gupta art and must be ranked among the great paintings of the world. The *Beautiful Bodhisattva Padmapani* in Cave I (FIG. **11-23**) moves with the subtle grace of the Deogarh sculptures, while the glow of color imparts an even more spiritual presence. The Ajanta paintings, however, are more than the manifestations of Buddhist devotion. Their genrelike scenes and worldly figures, although illustrating Buddhist texts, reflect a sophisticated and courtly art.

The Ajanta painting tradition, in all its colorful vitality, was continued under the Chola rule, as witnessed by the paintings in the Brihadesvara Temple at Thanjavur. The dancing figures in these paintings, although drawn in the vivacious postures familiar in

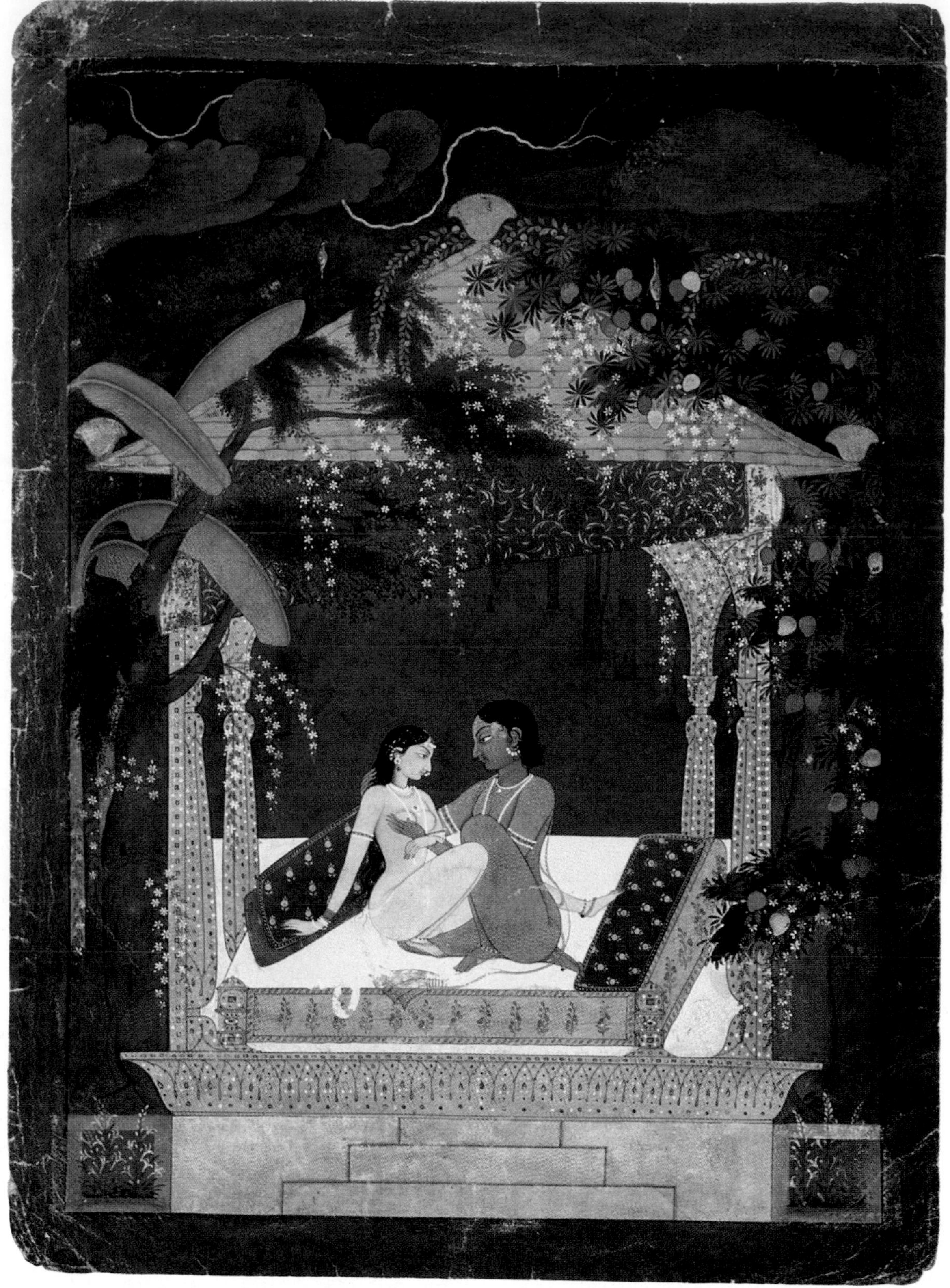

11-24 *Krishna and Radha in a Pavilion,* from Punjab, c. 1760. Opaque watercolor on paper, $11\frac{1}{8}'' \times 7\frac{3}{4}''$. National Museum, New Delhi.

the Chola bronzes, retain some of the modeling and the soft tonality of the Gupta style.

The Moslem conquests inhibited the evolution of Hindu sculpture and architecture in northern India after the thirteenth century but revitalized the art of painting. In the sixteenth century, especially under the reign of Akbar, who was sympathetic to Hinduism and Christianity as well as Islam, traditional Indian painters were exposed to the delicate and conventionalized miniatures of the great Persian artists. During the seventeenth and eighteenth centuries, painting responded vigorously to the interplay between foreign modes at the imperial capital and autochthonous idioms at isolated feudal courts.

Many delightful hybrids and innovations resulted—some delicate and lyrical, as at Bundi and Kishangarh (Rajasthan); some stark and bold, as at Basohli in the Himalayan foothills. Among others, the hill schools in Guler and Kangra developed their own idioms, emphasizing such subjects as elegant figures in serene landscapes, portraits of rulers, interpretations of musical modes *(ragamalas),* and religious themes. The joyous exuberance of these new styles was particularly well suited to newer Hindu cults, which were dedicated to the worship of Krishna, an avatar of Vishnu, whose praises were sung in the erotic poetry of the *Gita-Govinda.* The love of the lush and the sensuous, which the earliest Indian sculptures had expressed, thus found an entirely new medium in exquisitely colored, often tender paintings like the miniature *Krishna and Radha in a Pavilion* (FIG. **11-24**). Krishna, the "Blue God," gently caresses his favorite shepherdess, Radha. They are seated within a golden pavilion hung with a rich scarlet textile and wreathed with flowering vines and succulent mangoes. Above the pavilion a lightning bolt crackles in the dark heavens, symbolizing the physical and spiritual energy that unites the pair. The firm yet gentle delineation describes a myriad of colored shapes with perfect fidelity and evenness, integrating the luxuriant variety of all elements of the design into coherent unity. Yet, such is the cunning of the designer that the figures of the narrative are adroitly centered and not absorbed into the pattern (compare FIG. 11-24 with FIG. 7-85). In this masterful depiction, the erotic theme is rarified into a suprasensual ideal of the mutual and enduring affection between man and woman. At the same time, the gorgeously colored accessories and the sinuously curved and supple bodies of the young lovers pay homage to the substances and rhythms of material nature as the source of love and pleasure. The last native masterpieces of Indian art, flourishing in the courts of the art-loving magnates of the Punjab, are among the world's supreme exemplars of amorous vision, rendered with delicacy and subtlety, sweetness and grace.

THE SPREAD OF INDIAN ART

The vigorous culture that generated the great achievements of art in India overflowed its borders. The great tide of Buddhism in the early centuries of the Christian era carried Mahayana beliefs and Gandhara-Mathura art through Afghanistan, across the desert trade routes of Turkestan into China, and eventually into Japan.

The path of Hinayana Buddhism (see page 431), which was opened in the third century B.C. by the son of the emperor Asoka, led in another direction—south from Amaravati across the straits to Sri Lanka (formerly Ceylon). From that time on, Sri Lanka became a "little India"; its arts were influenced first by Amaravati and then, successively, by the Guptas, the Pallavas, and the Cholas. The largest concentrations of art were at two royal centers: Anuradhapura (virtually an extension of Amaravati), where most of what remains is from the second and third centuries, and Polonnaruwa, best known for the colossal 46-foot-long sculpture of the expiring Buddha found there (FIG. **11-25**), which dates from the eleventh and twelfth centuries. Sri Lanka also is the site of many

11-25 *Buddha,* from Gal Vihara, near Polonnaruwa, Sri Lanka, eleventh and twelfth centuries. Stone, whole figure 46′ long.

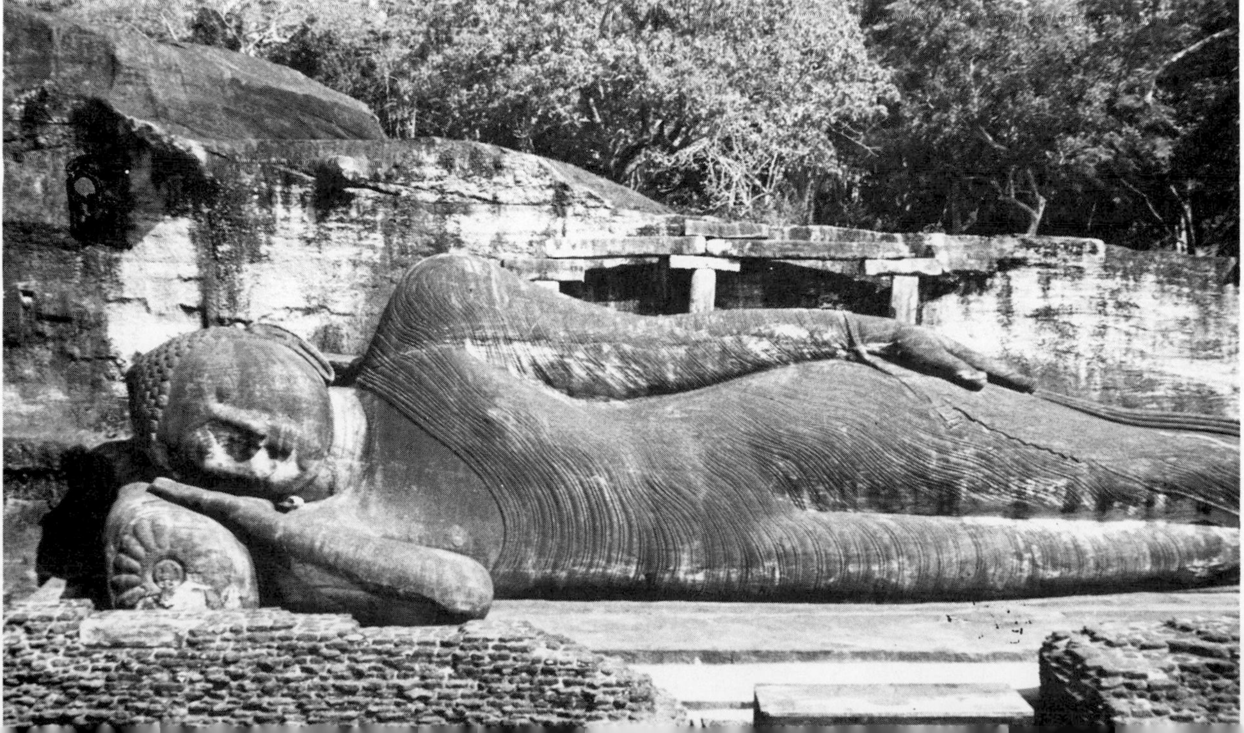

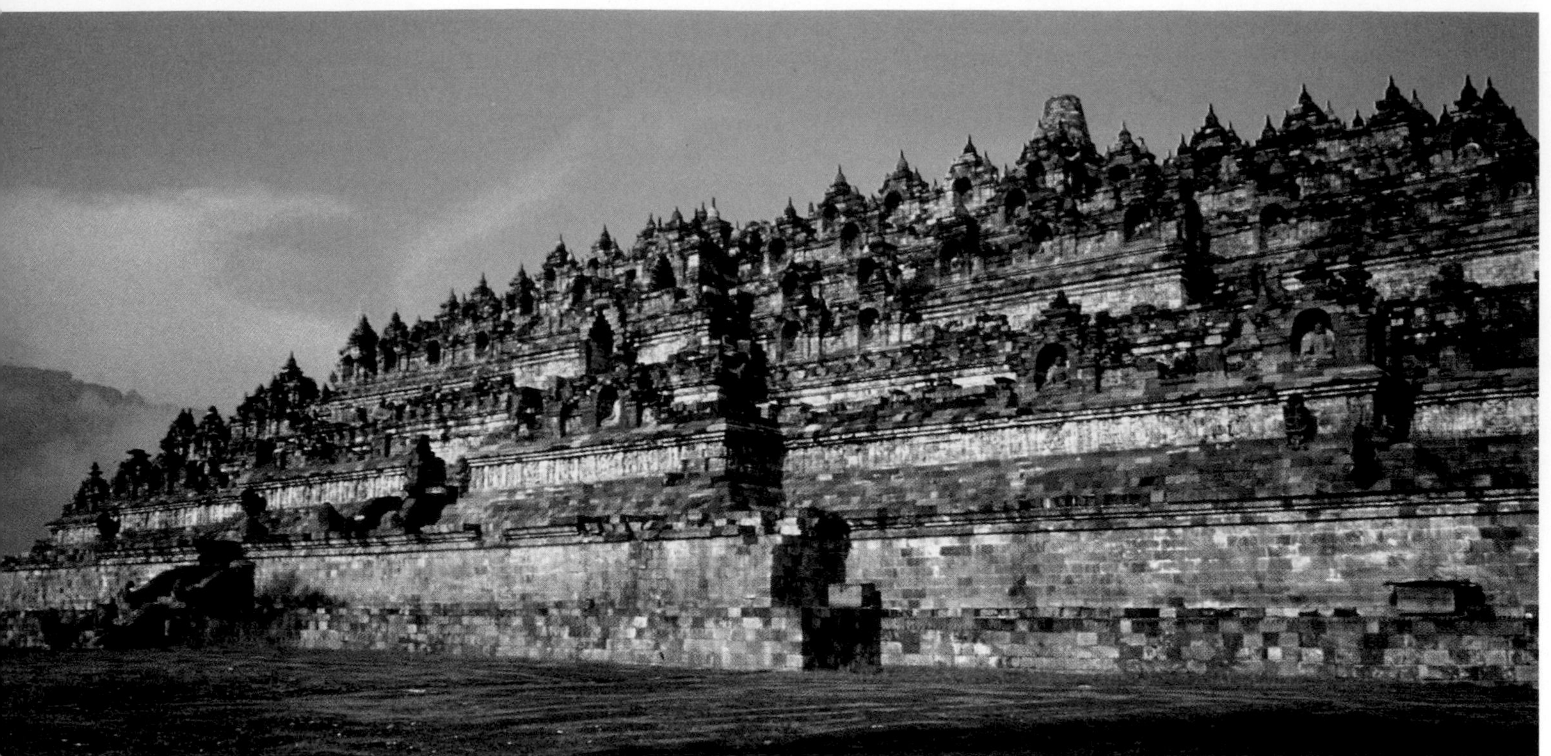

11-26 Stupa, Borobudur, Java, Indonesia, *c.* 800.

famous stupas that basically adhere to the Amaravati tradition but are simpler. Innovative carvings of guardian figures on stelae are placed at stupa entrances. Although some paintings have been discovered at Polonnaruwa, the earliest (fifth century) and most exquisite are the heavenly maidens on the escarpment of the fortress at Sigiriya.

By the fifth century, a series of emigrations from India began to bring the impact of Indian culture to Burma, Thailand, Cambodia, Sumatra, and Java. There, Buddhism and Hinduism continued their struggle for supremacy, with each introducing and fostering its arts. While Buddhism was under siege in India, one of its greatest monuments was rising at Borobudur in Java. There, around 800, a huge stupa (FIG. **11-26**), basically square and measuring over 400 feet across the base, was built of stone in nine terraced levels, with a central stairway in each of the four sides. The base and the first four tiers are rectilinear and signify the terrestrial world of sensation; the upper four tiers are circular and symbolize the heavens.

On the base, mostly covered by earth, 160 reliefs depict people trapped in the karmic cycle of life, death, and rebirth. Abundantly decorating the walls along the corridors of the next four tiers are over one thousand cautionary scenes from the *jatakas* and different *sutras* (scriptural accounts of the Buddha). But above, on the circular terraces, no narratives intrude. Here, ringing the pathways in solitary dignity, are latticed stupas, in each of which, barely visible, is a seated Buddha of gentle beauty (originally, seventy-two of these small stupas were constructed to crown the upper tiers). A larger stupa, rising at the pinnacle, may have enclosed a single Buddha, symbol of the Ultimate.

This architectural orchestration of sculptures is a mandala, a cosmic diagram perhaps representing the three spheres of Buddhist cosmology: the Human Sphere of Desire (didactic narratives crowded with figures and foliage); the Bodhisattva Sphere of Form; and the Buddha Sphere of Formlessness, where the simplicity and isolation of the individual stupas effect a serene release. The entire stupa has 505 Buddha figures. It is an eloquent statement of the Esoteric Buddhism that developed from Mahayana in Java.

The Buddhists in Java also erected *chandis* (temples). Two near the stupa of Borobudur that date to the same time period are Chandi Mendut and Chandi Pawon. Their dark sanctuaries, containing colossal Buddhist images, have the same awesome impact on the visitor as the shrines of the Buddhist cave temples in northwest India. Indeed, those caves, as well as other sacred sites throughout India, were well known to Indonesian pilgrims, whose exposure to Indian monuments and texts influenced their island culture.

The Hindus also were active in Java. On the Dieng Plateau, they erected single-celled Siva temples based on southern Indian Pallava models. At Prambanan in central Java, where structures and motifs were rap-

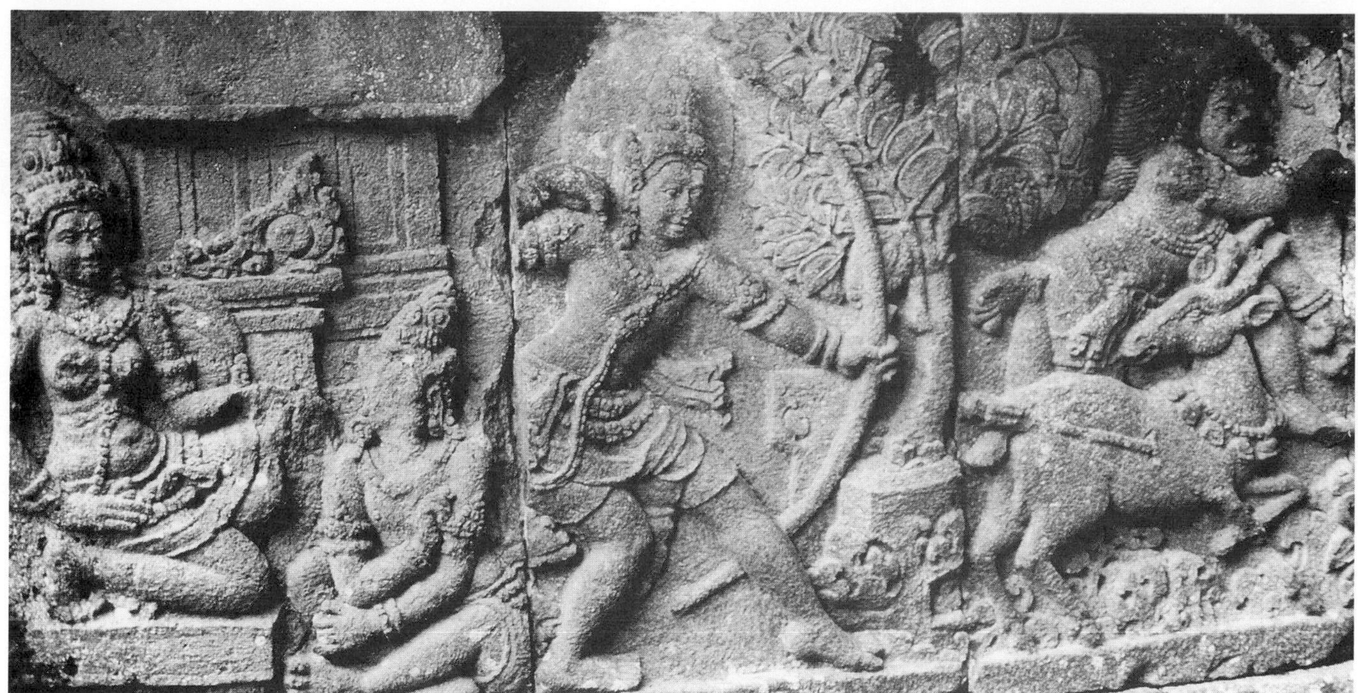

11-27 *Ramayana* scene, Siva temple, Lara Jonggrang, Java, Indonesia, ninth and tenth centuries.

idly Javanized, the tall and narrow Siva temple of Lara Jonggrang (ninth and tenth centuries), is characteristically a studied aggregate of piled-up stones, terraced peaks, and sanctuaries—a symbol of Mahameru, axis of the universe and mountain home of the gods. Reliefs on the temple balustrade illustrate the great Hindu epic *Ramayana*. Naturalistic yet decorative, these dramatic narratives (FIG. **11-27**) are a harmony of Indian forms and Javanese physical types.

The Indochinese mainland, in contact with India by the third century, also reacted to the stimuli of Indian culture. In Thailand, the softly modeled figures of bronze and stucco that were produced during the Dvaravati period (sixth to tenth centuries) were inspired by the Gupta style. During the pre-Angkor or Early Khmer period (fifth to ninth centuries), the Cambodians, too, borrowed the flowing planes and sensitive surfaces of Gupta. Around the seventh century, they also worked in the manner of the southern Indian Pallavas, as we can see in the figure of *Harihara* (a combined form of Siva and Vishnu) from Prasat Andet (FIG. **11-28**). The elegance of the Pallava prototypes at Mahabalipuram has been modified only slightly in this stone representation by the addition of a taut, almost springlike tension. Tall, broad shouldered, full-bodied, and slender legged, this is an idealized figure, more godly than human. We shall see later how the classical configuration of the pre-Angkor gods gradually was transformed into a distinctly more Cambodian type, with a broad face composed of full lips (doubly outlined), continuous eyebrows, and flat nose (FIG. 11-33).

11-28 *Harihara*, from Prasat Andet, Cambodia, seventh century. Stone, 6′ 3″ high. Musée Albert Sarraut, Phnom Penh.

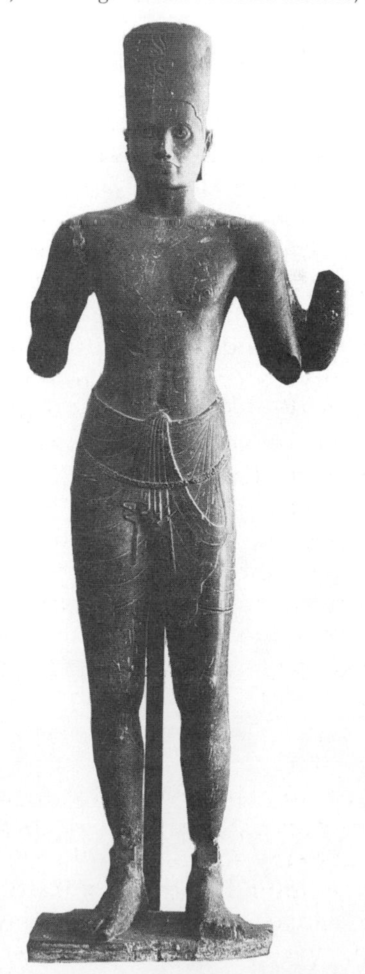

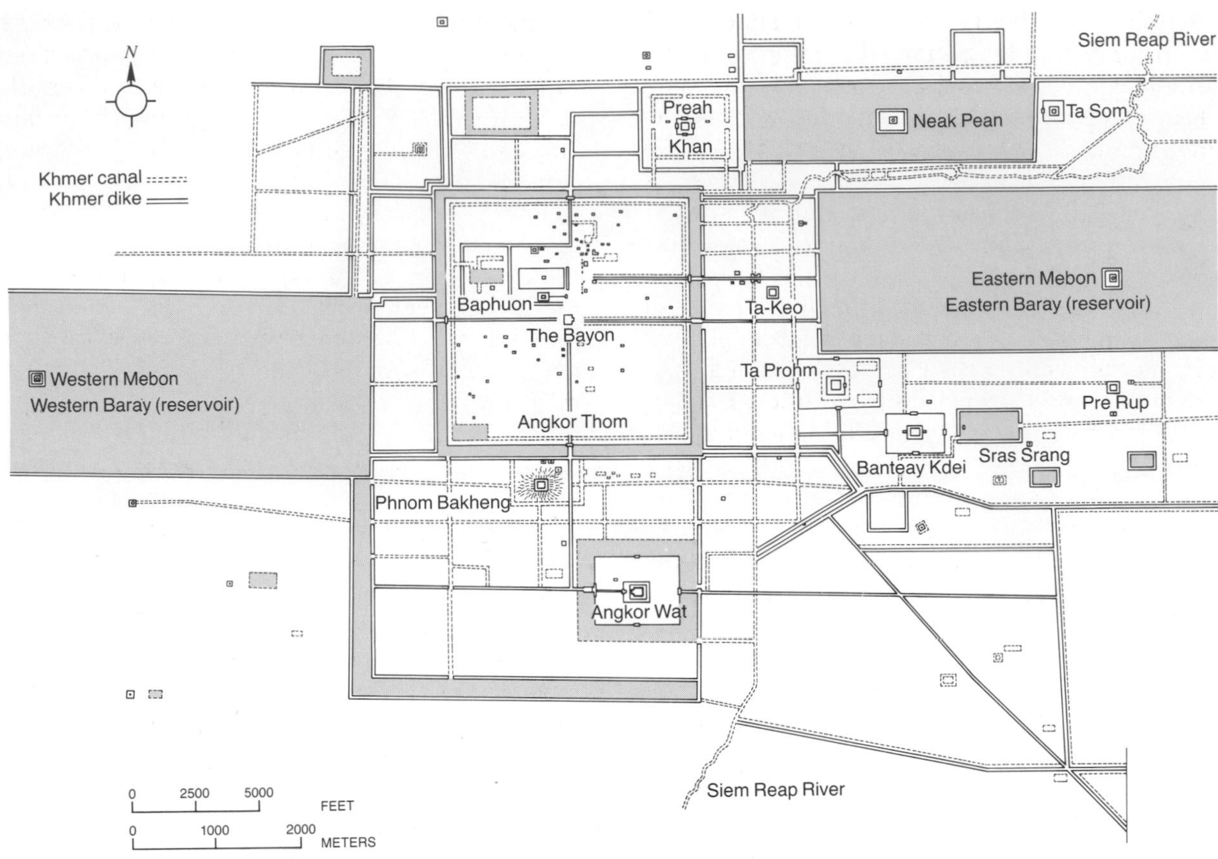

11-29 Overall plan of Angkor site, Cambodia, during the twelfth and thirteenth centuries.

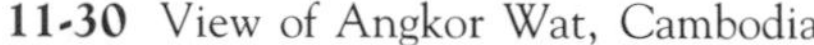

11-30 View of Angkor Wat, Cambodia.

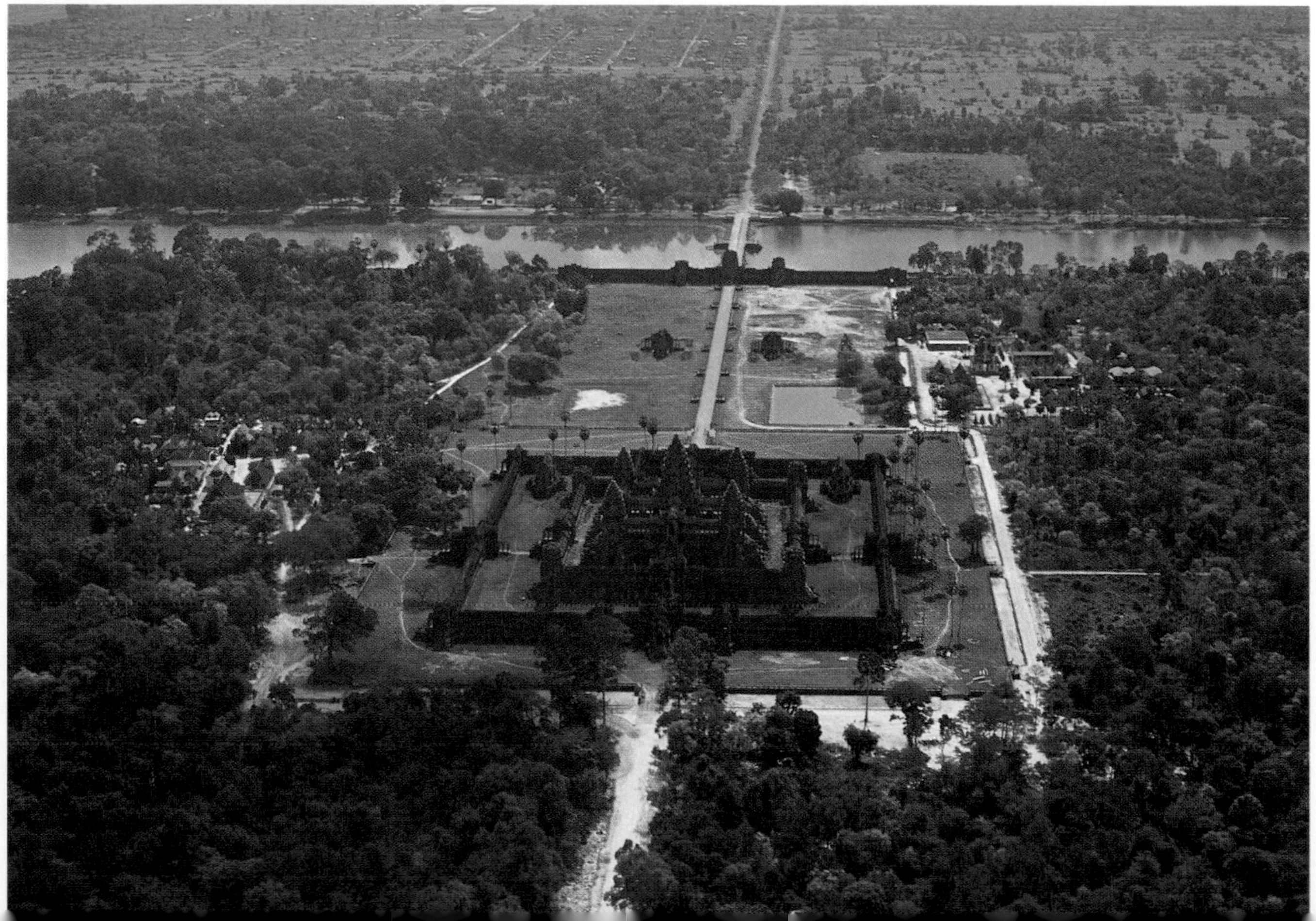

The temple in Cambodia was directly related to the Angkorian concept of kingship. Whereas in India the ideal king was the Universal Lord *(chakravartin)* who ruled through goodness, in Cambodia he was the god-king *(devaraja)* in life and after death. The temple the king built was dedicated to himself as the god. As the kings grew more powerful and ambitious, their temples were enlarged and the architectural and decorative elements multiplied.

At Angkor (meaning "the city" or "the capital" in the Khmer language), in the midst of a fertile plain, a dozen Khmer kings built their successive capitals between the ninth and the thirteenth centuries. Eventually, this agglomeration of capital cities spread across some seventy-five square miles and comprised many major brick and stone monuments amid a vast and intricate irrigation system (FIG. **11-29**). Only the temples were of stone or brick (materials reserved for the gods); other buildings, including the royal palaces, were constructed of wood and perished long ago. Laid out orthogonally, the network of canals, supported from large reservoirs *(barays)*, served as a means of transportation as well as of irrigation for the fertile rice fields that fed an estimated population of one million. The canals also interconnected and fed the moats around many of the major temples, including the two largest, Angkor Wat and Angkor Thom.

Angkor Wat (a *wat* is a Buddhist monastery; FIG. **11-30**) was originally a Hindu temple built between 1113 and 1150. Dedicated to Vishnu by its builder, King Suryavarman II, it is a physical representation of Hindu cosmology. The five central towers represent the peaks of Mount Meru, the Olympus of the Hindu gods and the center of the universe. The outer wall symbolizes the mountains at the edge of the world; the moat represents the oceans beyond. Recent study suggests that the layout also had astronomical significance and that the sections of the design were aligned to form a kind of solar calendar by which the summer and winter solstices and the spring and fall equinoxes could be fixed. Sight lines from vantage points within the temple complex can be constructed to show that the varying positions of the sun and moon throughout the year could be observed, predicted, and marked systematically. The dimensions of the complex are enormous. The moat is $2\frac{1}{2}$ miles long, and the circumference of the outer gallery measures half a mile and contains reliefs with literally thousands of figures representing the myths of Vishnu, Krishna, and Rama. The temples comprising this great complex are set at the corners of two concentric walls that gird the central shrine. Each of the temple towers repeats the form of the main spire, which rises in the center from a raised platform like the apex of a pyramid. The towers themselves resemble, in outline, the sikhara of northern Indian temples.

The relief carvings (FIG. **11-31**) express the Cambodian predilection for rhythmic design, the juxtaposition of two, three, or more identical figures, and the repetition of undulating contours. These graceful but stylized forms, thus locked together, move in a harmonious rhythm like their counterparts in Cambodian dance.

The Bayon at Angkor Thom (FIG. **11-32**), dating from the twelfth and thirteenth centuries, is, in many ways, the culmination of the Indian temple, particularly in its complete integration of sculpture and architecture. It also illustrates the syncretic relationship of Hinduism and Buddhism. The long, impressive approach to the Bayon, a Buddhist temple, is lined in

11-31 Dance relief, from Angkor Wat, twelfth century. Musée Guimet, Paris.

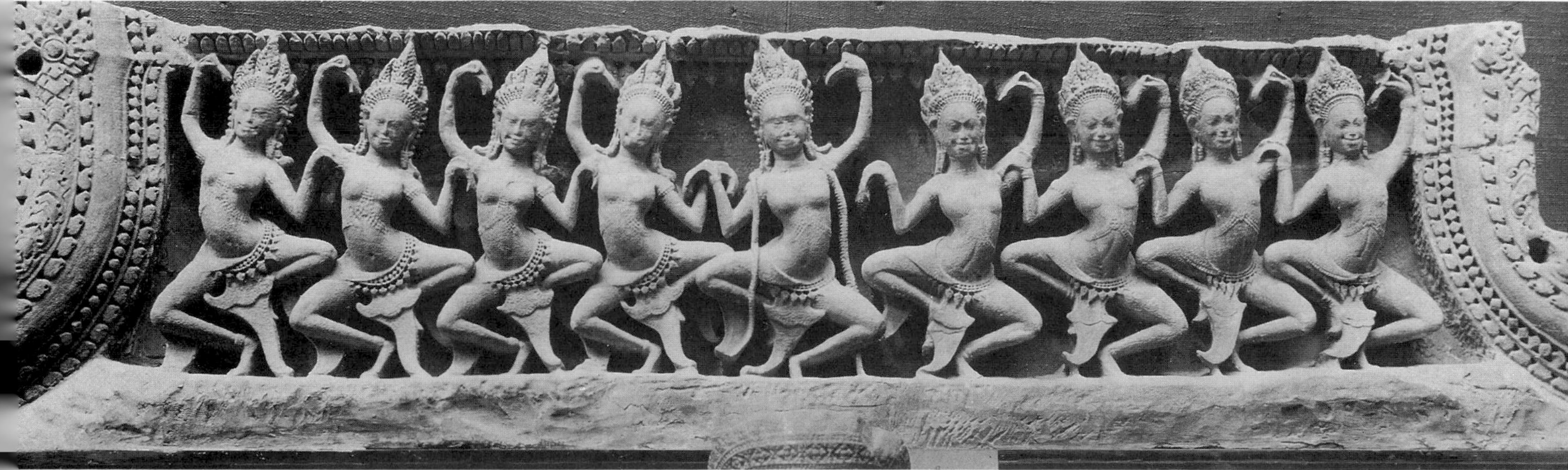

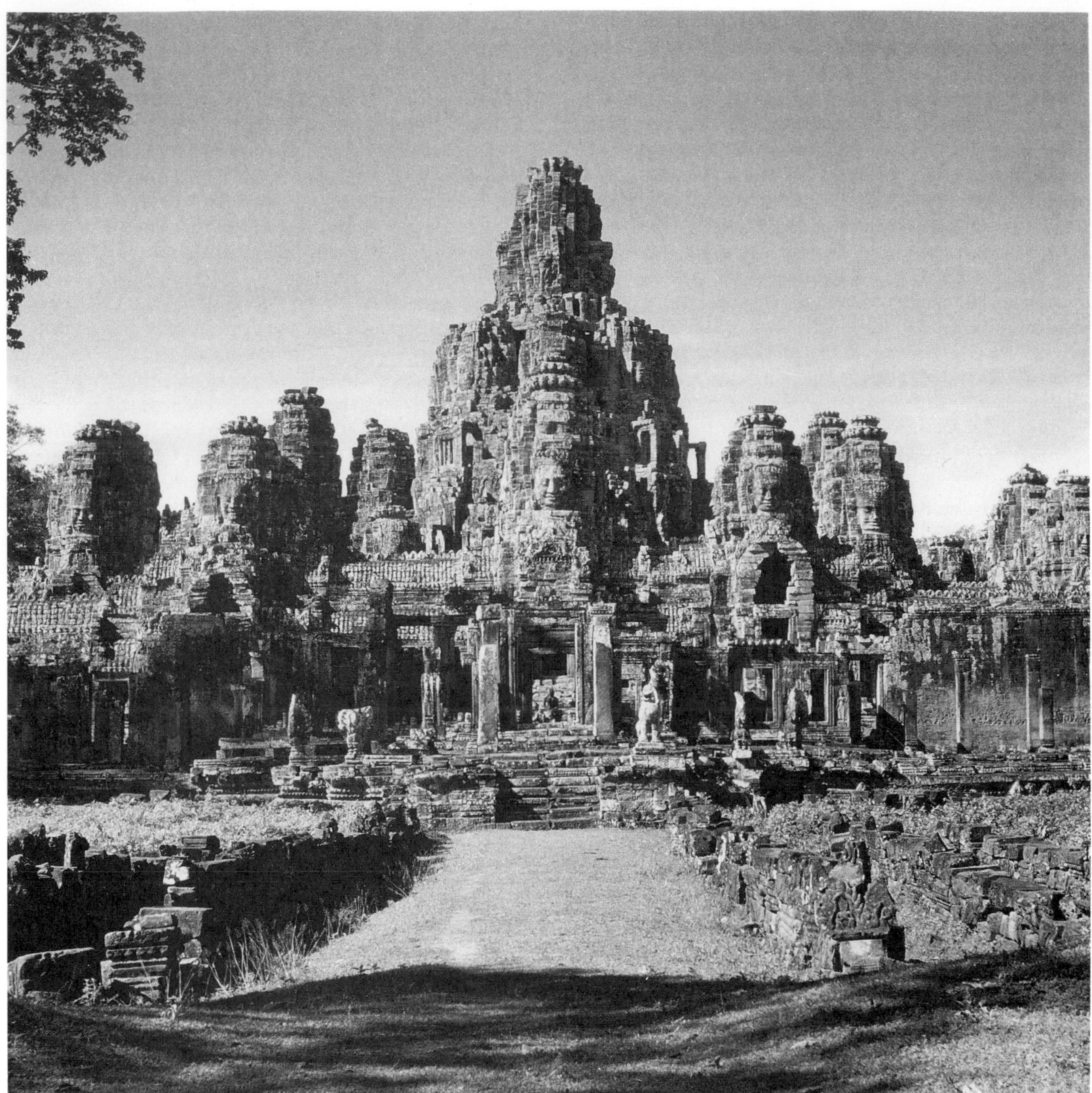

11-32 Bayon, Angkor Thom, Cambodia, twelfth and thirteenth centuries.

places with giant gods and demons holding onto the body of the serpent Vasuki in an enactment of a Hindu legend, the Churning of the Sea of Milk. But the uniqueness of the Bayon lies in the size and disposition of the colossal heads, one on each side of the square towers (FIG. **11-33**). These faces, their Cambodian features now fully stylized, smile enigmatically from a lofty height. They are the faces of the Bodhisattva Lokesvara, a god form of the reigning king and symbol of the inexhaustible powers of the Devaraja-Bodhisattva, which extend to all points of the compass. The Bayon was conceived as the world mountain. On it and around it, a luxuriance of decorative and narrative carvings intensifies its magic. The creative force that had been India left its last great record abroad in these compassionate faces of Lokesvara, surveying from eternity the legendary history carved on the walls below.

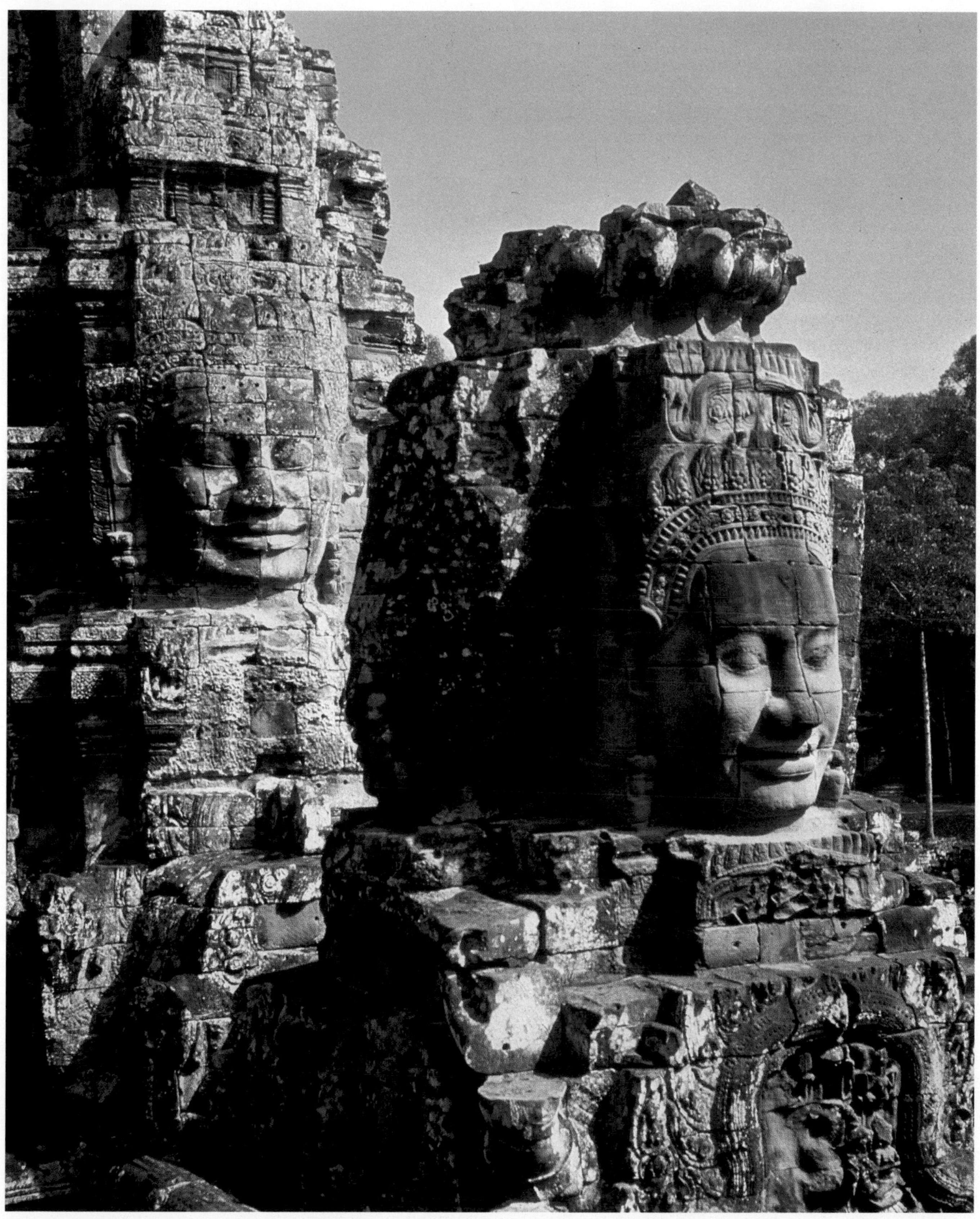

11-33 Tower of Bayon, Angkor Thom.

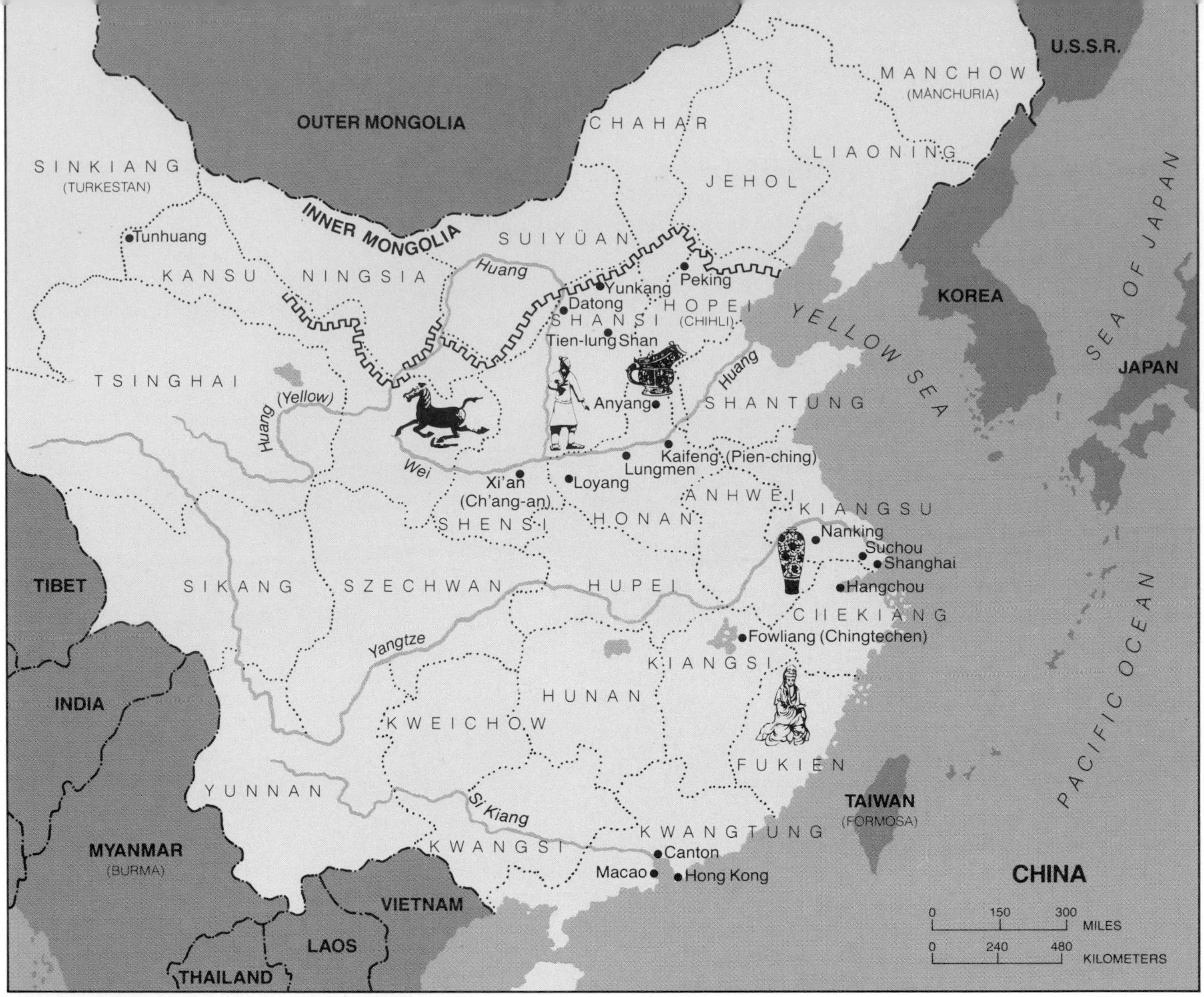

CHINA

U.S.S.R.
MANCHOW (MANCHURIA)
OUTER MONGOLIA
CHAHAR
LIAONING
SINKIANG (TURKESTAN)
JEHOL
SEA OF JAPAN
INNER MONGOLIA
SUIYÜAN
Tunhuang
KANSU
NINGSIA
Huang
Yunkang
Peking
Datong
HOPEI (CHIHLI)
SHANSI
KOREA
YELLOW SEA
Tien-lung Shan
TSINGHAI
Huang
JAPAN
Huang (Yellow)
Anyang
SHANTUNG
Kaifeng (Pien-ching)
Wei
Lungmen
Xi'an (Ch'ang-an)
Loyang
ANHWEI
KIANGSU
SHENSI
HONAN
Nanking
Suchou
Shanghai
TIBET
SIKANG
SZECHWAN
HUPEI
Hangchou
CHEKIANG
Yangtze
Fowliang (Chingtechen)
KIANGSI
INDIA
HUNAN
PACIFIC OCEAN
KWEICHOW
FUKIEN
YUNNAN
TAIWAN (FORMOSA)
Si Kiang
KWANGTUNG
MYANMAR (BURMA)
KWANGSI
Canton
Macao
Hong Kong
VIETNAM
LAOS
THAILAND

0 150 300 MILES
0 240 480 KILOMETERS

c. 1523 B.C.	1027	256	221	206	B.C. A.D.	A.D. 220	581
SHANG	CHOU		CH'IN	HAN		NORTHERN AND SOUTHERN DYNASTIES	SUI

Kuang
12th century B.C.

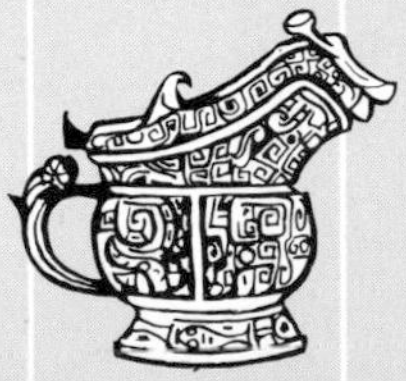

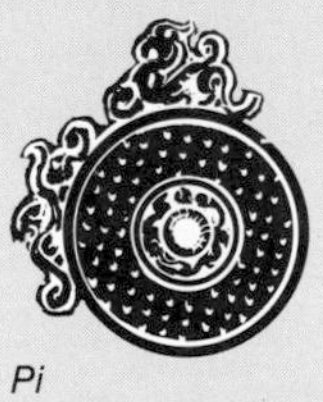

Pi
6th–3rd centuries B.C.

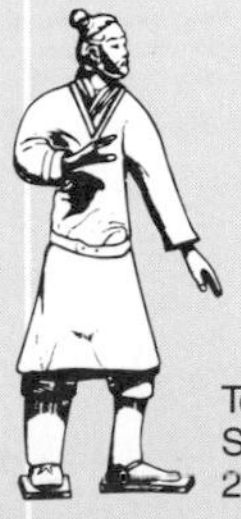

Tomb of Emperor Shih Huang Ti 221–206 B.C.

Flying Horse
2nd century

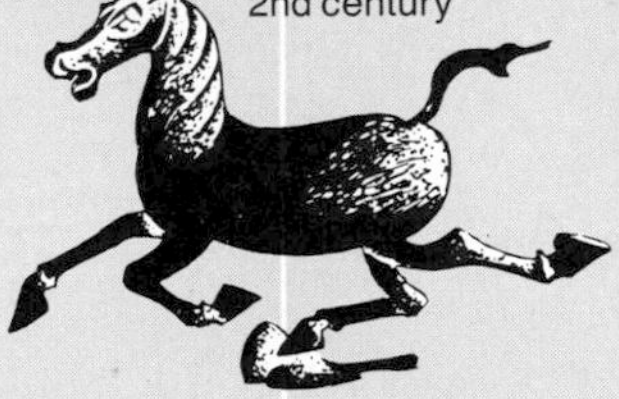

KU K'AI-CHIH
c. 344–406

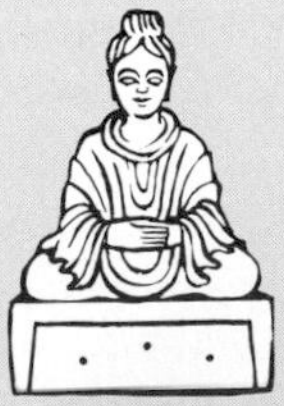

Sakyamuni Buddha 338

Shang dynasty overthrown by the Chou *c.* 1027 B.C.

Birth of Confucius *c.* 550

Shih Huang Ti *r.* 221–210

Great Wall begun

Introduction of Buddhism 1st century A.D.

Wei Tatars move court to Loyang 494

Hsieh Ho "Six Principles" late 5th century

Paradise Sects reach peak

12

THE ART OF CHINA

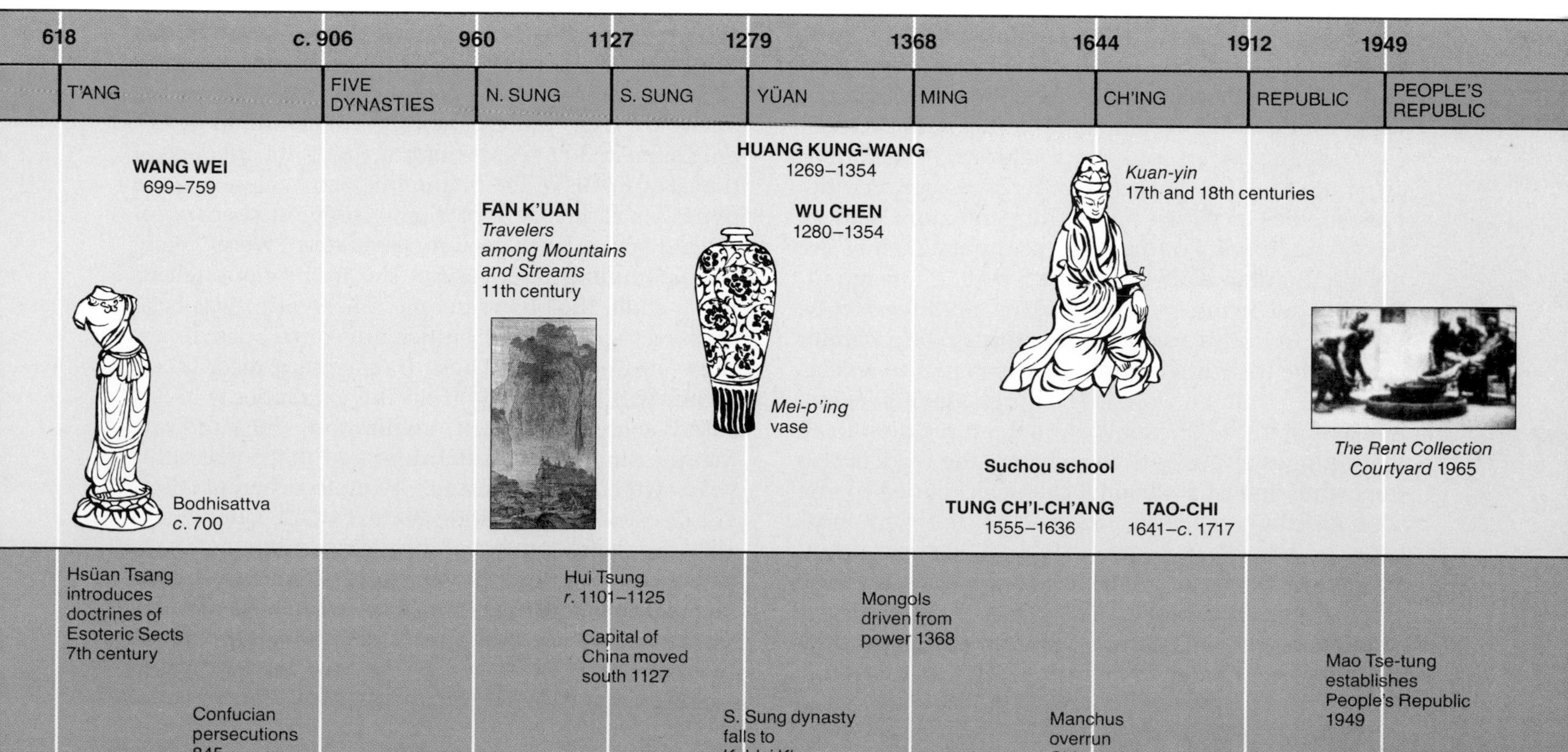

OF THE GREAT non-Western civilizations, that of China was the first to be known and appreciated in Europe. But only in the past half-century or so have the achievements of Chinese art and culture progressively been revealed and systematically been studied. Still, many in the West who now realize the extent and continuity of Chinese civilization and who recognize the striking beauty of its art are not fully aware of the complexity of either. Our task here is to identify the spirit of Chinese art and to trace, at least in outline, its major developments and styles.

China is a vast and topographically varied country about the size of the United States. Its political and cultural boundaries have spread, at times, to double that area, encompassing Tibet, Chinese Turkestan (Sinkiang), Mongolia, Manchuria, and parts of Korea. The country includes great stretches of sandy plains, mighty rivers, towering mountains, and fertile farmlands. North China, centered around Peking,* has a dry and moderate-to-cold climate, whereas south China is moist and tropical.

Although the spoken language of China varies so much as to be unrecognizable in different areas, the written language has remained uniform and intelligible in all parts of the country, permitting literary, philosophic, and religious traditions to be shared by people thousands of miles apart. Distinct regional styles of art did appear, especially in the early eras and during times of political fragmentation, but a broad cultural unity also permitted an easy flow of artistic ideas and influences throughout China.

The primarily expressive function of Chinese painting during the last millennium gradually has been made more comprehensible to the Western mind, partly by developments in the modern art of the West. Many of the fundamental differences between Chinese secular art and the traditional, premodern art of the West are based on differences between the philosophies of nature and of human nature held by the two cultures. For the Chinese, human beings are not dominant in nature; they are a part of it, responding, like all living creatures, to its rhythms. To be happy is to live in accord with nature; to be a painter is to be the instrument through which nature reveals itself. The painter's work is an expression of personal immersion in the flow of life and of attunement to all that changes and grows; in so being, the work is also the expression of a personal character refined by the contemplation of nature. Because nature is not measured and classified according to space and time, Chinese painters do not frame it off in perspective boxes with colors scaled in light and shade. They do not attempt to duplicate and fix natural appearances by such means. The asymmetry of growing things, the ceaseless and random movements of nature, the infinity of cosmic events—these forbid all enframements, rigid regularities, beginnings and ends. Appearance is transformed by the artist's passage through it. Each artist becomes part of the total expression of the art being produced, just as the art is the total expression of one's experience of nature.

This philosophical attitude of the Chinese toward secular painting can be seen even in the artists' almost ritualistic preparation of their medium, their materials. The best ink, for instance, was derived from soot or lampblack mixed with animal glue and pulverized clay, oyster shells or powdered jade, and various fragrances. From these ingredients, each of which had symbolic as well as physical properties, an ink stick (often carved) was formed that was treasured by the artist.

SHANG DYNASTY

A series of Neolithic cultures characterized by a variety of painted wares date back to the fourth millennium B.C. According to traditional Chinese history, the fourth millennium would have been the period of the Hsia. Although the Hsia state is still a matter of legend, the remains of a considerable kingdom, discovered within the last sixty years, have confirmed the existence of the Shang dynasty. As late as 1928, many scholars doubted the existence of the Shang dynasty, but excavations at Anyang in northern China in that year brought to light not only one of the last capitals of the Shang but also evidence of the dynasty's earlier development. Large numbers of inscribed bones, once used for divination, were among the astounding discoveries. The inscriptions tell us much about the Shang people. Their script was basically pictographic but sufficiently developed to express abstract ideas. These fragmentary records, together with other finds from the excavations, reveal an advanced, if barbaric, civilization. They indicate that the king was a feudal ruler and that some of his wives were also his vassals, living in different cities. Warfare with neighboring states was frequent, and all cities were protected by surrounding walls of pounded earth. Royal tombs were extensive, and the beheaded bodies of servants or captives accompanied deceased rulers to their graves. Chariots, trappings of horses buried alive, weapons, and ritual objects

*In the romanization system called *pinyin*, Peking presently is known as Beijing. This text, however, will use the place-name spellings more commonly recognized prior to the official 1979 adoption of the pinyin spellings for use in all texts in the Roman alphabet.

found in these graves help us to describe the art of this period.

Although sculpture in marble and small carvings in bone and jade exist, the great art of the Shang dynasty consisted of ritual bronze vessels. These bronzes were made in piece molds. They show a casting technique as advanced as any ever used in the East or West, indicating that this art must have been practiced for some centuries before the period of Anyang. The bronze vessels were intended to hold wine, water, grain, and meat for use in sacrificial rites. The major elements of decoration are zoomorphic, but usually the background and sometimes the animals themselves are covered with round or squared spirals. Conventions, which obviously evolved over a long period, rigidly governed the stylistic representation of animals, so that images or symbols often are involved and difficult to decipher. A major zoomorphic motif is that of an animal divided in half lengthwise, with the two halves spread out on the vessel body in a bilaterally symmetrical design. The two head parts, meeting in the center, often also can be read as a complete frontal animal mask with vestigial bodies at both sides. Such ambiguity of design occurs frequently on Shang vessels, with fragmentary parts of bodies taking on a life of their own.

The covered libation vessel, or *kuang*, shown here (FIG. **12-1**) is decorated with just such an animal. In this complex design, the representation (on the vessel's side) may be of the eyes of a tiger and the horns of a ram. (On other such Shang vessels, the eyes may be those of a sheep and the horns those of a bull, water buffalo, or deer.) The front of the lid is formed of a horned animal; the rear depicts a horned head with a bird's beak in its mouth. Another horned head is on the handle. Fish, birds, elephants, rabbits, and more abstract, composite creatures swarm over the surface against a background of spirals. Specific combinations of such animal motifs may have defined certain concepts; for example, an animal or bird in the mouth of another animal may signify generation. The multiple designs and their enigmatic fields of spirals are integrated so closely with the form of the vessel that they are not merely an external embellishment but an integral part of the sculptural whole. The tense outline of the bronze compactly encloses the forces symbolized on its surface. These vessels were not only ritual containers but also, in their very form and decoration, a kind of sculptural icon or visualization of the early Chinese attitude toward the powers of nature.

12-1 *Kuang*, Shang dynasty, twelfth century B.C. Bronze, $6\frac{1}{2}''$ high. Smithsonian Institution, Freer Gallery of Art, Washington, D.C.

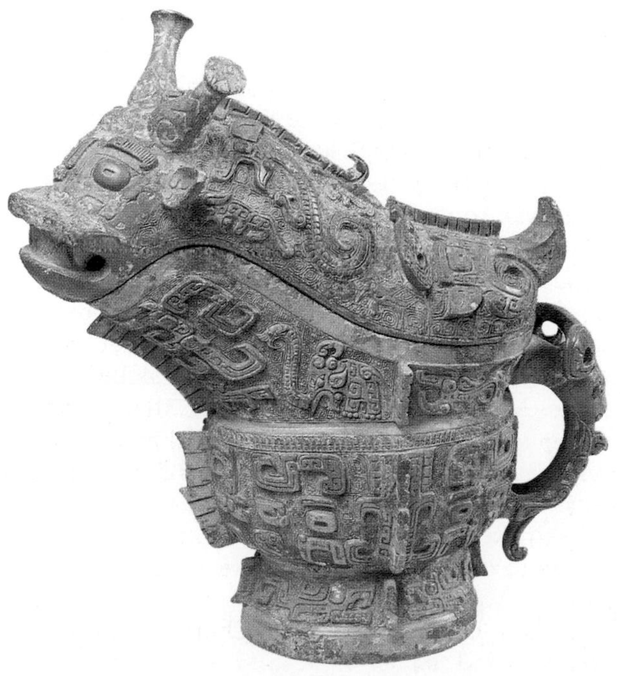

CHOU DYNASTY

About 1027 B.C., the Shang dynasty was overthrown by the Chou, whose dynasty endured until 256 B.C. Although the Chou were a more primitive people from the west, their culture apparently resembled that of the Shang.

The very earliest Chou bronzes are indistinguishable from those of the Shang. Indeed, they probably were made by the same craftsmen. But within a generation, the new and bolder spirit of the conquerors was imprinted unmistakably on the ritual vessels. Where the Shang silhouette had been suave and compact, the Chou (FIG. **12-2**) was explosive and dynamic. Gradually, this vitality diminished, and, in a hundred years, the shapes became more utilitarian and the zoomorphic designs more ornamental. The animal forms were distorted and twisted into interlaces until, by the beginning of the Late Chou period (600–256 B.C.), almost all evidence of the awesome original motifs was lost in an exuberance of playful rhythms over the surface of the bronzes. What once had expressed the power of magic and religion was transformed into a secular display of technical skill and fantasy.

During the sixth century B.C., the Chou Empire began to dissolve into a number of warring feudal states. As old values were forgotten, Confucius and other philosophers strove to analyze the troubles of

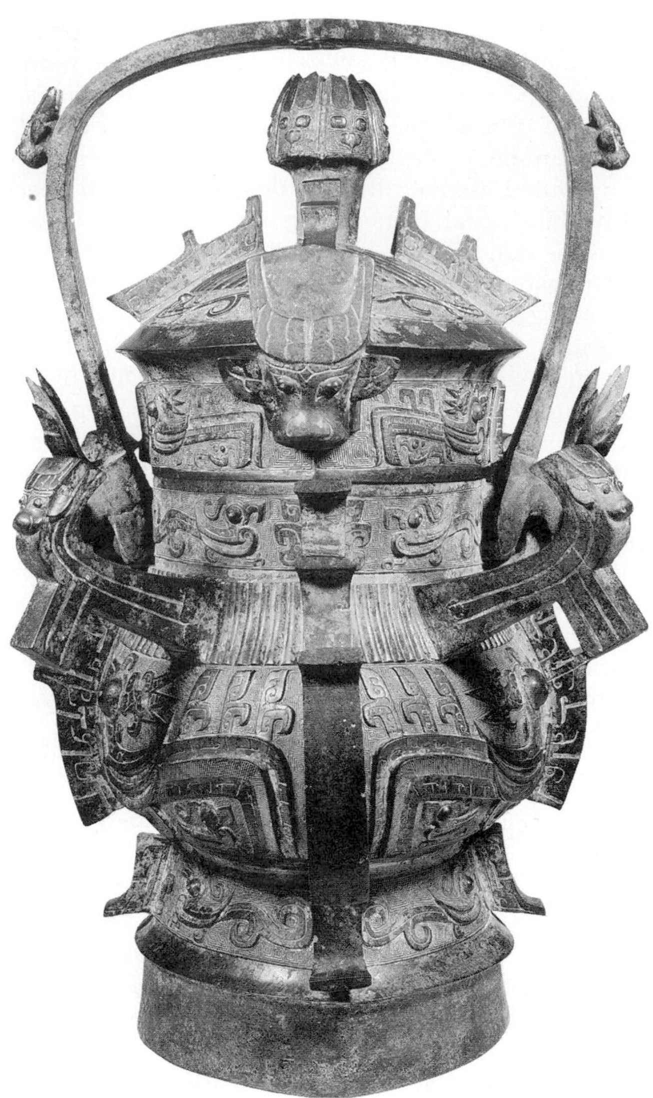

12-2 *Yu*, Early Chou dynasty, *c.* tenth century B.C. Bronze, $20\frac{1}{8}''$ high. Smithsonian Institution, Freer Gallery of Art, Washington, D.C.

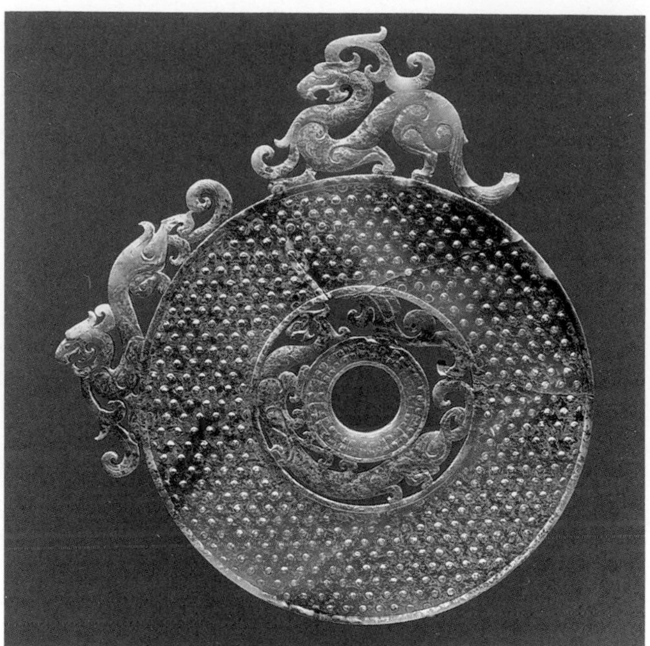

12-3 *Pi* (disc), Late Chou dynasty, sixth to third centuries B.C. Jade, $6\frac{1}{2}''$ in diameter. Nelson Gallery-Atkins Museum, Kansas City, Missouri (Nelson Fund).

their day. While Confucius urged intelligent and moral action on his followers, his famous contemporary, Lao-tzu, favored meditation, inaction, and withdrawal from society. Neither philosophy, however, was to affect Chinese art for several centuries.

The art of the Late Chou, whether in bronze, jade (FIG. 12-3), or lacquer, was produced to satisfy the elaborate demands of ostentatious feudal courts that vied with each other in lavish display. Bronzes inlaid with gold and silver were popular at this time as were mirrors highly polished on one side and decorated with current motifs on the other. About the fourth century B.C., ritual bronzes were embellished with an entirely new system of narrative designs. Scenes of hunting, religious rites, and magic practices, although small, nevertheless reveal subjects and compositions that probably are reflective of paintings lost but mentioned in the literature of the period.

In the Late Chou period, carvings of jade, a stone regarded with special reverence by the Chinese and often found in Neolithic tombs, reached a peak of technical perfection in the jewelry and ritual objects entombed with the dead (FIG. **12-3**). At this time, Confucius extolled the virtues of jade, in which, he said, superior men in ancient times "found the likeness of all excellent qualities." It was soft, smooth, and glossy (when polished), like benevolence; fine, compact, and strong, like intelligence; angular, but not sharp and cutting, like righteousness; and (when struck), like music. Like loyalty, its flaws did not conceal its beauty nor its beauty its flaws, and, like virtue, it was conspicuous in the symbols of rank.*

The culture that had produced the great bronzes and jades of the Shang and Chou periods was being transformed. The political turbulence of the Late Chou period, at times called the "period of the Warring States," was accompanied by an intellectual and artistic upheaval that coincided with the rise of conflicting schools of philosophy, and, in art, a new iconography and style combined with vestigial elements from the Shang and Early Chou periods. During the next four hundred years, a radically different art was to develop.

*From the *Li Chi* attributed to Confucius, translated by James Legge, *The Sacred Books of the East* (New York: Clarendon Press, 1966), Vol. 28, p. 464.

CH'IN AND HAN DYNASTIES

The political chaos of the last few hundred years of the Chou dynasty was halted temporarily by Shih Huang Ti, ruler of the state of Ch'in (hence, the name "China"), whose powerful armies conquered all rival states. Shih Huang Ti became the First Emperor of China, establishing totalitarian control over most of the country between 221 and 210 B.C. His reign was signalized by the building of the Great Wall and by his attempt to eradicate old traditions by destroying all historical books and burying alive thousands of Confucian scholars.

In 1974, the immense tomb mound of Shih Huang Ti was discovered in Shensi, and excavations in its vicinity, which are still proceeding, have revealed an astonishing collection of monuments, making this tomb mound one of the great archeological discoveries of modern times. More than six thousand life-size clay figures of soldiers and horses—and, more recently, bronze horses and chariots—have been found. Replicating the invincible hosts of the emperor, they serve as the immortal imperial bodyguard (FIGS. **12-4** and **12-5**), deployed outside a vast, underground funerary palace designed to match the fabulous palace occupied by the emperor in life. Both palaces were described by the ancient historian Sima Quian (136–85 B.C.), whose account was not taken seriously until these recent discoveries validated it. The statues, originally in vivid color, were arranged in long ranks and files, as if lined up for battle: infantry, cavalry, horses and chariots, archers, lancers, and hand-to-hand fighters. The style of the Ch'in warriors blends archaic formalism—simplicity of volume and contour, rigidity, and frontality—with sharp realism of detail. Set poses are repeated with little or no variation, as if from a single mold, but subtle differences in details of facial features, coiffures, and equipment are delineated. An unarmed warrior (FIG. 12-5) assumes the watchful stance of a fighter skilled in hand-to-hand combat, presumably similar to karate. He stands in line with scores of other figures exactly matching his pose and gesture.

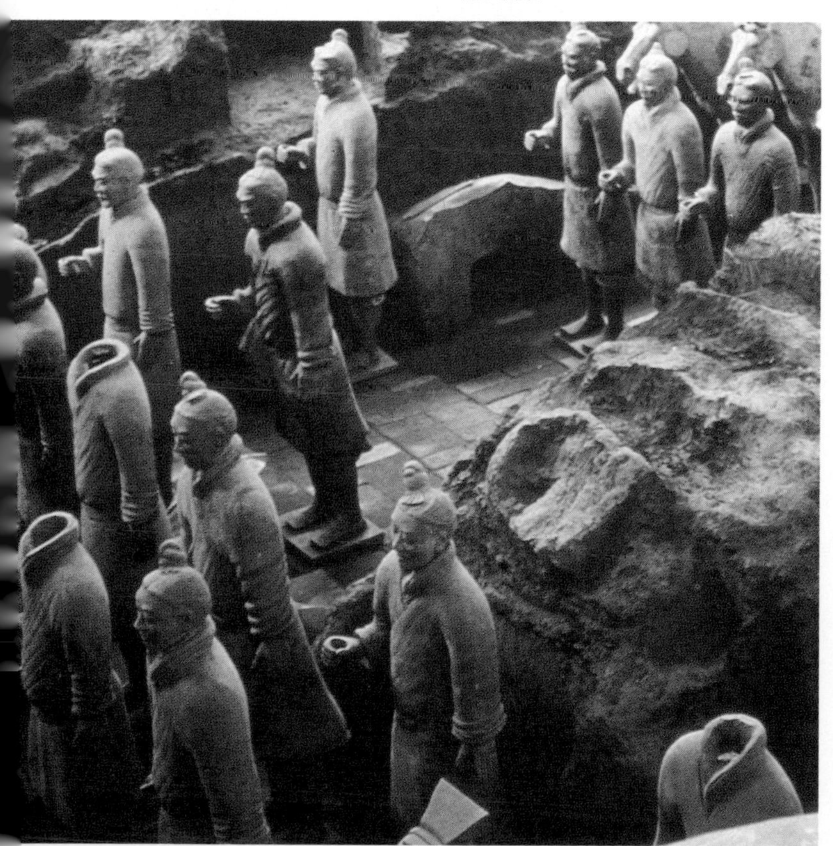

12-4 *Soldiers of the Imperial Bodyguard,* tomb of emperor Shih Huang Ti, Shensi, 221–206 B.C. Painted ceramic, life size.

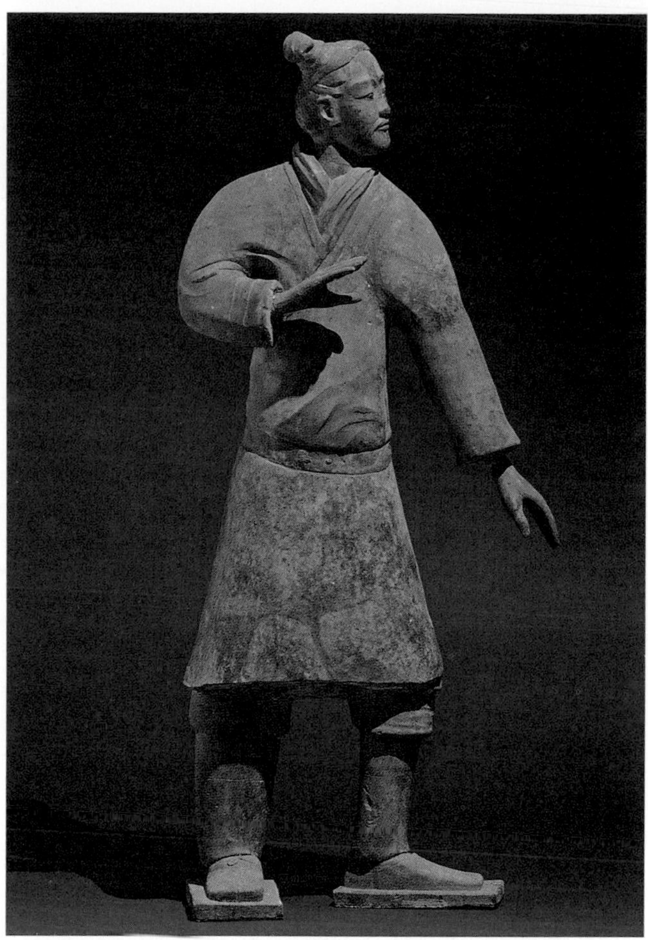

12-5 *Soldier Poised for Hand-to-Hand Combat,* tomb of emperor Shih Huang Ti. Painted ceramic, life size.

On the death of Shih Huang Ti, the people of Ch'in revolted, and a new dynasty, the Han, was founded in 206 B.C. A powerful, centralized government extended the southern and western boundaries of

China. Chinese armies penetrated far into Turkestan, and indirect trade was maintained with distant Rome. Confucianists struggled with Taoists (followers of the mystic philosophy of Lao-tzu) for control of governmental power. The Confucianists eventually won, although the formalized Confucianism that triumphed was far removed from the teachings of the master. The Confucian legends of filial piety and the folklore of Taoism together provided most of the subject matter of Han art.

The Han pictorial style is known from a few extant paintings and many stone reliefs as well as stamped pottery tiles. In some paintings, the outlines of figures are rendered in the characteristic Chinese line, with calligraphic elasticity that conveys not only outline but depth and mass as well. Overlapping of arms and drapery further emphasizes the third dimension, while flat colors, applied within contours, accent the rhythmic relationship between figures. Background and environment are not represented.

Numerous stone reliefs from the Wu family shrines in Shantung (*c.* A.D. 150) also reflect modes of Han pictorial representation. On the slabs, scenes from history and folklore depict mythological beings associated with Taoism as well as exemplars of Confucian piety. The story on each relief unfolds in images of flat polished stone against an equally flat, though roughly striated, ground (FIG. **12-6**). The rounded figures are related by the linear rhythms of their contours. In addition, buildings and trees now indicate a milieu. Space, however, is conceptual, as in Egyptian painting, and distance is suggested by the superposition of figures, although, curiously enough, chariot wheels overlap. Individuals of importance are shown hierarchically, in larger size than their subordinates. Most interesting are the trees, which are highly stylized as masses of intertwined branches bearing isolated, overlarge leaves. Yet within this schematic form, some accidental variation in a twisted branch or broken bough shows how the designer's generalization derived from the observation of specific trees and how a detail of the particular can individualize the general. It is this subtle relationship between the specific and the abstract that will become one of the most important esthetic attributes of later Chinese painting.

A group of reliefs from Szechwan, although similar to those of the Wu tombs and probably of the same date, are more advanced. Rhythms are more rapid, and space and the environment are stated more fully. Some subjects concern everyday life, in contrast to the earlier preoccupation with mythological or historical themes. A figure of the Buddha also appears—probably the earliest in China and therefore the first reference to the religion that was to dominate Chinese thought for the next one thousand years.

A superb example of Han bronze craft, in the tradition of the Chinese mastery of that metal prevalent since Shang times, is a figure of a horse (FIG. **12-7**) from a tomb in Kansu discovered in 1969. Although

12-6 *Mythological Scenes,* Wu family shrine, Shantung, Late Han dynasty, 147–168. Rubbing of stone relief approx. 60″ long.

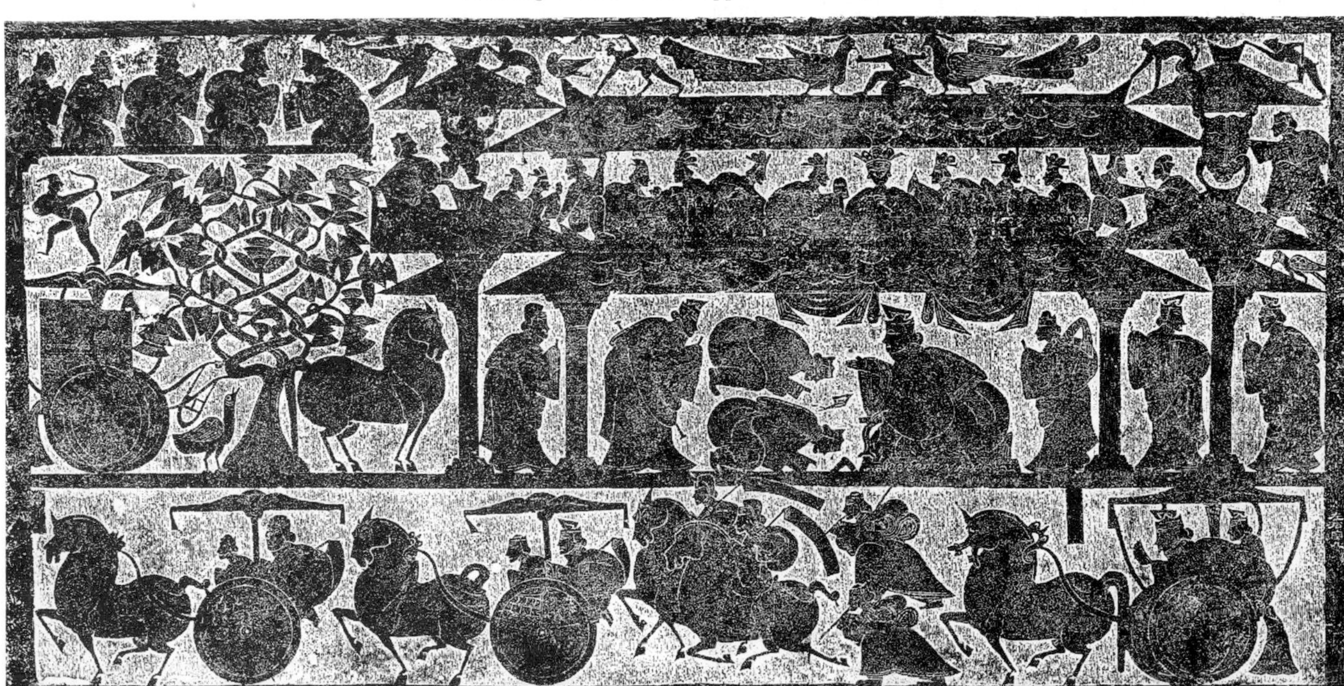

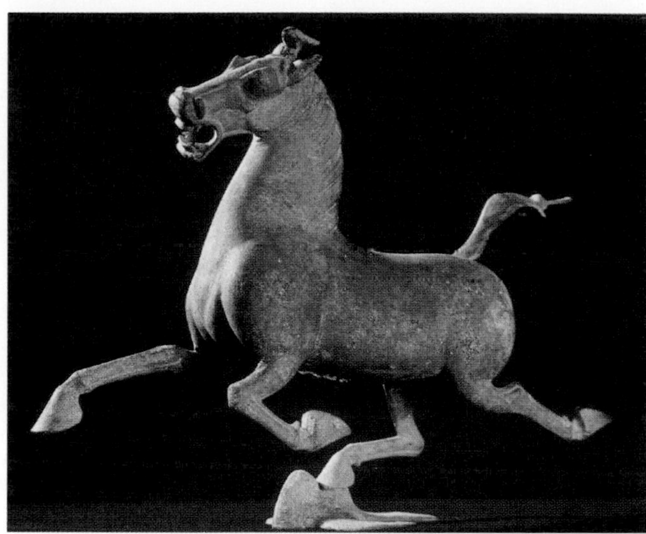

12-7 *Flying Horse Poised on One Leg on a Swallow,* from a tomb at Wuwei, Kansu, Late Han dynasty, second century. Bronze, $13\frac{1}{2}''$ high, $17\frac{3}{4}''$ long. The exhibition of archeological finds of the People's Republic of China.

its action is certainly that of a quick trot, the animal seems to be flying, one hoof lightly poised on a swallow, its single point of attachment to its pedestal. The horse, because it was revered for its power and majesty, has a prominence in Chinese art tantamount to that of the lion or bull in the art of the Near East.

THREE KINGDOMS AND SUI DYNASTY

Buddhism (pages 427–28), whose spirit differed profoundly from the ancient and native philosophies of China, was introduced by the first century of the Christian era. During the last century of Han rule and the succeeding Three Kingdoms period, China, splintered by strife, grasped eagerly at a new ideal by which to live. The Confucian system of ethics had proved itself incapable of adapting to the anarchy of the times, and Taoism, having degenerated into magic and superstition, no longer appealed to the philosophic mind. Buddhism offered the Chinese masses the promise of hope beyond the troubles of this world. In addition, the fully developed Buddhist system of logic, refined to the point of surpassing any previous Chinese system of thought, attracted the intellectuals. Buddhist missionaries from India, working at first with the ruling families, spread their gospel so successfully that their teachings ran like wildfire through China.

The arts flourished in the service of the imported religion. Following the brief Three Kingdoms period in the third century, China entered an era of political confusion known as the period of the Northern and Southern dynasties, which fostered many short-lived states. Native Chinese dynasties, centered at Nanking, ruled in the south. Most of the Buddhist art that survives from this period, however, originated in the northern states, which were ruled by barbarian peoples who rapidly adopted Chinese ways and culture. A new esthetic developed in imitation of Indian or central Asian models that harmonized with the prescribed formalism of Buddhist doctrine. The earliest important Buddhist image, a gilt-bronze statuette of *Sakyamuni Buddha* (FIG. **12-8**), dated, by inscription, to the year 338, is related clearly, in both style and iconography, to the prototype conceived and developed at Gandhara (FIG. 11-10).* The heavy concentric folds

*So new were the icon and its meaning that the Chinese craftsman, although endeavoring to make an image faithful to prescription, nevertheless erred in representing the canonical *mudra* of meditation: the Buddha's hands are clasped across his stomach; they should be turned palms upward, with thumbs barely touching (FIG. 11-12).

12-8 *Sakyamuni Buddha,* Northern and Southern dynasties, 338. Gilt bronze, $15\frac{1}{2}''$ high, $9\frac{5}{8}''$ wide. Asian Art Museum of San Francisco, The Avery Brundage Collection.

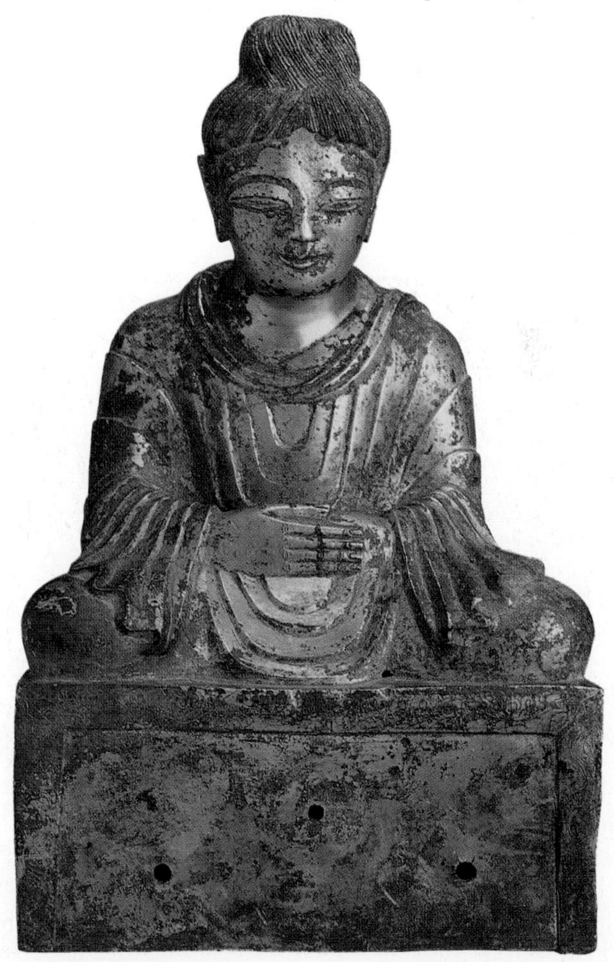

of the robe, the ushnisha on the head, and the cross-legged position all derived ultimately from the Indian prototype, examples of which were brought to China by pilgrims and priests who had made the hazardous trip along the desert trade routes of central Asia.

The Chinese artist transformed the basic Indian pattern during the following century or so. These changes are evident in a series of great cave temples that were carved into the hillsides after the fashion of the early Buddhists in India. At Tunhuang, westernmost gateway to China, over three hundred sanctuaries were cut into the loess cliffs, the walls decorated with paintings, and the chambers adorned with images of painted, unfired clay and stucco. This site was dedicated in 366, but the earliest extant caves date from the late fifth century. About the same time, in 460, sculptors at Yunkang, near Tatung in northern China, were carving temples in cliffs of sandstone. Although the materials are different, both sites have an archaic style similar to the sculpture of the sixth century B.C. in Greece and of the early twelfth century in France. Like their Western counterparts, the faces of the cave figures are carved in sharp planes and their drapery is conventionalized into angular patterns (FIG. **12-9**). Considered as a whole, they too express the intense and noble dignity of a deeply felt religion. The Buddhist concept of divinity may be seen in the caves of Yunkang, where the image of the Buddha—a blend of conventional restraint and religious fervor—became human enough for popular recognition but remained idealized enough to carry the worshiper beyond the image to the abstraction it symbolized.

12-9 Colossal Buddha, from Cave XX, Yunkang, Shansi, Northern and Southern dynasties, *c.* 460. Sandstone, 45′ high.

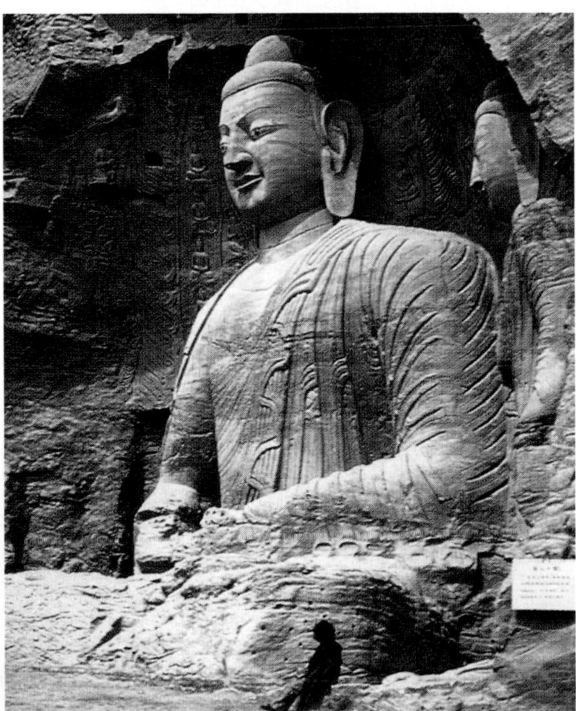

In 494, the Wei Tatars, staunch Buddhists who had supported the colossal program at Yunkang, moved their court southward to Loyang in Honan. Near there, in the limestone cliffs of Lungmen, another series of caves was started. The first phase of work here continued until the early part of the sixth century. The new carvings reveal elongated body and facial types and a fluid elegance in the rendering of drapery folds that reflect the influence of native Chinese styles, including those of painting. An air of courtly sophistication begins to appear, especially in some of the secular figures of imperial donors. The new linearity and elongation, combined with pure body volumes and balanced poses, result in many images that harmonize religious sincerity with extraordinary grace of design.

While the Lungmen caves were being worked on, the popular imagination was captured by a new form of Buddhism (promoted by various Paradise Sects) that promised rebirth in a Buddhist paradise rich in the material pleasures denied to most in this world. As an idyllic existence in this paradise could be gained merely by faith in the word of the Buddha, many who might have failed to appreciate the goal of nirvana and the ultimate extinction of personality were won over to Buddhism by the more tangible and attractive goal offered by the Paradise Sects. Glories beyond those even of the imperial court thus were offered to every person who placed trust in the Buddha. The pleasant aspirations of these Buddhists were reflected in the greater naturalism of their arts, particularly the humanization of the deity. It is no wonder, therefore, that by the time the Paradise Sects reached their peak in the Sui dynasty (581–618), the Buddha gradually had been transformed from an archaic image of divine perfection into a gentle and human savior. The transition is manifest in a gilt-bronze shrine (FIG. **12-10**), which also reflects the attenuated Lungmen style. Prabhutaratna (Buddha of the remote past) listens to the sermon by Sakyamuni, the most recent Buddha. Seated within flamelike aureoles, the graceful, slender figures are almost absorbed into the rhythmic fall and flow of linear drapery that is beginning to acquire the character of cloth. The humanization is manifest in the gentle, suave beauty of attitude and gesture, although the faces retain the characteristics of archaic formulas.

A comparable development of Buddhist images can be observed in the richly painted walls of the Tunhuang sanctuaries, which were calculated to inspire in the worshiper the splendor of Buddhism and (like Medieval paintings) to instruct the illiterate. Hieratic

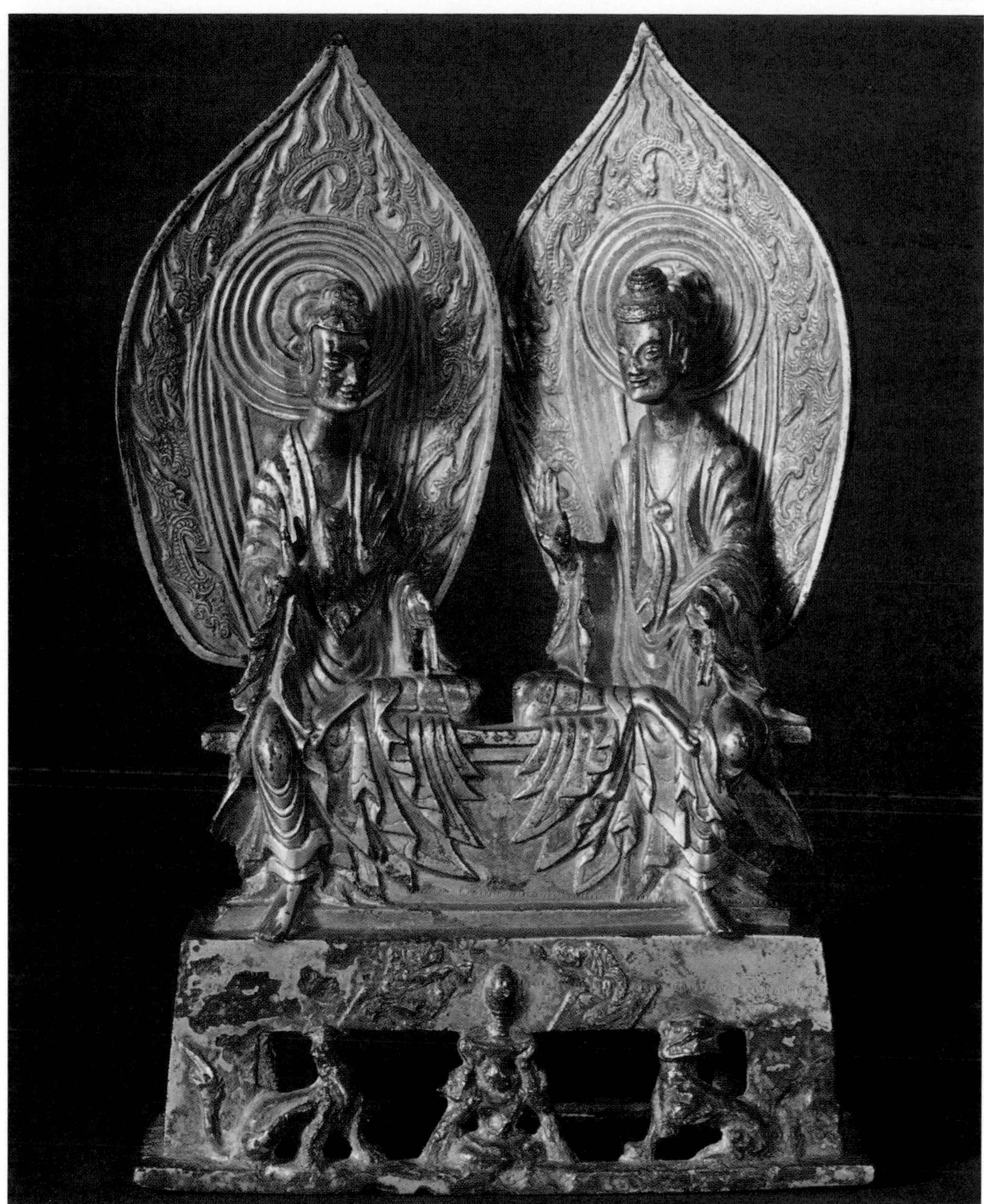

12-10 *Prabhutaratna and Sakyamuni,* Northern and Southern dynasties, c. 518. Gilt bronze, $10\frac{1}{2}''$ high. Musée Guimet, Paris.

figures of the Buddha are surrounded by illustrations of stories about past lives (*jataka*). The formalized patterns of the individual Buddhas are like those of the sculptured images at Yunkang and Lungmen, but the narrative scenes carry on the traditions of Han painting, especially in the cell-like composition, the leaping rhythms, and the disproportionate relationship of figures to diminutive, conventionalized settings.

By 539, most traces of central Asian influence had disappeared. Like the sculpture of the time, Buddhist painting responded to the happy credo of the Paradise Sects with increasing naturalism and grace. Although the Buddha groups retained the strict frontality and rigid balance of ritualistic art, the jataka tales expanded haphazardly over the temple walls. Their figures—now slim, elegant, and emancipated from their compartmental designs—moved freely over the plane surface. By the end of the century, the abstract environment of the painted figures began to be three-dimensional. Overlapping was used to create depth, and a sense of reality was heightened further by surrounding the celestial groups with such earthly phenomena as trees, pavilions, lotus ponds, and bridges.

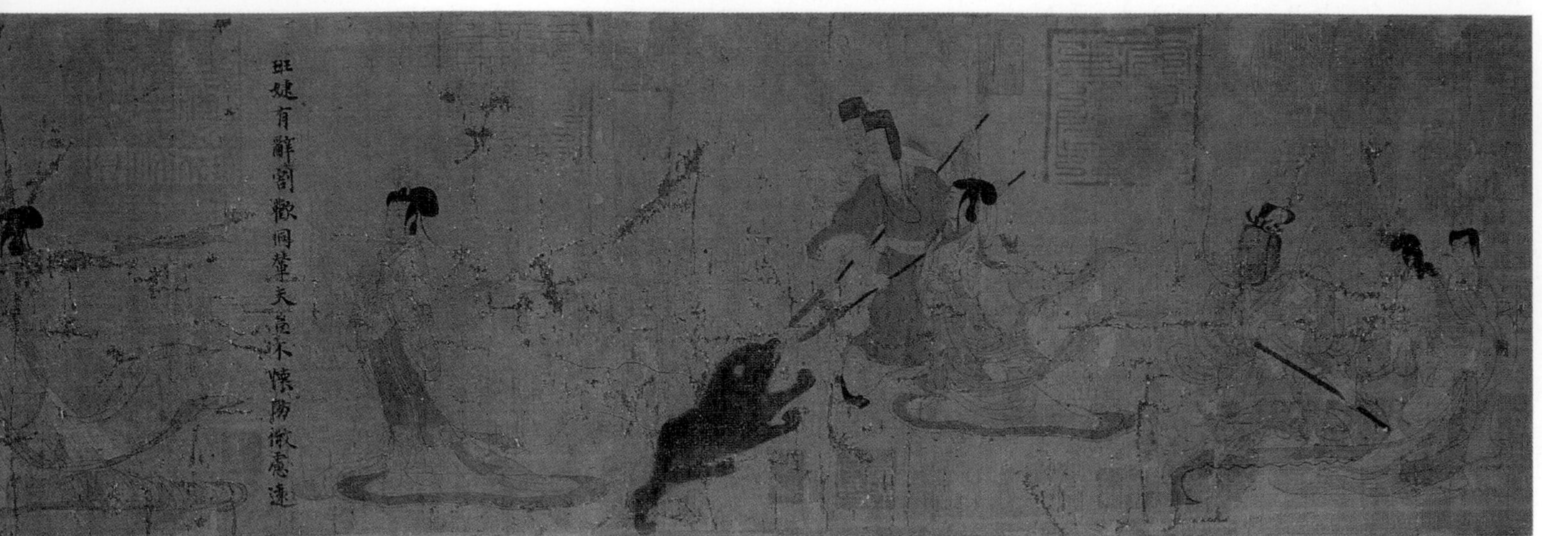

12-11 Attributed to Ku K'ai-chih, *Lady Feng and the Bear,* section of the *Admonitions of the Instructress to the Court Ladies.* Horizontal scroll, ink and colors on silk, 7⅝" high. British Museum, London.

Painting flourished at the courts of the Southern dynasties during this period. Taoist nature cults and a new appreciation of landscape themes in poetry provided the stimulus for the early development of landscape painting. No scrolls from the hands of individual masters have survived from this early era, but descriptive texts indicate that the almost magical potential of landscape painting to re-create and organize the experience of nature or to transport the viewer to an imaginary realm already was well appreciated. When the painter Tsung Ping (373–443), for example, became too old to continue his mountain wanderings, he re-created favorite landscapes on the walls of his studio so that he could take imaginary journeys. Of the representational power of painting, Tsung wrote:

> Nowadays, when I spread out my silk to catch the distant scene, even the form of the K'un-lun [Mountain] may be captured within a square inch of space; a vertical stroke of three inches equals a height of several thousand feet. . . . By such means as this, the beauty of the Sung and Hua Mountains and the very soul of the *Hsuan-p'in* [Dark Spirit of the Universe] may all be embraced within a single picture.[*]

Another fifth-century painter, Wang Wei, elaborated on the re-creative potential of landscape painting:

> I unroll a picture and examine it, and reveal mountains and seas unfamiliar to me. The wind scatters in the verdant forests, the torrent overflows in bubbling foam. Ah, how could this be achieved merely by the skillful use of hands and fingers? The spirit must also exercise control over it. For this is the essence of painting.[†]

The painter and essayist Ku K'ai-chih (*c.* 344–406) is one of the few individual artists from this period to whom extant paintings seriously have been attributed. In an essay on landscape painting couched in Taoist terms, he describes "crags, fanglike and tapering," and "rocks, split with fissures as though torn by lightning." But for Ku K'ai-chih and others of his time, the crucial aspect of painting was not mere imitation of appearance but transmission of "spiritual quality." Indeed, in the late fifth century, the critic Hsieh Ho named, as the first of the "Six Principles" of painting, "spirit-consonance engendering movement"—a sense of animation through transmission of the vital spirit that pervades both artist and object—which was to remain the cardinal principle for artists and critics in China until modern times.

Something of this vital spirit appears in a horizontal scroll attributed to Ku K'ai-chih called *Admonitions of the Instructress to the Court Ladies,* perhaps an early copy of a painting of Ku's era. Scrolls in this format were meant to be viewed slowly and in sections; in this case, scenes are illustrated between passages of explanatory text. One of the sections (FIG. **12-11**) depicts a well-known act of heroism in which the Lady Feng saved the life of her emperor by placing herself between him and an attacking bear. Although no background is shown and only a minimal setting for the scene is provided, fluid poses and fluttering ribbons of drapery, in concert with individualized facial expressions, convey the quality of animation called for in texts of the period.

*For this and other excerpts from essays on painting quoted subsequently, see Michael Sullivan, *The Birth of Landscape Painting in China* (Berkeley: University of California Press, 1962).

†Ibid.

T'ANG DYNASTY

The short-lived Sui dynasty was followed by the T'ang dynasty (618–906), under which China entered a period of unequaled magnificence. Chinese armies marched across central Asia, opening a path for the flow of wealth, ideas, and foreign peoples. Arab traders, Nestorian Christians, and other travelers journeyed to the cosmopolitan capital of the T'ang, and the Chinese, in turn, ventured westward. During the middle of the seventh century, Hsüan Tsang, a Chinese monk, visited India, as had some earlier devotees. He returned from the mother country of Buddhism with revolutionizing doctrines of the recently developed Esoteric Sects. These years were a critical time for Buddhism in China; Buddhist religious beliefs were being brought into disrepute by a lax court and a corrupt clergy. Under the notorious Empress Wu, who had usurped the throne, religion was used as an instrument for political power and as a cloak for personal excess. The material rewards promised in Heaven by the Paradise Sects offered no effective antidote to the troubles of the time. But the elaborate and mysterious rituals of the new Esoteric Sects attracted worshipers by giving them in their daily life many of the sensory pleasures that the Paradise Sects had promised in Heaven. As the new cult spread, Chinese craftsmen again looked to India, where they found appropriate models in Gupta sculpture.

The fluid style of art developed during the Gupta period in India (FIGS. 11-13 and 11-14) already had affected Chinese sculpture during the late sixth century, and, by the end of the seventh, Buddhist sculpture in China had lost much of its own character due to its borrowing from the sensuous carvings of India. Fleshiness increased even more, and drapery was made to cling, as if wet, against the body. The new wave of influence from India brought not only stylistic changes but also the iconography of the Esoteric Sects, which we see in figures with multiple arms and heads, symbolizing various aspects of the deities as described in the new gospels.

The Early T'ang style, heavily influenced by Indian prototypes, is exemplified admirably by the *Bodhisattva* (FIG. **12-12**). The sinuous beauty of this figure has been accented by the hip-shot pose and revealing drapery, as in Gupta sculpture. Executed at almost the same time as the *Bodhisattva* (around 700) were carvings in the caves of Ti'en-lung Shan, which anticipated the later T'ang style. These cave figures might seem gross were it not for the graceful postures and the soft drapery that falls in rhythmic patterns over the plump bodies.

Esoteric Buddhism, with its emphasis on detailed and complicated ritual, placed the deity in a formal relationship to the worshiper. The followers of Amitabha Buddha—one of the most important Buddhas of the Paradise Sects—in stressing salvation by faith, visualized a warm and human deity, but, by the ninth century, the arduous discipline of the Esoteric

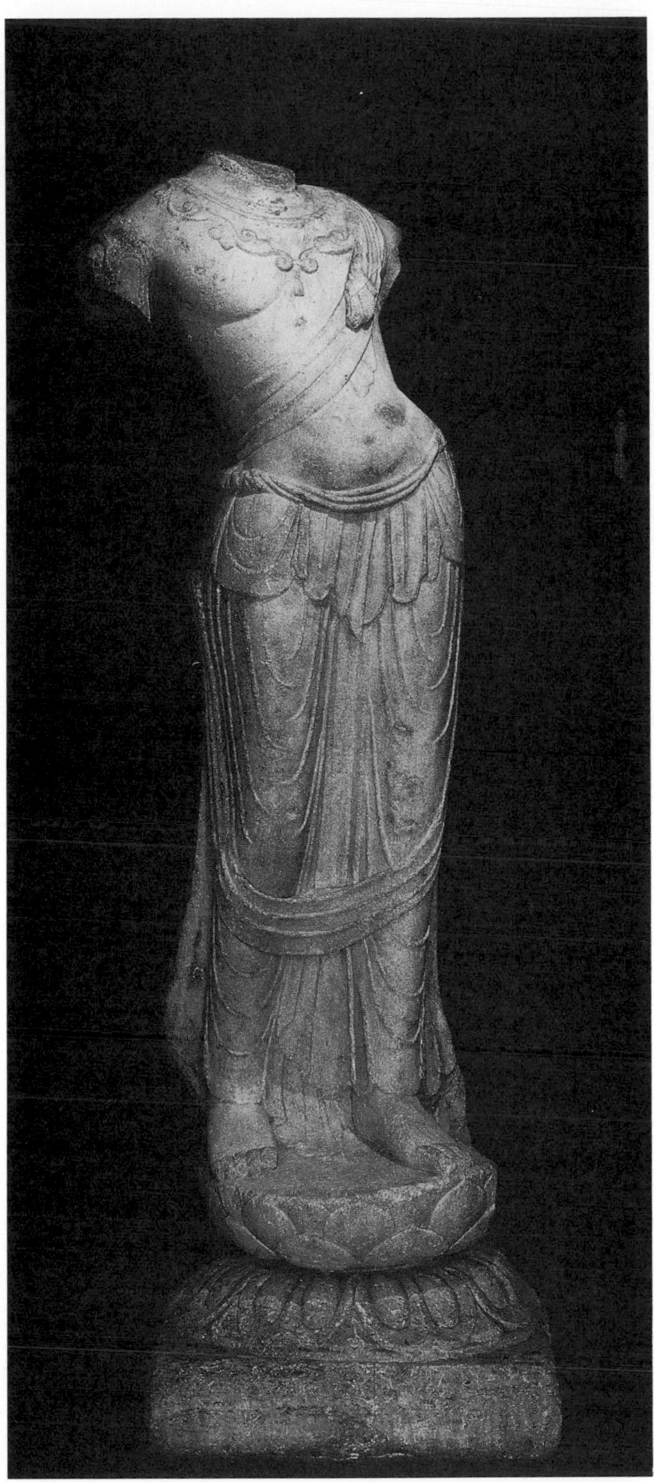

12-12 *Bodhisattva,* Early T'ang dynasty, seventh and eighth centuries. Marble. Private collection of Charles Uht, New York.

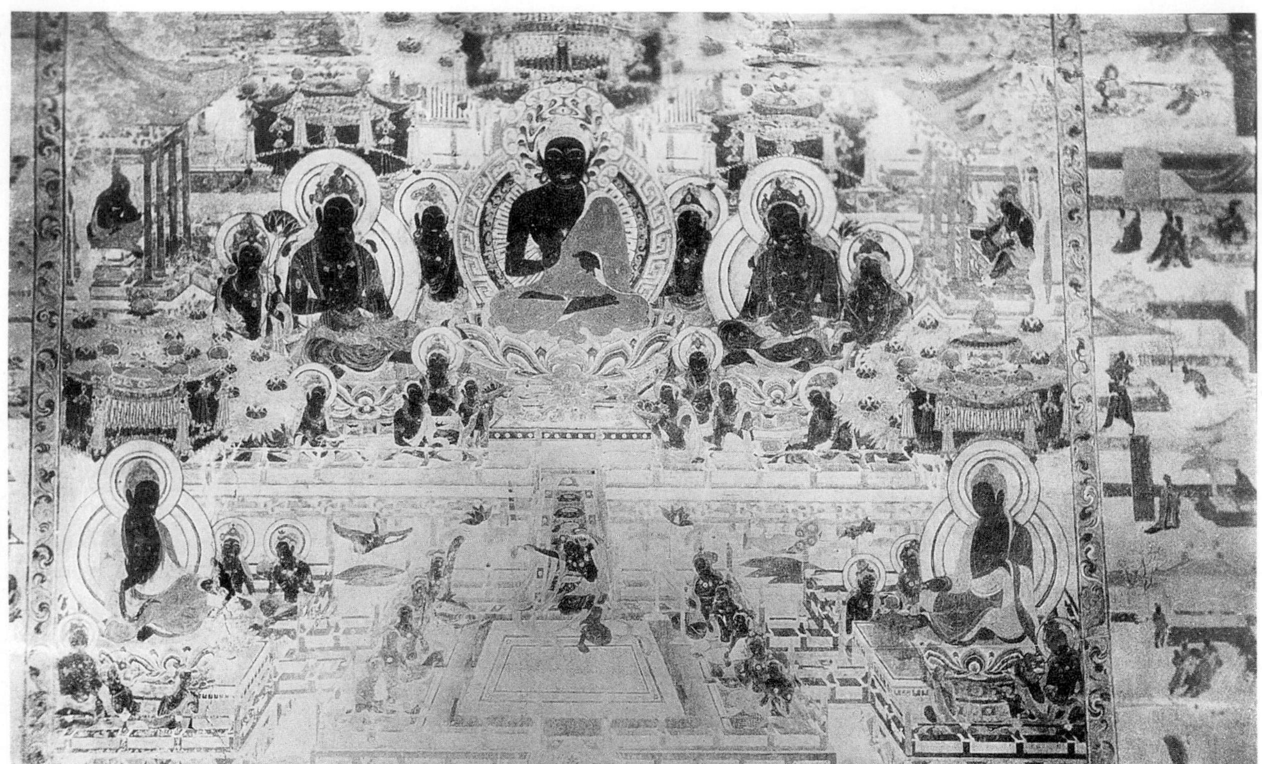

12-13 *Paradise of Amitabha,* Cave 139A, Tunhuang, Kansu, T'ang dynasty, ninth century. Wall painting.

Sects had inspired an austere, heavyset, almost repellent icon. At times, fleshiness was exaggerated almost to the point of obesity, and yet sufficient restraint lent the figures a somber dignity.*

The westward expansion of the T'ang Empire increased the importance of Tunhuang. Here, the desert routes converged and the cave temples profited from the growing prosperity of the people. By the eighth century, wealthy donors to Buddha were demanding larger and more elaborately decorated caves. The comparatively simple Buddha group in paintings of the previous century was enlarged to include crowds of attendant figures, lavish architectural settings, and minor deities who worshiped the resplendent Buddha with music and dance. The opulence of the T'ang style is reflected in the detailed richness of the brilliantly colored *Paradise Paintings* (shown is *Paradise of Amitabha,* FIG. **12-13**). Vignettes flanking the Buddha group illustrate incidents from specific *sutras.* These little scenes, like the jataka tales in earlier caves, usually are set in landscapes painted in an altogether different style from that of the hieratic groups. Mountains, for example, are stacked one behind the other and painted in graded washes to give the impression of distance. (Although each mountain is related to the adjacent peak through this device of atmospheric perspective, no continuous perspective yet gives a sense of recession into the distance.)

The Confucian persecutions of 845 did not affect Tunhuang, which was then under Tibetan rule. Numerous paintings (murals and scrolls) were produced in this region, but because the area was isolated from the mainstream of Chinese culture, the paintings remained stylistically static from the middle of the ninth century to the beginning of the eleventh century. Meanwhile, during the seventh and eighth centuries at the T'ang court in Ch'ang-an (modern Xi'an)—perhaps the greatest city in the world during this period—a brilliant tradition of figure painting developed that, in its variety and balance, reflected the worldliness and self-assurance of the T'ang Empire. Indeed, Chinese historians regard the Early T'ang dynasty as their golden age of figure painting. Glowing accounts by poets and critics and a few remaining examples of the paintings themselves permit us to understand this enthusiasm.

Wall paintings from the tomb of the T'ang princess Yung-t'ai (built in 706 near Ch'ang-an) allow us to view court painting styles unobscured by problems of authenticity and reconstruction. The figures of *Palace Ladies* (FIG. **12-14**) are arranged as if on a shallow

*Few sculptures survived the terrible persecutions of Buddhism during a revival of Confucianism in 845. Many wooden temples were destroyed by fire, and their bronze images were melted down. Fortunately, we are able to reconstruct the style of the period from Buddhist art in Japan, which was then under direct Chinese influence (see FIGS. 13-3 to 13-5).

stage; although no indications of background or setting are given, intervals between the two rows and the grouping of the figures in an oval suggest a consistent ground plane. The women are shown full-face and in three-quarter views from the front and the back. The device of paired figures facing into and out of the space of the picture in a near mirror image—an effective means of creating depth—appears often in paintings attributed to this period. Thick, even contour lines describe full-volumed faces and suggest solid forms beneath the drapery, all with the utmost economy. This simplicity of form and drawing, along with the measured cadence of the poses, results in an air of monumental dignity, as befits a daughter of the ruling house of the T'ang.

In perfect accord with descriptions of the robust T'ang style are the unrestored portions of *Portraits of the Emperors,* masterfully drawn in line and in colored washes by YEN LI-PEN (d. 673), a celebrated painter and statesman of the seventh century. Each emperor is represented as standing in undefined space, his eminence clearly indicated by his great size relative to that of his attendants. Yen Li-pen also made designs for a series of monumental and spirited stone horses that once flanked the approach to the tomb of the T'ang emperor T'ai Tsung.

The horse in Chinese art reflected the importance the emperors placed on the quality of their stables. Even Han emperors had sent missions westward to Bactria for blooded stock. Paintings of the finest among his forty thousand steeds were commissioned by the emperor Ming Huang (713–756), and one of these may be the picture of a tethered horse that is attributed to HAN KAN (active 742–756), Ming Huang's favorite painter of horses. The fiery stallion (FIG. **12-15**) evokes the dynamic "inner vitality" so stressed by Chinese critics.

Two of the most famous artists of the T'ang period were WANG WEI (699–759; not to be confused with Wang Wei of the fifth century) and WU TAO-TZŬ (active *c.* 725–750), both of whom have become almost legendary figures, although none of their paintings has survived. Wang was not only a painter, but like many other Chinese artists, he was also a poet. His poems are mellow and lyrical, as his paintings are said to have been. Numerous imitations of his painting style have the peaceful lyricism of his poems. Many of these copies are of snow scenes, a favorite subject of Chinese artists, probably due to its adaptability to monochrome painting, an art of infinite variation and contrast in black and white. Wu's work, according to reports of his time, was very different. He painted with such speed and "ferocious energy" and over such large surfaces that people are said to have watched with awe as astonishingly real images rapidly appeared. His bold brushwork and expansive

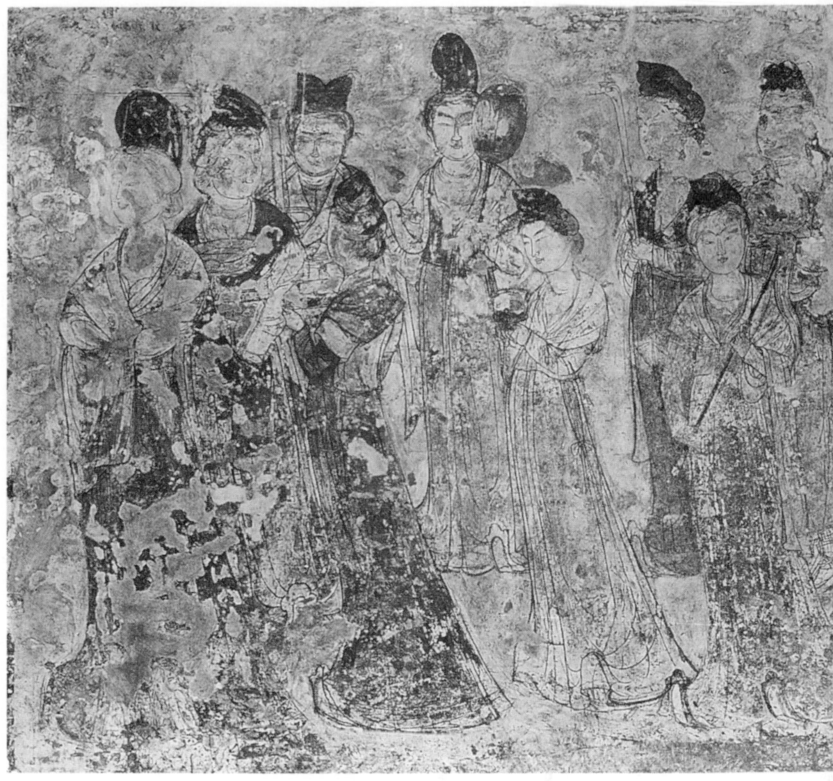

12-14 *Palace Ladies,* from the tomb of Princess Yung-t'ai, near Ch'ang-an (Xi'an), Shensi, T'ang dynasty, 706. Wall painting.

12-15 HAN KAN, *Horse,* T'ang dynasty, eighth century. Album leaf, ink on paper, $11\frac{13}{16}$" high. Metropolitan Museum of Art, New York.

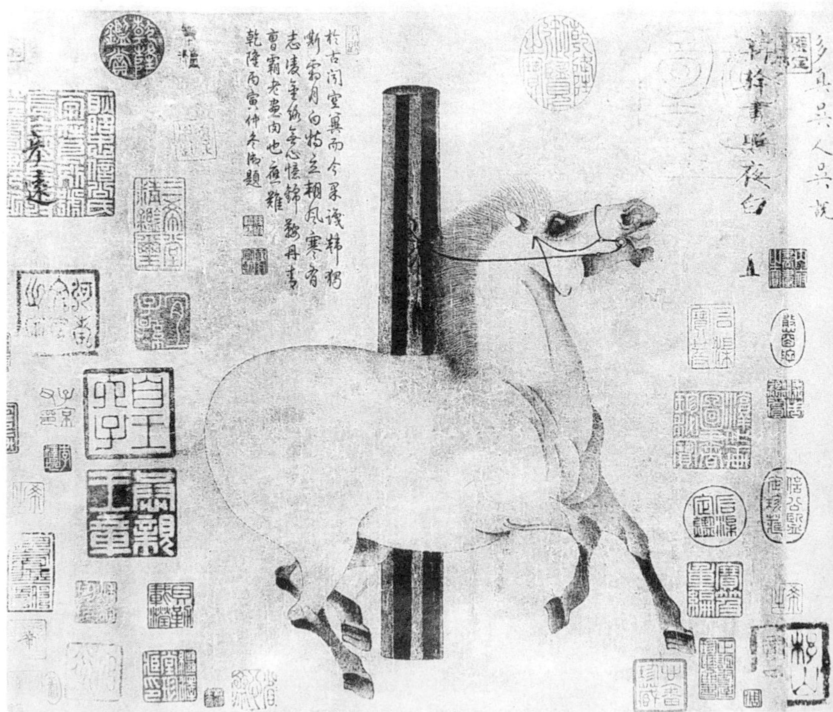

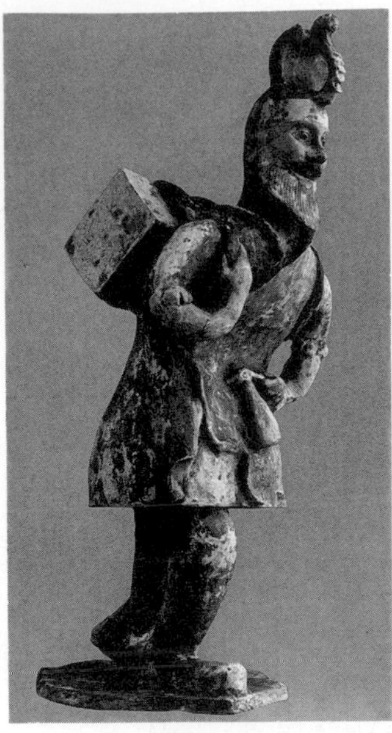
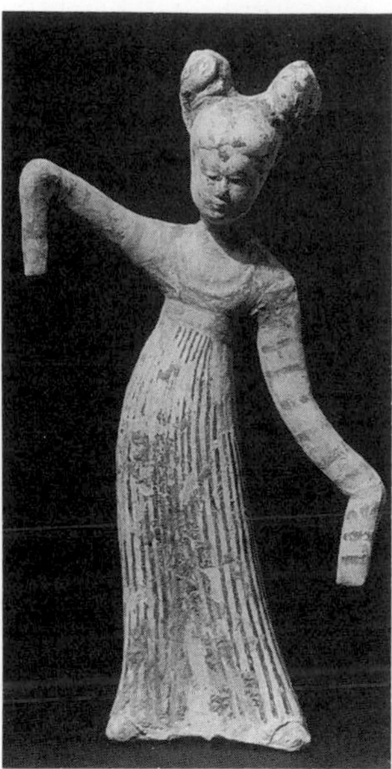
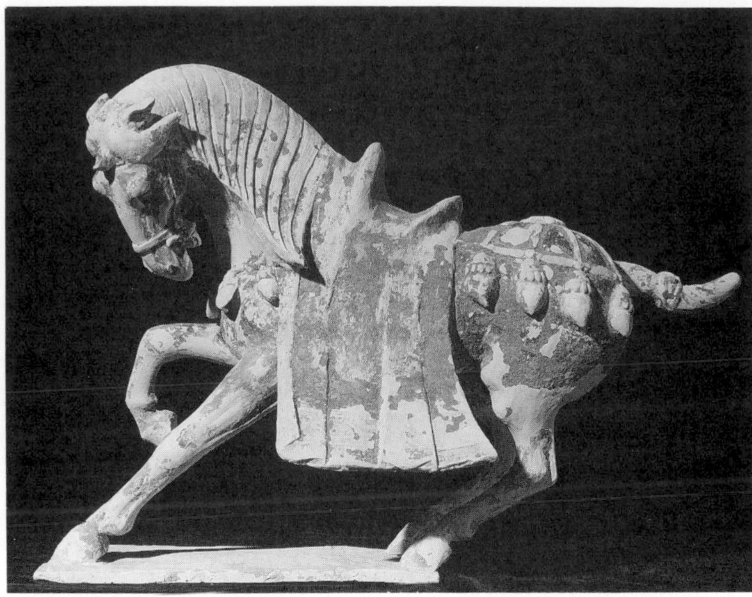

12-16 T'ang tomb figurines, seventh to ninth centuries: *(left)* Peddler, $24\frac{1}{2}''$ high, Portland Art Museum, Portland, Oregon; *(middle)* Dancer, $10\frac{3}{4}''$ high, Nelson Gallery-Atkins Museum, Kansas City, Missouri; *(right)* Horse, $14\frac{1}{2}''$ high, Fogg Art Museum, Harvard University, Cambridge, Massachusetts.

forms frequently were copied, and rubbings were made from engraved replicas. Later artists looked to Wu's virtuoso brushwork and to Wang's subtle harmonies for their models.

The T'ang rulers embellished their empire with extravagant wooden structures, all of which have disappeared. Judging from records, however, they were colorfully painted and of colossal size. Bronze mirrors with decorations in strong relief added to T'ang luxury and to the furnishings of a court already enriched by elaborate gold and silver ornaments.

The potter met the demand for display by covering his wares with colorful lead glazes and by inventing robust shapes with clearly articulated parts—base, body, and neck. Earlier potters had imitated bronze models, but T'ang craftsmen derived their forms directly from the character of the clay. Ceramic figures of people, domesticated animals, and fantastic creatures also were made by the thousands for burial in tombs (FIG. **12-16**). The extraordinarily delicate grace and flowing rhythms of these figures have a charm and vivacity seldom equaled in ceramic design. Their subject matter, which included such diverse figures as Greek acrobats and Semitic traders, is proof of the cosmopolitanism of T'ang China.

FIVE DYNASTIES AND NORTHERN SUNG DYNASTY

The last century of T'ang rule witnessed the gradual disintegration of the empire. When the dynasty finally fell in 906, China once more was left to the ravages of civil war. Conflicting claims between rival states were not resolved until the country was consolidated under the Sung, whose court was at Pienching (modern Kaifeng in Honan). During the interim of internal strife known as the Five Dynasties (906–960), a marked development took place in the styles and techniques of landscape painting. An analogy with events of the period of the Northern and Southern dynasties may be justified here; that earlier period of political and social turmoil also witnessed a turning away from portrayals of society toward an involvement with nature and an accompanying development of landscape art.

CHING HAO (*c.* 900–967) left an essay in which he listed his criteria for judging paintings. Under the classification of "divine," he grouped the greatest paintings. In these, he wrote, "there appears no trace of human effort; hands spontaneously reproduce natural forms." In the lowest category, he placed the "skillful" artist who "cuts out and pieces together fragments of beauty and welds them into the pretense of a masterpiece. . . ." "This," he added, "is owing to the poverty of inner reality and to the excess of outward form." Although these ideas were not original with Ching Hao, his restatement of them showed the continuity of thought underlying Chinese painting regardless of changing styles. The artist who painted the truth beneath surface appearances had to be imbued with *ch'i*, the "divine spirit" of the universe. Any artist who achieved this did so only through years of self-cultivation. Ching Hao and his equally famous contemporary LI CH'ENG (active *c.* 940–967), through the inherent power of their personalities, departed from T'ang landscape formulas, breathing life into every twig and rock they painted. Succeeding generations went to their works for inspiration—great artists, to catch the spirit; lesser painters, to copy tricks for drawing trees and hills.

We know enough about the art of this period to distinguish the styles of some individual masters, such as TUNG YUAN and CHU-JAN, of the mid-tenth century, and FAN K'UAN and KUO HSI, active early and late in the eleventh century, respectively. Paintings by the latter two artists, which exemplify the maturity of landscape painting styles in the Northern Sung period (960–1127), express very different personalities and yet exhibit a common feeling for monumentality. A characteristic painting in this style presents a vertical landscape of massive mountains rising from the distance (FIG. **12-17**). Human figures, reduced to minute proportions, are dwarfed by overwhelming forms in nature. Paths and bridges in the middle region vanish, only to reappear in such a way as to lead the spectator on a journey through the landscape—a journey facilitated by shifting perspective points. No single vanishing point organizes the entire perspective, as in many Western paintings; as a result, the observer's eye moves with freedom. But to appreciate these paintings fully, one must focus on intricate details and on the character of each line.

The full development of the horizontal handscroll occurred during this period. The scroll, which might measure as long as 50 feet or more, had to be unrolled from right to left; only a small section could be seen at a time and then, properly, by only two or three persons. The organization of these paintings has been compared to the composition of a symphony because of the way in which motifs are repeated and moods are varied in the different sections. The temporal sequence of the scroll involved memory as well as vision; it was an art of contemplation and leisure.

Among the versatile figures clustered around the court at Pien-ching was SU TUNG-P'O (1036–1101), one of China's greatest poets, a celebrated painter and statesman. Another, LI KUNG-LIN (1040–1106), was famous for his original Buddhist compositions and for his outline drawings of horses. These, along with the antiquarian and landscape artist MI FU (1052–1109), were the leading figures in a group of scholar-gentlemen painters who created an alternative to the emphasis on the skillful representation of nature then prevalent among professional and academy artists. These amateurs of the "literary" school, by contrast, saw painting as primarily expressive of the moods and personality of the artist. Representational accuracy was deemphasized, or even derided, in favor of learned allusions to antique styles, sometimes couched in deliberately awkward or naïve forms. Many paintings in this style concentrate on qualities inherent in the medium of brush and ink. In this, they are close to the expressiveness of calligraphy, which depends, for its effects, on the controlled vitality of individual brush strokes and on the dynamic relationships of strokes within a character and among the characters themselves. Training in calligraphy was a fundamental part of the education and self-cultivation of Chinese scholars and officials; with

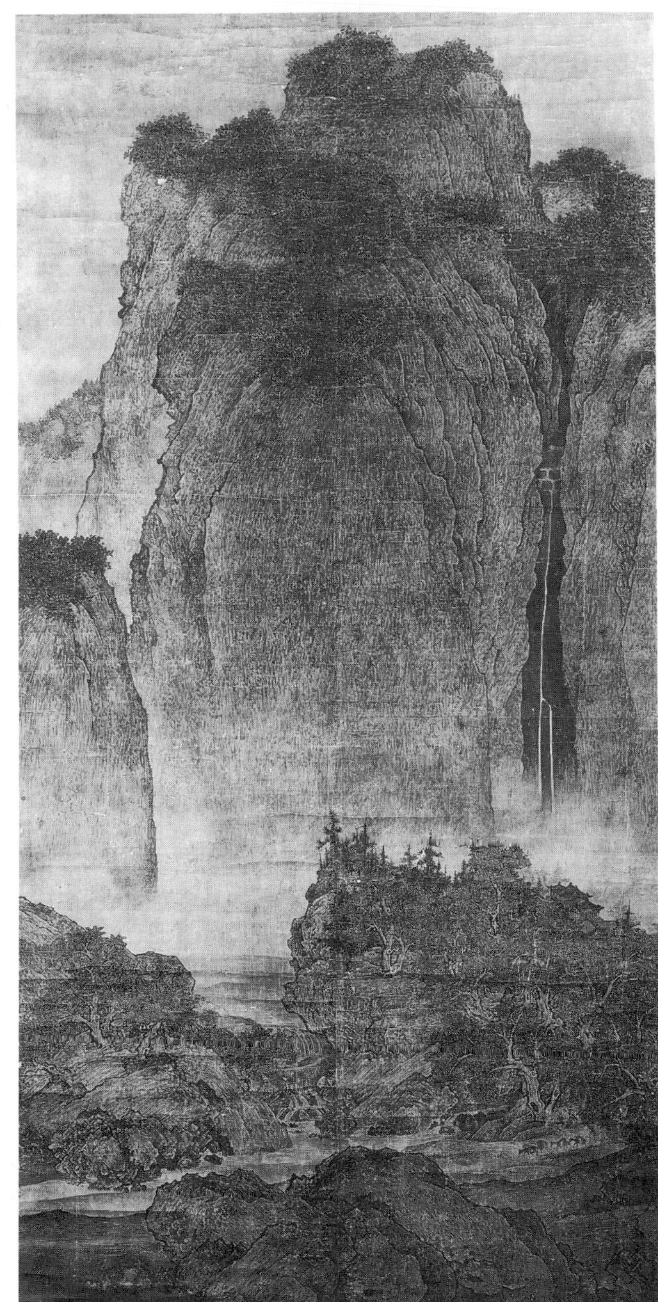

12-17 FAN K'UAN, *Travelers Among Mountains and Streams,* Northern Sung dynasty, early eleventh century. Hanging scroll, ink and colors on silk, 6′ 9″ × 2′ 5″. Collection of the National Palace Museum, Taipei, Taiwan.

Su Tung-p'o and Mi Fu ranked among the greatest of Northern Sung calligraphers, calligraphic qualities and effects became part of the repertory of many painters as well.

The emperor HUI TSUNG (ruled 1101–1125), an avid collector and patron of art, was himself an important painter. He is known particularly for his meticulous pictures of birds, in which almost every feather is carefully drawn in sharp lines. Lesser artists attached to the imperial court functioned as a sort of academy and, in general, followed the detailed and colorful style of the emperor. Illustrating some lines of poetry in painting often served as an examination for court office. Fans painted by master artists were treasured in albums. But while the court spent its energy on esthetic refinements, less cultured neighbors were assaulting the frontiers of China.

SOUTHERN SUNG DYNASTY

In 1127, as a result of increasing pressure from the Tatars and Mongols in the west and north, the capital of China was moved to the south. From then until 1279, the Southern Sung court lived out its days amid the tranquil beauty of Hangchou. Neo-Confucianism, a blend of traditional Chinese thought and some Buddhist concepts, became the leading philosophy. Accordingly, orthodox Buddhism declined. Buddhist art continued to develop in the north, where a Tatar tribe had established itself as the Chin dynasty (1115–1234), but it stagnated in the south. Buddhist sculpture in the Southern Sung period merely added grace and elegance to the T'ang style. Secular paintings and those associated with Ch'an (a meditative school of Buddhism), however, reflected a new and more intimate relationship between the human being and nature.

A typical Southern Sung landscape basically is asymmetrical. It is composed on a diagonal and consists of three parts: foreground, middle distance, and far distance. These parts are separated from each other by a field of mist. The first part is marked by a rock, which, by its position, emphasizes the distance of the other parts. The middle distance may be marked by a flat cliff or given over entirely to mist or water. In the far distance, mountain peaks, which are usually tinted in pale blue, suggest the infinity of space. The whole composition illustrates the manner in which the Sung artists used great voids to hold solid masses in equilibrium. The technique is one of China's unique contributions to the art of painting. To this basic composition, of which many variations were employed, the artist frequently added the figure of a scholar meditating under a gnarled pine tree, accompanied by an attendant. Such paintings were expressions of the artist's ideal of peace and pantheistic unity.

The chief painters in the Southern Sung style were MA YUAN (*c.* 1190–1224) and HSIA KUEI (*c.* 1180–1230). Ma was a master of suggestion, as demonstrated by a small, fan-shaped album leaf (FIG. **12-18**), a picture of tranquility stated in a few sensitively balanced and half-seen shapes. Hsia Kuei's misty landscapes were often so like those of Ma Yuan—though sometimes more delicate and sometimes bolder—that the Chinese refer to these artists and their followers as the Ma-Hsia school. But the Ma-Hsia tradition, despite its gentle beauty, could not be maintained. It perpetuated an ephemeral, classic moment, but the serenity of its beliefs soon was threatened by political realities.

As orthodox Buddhism lost ground under the Sung, the new school of Buddhism (called Ch'an in China, but better known by its Japanese name, Zen) gradually gained importance, until it was second only to Neo-Confucianism. The Zen sect traced its semi-legendary origins to Bodhidharma, an Indian missionary of the sixth century. By the time of the Sixth Ch'an Patriarch, who lived during the Early T'ang period, the pattern of the school already was established, and Zen remains an important religion in Japan today.

12-18 MA YUAN, *Bare Willows and Distant Mountains,* Southern Sung dynasty, thirteenth century. Album leaf, ink and colors on silk, $9\frac{1}{2}'' \times 9\frac{1}{2}''$. Museum of Fine Arts, Boston.

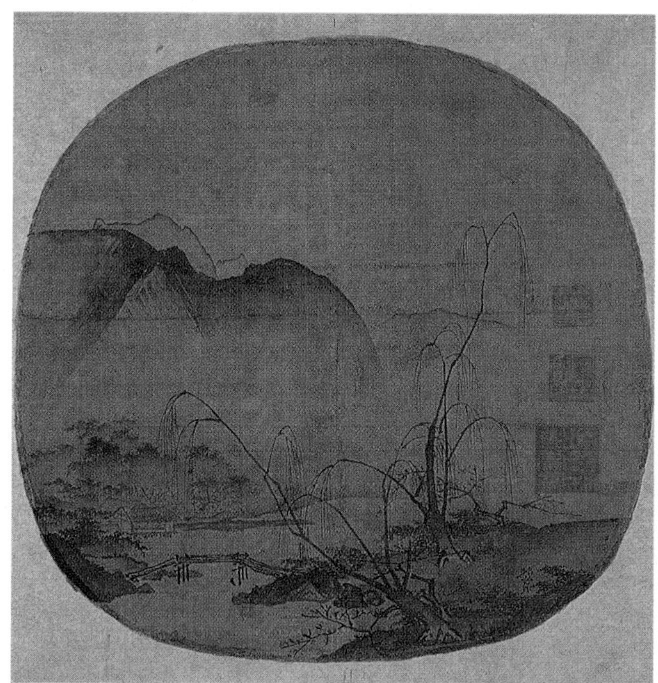

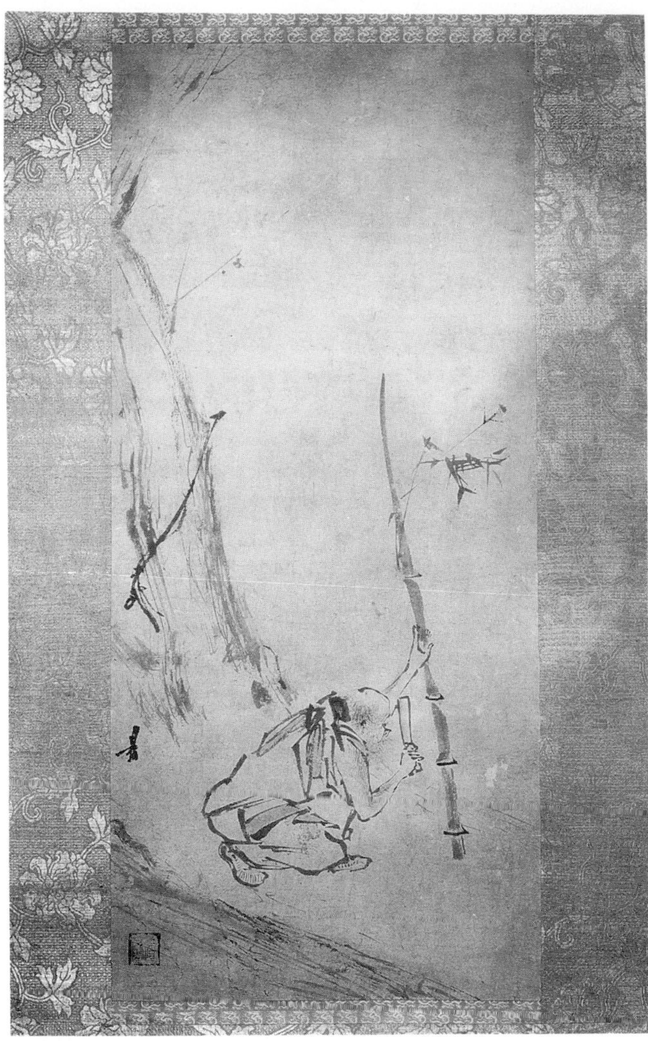

12-19 LIANG K'AI, *The Sixth Ch'an Patriarch Chopping Bamboo,* Southern Sung dynasty, thirteenth century. Hanging scroll, ink on paper, 29¼″ high. Tokyo National Museum.

The followers of Zen repudiate texts, ritual, and charms as instruments of enlightenment. They believe, instead, that the means of salvation lie within the individual, that meditation is useful, and that direct personal experience with some ultimate reality is the necessary step to enlightenment. Zen enlightenment is conceived of as a sudden, almost spontaneous act. These beliefs shaped a new art.

LIANG K'AI, a Zen painter of the thirteenth century, has left us two portraits of Hui Neng, the Sixth Ch'an Patriarch. In one (FIG. **12-19**), the patriarch is a crouching figure chopping bamboo; in the other, he is tearing up a Buddhist sutra. Both are informal sketches that look as though they were caricatures of the revered figure. The brush strokes are staccato and splintery, like the spontaneous process of Zen enlightenment. Each sketch probably was painted in a few minutes, but, like enlightenment, their execution required years of training. Their impact can be a shock, much like the shock of Zen understanding.

Southern Sung artists also produced superb ceramics with monochrome glazes. The most famous of the single-glaze wares are known as *celadon* (a mat gray-green), *ying-ch'ing* (a subtle pale blue), and *ting* (a fine, white protoporcelain). One type of the heavier *chun* ware employed a blue glaze, splashed with red and purple flowing over a stoneware body. A quite different kind of pottery, loosely classed as *tz'u-chou,* is a northern Chinese ceramic type. The subtle techniques of underglaze painting and incision of the design through a colored slip were developed for this pottery during the Sung period. The intricate black-white design of the *mei-p'ing* vase shown here (FIG. **12-20**) was produced by cutting through a black slip to a white slip. The tightly twining vine and petal motifs closely embrace the high-shouldered vessel in

12-20 *Mei-p'ing* vase, Sung dynasty. *Tz'u-chou* stoneware, carved black slip over white slip, 19½″ high, 7¾″ wide. Asian Art Museum of San Francisco, The Avery Brundage Collection.

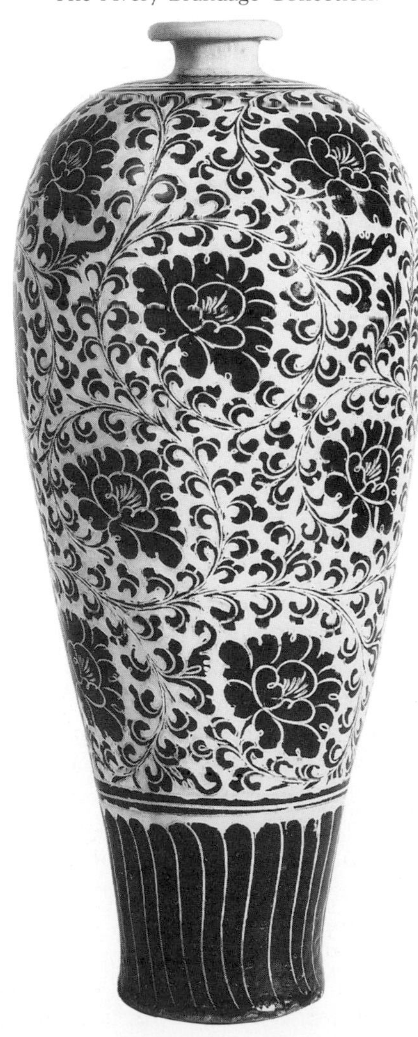

a perfect accommodation of surface design to vase shape—a common characteristic of Chinese pottery in its great periods. These shapes were generally more suave than those of the T'ang period; some, however, reflecting the prevailing interest in archeology, imitated the powerful forms of the Shang and Chou bronzes. Other crafts, particularly jade carving, also were subjected to the influence of archeological or antiquarian interests.

YÜAN DYNASTY

The artistic vitality of Southern Sung was not a reflection of the political conditions of the times. In 1279, the Sung dynasty crumbled beneath the continued onslaughts of Kublai Khan. Yüan, the dynasty of the Mongol invaders, dominated China only until 1368, yet it profoundly affected the culture of the country and particularly the art of painting. Many scholar-painters chose exile in the provinces to avoid service under the barbarian usurpers in Peking. Forced by their exile to reappraise their place in the world, these artists no longer looked at a landscape as an idyllic retreat; it had become part of a formidable environment. This new austerity is evident in a painting (FIG. **12-21**) by one of the great masters of Yüan, HUANG KUNG-WANG (1269–1354). Here, the misty atmosphere of the Southern Sung landscapes has been replaced by massive, textureful forms. The inner structure and momentum of the landscape is rendered by a rhythmic play of brush and ink.

Another leader of the Yüan scholar-artist movement was CHAO MENG-FU (1254–1322), whose paintings contain knowing allusions to old styles. The landscapes of his grandson, WANG MENG (d. 1385), reached a high level of dynamic, expressive intensity. Most of these painters rejected the mellow harmonies of Southern Sung as no longer valid; for their sources, they went back to the more monumental works of the tenth century. The degree to which styles could become personalized in this period is shown in the spare, almost brittle landscapes and bamboo-and-rock paintings of NI TSAN (1301–1374), which reveal an aloof and fastidious personality. These works contrast markedly with the paintings of WU CHEN (1280–1354), which are done in a softer and more relaxed manner. Paintings of bamboo (FIG. **12-22**), for which Wu Chen is famous, were particularly favored at this time, for that plant is a symbol of the ideal Chinese gentleman, who, in adversity, bends but does not break. Moreover, the pattern of leaves, like that of calligraphic script, provided an excellent opportunity for the display of brushwork.

The Mongol regime apparently did little to disturb the Chinese potters' increasing mastery of porcelain. A Late Yüan or Early Ming vase of white porcelain (FIG. **12-23**), discovered in 1961, exhibits brilliance in the use of the underglaze decoration that was so successful in the Sung period.

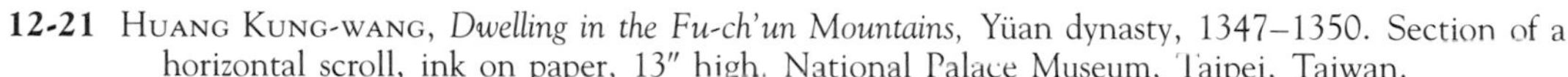

12-21 HUANG KUNG-WANG, *Dwelling in the Fu-ch'un Mountains,* Yüan dynasty, 1347–1350. Section of a horizontal scroll, ink on paper, 13″ high. National Palace Museum, Taipei, Taiwan.

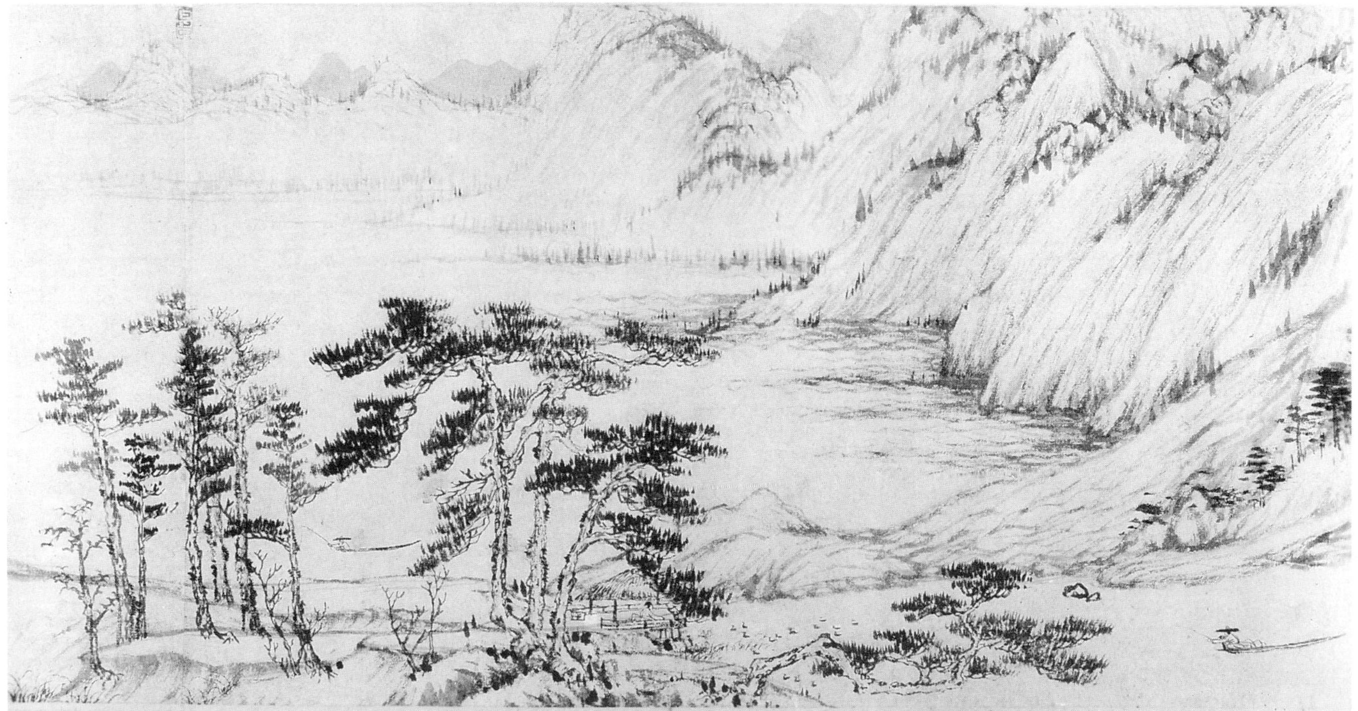

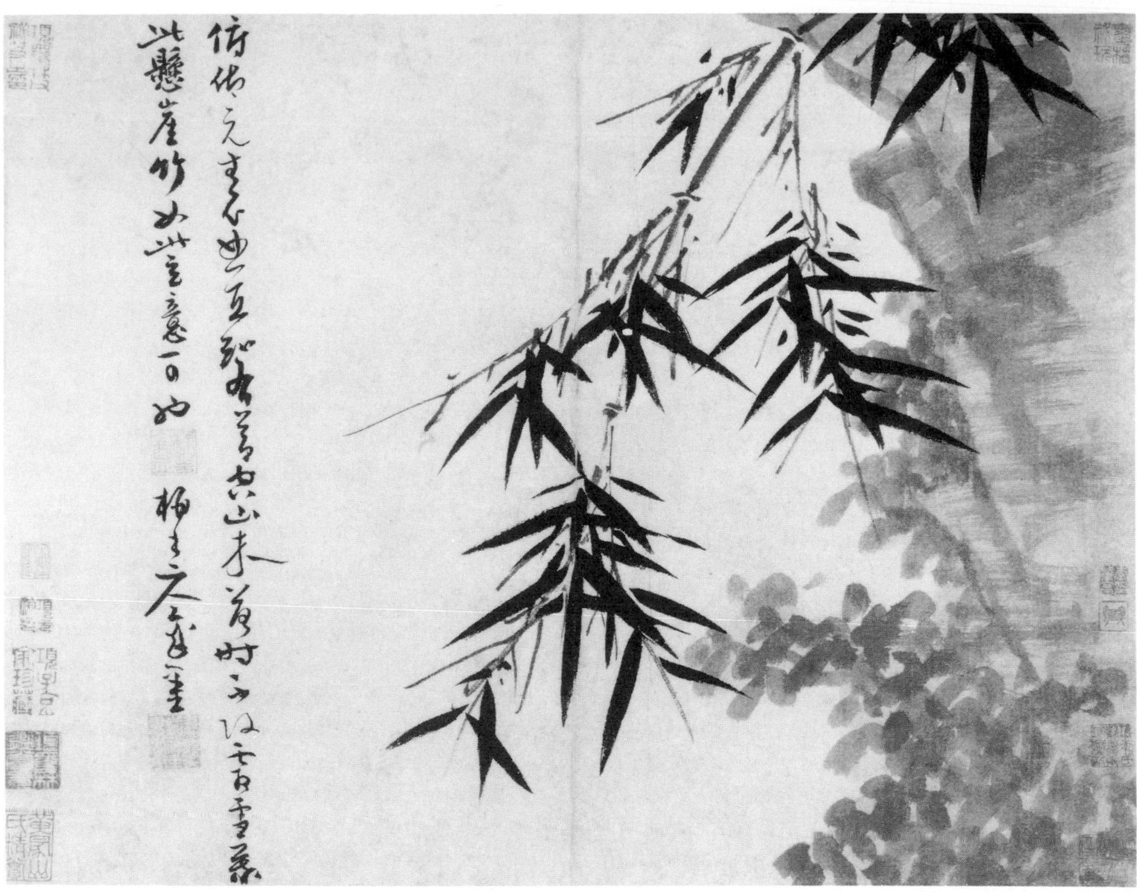

12-22 Wu Chen, *Bamboo,* Yüan dynasty, 1350. Album leaf, ink on paper, 16″ × 21″. Collection of the National Palace Museum, Taipei, Taiwan.

12-23 Covered vase (excavated at Peking), Late Yüan or Early Ming dynasty, late fourteenth century. White porcelain with underglaze decoration, 26½″ high. The exhibition of archeological finds of the People's Republic of China.

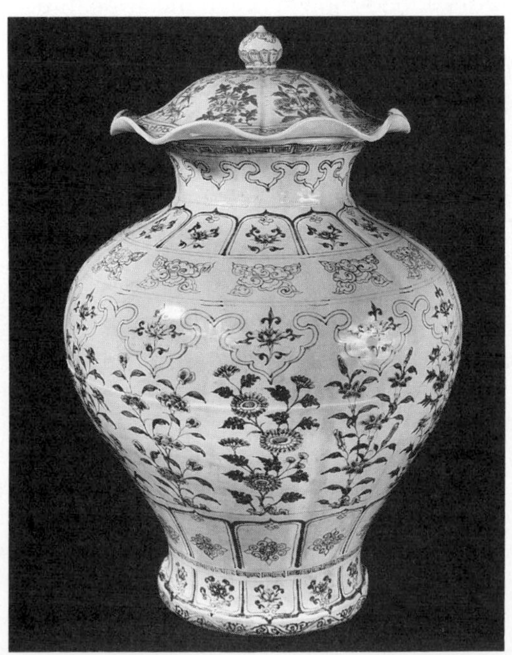

MING, CH'ING, AND LATER DYNASTIES

In 1368, a popular uprising drove out the hated Mongol overlords, and, from that time until 1644, China was ruled by the native Ming dynasty. Many of the fifteenth-century Ming masters, such as Tai Chin (1388–1452), reverted to Sung models. The court, where Tai Chin worked, was one center of patronage and activity; local schools of painting, such as those centered in Nanking and in Suchou, also became important. The Suchou school, under the leadership of Shen Chou (1427–1509) and Wen Cheng-ming (1470–1559), included many highly educated amateur painters who concentrated on refined re-creations of the styles of the masters of the preceding Yüan dynasty. Professional artists, active in Suchou and elsewhere, executed works that displayed great skill and spontaneity.

The distinction between scholar-amateur and academic-professional traditions was codified, rather artificially, in the writings of the influential critic, statesman, and artist Tung Ch'i-ch'ang (1555–1636),

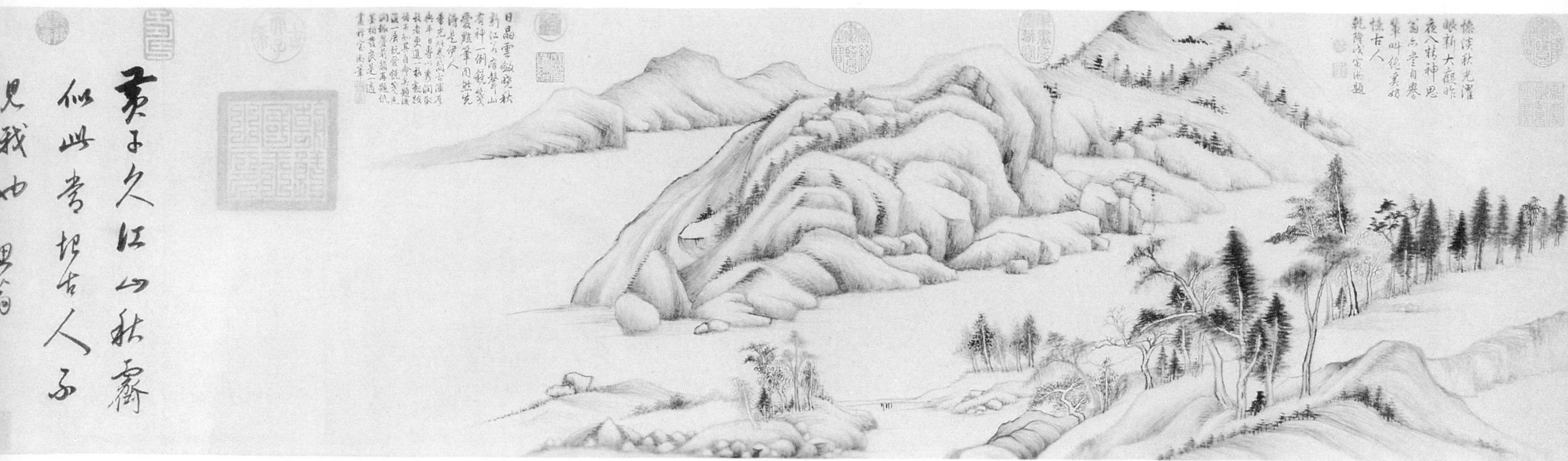

12-24 TUNG CH'I-CH'ANG, *Autumn Mountains,* Ming dynasty, early seventeenth century. Horizontal scroll, ink on paper, $15\frac{1}{8}'' \times 53\frac{7}{8}''$. Cleveland Museum of Art (purchase from the J. H. Wade Fund).

at the end of the Ming period. Tung's glorification of the amateur or literary school reflected his own voracious study and collecting of old paintings. His theories promoted the creation of an orthodoxy in later art that could be stifling, but his own works were true to his ideal of the transformation of old styles, rather than the sterile imitation of them. In Tung's landscapes, his attempts to reveal the inner structure and momentum of nature often result in a radical reorganization of forms (FIG. **12-24**). Ground planes are allowed to tilt or shift; this—and the bold arrangement of rocks and trees to emphasize repeated abstract shapes and textures, without regard for natural scale and surface qualities—may seem arbitrarily distorted, or even crude. What is lost in harmony of surface or representational accuracy, however, is more than made up in qualities of monumentality and power. Paintings by Tung and other masters during the period of social and intellectual readjustment at the end of the Ming dynasty created an atmosphere of artistic freedom. The artists who lived into the next dynasty were its beneficiaries.

The internal decay of Ming bureaucracy permitted another group of invaders, the Manchus, to overrun the country in the seventeenth century. Established as the Ch'ing dynasty (1644–1912), these northerners quickly adapted themselves to Chinese life. The early Ch'ing emperors cultivated a knowledge of China's arts, but their influence merely seems to have encouraged academic work. While the Yüan style continued to be fashionable among the conservatives, other painters experimented with extreme effects of massed ink or individualized patterns of brushwork. Bold and freely manipulated compositions that had a new, expressive force began to appear.

Two artists with intensely personal styles stand out against a mass of lesser painters during this period. The sketchy brush and wet-ink technique of CHU TA (1625–*c.* 1705) derived from sixteenth-century precursors, but his subjects—whimsical animals or petulant birds that are tensely balanced on an album page—demonstrated his discontent with conventional themes. The theoretical writings of Chu Ta's great contemporary TAO-CHI (1641–*c.* 1717) called for a return to wellsprings of creativity through use of the "single brush stroke" or "primordial line" that was the root of all phenomena and representation. The figure in a hut in one of Tao-chi's album leaves (FIG. **12-25**) is surrounded by the surging energy of free-floating colored dots and multiple, sinuous, contour lines that suggest the vital arteries of an organism. What is depicted is not so much the appearance of the landscape as the animating, molding forces that run through it—the prime focus of Chinese landscape art from the earliest times.

Some twentieth-century artists, such as CH'I PAI-SHIH, have found the free brush expressive and have maintained the calligraphic tradition with vitality. HSU PEI-HUNG (1895–1953), known for his boldly brushed pictures of horses, has imbued his work with social content, in keeping with China's political developments. The coming decades will reveal whether a popular art can assimilate the traditions of aristocratic painting that have dominated Chinese art for over a thousand years.

In ceramics, the technical ingenuity of the Ming and Ch'ing potters exceeded the skill of even the Sung potters. In general, porcelain was favored over stoneware and earthenware, with the exception of Ming stonewares, which were decorated broadly in

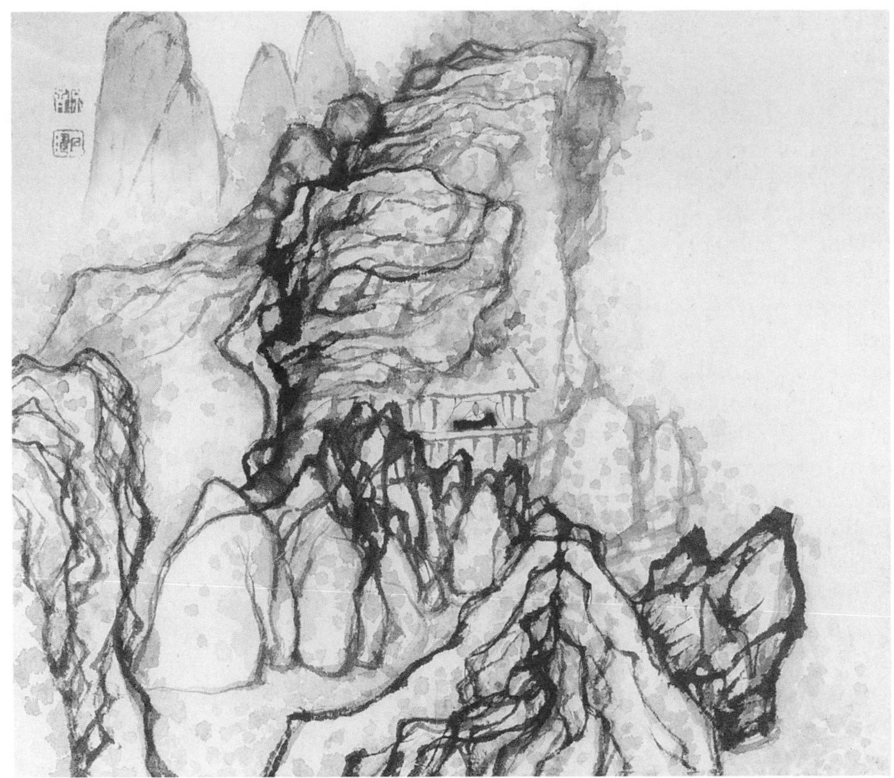

12-25 TAO-CHI, *Landscape,* Ch'ing dynasty, late seventeenth century. Album leaf, ink and colors on paper, 9½" × 11". C. C. Wang Collection, New York.

"three-color" enamels. More delicate designs were painted on "five-color" wares, fine clay forms decorated with enamels and underglaze painting. The celebrated blue-and-white porcelains (FIG. 12-26) owe their quality as much to the distinction of their painted decoration as to the purity of their imported cobalt pigments. Craftsmen also devised a "secret," barely visible decoration that was carved into paper-thin porcelain.

When the Manchus came to power in 1644, they continued to support the great kilns at Fowliang (ancient Chingtechen), where enormous quantities of excellent porcelains were made until the destruction of the kilns during warfare in the mid-nineteenth century. During the K'ang-hsi period (1662–1722), delicate glazes known as *clair de lune* (a silvery blue) and *peachbloom* (pink dappled with green) vied with the polychrome wares. Experiments with glazes led to the invention of the superb imperial yellow and oxblood monochromes. A brief revival of Sung simplicity occurred during the reign of Yung Chêng (1723–1735), but under Ch'ien Lung (1736–1795), a reaction against Sung simplicity led to a style that was sometimes more elaborate than artistic.

Fine embroidered and woven textiles, created for lavish court ceremonies, followed the general style of

12-26 Vase, Ming dynasty, fifteenth century. Porcelain with blue underglaze decoration. Musée Guimet, Paris.

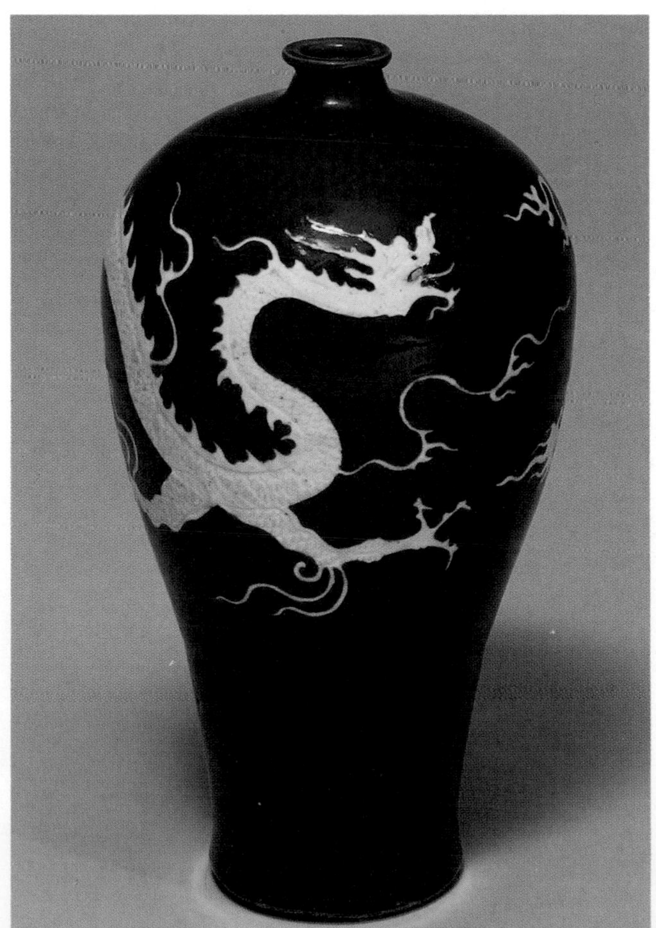

the age, becoming more intricate and, at the same time, more delicate.

During this long period, from the mid-seventeenth to the late eighteenth century, sculpture consisted primarily of charming but inconsequential porcelain bibelots and jade and ivory carvings of an almost unbelievable technical perfection. An example of this work is the white porcelain *Kuan-yin* (FIG. **12-27**), goddess of compassion, from the Early Ch'ing dynasty, which completes that long process of the humanization of the sacred Buddhist images that began even before the T'ang period (see FIG. 12-10). This lovely statuette, reflecting the culmination of the technical achievement of Chinese ceramists, embodies the Bodhisattva's quality of mercy in its softness of form. An easy play of line betrays the influence of painting on ceramics. This "white china ware" (*blanc-de-Chine*) was exported widely to Europe in the eighteenth century, and, in the West to this day, fine ceramic wares, especially porcelain, are called "china."

As the eighteenth century waned, huge workshops, much like our own production-line factories, continued to provide masses of materials for imperial use. Specialists, instead of designer-craftsmen, worked on each stage of manufacture. By the middle of the nineteenth century, this system had drained all vitality from the crafts.

The establishment of the People's Republic of China in 1949 produced a social realism in art that is familiar to the world of the twentieth century (see pages 1015–27) and that breaks drastically with traditional Chinese art. Some Chinese artists carry on cre-

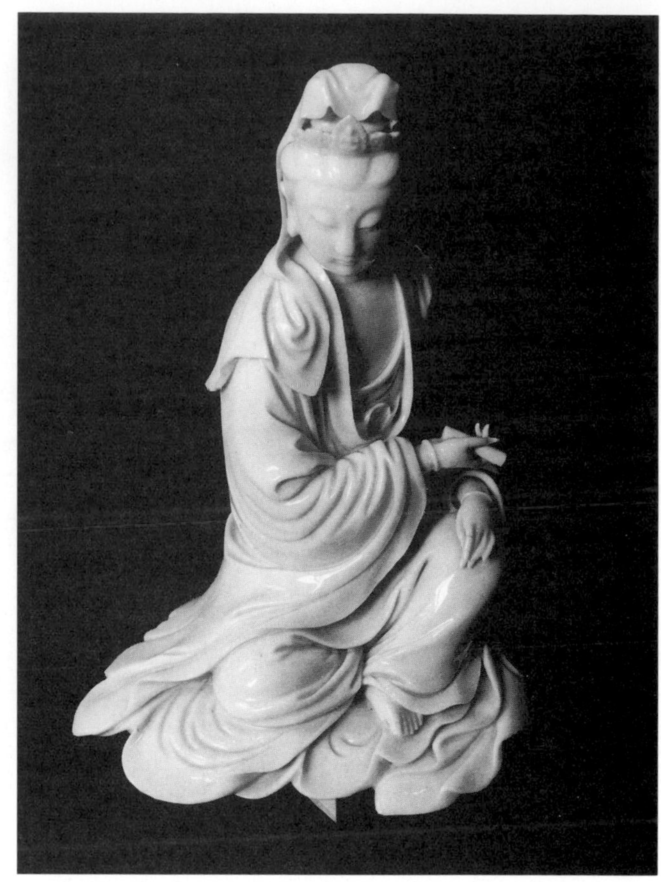

12-27 *Kuan-yin,* Early Ch'ing dynasty, seventeenth and eighteenth centuries. Fukien ware, white porcelain, $8\frac{7}{8}''$ high, $6\frac{1}{4}''$ wide. Trustees of the Barlow Collection, University of Sussex, England.

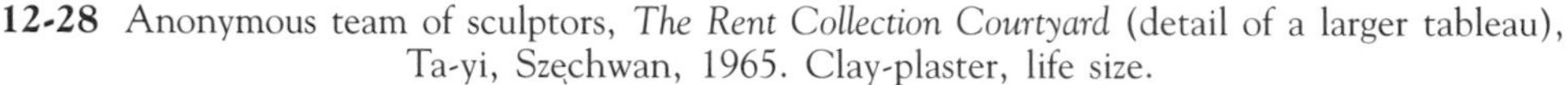

12-28 Anonymous team of sculptors, *The Rent Collection Courtyard* (detail of a larger tableau), Ta-yi, Szechwan, 1965. Clay-plaster, life size.

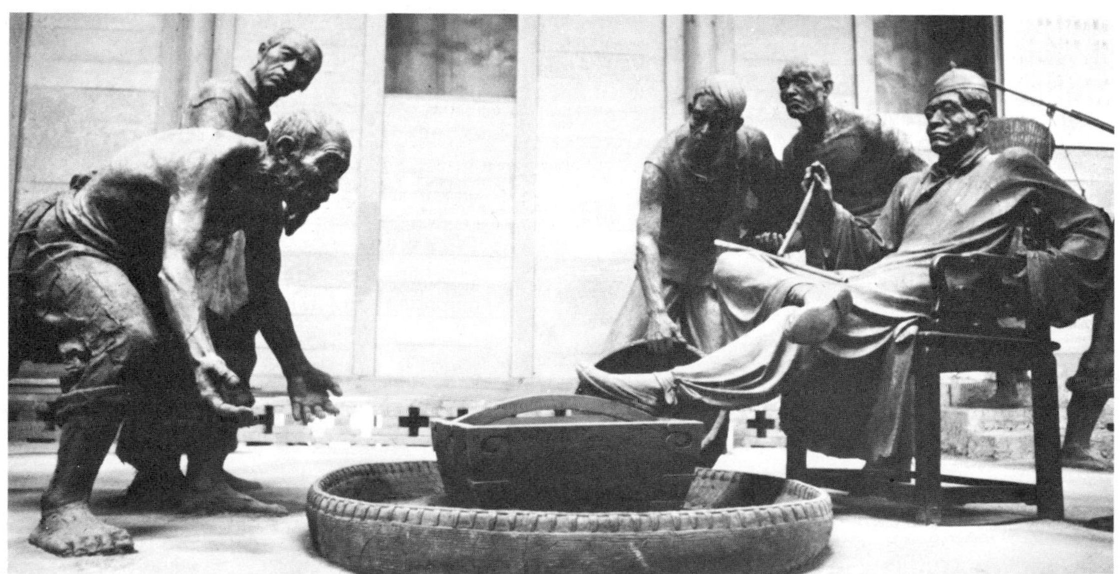

ative work based on the old traditions, but for most, the purpose of art now is, as the People's Republic would claim, to serve the people in the struggle to liberate and elevate the masses. In the work shown (FIG. **12-28**), a life-size tableau, the old times are depicted grimly in a scene common enough before the revolution. Peasants, worn and bent by toil, are bringing their taxes (in the form of produce) to the courtyard of their merciless, plundering landlord. The message is clear: this kind of thing must not happen again. Significantly, the artists who depict the event are an anonymous team. The "name" artist belongs to the past; only collective action, say its theoreticians, can bring about the transformations the People's Republic is seeking. Ironically, "collective action" by students protesting in Tiananmen Square in early June, 1989, produced not an image of an oppressed peasant or a militant worker, but an allegorical statue of "Liberty" based on the colossal one in New York Harbor. This was not at all the kind of art the leaders of the People's Republic wanted to see.

ARCHITECTURE

We have said little about Chinese architecture, partly because few early buildings exist and partly because Chinese architecture has not displayed distinctive changes in style over the centuries. The modern Chinese building closely resembles its prototype of a thousand years ago. Indeed, the dominant silhouette of the roof, which gives Chinese architecture much of its specific character, may go back to Chou or Shang times. Even the simple buildings depicted on Han stone carvings reveal a style and a method of construction still basic to China. The essentials consist of a rectangular hall, dominated by a pitched roof with projecting eaves supported by a bracketing system and wooden columns. The walls serve no bearing function but act only as screening elements.

Within this limited formula, the Chinese architect has focused his attention on the superstructure. As early as the Han dynasty, combinations of brackets, impost blocks, and columns were devised to support the weight of massive, tiled roofs (FIG. **12-29**). The architects gave animation to the exterior by varying the shapes of the brackets. From these simple beginnings, later architects developed very intricate systems of support. Some brackets were placed parallel to the walls; others reached outward to support a beam or other brackets, until the multiplication of units created a rich pattern of light and shade. The effect was intensified by decorations in red and gold lacquer (FIG. **12-30**). Function often was subordinated

12-29 Structural diagram of typical Chinese construction. (After Watson.)

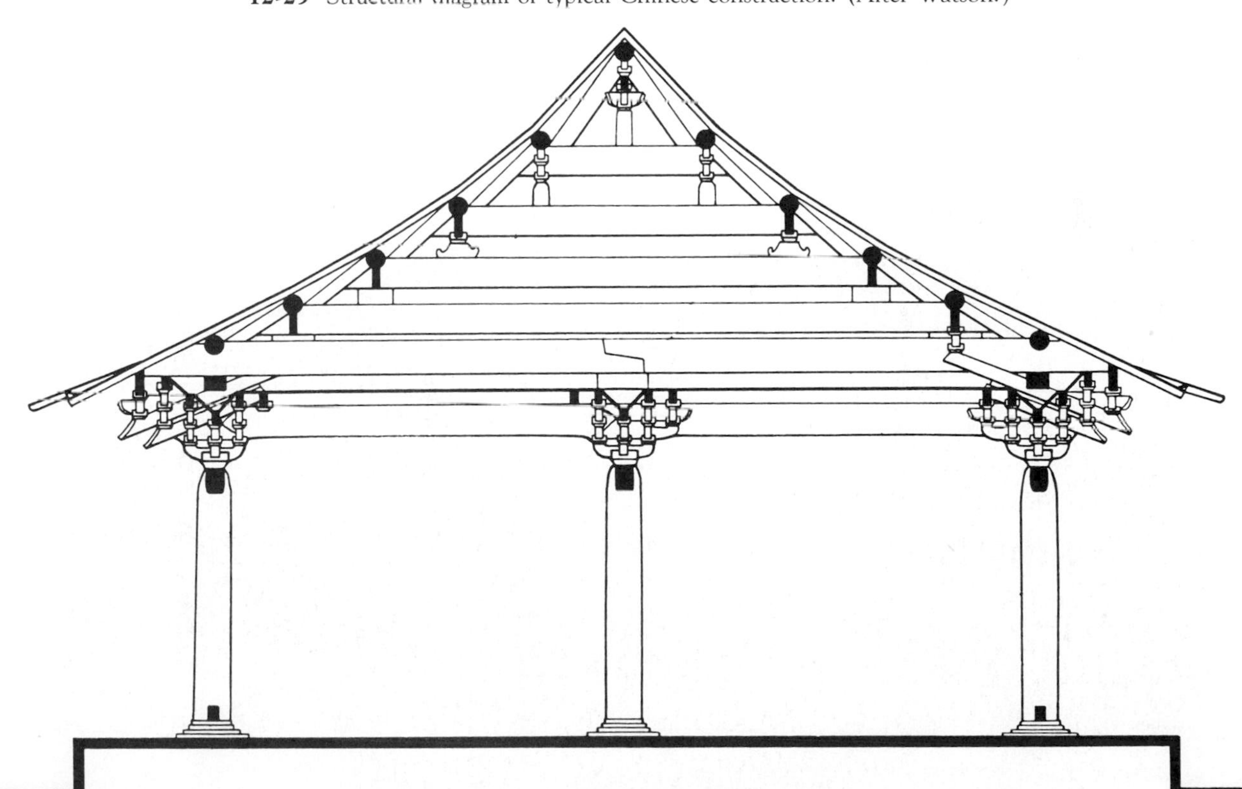

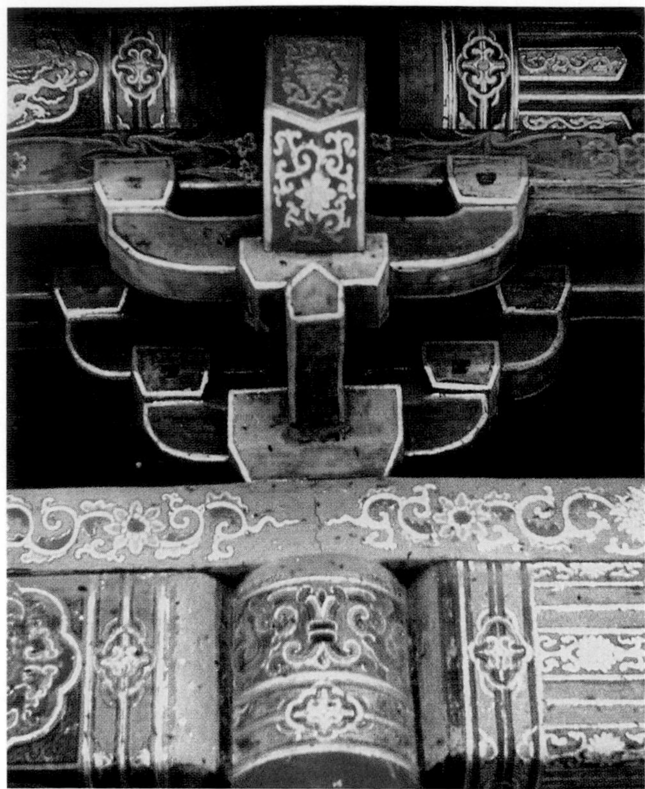

12-30 Console bracket cluster supporting eaves of a bell tower, Xi'an, Shensi.

to ornament; where only minimal support was required, complicated bracket systems sometimes were introduced for decoration.

On the exterior, the coloristic interplay of the supports formed a pleasing contrast to the uninterrupted sweep of the pitched roof. The overhanging eaves became even wider during the T'ang period, and builders began to turn up the corners. These slightly curving eaves were exaggerated in later buildings, especially in south China, where they produced a riotous fantasy of upswept lines. But in most areas, the gentle curves of the roofs give an air of grace to the otherwise severe rectangular form and rigid symmetry that were imposed by the plans of the buildings. The style was imported by Japan along with Buddhism, and the Phoenix Hall of the Byodo-in Temple at Uji, Japan (FIG. 13-11), may serve as a good example of the Chinese style. In China proper, the best-known building is the T'ai-ho Tien (Hall of Supreme Harmony, FIG. **12-31**) in the Forbidden City of Peking. Built in 1627, rebuilt in 1697, and restored in 1765, it is one of the less florid examples of Chinese architecture that impresses more through size (it is over 200 feet long) than gracefulness. Raised high on a terraced marble podium, the wooden structure is the largest of several similar buildings that are aligned along a central north–south axis that runs through the rectangu-

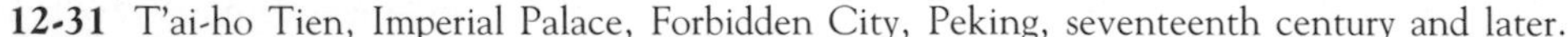

12-31 T'ai-ho Tien, Imperial Palace, Forbidden City, Peking, seventeenth century and later.

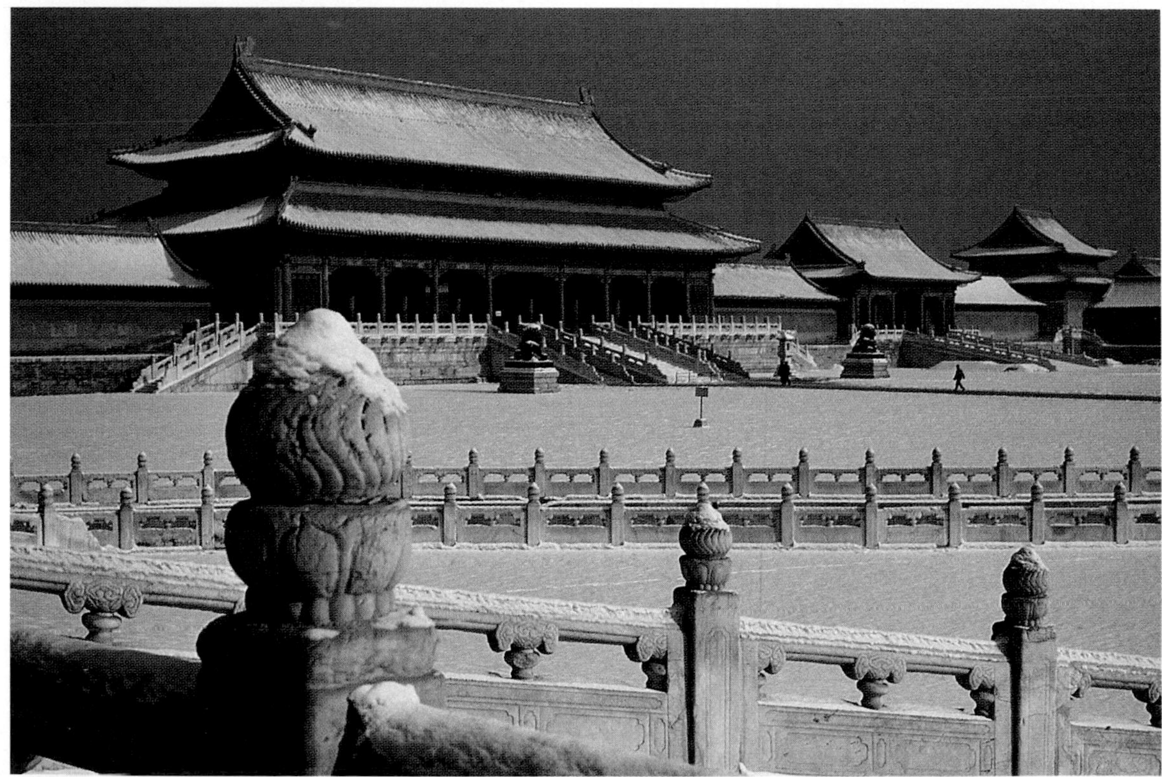

lar, moat-surrounded former imperial compound. Although here its exterior is somewhat blunt and massive in appearance, the building's proportions are pleasing enough and the upswept corners of the roof soften what otherwise might have been a rather heavy and forbiddingly stern appearance. For centuries, the orientation of buildings, even of whole cities, had been ordered on a strict north–south axis. Houses, palaces, temples, and official buildings all fell within one formal pattern. Even the seeming randomness of the varied bridges and pavilions in the informal gardens was carefully devised.

Buddhist architecture contributed a specific form—the *pagoda* (FIG. **12-32**)—which, to many, has become a symbol of China. These pagoda towers, which dot the countryside and seem so native to the land, were derived from the Indian stupa (FIG. 11-5). Most of the wooden pagodas, with their multiplicity of winged eaves, bear little resemblance to the solid domes of Sanchi or Amaravati, but their origin, like that of the Chinese Buddha, is to be found in Gandhara, where terraced and towering variants of the stupa once had impressed Chinese pilgrims with their grandeur. So quickly was the stupa structure assimilated by the Chinese that even the earliest pagodas (sixth to eighth centuries) show only a few traces of their Indian origin. In the Chinese wooden idiom, all that remained of the Indian stupa were the yasti and parasols, which crowned that structure. Instead of a circular plan, the Chinese preferred a four-, six-, or eight-sided one, and story was piled on story in order to form towers as high as 300 feet. Each story was marked by its own projecting eaves, the curved lines of which soared into the sky. Like other Chinese architectural forms, the pagoda was imported by Japan, where, stylistically modified, it marks the sites of many Buddhist temples.

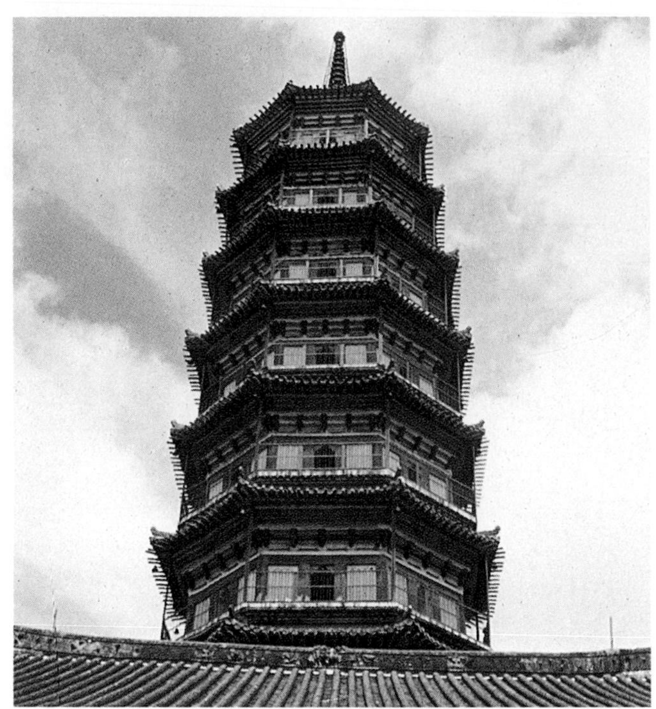

12-32 Pagoda of the Temple of the Six Banyan Trees, Canton, Kwangtung, 537 (rebuilt 1098). 180′ high.

It is curious that the architecture of China, the oldest continuing civilization in the world, should be represented by few surviving buildings older than the ninth century. This phenomenon is due largely to a flexible construction that is easily dismantled, moved to other sites, or simply replaced. The joinery, like cabinet-making in its exquisite fitting together of the component parts, almost invites taking apart. At the same time, this structural flexibility has permitted easy replication and the perpetuation of a style recognizable through the ages as indigenously and characteristically Chinese.

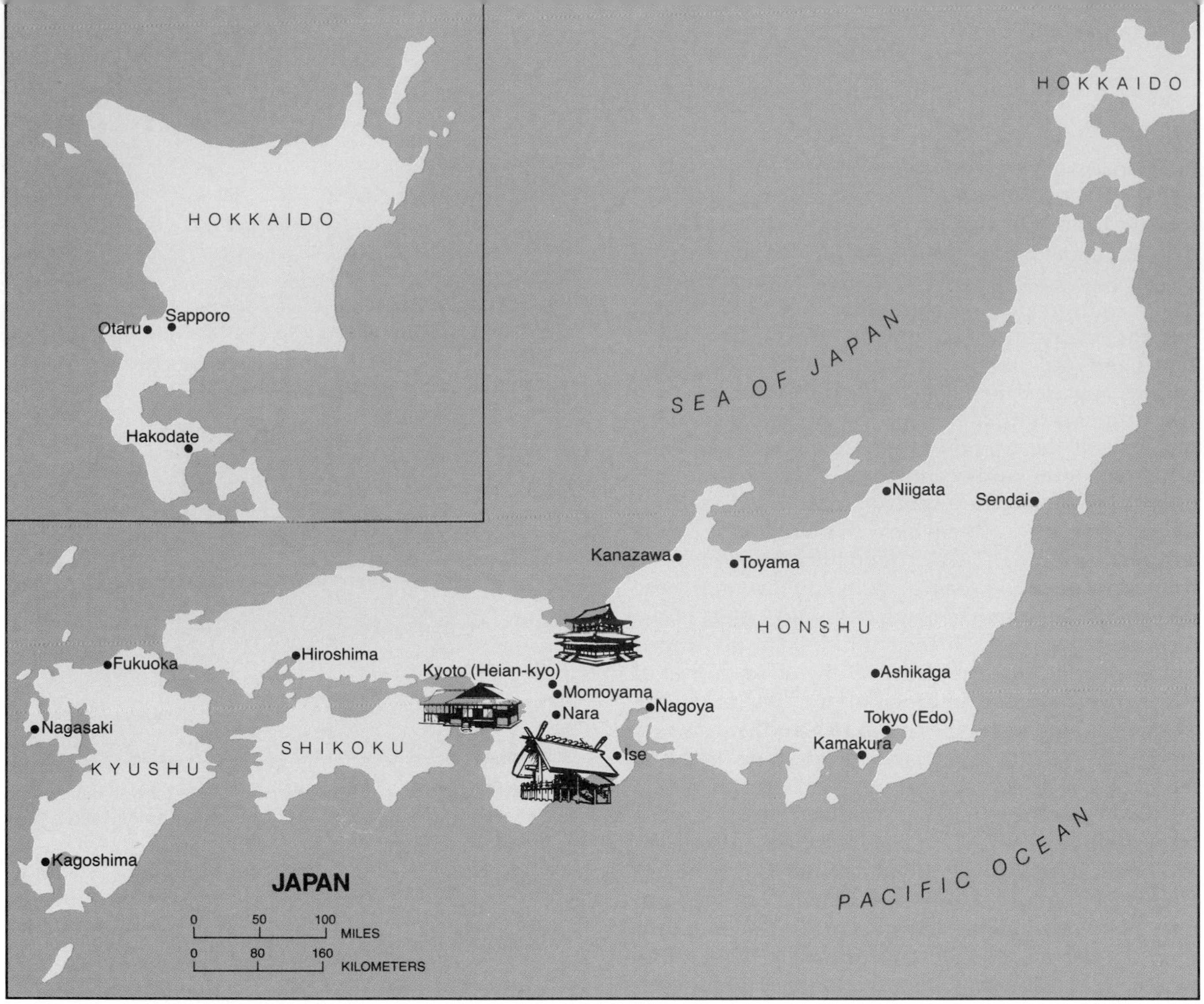

HOKKAIDO

HOKKAIDO
Otaru
Sapporo
Hakodate

SEA OF JAPAN
Niigata
Sendai
Kanazawa
Toyama
HONSHU
Hiroshima
Fukuoka
Kyoto (Heian-kyo)
Momoyama
Nara
Nagoya
Ashikaga
Tokyo (Edo)
Kamakura
Ise
Nagasaki
SHIKOKU
KYUSHU
Kagoshima
PACIFIC OCEAN

JAPAN

0 50 100 MILES
0 80 160 KILOMETERS

3000 B.C.	B.C.	A.D.	552	710	794	1185
JOMON CULTURE		ARCHAIC PERIOD	ASUKA AND HAKUHO PERIODS	NARA PERIOD	EARLY AND LATE HEIAN (FUJIWARA) PERIODS	KAMAKURA PERIOD

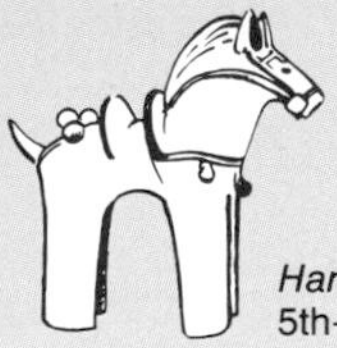

Haniwa figure 5th–6th century

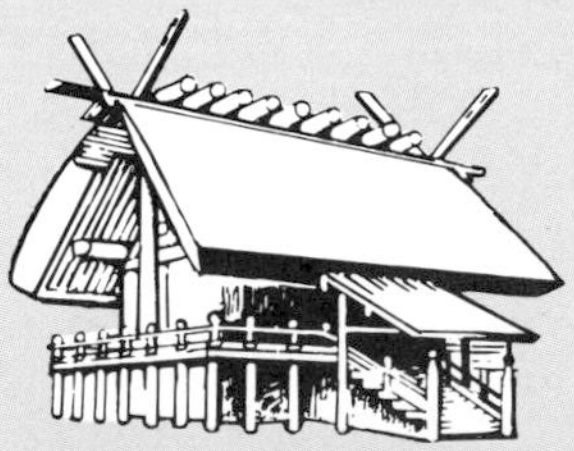

Ise Shrine 3rd-century type

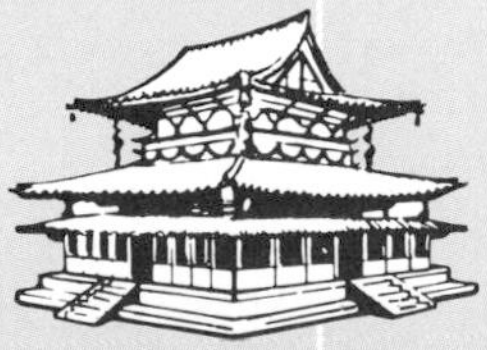

Kondo 7th century

TAKAYOSHI (?) *The Tale of Genji* 12th century

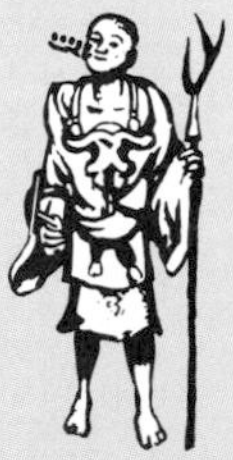

The Sage Kuya Invoking the Amida Buddha 13th century

Kimmei, Emperor of Japan 552

Introduction of Buddhism to Japan

Civil wars lead to end of Fujiwara rulers

Zen Buddhism begins rise

New capital established at Kamakura 1185

13
THE ART OF JAPAN

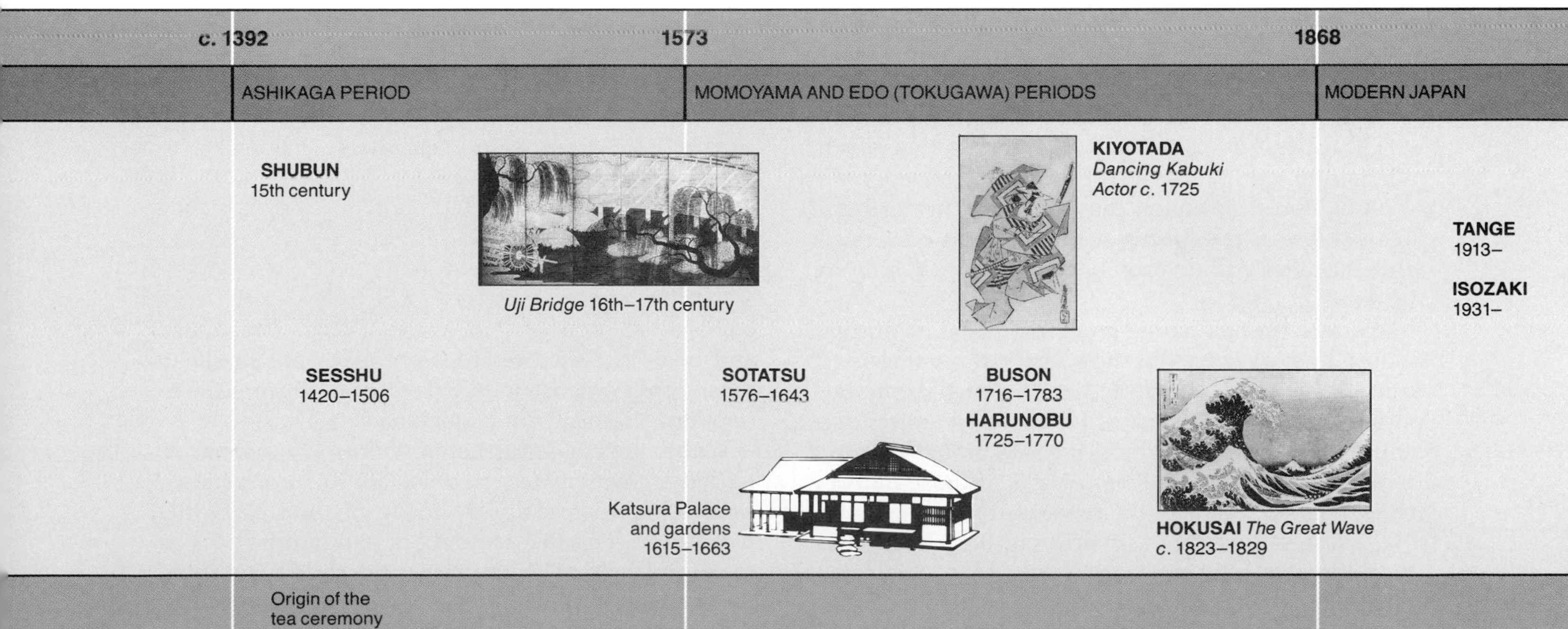

THE ARTS OF JAPAN have neither the progressive, stylistic continuity of the arts of India nor the wide variety of those of China. A series of foreign influences sporadically affected the course of Japan's artistic evolution. Yet, no matter how overwhelming the impact of new forms and styles, the indigenous tradition invariably reasserted itself. Hence, the artistic pattern evolved in a rhythmic sequence of marked periods of borrowing, absorption, and return to native patterns.

Because Japan and its nearby islands are of volcanic origin, little stone suitable for carving or building is available. In architecture, this scarcity led to the development of wooden construction carefully devised to withstand the frequent earthquakes and tempests. In sculpture, figures were modeled in clay, which was often left unfired, cast in bronze by the *cire perdue* process familiar to many other cultures, or constructed of lacquer. Although the lacquer technique originated in China, Japanese artists excelled in creating large, hollow, lacquer figures by placing hemp cloth soaked in the juice of the lacquer tree over wooden armatures. The surfaces gradually were added to and finished, but the technique remained one of modeling rather than of carving. Such figures were not only light but very durable, being hard and resistant to destructive forces. Hollow lacquer figures eventually were superseded by sculptures carved in wood, with unusual sensitivity for grain and texture.

ARCHAIC PERIOD

The first artifacts known in Japan are pottery vessels and figurines from a culture designated Jomon, which apparently flourished as early as the fourth millennium B.C. These objects are associated with Neolithic tools, although they persisted in northern Japan as late as the fourth or fifth century A.D., even while a metal culture was being developed fully in the south.

Japanese objects dating from about the beginning of the Christian era are of three kinds: those imported from the Asian mainland, those copied from imported articles, and those of Japanese invention. Examples, for instance, would include bronze mirrors from Han China, as well as replicas of these mirrors made in Japan. Some of the replicas are adorned with a Japanese innovation—spherical rattles attached to the perimeter. A gray pottery known as *sue* came from Korea, another source of continental influence. Sue soon was copied, and small, comma-shaped stones (*magatama*) were used in necklaces. A third area, Indochina, was the source of motifs used on bell-shaped bronzes, known as *dotaku*. The houses and boats depicted on these bronzes are similar to those on contemporaneous drums from Annam (modern Vietnam), in Indochina.

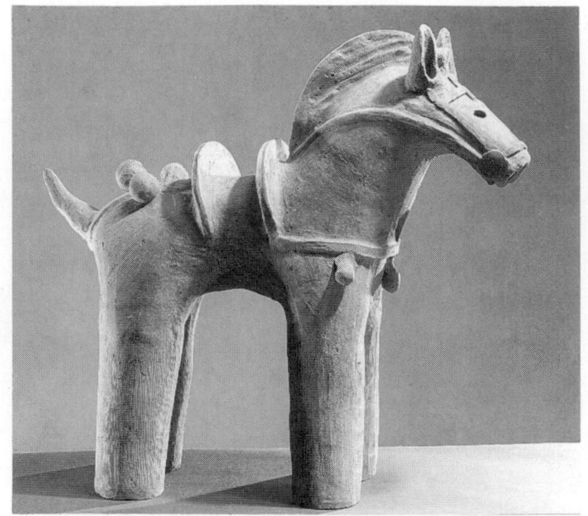

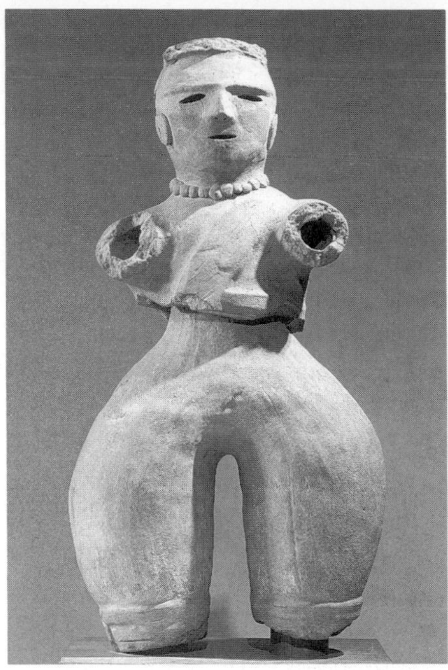

13-1 *Haniwa* figures, horse and peasant, fifth to sixth centuries. Clay. Horse, Cleveland Museum of Art (gift of The Norweb Collection); peasant, Cleveland Museum of Art (James Parmelee Fund purchase).

Within this heterogeneous culture, a specifically Japanese creativity asserted itself in the production of *haniwa*—tubular sculpture made of fired clay—that was placed fencelike around burial mounds, possibly to control erosion or to protect the dead. The upper parts of the haniwa are usually modeled in human form, but these sculptures also sometimes take the shape of a horse (FIG. **13-1**), a bird, or even a house. Simple pottery cylinders were used similarly in Indochina, but the sculptural modeling of haniwa is uniquely Japanese. The arms and legs, as well as the mass of the torso, in most instances, recapitulate the cylindrical base of the haniwa. The tubelike character of some later monumental sculpture—and even of a particular wooden doll common in Japan today—may derive from these remote ancestors.

Aside from colossal tomb mounds, reminiscent of those found in China, the earliest Japanese architecture was limited to pit dwellings and simple constructions of thatched roofs on bamboo or wooden stilts. From these primitive origins evolved what may be called the native Japanese style of architecture, as distinguished from the imported Chinese style. This native building style has survived into our time in some of the shrines of Shinto, the indigenous faith of the Japanese people.* The custom at the Ise Shrine in Mie Prefecture (FIG. **13-2**) has been to disassemble the buildings every twenty years and to replace them with exact copies. This process has been repeated since the third century, and we may assume that the structures there today reproduce the original ones with considerable accuracy.

The typical Shinto shrine, like the Buddhist temple, consists of several buildings within a rectangular, fenced enclosure. The buildings are disposed symmetrically along a central axis that leads from the outside, through one or more ceremonial gates *(torii),* into and through the compound. This axis is interrupted only by the off-center outermost gate and by the transversely placed main building. The main sanctuary was regarded as the dwelling place of the deity and was not accessible to worshipers, who said their prayers outside the innermost gate. The sanctuary was to be seen only from the outside (much like a Greek temple), and all of the builders' efforts were directed toward the refinement of the building's proportions and details.

*Shinto, or "the Way of the Gods," was based on love of nature, of the family, and, above all, of the ruling family, as direct descendents of the gods. Nationalistic in character, Shinto was embodied in symbolic forms and shunned pictorial representation.

13-2 Ise Shrine, Japan. Rebuilt in 1973, reproducing third-century type.

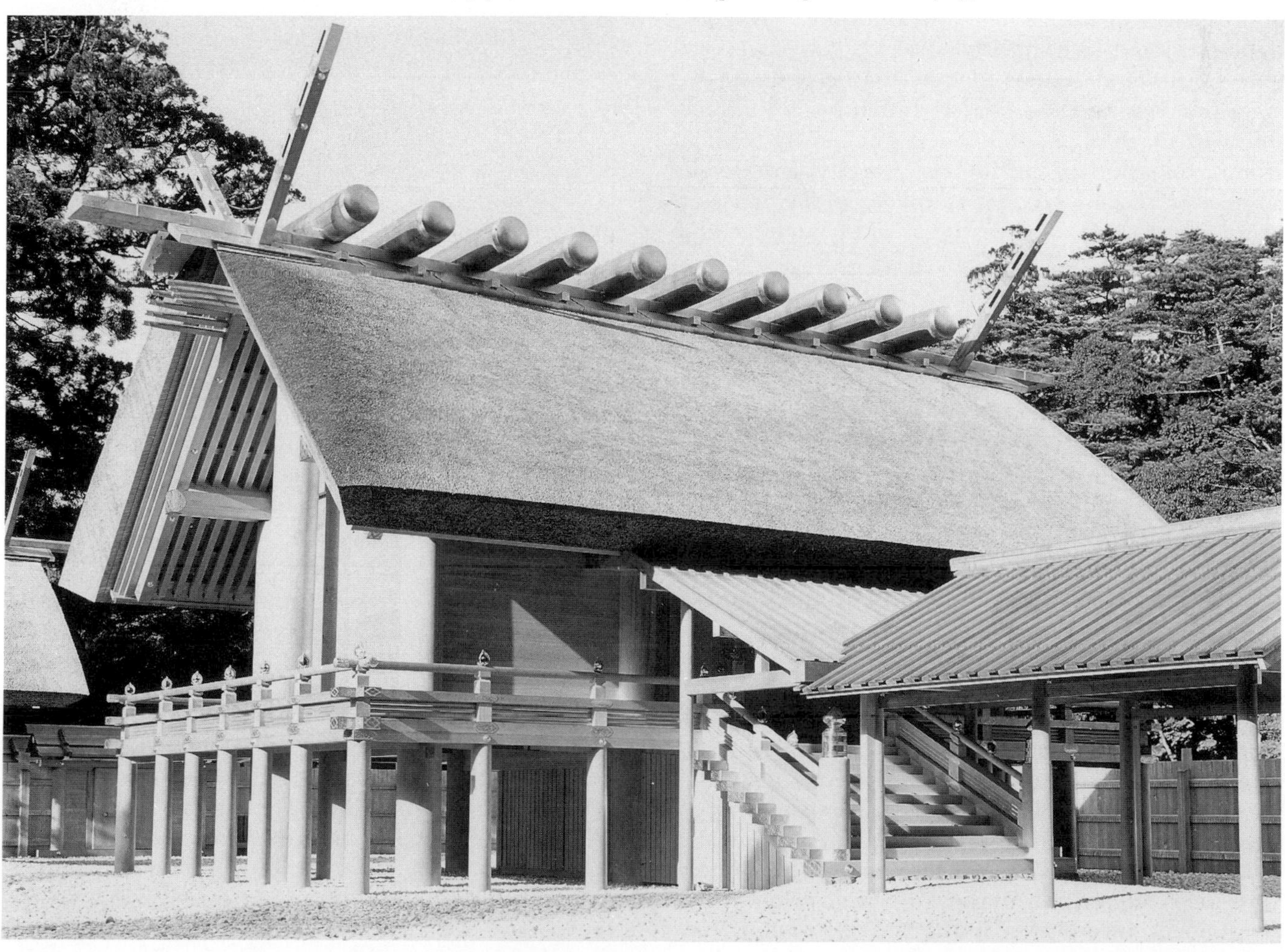

The Ise Shrine (FIG. 13-2), the greatest of all Shinto shrines, was rebuilt for the sixtieth time in 1973. It covers an area 55 by 127 yards and is enclosed by four concentric fences. Aside from their thatched roofs, the buildings are constructed entirely of wood fitted together in a mortise-and-tenon system (without nails), the wall boards being slipped into slots in the pillars. Two massive, freestanding posts (once great trunks of cypress trees), one at each end of the building, support most of the weight of the ridgepole. Golden-hued columns and planks of the same wood are burnished to mellow surfaces, their color and texture contrasting with the white gravel that covers the ground of the sacred precinct. In the characteristic manner of the Japanese artist, the thatched roof was transformed from a simple functional element into one that established the esthetic of the entire structure. Browned by a smoking process, the thatch was sewn into bundles and then carefully laid in layers that gradually decreased in number from the eaves to the ridgepole. The entire surface was then sheared smooth, and a gently changing contour resulted. The roofline was enhanced further by decorative elements that once had been structural—the *chigi* or crosspiece at the gables, and cylindrical, wooden weights placed at right angles across the ridgepole. The repeats and echoes of the various parts of the main building and the related structures are a quiet study in rhythmic form. The shrine, in its setting, is an expression of purity and dignity, effectively emphasized by the extreme simplicity of the precisely planned proportions, textures, and architectural forms employed.

ASUKA PERIOD

The development of native traditions was interrupted in 552 by an event of paramount importance to Japan. In that year, the ruler of Kudara (Korean: Paekche), a kingdom in Korea, sent a gilt bronze figure of the Buddha to Kimmei, emperor of Japan. With the image came the gospels. For half a century, the new religion met with opposition, but at the end of that time, Buddhism and its attendant arts were established firmly in Japan.

Among the earliest examples of Japanese art serving the cause of Buddhism is *The Shaka Triad* (FIG. **13-3**), a bronze sculpture of Shaka (Sanskrit: Sakyamuni) and attendant Bodhisattvas, made in 623 by TORI BUSSHI, a third-generation Korean living in Japan. Tori's style is that of the mid-sixth century in China. His work proved how tenaciously the formula for a "correct" representation of the icon had been maintained since the introduction of Buddhism almost a century earlier. Yet, at the same time, a new

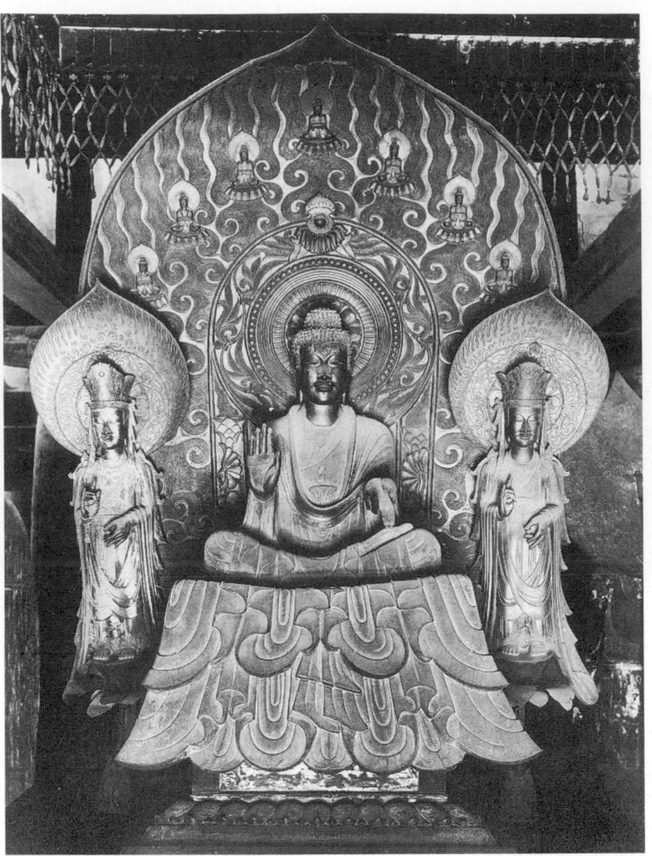

13-3 TORI BUSSHI, *The Shaka Triad,* Asuka period, 623. Bronze, 69½″ high. Hōryū-ji, Nara, Japan.

influence was coming from Sui China, which may be seen in the cylindrical form and flowing draperies of the wood sculpture known as the *Kudara Kannon* (Chinese: *Kuan-yin*). The two styles were blended, and, in the middle of the seventh century, they coalesced in one of Japan's finest sculptures, the *Miroku* (Sanskrit: *Maitreya*) of the Chugu-ji (the suffix *-ji* means "temple") nunnery near Nara (FIG. **13-4**). In this figure, the Japanese artist combines a gentle sweetness with formal restraint in a manner unknown in Chinese sculpture.

Within a little more than half a century, however, all the archaisms of the fused style (loosely called Suiko, after the empress who reigned from 593 to 628, or Asuka, after the site of the capital) were swept aside by a new influence from T'ang China. The T'ang style, which found its way to Japan at the end of the Hakuho period (645–710), dominated Japanese art during the following periods of late Nara (710–794) and Early Heian (794–897). Chinese models were followed not only in sculpture and painting but also in architecture, literature, and even etiquette.

The mature T'ang style appeared suddenly in Japan in the bronze *Shrine of Lady Tachibana* (FIG. **13-5**). The shrine consists of three full-round figures: the

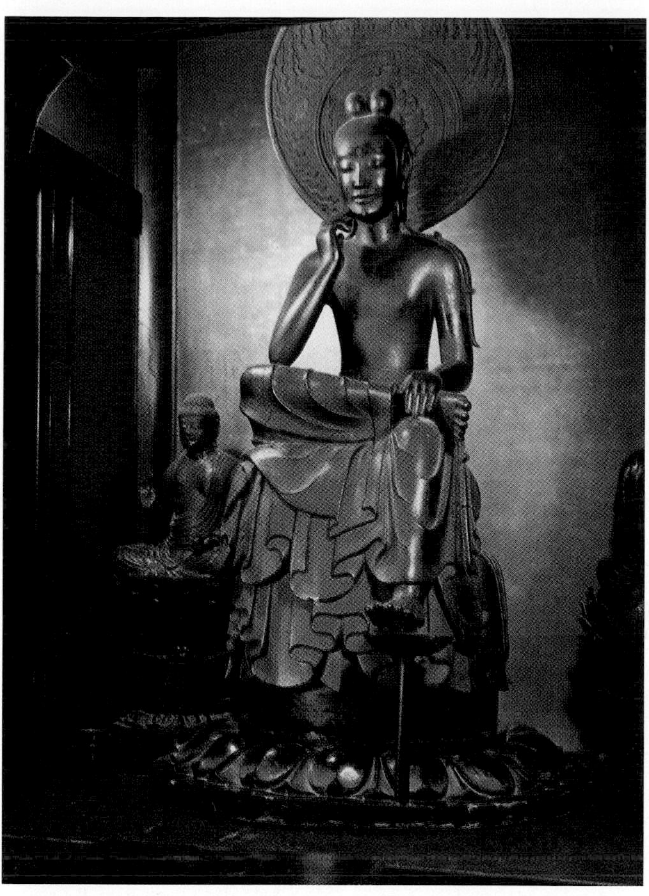

13-4 *Miroku,* Asuka period, mid-seventh century. Wood, 62″ high. Chugu-ji nunnery, Hōryū-ji, Nara.

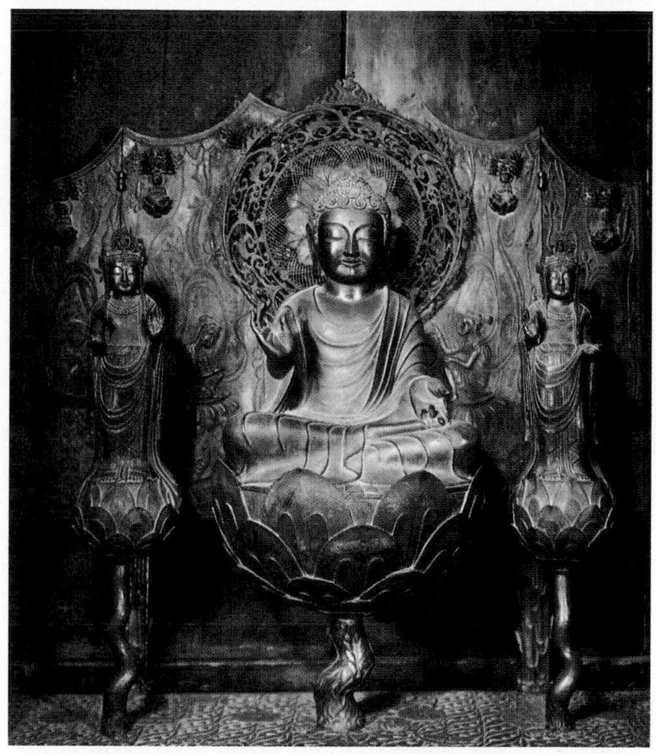

13-5 *The Amida Triad,* from the *Shrine of Lady Tachibana,* Nara period, early eighth century. Gilded bronze; Amida, 11″ high, attendants, 10″ high. Hōryū-ji, Nara.

Buddha Amida (Sanskrit: Amitabha) seated on a lotus between the smaller figures of Kannon and Dai Seishi (Bodhisattva attendants), each standing on a lotus. All three are rising from a platform that represents the stylized waters of the Sukhavati lake in the paradise of the Buddha. Behind them is a threefold screen on which are modeled, in relief, the graceful forms of *apsaras* (heavenly nymphs) seated on lotuses and the tiny figures of souls newly borne into heaven. The upswept scarves of the apsaras and the petals, tendrils, and pads of the lotuses create an exquisite background for the three divinities, while a detached, openwork halo of delicate design frames the head of the Buddha. The ensemble gives us some idea of the glorious T'ang bronzes that were melted down in China during the Buddhist persecutions of 845. It also clearly demonstrates the remarkable adaptability of the Japanese artist in seizing a new art form and making it his own.

The development of painting in Japan paralleled that of Buddhist sculpture. Some of the earliest surviving examples are found on the *Tamamushi* (beetlewing) *Shrine* (FIG. **13-6**), which dates from the first half of the seventh century. The shrine is in the form of a miniature temple on a high wooden base, which

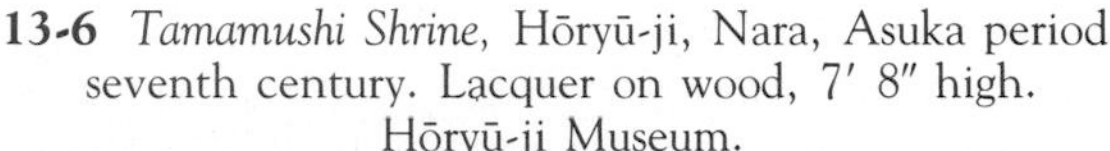

13-6 *Tamamushi Shrine,* Hōryū-ji, Nara, Asuka period, seventh century. Lacquer on wood, 7′ 8″ high. Hōryū-ji Museum.

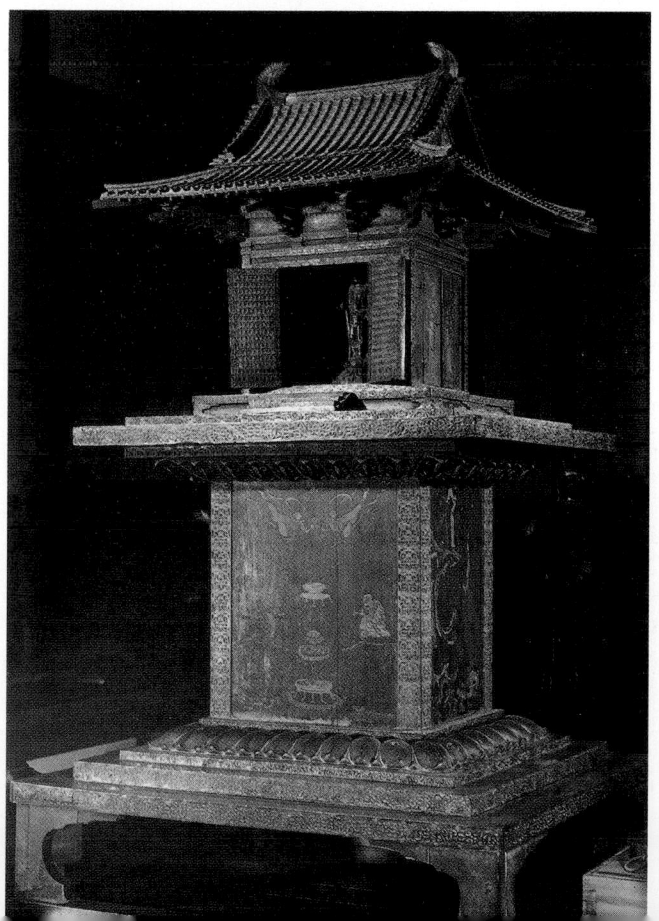

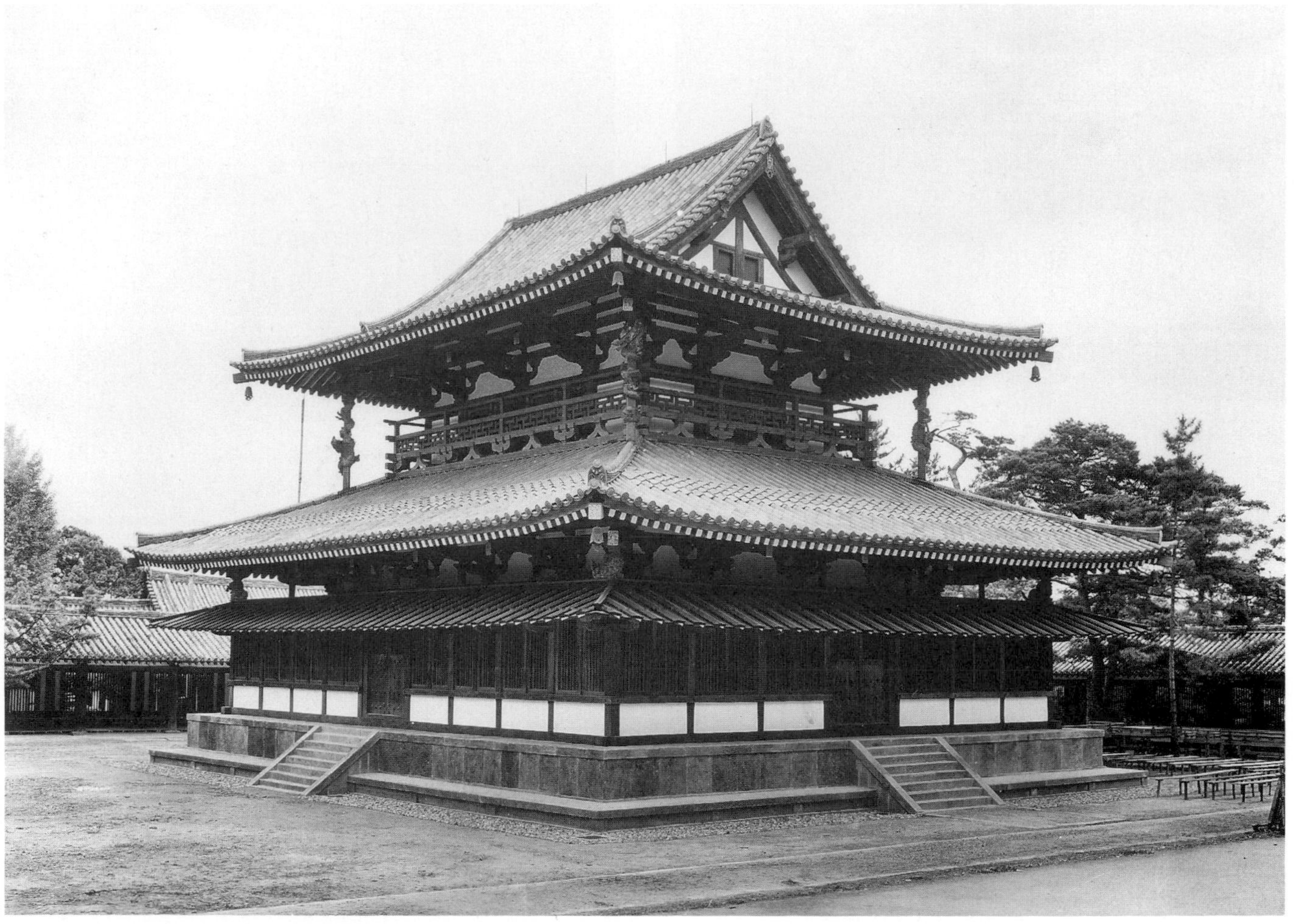

13-7 Kondo (Golden Hall), Hōryū-ji, Nara. Asuka period, seventh century.

was decorated with the iridescent wings of beetles. The four side panels of the base are painted with scenes from the *Jataka* in the style of the Chinese Tunhuang caves of a century earlier, as may be seen in the cell-like composition, the crystalline rock formations, the attenuated figures, and the free linear movement. The shrine paintings also manifest the same delight in surface pattern to the point of disregard of naturalism in scale and spatial relationships.

The Japanese dependence on China during the seventh and eighth centuries is not confined to sculpture and painting. Buddhist architecture adhered so closely to Chinese models that the lost T'ang style can be reconstructed from such temple complexes as the Hōryū-ji or the Todai-ji, which still stand in Japan. The Kondo (Golden Hall) of the Hōryū-ji (FIG. **13-7**), which dates from shortly after 670, is one of the oldest wooden buildings in the world. Although periodically repaired and somewhat altered (the covered porch was added in the eighth century; the upper railing, in the seventeenth), the structure retains the light and buoyant quality characteristic of the style of the Northern and Southern dynasties in China. A rather unusual feature of this building is the entasis of its wooden columns. The appearance of this feature here is said to be due to Greek influence, as third-hand knowledge of it may have reached Japan, along with Buddhism, from India by way of China. Although seemingly more appropriate to elastic wood than to brittle stone, entasis was a short-lived feature that soon disappeared again from Japanese architecture.

EARLY HEIAN AND LATE HEIAN (FUJIWARA) PERIODS

A new style of representation arrived in Japan at the beginning of the ninth century. Under the influence of Esoteric Buddhism (pages 459–60), a heavier image with multiple arms and heads was introduced—a type that, in China, was then replacing the earlier, classic grace of the T'ang style. The bloated forms of the new style, though they may be repellent, have

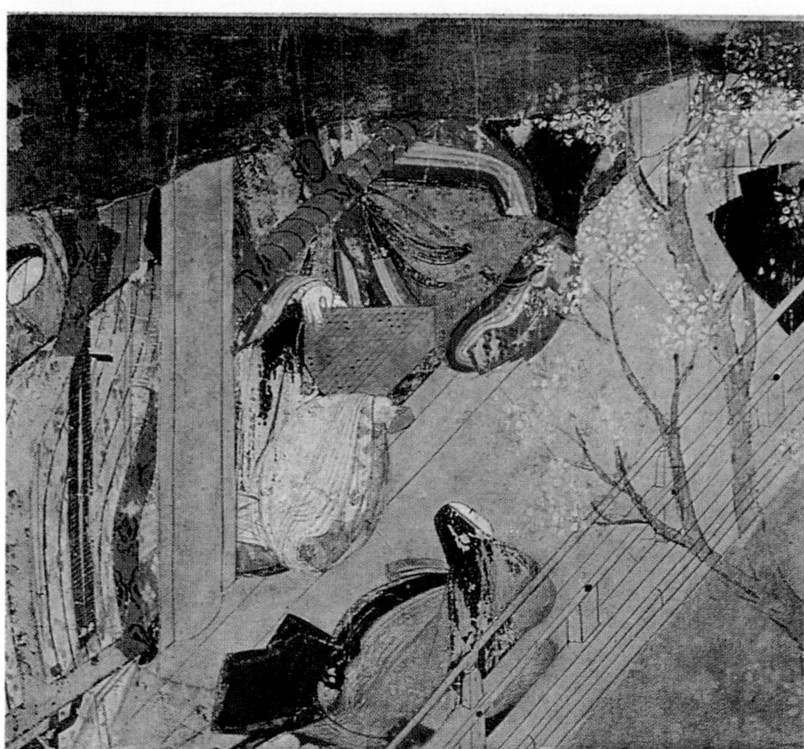
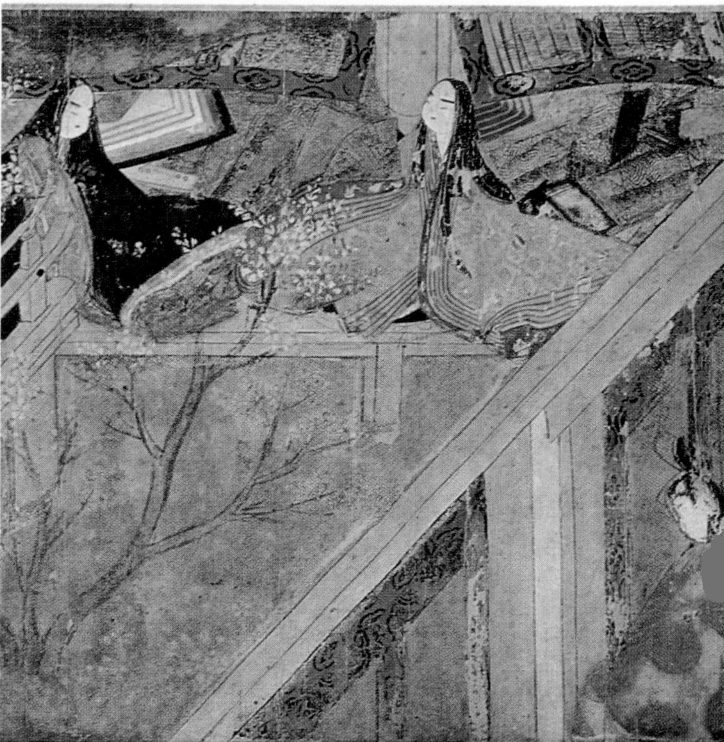

13-8 TAKAYOSHI(?), detail illustrating *The Tale of Genji,* Late Heian (Fujiwara) period, twelfth century. Scroll, color on paper, 8½″ × 15¾″. Tokugawa Museum, Nagoya, Japan.

the merit of somber dignity. In paintings, these bulky figures, often cut off at the sides, give the effect of a mighty force expanding beyond the pictorial format.

From the middle of the ninth century, relations between Japan and China deteriorated so rapidly that, by the end of that century, almost all intercourse had ceased. No longer able to reflect the fashions of China, the artists of Japan began to create their own forms during the Late Heian, or Fujiwara, period (897–1185). At this time, court practices at Heian-kyo (modern Kyoto) were refined to the point of preciosity. A vivid and detailed picture of the period appears in Lady Murasaki's eleventh-century novel, *The Tale of Genji,* a work of superb subtlety. The picture that emerges is one of a court in which etiquette overwhelmed morality, a society in which poor taste—in such matters as the color of a robe, the paper used in the endless writing of love letters, or the script itself—was considered a cardinal sin.

The essence of this court is reflected in a set of scrolls (illustrating *The Tale of Genji*) formerly attributed to the twelfth-century court artist TAKAYOSHI, but now considered to be an anonymous group effort. Painted in the horizontal-scroll (*makimono*) format, small pictures like the one shown here (FIG. **13-8**) alternate with sections of text. The artists, using a distinctly Japanese technique for representing space, view the scenes from an elevation, remove the ceilings to expose the interiors, and tilt the ground plane sharply toward a high horizon, or one that often is excluded altogether. Thus, the area of representation is expanded in terms of content and abruptly contracted by the resulting diminution of a sense of depth. Flat fields of unshaded color emphasize the painting's two-dimensional character, as do strong diagonal lines, which direct the eye more along the surface than into the picture space. Human figures have the appearance of being constructed of stiff layers of contrasting fabrics, and although they represent specific characters, their features are scarcely differentiated. A formula for such aristocratic faces, which produced a depersonalizing effect, called for a brush stroke for each eye and eyebrow, one for the nose, and a final stroke (sometimes omitted) for the mouth. Paintings in this purely Japanese style, known as *Yamato-e,** reflect the sophisticated taste of the Fujiwara nobility for whom these works were created.

A different facet of Yamato-e is represented by *The Shigisan Engi* (the *Legends of Mount Shigi*), painted at the end of the Fujiwara period. One of the first Japanese scrolls designed as a continuous composition, *The Shigisan Engi* illustrates the story of a Buddhist

*Yamato is the area around Kyoto and Nara regarded as the cradle of Japanese culture. The suffix *-e* means "picture."

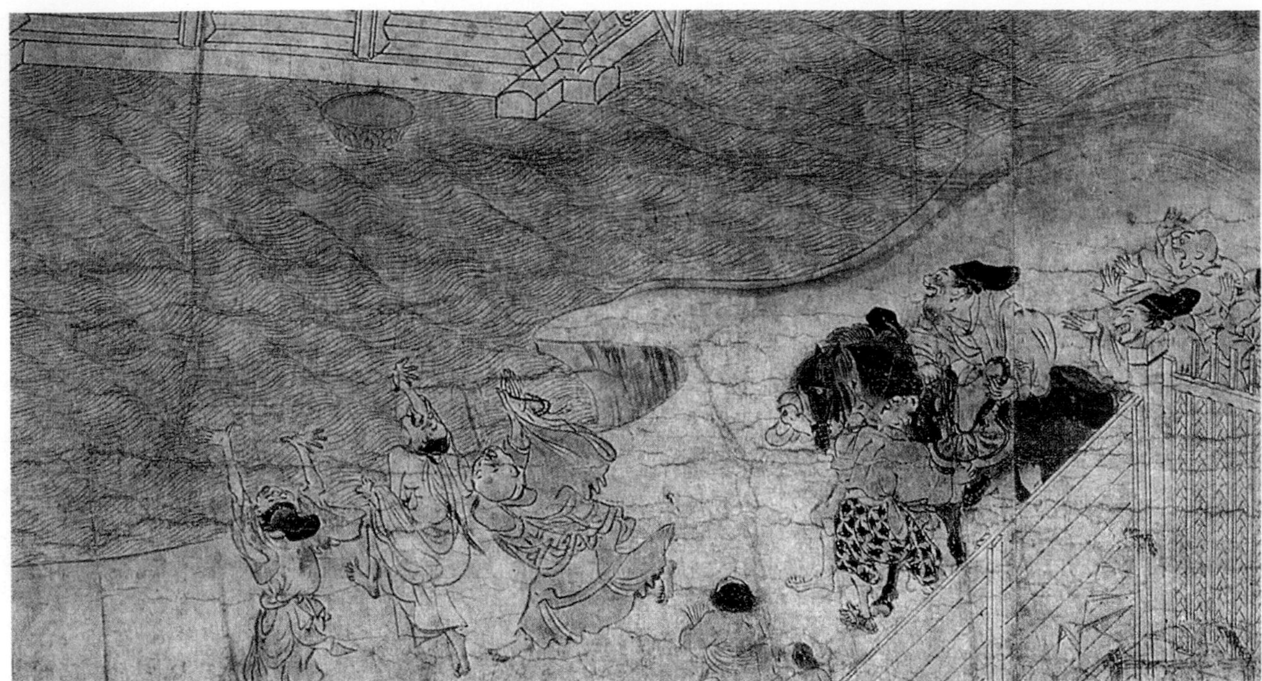

13-9 Detail of *The Shigisan Engi,* Late Heian (Fujiwara) period, late twelfth century. Horizontal scroll, ink and color on paper, 12½″ high. Chogosonshi-ji, Nara.

monk and his miraculous golden bowl. Our episode, called *The Flying Storehouse* (FIG. **13-9**), depicts the bowl lifting the rice-filled storehouse of a greedy landowner and carrying it off to the monk's hut in the mountains of Wakayama. The gaping landowner, his attendants, and several onlookers are shown in various poses—some grimacing, others gesticulating wildly and scurrying about in frantic astonishment. The Fujiwara aristocracy felt that only the crude and ill-bred would display such feelings and that they were therefore appropriate subjects for humorous caricature. The faces—so unlike the generalized masks in the *Genji* scrolls—are drawn with each feature exaggerated, conforming to a convention of the period to distinguish the lower classes from the nobility. Cartooning of this kind became an important element in Japanese pictorial art.

From the same general period (but of disputed date) are four horizontal scrolls of animal caricatures, which are more typical of Chinese Zen painting than of the refined style of Yamato-e. Painted in ink monochrome with a free calligraphic brush, one of these

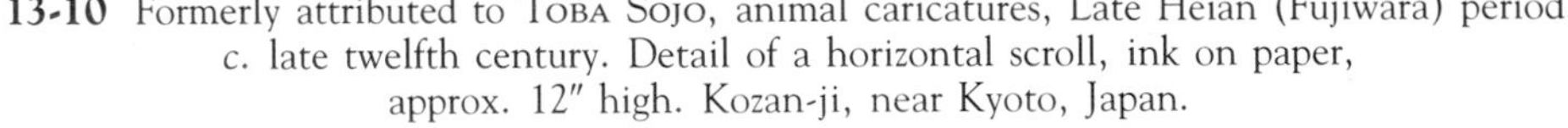

13-10 Formerly attributed to TOBA SOJO, animal caricatures, Late Heian (Fujiwara) period, c. late twelfth century. Detail of a horizontal scroll, ink on paper, approx. 12″ high. Kozan-ji, near Kyoto, Japan.

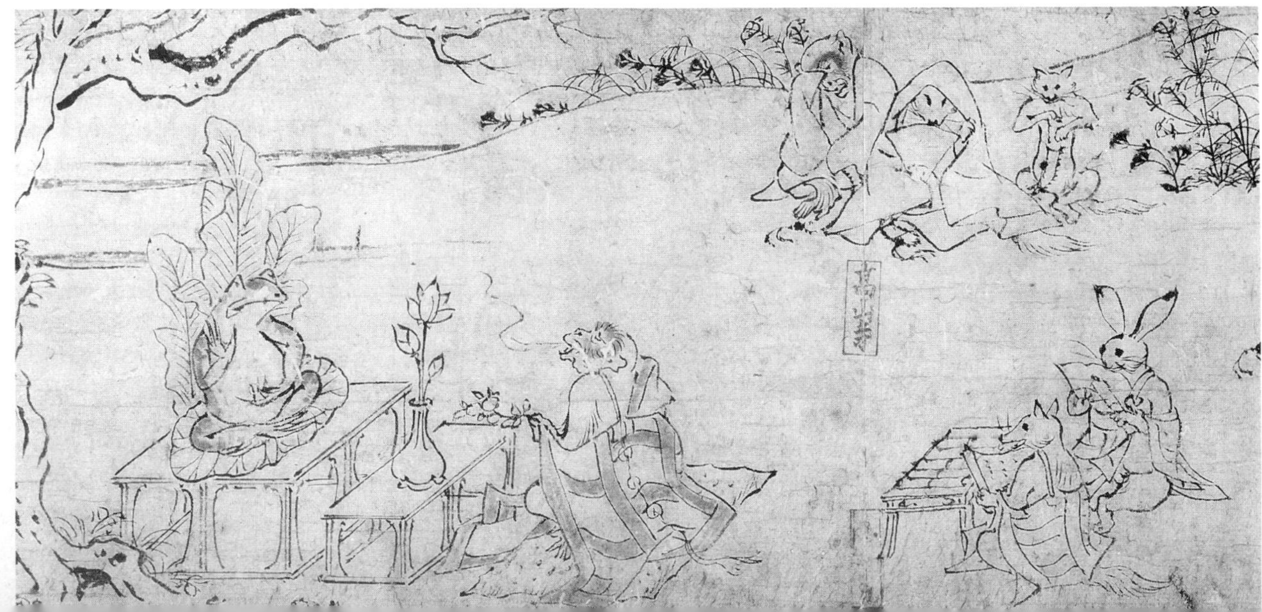

scrolls, previously attributed to the Buddhist Abbot Toba (TOBA SOJO), depicts a medley of frogs, monkeys, and hares in a hilarious burlesque of Buddhist practices. In one section (FIG. **13-10**), a monkey dressed as a priest pays homage to a Buddha in the shape of a frog seated pompously on a lotus throne with a nimbus of luxuriant banana leaves. In another, more animated passage, the animals tumble and frolic while washing each other in a river. Throughout this whimsical satire, the Japanese predilection for decoration asserts itself in charming clumps of foliage that play a delicate counterpoint to the vigorous movement of the animals.

A more conservative style of Buddhist art continued through the Late Heian period, but a new subject was added. This subject, known as *raigo*, portrayed the Buddha Amida descending through clouds amid a host of Bodhisattvas, welcoming deceased believers to his paradise. Such paintings, products of the Paradise Sects (page 456), eased the rigors of religion for the luxurious courtiers in Kyoto. A remarkable sculptural rendering of the raigo theme is housed at the Hoodo (Phoenix Hall) of the Byodo-in Temple at Uji, near Kyoto (FIG. **13-11**). The gilded wooden figure of *Amida* (FIG. 13-11) by the sculptor JOCHO (d. 1057) embodies a serene grace through the expanding curves of face and torso, stabilized into a triangular composition by the elongated legs below. The smaller

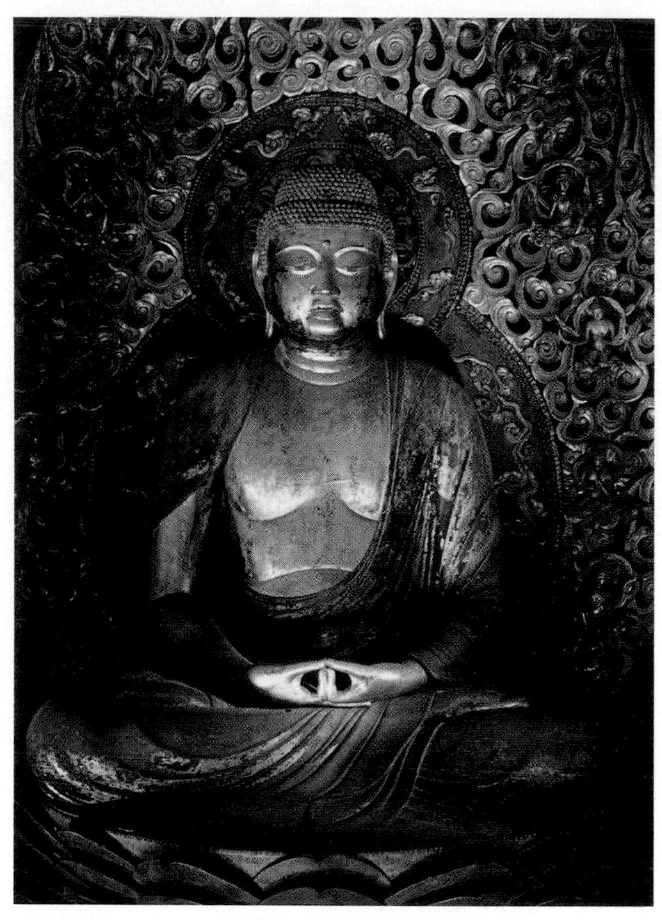

13-11 *Below:* Hoodo (Phoenix Hall), Byodo-in Temple at Uji, Japan, Heian period, eleventh century. *Above:* JOCHO, *Amida* (from the interior of the Hoodo), 1053; gilded wood, 9′ 4″ high.

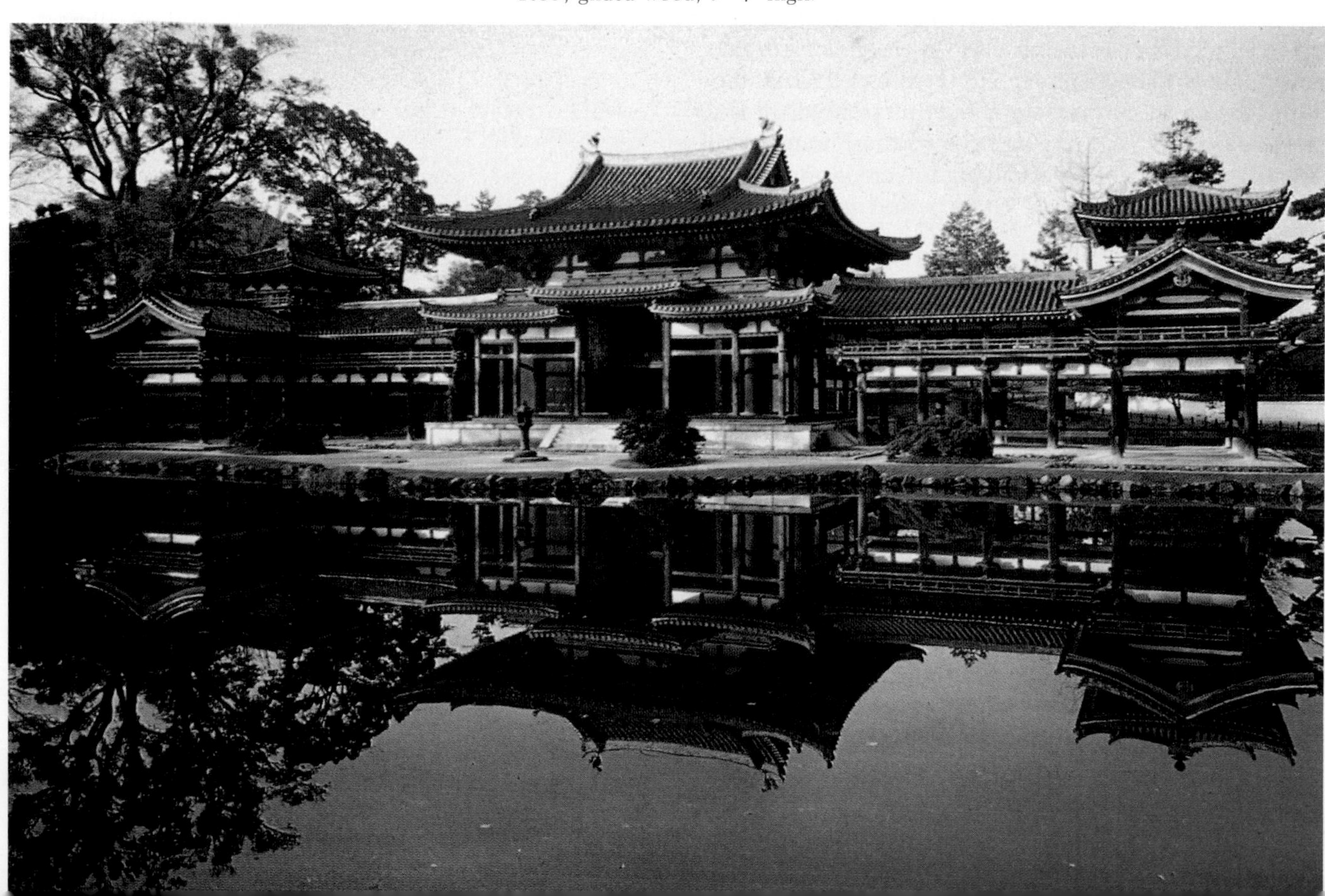

figures of angels and celestial musicians, floating on clouds as they accompany Amida Buddha on his descent, complete the impression of courtly elegance.

The building that shelters the *Amida* originally was a country villa inherited by Fujiwara Yorimichi (992–1074). In ancient Japan, villas could serve as temporary retreats from the pressures and turbulence of city life, but they often also were converted to temples by their owners and became their places of permanent interment. As explained by J. E. Kidder, Jr., "The transition from the city to the country, from a villa to a temple, from a recreation spot to a grave, from this world to the next, was seen hardly as a break in the pattern of human existence and only one more rite of passage." Yorimichi converted his villa into a monastery in 1053 and settled there in 1068, when he retired from politics.

The Phoenix Hall was inspired by aristocratic Chinese palace pavilions but was Japanized through greater integration with its natural surroundings. It is named after the two bronze phoenixes that decorate the ridgepole ends. The phoenix, rising to new life from its own ashes, is a symbol of immortality and thus appropriate for a tomb. Here, this symbolism is not confined to the two rooftop sculptures but seems to permeate the design of the entire building. The plan resembles a great bird in flight, and the swinging, multiple rooflines, with their widely overhanging eaves, suggest its beating wings. Carried by the slenderest of supports, the roofs convey a feeling of floating weightlessness that belies their mass and weight. This impression is enhanced when the building is viewed across the rippling surface of the reflection pond, where its image is put into perpetual motion. We cannot be sure whether this symbolism was intended or not; with or without it, the Phoenix Hall is the most delightful and elegant creation of Chinese-inspired architecture to be found in Japan.

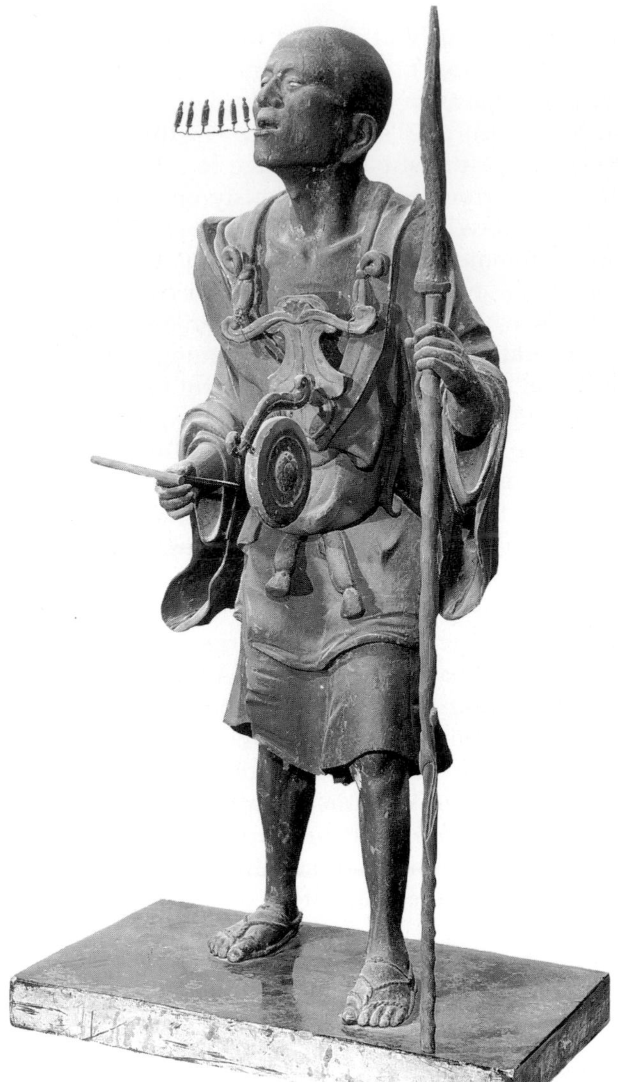

13-12 *The Sage Kuya Invoking the Amida Buddha,* Kamakura period, thirteenth century. Painted wood, approx. 46″. Rokuharamitsu-ji, Kyoto.

KAMAKURA PERIOD

A series of civil wars led to the downfall of the decadent Fujiwara rulers, and their successful rivals established a new capital at Kamakura, the city that gave its name to the period from 1185 to about 1392. The new rulers, reacting against what they considered to be the effeteness of the Fujiwaras, supported art that emphasized strength and realism. The style of the Nara period (710–794) was revived by UNKEI (d. 1223), perhaps the greatest sculptor of Japan. Unkei and his followers went even further than the earlier realists, carefully reproducing their observations of every accidental variation in the folds of drapery and using crystal for the eyes of their sculptures. That they were able, nonetheless, to keep a sensitive balance between the spiritual and the realistic is evident in the superb representation of Kuya (FIG. **13-12**), a priest who is shown as he walked about invoking the name of Amida Buddha. Not only is every detail meticulously rendered, but six small Buddha images issue from the sage's mouth, representing the syllables of a prayer in which Amida's name is evoked. Realism here is carried to the point at which the sculptor is attempting to invest his figures with speech.

Painting during the Kamakura period is most interesting for the advances made in the Yamato-e style, although all types of Fujiwara art also were continued. Perhaps the greatest Yamato-e of this time is *The Burning of the Sanjo Palace* (FIG. **13-13**), one of a series of horizontal scrolls illustrating tales of the Heiji In-

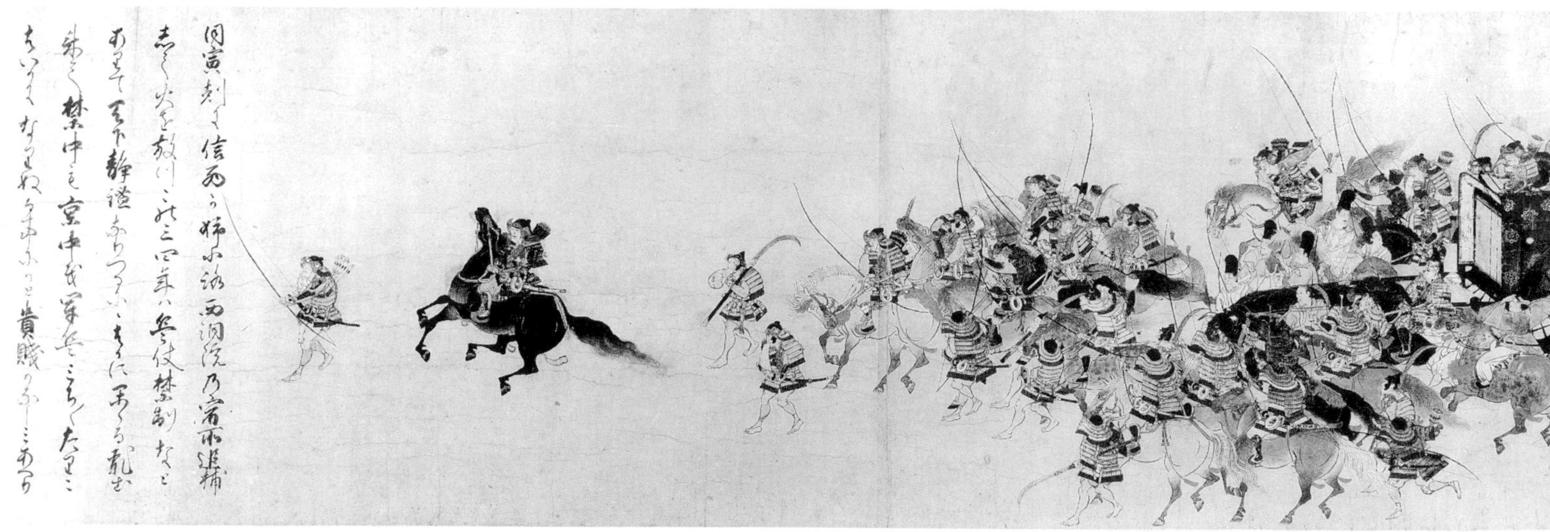

13-13 *The Burning of the Sanjo Palace,* Kamakura period, thirteenth century. Detail of a horizontal scroll, ink and color on paper, 1′ $4\frac{1}{4}$″ × 22′ 10″. Fenollosa-Weld Collection, Museum of Fine Arts, Boston.

surrection (*Heiji Monogatari*). Here, the artist, perfecting the symphonic composition of the Chinese landscape scroll, has added drama with swift and violent staccato brushwork and vivid flashes of color. At the beginning of the scroll (read from right to left), the eye is caught by a mass of figures rushing toward a blazing building—the crescendo of the painting—and is then led at a decelerated pace through swarms of soldiers, horses, and bullock carts. Finally, the viewer's gaze is arrested by a warrior on a rearing horse (FIG. 13-13), but the horse and rider are positioned to serve as a deceptive cadence (false ending). They are merely a prelude to the single figure of an archer, who picks up and completes the mass movement of the soldiers and so draws the turbulent narrative to a quiet close.

ASHIKAGA PERIOD

The power of the Kamakura rulers ceased in 1333, after which internal warfare persisted until 1392, when the Ashikaga shoguns (military dictators) imposed a brief peace. Civil war soon broke out again, although the shoguns managed to maintain control amid almost continuous insurrections, and lasted until 1573. A central government was formed, and, after centuries of suspension of diplomatic contact, official relations with China were once again established. The arts, under increased Chinese influence, flourished. New painting styles imported from China coexisted with conventional Buddhist pictures and with paintings in the Yamato-e style carried on by artists of the Tosa family. The monochrome landscape style of the thirteenth-century Sung masters Ma Yuan and Hsia Kuei was adopted by the painter-monk SHUBUN at the beginning of the fifteenth century. Shubun created evocative, idealized landscapes, sometimes with subjects and associated poems based on Chinese themes, which reflect the deep involvement of Japanese monasteries with Chinese culture during this period. MINCHO (1352–1431), also known as CHO DENSU, and other painters went directly to Yüan dynasty models. But the most powerful current to come from China was the one that accompanied Zen Buddhism and that accounts largely for the flowering of art despite the troubled times of the Ashikaga period. The new philosophy appealed to the *samurai,* a caste of professional warriors composed of men who held a relatively high position in society and who were supporters of the feudal nobility. They lived by rigid standards that placed high values on such virtues as loyalty, courage, and self-control. The self-reliance required of its adherents made Zen the ideal religion for the samurai.

Because the samurai found Zen attractive, the arts that had been associated with it in China swept Japan. Sculpture, as in China under the influence of Ch'an Buddhism, declined in importance, and painting imitated the bold brush of the Sung masters of the Ch'an school. Early in the Ashikaga period, the artist KAO (d. 1345) worked in the style of the thirteenth-century Chinese artist Liang K'ai, while his contemporary, MOKUAN (active *c.* 1323–1345), painted almost indistinguishably from a Chinese predecessor, Mu-ch'i. Of all the Zen artists in Japan at this time, SESSHU (1420–1506) is the most celebrated. He had several different styles but is best known for paintings in the Ma-Hsia manner (page 464). Sesshu greatly admired Sung painting, and, although he

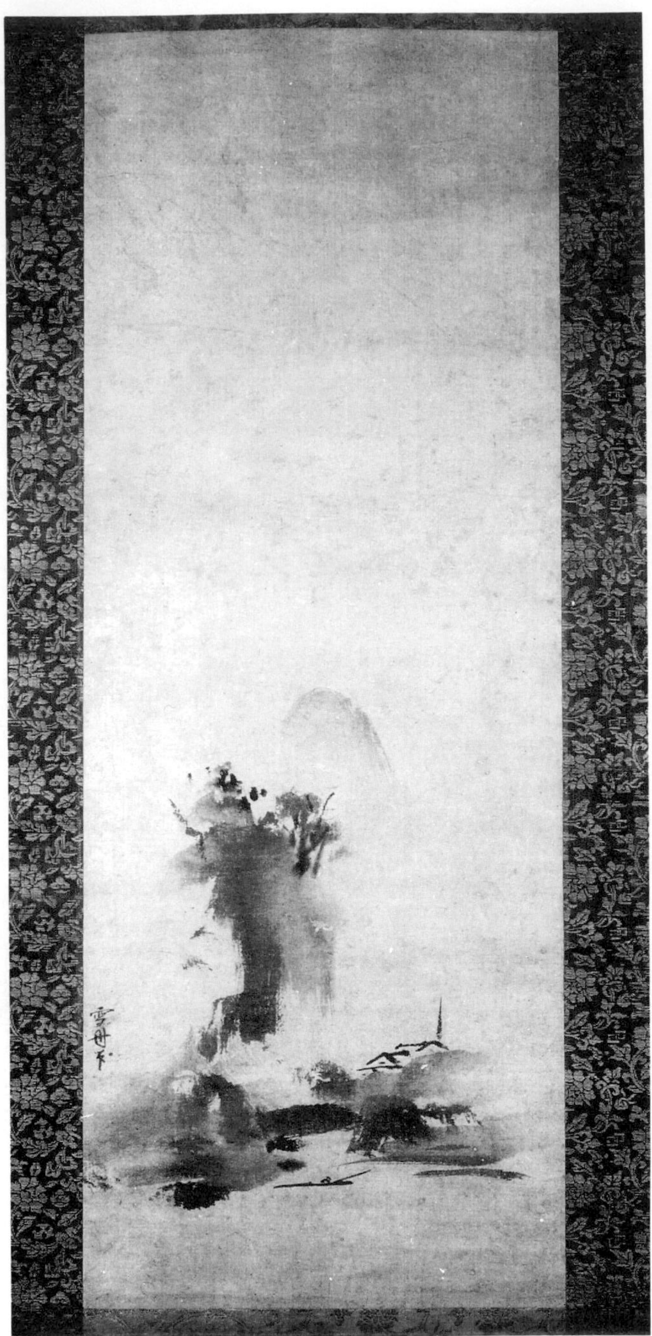

13-14 SESSHU, *Landscape,* Ashikaga period, 1495. Detail of a hanging scroll, ink on paper, approx. 55″ high. Tokyo National Museum.

studied in China, he decried the work of contemporary Ming painters. Nevertheless, he was affected by the Ming style; one of his masterpieces, an ink-splash landscape in the National Museum in Tokyo (FIG. **13-14**), contains elements basic to the Ming as well as to the Sung style. Although the landscape recalls the wet style characteristic of Ch'an painters of the Sung, the brushwork is more abstract and the tonal contrasts are more startling, after the Ming manner.

The Tea Ceremony

The influence of Zen went considerably beyond painting. It gave rise, during the Ashikaga period, to the *tea ceremony,* a unique custom that, among other things, provided a new outlet for the products of the Japanese artist-craftsman. This ceremony soon became a major social institution of the aristocracy in Japan. Its function and purpose are described by Father João Rodrigues (1562–1633), a Portuguese Jesuit who spent more than thirty years in Japan and who was a keen observer of Japanese customs and culture. Everything used in the tea ceremony, he reports, "is as rustic, rough, completely unrefined, and simple as nature made it, after the style of a solitary and rustic hermitage." The purpose of the ceremony was "to produce courtesy, politeness, modesty, moderation, calmness, peace of body and soul, without pride or arrogance, fleeing from all ostentation, pomp, external grandeur and magnificence."

The setting for the tea ceremony was appropriately unpretentious. Special, small teahouses, designed to give the appearance of refined simplicity, were placed into carefully planned and subtly arranged garden settings. The Shokintei (Pavilion of the Pine Lute, named after the sound of the wind in the surrounding trees, FIGS. **13-15** to **13-17**) in the gardens of the Katsura Palace, dating from the early Tokugawa period, is a charming example. Its exterior was planned carefully to blend with the calculated casualness of the gardens (FIG. 13-15). A flagstone path leads past moss-covered stone lanterns to an entrance where the guests washed their hands at a "natural" spring. In a rectangular room, scaled to create a feeling of intimacy and adorned only with a shallow alcove (*tokonoma*) in which a single painting and perhaps, a stylized flower arrangement might be displayed, the host would entertain his guests. The ritual of tea drinking in this setting imposed a set of mannered gestures and even certain topics of conversation on all participants. Every effort was made to prevent any jarring note that might disturb the perfectly planned occasion.

Although often emulated in modern times, originally no two teahouses were alike. According to an old teamaster, "beauty is lost through imitation," and originality was as important an aspect of the design as the perfection of its execution. Visual surprises were appreciated highly; for instance, the bold pattern of blue and white rectangles with which the tokonoma in our example (FIG. 13-16) is papered is an unusual and rather daring departure from the usually neutral and, at best, lightly textured treatment of these alcoves. Important also were the subtlety and finesse with which the building components were

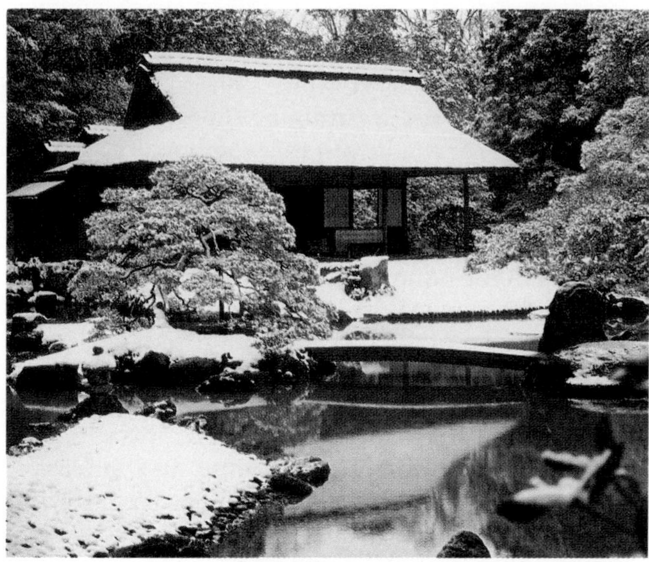

13-15 The Shokintei, Katsura Palace gardens, near Kyoto, early 1660s.

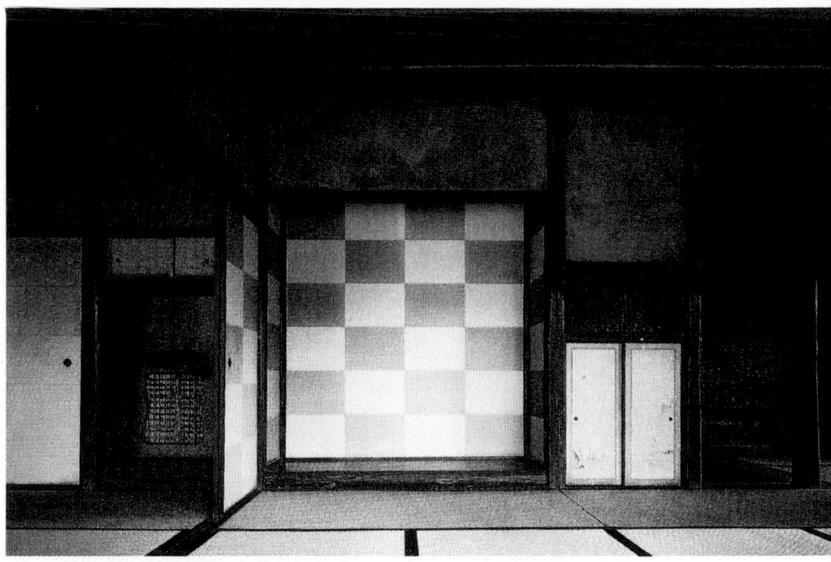

13-16 The first room of the Shokintei, Katsura Palace.

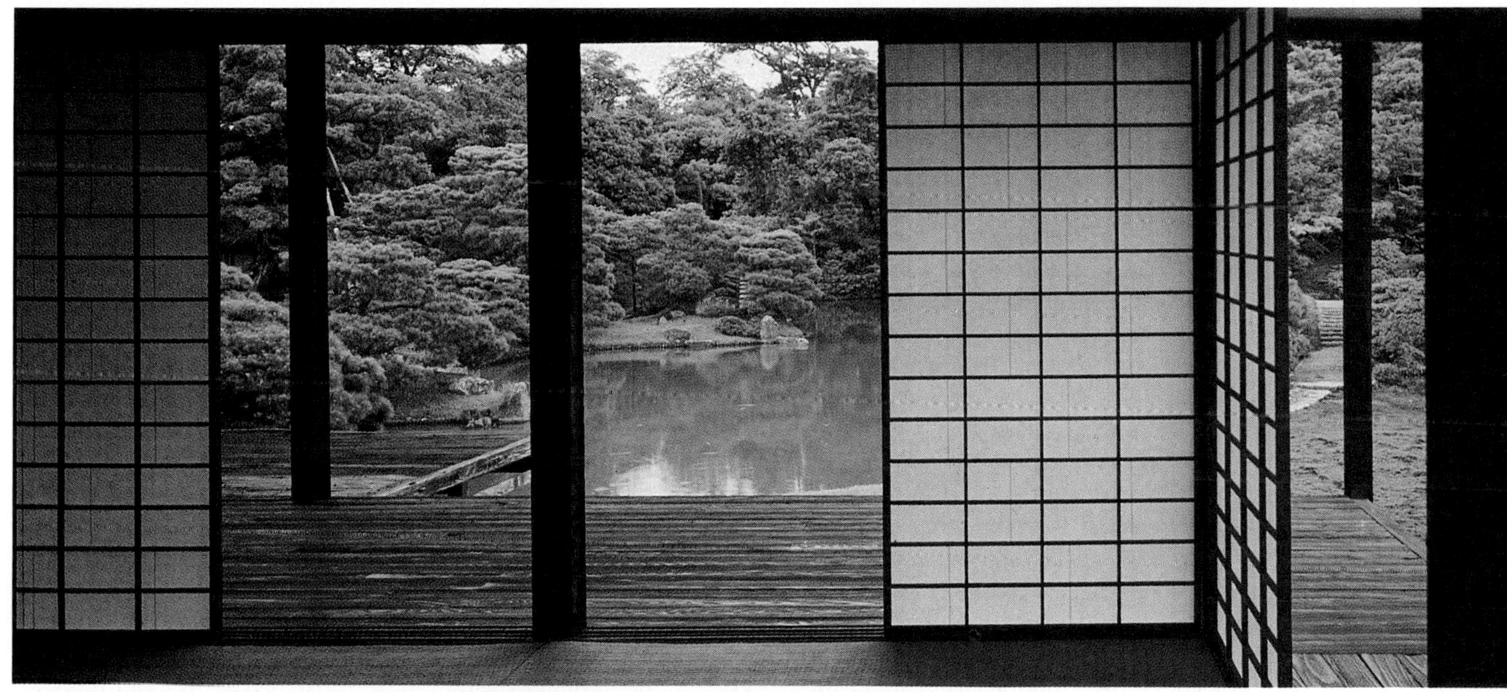

13-17 Pond and garden as seen from the second room of the Shokintei, Katsura Palace.

treated. Supporting posts were fashioned to keep their natural appearance, and they often remained rounded and knotty like tree trunks. All surfaces were painstakingly rubbed and burnished to bring out the natural beauty of their grains and textures. Common to all teahouses, and expressive of the Japanese love of nature, was the close integration of the building with its natural setting; when their translucent, paper-covered, sliding screens (*shoji*) are opened, the rooms become no more than roofed-over extensions of the garden (FIG. 13-17).

Although inspired and developed by Zen monks and subsequently adopted by the high and low aristocracy, the ritual of the tea ceremony, with its refined standards of taste, had a lasting influence on the style of living of the people at large. The studied simplicity, austerity, and understatement of the fifteenth-century teahouse were monumentalized in the Katsura Palace (see pages 490–91) and, from there, filtered down into domestic architecture to become what is now regarded as the traditional Japanese dwelling.

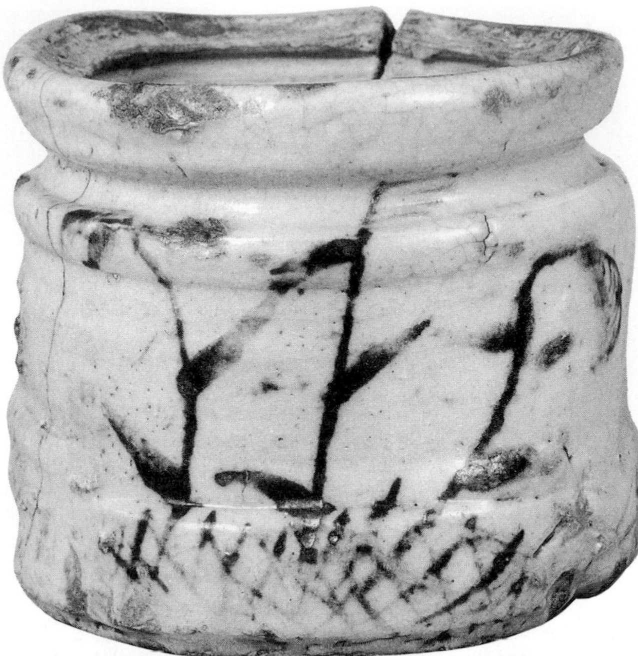

13-18 Tea-ceremony water jar, named *kogan* (ancient stream bank), Momoyama period, late sixteenth century. *Shino* ware with underglaze design, 7" high. Hatakeyama Memorial Museum, Tokyo.

The esthetics of the tea ceremony were found in the beauty of the commonplace, and each object employed in the ceremony was selected with the utmost discrimination. The connoisseur preferred a tea bowl, a flower container, or other ritual utensil that appeared to have been made without artifice. Potteries used in the ceremony (FIG. **13-18**) were covered with heavy glazes, seemingly applied in a casual manner, belying the skill that had controlled the colors and textures. The irregular, sometimes battered or flawed shapes of many Japanese tea wares provide an extreme contrast to the technical perfection common in Chinese ceramics (FIG. 12-26). Many Japanese wares of this type were given individual names based on literary or historical associations of their decor or on the visual and tactile qualities of the entire piece. Conferring such attention on an individual object and attaching such importance to it at this stage foreshadows the advent of major ceramic artists, who would sign, paint, and even inscribe poems on their wares as part of the development of this craft into a self-conscious and sophisticated art.

The Tosa and Kano Schools

The artistic understatement of the tea ceremony was counterbalanced by the continuing Yamato-e style of decorative painting. TOSA MITSUNOBU (1434–1525), the foremost exponent of Yamato-e during the Ashikaga period, retained the coloristic patterns of his native style but also emphasized ink outline after the fashion of Chinese painting. The new manner of painting that resulted from this combination is most apparent in pictures of the Kano school. KANO MOTONOBU (1476–1559), who was most likely the grandson of the founder of the Kano school, worked so closely in the Sung tradition that some of his paintings have been mistaken for those of Hsia Kuei (page 464). Motonobu had, however, a more personal style, in which we find a new emphasis on brushed outlines and strong tonal contrasts—features that became distinctive of the Kano school. In addition, Motonobu often used Tosa coloring and, at times, even painted in a purely Tosa manner. As a result, the Tosa and Kano schools became less distinguishable after the sixteenth century.

MOMOYAMA AND EDO (TOKUGAWA) PERIODS

In the Momoyama period (1573–1615), which followed the stormy Ashikaga, a succession of three dictators finally imposed peace on the Japanese people. Huge palaces were erected—partly as symbols of power, partly as fortresses. The grand scale of the period is typified by the Nagoya Castle, built about 1610. This castle also exemplifies how well the new style of decorative painting suited the tastes of the Momoyama nobility. The sliding doors and large screens within the mammoth structure were covered with gold leaf, on which were painted a wide range of romantic and historical subjects, even exotic portrayals of Dutch and Portuguese traders. Traditional Chinese themes were frequent, as were commonplace subjects of everyday experience. But all were transformed by an emphasis on two-dimensional design and striking color patterns (FIG. **13-19**). The anecdotal or philosophical content almost was lost in a grandiose decorative display.

Not every Momoyama artist worked exclusively in the colorful style exemplified by the Nagoya paintings. HASEGAWA TOHAKU (1539–1610), for instance, carried on the Zen manner of Mu-ch'i with brilliant success. His versatility, which was shared by most artists of the time, is evident in a brilliant, monochromatic screen painting, *Pine Trees* (FIG. **13-20**), whose strong verticals and diagonals are distinctively Japanese. In Japan, the decoration of screens was very highly developed and often exemplifies the highest quality of painting.

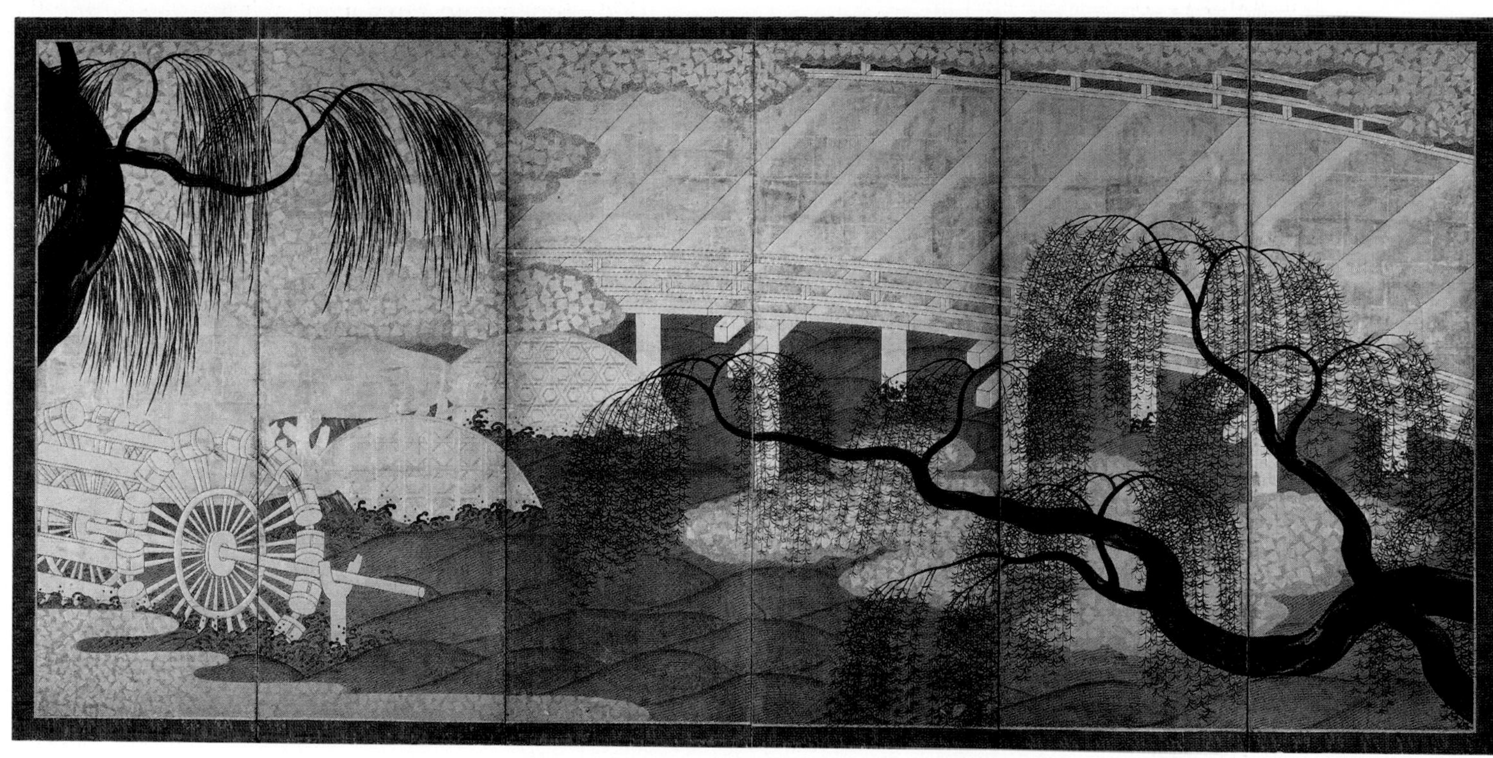

13-19 *Uji Bridge,* Momoyama period, sixteenth to seventeenth centuries. Six-fold screen, color on paper, 62″ high. Tokyo National Museum.

13-20 Hasegawa Tohaku, *Pine Trees,* Momoyama period, sixteenth to seventeenth centuries. Six-fold screen, ink on paper, 61″ high. Tokyo National Museum.

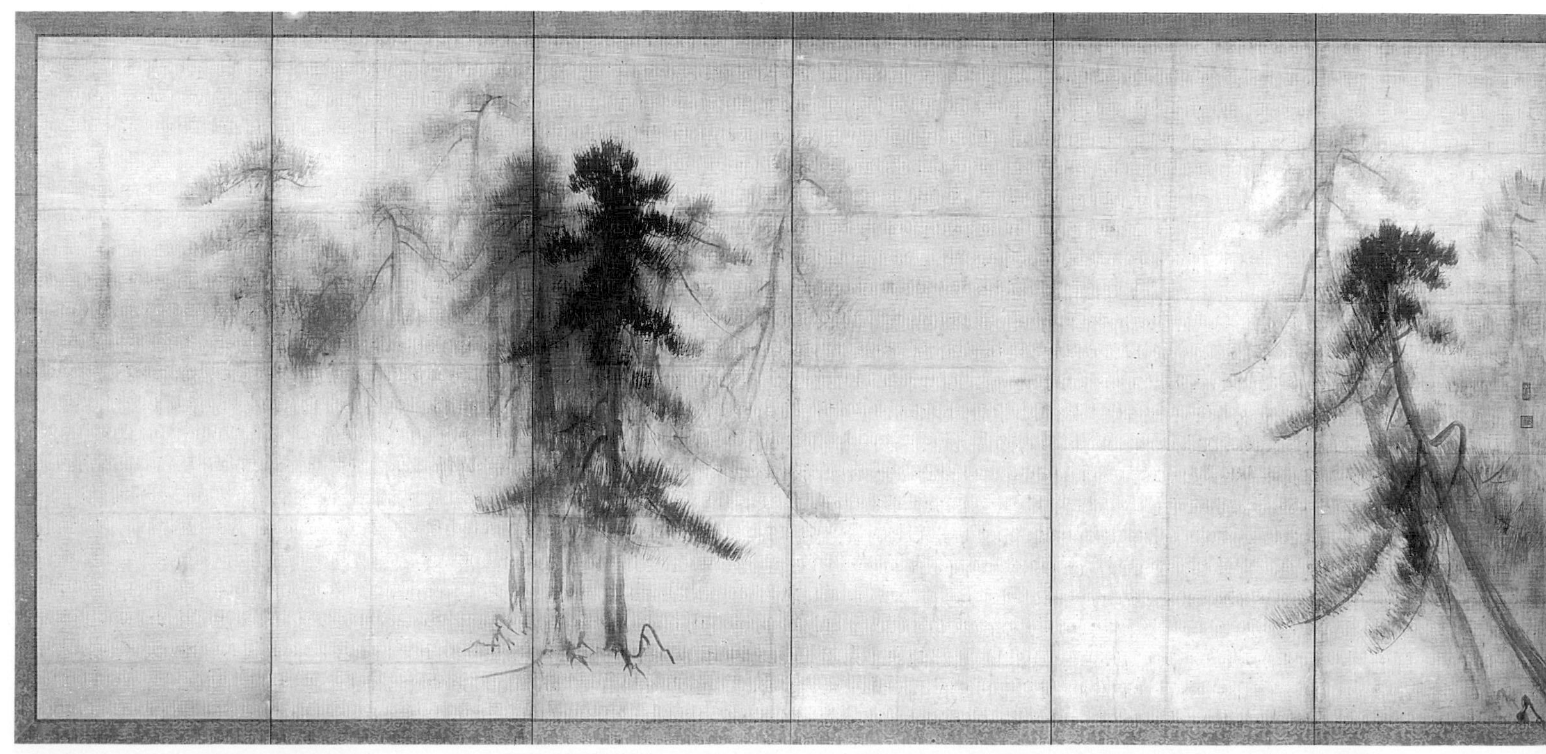

The Katsura Palace

In 1615, Tokugawa Ieyasu, the last of the Momoyama rulers, consolidated his power as shogun of Edo (modern Tokyo) and established the Tokugawa, or Edo, shogunate, which lasted until 1868. By this time, the emperors had lost their political power and independence and, under a succession of military dictators, had become little more than ceremonial figureheads. Still, in the hope of legitimizing their authority, the shoguns supported the traditional imperial institutions, and Ieyasu, in a magnanimous gesture, donated some land at Katsura (which was at that time a suburb of Kyoto) to members of the imperial family. There, over a period of some fifty years, successive generations of the Hachijo family developed a modest country retreat (*besso*) into a country palace that became the admired, but rarely equaled, standard for domestic Japanese architecture down to modern times.

The Katsura Palace (*c.* 1615–1663; FIGS. **13-21** to **13-23**) was built at a time when the tea ceremony was enjoying its greatest popularity, and many of the palace's design features and tasteful subtleties can be traced back to the earlier teahouses (see FIGS. 13-15 to 13-17). The straight rooflines of traditional Japanese architecture go back all the way to the Ise Shrine (FIG. 13-2) and stand in striking contrast to the swinging, curving ridgepoles and eaves of the Buddhist architecture imported from China, which originally served structural functions but by this time were overloaded and had become ostentatious decoration (compare FIGS. 13-7 and 13-11). At Katsura, the architectural forms express their function simply and without disguise, and the subtle adjustment of their pleasing proportions to each other and to the whole has produced a building of astonishing beauty. The main entrance to the palace, the so-called Palanquin Entry (FIG. 13-22), is a marvelously rich and subtle composition of juxtaposed solids and voids, of rectangular shapes of varying sizes and proportions, arranged along vertical, horizontal, and sloping planes. Lines, planes, and volumes are enriched by a variety of textures (stone, wood, tile, plaster) and by subdued colors and tonal values that build up toward and enframe the composition's focal point—the sliding panels of the doorway.

In the interior (FIG. 13-23), lacquered posts and wooden trim surround painted panels and screens to create settings more sumptuous than those of the teahouse, but just as refined and delicate. Everything is done with the utmost restraint. The rooms are not large by Western standards, but the screens between them can be slid apart, or removed completely, to create sweeping areas of rectangular spaces that also can be opened to the outside to achieve that harmonious integration of building and garden that we have seen, on a smaller scale, in the teahouse (FIG. 13-17).

13-21 Eastern façade of the Katsura Palace, *c.* 1615–1663.

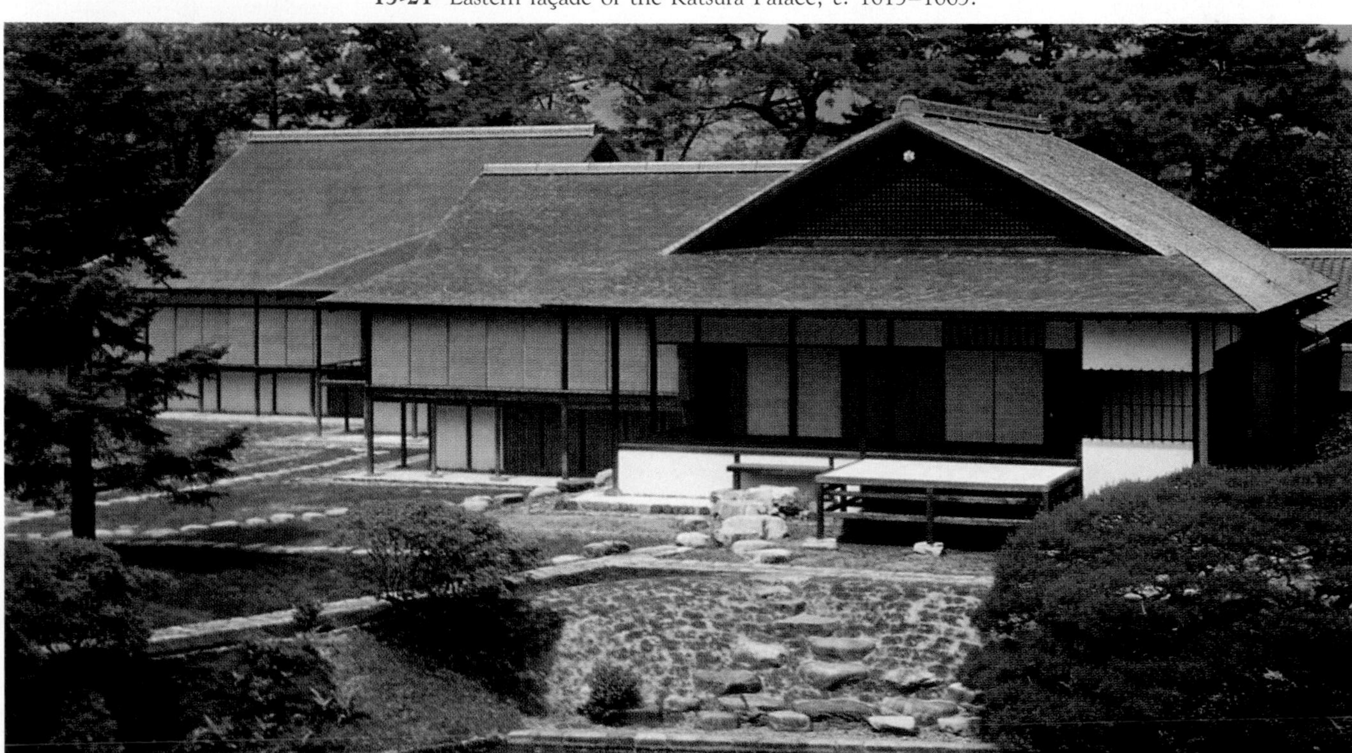

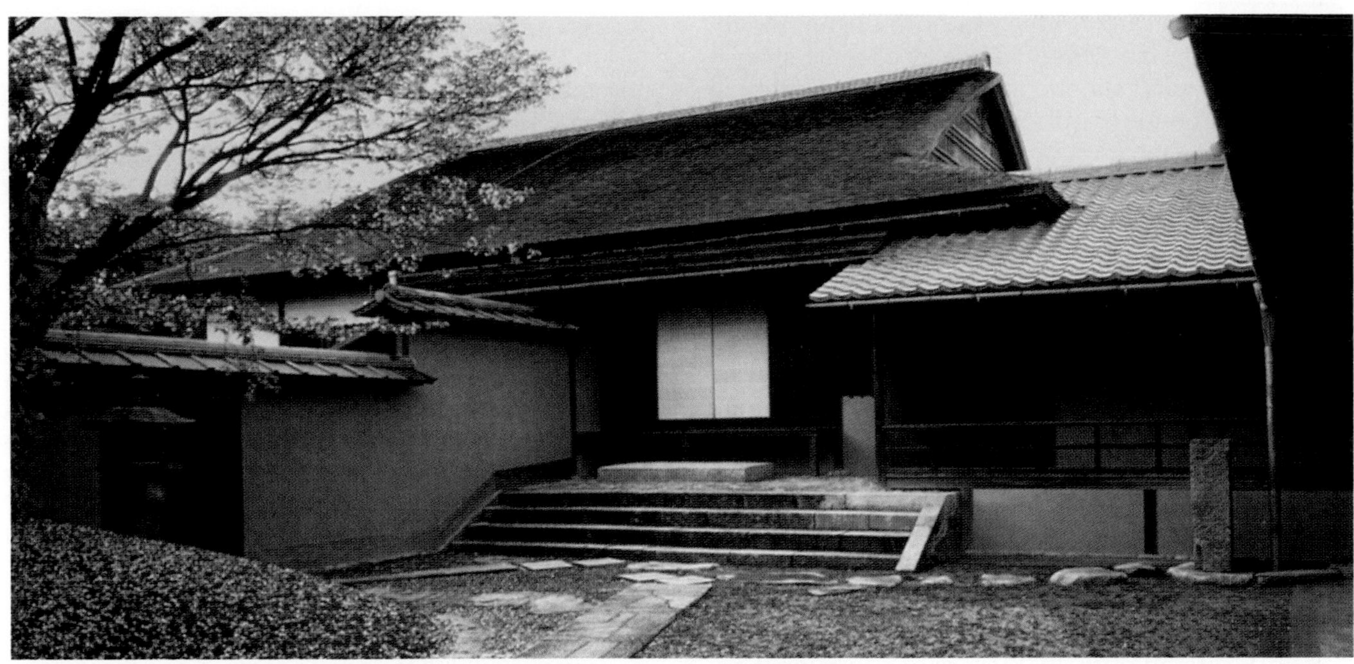

13-22 Palanquin Entry, Katsura Palace.

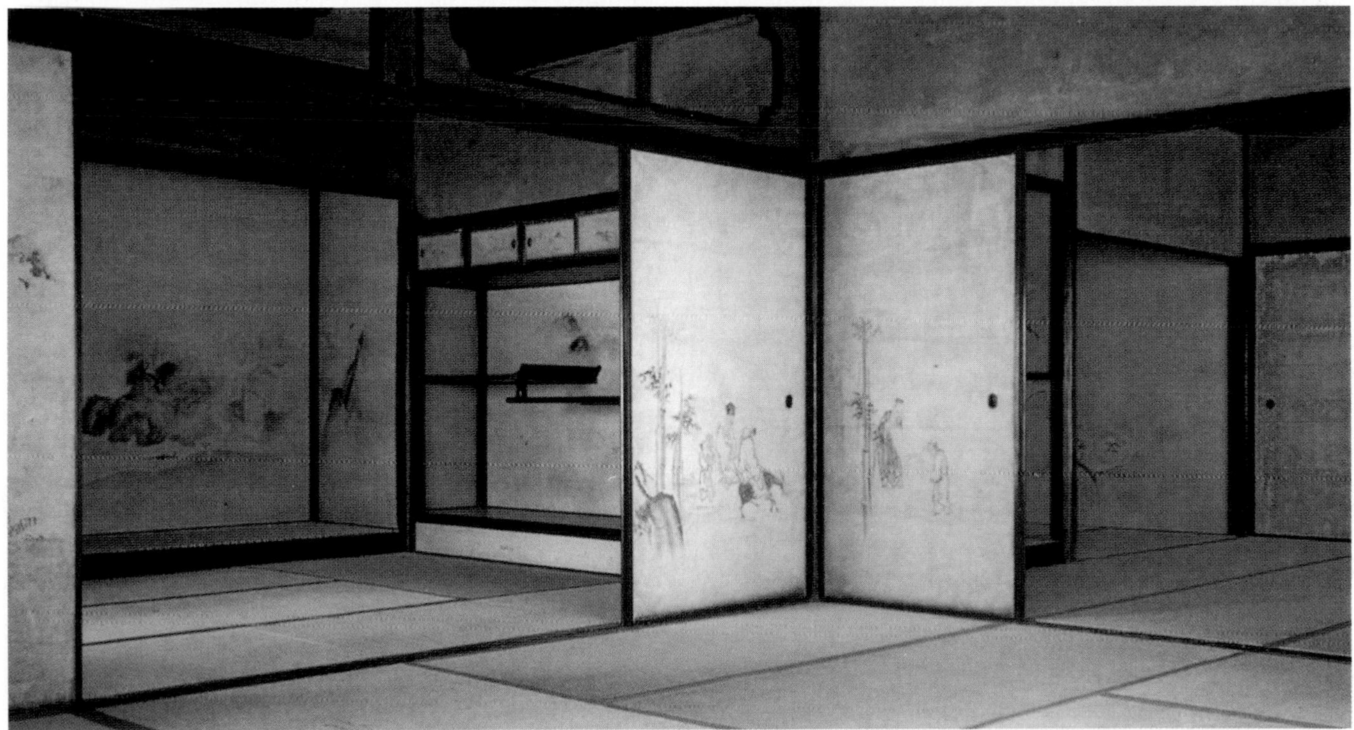

13-23 Interior, Katsura Palace.

Gardens

In Japanese garden design, as in architecture, man-made and natural elements are combined to create a sense of balance, proportion, and harmony. Japanese gardens are intended to be retreats in which one can enjoy peaceful seclusion and meditation. They create "landscape pictures" in which waterfalls, streams, lakes, bridges, and teahouses are artfully combined with stones, trees, and shrubs to simulate, in a restricted area, vistas of much larger landscapes. The Katsura gardens skillfully exploit the element of surprise. Long walkways suddenly are blocked by a wall of shrubbery that forces the visitor to turn in the direction of a designed view, such as a single shaped tree dramatically silhouetted against the glittering surface of a pond. Guests are led along carefully designed paths that present charming views of garden and landscape elements at planned intervals. The stepping stones along these paths are small and irregularly spaced, so that visitors must keep their eyes down in order not to stumble. Here and there, larger stones invite a rest and allow guests to lift their heads safely to view their surroundings and appreciate the designed prospect offered to their eyes.

The Katsura gardens cover several acres and are meant to be walked through. The Zen rock gardens, which originated in the thirteenth century, are much smaller and were intended to be viewed from a fixed position. The rock gardens consist of stone groupings in dry landscapes that are symbolic and suggestive of large landscape features. Level ground covered with raked sand or pebbles represents rivers, lakes, or oceans. Scattered over this surface and framing it are rocks, carefully placed singly or in groups: the vertical ones represent islands, cliffs, and mountain ranges; the horizontal ones denote embankments, bridges, and ships. Peninsulas and islands, carved out by the ocean, or a coastline with mountain ranges may be symbolized. The ensemble is intended to induce and facilitate intense meditation, to encourage the spirit to take off in free flight and transform the limited sphere of a tiny plot of soil into a cosmic universe without man-made boundaries.

Decorative Painting

Screen painting during the Tokugawa period was continued in all of its Momoyama magnificence by such artists as KANO SANRAKU (1561–1635), HON-AMI KOETSU (1558–1637), and TAWARAYA SOTATSU (1576–1643), whose lives spanned both periods. Koetsu and Sotatsu also composed numerous scrolls on which pictorial forms of flowers or animals were interlaced with strokes of a free-flowing calligraphy. One such collaborative effort is a deer scroll (FIG. **13-24**), in which the shapes of the animals, painted in decorative gold and silver, are repeated with subtle variations in pose and interval to create an almost musical effect.

OGATA KORIN (1658–1716) and his brother OGATA KENZAN (1663–1743) carried the decorative tradition that characterized the Momoyama on into the eighteenth century. Korin was primarily a decorative painter, who also worked as a lacquer designer; Kenzan was a master potter, whose line of "natural" wares is still produced today by the ninth artist to take his name. Korin is famous largely for his dramatic renderings of rocks, tree branches, and waves, which he combined in elegant and flowing compositions (FIG. **13-25**). Both artists harmonized the decorative styles of Momoyama and Early Edo with the studied simplicity required of art in the service of the tea ceremony.

Nanga and Realism

Although the decorative style of the Sotatsu-Korin schools continued to flourish until the nineteenth century, it had to share its popularity with several other trends in later Japanese painting. One, Nanga, "southern school painting," was inspired by the Chinese "literary" school painting of Su Shih and Mi Fu (pages 463–64). The Nanga painters transformed the techniques of their Chinese models into a style that combined virtuoso brushwork with decorative pattern and a strong sense of humor. Two outstanding

13-24 TAWARAYA SOTATSU and HON-AMI KOETSU, *Deer and Calligraphy*, Tokugawa period, early seventeenth century. Section of a horizontal scroll, ink and gold and silver on paper, 12½″ high. Seattle Art Museum (gift of Mrs. Donald E. Frederick).

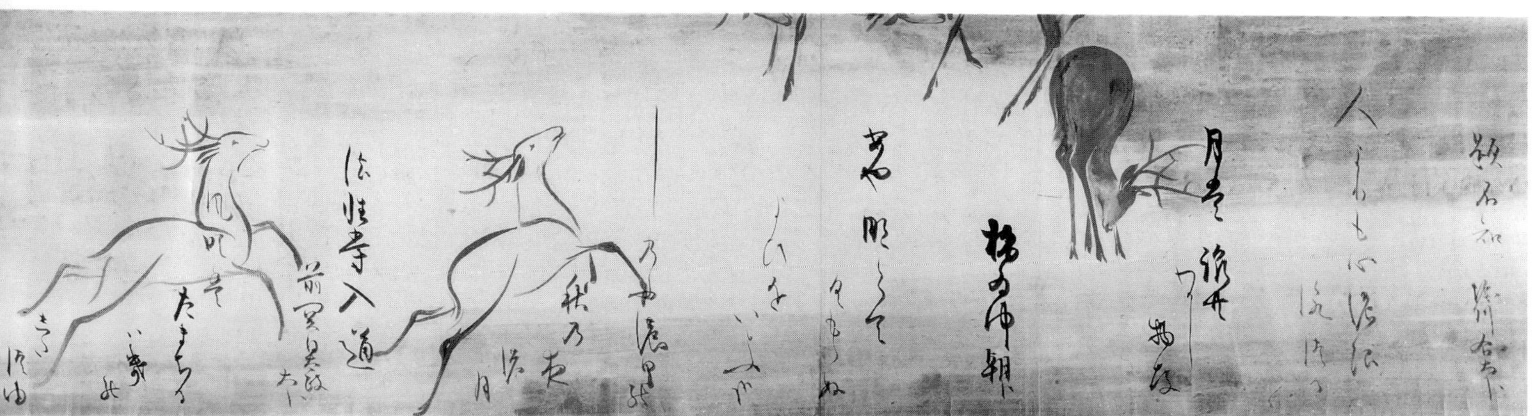

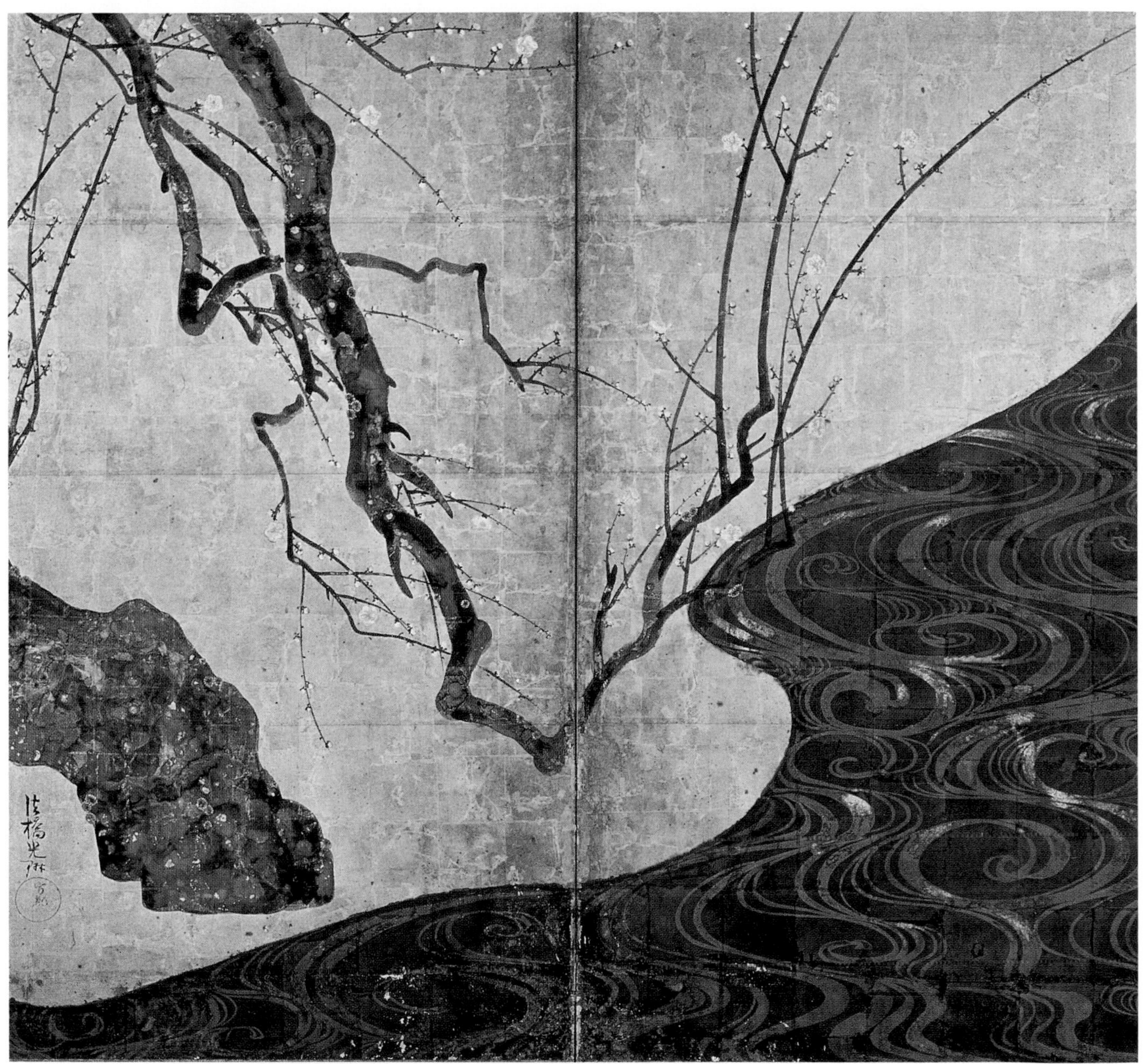

13-25 OGATA KORIN, *White Plum Blossoms in the Spring,* Tokugawa period, late seventeenth to early eighteenth centuries. Screen, color on gold paper, 62″ high. Tokyo National Museum.

early representatives of this style are IKENO TAIGA (1723–1776) and YOSA BUSON (1716–1783), who jointly illustrated an album entitled *The Ten Conveniences and the Ten Enjoyments of Country Life.* On one of the pages illustrated by Buson (FIG. **13-26**), a bulbous-nosed figure peering from a hut at richly textured summer foliage is shown with wistful humor by this master of the brush.

Another major style of later Japanese painting, which has been called realistic or naturalistic, is represented by MARUYAMA OKYO (1733–1795). His studies of animals, insects, and plants (FIG. **13-27**) combine an almost Western objectivity with an unusual handling of the brush to produce a style that follows the observed forms rather than established conventions. This kind of realism may well be due, in part, to Western influence. From the mid-sixteenth century on, Portuguese and Spanish missionaries and Dutch traders visited Japan, bringing with them paintings and illustrated books that, despite the efforts of the Tokugawa shoguns to bar foreign influences, had some effect on Japanese art.

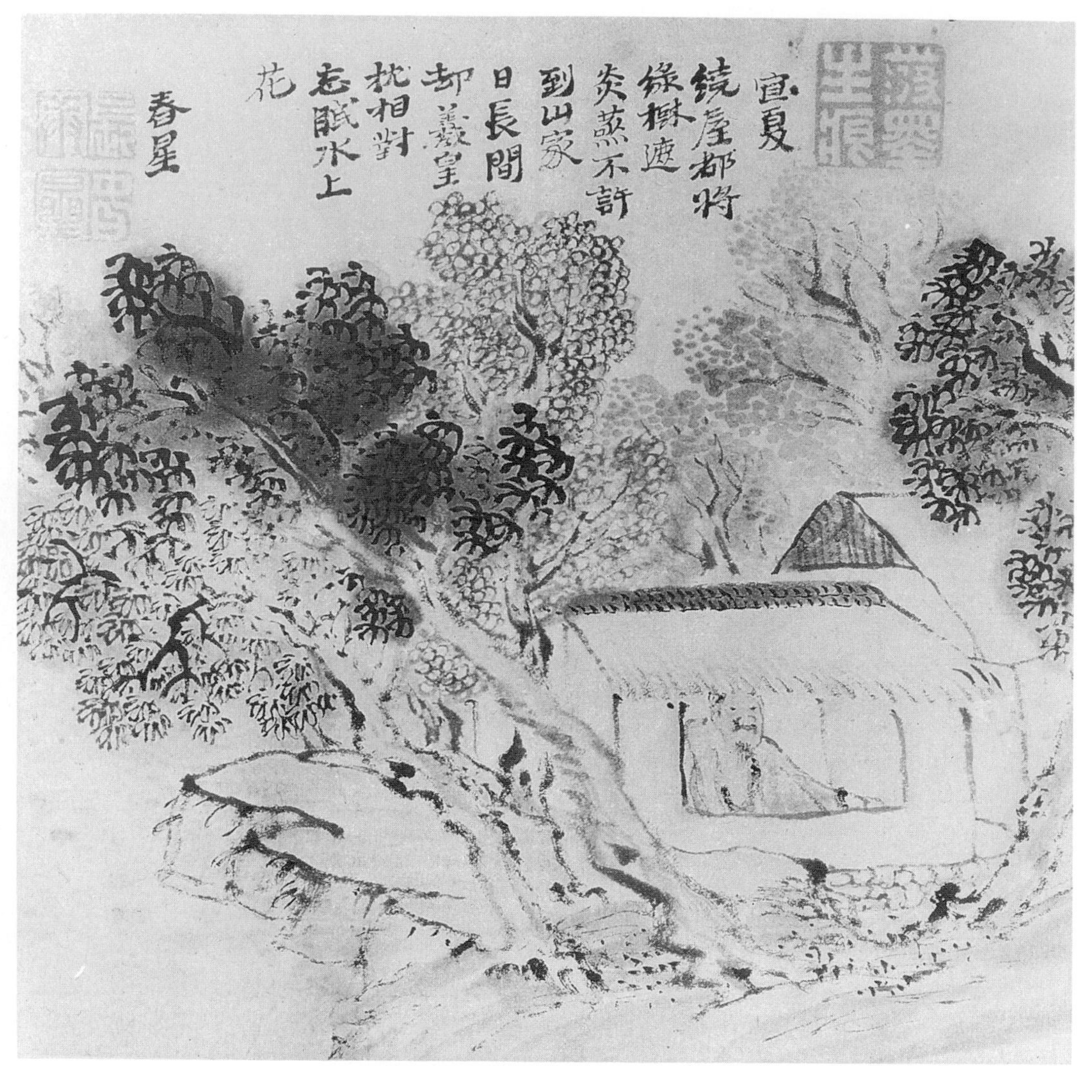

13-26 Yosa Buson, *Enjoyment of Summer Scenery,* from *The Ten Conveniences and the Ten Enjoyments of Country Life,* Tokugawa period, 1771. Album leaves, ink and color on paper, 7″ high. Yasunari Kawabata Collection, Kanagawa, Japan.

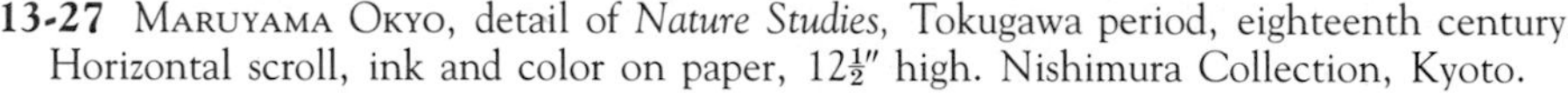

13-27 Maruyama Okyo, detail of *Nature Studies,* Tokugawa period, eighteenth century. Horizontal scroll, ink and color on paper, 12½″ high. Nishimura Collection, Kyoto.

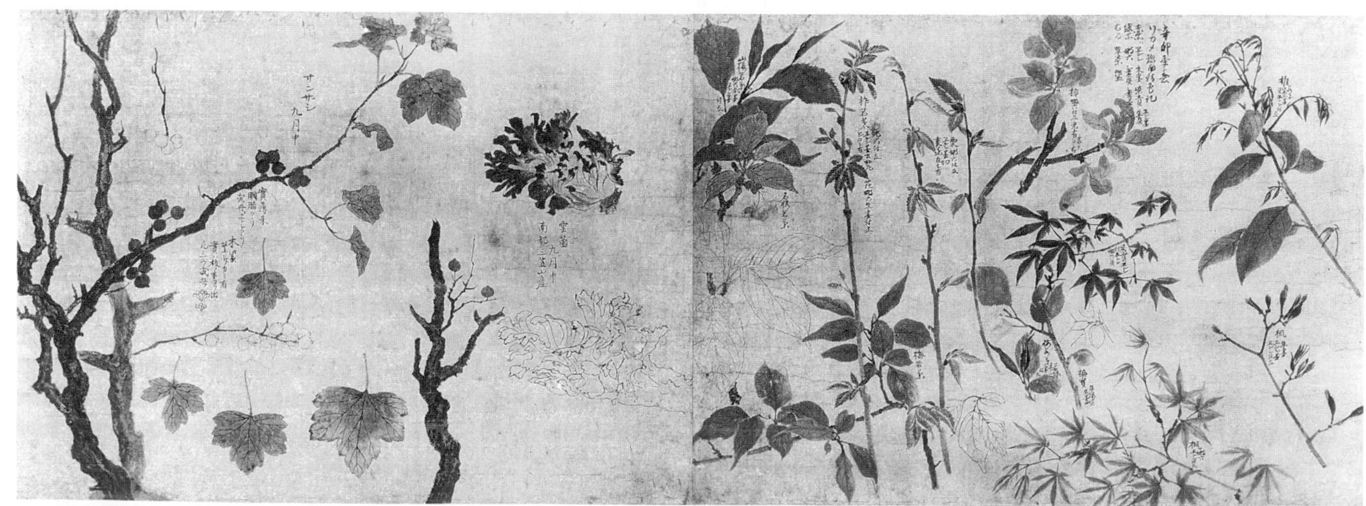

Ukiyo-e and Printmaking

The Tokugawa shoguns maintained a static and stratified society, and, as a result, each class developed its own distinctive culture. The center of the plebeian culture was the Yoshiwara entertainment area of Edo, where the popular idols were the talented courtesans of the teahouses and the actors of the Kabuki theater. Kabuki itself was a popular and lusty form of drama that developed in response to a demand for a more intelligible and more easily enjoyed theater than that of the highly stylized No plays, which were patronized exclusively by the nobility and a small number of the nouveau riche. Kabuki eventually provided endless subjects for a new art form—a style of genre painting (see FIG. 21-74) instituted in about 1600—that was to have considerable influence on Western art in the nineteenth century. This new art, known as *ukiyo-e,* or "pictures of the floating (or passing) world," was centered largely in Kyoto. Toward the end of the seventeenth century, the center of production shifted to Edo and the predominant medium soon became the woodblock print, which reflected the tastes and pleasures of a bourgeoisie emerging in a feudal society.

The woodblock as a device for printing had been invented in China during the T'ang dynasty. The technique was introduced in Japan during the eighth century, when it was employed chiefly to reproduce inexpensive religious souvenirs or charms. In the seventeenth century, Chinese woodblock book illustrations inspired the production of low-cost illustrated guidebooks of the Yoshiwara district.

The art of block printing, as it ultimately developed in the eighteenth century, was a triumph of collaboration. The artist, having been selected and commissioned by a publisher, prepared his design in ink, merely adding color notations. A specialist in woodcutting then transferred the lines to the blocks, and a third man did the printing. The quality of the finished picture depended as much on the often anonymous cutter and printer as on the painter of the original design.

HISHIKAWA MORONOBU (*c.* 1625–1694) was probably the first Japanese artist to employ the woodblock print to illustrate everyday subjects in books and to make and produce individual prints, which he started to do in about 1673. The woodblock quickly evolved as a medium for cheap reproduction and wide distribution. Moronobu's woodblock prints were executed simply in black outline against a plain white paper, as were the prints produced for the next fifty years, but often they were hand-colored by their purchasers. Moronobu's designs of large and simple forms had the exuberance of a young art. The same

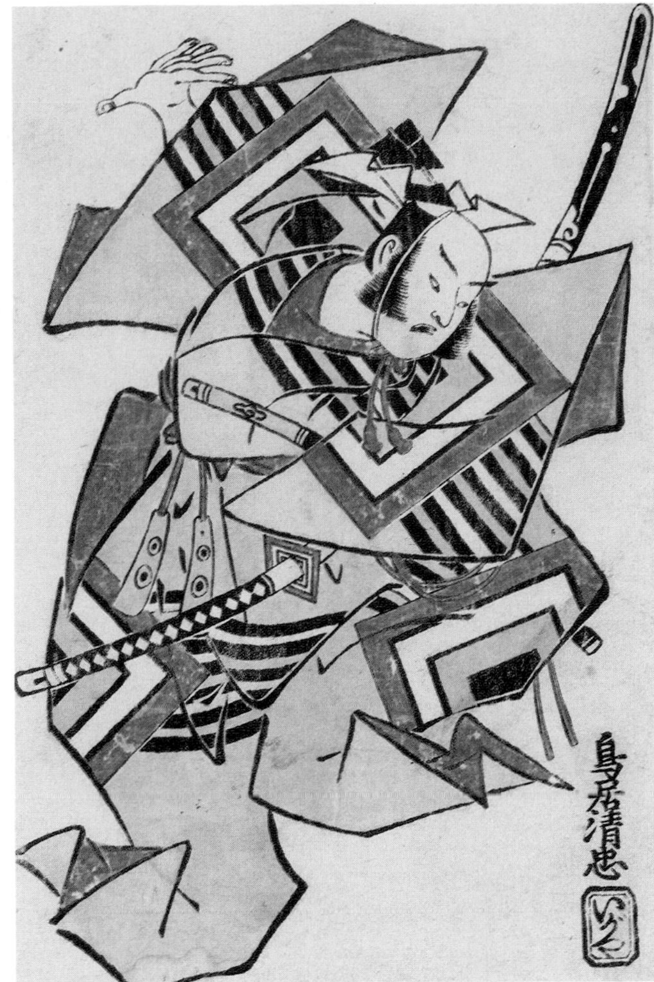

13-28 TORII KIYOTADA, an actor of the Ichikawa clan, *c.* 1710–1740. Hand-colored woodcut, $11\frac{1}{4}'' \times 6''$. Metropolitan Museum of Art, New York (Harris Brisbane Dick Fund, 1949).

vitality was expressed in prints of the Torii school by such artists as KIYONOBU I (1664–1729), KIYOMASU I (active 1694–1716), and TORII KIYOTADA (active in the early eighteenth century; FIG. **13-28**). These artists specialized in portraying Kabuki actors. (Kiyonobu I was an actor's son.) They worked with a broad rhythmic outline, and, for emphatic pattern, used the bold textile designs of the actors' robes.

At about the same time, members of the Kaigetsudo family were painting pictures and making designs for woodblock prints of elegant courtesans. The Kaigetsudo figures had more grace but somewhat less power than those of the Torii painters. In general, the print style gradually acquired more delicacy during the eighteenth century. The invention of a process of printing in color directly from blocks brought the "primitive" period of ukiyo-e printmaking to an end by about 1741.

OKUMURA MASANOBU (1686–1764) experimented with what is called lacquer technique in an effort to

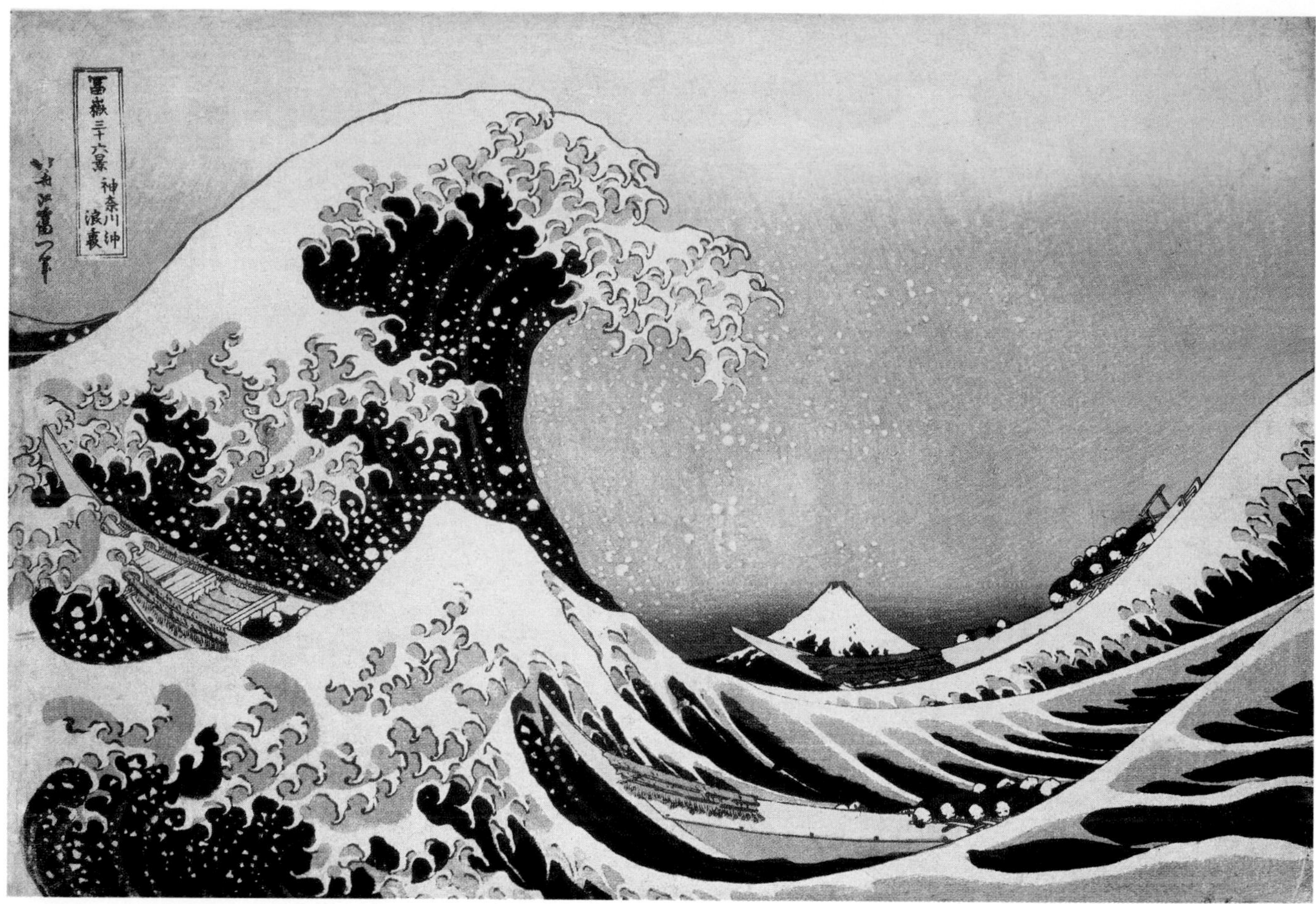

13-29 Katsushika Hokusai, *The Great Wave*, from *Thirty-Six Views of Mt. Fuji*, Tokugawa period, c. 1823–1829. Woodblock print, 14¾" wide. Museum of Fine Arts (Spaulding Collection), Boston.

increase the luster of the ink in his black-and-white prints. Later, he used a new, two-color method for printing in pink and green (*benizuri-e*), in which the dominant pink contrasts with patches of pale green and still smaller areas of black to produce a strong color vibration despite the very limited palette. Coincident with the use of color printing, the artists began to work in smaller, more delicate scale. In 1765, a device was introduced that permitted more accurate register and the successful use of even smaller color areas. This led to the development of the *nishiki-e* or "brocade picture," which was a true polychrome print. The new technique encouraged greater refinement and delicacy, evident in prints by the two leading print masters of the time—the incomparable Suzuki Harunobu (1725–1770) and Isoda Koryusai (active 1764–1788). In their work (see FIG. 21-74), a new loveliness replaces the monumentality of earlier compositions. The figures are of slighter proportions, the colors are more muted, and the line is lyric rather than dramatic.

After Harunobu died, prints changed rapidly in style, shape, subject, and color. Torii Kiyonaga (1752–1815) and Kitagawa Utamaro (1753–1806) revived the taste for tall, willowy figures. Utamaro, who later concentrated on half-length figures, was fortunate to have the services of craftsmen who were skilled enough in woodcutting to allow him to create extraordinary nuances in color, texture, and line. Buncho (active 1766–1790), working in another vein, made many striking portraits of well-known figures. Even more dramatic are the prints of Toshusai Sharaku, who, active for a brief ten months during 1794 and 1795, was a unique and enigmatic figure among print artists. About 160 of his prints survive—all of them piercing, rather acid, psychological studies of actors, wrestlers, or managers. Utagawa Toyokuni I (1769–1825) followed in a similar, less biting manner, but the strength of this style was dissipated in the hands of later artists.

Dozens of other artists contributed to the popular art of printmaking, but, during the nineteenth century, Katsushika Hokusai (1760–1849) and Ando Hiroshige (1797–1858) were outstanding. Increasing political and moral censorship, which was to contribute to the decline of this art, led Hokusai to select landscapes as his ukiyo-e subjects. His brilliant and ingenious compositions, such as his *Thirty-Six Views of Mt. Fuji* (FIG. **13-29**), make use of striking juxtapositions and bold, linear designs. Nature was his primary subject, but, in its setting, he also included genre and anecdote as minor themes. Hiroshige, too, specialized in landscape and, like Hokusai, painted birds, flowers, and legendary scenes. In general, however, Hiroshige's prints did not evoke the sense of grandeur implicit in Hokusai's work.

These prints, although sometimes influenced by European art, show the Japanese attitude toward nature—the regard for natural forms in their utmost simplicity as a point of departure for an interpretation of reality—which, in turn, will lead to abstract pictorial design.

DOMESTIC ARCHITECTURE

Until recently, the Japanese home—modest or pretentious—has been designed according to basically the same structural and esthetic principles that apply to the teahouse or the Katsura Palace. The traditional Japanese dwelling almost invariably is related intimately to the land around it, and, wherever possible, it is set in a garden closed off by a bamboo fence (a thing of beauty in itself), providing a sense of privacy and intimacy in even the most crowded environment.

The structure is essentially a series of posts supporting a roof. The walls, which are screens rather than supports, slide open from one room into the next or onto the outside. Space is treated as continuous yet harmoniously divisible—a concept that revolutionized architectural theory in the West. Uniformity and harmony of proportions are achieved by the use of the conventional straw mat (*tatami*) as a module. Its dimensions (3 feet by 6 feet) determine most measurements of both the plan and the elevation of the house, so that many of its structural elements can be prefabricated—another feature highly appreciated by Western architects.

In the traditional Japanese house, no furniture is used, except for some low tables and cushions (bedding is rolled up and kept in closets during the day). The various rooms of the house have no specific functions and can be used for any and all purposes. The main room, in which guests are received (FIG. **13-30**), is identified by the tokonoma, where works of art from the owner's collection are displayed one at a time. Quite unlike Western collectors, who tend to convert their homes into museums by displaying all of their objets d'art together, their Japanese counterparts rotate the works in their collections, showing a single work in the tokonoma to suit season or mood—an attitude that conforms with the simplicity and architectural understatement of the traditional Japanese dwelling.

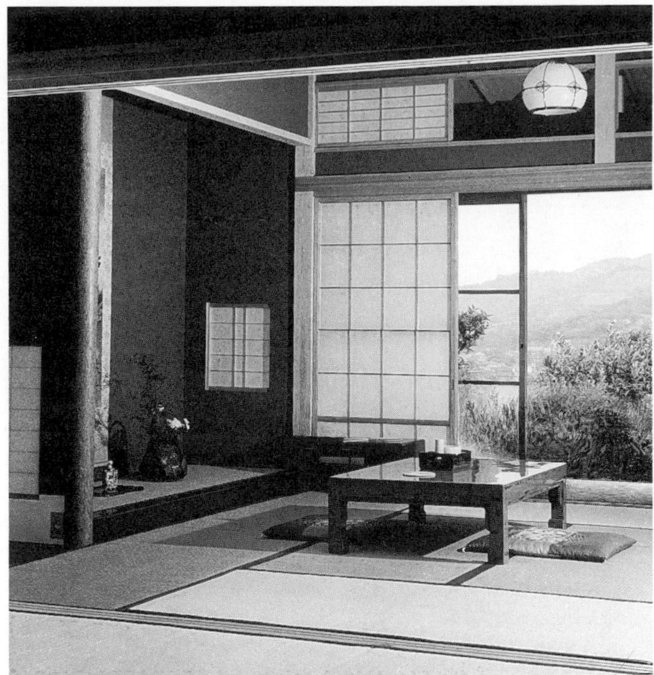

13-30 Main room of a traditional Japanese house.

Despite its sophistication and refinement, the traditional Japanese house suffers from the inconvenience that it cannot be heated adequately. Unlike their Korean neighbors, the Japanese never developed an efficient heating system for their homes. The Japanese love of nature has been cited as a partial explanation for this, to us, evident deficiency. Rather than shutting themselves off from nature's manifestations by retreating into hermetically sealed enclosures, the Japanese preferred to experience climatic changes and simply protected themselves against the winter cold with additional layers of clothing. No wonder, perhaps, that the modern Japanese, newly aware of and acquainted with Western standards of living, long to live in a Western-style house.

With the advent of the Meiji period in 1868, Japan has become increasingly exposed to Western influences. The process of adjusting not only its economy, but also its life-style, to Western standards accelerated after the turn of the century, to reach a crescendo after the end of World War II. The pace of Japan's recent development is awesome, not only in its industrial production, which is well known to us, but also in the arts. The Japanese excelled particularly in the fields of architecture and design in recent years and such men as KENZO TANGE and ARATA ISOZAKI now must be ranked among the foremost contemporary architects.

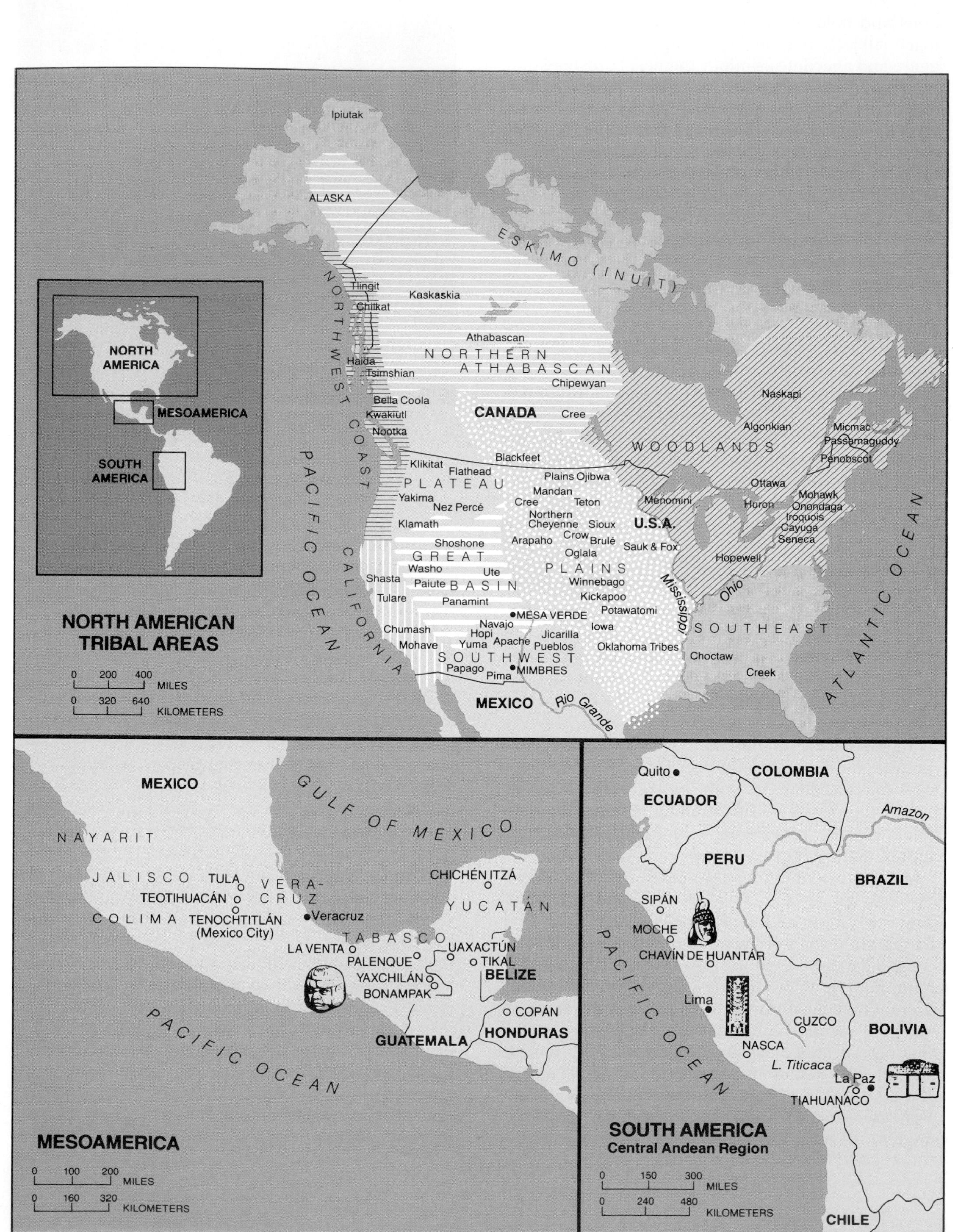

NORTH AMERICAN TRIBAL AREAS
0 200 400 MILES
0 320 640 KILOMETERS
NORTH AMERICA
MESOAMERICA
SOUTH AMERICA
Ipiutak
ALASKA
ESKIMO (INUIT)
NORTHWEST COAST
Tlingit
Chilkat
Kaskaskia
Athabascan
NORTHERN ATHABASCAN
Haida
Tsimshian
Chipewyan
Bella Coola
Kwakiutl
Nootka
CANADA
Cree
Naskapi
Algonkian
Micmac
Passamaquddy
Penobscot
WOODLANDS
Blackfeet
Klikitat
Flathead
PLATEAU
Plains Ojibwa
Mandan
Yakima
Nez Percé
Cree
Teton
Menomini
Ottawa
Huron
Mohawk
Onondaga
Iroquois
Cayuga
Seneca
Klamath
Northern Cheyenne
Sioux
U.S.A.
Shoshone
Arapaho
Crow
Brulé
Sauk & Fox
GREAT BASIN
Oglala
Hopewell
Washo
Ute
PLAINS
Shasta
Paiute
Winnebago
Mississippi
Ohio
Tulare
Panamint
Kickapoo
MESA VERDE
Potawatomi
Navajo
Iowa
Chumash
Hopi
Apache
Jicarilla
SOUTHEAST
Mohave
Yuma
Pueblos
Oklahoma Tribes
SOUTHWEST
Choctaw
Papago
Pima
MIMBRES
Creek
CALIFORNIA
PACIFIC OCEAN
ATLANTIC OCEAN
MEXICO
Rio Grande
MEXICO
GULF OF MEXICO
NAYARIT
JALISCO
TULA
VERA-CRUZ
CHICHÉN ITZÁ
TEOTIHUACÁN
YUCATÁN
COLIMA
TENOCHTITLÁN (Mexico City)
Veracruz
TABASCO
LA VENTA
UAXACTÚN
PALENQUE
TIKAL
YAXCHILÁN
BELIZE
BONAMPAK
COPÁN
PACIFIC OCEAN
GUATEMALA
HONDURAS
MESOAMERICA
0 100 200 MILES
0 160 320 KILOMETERS
Quito
COLOMBIA
ECUADOR
Amazon
PERU
BRAZIL
SIPÁN
MOCHE
CHAVÍN DE HUANTAR
PACIFIC OCEAN
Lima
CUZCO
BOLIVIA
NASCA
L. Titicaca
La Paz
TIAHUANACO
SOUTH AMERICA
Central Andean Region
0 150 300 MILES
0 240 480 KILOMETERS
CHILE

14

THE NATIVE ARTS OF THE AMERICAS, AFRICA, AND THE SOUTH PACIFIC

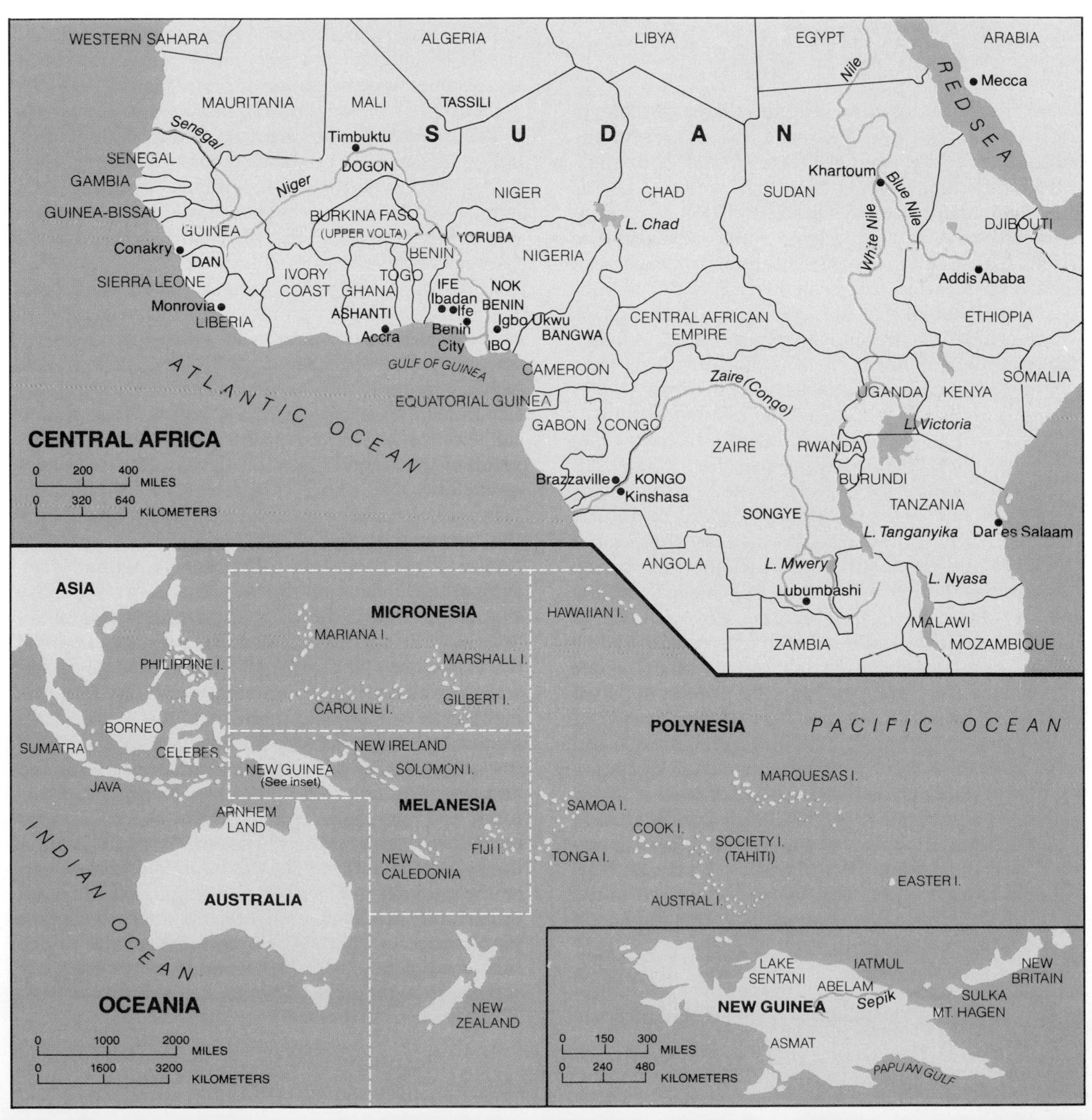

BY "NATIVE ARTS," WE understand those products of skilled craft that originate within an indigenous community, that are intended for its own use, and that are expressive of its own mentality and values. Opposed to native arts are those that are foreign, alien; they originate outside the community and are incomprehensible to it. In this chapter, we describe the arts of native peoples who were conquered and colonized by Europeans between the sixteenth and the twentieth centuries. It will be obvious to readers of this book how different—in principle, antagonistic—the art forms produced by the foreign conquerors and the conquered natives are in function, style, and meaning.

SIGNIFICANCE OF THE NATIVE ARTS

Europeans looked down on the native inhabitants of the New World, Africa, and the islands of the South Pacific; they thought them savage, barbarous, wild, and animallike. At best, they viewed them as childlike and backward, without religion or civilization. In every way, they were supposed inferior to white, Christian Europeans, who seriously believed it their duty to bring true religion and higher civilization to the benighted and unlettered heathen. This sense of mission to inferior peoples lasted well into the twentieth century. It was sloganized as "the white man's burden"; racial as well as religious superiority served as the fundamental assumptions justifying the entire colonial enterprise. In the early nineteenth century, the American historian, William H. Prescott, narrating the exploits of the first Europeans in "New Spain" in his *History of the Conquest of Mexico,* makes Cortés, the Spanish *conquistador,* the hero of the story and the instrument of Divine Providence: "It was beneficially ordered by Providence that the land [of Aztec Mexico] should be delivered over to another race who would rescue it from brutish superstition. . . . The debasing institutions of the Aztec furnish the best apology for their conquest." Two centuries earlier, Prescott's Puritan forebears had briefly and bluntly proclaimed the same religious and racial right, not only to the land they were disputing with the stubborn native tribes, but to the whole world. At a town meeting in Milford, Connecticut, in 1640, the Puritan fathers approved the following resolution: "Voted, that the earth is the Lord's and the fulness thereof; voted, that the earth is given to the saints; voted, that we are the saints."* This conviction doubtless was shared by generations of European colonizers as they suppressed native populations throughout the world.

It is not our aim to summarize the story of Europe's colonial imperialism here in these pages. For our purpose, the important assumption made by the European colonizers was that the natives and all their deeds and works were abjectly *inferior* to their colonial proprietors'. The native arts were thought to be ugly, outlandish toys, baubles, trinkets, fetishes, and idols fit only for travelers' souvenirs; native artworks were viewed as bizarre and grotesque curiosities of interest only to eccentric collectors. If such objects had any value at all, it was due to the precious stones or metals that composed them.

In the twentieth century, particularly in its later half, the status of native arts, if not of native peoples, has been upgraded dramatically. Three historical developments—one political, one scientific, and one esthetic—have promoted this new assessment.

The political development is obvious enough; it is still going on. The erstwhile colonial native peoples largely have won their independence as the colonial empires have dissolved. They have claimed a place and value in world civilization equal to that of their former European masters. The old labels ("savage," "barbarous," "wild") no longer have reference to them, and the label "primitive," which appeared to take the place of these earlier descriptions, is now an unpardonable slur. Yet "primitive" has been the heading under which the native arts have been classified in libraries and museums and grouped in exhibitions to this very day. This designation is in part the result of the second historical development—the scientific one.

In the colonial age, many Europeans did not share the contemptuous hostility toward native peoples typical of the rapacious colonizers. A neutral, even sympathetic, view of the inhabitants of the New World appeared in the work and writings of missionaries such as the Franciscan friars who accompanied the expeditions of Cortés. Missionary tolerance later was to be augmented by scientific curiosity. From the eighteenth century on, interest in the mysteries of human nature, its physical and social constitution, the origin, diffusion and interrelation of the races, and the seemingly infinite variety of religions, customs, and languages, ripened from the speculations of philosophers and the guesswork of explorers into the science of anthropology. The native populations of the colonial world gave anthropologists an ideal opportunity to observe and record scientifically the peculiarities of strange new societies in the undisturbed wholeness of their natural habitats. Early observers thought it possible to generalize the basic

*In R. C. Padden, *The Hummingbird and the Hawk: Conquest and Sovereignty in the Valley of Mexico, 1503–1541* (New York: Harper & Row, 1970), p. 137, n. 4.

traits of human nature from their elementary forms as seen in the pristine native condition, unobscured by the distorting influences of civilization.

In the process, anthropologists came up with a key concept—*culture*—by which they could classify and organize the observed data. "Culture" was a name for the sum of characteristics by which a given human community could be identified—race, physique, social organization, language, religion, technology, artifacts. The comparison of cultures led to the conclusion that cultures *as* cultures are equivalent in value, that they are not better or worse, but merely different. Scientific objectivity left no room for value judgments, certainly not the "superior" or "inferior" distinctions by which the colonizers had ruled the subjugated native populations.

Yet one distinction remained, not to be challenged until recently. Some cultures are more "advanced" than others—more successful in adapting to the environment, more flexible in responding to outside challenge, more in control of the conditions of life, more adept technologically or linguistically. Being more advanced meant being farther ahead and "later" in a progressive evolution of society; being less advanced meant being at an "earlier" stage. Consciously or unconsciously using European civilization as both the standard and the goal of human achievement, anthropologists classed native cultures as "early," that is to say, "primitive." And "primitive" could not escape a sense of "inferior."

Thus, the work of native hands came to be seen as *artifact*, not yet *art*. The great collections of artifacts made by anthropologists were not exhibited in museums of art, but in museums of "natural history." They were placed among relics of prehuman and prehistoric ages—markers on the path of progress to higher and later forms of existence. And when artifacts finally were acknowledged to be art, the label "primitive art," by which they were classified, still suggested backwardness. The prevailing theory of art as progressive could not fail to associate "backward" with "inferior."

The change in status from artifact to art was the consequence of the third historical development, the esthetic one. This was a profound change of taste, beginning in the late nineteenth century, by which artists, critics, and connoisseurs, along with a small public audience, came to perceive the intrinsic beauty and power of native arts. The story of that revelation and its effect on the rise of modern art is told in the last chapters of this book. In brief, this change of taste led to a full appreciation of the esthetic value of the arts of native peoples and to the acknowledgment of their right to a place in museums of art and in the history of the art of those museums. The arts of native peoples came to be viewed not as artifacts, nor as the primitive stage in the development of museum art, but rather as the coeval, equal, and rival of that art—perhaps its alternative, or perhaps, as some would suggest, its successor.

Stylistic Community of the Native Arts

Like the styles that make up other great areas of the history of art, those of the native arts have certain characteristics in common that allow us to recognize and group them as a stylistic community. These styles bear little resemblance to the art of the other areas, except for certain features that we shall note presently. It was their stylistic uniqueness and community in world art that drew the attention and the admiration of the moderns, leading to the adoption of radically new principles of design that contrasted sharply with Western tradition.

Small-scale works of native art, easily transportable and readily accessible in exhibitions, were the first to suggest a new design. With the exception of the pre-Columbian peoples of North and South America, native cultures rarely produced monumental architecture, sculpture, or painting. The native genius for design generally appeared in relatively small sculpture in stone, wood, metal, bone, and perishable materials of many kinds. Painting was done on a variety of framed and unframed surfaces and in a variety of media, and its ornamental systems were applied in ceramics, weaving, embroidery, basketry, jewelry, costume, and utensils. In this chapter, we are concerned primarily with works of this kind.

A remarkable consistency is maintained throughout the many variations among styles and substyles of native art. Native artists work almost by instinct in what we call *abstract* forms—nonobjective, nonrepresentational, stylized. We also have seen such forms in early Egyptian and Mesopotamian art, in the "idols" of Crete, in Islamic art, in the art of the European migrations, in the Early Romanesque, and in the haniwa art of Japan; we shall see them presently as an enormous influence on modern art. But the art of native peoples, with a few startling exceptions, remains consistently and conservatively abstract. In abstraction, the complex systems of color, light and shade, shape, and contour and surface that are given to the eye in optical perception are drastically simplified into basic, geometrical forms: in sculpture, *volumes*—spheroid, cuboid, conoid, pyramidal; in painting, *planes*—curvilinear, rectilinear, angular. In sculpture, shadow-casting projections are often much reduced, largely eliminating detail, except as it may be incised linearly upon surfaces. In painting, color-tone is laid on, without value gradations (chiaroscuro), within line-bound shapes, to make flat, hard-edged silhouettes. Colorful patterns on painted surfaces, textiles, pottery, and basketry are composed of motifs ingeniously repeated and expanded. Indeed, the formality of abstract shape and pattern dominates *all* the native arts; it is not, as in other world styles, confined primarily to ornament.

The consistency of style in native art finds its counterpart in the consistency of its modes of signification. Insofar as it signifies by images, native art can be said to be representational, but only to a degree strictly limited by convention (convention which, as we have noticed, largely eliminates detailed report of the optical world). Geometrical simplicity of form is best suited to the rendering of signs, symbols, and images that have unchanging attributes and general meaning, like "divinity," "royalty," and "kinship." In its simplicity of form, native art approaches the abstraction of pictographic and written figuration, although it incorporates much more information from the optical world. This information, altered to fit the meanings the artist wishes to signify, appears in characteristic distortions of the forms of nature. In the representation of the human figure, natural proportions are disregarded: the head may be larger than the torso, the features of the face may be exaggerated, abbreviated, misplaced, or partly eliminated. The face most often has the character of a mask; the body and limbs take on the aspect of a hinged mannikin, the motions of which have been arbitrarily twisted and fixed. In this connection, we must note the importance of the mask and the ceremonial dance in native cultures; both are crucial in the rituals of native religion. The powerfully exaggerated features of the mask are consistent with the patterned, abruptly repeated rhythms of the dance performed by the masked participants.

The consistency of style and signification in native art is reinforced by their conventionality and conservatism; the three characteristics are mutually reinforcing. Native art is overwhelmingly religious, and in religious art, as in religious rite, conventional forms, established from time immemorial, are conservatively retained, with only slight change. Thus, we find little of the *historical* development of style in native art that we have traced in the art of other periods. (The art of ancient Egypt, conservative as it was, moved from an earlier style resembling native art [see FIG. 3-2] to the standard style by which we easily identify it.) In native art, continuity does exist, but almost no traceable change could be called developmental. Great diversity is apparent in the working out of stylistic possibilities, but invention and experimentation remain within the limits imposed by the rules of convention. The astonishing realism of the African bronzes of Ife and Benin (FIGS. 14-44 and 14-45) seem inexplicable as part of any line of development. The power of convention that restrains innovation and conserves stylistic types is a brake on any developmental motion leading to new languages of form and signification. Within world art, the art of native peoples, in its consistency, conservatism, and conventionality, has preserved a timeless community resistant to the destructive influences of imported change.

THE PRE-COLUMBIAN ART OF THE AMERICAS

Among the native cultures of the world, those that flourished in the Americas before the coming of Columbus are exceptional in several important respects. We have remarked in passing that these New World cultures are distinguished by monumental architecture, sculpture, and painting, as well as the craft arts. In addition, some of these groups, like the Maya, had a highly developed writing system and knowledge of mathematical calculation that made possible the keeping of precise records and the creation of a sophisticated calendar and a highly accurate astronomy. Although they used Stone Age technology, did not use the wheel (except for toys), and had no pack animals but the llama, pre-Columbian peoples excelled in the engineering arts associated with the planning and construction of cities, civic and domestic buildings, roads and bridges, and irrigation and drainage systems. They mastered complex agricultural techniques using only rudimentary tools of cultivation. Their works, left in ruins by the Spanish invasions or abandoned to the forces of nature, are being reclaimed from erosion and the encroachment of tropical forests. Today, ever more important discoveries are being made, and now the ruined cities can be visited and marveled at as among the most prodigious creations of human hands.

The origins of these peoples are still a matter of some dispute, centering primarily about the chronology of their arrival in America from Asia. They crossed the now submerged land bridge, "Beringia," which connected the shores of the Bering Strait, sometime between 30,000 B.C. and 10,000 B.C. These Stone Age Asian nomads were hunters; their only tools were made of bone, pressure-flaked stone, and wood. They had no knowledge of agriculture but possibly some of basketry. They could control fire and probably built rude shelters. Over many centuries, they spread out until they occupied the two American continents. They were few in number: the total population of the hemisphere in 1492 may not have exceeded fifteen million. By about 3000 B.C., a number of the migrants had learned to cultivate wild grasses, setting the stage for the maize (corn) culture that was basic to the early peoples of the Americas. As agriculturists, the nomads became a settled people and learned to make pottery utensils and lively figurines of clay. Metals were used for ornament, not for tools; these cultures never developed a metal technology. With these skills as a base, many cultures arose over long periods of time. Several reached a high level of accomplishment by the early centuries of the Christian era.

MESOAMERICA

The term *Mesoamerica* (Middle America) names the region comprised of Mexico, Guatemala, Belize, and Honduras, triply referring to its geography, ethnology, and archeology. The Mexican highlands are a volcanic and seismic region. In highland Mexico, great reaches of arid plateau land, fertile for maize and wheat wherever water is available, lie between heavily forested mountain slopes, which at some places rise to perpetual snow. The moist tropical jungles of the coastal plains yield rich crops, when the land can be cleared. In Yucatán, a subsoil of limestone furnishes abundant material both for building and carving. The limestone tableland, covered with jungle, continues into the Petén region of Guatemala, which separates Mexico from Honduras. Some of the most spectacular of Maya ruins are located in the region of Yucatán and the Petén, where dense jungle is interspersed with broad stretches of savanna. The great mountain chains of Mexico and Guatemala extend into Honduras (which is 75 percent mountainous) and slope sharply down to tropical coasts. Highlands and mountain valleys, jungle and coastlines, with their chill, temperate, and humid climates, alternate dramatically.

The variegated landscape of Mesoamerica may have much to do with the diversity of languages spoken by its native populations; a very large number of different languages are distributed among no less than fourteen linguistic families. Many of the languages spoken in the pre-conquest periods survive to this day: the Maya tongue still can be heard in Guatemala; the Náhuatl of the Aztecs is spoken in the Mexican highlands; the Zapotec and Mixtec languages linger in Oaxaca and its environs. Diverse as the languages of these peoples were, their cultures otherwise had much in common (in this respect, the peoples of pre-Columbian Mesoamerica resemble the peoples of Europe): maize cultivation, religious rites, myths, traditions and folklore, social structures, customs and arts. Yet, some (like the Maya) were distinguished as rich in total achievement; the Toltecs were renowned as great builders and organizers; the Aztecs were reputedly implacable warriors; and the Mixtecs were known as master craftsmen in gold and turquoise. As their history becomes better known, the cultures of Mesoamerica, taken in sum, are revealed as rivaling more familiar great cultures of the world.

Archeological investigation, with ever increasing refinement of technique, has been uncovering, describing, and classifying Mesoamerican monuments for more than a century. Since 1960, when important steps were taken in the decipherment of the hieroglyphic script of the Maya and in the systematic interpretation of their pictorial imagery, evidence for a detailed account of Mesoamerican history and art has fallen into place. Like the pharaohs of ancient Egypt, many Maya rulers now can be listed by name and the dates of their reigns fixed with precision. This accomplishment reinforced the general Mesoamerican

MESOAMERICAN CHRONOLOGY

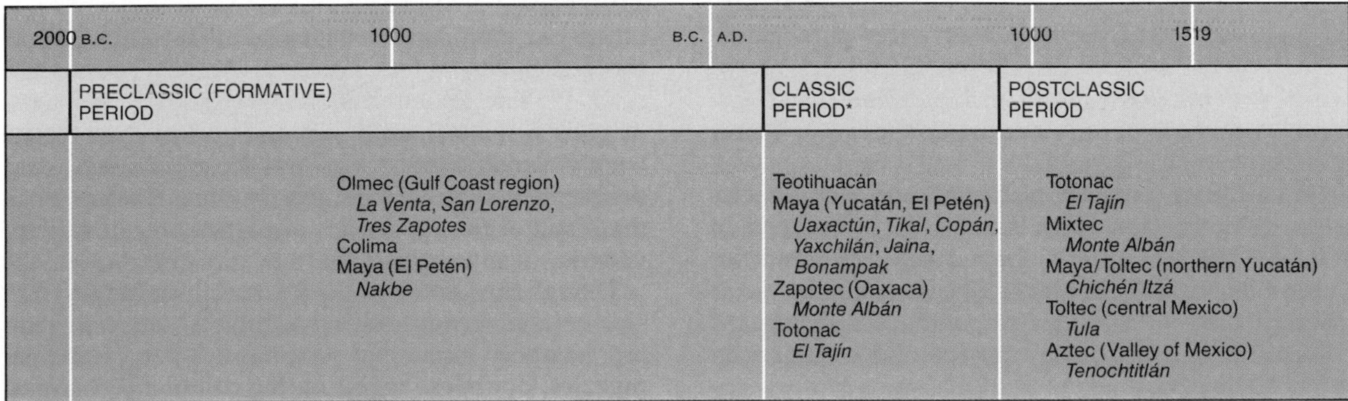

2000 B.C. — 1000 — B.C.	A.D. — 1000	— 1519
PRECLASSIC (FORMATIVE) PERIOD	CLASSIC PERIOD*	POSTCLASSIC PERIOD
Olmec (Gulf Coast region) *La Venta, San Lorenzo, Tres Zapotes* Colima Maya (El Petén) *Nakbe*	Teotihuacán Maya (Yucatán, El Petén) *Uaxactún, Tikal, Copán, Yaxchilán, Jaina, Bonampak* Zapotec (Oaxaca) *Monte Albán* Totonac *El Tajín*	Totonac *El Tajín* Mixtec *Monte Albán* Maya/Toltec (northern Yucatán) *Chichén Itzá* Toltec (central Mexico) *Tula* Aztec (Valley of Mexico) *Tenochtitlán*

*Many of the cultures listed in the Classic period actually originated during the later Preclassic. The Classic period was the period in which they achieved their unprecedented magnificence.

chronology, which is now well established and widely accepted. The standard chronology is divided into three epochs, with some overlapping of subperiods: the Preclassic (Formative) extends from 2000 B.C. to A.D. 300; the Classic period runs from A.D. 200 to 900; and the Postclassic begins in A.D. 900 and ends during the first several decades of the sixteenth century. The principal regions of pre-Columbian Mesoamerica are the Gulf Coast region (Olmec culture); Yucatán and the Petén (Maya culture); southwestern Mexico and the region of Oaxaca (Zapotec and Mixtec cultures); and the Valley of Mexico (Teotihuacán, Toltec, and Aztec cultures). The expansion and wide influence of the principal cultures, however, has made for a fairly even distribution of important archeological sites throughout Mesoamerica.

Preclassic: 2000 B.C.–A.D. 300

OLMEC

Olmec culture is known as the "mother culture" of Mesoamerica; the religious, social, and artistic traditions largely reach back to it. Though we know little of its origins and history, its influence is traced readily through the wide diffusion of its institutional forms, its monuments, arts, and artifacts.

Settling in the tropical lowlands of the Gulf of Mexico (the present-day states of Veracruz and Tabasco), the Olmec peoples cultivated a terrain of rain forest and alluvial lowland washed by numerous rivers that flowed into the Gulf. It was here that social organization assumed the form adapted and developed by later Mesoamerican cultures. The mass of the population—food-producing farmers scattered in hinterland villages—provided the sustenance and labor that maintained a hereditary caste of rulers, hierarchies of priests, functionaries, retainers, and artisans. These were located by rank within enclosed precincts that served ceremonial, administrative, and residential functions, and perhaps the economic purpose of marketplace as well. At regular intervals, the whole community convened for ritual observances at religious-civic centers such as San Lorenzo and La Venta, which now can be regarded as the formative architectural expressions of the structure and ideals of Olmec society.

At La Venta, earthen platforms and stone enclosures mark out two great courtyards; at one end of the larger was a volcano-shaped clay "pyramid" or mound almost 100 feet high. The La Venta layout is an early form of the temple-pyramid, plaza-courtyard complex that will be characteristic of Mesoamerican "urban" design.

Facing out from the plaza are four colossal heads of basalt that weigh about ten tons each and stand between 6 and 8 feet high (FIG. **14-1**). Almost as much of an achievement as the carving of these huge stones was their transportation across the sixty miles of swampland from the nearest known source of basalt. The heads are hallmarks of Olmec art; a number of others like them have been found at Tres Zapotes and the earlier site of San Lorenzo. Archeologists have not been able to determine whether they are images of gods or rulers. Both San Lorenzo and La Venta were violently overthrown, and the great heads were deliberately defaced, perhaps for ritual reasons or as the result of the vandalism of particularly hostile invaders.

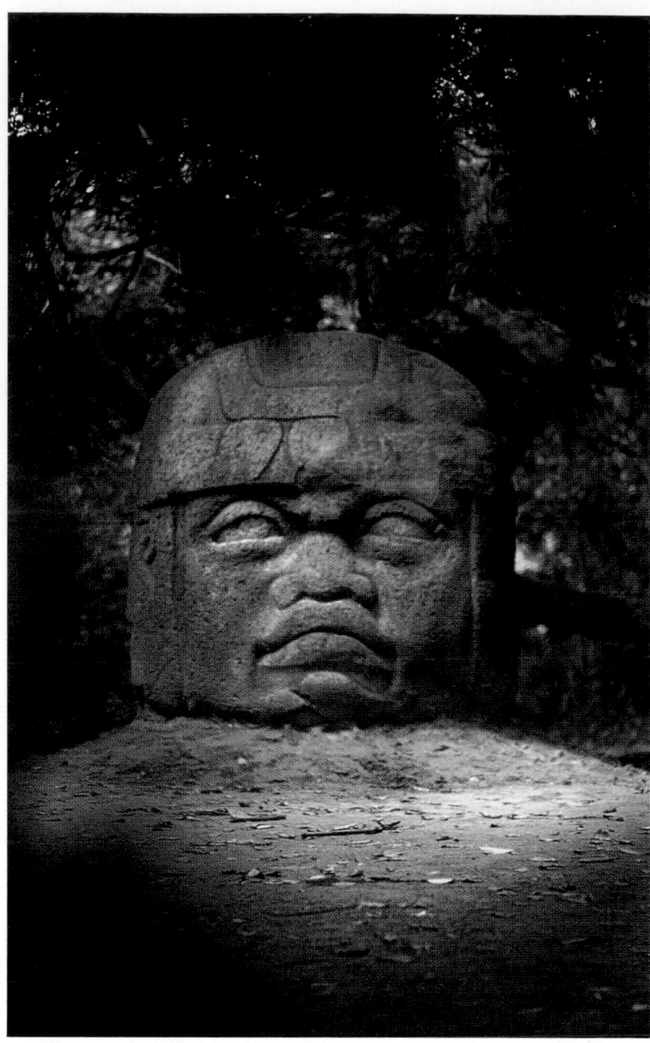

14-1 *Colossal Head,* Olmec, La Venta, Mexico, 1500–300 B.C. Basalt, 8′ high, 21′ in circumference.

Though the Olmec worked primarily in basalt, they also created beautifully wrought statuettes in jade representing humanoid creatures with jaguarlike muzzles, doubtless reflecting the cult of a jaguar-god (FIG. **14-2**). The Mesoamerican motif of the animal-man deity here makes an early appearance.

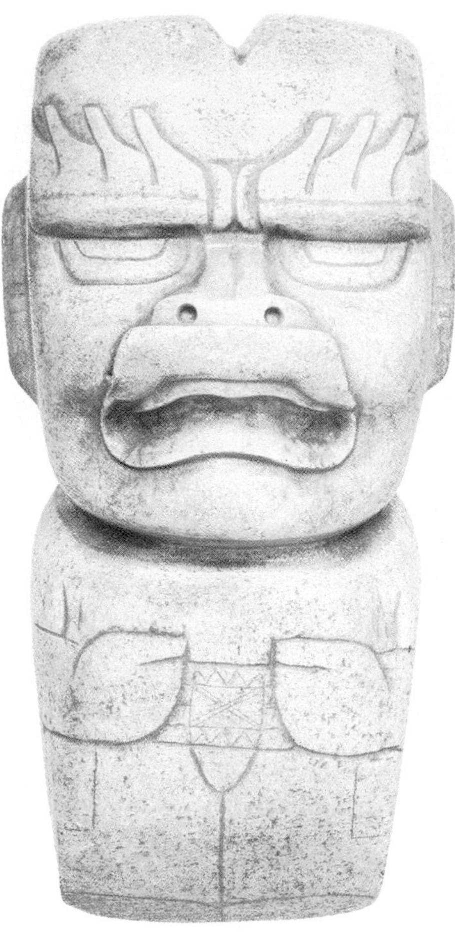

14-2 Ceremonial ax, Olmec, from La Venta, Mexico, 1500–300 B.C. Jadeite, 11½″ high. British Museum, London.

WEST MEXICO: COLIMA

In the area of Mexico far to the west of the tropical heartland of the Olmec, Preclassic sites along the country's Pacific coast have yielded small art of a distinctive kind. The pre-Columbian peoples of West Mexico produced neither massive architecture nor large-scale stone sculpture and, in general, did not share in the cultural achievements of the central and southern zones of Mesoamerica. In fact, the West Mexico states of Jalisco, Nayarit, and Colima frequently have been referred to as cultural "backwaters" relative to the "high" cultures for which Mesoamerica is most famous.

Yet West Mexico had a long and rich artistic tradition, principally in the medium of clay sculpture. Effigy figures of humans, animals, and mythological creatures have been encountered in distinctive tombs consisting of shafts (as deep as 50 feet) with chambers at their bottom end. Unfortunately, this area was long neglected by archeologists, and our limited knowledge of tomb contents derives primarily from the operations of grave robbers.

The large, hollow, ceramic figures found in these tombs exhibit a distinct sense of volume, particularly in the swollen torsos and limbs. The Colima figures are consistently a highly burnished red-orange, in contrast with the distinctive variegated surfaces of the majority of other West Coast ceramics. The area also is noted for small-scale clay scenes that include modeled houses or temples and numerous solid figurines, the latter shown in a variety of lively activities, some of which have been interpreted as festivals and battles.

The sculpture from this area frequently is described as exhibiting a secular quality seldom encountered in the arts elsewhere in Mesoamerica. To some degree this viewpoint may have been a result of our inability to discriminate religious from nonreligious objects. Many figures have been identified, for example, as "warriors" or as "shamans." The latter seems to be the correct identification for the seated figure shown here (FIG. **14-3**), especially since it is becoming increasingly clear that the arts of this area, with few exceptions, were largely connected with religion and mortuary ritual.

14-3 *Seated Figure with Raised Arms,* from Colima, Mexico, 1000–300 B.C. Terra-cotta, 13½″ high. Stendahl Collection, Los Angeles.

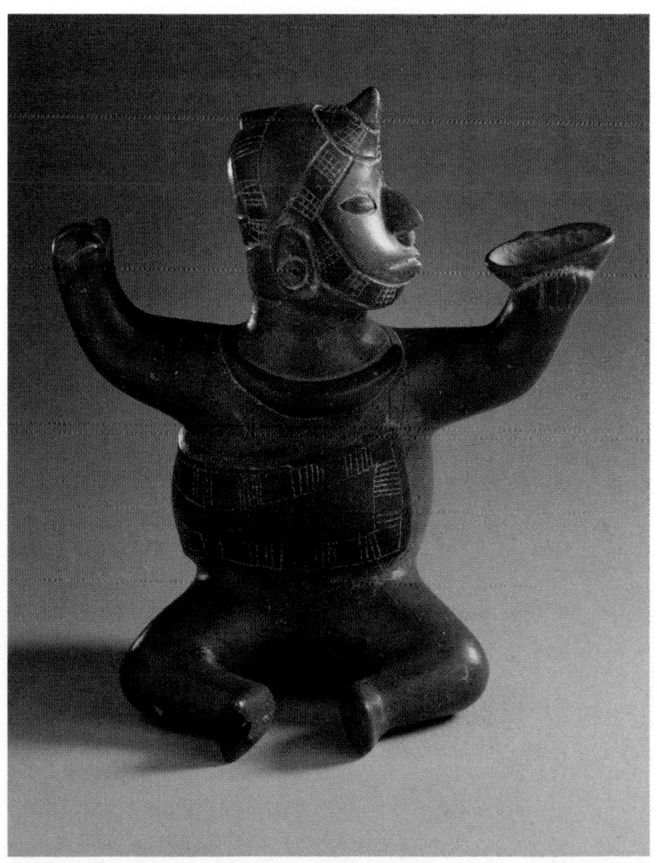

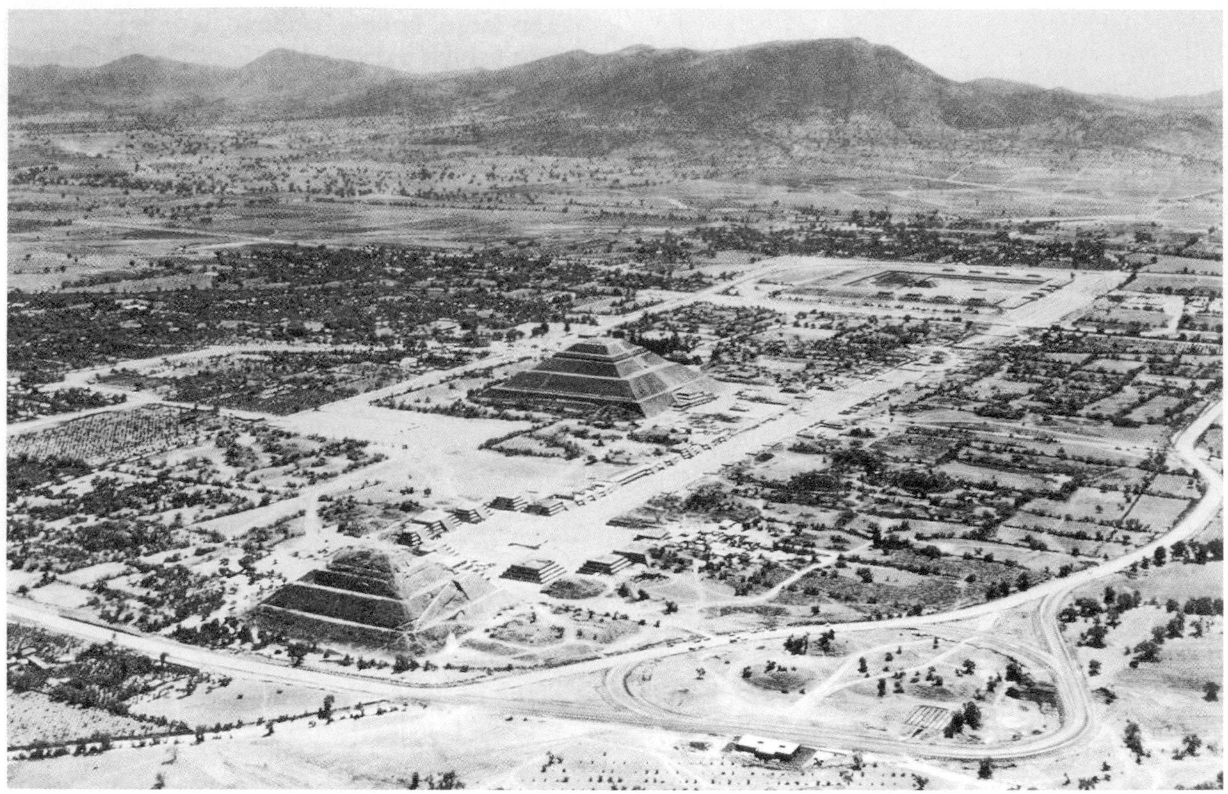

14-4 Teotihuacán, Valley of Mexico. Aerial view from the northwest. Pyramid of the Moon (*foreground*), Pyramid of the Sun (*center*), the Citadel (*right background*); all connected by the Avenue of the Dead; main structures c. A.D. 50–200, site c. 100 B.C.–A.D. 600.

Classic: A.D. 200–900

VALLEY OF MEXICO: TEOTIHUACÁN

The time period designated as the Classic period in Mesoamerica witnesses the rise and flourishing of great civilizations that are on a par with those of the ancient Near East, which in many respects they resemble. Though these advanced civilizations originate in the later Preclassic, it is in the Classic period that they achieve their unprecedented magnificence. We have seen at Olmec La Venta an embryonic form of the temple-pyramid-plaza layout. At the awe-inspiring site of Teotihuacán, northeast of modern Mexico City, we can observe the monumental expansion of the Olmec scheme into a genuine city. The carefully planned area covers nine square miles and is laid out in a grid pattern, the axes of which were oriented consistently by sophisticated surveying (FIG. **14-4**). At its peak, around A.D. 600, Teotihuacán may have had as many as two hundred thousand residents; it would have been at that time the sixth largest city in the world. Divided into numerous wardlike sectors, this metropolis must have had a uniquely cosmopolitan character, with Zapotec peoples located in the western wards of the city and Maya in the eastern. The city's urbanization did nothing to subtract from it as a religious center; its importance as such was vastly augmented. Teotihuacán was known throughout Mesoamerica as "the place of the gods"; it was visited regularly and reverently by later Aztec kings long after it had been abandoned.

The grid plan is quartered by a north–south and an east–west axis, each four miles in length (we are reminded of Hellenistic and Roman urban planning [FIGS. 5-88 and 6-44]). The main north–south axis, the Avenue of the Dead, is a thoroughfare 130 feet wide. It connects the Pyramid of the Moon complex with the Citadel, which houses the well-preserved Temple of Quetzalcóatl. The Pyramid of the Sun, the centerpiece of the city and its largest structure, is oriented to the west and rises on the east side of the Avenue of the Dead to a height of over 200 feet. The imposing mass and scale of the monuments at Teotihuacán are early indicators of the great feats of the Classic period.

Although the pyramids here do not yet have the regularity of shape characteristic of other Classic period pyramids, they do exhibit the basic elements of form: solid stone construction; superposed, squared platforms, diminishing in perimeter; and ramped stairways ascending to a crowning temple (the temple is missing at Teotihuacán). The pyramids at this

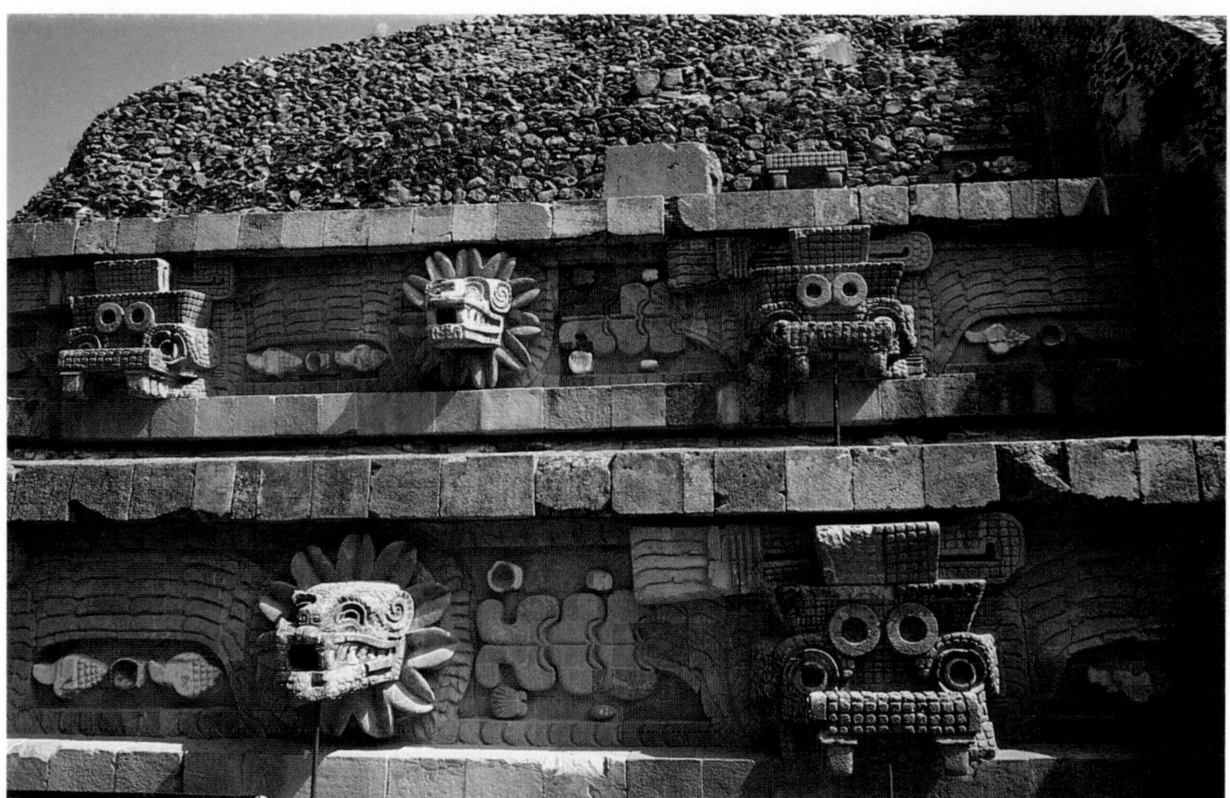

14-5 Detail of Temple of Quetzalcóatl, the Citadel, Teotihuacán, Mexico, third century (?).

site at once recall the ziggurat of Mesopotamia and the stepped pyramid of Egypt (FIGS. 2-13 and 3-6). Since these New World structures were built more than two millennia later than their Near Eastern counterparts, we have no good reason to suppose that they were influenced by the earlier works erected halfway around the world. Yet, it is interesting that intensely religious civilizations in two different hemispheres seem to agree in their selection of the pyramid form for the worship of their gods.

At the south end of the Avenue of the Dead is the great quadrangle of the Citadel. It encloses a smaller shrine, the Temple of Quetzalcóatl (a major god in the Mesoamerican pantheon). Its sculptured panels, protected by subsequent building, are well preserved (FIG. **14-5**). The six terraces of the temple are each decorated with massive, projecting stone heads of the feathered serpent, the mask-symbol of Quetzalcóatl, which alternate with heads of the goggle-eyed rain god, Tlaloc. Linking these alternating heads are low-relief carvings of feathered-serpent bodies and seashells, the latter reflecting Teotihuacán contact with the peoples of the Mexican coasts. The stone temple and its carved décor manifest that mutually reinforcing union of monumental sculpture and architecture that reminds us of the powerful ensembles distinguishing the art of the ancient Near East, Hellenic civilization, and the Gothic world.

The influence of Teotihuacán was all-pervasive in Mesoamerica. Colonies like Cholula, on the Mexican plateau, were established widely. Others adjoined the southern borders of Maya civilization, in the highlands of Guatemala, some eight hundred miles from Teotihuacán. Political and economic interaction between Teotihuacán and the Maya in southern Mexico and Guatemala linked the two outstanding cultures of the Early Classic.

GUATEMALA-HONDURAS-YUCATÁN: MAYA

A considerable number of strong cultural influences stemming from the Olmec tradition and from Teotihuacán were active in the development of Classic Maya culture, which has been called "the most advanced, sophisticated, and subtle civilization of the New World"; certainly, Maya culture is exemplary of the whole of Mesoamerican achievement. As with Teotihuacán, Maya civilization's foundations were laid in the Preclassic period, as early as 200 to 50 B.C.* At that time, the Maya, who occupied the moist lowland areas of Guatemala and Honduras, abruptly

*Archeologists working in the jungles of Guatemala at the site of Nakbe currently are excavating the ruins of an early Maya urban center dated about 800–600 B.C. This discovery pushes back dramatically the time at which Maya civilization is supposed to have begun and will alter significantly our historical picture of that society.

abandoned their early, more or less egalitarian pattern of village life and adopted a hierarchical, autocratic society. This system evolved into the typical Maya theocratic city-state, governed by hereditary rulers and ranked nobility. How and why this happened is still in doubt. The change was signalized by stupendous building projects. Stone structures rivaling those of Teotihuacán in scale rose dramatically, covering square miles of territory with vast, enclosed complexes of terraced temple-pyramids, tombs, palaces, plazas, ball courts, and residences of the governing elite. The new architecture, and the art that embellished it, advertised the power and interrelationship of rulers and gods and their absolute control of human as well as cosmic life. The unified institutions of religion and kingship were established so firmly, their hold on life and custom was so tenacious, and their meaning was so fixed in the symbolism and imagery of art, that the rigidly conservative system of the Classic Maya lasted almost a thousand years. Maya civilization collapsed in about the year 900, vanishing more abruptly and unaccountably than it had appeared.

Though the causes of the beginning and end of Classic Maya civilization are obscure, the events of its history, beliefs, ceremonies, conventions, and patterns of daily life presently are being revealed in minute detail. The Maya now enter upon the stage of world history as believably as the peoples of the other great civilizations we have been studying. The distorting lenses of myth and legend, which made this group almost akin to the fantastic characters of science fiction, have been removed. This more accurate picture is the consequence of the documentary bequest of the Maya on the one hand and the work of modern archeology on the other.

As we have seen, the Maya possessed an elaborate writing system and highly developed knowledge of arithmetical calculation. These accomplishments enabled them to keep exact records of important events, times, places, and people. They were able to establish the all-important genealogical lines of rulers, which certified their claim to rule, and could construct astronomical charts and tables. They contrived an intricate but astonishingly accurate calendar. Their calendric structuring of time, though radically different in form from ours, was just as sophisticated and efficient. The sixteenth-century Franciscan chronicler of the Maya of Yucatán, Bishop Diego de Landa, declared that time reckoning was "the science in which they believed most and which they valued most highly" of all their achievements. In addition, the Maya mirrored themselves in carved and painted imagery. Though strictly conventional in style, their images, with their hieroglyphic "captions," have great descriptive value.

With these ample documentary materials, modern archeologists have deciphered numerous additional elements of Maya writing in the last three decades. They have made a precise historical record from the calendar and have clarified the iconography of symbol and image. All of these advances have enabled them to bring into ever sharper focus a true picture of the civilization of the Maya.

Time reckoning, like all the arts and institutions of this civilization, was religious in purpose. It aimed to bring human life into the closest possible correspondence with the rhythmic pulse of the living cosmos—the movements of the stars, the diurnal career of the sun, the changes of the seasons, the fluctuations of the climate, and the growth of crops. Within the vital universe of the Maya, all things—animate and inanimate—were interlinked by occult affinities; arts like astrology and divination were practiced to recognize these affinities and determine their influence on human action, while rituals were performed to control them.

Whole populations of greater and lesser gods filled the Maya pantheon and were represented in their art: gods of the Overworld, the Middleworld, the Underworld; gods of the points of the compass; gods of wind and stone, of water lilies, trees, maize, jaguars, jade, serpents, hummingbirds; even a god of the number zero. The business of religion was to gain access to the gods, to propitiate them with sacrifice and manipulate them with magic. By rituals of sacrifice a god could be summoned up. The celebrants of the rituals, through a vision induced by hallucinogenic drugs or by massive letting of their own blood (usually both), could then unite their essence with that of the god, though only for the duration of the rite. In this mingling of human and divine, the distinction between natural and supernatural disappeared.

This commingling of human and divine also applied to Maya statecraft, for statecraft and religion were one. The ruler was not merely godlike; he (or at times, she) *was* a god. Kingship and deity shared the rule of the cosmos as well as the rule of the state. In art, the Maya ruler was shown holding the sky in his arms, controlling the motions of the sun and Venus (the morning and evening star), those most ancient and august twin gods of the Maya pantheon. Rulers and gods reciprocally existed, the rulers requiring the gods for the preservation of the state, the gods depending on the ruler for their honor and sustenance. One could not exist without the other. It was in the ritual ceremonies of bloodletting and human sacrifice that the natures of god and king, of divinity and humanity, were commingled.

In the mythology of the Maya, the gods created human beings by self-sacrifice. Fashioning them from maize and water, they brought them to life with their own blood. The reciprocal relationship between humans and gods required that human beings strengthen and nourish the gods. The blood of the gods had to be replaced by human blood; blood had to be perpetually supplied in order for the gods to survive. The most sacred and necessary function of Maya religion was, therefore, the procurement of human blood for the nourishment of the gods. The life of the gods, the state, and the cosmos demanded blood sacrifice.

On all occasions of state, public bloodletting was an integral part of Maya ritual. The ruler, his consort, and certain members of the nobility drew blood from their own bodies and sought union with deity in ecstatic vision (the vision quest). This ceremony was regularly accompanied by the wholesale slaughter of captives taken in war. Wars between the Maya city-states and foreigners were fought principally to provide victims for sacrifice. After prolonged participation in bloodletting rites, these individuals were stretched out on specially designed altars or bound to scaffolds placed on high temple platforms. Their hearts eventually were cut out, and their bodies hurled down the steep stairways. Many captives were forced to play the fatal ballgame in courts laid out adjacent to the temples. The losers of the game were decapitated or otherwise killed. The torture, mutilation, and execution of the victims of the blood ceremonies presented the public with spectacles of profoundly religious import. It has been said that blood was the very mortar of the structure of the Maya system.

Architecture The relationship of the Maya politico-religious system to Maya architecture is obvious. The enclosed, centrally located precincts, where the most sacred and majestic buildings of the Maya city were raised, were intended as settings for those religious-civic transactions that guaranteed the order of state and cosmos. The drama of the blood ritual took place within a sculptured and painted environment, where huge symbols and images proclaimed the nature and necessity of that order. The spacious plazas were designed for vast audiences, who, stimulated by drugs, drums, and dancing, were exposed to an overwhelming propaganda. The programmers of that propaganda, the ruling families and troops of priests, nobles, and retainers, carried its symbolism through in their costumes. They were clad in extravagant profusions of vividly colorful textiles and feathers, each ornamental article having meanings that linked it to supernatural persons and powers. On the different levels of the painted and polished temple platforms, before sanctuaries glittering in the sun, the ruling classes performed the offices of their rites in clouds of incense to the music of maracas, flutes, and drums.* The architectural complex at the center of the city was transformed into a theater of religion and statecraft.

The stagelike layout of a characteristic Maya city complex can be seen in a reconstruction of the site of Uaxactún (FIG. **14-6**). It is the setting for public art and activity. The plazas conspicuously occupy the major operational spaces; the buildings themselves are

*Though our knowledge of the music of the Maya is slight, elite tombs at the site of Pachitun in Belize have yielded a cache of musical instruments from the Late Classic period, some of which still can be played. Among them are a drum, flute-maracas, flutes, and "figurine ocarinas." The painted walls of Bonampak show processions of musicians beating drums, rattling maracas, and blowing wooden trumpets.

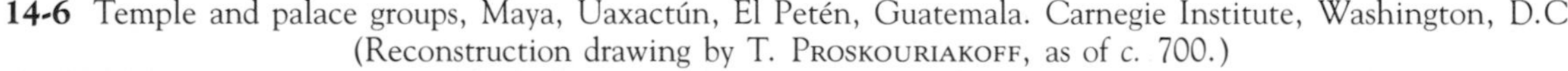

14-6 Temple and palace groups, Maya, Uaxactún, El Petén, Guatemala. Carnegie Institute, Washington, D.C. (Reconstruction drawing by T. PROSKOURIAKOFF, as of *c.* 700.)

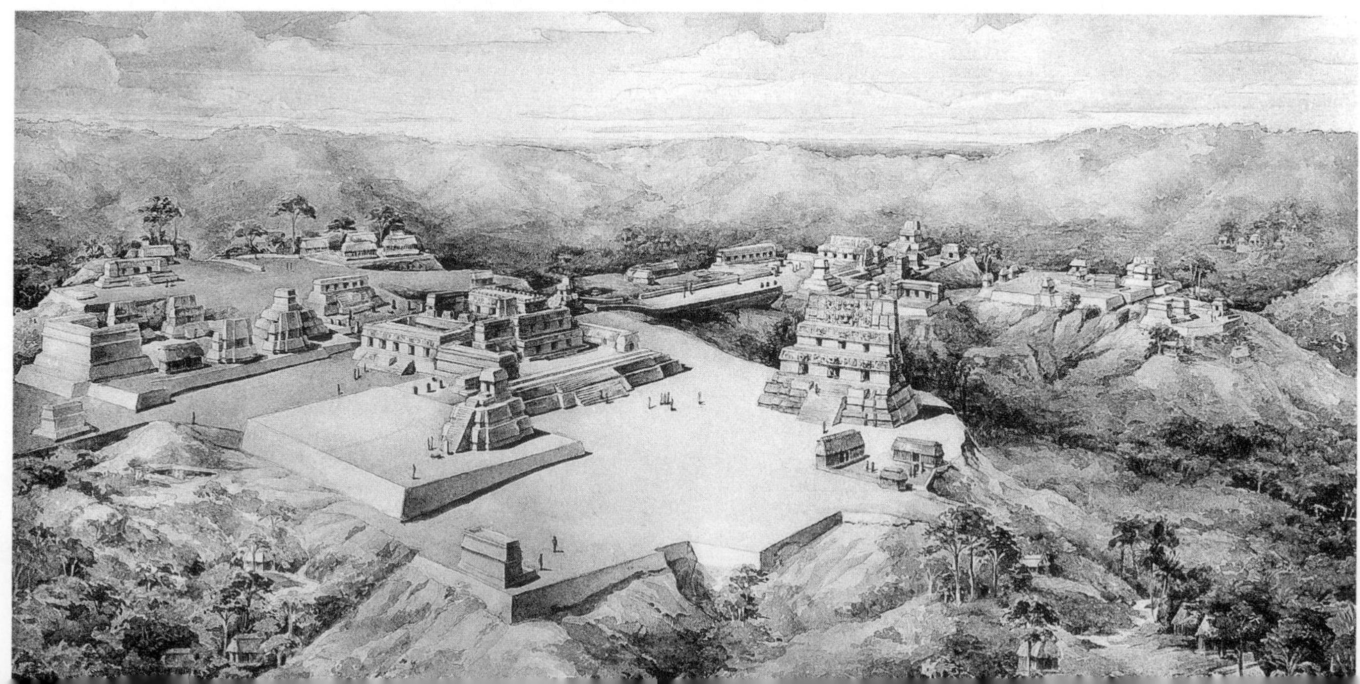

more like stage properties. Tall slabs of sculptured stone, anywhere from 5 feet to 25 feet in height, further define the space of the plazas. Permanent fixtures, these stelae describe in images and glyphs the history and meaning of the site and are characteristic features of Classic Maya urban composition. The temple group at Uaxactún was part of a larger assembly of temples and buildings on hilltops, all connected by roadways and covering many square miles. The base of the group was composed of receding terraces with stairways ascending to the temple court. The massive temple roofs were surmounted by ornate and towering roof combs painted in a variety of colors. The whole complex, contemporaneous with Teotihuacán, dates from the Late Preclassic period, 200 B.C. to A.D. 50.

The public character of Maya architecture is evident in its stress upon the exterior aspect of its principal buildings. The interiors were limited spatially by corbel vaulting, the structural form we have seen at Tiryns in Mycenean Greece (FIG. 4-22). Such chambers were rarely more than 15 feet in width, but might be of any length; temples constructed in this manner were aggregates of one or more long narrow compartments.

About twenty air miles from Uaxactún, Tikal, one of the oldest and largest of the Maya cities, rises above the thick tropical forest that once had invaded it completely. The city and its suburbs originally covered some seventy-five square miles and served as the ceremonial center of a population of perhaps seventy-five thousand. Central Tikal was not laid out on a grid plan like its contemporary, Teotihuacán; instead, irregular groupings were connected by causeways. Modern surveys have uncovered the remains of as many as three thousand separate constructions in an area of about six square miles. The site's nucleus, the Great Plaza, which is studded with sculptured stelae, contains numerous structures, the most prominent of which are two soaring pyramids facing each other across an open square. The larger construction (FIG. **14-7**), Temple I (also called the Temple of the Giant Jaguar after a motif on one of its lintels) reaches a height of 144 feet. It is the temple-mausoleum of a ruler of Tikal, whose tomb is encased in a vaulted chamber excavated at the level of the plaza. The structure is made up of nine sharply inclining platforms, culminating at the summit in a superstructure composed of a supplementary platform and stairway. These elements serve as a base for a three-chambered

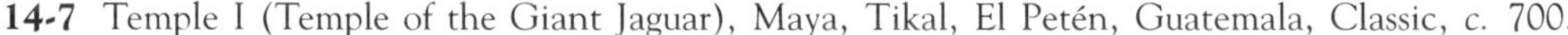

14-7 Temple I (Temple of the Giant Jaguar), Maya, Tikal, El Petén, Guatemala, Classic, *c.* 700.

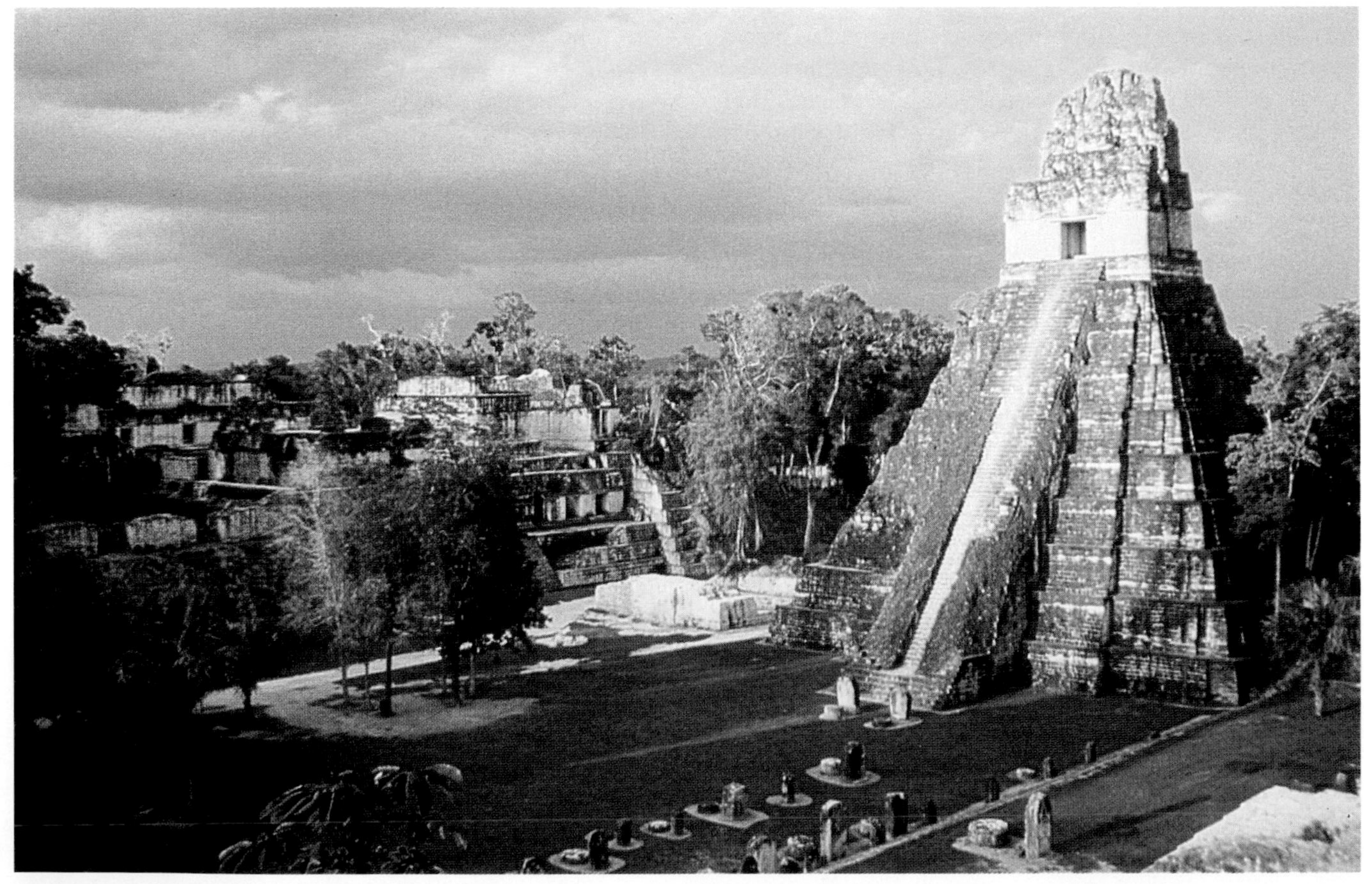

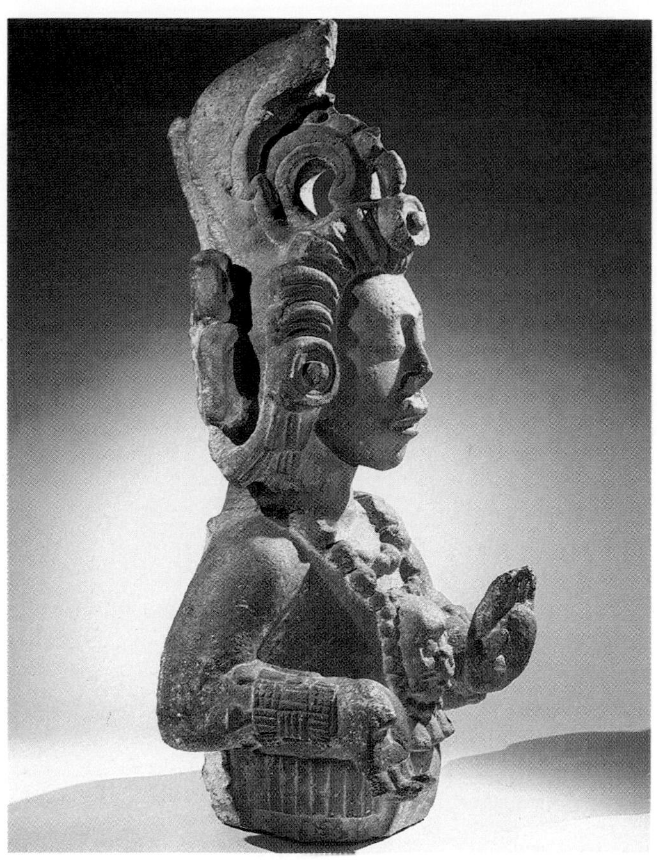

14-8 *Maize God,* from Temple 22, Maya, Copán, Honduras, c. 775. Limestone, 35⅓″ × 21⅓″. British Museum, London.

temple surmounted by an elaborately carved roof comb. The swift upward drive of the great staircase, forbiddingly steep (and perilous in descent!), forces these elements into the towerlike verticality of the pyramid, elevating the temple unit far above the public concourse. This structure exhibits most concisely the Mesoamerican formula for the stepped temple-pyramid and, freed from its dense jungle cover, the compelling esthetic and psychological power of Maya architecture.

Sculpture and Painting Architecture, the dominant Maya art, also provided the matrix of Maya sculpture and painting. Rarely do we have sculpture independent of architecture, whether in high relief, in the round, or freestanding. The sculptured stele resembles the detached panel of a wall, and freestanding sculpture, such as it is, is found on the scale of the ceramic figurine. Painting is bound to architecture; murals are the most common form. But considerable painting also has survived on the surfaces of ceramic receptacles, cups, bowls, and pots, which provide detailed information concerning Maya life and culture.

A striking sculptured head representing the maize god (FIG. **14-8**) was found in the ruins of a palace at the site of Copán. With others like it, it originally was tenoned into the architectural fabric, jutting out from the flat frieze of a cornice. We have noted the significance of maize as the basic foodstuff of Mesoamerica. The personification of natural elements and forces in Maya religion found embodiment in the figurative arts. Here, in the features of head and headdress, the sculptor alludes metaphorically to ripening corn: the face is the cob, the necklace the kernels, the hair the cornsilk, and the headdress the clustering foliage. The graceful motion of the hands suggests the waving of the stalks in the wind. The closed, heavy-lidded eyes turn inward to the young plant's interior life. In the youthful beauty and sensitivity of the face, we find expression of the very idea of spiritual composure. The work is executed with that deft simplification of appearances into plane and volume that we have seen to be characteristic of native arts. But here the simplifying process stops well short of total abstraction of form. The peculiar traits of Maya physiognomy are smoothed into a symmetry and regularity that subordinate the real to the ideal.

Farther along toward abstraction, but replete with descriptive detail, are the figures of a carved lintel from Yaxchilán (FIG. **14-9**). The calendrical glyphs surrounding the figures date the commemorated event

14-9 *Bird-Jaguar Taking a Prisoner,* Maya, Yaxchilán, from Chiapas, Mexico, Late Classic, 755–770. Limestone, 31″ × 30″ × 2¾″. British Museum, London.

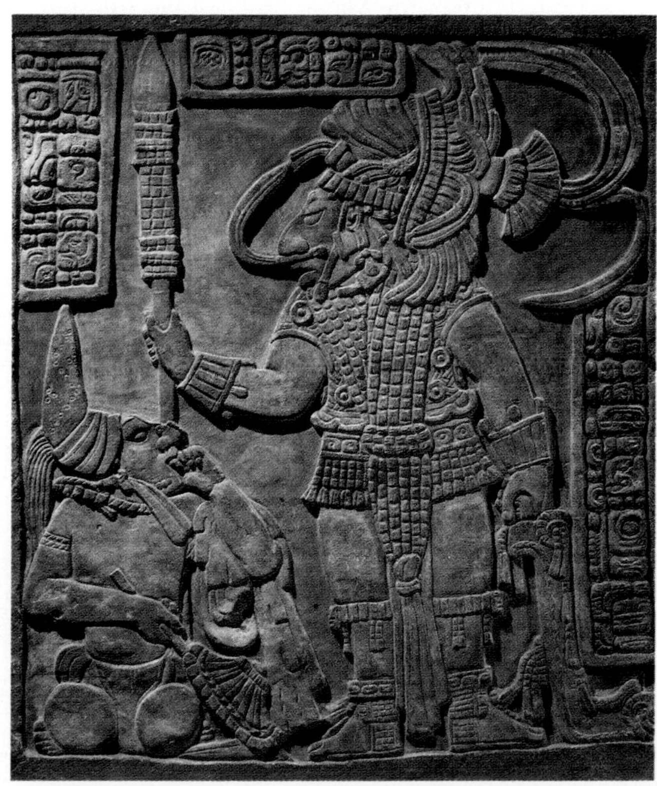

precisely at February 1, A.D. 752 (around the beginning of the Carolingian Empire in Europe). On that day, the Yaxchilán ruler Bird Jaguar (named for the form of his name glyph) took captive a rebellious local lord, who is seen crouching apprehensively at his feet. The capture of a nobleman, later to be sacrificed, was probably a feat prerequisite to the rite of Bird Jaguar's accession to the throne. The humbled captive, his face bloody, his parasol broken, makes the gesture of eating dirt. The king, with spear and feathered crown, looms threateningly above him. His facial features are accommodated to those of the jaguar mask, symbol of fierce authority. (The Maya inherited the jaguar cult from the Olmec and believed that the legitimacy of their titles descended from the same ancient source.)

The hard-edged, slablike carving recalls to a degree the low relief of ancient Assyria (FIG. 2-32), the slight projection being flat rather than round in cross section. This feature is characteristic of much Mesoamerican sculpture. Though Bird Jaguar's image is confined within the formal rigidity of pose befitting the representation of a ruler, considerable visual information is given in the figure of the captive. The sculptor has sharply observed the foreshortening of the legs, for example, and has been able to pose the figure in a convincing posture of shrinking abjection.

The almost unlimited variety of figural attitude and gesture permitted in the modeling of clay explains the profusion of informal ceramic figurines that illustrate the everyday life of the Maya. Small-scale, freestanding figures in the round, they are remarkably lifelike, carefully descriptive, shrewdly psychological, and often comic. A pair that might be called "an amorous couple" (FIG. **14-10**) shows a lecherous old man fondling a courtesan, who replies in kind; he lifts her skirt, she advances her knee. Though apparently no more than an amusing piece of sexual genre, the pair may have religious overtones. The female figure could be the inconstant goddess of the moon, the old man, the God N, a supporter of the arc of heaven. Figurines representing a great variety of subjects regularly are found in tombs among the funeral accessories. This pair comes from Jaina, the Maya necropolis, an island of the dead off the coast of Yucatán. Their mortuary function must be kept in mind as we appreciate their piquant liveliness.

The vivacity of the figurines and their variety of pose are not destructive of the formality of Maya art. Simplification of plane, volume, and contour still is to be seen in the overall form as well as in its details. This same unity of action with formality of design appears at Bonampak (Mayan for "painted walls"). Three chambers in one structure at this site contain mural paintings that are vivid vignettes of Maya court life (FIG. **14-11**). As in most Egyptian painting (FIGS. 3-36 and 3-45), the figures are rendered in line and flat tone without shading or perspective. They are arranged friezelike in superposed horizontal registers without background settings. Maya painting, like Maya sculpture, is mural; architecture is its matrix. But, again, the architectural limits do not in any way restrict the scope and circumstantial detail of the narrative; presented with great economy of means, the information given is comprehensive, explicit, and presented with the fidelity of an eye-witness report. At Bonampak, not only can we identify the royal personages who pass in review, but inscriptions give us the precise dates for the events recorded, the days and the months in the years A.D. 790 and 791. Like the inscribed dates on the Bird Jaguar lintel, these impress us with the almost obsessive Maya concern for accurate time reckoning.

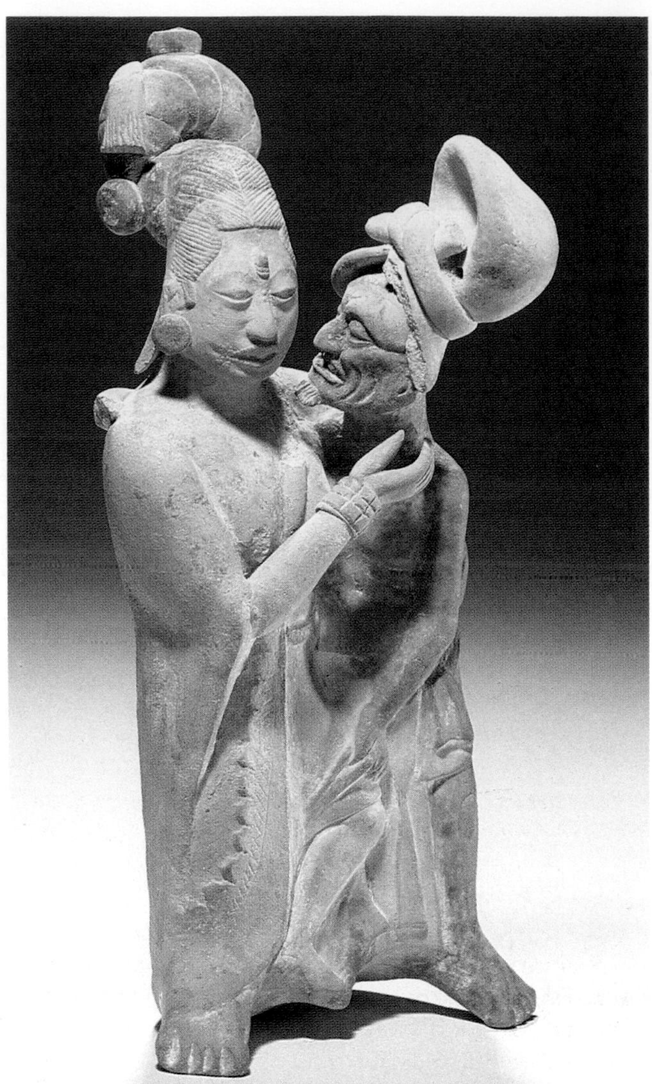

14-10 *Amorous Couple,* Maya, Late Classic, 700–900. Polychromed ceramic, $9\frac{3}{4}''$. Detroit Institute of the Arts, Detroit.

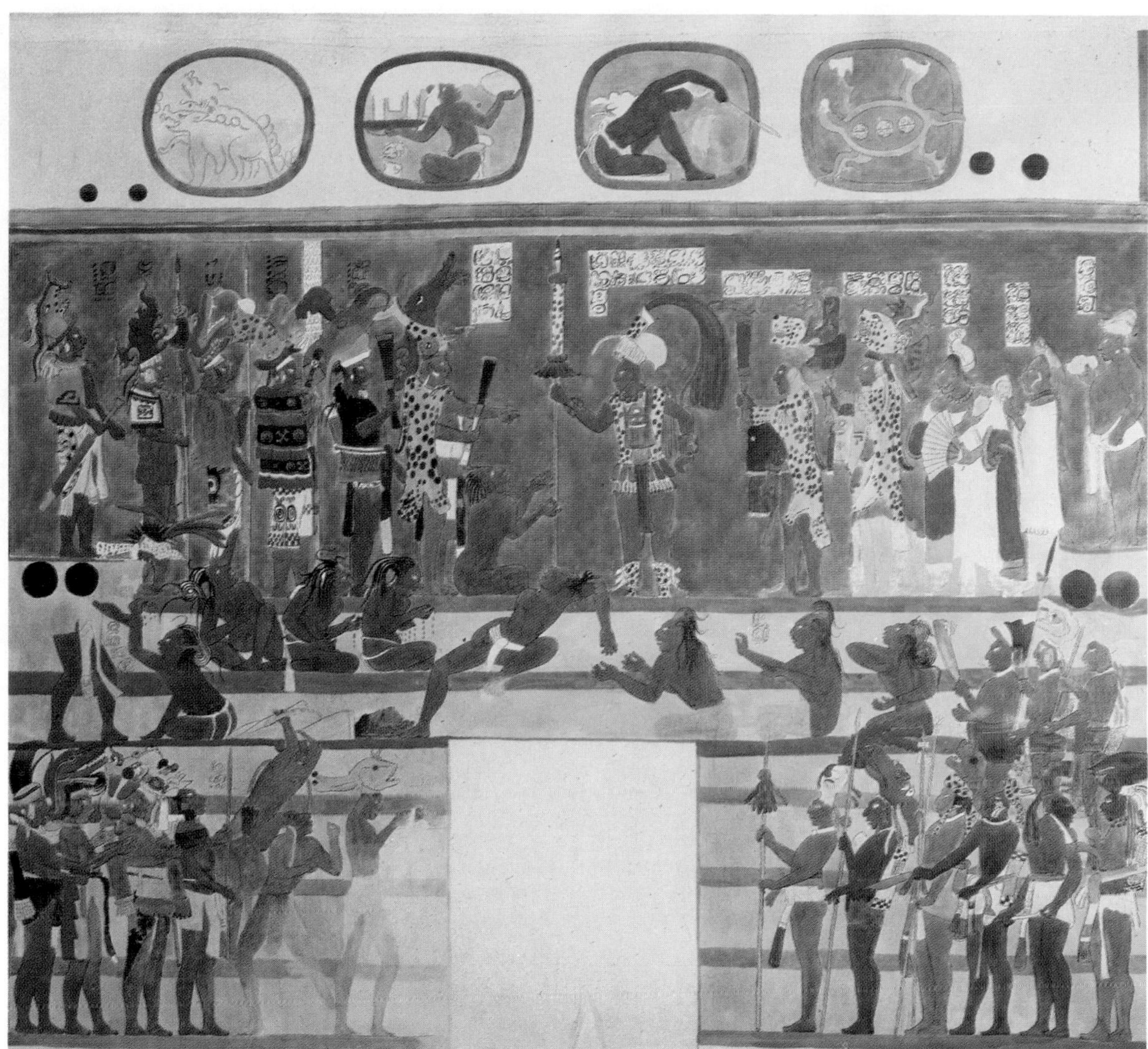

14-11 Temple mural of warriors surrounding captives on a terraced platform, Maya, from Bonampak, Mexico, *c.* sixth century. Peabody Museum, Harvard University, Cambridge, Massachusetts. (Watercolor copy by ANTONIO TEJEDA.)

The scenes recorded at Bonampak relate the ceremonies that welcome a new heir to the throne; they include presentations, preparations for a royal fête, dancing, battle, and the taking and sacrificing of prisoners. In the scene representing the arraignment of the prisoners (FIG. 14-11), the uppermost register depicts a file of gorgeously appareled nobility wearing animal headgear. Conspicuous among them on the right are retainers clad in jaguar pelts and jaguar heads. The ruler himself, in jaguar jerkin and buskins, is posed at the center and closely resembles Bird Jaguar in the Yaxchilán lintel (FIG. 14-9). Like the latter figure, he is accompanied by a crouching victim who appears to beg his mercy. The middle level is crowded with naked captives anticipating death. One of them, already dead, sprawls at the feet of the ruler; others dumbly contemplate the blood dripping from their mutilated hands. The lower zone, divided by a doorway, shows clusters of attendants who are doubtless of inferior rank to the lords of the upper zone. The stiff formality of the grandees and the attendants contrasts graphically with the supple, imploring attitudes and gestures of the hapless victims. In this single composition, we have a narrative of those appalling rituals of blood so central in the life of the Maya and throughout pre-Columbian civilizations in Mesoamerica.

The Postclassic: A.D. 900–1521

Throughout Mesoamerica, the Classic period culminated in the disintegration of the great civilizations. Teotihuacán's political and cultural empire was disrupted around 600, and its influence waned. In 700 the great city was destroyed by fire, presumably at the hands of invaders from the north. Around

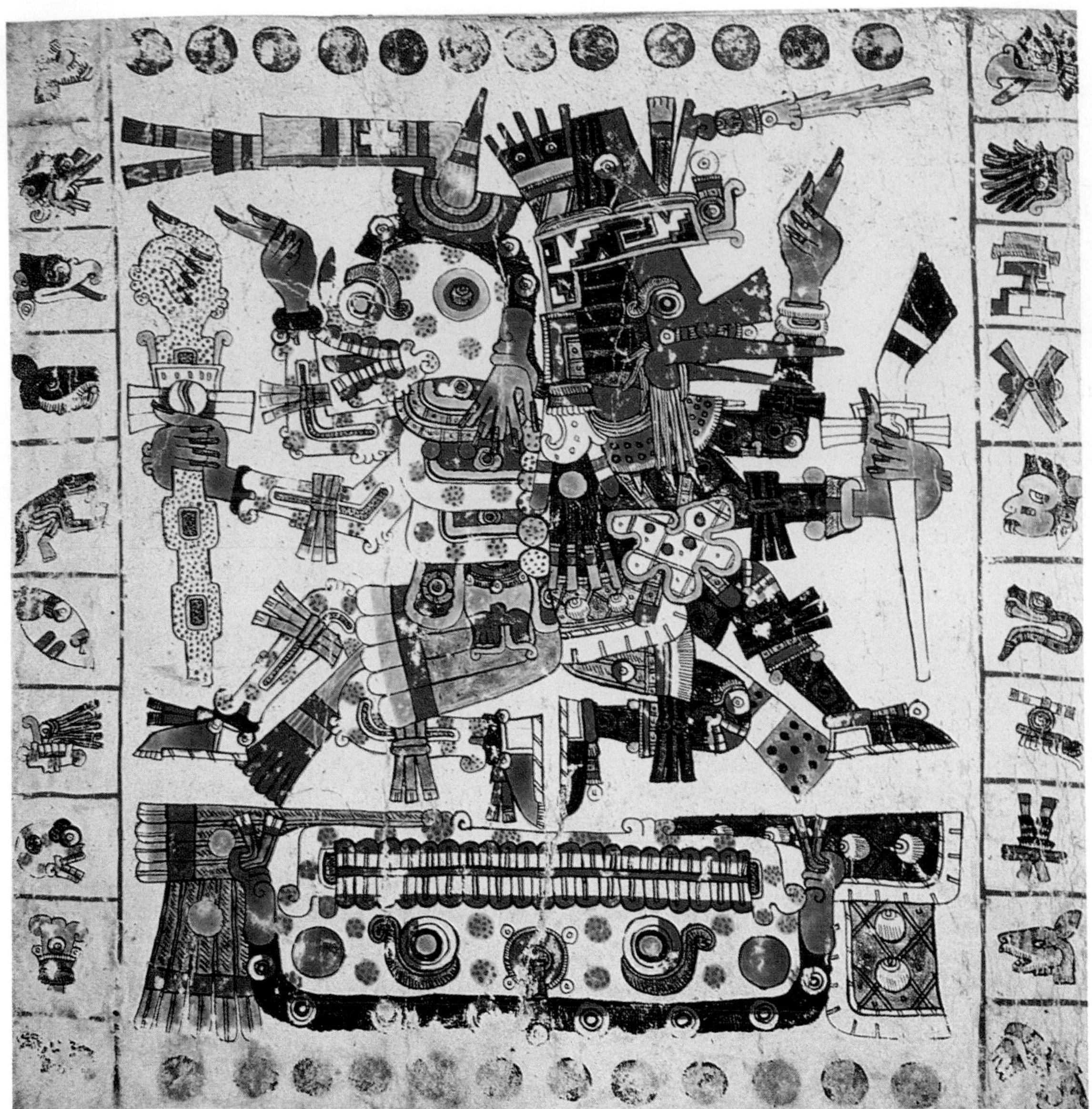

14-12 *Life God (Quetzalcóatl)* and *Death God (Mictlantecuhtli)*, from the *Borgia Codex*, Mixtec, Late Postclassic, *c.* 1400. Deerskin, 10⅝″ × 4″. Vatican Library, Rome.

A.D. 900, many of the great Maya sites were abandoned to the jungle. Though a later Maya culture continued in northern Yucatán during the Postclassic period, it was strongly subordinated by Toltec influences from central Mexico. The Classic culture of the Zapotecs, centered at Monte Albán in the state of Oaxaca, came to an end around A.D. 700, and the neighboring Mixtec peoples assumed supremacy in this area during the Postclassic. Classic El Tajín (Totonac culture), later heir to the Olmec in the Veracruz plain, survived the general crisis that afflicted the others but was burned out sometime in the twelfth century, again, by northern invaders.

The war and confusion that followed the collapse of the Classic civilizations broke the great states up into small, local political entities isolated in fortified sites. The collapse encouraged warlike regimes, chronic aggression, and expansion of the bloodletting rite. In Mexico, the Toltec and the Aztec peoples, ruthless migrants from the north, forged empires by force of arms and glorified militarism.

The Mixtecs, who succeeded to Zapotec Monte Albán, were exceptional in that they extended their political sway in Oaxaca by dynastic intermarriage rather than by war. The magnificent treasures found in the tombs at Monte Albán bear witness to Mixtec wealth, and the quality of these works demonstrates the high level of Mixtec artistic achievement. These people were accomplished in sculpture and ceramics. Metallurgy was introduced into Mexico in Late Classic times, and the Mixtec became the skilled goldsmiths of Mesoamerica. They were renowned for their turquoise mosaic, and, perhaps most important, they were producers of painted manuscripts.

The Classic Maya were preeminent in the art of writing and had libraries of painted books. The painted and inscribed book, somewhat inaccurately called a *codex* (plural *codices*), was the precious vehicle that recorded religious occurrences, historical events, genealogical charts, astronomical tables, calendric calculations, maps, and trade and tribute accounts. Codices were painted on long sheets of fig-bark paper or deerskin, which were coated with fine white lime plaster and folded into accordionlike pleats. These manuscripts were protected by wooden covers. Their hieroglyphs were designed to be read in zigzag fashion from left to right and top to bottom. Only four Maya codices survive. Bishop Diego de Landa, whom we have met as the Spanish chronicler of the Maya of Yucatán, explains why: "We found a great number of these books in Indian characters and because they contained nothing but superstition and the Devil's falsehoods we burned them all; and this they felt most bitterly and it caused them great grief."

Eight Mixtec codices survive. A "page" from one of them, the beautifully illuminated *Borgia Codex* (FIG. **14-12**), shows the god of life, Quetzalcóatl, seated back-to-back with the lord of death, Mictlantecuhtli. Below them is an inverted skull with a double keyboard of teeth. Both figures hold scepters in one hand and gesticulate with the other. Strings of flesh hang from the death god's red, triple jaws. The margins are paneled with symbols of the days of the year ruled by each of the two deities.

The fantastic image is an explosion of shapes. The design approaches complete abstraction of visual materials. Were the shapes in less confusion, they would resemble in their taut line and flat, sharp color the face cards of a playing deck. The artist's imagination conjures up and personifies the wild powers of the gods, producing a terrifying figment of the sort that might be experienced in the delirium of the vision quest. Reality vanishes in nightmare.

CHICHÉN ITZÁ: LATER MAYA

The flat, scrub-vegetation covered, low limestone peninsula of Yucatán lies north of the rolling and densely forested region of central Yucatán and the Petén. During the Classic period, this northern region was inhabited sparsely by Mayan-speaking peoples who settled around such centers as Uxmal. For unknown reasons, when the Classic sites were abandoned after A.D. 900, many new temples still were built in this area. A new art style, which can be seen in these late temples at Chichén Itzá, is contemporaneous with the political ascendancy in the Yucatán of the Toltecs from Tula (a site northwest of Mexico City). The Toltecs ruled at Chichén Itzá during the twelfth and thirteenth centuries.

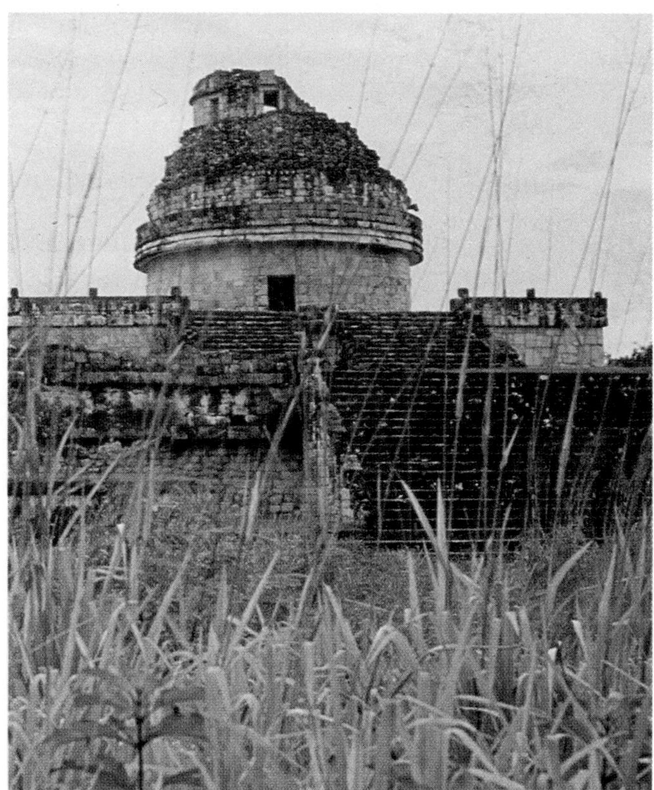

14-13 The Caracol (observatory), Chichén Itzá, Toltec-Maya, Yucatán, Mexico, Postclassic, *c.* 1050.

The northern Maya (under heavy influence from the Toltecs) experimented with building construction and materials to a much greater extent than the Maya farther south; piers and columns were placed in doorways, encrusted decoration of stone mosaic enlivened outer façades. The northern groups invented a new type of concrete construction: a solid core of coarse rubble faced inside and out with a veneer of square limestone plates. The region provided plenty of solid material to work with; Bishop Landa wrote of Yucatán: "The whole land is made of limestone!"

The design of the structure known as the Caracol at Chichén Itzá (FIG. **14-13**) suggests that the northern Maya were as inventive of architectural form as they were experimental with construction and materials. A cylindrical tower rests on a broad terrace, which is supported, in turn, by a larger platform measuring 169 by 232 feet. The tower is composed of two concentric walls enclosing a circular staircase that leads to a small chamber near the top of the structure. Windows along the staircase and an opening at the summit were doubtless used for astronomical observation, which has given the building another name—

"The Observatory." Observation of the stars and of their movements made possible the essential astrological calculations that charted their influence.

TULA: TOLTEC

The circular Caracol is but one of a number of impressive buildings constructed at the site of Chichén Itzá. Among the others, the colonnaded Temple of the Warriors resembles buildings excavated at Tula, the Toltec capital north of Mexico City. Detailed resemblances between the sculptures of the two sites support the inference that the builders of Tula worked for the same Toltec masters as those who ruled the Maya at Chichén Itzá.

The name Toltec, which signifies "makers of things," generally is applied to a powerful tribe of barbarian invaders from the north, whose arrival in south-central Mexico coincided with the great disturbances that, as we have seen, must have brought down the Classic civilizations. The Toltec capital at Tula flourished from about A.D. 900 to 1200. The Toltecs were great political organizers and military strategists and came to dominate large parts of north and central Mexico, Yucatán, and the highlands of Guatemala. They were respected as the masters of all that came to hand, and later peoples looked back on them admiringly, proud to claim descent from them.

Legend and history recount that in the city of Tula civil strife between the forces of peace and those of war and bloodletting resulted in the victory of the militarists. The grim, warlike regime that followed is personified in four colossal atlantids that portray armed warriors (FIG. **14-14**). Built up of four stone drums each, these sculptures loom above Pyramid B at Tula. They originally were designed to support a now missing temple roof and wear stylized feathered headdresses and, as breastplates, stylized butterflies, heraldic symbols of the Toltecs. In one hand they clutch a bundle of darts, in the other, an *atlatl* (throwstick). The architectural function of these support figures requires rigidity of pose, compactness, and strict simplicity of contour; where possible, all projecting details are suppressed. The unity and regularity of architectural mass and silhouette here combine perfectly with abstraction of form. The effect is that of overwhelming presence. These images of brutal and implacable authority, with "gaze blank and pitiless as the sun," stand eternally at attention, warning off all hostile threats to sovereign power, good or evil.

14-14 *Colossal Atlantids,* Pyramid B, Toltec, Tula, Hidalgo, Mexico, Early Postclassic, c. 1050. Stone, 16′ high.

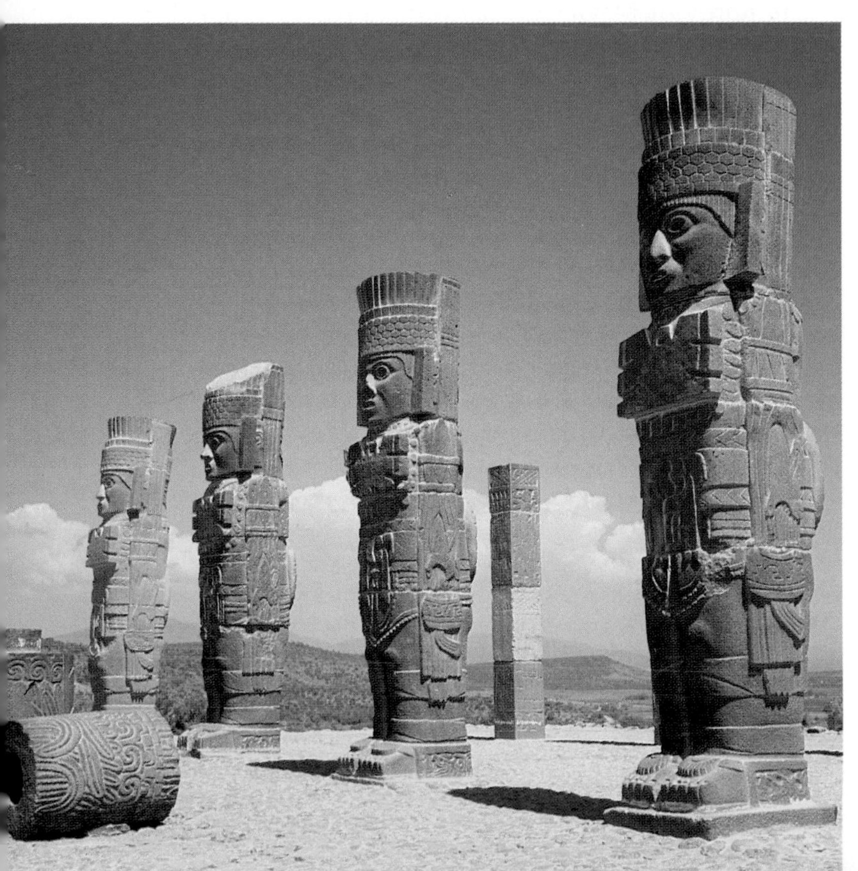

By 1180, the last Toltec ruler abandoned Tula and was followed by most of his people. Some years later, the city was catastrophically destroyed, its ceremonial buildings burnt to their foundations, its walls thrown down, and the straggling remainder of its population scattered throughout Mexico.

TENOCHTITLÁN: AZTEC

The destruction of Tula and the disintegration of the Toltec empire in central Mexico made for a century of anarchy in the Valley of Mexico. Barbaric northern invaders, who again must have wrought the destruction, gradually organized into small, warring city-states. Nevertheless, they civilized themselves on the cultural remains and traditions of the Toltecs. When the last wave of northern invaders appeared, they were regarded as detestable savages.

These "savages" were the Aztecs, the "people whose face nobody knows." With astonishing rapidity, they were transformed within a few generations from outcasts and serfs to mercenaries of the Tepanec imperialists, and then masters in their own right of the petty kingdoms of the Valley of Mexico. In the process, they acquired, like their neighbors, the culture of the Toltecs. They had begun to call themselves *Mexica,* and, following a legendary prophecy that they would build a city where they saw an eagle perched on a cactus with a serpent in its mouth, they settled in the marshes on the west shore of the great "Lake of the Moon," Lake Texcoco. Their settlement grew into the magnificent city of Tenochtitlán, which in 1519 so astonished the Spanish conqueror Cortés and his men.

The Aztecs were known by those they subdued as fierce in war and cruel in peace. Indeed, they gloried in warfare and in military prowess. They radically changed the social and political situation in Mexico. The cults of bloodletting and human sacrifice, though still practiced, had been waning in central Mexico since Toltec times. The Aztecs revived the rituals with a vengeance—and a difference. In the older civilizations, like the Classic Maya, the purposes of religion and statecraft were in balance. With the Aztec, the purpose of religion was to serve the policy of the state. The Aztecs believed that they had a divine mission to propagate the cult of their tribal god, Huitzilopochtli,* the hummingbird god of war. This goal meant forcing conformity on all peoples conquered by them. Subservient groups had not only to submit to Aztec military power but also were forced to accept the cult of Huitzilopochtli and to provide victims for sacrifices to him. Thus, Aztec statecraft used the god to achieve and maintain its ruthless political dominion. Human sacrifice was vastly increased in a reign of terror designed to keep the Aztec empire under control. To this end, tribute of sacrificial victims was regularly levied on unwilling subjects. It is no wonder that Cortés, in his conquest of the Aztec state, found ready allies among the peoples the Aztecs had subjugated.

The ruins of the Aztec capital, Tenochtitlán, lie directly beneath the center of Mexico City. The exact location of many of the most important structures within the Aztec "sacred precinct" was discovered in the late 1970s, and extensive excavations near the cathedral in Mexico City are ongoing. The principal building is the Great Temple (Templo Mayor), a double temple-pyramid honoring the gods Huitzilopochtli and Tlaloc, the rain god, whose image we have seen in the company of Quetzalcóatl on his pyramid at Teotihuacán. Two great staircases sweep upward from the plaza level to the double sanctuaries at the summit. The Great Temple is a remarkable example of superimposition, a common trait in Mesoamerica. The excavated structure is composed of five shells, the earlier walls nested within the later. The sacred precinct also contained palaces, the temples of other deities (the Aztec pantheon was as crowded as that of the Maya), a ball court, and a skull rack for the exhibition of thousands of the heads of victims killed in sacrificial rites.

Tenochtitlán was a city laid out on a grid plan in quarters and wards. Its location on an island in Lake Texcoco caused communication and transport to be conducted by canals and waterways; many of the Spaniards thought of Venice when they saw the city rising from the waters like a radiant vision. It was crowded with buildings, plazas, and courtyards, and was equipped with a vast and ever busy marketplace. The city proper had a population of more than one hundred thousand people; the total population of the area of Mexico dominated by the Aztecs at the time of the conquest has been estimated at eleven million.

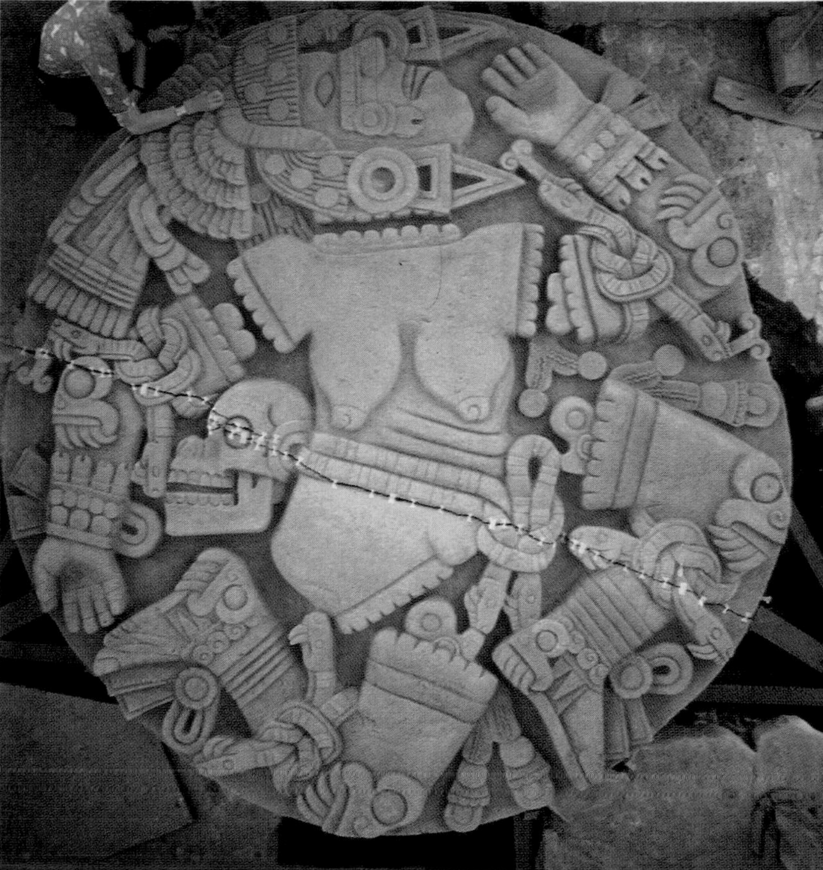

14-15 *Coyolxauhqui,* from the Great Temple of Tenochtitlán, Aztec, Mexico City, Late Postclassic, c. 1400–1500. Stone, diameter approx. 11′.

The Temple of Huitzilopochtli commemorates his victory over his brothers and sister; since he was a sun god, the nature myth reflects the sun's conquest of the stars and the moon. Revenging the death of his mother, Coatlicue,† at the hands of his siblings, he kills them and dismembers the body of his evil sister, Coyolxauhqui.‡ The macabre event is depicted in a work of sculpture, whose discovery in 1978 set off the ongoing archeological investigations near the main plaza in Mexico City. The huge stone disk (FIG. **14-15**), about 11 feet in diameter, was placed at the foot of the staircase leading up to the shrine of Huitzilopochtli. Carved on it is an image of the segmented body of Coyolxauhqui. The horror of the theme should not distract us from its artistic merit; the disk has a kind of dreadful, yet formal, beauty. At the same time, it is an unforgettable expression of Aztec temperament and taste, and the cruelty inculcated by

*weet-zeel-O-POCH-tlee

†kwah-TLEE-kway

‡ko-yol-SHOW-kee

ceremonies of blood. The image proclaimed the power of the god over his enemies and the inevitable fate that must befall them. As such, it was an awful reminder to sacrificial victims, as they were ritually halted beside it preparatory to mounting the stairs that led to the temples above and death.

The sculpture is marvelously composed. Within the circular space, the carefully enumerated, richly detailed components of the design are so adroitly placed that they seem to have a slow, turning rhythm, like some revolving constellation. (This presentation would be appropriate for a goddess of the sky, no matter her decrepitude!) The carving is confined to a single level, a smoothly even, flat surface raised from a flat ground. We have seen this kind of relief in the Bird Jaguar lintel from Yaxchilán (FIG. 14-9). It is the sculptural equivalent of the line and flat tone, figure and neutral ground, characteristic of Mesoamerican painting.

In addition to relief carving, the Aztecs, unlike the Maya, produced sculpture unbound to architecture, freestanding and in the round. The colossal monster statue of Coatlicue (Lady of the Skirt of Serpents), ancient earth mother of the gods Huitzilopochtli and Coyolxauhqui, is a massive apparition of dread congealed into stone (FIG. **14-16**). Sufficiently expressive of the Aztec taste for the terrible, the beheaded goddess is composed of an inventory of macabre and repulsive objects. Up from her headless neck writhe two serpents whose heads meet to form a tusked mask. The goddess wears a necklace of severed human hands and excised human hearts. The pendant of the necklace is a skull. Her skirt is formed of entwined snakes. Her hands and feet have great claws, with which she tears the human flesh she consumes. All of her loathsome attributes symbolize sacrificial death. Yet, in Aztec thought, this mother of the gods combines savagery and tenderness, for out of destruction arises new life. In this expression of the concept, the tenderness is missing.

The main forms are carved in high relief, the details are executed either in low relief or by incising. The overall aspect is of an enormous, blocky mass, the ponderous weight of which is in itself a threat to the awed viewer. In its original setting, where it may have functioned in the visual drama of sacrificial rites, it must have had a terrifying effect on victims.

It was impossible for the Spanish conquerors to reconcile the beauty of the great city of Tenochtitlán with its hideous cults. They wonderingly admired its splendid buildings, ablaze with color; its luxuriant and spacious gardens, sparkling waterways, teeming markets, and vivacious populace; its grandees resplendent in the feathers of exotic birds. But when Moctezuma, king of the Aztecs, brought Cortés and his entourage into the shrine of Huitzilopochtli's temple, the newcomers started back in horror and disgust from the huge statues clotted with dried blood. One of Cortés's party, Bernal Diaz del Castillo recorded: "There was on the walls such a crust of blood, and the whole floor bathed in it, that even in the slaughter houses of Castile there is not such a stench." Cortés was furious. Denouncing Huitzilopochtli as a devil, he proposed to put a high cross above the pyramid and a statue of the Virgin in the sanctuary to exorcise its evil.

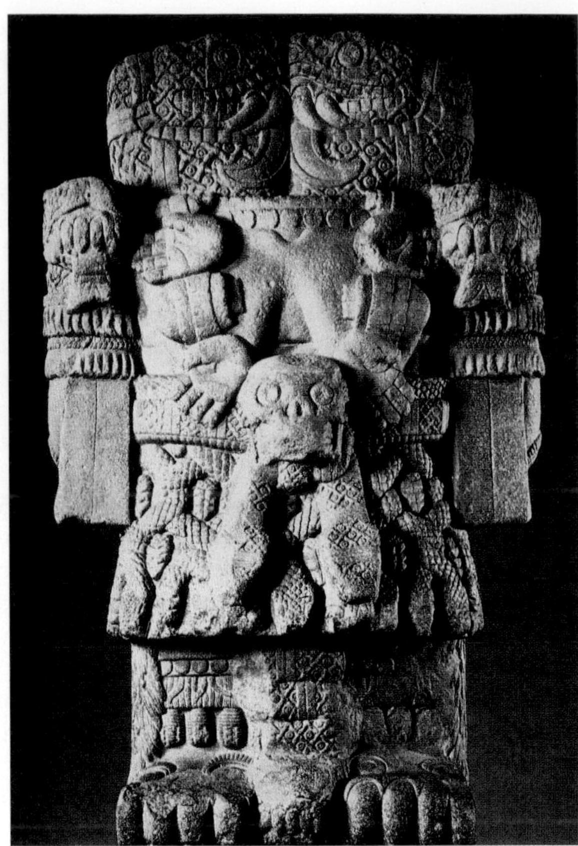

14-16 *Coatlicue (Lady of the Skirt of Serpents)*, Aztec, fifteenth century. Andesite, approx. 8′ 6″ high. Museo Nacional de Antropología, Mexico City.

This proposal would come to symbolize the avowed purpose and the historic result of the Spanish conquest of Mesoamerica. The cross and the Virgin, triumphant, would be venerated in new shrines raised upon the ruins of the plundered temples of the Indian gods, and the banner of the Most Catholic Kings of Spain would wave over new atrocities of a European kind.

SOUTH AMERICA: CENTRAL ANDES

The story of the great cultures of Andean South America was much the same as that of the pre-Columbian peoples of Mesoamerica: native civilizations jarring against and stimulating one another; production of distinctive architecture and art; extermination in violent confrontations with the Spanish *conquistadores*—Cortés in Mesoamerica and Pizarro in the Andes.

The central Andean region of South America lies between Ecuador and northern Chile. It consists of three well-defined geographic zones, running north and south, roughly parallel to one another: (1) a narrow western coastal plain, where a hot desert is crossed by rivers, creating habitable, fertile valleys; (2) the great Cordillera of the Andes, whose high peaks hem in plateaus of a temperate climate; and (3) the eastern slopes of the Andes, a hot, humid jungle. Highly developed civilizations flourished both on the coast and in the highlands, but their origins are still obscure. These civilizations and their arts succeeded one another with rough correspondence to the Mesoamerican chronology.

CHAVÍN

Evidence indicates that, in the first millennium B.C., a cult began to grow that, at its height, prevailed over great portions of the coast and highland areas.* The cult is called Chavín, after the ceremonial center of Chavín de Huantar, which is located in the northern highlands and consists of a number of stone-faced, pyramidal platforms penetrated by narrow passageways and small chambers, surrounding a sunken court.

Chavín de Huantar is famed, too, for its stone carvings. Associated with the architecture and consisting of much sunken relief on panels, lintels, and columns and some rarer instances of sculpture in the round, Chavín sculpture is essentially linear, hardly more than incision. Freestanding sculpture is represented by an immense cult image in the center of the oldest structure, as well as by heads of mythological creatures tenoned into the exterior walls. Although, at first glance, the subject matter of Chavín stone carving appears to exhibit considerable variety, the emphasis is most consistently on composite creatures that combine feline, avian, reptilian, and human features. The *Raimondi Stone* (FIG. **14-17**), which was

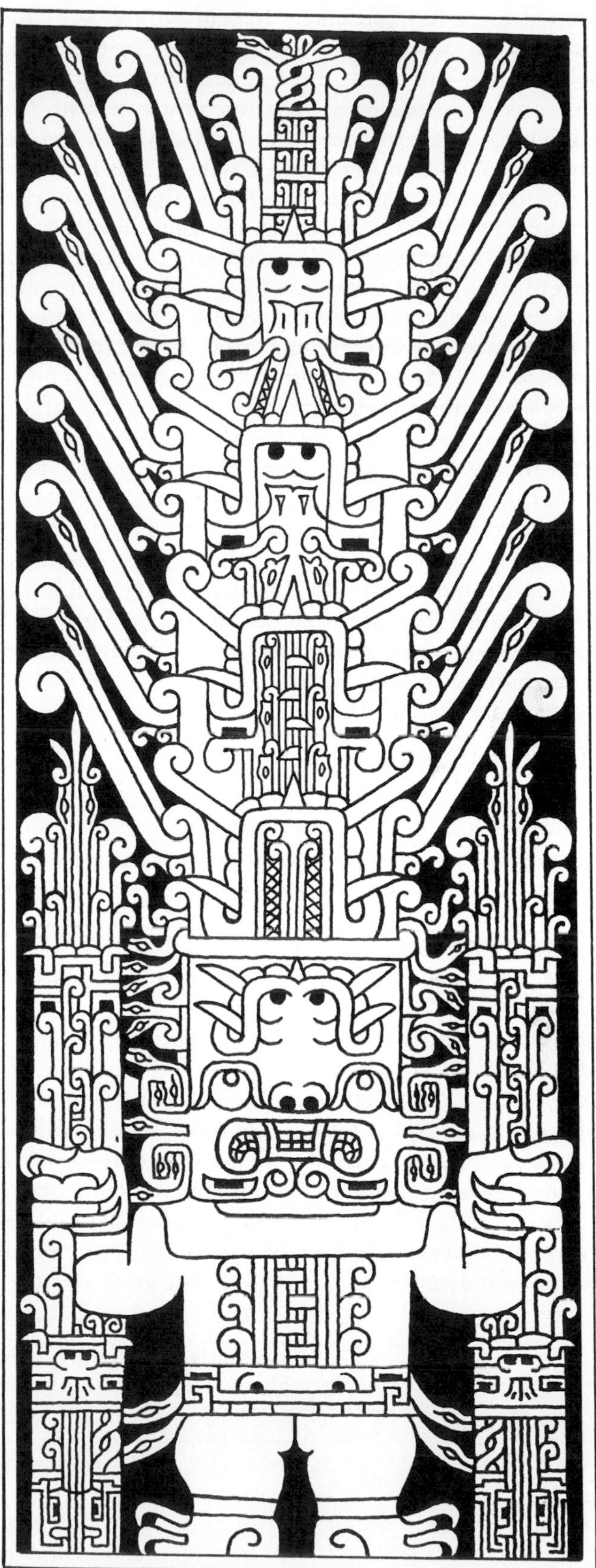

14-17 Drawing of the *Raimondi Stone,* from principal pyramid, Chavín de Huantar, Peru, first millennium B.C. Incised green diorite, 6′ high. Instituto Nacional de Cultura, Lima, Peru.

*On the basis of recent discoveries, archeologists are now concluding that Chavín culture was the culmination of developments that began some two thousand years earlier in other Andean regions. Complex ancient communities documented by radiocarbon dating as having been built from one thousand to twenty-five hundred years before Chavín are changing researchers' assessments of early New World cultures. Work at such sites as Aspero, Sechín Alto, and Pampa de las Llamas-Moxeke indicates that planned communities boasting monumental architecture, organized labor systems, and bright, multicolored adobe friezes dotted the narrow river valleys that drop from the Andes to the Pacific Ocean centuries earlier than previously thought.

named after its discoverer, is representative of the late variant of Chavín stone carving. On the lower third of the stone is a figure called the "staff god," versions of whom have been encountered from Colombia to northern Bolivia, but seldom with the degree of elaboration found at Chavín. In this instance, the squat, scowling deity, who is always depicted holding staffs, is shown with his gaze directed upward. An elaborate headdress dominates the upper two-thirds of the slab. Inverting the image reveals that the headdress is composed of a series of fanged, jawless faces, each emerging from the mouth of the one above it. Snakes abound; they extend from the deity's belt, forming part of the staffs; serve as whiskers and hair for the deity and the headdress creatures; and, finally, form a guilloche at the apex of the composition.

The ceramic vessels of the northern Chavín area are identified easily by their massiveness of chamber, spout, and surface relief. The motifs are much like those found on Chavín stone carvings. The stirrup spout became popular at this time and continued to be a commonly used North Coast form until the advent of the Spaniards.

MOCHE (MOCHICA)

The great variations within Peruvian art styles are exemplified by two coastal traditions that developed during the period between about 200 B.C. and A.D. 600 in the cultures of the Moche in the north and the Nasca in the south.

The Moche concern with ritual is reflected clearly in their ceremonial architecture and ceramic vessels. The former consisted of immense, pyramidal, supporting structures for temples that, due to the scarcity of stone, were constructed of sun-dried mud brick or adobe. Their scale may be surmised from the remains of the Temple of the Sun in the lower Trujillo Valley, which utilized millions of adobes. The temple atop it already had disappeared by the advent of the Spaniards. As a result of persistent treasure hunting by early colonial residents, only a remnant of the original pyramid remains.

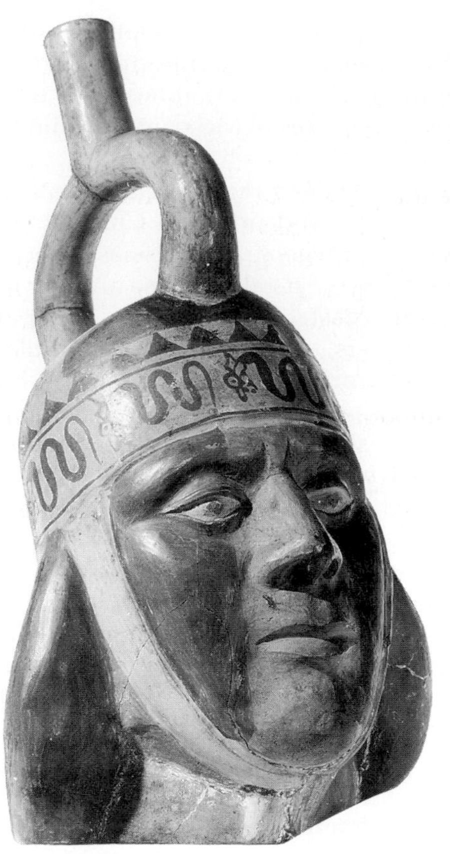

14-18 Portrait bottle, Moche, Peru, fifth to sixth century. Ceramic, $11\frac{1}{2}''$ high. American Museum of Natural History, New York.

Probably the most famous art objects produced by the ancient Peruvians are the ceramic vessels of the Moche, which were predominantly flat-bottomed, stirrup-spout jars, molded without the aid of a potter's wheel and generally decorated with a bichrome slip. (Their abundance can be credited to the ancient Peruvian practice of seeing that the dead were accompanied in the grave by many offerings.) Moche potters continued to employ the stirrup spout, making it an elegant tube much more slender than the Chavín prototype. This refinement may be seen in one of the famous Moche portrait bottles (FIG. **14-18**), believed to be either a warrior or a priest. In early bottles of this

SOUTH AMERICAN CHRONOLOGY: CENTRAL ANDES

	2000 B.C.	1000	B.C. A.D.		1000	1534
PRECERAMIC PERIODS	INITIAL PERIOD	EARLY HORIZON	EARLY INTERMEDIATE PERIOD	MIDDLE HORIZON	LATE INTERMEDIATE PERIOD	LATE HORIZON
		Chavín *Chavín de Huántar*	Moche (Mochica) *Sipán* *Moche* Nasca	Tiahuanaco	Inca *Machu Picchu*	

type, the sculptured form was dominant; in time, however, linear surface decoration came to be employed equally.

Warrior and priest are one and the same for the incumbent of a rich tomb recently (1988) excavated near the little village of Sipán on the arid northwest coast of Peru. The unlooted tomb and a pottery cache nearby have yielded a treasure of golden artifacts and more than a thousand ceramic vessels. The tomb's discovery has made a great stir in the world of archeology, contributing immensely to our knowledge of Moche culture, and elevating the Moche above the Inca in importance. Located beneath a large adobe platform adjacent to two high but greatly eroded pyramids, the tomb had escaped the attention of village grave robbers. The splendor of the funeral trappings that adorned the body of the "warrior-priest" (as he has been called), the quantity and quality of the sumptuous accessories, and the bodies of the retainers buried with him in this tomb indicate that he was a personage of the highest rank. Indeed, he may have been one of the warrior-priests so often pictured on Moche ceramic wares (and in this tomb, on a golden, pyramid-shaped rattle), assaulting his enemies and participating in sacrificial ceremonies, wherein victims' throats were slit and their blood drunk from ornamental cups.

An ear ornament of turquoise and gold found in the tomb shows a warrior-priest clad much like the dead man (FIG. **14-19**). Represented frontally, he carries a war club and shield and wears a necklace of owls' heads. The figure's bladelike, crescent-shaped helmet is a replica of the large golden one buried with the warrior-priest. The ear ornament of the image is a simplified version of the piece on which it is portrayed. The nose guard, which is removable, and the golden chin guard, also are like those worn by the deceased. Two retainers, with similar helmets and ear ornaments, are shown in profile.

Though the Andean cultures did not develop a system of writing, they had an advanced knowledge of metallurgy long before the Mesoamericans, who

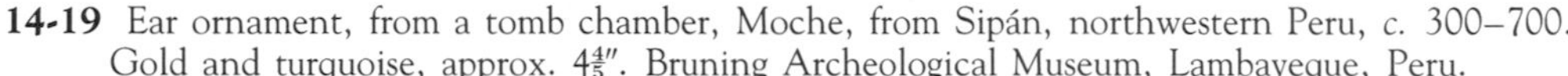

14-19 Ear ornament, from a tomb chamber, Moche, from Sipán, northwestern Peru, *c.* 300–700. Gold and turquoise, approx. $4\frac{4}{5}$". Bruning Archeological Museum, Lambayeque, Peru.

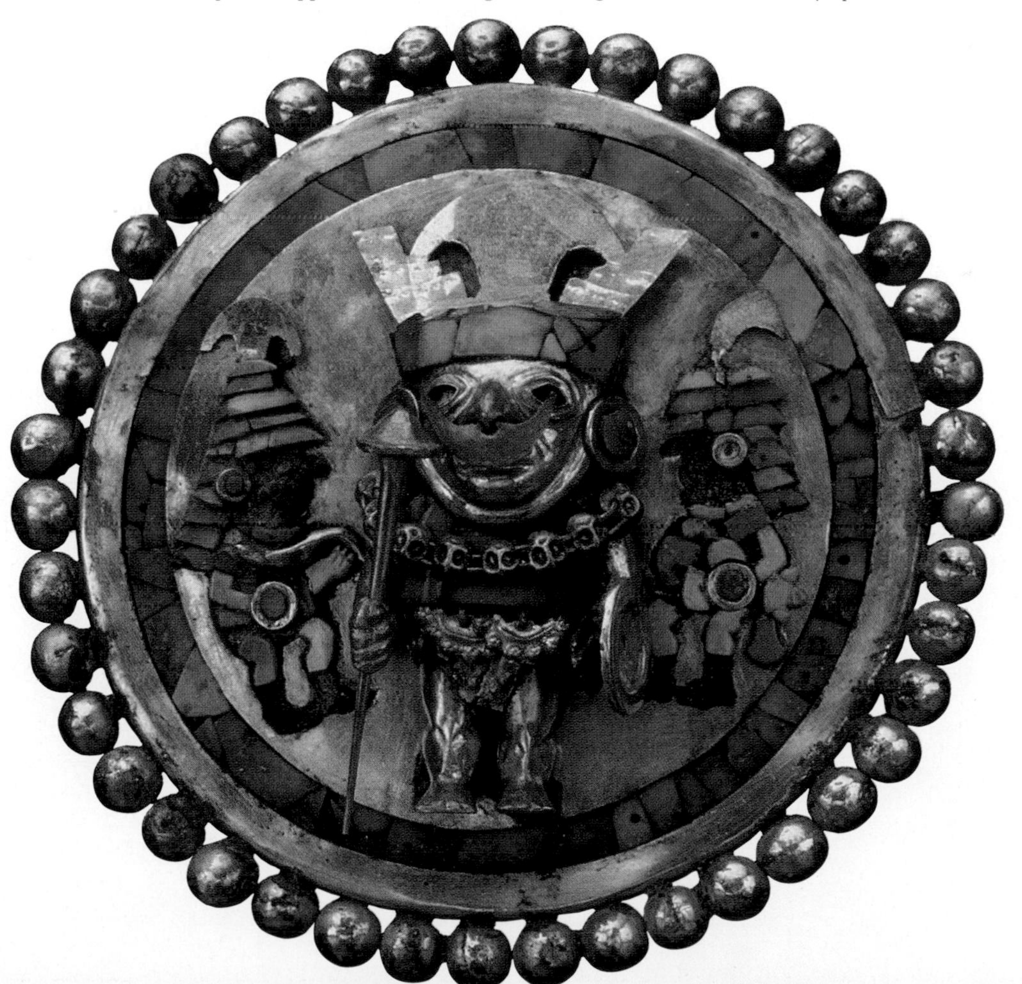

must have received it from them as late as the tenth century. Treasure of silver and gold, of course, lured the Spanish invaders to the Americas, and the wildcat plundering of pre-Columbian tombs by grave robbers, both foreign and domestic, continues to scatter precious artifacts worldwide. Needless to say, this hampers the work of archeology. The value of the Sipán find is incalculable for what it reveals about the Moche culture. Moche craftsmanship in gold and other metals and their sophisticated ceramic production place them among the most ingenious cultures of North and South America.

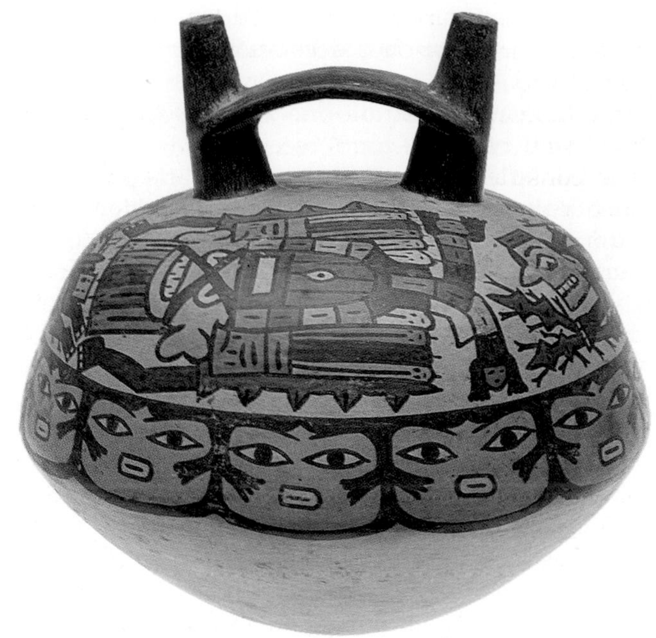

14-20 Bridge-spout vessel, Nasca, Peru, *c.* fifth and sixth centuries. Ceramic with slip, $5\frac{1}{2}''$ high. Museum of Cultural History, University of California, Los Angeles.

NASCA

Although the Nasca rarely produced ceremonial architecture on a large scale, they did create a comparable art form in their ceramic vessels, which, unlike their counterparts on the north coast, had round bottoms, double spouts connected with bridges, and smoothly burnished, polychrome surfaces. The subject matter is of great variety, with particular emphasis on plants, animals, and mythological creatures. The initially elegant simplicity of their depiction evolved into a style exhibiting a marked complexity and bold stylization (FIG. **14-20**).

Nasca is not known only for its polychrome pottery. Some 1,300 kilometers of lines, drawn in complex networks on the dry surface of the Nasca Valley in southwestern Peru, have long attracted world attention as the most mysterious and gigantic works of human art. The earliest of these works trace out biomorphic figures: birds, fish, plants, and, in our example, a hummingbird (FIG. **14-21**)—a motif that, incidentally, is almost identical to hummingbirds on contemporaneous Nasca pottery. The wingspan of the hummingbird is over 200 feet. To produce figures of this scale and accuracy of proportion required some rudimentary geometry and an elementary method of measurement. Geometric forms with miles-long straight lines were drawn later, perhaps as late as Inca times. Uniformly, the Nasca Lines appear light on a dark ground, an effect produced by scraping aside the sun-darkened desert pebbles to reveal the lighter layer of whitish clay and calcite beneath.

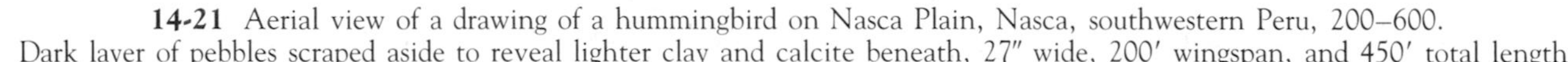

14-21 Aerial view of a drawing of a hummingbird on Nasca Plain, Nasca, southwestern Peru, 200–600. Dark layer of pebbles scraped aside to reveal lighter clay and calcite beneath, 27″ wide, 200′ wingspan, and 450′ total length.

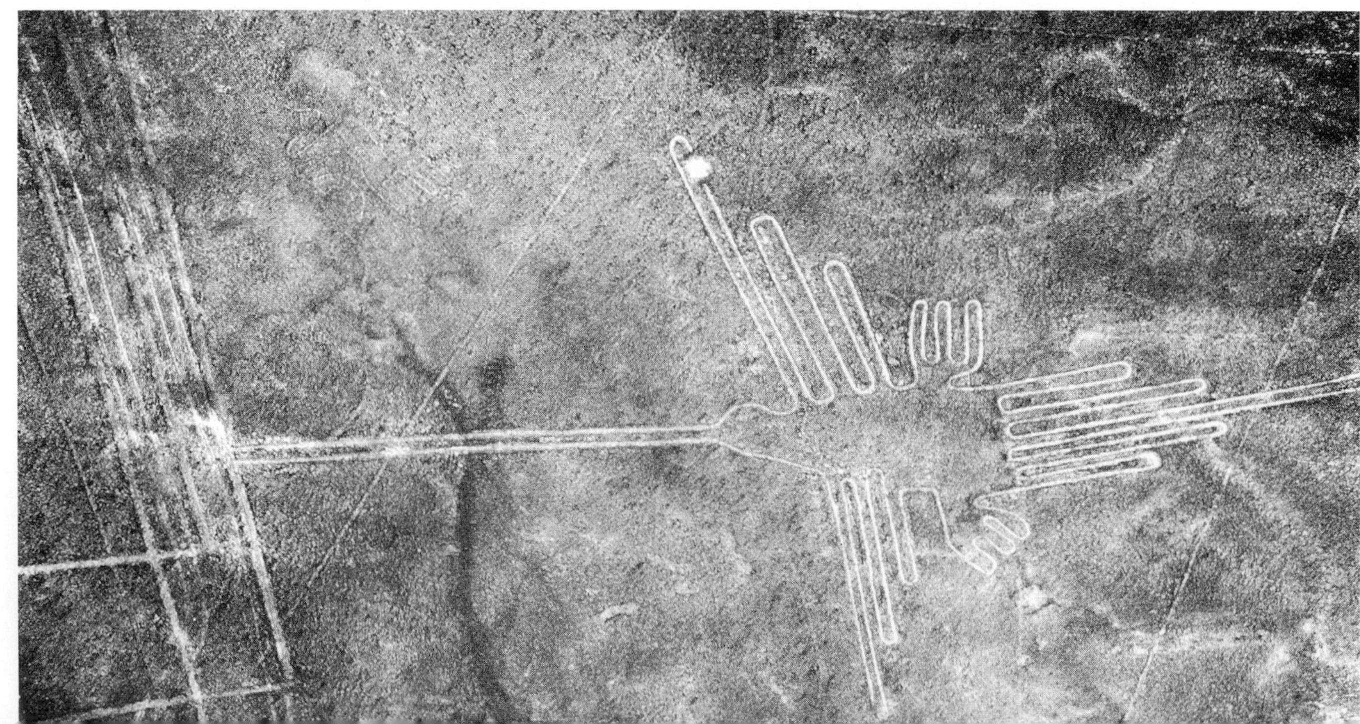

Speculation continues as to the source, construction, and meaning of the Nasca Lines. Some of the explanations are fantastic: the lines were the work of superhuman beings from outer space who arrived by spaceship or of designers of a colossal athletic field. The construction of such ingenious shapes and of such regular geometry seems nearly beyond mere human agency, especially since, given their immense length and bewildering intricacy, the lines were supposed visible only from the air. But, in fact, the lines are visible from the Andean foothills and the great coastal dunes. Moreover, they are constructed quite easily from available materials; simple stone-and-string methods can be used to lay out paths. Lines left uncompleted have guided the modern reproduction of them.

Indeed, the lines seem to be some sort of paths. They lead in traceable directions across the deserts of the Nasca drainage; they are punctuated by many shrinelike nodes, like the knots on a cord; and they converge at central places usually situated close to sources of water. They seem to be associated with water supply and irrigation, and may have become pilgrimage routes for those who journeyed to shrines by foot. They probably had astronomical and calendric functions, forecasting the onset of the planting seasons. Altogether, the vast arrangement of the Nasca Lines is a system—not a meaningless maze, but a traversable map that plotted out the whole terrain of the material and spiritual concerns of the Nasca.

TIAHUANACO

The bleak highland country surrounding Lake Titicaca in southeastern Peru contrasts markedly with the warm valleys of the coast. Isolated in these mountains, at a height of 12,500 feet, another culture developed semi-independently of the coastal cultures until 1000. The art style of this culture, named for Tiahuanaco, the principal archeological site on the southern shores of the lake, then spread to the adjacent coastal area as well as to other highland areas, extending from southern Peru to northern Chile.

Tiahuanaco was an important ceremonial center. The buildings of its Calasasaya sector were constructed of the fine stone of the region: sandstone, andesite, and diorite. Among these impressive structures is the imposing Gateway of the Sun, a huge, monolithic block of andesite, pierced by a single doorway and crowned with a sculptured lintel (FIG. **14-22**). Shrunken beneath an enormous head, the central figure, rigidly frontal, stands on a terraced step holding a staff in each hand. From the blocklike head project rays that terminate in circles and puma heads. The form recalls that of the *Raimondi Stone* (FIG. 14-17) in its frontality and in the symmetrical staffs, as well as in the geometrical conventions used for human and animal representation. The "staff-god" appears in art throughout the Tiahuanaco period, associated, as here, with smaller-scale attendant figures. On this lintel the god is carved in high relief and stands out prominently against the low-relief border of rows of condors and winged men with weapons who run toward the center. Each of the running figures fills a square panel, giving an effect of movement, which quickens slightly the otherwise static formality of the composition. A border of frets

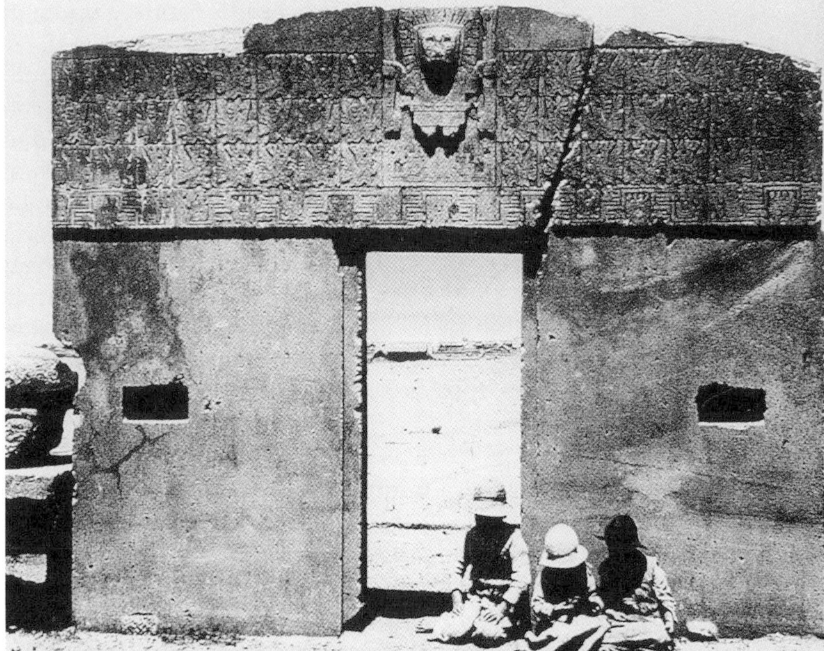

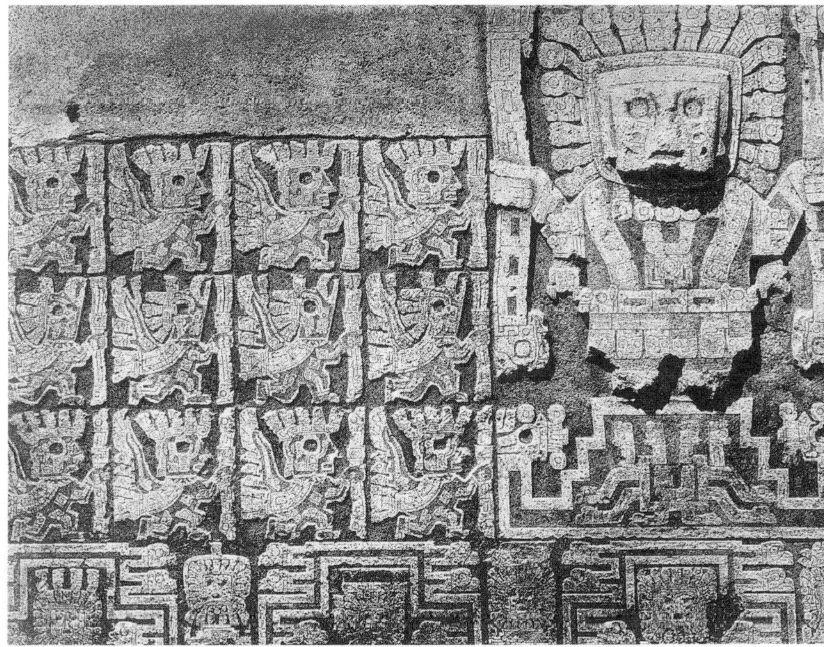

14-22 Monolithic gateway (*top*), detail (*bottom*), Tiahuanaco, Bolivia, ninth century (?).

interspersed with masklike heads forms a kind of supporting lower step.

The carving method should be compared with those of the Maya (FIG. 14-9) and the Aztecs (FIG. 14-15). Here, again, flat relief is carved on a flat ground, although as mentioned, the central panel on the Sun Gate projects an extra level beyond, casting a sharp shadow. But the Tiahuanaco figures are radically abstract, the sculptured equivalent of the linear painting in the *Borgia Codex* (FIG. 14-12). By abstractive distortion of bodily proportion and suppression of descriptive detail, the figures are reduced almost to pictographs; they are more symbols than images.

INCA

The Inca were a small highland tribe who established their rule in the valley of Cuzco, with the city of Cuzco as their capital. Between the thirteenth and the fifteenth centuries, they gradually extended their power until their empire stretched from Quito in Ecuador to central Chile, a distance of more than three thousand miles.

The dimensions of this vast empire required skillful organizational and administrative control, and the Inca had rare talent for both; in this respect, they resemble the imperial Romans. Without writing, but with ingenious maps and models, they divided the empire into sections and subsections, provinces and communities, the boundaries of which all converged on, or radiated from, Cuzco. Their organizational talent was matched by their constructional prowess; they were skillful engineers, who knitted together the fabric of empire with networks of roads and bridges. They established a highly efficient, swift communication system of runners who used their excellent road system to carry messages the length of the empire in relays. The Inca mastered the difficult problems of Andean agriculture with expert terracing and irrigation. They were metallurgists and mined extensively, accumulating the fabled troves of gold and silver that motivated Pizarro to conquer them.

Although the Inca aimed at imposition of their art style throughout their realm, objects of pure Inca style were confined to areas that came under the power of Cuzco. The Inca were concerned not so much with annihilating local traditions as with subjugating them to those of the empire. Local styles, although they sometimes came to employ a few Inca features, continued to be produced in areas marginal to the centers of Inca power.

Like the Romans, the imperial Inca were great architects. They valued the building art highly and drew their professionals from the nobility. Unlike the Romans, who built in concrete, the Inca were supreme masters of shaping and fitting stone. In addition, they had an almost instinctive grasp of the proper relation of architecture to site. As a militant, conquering people they selected sites fortified by nature and further strengthened them by building various defensive structures.

14-23 Aerial view of Machu Picchu, Inca, Peru, *c.* 1500.

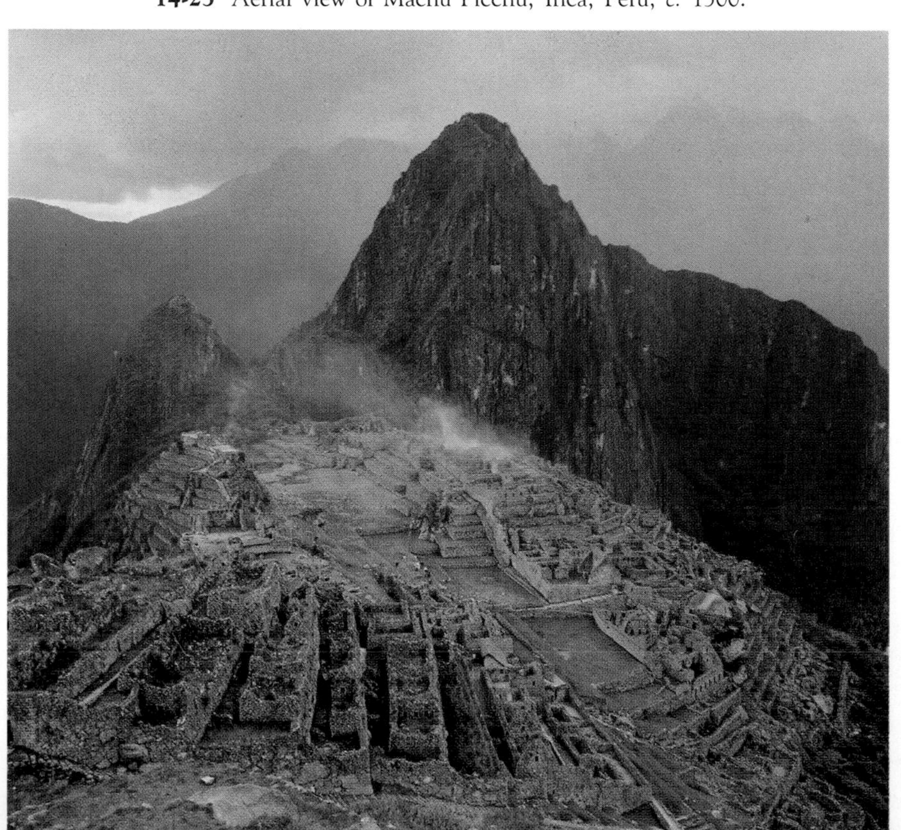

Machu Picchu (FIG. **14-23**) was an Inca city built to protect the highlanders from attacks by lowland tribes living in the Amazonian jungles to the east. One of the world's most awe-inspiring sights, the city perches on a ridge between two jagged peaks, 9,000 feet above sea level. Hiram Bingham, the American discoverer of Machu Picchu (1911), described one aspect of its wildly dramatic situation: "On both sides tremendous precipices fall away to the white rapids of the Urubamba River," some 1,600 feet below. In the very heart of the Andes, the site is about fifty miles north of Cuzco, and like other cities of the region, may have been part of a defensive pale around the capital. Though relatively small and insignificant among its neighbors (with a resident population of little more than a thousand), Machu Picchu is of great archeological importance as a site left undisturbed since Inca times. The accommodation of its architecture to the landscape is so complete that it seems a natural part of a geologically terraced mountain range.

We have noted the Inca as masters of stone masonry. Their technique of dry-joining ashlar construction is famous; blocks of stone were fitted together entirely without mortar. The joints of the ashlar could be beveled to show their tightness, or laid in courses with perfectly joined faces so that the lines of separation were hardly visible. The close joints of Inca masonry were produced by abrasion alone; each stone was swung in slings against its neighbor until the surfaces were ground to a perfect fit. Stones in the walls of more important buildings, like temples or administrative palaces, were usually laid in regular, horizontal courses; for lesser structures, they were laid in polygonal (mostly trapezoidal) patterns. (The trapezoid was a favorite architectural figure, commonly appearing as the shape of niches, doorways, and windows.) With Inca stonecraft, walls could be fashioned with curved surfaces, their planes as level and continuous as if they were a single form poured in concrete. It is interesting that building techniques similar to the Inca method of walling in stone were known across the Pacific (in Cambodian temples like Ankor Thom [FIG. 11-33], monumental stone sculpture is actually built up like shaped wall).

A prime example of the single-form effect is a surviving wall from the great Temple of the Sun in Cuzco (FIG. **14-24**). The most magnificent of all Inca shrines, this structure originally was known as Coricancha (Court of Gold) and was dedicated to the worship of the Supreme Being of the Inca, Viracocha. Viracocha ruled over all the gods of nature, the sun, moon, stars, and the elements. Sixteenth-century Spanish chroniclers wrote in awe of the gold and silver splendor of Coricancha: the interior was veneered with sheets of gold, silver, and "emeralds" (turquoise). "It was," wrote one, "one of the richest temples there was in the world." During the Inca revolt against the Spaniards in the 1530s, the temple was destroyed. Later, the church of Santo Domingo, in the Spanish colonial style, was erected on what remained of it, the curved section of wall serving as the foundation of the apse.

The hewn stones, precisely fitted and polished, form a curving, semiparabola (a sickle-shape) and are set in such a way as to be flexible in earthquakes, allowing for a temporary dislocation of the courses, which return to their original position. A violent earthquake in 1950 seriously damaged the church; the wall was left standing, and much of the original substructure of the temple came into view, with its chambers, courtyards, and trapezoidal niches and doorways. Santo Domingo has been rebuilt, and now the two contrasting architectural styles stand one atop the other (FIG. 14-24).

The Coricancha is of more than architectural and archeological interest. It is a symbol of the Spanish conquest of the Americas and serves as a composite

14-24 Temple of the Sun (now church of Santo Domingo, *left*), detail of wall showing Coricancha masonry (*right*), Inca, Cuzco, Peru, fifteenth century.

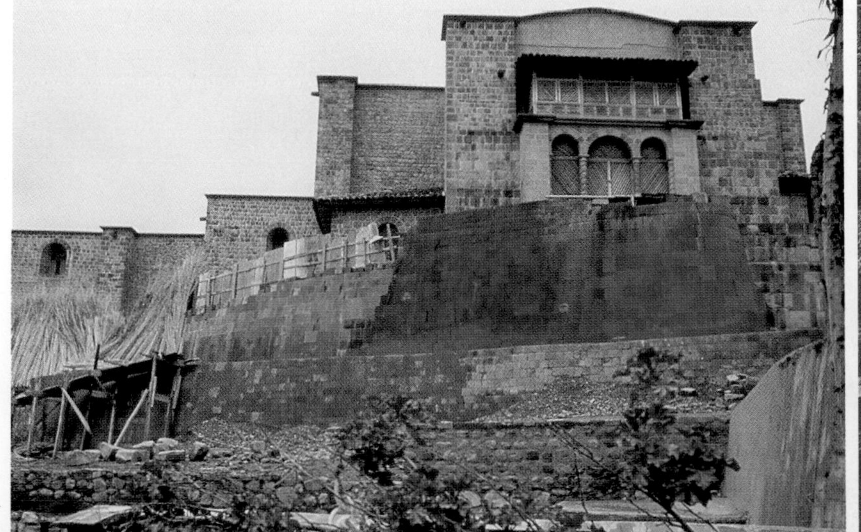

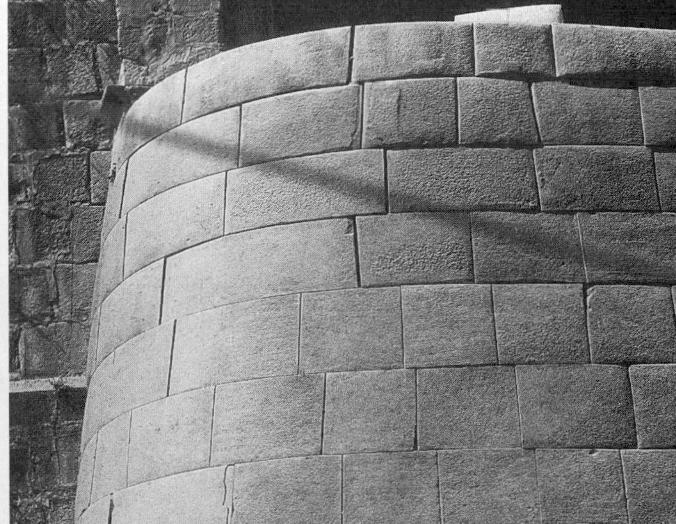

monument to it—one civilization built on the ruins of another. We perceive at once the enduring tension between the native and the foreign arts, the theme we stated at the beginning of this chapter.

NORTH AMERICA

The styles and objects of the cultures native to North America are well known, beginning with the period of prolonged contact with Europeans. We also have considerable knowledge of many earlier forms and styles, although our information is not nearly as extensive as our knowledge of earlier periods in South America and Mesoamerica. In many parts of the United States and Canada, "prehistoric" cultures have been discovered that reach back as far as twelve thousand years; most of the finer art objects, however, come from the last two thousand years. "Historic" cultures, beginning with the earliest date of prolonged contact with Europeans, which varies from the sixteenth to the nineteenth century, have been widely and systematically recorded by anthropologists. The material objects from these cultures usually reflect profound changes wrought by the impact of alien tools, materials, and values on the native peoples.

Scholars divide the vast and varied territory involved into a number of areas on the basis of relative homogeneity of language and culture patterns. We will briefly discuss both prehistoric and historic art forms from most of these culture areas in this section.

Prehistoric Era

Eskimo (Inuit) sculpture, often severely economical in the handling of form, is at the same time refined—even elegant—in the placement and precision of both geometric and representational incised designs. A carved ivory burial mask (FIG. **14-25**) from the Ipiutak culture (*c.* 300) is composed of nine carefully shaped parts that are interrelated to produce several faces, both human and animal, in the manner of a visual pun. The mask is a confident, subtle composition in shallow relief, a tribute to the artist's imaginative control over his materials. Over the centuries, Eskimos also have carved hundreds of small human and animal figures (usually in ivory) and highly imaginative "mobile" (with moving parts) masks used by shamans (FIG. **14-26**) that, due to their fanciful forms and odd juxtapositions of images and materials, were much appreciated by Surrealists in the 1920s.

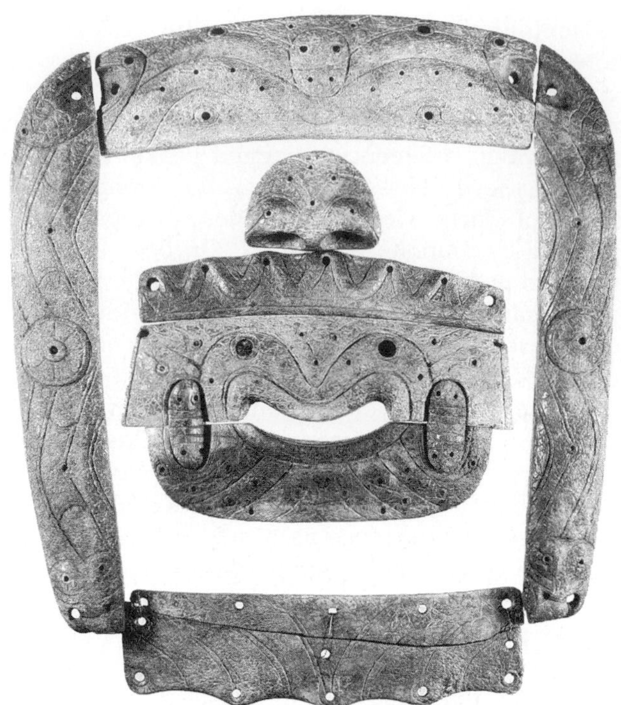

14-25 Set of burial carvings, Ipiutak, *c.* 300. Ivory, greatest width 9½″. American Museum of Natural History, New York.

Early Native American artists also excelled in working stone into a variety of utilitarian and ceremonial objects. The quite realistic handling of the so-called

NORTH AMERICAN CHRONOLOGY

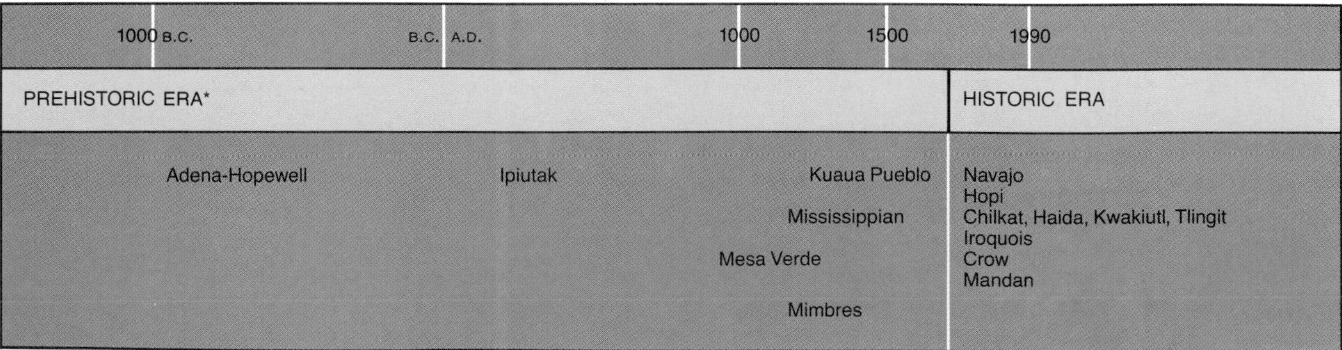

*Culture placements in the Prehistoric era reflect not just a period designation but actual chronological positioning.

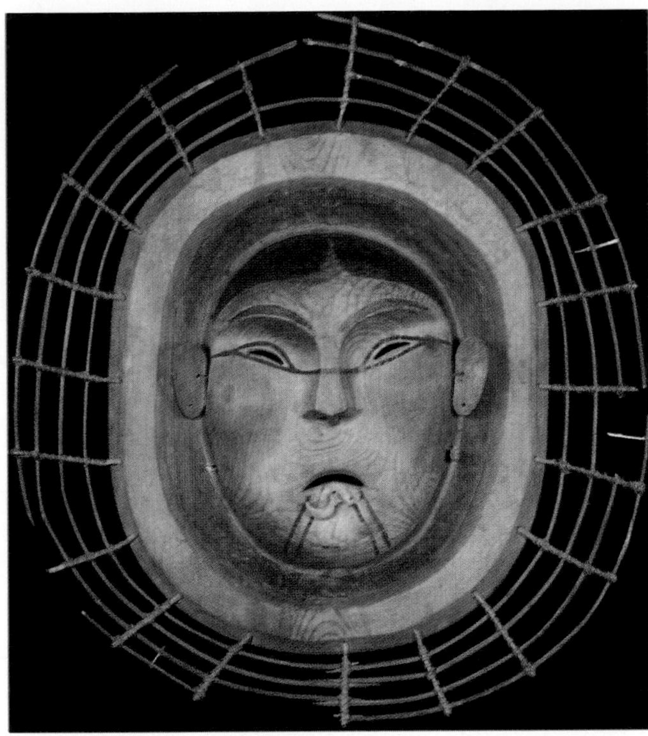

14-26 Eskimo mask representing a moon goddess, before 1900. The Robert H. Lowie Museum of Anthropology, Berkeley, California.

14-27 Adena pipe, Adena, *c.* 1000–300 B.C. Stone, 8″ high. Ohio Historical Society, Columbus.

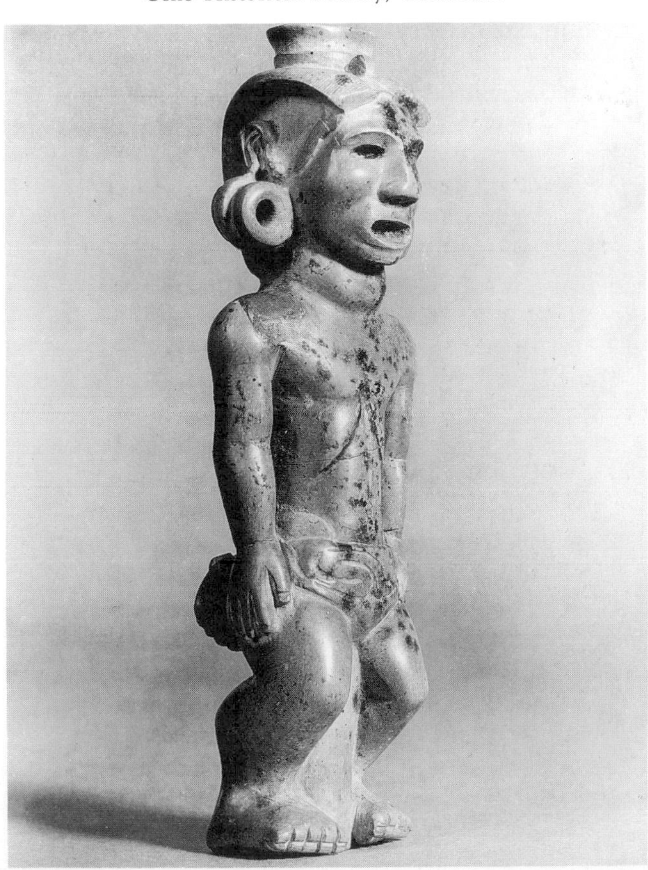

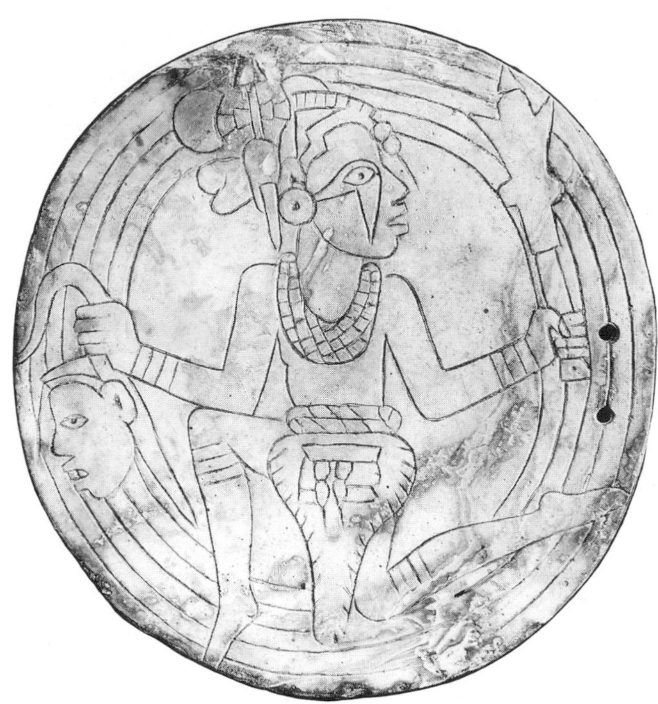

14-28 Incised shell gorget, Mississippian culture, from Sumner County, Tennessee, *c.* 1200–1500. 4″ wide. Museum of the American Indian, New York.

Adena pipe (FIG. **14-27**), a figural pipe bowl dated between 1000 and 300 B.C., provides an interesting contrast to the two-dimensional, more animated composition on a shell gorget (FIG. **14-28**) found at a Mississippian culture site in Tennessee and dating from the Temple Mound II period (*c.* A.D. 1200–1500). The standing pipe figure, although simplified, has naturalistic joint articulations and musculature, a lively, flexed-leg pose, and an alert facial expression—all of which combine to suggest movement. The incised shell gorget depicts a kneeling personage with an elaborate headdress, who carries a mace in his left hand and a severed human head in his right. Most Adena and Mississippian objects come from burial and temple mounds and are thought to have been gifts to the dead to ensure their safe, prosperous arrival in the land of the spirits. Other art objects found in such contexts include fine mica and embossed copper cut-outs of hands, bodies, snakes, birds, and other presumably symbolic forms.

Serpent Mound (FIG. **14-29**) in Adams County, Ohio, one of the larger Native American creations, is an artistic transformation of the natural environment. Undoubtedly made for spiritual purposes, this monument is a spectacular prehistoric example of the universal practice of creating visually impressive settings for ceremonial activities. The serpent, which has been restored, is about a quarter of a mile long. Other effigy mounds are known, and complex platformed

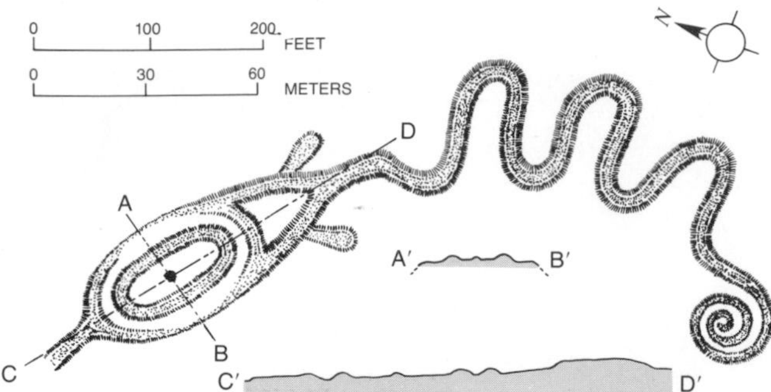

14-29 Serpent Mound, Adams County, Ohio. Approx. 1,400′ long.

temple mounds have been discovered. The latter, along with small, incised, shell reliefs, such as the Mississippian shell discussed earlier (FIG. 14-28), show strong influence from pre-Columbian Mesoamerica.

Engravings and paintings on rock are distributed widely across North America. Many of these are sacred sites and probably were used for communal rituals or the recording of personal spiritual experiences, which were very important in traditional Native American religions. Rock arts vary from lively naturalistic or schematic renderings of humans and animals to complex, convoluted compositions of as yet undeciphered symbols. The processions of linear, geometric, human (or spirit) figures picked into rock surfaces near Dinwoody, Wyoming (FIG. **14-30**), have overlays suggesting successive visits, probably for ritual purposes. Precise dating of rock art often is impossible, and, although the example shown probably was made prior to European contact, others depict horses and guns and have more naturalistic renderings, indicating a later date of execution.

Most Native American art forms (rock painting, pottery, architecture) span great periods of time. Detailed chronological sequences of pottery styles are, in fact, the historian's major tool in dating and reconstructing the cultures of the distant past, especially in the Southwest, where written records were unknown. Many fine specimens of ceramics from the Southwest date from before the Christian era until the present day, but pottery became especially fine, and its decoration most impressive, after about 1000.

A thirteenth-century bowl (FIG. **14-31**) from the Mimbres culture has an animated, graphic rendering of a warrior with a shield in a composition that creates a dynamic tension between the black figuring and the white ground. Thousands of different compositions are known from Mimbres in the Southwest. They range from lively and often complex geometric patterns to fanciful, often whimsical pictures of humans and animals; almost all are imaginative creations of artists who seem to have been bent on not repeating themselves. Designs are created by linear rhythms balanced and controlled within a clearly de-

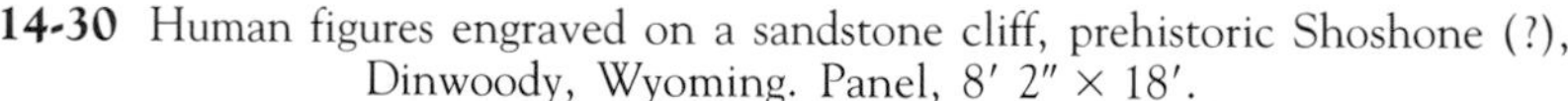

14-30 Human figures engraved on a sandstone cliff, prehistoric Shoshone (?), Dinwoody, Wyoming. Panel, 8′ 2″ × 18′.

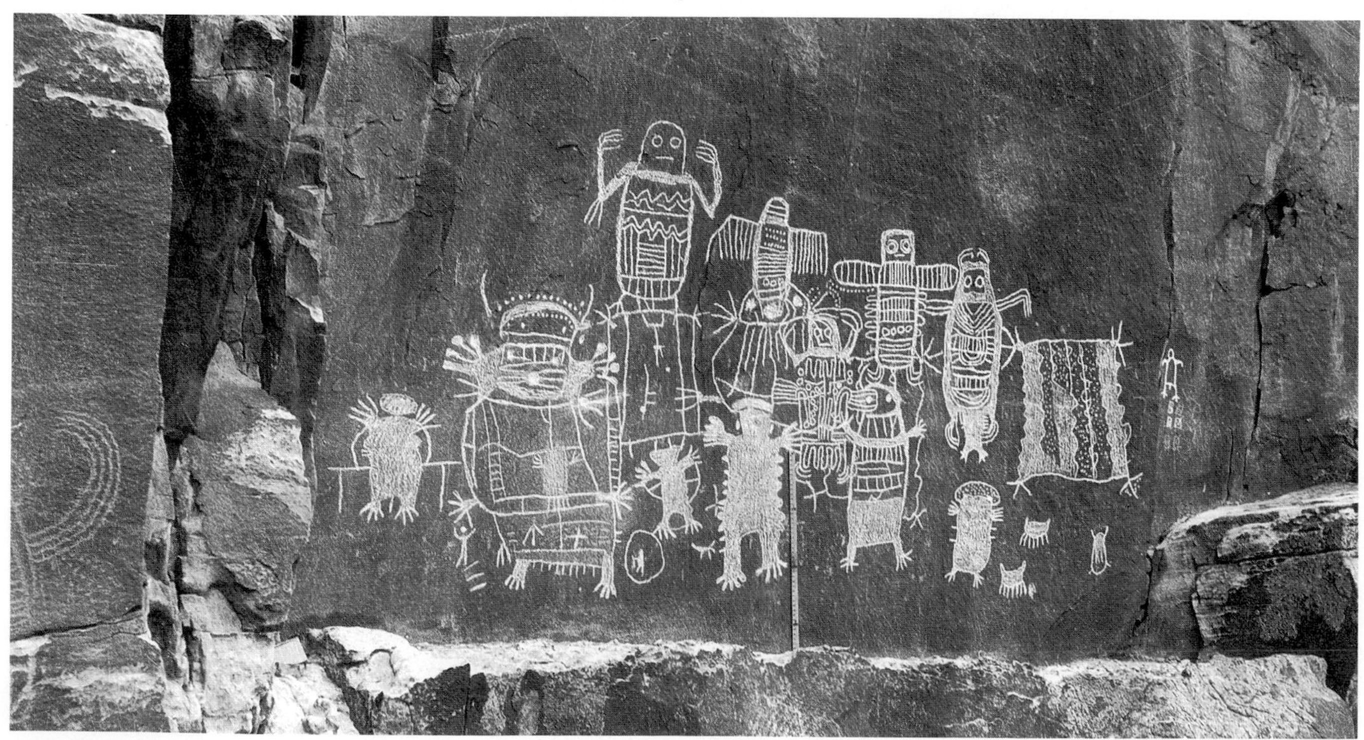

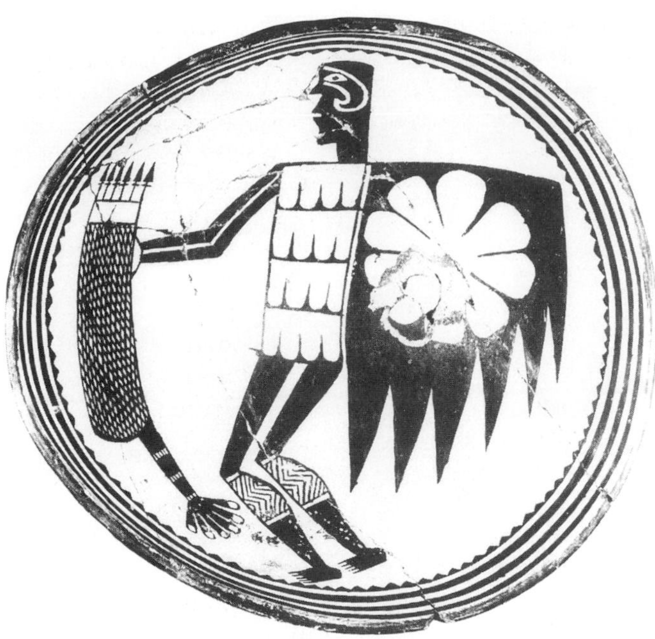

14-31 Bowl, Mimbres, thirteenth century. Ceramic, diameter 9″. Peabody Museum, Harvard University, Cambridge, Massachusetts.

fined border. Because the potter's wheel was unknown in the Southwest, countless sophisticated shapes of varied size were built by the coiling method. These ceramics are always characterized by technical excellence.

In the later centuries of the prehistoric era, Native Americans of the Southwest constructed many architectural complexes that reflect masterful building skills and impressive talents of spatial organization. Of the many ruins of such complexes, Cliff Palace at Mesa Verde, Colorado, and Pueblo Bonito at Chaco Canyon in New Mexico are among the best known. Cliff Palace (FIG. **14-32**) occupies a sheltered ledge above a valley floor and has about two hundred rectangular rooms (mostly communal dwellings) in several stories of carefully laid stone or adobe and timber; twenty larger circular underground structures, called *kivas,* were the spiritual and ceremonial centers of Pueblo life. Pueblo Bonito contains similar rooms but contrasts with Mesa Verde in its open site and, especially, in its superbly unified plan. The whole complex is enclosed by a wall in the shape of a giant D. The careful planning suggests that it was designed by a single architect or master builder and constructed by hundreds of workers under a firm, directing hand. Modern terraced pueblos, like Taos in New Mexico, although impressive, reflect neither such unified design nor such a massive, well-organized building effort.

Between 1200 and 1400, long before Europeans arrived in the New World, ancestors of the present-day Hopi and Zuñi decorated their kivas with elaborate mural paintings representing deities associated with agricultural fertility. The detail of the Kuaua Pueblo

14-32 Cliff Palace, Mesa Verde National Park, Colorado, c. 1100.

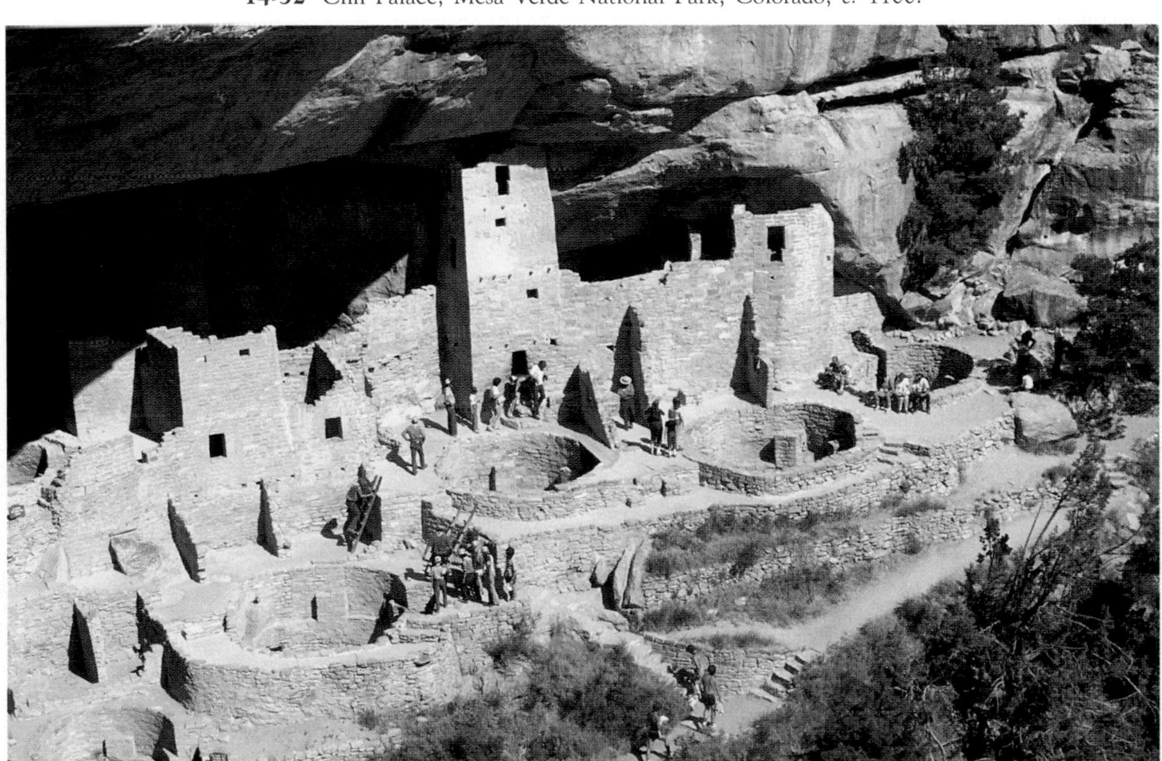

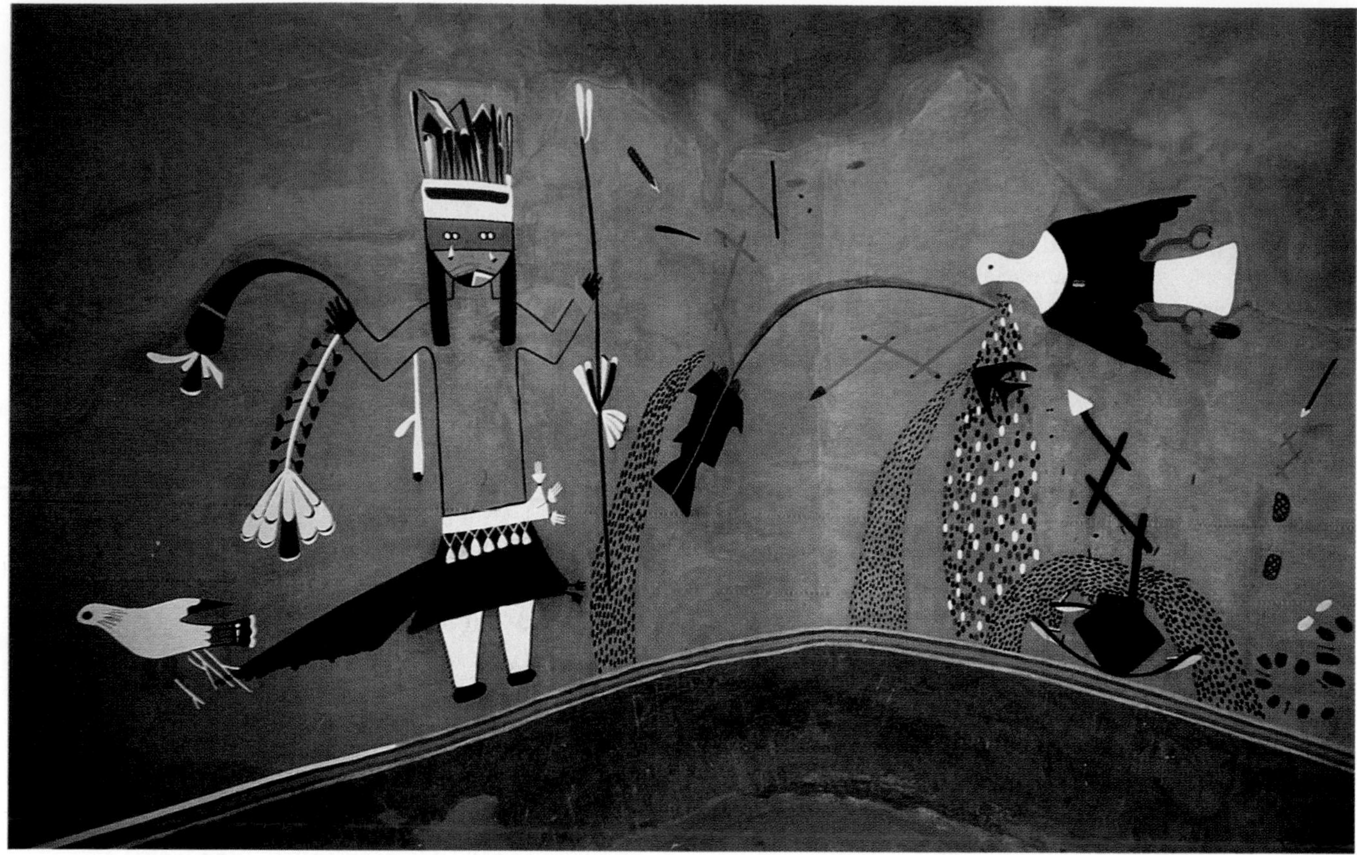

14-33 Detail of a kiva painting from Kuaua Pueblo (Coronado State Monument), New Mexico, c. 1300–1500. Museum of New Mexico, Santa Fe.

mural shown (FIG. **14-33**) depicts a "lightning man" on the left side. Fish and eagle images (associated with rain) appear on the right side. Seeds, a lightning bolt, and a rainbow stream from the eagle's mouth. All of these figures are associated with the fertility of the earth and the life-giving properties of the seasonal rains.

Historic Era

SOUTHWEST

Obviously, the motivations, functions, and means of art forms from the historic period are better known than those of the art forms from earlier eras; while the complex prehistoric religious murals from the Southwest are hard to interpret, Navajo sand painting, an art that still survives, is susceptible of detailed elucidation. The highly transient sand paintings, constructed by artist-priests to the accompaniment of prayers and chants, are an essential part of ceremonies for curing disease. (In the healing ceremony, the patient sits in the center of the painting to absorb the healing, life-giving powers of the gods and their representations.) Similar rites are performed to assure success in hunting and to promote fertility in human beings and nature alike. The natural materials used (corn pollen, charcoal, and varicolored, powdered stones) play a symbolic role that reflects the Native Americans' preoccupation with the spirits and the forces of nature. The paintings, which depict the gods and mythological heroes whose help is sought, are destroyed in the process of the ritual, so that no models exist; still, the traditional prototypes, passed on from artist to artist, must be adhered to as closely as possible. Mistakes can render the ceremony ineffective. Navajo dry-painting style is rigid—composed of simple curves, straight lines, and serial repetition—despite the potential freedom of freehand drawing (FIG. **14-34**). Navajo weaving and silver jewelry making are later developments that, until very recently, have met high technical and artistic standards.

Another art form from the Southwest, the Kachina spirit mask, contrasts markedly with the Northwest Coast and Eastern Woodlands masks. The Hopi spirit mask of a rain-bringing deity (FIG. **14-35**) is painted in geometric patterns based on rainbow, cloud, and flower forms. The more expressionistic handling of human physiognomy is quite obvious in the Northwest Coast and Eastern Woodlands masks (FIGS. 14-36 and 14-42).

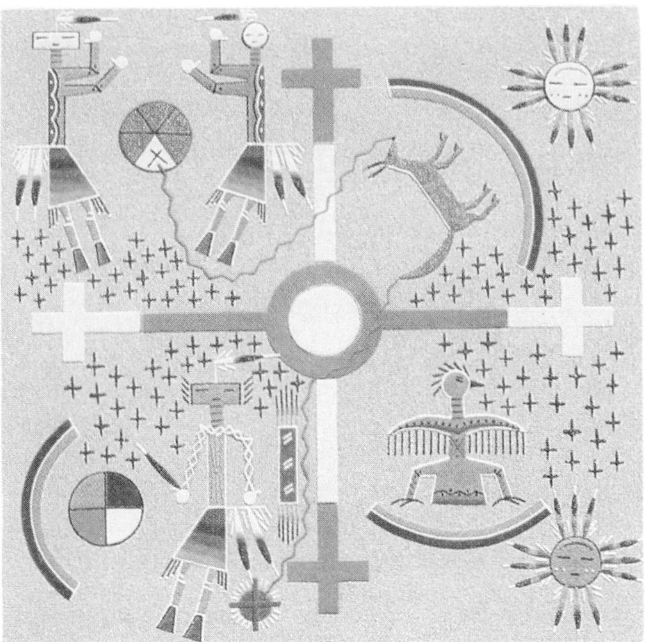

14-34 Ceremonial dry painting, Navajo, Arizona, modern.

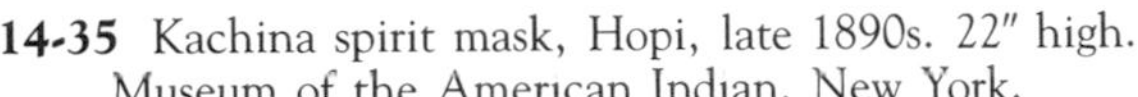

14-35 Kachina spirit mask, Hopi, late 1890s. 22" high. Museum of the American Indian, New York.

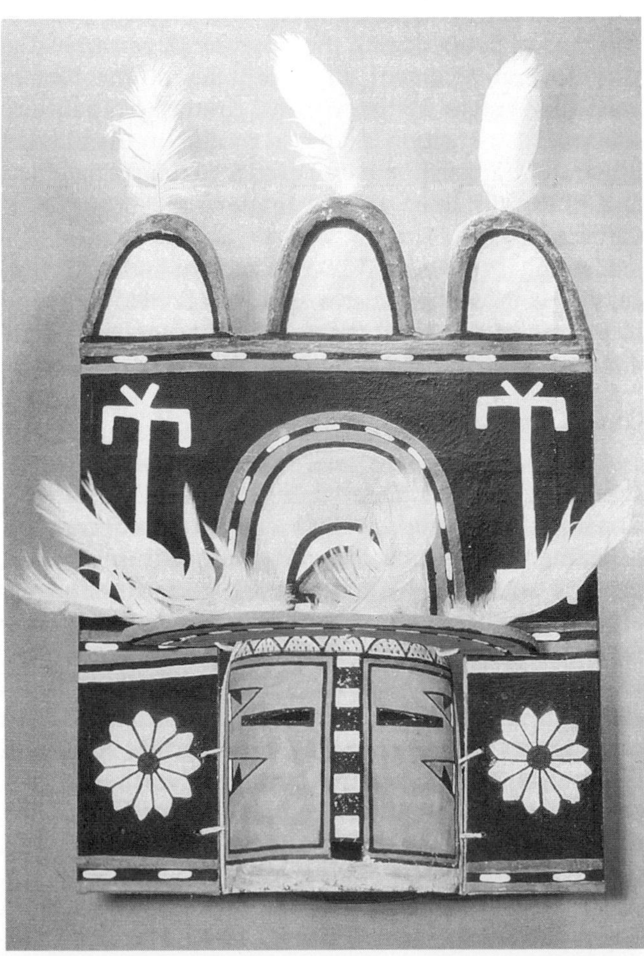

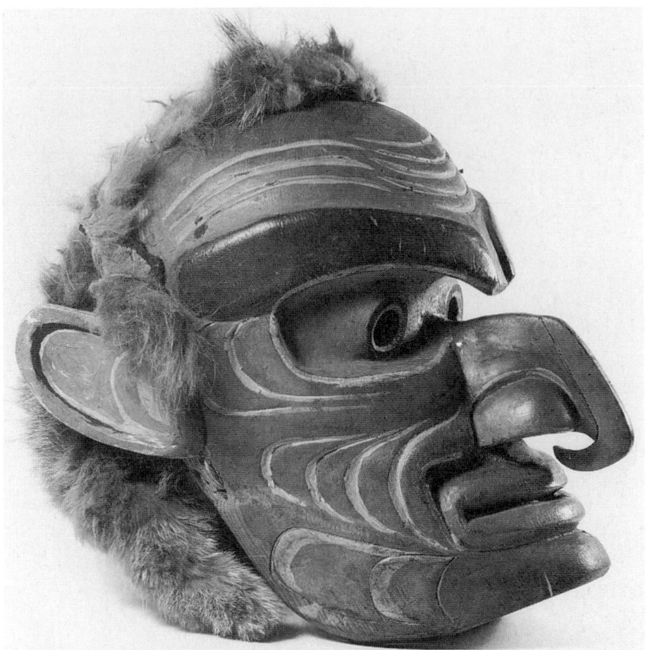

14-36 Mask, Kwakiutl, *c.* 1890. Approx. $13\frac{1}{4}$" high. Denver Art Museum.

NORTHWEST COAST

Working in a highly formalized, subtle style, the Native Americans of the Northwest Coast have produced a wide variety of art objects: totem poles, masks, rattles, chests, bowls, clothing, charms, and decorated houses and canoes. Masks were carved for use by shamans in their healing rites and by others in public reenactments of "spirit quests." The animals and mythological creatures encountered on such quests were, in turn, represented in masks and a host of other carvings. The mask from the Kwakiutl people (FIG. **14-36**) owes its dramatic character to the exaggeration of facial parts and to the deeply undercut curvilinear depressions, which result in strong shadows. It is a refined, yet forceful carving typical of the more expressionistic styles of the area. Others are more subdued, and some, like a wooden Tlingit helmet (FIG. **14-37**), are exceedingly naturalistic, probably actual portraits, almost as if the artist were proving that no restrictions could be set on artistic representation. Inherited motifs and styles usually were preferred, however, above radical new departures. Although Northwest Coast arts have a spiritual dimension, they are more important as expressions of social status, in that the art form one uses and, indeed, the things one may depict, are functions of that status. Haida mortuary poles and house frontal poles (FIG. **14-38**), used where totemic crest emblems of clan groups are displayed before the clan chief's house, are striking expressions of this interest in social status.

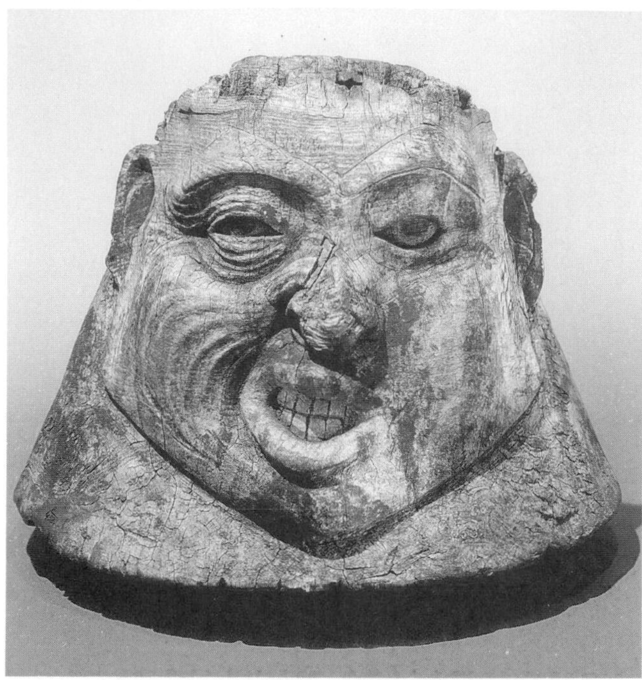

14-37 Helmet, Tlingit. Wood, 12″ high. American Museum of Natural History, New York.

14-38 Haida mortuary poles and house frontal poles at Skedans Village, British Columbia, 1878. National Archives, Canada. (After a photograph by George M. Dawson.)

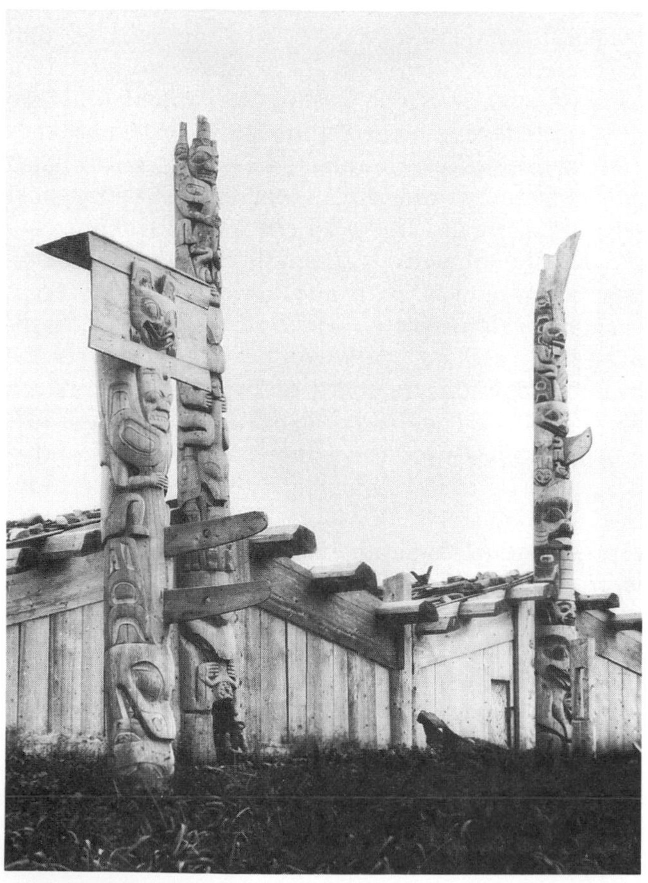

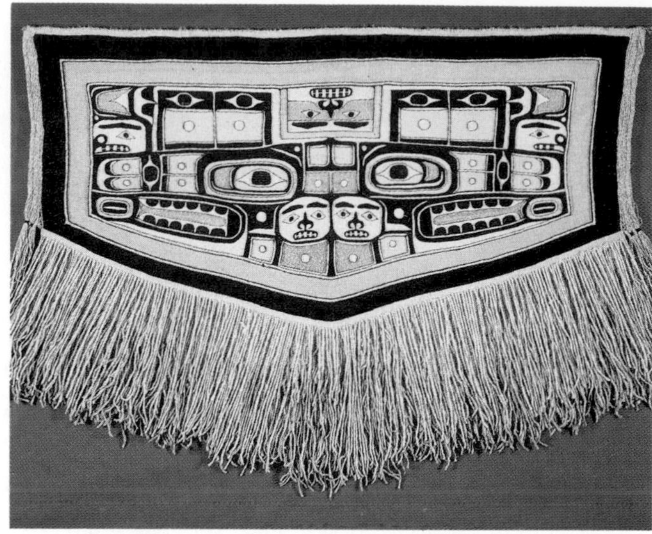

14-39 Chilkat blanket with stylized animal motifs, Tlingit, early twentieth century. Wild goat's wool and cedar bark in bright colors, 72″ × 35″. Southwest Museum, Los Angeles.

Another characteristic Northwest Coast art form is the Chilkat blanket (FIG. **14-39**). Male artists provided the designs for these blankets in the form of pattern boards from which female weavers worked. The blankets, which became widespread prestige items of ceremonial dress during the nineteenth century, display several recurrent characteristics of the Northwest Coast style: symmetry and rhythmic repetition, schematic abstraction of animal motifs (in the blanket illustrated, a bear), eye designs, a regularly swelling and thinning line, and a tendency to round off corners.

Elegant, precise, and highly accomplished technically, the art of the Northwest Coast is held by many to be one of the sophisticated high points of Native American artistic accomplishment.

GREAT PLAINS

Artists of the Great Plains worked in materials and styles quite different from those of the Northwest Coast. Much artistic energy went into the decoration of leather garments, first with compactly sewn quill designs and later with beadwork patterns. Tepees, tepee linings, and buffalo-skin robes were painted with geometric and stiff figural designs prior to about 1830; after that, naturalistic scenes, often of war exploits, in styles adapted from those of visiting European artists, were gradually introduced. After the Europeans introduced the horse to North America and the establishment of colonial governments disrupted settled indigenous communities on the east coast, a new, mobile Native American culture flourished for a short period of time on the Great Plains. The tepee lining illustrated (FIG. **14-40**) is of that later

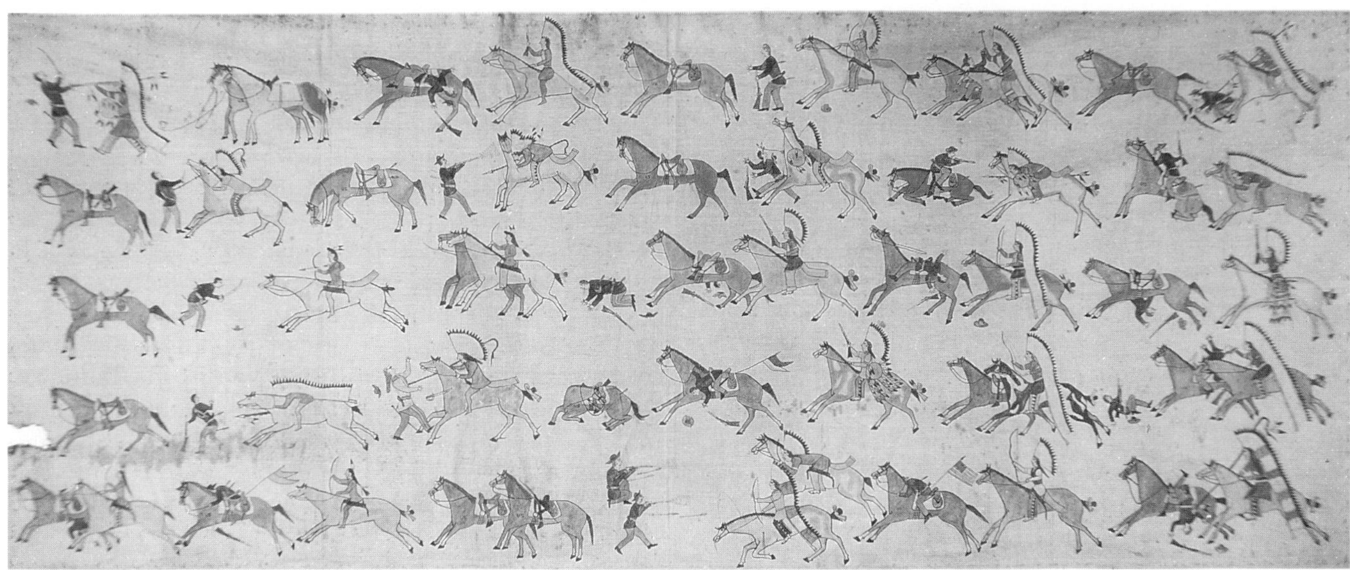

14-40 Tepee lining with pictograph of war scenes, Crow, late nineteenth century. Painted muslin, 2′ 11″ × 7′ 1″. Smithsonian Institution, Washington, D.C.

style, when realistic action and proportions, careful detailing, and a variety of colors were employed.

Because, at least in later periods, most Plains peoples were nomadic, their esthetic attention was focused largely on their clothing and bodies and on other portable objects, such as shields, clubs, pipes, tomahawks, and various containers. Transient but important Plains art forms sometimes can be found in the paintings and drawings of visiting white artists. The Swiss KARL BODMER, for example, accurately portrayed the personal decoration of Chief Four Bears (Mato-Tope, FIG. **14-41**), a Mandan warrior and chief. The chief's body paintings and feather decorations, all symbolic of his affiliations and military accomplishments, may be said to be his biography—a composite artistic statement in several media—which could be "read" easily by other Native Americans. Plains peoples also made shields and shield covers that were both artworks and "power images." Shield paintings often derive from religious visions; their symbolism, the pigments themselves, and added materials, such as feathers, provided their owners with magical protection and supernatural power.

14-41 KARL BODMER, *Mandan Chief Mato-Tope,* 1840. Lithograph, 14″ × 10″. The Thomas Gilcrease Institute of American History and Art, Tulsa, Oklahoma.

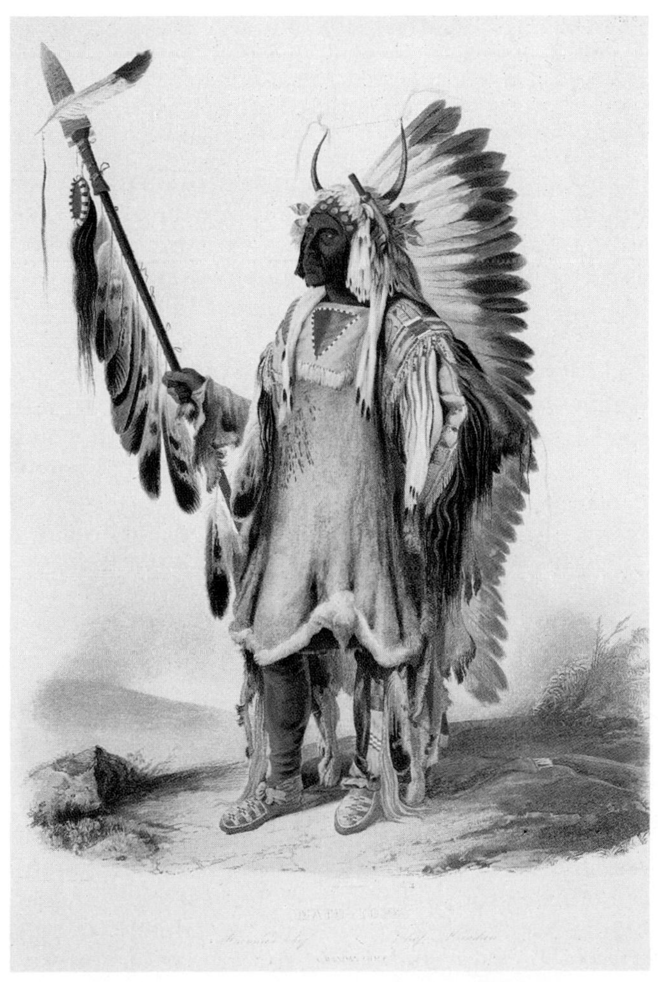

EASTERN WOODLANDS

Artists of the Eastern Woodlands made quilled and beaded objects and items of clothing, often decorated with curvilinear, floral motifs. The Iroquois also carved compelling, expressionistic masks (FIG. **14-42**) for use in the False Face Society ceremonies, which healed physical and psychological sickness and cleansed whole communities of destructive impurities. The spirit "faces" portray legendary supernaturals whose exploits are recounted in mythology. Bold

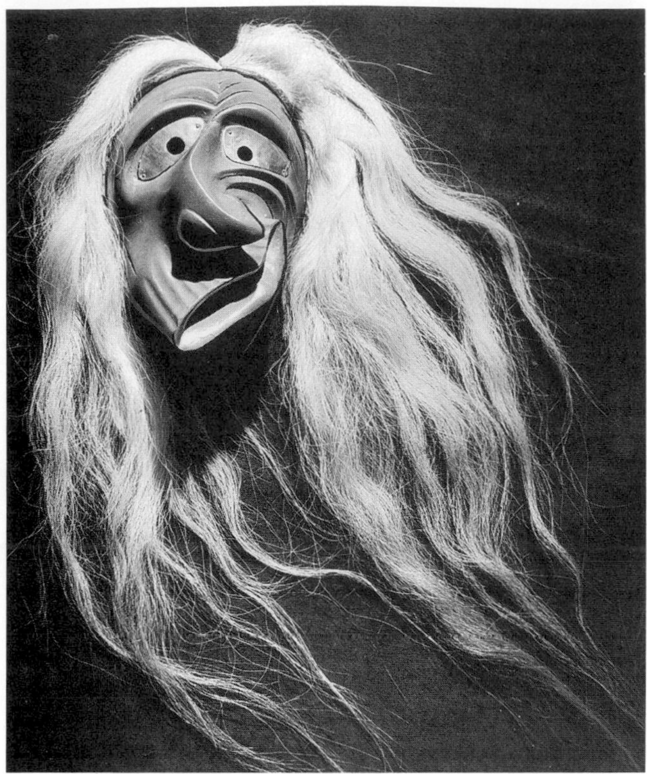

14-42 ELON WEBSTER, False Face mask, Iroquois, 1937. Wood. (The artist was an Onondaga of the Tonawanda Reservation.) Courtesy of Cranbrook Institute of Science, Bloomfield Hills, Michigan.

in conception, these masks rely on a dramatizing distortion and exaggeration of facial features for their strong effects. Like others used in Africa and Oceania, these masks must be hidden when not in use, lest their power inadvertently cause injury.

Whether secular and merely decorative or spiritual and highly symbolic, the diverse styles and forms of Native American art testify to the ancient and continuing artistic sensibility of the peoples of North America. Their creative use of local materials and pigments constitutes an artistic reshaping of nature that, in many cases, reflects the Native Americans' reliance on and reverence toward the environment that they considered it their privilege to inhabit.

AFRICA

The population of the huge continent of Africa is subdivided into several racial and linguistic groups. Although nearly all African peoples have produced artists (dancers, musicians, storytellers, rock painters, architects, and masters at personal decoration), only those groups dwelling in the vast areas drained by the Niger and Congo rivers—essentially, tropical Africa—have produced the extraordinary sculptures, mostly in wood, that deservedly have become famous as "African art." It is largely this art that we will survey here.

Africa is as widely varied artistically as it is sociopolitically, geographically, ecologically, linguistically, and racially. Divine rulers headed great kingdoms, and groups of elders governed small tribes; forest regions along the coast give way inland to grassy savannas and highlands and, in turn, to the semiarid lands south of the Sahara desert.

Like North America, Africa has hundreds of Neolithic rock painting sites, especially in the Tassili region of the Algerian Sahara, which contain the earliest examples of its art. These paintings and engravings, which are considerably more recent than the Paleolithic works found in Spain and southern France, are equally accomplished renderings of humans, animals, and a host of nonrepresentational patterns thought to be symbolic.

NIGERIA

From a number of archeological sites collectively labeled Nok, we have precise radiocarbon dates of between 500 B.C. and A.D. 200. The earliest African evidence of sculpture in the round was found at these sites. Because they are so confidently handled, Nok terra-cotta heads (FIG. **14-43**) and figures of humans

14-43 *Jemaa Head,* from Nok, fifth century B.C. Terra-cotta, $9\frac{13}{16}''$ high. National Museum, Lagos, Nigeria.

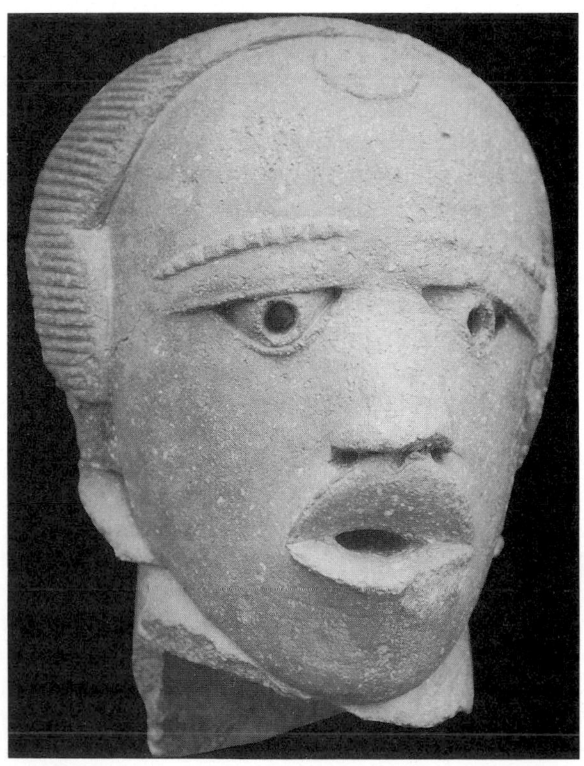

and animals suggest wooden or other clay prototypes, now lost. No "formative" prototypes are yet known. Volumes are full and surfaces are modeled smoothly in these terra-cotta sculptures, which some authorities believe to be direct ancestors of terra cottas and bronzes found at Ife (150 miles southwest of the Nok area) that date from 1000 to 1200.

By about the ninth century, at Igbo Ukwu in tropical Africa, sophisticated cire perdue (lost-wax) casting techniques had evolved, and, by the twelfth century, the most naturalistic style known for any tropical African era had appeared. Wood carvings certainly were made in the twelfth century, too, but no examples have survived. The bronze figure illustrated here (FIG. **14-44**) undoubtedly is an ancient, divine king of Ife, the city in western Nigeria that is still the spiritual capital of the numerous Yoruba peoples. The king figure, unlike most African wood sculpture, shows fleshlike modeling that attempts a realistic rendering of the human form. The idealized naturalism of the flesh and head in this figure approaches portraiture, although its proportions, which exaggerate the head, are not lifelike. The casting is fine, though somewhat weathered, and accurately records precise details of the costume and jewelry worn by ancient Ife kings.

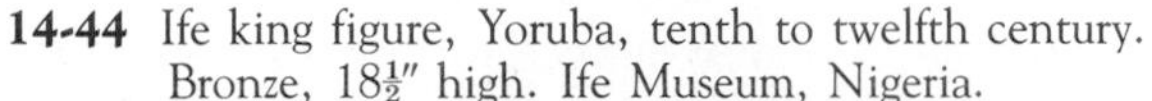

14-44 Ife king figure, Yoruba, tenth to twelfth century. Bronze, $18\frac{1}{2}$″ high. Ife Museum, Nigeria.

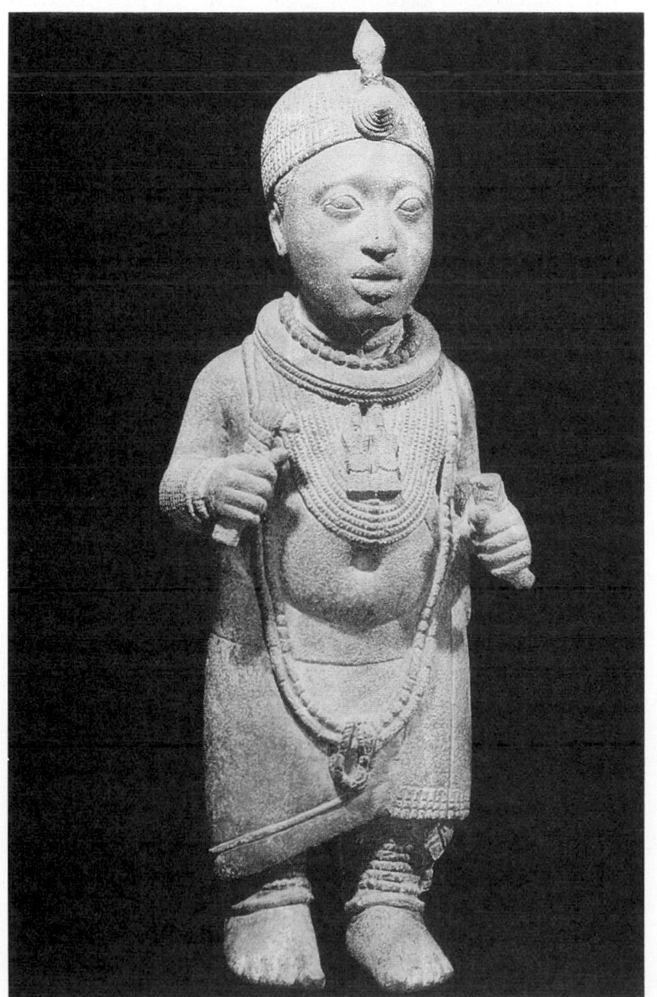

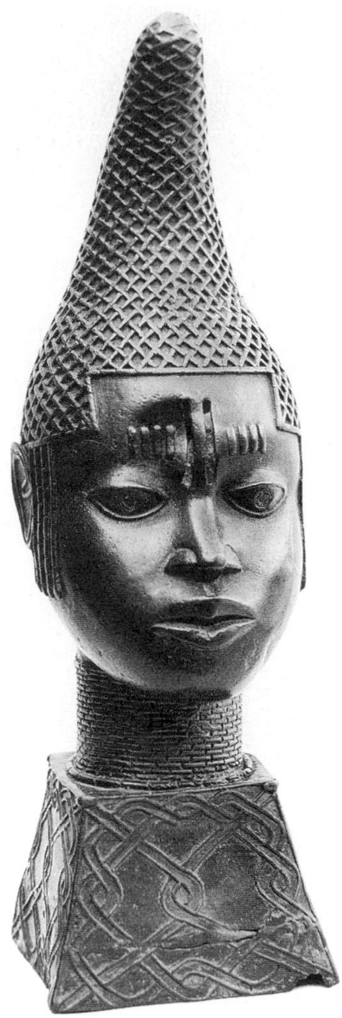

14-45 *Queen Mother Head,* from Benin, early sixteenth century. Bronze, 20″ high. National Museum, Lagos, Nigeria.

Numerous historical and ritual ties are known to have existed between the divine kings of Ife and those who presided over the kingdom of Benin, which was ascendant from the fifteenth to the eighteenth centuries. Many complex, finely cast bronzes, as well as ivory, wood, terra-cotta, and wrought-iron sculptures, were produced in Benin, where bronze casting and ivory carving were royal prerogatives carried out by guilds of highly trained professionals.

An exquisite bronze portrait of a royal lady (FIG. **14-45**) shows the Ife-Benin style at its classic height. Cast in the cire perdue process, the head seems to be designed on principles of form familiar in Greek idealizing art; the naturalistic traits of the subject are simplified into near-geometric volumes. In any event,

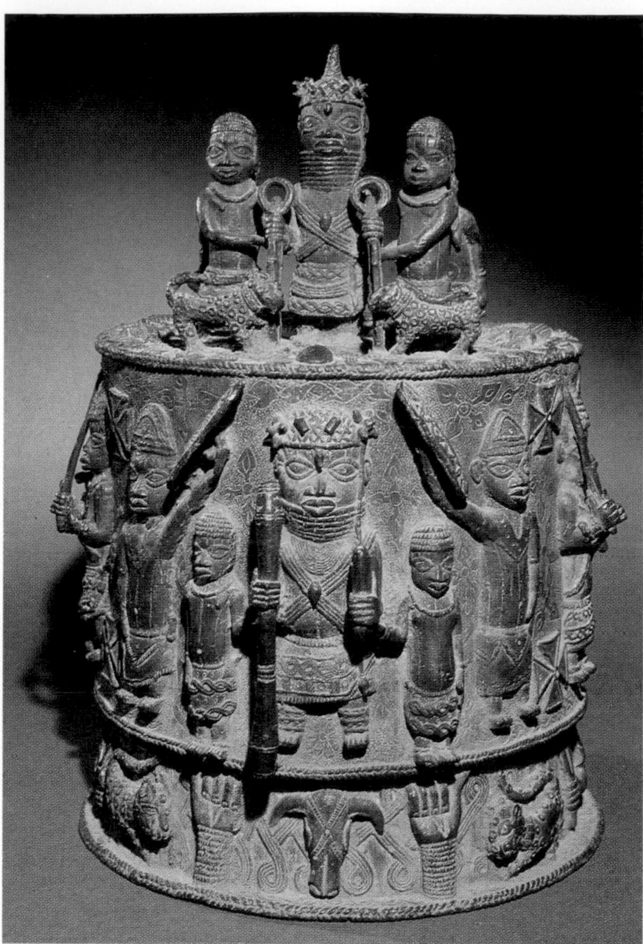

14-46 *Altar of the Hand,* 1550–1680, Benin, from Nigeria. Bronze, 17½″ high. British Museum, London.

the Benin queen and related portraits in clay and bronze contrast noticeably in their realism of proportion and likeness with much of the African sculpture we are surveying in this chapter. The queenly beauty wears a high, conoid, basket-weave headdress, plaited side curls, and a wide, tight choker; ornamental scars adorn her forehead. The serene and proud composure of her expression is reinforced by the formal control of the elegant surfaces and contours. The perfect unity of form and expression achieved here places this portrait sculpture among the masterpieces of world art.

Much Benin art, like the gilded objects of the Ashanti further west, glorifies the office and trappings of the divine king. The divine king is the central figure in the casting shown in FIG. **14-46** and in many other works. As in the Ife king figure (FIG. 14-44), the head here is greatly exaggerated, reflecting the view that it is the center of being and the source of power and intelligence. Taken together with the hieratic arrangement of the group, this distortion clearly affirms the importance of symbolism to the artist.

The Ijo Iphri sculpture (FIG. **14-47**) manifests the symbolism of power in a less centralized culture than that of Benin. The "owner of the power" is seen sitting atop a monstrous animal (symbolic of his own aggressiveness), holding a fan and libation vessel. This Ijo piece seems more expressionistic in form and freer in invention than the more court-regulated style at Benin (FIG. 14-46).

In understanding the range and quality of African art, customary definitions must be broadened to include more than monuments, more than objects that can be displayed in museums. This observation is especially true of the art of masquerade, which depends on music, dance, and costuming for its real vitality. Although many of the wooden masks used in

14-47 Iphri figure, Ijo, from Nigeria, nineteenth to twentieth century. Wood, 25½″ high. Metropolitan Museum of Art, New York (Michael C. Rockefeller Memorial Collection of Primitive Art, gift of the Matthew T. Mellon Foundation).

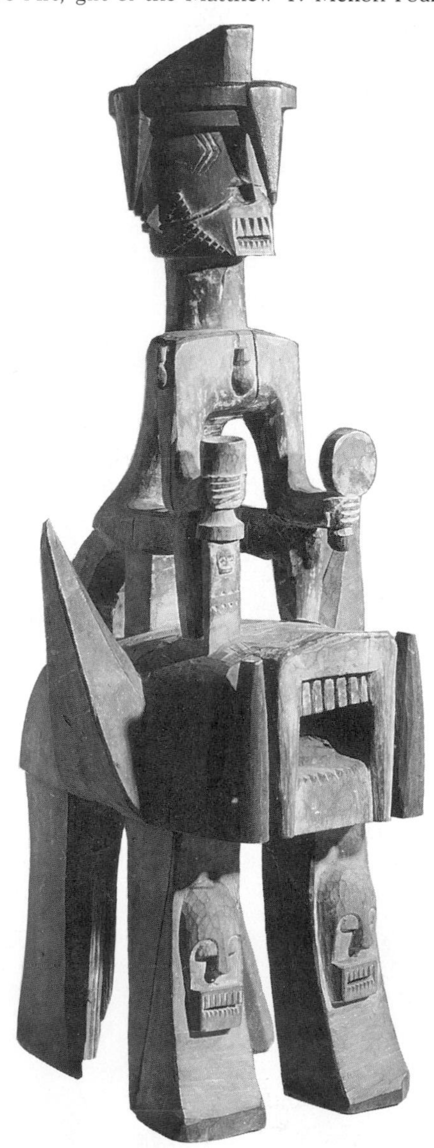

such performances are dramatic carvings in their own right, they should be seen as single, important elements in a complex of interacting artistic media that occupy time as well as space. (We noted earlier on page 502 the importance of dance and mask in the community of the native arts.)

The Yoruba Gelede masquerader from Nigeria (FIG. **14-48**), photographed in full costume and caught in motion, is a case in point. Gelede is a cult devoted to the propitiation and entertainment of powerful senior women in Yoruba communities and deities associated with witchcraft. The masqueraders perform in pairs, their rich, appliqué-panel costumes activated by vigorous dance movements. Theater and ritual combine in the dance, and the masked characters present a bewildering array of traditional and modern types: a motorcyclist, cloth seller, hunter, leopard, king, white man, prostitute, policeman. Performances involve considerable social criticism of the community at large, which is expressed in song, gesture, dance, and in the masks themselves.

14-48 Dancer of the Gelede Society of Meko, Yoruba, Nigeria, 1969.

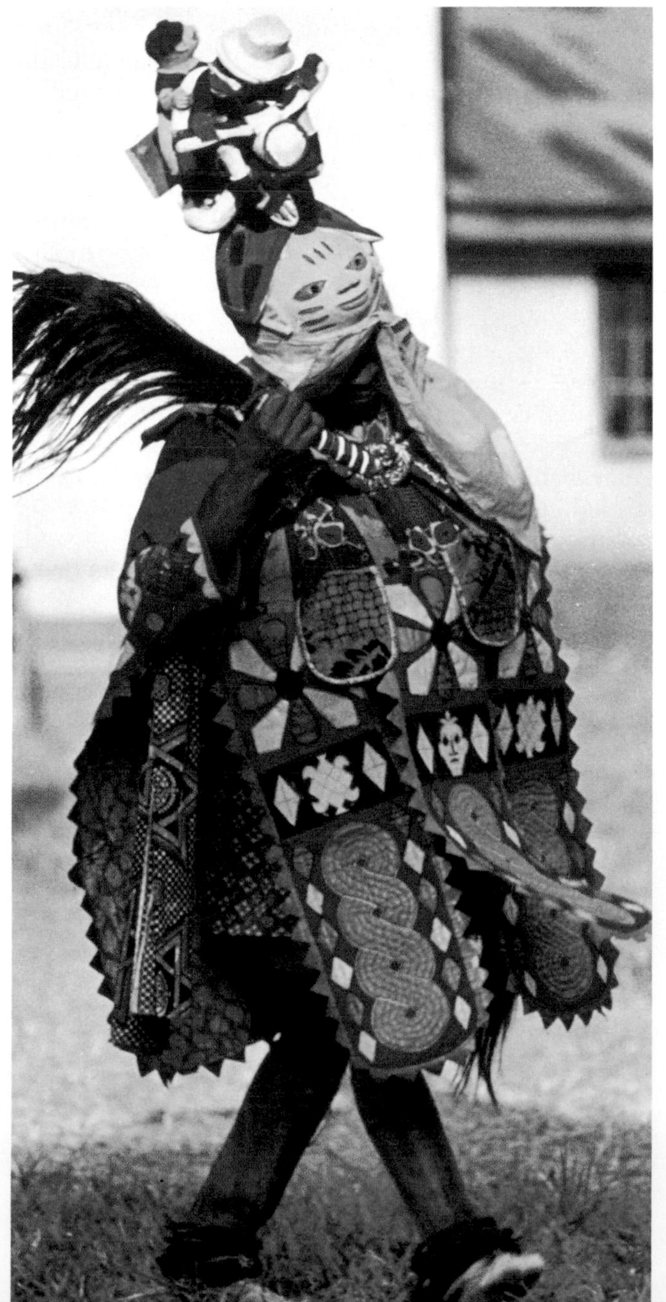

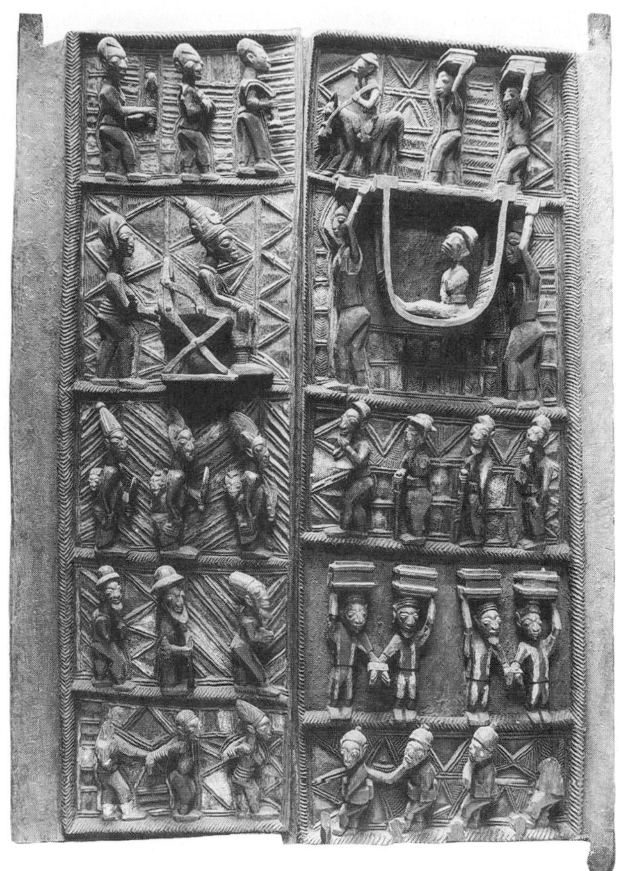

14-49 OLOWE of Ise, door from the king's palace at Ikerre, Yoruba, Nigeria, *c.* 1910. Wood, approx. 6′ high. Trustees of the British Museum, London.

The Yoruba, Africa's most prolific artists, have created an abundance of art forms other than masks: cult figures in wood, bronze, terra cotta, and iron; beaded objects and garments; as well as palace houseposts and doors designed to enhance the dignity and prestige of leaders. One such door (FIG. **14-49**), which stood at the king's palace at Ikerre, was carved by the master sculptor OLOWE of Ise (d. 1938), around 1910. It tells of the visit of a British colonial official, Captain Ambrose, to the king. In the panels on the right leaf of the door, the captain, carried in a litter, is accompanied by his guards and luggage bearers; on the left leaf, the king, his wives, and retainers await the visitor. Genre scenes and anecdotes of Yoruba life are represented in other panels. Olowe, a virtuoso woodcarver, sets his figures in such high relief that they stand almost free of the panel surface. Though recognizably of the Yoruba family, the style is distinctively

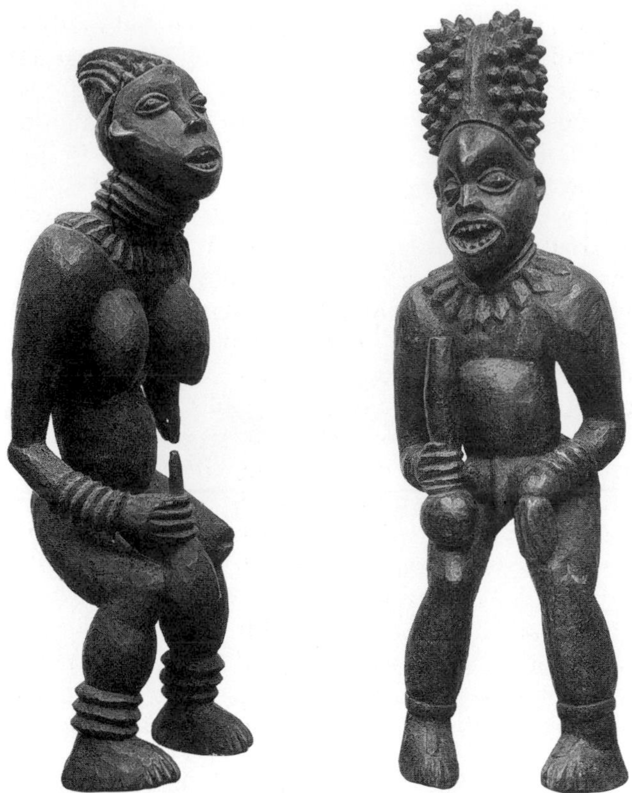

14-50 *Dancing Royal Couple,* Bangwa, from Cameroon, nineteenth century. Wood, female 33½" high, male 35½" high. Private collection.

Olowe's. The strong, elegant abstraction of the forms and the precise, facetlike carving yield the kind of expressive force that would fascinate European artists in the early decades of the twentieth century and generate a radically new, "expressionistic" style. Like many African artists, Olowe had a clearly recognizable personal style, although individuality and personal, idiosyncratic style are of less concern here than, for example, in the modern West.

As the prevalence of the multimedia art of masquerade suggests, dance may be the artistic medium most important and expressive to native Africans. Many sculptures are used in dance contexts, and many others depict people dancing. The vital, energetic figures from the Bangwa kingdom of the Cameroon grasslands (FIG. **14-50**) express the vigor of dance in several complementary ways: by active, asymmetrical posing; a head thrust back with open mouth; constrictions at the joints, which rhythmically energize the figures; and the use of rough textures (surfaces faceted with tool marks). The female figure is believed to portray a priestess and finder of witches. Both of these figures stood among dozens of royal carvings depicting ancestors, chiefs, and priests—those, whether living or dead, who were responsible for the continuity of life itself. Such figures, intended among the Bangwa to display the wealth, power, and taste of the ruler who presided over them, were gathered for rituals and given food and drink. The importance of artistic display to Cameroon leaders made them major patrons, as well as critics, of the arts.

Ibo *mbari* houses, like the Yoruba door (FIG. 14-49), are complex works of art. These elaborate, unified complexes consist of groupings of clay sculptures (often with more than a hundred pieces in one mbari) and paintings placed in a specially designed architectural setting. The houses are built to honor principal community deities, often the goddess of the earth. In the house shown (FIG. **14-51**), the goddess is seated with dignity in the center of the front side, her children close by; her servants, in high relief, stand guard behind her. The sculptor has enlarged and extended her torso, neck, and head to express her aloofness and power. She is the apex of a formalized, hieratic composition that is balanced on either side by seated couples.

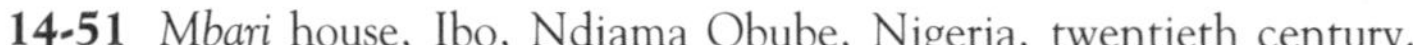

14-51 *Mbari* house, Ibo, Ndiama Obube, Nigeria, twentieth century.

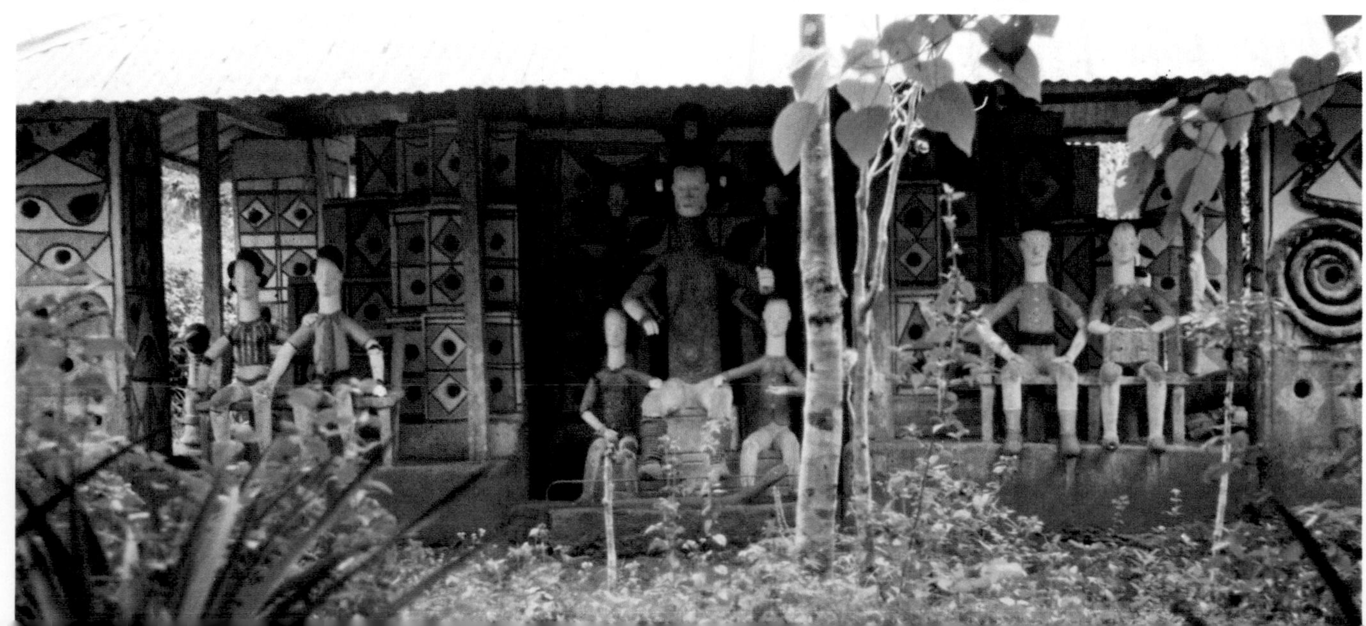

More informally posed figures and groups are found on the other sides of the house—beautiful, amusing, or frightening figures of animals, humans, and gods taken from history, mythology, and everyday life. The complex, secret mbari construction rituals, as well as the sculptural program, suggest that each house is in fact a cosmic symbol and that the building process itself is a stylized, world-renewal ritual. Ceremonies of opening the house to public view indicate that the god has accepted the offering (of the house) and, for a time at least, will be benevolent. The mbari is never repaired; instead, it is allowed to disintegrate and return to the earth from which it is made and to which it often is dedicated. These houses, then, are a relatively transient art form, as are the arts of masquerade, personal ornamentation, and festivals. (The last three are best seen on film, which preserves the movement inherent in their design.)

OTHER REGIONS

Ancestral or power images from Zaire (formerly the Belgian Congo) are more conventional sculptural forms, often carefully preserved by their owners for generations. The commemorative, ancestral mother-and-child carving from the Kongo peoples (FIG. **14-52**) has a smooth, refined delicacy, whereas the composite power figure from the Songye people several hundred miles to the east (FIG. **14-53**) deals with the human form more abstractly, in abrupt and forceful carving. The functions of the two works are comparable, both being visible manifestations of ancestral power, which can affect people's lives so materially. The Kongo piece, probably a symbolic repository of the soul of a deceased noblewoman, received prayers invoking her continuing care and beneficence; the Songye figure directed (for the benefit of the community) specific ancestral powers activated by (and to some extent contained in) various "medicines" positioned inside and on the figure. Such power figures most commonly were used to protect warriors in battle, to promote human and crop fertility, to cure disease, and to end drought.

The dramatic stylistic contrast between the Songye image and the Kongo mother and child suggests the wide range and variety of carving conventions present in Africa. Indeed, tendencies toward realism or

14-52 Ancestral figure, Kongo, from Zaire, nineteenth to twentieth century. Wood and brass, 16" high. Musée Royal de l'Afrique Centrale, Tervuren, Belgium.

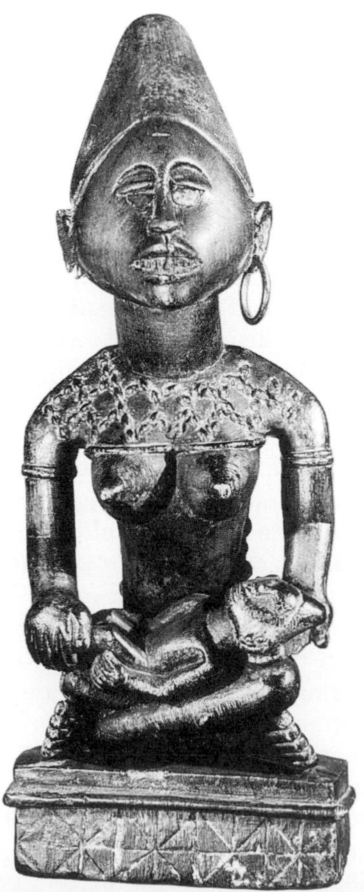

14-53 Power figure, Songye, from Zaire, nineteenth to twentieth century. Wood, iron, copper, horn, fibers, cowrie shells, feathers, and glass beads, 35" high. Musée Royal de l'Afrique Centrale, Tervuren, Belgium.

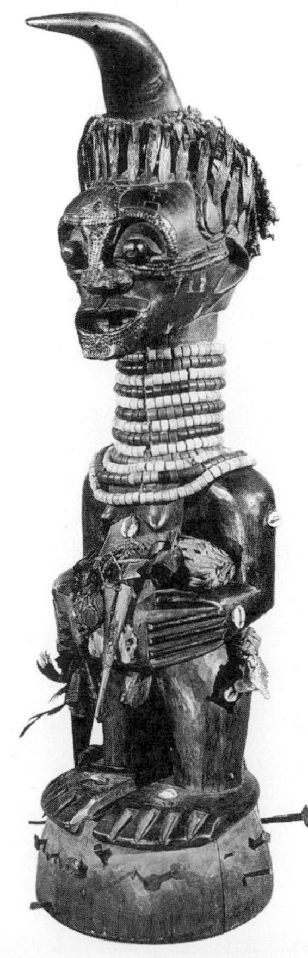

toward abstraction are not easily charted on the African map; deviations sometimes occur between neighboring tribes, within a tribe, and, occasionally, in the work of a single artist, as is the case among the Dan and related peoples of Liberia, Sierra Leone, and the Ivory Coast. Like many African peoples, the Dan evolved a great variety of masks representing judges, policemen, priests, and a host of other people, both harmful and helpful. In many cases, the role conferred by the mask was functionally real. A person wearing a judge or an executioner mask, for example, actually judged cases or executed criminals. Members of the men's masking society, armed with the power of the bush spirits and clothed in anonymous masking costumes, regulated the behavior of the community. The society also held masked entertainments, impersonating secular personages, whose behavior was held up for public scrutiny, or performing spectacular acrobatic and stilt dances.

Dan woodcarvers, required to make representations of varied spiritual and secular types, became skilled in several contrasting styles. The same artist could carve a refined, polished mask depicting a beautiful woman (FIG. **14-54**) and a rougher, highly abstracted mask called *kagle* (FIG. **14-55**). In fashioning the female mask, the carver has simplified facial planes and brought their smooth surfaces to a high polish, while retaining naturalistic shapes and the placement of features. The carver of kagle, on the other hand, simplifies and abstracts, creating a series of forceful thrusting and receding positive and negative shapes with great dramatic impact.

14-54 Mask, Dan, from Liberia, nineteenth to twentieth century. Wood, 8½" high. Metropolitan Museum of Art, New York.

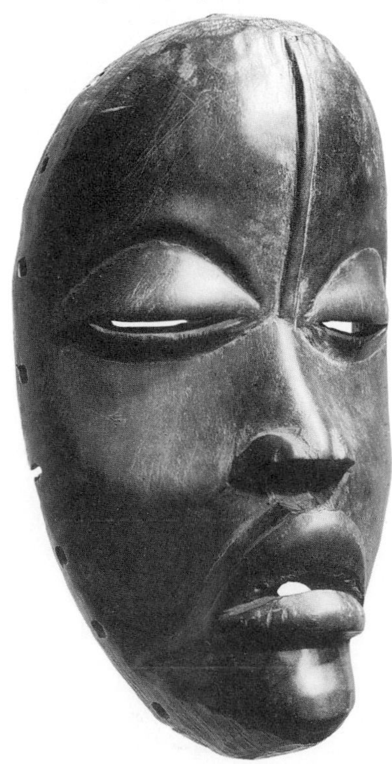

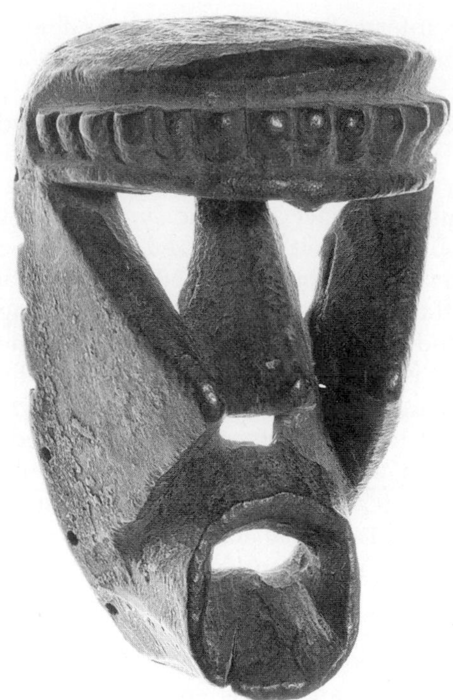

14-55 *Kagle* (mask), Dan, from Sierra Leone, *c.* 1775–1825. Wood, 9" high. Yale University Art Gallery, New Haven, Connecticut (gift of Mr. and Mrs. James M. Osborn for the Linton Collection of African Art).

The royal Kuba sculptors of central Zaire created an entirely different type of mask to represent a primordial ancestor who helps to oversee the ritual passage of boys into adulthood. (Many other African peoples use masks in analogous ceremonies.) The creator of the *mboom* mask illustrated here (FIG. **14-56**) employs a rich combination of beads, feathers, copper, fur, and raffia to embellish a carved, wooden helmet. A strong basic head shape with a bulging forehead is overlaid with visually complex textural effects that are Kuba symbols of royalty.

The seated male and female sculpture shown in FIG. **14-57** is an example of another well-known African style, that of the Dogon people of Mali. Depicting mythical ancestors of the human race, this group is a masterfully integrated composition of vertical forms enclosed by tubular shapes, with geometric incised decorations on the surfaces of both. Rejecting naturalistic rendering in this instance (though capable of it), the Dogon sculptor here seems to have dismantled the human body, straightening, simplifying, and distorting its parts before reassembling them. Body parts are present but often sharpened, attenuated, or reduced to suggestions. Perhaps it was this primordial couple's remoteness from life that prompted the

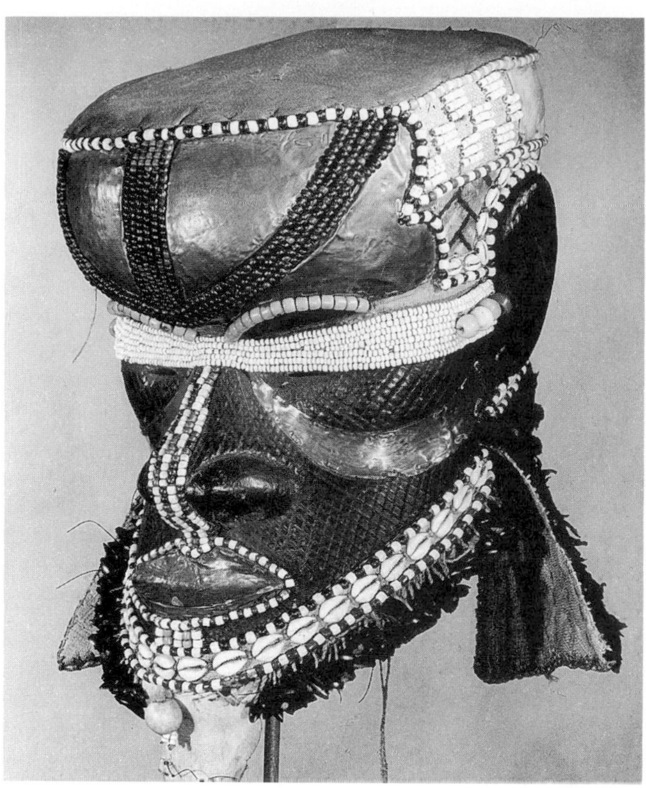

14-56 *Mboom* helmet mask, Kuba, from Zaire, nineteenth to twentieth century. Wood, brass, cowrie shells, beads, seeds, 13″ high. Musée Royal de l'Afrique Centrale, Tervuren, Belgium.

14-57 *Couple,* Dogon, Mali. Wood, 30″ high. Photograph copyright © 1975 by the Barnes Foundation.

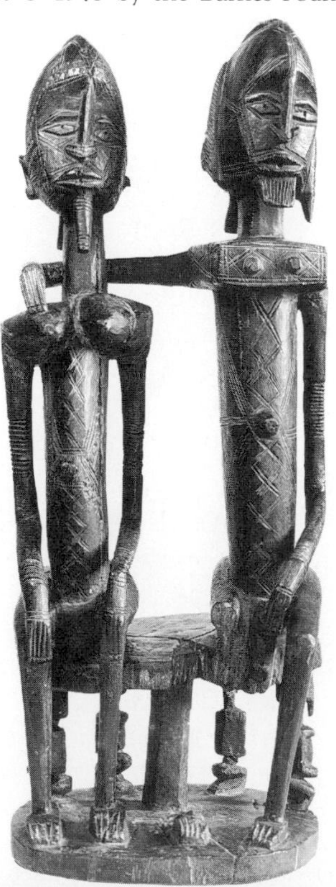

artist to work in such a schematic style. In any case, the group remains one of the great monuments of African creative genius, a strong and complex statement about human values—indeed, about the very origins of the human race itself.

Recent research among the Baule people of the Ivory Coast has led to new information regarding the male and female figures so popular in European and American private and public collections. Figures that represent spirit "marriage partners" (*blolo bla,* the male, and *blolo bia,* the female) differ neither formally nor conceptually from figures that represent wild bush spirits (*asie usu*). The main distinction is found in the surface. The asie usu (FIG. **14-58**) have a "sacrificial patina"—a surface thickly encrusted with matter accumulated when they are "fed" during sacrificial ritual; the spirit "marriage partners," on the other

14-58 *Wild Bush Spirit,* Baule, from the Ivory Coast, nineteenth to twentieth century. Wood, male figure approx. 22″ high. Metropolitan Museum of Art, New York (Michael C. Rockefeller Memorial Collection of Primitive Art, gift of Nelson A. Rockefeller, 1969).

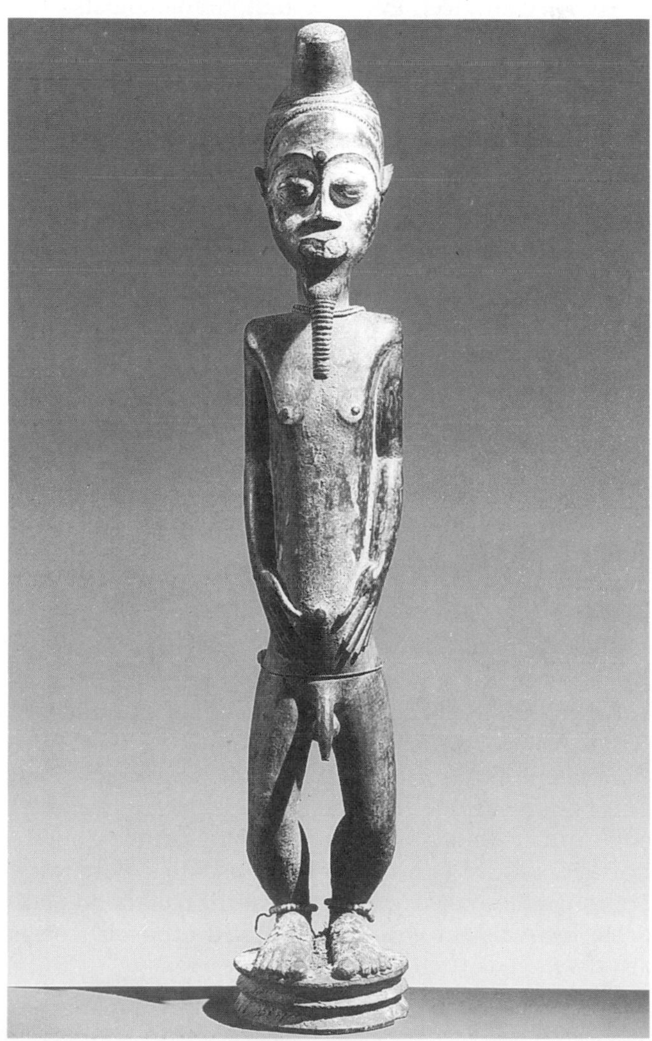

hand, are rubbed and polished, so that, in time, they acquire a smooth and shiny surface.

African arts also include beautifully decorated, utilitarian objects such as stools, chairs, pipes, and spoons; a host of sculptural as well as decorated buildings; body painting and scarification; miniature objects, such as the well-known Ashanti gold weights; finely crafted textiles and leatherwork; and countless forms of pottery and basketry. Subdivision of the arts into "fine," "decorative," and "craft" is a barrier to the understanding of African artistic sensibilities, for African arts often play a role in everyday affairs, as well as in the life-crisis rituals (initiations, funerals, and the countless other events) that punctuate human existence.

OCEANIA

Relative to the abundant records associated with Western art, only a vague chronology can be established for the arts of Oceania in the absence of documentary evidence, even though archeologists, linguists, and others have gone far in sorting out migration routes, language and racial distributions, and early aspects of Stone Age technology and social organization.

The thousands of islands that make up Oceania conventionally are divided into three cultural areas: Polynesia, Melanesia, and Micronesia. Polynesia was the last area in the world to be settled. Its inhabitants seem to have brought complex sociopolitical and religious institutions with them, and a general homogeneity of style (lacking in Melanesia) characterizes much Polynesian art, despite the relative isolation of various island groups during the several centuries prior to European exploration. Polynesian societies typically are aristocratic, with ritual specialists and elaborate political organizations headed by chiefs. Polynesian art forms often serve as a means of upholding spiritual power *(mana),* which is vested in the nobility and channeled by ancestral and state cults.

Melanesia certainly was settled early, and its art forms seem to suggest a variety of overlays of style and symbolism brought with a series of migrations. Art styles are numerous and extremely varied. Typical Melanesian societies are more democratic than Polynesian societies and relatively unstratified. Their cults and art forms address a host of legendary ancestral and nature spirits. Masks, absent in Polynesia, are central in many Melanesian spirit cults, and elaborate festivals, in which masks and other art forms are displayed, occur with some frequency.

Micronesia, in contrast to the other two areas, has little visual material and will not be discussed. The rich arts of Australia, though quite distinct from those of other areas, often are included in discussions of Oceanic art and will be mentioned briefly here.

Polynesia

Polynesian artists excelled in carving figural sculptures in wood, stone, and ivory in sizes that range from the gigantic fabled stone images of Easter Island to tiny ivory Marquesan ear plugs an inch long. These sculptures were generally full-volumed, monochromatic human figures, often dynamic in pose. Polynesians also were adept at making decorative bark cloth, called *tapa,* and the art of tattooing was highly developed (the word *tattoo* is of Polynesian origin).

Polynesian carving at its most dramatic is represented by the Hawaiian figure of the war god, *Kukailimoku* (FIG. **14-59**). Huge wooden images of this deity were erected on stone temple platforms that, in varied forms, were part of the apparatus of all Polynesian state religions. Although relatively small, the figure illustrated here is majestic in scale and forcefully carved to convey vigorous tensions; in short, the form possesses much of the ferocity attributed to the

14-59 *Kukailimoku,* from Hawaii. Wood, 30" high. British Museum, London.

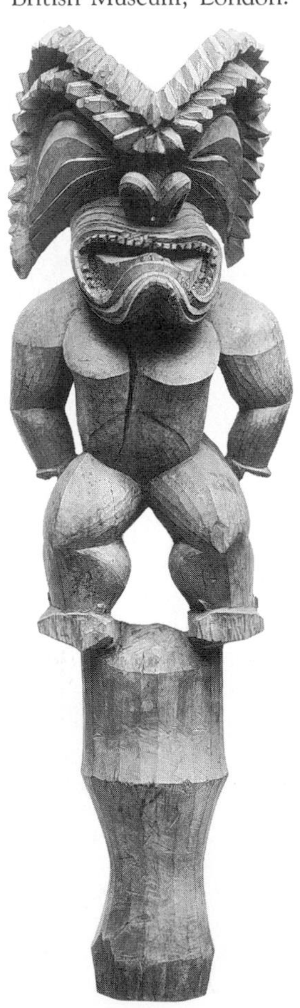

deity. Flexed limbs and faceted, conventionalized muscles combine with the aggressive, flaring mouth and serrated headdress to achieve a tense dynamism seldom rivaled in any art. This carving is the work of a master sculptor supremely confident with respect to materials and technique—a work that speaks forcefully across cultural barriers.

Even though Polynesians were skillful navigators, various island groups remained sufficiently isolated from one another to allow distinct regional styles to develop within a recognizable, general Polynesian style. Thus, the arts of central Polynesia, represented here by the contrasting art forms of a wooden *District God* (FIG. **14-60**) and a skeletalized, double-headed male figure from Easter Island (FIG. **14-61**), are quite different from the Hawaiian figures. The highly polished *District God* from the Cook Islands (FIG. 14-60) has a blade-shaped head and schematized features. Instead of a body, numerous tiny, abstracted figures—the god's progeny—are carved in the same geometric, angular style as the head above. Such carvings probably represented clan ancestors, revered for their protective and procreative powers. Analogous images from Mangaia in the Cook Islands and Rurutu in the Austral Islands also have multiple figures attached to their bodies. All such images refer ultimately to creator deities, who are revered for their central role in human fertility. The double-headed male figure (FIG. 14-61) may represent a mythological ancestor or deity of the early inhabitants of Easter Island. Its bent posture and the emphasis on skeletal structure reflect an esthetic quite different from that of the massively aggressive sculpture of the Hawaiian war god (FIG. 14-59).

Polynesians developed the painful but prestigious art of tattoo more fully than other Oceanic peoples. Nobles and warriors, especially, were concerned with increasing their status, mana, and personal beauty by accumulating various tattoo patterns over the years. An early nineteenth-century engraving (FIG. **14-62**) shows Marquesan tattoo patterns, with divided and subdivided geometric motifs covering most of the

14-60 *Below left: District God,* from the Cook Islands, nineteenth century. Wood, approx. 25″ high. Peabody Museum, Harvard University, Cambridge, Massachusetts.

14-61 *Below right:* Double-headed male figure (*moai kava-kava*), from Easter Island, before 1860. Wood, approx. 16″ high. Museum of Natural History, La Rochelle, France.

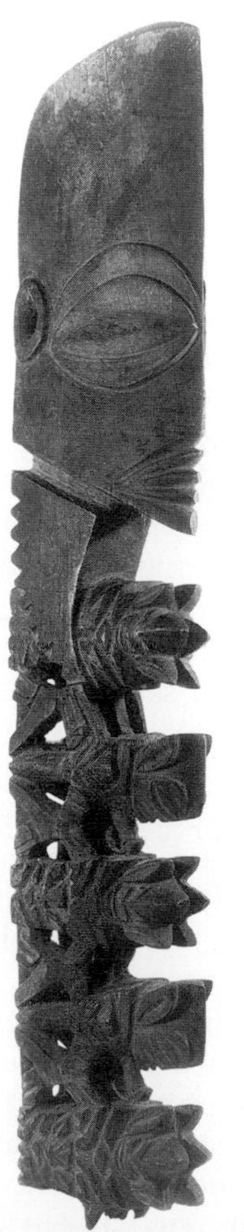

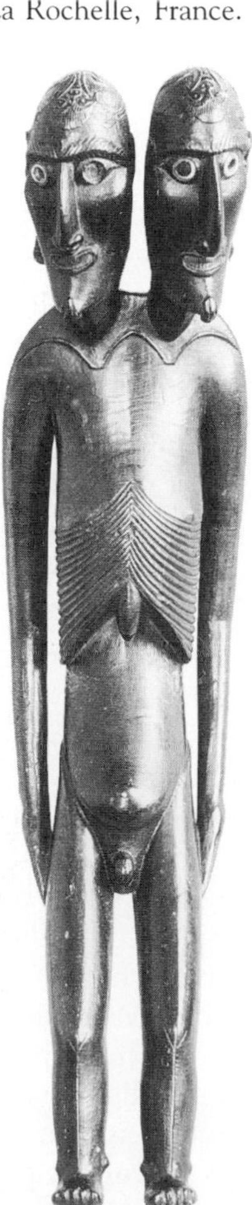

14-62 Tattooed Marquesan warrior, nineteenth century. Engraving.

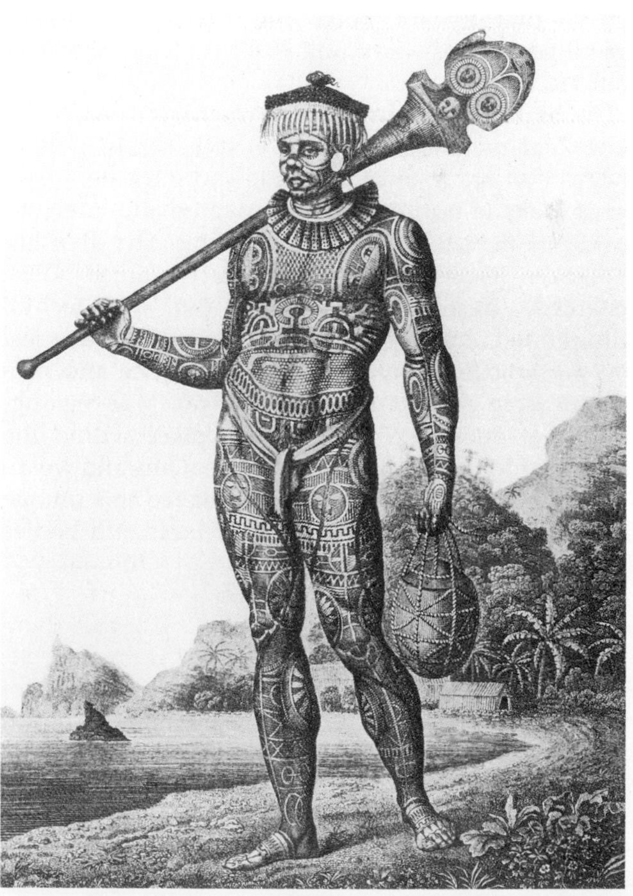

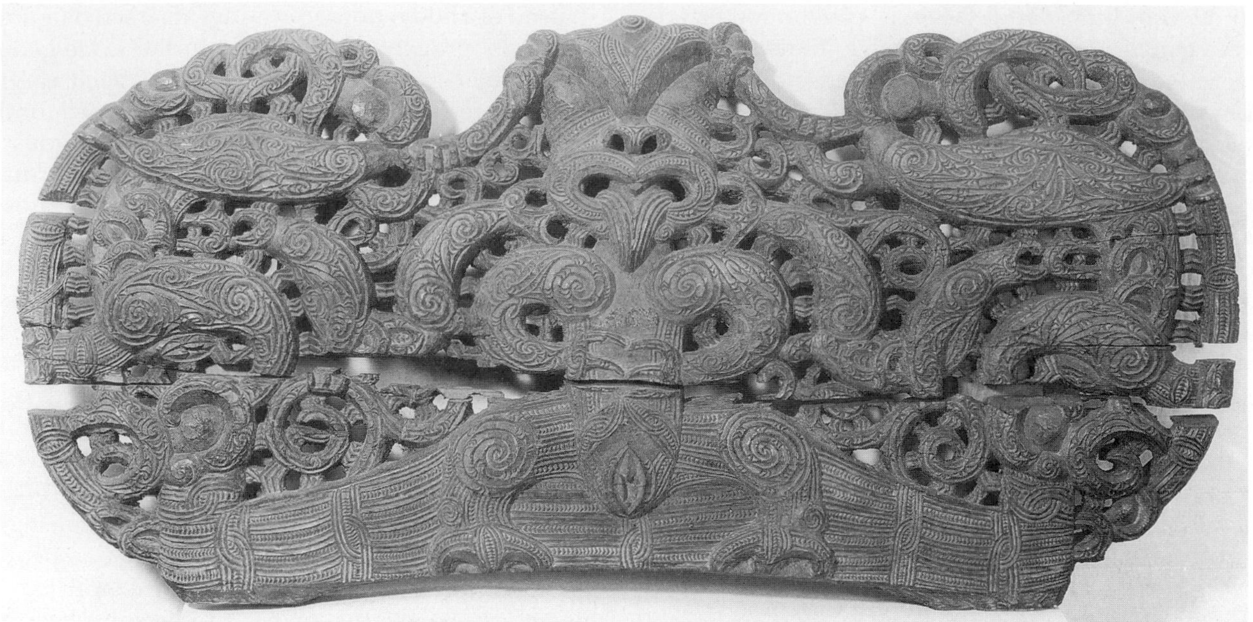

14-63 Door lintel, Maori, from New Zealand, late nineteenth century. Wood, 19″ × 45″. Peabody Museum of Salem, Massachusetts.

body. Such a multiplication of small, repetitive, abstract forms (a feature also seen in the "children" on the Cook Islands figure [FIG. 14-60]) is one major tendency in much Polynesian art. The other main tendency—that toward bold, full-volume, large-scale figural sculptures—is manifest in the Hawaiian war god (FIG. 14-59).

The highly distinctive arts of the Maori peoples of New Zealand merge these two stylistic currents in images that are at once dynamic and intricate; major forms are bold but surfaces are covered and interconnected by minute curvilinear detailing. The door lintel shown (FIG. **14-63**) comes from a council house generously decorated, inside and out, with technically refined, complex imagery. The subjects are real and mythological ancestors, whose advice and protection were sought for the political, war-making, and ritual deliberations that took place within the council structure. Countless prestige items and weapons used by the Maori nobility displayed this unique style, as did the tattooing on their faces and bodies (Introduction, FIG. 15).

Melanesia

Despite the aggressive poses of the figural art of Hawaii and the lively surface convolutions found in the art of New Zealand, Polynesian art generally is characterized by compactness, solidity, and restraint, as exemplified in the Cook Islands *District God* (FIG. 14-60). Melanesian art, on the other hand, has an insubstantial, colorful, flamboyant aspect, epitomized in wood carvings from New Ireland (FIG. **14-64**). The bewildering intricacy of the New Ireland wood carvings called *malanggan,* which are used in display ceremonies of the same name, stems from generous use of openwork and sliverlike projections and from over-painting in minute geometric patterns that further subdivide the image. The result is a "splintered" or fragmented and airy effect. This style is even more remarkable in view of the fact that most of these forms are carved from a single block of wood (a characteristic of all of the woodcarving considered in this chapter). In the dramatic scene shown, several malanggan showpieces are set up in a special house that was opened to the public; the associated rituals served both to commemorate ancestors and to initiate youths into adulthood. Dancers wearing a variety of intricate masks also performed during these rites.

The Melanesian penchant for color and drama in art is reflected too in the Abelam cult sculptures and paintings found on (and inside) the monumental Men's Houses in New Guinea (FIG. **14-65**). Rows of mythological creatures, intricately painted in contrasting bright colors, are portrayed in the gable paintings on these buildings. This kind of repetition and almost compulsive space-filling are common to the native arts.

In other Melanesian art forms from the Papuan Gulf and Asmat areas of New Guinea's south coast, the artists distort human forms according to local preferences, which here, as elsewhere, are not at all attuned to realistic proportions or modeling. The fact that remote spirits (Papuan Gulf, FIG. **14-66**) and

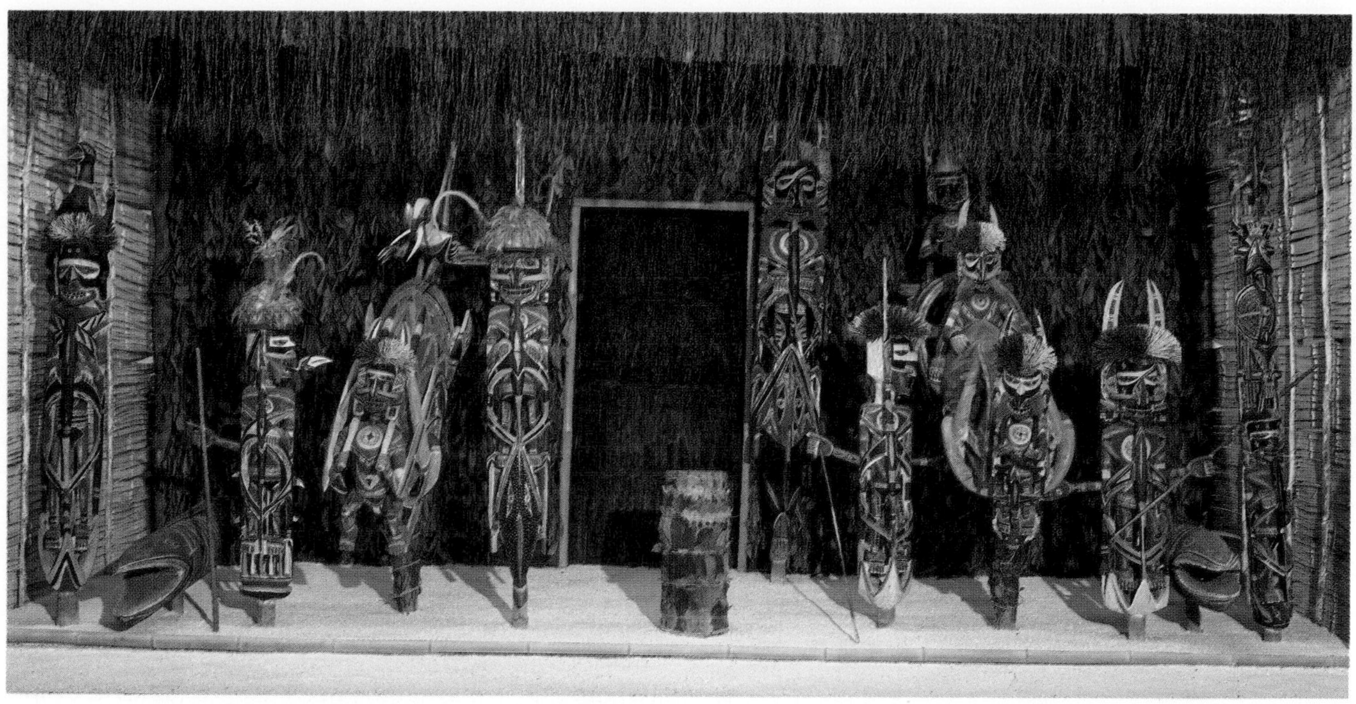

14-64 Malanggan tableau, from New Ireland, nineteenth to twentieth century. Bamboo, palm and croton leaves, painted wood, approx. 8′ high, 16′ 6″ wide, 10′ deep. Museum für Völkerkunde, Basel, Switzerland.

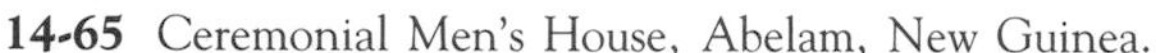

14-65 Ceremonial Men's House, Abelam, New Guinea.

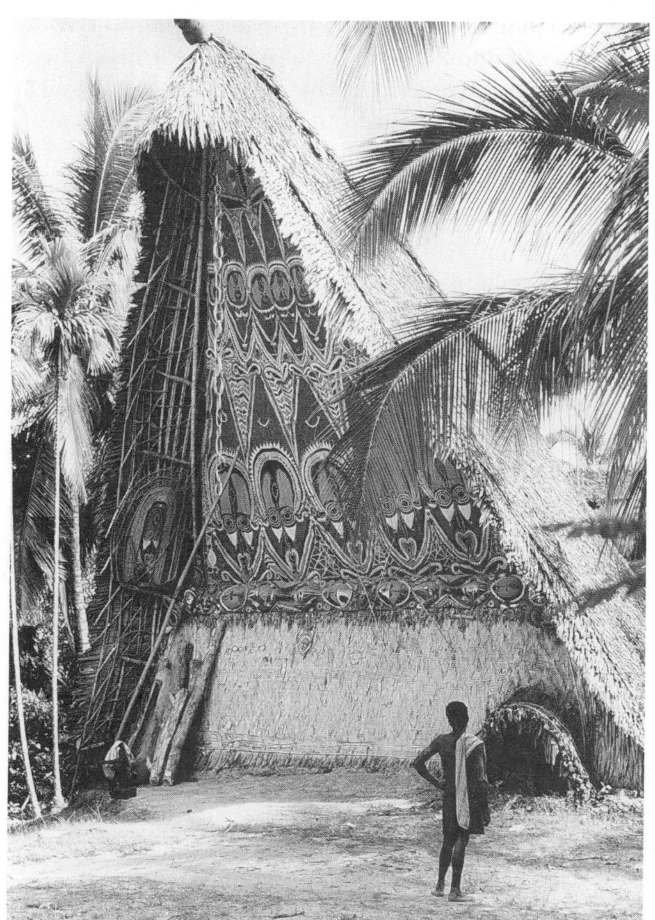

14-66 Spirit figure, from the Papuan Gulf, New Guinea. Wood, fibers, bark, red and white paint, 51″ long. Tropenmuseum, Amsterdam, Netherlands.

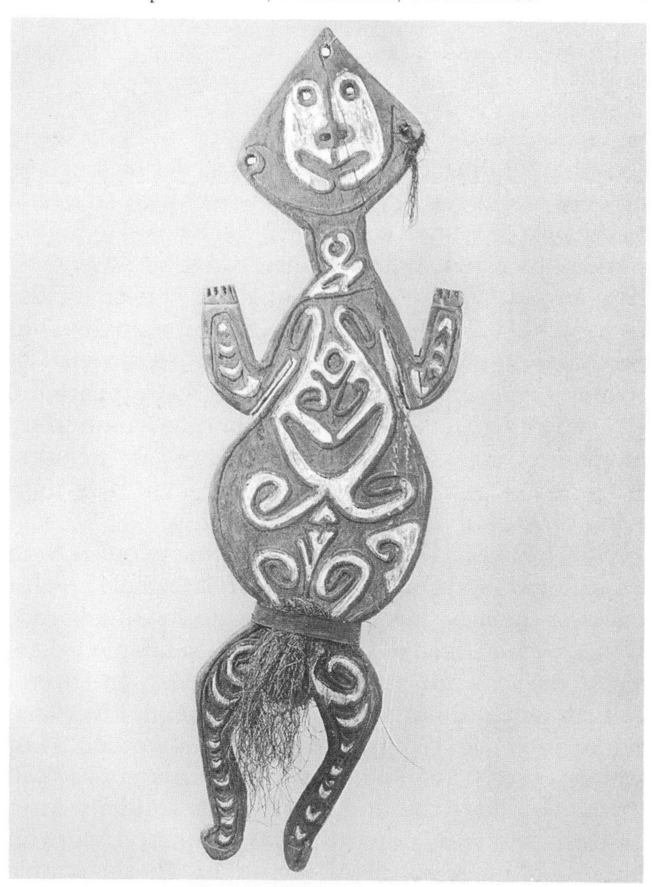

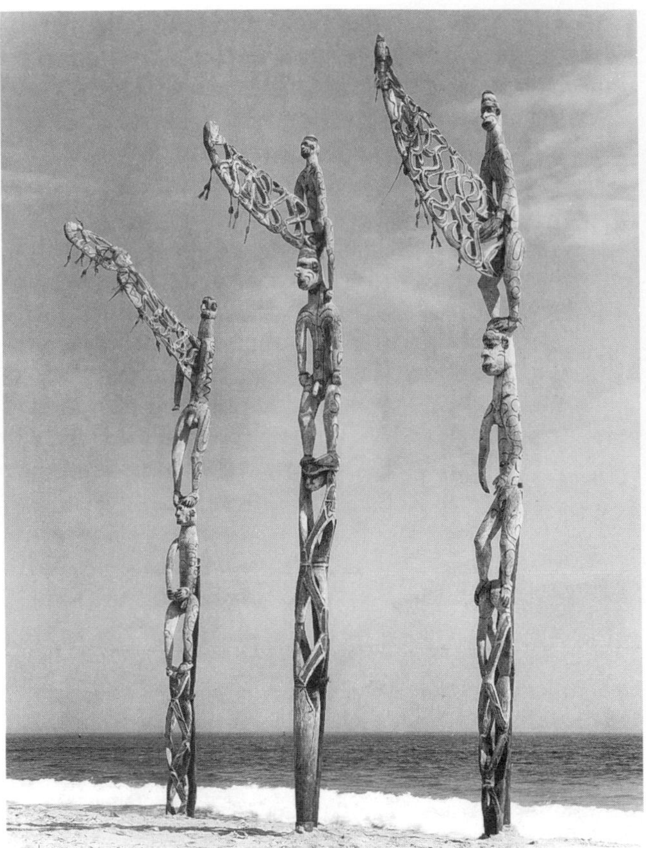

14-67 Ancestral poles, Asmat, from New Guinea, 1960. Wood, paint, sago palm leaves, approx. 18′ high. Metropolitan Museum of Art, New York.

ancestors (Asmat, FIG. **14-67**) are portrayed partially accounts for the lack of naturalism, as do the long traditions of repeating and renewing such spiritual images—a repetition that seems to give rise to highly conventionalized styles in conservative societies. The Papuan Gulf figure is a Melanesian version of the power image, whose in-dwelling spirit is invoked to protect and otherwise benefit the figure's owner. The Asmat pole is erected in ceremonies that prepare the participants to avenge the death of a community member in war. The openwork "flags" are penises, exaggerated in a reflection of the Asmat male's aggressive roles in sex and head-hunting.

The Asmat and many other Oceanic peoples were headhunters until early in the twentieth century, and many of their art forms were created for rituals concerned with head-hunting and attendant beliefs about the loss and gain of the life-force. In several cultures, including the Iatmul of the Sepik River, artists cleaned actual human skulls and reworked them into art objects (FIG. **14-68**) by modeling over the skull with a claylike paste and painting the resultant form with the kinds of flowing facial decoration worn in life, particularly on ritual occasions. These graphic images (a fascinating parallel to the "reconstructed" prehistoric skulls found at Jericho, FIG. 2-2) were believed to contain the life-force or power that men sought to increase by head-hunting; the heads were displayed in ceremonies preparing for war or celebrating its success, as well as at funerals.

Face and body decoration are still important art forms in several parts of New Guinea. Although of course extremely transient, such embellishments can be highly complex, colorful, multimedia assemblages of pigments, feathers, fur, leaves, shells, and other materials, which gain both symbolic significance and artistic impact from their combination. Men and women decorate themselves in this fashion to display their idealized beauty and to compete with rivals similarly embellished.

Varied types and styles of masks were worn in Iatmul ceremonies, as well as in ceremonies conducted by the peoples of New Britain, New Ireland, Abelam, the Papuan Gulf, Asmat, and other areas. These masks were used in ceremonies to materialize spirits whom the people felt the need to entertain and propitiate (uses similar to those for which masks were employed in Africa and the Americas). Elaborate festivals sometimes included over a hundred such "spirit impersonators," who danced to amuse the human community and, at the same time, to remind it of its obligations to supernatural ancestors and culture-bringers. Many of the same masked spirits played an important role in initiating and educating youths to be fully socialized, productive members of the group. Melanesian artists seem to have given free rein to their creativity and imagination, especially in

14-68 Skull, Iatmul, from New Guinea, nineteenth to twentieth century. Human skull, clay, paint, human hair, cuscus fur, 10″ high. Metropolitan Museum of Art, New York (gift of Mr. and Mrs. John J. Klijman).

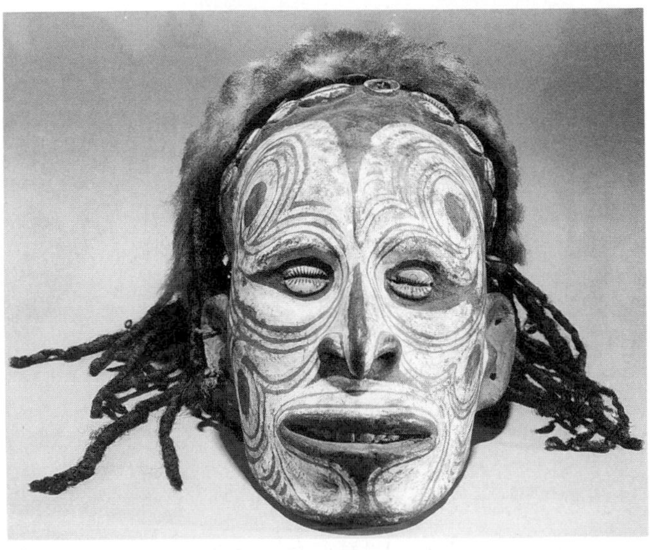

the design of the heads and bodies of spirits. A bizarre, flamboyant Sulka mask (FIG. **14-69**) is but one example of a type of mask made by stretching and sewing vegetable fibers over a light framework. These and other Melanesian masks were quite perishable; indeed, in some areas, the masks were destroyed ritually at the end of a ceremony, an act that banished the spirits until their next "invitation" to intervene in human affairs.

Some Melanesian styles, like that of the Solomon Islands, are more restrained than those just discussed. In the canoe-prow carving shown here (FIG. **14-70**), which served both practical and spiritual purposes of protection, the emphasis is on strong modeling, the enlargement of facial features, and very precise inlay patterns of seashell fragments that contrast with the solid dark color of the head itself. In several Melanesian areas, styles combine high-contrast, intricate surface patterns with bold sculpture. In some other areas, masks are not used, suggesting that these may be transitional cultures between those in which the wilder, less restrained Melanesian style prevails and those in which the more restrained Polynesian style, with its more solid, full-volumed sculpture, is dominant.

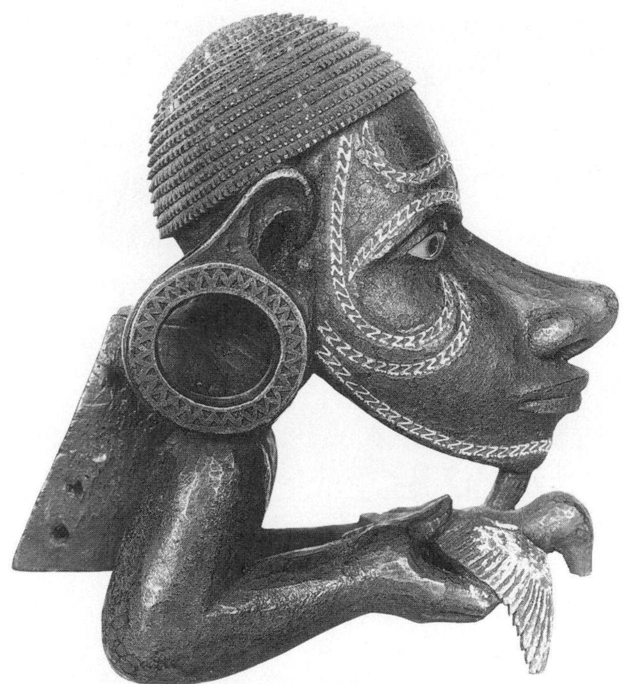

14-70 Canoe-prow figure, from the Solomon Islands, Melanesia, nineteenth to twentieth century. Wood with mother-of-pearl, 6½″ high. Museum für Völkerkunde und Schweizerisches Museum für Völkskunde, Basel, Switzerland.

14-69 Mask, Sulka, from Melanesia, 1900–1910. Fiber structure covered with pith, feathers, and pieces of wood, 27″ high (without leaf skirt). Übersee-Museum, Bremen, West Germany.

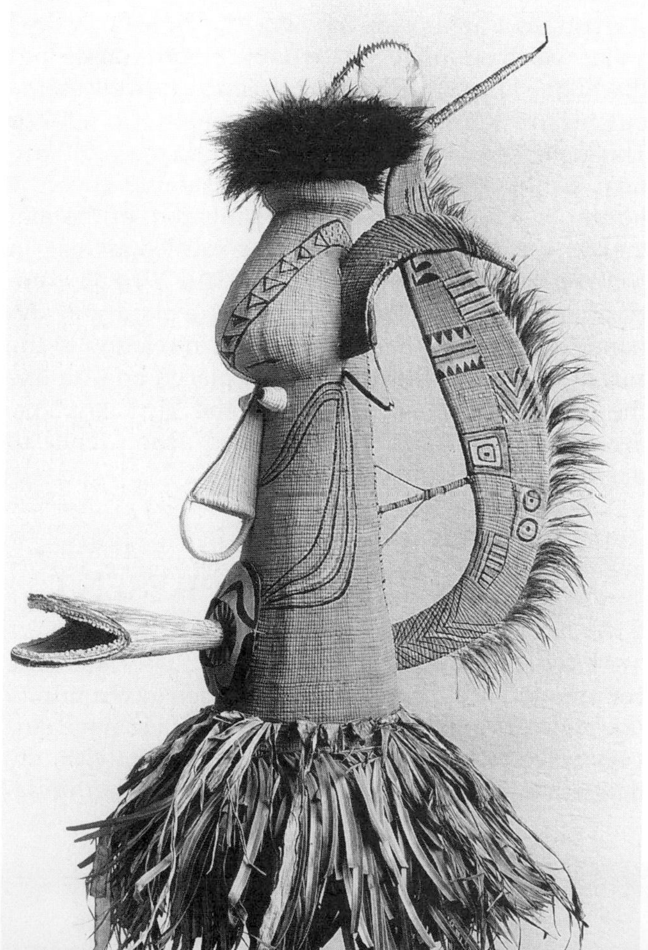

Australia

In Australia, a number of styles and object types bear little relationship to the arts of neighboring New Guinea. Most objects are ceremonial aids used to project the Australian people into the legendary past (Dream Time), when their world, its creatures, and its institutions were created. For the native Australian, the fertility of nature and humanity and the continuity of life itself depended on reenactments of the primordial events of the Dream Time. Cosmogonic myths were recited in concert with songs and dances, and many art forms (body painting, carved figures, decorated stones, rock and bark paintings) were essential props in these dramatic re-creations. A bark painting by MUNGARAWAI, entitled *The Djanggawul Sisters* (FIG. **14-71**), describes, in schematic form, the birth of the human race, along with other mythical episodes from the Dream Time. The Djanggawul sisters and brothers were the mythological progenitors of the Yirrkala people of Arnhem Land, a region on the north coast of Australia in the Northern Territory. Symbolic motifs include trees and pole emblems, the rising and setting sun, a Djanggawul brother, and (top right) the artist himself. The intricate style is representative of the main features of Yirrkala art: rhythmic repetition, subdivision into crowded panels, fine detailing, and lack of a ground line, perspective, or modeling.

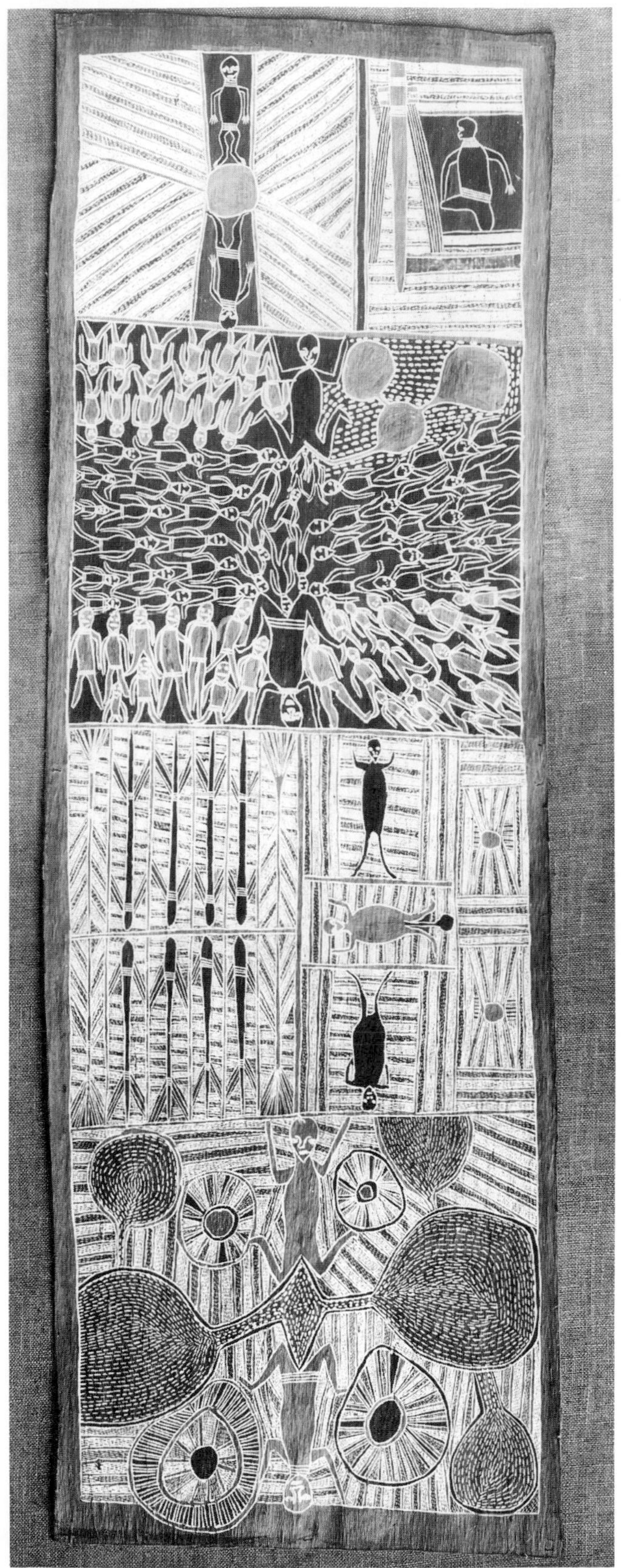

14-71 MUNGARAWAI, *The Djanggawul Sisters,* Yirrkala, from Arnhem Land, Australia. Bark and paint. Art Gallery of New South Wales, Australia.

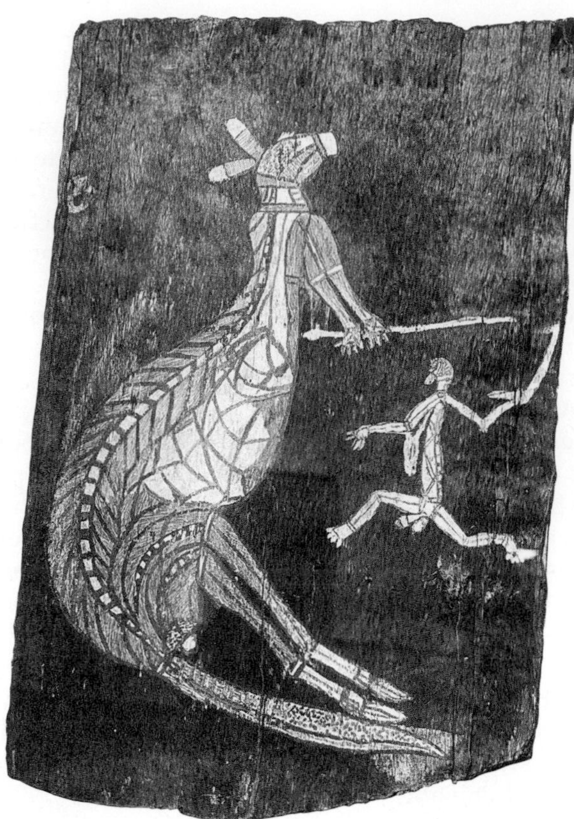

14-72 *Hunter and Kangaroo,* Oenpelli, from Arnhem Land, Australia, *c.* 1913. Paint on bark, 51″ × 32″. National Museum of Victoria, Melbourne, Australia.

Australian art is well known, too, for its "x-ray" style, which simultaneously depicts both the insides (backbone, heart, and other organs) as well as the outsides of human beings and animals (FIG. **14-72**). This style of painting is common to the area of Arnhem Land called Oenpelli. Our example shows a hunter and his quarry, a black kangaroo, at the moment a spear is about to strike the startled animal. In contrast to the rather static order of the Yirrkala composition, the Oenpelli painting has a fluid and dynamic quality. The figures are large in relation to the surface on which they have been placed and, unlike the distant, "bird's-eye" view of the Yirrkala painting, the immediacy of the depicted action tends to draw the viewer into its orbit.

AFTERWORD: THE PRESENT

At the beginning of this chapter, we noted the community of the native arts; that such a community does exist is apparent from the works we have surveyed. Despite the differences in regional styles, the native arts exhibit general agreement on the fundamentals of form and content. The almost exclusive motive and theme of art is religion, with all its symbols and ceremonials. The native arts have kinship with the religious art of many other cultural communities—India, Islam, East Asia, medieval Europe—in reinforcing this emphasis.

Of course, important differences do exist. Aside from the Mesoamerican and central Andean cultures, planned urban complexes, monumental architecture and sculpture in durable materials, mural painting, and other media are not, with some exceptions, conspicuous in the program of the native arts, nor primarily characteristic of them. These omissions by no means diminish the esthetic value of the native arts, their power of expression, nor the fascination with which we now can regard them.

Many of the traditional arts of the Native Americans and the Eskimo, of Africa, Oceania, and Australia are not now being practiced, for they no longer have critical roles in cultural continuity and survival. Ironically, only now, at a time when most of them no longer may be accessible to be appreciated and preserved, are we coming to acknowledge the variety and richness of the native traditions.

Yet an echo of these traditions persists in "folk art," the art that is made by unsophisticated, untaught, or self-taught persons as a kind of abstract version of the once dominant art of their societies. The native arts, on the other hand, predominate in their cultures. They are the products of trained, highly skilled professionals, who work in traditional styles and techniques that fully express the beliefs, ideals, and customs of their peoples. The patrons of the native artists are the powers that rule the society: kings and priests, nobility and merchants. Folk artists have no such official, privileged status, just as they have none of the specialized competence of the native artists whose forms they approximate. Folk art, existing as a substyle, can come into view when great traditions have been broken down or are exhausted. When this happens, we find that folk art does share some fundamental principles of design and representation with the native art of all times and places.

A contemporary example, a figured textile produced in Pakistan and offered for sale in an Islamabad bazaar, presents the recent Soviet war in Afghanistan with only a few representative objects (FIG. **14-73**). Their elegantly simplified shapes are linear, flat, and vividly colored. Silhouetted against monochrome ground and placed on superposed levels, the figures are painted in the mode of representation that we find in ancient Egyptian painting (FIG. 3-36), the Bayeux Tapestry (FIG. 9-35), the murals of Bonampak (FIG. 14-11), and the Crow tepee lining (FIG. 14-40). They distantly echo the style of Islamic book illumination (FIG.7-85). And the ironic contrast of old and new warfare, the Afghan horsemen and the Soviet helicopter, could hardly be a more poignant comment on the fatal impact of alien force upon native peoples.

In the faint replication of it in folk art, native art continues to live. Its vitality lies in the undying human instinct and capacity for making art that dramatizes and intensifies life itself. For native peoples, life without art was unknown.

14-73 *Horsemen and Helicopters,* from Islamabad, Pakistan, 1987. Fringed textile. (Courtesy of Mr. Todd Disotell.)

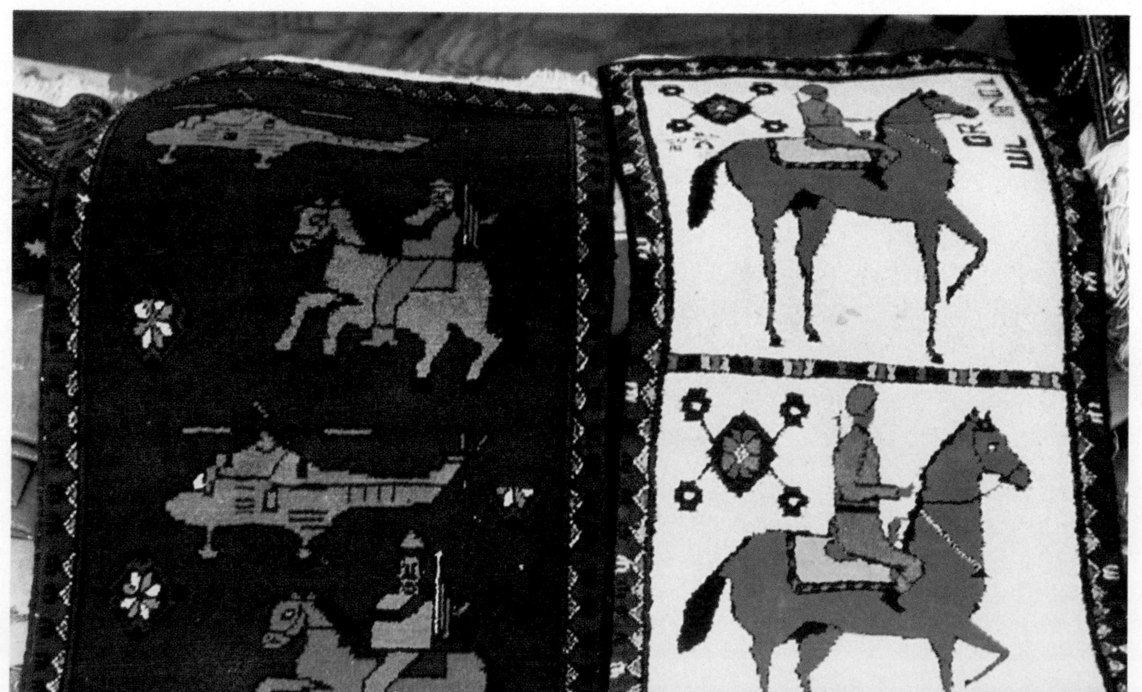

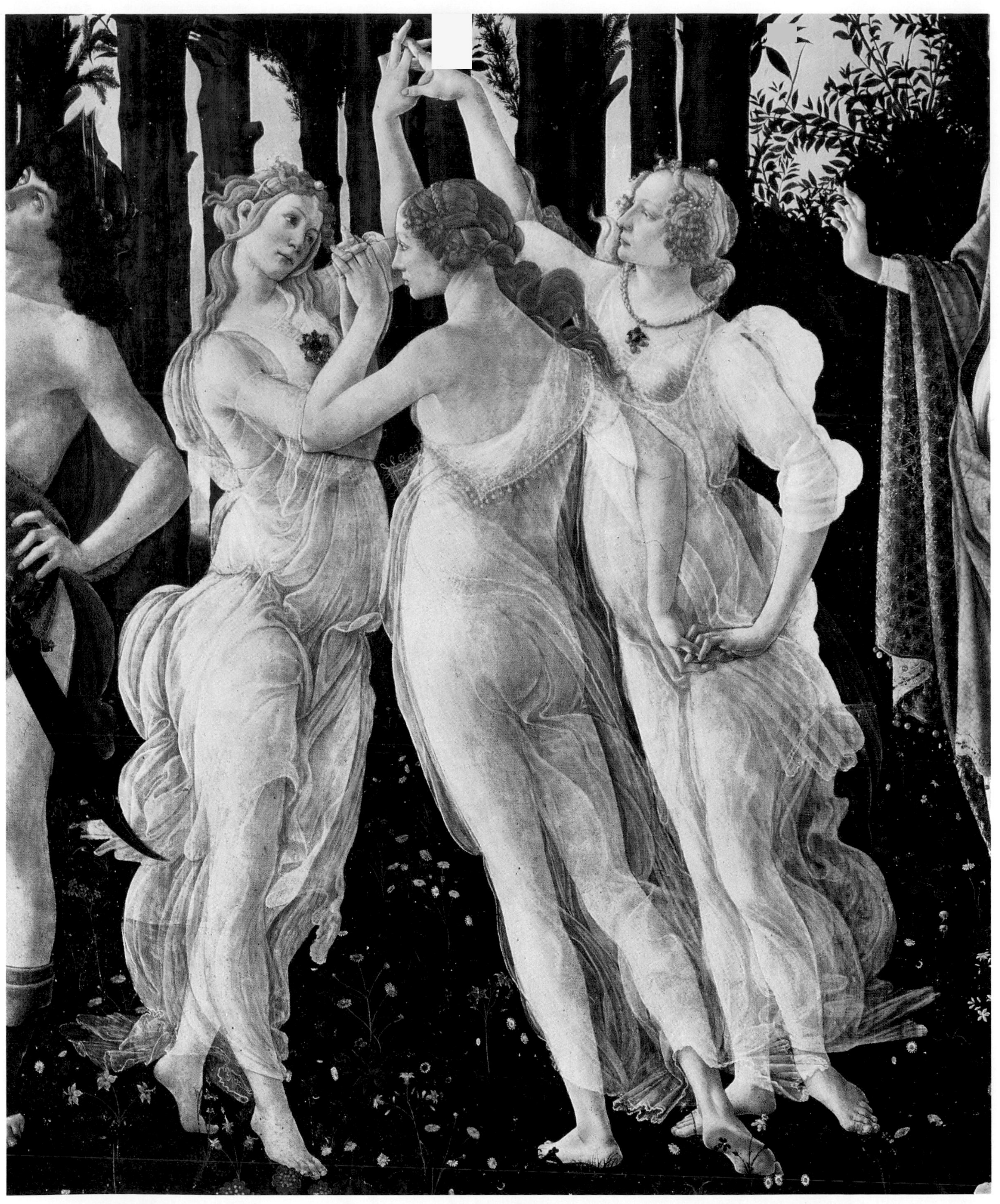

The new spirit of the Renaissance, a flowering of love for nature and human beauty, enlivens a detail of Botticelli's *La Primavera,* painted in the last quarter of the fifteenth century.

IV

THE RENAISSANCE AND THE BAROQUE AND ROCOCO

The Medieval period once was regarded as a thousand dark and empty years separating the "good" eras of classical antiquity and modern times; the Renaissance was thought of as "early modern." But beginning in the nineteenth century, a more cosmopolitan and tolerant taste and a more discerning and accurate historical method readjusted this view, and today the Middle Ages are no longer so "dark" as once depicted. In the same way, the Renaissance (rebirth), spanning roughly the fourteenth through the sixteenth centuries, no longer seems to be the abrupt onset of the modern era, suddenly shining forth in the fifteenth century to illuminate medieval darkness with the rekindled light of classical antiquity. Much of the Renaissance has its roots in epochs that long preceded the Middle Ages, and much that is medieval continues in the Renaissance and even in later periods. Since the mid-nineteenth century, when Jacob Burckhardt wrote his influential and still highly valuable work, *The Civilization of the Renaissance in Italy*, the precise dividing line between the Middle Ages and the Renaissance and the question of whether a Renaissance ever actually took place have been disputed. Without reopening these issues, it may be useful to examine those characteristics of the Renaissance that seem to have matured and to have become influential during the period from the fourteenth through the sixteenth centuries, even though they originated during the Middle Ages.

Medieval feudalism, with its patchwork of baronial jurisdictions and sprawling, inefficient local governments, yielded slowly to the competition of strong cities and city-states, which increasingly were in league with powerful kings, both being the natural political enemies of the countryside barons. The outlines of the modern state, with its centralized administrations, organized armies, aggressive expansionism, and "realistic" politics, began to firm up at about this time. The discovery of the world outside Europe—especially the Western Hemisphere and Africa, itself so dramatically expressive of Renaissance expansiveness—brought vast treasures of gold and silver into Europe, beginning its transformation into a money economy (a process already begun in the thirteenth century in the commercial cities of Italy). Religion increasingly came under the direction of the clergy of the cities. Particularly influential were the members of the Dominican and the Franciscan orders. The claims of the popes to temporal as well as spiritual supremacy were surrendered, and they became merely splendid Italian princes. Eventually, with the upheaval of the Protestant Reformation, which fractured medieval religious unity, religion became almost a branch of the state, with kings and princes in control of its secular manifestations. Dramatic events in science, like Nicolaus Copernicus's enunciation of the heliocentric theory of the solar system, set the stage for the development of the first successful empirical science—mathematical physics. The opening of the heavens to the scrutiny of scientific investigation was attended by the renewed physical exploration of the globe and, until recently, by the increasing subjugation of it to the will of Europe. Technological advances in navigation, metallurgy, mechanics, and warfare helped greatly to that end.

The religious fanaticism that had launched the Crusades, Europe's first extended contact with non-European civilizations, was replaced during the Renaissance by motives of calculated economic interest mingled with the genuine and fruitful curiosity of the explorer. Indeed, the Renaissance was precisely what it often has been called—an "age of discovery"—when Europe saw before it an almost fantastic realm of possibility open to all those of merit who could perceive it.

Accompanying the great events that quite clearly set the Middle Ages and the Renaissance apart were subtler changes of human attitude. Emphasis slowly was turned away from the ideas and values of a supernatural orientation and toward those concerned with the natural world and human life. The meaning of these new concerns came to be couched in terms that were not exclusively religious. The spirit and dogma of medieval religion, and even its emotional color, were modified as the worldly philosophy of the Greco-Roman tradition revived and took on new strength. But the process of humanization had begun well before the full influence of the pagan tradition was felt; humanizing tendencies began to appear in the twelfth century. In the thirteenth century, the teachings of St. Francis had humanized religion itself and had called attention to the beauty of the world and of all things in it. Even though St. Francis understood the physical beauty he celebrated as a manifestation of the spiritual, his emphasis, nevertheless, was clear, and the Franciscan message calls attention to the God-made beauties of the natural order. This message had special significance for the naturalism of proto-Renaissance art. In the Middle Ages, the focus of life was to procure the salvation of one's immortal soul through the sacred offices of the Church. In the Renaissance, however, though the obligation and concern remained and the institutions of the Church retained power, nature and the relations among human beings simply became *more interesting* than theological questions. Theology, like institutional Christianity, persisted, as did fervent Christian devotion. But these elements were affected by a new spirit—the spirit of pagan humanism—which curiously joined with and reinforced the Christian humanism of St. Francis. The intellectual and artistic history of the modern world is as much the history of Christianity's reaction to this new spirit as it is a history of the challenge of that spirit to Christianity. Actually, the challenge and the reaction interacted, modifying each other. The dialogue between the late Greco-Roman world and nascent Christianity commenced again in the Renaissance; since that time, it has been supplemented and amplified by other, even stronger voices, especially those of modern science.

Whereas the veritable face and body of the human being emerged in the transition from Romanesque to Gothic sculpture, Renaissance art brings

Western humanity rapidly into full view—a phenomenon that resembles the manifestation of the human figure in Greek art during the sixth and fifth centuries B.C. The Renaissance stresses the importance of the individual, especially individuals of merit. In life and in art, the focus is sharpened. At last, individuals are real and solid; they cast a shadow. During the Middle Ages, people saw themselves as corrupt and feeble of will, capable of acting only by the agency of God's grace. Although many thinkers, both Protestant and Catholic, insisted on this view for centuries, the Renaissance view is different: individuals may create themselves. They are assumed to have a power of agency—God-given, to be sure—that, in the greatest of achievers, becomes the divine gift of "genius." Thus, in the Renaissance, those who think may overcome the curse of original sin and, in so doing, rise above its devastating load of guilt to make themselves, if they will, what they will. In his *Oration on the Dignity of Man* (the very title of which constitutes a bold new claim), Giovanni Pico della Mirandola, an ingenious and daring Renaissance philosopher, represents God giving the following permission to every human being in a way that reflects a sharp departure from the medieval sense of humanity's natural helplessness:

> The nature of all other beings is limited and constrained within the bounds of laws prescribed by Us. Thou, constrained by no limits, in accordance with thine own free will . . . shalt ordain for thyself the limits of thy nature. We have set thee at the world's center . . . and have made thee neither of heaven nor of earth, neither mortal nor immortal, so that with freedom of choice and with honor . . . thou mayest fashion thyself in whatever shape thou shalt prefer.*

This option would have been almost unthinkable in the Middle Ages. Could one really aspire beyond the angels or debase oneself below the beasts and inanimate nature, given one's place in the carefully articulated "chain of being" that God had made permanent?

Whether or not one could indeed so rise or fall, the leaders of the Renaissance were acutely aware of the new possibilities open to their talents and did not fail to recognize, and often advertise, the powers they were confident they possessed. The wide versatility of many Renaissance artists, men like Alberti, Brunelleschi, Leonardo da Vinci and Michelangelo, led them to experimentation and to achievement in many of the arts and sciences. Their accomplishments gave substance to that concept of the archetypal Renaissance genius—*l'uomo universale* (the universal man). Class distinctions and social hierarchies had loosened, and the ambitious and talented now could take their places even as the friends, companions, and advisers of princes. Such persons could win the award of everlasting fame, and what has been called the "cult of fame" went naturally with the new glorification of individual genius. Indeed, the immortality won through fame may have been more coveted by many great men of the time than the spiritual immortality promised by religion. When the painter Fra Filippo Lippi died in 1469, the town of Spoleto requested that it be allowed to keep his remains. The town fathers argued that Florence, his native city, already had many celebrated men buried within the bounds of its walls.

Petrarch, the great Italian poet and scholar of the fourteenth century, who may be said to have first propounded those peculiarly Renaissance values of versatile individualism and humanism nourished by the study of classical antiquity, has been called the high priest of the "cult of fame" and, by many, the founder of the Renaissance. Petrarch himself was crowned with the ancient symbol of triumph and fame, the laurel wreath, on the Capitoline Hill

*Giovanni Pico della Mirandola, *Oratio de hominis dignitate* (1485), trans. by E. L. Forbes, in Ernst Cassirer et al., eds., *The Renaissance Philosophy of Man* (Chicago: University of Chicago Press, 1956), pp. 224–25.

in Rome; the occasion was a celebration of his superb sonnets (written in native Italian), which opened the age of Renaissance literature. Petrarch, in his development of the "cult of fame," postulated that public recognition never is given to an unworthy work of talent and that, therefore, public glory is proof of excellence. After Petrarch, it would be possible to call both great works and great men "divine," as if they belonged to a kind of religious congregation of a new elect; thus it was with *La Divina Commedia* of Dante and with Michelangelo after his death.

Petrarch's eager acceptance of a new concept of Humanism encouraged the resurrection of the spirit of classical antiquity from a trove of ancient manuscripts, which were hunted eagerly, edited, and soon to be reproduced in books made by the new process of mechanical printing. With the help of a new interest in and knowledge of Greek (stimulated by the immigration of Byzantine refugee-scholars after the fall of Constantinople to the Turks), the Humanists of the later fourteenth and fifteenth centuries recovered a large part of the Greek as well as the Roman literature and philosophy that had been lost, left unnoticed, or cast aside in the Middle Ages. The Humanists' greatest literary contribution was, perhaps, the translation of these works, but they also wrote commentaries on them, which they used as models for their own historical, rhetorical, poetic, and philosophical writings. What the Humanists perceived with great excitement in classical writing was a philosophy for living in *this* world, a philosophy primarily of human focus, that derived not from an authoritative and traditional religious dogma but from reason. The model for the Renaissance is thus no longer the world-despising holy man but rather the great-souled, intelligent man of the world.

Though the Humanism inspired by Petrarch matured and flourished between the late fourteenth and early sixteenth centuries in Renaissance Italy, it was a phenomenon of great complexity, with varying tendencies and emphases, diverging as well as converging doctrines, and personalities often in wordy conflict with one another. Thus, Humanism is not easy to define with comprehensive sureness. The modern philosophy called "humanism," for example, is quite different in many ways from that of the Renaissance. Yet we can say that the early Humanism embraced the ideal of a new kind of practical knowledge, extracted from the literature of classical antiquity and applied to the problems of secular and civil life prevailing in the city culture of the Renaissance. The Humanists thought of themselves as a new kind of professionals, distinct from the clergy, who could improve the human condition by propagating the new knowledge through education and public service. They were educators, publicists, administrators, secretaries, and advisers to princes just as much as they were philosophers, scholars, historians, and poets—and, as we shall see, they were very important for Renaissance art. Though they prized literature and scholarship for their own sake, they sought not so much to recover classical antiquity in all its completeness and correctness, but rather to use it as a basis for pointing a new way to the understanding, conduct, and enjoyment of life.

Medieval scholars possessed a vast body of knowledge that was embodied in the inherited culture of antiquity, but they had viewed this heritage in a different light from that prevalent in the Renaissance. The medieval scholar, usually a theologian, had valued classical learning mostly for its usefulness in arguing Christian dogma; thus, Aquinas could use Aristotle as the authority for arguments based on scriptural revelation, while others could point to secular classical literature as a tool for tempting souls to damnation through atheism and sensuality. The Renaissance Humanists found inspiration in the heroes of antiquity, especially in the accounts of their careers given in Plutarch's *Parallel Lives*. By the fifteenth and sixteenth centuries, even the lives

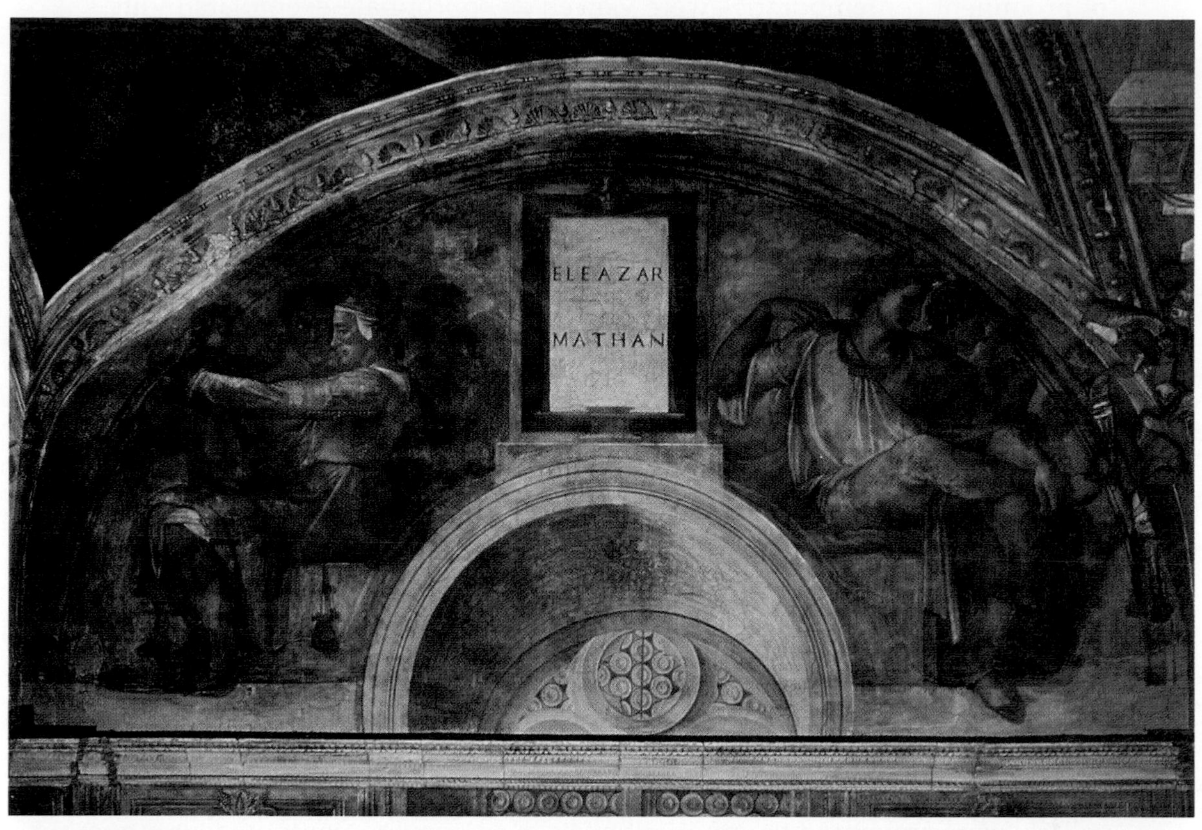

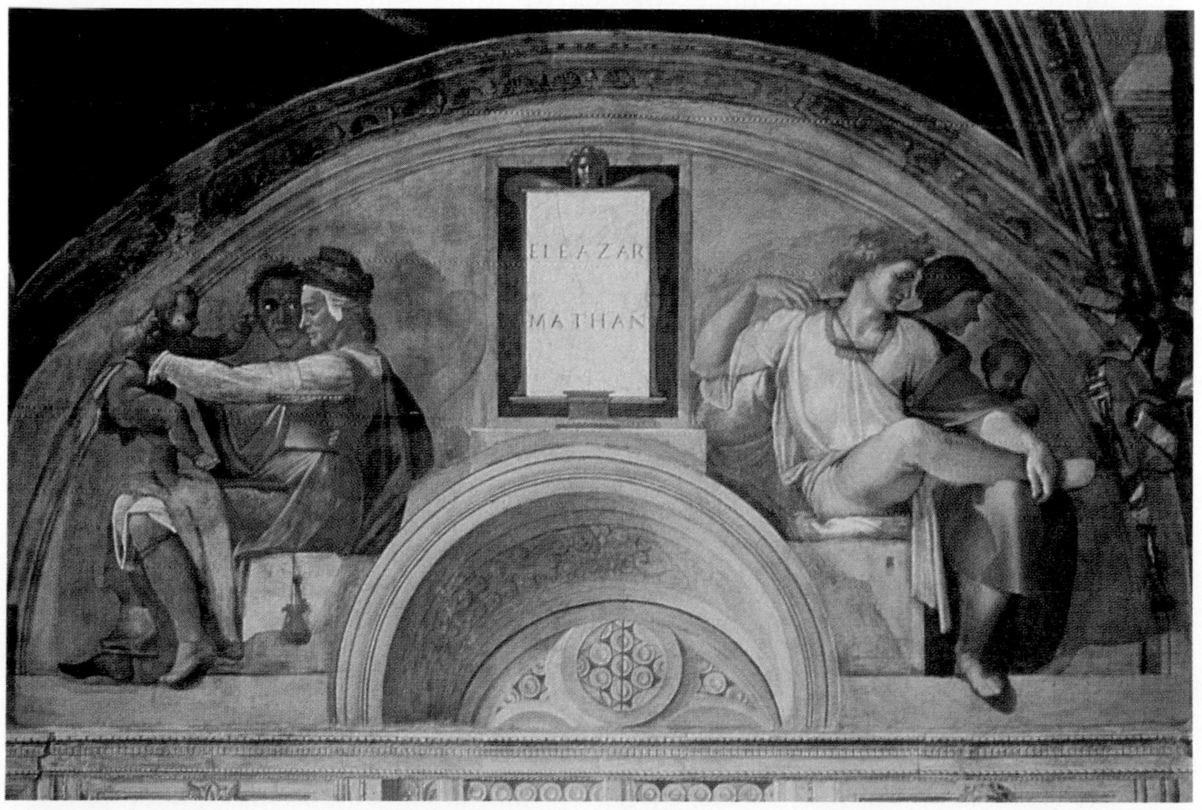

The lunette in the Sistine Chapel portraying Eleazar and Matthan, ancestors of Christ, has been restored after nearly a decade of meticulous cleaning.

of prominent contemporaries were viewed as appropriate exemplars of life's rule of reason intelligently and nobly followed. The biographies of famous men no longer dealt exclusively with the heroes of antiquity, and artists painted portraits of illustrious contemporaries. The confident, new, "modern" tone rings in Alberti's treatise *On Painting,* in which he congratulates his generation on its achievements:

> And I reveal to you, that if it was less difficult for the ancients, having as they had so very many to learn from and imitate, to rise to a knowledge of those supreme arts that are so toilsome for us today, then so much the more our fame should be greater if we, without teachers or any model, find arts and sciences unheard of and never seen.*

Almost prophetically, Alberti asserts that the moderns will go beyond the ancients, but the ancient example had first to be given—both as a model and as a point of departure.

Although the Humanists of the Renaissance received the new message from pagan antiquity with enthusiasm, they did not look on themselves as pagans. It was possible, for example, for the fifteenth-century scholar Lorenzo Valla to prove the forgery of the *Donation of Constantine* (an early medieval document purporting to record Constantine's bequest of the Roman Empire to the Church) without feeling that he had compromised his Christian faith. The two great religious orders founded in the thirteenth century, the Dominicans and the Franciscans, were as dominant in setting the tone of fourteenth- and fifteenth-century Christian thought as they had been earlier, and they continued to be patrons of the arts. Within these established religious orders, Humanist clerics strengthened rather than weakened the reputation of the Church. Humanists, sometimes while members of religious orders, were appointed to important posts in city government; the Florentine office of chancellor, for example, was held by distinguished men of letters. On the other hand, secular lords like Federigo da Montefeltro, Lord of Urbino (a skilled general, generous governor of his people, Humanist patron of the arts and letters, and renowned lover of books) chose to die in the arms of the Church after a long and pious spiritual preparation. Here and there, the antagonism between the pagan and the Christian traditions may have manifested itself—and certainly it was bound to continue to exist—but, in general, the Renaissance achieved a natural, sometimes effortless, reconciliation of the two.

Not least among the leaders of the new age were the artists who, it appears to a number of modern historians, were among its most significant producers. Indeed, the products of the plastic arts may have been the most characteristic and illustrious of the Renaissance. Although we now perceive much more of the value of Renaissance literature, philosophy, and science, these branches of human creativity seem, in comparison with the plastic arts, to have been less certain, complete, and developed. But it is noteworthy that the separation of the great disciplines was not as clear-cut as it now is; mathematics and art, especially went hand in hand, many Renaissance artists being convinced that geometry was fundamental to the artist's education and practice. In *The School of Athens* (FIG. 17-16, p. 647), Raphael places his portrait and the portraits of his colleagues among the mathematicians and philosophers, not among the poets. The medieval distinction of *ars* and *scientia* is replaced by a concept (now becoming current again) that views them as interrelated. Albrecht Dürer will insist that art without science—that is, technique without a theory relating the artist's skills and observations—is fruitless. The careful observations of the optical world made by Renaissance artists and the integration of

*In E. G. Holt, ed., *Literary Sources of Art History* (Princeton, NJ: Princeton University Press, 1947), p. 109.

these observations by such a mathematical system as perspective (derived from medieval optics) foreshadow the formulations of the natural sciences. The twentieth-century thinker and mathematician Alfred North Whitehead believed that the habit and temper of modern science are anticipated in the patient and careful observation of nature practiced by the artists of the Renaissance. The methodical pursuit of a system that could bring order to visual experience may necessarily precede the scientific analysis of what lies behind what we see. Thus, the art of the Renaissance may be said to be the first monument to the Western search for order in nature.

The search for order in nature continued in the seventeenth and early eighteenth centuries and was rewarded by the triumph of science in the revolutionary theories developed by Galileo, Kepler, and Newton—theories that stated universal laws of physical nature. In the history of human intelligence, this period has been called the Age of Reason or the Enlightenment. During the Enlightenment, answers to the age-old questions about the structure and causes of the world were sought not so much in the revelations of religion as in the deliverances of experimental science. The spiritual interpretation of nature was replaced by the mechanical, the dynamic. The world came to be seen as a magnificent machine contrived and set in motion by God, who, in the laws offered by the new physics, was thought to have revealed the secret operations that govern creation.

The Age of Reason was also the age of Europe's expansion around the globe, that period of roughly a century and a half between 1600 and 1750 in which the foundations of Europe's colonial empires were secured. It began with the last great wars of religion and closed with the world-transforming industrial, economic, social, and political revolutions that produced the secular, modern world.

For art, this period was the age of the Baroque and Rococo, when a great new surge of creativity took place. Architecture, sculpture, painting, and all the arts of design flourished magnificently throughout Europe, encouraged and patronized by sovereigns royal and aristocratic or republican. In Protestant, republican Holland, as in the lands of the Catholic dynasts of France, Spain, and papal Italy, and in the domains of the Hapsburg emperors, art reached the very highest peaks of accomplishment. The dynamism and expansiveness of the age are reflected in the very projects and principles of artistic design: in the scale and movement of composition, brilliance of color, profusion and opulence of ornament, and in stylistic variety and coherence. Rivaling the ambition and achievement of the scientists, artists in all fields—literature, drama, music, and the visual arts—created works of supreme perfection and imperishable worth. They produced and performed with a breadth of inspiration, skill, and virtuosity that emulated the great Renaissance, which indeed they continued. The Age of Reason, the Enlightenment, was also—as it has been called—the Age of Genius.

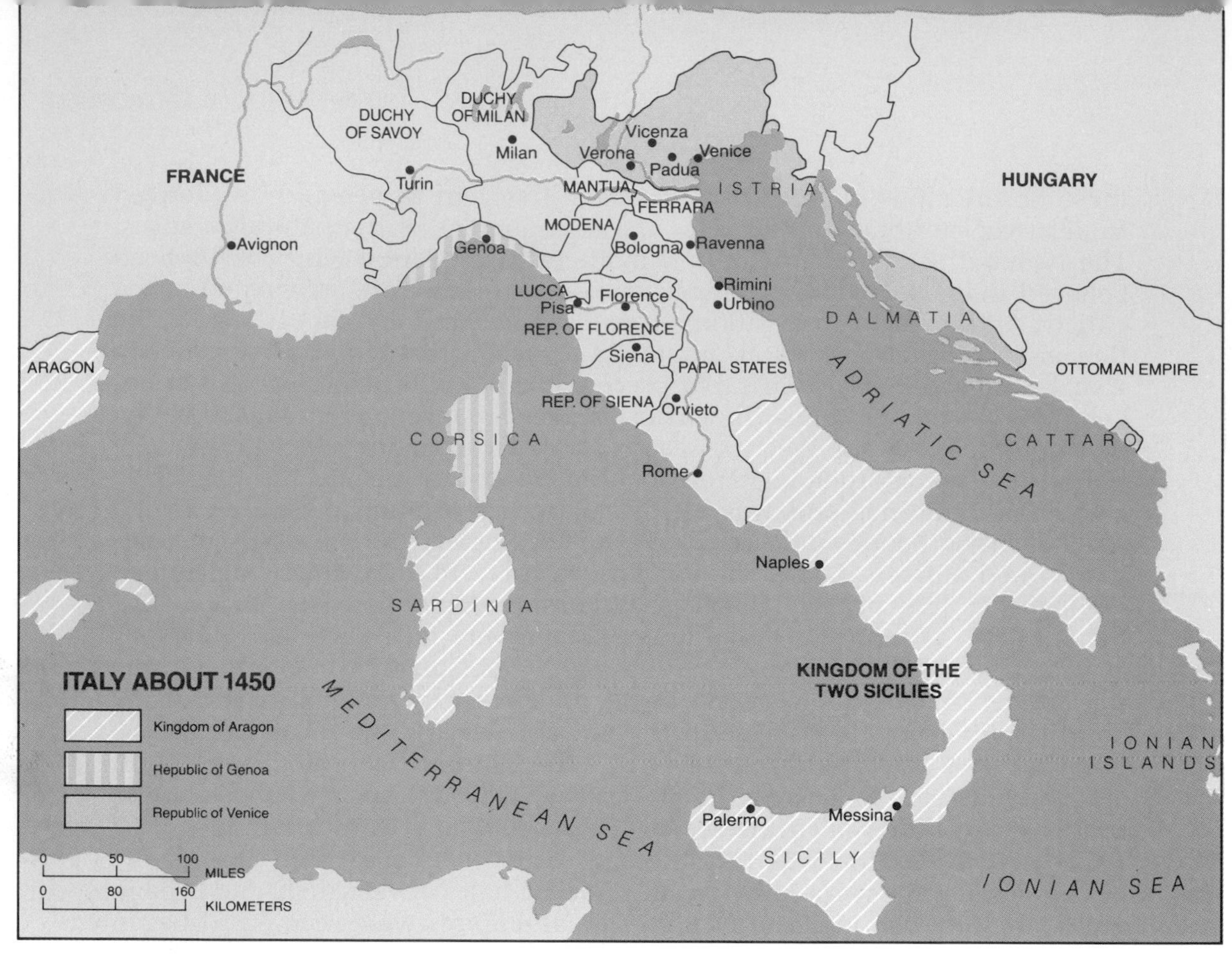

1200	1225	1250	1275

	FREDERICK II (HOLY ROMAN EMPEROR)	GREAT INTERREGNUM	

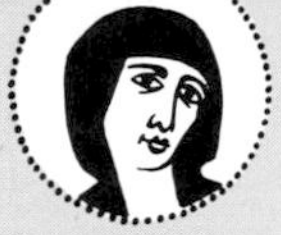

CIMABUE *Madonna Enthroned with Angels and Prophets*, detail *c.* 1280–1290

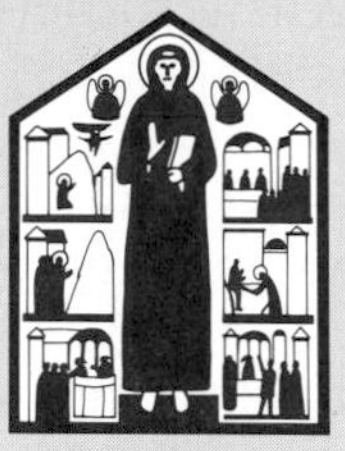

BERLINGHIERI
St. Francis Altarpiece
1235

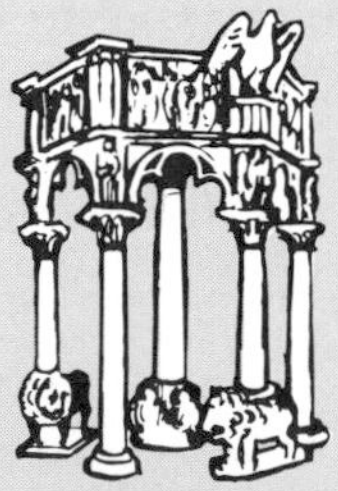

DUCCIO
active *c.* 1278–1319

CAVALLINI
active *c.* 1273–1308

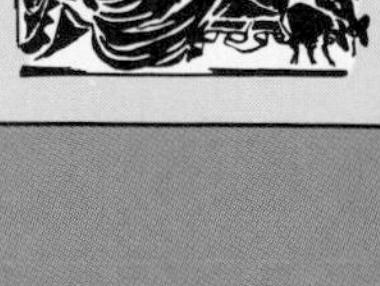

N. PISANO
Pulpit
1259–1260

G. PISANO *Nativity*, detail 1297–1301

St. Francis of Assisi
1182–1226
(Christian Humanism)

St. Thomas Aquinas
c. 1225–1274
(Scholasticism)

Roger Bacon
c. 1220–1292

Dante 1265–1321
Divina Commedia

15

THE "PROTO-RENAISSANCE" IN ITALY

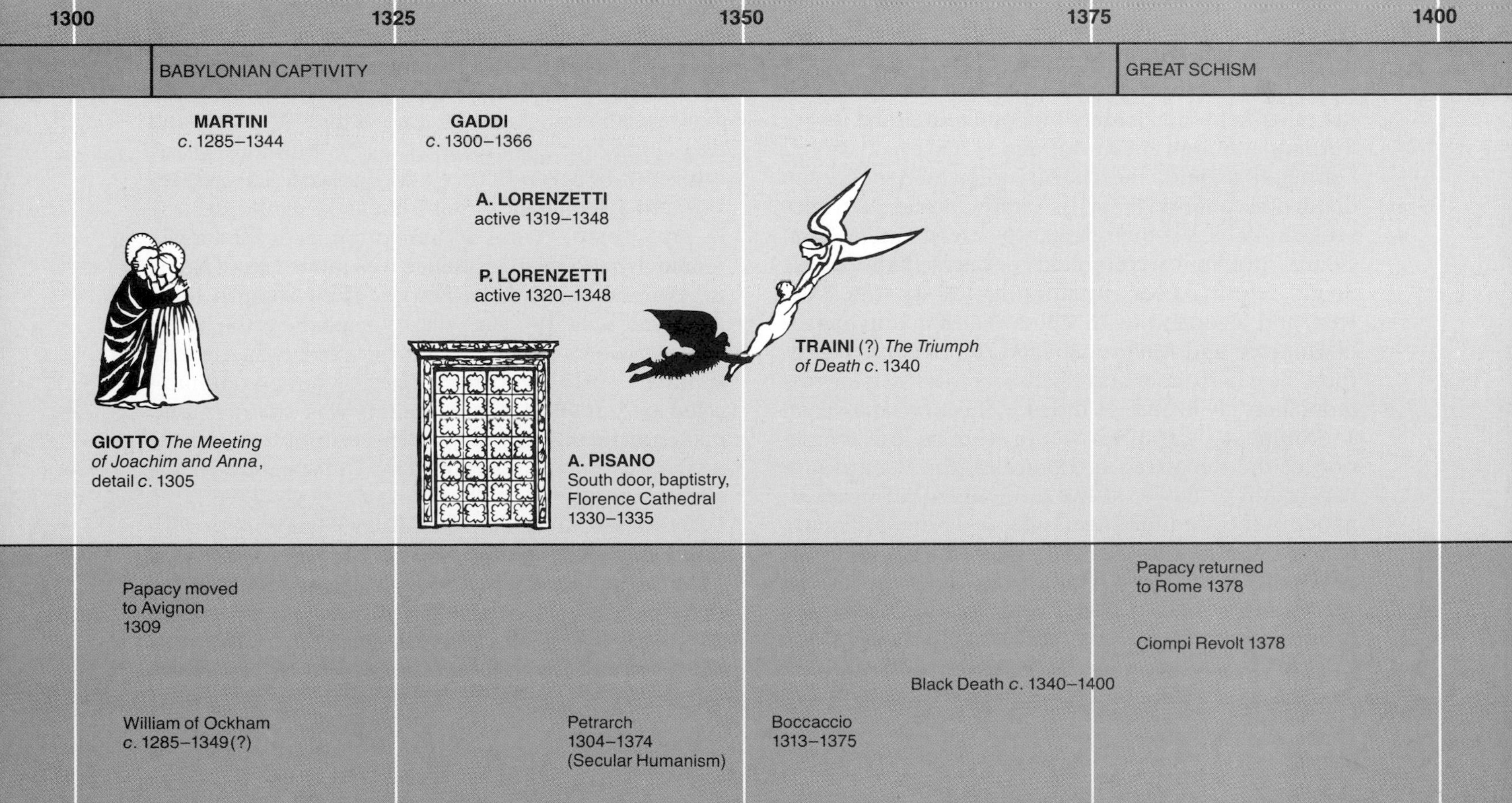

SCHOLARS HAVE LONG been uncertain about how to classify the art of the late thirteenth and the fourteenth centuries. Most of it still looks quite Byzantine or Gothic; in the countries outside Italy, Gothic traits last into the sixteenth century. In Italy, however, a new spirit begins to be felt in art in the late thirteenth century. As this new spirit is in fact that of the emerging Renaissance, it is misleading to define its monuments exclusively as "Gothic," even though Gothic traits are obvious in them. (To be sure, Gothic art itself represents a quickening of naturalism, although not the naturalism of the Renaissance; Gothic naturalism is a principal ingredient in the stylistic complex of the late Medieval world.) What appears in Italy in the thirteenth century is destined to commence a new epoch, one that will have a quite recognizable continuity for centuries—indeed, almost until our own times. To stress the initiative that Italian art takes at this time and to prevent the new epoch from being cut off from its beginnings, we have classified Italian art of the later thirteenth and the fourteenth centuries as "proto-Renaissance." Although it is not until the fifteenth century that Renaissance art makes its not always clear break with the Gothic, one can discern in the proto-Renaissance the advance of novel tendencies that will lead to the new era.

Of course, Italy does not come into historical view only with the Renaissance. After the long period of disorganization in Europe, attendant on the passing of Rome and the age of the migrations, the Italian peninsula held a commanding position in the Mediterranean world, commercially and politically, from the eleventh until the fifteenth century. The power of its city-states on the one hand and of the papacy on the other kept Italy largely independent of the rest of Europe, although Italian influence remained strong. During this time, the country remained politically divided. Economic life as we know it had its beginnings in Italy. Via their fleets, the merchants of Pisa, Genoa, and Venice controlled commerce with Islamic Spain, North Africa, Byzantium, Russia, the Near East, and, overland, with China. The banking houses of Florence and Milan managed the finances of Europe. Southern Italy and Sicily were the sites of cosmopolitan civilizations. Indeed, Italy was powerful and influential centuries before what we call the period of the Renaissance. Ironically, the Renaissance had begun to flower at the time when Italian dominance in the Mediterranean was declining in the face of the expanded role being played by the Ottoman Turks in the east and Spain in the west.

French Gothic art developed and flourished in the regions around Paris under the patronage of the kings of France. In Italy, the art of the Renaissance was supported by the prosperous merchant classes that ruled the cities after ousting the aristocracies. The reconstitution and expansion of city culture, which began as early as the eleventh century, increasingly had broken down old feudal barriers to the advancement of ambitious people of merit from all classes. Communal government (the Italian city-republics were called *communes*) came into the hands of guilds of merchants and bankers. These magnates and their families ruled not by hereditary right but by the authority of power—a power that, often as not, favored republican institutions; thus, the Medici came to rule in Florence, not as raw tyrants but as a kind of "first among equals." Behind their power was commercial success (their own as well as the city's) and their skill in business government. During the proto-Renaissance, the growth in wealth and power of many Italian cities corresponded with a rise in their wool trade. Florence, in particular, was noted for finished cloth that was sold all over Europe. As their wealth increased, the guilds, including the powerful wool guild, commanded ever-greater political influence; eventually the city, and, with it, much of the patronage of art, was in their hands. Commercial setbacks or jealousies within the guild coalitions created a highly unstable government in which authority frequently changed hands overnight.

In 1378, workmen in Florence attempted to wrest the government from the merchant guilds. This rebellion (the Ciompi revolt) was only one of many social upheavals that followed the disaster of the great plague (the "Black Death"), which almost depopulated the continent in the years 1348–1351. Peasants revolted all over Europe and unrest was widespread among laboring men in the cities. A great and desolating war, destined to last a hundred years, broke out between France and England. The papacy suffered a humiliation that ultimately would destroy its prestige; the popes became puppets of the French monarchy and their residence was moved from Rome to Avignon in southern France. Their sojourn there for some seventy years was climaxed by the Great Schism, when the throne of St. Peter was claimed simultaneously by three popes, who excommunicated one another. Christendom was changed permanently by this scandal, which contributed mightily to the advent of the Protestant Reformation in the sixteenth century.

Yet, despite turbulence and devastation, a powerful vitality was stirring, and confusion was but one aspect of significant and beneficial change. Old ideas and institutions were being challenged and, to a degree, discredited, and people of merit—in this age of

Petrarch and Giotto—could feel that the times encouraged setting off in new directions.

Events from the twelfth to the fourteenth centuries constitute a kind of long overture, announcing the advent of full, naturalistic representation in European art. Whether we regard the proto-Renaissance as the end of the overture or the raising of the curtain on the first act, the event, especially in painting, is singularly dramatic. Medieval artists had for centuries depended chiefly on prototypes (pictures and carvings) for representations of the human figure, with an occasional searching glance at objects and persons in the optical world. In the proto-Renaissance, it is the optical world that offers prototype and authority to the artist, though not all at once, of course. Not until the fifteenth century will the "imitation of nature" as an objective give artists direction, and not until the sixteenth will it become theory and doctrine. In the proto-Renaissance, artists' procedures are tentative, as if many were suspicious of an approach that involves fleeting appearances and is devoid of traditionally authoritative formulations. Nevertheless, the experimental groping of artists carefully treading the threshold of discovery infuses the art of the period with a spirit that is hopeful and often confident, if somewhat unsystematic.

Artists are not philosophers, although in the Renaissance they come very close to sharing in the philosophical enterprise. Certainly, in the fourteenth century, the way was opening to tremendous new possibilities that would have to be thought through as well as worked through. In many ways, the situation was similar to that of art today: so many possibilities and such diverse directions that, though rich conclusions may be anticipated, the way to them seems confused.

As the Christian Middle Ages evolved out of the disintegration of the Roman Empire, so a new way of looking at the world emerged from the disintegration of what might be called the medieval style of thought. Distinct from and in opposition to the balanced Scholasticism of Aquinas, the new views were only in part products of the Christian humanism of St. Francis and the secular humanism of Petrarch and the classicizing scholars. The attack on the rationalism of Aquinas made by the *later* Scholastics and theologians led to the discrediting of philosophy as a valid form of knowledge and to the unseating of reason, with its logical method, as the ruling faculty that produces knowledge. The unity of theology and philosophy, which Aquinas had achieved by bringing together Christian dogma and Aristotelian thought, was broken with theology going off in the direction of mysticism and pure faith, and philosophy yielding to skepticism and the first faint manifestation of that inquisitive bent of mind that would later mature into experimental science. If knowledge of God was impossible to achieve through philosophy and pure reason, so also was knowledge of nature and the world, God's creation. Thus, pure reason came to be despised for its failure to make the mysteries of faith or the world intelligible. In the fifteenth century, Nicholas of Cusa would disparage philosophy as mere "learned ignorance"; in the sixteenth, Martin Luther would call reason a "whore."

A new approach was needed to understand and explain nature and God, and it is necessary to examine the great changes in the Western view of nature that lie behind and accompany fundamental changes in art. William of Ockham, one of the most subtle and ingenious Scholastics who attacked the rationalism of Aquinas, seemed to be providing such an approach when, on the verge of a great insight, he stressed the importance of the role of intuitive knowledge and individual experience in the process of knowing: "Everything outside the soul is individual . . . [and] knowledge which is simple and peculiarly individual . . . is intuitive knowledge. . . . Abstractive individual knowledge presupposes intuitive knowledge . . . our understanding knows sensible things intuitively."

The placement of intuition before abstraction was common to *both* the mystical and skeptical critics of Aquinas in the fourteenth century and, in effect, put human intuition squarely in front of individual knowledge, whether of God (for the mystic) or of the world (for the skeptic). This elevation of direct human experience constitutes a kind of exaltation of the knowing, human agent. Of course, since Early Christian times and especially since St. Augustine in the fifth century, the tradition of Christian mysticism had been that the experience of God must be personal; knowledge otherwise must be the result of divine illumination. The fourteenth-century advocacy of intuitive experience, therefore, is a kind of renewal of the idea that prevailed before the conviction held by Abelard and Aquinas in the twelfth and thirteenth centuries that truth could be achieved by the intellect only by following rules of rational demonstration. Even in the thirteenth century, the importance of experience in acquiring knowledge had been stressed by the remarkable Roger Bacon, the English philosopher, who bore out his convictions on this point with many astonishingly precocious discoveries and inventions in what now would be called the physical sciences and technology. Calling attention to the existence and necessity of experimental science, Bacon insisted that the experimenter "should first examine visible things . . . without experience nothing can be known sufficiently . . . argumentation [that is, logical, rational demonstration in Aquinas's manner] does not suffice, but experience does." In the universities of the fourteenth century (especially Oxford), the followers of men like Bacon and Ockham discussed questions in physics (the acceleration of freely falling bodies, inertia, the center of gravity, and the like)—anticipating by centuries the age of Galileo.

Interestingly, many of the later thirteenth- and fourteenth-century mystical and skeptical thinkers who emphasized personal intuition and experience in seeking divine and natural knowledge were Franciscans. In view of St. Francis's humanizing of medieval religion—making it a matter of intense personal experience and drawing attention to the handiwork of God in the beauty of natural things—it is natural that his successors should inspect nature more closely, with a curiosity that would lead to scientific inquiry. St. Francis's independence and his critical posture toward the religious establishment were passed down to many Franciscans, the more radical of whom often were accused by the Church of association with outright heretics. The Franciscans—conspicuously, William of Ockham—challenged the papacy itself, especially its claim of secular lordship over all Christendom. In these challenges, the rebelliousness that will take mature shape in the Protestant Reformation already is being sounded.

What might be called Franciscan "radicalism," then, stresses the primacy of personal experience, the individual's right to know by experiment, the futility of formal philosophy, and the beauty and value of things in the external world. It was in the stimulating intellectual and social environment created in part by the Franciscans that the painters and sculptors of the proto-Renaissance began a new epoch—an epoch in which the carved and painted image took its shape from the authority of the optical world and what could be found of that authority in the Classical antique. Individual artists, breaking with the formal traditions of a thousand years, now came to depend on their own inspection of the world before their eyes. Applying the Baconian principle of personal discovery through experience—in the artist's case, the experience of *seeing*—artists began to project in painting and sculpture the infinitely complex and shifting optical reticulum that we experience as the world.

SCULPTURE

Many imitations of the art of classical antiquity may be encountered during the Carolingian, Ottonian, Romanesque, and French Gothic periods. The statues of the *Visitation* group on the west façade of Reims Cathedral (FIG. 10-33) show an unmistakable interest in Late Roman sculpture, even though the modeling of the faces reveals their Gothic origin. However, the thirteenth-century sculpture of NICOLA PISANO (active *c.* 1258–1278), contemporary with the Reims statues, exhibits an interest in the forms of the Classical antique unlike that found in the works of his predecessors. This interest was perhaps due in part to the influence of the humanistic culture of Sicily under its brilliant king, Holy Roman Emperor Frederick II, who, for his many intellectual gifts and other talents, was known in his own time as "the wonder of the world." Frederick's nostalgia for the grandeur that was Rome fostered a revival of Roman sculpture and decoration in Sicily and southern Italy before the mid-thirteenth century. Nicola may have received his early training in this environment, although recently scholars have suggested that his style merely continues that of Romanesque Pisa. After Frederick's death in 1250, Nicola traveled northward and eventually

15-1 NICOLA PISANO, pulpit of the baptistry of Pisa Cathedral, 1259–1260. Marble, approx. 15′ high.

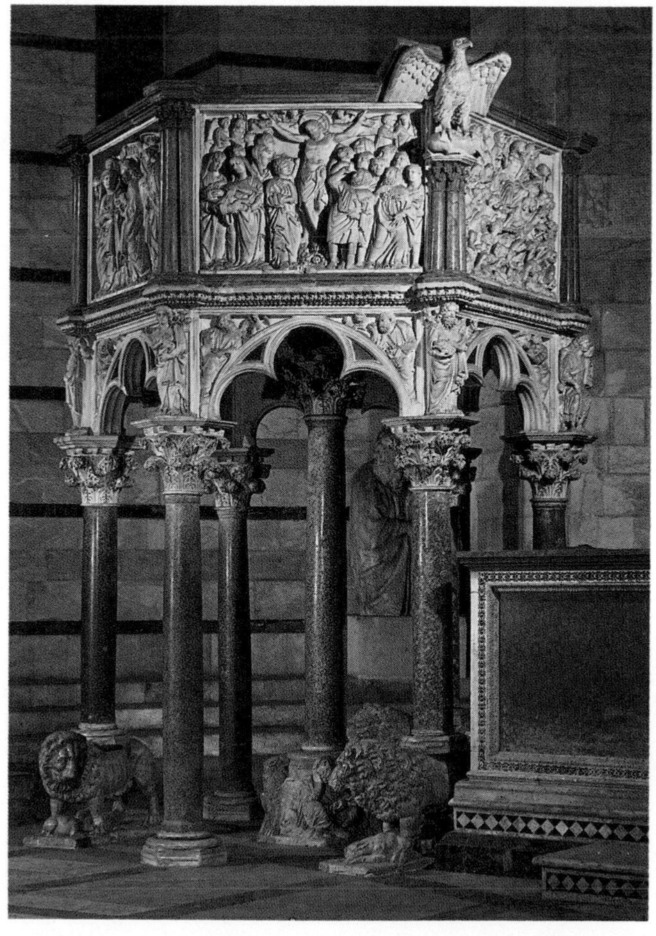

settled in Pisa, which was then at the height of its political and economic power and was clearly a place where a proficient artist could hope to find rich commissions.

In typically Italian fashion, Nicola's sculpture was not applied in the decoration of great portals; it is, therefore, quite unlike the French sculpture of the period. Nicola carved marble reliefs and ornament for large pulpits, the first of which he completed in 1260 for the baptistry of Pisa Cathedral (FIG. **15-1**). Some elements of the pulpit's design carry on Medieval traditions (for example, the lions supporting some of the columns and the tri-lobed arches), but Nicola evidently is trying to retranslate a Medieval type of structure into Classical terms. The large, bushy capitals are a Gothic variation of the Corinthian; the arches are round rather than ogival; and the large, rectangular relief panels, if their proportions were altered slightly, could have come from the sides of Roman sarcophagi. The densely packed, large-scale figures of the individual panels also seem to derive from the compositions found on Late Roman sarcophagi. In one of these panels, representing *The Annunciation and the Nativity* (FIG. **15-2**), the Virgin of the Nativity reclines in the ancient fashion seen in Byzantine ivories, mosaics, and paintings. But the face-types, beards, coiffures, and draperies, as well as the bulk and weight of the figures are inspired by Classical models and impart a Classical flavor to the relief that is stronger than anything seen in several centuries.

Nicola's classicizing manner was reversed strongly by his son GIOVANNI PISANO (*c.* 1250–1320). Giovanni's version of *The Annunciation and the Nativity* (FIG. **15-3**), from his pulpit in Sant' Andrea of Pistoia, was finished some forty years after the one by his father in the Pisa baptistry and offers a striking contrast to Nicola's thick carving and placid, almost stolid presentation of the theme. Giovanni's figures are arranged loosely and dynamically; an excited animation twists and bends them, and their activeness is emphasized by spaces that open deeply between them, through which they hurry and gesticulate. In the Annunciation episode, which is combined with the Nativity (as in the older version), the Virgin shrinks from the sudden apparition of the angel in an alarm touched with humility. The same spasm of diffidence contracts her supple body as she reclines in the Nativity scene. The principals of the drama share in a peculiar, nervous agitation, as if they all suddenly are moved by spiritual passion; only the shepherds and the sheep, appropriately, do not yet share in the miraculous event. The swiftly turning, sinuous draperies, the slender figures they enfold, and the general emotionalism of the scene are features to be found not in Nicola's interpretation but in the Gothic art of the north in the fourteenth century. (These linear rhythms and deep currents of Gothic naturalism are evident in most sculpture in Italy throughout the fourteenth century.)

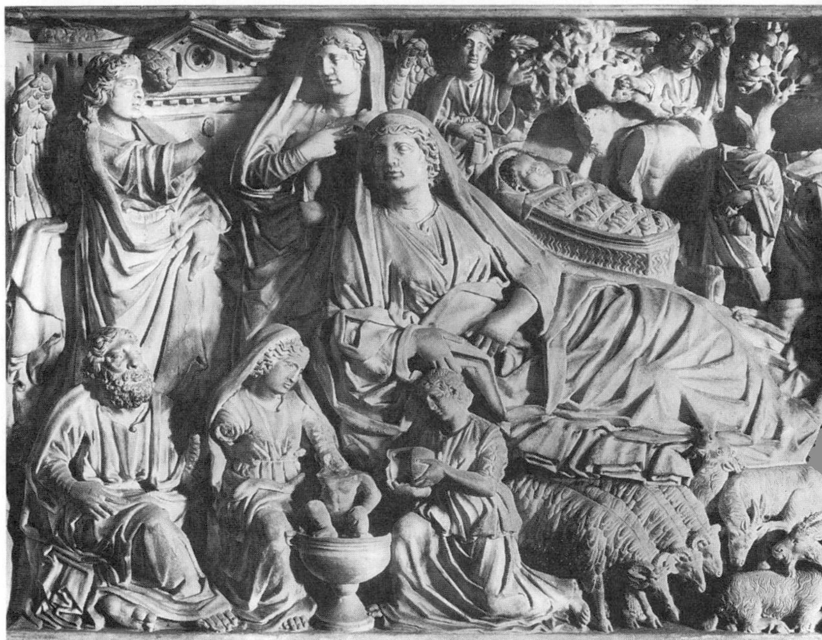

15-2 NICOLA PISANO, *The Annunciation and the Nativity* (detail of FIG. 15-1). Marble relief, approx. 34″ × 45″.

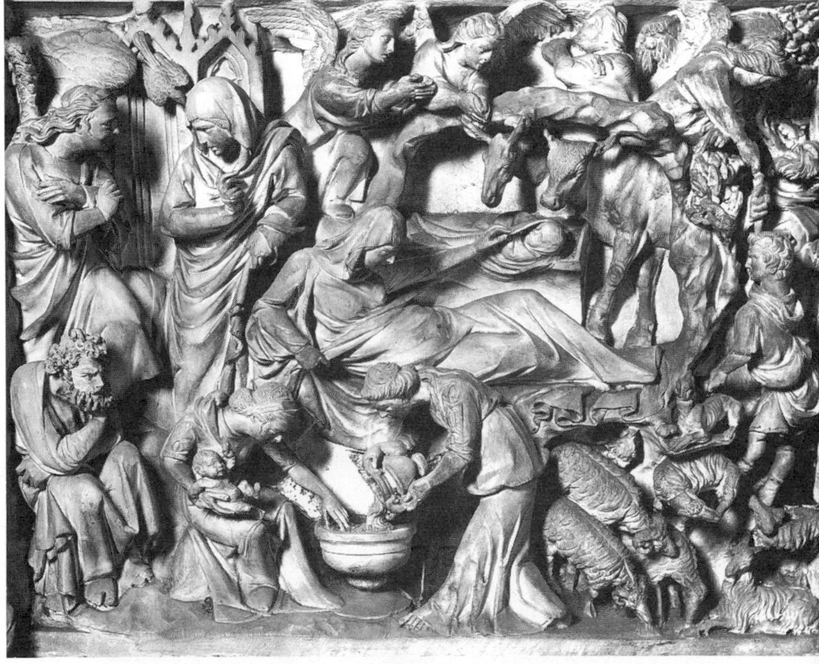

15-3 GIOVANNI PISANO, *The Annunciation and the Nativity*, 1297–1301, detail of the pulpit of Sant' Andrea, Pistoia. Marble relief, approx. 34″ × 40″.

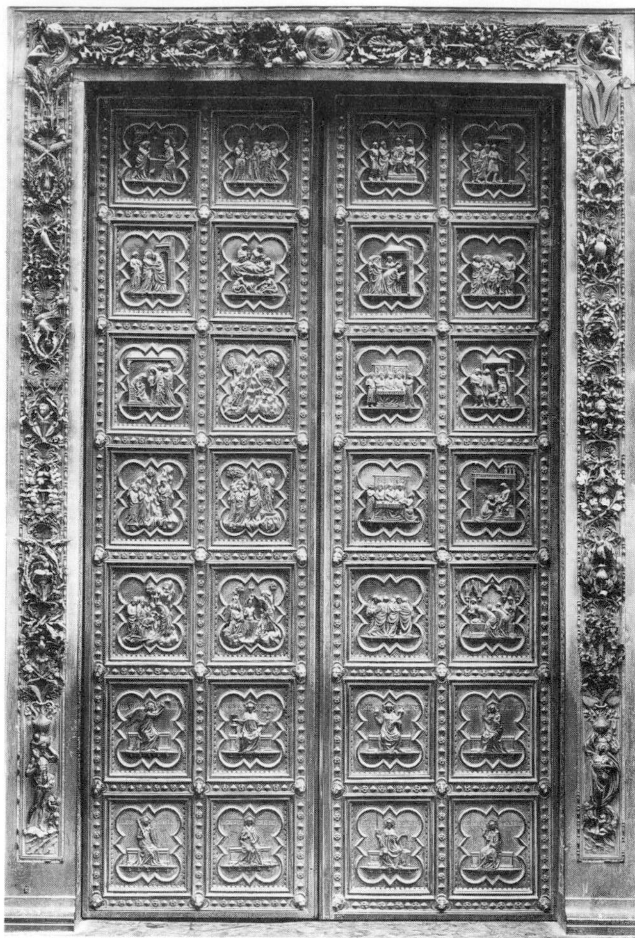

15-4 ANDREA PISANO, south door of the baptistry of Florence Cathedral, 1330–1335. Gilt bronze, approx. 17′ high.

15-5 ANDREA PISANO, *The Visitation* (detail of FIG. 15-4). Gilt bronze, approx. 20″ high.

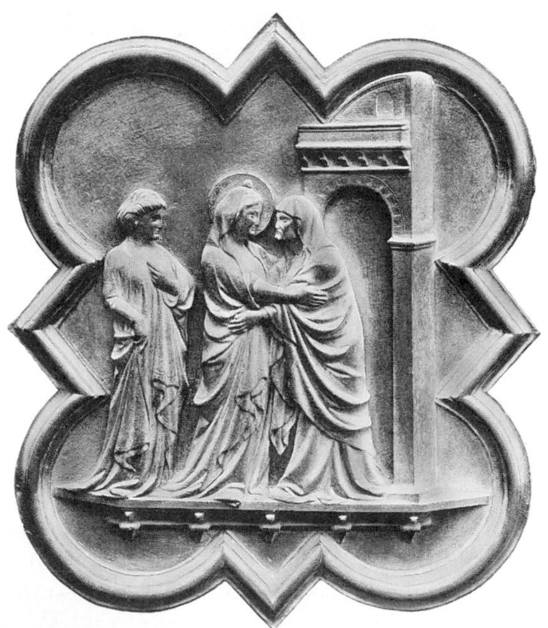

Thus, the works of Nicola and of Giovanni show, successively, two novel trends of great significance for Renaissance art: a new contact with the Classical Antique and a burgeoning, native Gothic naturalism.

Sculpture seems to have been pursued more actively in centers other than Florence until ANDREA PISANO (*c.* 1270–1348), unrelated to Nicola and Giovanni, was commissioned by the city to make bronze doors for the cathedral baptistry (FIG. **15-4**). Each door has fourteen panels, and each panel enframes a quatrefoil, a motif found in Gothic sculpture and illuminations. Within these, as in *The Visitation* panel (FIG. **15-5**), Andrea placed low reliefs with smoothly flowing lines admirably adapted to the complex space of the Gothic frame. The gentle sway of the figures and the bladelike folds of their drapery are quite in the general Late Gothic manner, but Andrea's skill at composition and the quiet eloquence of his narrative make him an outstanding master among the fourteenth-century sculptors who followed the earlier Pisani. The simplicity of Andrea's statements and the amplitude and clear placement of his forms in shallow space also point to the influence of his great contemporary, the painter Giotto di Bondone.

PAINTING

Maniera Greca

Throughout the Middle Ages, Italian painting was strongly dominated by the Byzantine style. This Italo-Byzantine style, or *maniera greca,* is shown in a panel of the *St. Francis Altarpiece* (FIG. **15-6**) and is a descendant of those tall, aloof, austere figures that people the world of Byzantine art. Painted in tempera (a water-base paint that uses a binder such as glue or egg yolk) on wood panel, St. Francis wears the cinctured canonicals of the order that he founded. He holds a large book and displays the stigmata—the wounds of Christ, imprinted as a sign of Heavenly favor—on his hands and feet. The saint is flanked by two very Byzantine angels and by scenes from his life that strongly suggest that their source is in Byzantine illuminated manuscripts. The central scene on the saint's right represents *St. Francis Preaching to the Birds.* The figures of St. Francis and his two attendants are aligned carefully against a shallow, stage-property tower and wall, a stylized symbol of a town or city from Early Christian times. In front of the saint is another stage-scenery image of nested, wooded hills populated by alert and sprightly birds and twinkling plants. The strict formality of the composition (relieved somewhat by the sharply observed birds and the lively stippling of the plants), the shallow

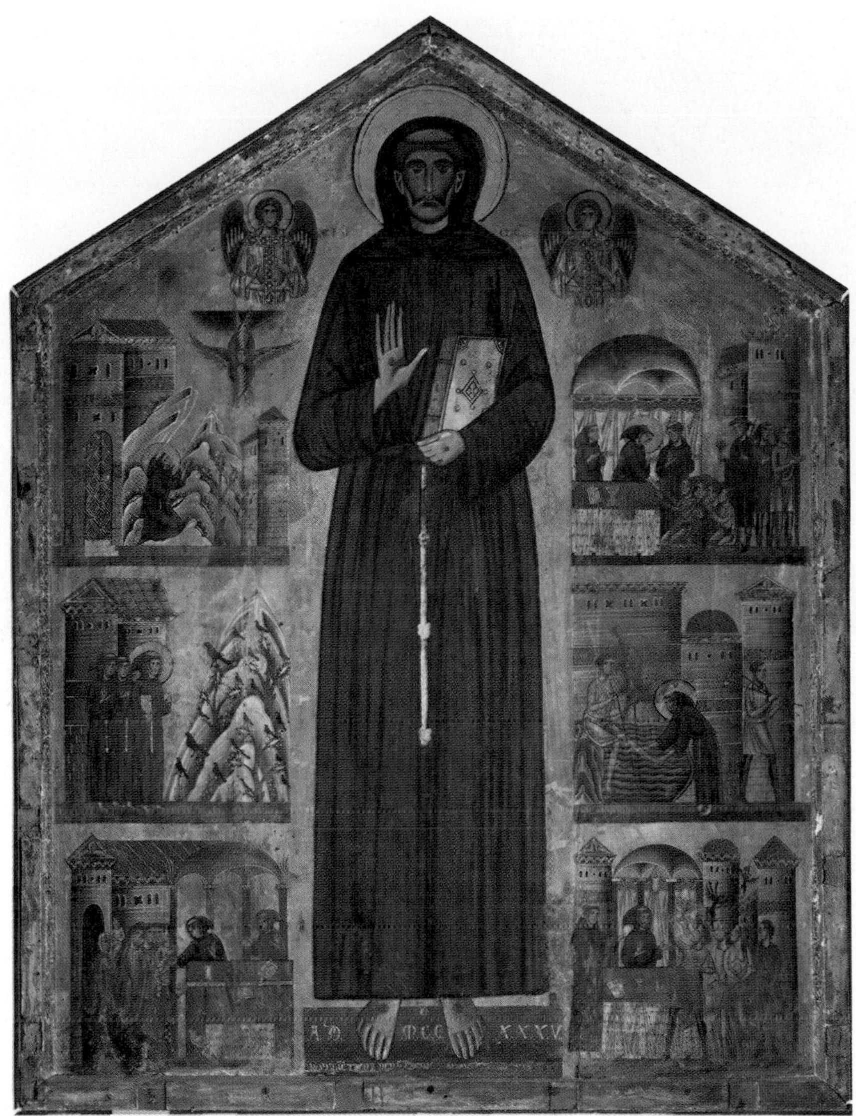

15-6 Bonaventura Berlinghieri, panel from the *St. Francis Altarpiece,* 1235. Tempera on wood, approx. 60″ × 42″. San Francesco, Pescia.

space, and the linear flatness in the rendering of the forms are all familiar traits of a long and august tradition, soon suddenly and dramatically to be replaced.

Bonaventura Berlinghieri, artist of the *St. Francis Altarpiece,* was one of a family of painters in the Tuscan city of Lucca. The stirrings of the new artistic movement began largely in the busy cities of Tuscany (Lucca, Pisa, Siena, Florence). Florence was destined to lead the great development toward the new pictorial manner of the Renaissance, just as politically it gradually absorbed the other cities in Tuscany to form the Florentine republic. But during the fourteenth century, its defiant rival, Siena, which had long and stubbornly resisted the encroachment of Florence, was the seat of a rich and productive school of painting of its own.

Duccio

The works of Duccio (Duccio di Buoninsegna, active *c.* 1278–1319) represent the Sienese tradition at its best. Among his large altarpieces, the *Maestà,* showing the Madonna enthroned in majesty as Queen of Heaven amidst choruses of angels and saints, was commissioned for the high altar of Siena Cathedral in 1308 and completed in 1311. As originally executed, it consisted of a seven-foot-high panel with seven pinnacles above and a *predella* below it, all painted on both sides. Unfortunately, the work no longer can be seen in its entirety; it was dismantled in the sixteenth century, and its panels now are scattered throughout the museums of the world. On the front side, the predella showed seven scenes depicting the early life of Christ. Scenes from the last days

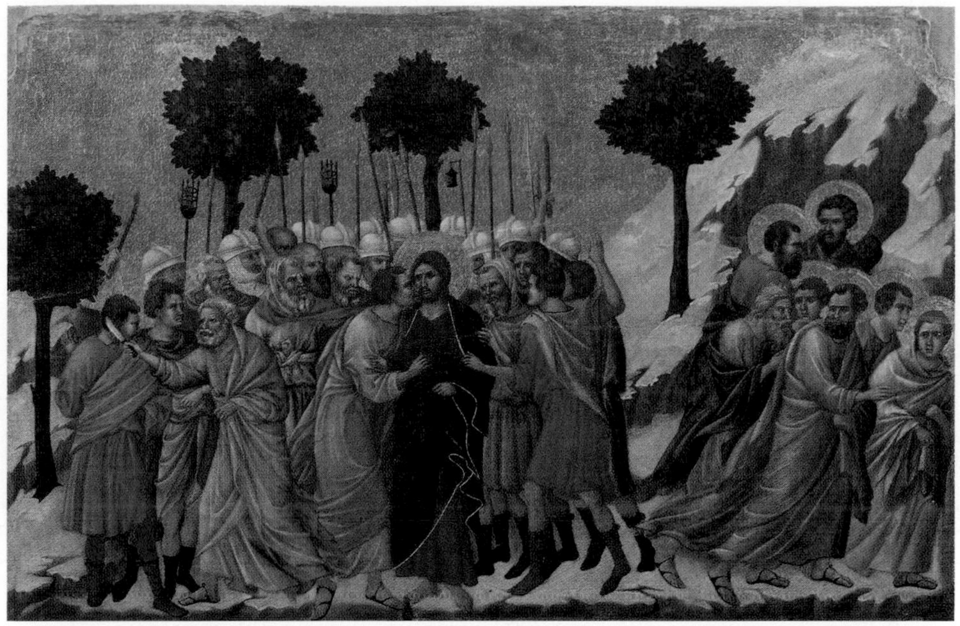

15-7 Duccio, *The Betrayal of Jesus,* detail from the back of the *Maestà Altarpiece,* 1309–1311. Tempera on wood, size of detail approx. $22\frac{1}{2}'' \times 40''$. Museo dell'Opera del Duomo, Siena.

of the Virgin were represented on the pinnacles. In the numerous panels on the back, Duccio illustrated the later life of Christ—his ministry (on the predella), Passion (on the main panel), the Resurrection and appearances to his disciples (on the pinnacles). On this single large altarpiece, Duccio rivaled the scope and complexity of monumental fresco cycles, such as Giotto's stunning works in the Arena Chapel (see FIG. 15-12).

The altarpiece illustrates the two major aspects of Duccio's mature style. The main panel on the front, showing the Madonna in majesty, represents the formal, monumental side of his art, which remains essentially Byzantine. In the accompanying small narrative pictures, on the other hand, Duccio relaxed the formalism appropriate to the iconic, symbolic representation of the *Maestà* and revealed his ability not only as a narrator but as an experimenter with new pictorial ideas. In a synoptic sequence on one of the small panels, *The Betrayal of Jesus* (FIG. **15-7**), the artist represents several episodes of the event: the betrayal of Jesus by Judas's false kiss, the disciples fleeing in

15-8 Duccio, *The Annunciation of the Death of Mary,* detail from the *Maestà Altarpiece,* 1309–1311. Tempera on wood, size of detail approx. $16'' \times 21''$. Museo dell'Opera del Duomo, Siena.

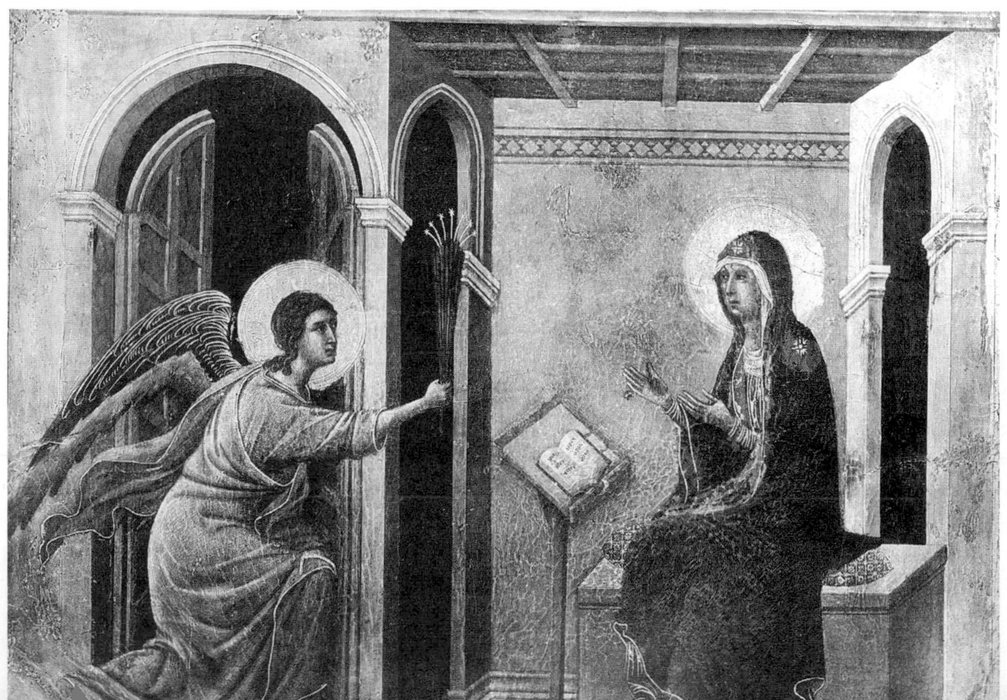

terror, St. Peter cutting off the ear of the high priest's servant. Although the background, with its golden sky and its cheeselike rock formations, remains traditional, the figures before it have changed quite radically. They are no longer the flat, frontal shapes of Byzantine art but have taken on mass; they are modeled through a range from light to dark, and their draperies articulate around them convincingly. Only their relation to the ground on which they stand remains somewhat in doubt, as they tend to sway, glide, and incline with a kind of disembodied instability. Even more novel and striking is the manner in which the figures seem to react to the central event. Through posture, gesture, and even facial expression, they display a variety of emotions, as Duccio extends himself to differentiate between the anger of Peter, the malice of Judas (echoed in the faces of the throng about Jesus), and the apprehension and timidity of the fleeing disciples. No longer the abstract symbols of Byzantine art, these figures have become actors in a religious drama, which, in a lively performance, is interpreted in terms of thoroughly human actions and reactions. In this and similar narrative panels, Duccio takes a decisive step toward the humanization of religious subject matter—an approach that will become an ever-stronger undercurrent in the development of painting in the centuries to follow.

In *The Annunciation of the Death of Mary* (FIG. **15-8**), from one of the pinnacles of the same altarpiece, Duccio shows that, in the study of interior space, he is the equal of his contemporaries. Although his perspective is approximate, he creates the illusion of an architectural space that *encloses* a human figure. If we could be sure that the sophisticated ancient Roman painters had not achieved this effect also, we might say that it had never been done before. Certainly, nothing like it is to be found in painting during the nine hundred years preceding Duccio, and it must be regarded as epoch-making even though it was accomplished in a similar manner by Giotto in the Arena Chapel in Padua (FIG. 15-16) a few years before Duccio painted his *Maestà*. While the angel's position remains ambiguous, the Virgin clearly has been placed in a cubical space that recedes from the picture plane. The illusion is made quite emphatic by the convergence of the three beams in the ceiling, a phenomenon that Duccio observed and recorded. As yet the perspective is not entirely unified, each of Duccio's planes tending to have its own point of convergence. Nevertheless, the illusion is convincing enough and represents the first step in the progressive construction of a true, geometrically ordered, perspective space—an achievement that will be completed in the next century.

Giotto

Duccio resolved his problems within the general framework of the Byzantine style, which he never really rejected. His great Florentine contemporary, GIOTTO (Giotto di Bondone, *c.* 1266–1337), made a much more radical break with the past. The sources of Giotto's style still are debated, although one must have been the style of the Roman school of painting represented by PIETRO CAVALLINI (active *c.* 1273–1308). As is shown in a detail from Cavallini's badly damaged fresco of *The Last Judgment* in the church of Santa Cecilia in Trastevere (FIG. **15-9**), the style is

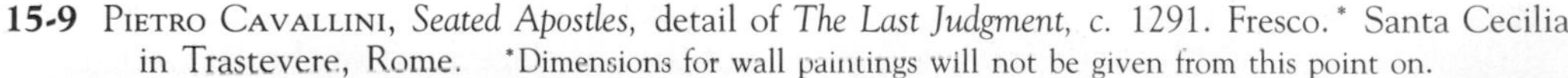

15-9 PIETRO CAVALLINI, *Seated Apostles*, detail of *The Last Judgment*, *c.* 1291. Fresco.* Santa Cecilia in Trastevere, Rome. *Dimensions for wall paintings will not be given from this point on.

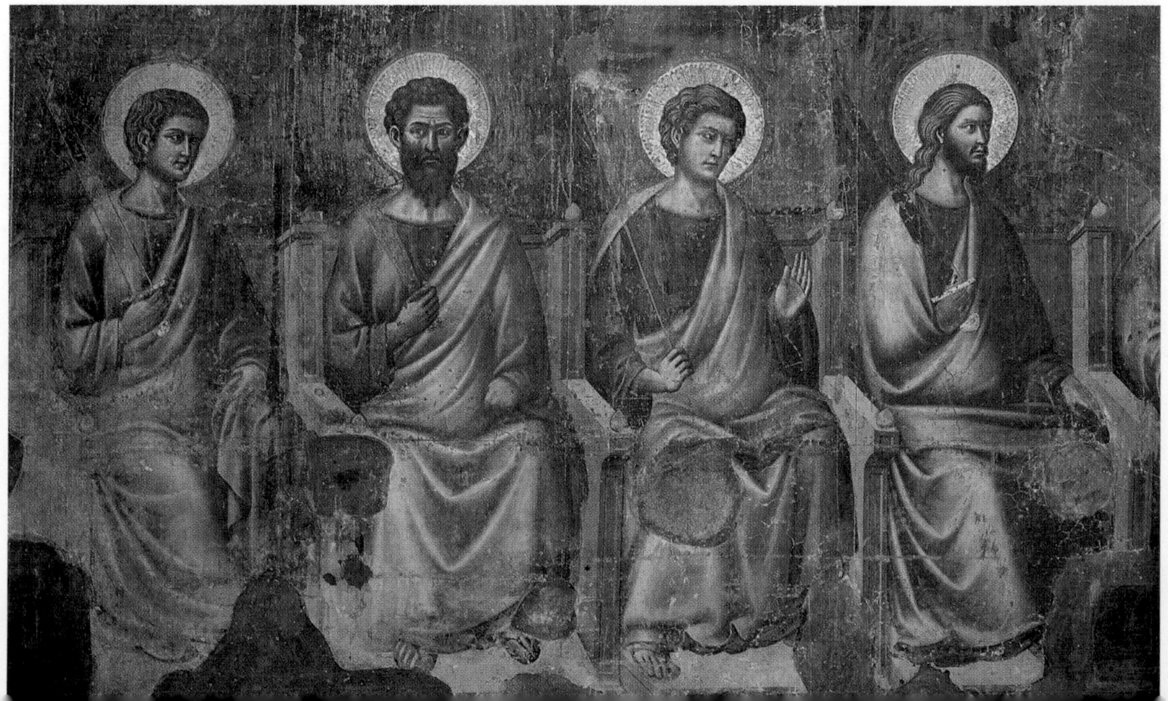

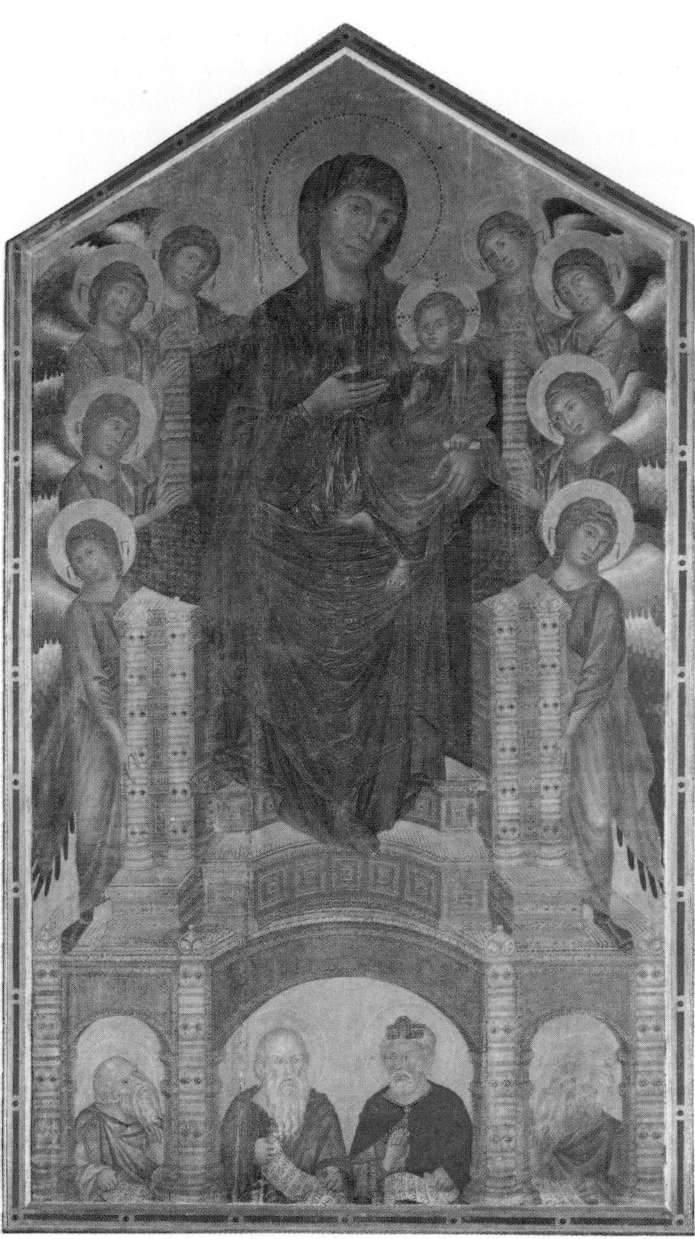

15-10 GIOVANNI CIMABUE, *Madonna Enthroned with Angels and Prophets*, c. 1280–1290. Tempera on wood, 12′ 7″ × 7′ 4″. Galleria degli Uffizi, Florence.

characterized by a great interest in the sculptural rendering of form. Cavallini, perhaps under the influence of Roman paintings now lost, abandons Byzantine linearism for a soft, deep modeling from light to dark and achieves an imposing combination of Byzantine hieratic dignity with a long-lost impression of solidity and strength.

Another, perhaps less significant, formative influence on Giotto may have been the work of the man presumed to be his teacher, GIOVANNI CIMABUE (*c.* 1240–1302). A Florentine, Cimabue must have been an older rival of Giotto, as Dante suggests in *Il Purgatorio* (XI, 94–96): "Cimabue thought to hold the field in painting, and now Giotto has the cry, so that the fame of the other is obscured." Inspired by the same impulse toward naturalism as Giovanni Pisano and also influenced, no doubt, by Gothic sculpture, Cimabue (like Cavallini) pushed well beyond the limits of the Italo-Byzantine style. In an almost ruined fresco of the Crucifixion in San Francesco in Assisi, Cimabue's style (like Giovanni Pisano's) can be seen to be highly dramatic; the figures are blown by a storm of emotion. On the other hand, Cimabue is much more formal in his *Madonna Enthroned with Angels and Prophets* (FIG. **15-10**), as the theme here naturally calls for unmoving dignity and not for dramatic presentation. Despite such progressive touches as the three-dimensional appearance of the throne, this vast altarpiece is a final summing-up of centuries of Byzantine art before its utter transformation. Giotto's version of the same theme (FIG. 15-11) shows us what that transformation looked like in its first phase.

The art of Cimabue, the art of Cavallini and of the Roman painters like him (whom Giotto must have seen at work in San Francesco at Assisi), the art of the Gothic sculptors of France (perhaps seen by Giotto himself, but certainly received by him from the sculpture of Giovanni Pisano), and the ancient art of Rome, both sculpture and painting—all must have provided the elements of Giotto's artistic education. Yet no synthesis of these varied influences could have sufficed to produce the great new style that makes Giotto the father of Western pictorial art. Renowned in his own day, his reputation never has faltered. No matter the variety of his materials of instruction, his true teacher was nature—the world of visible things.

Giotto's revolution in painting did not consist only of the displacement of the Byzantine style, the establishment of painting as a major art for the next six centuries, and the restoration of the naturalistic approach invented by the ancients and lost in the Middle Ages. He also inaugurated a firm method of pictorial experiment through observation, and, in the spirit of the experimenting Franciscans, initiated an age that might be called "early scientific." Giotto and his successors, by stressing the preeminence of the faculty of sight in gaining knowledge of the world, laid the trails that empirical science would follow. They recognized that the visual world must be observed before it can be analyzed and understood. Praised in his own and later times for his fidelity to nature, Giotto is more than an imitator of it; he *reveals* nature in the process of observing it and divining its visible order. In fact, he showed his generation a new way of seeing. With Giotto, Western artists turned

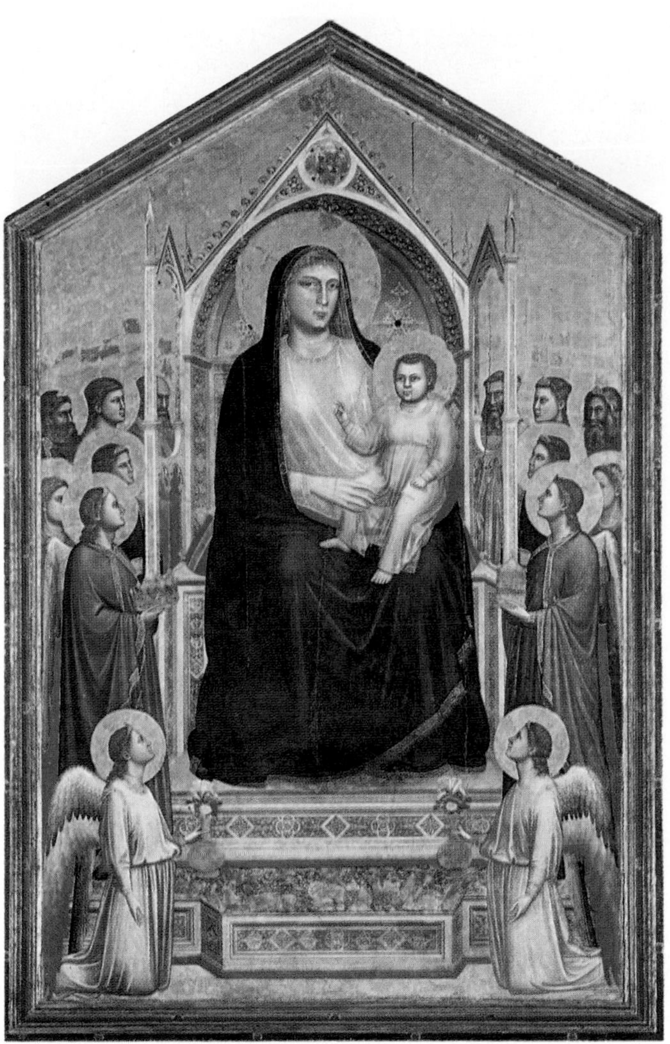

15-11 GIOTTO, *Madonna Enthroned,* c. 1310. Tempera on wood, 10′ 8″ × 6′ 8″. Galleria degli Uffizi, Florence.

resolutely toward the visible world as the source of knowledge of nature. This new *outward* vision replaced the medieval *inward* vision that searched not for the secrets of nature but for union with God.

In nearly the same great scale as the Madonna painted by Cimabue, Giotto presents her (FIG. **15-11**) in a work that offers an opportunity to appreciate his perhaps most telling contribution to representational art—sculptural solidity and weight. The Madonna, enthroned with angels, rests within her Gothic throne with the unshakable stability of a marble goddess out of antiquity. The slender Virgins of Duccio and Cimabue, fragile beneath the thin ripplings of their draperies, are replaced by a sturdy, queenly mother, corporeally of this world, even to the swelling of the bosom. The body is not lost; it is asserted. The new art aims, before all else, to construct a figure that will have substance, dimensionality, and bulk. Works painted in the new style portray figures, like those in sculpture, which project into the light and throw a shadow or give the illusion that they do. In this work of Giotto, the throne is deep enough to contain the monumental figure and breaks away from the flat ground to project and enclose it.

In Roman painting, we have seen formulas for creating perspective illustration of the spatial world (see FIGS. 6-27, 6-29, 6-32, 6-36, 6-37). But the arrangement of figures in relation to the space they are supposed to occupy is not consistent; most often figures are crowded into the front plane, or seem to move in haphazardly placed planes, much like stage flats. In the art of Byzantium, perspective space is discarded and the figures are set against a flat and often featureless ground (see FIGS. 7-28, 7-36, 7-39, 7-53). Details of the environment, when they are included, are all inscribed, as it were, on the same plane (see FIGS. 7-30 and 7-56). The Islamic illuminated page presents spatial cues, diagonal screens fitted to the surface of the page as color fields to which the figures are attached (see FIG. 7-85). Romanesque painting shows the same disregard of perspective illusion; the figures are simply silhouetted on the neutral space of the picture plane (see FIGS. 9-38, 9-39, 9-40, 9-41, 9-42). Gothic stained glass exhibits similar nonspatial representation (see FIGS. 10-35 and 10-36), though in illumination we begin to feel the painter's concern with spatial description of the environment of the narrative in settings not yet perspectively ordered (see FIG. 10-38). When we match these nonspatial representations of Western figural art between late Roman times and Giotto, we may appreciate the revolutionary character of his work.

THE ARENA CHAPEL

The projection on a flat surface of an illusion of solid bodies moving through space presents a double problem. The construction of the illusion of a body requires, at the same time, the construction of the illusion of a space sufficiently ample to contain that body. In Giotto's fresco cycles (he was primarily a muralist), he constantly is striving to reconcile these two aspects of illusionistic painting. His frescoes in the Arena Chapel (Cappella Scrovegni) at Padua (FIG. **15-12**) show us his art at its finest. The Arena Chapel, which takes its name from an ancient Roman amphitheater nearby, was built for Enrico Scrovegni, a wealthy Paduan merchant, on a site adjacent to his now razed palace. This small building, intended for the private use of the Scrovegni family, was consecrated in 1305, and its design is so perfectly suited to its interior decoration that some scholars have suggested that Giotto himself may have been its architect.

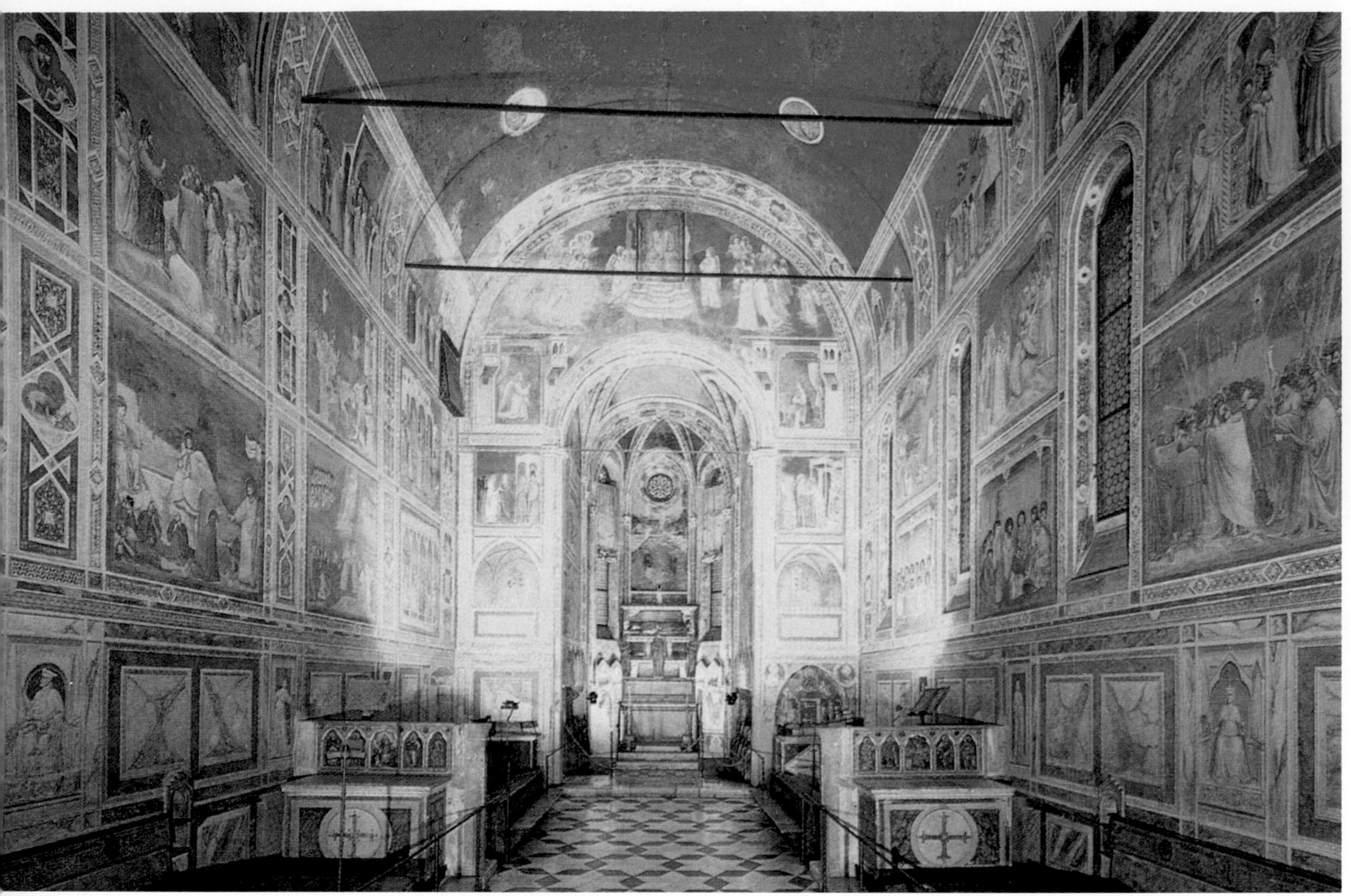

15-12 Interior of the Arena Chapel (Cappella Scrovegni), Padua, 1305–1306.

The rectangular, barrel-vaulted hall has six narrow windows in its south wall only, leaving the entire north wall an unbroken and well-illuminated surface for painting. The entire building seems to have been designed to provide Giotto with as much flat surface as possible for his presentation of one of the most impressive and complete pictorial cycles of Christian Redemption ever rendered. With thirty-eight framed pictures, arranged on three levels, the artist relates the most poignant incidents from the lives of the Virgin and her parents, Joachim and Anna *(top),* the life and mission of Christ *(middle),* and his Passion, Crucifixion, and Resurrection *(bottom).* These three pictorial levels rest on a coloristically neutral base on which imitation marble veneer (reminiscent of the incrustation style of ancient Roman wall decoration [see page 206], which Giotto must have seen) alternates with representations of the Virtues and Vices, which are painted in *grisaille* (monochrome greys) to resemble sculpture. The climactic event of the cycle of human salvation, the Last Judgment, covers most of the west wall above the chapel's entrance.

The hall's vaulted ceiling is blue—an azure sky symbolic of Heaven; it is dotted with golden stars and medallions bearing images of Christ, Mary, and various prophets. The blue of the sky is the same as the color in the backgrounds of the narrative panels on the walls below and functions as a powerful unifying agent for the entire decorative scheme; it serves as visual reinforcement for the spiritual unity and the thematic continuity of the numerous pictured episodes. For the visitor to this remarkable little chapel, the formal and coloristic unity of the decorative ensemble become memorable standards against which other decorative schemes must be measured.

The individual panels are framed with decorative borders, which, with their delicate tracery, offer a striking contrast to the sparse simplicity of the figured representations they surround. Subtly scaled down to the chapel's limited space (the figures are

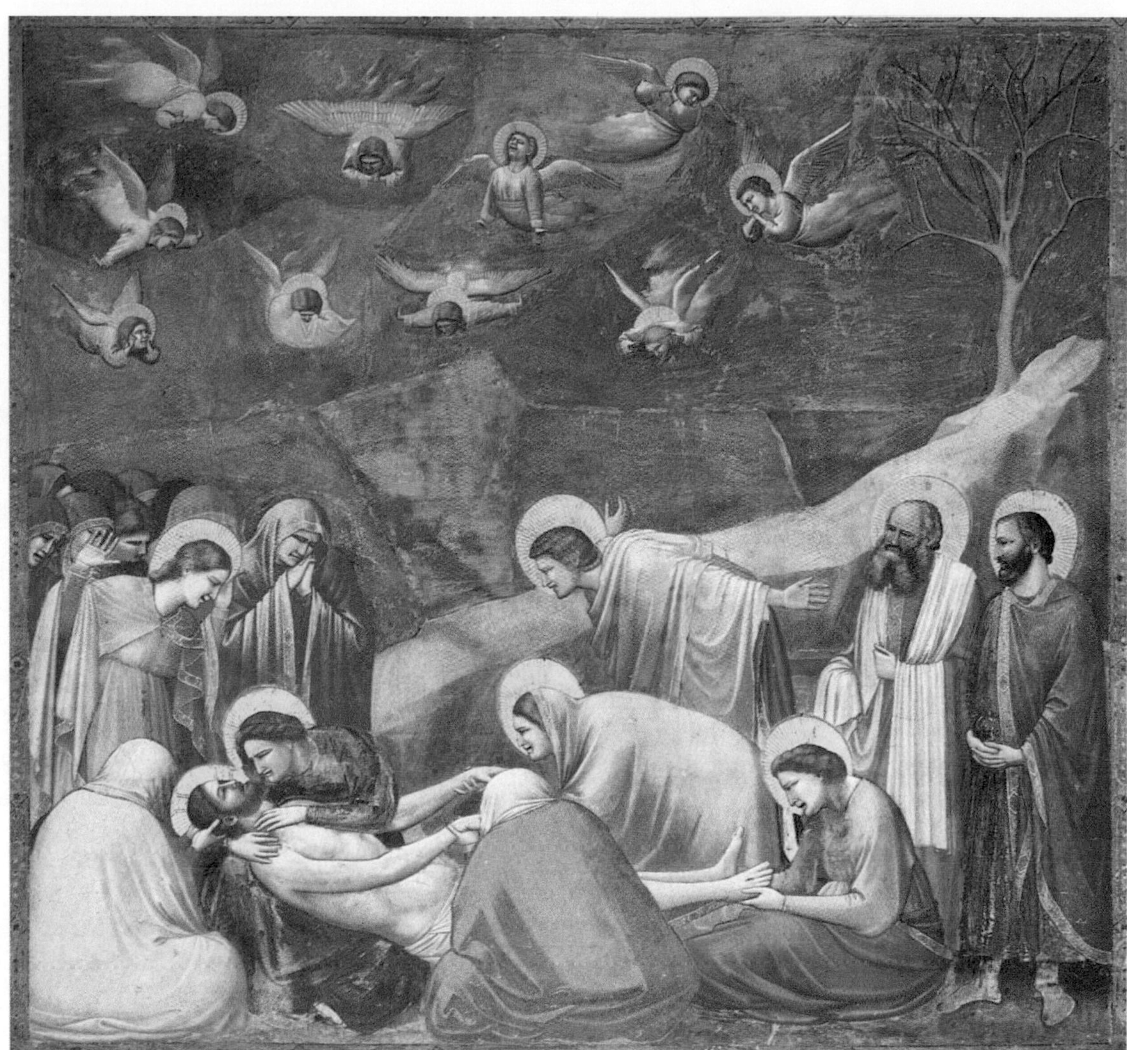

15-13 GIOTTO, *Lamentation,* c. 1305. Fresco. Arena Chapel.

only about one-half life size), Giotto's stately and slow-moving actors present their dramas convincingly and with great restraint. The essentials of his style are well illustrated by the *Lamentation* (FIG. **15-13**). In the presence of angels, who dart about in hysterical grief, Christ's mother, his disciples, and the holy women mourn over the dead body of the Savior just before its entombment. Giotto has arranged a shallow stage for the figures, bounded by a thick, diagonal scarp of rock that defines a horizontal ledge in the foreground. The rocky landscape links this scene with the adjoining one. Giotto connects the framed scenes throughout the fresco cycle, much as Dante joins the cantos in his epic poem, the *Divina Comedia.* Though rather narrow, the ledge provides the figures with firm visual support, while the scarp functions as an indicator of the picture's dramatic focal point at the lower left. The centralizing and frontalizing habits of Byzantine art are dismissed here. The figures are sculpturesque, simple, and weighty, but they are not restrained by their mass from appropriate action. Postures and gestures that might have been only rhetorical and mechanical now convincingly express a broad spectrum of grief that ranges from Mary's almost fierce despair through the passionate outbursts of Mary Magdalene and John, to the philosophical resignation of the two disciples at the right and the mute sorrow of the two hooded mourners in the foreground. Although Duccio makes an effort to distinguish shades of emotion in *The Betrayal of Jesus* (FIG. 15-7), he does not match Giotto in his stage management of a great tragedy. Giotto, indeed, has constructed a kind of stage, which will serve as a model for those on which many human dramas will be depicted in subsequent paintings. He is now far removed from the old isolation of episodes and actors seen in art until the late thirteenth century. In the *Lamentation,* a single event provokes a single, intense response within which degrees of psychic vibration, so to speak, are quite apparent. This integration of the formal with the emotional composition was rarely attempted, let alone achieved, in art before Giotto.

The formal design of the *Lamentation* fresco, the way the figures are grouped within the contrived space, is worth close study. Each group has its own definition, and each contributes to the rhythmic order of the composition. The strong diagonal of the rocky ledge, with its single dead tree (the tree of knowledge of good and evil, which withered at the fall of Adam), concentrates our attention on the group around the head of Christ, whose positioning is dynamically off-center. All movement beyond this group is contained, or arrested, by the massive bulk of the seated mourner in the left corner of the painting. The seated mourner to the right establishes a relation with the center group, the members of which, by their gazes and gestures, draw the viewer's attention back to the head of Christ. Figures seen from the back, which are frequent in Giotto's compositions, emphasize the foreground, helping visually to place the intermediate figures further back in space. This device, the very contradiction of the old frontality, in effect puts the viewer behind the "observer" figures, which, facing the action as spectators, reinforce the sense of stagecraft as a model for paintings with a human "plot." In this age of dawning Humanism, the old Medieval, hieratic presentation of holy mysteries evolved into full-fledged dramas employing a plot. By the thirteenth century, the drama of the Mass was extended first into one- and two-act tableaus and scenes and then into simple shows, often presented at the portals of churches. (The portal statuary of the Gothic period suggests a discourse among the represented saints, and the architectural settings serve to enframe and enclose them, as a stage does the movement of its actors.) Thus, the arts of illusionistic painting and of drama were developing simultaneously, and the most accomplished artists of the Renaissance and later periods became masters of a kind of stage rhetoric of their own. Giotto, the first master of the tradition, was one of the most expert in the matching of form and action; it is difficult to exaggerate his trailblazing achievement.

SANTA CROCE

For the Franciscan church of Santa Croce in Florence, Giotto painted a St. John cycle and frescoes of

15-14 GIOTTO, *Death of St. Francis,* c. 1320. Fresco. Bardi Chapel, Santa Croce, Florence.

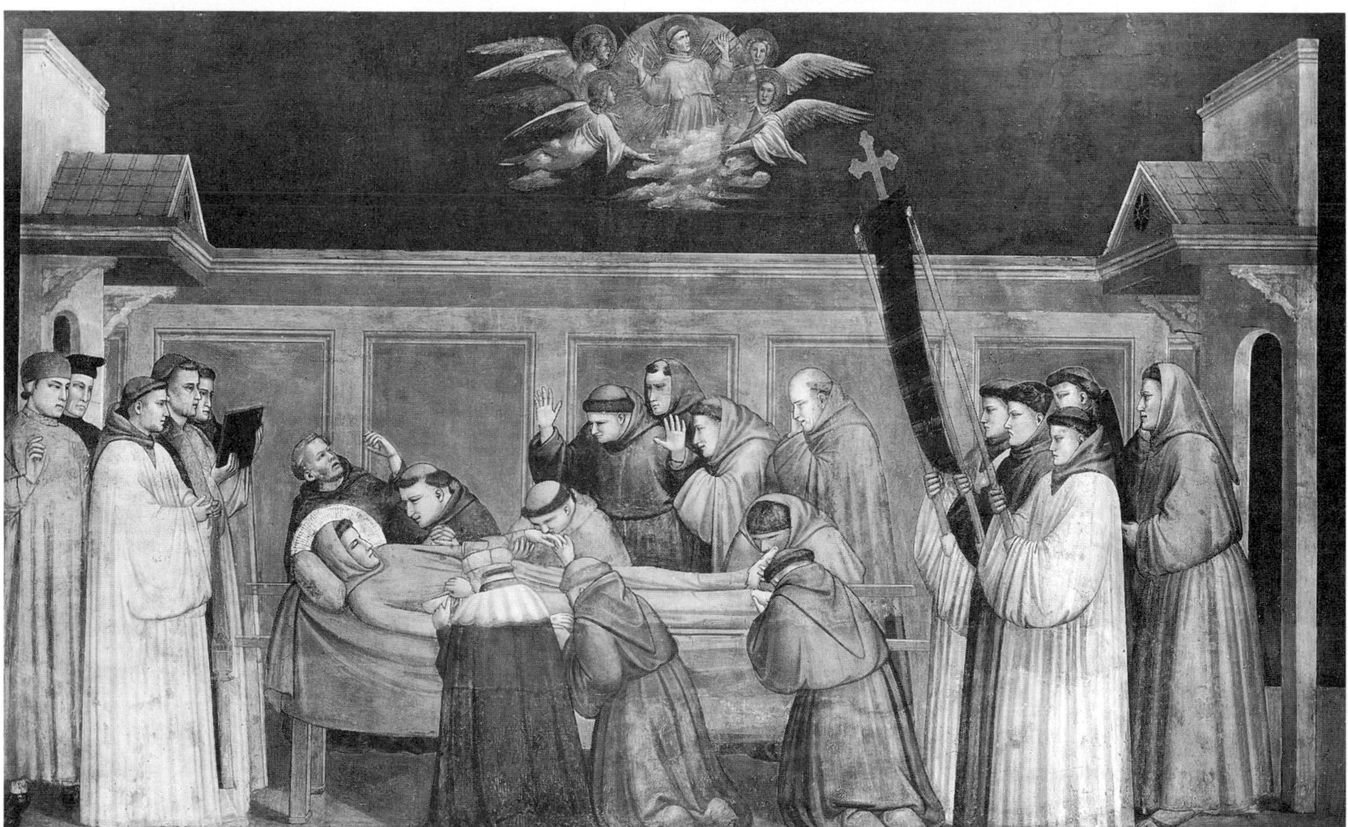

the life and death of St. Francis. Our illustrations show the *Death of St. Francis,* as restored in the nineteenth century (FIG. **15-14**) and with the restorations removed (FIG. **15-15**).* Fortunately, despite the removal of the restorations and the resultant gaps in the composition, enough of the original *Death of St. Francis* remains to give us an idea of the later style of Giotto. Although the St. Francis painting has considerable spiritual affinity with the *Lamentation,* it also shows significant changes. The Gothic agitation has quieted, and the scene has little of the jagged emotion of the *Lamentation.* It seems, indeed, as if the artist had watched the solemn obsequies from offstage. We see the saint, at center on his bier, flanked by kneeling and standing monks; the kneeling figures are seen from behind, in Giotto's fashion. Stately processions of friars in profile come from left and right, as they would be seen in actuality—not frontally, as in a Byzantine procession like that of *Justinian and Attendants* at San Vitale (FIG. 7-36). The figures are accommodated carefully on an architecture-enclosed, stagelike space that has been widened and no longer leaves any doubt that the figures have sufficient room in which to move about. They are taller and have lost some of their former sacklike bulk; Giotto now makes a distinction between the purely form-defining function of the robes and the fact that they are draped around articulated bodies. The impressive solemnity of the procession is enhanced by the omission of the casual and incidental beauties of the world so dear to Sienese and Gothic painters. Giotto sees and records nature in terms of its most basic facts: solid volumes resting firmly on the flat and horizontal surface of the earth. He arranges his figures in meaningful groups and infuses them with restrained emotions that are revealed in slow and measured gestures. With the greatest economy of means, Giotto achieves unsurpassed effects of monumentality, and his paintings, because of the simplicity and directness of their statements, are among the most memorable in world art.

*This painting exemplifies another aspect of the problem of attribution and authenticity. Until the historically sensitive twentieth century, it had long been the custom to "renew" old pictures by painting over damaged or faded areas. Modern scholars, in their zeal to know the "real" painter, have advocated stripping even where this leaves only fragments that are perhaps esthetically unsatisfactory. The practice remains controversial, and the historian of art, the expert, the connoisseur, and, ultimately, the layman always have before them the question of the authenticity of the given work.

15-15 GIOTTO, *Death of St. Francis* (FIG. 15-14 after removal of nineteenth-century restorations).

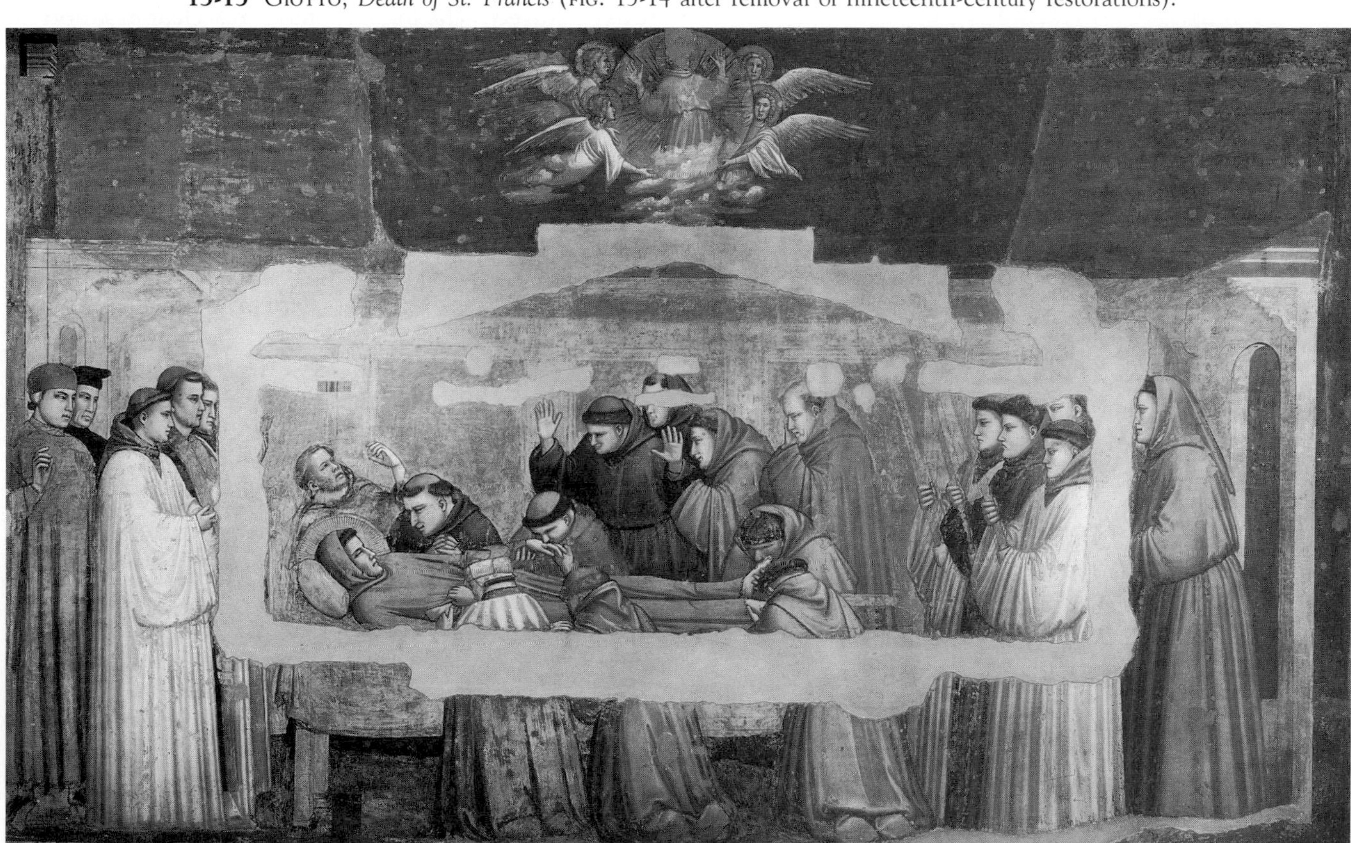

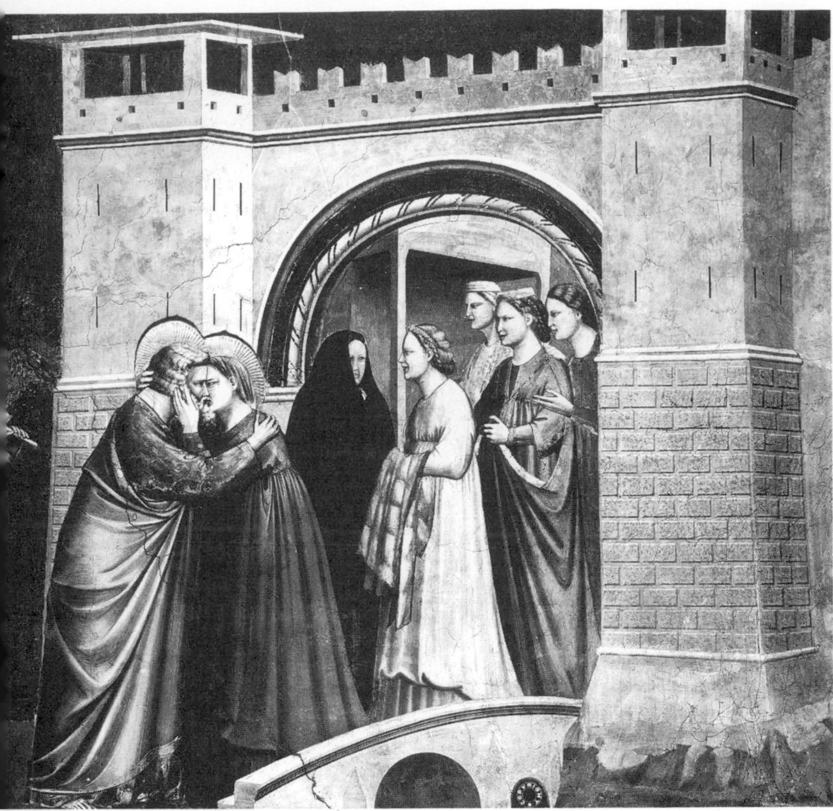

15-16 GIOTTO, *The Meeting of Joachim and Anna*, c. 1305. Fresco. Arena Chapel.

15-17 TADDEO GADDI, *The Meeting of Joachim and Anna*, 1338. Fresco. Baroncelli Chapel, Santa Croce, Florence.

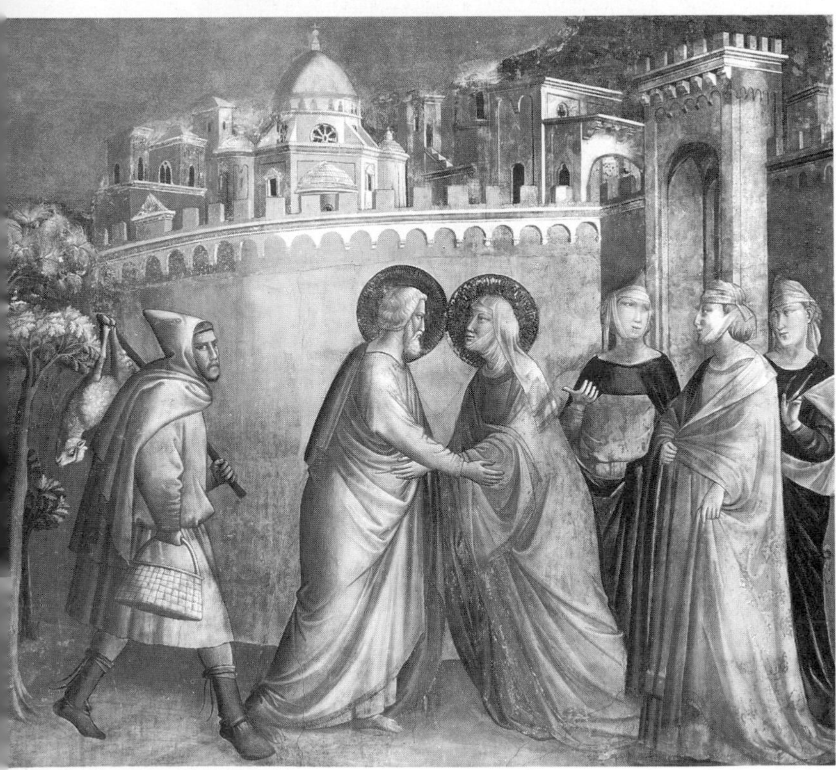

Giotto's murals in the Bardi and Peruzzi chapels of Santa Croce served as textbooks for generations of Renaissance painters from Masaccio to Michelangelo and beyond. These later artists were able to understand the greatness of Giotto's art better than his immediate followers, who never were capable of absorbing more than a fraction of his revolutionary innovations. Their efforts usually remained confined to the emulation of his plastic figure description. Giotto's foster son and his assistant for many years, TADDEO GADDI (*c.* 1300–1366), is a good example of a diligent follower. The differences between the work of a great artist and that of a competent one are readily apparent if we compare Giotto's *The Meeting of Joachim and Anna* in the Arena Chapel (FIG. **15-16**) with Taddeo's version of the same subject in the Baroncelli Chapel in Santa Croce (FIG. **15-17**). Giotto's composition is simple and compact. The figures are related carefully to the single passage of architecture (the Golden Gate), where the parents of the Virgin meet in triumph in the presence of splendidly dressed ladies. The latter mock the cloaked servant who refused to believe that the elderly Anna (St. Anne) would ever bear a child. The story, related in the Apocrypha, is managed with Giotto's usual restraint, clarity, and dramatic compactness. Taddeo allows his composition (FIG. 15-17) to become somewhat loose and unstructured. The figures have no clear relation to the background; the elaborate cityscape, though pleasant in itself, demands too much attention and detracts from the action in the foreground. Gestures have become weak and theatrical, and the hunter (discreetly cut off and unobtrusive in Giotto's painting) here strides boldly toward the center of the scene—a picturesque genre subject that weakens the central theme. Although his figures retain much of Giotto's solidity, Taddeo's painting weakens the dramatic impact of the story by elaborating its incidental details. Giotto stresses the essentials and, by presenting them with his usual simplicity and forceful directness, gives the theme a much more meaningful interpretation. Yet we must not seem to disparage Giotto's contemporaries and followers. Taddeo presses forward the investigation of perspective, as his cityscape reveals, and the genre figure attests to the development of a keen interest in realism.

Simone Martini and the International Style

Duccio's successors in the Siena school display even greater originality and assurance than did Duccio himself. SIMONE MARTINI (*c.* 1285–1344) was a

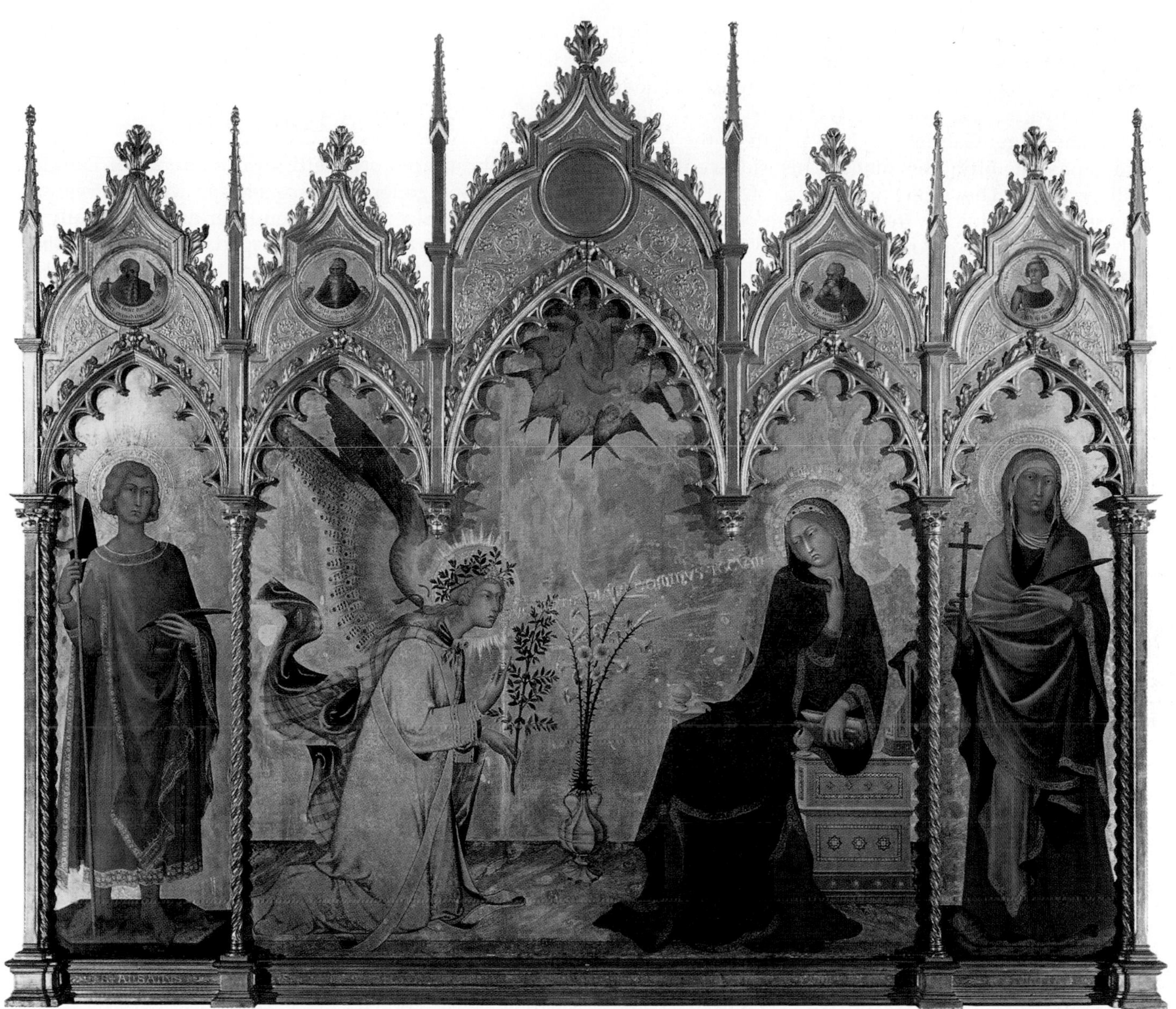

15-18 Simone Martini, *The Annunciation,* 1333. Tempera on wood, approx. 10′ 1″ × 8′ 8¾″ (frame reconstructed in the nineteenth century). Galleria degli Uffizi, Florence.

pupil of Duccio and a close friend of Petrarch, who praised him highly for his portrait of "Laura" (the woman to whom Petrarch dedicated his sonnets). Simone worked for the French kings in Naples and Sicily and, in his last years, was employed at the papal court at Avignon, where he came in contact with northern painters. By adapting the insubstantial but luxuriant patterns of the French Gothic manner to Sienese art and, in turn, by acquainting northern painters with the Sienese style, Simone became instrumental in the formation of the so-called International style, which swept Europe during the late fourteenth and early fifteenth century. This style appealed to the aristocratic taste for brilliant color, lavish costume, intricate ornament, and themes involving splendid processions in which knights and their ladies, complete with entourages, horses, and greyhounds, could glitter to advantage.

Simone's own style does not quite reach the full exuberance of the developed International style, but his famous *Annunciation* altarpiece (FIG. **15-18**) is the perfect antithesis of the style of Giotto, whose work Simone certainly must have been aware of, but whose art just as certainly left him untouched. The

Annunciation is characterized by elegant shapes and radiant color; flowing, fluttering line; and weightless figures in a spaceless setting. The complex etiquette of the chivalric courts of Europe dictates the presentation. The angel Gabriel has just alighted, the breeze of his passage lifting his mantle, his iridescent wings still beating. The white and gold of his sumptuous gown heraldically represent the celestial realm whence he bears his message. The Virgin, putting down her book of devotions, shrinks demurely from Gabriel's reverent genuflection, an appropriate gesture in the presence of royalty. She draws about her the deep blue, golden-hemmed mantle, the heraldic colors she wears as the Queen of Heaven. Despite the Virgin's modesty and diffidence and the tremendous import of the angel's message, the scene subordinates drama to court ritual and structural experiments to surface splendor. The painted splendor is matched by the intricate tracery of the richly tooled, late Gothic frame. Of French inspiration, it replaces the more sober, clean-cut shapes that were traditional in Italy, and its appearance here is eloquent testimony to the two-way flow of transalpine influences that fashioned the International style.

The altarpiece is dated 1333 and signed by Simone Martini and his student and assistant, Lippo Memmi. Lippo's contribution to the *Annunciation* is still a matter of debate, but historians now generally subscribe to the theory that he painted the two lateral saints, St. Ansano and his godmother, St. Maxima (?). These figures, which are reminiscent of the jamb statues of Gothic church portals, are drawn a little more solidly and lack the linear elegance of Simone's central pair. Given medieval and Renaissance workshop practices, it is often next to impossible to distinguish the master's hand from that of his assistants, especially if part of the latters' work was corrected or partially redone by the master. Generally, assistants were charged with the gilding of frames and backgrounds, the completion of decorative work, and, occasionally, the rendering of architectural settings. Figures, especially those that were central to the represented subject, were regarded as the most important and difficult parts of a painting and were the master's responsibility. Assistants might be allowed to paint some of the less important, marginal figures, but only under the master's close supervision. Among the numerous contracts for paintings that have survived from this period some are quite specific in spelling out the master's responsibilities, stipulating that the major parts of the work be executed by his hand and his alone. As we move from the anonymity of Medieval art toward the artist's emancipation during the Renaissance (when he rises from the rank of artisan to that of artist-scientist), the value of his individual skills—and his reputation—become increasingly important to his patrons and clients.

The Lorenzetti

The brothers Lorenzetti, also students of Duccio, share in the general experiments in pictorial realism that characterize the fourteenth century, especially in their seeking of convincing spatial illusions. Going well beyond his master, PIETRO LORENZETTI (active 1320–1348) achieved remarkable success in a large panel representing *The Birth of the Virgin* (FIG. **15-19**). The wooden architectural members that divide the panel into three compartments are represented as extending back into the painted space, as if we were looking through the wooden frame (apparently added later) into a boxlike stage, where the event takes place. The illusion is strengthened by the fact that one of the vertical members cuts across one of the figures, blocking part of it from view. Whether this architecture-assisted perspective illusion was intentional is problematical; in any case, the full significance of the device of pictorial illusion enhanced by applied architectural parts was not realized until the next century. No precedent for it exists in the history of Western art, but a long, successful history of such visual illusions produced by a union of real and simulated architecture with painted figures was to develop during the Renaissance and Baroque periods. Pietro did not make just a structural advance here; his very subject represents a marked step in the advance of worldly realism. St. Anne, reclining wearily as the midwives wash the child and the women bring gifts, is the center of an episode that takes place in an upper-class Italian house of the period. A number of carefully observed domestic details and the scene at the left, where Joachim eagerly awaits the news of the delivery, place the events in an actual household, as if we had moved the panels of the walls back and peered inside. The structural innovation in illusionistic space becomes one with the new curiosity that leads to careful inspection and recording of what lies directly before our eyes in the everyday world.

Pietro's brother, AMBROGIO LORENZETTI (active 1319–1348), elaborated the Sienese advances in illusionistic representation in spectacular fashion in a vast mural in the Palazzo Pubblico. The effects of good and bad government are allegorically juxtaposed here in the *Good Government* fresco. Good Government is represented as a majestic, enthroned figure flanked by the virtues of Justice, Prudence, Temperance, and Fortitude, as well as by Peace and Magnanimity; above hover the theological virtues of Faith, Hope, and Charity. In the foreground, the citizens of Siena advance to do homage to Good Govern-

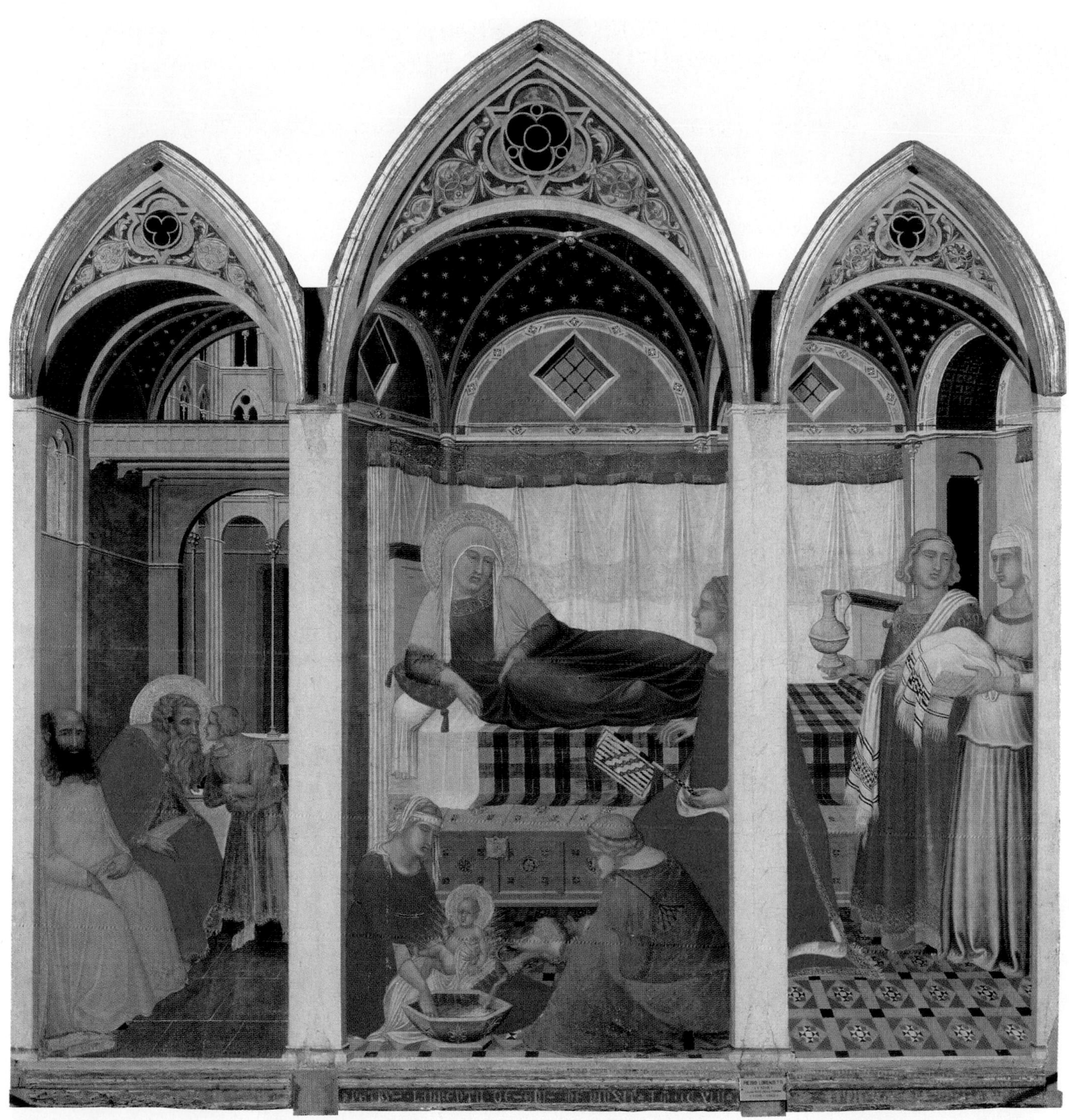

15-19 PIETRO LORENZETTI, *The Birth of the Virgin*, 1342. Tempera on wood, approx. 6′ 1″ × 5′ 11″. Museo dell'Opera del Duomo, Siena.

ment and all the virtues that accompany it. The turbulent politics of the Italian cities, the violent party struggles, the overthrow and reinstatement of governments would certainly have called for solemn reminders of the value of justice in high places, and the city hall would be just the place for a painting like Ambrogio's. Beyond the allegories and the dedication scene stretch the depictions of the fruits of Good Government, both in the city and the countryside. The *Peaceful City* (FIG. **15-20**) is a panoramic view of Siena itself, with its clustering palaces, markets, towers, churches, streets, and walls. The traffic of the city moves peacefully, the guildsmen ply their trades and crafts, and a cluster of radiant maidens, hand in

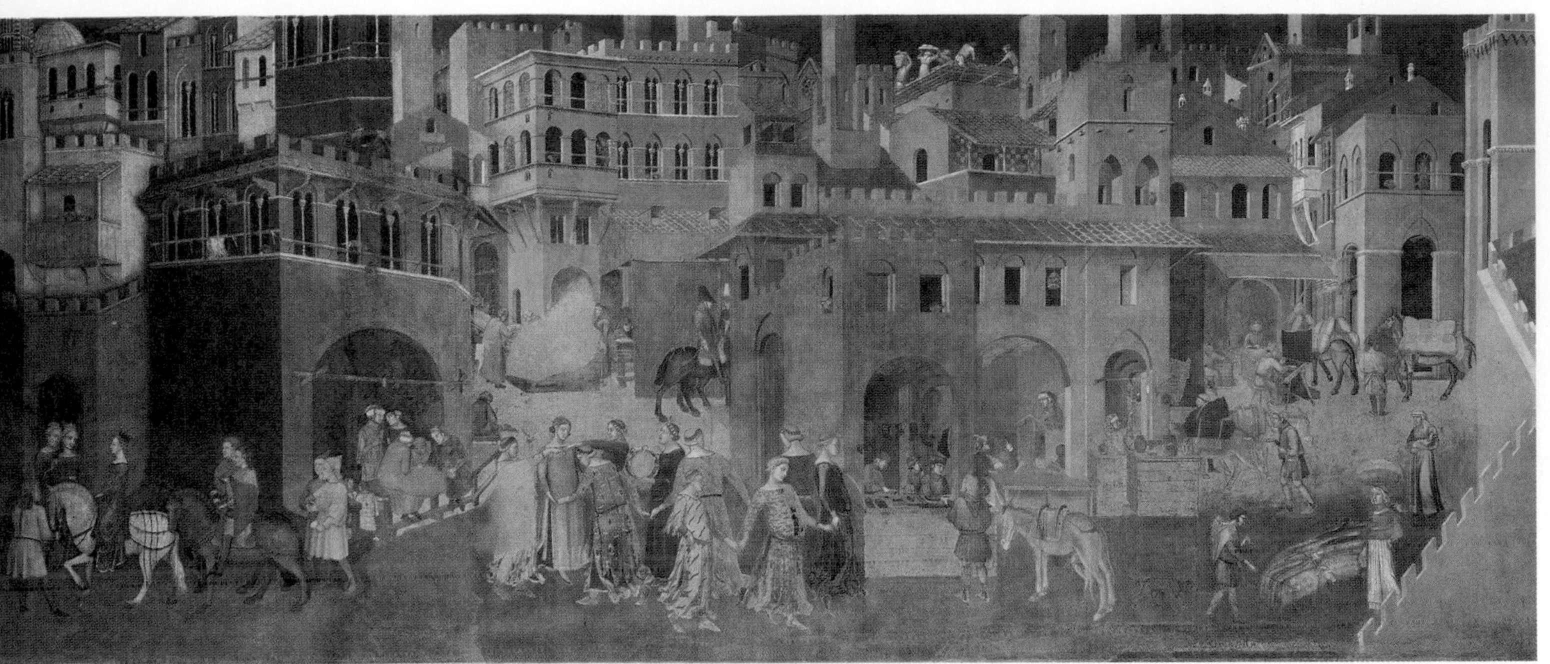

15-20 Ambrogio Lorenzetti, *Peaceful City,* detail from the fresco *Allegory of Good Government: The Effects of Good Government in the City and the Country,* Sala della Pace, Palazzo Pubblico, Siena, 1338–1339.

hand, perform a graceful, circling dance. The artist fondly observes the life of his city, and its architecture gives him an opportunity to apply Siena's rapidly growing knowledge of perspective. Passing through the city gate to the countryside beyond its walls, Ambrogio's *Peaceful Country* (FIG. **15-21**) presents a bird's-eye view of the undulating Tuscan countryside—its villas, castles, plowed farmlands, and peasants going about their seasonal occupations. An allegorical figure of Security hovers above the landscape, unfurling a scroll that promises safety to all who live under the rule of the law. In this sweeping view of an actual countryside, we have the first appearance of landscape since the ancient world. The difference is

15-21 Ambrogio Lorenzetti, *Peaceful Country,* detail from the fresco *Allegory of Good Government: The Effects of Good Government in the City and the Country.*

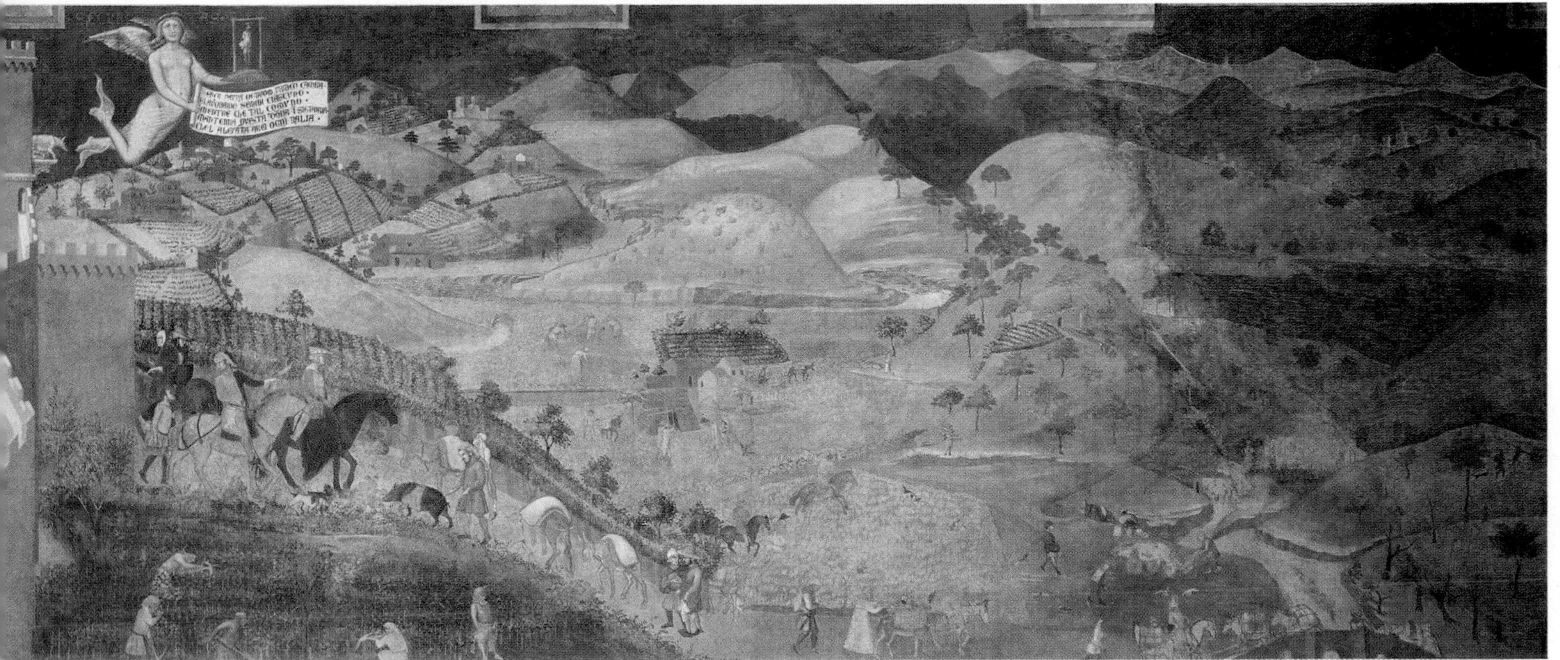

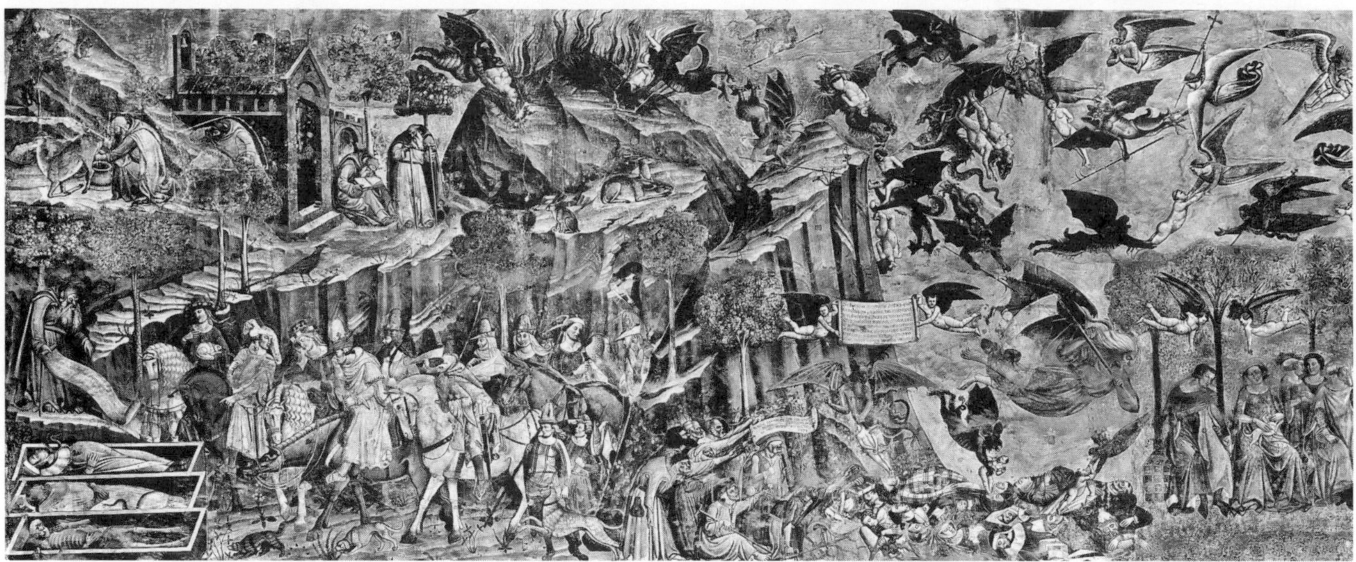

15-22 BUONAMICO BUFFALMACCO or FRANCESCO TRAINI (?), *The Triumph of Death*, *c.* 1340. Fresco. Campo Santo, Pisa.

that now the landscape—as well as the view of the city—is particularized by careful observation, being given almost the character of a portrait of a specific place and environment in a desire for authenticity. By combining some of Giotto's analytical powers with the narrative talent of Duccio, Ambrogio is able to achieve more spectacular results than those of either of his two great predecessors.

The Black Death may have ended the careers of both Lorenzettis; nothing is heard of them after 1348, the year that brought so much horror to defenseless Europe. An unusual and fascinating painting relates this common late Medieval theme. In *The Triumph of Death* (FIG. **15-22**) in the Campo Santo at Pisa, attributed to FRANCESCO TRAINI (active *c.* 1321–1363) and, more recently, to BUONAMICO BUFFALMACCO (active during the early fourteenth century), three young aristocrats and their ladies, mounted in a stylish cavalcade, encounter three coffin-encased corpses in differing stages of decomposition. As the horror of the confrontation with death strikes them, the ladies turn away with delicate and ladylike disgust and a gentleman holds his nose (the animals, horses and dogs, sniff excitedly). A holy hermit unrolls a scroll that demonstrates the folly of pleasure and the inevitability of death. In another section to the right, the ladies and gentlemen, wishing to forget dreadful realities, occupy themselves in an orange grove with music, gallantries, and lapdogs, while all around them death and judgment occur and angels and demons struggle for souls. The medieval message is as strong as ever, but gilded youth refuses to acknowledge it. The painting applies all the stock of Florentine-Sienese representational craft to present the most worldly—and mortal—picture of the fourteenth century. It is an irony of history that, as Western humanity draws both itself and the world into ever-clearer visual focus, it perceives ever more clearly that corporeal things are perishable.

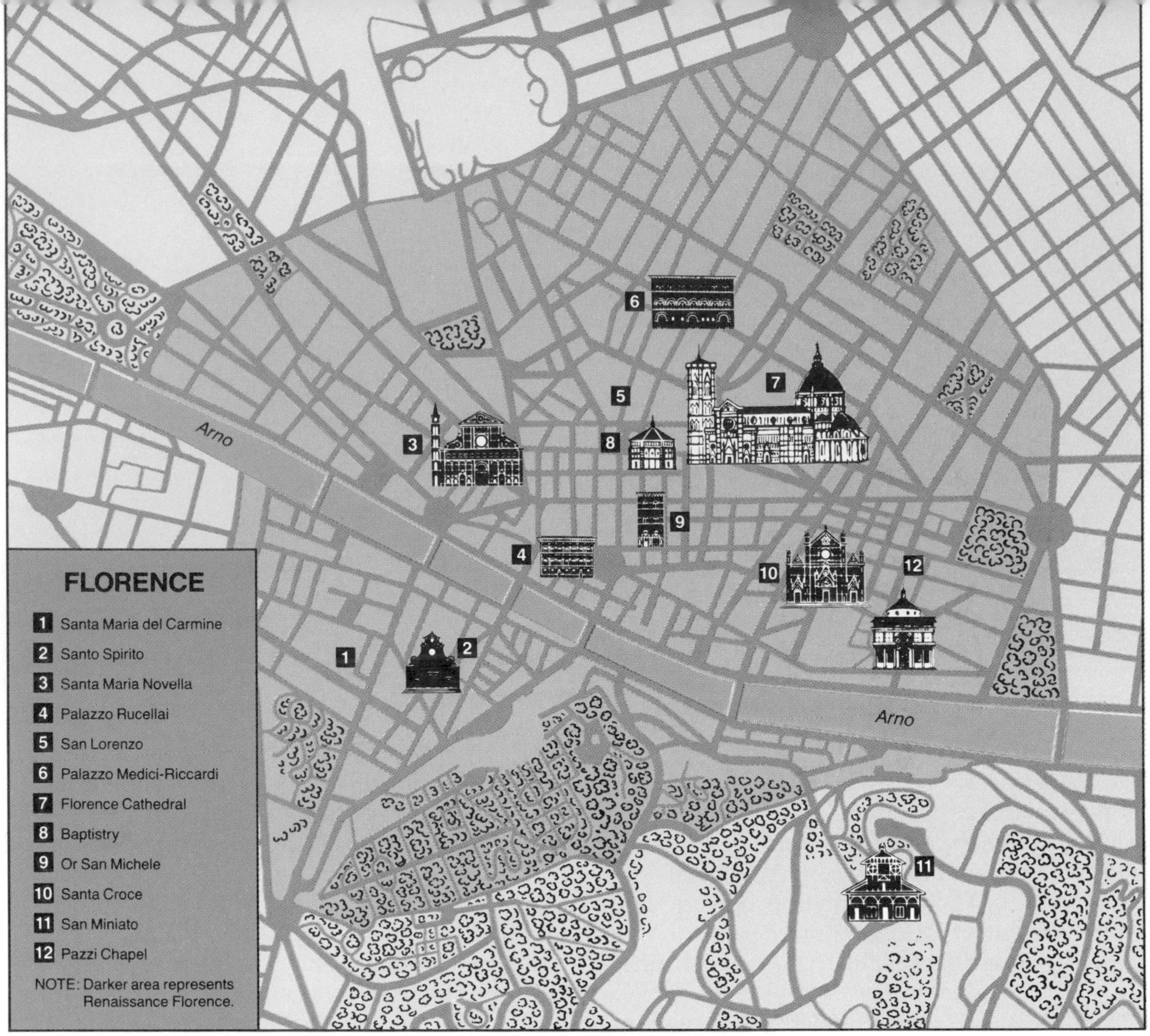

Arno

Arno

FLORENCE

1 Santa Maria del Carmine
2 Santo Spirito
3 Santa Maria Novella
4 Palazzo Rucellai
5 San Lorenzo
6 Palazzo Medici-Riccardi
7 Florence Cathedral
8 Baptistry
9 Or San Michele
10 Santa Croce
11 San Miniato
12 Pazzi Chapel

NOTE: Darker area represents Renaissance Florence.

1400 1410 1420 1430 1440

EARLY RENAISSANCE

NANNI DI BANCO
Quattro Santi Coronati
c. 1408–1414

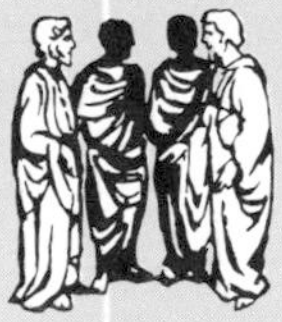

MASACCIO
1401–1428

BRUNELLESCHI
Dome of Florence Cathedral
1420–1436

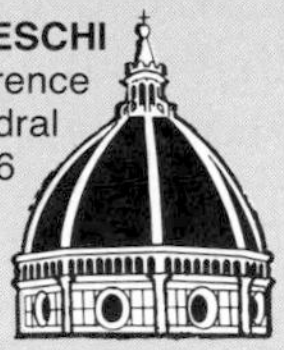

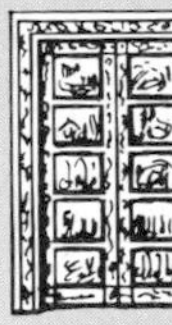

GHIBERTI
Gates of Paradise
1425–1452

BRUNELLESCHI
Pazzi Chapel
begun *c.* 1440

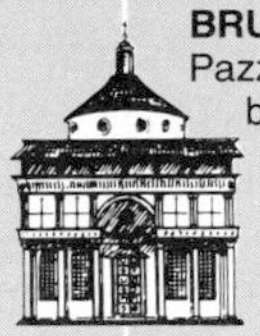

LUCA DELLA ROBBIA
1400–1482

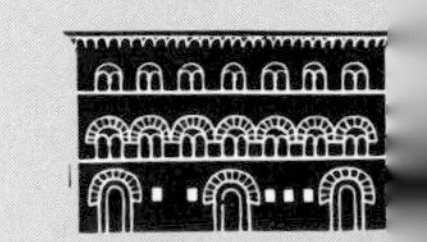

FRA FILIPPO LIPPI
c. 1406–1469

MICHELOZZO
Palazzo Medici-Riccardi
begun 1444

JACOPO DELLA QUERCIA
c. 1375–1438

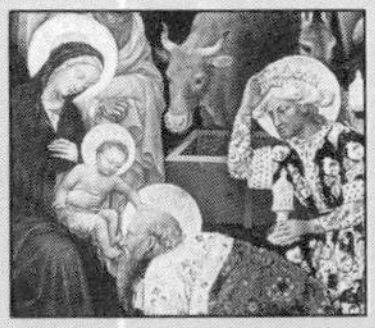

GENTILE DA FABRIANO
The Adoration of the Magi, detail 1423

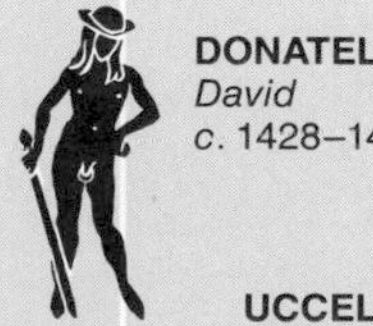

DONATELLO
David
c. 1428–1432

UCCELLO
1397–1475

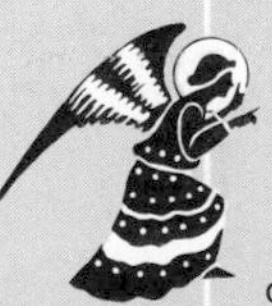

FRA ANGELICO
Annunciation, detail *c.* 1440–1445

Rise of House of Medici early 15th century

Pisa ruled by Florence 1406

End of Great Schism 1417

16
FIFTEENTH-CENTURY ITALIAN ART

1450 | 1460 | 1470 | 1480 | 1490 | 1500

EARLY RENAISSANCE

PIERO DELLA FRANCESCA *Resurrection*, detail *c.* 1463

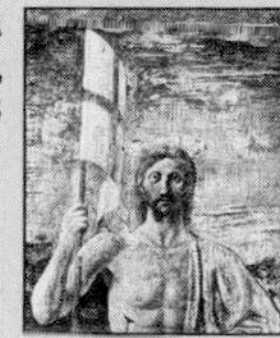

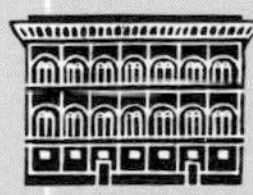

ALBERTI Palazzo Rucellai *c.* 1452–1470

ALBERTI Santa Maria Novella, façade *c.* 1458–1470

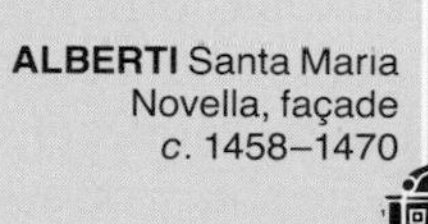

Alberti's Treatises 1436–1464

MANTEGNA *c.*1431–1506

GHIRLANDAIO 1449–1494

POLLAIUOLO *Hercules and Antaeus c.* 1475

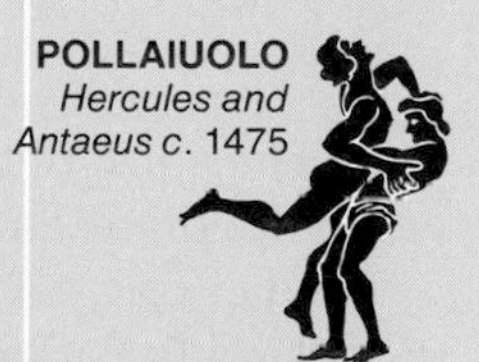

VERROCCHIO *David c.* 1465

A. ROSSELLINO *Matteo Palmieri* 1468

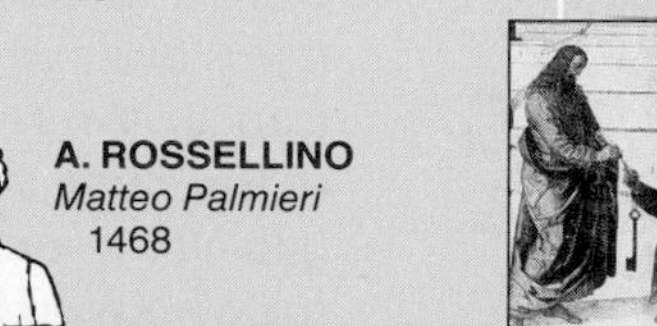

BOTTICELLI *The Birth of Venus*, detail *c.* 1482

Sistine Chapel frescoes, painted 1481–1483

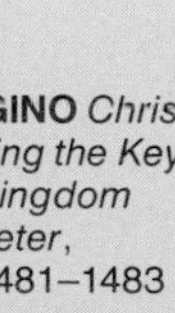

PERUGINO *Christ Delivering the Keys of the Kingdom to St. Peter*, detail 1481–1483

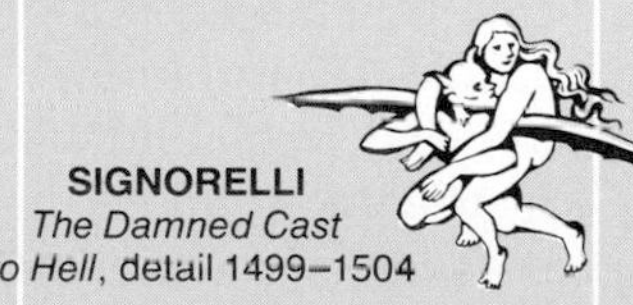

SIGNORELLI *The Damned Cast into Hell*, detail 1499–1504

Cosimo de' Medici 1389–1464

Conquest of Constantinople by Turks 1453

Lorenzo de' Medici 1449–1492

Pico della Mirandola 1463–1494 *Oration on the Dignity of Man*

Medici expelled from Florence 1494

Girolamo Savonarola assumes power 1496, is burned at stake 1498

France captures Milan 1499

FLORENCE took cultural command of Italy early in the fifteenth century, inaugurating the Renaissance and establishing itself as the intellectual and artistic capital of southern Europe—a position of dominance it was to retain until the end of the century. According to John Addington Symonds, a nineteenth-century historian of the Renaissance:

> Nowhere else except at Athens has the whole population of a city been so permeated with ideas, so highly intellectual by nature, so keen in perception, so witty and so subtle, as at Florence. . . . The primacy of the Florentines in literature, the fine arts, law, scholarship, philosophy, and science was acknowledged throughout Italy.*

The power and splendor of Florence had been building for many years; the fifteenth century marked its perfection. Like the Athenians after the repulse of the Persians, the citizens of Florence (who felt a historical affinity with the Athenians) responded with conscious pride to the repulse of the dukes of Milan, who had attempted the conquest of Tuscany. The Florentines also developed a culture that was stimulated and supported by a vast accumulation of wealth, a situation much like that in Athens, but only a few illustrious Florentine families controlled that wealth.

The Medici, bankers to all Europe, became such lavish patrons of art and learning that, to this day, the name "Medici" means a generous patron of the fine arts. For centuries, the history of Florence is the history of the House of Medici. Early in the fifteenth century, Giovanni de' Medici had established the family fortune. His son Cosimo, called the "father of his country" by the Florentines, secured the admiration and loyalty of the people of Florence against the noble and privileged. With this security, the Medici gradually became the discreet dictators of the Florentine republic, disguising their absolute power behind a mask of affable benevolence. Scarcely a great architect, painter, sculptor, philosopher, or Humanist scholar was unknown to the Medici. Cosimo began the first public library since the ancient world, and historians estimate that in some thirty years he and his descendants expended almost $20 million for manuscripts and books; such was the financial power behind the establishment of Humanism in the Renaissance. Careful businessmen that they were, the Medici were not sentimental about their endowment of art and scholarship. Cosimo declared that his good works were "not only for the honor of God but . . . likewise for my own remembrance." Yet the astute businessman and politician had a sincere love of learning, reading Plato in his old age and writing to his tutor, the Neo-Platonic philosopher Marsilio Ficino, "I desire nothing so much as to know the best road to happiness."

Cosimo is the very model of the cultivated, Humanist grandee. His grandson, Lorenzo the Magnificent, went even beyond his grandfather in munificence, as his name suggests. A talented poet himself, he gathered about him a galaxy of artists and gifted men in all fields, extending the library Cosimo had begun, revitalizing his academy for the instruction of artists, establishing the Platonic Academy of Philosophy, and lavishing funds (often the city's own) on splendid buildings, festivals, and pageants. If his prime motive was to retain the affection of the people and, thus, the power of the House of Medici, he nevertheless made Florence a city of great beauty, the capital of all the newly flourishing arts. His death, in 1492, brought to an end the golden age of Florence, and the years immediately following saw Italy invaded by the "barbarian" nations (as the Italians called them) of France, Spain, and the Holy Roman Empire. The Medici were expelled from Florence; the reforming, fanatical Girolamo Savonarola preached repentance in the cathedral of Florence; and the Renaissance moved its light and its artists from Florence to Rome. But one of the most prominent patrons of the Roman Renaissance, Pope Leo X, benefactor of Raphael and Michelangelo, was himself a Medici, the son of Lorenzo the Magnificent. Never in history was a family so intimately associated with a great cultural revolution. We may safely say that the Medici subsidized and endowed the Renaissance.

THE FIRST HALF OF THE FIFTEENTH CENTURY

Sculpture

The spirit of the Medici and of the Renaissance was competitive and desirous of fame. But even before Medici rule, civic competitiveness and pride had motivated the adornment of Florence. The history of the Early Renaissance in art begins with an account of a competition for a design for the east doors of the baptistry of Florence (doors later moved to the north entrance). Andrea Pisano had designed the south doors of the same structure almost three generations earlier (FIG. 15-4). LORENZO GHIBERTI (1378–1455), the sculptor who won the competition, describes his victory in terms that reflect the egoism and the "cult of fame" characteristic of the period and of Renaissance artists in general:

*John Addington Symonds, *Renaissance in Italy* (New York: Modern Library, 1935), Vol. 1, p. 125.

> To me was conceded the palm of the victory by all the experts and by all . . . who had competed with me. To me the honor was conceded universally and with no exception. To all it seemed that I had at that time surpassed the others without exception, as was recognized by a great council and an investigation of learned men . . . highly skilled from the painters and sculptors of gold, silver, and marble. There were thirty-four judges from the city and the other surrounding countries. The testimonial of the victory was given in my favor by all. . . . It was granted to me and determined that I should make the bronze door for this church.*

This passage also indicates the esteem and importance now attached to art, with leading men of a city bestowing eagerly sought-for commissions and great new programs of private and public works being undertaken widely.

The contestants seeking to design the doors represented the assigned subject, *The Sacrifice of Isaac,* within panels shaped like the Gothic quatrefoil used by Andrea Pisano for the south doors of the baptistry. Only the panels by FILIPPO BRUNELLESCHI and Ghiberti have survived. Brunelleschi's panel (FIG. **16-1**) shows a sturdy and vigorous interpretation of the theme, with something of the emotional agitation of the tradition of Giovanni Pisano (FIG. 15-3). Abraham seems suddenly to have summoned the dreadful courage needed to kill his son at God's command; he lunges forward, draperies flying, exposing Isaac's throat to the knife with desperate violence. Matching Abraham's energy, the saving angel darts in from the left, arresting the stroke just in time. Brunelleschi's figures are carefully observed and display elements of a new realism. Yet his composition is perhaps overly busy, and the figures of the two servants and the donkey are not subordinated sufficiently to the main action.

We can make this criticism more firmly when we compare Brunelleschi's panel to Ghiberti's (FIG. **16-2**). In the latter, vigor and strength of statement are subordinated to grace and smoothness; little of the awfulness of the subject appears. Abraham sways elegantly in the familiar Gothic S-curve and seems to feign a deadly thrust rather than aim it. The figure of Isaac, beautifully posed and rendered, recalls ancient Classicism and could be regarded as the first really classicizing nude since antiquity. Ghiberti was trained as both a goldsmith and a painter, and his skilled treatment of the fluent surfaces, with their sharply and accurately incised detail, evidences his goldsmith's craft. As a painter, he shares the painter's interest in spatial illusion. The rocky landscape seems to emerge from the blank panel toward us, as

*In E. G. Holt, ed., *Literary Sources of Art History* (Princeton, NJ: Princeton University Press, 1947), pp. 87–88.

16-1 FILIPPO BRUNELLESCHI, *The Sacrifice of Isaac,* competition panel for the east doors of the baptistry of Florence, 1401–1402. Gilt bronze relief, 21″ × 17″. Museo Nazionale del Bargello, Florence.

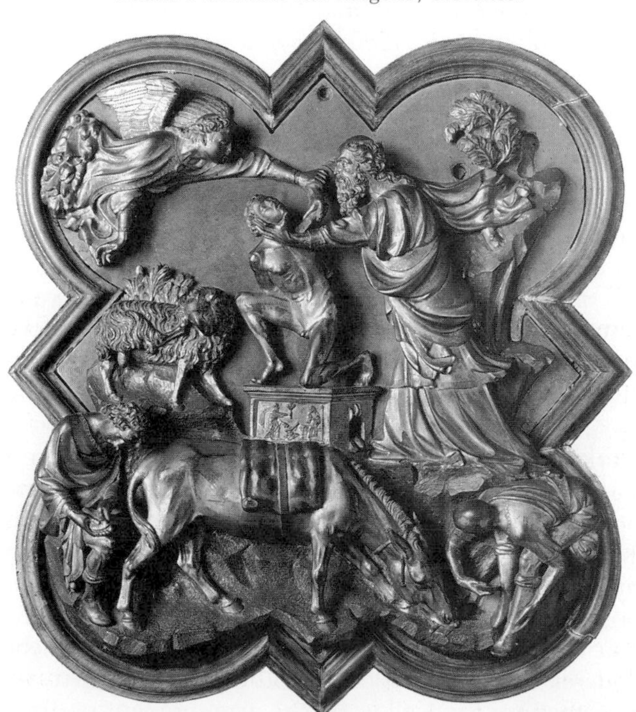

16-2 LORENZO GHIBERTI, *The Sacrifice of Isaac,* competition panel for the east doors of the baptistry of Florence, 1401–1402. Gilt bronze relief, 21″ × 17″. Museo Nazionale del Bargello, Florence.

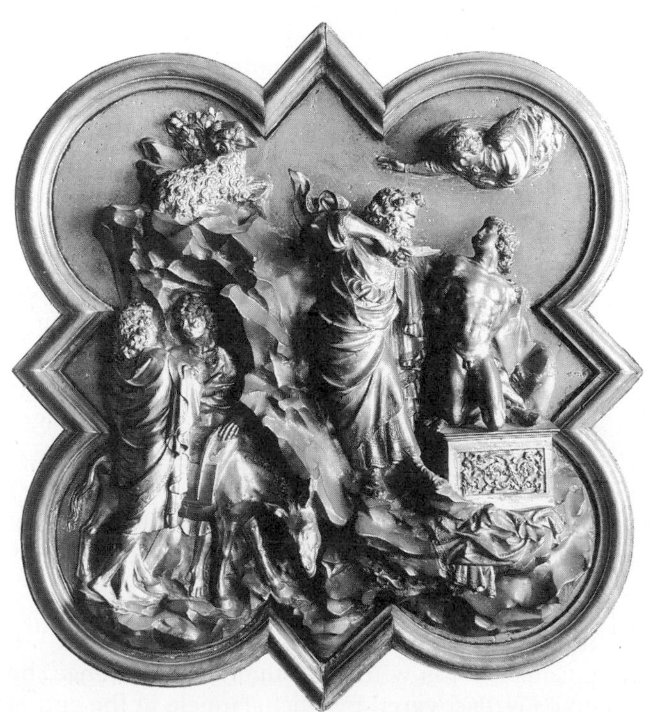

does the strongly foreshortened angel. These pictorial effects, sometimes thought alien to sculpture, are more developed in Ghiberti's later work. The execution of a second pair of doors for the baptistry (FIG. 16-10) testifies to his extraordinary skill in harmonizing the effects peculiar to sculpture and painting. Here, however, within the limits of the awkward shape of the *Isaac* panel, Ghiberti achieves a composition that is perhaps less daring than Brunelleschi's but more cohesive and unified, and the jury's choice probably was fortunate for the course of art, despite accusations of collusion by Brunelleschi's biographer, Manetti. One result of the decision was, apparently, that it helped Brunelleschi to resolve his indecision about his proper calling. Subordinating sculpture to a less important role, he became the first great architect of the Renaissance. As for Ghiberti, his conservative style would be modified greatly by the discoveries of his contemporaries, and their influence on him would be visible in the set of doors he designed later for the east entrance of the baptistry.

The artists of Florence in the early Renaissance sometimes are classified as "conservative" or "progressive," depending on whether they cling to the International Gothic style or take up the new pictorial experimentalism. The classification cannot be applied consistently, however, for some artists who keep to the old conventions still occasionally adopt what they can use from their more experimental contemporaries when they can make it consistent with their own styles. Both conservative and progressive works may be of the highest quality, and we should not think that their excellence is merely a function of their being up to date or avant-garde. In some cases, too fertile and inventive an imagination may outrace the artist's powers to systematize his efforts and become detrimental to his development.

JACOPO DELLA QUERCIA (*c.* 1375–1438), a Sienese sculptor competing for the baptistry commission, was perhaps the only non-Florentine sculptor of first rank in the fifteenth century. In comparison with the early work of Ghiberti, Jacopo's is progressive. His panel, *The Expulsion from the Garden of Eden* (FIG. **16-3**), from a series of reliefs enframing the portal of San Petronio in Bologna, is carved in shallow relief and set into the frame in a closely knit pattern of curves and diagonals. The figures are constructed so that they seem capable of breaking out of the confines of the relief. A robust energy animates the powerful, heavily muscled forms and recalls the ideal Classical athletes. The conventional Gothic slenderness and delicacy are gone, and Jacopo's massive, monumental forms herald the grand style of the Renaissance. Indeed, although his style is without influence in Florence, he was to be rediscovered by Michelangelo at the end of

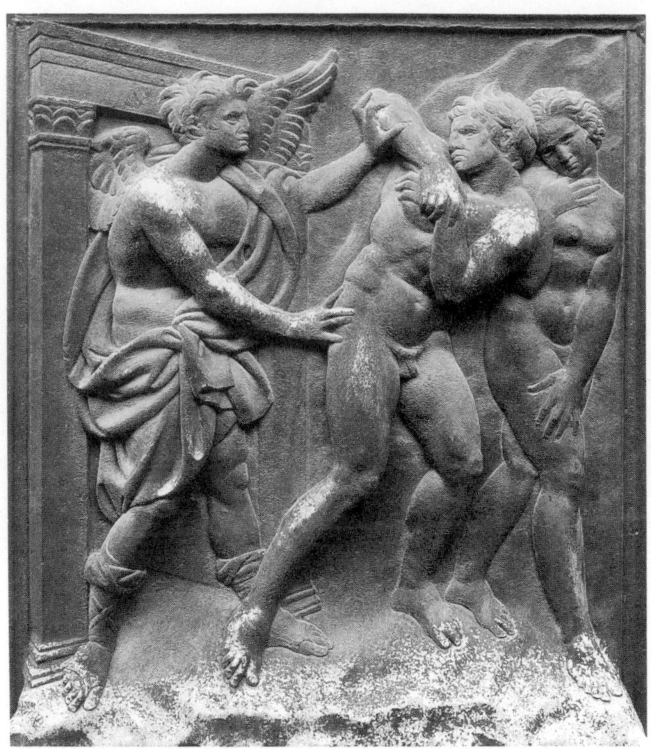

16-3 JACOPO DELLA QUERCIA, *The Expulsion from the Garden of Eden*, *c.* 1430. Istrian stone, 34″ × 27″. Main portal, San Petronio, Bologna, Italy.

the fifteenth century; the latter's debt to Jacopo is clearly visible in the great Florentine's painting of the same subject in the Sistine Chapel ceiling.

As the Sienese artist turned to the observation of the mechanics of the human body, a Florentine artist, NANNI DI BANCO (*c.* 1380–1421), began to explore that other popular avenue of Humanistic research, the antique. His life-size figures of four martyred saints, *Quattro Santi Coronati* (FIG. **16-4**), represent the patron saints of the Florentine guild of sculptors, architects, and masons. The group, set into the outside wall of the Medieval church of Or San Michele in Florence, is an early near-solution to the Renaissance problem of integrating figures and space on a monumental scale. With these figures, we are well on the way to the great solutions of Masaccio and of the masters of the High Renaissance. The emergence of sculpture from the architectural matrix, a process that began in such works as the thirteenth-century statues of the west front of Reims Cathedral (FIG. 10-33), is almost complete in Nanni's figures, which stand in a niche that is *in* but that confers some separation *from* the architecture. This spatial recess permits a new and dramatic possibility for the interrelationship of the figures. By placing them in a semicircle within their deep niche and relating them to one another by their postures and gestures, as well as by the arrangement of draperies, Nanni has achieved a wonderfully unified spatial composition. The persisting dependence on the architecture may be seen in the abutment of the two forward figures and the enframement of the niche and in the position of the two recessed figures, each in front of an engaged half-column. Nevertheless, these unyielding figures, whose bearing (as in Roman art and stoicism) expresses the discipline through which men of passionate conviction attain order and reason, are joined in a remarkable psychological unity. While the figure on the right speaks, pointing to his right, the two men opposite listen and the one next to him looks out into space, pondering the meaning of the words. Such reinforcement of the formal unity of a figural group with psychological cross-references will be exploited by later Renaissance artists, particularly Leonardo da Vinci.

16-4 Nanni di Banco, *Quattro Santi Coronati*, c. 1408–1414. Marble, figures approx. life size. Or San Michele, Florence.

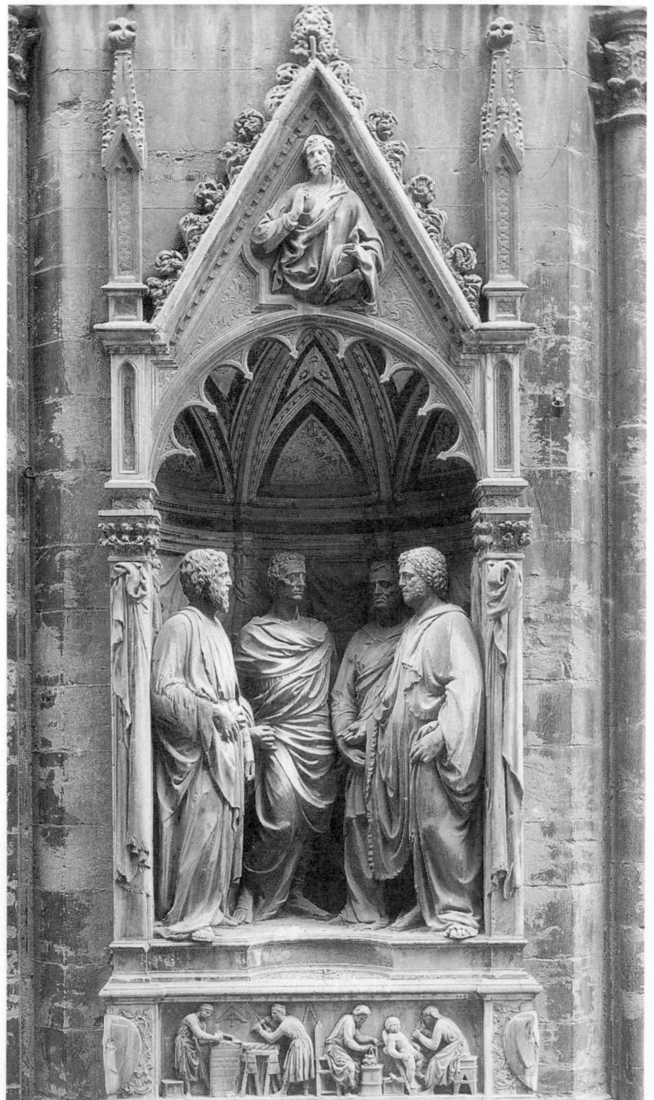

Nanni has before him the example of the sculpture of antiquity. If we compare his statues with those of the *Visitation* group at Reims (FIG. 10-34) or of Nicola Pisano (FIG. 15-2), we find the Classicism of the older works lacking in authority and, as yet, unsure. The *Quattro Santi Coronati* figures have achieved a level of accomplishment that, if not identical with the Roman norm, is at least its equal. Renaissance artists have begun to comprehend the Roman meaning, even if they do not duplicate the Roman form. But duplication is not their purpose; rather, they strive to interpret or offer commentary in the manner of the Humanist scholars dealing with Classical texts.

DONATELLO

The Humanist, Roman Classicism expressed in the sculpture of Nanni was not exclusively of his devising. The whole city of Florence, in its last, fierce war with the Visconti of Milan at the turn of the century, modeled itself on the ancient Roman republic. The Humanist chancellor of Florence, Coluccio Salutati, whose Latin style of writing was widely influential, exhorted his fellow citizens to take as their own the republican ideal of civil and political liberty they believed to be that of Rome, and to identify themselves with its spirit. To be Florentine was to be Roman; freedom was the distinguishing virtue of both.

A new realism based on the study of humanity and nature, an idealism found in the study of Classical forms, and a power of individual expression characteristic of genius are the elements that define the art and the personality of the sculptor Donatello (1386–1466). In the early years of the century, he carried forward most dramatically the search for innovative forms capable of expressing the new ideas of the Humanistic Early Renaissance. Working side by side, Donatello and Nanni collaborated on sculpture for the cathedral of Florence and the church of Or San Michele. They shared the Humanistic enthusiasm for Roman virtue and form; their innovations in style, expressive of a new age, are parallel. Donatello's greatness lies in an extraordinary versatility and depth that led him through a spectrum of themes fundamental to human experience and through stylistic variations that express these themes with unprecedented profundity and force.

A principal characteristic of greatness is authority. Great artists produce work that their contemporaries and posterity accept as authoritative; their work becomes a criterion and a touchstone for criticism. Judgments of what is authoritative and "best" will of course vary with time and place, but the greatest artists seem to survive this relativity of judgment, apparently because they reveal something deeply and permanently true about human nature and broadly applicable to human experience. Shakespeare, for example, seems miraculously familiar with almost the whole world of human nature. Similarly, Donatello is at ease not only with the real, the ideal, and the spiritual, but with such diverse human forms and conditions as childhood, the idealized human nude, practical men of the world, military despots, holy men, derelict prelates, and ascetic old age. Others who follow Donatello in the school of Florence may specialize in one or two of these human types or moods, but none commands them so completely and convincingly. In the early fifteenth century, Donatello defined and claimed as his province the whole terrain of naturalistic and Humanistic art.

Early in his career, he took the first fundamental and necessary step toward the depiction of motion in the human figure—recognition of the principle of weight shift (*ponderation*). His *St. Mark* (FIG. **16-5**), commissioned for Or San Michele, was completed in 1413. With it, Donatello closed a millennium of Medieval art and turned a historical corner into a new era. We have seen the importance of weight shift in the ancient world, when Greek sculptors, in works like the *Kritios Boy* (FIG. 5-19) and the *Doryphoros* (FIG. 5-58), grasped the essential principle that the human body is not rigid, but a flexible structure that moves by continuously shifting the weight from one supporting leg to the other with the main masses of the body moving in consonance. An illuminating comparison may be made between Donatello's *St. Mark* and Medieval portal statuary, the sculpture of Nicola and Giovanni Pisano, or even the early work of Ghiberti. The principle of weight shift has not been grasped in any of these figures except Donatello's *St. Mark.* All at once, with the same abruptness with which it appeared in ancient Greece in Early Classical art (FIG. 5-19), this crucial concept has been rediscovered. In sculpture and painting, Donatello's successors gradually mastered the representation of bodily motion of the most complex kind.

As the body now "moves," its drapery "moves" with it, hanging and folding naturally from and around bodily points of support, so that we sense the figure as a draped nude, not simply as an integrated column with arbitrarily incised drapery. This development further contributes to the independence of the figure from its architectural setting. We feel that *St. Mark* can and is about to move out of the deep niche in which he stands, as the stirring limbs, the shifting weight, and the mobile drapery suggest. It is easy to imagine the figure as freestanding, unenframed by architecture, without loss of any of its basic qualities.

In his *St. George* (FIG. **16-6**), also designed for Or San Michele (between 1415 and 1417), Donatello provides an image of the proud idealism of youth. The armored soldier-saint, patron of the guild of armorers (for whom the statue was commissioned), stands with bold firmness—legs set apart, feet strongly planted, the torso slightly twisting so that the left shoulder and arm advance with a subtle gesture of haughty and challenging readiness. As the dragon approaches, St. George's head is erect and turned slightly to the left; the noble features beneath the furrowed brows are intent, concentrated, yet composed in the realization of his power, intelligence, and reso-

16-5 DONATELLO, *St. Mark,* 1411–1413. Marble, approx. 7′ 9″ high. Or San Michele, Florence.

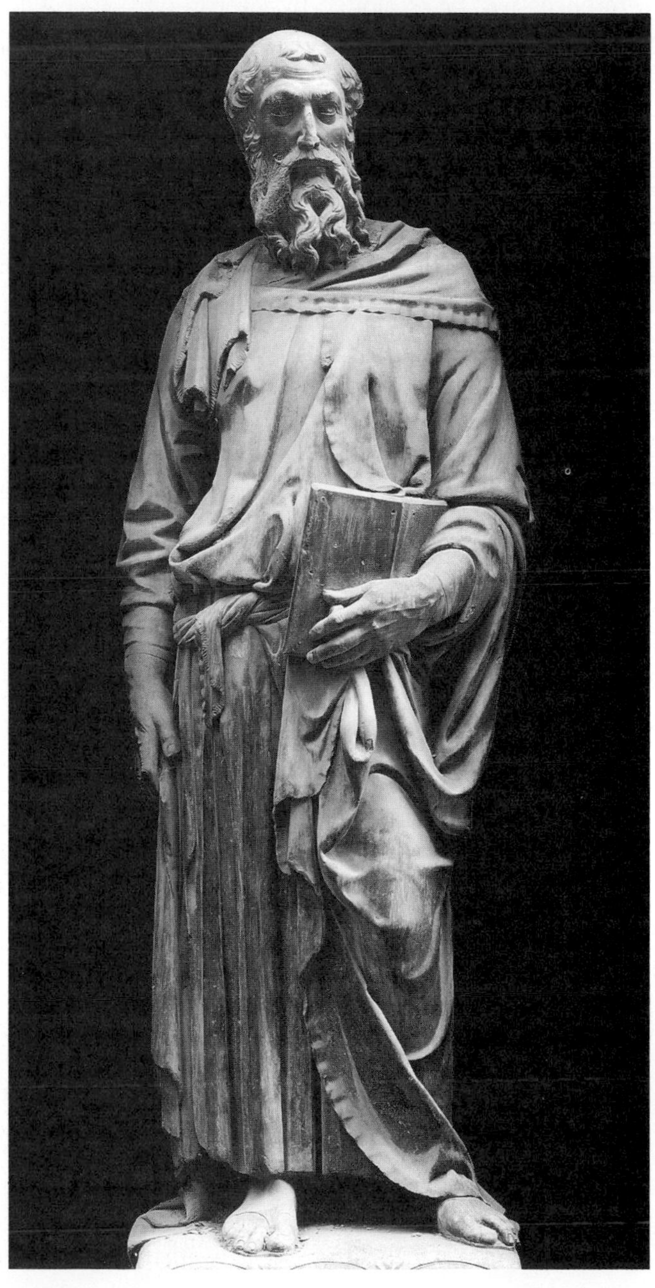

lution. In its regal poise and tense anticipation, the figure contrasts strikingly with its earlier Gothic counterpart, *St. Theodore* (FIG. **16-7**), from Chartres Cathedral. *St. Theodore*, the soldier, appearing essentially weightless, seems lost in some mystic reverie, removed from the world and unaware of his surroundings. The elements of his body are not coordinated in the unity of action we find in *St. George*. The Medieval figure conveys the *idea* of the chivalric knight but nothing of the *fact* of the soldier confronting his enemy.

Between 1416 and 1435, Donatello carved five statues for the niches on the campanile of Florence Cathedral—a project that, like the figures for Or San Michele, had originated in the preceding century. Unlike the Or San Michele figures, however, which were installed only slightly above eye level, those for the campanile were placed in niches at least 30 feet above the ground. At that distance, delicate descriptive details (hair, garments, and features) no longer can be recognized readily and become meaningless. Massive folds that can be read from afar and a much

16-6 DONATELLO, *St. George*, 1415–1417, from Or San Michele. Marble (has been replaced by a bronze copy), approx. 6′ 10″ high. Museo Nazionale del Bargello, Florence.

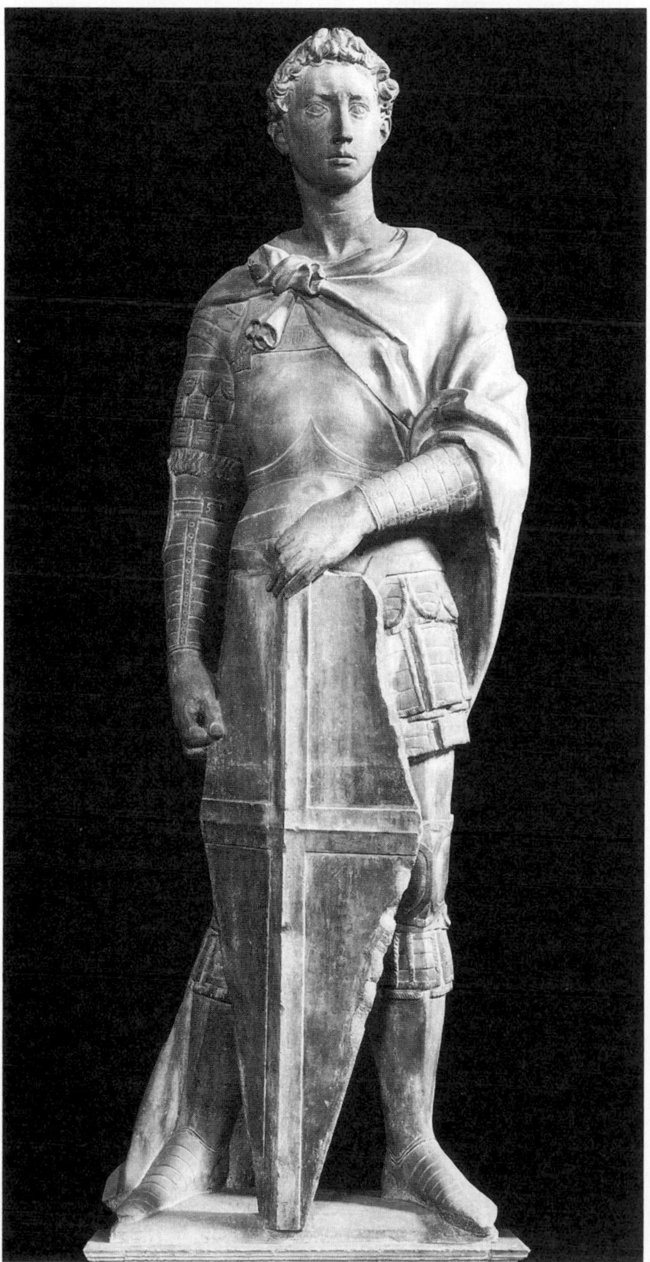

16-7 *St. Theodore*, jamb statue, c. 1215–1220. Stone, over life size. South portal, Chartres Cathedral, Chartres, France.

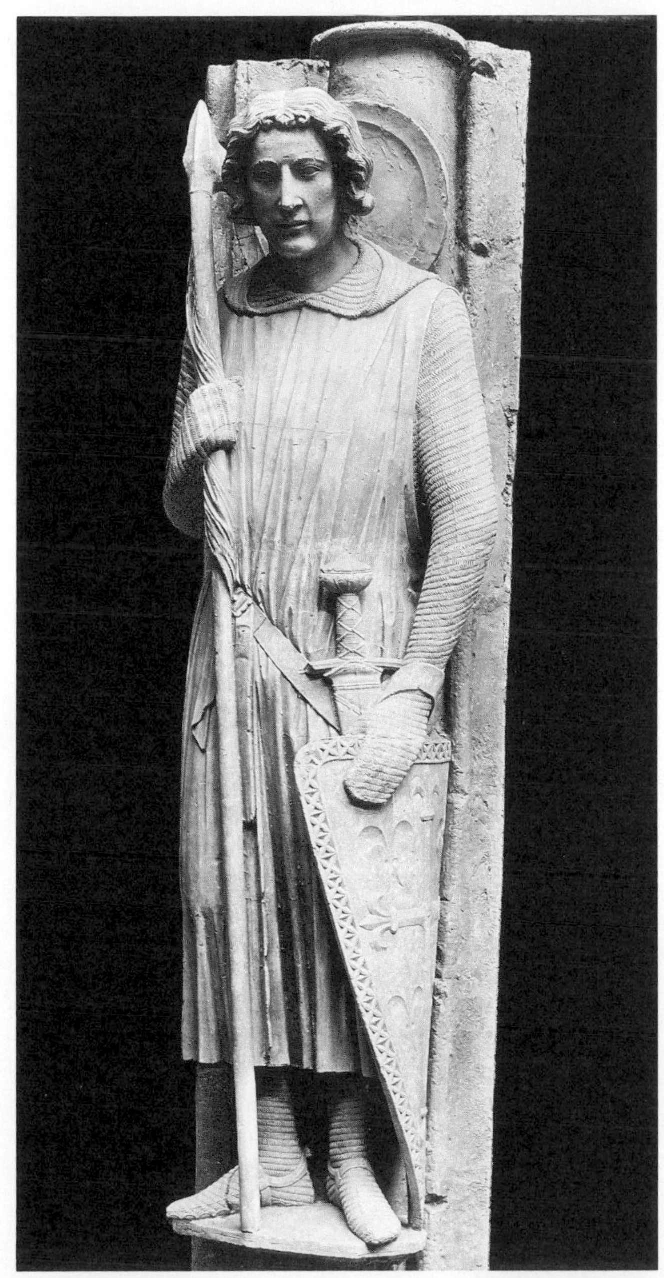

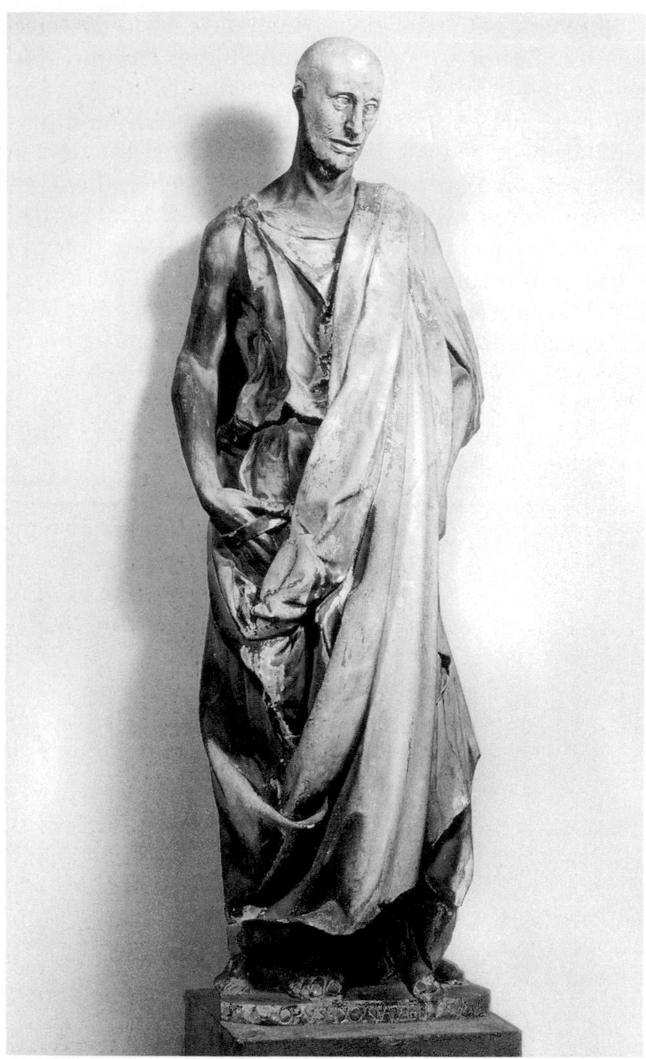

16-8 DONATELLO, prophet figure *(Zuccone)*, 1423–1425, from the campanile of Florence Cathedral. Marble, approx. 6′ 5″ high. Museo dell'Opera del Duomo, Florence.

broader, summary treatment of facial and anatomical features are required for the campanile figures and are used effectively by Donatello. In addition, he takes into account the elevated position of his figures and, with subtly calculated distortions, creates images that are at once realistic and dramatic when seen from below (see also Introduction, FIG. 9).

The most striking of the five figures is that of a prophet, generally known by the nickname *Zuccone*, or "pumpkin-head" (FIG. **16-8**). This figure shows Donatello's peculiar power for characterization at its most original. All of his prophets are represented with a harsh, direct realism reminiscent of ancient Roman portrait sculpture. Their faces are bony, lined, and taut; each is strongly individualized. The *Zuccone* is also bald, a departure from the conventional representation of the prophets. He is dressed in an awkwardly draped and crumpled togalike garment with deeply undercut folds. At first view, one might suspect Donatello of simply draping a gaunt, uncouth assistant, placing him in a casual stance, and rendering the subject just as he saw it. The head discloses an appalling personality—full of crude power, even violence. The deep-set eyes glare under furrowed brows, nostrils flaring, the broad mouth agape, as if the prophet were in the very presence of disasters that would call forth his declamation.

In a bronze relief, *The Feast of Herod* (FIG. **16-9**), on the baptismal font in the baptistry at Siena, Donatello carries his talent for characterization of single figures to the broader field of dramatic groups. Salome (toward the right), still seems to be dancing, even though she already has delivered the severed head of John the Baptist, which the kneeling executioner offers to King Herod. The other figures recoil in horror into two groups: at the right, one man covers his face with his hand; at the left, Herod and two terrified children shrink back in dismay. The psychic explosion that has taken place drives the human elements apart, leaving a gap across which the emotional electricity crackles. This masterful stagecraft obscures the fact that on the stage itself another drama is being played out—the advent of rationalized perspective space, long prepared for in the proto-Renaissance and recognized by Donatello and his generation as a means of intensifying the reality of the action and the characterization of the actors.

Proto-Renaissance artists, like Duccio and the Lorenzetti brothers, used several devices to give the effect of distance, but with the invention of "true" linear perspective (a discovery generally attributed to Brunelleschi), Early Renaissance artists were given a way to make the illusion of distance mathematical and certain. In effect, they had come to understand the picture plane as a transparent window through which the observer looks *into* the constructed, pictorial world. From the observer's fixed standpoint, all orthogonals (lines perpendicular to the picture plane) meet in a single point on the horizon (a horizontal line that corresponds to the viewer's eye level) and all objects are unified within a single space system—the perspective. This discovery was of enormous importance, for it made possible what has been called the "rationalization of sight." It brought all of our random and infinitely various visual sensations under a simple rule that can be expressed mathematically.

Indeed, the discovery of perspective by the artists of the Renaissance reflects the emergence of science itself, which is, put simply, the mathematical ordering of our observations of the physical world. The artists of the Renaissance were often mathematicians, and one modern mathematician asserts that the most creative work in mathematics in the fifteenth century

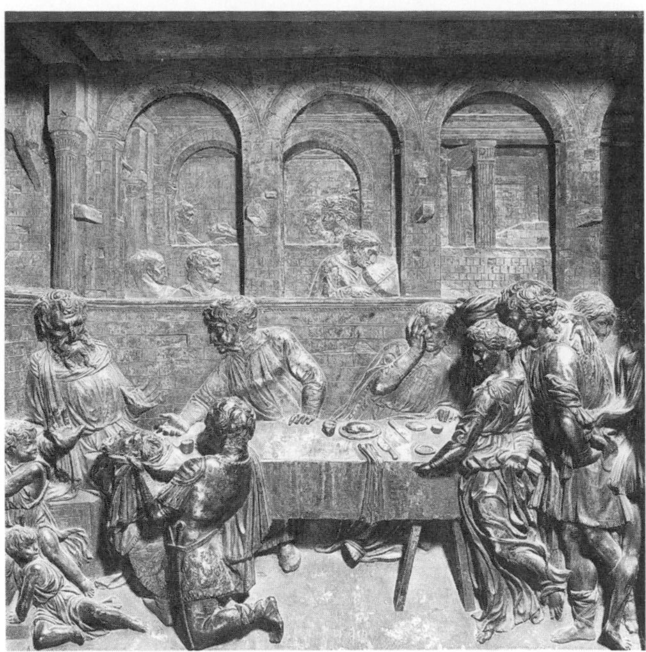

16-9 DONATELLO, *The Feast of Herod,* from the baptismal font, c. 1425. Gilt bronze relief, approx. 23″ × 23″. Siena Cathedral, Siena, Italy.

was done by artists. The experimental spirit that had animated many Franciscans, like Roger Bacon, now came firmly to earth; indeed, Bacon's essays on optics had considerable influence on Renaissance theorists like Alberti. The position of the observer of a picture, who looks "through" it into the painted "world," is precisely that of any scientific observer fixing his gaze on the carefully placed or located datum of his research. Of course, the Early Renaissance artist was not primarily a scientist; he simply found perspective a wonderful way to order his composition and to clarify it. Nonetheless, we cannot doubt that perspective, with its new mathematical authority and certitude, conferred a kind of esthetic legitimacy on painting by making the picture *measurable* and exact. According to Plato, "the excellence of beauty of every work of art is due to the observance of measure." This dictum certainly is expressed in the art of Greece, and in the Renaissance, when Plato was discovered anew and read eagerly, artists once again exalted the principle of measure as the foundation of the beautiful in the fine arts. The projection of measured shapes on flat surfaces now influenced the character of painting and made possible scale drawings, maps, charts, graphs, and diagrams—those means of exact representation without which modern science and technology would be impossible. Mathematical truth and formal beauty became conjoined in the minds of Renaissance artists. In his relief panel *The Feast of Herod* (FIG. 16-9), Donatello, using the device of pictorial perspective, opens the space of the action well into the distance, showing two arched courtyards and groups of attendants in the background. This penetration of the panel surface by spatial illusion replaces the flat grounds and backdrop areas of the Medieval past. The ancient Roman illusionism returns, but it is now based on a secure principle never possessed by the ancients.

It is worth comparing Donatello's Siena panel with a panel from Ghiberti's famous east doors of the baptistry of Florence Cathedral (FIG. **16-10**), which were later declared by Michelangelo to be "so fine that they might fittingly stand as the Gates of Paradise." The east doors (1425–1452) were composed differently from Ghiberti's earlier north doors. Three sets of doors provide access to the baptistry. The first set was made by Andrea Pisano for the east doorway (1330–1335), which faces the cathedral and is the most important entrance. This set of doors was moved to the south doorway to make way for Ghiberti's first pair of doors (1403–1424), which, in turn, was moved to the north doorway so that Ghiberti's second pair of doors, the "Gates of Paradise," could be

16-10 LORENZO GHIBERTI, east doors (Gates of Paradise), 1425–1452. Gilt bronze relief, approx. 17′ high. Baptistry of Florence.

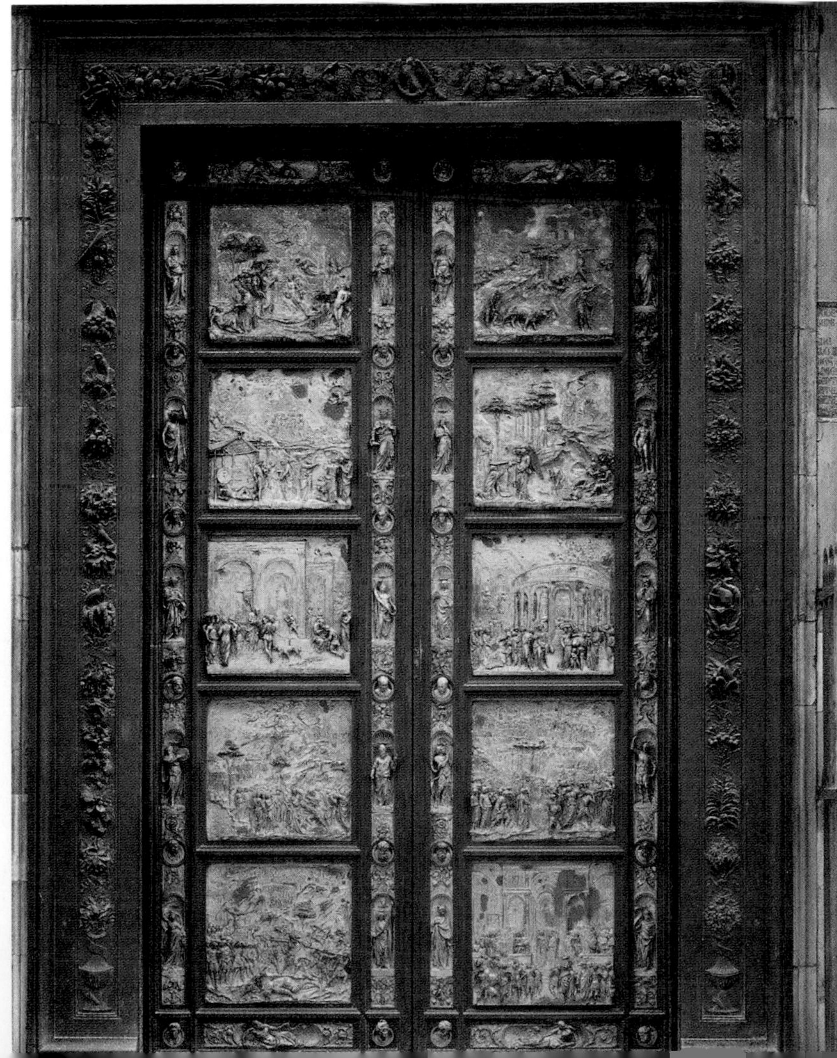

placed in the east doorway. After 1425, Ghiberti abandoned the quatrefoil pattern of the earlier doors and divided the space into ten square panels, each containing a relief set in plain moldings. When gilded, the glittering movement of the reliefs created an effect of great splendor and elegance.

The individual panels of Ghiberti's doors, such as *Isaac and His Sons* (FIG. **16-11**), clearly recall painting in their depiction of space as well as in their treatment of the narrative. Some exemplify more fully than painting many of the principles Alberti formulated in his treatise, *On Painting*. In his relief, Ghiberti creates the illusion of space partly by pictorial perspective and partly by sculptural means. Buildings are represented according to the painter's one-point perspective construction, but the figures (in the lower section of the relief, which actually projects slightly toward the viewer) appear almost in the full round, some of their heads standing completely free. As the eye progresses upward, the relief increasingly becomes flatter until the architecture in the background is represented by barely raised lines, creating a sort of "sculptor's aerial perspective" in which forms are less distinct the deeper they are in space. Ghiberti describes the work as follows:

> I strove to imitate nature as closely as I could, and with all the perspective I could produce [to have] excellent compositions rich with many figures. In some scenes I placed about a hundred figures, in some less, and in some more. I executed that work with the greatest diligence and the greatest love. There were ten stories, all [sunk] in frames because the eye from a distance measures and interprets the scenes in such a way that they appear round. The scenes are in the lowest relief and the figures are seen in the planes; those that are near appear large, those in the distance small, as they do in reality. . . . Executed with the greatest study and perseverance, of all my work it is the most remarkable I have done and it was finished with skill, correct proportions, and understanding.*

Thus, an echo of the ancient and Medieval past is harmonized by the new science: "proportion" and "skill" are perfected by "understanding." Ghiberti has achieved a greater sense of depth than has ever before been possible in a relief. However, his principal figures do not occupy the architectural space he has created for them; rather, they are arranged along a parallel plane in front of the grandiose architecture. (According to Alberti, in his *De re aedificatoria*, the grandeur of the architecture reflects the dignity of events shown in the foreground.) Ghiberti's figure style mixes a Gothic patterning of rhythmic line,

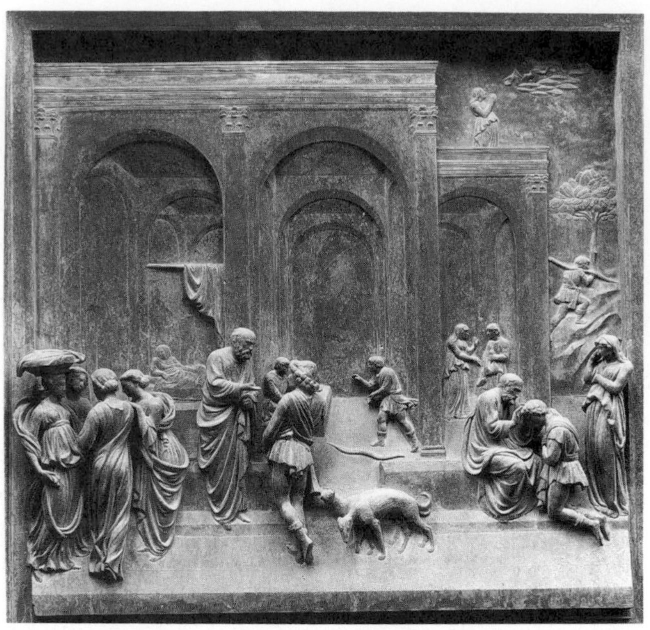

16-11 LORENZO GHIBERTI, *Isaac and His Sons* (detail of FIG. 16-10). Approx. 31½" × 31½".

Classical poses and motifs, and a new realism in characterization, movement, and surface detail. The Medieval narrative method of arranging several episodes within a frame persists. In *Isaac and His Sons* (FIG. 16-11), the group of ladies in the left foreground attends the birth of Esau and Jacob in the left background; Isaac sends Esau and his hunting dogs on his mission in the central foreground; and, in the right foreground, Isaac blesses the kneeling Jacob as Rebecca looks on (Genesis 25–27). Yet the groups are so subtly placed that no crowding or confusion is apparent. The figures, in varying degrees of projection, gracefully twist and turn, appearing to occupy and move through a convincing stage space, which is deepened by showing some figures from behind. The Classicism, particularly of the group of visiting ladies, derives from Ghiberti's close study of ancient art. From his biography, we know that he admired and collected Classical sculpture, bronzes, and coins, and their influence is seen throughout the panel. The beginning of the practice of collecting Classical art in the fifteenth century had much to do with the appearance of Classicism in the Humanistic art of the Renaissance.

For a time, Donatello forgot his earlier realism under the spell of Classical Rome, the ruins and antiquities of which he studied at some length. His bronze statue of *David* (FIG. **16-12**), designed between about 1428 and 1432, is the first freestanding nude statue since ancient times, and here Donatello shows himself once more to be an innovator. The nude, as such, proscribed in the Christian Middle Ages as both

*In E. G. Holt, ed., *Literary Sources of Art History* (Princeton, NJ: Princeton University Press, 1947), pp. 90–91.

indecent and idolatrous, had been shown only rarely—and then only in biblical or moralizing contexts, like the story of Adam and Eve or descriptions of sinners in Hell. Donatello reinvented the Classical nude, even though, in this case, we have neither god nor athlete but the young David, slayer of Goliath, biblical ancestor and antitype of Christ, and symbol of the Florentine love of liberty. The classically proportioned nude—a balance of opposing axes, of tension and relaxation—recalls, and perhaps is derived from, Roman copies of Hellenic statues. Although the body has an almost Praxitelean radiance and a sensuous quality unknown to Medieval figures, David is involved in a complex psychological drama unknown to Antique sculpture. The glance of this youthful, still adolescent hero is not directed primarily toward the severed head of Goliath, which lies between his feet, but toward his own graceful, sinuous body, as though, in consequence of his heroic deed, he is becoming conscious for the first time of its beauty, its vitality, and its strength. This self-awareness, this discovery of the self, is a dominant theme in Renaissance art.

16-12 Donatello, *David,* c. 1428–1432. Bronze, $62\frac{1}{4}''$ high. Museo Nazionale del Bargello, Florence.

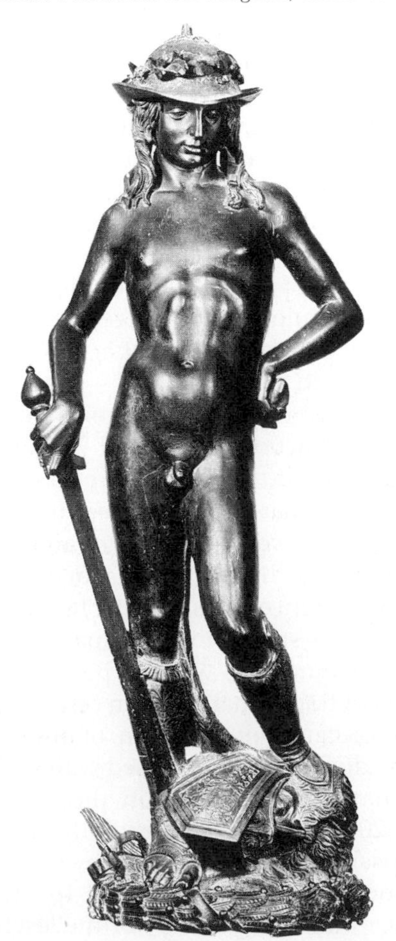

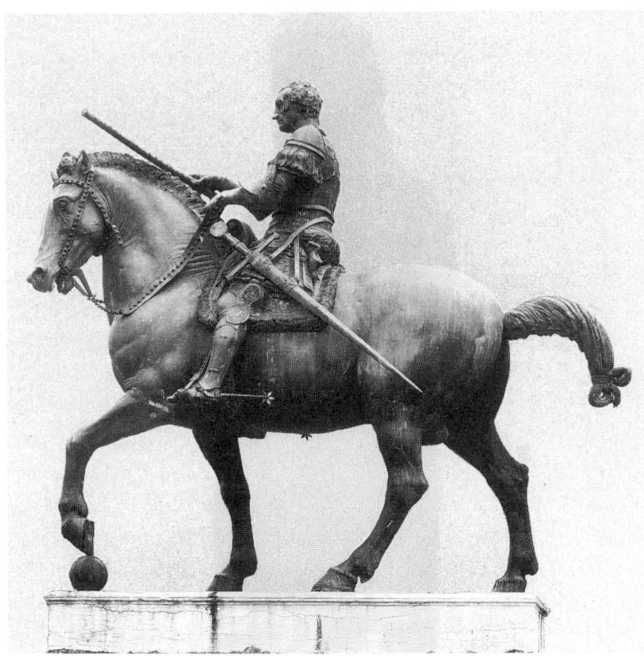

16-13 Donatello, *Gattamelata,* equestrian statue of Erasmo da Narni, c. 1445–1450. Bronze, approx. 11′ × 13′. Piazza del Santo, Padua, Italy.

In 1443, Donatello left Florence for northern Italy to accept the rewarding commission of an equestrian statue of the Venetian *condottiere* Erasmo da Narni, for the square of San Antonio in Padua. With this work (FIG. **16-13**), called *Gattamelata* (slick cat), Donatello recovered the grandeur of the mounted leader as it existed in the great Roman equestrian statue of Marcus Aurelius (FIG. 6-77), which the artist must have seen in Rome. The figure stands high on a lofty, elliptical base to set it apart from its surroundings and becomes almost a celebration of the liberation of sculpture from architecture. Massive and majestic, the great horse bears the armored general easily; together, they make an overwhelming image of irresistible strength and unlimited power. Compared to the *Gattamelata,* a Medieval equestrian statue like the *Bamberg Rider* (FIG. 10-55), still attached to the wall, looks positively fragile, even ghostlike. The Italian rider, his face set in a mask of dauntless resolution and unshakable will, is the very portrait of the Renaissance individualist: a man of intelligence, courage, and ambition, frequently of humble origin, who, by his own resourcefulness and on his own merits, rises to a commanding position in the world.

Donatello's ten-year period of activity in Padua (he received additional commissions for statues and reliefs for the high altar of the church of San Antonio) made a deep and lasting impression on the artists of the region and contributed materially to the formation of a Renaissance style in northern Italy. After his

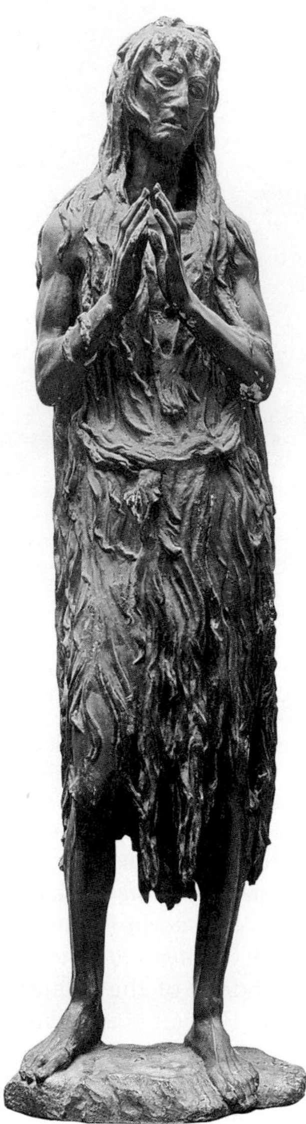

16-14 DONATELLO, *Mary Magdalene*, c. 1454–1455. Polychromed and gilded wood, approx. 6′ 2″ high. Baptistry of Florence.

return to Florence in 1453, Donatello's style changes once more. His last period is marked by an intensely personal kind of expression, in which his earlier realism returns, but with purposeful exaggeration and distortion. He turns away from Classical beauty and grandeur toward a kind of expressionism that seems deliberately calculated to jar the sensibilities; he gives us the ugly, the painful, and the violent. He may, in his last years, have felt religious remorse for such works as his *David* and may have set about to achieve a kind of anti-esthetic manner, well exemplified in his *Mary Magdalene* (FIG. **16-14**). The repentant saint in old age, after years of wasting mortification, stands emaciated, hands clasped in prayer. Donatello, in what appears to be a rekindling of Medieval piety, here rejects the body as merely the mortal shell of the immortal soul. The beautiful woman has withered, but her soul has been saved by her denial of physical beauty. Donatello's originality, independence, and insight into the meaning of religious experience are asserted here as he reinterprets Medieval material in his own terms. But Medieval as *Mary Magdalene* might first appear, we realize that this work also was carved by the man who created the *David*, and Donatello again is best characterized as we first described him—a man with the vast versatility that distinguishes the great artist from the good artist.

Architecture

BRUNELLESCHI

FILIPPO BRUNELLESCHI (1377–1446), one of the unsuccessful competitors for the commission to design the doors of the baptistry of Florence in 1401, was (like Ghiberti) trained as a goldsmith, but his ability as a sculptor must have been well known even at the time of the baptistry competition. Although his biographer, Manetti, tells us that Brunelleschi turned to architecture out of disappointment over the loss of the baptistry commission, he continued to work as a sculptor for several years and received commissions for sculpture as late as 1416. In the meantime, however, his interest turned more and more toward architecture, spurred by several trips to Rome (the first in 1402, probably with his friend Donatello), where he too was captivated by the Roman ruins. It may well be in connection with his close study of Roman monuments and his effort to make an accurate record of what he saw that Brunelleschi developed the revolutionary system of geometric, linear perspective that was so eagerly adopted by fifteenth-century artists and that has made him the first acknowledged Renaissance architect.

Brunelleschi's broad knowledge of the principles of Roman construction, combined with an analytical and inventive mind, permitted him to solve an engineering problem that no other fifteenth-century architect could have solved—the design and construction of a dome for the huge crossing of the unfinished cathedral of Florence (FIGS. **16-15, 16-16,** and 10-58). The problem was staggering; the space to be spanned (140 feet) was much too wide to permit construction with the aid of traditional wooden centering. Nor was it possible (because of the plan of the crossing) to support the dome with buttressed walls. Brunelleschi seems to have begun work on the problem about 1417; in 1420, he and Ghiberti jointly were awarded the commission. The latter, however, soon retired from the project and left the field to his associate.

With exceptional ingenuity, Brunelleschi not only

bristling with insolent challenge. The figure is meant to be seen as standing in a *loggia*, the space of which is continuous with that occupied by the spectator. The illusion is reinforced by the heavy, armored, foreshortened foot that seems to protrude over a sill of the opening. If Masaccio first "made his figures stand upon their feet," then Andrea followed him faithfully and made the point more emphatically in this splendid figure, which is alive with truculent energy. And by having parts of the figure appear to project into the space of the viewer, Andrea takes a step beyond Masaccio's *Holy Trinity* in the direction of Baroque illusionism.

Andrea's sometime collaborator DOMENICO VENEZIANO (*c.* 1420–1461) was born and trained in Venice, but settled in Florence in the late 1430s. The sixteenth-century architect, painter, and biographer Giorgio Vasari tells us that Andrea, in a fit of jealous rage, killed Domenico by hitting him with an iron bar; in fact, Andrea fell victim to the plague some four years before Domenico died. Vasari also claims that Domenico introduced the mixed-oil technique to Florence, but the artist himself seems to have painted in the traditional tempera. Although he fully assimilates Florentine forms, Domenico retains some International-style traits that he may have acquired from northern painters active in Venice. He also may have brought from Venice his sensitivity to color and outdoor light, which goes well beyond that of his Florentine contemporaries; indeed, Domenico makes his major contribution to Florentine art of the mid-century in connection with considerations of color and light. His *St. Lucy Altarpiece* (FIG. **16-32**) is one of the earliest examples of a type of painting that will enjoy great popularity from this time on. In a *sacra conversazione* (holy conversation), saints from different epochs are joined in a unified space to form a company and seem to be conversing either with each

16-32 DOMENICO VENEZIANO, *The St. Lucy Altarpiece*, center panel, *c.* 1445. Tempera on wood, approx. 6′ 7½″ × 7′. Galleria degli Uffizi, Florence.

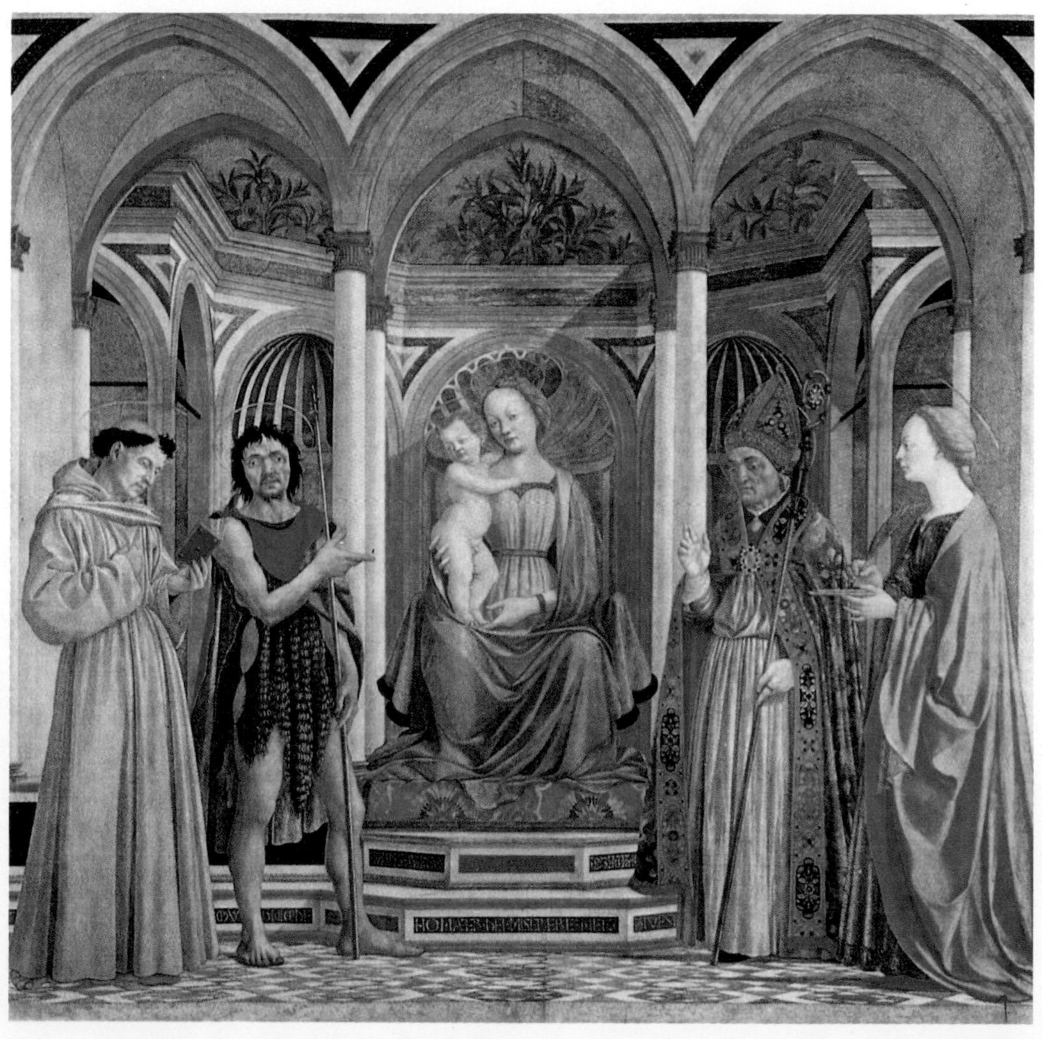

other or with the audience. Here, in the presence of the enthroned Madonna, are St. Francis, John the Baptist, St. Zenobius, and St. Lucy. The clarity and precision of the architectural setting and the individualization, weight, and solemn dignity of the figures show Domenico to be a worthy heir to both Masaccio and Donatello. The composition recalls Nanni di Banco's *Quattro Santi Coronati* (FIG. 16-4); here, however, the vaulted niche has been converted to an airy loggia open to the sky and flooded with bright, outdoor light. The brilliant local colors and ornate surfaces of the International style are muted by this directed light, which falls into the loggia from the upper right and bathes the scene with atmospheric luminosity. Reflected from the architecture, it lightens the shadows, and the modeling of the figures becomes less harsh than that in Masaccio, to whom effects of relief were more important than those of color. The resultant overall blonde tonality is characteristic of the paintings of Domenico and his followers.

PIERO DELLA FRANCESCA

Domenico's most important disciple and his assistant in Florence during the early 1440s was PIERO DELLA FRANCESCA (*c.* 1420–1492). Piero's art is the projection of a mind cultivated by mathematics and convinced that the highest beauty is found in forms that have the clarity and purity of geometric figures. Toward the end of his long career, Piero, who was a skilled geometrician, wrote the first theoretical treatise on systematic perspective, after having practiced the art with supreme mastery for almost a lifetime. His association with the architect Alberti at Ferrara and at Rimini around 1450–1451 probably turned his attention fully to perspective (a science in which Alberti was an influential pioneer) and helped to determine his later, characteristically architectonic compositions. One can fairly say that Piero's compositions are determined almost entirely by his sense of the exact and lucid structures defined by mathematics. Within this context, he developed Domenico's sophistication in the handling of light and color, so that color became the matrix of his three-dimensional forms, lending them a new density as well as fusing them with the surrounding space.

A damaged but still beautiful panel, Piero's *The Flagellation of Christ* (FIG. **16-33**), is almost a painted exposition of the rules of linear perspective and its inherent pictorial possibilities. The painting has been designed with such precision that modern architects, using the division of the brick floor paneling along the painting's baseline as a module, have been able to

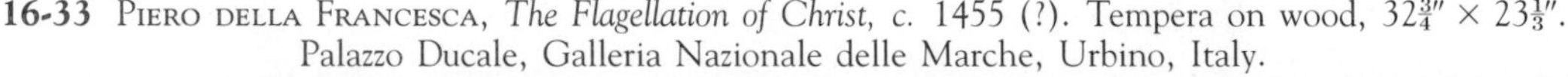

16-33 PIERO DELLA FRANCESCA, *The Flagellation of Christ*, *c.* 1455 (?). Tempera on wood, 32¾″ × 23⅓″. Palazzo Ducale, Galleria Nazionale delle Marche, Urbino, Italy.

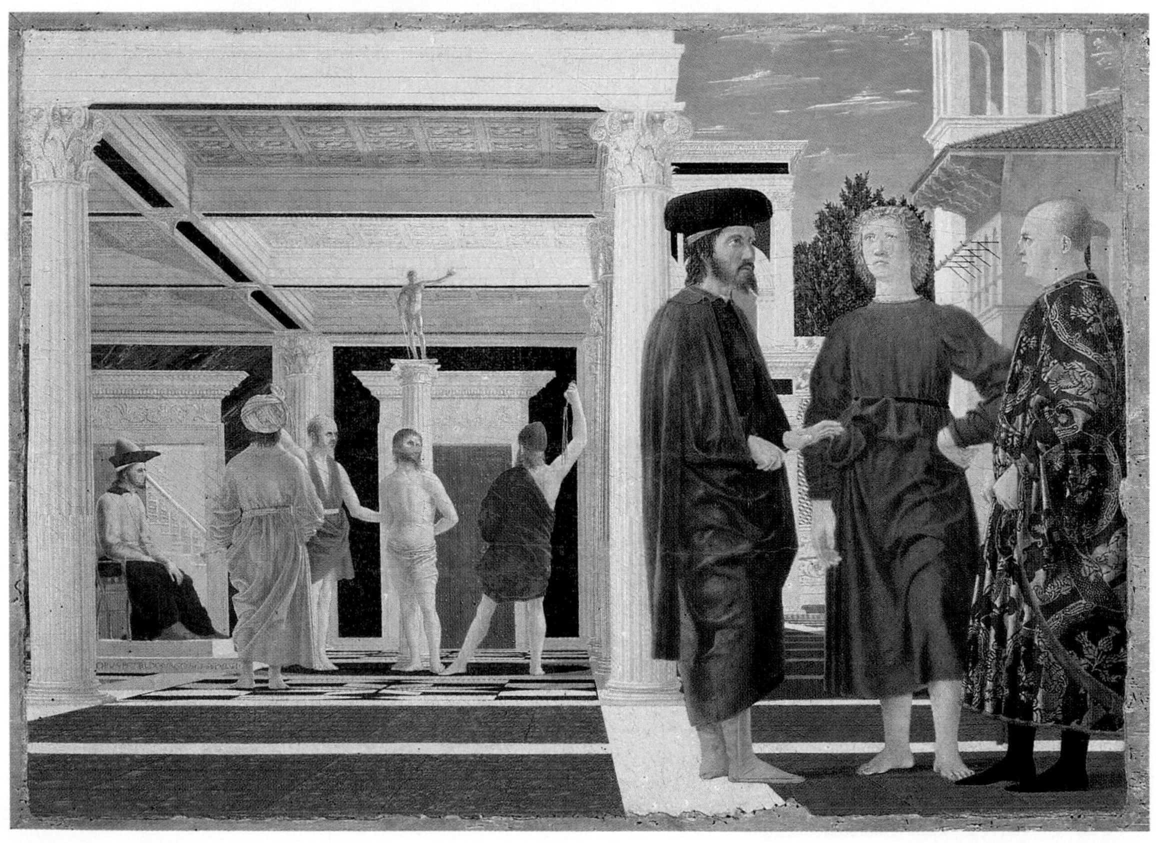

reconstruct accurately the floor plans of the depicted court and building and the positions of the figures within them.

The dating of the panel is uncertain; historians have assigned dates that range from 1445 to 1472. Since the depicted loggia has a distinctly "modern" (that is, Albertian) look, the painting seems to presuppose Piero's contact with the architect Alberti in the early 1450s, so that its date might fall into the middle of that decade. As exact as the architectural rendering of the portico appears to be, its structure has been modified for pictorial reasons. Stalactite-shaped forms at the beam crossings denote the positions from which two interior columns have been removed in order to create a continuous space that encloses the martyrdom scene and permits a full view of Pontius Pilate, who watches impassively as the executioners raise their whips to chastise Christ. The column to which Christ is tied is topped by a golden statue of a nude man holding a rod in one hand and a ball in the other, attributes that appear on coins portraying Roman emperors. The meaning of this figure within the context of the flagellation scene is uncertain; apparently a pagan symbol, it may represent the pagan power that Christianity had to confront and overcome.

The lighting is not as clearly legible as the perspective rendering. All outdoor forms are illuminated from the left, but the interior of the loggia receives its light from the right, either reflected from the buildings across the court or from a stipulated secondary light source behind the second column of the right colonnade. Even more ambiguous are the identities of the three figures in the right foreground and their relation to the central event; none of many tentative identifications, nor their meanings in relation to the central event, have found universal acceptance. Perhaps we should be content with viewing and experiencing the formal aspects of a masterful painting. In a composition that is at once clear, complex, and marvelously subtle, the perspective design is reinforced by visual cross-references that create a compact, pictorial unity. In the foreground figure group, which, at first glance, seems to have little relation to the depicted event, the pose of the central figure is almost identical to that of Christ. In addition, the relation of the turbaned man with his back to us (Herod?) to the flagellation scene is the same as that of the viewer of the painting to the foreground figure group. Thus, in a unique and ingenious manner, the artist draws the spectator past the foreground triad toward the main subject in the middle ground. By manipulating perspective and the disposition of volumes and voids, Piero creates pictorial tension using forms that are essentially static, in a composition that is firmly contained within its frame and, at the same time, highly dynamic. By placing the massed volumes of his three foreground figures off-center into a relatively restricted space, Piero poses the question of how much mass balances how large an empty space. The proportional relationships Piero shows us in this painting provide one possible (and certainly most satisfying) answer.

Piero's most important work is the fresco cycle in the apse of the church of San Francesco in Arezzo, which represents ten episodes from the legend of the True Cross (the cross on which Christ died). Painted between 1452 and 1456, the cycle is based on a thirteenth-century popularization of the Scriptures, the *Golden Legend* by Jacobus de Varagine. The *Annunciation* from this cycle (FIG. **16-34**) perhaps best illustrates Piero's manner. One of the problems that occupied him all his life was how to establish a convincing architectonic relation between animate and inanimate objects. The key to Piero's solution in this painting is the conspicuously placed column that divides the depicted space into two vertical, cubic sections. The cylindrical shape of the column is echoed in the simplified, solemn, and immobile form of the Virgin. To

16-34 PIERO DELLA FRANCESCA, *Annunciation* from the *Legend of the True Cross*, c. 1455. Detail of fresco. San Francesco, Arezzo, Italy.

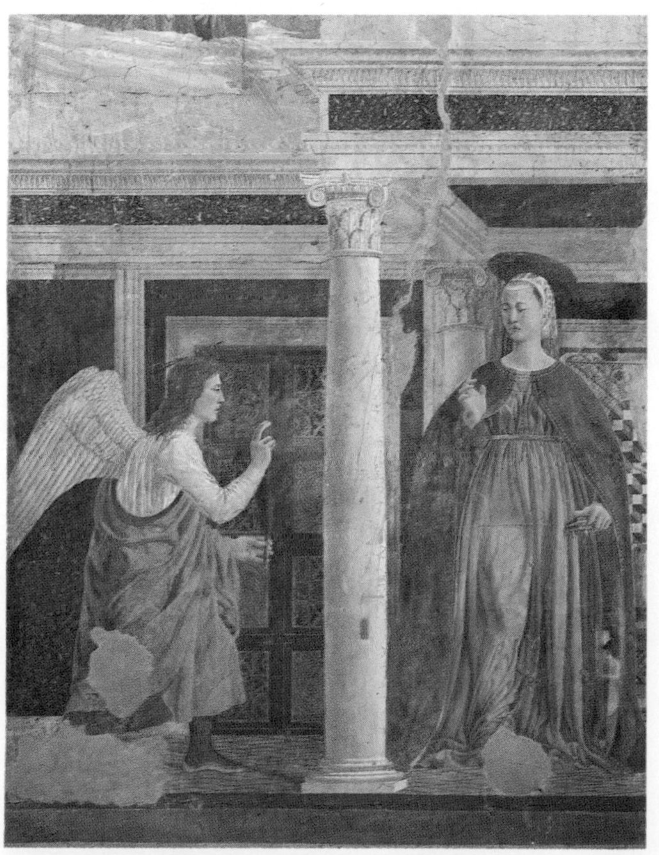

make his figures conform to the static quality of the architecture that surrounds them, Piero reduces all actions and gestures to the slowest, simplest signals; all emotion is banished. The composition is essentially a cylinder inscribed in a cubic void, and this geometricality of the forms gives the depiction of the event a trancelike and abstract quality.

In addition, of course, Piero's work shows an unflagging interest in the properties of light and color. He suspects that one is the function of the other; he observes that colors turn cool (bluish) in shadow and that they lose intensity with increasing distance from the observer. In his effort to make the clearest possible distinction between forms, he floods his pictures with light, imparting a silver-blue tonality. To avoid heavy shadows, he illumines the dark sides of his forms with reflected light. By moving the darkest tones of his modeling toward the centers of his volumes, he separates them from their backgrounds. As a result, Piero's paintings lack some of Masaccio's relieflike qualities but gain in spatial clarity as each shape becomes an independent unit, surrounded by an atmospheric envelope and movable to any desired position, like a figure on a chessboard.

In the *Resurrection* fresco in the town hall of Borgo San Sepolcro (FIG. **16-35**), Piero introduces a compositional device—the figure triangle—that will enjoy great favor with later Renaissance artists. To stabilize his composition, Piero arranges his figures in a group that can be circumscribed by a triangle centrally placed in the painting. The figure of the risen Christ, standing with columnar strength in the attitude of eternal triumph at the edge of the sepulcher, occupies the upper portion of a triangular arrangement that rests on the broad base of the sleeping soldiers in the foreground. This triangular massing of volumes around a picture's central axis gives a painting great compositional stability and is one of the keys to the symmetry and self-sufficiency that Renaissance artists strove for in their work.

16-35 PIERO DELLA FRANCESCA, *Resurrection*, c. 1463. Fresco. Palazzo Comunale, Borgo San Sepolcro, Italy.

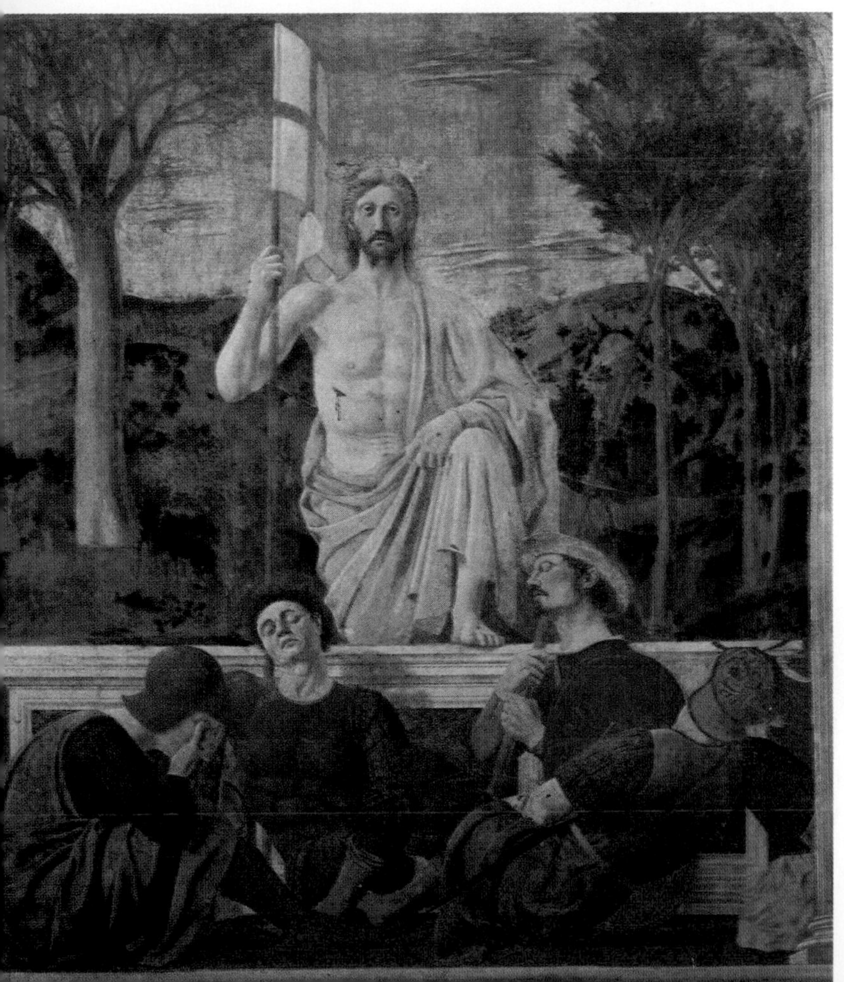

Piero was at home with realism and could paint exact and unflattering likenesses of human subjects, quite unlike the generalized heads and features of his customary type. His work summarizes most of the stylistic and scientific developments in painting during the first half of the fifteenth century: realism, descriptive landscape, the structural human figure, monumental composition, perspective, proportionality, and light and color.

FRA ANGELICO AND FRA FILIPPO LIPPI

But other good artists were active during this period whose styles remain rooted in an earlier age and whose interest in the new tendencies remained marginal. One of these, the Dominican painter-monk FRA ANGELICO (*c.* 1387–1455), was conservative by training and inclination. Although he was fully aware of what was being done by his more experimentally inclined contemporaries, Fra Angelico adopted into his essentially conservative style only those innovations he could incorporate without friction. While accepting realistic details in anatomy, drapery, perspective, and architecture, he rejected Masaccio's heavy modeling, which would have dulled his bright Gothic coloring. In the *Annunciation* (FIG. **16-36**), one of numerous frescoes with which Fra Angelico decorated the Dominican convent of San Marco in Florence between 1435 and 1445, the Brunelleschian loggia is neatly designed according to the rules of linear perspective, but the fact that the vault is too low to allow the figures to stand would have been unacceptable to Piero della Francesca and other less conservative artists. However, such considerations were secondary to Fra Angelico; what he wanted above all was to stress the religious content of his paintings, and he did so by using the means, past and present, that he felt were most appropriate. In our example, the simplicity of the statement recalls Giotto, as does the form of the kneeling, rainbow-winged angel; the elegant silhouette of the sweetly shy Madonna descends from Sienese art, and the flower-carpeted, enclosed

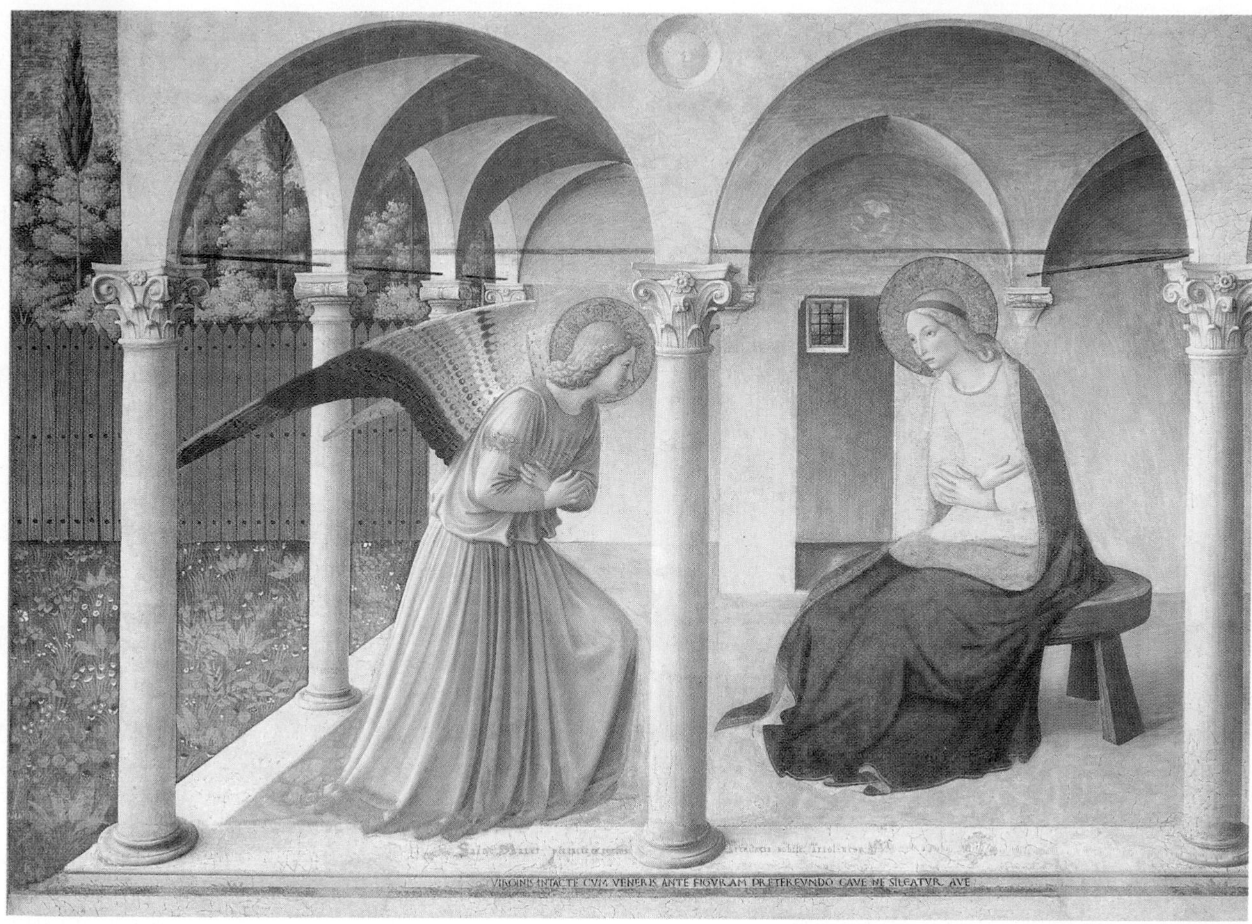

16-36 Fra Angelico, *Annunciation*, c. 1440–1445. Fresco. San Marco, Florence.

garden (symbolic of the virginity of Mary) is a bit of International Gothic. All these elements have been combined with lyrical feeling and a great sense for decorative effect, so that nothing seems incongruous. Like most of Fra Angelico's paintings, the naïve and tender charm of the *Annunciation* still has an almost universal appeal and fully reflects the character of the artist, who, as Giorgio Vasari tells us, "was a simple and most holy man . . . most gentle and temperate, living chastely, removed from the cares of the world . . . humble and modest in all his works."

A strong, though perhaps somewhat unlikely, contributor to the pictorial humanization of religious subject matter was Fra Filippo Lippi (c. 1406–1469). Like Fra Angelico, Fra Filippo was a monk, but there all resemblance ends. From reports, he seems to have been a kind of amiable scapegrace quite unfitted for monastic life, who indulged in misdemeanors ranging from forgery and embezzlement to the abduction of a pretty nun, Lucretia, who became his mistress and the mother of his son, the painter Filippino Lippi. Only the Medici's intervention on his behalf at the papal court preserved Fra Filippo from severe punishment and total disgrace. An orphan, Fra Filippo was raised in a monastery adjacent to the church of Santa Maria del Carmine, and, when about eighteen, he must have met Masaccio there and witnessed the decoration of the Brancacci Chapel. Fra Filippo's early work survives only in fragments, but these show that he tried to work with Masaccio's massive forms. Later, probably under the influence of Ghiberti's and Donatello's relief sculptures, he developed a linear style that emphasizes the contours of his figures and permits him to suggest movement through flying and swirling draperies.

A fresh and inventive painting from Fra Filippo's later years, a *Madonna and Child with Angels* (fig. **16-37**) shows his skill in manipulating line. Beyond noting its fine contours and modeling, we soon become aware of the wonderful flow of line throughout the picture; the forms are precisely yet smoothly delineated, whether they are whole figures or the details within them. Even without the reinforcing modeling, the forms would look three-dimensional and plastic, as the line is handled in a sculptural rather than in a two-dimensional sense. Fra Filippo's skill in the use of line is rarely surpassed; in the immediate future, only his most famous pupil, Botticelli, will use

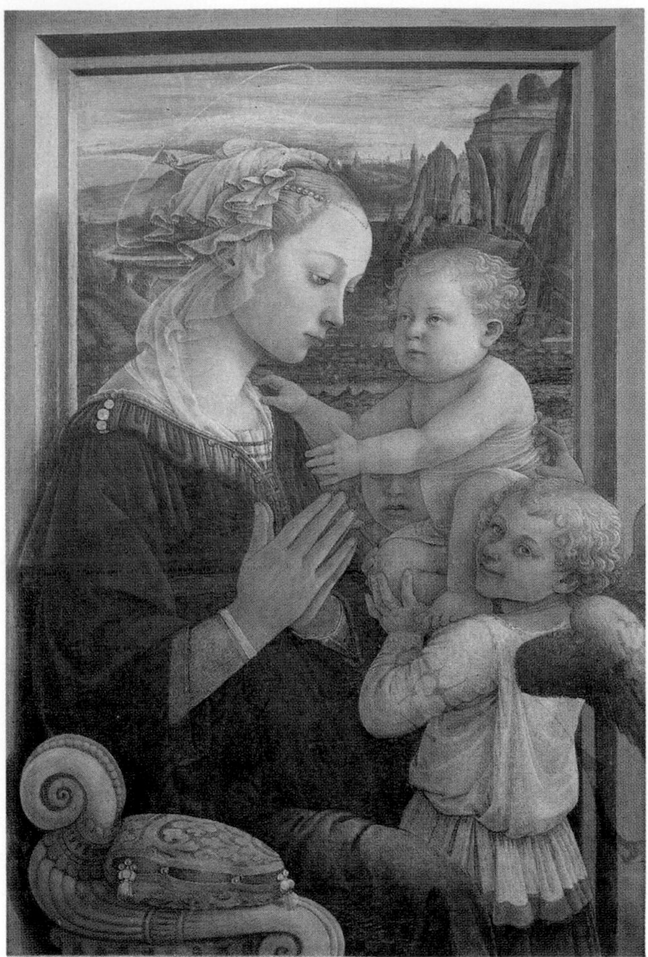

16-37 FRA FILIPPO LIPPI, *Madonna and Child with Angels*, c. 1455. Tempera on wood, approx. 36″ × 25″. Galleria degli Uffizi, Florence.

it with greater subtlety. Fra Filippo has interpreted his subject here in a surprisingly worldly manner. The Madonna, a beautiful young mother, is not at all spiritual or fragile, and neither is her plump bambino, the child Christ, who is held up to her by two angels, one of whom turns toward us with the mischievous, puckish grimace of a boy refusing to be subdued by the pious occasion. Significantly, all figures reflect the use of models (that for the Madonna may even have been Lucretia). Fra Filippo plainly relishes the charm of youth and beauty as he finds it in this world. He prefers the real in landscape also, and the background, seen through the window, has, despite some exaggerations, recognizable features of the Arno River valley. Compared with the earlier Madonnas by Duccio (FIG. 15-8) and Giotto (FIG. 15-11), this work shows how far the humanization of the theme has been carried. Whatever the ideals of spiritual perfection may have meant to artists in past centuries, those ideals now are realized in terms of the sensuous beauty of this world.

THE SECOND HALF OF THE FIFTEENTH CENTURY

In the early fifteenth century, Florence led Italy in the development of the new Humanism; later, the city shared its leadership role with other Italian cities. Under the sponsorship of local rulers, important cultural centers developed in other parts of Italy and began to attract artists and scholars: Urbino under the Montefeltri, Mantua under the Gonzaga, Milan under the Sforza, Naples under the kings of Aragon, and so forth.

This later period of Humanism is marked by a new interest in the Italian language and literature, the beginnings of literary criticism (parallel to the development of theory in art and architecture), the foundation of academies (especially the Platonic Academy of Philosophy in Florence), and the introduction of the printing press—and all that these elements could mean for the dissemination of culture.

The conquest of Constantinople by the Turks in 1453 caused an exodus of Greek scholars, many of whom fled to Italy, bringing with them knowledge of ancient Greece to feed the avid interest in Classical art, literature, and philosophy. That same conquest closed the Mediterranean to Western shipping, making it necessary to find new routes to the markets of the East. Thus began the age of navigation, discovery, and exploration.

In art and architecture, a theoretical foundation could now be placed under the more or less "intuitive" innovations of the earlier generation of artists. We must emphasize again the high value that Renaissance artists placed on *theory*. In their view, if any occupation or profession were to have dignity and be worthy of honor, it must have an intellectual basis. We still recognize this requirement; a "scientific" pursuit wins utmost respect in our age, and, for somewhat similar reasons, "fine" artists today are likely to consider their pursuits superior to those of "commercial" artists. Renaissance artists strove to make themselves scholars and gentlemen, to associate with princes and the learned, and to rise above the longstanding ancient and medieval prejudice that saw them as mere handicraftsmen.

Beginning with Alberti's treatises on painting and architecture, theoretical studies multiplied. The rediscovered text of the ancient Roman architect and theoretician, Vitruvius, became the subject of exhaustive examination and interpretation (partly because the recovered text was only a copy, which, unlike the original, was not illustrated, rendering passages that referred to illustrations obscure and subject to varying interpretations). Brunelleschi's invention of perspective and Alberti's and Piero's treatises on the subject provided the Renaissance artist with the opportunity to demonstrate the scientific basis of the visual arts.

The genius and creative energy required to achieve the new social and intellectual status claimed by the artist were available in abundance. The Renaissance ideal of *l'uomo universale* (the universal man) here finds its full realization; indeed, in LEON BATTISTA ALBERTI (1407–1472), it finds one of its first personifications. Writing of himself in the third person, Alberti gives us a most revealing insight into the mind of the brilliant Renaissance man—his universal interests, broad capabilities, love of beauty, and hope of fame:

> In everything suitable to one born free and educated liberally, he was so trained from boyhood that among the leading young men of his age he was considered by no means the last. For, assiduous in the science and skill of dealing with arms and horses and musical instruments, as well as in the pursuit of letters and the fine arts, he was devoted to the knowledge of the most strange and difficult things. And finally he embraced with zeal and forethought everything which pertained to fame. To omit the rest, he strove so hard to attain a name in modeling and painting that he wished to neglect nothing by which he might gain the approbation of good men. His genius was so versatile that you might almost judge all the fine arts to be his. . . . He took extraordinary and peculiar pleasure in looking at things in which there was any mark of beauty. . . . Whatever was done by man with genius and with a certain grace, he held to be almost divine.*

It is probably no accident that this autobiography sounds like a funeral oration on a great man.

Architecture

ALBERTI

Alberti scarcely mentioned architecture as a prime interest. He entered the profession rather late in life, but today we know him chiefly as an architect. He was the first to seriously study the treatise of Vitruvius *(De architectura),* and his knowledge of it, combined with his own archeological investigations, made him the first Renaissance architect to understand Roman architecture in depth. Alberti's most important and influential theoretical work, *De re aedificatoria,* although inspired by Vitruvius, contains much new and original material. For later architects, some of Alberti's most significant observations were the advocations of a system of ideal proportions, a central-type plan as the ideal Christian church, and the avoidance of the column-arch combination (which had persisted from Spalatum in the fourth century to Brunelleschi in the fifteenth) as incongruous. By arguing that the arch is a wall-opening that should be supported only by a section of wall (a pier), not by an independent sculptural element (a column), Alberti (with a few exceptions) disposed of the Medieval arcade for centuries.

Alberti's own architectural style represents a scholarly application of Classical elements to contemporary buildings. His Palazzo Rucellai in Florence (FIG. **16-38**) probably dates from the mid-1450s. The façade, built over a group of three Medieval houses, is much more severely organized than that of the Palazzo Medici-Riccardi (FIG. 16-24). Each story of the Palazzo Rucellai is articulated by flat pilasters, which support full entablatures. The rustication of the wall surfaces between the smooth pilasters is subdued and uniform, and the suggestion that the structure becomes lighter toward its top is made in an adaptation of the ancient Roman manner by using different articulating orders for each story: Tuscan (resembling the Doric order) for the ground floor, Composite (combining Ionic volutes with the acanthus leaves of the Corinthian) for the second story, and Corinthian

16-38 LEON BATTISTA ALBERTI, Palazzo Rucellai, Florence, c. 1452–1470.

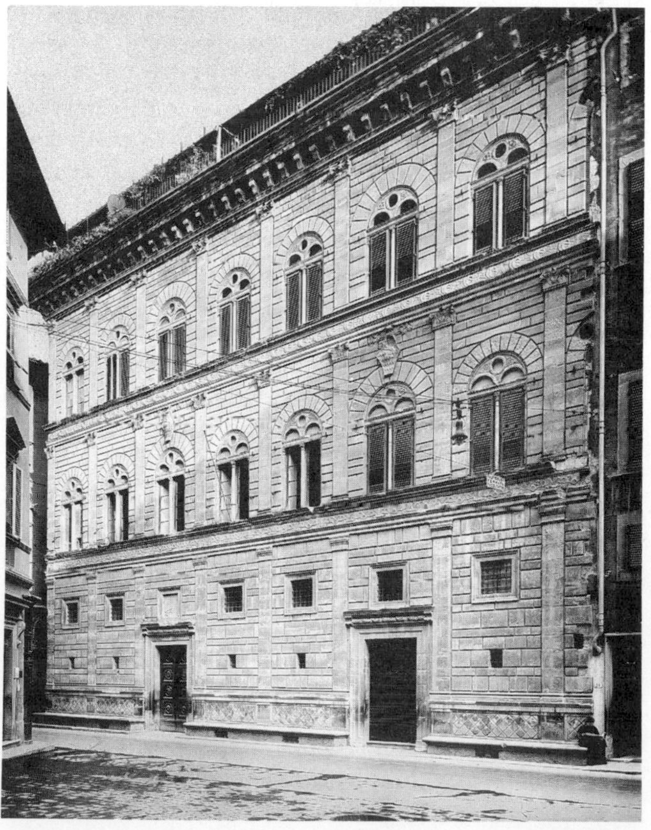

*In J. B. Ross and M. M. McLaughlin, eds., *The Portable Renaissance Reader* (New York: Viking, 1953), pp. 480ff.

for the third floor. Here, Alberti has adapted the articulation of the Colosseum (FIG. 6-48) to a flat façade, which does not allow the deep penetration of the building's mass that is so effective in the Roman structure. By converting the plastic, engaged columns of the ancient model into shallow pilasters that barely project from the wall, Alberti has created a large-meshed, linear net that, stretched tightly across the front of his building, not only unifies its three levels but also emphasizes the flat, two-dimensional qualities of the wall.

The design for the façade of the Gothic church of Santa Maria Novella in Florence (FIG. **16-39**) also was commissioned by the Rucellai family. Here, Alberti takes his cue (just as Brunelleschi did occasionally) from a pre-Gothic Medieval design—that of San Miniato al Monte (FIG. 9-20). Following his Romanesque model, he designs a small, pseudo-Classical portico for the upper part of the façade and supports it with a broad base of pilaster-enframed arcades that incorporate the six tombs and three doorways of the extant Gothic building. But in the organization of these elements (FIG. **16-40**), Alberti takes a long step beyond the Romanesque planners. The height of Santa Maria Novella (to the tip of the pediment) equals its width, so that the entire façade can be inscribed in a square. The upper structure, in turn, can be encased in a square one-fourth the size of the main square; the cornice of the entablature that separates the two levels halves the major square, so that the lower portion of the building becomes a rectangle that is twice as wide as it is high; and the areas outlined by the columns on the lower level are squares with sides that are about one-third the width of the main unit. Throughout the façade, Alberti defines areas and relates them to each other in terms of proportions that can be expressed in simple numerical ratios (1:1, 1:2, 1:3, 2:3, and so on). In his treatise, Alberti uses considerable space to propound the necessity of such harmonic relationships for the design of beautiful buildings. He shares this conviction with Brunelleschi, and it is basically this dependence on mathematics—a belief in the eternal and universal validity of numerical ratios as beauty-producing agents—that distinguishes the work of these two architects from that of their predecessors.

The façade of Santa Maria Novella is an ingenious solution to a difficult design problem. On one hand, it adequately expresses the organization of the structure to which it is attached; at the same time, it subjects diffused and preexisting features, including the large round window on the second level, to a rigid geometrical order that instills a quality of Classical calm and reason. This façade also introduces a feature of great historical consequence: the scrolls that form the transition from the broad lower level to the narrow upper level and that screen the sloping roofs over the aisles solve a problem that had vexed architects for centuries. With variations, such spirals will appear in literally hundreds of church façades throughout the Renaissance and Baroque periods.

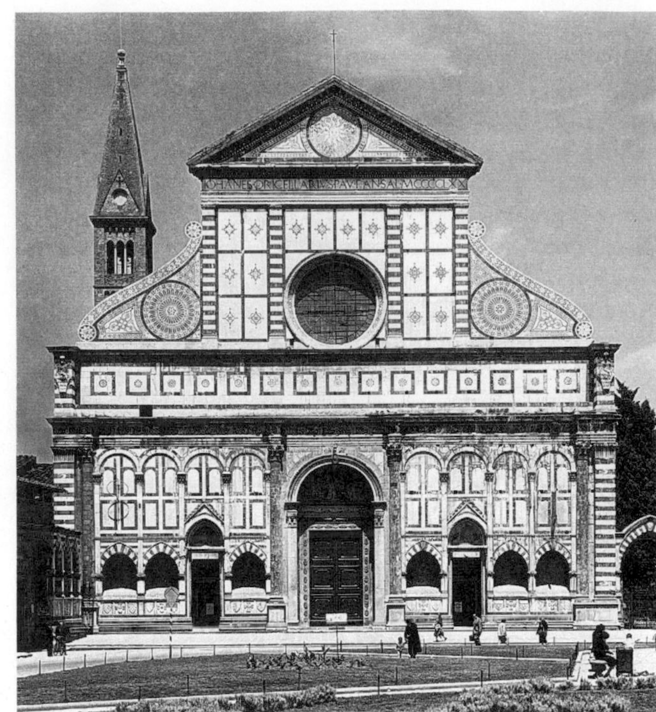

16-39 LEON BATTISTA ALBERTI, west façade of Santa Maria Novella, Florence, c. 1458–1470.

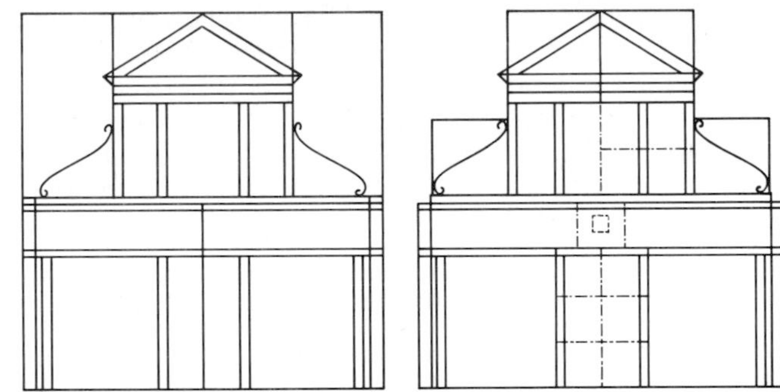

16-40 West façade, Santa Maria Novella.

At San Francesco in Rimini (FIG. **16-41**), Alberti again modernized a Gothic church—in this case, at the behest of one of the more sensational tyrants of the Early Renaissance, Sigismondo Pandolfo Malatesta, Lord of Rimini. Malatesta wanted a temple in which to enshrine the bones of great Humanist scholars like Gemistus Pletho, who dreamed of a neopagan religion that would supersede Christianity and whose remains Malatesta had brought from Greece. He intended his "temple" also to memorialize his

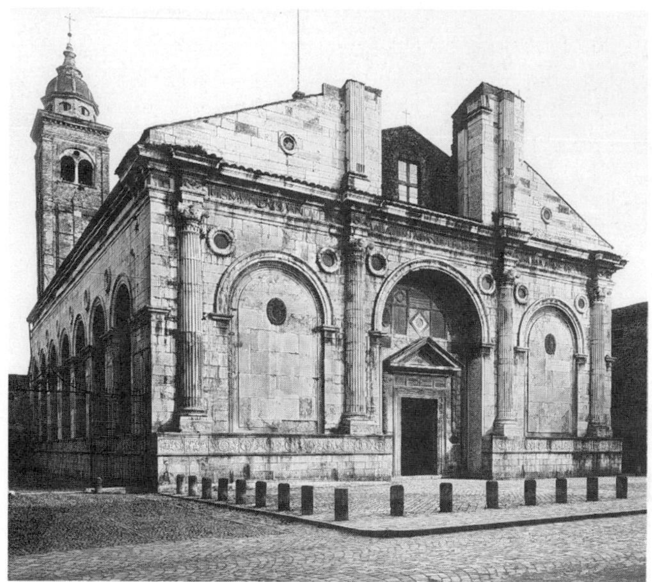

16-41 Leon Battista Alberti, San Francesco, Rimini, Italy, begun 1451 (view from the northwest).

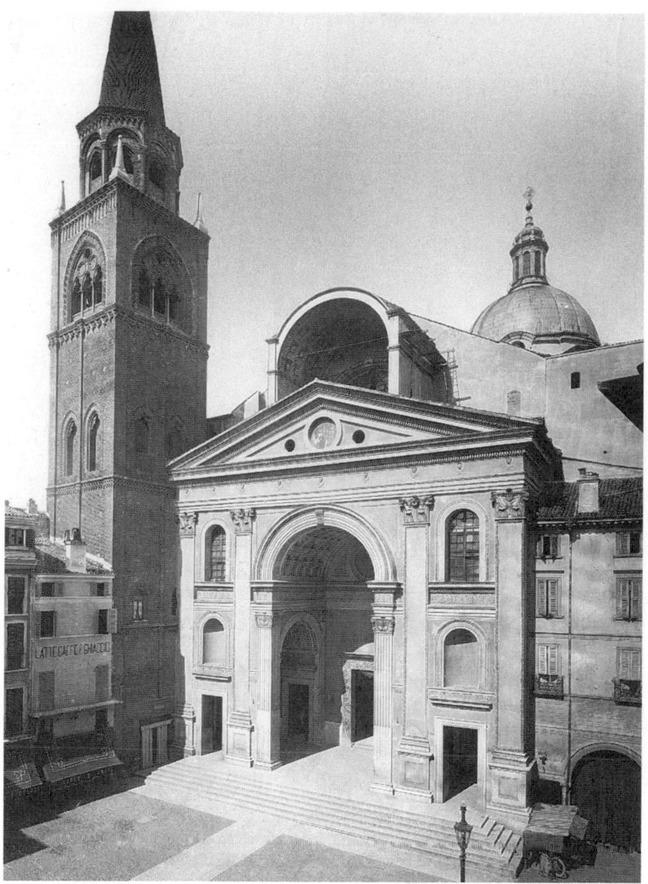

16-42 Leon Battista Alberti, west façade of Sant' Andrea, Mantua, Italy, designed c. 1470.

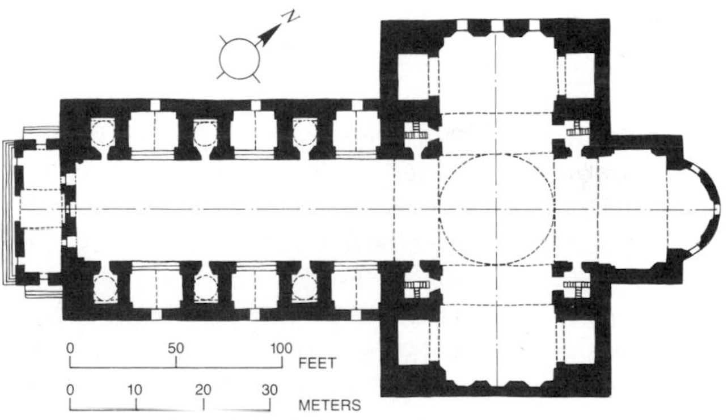

16-43 Leon Battista Alberti, plan of Sant' Andrea.

mistress, Isotta. Alberti's thoroughly Roman design is a monument both to the tyrant's love of Classical learning and to his arrant paganism. Alberti redesigned the exterior shell of San Francesco, making a cubic structure, complete within itself, and fronting it with a façade like a Roman triumphal arch. Four massive engaged columns frame three recessed arches and carry a flat entablature that projects sharply, making a *ressaut,* or "jump," above each capital. Alberti intended the second story, which remains incomplete, to have an arched window framed by pilasters. The heavy relief of this façade contrasts with the flat, bandlike elements in most of Alberti's other buildings. The deep, arched niches, rhythmically deployed along the flanks of the building, which contain sarcophagi for the remains of famous men, are in keeping with Alberti's conviction that arches should be carried on piers, not columns. These niches, along with the elements of the façade, provide an effect of monumental scale and grandeur that approaches ancient Roman architecture.

Adjusting the Classical orders to façade surfaces occupied Alberti throughout his career. In 1470, in his last years, he designed the church of Sant' Andrea in Mantua (FIGS. **16-42** to **16-44**) to replace an older eleventh-century church. In the ingeniously planned façade, which illustrates the culmination of Alberti's experiments, he locks together two complete Roman architectural motifs—the temple front and the triumphal arch. His concern for proportion made him equalize the vertical and horizontal dimensions of the façade, which leaves it considerably lower than the church behind it. This concession to the demands of a purely visual proportionality in the façade and to the relation of the façade to the small square in front of it, even at the expense of continuity with the body of the building, is frequently manifest in Renaissance architecture, where considerations of visual appeal are of first importance. On the other hand, structural correspondences do exist in the Sant' Andrea façade. The façade pilasters are the same height as those on the interior walls of the nave, and the central barrel vault over the main entrance, from which smaller barrel

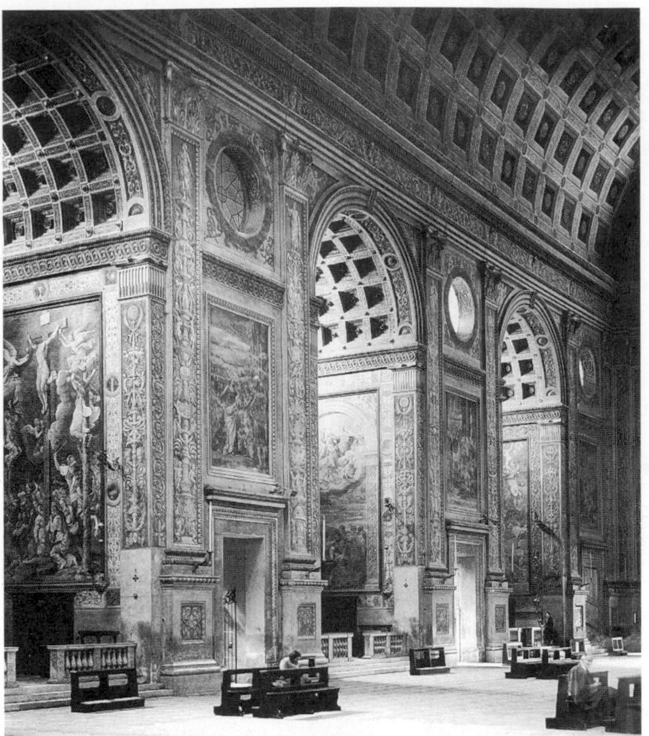

16-44 LEON BATTISTA ALBERTI, interior of Sant' Andrea.

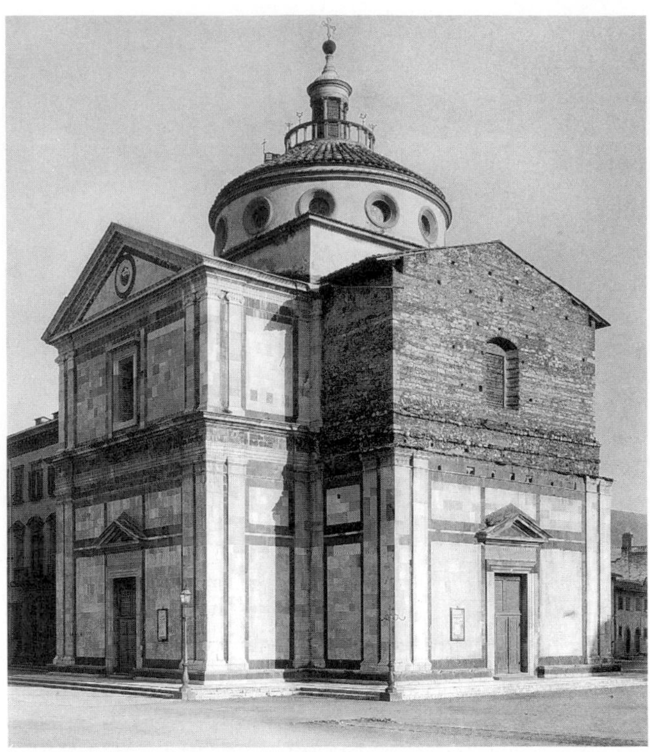

16-45 GIULIANO DA SANGALLO, Santa Maria delle Carceri, Prato, Italy, 1485 (view from the northwest).

vaults branch off at right angles, introduces (in proportional arrangement but on a smaller scale) the system used on the interior. The façade pilasters, becoming part of the wall, run uninterrupted through three stories in an early application of the "colossal" or "giant" order that will become a favorite motif of Michelangelo.

The interior of Sant' Andrea (FIG. 16-44) suggests that Alberti may have been inspired by the tremendous vaults of the ruined Basilica of Constantine (FIG. 6-91). The Medieval columned arcade, still used by Brunelleschi in Santo Spirito, now is forgotten, and the huge barrel vault, supported by thick walls alternating with vaulted chapels and interrupted by a massive dome over the crossing,* returns us to the vast interior spaces and dense enclosing masses of Roman architecture. In his treatise, Alberti calls the traditional basilican plan (in which continuous aisles flank the central nave) impractical, because the colonnades conceal the ceremonies from the faithful in the aisles; for this reason, he designed a single, huge hall, from which independent chapels branch off at right angles. This break with a Christian building tradition that had endured for a thousand years was extremely influential in later Renaissance and Baroque church planning.

*No one knows what kind of dome Alberti planned for the crossing; the present dome was added by FILIPPO JUVARA in the eighteenth century.

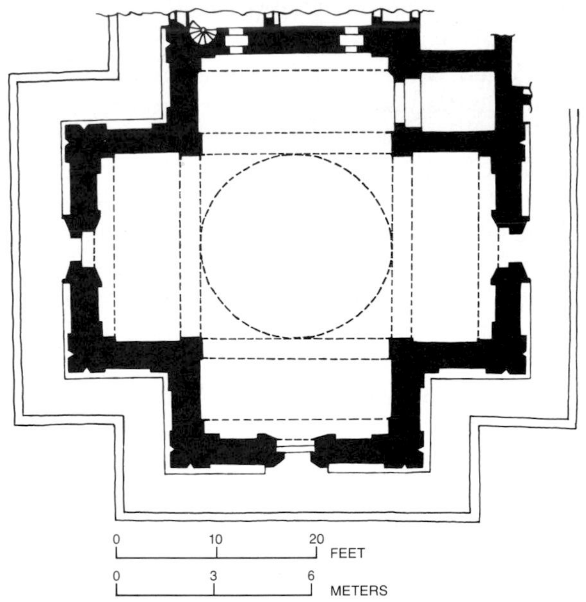

16-46 GIULIANO DA SANGALLO, plan of Santa Maria delle Carceri.

For many Renaissance architects and theoreticians, the circle was the ideal geometric figure; without a beginning or an end and with all points equidistant from a common center, it seemed to reflect the nature of the universe. This is one reason why the central plan was felt to be so appropriate for religious architecture. (Figures that approached the circle, such as

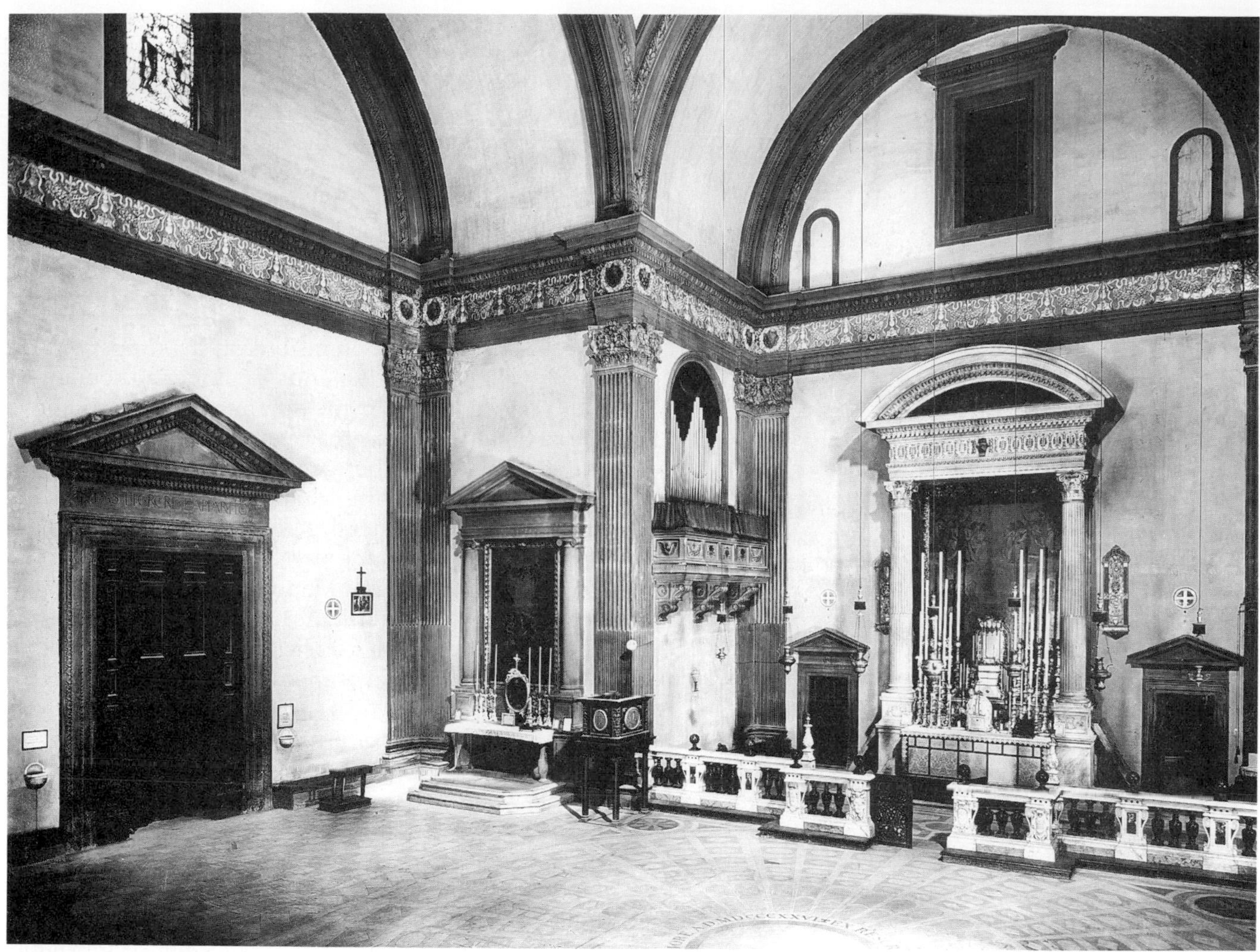

16-47 Giuliano da Sangallo, interior of Santa Maria delle Carceri (view facing northeast).

polygons, were considered adequate.) But as firm as this conviction of the architects may have been, the clergy was almost as firm in its demands for traditional longitudinal churches, which, of course, are much more practical for Christian religious services. In addition to the question of how to accommodate the congregation in central-plan churches, architects were confronted with the question of where to put the main altar, and they were permitted to realize their ideal relatively rarely.

A compromise solution, suggested first in Alberti's San Sebastiano in Mantua (his one, abortive attempt at building a central-plan church), was realized by Giuliano da Sangallo (1443–1516) in Santa Maria delle Carceri in Prato (figs. **16-45** to **16-47**). This building was built according to the plan of a Greek cross, with the cross arms so short that the emphasis is on the central, dome-covered square, very closely approaching the central-plan ideal. Blocklike, the structure is as high as it is wide, the cross arms are twice as wide as they are deep, and the Ionic second story is two-thirds the height of the Doric first floor. The whole building can be read in terms of the simple numerical relations that Alberti advocates. Interior articulation, however, is much closer to Brunelleschi and resembles that of the Pazzi Chapel (fig. 16-22). The building seems to be a hybrid of the styles of Giuliano's two great predecessors, but it is also a neat and compact near-realization of an ideal central-plan Renaissance church.

Sculpture

Like the work of Alberti in the latter half of the fifteenth century, the sculpture of the Florentine school realizes new triumphs of Humanist Classicism. Donatello's successors refined his innovating art and each specialized in one of its many forms and subjects. No monument made by the next generation expresses more beautifully and clearly this dedication to the values of pagan antiquity than the tomb of Leonardo Bruni in Florence (fig. **16-48**). Its sculptor,

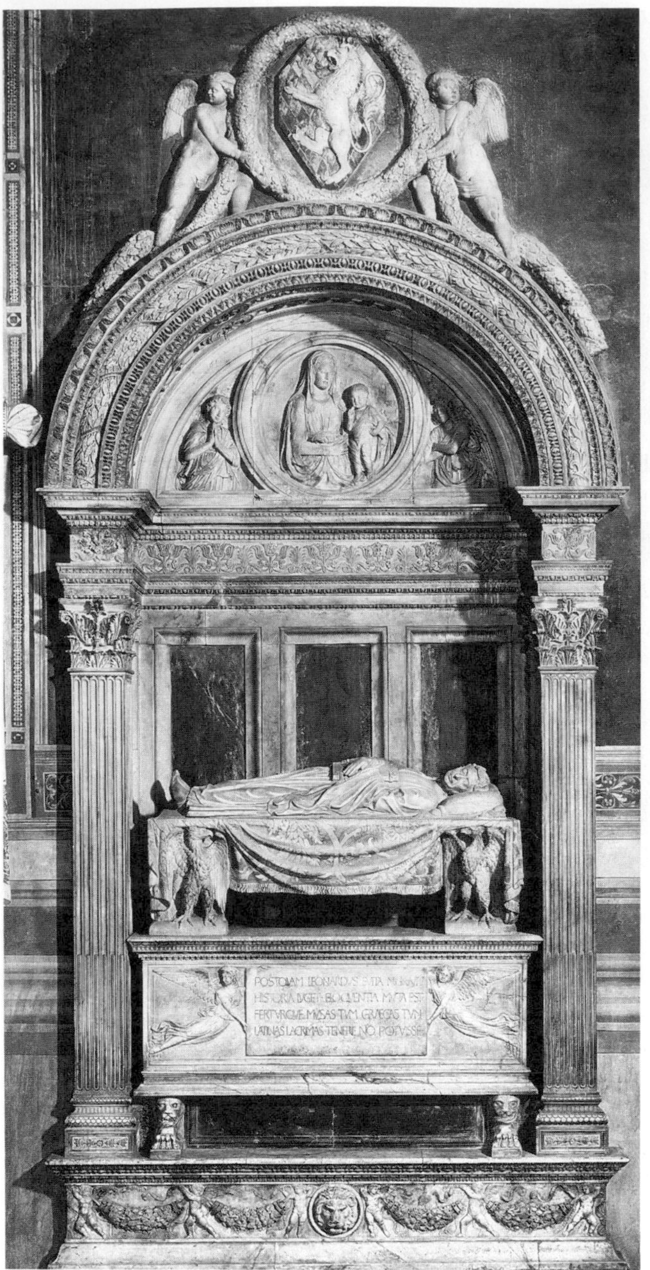

16-48 Bernardo Rossellino, tomb of Leonardo Bruni, *c.* 1445–1450. Marble, approx. 20′ high to top of arch. Santa Croce, Florence.

Bernardo Rossellino (1409–1464), like the man whose tomb he built in Santa Croce, was at one time a resident of Arezzo. Rossellino strove mightily to immortalize his fellow citizen. The wall tomb has a history that reaches back into the Middle Ages, but Rossellino's version is new and definitive and the expression of an age deliberately turning away from the medieval past.

Leonardo Bruni was one of the most distinguished men of Italy, and his passing was mourned widely. As an erudite scholar in Greek and Latin, a diplomat and apostolic secretary to four popes, and a member of the chancery of the city of Florence, Bruni's career sums up the Humanistic ideal. The Florentines particularly praised him for his *History of Florence.* In his honor, the practice of the funeral oration was revived, as was the ancient custom of crowning the deceased with laurel. The historic event of the crowning of the dead Humanist may have given Rossellino his theme and the tomb may have been intended as a kind of memorialization of the laureate scene.

The deceased lies on the catafalque in a long gown, the *History of Florence* on his breast, the drapery of his couch caught up at the ends by imperial Roman eagles. Winged genii at the summit of the arch above the catafalque hold a great escutcheon; on the side of the sarcophagus, other genii support a Latin inscription that describes the Muses' grief at the scholar's passing. Roman funeral garlands are carved on the narrow platform at the base of the niche. The only Christian reference is a Madonna and Child with angels in the tympanum. As in Alberti's churches, a Humanist and pagan Classicism controls the mood of the design in an evocation of the ancient Greco-Roman world.

Few could hope for a funeral and tomb like those given Leonardo Bruni, but in a Humanistic age, many people wanted to see their memory, if not their fame, perpetuated. In addition, Renaissance man probably enjoyed seeing likenesses of himself. Roman portrait busts were being found and preserved in ever-greater numbers during the latter half of the fifteenth century, and, given this model, it was almost inevitable that the Renaissance would develop a similar portrait type. The form may have originated in the shop of Antonio Rossellino (*c.* 1427–1479), the younger brother of Bernardo. The portrait bust of *Matteo Palmieri* (FIG. **16-49**), apostolic delegate for Pope Sixtus IV, is an example of Antonio's work. Palmieri, who held high rank in Florence, was a learned man and author of a theological poem, *City of Life,* based formally on Dante's writing. After his death, parts of the poem were declared heretical because the souls of men originally were represented as fallen angels. However, at the time of his death, Palmieri received a state funeral like Bruni's; his book was placed on his breast and a funeral oration was delivered. Antonio's portrait of Palmieri is extremely realistic but avoids the hardness of Roman Republican visages, which suggest the lifeless exactitude of the death mask—from which, indeed, they must have been made. Palmieri's almost clownlike face, with its enormous nose and endless mouth, is filled with a bright, intelligent animation, and the fine eyes seem those of a man engaged in a quick and subtle dialogue. The unsparing realism in the depiction of the ugly yet beguiling

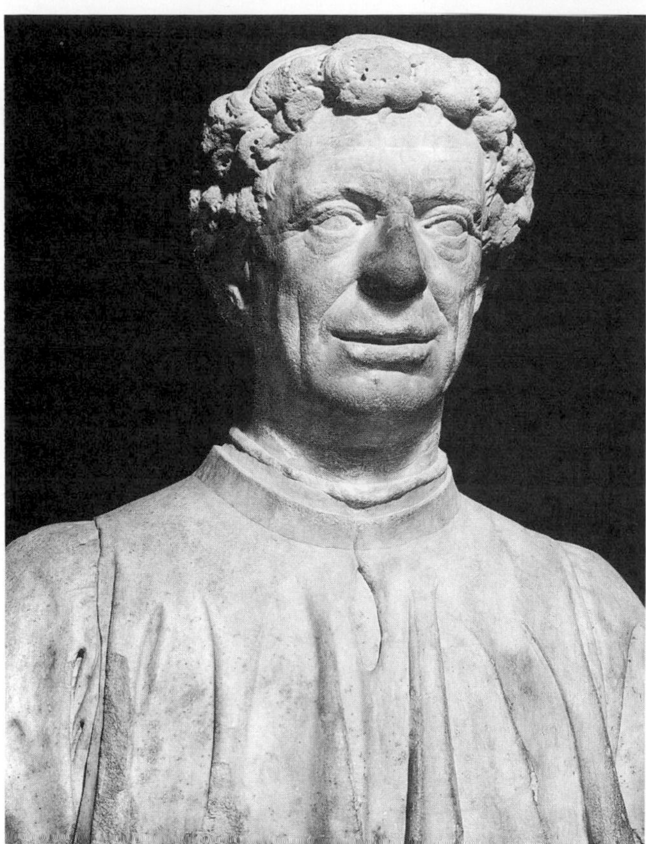

16-49 Antonio Rossellino, *Matteo Palmieri,* 1468. Marble, life size. Museo Nazionale del Bargello, Florence.

16-50 Desiderio da Settignano, *Bust of a Little Boy,* c. 1455. Marble, life size. National Gallery of Art, Washington, D.C. (Andrew W. Mellon Collection).

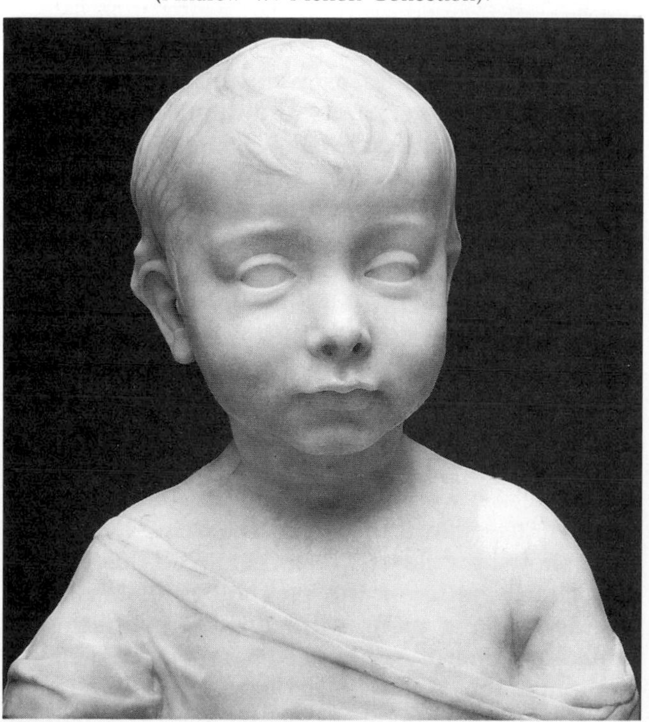

face is not surprising for a subject who probably had little difficulty in detecting flattery and rejecting it.

Donatello has shown the sternly real and the gently idealized in his forms; indeed, realism and idealism are parallel tendencies in the later fifteenth century. Desiderio da Settignano (1428–1464) specialized in the sensitive reading of the faces of women and children, which he idealized without diminishing character, as we may see in his *Bust of a Little Boy* (fig. **16-50**). The proportions and soft contours of the head are wonderfully understood, as is the psychological set—a wondering innocence—captured by Desiderio in the ambiguous pout and in the uplifted brows and large eyes directed wide at an adult world. The marble has been carved to give a remarkable smoothness to the planes, so that the light will be modulated softly and the impression of living, tender flesh conveyed. The subtlety of Desiderio's surfaces and the consequent effect of life they give have long been admired by the Italians, as is evident in their phrase, *il vago Desiderio, si dolce bello* (the charming Desiderio, so sweetly beautiful). A whole school of sculptors worked in this manner, and attributions, often quite uncertain, range from Desiderio to the young Leonardo da Vinci. The soft, misty, shadow effects certainly point ahead to the *sfumato* ("smoky" light and shade) in Leonardo's paintings.

Since the thirteenth and fourteenth centuries, the Madonna and Child theme has become increasingly humanized, until, in the fifteenth century, we might almost speak of a school of sweetness and light in which many sculptors attempt to outdo each other in rendering the theme ever gentler and prettier, especially in relief. In the latter half of the fifteenth century, increasing demand for devotional images for private chapels and shrines (rather than for large public churches) contributed to an increasing secularization of traditional religious subject matter. Luca della Robbia (1400–1482), a sculptor in the generation of Donatello and a leader of the trend toward sweetness and light, discovered a way to multiply the images of the Madonna so that they would be within the reach of persons of modest means. His discovery (around 1430), involving the application of vitrified potters' glazes to sculpture, led to his production, in quantity, of the glazed terra-cotta reliefs for which he is best known. Because they were cheap, durable, and decorative, these works became extremely popular and provided the basis for a flourishing family business. The tradition was carried on by Luca's nephew Andrea, whose colors tend to become a little garish, and by the latter's sons, Giovanni and Girolamo, whose activity extends well into the sixteenth century, when the product tends to become purely commercial; we still speak today of "della

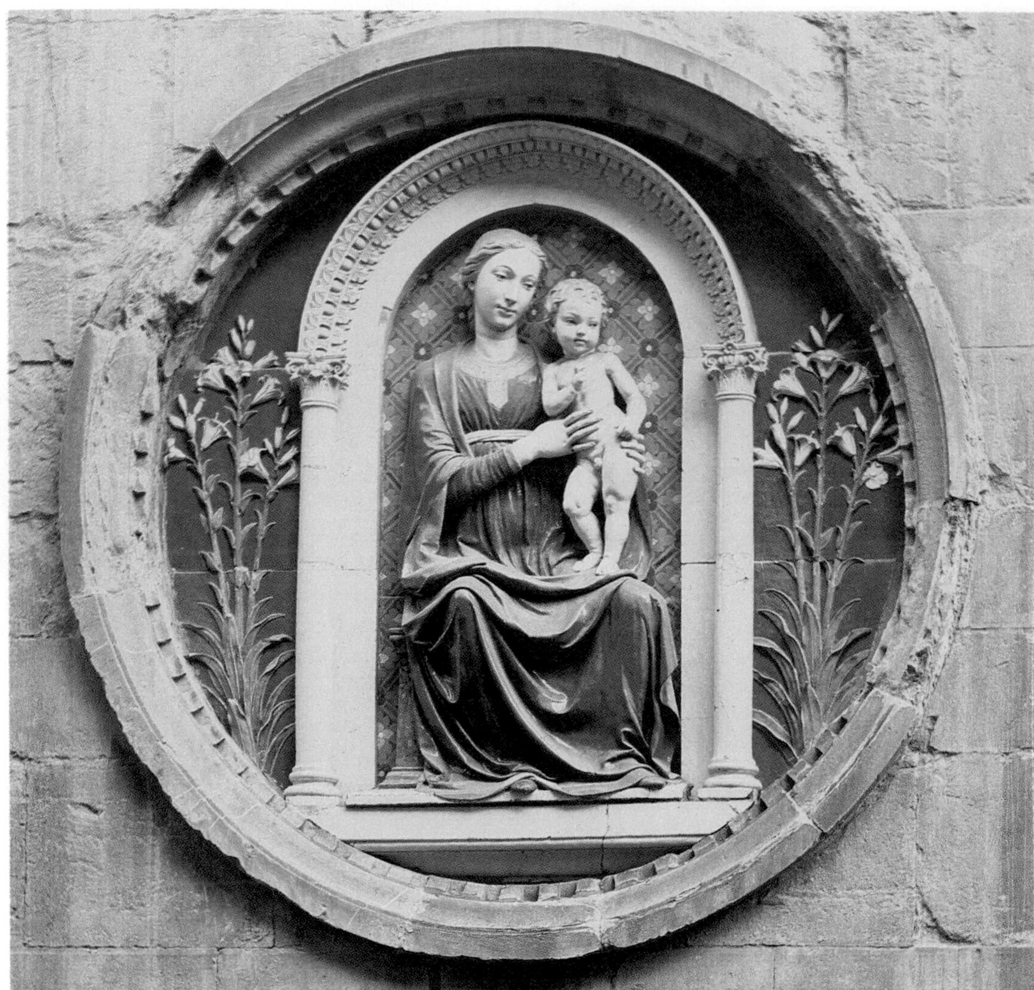

16-51 Luca della Robbia, *Madonna and Child,* c. 1455–1460. Terra-cotta with polychrome glaze, diameter approx. 6′. Or San Michele, Florence.

Robbia ware." An example of Luca's specialty is the *Madonna and Child* set into a wall of Or San Michele (FIG. **16-51**). The figures are composed within a *tondo,* a circular frame that will become popular with both sculptors and painters, particularly within the della Robbia family, in the later part of the century. The introduction of high-key color into sculpture adds a certain worldly gaiety to the theme, and the customary light blue grounds (and here the green and white of lilies and the white architecture) suggest the festive season of Easter and the freshness of May, the month of the Virgin. Of course, the somber majesty of the old Byzantine style has long since disappeared. The young mothers who prayed before images like this new form easily could identify with the Madonna, and doubtless did. The distance between the observed and the observer has vanished.

VERROCCHIO

The most important sculptor during the second half of the century was Andrea del Verrocchio (1435–1488). A painter as well as a sculptor, with something of the versatility and depth of Donatello, Verrocchio directed a flourishing *bottega* (studio-shop) in Florence that attracted many students, among them Leonardo da Vinci. Verrocchio, like Donatello, also had a broad repertory. He too made a figure of *David* (FIG. **16-52**), one that contrasts strongly in its narrative realism with the quiet, esthetic Classicism of Donatello's *David* (FIG. 16-12). Verrocchio's *David,* a sturdy, wiry young apprentice clad in a leathern doublet, stands with a jaunty pride, the head of Goliath at his feet. He poses like any sportsman who has just won a game, or a hunter with his kill. The easy balance of the weight and the lithe, still thinly adolescent musculature, in which the veins are prominent, show how closely Verrocchio read the text and how clearly he knew the psychology of brash and confident young men. Although the contrast with Donatello's interpretation need hardly be labored, we might note the "open" form of the Verrocchio *David,* the sword and pointed elbow sharply breaking

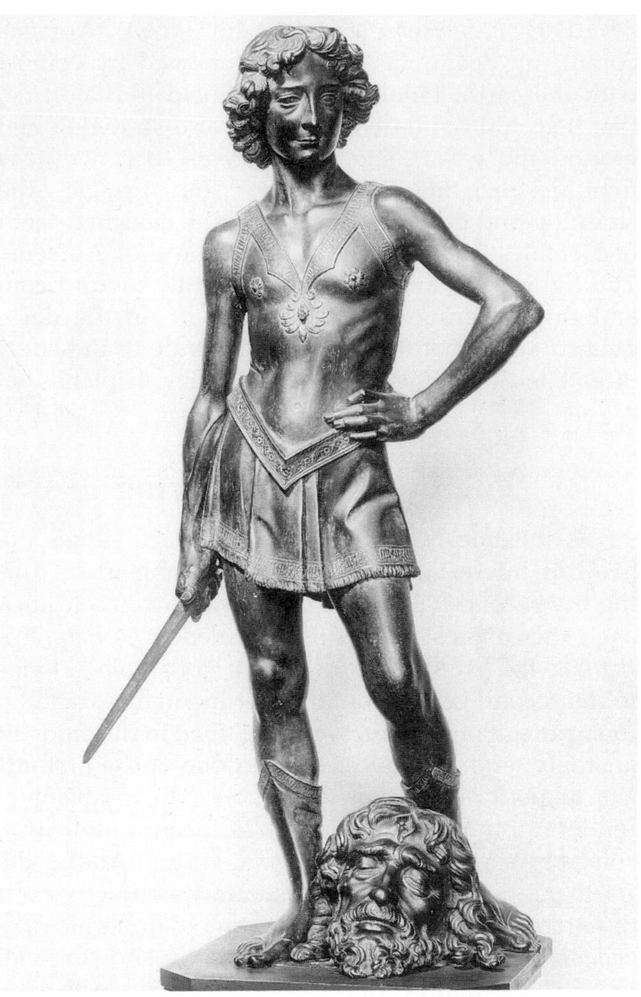

16-52 Andrea del Verrocchio, *David*, c. 1465. Bronze, approx. 49″ high. Museo Nazionale del Bargello, Florence.

through the figure's silhouette and stressing the live tension of the still alert victor. Donatello's *David*, on the other hand, has a "closed" silhouette that emphasizes its Classical calm and relaxation. The description of the anatomy of the two figures—specific in the former, generalized in the latter—puts further accent on the difference between them. Both statues are masterpieces and show how two skillful and thoughtful men approach the same theme very differently.

Verrocchio competes with Donatello again in an equestrian statue of another *condottiere* of Venice, *Bartolommeo Colleoni* (FIG. **16-53**), who, eager to emulate the fame and the monument of Donatello's *Gattamelata* (FIG. 16-13), provided for the statue in his will. Both Donatello's and Verrocchio's statues were made after the deaths of their subjects, so that neither artist knew the person being portrayed. The result is a fascinating difference of interpretation (like that between the two *Davids*) as to what a professional captain of armies would look like. On a pedestal even higher than that used in Donatello's *Gattamelata*, Verrocchio's statue of the bold equestrian general is placed so that the dominating, aggressive figure can be seen above the rooftops, silhouetted against the sky, its fierce authority unmistakably present from all major approaches to the piazza (the Campo dei Santi Giovanni e Paolo). In contrast with the near repose of the *Gattamelata*, the Colleoni horse moves in a prancing stride, arching and curving its powerful neck, while the commander seems suddenly to shift his whole weight to the stirrups and, in a fit of impassioned anger, to rise from the saddle with a violent twist of his body. The figures are charged with an exaggerated tautness; the bulging muscles of the animal and the fiercely erect and rigid body of the man unify brute strength and rage. The commander, represented as delivering the battle harangue to his troops before they close with the enemy, has worked himself into a frenzy that he hopes to communicate to his men. In the *Gattamelata*, Donatello gives us a portrait of grim sagacity; Verrocchio's *Bartolommeo Colleoni* is a portrait of savage and merciless might. Machiavelli writes that the successful ruler must combine the traits of the lion and the fox; one feels that Donatello's *Gattamelata* is a little like the latter and that Verrocchio's *Bartolommeo Colleoni* is much like the former.

16-53 Andrea del Verrocchio, *Bartolommeo Colleoni*, c. 1483–1488. Bronze, approx. 13′ high. Campo dei Santi Giovanni e Paolo, Venice.

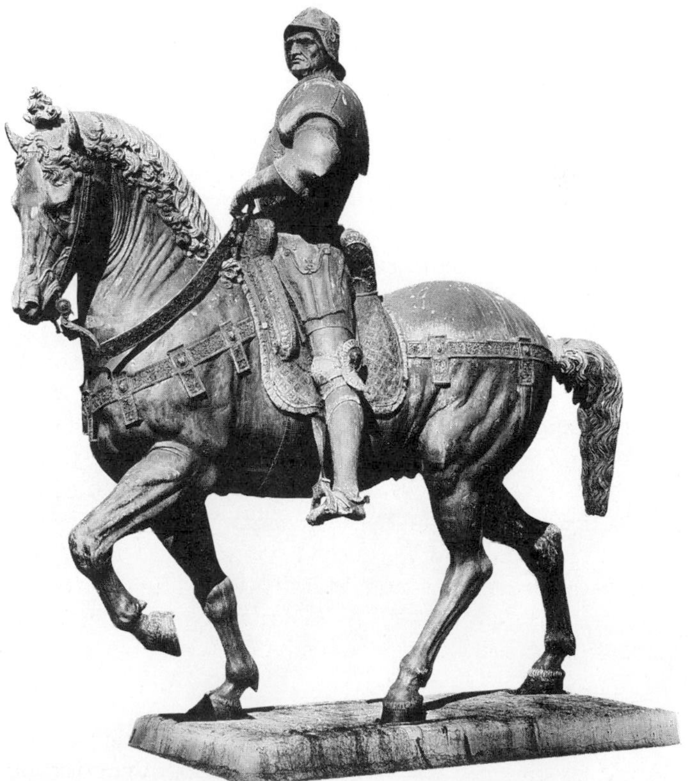

POLLAIUOLO

Closely related in stylistic intent to the work of Verrocchio is the work of ANTONIO POLLAIUOLO (*c.* 1431–1498). Pollaiuolo, who is also important as a painter and engraver, infuses the nervous movement and emotional expressiveness of Donatello's late style with a new linear mobility, spatial complexity, and dramatic immediacy. He has a realistic concern for movement in all its variety and for the stress and strain of the human figure in violent action. These qualities are apparent in Pollaiuolo's small-scale group of *Hercules and Antaeus* (FIG. **16-54**); not quite 18 inches high, it embodies the ferocity and vitality of elemental, physical conflict. The group illustrates the legend of a wrestling match between Antaeus (Antaios), a giant and son of the earth, and Hercules (Herakles). We already have seen this story represented by Euphronios on an ancient Greek vase (FIG. 5-9). Each time Hercules threw him down, Antaeus sprang up again, his strength renewed by contact with the earth. Finally, Hercules held him aloft, so that he could not touch the earth, and strangled him around the waist. The artist strives to convey the final, excruciating moments of the struggle—the straining and cracking of sinews, the clenched teeth of Hercules, the kicking and screaming of Antaeus. The figures are interlocked in a tightly wound coil, and the flickering reflections of light on the dark, gouged surface of the bronze contribute to the effect of agitated movement and a fluid play of planes.

16-54 ANTONIO POLLAIUOLO, *Hercules and Antaeus*, *c.* 1475. Bronze, approx. 18″ high with base. Museo Nazionale del Bargello, Florence.

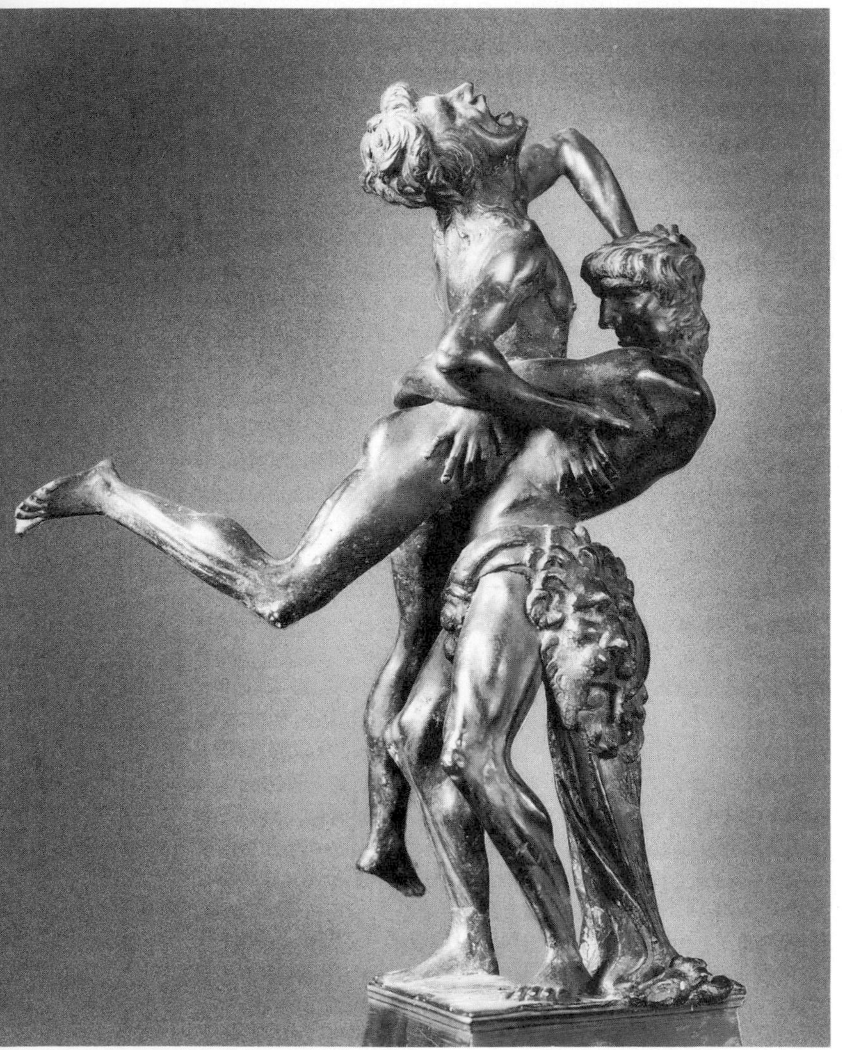

Painting and Engraving

The twisting of figures through space shows the growing interest in realistic action among artists during the second half of the century. Now an enthusiasm, this interest is further revealed in Pollaiuolo's *Battle of the Ten Nudes* (FIG. **16-55**). Pollaiuolo belongs to the second generation of experimentalists, who, in their pursuit of realism, were absorbed in the study of anatomy, and he may have been one of the first artists to perform human dissection. The problem of rendering human anatomy had been rather well solved by earlier artists like Donatello and Andrea del Castagno, but their figures usually are shown at rest or in restrained motion. As we can see in his *Hercules and Antaeus,* Pollaiuolo takes delight in showing violent action and finds his opportunity in subjects dealing with combat. He conceives the body as a powerful machine and likes to display its mechanisms; knotted muscles and taut sinews activate the skeleton as ropes pull levers. To show this to best effect, Pollaiuolo developed a figure so thin and muscular that it appears *écorché* (as if without skin or outer tissue), with strongly accentuated articulations at the wrists, elbows, shoulders, and knees. His *Battle of the Ten Nudes* shows this figure type in a variety of poses from numerous points of view. If the figures, even though they hack and slash at one another without mercy, seem somewhat stiff and frozen, it is because Pollaiuolo shows *all* the muscle groups at maximum tension. The fact that only part of the body's muscle groups are involved in any one action, while the others are relaxed, was to be observed only several decades later by an even greater anatomist, Leonardo da Vinci.

Pollaiuolo's *Battle of the Ten Nudes* is an *engraving*, a print made by pressing an inked metal plate, into which a drawing has been incised, against a sheet of paper. Developed around the middle of the fifteenth century, probably in northern Europe, engraving proved to be more flexible and durable than the older

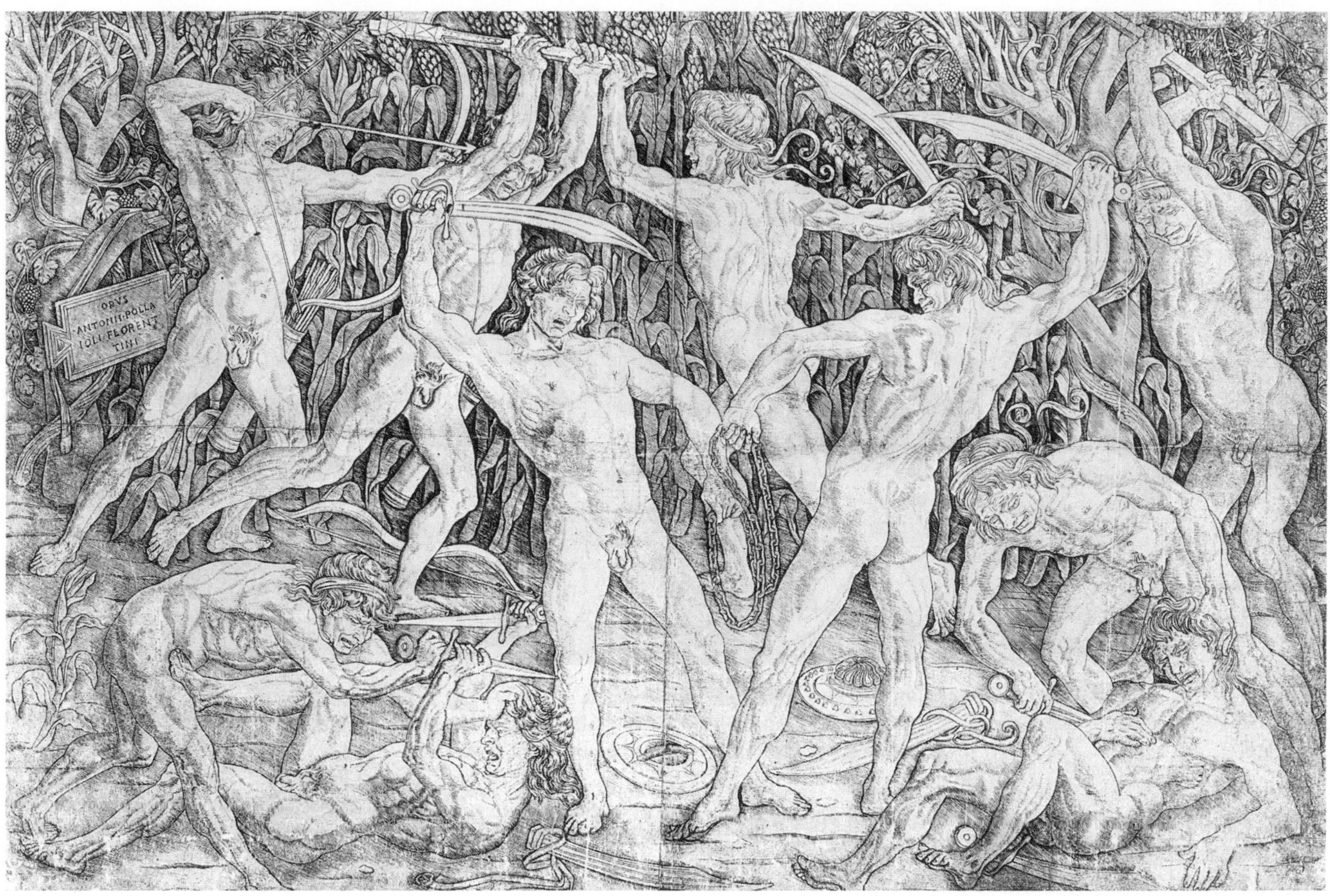

16-55 Antonio Pollaiuolo, *Battle of the Ten Nudes*, c. 1465. Engraving, approx. 15″ × 23″. Metropolitan Museum of Art, New York (bequest of Joseph Pulitzer, 1917).

woodcut, which it gradually replaced during the later part of the century. As numerous prints could be made from the same plate, they were cheap and could be circulated widely, bringing art to all levels of society and spreading new and stimulating pictorial ideas among artists. Because they were easy to transport, prints were a quick and easy means of interartist communication. Italian prints had important influence on such northern painters as Albrecht Dürer, and the prints of that great master of engraving were admired widely by Italian artists.

The versatile Pollaiuolo experimented in painting, especially with the problem of representing figures in a landscape setting. The problem of relating figures to architecture already had been solved by Piero della Francesca, but the landscape setting presented a different set of requirements, some of which had been met by Masaccio. The panel representing *Hercules and Deianira* (FIG. **16-56**), a work contemporaneous with the sculptured group of *Hercules and Antaeus*, indicates that Pollaiuolo is a master not only of anatomy but also of landscape and light. In this, one of three paintings (the subjects of which were the labors of Hercules, the legendary Greek hero) commissioned by Piero de' Medici for the Medici palace, the centaur Nessus has abducted Deianira, the bride of Hercules, and Hercules is in the act of slaying him with a poisoned arrow. The dramatic action and play of muscle and sinew is what we would expect of Pollaiuolo, but here he sets the bounding Nessus, the gesticulating Deianira, and the bow-taut Hercules in a broad landscape, the valley of the river Arno. The winding river takes the viewer's gaze all the way to the horizon, past the city of Florence, dim in the distance (the cathedral can be seen just beyond Deianira's left hand). Pollaiuolo's observation of deep landscape space and atmospheric effects, like the luminous glaze on the river and the fade-out of the contours of the far distant hills, complements his knowledge of the human figure; the broad, quiet, natural perspective serves to set off the tense movements of the figures. From midcentury on, a sharply increased interest developed in the pagan mythologies as subjects for painting and sculpture, an interest that will persist well into the nineteenth century. Here, a mythological subject has been imagined so vividly that it has been made part

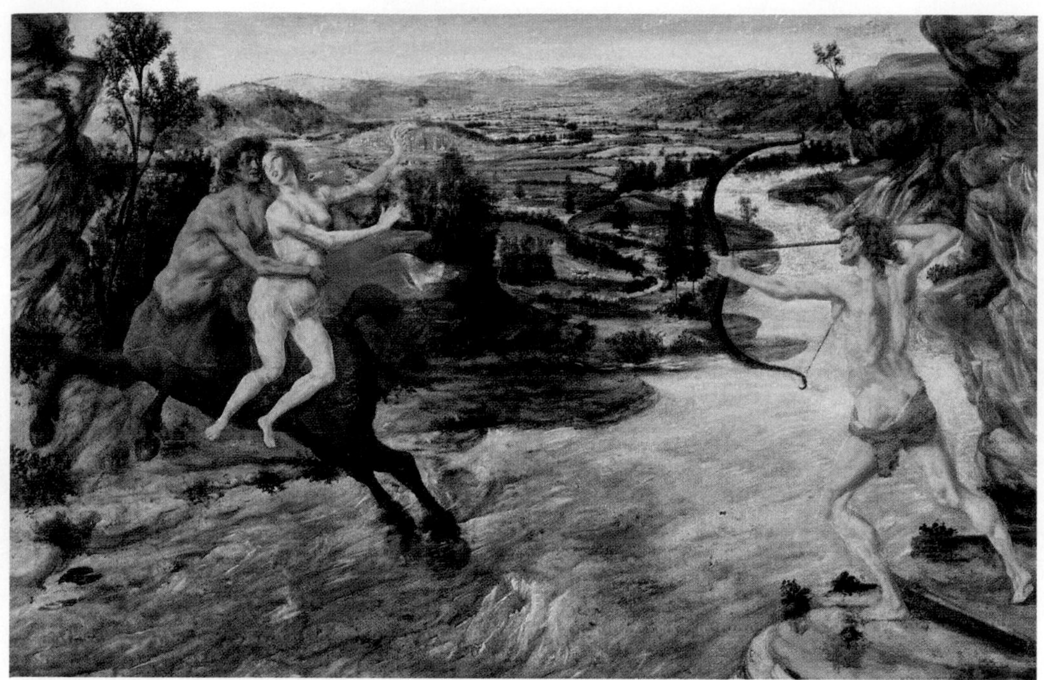

16-56 ANTONIO POLLAIUOLO, *Hercules and Deianira,* c. 1470. Egg tempera and oil (?) on canvas, $21\frac{1}{2}'' \times 31\frac{3}{16}''$. Yale University Art Gallery, New Haven, Connecticut (university purchase from James Jackson Jarves).

of the actual Florentine scene. Instead of relating figures and space in a rationally clear perspective, abstracted from nature, Pollaiuolo represents human figures in their natural environment. This image of the world is not fixed, like Piero della Francesca's, but is fluid and changing.

DOMENICO GHIRLANDAIO (1449–1494) differs in character from Pollaiuolo. Neither an innovator nor an experimenter, Ghirlandaio is rather a synthesizer who, profiting from everything done before, summarizes the state of Florentine art by the end of the century. His works express his times to perfection, and, for this, he enjoyed great popularity among his contemporaries. Ghirlandaio's paintings also show a deep love for the city of Florence, its spectacles and pageantry, its material wealth and luxury. His most representative pictures, a cycle of frescoes representing scenes from the lives of the Virgin and St. John the Baptist, are found in the choir of Santa Maria Novella. In our illustration, *The Birth of the Virgin* (FIG. **16-57**), Mary's mother, St. Anne, reclines in a palace room embellished with fine *intarsia* (wooden mosaic)

16-57 DOMENICO GHIRLANDAIO, *The Birth of the Virgin,* 1485–1490. Fresco. Cappella Maggiore, Santa Maria Novella, Florence.

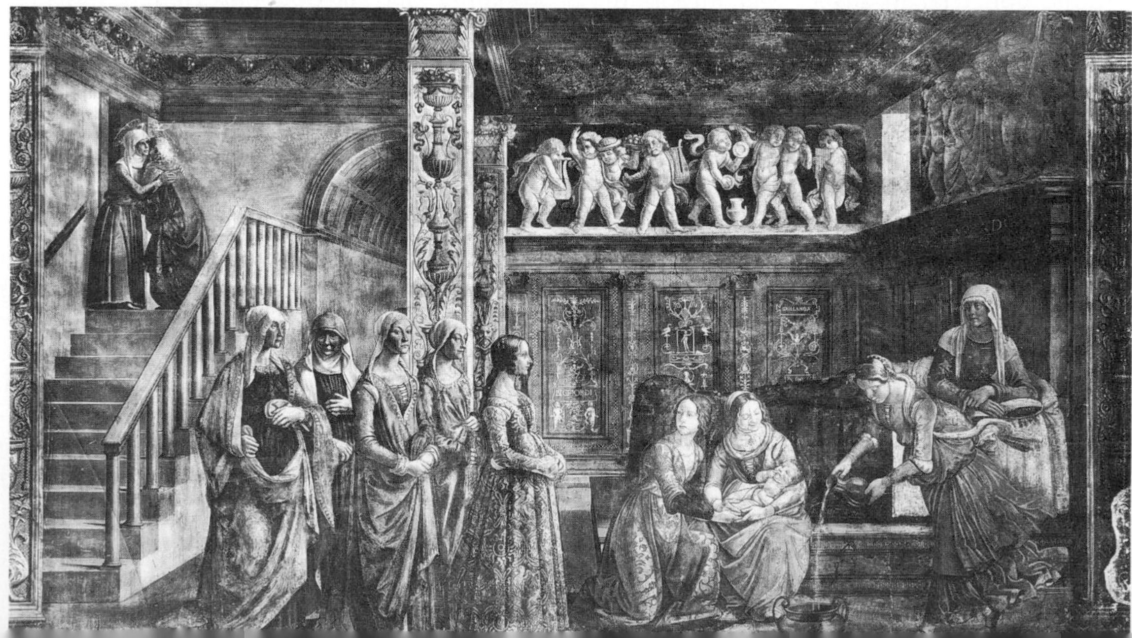

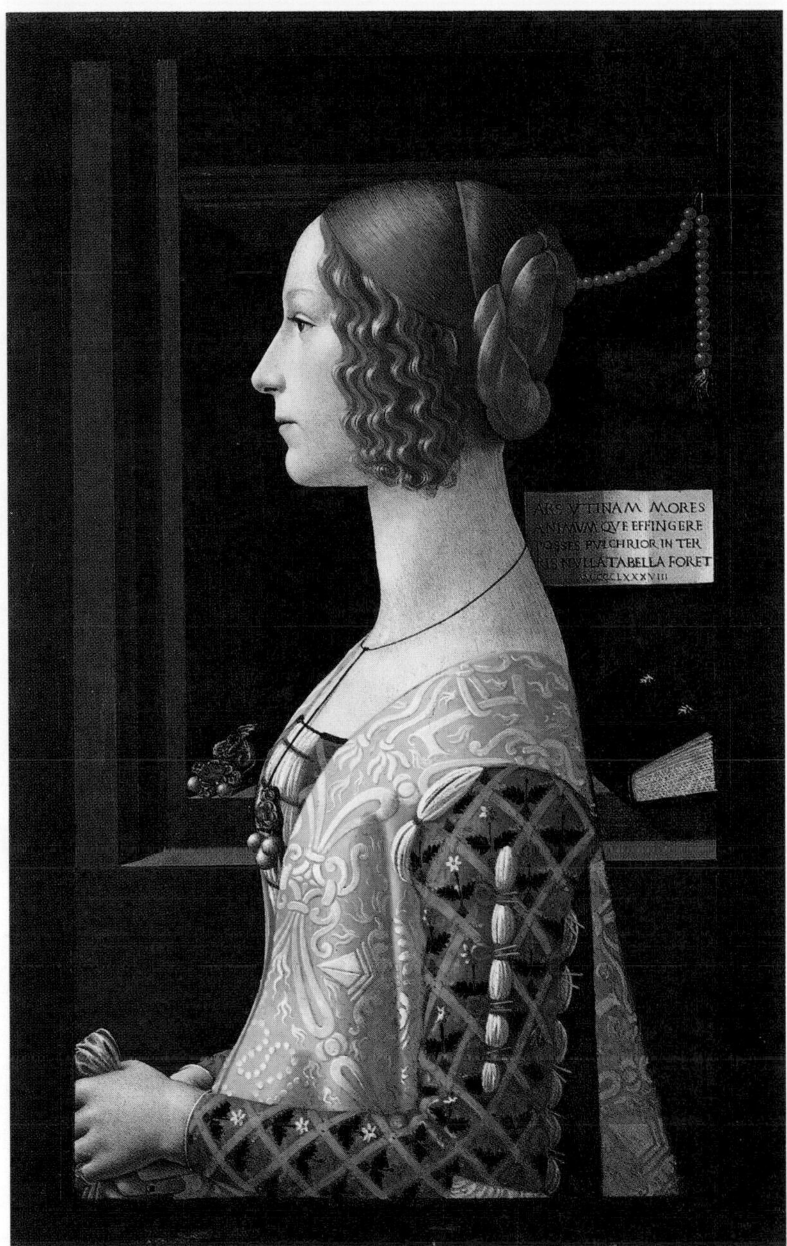

16-58 Domenico Ghirlandaio, *Giovanna Tornabuoni* (?), 1488. Oil and tempera on wood, approx. 30″ × 20″. Sammlung Thyssen-Bornemisza, Lugano, Switzerland.

and sculpture, while midwives prepare the infant's bath. From the left comes a grave procession of ladies, led by a member of the Tornabuoni family (the donors of the paintings). This splendidly dressed young woman holds as prominent a place in the composition (close to the central axis) as she must have held in Florentine society; her appearance in the painting (a different female member of the house appears in each of the frescoes) is conspicuous evidence of the secularization of sacred themes commonplace in art by this time. Living persons of high rank now are not only represented as present at biblical dramas but, as here, often steal the show from the saints. The display of patrician elegance absorbs and subordinates the devotional tableau.

The composition epitomizes the achievements of Early Renaissance painting: clear spatial representation; statuesque, firmly constructed figures; and rational order and logical relation among these figures and objects. If anything of earlier traits remains, it is in the arrangement of the figures, which still somewhat rigidly cling to layers parallel to the plane of the picture.

Giovanna Tornabuoni may be the subject of a portrait by Ghirlandaio (FIG. **16-58**), the cool formality of which recalls the lady in the fresco and sets off the

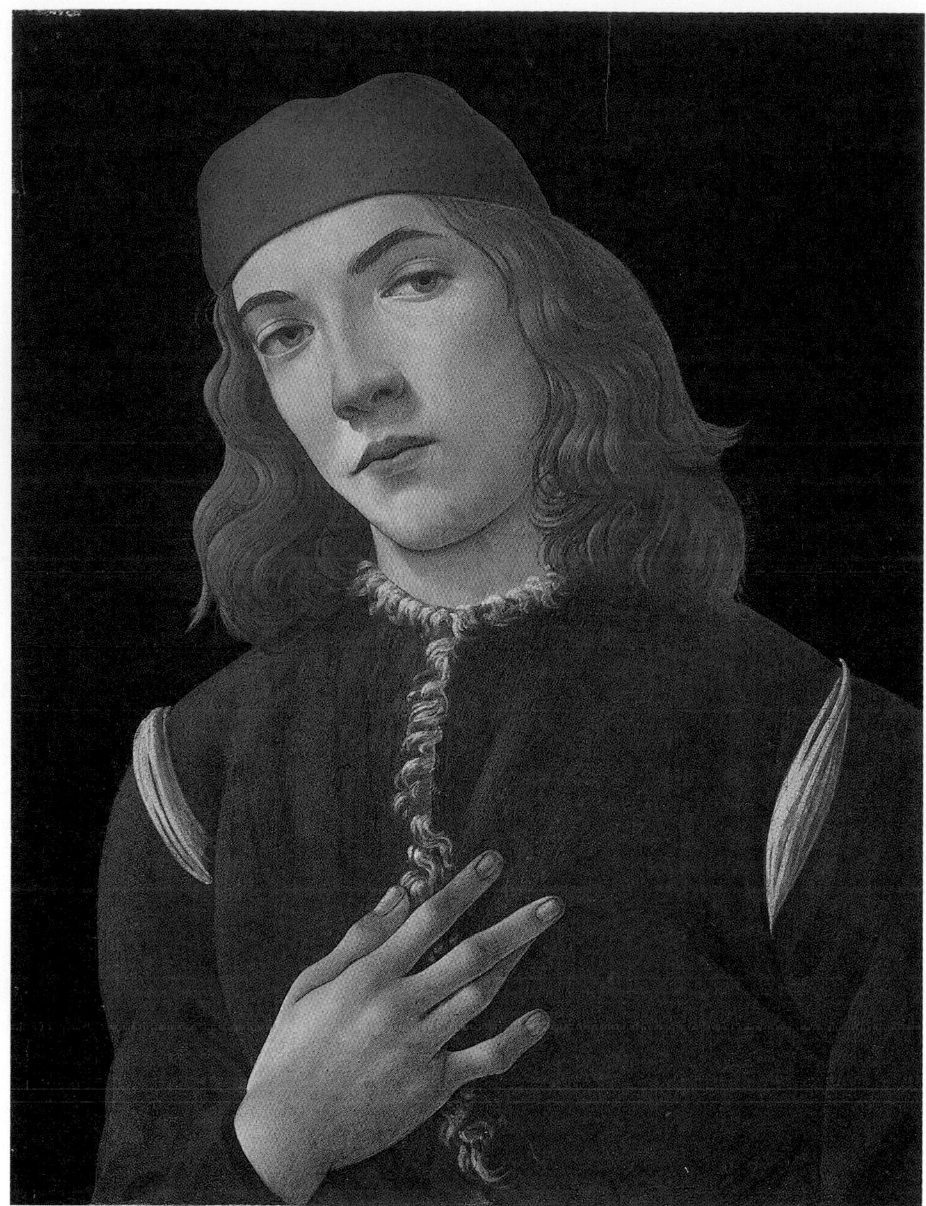

16-59 SANDRO BOTTICELLI, *Portrait of a Young Man*, c. 1489–1490. Tempera on panel, approx. $16\frac{1}{8}'' \times 12\frac{1}{4}''$. National Gallery of Art, Washington, D.C. (Andrew W. Mellon Collection).

proud, sensitive beauty of the aristocratic features. Although the profile pose is not intended primarily to convey a reading of character, this portrait tells us much about the high state of human culture achieved in Florence, the value and careful cultivation of beauty in life and art, the breeding of courtly manners, and the great wealth behind it all.

BOTTICELLI

The profile pose was customary in Florence until about 1470, when three-quarter and full-face portraits began to replace it. In about the last decade of the fifteenth century, SANDRO BOTTICELLI (Alessandro di Mariano dei Filipepi, 1444–1510) painted the nearly full-face *Portrait of a Young Man* (FIG. **16-59**). Three-quarter and full-face views were made common earlier in the century by the painters of northern Europe. The Italian painters now adopt them, perceiving that they increase the viewer's information about the subject's appearance and allow the artist to reveal the subject's character, although Italian artists will long prefer an impersonal formality that conceals the private, psychological person. An apparent exception, Botticelli's young man is highly expressive psychologically. The delicacy of the pose, the graceful tilt of the head, the sidelong glance, and the elegant gesture of the hand compose an equivocal expression half-musing and half-insinuating. Feminine and masculine traits are merged to make an image of rarified, epicene beauty.

Botticelli was the pupil of Fra Filippo Lippi, from whom he must have learned the method of "drawing" firm, pure outline with light shading within the contours. The effect clearly is apparent in the explicit and sharply elegant form of the portrait. In the hands of Botticelli, this method will be refined infinitely, and he is known in world art as one of the great masters of line. One of the most important monographs on Botticelli was written by a Japanese;* in Botticelli, the Orient recognizes a master from the West.

No discussion of Botticelli can be fully meaningful without some reference to the environment that peculiarly encouraged him—the circle of Lorenzo de' Medici and the Platonic Academy of Philosophy. Here, he studied the philosophy of Plato, or rather of Neo-Platonism, for scholars had not yet developed the critical sense that would distinguish between Plato and the Neo-Platonic mystics of Alexandria, who came centuries after and quite transformed Plato's thought in the direction of a religious system. It was this spiritualized and mystical Platonism that Botticelli absorbed, believing that it was close to Christianity in essence and that the two could be reconciled. He must have heard the Humanists gathered around Lorenzo discoursing on these new mysteries in one of the Medici villas—surroundings highly conducive to reflection. A modern historian writes:

> In a villa overhanging the towers of Florence, on the steep slope of that lofty hill crowned by the mother city, the ancient Fiesole, in gardens which Cicero might have envied, with Ficino, Landino, and Politian at his side, he [Lorenzo] delighted his hours with the beautiful visions of Platonic philosophy, for which the summer stillness of an Italian sky appears the most genial accompaniment.†

Botticelli had the power to materialize the "beautiful visions," and this he did in a number of works for the Medici villas, among them the famous *Birth of Venus* (FIG. **16-60**), inspired, it is believed, by a poem by Politian on that theme. Botticelli is of his generation in his enthusiasm for themes from Classical mythology as well as in his suiting of the ancient pagan materials to a form prepared by the Early Renaissance, a form realistic yet still modified by something of the Medieval past. Competent in all the new representational methods, he seems deliberately to sacrifice them in the interest of his own original manner, rarefying the realism of the Early Renaissance into an inimitable decorative and linear system that generates its own kind of figure and space.

Venus, born of the sea foam, is wafted on a cockle shell, blown by the Zephyrs, to her sacred island, Cyprus, where the nymph Pomona, descended from the ancient goddess of fruit trees, runs to meet her with a brocaded mantle. The lightness and bodilessness of the Zephyrs move all the figures without effort. Draperies undulate easily in the gentle gusts, perfumed by rose petals that fall on the whitecaps stirred by the Zephyrs' toes. The presentation of the figure of Venus nude was, in itself, an innovation; as we have seen, the nude, especially the female nude, had been proscribed in the Middle Ages. Its appearance on such a scale and the use of an ancient Venus statue of the *Venus pudica* (modest Venus) type as a model could have drawn the charge of paganism and infidelity. But under the protection of the powerful Medici, a new world of imagination could open freely with the new Platonism.

In Botticelli's hands, the pagan myth is transmuted into a Neo-Platonic allegory of the human soul. The high priest of the Neo-Platonic cult (for which *The Birth of Venus* almost could have been an altarpiece) was the Humanist Marsilio Ficino, certainly known to Botticelli through Lorenzo de' Medici's circle. Ficino taught that God, the Supreme One, had created the universe as a hierarchy of descending orders of being that extended from the perfection of the angelic spheres down to the inert being of base matter. The human soul, before its birth, had perfect existence; coming into the world of matter, it had become corrupt. Now it occupied the central place in the great chain of being. It could regain its original perfection and ascend to fullest being only by the love of God as manifested in the beauty of creation. By the contemplation of beauty, the soul could progress from the love of the material to the love of the abstract, and then to the love of the spiritual. The goal of the quest is the vision of God—Dante's experience at the end of the *Comedia*. Venus, the pagan goddess of beauty, is transformed into the Heavenly Venus, purged of all mundane sensuality; it is she whom the soul must contemplate.

Botticelli gives us the Heavenly Venus. The lovely figure of the goddess, strangely weightless and ethereal, is the intellectual or spiritual apparition of beauty. At the same time, she personifies the human soul. The *Birth of Venus* is an allegory of the primal innocence and truth of the soul, before its birth into gross matter, its fall into lesser being. Here, the soul—naked as truth is naked—is blown upon by the winds of passion but is soon to be clothed in the robe of

*Y. Yashiro, *Sandro Botticelli and the Florentine Renaissance*, rev. ed. (Boston: Hale, 1929).

†Henry Hallam, in J. A. Symonds, *Renaissance in Italy* (New York: Modern Library, 1935), Vol. 1, p. 477.

reason. The coarse, pagan myth of the goddess is conflated with the Neo-Platonic account of the journey of the soul to God through the contemplation of beauty. The ascent of the soul to the ultimate ecstasy, the vision of God, is the main theme of Christian mysticism; the concept that the ascent is made possible by the contemplation of beauty is Neo-Platonic. The beauty of the pagan goddess becomes the beauty of the perfected soul.

This kind of mystical approach, so different from the earnest search of the early fifteenth century to comprehend humanity and the natural world through a rational and empirical order, finds expression in Botticelli's strange and beautiful style, which seems to ignore all of the scientific ground gained by experimental art. His style parallels the allegorical pageants in Florence, which were staged as chivalric tournaments but revolved completely around allusions to Classical mythology; the same trend is evident in the poetry of the 1470s and 1480s. Artists and poets at this time did not directly imitate classical antiquity, but used the myths, with delicate perception of their charm, in a way still tinged with medieval romance.

Botticelli's style, the sensitive vehicle of an intensely sensitive mind, changed with the fortunes of Florence; as he responded to the Humanist and Neo-Platonic ideas of the circle of Lorenzo de' Medici, so he responded to the overthrow of the Medici, the incursion of the French armies, and especially to the preaching of the Dominican monk Girolamo Savonarola, the reforming priest-dictator who denounced the paganism of the Medici and their artists, philosophers, and poets. Savonarola called on the citizens of Florence to repent their iniquities, and, when the Medici fled, he prophesied the doom of the city and of Italy and took absolute power over the state. Together with a large number of citizens, Savonarola believed that the Medici had been a political, social, and religious influence for the worse—corrupting Florence and inviting the scourge of foreign invasion. Modern scholars still debate the significance of Savonarola's brief span of power. Apologists for the undoubtedly sincere monk deny that his actions played a role in the decline of Florentine culture at the end of the century. But he did rail at the Neo-Platonist Humanists as heretical gabblers, and his banishing of the Medici, Tornabuoni, and other noble families from

16-60 SANDRO BOTTICELLI, *The Birth of Venus*, c. 1482. Tempera on canvas, approx. 5′ 8″ × 9′ 1″. Galleria degli Uffizi, Florence.

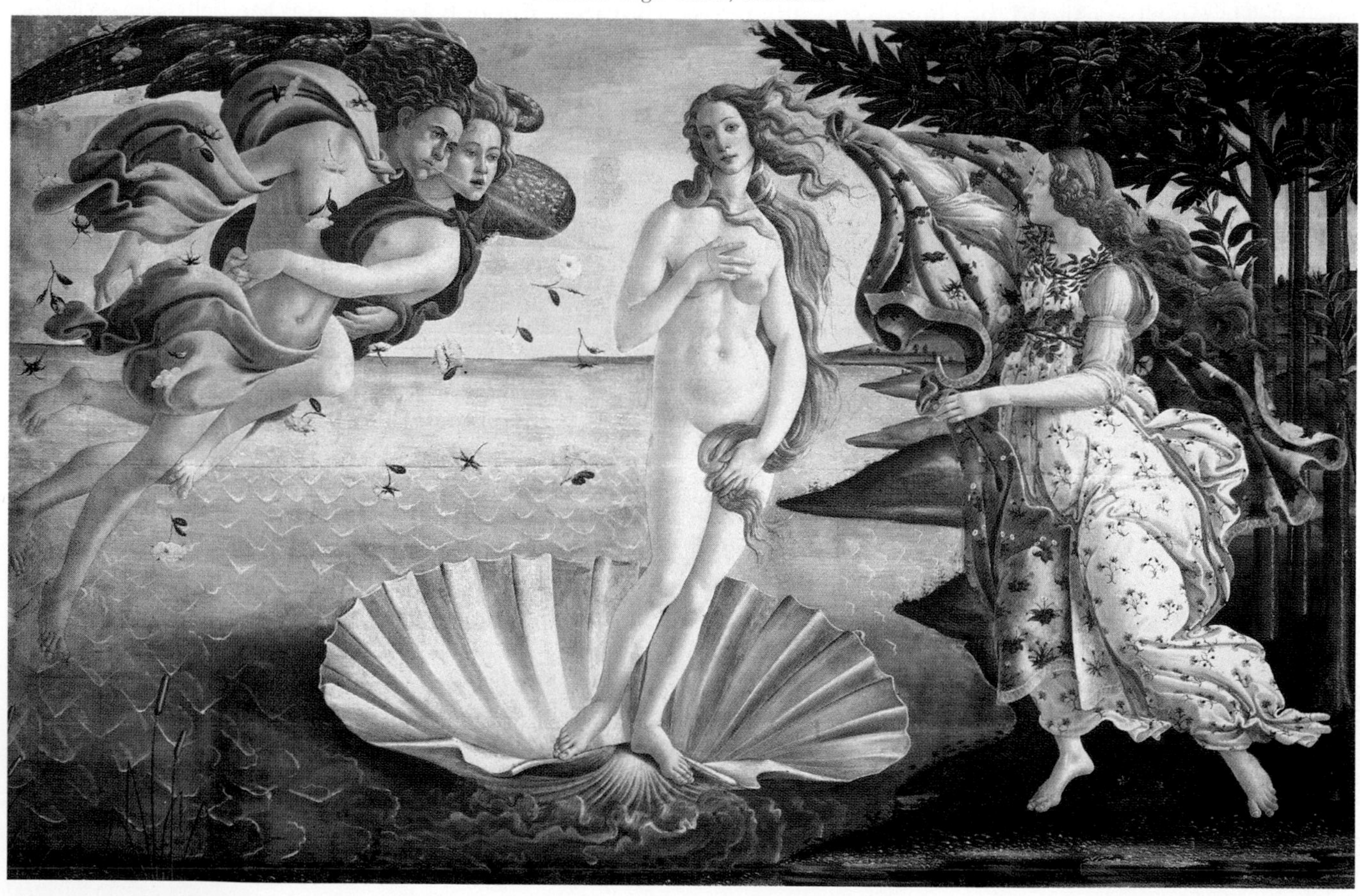

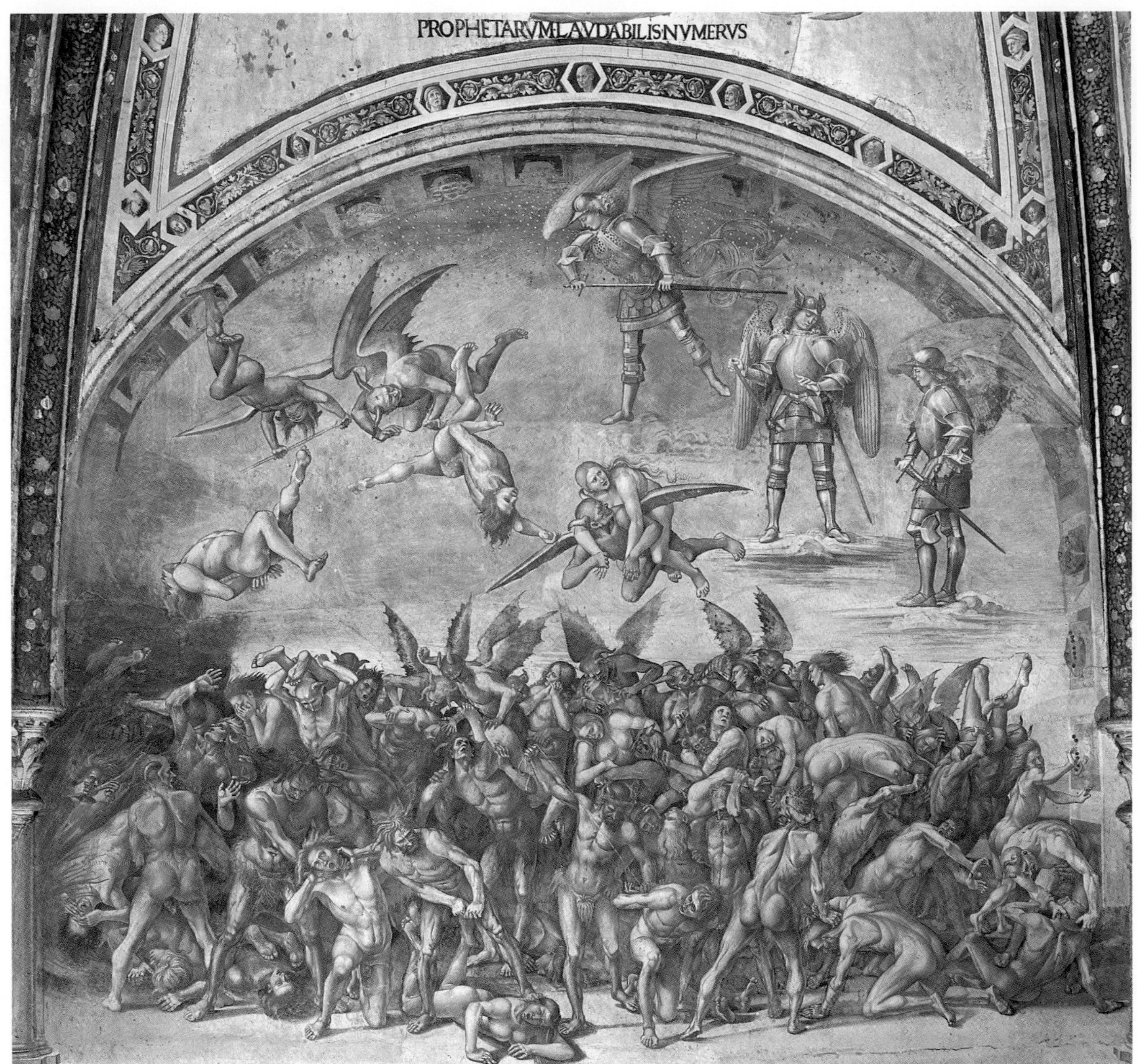

16-61 Luca Signorelli, *The Damned Cast into Hell,* 1499–1504. Fresco. San Brizio Chapel, Orvieto Cathedral, Orvieto, Italy.

Florence deprived local artists of some of their major patrons. Florence lost its position of cultural leadership at the end of the century and never regained it. Certainly, the puritanical spirit that moved Savonarola—and that was soon to appear throughout Europe in the reforming preachments of the Protestant Reformation—must have dampened considerably the neopagan enthusiasm of the Florentine Early Renaissance.

The sensitive, highly personal, and exotic style of Botticelli closed the great age of Florentine art on an exquisitely refined note. Artists of his generation outside Florence, but within the circuit of its influence, elaborated on the experiments introduced earlier in the century. An Umbrian painter, Luca Signorelli (*c.* 1445–1523), further developed the interest of Antonio Pollaiuolo in the depiction of muscular bodies in violent action in a wide variety of poses and foreshortenings. In the San Brizio Chapel in Orvieto Cathedral, Signorelli's painted scenes depicting the end of the world include *The Damned Cast into Hell* (fig. **16-61**). Few figure compositions of the fifteenth century have the same awesome psychic impact. St. Michael and the hosts of Heaven hurl the damned

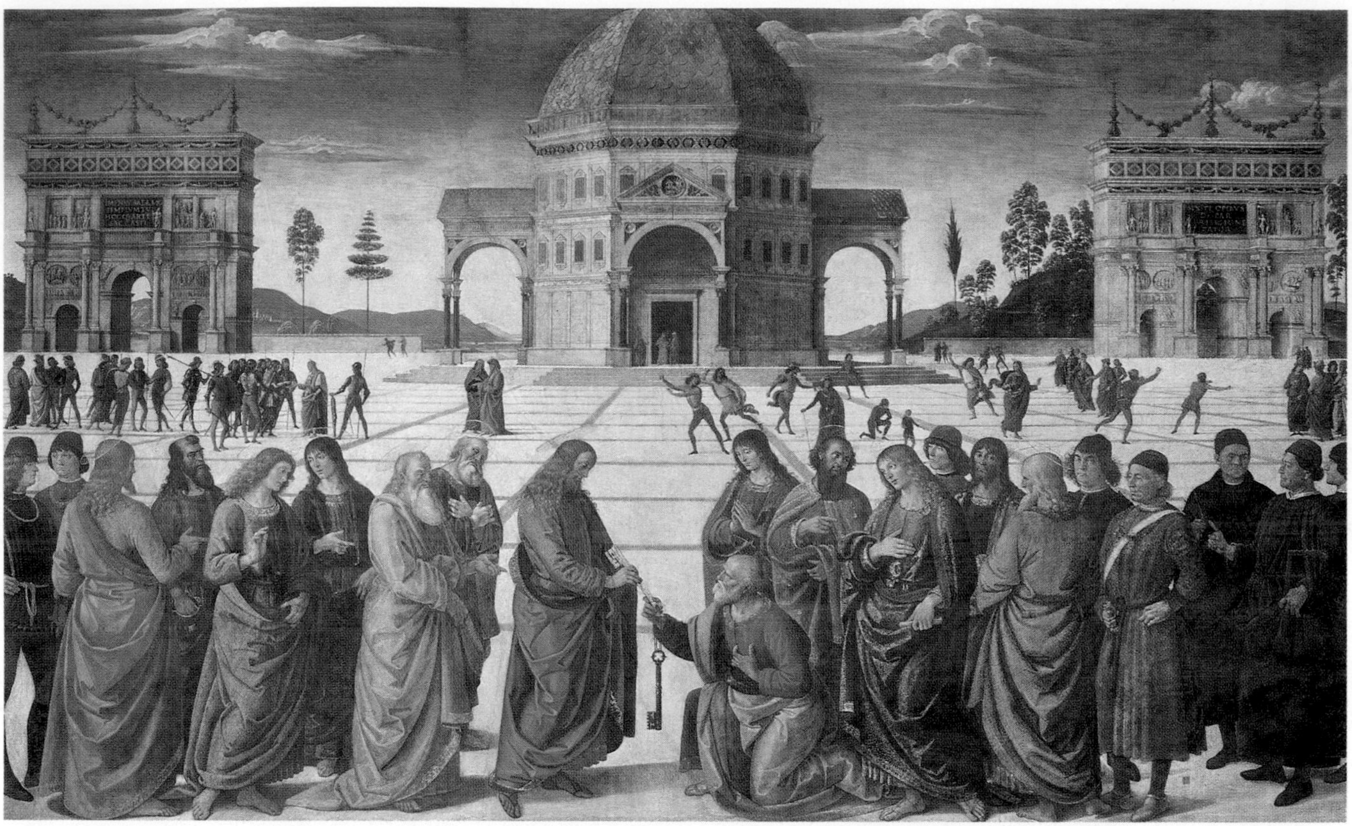

16-62 PERUGINO, *Christ Delivering the Keys of the Kingdom to St. Peter,* 1481–1483. Fresco. Sistine Chapel, Vatican, Rome.

into Hell, where, in a dense, writhing mass, they are tortured by vigorous demons. The figures—nude, lean, and muscular—assume every conceivable posture of anguish. Signorelli's skill at foreshortening the human figure is one with his mastery of its action, and although each figure is clearly a study from a model, he fits his theme to the figures in an entirely convincing manner. Terror and rage pass like storms through the wrenched and twisted bodies. The fiends, their hair flaming and their bodies the color of putrefying flesh, lunge at their victims in ferocious frenzy. Not even Pollaiuolo achieves such virtuosity in the manipulation of anatomy for dramatic purpose. Doubtless, Signorelli influenced Michelangelo, who makes the human nude his sole and sufficient expressive motif. In *The Last Judgment* in the Sistine Chapel, Michelangelo shows that he was much aware of Signorelli's version of the theme.

Signorelli's fellow Umbrian, PERUGINO (Pietro Vannucci, *c.* 1450–1523), was concerned not with the human figure in violent action, as Signorelli was, but with the calm, geometric ordering of pictorial space. Between 1481 and 1483, Perugino, Botticelli, Ghirlandaio, and Signorelli were among a group of artists summoned to Rome to decorate the walls of the newly completed Sistine Chapel with frescoes. Perugino painted *Christ Delivering the Keys of the Kingdom to St. Peter* (FIG. **16-62**), the event on which the papacy had, from the beginning, based its claim to infallible and total authority over the Church. Christ hands the keys to St. Peter, standing at the center of solemn choruses of saints and citizens, who occupy the apron of a great stage space that marches into the distance to a point of convergence in the doorway of a central-plan temple. (The intervening space is stepped off by the parallel lines of the pavement.) Figures in the middle distance complement the near group, emphasizing its density and order by their scattered arrangement. At the corners of the great piazza, triumphal arches resembling the Arch of Constantine (FIG. 6-95) mark the base angles of a compositional triangle having its apex in the central building. Christ and Peter are placed on the central axis, which runs through the temple's doorway, within which is the vanishing point of the perspective. Thus, the composition interlocks both two-dimensional and three-dimensional space, and the central actors are integrated carefully with the axial center. This spatial science provides a means for organizing the action systematically. Perugino, in this single picture, incor-

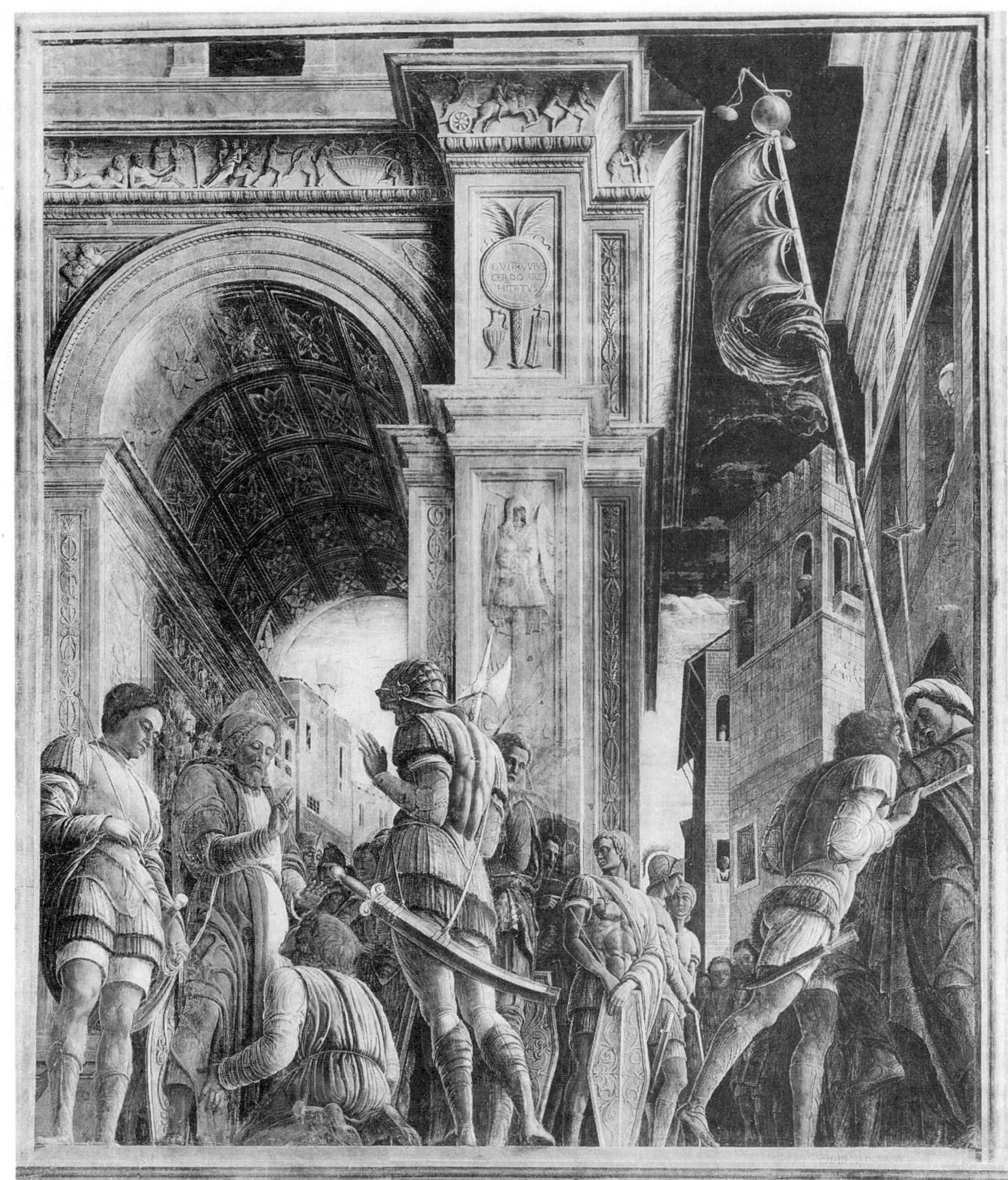

16-63 ANDREA MANTEGNA, *St. James Led to Martyrdom,* c. 1455. Fresco. Ovetari Chapel, Church of the Eremitani, Padua (largely destroyed, 1944).

porates the learning of generations. His coolly rational, orderly style and the uncluttered clarity of his compositions left a lasting impression on his best-known student, Raphael.

MANTEGNA

Many Florentine artists worked in northern Italy: Donatello in Padua; Paolo Uccello, Andrea del Castagno, and Fra Filippo Lippi in Venice. Gradually, the International style, which lingered long in the north, yielded to the new Florentine art. Around mid-century, one of the most brilliant talents of the entire Renaissance, ANDREA MANTEGNA (*c.* 1431–1506) of Padua, appeared in northern Italy; there he must have met Donatello, who greatly stimulated and influenced his art. Mantegna's frescoes in the Ovetari Chapel in the Church of the Eremitani in Padua (largely destroyed in World War II) bring northern Italian painting into line with the Humanist art of Florence. *St. James Led to Martyrdom* (FIG. **16-63**) reveals the breadth of Mantegna's literary, archeological, and pictorial learning. The motifs that appear on

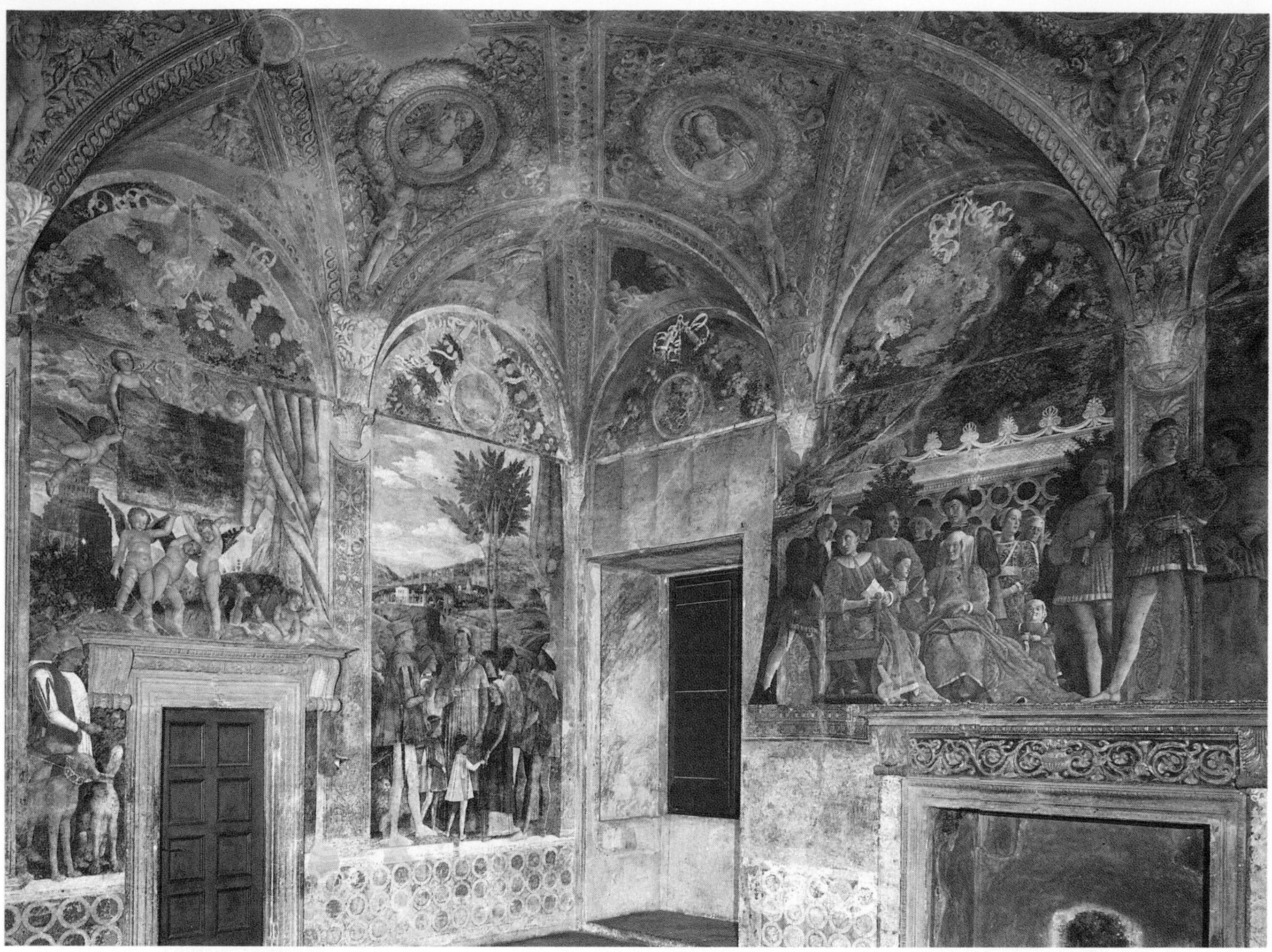

16-64 ANDREA MANTEGNA, Camera degli Sposi, 1474. Ducal palace, Mantua.

the barrel-vaulted triumphal arch are taken from the Classical ornamental vocabulary. The soldiers' costumes are studied from antique models; the painter strives for historical authenticity, much as did the antiquarian scholars of the University of Padua. Mantegna sets himself difficult problems in perspective for the joy of solving them. Here, the observer views the scene from a very low point, almost as if looking up out of a basement window at the vast arch looming above. The lines of the building to the right plunge down dramatically. Several significant deviations from true perspective are apparent, however. Using artistic license, Mantegna ignores the third vanishing point (seen from below, the buildings should converge toward the top). Disregarding the facts of perspective, he prefers to work toward a unified, cohesive composition in which pictorial elements are related to the picture frame. The lack of perspective logic is partly compensated for by the insertion of strong diagonals in the right foreground (the staff of the banner, for example).

From about 1460 onward, Mantegna worked predominantly for the Gonzaga family of Mantua, who were great art patrons like the Medici. Unlike the Medici, however, who were the most powerful members of a merchant oligarchy, the Gonzaga were hereditary dukes. In the ducal palace at Mantua, Mantegna performed a triumphant feat of pictorial illusionism, producing the first completely consistent illusionistic decoration of an entire room—the so-called Camera degli Sposi (Room of the Newlyweds, FIG. **16-64**). Utilizing actual architectural elements, Mantegna paints away the walls of the room in a manner that forecasts later Baroque decoration. He represents members of the House of Gonzaga welcoming home a son, a prince of the Church, from Rome. The family members, magnificently costumed, are shown in both domestic and landscape settings and are rendered carefully in portrait realism. The poses are remarkably unstudied and casual, conveying the easy familiarity of a family reunion. The painting is a celebration of fifteenth-century court life

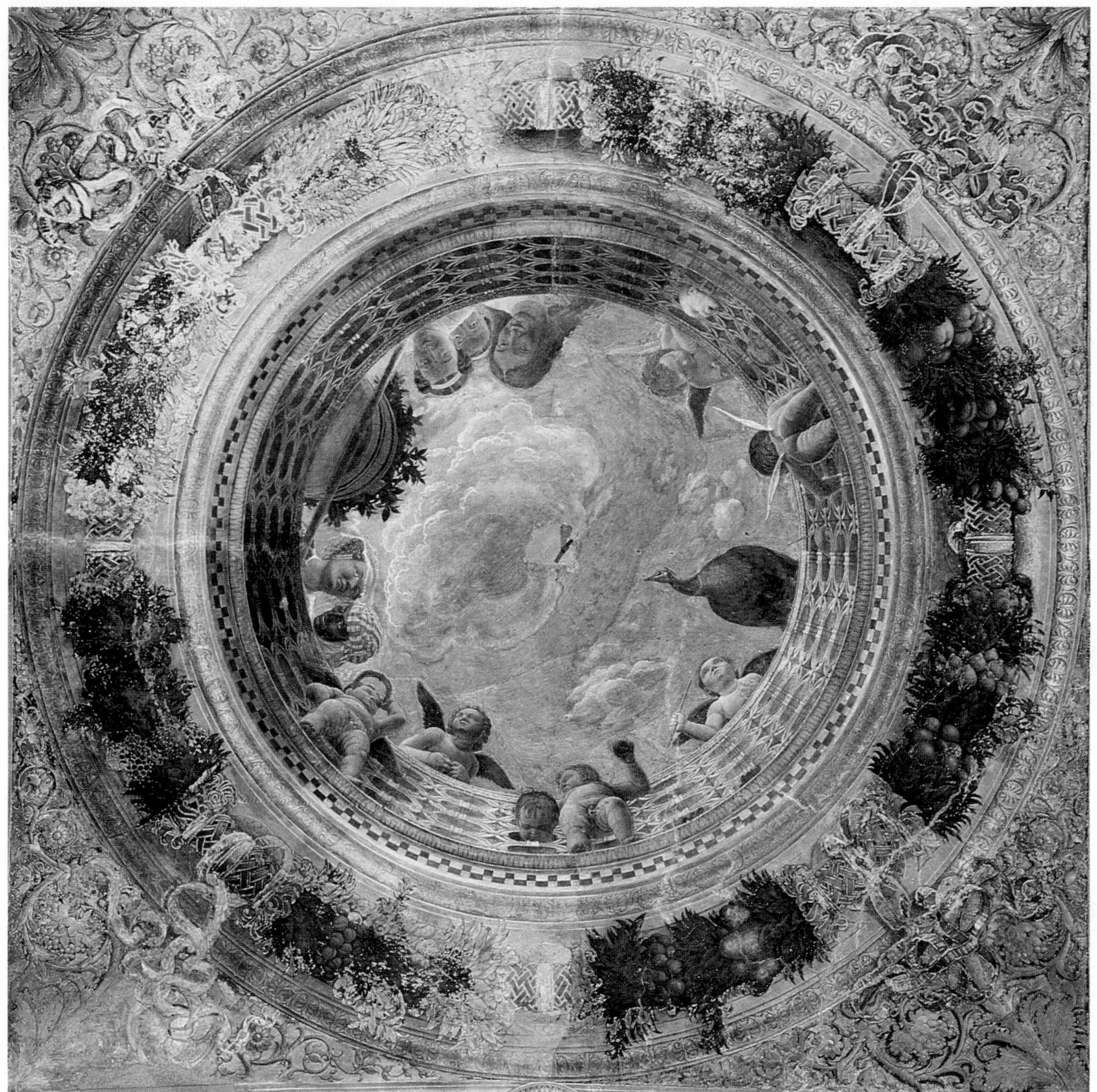

16-65 ANDREA MANTEGNA, ceiling of the Camera degli Sposi, 1474. Fresco. Ducal palace.

and a glorification of the Gonzaga, as well as the century's major depiction of a current event. The lunettes are filled with garlands and medallions *all' antica* (in the antique manner), motifs that are standard features in northern Italian painting.

Mantegna's daring experimentalism leads him to complete the room's decoration with the first *di sotto in sù* (Italian: from below upwards) perspective of a ceiling (FIG. **16-65**). This technique was broadly developed later by the northern Italian painter, Correggio, and the Baroque ceiling decorators. In the Room of the Newlyweds, we look directly up at figures looking down at us. Italians traditionally have a great deal of fun with newlyweds; spying on them is part of the fun. The dome of the room is positioned directly over the marriage bed. The oculus is itself an "eye" looking down. Cupids (the sons of Venus), strongly foreshortened, set the amorous mood, as the painted spectators (who are not identified) smile down on the scene. The peacock is an attribute of Juno, the bride of Jupiter, who is the patroness of lawful marriage and the goddess of women. This tour de force of illusionism climaxes almost a century of experiment in perspective.

One of Mantegna's later paintings, *The Dead Christ* (FIG. **16-66**), is a work of overwhelming power, despite the somewhat awkward insertion of the two mourning figures on the left. What seems to be a strikingly realistic study in foreshortening, however, is modified by a reduction in the size of the figure's feet, which, as every photographer knows (and as Mantegna must have known), would cover the body if properly represented. Thus, tempering naturalism with artistic license, Mantegna presents both a harrowing study of a strongly foreshortened cadaver and an intensely poignant presentation of a cosmic tragedy. The harsh, sharp line seems to cut the surface as if it were metal and conveys, by its grinding edge, the corrosive emotion of the theme; the observer thinks immediately of Ernest Hemingway's "the bitter nail holes in Mantegna's Christ." Mantegna's presentation is unrelievedly bitter, an unforgiving reproach to guilty mankind. What is remarkable is that all the science of the fifteenth century here serves the purpose of devotion. A Gothic religious sensitivity of great depth and intensity still lingers in northern Italy at the end of the Middle Ages and is embodied in an image created by a new science.

Mantegna's work was highly influential in northern Italy, especially in the school of Ferrara—but also in Venice, where his style had a strong, formative influence on Giovanni Bellini, who may be viewed as the progenitor of Venetian painting (see FIG. 17-55). Mantegna's influence went even further, however, for he was a great engraver (the line in *The Dead Christ* certainly suggests engraving), and his prints found their way across the Alps to where they influenced Albrecht Dürer, German father of the Northern Renaissance.

By itself, the influence of Mantegna might have stunted Giovanni Bellini's development, and the arrival in Venice of an artist with a style very different

16-66 ANDREA MANTEGNA, *The Dead Christ*, c. 1501. Tempera on canvas, approx. 26″ × 31″. Pinacoteca di Brera, Milan.

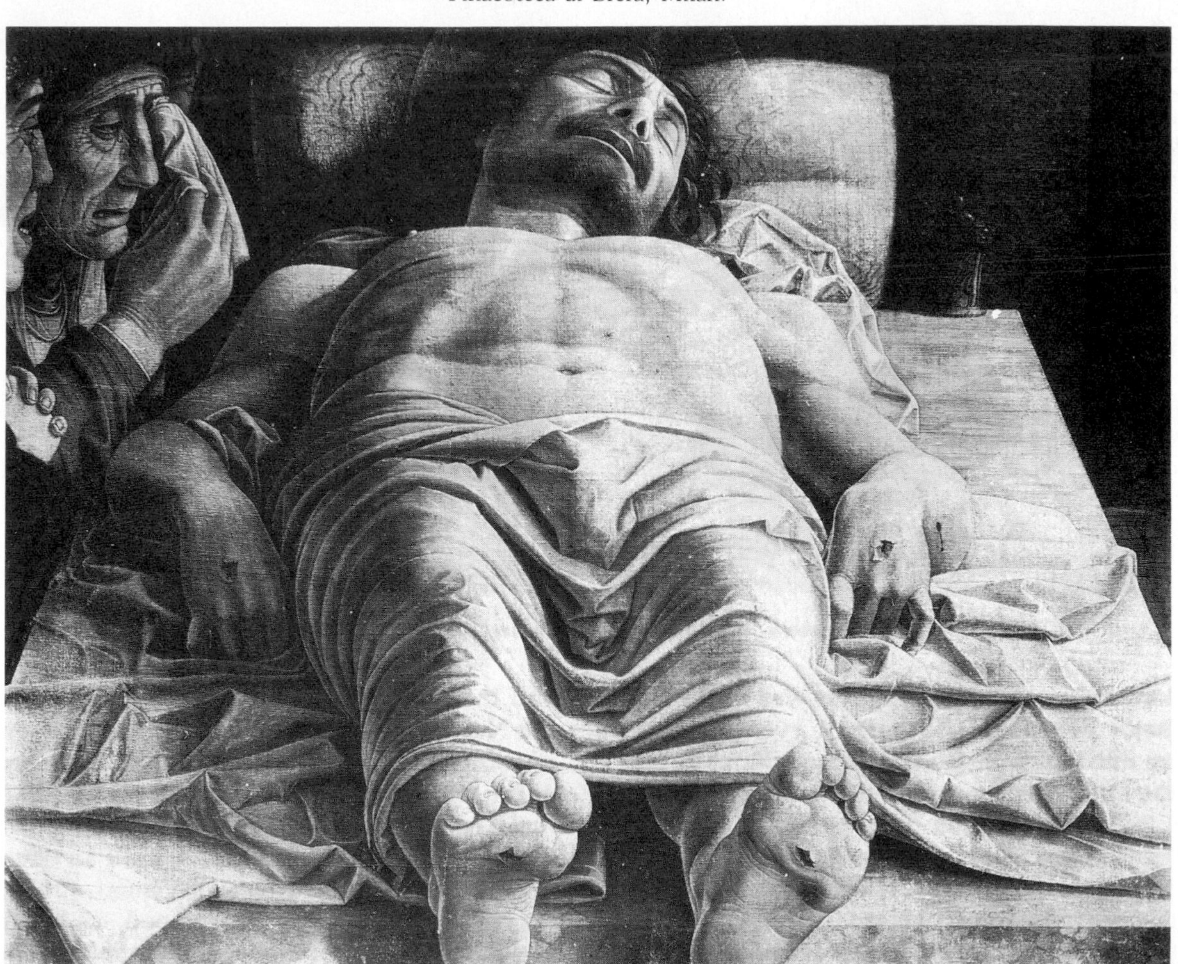

from Mantegna's probably was most opportune for Bellini's artistic growth. ANTONELLO DA MESSINA (*c.* 1430–1479) is an enigmatic figure about whose background little is known. He was born in Sicily (the only major artist of the fifteenth century to be born south of Rome) and received his early training in Naples, where he must have come in close contact with Flemish painting. The Flemish influence in some of his works is so strong that it has long been assumed that Antonello actually spent some time in Flanders, a possibility that now seems unlikely. Historians also have speculated that Antonello may have had direct contact with the Flemish artist Petrus Christus in Milan during the mid-1450s—a most intriguing possibility, as the styles of the two artists have many similarities. But the presence of either man in Milan at that time cannot definitely be proved. In any case, Antonello arrived in Venice in 1475, with a full mastery of the mixed-oil technique, and made a strong impression there during his two-year stay.

How greatly Antonello's style differs from Mantegna's can be seen in one of his later works, *The Martyrdom of St. Sebastian* (FIG. **16-67**), which has none of Mantegna's brittle, sometimes harsh linearity. The forms are modeled in broad, simplified planes, reminiscent of the style of Piero della Francesca, whose work Antonello must have studied very closely. The crisp clarity of the spatial composition, the subdued emotion, and the solemn calm with which the saint suffers his martyrdom are also suggestive of Piero's work. But Antonello goes even beyond Piero in bathing his painting in atmospheric luminosity, and his colors tend to be warm rather than cool, with golden brown tones dominating. Compared to earlier works, the painting has a "juicy" colorism that is due, in good part, to Antonello's use of mixed oil—a more flexible medium that is wider in coloristic range than tempera or fresco. Thus, by combining elements of Piero's style with Flemish painting techniques, Antonello fuses monumental qualities with coloristic effects of unrivaled richness. Giovanni Bellini was one of the first to appreciate the value of Antonello's gift to Venice and to abandon Mantegna's "hard" style, which, within a decade of Antonello's visit to Venice, became hopelessly outdated.

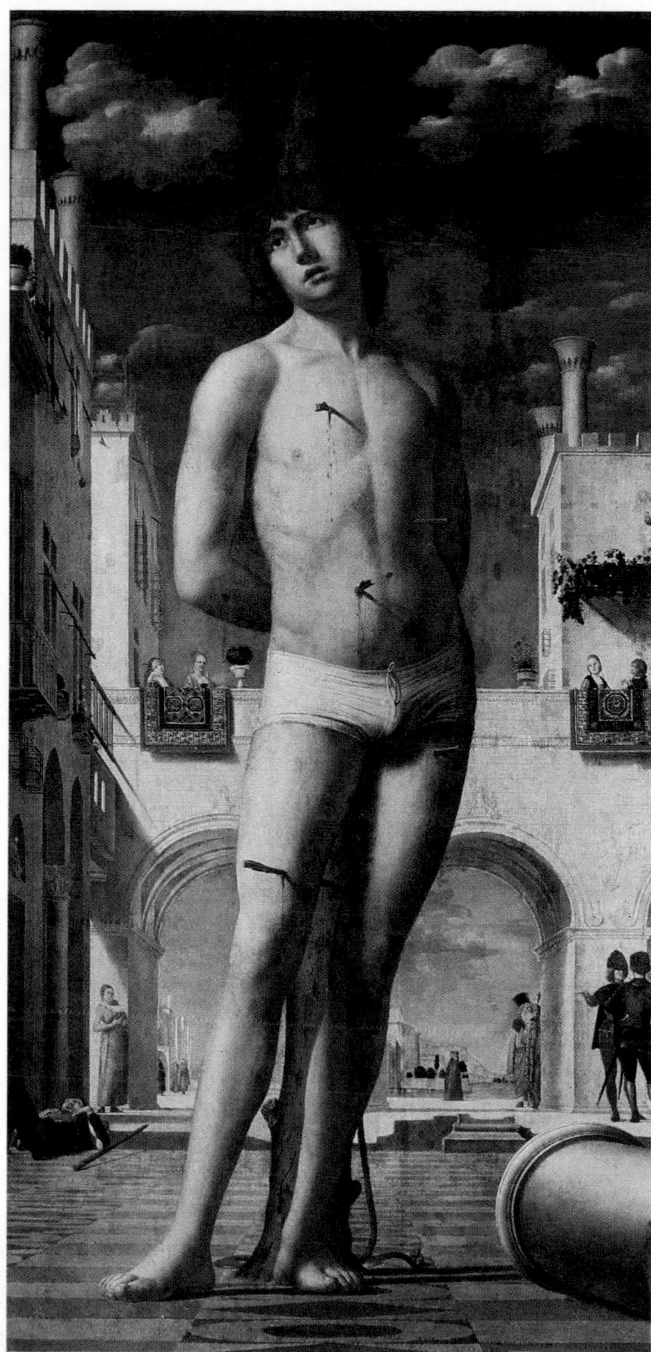

16-67 ANTONELLO DA MESSINA, *The Martyrdom of St. Sebastian*, *c.* 1475–1477. Oil on wood, approx. 68″ × 34″. Gemäldegalerie, Abt. Alte Meister, Staatliche Kunstsammlungen, Dresden, East Germany.

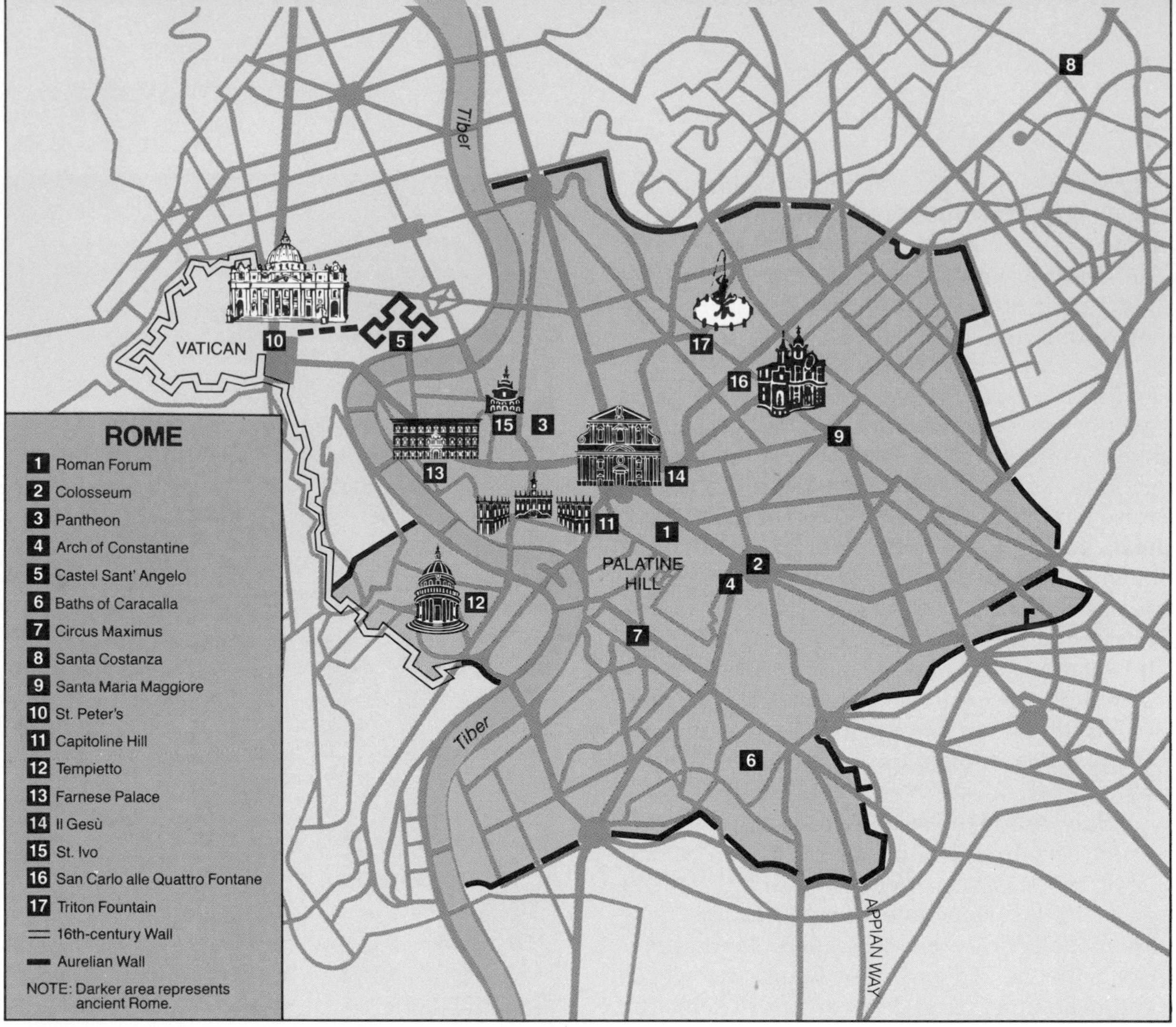

ROME

1 Roman Forum
2 Colosseum
3 Pantheon
4 Arch of Constantine
5 Castel Sant' Angelo
6 Baths of Caracalla
7 Circus Maximus
8 Santa Costanza
9 Santa Maria Maggiore
10 St. Peter's
11 Capitoline Hill
12 Tempietto
13 Farnese Palace
14 Il Gesù
15 St. Ivo
16 San Carlo alle Quattro Fontane
17 Triton Fountain
16th-century Wall
Aurelian Wall

NOTE: Darker area represents ancient Rome.

VATICAN
Tiber
PALATINE HILL
APPIAN WAY

1475 | 1500 | 1525

EARLY RENAISSANCE | HIGH RENAISSANCE

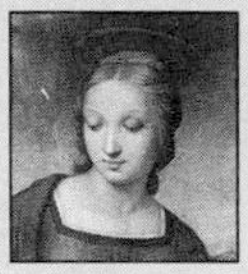

ANDREA DEL SARTO
1486–1531

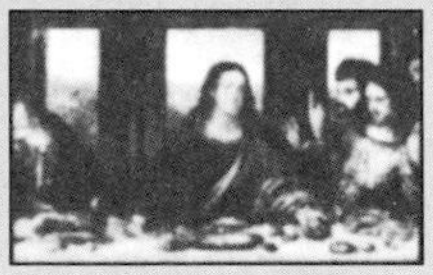

RAPHAEL *Madonna with the Goldfinch*, detail 1505–1506

LEONARDO
The Last Supper, detail
c. 1495–1498

BELLINI
c. 1430–1516

MICHELANGELO
David 1501–1504

Sistine Chapel ceiling 1508–1512

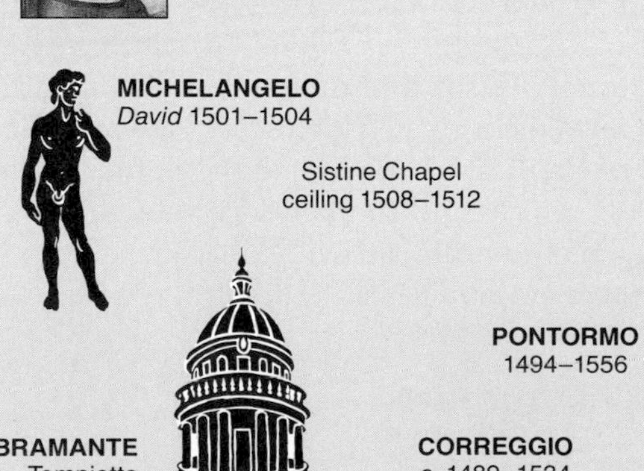

GIORGIONE
1478–1510

PONTORMO
1494–1556

BRAMANTE
Tempietto
1508 (?)

CORREGGIO
c. 1489–1534

Pope Alexander VI (Borgia) 1492–1503

Pope Julius II (della Rovere) 1503–1513

Pope Leo X (Medici) 1513–1521

Machiavelli
1469–1527
The Prince

Castiglione
1478–1529
Book of the Courtier

Protestant Reformation begins 1517

17
SIXTEENTH-CENTURY ITALIAN ART

1550 | 1575 | 1600

LATE RENAISSANCE

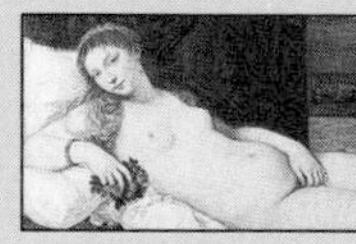

TITIAN *Venus of Urbino,* detail 1538

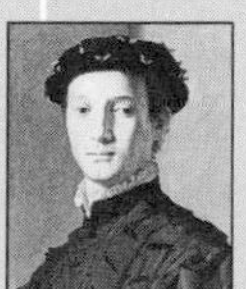

BRONZINO *Portrait of a Young Man c.* 1550

ANGUISSOLA 1532–1625

GIOVANNI DA BOLOGNA 1529–1608

CELLINI 1500–1571

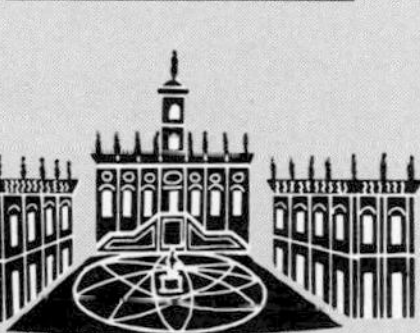

MICHELANGELO Campidoglio *c.* 1537

TINTORETTO 1518–1594

VERONESE 1528–1588

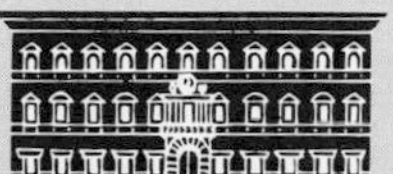

A. DA SANGALLO THE YOUNGER Farnese Palace *c.* 1530–1546

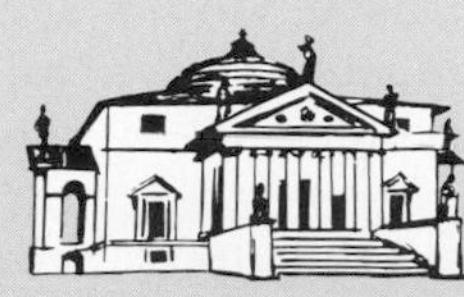

PALLADIO Villa Rotonda *c.* 1566–1570

GIULIO ROMANO Palazzo del Tè 1525–1535

Pope Clement VII (Medici) 1523–1534

Pope Paul III (Farnese) 1534–1549

Pope Pius IV (Medici) 1559–1565

Pope Gregory XIII (Buoncompagni) 1572–1585

Pope Sixtus V (Peretti) 1585–1590

Sack of Rome by Charles V 1527

Vasari 1511–1574 *Lives of the Most Eminent . . .*

Council of Trent 1545–1563

BEFORE THE END of the fifteenth century, Florence had lost her unique position of leadership in the arts, and the innovations of her artists had become the property of Italian artists, regardless of local political boundaries. We do not mean to suggest that Florence no longer produced the artistic giants of an earlier age. Leonardo and Michelangelo called themselves Florentines, even though they spent a great part of their lives outside the city, and the turning point in Raphael's artistic education occurred as a result of his experience of Florentine art. In addition, Florence, with the early work of Leonardo, already had become the source of sixteenth-century style and later shared with Rome the beginnings and growth of Mannerism, a style that was to dominate western European art during much of the sixteenth century. But Florence was faced with a time of crisis that began with the expulsion of the Medici and the brief and stormy dictatorship of Girolamo Savonarola and ended with the subversion of the Florentine republic by the Spanish and the return of the Medici (a collateral line of the original family) as tyrants under Spanish protection. Finally, in the 1530s, Florentine independence became a thing of the past when the state was made into a grand duchy under the crown of the Hapsburgs.

THE HIGH RENAISSANCE

Between about 1495 and the date of its own invasion and sack in 1527, Rome took the place of Florence and laid claim to its artistic preeminence. A series of powerful and ambitious popes—Alexander VI (Borgia), Julius II (della Rovere), Leo X (Medici), and Clement VII (Medici)—created a new power in Italy: a papal state, with Rome as its capital. At the same time, Rome became the artistic capital of Europe. The popes, living in the opulent splendor of secular princes, embellished the city with great works of art, inviting artists from all over Italy and providing them with challenging tasks. In its short duration, the artists of this High Renaissance produced works of such authority that generations of later artists were instructed by them. The art of Leonardo, Raphael, Michelangelo, and Titian belongs to no school but is, in the case of each, something unique. The masters had of course inherited the pictorial science of the fifteenth century, and they learned from one another. Yet they made a distinct break from the past, occupying new and lofty ground—so lofty as to discourage emulation by their successors.

The High Renaissance produced a cluster of extraordinary geniuses and found in divine inspiration the rationale for the exaltation of the artist-genius. The Neo-Platonists found in Plato's *Ion* his famous praise of the poet: "All good poets compose their beautiful poems not by art, but because they are inspired and possessed. . . . for not by art does the poet sing, but by power divine." And what the poet could claim, the Renaissance artist claimed also, raising visual art to the status formerly held only by poetry. Thus, at the threshold of the modern world, painters, sculptors, and architects came into their own, successfully claiming for their work a high place among the fine arts. In the High Renaissance, the masters in a sense created a new profession, having its own rights of expression, its own venerable character, and its own claims to recognition by the great. The "fine" artist today lives, often without realizing it, on the accumulated prestige won by preceding artists, beginning with those who made the first great gains of the High Renaissance.

Leonardo da Vinci

A man who is the epitome of the artist-genius as well as of the "universal man," LEONARDO DA VINCI (1452–1519) has become a kind of wonder of the modern world, standing at the beginning of a new epoch like a prophet and a sage, mapping the routes that art and science are to take. The scope and depth of his interests were without precedent—so great as to frustrate any hopes he might have had of realizing all that his feverishly inventive imagination could conceive. We still look with awe on his achievements and, even more, on his unfulfilled promise. His mind and personality seem to us superhuman; the man himself was mysterious and remote. Jacob Burckhardt writes: "The colossal outlines of Leonardo's nature can never be more than dimly and distantly conceived."

Although we are concerned here primarily with Leonardo as an artist, we scarcely can hope to do his art credit in isolation from his science; his scientific drawings are themselves works of art, as well as models for that exact delineation of nature that is one of the aims of science. Leonardo's unquenchable curiosity is revealed best in his voluminous notes, liberally interspersed with sketches dealing with matters of botany, geology, zoology, hydraulics, military engineering, animal lore, anatomy, and aspects of physical science, including mechanics, perspective, light, optics, and color. Leonardo's great ambition in his painting, as well as in his scientific endeavors, was to discover the laws underlying the flux and processes of nature. With this end in mind, he also studied the human body and contributed immeasurably to our knowledge of physiology and psychology. Leonardo believed that reality in an absolute sense is inaccessible and that we can know it only through its changing images. He considered the eyes to be the most vital organs and sight the most essential function, as, through these, the images of reality could be grasped most directly and profoundly. He stated many times in his notes that all his scientific investigations merely were aimed at making himself a better painter.

Leonardo was born near Florence and was trained in the studio of Andrea del Verrocchio, but he left Florence around 1481, offering his services to Ludovico Sforza, Duke of Milan. The political situation in Florence was uncertain, and the Neo-Platonism of Lorenzo de' Medici and his brilliant circle may have proved uncongenial to the empirical and pragmatic Leonardo. It also may be that Leonardo felt that the artistic scene in Milan would be less competitive. He devoted most of a letter to the Duke of Milan to advertising his competence and his qualifications as a military engineer, mentioning only at the end his supremacy as a painter and sculptor:

> And in short, according to the variety of cases, I can contrive various and endless means of offence and defence. . . . In time of peace I believe I can give perfect satisfaction and to the equal of any other in architecture and the composition of buildings, public and private; and in guiding water from one place to another. . . . I can carry out sculpture in marble, bronze, or clay, and also I can do in painting whatever may be done, as well as any other, be he whom he may.*

The letter illustrates the new relation of the artist to his patron, as well as Leonardo's breadth of competence. That he should select military engineering and design to interest a patron is an index of the dangerousness of the times. Weaponry now had been developed to the point, especially in northern Europe, that the siege cannon was a threat to the feudal castles of those attempting to resist the wealthy and aggressive new monarchs. When, in 1494, Charles VIII of France invaded Italy, his cannon easily smashed the fortifications of the Italian princes. By the turn of the century, when Italy's liberties and unity were being trampled by the aspiring kingdoms of Europe, not only soldiers and architects, but artists and Humanists, were deeply concerned with the problem of designing a system of fortifications that might withstand the terrible new weapon.

During his first sojourn in Milan, Leonardo painted *The Virgin of the Rocks* (FIG. **17-1**), a group that, although it may derive ultimately from Fra Filippo Lippi, is well on its way out of the older tradition. The old triangular composition now broadens out into three dimensions, making a weighty pyramid. The linear approach, with its musical play of undulating contours and crisp edges, is abandoned, as Leonardo journeys back through the generations of the fifteenth century to Masaccio's great discovery of chiaroscuro, the subtle play of light and dark. What we see is the result of the moving together and interpenetration of lights and darks. "Drawn" representations, consisting of contours and edges, can be beautiful, but they really are not true to the optical facts. Moreover, a painting must embody not only physical chiaroscuro but the lights and darks of human psychology as well. Modeling with light and shadow and the expression of emotional states were, for Leonardo, the heart of painting:

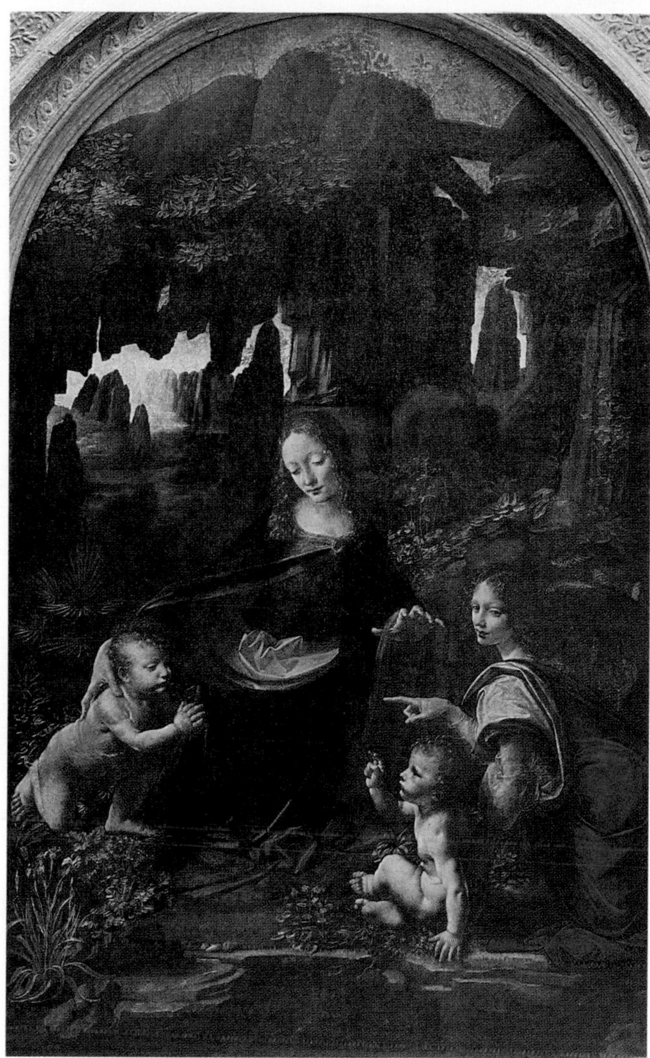

17-1 LEONARDO DA VINCI, *The Virgin of the Rocks,* c. 1485. Oil on wood (transferred to canvas), approx. 6′ 3″ × 3′ 7″. Louvre, Paris.

*In E. G. Holt, ed., *Literary Sources of Art History* (Princeton, NJ: Princeton University Press, 1947), p. 170.

> A good painter has two chief objects to paint—man and the intention of his soul. The former is easy, the latter hard, for it must be expressed by gestures and the movement of the limbs. . . . A painting will only be wonderful for the beholder by making that which is not so appear raised and detached from the wall.*

The figures in *The Virgin of the Rocks* are knit together not only as a pyramidal group but as figures sharing the same atmosphere, a method of unification first seen in Masaccio's *The Tribute Money* (FIG. 16-27). The Madonna, Christ Child, infant John the Baptist, and angel emerge through subtle gradations and nuances of light and shade from the half-light of the cavernous, visionary landscape. Light simultaneously veils and reveals the forms of things, immersing them in a layer of atmosphere between them and our eyes. The ambiguity of light and shade (familiar in the optical uncertainties of dusk) functions here in the service of the psychological ambiguity of perception. The group depicted, so strangely wrapped in subtle light and shade, eludes our precise definition and interpretation. The figures pray, point, and bless, and these acts and gestures, although their meanings are not certain, visually unite the individuals portrayed. The angel points to the infant John, who is blessed by the Christ Child and sheltered by the Virgin's loving hand. The melting mood of tenderness, enhanced by the caressing light, is compounded of yet other moods. What the eye sees is fugitive, as are the states of the soul, or, in Leonardo's term, its "intentions."

*In Anthony Blunt, *Artistic Theory in Italy, 1450–1600* (London: Oxford University Press, 1964), p. 34.

17-2 LEONARDO DA VINCI, cartoon for *The Virgin and Child with St. Anne and the Infant St. John*, 1498 (?). Charcoal heightened with white on brown paper, approx. 54″ × 39″. Reproduced by courtesy of the Trustees of the National Gallery, London.

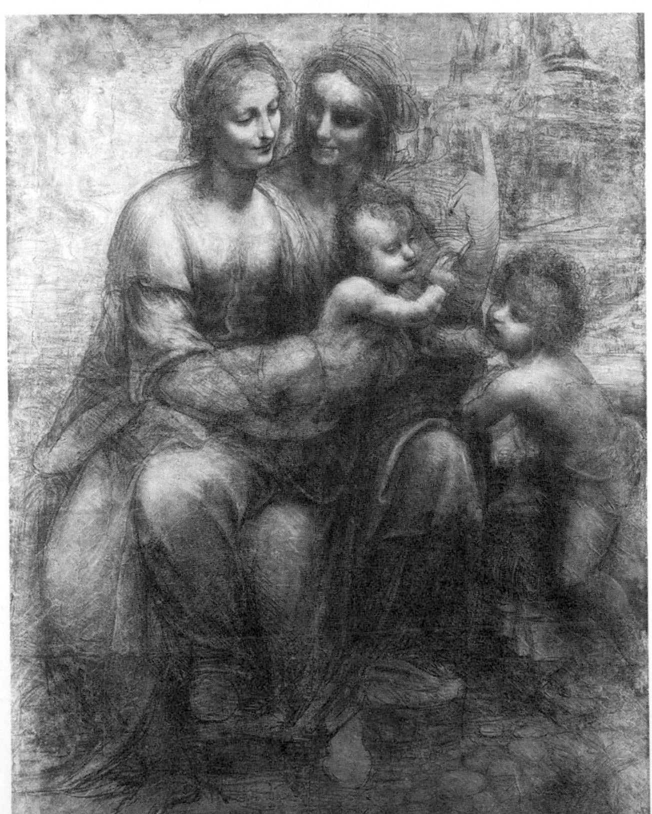

The style of the High Renaissance fully emerges in a *cartoon* (a full-size drawing) for a painting of *The Virgin and Child with St. Anne and the Infant St. John* (FIG. **17-2**). The glowing light falls gently on the majestic forms and on a tranquil grandeur, order, and balance. The figures are robust and monumental, moving with a stately grace reminiscent of the Phidian sculptures of the Parthenon. Every part is ordered by an intellectual, pictorial logic into a sure unity. The specialized depiction of perspective, anatomy, light, and space is a thing of the past. Leonardo has assimilated the learning of two centuries and applies it wholly, in a manner that is Classical and complete. This High Renaissance style, as Leonardo authoritatively presents it here, is stable without being static, varied without being confused, and dignified without being dull. As was the case in Greece, this brief, Classical moment inaugurated by Leonardo unifies and balances the conflicting experiences of an entire culture. This style will prove difficult to maintain. In a rapidly changing world, the artist may either repeat the compositions and forms of the day in a sterile, academic manner or revolt against the practices of the time by denying or exaggerating their principles. For these reasons, the High Renaissance was of short duration—even shorter than the brief span of the golden age of Athens in the fifth century B.C.

For the refectory of the church of Santa Maria delle Grazie in Milan, Leonardo painted *The Last Supper* (FIG. **17-3**). Despite its ruined state (in part the result of the painter's own unfortunate experiments with his materials), and although it has often been ineptly restored, the painting is both formally and emotionally his most impressive work.† It is the first great

†Since 1977, the painting has been undergoing painstaking, scientifically controlled restoration (a square inch at a time!). Although much of it is lost permanently, enough already has been recovered and repaired to reveal Leonardo's actual intentions and performance. The restored portions, freed from five hundred years' dark accumulation of dirt, mold, glue, and overpainting, reveal bright and strong colors and firm and elegant contours. Restoration also shows that Leonardo's style is rooted firmly in the practice of fifteenth-century Italian painting. Beneath the many mistaken overpaintings, the true characters of the disciples emerge from the blurred, murky, out-of-focus forms of the damaged picture. They are vividly realized individuals, of the kind we find in Leonardo's preserved preparatory drawings. Through their attitudes, gestures, personal traits, and facial expressions, they compellingly play the roles Leonardo designed for them, consistent with his own highly personal conception of this drama and its protagonists.

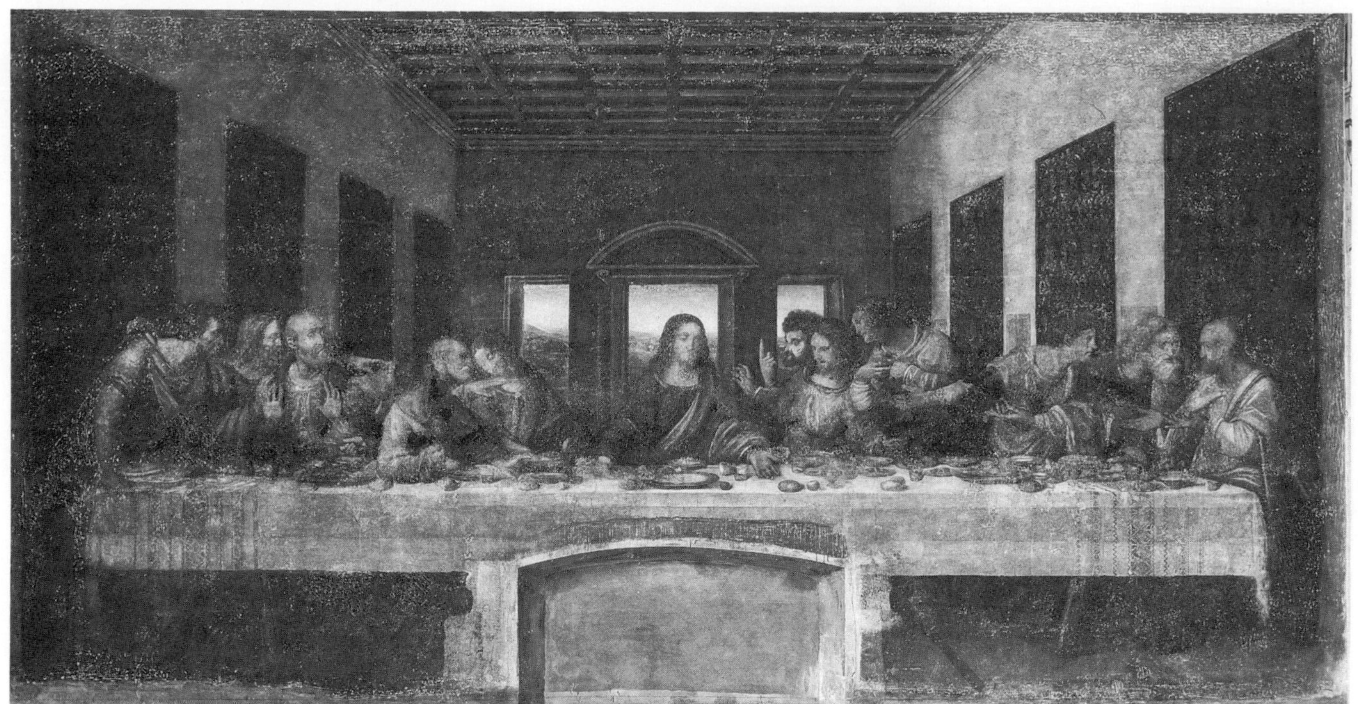

17-3 LEONARDO DA VINCI, *The Last Supper*, c. 1495–1498. Fresco (oil and tempera on plaster). Refectory, Santa Maria delle Grazie, Milan.

figure composition of the High Renaissance and the definitive interpretation of its theme. Christ and the Twelve Disciples are seated at a long table set parallel to the picture plane in a simple, spacious room. The highly dramatic action of the painting is made still more emphatic by the placement of the group in the austerely quiet setting. Christ, with outstretched hands, has just said, "One of you will betray me." A wave of intense excitement passes through the group, as each disciple asks himself and, in some cases, his neighbor, "Is it I?" Leonardo has made a brilliant conjunction of the dramatic "One of you will betray me" with the initiation of the ancient liturgical ceremony of the Eucharist, when Christ, blessing bread and wine, said "This is my body and this is my blood: do this in remembrance of me." The force and lucidity with which this dramatic moment is expressed are due to the abstract organization of the composition.

In the center, Christ is in perfect repose, the still eye of the swirling emotion around him. Isolated from the disciples, his figure is framed by the central window at the back, the curved pediment of which arches above his head. The pediment is the only curve in the architectural framework, and it serves here as a halo. Christ's head is the focal point of all perspective lines in the composition. Thus, the still, psychological focus and cause of the action is, at the same time, the perspective focus as well as the center of the two-dimensional surface. One could say that the two-dimensional, the three-dimensional, and the psychodimensional focuses are one and the same. The agitated disciples, registering a whole range of rationally ordered, idealized, and proportionate responses, embracing fear, doubt, protestation, rage, and love, are represented in four groups of three, united among and within themselves by the gestures and postures of the figures. Leonardo sacrifices traditional iconography to pictorial and dramatic consistency by placing Judas on the same side of the table as Jesus and the other disciples. His face in shadow, Judas clutches a money bag in his right hand and reaches his left forward to fulfill the Master's declaration: "Behold, the hand of him that betrayeth me is with me on the table." The two disciples at either end of the table are more quiet than the others, as if to enclose the overall movement, which is more intense closer to the figure of Christ, whose calm at the same time halts and intensifies it.

We know from numerous preparatory studies that Leonardo thought of each figure as carrying a particular charge and type of emotion. Like a skilled stage director (perhaps the first, in the modern sense), he has read the gospel story carefully and scrupulously cast his actors as their roles are described. With him begins that rhetoric of Classical art that will direct the compositions of generations of painters until the nineteenth century. The silence of Christ is one such powerful rhetorical device. Indeed, Heinrich Wölfflin saw that the Classical element is precisely here, for in

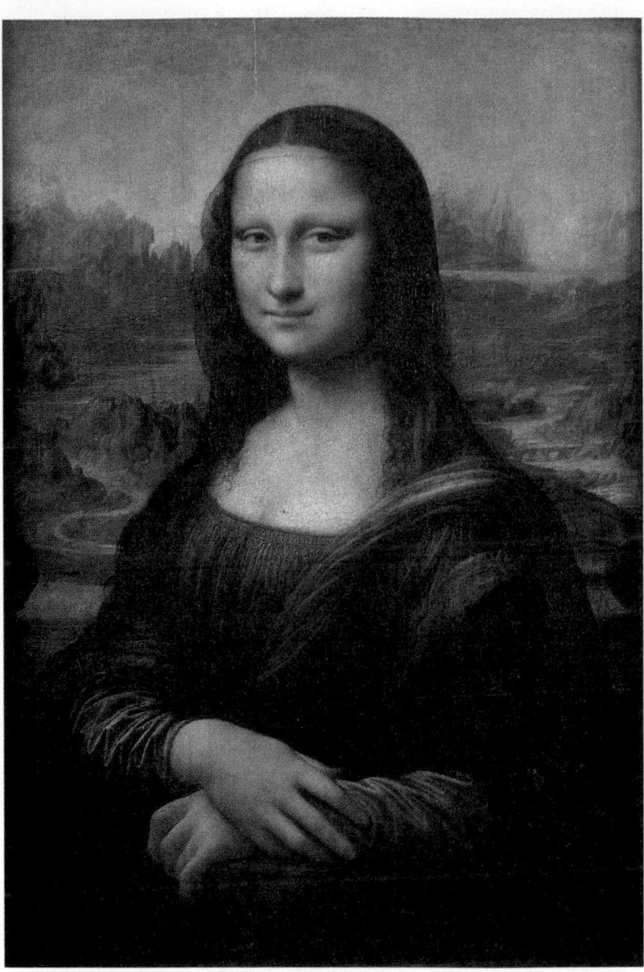

17-4 LEONARDO DA VINCI, *Mona Lisa*, c. 1503–1505. Oil on wood, approx. 30″ × 21″. Louvre, Paris.

the silence following Christ's words, "the original impulse and the emotional excitement continue to echo and the action is at once momentary, eternal and complete."* The two major trends of fifteenth-century painting—monumentality and mathematically ordered space at the expense of movement, and freedom of movement at the expense of monumentality and controlled space—are here harmonized and balanced. *The Last Supper* and Leonardo's career leading up to it are at once a synthesis of the artistic developments of the fifteenth century and a first statement of the High Renaissance style in Italy during the early sixteenth century.

If Leonardo's *Last Supper* is the world's most famous religious picture, the *Mona Lisa* (FIG. **17-4**) is probably the world's most famous portrait. Since the nineteenth century and perhaps earlier, this enigmatic face has been a part of Western folklore. Painted after Leonardo returned from Milan to Florence, the lady (thought by many to be La Gioconda, wife of the banker Zanobi del Giocondo) originally was represented in a loggia with columns that have been cut from the painting. She is shown in half-length view, her hands quietly folded and her gaze directed at the observer. The ambiguity of the famous "smile" is really the consequence of Leonardo's fascination and skill with atmospheric chiaroscuro, which we have seen in his *Virgin of the Rocks* and *Virgin and St. Anne* groups and which here serve to disguise rather than reveal a human psyche. The light is adjusted subtly enough, but the precise planes are blurred (a useful comparison can be made between the *Mona Lisa* and the portraits by Domenico Ghirlandaio and Sandro Botticelli that we saw in Chapter 16) and the facial expression is hard to determine. Commentators during the romantic nineteenth century made perhaps too much of the enigma of the "smile," without appreciating Leonardo's quite scientific concern with the nature of light and shadow. On the other hand, Leonardo himself must have enjoyed the curious effect he achieved here. This was one of his favorite pictures—one with which he could not bear to part. The superb drawing present beneath the fleeting shadow is a triumph in its rendering of both the head and the hands, the latter exceptionally beautiful. The artist's intention may well have been to confuse observers or to enchant them by allowing them to interpret the secret personality as they pleased.

Leonardo completed very few paintings; his perfectionism, restless experimentalism, and far-ranging curiosity scattered his efforts. Yet an extensive record of his ideas is preserved in the drawings in his notebooks, one of which was discovered in Madrid in the 1960s. Science interested him increasingly in his later years, and he took knowledge of all nature (given first to the eye) as his proper province. His investigations in anatomy yielded drawings of great precision and beauty of execution. The *Embryo in the Womb* (FIG. **17-5**) is so true to fact that, despite some inaccuracies, it could be used in medical instruction today. Although Leonardo may not have been the first scientist of the modern world (at least not in the modern sense of "scientist"), he certainly originated the method of scientific illustration, especially cutaway and exploded views. The importance of this has been stressed by Erwin Panofsky: " . . . anatomy as a science (and this applies to all the other observational or descriptive disciplines) was simply not possible without a method of preserving observations in graphic records, complete and accurate in three dimensions."†

*Heinrich Wölfflin, *Classic Art*, 2nd ed. (London: Phaidon, 1953), p. 27.

†Erwin Panofsky, "Artist, Scientist, Genius," in *The Renaissance*, ed. Wallace K. Ferguson (New York: Harper & Row, 1962), p. 147.

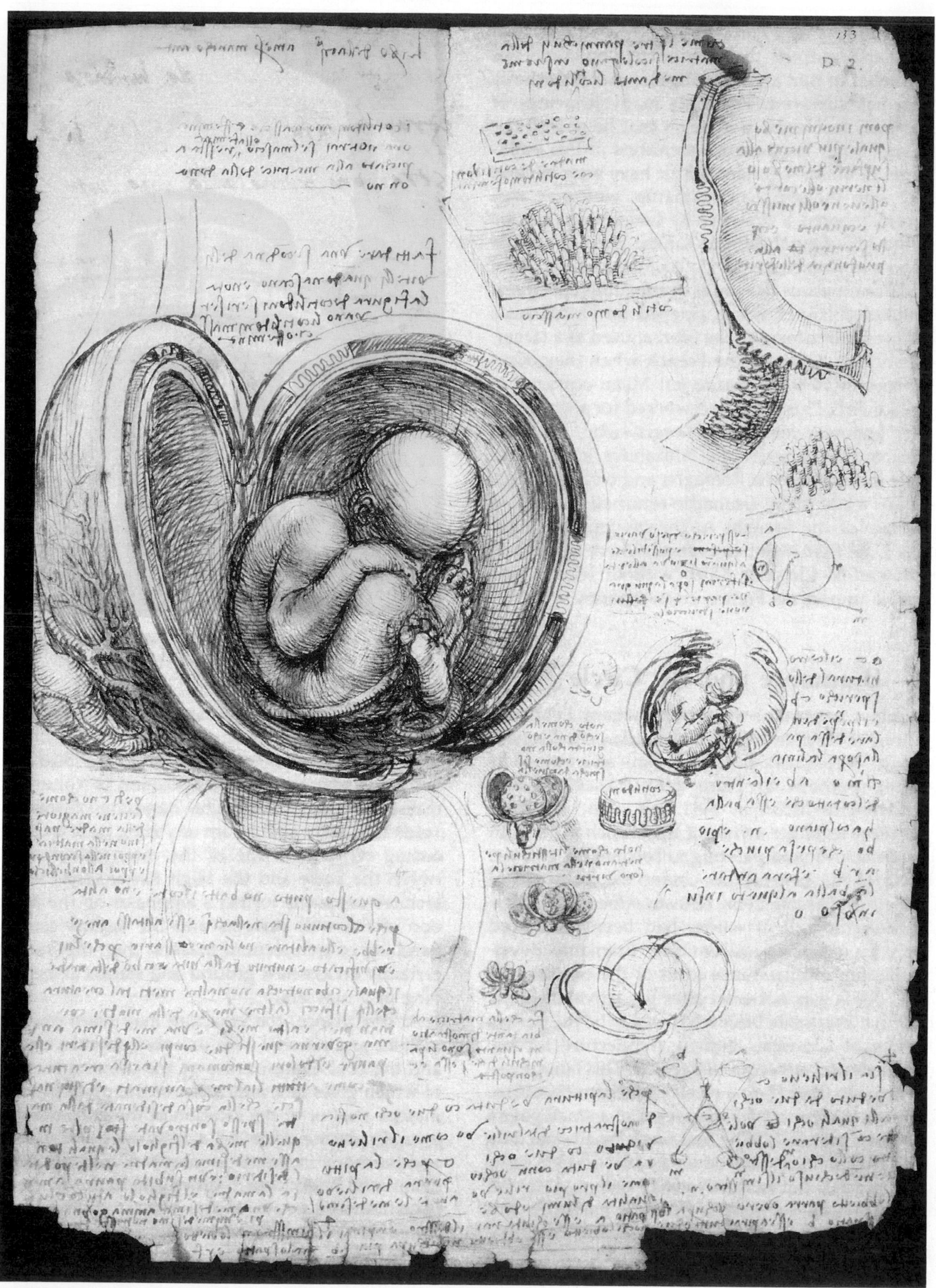

17-5 LEONARDO DA VINCI, *Embryo in the Womb, c.* 1510. Pen and ink. Royal Collection, Windsor Castle. Windsor Castle, Royal Library, copyright 1990 Her Majesty Queen Elizabeth II.

Leonardo was well known in his own time as both architect and sculptor, though no actual buildings can be attributed to him and no sculpture that is certainly by him has survived. From his many drawings of central-plan buildings, it appears that he shared the interest of other Renaissance architects in this building type. In Milan, Leonardo must have been in close contact with the architect Bramante, who may well have remembered a drawing by Leonardo when he prepared his original designs for the great church of St. Peter's in Rome (FIG. 17-7). As for sculpture, Leonardo left numerous drawings of monumental equestrian statues, one of which ripened into a full-scale model for a monument to the Sforza; used as a target, it was shot to pieces by the French when they occupied Milan in 1499. Leonardo left Milan outraged at this treatment of his work and worked for a while as a military engineer for Cesare Borgia, who, with the support of his father, Pope Alexander VI, tried to conquer the cities of the Romagna and create a Borgia duchy. At a later date, Leonardo returned to Milan in the service of the French. At the invitation of King Francis I, he then went to France, where he died at the château of Cloux in 1519, without leaving any noticeable impact on French contemporary art.

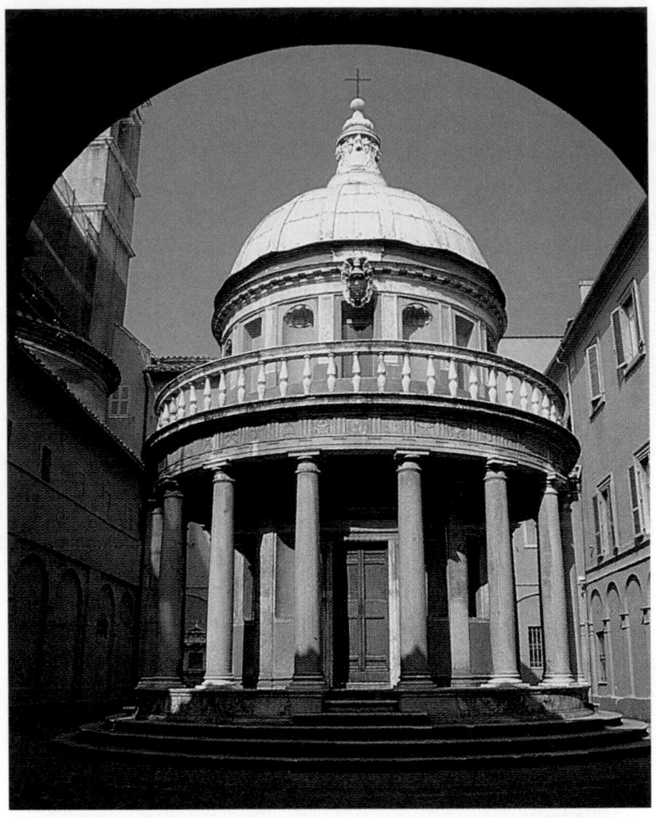

17-6 BRAMANTE, the Tempietto, 1504 (?). San Pietro in Montorio, Rome.

Bramante and His Circle

The most important artist with whom Leonardo came into contact in Milan was BRAMANTE (Donato d'Angelo, 1444–1514). Born in Urbino and trained as a painter (perhaps by Piero della Francesca), Bramante went to Milan in 1481 and, like Leonardo, stayed there until the arrival of the French in 1499. In Milan, he abandoned painting to become the greatest architect of his generation. Under the influence of Filippo Brunelleschi, Leon Battista Alberti, and perhaps Leonardo, all of whom had been influenced strongly by the Classical antique, Bramante developed the High Renaissance form of the central-plan church. But it was not until after his arrival in Rome in 1499 that Bramante built what was to be the perfect prototype of Classical, domed architecture for the Renaissance and subsequent periods. This building—the Tempietto (FIG. **17-6**)—received its name because, to contemporaries, it had the aspect of a small pagan temple from antiquity. The building's traditional date of 1502 is disputed, and dates as late as 1508 have been advanced, but not universally accepted. It was commissioned by the king of Spain to mark the conjectural location of St. Peter's crucifixion. Standing inside the cloister alongside the church of San Pietro in Montorio, the Tempietto resembles a sculptured reliquary and would have looked even more like one inside the circular, colonnaded courtyard that was planned for it but never executed.

All but devoid of ornament, this little building relies for its effect on the composition of volumes and masses and on a sculptural handling of solids and voids that set it apart from anything built in the preceding century. If one of the main differences between the Early and the High Renaissance styles of architecture is the former's emphasis on the articulation of flat wall surfaces and the latter's sculptural handling of architectural masses, then the Tempietto certainly breaks new ground and stands at the beginning of a new era.

At first glance, the structure may seem overly formalistic and rational with its sober, circular stylobate and the cool Tuscan order of the colonnade, neither of which gives any indication of the placement of an interior altar or of the location of the entrance. However, Bramante achieved a truly wonderful balance and harmony in the relationship of the parts (dome, drum, and base) to each other and to the whole. The balustrade echoes, in shorter beats, the rhythm of the colonnade and averts a too-rapid ascent to the drum, while the pilasters of the drum itself repeat the ascending motif and lead the eye past the cornice to the exposed ribs of the dome. The play of light and shade around columns and balustrade and across alternating deep-set, rectangular windows and shallow, shell-capped niches in cella walls and drum enhances the experience of the building as an articulated sculptural mass. Although the Tempietto, superficially at least, may resemble a Classical tholos, and although all of its details have been studied closely from antique models, the combination of parts and details is new and original (Classical tholoi, for instance, had neither drum nor balustrade!). Conceived as a tall, domed cylinder projecting from the lower, wider cylinder of its colonnade, this small building incorporates all the qualities of a sculptured monument.

The significance of the Tempietto was well understood in the sixteenth century. The architect Andrea Palladio, an artistic descendant of Bramante, included it in his survey of ancient temples because "Bramante was the first who brought good and beautiful architecture to light, which from the time of the ancients to his day had been forgotten. . . ." Round in plan, elevated on a base that isolates it from its surroundings, the Tempietto conforms with Alberti's and Palladio's strictest demands for an ideal church, demonstrating "the unity, the infinite essence, the uniformity, and the justice of God."

The same architectural concept guided Bramante's plans for the new St. Peter's, which was commissioned by Pope Julius II in 1505 to replace the Constantinian basilica, Old St. Peter's (FIG. 7-6). The earlier structure had fallen into considerable disrepair and, in any event, did not suit this ambitious and warlike pope's taste for the colossal; Julius wanted to gain sway over the whole of Italy and to make the Rome of the popes more splendid than the Rome of the caesars. As originally designed by Bramante, the new St. Peter's (FIG. **17-7**) was to have consisted of a cross with arms of equal length, each terminated by an apse. The new building was intended as a martyrium to mark St. Peter's grave; Julius also hoped to have his own tomb in it. The crossing would have been covered by a large dome, and smaller domes over subsidiary chapels would have covered the diagonal axes of the roughly square plan. Bramante's ambitious plan called for a boldly sculptural treatment of the walls and piers under the dome. The interior space is complex in the extreme, with the intricate symmetries of a crystal. It is possible to detect in the plan some nine interlocking crosses, five of which are domed. The scale was titanic; Bramante is said to have boasted that he would place the dome of the Pantheon over the Basilica of Constantine. A commemorative medal by CARADOSSO (FIG. **17-8**) shows how Bramante's scheme would have attempted to do just that. The dome is hemispherical, like the Pantheon's, but otherwise the exterior, with two towers and

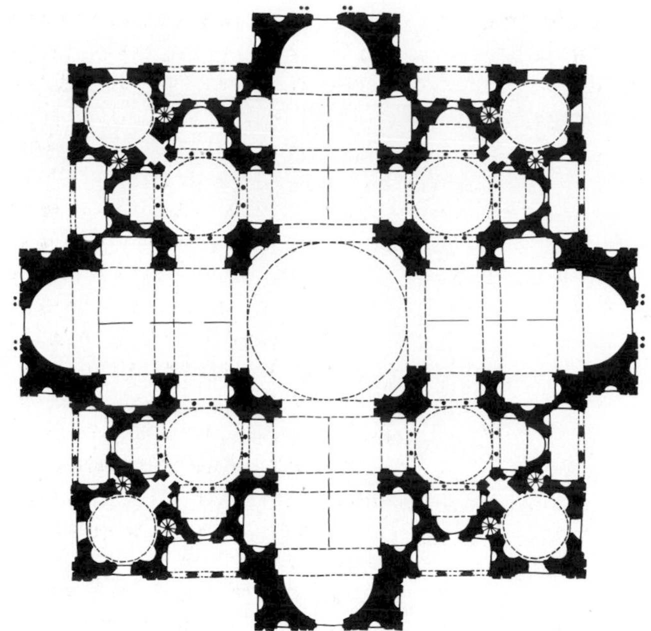

17-7 BRAMANTE, plan for the new St. Peter's, the Vatican, Rome, 1505.

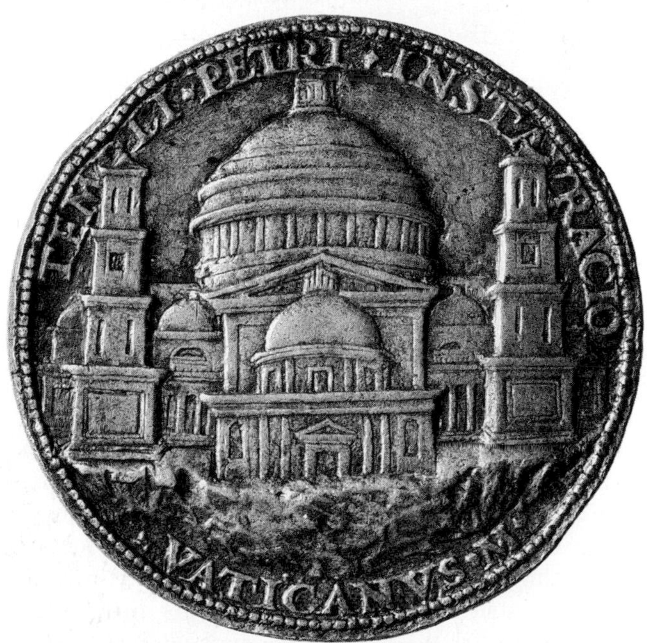

17-8 CHRISTOFORO FOPPA CARADOSSO, medal showing Bramante's design for the new St. Peter's, 1506. British Museum, London.

a medley of domes and porticoes, breaks the massive unity, resulting in a still essentially anthropometric design scaled down to human proportions in the Early Renaissance manner. During Bramante's lifetime, the actual construction did not advance beyond the building of the piers of the crossing and the lower walls of the choir. With his death, the work passed

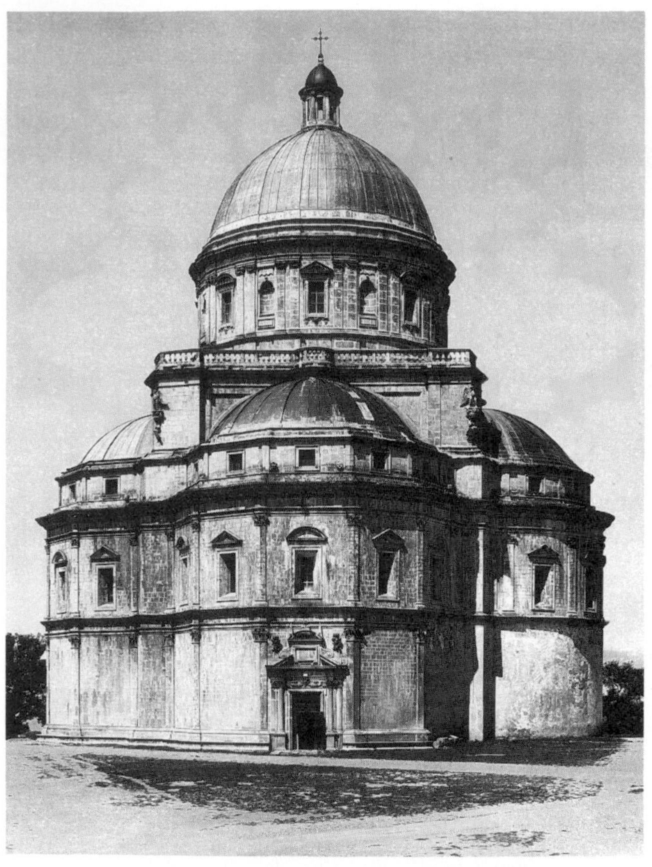

17-9 Santa Maria della Consolazione, Todi, Italy, begun 1508 (view from the south).

from one architect to another and finally to Michelangelo, who was appointed by Pope Paul III in 1546 to complete the building.

After Bramante's Tempietto, the closest realization of the High Renaissance Classical ideals—order, clarity, lucidity, simplicity, harmony, and proportion—is found in the pilgrimage church of Santa Maria della Consolazione at Todi, begun in 1508 (FIG. **17-9**). This church's hillside site outside the town makes it visible from far away, and its sturdy, carefully proportioned silhouette offers an attractive goal for the faithful approaching through the valley below. Although the identity of its designer is uncertain, it is quite clearly in the manner of Bramante, and we can call it "Bramantesque."

In its plan, the church takes the form of a domed cross, with its lobelike arms ending in polygonal apses. The interior space, showing a Classical purity of arrangement in which the layout is immediately open to the eye and volumes and spaces are in exquisite adjustment, finds its exact expression on the exterior. Here, each level is carefully marked off by projecting cornices, and the rhythm increases steadily from bottom to top. The unfenestrated first story, marked off into blank panels by pilasters, provides a firm base for the upper structure. The second story is fenestrated, the windows topped by alternating triangular and segmental pediments. The attic story makes a transition to the half-domes, and the half-domes serve the same function in relation to the balustraded platform that sets off drum and dome as it makes a transition to them. The rhythm of fenestration of the second floor reappears in the drum, where it is quickened by the interpolation of round-headed niches between the windows, like the appearance of a second voice in a fugue.

Regardless of the side from which it is seen, the building presents a completely balanced and symmetrical aspect. Like a three-dimensional essay in rational order, all of its parts are in harmonious relation to each other and to the whole, yet each is complete and independent. To appreciate the wide difference between the Medieval and the High Renaissance views of the nature of architecture, one need only recall the design of a typically Gothic building. In both scale and complexity, Santa Maria della Consolazione stands between the Tempietto and the design for the new St. Peter's. More amply than the former, with greater purity than the latter, it expresses the architectural ideals of the High Renaissance. Its spirit is that of classical antiquity and, though it is modern, it speaks only the Classical language.

The palaces designed by Bramante have been preserved only in drawings or engravings. His Palazzo Caprini (FIG. **17-10**), bought by Raphael in 1517, was

17-10 BRAMANTE, Palazzo Caprini (House of Raphael), Rome. (Drawing attributed to ANDREA PALLADIO.)

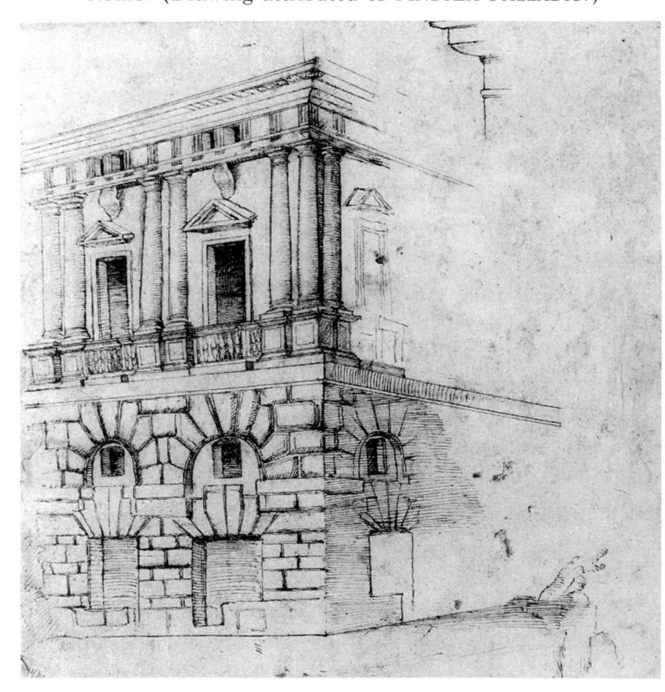

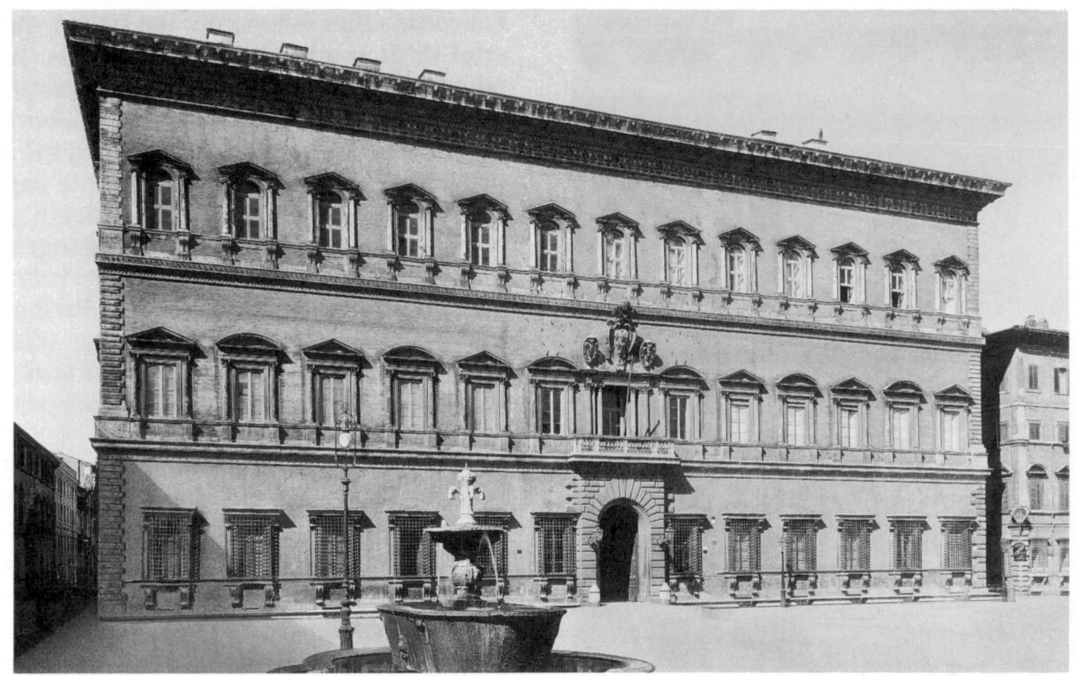

17-11 ANTONIO DA SANGALLO THE YOUNGER, Farnese Palace, Rome, c. 1530–1546 (view from the northwest).

torn down during the rebuilding of the area around St. Peter's. Still, it was one of the most important and influential palace designs of the sixteenth century. In it, Bramante reduced the typical three-story façade of the fifteenth century to two stories, with the strongly rusticated first story serving as a robust support for the elegantly articulated *piano nobile.* This arrangement not only differentiates the two stories, but emphatically puts the residential level of the building above the commercial. (The ground floor was occupied by shops and offices.) The pedimented windows of the second story are flanked by pairs of engaged Tuscan columns supporting an entablature in which the frieze is pierced by the windows of an attic story. The total aspect of the building is one of rugged plasticity, and its influence on contemporary and later architects, including Palladio and Inigo Jones, was lasting. With Baroque modifications, Bramante's scheme can be recognized in Claude Perrault's Louvre façade (FIG. 19-64), erected almost two centuries later.

Less plastic, perhaps, than Bramante's design, but equally imposing, is the Farnese Palace in Rome (FIGS. **17-11** to **17-13**), designed by ANTONIO DA SANGALLO THE YOUNGER (1483–1546), which fully expresses the Classical order, regularity, simplicity, and dignity of the High Renaissance. Antonio, the youngest of a family of architects, received his early training from his uncles Giuliano, the designer of Santa Maria delle Carceri in Prato (FIG. 16-45), and Antonio the Elder. Antonio the Younger went to Rome around 1503 and became Bramante's draftsman

17-12 ANTONIO DA SANGALLO THE YOUNGER, plan of the Farnese Palace.

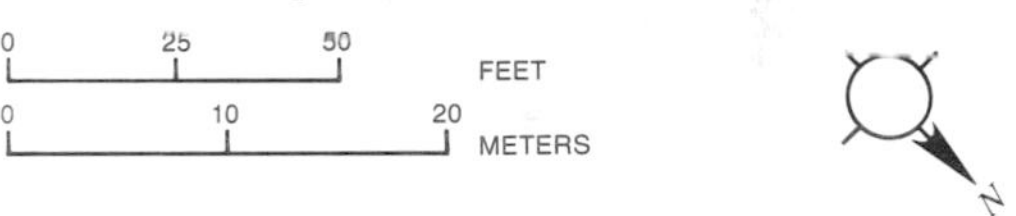

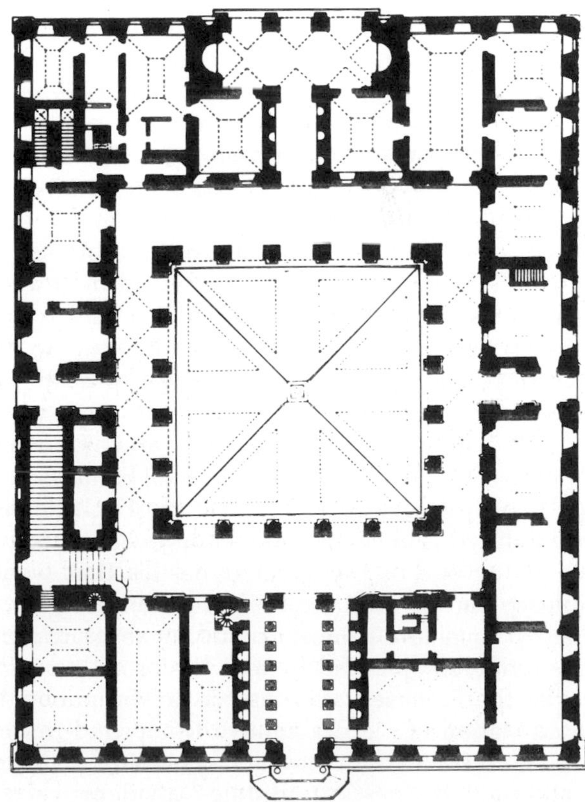

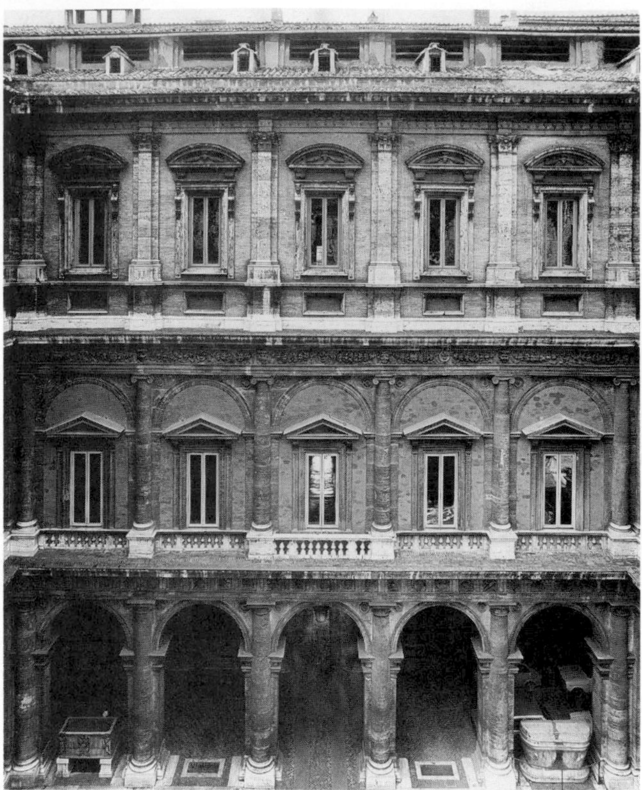

17-13 Antonio da Sangallo the Younger, courtyard of the Farnese Palace. Third story and attic by Michelangelo in 1548.

and assistant. As Paul III's favorite architect, he received many commissions that might have gone to Michelangelo. He is the perfect example of the professional architect, and his family constituted an architectural firm, often working up the plans and doing the drafting for other architects. Essentially a developer, Antonio frequently has been criticized as unimaginative, but if this is so, it is only by comparison with Michelangelo. He built fortifications for almost the entire papal state and received more commissions for military than for civilian architecture. Although he may not have invented it, Antonio certainly developed the modern method of bastioned fortifications to a high degree and, in this accomplishment, he demonstrated his ingenuity and originality.

The Farnese Palace, built for Cardinal Farnese (later Pope Paul III), sets a standard for the High Renaissance palazzo. The sixteenth century was the beginning of the age of the great dynasties that would dominate Europe until the French Revolution. It was an age of royal and princely pomp, of absolute monarchy rendered splendid by art. The broad, majestic front of the Farnese Palace asserts to the public the exalted station of a great family. This proud frontispiece symbolizes the aristocratic epoch that followed the stifling of the nascent, middle-class democracy of European cities (especially the Italian cities) by powerful kings heading centralized states. It is thus significant that the original, rather modest palace was greatly enlarged to its present form after Paul's accession to the papacy in 1534, reflecting the ambitions of the pope both for his family and the papacy. Unfinished at the time of Antonio's death in 1546, the building was completed by Michelangelo.

The façade (FIG. 17-11) is the very essence of princely dignity in architecture. Facing a spacious paved square, the rectangle of the smooth front is framed and firmly anchored by the *quoins* (rusticated building corners) and cornice, while lines of windows (with alternating triangular and segmental pediments, in Bramante's fashion) mark a majestic beat across it. The window casements are no longer flush with the wall, as in the Palazzo Medici-Riccardi (FIG. 16-24), but project from its surface, so that instead of being a flat, thin plane, the façade becomes a spatially active, three-dimensional mass. Each casement is a complete architectural unit, consisting of a *socle* (a projecting under-member), engaged columns, entablature, and pediment. The variations in the treatment of these units prevent the symmetrical scheme from becoming rigid or monotonous. The rusticated doorway and second-story balcony, surmounted by the Farnese coat of arms, emphasize the central axis and bring the horizontal and vertical forces of the design into harmony. This centralizing feature, not present in the palaces of Alberti or Michelozzo di Bartolomeo, is the external opening of a central-corridor axis (FIG. 17-12) that runs through the whole building and continues in the garden beyond; around this axis, the rooms are disposed with strict regularity. The interior courtyard (FIG. 17-13) displays stately Colosseum arch-orders on the first two levels and, on the third, Michelangelo's sophisticated variation on that theme, with overlapping pilasters replacing the weighty columns of Antonio's design.

Raphael

The artist most typical of the High Renaissance is Raphael (Raffaello Santi, 1483–1520). The pattern of his growth recapitulates the sequence of artistic tendencies of the fifteenth century, and although strongly influenced by Leonardo and Michelangelo, Raphael developed an individual style that, in itself, clearly states the ideals of High Renaissance art. His powerful originality prevailed while he learned from everyone; he assimilated what he best could use and rendered into form the Classical instinct of his age. He worked so effortlessly in the Classical mood that his art is almost the resurrection of Greek art at its height. Goethe, the renowned German poet and critic, said of Raphael that he did not have to imitate the Greeks, for he thought and felt like them.

Born in a small town in Umbria near Urbino, Raphael probably learned the rudiments of his art from his father, GIOVANNI SANTI, a provincial painter connected with the court of Federigo da Montefeltro. While still a child, Raphael was apprenticed to Perugino, who had been trained in Verrocchio's shop with Leonardo. We have seen in Perugino's *Christ Delivering the Keys of the Kingdom to St. Peter* (FIG. 16-62) that the most significant formal quality of his work is the harmony of its spatial composition. While Raphael was still in the studio of Perugino, the latter painted a panel of *The Marriage of the Virgin* (not shown), which, in its composition, very closely resembles the central portion of his Sistine Chapel fresco. Perugino's panel, now in the Museum of Caen, probably served as the model for Raphael's *Marriage of the Virgin* (FIG. **17-14**). Although scarcely twenty-one, Raphael was able to recognize and to remedy some of the weaknesses of his master's composition. By relaxing the formality of Perugino's foreground figure screen and disposing his actors in greater depth, the young artist not only provides them with greater freedom of action but also bridges the gap between them and the building in the background more successfully. The result is a painting that, although it resembles its model very closely, is nevertheless more fluid and better unified.

17-14 RAPHAEL, *The Marriage of the Virgin*, 1504. Oil on wood, 67″ × 46½″. Pinacoteca di Brera, Milan.

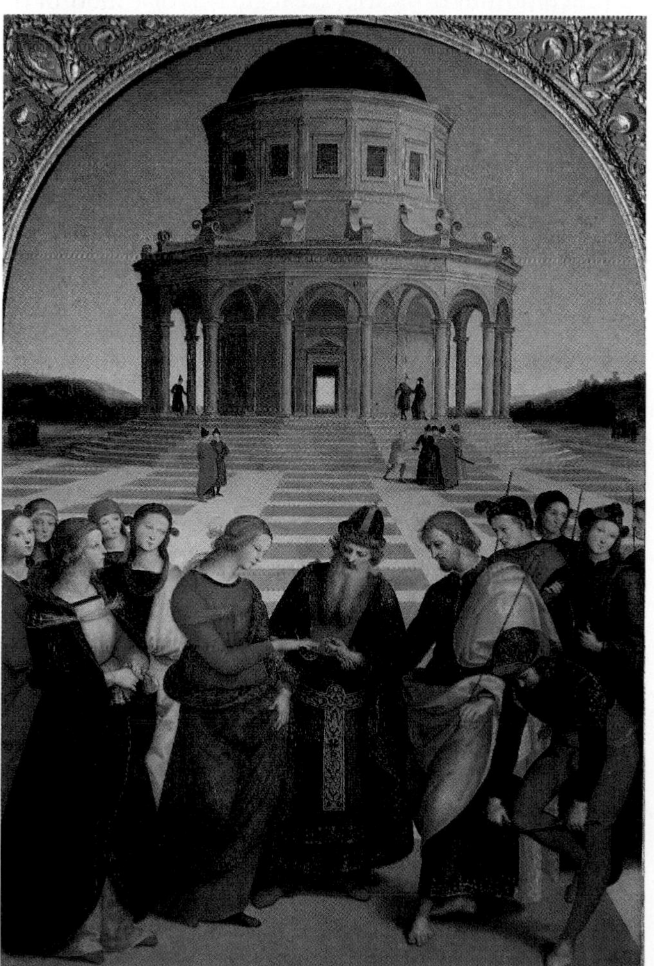

Raphael spent the four years from 1504 to 1508 in Florence. Here, in the home of the Renaissance, he discovered that the style of painting he had learned so painstakingly from Perugino already was outmoded. The two archrivals, Leonardo and Michelangelo, were engaged in an artistic battle. Crowds flocked to Santissima Annunziata to see the recently unveiled cartoon for Leonardo's *Virgin and Child with St. Anne and the Infant St. John* (FIG. 17-2), the original version of which was done about 1498. Michelangelo responded with the *Doni Madonna*. Both artists were commissioned to decorate the council hall in the Palazzo Vecchio with pictures memorializing Florentine victories of the past. Although only Leonardo completed this task and although only some small preparatory sketches and small copies survive, the effect on artists in Florence, especially on one as gifted as Raphael, must have been considerable.

Under the influence of Leonardo, Raphael began to modify the Madonna compositions he had learned in Umbria. In the *Madonna with the Goldfinch (Madonna del Cardellino)* of 1506 (FIG. **17-15**), Raphael uses the pyramidal composition of Leonardo's *Virgin of the Rocks* (FIG. 17-1). The faces and figures are modeled in subtle chiaroscuro, and Raphael's general application of this technique is based on Leonardo's cartoon for *The Virgin and Child with St. Anne and the Infant St. John* (FIG. 17-2). At the same time, the large, substantial figures are placed in a Peruginesque landscape, with the older artist's typical feathery trees in the middle ground. Although Raphael experimented with Leonardo's dusky modeling, he tended to return to Perugino's lighter tonalities. Raphael preferred clarity to obscurity, not being, as Leonardo was, fascinated with mystery. His great series of Madonnas, of which this is an early example, unify Christian devotion and pagan beauty; no artist ever has rivaled Raphael in his definitive rendering of this sublime theme of grace and dignity, sweetness and lofty idealism.

Had Raphael painted nothing but his Madonnas, his fame still would be secure. But he was also a great muralist, a master in the grand style begun by Giotto and carried on by Masaccio and other artists of the fifteenth century. In 1508, Raphael was called to the court of Pope Julius II in Rome, perhaps on the recommendation of his fellow townsman, Bramante. There, in competition with older artists like Perugino and Luca Signorelli, Raphael received one of the largest commissions of the time: the decoration of the

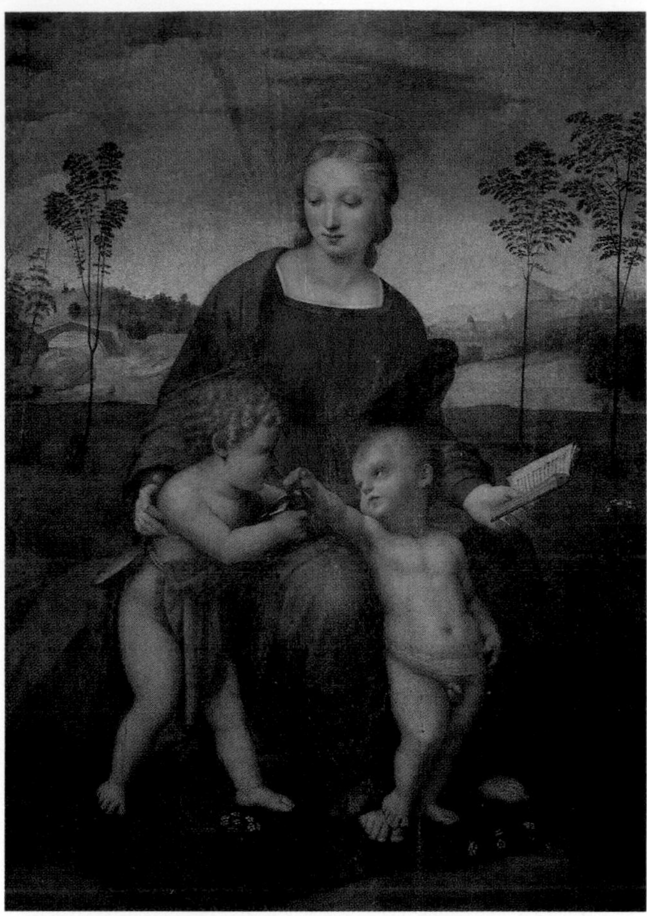

17-15 RAPHAEL, *Madonna with the Goldfinch (Madonna del Cardellino)*, 1505–1506. Oil on wood, 42″ × 29½″. Galleria degli Uffizi, Florence.

papal apartments in the Vatican. Of the several rooms *(stanze)* of the suite, Raphael painted the first, the Stanza della Segnatura; the others were done mostly by his pupils, following his sketches. On the four walls of the Stanza della Segnatura, under the headings of Theology, Law, Poetry, and Philosophy, Raphael deploys a host of magnificent figures that symbolize and sum up Western learning as it was understood in the Renaissance. His intention was to indicate the four branches of human knowledge and wisdom, while pointing out the virtues and the learning appropriate to a pope.

The iconographic scheme is most complex, and Raphael probably received advice from the brilliant company of Classical scholars surrounding Julius. On one wall, in the so-called *School of Athens* (FIG. **17-16**), the artist presents a composition that, in and of itself, constitutes a complete statement of the High Renaissance in its artistic form and spiritual meaning. The setting is not a "school" but rather a concourse of the great philosophers and scientists of the ancient world, who—rediscovered by the Renaissance—hold a convention, where they teach one another once more and inspire a new age. In a vast hall covered by massive vaults that recall Roman architecture (and approximate the appearance of the new St. Peter's in the year the painting was executed [1509]), the figures are arranged ingeniously around the central pair, Plato and Aristotle. The ancient philosophers, men concerned with the ultimate mysteries that transcend this world, stand on Plato's side; on Aristotle's side are the philosophers and scientists concerned with nature and the affairs of men. At the lower left, Pythagoras writes as a servant holds up the harmonic scale. In the foreground, Heraclitus (probably a portrait of Michelangelo) broods alone. Diogenes sprawls on the steps. At the right, students surround Euclid, who demonstrates a theorem. This group is especially interesting; Euclid may be a portrait of the aged Bramante. At the extreme right, Raphael includes his own portrait. The groups move easily and clearly, with eloquent poses and gestures that symbolize their doctrines and are of the greatest variety. Their self-assurance and natural dignity bespeak the very nature of calm reason, that balance and measure so much admired by the great minds of the Renaissance as the heart of philosophy.

Significantly, in this work, Raphael places himself among the mathematicians and scientists, and certainly the evolution of pictorial science comes to its perfection in *The School of Athens*. A vast perspective space has been created, in which human figures move naturally, without effort—each according to his own intention, as Leonardo might say. The stage setting, so long in preparation, is finally complete; the Western artist knows now how to produce the human drama. That this stagelike space is projected onto a two-dimensional surface is the consequence of the union of mathematics with pictorial science, which yields the art of perspective, here mastered completely.

The artist's psychological insight has matured along with his mastery of the problems of physical representation. Each character in Raphael's *School of Athens*, like those in Leonardo's *The Last Supper* (FIG. 17-3), is intended to communicate a mood that reflects his beliefs, and each group is unified by the sharing of its members in the mood. The design devices by which individuals and groups are related to each other and to the whole are wonderfully involved and demand close study. From the center, where Plato and Aristotle stand, silhouetted against the sky within the framing arch in the distance, the groups of figures are rhythmically arranged in an elliptical movement that swings forward, looping around the

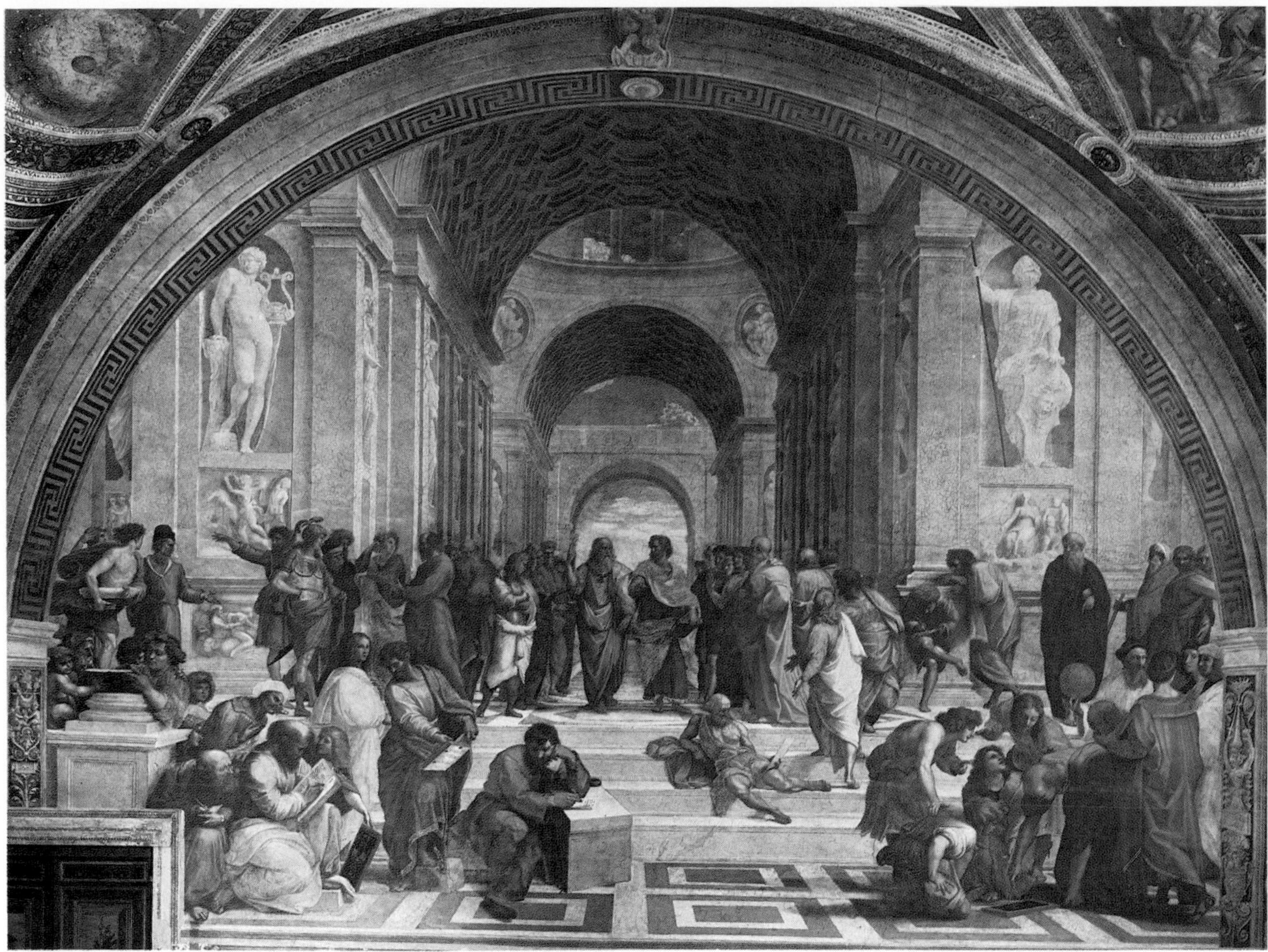

17-16 Raphael, *The School of Athens*, 1509–1511. Fresco. Stanza della Segnatura, Vatican Palace, Rome.

two forward groups to either side, and then back again to the center. Moving through the wide opening in the foreground along the perspective pattern of the floor, we penetrate the assembly of philosophers and are led, by way of the reclining Diogenes, up to the here-reconciled leaders of the two great opposing camps of Renaissance philosophy. In the Stanza della Segnatura, Raphael reconciles and harmonizes not only the Platonists and Aristotelians, but paganism and Christianity, in the same kind of synthesis manifest in his Madonnas.

Pope Leo X, the son of Lorenzo de' Medici, succeeded Julius II as Raphael's patron. During Leo's pontificate, Rome achieved a splendor it had not known since ancient times. Leo was a worldly, pleasure-loving prince, who spent huge sums on the arts, of which, as a true Medici, he was a sympathetic connoisseur. Raphael moved in the highest circles of the papal court, the star of a brilliant society. He was young, handsome, wealthy, and adulated, not only by his followers but by the city of Rome and all Italy. His personality contrasts strikingly with that of the aloof, mysterious Leonardo or the tormented and intractable Michelangelo. Genial, even tempered, generous, and high-minded, Raphael was genuinely loved. The pope was not his only patron. His friend, Agostino Chigi, an immensely wealthy banker who managed the financial affairs of the papal state, commissioned Raphael to decorate his palace on the Tiber with scenes from Classical mythology. Outstanding among the frescoes painted by Raphael in the small but splendid Villa Farnesina is the *Galatea* (FIG. **17-17**), which takes its theme from the popular Italian poem "La giostra," by Politian. Botticelli took the theme for his *Birth of Venus* (FIG. 16-60) from the same work.

In Raphael's fresco, Galatea flees from her uncouth lover, the giant Polyphemus, on a shell drawn by leaping dolphins. She is surrounded by sea creatures

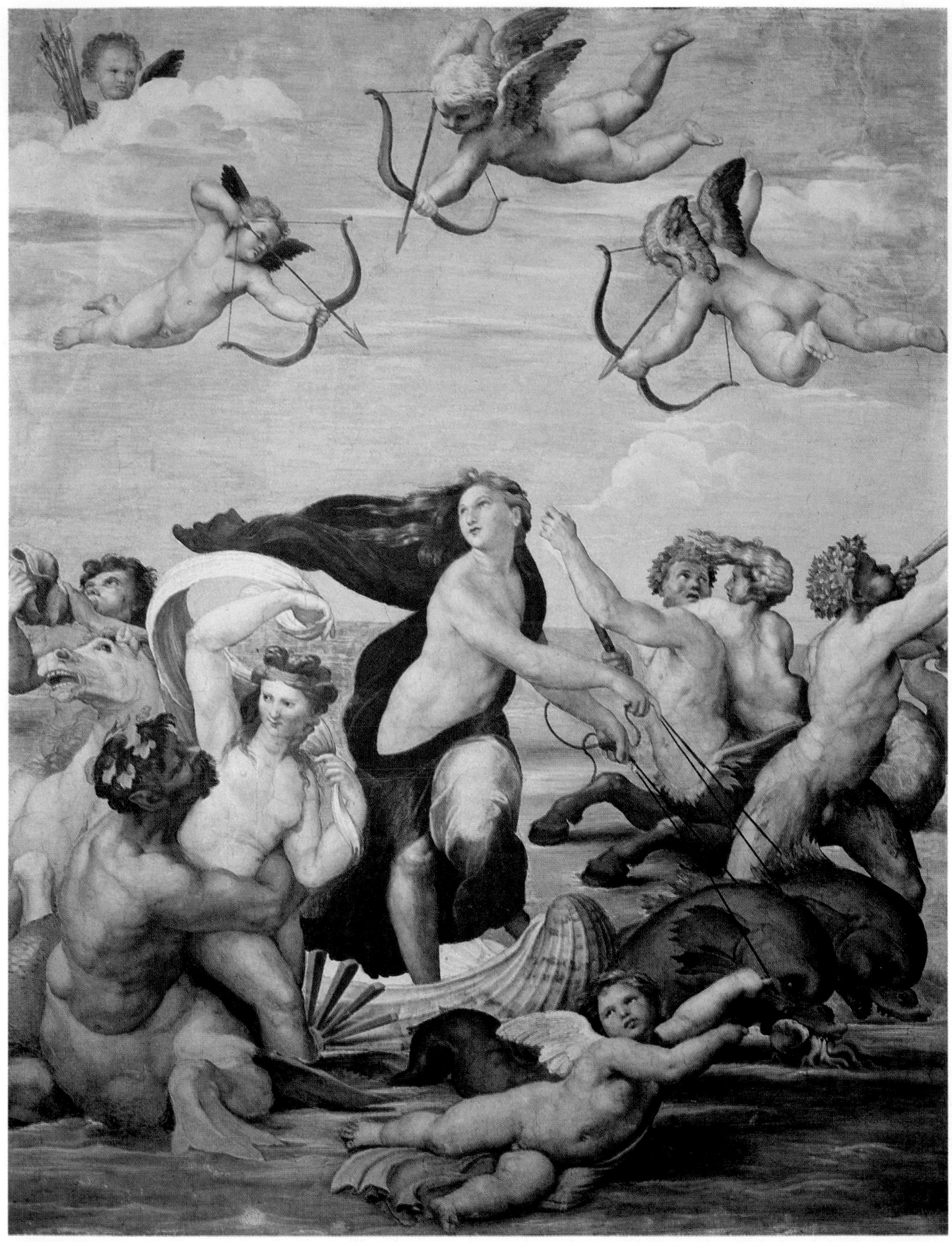

17-17 RAPHAEL, *Galatea,* 1513. Fresco. Villa Farnesina, Rome.

and playful cupids. The painting erupts in unrestrained pagan joy and exuberance, an exultant song in praise of human beauty and zestful love. The composition artfully wheels the sturdy figures around Galatea in bounding and dashing movements that always return to her as the energetic center. The cupids, skillfully foreshortened, repeat the circling motion. Raphael's figures are sculpturally conceived, and the body of Galatea—supple, strong, and vigorously in motion—should be compared with Botticelli's delicate, hovering, almost dematerialized Venus. Pagan myth presented in monumental form, in vivacious movement, and in a spirit of passionate delight brings back the seminal substance of which the naturalistic art and poetry of the Classical world was made. Raphael revives the gods and heroes and the bright world they populated, not to venerate them but to make of them the material of art. From Raphael almost to the present, Classical matter will hold as prominent a place in art as religious matter. So completely does the new spirit embodied in the *Galatea* take control that it is as if the Middle Ages had never occurred.

Raphael was also an excellent portraitist. His subjects were the illustrious scholars and courtiers who surrounded Pope Leo X, among them Count Baldassare Castiglione, a close friend of Raphael and the author of a handbook on High Renaissance criteria of genteel behavior. In the *Book of the Courtier*, Castiglione portrays an ideal type of the High Renaissance, a courageous, sagacious, truth-loving, skillful, and cultivated man—in a word, the completely civilized man, a culmination of the line that runs from the rude barbarian warriors who succeeded to the Roman Empire through the half-literate knights and barons of the Middle Ages. Castiglione goes on to describe a way of life based on cultivated rationality in imitation of the ancients. In Raphael's portrait of him (FIG. **17-18**), Castiglione, splendidly yet soberly garbed, looks directly at us with a philosopher's grave and benign expression, clear-eyed and thoughtful. The figure is in half-length and three-quarter view, in the pose made popular by the *Mona Lisa* (FIG. 17-4), and we note in both portraits the increasing attention paid by the High Renaissance artist to the personality and psychic state of the subject. The tones are muted and low-keyed, as would befit the temper and mood of this reflective, middle-aged man; the background is entirely neutral, without the usual landscape or architecture. The head and the hands are both wonderfully eloquent in what they report of the man, who himself had written so eloquently in the *Courtier* of the way to enlightenment by the love of beauty. Raphael, Castiglione, and other artists of their age were animated by such love, and we know from his poetry that Michelangelo shared in this widely held Neo-Platonic belief that the soul rises to its enlightenment by the progressively rarefied experience of the beautiful.

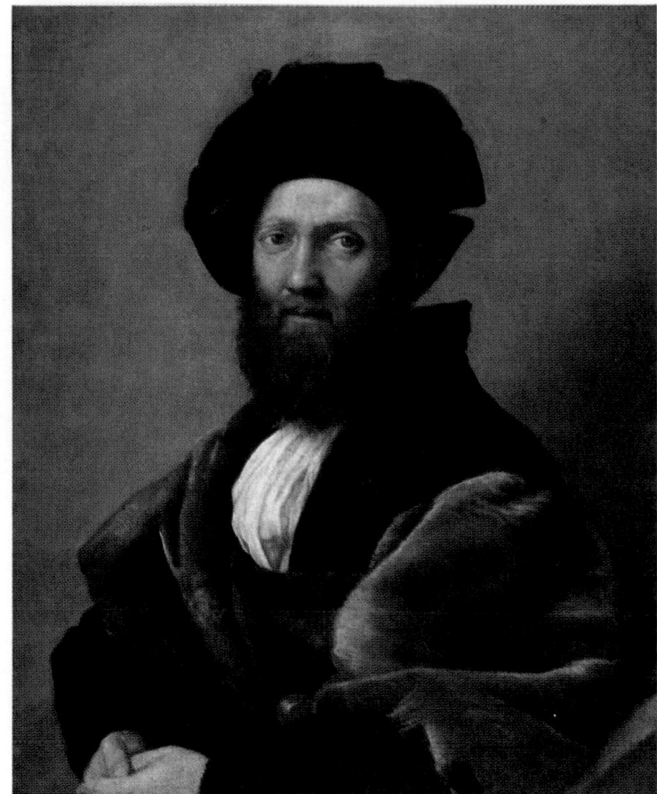

17-18 RAPHAEL, *Baldassare Castiglione*, c. 1514. Oil on wood transferred to canvas, approx. $30\frac{1}{4}'' \times 26\frac{1}{2}''$. Louvre, Paris.

Michelangelo

MICHELANGELO (Michelangelo Buonarroti, 1475–1564) is a far more complex personality than Raphael, and his art is not nearly so typical of the High Renaissance as that of his somewhat younger contemporary. Frequently irascible, Michelangelo was as impatient with the shortcomings of others as he was with his own. His jealousy of Raphael, his dislike of Leonardo, and his almost continuous difficulties with his patrons are all well known. Perhaps these personal problems arose out of his strong and stern devotion to his art, for he was always totally absorbed in the work at hand. He identified himself completely with the task of artistic creation, and his reactions to his rivals often were impulsive and antagonistic. In this respect, Michelangelo's character often has been compared with Beethoven's, but the personal letters of both reveal a deep sympathy and concern for those close to them, and a profound understanding of humanity informs their works.

Whatever his traits of character, Michelangelo's career realizes all those Renaissance ideals that we conceptualize as being characteristic of an "inspired genius" and a "universal man." His work has the authority of greatness we already have attributed to Donatello. His confidence in his genius was unbounded; the demands of that genius determined his choices absolutely, often in opposition to the demands of his patrons. His belief that nothing worth preserving could be done without genius was attended by the conviction that nothing could be done without persevering study.

Although he was an architect, a sculptor, a painter, a poet, and an engineer, Michelangelo thought of himself first as a sculptor, regarding that calling as superior to that of a painter because the sculptor shares in something like the divine power to "make man." In true Platonic fashion, he believed that the *image* produced by the artist's hand must come from the *idea* in the artist's mind; the idea is the reality that has to be brought forth by the genius of the artist. But artists are not the *creators* of the ideas they conceive; rather they find their ideas in the natural world, reflecting the absolute idea, which, for the artist, is *beauty*. In this way, the strongly Platonic strain makes the Renaissance theory of the imitation of nature a *revelation* of the high truths hidden within nature. The theory that guided Michelangelo's hand, though never complete or entirely consistent, appears in his poetry:

> Every beauty which is seen here below by persons of perception resembles more than anything else that celestial source from which we all are come . . .
>
> My eyes longing for beautiful things
> together with my soul longing for salvation
> have no other power
> to ascend to heaven than the contemplation of beautiful things.*

One of the best-known observations by Michelangelo is that the artist must proceed by finding the idea—the image, locked in the stone, as it were—so that, by removing the excess stone, he extricates the idea, like Pygmalion bringing forth the living form:

> The best artist has no concept which some single marble does not enclose within its mass, but only the hand which obeys the intelligence can accomplish that. . . . Taking away . . . brings out a living figure in alpine and hard stone, which . . . grows the more as the stone is chipped away.†

*In Robert J. Clements, *Michelangelo's Theory of Art* (New York: New York University Press, 1961), p. 9. © 1961 by Robert J. Clements. Reprinted by permission of the publisher.

†Ibid., p. 16.

The artist, Michelangelo felt, works through many years at this unceasing process of revelation and "arrives late at lofty and unusual things and . . . remains little time thereafter."

Michelangelo did indeed arrive "at lofty and unusual things," for he broke sharply from the lessons of his predecessors and contemporaries in one important respect: he mistrusted the application of mathematical methods as guarantees of beauty in proportion. Measure and proportion, he believed, should be "kept in the eyes." Giorgio Vasari quotes Michelangelo as declaring that "it was necessary to keep one's compass in one's eyes and not in the hand, for the hands execute, but the eye judges." Thus, he would set aside Vitruvius, Alberti, Leonardo, Albrecht Dürer, and others who tirelessly sought the perfect measure, being convinced that the inspired judgment could find other pleasing proportions and that the artist must not be bound, except by the demands made by the realization of the idea. This insistence on the artist's own authority is typical of Michelangelo and anticipates the modern concept of the right of talent to a self-expression limited only by its own judgment. The license thus given to genius to aspire far beyond the "rules" led Michelangelo to create works in architecture, sculpture, and painting that depart from High Renaissance regularity and put in its stead a style of vast, expressive strength with complex, eccentric, often titanic forms that loom before us in tragic grandeur. His self-imposed isolation (Raphael described him as "lonely as the hangman"), his creative furies, his proud independence, and his daring innovations led Italians to speak of the dominating quality of the man and his works in one word: *terribilità*, the sublime shadowed by the awesome and the fearful.

As a youth, Michelangelo was apprenticed to the painter Domenico Ghirlandaio, whom he left before completing his training. He soon came under the protection of Lorenzo the Magnificent and must have been a young and thoughtful member of the famous Neo-Platonic circle. He studied sculpture under one of Lorenzo's favorite artists, Bertoldo di Giovanni, a former collaborator of Donatello who specialized in small-scale bronzes. When the Medici fell in 1494, Michelangelo fled from Florence to Bologna, where he was impressed by the sculpture of Jacopo della Quercia (FIG. 16-3). Besides his study of Jacopo's works, although he claimed that in his art he owed nothing to anyone, Michelangelo made studious drawings after the great Florentines, Giotto and Masaccio, and his consuming interest in representing the male nude both in sculpture and painting in all likelihood was much stimulated by Signorelli (FIG. 16-61).

Michelangelo's wanderings took him to Rome, from which he returned to Florence in 1501, partly because the city might permit him to work a great block of marble, called the Giant, left over from an earlier, abortive commission. With his sure insight into the nature of stone and a proud, youthful confidence that he could perceive its idea, Michelangelo added to his already great reputation by carving his *David* (FIG. **17-19**). This colossal figure again takes up the theme that Donatello and Verrocchio had used successfully, but it reflects Michelangelo's own highly original interpretation of the subject. David is represented not after the victory, with the head of Goliath at his feet, but rather turning his head to his left, sternly watchful of the approaching foe. His whole muscular body, as well as his face, is tense with gathering power. The ponderated pose, suggesting the body at ease, is misleading until we read in the tightening sinews and deep frown what impends.

Here is the characteristic representation of energy in reserve that gives the tension of the coiled spring to Michelangelo's figures. The anatomy plays an important part in this prelude to action. The rugged torso and sturdy limbs of the young David and the large hands and feet, giving promise of the strength to come, are not composed simply of inert muscle groups, nor are they idealized by simplification into broad masses. They serve, by their active play, to make vivid the whole mood and posture of tense expectation. Each swelling vein and tightening sinew amplifies the psychological vibration of the monumental hero's pose.

Michelangelo doubtless had the Classical nude in mind—Antique statues, which were being found everywhere, were greatly admired by Michelangelo and his contemporaries for their skillful and precise rendering of heroic physique—but if we compare the *David* with the *Doryphoros* (FIG. 5-58), we realize how widely his intent diverges from the measured, almost bland quality of the Antique statue. As early as the *David*, then, Michelangelo's genius, unlike Raphael's, is dedicated to the presentation of towering, pent-up passion rather than to calm, ideal beauty. His own doubts, frustrations, and torments of mind passed easily into the great figures he created or planned.

The tomb of Julius II, a colossal structure that would have given Michelangelo the room he needed for his superhuman, tragic beings, became one of the great disappointments of Michelangelo's life when the pope, for unexplained reasons, interrupted the commission, possibly because funds had to be diverted for Bramante's rebuilding of St. Peter's. The original project called for a freestanding, two-story structure with some twenty-eight statues. After the pope's death in 1513, the scale of the project was reduced step by step until, in 1542, a final contract specified a simple wall tomb with less than one-third of the originally planned figures.

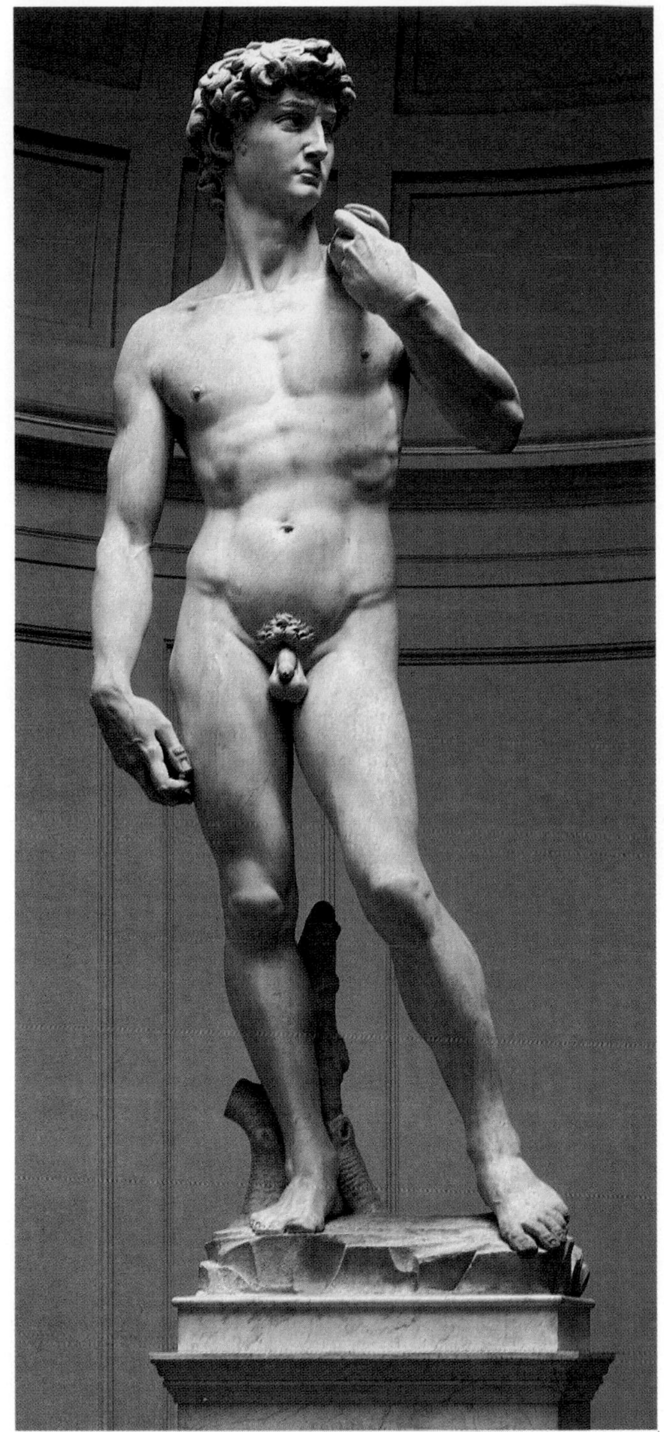

17-19 MICHELANGELO, *David*, 1501–1504. Marble, approx. 13′ 5″ high. Galleria dell' Accademia, Florence.

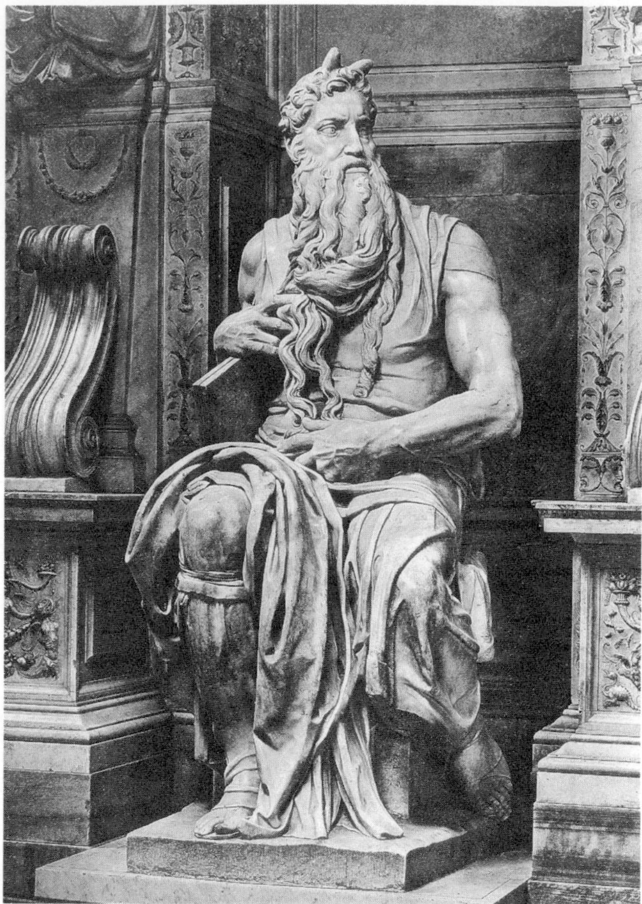

17-20 MICHELANGELO, *Moses,* c. 1513–1515. Marble, approx. 8′ 4″ high. San Pietro in Vincoli, Rome.

The spirit of the tomb may be summed up in the figure of *Moses* (FIG. **17-20**), which was completed during one of the sporadic resumptions of the work in 1513. Meant to be seen from below, and balanced with seven other massive forms related in spirit to it, the *Moses* now, in its comparatively paltry setting, can hardly have its full impact. The leader of Israel is shown seated—the tables of the Law under one arm, his other hand gripping the coils of his beard. We may imagine him pausing after the ecstasy of receiving the Law on Mount Sinai, while, in the valley below, the people of Israel give themselves up once more to idolatry. Here again, Michelangelo uses the turned head (as in the *David*), which concentrates the expression of awful wrath that now begins to stir in the mighty frame and eyes. One must study the work closely to appreciate Michelangelo's sense of the relevance of each detail of body and drapery in forcing up the psychic temperature. The muscles bulge, the veins swell, the great legs begin slowly to move. If this titan ever rose to his feet, says one writer, the world would fly apart. The holy rage of *Moses* mounts to the bursting point, yet must be contained, for the free release of energies in action is forbidden forever to Michelangelo's passion-stricken beings.

Two other figures, *The Dying Slave* (FIG. **17-21**) and *The Bound Slave* (FIG. **17-22**), believed to have been intended for the Julius tomb (although this is now doubted by some), may represent the enslavement of the human soul by matter when the soul falls from Heaven into the prison house of the body. With the imprisoned soul slumbering, our actions, as Marsilio Ficino says, are "the dreams of sleepers and the ravings of madmen." Certainly, the dreams and ravings are present in these two figures. Originally, some twenty slaves, in various attitudes of revolt and exhaustion, were to have been designed for the tomb.

17-21 MICHELANGELO, *The Dying Slave,* 1513–1516. Marble, approx. 7′ 5″ high. Louvre, Paris.

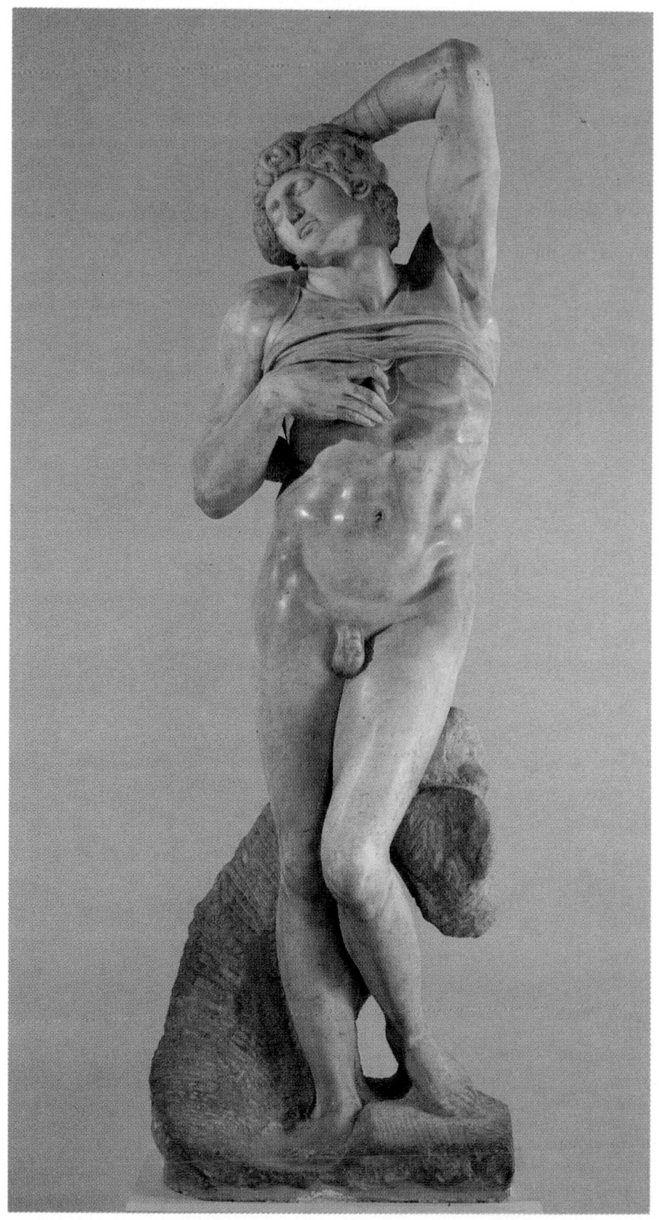

In the two slaves shown, as in the *David* and the *Moses*, Michelangelo makes each body a total expression of the idea, so that the human figure serves not so much as a representation of a concept, as in Medieval allegory, but as the concrete realization of an intense feeling. Indeed, Michelangelo's own powerful imagination communicates itself in every plane and hollow of the stone. The beautiful, Praxitelean lines of the swooning captive present—in their slow, downward pull—the weight of exhaustion; the violent contrapposto of the defiant captive is the image of frantic, impotent struggle. Michelangelo's whole art depends on his conviction that whatever can be said greatly through sculpture and painting must be said through the human figure.

17-22 Michelangelo, *The Bound Slave*, 1513–1516. Marble, approx. 6′ 10½″ high. Louvre, Paris.

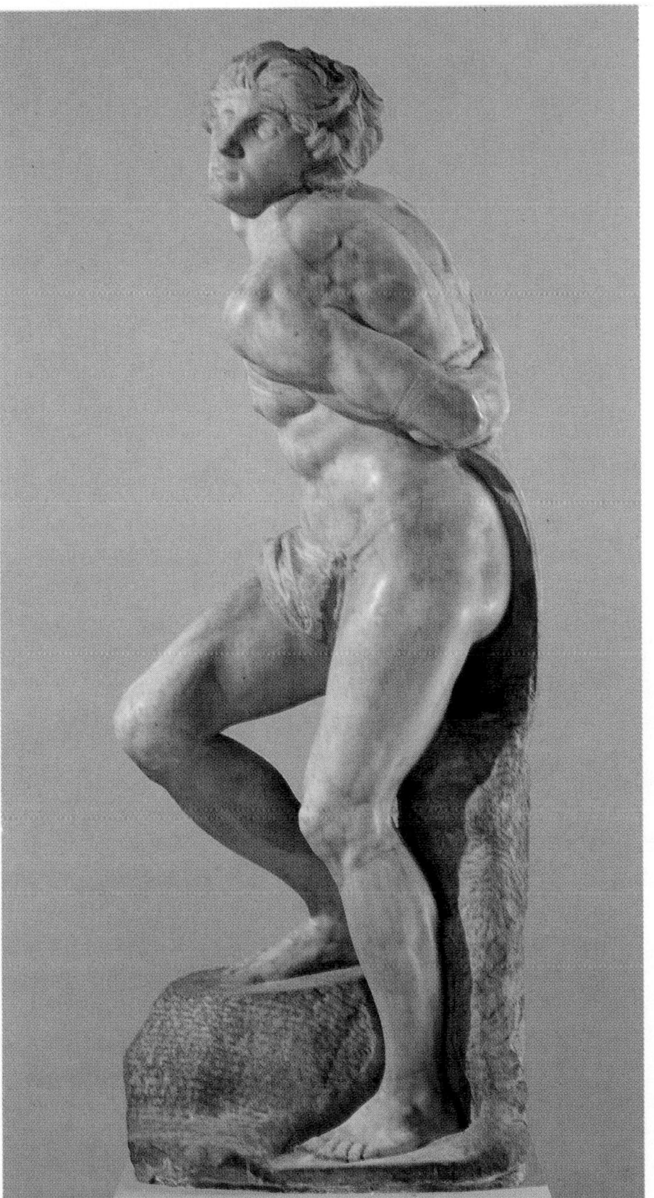

A group of four unfinished slaves, one of which is illustrated in the Introduction (FIG. 10), was probably meant for one of the later versions of the Julius tomb. These figures serve not only as object lessons in the subtractive method of sculpture, but also as revelations of the creative process in which abstract ideas—in effect, encased in blocks of stone—are converted into dynamically expressive, concrete forms. If Michelangelo's slaves indeed symbolize the struggle of the human soul to find release from the bonds of its material body, then this idea can find no fuller expression than in these partly finished figures that, with superhuman effort, struggle to cast off the inert masses of stone that imprison them.

With the failure of the tomb project, Julius II gave the bitter and reluctant Michelangelo the commission to paint the ceiling of the Sistine Chapel (FIG. **17-23**). The artist, insisting that painting was not his profession, assented only in the hope that the tomb project could be revived. The difficulties facing Michelangelo were enormous: the inadequacy of his training in the

17-23 Interior of the Sistine Chapel (view facing east). The Vatican, Rome.

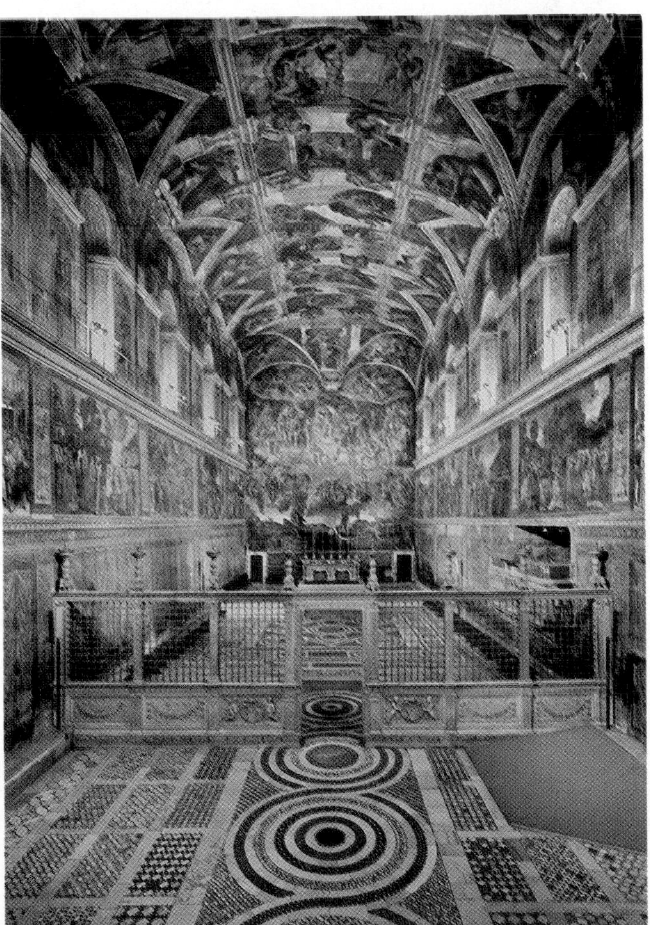

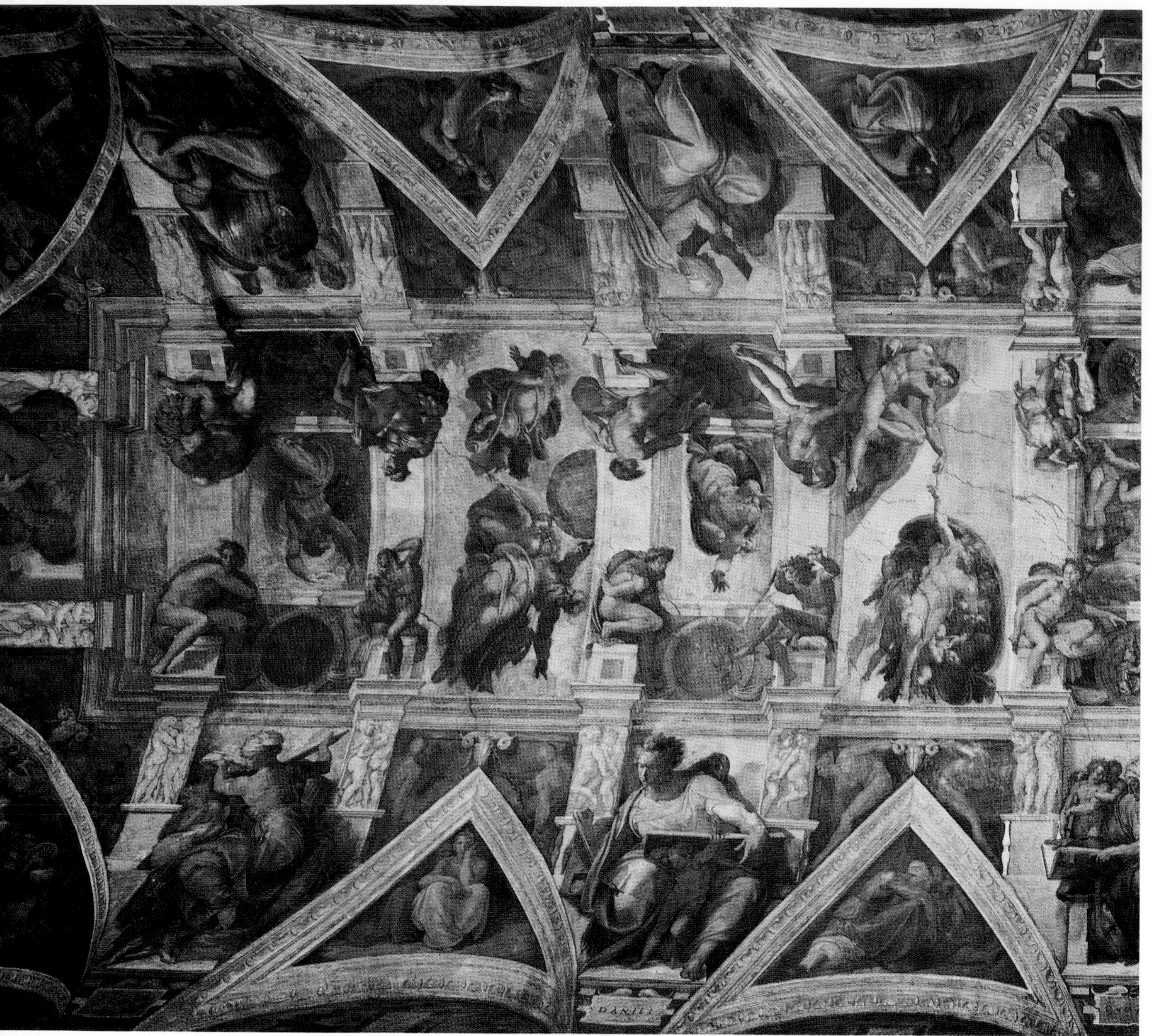

17-24 MICHELANGELO, ceiling of the Sistine Chapel (unrestored and recently restored views), 1508–1512. Fresco.

art of fresco; the dimensions of the ceiling (some 5,800 square feet); its height above the pavement (almost 70 feet); and the complicated perspective problems presented by the height and curve of the vault. Yet, in less than four years, Michelangelo produced an unprecedented work—a one-man masterpiece without parallel in the history of world art (FIG. **17-24**). Taking the most august and solemn themes of all, the Creation, Fall, and Redemption of man, Michelangelo spread a colossal decorative scheme across the vast surface, weaving together more than three hundred figures in an ultimate grand drama of the human race. A long corridor of narrative panels describing the creation recorded in Genesis runs along the crown of the vault, from God's *Separation of Light and Darkness* (above the altar) to the *Drunkenness of Noah* (nearest the entrance). The Hebrew prophets and pagan sibyls who foretold the coming of Christ

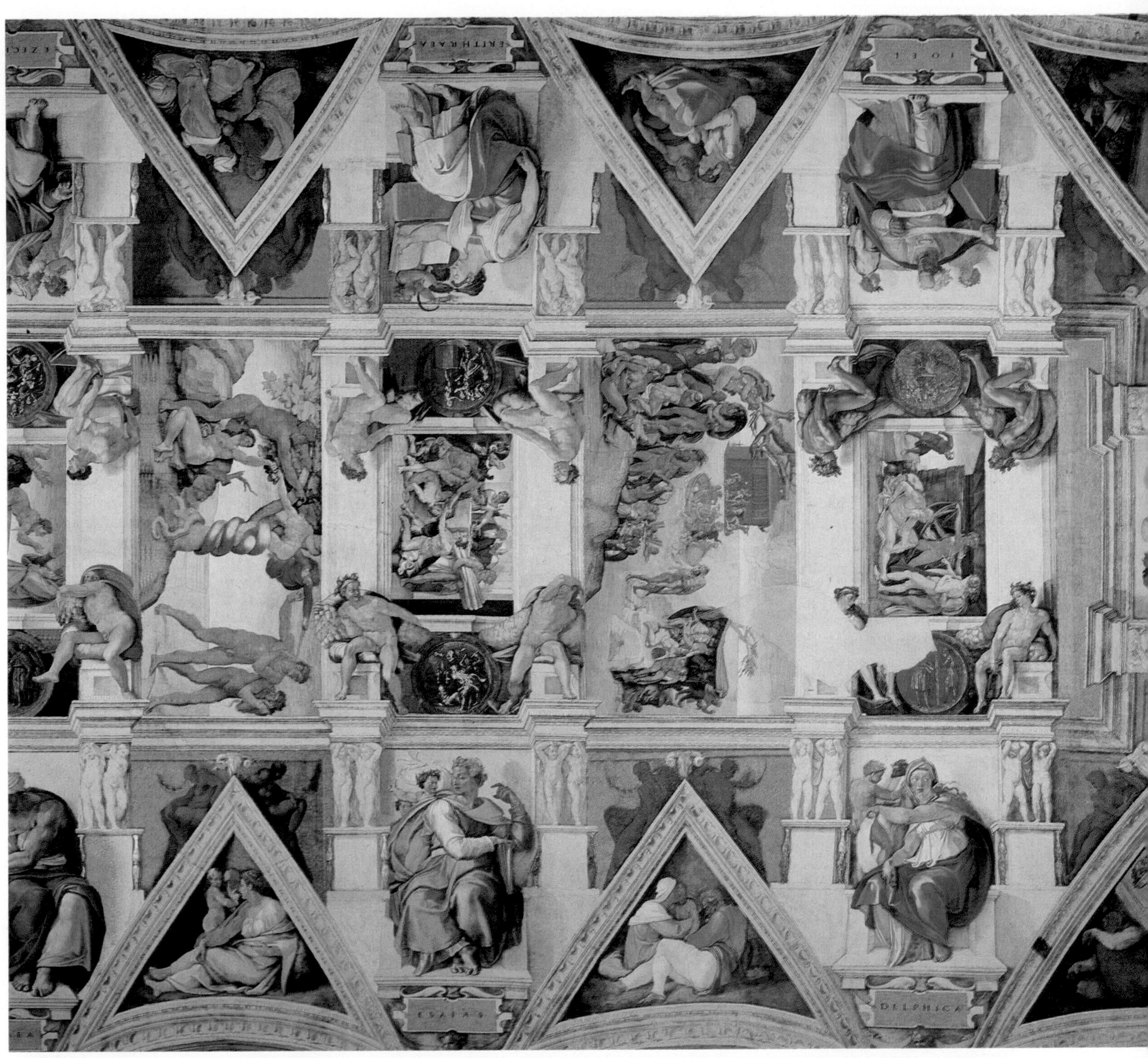

The left half in this view is unrestored, the right restored as part of a twelve-year project begun in 1980.

are seated on either side, where the vault curves down. At the four corner pendentives Michelangelo placed four Old Testament scenes with David, Judith, Haman, and the Brazen Serpent. Scores of lesser figures also appear: the ancestors of Christ in the triangular compartments above the windows, the nude youths who punctuate the corners of the central panels, and the small pairs of putti in grisaille (grey monochrome to imitate sculpture), who support the painted cornice surrounding the whole central corridor. The conception of the whole design is astounding enough in itself; the articulation of it in its thousand details is a superhuman achievement. But Michelangelo *was* human; in the first few months of work, he made mistakes in the technical application of the fresco that spoiled all he had done up to that time. In the first three panels, beginning at the entrance with the *Drunkenness of Noah,* he did not estimate the scale properly, and the compositions are crowded, without the simplicity of the panels beginning, in the center, with the *Temptation and Fall.*

Unlike Andrea Mantegna's decoration of the Camera degli Sposi in Mantua (FIG. 16-64), the strongly marked, unifying architectural framework in the Sistine Chapel is not used to construct "picture windows" through which we may look up into some illusion just above. Rather, our eyes seize on figure after figure, each sharply outlined against the neutral tone of the architectural setting or the plain background of the panels. Here, as in his sculpture, Michelangelo relentlessly concentrates his expressive purpose on the human figure. To him, the body is beautiful not only in its natural form but also in its spiritual and philosophical significance; the body is simply the manifestation of the soul or of a state of mind and character. Michelangelo represents the body in its most simple, elemental aspect: in the nude or simply draped, with no background and no ornamental embellishment, and always with a sculptor's sense that the figures could be tinted reliefs or full-rounded statues.

One of the central panels of the ceiling will evidence Michelangelo's mastery of the drama of the human figure. *The Creation of Adam* (FIG. **17-25**) is not the traditional representation but a bold, entirely Humanistic interpretation of the primal event. God and Adam, members of the same race of superbeings, confront each other in a primordial, unformed landscape of which Adam is still a material part, heavy as earth, while the Lord transcends it, wrapped in his billowing cloud of drapery and borne up by his genius powers. Apprehensively curious but as yet uncreated, the female figure beneath his sheltering arm, long held to represent Eve, recently has been interpreted as the Virgin Mary (with the Christ Child at her knee). Life leaps to Adam like an electric spark from the extended and mighty hand of God. The communication between gods and heroes, so familiar in Classical myth, is here concrete: both are made of the same substance; both are gigantic. This blunt depiction of the Lord as ruler of Heaven in the Olympian, pagan sense is an indication of how easily the High Renaissance joined pagan and Christian traditions; we could imagine Adam and the Lord as Prometheus and Zeus.

The composition is dynamically off-center, its focus being the two hands that join the great bodies by the energy that springs between their fingers. The bodies themselves are complementary—the concave body of Adam fitting the convex body of the Lord. The straight, architectural axes we find in the compositions of Leonardo and Raphael are replaced by curves and diagonals; thus, motion directs not only the figures but the whole composition. The reclining poses, the heavy musculature, and the twisting contrapposto are all a part of Michelangelo's stock, which he will show again later in the sculptured figures of the Medici tombs.

The *Creation of Adam* soon will present a new appearance; the paintings of the Sistine Chapel, like Leonardo's *Last Supper,* are in the process of being restored. Centuries of accumulated grime, overpainting, and protective glue are being removed, and restorers have uncovered much of the artist's original

17-25 MICHELANGELO, *The Creation of Adam* (detail of FIG. 17-24).

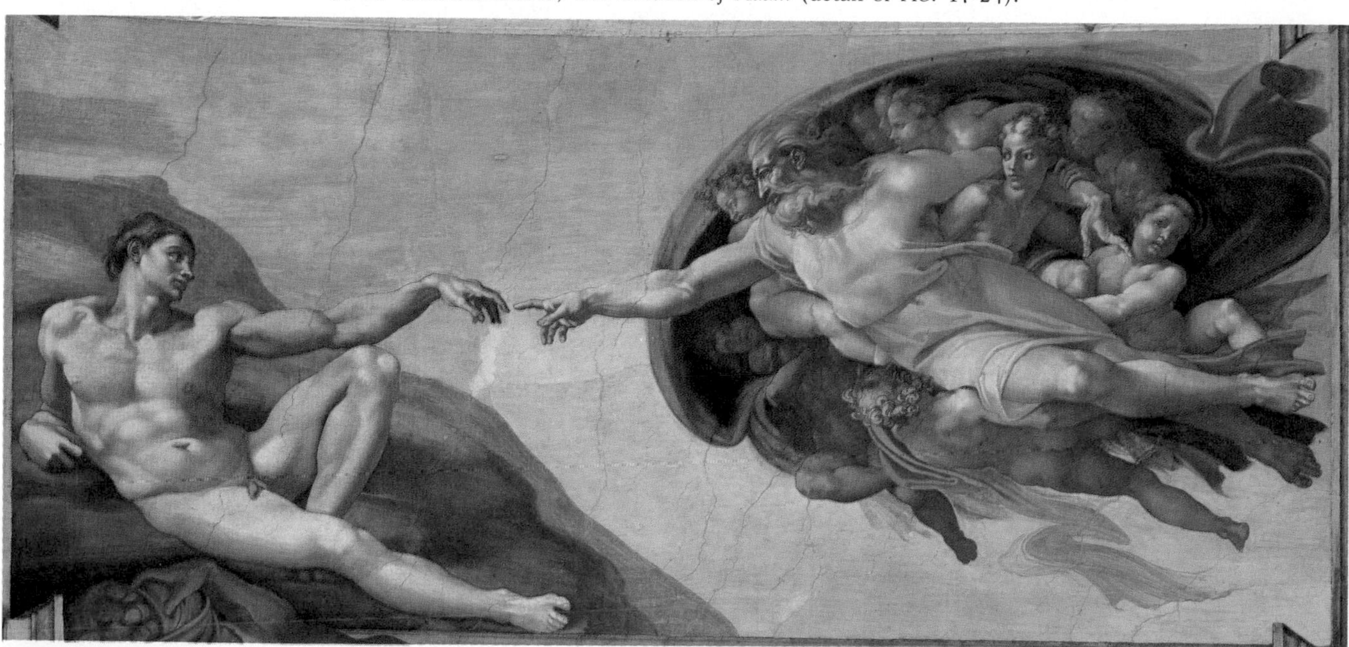

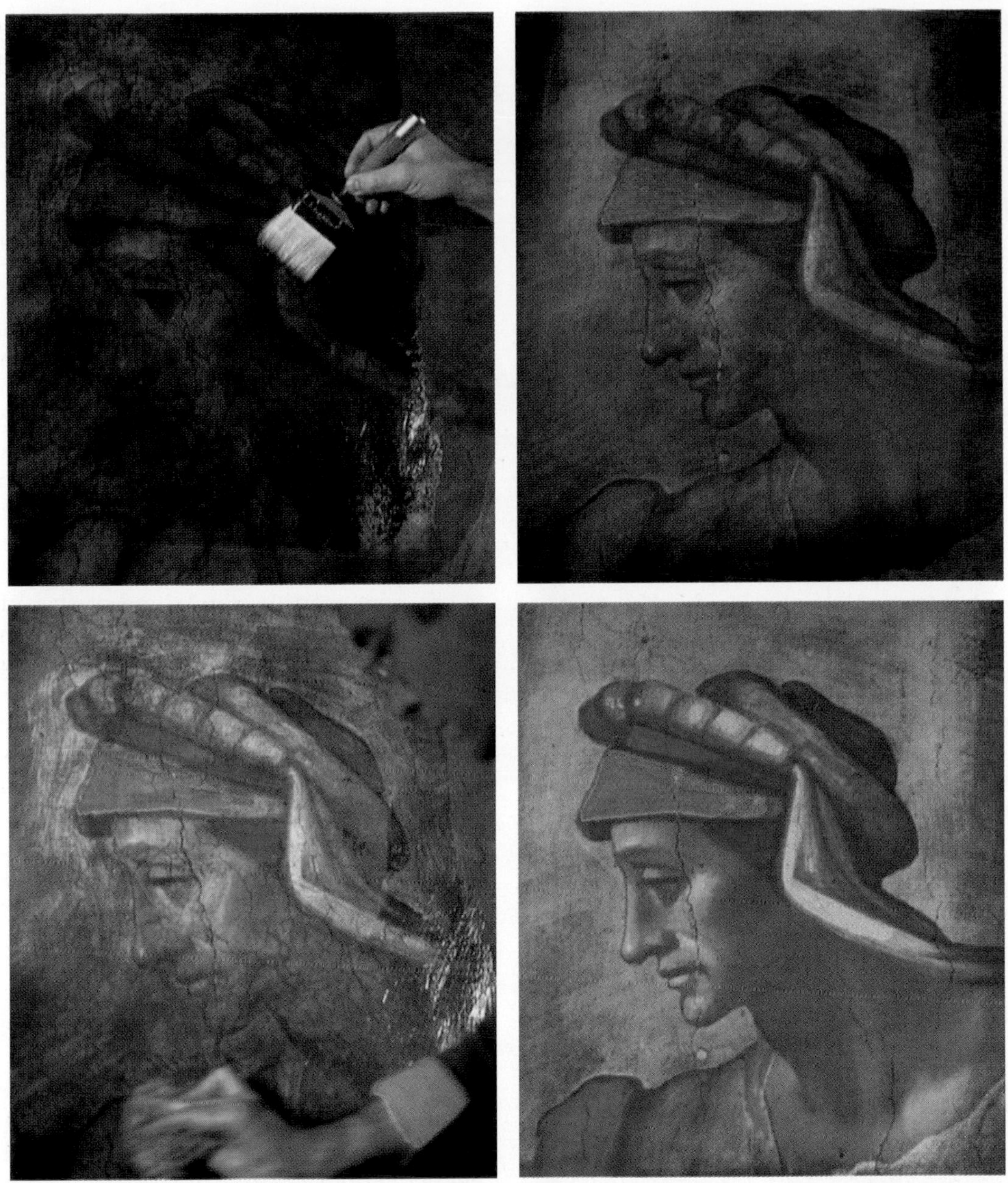

17-26 Detail of the left side of the *Azor-Sadoch* lunette at various stages of the restoration process, lunettes over the windows of the Sistine Chapel.

craft in form, color, style, and procedure. The restoration work, part of a twelve-year program (1980–1992), began on the lunettes above the windows (FIG. 17-23). In these semicircular spaces, Michelangelo painted figures representing the ancestors of Christ (Matthew 1:1–17). These figures, once thought to be purposefully dark, now show brilliant colors of high intensity, brushed on with an astonishing freedom and verve. A detail from the *Azor-Sadoch* lunette (FIG. **17-26**) shows the startling result of the restorers' procedure, as the original work emerges from the dark film laid down by time and faulty repair. The fresh, luminous hues, boldly joined in unexpected harmonies, have seemed uncharacteristically dissonant to some experts and have aroused brisk controversy. Some believe the restorers are removing Michelangelo's work along with the accumulated layers and that the apparently strident coloration cannot possibly be his. Others insist that the artist's real intentions and effects only now are being revealed to modern eyes. The issues raised are similar to those we have noted (in a footnote on page 573) with reference to Giotto's paintings in the Bardi Chapel (FIG. 15-15). In any event, when the restoration is completed, it is likely that the pictorial art of Michelangelo and its influence will have to be restudied and reassessed.

LATER WORKS

Following the death of Julius II, Michelangelo went once again into the service of the Medici popes, Leo X and Clement VII. These pontiffs were not interested in perpetuating the fame of their predecessor by letting Michelangelo complete Julius's tomb; instead, they commissioned him to build a funerary chapel, the New Sacristy, in San Lorenzo in Florence. Brunelleschi's Old Sacristy was off the left transept of San Lorenzo, and Michelangelo built the new addition off the right. He attempted a unification of architecture and of sculpture, designing the whole chapel as well as the tombs. This relationship between the two arts (and, in this case, painting as well) was a common Medieval feature; we think of the sculptured portals and stained glass of the Gothic cathedral. But the relationship had been broken in the fifteenth century, when sculpture fought free of its architectural matrix and asserted its independence—so much so that Brunelleschi could complain that Donatello's architectural and sculptural additions to his Old Sacristy spoiled the purity of his design. This new integration by Michelangelo, though here unfinished, pointed the way to Baroque art, in which the architectural-sculptural-pictorial ensemble again will become an effective standard.

17-27 MICHELANGELO, tomb of Giuliano de' Medici, 1519–1534. Marble, central figure approx. 71″ high. New Sacristy (Medici Chapel), San Lorenzo, Florence.

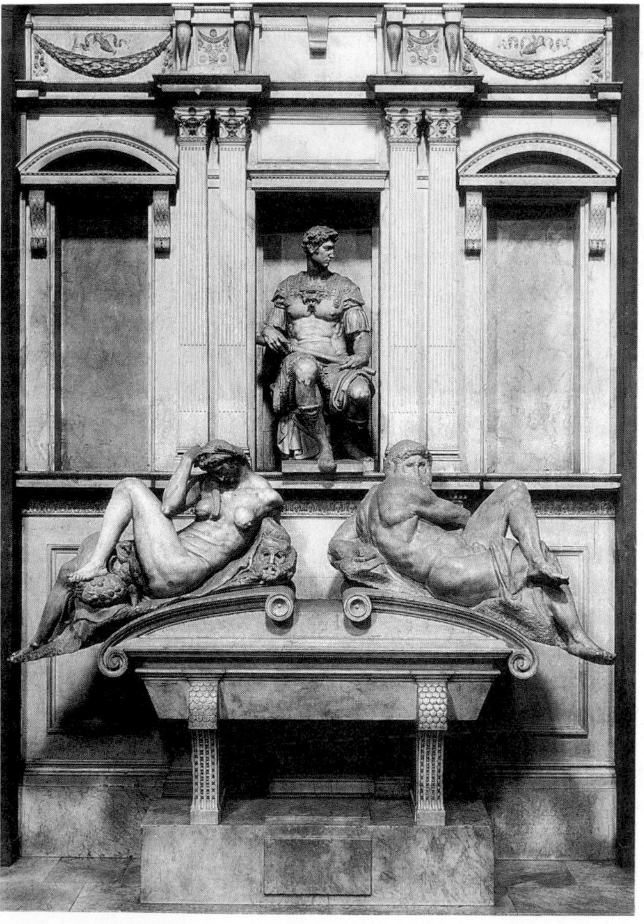

At opposite sides of the New Sacristy stand the tombs of Giuliano, Duke of Nemours, and Lorenzo, Duke of Urbino, son and grandson of Lorenzo the Magnificent. The tomb of Giuliano (FIG. **17-27**) is compositionally the twin of Lorenzo's. Both are unfinished; scholars believe that pairs of recumbent river gods were to be placed at the bottom of the sarcophagi, balancing the pairs of figures that rest on the sloping sides. The composition of the tombs has been a long-standing puzzle. How were they ultimately to look? What is their relationship to one another? What do they signify? The present arrangement seems quite unstable. Were the sloping figures meant to recline on a flat surface, or were they to be partly supported by the river-gods below them? We can do little more here than to state some of the questions; we cannot answer them in full. Art historians have suggested that the arrangement planned by Michelangelo, but never completed, can be interpreted as the ascent of the soul through the levels of the Neo-Platonic universe. The lowest level, represented by the river-gods, would have signified the underworld of brute matter, the source of evil. The two statues on the sarcophagi would then symbolize the realm of time: the specifically human world of the cycles of dawn, day, evening, and night. Man's state in this world of time is one of pain and anxiety, frustration and exhaustion. At left, the female figure of Night and, at right, the male figure of Day appear to be chained into never-relaxing tensions. Both exhibit that anguished twisting of the masses of the body in contrary directions seen in *The Bound Slave* (FIG. 17-22) and in the Sistine Chapel paintings. This contrapposto is the signature of Michelangelo. Day, with a body the thickness of a great tree and the anatomy of Hercules, strains his huge limbs against each other, his unfinished visage rising menacingly above his shoulder. Night, the symbol of rest, twists as if in troubled sleep, her posture wrenched and feverish. The artist has surrounded her with an owl, poppies, and a hideous mask symbolic of nightmares.

On their respective tombs, the figures of Lorenzo and Giuliano, rising above the troubles of the realm of time, represent the two ideal human types: the contemplative man (Lorenzo) and the active man (Giuliano). They thus become symbols for the two means by which human beings might achieve union with God: meditation or the active life fashioned after that of Christ. Michelangelo disdained to make portraits of the actual persons; who, he asked, would care what they looked like in a thousand years? What counted was the contemplation of what was beyond the corrosion of time. Giuliano, the active man (FIG. 17-27), his features quite generalized, sits clad in the armor of a Roman emperor, holding the baton of a commander, his head turned alertly, as if in council (he looks toward the statue of the Virgin at one end of the chapel). Across the room, Lorenzo, the contemplative man, sits wrapped in thought, his face in deep shadow. In these works, as in many others, Michelangelo suggests powerful psychic forces that cannot be translated into action but are ever on the verge of it. His prevailing mood is tension and constraint, even in the figures that seem to aspire to the ideal, to the timeless, perfect and unmoving. Michelangelo's style was born to disturb. It brings the serene, brief High Renaissance to an end.

The tensions and ambiguities of Michelangelo's style, which will pass over into the general style called Mannerism, are felt strongly in his architecture. His building activity for the Medici in Florence centered in and around San Lorenzo, and his Laurentian Library, built to house the great collections of the Medici, adjoins it. The building's peculiar layout was dictated by its special function and by its rather constricted site. Michelangelo had two contrasting spaces to work with: the long horizontal of the library proper, and the vertical of the vestibule. In the latter, everything is massive and plastic, but the planes and solids of the reading room are shallow and played down (perhaps so as not to distract the readers). The need to place the vestibule windows up high determined the narrow verticality of its elevation and proportions (FIG. **17-28**).

The vestibule, much taller than it is wide or long, gives the impression of a vertically compressed, shaftlike space. A vast, flowing stairway that almost fills the interior greatly adds to a sense of oppressiveness. Anyone schooled exclusively in the Classical architecture of Bramante and the High Renaissance would have been appalled by Michelangelo's indifference here to Classical norms in the use of the orders or in proportion. He uses columns in pairs and sinks them into the walls. He breaks columns around corners. He places consoles beneath columns that are

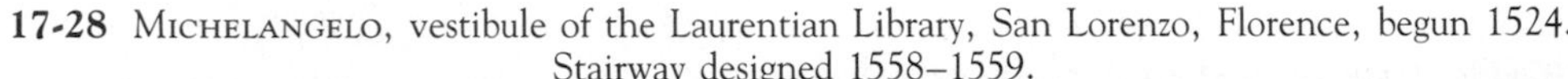

17-28 MICHELANGELO, vestibule of the Laurentian Library, San Lorenzo, Florence, begun 1524. Stairway designed 1558–1559.

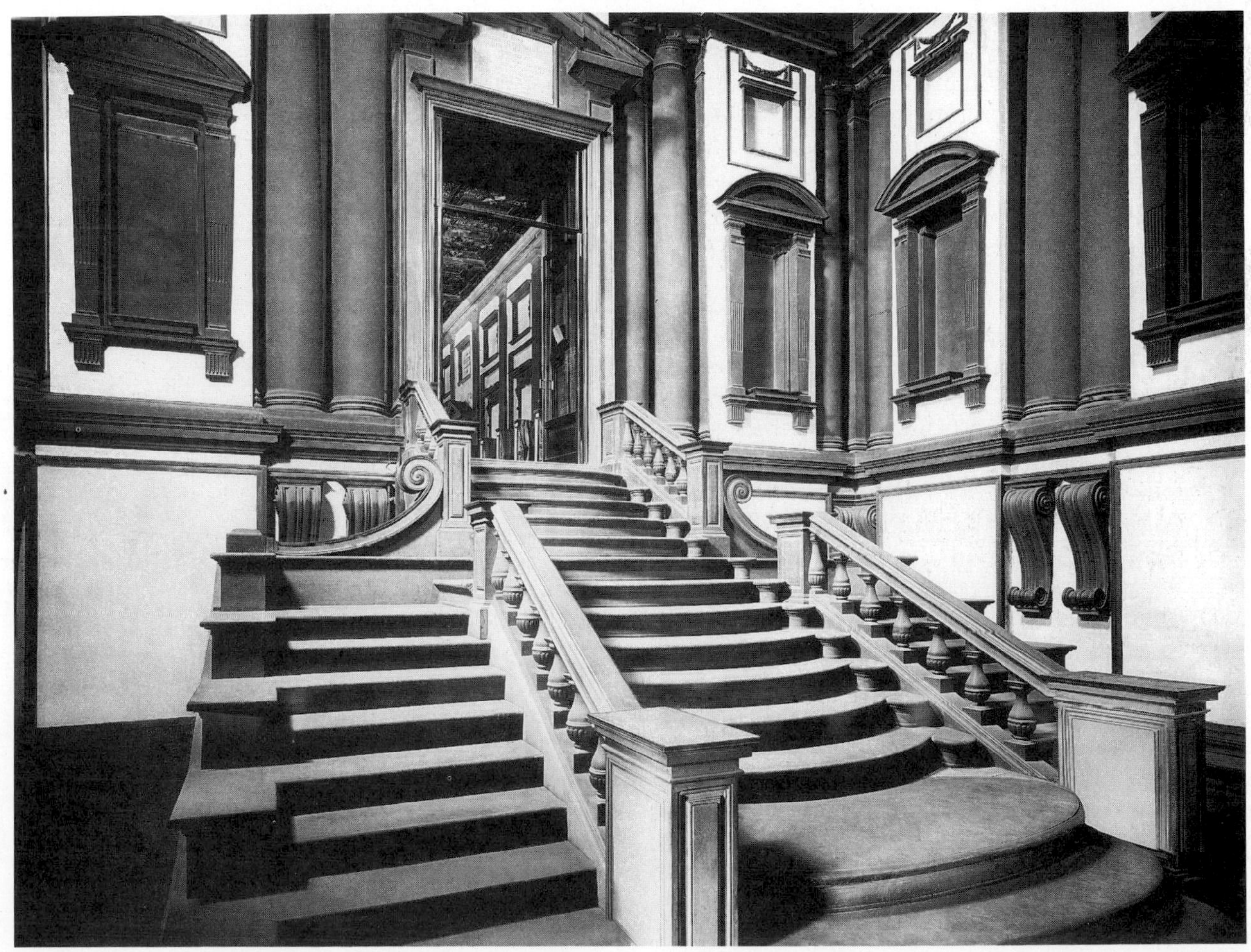

not meant to support them. He arbitrarily breaks through pediments, as well as through cornices and stringcourses. In short, Michelangelo disposes willfully and abruptly of Classical architecture as it was valued by other artists of the High Renaissance. But some features, often called Manneristic, were dictated by structural necessity. The recessed columns, for example, which seem neither to support nor to be supported, recently have been shown to perform a supporting function, in contrast with the standard, applied Classical orders, which are purely decorative. These paired stone columns, due to their greater compressive strength, actually add rigidity to the relatively thin brick walls and support the upper part of the structure. The "ambiguity" of the resulting wall surface is illusory, as the columns clearly have been recessed *into* the wall.

In any event, with his usual trailbreaking independence of mind, Michelangelo has sculptured an interior space that conveys all the strains and tensions we find in his statuary and in his painted figures. But, unlike Mannerist architects, especially his contemporary, Giulio Romano, in the Palazzo del Tè (FIGS. 17-47 and 17-48), he never tried to baffle or to confuse. His style in all three arts is wonderfully consistent. The key to that consistency may be found in his own words: "The members of an architectural structure follow the laws exemplified in the human body. He who . . . is not a good master of the nude . . . cannot understand the principles of architecture." His whole inspiration came from the beauty and majesty of the human body—the visible aspect of the human soul.

THE CAPITOLINE HILL

In his later years, Michelangelo turned increasingly to architecture. In 1537, he undertook to reorganize the Capitoline Hill (the Campidoglio) in Rome (FIGS. **17-29** and **17-30**), receiving from Pope Paul III a flattering and challenging commission. The pope wished to transform the ancient hill, which once had been the spiritual as well as the political capitol of Rome, into a symbol of power of the new Rome of the popes. The great challenge of the project was that Michelangelo was required to incorporate into his design two existing buildings—the medieval Palazzo dei Senatori (Palace of the Senators) on the east, and the fifteenth-century Palazzo dei Conservatori (Palace of the Conservators) on the south. These buildings formed an eighty-degree angle. Such preconditions might have defeated a lesser architect, but Michelangelo converted what seemed to be a limitation into the most impressive design for a civic unit formulated during the entire Renaissance.

Michelangelo reasoned that architecture should follow the form of the human body to the extent of

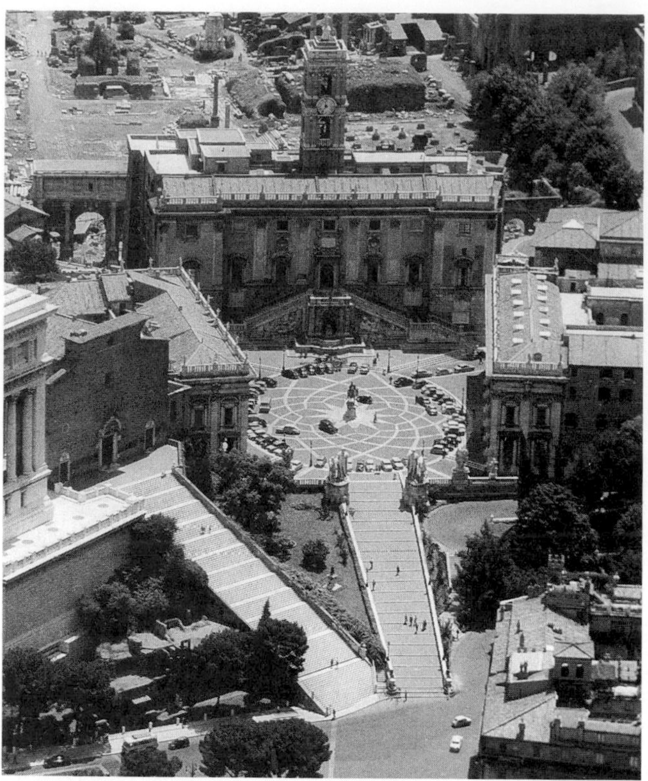

17-29 MICHELANGELO, the Capitoline Hill (the Campidoglio), Rome, designed *c.* 1537.

17-30 MICHELANGELO, plan for the Capitoline Hill. (Engraving by ÉTIENNE DUPÉRAC, *c.* 1569).

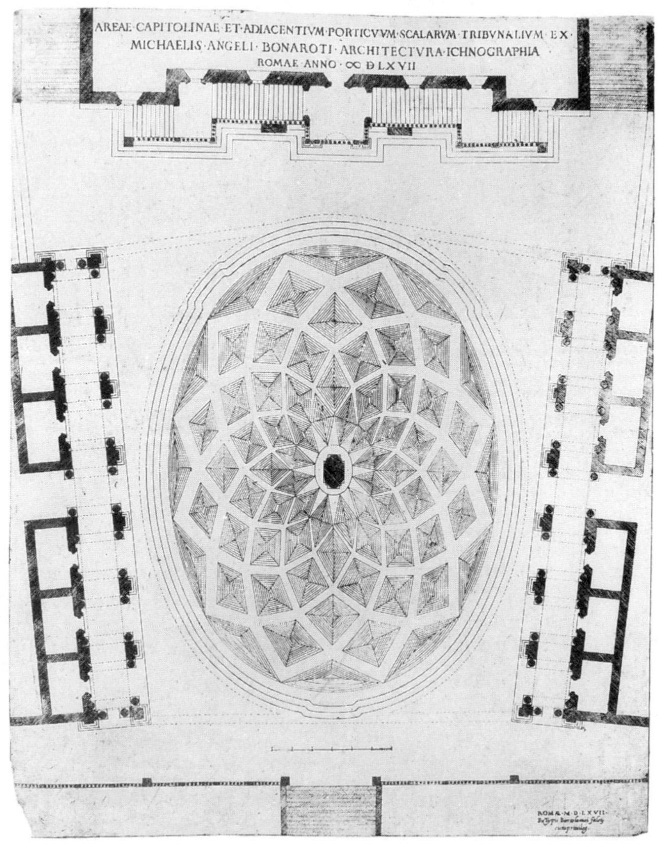

disposing units symmetrically around a central and unique axis, as the arms are related to the body or the eyes to the nose. It must have been with arguments like this that he convinced his sponsors of the necessity of balancing the Palazzo dei Conservatori, for which he was going to redesign the façade, with a similar unit on the north side of the square. To achieve balance and symmetry in his design, Michelangelo placed the new building (the Museo Capitolino, originally planned only as a portico with single rows of offices above and behind it) so that it stood at the same angle to the Palazzo dei Senatori as the Palazzo dei Conservatori, yielding a trapezoidal rather than a rectangular plan for the piazza (FIG. 17-30). All other design elements subsequently were adjusted to this unorthodox but basic feature.

The statue of Marcus Aurelius (FIG. 6-77), the only one of many equestrian statues of Roman emperors to survive the Middle Ages, became the focal point for the whole design. It was brought to the Capitoline Hill on the pope's orders and against the advice of Michelangelo, who might have preferred to carve his own centerpiece. The symbolic significance of the statue, which seemed to link the Rome of the caesars with the Rome of the popes, must have appealed to Paul III. To connect this central monument with the surrounding buildings, Michelangelo provided it with an oval base and placed it centrally in an oval pavement design (FIG. 17-30), the twelve points of which may have had ancient or medieval cosmological connotations. Michelangelo's choice of the oval is significant, as it was considered to be an unstable geometric figure and was shunned by earlier Renaissance architects. Given the trapezoidal shape of the piazza, however, the oval (which combines centralizing with axial qualities) was the figure best suited to relate the various elements of the design to one another. The oval later was to become the favorite geometric figure of the Baroque period.

Facing the piazza, the two lateral palazzi have identical, two-story façades (FIG. **17-31**). They introduce us again to the giant order, first seen in somewhat timid fashion in Alberti's Sant' Andrea in Mantua (FIG. 16-42). Michelangelo uses the giant order with much greater gusto and authority. The huge pilasters not only tie the two stories of the building together but provide a sturdy skeleton that actually functions as the main support of the structure. Walls have been all but eliminated. At ground level, the transition from the massive bulk of the pilaster-faced piers to the deep voids between them has been softened by the interposed columns. These columns carry straight lintels, in the manner earlier advocated by Alberti, but Michelangelo uses them with even greater logic and consistency than Alberti did. The façade of the third building on the piazza, the three-storied Palazzo dei Senatori, uses the same design elements as the other two palazzi, but in a less plastic fashion. The axial building, with its greater height, thus becomes a distinctive and commanding accent for the ensemble, providing variety within the design without disrupting its unity.

17-31 MICHELANGELO, Museo Capitolino, Capitoline Hill.

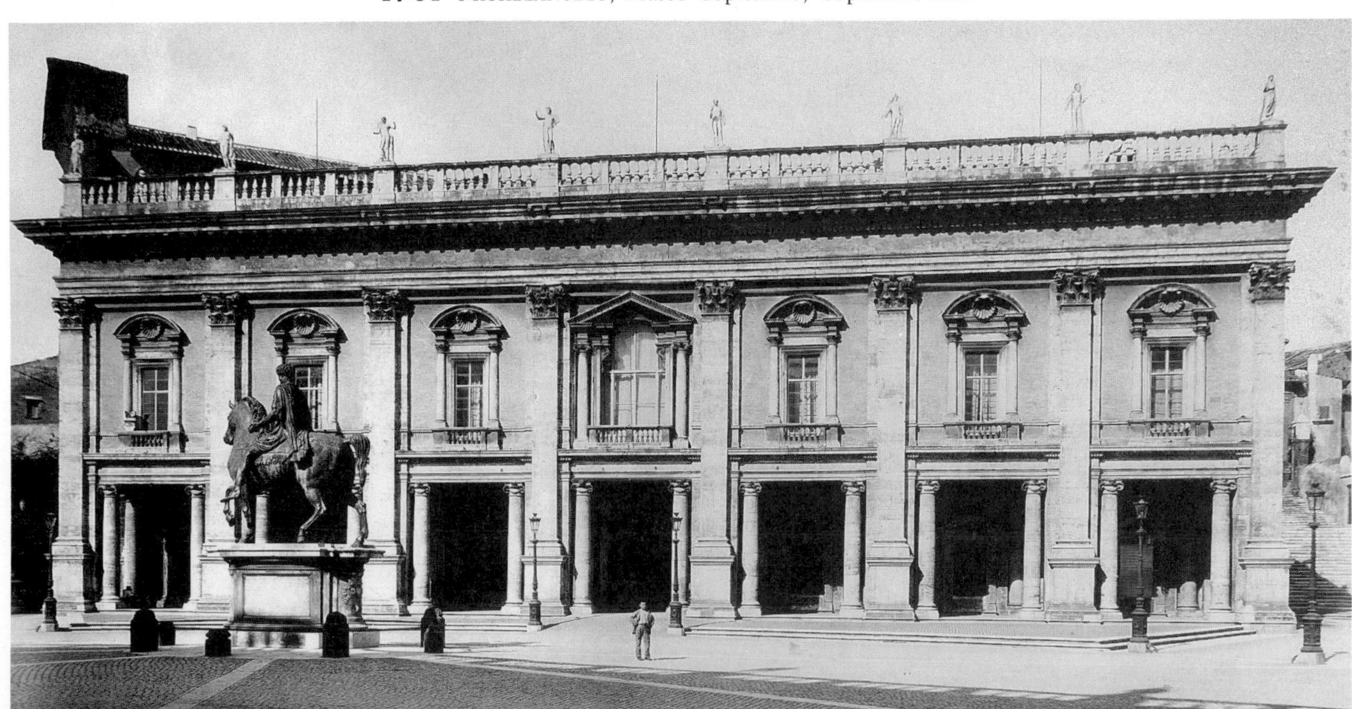

The piazza might have become a roomlike enclosure, as Renaissance squares often were and as Alberti, in his treatise, had advised that they be. But again Michelangelo parts with tradition and points to the future. Instead of enclosing his piazza with four walls punctuated by entrances leading through their centers, as a roomlike enclosure would seem to demand, he left the fourth side open. A fourth wall is merely suggested by a balustrade and a thin screen of Classical statuary that effectively defines the limits of the piazza without obstructing a panoramic view across the city's roofs toward the Vatican. The accidental symbolism of this axis must have pleased the pope just as much as the piazza's dynamic design, and the sweeping vista must have pleased later Baroque planners.

ST. PETER'S

Michelangelo took over the supervision of the building of the new St. Peter's a few years after he had designed the Capitoline Hill; neither project was finished at the time of his death. His work on St. Peter's, after efforts by a succession of architects following the death of Bramante, apparently became a show of dedication, thankless and without pay, on his own decision. Writing in May 1557 to his friend Giorgio Vasari, Michelangelo complained:

> God is my witness how much against my will it was that Pope Paul forced me into this work on St. Peter's in Rome ten years ago. If the work had been continued from that time forward as it was begun, it would by now have been as far advanced as I had reason to hope.*

Among Michelangelo's difficulties had been his struggle to preserve and carry through Bramante's original plan (FIG. 17-7), which he praised even as he changed it:

> It cannot be denied that Bramante was a skillful architect and the equal of any one from the time of the ancients until now. It was he who drew up the original plan of St. Peter's, not full of confusion but clear and straightforward. . . . It was considered to be a fine design, and there is still evidence that it was so: indeed, every architect who has departed from Bramante's plan . . . has departed from the right way.†

We already have seen Michelangelo's respect for a good plan in his willingness to carry out Sangallo's design for the Farnese Palace (FIG. 17-12) with only minor modifications. With Bramante's plan for St. Peter's, Michelangelo managed a major concentration, reducing the central fabric from a number of interlocking crosses to a compact, domed Greek cross inscribed in a square and fronted with a Pantheon-like, double-columned portico (FIG. **17-32**). Without destroying the centralizing features of Bramante's plan, Michelangelo, with a few strokes of the pen, converted its snowflake complexity into massive, cohesive unity.

The same striving for a unified and cohesive design is visible in Michelangelo's treatment of the building's exterior. Later changes to the front of the church make the west (apse) end (FIG. **17-33**) the best place to see his style and intention. The colossal order again serves him nobly, as the giant pilasters march around the undulating wall surfaces, confining the movement without interrupting it. The architectural sculpturing, which Michelangelo began in the Laurentian Library (FIG. 17-28), here extends up from the ground through the attic stories and moves on into the drum and the dome, pulling the whole building together into a unity from base to summit. Baroque architects will learn much from this kind of integral design, which ultimately is based on Michelangelo's conviction that architecture is one with the organic beauty of the human form. The domed west end—as majes-

17-32 MICHELANGELO, plan for St. Peter's, the Vatican, Rome.

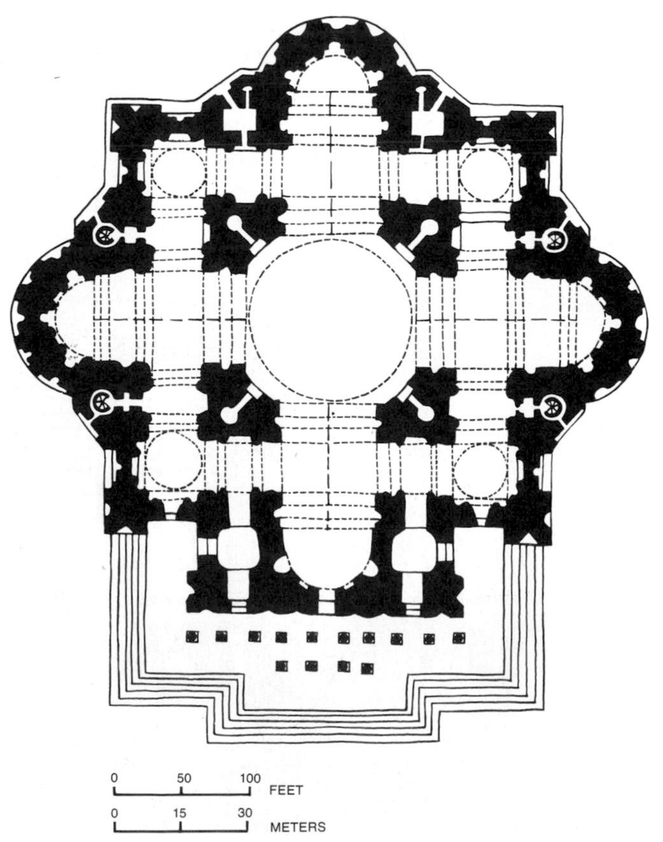

*In Robert J. Clements, ed., *Michelangelo: A Self-Portrait* (Englewood Cliffs, NJ: Prentice-Hall, 1964), p. 57.

†In E. G. Holt, ed., *Literary Sources of Art History* (Princeton, NJ: Princeton University Press, 1947), p. 195.

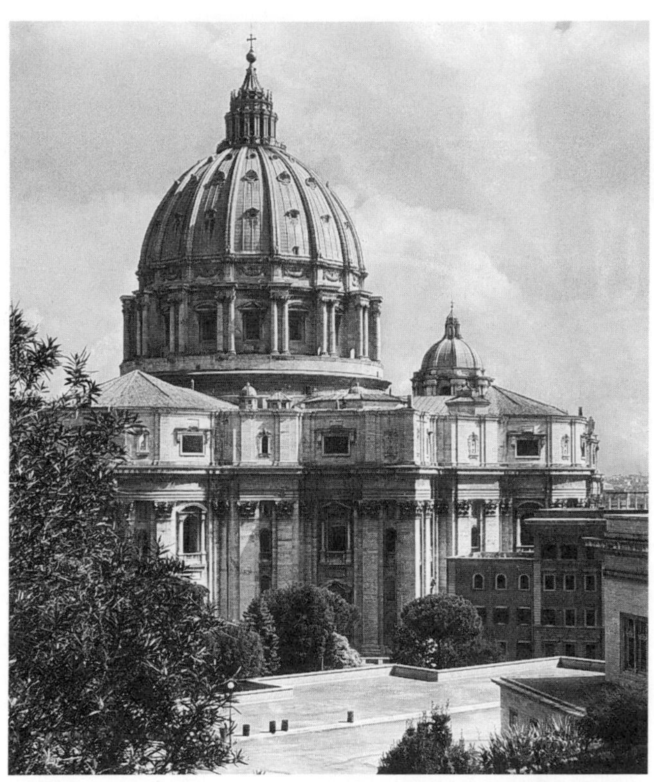

17-33 MICHELANGELO, St. Peter's, 1546–1564 (view from the northwest). Dome completed by GIACOMO DELLA PORTA in 1590.

tic as it is today and as influential as it has been on architecture throughout the centuries—is not quite as it was intended to be. Originally, Michelangelo had planned a dome with a raised silhouette, like that of Florence Cathedral. But in his final version he decided on a hemispheric dome (FIG. **17-34**) to moderate the verticality of the design of the lower stories and to establish a balance between dynamic and static elements. However, when GIACOMO DELLA PORTA executed the dome after Michelangelo's death, he restored the earlier high design, ignoring Michelangelo's later version. Giacomo's reasons were probably the same ones that had impelled Brunelleschi to use an ogival section for his Florentine dome (FIG. 16-15): greater stability and ease of construction. The result is that the dome seems to be rising from its base, rather than resting firmly on it—an effect that Michelangelo might not have approved. Nevertheless, the dome of St. Peter's is probably the most impressive and beautiful in the world and has served as a model to generations of architects to this day.

THE LAST JUDGMENT

While Michelangelo endured the tribulations of age and the long frustrations of art, his soul was further oppressed by the events that had been erupting

17-34 MICHELANGELO, south elevation of St. Peter's. (Engraving by ÉTIENNE DUPÉRAC, c. 1569.)

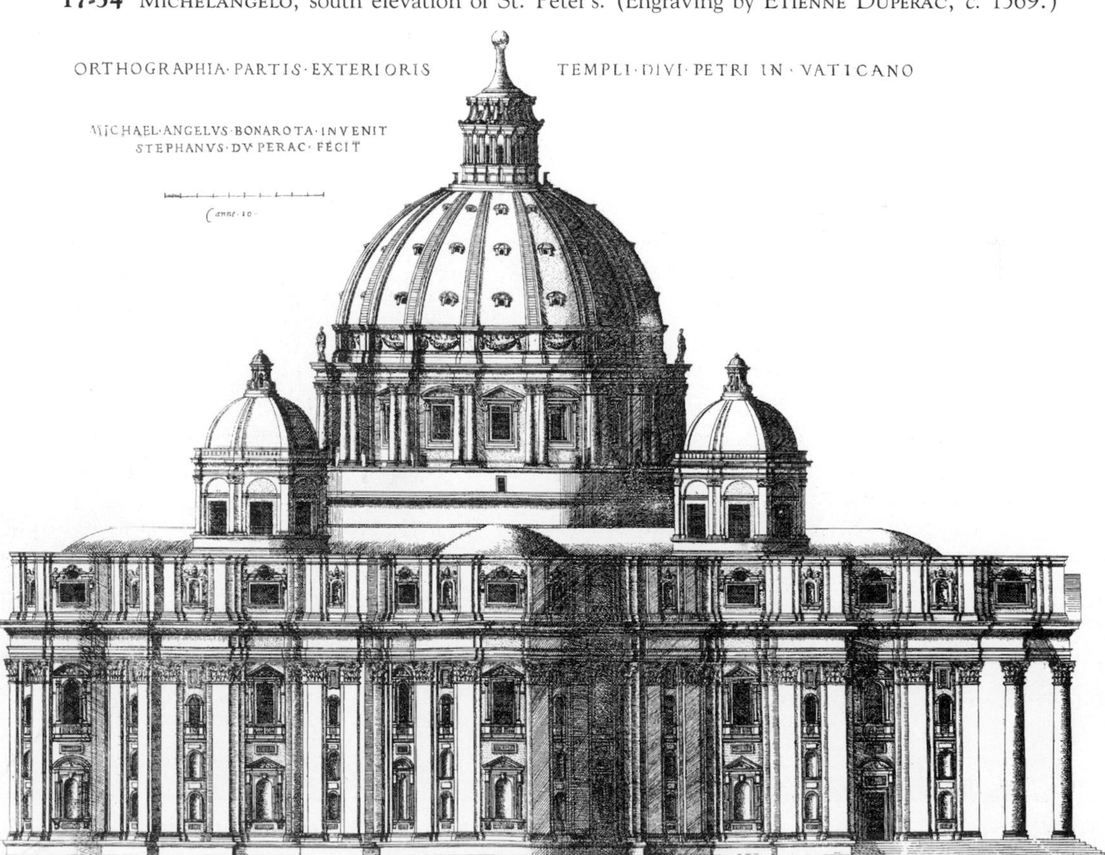

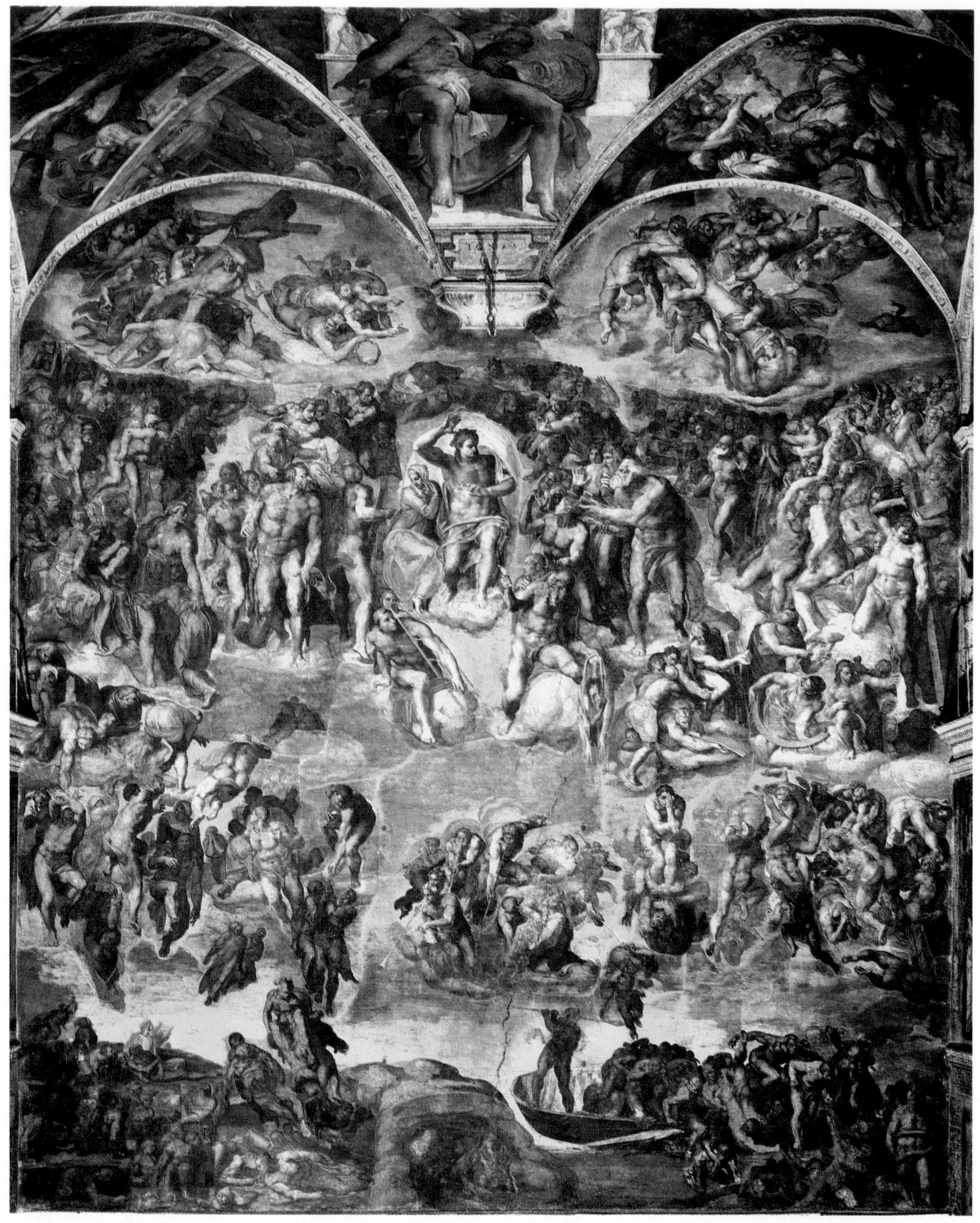

17-35 MICHELANGELO, *The Last Judgment,* fresco on the altar wall of the Sistine Chapel (before restoration), 1534–1541. The Vatican, Rome.

around him from the time he fled Florence as a young man after the fall of the Medici. The liberties of Florence were destroyed; the Medici had returned as tyrants, and Michelangelo felt himself an exile, even while he worked for them. Italy was laid to waste by the French and Spanish invasions, and the Protestant Reformation divided Christendom into warring camps. The Catholic Counter-Reformation gained force, and Europe was to be racked by religious war for more than a century. The glories of the High Renaissance faded, and the philosophy of Humanism retreated before the resurgence of a religious spirit that was often pessimistic, moralizing, and grimly fanatical, whether Protestant or Catholic. Michelangelo himself turned from his Humanist beginnings to a deep religious preoccupation with the fate of man and of his own soul. His sense that the world had gone mad and that man, forsaking God, was doomed must have been sharpened by his still vivid memory of Savonarola's foreboding summons of sinners to repent and by his very close reading of Dante.

In this spirit, Michelangelo undertook the great *Last Judgment* fresco on the altar wall of the Sistine Chapel (FIG. **17-35**). The change in this fresco from the mood of the ceiling paintings of twenty years before is radical. In the ceiling frescoes, fallen man was to have been exalted by the coming of the Redeemer, announced everywhere in the thronging figures of the ceiling panels. Now, on the altar wall, Christ indeed has come, but as the medieval judge of the world—a giant whose mighty right arm is lifted in a gesture of damnation so broad and universal as to suggest he will destroy all creation, Heaven and earth alike. The choirs of Heaven surrounding him pulse with anxiety and awe. The spaces below are crowded with trumpeting angels, the ascending figures of the just, and the downward-hurtling figures of the damned. On the left, the dead awake and assume flesh; on the right, the damned are tormented by demons whose gargoyle masks and burning eyes revive the demons of the Romanesque tympana (FIG. 9-31). Martyrs who suffered especially agonizing deaths crouch below the Judge. One of them, St. Bartholomew, who was skinned alive, holds the flaying knife and the skin, in which hangs a grotesque self-portrait of Michelangelo. We cannot find any trace of the old Neo-Platonic aspiration to beauty anywhere in this fresco. The figures are grotesquely huge and violently twisted, with small heads and contorted features. The expressive power of ugliness and terror in the service of a terrible message reigns throughout the composition.

Michelangelo's art began in the manner of the fifteenth century, rose to an idealizing height in the High Renaissance, and, at the end, moved toward the Baroque. Like a colossus, he bestrides three centuries. He became the archetype of the supreme genius who transcends the rules by making his own. Few artists could escape his influence, and variations on his style will constitute much of artistic experiment for centuries.

Andrea del Sarto and Correggio

The towering achievements of Raphael and Michelangelo in Rome tend to obscure everything else that was done during their time. Nevertheless, aside from the flourishing Venetian school, some excellent artists were active in other parts of Italy during the first part of the sixteenth century. One of these, the Florentine ANDREA DEL SARTO (1486–1531), expresses, in his early paintings, the ideals of the High Renaissance with almost as much clarity and distinction as does Raphael.

Andrea's *Madonna of the Harpies* (FIG. **17-36**) shows the Madonna standing majestically on an altarlike base decorated with sphinxes (figures misidentified by Vasari as harpies—hence, the name of the painting). The composition is based on a massive and imposing figure pyramid, the static qualities of which are relieved by the opposing contrapposto poses of the flanking saints—a favorite and effective High

17-36 ANDREA DEL SARTO, *Madonna of the Harpies*, 1517. Oil on wood, approx. 6′ 9″ × 5′ 10″. Galleria degli Uffizi, Florence.

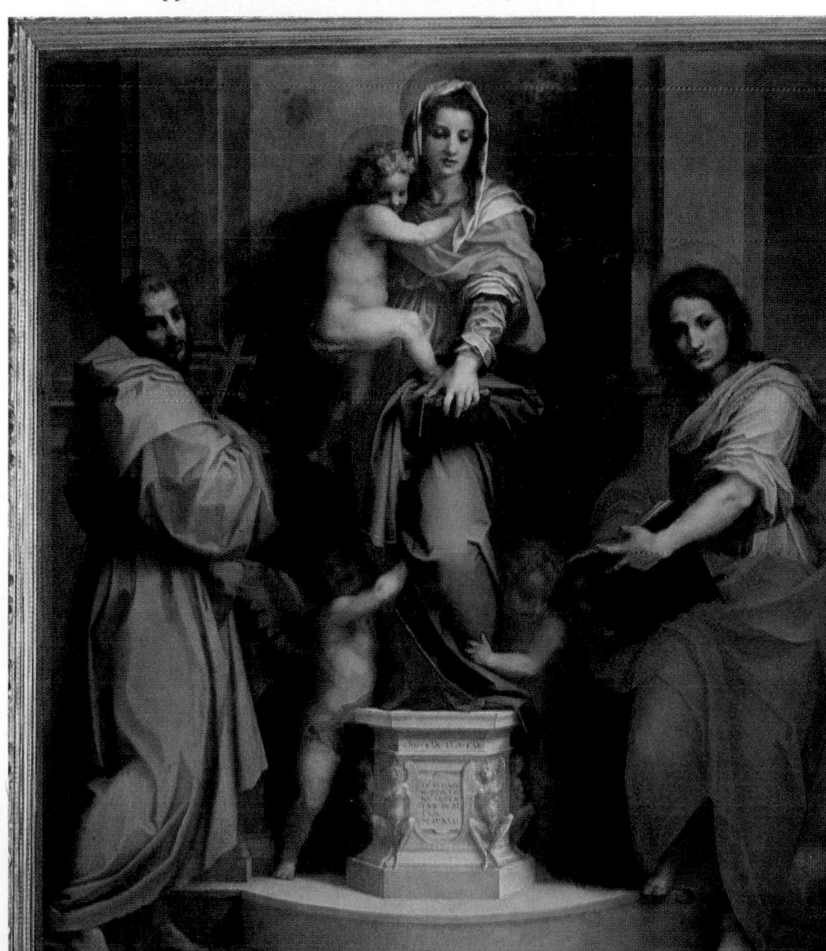

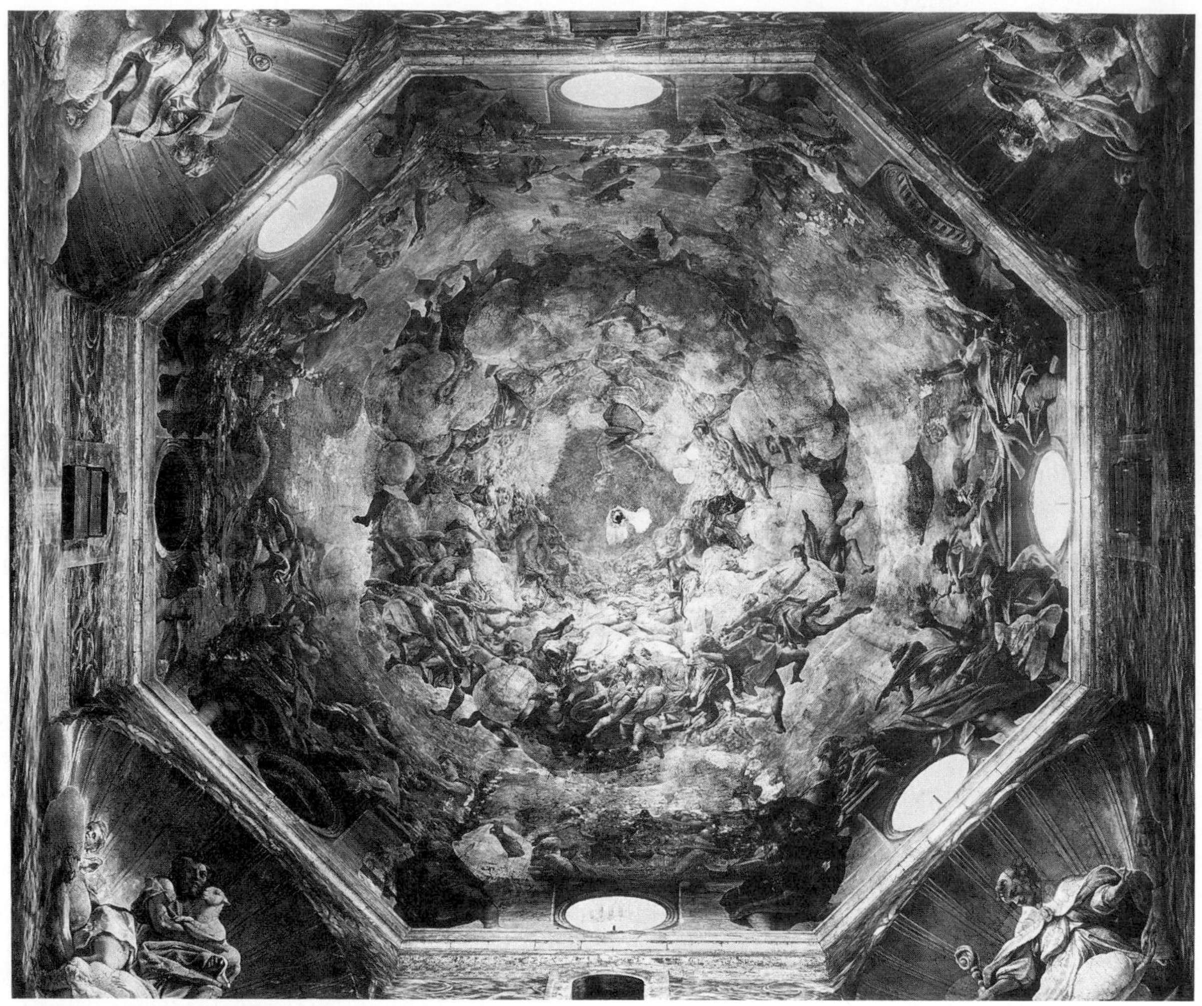

17-37 CORREGGIO, *The Assumption of the Virgin,* 1526–1530. Fresco. Dome of Parma Cathedral, Italy.

Renaissance device to introduce variety into symmetry. The potentially rigid pyramid is softened further by the skillful coordination of the figures' poses into an organic movement that leads from St. Francis (on the left) to the Virgin, to St. John the Evangelist, and downward from him toward the observer. This main movement is either echoed or countered by numerous secondary movements brought into perfect formal balance in a faultless compositional performance. The soft modeling of the forms is based on Leonardo but does not affect the colors, which are rich and warm. Andrea's sense of and ability to handle color set him apart from his central Italian contemporaries; he is perhaps the only Renaissance artist to transpose his rich color schemes from panels into frescoes. Andrea's later compositions tend to be less firmly knit and his color schemes move toward the cool harshness that will become typical of Mannerist painting. Although he was greatly admired in the sixteenth and seventeenth centuries, Andrea's fame has waned; today, he seems to be remembered primarily as the teacher of Jacopo da Pontormo, Rosso Fiorentino, and Vasari and, thus, as one of the forerunners of Mannerism.

Andrea del Sarto may still be placed firmly in the High Renaissance, but his northern Italian contemporary, CORREGGIO (Antonio Allegri da Correggio, *c.* 1489–1534), of Parma, is almost impossible to classify. A solitary genius, Correggio brings together many stylistic trends, including those of Leonardo, Raphael, and the Venetians. Yet he developed a unique personal style, which, if it must be labeled, might best be called "proto-Baroque." Historically, his most enduring contribution was the development of illusionistic ceiling perspectives to a point seldom surpassed by his Baroque emulators. At Mantua, Mantegna had painted a hole into the ceiling of the Camera degli Sposi (FIG. 16-65); some fifty years later, Correggio painted away the entire dome of the cathedral of Parma (FIG. **17-37**). Opening up the cupola, the artist shows his audience a view of the sky, with concentric rings of clouds among which hundreds of soaring figures perform a wildly pirouetting dance in celebration of *The Assumption of the Virgin.* These angelic creatures will become permanent tenants of numerous Baroque churches in later centuries. Correggio was also an influential painter of religious panels, in which he forecast many other Baroque compositional devices. As a painter of erotic mythological subjects, he had few equals. *Jupiter and Io* (FIG. **17-38**) depicts a suavely sensual vision out of the pagan past. The painting is one of a series on the loves of Jupiter that Correggio painted for the Duke of Mantua, Federigo Gonzaga. The god, who assumed many disguises to hide his numerous liaisons from his wife, Juno, appears here as a cloud that embraces the willing nymph. The soft, smoky modeling (sfumato), derived from Leonardo, is fused with glowing color and renders the voluptuous moment with exquisite subtlety. Even Titian, in his mythological paintings, rarely was able to match the sensuous quality expressed here by Correggio. Unlike Andrea del Sarto, Correggio was little appreciated by his contemporaries; later, during the seventeenth century, Baroque painters recognized him as a kindred spirit.

17-38 CORREGGIO, *Jupiter and Io,* c. 1532. Oil on canvas, approx. 64½″ × 29¾″. Kunsthistorisches Museum, Vienna.

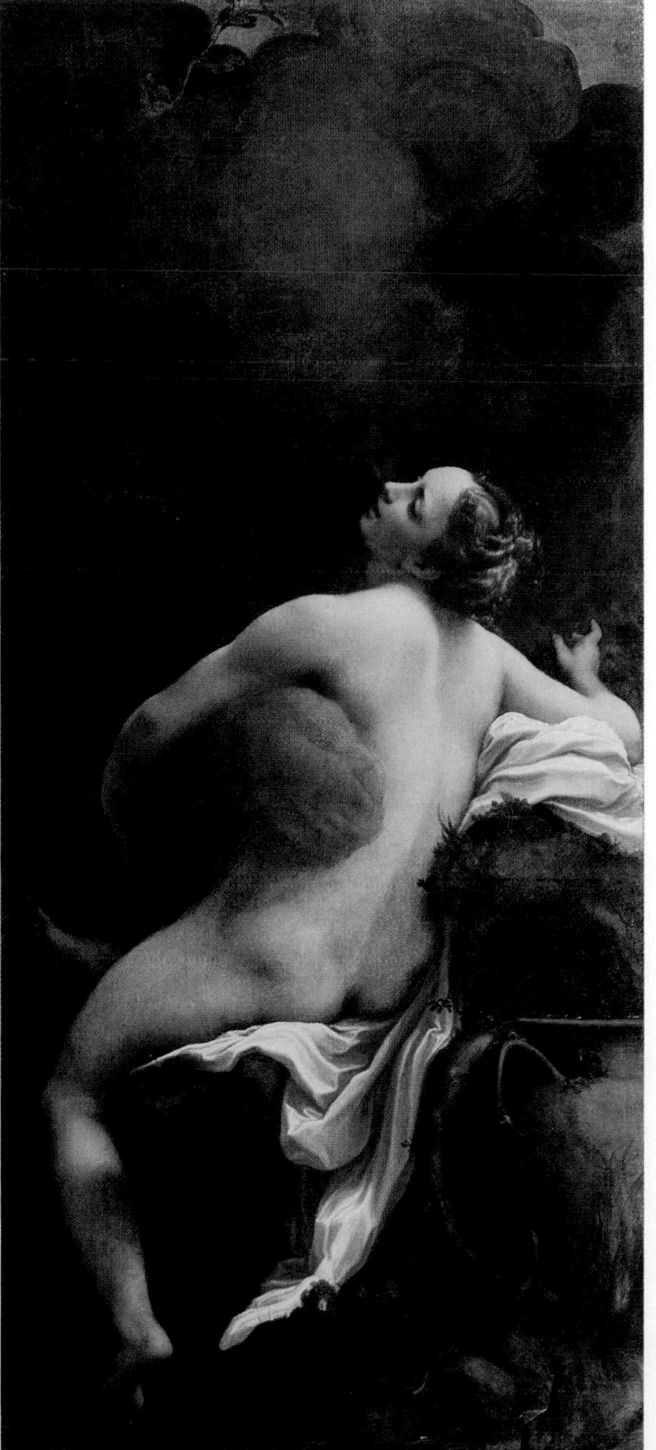

MANNERISM

The term *Mannerism* refers to certain tendencies in the art of the Late Renaissance—the period from the death of Raphael (1520) to the end of the sixteenth century. In its broadest sense, the word means excessive or affected adherence to a distinctive manner, especially in art and literature. In its early application to these tendencies, it also carried the pejorative connotation of the term when applied to a description of individual behavior. Today, we view these styles in art and literature more objectively and appreciate much that is excellent in them.

The artists of the Early Renaissance and the High Renaissance developed their characteristic styles from the studious observation of nature and the formulation of a pictorial science. By the time Mannerism matured (after 1520), all the representational problems had been solved; a vast body of knowledge was there to be learned from. In addition, an age of antiquarianism and archeology now was bringing to light thousands of remnants of ancient Roman art. The Mannerists, instead of continuing the earlier research into nature and natural appearance, turned for their models to the masters of the High Renaissance (especially Michelangelo) and to Roman sculpture (especially relief sculpture). Instead of nature as their teacher, they took art. One could say that whereas their predecessors sought nature and found their style, the Mannerists looked first for a style and found a manner.

Following Michelangelo's example in one respect, the Mannerists declared each artist's right to a personal interpretation of the rules, looking for inspiration to the Platonic Idea, which they referred to as the *disegno interno* and with which they fired their creative fervor. They saw a roughness in nature that needed refining, and they turned to where it had already been refined in art.

From the Antique and the High Renaissance, artists, to the limits of their own ingenuity and skill, abstracted forms that they idealized further, so that the typical Mannneristic picture or statue looks like an original essay in human form somewhat removed from nature. As *maniera* (the name given the style by Mannerist theorists) is almost exclusively an art of the human figure, its commonest expression is in paintings of numerous figures performing what appears to be a complicated dance and pantomime, in which the compositions, as well as the fanciful gestures and attitudes, are deliberately intricate. The movements are so studied and artificial that they remind us not of the great stage dramatics of the High Renaissance but of an involved choreography for interpretive dancers. Where the art of the High Renaissance strives for balance, Mannerism seeks instability. The calm equilibrium of the former is replaced by a restlessness that leads to distortions, exaggerations, and bizarre posturings on the one hand and sinuously graceful, often athletic attitudes on the other. The positions and actions of the figures often have little to do with the subject. The Mannerist requirement of "invention" leads its practitioner to the maniera, a self-conscious stylization involving complexity, caprice, bizarre fantasy (the "conceit"), elegance, preciosity, and polish. Mannerism is an art made for aristocratic patrons by artists who sense that their profession is worthy of honor and the admiration of kings. It is an age when monarchs and grandees would plead for anything from the hands of Raphael and Michelangelo, if only a sketch. The concepts of "classic" and "old master" are abroad, and artists are being called *divino*. Artists become conscious of their own personalities, powers of imagination, and technical skills; they acquire learning and aim at virtuosity. They cultivate not the knowledge of nature but the intricacies of art.

In Painting

The Descent from the Cross (FIG. **17-39**) by JACOPO DA PONTORMO (1494–1556) exhibits almost all the stylistic features characteristic of the early phase of Mannerism in painting. The figures crowd the composition, pushing into the front plane and almost completely blotting out the setting. The figure masses are disposed around the frame of the picture, leaving a void in the center, where High Renaissance artists had concentrated their masses. The composition has no focal point, and the figures swing around the edges of the painting without coming to rest. The representation of space is as strange as the representation of the human figure. Mannerist space is ambiguous; we are never quite sure where it is going or just where the figures are in it. We do not know how far back the depicted space extends, although its limit is defined by the figure at the top. But we do know that the space is really too shallow for what is taking place in it. For example, Pontormo does not provide any space for the body belonging to the head that appears immediately over Christ's.

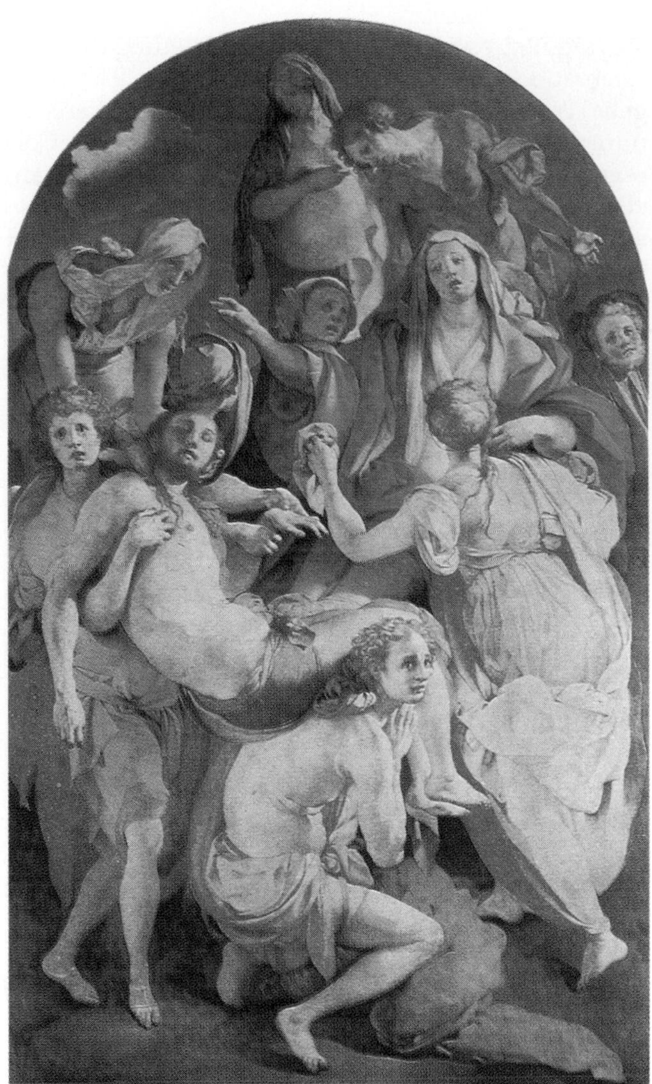

17-39 JACOPO DA PONTORMO, *The Descent from the Cross*, 1525–1528. Oil on wood, approx. 10′ 3″ × 6′ 6″. Capponi Chapel, Santa Felicità, Florence.

The centrifugal effect of the positions of the figures is strengthened by the curiously anxious glances that the actors cast out of the picture in all directions. Many figures are characterized by an athletic bending and twisting, with distortions (a torso cannot bend at the point at which the foreground figure's does), an elastic elongation of the limbs, and a rendering of the heads as uniformly small and oval. The composition is jarred further by clashing colors, which are unnatural and totally unlike the sonorous primary color chords used by painters of the High Renaissance. The mood of the painting is hard to describe; it seems the vision of an inordinately sensitive soul, perhaps itself driven, as are the actors, by nervous terrors. The psy-

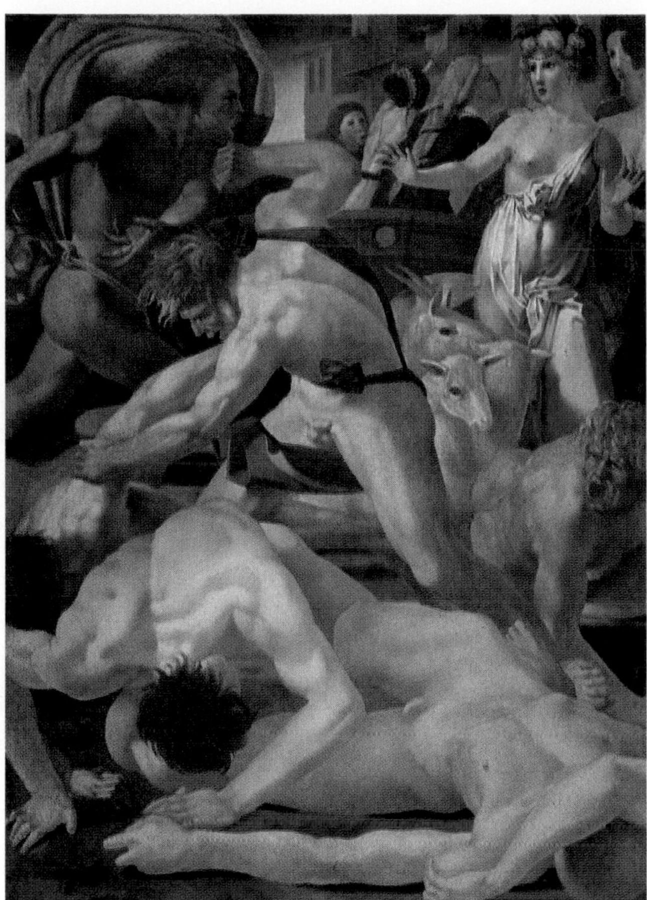

17-40 Rosso Fiorentino, *Moses Defending the Daughters of Jethro,* 1523. Oil on canvas, approx. 63″ × 46″. Galleria degli Uffizi, Florence.

chic dissonance of the composition would indeed appear out of tune to a Classical artist.

Rosso Fiorentino (1494–1540), who was, like Pontormo, a pupil of Andrea del Sarto, compresses space in a manner similar to that used by Pontormo but fills it with turbulent action. Rosso's painting of *Moses Defending the Daughters of Jethro* (fig. **17-40**) recalls the titanic struggles and powerful musculature of Michelangelo's figures on the Sistine Chapel ceiling, but Rosso's purpose is not so much expressive as it is inventive of athletic poses. At the same time, although the figures are modeled for three-dimensional effect, they are compressed within a limited space, so that surface is emphasized as a two-dimensional pattern. By 1530, when Francis I of France called him to decorate the palace at Fontainebleau, Rosso had all but forsaken this early furor for more graceful, elongated forms (fig. 18-49).

Correggio's pupil Parmigianino (Girolamo Francesco Maria Mazzola, 1503–1540), in his best-known work, *Madonna with the Long Neck* (fig. **17-41**), achieves the elegance that is a principal aim of Mannerism. He smoothly combines the influences of Correggio and Raphael in a picture of exquisite grace and precious sweetness. The small, oval head of the Madonna; her long, slender neck; the unbelievable length and delicacy of her hand; and the sinuous, swaying elongation of her frame are all marks of the aristocratic, gorgeously artificial taste of a later phase of Mannerism. Here is Leonardo distilled through Correggio. On the left stands a bevy of angelic creatures, melting with emotions as soft and smooth as their limbs (the left side of the composition is quite in the manner of Correggio). On the right, the artist has included a line of columns without capitals—an enigmatic setting for an enigmatic figure with a scroll, whose distance from the foreground is immeasurable and ambiguous.

The Mannerists sought a generally beautiful style that had its rules, but rules, as we have seen, that still

17-41 Parmigianino, *Madonna with the Long Neck,* c. 1535. Oil on wood, approx. 7′ 1″ × 4′ 4″. Galleria degli Uffizi, Florence.

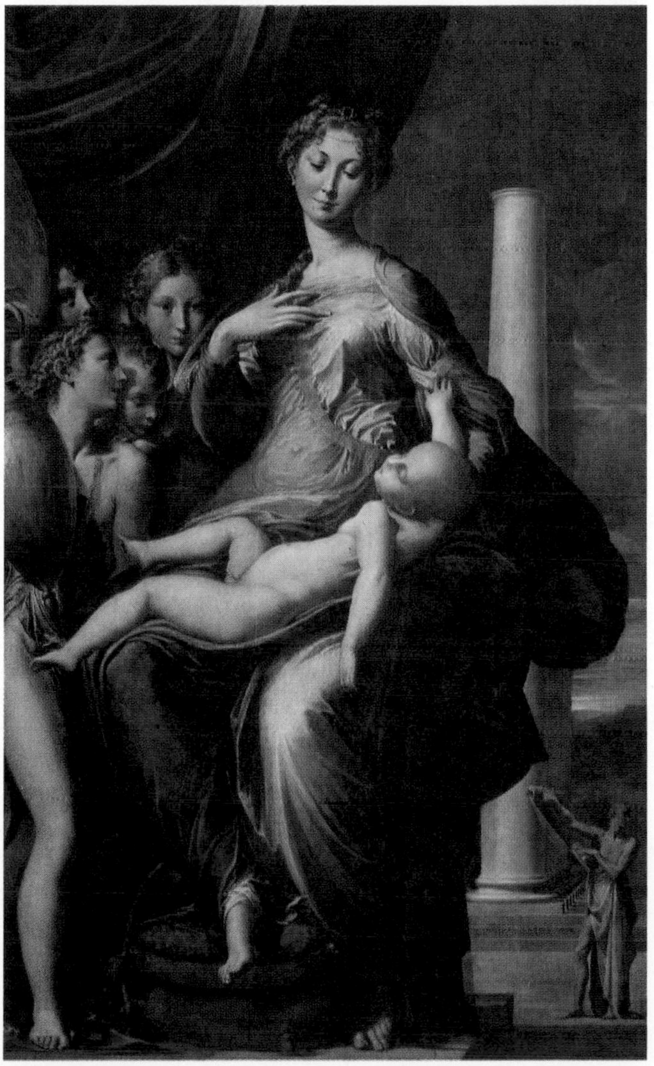

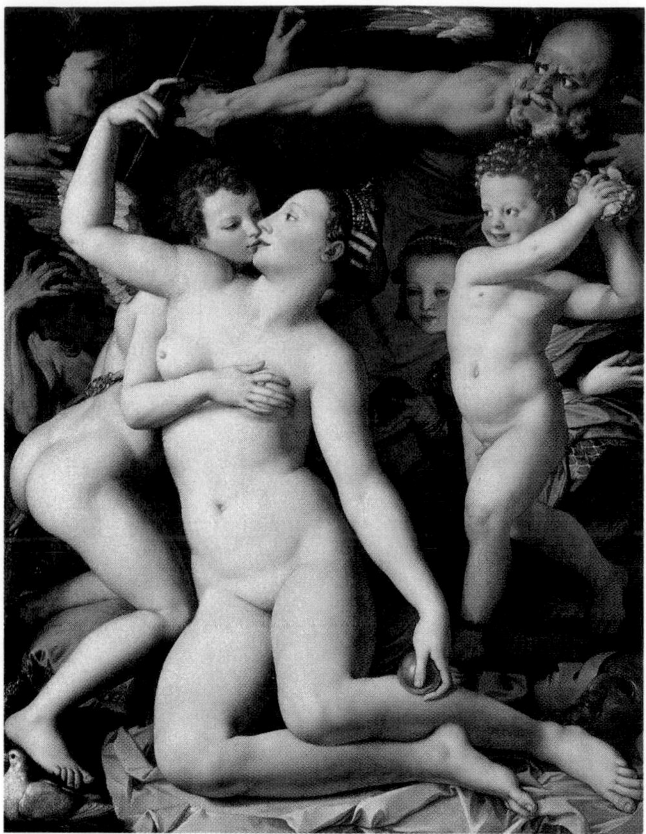

17-42 BRONZINO, *Venus, Cupid, Folly, and Time (The Exposure of Luxury)*, c. 1546. Oil on wood, approx. 61″ × $56\frac{3}{4}$″. Reproduced by courtesy of the Trustees of the National Gallery, London.

permitted artists the free play of their powers of invention. Thus, although all Mannerist paintings share common features, each artist, as it were, has an individualized, recognizable signature.

All the points made thus far about Mannerist composition are recognizable in *Venus, Cupid, Folly, and Time* (or *The Exposure of Luxury*, FIG. **17-42**) by BRONZINO (Agnolo di Cosimo, 1503–1572). A pupil of Pontormo, Bronzino was a Florentine and painter to Cosimo I, first Grand Duke of Tuscany. In this painting, he manifests the Mannerist fondness for extremely learned and intricate allegories that often have lascivious undertones; we are now far from the simple and monumental statements and forms of the High Renaissance. Venus, fondled by her son Cupid, is uncovered by Time, while Folly prepares to bombard them with roses; other figures represent Hatred and Inconstancy. The masks, a favorite device of the Mannerists, symbolize falseness. The picture seems to convey that love—accompanied by its opposite, hatred, and plagued by inconstancy—is foolish, and its folly will be discovered in time. But, as in many Mannerist paintings, the meaning is ambiguous, and interpretations vary. The figures are drawn around the front plane and almost entirely block the space, although there really is no space. The contours are strong and sculptural, the surfaces, of enamel smoothness. Of special interest are the heads, hands, and feet, for the Mannerists considered the extremities to be the carriers of grace and the clever depiction of them evidence of skill in maniera.

The sophisticated elegance sought by the Mannerist painter most often was achieved in portraiture, in which the Mannerists excelled. Bronzino's *Portrait of a Young Man* (FIG. **17-43**) is exemplary of Mannerist portraiture. The subject is a proud youth—a man of books and intellectual society, rather than a man of action or a merchant. His cool demeanor is carefully affected, a calculated attitude of nonchalance toward the observing world. This austere and incommunicative formality is standard for the Mannerist portrait. It asserts the rank and station of the subject, but not his personality. The haughty poise, the graceful, long-fingered hands, the book, the masks, and the severe architecture all suggest the traits and environment of the high-bred, disdainful patrician. The somber Spanish black of the young man's doublet and cap (this is the century of Spanish etiquette) and the

17-43 BRONZINO, *Portrait of a Young Man*, c. 1550. Oil on wood, approx. $37\frac{5}{8}$″ × $29\frac{1}{2}$″. Metropolitan Museum of Art, New York (H. O. Havemeyer Collection, bequest of Mrs. H. O. Havemeyer, 1929).

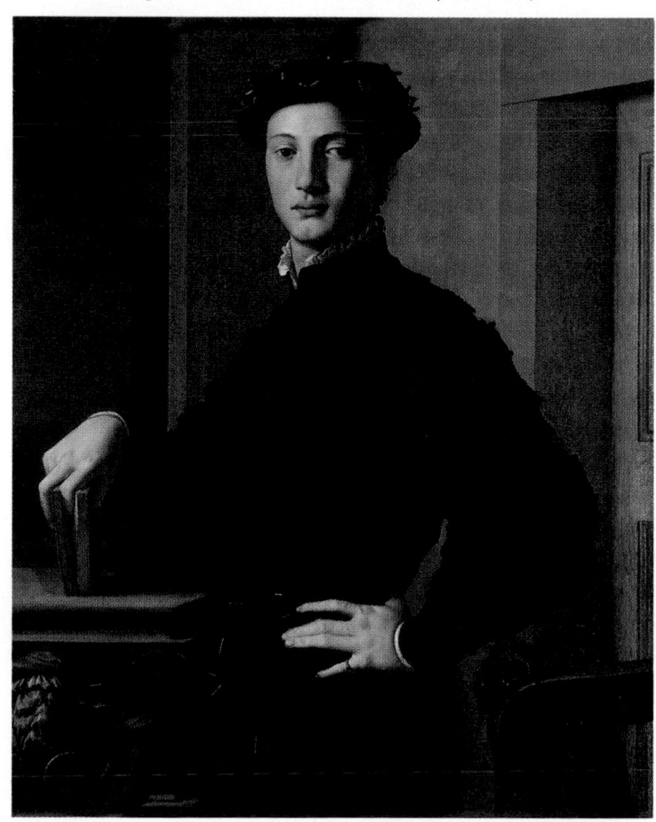

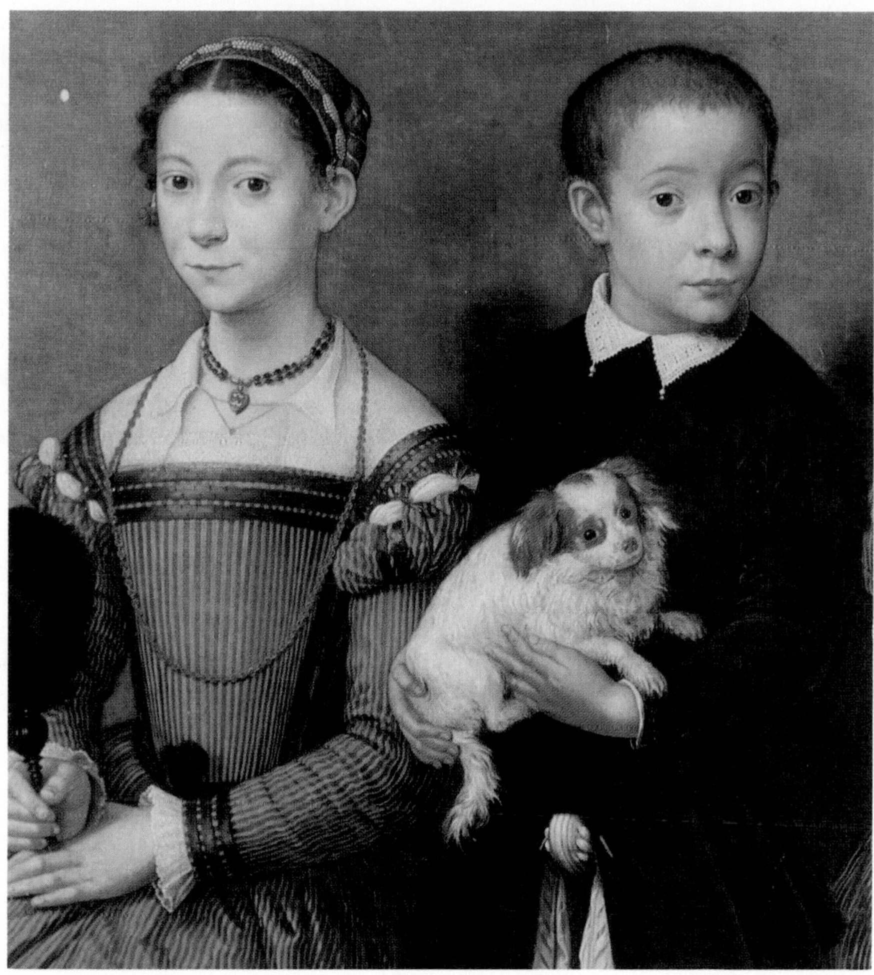

17-44 SOFONISBA ANGUISSOLA, detail of *Portrait of the Artist's Sisters and Brother,* c. 1555. Methuen Collection, Corsham Court, Wilshire, England.

slightly acid olive green walls of the room make for a deeply restrained color scheme—a muted background for the sharply defined, busily active, Manneristic silhouette that contradicts the subject's impassive pose.

The aloof formality of Bronzino's portrait is much relaxed in the portraiture of SOFONISBA ANGUISSOLA (1532–1625). A northern Italian from Cremona, Anguissola uses the strong contours, muted tonality, and smooth finish familiar in Mannerist portraits. But she introduces, in a group portrait of irresistible charm (detail, FIG. **17-44**), an informal intimacy of her own. Like many of her other works done before 1559, this is a portrait of members of her family. Against a neutral ground, she places one of her sisters and her brother in an affectionate pose meant not for official display but for private showing, much as they might be posed in a modern photo-studio portrait. The sister, wearing a striped gown, flanks her brother, who caresses a lap dog. The young girl has summoned up the dignity required for the occasion, while the boy looks quizzically at the portraitist with an expression of naive curiosity.

The naturalness of poses and expressions, the sympathetic, personal presentation, and the graceful treatment of the forms did not escape the attention of famous contemporaries. Vasari praised Anguissola's art as wonderfully lifelike, and declared that she "has done more in design and more gracefully than any other lady of our day." She was praised, moreover, for her "invention," and, though the word does not now have quite the meaning it had then, Anguissola can be considered to have introduced the intimate, anecdotal, and realistic touches of genre painting into formal portraiture. This group portrait could be simply a good-natured portrayal of the members of any happy, middle-class family; names, titles, and elegance of dress are not flourished to gain public respect. Anguissola lived long and successfully. She knew and learned from the aged Michelangelo, was court painter to Philip II of Spain, and, at the end of her life, gave advice on art to a young admirer of her work, Anthony Van Dyck, the great Flemish master. Circumstances generally prevented women artists from having the training and renown that favored Anguissola's career in Italy. We have knowledge of women who were painters as far back as the thirteenth century, and although they came into their own in the sixteenth century, they were few in number and did not achieve prominence. Social conventions, restricted education, and guild rules tended to exclude women from training and practice in the arts.

In Sculpture

With Bronzino, Florentine Mannerism in painting passed its high-water mark. But a remarkable person, as Mannerist in his action as in his art, has left us, in his sculpture, the mark of the prevailing style. To judge by his fascinating *Autobiography*, BENVENUTO CELLINI (1500–1571) had an impressive proficiency as an artist, statesman, soldier, lover, and many other things. He was, first of all, a goldsmith. The influence of Michelangelo led him to attempt larger works, and, in the service of Francis I, he cast in bronze the *Diana of Fontainebleau* (FIG. **17-45**), which sums up Italian and French Mannerism. The figure is derived from the reclining tomb figures in the Medici Chapel (FIG. 17-27), but it exaggerates their characteristics. The head is remarkably small, the torso stretched out, and the limbs elongated. The contrapposto is more apparent than real, for it is flattened out almost into the forward plane, as Mannerist design sense dictates. This almost abstract figure, along with Mannerist works by Rosso and others, greatly influenced the development of French Renaissance art, particularly in the school of Fontainebleau.

Italian influence, working its way into France, had strength enough to draw a brilliant, young French sculptor, Jean de Boulogne, to Italy, where he practiced his art under the Italian cognomen GIOVANNI DA BOLOGNA (1529–1608). Although Giovanni's quality and importance have not always been recognized, he is the most important sculptor in Italy after Michelangelo and his work provides the stylistic link between the sculpture of that great master and that of the Baroque sculptor Gianlorenzo Bernini. Giovanni's *Rape of the Sabine Women* (FIG. **17-46**) wonderfully exemplifies the Mannerist principles of figure composition and, at the same time, shows an impulse to break out of the Mannerist formulas of representation.

The title was given to the group after it was raised

17-45 BENVENUTO CELLINI, *Diana of Fontainebleau,* 1543–1544. Bronze, over life size. Louvre, Paris.

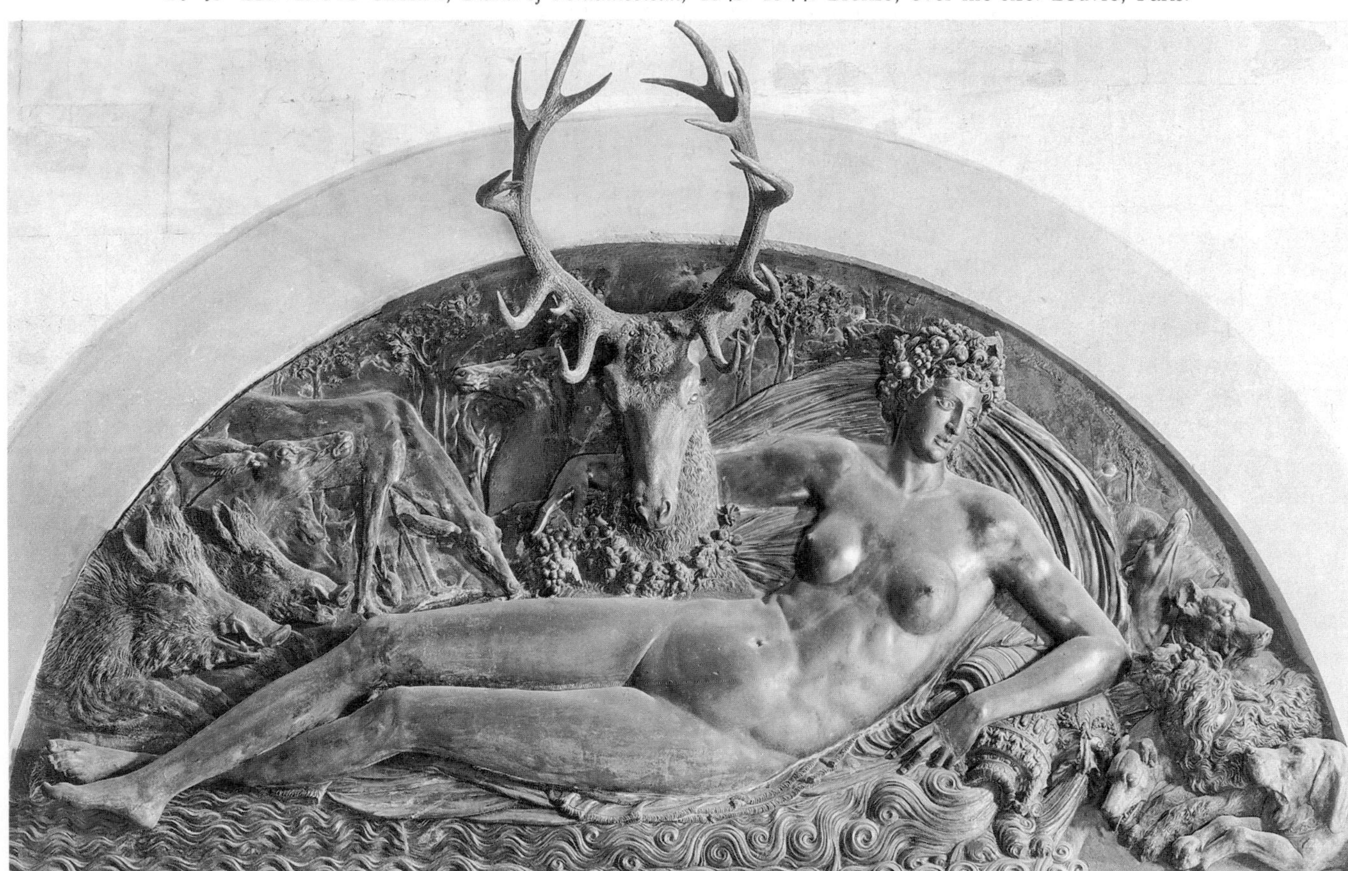

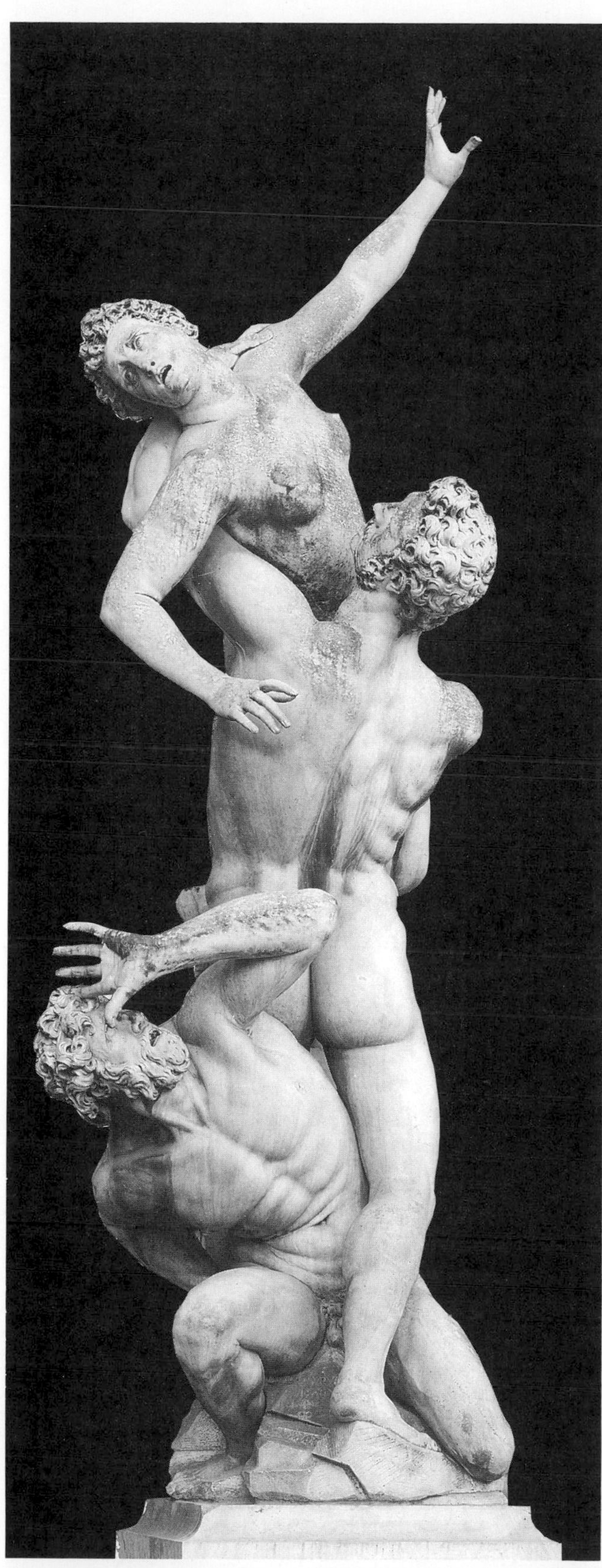

17-46 GIOVANNI DA BOLOGNA, *Rape of the Sabine Women*, completed 1583. Marble, approx. 13′ 6″ high. Loggia dei Lanzi, Piazza della Signoria, Florence.

(Giovanni probably intended to present only an interesting figure composition involving an old man, a young man, and a woman). The story, derived from mythic Roman history, tells how the Romans took wives for themselves from the neighboring Sabines. The amateurs, critics, and scholars who flocked around works of art in this age of Mannerism, naming groups in any way they found appropriate, serve to indicate how important and how valued the visual arts had become. The artist himself is learned in his artistic sources; here, Giovanni twice adapts the *Laocoön* (FIG. 5-79) discovered early in the century—once in the figure of the crouching old man and again in the gesture of the woman with one arm flung up. The three bodies interlock on an axis, along which a spiral movement runs; significantly, the figures do not break out of this vortex but remain as if contained within a cylinder. The viewer must walk around the sculpture to appreciate that, despite its confinement, the aspect of the group changes radically according to the point from which it is viewed. One reason is that the open spaces that pass through the masses (for example, the space between an arm and a body) have as great an effect as the solids. This sculpture is the first large-scale group composed to be seen from multiple points of view, but, as yet, the figures do not reach freely out into space and relate to the environment. The fact that they remain "enclosed" prevents our calling them Baroque. Yet the Michelangelesque potential for action and the athletic flexibility of the figures are there. The Baroque period will see sculptured figures released into full action.

In Architecture

Mannerism in painting and sculpture has been studied fairly extensively since the early decades of this century, but only in the 1930s was it discovered that the term also could be applied to much of sixteenth-century architecture. The corpus of Mannerist architecture that has been compiled since then, however, is far from homogeneous and includes many works that really do not seem to fit the term "Mannerist." The fact that Michelangelo was using Classical architectural elements in a highly personal and unorthodox manner does not necessarily make him a Mannerist architect. In his designs for St. Peter's, he certainly was striving for those effects of mass, balance, order, and stability that are the very hallmarks of High Renaissance design, and even some of the most unusual features in the Laurentian Library (FIG. 17-28) were dictated by structural necessity. As we have seen, Michelangelo never really aimed to baffle or to confuse, but this was the precise goal of GIULIO ROMANO when he designed the Palazzo del Tè in

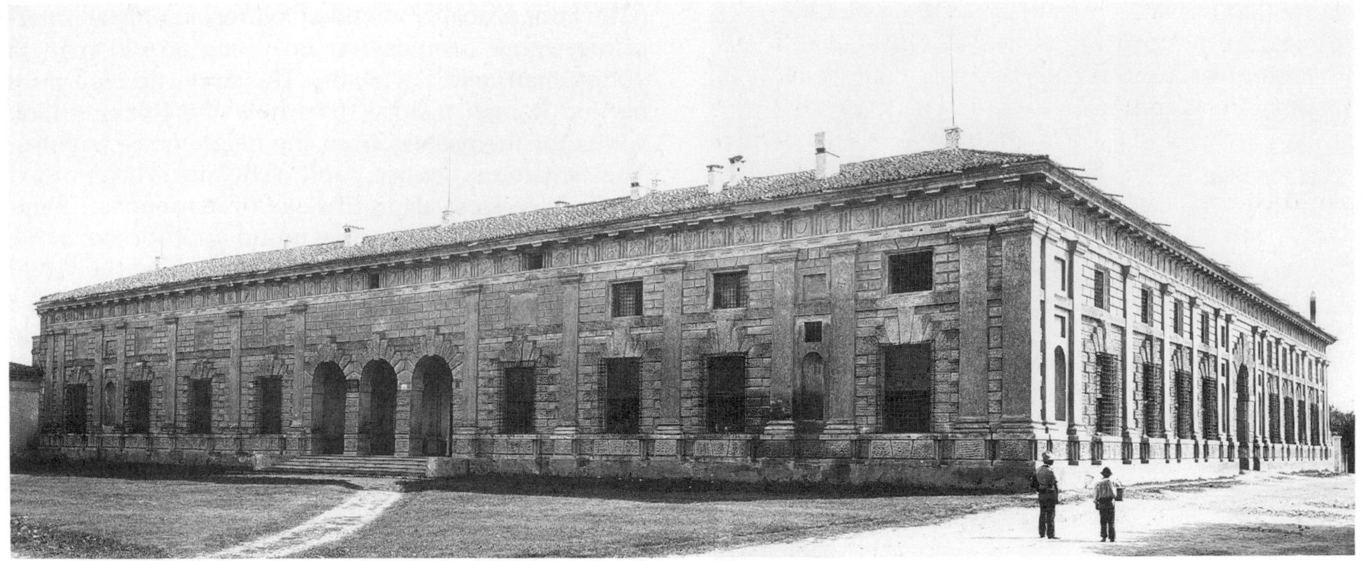

17-47 Giulio Romano, north façade of the Palazzo del Tè, Mantua, Italy, 1525–1535.

Mantua (FIGS. **17-47** and **17-48**) and, with it, formulated almost the entire architectural vocabulary of Mannerism.

GIULIO ROMANO AND THE PALAZZO DEL TÈ

Giulio Romano was born either in 1492, if we accept Vasari's suggestion, or in 1499, if we disallow the possibility of error in a document that states that he died in Mantua in 1546 at the age of forty-seven. If we give credence to the latter birthdate, however, Giulio must have been one of the most precocious young prodigies in the history of world art, as he could then have been little more than sixteen when he became Raphael's chief assistant in the decoration of the Vatican stanze. After Raphael's premature death in 1520, Giulio became his master's artistic executor, completing Raphael's unfinished frescoes and panel paintings. In 1524, Giulio went to Mantua, where he found a patron in Federigo Gonzaga, for whom he built and decorated the Palazzo del Tè between 1525 and 1535.

The Palazzo del Tè was intended to combine the functions of a suburban summer palace with those of a stud farm for the duke's famous stables. Originally

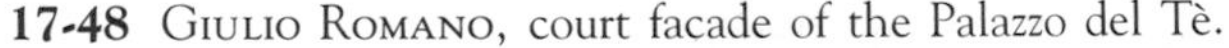

17-48 Giulio Romano, court facade of the Palazzo del Tè.

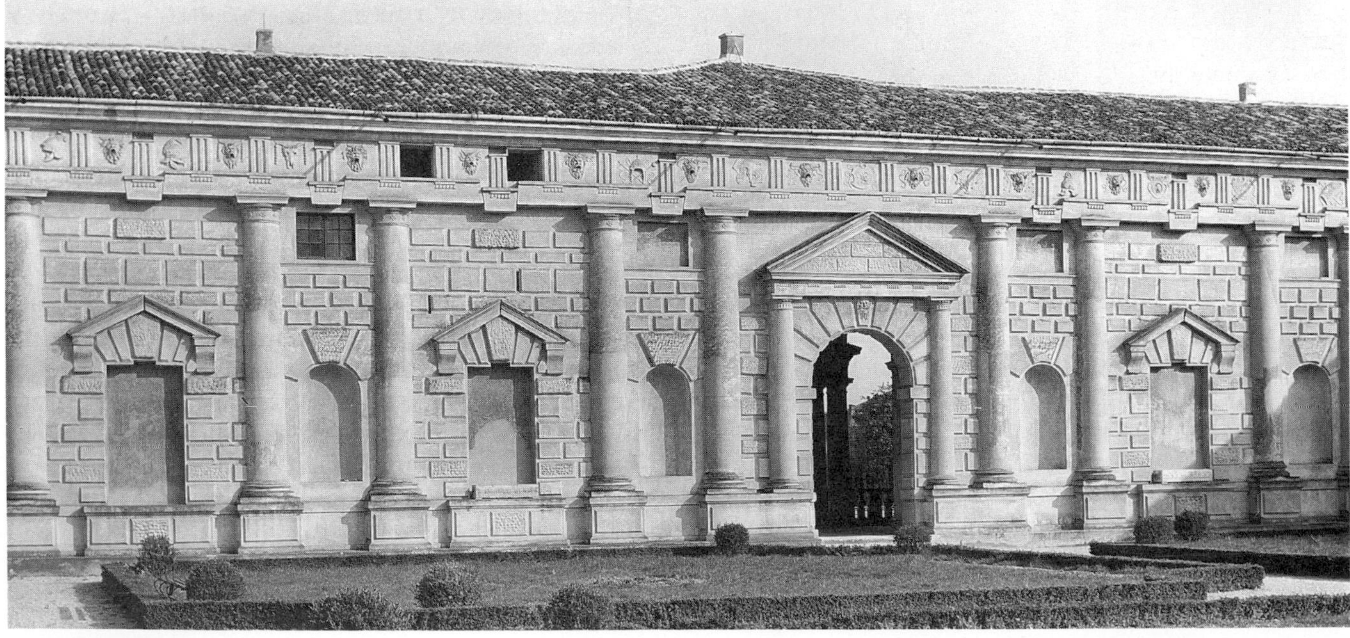

planned as a relatively modest country villa, Giulio's building so pleased the duke that he soon commissioned his architect to enlarge the structure. In a second building campaign, the villa was expanded to a palatial scale by the addition of three wings, which were placed around a square central court. This once-paved court, which serves both as a passage and as the focal point of the design, has a near-urban character and, with its surrounding buildings, forms a self-enclosed unit to which a large, stable-flanked garden has been attached on the east side.

The first impression of the north façade (FIG. 17-47) is that of a fairly standard Renaissance structure with rusticated walls that have been articulated with smooth Doric pilasters. Closer study reveals a number of startling departures from the Renaissance norm. Most immediately noticeable is the ambiguity of the elevation, which can be read either as a one-story or a two-story system. Other discrepancies gradually reveal themselves. The distances from the central loggia to the corners of the building are unequal; the windows are located eccentrically between pilasters; the pilasters are paired at varying distances from each other; and the voussoirs above the windows and portals are handled in a way that makes them seem to tumble outward from the building. These divergences from convention serve as an overture to a building so laden with structural surprises and contradictions that, taken all together, it becomes an enormous parody on the Classical style of Bramante. To be sure, the appreciation of the joke required a highly sophisticated audience, and the recognition of some quite subtle departures from the norm presupposed a thorough familiarity with the established rules of Classical architecture. It speaks well for the duke's sophistication that he accepted Giulio's form of architectural humor.

It has recently been claimed that the irregularities of the north façade were forced on Giulio by the need to adjust the design of the façade to the features of the already completed villa behind it. Such impediments, however, rarely kept Renaissance architects from designing regular and symmetrical façades (compare Alberti's Palazzo Rucellai, FIG. 16-38). In any case, Giulio's intent seems to be expressed clearly enough in the palace's garden façade, where the irregularly spaced arches do not have to conform to any preexisting conditions. Even more chaotic is the design of the façades that face the interior courtyard (FIG. 17-48), where keystones (central voussoirs) either have not fully settled or seem to be slipping from the arches. The massive Tuscan columns carry incongruously narrow architraves whose structural insufficiency is stressed by the fact that they break midway between the columns, evidently unable to support the weight of the triglyphs above. And if this architectural chaos does not suffice to shock the visitor, Giulio delivers the coup de grace in the Sala dei Giganti (FIG. **17-49**). In a panoramic sequence that covers the ceiling and all the walls of this room, Giulio has represented Jupiter destroying the palaces of the rebellious giants with thunderbolts. Viewers cringe involuntarily as the entire universe appears to be collapsing around them in a tour de force of pictorial illusionism and wild Mannerist convulsion.

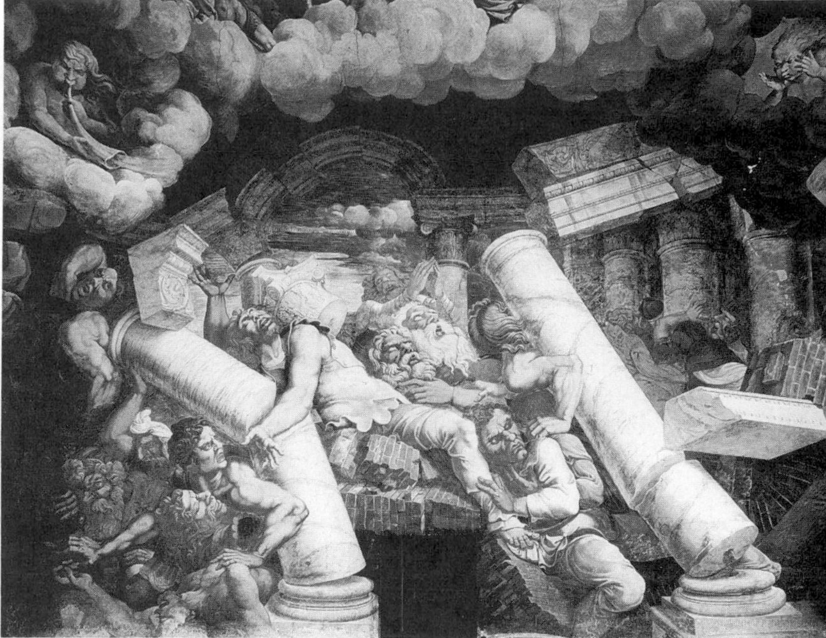

17-49 GIULIO ROMANO, *The Fall of the Giants* (detail), 1532–1534. Fresco. Sala dei Giganti, Palazzo del Tè.

In short, in the Palazzo del Tè, most of the Classical rules of order, stability, and symmetry have been flouted deliberately, and every effort has been made to startle and shock the beholder. This desire to create ambiguities and tensions is as typical of Mannerist architecture as it is of Mannerist painting, and many of the devices invented by Giulio Romano for the Palazzo del Tè will become standard features in the formal repertoire of later Mannerist building.

VENICE

In the sixteenth century, Venetian art became a strong, independent, and influential school in its own right, touched only very slightly (if at all) by the fashions of Mannerism sweeping Western Europe. Venice had been the proud maritime mistress of the Mediterranean and its coasts for centuries; as the gateway to the Orient, it "held the gorgeous east in fee; and was the safeguard of the west." At the height of its commercial and political power during the fifteenth century, Venice saw its fortunes decline in the sixteenth century. Even so, Venice and the papal state were the only Italian sovereignties to retain their independence during the century of strife; all others were reduced to dependency on either France or Spain. Although the fundamental reasons for the decline of Venice were the discoveries in the New World and the economic shift from Italy to the Hapsburg Germanies and Netherlands, other even more immediate and pressing events drained her wealth and power. Venice was constantly embattled by the Turks, who, after their conquest of Constantinople, began to contest with Venice over control of the eastern Mediterranean. Early in the century, Venice also found itself attacked by the European powers of the League of Cambrai, formed and led by Julius II, who coveted Venetian holdings on the mainland. Although this wearing, two-front war sapped its strength, Venice's vitality endured, at least long enough to overwhelm the Turks in the great sea battle of Lepanto in 1571. This time, Europe was on Venice's side.

Architecture: Sansovino and Palladio

Venice was introduced to the High Renaissance style of architecture by a Florentine called JACOPO SANSOVINO (Jacopo Tatti, 1486–1570). Originally trained as a sculptor under ANDREA SANSOVINO, whose name he adopted, Jacopo went to Rome in 1518, where, under the influence of Bramante's circle, he increasingly turned toward architecture. When he arrived in Venice as a refugee from the Sack of Rome in 1527, he quickly established himself as that city's leading and most admired architect; his buildings frequently inspired the architectural settings of the most prominent Venetian painters, including Titian and Veronese (FIG. 17-67).

Sansovino's largest and most rewarding public commissions were La Zecca (Mint) and the adjoining State Library (FIG. **17-50**) in the heart of the island city. The Zecca, begun in 1535, faces the Canale San Marco with a stern and forbidding three-story façade. Its heavy rustication gives it an intended air of strength and impregnability. This fortresslike look is emphasized by a boldly projecting, bracket-supported cornice reminiscent of the machicolated galleries of medieval castles.

A very different spirit is expressed by the neighboring State Library of San Marco, begun a year after the Zecca, which Palladio referred to as "probably the richest and most ornate edifice since ancient times." With twenty-one bays (only sixteen of which were completed during Sansovino's lifetime), the library faces the Gothic Doge's Palace (FIG. 10-64) across the Piazzetta, a lateral extension of Venice's central Piazza San Marco. The relatively plain ground-story arcade has Doric columns attached to the arch-supporting piers in the manner of the Roman Colosseum (FIG. 6-48). It serves as a sturdy support for the higher, lighter, and much more decorative Ionic second story, which housed the reading room, with its treasure of manuscripts, keeping them safe from not-uncommon flooding. On this second level, the stern system of the ground story has been softened by the introduction of Ionic colonnettes that flank the piers and are paired in depth, rather than in the plane of the façade. Two-thirds the height of the main columns, they rise to support the springing of arches, the spans of which are two-thirds those of the lower arcade. The main columns carry an entablature with a richly decorated frieze on which, in strongly projecting relief, putti support garlands. This favorite decorative motif of the ancient Romans is punctuated by the oval windows of an attic story. Perhaps the most striking feature of the building is its roofline, where Sansovino replaces the traditional straight and unbroken cornice with a balustrade (reminiscent of the one on Bramante's Tempietto, FIG. 17-6) interrupted by statue-bearing pedestals. The spacing of the latter corresponds to that of the orders below, so that the sculptures become the sky-piercing finials of the building's vertical design elements. The deft application of sculpture to the massive framework of the building (no walls are visible) mitigates the potential severity of its design and gives its aspect an extraordinary plastic richness.

One feature rarely mentioned is the subtlety with which the library echoes the design of the lower two stories of the Doge's Palace (FIG. 10-64) opposite it. Although he uses a vastly different architectural vocabulary, Sansovino manages admirably to adjust his building to the older one. Correspondences include the almost identical spacing of the lower arcades, the rich and decorative treatment of the second stories (including their balustrades), and the dissolution of the rooflines (by use of decorative battlements in the palace and a statue-surmounted balustrade in the library). It is almost as if Sansovino set out to translate the Gothic architecture of the Doge's Palace into a "modern" Renaissance idiom. If so, he was eminently successful; the two buildings, although of different spiritual and stylistic worlds, mesh and combine to make the Piazzetta one of the most elegantly framed urban units in Europe.

When Jacopo Sansovino died, he was succeeded as chief architect of the Venetian Republic by ANDREA

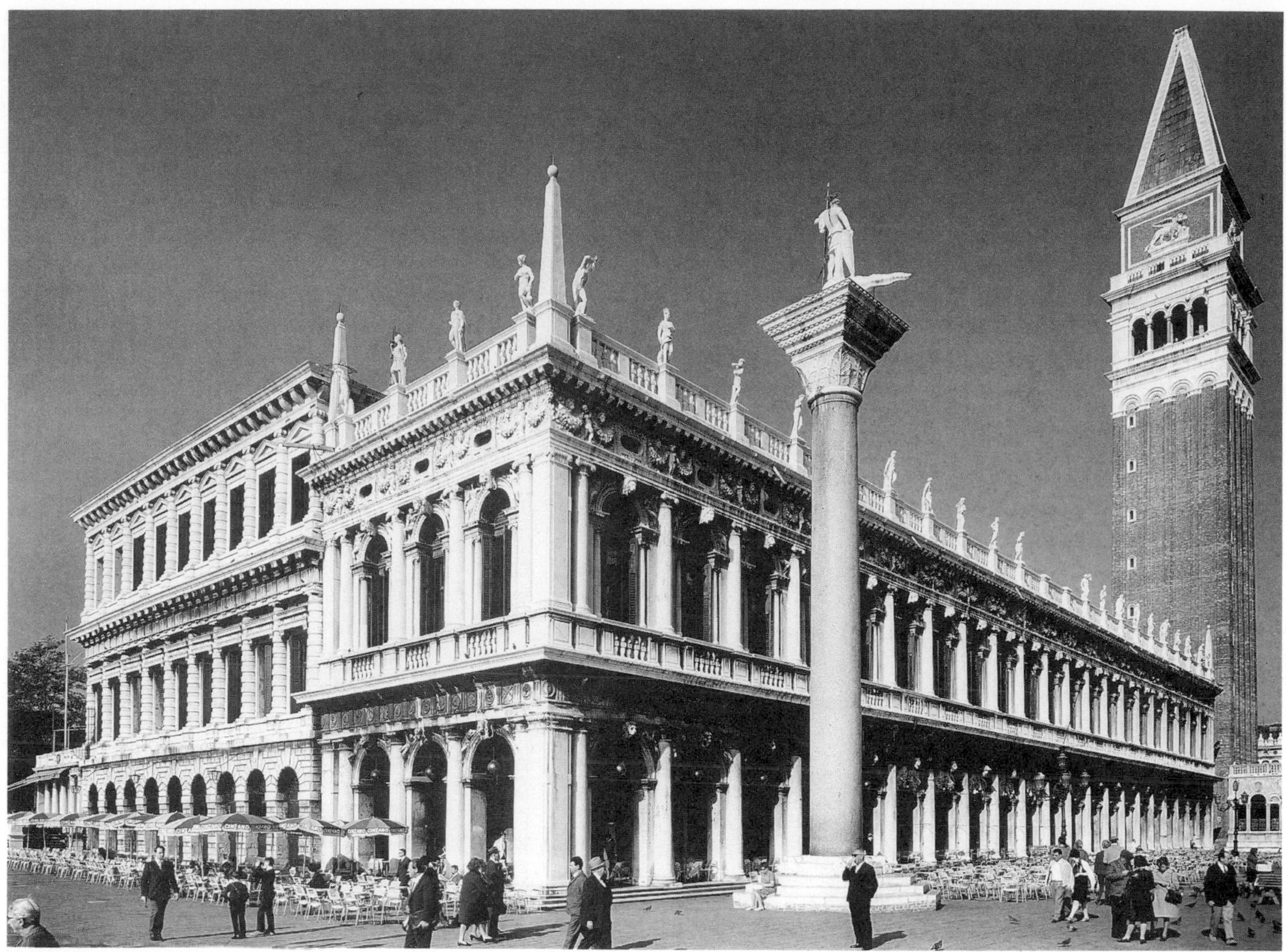

17-50 Jacopo Sansovino, La Zecca (Mint), 1535–1545 *(left)* and State Library, begun 1536, San Marco, Venice.

Palladio (1508–1580). Beginning as a stonemason and decorative sculptor, at the age of thirty, Palladio turned to architecture, the ancient literature on architecture, engineering, topography, and military science. Unlike the universal scholar, Alberti, Palladio became more of a specialist. He made several trips to Rome to study the ancient buildings at first hand. He illustrated Daniele Barbaro's edition of *Vitruvius* (1556), and he wrote his own treatise on architecture, *I quattro libri dell' architettura (Four Books on Architecture)*, originally published in 1570, which had a wide-ranging influence on succeeding generations of architects throughout Europe. Palladio's influence outside Italy, most significantly in England and in colonial America, was stronger and more lasting than that of any other architect.

Palladio is best known for his many villas built on the Venetian mainland, of which nineteen still stand; the villas were especially influential on later architects. The same Arcadian spirit that prompted the ancient Romans to build villas in the countryside, and that will be expressed so eloquently in the art of the Venetian painter Giorgione, motivated a similar villa-building boom in the sixteenth century. One can imagine that Venice, with its very limited space, must have been more congested than any ancient city. But a longing for the countryside was not the only motive; declining fortunes prompted the Venetians to develop their mainland possessions with new land investment and reclamation projects. Citizens who could afford it were encouraged to set themselves up as gentlemen farmers and to develop swamps into productive agricultural land. Wealthy families could look on their villas as providential investments. The villas were thus gentleman farms (like the much later American plantations, which were architecturally influenced by Palladio) surrounded by service outbuildings that Palladio generally arranged in long, low wings branching out from the main building and enclosing a large, rectangular court area.

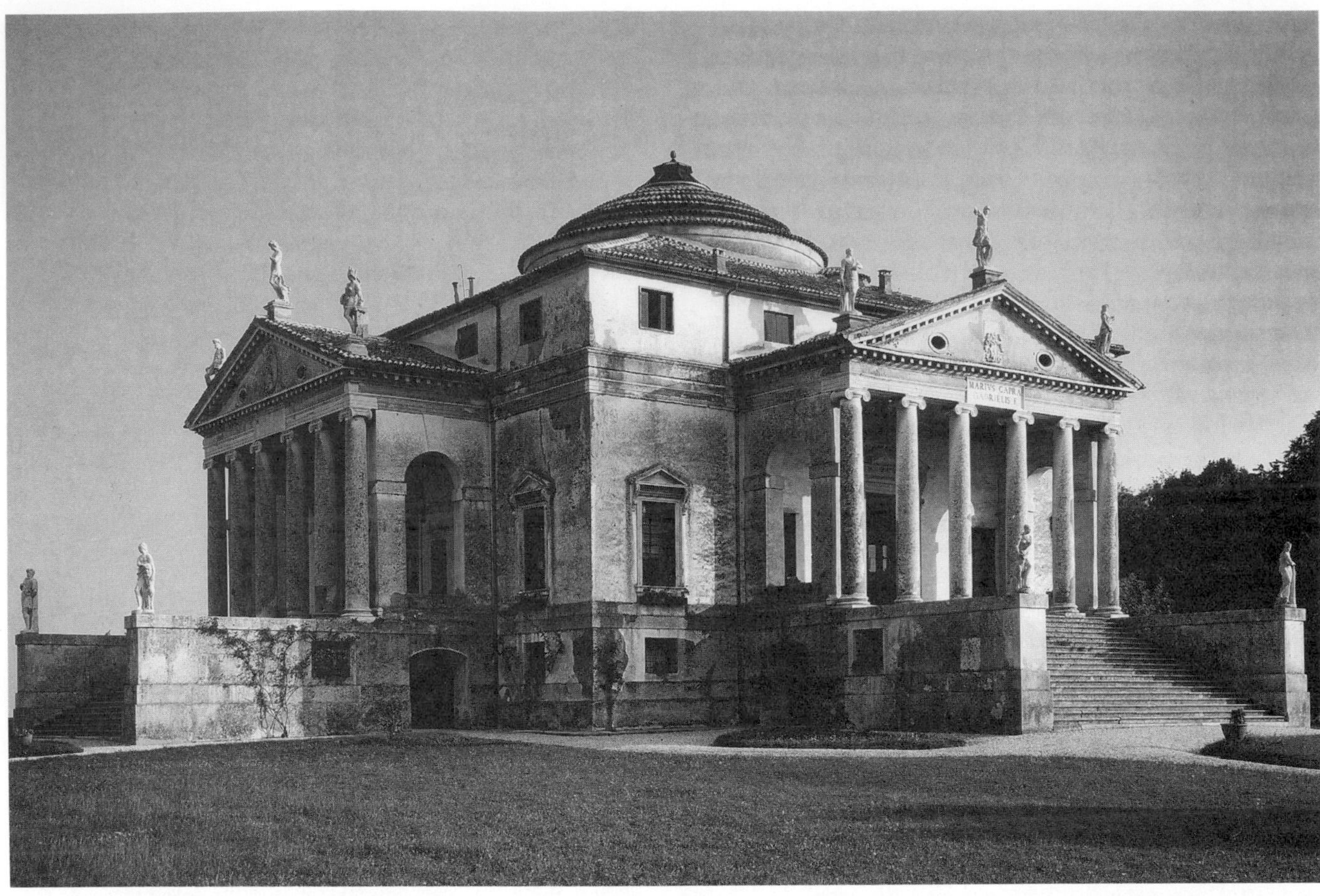

17-51 ANDREA PALLADIO, Villa Rotonda (formerly Villa Capra), near Vicenza, Italy, *c.* 1566–1570.

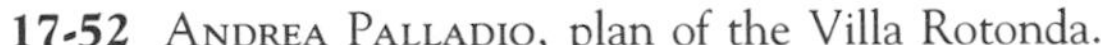

17-52 ANDREA PALLADIO, plan of the Villa Rotonda.

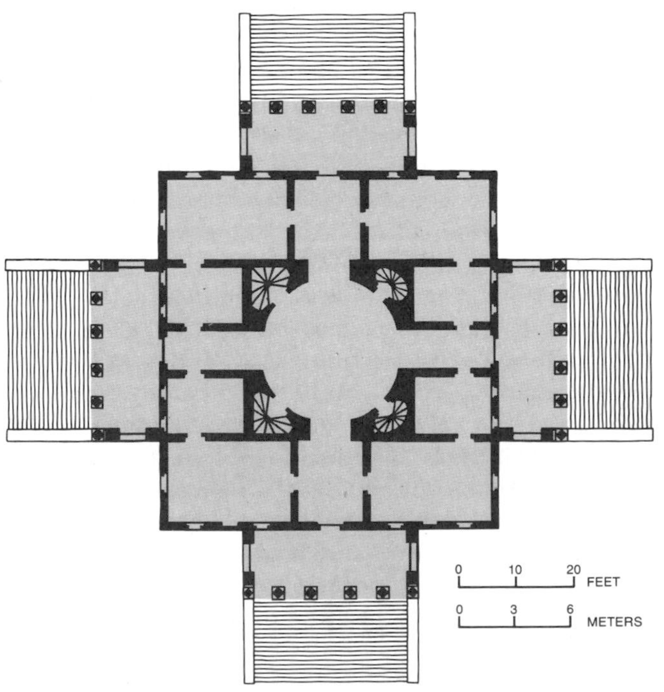

Although it is the most famous, Villa Rotonda (FIG. **17-51**), near Vicenza, is not really typical of Palladio's villa style. It was not built for an aspiring gentleman farmer, but for a retired monsignor who wanted a villa for social events. Located on a hilltop, Villa Rotonda was planned and designed as a kind of belvedere, without the usual wings of secondary buildings. Its central plan (FIG. **17-52**), with four identical façades and projecting porches, is therefore both sensible and functional; each of the porches can be used as a platform from which to enjoy a different view of the surrounding landscape. In this design, the central dome-covered rotunda logically functions as a kind of revolving platform, from which the visitor can turn in any direction for the preferred view. The result is a building with parts that are functional and systematically related to one another in terms of calculated mathematical relationships. Villa Rotonda, like Santa Maria della Consolazione at Todi (FIG. 17-9), thus embodies all the qualities of self-sufficiency and formal completeness that most Renaissance architects dreamed of. In his formative years, Palladio was influenced by Alberti, by Bramante, and, briefly, by Giulio Romano. By 1550, however, he had developed

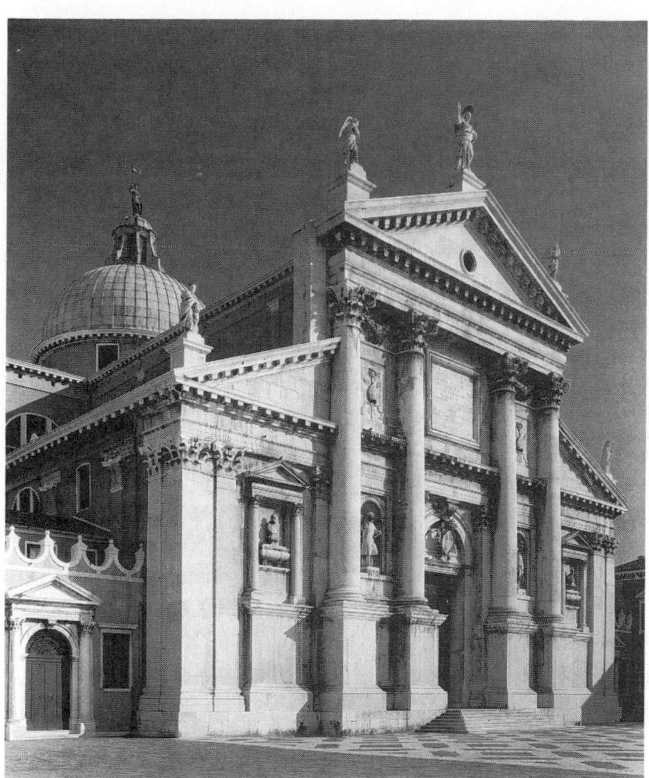

17-53 ANDREA PALLADIO, west façade of San Giorgio Maggiore, Venice, 1565.

17-54 ANDREA PALLADIO, interior of San Giorgio Maggiore (view facing east).

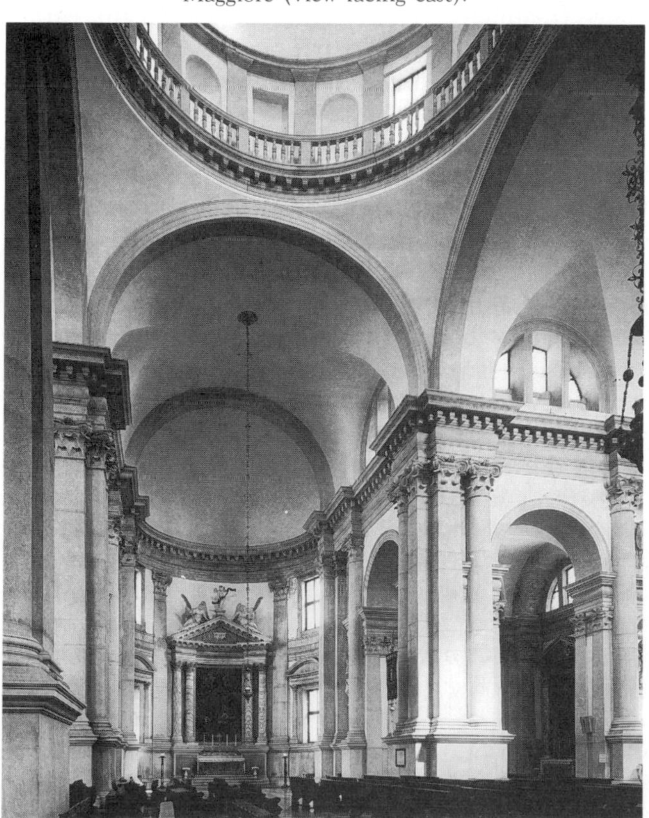

his own personal style, which, in its clarity and lack of ambiguity, was as different from contemporary Mannerism as it was, in its static qualities and rather dry, "correct" Classicism, from the dynamic style of Michelangelo.

San Giorgio Maggiore (FIG. **17-53**), directly across a broad canal from the Piazza San Marco, is one of the most dramatically placed buildings in Venice. Dissatisfied with earlier solutions to the problem of integrating a high central nave and lower aisles into a unified façade design, Palladio solved it by superimposing a tall, narrow, Classical porch on a low, broad one. This solution not only reflects the interior arrangement of the building, but also introduces the illusion of three-dimensional depth, an effect that is intensified by the strong projection of the central columns and the shadows they cast. Although at first the result seems to be a rigid formalism, the play of shadow across the building's surfaces, its reflection in the water, and its gleaming white against sea and sky create a remarkably colorful effect. The interior of the church (FIG. **17-54**) is flooded with light, which crisply defines the contours of the rich wall articulations (pedestals, bases, shafts, capitals, entablatures), all beautifully and "correctly" profiled—the exemplar of what Classical architectural theory means by "rational" organization.

Painting: Giovanni Bellini and Giorgione

The soft, colored light of Venice, which relaxes the severe lines of Palladio's architecture, lives at its fullest in Venetian painting. In the career of GIOVANNI BELLINI (*c.* 1430–1516), we find the history of that style. In his long productive life, Bellini, always alert to what was new, never ceased to develop artistically and, almost by himself, created what is known as the Venetian style, which will be so important to the subsequent course of painting. Trained in the tradition of the International style by his father, a student of Gentile da Fabriano, Bellini worked in the family shop and did not develop his own style until after his father's death in 1470. His early independent works show him to be under the dominant influence of his brother-in-law, Andrea Mantegna. But in the late 1470s, impressed by the possibilities offered by the new oil technique that Antonello da Messina (FIG. 16-67) introduced during a visit to Venice, Bellini abandoned the Paduan's harsh, linear style and developed a sensuous, coloristic manner that was to become characteristic of Venetian painting.

Bellini is best known for his many Madonnas, which he painted both in half-length (with or without accompanying saints) on small devotional panels and

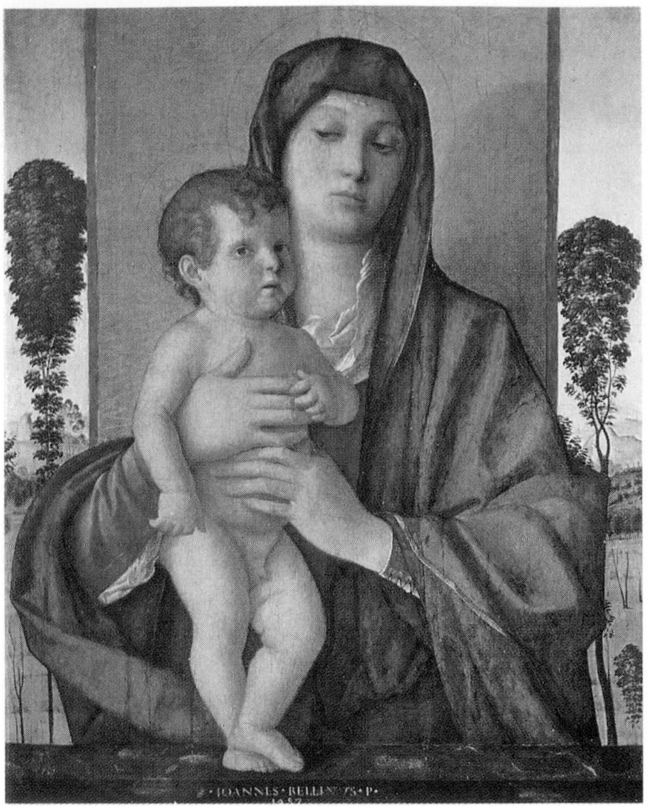

17-55 Giovanni Bellini, *Madonna of the Trees,* c. 1487. Oil on wood, 29" × 22". Galleria dell' Accademia, Venice.

on large, monumental altarpieces of the sacra conversazione type (FIG. 16-32). Judging by what appears to have been an unending string of commissions, his half-length Madonnas were especially popular. More than eighty of these are still extant, and, if arranged chronologically, they provide an almost gapless overview of the painter's artistic development. Our example, *Madonna of the Trees* (FIG. **17-55**) dates from 1487 (a year or two after Bellini's adoption of the oil technique) and stands about halfway between his early linear, Mantegnesque approach and the fully developed, painterly style of his later years.* Placed before a wide strip of green satin, the grave and pensive Madonna steadies her child's uneasy pose, her somber expression suggesting foreknowledge of the infant's eventual fate. Although firmly modeled, the forms are softly rounded and, combined with warm and luminous colors, instill the painting with a quality of subdued voluptuousness that will become a trademark of much later Venetian painting.

Despite the large number of similar works he painted, Bellini never repeated himself and always found some new variation on his Madonna theme. In most of his versions, the Madonna is placed behind a low parapet and, quite often, before a hanging drapery—devices that detach without completely isolating the sacred subject from its worldly surroundings. The Christ Child is shown standing or sitting on the parapet, cradled in the Madonna's arms, or seated on her lap; he is shown facing his mother or the viewer. At times, the drapery in back of the figures is moved off-center and its width is varied to show more or less of the background landscape. The drapery may extend into the picture from either the left or the right frame to permit a view into the distance on one side only, creating the kind of asymmetrical composition that will enjoy great favor with Bellini's most illustrious student, Titian. After 1500, the landscape backgrounds become more and more important, to the point that the artist often omits the middle-ground drapery and sometimes changes his format from vertical to horizontal to show a greater expanse of landscape behind his Madonnas. His landscapes also take on an increasingly Arcadian character.

If the long series of Bellini's half-length Madonnas reveals the gradual change in his painting style, two of his large altarpieces, the *San Giobbe Altarpiece,* c. 1490 (FIG. **17-56**), and the *San Zaccaria Altarpiece,* 1505 (FIG. **17-57**), illustrate not only two stages in the artist's stunning development but also the essential differences between the Early and the High Renaissance treatments of the same subject. In the earlier work, the *San Giobbe Altarpiece,* although the space is large, airy, and clearly defined, the figures seem to be crowded. They cling to the foreground plane and are seen in a slightly forced, Mantegnesque, "worm's eye" perspective. The drawing remains sharp and precise, particularly in that charming Venetian trademark, the group of angel-musicians at the foot of the Madonna's throne. The figures already are arranged in the pyramidal grouping preferred by the High Renaissance, but they tend to exist as individuals rather than as parts of an integrated whole. Seen by itself, the *San Giobbe Altarpiece* is an orderly, well-balanced painting that can hold its own with any produced during the Early Renaissance, but side by side with the subsequent *San Zaccaria Altarpiece,* it suddenly seems cluttered and overly busy. By adding simplicity to the order, balance, and clarity of the earlier painting, Bellini takes the long step into the High Renaissance.

In the *San Zaccaria Altarpiece,* in contrast to his earlier treatment of the theme, Bellini raises the observer's viewpoint and deemphasizes the perspective. The number of figures is reduced, and they are more closely integrated with each other and with the space that surrounds them. Combined into a single, cohe-

*The painting suffered some damage during restoration in 1902, when the Madonna's veil was repainted in a style that does not conform with that of the rest of the painting.

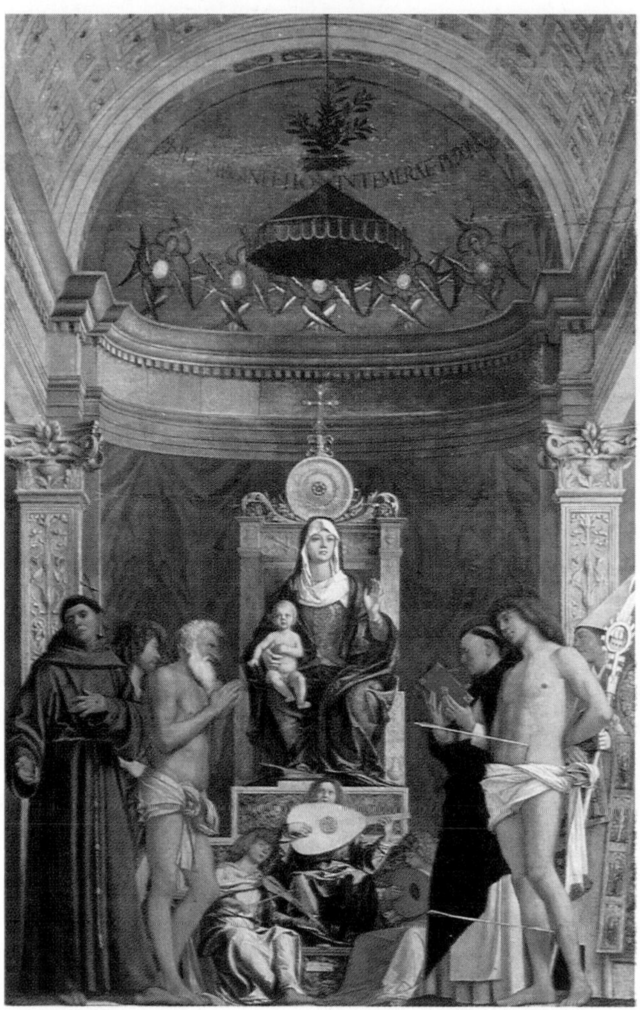

17-56 Giovanni Bellini, *San Giobbe Altarpiece*, c. 1490. Oil on wood, 15′ 4″ × 8′ 4″. Galleria dell' Accademia, Venice.

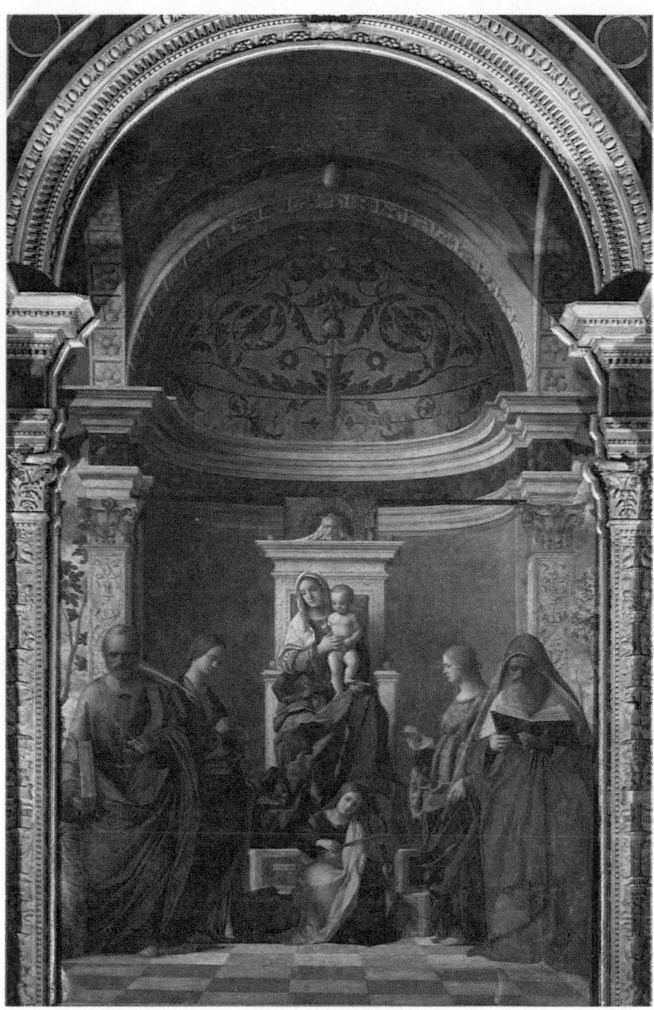

17-57 Giovanni Bellini, *San Zaccaria Altarpiece*, 1505. Oil on wood transferred to canvas, approx. 16′ 5″ × 7′ 9″. San Zaccaria, Venice.

sive group, the figures no longer cling to the front of the painting; disposed in depth, they now move in and out of the apse instead of standing before it. Their attitudes produce a rhythmic movement within the group, but all obvious gestures have been eliminated and the former busyness has changed to serene calm. In addition, Bellini's method of painting has become softer and more luminous. Line is no longer the chief agent of form but has been submerged in a sea of glowing color—a soft radiance that envelops the forms with an atmospheric haze and enhances their majestic serenity.

The San Zaccaria Madonna is the mature work of an old man whose paintings spanned the development of three artistic generations in Florence. Departing from the Gothic, Bellini moved through the Early Renaissance and arrived in the High Renaissance even before Raphael and Michelangelo. At the very end of his long life, this astonishingly apt artist was still willing and able to make changes in his style and approach to keep himself abreast of his times; he began to deal with pagan subjects.

The Feast of the Gods (FIG. **17-58**) was influenced by one of Bellini's own students, Giorgione (see page 683), who developed his master's landscape backgrounds into poetic, Arcadian reveries. (In this case, Titian, another of Bellini's pupils, repainted the right background after his master's landscape had been painted over by a lesser craftsman, Dosso Dossi, at the behest of the Duke of Ferrara.) After Giorgione's premature death, Bellini embraced his student's interests and, in *The Feast of the Gods,* developed a new kind of mythology in which the Olympian gods appear as peasants enjoying a heavenly picnic in a shady northern Italian glade. His source is Ovid's *Fasti,* which describes a banquet of the gods. The figures are spread across the foreground: satyrs attend the gods, nymphs bring jugs of wine, a child draws

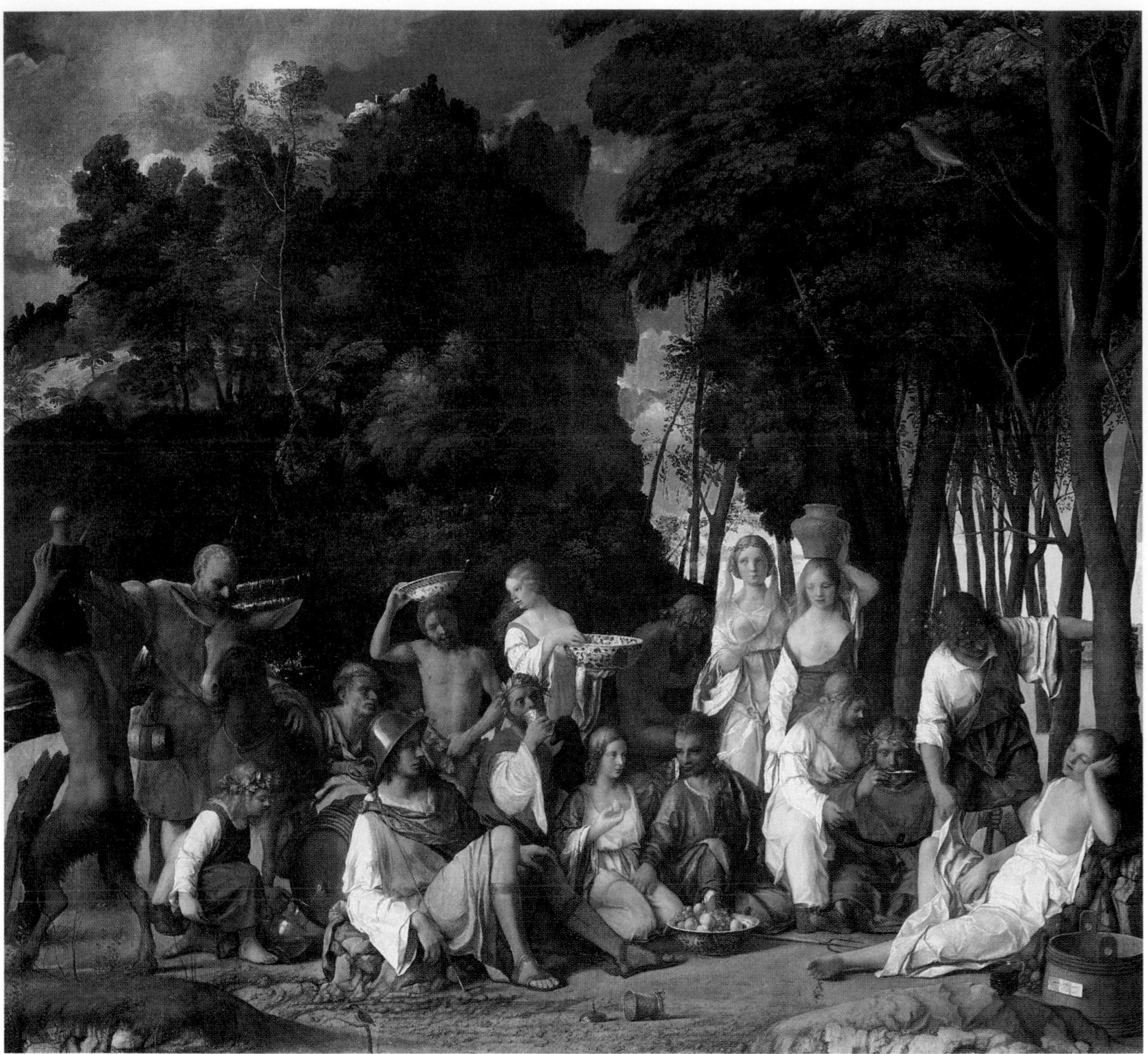

17-58 Giovanni Bellini (and Titian), *The Feast of the Gods,* 1514. Oil on canvas, approx. 5′ 7″ × 6′ 2″. National Gallery of Art, Washington, D.C. (Widener Collection).

from a keg, couples engage in love play, and the sleeping nymph at the right receives amorous attention. The mellow light of a long afternoon glows softly around the gathering, touching the surfaces of colorful draperies, smooth flesh, and polished metal. Here, Bellini announces the delight the Venetian school will take in the beauty of texture revealed by the full resources of gently and subtly harmonized color. Behind the warm, lush tones of the figures, a background of cool, green, tree-filled glades reaches into the distance; at the right, a screen of trees makes a verdant shelter. The atmosphere is idyllic, a floral countryside making a setting for the never-ending pleasure of the immortal gods. The poetry of Greece and Rome, as well as that of the Renaissance, is filled with this pastoral mood, and the Venetians make a specialty of its representation. Its elements include the smiling landscape, eternal youth, and song and revelry, always with a touch of the sensual.

Thus, with Bellini, Venetian art becomes the great complement of the schools of Florence and Rome. The Venetians' instrument is color; that of the Florentines and Romans is sculpturesque form. These two schools run parallel—sometimes touching and engaging—through the history of Western art from the Renaissance on. Their themes are different. Venice paints the poetry of the senses and delights in the beauty of nature and the pleasures of mankind. Florence and Rome attempt the sterner, intellectual themes—the epic of man, the masculine virtues, the grandeur of the ideal, the lofty conceptions of religion as they involve the heroic and the sublime. The history of later Western art broadly can be understood as a dialogue between these two traditions.

The inspiration for Bellini's late Arcadianism is to be found in paintings like the so-called *Pastoral Symphony* (FIG. **17-59**) by his illustrious student GIORGIONE (Giorgione da Castelfranco, 1478–1510), a work held by some to be an early Titian. Out of dense color shadow emerge the soft forms of figures and landscape. The theme is as mysterious as the light. Two nude females, accompanied by two clothed young men, occupy the rich, abundant landscape through which a shepherd passes. In the distance, a villa crowns a hill. The pastoral mood is so eloquently evoked here that we need not know (as we do not) the precise meaning of the picture; the mood is enough. The shepherd is symbolic of the poet; the pipes and the lute symbolize his poetry. The two nymphs accompanying the young men may be thought of as their invisible inspiration, their muses. One turns to lift water from the sacred well of poetic inspiration. The great, golden bodies of the nymphs, softly modulated by the smoky shadow, become the standard Venetian type. It is the Venetian school that resurrects the Venus figure from antiquity, making her the fecund goddess of nature and of love. The full opulence of the figures should, of course, not be read according to modern preferences in womanly physique but as poetic personifications of the abundance of nature.

As a pastoral poet in the pictorial medium and one of the greatest masters in the handling of light and color, Giorgione praises the beauty of nature, music, woman, and pleasure. Vasari reports that Giorgione was an accomplished lutist and singer, and adjectives from poetry and music seem best suited to describe the pastoral air and muted chords of his painting. He

17-59 GIORGIONE (and/or TITIAN ?), *Pastoral Symphony*, c. 1508. Oil on canvas, approx. 43″ × 54″. Louvre, Paris.

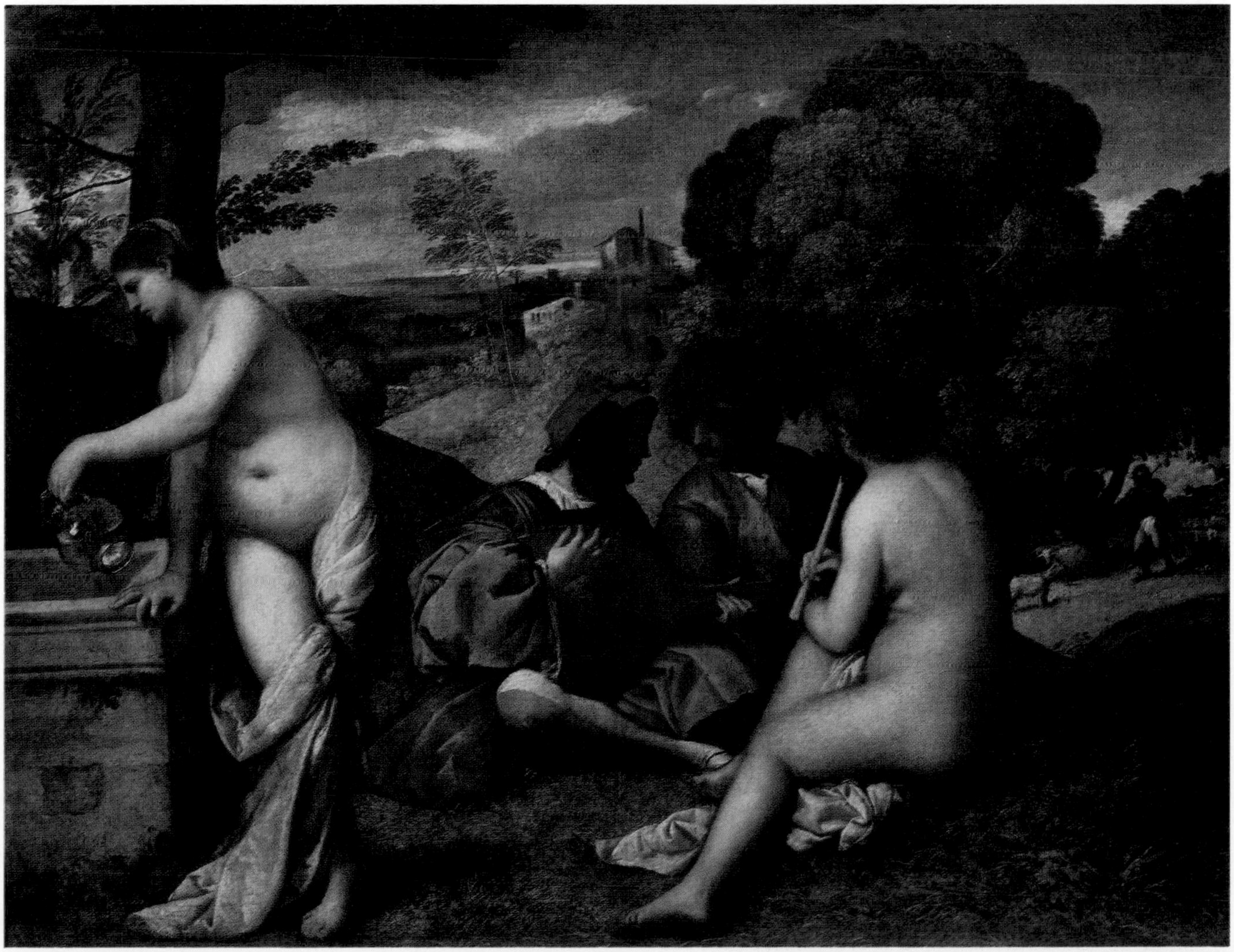

casts a mood of tranquil revery and dreaminess over the whole scene, evoking the landscape of a lost but never forgotten paradise. Arcadia and its happy creatures persist in the subconscious memory and longing of humankind. Among the Italians, the Venetians were the first to express a love of nature and a realization of its potentialities for the painter, although they never represent it except as humanly inhabited. The ancient spirits, the deities of field and woodland, still inhabit it too, and landscape—manifesting the bounty of Venus and sanctified by her beauty—as yet simply provides the inspiring setting for the poet, without whom it would be incomplete.

Titian

Giorgione's Arcadianism passed not only to his much older yet constantly learning master, Bellini, but also to Tiziano Vecelli, whose name we anglicize into Titian (*c.* 1490–1576). Titian is the most prodigious and prolific of the great Venetian painters. He is among the very greatest painters of the Western world—a supreme colorist and, in a broad sense, the father of the modern mode of painting. An important change that took place in Titian's time was the almost universal adoption of canvas, with its rough-textured surface, in place of wood panels for paintings. The works of Titian establish oil color on canvas as the typical medium of our pictorial tradition. According to a contemporary of Titian, Palma Giovane:

> Titian [employed] a great mass of colors, which served . . . as a base for whatever he was going to paint over it . . . I myself have seen his determined brushstrokes laden with color, sometimes a streak of pure earth-red which served him (one might say) as a half-tone, other times with a brushstroke of white lead; and with the same brush colored with a red, black, and yellow, he formed a highlight; and with these rules of technique made the promise of an excellent figure appear in four brushstrokes.
>
> After having laid these important foundations, he then used to turn the pictures to the wall, and leave them—sometimes for as long as several months—without looking at them; and when he wanted to apply his brush to them again, he [examined] them most rigorously . . . whether he could find any defects in them or discover anything which would not be in harmony with the delicacy of his intentions. . . . Working thus, and redesigning his figures, Titian brought them into a perfect symmetry which could represent the beauty of Art as well as of Nature. After this was done, he put his hand to some other picture until the first was dry, working in the same way with this other; thus gradually he covered those quintessential outlines of his figures with living flesh. . . . He never painted a figure all at once, and used to say that he who improvises his song can form neither learned nor well-turned verses. But the final polish . . . was to unite now and then by a touch of his fingers the extremes of the light areas, so that they became almost half-tints . . . at other times, with a stroke he would place a dark streak in a corner; to reinforce it he would add a streak of red, like a drop of blood. . . . in the final phase [he] painted more with his fingers than with his brushes.

Trained by both Bellini and Giorgione, Titian learned so well from them that even today no general agreement exists as to the degree of his participation in their later works. He completed several of Bellini's and Giorgione's unfinished paintings. One of his own early works, *Sacred and Profane Love* (FIG. **17-60**), is very much in the manner of Giorgione, with its

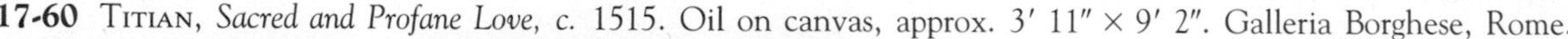

17-60 Titian, *Sacred and Profane Love,* *c.* 1515. Oil on canvas, approx. 3′ 11″ × 9′ 2″. Galleria Borghese, Rome.

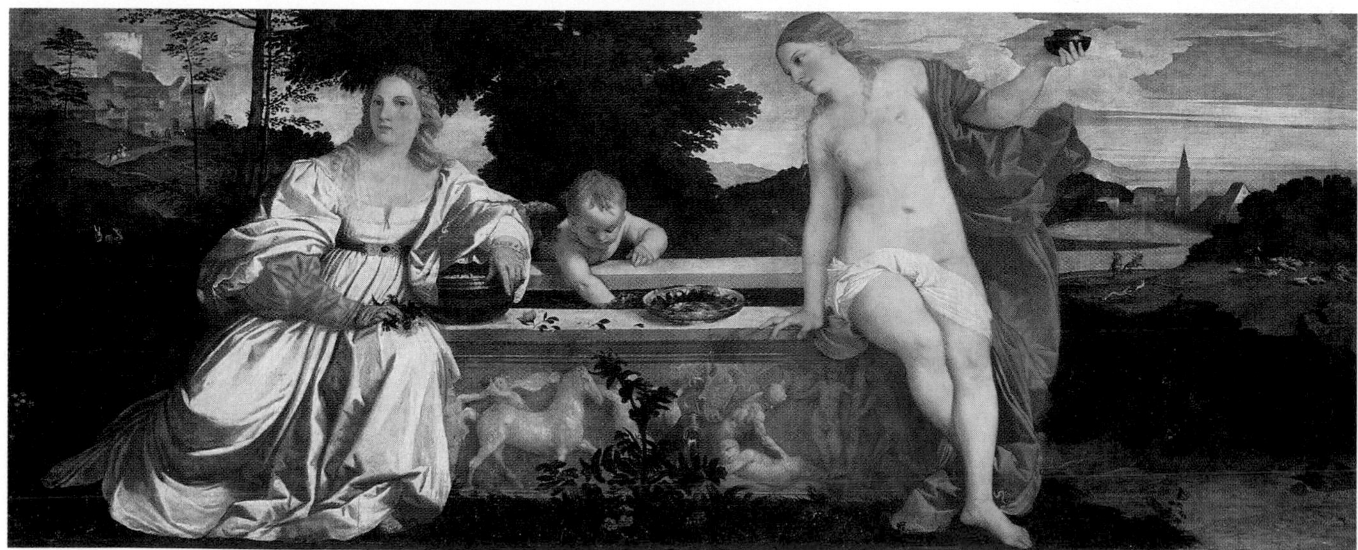

Arcadian setting, its allegory, and its complex and enigmatic meaning. Two young women, one draped, the other nude, flank a sarcophagus into which a cupid reaches. Behind them is a screen of trees and, to left and right, deep vistas into different landscapes. The two figures may represent the different levels of Neo-Platonic love: the sumptuously draped woman is a kind of allegory of vanity and the love of this world; the nude who holds aloft her lamp represents the highest level of love that can be reached (love of the divine, nudity being symbolic of truth). Titian's figures are not suffused with Giorgione's glowing, mysterious tones; they are drawn firmly and boldly and brilliantly colored, and the artist manifests his chief interest in the play of light over the rich satins and the smooth volumes of the body and glossy flesh. The world given to the eye is a world of color before it is a world of solid forms, and this truth is one that the Venetians were the first to grasp.

On the death of Giovanni Bellini in 1516, Titian was appointed painter to the republic of Venice. Shortly thereafter, he painted the *Madonna of the Pesaro Family* (FIG. **17-61**) for the church of the Frari. This great work, which furthered Titian's reputation and established his personal style, was presented to the church by Jacopo Pesaro, Bishop of Paphos in Cyprus and commander of the papal fleet, in thanksgiving for a successful expedition in 1502 against the Turks during the Venetian-Turkish war. In a stately, sunlit setting, the Madonna receives the commander, who kneels dutifully at the foot of her throne. A soldier (St. George?) behind the commander carries a banner with the arms of the Borgia (Pope Alexander VI); behind him is a turbaned Turk, a captive of the Christian forces. St. Peter occupies the steps of the throne, and St. Francis introduces other members of the Pesaro family, who kneel solemnly in the right foreground.

The massing of monumental figures, singly and in groups, within a weighty and majestic architecture is, as we have seen, characteristic of the High Renaissance. But Titian does not compose a horizontal and symmetrical arrangement, as Leonardo did in *The Last Supper* (FIG. 17-3) or Raphael in *The School of Athens* (FIG. 17-16). Rather, he places the figures in occult balance on a steep diagonal, positioning the Madonna, the focus of the composition, well off the central axis. Attention is directed to her by the perspective lines, by the inclination of the figures, and by the directional lines of gaze and gesture. The design is beautifully brought into poise by the banner that inclines toward the left, balancing the rightward and upward tendencies of the main direction.

This kind of composition is more dynamic than what we have seen so far in the High Renaissance.

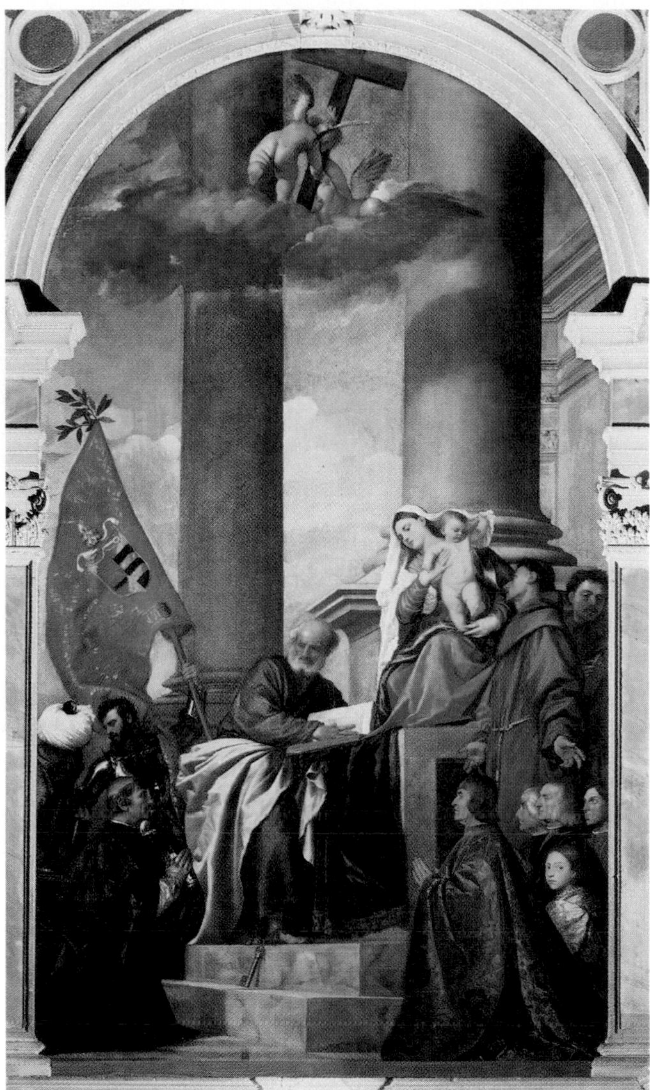

17-61 TITIAN, *Madonna of the Pesaro Family*, 1519–1526. Oil on canvas, approx. 16′ × 9′. Santa Maria dei Frari, Venice.

The forces already moving in it promise a new kind of pictorial design—one built on movement rather than rest. In his rendering of the rich surface textures, Titian gives a dazzling display of color in all its nuances. The human—especially the Venetian—scene is one with the heavenly, as the Madonna and saints find themselves honoring the achievements of particular men in this particular world. A quite worldly transaction is taking place between a queen, her court, and her loyal servants; the tableau is constructed in terms of Renaissance protocol and courtly splendor.

As Praxiteles brought the motif of the feminine nude into ancient Greek art, so Giorgione and Titian re-create it for the art of the modern West. In 1538, at the height of his powers, Titian painted the *Venus of*

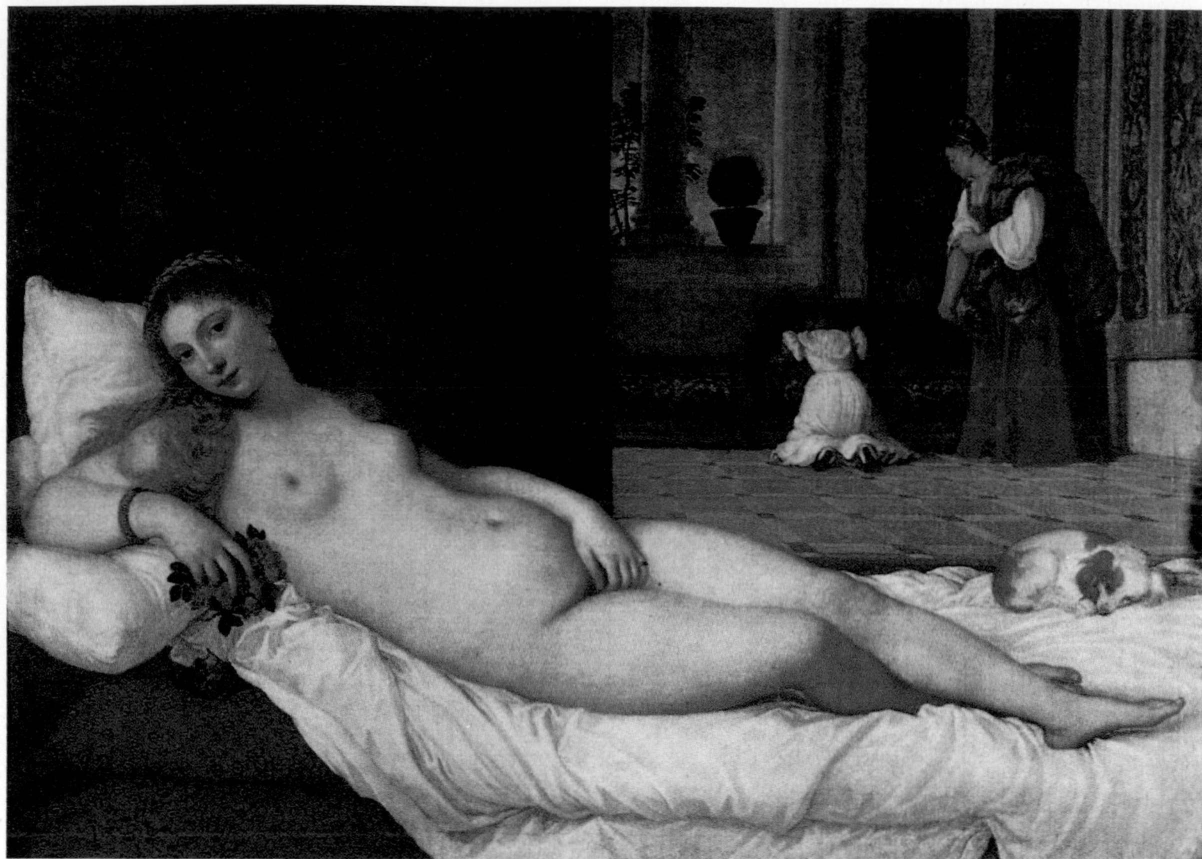

17-62 TITIAN, *Venus of Urbino,* 1538. Oil on canvas, approx. 48″ × 66″. Galleria degli Uffizi, Florence.

Urbino (FIG. **17-62**), for Guidobaldo II, the Duke of Urbino. This work gives us the compositional essentials for the representation of a theme that will be popular for centuries. Titian's version, based on an earlier (and pioneering) one painted by Giorgione, was to become official for paintings of the reclining nude, regardless of the many variations that would later ensue. Venus reclines on a gentle slope made by her luxurious, pillowed couch, the linear play of the draperies contrasting with the sleek, continuous volume of her body. At her feet is a pendant (balancing) figure—in this case, a slumbering lapdog. Behind her, a simple drape serves both to place her figure emphatically in the foreground and to press a vista into the background at the right half of the picture. In the vista, two servants bend over a chest; beyond them, a smaller vista opens into a landscape. The steps backward into space and the division of the space into progressively smaller units are beautifully contrived. All of the resources of pictorial representation are in Titian's hands, and he uses them here to create original and exquisite effects of the sort that will inspire generations of painters in Italy and the north.

Deep Venetian reds set off against the pale, neutral whites of the linen and the warm ivory-gold of the flesh are echoed in the red tones of the matron's skirt, the muted reds of the tapestries, and the neutral whites of the matron's sleeves and the kneeling girl's gown. One must study the picture carefully to realize what subtlety of color planning is responsible, for example, for the placing of the two deep reds (in the foreground cushions and in the background skirt) that function so importantly in the composition as a gauge of distance and as terminals of an implied diagonal opposed to the real one of the reclining figure. Here, color is used not simply for the tinting of preexisting forms but as a means of organization that determines the placement of forms.

Titian could paint a Virgin Mary or a nude Venus with equal zeal. Neither he nor the connoisseurs of his time were aware of any contradiction. Yet it is significant that the female nude reappears in Western art as Venus, the great goddess of the ancient world, whom medieval Christianity had especially feared and whom it damned in exalting virginity and chastity as virtues. Now Venus returns, and the great Venetian paintings of her almost constitute pagan altarpieces. The Venetian Renaissance resurrects a formidable competitor for the saints.

Titian was not only a prolific painter of mythological and religious subjects but also a highly esteemed portraitist, and one of the very best. Of the well over fifty portraits by his hand to survive, an early example, *Man with the Glove* (FIG. **17-63**), will suffice to illustrate his style. The portrait is a trifle more than half-length. The head is turned slightly away from the observer; the right hand gathers the drapery of a mantle, and the gloved left hand holds another glove. The blade-shaped shirtfront directs attention to the right hand; the direction of the subject's gaze controls the left. These dexterous compositional arrangements, creating a kind of "three-spot" relationship among head and hands, had already been made by Leonardo in his *Mona Lisa* (FIG. 17-4). Titian's portraits, as well as those of many of the Venetian and subsequent schools, generally make much of the psychological reading of the most expressive parts of the body—the head and the hands. We are not immediately aware that these subtle placements influence our response to the portrait subject. In fact, a portrait must be as skillfully composed as a great figure composition. The mood of this portrait is Giorgionesque—one of dreamy preoccupation. The eyes turn away from us, as if, in conversation, the subject has recalled something that sets him musing in silence. Titian's *Man with the Glove* is as much the portrait of a cultivated state of mind as of a particular individual. It is the meditative, poetic youth, who is at the same time Baldassare Castiglione's ideal courtier, perfectly

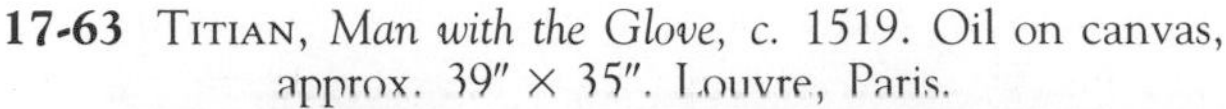

17-63 TITIAN, *Man with the Glove,* c. 1519. Oil on canvas, approx. 39″ × 35″. Louvre, Paris.

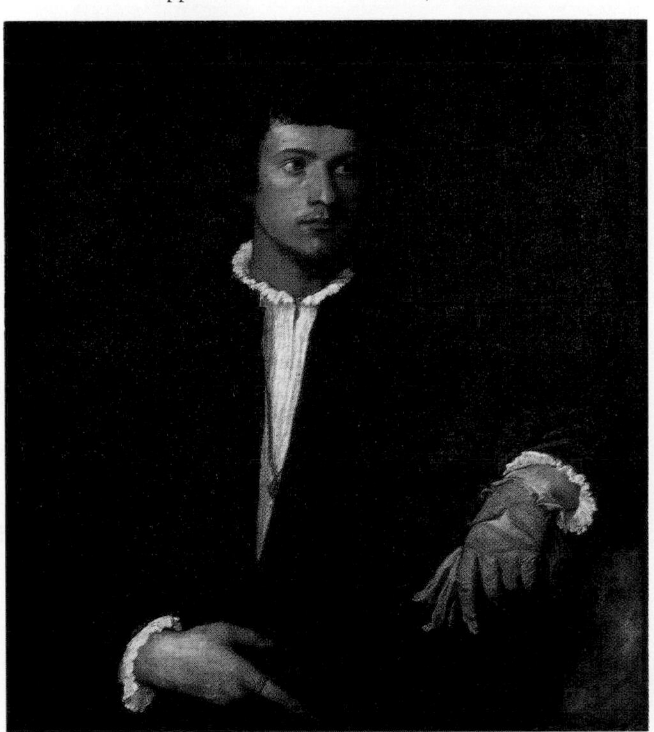

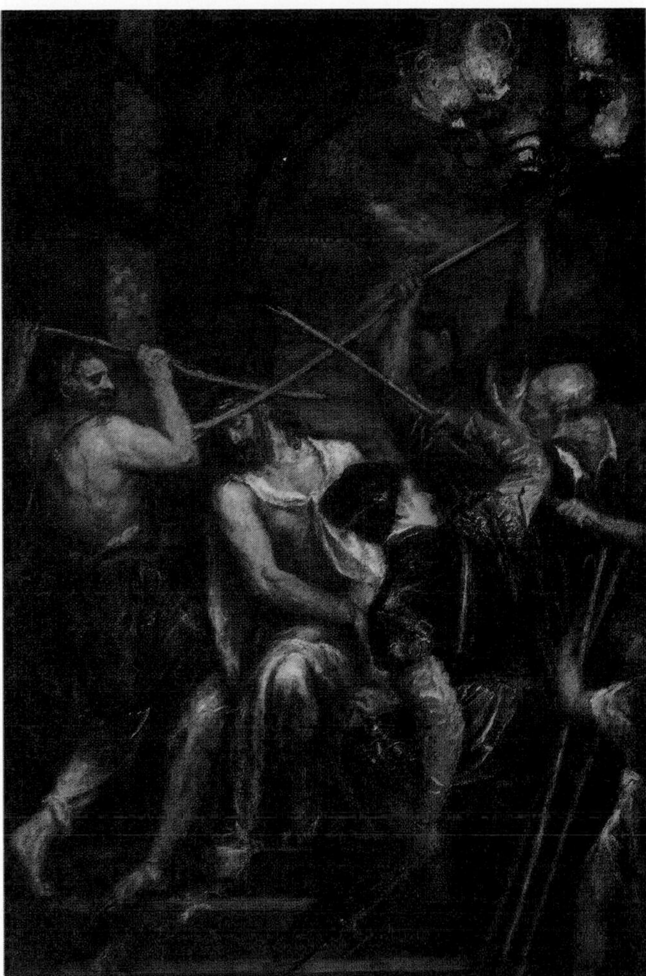

17-64 TITIAN, *Christ Crowned with Thorns,* c. 1573–1575. Oil on canvas, approx. 9′ × 6′. Alte Pinakothek, Munich.

poised and self-assured, handsome, gallant, debonair, the "glass of fashion and the mold of form." No portrait gives us so much of the Renaissance manner in a single individual, unless it be Raphael's *Castiglione* (FIG. 17-18).

Honor and glory attached to Titian as he grew older. He was known and sought after by all the great of Europe. He was painter to and close friend of Emperor Charles V, who made him a knight of the Holy Roman Empire; afterward, he painted numerous pictures for Charles's son, Philip II of Spain. The great Hapsburg painting collections centered around Titian's works, and his fame and wealth recall the success of Raphael. Toward the end of his life, his work became increasingly introspective, and a religious picture like the *Christ Crowned with Thorns* (FIG. **17-64**) seems to be a sincerely devotional theme repudiating the paganism of the artist's prime. In this picture, Titian shows Christ tormented by the soldiers of Pilate, who twist a wreath of thorns around his head. The drama is achieved by the limited number of figures, the emphasis on the figure of Christ, and the muted, flickering light that centers the action. The color scheme is almost monochromatic; the light and color play freely within and beyond the contours, making a patchy, confused mixture of lights and darks, in which it is difficult to read the forms with precision. But this effect only enhances the mystery, the gloomy environment, and the mood of torment. Titian's intention is not so much to stage the event as to present his religious and personal response to it. His very brushstroke—broad, thick, and freely applied—bespeaks the directness of his approach. It melts and scatters solid form to produce the wavering, supernatural glow that encircles spiritual vision. Here Titian's art looks forward to the painting of Rembrandt in the next century.

Tintoretto and Veronese

TINTORETTO (Jacopo Robusti, 1518–1594) claimed to be a student of Titian and aspired to combine the color of Titian with the drawing of Michelangelo. He usually is referred to as the outstanding Venetian representative of Mannerism. He adopts many Mannerist pictorial devices, but his dramatic power, depth of spiritual vision, and glowing Venetian color schemes do not seem to fit the Mannerist mold. We need not settle here the question of whether or not Tintoretto is a Mannerist; we need only mention that he shares some common characteristics with central Italian Mannerism and that, in other respects, his work really anticipates the Baroque.

The art of Tintoretto is always extremely dramatic. In his *Miracle of the Slave* (FIG. **17-65**), we find some of his typical stageplay. St. Mark hurtles downward to the assistance of a Christian slave, who is about to be martyred for the faith, and shatters the instruments of torture. These are held up by the executioner to the startled judge as the throng around the central action stares. The dynamism of Titian is greatly accelerated, and the composition is made up of contrary and opposing motions; for any figure leaning in one direction, another figure counters it. At the extreme left, a group of two men, a woman, and a child winds contrapuntally about a column, resembling the later Mannerist twisting of Giovanni da Bologna's *Rape of*

17-65 TINTORETTO, *The Miracle of the Slave*, 1548. Oil on canvas, approx. 14′ × 18′. Galleria dell' Accademia, Venice.

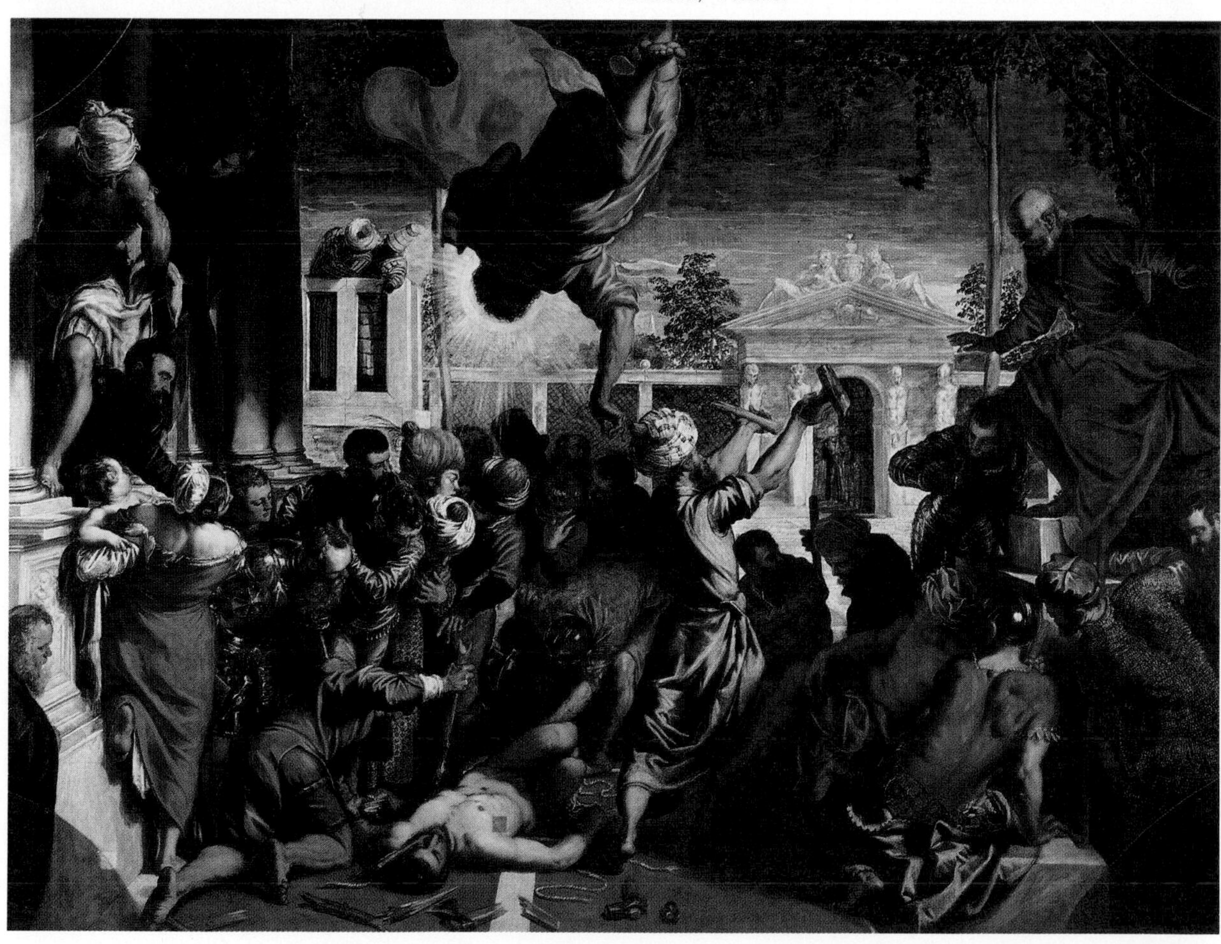

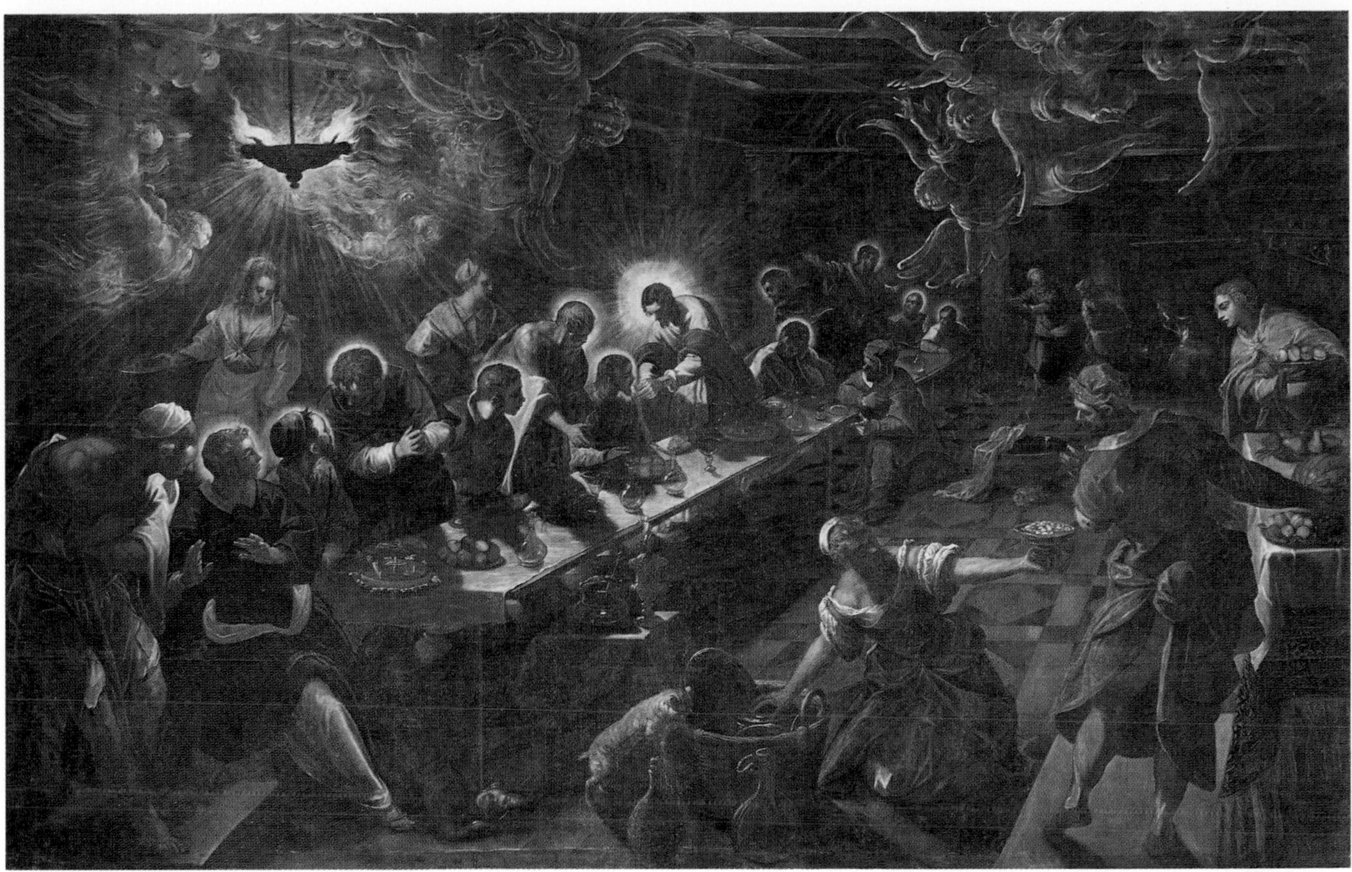

17-66 TINTORETTO, *The Last Supper,* 1594. Oil on canvas, 12′ × 18′ 8″. Chancel, San Giorgio Maggiore, Venice.

the Sabine Women (FIG. 17-46). The main group curves deeply back into space, but the most dynamic touch of all is made by the central trio of the slave, the executioner, and the inverted St. Mark. The three figures sweep together in a great, upward, serpentine curve, the motion of which is checked by the plunging figure of St. Mark, moving in the opposite direction. The entire composition is a kind of counterpoint of motion characteristic of Mannerism. The motion, however, is firmly contained within the picture frame, and the robustness of the figures, their solid structure and firm movement, the clearly composed space, and the coherent action have little to do with Manneristic presentation. There is nothing hesitant or ambiguous in the depiction of the miraculous event, which is dramatized forcefully and with conviction. Tintoretto's skillful theatricality and sweeping power of execution set him apart from the Mannerists and make him a forerunner of the Baroque, the age of theater and opera. And the tonality—the deep golds, reds, and greens—is purely Venetian.

Toward the end of his life, Tintoretto's art, like Titian's, becomes spiritual, even visionary, as solid forms melt away into swirling clouds of dark, shot through with fitful light. In Tintoretto's *Last Supper* (FIG. **17-66**), painted for Palladio's church of San Giorgio Maggiore (FIG. 17-54), the actors take part in a ghostly drama; they are as insubstantial as the shadows cast by the faint glow of their halos and the flame of a single lamp that seems to breed phosphorescent spirits. All are moved by an intense, psychic commotion. The space speeds away into an unearthly darkness peopled by phantoms. Only the incandescent nimbus around his head identifies Jesus as he administers the Sacrament to his disciples.

The contrast with Leonardo's *Last Supper* (FIG. 17-3) is both extreme and instructive. Leonardo's composition, balanced and symmetrical, parallels the picture plane in a geometrically organized and closed space; Christ's figure is the tranquil center of the drama and the focus of the perspective. In Tintoretto's painting, Christ is above and beyond the converging perspective lines that race diagonally away from the picture surface, creating disturbing effects of limitless depth and motion. Tintoretto's Christ is located by light flaring beaconlike out of darkness; Leonardo's is placed by geometric and perspectival centralization. The contrast of the two expresses the direction Renaissance painting takes in the sixteenth century, as it moves away from architectonic clarity of space and neutral lighting toward the dynamic perspectives and dramatic chiaroscuro of the coming Baroque.

The last of the great Venetian masters was Veronese (Paolo Cagliari, 1528–1588). Where Tintoretto glories in monumental drama and deep perspectives, Veronese specializes in splendid pageantry painted in superb color and set within a majestic, Classical architecture. Like Tintoretto, Veronese painted on a huge scale, with canvases often as large as 20 by 30 feet. His usual subjects, painted for the refectories of wealthy monasteries, afforded him an opportunity to display magnificent companies at table. *Christ in the House of Levi* (fig. **17-67**), originally called *The Last Supper,* is a good example. Here, in a great open loggia framed by three monumental arches (the style of the architecture closely resembles the upper arcades of Jacopo Sansovino's library; fig. 17-50), Christ is seen seated at the center of splendidly garbed grandees of Venice, while with a courtly gesture, the very image of gracious grandeur, the chief steward welcomes guests. The spacious loggia is crowded not only with robed magnificoes but with their colorful retainers, clowns, dogs, and dwarfs. The Holy Office of the Inquisition accused Veronese of impiety in painting such creatures so close to the Lord, and he was ordered to make changes at his own expense. Reluctant to do so, he simply changed the painting's title, converting the subject to a less solemn one. As Palladio looks to the example of the Classical architecture of the High Renaissance, so Veronese returns to High Renaissance composition, its symmetrical balance, and its ordered architectonics. His shimmering color is drawn from the whole spectrum, although he avoids solid colors for half shades (light blues, sea greens, lemon yellows, roses, and violets), creating veritable flower beds of tone.

Tintoretto and Veronese were employed by the republic of Venice to decorate the grand chambers and council rooms of the Doge's Palace. A great and popular decorator, Veronese shows himself to be a master of imposing, illusionistic ceiling compositions like *The Triumph of Venice* (fig. **17-68**), where within an oval frame, he presents Venice, crowned by Fame, enthroned between two great, twisted columns in a balustraded loggia, garlanded with clouds, and attended by figures symbolic of her glories. This work represents one of the very first modern, pictorial glorifications of a state—a subject that will become very popular during the Baroque period. Veronese's perspective is not, like Mantegna's or Correggio's, projected directly up from below; rather, it is a projection of the scene at a forty-five degree angle to the spectator, a technique that will be used by many later Baroque decorators, particularly the Venetian Tiepolo in the eighteenth century.

It is fitting that we close our discussion of Italian art in the sixteenth century with a scene of triumph, for indeed the century witnessed the triumph of architecture, sculpture, and painting. They achieve the status of fine arts, and a tradition is established by these masters of prodigious genius, whose works inspire all artists who follow but never surpass them.

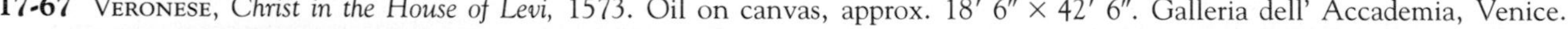

17-67 Veronese, *Christ in the House of Levi,* 1573. Oil on canvas, approx. 18′ 6″ × 42′ 6″. Galleria dell' Accademia, Venice.

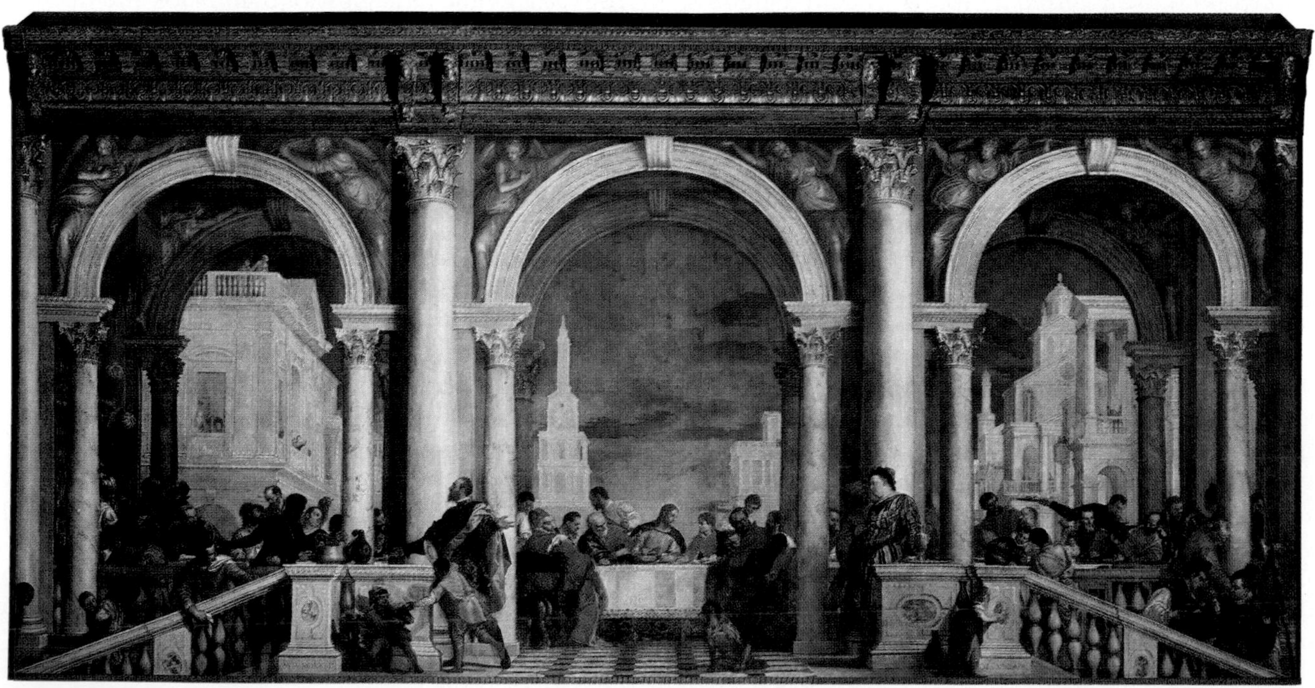

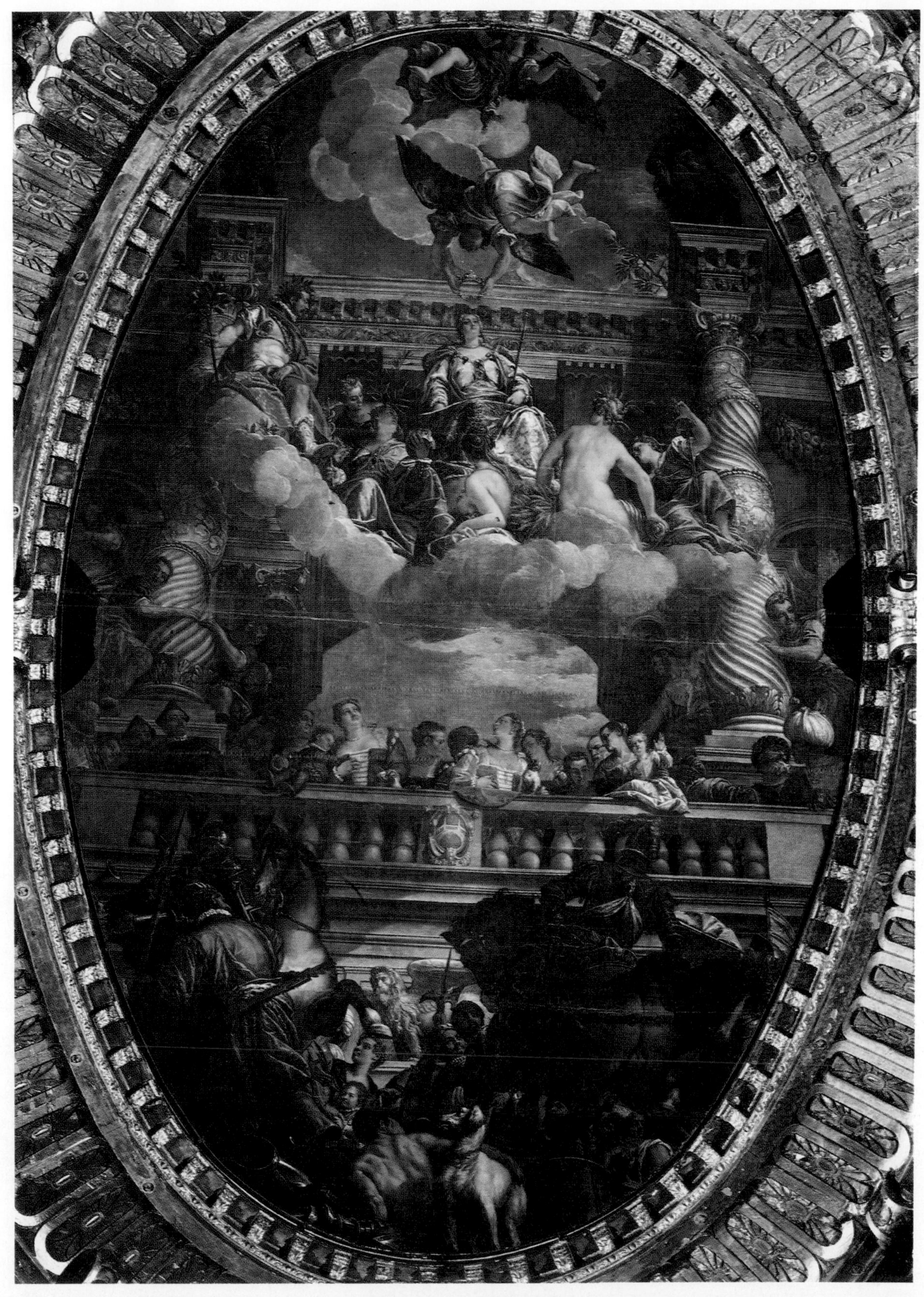

17-68 Veronese, *The Triumph of Venice, c.* 1585. Oil on canvas. Ceiling of the Hall of the Grand Council, Palazzo Ducale, Venice.

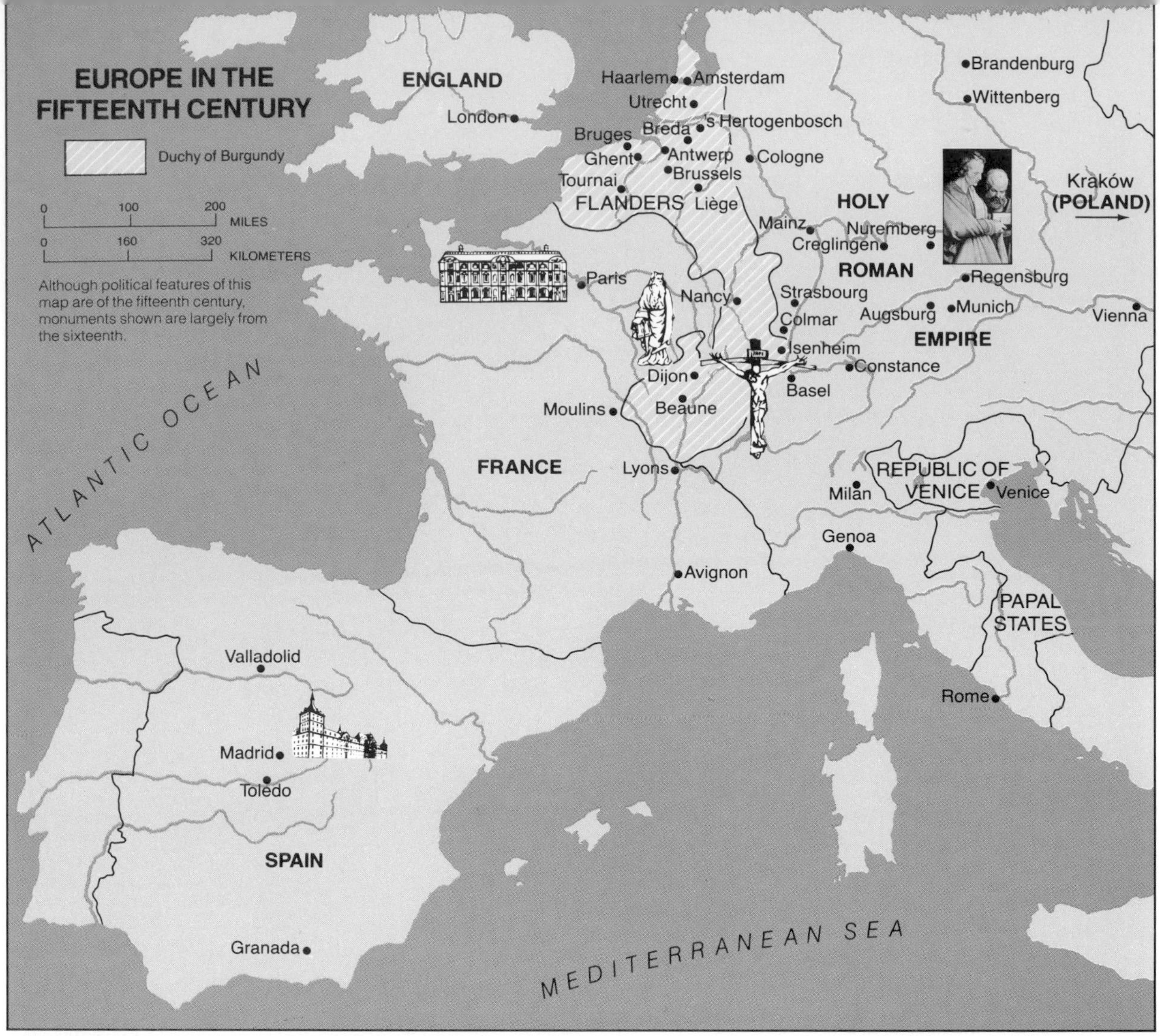

EUROPE IN THE FIFTEENTH CENTURY

Duchy of Burgundy

0 100 200 MILES

0 160 320 KILOMETERS

Although political features of this map are of the fifteenth century, monuments shown are largely from the sixteenth.

ENGLAND
London
Haarlem
Amsterdam
Utrecht
Bruges
Breda
's Hertogenbosch
Ghent
Antwerp
Cologne
Tournai
Brussels
FLANDERS
Liège
Brandenburg
Wittenberg
HOLY
ROMAN
EMPIRE
Mainz
Nuremberg
Creglingen
Regensburg
Kraków
(POLAND)
Paris
Nancy
Strasbourg
Colmar
Augsburg
Munich
Vienna
Isenheim
Constance
Basel
Dijon
Beaune
Moulins
ATLANTIC OCEAN
FRANCE
Lyons
Milan
REPUBLIC OF VENICE
Venice
Genoa
Avignon
PAPAL STATES
Rome
Valladolid
Madrid
Toledo
SPAIN
Granada
MEDITERRANEAN SEA

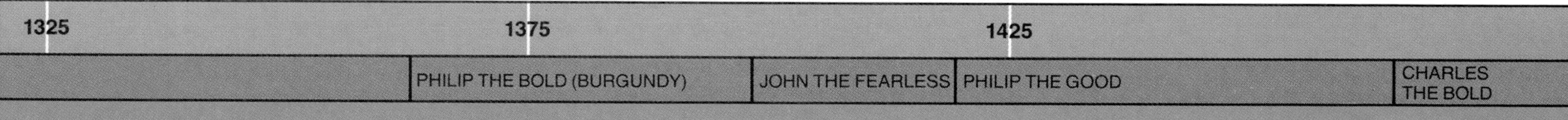

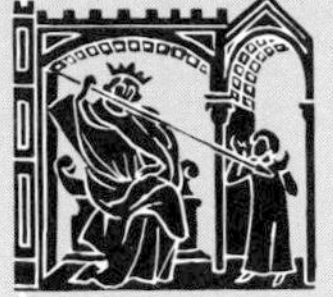

PUCELLE
Belleville Breviary
c. 1325

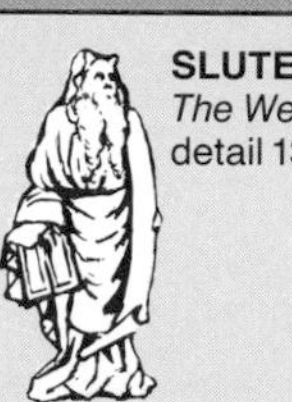

SLUTER
The Well of Moses,
detail 1395–1406

CAMPIN
c. 1378–1444

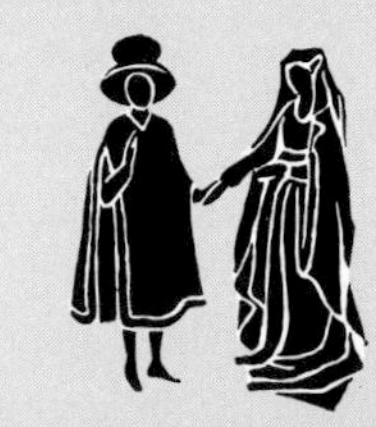

VAN EYCK
Giovanni Arnolfini and His Bride,
detail 1434

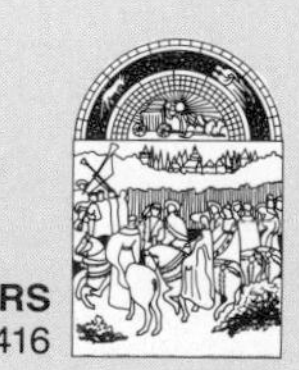

LIMBOURG BROTHERS
May c. 1413–1416

FOUQUET
c. 1420–1481

BROEDERLAM
active 1385–1409

VAN DER WEYDEN
c. 1400–1464

Hundred Years' War begins 1337

The Papacy in Avignon 1305–1376

Chaucer *The Canterbury Tales* 1387–1400

The Great Schism in the Church 1376–1415

The Netherlands under the Dukes of Burgundy 1384–1477

Hundred Years' War ends 1453

18
THE RENAISSANCE OUTSIDE OF ITALY

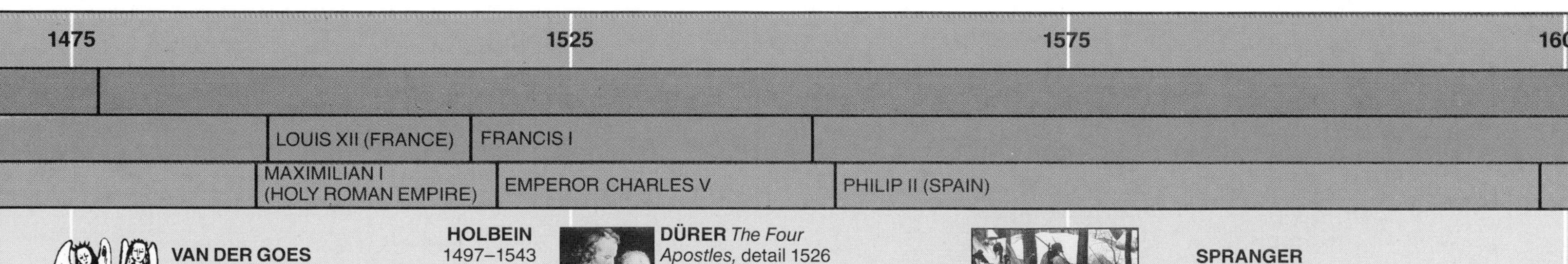

VAN DER GOES *The Portinari Altarpiece,* detail *c.* 1476

HOLBEIN 1497–1543

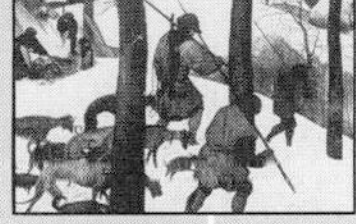

DÜRER *The Four Apostles,* detail 1526

PRIMATICCIO 1504–1570

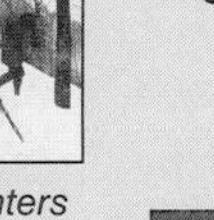

BRUEGEL *Hunters in the Snow,* detail 1565

SPRANGER 1546–1611

PATINIR 1475–1524

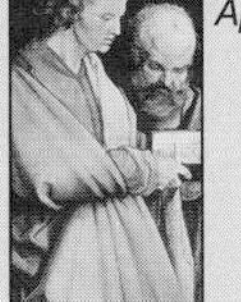

SCHONGAUER *c.* 1450–1491

CLOUET *c.* 1485–1541

GRÜNEWALD *The Isenheim Altarpiece,* detail *c.* 1510–1515

GOUJON 1510–1565

PILON *c.* 1535–1590

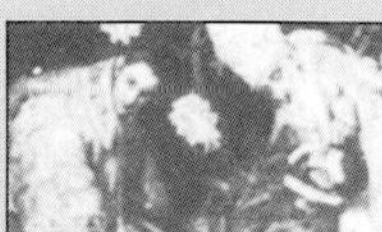

EL GRECO *The Burial of Count Orgaz,* detail 1586

MEMLING *c.* 1430–1494

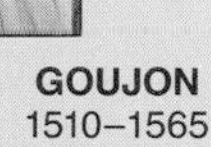

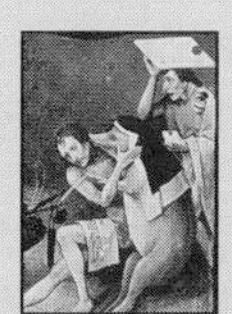

BOSCH *The Garden of Earthly Delights,* detail 1505–1510

STOSS 1447–1533

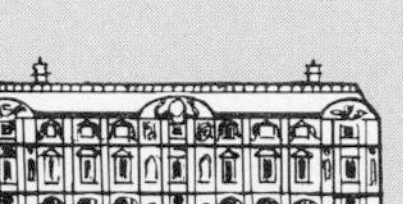

LESCOT Louvre Square Court begun 1546

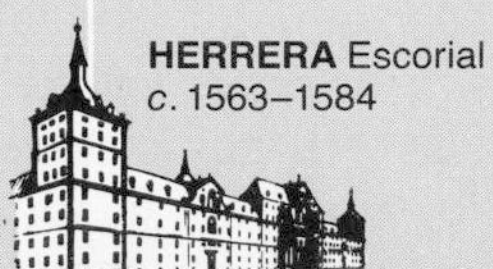

HERRERA Escorial *c.* 1563–1584

Henry VIII of England *r.* 1509–1547

Protestant Reformation begins 1517

Council of Trent 1545–1562

Copernicus announces planetary theory 1543

Netherlands proclaims independence from Spain 1581

Columbus arrives in West Indies 1492

Erasmus *c.* 1466–1536

Catholic Counter-Reformation begins

Birth of Galileo and Shakespeare 1564

Europe colonizes North and South America 1519–1600

While great artistic events were happening in Renaissance Italy, the lands beyond the Alps still were immersed in the Gothic style that Italy never had really accepted as its own. Strictly speaking, the term *Renaissance* refers to the revival of ancient Roman ideals and forms in Italian art of the fifteenth century and later, and the applicability of the term to the contemporaneous art of non-Italian Europe has been questioned. Gothicism in architecture persisted well into the sixteenth century in the north, which never knew classical antiquity as the Italians knew it. In Italy, the remains of the Classical world were everywhere, and the Italians believed themselves to be descendants of the ancient Romans. The Gothic International style of the fourteenth century was, for the Italians, only a passing fashion; coming between Giotto and Masaccio, it hardly constitutes more than a brief interruption of a new stylistic movement that will carry along with it the future of European art. In the north, too, the International style will pass, giving way to a powerful realism that, even without the inspiration of the Classical Antique style, will break with the past and point directions of its own. New artistic and socioeconomic developments in northern Europe usher in changes that set the fifteenth century apart from the Middle Ages just as much as in Italy and justify the use of the term *Renaissance* for northern art as well.

The northern painter, evolving out of the illuminator, finds, as did the artist in Italy, a new prestige and place. Although it coexisted with a development of commerce and wealth almost modern in tone, the social structure of the north in the fifteenth century adhered to the hierarchies of the Middle Ages. The nobles and clergy continued to rule, even though the true source of wealth and power was the bourgeoisie. This large middle class, in turn, still was organized and controlled by the guild system that had taken form in the Middle Ages.

In the north, the guild dominated the life of the average man to an even greater extent than in Italy. To pursue a craft, a man had to belong to the guild controlling that craft. Painters, for example, sought admission to the Guild of St. Luke, which included the saddlers, glassworkers, and mirrorworkers as well. To secure membership in the guild, the aspiring painter was apprenticed in boyhood to a master, with whom he lived as a son and who taught him the fundamentals of his craft: how to make implements; how to prepare panels with gesso (plaster mixed with a binding material); and how to mix colors, oils, and varnishes. Once the youth mastered these procedures and learned to work in the traditional manner of his master, he usually spent several years working as a journeyman in various cities, observing and gaining ideas from other masters. He was then eligible to become a master and was admitted to the guild. Through the guild, he obtained commissions; the guild inspected his painting for honest materials and workmanship and secured him adequate payment for his labor. The result was the solid craftsmanship that characterizes the best work of Flanders and of Italy.

We know much less about the training of women artists than we do about that of men. Certainly, far fewer women were involved in the professions of art, although a substantial number of women are recorded in the membership of the art guilds of Flemish cities like Bruges in the fifteenth century and later. Albrecht Dürer recounts women's participation in parades of the guilds as persons earning a livelihood by their art.

Women most often were tutored in art by fathers and husbands who were professionals, and whom they assisted in all technical procedures of the craft. Social and moral restraints would have forbidden women's apprenticeship in the homes of male masters and would have stringently limited their freedom of movement. Moreover, from the sixteenth century on, when academic courses of training supplement and then replace guild training, women would not as a rule expect or be permitted instruction in figure painting, insofar as it involved dissection of cadavers and study of the nude, male model. Most women, as we have seen, did not have access to the training and experience enjoyed by many male artists. Yet Lavinia Teerlinc, a Flemish counterpart of Anguissola, was an accomplished professional in Bruges before she was invited to England to paint miniatures for the courts of Henry VIII and his successors. There, she was a formidable rival of Hans Holbein the Younger and received greater compensation for her work than he did for his.

The craftsmanship that gave such distinction to men and to women artists involved mastery of the new oil medium, which had such great influence on Venetian painters at the end of the fifteenth century; we have spoken of Titian's management of it (page 684). Traditionally, Jan van Eyck is credited with the invention of oil painting a century before Titian, although the facts surrounding the early history of the medium still remain mysterious. Flemish painters built up their pictures by superimposing translucent paint layers, called *glazes,* on a layer of opaque monochrome underpainting, which in turn had been built up from a carefully planned drawing made on a white-grounded panel of wood. The base of the binding medium for the pigments was a fast-drying oil that had been known and used by certain painters in the Late Middle Ages. The secret of the new technique appears to have been an unidentified supplement to the usual composition of the glazes. With the new medium, painters were able to create richer colors than previously had been possible. As a result, northern painting of the fifteenth century is characterized by a deep, intense tonality, glowing light (the new colors were seemingly lit from within), and hard, enamel-like surfaces, quite unlike the high-keyed color, sharp light, and rather matte surfaces of Italian tempera.

The brilliant and versatile new medium was exactly right for the formal intentions of the northern painters, who aimed for sharply focused, hard-edged, sparkling clarity of detail in their representation of thousands of objects ranging in scale from large to almost invisible. The Italians were interested primarily in the *structure* behind the appearances given to the eye—that is, in perspective, composition, anatomy, the mechanics of bodily motion, and proportion through measure. The northern painters were intent on rendering the *appearances* themselves—the bright, colored surfaces of things touched by light. Their traditions of stained glass and miniatures made their realism one of radiant, decorative color rather than of sculpturesque form. The differences between the painting of Italy and of northern Europe are emphasized by the fact that, when oil painting spread to Italy after the mid-century, it did not radically affect Italian sensibility to form. Although the color of Italian painting became richer, particularly in Venice, the new medium—which, in time, completely replaced tempera—was exploited in the service of the structural purposes of Italian art. On the whole, until the early sixteenth century, artistic communication between northern and southern Europe seems to have been limited to a relatively few individuals, and both areas tended to develop independently of each other.

The political background against which the development of northern art took place in the fifteenth century was not unlike that of Italy. The commercial free cities that dominated the political scene at the beginning of the fifteenth century gradually fell under the rule of princes until the beginning of the sixteenth century, when powerful states like France, England, and the Hapsburg empire, comprising Spain, the Germanies, and the Netherlands, began to emerge. As in Italy, the wealth and leisure necessary to encourage the growth of the arts were based on commerce and on the patronage of the powerful princes and rich merchants who controlled it.

THE FIFTEENTH CENTURY

Flanders

The most important of the prosperous commercial cities of the north was Bruges, which, like Florence, derived its wealth from the wool trade and from banking. Until late in the fifteenth century, an arm of the North Sea, now silted up, reached inland to Bruges. Here, ships brought raw wool from England and Spain and carried away the fine woolen cloth that became famous throughout Europe. The wool trade brought bankers, among them representatives of the House of Medici, and Bruges became the financial clearinghouse for all of northern Europe. In its streets, merchants from Italy and the Near East rubbed shoulders with traders from Russia and Spain. Despite the flourishing economies of its sister cities—Ghent, Louvain, and Ypres—Bruges so dominated Flanders that the Duke of Burgundy chose to make the city his capital and moved his court there from Dijon in the early fifteenth century.

The dukes of Burgundy were probably the most powerful rulers in northern Europe during the first three quarters of the fifteenth century. Although cousins of the French kings, they usually supported England (on which they relied for the raw materials used in their wool industry) during the Hundred Years' War and, at times, were in control of much of northern France, including Paris. Through intermarriage with the House of Flanders, they annexed the Low Countries, and, at the height of their power, their lands stretched from the Rhône River to the North Sea. Only the rash policies of the last of their line, Charles the Bold, and his death at the battle of Nancy in 1477 brought to an end the Burgundian dream of forming a strong middle kingdom between France and the Holy Roman Empire. After Charles's death, the southern Burgundian lands were reabsorbed by France, and the Netherlands passed to the Holy Roman Empire by virtue of the dynastic marriage of Charles's daughter, Mary of Burgundy, to Maximilian of Hapsburg.

Philip the Bold of Burgundy, who ruled from 1364 to 1404, and his brother John, Duke of Berry, were the greatest sponsors of the arts of their time in northern Europe. Their interests centered on illuminated manuscripts, Arras tapestries, and rich furnishings for their numerous castles and town houses, which were located throughout their duchies. Philip's largest artistic enterprise was the foundation of the Chartreuse (Carthusian monastery) de Champmol, near Dijon. Intended as a repository of the tombs of the grandees of the House of Burgundy, its magnificent endowment attracted artists from all parts of northern Europe. The outstanding representative of this short-lived Burgundian school was the sculptor CLAUS SLUTER (active *c.* 1380–1406).

For the cloister of the Chartreuse de Champmol, Sluter designed a symbolic well in which Moses and five other prophets surround a base that once supported a Crucifixion group. The six prophets of *The*

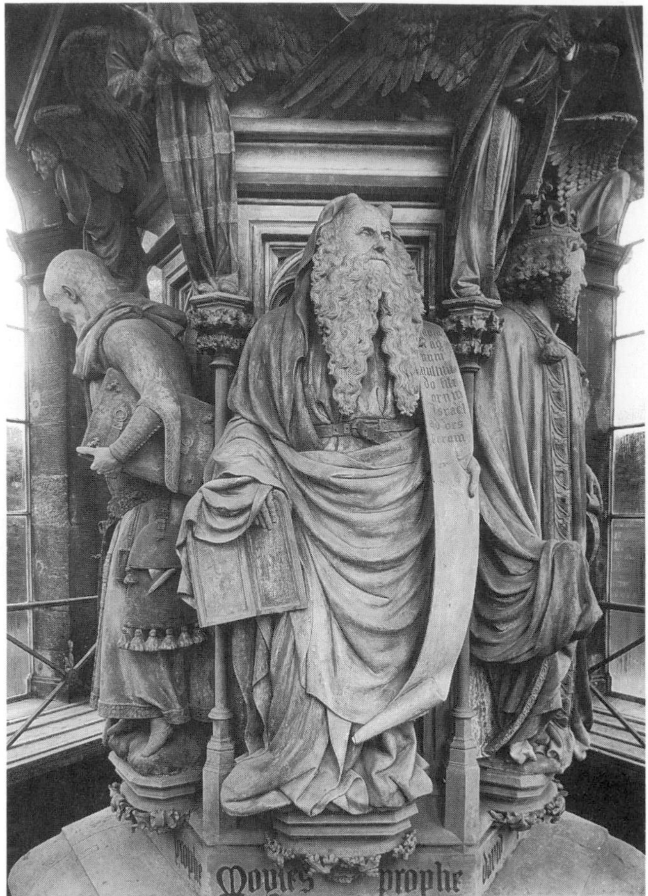

18-1 Claus Sluter, *The Well of Moses,* 1395–1406. Figures approx. 6′ high. Chartreuse de Champmol, Dijon, France.

Well of Moses (fig. **18-1**) recall the jamb figures of the Gothic portals, but they far surpass even the most realistic of those (fig. 10-34) in the artist's intense observation of natural appearance, in the rendering of minute detail, and in their bulk, which manages to contain a wealth of descriptive information that might otherwise be distracting. The life-size figures are swathed in heavy draperies with voluminous folds, characteristic of Sluter's style, and the artist manages to make their difficult, complex surfaces seem remarkably lifelike. This effect is enhanced by the skillful differentiation of textures, from coarse drapery to smooth flesh and silky hair, and by the paint, which still is partly preserved. This fascination with the specific and tangible in the visible world will be one of the chief characteristics of fifteenth-century Flemish painting. But despite the realism of Sluter's figures, a comparison of his *Moses* (fig. 18-1) and Donatello's *St. Mark* (fig. 16-5) reveals what is still missing in the northern concept of the figure: the principle of interior movement, or weight shift.

The Chartreuse de Champmol must have been furnished with numerous altarpieces, but only a carved altarpiece representing the Adoration of the Magi survives. The odd-shaped wings for this altarpiece were painted by Melchior Broederlam (active 1385–1409), a Flemish painter who had been drawn to Dijon. On the left wing are *The Annunciation* and *The Visitation* (fig. **18-2**); on the right wing, Broederlam depicts *The Presentation* and *The Flight into Egypt.* The paintings show that Broederlam was a major northern exponent of the International style. His compositional devices—the uptilted plane of the landscape in the *Visitation* scene, with its horizon topped by a castle; the serpentine recession into the background; and the elegant silhouettes of the figures, reminiscent of Sienese art—already have been seen in such southern works as Gentile da Fabriano's *Adoration of the Magi* (fig. 16-26). Also suggestive of Sienese art is Broederlam's modest essay into perspective and the delicate architectural enframement of the *Annunciation* scene. All of these elements have been combined with the minutest observation and rendering of realistic details. Broederlam, working at Dijon, must have seen Sluter's sculptures and was influenced by them in the handling of the voluminous drapery. But

18-2 Melchior Broederlam, *The Annunciation* and *The Visitation* (wing of an altarpiece), 1394–1399. Tempera and oil on wood, approx. 66″ × 49″. Musée des Beaux-Arts, Dijon.

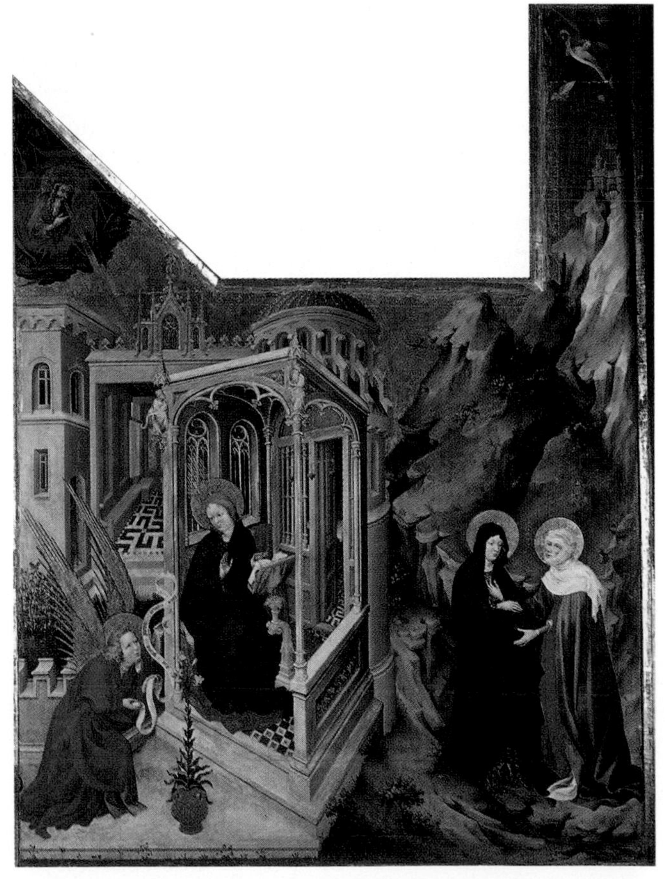

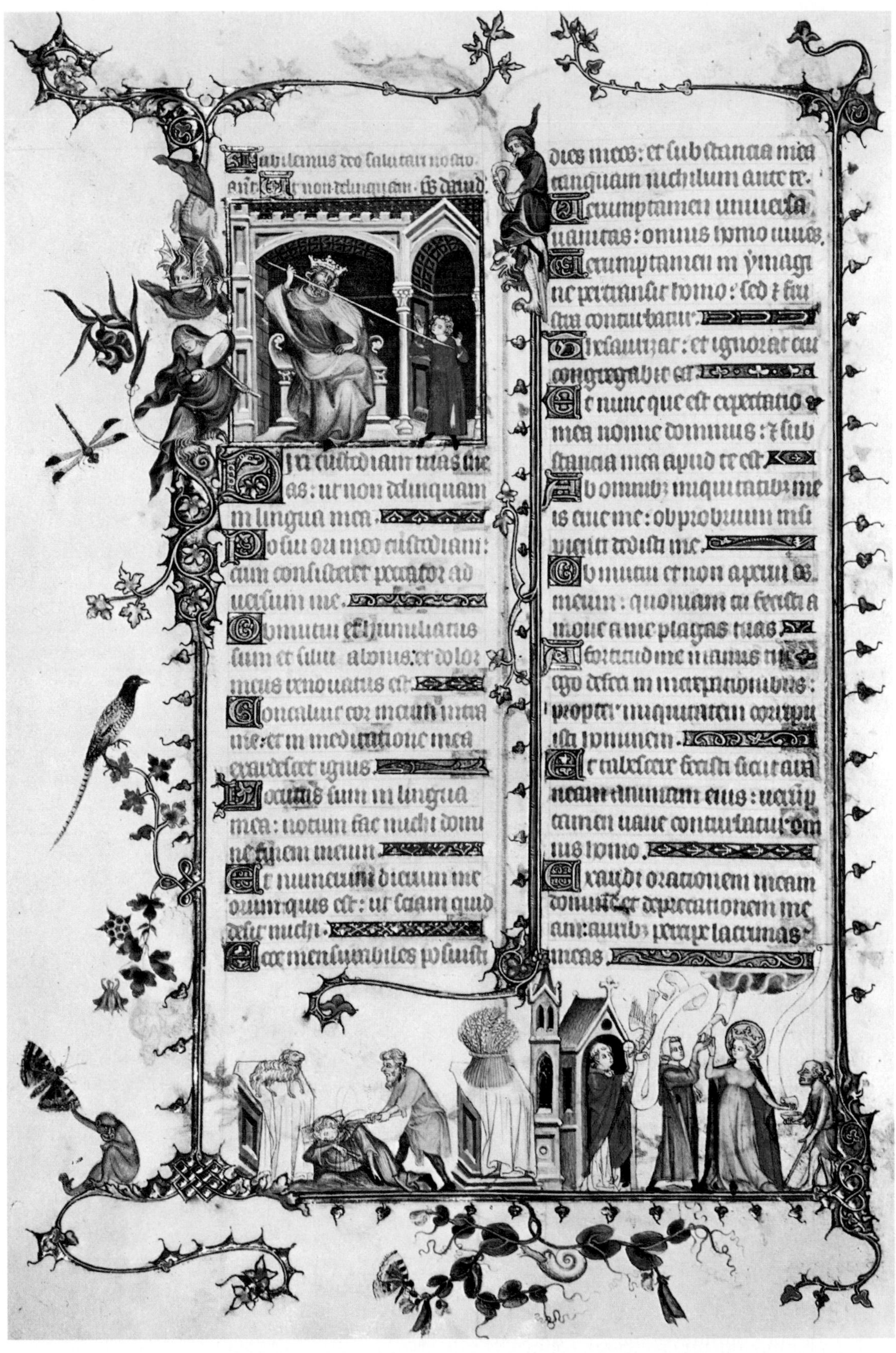

18-3 Jean Pucelle, *David before Saul*, page from the *Belleville Breviary*, c. 1325. Illumination, approx. 9½″ × 6¾″. Bibliothèque Nationale, Paris.

despite the large scale of the panels, the pattern-like composition fixed to the picture plane, the traceried screens of the architecture, the overall linearity, and the meticulous details still place the work within the tradition of Gothic illumination.

Critics sometimes point out that Broederlam's miniaturistic style is ill-suited to the size of these panels, which are some 5 feet high. This disproportion is attributable to the fact that, as some of the earliest surviving examples of northern panel paintings, these works still reflect a number of the long-standing northern painting traditions from which they are a revolutionary departure. For centuries, the characteristic painted surface in the north had been either stained glass or the illuminated manuscript page. Gothic architecture in northern Europe had eliminated solid walls and had left few continuous, blank surfaces that invited painted decorations, unlike the case in Italy, where climate and architecture favored mural painting in fresco. Northern artists were accustomed to working not only in miniature but with rich, jewel-like color, which, especially in stained glass, has a profound luminosity, with light seemingly irradiating the forms. Thus, they came into the fifteenth century habituated to deep color worked into exquisitely tiny and intricate shapes and patterns. When northern miniaturists became acquainted, through the International style, with Italian forms and ideas, they were forced to reduce to page size, or smaller, the inventions used in large compositions by Italian wall and panel painters like Duccio, Giotto, Simone Martini, and others. This development, which led to a kind of "perspective naturalism," was inconsistent with the basic function of book illumination—page decoration and the illustration of the written text. Toward the end of the fourteenth century, illuminations began to take on the character of independent paintings, expanding on the page until they occupied it completely. By about 1400, these new forces generated in miniatures seemed to demand larger surfaces, and the shift was made to panel painting.

The first steps toward the illumination's expansion within the text appear in the work of JEAN PUCELLE (active *c.* 1320–1370), a Parisian illuminator who revitalized the stagnating Gothic manner of the Paris school. A page from the so-called *Belleville Breviary*, about 1325 (FIG. **18-3**), shows how the entire page has become the province of the illuminator. The borders, extended to invade the margins, include not only decorative tendrils and a profusion of spiky ivy and floral ornaments, but also a myriad of insects, small animals, and grotesques. In addition, three narrative scenes encroach on the columns of the text, the graceful postures and flowing draperies of the figures reflecting Sienese influence. One feels that any of these narratives could have been expanded into a full-page illustration or even a panel painting.

Such an expansion has occurred in the calendar pages of a gorgeously illustrated Book of Hours made for the Duke of Berry, brother of the king of France and of Philip the Bold of Burgundy. The manuscript, *Les Très Riches Heures du Duc de Berry*, was completed in 1416 by the three LIMBOURG BROTHERS—Pol, Hennequin, and Herman. Such books became favorite possessions of the northern aristocracy during the fourteenth and fifteenth centuries. As prayer books, they replaced the traditional psalters, which had been the only liturgical books in private hands until the mid-thirteenth century. The heart of the Book of Hours is the "Office of the Blessed Virgin," which contains liturgical passages to be read privately at eight set points during the day, from matins to compline. This part of these books usually is preceded by an illustrated calendar containing local religious feast days; it is followed by penitential psalms, devotional prayers, litanies to the saints, and other offices, including those of the dead and of the Holy Cross.

The calendar pictures of *Les Très Riches Heures* are perhaps the most famous in the history of manuscript illumination. They represent the twelve months of the year in terms of the associated seasonal tasks, alternating the occupations of nobility and peasantry. Above each picture is a lunette representing the chariot of the sun as it makes its yearly round through the twelve months and signs of the zodiac; numerical notations designate the zodiacal degree passed through in the course of the year. Representative is the colorful calendar picture for the month of May (FIG. **18-4**). Here, a cavalcade of patrician ladies and gentlemen, preceded by trumpeters, rides out to celebrate the first day of May, a spring festival observed by courts throughout Europe. They are clad in springtime green, garlanded with fresh leaves, and sparkle with ornate finery. Behind them is a woodland and the château of Riom. These great country estates, most of which belonged to the Duke of Berry, loom in the backgrounds of most of the calendar pictures and are represented so faithfully that those that still survive today are easily recognized. The spirit of the picture is Chaucerian—lightsome, artificial, chivalric, and pleasure-loving. (*The Canterbury Tales* is hardly a generation older.) The elegant silhouettes, rich colors, and decorative linear effects again recall Sienese art. The varying scenes evidently were painted by different artists, but historians have never been able to assign specific pictures to the different Limbourg brothers. Nevertheless, although the artists' styles may differ, their main interests were the same. Within the confines of the International style,

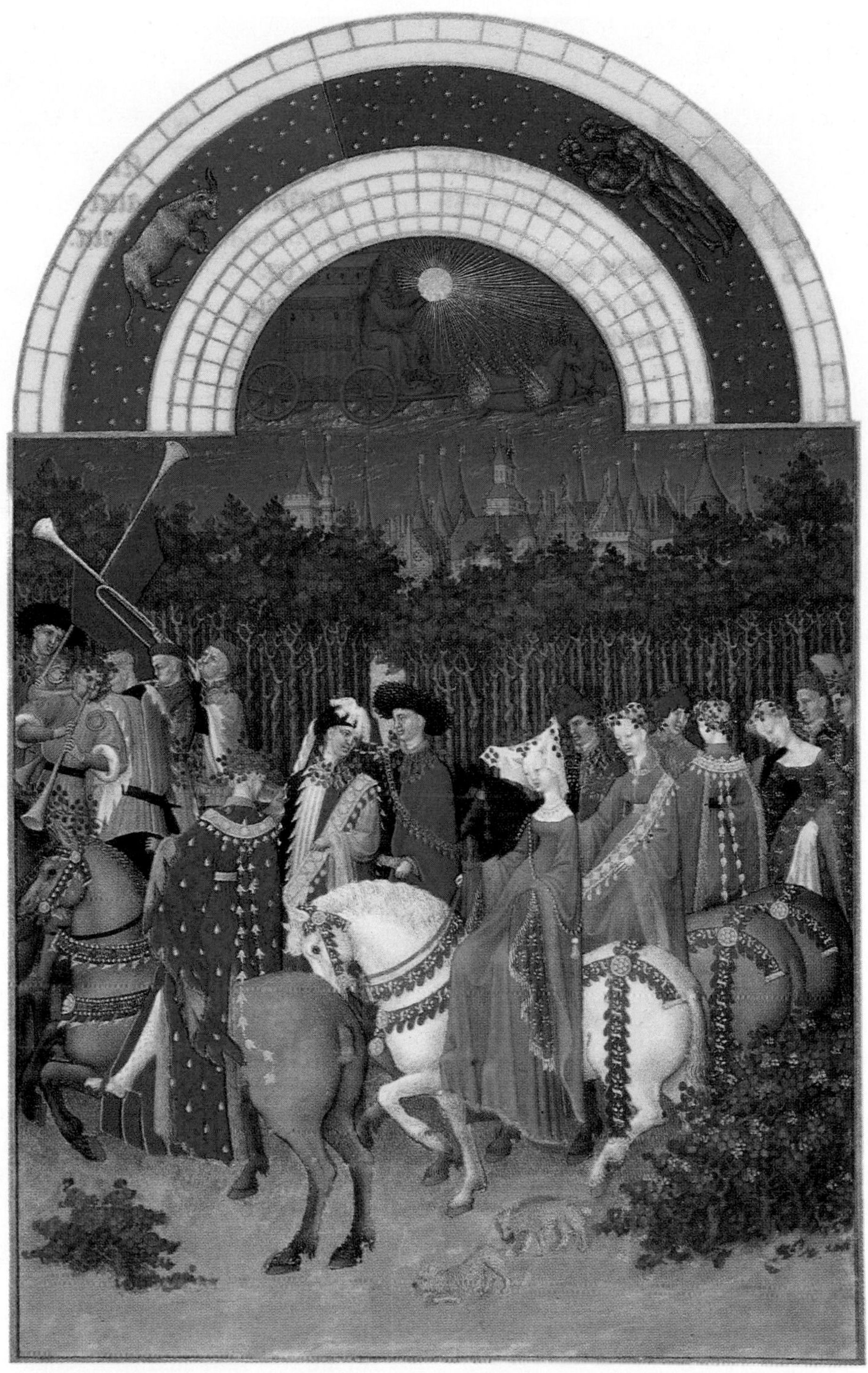

18-4 THE LIMBOURG BROTHERS, *May*, from *Les Très Riches Heures du Duc de Berry*, 1413–1416. Illumination, approx. 8½″ × 5½″. Musée Condé, Chantilly, France.

they represented as accurately as possible the actual world of appearances and the activities of men and women, peasants and aristocrats, in their natural surroundings at specific times of the year. Thus, the traditional field of subject matter has been expanded to include genre subjects; they are given a prominent place, even in a religious book. Secular and religious subjects remain neatly separated, but they will encroach on each other increasingly during the fifteenth century to produce as thorough a humanization of religious subject matter as we saw in Italy.

Hardly a decade after *Les Très Riches Heures*, an example of the International style at its peak, we have a work of quite different and novel conception, *The*

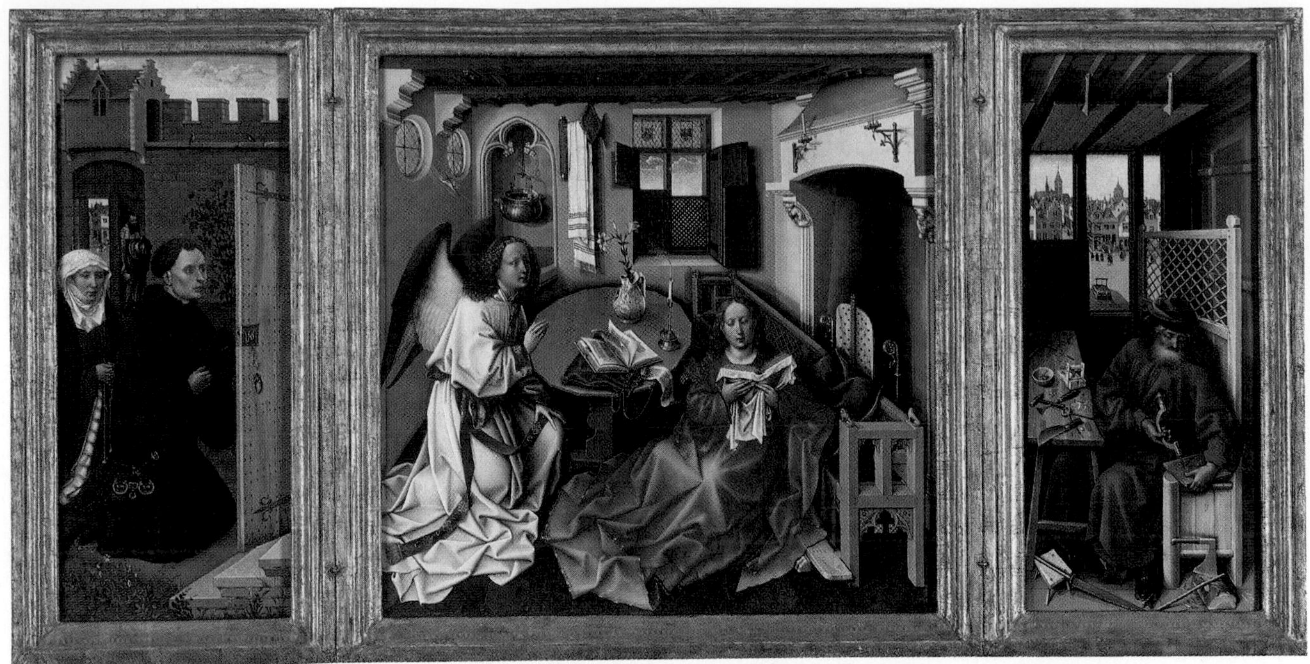

18-5 ROBERT CAMPIN (Master of Flémalle), *The Mérode Altarpiece* (open), *c.* 1425–1428. Tempera and oil on wood, center panel approx. 25″ × 25″. Metropolitan Museum of Art, New York (Cloisters Collection purchase).

Mérode Altarpiece (FIG. **18-5**) by the Master of Flémalle, now identified as ROBERT CAMPIN (*c.* 1378–1444), the leading painter of the city of Tournai. Here, the aristocratic taste, romantic mood, and ornamental style of the International painters are replaced with a relatively blunt, sober realism in setting and characterization. The old theme of the Annunciation occupies the central panel of the triptych, and something of Internationalism remains in its decorative line play, but the donors, depicted in the left panel, set the tone. Man and wife, they are of the grave and sedate middle class; unostentatiously prosperous, quietly attired, they kneel in a little courtyard, the man peering through the door at the mystery taking place in the central scene. Discreetly set apart from it, they take the mystery as a fact, and factualness determines the artist's whole approach.

All the objects in the Annunciation scene are rendered with careful attention to their actual appearance, and the event takes place in an everyday, middle-class Flemish interior, in which all accessories, furniture, and utensils are indicated, lest the setting be incomplete. But the objects represented are not merely that; book, candle, flowers, sink (in the corner niche), fire screen, polished pot, towels, and bench symbolize, in different ways, the Virgin's purity and her divine mission. In the right panel, Joseph has made a mousetrap, symbolic of the theological tradition that Christ is bait set in the trap of the world to catch the Devil. The carpenter's shop is completely inventoried by the painter, down to the vista into a distant city street. Thus, we have a thorough humanizing of a traditional religious theme—a transformation of it in terms of a particular time and place: a middle-class house, courtyard, and shop in a fifteenth-century city of Flanders. So close is the status of the sacred actors to the human level that they are even represented without halos; this does not happen in Italy until the end of the fifteenth century.

We have been tracing the humanization of art from the thirteenth century. The distance between the sacred and the secular has now narrowed to such a degree that they become intermixed. As Johan Huizinga, renowned modern historian of the fifteenth century, describes it:

> Individual and social life, in all their manifestations, are imbued with the conception of faith. There is not an object nor an action, however trivial, that is not constantly correlated with Christ or salvation. . . . All life was saturated with religion to such an extent that the people were in constant danger of losing sight of the distinction between things spiritual and things temporal. If, on the one hand, all details of ordinary life may be raised to a sacred level, on the other hand, all that is holy sinks to the commonplace, by the fact of being blended with everyday life . . . the demarcation of the spheres of religious thought and that of worldly concerns was nearly obliterated.*

*Johan A. Huizinga, *The Waning of the Middle Ages* (Garden City, NY: Doubleday, 1954), p. 156.

Hence, the realistically rendered, commonplace objects in a Flemish painting become suffused with religious significance and take on the nature of sacramental things. With this justification for their existence in art, the ordinary things that surround us—and we ourselves—share the realm of the saints; conversely, the saints now occupy our realm. But we, as well as our things will remain when, with the secularization of art, the saints and sanctity have disappeared.

JAN VAN EYCK

One of the largest and most admired Flemish altarpieces of the fifteenth century is *The Ghent Altarpiece* in the Cathedral of St. Bavo in Ghent (FIGS. **18-6** and **18-7**). It also has been one of the most controversial ever since the discovery, in 1832, of a partly damaged, four-line Latin poem on the frame of one of the outside panels which, in part, translates: "The painter Hubert van Eyck, greater than whom no one was found, began [this work]; Jan, second in art, completed it at the expense of Jodocus Vyt. . . ." The last line of the quatrain gives the date of 1432.

For more than a century after the discovery of this inscription under a coat of greenish paint, the altarpiece was believed to be the product of a collaboration between JAN VAN EYCK (*c.* 1390–1441) and his older brother HUBERT (*c.* 1370–1426). But none of the numerous attempts to assign different parts of the many-paneled work to one or the other brother found more than partial acceptance among art historians. Even Erwin Panofsky's tightly argued conclusion that the present altarpiece is the result of an artful combination of three independent works, begun by Hubert and finished by Jan, that originally were not meant to be seen together, left considerable room for doubt and argument.*

An entirely new light was thrown on the controversy with the more recent suggestion that Hubert may not have been a painter at all, but rather a sculptor, who carved an elaborate, now lost framework for the painted panels. Lotte Brand Philip points out that the damaged word *-ictor* in the inscription, which precedes Hubert's name and had been restored to read *pictor* (painter), could also be read *fictor* (sculptor).† "Second in art" would then not mean that Jan was a less accomplished painter than his brother but would be a chronological reference to the fact that Jan worked on the altarpiece *after* Hubert. Judging from surviving contracts and commissions of the period, it seems to have been fairly common practice for a painter to begin work on panels after their frames had been completed.

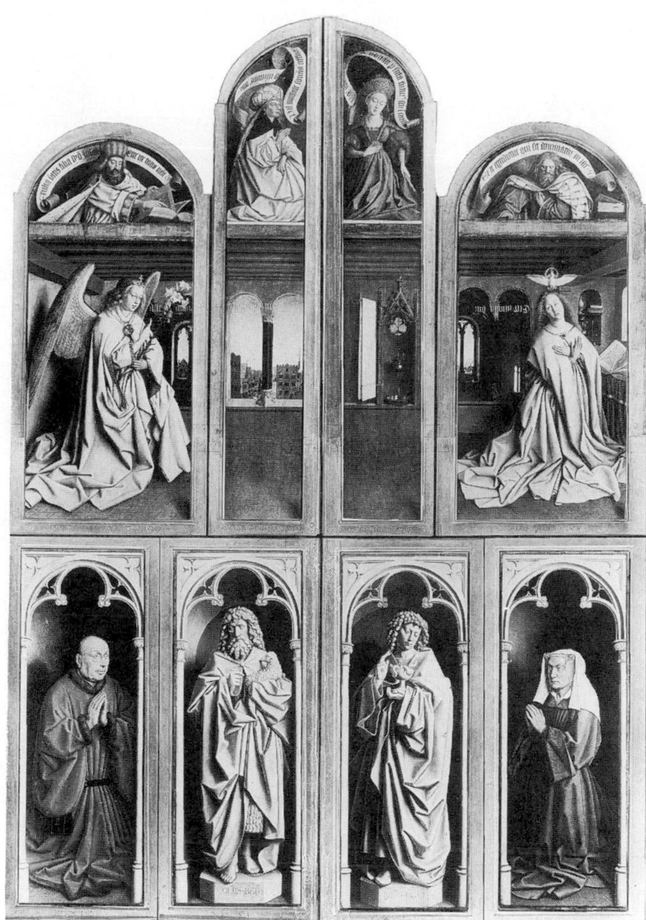

18-6 HUBERT and JAN VAN EYCK, *The Ghent Altarpiece* (closed), completed 1432. Tempera and oil on wood, approx. 11′ 6″ × 7′ 3″. Cathedral of St. Bavo, Ghent, Belgium.

In 1566, the panels of the altarpiece were removed from the original frame and hidden, to protect them from Protestant iconoclasts who probably destroyed the frame. The panels were reinstalled in 1587, but without the original framework, which Lotte Brand Philip envisions to have been in the form of a richly carved, two-storied, Gothic reliquary front. Her ingenious theory and imaginative reconstruction would give sole authorship of the paintings to Jan van Eyck and solve the problem of attribution that has vexed art historians for almost a century and a half. It also would tend to explain the disparity of the scale used on the inner panels, which has disturbed some modern observers. If, indeed, the panels were originally more widely spaced and separated by richly carved, Gothic architectural elements, the formal unity of the altarpiece may have been stronger and more cohesive, especially if perspective devices in the lower level created the illusion that the smaller-scale scenes receded and were seen through, and at some distance

*Erwin Panofsky, *Early Netherlandish Painting* (Cambridge, MA: Harvard University Press, 1953).

†Lotte Brand, Philip, *The Ghent Altarpiece and the Art of Jan van Eyck* (Princeton, NJ: Princeton University Press, 1972).

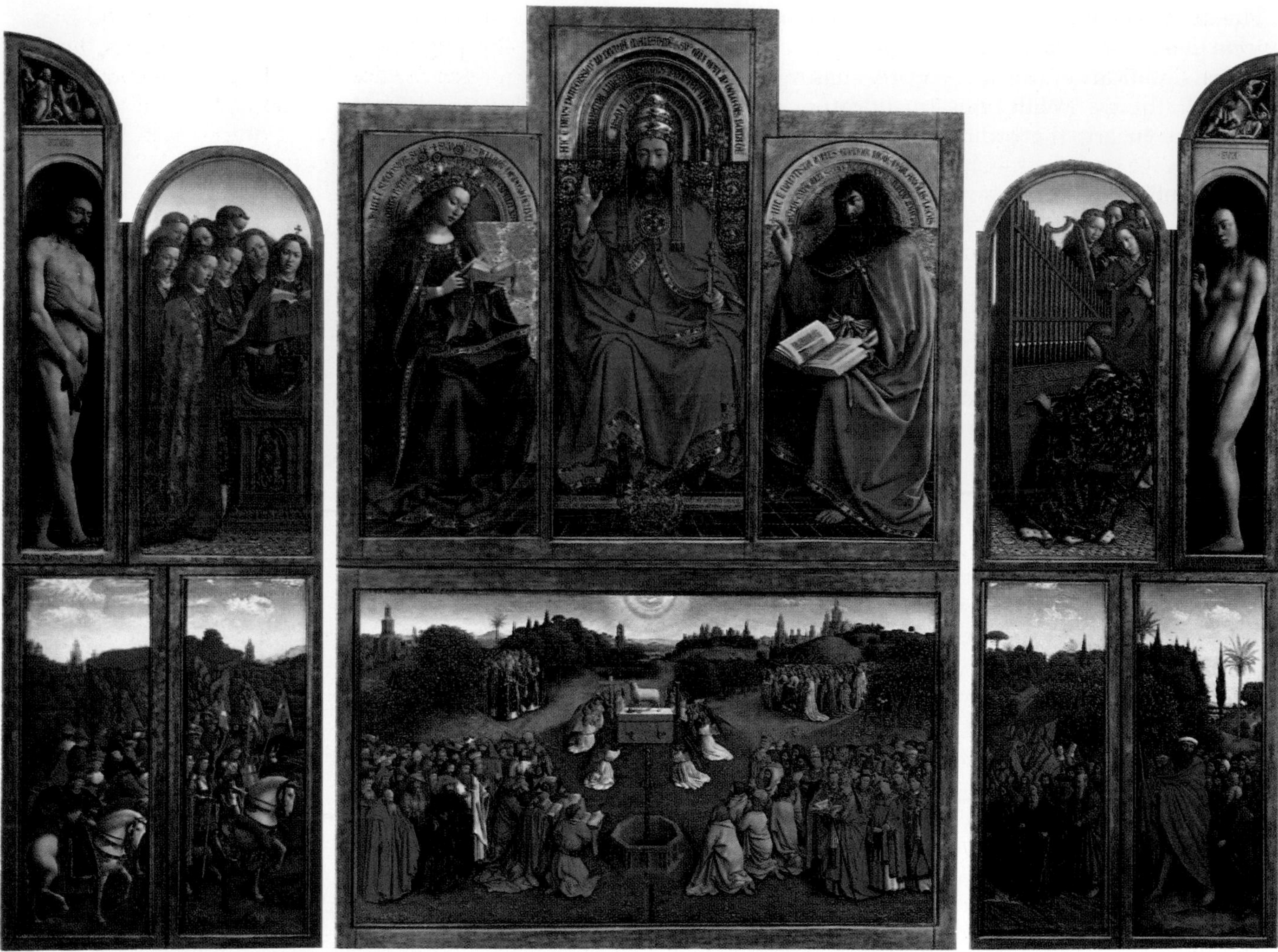

18-7 HUBERT and JAN VAN EYCK, *The Ghent Altarpiece* (open). Approx. 11′ 6″ × 15′ 1″.

behind, the architectural screen. On the other hand, it may well be that fifteenth-century viewers paid much less attention to formal unity than we do today and that the spiritual unity of the work was their real concern.

The Ghent polyptych remains an outstanding example of the large, folding altarpiece, typical of the north, that discloses new meanings to the observer as the unfolding panels reveal new subjects in sequence. The very form of the folding altarpiece expresses the medieval tendency to uncover truth behind natural appearances, to clothe thought in allegory, to find "essential" meaning hidden beneath layers of secondary meanings. When closed (FIG. 18-6), *The Ghent Altarpiece* shows the Annunciation and simulated statues of St. John the Baptist and St. John the Evangelist, flanked by the donors, Jodoc Vyt and his wife; above, in the lunettes, are the Prophet Zechariah with the Erythraean sibyl and the Prophet Micah with the Cumaean sibyl. All these are symbolic references to the Coming of Christ. The Annunciation figures are set in a raftered room in which the Romanesque and Gothic architectural elements may symbolize the Old and the New Testaments, respectively. As in *The Mérode Altarpiece* (FIG. 18-5), a vista opens on a distant street. The angel and the Virgin are bundled in the heavy flannel draperies of the Burgundian school, resembling those of Sluter's *Moses* (FIG. 18-1). Although the architecture is spacious, the figures are in ambiguous relation to it and quite out of scale; as yet, the artist shows little concern for a proportioned space adjusted to the human figure.

When opened (FIG. 18-7), the altarpiece reveals a sumptuous, superbly colored representation of the medieval conception of the Redemption of man. In the upper register, God the Father—wearing the triple tiara of the papacy, with a worldly crown at his feet and resplendent in a deep-scarlet mantle—is flanked on the left by the Virgin, represented as the

Queen of Heaven, with a "crown of twelve stars upon her head," and on the right by St. John the Baptist. To either side is a choir of angels and, on the right, St. Cecilia at her organ. Adam and Eve are in the far panels. The inscriptions in the arches above Mary and St. John extol the virtue and purity of the Virgin and the greatness of St. John as the forerunner of Christ. The particularly significant inscription above the head of the Lord translates: "This is God, all-powerful in his divine majesty; of all the best, by the gentleness of his goodness; the most liberal giver, because of his infinite generosity." The step behind the crown at the Lord's feet bears the inscription: "On his head, life without death. On his brow, youth without age. On his right, joy without sadness. On his left, security without fear." This inscription is a most concise and beautiful statement of the change from the concept of God as a stern, medieval judge of mankind to the benevolent Franciscan father of the human race. This Franciscan concept of the benevolent nature of God is reinforced by the pelicans embroidered on the tapestry draped over the back of his throne, for pelicans (then thought to tear open their breasts to feed their starving young with their own blood) were symbols of self-sacrificing love. The entire altarpiece amplifies this central theme; though man, symbolized by Adam and Eve, is sinful, he will be saved because God, in his infinite love, will sacrifice his own son for this purpose.

The figures are rendered in a shimmering splendor of color that defies reproduction. Both Hubert and Jan van Eyck were trained miniaturists, and not the smallest detail has escaped their eyes. They amplify the beauty of the most insignificant object as if it were a work of piety as much as a work of art. The soft texture of hair, the glitter of gold in the heavy brocades, the luster of pearls, and the flashing of gems are all given with tireless fidelity to appearance. The new medium of oil paint shows its marvelous magic.

The panels of the lower register extend the symbolism of the upper. In the central panel, the community of saints comes from the four corners of the earth through an opulent, flower-spangled landscape. They move toward the altar of the Lamb, from whose heart blood flows into a chalice, and toward the octagonal fountain of life into which spills the "pure river of water of life, clear as crystal, proceeding out of the throne of God and of the Lamb" (Revelation 22:1). On the right, the Twelve Apostles and a group of martyrs in red robes advance; on the left, with minor prophets, the Four Evangelists arrive carrying their Gospels. In the right background come the holy virgins, and in the left background, the holy confessors. On the lower wings, other approaching groups symbolize the four cardinal virtues: the hermits, Temperance; the pilgrims, Prudence; the knights, Fortitude; the judges, Justice. The altarpiece celebrates the whole Christian cycle from the Fall to the Redemption, presenting the Church triumphant in heavenly Jerusalem. The uncanny naturalism and the precise rendering, in the miniaturist tradition, make the great event as concrete and credible as possible to the observer. The realism is so saturated with symbolism that we almost think of it as a kind of superreality or "surrealism," for what is given to the eye is more than the eye alone can report.

Jan van Eyck's matchless color craft also is evident in *The Virgin with the Canon van der Paele* (FIG. **18-8**), painted in 1436. The figures are grouped in a manner reminiscent of the sacra conversazione paintings that appear in Florence about the same time (FIG. 16-32). The architecture, the elaborately ornamented rug, and the placement of the figures all lead the observer's eye to the Madonna and Child, who sit on a throne in the apse of a church. The rich texture of the Virgin's red robes strongly contrasts with the white surplice of the painting's donor, the kneeling Canon van der Paele. A similar contrast plays across the space between the dull glint from the armor of St. George, the patron saint of the canon, and the rich brocades of St. Donatian, the patron of the church for which the painting was commissioned. The incredibly brilliant profusion of color is controlled carefully, so that the forms are distinguished clearly in all detail. The symbolism is as profuse and controlled as the color, incorporating again the complete cycle of the Fall and the promise of Redemption. The arms of the Virgin's throne and the historiated capitals of the pilasters behind her make reference to the Old Testament prefiguration of the Coming of Christ, so well known in the Middle Ages.

Van Eyck's use of perspective is evident in the picture; he uses not a single perspective that would consistently unify the space, but several. His intention here once again appears to be accomplished indirectly, the multiple perspectives directing attention to the principal figures. For example, a projection of the line of the column base at the far right leads to the head of the canon; the orthogonals of the floor tiles converge on the midpoint of the figure of the Virgin; and the base of the throne can be projected to the infant Christ. No real spatial unification can be found here. The figures do not interrelate as we might expect. Each fills its own space with, as it were, its own perspective. Although St. George lifts his helmet to the Virgin, the direction of his gaze goes well beyond her; this disorientation is also true of the other figures. Jan van Eyck and his generation still essentially

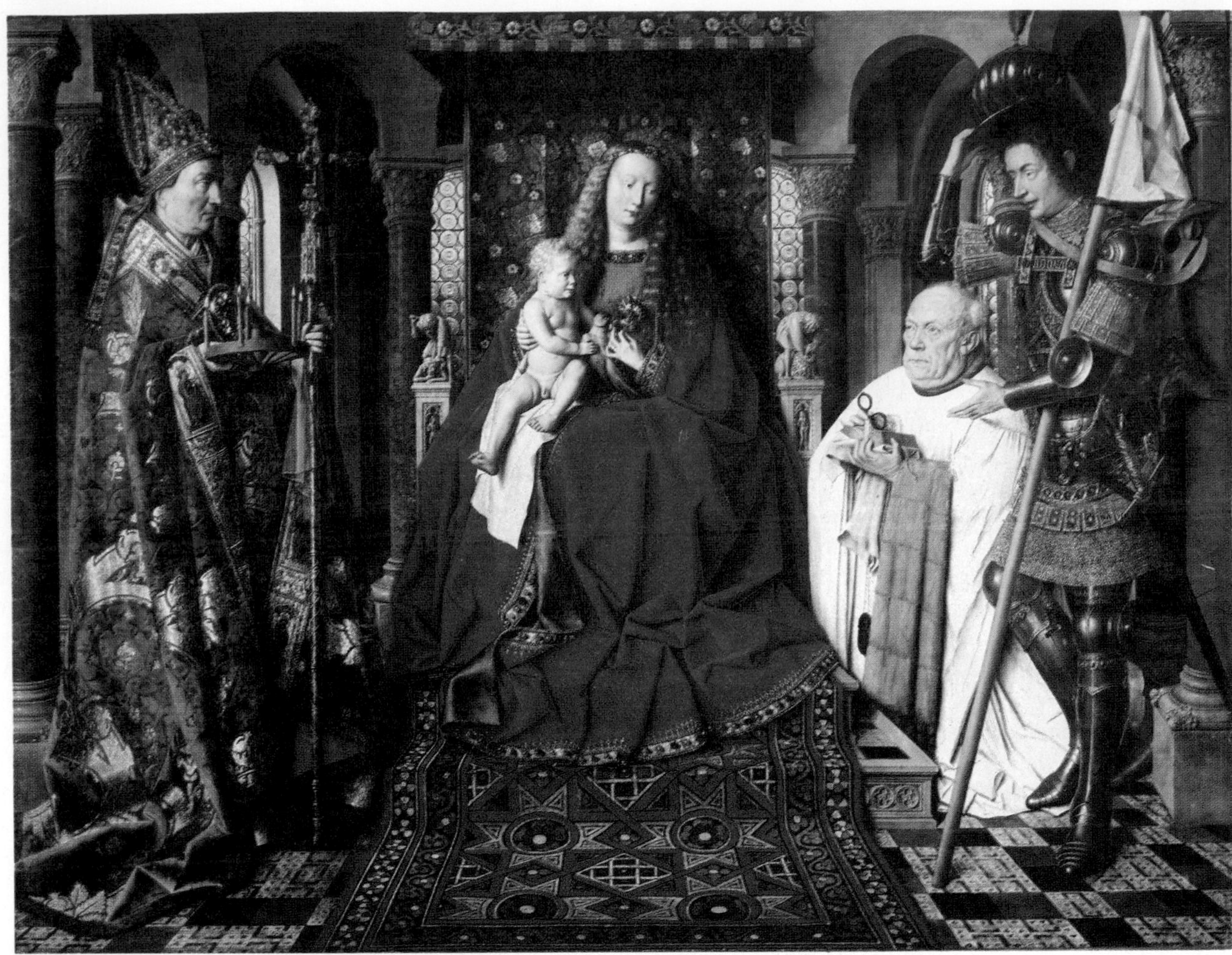

18-8 JAN VAN EYCK, *The Virgin with the Canon van der Paele*, 1436. Tempera and oil on wood, approx. 48″ × 62″. Musées Communaux, Bruges, Belgium.

conceive the organization of the two-dimensional picture surface in terms of shape, color, and symbol; they have not yet thought of it as a window into a constructed illusion of the third dimension, as the painters of the later Flemish schools will.

The portrait head of Canon van der Paele shows the same nonstructural approach. The heavy, wrinkled visage of the canon is recorded in precise detail, almost to the pores. The artist makes a relief map of his subject, delineating every minute change of the facial surface. Unlike the Italian portraitists, who think first of the structure of the head and then draw the likeness over it, Jan van Eyck works from the outside inward, beginning with the likeness and shaping the head incidentally. This procedure is what gives the masklike aspect to the canon's face, despite the portrait's fidelity to physiognomy; the surface is all there, but the illusion of three-dimensional mass is only implied.

We have seen three works that included painted portraits of their donors: *The Mérode Altarpiece* (FIG. 18-5), *The Ghent Altarpiece* (FIG. 18-6), and *The Virgin with Canon van der Paele* (FIG. 18-8). These portraits mark a significant revival of portraiture, a genre unknown since antiquity. A fourth portrait, Jan van Eyck's *Man in a Red Turban* (FIG. **18-9**) takes another step toward the complete secularization of the portrait. In the Mérode and Ghent altarpieces, the donors were depicted apart from the saints; in the Canon van der Paele portrait, the donor associates with the saints at the throne of the Virgin. In this portrait of a man wearing a turban (possibly a depiction of the artist himself), the image of a living individual apparently needs no religious purpose for being—only a personal one; the portrait is simply a personal record of one's features interesting to the subject himself or to someone who knows him. These private portraits now begin to multiply, as both artist and patron become interested in the reality they reveal, for the painter's close observation of the lineaments of a human face is as revealing of the real world as his observation of objects in general. As human beings confront themselves in the painted portrait, they objectify themselves as selves, as people. In this confrontation, the otherworldly anonymity of the Middle Ages must fade away. The *Man in a Red Turban* looks directly at us, or perhaps at himself in a mirror. So far as is known, this depiction is the first painted portrait in a thousand years to do so. The level, composed gaze, directed from a true three-quarter pose of the head, must have impressed observers deeply. The painter gives us the illusion that from whatever angle we observe the face, the eyes still fix us. A painting of this kind by the great Rogier van der Weyden must have inspired the writing of *The Vision of God* (1453) by Nicholas of Cusa, who says, in the preface to that work:

> To transport you to things divine, I must needs use a comparison of some kind. Now among men's works I have found no image better suited to our purpose than that of an image which is *omnivoyant* [all-seeing]—its face, by the painter's cunning art, being made to appear as though looking on all around it—for example . . . that by the eminent painter, Roger [*sic*], in his priceless picture in the governor's house at Brussels. . . . this I call the icon of God.

Nicholas goes on with a praise of sight and vision that amounts to a sanctification of them:

> Thou, Lord . . . lovest me because Thine eyes are so attentively upon me . . . where the eye is, there is love. . . . I exist in that measure in which Thou art with me, and since Thy look is Thy being, I am because Thou dost look at me, and if Thou didst turn Thy glance from me I should cease to be.
>
> Apart from Thee, Lord, naught can exist. If, then, Thine essence pervade all things, so also does Thy sight, which is Thine essence. . . . Thou Lord, seest all things and each thing at one and the same time.

Nicholas of Cusa is a contemporary of the great Flemish painters, and it is likely that he spoke in a sense they could understand and in a mood they could share. The exaltation of sight to divine status and the astonishing assertion that the essence of God is sight—not being, as St. Thomas tells us—are entirely in harmony with the new vision in painting. As sight and being in God are essentially the same, so the painter's sight, which is instrumental in making likenesses, brings them into being. As the contemplative man achieves union with God by making himself like God, the imitation of objects in the sight of (hence, caused by) God must be a holy act on the part of the painter: seeing what God sees, he achieves the reality of God's vision and reveals it to others. The minute realism of the Flemish painters can be understood in the light of Nicholas's doctrine. God sees everything, great and small alike, and Nicholas's fundamental doctrine that all opposites and contradictions are resolved and harmonized in God makes God present in the greatest and in the smallest, in the macrocosm and in the microcosm, in the whole earth and in a drop of water. In the whole world of vision *caused* by God's sight, everything is worthwhile because it is seen by God—even the "meanest flower that blows." Nicholas's sanctification of the faculty of sight provides Flemish painters with a religious warrant to apply sight in the investigation of the given world; painters in the north will continue the investigation long after the original religious motive is gone.

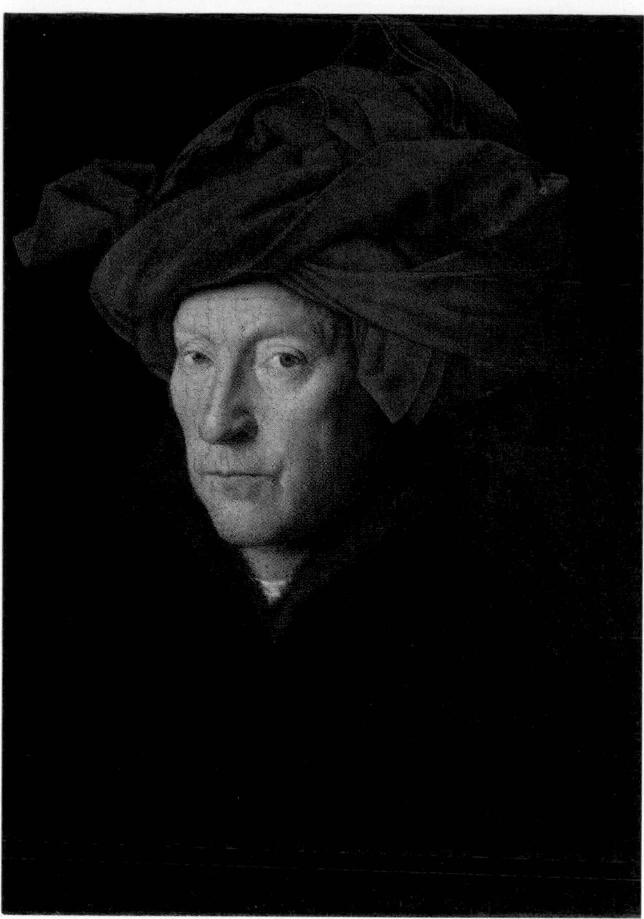

18-9 JAN VAN EYCK, *Man in a Red Turban (Self-Portrait?)*, 1433. Tempera and oil on wood, approx. $10\frac{1}{4}'' \times 7\frac{1}{2}''$. Reproduced by courtesy of the Trustees of the National Gallery, London.

Above all, an age had begun in both the Netherlands and Italy in which people gloried in the faculty of sight for what it could reveal of the world around them. Artists now began to show the Western public "what things look like," and it took extreme pleasure in recognizing a revelation. The level gaze of the *Man in a Red Turban,* in all its quiet objectivity, is not only the omnivoyant "icon of God"; in its historical destiny, it is the impartial, eternally observant face of science. It is also, significantly, humanity beginning

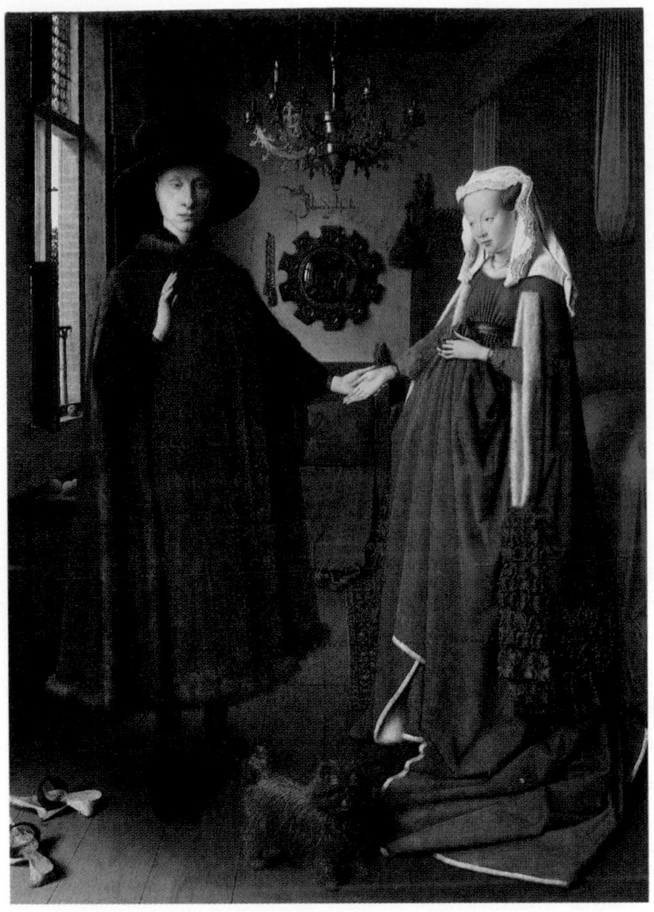

18-10 Jan van Eyck, *Giovanni Arnolfini and His Bride,* 1434. Tempera and oil on wood, approx. 32″ × 23½″. Reproduced by courtesy of the Trustees of the National Gallery, London.

to confront nature in terms of the human component. This step is the climax of the slow but mighty process that will bring the artist's eyes down from the supernatural to the natural world—a process that is expressed with just as much conviction and vigor in the north as it is in Italy.

The humanization of pictorial themes advances another step in Jan van Eyck's double portrait of *Giovanni Arnolfini and His Bride* (fig. **18-10**). The Lucca financier (who had established himself in Bruges) and his lady occupy a scene that is empty of saints but charged with the spiritual. Almost every object depicted is in some way symbolic of the holiness of matrimony. Giovanni and his bride, hand in hand, take the marriage vows. Their shoes have been removed, for the sacrament of matrimony makes the room a holy place. The little dog symbolizes fidelity (the origin of the common canine name *Fido*). Behind the pair, the curtains of the marriage bed have been opened. The finial of the bedpost is a tiny statue of St. Margaret, patron saint of childbirth; from the finial hangs a whisk broom, symbolic of domestic care (fig. **18-11**). The oranges on the chest below the window may refer to the golden apples of the Hesperides, representing the conquest of death, and the presence of the omnivoyant eye of God seems to be referred to twice: once in the single candle burning in the ornate chandelier and again in the mirror, in which the entire room is reflected (fig. 18-11). The small medallions set into the mirror's frame show tiny scenes from the Passion of Christ and represent Van Eyck's ever-present promise of salvation for the figures reflected on the mirror's convex surface. These figures include not only the principals, Arnolfini and his wife, but two persons who look into the room through the door. One of these must be the artist himself, as the florid inscription above the mirror, *Johannes de Eyck fuit hic,* announces that he was present. The purpose of the picture, then, is to document and sanctify the marriage of two particular persons. In this context, human beings come to the fore of their own setting; the spiritual is present, but in terms of symbol, not image.

The paintings of Jan van Eyck have a weighty formality that banishes movement and action. His symmetrical groupings have the stillness and rigidity of the symbol-laden ceremony of the Mass; each person and thing has its prescribed place and is adorned as

18-11 Detail of fig. 18-10.

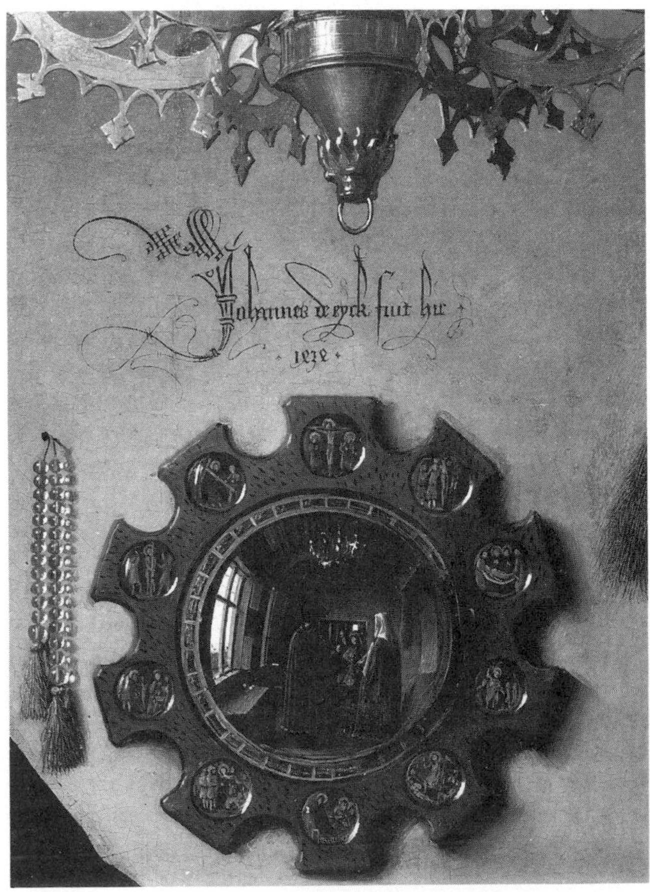

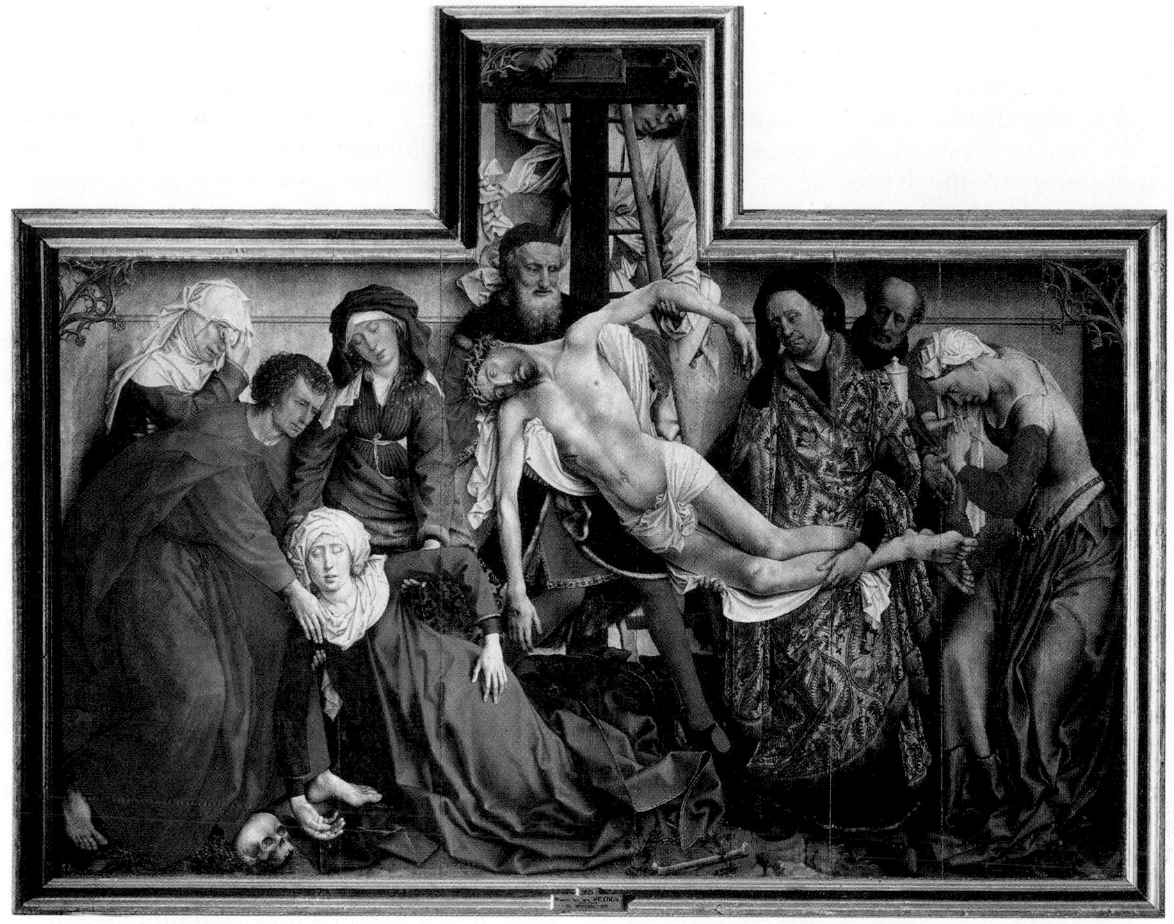

18-12 ROGIER VAN DER WEYDEN, *The Escorial Deposition*, c. 1435. Tempera and oil on wood, approx. 7′ 3″ × 8′ 7″. Museo del Prado, Madrid.

befits the sacred occasion. The long tradition of manuscript illumination accepted that the Holy Book must be as precious as the words it contains. Jan van Eyck, himself a miniaturist and illuminator, instinctively created a rich and ornamental style in which to proclaim his optimistic message of human salvation. In their own way, the paintings of Jan van Eyck are perfect and impossible to surpass. After him, Flemish painting looked for new approaches, and Van Eyck had few, if any, emulators.

VAN DER WEYDEN, CHRISTUS, AND BOUTS

The art of ROGIER VAN DER WEYDEN (*c.* 1400–1464) had a much greater impact on northern painting during the fifteenth century. A student of Robert Campin, Rogier evidently recognized the limitations of Van Eyck's style, although it had not been without influence on his early work. By sweeping most of the secondary symbolism from his paintings, Rogier cleared his pictorial stage for fluid and dynamic compositions stressing human action and drama. He concentrates on themes like the Crucifixion and the Pietà, in which he moves the observer by relating the sufferings of Christ. For Van Eyck's symbolic bleeding lamb, Rogier substitutes the tortured body of the Redeemer and his anguished mother. His paintings are filled with deep religiosity and powerful emotion, for he conceived his themes as expressions of a mystic yearning to share in the Passion of Jesus.

The great *Escorial Deposition* (FIG. **18-12**) sums up Rogier's early style and content. Instead of creating a deep landscape setting, as Jan van Eyck might have, he compresses the figures and action onto a shallow stage to concentrate the observer's attention. Here, Rogier imitates the large, sculptured shrines so popular in the fifteenth century, especially in Germany, and the device serves well his purpose of expressing maximum action within disciplined structure. The painting resembles a stratified relief carving in the crisp drawing and precise modeling of its forms. A series of lateral, undulating movements gives the group a unity, a formal cohesion, that is underlined by psychological means—by the desolating anguish common to all the figures. Few painters have equaled Rogier in the rendering of passionate sorrow as it vibrates through a figure or distorts a tear-stained face.

His depiction of the agony of loss is the most authentic in religious art; in a painting as bare of secondary symbolism as the *Deposition,* the emotional impact on the observer is immediate and direct. From this single example, we can understand why Rogier's art became authoritative for the whole fifteenth century outside of Italy.

His portraits were no less important than his altarpieces. Campin and Van Eyck had established portraiture among the artist's principal tasks. Great patrons were ready to have their likenesses painted for many different reasons: to memorialize themselves in their dynastic lines; to establish their identity, rank, and station by an image far more concrete than a heraldic coat of arms; to represent themselves at occasions of state when they could not be present; even as a kind of photograph of the betrothed to be exchanged by families who had arranged their children's marriages. Royalty, nobility, and the very rich might send painters to "take" the likeness of a prospective bride or groom. It is reported that when a bride was sought for young King Charles VI of France, a painter was sent to three different royal courts to make portraits of the candidates, on the basis of which the king then made his choice.

18-13 ROGIER VAN DER WEYDEN, *Portrait of a Lady,* c. 1460. Oil on wood, 14½" × 10¾". National Gallery, Washington, D.C. (Andrew W. Mellon Collection).

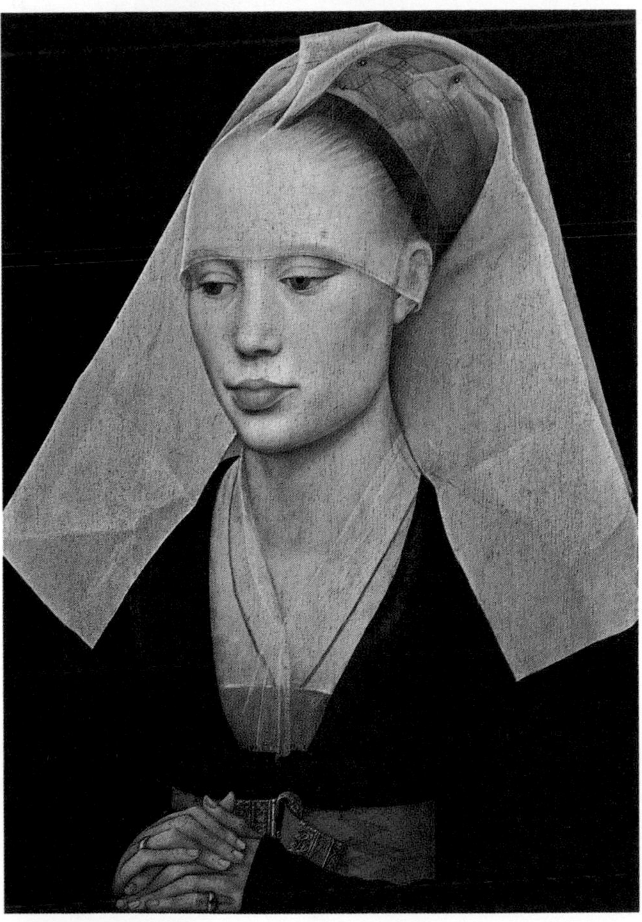

We are not sure for what specific purpose Rogier's portrait of an unknown young lady (FIG. **18-13**) was painted. From her dress and bearing, she was probably of noble rank. The artist is at pains to realize not only a faithful likeness of her somewhat plain features, but to read, with his uncommon perception, her individual character. Her lowered eyes, tightly locked, thin fingers, and fragile physique bespeak a personality reserved, introverted, and devout. The unflattering honesty and directness, typical in the Flemish artist's approach, reveals much, despite the formality of pose and demeanor. This style contrasts with the formality of the Italian approach (FIG. 16-58), derived from the profiles common to coins and medallions, which is more stern and admits little revelation of personality. The Italian patron and portraitist will prefer the profile view throughout most of the century, rather than the full-face and three-quarter views favored by the Flemish. Rogier is perhaps chief among the Flemish in his penetrating readings of his subjects, and, great pictorial composer that he is, he makes beautiful use here of flat, sharply pointed angular shapes that themselves so powerfully suggest an "angularity" (rigidity) of this subject's personality. Unlike Jan van Eyck, Rogier lays little stress on minute description of surface detail. Instead, he defines large, simple planes and volumes, achieving an almost "abstract" effect, in the modern sense, of dignity and elegance.

Although evidence that Rogier traveled to Italy is not unequivocal, some of his paintings clearly show his acquaintance with Italian pictorial devices. His religious sincerity and concern with sin and guilt, however, remained undimmed by them. The appearance of these mid-century Italian influences in Rogier's paintings was not an isolated instance in Flemish art. The work of PETRUS CHRISTUS (*c.* 1410–1472) shows so marked an interest in the depiction of space and cubic form that, although the idea now largely is discounted, he too was often felt to have traveled to Italy. Little is known of Christus's life, except that he may have been Van Eyck's student and that he settled and worked in Bruges. His style vacillates between Van Eyck's and Rogier's. Still, his interests are quite different from those of his models.

His painting of *The Legend of Saints Eligius and Godeberta* (FIG. **18-14**) seems, at first glance, to exhibit all of Van Eyck's miniaturistic traits, from the stitching on the lady's gown to the carefully enumerated attributes that identify the seated saint as a patron of the goldsmith's guild. Even the convex mirror on the table seems to have been extracted from Van Eyck's

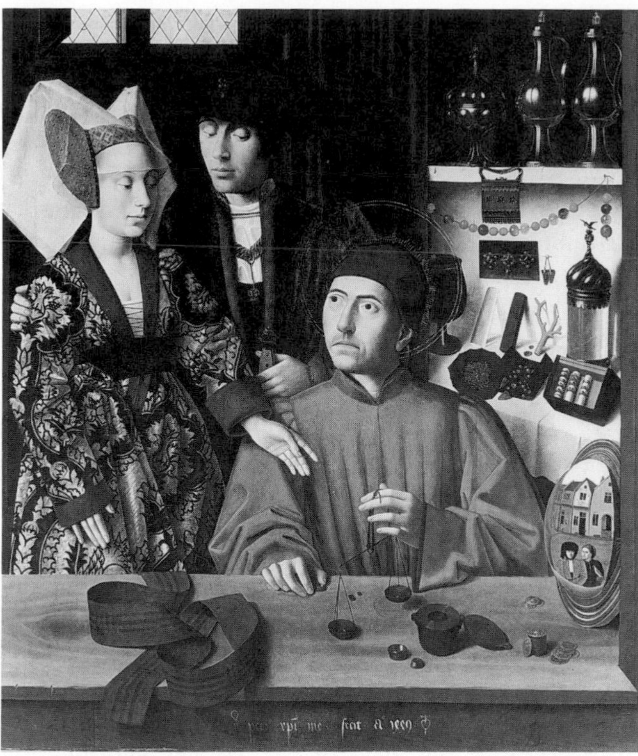

18-14 PETRUS CHRISTUS, *The Legend of Saints Eligius and Godeberta*, 1449. Tempera and oil on wood, approx. 39″ × 34″. Metropolitan Museum of Art, New York (the Lehman Collection).

portrait of Arnolfini and his bride (FIG. 18-10), and the two "witnesses" reflected in it suggest that this also may be a wedding picture. But Christus's concept of reality and his approach to it are quite different from Van Eyck's; he is much more concerned with the underlying structure of an object's appearance and, in this respect, is more closely related to the Italian than to the northern approach. The three solidly constructed figures within the cubic void defined by the desk and the room corner represent an essentially southern essay in pictorial form that has been overlaid with Van Eyck's surface realism. Curiously, in his effort to make the structure of his picture clear, Christus resorts to the same kind of simplification of forms seen in the paintings of Paolo Uccello and Piero della Francesca (FIGS. 16-29 and 16-33). Even more striking, perhaps, is the similarity of Christus's "volumetric" portrait heads to those by Antonello da Messina (FIG. 16-67). The speculation that these two artists may have met, either in Flanders or in Italy, remains tempting, despite the lack of solid documentation.

Christus may have had some contact with DIRK BOUTS (*c.* 1415–1475), a slightly younger artist of similar temperament and interests. For a long time, the central panel of Bouts's *The Altarpiece of the Holy Sacrament* was believed to be the first northern painting in which the use of a single vanishing point for the construction of an interior could actually be demonstrated. Although Rogier may have known about the Italian science of linear perspective, he apparently did not use it in his paintings. Recent studies tend to give precedence in this field to Petrus Christus, from whom, in fact, Bouts may have acquired his knowledge. The setting for the altarpiece's *Last Supper* (FIG. **18-15**) is probably the refectory of the headquarters of the Louvain Confraternity of the Holy Sacrament, by which the painting was commissioned. All the orthogonals of the depicted room lead to a single vanishing point in the center of the mantelpiece above the head of Christ. This painting is not only the most successful northern fifteenth-century representation of an interior, but it is also the first in which the scale of the figures has been adjusted realistically to the space they occupy. So far, however, the perspective unity is confined to single units of space only; the small side room has its own vanishing point, and neither it nor the vanishing point of the main room falls on the horizon of the landscape seen through the windows. The tentative manner with which Bouts solves his spatial problems suggests that he arrived at his solution independently and that the Italian science of perspective had not yet reached the north, except perhaps in small fragments. Nevertheless, the

18-15 DIRK BOUTS, *The Last Supper* (center panel of *The Altarpiece of the Holy Sacrament*), 1464–1468. Tempera and oil on wood, approx. 6′ × 5′. St. Peter's, Louvain, Belgium.

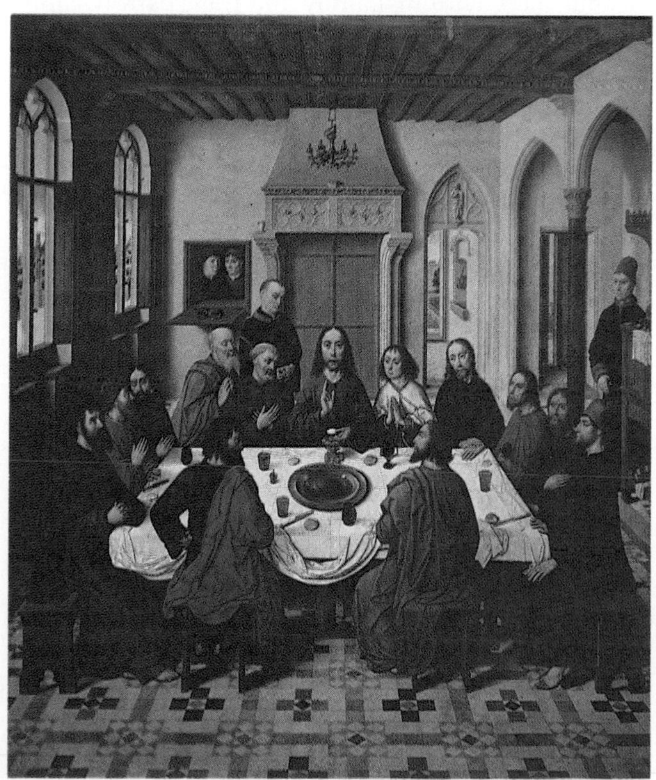

works of Christus and Bouts clearly show that, by mid-century, northern artists had become involved with the same scientific, formal problems that concerned Italian artists during most of the fifteenth century.

The mood of Bouts's *Last Supper* is neutral. The gathering is solemn enough, but it lacks all pathos and dramatic tension, almost as if the artist was more concerned with the solution of a difficult formal problem than with the pictorial interpretation, either personal or traditional, of the sacred event.

VAN DER GOES AND MEMLING

The highly subjective and introspective paintings of HUGO VAN DER GOES (*c.* 1440–1482) seem to express a discontent with the impersonal quality that the artist must have felt was a loss of religious meaning in the paintings of his older contemporaries. Hugo was dean of the painter's guild of Ghent from 1468 to 1475 and an extremely popular painter. At the height of his success and fame, he entered a monastery as a lay brother. While there, he suffered a mental breakdown, and a year later, in 1482, he died. His retirement to the monastery did not interrupt Hugo's career as a painter immediately; he continued to receive commissions and probably completed his most famous work, *The Portinari Altarpiece* (FIG. **18-16**), within the monastery's walls.

Hugo painted the triptych for Tommaso Portinari, an agent of the Medici, who appears on the wings of the altarpiece with his family and their patron saints. The central panel (FIG. **18-17**) represents *The Adoration of the Shepherds*. On this large surface, Hugo displays a scene of solemn grandeur, muted by the artist's introspective nature. The high drama of the joyous occasion is stilled; the Virgin, Joseph, and the angels seem to brood on the suffering that is to come rather than to meditate on the miracle of the Nativity. The Virgin kneels, somber and monumental, on a tilted ground that has the expressive function of centering the main actors. From the right rear enter three shepherds, represented with powerful realism in attitudes of wonder, piety, and gaping curiosity. Their lined, plebeian faces, work-worn hands, and uncouth dress and manner are so sharply characterized as to make us think of the characters in such literature of the poor as *Piers Plowman* and the *Second Shepherd's Play*. The three panels are unified by the symbolic architecture and a continuous, wintry, northern landscape. Symbols are scattered plentifully throughout the altarpiece: iris and columbine symbolize the Sorrows of the Virgin; the fifteen angels represent the Fifteen Joys of Mary; a sheaf of wheat stands for Bethlehem (the "house of bread" in Hebrew), a reference to the Eucharist; and the harp of David, emblazoned over the portal of the building in the middle distance (just to the right of the head of the Virgin), signifies the ancestry of Christ.

To stress the meaning and significance of the depicted event, Hugo revives Medieval pictorial devices and casts aside the unities of time and action so treasured by other Renaissance artists, wherein a single episode in time is confined to a single framed piece. Small scenes shown in the background of the altarpiece represent (from left to right across the three panels) the Flight into Egypt, the Annunciation to the

18-16 HUGO VAN DER GOES, *The Portinari Altarpiece* (open), *c.* 1476. Oil on wood, center panel 8′ $3\frac{1}{2}$″ × 10′. Galleria degli Uffizi, Florence.

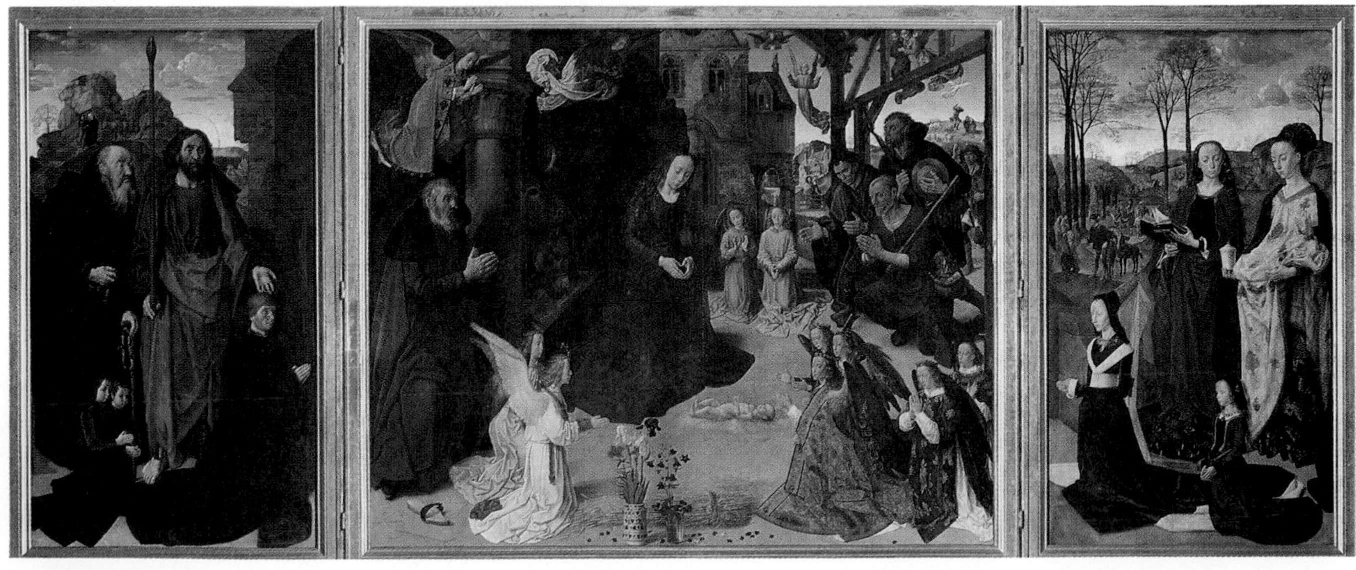

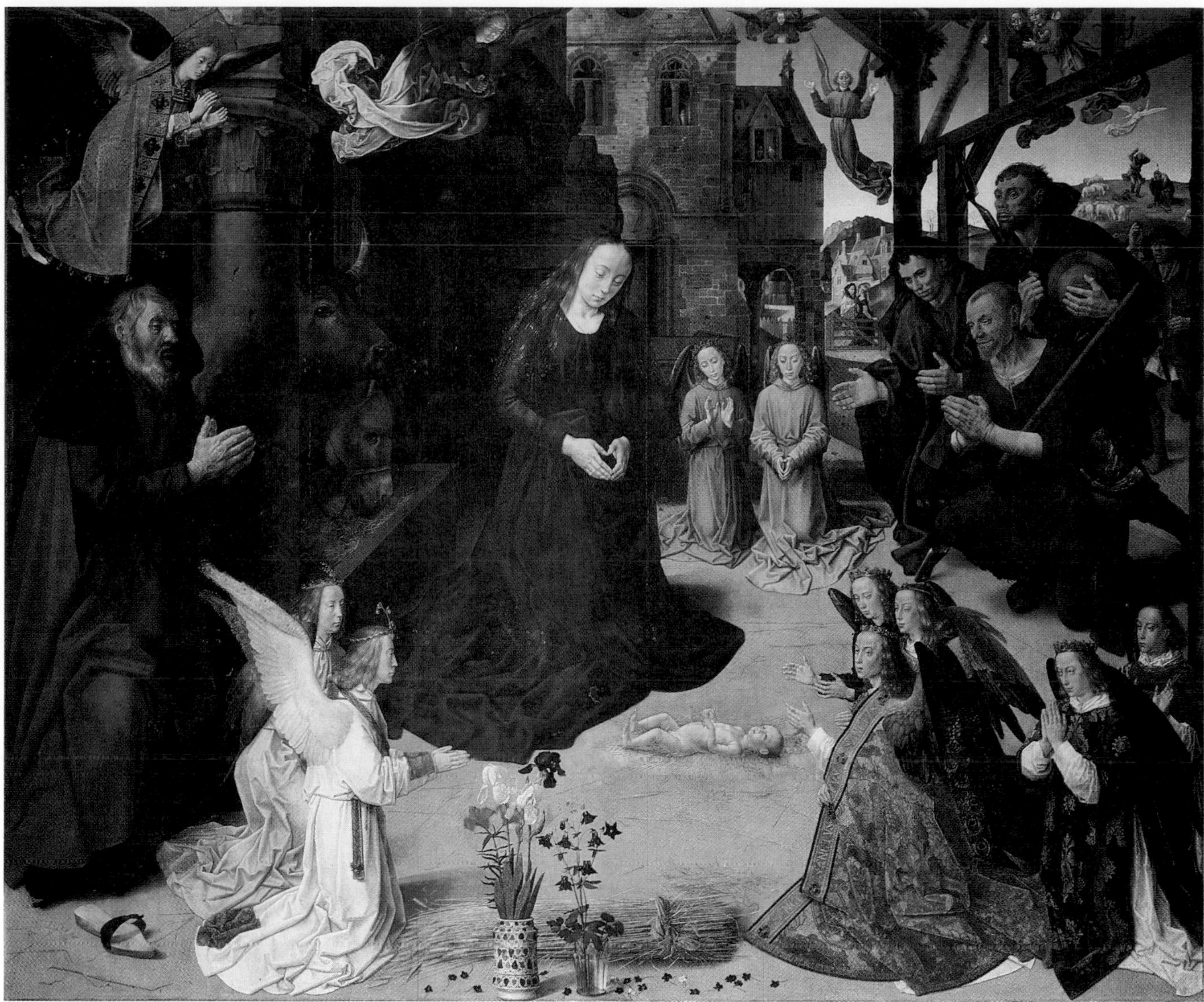

18-17 Hugo van der Goes, *The Adoration of the Shepherds,* center panel of *The Portinari Altarpiece* (fig. 18-16).

Shepherds, and the Arrival of the Magi—the "prelude and epilogue to the Nativity." Also reflective of older traditions is the manner in which Hugo varies the scale of his figures to differentiate them according to their importance in relation to the central event. At the same time, he puts a vigorous, penetrating realism to work in a new direction, characterizing human beings according to their social level while showing their common humanity, and thus the painting becomes a plea for all to join the Brotherhood of Man.

Portinari placed his altarpiece in the church of Sant' Egidio in Florence, where it created a considerable stir among Florentine artists. Although the painting as a whole must have seemed unstructured to them, Hugo's brilliant technique and what they thought of as incredible realism in representing drapery, flowers, animals, and, above all, human character and emotion made a deep impression on them. At least one Florentine artist, Domenico Ghirlandaio, paid tribute to the northern master by using Hugo's most striking motif, the adoring shepherds, in one of his own Nativity paintings.

Hugo's contemporary, Hans Memling (*c.* 1430–1494), who, although like Hugo, was esteemed by all and called, at his death, the "best painter in all Christendom," was of a very different temperament. Gentle and genial, he avoided the ambitious, dramatic compositions of Rogier and Hugo, and his sweet, slightly melancholy style fits well into the twilight of the waning fifteenth century. Memling's speciality is the Madonna; the many that have survived are slight, pretty, young princesses. His depictions of the infant Christ are doll-like. A good example of his work is the center panel of a triptych representing *The Mystic*

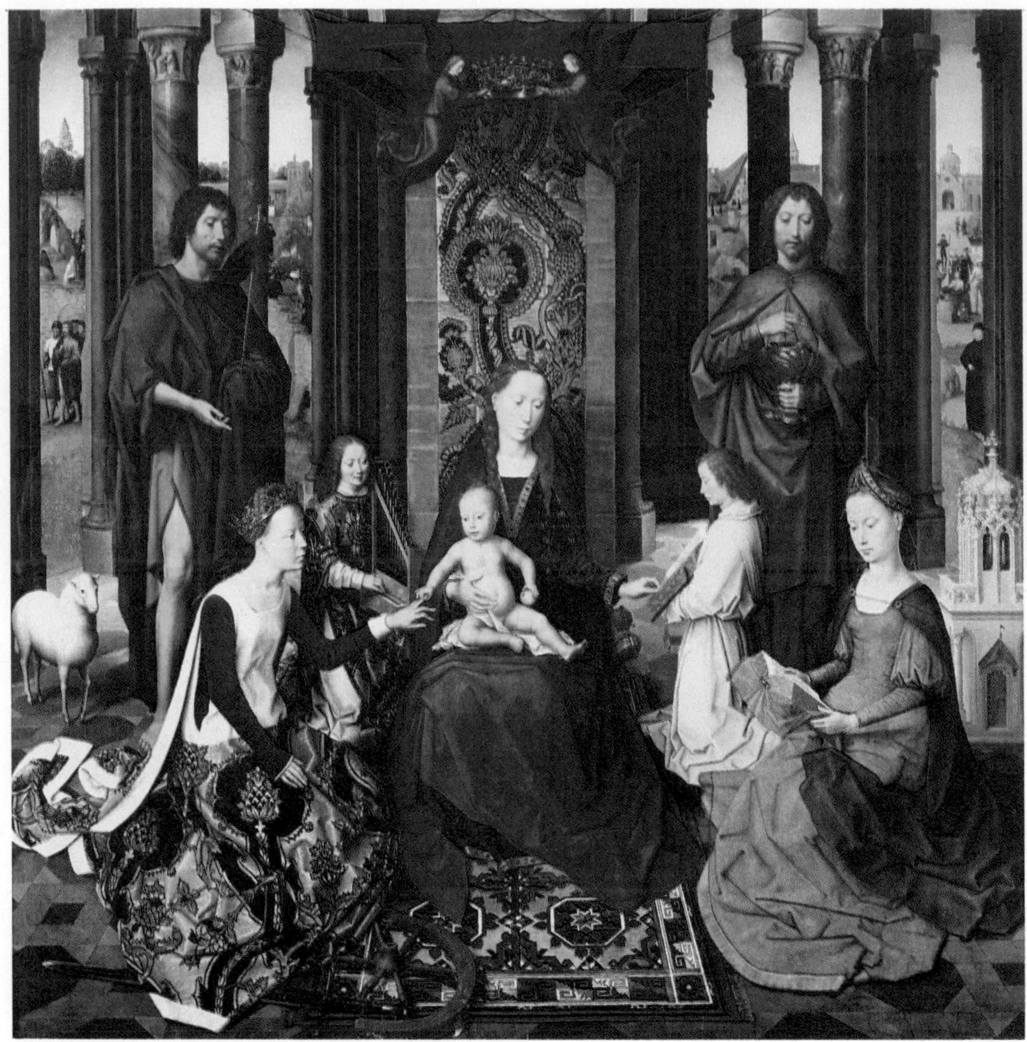

18-18 HANS MEMLING, *The Mystic Marriage of St. Catherine,* center panel of *The St. John Altarpiece,* 1479. Oil on wood, approx. 67¾" × 67¾". Hospitaal Sint Jan, Bruges.

Marriage of St. Catherine (FIG. **18-18**). The composition is balanced and serene; the color, sparkling and luminous; the execution, of the highest technical quality (Memling's paintings are among the best preserved from the fifteenth century). The prevailing sense of isolation and the frail, spiritual human types contrast not only with Hugo's monumental and somber forms but also with Van Eyck's robust and splendid ones. The century began, with Van Eyck's sumptuous art, on a note of humanistic optimism. It ends with a waning strength of spirit, an erosion of confidence in the moral and religious authority of the Church. Contemporary poetry is filled with dreary pessimism and foreboding, almost in anticipation of another fall of man and the disasters that will lie ahead for Christendom in the Reformation.

HIERONYMUS BOSCH

This time of pessimistic transition finds its supreme artist in one of the most fascinating and puzzling painters in history, HIERONYMUS BOSCH (*c.* 1450–1516). Interpretations of Bosch differ widely. Was he a satirist, an irreligious mocker, or a pornographer? Was he a heretic or an orthodox fanatic like Girolamo Savonarola? Was he obsessed by guilt and the universal reign of sin and death? Certainly, his art is born of the dark pessimism of his age, burdened with the fear of human fate and the conviction that man's doom is approaching. A contemporary poet, Eustache Deschamps, writes:

> Now the world is cowardly, decayed and weak,
> Old, covetous, confused of speech:
> I see only female and male fools. . . .
> The end approaches . . .
> All goes badly.

In a much copied and imitated series of small panels with half-length figures, Bosch describes the Passion of Christ. *The Carrying of the Cross* (FIG. **18-19**) from this group is a bitter judgment of humanity.

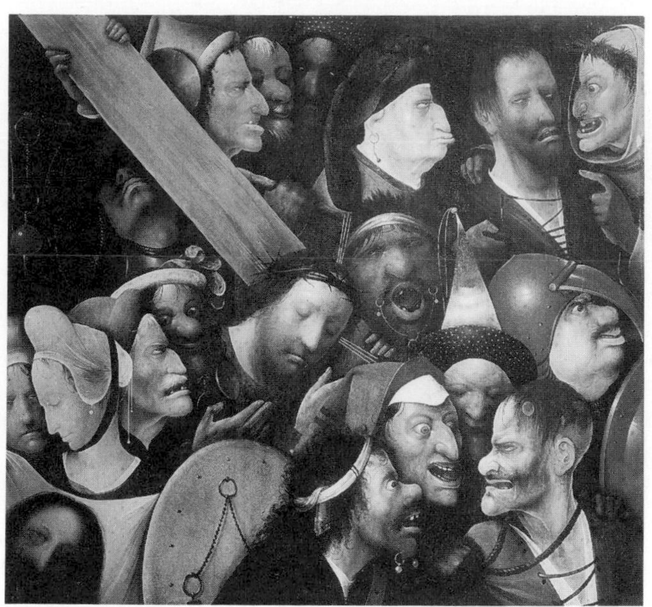

18-19 Hieronymus Bosch, *The Carrying of the Cross,* c. 1510 (?). Oil on wood, approx. 30″ × 32″. Musée des Beaux-Arts, Ghent.

Christ is surrounded by hate and evil. His executioners show a sadistic delight in the suffering of their victim. Heedless of spatial effects, Bosch packs the entire surface of his panel with hate-distorted faces. In the upper right corner, a grinning scoundrel in a monk's habit exhorts the repentant thief; in the lower right corner, the unrepentant thief grimaces at two leering comrades, forming with them a triad of stupidity, bestiality, and hate. At the lower left, St. Veronica, representing the Church, turns away from Christ and becomes a symbol of vanity. No further interpretation of this panel seems needed; Bosch not only makes his meaning clear but expresses it with unrivaled ferocity.

Much more difficult to understand are Bosch's large altarpieces, which are packed with obscure meaning and symbolism. But even if we do not fully understand his teeming fantasies, we can appreciate the incredible scope of an imagination that makes him the poet of the nightmarish subconscious. The dreaming and waking worlds are one in Bosch, as he draws on the tradition of beast and monster that we have followed from Mesopotamia to the Gothic gargoyle.

His most famous work, the so-called *Garden of Earthly Delights* (FIGS. **18-20** to **18-22**), is also his most puzzling, and no interpretation of it is universally accepted. The left wing of the triptych shows the *Creation of Eve* in the Garden of Eden. However, here Eve is not the mother of mankind, as she is in Van Eyck's *Ghent Altarpiece* (FIG. 18-7), but rather the seductress whose temptation of Adam resulted in the original sin, the central theme of the main panel. Evil lurks even in Bosch's paradise: a central fountain of life is surrounded by ravens, the traditional symbols for

18-20 Hieronymus Bosch, triptych of *The Garden of Earthly Delights, Creation of Eve* (left wing), *The Garden of Earthly Delights* (center panel), *Hell* (right wing), 1505–1510. Oil on wood, center panel 86⅝″ × 76¾″. Museo del Prado, Madrid.

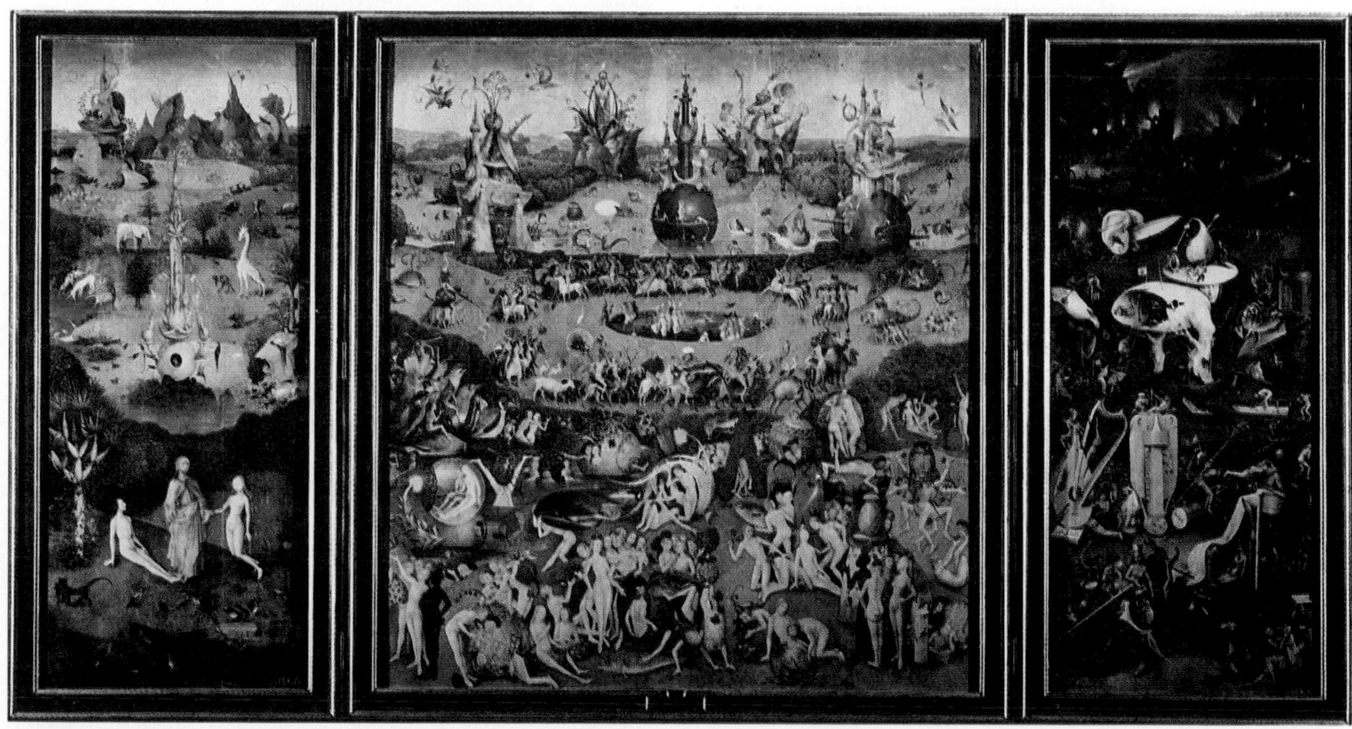

nonbelievers and magicians; an owl, hiding in the dark hole in the center of the fountain, represents witchcraft and sorcery.

The central panel, *The Garden of Earthly Delights,* swarms with the frail nude figures of men and women sporting licentiously in a panoramic landscape that is studded with fantastic growths of a quasisexual form. Bosch seems to be showing erotic temptation and sensual gratification as a universal disaster and the human race, as a consequence of original sin, succumbing to its naturally base disposition. The themes are derived in part from three major sources: Medieval bestiaries, Flemish proverbs, and the then very popular dream books, all mixed in the melting pot of Bosch's astoundingly inventive imagination. In addition, the artist includes frequent allusions to magic and alchemy and mingles animal and vegetable forms in the most absurd combinations. Symbols are scattered plentifully throughout the panel: fruit for carnal pleasure, eggs for alchemy and sex, the rat for falsehood and lies, dead fish for memories of past joys. A couple in a glass globe may illustrate the proverb "Good fortune, like glass, is easily broken." We have lost the key to many of Bosch's symbols, but it may be assumed that they were well known to his contemporaries.

In the right wing, the fruits of license are gathered in *Hell* (FIG. 18-21). There, sinful mankind undergoes hideous torments to diabolic music, while the hellish landscape burns. This symphony of damnation apparently comments on the wickedness of music, with which the Devil lures souls away from God. In this context, the ears and the musical instruments would represent the erotic, soul-destroying thoughts engendered by music. A man is crucified on a harp; another is shut up in a drum. A gambler is nailed to his own table. A girl is embraced by a spidery monster and bitten by toads. The observer must search through the hideous enclosure of Bosch's *Hell* to take in its fascinating though repulsive details. The great modern poet Charles Baudelaire catches the mood in his *Flowers of Evil:*

> Who but the Devil pulls our walking-strings!
> Abominations lure us to their side;
> Each day we take another step to hell,
> Descending through the stench, unhorrified . . .
>
> Packed in our brains incestuous as worms
> Our demons celebrate in drunken gangs . . .
>
> . . . in this den of jackals, monkeys, curs,
> Scorpions, buzzards, snakes . . . this paradise
> Of filthy beasts that screech, howl, grovel, grunt—
> In this menagerie of mankind's vice. . . .

The triptych as a whole may represent the false paradise of this world between Eden and Hell, but

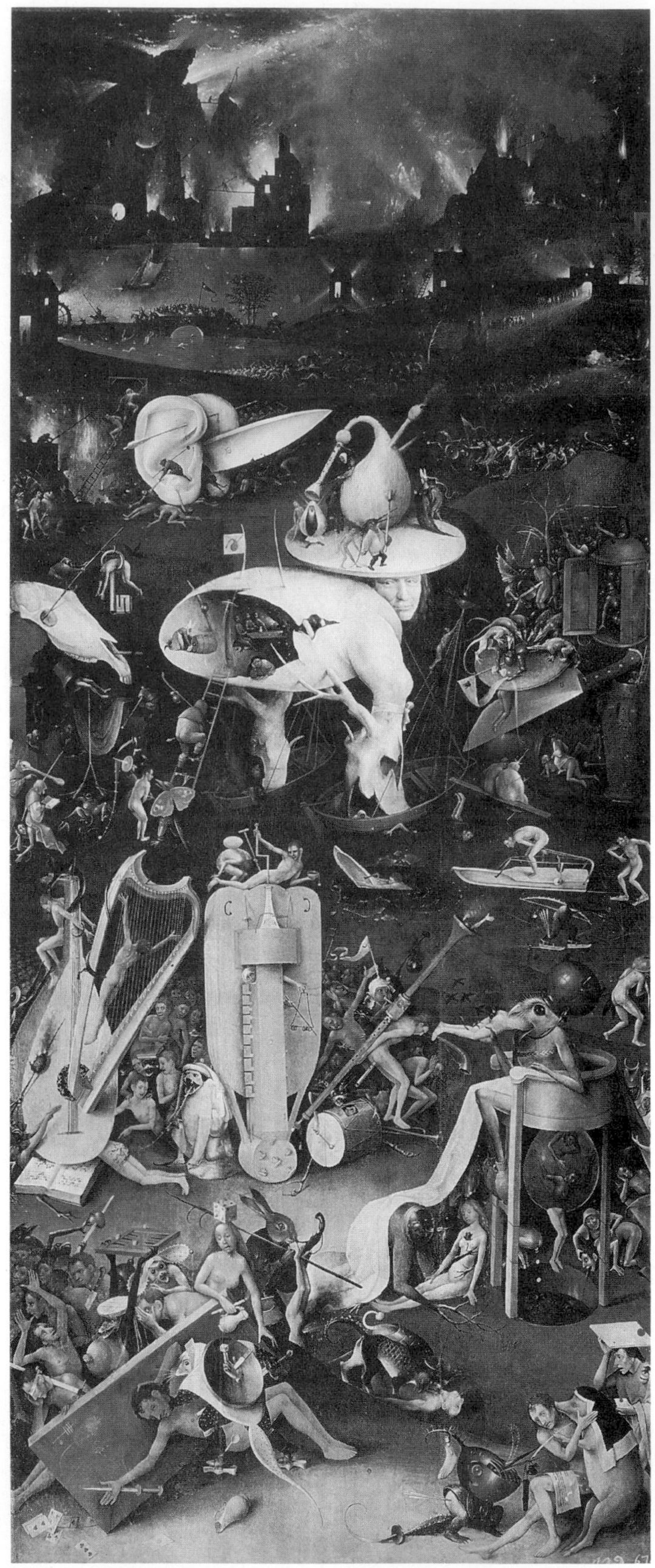

18-21 HIERONYMUS BOSCH, *Hell,* right wing of the triptych of *The Garden of Earthly Delights* (detail of FIG. 18-20).

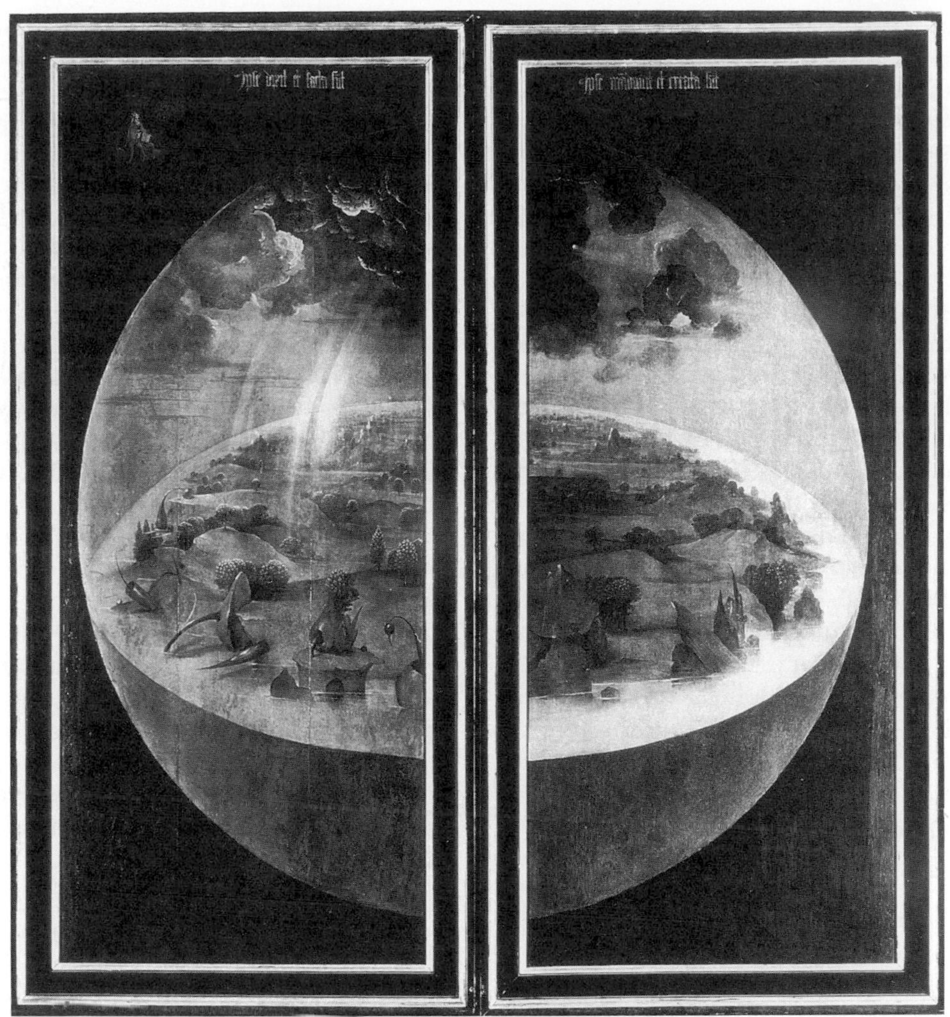

18-22 Hieronymus Bosch, *The Third Day of Creation* (?), exterior of the closed wings of the triptych of *The Garden of Earthly Delights.*

this is only one interpretation. Another explanation has it that Bosch belonged to a secret, heretical sect, the Adamites, and that the central panel was thought of as a kind of altarpiece symbolically celebrating its rites and practices. A fairly strong case has been made for an interpretation in terms of contemporaneous alchemical knowledge and practice.* In this connection, it should be pointed out that alchemy, in Bosch's time, was not an illegal and occult art but a practical and legitimate science practiced to make artist's paints, women's cosmetics, herbal cooking preparations, and healing potions. The alchemical science of distillation is basic to modern chemistry, and Philippus Aureolus Paracelsus, a physician of the early sixteenth century, stated emphatically that the true and only purpose of alchemy is to heal the sick, not to make gold.

*See Laurinda S. Dixon, "Bosch's *Garden of Delights* Triptych: Remnants of a 'Fossil' Science," *The Art Bulletin,* Vol. LXIII, No. 1 (March 1981), pp. 96–113.

Numerous alchemical treatises circulated during Bosch's time, and some of them may well have been known to him. Many observers have noted that the triptych is punctuated by forms and shapes similar to diagrams found in distillation texts. The most striking of these, perhaps, is the beaker-shaped "fountain of life" that appears once in the center of the left wing and again in the background of the central panel. In form, this shape strongly resembles an alchemical mixing retort. Many other distillation apparatus appear, especially in the central panel, including glass pipes and lids and transparent globes and funnels. Numerous egg shapes seem to refer to the ovoid mixing vessels in which ingredients were combined to produce the hoped-for transmutations. These vessels, called "eggs" in the symbolic language of alchemy, were considered microcosmic models of the world, which contained all the qualities of life and in which "the four elements [earth, air, fire, water] were perfectly conjoined." Egg shapes appear on all three panels of Bosch's altarpiece; the most prominent one, on the right panel (FIG. 18-21), forms the body of a grotesque, human-headed monster. This creature has been called the "alchemical man," and the tiny figures inside his eggshell torso, usually interpreted as embodying the sins of gluttony and lust, are seen as gathered around a table to watch the glow of an alchemical furnace hidden by the broken shell of the egg man's body.

According to this interpretation, the subject and organization of the triptych correspond to the basic (and, at the time, current) alchemical allegory, in which the distillation process—seen as the cyclical and self-perpetuating creation, destruction, and rebirth of the world and its inhabitants—takes place in four stages: "conjunction" (the marriage of opposites); "coagulation" (the multiplication of Adam and Eve into the peoples of the earth); "putrification" (the separation of the opposing elements previously joined in "matrimony"); and "cleansing" (the washing and purifying of the separated ingredients, a process compared to the Christian resurrection and purification of the soul). The final outcome of this entire allegorical distillation—union with God—is symbolized by the circle and the globe.

If interpreted in these terms, the first three stages of the distillation process are represented symbolically in sequence from left to right on the interior of the three altarpiece panels. The fourth and final stage appears on the outside of the closed wings (FIG. 18-22), where a transparent globe containing earth, water, and clouds, painted in grisaille (tones of gray), represents God's creation of the earth, which the alchemists tried to imitate in their operations.

In keeping with the cyclical and self-perpetuating process of distillation, the exterior of the altarpiece can be read either as the beginning or as the end of the cycle depicted on the interior. Placed at the end, it would provide the altarpiece with a comforting conclusion, a consolatory postscript promising that the sufferings of Hell may not be the end of everything after all. Most scholars, however, place the outside panels at the beginning of the sequence. To them, the grisaille represents the third day of Creation, when dark, light, water, land, and flora (but not the fauna) had been created. The outside thus becomes the natural prelude to the altarpiece's interior, where the remainder of Genesis is recorded on the left wing. On the central panel, the descendants of the first parents abandon themselves to the delights of the flesh, oblivious to the eventual but inevitable consequences recorded on the right wing—the apocalyptic results of the Last Judgment in the form of the fearsome destruction and tortures suffered in Hell. And if we realize how far God—a tiny figure in the upper left corner of the left exterior panel—has been removed from his creation, then Bosch's message seems to become quite clear: humanity, left to its own devices, is destined for damnation. Although far from being universally accepted, this last interpretation of *The Garden of Earthly Delights* appears to conform best with the remainder of the artist's oeuvre. Neither in this, nor in Bosch's other works, does humankind appear to advantage. Abandoned to evil by the Fall, humanity merits Hell.

Bosch was a supreme narrative painter, and the visions of his bubbling imagination demanded quick release. His technique is more rapid and spontaneous than the labored traditional Flemish manner. He seems to have had no time for the customary monochrome underpaintings or careful modeling of figures. His method forecasts the *alla prima* technique of the seventeenth and eighteenth centuries, as he puts down with quick and precise strokes the myriad creatures that populate his panels. His use of *impasto,* which did not require the traditional laborious application of numerous glazes, was ideally suited to the spinning of his mordant fantasies, and if he extends no hope of salvation for man, he only anticipates Michelangelo, who, in his *Last Judgment* fresco (FIG. 17-35), arrived at the same conclusion some thirty years later.

France and Germany

The bourgeoisie in France, unlike that in the Netherlands, was not wealthy, localized in strong towns, nor interested in fostering the arts. In France, the Hundred Years' War had wrecked economic enterprise and prevented stability. During the fifteenth century, the anarchy of war and the weakness of the kings resulted in a group of rival duchies. The strongest of these, as we have seen, was the duchy of Burgundy; through marriage and political alliance, it occupied the Netherlands and became essentially Flemish, particularly in art commissioned by the court. In France, artists joined the retinues of the wealthier nobility, the dukes of Berry, Bourbon, and Nemours, and sometimes the royal court, where they were able to continue to develop an art that is typically French despite its regional variations. But no artist of the fifteenth century north of the Alps could escape the influence of the great artists of Flanders. French art accepted it, and works of high quality were produced, although only one really major figure emerged.

JEAN FOUQUET (*c.* 1420–1481) is the outstanding French artist of the fifteenth century. During his career, he worked for the king, Charles VII, for the Duke of Nemours, and for Étienne Chevalier, the

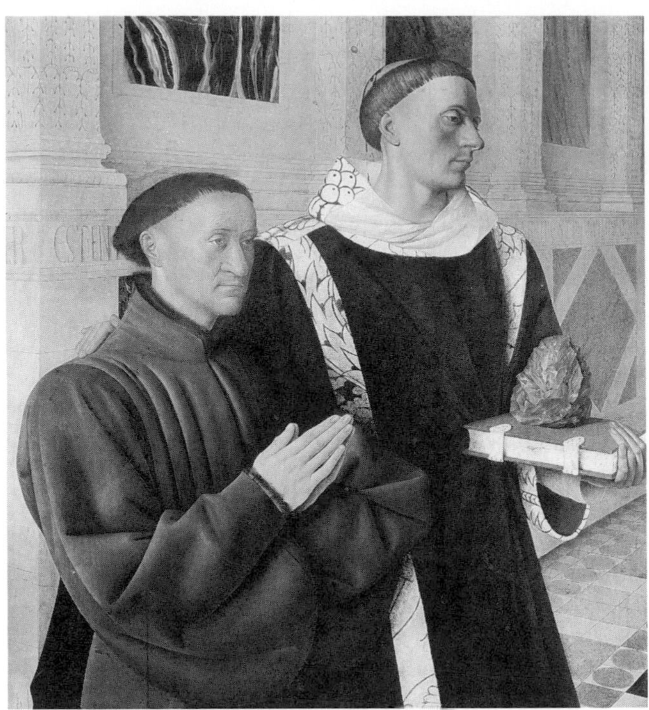

18-23 JEAN FOUQUET, *Étienne Chevalier and St. Stephen* (from a diptych now divided), c. 1450. Tempera on wood, 36½″ × 33½″. Gemäldegalerie, Staatliche Museen, Berlin-Dahlem.

king's minister of finance. Fouquet's portrait of Chevalier with his patron, St. Stephen (FIG. **18-23**), shows, in addition to Flemish influence, the effect of the two years the artist spent in Italy, between 1445 and 1447. The kneeling donor with his standing saint is familiar in Flemish art, as are the three-quarter stances and the sharp, clear focus of the portraits. The reading of the surfaces, however, is less particular than in the Flemish practice; the artist is trying to represent the forms underneath the surfaces, in the Italian manner. Also of Italian inspiration are the architectural background and its rendering in perspective. The secularizing tendency that advanced so rapidly in the fifteenth century is apparent in the familiar, comradely demeanor of the two men. Nothing whatever distinguishes them as being of different worlds, except possibly that St. Stephen, who holds the stone of his martyrdom, is dressed as a priest.

*The Avignon Pietà** (FIG. **18-24**), which has both Flemish and Italian elements, is an isolated masterpiece of great power, painted in the extreme south of France by an anonymous artist. Rogier van der Weyden's great *Escorial Deposition* (FIG. 18-12) comes

*Now attributed to ENGUERRAND QUARTON (*c.* 1410–1466), a French artist active in Provence in the south of France.

18-24 Attributed to ENGUERRAND QUARTON, *The Avignon Pietà,* c. 1455. Tempera on wood, approx. 5′ 4″ × 7′ 2″. Louvre, Paris.

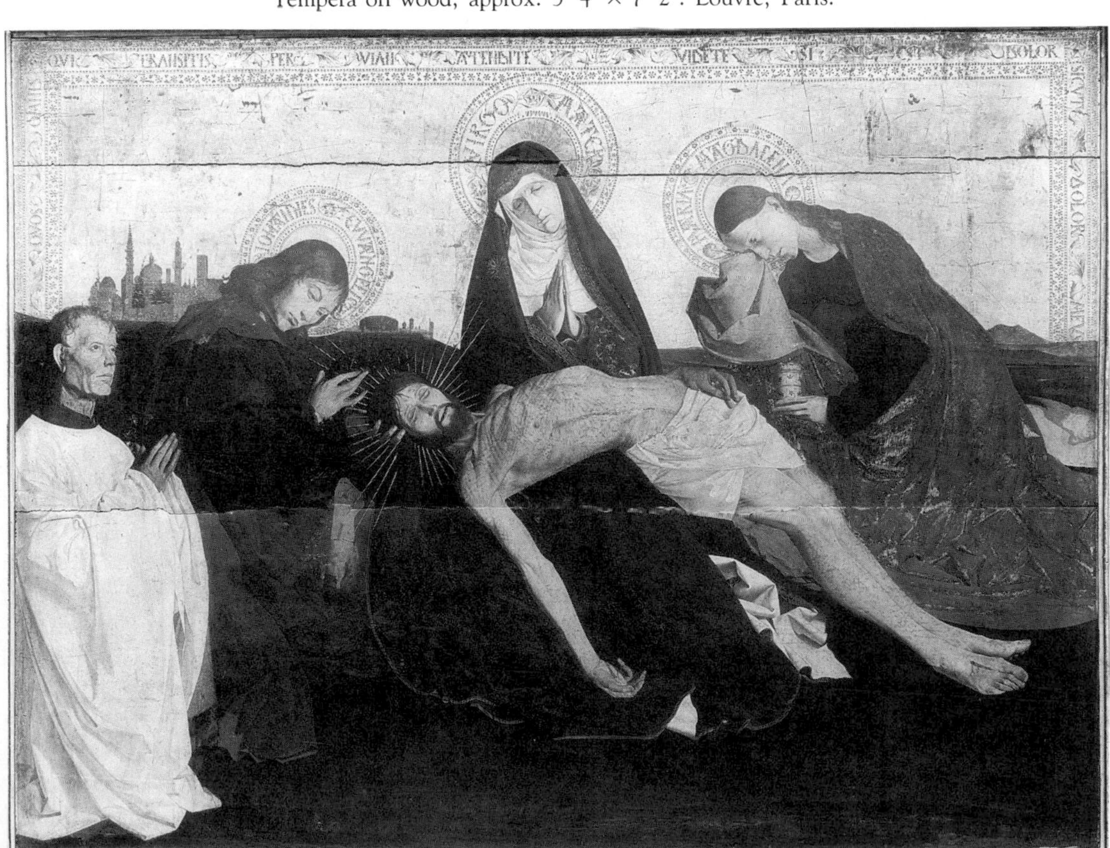

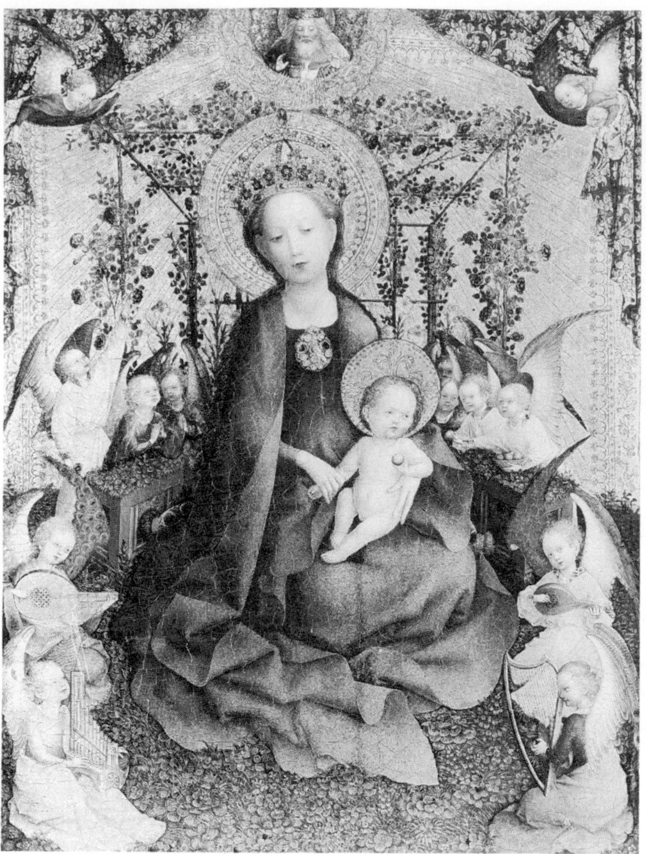

18-25 Stephan Lochner, *Madonna in the Rose Garden*, c. 1430–1435. Tempera on wood, approx. 20″ × 16″. Wallraf-Richartz Museum, Cologne.

to mind at once when we see the Avignon work, although the balanced, almost symmetrical massing clearly reflects the Italian Renaissance. (The subdued color scheme also has suggested Iberian influence to some writers.) The donor, now familiarly present at the sacred event, kneels at the left. His is a strikingly characteristic portrait, the face gnarled, oaken, and ascetic. The group of Christ and saints is united by the splendidly painted figure of Christ and by the angular shapes that seem deliberately simplified for graphic emphasis. As in Italian art, surface ornament is suppressed in the interest of monumental form. The luminous gold background, against which the figures are silhouetted and into which the halos are incised, is a strangely conservative feature, contrasting with the detailed background landscape reminiscent of Flemish paintings. No matter what his sources, the painter is deeply sensitive to his theme. Along with Rogier's version, *The Avignon Pietà* is one of the most memorable in the history of religious art.

To an even greater extent than in France, the development of German painting in the fifteenth century was strongly colored by the achievements of Flemish painting. In northern Germany, the influence of Jan van Eyck joined the tradition of the International style to produce the gentle, pictorially ornate world of delicacy and charm portrayed by Stephan Lochner (*c.* 1400–1451), the leading master of the school of Cologne. Lochner is noted for his compositions on the idyllic theme of the *Madonna in the Rose Garden* (fig. **18-25**), which seems particularly well suited to his sophisticated and refined sensibilities.

Sometimes referred to as the "soft" style because of its feminine suavity and curvilinear rhythm, Lochner's manner was very different from the sculptural, blocky, "hard" style of southern Germany as we find it in the work of the Swiss painter Conrad Witz (*c.* 1400–1447). Although *The Miraculous Draught of Fish* (fig. **18-26**) by this remarkable painter also shows Flemish influence, particularly that of Van Eyck, the painting demonstrates Witz's powerful and original sense of realism. Witz shows precocious skill in the study of water effects: the sky-glaze on the slowly moving lake surface, the mirrored reflections of the figures in the boat, and the transparency of the shallow water in the foreground. This painting is one of the first Renaissance pictures in which the landscape not only dominates the figures but is also the representation of a specific place—the shores of Lake Geneva, with the town of Geneva on the right and the ranges of the Alps in the distance.

The Late Gothic style is seen to best advantage in the works of German artists, who specialized in the carving of large retables (altar screens) in wood. The sculptor Veit Stoss (1447–1533) carved a great altar for the church of St. Mary in Kraków, Poland (fig. **18-27**), no element of which is recognizable as having been influenced by the Italian Renaissance. Typically, the altar consists of a central, boxlike space; the shrine is flanked by hinged, movable wings—an inner pair (shown here) and an outer pair. In the shrine, huge figures (some 9 feet high) represent *The Death and Assumption of the Virgin*, and, in the wings, scenes from the lives of Christ and the Virgin are portrayed. The altar expresses the intense piety of Gothic culture in its late phase, when every resource of figural and ornamental design from the vocabulary of Gothic art is drawn on to heighten the emotion and to glorify the apparition of the sacred event. The disciples of Christ are gathered about the Virgin, who sinks down in death. One of them supports her; another, just above her, wrings his hands in grief; others are posed in attitudes of woe and psychic shock. The sculptor strives for minute realism in every detail. At the same time, he enwraps the figures in an almost abstract pattern of restless, twisting, curving swaths of drapery, which, by their broken and writhing lines, unite the whole tableau in a vision of agitated emotion. The massing of sharp, broken, and

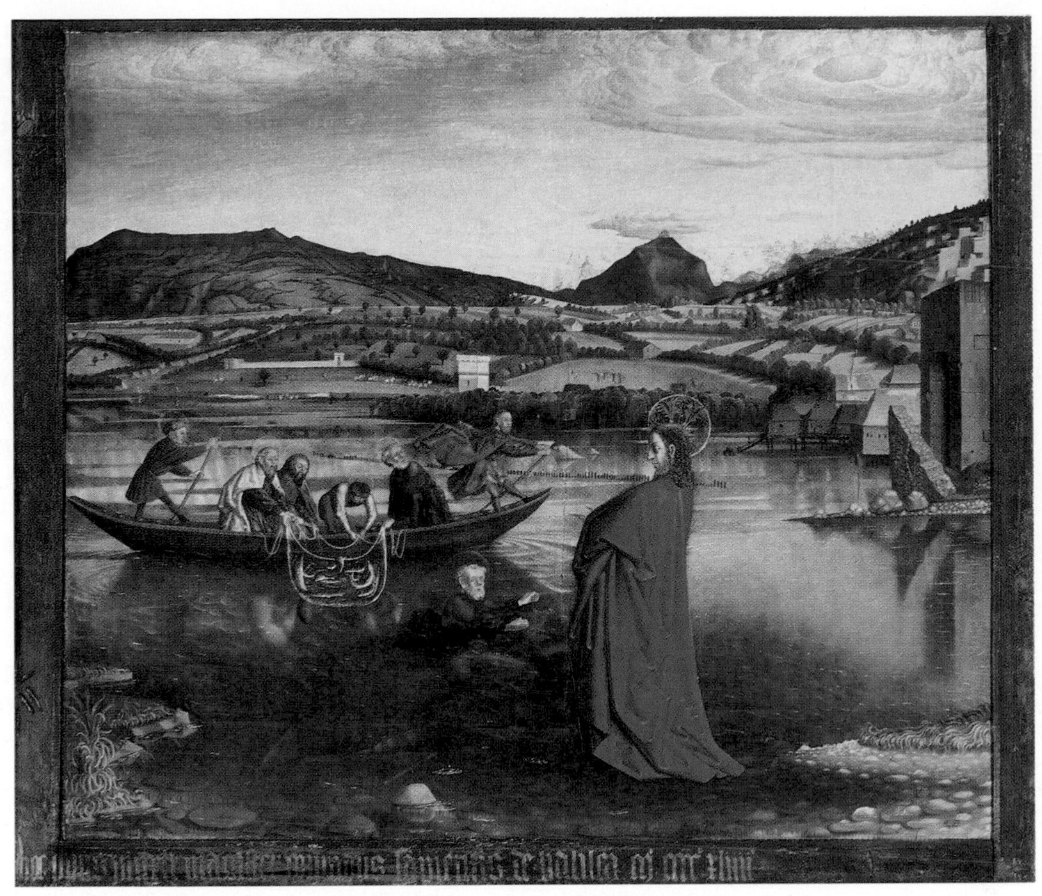

18-26 CONRAD WITZ, *The Miraculous Draught of Fish,* from the *Altarpiece of St. Peter,* 1444. Tempera on wood, approx. 51″ × 61″. Musée d'Art et d'Histoire, Geneva.

18-27 VEIT STOSS, *The Death and Assumption of the Virgin,* from the Altar of the Virgin Mary, 1477–1489. Painted and gilded wood, triptych (wings open) 43′ × 35′. Church of St. Mary, Kraków, Poland.

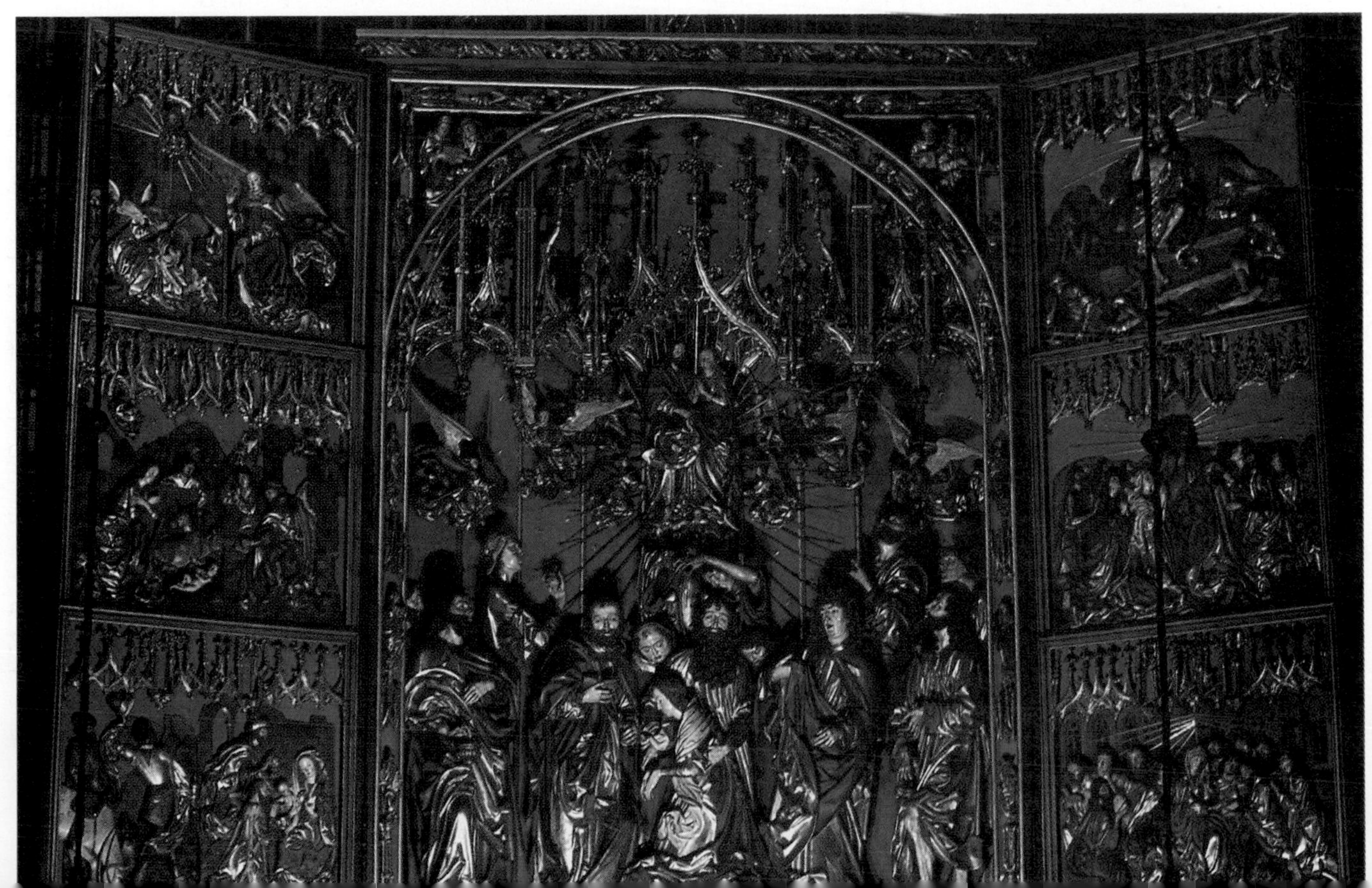

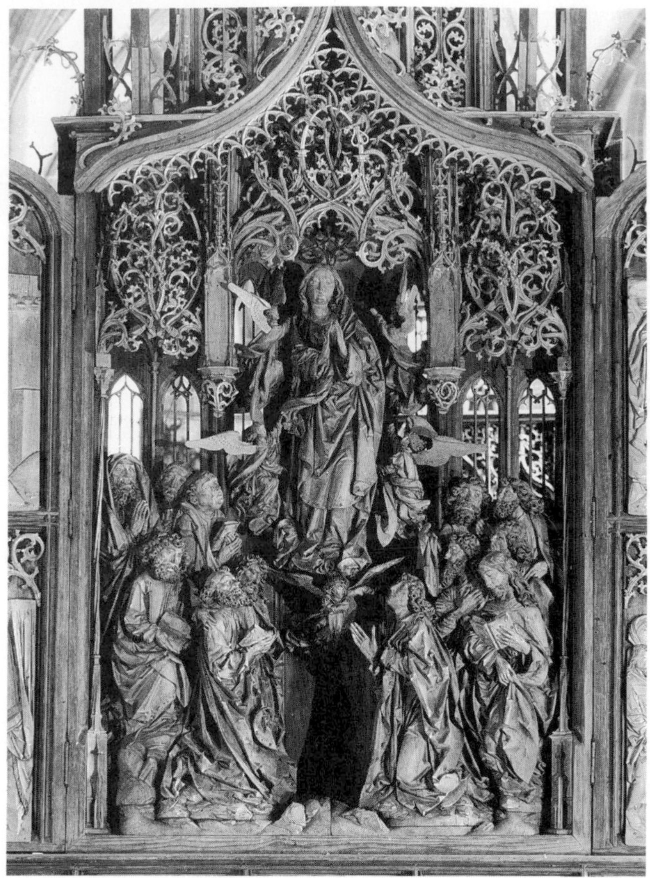

18-28 Tilman Riemenschneider, *The Assumption of the Virgin,* center panel of *The Creglingen Altarpiece,* c. 1495–1499. Carved lindenwood, 6′ 1″ wide. Parish church, Creglingen, West Germany.

pierced forms, which dart flamelike through the composition—at once unifying and animating it—recalls the design principles of Late Gothic "flamboyant" architecture (fig. 10-40). Indeed, in the Kraków altarpiece, sculpture and architecture are amalgamated, and their union is enhanced by painting and gilding. The distinction of the different media, familiar in Italian Renaissance art and furthered by it, is as yet unknown to this Late Gothic artist, even though, like the Italian artist, his eye focuses ever more sharply on natural appearance.

In the work of Tilman Riemenschneider (1460–1531), we find (as we do in the work of Veit Stoss) scarcely a trace of the Italian Renaissance. The canopy of Tilman's *Creglingen Altarpiece* (fig. **18-28**) is an intricate weaving of flamboyant Gothic forms, and the endless and restless line is communicated to the draperies of the figures. The whole design is thus in motion and complication, and no element functions without the rest. The draperies float and flow around bodies lost within them, serving not as descriptions but as design elements that tie the figures to each other and to the framework. The spirituality of the figures, immaterial and weightless as they appear, is heightened by a look of psychic strain, a facial expression common to Tilman's figures and consonant with the age of troubles that is coming. They brood in pensive melancholy, their brows often furrowed in anxiety. A favorite theme in Late Gothic German sculpture was the *Schmerzensmann* (man of sorrows); for Tilman, all his actors were men of sorrow—weary, grave, and unsmiling.

With the works of sculptor-painter Michael Pacher (*c.* 1435–1498), we come to the first important meeting of German art with the Italian Renaissance. Pacher, a Tyrolean, must have journeyed down the Po Valley and become familiar with the style of Andrea Mantegna and his school. In his painting *St. Wolfgang Forces the Devil to Hold His Prayerbook* (fig. **18-29**), we find the hard, wiry linearity of Mantegna and a combination of Late Gothic and Mantegna's drapery style. The figure of St. Wolfgang now has the monumental solidity of Italian form. The whole setting is Italian Renaissance. Perspective views down a street are familiar in northern Italian and Venetian compositions (the plunging orthogonals remind us of Mantegna's architecture in the *St. James Led to Martyrdom* fresco [fig. 16-63]), and the figures standing on a fretted balcony, which slow the swift recession of the

18-29 Michael Pacher, *St. Wolfgang Forces the Devil to Hold His Prayerbook,* panel from the Altar of the Fathers of the Church, *c.* 1481. Tempera and oil on wood, approx. 40″ × 37″. Alte Pinakothek, Munich.

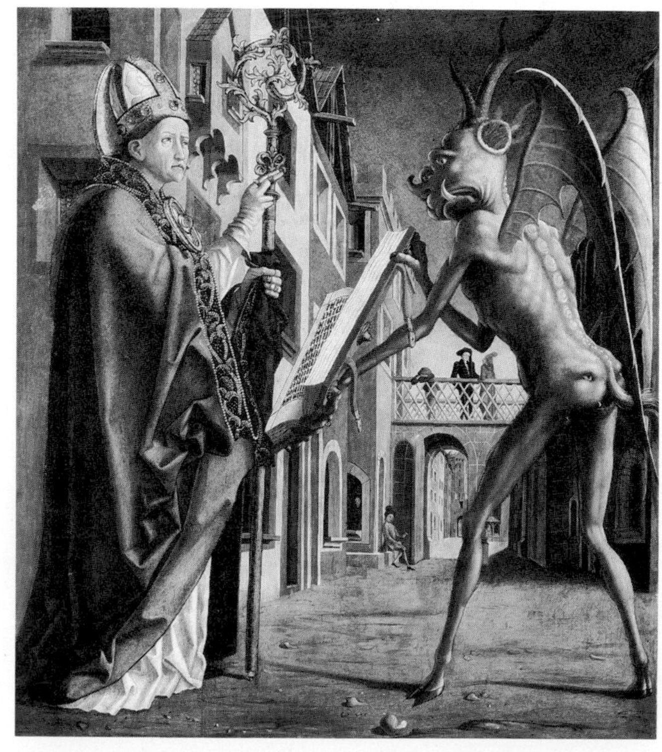

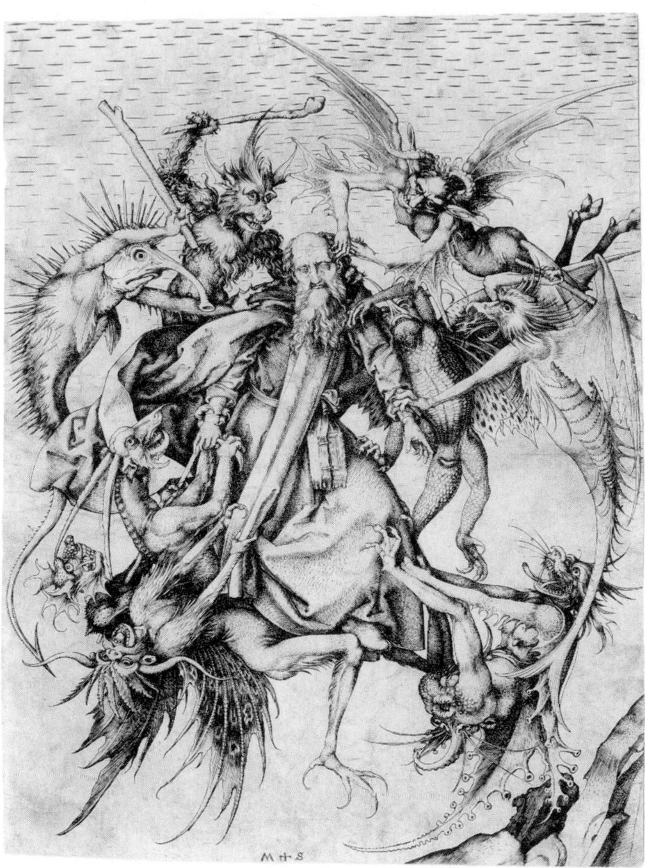

18-30 Martin Schongauer, *St. Anthony Tormented by the Demons,* c. 1480–1490. Engraving, approx. 13″ × 11″. Metropolitan Museum of Art, New York (Rogers Fund, 1920).

perspective to the horizon, are another Italian Renaissance trait. Only the gargoylish Devil tells us that the Gothic is still very much in the northern environment.

In Germany, where printing with movable type was developed, we would expect the graphic arts to be well represented by competent masters, and indeed, Martin Schongauer (*c.* 1450–1491) was the century's most skilled and subtle northern master of the new metal engraving technique. The process of printing pictures from woodblocks was developed in Europe around 1400 (the Chinese had known the technique centuries before) and remained popular, especially for book illustration, well into the 1500s. But engraving on metal surfaces—begun, as we have seen, in the 1430s and well developed by 1450—proved a much more flexible technique and, in the second half of the century, widely replaced the woodcut. Schongauer's *St. Anthony Tormented by the Demons* (FIG. **18-30**) shows both the versatility of the medium and the artist's mastery of it. Although better known for his gentle Madonnas in a style based on that of Rogier van der Weyden, here Schongauer displays almost the same taste for the diabolical as Hieronymus Bosch; his stoic saint is caught in a revolving thornbush of spiky demons, who claw and tear at him furiously. With unsurpassed skill and subtlety, the artist makes marvelous distinctions of tonal values and textures—from smooth skin to rough cloth, from the furry and feathery to the hairy and scaly. The method of describing forms with hatching that follows the forms, probably developed by Schongauer, became standard with German graphic artists. The Italians preferred parallel hatching (compare Antonio Pollaiuolo's engraving, FIG. 16-55) and rarely adopted this method, which, in keeping with the general northern approach to art, tends to describe the surfaces of things rather than their underlying structures.

THE SIXTEENTH CENTURY

Germany

The art of northern Europe during the sixteenth century is characterized by a sudden awareness of the advances made by the Italian Renaissance and by a desire to assimilate this new style as rapidly as possible. Many artists traveled to Italy to study the new art first hand; others met it either directly, in the form of Italian artists who came to the north, or indirectly, through the numerous Italian engravings that circulated throughout northern Europe. One of the most prolific Italian engravers, Marcantonio Raimondi, rarely invented his own compositions but copied those of other artists, particularly Raphael. In this way, many panel paintings and frescoes by Italian Renaissance artists became the common property of all Europe. Naturally, the impact of Italian art varied widely, according to the artist, the time, and the place. Many artists never abandoned existing local traditions; others frequently were content to borrow only single motifs or the general form of a composition. In Germany, the wealthy merchant class maintained close commercial relations with Venice, and German Humanists were in contact with the Neo-Platonic academy of Florence. As a result, Albrecht Dürer often illustrated Florentine thought clothed in Venetian and German forms.

During the fifteenth century, painting in the wealthy towns of southern Germany developed along its own expressionistic lines under the dominant influences of Flemish art. Around the turn of the century, it suddenly burst into full bloom. By 1528, with the deaths of its two greatest exponents, Dürer and Matthias Grünewald, it had spent itself. Thus, its most brilliant period corresponds almost exactly to the High Renaissance in Italy. Its decline around 1530 was just as abrupt as its rise, and the reason for this is

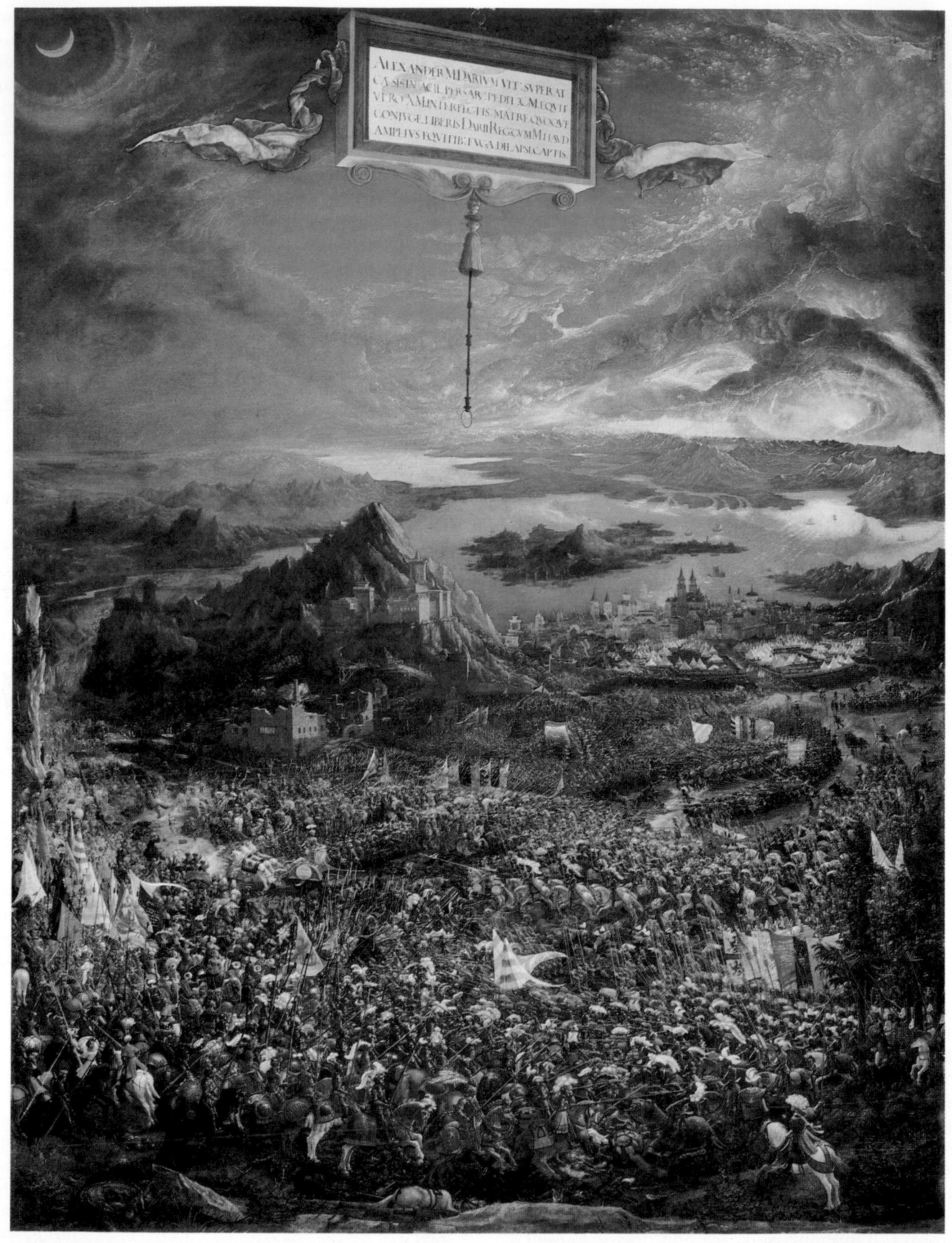

18-31 ALBRECHT ALTDORFER, *The Battle of Issus,* 1529. Oil on wood, 52¼″ × 47¼″. Alte Pinakothek, Munich.

uncertain. The almost incessant religious wars devastated the German lands, and puritanism, which accompanied the triumph of Protestantism in the north, may have opposed Humanistic paganism in the figurative arts. With the exception of Hans Holbein the Younger, the main representatives of the German school were born within ten years of one another and were contemporaries of Michelangelo, Raphael, Giorgione, and Titian.

ALTDORFER AND CRANACH

ALBRECHT ALTDORFER (*c.* 1480–1538) is the primary representative of the *Donaustil* (Danube style), which flourished along the Danube River from Regensburg (Altdorfer's hometown) eastward into Austria. The style is formed around the depiction of landscape and stresses mood, sometimes heightened to passion. Altdorfer's own style is highly personal and only occasionally modified by the influence of Dürer. As a gifted colorist and observer of atmospheric and light effects, Altdorfer loved to paint forests and ruins, in which his figure groups are half-submerged. He painted at least one landscape without figures, making *Danube Landscape, Near Regensburg* (*c.* 1522; not shown) perhaps the first landscape in Western art painted entirely for its own sake.

His most renowned work, *The Battle of Issus* (FIG. **18-31**), bears little resemblance to a Danube setting, although it does give a bird's-eye view of an Alpine landscape. Here, Altdorfer spreads out in awesome detail the battle in which Alexander the Great overthrew the Persian king, Darius. A huge inscription hanging in the clouds relates this. Swarms of warriors from both sides contest on a plain backed by cities, mountains, seas, and the opposed forces of nature: the sun and the moon in an illuminated sky. This sudden opening up of space, with its subordination of the human figure to the cosmic landscape, bespeaks a new view of nature—a view that will see human beings as insignificant motes in an infinite universe. We need not suppose that German artists knew of the work of the contemporary astronomer, Copernicus, who was about to revise the age-old view that the earth is fixed and to suggest instead that the earth and the other "fixed" planets revolve about the sun. It is interesting that such high-horizoned, "topographical" landscapes (we might better call them "cosmographical") anticipate the coming cosmic view that the sciences of physics and physical astronomy will open to the Western world. Altdorfer's technique is still that of the miniaturist, yet his setting is no longer a page but a world, one in which his insectlike combatants are all but lost. In this first vision of the immense space and power of the cosmos, Altdorfer seems to suggest a theme that all subsequent philosophers, scientists, and churchmen, as well as artists, will confront—the insignificance of human life.

The early works of LUCAS CRANACH THE ELDER (1472–1553) are close to the Donaustil, which immerses human beings in the breadth of nature. At Wittenberg, where he was summoned by the elector of Saxony, Cranach became a friend and follower of Luther, and he has been called the outstanding representative of German Protestant painting. His later works are marked by a shift from religious to humanistic subject matter: mythology, history, and portraits. Best known are his figure compositions featuring the nude, which he renders with a charming, provincial naïveté. A good example is *The Judgment of Paris* (FIG. **18-32**). Here, Paris and Mercury consult, while three spindly little goddesses show off their pretty contours. One of them bashfully stands on one foot; another coquettishly calls attention to her charms; the third stands by, wearing a fashionable

18-32 LUCAS CRANACH THE ELDER, *The Judgment of Paris*, 1530. Oil on wood, approx. $14\frac{1}{2}'' \times 9\frac{7}{8}''$. Staatliche Kunsthalle, Karlsruhe, West Germany.

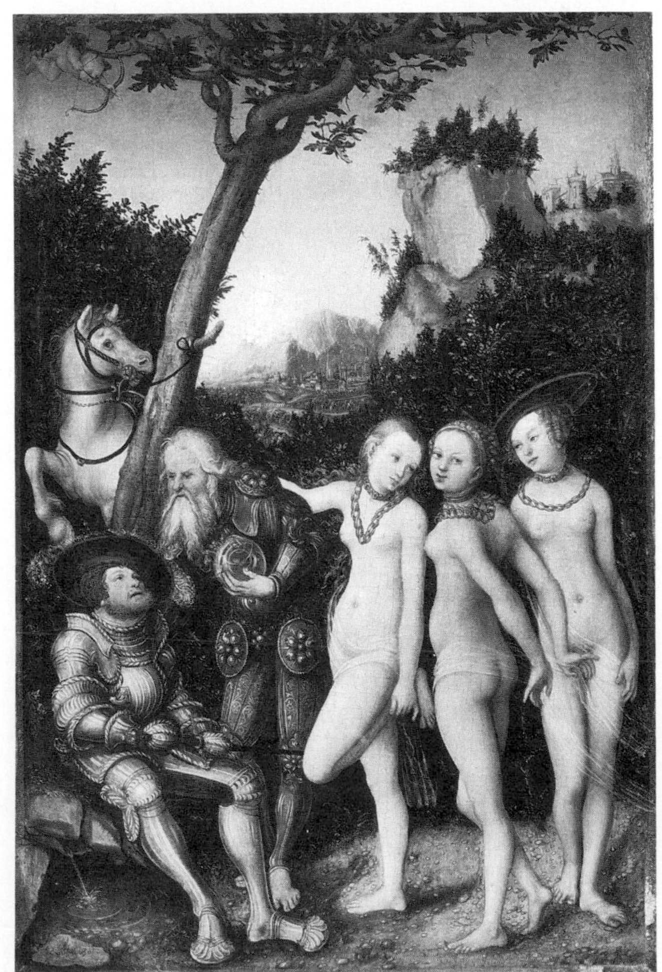

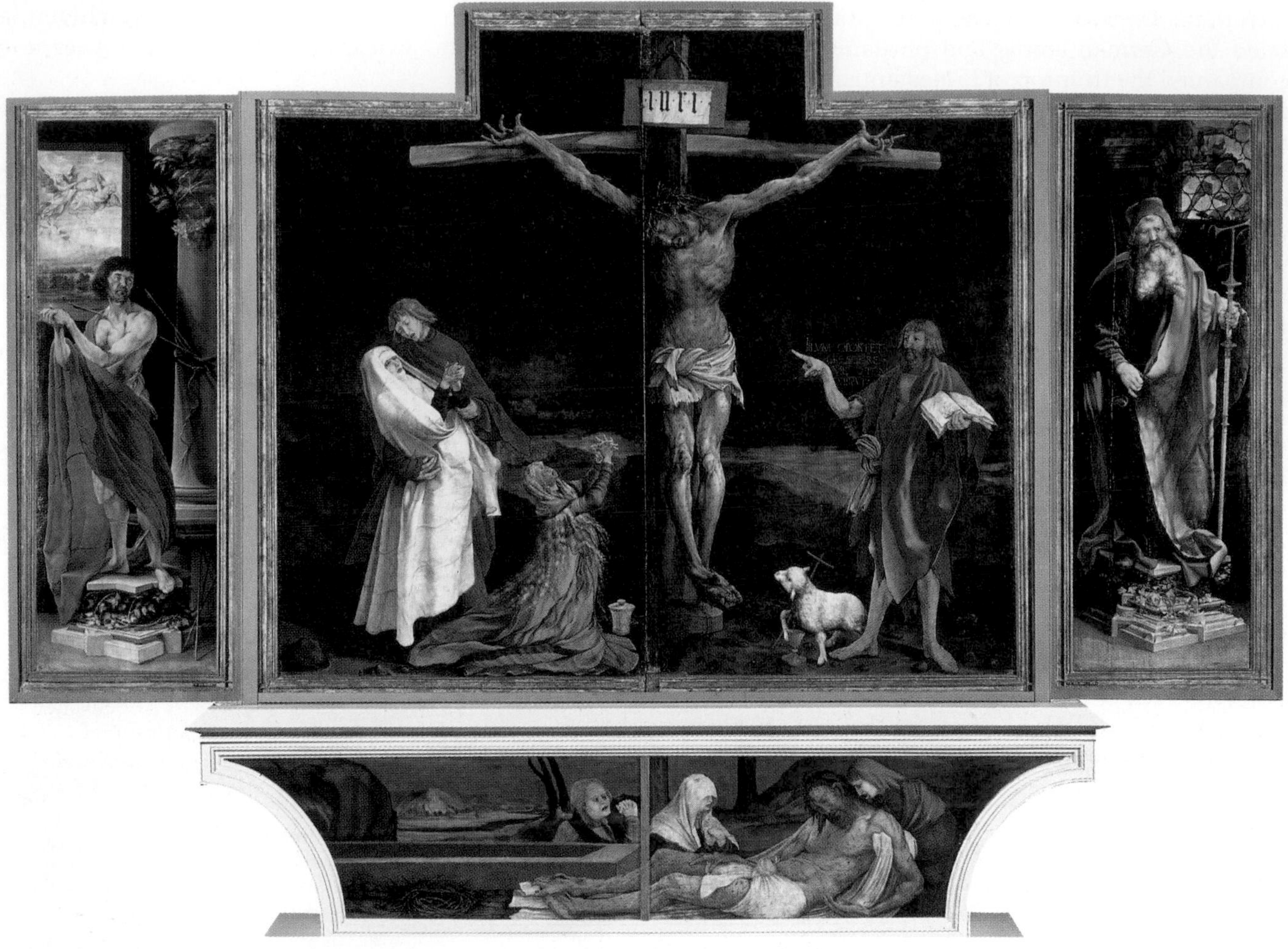

18-33 MATTHIAS GRÜNEWALD, *The Isenheim Altarpiece* (closed), *Crucifixion* (center panel), *c.* 1510–1515. Oil on wood, center panel 9′ 9½″ × 10′ 9″, each wing 8′ 2½″ × 3′ ½″, predella 2′ 5½″ × 11′ 2″. Musée d'Unterlinden, Colmar, France.

hat. Cranach makes no effort to dress his gods after the Antique manner. They wear the functional armor of German knights attached to provincial courts. Doughty and square-faced, they could have just come in from the field of honor. The background landscape reflects Cranach's earlier Donaustil in its meticulous description of foliage. And so far, only Dürer's approach to the nude (FIG. 18-36) is tutored by Italian art.

MATTHIAS GRÜNEWALD

One of the greatest individualists of the Renaissance and an artist of highly original genius is Matthias Neithardt, known conventionally as MATTHIAS GRÜNEWALD (*c.* 1480–1528). Forgotten until our time, he appears to have had the wide interests of the individualistic Renaissance artists. Working for the archbishops of Mainz from 1511 on as court painter and decorator, he also served them as architect, hydraulic engineer, and superintendent of works. Undoubtedly, he had Lutheran sympathies. He participated in the Peasant Revolt in 1525, and, after its collapse, had to flee to northern Germany, where he settled at Halle in Saxony. The sources of Grünewald's style are not certain. He may have been to Italy, but few indications of Renaissance Classicism appear in his art. He knew the work of Dürer and perhaps of Bosch. A brilliant colorist, he was not interested in the construction of the monumental, idealized figure in the Italian manner. His color is characterized by subtle tones and soft harmonies on the one hand and shocking dissonance on the other. Uninterested in natural landscape, Grünewald shows us either the celestial or the infernal.

In his appalling *Crucifixion* from *The Isenheim Altarpiece* (FIG. **18-33**), Grünewald gives us perhaps the most memorable interpretation of the theme in the history of art. The altar is composed of a carved wooden shrine with two pairs of movable panels, one directly in back of the other. Painted by Grünewald between 1510 and 1515 for the monastic hospital order of St. Anthony of Isenheim, the panels show three scenes, with the *Crucifixion* outermost, when the altar is closed. The dreadful aspect of the painting may be due in part to its placement in a house of the sick, where it may have admonished the inmates that Another has suffered more. It also may have had a therapeutic function, in that it offered some hope to the afflicted. Two saints are represented on the wings flanking the central panels: on the left, St. Sebastian, whose intercession was invoked to ward off disease (especially the plague); on the right, St. Anthony, the patron saint of the order, who was identified with miraculous cure. Together, the saints establish the theme of disease and healing that is reinforced by the paintings on the inner wings.

One of the main illnesses treated at the hospital was ergotism (called "St. Anthony's Fire"), a disease caused by ergot, a fungus that grows especially on rye. Although the cause of this disease was not discovered until about 1600, its symptoms (convulsions and gangrene) were well known. The gangrene often compelled amputation, and it has been noted in this connection that the two movable halves of the predella of the altarpiece, if slid apart, make it appear as if the legs of Christ have been amputated. The same observation can be made of the two main panels. Due to the off-center placement of the cross, the opening of the left center panel would "sever" one arm from the crucified figure.

Much of this symbolism may have been dictated by his patrons, but Grünewald's own inflamed imagination produced the terrible image of the suffering Christ. Against the pall of darkness lowered on the earth, the devasted body looms—dead, the flesh already discolored by decomposition and studded with the thorns of the lash. In death, the strains of the superhuman agony twist the blackening feet, tear at the arms, wrench the head to one side, and turn the fingers into crooked spikes. One has only to tense one's fingers in the position of Christ's to experience the shuddering tautness of nerves expressed in every line of the figure. No other artist has produced such an image of the dreadful ugliness of pain. The sharp, angular shapes of anguish appear in the figures of the swooning Virgin and St. John and in the shrill delirium of the Magdalene. On the other side, the gaunt, spectral form of John the Baptist stands in ungainly pose, pointing with a finger sharp as a bird's beak to the dead Christ and indicating in a Latin inscription Christ's destiny as Redeemer and his own as mere precursor: "It is fitting that he increase and I diminish." The bright, harsh, dissonant colors—black, blood-red, acid-yellow, and the dreadful green of death—suit the flat, angular shapes. Placed in a wilderness of dark mountains, the scene is relieved by a flood of glaring light that holds the figures in a tableau of awful impact.

Death and suffering seem to be the dominant themes shown by the altarpiece in its closed state. Yet they are combined with symbols offering hope and comfort to the viewer. Behind St. John is a body of water (the river Jordan?), which signifies baptism—the healing action of water, which symbolically washes away sin. (It may also refer to the growing contemporary interest in hydrotherapy, as numerous handbooks advertising local thermal and mineral baths were being published at the beginning of the sixteenth century.) The wine-red sky behind the cross evokes the blood of Christ and may symbolize the Eucharist. These references to the sacraments of baptism and the Eucharist offer the viewer the hope of salvation through the sacrifice of Christ, should earthly cures fail.

When we turn from the Good Friday of the *Crucifixion* to the Easter Sunday of the *Resurrection* (FIG. **18-34**), an inner panel of *The Isenheim Altarpiece,* the mood changes from disaster to triumph. Christ, in a

18-34 MATTHIAS GRÜNEWALD, *Resurrection,* detail of the inner right panel of the first opening of *The Isenheim Altarpiece.* Approx. 8′ 8⅜″ × 4′ 6¾″.

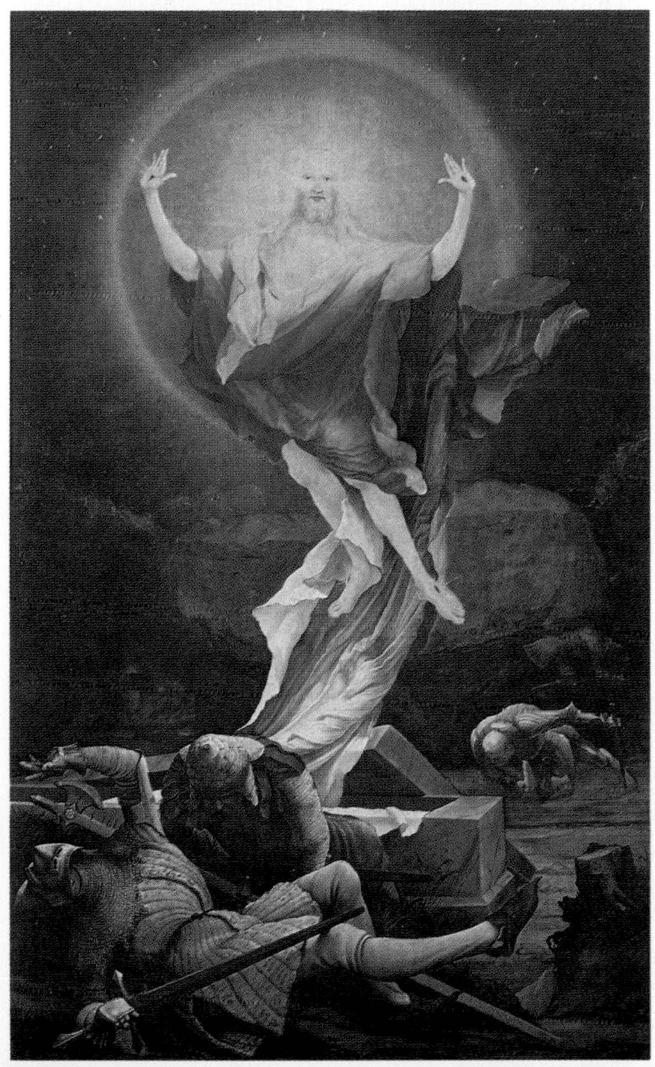

blazing aureole of light so incandescent that it dissolves his form and overwhelms the guards, rises like a great flame into the starlit heavens. The fluttering Gothic line prevails in the ascending Christ, and something of the awkward angularity of the *Crucifixion* scene shapes the fallen soldiers. The highly expressive light in both scenes is supernatural, not the light of common day. It is certainly not the even, flat light that models Piero della Francesca's *Resurrection* fresco (FIG. 16-35). Indeed, in these two pictures, we find the fundamental differences that set the German school apart from the Italian school in the Renaissance. Piero's *Resurrection* typically represents the event in terms of a static grouping of solidly rendered figures in a completely balanced, measured composition; the central figure of Christ stands solid as a column, one foot placed weightily on the edge of the sarcophagus. Grünewald converts everything into flowing motion; his Christ is disembodied, almost formless, and the composition has the irregularity and free form of a flaming cloud. Color determines everything here—not sculpturesque form and geometric composition, as with Piero's works. Moreover, Grünewald's intention is to render the supernatural in a bodiless way appropriate to it. Piero makes Christ as massive and corporeal as the stone sarcophagus on which he stands. From the Italian point of view, the visionary flashing and flickering of Grünewald's *Resurrection* must have appeared crude, formless, and utterly devoid of the order that theory, based on the study of nature and measurement, could confer.

ALBRECHT DÜRER

We know that Grünewald's great contemporary, ALBRECHT DÜRER (1471–1528), felt that much of the art of the north was crude and devoid of order and that, in comparison with Italian art, it appeared to him old-fashioned, clumsy, and without knowledge. In the introduction to an unfinished and unpublished treatise on painting, Dürer wrote:

> Now, I know that in our German nation, at the present time, are many painters who stand in need of instruction, for they lack all real art theory. . . . For as much as they are so numerous, it is very needful for them to learn to better their work. He that works in ignorance works more painfully than he who works in understanding; therefore let all learn to understand art aright.

While still a journeyman, Dürer became acquainted with, and began to copy, prints by Mantegna and Pollaiuolo. Fascinated with Classical ideas, as transmitted through Italian Renaissance artists, he was the first northern artist to travel to Italy expressly to study Italian art and its underlying theories at their source. After his first journey in 1495 (he made a second trip in 1505–1506), it became his life mission to bring the modern—the Italian Renaissance—style north and establish it there. Although Dürer did not always succeed in fusing his own native German style with the Italian manner, he was the first northern artist who fully understood the basic aims of the southern Renaissance.

Dürer was also the first artist outside of Italy to become an international art celebrity. Well traveled and widely admired, he knew many of the leading Humanists and artists of his time, among them Erasmus of Rotterdam and Giovanni Bellini. A man of wide talents and tremendous energy, he became the "Leonardo of the North," achieving fabulous fame in his own time and a firm reputation ever since. Like Leonardo da Vinci, Dürer wrote theoretical treatises on a variety of subjects, such as perspective, fortification, and the ideal in human proportions. Through his prints, he exerted strong influence throughout Europe, especially in Flanders, but also in Italy. Moreover, he was the first northern artist to make himself known to posterity through several excellent self-portraits, through his correspondence, and through a carefully kept, quite detailed and immanently readable diary.

In his own time, Dürer's fame and influence depended on his mastery of the graphic arts, and we still think that his greatest contribution to Western art lies in this field. Trained as a goldsmith before he took up painting and printmaking, he developed an extraordinary proficiency in the handling of the burin, the engraving tool. This technical ability, combined with a feeling for the form-creating possibilities of line, enabled him to create a corpus of graphic work in woodcut and engraving that has seldom been rivaled for quality and number. In addition to illustrations for books, Dürer circulated and sold prints in single sheets, which people of ordinary means could buy and which made him a "people's artist" quite as much as a model for professionals. It also made him a rich man.

An early and very successful series of woodblock prints on fourteen large sheets illustrates the Apocalypse, or the Revelation of St. John, the last book of the Bible. With great force and inventiveness, Dürer represents terrifying visions of doomsday and of the omens preceding it. The fourth print of the series, *The Four Horsemen* (FIG. **18-35**), represents, from foreground to background, Death trampling a bishop, Famine swinging scales, War wielding a sword, and

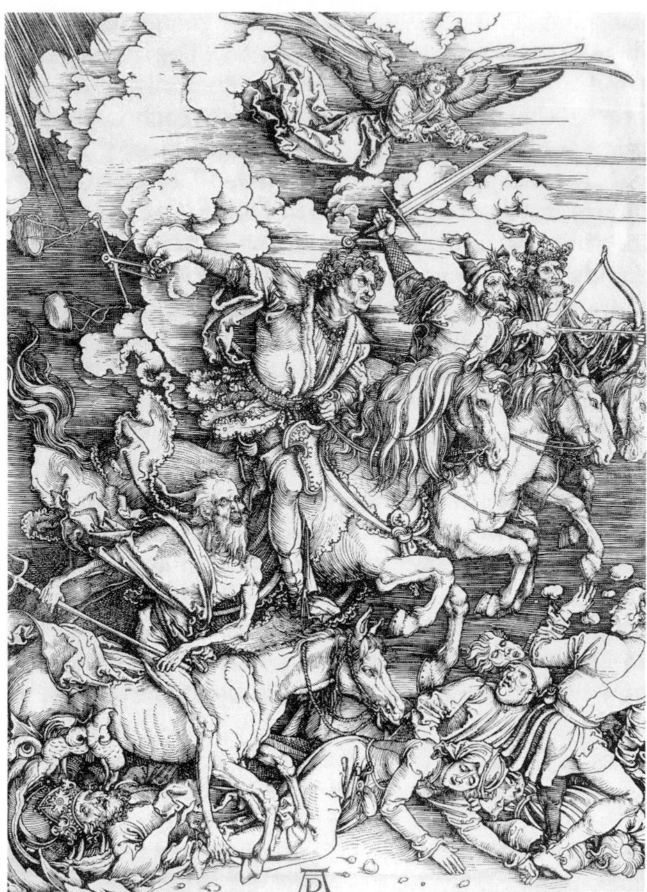

18-35 ALBRECHT DÜRER, *The Four Horsemen,* from the *Apocalypse* series, c. 1498. Woodcut, approx. $15\frac{1}{4}'' \times 11''$. Metropolitan Museum of Art, New York (gift of Junius S. Morgan, 1919).

Pestilence drawing his bow. The human race, in the last days of the world, is trampled by the grim quartet.

Technically, the virtuosity of Dürer's woodcuts never has been surpassed. By adapting to the woodcut the form-following hatching from Schongauer's engravings (FIG. 18-30), Dürer converts the former's primitive contrasts of black and white into a gliding scale of light and shade, achieving a quality of luminosity never before seen in woodblock prints. *The Four Horsemen* retains some Late Gothic characteristics in the angularity of shapes and the tendency of forms to merge into one another. On the other hand, Mantegna's influence can be found in the plastic and foreshortened poses of the trampled victims in the right foreground and in the head of Famine. But despite such Italicisms, the dramatic complexity of the composition remains essentially northern.

From 1500 on, Dürer increasingly became interested in the theoretical foundations of Italian Renaissance art. An engraving of *The Fall of Man (Adam and Eve)* (FIG. **18-36**) represents the first distillation of his studies of the Vitruvian theory of human proportions. Clearly outlined against the dark background of a northern forest, the two idealized figures of Adam and Eve stand in poses reminiscent of the *Apollo Belvedere* and the *Medici Venus*—two Hellenistic statues probably known to Dürer through graphic representations. Preceded by numerous geometric drawings, in which he tried to systematize sets of ideal human proportions in balanced contrapposto poses, the final print presents Dürer's 1504 concept of the "perfect" male and female figures. Adam does, in fact, approach the southern ideal quite closely, but the fleshy Eve remains a German matron, her individualized features suggesting the use of a model. The elaborate symbolism of the background "accessories" to the main figures is also a northern trait. The choleric cat, the melancholic elk, the sanguine rabbit, and the phlegmatic ox represent the four humors of man, and the relation between Adam and Eve at the crucial moment of *The Fall of Man* is symbolized by the tension between cat and mouse in the foreground.

Dürer's *The Fall of Man* shows idealized forms and strongly naturalistic ones in a close combination that, depending on the viewer's attitude, may be regarded

18-36 ALBRECHT DÜRER, *The Fall of Man (Adam and Eve)*, 1504. Engraving, approx. $10'' \times 7\frac{1}{2}''$. Centennial Gift of Landon T. Clay. Courtesy of Museum of Fine Arts, Boston.

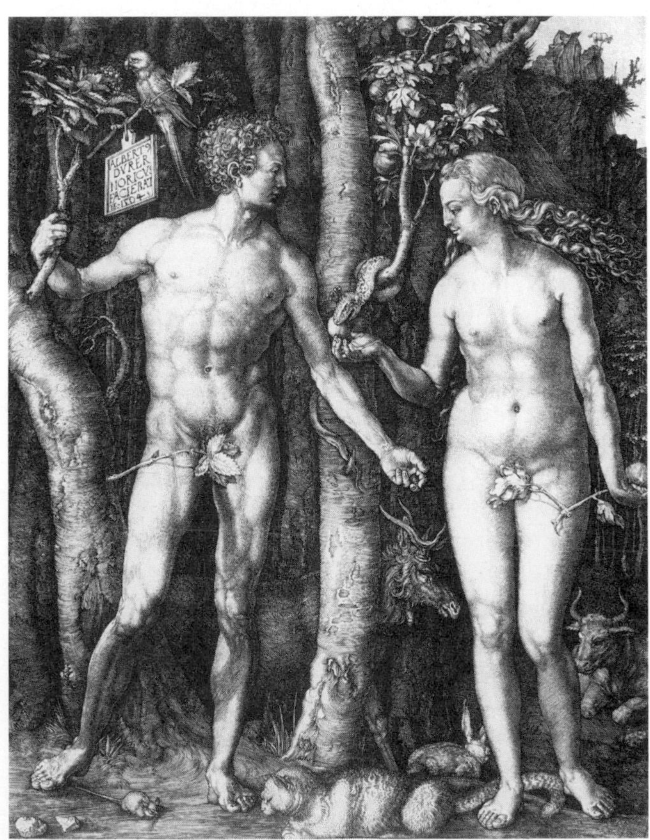

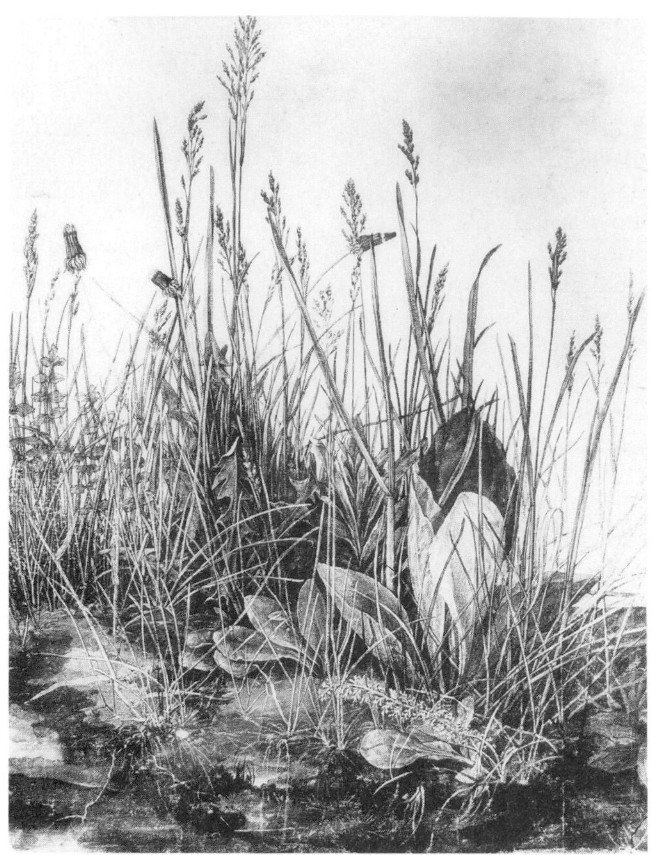

18-37 ALBRECHT DÜRER, *The Great Piece of Turf,* 1503. Watercolor, approx. 16″ × 12¼″. Graphische Sammlung Albertina, Vienna.

as complementary or conflictive elements—closely allied ingredients in most of Dürer's works. Dürer agreed with Aristotle (and the new critics of the Renaissance) that "sight is the noblest faculty of man" and that "every form brought before our vision falls upon it as upon a mirror." "We regard," said Dürer, "a form and figure out of nature with more pleasure than any other, though the thing itself is not necessarily altogether better or worse." This idea is a new and important one for artists. Nature holds the beautiful, said Dürer, for him who has the insight to extract it. Thus, beauty lies even in humble, perhaps ugly things, and the ideal, which bypasses or improves on nature, may not be the truly beautiful in the end: uncomposed and ordinary nature might be a reasonable object of the artist's interest, quite as much as its composed and measured aspect. With an extremely precise watercolor study of a piece of turf (FIG. **18-37**), Dürer allies himself to the scientific studies of Leonardo; for both artists, observation yields truth. Sight, sanctified by mystics like Nicholas of Cusa and artists like Jan van Eyck, becomes the secularized instrument of modern knowledge. The "mirror" that is our "vision" will later become telescope, microscope, and television screen. The remarkable *Great Piece of Turf* is as scientifically accurate as it is poetic; the botanist can distinguish each springing plant and variety of grass: dandelions, great plantain, yarrow, meadow grass, heath rush. "Depart not from nature in your opinions," said Dürer, "neither imagine that you can invent anything better. . . . for art stands firmly fixed in nature, and he who can find it there, he has it." The exquisite still life one finds in the northern paintings of the fifteenth century is irradiated with religious symbolism. Dürer's still life is of and for itself; he has found it in nature, and its representation no longer requires religious justification.

As Dürer's floral studies reveal the natural world, so he makes his portraits readings of character. The fifteenth-century portrait, like Van Eyck's *Man in a Red Turban* (FIG. 18-9) or his *Canon van der Paele* (FIG. 18-8), is a graphic description of features; Dürer's portraits, like that of *Hieronymus Holzschuher* (FIG. **18-38**), are interpretations of personality. It may be, however, that they are as much projections of Dürer's

18-38 ALBRECHT DÜRER, *Hieronymus Holzschuher,* 1526. Oil on wood, approx. 19″ × 14″. Gemäldegalerie, Staatliche Museen, Berlin-Dahlem.

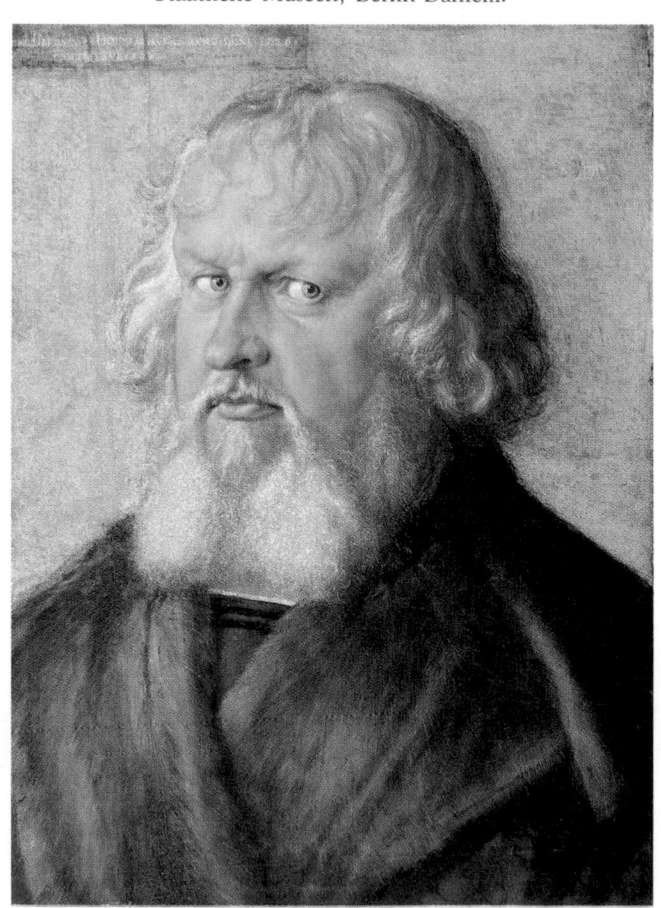

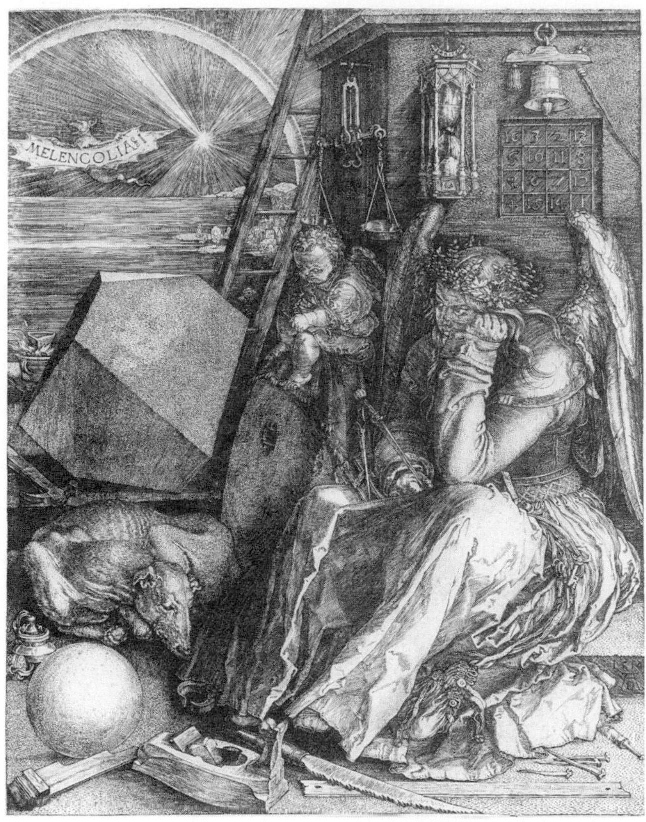

18-39 Albrecht Dürer, *Melencolia I*, 1514. Engraving, approx. 9⅜" × 6⅝". Fogg Museum of Art, Harvard University, Cambridge, Massachusetts (bequest of Francis Calley Gray).

own personality as they are readings of his subjects', for his portraits of men all show the subject as bold and virile, square-jawed, flashing-eyed, and truculent. All the subjects appear intense and intently aware of the observer. This strong psychic relationship to the external world, when the features are precisely particularized, makes for an extremely vivid presence. Holzschuher, a friend of Dürer's and town councilor of Nuremberg, fairly bristles with choleric energy and the burly belligerence of Nuremberg citizens, who, on many an occasion, had defended the city against all comers, including the emperor himself. Leaving the background blank, except for an inscription, the artist achieves a remarkable concentration on the forceful personality of his subject. The portrait in Italy never really brings the subject into such a tense personal relationship with the observer.

Dürer always found it quite difficult to reconcile his northern penchant for precise naturalism with his intellectual, theoretical pursuits and with the demands of southern High Renaissance art for simplified monumentality. This life-long dilemma seems to be expressed in *Melencolia I* (FIG. **18-39**), one of three so-called master prints Dürer made between 1513 and 1514. These works (the other two are *Knight, Death, and the Devil* and *St. Jerome in His Study*) were probably intended to symbolize the moral, theological, and intellectual virtues. They clearly carry the art of engraving to the highest degree of excellence. Dürer used his burin to render differences in texture and tonal values that would be difficult to match even in the much more flexible medium of etching, which was developed later in the century.

The complex symbolism of *Melencolia I* is based primarily on concepts derived from Florentine Neo-Platonism. The instruments of the arts and sciences lie strewn in idle confusion about the seated, winged figure of Melancholy; she is the personification of knowledge that, without divine inspiration, lacks the ability to act. According to then current astrological theory, the artist, or any individual engaged in creative activity, is the subject of Saturn. Such a person is characterized by a melancholia bordering on madness that either plunges him into despondency or raises him to the heights of creative fury; Michelangelo was regarded as subject to this humor. Dürer and Michelangelo both conceived of artists (and thus of themselves) as geniuses who struggle to translate the pure idea in their minds into gross but visible matter. Thus, the monumental image of the winged genius, with burning eyes in a shaded face and wings that do not fly, becomes the symbol for divine aspirations defeated by human frailty and, in a way, is a "spiritual self-portrait of Albrecht Dürer."

Only toward the very end of his life, and in one of his very last paintings, was Dürer finally able to reconcile the two opposing tendencies of northern naturalism and southern monumentality that had struggled for dominance in his entire oeuvre. He painted *The Four Apostles* (FIG. **18-40**) without commission and presented the two panels to the city fathers of Nuremberg in 1526 to be hung in the city hall. The work has been called Dürer's religious and political testament, in which he expresses his sympathies for the Protestant cause and warns against the dangerous times, when religion, truth, justice, and the virtues all will be threatened. The four apostles (John and Peter on the left panel; Mark and Paul on the right) stand on guard for the city. Quotations from each of their books, in the German of Luther's translation of the New Testament, are written on the frames. They warn against the coming of perilous times and the preaching of false prophets who will distort the word of God. The figures of the apostles summarize Dürer's whole craft and learning. Representing the four temperaments, or humors, of the human soul, as well as the four ages of man and other quaternities, these portraitlike characterizations of the apostles

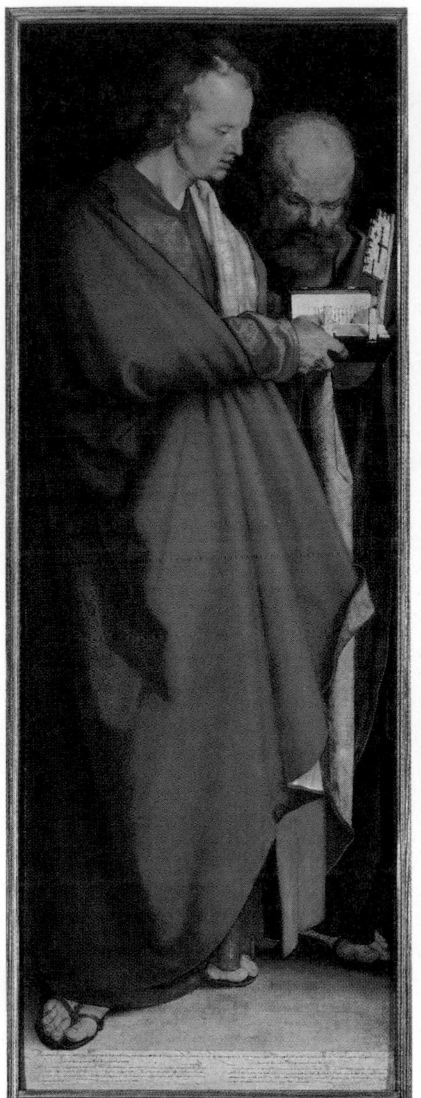
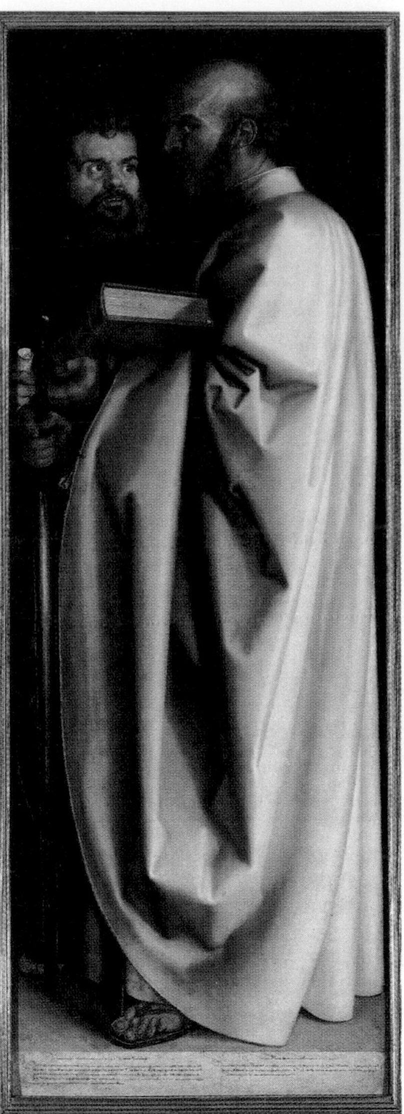

18-40 ALBRECHT DÜRER, *The Four Apostles,* 1526. Oil on wood, each panel 7′ 1″ × 2′ 6″. Alte Pinakothek, Munich.

have no equal in the idealized representations of Italian saints. At the same time, the art of the Italian Renaissance is felt in the monumental grandeur and majesty of the figures, which are heightened by a vivid color and sharp lighting. Here, Dürer unites the northern sense of minute realism with the Italian tradition of balanced forms, massive and simple. The result is a vindication of the artist's striving toward a new understanding—a work that stands with the greatest of the masterpieces of Italian art.

HANS HOLBEIN THE YOUNGER

What Dürer had struggled all his life to formulate and construct was achieved almost effortlessly by his younger contemporary, HANS HOLBEIN THE YOUNGER (1497–1543). Holbein's speciality was portraiture, in which he displayed a thorough assimilation of all that Italy had to teach of monumental composition, bodily structure, and sculpturesque form. He retains the northern traditions of close realism elaborated in fifteenth-century Flemish art. The color surfaces of his paintings are as lustrous as enamel; his detail, exact and exquisitely drawn; and his contrasts of light and dark, never heavy.

Holbein was first active in Basel, where he knew Erasmus of Rotterdam. Because a religious civil war was imminent in Basel, Erasmus suggested that Holbein leave for England and gave him a recommendation to Thomas More, chancellor of England under Henry VIII. Holbein did leave and became painter to the English court. While there, he painted a superb double portrait of the French ambassadors to England, Jean de Dinteville and Georges de Selve (FIG. **18-41**). The two men, both ardent Humanists, stand

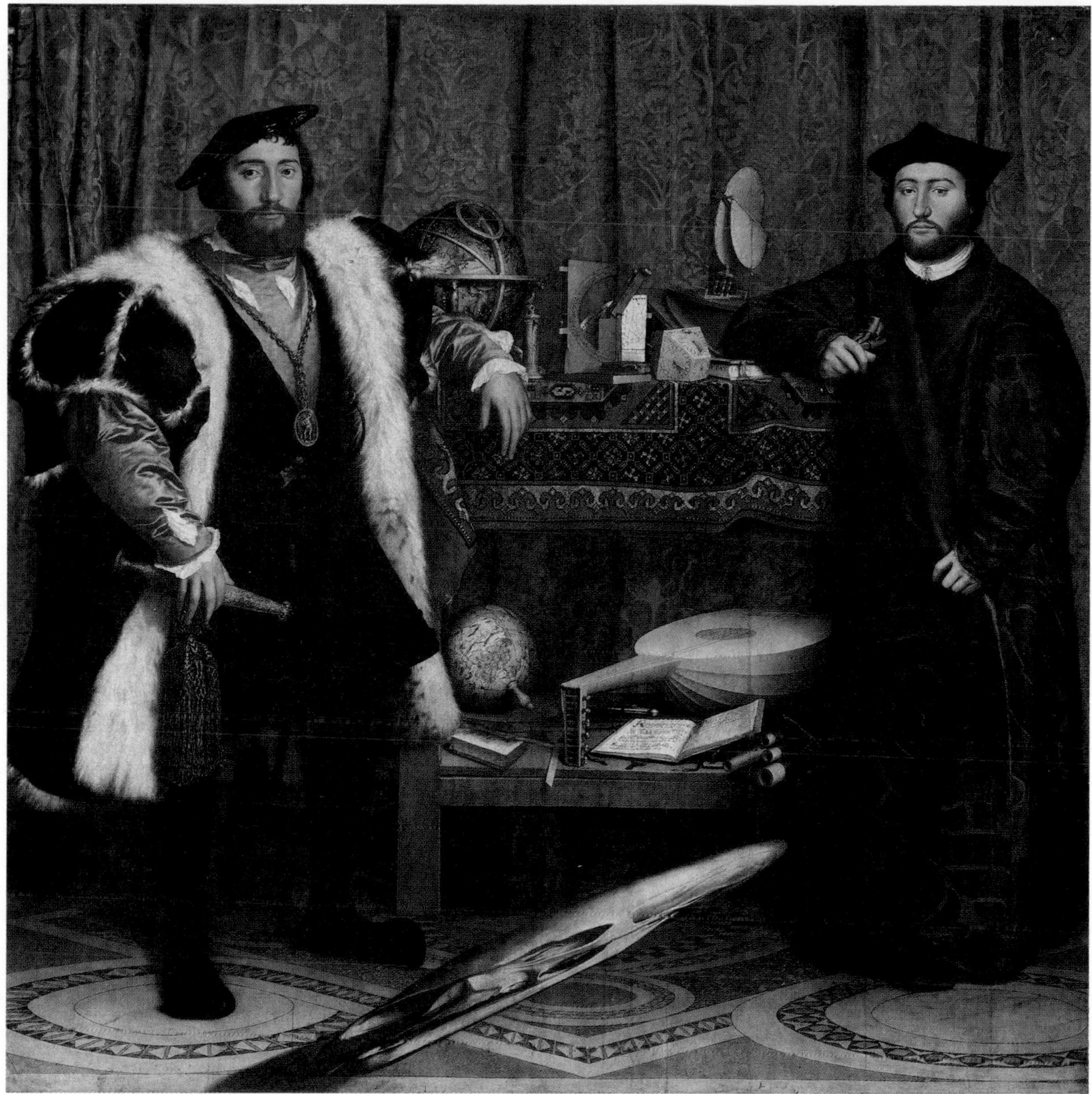

18-41 Hans Holbein the Younger, *The French Ambassadors,* 1533. Oil and tempera on wood, approx. 6′ 8″ × 6′ 9½″. Reproduced by courtesy of the Trustees of the National Gallery, London.

at either end of a side table covered with an oriental rug and a collection of objects reflective of their interests: mathematical and astronomical models and implements, a lute with a broken string, compasses, a sundial, flutes, globes, and an open hymnbook with Luther's translation of *Veni, Creator Spiritus* and of the Ten Commandments. The still-life objects are rendered with the same meticulous care as the men themselves, the woven design of the deep emerald curtain behind them, and the floor tiles, constructed in faultless perspective. The stable, balanced, serene composition is interrupted only by a long, gray shape that slashes diagonally across the picture plane. This form is an *anamorphic* image that needs to be viewed by some special means (for example, reflected in a cylindrical mirror) if it is to be recognizable. In this case, the image is of a death's-head, for Holbein, like Dürer, was interested in symbolism as well as in radical perspectives. The color harmonies are adjusted in symphonic complexity and richness. The grave, even somber portraits indicate that Holbein follows the Italian portrait tradition, which gives the face a neutral expression, rather than Dürer's practice of giving it an expression of keen intensity. *The French Ambassadors* exhibits Holbein's peculiar talents: his strong sense of composition, his subtle linear patterning, his gift for portraiture, his marvelous sensitivity to color, and his faultlessly firm technique. This painting may have been Holbein's favorite; it is the only one signed with his full name.

Holbein died prematurely in 1543 and, with him, the great German school of the Renaissance. But in 1532, when he left Basel for England, he already had taken the Renaissance with him. He had no significant successors, and German art faded in the uproar of a century of religious war.

The Netherlands

The resurgence of France and the eclipse of the House of Burgundy robbed the Flemish schools of their precedence. The tremendous acclaim of Albrecht Dürer, when he visited Antwerp in 1520, indicates a reverse for Flanders; Germany, which had followed Flanders, now led developments in the north. The decay of the old Flemish tradition, both in form and content, left a void that was filled by the confusing appearance of Italian ideas, received secondhand through Dürer. As with any new, inspiring, but ill-understood fashion, a number of conflicting mannerisms arose, which, if anything, had in common only their misunderstanding of the principles behind the novel forms. This period is characterized by a great delight in decorative extravagance, in which pedantic allusion to the classics is combined with exotic settings made of piled-up fragments of Italianate ornament. For a generation or so, the north, as it has been said, "simply could not get its Renaissance on straight."

But from all this confusion, new and confident movements could begin. In a first step toward new beginnings, remnants of the Medieval tradition had to be swept away. The dominance of religious conventions yielded to experiments in subject matter and form; although religious material persisted, it no longer prevailed in art. We have seen how religious themes were modified by humanization over a period of more than a century; now they had to share the artist's interest in portraiture, mythology, landscape, and genre. The structural basis for a new, Humanistic realism had been introduced by the great German painters. It was on this foundation that an international, European art, dealing primarily with human interests, had to be built.

Changing views and attitudes were accompanied by a geographical shift in the region's commercial center. Partly as a result of the silting-up of the Bruges estuary, traffic was diverted to Antwerp, which became the hub of economic activity in the Low Countries after 1510. By mid-century, a jealous Venetian envoy had to admit that more business was transacted in Antwerp in a few weeks than in a year in Venice. As many as five hundred ships a day passed through Antwerp's harbor, and large trading colonies from England, Germany, Italy, Portugal, and Spain established themselves in the city.

QUENTIN METSYS

Antwerp's growth and prosperity, along with the propensity of its wealthy merchants for collecting and purchasing art, attracted artists to the city. Among them was QUENTIN METSYS (*c.* 1465–1530), who became Antwerp's leading master after 1510. Son of a Louvain blacksmith, Metsys may have been largely self-taught, which would explain, in part, his susceptibility to outside influences and his willingness to explore the styles and modes of a variety of models, from Van Eyck to Bosch, and from Van der Weyden to Dürer and Leonardo. Yet his eclecticism was subtle and discriminating and enriched by an inventiveness that gave a personal stamp to his paintings and made him a popular as well as important artist. Quentin Metsys represents both the bad and the good aspects of early sixteenth-century Flemish art in its struggle to shed fifteenth-century traditions in favor of a more "modern" Renaissance mode of expression.

Metsys painted *The St. Anne Altarpiece* for the Louvain Brotherhood of St. Anne between 1507 and 1509. Its central panel (FIG. **18-42**) shows a stable and orderly grouping of figures before a triple-vaulted loggia, through which a finely painted distant landscape can be seen. The round-arched architecture, complete with tie-rods and a central dome, seems functional enough (except for the rectangular window, which intrudes illogically into the hemispheric dome), but it has little to do with Italian Renaissance architecture, which Metsys evidently tried to emulate. In this respect, he was no more successful than his Romanist contemporaries, whose attempts to provide their paintings with "modern" (Italian Renaissance) settings produced little more than architectural fantasies. On the other hand, the triple loggia effectively unifies the solemn, softly draped figures, whose heads are grouped in three inverted triangles. The compression of the composition may have been inspired by one of the late paintings of Hugo van der Goes, and the calm serenity of the scene evokes memories of Hans Memling's paintings (FIG. 18-18). But these and other possible sources of inspiration are thoroughly assimilated and synthesized by Metsys into a personal style. The regularized composition and the light coloration of his forms produce a tapestry-like effect that is decorative and memorable.

Metsys's explorations of the past are liberally mixed with forward-looking genre and moralizing subjects to give his oeuvre a highly diversified aspect. The variety of his inventions provides a bridge from the fifteenth into the sixteenth century and makes

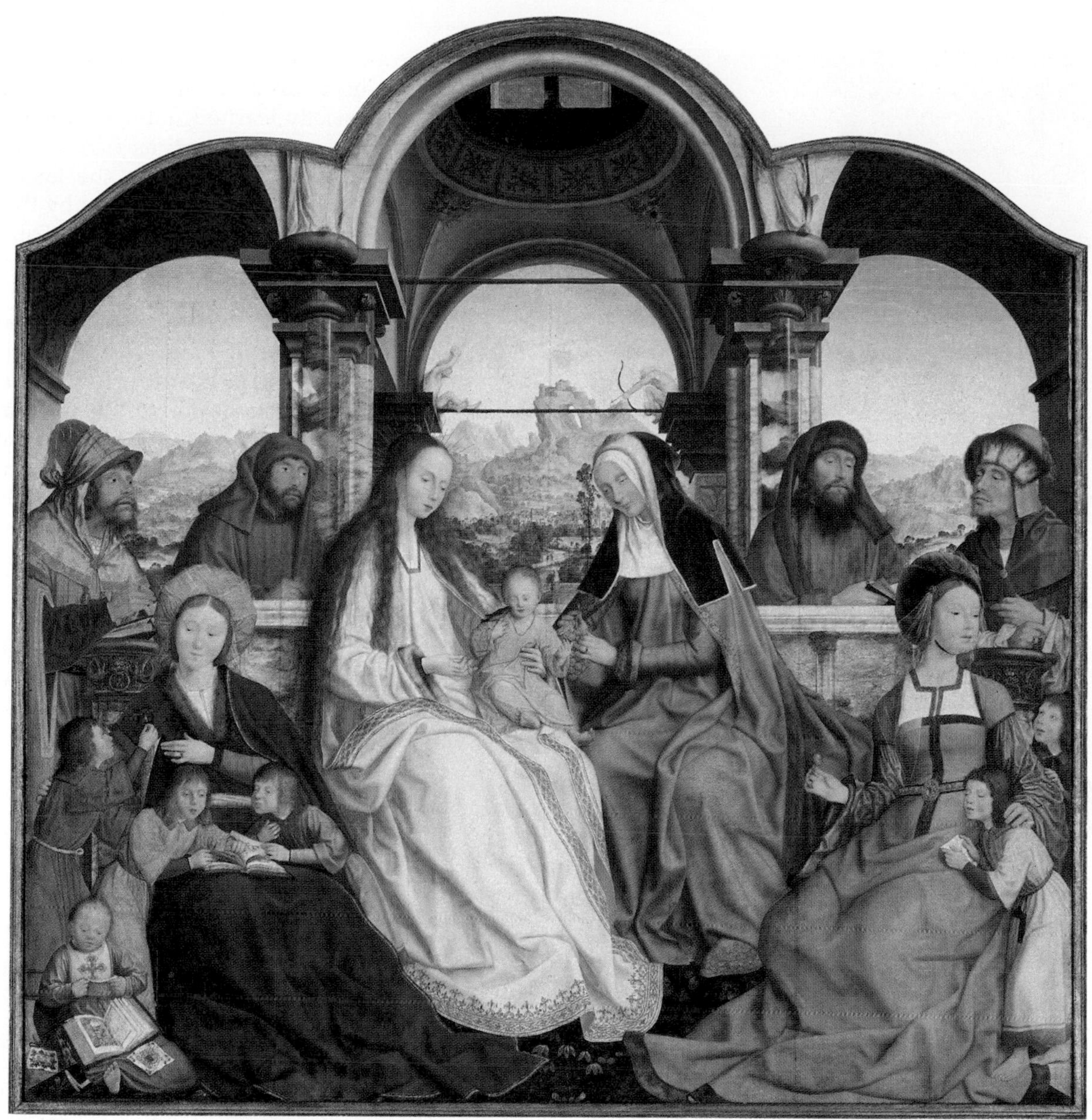

18-42 Quentin Metsys, *The St. Anne Altarpiece,* center panel, 1507–1509. Oil on wood, 7′ 4½″ × 7′ 2¼″. Musées Royaux des Beaux-Arts de Belgique, Brussels.

him an influential inspiration to many of his contemporaries.

JAN GOSSAERT

More single-minded, although no more successful than Metsys in his exploration of Italian Renaissance art, was Jan Gossaert (*c.* 1478–1535), who worked for the later Philip of Burgundy, associated with Humanist scholars, and visited Italy. There, Gossaert (who adopted the name Mabuse, after his birthplace of Maubeuge) became fascinated with the Antique and its mythological subject matter. Giorgio Vasari, the Italian historian and Gossaert's contemporary, wrote that "Gossaert was almost the first to bring the true method of representing nude figures and mythologies from Italy to the Netherlands," although it is obvious that he derived much of his Classicism from Dürer.

The composition and poses in Gossaert's *Neptune and Amphitrite* (fig. **18-43**) are borrowed from Dürer's *Adam and Eve* (fig. 18-36), although Gossaert's figures have been inflated, giving an impression of ungainly weight. The artist approximates the Classical stance but seems to have been more interested in nudity than in a Classical, ideal canon of proportions. The setting for the figures is a carefully painted architectural fantasy that illustrates a complete lack of understanding of the Classical style. Yet the painting is executed with traditional Flemish polish, and the figures are skillfully drawn and modeled. Although Gossaert also painted religious subjects in the traditional style, attempting unsuccessfully to outshine the fifteenth-

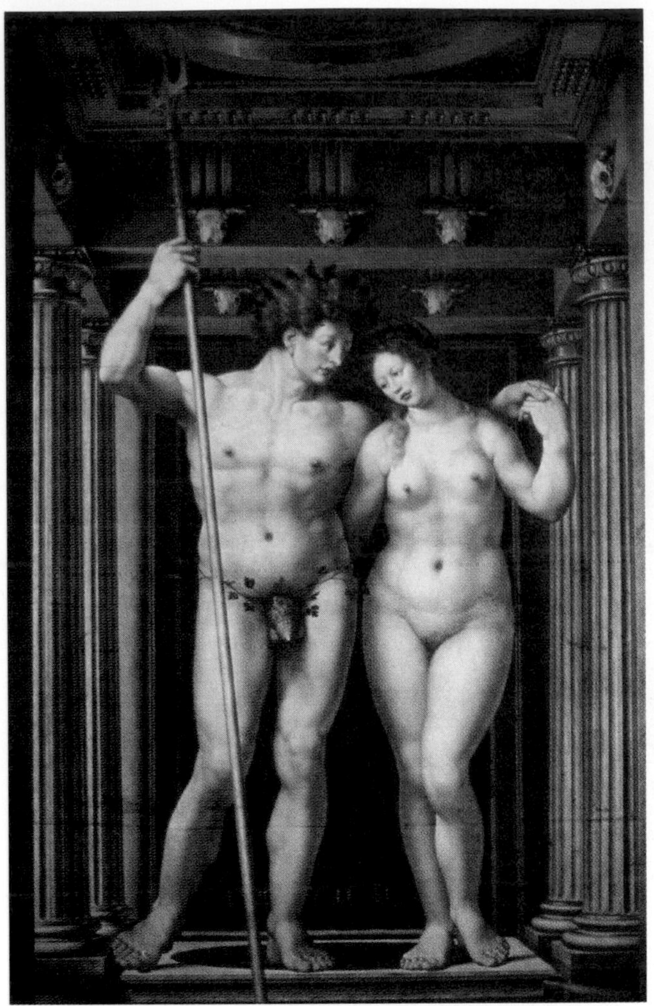

18-43 JAN GOSSAERT (MABUSE), *Neptune and Amphitrite*, c. 1516. Oil on wood, 7′ 2″ × 4′ 1″. Gemäldegalerie, Staatliche Museen, Berlin-Dahlem.

century Flemish masters, his *Neptune and Amphitrite* aligns him firmly with the so-called Romanists, in whose art Italian Mannerism joins with fanciful native interpretations of the Classical style to form a highly artificial, sometimes decorative, and often bizarre and chaotic style.

BARTHOLOMEUS SPRANGER

Much more the Romanist than Jan Gossaert, the Netherlandish painter BARTHOLOMEUS SPRANGER (1546–1611) exaggerates the stylistic peculiarities of Italian Mannerism almost to the point of caricature. Spranger traveled widely in Italy and France, studying a variety of pictorial styles that ranged from those of Jacopo da Pontormo and Parmigianino to the painters of the school of Fontainebleau (FIG. 18-49). What he learned from them merged with his earlier training in the Netherlands to form a highly sophisticated and imaginative style.

For the connoisseur Emperor Rudolph II, whose court painter he became at Prague, Spranger fashioned such classically learned, intricately composed, and suggestively erotic pictures as *Hercules and Omphale* (FIG. **18-44**), a work much to the taste of his bachelor patron. Hercules was enslaved by the beautiful Omphale, who garbed him in the attributes of womanhood. Here, he wears women's satins and jewels and does women's work, spinning with distaff and spindle. His massive wrist is braceleted, and his hand is bent in an effeminate movement. Behind him, an ugly hag makes the gesture of cuckoldry. The nude Omphale, her form androgynous (the emperor had a penchant for the epicene), smiles coquettishly over her shoulder. She carries Hercules' club and wears his lion's skin teasingly. Spranger's themes, lascivious and pagan, find their appropriate vehicle of expression in Italian Mannerism. The Manneristic traits are all here: the gliding, bending, turning poses; the constricted space; the crowded surface; the bright, decorative colors. Worldly, sensuous, and ornamental, these pictures express a luxurious, courtly taste that contrasts markedly with the reverent art of the bourgeois towns in which the Netherlandish master painters worked.

18-44 BARTHOLOMEUS SPRANGER, *Hercules and Omphale*, c. 1598. Paint on copper, $9\frac{1}{4}'' \times 7\frac{1}{2}''$. Kunsthistorisches Museum, Vienna.

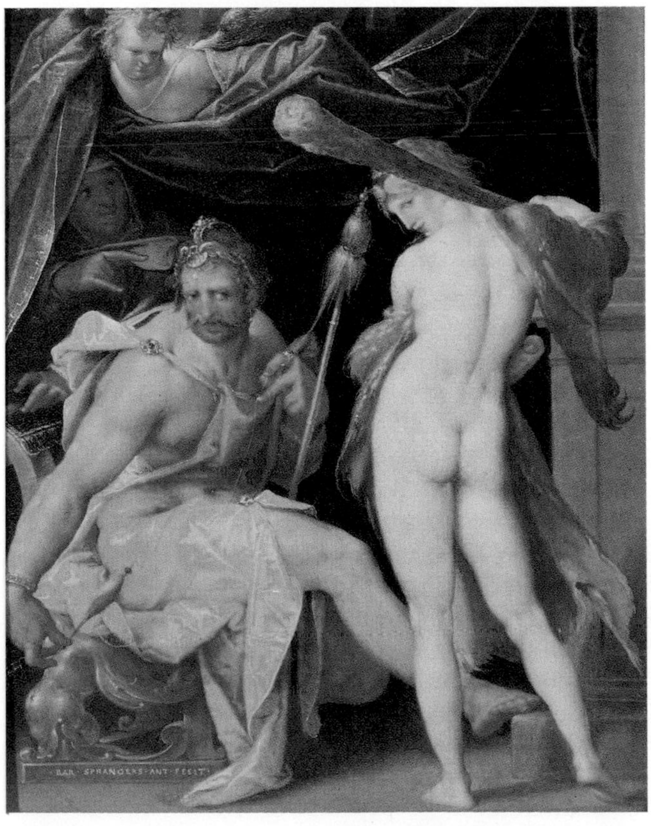

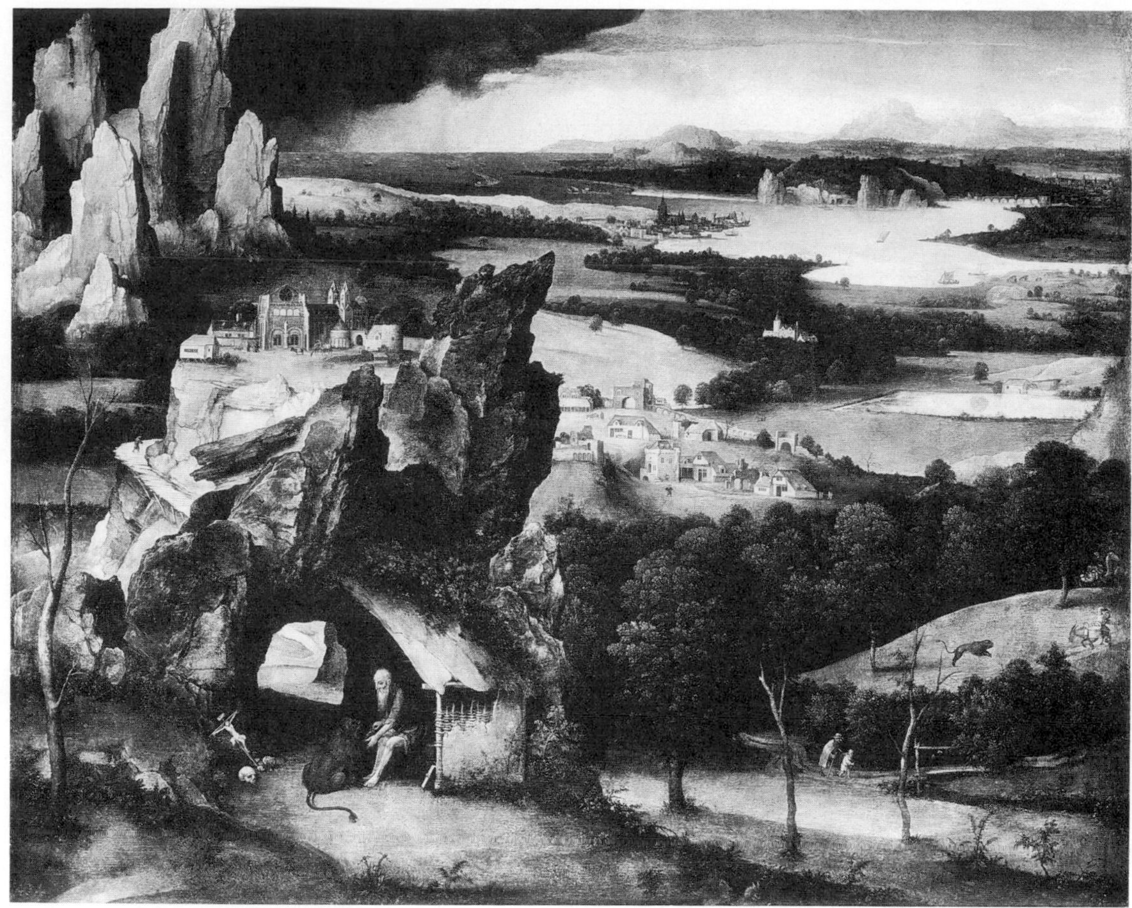

18-45 Joachim Patinir, *Landscape with St. Jerome*, c. 1520 (?). Oil on wood, 30″ × 36″. Museo del Prado, Madrid.

JOACHIM PATINIR

An outstanding representative of a very different trend in sixteenth-century Flemish art is Joachim Patinir (1475–1524), the first Netherlandish landscape painter and the counterpart of the German Albrecht Altdorfer. A highly valued specialist in this field, Patinir often collaborated with other artists, letting them paint figures into his landscapes. Little is known of his background, and, although no definite links can be established between the two artists, Bosch may well have provided the initial inspiration for Patinir's panoramic vistas. Significantly, however, the landscapes in Bosch's paintings are of secondary importance and serve only as broad stages on which his figures perform their fantastic frolics; in Patinir's works, the landscapes take on primary importance, and the figures become mere accessories.

In his *Landscape with St. Jerome* (fig. **18-45**), the insignificant figure of Patinir's title saint is almost hidden in the left middle ground. The vast panorama is seen from a mountaintop, and the artist works like a cartographer, building up his landscape in strips or layers parallel to the picture plane. The effect of recession is achieved by the careful diminution of familiar things (houses, trees, figures) and by the emphatic use of aerial perspective, in which the generally warm foreground colors shift to greens in the middle distance and to cool blues in the far distance. Realism is confined to the description of details. Plants are painted with botanical accuracy, and trees and rock formations are rendered with great feeling for their textural differences. The rich multiplicity of Patinir's paintings, with activity almost everywhere, is drawn together by a strong design and an extremely effective dark–light pattern. The tiny figures scattered throughout his landscape effectively contrast human frailty and the power of nature.

PIETER BRUEGEL THE ELDER

A similar interest in the interrelationship of human beings and nature is expressed in the works of the greatest and most original Flemish painter of the sixteenth century, Pieter Bruegel the Elder (*c.* 1525–1569), whose early, high-horizoned, "cosmographical" landscapes probably were influenced by Patinir. But in Bruegel's paintings, no matter how huge a slice

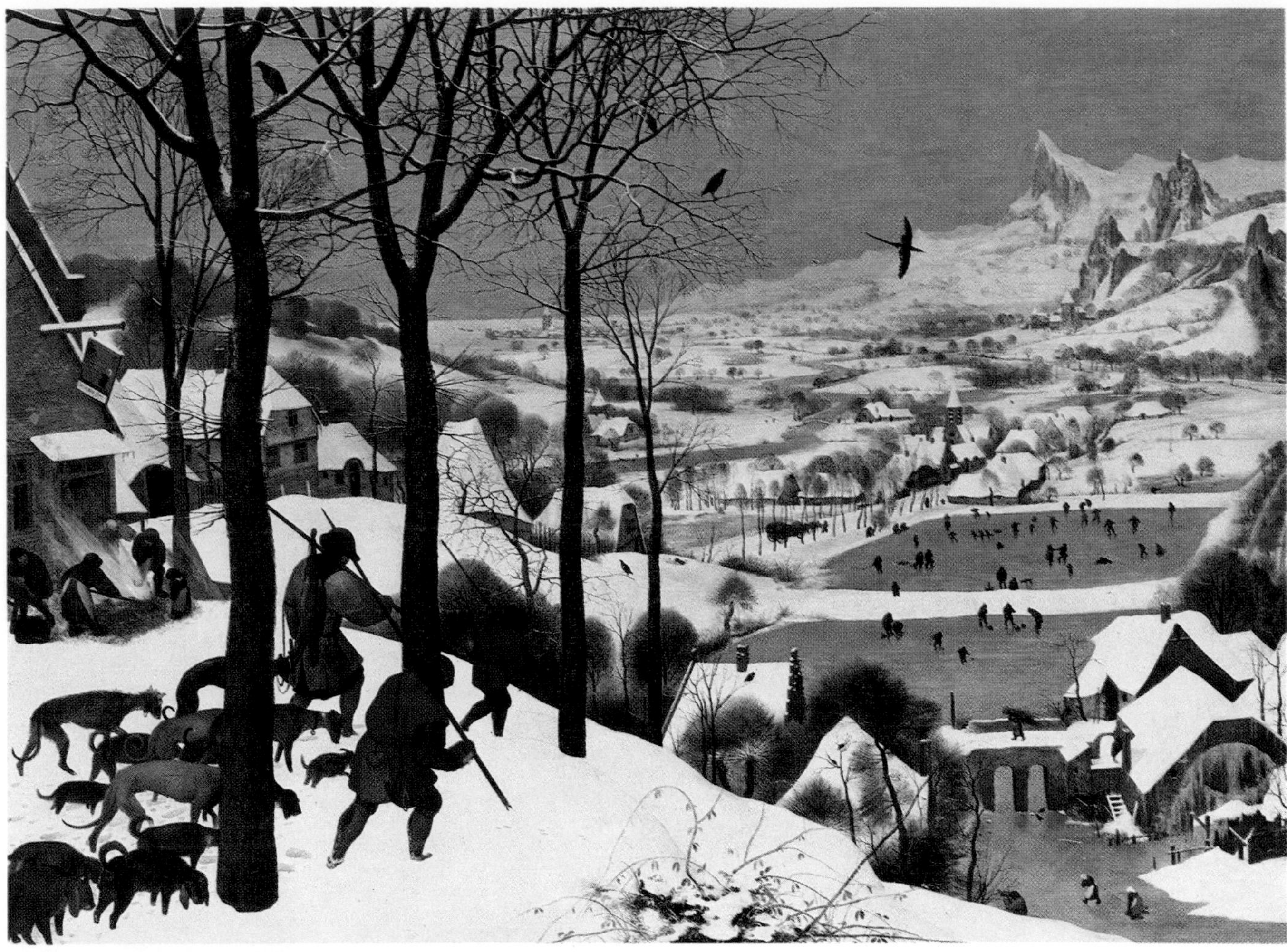

18-46 Pieter Bruegel the Elder, *Hunters in the Snow*, 1565. Oil on wood, approx. 46″ × 64″. Kunsthistorisches Museum, Vienna.

of the world he shows, human activities remain the dominant theme. Bruegel was apprenticed to a "Romanist," Pieter Coecke, and, like many of his contemporaries, traveled to Italy, where he seems to have spent almost two years, going as far south as Sicily. Unlike his contemporaries, however, Bruegel was not overwhelmed by Classical art, and his Italian experiences are reflected only incidentally in his paintings, usually in the form of Italian or Alpine landscape features that he recorded in numerous drawings made during his journey. On his return from Italy, Bruegel was exposed to Bosch's works, and the influence of that strange master, strongly felt in Bruegel's early paintings, must have swept aside any Romanist inclinations he may have had.

Hunters in the Snow (fig. **18-46**) is one of five surviving paintings of a series of six in which Bruegel illustrated seasonal changes in the year. It shows human figures and landscape locked in winter cold. The weary hunters return with their hounds, wives build fires, skaters skim the frozen pond, the town and its church huddle in their mantle of snow, and beyond this typically Flemish winter scene lies a bit of alpine landscape. Aside from this trace of fantasy, however, the landscape is realistic and quite unlike Patinir's. It develops smoothly from foreground to background and draws the viewer diagonally into its depths. The artist's consummate skill in the use of line and shape and his subtlety in tonal harmony make this one of the great landscape paintings in history and an Occidental counterpart of the masterworks of classical Chinese landscape.

Bruegel, of course, is not simply a landscapist. In his series of the months, he presents—in a fairly detached manner, occasionally touched with humor—human activities at different times of the year. And he chooses for his purpose the social class that is most directly affected by seasonal changes, the peasantry. But usually Bruegel is much more personal as he makes satirical comments on the dubious human

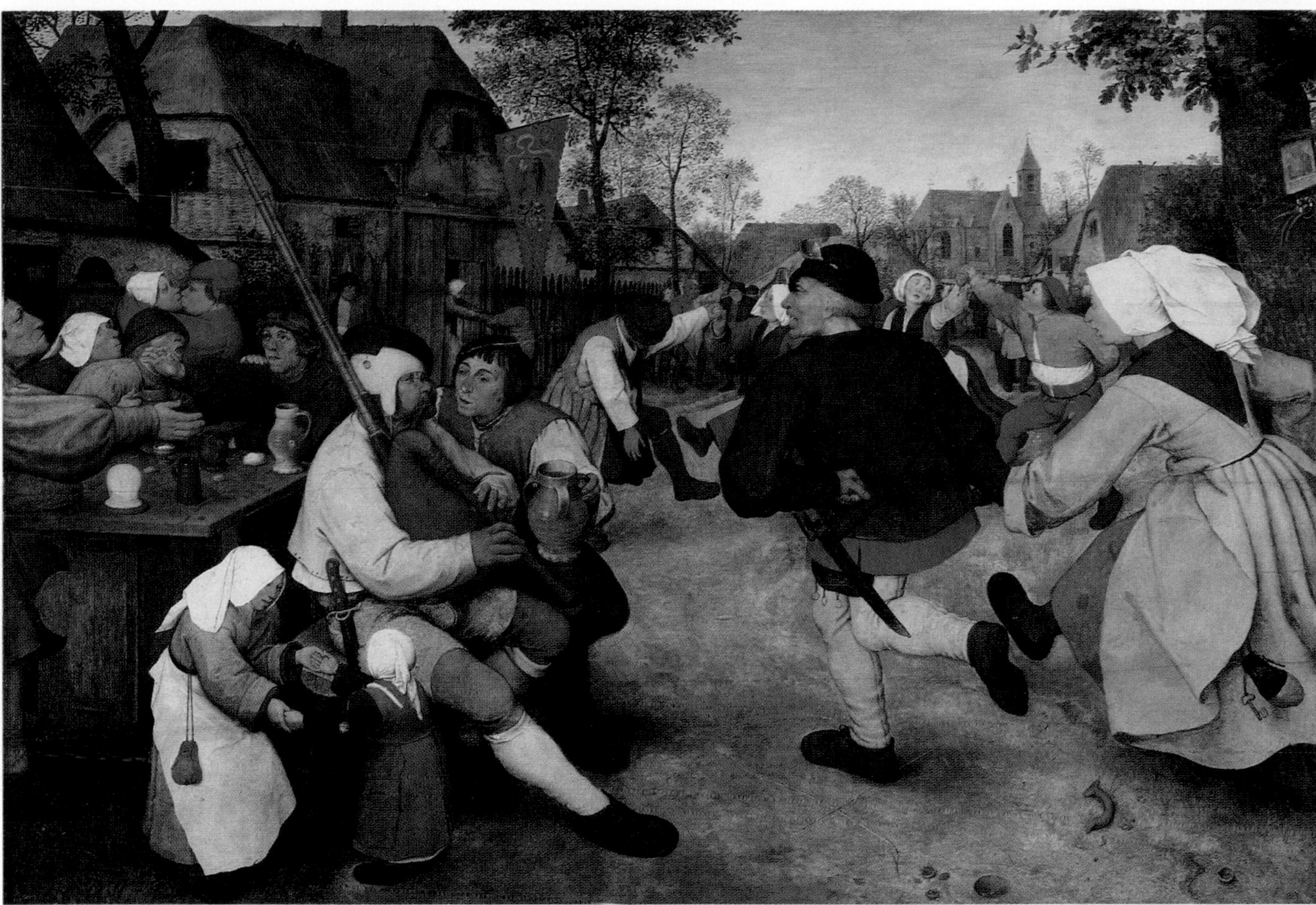

18-47 Pieter Bruegel the Elder, *The Peasant Dance,* c. 1567. Oil on wood, approx. 45″ × 65″. Kunsthistorisches Museum, Vienna.

condition. His meaning in specific cases is often as obscure as Bosch's, and he seems to delight in leading us into his pictures through devious paths and confronting us with mystery, with an appalling revelation. As a vehicle for his sarcasm, he again chooses the peasant, whom he sees as an uncomplicated representative of humanity—a member of society whose actions and behavior are open, direct, and unspoiled by the artificial cultural gloss that disguises but does not alter the city dweller's natural inclinations.

These good countryfolk are shown enjoying themselves in *The Peasant Dance* (FIG. **18-47**), which is no mincing quadrille, but a boisterous, whirling, hoedown in which plenty of sweat is shed. One can almost hear the feet stomping to the rhythm of the bagpipe. With an eye much more incisive than any camera lens, the artist grasps the entire scene in its most characteristic aspect and records it in a broad technique that discards most of the traditional Flemish concern for detail. Strong but simplified modeling emphasizes the active, solidly drawn silhouettes, which, combined with strong local colors, give the painting the popular robustness so suited to its subject. From the hilltop that he shared with the *Hunters,* Bruegel descends into the village to look more closely at its life and amusements, and he finds that all is not well in this rustic paradise. A fight is brewing at the table on the left; everyone's back is turned to the church in the background; nobody is paying the least attention to the small picture of a Madonna tacked to the tree on the right; the man next to the bagpiper is wearing the feather of a peacock (a symbol of vanity) in his cap; and what about the young couple kissing unashamedly in public in the left middle ground? Is Bruegel telling us, like Bosch in his *Hell* (FIG. 18-21), that music is an instrument of the Devil and a perverter of morals? A closer inspection of the painting reveals that Bruegel is telling much more than the simple story of a country festivity. He is showing that a *kermess,* a festival celebrating a saint, has become a mere pretext for people to indulge their lust, anger, and gluttony.

Toward the end of his life, Bruegel's commentary on the human condition takes on an increasingly bitter edge. The Netherlands, racked by religious conflict, had become the seat of cruel atrocities, made even more cruel by the coming of the power of Catholic Spain to put down the Reformation. We do not know whether Bruegel took sides; like the great satirist he was, he may have preferred to make all mankind, not just partisans, the object of his commentary. His secret meanings may be explained partly by the danger of too much outspokenness. His biographer, Karel van Mander* (1548–1606), writes:

> Many of Bruegel's strange compositions and comical subjects one may see in his copper engravings . . . he supplied them with inscriptions which, at the time, were too biting and too sharp, and which he had his wife burn during his last illness, because of . . . fear that most disagreeable consequences might grow out of them.

Bruegel knew well how to disguise his intent—so well that in his day he was called "Peter the Droll," because, as Van Mander writes, "there are very few works from his hand that the beholder can look at seriously, without laughing."

France

Divided and harried during the fifteenth century, France was reorganized by decisive kings and was strong enough to undertake an aggressive policy toward her neighbors by the end of the century. Under the rule of Francis I, the French held a firm foothold in Milan and its environs. The king eagerly imported the Renaissance into France, bringing Leonardo da Vinci and Andrea del Sarto to his court, but they left no permanent mark on French art. It was Florentine Mannerists like Rosso Fiorentino and Benvenuto Cellini who implanted the Italianate style that replaced the Gothic in France. Francis's attempt to glorify the state and himself meant that the religious art of the Middle Ages finally was superseded, for it was the king and not the Church who now held power.

A portrait of *Francis I* (FIG. **18-48**), painted by JEAN CLOUET (*c.* 1485–1541) in the Franco-Italian manner, shows a worldly prince magnificently bedizened in silks and brocades, wearing a gold chain, and caressing the pommel of a dagger. One would not expect the king's talents to be directed to spiritual matters, and legend has it that the "merry monarch" was a great lover and the hero of hundreds of "gallant" situations. The flat light and suppression of modeling give equal emphasis to head and costume, so that the king's finery and his face enter equally into the effect

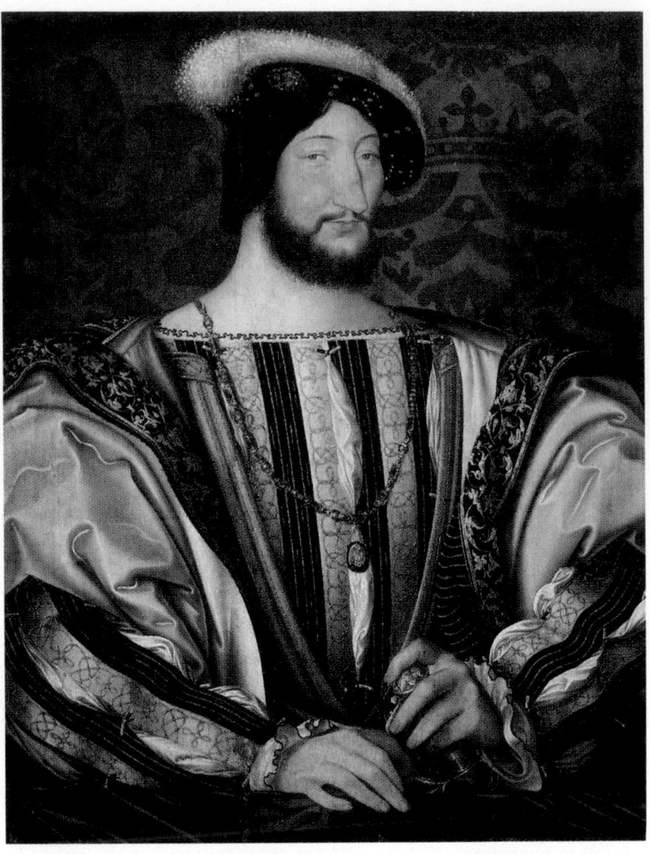

18-48 JEAN CLOUET, *Francis I*, *c.* 1525–1530. Tempera and oil on wood, approx. 38″ × 29″. Louvre, Paris.

of royal splendor. Yet, despite this Mannerist formula for portraiture, the features are not entirely immobile; the faintest flicker of an expression that we might read as "knowing" lingers on the king's features.

The personal tastes of Francis and his court must have run to an art at once suave, artificial, elegant, and erotic. The sculptors and painters working together on the decoration of the new royal palace at Fontainebleau, under the direction of Florentines Rosso and FRANCESCO PRIMATICCIO (1504–1570), are known as the school of Fontainebleau. Rosso became the court painter of Francis I shortly after 1530. In France, his style no longer showed the turbulent harshness of *Moses Defending the Daughters of Jethro* (FIG. 17-40) but became consistently more elegant and graceful. When Rosso and Primaticcio decorated the Gallery of Francis I at Fontainebleau, they combined painting, fresco, imitation mosaic, and stucco sculpture in low and high relief (FIG. **18-49**). The abrupt changes in scale and texture are typically Mannerist, as is the composition of the central painting, which shows *Venus Reproving Love* in compressed Mannerist space with elongated grace and mannered poses. The same artificial grace can be seen in the stucco relief figures of Hermes and caryatids flanking the central

*Karel van Mander's *Het Schilderboeck (The Painter's Book)* was published in Haarlem in 1604. It contains a section with biographies of Netherlandish and German painters that is the northern equivalent of Giorgio Vasari's *Vite*.

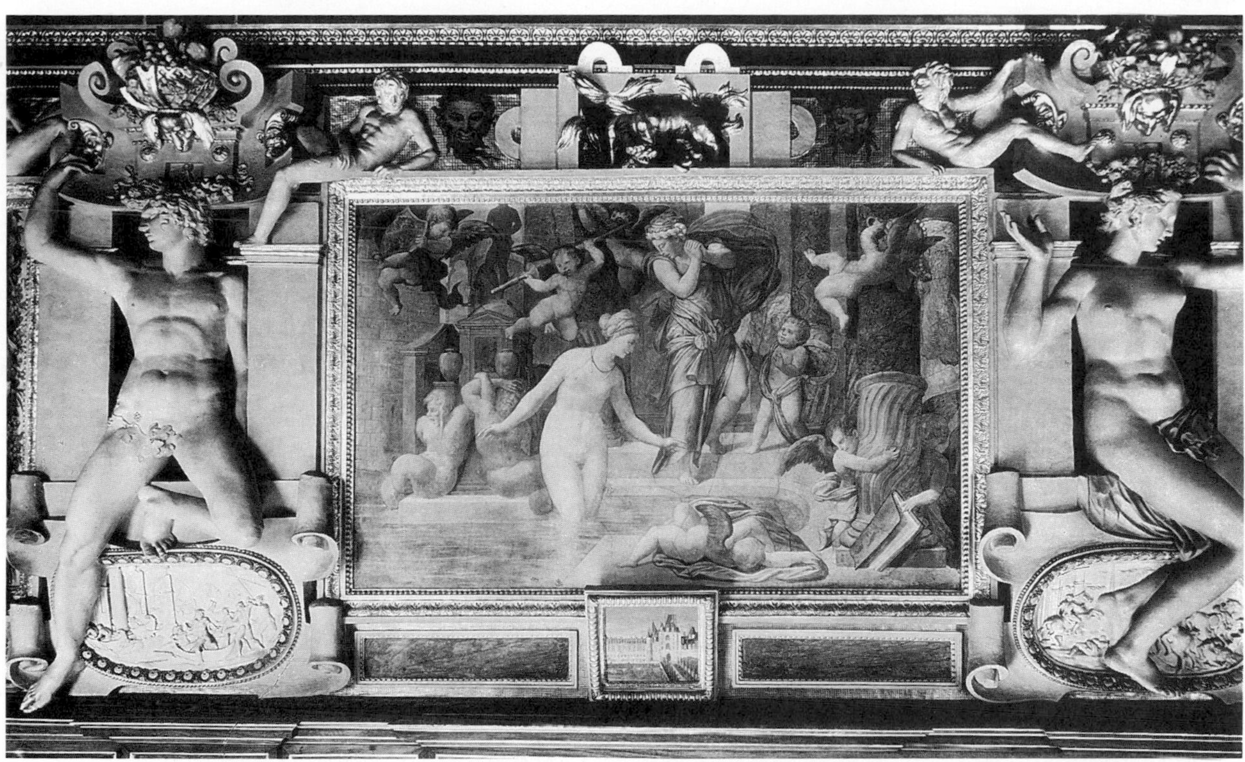

18-49 Rosso Fiorentino and Francesco Primaticcio, *Venus Reproving Love,* c. 1530–1540. Gallery of Francis I, Fontainebleau, France.

painting, and the viewer is jarred by the shift in scale between the painted and the stucco figures. However, the combination of painted and stucco relief decorations became extremely popular from this time on and remained a favorite decorative technique throughout the Baroque and Rococo periods.

It has been said of Francis I that, besides women, his one obsession was building. During his reign, which lasted from 1515 to 1547, several large-scale châteaux were begun, among them the Château de Chambord (FIG. **18-50**), on which construction was started in 1519. Reflecting the more peaceful times, these châteaux, developed from the old countryside fortresses, served as country houses for royalty, and usually were built near a forest, for use as hunting lodges. The plan of Chambord, originally drawn by a pupil of Giuliano da Sangallo, imposes Italian concepts of symmetry and balance on the irregularity of the old French fortress. A central square block with four corridors, in the shape of a cross, leads to a broad, central staircase that gives access to groups of rooms—ancestors of the modern suite of rooms or apartments. The square plan is punctuated at each of the four corners by a round tower, and the whole is surrounded by a moat. From the exterior, Chambord presents a carefully contrived horizontal accent on three levels, its floors separated by continuous moldings. Windows are placed exactly over one another. This matching of horizontal and vertical features is, of course, derived from the Italian palazzo, but above the third level, the lines of the structure break chaotically into a jumble of high dormers, chimneys, and lanterns that recall soaring, ragged, Gothic silhouettes on the skyline.

18-50 Château de Chambord, France, begun 1519.

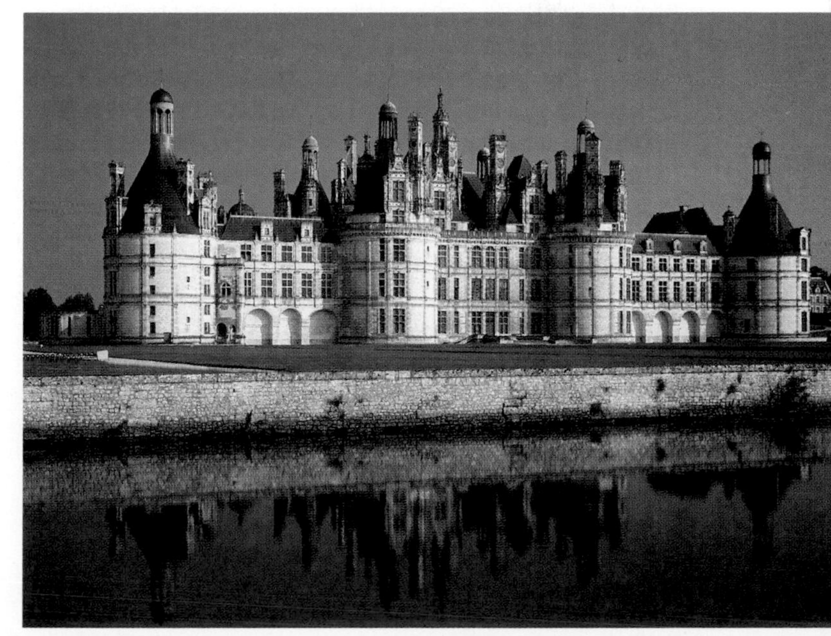

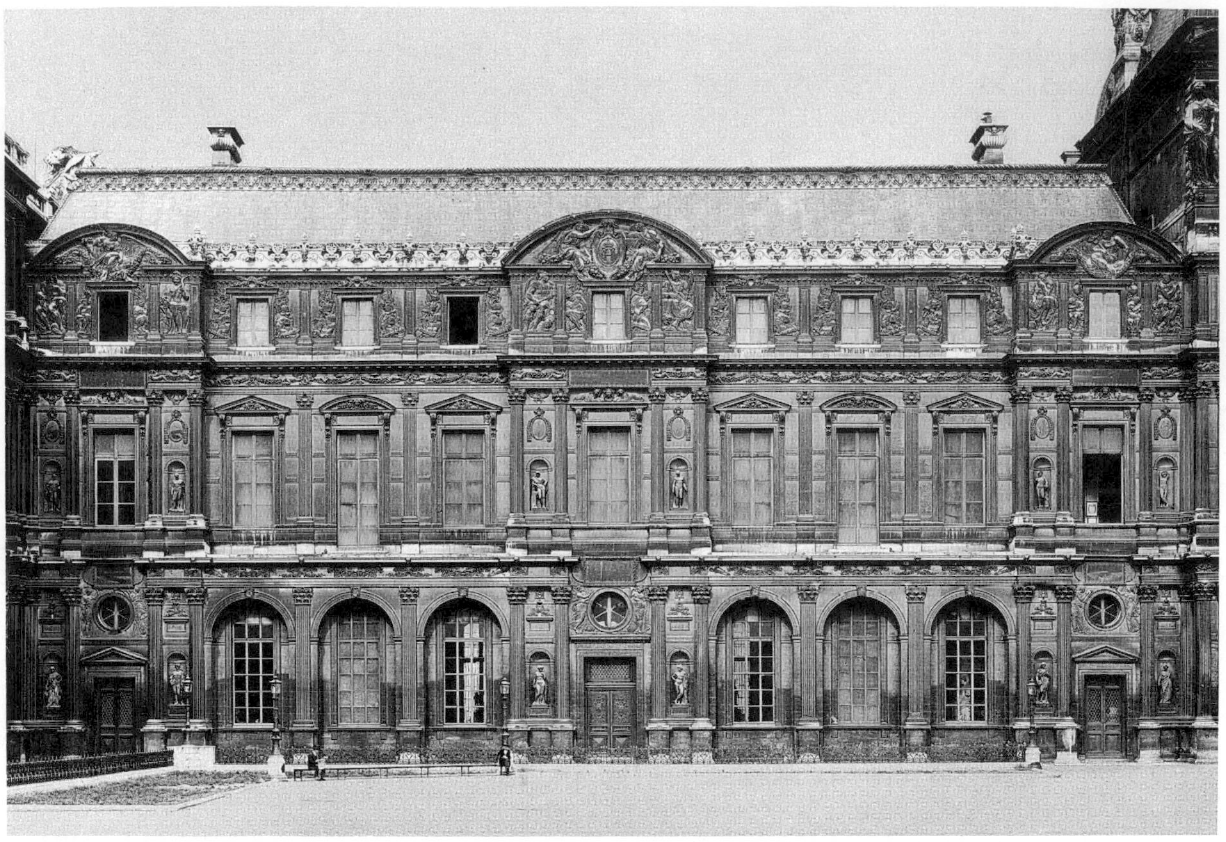

18-51 Pierre Lescot, west façade of the Square Court of the Louvre, Paris, begun 1546.

The architecture of Chambord is still French at heart. During the reign of Francis's successor, Henry II (1547–1559), however, treatises by Italian architects were translated and Italian architects came to work in France; at the same time, the French turned to Italy for study and travel. This interchange brought about a more thoroughgoing revolution in style, although it never eliminated certain French elements that persisted from the Gothic tradition. Francis began the enlargement of the Louvre in Paris (FIG. **18-51**) to make a new royal palace, but he died before the work was well begun. His architect, Pierre Lescot (1510–1578), continued under Henry II and, with the aid of the sculptor Jean Goujon (*c.* 1510–1565), produced the Classical style of the French Renaissance. Although Chambord incorporated the formal vocabulary of the Early Renaissance, particularly from Lombardy, Lescot and his associates were familiar with the High Renaissance of Bramante and his school. Each of the stories of the Louvre forms a complete order, and the cornices project enough to furnish a strong horizontal accent. The arcading on the ground story reflects the ancient Roman arch-order and is recessed enough to produce more shadow than in the upper stories, strengthening the visual base of the design. On the second story, the pilasters rising from bases and the alternating curved and angular pediments supported by consoles have direct antecedents in several Roman High Renaissance palaces. On the other hand, the decreased height of the stories, the proportionately much larger windows (given the French weather!), and the steep roof are northern. Especially French are the pavilions that jut from the wall. These are punctuated by a feature that the French will long favor—double columns framing a niche. The vertical lines of the building remain strong. The wall is deeply penetrated by openings and (in un-Italian fashion) profusely sculptured. This French Classical manner—double-columned pavilions, tall and wide windows, profuse statuary, and steep roofs—will be imitated widely in other northern countries, with local variations. The mannered Classicism produced by the French will be the *only* Classicism to serve as a model for northern architects through most of the sixteenth century. The west courtyard façade of the Louvre is the best of French Renaissance architecture; eventually, the French will develop a quite native Classicism of their own, cleared of Italian Mannerist features.

The statues of the Louvre courtyard façade, now much restored, are the work of Goujon. We can appreciate the quality of Goujon's style best by examin-

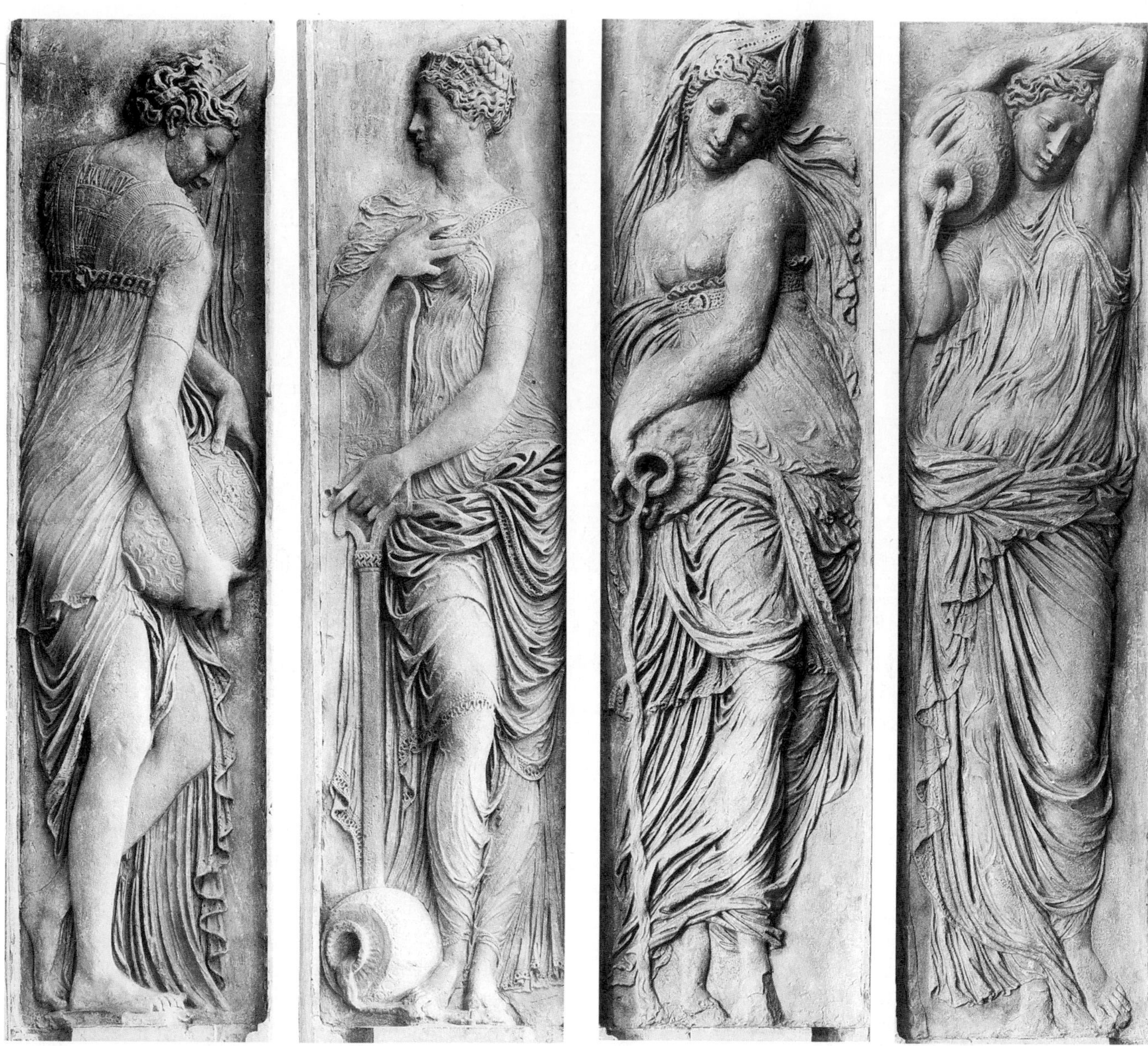

18-52 Jean Goujon, *Nymphs*, from the dismantled Fountain of the Innocents, Paris, 1548–1549. Marble reliefs. Louvre, Paris.

ing his *Nymphs* reliefs from the Fountain of the Innocents in Paris (fig. **18-52**). Like the architecture of the Louvre, Goujon's nymphs are intelligent and sensitive French adaptations of the Italian Mannerist canon of figure design. Certainly, they are Mannerist in their ballet-like contrapposto and in their flowing, clinging draperies, which recall the ancient "wet" drapery of Hellenic sculpture—the figures on the parapet of the Temple of Athena Nike (fig. 5-57), for example. Goujon's slender, sinuous figures perform their steps within the structure of Mannerist space, and it is interesting that they appear to make one continuous motion, an illusion produced by reversing the gestures, as they might be seen in a mirror. The style of Fontainebleau, and ultimately of Primaticcio and Cellini, guides the sculptor here, but Goujon has learned the manner so well that he can create originally within it. The nymphs are truly French masterpieces, with lightness, ease, grace, and something of a native French chic that saves them from being mere lame derivatives of the Italian Mannerist norm.

In France, as in all of Europe in the sixteenth century, the influence of Italian art was direct and overpowering. But as the century progressed, native French artists adapted the new elements to the strong Gothic traditions and created a distinctively French expression. An example of this maturing style is seen in the works of the sculptor Germain Pilon (*c.* 1535–1590), who made his reputation with monumental tomb sculpture, especially that he created for the

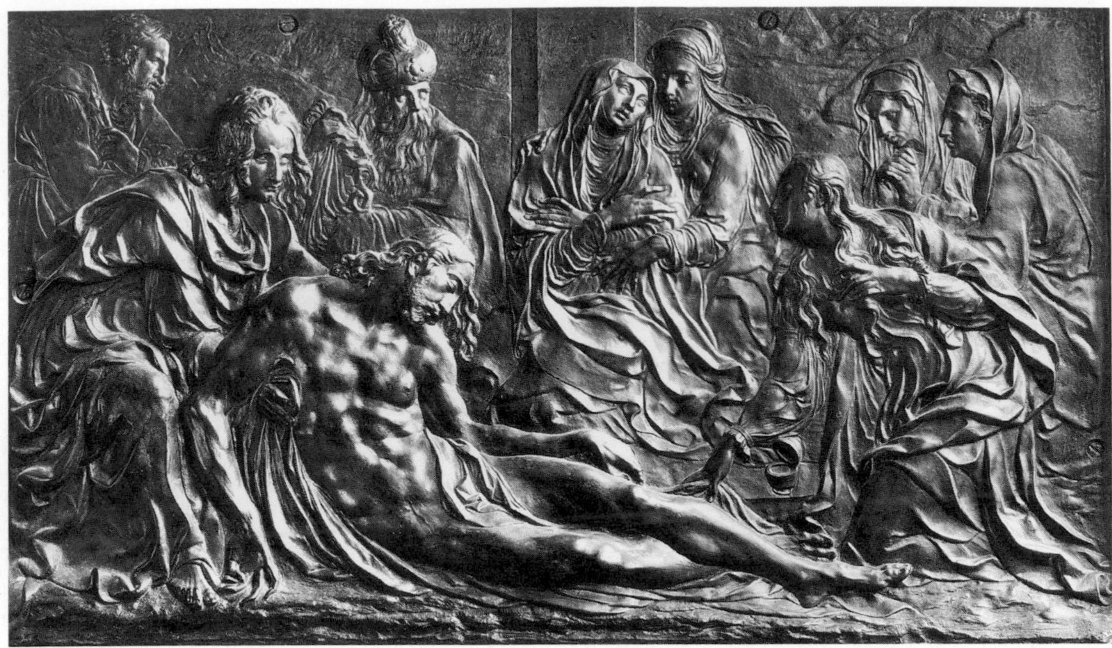

18-53 GERMAIN PILON, *Descent from the Cross,* 1583. Bronze relief, 19″ × 32½″. Louvre, Paris.

monument of Henry II and Catherine de' Medici in St. Denis, Paris. Like Goujon and other French sculptors, Pilon began in the Fontainebleau style, emphasizing artifice in pose and gesture and graceful, sinuous contour. Gradually, his style changed as he made contact with the still strong tradition of Late Gothic realism. A bronze relief, *Descent from the Cross* (FIG. **18-53**), recalls monumental compositions of Rogier van der Weyden (FIG. 18-12) and the master of *The Avignon Pietà* (FIG. 18-24). Unlike them, Pilon shows the influence of Mannerism in the great, elongated, muscular Christ; like them, he expresses a quiet yet profound pathos that Mannerism could not convey sincerely. The realistic element appears in the very staging of the drama. The Virgin, consoled by a holy woman, is removed from the center of the action. Those in authority stand at the head and feet of Christ. Pilon presents a curiously steady, almost serene reading of the emotions of those portrayed. The curving lines of the draperies have lost the angularity of the Gothic but are not arranged in the contrived patterns of Mannerism. Pilon, from a fusion of the old tradition with the new fashion, has risen to a bold statement of his own—a statement that makes use of both while transcending them in a moving, personal interpretation of the Medieval theme.

Spain

In some respects, the sixteenth century is the Spanish century. Under Charles V of Hapsburg and his son, Philip II, the Spanish Empire dominated a territory greater in extent than any ever known: a large part of Europe, the western Mediterranean, a strip of North Africa, and vast expanses in the newly discovered Western Hemisphere. The Hapsburg empire, enriched by the plunder of the New World, supported the most powerful military force in Europe, which backed the ambitions and the ventures of the "Most Catholic Kings." Spain defended and then promoted the interests of the Catholic church in its battle against the inroads of the Protestant Reformation. What we call the Catholic Counter-Reformation was funded, directed, fought for, and then enforced by Spain. By force and influence—by the preaching and the propaganda of the newly founded Spanish order of the Society of Jesus (the Jesuits)—Spain drove Protestantism from a large part of Europe and sponsored the internal reform of the Catholic church at the great Council of Trent. The Spaniards humbled France; trampled the Netherlands; reclaimed much of Germany, Poland, and Hungary for Catholicism; and held England at bay (until the end of the century), while they converted the native empires of the New World to the Catholic faith and destroyed them in a relentless search for treasure. The material and the spiritual exertions of Spain—the fanatical courage of Spanish soldiers and the incandescent fervor of the great Spanish mystical saints—went together. The former became the terror of the Protestant and pagan worlds, while the latter served as the inspiration of the Catholic faithful. The crusading spirit of Spain, nourished by centuries of war with Islam, engaged body and soul in the formation of the most Catholic civilization of Europe and the Americas. In the sixteenth century, for good or for ill, Spain left the mark of Spanish power, religion, language, and culture on two hemispheres.

Yet Spain, like all of Europe at this time, came under the spell of Renaissance Italy; Spanish architecture especially shows that influence, but not all at once. During the fifteenth century and well into the sixteenth, a Late Gothic style of architecture, the Plateresque, prevailed side by side with buildings influenced by Italy. ("Plateresque" is derived from the Spanish *platero*, meaning silversmith, and is applied to the style because of the delicate execution of its ornament.) The Colegio de San Gregorio (FIG. **18-54**) in the Castilian city of Valladolid handsomely exemplifies the Plateresque manner. The Spanish were particularly fond of great carved retables, like the German altar screens that influenced them (FIGS. 18-27 and 18-28)—so much so that they made them a conspicuous decorative feature of their exterior architecture, dramatizing a portal set into an otherwise blank wall. The Plateresque entrance of San Gregorio is a lofty, sculptured stone screen that bears no functional relation to the architecture behind it. On the entrance level, ogival, flamboyant arches are hemmed with lacelike tracery reminiscent of Moorish design. A great screen, paneled into sculptured compartments, rises above the tracery; in the center, the coat of arms of Ferdinand and Isabella is wreathed by the branches of a huge pomegranate tree (symbolizing Granada, the Moorish capital of Spain, captured by the "Catholic Kings" in 1492). Cupids play among the tree branches, and, flanking the central panel, niches enframe armed pages of the court, heraldic wildmen, and armored soldiers, attesting to the new, proud militancy of the united kingdom of Spain. In typical Plateresque and Late Gothic fashion, the whole design is unified by the activity of a thousand intertwined motifs, which, in sum, create an exquisitely carved panel greatly expanded in scale.

A sudden and surprising Italianate Classicism makes its appearance in the unfinished palace of Charles V in the Alhambra in Granada (FIG. **18-55**), the work of the painter-architect PEDRO MACHUCA (active 1520–1550). The circular central courtyard is ringed with superposed Doric and Ionic orders, which support continuous horizontal entablatures rather than arches. Ornament consists only of the details of the orders themselves, which are rendered with the simplicity, clarity, and authority we find in the work of Bramante and his school. The lower story recalls the ring colonnade of the Tempietto (FIG. 17-6), although here, of course, the curve is reversed. This pure Classicism, entirely exceptional in Spain at this time, may be a reflection of Charles V's personal

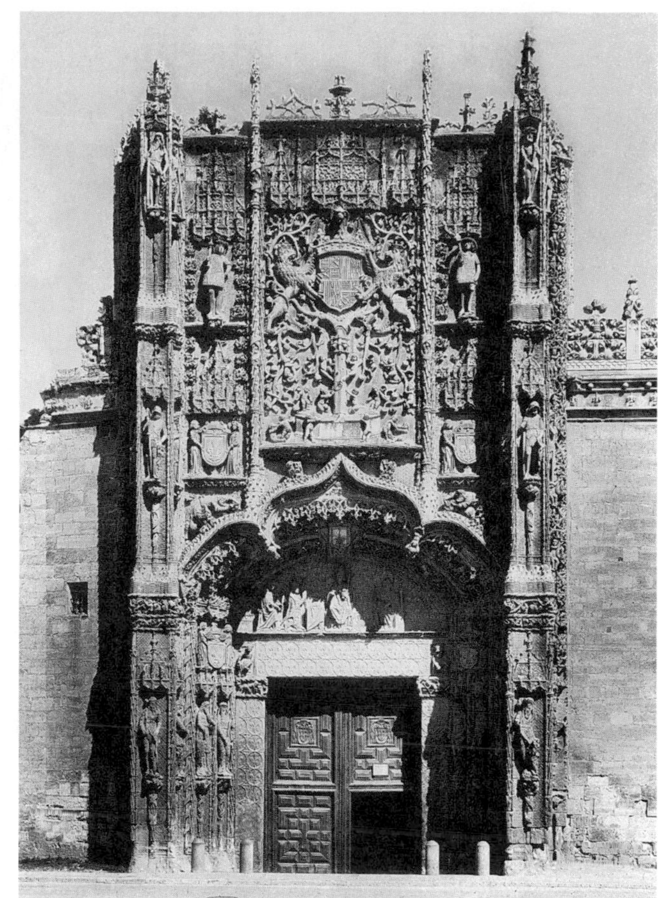

18-54 Portal, Colegio de San Gregorio, Valladolid, Spain, *c.* 1498.

18-55 PEDRO MACHUCA, courtyard of the palace of Charles V, Alhambra, Granada, Spain, *c.* 1526–1568.

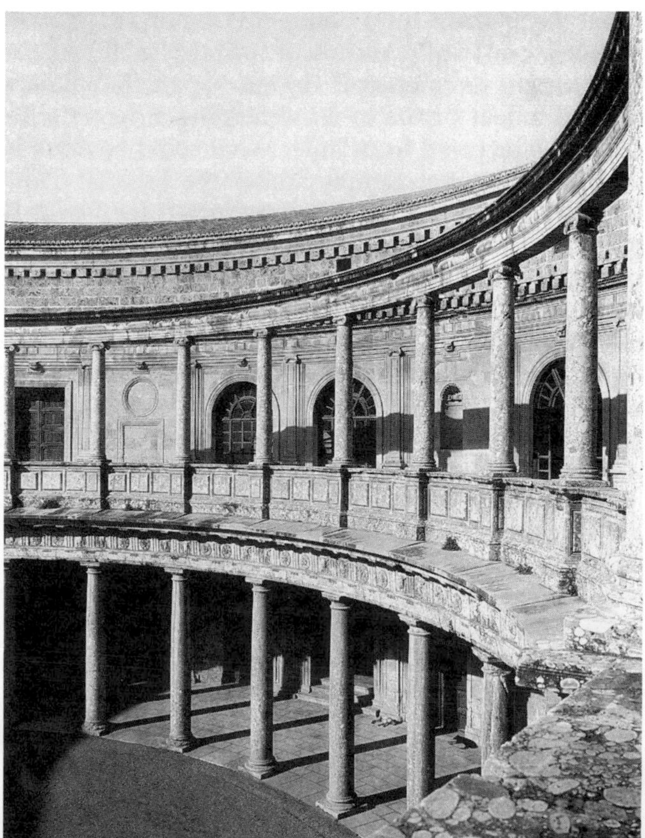

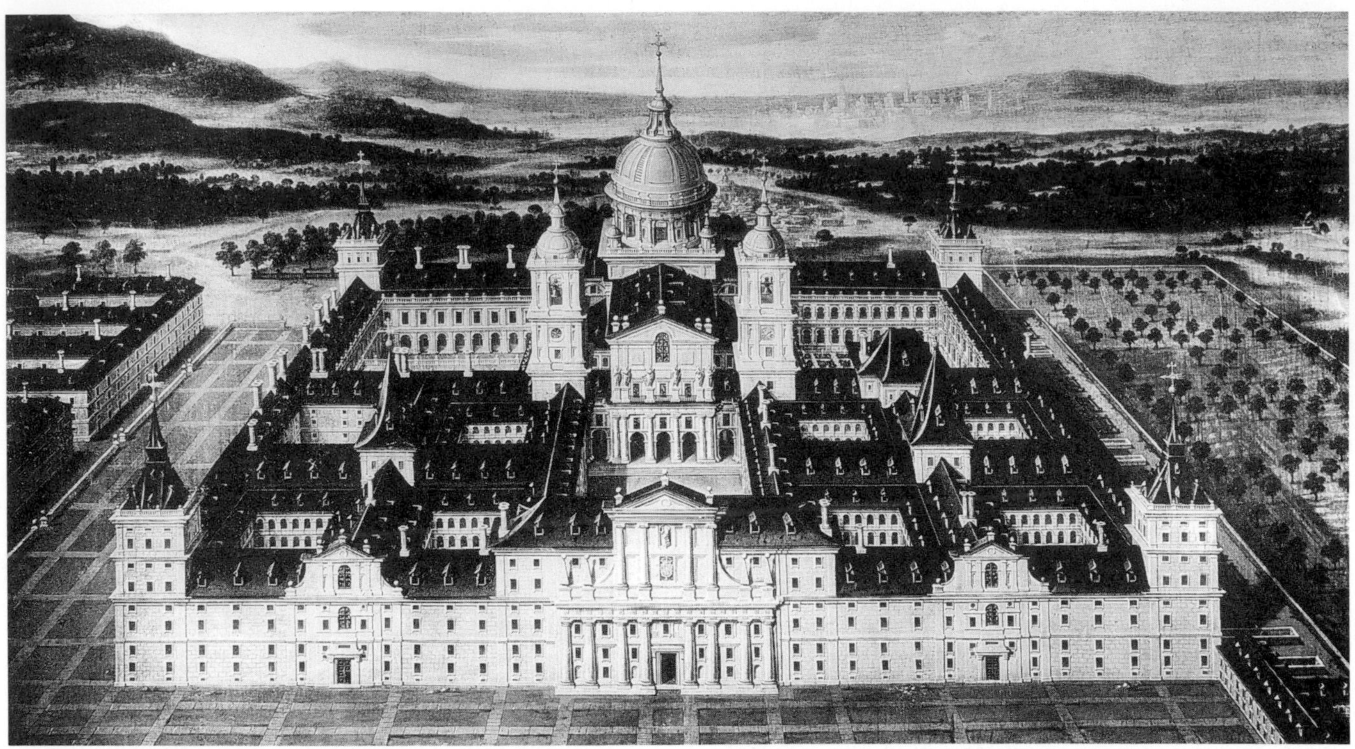

18-56 JUAN DE HERRERA, the Escorial (bird's-eye view after an anonymous eighteenth-century painting), near Madrid, Spain, *c.* 1563–1584.

taste, acquired on one of his journeys to Italy. (It should be remembered that the emperor was an enthusiastic patron of Titian.) Machuca himself had sojourned in Italy, and the courtyard may be the consequence of his endeavor to revive this feature of the ancient Classical palace.

But the Spanish spirit of the time seemed to disdain the ideal purity of feature and correctness of proportion sought in Classical design. Spanish builders seemed to feel a need to do something different with what was received from Italy. What could be done is visible in the great complex called the Escorial (FIGS. **18-56** to **18-58**), which was constructed for Philip II by JUAN BAUTISTA DE TOLEDO (d. 1567) and JUAN DE HERRERA (1530–1597), principally the latter. The king, perhaps the greatest in Spanish history, must have had much to do with the design. Certainly Philip and his architects collaborated closely. The whole vast structure is in keeping with his austere and conscientious character, his passionate Catholic religiosity, his proud reverence for his dynasty, and his stern determination to impose his will worldwide. Philip wrote to Herrera to outline what he expected from him: "Above all, do not forget what I have told you—simplicity of form, severity in the whole, nobility without arrogance, majesty without ostentation." The result is a Classicism of Doric severity, ultimately derived from Italian architecture and with the grandeur of St. Peter's implicit in the scheme, but unique in Spanish and European architecture—a style inimitably of itself, even though later structures will reflect it.

In his will, Charles V stipulated that a "dynastic pantheon" be built to house the remains of past and future monarchs of Spain. Philip II, obedient to his father's wishes, chose a site some thirty miles northwest of Madrid, in rugged terrain with barren mountains. Here, he built the Escorial, not only a royal mausoleum, but a church, a monastery, and a palace. Legend has it that the gridlike plan for the enormous complex, 625 feet wide and 520 feet deep, was meant to symbolize the gridiron on which St. Lawrence, patron of the Escorial, was martyred.

The long sweep of the severely plain walls of the complex is broken only by the three entrances, with the dominant central portal framed by superposed orders and topped by a pediment in the Italian fashion. The corners of the wall are punctuated by massive square towers. The stress on the central axis, with its subdued echoes in the two flanking portals, forecasts the three-part organization of later Baroque palace façades. Like the whole complex of buildings, the domed-cross church, with similarly heavy towers, is constructed of granite, expressing, in its grim starkness of mass, the obdurate quality of a material most difficult to work. The massive façade of the

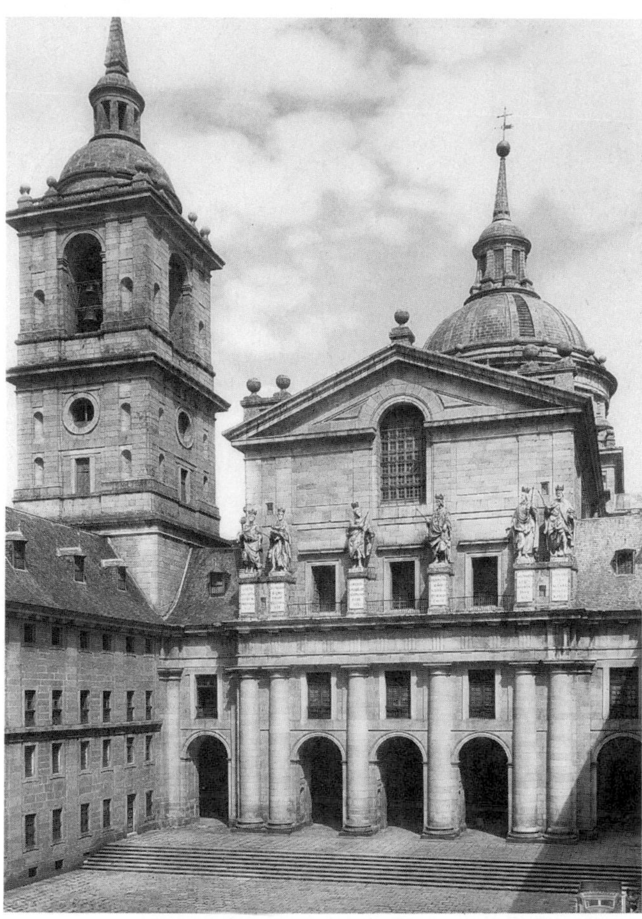

18-57 JUAN DE HERRERA, the Escorial, façade of church.

18-58 JUAN DE HERRERA, the Escorial, interior of church.

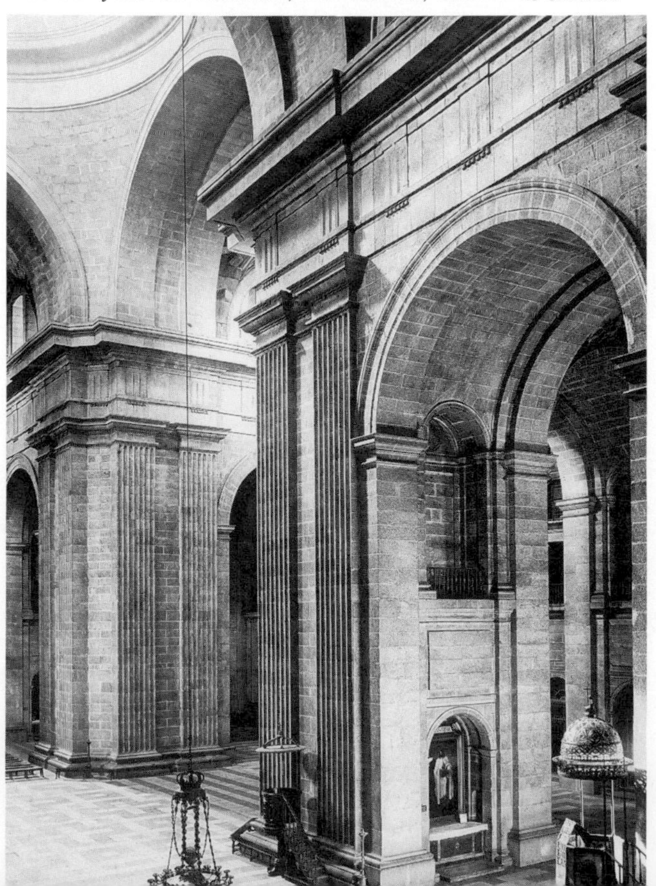

church (FIG. 18-57) and the austere geometry of its interior, with its blocky walls and ponderous arches (FIG. 18-58), dominate the Classical forms, producing an effect of overwhelming strength and weight that contradicts the grace and elegance we associate with much of the Renaissance architecture of Italy.

The Escorial is a monument to the collaboration of a great king and a remarkably understanding architect, who made of it an original expression of a unique idea and personality—the embodiment of the stern virtues of a monarch, a realm, and an age conscious of their peculiar power and purpose. The visitor to the Escorial is awed by the overpowering architectural expression of the spirit of Spain in its heroic epoch and of the character of Philip II, the extraordinary monarch who directed it.

EL GRECO

There appear to be two sides to the Spanish genius in the period of the Counter-Reformation: fervent religious faith and ardent mysticism, on the one hand, and an iron realism on the other. St. Theresa of Ávila and St. John of the Cross can be considered representative of the first; the practical St. Ignatius of Loyola, founder of the Jesuit order, represents the latter. It is possible for the two tempers to be found in the same persons and works of art, but it is more common to find them apart. Interestingly enough, a painter of foreign extraction was able to combine them in a single picture.

Doménikos Theotokopoulos (*c.* 1547–1614), called EL GRECO, was born in Crete but emigrated to Italy as a young man. In his youth, he was trained in the traditions of Late Byzantine frescoes and mosaics. While still young, El Greco went to Venice, where he was connected with the shop of Titian, although Tintoretto's painting seems to have made a stronger impression on him. A brief trip to Rome explains the influences of Roman and Florentine Mannerism on his work. By 1577, he had left for Spain to spend the rest of his life in Toledo.

El Greco's art is a strong, personal blending of Late Byzantine and Late Italian Mannerist elements. The intense emotionalism of his paintings, which naturally appealed to the pious fervor of the Spanish; the dematerialization of form; and a great reliance on color bind him to sixteenth-century Venetian art and to Mannerism. His strong sense of movement and use of light, however, prefigure the Baroque. El Greco's art is not strictly Spanish (although it appealed to certain sectors of that society), for it had no Spanish antecedents and little effect on later Spanish painters. Nevertheless, the paintings of this hybrid genius interpret Spain for us in its Catholic zeal and yearning spirituality. This statement is especially true

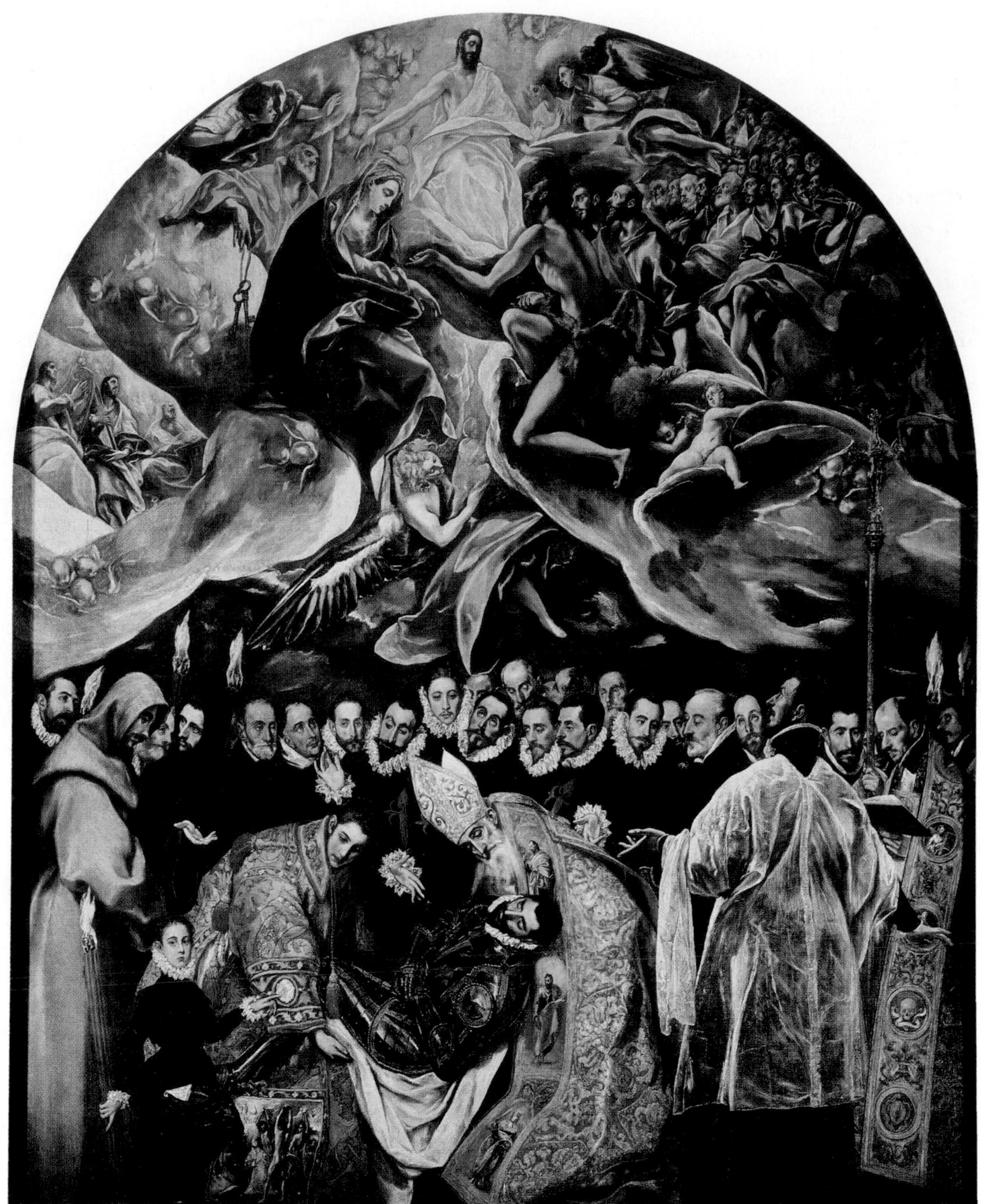

18-59 El Greco, *The Burial of Count Orgaz,* 1586. Oil on canvas, approx. 16′ × 12′. Santo Tomé, Toledo, Spain.

of the artist's masterpiece, *The Burial of Count Orgaz* (FIG. **18-59**), painted in 1586 for the church of Santo Tomé in Toledo. The theme illustrates the legend that the Count of Orgaz, who had died some three centuries before and who had been a great benefactor of the church of Santo Tomé, was buried in the church by Saints Stephen and Augustine, who miraculously descended from heaven to lower the count's body into its sepulcher. The earthly scene is irradiated by the brilliant heaven that opens above it, as El Greco carefully distinguishes the terrestrial and celestial spheres. The terrestrial is represented with a firm realism; the celestial, in his quite personal manner, is shown with elongated, undulant figures, fluttering draperies, cold highlights, and a peculiar kind of ectoplasmic, swimming cloud. Below, the two saints lovingly lower the count's armor-clad body, the armor and heavy draperies painted with all the rich sensuousness of the Venetian school. The background is filled with a solemn chorus of black-clad

Spanish grandees, in whose carefully individualized features El Greco shows us that he was also a great portraitist. These are the faces that looked on the greatness and glory of Spain when it was the leading power of Europe—the faces of the *conquistadores,* who brought Spain the New World and who, two years after this picture was completed, would lead the Great Armada against both Protestant England and Holland.

The lower and upper spheres of the painting are linked by the upward glances of the figures below and by the flight of an angel above, who carries the soul of the count in his arms as St. John and the Virgin intercede for it before the throne of Christ. El Greco's deliberate change in style to distinguish between the two levels of reality gives the viewer the opportunity to see the artist's early and late manners in the same work, one above the other. The relatively sumptuous and realistic presentation of the earthly sphere is still strongly rooted in Venetian art, but the abstractions and distortions that El Greco uses to show the immaterial nature of the Heavenly realm will become characteristic of his later style. Pulling Heaven down to earth, he will paint worldly inhabitants in the same abstract manner as celestial ones. His elongated figures will exist in undefined spaces, bathed in a cool light of uncertain origin. For this, El Greco has been called the last and greatest of the Mannerists, but it is difficult to apply that label to him without reservations. Although he used Manneristic formal devices, El Greco was not a rebel, nor was he aiming for elegance in his work. He was concerned primarily with emotion and with the effort to express his own religious fervor or to arouse the observer's. To make the inner meaning of his paintings forceful, he developed a highly personal style in which his attenuated forms become etherealized in dynamic swirls of unearthly light and color. Some ambiguity may be found in El Greco's forms, but none exists in his meaning, which is mystical, spiritual, ecstatic devotion.

Toward the end of his life, El Greco painted a portrait of his friend, the theologian, poet, and Trinitarian priest, *Fray Hortensio Félix Paravicino* (FIG. **18-60**). It is one of the most distinguished portraits of the age. Father Hortensio, clad in the black-and-white vesture of his order, is represented seated, which,

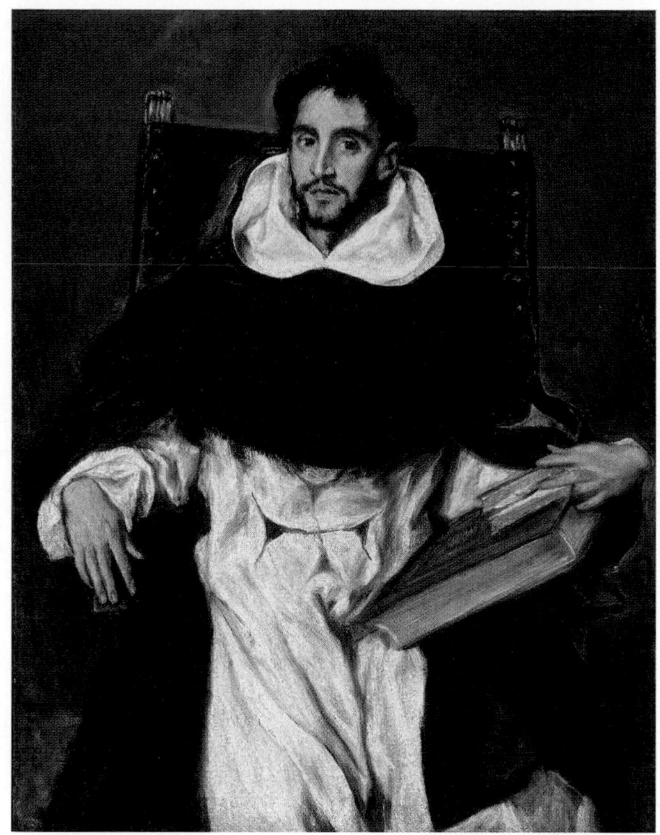

18-60 EL GRECO, *Fray Hortensio Félix Paravicino,* 1609. Oil on canvas, $44\frac{1}{2}'' \times 33\frac{3}{4}''$. Isaac Sweetser Fund, Museum of Fine Arts, Boston.

since the time of Raphael, was the customary pose used in portraits of ecclesiastics of high rank. In his left hand, he holds books, attributes of intellectual dedication and accomplishment. The vividly contrasting black and white of his canonicals and the square-backed leather chair, with its gilt bronze studs and finials, magnificently set off the pale, ascetic face, accented by the dark hair, eyebrows, and beard. El Greco renders the character of a man given wholly to other-worldly concerns as a kind of apparition not quite of this world. The likeness fades into the image of a typical El Greco saint. As is often the case when a great painter makes the likeness of a great-souled subject, the latter becomes more than an individual person. He becomes, as here, generalized into a type, that of the spiritually exalted priest, protagonist in the drama of Spanish history in its great century.

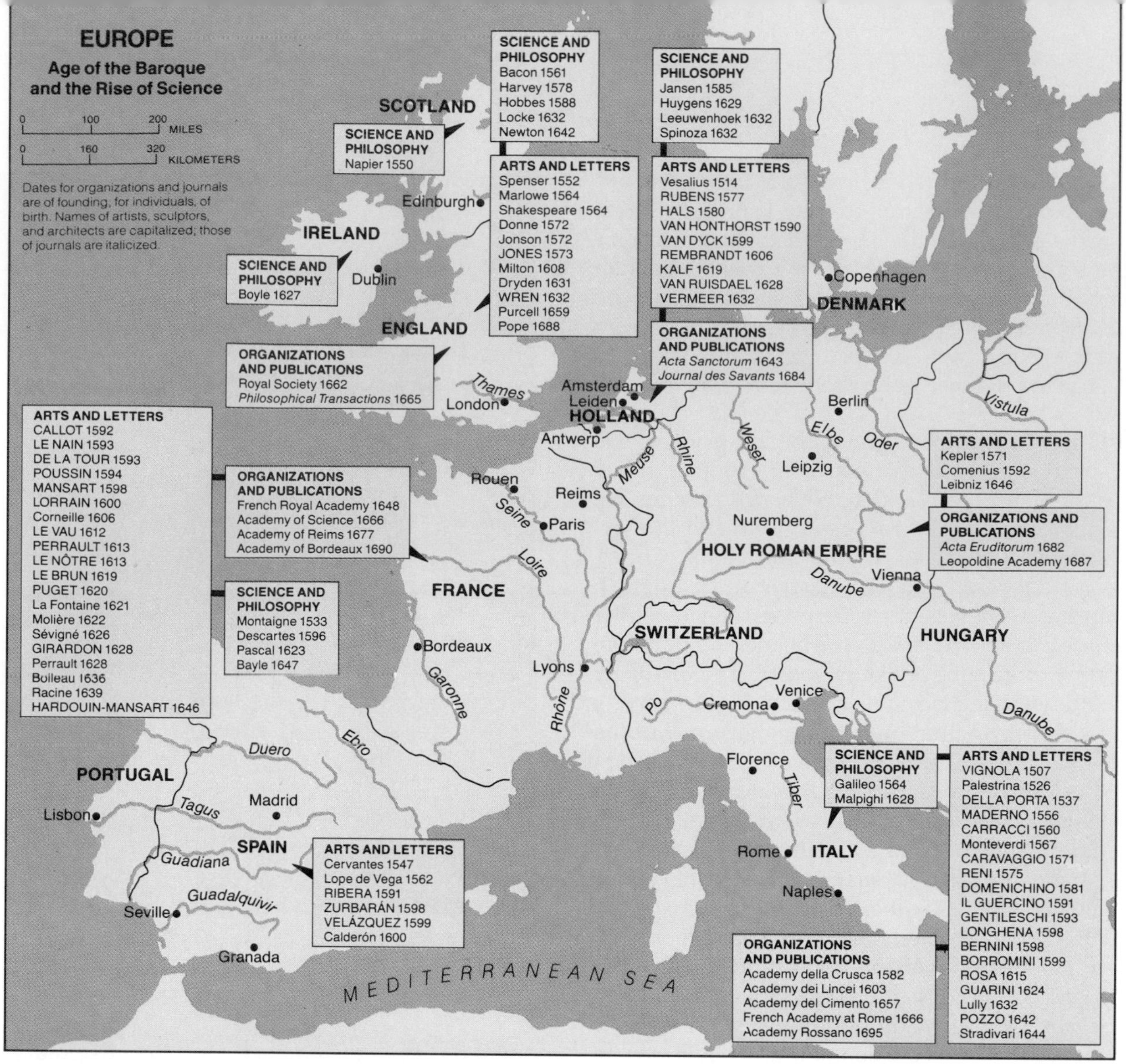

EUROPE
Age of the Baroque and the Rise of Science

0 100 200 MILES
0 160 320 KILOMETERS

Dates for organizations and journals are of founding; for individuals, of birth. Names of artists, sculptors, and architects are capitalized; those of journals are italicized.

SCOTLAND

SCIENCE AND PHILOSOPHY
Napier 1550

Edinburgh

IRELAND

SCIENCE AND PHILOSOPHY
Boyle 1627

Dublin

ENGLAND

SCIENCE AND PHILOSOPHY
Bacon 1561
Harvey 1578
Hobbes 1588
Locke 1632
Newton 1642

ARTS AND LETTERS
Spenser 1552
Marlowe 1564
Shakespeare 1564
Donne 1572
Jonson 1572
JONES 1573
Milton 1608
Dryden 1631
WREN 1632
Purcell 1659
Pope 1688

ORGANIZATIONS AND PUBLICATIONS
Royal Society 1662
Philosophical Transactions 1665

London Thames

HOLLAND

SCIENCE AND PHILOSOPHY
Jansen 1585
Huygens 1629
Leeuwenhoek 1632
Spinoza 1632

ARTS AND LETTERS
Vesalius 1514
RUBENS 1577
HALS 1580
VAN HONTHORST 1590
VAN DYCK 1599
REMBRANDT 1606
KALF 1619
VAN RUISDAEL 1628
VERMEER 1632

ORGANIZATIONS AND PUBLICATIONS
Acta Sanctorum 1643
Journal des Savants 1684

Amsterdam
Leiden
Antwerp

Copenhagen
DENMARK

FRANCE

ARTS AND LETTERS
CALLOT 1592
LE NAIN 1593
DE LA TOUR 1593
POUSSIN 1594
MANSART 1598
LORRAIN 1600
Corneille 1606
LE VAU 1612
PERRAULT 1613
LE NÔTRE 1613
LE BRUN 1619
PUGET 1620
La Fontaine 1621
Molière 1622
Sévigné 1626
GIRARDON 1628
Perrault 1628
Boileau 1636
Racine 1639
HARDOUIN-MANSART 1646

ORGANIZATIONS AND PUBLICATIONS
French Royal Academy 1648
Academy of Science 1666
Academy of Reims 1677
Academy of Bordeaux 1690

SCIENCE AND PHILOSOPHY
Montaigne 1533
Descartes 1596
Pascal 1623
Bayle 1647

Rouen
Reims
Paris
Seine
Loire
Bordeaux
Garonne
Lyons
Rhône
Meuse
Rhine

HOLY ROMAN EMPIRE

ARTS AND LETTERS
Kepler 1571
Comenius 1592
Leibniz 1646

ORGANIZATIONS AND PUBLICATIONS
Acta Eruditorum 1682
Leopoldine Academy 1687

Berlin
Leipzig
Nuremberg
Vienna
Weser
Elbe
Oder
Vistula
Danube

SWITZERLAND
HUNGARY

PORTUGAL
Lisbon

SPAIN

ARTS AND LETTERS
Cervantes 1547
Lope de Vega 1562
RIBERA 1591
ZURBARÁN 1598
VELÁZQUEZ 1599
Calderón 1600

Madrid
Seville
Granada
Duero
Ebro
Tagus
Guadiana
Guadalquivir

ITALY

SCIENCE AND PHILOSOPHY
Galileo 1564
Malpighi 1628

ARTS AND LETTERS
VIGNOLA 1507
Palestrina 1526
DELLA PORTA 1537
MADERNO 1556
CARRACCI 1560
Monteverdi 1567
CARAVAGGIO 1571
RENI 1575
DOMENICHINO 1581
IL GUERCINO 1591
GENTILESCHI 1593
LONGHENA 1598
BERNINI 1598
BORROMINI 1599
ROSA 1615
GUARINI 1624
Lully 1632
POZZO 1642
Stradivari 1644

ORGANIZATIONS AND PUBLICATIONS
Academy della Crusca 1582
Academy dei Lincei 1603
Academy del Cimento 1657
French Academy at Rome 1666
Academy Rossano 1695

Venice
Cremona
Po
Florence
Tiber
Rome
Naples

MEDITERRANEAN SEA

1600 | 1610 | 1620 | 1630 | 1640 | 1650

JAMES I OF ENGLAND — CHARLES I OF ENGLAND

PHILIP III OF SPAIN — PHILIP IV OF SPAIN

HENRY IV OF FRANCE — LOUIS XIII OF FRANCE (dominated by Cardinal Richelieu)

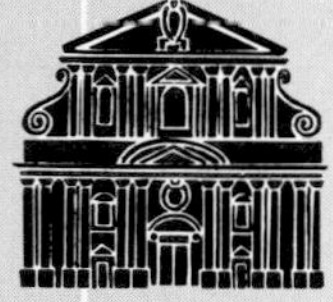

GIACOMO DELLA PORTA
Il Gesù façade
c. 1575–1584

ANNIBALE CARRACCI
1560–1609

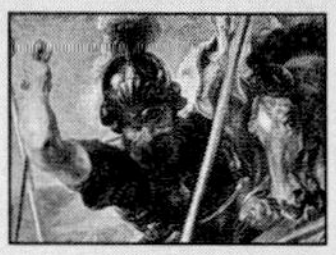

DOMENICHINO
1581–1641

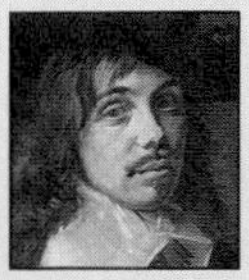

CARAVAGGIO
1571–1610

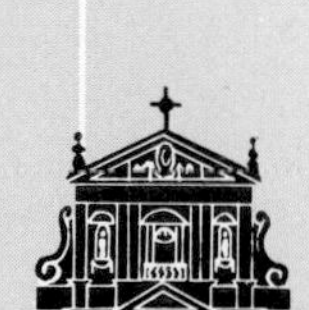

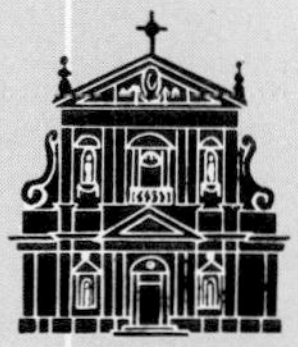

MADERNO
Santa Susanna
1597–1603

GENTILESCHI
1593–1653

RUBENS
The Lion Hunt,
detail 1617–1618

JONES Banqueting
House 1619–1622

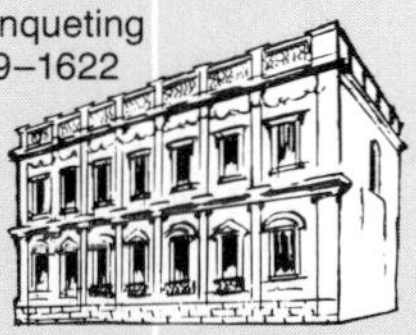

VAN DYCK
1599–1641

RIBERA
1591–1652

POUSSIN
1594–1665

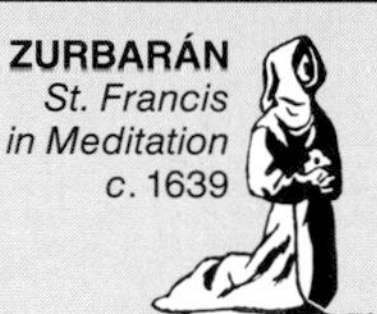

ZURBARÁN
*St. Francis
in Meditation*
c. 1639

REMBRANDT
1606–1669

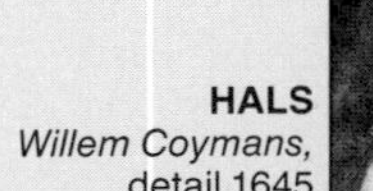

HALS
Willem Coymans,
detail 1645

Pope Paul V
1605–1621

Kepler's laws of
planetary motion
1609, 1619

Thirty Years'
War begins
1618

Pope Urban VIII
1623–1644

William Harvey
discovers blood
circulation 1628

Galileo's laws of
falling bodies,
projectile motion 1638

Descartes's *Discourse
on Method* 1637

French Royal Academy
of Painting and Sculpture
founded 1648

Thirty Years' War
ends 1648

19
BAROQUE ART

1660 · 1670 · 1680 · 1690 · 1700

ENGLAND UNDER CROMWELL | CHARLES II OF ENGLAND | JAMES II | WILLIAM AND MARY

CHARLES II OF SPAIN

LOUIS XIV OF FRANCE (dominated by Cardinal Mazarin until 1661)

VAN RUISDAEL
1628–1682

BERNINI
Scala Regia
1663–1666

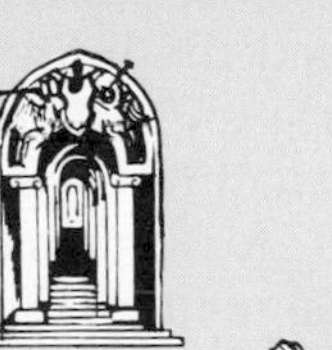

BORROMINI
San Carlo alle
Quattro Fontane
1665–1676

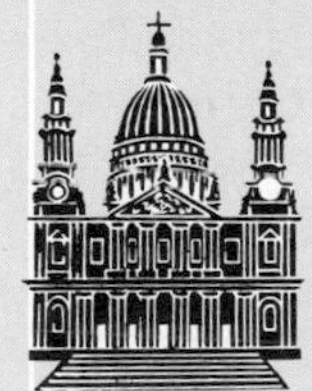

WREN St. Paul's
1675–1710

VELÁZQUEZ
Las Meninas,
detail 1656

GIRARDON
Apollo Attended by the Nymphs,
detail *c.* 1666–1672

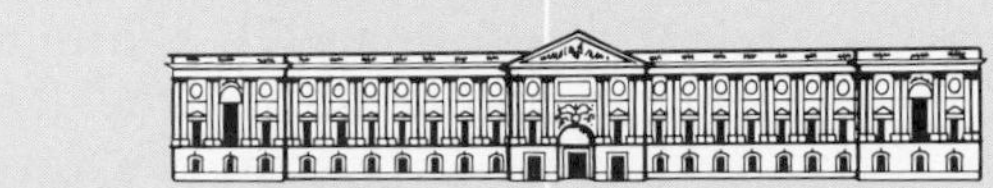

PERRAULT, LE VAU, and **LE BRUN**
Louvre, east façade 1667–1670

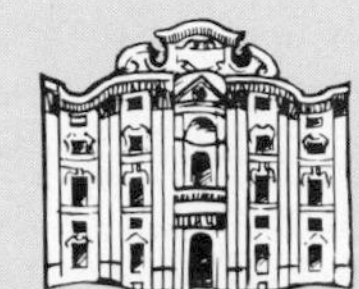

GUARINI Palazzo Carignano
1679–1692

VERMEER
1632–1675

Pope Innocent X
1644–1655

Dutch-English-
French rivalry
in North America

Pope Alexander VII
1655–1667

Royal Society
founded in
London 1662

Great Fire
of London
1666

Jean Baptiste Racine
French Dramatist
1639–1699

The wars of Louis XIV
begin 1667 . . . (1713)

Sir Isaac Newton's
laws of motion;
gravitation 1687

"Glorious Revolution"—
movement towards
parliamentary government
begins in England 1688

Emergence of
Rococo style
in France

THE GENERAL PERIOD we have labeled "Renaissance" continues without any sharp stylistic break (except for the interrupting episode of Mannerism) into the seventeenth and eighteenth centuries. We call the art of this later period *Baroque,* although no one Baroque style or set of stylistic principles actually has been defined. The origin of the word is not clear. It may come from the Portuguese word *barroco,* meaning an irregularly shaped pearl. Certainly, the term originally was used in a disparaging sense, especially in connection with post-Renaissance architecture, which nineteenth-century critics perceived as decadent Classical: unstructural, overornamented, theatrical, and grotesque. The use of "Baroque" as a pejorative has faded, however, and the term has been included in the art-historical vocabulary for many years as a blanket designation for the art of the period roughly covering 1600 to 1750.

Scholars gradually came to see that the Baroque styles were quite different from those of the Renaissance. The Baroque, for example, looks dynamic; Renaissance styles are relatively static. This basic difference led to the claim that the two are fundamentally in opposition; scholars still disagree about the historical and formal relation of the two stylistic periods, especially since it is clear that the Classicism of the High Renaissance is restored and flourishes in the Baroque. The historical reality lies in the flow of stylistic change, and Baroque is a useful classification for isolating the tendencies and products of stylistic change. We shall designate as Baroque those traits that the styles of the seventeenth and earlier eighteenth centuries seem to have in common.

Like the art it produced, the Baroque era was manifold—spacious and dynamic, brilliant and colorful, theatrical and passionate, sensual and ecstatic, opulent and extravagant, versatile and *virtuoso.* It was an age of expansion following on an age of discovery, and its expansion led to still further discovery. The rising national powers colonized the globe. Wars between Renaissance cities were supplanted by wars between continental empires, and the history of Europe was influenced by battles fought in the North American wilderness and in India.

Baroque expansiveness extended well beyond earth in the conceptions of the new astronomy and physics proposed by Galileo, Kepler, and Newton. The same laws of mechanics were found to govern a celestial body moving at great velocity and a falling apple. Humanity's optical range was expanding to embrace the macroscopic spaces of the celestial world and the microscopic spaces of the cellular. The Baroque is almost obsessively interested in the space of the unfolding universe. Descartes makes extension (space and what occupies it) the sole physical attribute of being; only mind and extension exist, the former proving the reality of the latter in Descartes's famous phrase, *Cogito, ergo sum* (I think, therefore I am). Pascal confesses in awe that "the silence of these infinite spaces frightens me." Milton expresses the Baroque image of space in a phrase: "the vast and boundless deep."

The Baroque scientist comes to see physical nature as matter in motion through space and time; the latter two are thought of as the conditions of the first. The measurement of motion is made possible by the new mathematics of analytical geometry and the infinitesimal calculus, and experiment comes to be accepted as the prime method for getting at the truth of physical nature. Time, like space and motion, is a preoccupation of the creative Baroque mind, in art as well as in science. The age-old sense of time, rich with religious, philosophical, psychological, and poetic import, persists alongside the new concept of it as a measurable property of nature. Time, "the subtle thief of youth" that steals away the lives of all of us; that, in the end, reveals the truth, vindicates goodness, and rescues innocence; that demolishes the memory of great empires; and that points to the ultimate judgment of humankind by God—this sense of time pervades the art and literature of the Baroque. The sonnets of Shakespeare dwell on the mutability and brevity of life and on time's destruction of beauty ("that time will come/and take my love away"). The great landscapes of Van Ruisdael suggest the passage of time in hurrying clouds, restless sea, and ever-changing light. Painters and sculptors, eager to make action explicit and convincing, depict it at the very moment it is taking place, as in Bernini's *David* (FIG. 19-10). Countless allegorical representations portray time as the fierce old man carrying his scythe or devouring his children. For the Baroque artist, then, time has acquired its new "scientific" connotations of the instantaneous and the infinite, yet without any loss of its significance for each human life.

Scarcely less fascinating to the Baroque mind is light. Light, which for thousands of years was thought of and worshiped as the godlike sun or the truth of the Holy Spirit, now becomes a physical entity, propagated in waves (or corpuscles) through Pascal's "infinite spaces," capable of being refracted into color by a prism. But, as with time, the newfound materiality of light by no means diminishes its ancient association with spirituality in the religion, poetry, and art of the Baroque. It still stands for inspiration, truth of dogma, the mystical vision of the transcendental world, the presence of the Divine, the "inner light" (FIG. 19-12). And it can have these associations in a commonplace setting or in one of splendor and magnificence (FIG. 19-9). Yet the age of the new science, adapting the old metaphor of light to the dawn of a new day, would be called the "Enlightenment," signifying that the old, dark, mythical way of reading the world has been given up and that the light of knowledge brings a new day. Alexander Pope, expressing the enthusiasm of his day for the discoveries of Newton, makes them out to be a kind of second revelation:

> Nature, and Nature's laws lay hid in night.
> God said: "Let Newton be!" and all was Light!

The elements of perception in naturalistic Baroque art are the elements of nature described by Baroque science: matter in motion through space, time, and light. And the ingredients of an increasingly precise method for the scientific study of nature—observation and measurement, representation and experimental testing—are analogous to the naturalistic artist's careful study and reproduction of natural appearances.

Although the exclusive and exacting report of these elements is a most important enterprise in the age of the Baroque, the mechanical simulation of appearances for its own sake is by no means the naturalistic artist's intention. Although each artist obviously delights in the achievement of astonishing illusion, the images that are rendered embody spiritual and metaphysical meanings of nature so persuasively real and present that their significance and truth are strongly reinforced. In this way, the artist brings before us the reality of the unseen world by means of the seen, the visible objects that are regarded as symbolic or emblematic of invisible and unchanging truth. Baroque naturalism remains largely religious in content.

While naturalism thrived in Baroque art, Classicism was revised and further developed, and the two styles divided the taste of the age with a third: the dynamic, colorful, sensuous style characteristic of Rubens and Bernini. The differences among these three styles were not so definitive as to disallow exchanges of influence or even occasional collaboration, although the esthetic doctrines or presuppositions of naturalism were fundamentally opposed to those of the other two, and the French Academy could debate the virtues of the Classical (formalistic) Poussin over the coloristic Rubens. Art theory flourished, and most of it was on the side of Classicism. The cause of Classicism also was favored by an increasing antiquarian literature, the fruit of an expanding enthusiasm for ancient civilization and art and an increasingly sophisticated and systematic study of it. The Classical masters of the Baroque took as their models the great artists of the High Renaissance, Antique statuary, and nature; artists of whatever stylistic bent often were learned in Classical literature and antiquities. Although the Classical masters' philosophy of art proclaimed the ideal rather than the real as the only worthy subject and form for painting and sculpture, they believed that study of nature was essential to the full and valid realization of the idea in its purity and perfection. This concept was manifest in their insistence on the careful observation and depiction of the human figure from life.

Nevertheless, the opposition of Classicism to the dramatic dynamism of painters like Rubens becomes conscious and fixed in the Baroque. This dualism will hold well into the nineteenth and even the twentieth century. Indeed, it reaches through the entire Western tradition, exclusive of the Middle Ages; an ancient statement of it may be seen in the art of Greece and Rome (compare FIGS. 5-50 and 5-78). Classicism in art and thought amounts to calm rationality; we see it in the landscapes of Poussin (FIG. 19-61). Its opposite—turbulent action stirred by powerful passions—(later, we shall call it "Romanticism") appears in the painting of Rubens (FIG. 19-41) and in the sculpture of Bernini (FIG. 19-12). A central theme of Baroque art and literature is the conflict of reason with passion. The representation of that conflict is, of course, as ancient as Plato and survives as a great dualism in Western thinking about human nature.

The exploration of the elementary structure of physical nature is accompanied, quite consistently, by the exploration of human nature, the realm of the senses and the emotions. The function of the representational arts is to open that realm to full view. The throwing open to human scrutiny of the two physical universes of macrocosm and microcosm did not distract Baroque humanity from the age-old curiosity about the nature of humankind. After all, it was now perceived that if we are one with nature, the knowledge of ourselves must be part of the knowledge of nature. The new resources given to Baroque artists allow them to render, with new accuracy and authority, the appearances of the world and of the beings that people it. Painting and sculpture, equipped with every device of sensuous illusion now available, provide a stage for the enactment of the drama of human life in all its variety. Baroque is preeminently the age of theater. Art shares with the actor's stage the purpose (as Shakespeare puts it in *Hamlet*)

> to hold, as 'twere, the mirror up to nature, to show virtue her own feature, scorn her own image, and the very age and body of the time his form and pressure. (III:2)

Shakespeare urges us to present and analyze the spectrum of human actions and passions in all its degrees of lightness, darkness, and intensity. In this great era of the stage, tragedy and comedy are reborn. At the same time, the resources of music greatly expand, creating the opera and refining the instruments of the modern orchestra. All the arts approve the things of the senses and the delights of sensuous experience. Although here and there the guilty fear of pleasure lingers from the times of Hieronymus Bosch, poetry and literature in all countries acquire a richly expressive language capable of rendering themes that involve the description, presentation, conflict, and resolution of human emotions. In the Catholic countries, every device of art is used to stimulate pious emotions—sometimes, to the pitch of ecstasy. Luxurious display and unlimited magnificence and splendor frame the extravagant life of the courts, cost notwithstanding; the modes of furniture and dress are perhaps the most ornate ever designed. Even in externals, a dramatic, sensuous elaborateness is the rule. However, what people wear and what they do must approach perfection, with the added flourish of seeming effortlessness. Courtiers, at one end of Baroque society, and brigands and pirates at the other, are brilliant performers, as are those who fashion the arts and the sciences. All are virtuosi, proud of their technique and capable of astonishing quantities of work.

ITALY

The age of the Baroque has been identified with the Catholic reaction to the advance of Protestantism. Although it extends much more widely in time and place than seventeenth-century Italy and is by no means only a manifestation of religious change, Baroque art doubtless had papal Rome as its birthplace. Between the pontificates of Paul III (Farnese) from 1534 to 1549 and of Sixtus V (Peretti) in the 1580s, the popes led a successful military, diplomatic, and theological campaign against Protestantism, wiping out many of its gains in central and southern Europe. The great Council of Trent, which met in the early 1540s and again in the early 1560s, was sponsored by the papacy in an effort to systematize and harden orthodox Catholic doctrine against the threat of Protestant persuasion. The Council firmly resisted Protestant objection to the use of images in religious worship, insisting on their necessity in the teaching of the laity. This implied separation of the priest from an unsophisticated congregation was to be reflected in architecture as well, the central type of church plan being rejected in favor of the long church and of other plans that maintained the distinction between clergy and laity; an example is the addition of the nave to the central plan of Bramante and Michelangelo for St. Peter's (FIGS. 19-3 and 19-6).

Interrupted for a while, the building program begun under Paul III (with Michelangelo's Capitoline Hill design) was taken up again by Sixtus V, who had augmented the papal treasury and who intended to construct a new and more magnificent Rome, an "imperial city that had been subdued to Christ and purged of paganism." Sixtus was succeeded by a number of strong and ambitious popes—Paul V (Borghese), Urban VIII (Barberini), Innocent X (Pamfili), and Alexander VII (Chigi)—the patrons of Bernini and Borromini and the builders of the modern city of Rome, which bears their Baroque mark everywhere. The energy of the Catholic Counter-Reformation, transformed into art, radiated throughout Catholic countries and even into Protestant lands, which found a response to it in their own art.

Architecture and Sculpture

The Jesuit order, newly founded (in 1534, in the pontificate of Paul III), needed an impressive building for its mother church. Because Michelangelo was dilatory in providing the plans, the church, called Il Gesù (Church of Jesus, FIG. **19-1**), was designed and built between 1568 and 1584 by GIACOMO DA VIGNOLA (1507–1573), who designed the ground plan, and GIACOMO DELLA PORTA (1537–1602), who is responsible for the façade. Chronologically and stylistically,

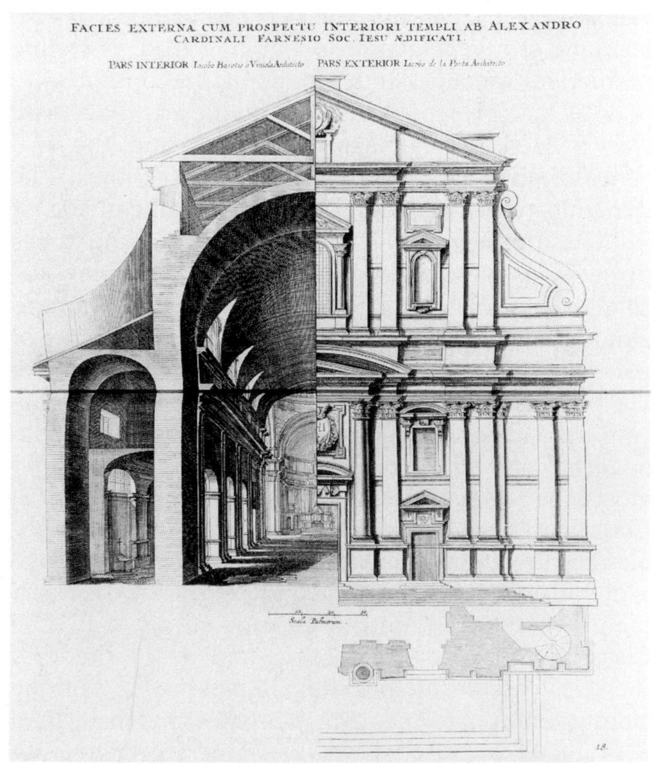

19-1 GIACOMO DELLA PORTA, façade of Il Gesù, Rome, c. 1575–1584. Interior by GIACOMO DA VIGNOLA, 1568. (Engraving by JOACHIM VON SANDRART.)

the building belongs to the Late Renaissance, but its enormous influence on later churches marks it as one of the major seminal monuments for the development of Baroque church architecture. Its façade is an important model and point of departure for the façades of Roman Baroque churches for two centuries, and its basic scheme is echoed and reechoed throughout the Catholic countries, especially in Latin America. The design of the façade is not entirely original; the union of the lower and upper stories, effected by scroll buttresses, goes back to Leon Battista Alberti's Santa Maria Novella in Florence (FIG. 16-39); its Classical pediment is familiar in Alberti and Andrea Palladio; and its paired pilasters appear in Michelangelo's design for St. Peter's. But the façade is a skillful synthesis of these already existing motifs; the two stories are well unified, the horizontal march of the pilasters and columns builds to a dramatic climax at the central bay, and the bays of the façade snugly fit the nave-chapel system behind them. The many dramatic Baroque façades of Rome will be architectural variations on this basic theme.

In plan (FIG. **19-2**), a monumental expansion of Alberti's scheme for Sant' Andrea in Mantua (FIG. 16-43), the nave takes over the main volume of space, so that the structure becomes a great hall with side chapels. The approach to the altar is emphasized by a dome. The wide acceptance of the Gesù plan in the Catholic world, even until modern times, seems to attest that it is ritually satisfactory. The opening of the church building into a single great hall provides an almost theatrical setting for large promenades and processions (that seemed to combine social with sacerdotal functions) and, above all, a space adequate to accommodate the great crowds that gathered to hear the eloquent preaching of the Jesuits. The Jesuits had a strong, indirect influence on art and architecture through the teachings of Saint Ignatius of Loyola, their Spanish founder. Loyola, in his *Spiritual Exercises,* advocated that the spiritual experience of the mysteries of the Catholic faith be intensely imagined, so much so as to be visible to the eye. The content of faith was to be visualized, and the sacred objects of the Church were to be venerated as defenses against false doctrine and the powers of Hell. This is still the function and warranty of religious art throughout the Roman Catholic world.

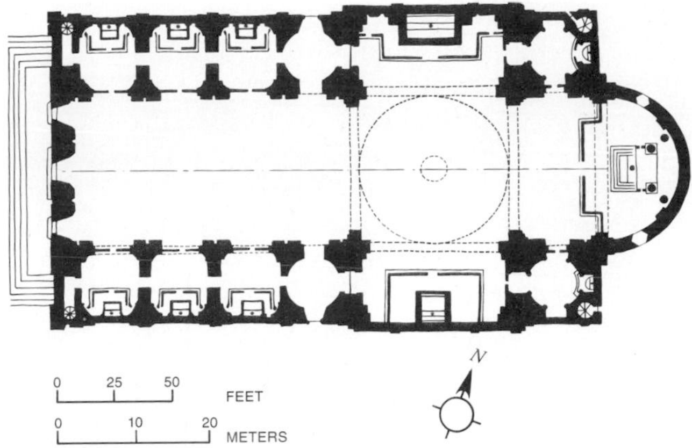

19-2 GIACOMO DA VIGNOLA, plan of Il Gesù.

The great Baroque project in Rome was the completion of St. Peter's (FIG. **19-3**). Bramante's and Michelangelo's central plan was unsatisfactory to the clergy

19-3 Aerial view of St. Peter's, the Vatican, Rome.

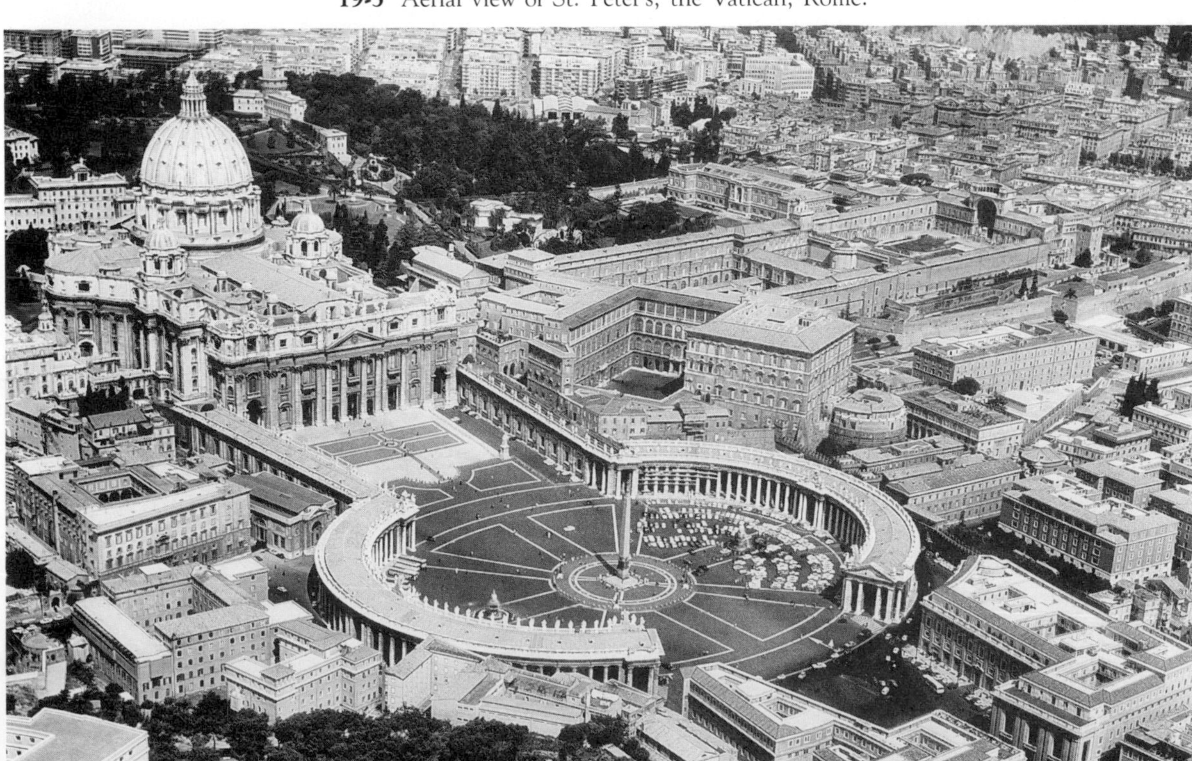

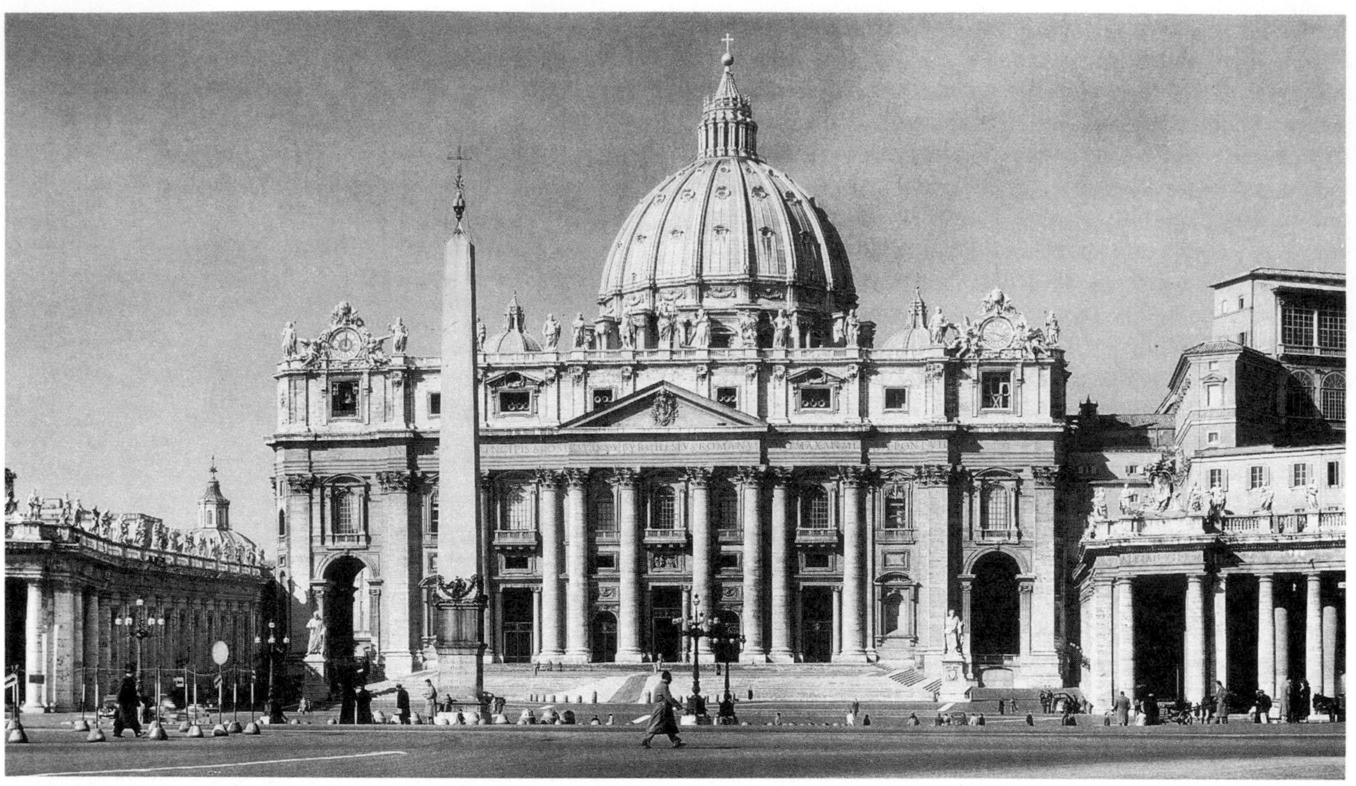

19-4 Carlo Maderno, façade of St. Peter's, 1606–1612.

of the seventeenth century, who thought it smacked of paganism and who felt it was inconvenient for the ever-growing assemblies. Under Paul V, Carlo Maderno (1556–1629) was commissioned to add three bays of a nave to the earlier nucleus and to provide the building with a façade (FIG. **19-4**). Before he received the St. Peter's commission, Maderno had designed the façade of Santa Susanna (FIG. **19-5**), concentrating and dramatizing in it the major features of the façade of Il Gesù. Strong shadows cast by the vigorously projecting columns and pilasters of Santa Susanna mount dramatically toward the emphatically stressed central axis; the sculptural effect is enhanced by the recessed niches, which contain statues.

The façade of St. Peter's (FIG. 19-4) is a gigantic expansion of the elements of Santa Susanna's first level, but Maderno overextends his theme, and the compactness of Santa Susanna's façade is lost. The elements are spread too wide, and the quickening rhythm of pilasters and columns from the sides toward the center becomes slack. The role of the central pediment is reduced to insignificance by the façade's excessive width. In fairness to Maderno, it must be pointed out that his design for the façade never was completely executed. The two outside bays are the first stages of two flanking towers, which never were built; their vertical accents might have visually compressed the central part of the façade. As it stands,

19-5 Carlo Maderno, Santa Susanna, Rome, 1597–1603.

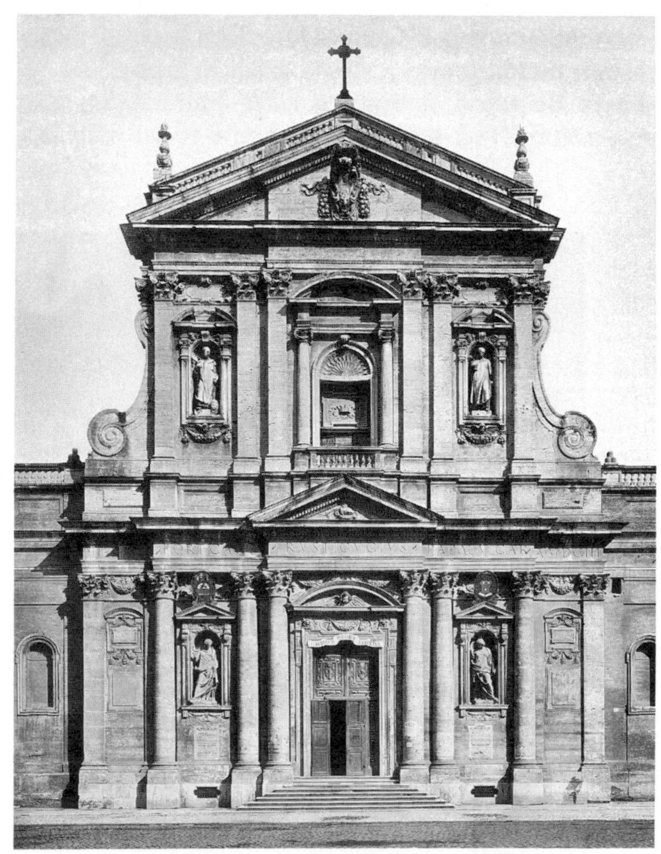

this unfinished, watered-down frontispiece is criticized almost universally by artists and historians and has, unfortunately, become the dominant feature of the church's exterior. Lengthening the nave moves the façade outward and away from the dome, and the effect that Michelangelo had planned—a structure pulled together and dominated by its dome—is seriously impeded. When viewed at close range, the dome hardly emerges above the soaring cliff of the façade; seen from farther back, it appears to have no drum. One must go back beyond the piazza to see the dome and drum together and to experience the effect that Michelangelo intended. Today, to see the structure as it was originally planned, it must be viewed from the back (FIG. 17-33).

BERNINI

The design of St. Peter's, which had been evolving since the days of Bramante and Michelangelo and had engaged all of the leading architects of the Renaissance and Baroque periods, was completed (except for details) by GIANLORENZO BERNINI (1598–1680). Bernini was an architect, a painter, and a sculptor—one of the most brilliant and imaginative artists of the Baroque era and, if not the originator of the Baroque style, probably its most characteristic and sustaining spirit. Bernini's largest and most impressive single project was the design for a monumental piazza in front of St. Peter's (FIGS. 19-3 and **19-6**). In much the way that Michelangelo was forced to reorganize the Capitoline Hill, Bernini had to adjust his design to some preexisting structures on the site: an ancient obelisk brought from Egypt and a fountain designed by Maderno. He used these features to define the long axis of a vast oval embraced by colonnades that are joined to the façade of St. Peter's by two diverging wings. Four files of huge Tuscan columns make up the two colonnades, which terminate in severely Classical temple fronts. The dramatic gesture of embrace made by the colonnades (FIG. 19-3) symbolizes the welcome given its communicants by the Roman Catholic church. Thus, the compact, central designs of Bramante and Michelangelo are expanded by a Baroque transformation into a dynamic complex of axially ordered elements that reach out and enclose spaces of vast dimension. Where the Renaissance building stood in self-sufficient isolation, the Baroque design expansively relates it to its environment.

19-6 Plan of St. Peter's, with adjoining piazza designed by GIANLORENZO BERNINI.

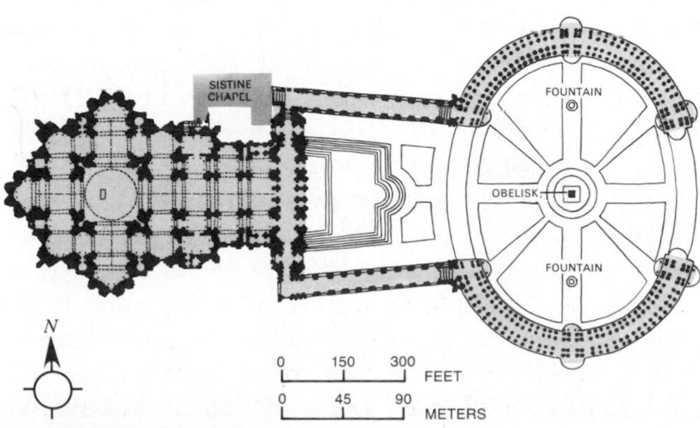

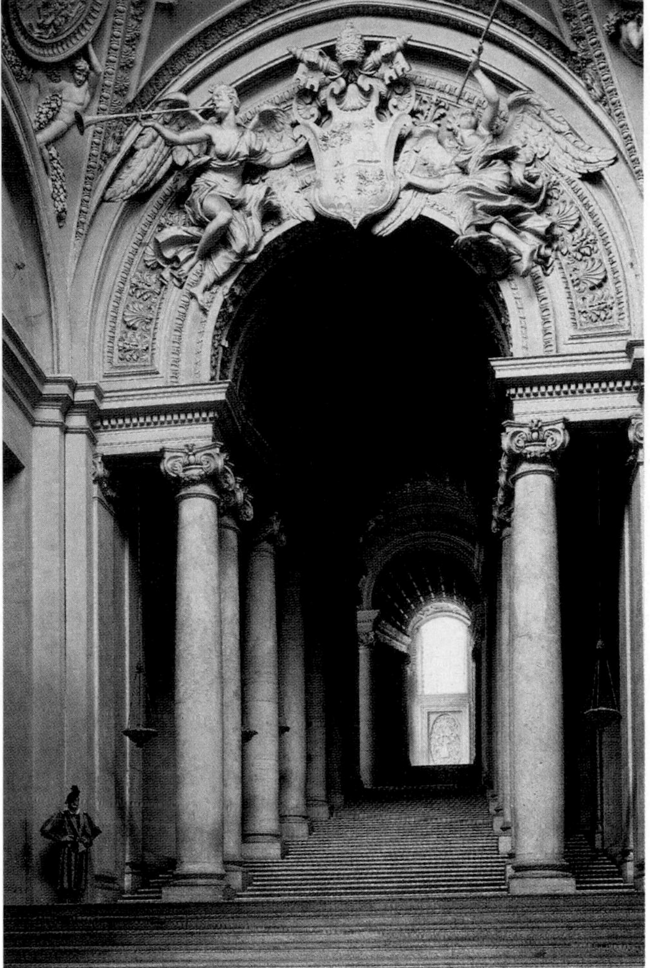

19-7 GIANLORENZO BERNINI, Scala Regia, the Vatican, Rome, 1663–1666.

The wings that connect St. Peter's façade with the oval piazza flank a trapezoidal space also reminiscent of the Capitoline Hill, but here the latter's visual effect is reversed; as seen from the piazza, the diverging wings counteract the natural perspective and tend to bring the façade closer to the observer. Emphasizing the façade's height in this manner, Bernini subtly and effectively compensates for its excessive width.

The Baroque delight in illusionistic devices is expressed again in the Vatican in the Scala Regia (FIG. **19-7**), a monumental stairway connecting the papal apartments and the portico and narthex of the

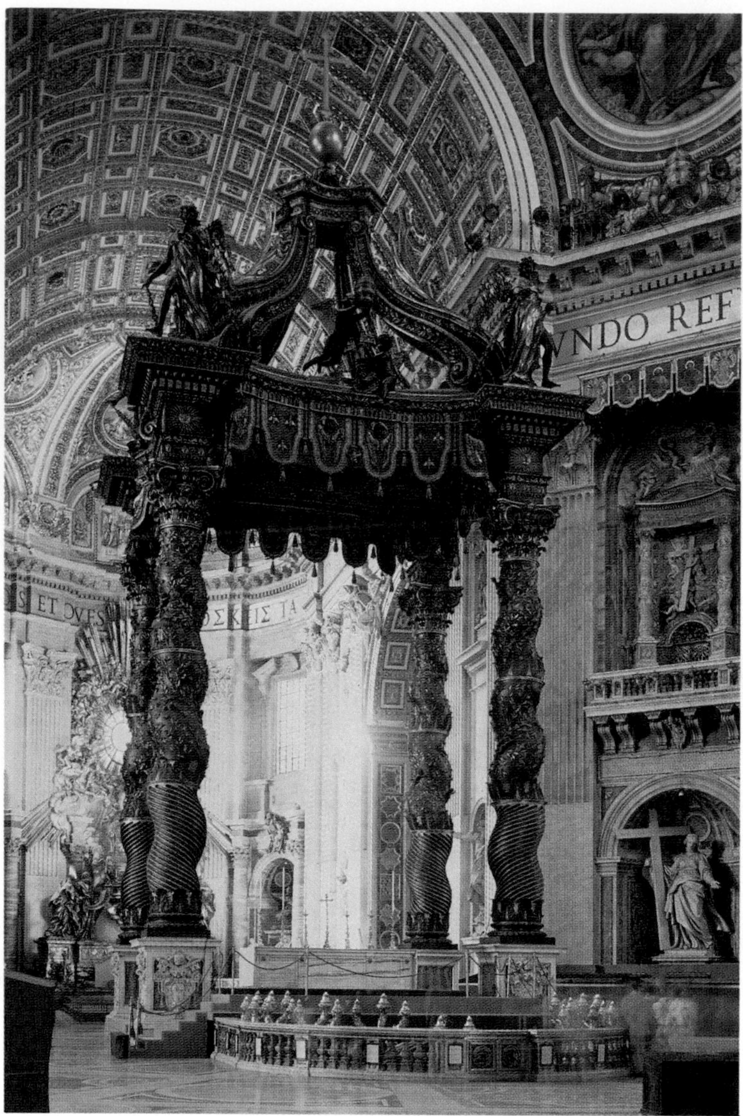

19-8 Gianlorenzo Bernini, baldacchino for St. Peter's, 1624–1633. Gilded bronze, approx. 100′ high.

church. Because the original passageway was irregular, dark, and dangerous to descend, Pope Alexander VII commissioned Bernini to replace it. Bernini, like Michelangelo at the Campidoglio, here makes architectural virtue of necessity by using illusionistic techniques characteristic of stagecraft. The stairway, its entrance crowned by a sculptural group of trumpeting angels and the papal arms, is covered by a barrel vault (in two stages) carried on columns that form aisles flanking the central corridor. By gradually reducing the distance between columns and walls as the stairway ascends, Bernini actually eliminates the aisles on the upper levels, while creating an illusion of uniformity of width and continuity of aisle for the whole stairway. At the same time, the space between the colonnades also narrows with ascent, reinforcing the natural perspective and making the stairs appear to be longer than they actually are. To minimize this effect, Bernini made the lighting at the top of the stairs brighter, exploiting the natural human inclination to move from darkness toward light. To make the long ascent more tolerable, he provided an intermediate goal in the form of an illuminated landing that promises a midway resting point. The result is a highly sophisticated design, both dynamic and dramatic, which repeats on a smaller scale, but perhaps even more effectively, the processional sequence found inside St. Peter's.

Long before the planning of the piazza and the completion of the Scala Regia, Bernini had been at work decorating the interior of St. Peter's. His first commission, completed between 1624 and 1633, called for the design and erection of the gigantic bronze *baldacchino* above the main altar under the cathedral's dome (FIG. **19-8**), which was built to mark and memorialize the tomb of St. Peter. Almost

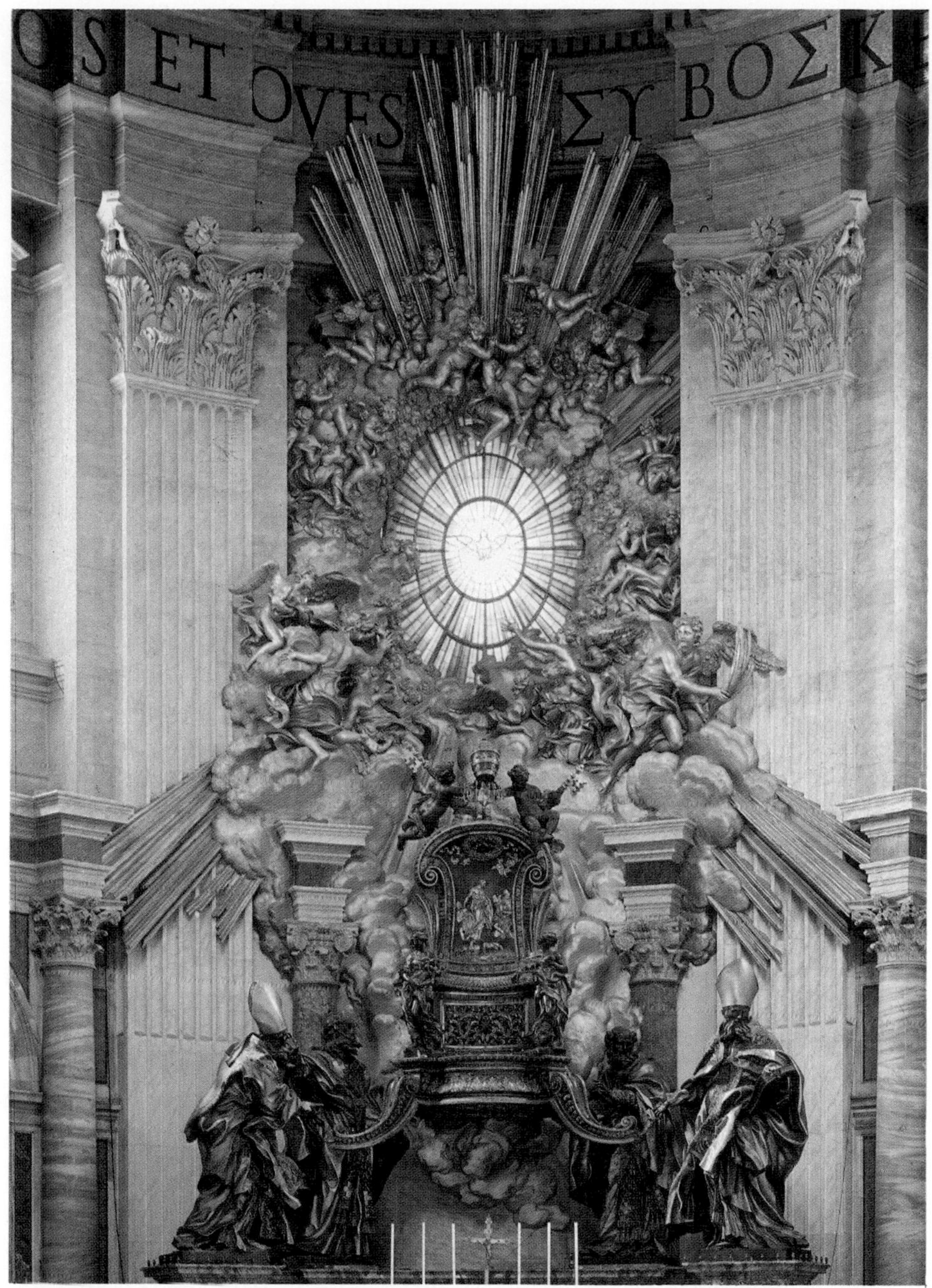

19-9 Gianlorenzo Bernini, Cathedra Petri, 1656–1666. Gilded bronze, marble, stucco, and stained glass. St. Peter's.

100 feet high (the height of an average eight-story building), this canopy is in harmony with the tremendous proportions of the new church and is a focus of its splendor. Its four spiral columns recall those of the ancient baldacchino over the same spot in Old St. Peter's. Partially fluted and wreathed with vines, they seem to deny the mass and weight of the tons of bronze resting on them. At the same time, they communicate their Baroque energy to the four colossal angels standing guard at the upper corners and to the four serpentine brackets that elevate the orb and the cross, symbols of the triumph of the Church.

Indeed, it is this theme of triumph that dictates the architectural as well as sculptural symbolism both inside and outside St. Peter's. Suggesting a great and solemn procession, the main axis of the complex traverses the piazza (slowed by the central obelisk) and enters Maderno's nave. It comes to a temporary halt at the altar beneath the baldacchino, but it continues on toward its climactic destination at another great altar in the apse, the Cathedra Petri (FIG. **19-9**), also the work of Bernini. In this explosively dramatic composition, the Chair of St. Peter is exalted in a burst of light, in which the Dove of the Holy Ghost appears amidst flights of angels and billowing clouds. Four colossal figures in gilt bronze seem to support the chair miraculously, for they scarcely touch it. The two in the foreground represent two fathers of the Latin church, Saints Ambrose and Augustine. Behind them, less conspicuously, stand Saints Athanasius and Chrysostom, representing the Greek church. The grouping of the figures constitutes an appeal for unity within Christianity and, at the same time, suggests the subservience of the Eastern church to the Western. The Cathedra Petri is the quintessence of Baroque composition. Its forms are generated and grouped not by clear lines of structure but by forces that unfold from a center of violent energy. Everything moves, nothing is distinct, light dissolves firmness, and the effect is visionary. The vision asserts the triumph of Christianity and the papal claim to doctrinal supremacy.

Much of Bernini's prolific career was given to the adornment of St. Peter's, where his works combine sculpture with architecture. Although Bernini was a great and influential architect, his fame rests primarily on his sculpture, which, like his architecture, expresses the Baroque spirit to perfection. It is expansive and dramatic, and the element of time usually plays an important role in it. Bernini's version of *David* (FIG. **19-10**) aims at catching the split-second action of the figure and differs markedly from the restful and tense figures of *David* portrayed by Donatello (FIG. 16-12), Verrocchio (FIG. 16-52), and Michelangelo (FIG. 17-19). Bernini's *David,* his muscular legs widely and firmly planted, is beginning the violent, pivoting motion that will launch the stone from his sling. A moment before, his body was in one position; the next moment, it will be in a completely different one. Bernini selects the most dramatic of an implied sequence of poses, so that the observer has to think simultaneously of the continuum and of this tiny fraction of it. The implied continuum imparts a dynamic quality to the statue that suggests a bursting forth of the energy one sees confined in Michelangelo's figures (FIGS. 17-19 and 17-20). Bernini's statue seems to be moving through time and through space. This is not the kind of statue that can be inscribed in a cylinder or confined to a niche; its implied action demands space around it. Nor is it self-sufficient in the Renaissance sense, as its pose and attitude direct the observer's attention beyond itself and to its surroundings (in this case, toward an unseen Goliath). For the first time since the Hellenistic era (FIG. 5-75), a sculptured figure moves out into and partakes of the physical space that surrounds it and the observer.

The expansive quality of Baroque art and its refusal to limit itself to firmly defined spatial settings are

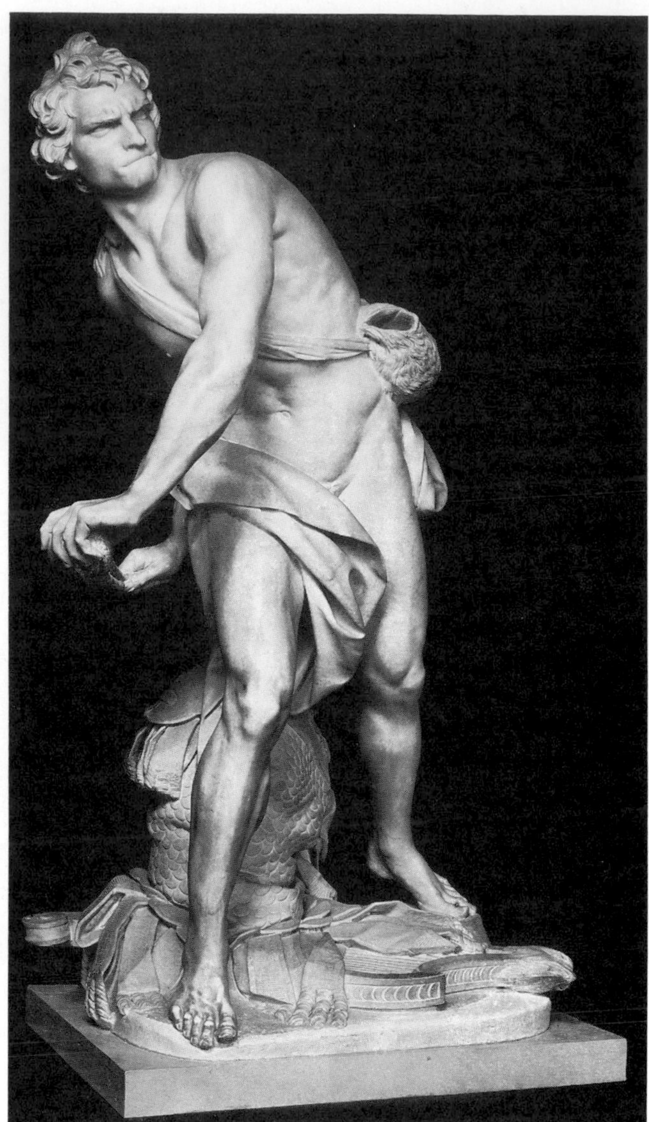

19-10 GIANLORENZO BERNINI, *David,* 1623. Marble, life size. Galleria Borghese, Rome.

encountered again in *The Ecstasy of St. Theresa* in the Cornaro Chapel of the church of Santa Maria della Vittoria (FIG. **19-11**). In this chapel, Bernini draws on the full resources of architecture, sculpture, and painting to charge the entire area with crosscurrents of dramatic tension. St. Theresa was a nun of the Carmelite order and one of the great mystical saints of the Spanish Counter-Reformation. Her conversion took place after the death of her father, when she fell into a series of trances, saw visions, and heard voices. Feeling a persistent pain in her side, she came to believe that its cause was the fire-tipped dart of Divine love, which an angel had thrust into her bosom and which she described as making her swoon in delightful anguish. The whole chapel becomes a theater for the production of this mystical

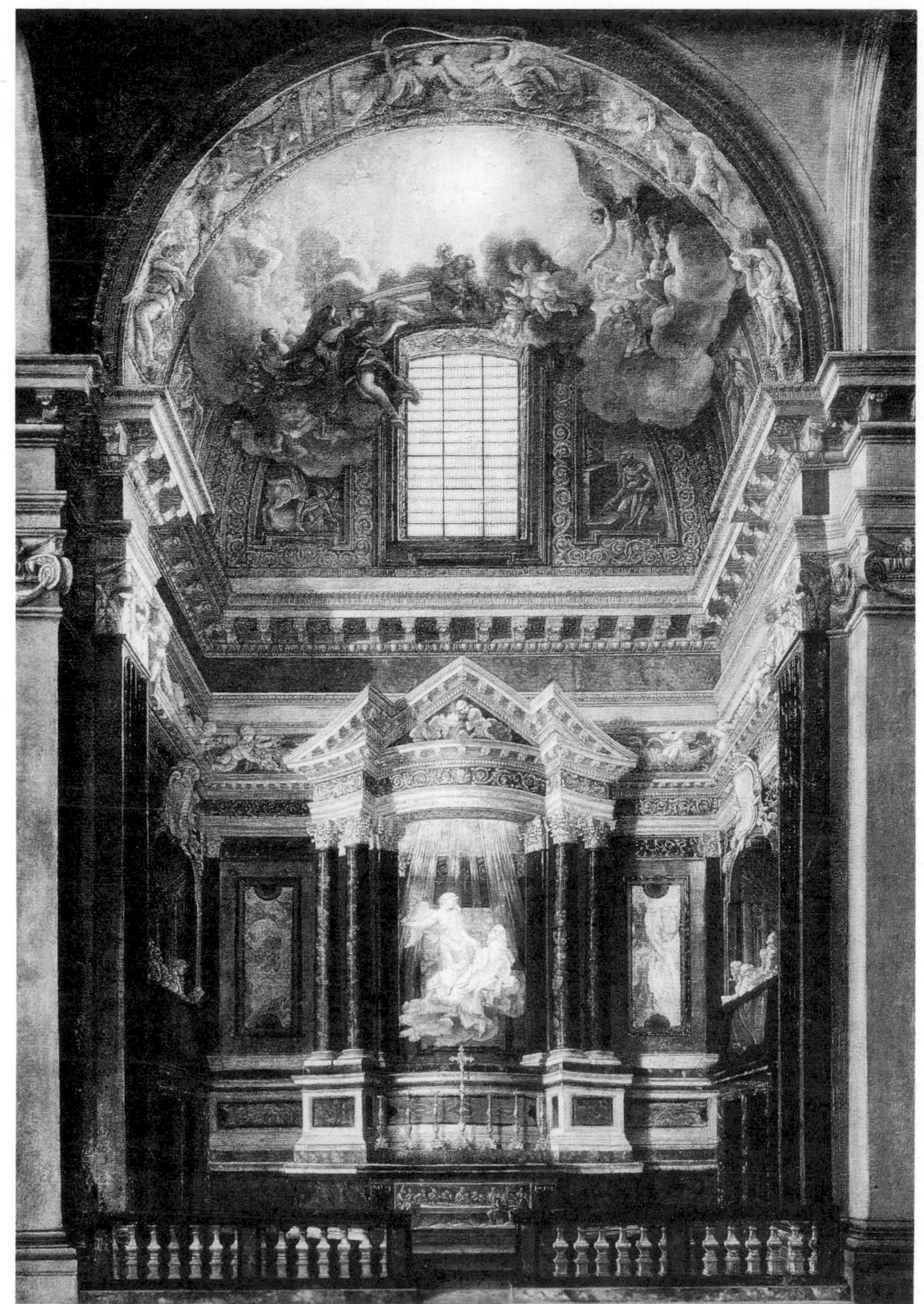

19-11 GIANLORENZO BERNINI, interior of the Cornaro Chapel, 1645–1652, Santa Maria della Vittoria, Rome. Eighteenth-century painting, Staatliches Museum, Schwerin, East Germany.

drama. The niche in which it takes place is a proscenium crowned with a broken Baroque pediment and ornamented with polychrome marble (FIG. 19-11). On either side of the chapel, portraits of the Cornaro family in sculptured opera boxes represent an audience watching the denouement of the heavenly drama with intent piety. Bernini shows the saint in ecstasy (FIG. **19-12**), unmistakably a mingling of spiritual and physical passion, swooning back on a cloud, while the smiling angel aims his arrow. The group is of white marble, and the artist goes to extremes of virtuosity in his management of textures: the clouds, rough monk's cloth, gauzy material, smooth flesh, and feathery wings are all carefully differentiated, yet harmonized in visual and visionary effect. Light from a hidden window pours down bronze rays that are meant to be seen as bursting forth from a painting of Heaven in the vault (FIG. 19-11). Several tons of marble seem to float in a haze of light, the winds of Heaven buoying draperies as the cloud ascends. The

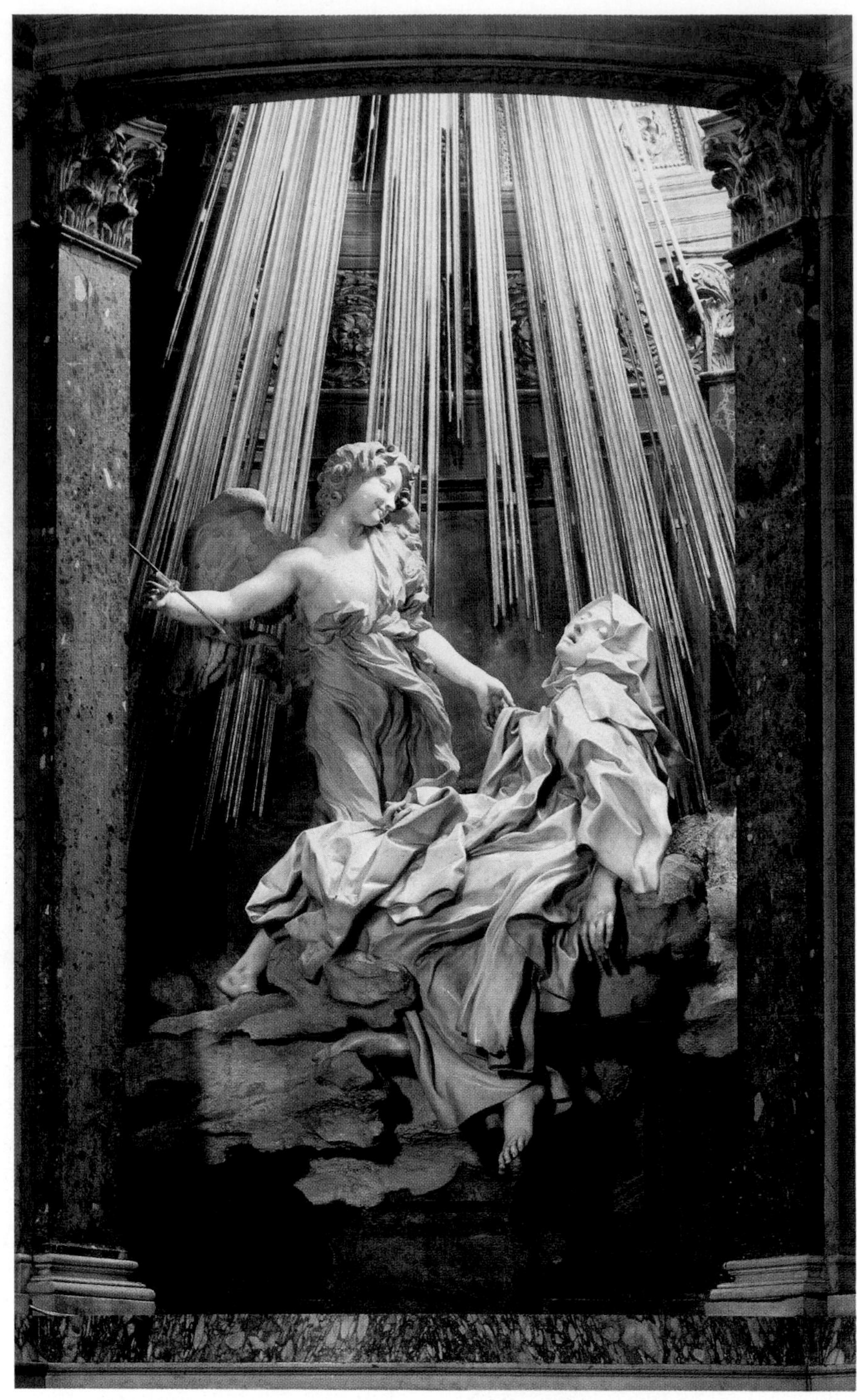

19-12 Gianlorenzo Bernini, *The Ecstasy of St. Theresa,* 1645–1652. Marble, height of group 11′ 6″. Cornaro Chapel, Santa Maria della Vittoria.

remote mysteries of religion, taking on recognizable form, descend to meet the human world halfway, within the conventions of Baroque art and theater. Bernini had much to do with the establishment of the principles of visual illusion that guided both. He was perfectly familiar with the writing of plays, theatrical production, and stagecraft. The young English traveler, John Evelyn, sojourning in Rome in 1644, wrote that "Bernini, a Florentine sculptor, architect, painter, and poet, gave a public opera . . . wherein he painted the scenes, cut the statues, invented the engines, composed the music, writ the comedy and built the theater." The community of the Baroque arts is reflected in the universal genius of Bernini.

Given the virtuosity, versatility, and vast output of Bernini, we should not suppose that he carried out the execution of each piece unaided. He presided over a whole corps of assistants who performed the heavy manual labor involved in rough shaping of the stone, transferring the figure from clay model to marble block, cutting the main forms and outlines, and casting the bronze. The essential tasks were always under the supervision of the master, who would direct each stage of production and place the finishing touches himself. Rudolf Wittkower observes that "in a critical study of Bernini's work, one would have to differentiate between works designed by him and executed by his own hand; those to a greater or lesser extent carried out by him; others where he firmly held the reins but contributed little or nothing to the execution; and finally, those works for which he did no more than a few preliminary sketches."*

The evident desire of the time to instill designs with dynamic qualities finds expressive release in the design of monumental fountains. The challenge of working with an element that actually *is* in motion fascinated Baroque artists, and not surprisingly, Bernini was one of the most inventive and most widely imitated designers in this field. It is largely his doing that Rome is a city of fountains. One of his most charming inventions is the Triton Fountain (FIG. **19-13**), in which Bernini shows the male counterpart of the mermaid, seated on a shell supported by dolphins, blowing a jet of water toward the sky. The jet falls back into the shell, and the water dribbles in thin rivulets from its corrugated edges into the collecting basin below. The maritime group, risen from the depths of the ocean, is enveloped in rising and falling sprays of water. Sunlight reflected from the constantly agitated surface of the collecting pool around the base of the monument ripples across the stone surfaces of the sculptured group in ever-changing patterns that make the Triton seem alive, his bellowslike chest heaving with the effort of blowing into his shell. For centuries, he has performed his task for Urban VIII, the Barberini Pope, whose emblems (the bees) decorate the fountain's base.

*Rudolf Wittkower, *Sculpture: Processes and Principles* (New York: Harper & Row, 1977), p. 181.

19-13 GIANLORENZO BERNINI, Triton Fountain, 1642–1643. Travertine. Piazza Barberini, Rome.

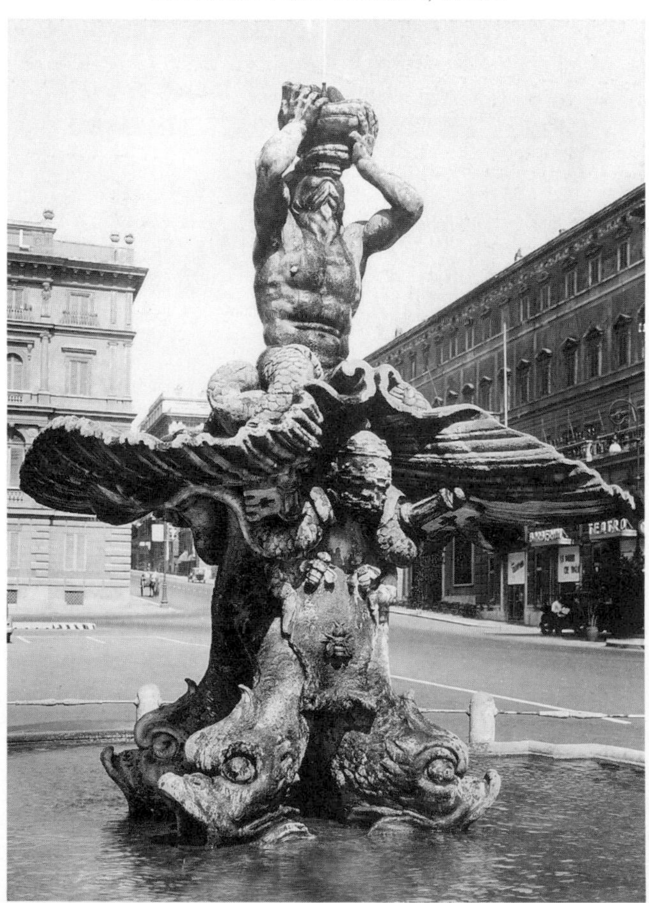

BORROMINI

It seems curious that Bernini, whose sculpture expresses the very essence of the Baroque spirit, should remain relatively conservative in his architecture. Frequently planning on a vast scale and employing striking illusionistic devices, Bernini tends to use the Classical orders in a fairly sober and traditional manner. Obvious exceptions include his baldacchino in St. Peter's and the St. Theresa altar (FIGS. 19-8 and 19-11). One might call his architectural style academic, in comparison with the unorthodox and quite revolutionary manner of his contemporary, FRANCESCO BORROMINI (1599–1667). A new dynamism appears in the little church of San Carlo alle Quattro Fontane (FIGS. **19-14** and **19-15**), where Borromini goes well beyond any of his predecessors or contemporaries in the plastic handling of a building. Maderno's façades of St. Peter's and Santa Susanna (FIGS. 19-4 and 19-5) are deeply sculptured, but they develop along straight, lateral planes. Borromini, perhaps thinking of Michelangelo's apse wall in St. Peter's (FIG. 17-33), sets his whole façade in serpentine motion forward and back, making a counterpoint of concave and convex on two levels (note the sway of the cornices), and emphasizes the sculptured effect by deeply recessed niches. This façade is no longer the traditional, flat frontispiece that defines a building's outer limits; it is a pulsating membrane inserted between interior and exterior space, designed not to separate but to provide a fluid transition between the two. This functional interrelation of the building and its environment is underlined by the curious fact that it has not one but two façades. The second, a narrow bay crowned with its own small tower, turns away from the main façade and, following the curve of the street, faces an intersection. (The upper façade was completed seven years after Borromini's death, and we cannot be sure to what degree the present supplemented and complex structure reflects his original intention.)

The interior is not only an ingenious response to an awkward site, but also a provocative variation on the theme of the centrally planned church. In plan (FIG. 19-15) it looks like a hybrid of a Greek cross and an oval, with a long axis between entrance and apse. The side walls move in an undulating flow that reverses the motion of the façade. Vigorously projecting columns articulate the space into which they protrude just as much as they do the walls to which they are attached. This molded interior space is capped by a deeply coffered, oval dome that seems to float on the light entering through windows hidden in its base. Rich variations on the basic theme of the oval, dynamic relative to the static circle, create an interior that appears to flow from entrance to altar, unimpeded by the segmentation so characteristic of Renaissance buildings.

The unification of interior space is carried even further in Borromini's Chapel of St. Ivo in the courtyard of the College of the Sapienza (wisdom) in Rome (FIG. **19-16**). In his characteristic manner, Borromini plays concave off against convex forms on the upper level of the exterior of his chapel. The lower stories of the court, which frame the bottom façade, were already there when Borromini began work. Above the inward curve of the façade—its design adjusted to the earlier arcades of the court—rises a convex, drumlike structure that supports the lower parts of the dome. Powerful pilasters restrain the forces that seem to push the bulging forms outward. Buttresses above the angle pilasters curve upward to brace a tall, plastic lantern topped by a spiral that seems to fasten the structure, screwlike, to the sky.

The centralized plan (FIG. **19-17**) is that of a star, having rounded-off points and apses on all three sides. Indentations and projections along the angled, curving walls create a highly complex plan, all the elements of which are fully reflected in the interior elevation. From floor to lantern, the wall panels rise in a continuously tapering sweep that is halted only momentarily by a single, horizontal cornice (FIG. **19-18**). The dome is thus not, as in the Renaissance, a separate unit placed on the supporting block of a

19-14 FRANCESCO BORROMINI, façade of San Carlo alle Quattro Fontane, Rome, 1665–1676.

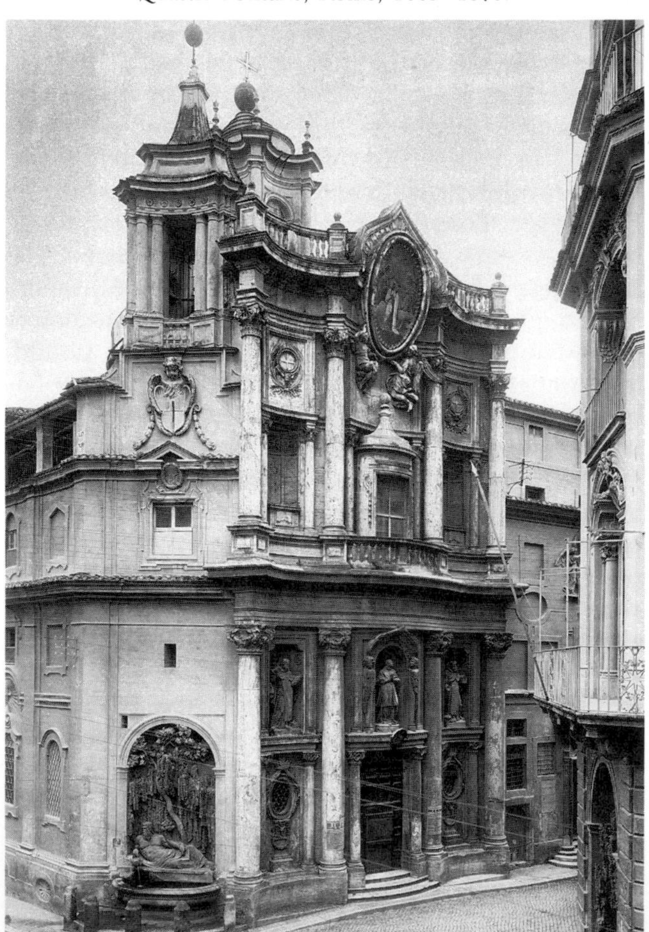

19-15 FRANCESCO BORROMINI, plan of San Carlo alle Quattro Fontane, 1638–1641.

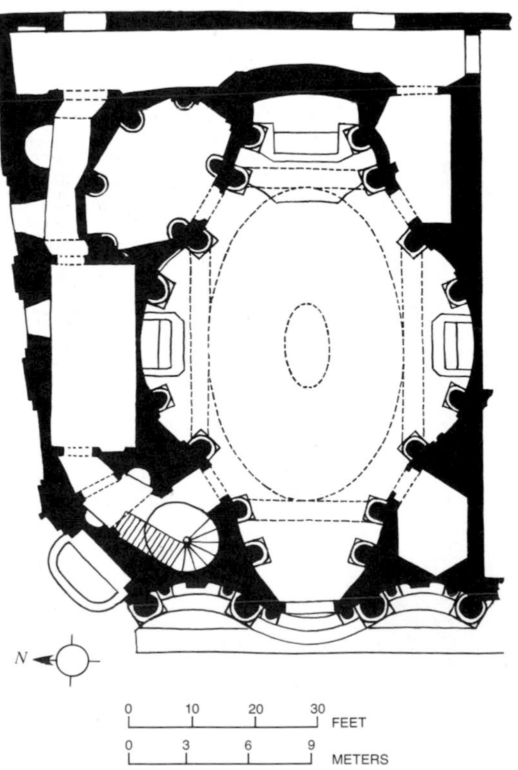

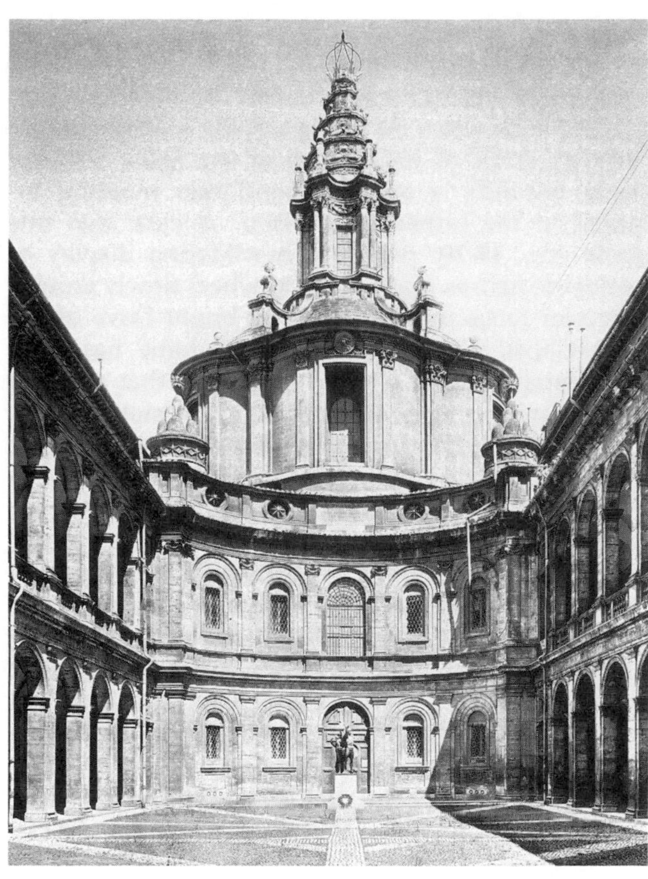

19-16 FRANCESCO BORROMINI, Chapel of St. Ivo, begun 1642. College of the Sapienza, Rome.

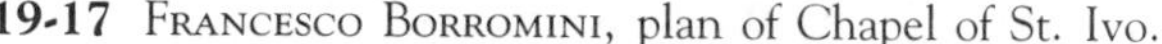

19-17 FRANCESCO BORROMINI, plan of Chapel of St. Ivo.

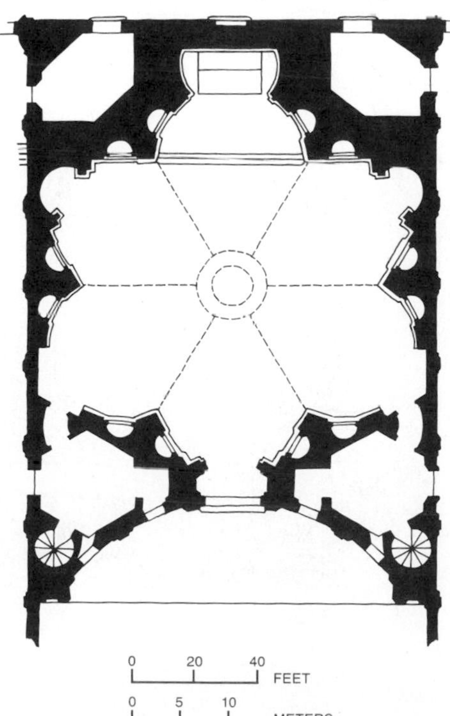

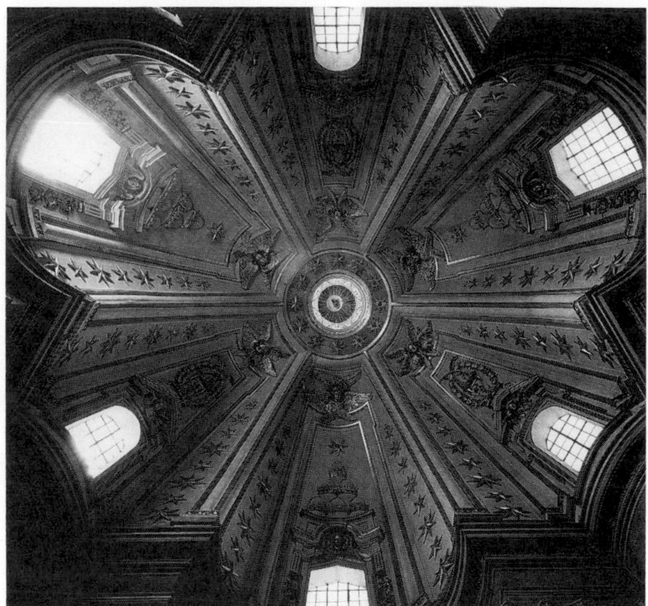

19-18 View into the dome of Chapel of St. Ivo.

building; rather it is an organic part that evolves out of and shares the qualities of the supporting walls, from which it cannot be separated. The complex, horizontal motion of the walls is transferred fully into the elevation, creating a dynamic and cohesive shell that encloses and energetically molds a scalloped fragment of universal space. Few architects have matched Borromini's ability to translate extremely complicated designs into such masterfully unified and cohesive structures as that of St. Ivo.

GUARINI AND LONGHENA

The heir to Borromini's sculptured architectural style was GUARINO GUARINI (1624–1683), a priest, mathematician, and architect who spent the last seventeen years of his life in Turin, converting that provincial Italian town into a fountainhead of architectural theories that would sweep much of Europe. In his Palazzo Carignano (FIG. **19-19**), Guarini effectively applies Borromini's principle of undulating façades. He divides his long façade into three units, the central one of which curves much like the façade of San Carlo alle Quattro Fontane (FIG. 19-14) and is flanked by two blocklike wings. This lateral, three-part division of façades, characteristic of most Baroque palazzi, probably is based on the observation that the average human instinctively can recognize up to three objects as a unit; a greater number will require the observer to count each object individually. A three-part organization of extended surfaces thus gives the artist the opportunity to introduce variety into his design without destroying its unity. It also

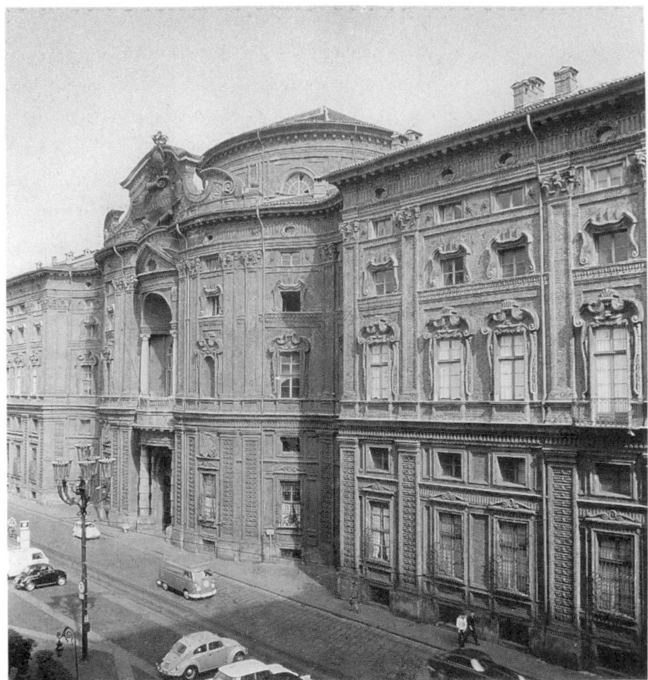

19-19 GUARINO GUARINI, Palazzo Carignano, Turin, Italy, 1679–1692.

permits him to place added emphasis on the central axis, which Guarini has done here most effectively by punching out deep cavities in the middle of his convex central block. The variety of his design is enhanced by richly textured surfaces (all executed in brick) and by pilasters, which further subdivide his units into three bays each. High and low reliefs create shadows of different intensities and add to the decorative effect, making this one of the finest façades of the late seventeenth century.

Guarini's mathematical talents must have been guiding him when he designed the extraordinarily complex dome of the Chapel of the Santa Sindone (Holy Shroud), a small, central-plan building attached to the cathedral of Turin. A view into this dome (FIG. **19-20**) reveals a bewildering display of geometric figures that appear to wheel slowly around a circular focus that contains the bright Dove of the Holy Ghost. Here, the traditional dome has been dematerialized into a series of figures that seem to revolve around each other in contrary motion; they define it, but they no longer limit the interior space. A comparison of Guarini's dome with that of the church of Sant' Eligio degli Orifici in Rome (FIG. **19-21**), attributed both to Bramante and to Raphael and reconstructed about 1600, indicates that a fundamental change has taken place. The static "dome of heaven" of architecture and philosophy has been converted into the dynamic apparition of a mathematical heaven of calculable motions.

The style of Borromini and Guarini will move across the Alps to inspire architecture in Austria and South Germany in the late seventeenth and early

19-20 GUARINO GUARINI, Chapel of the Santa Sindone, Turin, 1667–1694 (view into dome).

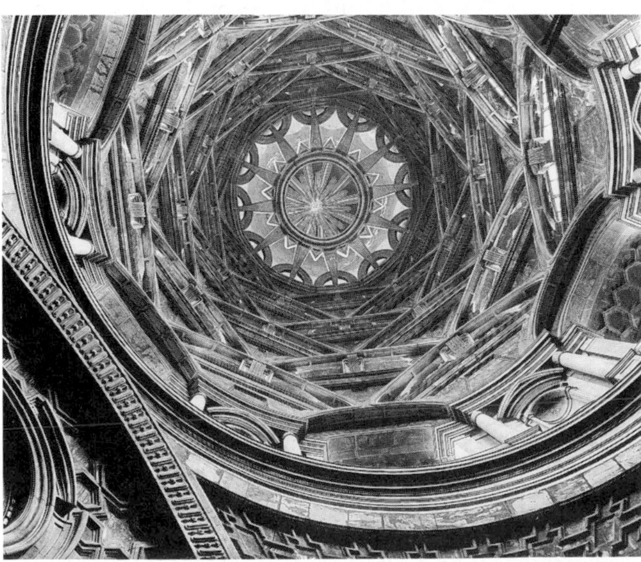

19-21 Dome of Sant' Eligio degli Orifici, Rome, attributed to BRAMANTE and RAPHAEL, c. 1509 (reconstructed c. 1600; view into dome).

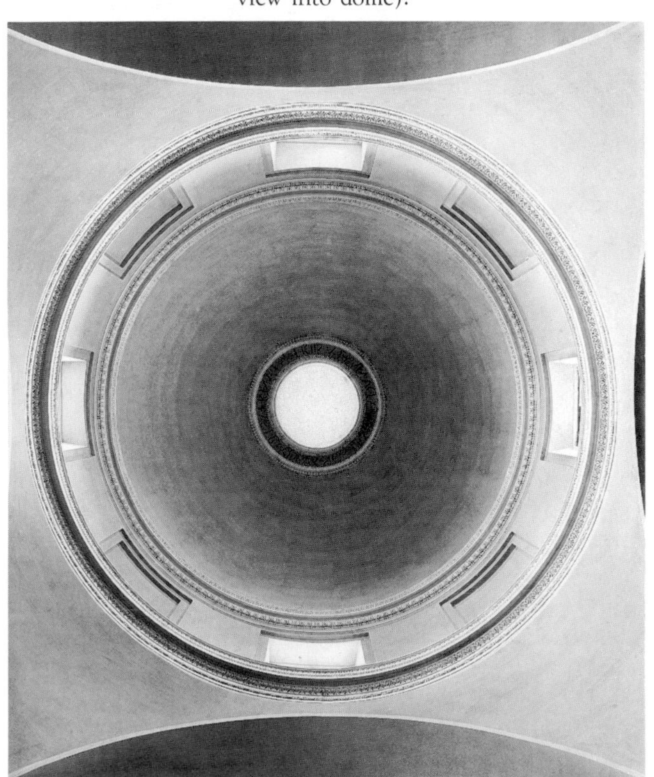

eighteenth centuries. Popular in the Catholic regions of Europe and the New World (especially in Brazil), it will exert little influence in France, where the more conservative style of Bernini will be favored.

In Venice, something of the Late Renaissance Classicism of Andrea Palladio survives, paradoxically, in the very Baroque church of Santa Maria della Salute (FIGS. **19-22** and **19-23**), often called simply the "Salute" (health). Built by BALDASSARE LONGHENA (1598–1682), the church was commissioned by the republic in thanksgiving to the Virgin Mary for ridding the city of plague. Standing at the head of the Grand Canal, the main thoroughfare of Venice, the Salute has for centuries dominated it like a gorgeous crown, the admiration of generations of travelers and artists. Longhena was well aware of the architectural value of the site; the two domes of the Salute harmonize with the family of domes in its vicinity, among them those of St. Mark's (FIG. 7-47) and of the Palladian churches of San Giorgio Maggiore (FIG. 17-53) and Il Redentore (The Redeemer). Together, they make a skyline of surpassing beauty, floating above the city or reflected in its waters in ever-changing groupings as the admiring visitor moves.

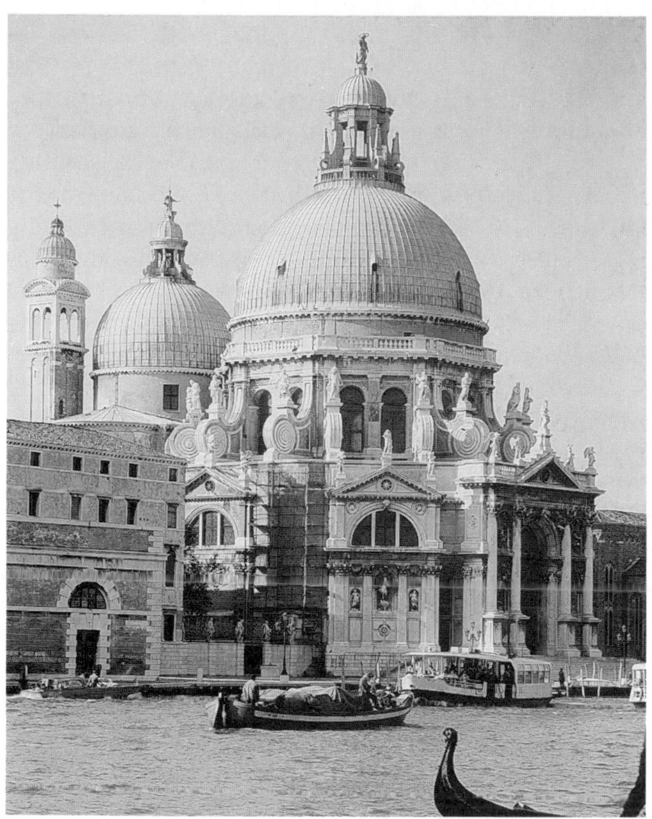

19-22 BALDASSARE LONGHENA, Santa Maria della Salute, Venice, 1631–1648 (consecrated 1687).

19-23 BALDASSARE LONGHENA, plan of Santa Maria della Salute. (After Christian Norberg-Schulz.)

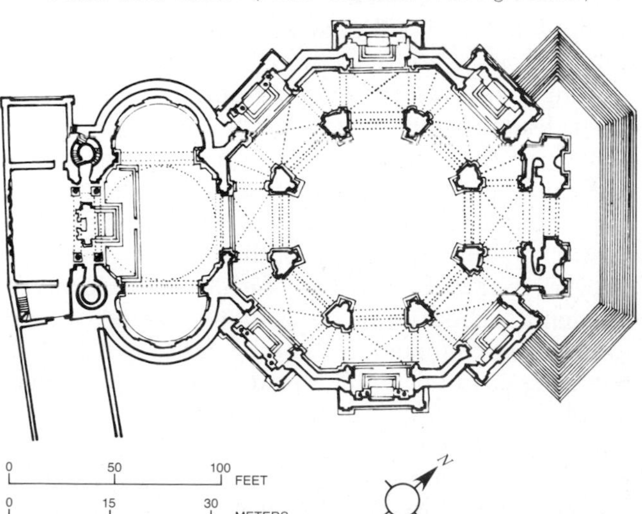

Central plans were largely foreign to Venice, and it may be that the domes and central plan of St. Mark's suggested the design of the Salute, although Longhena insisted his design had not been done before. The plan of the building (FIG. 19-23) is an octagon with an auxiliary choir. The greater of the two domes is over the octagon; the lesser is over the choir and is flanked by campaniles. Both in plan and elevation, the grouping of the masses and spaces is essentially Renaissance, without the intricacies of Bernini, Borromini, or Guarini. This observation is especially true of the interior, which has the clear arrangement, the correct orders, and the steady grey-white color of Palladio's wall-and-column features, as in San Giorgio Maggiore (FIG. 17-54). But the exterior elevation is dramatic. The façadelike faces of the octagon play counterpoint with the main façade, and the highest excitement of Baroque invention is apparent in the great scroll buttresses that seem to open organically from the main body and to sprout statuary (FIG. 19-22). The Salute is a splendid example of an architecture rooted in a native (Venetian) tradition, yet flowering successfully in a new stylistic climate.

The style of Palladio and the Venetian Renaissance could be and was transplanted into a widely different environment. While Longhena was building the Salute, the Palladian style was already being naturalized in the distant north, in England (FIG. 19-74).

Painting

Italian painters of the seventeenth century, with the possible exception of Caravaggio and the later decorators, were somewhat less adventurous than the sculptors and architects. The painters of the High Renaissance had bequeathed to them an authoritative tradition as great as that of classical antiquity. After the sixteenth century, European artists drew from both sources, and the history of painting well into the nineteenth century—that is, well into modern times—is an account of the interpretation, development, and modification of these two great traditions. The three most influential stylistic bequests of the High Renaissance were the styles of Raphael, Michelangelo, and Titian, with an additional subdominant trend inspired by Correggio. Baroque painting is the consequence of the many varied interchanges among these styles, with the Antique sometimes supplementing them and sometimes used against them. A style that seems hostile to both authorities and that is based on the assumption that the artist should paint what he sees, without regard for either the Antique or the Renaissance masters, might be called "native naturalism." This native naturalism appears as a minority style in Italy and France but plays an important role in Spain and a predominant one in the Dutch school.

THE CARRACCI AND THE BOLOGNESE ACADEMY

The Baroque gets well under way in Italian painting around the year 1600, with the decoration of the gallery of the Farnese Palace by ANNIBALE CARRACCI (1560–1609). His generation, weary of the strained artifice of Mannerism, returned for a fresh view of nature, but only after they had studied the Renaissance masters carefully. Annibale had attended an academy of art in his native city of Bologna. Founded cooperatively by members of his family, among them LODOVICO and AGOSTINO CARRACCI, the Bolognese academy is the first significant institution of its kind in the history of Western art. It was founded on the premises that art can be taught—the basis of any academic philosophy of art—and that the materials of instruction must include the Antique and the Renaissance traditions, in addition to the study of anatomy and life drawing. The Bolognese painters were long called academics, and sometimes eclectics, for they appeared to assume that the development of a correct style in painting is learned and synthetic. In any event, we can tell from the gallery of the Farnese Palace that Annibale was familiar with Michelangelo, Raphael, and Titian, and also that he could make clever, illusionistic paintings. The Farnese ceiling (FIG. **19-24**) is a brilliant and widely influential revision of High Renaissance painting. It restores the Renaissance interest in human themes and emotions, renouncing the artificialities of Mannerism to return to the study of nature, and forming a firm bridge between the Renaissance and the Baroque. The style is a vigorous, sensuous, and adroit naturalism, modified by the Classical form inherited from the masters.

The iconographical program of the ceiling is the *Loves of the Gods,* interpretations of the subtle and various stages and degrees of earthly and Divine love (see Titian's treatment of the theme in *Sacred and Profane Love,* FIG. 17-60). Despite the apparent paganism of the subjects here, we find them to have Christian overtones. The human nude is the principal motif, as it is in Michelangelo's frescoes and in much of Venetian art. Luxuriantly pagan images from classical literature, especially Ovid's *Metamorphoses,* throng the vault (FIG. 19-24), binding the composition together and filling it with exuberant and passionate life.

The scenes are arranged in panels resembling framed paintings on a wall, but here they are on the surfaces of a shallow, curved vault; the Sistine Ceiling (FIG. 17-24), of course, comes to mind, although it is not an exact source. This type of simulation of wall painting for ceiling design is called *quadro riportato* (carried picture). The great influence of the Carracci will make it fashionable for more than a century. The framed pictures are flanked by seated, nude youths, who turn their heads to gaze at the scenes above them, and by standing giants—motifs taken directly from Michelangelo's Sistine Ceiling. It is noteworthy that the chiaroscuro is not the same for both the pictures and the painted figures surrounding them. The figures inside the pictures are modeled in an even, sculptured light; the outside figures are lit from beneath, as if they were three-dimensional statues illuminated by torches in the gallery below. This interest in illusion, already manifest in the Renaissance, will continue in the grand ceiling compositions of the seventeenth century. In the crown of the vault, a long panel representing the Triumph of Bacchus is a quite ingenious mixture of Raphael and Titian and represents Annibale's adroitness in adjusting their authoritative styles to make something of his own.

Another artist trained in the Bolognese academy, GUIDO RENI (1575–1642), selected Raphael for his inspiration, as we see in his *Aurora* (FIG. **19-25**), a ceiling painting conceived in quadro riportato. *Aurora,* the dawn, leads the chariot of Apollo, while the Hours dance about it. The fresco exhibits a suave, almost swimming motion, soft modeling, and sure composition, without Raphael's sculpturesque strength. It is an intelligent interpretation of the master's style, but in every sense learned, or "academic." However, "academic" should not be burdened here with the unfortunate connotation it will later acquire as art that is mechanical, imitative, dull, and uninspired. The *Aurora* is a masterpiece of the Bolognese style and of its age. Guido was so much admired in his own day and well into the nineteenth century that he was known as "the divine Guido."

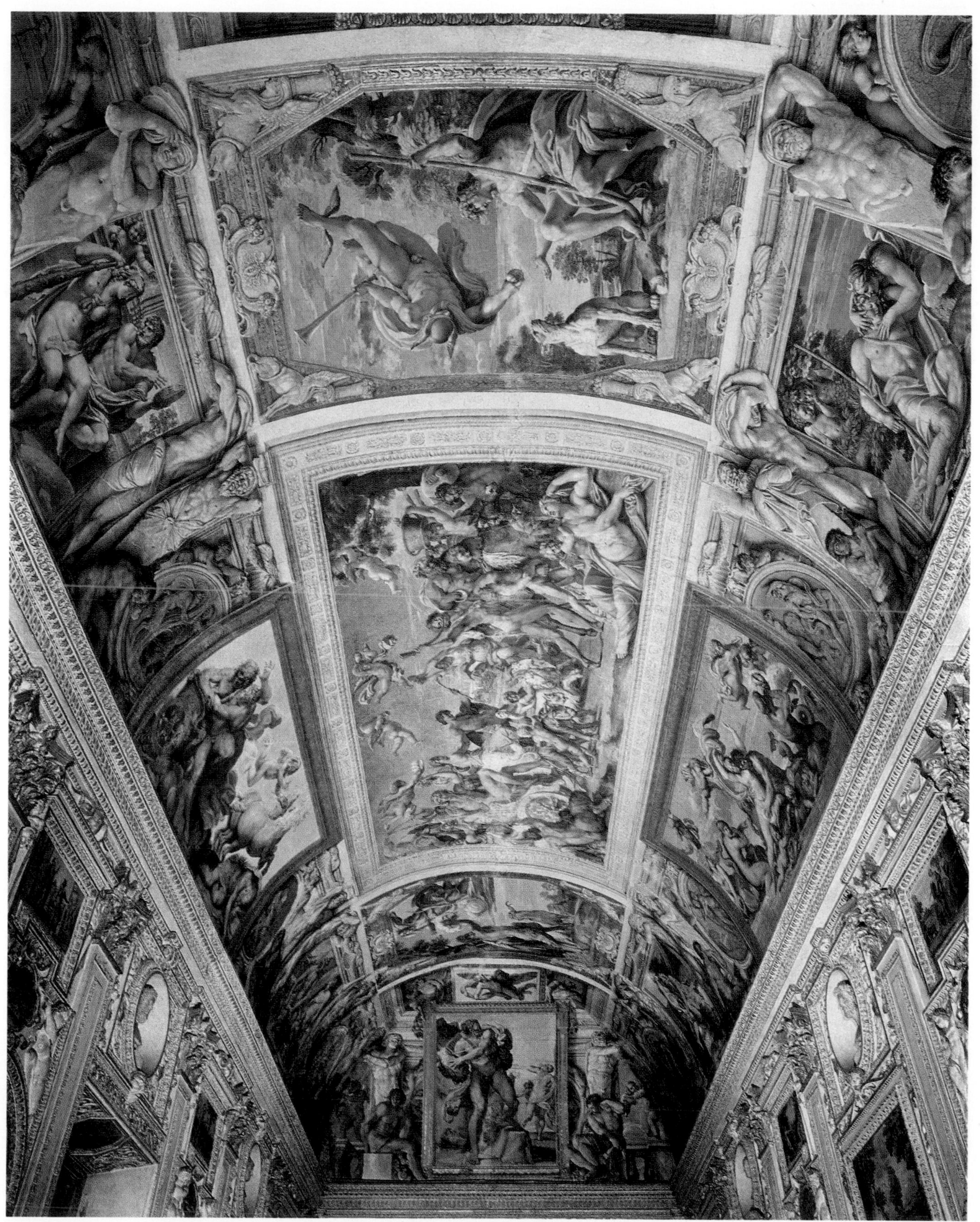

19-24 Annibale Carracci, ceiling frescoes in the Palazzo Farnese, Rome, 1597–1601.

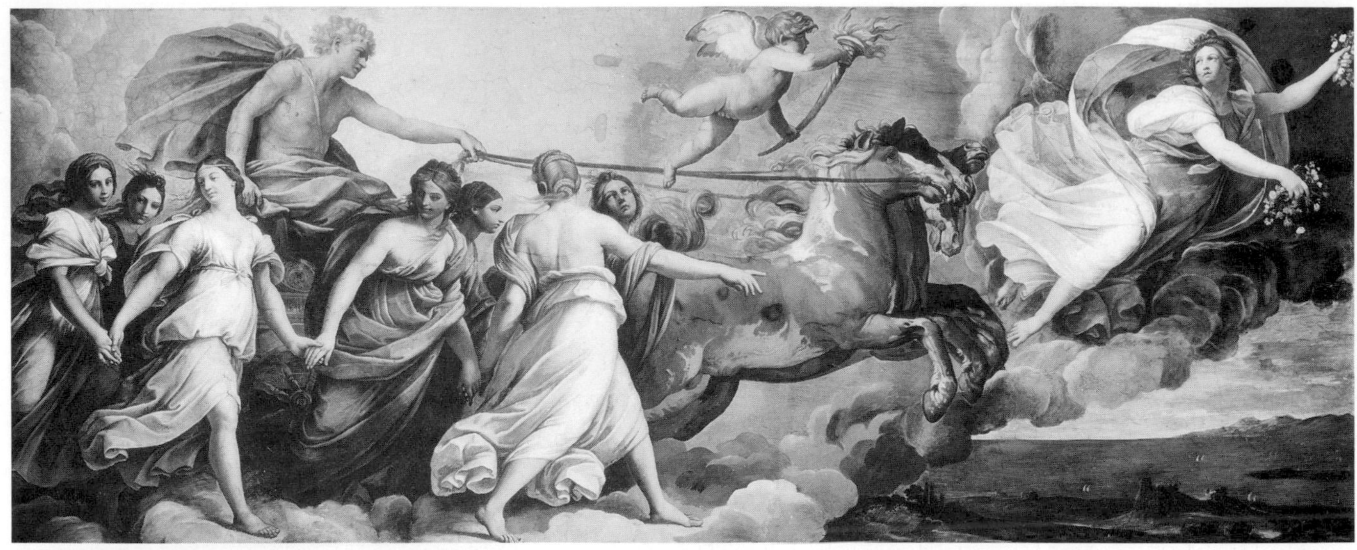

19-25 Guido Reni, *Aurora,* 1613–1614. Ceiling fresco in the Casino Rospigliosi, Rome.

Another member of the Bolognese school, Giovanni Francesco Barbieri, called Il Guercino (1591–1666), also painted a ceiling *Aurora* (fig. **19-26**), but with a very different effect. Guercino abandons the method of quadro riportato to emulate that of Veronese, whose figures are seen from below at a forty-five-degree angle (fig. 17-68). By this method, the subject of the picture is painted as if happening above our heads and seen from beneath; it is not simply a transfer of a painting from wall to ceiling. Taking his cue from the illusionistic figures in the Farnese Gallery and from its central ceiling panel (fig. 19-24), Guercino converts the ceiling into a limitless space, through which the procession sweeps past. The observer's eye is led toward the celestial parade by converging, painted extensions of the room's architecture. While the perspective may seem a little forced, Guercino's *Aurora* inspired a new wave of enthusiasm for illusionistic ceiling paintings that culminated in some of history's most stupendous decorations.

19-26 Il Guercino, *Aurora,* 1621–1623. Ceiling fresco in the Villa Ludovisi, Rome.

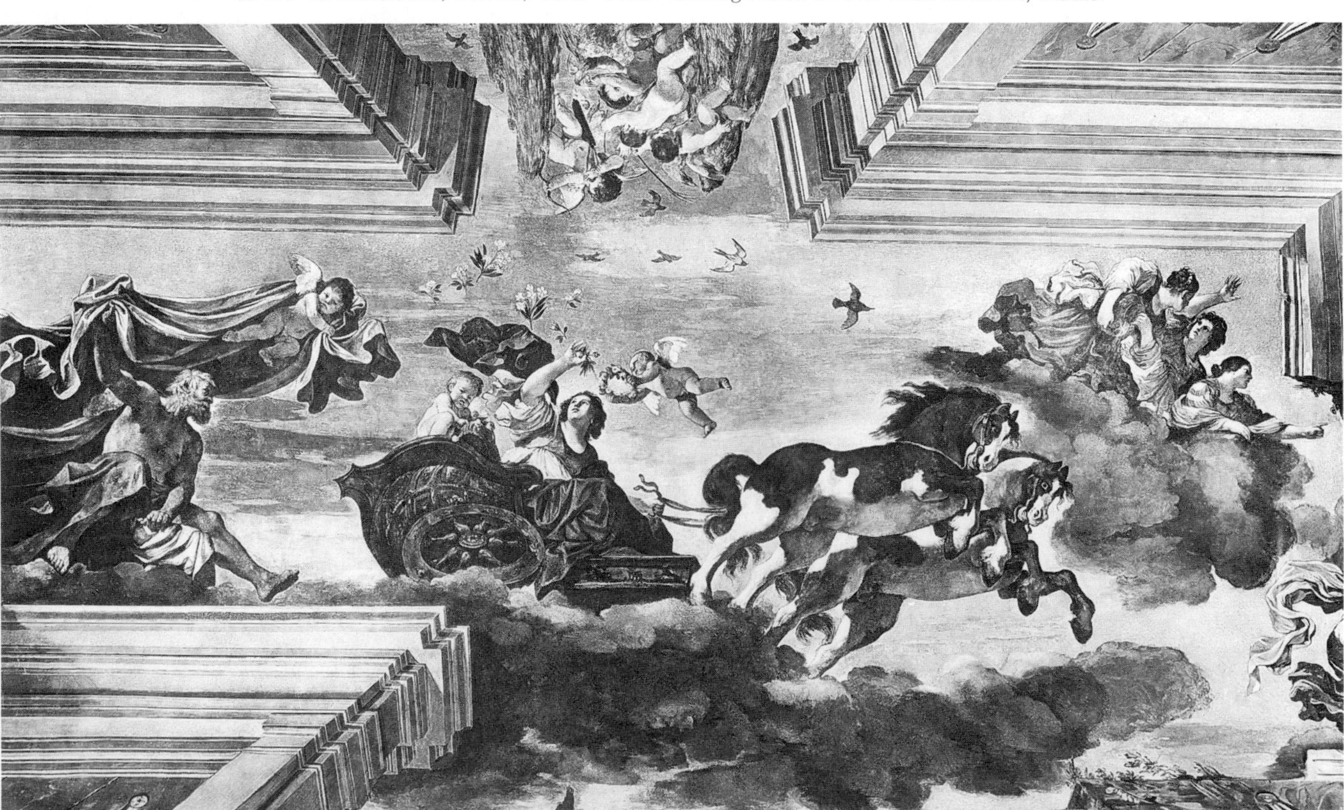

CARAVAGGIO

Although the Bolognese painters were willing to imitate nature as directly as possible, they believed that the Renaissance and the Antique masters already had captured much of nature's essence and that the works of the Renaissance and of the Antique masters would prepare them for the study of nature. Michelangelo Merisi (1571–1610), called CARAVAGGIO after the northern Italian town from which he came, thought very much otherwise. His outspoken disdain for the Classical masters (probably more vocal than real) drew bitter criticism from many painters, one of whom denounced him as the "anti-Christ of painting." Yet many paid him the genuine compliment of borrowing from his innovations.

The unconventional life of this great painter was consistent with the defiant individualism of his art. We know almost as much about Caravaggio from police records as from other documents. Violent offenses and assaults reaching to murder trace his tragic, antisocial career through restless, tormented wanderings, which, nevertheless, did not prevent him from producing a large number of astonishing works. His very association with lowlifes and outcasts may help to account for his unglorified and unfashionable view of the great themes of religion, as well as his indifference to the Renaissance ideals of beauty and decorum. In his art, he secularizes both religion and the classics, reducing them to human dramas that might be played out in the harsh and dingy settings of his time and place. He employs a cast of unflattering characters selected from the fields and the streets; these, he was proud to declare, were his only teachers—to paint from them gave him sufficient knowledge of nature.

We easily can appreciate how startling Caravaggio's methods must have been for his contemporaries when we look at *The Conversion of St. Paul* (FIG. **19-27**), which he painted for the Roman church of Santa Maria del Popolo. The scene illustrates the conversion of the Pharisee Saul by a light and a voice from Heaven (Acts 9:3–9). The saint-to-be is represented flat on his back, his arms thrown up, while an old ostler appears to maneuver the horse away from its fallen master. At first inspection, little here suggests the awful grandeur of the spiritual event that is taking place. We seem to be witnessing a mere stable accident, not a great saint overcome by a great miracle. The saint is not specifically identified; he could be anyone. The ostler is a swarthy, bearded old man, who looks well acquainted with stables. The horse

19-27 CARAVAGGIO, *The Conversion of St. Paul*, c. 1601. Oil on canvas,* approx. 7′ 6″ × 5′ 9″. Cerasi Chapel, Santa Maria del Popolo, Rome.

*Unless stated otherwise, all subsequent paintings are in oil on canvas.

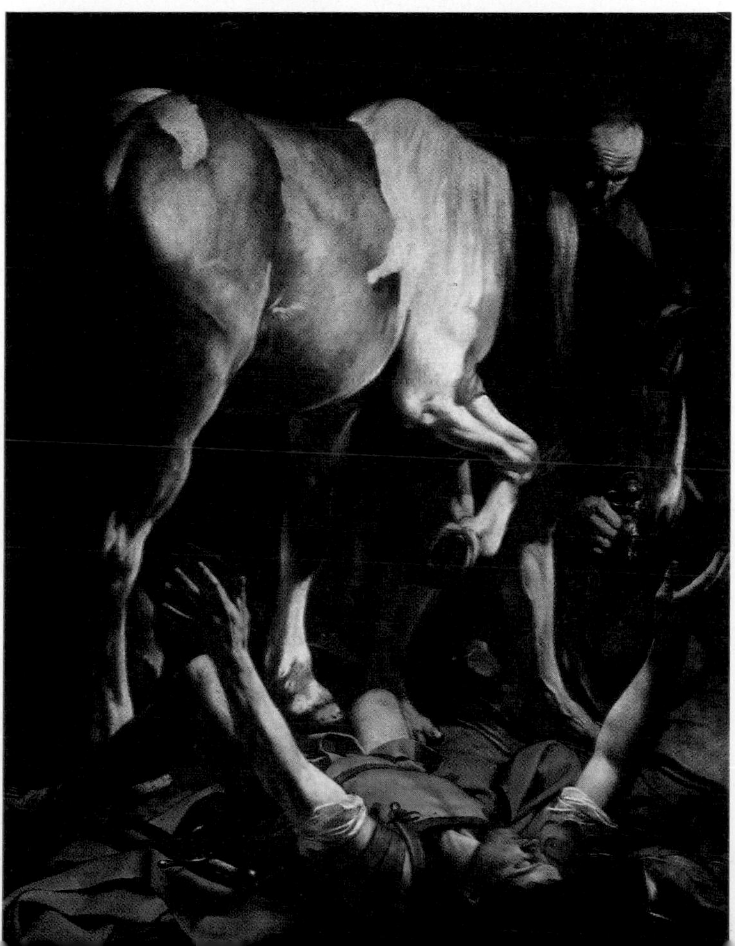

fills the picture as if it were the hero, and its explicitness and the angle from which it is viewed might betray some irreverence on the part of the artist for this subject. Although Caravaggio found numerous sympathetic patrons in both church and state, a number of his works were refused on the ground that they lacked propriety (that is to say, decorum). He sometimes appears to pay no attention to the usual dignity appointed to scenes from scripture and to go too far in dismissing the formal graces of Renaissance figure composition and color.

The fact is that, above all, Caravaggio seeks to create a convincing copy of the optical world as a vehicle of spiritual meanings; his intention in this respect is like Bernini's in the *St. Theresa* (FIG. 19-12). To this end, he uses a perspective and a chiaroscuro designed to bring viewers as close as possible to the space and action of the scene, almost as if they were participating in it. *The Conversion of St. Paul* is placed on the chapel wall and is composed with an extremely low horizon or eye level; the painting is intended to be on the viewers' line of sight as they stand at the entrance of the chapel. The sharply lighted figures are meant to be seen as emerging from the dark of the background. The actual light from windows outside the chapel functions as a kind of stage lighting for the production of a vision, analogous to the rays in Bernini's *St. Theresa.* Thus, Caravaggio, like Bernini, makes use of the world of optical experience to stage the visionary one. In *The Conversion of St. Paul,* what we see first as merely commonplace is in fact the elevation of the commonplace to the miraculous.

The stark contrast of light and dark was the feature of Caravaggio's style that first shocked and then fascinated his contemporaries. The sharp and sudden relief it gives to the forms and the details of form emphasizes their reality in a way that an even or subtly modulated light never could. Dark next to light is naturally dramatic; we do not need a director of stage lighting to tell us this. Caravaggio's device, a profound influence on European art, has been called *tenebrism* (Italian: *tenebroso*) or the "dark manner." This technique goes quite well with material that is realistic and is another mode of Baroque illusionism by which the eye is almost forced to acknowledge the visual reality of what it sees. Although tenebrism is widespread in Baroque art, it will have its greatest consequences in Spain and the Netherlands.

A contemporary observed that Caravaggio had "abandoned beauty and was interested in depicting reality," and Giovanni Pietro Bellori, the most influential critic of the age and an admirer of the Carracci, wrote: "Caravaggio deserves great praise, as he was the only one who attempted to imitate nature as opposed to the general trend in which painters imitated other painters." The instrumentalities of this unorthodox realism find full orchestration in Caravaggio's *Death of the Virgin* (FIG. **19-28**). The painting, refused as an altarpiece for Santa Maria della Scala in Rome (on the grounds of irreverence), represents the dead Virgin Mary, mourned by the disciples and friends of Christ. The Virgin is indeed unceremoniously laid out in the awkward stiffness of death, her body swollen, limbs uncomposed, and feet uncovered (the last feature considered indecent at the time). Contemporaries complained that Caravaggio had used as his model for the mother of Christ the corpse of a young woman who had drowned. Around the dead woman, in attitudes of genuine if uncouth grief, without rhetoric or declamation, Caravaggio portrays the customary plebeian types that he usually casts in his pictorial dramas of reality. The drawn curtain emphasizes the stagelike setting, into which the grouping of the figures invites the viewer as participant. The harsh light plunges into the space from a single source, shattering the darks into broken

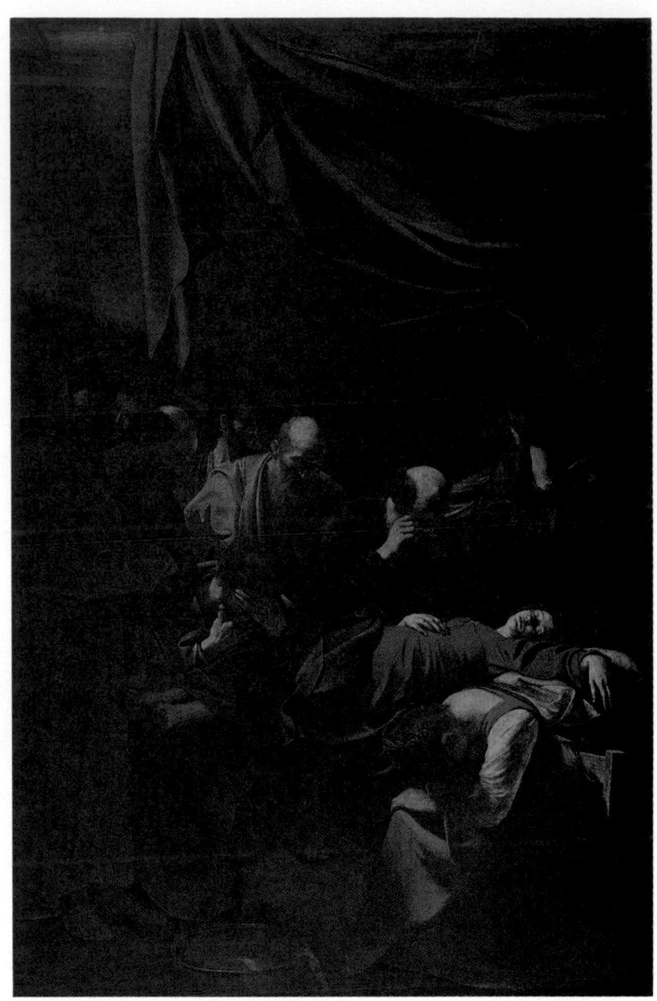

19-28 CARAVAGGIO, *Death of the Virgin,* 1605–1606. Approx. 12′ × 8′. Louvre, Paris.

areas of illumination that reveal the coarse materialities of the scene. But again (as in *The Conversion of St. Paul,* although in a different way) we can read the artist's interpretation not as diminishing the spiritual import of the theme but rather as informing it with a simple, honest, unadorned piety that is entirely sincere—the very piety that moves the humble watchers of the dead to tears.

DOMENICHINO AND GENTILESCHI

One would think that Annibale and Ludovico Carracci and their colleagues at the Bolognese academy would have carefully avoided the dangerous art of Caravaggio. To the contrary, many borrowed from it (some more than others), unconsciously integrating it into the tradition and into their own work. *The Last Communion of St. Jerome* (FIG. **19-29**) is a painting so typical of the Catholic Baroque—so expressive of the Counter-Reformation and its ideals—that we can hardly find its equal as a document of the times. The artist is another Bolognese disciple, DOMENICHINO (Domenico Zampieri, 1581–1641). In a Renaissance loggia that opens into a Venetian landscape background, St. Jerome, propped up to receive the viaticum (Eucharist), is surrounded by sorrowing friends. The realism of Caravaggio stamps the old man's sagging features, his weakened, once-rugged body, and the faces of at least three of his attendants and of the grave old priest. The sharpened darks and lights are also out of Caravaggio; the general composition, the architecture, the floating putti, and the turbaned spectator echo Titian, Correggio, and the mood of the High Renaissance. A painting like this would seem to be, of necessity, an academic pastiche, but all of its borrowed elements are synthesized successfully in a rare, effective unity. Domenichino's *St. Jerome* is a successful "school" picture, nourished as it is by all the sources, traditional and contemporary, available to him.

19-29 DOMENICHINO, *The Last Communion of St. Jerome,* 1614. Approx. 13′ 9″ × 8′ 5″. Vatican Museums, Rome.

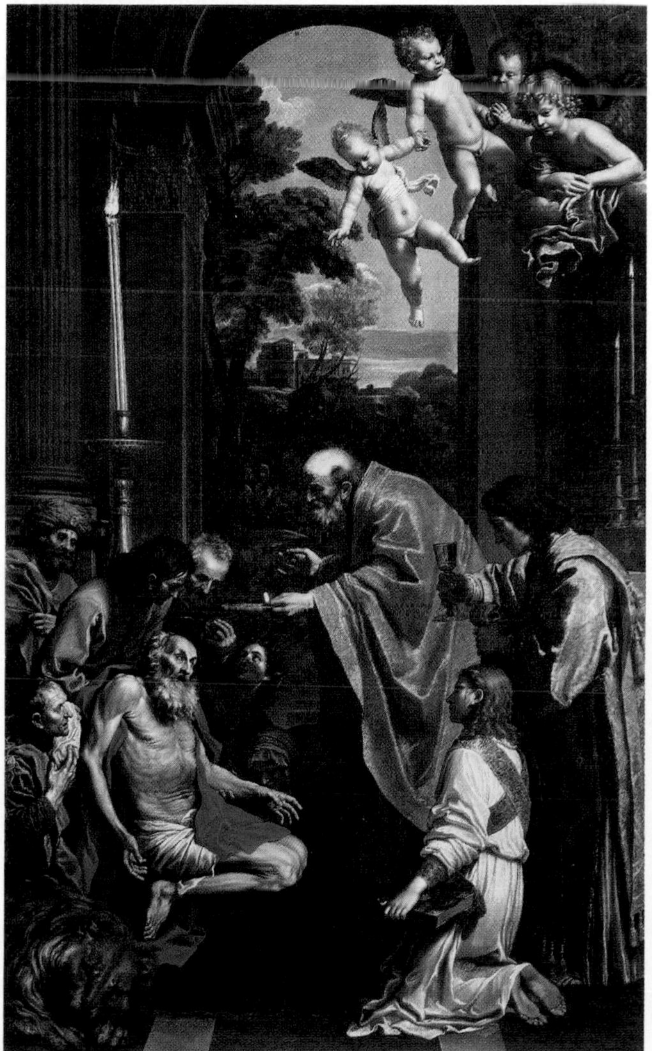

We already have mentioned the spread of Caravaggio's style outside Italy. Of course, he had many followers within its borders also, and they were artists more directly in tune with his message than eclectics like Domenichino. One of the best, whose work is increasingly appreciated by many modern critics, is ARTEMISIA GENTILESCHI (1593–1653). Gentileschi was instructed by her artist father, ORAZIO, who was himself strongly influenced by Caravaggio. Her successful career, pursued in Florence, Venice, Naples, and Rome, helped to propagate Caravaggio's manner throughout the peninsula. In her *Judith and Maidservant with the Head of Holofernes* (FIG. **19-30**), we find the dark manner (tenebroso) and what might be called the "dark" subject matter favored by the "Caravaggisti," the painters of "night pictures." The heroism of Judith, often a subject in Italian painting and sculpture, is depicted here. The story, which is told in an Apocryphal work of the Old Testament, the Book of Judith, relates the delivery of Israel from its enemy Holofernes. Having succumbed to the charms of Judith, Holofernes invites her to his tent for the night. When he has fallen asleep, Judith cuts off his head. Here, the act performed, her maidservant is putting the severed head in a sack. The action takes place in a curtained, oppressively closed space. The atmosphere of menace and horror is thickened by the heavy darks, scarcely relieved by the feeble candle, the sole source of light. Yet the light falls on the courtly splendor of the women's raiment and exhibits forms and characters intended by the artist to be convincingly real. The light is interrupted dramatically by Judith's hand, which casts a shadow on her face. This device is a favorite of the "night painters": a single source of illumination within the painting—partly or wholly concealed by an object in front of it or, as in

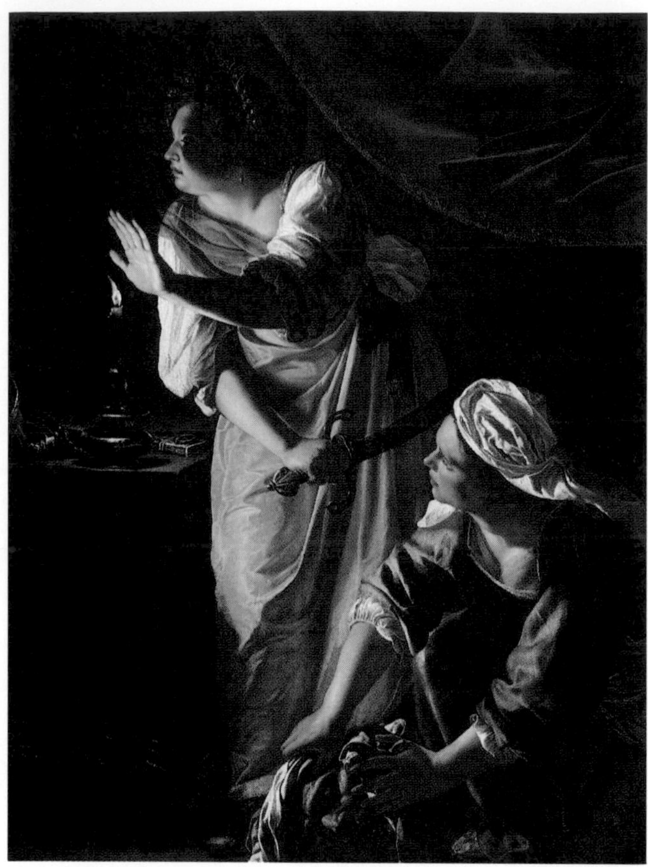

19-30 ARTEMISIA GENTILESCHI, *Judith and Maidservant with the Head of Holofernes,* c. 1625. Approx. 6′ × 4′ 8″. Detroit Institute of the Arts (gift of Leslie H. Green).

this case, intercepted by an object—casting an abrupt shadow. The effect is like opening the shutter of a lantern for a brief moment in a pitch-black cellar where unspeakable things are happening.

LANDSCAPE: ANNIBALE CARRACCI AND ROSA

The Carracci and Caravaggio powerfully influenced the art of figure painting for two centuries, but the Carracci largely determined the dominant course taken by landscape painting over the same period. In his *Flight into Egypt* (FIG. **19-31**), Annibale Carracci created the "ideal" or "classical" landscape. Adopted and developed in France by Nicolas Poussin and Claude Lorrain (FIGS. 19-61 and 19-62), this kind of landscape would come to prevail as the accepted pictorial representation of nature ordered by Divine law and human reason. The roots of the style are in the landscape backgrounds of Venetian paintings of the Renaissance (compare FIGS. 19-31 and 17-59). Tranquil hills and fields, quietly gliding streams, serene skies, unruffled foliage, shepherds with their flocks—all the props of the pastoral scene and mood—expand to fill the picture space. They are introduced regularly by a screen of trees in the foreground, dark against the even light of the sky. Attenuated streams or terraces, carefully placed one above the other, make a compositional direction left or right through the terrain. In the middle ground, many landscape artists place compositions of architecture (as in FIG. 19-31) —walled towns or citadels, towers, temples, monu-

19-31 ANNIBALE CARRACCI, *Flight into Egypt,* 1603–1604. Approx. 4′ × 7′ 6″. Galleria Doria Pamphili, Rome.

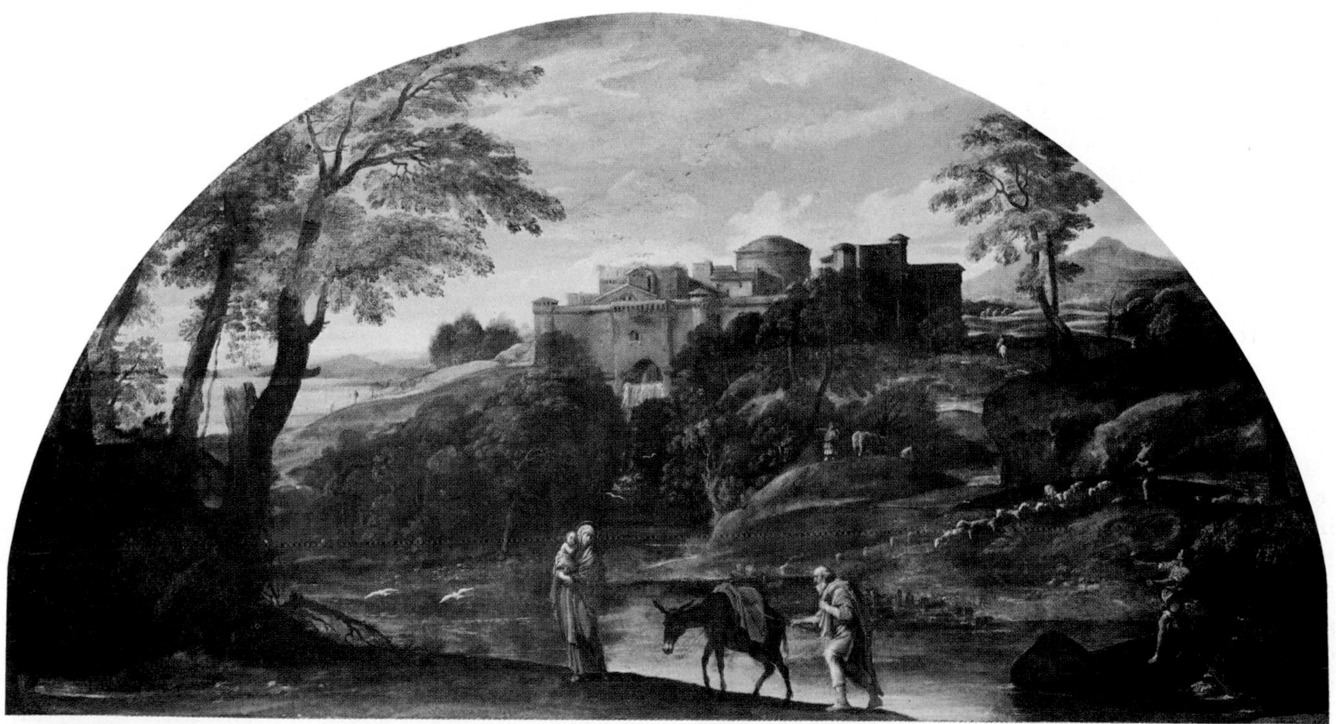

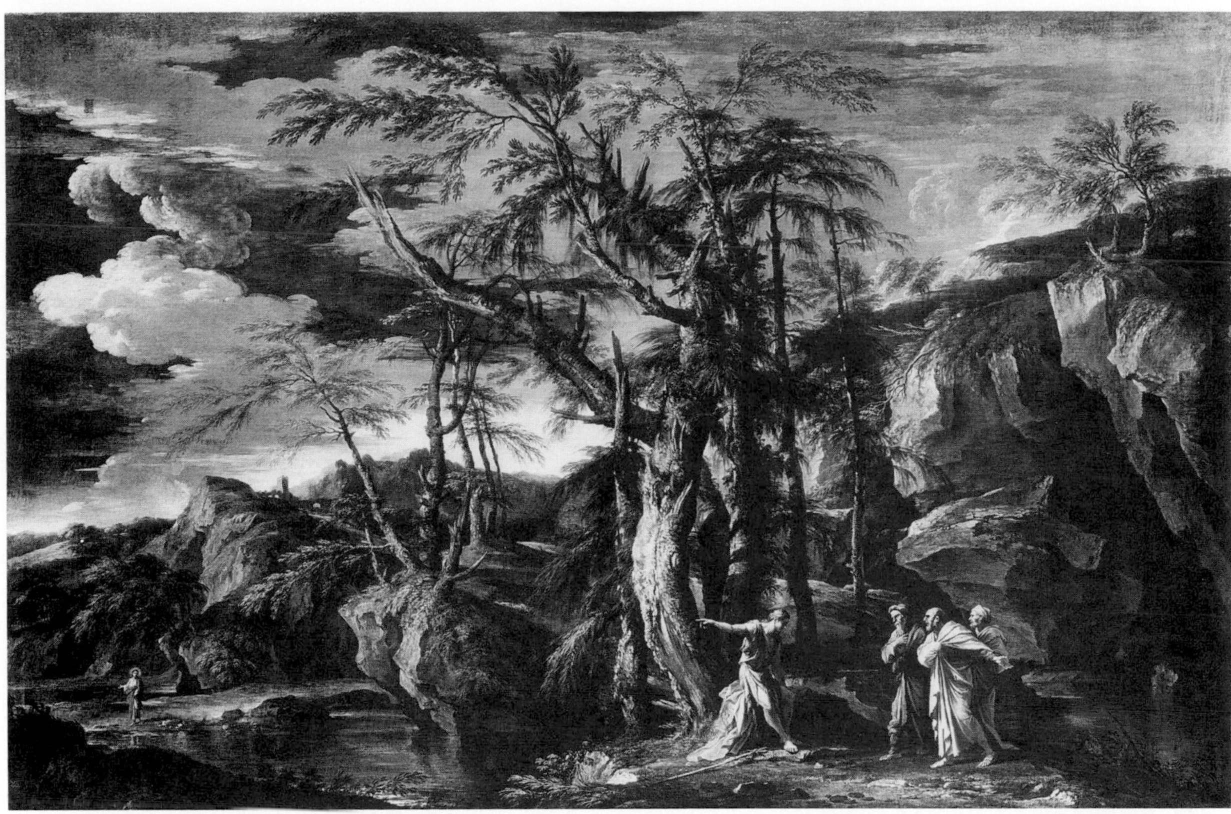

19-32 SALVATOR ROSA, *St. John the Baptist in the Wilderness,* c. 1640. Approx. 5′ 8″ × 8′ 6″. Glasgow Art Gallery and Museum, Scotland.

mental tombs, villas—the constructed environment of idealized antiquity and the idyllic life, undisturbed by the passions. The subjects are drawn from religious or heroic story; here, Mary, with the Christ Child, and St. Joseph wend their slow way to Egypt, after having been ferried across a stream (Matthew 2:13–14). The figures shrink in scale and importance, relative to the landscape, and are sometimes simply its excuse. Now, in the seventeenth century, landscape comes fully into its own as a major subject for the painter.

But there are landscape types other than the Classical during the seventeenth century. A landscape by SALVATOR ROSA (1615–1673), *St. John the Baptist in the Wilderness* (FIG. **19-32**), contrasts dramatically with Carracci's *Flight into Egypt.* Rosa's painting also has a sacred theme, and the figures in it are subordinate to the landscape, but the two paintings obviously have nothing else in common. Instead of the calm of idealized nature in Annibale's landscape, in Rosa, we have nature in a violent mood, a savage wilderness abandoned by Heaven. A ragged tree, blasted by generations of thunderbolts, writhes before a chaos of barren rocks. For Rosa, nature appears malevolent, the home only of wild beasts, of holy or of desperate men. The broken surfaces, jagged contours, and harsh textures in confused arrangement here should be compared with the smooth volumes and contours and regular placement of forms that characterize the Classical landscape. The alternative style of Rosa will exercise a great deal of influence on the next century's taste for the "picturesque"—sublime and awesome scenes, filled with terror and foreboding, which will indulge the Romantic temperament and fuel its enthusiasm.

PERSPECTIVE ILLUSIONISM

The development of landscape painting was contemporary with that of ceiling painting, the latter form being stimulated anew by the large, new churches of Baroque Rome. The problems associated with ceiling painting are, of course, special. Looking *up* at a painting is different from simply looking *at* a painting. The experience of looking at what is above us carries with it an element of awe, particularly when we are viewing something located at considerable height. Guercino recognized this when he painted his *Aurora* (FIG. 19-26), but Guido Reni apparently did not. In his *Aurora* fresco (FIG. 19-25), he either did not realize the special power of ceiling painting, or perhaps preferred or was required to use the quadro riportato method. The Baroque artist found a

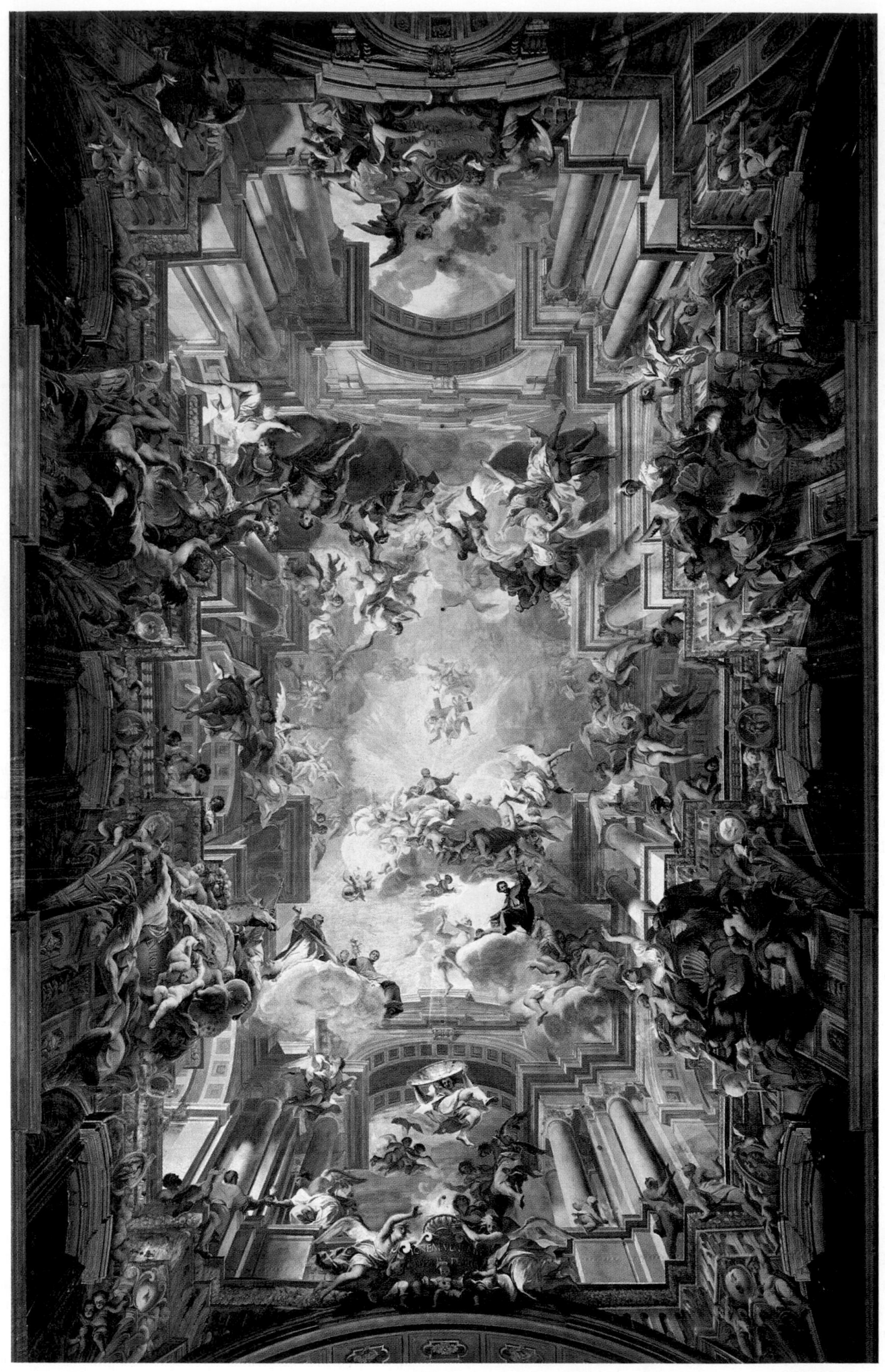

19-33 Fra Andrea Pozzo, *The Glorification of St. Ignatius,* 1691–1694. Ceiling fresco in the nave of Sant' Ignazio, Rome.

ceiling surface high above the ground a natural field for the projection of visual illusion. The devout Christian, thinking of Heaven as "up," must be overwhelmed with emotion when, looking up, he sees its image before his eyes. In the Sistine Ceiling, Michelangelo made no attempt to project an image of the skies opening into Heaven; rather, he represented an epic narrative of events of no physical place or time that could be read almost as well from walls as from ceilings. The *illusion* of bodies actually soaring above was of no interest to him; the truth of certain events in the history of Genesis was, and these events and figures could be shut off in their own compartments, self-contained.

A Baroque master of ceiling decoration like Fra Andrea Pozzo (1642–1709) takes an entirely different approach. A lay brother of the Jesuit order and a master of perspective, on which he wrote an influential treatise, Pozzo designed and executed the vast ceiling fresco depicting *The Glorification of St. Ignatius* (FIG. **19-33**) for the church of Sant' Ignazio in Rome. This fresco is indeed the culmination of the di sotto in sù (from below upwards) experiments of Mantegna (FIG. 16-65) and Correggio (FIG. 17-37). The artist intends to create the illusion that Heaven is opening up above the heads of the congregation—indeed, of the very congregation that fills this church of Sant' Ignazio. For, in painted illusion, Pozzo continues the actual architecture of the church into the vault, so that the roof seems to be lifted off, as Heaven and earth commingle and St. Ignatius is carried to the waiting Christ in the presence of figures personifying the four corners of the world. A metal plate in the nave floor marks the standpoint for the whole perspective illusion. Looking up from this point, the observer takes in the celestial-terrestrial scene as one, for in Pozzo's design the two are meant to fuse without the interruption of a boundary. To achieve his visionary effects, the artist employs all means offered by architecture, sculpture, and painting and unites them in a fusion that surpasses even the Gothic effects of total integration.

Sound, as well as light, is a vehicle of ecstasy and vision in the Baroque experience. We know that churches were designed with acoustical effect in mind, and, in a Baroque church filled with Baroque music, the power of both light and sound would be vastly augmented. Through simultaneous stimulation of both the visual and auditory senses, the faithful might be transported into a trancelike state that would indeed, in the words of Milton, "bring all Heaven before [their] eyes." But this transport always would have to be effected by physical means; although the devout in the Middle Ages were able to find the vision within, in the Baroque period they demanded that that mystery be made visible to the outward sight. To be credible, Heaven must more and more visually resemble the domain of earth. Dante could see Heaven in a dream, but Pozzo wanted to see it unfold above him while he was awake and walking in a church. Medieval humanity aspired to Heaven; Baroque humanity wanted Heaven to come down to their station, where they might see it, or even inspect it. Optical vision is the supreme faculty in seventeenth-century art and science.

Baroque expansiveness is expressed not only in the characteristic movement toward the infinite horizontal but in an emphasis on the vertical as well. The heavens are more and more within reach; Galileo and Newton will penetrate them to find the laws of their movement. The clouds of Heaven are not simply the seat of angels; seventeenth-century scientists discover that they are water vapor. The bright air through which light is propagated has density and weight. As the heavens become physical, human beings begin to dream of taking possession of them someday by flight—not the flight of the soul, but the flight of the body. The Baroque period transforms spirit into matter in motion, as Pozzo's ceiling relates.

SPAIN

In Spain, as in the other countries of Europe, Italianate Mannerism was adopted in the sixteenth century and cast off in the Baroque period. But along with Mannerism, Spain seemed to reject most of what the Italian Renaissance stood for, just as it would reject, for a long time, the scientific revolution and the Enlightenment. Since the Middle Ages, Spain had maintained a proud isolation from the events of Europe—an isolation that today has apparently ended.

In the art of El Greco, we have seen the mystical side of the Spanish character (FIG. 18-59). The hard, unsentimental realism that is the other side appears in the painting of José de Ribera (1591–1652), who, because he emigrated to Naples as a young man and settled there, is sometimes called by his Italian nickname, Lo Spagnoletto, "the little Spaniard." The realism of his style, a mixture of a native Spanish strain and the "dark manner" of Caravaggio, gives shock value to Ribera's often brutal themes, which express at once the harsh times of the Counter-Reformation and a Spanish taste for the representation of courageous resistance to pain. His *Martyrdom of St. Bartholomew* (FIG. **19-34**) is grim and dark in subject and form. St. Bartholomew, who suffered the torture of being skinned alive, is being hoisted into position by

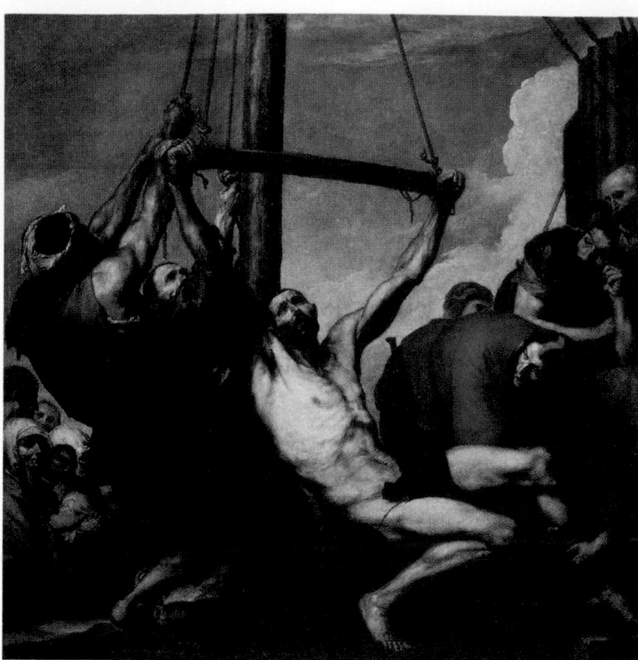

19-34 José de Ribera, *The Martyrdom of St. Bartholomew,* c. 1639. Approx. 92⅛" × 92⅛". Museo del Prado, Madrid.

19-35 Francisco de Zurbarán, *St. Francis in Meditation,* c. 1639. Approx. 60" × 39". Reproduced by courtesy of the Trustees of the National Gallery, London.

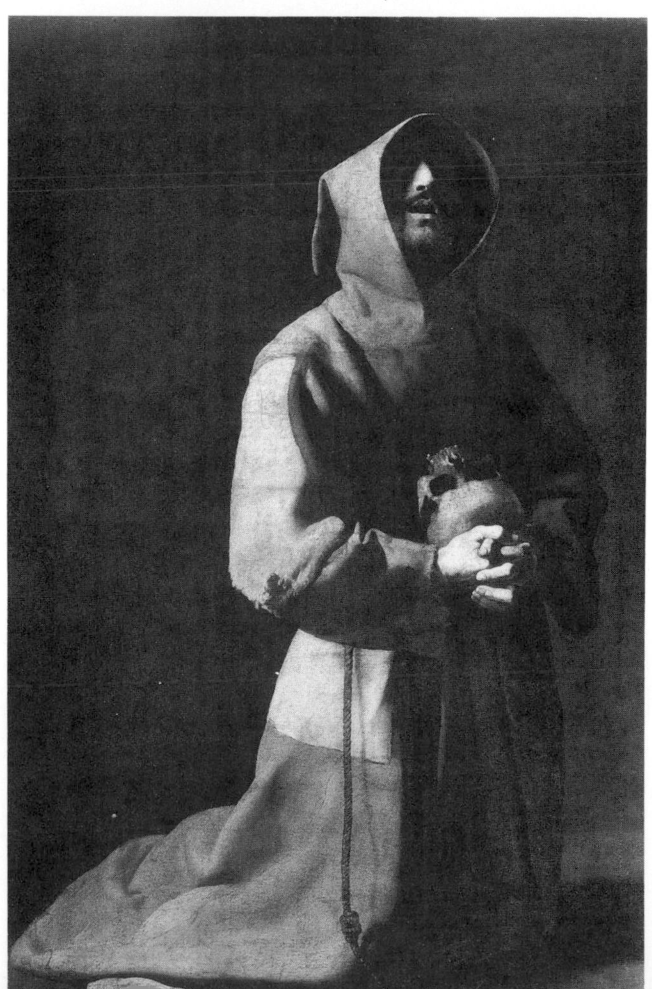

his executioners. The saint's rough, heavy body and swarthy, plebeian features express a kinship between him and his tormentors, who are members of the same cast of characters we found in the painting of Caravaggio and the Neapolitan school he so strongly influenced. In this painting, Ribera scorns idealization of any kind, and we have the uncomfortable feeling that he is recording rather than imagining the grueling scene. In an age of merciless religious fanaticism, torture, as a means of saving stubborn souls, was a common and public spectacle.

Francisco de Zurbarán (1598–1664) softens realism with an admixture of the mystical. His principal subjects are austere saints, represented singly in devotional attitudes and usually sharply lighted from the side. He shows us *St. Francis in Meditation* (fig. **19-35**), his uplifted face almost completely shadowed by his cowl, clutching a skull to his body. The skull is the *memento mori,* a constant reminder to the contemplative individual of his own mortality. The bare, unfurnished setting and the stark light and somber dark are the bleak environment of this entranced soul. We see enough to read this as an image of rapt meditation—the parted lips, the tensely locked fingers, the rigid attitude of a devotee utterly unaware of his surroundings and mystically in contact with God. Here, Zurbarán gives us a personification of the fierce devotion of Catholic Spain.

VELÁZQUEZ

In the Baroque age, visions and the visual go together. Diego Velázquez (1599–1660), an artist who set aside visions in the interest of what is given to the eye in the optical world, stands among the great masters of visual realism. Although he painted religious pictures, he was incapable of idealism or high-flown rhetoric, and his sacred subjects are bluntly real. Velázquez, who trained in Seville, came to the attention of the king, Philip IV, as a young man, and became the court painter at Madrid, where, save for two extended trips to Italy and a few excursions, he remained for the rest of his life. His close personal relationship with Philip and his high office of marshal of the palace gave him prestige and a rare opportunity to fulfill the promise of his genius with a variety of artistic assignments.

In an early work, *Los Borrachos* (*The Drinkers,* fig. **19-36**), Velázquez shows his cool independence of the ideals of Renaissance and Baroque Italy in a native naturalism that has the strength and something of the look of Caravaggio. Commissioned to paint Bacchus among his followers, presenting them the liberating gift of wine, Velázquez seems to mock Classical conventions in both theme and form. He burlesques the stately, Classical Bacchic scenes, making the god

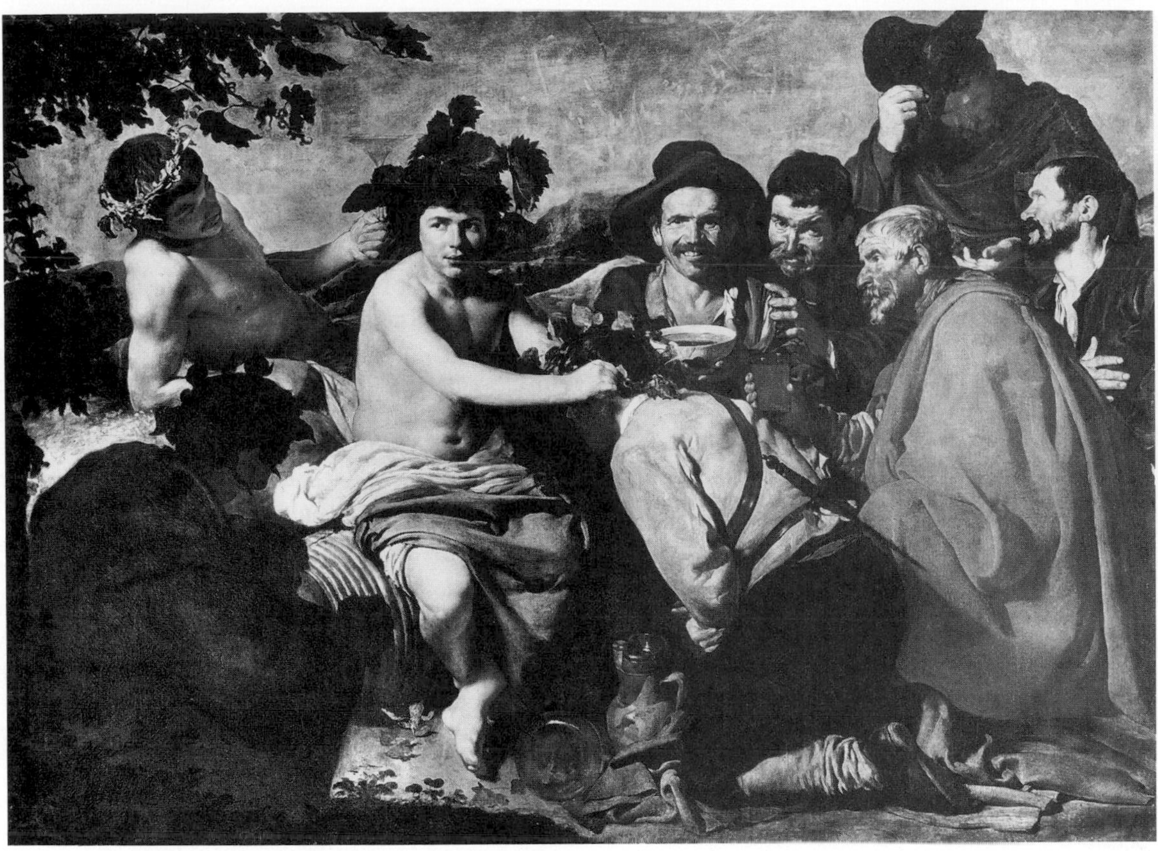

19-36 DIEGO VELÁZQUEZ, *Los Borrachos,* c. 1628. Approx. 5′ 6″ × 7′ 6″. Museo del Prado, Madrid.

a mischievous young *bravo,* stripped to the waist, crowning a wobbly tippler who kneels before him. The rest of the company is of the same type: weather-beaten, shabby roisterers of the tavern crowd, who grin and jape at the event uncouthly, enjoying the game for what it is. Painting the crude figures in strong light and dark that is evenly distributed so as not to obscure them, Velázquez makes sharp characterizations of each person, showing not only his instinct for portraiture but a Baroque interest in human "types." And, typically Spanish, he caricatures, through realism, an Italianate subject that ordinarily would be idealized. Enrique Lafuente, a modern critic, states the Spanish attitude, as he perceives it:

> Spain refuses to accept the basic ideas which inspire the Italian Renaissance because they are repugnant to its sense of the life of the Spanish man. The Spaniard knows that reality is not Idea, but Life. . . . The supreme value of life is linked with experience and the moral values that are based on personality. Idea, beauty, formal perfection, are abstractions and nothing more. Art, in its turn, is bound to concern itself with realities and not with dreams.*

*Enrique Lafuente, *Velázquez* (New York: Oxford University Press, 1943), p. 6.

To Velázquez, as to many Spanish artists, the academic styles of Baroque Italy must have seemed pretentious and insincere, not to say pagan. He turned away from them to concentrate instead on the world before his eyes.

One could hardly find in art a better example of Lafuente's dictum that "reality is not Idea, but Life" than Velázquez's portrait of *Juan de Pareja* (FIG. **19-37**). At the height of his powers, Velázquez painted his assistant when they were in Rome together in 1650. He was intending to paint a portrait of Pope Innocent X, a patron of Bernini, and he did the study of Pareja as a kind of trial run. Today, we probably would agree that it is a masterpiece in its own right. The work was exhibited in the Pantheon and drew the admiration of the many artists in Rome, Italian and foreign alike. They perceived in it an almost incredible knowledge of the structure of appearance, a matchless technique of execution, and an eloquent simplicity of composition that rejected conventional Baroque props and rhetoric. The apparent simplicity of the formal means matches the simplicity of presentation. Placed before an entirely neutral ground, Pareja looks directly at us with a calm dignity and quiet pride, a man perfectly self-contained. His character

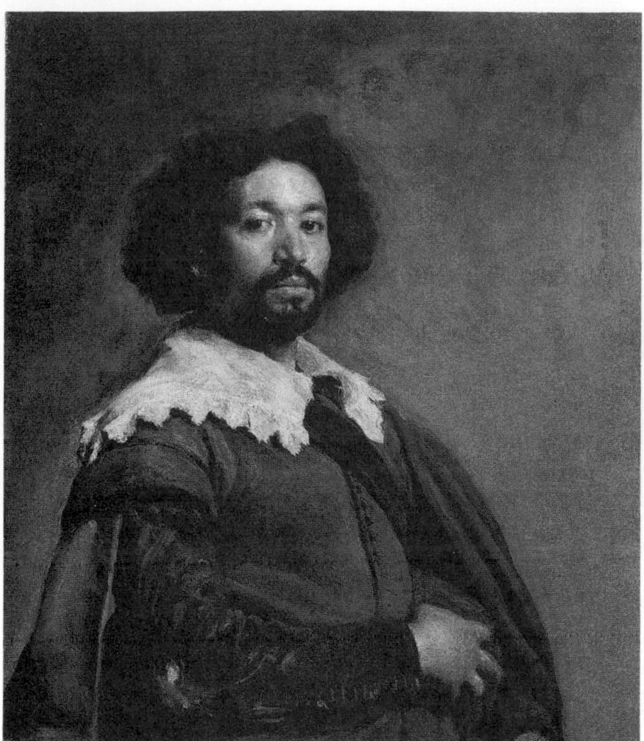

19-37 DIEGO VELÁZQUEZ, *Juan de Pareja,* 1649–1650. Approx. 33″ × 28″. Metropolitan Museum of Art, New York.

gives him a natural poise, utterly without arrogance or affectation. His level gaze, the easy gesture of arm and hand, and his erect carriage place him directly in front of us, and Velázquez introduces him.

Velázquez's uncanny power of penetration of the form and meaning before him, though in some ways unique, was not entirely untaught. He had studied the works of other artists carefully and was fully aware of the achievements of the great masters like Michelangelo and the Venetians. He knew the latter from the king's collections, of which he had charge, and he also studied them in Italy, where he journeyed at the suggestion of the great Flemish painter Peter Paul Rubens, whom he met when the older Rubens was copying the Venetians in the collections at the Madrid court. His studies in Italy did not make a "Romanist" of Velázquez, however. Their most notable effects were a softening of his earlier, somewhat heavy-handed realism (seen in *Los Borrachos*) and a lighter palette, which gave his paintings brighter and subtler tonality.

Looking at his masterpiece, *Las Meninas* (*The Maids-in-waiting*, FIG. **19-38**), with our experience of his portrait of *Juan de Pareja,* we recognize Velázquez as a master of a brilliant optical realism that seldom has been approached and never has been surpassed. The painter represents himself in his studio before a large canvas, on which he may be painting this very picture or, perhaps, the portraits of the king and queen, whose reflections appear in the mirror on the far wall. The little infanta, Margarita, appears in the foreground with her two maids in waiting, her favorite dwarfs, and a large dog. In the middle ground are a duenna and a male escort; in the background, a gentleman is framed in a brightly lit open doorway. The personages present have been identified, though we need not enumerate them here. On the wall above the doorway and mirror, two faintly recognizable pictures represent the immortal gods as the source of art. Our first impression of *Las Meninas* is of an informal family group (the painting was long called "The Family" by the Austrian kings of Spain), casually arranged and miraculously lifelike; one could think of it as a genre painting—"A Visit to the Artist's Studio"—rather than as a group portrait.

As first painter to the king and as chief steward of the palace, Velázquez was conscious not only of the importance of his court office but of the honor and dignity belonging to his profession as painter. In this painting, he appears to bring the roles together, asserting their equivalent value. A number of pictures from the seventeenth century show painters with their royal patrons, for painters of the time continually sought to aggrandize their profession among the arts and to achieve by it appropriate rank and respect. Throughout his career, Velázquez hoped to be ennobled by royal appointment to membership in the ancient and illustrious Order of Santiago, from which, he must have expected, his profession as painter would not disqualify him. Because some of the required patents of nobility were lacking in his background, he achieved this only with difficulty at the very end of his life, and then only through a dispensation from the pope. In the painting, he wears the red cross of the order on his doublet, painted there, legend tells us, by the king himself; the truth is that the artist painted it. In Velázquez's mind, *Las Meninas* might have embodied the idea of the great king visiting his artist's studio, as Alexander the Great visited the studio of Apelles in ancient times. We now know that the room represented in the painting was in the palace of the Alcázar in Madrid. After the death of Prince Baltasar Carlos in 1646, his chambers were partly converted into a studio for the use of Velázquez. The picture was designed to hang in the personal office of King Philip, in another part of the palace. It was intended for the king as private viewer and was not to be displayed in a gallery for general viewing. The figures in the painting all acknowledge the royal presence. Placed among them in equal dignity is Velázquez, face-to-face with his sovereign. The

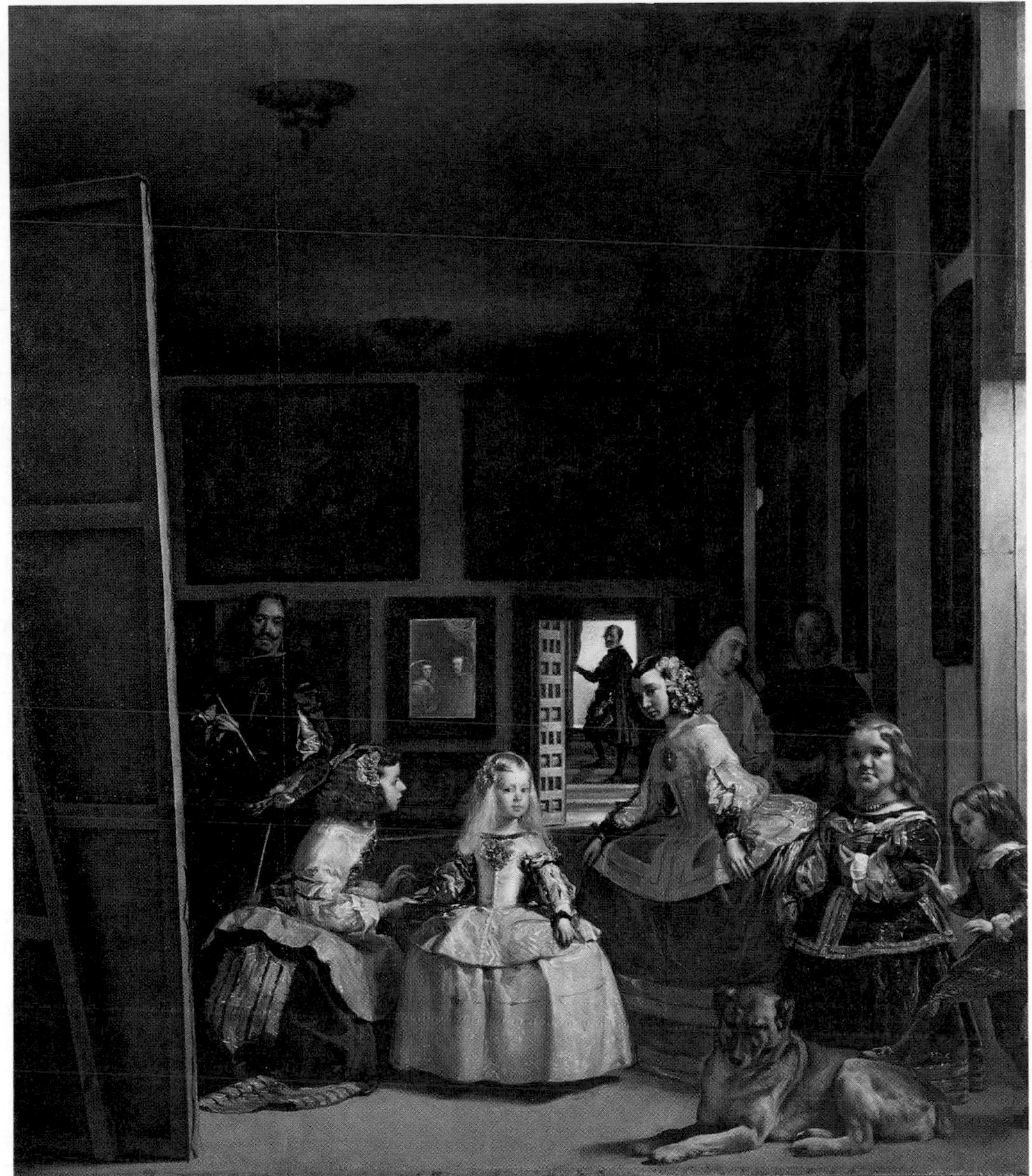

19-38 Diego Velázquez, *Las Meninas,* 1656. Approx. 10′ 5″ × 9′. Museo del Prado, Madrid.

art of painting, in the person of the painter, is elevated to the highest status. Velázquez sought ennoblement not for himself alone, but for his art.

Although Velázquez intends an optical report of the event, authentic in every detail, he also seems to intend a pictorial summary of the various kinds of images in their different levels and degrees of "reality"—the "reality" of canvas image, of mirror image, of optical image, and of the two imaged paintings. This work—with its cunning contrasts of mirrored spaces, "real" spaces, picture spaces, and pictures within pictures—itself appears to have been taken from a large mirror reflecting the whole scene, which would mean the artist has not painted the princess and her suite, but himself in the process of painting them. In the Baroque period, when artists were taking Leonardo's dictum that "the mirror is our master" very seriously, it is not surprising to find mirrors and primitive cameralike devices used to achieve optimum visual fidelity in painting. *Las Meninas* is a pictorial summary as well as a commentary on the essential mystery of the visual world and on the ambiguity that results when we confuse its different states or levels.

How does Velázquez achieve this stunning illusion? He opens the spectrum of light and the tones that compose it. Instead of putting lights abruptly beside darks, as Caravaggio, Ribera, and Zurbarán would do or as he himself had done in earlier works like *Los Borrachos* (FIG. 19-36), Velázquez allows a great number of intermediate values of grey to come between the two extremes. Thus, he carefully observes and records the subtle gradations of tone, matching with graded glazes what he sees in the visible spread of light and dark, using strokes of deep dark and touches of highlight to enliven the neutral tones in the middle of the value scale. This essentially cool, middle register of tones is what gives the marvelous effect of daylight and atmosphere to the painting. Velázquez's matching of tonal gradations approaches effects that the age of the photograph later will discover. His method is an extreme refinement of Titian's. Velázquez does not think of figures as first drawn, then modeled into sculptural effects, and then colored. He thinks of light and tone as the whole substance of painting—the solid forms being only *suggested,* never really constructed. Observing this reduction of the solid world to purely optical sensations in a floating, fugitive skein of color tones, one could say that the old, sculpturesque form has disappeared. The extreme thinness of Velázquez's paint and the light, almost accidental touches of thick pigment here and there destroy all visible structure; we examine his canvas closely, and everything dissolves to a random flow of paint. As a wondering Italian painter exclaimed of a Velázquez painting, "It is made of nothing, but there it is!" And viewing *Las Meninas,* the artist's biographer, Palomino, exclaimed, "It is truth, not painting!" Painters three hundred years later will realize that Velázquez's optical realism constitutes a limit. Their attempts to analyze it and to take it further will lead in an opposite direction to the one taken by the great Spanish master—to the abstract art of our own time.

FLANDERS

In the sixteenth century, the Netherlands came under the crown of Hapsburg Spain when the emperor Charles V retired, leaving the Spanish throne and his Netherlandish provinces to his only son, Philip II. Philip's repressive measures against the Protestants led to the breaking away of the northern provinces from Spain and the setting up of the Dutch republic under the House of Orange. The southern provinces remained with Spain, and their official religion continued to be Catholic. The political distinction between modern Holland and Belgium more or less reflects this original separation, which, in the Baroque period, signalized not only religious but also artistic differences. The Baroque art of Flanders (the Spanish Netherlands) remained in close contact with the Baroque art of the Catholic countries, while the Dutch schools of painting developed their own subjects and styles, consonant with their reformed religion and the new political, social, and economic structure of the middle-class Dutch republic.

RUBENS

The brilliant Flemish master PETER PAUL RUBENS (1577–1640) preceded Bernini in the development and dissemination of the Baroque style. Rubens's influence was international; he drew together the main contributions of the masters of the Renaissance (Michelangelo and Titian) and of the Baroque (the Carracci and Caravaggio) to synthesize in his own style the first truly European manner. Thus, Rubens completes the work begun by Albrecht Dürer in the previous century. The art of Rubens, even though it is the consequence of his wide study of many masters, is no weak eclecticism but an original and powerful synthesis. From the beginning, his instinct was to break away from the provincialism of the old Flemish Mannerists and to seek new ideas and methods abroad. His aristocratic education, his courtier's manner, diplomacy, and tact, as well as his classical learning made him the associate of princes and scholars. He became court painter to the dukes of Mantua (descended from the patrons of Mantegna), friend of the king of Spain and his adviser on art collecting, painter to Charles I of England and Marie de' Medici, queen of France, and permanent court painter to the Spanish governors of Flanders. Rubens also won the confidence of his royal patrons in matters of state, and he often was entrusted with diplomatic missions of the highest importance. In the practice of his art, he was assisted by scores of associates and apprentices, turning out large numbers of paintings for an international clientele. In addition, he functioned as an art dealer, buying and selling works of contemporary art and classical antiquities. His numerous enterprises made him a rich man, with a magnificent town house and a château in the countryside. Wealth and honors, however, did not spoil his amiable, sober, self-disciplined character. We have in Rubens, as in Raphael, the image of the successful, renowned artist, the consort of kings, and the shrewd man of the world, who is at the same time the balanced philosopher. Rubens more than makes good the Renaissance claim for the preeminence of the artist in society.

Rubens became a master in 1598 and went to Italy two years later, where he remained until 1608. During these years, he formulated the foundations of his style. Shortly after his return from Italy, he painted *The Elevation of the Cross* (FIG. **19-39**) for Antwerp Cathedral. This work shows the result of his long study

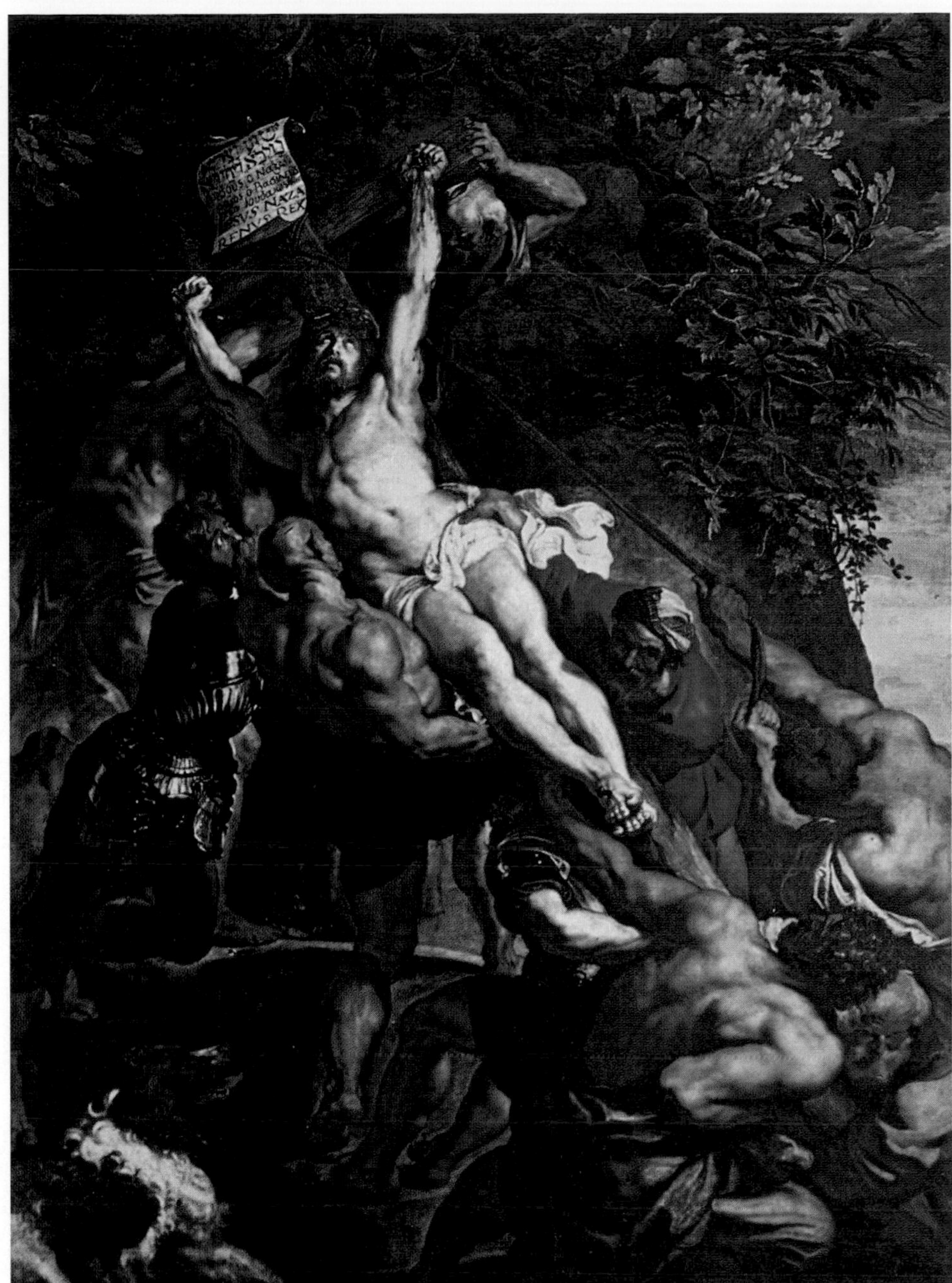

19-39 Peter Paul Rubens, *The Elevation of the Cross,* 1610. 15′ 2″ × 11′ 2″. Antwerp Cathedral, Belgium.

of Italian art, especially of Michelangelo, Tintoretto, and Caravaggio. The scene is a focus of tremendous, straining forces and counterforces, as heavily muscled giants strain to lift the cross. Here, the artist has the opportunity to show foreshortened anatomy and the contortions of violent action—not the bound action of Mannerism, but the tension of strong bodies meeting resistance outside themselves. The body of Christ is a great, illuminated diagonal that cuts dynamically across the picture and, at the same time, inclines back into it. The whole composition seethes with a power that we feel comes from genuine exertion, from elastic human sinew taut with effort. Strong modeling in dark and light marks Rubens's work at this stage of his career; it gradually will give way to a much subtler, coloristic style.

The vigor and passion of Rubens's early manner never leave his painting, although the vitality of his work is modified into less strained and more subtle forms, depending on the theme. Yet Rubens has one general theme—the human body, draped or undraped, male or female, freely acting or free to act in an environment of physical forces and other interacting bodies. Rubens's conception of the human scene

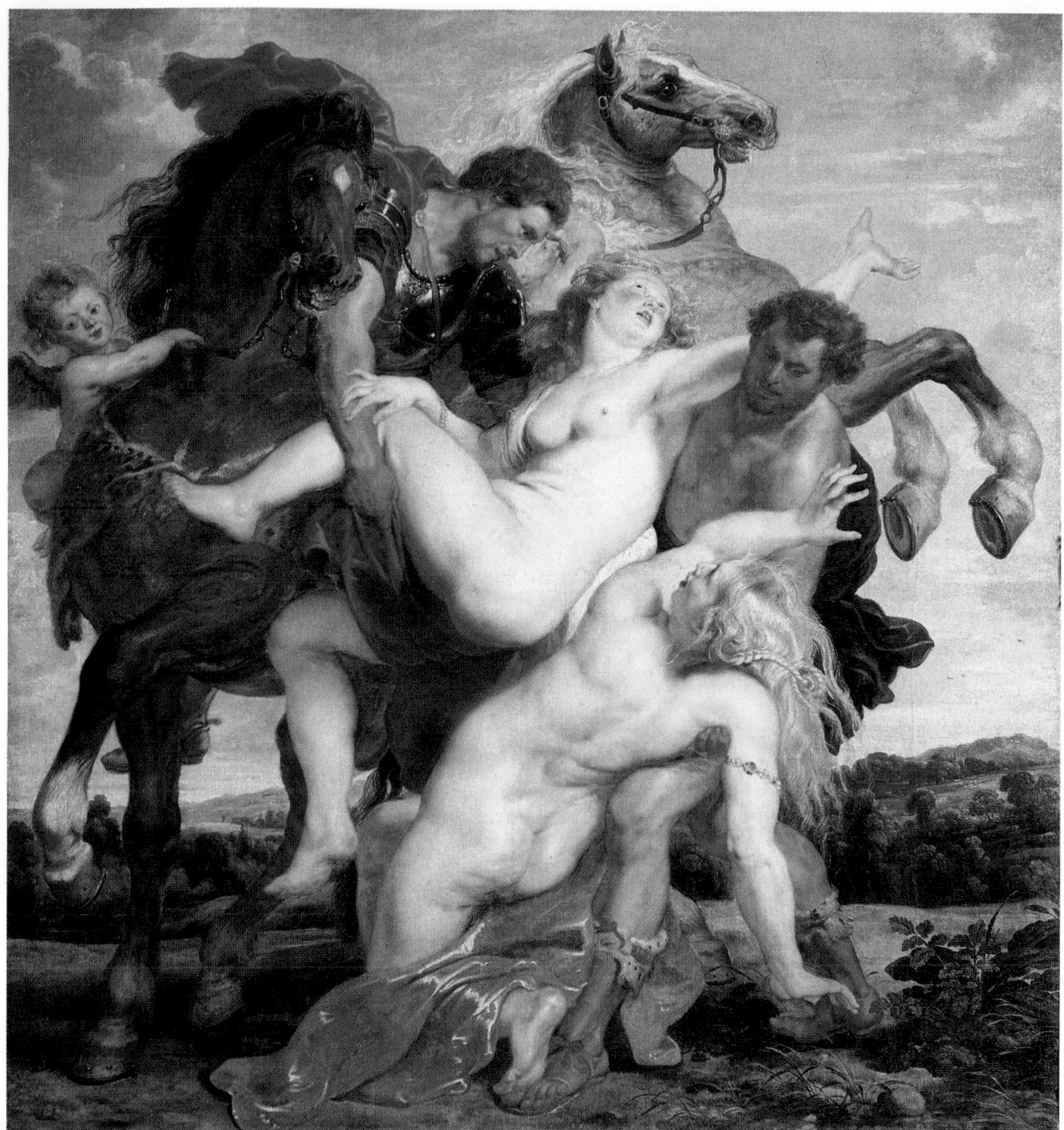

19-40 PETER PAUL RUBENS, *The Rape of the Daughters of Leucippus*, 1617. Approx. 7′ 3″ × 6′ 10″. Alte Pinakothek, Munich.

does not contain profoundly tragic elements nor anything manneristically intellectual, enigmatic, or complex. His forte is the strong animal body described in the joyful, exuberant motion natural to it. His *Rape of the Daughters of Leucippus* (FIG. **19-40**) describes the abduction of two young mortals by the gods Castor and Pollux, who have fallen in love with them. The amorous theme permits departures from realism, especially in the representation of movement and exerted strength. The gods do not labor at the task of sweeping up the massive maidens—descendants of the opulent Venuses of Giorgione and Titian (FIGS. 17-59 and 17-62)—nor do the maidens energetically resist. The figures are part of a highly dynamic, slowly revolving composition that seems to turn on an axis; they form a diamond-shaped group that defies stability and the logic of statics. The surface pattern, organized by intersecting diagonals and verticals, consists of areas of rich, contrasting textures: the soft luminous flesh of the women, the bronzed tan of the muscular men, lustrous satins, glinting armor, and the taut, shimmering hides of the horses. All around this surface pattern, a tight massing of volumes moves in space. The solid forms are no longer described simply in terms of the dark-light values of Florentine draftsmanship but are now built up in

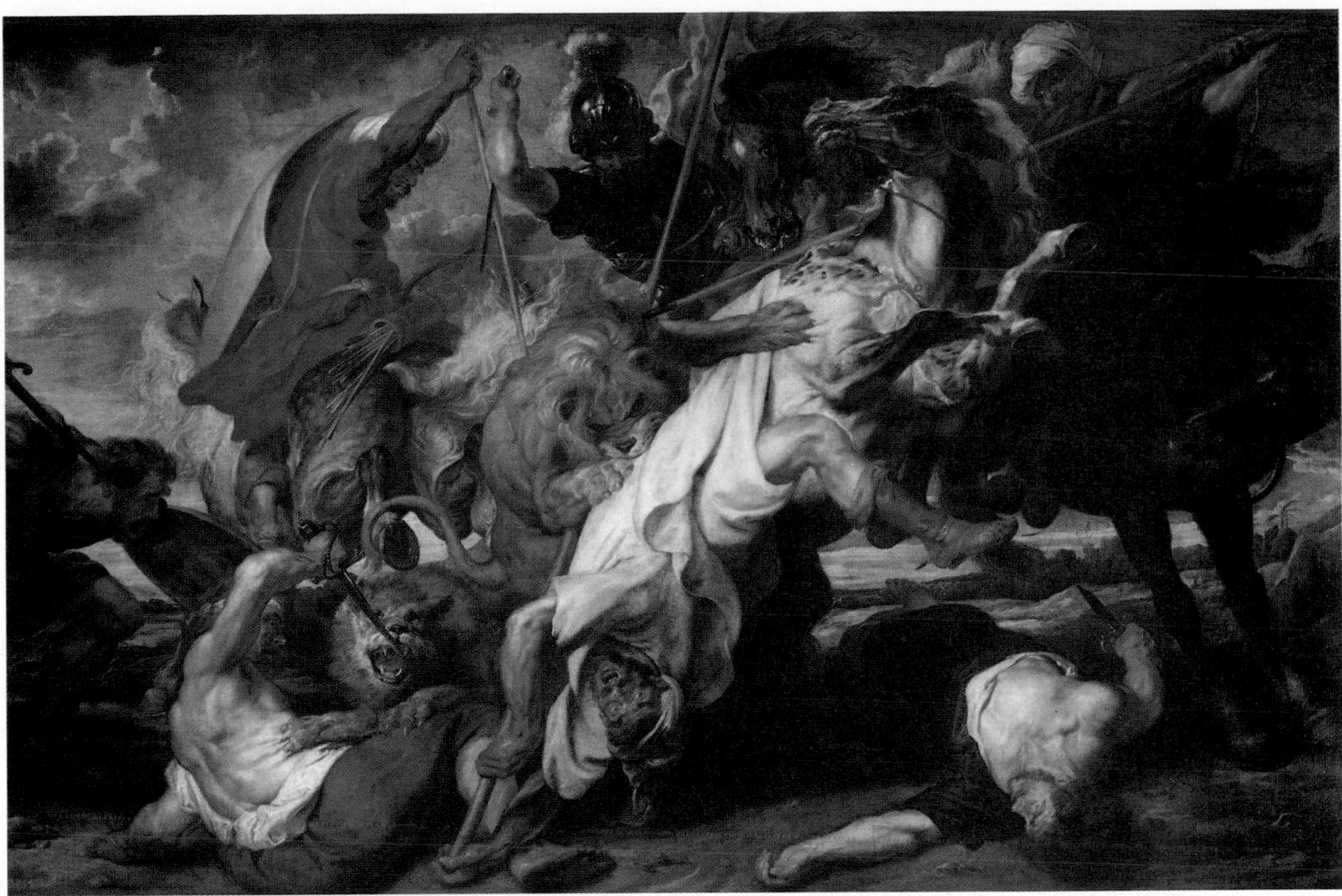

19-41 Peter Paul Rubens, *The Lion Hunt*, 1617–1618. Approx. 8′ 2″ × 12′ 5″. Alte Pinakothek, Munich.

color and defined by light, as in Venetian painting.

The impact of Rubens's hunting pictures lies in their depiction of ferocious action and vitality. In *The Lion Hunt* (FIG. **19-41**), a cornered lion, three lances meeting in his body, tears a Berber hunter from his horse. A fallen man still grips his sword, while another, in a reversed position, stabs at a snarling cat. Horsemen plunge in and out of the picture space, and the falling Berber makes a powerful, diagonal cut across the composition. The wild melee of thrusting, hacking, rearing, and plunging is almost an allegory of the confined tensions of Mannerism exploding into the extravagant activity that characterized the Baroque.

Rubens shared heartily in the Baroque love of magnificent pomp, especially as it set off the majesty of royalty, in which Rubens, born courtier that he was, heartily believed. The Baroque age saw endless, extravagant pageants and festivals produced whenever the great or even lesser dynasts moved. Their authority and right to rule were forever being demonstrated by lavish display. We have seen that the popes themselves, the princes of the Church, made of St. Peter's a permanently festive monument to papal supremacy. And Marie de' Medici, a member of the famous Florentine house, commissioned Rubens to paint a cycle memorializing and glorifying her career and that of her late husband, the first of the Bourbon kings, Henry IV. Between 1622 and 1626, Rubens, working with amazing creative energy, produced by his own hand twenty-one huge historical-allegorical pictures, designed to hang in the queen's new palace, the Luxembourg, in Paris.

Perhaps the most vivacious and dexterously composed of the series is the *Arrival of Marie de' Medici at Marseilles* (FIG. **19-42**); it can be taken as exemplary of the mood and style of the others. Marie has arrived in France after the sea voyage from Italy. Surrounded by her splendid ladies, she is welcomed by an allegory of France, a figure draped in the fleur-de-lis. The sea and sky rejoice at her safe arrival; Poseidon and the Nereids salute her, and a winged, trumpeting Fame swoops overhead. Conspicuous in the opulently carved stern-castle of the Baroque galley, under the coat of arms of the Medici, stands the imperious commander of the vessel. In black and silver, his figure makes a sharp accent in the midst of the swirling tonality of ivory, gold, and red. He wears the cross of a Knight of Malta, which may identify this as a ship belonging to that order. The only immobile figure in the composition, he could be director of and witness to the boisterous ceremonies. Broad and florid

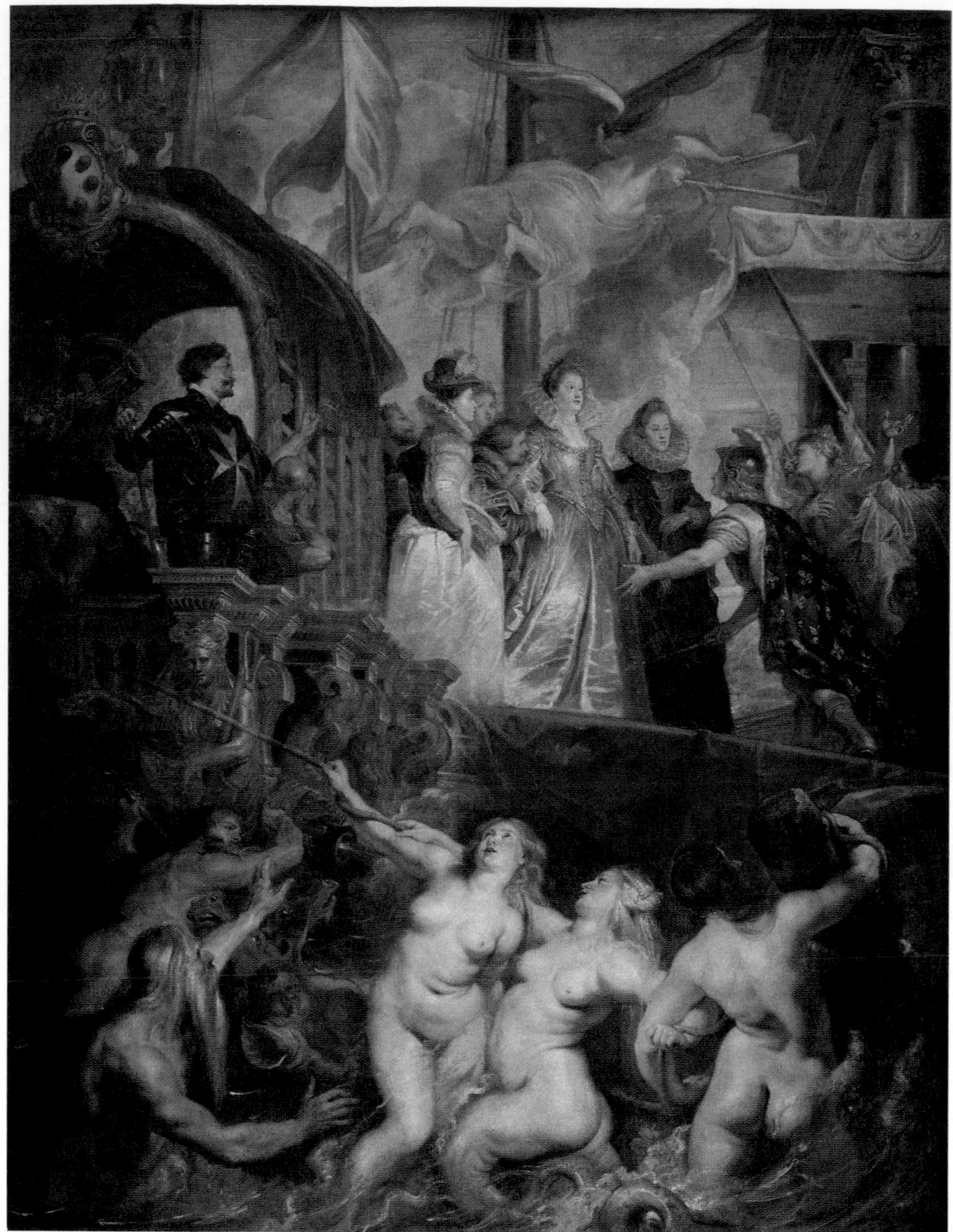

19-42 PETER PAUL RUBENS, *Arrival of Marie de' Medici at Marseilles,* 1622–1625. Approx. 61″ × 45⅜″. Louvre, Paris.

compliments, in which Heaven and earth join, are standard in Baroque pageantry, where honor is done to royalty. (We already have met the collaboration of the celestial and earthly spheres in the glorification of religious themes in Italian Baroque art.) The artist enriches his surfaces here with a decorative splendor that pulls the whole composition together, and the audacious vigor that customarily enlivens Rubens's figures, beginning with the monumental, twisting sea creatures, vibrates through the entire design.

Rubens's imposing, dynamic figure compositions were not his only achievement; he also produced rich landscapes and perceptive portraits. His portrait of *Thomas Howard, Earl of Arundel* (FIG. **19-43**), is a painting of singular power. This great English nobleman played a leading role in the complicated diplomacy and statecraft of the age of Charles I, when England was on the verge of a tragic civil war between the Stuart king and Parliament. Arundel is best remembered, however, as a lover of art, who built a collection of ancient statuary and other works of art unsurpassed in the Europe of his time. Rubens was a friend of Arundel and an admirer of his taste and learning. The artist's admiration for the man himself, regarded by contemporaries as the bringer of "true virtu"—knightly gallantry and magnanimity—to England, is clearly expressed in the portrait. The earl is posed in an attitude of regal majesty. He directs a sharp, stern, haughty glance over his shoulder, creating instant distance between *his* rank and that of the observer. The look given by the aquiline features is that of a commander of armies silencing a subordinate; it is full of an authority not to be questioned. Rubens gives us not the sensitive lover of art but the fearless captain. We realize that the earl himself must have stipulated that this aspect of his character and career be shown. To this end, Rubens has garbed him in magnificent ceremonial armor. His gauntleted hand rests on the commander's staff; his plumed helmet sits on a table at his side. Behind him, a curtain is drawn aside, revealing a severe Classical architecture that echoes his mood. Rubens lavishes all of his rich resources of color tone in the rendering of the splendid accoutrements of high rank and latter-day chivalry. This imperious image speaks for an autocratic age—for the great dynasts of the Baroque, whom Rubens knew well and who were his patrons.

19-43 PETER PAUL RUBENS, *Thomas Howard, Earl of Arundel*, c. 1630. Approx. 54″ × 45″. Isabella Stewart Gardner Museum, Boston.

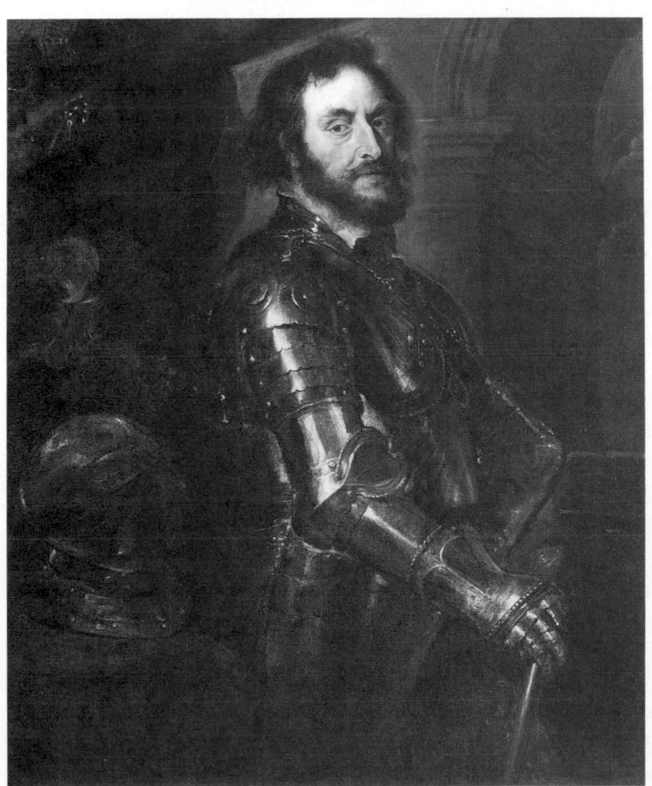

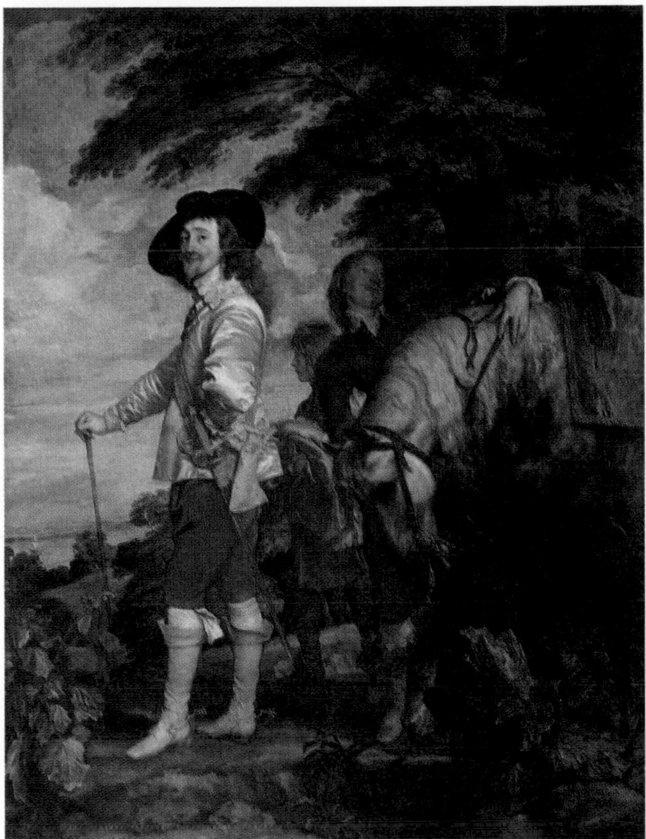

19-44 ANTHONY VAN DYCK, *Charles I Dismounted*, c. 1635. Approx. 9′ × 7′. Louvre, Paris.

Most of Rubens's successors in Flanders had been his assistants. The most famous, ANTHONY VAN DYCK (1599–1641), probably worked with his master on the canvas of *The Rape of the Daughters of Leucippus*. Quite early, the younger man, unwilling to be overshadowed by the undisputed stature of Rubens, left his native Antwerp for Genoa and then London, where he became court portraitist to Charles I. Although Van Dyck created dramatic compositions of high quality, his specialty became the portrait, and he developed a courtly manner of great elegance that would be influential internationally. His style is felt in English portrait painting down to the nineteenth century. In one of his finest works, *Charles I Dismounted* (FIG. **19-44**), he shows the ill-fated Stuart king standing in a Venetian landscape (with the river Thames in the background), attended by an equerry and a page. Although the king impersonates a nobleman out for a casual ride in his park, no one can mistake the regal poise and the air of absolute authority that his Parliament resented and was soon to rise against. The composition is exceedingly artful in the placement of the king. He stands off-center, but balances the picture with a single keen glance at the observer. The full-length portraits by Titian and the cool composure of the Mannerists both contribute to Van Dyck's sense of pose and arrangement of detail. For centuries to come, artists who make portraits of the great—Thomas Gainsborough, Joshua Reynolds, and John Singer Sargent, among them—will keep Van Dyck very much in mind.

HOLLAND

For all intents and purposes, the style of Peter Paul Rubens is the style of Baroque Flanders; he had few rivals of significance and held a monopoly on commissions. The situation is so completely different in Holland that it is difficult to imagine how, within such a tiny area, two such opposite artistic cultures could flourish. The Dutch Protestants and the Flemish Catholics went their separate ways after the later sixteenth century. Although closer in outlook to the Germans, the Dutch were ethnically the same as the Flemish, who were, in turn, closer in viewpoint to their neighbors to the south—the French. A Catholic, aristocratic, and traditional culture reigned in the Flanders of Rubens. In Holland, severe, Calvinistic Protestantism was puritanical toward religious art, sculptural or pictorial, although many of the Dutch were Catholics, including a number of painters. The churches were swept clean of images, and any recollection of the pagan myths, the material of Classicism, or even historical subjects, was proscribed in art. During the Middles Ages and the Renaissance, religious subjects and, later, Classical and historical subjects had been the major stimuli for artistic activity. Divested of these sources, what remained to enrich the lives of wealthy Hollanders? For they *were* wealthy! During the early part of the Spanish rule, the Dutch, like the Flemish, prospered. The East India Company was formed, and the discovery of the New World opened up further opportunities for trade and colonization. The wars of independence from Spain made Holland the major maritime country of Europe; its closest rival was England, another Protestant power in the times of the Spanish decline. The great Dutch commercial cities, such as Haarlem and Amsterdam, had been stimulated and enriched, and civic pride was strong. Although it was not internationally recognized until the Peace of Westphalia in 1648, Holland in fact had been independent from Spain since about 1580 and was extremely proud of its hard-won freedom. Under these circumstances, writes the nineteenth-century French painter Eugène Fromentin,

> Dutch painting . . . was and could be only the portrait of Holland, its exterior image, faithful, exact, complete, with no embellishments. Portraits of men and places, citizen habits, squares, streets, countryplaces, the sea and the sky—such was to be . . . the program followed by the Dutch school, and such it was from its first day to the day of its decline.*

Dutch painters increasingly pried into the pictorial possibilities of everyday life and kept an eye on their customers, the middle-class burghers, who wanted paintings to hang on their walls as evidence of their growing wealth and social position.

We have followed the secularization and humanization of religious art since the thirteenth century. In the Dutch school of the seventeenth century, the process is completed. A thousand years and more of religious iconography are dismissed by a European people who ask for a view of the world from which angels, saints, and deities have been banished. The old Netherlandish realism remains, but it no longer serves religious purposes. The Dutch artists rise to the occasion, matching the open, competitive, Dutch society, which is thoroughly middle-class, with an equally open arrangement of their own, in which the painter works not for a patron but for the market. Dutch artists become specialists in any one of a number of subjects—genre, landscape, seascape, cattle and horses, table still life, flower still life, interiors, and so on. In short, they paint subjects that they feel will appeal to the public and therefore be marketable. This independence from the patron gives the Dutch painter a certain amount of freedom, even if it is only the freedom to starve on the free-picture market. With respect to the artist–market relationship, the contrast between Flanders and Holland in the seventeenth century is poignantly reflected in the careers of Rubens and Rembrandt. The former *is* the market in Flanders; his genius determines it. The latter, after finding a place in the market, is rejected by it when his genius is no longer marketable.

The realism of Dutch art is made up of the old tradition, which goes back to Hubert and Jan van Eyck, and of the new "realism of light and dark," brought back to Holland by Dutch painters who had studied Caravaggio in Italy. One of these "night painters" (as they were called), GERARD VAN HONTHORST (1590–1656) of Utrecht, spent several years in Italy absorbing Caravaggio's style. He is best known for merry genre scenes like *The Supper Party* (FIG. **19-45**), in which unidealized, human figures are shown in an informal gathering. Although these "merry companies," naturalistically rendered in night settings, were popular and widely produced in the Baroque

*Eugène Fromentin, *The Masters of Past Time: Dutch and Flemish Painting from Van Eyck to Rembrandt,* trans. A. Boyle (London: Phaidon, 1948), p. 130.

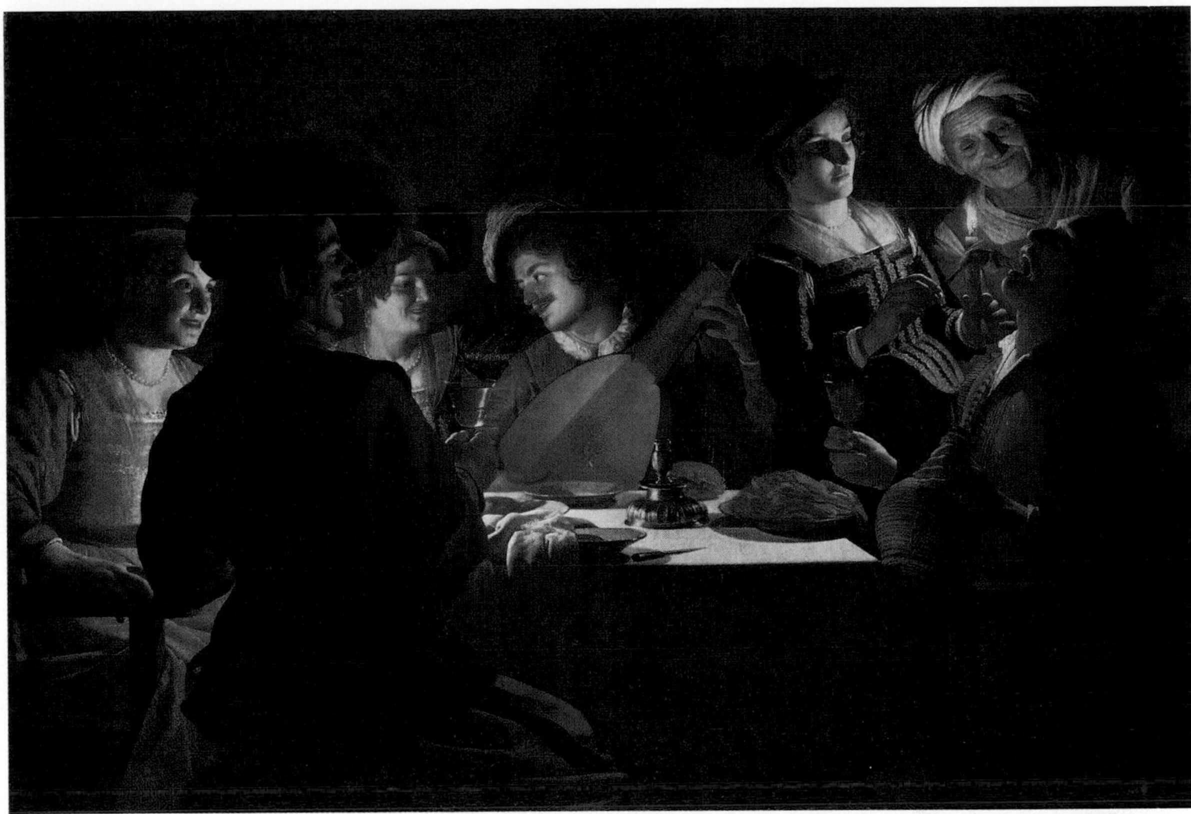

19-45 GERARD VAN HONTHORST, *The Supper Party*, 1620. Approx. 7′ × 4′ 8″. Galleria degli Uffizi, Florence.

period, they were not necessarily taken simply as pictures of people enjoying themselves. We must remember the Baroque mental habit of allegorizing and symbolizing even the most realistic images. Here, for example, we may be expected to witness the loose companions of the Prodigal Son (Luke 15:13)—panders and prostitutes, drinking, singing, strumming, laughing. Perhaps, at the same time, we have an allegory of the Five Senses through which sin can enter the soul: taste, touch, sight, sound, scent. Fascinated by nocturnal effects, Van Honthorst frequently places a hidden light source (two, in this case) in his pictures and uses it as a pretext to work with dramatic and violently contrasted dark-light effects. Without the incisive vision of Caravaggio, Van Honthorst nevertheless is able to match, and sometimes to surpass, the former's tenebristic effects.

FRANS HALS

The Dutch schools were centered in various cities (Utrecht, Haarlem, Leiden, Amsterdam), but all had in common the lesson of Caravaggio as interpreted by Dutch Caravaggisti like Van Honthorst. FRANS HALS (*c.* 1580–1666) was the leading painter of the Haarlem school and one of the great realistic painters of the Western tradition. Hals appropriates what he needs from the new lighting to make portraiture (his specialty) an art of acute psychological perception as well as a kind of comic genre. The way light floats across the face and meets shadow can be arranged by the artist, as can the pose and the details of costume and facial expression. Hals shows himself to be a master of all the devices open to a portraitist who no longer needs to maintain the distance required by the strictly formal portrait.

The relaxed relationship between the portraitist and his subject is apparent in the engaging portrait of *Willem Coymans* (FIG. **19-46**), dated 1645. Although the subject is a young man of some importance, the artist seems to be taking a great many liberties with his portrait. The young man leans on one arm with a jaunty air of insolence, his hat cocked at a challenging angle, a look of contemptuous drollery in his eyes. The illusion of life is such that we take cues from the subject's expression as if we were face to face with him. Hals's genius lies in capturing the minute, expressional movements by which we appraise the man across from us in everyday life. Until now, this kind of intimate confrontation rarely had been seen in painting. It is a kind of contradiction of the masks of

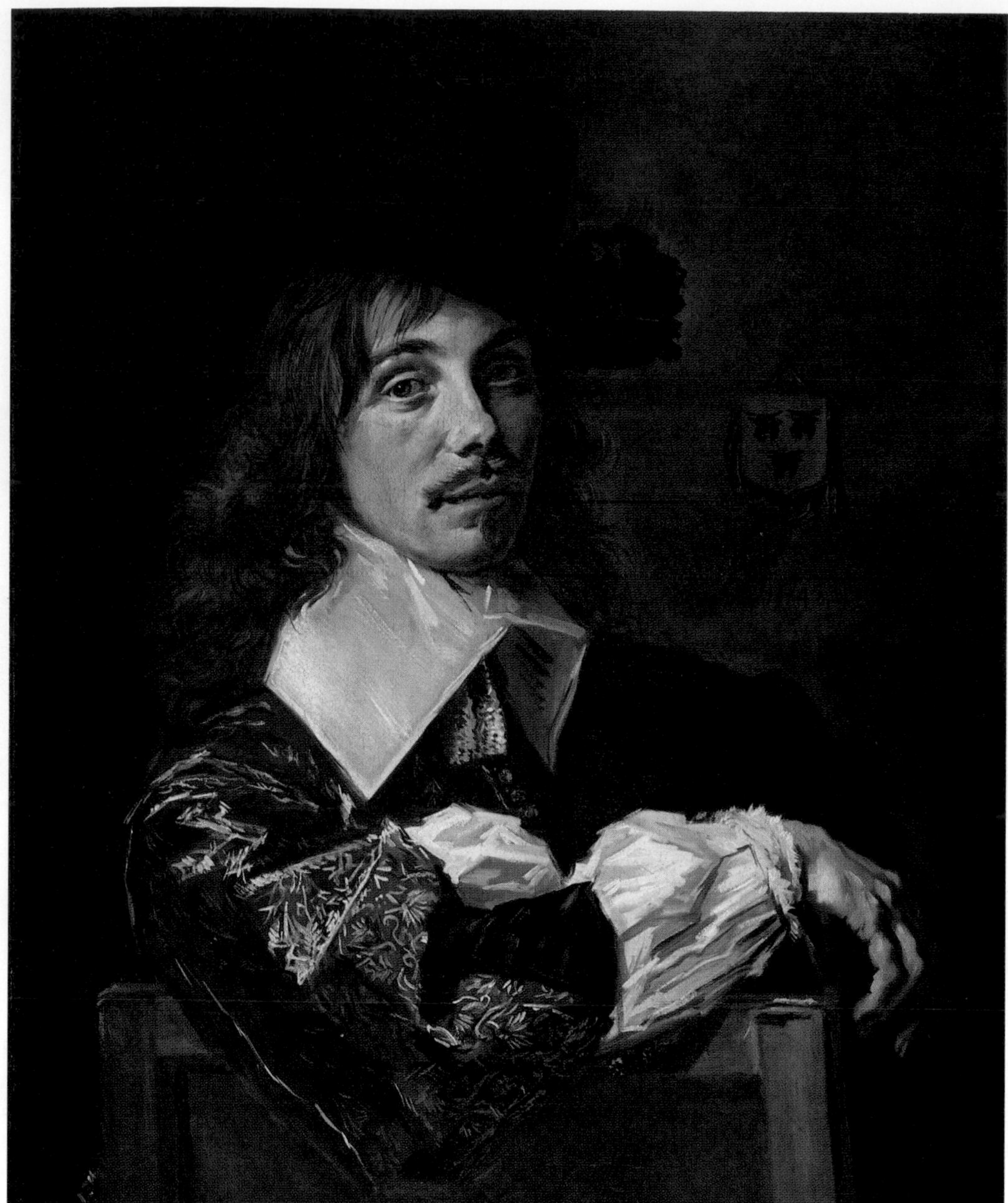

19-46 FRANS HALS, *Willem Coymans,* 1645. Approx. $30\frac{1}{4}'' \times 25''$. National Gallery of Art, Washington, D.C. (Andrew W. Mellon Collection).

formal portraiture created in the Renaissance. We are in the presence of an individual without formal introduction; the gap between us and the subject is reduced until we are almost part of his physical and psychological environment. The casualness, immediacy, and intimacy are intensified by the manner in which the painting is executed. The touch of the painter's brush is as light and fleeting as the moment in which the pose is caught; the pose of the figure, the highlights on the sleeve, the reflected lights within face and hand, and the lift of the eyebrow are all the instant prey of time. Thus, the evanescence of time that Bernini caught in his *David* (FIG. 19-10) is recorded far to the north a few years later in a different subject and medium. Both are Baroque.

Frans Hals is a genius of the comic. He had precedents in the gargoylism and grotesquerie of the northern Middle Ages and, in later times, in the works of Hieronymus Bosch and Pieter Bruegel. But Hals's comedy is that of character rather than situation. He shows us—as Aristotle would demand of comedy—people as they are and somewhat less than they are; this puts us at ease, out of superiority, so that we can laugh at others and at ourselves. Hals takes his comic characters, as did Shakespeare, his contemporary, from the lower levels of society.

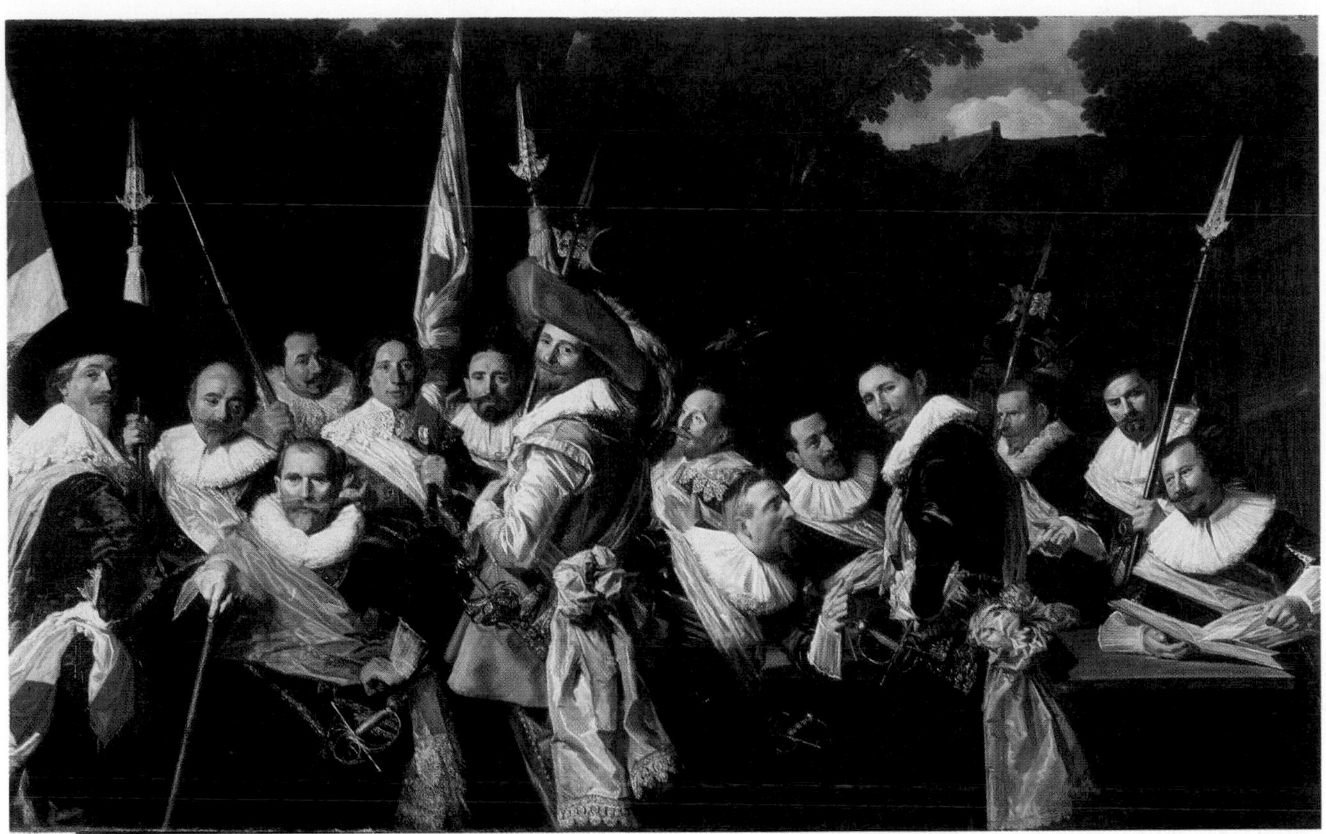

19-47 Frans Hals, *Archers of St. Adrian (Assembly of Officers and Subalterns of the Civic Guard)*, c. 1633. Approx. 6′ 9″ × 11′. Frans Halsmuseum, Haarlem, Netherlands.

Good-humored stageplay also brightens Hals's great canvases of units of the Dutch civic guard, which played an important part in the liberation of Holland. These companies of archers and musketeers met on their saints' days in dress uniform for an uproarious banquet, giving Hals an opportunity to attack the problem of adequately representing each subject of a group portrait while retaining action and variety in the composition. Earlier group portraits in the Netherlands represent the sitters as so many jugs on a shelf. Hals undertakes to correct this and, in the process, produces dramatic solutions to the problem, like that found in his *Archers of St. Adrian* (FIG. **19-47**). Here, the troopers have finished their banquet, the wine has already gone to their heads, and each in his own way is sharing the abundant high spirits. As a stage director, Hals has few equals. In quite Baroque fashion, he balances direction of glance, pose, and gesture, making compositional devices of the white ruffs, broad-brimmed black hats, and banners. Although the instantaneous effect—the preservation of every detail and facial expression—is, of course, the result of careful planning, Hals's vivacious brush seems to have moved spontaneously, directed by a plan in the artist's mind but not traceable in any preparatory scheme on the canvas. The bright optimism of this early period of Dutch freedom is caught in the swaggering bonhomie of the personalities, each of whom plays his particular part within the general unity of mood. This gregariousness goes with the new democracy, as well, perhaps, as with the fellowship that grows from a common experience of danger.

REMBRANDT

With Hals, Baroque realism concentrates on the human subject so intimately that we are forced to relate it to ourselves. We and the subject look at each other, as if in a sharing of mood; Hals purposely attempts to set up a confrontation of personalities. Yet most subjects still prefer to present only a public image, and even Hals has not entirely broken away from the tradition of formal portraiture that goes back to the fifteenth century. The first deep look into the *private* person will be made by Hals's younger contemporary, Rembrandt van Rijn (1606–1669).

Rembrandt's way was prepared spiritually by the Protestant Reformation and the Dutch aspiration to freedom, and formally by the Venetian painters, Rubens, and Caravaggio and his Dutch imitators. The richness of this heritage alone, however, cannot account for the extraordinary achievement of this artist, one of the very greatest among those geniuses who excel in revealing Western humanity to itself. Rembrandt used painting as a method for probing the states of the human soul, both in portraiture and in his uniquely personal and authentic illustrations of the Scriptures. The abolition of religious art by the Reformed church in Holland did not prevent him from making a series of religious paintings and prints that synopsize the Bible from a single point of view. His art is that of a believing Christian, a poet of the spiritual, convinced that the biblical message must be interpreted for human beings in human terms. In Rembrandt, the humanization of medieval religion is now completed in the vision of a single believer. In the Baroque age, this is roughly parallel to the sighting of a new planet by some single "watcher of the skies."

Rembrandt's pictorial method involves refining light and shade into finer and finer nuances, until they blend with one another. (Caravaggio's "absolute" light has, in fact, many shadows; his "absolute" dark is brightened by many lights.) We have seen that Velázquez renders optical reality as a series of values—a number of degrees of lightness and darkness. The use of abrupt lights and darks gives way in the works of men like Rembrandt and Velázquez to gradation, and, although the dramatic effects of violent chiaroscuro may be sacrificed, the artist gains much of the truth of actual appearances. This happens because the eye perceives light and dark not as static but as always subtly changing. Changing light and dark can suggest changing human moods; we might say that the *motion* of light through a space and across human features can express *emotion*, the changing states of the psyche.

The Renaissance represents forms and faces in a flat, neutral, modeling light (even Leonardo da Vinci's shading is of a standard kind), just as it represents action in a series of standard poses. The Renaissance painter represents the *idea* of light and the *idea* of action, rather than the actual *look* of either. Light, atmosphere, change, and motion are all concerns of Baroque art, as well as of Baroque mathematics and physics. The difference between the Baroque view and what went before lies largely in the new desire to *measure* these physical forces. For example, as the physicist in the seventeenth century is concerned not just with motion, but with acceleration and velocity—degrees of motion—so Baroque painters discover degrees of light and dark, of differences in pose, in the movements of facial features, and in psychic states. They arrive at these differences *optically*, not conceptually or in terms of some ideal. Rembrandt found that by manipulating light and shadow in terms of direction, intensity, distance, and texture of

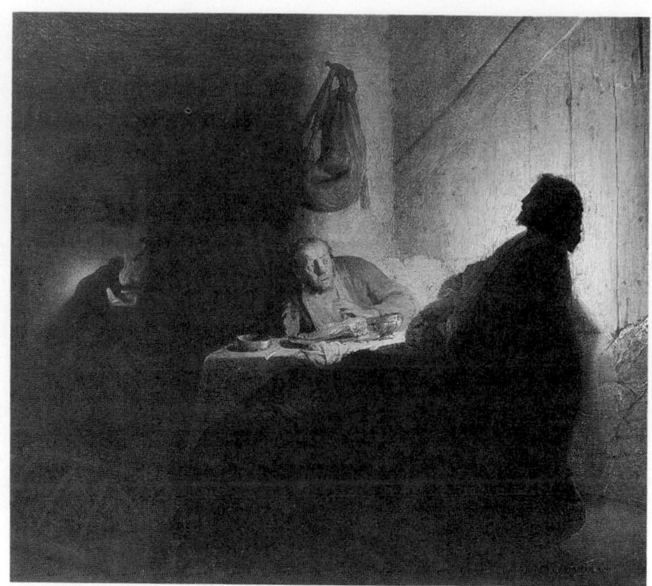

19-48 REMBRANDT VAN RIJN, *Supper at Emmaus*, c. 1628–1630. $14\frac{1}{2}'' \times 16\frac{1}{8}''$. Musée Jacquemart-André, Paris.

surface, he could render the most subtle nuances of character and mood, of persons, or of whole scenes. Rembrandt discovers for the modern world that differences of light and shade, subtly modulated, can be read as emotional differences. In the visible world, light, dark, and the wide spectrum of values between the two are charged with meanings and feelings that sometimes are independent of the shapes and figures they modify. The lighted stage and the photographic arts have accepted this for many decades as the first assumption behind all their productions. What Masaccio and Leonardo began, the age of Rembrandt completes.

In his early career in Amsterdam, Rembrandt's work was influenced by Rubens and by Dutch Caravaggesque painters like Van Honthorst. Thus, in a work like his early *Supper at Emmaus* (FIG. **19-48**), which dates from about 1630, he represents the subject with high drama—in sharp light and dark contrast—even using the device, familiar among his contemporaries, of placing the source of illumination behind an obstructing form (in this case, the head of Christ). This placement puts the darkest shadow in front of the brightest light, creating an emphatic, if obvious, dramatic effect. The poses of the two alarmed disciples to whom the risen Christ reveals himself are likewise a studied stage maneuver. Some eighteen years later, in another painting of the same subject (FIG. **19-49**), the mature Rembrandt forsakes the earlier melodramatic means for a serene and untroubled setting. Here, with his highly developed instinct for light and shade, he gives us no explosive contrasts; rather, a gentle diffusion of light mellows

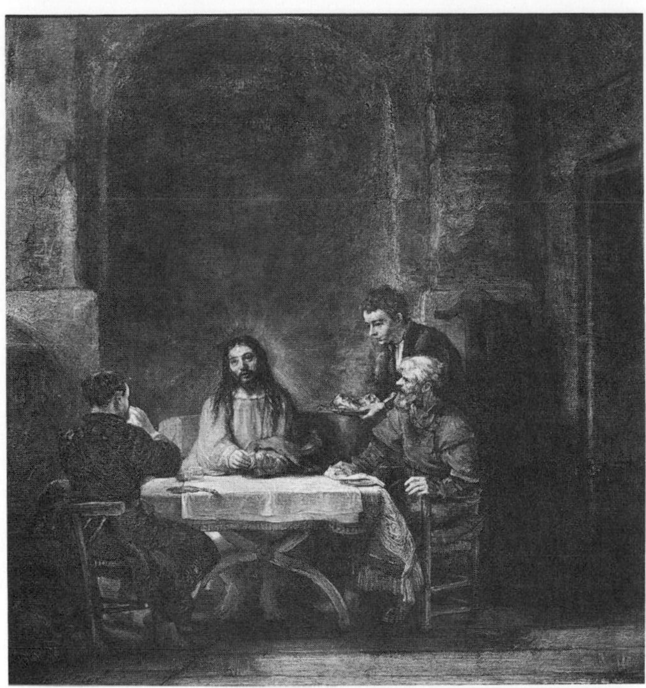

19-49 Rembrandt van Rijn, *Supper at Emmaus*, c. 1648. Approx. 27″ × 26″. Louvre, Paris.

the whole interior, condensing just slightly to make an aureole behind the head of Christ. The disciples only begin to understand what is happening; the servant is unaware. This Christ is Rembrandt's own interpretation of the biblical picture of the humble Nazarene—gentle, with an expression both loving and melancholy.

The spiritual stillness of Rembrandt's religious painting is that of inward-turning contemplation, far from the choirs and trumpets and the heavenly tumult of Bernini or Pozzo. Rembrandt gives us not the celestial triumph of the Church, but the humanity and humility of Jesus. His psychological insight and his profound sympathy for human affliction produce, at the very end of his life, one of the most moving pictures in all religious art, *The Return of the Prodigal Son* (FIG. **19-50**). Tenderly embraced by his forgiving father, the son crouches before him in weeping contrition while three figures, immersed in varying degrees in the soft shadows, note the lesson of mercy. The scene is determined wholly by the artist's inward vision of its meaning. The light, everywhere mingled with shadow, controls the arrangement of the figures, illuminating the father and son and largely veiling the witnesses. Its focus is the beautiful, spiritual face of the old man; secondarily, it touches the contrasting, stern face of the foremost witness. There is no flash or glitter of light or color; the raiment is as sober as the characters are grave. Rembrandt, one feels, has put the official Baroque style far behind him and has developed a personal style completely in tune with the simple eloquence of the biblical passage. One could not help but read the Bible differently, given the authority of Rembrandt's pictorial interpretations of it.

Rembrandt carries over the spiritual quality of his religious works into his later portraits by the same means—what we might call the "psychology" of light. Light and dark are not in conflict in his portraits; they are reconciled, merging softly and subtly to produce the visual equivalent of quietness. The prevailing mood is that of tranquil meditation, of philosophical resignation, of musing recollection—indeed, a whole cluster of emotional tones heard only in silence. He records the calamities of his own life and the age-old tragedies of the Jewish people (he had many friends in the Jewish quarter of Amsterdam) in the worn faces of aged and silent men. His study of the influence of time on the human features was one with his study of light. The mood of reflection conveyed by the slow movement of lights and darks complements the appearance of the aged face in slanting light: a sunken terrain crisscrossed with deep lines. In a long series of self-portraits, Rembrandt preserved his own psychic history from the

19-50 Rembrandt van Rijn, *The Return of the Prodigal Son*, c. 1665. Approx. 8′ 8″ × 6′ 8¾″. Hermitage Museum, Leningrad.

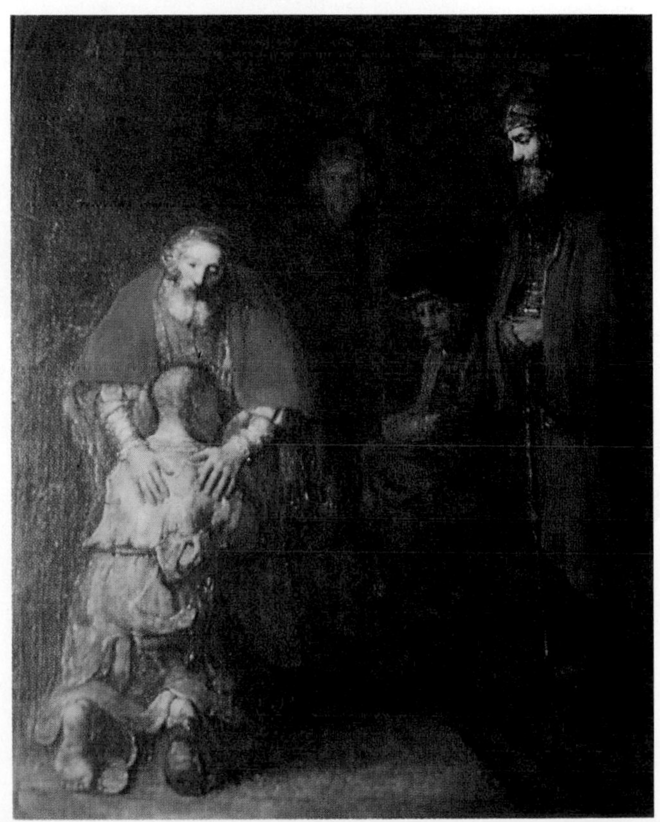

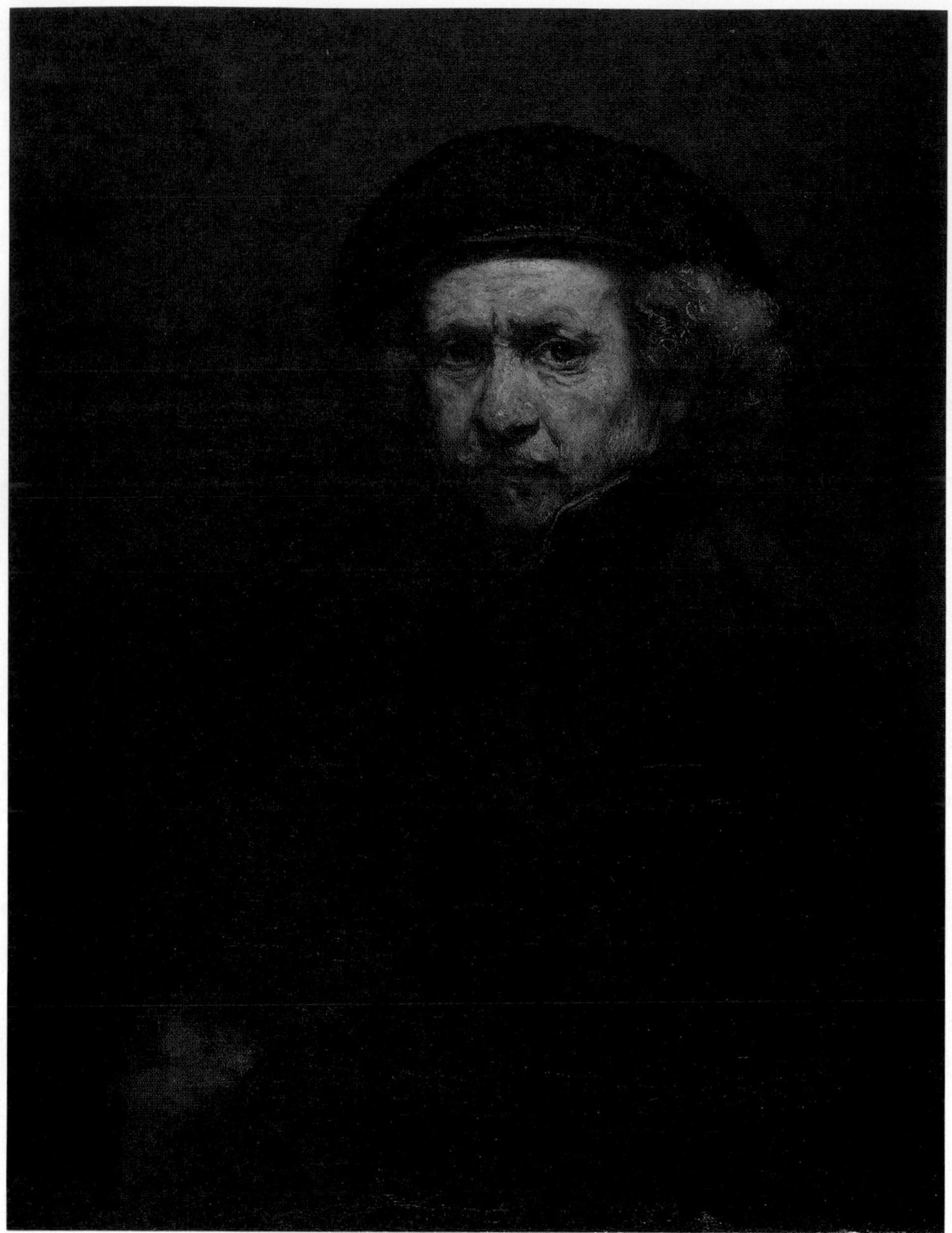

19-51 Rembrandt van Rijn, *Self-Portrait,* c. 1659. Approx. 33″ × 26″. National Gallery of Art, Washington, D.C. (Andrew W. Mellon Collection).

bright alert optimism of youth to the worn resignation of his declining years. These last years, when he was at the height of his artistic powers, cost him much physically.

In a late self-portrait (FIG. **19-51**), the light from above and from the artist's left pitilessly reveals a face ravaged by anxiety and care. The pose is that of Raphael's *Baldassare Castiglione* (FIG. 17-18), which Rembrandt had seen in Holland and copied in an earlier self-portrait. The difference between Raphael's and Rembrandt's portraits tells us much about the difference between the approaches of the artists and the philosophies of their times. In Raphael's subject, the ideal has modified the real. Rembrandt, on the other hand, shows himself as he appears to his own searching and unflattering gaze. Here, an elderly man is not idealized into the image of the courtly philosopher; he is shown merely as he is, a human being in the process of dwindling away. For some, the portrait and the self-portrait, which began as a medium for the recording of likeness, came to be painted out of motives of vanity. With Rembrandt, they are the history of Everyman's painful journey through the world.

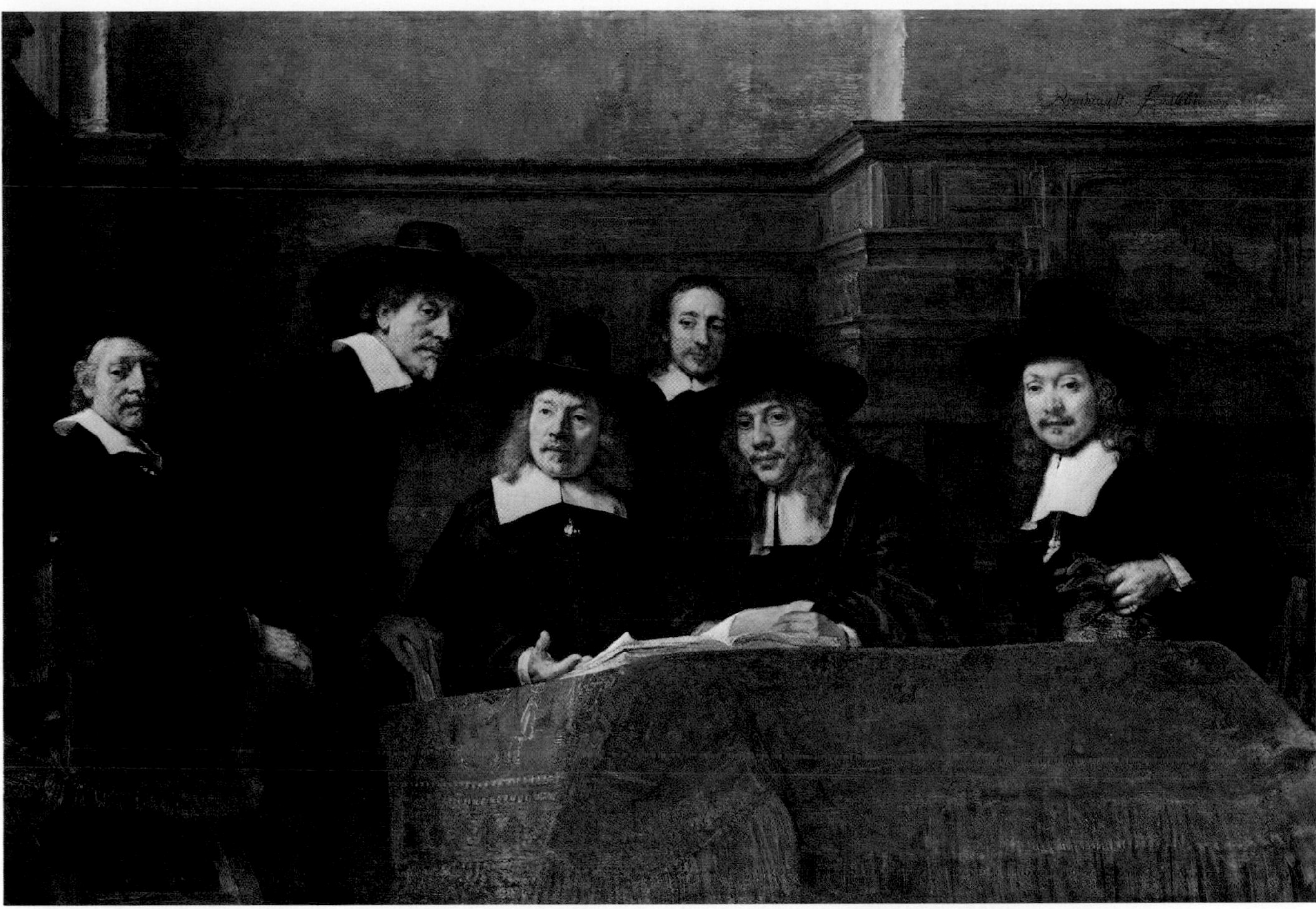

19-52 Rembrandt van Rijn, *Syndics of the Cloth Guild*, 1662. Approx. 6′ 2″ × 9′ 2″. Rijksmuseum, Amsterdam.

In the group portrait, an area of painting in which Frans Hals excelled, Rembrandt shows himself to be the supreme master. In *Syndics of the Cloth Guild* (FIG. **19-52**), representing an archetypal image of the new businessmen, Rembrandt applied all that he knew of the dynamics and the psychology of light, the visual suggestion of time, and the art of pose and facial expression. The syndics, or board of directors, are going over the books of the corporation. It would appear that someone has entered the room and they are just at the moment of becoming aware of him, each head turning in his direction. Rembrandt gives us the lively reality of a business conference as it is interrupted; yet he renders each portrait with equal care and with a studied attention to personality that one would expect to be possible only from a long studio sitting for each man. Although we do not know how Rembrandt proceeded, this harmonizing of the instantaneous action with the permanent likeness seems a work of superb stage direction that must have needed long rehearsal. The astonishing harmonies of light, color, movement, time, and pose have few rivals in the history of painting.

Rembrandt's virtuosity also extends to the graphic media, in particular, to etching. Here again, he ranks at the summit, alongside the original master, Dürer, who was actually an engraver. Etching, perfected early in the seventeenth century, rapidly was taken up by many artists; it was far more manageable than engraving and allowed greater freedom in drawing the design. In etching, a copper plate is covered with a layer of wax or varnish in which the design is drawn with an etching needle or any pointed tool, exposing the metal below but not cutting into its surface. The plate is then immersed in acid, which etches, or eats away, the exposed parts of the metal, acting in the same capacity as the burin in engraving. The softness of the medium gives the etcher greater freedom than the woodcutter and the engraver, who work directly in their more resistant media of wood and metal. Thus, prior to the invention of the lithograph in the nineteenth century, etching was the most facile of the graphic arts and the one that offered the greatest subtlety of line and tone.

If Rembrandt had never painted, he still would be renowned, as he principally was in his lifetime, for

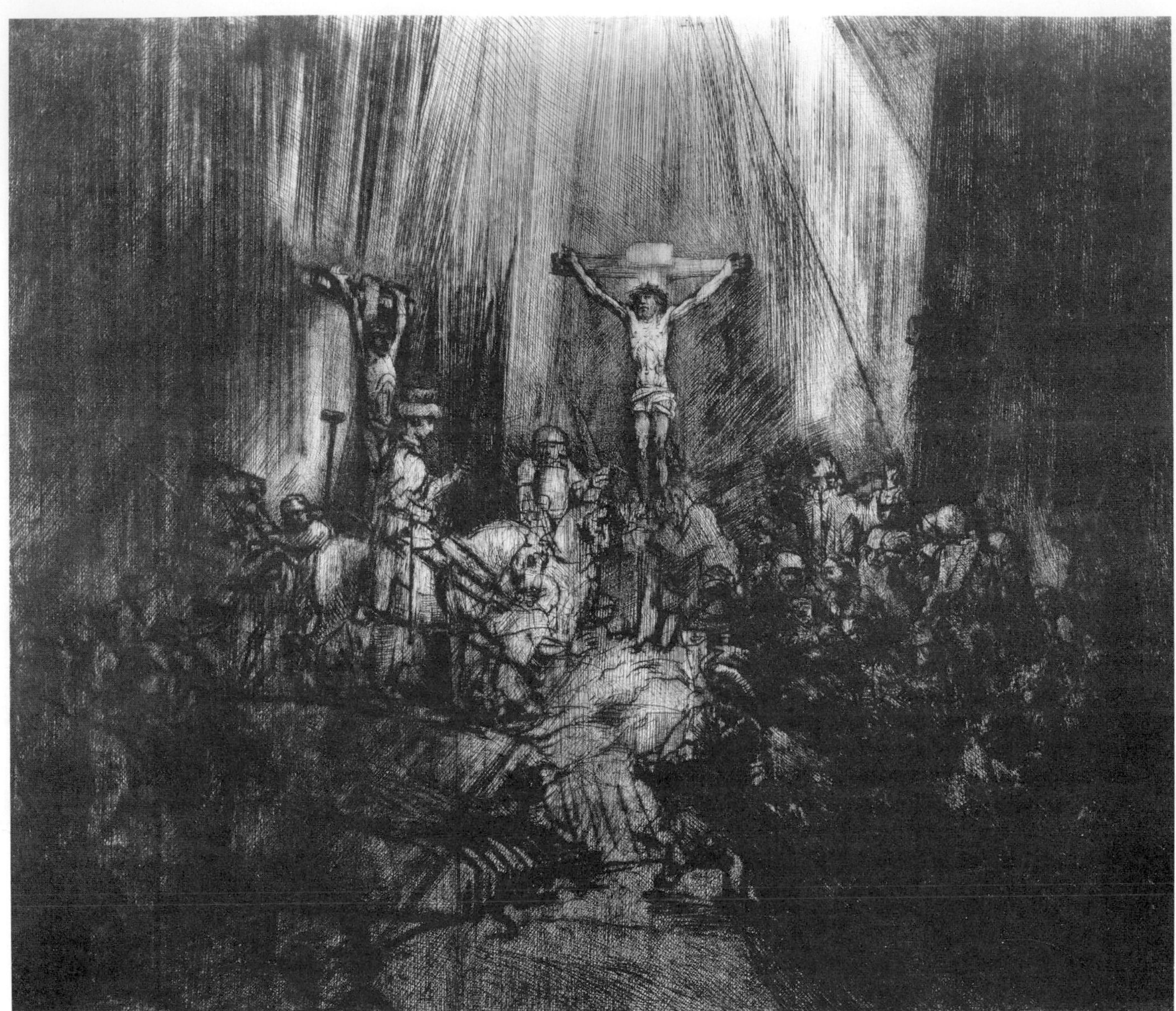

19-53 Rembrandt van Rijn, *The Three Crosses,* 1653. Fourth-state etching, approx. 15″ × 18″. British Museum, London.

his prints. Prints were a major source of income for him, and he often reworked the plates so that they could be used to produce a new issue or edition. The illustration here shows the fourth state, or version, of his *The Three Crosses* (FIG. **19-53**). In the earlier states, he represents the hill of Calvary in a quite pictorial, historical way, with crowds of soldiers and spectators, all descriptively and painstakingly rendered. In this last state, not the historical but the symbolic significance of the scene comes to the fore. As if impatient with the earlier detail, Rembrandt furiously eliminates most of it with hard, downward strokes of the needle, until what appears like a storm of dark lines pours down from Heaven, leaving a zone of light on the lonely figure of the crucified Christ. Here, Rembrandt seems clearly to show that, in the words of theologian William Vischer-T'Hooft, "the entire biblical story is meant to lead us to the cross."

The art of his later years was not really acceptable to Rembrandt's contemporaries (although he occasionally received important commissions, like that for *Syndics of the Cloth Guild*). It was too personal, too eccentric. Many, like the Italian biographer Filippo Baldinucci, thought Rembrandt was a tasteless painter, concerned with the ugly and ignorant of color. This prejudice lasted well into the nineteenth century, when Rembrandt's genius finally was acknowledged. We see him now as one of the great masters of the whole tradition, an artist of great versatility, and the unique interpreter of the Protestant conception of scripture.

At the same time, modern scholarship and connoisseurship are revising our notion of Rembrandt's uniqueness and our view of him as an isolated and courageous master, who found his own way to new heights of expression, no matter the barriers of misunderstanding raised against him. Though his greatness is still conceded, Rembrandt now is understood to have been very much a part of his time, society, and stylistic school. He had numerous colleagues and pupils, with whom he shared stylistic traits and technical methods—so much so, that it is often difficult and sometimes impossible to determine which of the many paintings attributed to him are actually his. For twenty years, a team of Dutch scholars, the Rembrandt Research Project, has been carefully examining paintings attributed to Rembrandt in museums and private collections throughout the world. The results of their investigation, which still continues, have raised vehement debate, controversy, and consternation among art historians, museum curators, collectors, and dealers. Millions of dollars are at stake. The Rembrandt research team does not seem willing to allow more than 350 pictures to be credited with certainty to Rembrandt; at one time, twice that number had been so attributed. None of this subtracts, of course, from the esthetic value of Rembrandt's contribution, which certainly is inestimable; nor does it in any way diminish his stature in the history of world art. It *does* remind us once again that the facts of art history are always open to review, and our interpretations of them to revision.

THE "LITTLE DUTCH MASTERS"

The pictorial genius of the Dutch masters of the seventeenth century surpassed all others in its comprehensiveness of subject, taking all that is given to the eye as its province. The whole world of sight is explored, but especially the things of ordinary use and aspect with which human beings surround themselves. In some ways, the old Netherlandish tradition of Jan van Eyck lives on in the rendering of things in the optical environment with a loving and scrupulous fidelity to their appearances. Dutch painters came to specialize in portraiture, genre, interiors, still life, landscape and seascape, and even in more specialized subdivisions of these. With many, the restriction of their professional interest is all to the good; they may not create works of grand conception, but, within their small compass, they produce exquisite art.

JAN VERMEER

The best-known and most highly regarded of these painters, once referred to as the "little Dutch masters," is JAN VERMEER (1632–1675) of Delft, who was rediscovered in the nineteenth century. Vermeer's pictures are small, few, and perfect within their scope. While the fifteenth-century Flemish artists usually painted interiors of houses occupied by persons of sacred significance, Vermeer and his contemporaries composed neat, quietly opulent interiors of Dutch middle-class dwellings, in which they placed men, women, and children engaged in household tasks or some little recreation—totally commonplace actions, yet reflective of the values of a comfortable domesticity that has a simple beauty. Vermeer usually composed with a single figure, but sometimes with two or more. His *Young Woman with a Water Jug* (FIG. **19-54**) can be considered typical, although we cannot be sure of the precise action being depicted or the precise moment of action. The girl may be opening the window to water flowers in a window box outside. This action is insignificant in itself and only one of hundreds performed in the course of a domestic day. Yet Vermeer, in his lighting and composing of the scene, raises it to the level of some holy, sacramental act. The old Netherlandish symbolism that made every ordinary object a religious sign is gone, but this girl's slow, gentle gesture is almost liturgical. The beauty of humble piety, which Rembrandt finds in human faces, is extended here to a quite different context. The Protestant world, renouncing magnificent churches, finds a sanctuary in a modest room illuminated by an afternoon sun. Yet the light is not the mysterious, spiritual light that falls on the face in a Rembrandt portrait as an outward manifestation of the "inner light" of grace stressed in Protestant mysticism; it is instead ordinary daylight, observed with a keenness of vision unparalleled in the history of art, unless we think of Velázquez.

Vermeer is master of pictorial light and so comprehends its functions that it is completely in the service of the artist's intention, which is to render a lighted depth so faithfully that the picture surface is but an invisible glass through which we look immediately into the constructed illusion. We know that Vermeer made use of mirrors and of the *camera obscura*, an ancestor of the modern camera in which a tiny pinhole, acting as a lens, projected an image on a screen or the wall of a room. (In later versions, the image was projected on a ground-glass wall of a box, the opposite wall of which contained the pinhole.) This does not mean that Vermeer merely copied the image; these aids helped him to obtain results that he reworked

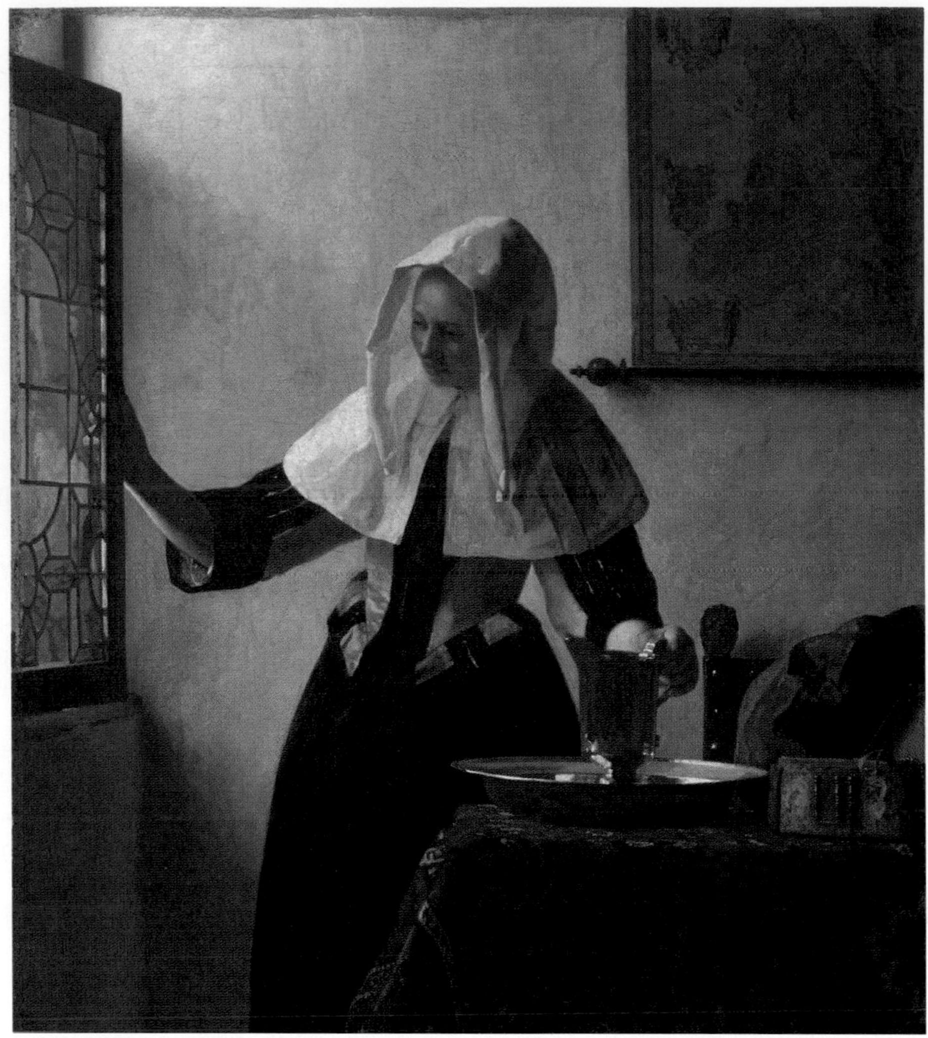

19-54 Jan Vermeer, *Young Woman with a Water Jug,* c. 1665. Approx. 18″ × 16″. Metropolitan Museum of Art, New York (gift of Henry G. Marquand, 1889).

compositionally, placing his figures and the furniture of the room in a beautiful stability of quadrilateral shapes that gives his designs a matchless Classical calm and serenity. This quality is enhanced by a color so true to the optical facts and so subtly modulated that it suggests Vermeer was far ahead of his time in color science. A detail of fig. 19-54 would show, for one thing, that Vermeer realized that shadows are not colorless and dark, that adjoining colors affect one another,* and that light is composed of colors. Thus, the blue drape is caught as a dark blue on the side of the brass pitcher, and the red of the carpet is modified in the low-intensity gold hue of the basin. It has been suggested that Vermeer also perceived the phenomenon photographers call *circles of confusion,* which appear on out-of-focus films; Vermeer could have seen them in images projected by the primitive lenses of the camera obscura. He approximates these effects in light dabs and touches that, in close view, give the impression of an image slightly "out of focus"; when we draw back a step, however, as if adjusting the lens, the color spots cohere, giving an astonishingly accurate illusion of a third dimension. All of these technical considerations reflect the scientific spirit of the age, but they do not explain the exquisite poetry of form and surface, of color and light, that could come only from the sensitivity of a great artist. In Marcel Proust's *Swann's Way,* the connoisseur hero, trying unsuccessfully to write a monograph on Vermeer, admits that no words could ever do justice to a single patch of sunlight on one of Vermeer's walls.

*Due to the phenomenon of *complementary afterimage,* in which, for example, the eye retains briefly a red image of a green stimulus; thus, a white area adjoining a green will appear "warm" (slightly pink), and a blue adjoining the same green will shift toward violet (blue plus the afterimage red).

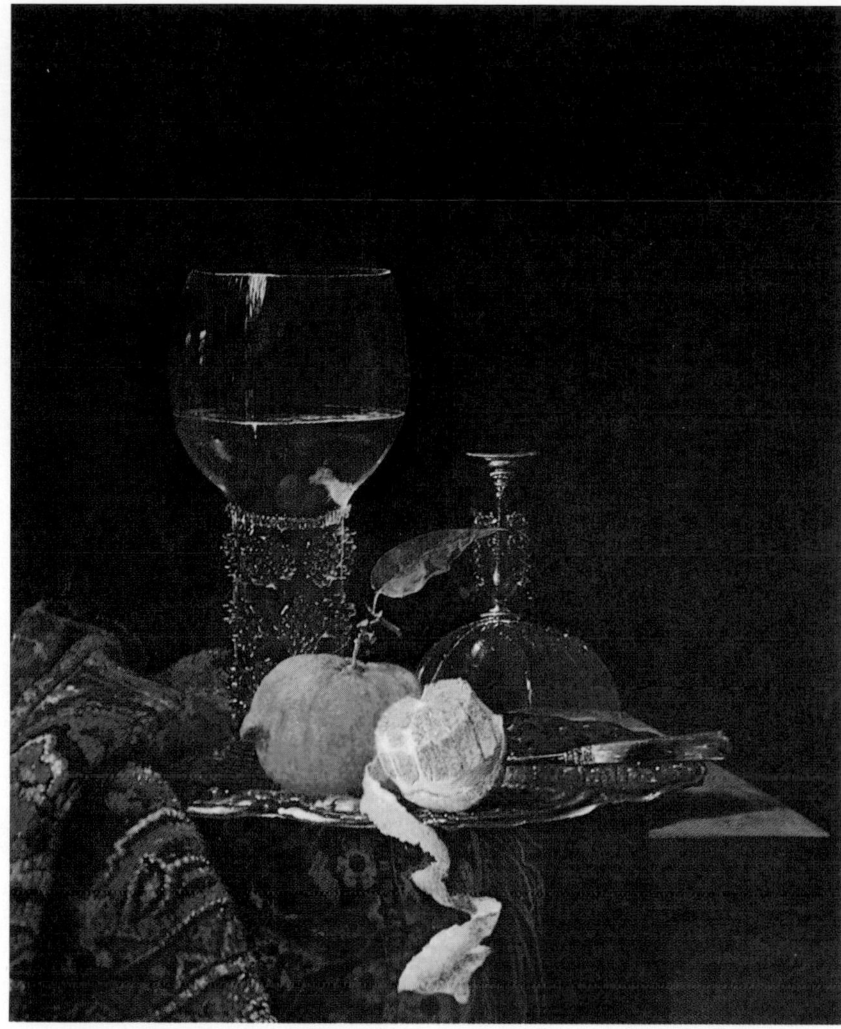

19-55 WILLEM KALF, *Still Life*, 1659. Approx. 20″ × 17″. Royal Picture Gallery (Mauritshuis), The Hague, Netherlands.

STILL LIFE: KALF

The "little Dutch masters" treat the humblest objects, which receive their meaning by their association with human uses, as reverently as if they were sacramentals. The Dutch painters of still life isolate these objects as profoundly interesting in themselves, making of their representation both scientific and poetic exercises in the revelation of the functions and the beauties of light. Many fine examples of Dutch still life have come down to us, each painted with the expertness of the specialist in analytical seeing. A still life (FIG. **19-55**) by WILLEM KALF (1619–1693) can serve as exemplary of the school. Here, against a dark ground, the artist arranges glass goblets, fruit, a silver salver, and a Turkish carpet, making a rich, luminous counterpoint of absorptive and reflective textures. The glossy, transparent shells of the goblets gleam like night skies with galaxies of sparklets and light filaments, contrasting with the duller highlights that edge the salver's rim. There is a textural gradation from the glass to the silver, from a lemon to a pomegranate to the muted glow of the light-absorbing Turkish carpet. The luminous flesh of the peeled lemon gleams as if lighted from within. (Oranges, emblem of the ruling House of Orange, occur more frequently in Dutch still life than do lemons.) This little masterpiece shows how this age of seeing must have taken pleasure in the infinite variety of the play of light in the small universe as well as the large. Such work is not dull imitation; it is revelation of what can be seen if the eye will learn to see it.

LANDSCAPE: VAN RUISDAEL

The Baroque world discovers the infinite, whether it is the infinitely small or the infinitely great. The minute spark of light that lifts the rim of a glass out

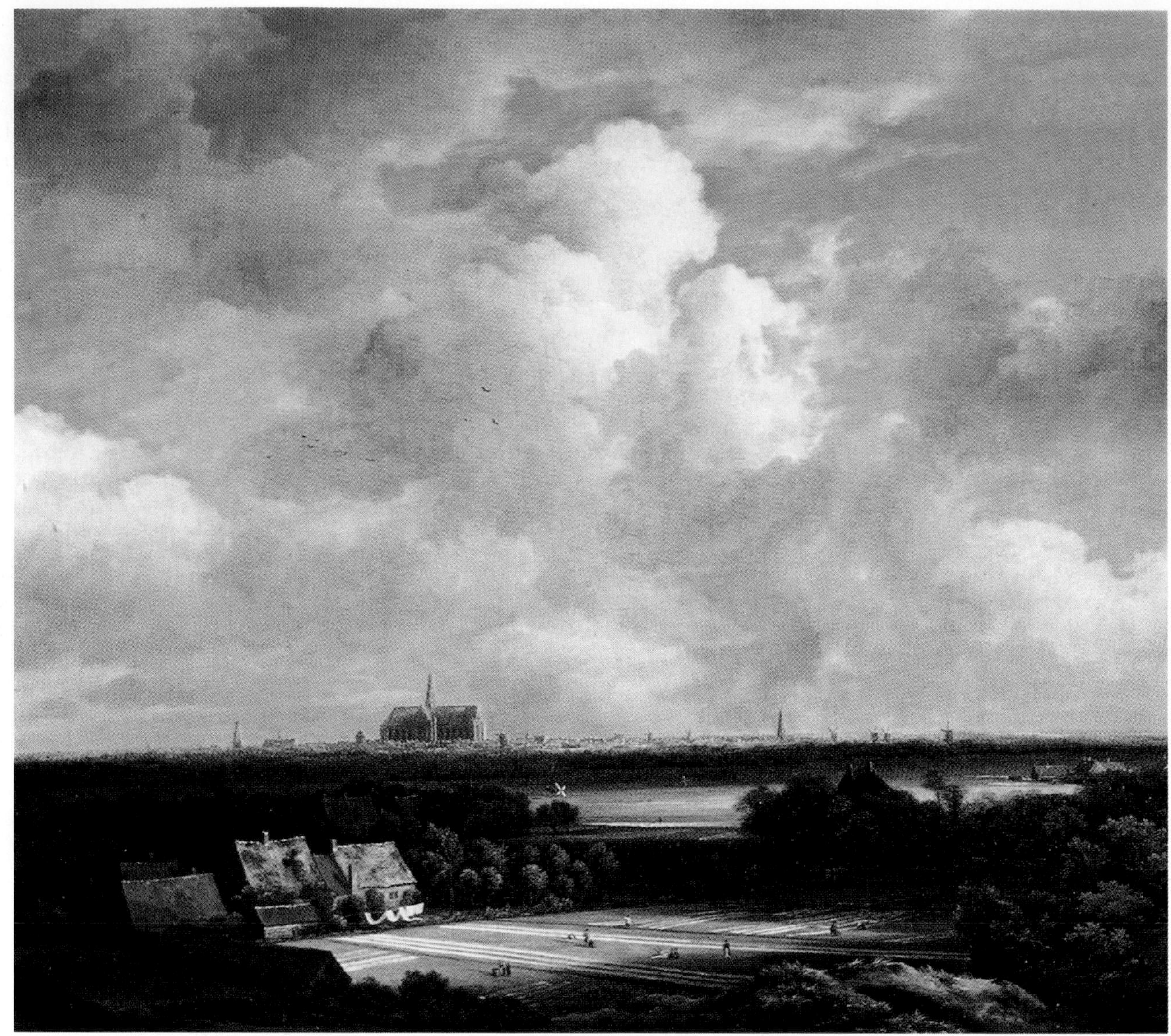

19-56 JACOB VAN RUISDAEL, *View of Haarlem from the Dunes at Overveen*, c. 1670. Approx. 22″ × 25″. Royal Picture Gallery (Mauritshuis), The Hague, Netherlands.

of darkness becomes, when expanded, the sunlit heavens. The globule of dew on a leaf in a Dutch flower becomes the aqueous globe of Earth itself. The space that began to open behind the figures of Giotto (FIG. 15-14) now, in Dutch landscape, takes flight into limitless distance, and the human being dwindles to insignificance—"his time a moment, and a point his place." In some of the works of JACOB VAN RUISDAEL (1628–1682), the human figure does not appear at all or appears only minutely. In *View of Haarlem from the Dunes at Overveen* (FIG. **19-56**), Van Ruisdael gives us almost a portrait of the newly discovered, infinite universe, allowing the sky to take up two-thirds of the picture space. One of the great landscape painters of all time, the artist turns to the vast and moody heavens that loom above the flat dunelands of Holland. His sullen clouds, in great droves never quite scattered by the sun, are herded by the winds that blew the fortunes of Holland's fleets as well as the disasters of the invading sea. Storms always are breaking up or gathering; the earth always is drenched, or about to be. As Rembrandt reads the souls of men in their faces, so Van Ruisdael reads the somber depths of the heavens. No angels swoop through his skies or recline on his clouds, for clouds now are simply water vapor. Like Rembrandt's, his is a "Protestant" reading of nature. The difference between northern and southern Baroque is evident at once in a comparison of Pozzo's *Glorification of St. Ignatius* (FIG. 19-33) and Van Ruisdael's *View of Haarlem*. It is the difference between the heavens of Jesuit vision and the heavens of Newton and Leibniz.

FRANCE

In the second half of the seventeenth century, the fortunes of both Holland and Spain sank before those of France, whose "Sun King," Louis XIV, dominated the period of European history between 1660 and 1715. The age of Louis XIV saw the ascendancy of French power in Europe, politically and culturally, and the achievement of an international influence in taste that France still has not entirely lost. The French regard this period as their golden age, a time when Paris began to replace Rome as the art center of Europe; when the French language became the polished instrument of discourse in diplomacy and in the courts of all countries; and when French art and criticism, fashion and etiquette, were imitated universally. Art and architecture came into the service of the king, as once they had been in the service of the Church, and the unity of style so conspicuous in them is the result of the taste of Louis XIV himself—imposed on the whole nation through his able minister Jean Baptiste Colbert and through the new academies Colbert set up to regularize style in all the arts.

The king's taste and, therefore, the taste of France favored a stately and reserved Classicism in place of the lavish and emotional Baroque of Italy and most of the rest of Europe. The severe Classical regularity of form—in the plays of Pierre Corneille and Jean Baptiste Racine, in the Corinthian colonnade of the Louvre (FIG. 19-64), and in the paintings of Nicolas Poussin (FIGS. 19-60 and 19-61)—is exceptional in the age of the Baroque. Even though we can find much that is Baroque in the "Classical" art produced in the time of *le Roi Soleil,* Classicism came to be thought of as standard by the French, and continued to be so for centuries.

Painting

During the earlier part of the seventeenth century, France began a slow recovery from the anarchy of the religious wars. While Cardinals Richelieu and Mazarin painfully rebuilt the power and prestige of the French throne, French art remained under the influence of Italy and Flanders. Even so, artists of originality emerged. Among them was GEORGES DE LA TOUR (1593–1652), a painter who learned of Caravaggio possibly through the Dutch school of Utrecht. Much as De La Tour uses the devices of the northern Caravaggisti, his effects are strikingly different from theirs. His *Adoration of the Shepherds* (FIG. **19-57**) shows us the night setting favored by that

19-57 GEORGES DE LA TOUR, *Adoration of the Shepherds,* 1645–1650. Approx. 42″ × 54″. Louvre, Paris.

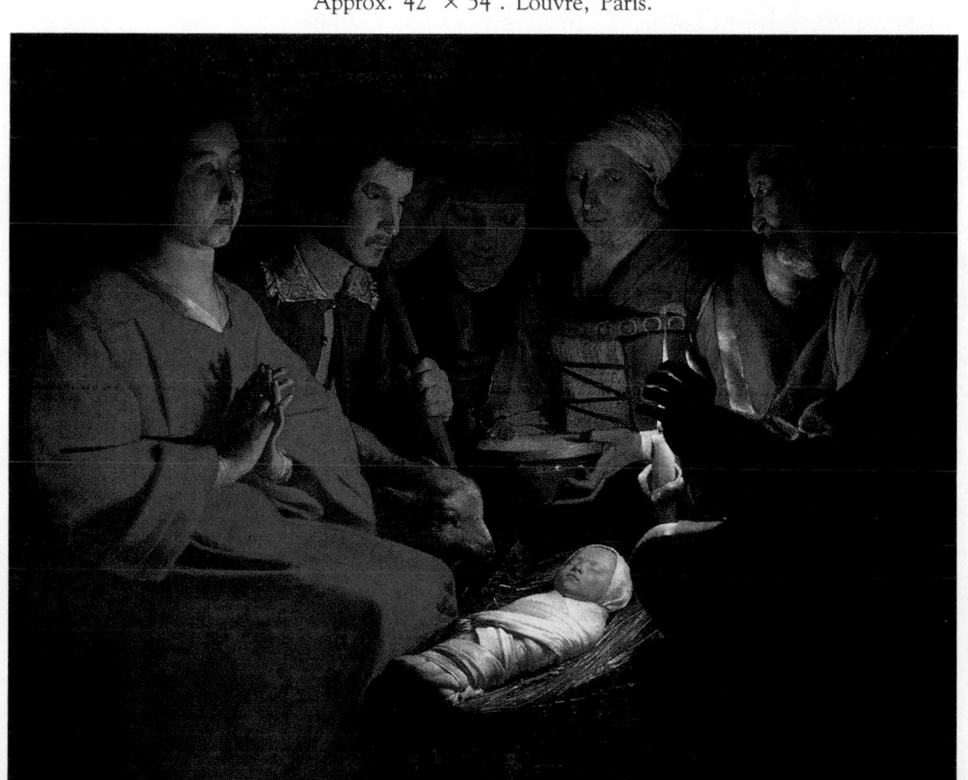

school, much as we have seen it in Van Honthorst (FIG. 19-45). But here, the light, its source shaded by the hand of an old man, falls upon a very different company in a very different mood. We see a group of humble men and women, coarsely clad, gathered in prayerful vigil around a luminous infant. If we did not know that this is a representation of the sacred event of the Nativity, we would consider it a genre piece, a narrative of some happening from peasant life. Nothing in the environment, placement, poses, dress, or attributes of the figures might distinguish them as the scriptural Virgin Mary, Joseph, Christ Child, or shepherds. The artist has not portrayed haloes, choirs of angels, stately architecture, or resplendent grandees (FIGS. 16-26, 18-17). The light is not spiritual but material; it comes from a candle. De La Tour's scientific scrutiny of the effects of material light, as it throws precise shadows on surfaces that intercept it, nevertheless, has religious intention and consequence. It illuminates a group of ordinary people, held in a mystic trance induced by their witnessing of the miracle of the Incarnation. The dogmatic significance and traditional iconography of the Incarnation are absorbed without trace in this timeless tableau of simple people, who are in reverent contemplation of something they regard as holy. As such, the painting is readable to the devout of any religious persuasion, whether or not they know of this central mystery of the Christian faith. Yet the effect of rapt religiosity is created by essentially the same devices of composition, chiaroscuro, and commonplace subject that we find in the worldly art of the Dutch Caravaggisti.

The supernatural calm that pervades this picture is characteristic of the mood of the art of Georges de La Tour. It is achieved by the elimination of motion and emotive gesture (only the light is dramatic), by the suppression of surface detail, and by the simplification of body volumes. These traits of style we associate with art of Classical substance or tendency—for example, that of Piero della Francesca (FIG. 16-34). Several apparently contrary elements meet in the work of De La Tour: Classical composure, fervent spirituality, and genre realism.

LOUIS LE NAIN (*c.* 1593–1648) and his contemporary, De La Tour, bear comparison with the Dutch. Subjects that in Dutch painting are an opportunity for boisterous good humor are managed by the French with a cool stillness. *Family of Country People* (FIG. **19-58**) expresses the grave dignity of a family close to the soil, one made stoic and resigned by hardship. Obviously, Le Nain sympathizes with his subjects and seems here to want to emphasize their rustic virtue, far from the gorgeous artificiality of the courts.

19-58 LOUIS LE NAIN, *Family of Country People*, c. 1640. Approx. 44″ × 62″. Louvre, Paris.

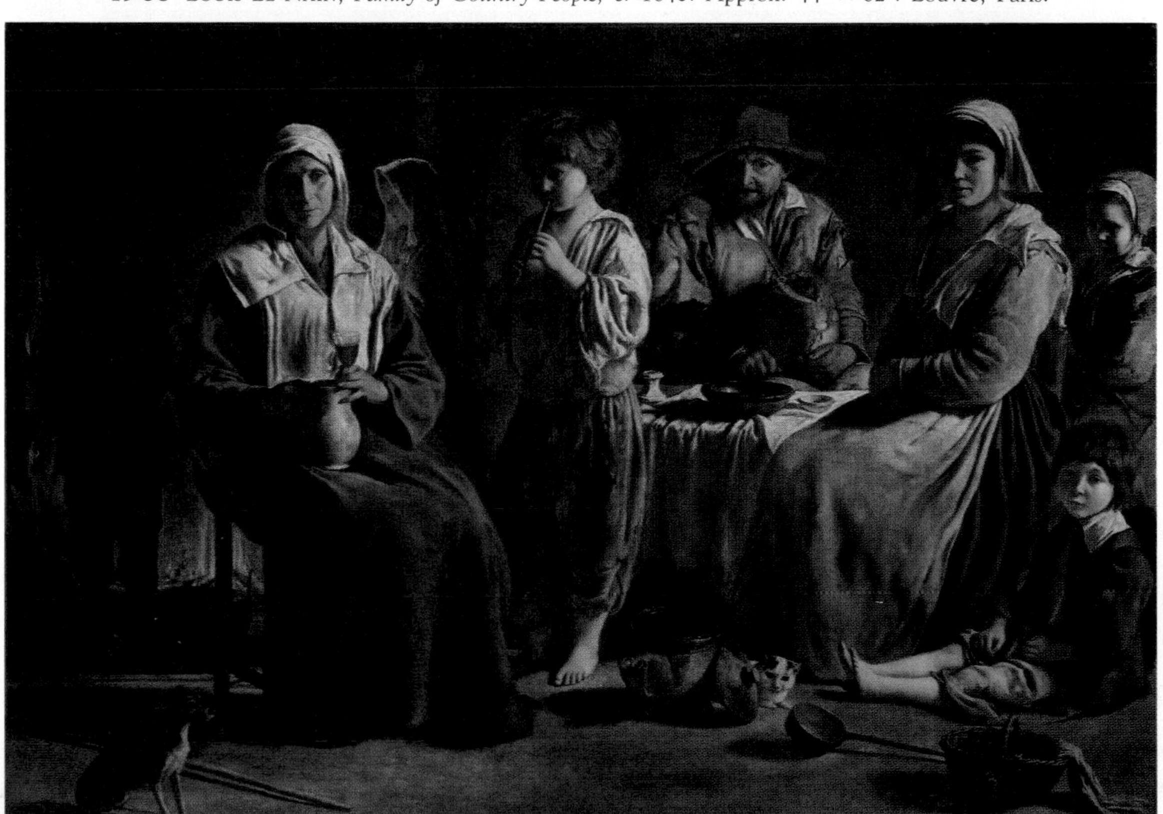

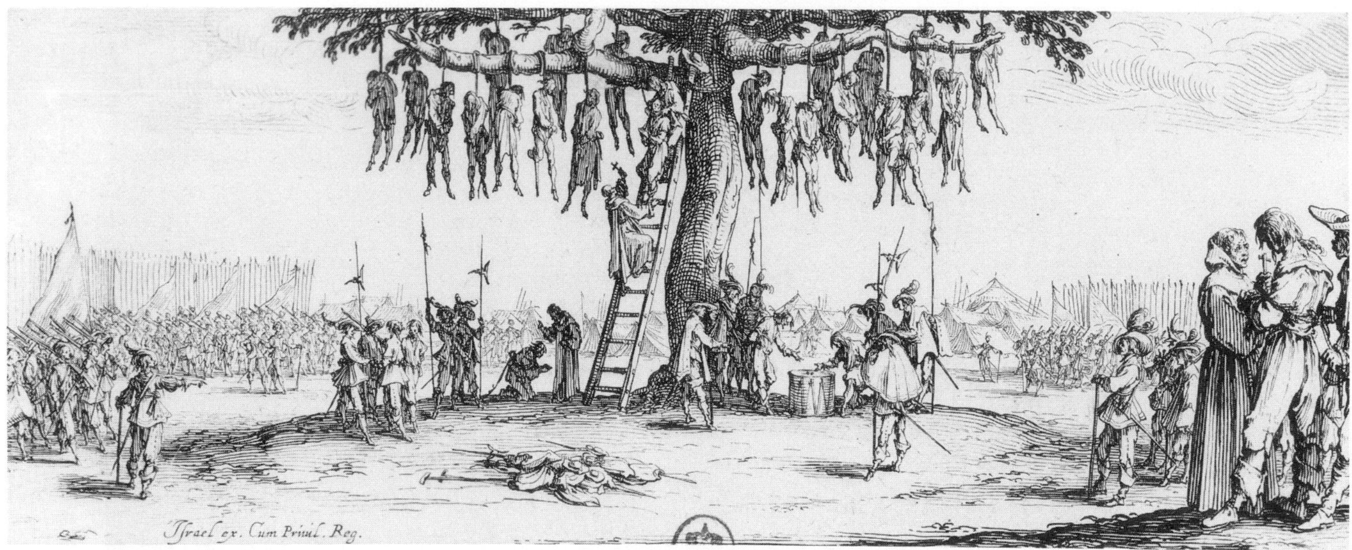

19-59 JACQUES CALLOT, *Hanging Tree,* etching from the *Miseries of War* series, 1621. Bibliothèque Nationale, Paris.

Stress on the honesty, integrity, and even innocence of uncorrupted country folk in the following century will become sentimentality. However, Le Nain's objectivity permits him to record a group of such genuine human beings that the picture rises above anecdote and the picturesqueness of genre. These still, sombre country folk could have had little reason for merriment. The lot of the peasant, never easy, was miserable during the time Le Nain painted. The terrible conflict we call the Thirty Years' War (1618–1648) was raging. The last and most devastating of the wars of religion between Protestants and Catholics, which had begun a century before, spread atrocity and ruin throughout France, Italy, and the Germanies. The anguish and frustration of the peasantry, suffering from the cruel depredations of unruly armies living off the country, often broke out in savage revolts that were savagely put down.

A record of the times appears in a series of etchings by JACQUES CALLOT (1592–1635) called *Miseries of War.* Callot, the first great master of the art of etching, a medium to which he confined himself almost exclusively, was widely influential in his own time and since; Rembrandt was among those who knew and learned from his work. Callot perfected the medium and the technique of etching, developing a very hard surface for the copper plate, to permit fine and precise delineation with the needle. In one small print, he may assemble as many as twelve hundred figures, which only close scrutiny can discriminate. His quick, vivid touch and faultless drawing produce a panorama sparkling with sharp details of life—and death. In the *Miseries,* he observes these coolly, presenting without comment things he himself must have seen in the wars in his own country, Lorraine. In one etching, he depicts a mass execution by hanging (FIG. **19-59**). The unfortunates may be war prisoners or defeated peasant rebels. The event takes place in the presence of a disciplined army, drawn up on parade, with banners, muskets, and lances, their tents in the right background. Hanged men sway in clusters from the branches of a huge, cross-shaped tree. A monk climbs a ladder, holding up a crucifix to a man, around whose neck the noose is being adjusted. At the foot of the ladder, another victim kneels to receive absolution. Under the tree, men roll dice on a drumhead for the belongings of the executed. (This may be an allusion, in the Baroque manner, to the soldiers who cast lots for the garments of the crucified Christ.) In the right foreground, a bound man is consoled by a hooded priest. Callot's *Miseries* are the first realistic, pictorial record of the human disaster of war. They foreshadow Goya's great prints on the same theme (not shown).

POUSSIN

The brisk animation of Callot's manner contrasts with the quiet composure in the art of De La Tour and Le Nain, his exact contemporaries. Yet although calm simplicity and restraint characterize the latter two, in comparison with other northern painters inspired by Caravaggio, and although these qualities suggest the Classical, it remains for another contemporary, NICOLAS POUSSIN (1594–1665), to establish Classical painting as peculiarly expressive of French taste and genius in the seventeenth century. Poussin, born in Normandy, spent most of his life in Rome. There, inspired by its monuments and the landscape of the Campagna, he produced his grandly severe and regular canvases and carefully worked out a theoretical

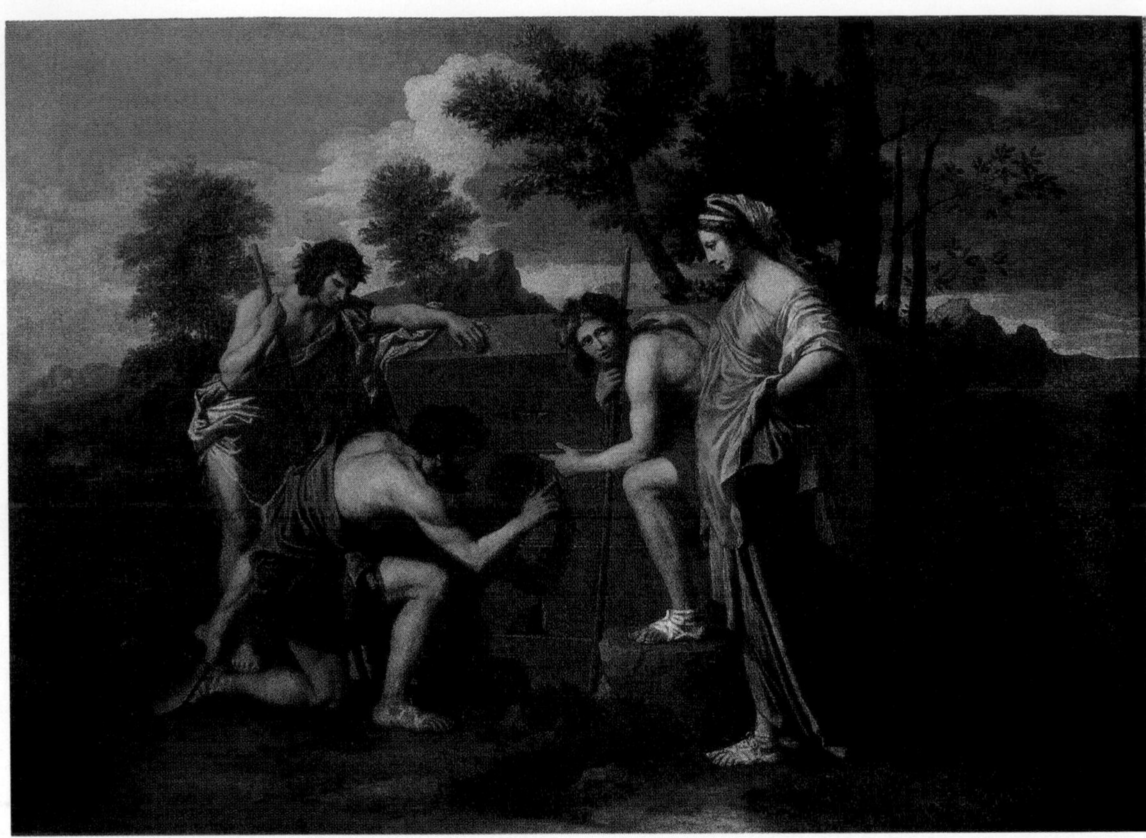

19-60 Nicolas Poussin, *Et in Arcadia Ego,* c. 1655 (?). Approx. 34″ × 48″. Louvre, Paris.

explanation of his method. He worked for a while under Domenichino but shunned the exuberant Italian Baroque; Titian and Raphael were the models that he set for himself. Of his two versions of a single theme titled *Et in Arcadia Ego* (*I, too, in Arcadia* or *Even in Arcadia, I* [am present]), the earlier is strikingly Titianesque, with all the warm, rich tonality of the Venetian master and the figure types familiar in Titian's idyllic "bacchanals." But, in the end, the rational order and stability of Raphael proved most appealing to Poussin. His second version of *Et in Arcadia Ego* (FIG. **19-60**) shows what he learned from Raphael, as well as from Antique statuary; landscape, of which Poussin became increasingly fond, expands in the picture, reminiscent of Titian but also indicative of Poussin's own study of nature. The theme is somewhat obscure and of interest to some modern scholars. As three shepherds living in the idyllic land of Arcadia spell out an enigmatic inscription on a tomb, a stately female figure quietly places her hand on the shoulder of one of them. She may be the spirit of death, reminding these mortals, as does the inscription, that death is found even in Arcadia, where naught but perfect happiness is supposed to reign. The compact, balanced grouping of the figures, the even light, and the thoughtful, reserved, elegiac mood set the tone for Poussin's art in its later, Classical phase.

In notes for an intended treatise on painting, Poussin outlines the "grand manner" of Classicism, of which he became the leading exponent in Rome. One must first of all choose great subjects: "The first requirement, fundamental to all others, is that the subject and the narrative be grandiose, such as battles, heroic actions, and religious themes." Minute details should be avoided, as well as all "low" subjects, like genre ("Those who choose base subjects find refuge in them because of the feebleness of their talents"). This dictum rules out a good deal of both the decorative and realistic art of the Baroque, and will lead to a doctrinaire limitation on artistic enterprise and experiment in the rules of the French Royal Academy, which, under Charles Le Brun in the 1660s, will take Poussin as its greatest modern authority. Although Poussin can create with ease and grandeur within the scope of his rather severe maxims, his method can become wooden and artificial in the hands of academic followers.

Poussin represents that theoretical tradition in Western art that goes back to the Early Renaissance and that asserts that all good art must be the result of good judgment—a judgment based on sure knowledge. In this way, art can achieve correctness and propriety, two of the favorite categories of the classicizing artist or architect. Poussin praises the ancient Greeks for their musical "modes," by which, he says,

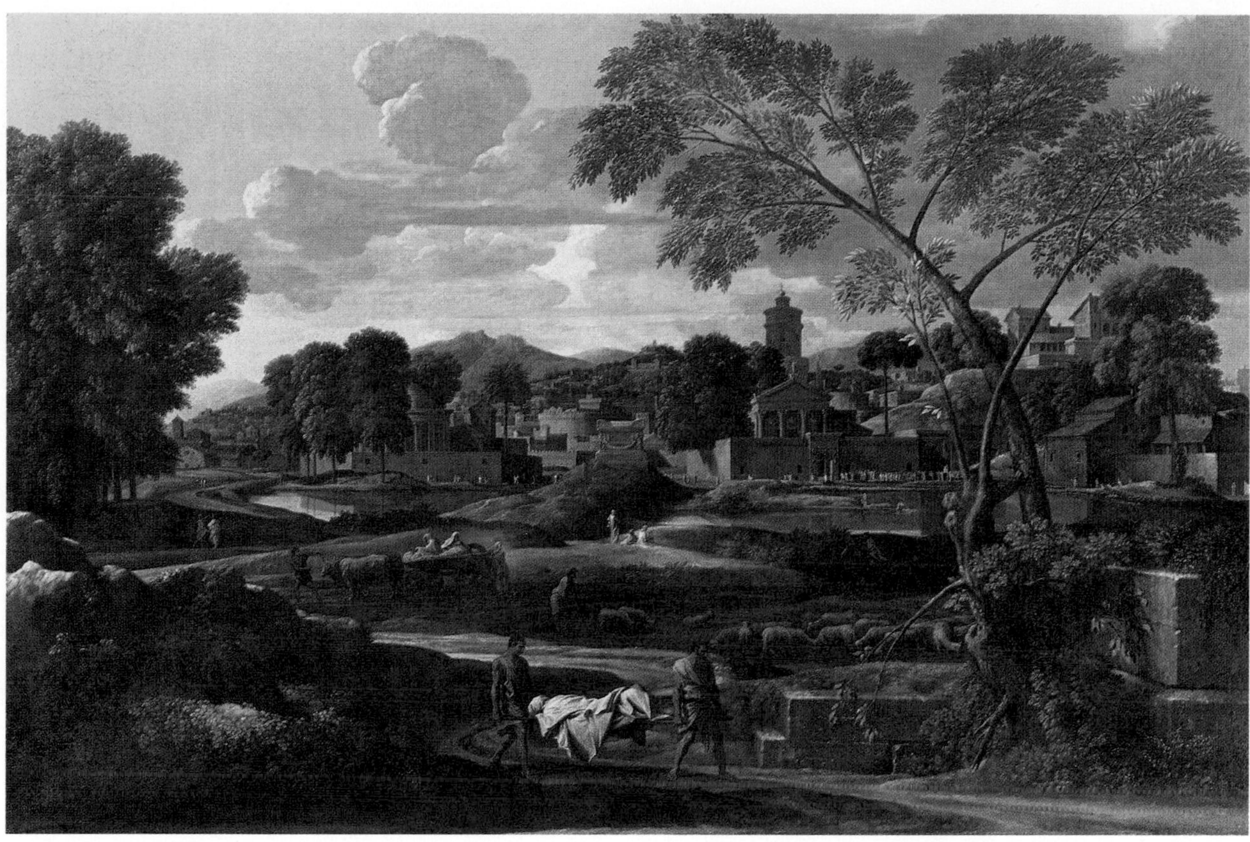

19-61 NICOLAS POUSSIN, *The Burial of Phocion,* 1648. Approx. 47″ × 70″. Louvre, Paris.

"they produced marvelous effects." He observes that "this word 'mode' means actually the rule or the measure and form which serves us in our production. This rule constrains us not to exaggerate by making us act in all things with a certain restraint and moderation." "Restraint" and "moderation" are the very essence of French Classical doctrine; in the age of Louis XIV, we find this doctrine preached as much for literature and music as for art and architecture. Poussin tells us further that

> the Modes of the ancients were a combination of several things . . . in such a proportion that it was made possible to arouse the soul of the spectator to various passions. . . . the ancient sages attributed to each style its own effects. Because of this they called the Dorian Mode stable, grave, and severe, and applied it to subjects which are grave and severe and full of wisdom.*

Poussin's finest works, like *The Burial of Phocion* (FIG. **19-61**), are instances of his obvious preference for the "Dorian Mode." His subjects are chosen carefully from the literature of antiquity, where his age would naturally look for the "grandiose," and it is with Poussin that the visual arts draw closer to literature than ever before. Here, he takes his theme from Plutarch's life of Phocion, an Athenian hero who was unjustly put to death by his countrymen but then given a public funeral and memorialized by the state. In the foreground, Poussin represents the body of the hero being taken away, his burial on Athenian soil having at first been forbidden. The two massive bearers and the bier are starkly isolated in a great landscape that throws them into solitary relief, eloquently expressive of the hero abandoned in death. The landscape is composed of interlocking planes that slope upward to the lighted sky at the left, carefully arranged terraces that bear slowly moving streams, shepherds and their flocks, and, in the distance, whole assemblies of solid geometric structures (temples, towers, walls, villas). The skies are untroubled and the light is even and form-revealing. The trees are few and carefully arranged, like curtains lightly drawn back to reveal a nature carefully cultivated as a setting for a single human action. Unlike Van Ruisdael's *View of Haarlem* (FIG. 19-56), this scene is not intended to represent a particular place and time; it is the construction of an *idea* of a noble landscape to frame a noble theme, much as we have seen it in Annibale Carracci's Classical landscape (FIG. 19-31). The *Phocion* landscape is nature subordinated to a

*In E. G. Holt, ed., *Literary Sources of Art History* (Princeton, NJ: Princeton University Press, 1947), p. 380.

rational plan, much like the gardens of Versailles (FIG. 19-66); it is eminently of the Age of Reason.

CLAUDE LORRAIN

The disciplined, rational art of Poussin, with its sophisticated revelation of the geometry of landscape, is modulated in the softer style of Claude Gellée, called CLAUDE LORRAIN (1600–1682) and sometimes only Claude. Unlike Poussin's pictures, Claude's are not "Dorian." The figures in his landscapes tell no dramatic story, point out no moral, and praise no hero; indeed, they often appear added as mere excuses for the radiant landscape itself. For Claude, painting involves essentially one theme: the beauty of a broad sky suffused with the golden light of dawn or sunset that makes its glowing way through a hazy atmosphere, and reflects scintillatingly from the rippling water. In one realization of Claude's landscape ideal the setting is a seaport, where the Queen of Sheba is embarking for home (FIG. **19-62**). Servants are loading boats with the rich gifts bestowed upon the queen by King Solomon (1 Kings 10:1–10, 13). The queen, with her stately entourage, descends to the quay from a majestic palace, the style of which is familiar in the classicizing architecture of the seventeenth century. Occupying the dark left foreground is a lofty fragment of a Roman ruin. The ships, their sails still furled, await their cargoes. A tower, arched bridge, and tall trees are grouped in the distance. These are the stage properties invented by Claude to set off his theme; they are not to be thought of as authentic representations of the time and place of his narrative. The firm architectural shapes, the busy diagonals of the ships' rigging, and the perfunctory, small figures are meant solely to frame (like the wings of a stage) the central actor and the pictorial focus, which is the effulgent sun and the trail of sparkling accents it leaves upon the sea. The dark foreground, lighter middleground, and dim background recede in serene orderliness, until all form dissolves in a luminous mist. Atmospheric and linear perspective reinforce one another to turn a vista into a typical Claudian vision, an ideal Classical world conjured up in the sunlit infinity of Baroque space.

In formalizing nature with balanced groups of architectural masses, screens of trees, and sheets of water, Claude is working in the great tradition of

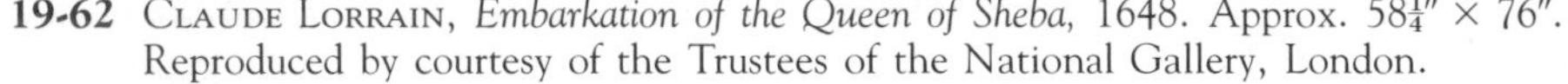

19-62 CLAUDE LORRAIN, *Embarkation of the Queen of Sheba*, 1648. Approx. $58\frac{1}{4}'' \times 76''$. Reproduced by courtesy of the Trustees of the National Gallery, London.

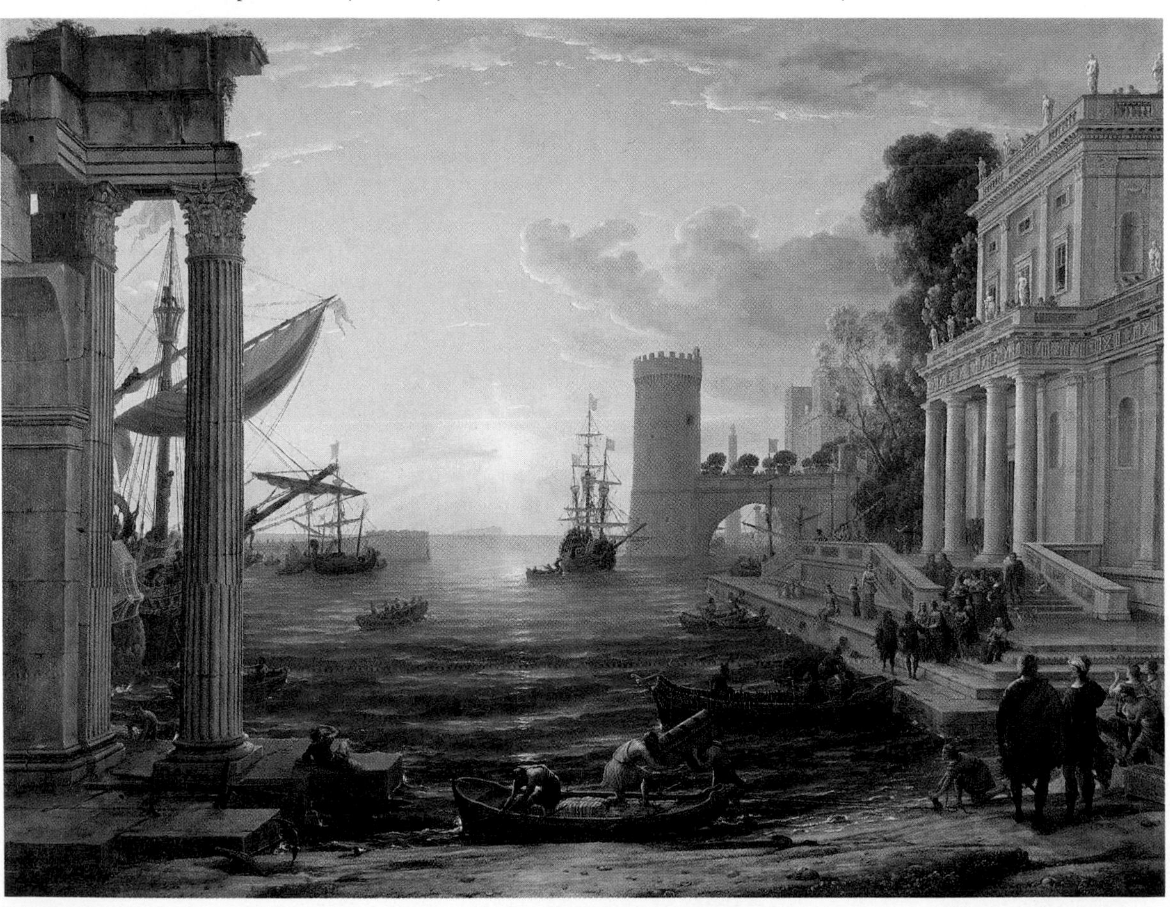

Classical landscape that opens in the backgrounds of Venetian painting (FIGS. 17-58 and 17-59) and continues in the art of Annibale Carracci (FIG. 19-31) and Poussin (FIG. 19-61). At the same time, Claude, like the Dutch painters, studies the actual light and the atmospheric nuances of nature, making a unique contribution. He recorded carefully in hundreds of sketches the veritable look of the Roman Campagna, its pellucid air, its gentle terrain variegated by stone-pines, cypresses, and poplars, and by ever-present ruins of ancient aqueducts, tombs, and towers. He made these the fundamental accessories of his compositions; travelers could learn of and could recognize the picturesque beauties of the Campagna in Claude's landscapes.

His marvelous effects of light were achieved by painstaking placement of infinitesimally small value gradations, which imitated, though on a very small scale, the actual range of values of out-of-door light and shade. Avoiding the problem of high noon, Claude preferred, and could convincingly represent, the disc of the sun as it gradually radiates the morning sky, or with its dying glow sets the pensive mood of evening. Thus he matches the moods of nature and of the human subject. Claude's infusion of nature with human feeling, while re-composing it in a calm equilibrium, would have great appeal to the landscape painters of the eighteenth and earlier nineteenth centuries, especially Turner, whose lifelong admiration of Claude's art was almost obsessive.

The softening of Poussin's stern manner in Claude parallels the reaction of other painters of the time against the severe rules and regulations of the French Royal Academy under the dictatorial administration of Le Brun. Established in 1648, the Academy had been intended to free artists from the constraints of the old guild system of art training; to improve the social status of painters and sculptors, so that they would be seen as more than mere handicraftsmen; to regularize instruction in the arts; and to centralize art production in the interest of the absolute monarchy. Above all, the Academy was to develop and propagate a Classical taste, based on the study and imitation of ancient works of art and such classicizing modern masters as Raphael, the Carracci, and Poussin himself. Students were taught the supremacy of drawing over coloring, of sculpturesque form over painterly tonality, of symmetrical and closed composition over the dynamic and open—in short, the superiority of Poussin over Rubens. Yet well before the end of the century, the painting of Rubens was increasingly admired, and his influence would weaken the doctrine of the Academy and shape the taste of eighteenth-century Rococo.

Architecture

In architecture, as in painting, France maintained an attitude of cautious selectivity toward the Italian Baroque. The Classical bent asserted itself early in the work of FRANÇOIS MANSART (1598–1666), as seen in the Orléans wing of the Château de Blois (FIG. **19-63**), built between 1635 and 1638. The polished dignity and sobriety evident here will become the hallmarks

19-63 FRANÇOIS MANSART, Orléans wing of the Château de Blois, France, 1635–1638.

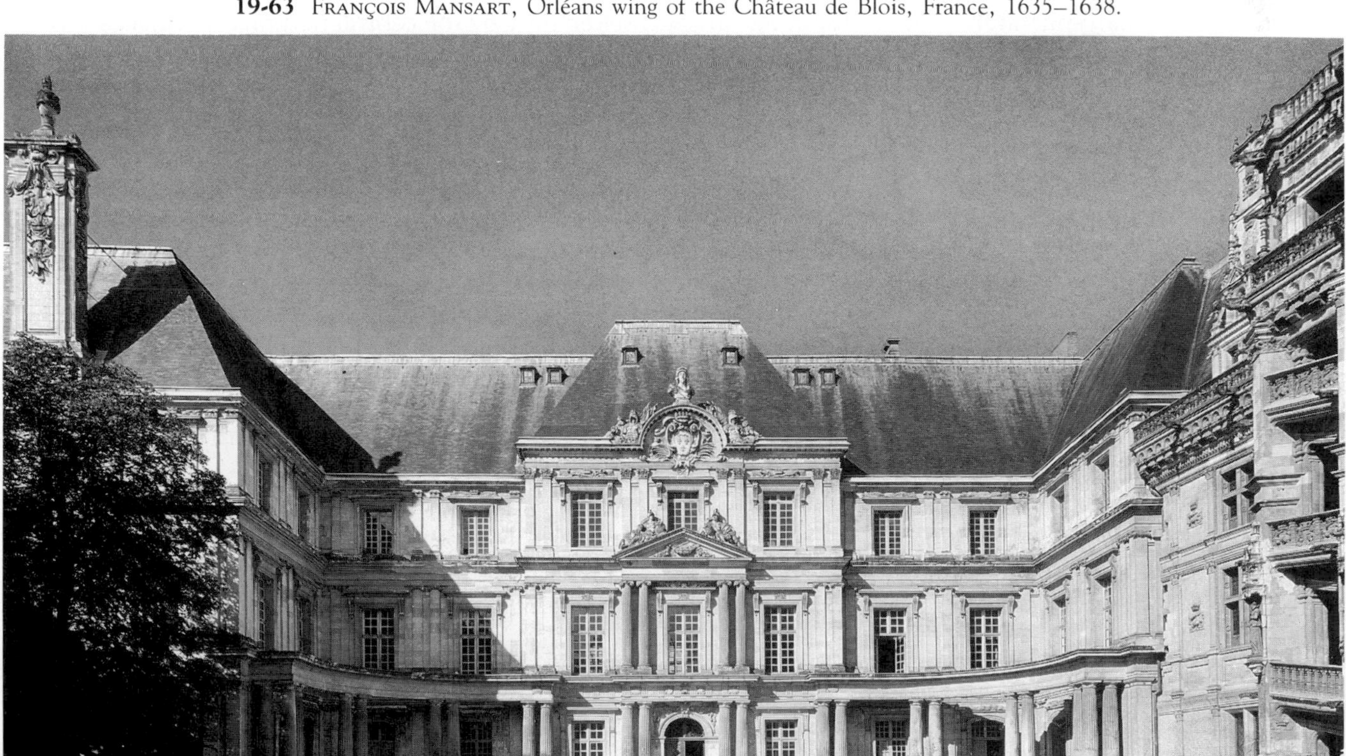

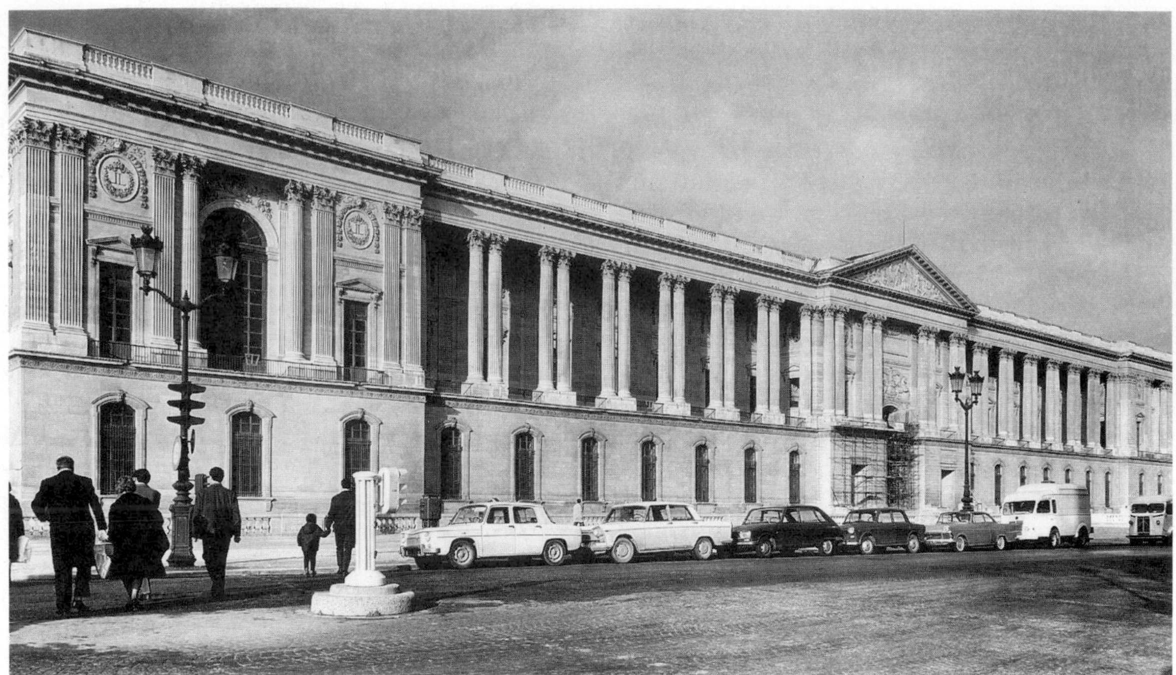

19-64 Claude Perrault, Louis Le Vau, and Charles Le Brun, east façade of the Louvre, Paris, 1667–1670.

of French "classical-baroque," contrasting with the more daring, excited, and fanciful styles of the Baroque in Italy and elsewhere. The strong, rectilinear organization and a tendency to design in terms of repeated units remind us of Italian Renaissance architecture, as does the insistence on the purity of line and sharp relief of the wall articulations. Yet the emphasis on a focal point—achieved through the curving colonnades, the changing planes of the walls, and the concentration of ornament around the portal—is characteristic of Baroque architectural thinking in general.

The formation of the French Classical style accelerated with the foundation of the Royal Academy of Painting and Sculpture in 1648, of which Poussin was a director, and with the determination of Louis XIV and Colbert to organize art and architecture in service of the state. No pains were spared to raise great symbols and monuments to the king's absolute power and to regularize taste under the academies. The first project undertaken by the young king and Colbert was the closing of the east side of the Louvre court, left incomplete by Lescot in the sixteenth century. Bernini, as the most renowned architect of his day, was summoned from Rome to submit plans, but he envisioned an Italian palace on a monumental scale that would have involved the demolition of all previous work. His plan rejected, Bernini returned to Rome in high indignation. The east façade of the Louvre (FIG. **19-64**) is the result of a collaboration between Claude Perrault (1613–1688), Louis Le Vau (1612–1670), and Charles Le Brun (1619–1690), with Le Vau probably playing a preponderant role. The design is a brilliant adjustment of French and Italian Classical elements, culminating in a new and definitive formula. The French pavilion system is retained; the central pavilion is in the form of a Classical temple front, and a giant colonnade of paired columns, resembling the columned flanks of a temple folded out like wings, is contained by the two salient pavilions at either end. The whole is mounted on a stately basement, or podium. An even roof line, balustraded and broken only by the central pediment, replaces the traditional French pyramidal roof. All memory of Gothic verticality is brushed aside in the emphatically horizontal sweep of this façade. Its stately proportions and monumentality are both an expression of the new official French taste and a symbol for centrally organized authority.

VERSAILLES

Work on the Louvre hardly had begun when Louis XIV decided to convert a royal hunting lodge at Versailles, a few miles outside Paris, into a great palace. A veritable army of architects, decorators, sculptors, painters, and landscape architects was assembled under the general management of former Poussin student Le Brun, the king's impresario of art and dictator of the Royal Academy. In their hands, the conversion of a simple hunting lodge into the Palace of Versailles (FIGS. **19-65** and **19-66**) became the greatest architectural project of the age.

Planned on a gigantic scale, the project called not only for a large palace facing a vast park but also for

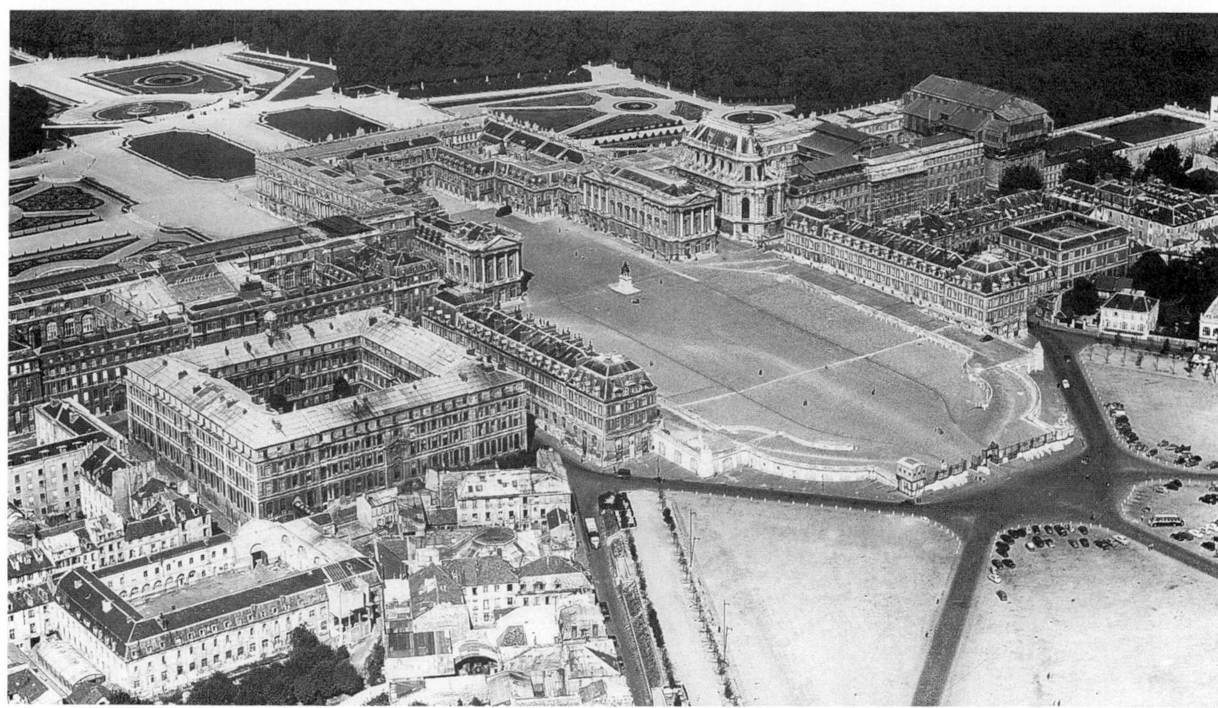

19-65 Aerial view of the Palace of Versailles, France, and a small portion of the surrounding park. The white trapezoid in the lower part of the plan (FIG. 19-66) outlines the area shown here.

19-66 Plan of the park, palace, and town of Versailles (after a seventeenth-century engraving by FRANÇOIS BLONDEL). The area outlined in the white trapezoid (lower center) is shown in FIG. 19-65.

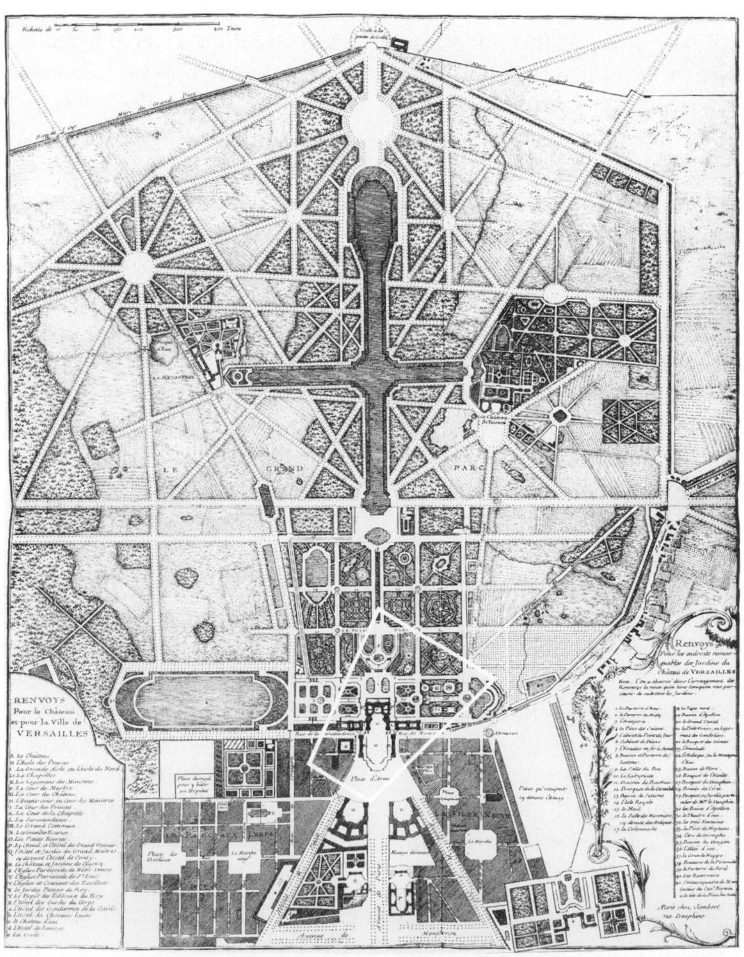

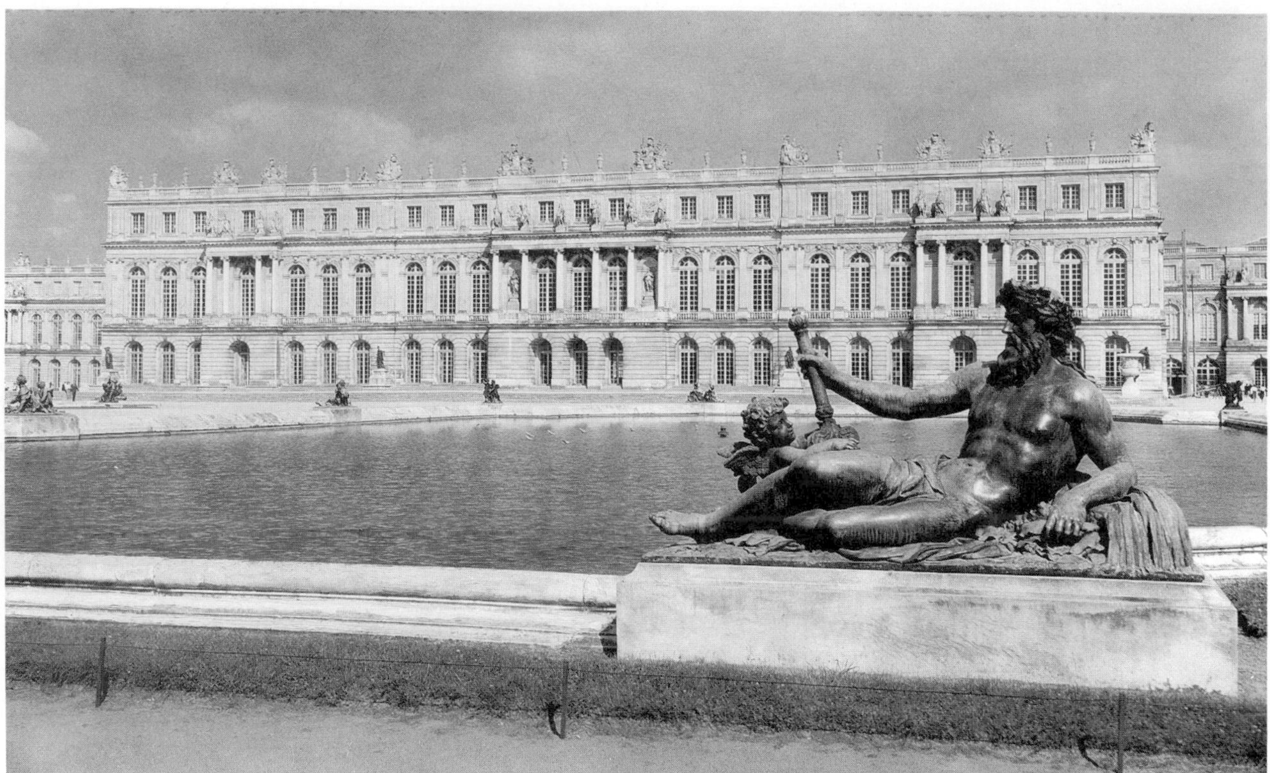

19-67 LOUIS LE VAU and JULES HARDOUIN-MANSART, garden façade of the Palace of Versailles, 1669–1685.

the construction of a satellite city to house court and government officials, military and guard detachments, courtiers, and servants. This town is laid out to the east of the palace along three radial avenues that converge on the palace structure itself; their axes, in a symbolic assertion of the ruler's absolute power over his domains, intersect in the king's bedroom. (As the site of the king's morning levée, this bedroom was actually an audience room, a state chamber.) The palace itself, over a quarter of a mile long, is placed at right angles to the dominant east–west axis that runs through city and park. Its most impressive feature is the garden façade (FIG. **19-67**), which was begun by Le Vau and continued in his style by JULES HARDOUIN-MANSART (1646–1708, a great-nephew of François Mansart), who took over the project after Le Vau's death in 1670. In typical Baroque fashion, the vast lateral extension of the façade has been broken up into units and subunits of threes, an effective organizational device even on this scale.

Careful attention has been paid to every detail of the extremely rich decoration of the palace's interior; everything from wall paintings to doorknobs is designed in keeping with the whole and is executed with the very finest sense of craftsmanship. Of the literally hundreds of rooms within the palace, the most famous is the Galerie des Glaces, or Hall of Mirrors (FIG. **19-68**), which overlooks the park from the second floor and extends along most of the width of the central block. Although deprived of its original sumptuous furniture, which included gold and silver chairs and bejeweled trees, the Galerie des Glaces retains much of its splendor today. Its tunnel-like quality is alleviated by hundreds of mirrors, set into the wall opposite the windows, that illusionistically extend the width of the room. The mirror, that ultimate source of illusion, was a favorite element of Baroque interior design; here, it must have harmonized as it augmented the flashing splendors of the great festivals of which Louis XIV was so fond.

The enormous palace might appear unbearably ostentatious, were it not for its extraordinary setting in the vast park to which it becomes almost an adjunct. The Galerie des Glaces, itself a giant perspective, is dwarfed by the sweeping vista (seen from its windows) down the park's tree-lined central axis and across terraces, lawns, pools, and lakes toward the horizon. The park of Versailles (FIG. 19-66), designed by ANDRÉ LE NÔTRE (1613–1700), must rank among the world's greatest works of art, not only in size but also in concept. Here, an entire forest has been transformed into a park. Although the geometric plan may appear stiff and formal, the park, in fact, offers an almost unlimited variety of vistas, as Le Nôtre uti-

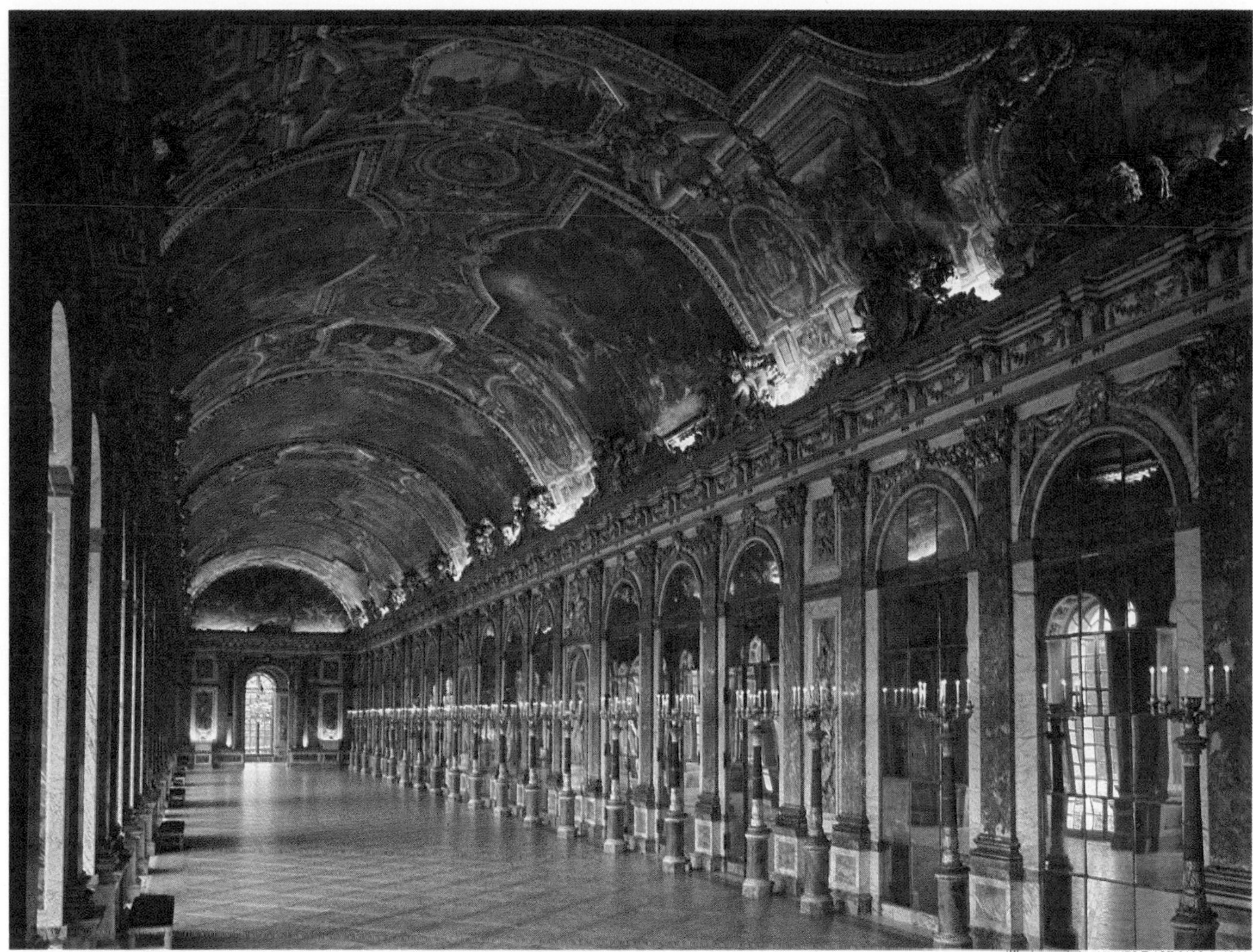
(Photograph by HENRI DAUMAN © 1966.)

19-68 JULES HARDOUIN-MANSART and CHARLES LE BRUN, Galerie des Glaces, Palace of Versailles, *c.* 1680.

lized not only the multiplicity of natural forms but also the slightly rolling contours of the terrain with stunning effectiveness.

A rational transition from the frozen forms of the architecture to the living ones of nature is provided by the formal gardens near the palace. Here, tightly designed geometric units are defined by the elegant forms of trimmed shrubs and hedges, each one different from its neighbor and having a focal point in the form of a sculptured group, a pavilion, a reflecting pool, or perhaps a fountain. Farther away from the palace, the design becomes looser as trees, in shadowy masses, screen or frame views into bits of open countryside. All vistas are composed carefully for maximum effect. Dark and light, formal and informal, dense growth and open meadows—all are played off against each other in unending combinations and variations. No photograph or series of photographs can reveal the full richness of the design; the park unfolds itself only to the person who actually walks through it. In this respect, it is a temporal work of art; its aspects change with time and with the relative position of the observer.

As a symbol of the power of absolutism, Versailles is unsurpassed. It also expresses, in the most monumental terms of its age, the rationalistic creed, based on the mathematical philosophy of Descartes, that all knowledge must be systematic and all science must be the consequence of the imposition of the intellect on matter. The whole stupendous design of Versailles proudly proclaims the mastery of human intelligence over the disorderliness of nature.

On the garden façade of Versailles, Hardouin-Mansart follows the style of his predecessor, Le Vau. When commissioned to add a Royal Chapel to the palace in 1698, he was in a position to give full play to his talents. The chapel's interior (FIG. **19-69**) is a masterful synthesis of Classical and Baroque elements. It

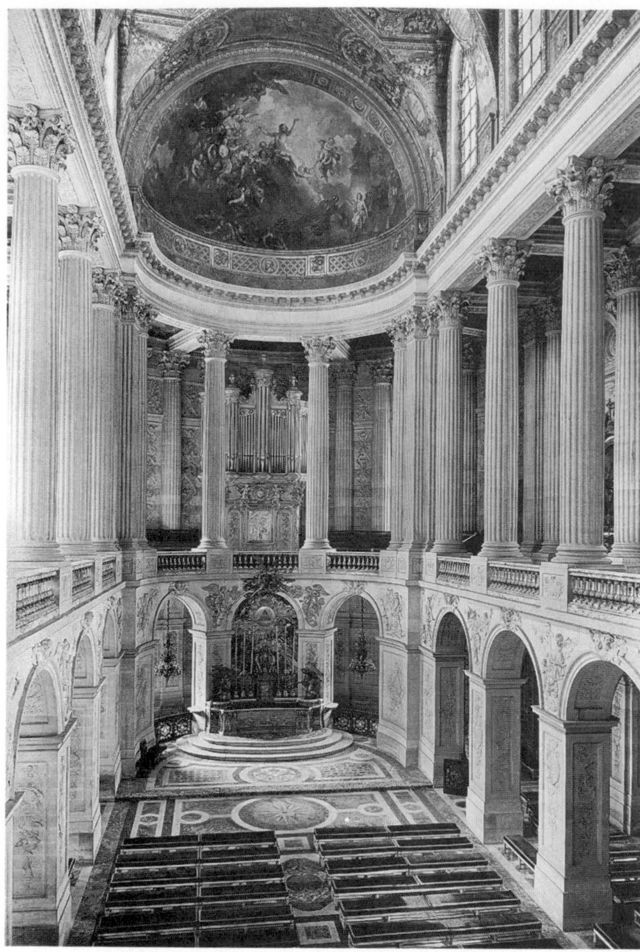

19-69 Jules Hardouin-Mansart, Royal Chapel of the Palace of Versailles, 1698–1710. (Ceiling decorations by Antoine Coypel.)

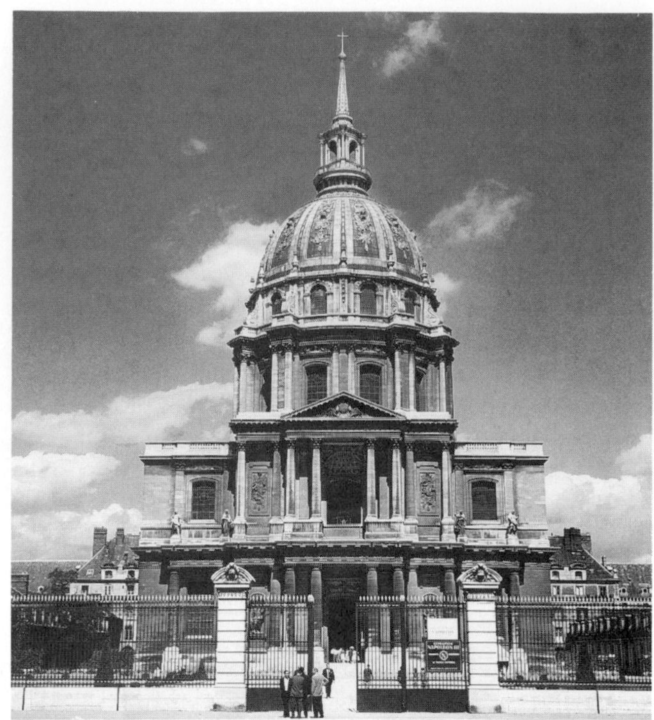

19-70 Jules Hardouin-Mansart, Église de Dôme, Church of the Invalides, Paris, 1676–1706.

19-71 Jules Hardouin-Mansart, interior of the Église de Dôme, Church of the Invalides.

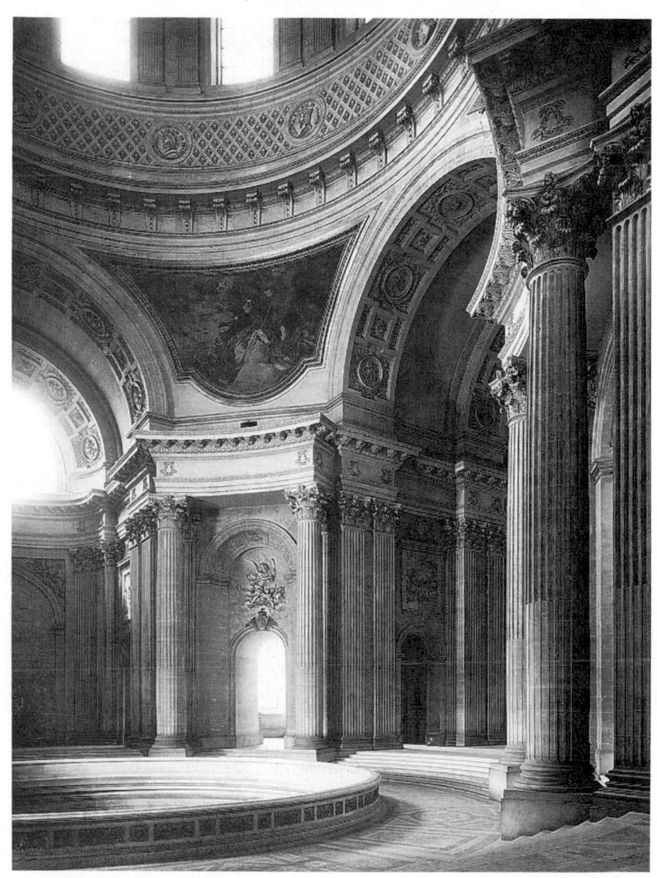

is essentially a rectangular building with an apse as high as the nave, which gives the fluid central space a curved Baroque quality. But the light entering through the large clerestory windows lacks the directed, dramatic effect of the Italian Baroque and illuminates the precisely chiseled details of the interior brightly and evenly. Pier-supported arcades carry a majestic row of Corinthian columns that define the royal gallery, the back of which is occupied by the royal pew, accessible directly from the king's apartments. The decoration is restrained and, in fact, only the illusionistic ceiling decorations, added in 1708–1709 by Antoine Coypel, can be called Baroque without reservation. Throughout the architecture, Baroque tendencies are severely checked by Classicism.

Although checked, such tendencies are not suppressed entirely in Hardouin-Mansart's masterwork, the Église de Dôme, Church of the Invalides in Paris (FIGS. **19-70** and **19-71**). An intricately composed domed square of great scale, the church is attached to the veterans' hospital set up by Louis XIV for the disabled soldiers of his many wars. The frontispiece is composed of two firmly separated levels, the upper pedimented. The grouping of the orders and the bays they frame is not unlike that in Italian Baroque. The compact façade is low and narrow in relation to the vast drum and dome, for which it seems to serve simply as a base. The overpowering dome, conspicuous on the skyline of Paris, is itself expressive of the Baroque love for dramatic magnitude. The way that its design aims for theatrical effects of light and space is especially Baroque. The dome is built of three shells, the lowest cut off so that the visitor looks up through it to the one above, which is painted illusionistically with an apotheosis of St. Louis, patron of France. This second dome, filled with light from hidden windows in the third, outermost dome, creates an impression of the open, limitless space and brightness of the heavens. Below, the building is only dimly illuminated and is designed in a Classicism only less severe than that of the Escorial (FIG. 18-56). The rapid vertical gradation from the austerely membered masses below to the ethereal light and space above is entirely Baroque. Yet we feel here the dominance of the Classical style in substance, despite the soaring illusion for which it serves as a setting.

Sculpture

The stylistic dialogue between Classicism and the Italian Baroque in seventeenth-century French sculpture also ends with a victory for Classicism. The strained dramatic and emotional qualities in the work of PIERRE PUGET (1620–1694) were not at all to the court's taste. His *Milo of Crotona* (FIG. **19-72**)

19-72 PIERRE PUGET, *Milo of Crotona,* 1671–1682. Marble, approx. 8′ 10″ high. Louvre, Paris.

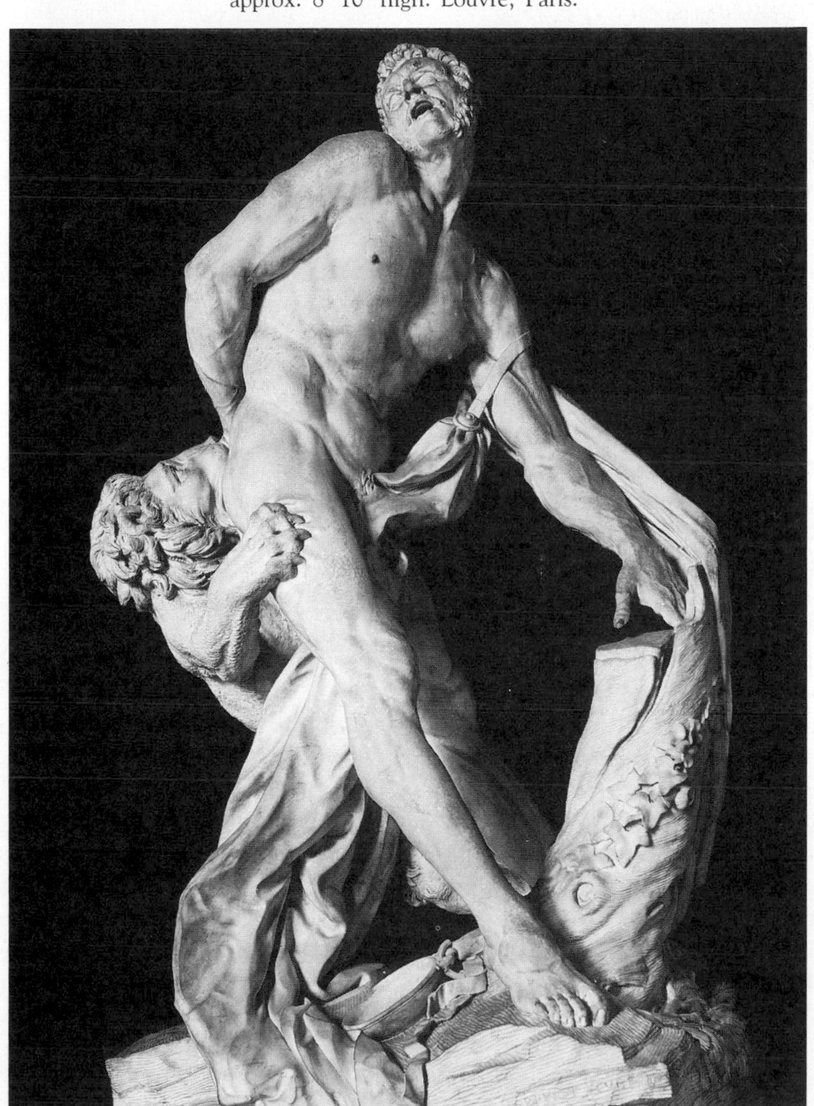

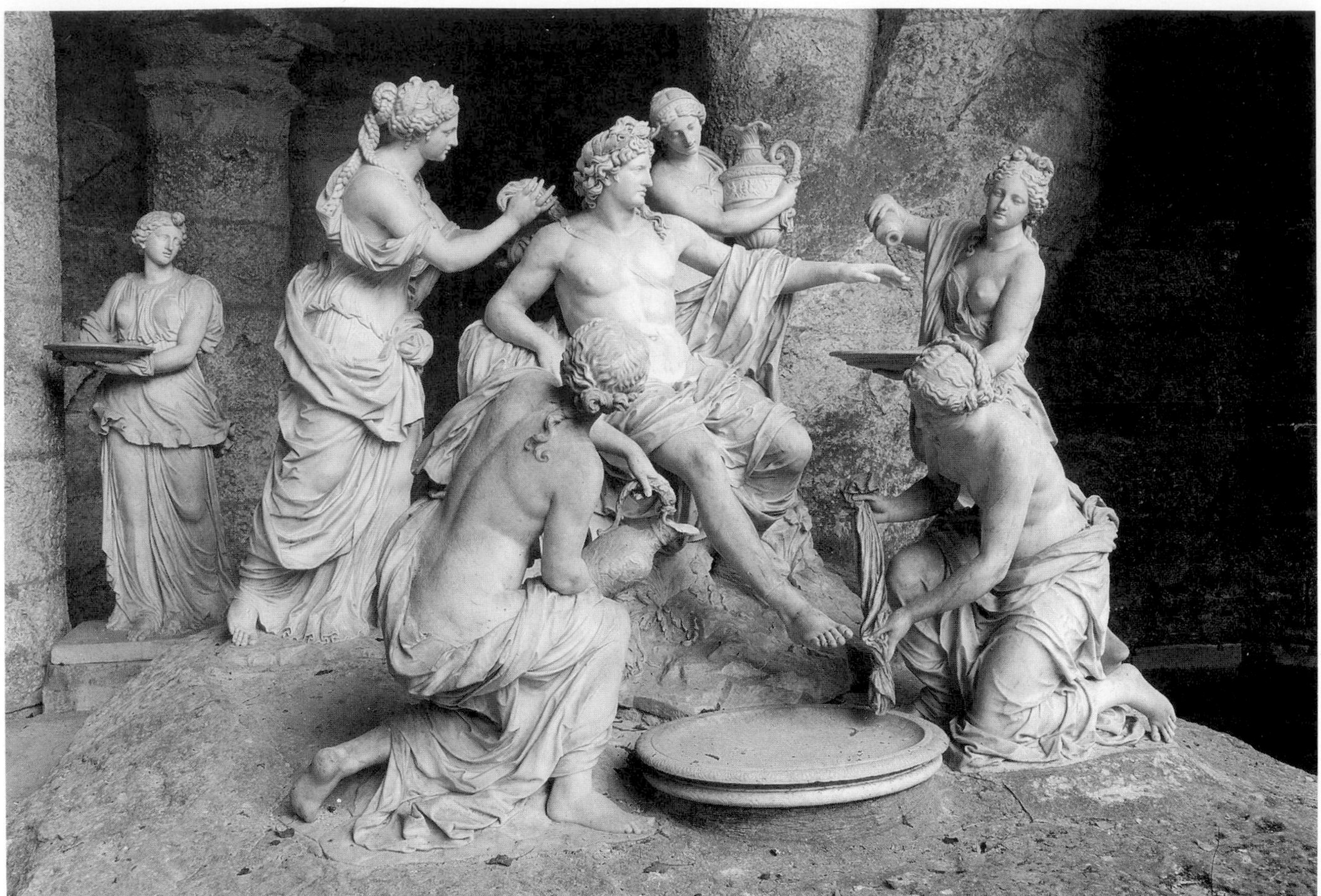

19-73 François Girardon, *Apollo Attended by the Muses,* c. 1666–1672. Marble, life size. Park of Versailles.

represents the powerful ancient hero, his hand trapped in a split stump, helpless before the attacking lion. With physical and psychic realism, Puget presents a study of immediate and excruciating agony—an attitude that ran counter to the official taste for heroic design dictated by the king and Le Brun. Although Puget was very briefly in vogue, the most original French sculptor of his time never found acceptance at the French court.

Much more fortunate was François Girardon (1628–1715), who admirably adjusted his style to the taste of his sponsors. His *Apollo Attended by the Muses* (fig. **19-73**) was designed as a tableau group for the Grotto of Thetis in the gardens of Versailles. (The arrangement of the figures was altered slightly when the group was moved to a different grotto in the eighteenth century.) Both stately and graceful, the Muses have a compelling charm as they minister to the god-king at the end of the day. The style of the figures is heavily conditioned by the artist's close study of Hellenistic sculpture, the central figure imitating the ancient Apollo Belvedere in the Vatican; the arrangement is inspired by Poussin's figure compositions (fig. 19-60). And if this combination did not suffice, the group's rather florid reference to Louis XIV as the "god of the sun" was bound to assure its success at court. Girardon's style and symbolism were well suited to the glorification of royal majesty.

ENGLAND

English art has been mentioned little since the Middle Ages because, except for its architecture, England stands outside the main artistic streams of the Renaissance and the Baroque periods. It is as if the English genius were so occupied with its prodigious creation in dramatic literature, lyric poetry, and music, that it did not find itself particularly suited to the purely visual arts. Not until the eighteenth century does England develop an important native school of painting and extend its distinguished architectural tradition.

Gothic practices lived on in English, as in French, building, long after Renaissance architects in Italy

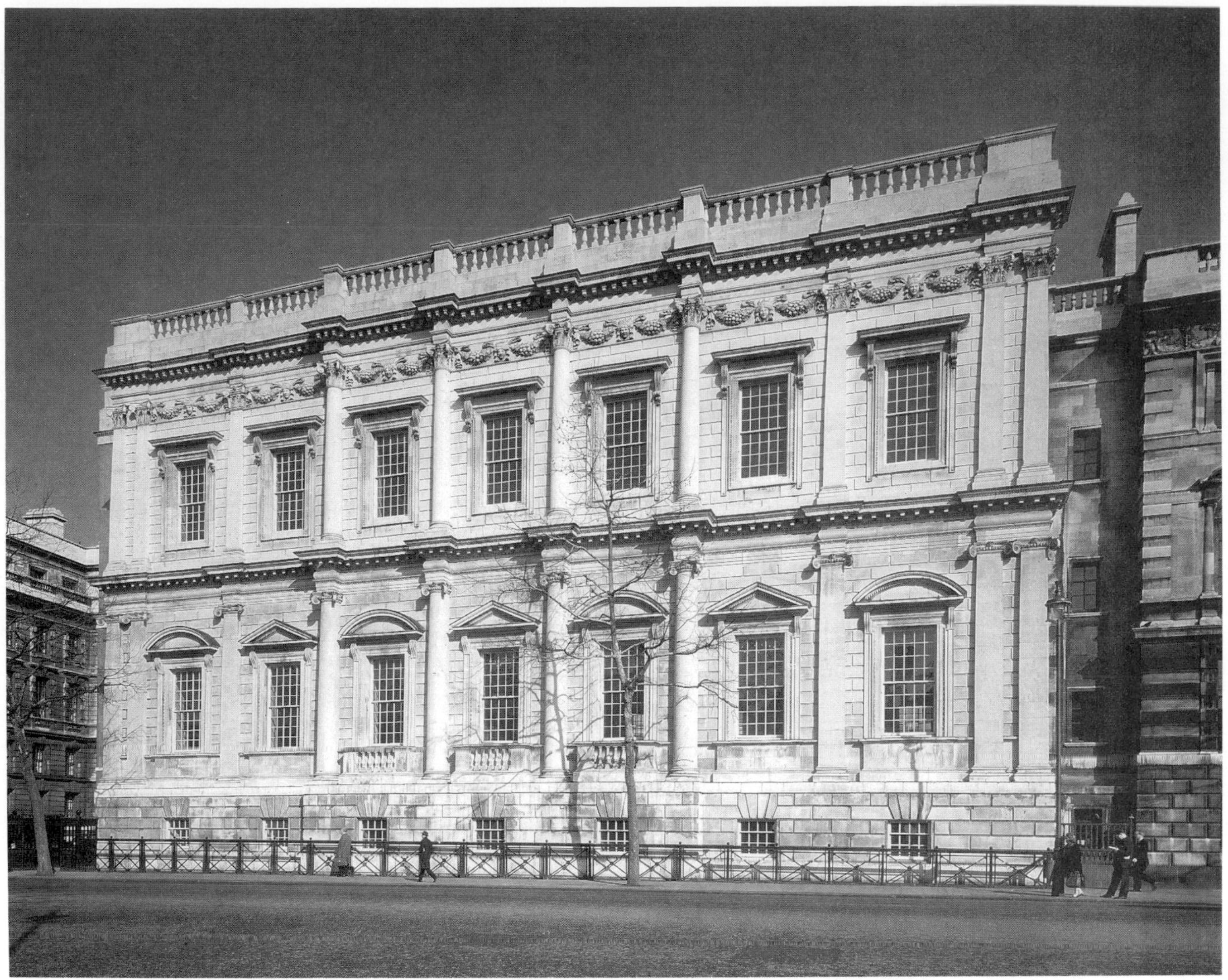

19-74 Inigo Jones, Banqueting House at Whitehall, London, 1619–1622. British Crown Copyright.

struck out in new directions. During the sixteenth century, the English made minor concessions to Italian architectural ideas. Classical ornament appeared frequently in the decoration of buildings, and a distinct trend developed toward more regular and symmetrical planning. But not until the early seventeenth century did England wholeheartedly accept the principles that govern Italian architectural thinking. The revolution in English building was primarily the work of one man, Inigo Jones (1573–1652), surveyor (architect) to James I and Charles I. Jones spent considerable time in Italy. He disliked Michelangelo's work as intensely as he admired Palladio's, whose treatise on architecture he studied with great care. From the stately palaces and villas of Palladio, Jones selected certain motifs and systems of proportion to use as the basis of his own architectural designs. The nature of his achievement is evident in the Banqueting House at Whitehall (fig. **19-74**). In this structure, a symmetrical block of great clarity and dignity, Jones superimposes two orders, using columns in the center and pilasters near the ends. The balustraded roof line, uninterrupted in its horizontal sweep, anticipates the façade of the Louvre (fig. 19-64) by more than forty years. There is almost nothing here that Palladio would not have recognized and approved, but the building as a whole is not a copy. While working within the architectural vocabulary and syntax of the revered Italian, Jones retained his own independence as a designer; for two centuries his influence was almost as authoritative in English architecture as Palladio's. In a fruitful collaboration recalling the combination of painting by Veronese and architecture by Palladio in northern Italian villas, Jones's interior at

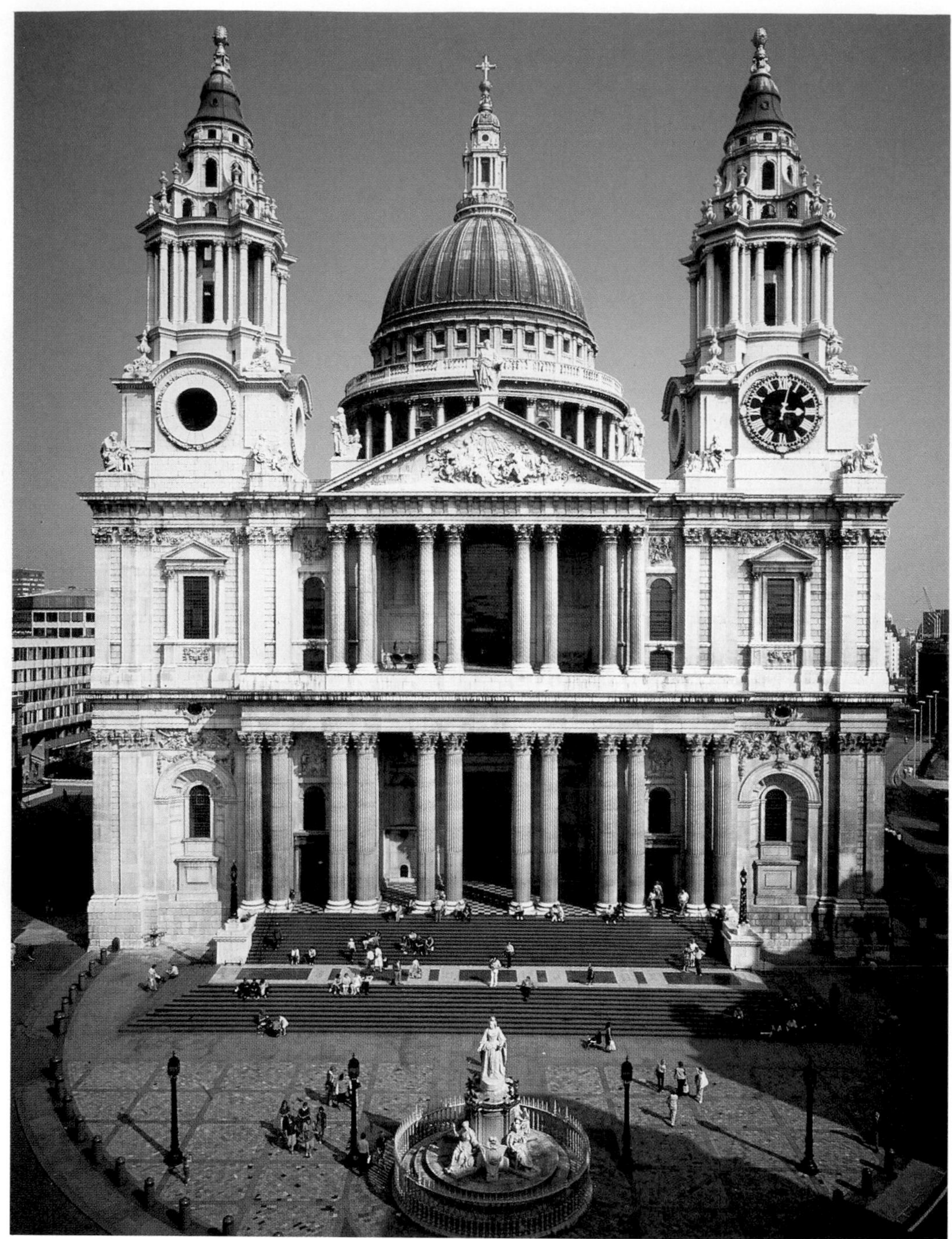

19-75 CHRISTOPHER WREN, new St. Paul's Cathedral, London, 1675–1710.

Whitehall is adorned with several important paintings by Rubens.

Until almost the present day, the dominant feature of the London skyline has been the majestic dome of St. Paul's (FIG. **19-75**), the work of England's most renowned architect, CHRISTOPHER WREN (1632–1723). A mathematical genius and skilled engineer, whose work won the praise of Isaac Newton, Wren began as a professor of astronomy and took an amateur's interest in architecture. Asked by Charles II to prepare a plan for the restoration of the old Gothic church of St. Paul, he proposed to remodel the building "after a good Roman manner" rather than "to follow the Gothic rudeness of the old design." Within a few months, the Great Fire of London, which destroyed the old structure and many churches in the city in 1666, gave Wren his opportunity. He built not only the new St. Paul's but numerous other churches as well. Wren was a Baroque virtuoso of many talents, the archetype of whom we see in Bernini. He was strongly influenced by the work of Jones, but he also traveled in France, where he must have been much impressed by the splendid palaces and state buildings being created in and around Paris at the time of the competition for the Louvre design. Wren also must have closely studied prints illustrating Baroque architecture in Italy, for Palladian, French, and Italian Baroque features are harmonized in St. Paul's. In view of its size, the cathedral was built with remarkable speed—in a little over thirty years—and Wren lived to see it completed. The form of the building was constantly refined as it went up, and the final appearance of the towers was not determined until after 1700. The splendid skyline composition, with the two foreground towers acting effectively as foils to the great dome, must have been suggested to Wren by similar schemes devised by Italian architects to solve the problem of the façade–dome relation of St. Peter's in Rome (FIGS. 17-34 and 19-4). Perhaps Borromini's solution at Sant' Agnese in Piazza Navona influenced him. Certainly, the upper levels and lanterns of the towers are Borrominesque, the lower levels are Palladian, and the superposed, paired columnar porticoes remind us of the Louvre façade. Wren's skillful eclecticism brings all of these foreign features into a monumental unity.

Wren's designs for the city churches are masterpieces of Baroque planning ingenuity. His task was never easy, for the churches often had to be fitted into small, irregular areas. Wren worked out a rich variety of schemes to meet awkward circumstances. In designing the exteriors of the churches, he concentrated his attention on the towers, the one element of the structure that would set the building apart from its crowding neighbors. The skyline of London, as left by Wren, is punctuated with such towers, which will serve as prototypes for later buildings both in England and in colonial America.

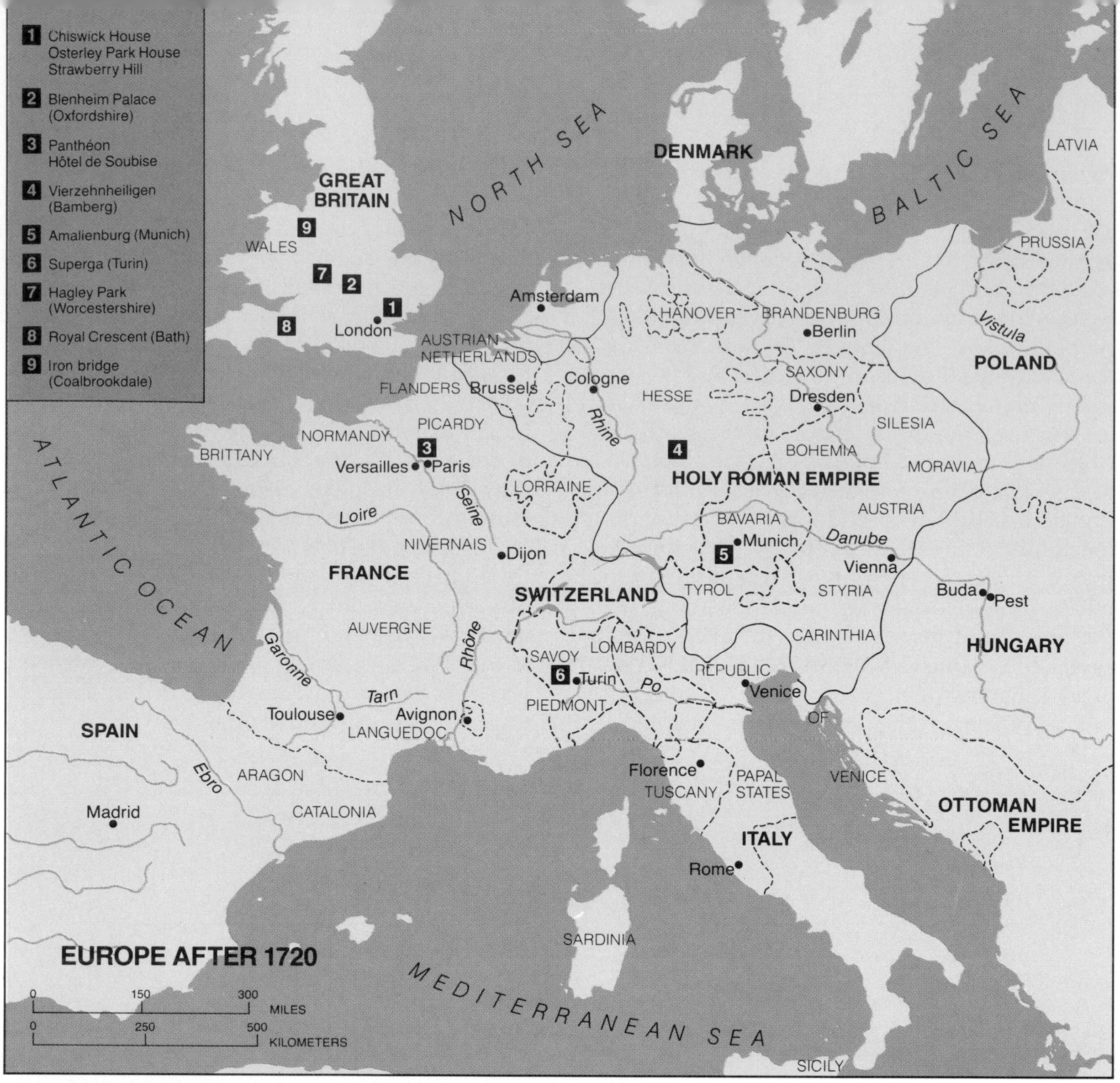

EUROPE AFTER 1720

1. Chiswick House, Osterley Park House, Strawberry Hill
2. Blenheim Palace (Oxfordshire)
3. Panthéon, Hôtel de Soubise
4. Vierzehnheiligen (Bamberg)
5. Amalienburg (Munich)
6. Superga (Turin)
7. Hagley Park (Worcestershire)
8. Royal Crescent (Bath)
9. Iron bridge (Coalbrookdale)

GREAT BRITAIN
WALES
London
NORTH SEA
DENMARK
BALTIC SEA
LATVIA
PRUSSIA
Amsterdam
HANOVER
BRANDENBURG
Berlin
Vistula
POLAND
AUSTRIAN NETHERLANDS
FLANDERS
Brussels
Cologne
HESSE
SAXONY
Dresden
SILESIA
NORMANDY
PICARDY
BRITTANY
Versailles
Paris
Rhine
BOHEMIA
MORAVIA
HOLY ROMAN EMPIRE
LORRAINE
Seine
Loire
AUSTRIA
BAVARIA
Danube
Munich
NIVERNAIS
Dijon
Vienna
ATLANTIC OCEAN
FRANCE
SWITZERLAND
TYROL
STYRIA
Buda
Pest
AUVERGNE
Garonne
Rhône
CARINTHIA
HUNGARY
SAVOY
LOMBARDY
Turin
Po
REPUBLIC OF VENICE
Tarn
PIEDMONT
Venice
Toulouse
Avignon
LANGUEDOC
SPAIN
Ebro
ARAGON
Florence
PAPAL STATES
TUSCANY
Madrid
CATALONIA
OTTOMAN EMPIRE
ITALY
Rome
SARDINIA
MEDITERRANEAN SEA
SICILY

0 150 300 MILES
0 250 500 KILOMETERS

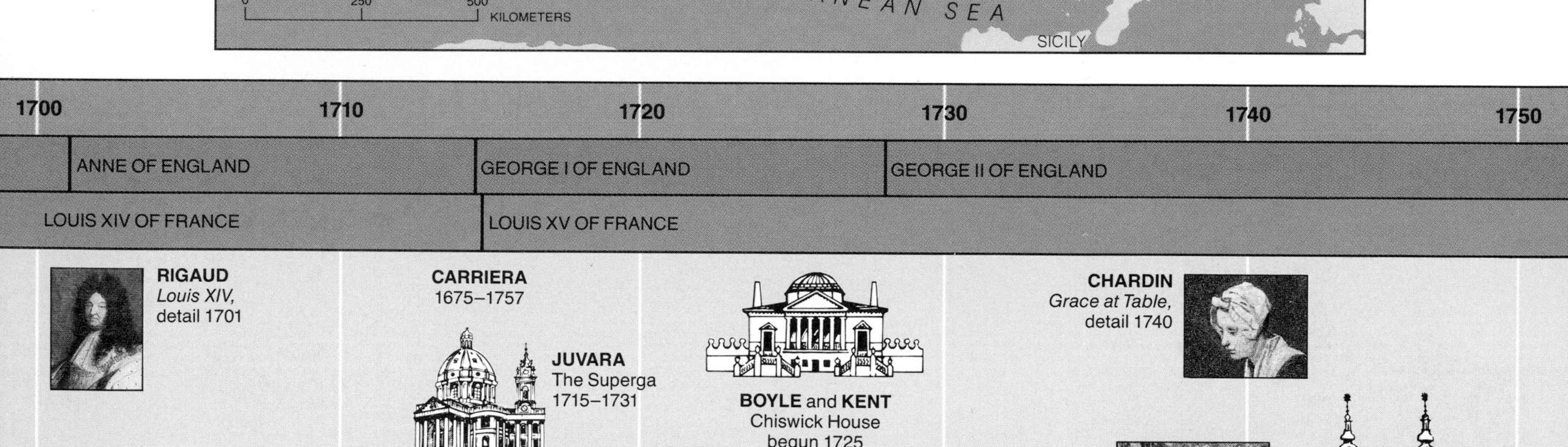

1700	1710	1720	1730	1740	1750

ANNE OF ENGLAND — GEORGE I OF ENGLAND — GEORGE II OF ENGLAND

LOUIS XIV OF FRANCE — LOUIS XV OF FRANCE

RIGAUD *Louis XIV*, detail 1701

CARRIERA 1675–1757

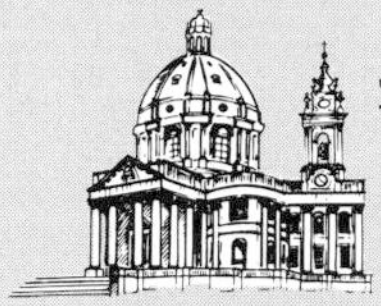

JUVARA The Superga 1715–1731

BOYLE and **KENT** Chiswick House begun 1725

CHARDIN *Grace at Table*, detail 1740

BOFFRAND Decorations of Salon de la Princesse, Hôtel de Soubise 1737–1740

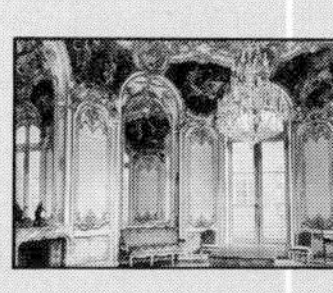

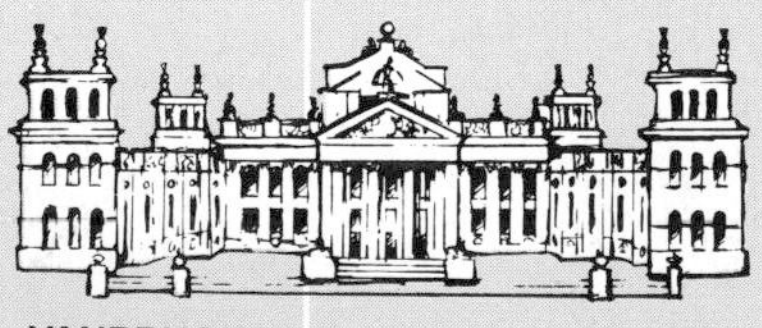

VANBRUGH Blenheim Palace 1705–1722

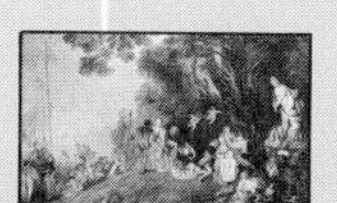

WATTEAU *Return from Cythera* 1717–1719

CANALETTO 1697–1768

HOGARTH 1697–1764

BOUCHER 1703–1770

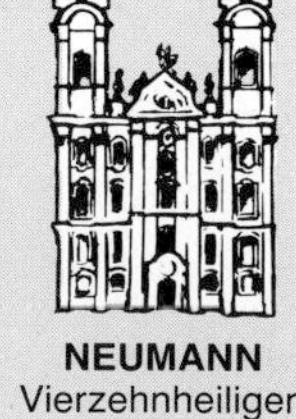

NEUMANN Vierzehnheiligen 1743–1772

Newton 1642–1727

Bach 1685–1750

Pope 1688–1744

First copyright act passed in England 1735

Voltaire 1694–1778

Diderot 1713–1784 *Encyclopedia*

Rousseau 1712–1778

Excavation of Pompeii 1748

20

THE EIGHTEENTH CENTURY: ROCOCO AND THE BIRTH OF THE MODERN WORLD

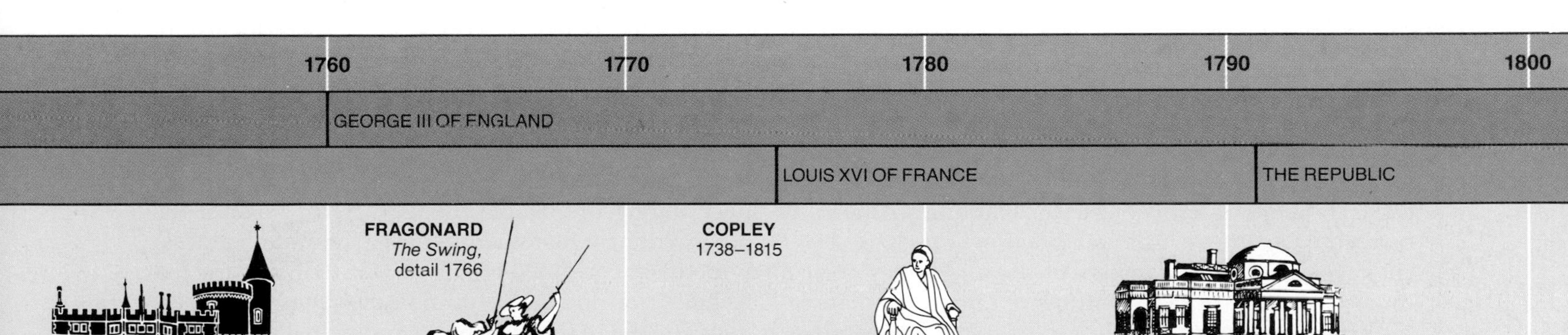

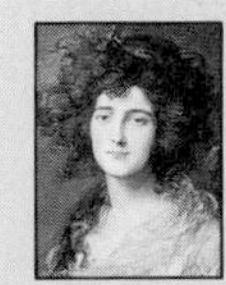

GAINSBOROUGH *Mrs. Richard Brinsley Sheridan,* detail *c.* 1785

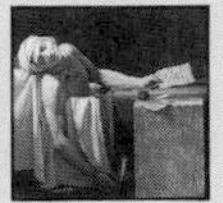

DAVID *The Death of Marat* 1793

THE EIGHTEENTH CENTURY had a dual character; its two parts corresponded chronologically to an earlier and a later stage. The earlier stage was a continuation of the Baroque seventeenth century, with a number of distinctive differences; the later stage was the period in which the foundations of the modern world were laid. The present chapter, in its title and arrangement, reflects this bipartite division. However, a brief view of the century as a whole also can be useful.

The political world took new shapes in the eighteenth century. The maritime British Empire achieved great power and pursued disputes with France over the continent of North America and the subcontinent of India. The majority of Europe was divided into small political units governed by princes, by high-ranking priests, or, in a few cases, by democratic councils. Once-powerful Spain was crippled by war and corrupt rule. Italy and much of Germany, as we now know them, were patchworks of principalities, duchies, and other small governing bodies. Against the awkward and shaky Holy Roman (later Austrian) Empire rose the small but aggressive state of Prussia, soon to become a significant military power. Farther to the east loomed the still dormant might of half-Asiatic Russia, accelerating its slow turn toward the West under Peter the Great.

Older patterns of life and society continued and obscured for a time the emergence of the new forces of change. On the continent, the decades between the death of Louis XIV in 1715 and the middle of the century were a period of relative relaxation after the exhausting "world" wars conducted by the great kings. Wars still were fought, but they were more often balancing maneuvers among the various states, waged by professional soldiers, with a kind of chessboard formality. In the arts, the wealthy remained eager to follow the royal taste for Baroque splendor, but this eagerness was modified everywhere by changes in society. Members of the aristocracy continued to be the primary patrons of the arts in many countries, and much of the century's art made before the French Revolution expressed their philosophy. The art that won aristocratic favor was luxurious, frivolous, sensual, and clever. The great religious and Classical themes and the grand manner of the Baroque gradually were overshadowed. Intricate and witty artifice now became the objective in all the arts—drama, music, painting, sculpture, architecture. The French were leaders in creating this art. In France, members of the court increasingly lived more in Paris than at Versailles, and they surrounded themselves with objects created in a delicately elegant Late Baroque variant called the *Rococo* style. Something of the quality of the Rococo also spread to the rest of Europe, competing in Italy with a lingering enjoyment of the heavier monumentality of the Classical Baroque, and being transformed in Germany and Austria by a distinctively buoyant and festive air.

The Rococo style had little effect in England, where an appetite for Palladian Classicism reflected to some degree developments in society and thought that were to inaugurate the modern age throughout Europe later in the century. At the beginning of the century, England already had started to point the way to the future with a parliamentary form of government, a free press, and a high degree of religious toleration, all of which tempered the power of the monarchy. Throughout the century, England enjoyed great material prosperity, generated by inventions in industry and agriculture, and by international trade. Englishmen set the tone of much of the new thinking as well. In John Locke's *Essay Concerning Human Understanding* (1690), he argued that all true knowledge is derived from perceptions of the sense organs and from the mind's reflections on those perceptions. Sir Isaac Newton's theories of gravity and the laws of motion reinterpreted physical nature to demonstrate that it was mechanically (rather than spiritually or organically) constituted.

From such sources, new ideas were propagated that would threaten the authority of both church and state. As the result of a visit to England in 1726, the French writer Voltaire "discovered" England for the rest of Europe. In writings such as his *Philosophical Letters on the English* (1734), the ideas of English thought, science, and government became matters for general discussion. These ideas were to inspire campaigns to reform the abuses and limit the privileges of royalty, the aristocracy, and the clergy. In 1762, Jean Jacques Rousseau wrote in his *Social Contract* that organized society should be based not on a contract between a ruler and a people, but on a contract among the people themselves. In most of his other writings, he touted people's natural goodness, a goodness corrupted only by civilization. He trusted feelings over thought, intuition over reason. Adhering as he did to the ideal of the individual as a person guided by an innate "natural" intuition or conscience, Rousseau was feared by churches as a dangerous influence. He was also a forerunner to Romanticism and a source of the modern world's interest in the nonrational and the subconscious.

The eighteenth century in Europe is known as the Age of Enlightenment, an age in which reason and common sense were put forth as the real remedies of society's ills and "progress" was seen as a law of human development. In support of this philosophy of progress, knowledge burgeoned in all fields. Important advances from the emerging natural sciences dealt with the nature of such phenomena as living matter, electricity, combustion, and oxygen. For its immediate application, the most important practical invention of the age was, undoubtedly, the development of steam power, with its enormous significance as a substitute for human labor. The use of steam engines for production and, later, for transportation, began in England, as part of the initial phase of the machine age. Soon, England and all of Europe were transformed by the harnessed power of steam, coal, oil, iron, and steel.

The political, economic, and social consequences of these changes were tremendous. The era of industrial capital and labor was born, as people flocked to cities to take jobs in the new steam-powered factories. The growth of the urban working class was so swift that social services could not evolve fast enough to serve new city residents. A split between employer and employee widened. The merchant rich became captains of industry, demanding that production and trade be free from government regulation and, at the same time, that the heads of industry participate in the fiscal decisions of government. Antagonisms between the powerful, wealthy few and the workers helped to fuel political revolutions organized under the banners of democracy and free trade later in the century. All of these developments helped to initiate the era we call "modern," and many of the ideas and institutions that originated mid-century are still with us today.

The ruling aristocracies, as if conscious of their waning historical significance, gradually abandoned their administrative and executive functions to members of the increasingly wealthy and influential middle class, the Third Estate. Without fully realizing it, royalty and the nobility were slowly becoming obsolete. Stubbornly insisting on their ancient privileges, the nobility helped precipitate the French Revolution. Still, earlier in the century, these patrons of the arts and sciences followed with great interest the theories and discoveries exchanged by scholars in official groups like England's Royal Society and Royal Academy of Arts and France's Academies of science and painting, and joined intellectuals and members of the wealthy middle class in "salons" to discuss the latest ideas. Aristocrats helped fund the scientists and artists who accompanied Captain James Cook on his round-the-world voyages of discovery. They also encouraged the production of vast compendia of knowledge, such as Georges Louis Leclerc Buffon's *Natural History,* which contained descriptions of all known animals, and the vast *Encyclopedia* compiled by Denis Diderot and a group of fellow intellectuals (known as the *philosophes*), which included knowledge in many disciplines.

Art reflected all of these changes. By mid-century, the marked changes in culture and society had begun to produce new forms of art that reflected the beginnings of the modern era. A reaction against the Rococo style generated a new "naturalness," especially in portraits and landscapes. The Enlightenment brought with it a desire for art that would help to better the world by using new technology to create an improved physical environment, by providing people with facts about their world, and by instructing viewers about correct moral conduct. Yet the last half of the century also saw the return of nostalgia for the past, in part inspired by the excitement accompanying the archeological excavations of the ancient Roman communities of Pompeii and Herculaneum, and in part connected to the convulsive changes in society that resulted from the American and French revolutions and the rise of Napoleon. The excitement over the discovery of ancient ruins was accompanied by a renewed interest in things Classical. The upheavals in society sparked a taste for "Gothic" in architecture and an investigation in painting of sublime and terrible subjects that reflected human fantasies and nightmares.

THE EARLY EIGHTEENTH CENTURY: LATE BAROQUE AND ROCOCO

During the first half of the eighteenth century, royalty and the members of the European aristocracy still held much economic and social power, although their political power was in decline. Monarchs and nobles still wished to surround themselves with visible signs of their wealth and position. In England, a bent for austerity tempered aristocratic desires for opulent grandeur. In France, the monumentality of Louis XIV's Baroque taste was recast in a more intimate and enjoyable guise—the Rococo style. Rococo proved so appealing to the nobility that it spread rapidly throughout Europe, replacing the earlier, heavier Baroque style.

Late Baroque and Palladian Classicism in England

In England, early in the century, the monumentality of the Baroque inspired one vast palace, Blenheim (FIG. **20-1**), which was commissioned by the government to commemorate the British victory over the French led by John Churchill, Duke of Marlborough. Designed by JOHN VANBRUGH (1664–1726), Blenheim was one of the largest of the splendid country houses built during the period of prosperity that resulted from Great Britain's expansion into the New World.

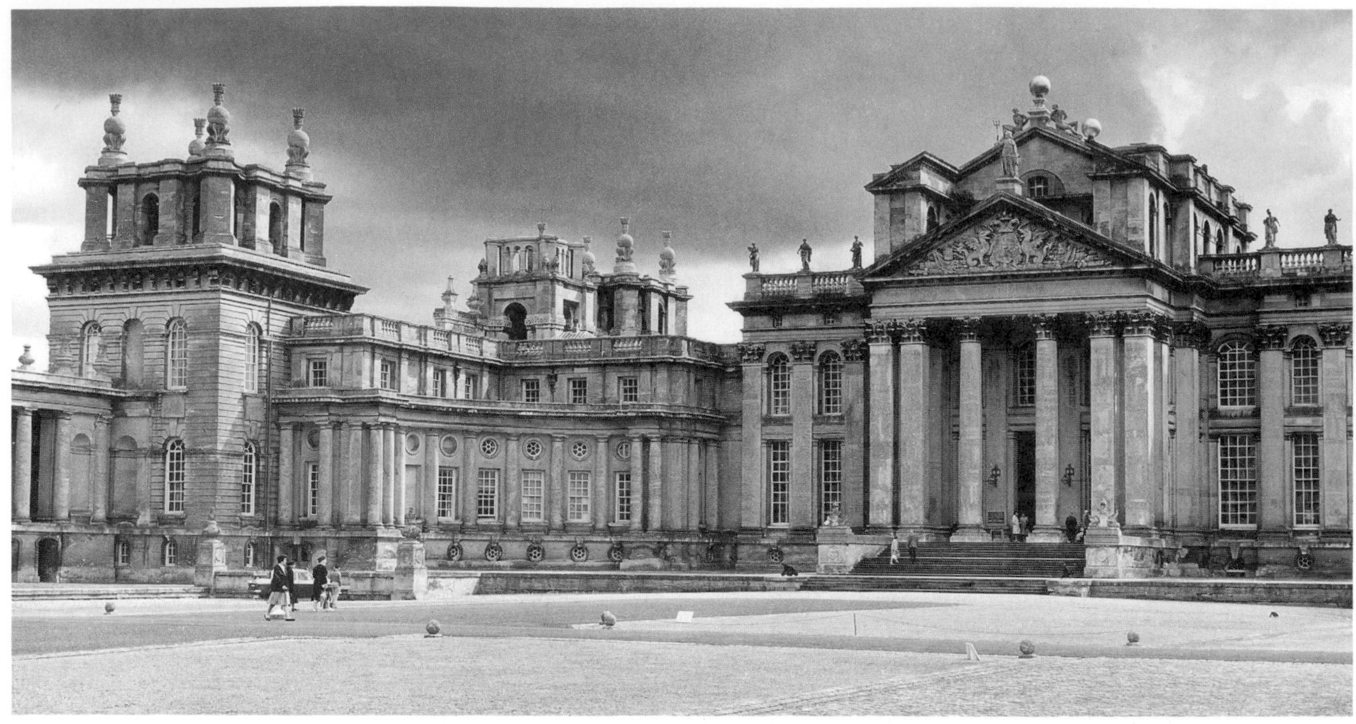

20-1 JOHN VANBRUGH, Blenheim Palace, Oxfordshire, England, 1705–1722.

During this period, a small group of architects associated with the aging Sir Christopher Wren were responsible for a brief return to favor of the Baroque over the Palladian Classicism of Inigo Jones. Vanbrugh was the best known of this group. The picturesque silhouette he created for Blenheim, with its massing and its inventive architectural detail, is thoroughly Baroque. The design demonstrates his love of variety and contrast, tempered by his ability to create areas of focus like those found so frequently in the Baroque architecture of the seventeenth century. The tremendous forecourt, the hugely projecting pavilions, and the extended colonnades simultaneously recall St. Peter's and Versailles (FIGS. 19-3 and 19-65). Perhaps because Vanbrugh had begun his career as a writer of witty and popular comedies and as the builder of a theater in which to produce them, all of his architecture tended toward the theatrical on a mighty and extravagant scale. Like many Baroque architects, he even sacrificed convenience to dramatic effect, as in the placement of the kitchen at Blenheim some 400 yards from the majestic dining salon. Vanbrugh's architecture pleased his patrons in the beginning, but even before Blenheim was completed, critics were condemning what they considered its ponderous and bizarre qualities.

The criticism of buildings like Blenheim gradually was broadened to encompass the defects of the Baroque style in general. Soon, preference swung from the "irrationality" and "artificiality" of Baroque pomp, vast scale, theatrical effects, irregular forms, exuberant details, and grandiose rhetoric toward the "good sense" found in simple, harmonious, and useful Palladian designs. The British may also have come to connect the Baroque style with the showy rule of absolute monarchy—something to be played down in parliamentary England. In English architecture, the instinct for an unostentatious and commonsensical style led straight from the authority of Vitruvius, through the work of Andrea Palladio (FIG. 17-51), and on to that of Inigo Jones (FIG. 19-74). As Alexander Pope, in his "Fourth Moral Epistle" (1731), advised his friend, the statesman and architectural amateur RICHARD BOYLE, Earl of Burlington (1695–1753):

> You, too, proceed! make falling arts your care,
> Erect new wonders, and the old repair;
> Jones and Palladio to themselves restore
> And be whate'er Vitruvius was before.

Lord Burlington took the advice and strongly restated the Palladian doctrine of Inigo Jones in a new style in Chiswick House (FIG. **20-2**), which he built on the outskirts of London with the help of the talented professional WILLIAM KENT (1685–1748). The way had been paved for this shift in style by, among other things, the publication of Colin Campbell's *Vitruvius Britannicus* (1715), three volumes of engravings of ancient buildings in Britain, prefaced by a denunciation of Italian Baroque and high praise for Palladio and Inigo Jones.

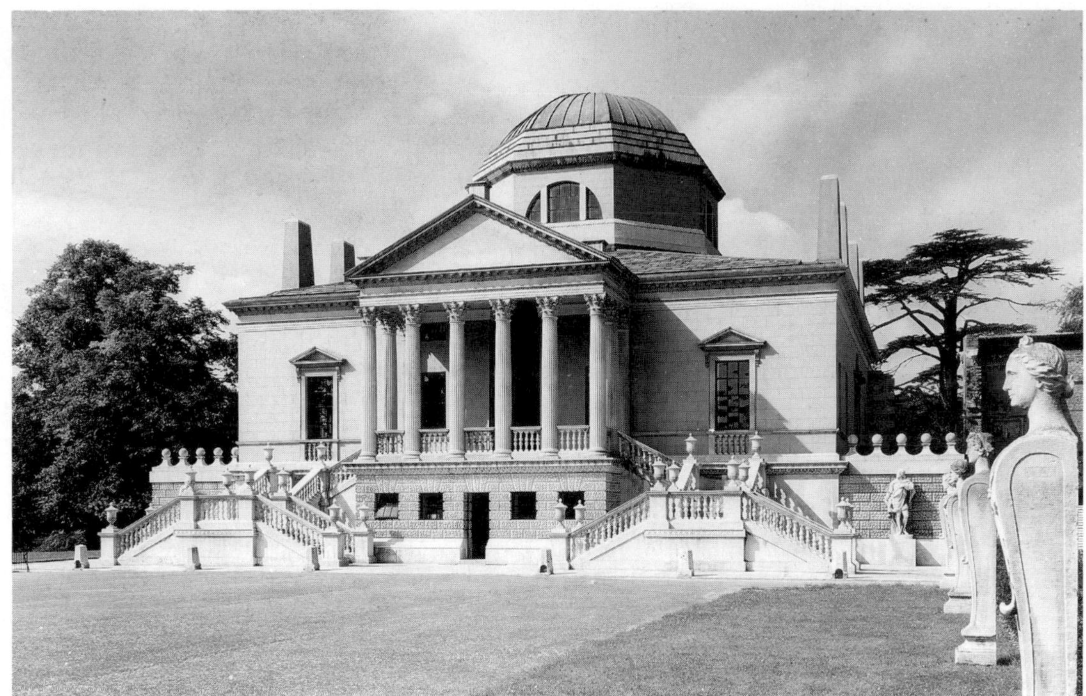

20-2 RICHARD BOYLE (Earl of Burlington) and WILLIAM KENT, Chiswick House, near London, begun 1725. British Crown Copyright.

Chiswick House is a free variation on the theme of Palladio's Villa Rotonda (FIG. 17-51). The exterior design provided a clear alternative to the colorful splendors of Versailles. In its simple symmetry, unadorned planes, right angles, and stiffly wrought proportions, Chiswick looks very Classical and "rational," but, like so many Palladian villas in England, the effect is modified by its setting within informal gardens, where a charming irregularity of layout and freely growing, uncropped foliage dominate the scene. The development of the "English garden" as a rival to the formality of the continental garden is an important chapter in the history of eighteenth-century taste about which we will say more later. Just as irregularity was cultivated in the landscaping surrounding English Palladian villas, so the interiors of buildings sometimes were ornamented in a style more closely related to the Rococo decoration fashionable on the continent than to the severity of the Classical Palladian exteriors. At Chiswick, the interior design created a luxurious Late Baroque foil to the stern symmetry of the exterior and the plan. Despite such "lapses," Palladian Classicism prevailed in English architecture until about 1760, when it began to evolve into Neoclassicism.

Rococo: The French Taste

The death of Louis XIV in 1715 brought many changes in French high society. The court of Versailles was at once abandoned for the pleasures of town life. The *hôtels* (town houses) of Paris soon became the centers of a new, softer style we call Rococo. The sparkling gaiety cultivated by the new age, associated with the regency that followed Louis XIV's death and with the reign of Louis XV, found perfectly harmonious expression in this new style. Rococo appeared in France in about 1710, primarily as a style of interior design. The French Rococo exterior was most often simple, or even plain, but Rococo exuberance took over the interior. The word *Rococo* came from the French *rocaille,* which literally means "pebble," but the term referred especially to the small stones and shells used to decorate the interiors of grottoes. Such shells or shell forms were the principal motifs in Rococo ornament.

The feminine look of the Rococo style suggests that the age was dominated by the taste and the social initiative of women—and, to a large extent, it was. Women—Madame de Pompadour in France, Maria Theresa in Austria, Elizabeth and Catherine in Russia—held some of the highest positions in Europe, and female influence was felt in any number of smaller courts. The Rococo salon was the center of early eighteenth-century Parisian society, and Paris was the social capital of Europe. Wealthy, ambitious, and clever society hostesses competed to attract the most famous and the most accomplished people to their salons. The medium of social intercourse was conversation spiced with wit, repartee as quick and

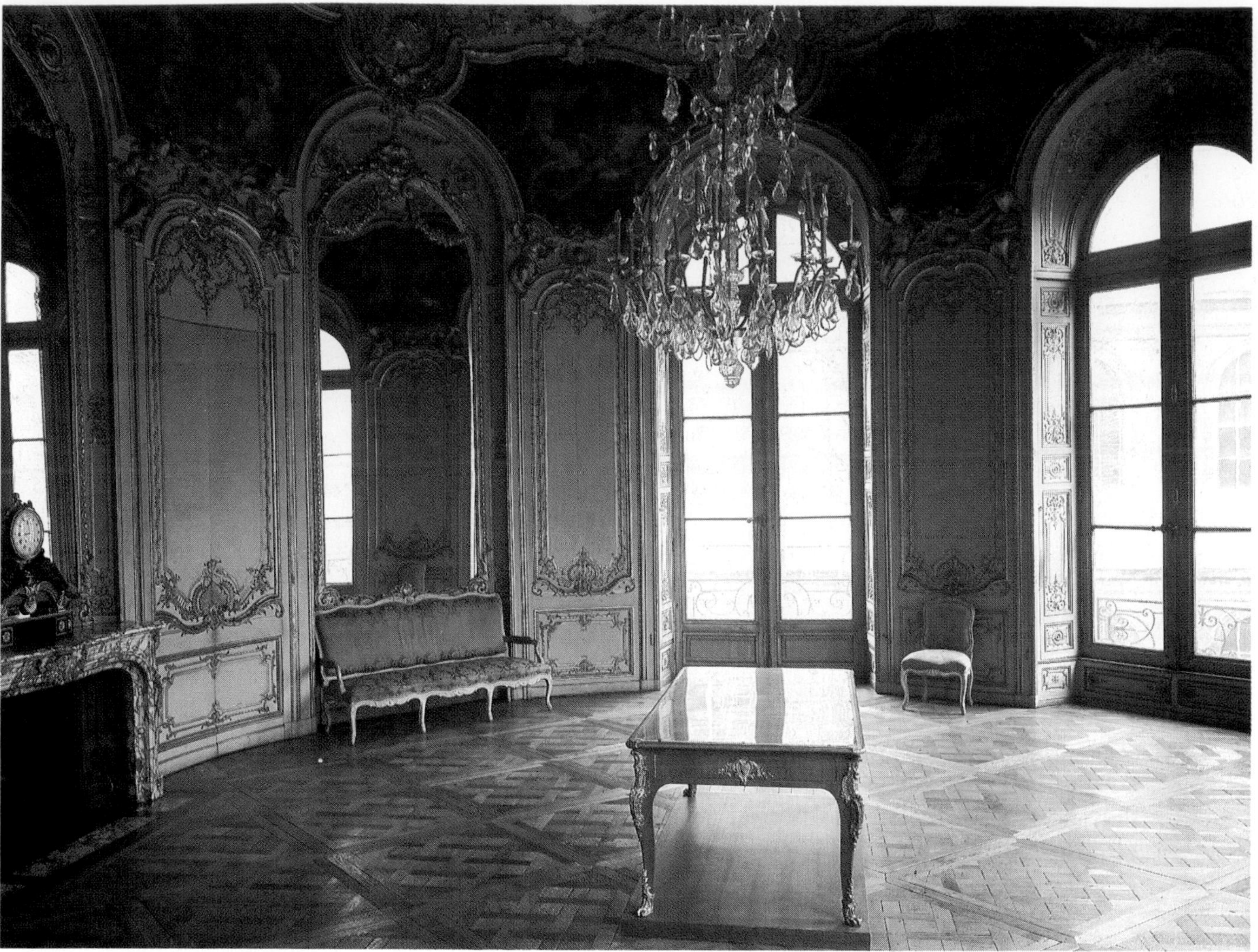

20-3 Salon de la Princesse, Hôtel de Soubise, Paris, 1737–1740. Decorations by GERMAIN BOFFRAND. © Arch. Photo. Paris/S.P.A.D.E.M.

deft as a fencing match. The masculine heroics and rhetoric of the Baroque era were replaced by dainty gallantries and pointed sallies of humor. Artifice reigned supreme, and it was considered in bad taste to be enthusiastic or sincere.

A typical French Rococo room is the Salon de la Princesse (FIG. **20-3**) in the Hôtel de Soubise in Paris, decorated by GERMAIN BOFFRAND (1667–1754). If we compare this room with the Galerie des Glaces at Versailles (FIG. 19-68), we see the fundamental difference at once. The strong architectural lines and panels of the earlier style were softened here into flexible, sinuous curves. The walls melt into the vault; the cornices are replaced by irregular painted shapes, surmounted by sculpture and separated by the typical shells of rocaille. Painting, architecture, and sculpture make a single ensemble. The profusion of curving tendrils and sprays of foliage combine with the shell forms to give an effect of freely growing nature and to suggest that the Rococo room is permanently decked for a festival. Rococo was a style preeminently evident in small art; furniture, utensils, and accessories of all sorts were exquisitely wrought in the characteristically delicate, undulating Rococo line. French Rococo interiors were designed as lively, total works of art in which the architecture, relief sculptures, and wall paintings were complemented by elegant furniture, enchanting small sculpture, delightful ceramics and silver, a few "easel" paintings, and decorative tapestry. As we see them today, French Rococo interiors, like that of the Salon de la Princesse, have lost most of the moveable "accessories" that once adorned them. We can imagine, however, how such rooms, with their alternating gilded moldings, vivacious relief sculptures, and daintily colored ornament of flowers and garlands, must have harmonized with the chamber music played in them, with the elaborate costumes of satin and brocade, and with the equally elegant etiquette and sparkling wit of the people who graced them.

The painter above all others whom we associate with the French Rococo is ANTOINE WATTEAU (1684–1721). The differences between the age of the Baroque and the age of Rococo can be seen clearly if we contrast the portrait of Louis XIV (FIG. **20-4**) by HYACINTHE RIGAUD (1659–1743) with one of Watteau's paintings, *L'Indifférent* (FIG. **20-5**). Rigaud portrays pompous majesty in slow and stately promenade, as if the French monarch were reviewing throngs of bowing courtiers at Versailles. The other painting represents a languid, gliding dancer, whose mincing minuet might be seen as mimicking the monarch's solemn pacing. In Rigaud's portrait, stout architecture, bannerlike curtains, flowing ermine, and fleur-de-lis exalt the king, while fanfares of trumpets blast. In Watteau's painting, the dancer moves in a rainbow shimmer of color, emerging onto the stage of the intimate comic opera to the silken sounds of strings. The portrait of the king is very large, the "portrait" of "the indifferent one," quite small. The first painting is Baroque; the second is Rococo.

20-4 HYACINTHE RIGAUD, *Louis XIV*, 1701. Approx. 9′ 2″ × 6′ 3″. Louvre, Paris.

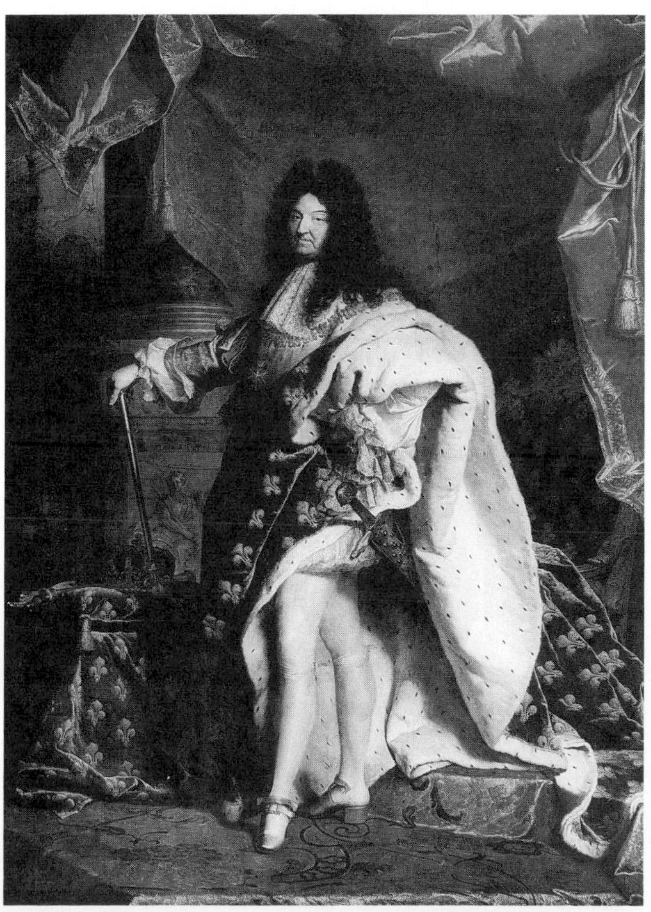

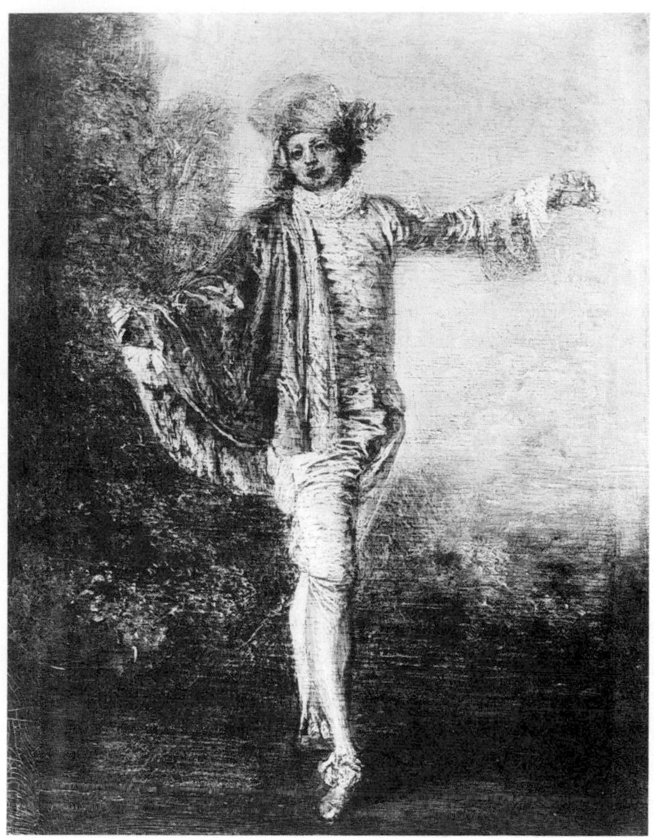

20-5 ANTOINE WATTEAU, *L'Indifférent*, c. 1716. Approx. 10″ × 7″. Louvre, Paris.

Watteau's masterpiece (of which he painted two different versions) is *Return from Cythera* (FIG. **20-6**), completed between 1717 and 1719 as the artist's acceptance piece for admission to the French Royal Academy. Watteau was Flemish, and his style was a beautiful derivative of the style of Rubens—a kind of rarefaction and refinement of it. At the turn of the century, the French Royal Academy was rather sharply divided between two doctrines. One doctrine upheld the ideas of Le Brun (the major proponent of French Baroque under Louis XIV), who followed Nicolas Poussin in teaching that form was the most important element in painting, while "colors in paintings were . . . blandishments to lure the eyes," something added for effect, and not really essential. The other doctrine, with Rubens as its model, proclaimed the supremacy of color as natural and the coloristic style as the proper guide to the artist. Depending on which side they took, members of the Academy were called "Poussinistes" or "Rubénistes." With Watteau, the Rubénistes carried the day, and the Rococo style in painting was established on the colorism of Rubens and the Venetians.

Watteau's *Return from Cythera* represents a group of lovers preparing to depart from the island of eternal

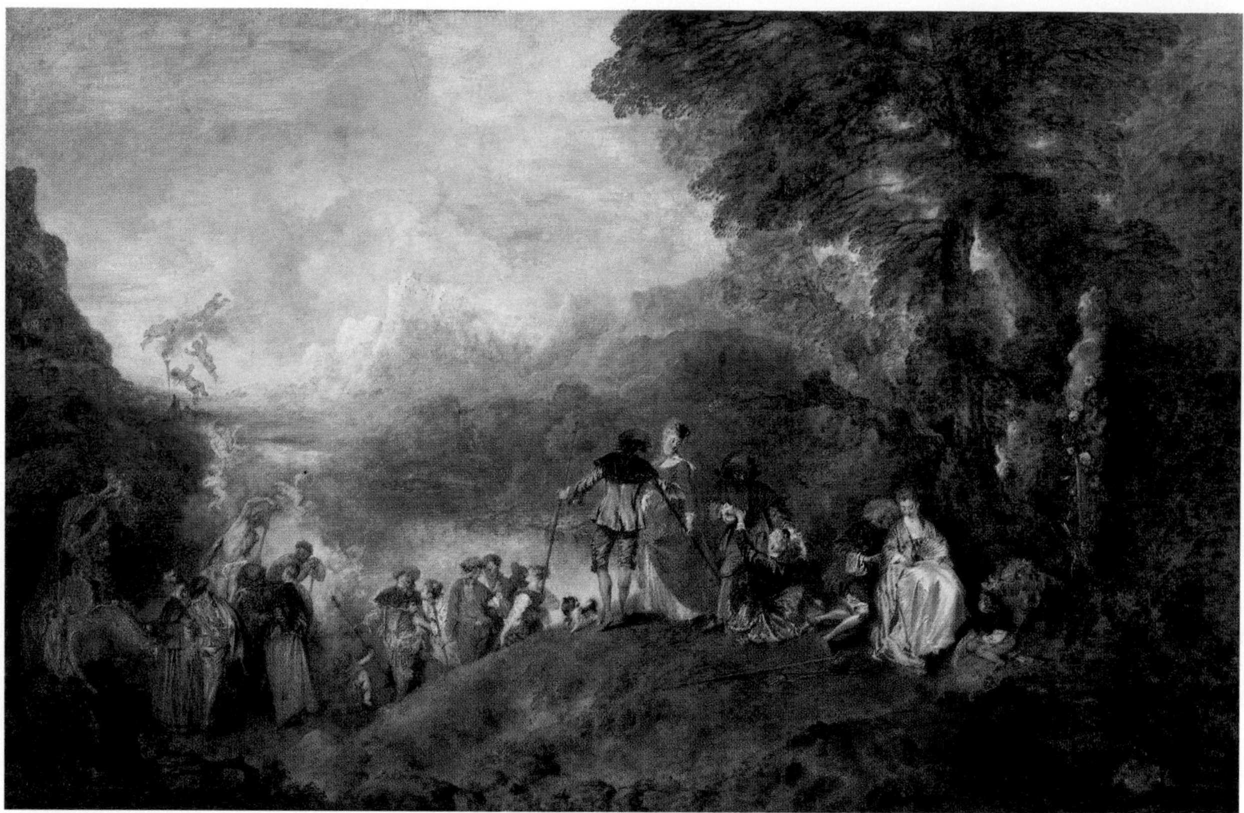

20-6 Antoine Watteau, *Return from Cythera,* 1717–1719. Approx. 4′ 3″ × 6′ 4″. Louvre, Paris.

youth and love, sacred to Aphrodite. Young and luxuriously costumed, they perform, as it were, an elegant, tender, graceful ballet, moving from the protective shade of a woodland park, peopled with amorous cupids and voluptuous statuary, down a grassy slope to an awaiting golden barge. The attitudes of the figures were studied carefully; Watteau has never been equaled for his distinctive poses, which combine elegance and sweetness. He composed his generally quite small paintings from albums of superb drawings that have been preserved and are still in fine condition. In these, we find him observing slow movement from difficult and unusual angles, obviously with the intention of finding the smoothest, most poised, and most refined attitudes. As he sought nuances of bodily poise and movement, Watteau also strove for the most exquisite shades of color difference, defining in a single stroke the shimmer of silk at a bent knee or the iridescence that touches a glossy surface as it emerges from shadow. Art historians have noted that the theme of love and Arcadian happiness in Watteau's pictures (which we have seen since Giorgione and which Watteau may have seen in works by Rubens) is slightly shadowed with wistfulness, or even melancholy, as if Watteau, during his own short life, meditated on the swift passage of youth and pleasure. The haze of color, the subtly modeled shapes, the gliding motion, and the air of suave gentility were all to the taste of the Rococo artist's aristocratic patronage. The unifying power of that taste drew the arts together. The titles, as well as the mood of many musical compositions by Watteau's contemporary, Jean Philippe Rameau, are perfectly suited to Watteau's pictures. The mood is also wonderfully echoed in a passage from Alexander Pope's *Rape of the Lock* (1714), showing that Rococo taste touched even the English arts on occasion:

> But now secure the painted vessel glides,
> The sunbeams trembling on the floating tides;
> While melting music steals upon the sky,
> And softened sounds along the waters die.
> . . . .
> The lucid squadrons round the sails repair:
> Soft o'er the shrouds aërial whispers breathe,
> That seemed but zephyrs to the train beneath.
> Some to the sun their insect wings unfold,
> Waft on the breeze, or sink in clouds of gold;
> Transparent forms too fine for mortal sight,
> Their fluid bodies half dissolved in light,
> Loose to the wind their airy garments flew,
> Thin glittering textures of the filmy dew.

Watteau's successors never quite matched his taste and subtlety. Their themes were concerned with love, artfully and archly pursued through erotic frivolity and playful intrigue. After Watteau's untimely death, his follower, FRANÇOIS BOUCHER (1703–1770), painter to Madame de Pompadour, rose to the dominant position in French painting. Although he was an excellent portraitist, Boucher's fame rests primarily on his gay and graceful allegories, in which Arcadian shepherds, nymphs, and goddesses cavort in shady glens, engulfed in pink and sky-blue light. *Cupid a Captive* (FIG. **20-7**) presents the viewer with a rosy pyramid of infant and female flesh, set off against a cool, leafy background, with the nudity of the figures

20-7 FRANÇOIS BOUCHER, *Cupid a Captive,* 1754. Approx. 66″ × 34″. Reproduced by permission of the Trustees of the Wallace Collection, London.

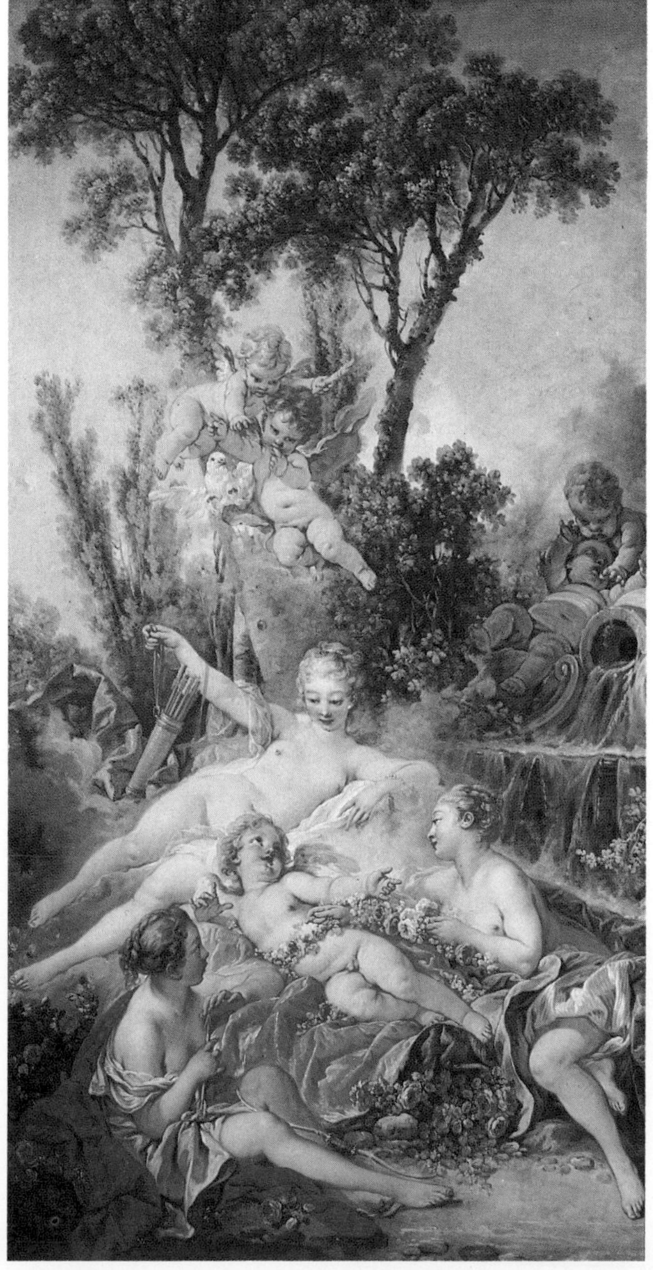

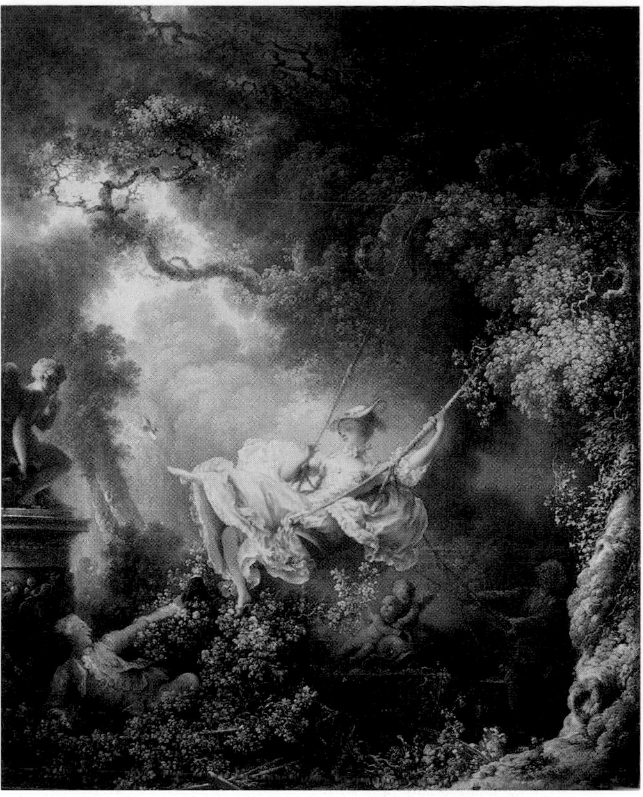

20-8 JEAN HONORÉ FRAGONARD, *The Swing,* 1766. Approx. 35″ × 32″. Reproduced by permission of the Trustees of the Wallace Collection, London.

both hidden and revealed by fluttering draperies. Boucher used the full range of Baroque devices to create his masterly composition: the dynamic play of crisscrossing diagonals, curvilinear forms, and slanting recessions. But powerful Baroque curves in his work were dissected into a multiplicity of decorative arabesques, and Baroque drama dissipated into sensual playfulness. Gay and superficial, Boucher's artful Rococo fantasies became mirrors in which his patrons, the French aristocracy, could behold the ornamental reflections of their cherished pastimes.

JEAN HONORÉ FRAGONARD (1732–1806), Boucher's student, was a first-rate colorist whose decorative skill almost surpassed his master's. An example of his manner can stand as characteristic not only of him, but of the later Rococo in general. *The Swing* (FIG. **20-8**) is a typical "intrigue" picture. A young gentleman has managed an arrangement by which an unsuspecting old bishop swings the young man's pretty sweetheart higher and higher, while her lover stretches out to admire her ardently from a strategic position on the ground. The young lady flirtatiously and boldly kicks off her shoe at the little statue of the god of discretion, who holds his finger to his lips. The landscape setting is out of Watteau—a luxuriant, perfumed bower in a park that very much resembles a

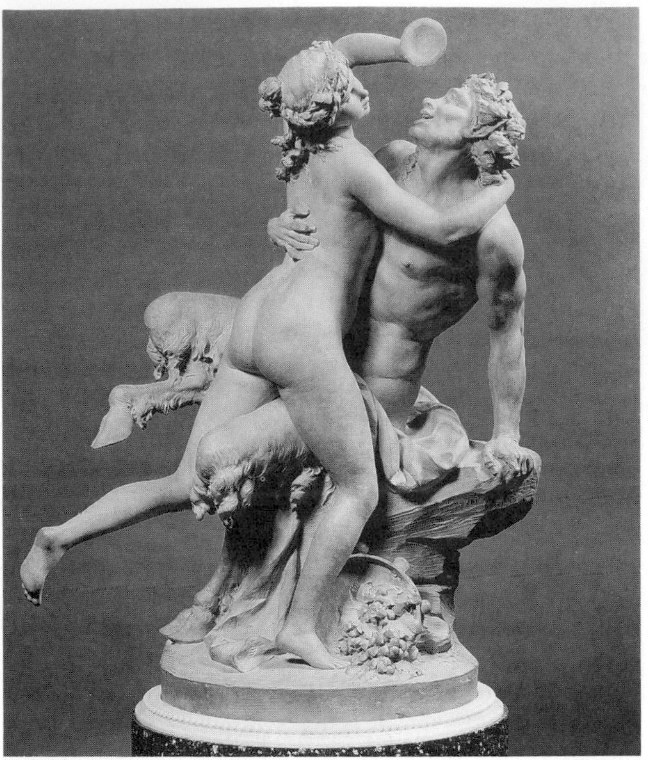

20-9 CLODION, *Nymph and Satyr*, c. 1775. Terra-cotta, approx. 23″ high. The Metropolitan Museum of Art, New York (bequest of Benjamin Altman, 1913).

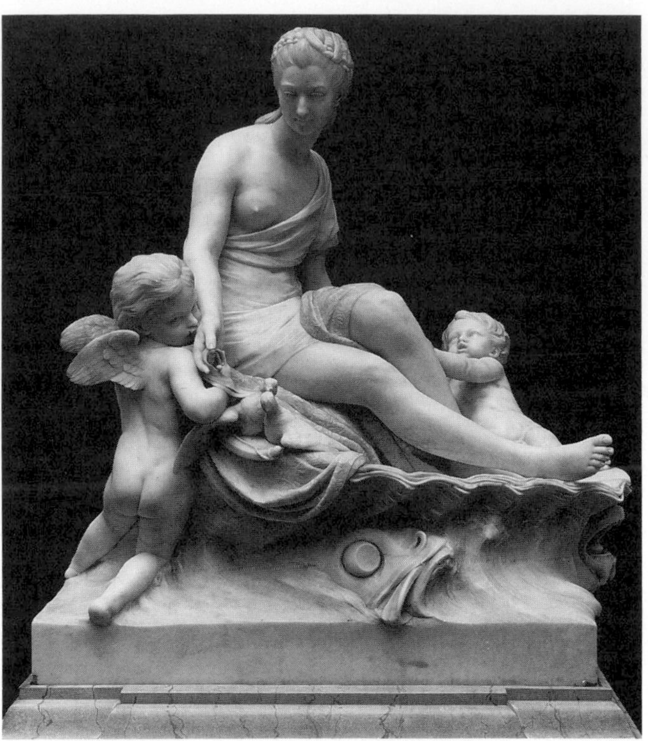

20-10 ÉTIENNE-MAURICE FALCONET, *Madame de Pompadour as the Venus of the Doves*, date unknown. Marble, 29½″ × 28″ × 18″. National Gallery of Art, Washington, D.C. (Samuel H. Kress Collection).

stage scene for the comic opera. The glowing pastel colors and soft light convey, almost by themselves, the sensuality of the theme.

The Rococo mood of sensual intimacy also permeated much of the small sculpture designed for the salons of the day. Artists like CLODION (Claude Michel, 1738–1814) specialized in small, lively sculptures that combined the sensuous fantasies of the Rococo with lightened echoes of Bernini's dynamic Baroque figures. Perhaps we should expect such influence in the works of Clodion; he lived and worked in Rome for some years after discovering the charms of the city during his tenure as the recipient of the cherished Prix de Rome. Clodion's small group, *Nymph and Satyr* (FIG. **20-9**), has an open and vivid composition suggestive of its dynamic Baroque roots, but the artist has overlaid that source with the erotic playfulness of Boucher and Fragonard to energize his eager nymph and the laughing satyr into whose mouth she pours a cup of wine. Here, the sensual exhilaration of the Rococo is caught in diminutive scale and fragile terra-cotta; as with so many Rococo artifacts, and most of Clodion's best work, this group was designed for a tabletop.

The Rococo style in small sculpture was so popular with patrons at court that it was even used to transform portraiture into incidents from dream fêtes. In *Madame de Pompadour as the Venus of the Doves* (FIG. **20-10**) by ÉTIENNE-MAURICE FALCONET (1716–1791), the artist demonstrated his special gift for portraying the soft, warm qualities of the human body. As the director of sculpture at the Sèvres Porcelain Manufactory, Falconet developed great skill in designing compositions in small scale. In this graceful marble piece, he fitted the portrait head of his famous patroness onto an idealized nude body, which sits gracefully between two attendant putti. The lyrical linking in this work between the Classical goddess of love and the eighteenth-century ex-mistress of the king of France, who remained the powerful arbiter of court taste in France for many years, must have pleased its subject as a particularly appropriate concept and design.

Rococo and Late Baroque in Italy and Germany

French Rococo did not immediately penetrate into Italy and other places where the titled grandees of Europe sought to emulate the Baroque splendor of Versailles or the glories of Counter-Reformation Italian Baroque churches designed by architects like Bernini, Borromini, and Guarini. One of the finest early eighteenth-century ecclesiastical structures is the

Superga (FIG. **20-11**), located near Turin in northwestern Italy. This church was designed by FILIPPO JUVARA (1678–1736) for Victor Amadeus II, king of Savoy, to commemorate Savoy's victory over the French in 1706 during the War of the Spanish Succession. Juvara had begun his career as royal architect at Turin by practicing the lavish Baroque style of his predecessor, Guarino Guarini (FIG. 19-19), but a period of study in Rome turned Juvara toward a more Classical approach. The style of the Superga reflects this shift, although the building's setting is entirely Baroque. The layout of the church and the monastery, of which it is the frontispiece, is similar to that of the Church of the Invalides in Paris (FIG. 19-70). The great dome and drum of the Superga are close to the dimensions of the Invalides and may reflect Juvara's knowledge of that building. At the same time, the Superga's deep, four-columned portico, surmounted by a balustrade that continues around the building, echoes Palladian Classicism, and the relation of the portico to the rotunda-like structure behind it recalls the ancient Pantheon (FIG. 6-56). The severity of the portico and of the colossal orders that articulate the walls is offset by the light, fanciful bell towers that flank the dome. In its adroit adjustment of Classical features and Baroque grouping, the building is an impressive example of Juvara's intelligent eclecticism.

By the second quarter of the century, the grandeur of the Late Baroque was being modified by French Rococo overtones in much of Germany and Austria. A brilliant example of French Rococo in Germany is the Amalienburg (FIGS. **20-12** and **20-13**), a small lodge built by FRANÇOIS DE CUVILLIÉS (1698–1768) in the park of the Nymphenburg Palace in Munich. Although we have seen that the Rococo was essentially a style of interior design, the Amalienburg beautifully harmonizes the interior and exterior elevations through the curving flow of lines and planes that cohere in a plastic unity of great elegance. The *bombé* (outward-bowed) shape of the central bay of the Amalienburg façade was a common feature of Rococo

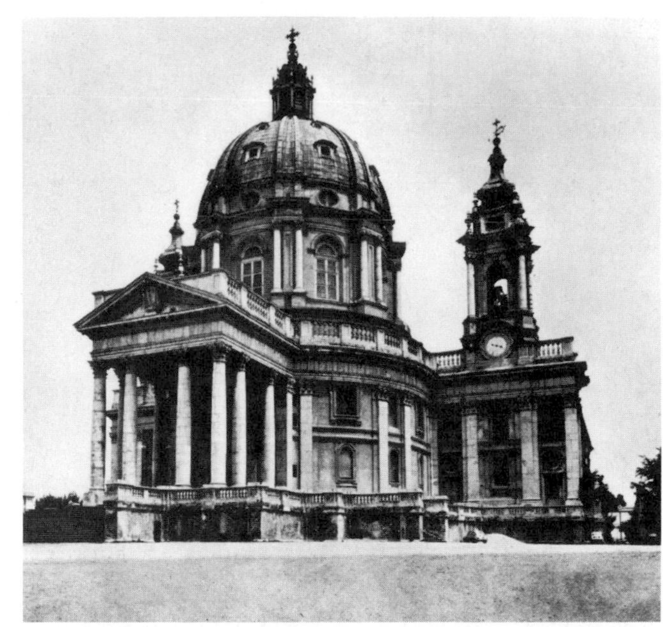

20-11 FILIPPO JUVARA, the Superga, near Turin, Italy, 1715–1731.

20-12 FRANÇOIS DE CUVILLIÉS, the Amalienburg, Nymphenburg Park, Munich, West Germany, 1734–1739.

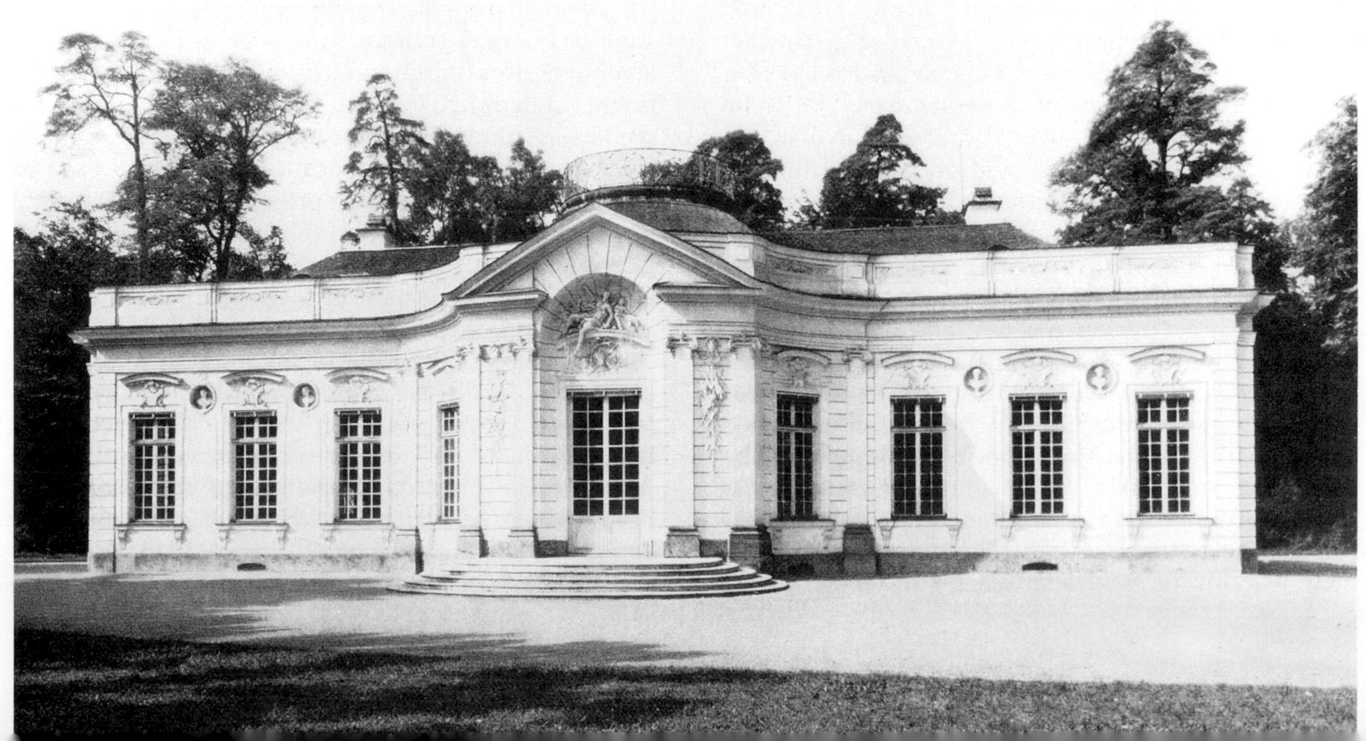

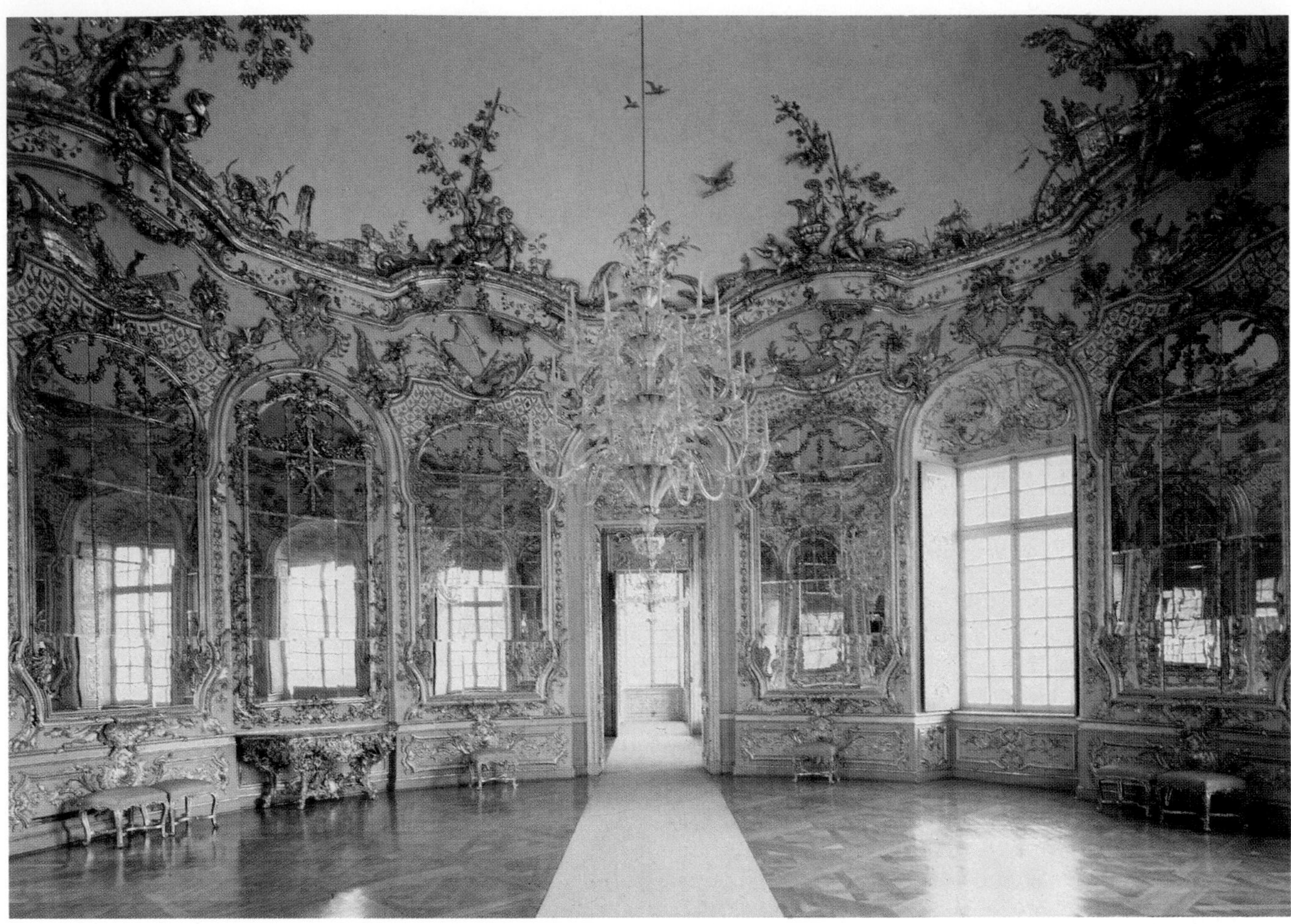

20-13 François de Cuvilliés, Hall of Mirrors, the Amalienburg.

furniture design; indeed, the compactness, diminutive scale, graceful lines, and exquisite detail invest the Amalienburg with the appearance of a kind of precious furnishing set down on the manicured greensward of its park setting. The most spectacular interior room in the lodge is the circular Hall of Mirrors (FIG. 20-13), a silver and blue ensemble of architecture, stucco relief, silvered-bronze mirrors, and crystal that dazzles the eye with myriad scintillating motifs, forms, and figurations borrowed from the full Rococo repertory of ornament. This is the zenith of the style. Facets of silvery light, multiplied by windows and mirrors, sharply or softly delineate the endlessly proliferating shapes and contours that weave rhythmically around the upper walls and the coves of the ceiling. Everything seems organic, growing and in motion, an ultimate rarefaction of illusion created with virtuoso flourishes by the team of architect, artists, and artisans, all magically in command of the resources of their varied media.

Even the ceilings of Late Baroque palaces sometimes became painted festivals for the imagination. The master of such works, Giambattista Tiepolo (1696–1770), was the last great Italian painter to have an international impact until the twentieth century. Of Venetian origin, Tiepolo worked for patrons in Austria, Germany, and Spain, as well as in Italy, leaving a strong impression wherever he went. His bright, cheerful colors and his relaxed compositions are ideally suited to Rococo architecture. *The Apotheosis of the Pisani Family* (FIG. **20-14**), a ceiling fresco in the Villa Pisani at Stra in northern Italy, shows airy populations fluttering through vast sunlit skies and fleecy clouds, their figures making dark accents against the brilliant light of high noon. As the word *apotheosis* indicates, members of the Pisani family are elevated here to the rank of the gods in a heavenly scene that recalls the ceiling paintings of Correggio (FIG. 17-37) and Pozzo (FIG. 19-33). While retaining the illusionistic tendencies of the seventeenth century, Tiepolo discards all rhetoric to create gay and brightly colored pictorial schemes of great elegance and grace, which, for sheer effectiveness as decor, are unsurpassed.

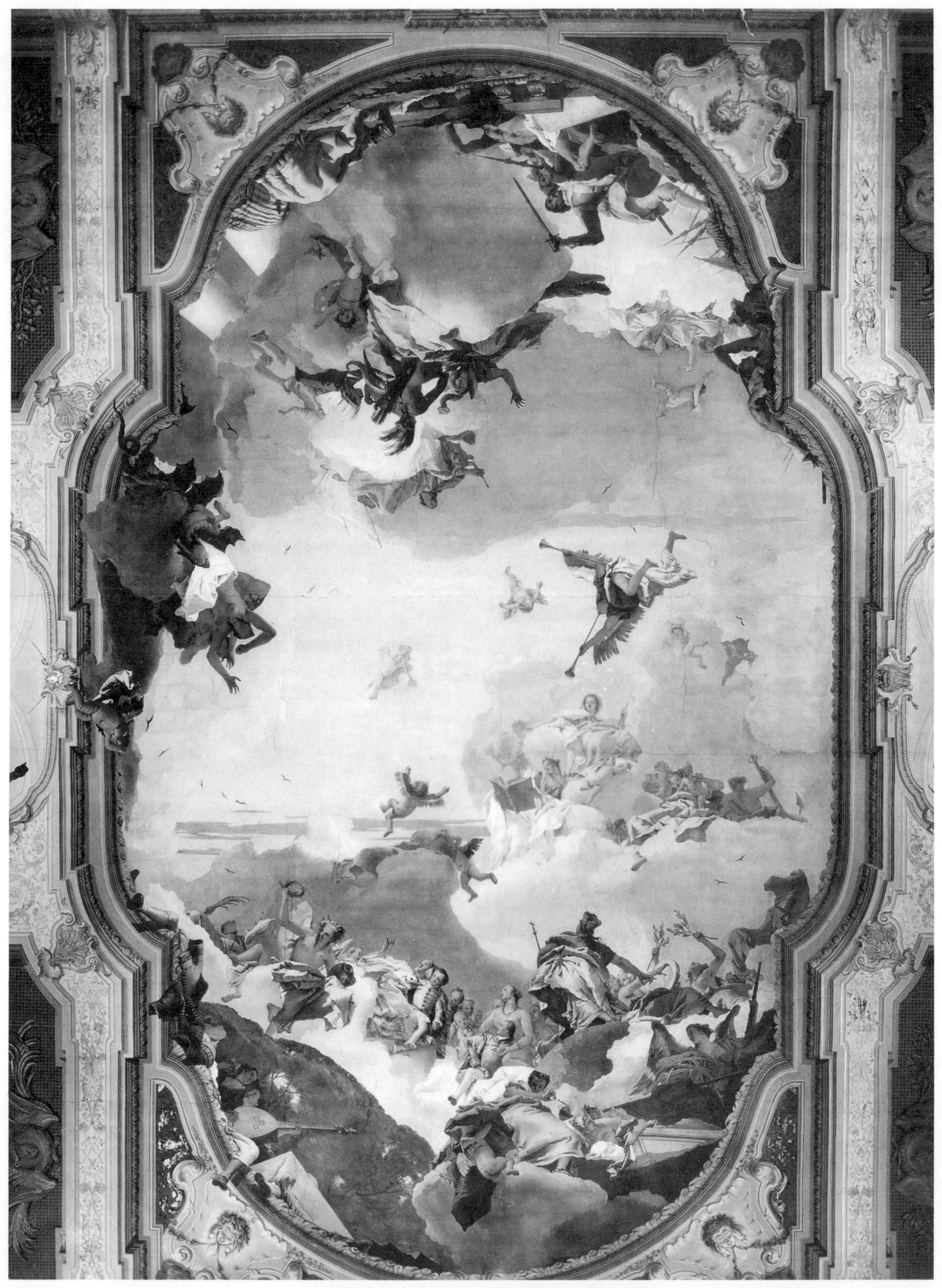

20-14 Giambattista Tiepolo, *The Apotheosis of the Pisani Family,* 1761–1762. Ceiling fresco in the Villa Pisani, Stra, Italy.

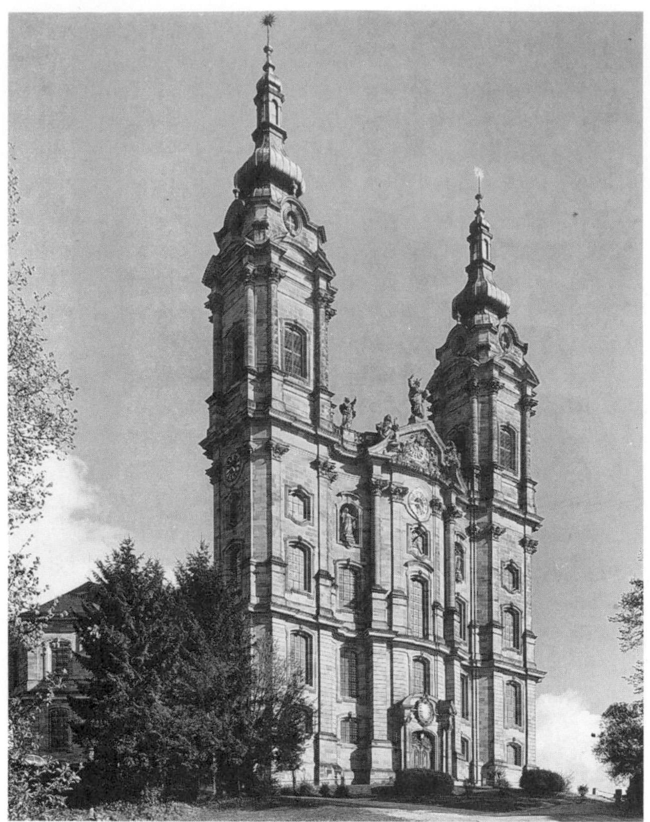

20-15 BALTHASAR NEUMANN, façade of the pilgrimage chapel of Vierzehnheiligen, near Staffelstein, West Germany, 1743–1772.

20-16 BALTHASAR NEUMANN, interior of Vierzehnheiligen.

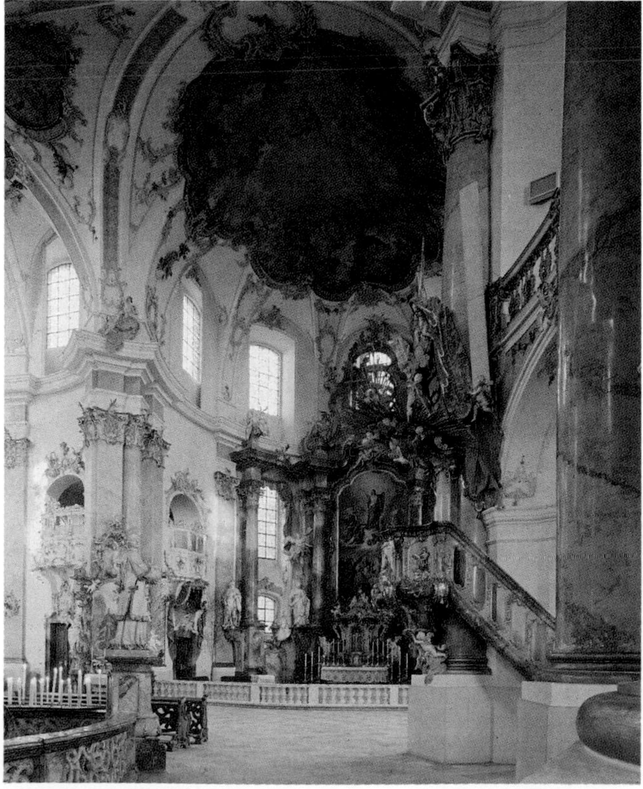

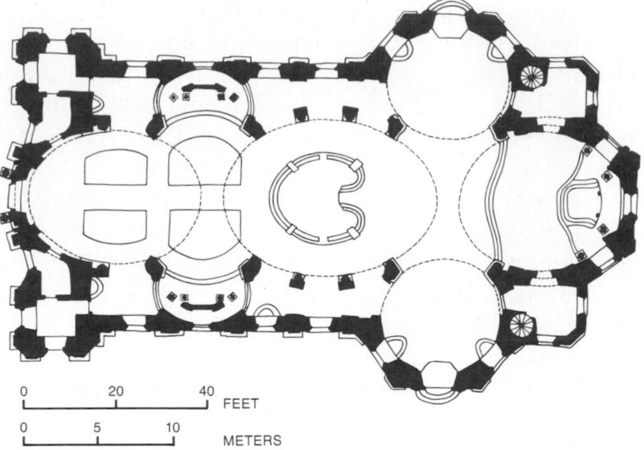

20-17 BALTHASAR NEUMANN, plan of Vierzehnheiligen.

The Rococo style spread beyond palaces to ecclesiastical architecture in an area of southern Germany and Austria that had lain dormant artistically throughout the seventeenth century. In a great wave of church building here in the eighteenth century, the new style was not confined to interiors but appeared in exteriors and plans as well. The chief influence, moreover, was not French but Italian, stemming from the architecture of Borromini and Guarini, so that it is perhaps more accurate to think of this style as Late Baroque with strong stylistic affinities to Rococo. One of the most splendid of the German buildings is the pilgrimage church of Vierzehnheiligen (Fourteen Saints), designed by BALTHASAR NEUMANN (1687–1753). Born in the German part of Bohemia, Neumann traveled in Austria and northern Italy and studied in Paris before returning home to become one of the most active architects working in his native land. The rounded corners and the undulating center of the façade of Vierzehnheiligen (FIG. **20-15**) recall the style of Borromini, without approaching his dramatic intensity. Numerous large windows in the richly articulated but continuous walls flood the interior with an even, bright, and cheerful light. The pilgrimage church sanctuary (FIG. **20-16**) exhibits a vivacious play of architectural fantasy that retains the dynamic energy but banishes all the dramatic qualities of Italian Baroque. The complexity of Vierzehnheiligen is readable in its ground plan (FIG. **20-17**), which has been called "one of the most ingenious pieces of architectural design ever conceived." The straight line deliberately seems to have been banished. The composition is made up of tangent ovals and circles, so that, within the essential outlines of the traditional Gothic church (apse, transept, nave, and western towers), a quite different interior effect is achieved, one of undulating space in continuous motion, creating unlimited vistas bewildering in their variety and surprise effects. The features of the structure pulse, flow, and commingle as if they were ceaselessly in the process of being molded. The fluency of line, the floating, hovering surfaces, the interwoven spaces, and dematerialized masses of the design combine to suggest a "frozen" counterpart to the intricacy of voices in a fugue by Bach. We must think of this kind of church as a brilliant ensemble of architecture, sculpture, music, and painting, in which the boundaries of the arts dissolve in a visionary unity.

Pictorial embellishment of German and Austrian churches, often in the style of Tiepolo, was supplemented by sculpture conceived to produce entirely pictorial effects. The group of the *Assumption of the Virgin* (FIG. **20-18**) was created by EGID QUIRIN ASAM (1692–1750) for the space above the altar in the monastery church at Rohr, Germany. The church was designed with his brother COSMAS DAMIAN ASAM (1680–1739). The brothers were influenced in their building designs by the Late Baroque architecture they saw on a trip to Rome. What they brought home was a feeling for the illusionistic spectacle we have just seen in Tiepolo's ceiling painting (FIG. 20-14). In Egid Quirin Asam's *Assumption of the Virgin,* as in Bernini's *Ecstasy of St. Theresa* (FIG. 19-12), the miraculous is made real before our eyes, a spiritual vision materially visible. The Virgin, effortlessly borne aloft by angels, soars to the glowing paradise above her, while the apostolic witnesses below gesticulate in astonishment around her vacant tomb. The figures ascending to Heaven have gilded details that set them apart from those that remain on earth. The setting is a luxuriously ornamented theater; the scene itself, pure opera—an art that was perfected and became very popular in the eighteenth century. One can imagine the Virgin as the protagonist in an operatic production, singing the climactic aria, with all appropriate gestures, to the excited accompaniment of a chorus, while a virtuoso designer directs the stagecraft. Here, sculpture dissolves into painting, theater, and music, its mass rendered weightless, its natural compactness of composition broken up and diffused. In this instance, the art of the sculptor was used, paradoxically, to disguise substance and function, weight and tactility, in the interest of eye-deceiving mystical illusion.

20-18 EGID QUIRIN ASAM, *Assumption of the Virgin,* monastery church at Rohr, West Germany, 1723.

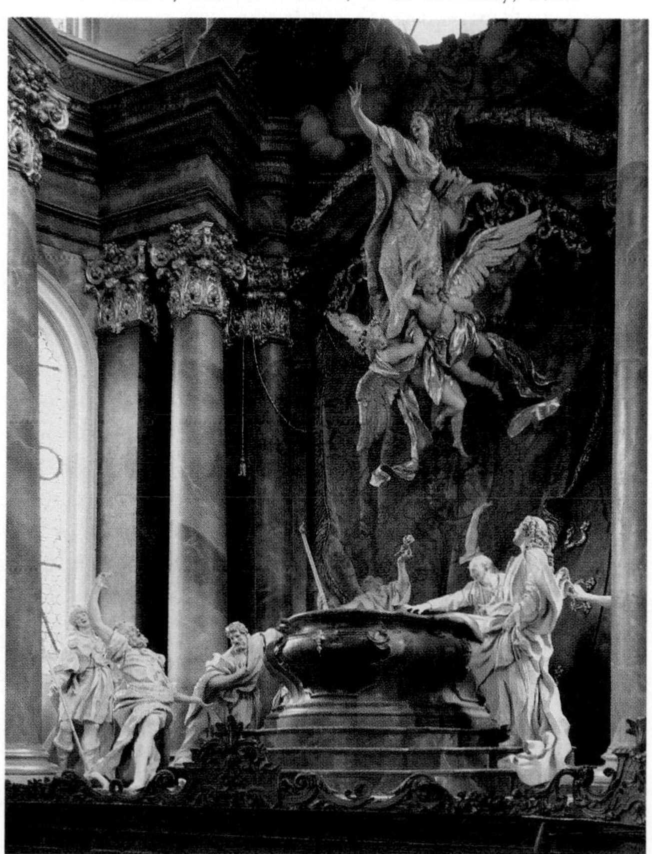

THE LATER EIGHTEENTH CENTURY: THE BIRTH OF THE MODERN WORLD

The second half of the eighteenth century quickened in tempo and changed in mood as the course of history swept toward the climax of the revolutions that opened the modern epoch. An uneasiness and then an impatience with the status quo bred a new and restless spirit of criticism that, here and there, edged toward rebellion against what was thought to be the wanton lavishness and profligacy of the Rococo. An impulse toward the simple, the earnest, and the moral began to rise. Side by side with the waning of the Rococo ran a rising belief in the importance of using reason and one's senses in free inquiry to achieve a better understanding of oneself and the world. These ideas were part of the "enlightened" thinking of Voltaire and Diderot, who taught the importance of understanding gained by the systematic gathering and ordering of data about the physical world. Related to these teachings was a belief in the power of knowledge and education to improve human life. A renewed taste for naturalism in art arose, bringing with it a resurgence of interest in carefully detailed landscapes and cityscapes, and a desire for natural effects in portraiture that recalled those of seventeenth-century Holland.

The later eighteenth century was also the time of Rousseau, the "age of sensibility" whose leading thinkers preached the value of sincere feeling and natural human sympathy over artful reason and the cold calculations of courtly societies. The slogan of sensibility was "Trust your heart rather than your head," or, as Goethe put it, "Feeling is all!" Werther, the young Goethe's archetype of Romantic sensibility, cried: "We desire to surrender our whole being, that it may be filled with the perfect bliss of one glorious emotion!" All that was false and artificial was to be banished as the enemy of honest emotion. In art, sensibility joined with the idea of Enlightenment thinkers that paintings with a moral theme could move the hearts of viewers toward correct social behavior.

Sensibility was swiftly overtaken by the heroic emotions of the revolutionary age. Archeological discoveries of ancient Roman cities in the early and mid-eighteenth century helped to reinforce a rising belief that people in the days of ancient Greece and Rome had lived by a splendid moral code, which had governed their behavior and their allegiance to the wider society. Eighteenth-century thinkers were quick to link models of self-sacrificing virtue from the Greek and Roman past with some from the rebellious present—heroes like Cato and Washington, Regulus and Marat—to touch the hearts of viewers and readers and to inspire thoughts and deeds of civic idealism. A revived Classical style was developed in architecture, painting, and sculpture to help encourage modern citizens toward exemplary acts of civic behavior.

Contemporary with both the sentimental and the heroic came the taste for the sublime in art and nature. The sublime inspired feelings of awe mixed with terror—the feelings we experience when we look on vast, impassable mountain peaks or great storms at sea. Accompanying the taste for the sublime was the taste for the fantastic, the occult, the grotesque, the macabre—for the adventures of the soul voyaging into the dangerous reaches of consciousness. Images of the sublime and the terrible often combined something of Baroque dynamism with natural details in their quest for the presentation of grippingly convincing visions.

Everything that moved the emotions of artists and their audience—the sentimental, the heroic, the sublime, the "Gothic," or combinations of them—was marked by a shift in emphasis from reason to feeling, from calculation to intuition, from objective nature to subjective emotion. Here, that attitude of the modern mind we call Romanticism first emerges.

J. P. Eckermann's *Conversations with Goethe* throw a strong, revealing light on the emotional side of Romanticism, especially on its supposed opposition to Classicism. Goethe is recorded as declaring:

> The distinction between Classical and Romantic poetry, which is now spread over the whole world and occasions so many quarrels and divisions, came originally from Schiller and myself. [Goethe is looking back some forty years in time.] I laid down the maxim of objective treatment in poetry, and would allow no other; but Schiller, who worked quite in the subjective way, deemed his own fashion right, and to defend himself against me, wrote the treatise upon *Naïve and Sentimental Poetry*. He proved to me that I, against my will, was romantic, and that my *Iphigenia*, through the predominance of sentiment, was by no means so much in the Antique spirit as some people supposed. The Schlegels took up this idea, and carried it further, so that it has now been diffused over the whole world; and everybody talks about Classicism and Romanticism—of which nobody thought fifty years ago.*

Goethe wanted his drama, *Iphigenia*, to be in the Antique spirit and, "against his will," discovered that he had been romantic all the time. This discovery was probably made by many artists throughout the era of Romanticism. The break with tradition forced the artist to look at tradition historically; if Classical art was preferred, then a "classic" bent of mind must be assumed or affected, but the artist would still be representing Classical form, not *creating* it. In the end, it was the emotional response to Classical form that counted, and the emotional response to Classical form was precisely Romantic!

Reaction Against the Rococo: "Naturalness" in Landscape and Portraiture

By mid-century, accompanying the diminishing power of the aristocracy and the rise of a new moneyed bourgeois class, a reaction had developed against the sweet sensual fantasies of Rococo art. A desire for "naturalism" in art complemented the increased interest in the workings of the natural world that was fostering scientific attempts to assemble and organize data about every aspect of the earth and the universe beyond it. Documentation of particular places became popular, both to serve the needs of the many scientific expeditions mounted during the century, and to satisfy the desires of genteel tourists for mementos of their journeys. By this time, a "grand tour" of the major sites of Europe was considered part of every well-bred person's education. Naturally, those on tour wished to bring home things that

*John Oxenford, trans., and J. K. Moorehead, ed., *Conversations of Goethe with Eckermann* (New York: Dutton, 1935), p. 366.

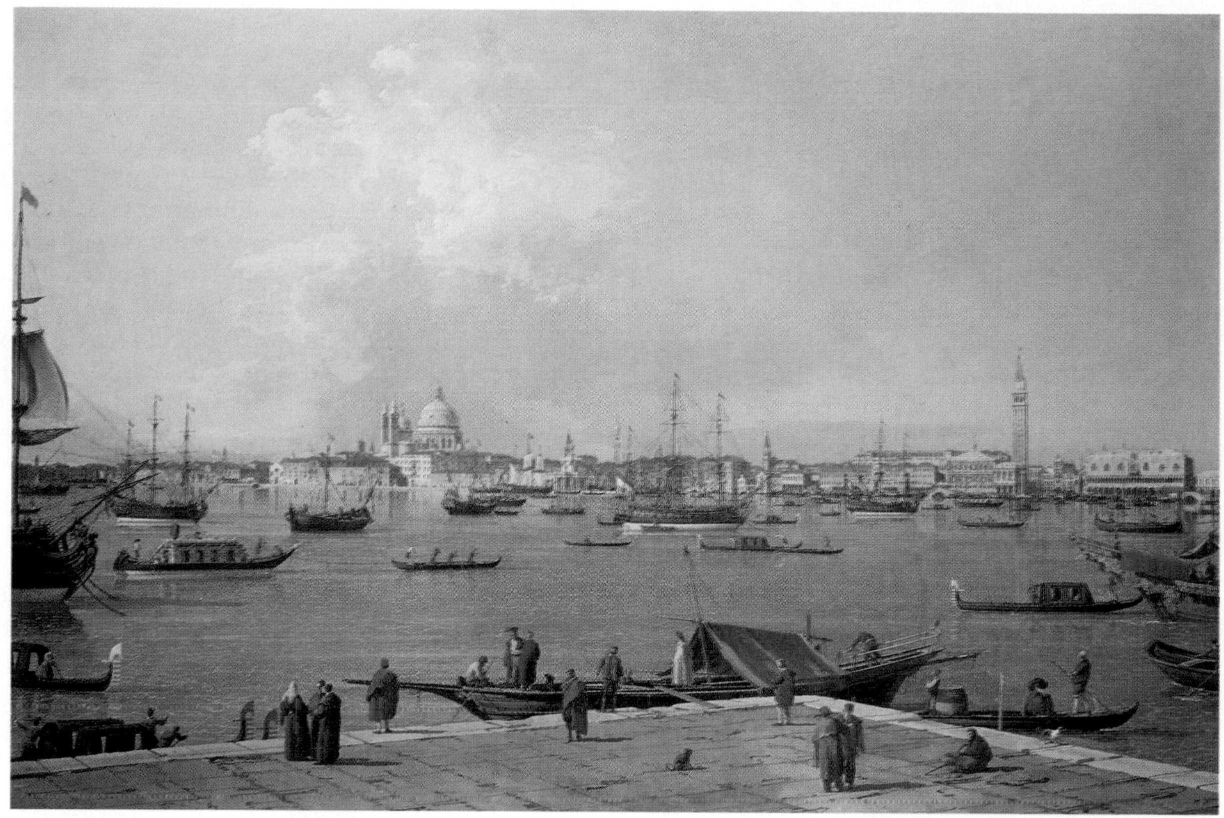

20-19 ANTONIO CANALETTO, *Basin of San Marco from San Giorgio Maggiore.* Wallace Collection, London.

would help them remember their experiences and would impress those at home with the wonders they had seen.

The English were especially eager collectors of pictorial souvenirs. Certain artists in Venice specialized in painting the most characteristic scenes *(veduta)* of that city to sell to British visitors. The veduta paintings of (GIOVANNI) ANTONIO CANALETTO (1697–1768) were eagerly acquired by English tourists, who hung them on the walls of homes like Chiswick and Blenheim as visible evidence of their visit to the city of the Grand Canal. It must have been very cheering in the midst of a grey winter afternoon in England to look up and see a sunny, panoramic view like that in Canaletto's *Basin of San Marco from San Giorgio Maggiore* (FIG. **20-19**), with its cloud-studded sky, calm harbor, varied water traffic, picturesque pedestrians, and well-known Venetian landmarks all picked out in scrupulous perspective and minute detail. Canaletto had trained as a scene-painter with his father, but his easy mastery of detail, light, and shadow soon made him one of the most popular "vedutista" in Venice. Occasionally, he painted his scenes directly from life, but usually he made drawings "on location" to take back to his studios as sources for canvases to be painted there. To help make the on-site drawings true to life, he often used a camera obscura (see page 795). Like Van Ruisdael (FIG. 19-56), Canaletto was interested in painting the visible facts of the scene he had chosen, but unlike the Dutch painter, the Venetian artist's main subject was the architectural setting and the space it created. His paintings give the impression of capturing every detail, with no "editing." Actually, he presented each site within the rules of Renaissance perspective and exercised great selectivity about which details to include and which to omit to make a coherent and engagingly attractive picture. In addition, the mood in each of his works was carefully constructed to be positive and alluring. Everything in the world presented by Canaletto is clean, orderly, and tidy. The sun always shines, and every aspect of the weather is serene.

Perhaps not surprisingly, the desire for naturalism in art was felt most strongly in the area of portraiture. Even many of the powerful and noble patrons of Rococo art were delighted to see themselves portrayed in a more natural guise. The Venetian artist ROSALBA CARRIERA (1675–1757) made an international reputation for herself with vividly natural pastel portraits of the gentry, nobility, and royalty of Europe. Pastels are chalklike crayons made of ground color pigments mixed with water and a binding medium. They lend

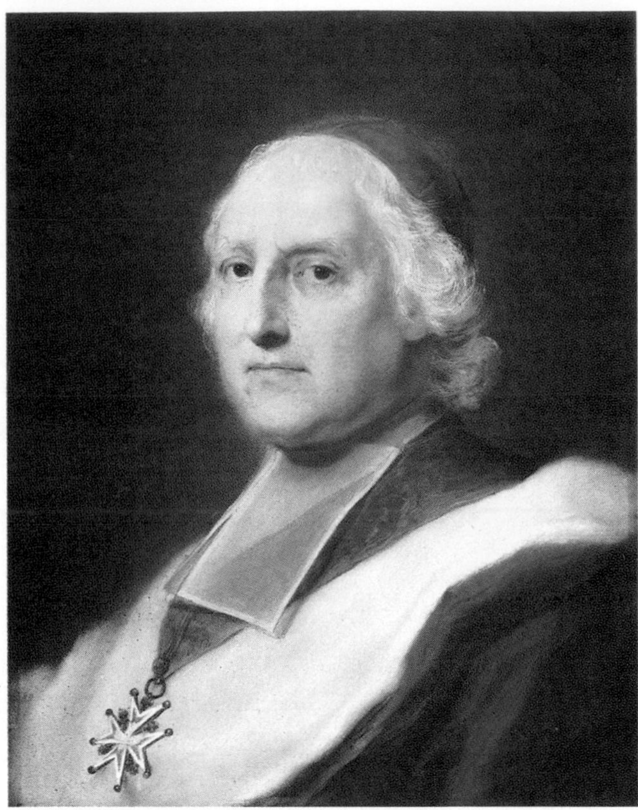

20-20 ROSALBA CARRIERA, *Cardinal de Polignac,* 1732. Pastel. Gallerie dell' Accademia, Venice.

themselves to quick execution, particularly of portraits, and provide the artist with a wide range of colors and subtle variations of tone, characteristics well suited to the rendering of nuances of value and fleeting expressions of feature. Carriera was a pioneer of the pastel medium, and her art became the fashion in Paris, so much so that she had offers for more commissions than she could accept. Her efforts raised the medium of pastel to the level of the art of painting from its hitherto exclusive use for preliminary drawings. Her pastel portrait of *Cardinal de Polignac* (FIG. **20-20**), diplomat and collector of ancient art, shows her portrait method. Essentially informal, the composition includes only the head and bust, eliminating all details not needed to record the features and status of the subject. The design is simple; the pose and presentation are forthright and unpretentious. The pomp and rhetorical flourishes of the Baroque and the sensual playfulness of the Rococo are missing. As is typical for the pastel medium, the colors are high-keyed and luminous, shading is minimal, and the cardinal's grave features are modulated by a slightly hazed, soft focus, suggestive of sunlit atmosphere. By the end of her life, esteem for works such as this had won Carriera election to membership in both the Accademia de San Luca in Rome and the French Royal Academy in Paris.

In England, the tradition of Van Dyck was still strong, but now it was taken up by a whole school of painters, who gradually modified it for the more modern taste. SIR JOSHUA REYNOLDS (1723–1792) specialized in portraits of contemporaries who participated in the great events that ushered in modern times. Reynolds was an influential theorist. In his *Discourses* and as the first president of the British Royal Academy of Arts, founded in 1768, he expounded a doctrine close to that of the academic Baroque, maintaining that "general" nature, as represented by the Carracci and others, was always superior to "particular" nature, as rendered by the Dutch. Yet Reynolds could respond to a portrait subject like *Lord Heathfield* (FIG. **20-21**) by combining careful attention to appearance with a dramatic pose and setting that owed much to the Baroque, while dynamically expressing the character of the sitter. Reynolds was at his best with a subject like this burly, brandy-flushed English officer, commandant of the fortress of Gibraltar during the American Revolution. Lord Heathfield had doggedly defended the great

20-21 SIR JOSHUA REYNOLDS, *Lord Heathfield,* 1787. Approx. 56″ × 45″. Reproduced by courtesy of the Trustees of the National Gallery, London.

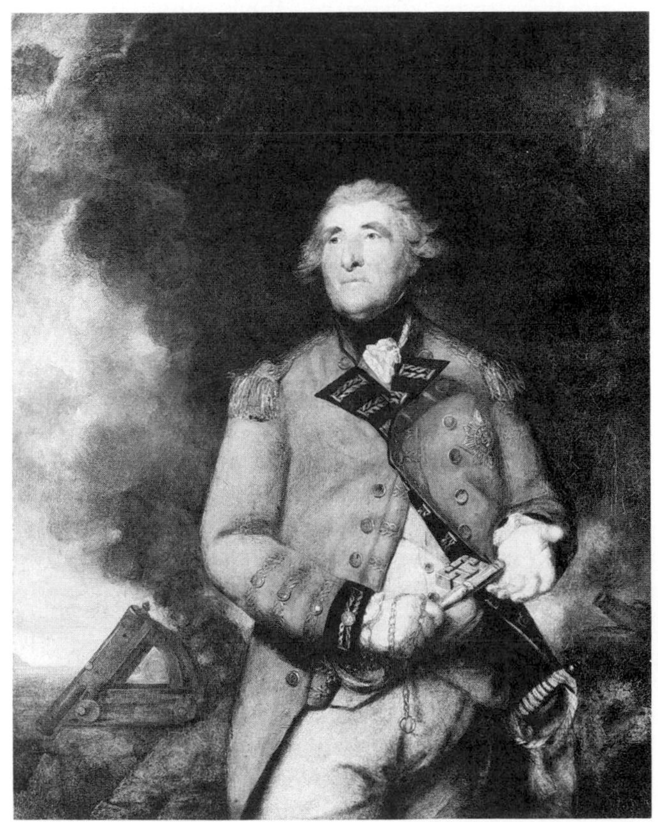

rock against the Spanish, and his victory is symbolized here by the huge key to the fortress, which he holds thoughtfully. He stands in front of a curtain of dark smoke rising from the battleground, flanked by one cannon that points ineffectively downward and another whose tilted barrel indicates that it lies uselessly on its back. The features of the general's heavy, honest face and his uniform are portrayed with a sense of unidealized realism, but his posture and the setting dramatically suggest the heroic theme of battle and also refer to the actual revolutions then taking shape in deadly earnest, as the old regime faded into the past.

A contrasting blend of naturalistic representation and Romantic mood is found in the portrait of *Mrs. Richard Brinsley Sheridan* (FIG. **20-22**) by THOMAS GAINSBOROUGH (1727–1788). This portrait shows the lovely lady, dressed informally, seated in a rustic landscape faintly reminiscent of Watteau in its soft-hued light and feathery brushwork. Gainsborough intended to match the unspoiled beauty of the natural landscape with the natural beauty of the subject, whose dark brown hair blows freely in the slight wind and whose clear, unassisted "English" complexion and air of ingenuous sweetness contrast sharply with the pert sophistication of continental Rococo portraits. The artist originally had planned to give the picture "an air more pastoral than it at present possesses" by adding several sheep, but he did not live long enough to paint them in. Even without this element, we can sense Gainsborough's deep interest in the landscape setting; although he won greater fame in his time for his portraits, he had begun as a landscape painter and always preferred painting scenes of nature to the depiction of human likenesses.

20-22 THOMAS GAINSBOROUGH, *Mrs. Richard Brinsley Sheridan*, c. 1785. Approx. 7′ 2″ × 5′. National Gallery of Art, Washington, D.C. (Andrew W. Mellon Collection).

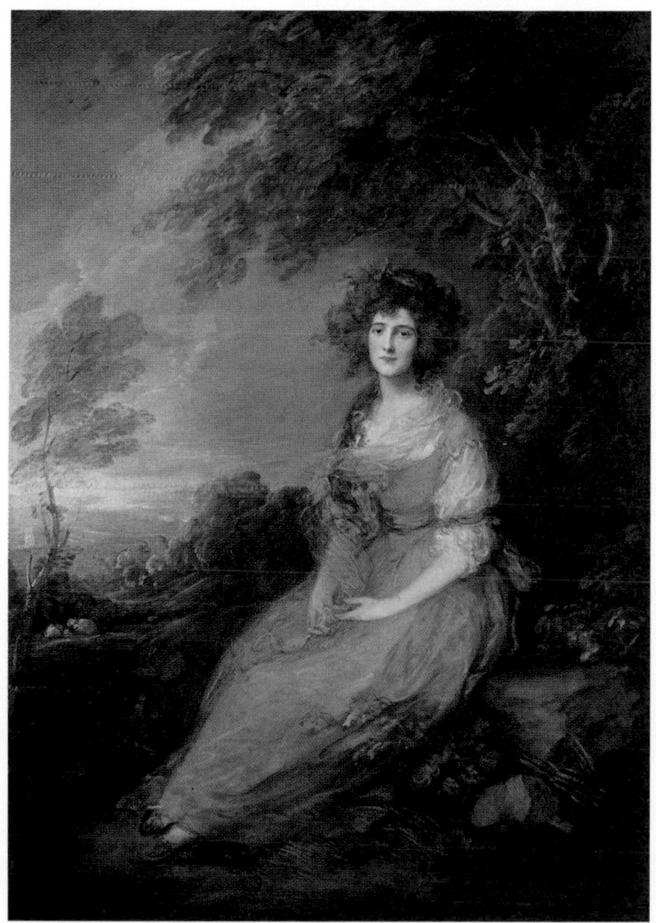

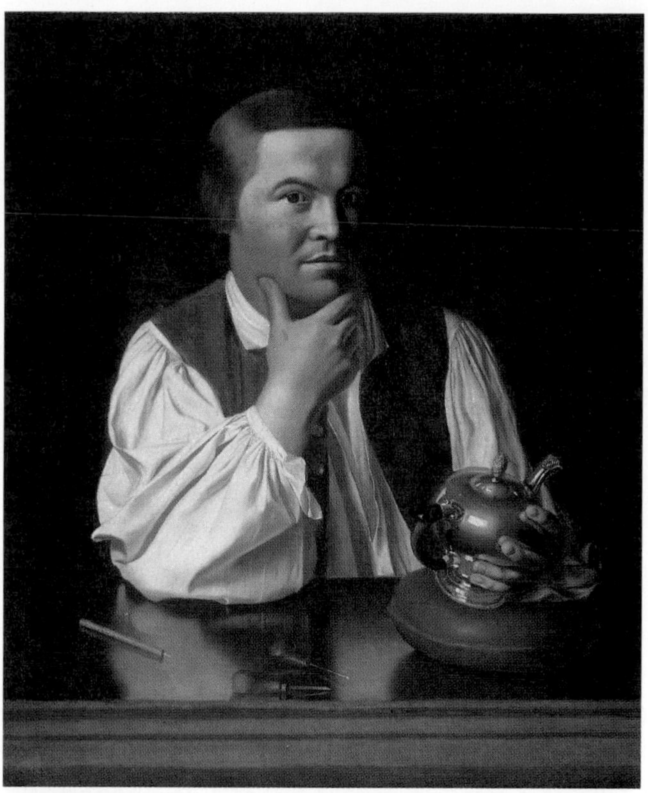

20-23 JOHN SINGLETON COPLEY, *The Portrait of Paul Revere*, c. 1768–1770. 35″ × 28½″. Museum of Fine Arts, Boston (gift of Joseph W., William B., and Edward H. R. Revere).

The Portrait of Paul Revere (FIG. **20-23**), by the American artist JOHN SINGLETON COPLEY (1738–1815), is a painting in a different vein. Revere, like Carriera's Cardinal de Polignac, gazes directly out at the viewer. In contrast to the Cardinal's softened forms, however, everything in Copley's painting is in sharp focus. Each texture is carefully rendered, and every millimeter of the surface is given equal attention. Copley had matured as a painter in Massachusetts and later emigrated to England, where he absorbed

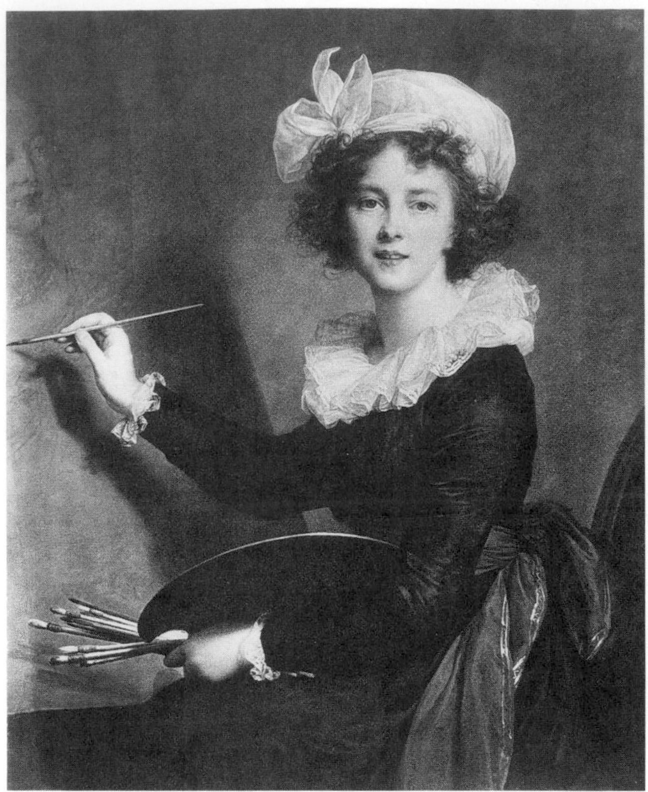

20-24 Élisabeth Louise Vigée-Lebrun, *Self-Portrait,* 1790. 8′ 4″ × 6′ 9″. Galleria degli Uffizi, Florence.

the fashionable English style of Gainsborough and others. *The Portrait of Paul Revere,* painted before Copley left Boston, conveys a sense of no-nonsense directness and faithfulness to visual fact that marked the taste for "downrightness" and plainness noticed by many visitors to America during the eighteenth and nineteenth centuries. At the time the portrait was painted, Revere was not yet the familiar hero of the American Revolution. In the picture, he is working at his everyday profession of silversmithing. The setting is plain, the lighting clear and revealing. The subject sits in his shirtsleeves, bent over a teapot in progress; he pauses and turns his head to look the observer straight in the eye. The artist has treated the reflections in the polished wood of the tabletop with as much care as Revere's figure, his tools, and the teapot resting on its leather graver's pillow. Special prominence was given to the figure's eyes by means of the intense reddish light that reflects onto the darkened side of the face and hands. The informality and the sense of the moment link this painting to contemporaneous English and European portraits, but the spare style and the emphasis on the sitter's down-to-earth character differentiate this American work from its British and continental counterparts.

The *Self-Portrait* (FIG. **20-24**) by Élisabeth Louise Vigée-Lebrun (1755–1842) is a fifth variation of the naturalistic impulse in eighteenth-century portraiture. In the new mode, Vigée-Lebrun looks directly at the viewer like Cardinal de Polignac and Paul Revere; like Revere, she pauses in her work to return our gaze. Although her mood is more light-hearted than that of either de Polignac or Revere and details of her costume echo the serpentine curve beloved by Rococo artists and aristocratic patrons, nothing about Vigée-Lebrun's pose or her mood speaks of Rococo frivolity. Hers is the self-confident stance of a woman whose art has won her an independent role in her society. Like many of her contemporaries, Vigée-Lebrun lived a life of extraordinary personal and economic independence, working for the nobility throughout Europe. She was famous for the force and grace of her portraits, especially those of high-born ladies and royalty. Although she was successful during the age of the late monarchy in France, she survived the fall of the French aristocracy through her talent, her wit, and her ability to forge connections with those in power in the post-revolutionary period. In her *Self-Portrait*, Vigée-Lebrun shows herself to us, in a close-up, intimate view, at work on one of the portraits that won her renown. The naturalism and intimacy of her expression are similar to those in Houdon's *Voltaire* (FIG. 20-25), reflecting the ideals of the French leaders of the Enlightenment, while the independence and self-reliance she exhibits here as a woman point the way to the modern world.

20-25 Jean Antoine Houdon, *Voltaire Seated,* 1781. Marble, 65″ high. Comédie-Française, Paris.

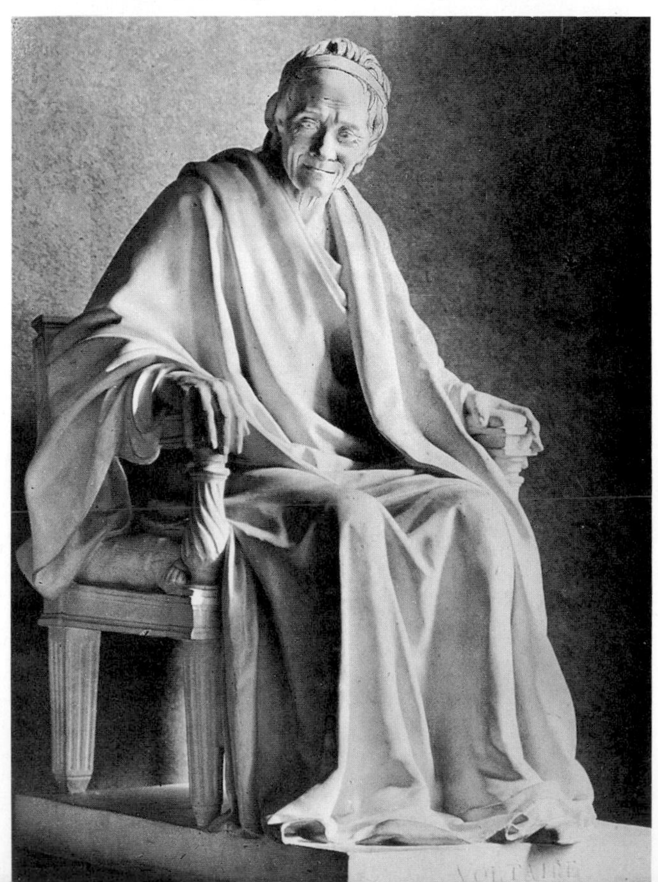

The Enlightenment: Science, Technology, and Moral Education

The second half of the eighteenth century is often called the Age of Enlightenment or the Age of Reason. In this period, many thinkers came to believe that the world operated rationally, according to natural laws that could be discovered through the systematic collection and organization of facts. Leading philosophers of the Enlightenment even encouraged the taking of a scientific, rational approach to political, religious, and socioeconomic matters, holding that people were, above all, reasonable beings who would behave with exemplary civic and social virtue if provided with proper facts and educational examples. Enlightenment ideas appealed almost immediately to those tired of the excesses of the Rococo age, and the teachings spread rapidly as former Rococo salons turned their attention to the new concepts.

The center of the Age of Reason on the continent was Paris, and, as already noted, a leading figure in the development of Enlightenment thinking in France was Voltaire. Voltaire was at the center of a group of thinkers who championed the power of reason, education, and enlightened action. His image was captured by the French sculptor JEAN ANTOINE HOUDON (1741–1828) in *Voltaire Seated* (FIG. **20-25**). The artist has dressed the aging philosopher in a flowing robe, like that of a Greek or Roman sage, and seated him in a chair reminiscent of the earlier Classical age. Houdon's training in Paris and Rome inspired him to create a host of sculptures with Classical themes, like *Minerva, Diana,* and *Morpheus,* but his mastery of the three-dimensional portrait brought him special fame and many commissions to portray the great men of his time. In addition to Voltaire, Houdon completed sculptural portraits of Rousseau, Benjamin Franklin, George Washington, Thomas Jefferson, and the Marquis de Lafayette. In all his portraits, Houdon's strong, perceptive realism penetrates at once to personality, catching its most subtle shade. Voltaire is captured in a thoughtful moment. His hands suggest that he is about to gesture in response to something that has just made him smile. This lively depiction of Voltaire, with its blend of naturalism and a reference to Classical values, remains a telling embodiment of his beliefs.

Enlightenment thinking's urge toward the rational, pragmatic uses of science led to inventions that modified and changed everyday life. Eighteenth-century engineering foreshadowed the future, particularly in its use of industrial materials. The first use of iron in bridge design came when a cast-iron bridge was built in England over the river Severn, near the site at Coalbrookdale where ABRAHAM DARBY III (1750–1789) ran his family's cast-iron business. The Darby family had spearheaded the evolution of the iron industry in England, and they vigorously supported the investigation of new uses for the material. The fabrication of cast-iron rails and bridge elements inspired Darby to work with architect THOMAS F. PRITCHARD (1723–1777) in designing the Coalbrookdale bridge (FIG. **20-26**). The utilitarian shapes in this structure are still breathtakingly beautiful. The cast-iron armature that supports the roadbed springs from stone pier to stone pier until it leaps the final 100 feet

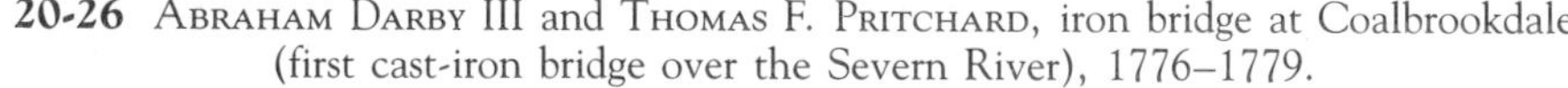
20-26 ABRAHAM DARBY III and THOMAS F. PRITCHARD, iron bridge at Coalbrookdale (first cast-iron bridge over the Severn River), 1776–1779.

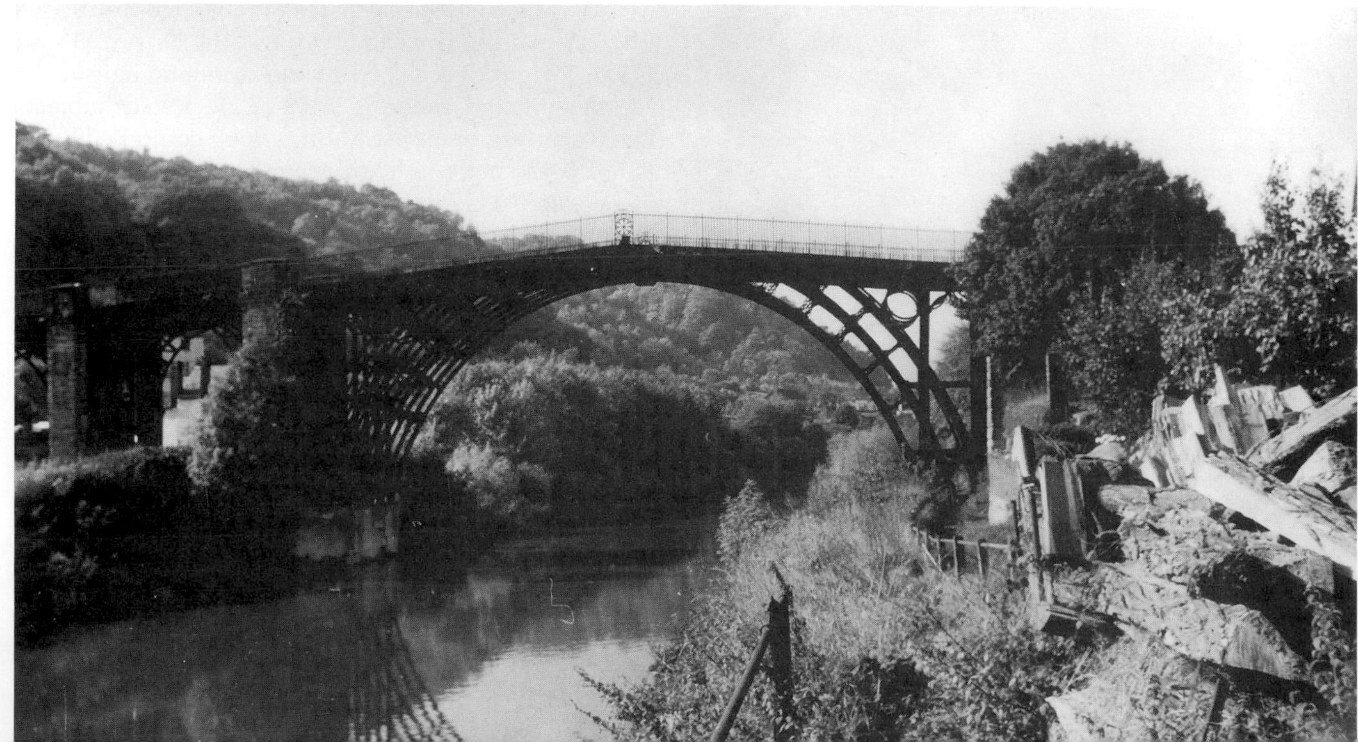

across the Severn River gorge. The style of the graceful center arc echoes the grand arches of Roman aqueducts (FIG. 6-42). At the same time, the exposed structure of the cast-iron parts of the bridge prefigures the skeletal use of iron and steel in the nineteenth century, when visible structural armatures will be expressive factors in the design of buildings like the Crystal Palace (FIG. 21-95) and the Eiffel Tower (FIG. 21-96).

The vast *Encyclopedia* published in France under the direction of Denis Diderot was representative of the thirst for accumulated and organized knowledge that characterized the Enlightenment. Its model was echoed elsewhere in Europe in vast compendia of facts and in more narrowly focused collections of information about individual sectors of learning, such as anatomy. A few gifted artists like BERNARD SIEGFRIED ALBINUS (1697–1770) were able to combine their interest in creating anatomy "textbooks" with a talent for dramatic poses and settings that linked their scientific illustrations with the blend of naturalism and drama developed by artists like Hogarth and Greuze (FIGS. 20-30 and 20-31). Albinus was a professor of anatomy at Leyden University in Holland. His special interest was in comparing the proportions of the human skeleton with those of other fauna, and his masterpiece was the multiple-volume *Tables of the Skeleton and Muscles of the Human Body (Tabulae skeleti et musculorum corporis humani).* Working with the engraver Jan Wandelaar, Albinus created a series of illustrations that combine the meticulous dissection-based realism of Leonardo da Vinci's remarkable anatomical drawings (FIG. 17-5) with an enchanting mid-eighteenth-century sense of the fantastic. Any student of medicine would find in Albinus's books the exact details of human structure, but Albinus was not content to depict his human subjects in static isolation. Instead, he created a series of theatrical moments in which his skeletal actors—in various stages of skin and muscle dress or undress—pose in lively landscape settings that might have graced a painting by Boucher or Fragonard. In *Plate IV, The Fourth Table of the Human Muscles (frontal view)* (FIG. **20-27**) of Albinus's book, a partially muscle-clad skeleton strikes a pose reminiscent of both Watteau's *L'Indifférent* (FIG. 20-5) and of the Roman statue of *Augustus of Primaporta* (FIG. 6-62). Albinus's figure has a companion, however; a rhinoceros munches placidly on a patch of grass nearby, as unperturbed as any less animate detail of this outdoor scene. The comparative anatomy here has a witty edge, but the plates of rhinoceros armor are depicted as carefully as the muscle coverings of the human form.

20-27 BERNARD SIEGFRIED ALBINUS, Plate IV, *The Fourth Table of the Human Muscles (frontal view)*, from *Tabulae skeleti et musculorum corporis humani,* 1749 edition. Alfred H. Taubman Medical Library, University of Michigan (the Crammer Collection).

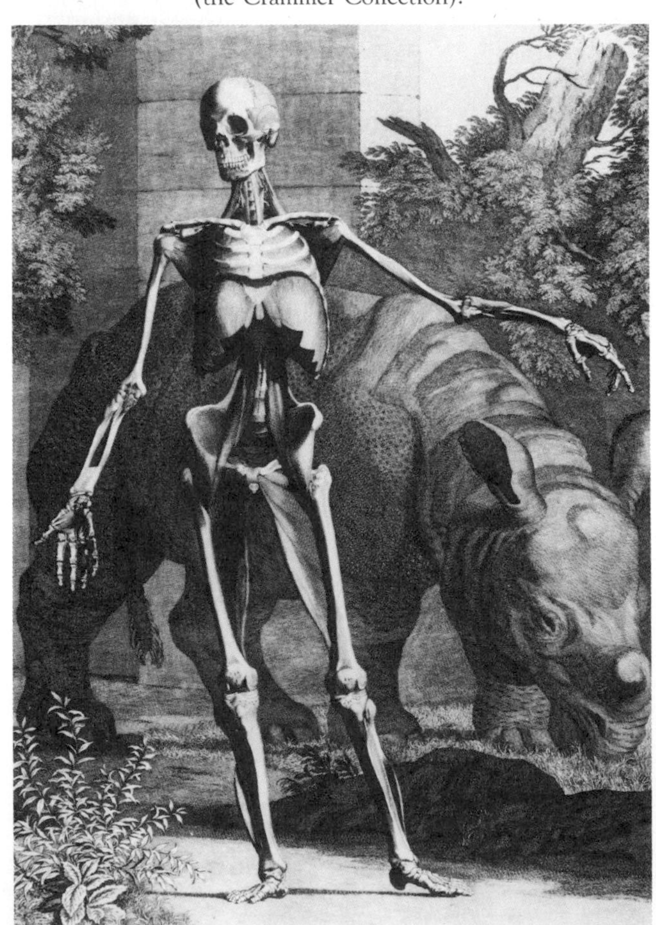

The excitement and awe that scientific knowledge held for many mid-eighteenth-century viewers is the subject of *A Philosopher Giving a Lecture at the Orrery (in which a lamp is put in place of the sun)* (FIG. **20-28**), by the English painter JOSEPH WRIGHT OF DERBY (1734–1797). Wright specialized in the dramatic lighting of candlelight and moonlit scenes. He loved subjects like the orrery demonstration, which could be illuminated by a single light from within the picture. The effect recalls Gerard van Honthorst's *Supper Party* (FIG. 19-45), but Wright's subject is thoroughly one from the Age of Reason. A scholar uses a special scientific model (called an "orrery") to demonstrate the theory that the universe operates like a gigantic clockwork mechanism. Light from the lamp used to represent the sun pours forth from behind the figure of the boy silhouetted in the foreground to create dramatic light and shadows that heighten the drama of the scene. Awed children crowd close to the tiny metal orbs that represent the planets within the arcing bands that symbolize their orbits. An earnest listener makes notes, while the lone woman seated at the left

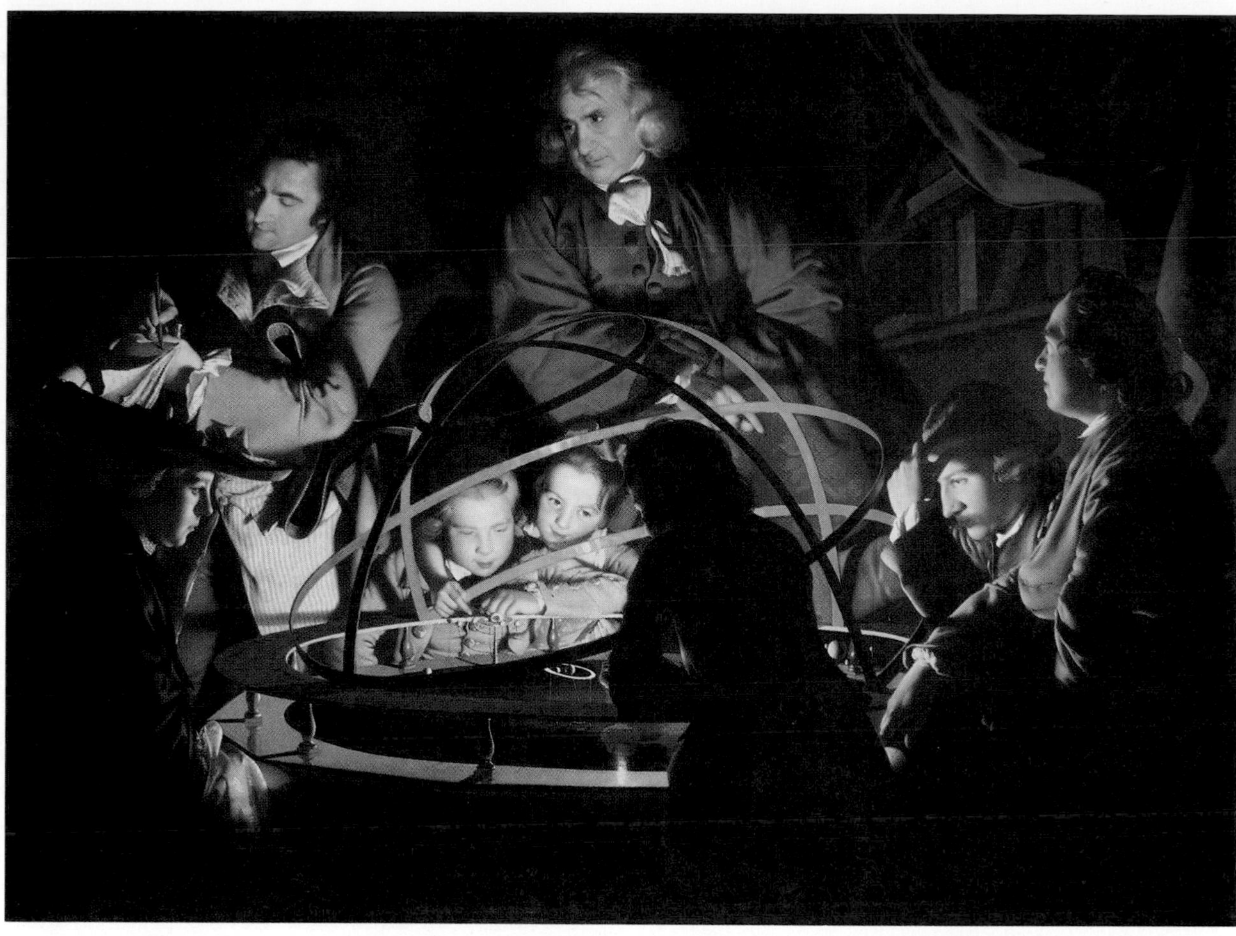

20-28 Joseph Wright of Derby, *A Philosopher Giving a Lecture at the Orrery (in which a lamp is put in place of the sun)*, c. 1763–1765. Derby Museums and Art Gallery, Derby, England.

and the two gentlemen at the right look on with rapt attention. Everyone in Wright's painting is caught up in the wonders of scientific knowledge; an ordinary lecture takes on the qualities of a grand "history painting." Wright has scrupulously rendered with careful accuracy every detail of the figures, the mechanisms of the orrery, and even the books and curtain in the shadowy background. The mood created by the lighting and the intensity of the poses, however, suffuse this realistic rendering with an aura of larger-than-life energy that is linked to the sense of emotional drama underlying much of the evolving vision of Romanticism. Wright's blend of Romanticism and realism appealed to the great industrialists of his day. Works like *Orrery* were often purchased by scientific-industrial innovators like Josiah Wedgwood (who pioneered many techniques of mass-produced pottery) and Sir Richard Arkwright (whose spinning frame revolutionized the textile industry). To them, Wright's elevation of the theories and inventions of the Industrial Revolution to the plane of history painting was excitingly and appropriately in tune with the future.

The ideas of the Enlightenment fostered a genre of painting in which pictures were constructed for the purpose of instructing and inspiring viewers. Such art appealed especially to those who disapproved of the licentious gallantries of Fragonard and other courtly Rococo artists. Early examples of such morally inspiring Enlightenment works come from both France and England. The moral paintings of Jean Baptiste Siméon Chardin and William Hogarth are filled with details based on accurate observations from life, but such natural particulars are submerged in compositions that follow the Rococo spirit. Rococo colors, however, were exchanged for naturalistic and earthy hues more appropriate to images intended to provide viewers with telling examples of correct social and moral behavior.

The Frenchman Jean Baptiste Siméon Chardin (1699–1779), who very briefly served as Fragonard's teacher, made a specialty of simple interiors and still lifes, which he painted masterfully in his own mode, rivaling the Dutch masters of the previous century. In *Grace at Table* (fig. **20-29**), Chardin gives us an unpretentious room in which a mother and her small

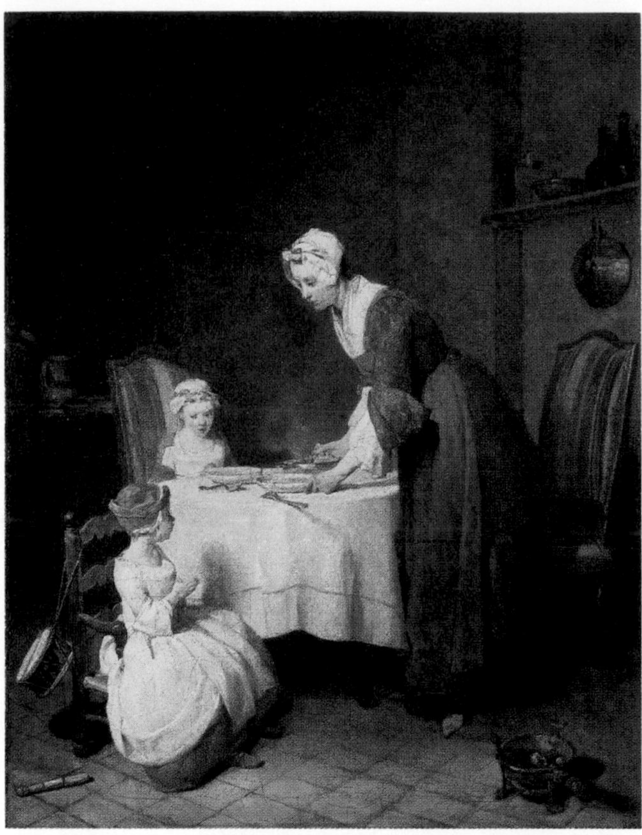

20-29 JEAN BAPTISTE SIMÉON CHARDIN, *Grace at Table,* 1740. 19″ × 15″. Louvre, Paris.

daughters are about to dine. The mood of quiet attention is at one with the hushed lighting and mellow color and the closely studied still-life accessories, with worn surfaces that tell their own humble domestic history. We are witnesses to a moment of social instruction, when mother and older sister supervise the younger sister in the simple, pious ritual of giving thanks to God before a meal. The mood of attendant maternal devotion will surface again late in the nineteenth century in the works of Gertrude Käsebier (FIG. 21-62) and Mary Cassatt (FIG. 21-77). In his own way, Chardin was the poet of the commonplace and the master of its nuances. A gentle sentiment prevails in all of his pictures, an emotion not contrived and artificial but born of the painter's honesty, insight, and sympathy.

The taste of the newly prosperous and confident middle classes was expressed in the art of WILLIAM HOGARTH (1697–1764), who satirized contemporary life with comic zest and with only a modicum of Rococo "indecency." With Hogarth, a truly English style of painting emerged. England had had few painters or sculptors who could match the accomplishments of English architects; traditionally, painters (such as Holbein, Rubens, and Van Dyck) were imported from the continent. Hogarth waged a lively campaign throughout his career against the English feeling of dependence on, and inferiority to, continental artists. Although Hogarth himself would have been the last to admit it, his own painting owed much to the work of his contemporaries across the channel in France, the artists of the Rococo. Yet his subject matter, frequently moral in tone, is distinctively English. It was the great age of English satirical writing, and Hogarth (who knew and admired this genre and included Henry Fielding, the author of *Tom Jones,* among his closest friends) clearly saw himself as translating satire into the visual arts:

> I therefore turned my thoughts to . . . painting and engraving modern moral subjects. . . . I have endeavored to treat my subjects as a dramatic writer; my picture is my stage, and men and women my players, who by means of certain actions and gestures, are to exhibit a dumb show.

Hogarth's favorite device was to make a series of narrative paintings and prints, in a sequence like chapters in a book or scenes in a play, that follow a character or group of characters in their encounters with some social evil. He is at his best in pictures like the *Breakfast Scene* (FIG. **20-30**) from *Marriage à la Mode,* in which the marriage of a young viscount, arranged through the social aspirations of one father and the need for money of the other, is just beginning to founder. The anglicized Rococo style is admirably suited to the scene, but we must read the situation carefully from its large inventory of naturalistic detail if we are to enjoy it fully. The moment portrayed is just past noon; husband and wife are tired after a long night spent in separate pursuits. The music and the musical instrument on the overturned chair in the foreground and the disheveled servant straightening the chairs and tables in the room at the back indicate that the wife has stayed at home for an evening of cards and music making. She stretches with a mixture of sleepiness and coquettishness, casting a glance toward her young husband, who clearly has been away from the house for a night of suspicious business. Still dressed in hat and social finery, he slumps in discouraged boredom on a chair near the fire. His hands are thrust deep into the empty money-pockets of his breeches, while his wife's small dog sniffs inquiringly at a lacy woman's cap protruding from his coat pocket. A steward, his hands full of unpaid bills, raises his eyes to heaven in despair at the actions of his noble master and mistress. The house is palatial, but Hogarth has filled it with witty clues to the dubious taste of its occupants. The mantelpiece is crowded with tiny statuettes and a Classical bust, which hide everything in the architecturally framed painting on the wall behind except a winged Eros fig-

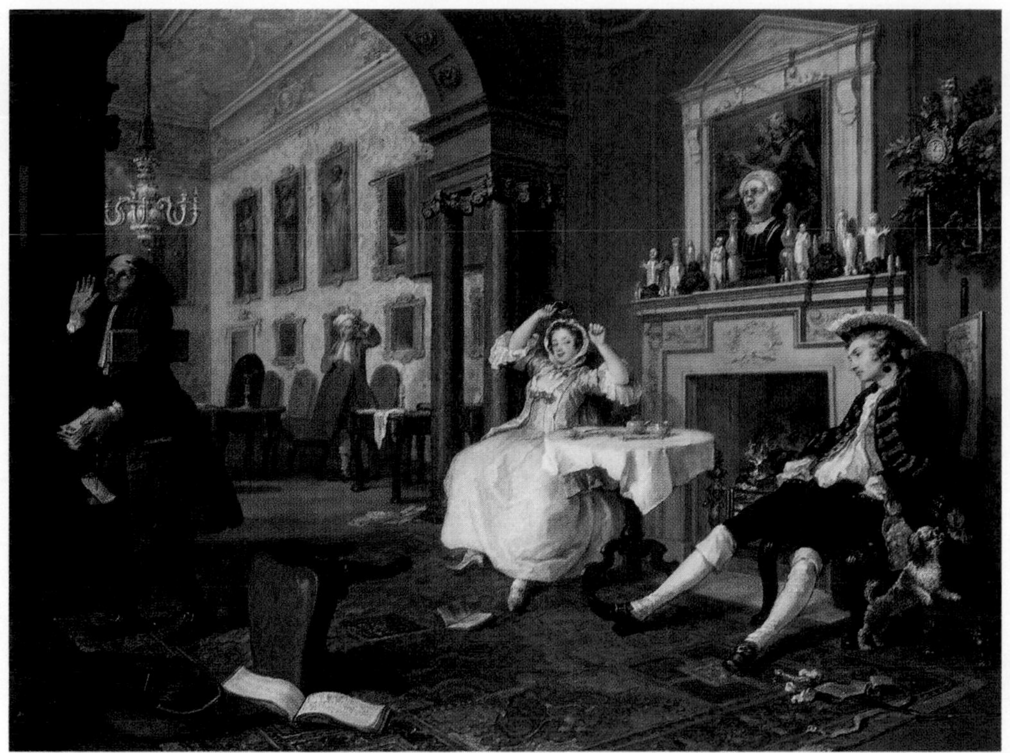

20-30 WILLIAM HOGARTH, *Breakfast Scene,* from *Marriage à la Mode,* c. 1745. Approx. 28″ × 36″. Reproduced by courtesy of the Trustees of the National Gallery, London.

ure. Paintings of religious figures hang on the upper wall of the distant room, contradicted by the curtained canvas at the end of the row (partially hidden by the columnar supports of the arched doorway). The curtain undoubtedly covers a canvas with an erotic subject, discretely hidden from the eyes of casual visitors and ladies, according to the custom of the day, but available at the pull of a curtain cord for the gaze of the master and his male guests. In this composition, as in all his work, Hogarth proceeded as a novelist might, elaborating on his subject with carefully chosen detail, which, as we continue to discover it, heightens the comedy. This scene is one in a sequence of six paintings that satirize the immoralities practiced within marriage by the moneyed classes in England. Hogarth designed the marriage series to be published as a set of engravings. The prints of this and his other moral narratives were so popular that unscrupulous entrepreneurs produced unauthorized versions almost as fast as the artist created his originals.*

*To protect himself against the loss of revenue from such theft, Hogarth helped write and win support for a proposal to include prints in the protections provided by the Copyright Act, which finally was passed by the British Parliament in 1735. Unfortunately, the Act could not prevent rival printers from sending spies to memorize details of Hogarth's latest paintings and rush them into mimicking versions before he had a chance to issue them as prints.

By the 1760s, Hogarth's example had helped to spur a taste in France for the new moral seriousness, which generated praise for the kind of sober, moralizing, narrative paintings that were the speciality of JEAN BAPTISTE GREUZE (1725–1805). Greuze's art expressed perfectly the transition of taste from the Rococo to nineteenth-century Romanticism. Almost overnight, many people in France—and Europe—abandoned the wanton frivolity and luxuriance of the Rococo and became not only serious and moralistic but especially "sensible" and "feeling," which is to say "emotional." Jean Jacques Rousseau called for the sincere expression of sympathetic and tender emotions to counter what he saw as the cold, heartless, selfish culture of courts. He exalted the simple life of the peasant as the most "natural" and set it up as a model to be imitated. The joys and sorrows of uncorrupted, "natural" people, now described everywhere in novels, soon drowned Europe in a flood of tears; it became fashionable to weep, to fall to one's knees, to swoon, and to languish in hopeless love. This kind of contrived and melodramatic emotion—this sentimentality—has remained a fundamental ingredient of popular art from the time of its appearance in the eighteenth century until the present. Greuze won wide acclaim with paintings entitled *The Father of the Family Reading the Bible to His Children, The Village Bride,* and *The Father's Curse,* in all of which he

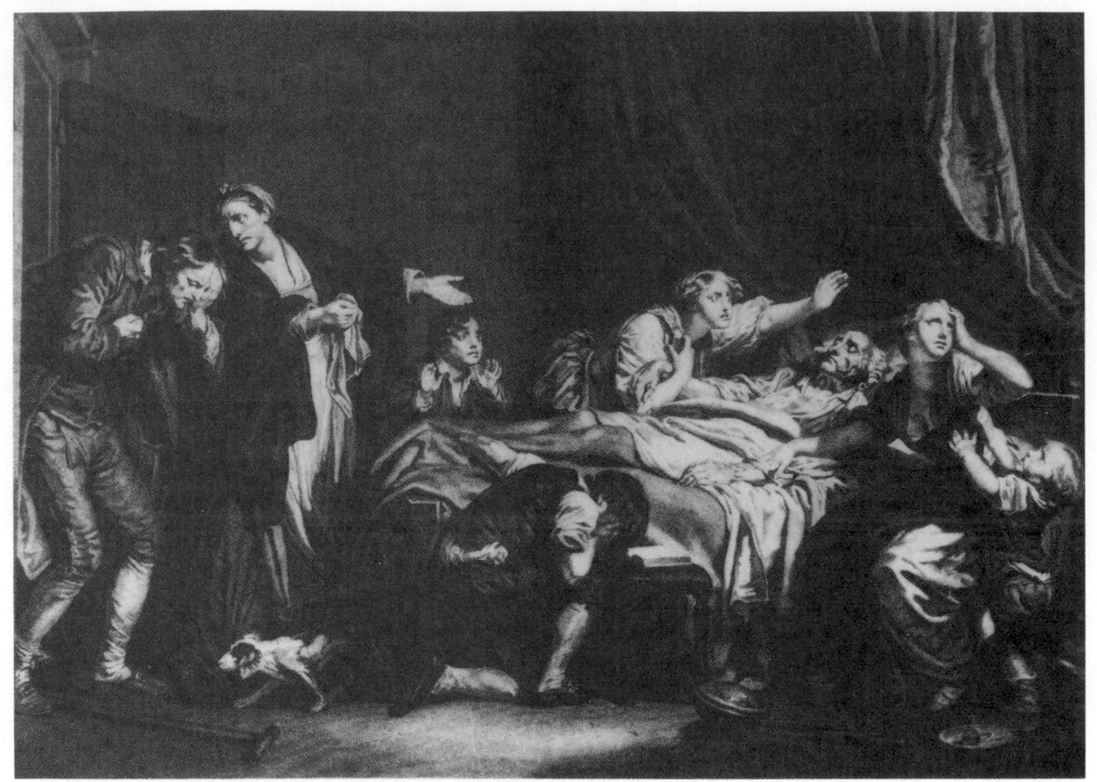

20-31 Jean Baptiste Greuze, *The Son Punished,* 1765–1777, from studies for the painting *The Return of the Prodigal Son,* 1777–1778.

pointed out a moral and sentimentalized his characters. Denis Diderot, the great Enlightenment philosophe and scholar, praised Greuze for his high moral themes. In the Salon of 1765, Diderot described Greuze's sketch for *The Return of the Prodigal Son:*

> This is the sight which meets the eyes of the ungrateful son. He comes forward, he is on the threshold. . . . His mother meets him at his entrance; she is silent, but with her hand points to the corpse as if to say: "See what you have done."
>
> The ungrateful son is struck with amazement; his head falls forward, and he strikes his forehead with his hand. What a lesson is here depicted for fathers and children! . . . I do not know what effect this short and simple description . . . will produce on others, but for my own part I could not write it without emotion.*

The public took Greuze so much to their hearts that, following Hogarth's custom in England, he made the scenes of his most popular designs available to a wide audience by having them copied in engravings. *The Son Punished* (FIG. **20-31**) is the engraved version of the studies for *The Return of the Prodigal Son.* The scene in the engraving duplicates that of the painting, but the design in the print reverses the original from left to right. Hogarth and Greuze sought through their art to prompt individual viewers to improved personal conduct. Their goals would soon be expanded by Neoclassical painters like Jacques Louis David in paintings intended to teach citizens how better to serve their nation state.

A moral of a very different sort underlies the history paintings based on the events of his time created by the expatriate American artist Benjamin West (1738–1820). Born in Pennsylvania, on what was then the colonial frontier, West was sent to Europe early in life to study art and then went to England, where he had almost immediate success. He was a cofounder of the Royal Academy of Arts and succeeded Sir Joshua Reynolds as its president. He became official painter to King George III and retained that position during the strained period of the American Revolution. In *The Death of General Wolfe* (FIG. **20-32**), West depicted the mortally wounded young English commander just after his defeat of the French in the decisive battle of Quebec in 1759, which gave Canada to Great Britain. Unlike Renaissance, Baroque, and Rococo artists, West chose to portray a contemporary historical subject, and his characters wear contemporary costume (although the military uniforms are not completely accurate in all details). However, West

*In E. G. Holt, *A Documentary History of Art* (Princeton, NJ: Princeton University Press, 1958), vol. 2, p. 319.

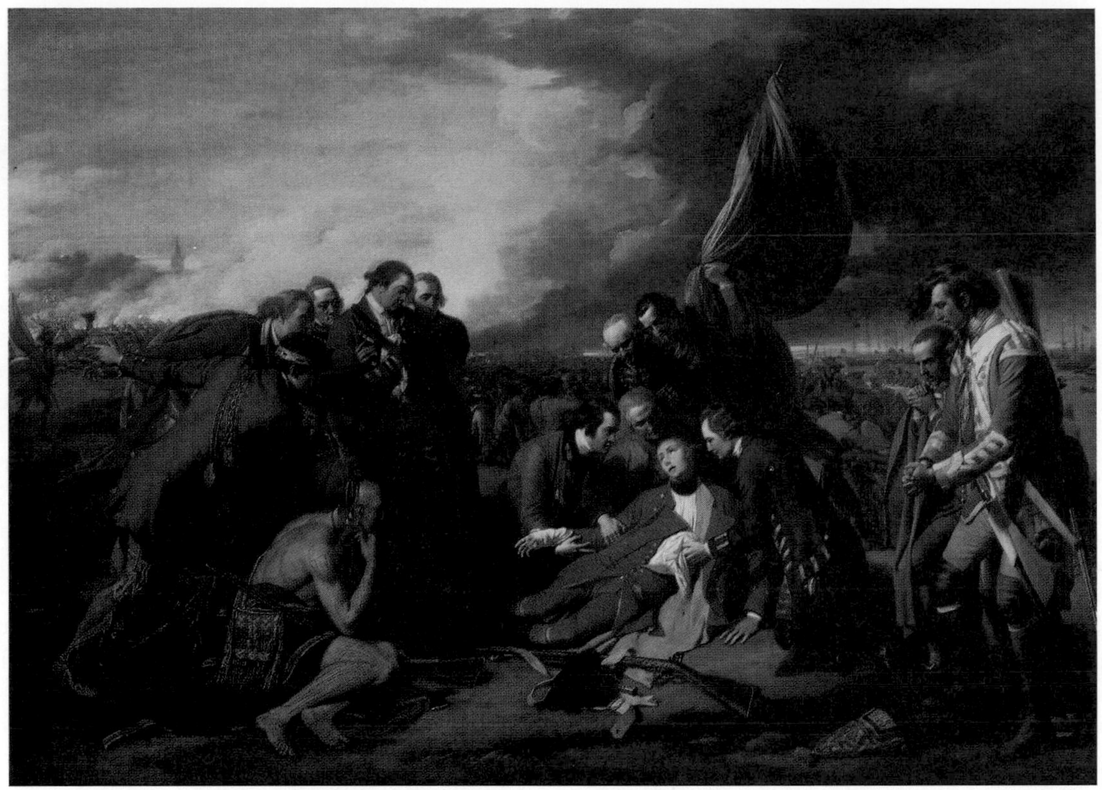

20-32 BENJAMIN WEST, *The Death of General Wolfe*, 1771. Approx. 5′ × 7′. National Gallery of Canada, Ottawa (gift of the Duke of Westminster, 1918).

blended this realism of detail with the grand tradition of history painting by arranging his figures in an essentially Baroque composition, and his modern hero dies among grieving officers on the field of victorious battle in a way that suggests the familiar Pietà theme found in earlier works like Giotto's *Lamentation* (FIG. 15-13) and Quarton's *The Avignon Pietà* (FIG. 18-24). West wanted to present this hero's death in the service of the state as a martyrdom, and his innovative combination of the conventions of traditional heroic painting with a look of modern realism was so effective that it won the hearts of viewers in his own day and continued to influence history painting well into the nineteenth century.

The Onset of Romanticism: "Gothic" and Neoclassical Taste

The late eighteenth century was increasingly a period under the spell of Romanticism. For almost two centuries, scholars have debated the definition and the historical scope of Romanticism; to this day, the controversy has not ended. The very widest definition would equate Romanticism and Modernism, making Romanticism the mood of the modern world and coextensive with its history. More narrowly, Romanticism was a phenomenon that began around 1750 and ended about 1850. Still more narrowly, Romanticism was just another among a miscellany of styles that rose and declined in the course of modern art, flourishing from about 1800 to 1840 and coming between Neoclassicism and Realism. In this book, we take the middle position, defining Romanticism as a way of perceiving the world, above all, with strong feelings. This attitude influenced art most strongly between 1750 and 1850.

The term *Romanticism* originated toward the end of the eighteenth century among German literary critics, who aimed to distinguish peculiarly "modern" traits from the Classical traits that already had displaced elements of Baroque and Rococo design. "Romance," which could refer as much to the novel, with its sentimental hero, as it does to the old medieval tales of fantastic adventure written in the "romance" languages, never quite fit with the broader term "romantic," nor has "romantic" ever comfortably covered all that might be understood by it.

In art, Romanticism might be said to wear two faces: one connected to the renewed interest in Classicism, and the other, less controlled and more associated with the emotions of mystery, the exotic, terror, and the sublime. The diversity of Romantic styles developed partly as a result of the fact that Enlightenment thinkers believed in the good of nature and the natural human being but had no universally agreed-upon meaning for "nature." Some considered nature to be, in the Classical sense, a regularity of proportion. Others argued that it meant the irregularity of growing things, with their wildness and accidents, their picturesqueness, and even their primitiveness. In the end, *all* historical styles were declared to be "natural," as each had evolved historically from the artistic instinct of people, who were, after all, part of nature. In the eighteenth century, this position led to a number of almost simultaneous "revival" styles, which tantalized the eyes, imaginations, and feelings of the public with visions of the past.

An attraction to faraway places and societies produced the enjoyment of exotic styles that suggested distant cultures and periods. This Romantic taste emerged first in garden design. In England, a revolt against the "regularity" of French Classical architecture had begun as early as the late seventeenth century, with the growth of an enthusiasm for Chinese art, especially the Chinese garden. An English critic of the time, Sir William Temple, described the Chinese garden as "without . . . order or disposition of parts that shall be commonly or easily observed," clearly unlike the carefully ordered gardens of France and other European countries. Within a generation of Temple's observation, gardens in England were being designed along informal, "naturalizing," Oriental lines. In the eighteenth century, the "English" garden became a vogue throughout Europe, while the formality of such gardens as those at Versailles was now thought unnatural. Similarly, "naturalness" was soon prized over formal order in architecture, and "natural" styles, like the Gothic, which had never entirely died out in England, became very popular.

Horace Walpole (1717–1797), a novelist and wealthy architectural dilettante, renovated Strawberry Hill, his "villa" at Twickenham (FIG. **20-33**), in the rising "Gothic" fashion, converting it into a sprawling "castle" with turrets, towers, battlements, galleries, and corridors. Sir Walter Scott was captivated by the effect and wrote that the structure's "fretted roofs, carved panels, and illuminated windows were garnished with the appropriate furniture of escutcheons, armorial bearings, shields, tilting lances, and all the panoply of chivalry." At Strawberry Hill, the master (and any visitor) could fully enjoy Walpole's favorite pastime, which was "to gaze on Gothic toys through Gothic glass." The features of the structure are, of course, pseudo-Gothic, but Walpole's version of Gothic architecture would be as influential for later architecture as his gothic novels would be for subsequent literature.

Strawberry Hill provided a setting that encouraged romantic flights of fancy about damsels in distress, ghouls, and other imaginings of the darker side of the psyche. These things were part of the sensibility for sublime terror that would become an important part of nineteenth-century Romanticism. The thrill produced by contemplating the supposed remains of a vanished past was cultivated by garden designers in England, who inserted replicas of period architecture

20-33 Horace Walpole, Strawberry Hill, Twickenham, near London, 1749–1777.

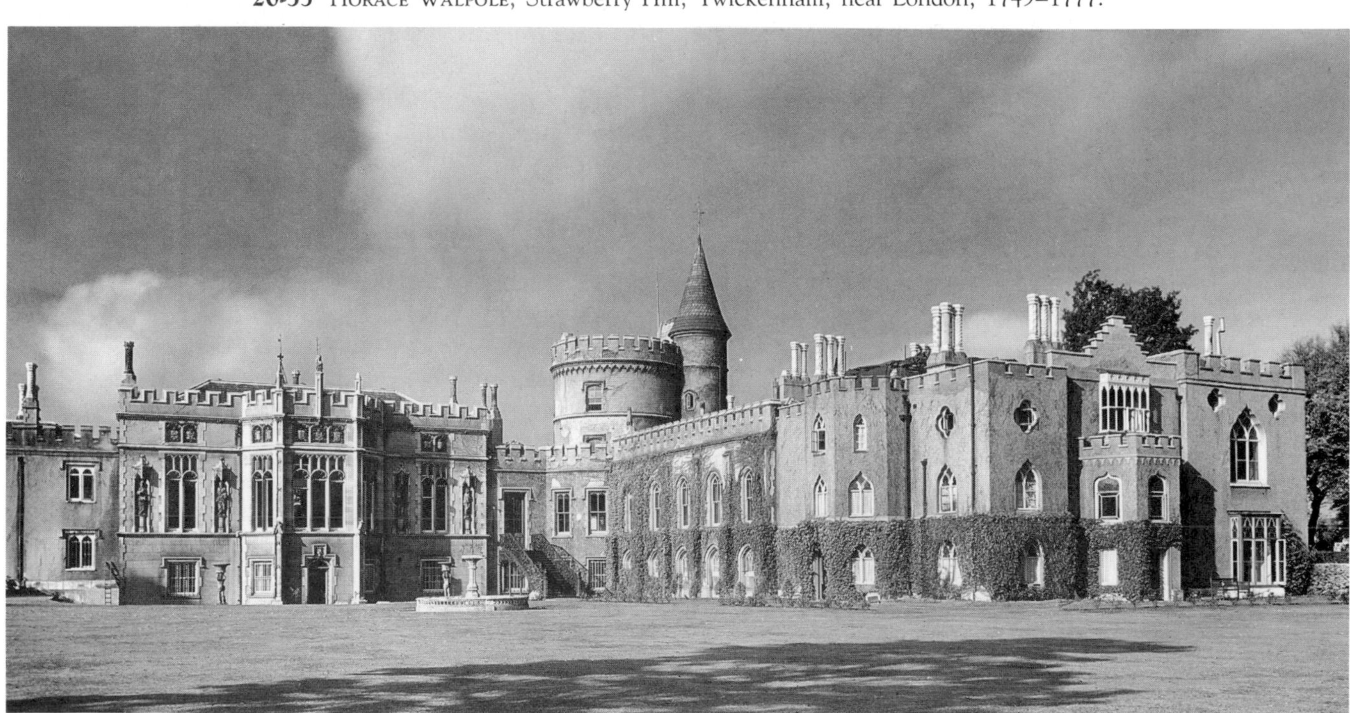

amid the random copses of trees, rustic bridges, and winding streams that filled the stately gardens of the time. Sometimes a single garden would boast structures in four or five different styles. Typical are the gardens at Hagley Park, where a sham Gothic ruin erected in 1747 (FIG. **20-34**) stands near a Doric portico built in 1758 (FIG. **20-35**). The portico is of special interest as the work of JAMES STUART (1713–1788), who, with Nicholas Revett, introduced to Europe the splendor and originality of Greek art in the enormously influential *Antiquities of Athens,* the first volume of which appeared in 1762. These volumes firmly distinguished Greek art from the "derivative" Roman style that had served as the model for Classicism since the Renaissance. Stuart's efforts, as shown in the Doric portico, were greeted with enthusiasm by those who had no use for the Rococo or any of the later "irregular" styles in art. A contemporary journal voiced the hope that the writings of Stuart and Revett and Robert Wood's magnificently illustrated *Ruins of Palmyra* (1753) and *Ruins of Baalbek* (1757) would "expel the littleness and ugliness of the Chinese and the barbarity of the Goths, that we may see no more useless and expensive trifles; no more dungeons instead of summer houses." Instead, the journal's author hoped that all eyes would rest only on the tantalizing echoes of proper Classical civilization.

As the presence of a Doric building in the gardens at Hagley Park indicates, a renewed interest in the style of ancient art developed side by side with the "Gothic" and other exotic styles. By mid-century, the rediscovery of Greek art and architecture had inspired a renewed taste for a serenely Classical style. The expanding desire for things connected with ancient Greece and Rome sparked the style we call Neoclassicism, which is based on the idea of a changeless generality that transcends the accidents of time. Neoclassicism, once thought of as a style in opposition to Romanticism, is now understood as simply one of the many fashions within that general movement but opposed to the "irregularity" of styles like Neo-Gothic, Neo-Baroque, and Chinese. By the late eighteenth and early nineteenth centuries, a Neoclassical taste for the more or less exact replication of Greek and Roman buildings spread rapidly throughout Europe and America.

The enthusiasm for classical antiquity permeated much of the scholarship of the time. More and more in the late eighteenth century, attention turned toward the ancient world. Edward Gibbon was stimulated on a visit to Rome to begin his monumental *Decline and Fall of the Roman Empire,* which appeared between 1776 and 1788. Earlier, in 1755, Johann Winckelmann, the first modern historian of art, published his *Thoughts on the Imitation of Greek Art in Painting and Sculpture,* in which he uncompromisingly designated Greek art as the most perfect to come from the hands of man, and a model that, if followed, would confer "assurance in conceiving and designing works of art, since they [the Greeks] have marked for us the utmost limits of human and divine beauty." Winckelmann characterized Greek sculpture as manifesting a "noble simplicity and quiet grandeur." In his *History of Ancient Art* (1764), he undertook to describe each monument as an element in the development of a single grand style. Before Winckelmann, the history of art had been a matter of biography, as with Giorgio Vasari. Winckelmann thus initiated one

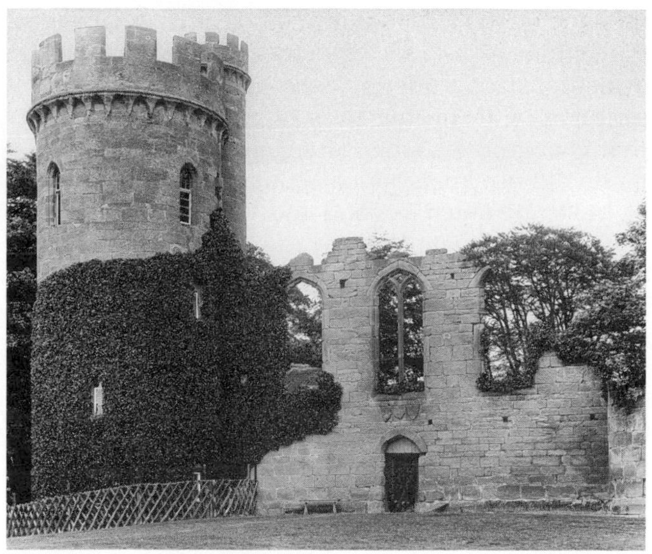

20-34 SANDERSON MILLER, sham Gothic ruin, Hagley Park, Worcestershire, England, 1747. Copyright, *Country Life,* London.

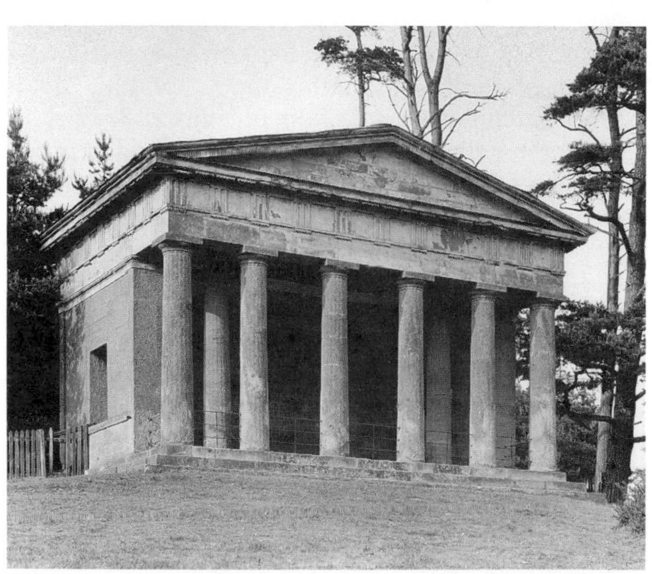

20-35 JAMES STUART, Doric portico, Hagley Park, 1758. Copyright, *Country Life,* London.

modern method thoroughly in accord with Enlightenment ideas of ordering knowledge; his was clearly a method that undertook the classification and description of art on the basis of general stylistic traits that change over time. Strangely enough, Winckelmann did not know much about original Greek art—at least not much beyond the Laocoön group (FIG. 5-79) and other late Greek works in the Vatican collections, of which he was custodian. For the most part, he had only late Roman copies for study, and he never visited Greece, where he might have seen the genuine thing. Despite the obvious defects of his work, however, its pioneering character cannot be overlooked. Winckelmann had wide influence, and his writings laid a theoretical and historical foundation for the enormously widespread taste for Neoclassicism that was to last well into the nineteenth century.

The Romantic fascination with ruins like those in Hagley Park was combined with an Enlightenment curiosity about archeological facts to create a taste for images like Giovanni Battista Piranesi's *Views of Rome* (FIG. 7-5) and Giovanni Pannini's meticulously painted scenes of ancient Roman buildings (FIG. 6-58). In architecture, the Roman ruins at Baalbek in Syria, especially a titanic colonnade, provided much of the inspiration for the Neoclassical portico of the church of Ste. Geneviève (FIG. **20-36**), now the Panthéon, in Paris, designed by JACQUES-GERMAIN SOUFFLOT (1713–1780). The columns, reproduced with studied archeological exactitude, are the first revelation of Roman grandeur in France. The walls are severely blank, except for a repeated garland motif in the attic level. The colonnaded dome, a Neoclassical version of the domes of St. Peter's in Rome, the Church of the Invalides in Paris, and St. Paul's in London (FIGS. 17-33, 19-70, 19-75), rises above a Greek-cross plan. Both dome and vaults rest on an interior grid of splendid, freestanding Corinthian columns, as if the colonnade of the portico were continued within. Although the whole effect, inside and out, is Roman, the structural principles employed are essentially Gothic. Soufflot was one of the first eighteenth-century builders to suggest that Gothic engineering was highly functional structurally and could be applied in modern building. In his work, we have the curious, but not unreasonable conjunction of Gothic and Classical in a structural integration that foreshadows nineteenth-century admiration of Gothic engineering.

20-36 JACQUES-GERMAIN SOUFFLOT, the Panthéon (Ste. Geneviève), Paris, 1755–1792.

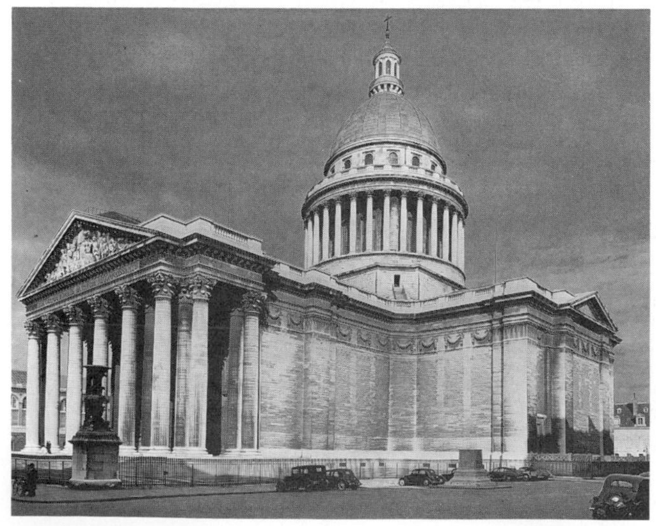

Eighteenth-century Neoclassical interiors were directly inspired by new discoveries of "the glory that was Greece / And the grandeur that was Rome," and summarized the conception of a noble Classical world. The first great archeological event of modern times, the discovery and initial excavation of the ancient buried Roman cities of Pompeii (FIGS. 6-21 and 6-23) and Herculaneum in the 1730s and 1740s, startled and thrilled all of Europe. The excavation of these cities was the veritable resurrection of the ancient world, not simply a dim vision of it inspired by a few moldering ruins; historical reality could now replace fancy with fact. The wall paintings and other artifacts of Pompeii inspired the slim, straight-lined, elegant "Pompeian" style that, after mid-century, almost entirely displaced the curvilinear Rococo. In France, the new Pompeian manner was associated with Louis XVI; in England, it took the name of its most artful practitioner, ROBERT ADAM (1728–1792), whose interior architecture was influential throughout Europe. The Etruscan Room in Osterley Park House (FIG. **20-37**) was begun in 1761. If compared with the Rococo salons of the Hôtel de Soubise (FIG. 20-3) and the Amalienburg (FIG. 20-13), this room shows how completely symmetry and rectilinearity have returned, but this return is achieved with great delicacy and none of the massive splendor of the style of Louis XIV. The decorative motifs (medallions, urns, vine scrolls, sphinxes, and tripods) were taken from Roman art and, as in Roman stucco work, are arranged sparsely within broad, neutral spaces and slender margins. Adam was an archeologist as well as an architect, and he had explored and written accounts of the ruins of the palace of Diocletian at Split (FIG. 6-80). Kedleston House in Derbyshire, Adelphi Terrace in London, and a great many other structures that he designed also show the influence of Split on his work.

The eighteenth century's Neoclassical taste in architecture also affected city planning. Designs for

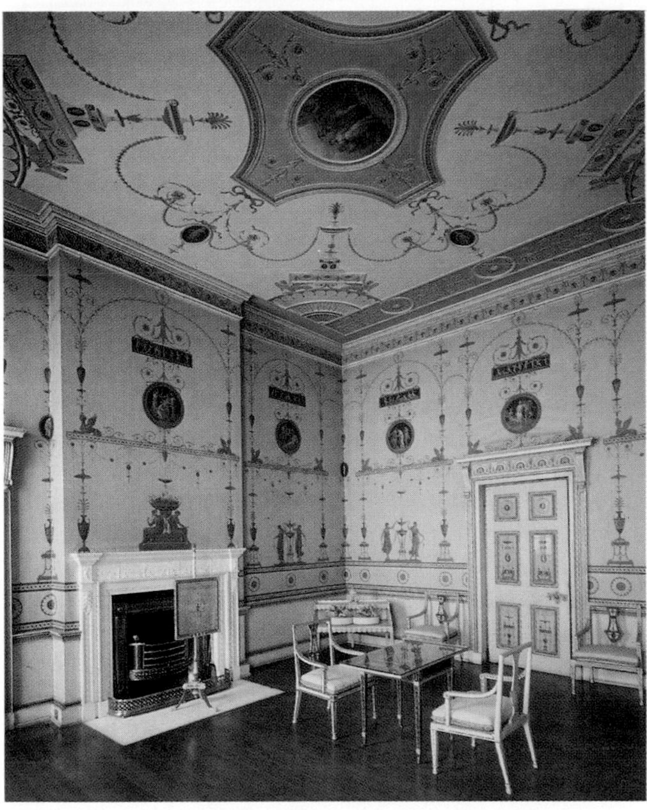

20-37 Robert Adam, Etruscan Room, Osterley Park House, Middlesex, England, begun 1761. By courtesy of the Board of Trustees of the Victoria and Albert Museum, London.

entire city sections, like the Circus and the Royal Crescent in Bath, England (FIG. **20-38**), by John Wood the Younger (1728–1782), reflect this Neoclassical influence. The town square was a keynote of eighteenth-century city planning. Throughout Europe, community after community was rebuilt to include gracious sequences of open-air plazas, designed on a more intimate scale than the grand spaces commanded by Baroque princes and popes. The Circus (begun by Wood's father) and the Royal Crescent at Bath integrated inviting park spaces with luxurious housing for the well-to-do members of society who came to "take the waters" at the city's hot springs, which had been famous since Roman times. In both the Circus and the Royal Crescent, the houses are linked into rows behind a single Palladian façade, which transforms each complex into a monumental palatial edifice. The design is especially felicitous in the Royal Crescent (entirely the younger Wood's work), where giant Ionic columns are attached to the walls along the entire length of the façade, setting up a regular rhythm and rising through two tall stories to create a central body resting between an unornamented basement story and the area where the architrave and the balustrade rail mark the beginning of the steeply sloped roof level. The roof is punctuated every four bays by a regular, crowning mini-wall of chimney pots.

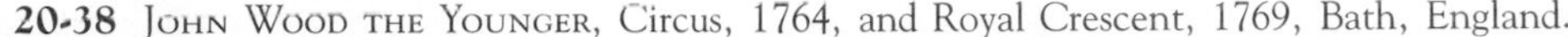

20-38 John Wood the Younger, Circus, 1764, and Royal Crescent, 1769, Bath, England.

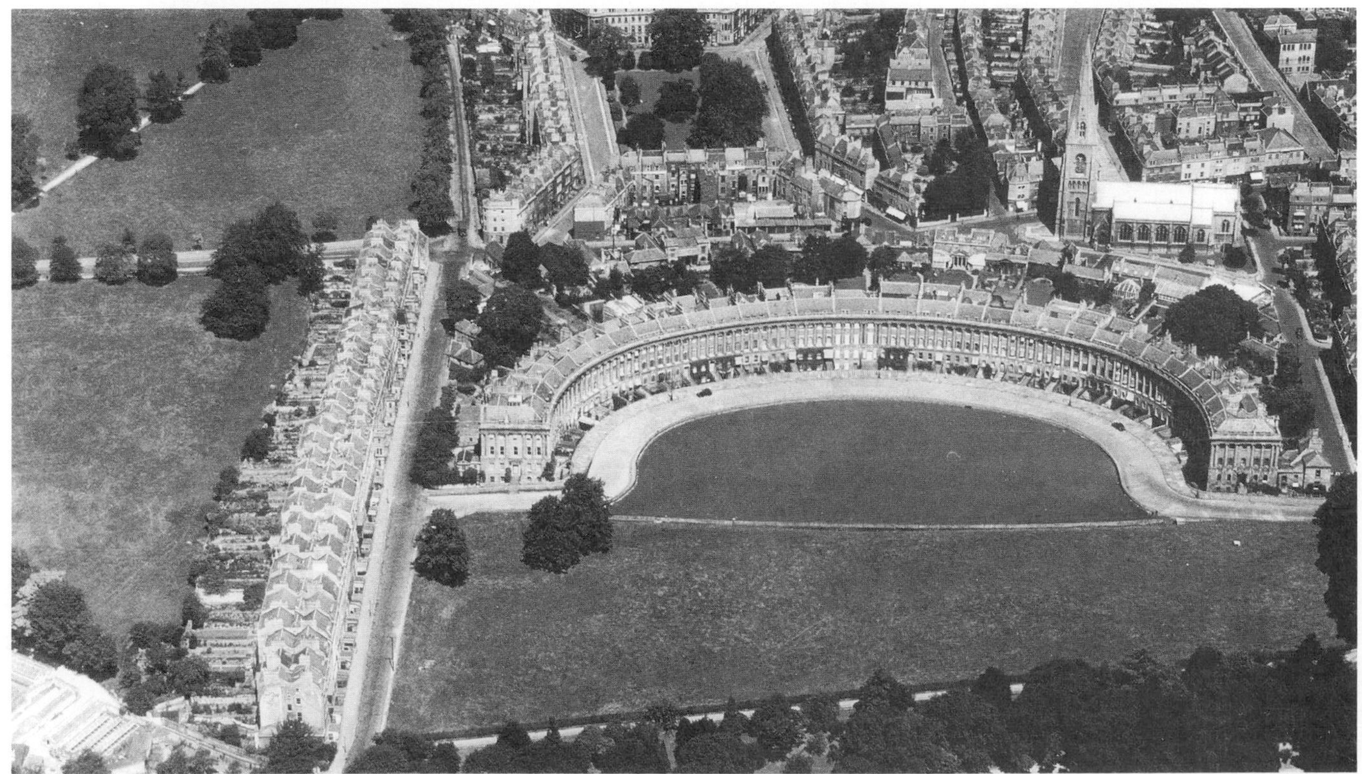

In painting, the sober Neoclassical manner was adopted eagerly by many late eighteenth-century painters who wished to include moral teaching in their art. In France, with the approaching revolution, the temper of the times was more severe and the type and quality of emotion changed. At the end of the "age of sensibility," the stern values of moral virtue, civic dedication, heroism, and self-sacrifice replaced romance, gentleness, and the expression of tenderness. Interest shifted from the intimate world of private life to the public theater of action. Noble attributes of human nature were now supposed to emerge naturally, cleansed of those past and present corruptions denounced by writers like Rousseau. Naturalness of behavior, formerly associated with the simple people of the French countryside, now came to be identified with the heroes of Classical Greece and Rome, who were considered to be natural paragons of goodness, truth, beauty, and "right" action. "Natural" and "Classical" were considered identical in much Neoclassical thinking.

In the art of ANGELICA KAUFFMANN (1741–1807), the simple figure types, homely situations, and contemporary settings of Greuze's moral pictures were transformed by a Neoclassicism that still contained elements of the Rococo style. Born in Switzerland and trained in Italy, Kauffmann spent many of her productive years in England. A protégeé of Sir Joshua Reynolds and the decorator of the interiors of many houses built by Robert Adam, she was a founding member of the British Royal Academy of Arts and enjoyed a fashionable reputation. Her *Cornelia, Pointing to Her Children as Her Treasures* (FIG. **20-39**) is a kind of "set piece" of early Neoclassicism. Its subject is an *exemplum virtutis* (example or model of virtue) of the didactic kind, drawn from the history and literature of Greece and Rome. This turning away from the frivolous and sensuous subjects of the Rococo to themes thought to be noble and elevating became general in the late eighteenth century. The moralizing pictures of Hogarth and Greuze had already marked a change in taste, but the modern setting of their works was replaced by Kauffmann, who clothed her actors in ancient Roman garb and posed them in classicizing Roman attitudes within Roman interiors. The theme in this painting is the virtue of Cornelia, mother of the future political leaders Tiberius and Gaius Gracchus, who, in the second century B.C., attempted to reform the Roman republic. Cornelia's character is revealed in this scene, which takes place after a lady

20-39 ANGELICA KAUFFMANN, *Cornelia, Pointing to Her Children as Her Treasures,* or *Mother of the Gracchi,* c. 1785. 40″ × 50″. Virginia Museum of Fine Arts, Richmond (the A. D. and W. C. Williams Fund).

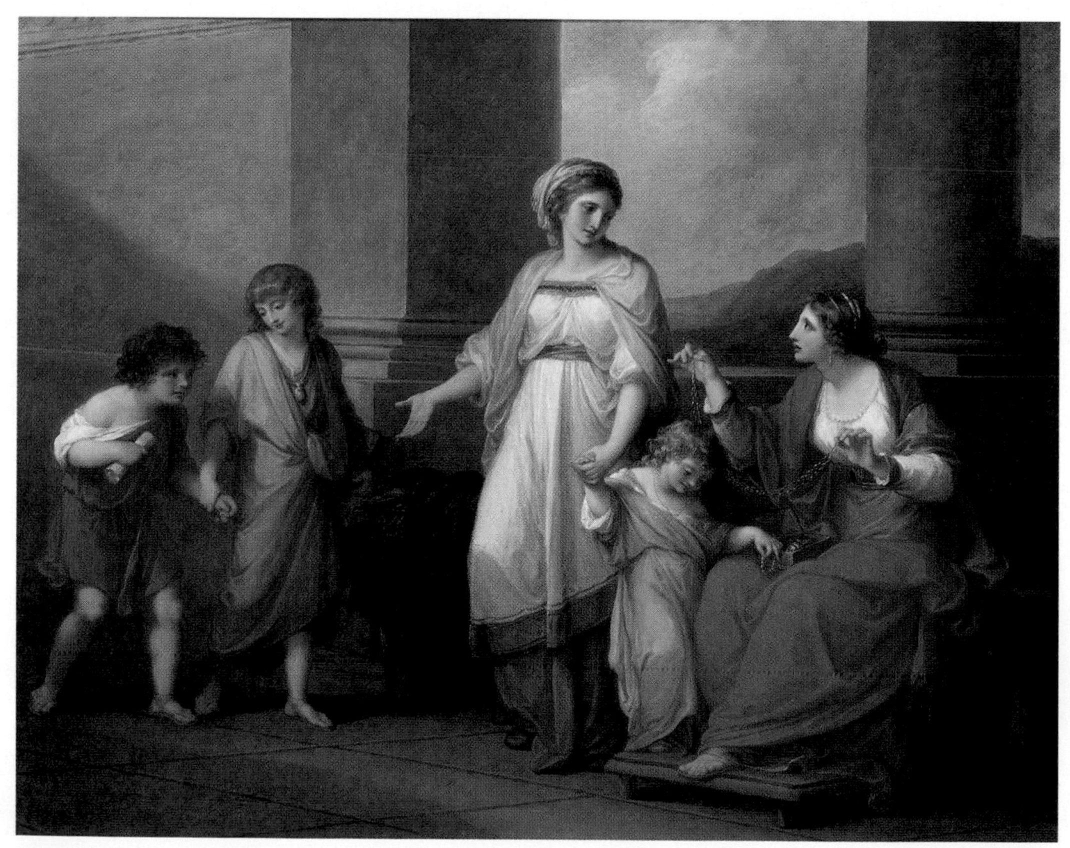

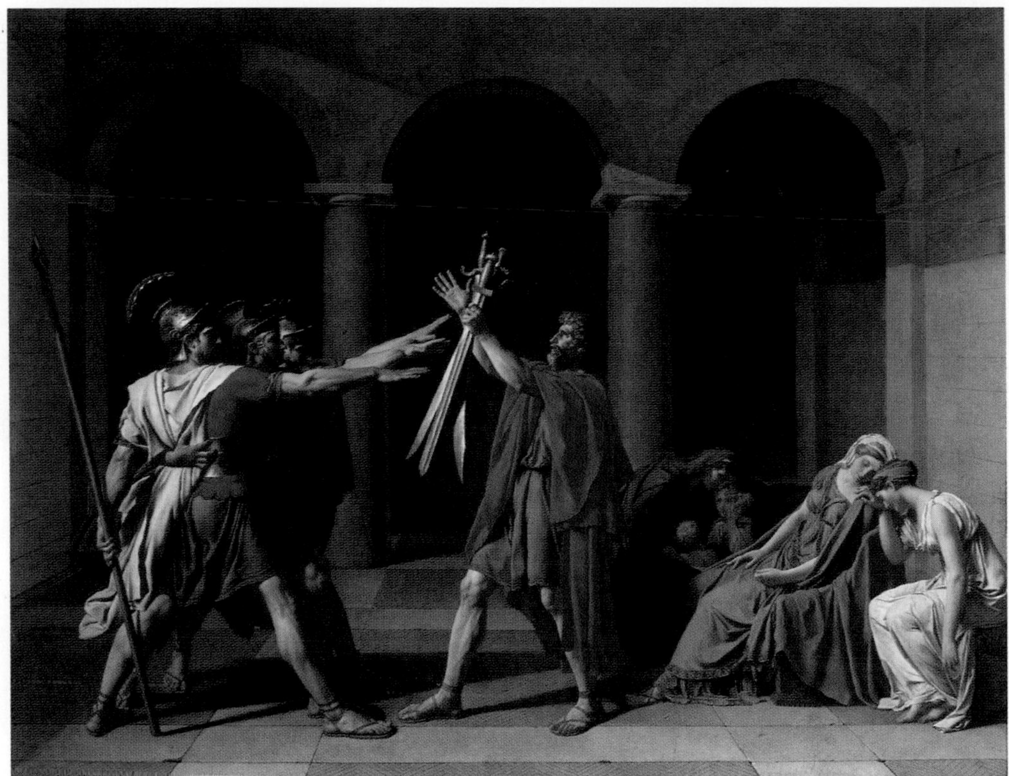

20-40 Jacques Louis David, *Oath of the Horatii,* 1784. Approx. 11′ × 14′. Louvre, Paris.

visitor has shown off her fine jewelry and then haughtily requested that Cornelia show hers. Instead of rushing to get her own precious adornments, Cornelia brings her sons forward, saying, "*These* are my jewels!" The architectural setting is severely Roman, with no Rococo motif in evidence, and the composition and drawing have the simplicity and firmness of low relief carving. Only the charm and grace of the Rococo style linger—in the arrangement of the figures, the soft lighting, and in Kauffmann's own tranquil manner.

Within a few years, Kauffmann's sentimental Neoclassicism had hardened into the public, programmatic stoicism of Jacques Louis David (1748–1825), the painter-ideologist of the Neoclassical art of the French Revolution and the Napoleonic empire. David was a distant relative of Boucher and followed Boucher's style until a period of study in Rome won the younger man over to the tradition of Classical art and to the academic teachings about the elements of art based on rules taken from the ancients and from the great masters of the Renaissance. In his own quite individual and often non-Classical style, David reworked the Classical and academic traditions. He rebelled against the Rococo as an "artificial taste" and exalted Classical art as, in his own words, "the imitation of nature in her most beautiful and perfect form." He praised Greek art enthusiastically, although he, like Winckelmann, knew almost nothing about it firsthand: "I want to work in a pure Greek style. I feed my eyes on ancient statues; I even have the intention of imitating some of them." David's doctrine of the superiority of Classical art was not based solely on an isolated esthetic, however. Believing that "the arts must . . . contribute forcefully to the education of the public," he was prepared both as an artist and as a politician when the French Revolution offered him the opportunity to create a public art—an art of propaganda.

David played many roles in the French Revolution: he was a Jacobin friend of the radical Maximilien Robespierre, a member of the National Convention that voted for the death of King Louis XVI, and the quasi dictator of the Committee on Public Education. David joined scholars and artists in persuading the revolutionary government to abolish the old French Royal Academy and to establish in its place panels of experts charged with reforming public taste. His position of power made him dominant in the transformation of style, and his own manner of painting was the official model for many years.

Although painted in 1784, before the French Revolution, David's *Oath of the Horatii* (fig. **20-40**) reflects his politically didactic purpose, his doctrine of the educational power of Classical form, and his method of composing a Neoclassical picture. David agreed with the Enlightenment belief that subject matter should have a moral and should be presented so that the "marks of heroism and civic virtue offered the eyes of the people will electrify its soul, and plant the seeds of glory and devotion to the fatherland." The *Oath of the Horatii* depicts a story from pre-Republican Rome, the heroic phase of Roman history that had been pushed to the foreground of public interest by the sensational archeological discoveries at Pompeii and Herculaneum. The topic was not an arcane one for David's audience. This story of conflict between love and patriotism, first recounted by the ancient Roman historian Livy, had been retold in a play by Pierre Corneille that was performed in Paris several years earlier, making it familiar to David's viewing public. According to the story, the leaders of the Roman and Alban armies, poised for battle, decided to resolve their conflicts in a series of encounters waged by three representatives from each side. The Roman champions, the three Horatius brothers, would face the three sons of the Curatius family, the Alban warriors. A sister of the Horatii, Camilla, was the bride-to-be of one of the Curatius sons.

David's painting shows the Horatii as they swear on their swords to win or die for Rome, oblivious to the anguish and sorrow of their sisters. In its form, *Oath of the Horatii* is a paragon of the Neoclassical style. The theme is stated with admirable force and clarity. In a shallow picture box, defined by a severely simple architectural framework, the statuesque and carefully modeled figures are deployed across the space, close to the foreground, in a manner reminiscent of ancient relief sculpture. The rigid and virile forms of the men effectively eclipse the soft, curvilinear shapes of the mourning women in the right background. Such manly virtues as courage, patriotism, and unwavering loyalty to a cause are emphasized over the less heroic emotions of love, sorrow, and despair symbolized by the women. The message is clear and of a type with which the prerevolutionary French public could readily identify. The picture created a sensation when it was exhibited in Paris in 1785, and, although it had been painted under royal patronage and was not at all revolutionary in its original intent, its Neoclassical style soon became the semiofficial voice of the revolution. David may have been painting in the academic tradition, but he made something new of it; he created a program for arousing his audience to patriotic zeal. From David's *Oath of the Horatii* onward, art became increasingly political—if not often in the strict sense of serving a state or party, then at least in its passionate adherence to selected trends, movements, and ideologies.

In David's later paintings, like *The Death of Marat* (FIG. **20-41**), the Classical elements of closed outline

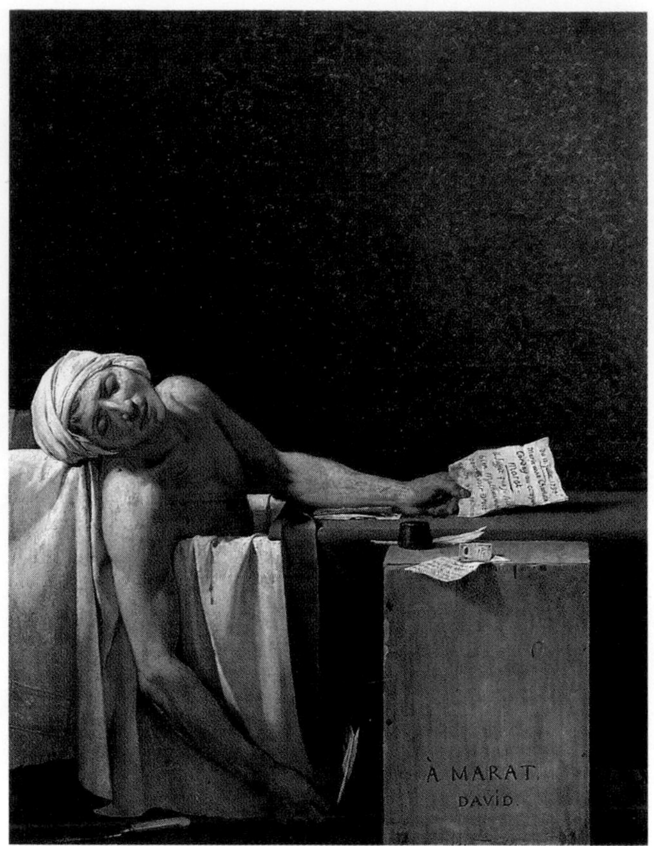

20-41 JACQUES LOUIS DAVID, *The Death of Marat*, 1793. Approx. 63″ × 49″. Musées Royaux des Beaux-Arts de Belgique, Brussels.

and compact composition, though present, are made to serve the ends of a carefully controlled dramatic realism, investing an event from David's own time with a strong, psychic impact. Marat, a revolutionary radical and a personal friend of David, had been stabbed to death in his bath by Charlotte Corday, a political enemy. David depicted the aftermath of the fatal attack with the directness and simple clarity of Zurbarán's painting of *St. Francis* (FIG. 19-35). The cold, neutral space above Marat's figure, slumped in the tub, makes for a chilling oppressiveness. Narrative details—the knife, the wound, the blood, the letter by which the young woman gained entrance—are vividly placed to sharpen the sense of pain and outrage, and to confront the viewer with the scene itself. David's depiction was shaped by historical fact, not Neoclassical theory, but his stele-like composition reveals his close study of Michelangelo, especially the Renaissance master's Christ in the *Pietà* in St. Peter's in Rome (not illustrated in this volume). *The Death of Marat* is convincingly real, yet it is masterfully composed to present Marat to the French people as a tragic martyr who died in the service of their state. In this way, the painting was meant to function as an "altarpiece" for the new civic "religion"; it was designed to inspire viewers with the saintly dedication of their slain leader. This depiction is a more severe version of modern martyrdom than *The Death of General Wolfe* by Benjamin West (FIG. 20-32). West's *Wolfe* was imbued with the grandeur of spectacle in a way that foreshadowed the dramatic and demonstrative side of nineteenth-century history painting. David's *Marat* has been stripped to a severe Neoclassical spareness that may appeal more to our late twentieth-century taste for minimalism.

In architecture, Neoclassicism proved to be such an expressively versatile style that it continued well into the nineteenth century, as we will see. By the end of the eighteenth century, however, in architecture, as in painting and sculpture, Neoclassicism was being used to symbolize moral and heroic links with the ancient past. Napoleon supported its use as appropriate for new buildings in his imperial state. In the new American republic, THOMAS JEFFERSON (1743–1826) spearheaded a movement for the adoption of a symbolic Neoclassicism (a style he saw as representative of the democratic qualities of the United States) as the national architecture. Scholar, economist, educational theorist, statesman, and gifted amateur architect, Jefferson was, by nature, attracted to Classical architecture. He worked out his ideas in his design for his own home, Monticello (FIG. **20-42**), which was begun in 1769. Jefferson admired Palladio immensely and read carefully the Italian architect's *Four Books of Architecture*. While minister to France, Jefferson studied French eighteenth-century Classical architecture and city planning, and visited Maison Carrée, the Roman temple at Nîmes (FIG. 6-46). After his European trip, Jefferson completely remodeled Monticello, which had first been designed in an English Georgian style. In his remodeling, he emulated the manner of Palladio, with a façade inspired by the work of Robert Adam. The final version of Monticello is somewhat reminiscent of the Villa Rotonda (FIG. 17-51) and of Chiswick House (FIG. 20-2), but its materials are the local wood and brick used in Virginia. Its hilltop setting was originally designed to open onto a garden façade designed in a less Classical style, and to provide an extended view over the surrounding countryside, linking people and nature in a manner that anticipated nineteenth-century ideas of the sublime in the picturesque.

Turning from the private domain to that of public space, Jefferson began to carry out his dream of developing a Classical style for the official architecture of the United States. Here, his Neoclassicism was an extension of the Enlightenment belief in the perfectability of human beings and in the power of art to help bring about that perfection. As Secretary of State to George Washington, Jefferson supported the logically ordered city plan for Washington, D.C., created in 1791 by Major Pierre L'Enfant, which extended

20-42 THOMAS JEFFERSON, Monticello, Charlottesville, Virginia, 1770–1806.

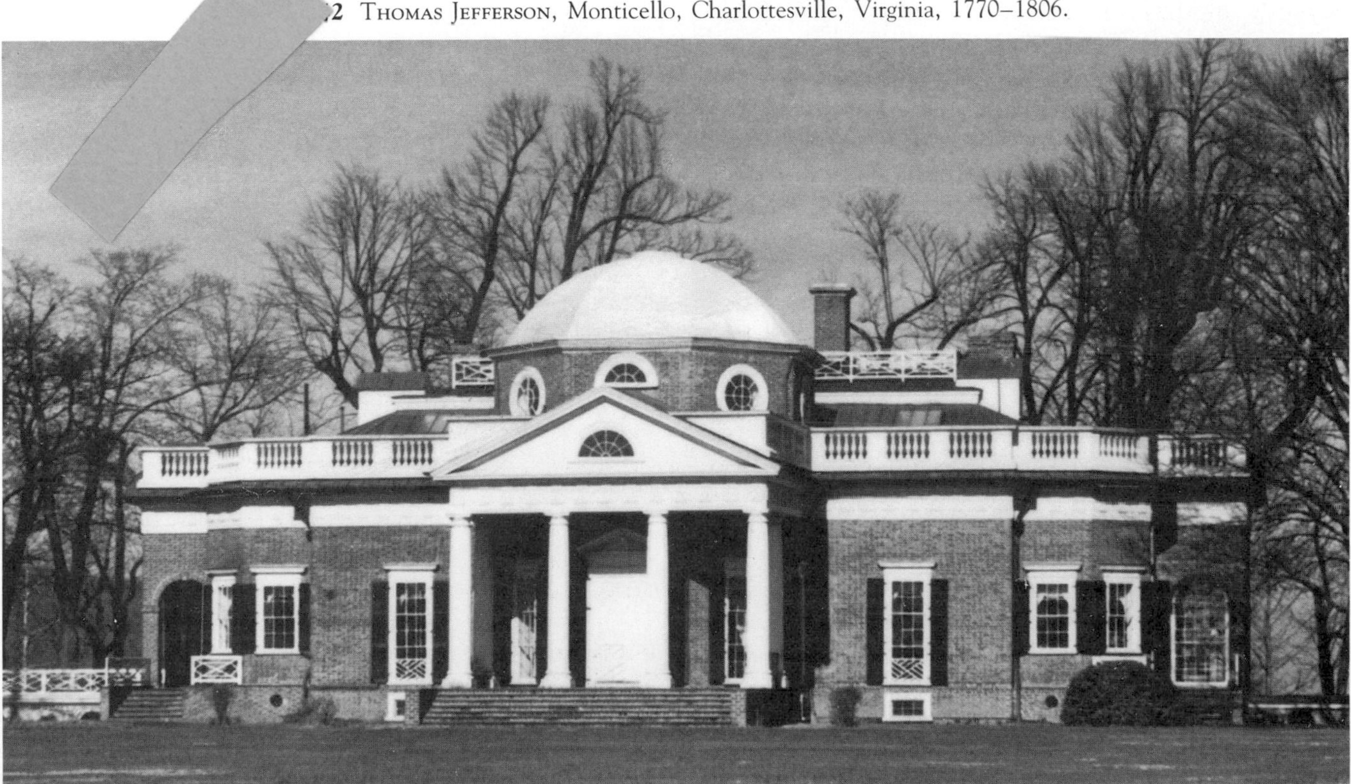

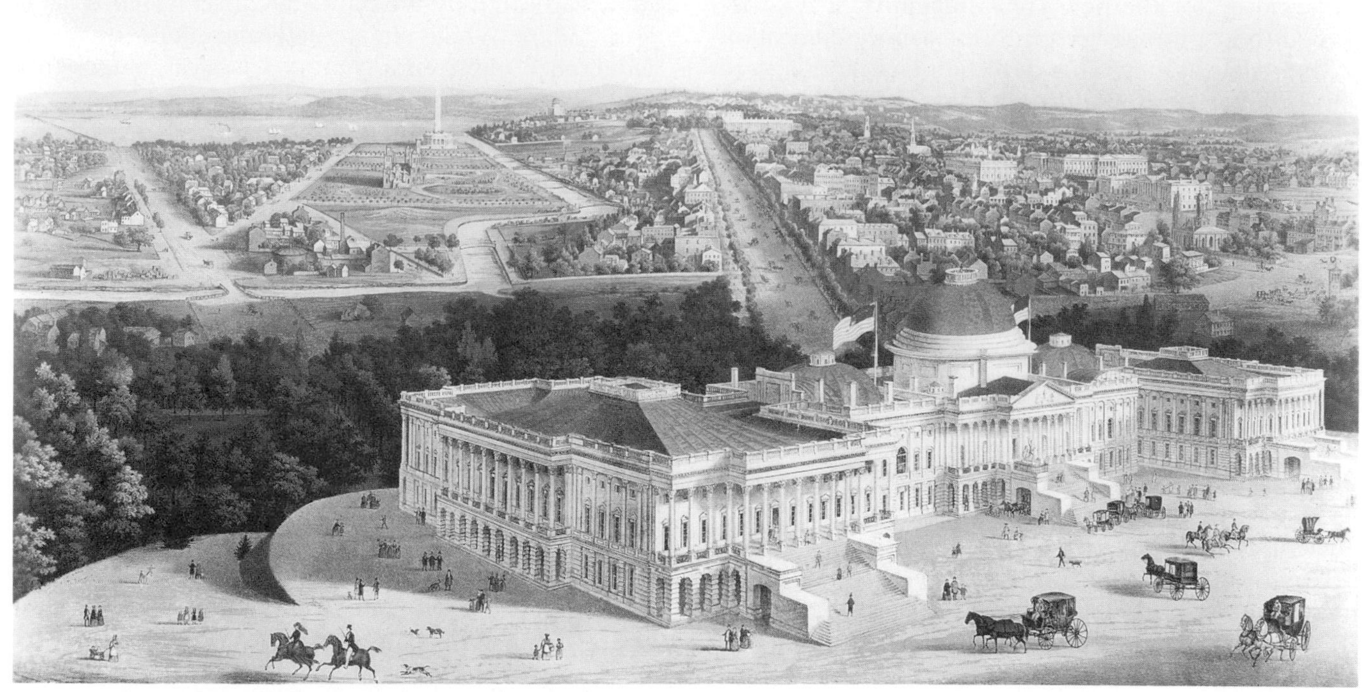

20-43 View of Washington, 1852, showing BENJAMIN LATROBE's Capitol and Major L'Enfant's plan of the city.

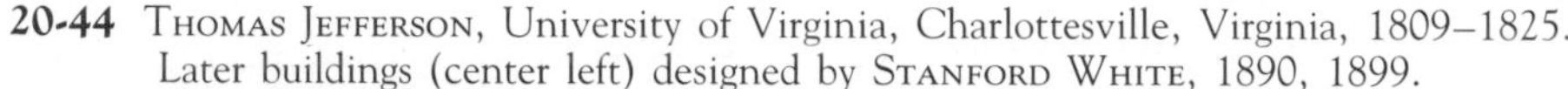

20-44 THOMAS JEFFERSON, University of Virginia, Charlottesville, Virginia, 1809–1825. Later buildings (center left) designed by STANFORD WHITE, 1890, 1899.

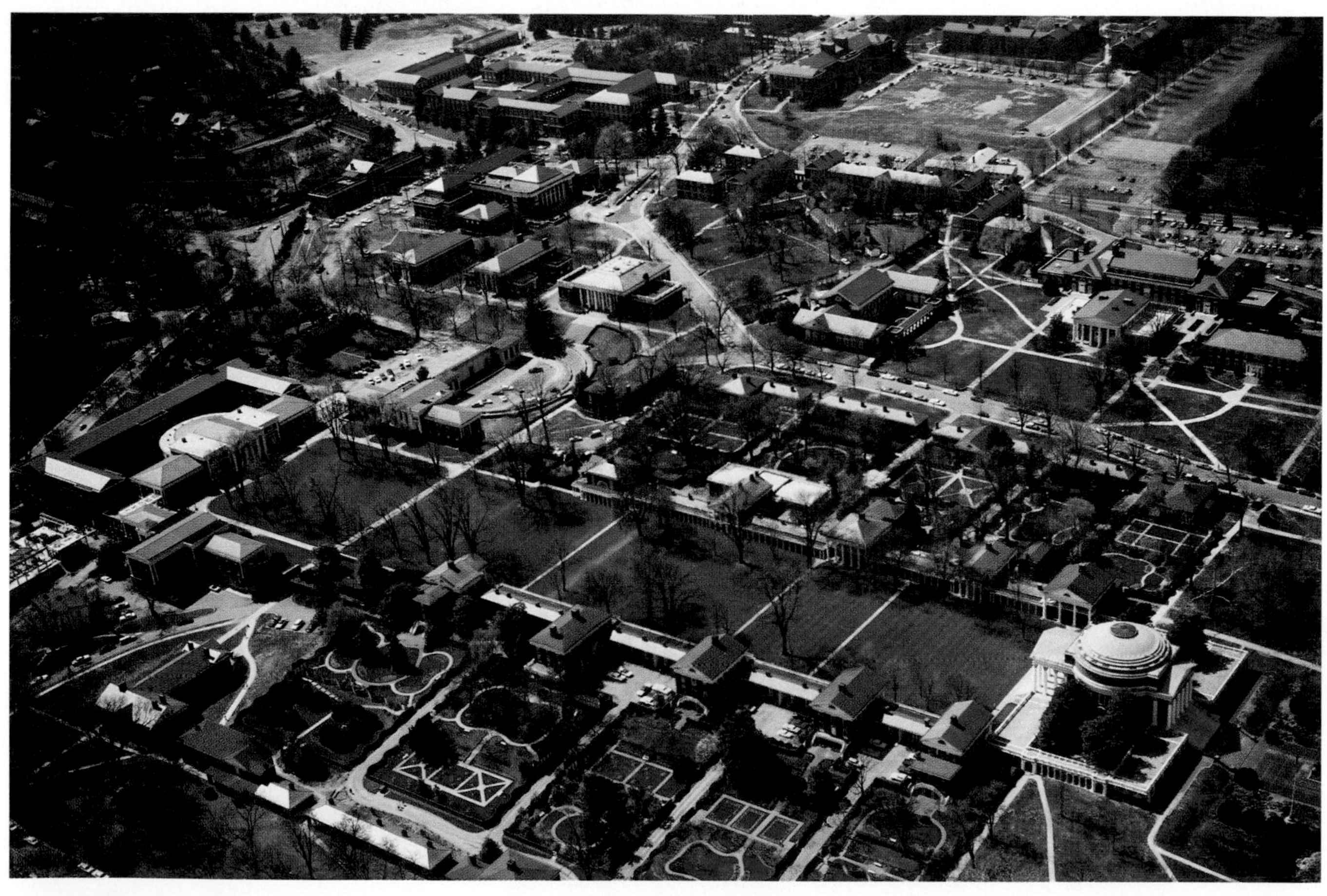

earlier ordered designs for city sections, like Woods's designs for Bath (FIG. 20-38), to an entire community. As an architect, Jefferson also incorporated the specific look of the Maison Carrée into his design for the Virginia State Capitol building in Richmond. He approved William Thornton's initial Palladian design for the federal Capitol building in 1793, and in 1803, as President, he selected B. H. LATROBE (1764–1820) to take over the design of the structure (FIG. **20-43**), with the goal of creating "a building that should . . . stand out as a superb visible expression of the ideals of a country dedicated to liberty." Jefferson's choice of a Roman-Classical style was influenced partly by his admiration for its beauty and partly by his associations of it with an idealized Roman republican government, and, through that, with the democracy of ancient Greece. Latrobe wrote that he wanted in his design for the Capitol to recreate "the glories of the Greece of Pericles in the woods of America." To that end, in the architecture of the Capitol, the symbol of the Roman Eagle became the American bald eagle, a special new Corinthian order was devised in which corn plants replaced acanthus leaves, and the sculptured representation of Liberty was designed to abandon traditional trappings and to hold a liberty cap in one hand and rest her other hand on the Constitution.

For Jefferson, if Classical architecture could embody the ideals of a new country, it also could help educate the young, especially when placed in a proper relationship to nature. In 1817, with help from Thornton and Latrobe, he began designing the University of Virginia (FIG. **20-44**) in Charlottesville as an "academical village." The original plan was a rectangle. A library modeled on the Roman Pantheon stood at one end. The other end originally was open, providing an extended vista into a panorama of wooded hills, a design element intended to indicate the perfect and balanced relationship between the works of human beings and those of nature. Along the sides of the rectangle, the designer placed pavilions, each built in a different Classical style and arranged with the goal of providing living architectural lessons to the students.

Romanticism of the Sublime and the Terrible

While some Enlightenment thinkers and proponents of the Age of Reason found a rational ideal in Neoclassical art, many artists felt that neither reason nor Neoclassical art could do justice to human reality. For these individuals, imagination could reach farther to find (by suprarational intuition and enkindled emotion) a higher and a deeper experience. Rather than produce images that could edify or educate their viewers, these artists chose to portray subjects that evoked feelings of the sublime and the terrible. The Romantic esthetic of the sublime was shaped in large part by ideas in Edmund Burke's *A Philosophical Enquiry into the Origin of Our Ideas of the Sublime and the Beautiful* (1757). For Burke, the sublime was related to our instinct for self-preservation.

> The passions which concern self-preservation turn mostly on *pain* or *danger*. The ideas of *pain, sickness,* and *death* fill the mind with strong emotions of horror; but *life* and *health,* though they put us in a capacity of being affected with pleasure, they make no such impression. . . . The passions therefore which are conversant about the preservation of the individual, turn chiefly on *pain* and *danger,* and they are the most powerful of all the passions. . . . Whatever is fitted in any sort to excite the ideas of pain and danger . . . is a source of the *sublime*. The passions which belong to self-preservation . . . are simply painful when their causes immediately affect us; they are delightful when we have an idea of pain and danger, without being actually in such circumstances. . . . Whatever excites this delight, I call *sublime*.*

Burke named the qualities that arouse feelings of the sublime: terror, obscurity, power, privation, vastness, infinity, magnificence, suddenness, feeling, pain—and also, special conditions of light, color, sound, smell, and taste. These qualities, in various combinations, suffused much Romantic art of the late eighteenth century and inspired much nineteenth-century Romantic art as well.[†]

For some artists, excursions into the sublime were only part of their activity. We already have noted how the etched *Views of Rome* by GIOVANNI BATTISTA PIRANESI (1720–1788) appealed to the Romantic taste for subjects from Rome's ancient past. His dramatic presentations of the city's majestic Classical ruins in this series of prints were so convincing that they have served for generations as the standard image of Roman grandeur, but Piranesi also exercised his imagination to create fantastic interiors that could not exist in the real world. No aid to the recording of nature could help the master etcher when he turned from the printing of dramatic scenes of existing Roman buildings to the creation of eerie prison interiors *(carceri)* that stirred the viewer's imagination with their sublime suggestions of vastness, power, and terror. Piranesi's early experience as an architect

*In J. T. Boulton, ed., (Oxford, UK: Basil Blackwell Ltd., 1987), pp. 38–39, 51ff.

†Burke saw beauty linked to passions connected with love—both sexual (mixed with lust) and societal. Burke's ideas about beauty were of less importance for Romantic art than his ideas about the sublime.

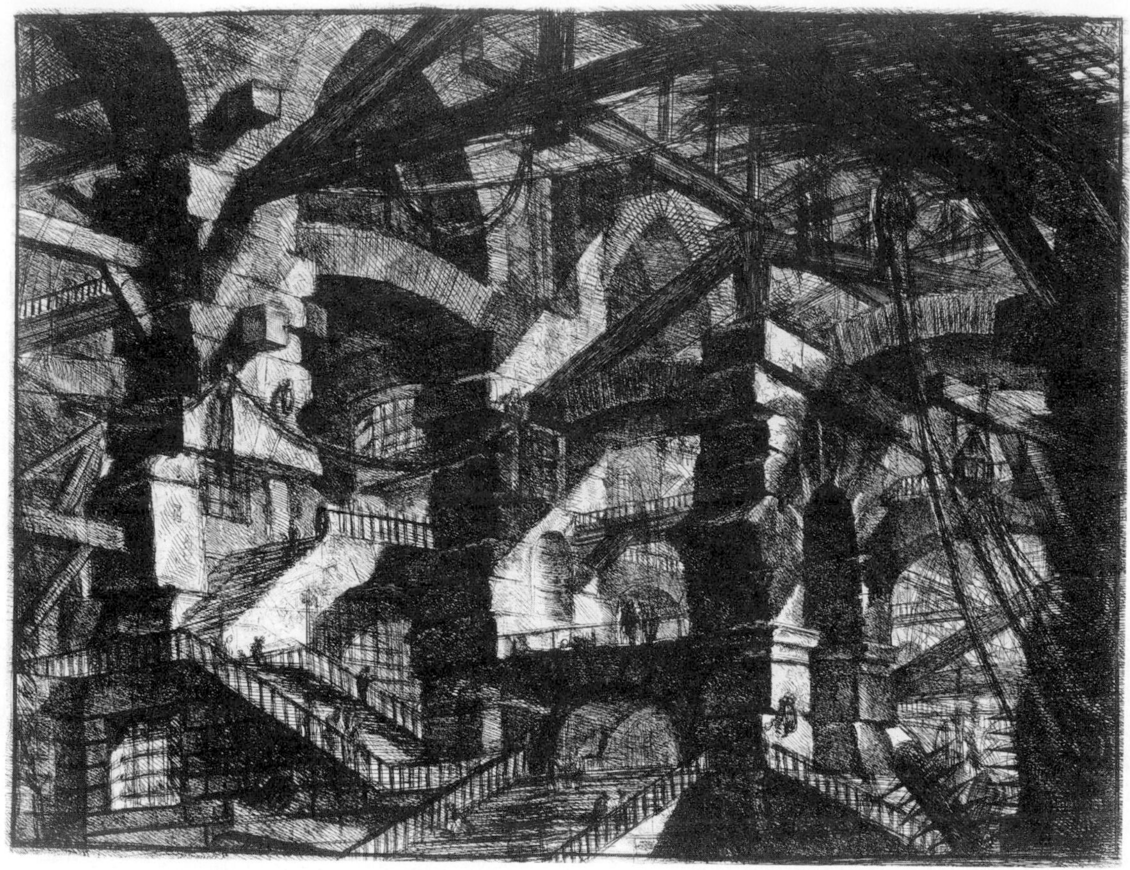

20-45 GIOVANNI BATTISTA PIRANESI, *Carceri 14*, c. 1750. Etching, second state, approx. 16″ × 21″. Ashmolean Museum, Oxford.

in Venice, which may have provided the inspiration for his project recording the monuments of Rome, began shortly after he moved to the Eternal City in 1740. He was not satisfied for long, however, with simply dramatizing existing Roman buildings with patterns of light and shadow. Soon he was conjuring up awe-inspiring visions of bafflingly complicated architectural masses, piled high and spread out through gloomy spaces. In such pictures, vistas are multiplied and broken by a seeming infinity of massive arches, vaults, piers, and stairways, through which small, insectlike human figures move stealthily. Despite wandering, soaring perspectives, the observer is overwhelmed by a suffocating sense of enclosure; the spaces are locked in, and no exit is visible. These grim places are filled with brooding menace and hopelessness. Piranesi etched a series of them, often darkening subsequent editions to make them even more sinister. Our picture, *Carceri 14* (FIG. **20-45**), is one of these. It reminds us that the gaiety of the Rococo and the rationality of the Enlightenment coexisted with an eighteenth-century sensibility for the sublime that returned to haunt the night imaginings of many a Romantic artist and poet in the nineteenth century.

Like Piranesi, many painters at the end of the eighteenth century worked in more than one mode. The Englishman GEORGE STUBBS (1724–1806) won a reputation for his naturalistic paintings of horses, but he also enjoyed creating scenes of natural struggle and horror. Stubbs began his career painting human portraits to support himself while he studied his lifelong passion, anatomy. Soon, he was specializing in the anatomy of horses and using this knowledge to create "portraits" of the mares, stallions, and foals owned by the English gentry. These were naturalistic images linked in spirit to the works of Canaletto (FIG. 20-19), but Stubbs was not content to remain tied always to a careful rendering of visual facts. He also invented a new type of picture, the "animal history painting," which depicted dramatic episodes from the lives of wild animals. This type of subject fit well with the teachings of Rousseau and others who idealized life far from any taint of civilization, which they believed distorted the innate "goodness" of the natural order. *Horse Being Devoured by a Lion* (FIG. **20-46**) shows the

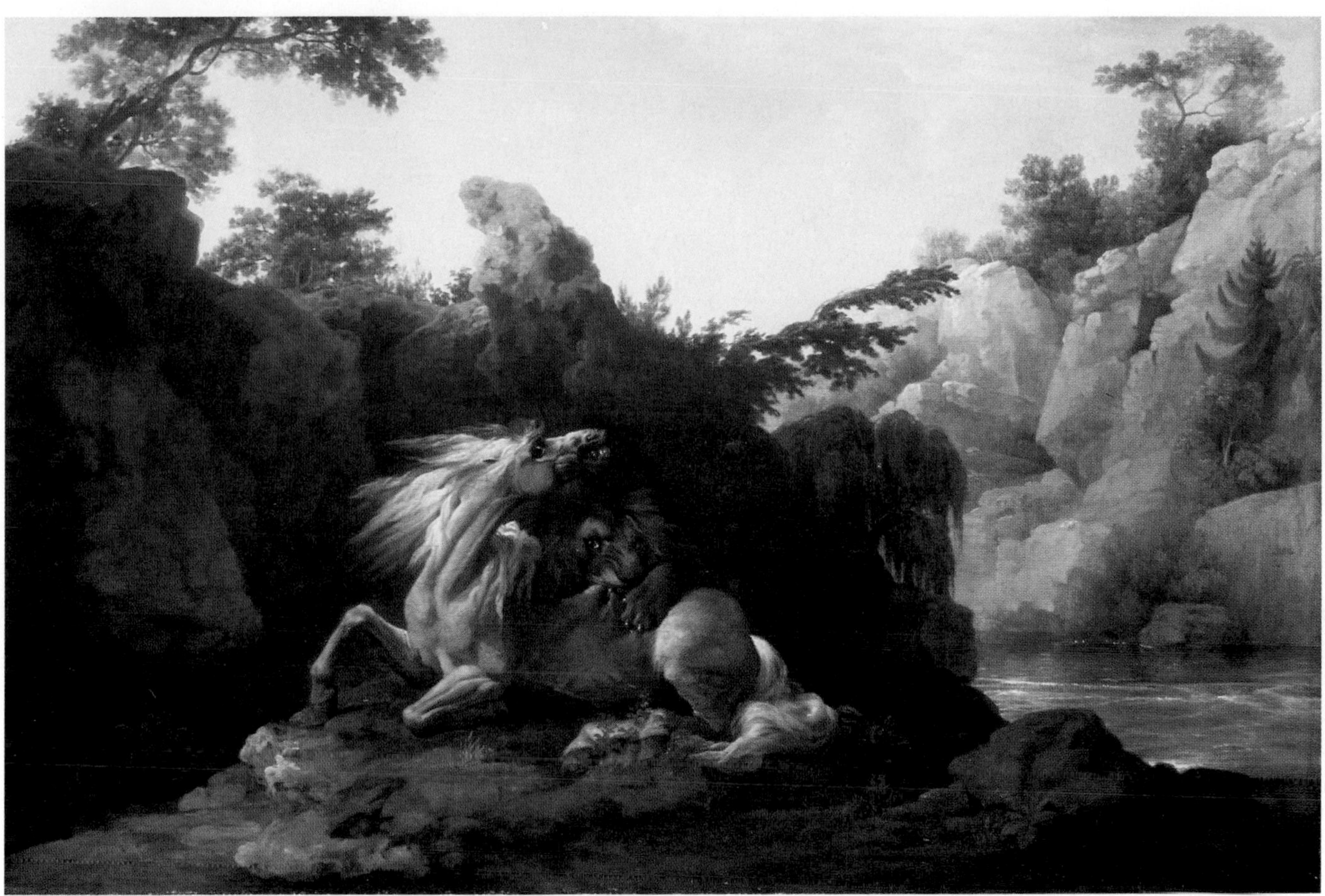

20-46 GEORGE STUBBS, *Horse Being Devoured by a Lion*, 1763. Enamel on metal. Tate Gallery, London.

violent side of nature in the raw. A flash of light illuminates the struggle of a terrified white horse, trying in vain to shake off a hungry lion that is already biting deeply into the horse's vulnerable back. The composition of *Horse Being Devoured by a Lion* may seem a "wilder" version of the lion attack on a man in Puget's *Milo of Crotona* (FIG. 19-72), but Stubbs's animal struggle also resembles an ancient Classical sculpture of a lion on the back of a horse, which the artist could have seen in Rome during a visit there. The scene also may have been inspired in part by an attack Stubbs witnessed in North Africa on his way back to England after studying Classical and Renaissance art in Italy. Whatever the source, the subject was so popular that Stubbs did nine versions of this Romantic scene. For the eighteenth-century viewer, the emotional shudders aroused by the horse-lion confrontation would have sweetened philosophical thoughts about the nobility of the natural state and the inevitable connections between life and death. In the nineteenth century, the emotions in such sublime Romantic themes will be fused into a fuller exploration of the qualities of the sublime in nature.

HENRY FUSELI (1741–1825) attempted to arouse delectable terror of a different sort. He specialized in night moods of horror and in "gothic" fantasies—in the demonic, the macabre, and often the sadistic. Swiss by birth, Fuseli settled in England and eventually became a member of the Royal Academy and an instructor there. Largely self-taught, he contrived a distinctive manner compounded of the influence of Michelangelo, the Antique style, and his own extravagant invention to express the fantasies of his vivid imagination. The twisted poses and frantic gestures of his figures go well beyond exaggeration and often suggest the influence of Italian Mannerism. *The Nightmare* (FIG. **20-47**) was the first of four versions of this terrifying theme. The beautiful young woman, tormented by some terrible dream and still not awake, has thrown herself partly from her couch. She lies helpless beneath the incubus that squats malignantly on her body, as a horse with flaming eyes bursts into the scene from beyond the curtain. The sublime vein of violent emotion and of perverse and tragic action in this composition will be heavily mined in the nineteenth century. Fuseli's art was among the

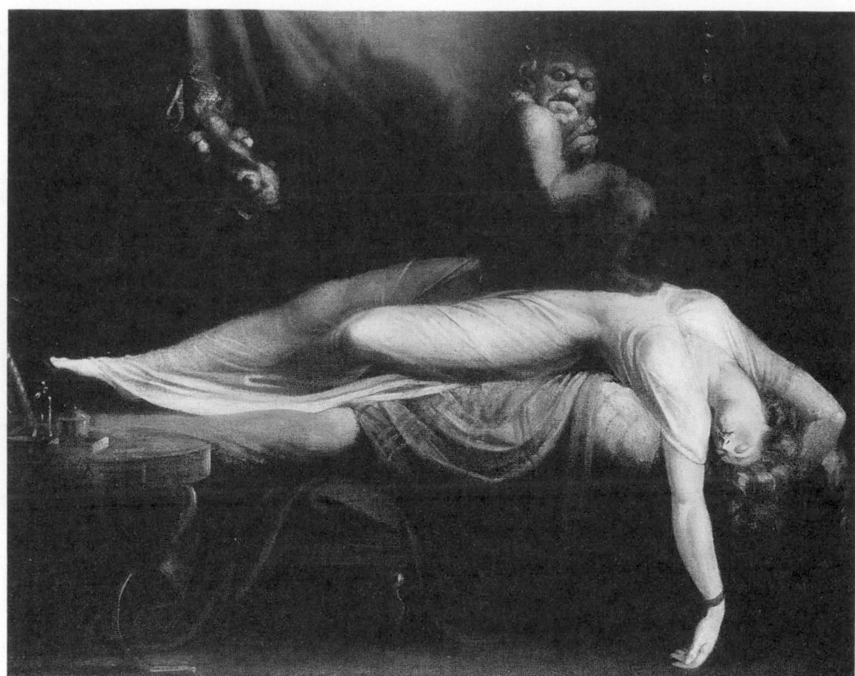

20-47 HENRY FUSELI, *The Nightmare,* 1781. Approx. $57\frac{1}{2}'' \times 47\frac{1}{2}''$. The Detroit Institute of the Arts (gift of Mr. and Mrs. Bert L. Smokler and Mr. and Mrs. Lawrence A. Fleishman).

first that attempted to depict the dark terrain of the human subconscious.

The visionary English poet, painter, and engraver, WILLIAM BLAKE (1757–1827), combined in his art calm Neoclassicism and the storm and stress of late eighteenth-century sublime Romanticism. Blake greatly admired both the art of ancient Greece and Gothic art. Gothic for him was the style best suited to the expression of personal religious emotions, while Classical Greek art exemplified the mathematical, and thus eternal, in a different way. Yet Blake joined neither the prominent figures of the Age of Reason nor any organized religious group. He would have been an uneasy member of any group because he treasured the fact that the compositions of many of his paintings and poems were given to him by spirit visitors in dreams. The importance he attached to these experiences led him to believe that rationalism's search for material explanations of the world stifled the spiritual side of human nature, while the stringent rules of behavior imposed by orthodox religions killed the individual creative impulse. Blake's vision of the Almighty in *Ancient of Days* (FIG. **20-48**) combines his ideas and interests in a highly individual way. For Blake, this figure combined the concept of the Creator with that of Wisdom as a part of God. The *Ancient of Days,* printed as the frontispiece for Blake's book, *Europe: A Prophesy,* was published with a quote ("When he set a compass upon the face of the deep") from the Book of Proverbs (8:22–23, 27–30) in the Old Testament of the Bible. Most of that chapter is spoken

20-48 WILLIAM BLAKE, *Ancient of Days,* frontispiece of *Europe: A Prophesy,* 1794. Metal relief etching, hand-colored. Whitworth Art Gallery, University of Manchester, England.

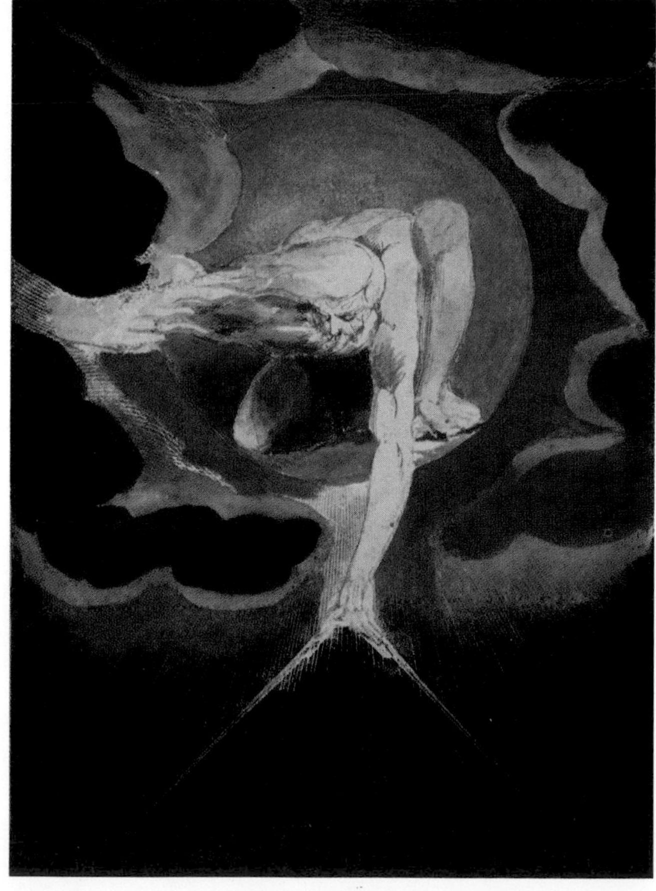

by Wisdom, identified as a female, who tells the reader how she was with the Lord through all the time of the Creation:

> The Lord possessed me in the beginning of his way, before his works of old. I was set up from the everlasting, from the beginning, or ever the earth was. . . . When he prepared the heavens, I *was* there; when he set a compass upon the face of the deep; When he established the clouds above; when he strengthened the fountains of the deep; When he gave to the sea his decree, that the waters should not pass his commandment; when he appointed the foundations of the earth; Then I was by him, I as one brought up with him; and I was daily his delight, rejoicing always before him.

Energy fills this composition. The Ancient of Days leans forward from a fiery orb, peering toward earth and unleashing power through his outstretched left arm into twin rays of light, which emerge between his spread fingers like an architect's measuring instrument. A might wind surges through his thick hair and beard. Only the strength of his Michelangelesque physique keeps him firmly planted within his heavenly perch. Here, Baroque vigor and ideal Classical anatomy merge with the inner, dark dreams of Romanticism, which we will meet often in the nineteenth century. In his independence and in the individuality of his artistic vision, Blake was very much a man of the modern age.

The world of dreams and visions provided wonderful sublime materials for artists who yearned to escape the rules of reason. Blake wrote: "I will not reason and compare, my business is to create. . . . The road of excess leads to the palace of wisdom." Yet, grave risks imperiled such an approach. Raw feeling could lead the soul astray, perhaps beyond the limits of sanity. The Spanish master FRANCISCO GOYA (1746–1828), whose works we will consider at greater length in the next chapter, graphically pictured this danger in a print he captioned *The Sleep of Reason Produces Monsters* (FIG. **20-49**), from a series called *Los Caprichos*. Here, the rational mind is stilled as the human figure sleeps, while around him throng the winged monsters who have sprung easily into being in the absence of thoughtful control.

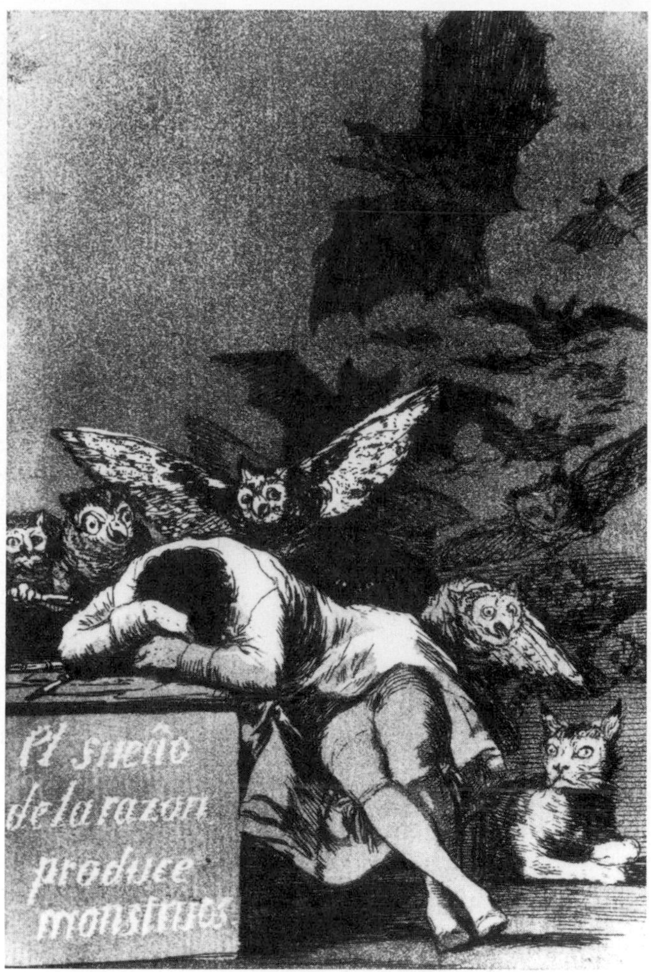

20-49 FRANCISCO GOYA, *The Sleep of Reason Produces Monsters*, from *Los Caprichos* (Plate 43), c. 1794–1799. Etching and aquatint, approx. 5″ × 8″. Pomona College, Claremont, California (gift of Norton Simon).

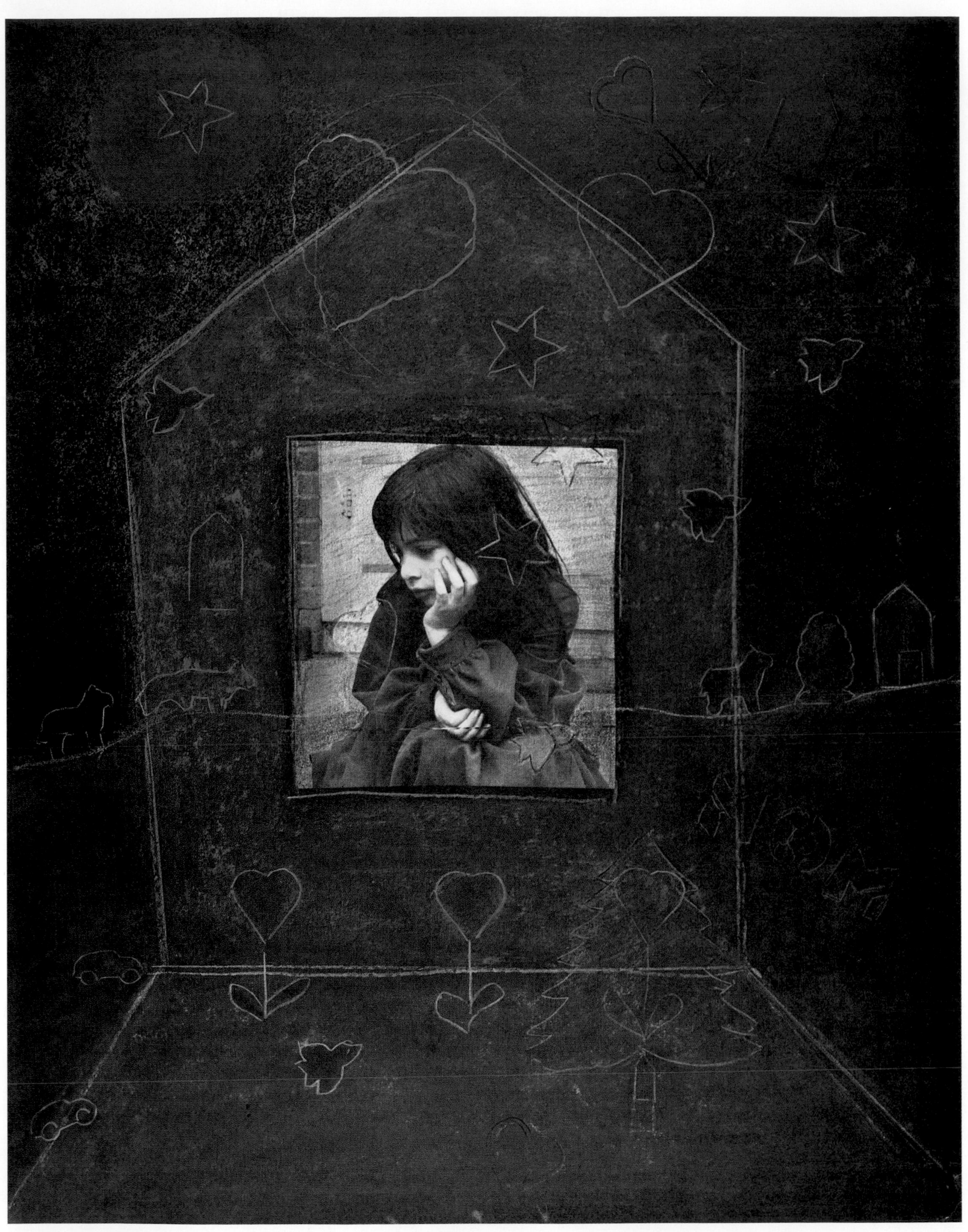

At the heart of the modern artistic experience, as seen in Joanne Leonard's *Julia and the Window of Vulnerability,* lie many personal reflections of our new knowledge of the vastness of the universe and both the fragility and enormous potential of human existence.

V
THE MODERN WORLD

Our era, the modern era, began to take form in the eighteenth century. As we saw in Chapter 20, the beginning of the modern age was influenced by political, economic, and social revolutions more widespread than any change affecting human society since prehistoric times, when agriculture replaced hunting and gathering as a major way of life. By the end of the eighteenth century, political revolutions had relegated royalty to positions of diminished influence in the power structure, allowing many nations to establish political systems with broader and more democratic power bases. The Industrial Revolution, initiated in the inventions and ideas of the eighteenth century, was transforming the social order in industrializing nations. Scientific investigation was providing new knowledge about the world as the accumulation of facts, begun during the Enlightenment, accelerated, and interest in distant cultures was awakened.

During the nineteenth century, many countries reorganized to fit a pattern that would become the modern nation-state. Nationalistic attitudes spurred ambitious governments in Europe to extend their authority and the influence of European culture to overseas colonies in Asia, Africa, and the Americas. The pace of discovery and development quickened, bringing other major changes in society. The Renaissance belief in a human capacity for rational control over self and nature was increasingly undermined as the social sciences adapted biological concepts to explain human culture and individual differences. Machines began to replace physical labor, which altered the nature of work, while new technologies began to revolutionize transportation and communication.

In the twentieth century, political power has continued to shift; the old Eurocentric view of the world has changed as former colonies have become nations in their own right, and countries like the Soviet Union, China, and Iran have gradually assumed new political importance. Marxist and capitalist philosophies and government structures based on totalitarianism or democratic models have continued to vie for dominance. New theories from the sciences and social sciences have continually altered our views of ourselves and our planet. The physical and biological sciences have delved more deeply than ever before into the basic structures of matter and the universe. Theories proposed by Albert Einstein have shown that everything has existence only in relation to everything else and that all life takes place in a continuum of space and time. The printed media have largely been supplanted by radio, television, and electronic telecommunications, affecting our perception of the reality of events. Psychiatry and psychology have probed the inner workings of the human mind, showing us how individual the "reality" each of us perceives really is. Old conventions and beliefs have been abandoned and traditional values have been called into question. Our comprehension of reality also has shifted to accommodate the ways in which new technologies have expanded our range of sensory perception. The multitude of changes that have taken place since the late eighteenth century have contributed to the problematic quality of modern life. Nothing is certain and everything is in question—especially the definition of what is real. Reality is now understood to be infinitely complex and, perhaps, ultimately elusive. Although people continue to believe in the potential of innovation, invention, and science to create a better world, a mood of doubt, restlessness, and challenge to authority persists.

The shifting conditions of society have been accompanied by a shift in the position of the artist within society. Eighteenth-century artists, content in their belief that knowledge, science, and industry could help individuals to achieve their full potential for happy, productive lives, held secure places in the social hierarchy. In the nineteenth century, many artists criticized society and its values. Others saw self-expression in art as a vehicle for realization of the whole self. In the twentieth century, artists have worked more and more apart from the mainstream, creating works based on personal inspiration. Artists with individual vision gradually came to consider themselves as prophets or seers with particular gifts for creating culturally revolutionary art.

Most of the art in the modern era has fallen into "movements" whose adherents have sought to establish the authority of their particular beliefs about the role of art. The names for many of these movements were bestowed by outsiders—critics or scholars—attempting to describe something about the content, form, or intention of the pieces created by artists working from a particular esthetic position. "Neoclassicism," "Romanticism," "Realism," "Impressionism," and "Post-Impressionism" are major nineteenth-century movements; "Fauvism," "Cubism," "Expressionism," "Futurism," and "Surrealism" are some early twentieth-century movements.* Each movement had a commonly held set of principles and positions on all issues involving art. Most recently, Postmodern artists have tended to avoid group doctrines, basing their art instead on a personal analysis of the whole history of art and learning. During the modern era, works have been marketed after completion; salon exhibitions and private dealers have grown steadily more important, and art has become more of a commercial business.

Throughout the modern period, the expression and fabric of art have been affected by the introduction of new media. The invention of photography in the late 1830s provided a new tool for recording reality and challenged painters to reassess what they would represent in their work and how they would represent it. New theories of color and optics, synthetic pigments, primed canvas, and paint packaged in tubes allowed artists to paint more easily and rapidly. In the twentieth century, modern media, ferroconcrete,

*In this text, when words such as these are used to designate art movements, they are capitalized. Some of these terms, however, also can be used more broadly. For example, *realism* might be used to describe all art that emphasizes a literal reproduction of the appearance of the physical world, as with the works of Velázquez or Vermeer during the Baroque period. When a word is used with this broader sense, it will not be capitalized.

new welding techniques, and electronic tools have provided new possibilities for form in architecture, sculpture, and image-making that have allowed expressions impossible with the older media of painting and drawing. One notable characteristic of art in the modern period has been its emphasis on the expressive power of each medium in itself. In the words of the Canadian theorist Marshall McLuhan, more and more in Modern art, "the medium has become the message."

Both Modern art and Postmodern art have tended to be international in their sources and influence, as have modern science, technology, scholarship, and politics. Beginning in the late nineteenth century, modern artists were increasingly inspired by the physical forms of non-Western art—the art of Islam, India, China and Japan and artworks brought to European collections from Africa and Oceania. In the twentieth century, more and more people have turned away from a view of Western culture as the culmination of societal evolution and toward a belief that all cultures have an important place in the world and its history. In addition, art made by non-Europeans, women, African-Americans, Latinos, and Native Americans has become increasingly visible.

What we have said here to provide background to the ensuing discussion of the art of the modern world is a simplification; it should be viewed as only a partial explanation of the ways in which Modern (and Postmodern) art either looks different from the art of the past or plays a role very different from that played by art in the past. The story of the artist in the modern period is the story of a multistranded search for the means to express what it is like to be alive in a complex and rapidly changing era.

Interrelation of Major Movements and Styles in the Art of the Nineteenth Century

Solid black lines indicate direct influence; dashed lines, indirect

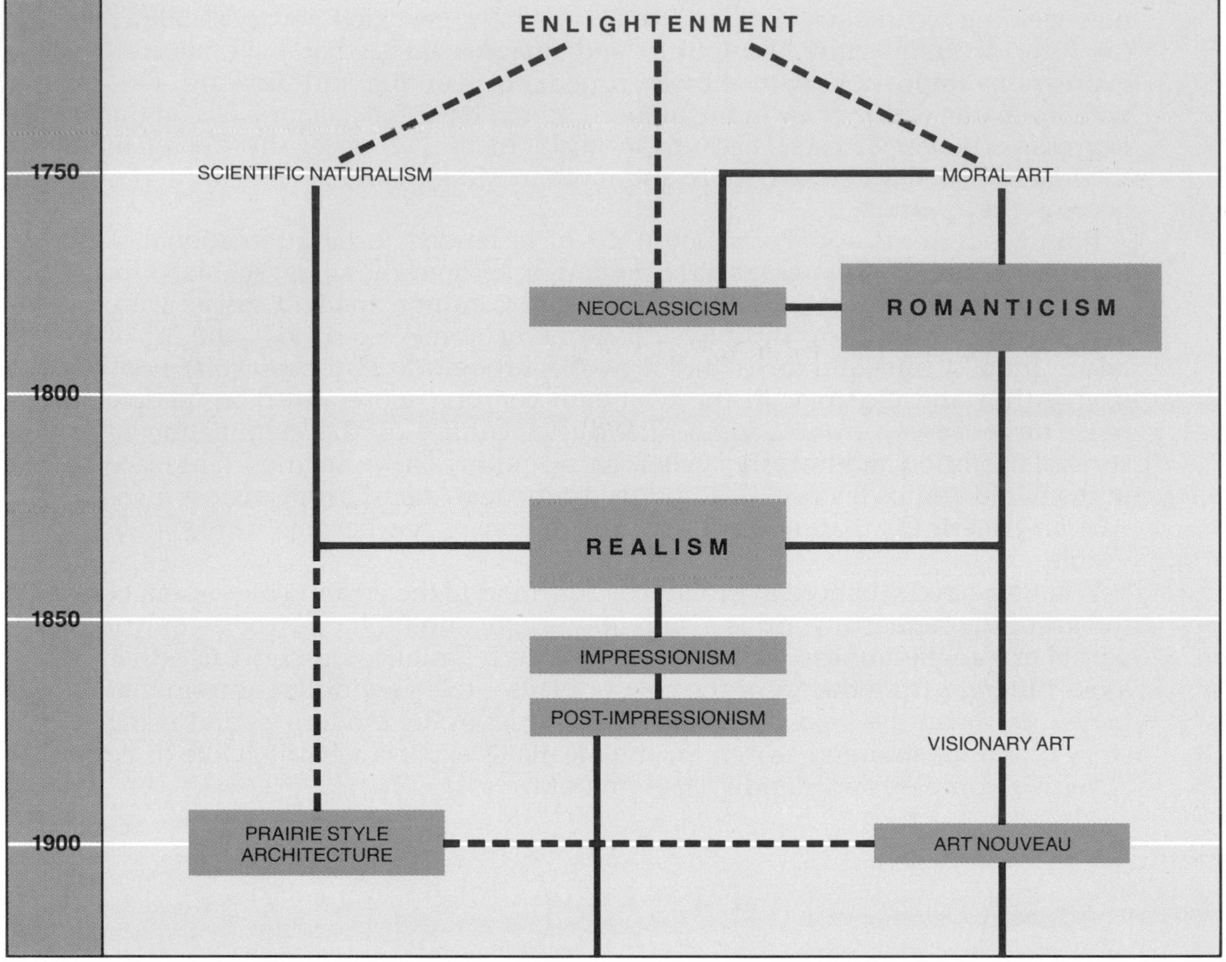

ENLIGHTENMENT

1750 — SCIENTIFIC NATURALISM — MORAL ART

NEOCLASSICISM — ROMANTICISM

1800

REALISM

1850

IMPRESSIONISM

POST-IMPRESSIONISM

VISIONARY ART

1900 — PRAIRIE STYLE ARCHITECTURE — ART NOUVEAU

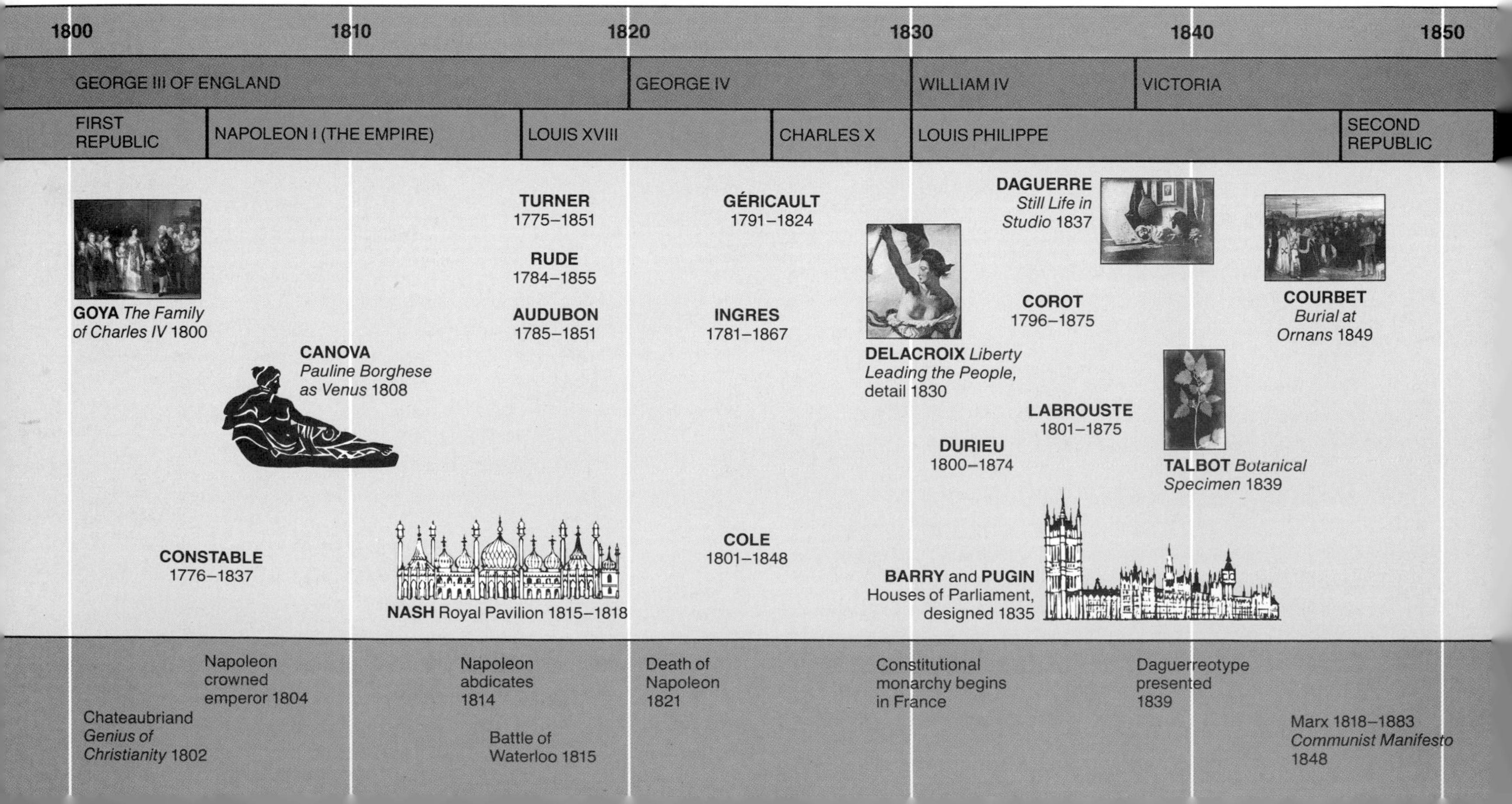

1800	1810	1820	1830	1840	1850

GEORGE III OF ENGLAND | GEORGE IV | WILLIAM IV | VICTORIA

FIRST REPUBLIC | NAPOLEON I (THE EMPIRE) | LOUIS XVIII | CHARLES X | LOUIS PHILIPPE | SECOND REPUBLIC

GOYA *The Family of Charles IV* 1800

CANOVA *Pauline Borghese as Venus* 1808

CONSTABLE 1776–1837

TURNER 1775–1851

RUDE 1784–1855

AUDUBON 1785–1851

NASH Royal Pavilion 1815–1818

GÉRICAULT 1791–1824

INGRES 1781–1867

COLE 1801–1848

DELACROIX *Liberty Leading the People*, detail 1830

DURIEU 1800–1874

BARRY and **PUGIN** Houses of Parliament, designed 1835

DAGUERRE *Still Life in Studio* 1837

COROT 1796–1875

LABROUSTE 1801–1875

TALBOT *Botanical Specimen* 1839

COURBET *Burial at Ornans* 1849

Napoleon crowned emperor 1804

Chateaubriand *Genius of Christianity* 1802

Napoleon abdicates 1814

Battle of Waterloo 1815

Death of Napoleon 1821

Constitutional monarchy begins in France

Daguerreotype presented 1839

Marx 1818–1883 *Communist Manifesto* 1848

21

THE NINETEENTH CENTURY: PLURALISM OF STYLE

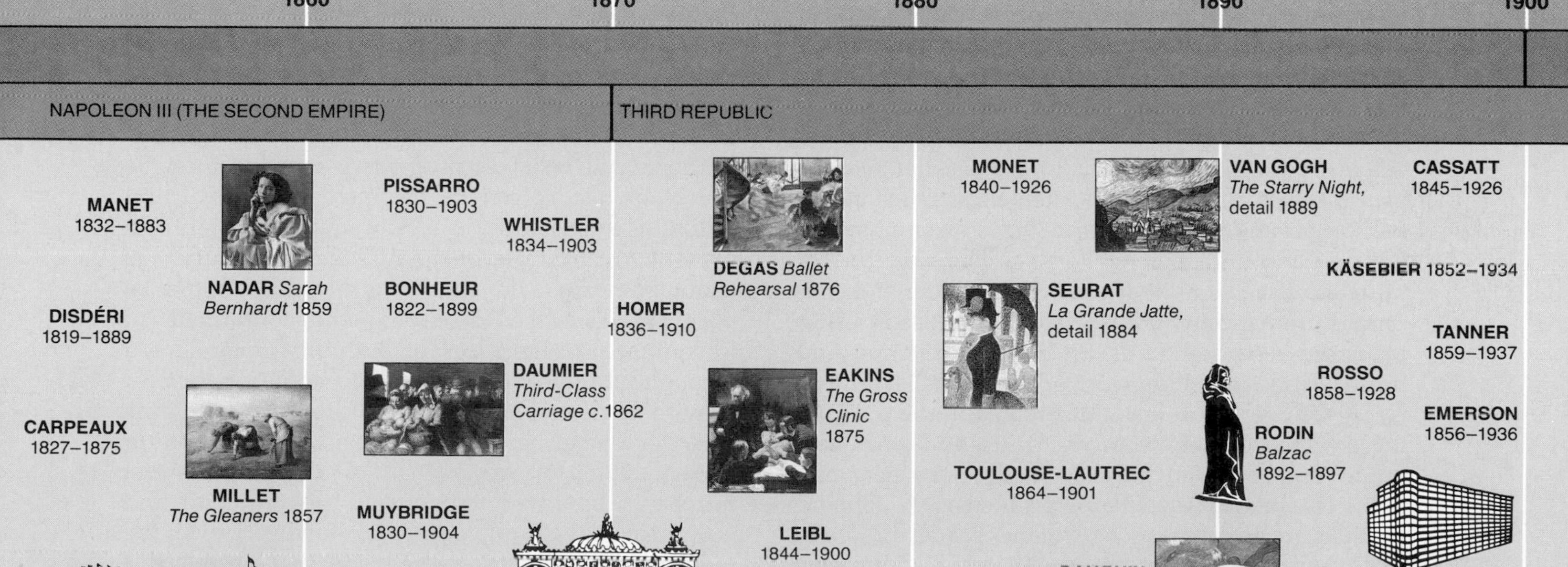

FOR EUROPE, the nineteenth century was an age of radical change during which the modern world took shape. In a world that was experiencing a population explosion of unparalleled magnitude, revolution followed revolution, a pattern punctuated by counterrevolution and conservative reaction. This was the era in which the modern nation-state and accompanying ideas of nationalism were born. European governments extended their rule to virtually every part of the globe, spreading the influence of European culture into colonies in Africa, the Americas, India, Asia, and Australasia, and clearing the way for influences from those areas to flow back to Europe. The formation of empires abroad was supported by the enthusiasm of popular nationalism at home, and patriotism and imperialism went hand in hand.

Social and economic struggle pitted industrial capitalism and the bourgeoisie (the middle class) against the widely impoverished masses. The rapid industrialization initiated in the eighteenth century created abrupt changes in age-old living patterns and an acute sense of dislocation for many. The Industrial Revolution, which mechanized agriculture, and periodic crop failures brought thousands of people from the countryside to the city in search of jobs and sent thousands of others overseas. The result of these changing patterns was that in urban and rural areas alike, the disparity between the rich and the poor widened unprecedentedly.

In thought as well as science, the nineteenth century was an era of grand new theories through which visionary thinkers attempted to unify whole bodies of knowledge into precise, well-ordered systems. These efforts can largely be seen as a natural extension of the Enlightenment thirst for encyclopedic collections of facts. Practitioners of psychiatry and psychology, sciences both in their infancy during the later decades of the century, attempted systematic studies of the human psyche to discover the "laws" of human behavior. On a more material level, science was contributing advancements that would improve living conditions dramatically. Louis Pasteur and Joseph Lister produced new standards for public sanitation and health, while the combined work of several scientists, Georg Ohm and Thomas Edison among them, led to the development of electricity for use in homes, factories, and theaters, making possible the new medium of cinema. Due to an ever-increasing demand on the part of government, business, and the scientific community for documentary information of all kinds, ambitious explorers in this expansionist period made meticulous records of what they discovered in lands then little known to the centers of Western civilization. Revolutionary new theories about life and society were formulated on the basis of some of this information. While many of these theories challenged accepted views, none caused more widespread controversy than Charles Darwin's theory of evolution as put forth in the *Origin of Species* (1859). In this seminal work, Darwin hypothesized that humans evolved from simian ancestors, thus contradicting and threatening Judeo-Christian beliefs and teachings.

A profound sense of history pervaded the century. The past was rapidly receding, and a unique present was asserting its originality as decisively as the early Christian world had asserted *its* values against the defeated and devalued pagan past. The new age, created by the great revolutions, was *modern,* and modern, for many, was good. What was not modern was rejected, for what was to come would be better. These concepts constituted the "doctrine of progress," whose supporters maintained the permanency of change for the better. As early as 1750, Turgot had predicted that the doctrine of progress would replace that of the will of God.

Many in the nineteenth century did not accept the doctrine of progress; others did so with reservations or with grave misgivings. Such critics saw much of value being lost through change and feared for the traditions, institutions, customs, and mores that knit society together and gave meaning to life. They could accept neither the depreciation of human value implicit in scientific explanations of human nature like Darwin's, nor the alienation and degradation of human beings by a mechanized and impersonal industry. They had a special distaste for the type of modern society built by new wealth, with all its ostentatious materialism. Many of those who objected to the vulgarity and banality of taste predominant in such a society were artists—some of them, the best artists of the century.

The liberal belief in progress is a belief that the course of history can be changed by thought and action, as long as people are not impeded by authority. The great debate of the nineteenth century was about authority—the questions of what should be believed, respected, defended, and conformed to. Revolutionary shake-ups of authority reverberated throughout the century, carrying people's hopes for something newer, better, truer, and purer. Humanity was thought to be perfectible, and the principle of utility, calling for the greatest good for the greatest number, was advocated for law, government, and economic life. Confusion arose, however, over the means to these ends, a confusion that produced a wide variety of philosophies rationalizing change and the reactions to change. These ideologies, which provided the maxims and slogans of the countless movements that agitated the nineteenth century and remain current today, are the "-isms": liberalism, radicalism, socialism, communism, conservatism, nationalism. We will presently meet their counterparts in the world of art: Romanticism, Realism, Impressionism, and the rest.

The element that all of these ideologies had in common was dissatisfaction with a status quo in which the past lingered, and disagreement about how it should be corrected—that is, modernized. For the arts, this meant continuing debate over the relative values of the "traditional" and the "modern"—a debate restimulated as each new style was itself rapidly superseded by yet a newer one. This rapid appearance and obsolescence of a variety of artistic styles (analogous to the concurrent rapid turnover in types of mechanically produced commodities and to the quick progression of scientific and technological discoveries and inventions) transformed painting, the graphic arts, sculpture, and architecture so radically that the transformations amounted to a dismantling of tradition altogether and the appearance of something utterly novel. This process was the reverse of the development of science, which built on its tradition in largely unbroken continuity within the expanding language of mathematics.

The nineteenth-century artist had to face formidable changes on all sides. The church and the secular nobility were replaced as sources of artists' commissions by the triumphant middle class, the national state, and national academies. The uncultivated taste of a vast new audience, concerned, above all, with money and property and guided and manipulated by professional critics writing in the press created an uncertain and risky market for the artist working alone. Competition forced crowds of artists, whose numbers had more than doubled since the end of the previous century, to bid for the public's attention by flattering its taste. Like small, independent capitalists with their own stocks and stores, artists took chances in the market, aiming to please. If they were unwilling to take such chances, they risked the suspicion and the hostility of the public. These developments contributed to the gradual alienation of artists and the emergence of their often isolated and difficult situation in modern society.

Artists who were dissatisfied with standards of public taste and the kind of art designed to satisfy it used their own work and the writings of friendly critics to protest what they viewed as the degeneration of art into shallow entertainment. Imbued with the romantic ideals of self-expression, they called for a new, highly individualistic vision, one that was original and sincere, free from the sentimentalities, trivialities, and hypocrisies of conventional taste. Rejecting the authority of prevailing taste and of the institutions backing it, these artists claimed the right to an authority of their own, often with a sense of mission not unlike that of the seer and prophet; they would restore or re-create art. These artists tended to group or be grouped into parties or "movements" analogous to those in political life and recognizable by their opposition to the status quo. Whichever side they occupied in the complex, stylistic dialogues that took place, they were, in fact, debating in a new way the very nature of art and the function of the artist. As it turns out, they were dealing with the question of a *modern* art, one fundamentally different from that of the past, even though it might be constructed out of the "tradition" of the past to a greater or lesser degree.

The Tradition, as we will refer to it, was the whole corpus of art acknowledged to be good or great: the art of Greece and Rome, of the Renaissance, and of the Baroque. Such art spanned a stylistic spectrum from "classical idealism" to "optical realism" and seemed to exhaust the physical possibilities of the media as well as their thematic content. The Tradition was first challenged and, by the end of the century, rejected for an art "of our own times," a modern art. In the course of the century, challenge was met by response, and response by new challenge, so that the modes of traditional and modern were interwoven, combined, recombined, and separated by independent artists, producing a bewildering plurality of individual styles not easily categorized. Although we will use the conventional categories of art history—Romanticism, Realism, Impressionism, and so on—as markers, these terms cannot help but be indefinite and often misleading. What we *do* perceive by mid-century is a bifurcation not seen previously in the arts. It is a bifurcation of emphasis and purpose: one branch, optical realism, is linked to scientific discoveries about the physical world and to the development of photography and the motion picture; the other branch is connected with psychological and spiritual investigations leading to the abstract art of the twentieth century. The former is directed to the public and popular taste; the latter is aimed, for the most part, at a select, specially trained audience.

Various factors contributed to this historical division. Artists in the nineteenth century were confronted by three innovations that fatefully affected their craft: the camera, the mass-produced print, and the printed reproduction. The almost infinite proliferation of the products of these new media flooded the world with images that became formidable rivals of the unique work made by hand. In a way, the nineteenth-century artist was technologically displaced, much as the manuscript illuminator of the sixteenth century had been displaced by the printer. Moreover, the collective techniques of an industrial age forced nineteenth-century artists, as individual craftspeople, to analyze their function and to study closely the physical nature of their medium. Photographic images challenged the iconic function of traditional art by accurately capturing the optical world of human experience. Toward the end of the century, artists found themselves using the elements of line, shape, and color to represent their private world, the realm of imagination and feeling. The functions of the artist and of the artist's medium were decisively transformed by the modern world, and the art of that world broke firmly away from the Tradition.

NINETEENTH-CENTURY ROMANTICISM

In art, stylistic change never occurs neatly at the beginning of a new century. The revolutions that ushered in the modern world were accompanied by a widespread agitation of spirit, a kind of collective mental revolution—the emotional response to accelerating change. We have already been introduced to Romanticism in the eighteenth century and have examined its onset, its rise, and the problems of defining its period. In the nineteenth century, Romanticism continued to center around concerns for the abrogation of traditions, institutions, and privileges that were seen to have impeded human progress. Romanticism as a view of life, as well as a state of mind, inherited the Enlightenment's admiration of nature and the natural over convention and artifice, and continued to uncover history as a storehouse of natural lessons for correcting the defects of the present.

The emphasis on human rights in the public sphere was accompanied by the assertion of the value of feeling and emotion in private experience. Truth could be sought and found inwardly more surely than in doctrines of religion or rules of reason; Romanticism's orientation was subjective, and the intensity of the religious and mystical emotions associated with traditional Christianity could live on in the individual, with or without reference to specific creeds. The ardor of Romanticism was also religious, as were its soul-searching and truth-seeking through feeling and vision. The pantheistic union of the soul with nature—nature, for many, replacing the Christian God—was part of the Romantic ritual and excitement. T. E. Hulme defined Romanticism as "spilled religion": the old doctrinal vessels were broken, and their volatile contents spread widely and indefinitely.

The contents spread indefinitely, because no fixed doctrines for Romanticism could really be identified. How could such doctrines be defined in a world of decisive change in which all that was fixed, dogmatic, and categorical was challenged? On issues of the day, we can find Romantic spirits on opposing sides: progressive and conservative, democratic and monarchistic, religious and agnostic, hoping and despairing, satanic and angelic. The world of history, for example, in the process of being systematically recovered, could be valued as serving the hopes of new nations by showing them the heroic past, by supplying them with an identity. Or it could be regarded as a nightmare from which the present was trying to wake: "The world," wrote Percy Bysshe Shelley, in *Hellas,* "is weary of the past / Oh, might it die, or rest at last!"

Romanticism, protean as the modern world it reflected and, like the modern mind, incorrigibly romantic, had one firm conviction at its center. This belief was the identification of reality as rooted in the self, not in the external, man-made world. The search for this identity—the revelation and expression of it in art and life—was the objective and meaning of personal existence. Jean Jacques Rousseau preached the religion of the value of the individual in a single assertion: "I may be no better than anyone else; at least I am different." For the Romantic, it was the difference that counted.

Despite the plurality of styles in the nineteenth century, the artist's claim of autonomy was a constant, and this individualism sometimes resulted in alienation. The right to be an individual authority justified this procedure, even when an artist chose to accept the authority of, say, the academies. The broad right to select a mode of expression was then matched by the broad range of materials supplied by the Tradition, which the artist could either adopt or turn aside. The artist's motives might be various: to stir an audience with drama or melodrama; to reconstruct historical incident; to exhibit the beauty of the human figure, a landscape, a still life, or other traditional subjects; to present the genre of modern life; to paint the inventions of a fertile imagination; to externalize dreams as images, private and strange. The subjects, modes of representation, and techniques of the artists of the nineteenth century, various as they may have been, were all derived from a common attitude and claim of autonomy.

In this earlier century of the modern era, then, much of the subject matter in art was mainly romantic, in that the artist stressed dramatic emotion or ideal beauty, or combinations of these with other material. Romantic artists discovered their themes in history, literature, nature and religion, the exotic, and the esoteric, and drew on the pictorial modes of the Tradition—the Classical, the Renaissance, and the Baroque. Romantic architects recovered the historical styles of Western architecture and those of the non-European world and paraded them dramatically. Historical and literary material, often produced with a photographic realism, predominated. It is this retrospective subject matter, seeming separate or escaping from the specifically modern scene, that, in part, invites the use of the term *Romanticism*. Yet we will see that some aspects of Romanticism survived into the twentieth century and that much contemporary art has been, in essence, subjective—an intellectual and emotional reflection of challenging and continual change.

Continuation of Neoclassicism

The Romantic Neoclassical taste for the more or less exact replication of Greek and Roman buildings, as we have seen it expressed in Thomas Jefferson's University of Virginia buildings (FIG. 20-44), spread throughout Europe and America. From Virginia to Munich, from Paris to St. Petersburg, Neoclassicism was associated with everything from revolutionary aspirations for democratic purity to imperial ambitions for unshakable authority. In France, the early years of the century were dominated by Napoleon Bonaparte, a figure of romantically enlightened temperament and enormous ego, who embraced all links with the Classical past as sources of symbolic authority for his short-lived imperial state. La Madeleine (FIG. **21-1**) was briefly intended to be a "temple of glory" for Napoleon's armies and a monument to the newly won glories of France. Begun as a church in 1807, at the height of Napoleon's power (some three years after he proclaimed himself emperor), the structure reverted again to a church after his defeat and long before its completion in 1842. Designed by PIERRE VIGNON (1763–1828) as an octastyle peripteral temple, its high podium and the broad flight of stairs leading to a deep porch simulate the buildings of the time of the first caesars, making La Madeleine a symbolic link between the Napoleonic and the Roman empires. Curiously, the building's Classical shell surrounds an interior that is covered by a sequence of three domes, a feature found in Byzantine and Aquitanian Romanesque churches, as though this Christian church had been clothed in the costume of pagan Rome.

Under Napoleon, Classical models were apparent in all the arts. The emperor's favorite sculptor was ANTONIO CANOVA (1757–1822), who somewhat reluctantly left a successful career in Italy to settle in Paris and serve the emperor. Once in France, Canova became an admirer of Napoleon and made numerous portraits, all in the Classical mode, of the emperor and his family. Perhaps the best known of these works is the portrait of Napoleon's sister, *Pauline Borghese as Venus* (FIG. **21-2**). The sensuous pose and form of Canova's figure recall the Greek sculpture of Praxiteles (FIG. 5-62), while the sharply detailed rendering of the couch and drapery echo a later Hellenistic style. With remarkable discretion, Canova created a daring image of seductive charm, generalized enough to personify the goddess of love, yet still suggestive of the living person. Despite a lingering Rococo charm, this work shows the artist to have been

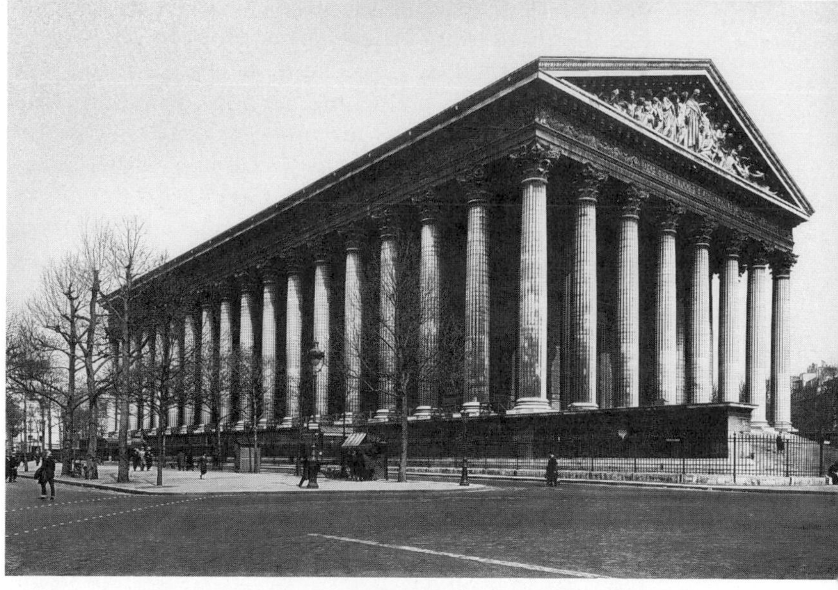

21-1 PIERRE VIGNON, La Madeleine, Paris, 1807–1842.

21-2 ANTONIO CANOVA, *Pauline Borghese as Venus*, 1808. Marble, life size. Galleria Borghese, Rome.

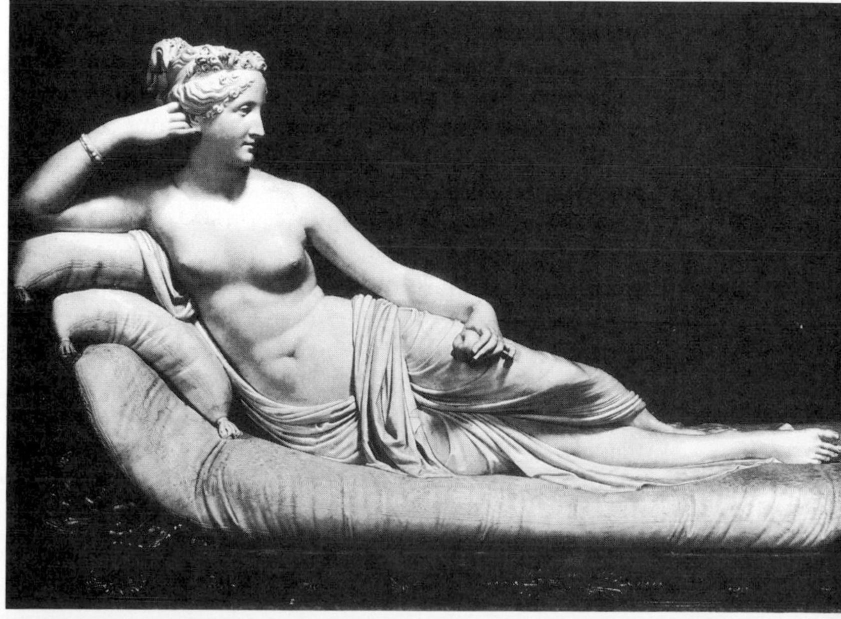

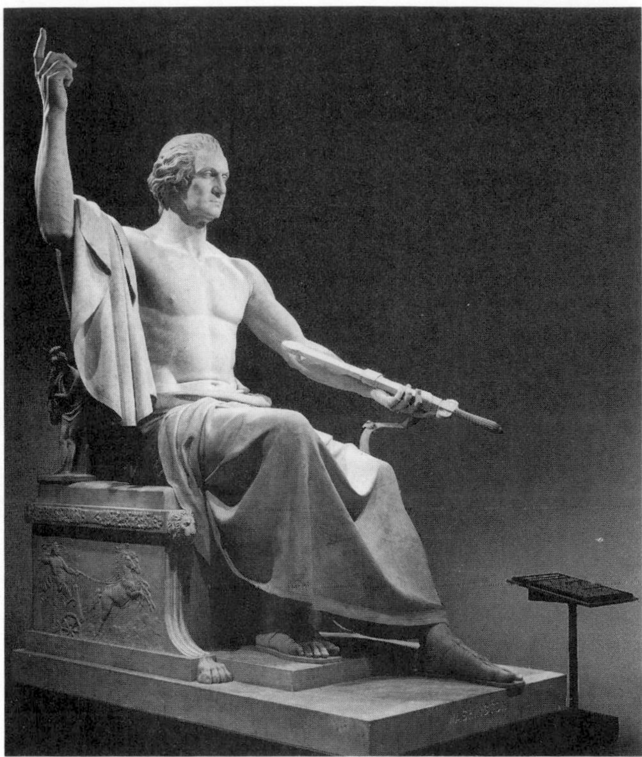

21-3 Horatio Greenough, *George Washington*, 1832–1841. Marble, approx. 11′ 4″ high. National Museum of American Art, Smithsonian Institution, Washington, D.C.

firmly Neoclassical in his approach. Canova was considered to be the greatest sculptor of his time, but suffered greatly in reputation later. Current criticism has restored him somewhat, although he still carries, as the most typical of the Neoclassicists, something of the burden of negative criticism leveled against this often doctrinaire style.

The defects of the Neoclassical style are apparent in a statue of *George Washington* (FIG. **21-3**) by the American sculptor Horatio Greenough (1805–1852). Here, the Neoclassical style Jefferson had championed so successfully for the architecture of the new democracy (FIG. 20-43) turned out to be less suitable for commemorative portraits. Commissioned by the United States Congress to honor Washington as the country's first president, the sculptor used as a model for the head a popular bust of Washington by Houdon (a work with the same lively realism as Houdon's *Voltaire Seated* [FIG. 20-25]). In the body of the statue, Greenough aimed at the monumental majesty inspired by a lost, but famous, sculpture by Phidias of the Greek god Zeus. The sheathed sword, offered hilt forward, was intended to symbolize "Washington the peacemaker," rather than "Washington the revolutionary war general." The representation of the "father of his country," deified as a half-naked pagan god, however, was, at the time, beyond the taste of the American public. As social observer and commentator Alexis de Tocqueville wrote: "Americans will habitually prefer the useful to the beautiful, and they will require that the beautiful be useful." The statue was considered to be a failure in Greenough's time precisely because it manifested, more than many sculptures of the Neoclassical style, the contradictions that sometimes develop when idealistic and realistic illusion meet. Canova appeared to harmonize these two trends; Greenough put them in opposition. Although Greenough's statue was never thrown into the Potomac river, "to hide it from the world," as one Congressman suggested, it also was never placed in its intended site beneath the Capitol dome. Today, the work is more highly regarded and is displayed at the National Museum of American History in Washington, D.C. While to some, it may seem stiff, cold, or simply unconvincing, it does have an imperious majesty appropriate to the national memory of its subject.

Eclectic Romanticism in Architecture and Sculpture

While Romantic Neoclassicism flourished, the Romantic Gothic taste begun in the eighteenth century by Walpole and others, in places like Strawberry Hill, was by no means extinguished. On the contrary, its development paralleled that of Romantic Neoclassicism and took on new significance in connection with religious meanings and the century's rising tide of nationalism. In 1802, the eminent French writer François René de Chateaubriand published his influential *Genius of Christianity*, a defense of religion on the grounds not of its truth, but of its beauty and mystery. A work such as this was in direct opposition to the skeptical rationalism of the Enlightenment and many of the ideals of the French Revolution. In this treatise, Chateaubriand says, "There is nothing of beauty, sweetness, or greatness in life that does not partake in mystery." (How different this statement is from the Age of Reason's injunction, "Be thou clear!") Christian ritual and Christian art, born of mystery, could move adherents by their strange and ancient beauty. Gothic cathedrals, according to Chateaubriand, were translations into stone of the sacred groves of the Druidical Gauls and must be cherished as manifestations of France's holy history. In his view, the history of Christianity and that of France merged in the Middle Ages. As the nineteenth century gathered the documentary materials of European history in stupendous historiographic enterprises, each nation came to value its past as evidence of the validity of its ambitions and claims to greatness. The art of the remote past was now appreciated as a product of racial and national genius. In 1773, Goethe, praising the Gothic cathedral of Strasbourg in *Of German Architecture,* announced the theme by declaring that the German art scholar "should thank God to be able to proclaim aloud that it is German architecture, our architecture"; he also bid the observer, "approach and recognize the deepest feeling of truth and beauty of proportion emanating from a strong, vigorous German soul."

Modern nationalism thus helped to bring about a new evaluation of the art in each country's past. In London, when the old Houses of Parliament burned in 1834, the Parliamentary Commission decreed that designs for the new building should be either "Gothic or Elizabethan." CHARLES BARRY (1795–1860), with the assistance of A. W. N. PUGIN (1812–1852), submitted the winning design (FIG. **21-4**) in 1835. By this time, style had become a matter of selection from the historical past. Barry had traveled widely in Europe, Greece, Turkey, Egypt, and Palestine, studying the architecture in each place. He preferred the Renaissance Classical styles, but he had designed some earlier Neo-Gothic buildings, and Pugin influenced him successfully in the direction of English Late Gothic. Pugin was one of a group of English artists and critics who saw moral purity and spiritual authenticity in the religious architecture of the Middle Ages and glorified the careful medieval craftsmen who had produced it. The Industrial Revolution was now flooding the market with cheaply made and ill-designed commodities. Handicraft was being replaced by the machine. Many, like Pugin, believed in the necessity of restoring the old craftsmanship, which had honesty and quality. The design of the Houses of Parliament, however, is not genuinely Gothic, despite its picturesque tower groupings (the Clock Tower, containing Big Ben, at one end, and the Victoria Tower at the other). The building has a formal axial plan and a kind of Palladian regularity beneath its Tudor detail. Pugin himself is reported to have said of it: "All Grecian, Sir. Tudor details on a classic body."*

While the Neoclassical and Neo-Gothic styles were dominant in the early nineteenth century, exotic new styles of all types soon began to appear, in part as a result of European imperialism. Great Britain's forays into all areas of the world, particularly India, had exposed English culture to a broad range of non-Western artistic styles. The Royal Pavilion (FIG. **21-5**), designed by JOHN NASH (1752–1835), exhibits a wide variety of these styles. Nash was an established architect, known for Neoclassical buildings in London, when he was asked to design a royal pleasure palace in the seaside resort of Brighton for the prince regent (later King George IV). The structure's fantastic exterior is a confection of Islamic domes, minarets, and screens that has been called "Indian Gothic," while the decor of the interior rooms was influenced by sources ranging from Greece and Egypt to China. Underlying the exotic façade is a cast-iron skeleton, an early (if hidden) use of this material in noncommercial building. Nash also put this metal to fanciful use in its own right, creating life-size, cast-iron palm-tree columns to support the Royal Pavilion's kitchen ceiling. The building, an appropriate enough backdrop for gala throngs pursuing pleasure by the seaside, served as the prototype for numerous playful

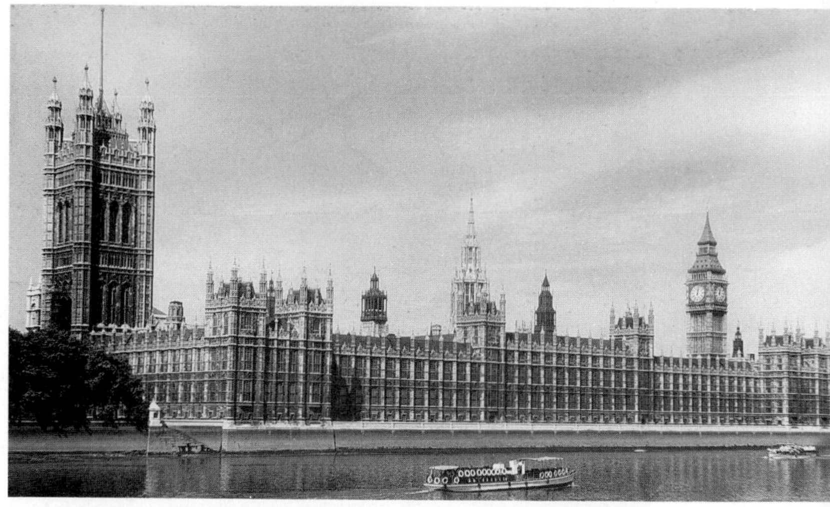

21-4 CHARLES BARRY and A. W. N. PUGIN, Houses of Parliament, London, designed 1835.

21-5 JOHN NASH, Royal Pavilion, Brighton, England, 1815–1818.

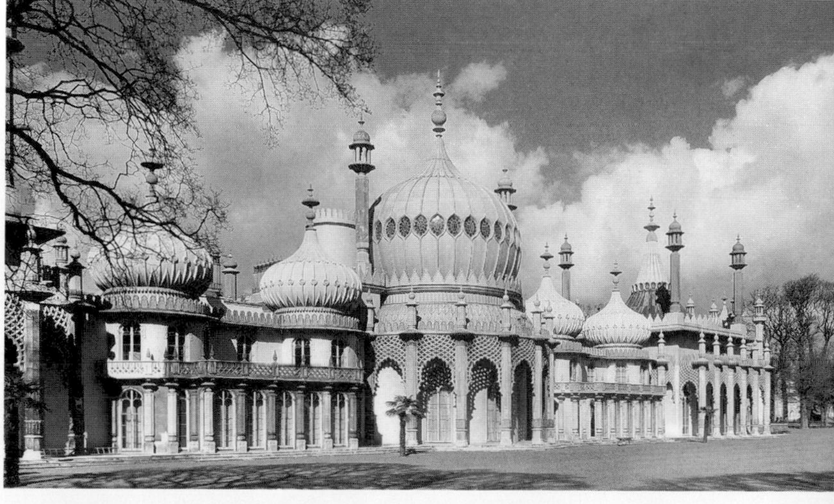

*In Nikolaus Pevsner, *An Outline of European Architecture* (Baltimore, MD: Penguin, 1960), p. 627.

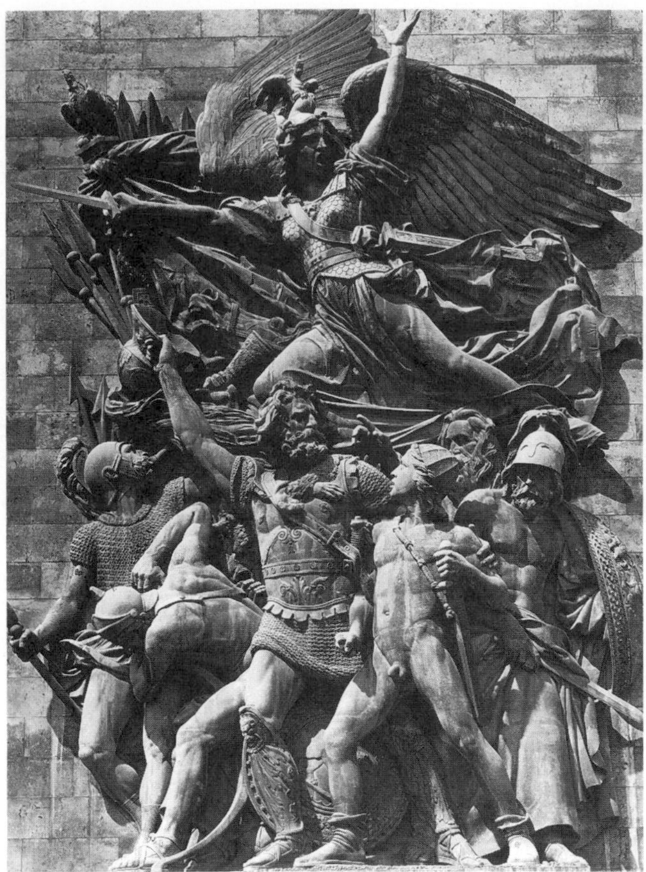

21-6 François Rude, *La Marseillaise,* Arc de Triomphe, Paris, 1833–1836. Approx. 42′ × 26′.

architectural exaggerations still to be found in European and American resorts.

Among the styles renewed with enthusiasm to express heroic and dramatic themes was the Baroque. In Paris, the Baroque was merged with a certain Classical rigor in *La Marseillaise* (fig. **21-6**), a sculpture by François Rude (1784–1855) that exhibited the national glories of France's more recent past. The colossal figures, in bold relief against the Arc de Triomphe, represent French volunteers leaving to defend the borders of France against the foreign enemies of the revolution in 1792. The volunteers are dressed in Classical armor, and the Roman war goddess Bellona (who may be thought of here as La Marseillaise, or the Goddess of Liberty) shouts the battle cry as she rallies the militia forward. The Classical accessories do not disguise the essentially Baroque qualities of the group: densely packed masses, jagged contours, violence of motion. If we were to think here of the Classical at all, it would be of the "post-classical baroque" of Hellenistic works like the great frieze at Pergamon (fig. 5-78).

A different variation of the renewed Baroque taste for the exotic is found in *Jaguar Devouring a Hare* (fig. **21-7**) by Antoine Louis Barye (1795–1875). Painful as the subject is, Barye draws us irresistibly to it by the work's fidelity to brute nature. The belly-crouching cat's swelling muscles, hunched shoulders, and tense spine—even the switch of the tail—tell of the sculptor's long sessions observing the animals in the Jardin des Plantes in Paris. This work shows the influence of the vast new geographies opening before the naturalistic eyes and temper of the nineteenth century, while demonstrating Romanticism's obsession with strong emotion and untamed nature. Nineteenth-century sensibility generally prevented animal ferocity from being shown in human beings but enthusiastically accepted its portrayal in Romantic depictions of wild beasts. Barye's portrayal of a beast with its dead prey contrasts with the more sublime depiction by Stubbs of a ferocious struggle to the death between two more equal natural enemies (fig. 20-46).

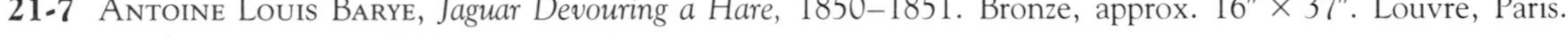

21-7 Antoine Louis Barye, *Jaguar Devouring a Hare,* 1850–1851. Bronze, approx. 16″ × 37″. Louvre, Paris.

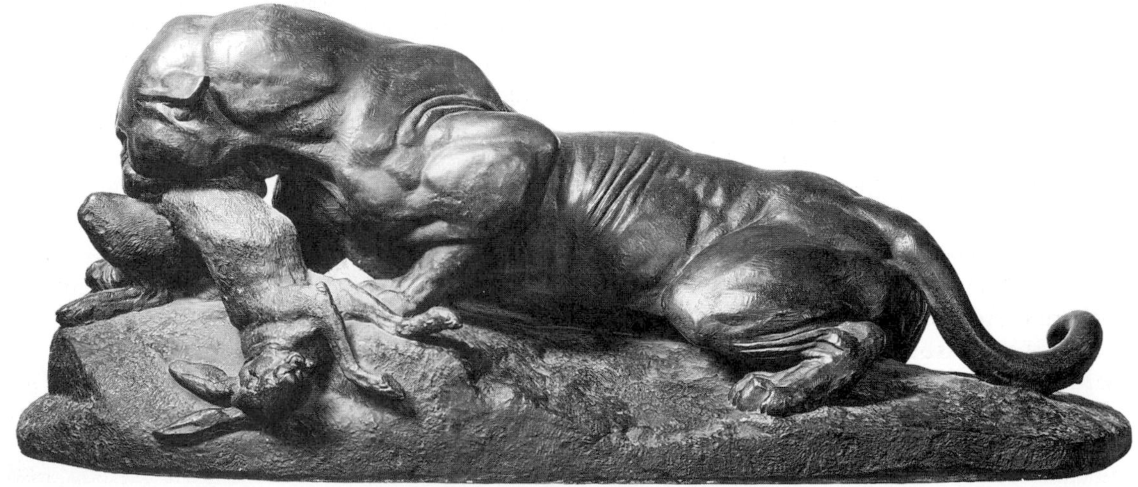

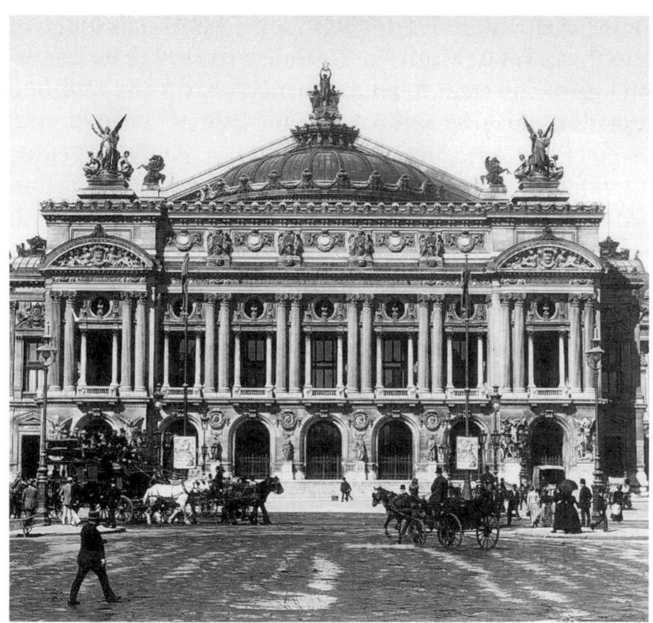

21-8 J. L. Charles Garnier, the Opéra, Paris, 1861–1874.

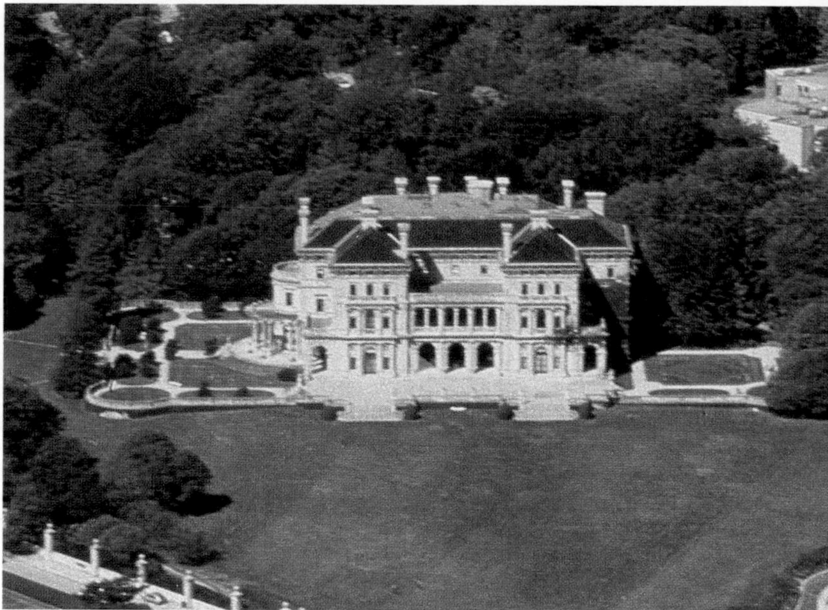

21-9 Richard Morris Hunt, The Breakers, Newport, Rhode Island, 1892.

The Baroque was also adapted in architecture, to convey a new grandeur worthy of the riches acquired during this age of expansion by those who heeded the advice of the French historian and statesman François Guizot to "get rich." The opulence reflected in the lives of these few was mirrored in the Paris Opéra (FIG. **21-8**), designed by J. L. Charles Garnier (1825–1898). The Opéra parades a festive and spectacularly theatrical Neo-Baroque front that should be compared with the façade of the Louvre (FIG. 19-64), which it mimics to a degree. The interior is ingeniously planned for the convenience of human traffic. Intricate arrangements of corridors, vestibules, stairways, balconies, alcoves, entrances, and exits facilitate easy passage throughout the building and provide space for entertainment and socializing at intermissions. The Baroque grandeur of the layout and of the ornamental appointments of the opera house proclaims and enhances its function as a gathering place for glittering audiences in an age of conspicuous wealth. The style was so attractive to the moneyed classes who supported the arts that theaters and opera houses continued to reflect the design of the Paris Opéra until World War I transformed society.

Near the end of the nineteenth century, Richard Morris Hunt (1828–1895) brought European Baroque and Renaissance style to the mansions he designed for members of America's "aristocracy"—entrepreneurs and industrialists whose enormous wealth had been derived from the profits of the era's new industries. Hunt had developed his architectural knowledge through study in Switzerland and Paris. The Breakers (FIG. **21-9**), built by Hunt for Cornelius Vanderbilt II, is a splendid private palace in Newport, Rhode Island, a favorite summer vacation spot for the affluent. Occupying a glorious promontory, the residence resembles a sixteenth-century Italian palazzo more than a large summer cottage. The interior rooms are grand in scale and sumptuously rich in decor, each having its own variation of Classical columns, painted ceilings, lavish fabrics, and sculptured furbelows. The entry hall, rising some 45 feet above the majestic main stairway, signals the opulence of the rooms beyond. This hall and most of the main rooms of the house offer a magnificent view over the grounds and the ocean, a view assured by Hunt's siting of the building. As Garnier's Opéra influenced theater design well into the twentieth century, so the grandeur and lavishness of Hunt's palatial domestic style were to remain popular with the ultra-rich until World War I shattered the bright period known as *la belle époque.* As we will see, however, architecture at this time was also developing along a very different line, one that would break finally with the Romantic styles to forge a new direction based on other themes and materials of the industrial and technological age.

Romanticism in Figure Painting

Painting, in the early nineteenth century, proved to be an extraordinarily sensitive medium for the romantically subjective, personal expression of the time. In France, Jacques Louis David demanded that his pupils select their subjects from Plutarch, the ancient author of *Lives of the Great Greeks and Romans* and a principal source of standard Neoclassical subject

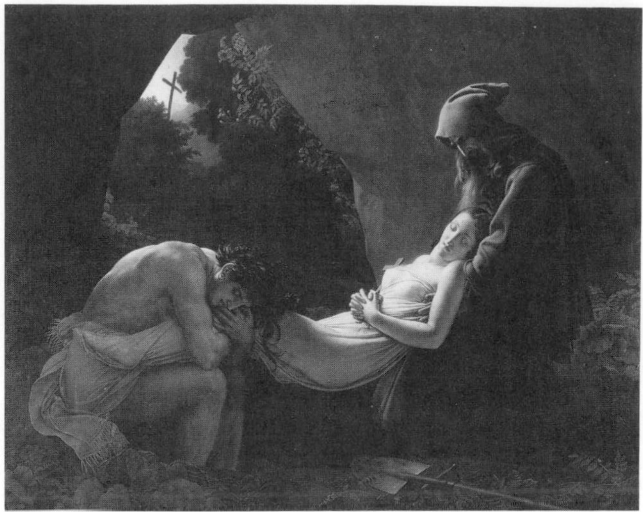

21-10 Anne Louis Girodet-Trioson, *The Burial of Atala,* 1808. Approx. 6′ 11″ × 8′ 9″. Louvre, Paris.

matter. David's students, however, often found their subjects elsewhere, and it was this distinction in subject matter that divided his style from the Romanticism of his successors.

One of David's students, Anne Louis Girodet-Trioson (1767–1824), turned to a popular novel by Chateaubriand (*Atala*) for the subject of his *Burial of Atala* (fig. **21-10**). This painting could be a set piece for Romanticism. Atala, sworn to lifelong virginity, falls passionately in love with a wild, young savage of the Carolina wilderness. Rather than break her oath, she commits suicide and is buried in the shadow of a cross by her grief-stricken lover. By representing the Holy Church in the person of the cloaked priest, Girodet daringly puts religion and sexual passion side by side, binding them with the theme of death and burial. Hopeless love, perished beauty, the grave, the purity of primitive life, and the consolation of religion are some of the Romantic themes Girodet successfully showed in this work. The picture's composite style combines classicizing contours and modeling with a dash of the erotic sweetness of the Rococo and the dramatic illumination of the Baroque. Unlike David's appeal to the feelings that manifest themselves in public action in the *Oath of the Horatii* (fig. 20-40), the appeal here is to the viewer's private world of fantasy and emotion. If David's purpose was to "electrify the soul," Girodet's was, in the language of Rousseau, to "wring the heart." The artist speaks here to our emotions, rather than inviting philosophical meditation or revealing some grand order of nature and form. The Romantic artist, above all else, wanted to excite the emotions of the audience.

Another pupil of David, the Baron Antoine Jean Gros (1771–1835), deviated from his master's teachings as much as Girodet did but in a much more influential way for the development of the Romantic style. In his *Pest House at Jaffa* (fig. **21-11**), painted in 1804,

21-11 Antoine Jean Gros, *Pest House at Jaffa,* 1804. Approx. 17′ 5″ × 23′ 7″. Louvre, Paris.

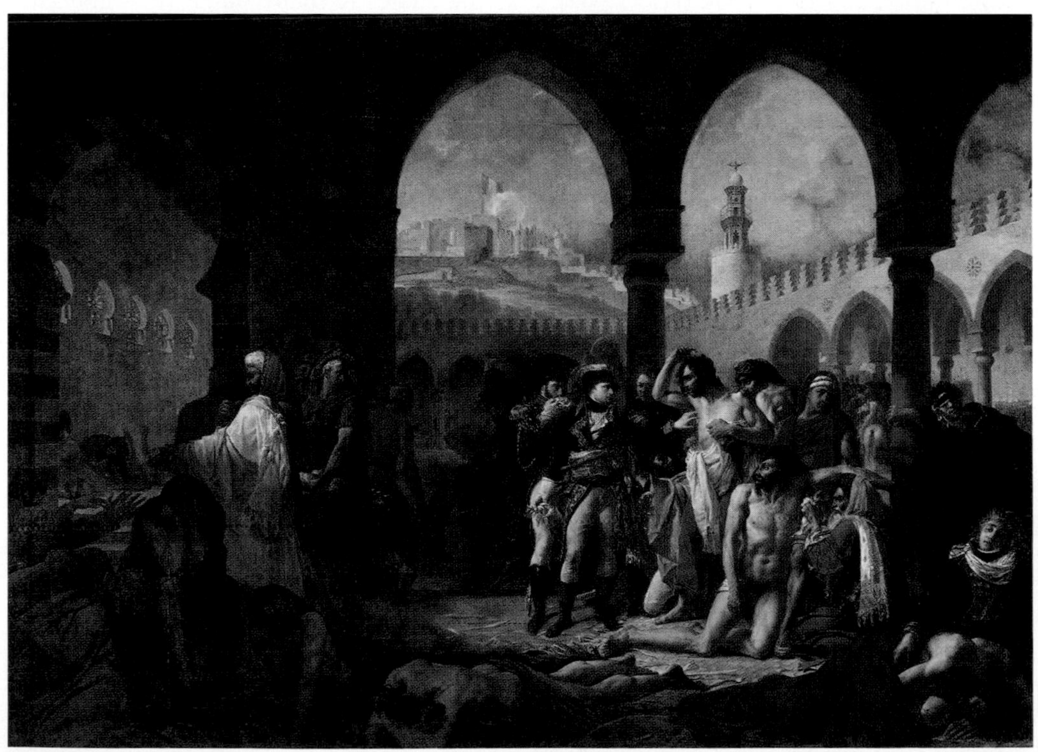

Gros took a then radically independent tack, sorting through and selecting numerous Baroque pictorial devices of light, shade, and perspective to create a dramatic tableau testifying to the superhuman power and glory of Napoleon Bonaparte. This work is similar to David's *Oath of the Horatii* in that both artists stage the action within an architectural enframement, deploying the figures in front of an arcade. Where David's arcade is Roman, however, Gros's is Moorish. The vista through Gros's arcade is of a distant landscape dominated by a fortress flying the French tricolor. Time has changed the setting, and the painter's means have changed to suit the present. In *Pest House,* Gros dismissed theoretical considerations of Classical balance and modeling by depicting Napoleon as a stage director might and making the fullest use of stage lighting and dramatic darkness to center attention on the figure of the chief protagonist. The result is the elevation of history painting to an art of almost religious significance and solemnity—one in which Napoleon, the Messiah of democracy, simultaneously plays the roles of Alexander, Christ, and Louis XIV.

Napoleon, portrayed here as the First Consul and not yet as Emperor Napoleon I, is at the end of the disastrous Egyptian campaign and in the process of retreating with his troops up the coast of Palestine (modern Israel). His army is stricken with the plague. He is shown visiting his sick and dying soldiers in a hospital in the ancient city of Jaffa. In the midst of the dead and dying, the fearless genius of the New Order touches the plague sores of a sick soldier, who stares at him in awe, as if he were the miracle-working Christ. Napoleon's staff officers cover their noses against the stench of the place, but the general is calm and unperturbed, like the king curing by the King's Touch. In the left foreground, men brood, crouch, and sprawl in a gloom of misery and anguish; these figures will be of special interest to later Romantic artists like Théodore Géricault and Eugène Delacroix. The entire scene is wrapped in the glamor of its Near Eastern setting. As in the work of Girodet, identifiable Romantic themes are evident—suffering and death, faith and personal heroism, the allure of distant places, patriotism. All of these held a certain appeal to the modern need for emotional stimulation.

THÉODORE GÉRICAULT (1791–1824) studied with an admirer of David (P. N. Guérin), but in the pupil the rigid Neoclassicism of the Davidian school receded to allow David's use of sharp light and shade to come to the fore. Géricault's work is also characterized by a maturing of the naturalistic element and further movement toward the dramatic presentation of contemporary events on huge canvases. For Géricault (unlike his predecessors), these events did not always demand a central hero. His masterpiece, *Raft of the Medusa* (FIG. **21-12**), shows these influences as well as those of Michelangelo and Peter Paul Rubens.

21-12 THÉODORE GÉRICAULT, *Raft of the Medusa,* 1818–1819. Approx. 16′ × 23′. Louvre, Paris.

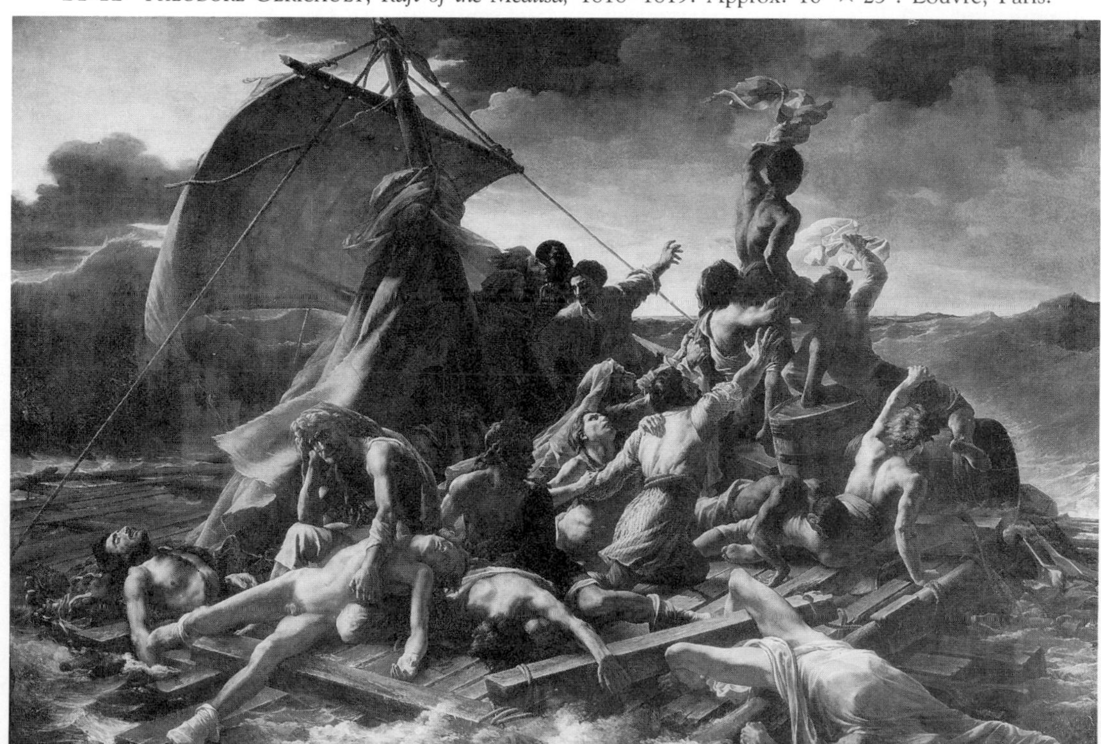

Géricault took for his subject the ordeal of the survivors of the French ship *Medusa,* which had foundered off the west coast of Africa in 1816, laden with Algerian immigrants. This incident was the result of tragic mismanagement and provoked scandal in France when the survivors were able to tell their stories. Géricault's depiction of the anguish of the event also was construed by the government as an outright political attack. The artist avoided showing the most horrific aspects of the tragedy—murder, cannibalism, and immense hardship—in choosing to depict the dramatic moment when the frantic castaways attempted to attract the attention of the distant ship that was eventually to rescue them. Fifteen survivors and several corpses are piled onto one another in every attitude of suffering, despair, and death (recalling Gros's *Pest House*) and are arranged in a powerful X-shaped composition. One light-filled diagonal axis stretches from bodies at the lower left up to the figure of the black man, raised on the shoulders of his comrades and waving a piece of cloth toward the horizon. The cross-axis descends from the storm clouds and dark, wind-filled sail at the upper left to the shadowed upper torso of the body trailing in the open sea.

Although Baroque devices abound, Géricault's use of shock tactics, stunning the viewer's sensibilities, amounted to something new—a new tone and intention that distinguished the "high" phase of Romanticism. In this phase, an instinct for the sublime and the terrible, qualities celebrated in the esthetic theory and art of the eighteenth century (see, for example, Fuseli's *Nightmare* [FIG. 20-47]), found sharpest expression in a method of reportorial accuracy far more stringent than that found in certain works by David (FIG. 20-41). The value Géricault placed on accuracy in *Raft of the Medusa* is indicated by the fact that he carried out prodigious research and completed numerous preliminary studies for the work, even going so far as to interview survivors of the wreck.

An interest in mental aberration, which contributed to the development of modern psychopathology later in the nineteenth century, was part of another Romantic fascination—an interest in the irregular and the abandoned. The inner storms that overthrow rationality could hardly fail to be of interest to the rebels against the Age of Reason. Géricault, like many of his contemporaries, examined the influence of mental states on the human face and believed, as others did, that a face accurately revealed character, especially in madness and at the instant of death. He made many studies of the inmates of hospitals and institutions for the criminally insane (indeed, he spent some time as a patient in such places), and he studied the severed heads of victims of the guillotine. Scientific and artistic curiosity were not easily separated from the morbidity of the Romantic interest in derangement and death. Géricault's *Insane Woman (Envy)* (FIG. **21-13**)—her mouth tense, her eyes red-rimmed with suffering—is one of several "portraits" of insane subjects that have a peculiar, hypnotic power and present the psychic facts with astonishing authenticity. *Insane Woman* is only another example of the increasingly realistic core of Romantic painting. The closer the Romantics became involved with nature, sane or mad, the more they hoped to get at the truth. For painting, this increasingly came to mean the *optical* truth, as well as the truth of "the way things are." Meanwhile, for the Romantic, the real was nature, wild and untamed. In Géricault's paintings, suffering, death, and madness amounted to nature itself, for nature, in the end, is formless and destructive.

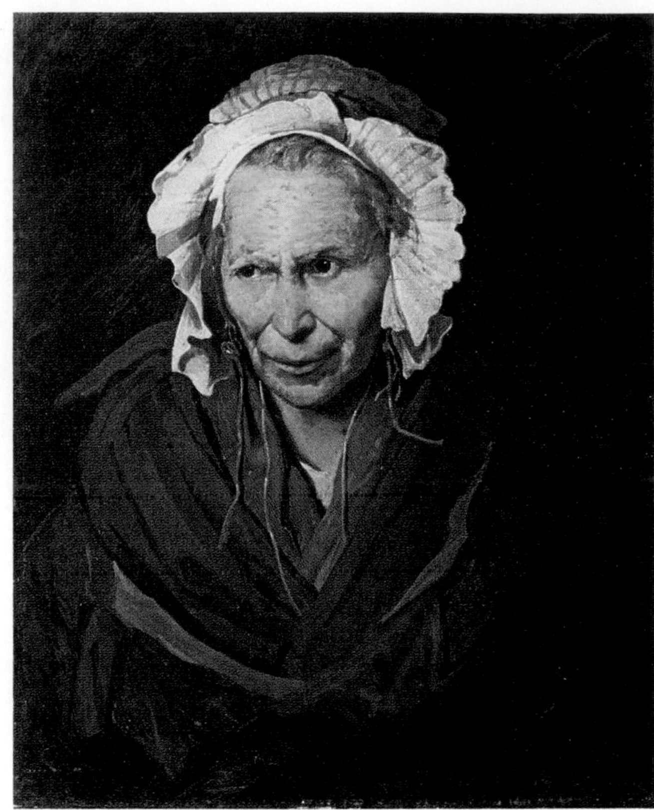

21-13 THÉODORE GÉRICAULT, *Insane Woman (Envy),* 1822–1823. Approx. 28″ × 21″. Musée des Beaux-Arts, Lyons.

JEAN AUGUSTE DOMINIQUE INGRES (1781–1867) arrived at David's studio after Gros and Girodet-Trioson had left to establish independent careers of their own. His study there was to be short-lived, however, as he soon broke with David on matters of style. This difference of opinion involved Ingres's adoption of a manner based on what he believed to be a truer and purer Greek style than that employed by David. The younger man adopted flat and linear forms approximating those found in Greek vase painting. In a good deal of Ingres's work, the figure is placed in the foreground, much like a piece of low-relief sculpture. The value Ingres placed on the flow of the contour is a characteristic of his style throughout his career. Contour, which is simply shaded line, was *everything* for Ingres, and drawing was the means of creating contour. Ingres has been credited with the famous slogan that became the battle cry of his school: "Drawing is the probity of art." In content, Ingres first adopted David's Neoclassical subjects, but he later also traversed the complete range of Romantic sources.

It was this rather strange mixture of artistic allegiances—the precise adherence to Classical form conveyed in Romantic content—that provoked one critic to ridicule Ingres's work as the vision of "a Chinaman wandering throughout the ruins of Athens." In both form and content, Ingres initially was seen by critics as a kind of rebel; they did not cease their attacks until the mid-1820s, when another enemy of the official style, Eugène Delacroix, appeared. Then they suddenly perceived that Ingres's art, despite its innovations and deviations, still contained many elements that adhered to the official Neoclassicism. Ingres soon was to become the leader of the academic forces in their battle against the "barbarism" of Géricault, Delacroix, and their "movement." Gradually, Ingres warmed to the role in which he had been cast by the critics, and he came to see himself as the conservator of good and true art, a protector of its principles against its would-be "destroyers."

While the painting drew acid criticism when first shown in 1814 ("She has three vertebrae too many," "No bone, no muscle, no life"), Ingres's *Grande Odalisque* (FIG. **21-14**) seems today to sum up the painter's artistic intentions. Ingres treats the figure in his own "sculpturesque style"—polished surfaces and simple, rounded volumes controlled by rhythmically flowing contours. The smoothness of the planes of the body is complemented by the broken, busy shapes of the drapery. His subject, the reclining nude figure, is traditional enough and goes back to Giorgione and Titian (FIG. 17-62), but by converting the figure to an odalisque (a member of a Turkish harem), Ingres made a strong concession to the contemporary Romantic taste for the exotic. The work also shows his admiration for Raphael in his borrowing of that master's type of female head, but Ingres did not draw only from the period of the High Renaissance. His figure's languid pose, her proportions (small head and elongated limbs), and the generally cool color scheme also reveal his debt to such Mannerists as Parmagianino (FIG. 17-41). Often criticized for not being a colorist, Ingres, in fact, had a superb color sense. It is true that he did not seem to think of his paintings primarily in terms of their color, as did Delacroix, but he did far more than simply tint his drawings for emphasis, as recommended by the Academy. In his best paintings, Ingres created color and tonal relationships so tasteful and subtle as to render them unforgettable.

Although he always aspired to become a history painter in the academic sense, Ingres never really was successful with multifigured compositions. He was at

21-14 JEAN AUGUSTE DOMINIQUE INGRES, *Grande Odalisque*, 1814. Approx. 35″ × 64″. Louvre, Paris.

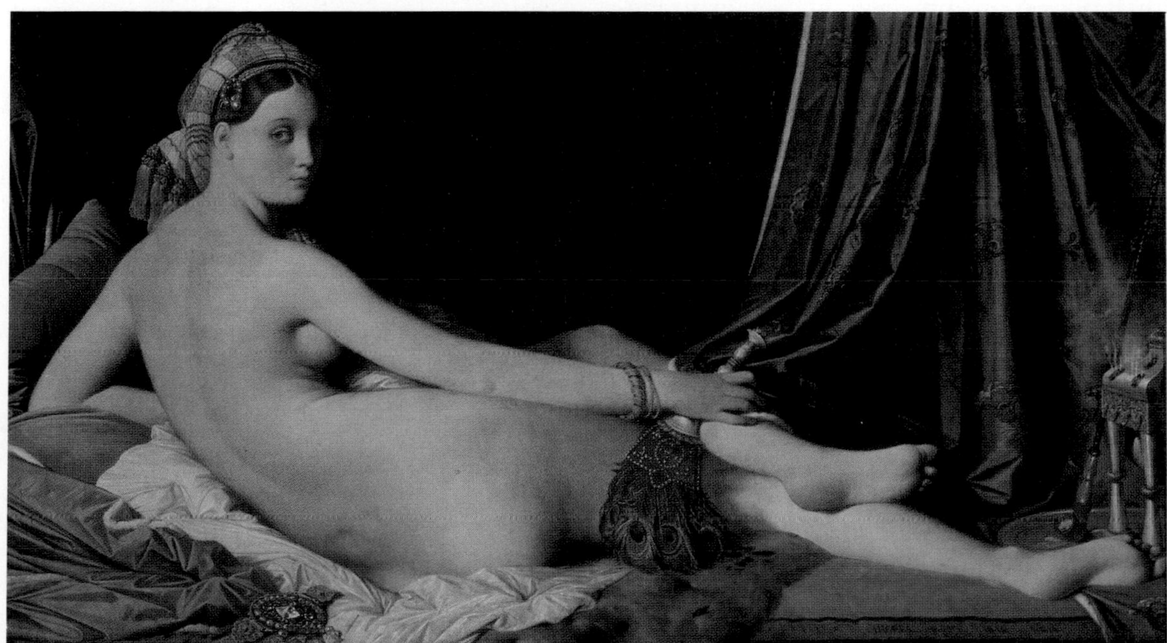

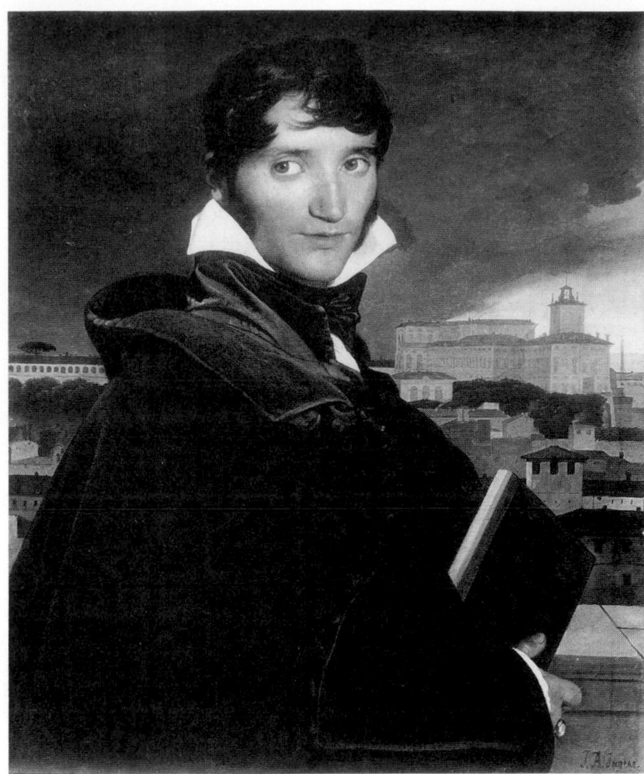

21-15 JEAN AUGUSTE DOMINIQUE INGRES, *François Marius Granet,* 1807. Approx. 28″ × 24″. Musée Granet, Aix-en-Provence.

his best with single figures and portraits. It is as a portraitist that he must be ranked among the greatest masters in a field that would soon be dominated by the camera. The portrait of his friend, the painter *François Marius Granet* (FIG. **21-15**), is not by itself sufficient to demonstrate Ingres's great distinction in this genre. It does show, however, his skill in arranging the pose and adjusting the costume to highlight Granet's sensitively introspective face and cap of picturesquely tousled hair. In this work, Ingres infused a clear Neoclassical style with a Romantic energy, an energy heightened by the dramatically draped cape and the stormy sky threatening the city in the background. In his portraits, as with his nudes, Ingres also contrasted the simple and regular volume of the head with the broken, irregular, and complicated folds of costume. His apparently cool detachment from his models, and his search for "pure form" commend him to the twentieth-century taste for the "abstract."

The history of nineteenth-century painting in its first sixty years has often been interpreted as a contest between two major artists—Ingres, the draftsman, and Delacroix, the colorist. Their dialogue reached back to the end of the seventeenth century in the quarrel between the Poussinistes and the Rubénistes, a quarrel most recently alluded to in the discussion of Rigaud and Watteau (FIGS. 20-4 and 20-5). The Poussinistes were conservative defenders of academism who held drawing to be superior to color, while the Rubénistes proclaimed color's importance over line (the quality of line being more intellectual and thus more restrictive than color). While their differences were clear, Ingres and his great rival Delacroix, in the end, complemented rather than contradicted each other, their work being a part of the great Romantic dialogue.

A comparison of Ingres's pencil portrait of the great violin virtuoso Niccolò Paganini (FIG. **21-16**) with Delacroix's painted version of the same personality (FIG. **21-17**) discloses the difference in approach that separated the two artists. Both painters were passionately fond of music, and Ingres was a creditable violin amateur who knew Paganini personally. His portrait, executed with that marvelously crisp precision of descriptive line that we find in all of his pencil portraits, is quite literal, relative to Delacroix's. Ingres gives us the man's appearance and public deportment—one might say his official likeness—enhanced by a suggestive characterization and sense of setting.

21-16 JEAN AUGUSTE DOMINIQUE INGRES, *Paganini,* 1819. Pencil drawing, approx. 12″ × 8½″. Louvre, Paris.

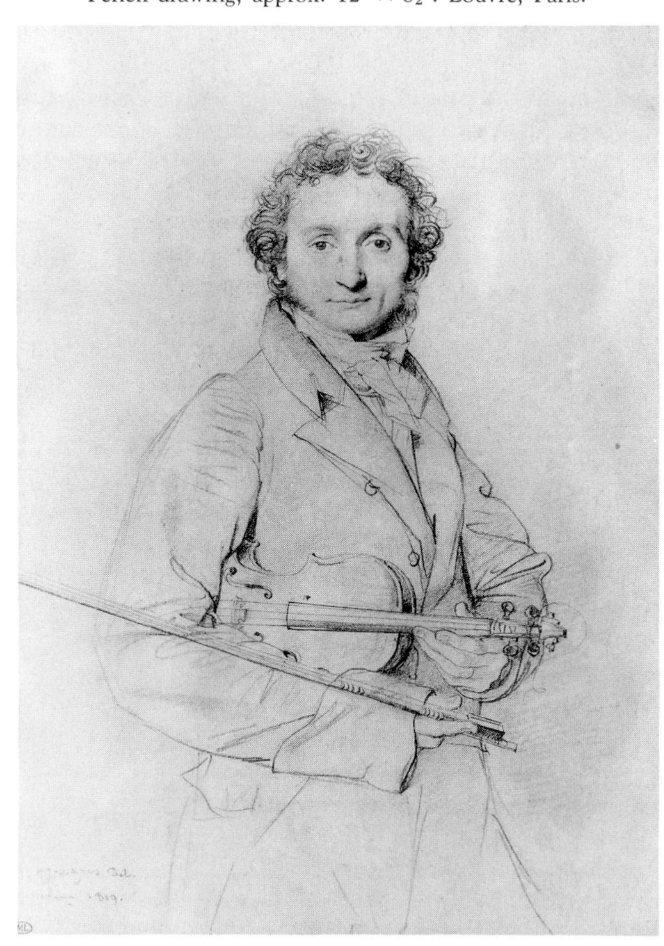

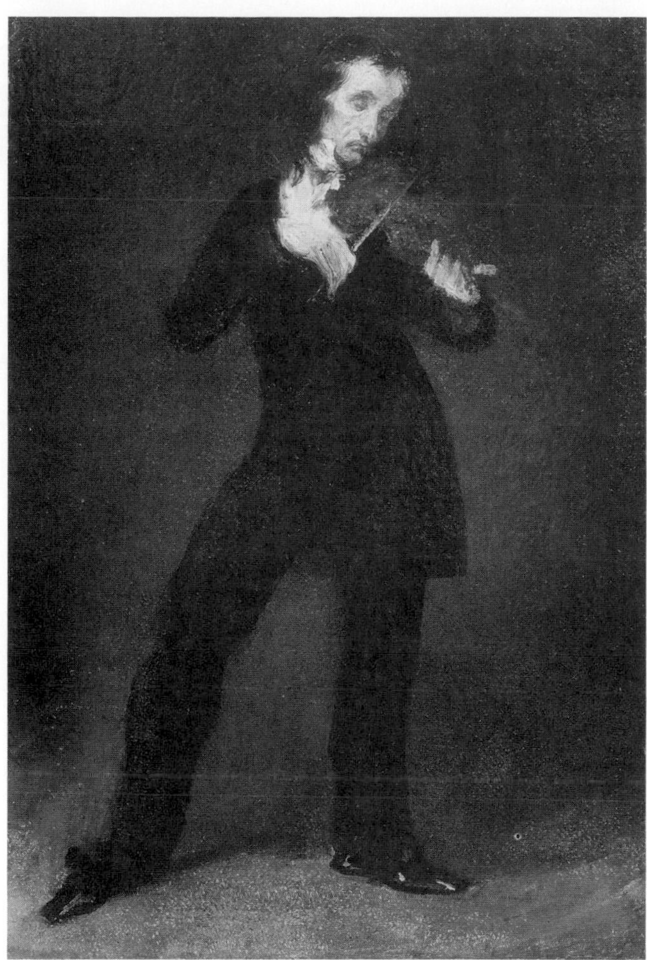

21-17 EUGÈNE DELACROIX, *Paganini*, c. 1832. Approx. 17″ × 11½″. The Phillips Collection, Washington, D.C.

Paganini, sharing a certain fragility and suppleness with his violin and bow, seems about to make his introductory obeisance to his audience. Above all, Ingres's portrait is *formal*, as is his subject, face to face with the public world; it is a graceful, not a stiff formality, however. Delacroix's *Paganini* presents a likeness not of the virtuoso's *form* but of his *performance*. Forgetting his audience, no longer in formal confrontation with his listeners, Paganini yields himself completely to the whirlwind of his own inspiration, which envelopes his reedlike frame, making it vibrate in tune to the quivering strings of his instrument. Delacroix tries to suggest the portrait, as it were, of Paganini's music, as it plays to his own ear and spirit. Where Ingres gave us the outside aspect of his subject and tried to perfect the form as presented to the eye, Delacroix represented the inner substance—the musician transformed by his music—in an attempt to realize the truth as given to the imagination.

While critics now regard both masters as equally great, it was this celebration of the imagination, the faculty that captures the essential in life and transforms mundane experience, that defined the fundamental difference between Ingres and EUGÈNE DELACROIX (1798–1863). Delacroix called the art of Ingres "the complete expression of an incomplete intellect," incomplete because it was unleavened with imagination. In a passage from his famous *Journal*, Delacroix wrote: "Baudelaire . . . says that I bring back to painting . . . the feeling which delights in the terrible. He is right."* Delacroix, who knew and admired Géricault, greatly expanded the expressive possibilities of Romantic art by developing its themes and elaborating its forms in a direction of ever-greater emotional power—in Romantic parlance, of "sublimity." While Delacroix denigrated Ingres's art, he also found much to admire in his rival's work, especially the drawings. The two artists continued to go their separate ways, Ingres even being instrumental in preventing Delacroix's election to the Académie des Beaux Arts until 1857.†

Although the faculty of mind most valued by the Romantic was imagination (to be intensely imaginative was to be intensely alive), Delacroix realized that skill and restraint must accompany it. Baudelaire, writing of Delacroix, observed that "in his eyes imagination was the most precious gift, the most important faculty, but [he believed] that this faculty remained impotent and sterile if it was not served by a resourceful skill which could follow it in its restless and tyrannical whims." Nevertheless, Delacroix's works were products of his view that the artist's powers of imagination would in turn capture and inflame the imagination of the viewer.

Literature of similar imaginative power served Delacroix (and many of his contemporaries) as a useful source of subject matter. Since David, literature and the other arts had been developing in ever-more intimate association. Baudelaire remarked that Delacroix "inherited from the great Republican and Imperial school [of David] a love of the poets and a strangely impulsive spirit of rivalry with the written word. David, Guérin, and Géricault kindled their minds at the brazier of Homer, Vergil, Racine, and Ossian. Delacroix was the soul-stirring translator of Shakespeare, Dante, Byron, and Ariosto." The relationship between the arts went back as far as the Renaissance,

*In *The Journal of Eugène Delacroix*, trans. Walter Pach (New York: Grove Press, 1937, 1948). Charles Baudelaire (1821–1867), one of the nineteenth century's finest and most influential poets, was also a perceptive art critic.

†The personal antagonisms between the two artists may have softened eventually. Of an accidental encounter between them late in their careers on the steps of the French Institute, the painter Paul Joseph Chevanard recounted that, after an awkward pause, Ingres impulsively extended his hand to Delacroix, who shook it sincerely.

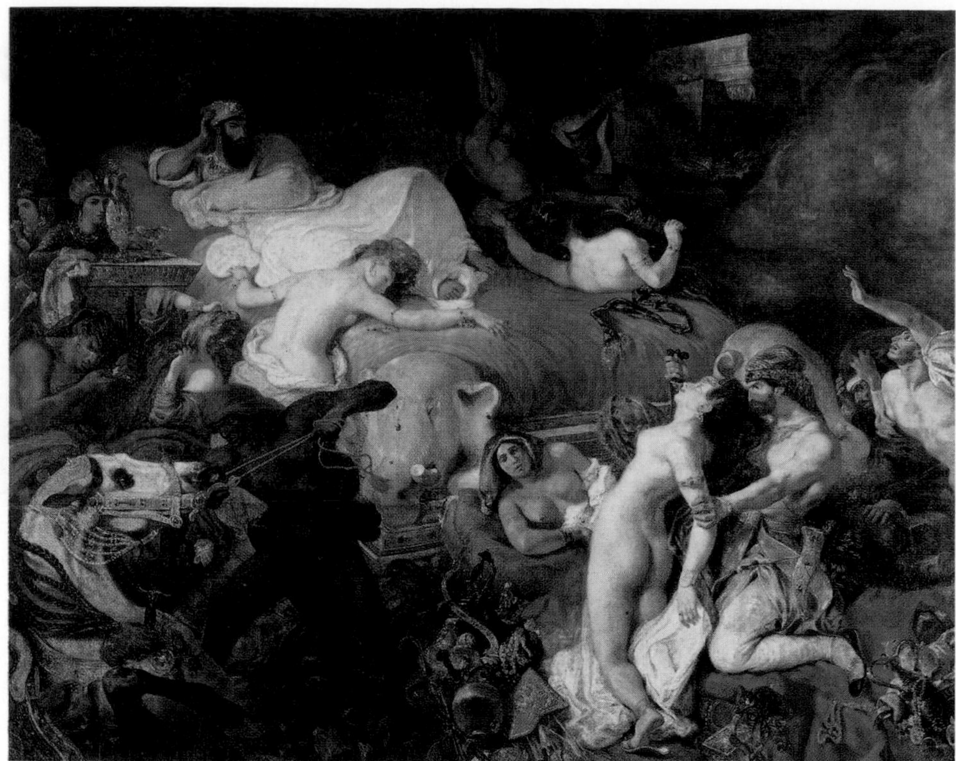

21-18 Eugène Delacroix, *The Death of Sardanapalus,* 1826. Approx. 12′ 1″ × 16′ 3″. Louvre, Paris.

but in the Romantic age, the association became so close that the paintings it produced could almost be said to be "programmed" by literature. The same held for music, as attested by Hector Berlioz's *Harold in Italy,* patterned after Lord Byron's *Childe Harold.* This trend that began with David culminated with Delacroix in the literature-inspired staging of exciting and disturbing human events, real or imaginary, and in a concern for the most accurate visual means of conveying them. The belief inherent in this practice was that the purpose of art was to stir, to "electrify," and to render the modern spirit with a modern look, accurately and sympathetically. It was an art also meant to appeal to the new, rapidly expanding democratic society. The "story picture" resulting from the painter's translation of literature into art, when further merged with the dramatic and musical theater, would evolve into the new medium of the motion picture—a composite of drama, narrative, sound, and pictures.

Delacroix's *The Death of Sardanapalus* (FIG. **21-18**), which he painted in 1826, is an example of pictorial grand opera on a colossal scale. Undoubtedly, Delacroix was inspired by Lord Byron's narrative poem *Sardanapalus,* but the painting does not illustrate that text. Instead, Delacroix depicted the last hour of the ancient king in a much more tempestuous and crowded setting than Byron described, with orgiastic destruction replacing the sacrificial suicide found in the poem. In the painting, on hearing of the defeat of his armies and the enemies' entry into his city, the king orders all of his most precious possessions—his women, slaves, horses, and treasure—destroyed in his sight while he watches gloomily from his funeral pyre, soon to be set alight. The king presides like a genius of evil over the panorama of destruction, most conspicuous in which are the tortured and dying bodies of his Rubenesque women, the one in the foreground dispatched by an ecstatically murderous slave. This carnival of suffering and death is glorified by superb drawing and color, by the most daringly difficult and tortuous poses, and by the richest intensities of hue and contrasts of light and dark. The king is the center of the calamity, the quiet eye of a hurricane of form and color. It is a testament to Delacroix's genius that his center of meaning is placed away from the central action yet entirely controls it.

Delacroix's composition in *Death of Sardanapalus* is an early example in painting of the newly invented Romantic picture type called the *vignette,* an image with a strong center that becomes less defined at its edges. In *Death of Sardanapalus,* everything swirls around the empty foot of the bed, but details fade toward the edge of the canvas. Similarly vertical com-

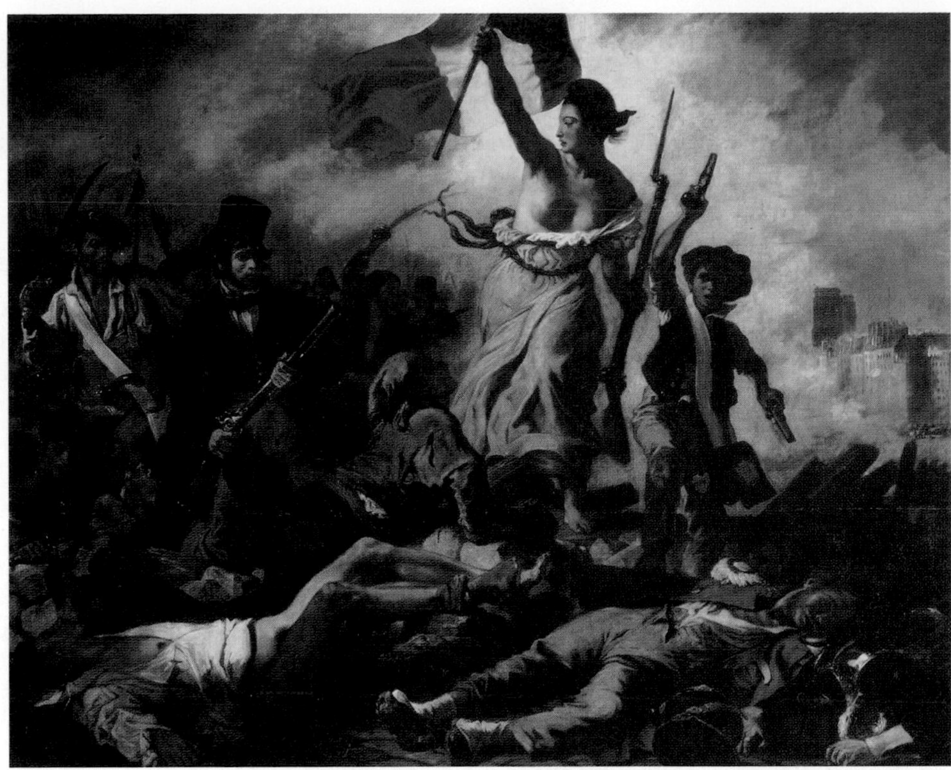

21-19 EUGÈNE DELACROIX, *Liberty Leading the People,* 1830. Approx. 8′ 6″ × 10′ 8″. Louvre, Paris.

positions were common in painters of the dynamic Baroque (FIG. 19-40), but in Delacroix's work this device extended its effect to a then unknown, and not entirely appreciated, degree (the work pleased none of the critics of the day). The Romantic vignette first appeared in book illustrations in which Romantic artists attempted to recapture the kind of total unity of text and illustration that they admired in medieval illuminated manuscripts. Cultural historians Charles Rosen and Henri Zerner offer an explanation for the vignette's eager adoption by painters:

> The vignette, by its general appearance, presents itself both as a global metaphor for the world and as a fragment. Dense at its center, tenuous on the periphery, it seems to disappear into the page: this makes it a naïve but powerful metaphor of the infinite, a symbol of the universe; at the same time, the vignette is fragmentary, . . . incomplete, mostly dependent upon the text for its meaning. . . . The vignette launches a powerful attack on the classical definition of representation, a window on the world. The vignette is not a window because it has no limit, no frame. The image, defined from its center rather than its edges, emerges from the paper [or canvas] as an apparition or a fantasy.*

*Charles Rosen and Henri Zerner, *Romanticism and Realism: The Mythology of Nineteenth-Century Art* (London: Faber and Faber, 1984), p. 81.

Generally, Delacroix chose his subjects from either non-Classical or post-Classical periods and literature, but sometimes he dealt with a Greek subject that moved him. Other sources of subjects were the events of his own time, notably popular struggles for freedom: the ill-fated revolt of the Greeks against Turkish rule in the 1820s; the Parisian revolution of 1830, which overthrew the restored Bourbons and placed Louis Philippe on the throne of France. In *Liberty Leading the People* (FIG. **21-19**), done in 1830, Delacroix makes no attempt to represent a specific incident seen in actuality. Instead, he gives us a full-blown allegory of revolution itself, teeming with unidealized and carefully presented details. Liberty, a majestic, partly nude woman, whose beautiful features wear an expression of noble dignity, waves the people forward to the barricades, the familiar revolutionary apparatus of Paris streets. She carries the tricolor banner of the republic and a musket with a bayonet and wears the cap of liberty. Her advance is over the dead and dying of both sides—the people and the royal troops. Arrayed around her are bold Parisian types: the street boy brandishing his pistols, the menacing *prolétaire* with a cutlass, the intellectual dandy in plug hat with sawed-off musket. In the background, the towers of Notre Dame rise through the smoke and clamor, witnessing the tradition of liberty

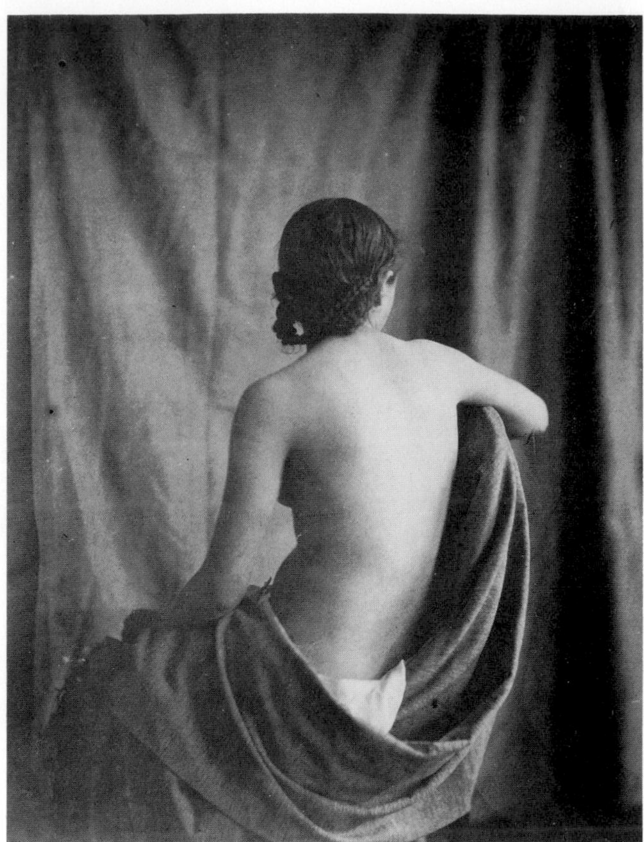

21-20 Eugène Durieu and Eugène Delacroix, *Draped Model (back view)*, c. 1854. Albumen print, $7\frac{5}{16}'' \times 5\frac{1}{8}''$. The J. Paul Getty Museum, Malibu.

that has been cherished by the people of Paris throughout the centuries.

In terms of form, *Liberty Leading the People* still reflected the strong impression made on Delacroix by the art of Géricault, especially *Raft of the Medusa* (FIG. 21-12); the fact that Delacroix made an allegory of *Liberty* shows that he was familiar with traditional conventions. The clutter of sprawling bodies in the foreground provides a kind of base for the pyramid of figures in the center, which builds from the heavy, inert forms of the dead and dying to the frantic energy of Liberty and the citizens still engaged actively in the struggle. The flashes of light suggest gunfire, while the intermingling of light and shadow echoes the confusion of battle and the dense atmosphere stirred up by the conflict. The forms were generated from the Baroque, as they were in Géricault, but Delacroix's sharp agitation of them created his own special brand of tumultuous excitement.

Delacroix's early use of the vignette shows him to have been an innovator. He was always studying the problems of his craft and always searching for fresh materials to supply his imagination. These were conscious efforts on his part; he said, "style can only result from great research." He made numerous studies for each of his projects and even worked with the photographer Eugène Durieu (1800–1874) to create photographic studies for paintings. A camera study was a supremely practical tool, if only because a photographic model would pose untiringly for just the cost of making the initial print. More important to the Romantic (and later Realist) interest in the depiction of nature was the camera's ability to record, with absolute fidelity, the physical facts of what was before it. *Draped Model (back view)* (FIG. **21-20**) is an early example of the photographic nudes Delacroix used for this purpose. Although such images were sought for their accuracy of detail, Durieu was able to create a romantic mood through careful lighting and the draping of the cloth. On one occasion, Delacroix shared some of the photographic studies he had made with visitors and then showed them some engravings by the famous Renaissance artist Marcantonio Raimondi. Writing of this event in his *Journal*, Delacroix recorded that

> [After] they had studied these photographs of nude models, some of whom were poorly built, oddly shaped in places and not very attractive generally, I put before their eyes engravings by Marcantonio. We all experienced a feeling of revulsion, almost disgust, for their incorrectness, their mannerisms, and their lack of naturalness, despite their quality of style. . . . Truly, if a man of genius should use the daguerreotype as it ought to be used, he will raise himself to heights unknown to us.*

An enormously influential event in Delacroix's life, and one that affected his art in both subject and form, was his visit to North Africa in 1832. Things he saw there shocked his imagination with fresh impressions that would last throughout the rest of his life. He discovered, in the sun-drenched landscape and in the hardy and colorful Arabs dressed in robes reminiscent of the Roman toga, new insights into a culture built on proud virtues—a culture that he believed to be more Classical than anything European Neoclassicism could conceive. "The Greeks and the Romans," he wrote to a friend, "they are here, within my reach. I had to laugh heartily about the Greeks of David." The gallantry, hardihood, valor, and fierce love of liberty made the Arabs, in Delacroix's eyes, "nature's noblemen"—unspoiled heroes, uninfected by European decadence.

Delacroix's African experience also further heightened his already considerable awareness of the expressive power of color and light. What Delacroix knew about color he passed on to later painters of the

*In Aaron Scharf, *Art and Photography* (Baltimore: Penguin, 1974), p. 122.

nineteenth century, particularly to the Impressionists. He observed that pure colors are as rare in nature as lines, that color appears only in an infinitely varied scale of different tones, shadings, and reflections, which he tried to re-create in his paintings. He recorded his observations in his *Journal,* which became a veritable corpus of pre-Impressionistic color theory and was acclaimed as such by the Post-Impressionist painter Paul Signac in 1898–1899. Delacroix anticipated the later development of Impressionist color science, but that art-science had to await the discoveries by Michel Eugène Chevreul and Hermann von Helmholtz of the laws of light decomposition and the properties of complementary colors before the problems of color perception and juxtaposition in painting could be properly formulated. Nevertheless, Delacroix's observations were significant: "It is advisable not to fuse the brushstrokes," he wrote, "as they will [appear to] fuse naturally at [a] . . . distance. In this manner, color gains in energy and freshness." This observation, suggested to him by his examination of a group of landscapes by John Constable, the great English landscape painter (FIG. 21-30), had strongly impressed Delacroix even before his color experiences in Morocco. He wrote:

> Constable said that the superiority of the green he uses for his landscapes derives from the fact that it is composed of a multitude of different greens. What causes the lack of intensity and of life in verdure as it is painted by the common run of landscapists is that they ordinarily do it with a uniform tint. What he said about the green of meadows can be applied to all other tones.

Inspired by Constable's example, Delacroix developed a more radical colorism, which he described forcibly in the following statement: "Speaking radically, there are neither lights nor shades. There is only a color mass for each object, having different reflections on all sides." These observations were stimulated by Delacroix's Moroccan visit and do not consistently apply to the early works he did under the influence of Géricault. His conception of the optical world as planes of color would find a new realization in the art of Paul Cézanne (FIG. 21-81), who made color planes serve a structural purpose in locking the composition together.

No other painter of the time explored the domain of Romantic subject and mood as thoroughly and definitively as Delacroix, and none matched his style and content. Delacroix's technique—impetuous, improvisational, and instinctive, rather than deliberate, studious, and cold—epitomizes Romantic painting, catching the impression at the very beginning and developing it in the process of execution. We know how furiously Delacroix worked once he had an idea, keeping the whole painting progressing at once. The fury of his attack matched the fury of his imagination and his subjects. He was indeed the artist of passion. Baudelaire sums him up as "passionately in love with passion . . . an immense passion, reinforced with a formidable will—such was the man." In the end, his friend Silvestre, in the language of Romanticism, delivered a eulogy that amounts to a definition of the Romantic artist:

> Thus died, almost with a smile on August 13, 1863, that painter of great race, Ferdinand Victor Eugène Delacroix, who had a sun in his head and storms in his heart; who for forty years played upon the keyboard of human passions and whose brush—grandiose, terrible, or suave—passed from saints to warriors, from warriors to lovers, from lovers to tigers, and from tigers to flowers.

The Romantic Landscape

Romanticism elevated the previously minor genre of landscape painting to a level of first importance, a level once occupied exclusively by figure painting. Early in the century, most landscape painting to some degree expressed the Romantic, pantheistic view (first extolled by Jean Jacques Rousseau) of nature as a "being" that included the totality of existence in organic unity and harmony. It was in nature—"the living garment of God," as Goethe called it—that the artist found an ideal subject to express the Romantic theme of the soul in union with the natural world. Romanticism in the arts, it could be said, made a kind of personal religion of nature, a religion based in profound esthetic emotion—of mystery and beauty, to recall the ideas of Chateaubriand. If nature was akin to religion, the artist could be likened (in the thought of the Idealist philosopher Schiller) to a priest, who in the act of creation duplicates or becomes one with the creative powers of nature itself, thus resolving the contradictions of the inner (subjective) and the outer (objective) worlds. The landscape would reveal the divine being of nature to the artist who was prepared by innocence, sincerity, and intuitive insight to receive the revelation. As all nature was mysteriously permeated by "being," the landscape artist had the task of interpreting the signs, symbols, and emblems of universal "spirit" disguised within visible material things. The artist was no longer a mere beholder of the landscape but a participant in its spirit, no longer a painter of mere things but the translator of nature's transcendent meanings, arrived at through feelings inspired by the landscape.

Artists in northern Europe were the first to depict the Romantic transcendental landscape. One, PHILIPP

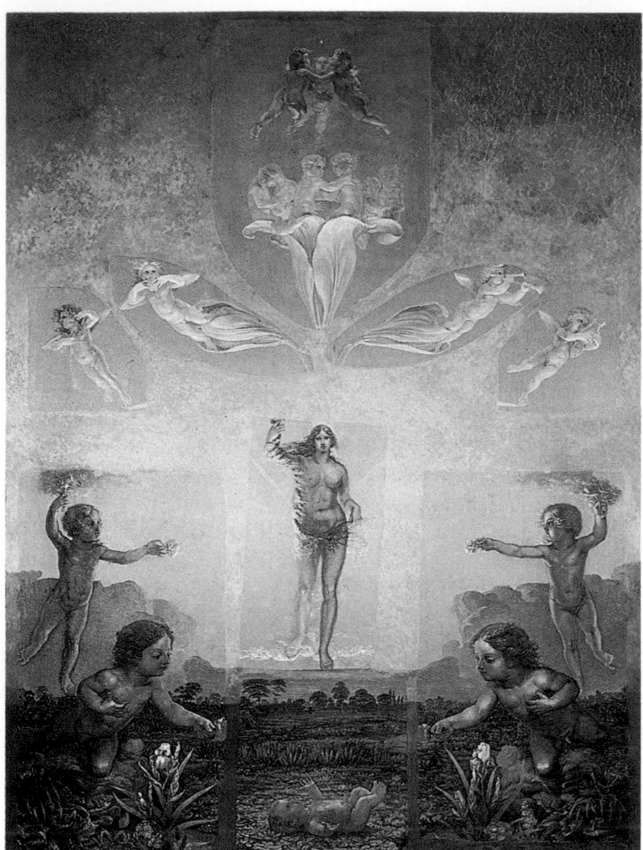

21-21 PHILIPP OTTO RUNGE, *The Times of Day: Morning* (large version), 1809. Approx. 60″ × 45″. Kunsthalle, Hamburg.

OTTO RUNGE (1777–1810) declared that true art could be understood only through the deepest mystical experience of religion. In words, as well as images, he celebrated

> the feeling of the whole universe with us; this united chord which in its vibrations touches every string of our heart; the love which keeps us and carries us through life. . . . each leaf and each blade of grass teems with life and stirs beneath me, all resounds together in a single chord. . . . I hear and feel the living breath of God who holds and carries the world, in whom all lives and works; here is the highest that we divine—God!*

Considering nature to be a part of God, and human beings to be part of nature, Runge said, "Once we see in all of nature only our own life, then it follows clearly, the right landscape can come about." Runge designed a four-part series, *The Times of Day,* as sacred pictures for a chapel dedicated to a new religion of nature. In *Morning* (FIG. **21-21**), from this series, he created an allegory of dawn enriched with his personal flower and color symbolism. In this piece, all plants are descended from Paradise and are emblematic of the states of the human soul, as are colors and musical harmonies. The image of the great lily floating in the sky is the floral manifestation of light and the symbol of Divine knowledge and purity. The morning star, Venus, glows above, under the arc of the earth; below it, on the central axis, is the graceful figure of the goddess herself in the guise of Aurora. On the ground below, the supine figure of an infant is an allusion to the Christ Child, as well as a symbol of regeneration and redemption and all the promise of the newborn day. The composition has the symmetry and formality of traditional religious painting and the mood of supernatural mystery, but the careful, objective study of color tone—the actual hues of dawn, with its tincture of rose turning to radiance—shows Runge's concern for the truth of appearance as the vehicle of symbolic truth. Fusing the empirical world with the transcendental, he gives us an apparition of the supernatural in a natural sky. Like William Blake, whose work he must have known (FIG. 20-48), Runge was a religious visionary who believed in angels; unlike Blake, Runge revered nature as given to the eye.

Runge's ideas are believed to have influenced the art of his great contemporary, CASPAR DAVID FRIEDRICH (1774–1840); in the work of both, as art historian Robert Rosenblum has remarked, "the experience of the supernatural has . . . been transposed from traditional religious imagery to nature."† Nature, as immanent God, requires no personifications other than its organic and inorganic subjects and objects, things visible to the eye, which symbolically express through their forms the truth of nature, which is to say, Divine truth. For Friedrich, landscapes were temples; his paintings themselves were altarpieces. His reverential mood demands from the viewer the silence appropriate to sacred places filled with a divine presence. *Cloister Graveyard in the Snow* (FIG. **21-22**) is like a solemn requiem. Under a winter sky, through the leafless oaks of a snow-covered cemetery, a funeral procession bears a coffin into the ruins of a Gothic chapel. The emblems of death are everywhere: the desolation of the season, leaning crosses and tombstones, the black of mourning worn by the grieving and by the skeletal trees, the destruction wrought by time on the chapel. The painting is a kind of meditation on human mortality, as Friedrich himself remarked: "Why, it has often occurred to me to ask myself, do I so frequently choose death, tran-

*From letters translated in R. M. Bisanz, *German Romanticism and Philipp Otto Runge* (De Kalb: Northern Illinois University Press, 1970), pp. 48–51.

†Robert Rosenblum, *Modern Painting and the Northern Romantic Tradition: Friedrich to Rothko* (New York: Harper & Row, 1975), p. 22.

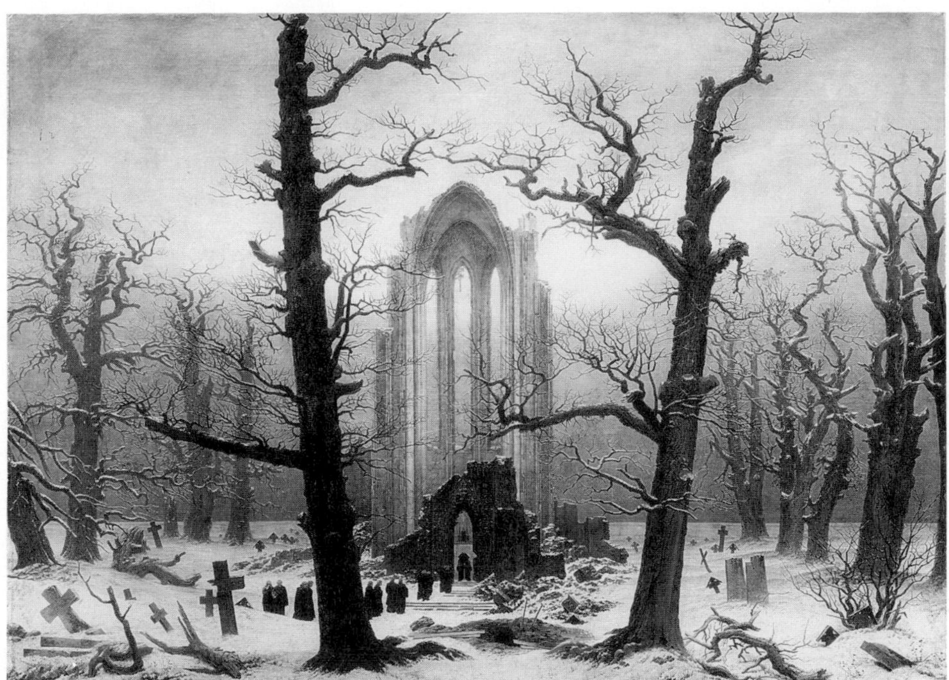

21-22 CASPAR DAVID FRIEDRICH, *Cloister Graveyard in the Snow,* 1810. Approx. 47″ × 70″. (Painting destroyed during World War II.)

sience, and the grave as subjects for my paintings? One must submit oneself many times to death in order some day to attain life everlasting."* The sharp-focused rendering of details demonstrates the artist's keen perception of everything in the physical environment relevant to his message. In the work of Friedrich, we find a balance of inner and outer experience. "The artist," he wrote "should paint not only what he sees before him, but also what he sees within him. If, however, he sees nothing within him, then he should also refrain from painting that which he sees before him."

A very different kind of natural symbolism is found in the widely influential school of English landscape painting. Just as literature and history are keys to the art of the French Romantics, English Romantic poetry is key to the paintings of the English landscapists. In the works of JOSEPH MALLORD WILLIAM TURNER (1775–1851), we find readings of nature in its terror and grandeur somewhat more often than in its peace and serenity, although the artist was capable of realizing all of nature's emotions. The critic John Ruskin wrote of Turner's *The Slave Ship* (FIG. **21-23**) in *Modern Painters* (1846):

> But I think the noblest sea that Turner has ever painted, and if so, the noblest certainly ever painted by man, is that of *The Slave Ship,* the chief Academy picture of the exhibition of 1840. . . . I believe, if I were reduced to rest Turner's immortality upon any single work, I should choose this.

The full title of the painting is *Slavers Throwing Overboard the Dead and Dying—Typhoon Coming On.* Its subject is an incident that took place in 1783 in which the captain of a slave ship threw sick and dying slaves overboard in hopes of collecting insurance on the claim that they were "lost at sea." The horror of the event is matched by Turner's turbulently emotional depiction of it. The sun is transformed into an incandescent comet amid flying, scarlet clouds that swirl above a sea choked with the bodies of slaves jettisoned from the ship by its ruthless master. The particulars of the event are almost lost in the boiling colors of the work. Turner was a great innovator whose special invention in works like *The Slave Ship* was to release color from any defining outlines in order to express the forces of nature, as well as the painter's emotional response to them. In works like this, the reality of color is one with the reality of feeling. Turner's methods had an incalculable effect on the development of modern art. His discovery of the esthetic and emotive power of pure color (the most fundamental element of the painting medium), and his pushing of the fluidity of the medium to a point at which the subject is almost manifest through the paint itself, were important steps toward twentieth-century abstract art, which dispenses with shape and form altogether.

*In H. Börsch-Supan, *Caspar David Friedrich* (New York: Braziller, 1974), p. 7.

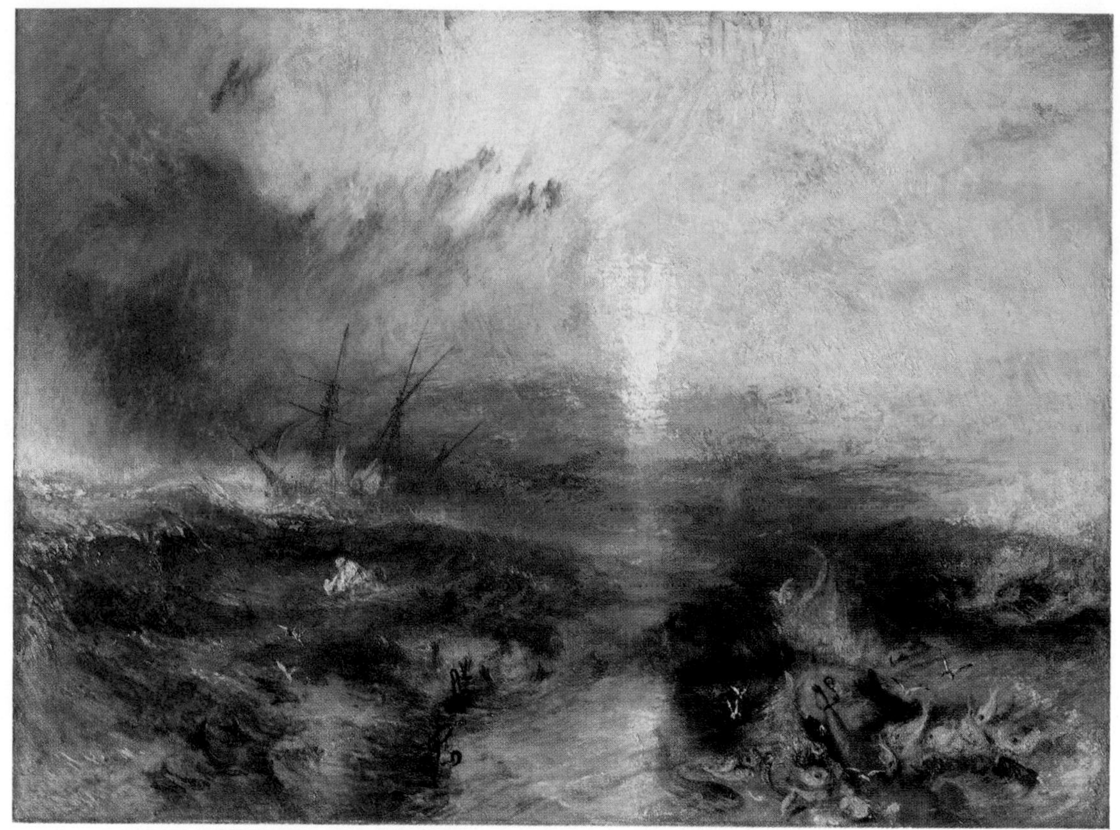

21-23 Joseph Mallord William Turner, *The Slave Ship,* 1840. $35\frac{3}{4}'' \times 48\frac{1}{4}''$. Museum of Fine Arts, Boston (Henry Lillie Pierce Fund).

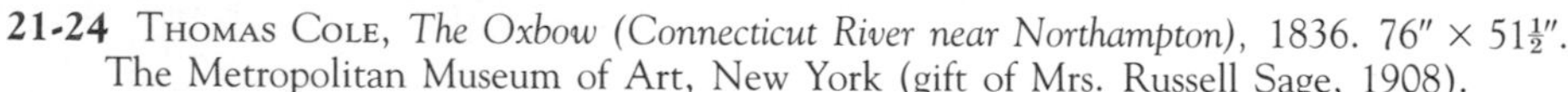

21-24 Thomas Cole, *The Oxbow (Connecticut River near Northampton),* 1836. $76'' \times 51\frac{1}{2}''$. The Metropolitan Museum of Art, New York (gift of Mrs. Russell Sage, 1908).

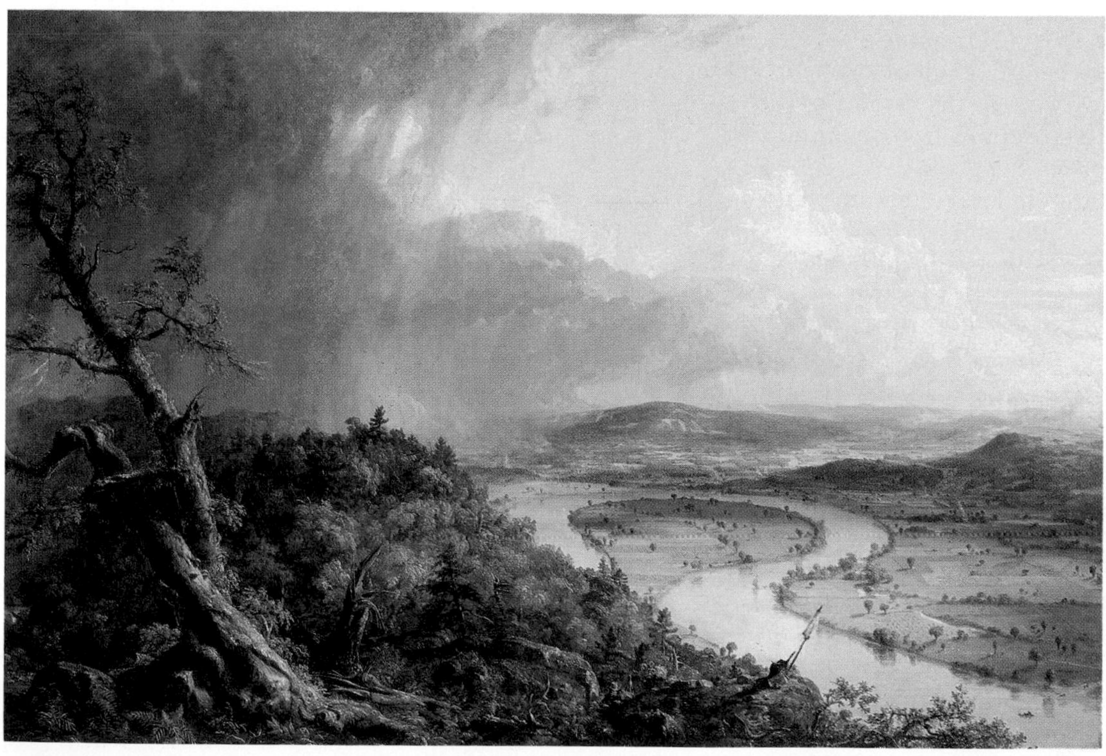

The American painter THOMAS COLE (1801–1848) was less concerned with pioneering advances in color and technique, and his work typified the landscape of reflection and mood so romantically appealing to the public, especially in the English-speaking world. Best known as the leading painter of the Hudson River school, whose members drew their subjects from the uncultivated regions of the Hudson River valley, Cole celebrated the wonders of the North American landscape in many of his works. He wrote:

> Whether he [the American] beholds the Hudson mingling waters with the Atlantic, explores the central wilds of this vast continent, or stands on the margin of the distant Oregon, he is still in the midst of American scenery—it is his own land; its beauty, its magnificence, its sublimity—all are his; and how undeserving of such a birthright, if he can turn towards it an unobserving eye, an unaffected heart!*

In *The Oxbow (Connecticut River near Northampton)* (FIG. **21-24**), the viewer looks out from a high promontory over a peaceful plain dotted with signs of human habitation and dominated by the lazy oxbow turning of the Connecticut River. Our hilly perch is densely forested; at the near left is an ancient, craggy tree. In contrast with the valley below, this high realm seems still part of the untouched wilderness. Just below, on a rock to the right, are the artist's stool and parasol; nearby we see the artist himself at work on a painting. The broad vista suggests the public fascination with the panorama, which Cole shared. Originally, "panoramas" were specially designed buildings that housed colossal circular murals; the buildings' curved walls surrounded spectators who stood on a central platform to view vast paintings of historical scenes or landscapes. Soon, the panorama experience was translated outdoors in Europe and America to viewing platforms overlooking spectacular landscape vistas. In his affection for his adopted country (Cole was born in England), the artist may have combined the natural drama of the panoramic view with the widely held notion that America was a New Eden, which, in its unspoiled and pristine virtue, might avoid the fateful cycle of European decay and decadence that had doomed earlier empires. This thoroughly Romantic myth of the innocence of America in contrast to the corruption of Europe was widely believed on both sides of the Atlantic in the nineteenth century.

*In John W. McCoubrey, *American Art 1700–1960: Sources and Documents* (Englewood Cliffs, NJ: Prentice-Hall, 1965), pp. 98, 106 and passim. Cole's sensitivity for the sublime quality of landscape also inspired him to produce heroic symbolic landscape cycles with themes like "The Voyage of Life."

THE RISE OF REALISM: THE RECORDING EYE

While Romanticism dominated the early decades of the century with its goals of expressing dramatic emotion or ideal beauty and its subject matter, taken for the most part from scenes outside common, everyday experience, another vein of expression also was beginning to address the century's growing appetite for optical reality in art. Increasingly during this period, real events were becoming subjects for artists who were willing to report or reconstruct scenes in visual modes faithful to appearance. These artists produced images that invited comparison to everyday optical experience in life, using simple recognition as a new criterion for judgment.

A technological device of immense consequence for the modern experience was invented at precisely this time: the camera, with its attendant art of photography. We are all familiar with what the camera equips us to do—report and record optical experience at will. We assume that a very close correlation exists between the photographic image and the fragment of the visual world it records. The evidence of the photograph is proof that what we think we see is really there. In other words, the camera can be a check on what is "real," "true," or "factual" in our visual experience. Photography was celebrated as embodying a kind of revelation of visible things from the time Louis J. M. Daguerre and Henry Fox Talbot announced the first practical photographic processes in 1839. The medium, itself a product of science, was an enormously useful tool for recording the discoveries of the century. The relative ease of the process seemed a dream come true for scientists and artists, who for centuries had grappled with less satisfying methods for capturing accurate images of their subjects. Photography was also perfectly suited to an age that saw artistic patronage continue to shift away from the elite few and toward a broader base of support, away from noble patronage and toward that of the growing and increasingly powerful middle class, who embraced the more practical and immediately comprehensible images of the new medium, and also its lower cost.

For the traditional artist, photography suggested new answers to the great debate about what is real and how to represent the real in art, but it also presented a challenge to the place of traditional modes of pictorial representation that had originated in the Renaissance. Artists as diverse as Delacroix, Ingres, Courbet, and Degas welcomed photography as a helpful auxiliary to painting and were increasingly intrigued by the manner in which photography translated three-dimensional objects onto a two-dimensional surface. Other artists, however, saw photography as a mechanism capable of displacing the painstaking work of a skilled painter dedicated to representing the truth of a chosen subject. The challenge of photography to painting, both historically and technologically, seemed to some an expropriation of the realistic image, until then the exclusive property of painting. As one painter, Maurice de Vlaminck, declared at the end of the century: "We [painters] hate everything that has to do with the photograph." But just as some painting looked to the new medium of photography for answers on how best to render an image in paint, so some photographers looked to painting for suggestions about ways to imbue the photographic image with qualities beyond simple reproduction—the near-symbiotic relationship already seen in the collaborative efforts of Delacroix and Durieu's *Draped Model* (FIG. 21-20).

In any event, at this time, painting and photography, whether in collaboration or opposition, were destined to replace the Tradition altogether—a tradition still very much alive in Romanticism. In substance and direction, in subject matter, and in form and technique, painting and photography were to topple the conventions of the Tradition through visual means faithful to Realism's new concerns with the optically real. Realism, the style of art that would dominate the latter part of the nineteenth century, came into being slowly. At first, it was combined with some of the qualities of Romanticism.

Seeds of Realism in Painting

At the very beginning of the modern period stood the imposing figure of FRANCISCO GOYA (1746–1828), the great independent painter of Spain. Founder of no school and acknowledging indebtedness to Velázquez, Rembrandt, and "nature," Goya was a great transitional figure who changed the Tradition while he manifested the present and prophesied the future. In his long life, he produced masterworks in a variety of artistic styles, and, from a higher vantage point than most of his contemporaries, he often depicted humanity's capacity for evil in bitter and unsparing revelation. Great Spanish painting has rarely been sentimental; it has insisted, often with ruthless honesty, on the cruel facts of life.

Little of the grim account of humanity foreshadowed in *The Sleep of Reason* (FIG. 20-49), a visionary work linked to the art of William Blake (FIG. 20-48), can be seen in Goya's early, vivacious manner, which

21-25 FRANCISCO GOYA, *The Family of Charles IV,* 1800. Approx. 9′ 2″ × 11′. Museo del Prado, Madrid.

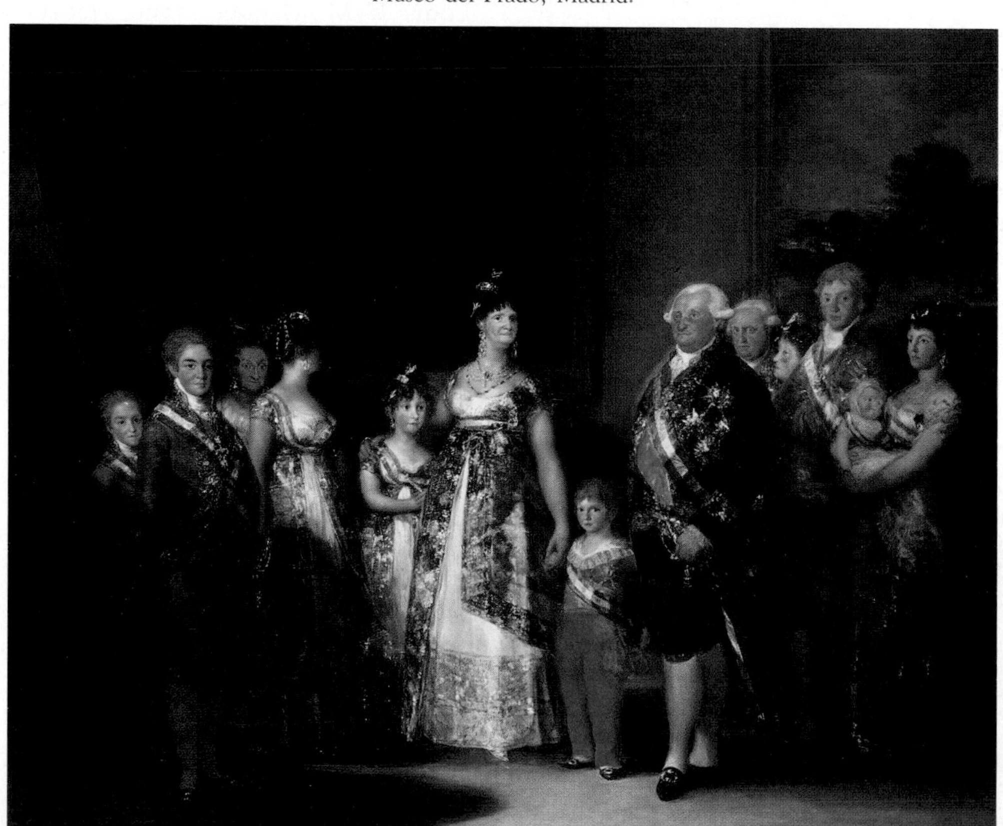

was brilliantly adapted from Tiepolo. At the royal court in Madrid, where his precocious talent had brought him early in his career, Goya produced a series of genre paintings (not illustrated) designed to serve as models for tapestries. Their prevailing mood of gaiety was the mood of the Rococo, but the blitheness of Goya's early style soon waned. His experiences as painter to Charles IV, at whose sensationally corrupt court he lived, must have fostered the unsentimental, hard-eyed realism of his later style. In his large painting of *The Family of Charles IV* (FIG. **21-25**), probably inspired by Velázquez's *Las Meninas* (FIG. 19-38), Goya presented, with a straight face, a menagerie of human grotesques who, critics have long been convinced, must not have had the intelligence to realize that the artist was presenting them with unflinching and unflattering truth. This superb revelation of stupidity, pomposity, and vulgarity, painted in 1800, led a later critic to summarize the subject as the "grocer and his family who have just won the big lottery prize." The painter, behind his canvas, is dimly discernible at the left; his features impassively ironical, he looks beyond his subjects to the observer. In this work, Goya exhibited his extraordinary skill as a colorist and manager of the oil medium. The colors float with a quiet iridescence across the surface, and the paint is applied with deft economy. Great solidity is suggested by the most transparent tones. A magician of optical pictorialism, Goya used the methods of his great predecessor, Velázquez.

The Third of May, 1808 (FIG. **21-26**) is perhaps the most compelling of all Goya's works. The subject is an incident that took place in 1808 during Napoleon's intervention in Spain when a French firing squad executed a "token" number of civilians in Madrid in retaliation for the murder of some of Napoleon's troops by Spanish troops the day before. Here, Goya showed the horrors of war without national bias (although he was a patriot) and without mercy for the viewer's sensibilities. Goya was in Madrid at the time the execution took place and visited the site later to make sketches of it to ensure the accuracy of his depiction of the bleak hillside and distant city. His main concern, however, was not the accurate recording of fact, but the expression of empathetic horror for the psychological agonies of men facing execution. Unlike the subtle, even suave realism of *The Family of Charles IV,* Goya's method here is coarse and extreme in its departure from optical fact. The postures and gestures of the figures are shockingly distorted to signal defiance and terror. The French firing squad has

21-26 FRANCISCO GOYA, *The Third of May, 1808,* 1814. Approx. 8′ 8″ × 11′ 3″. Museo del Prado, Madrid.

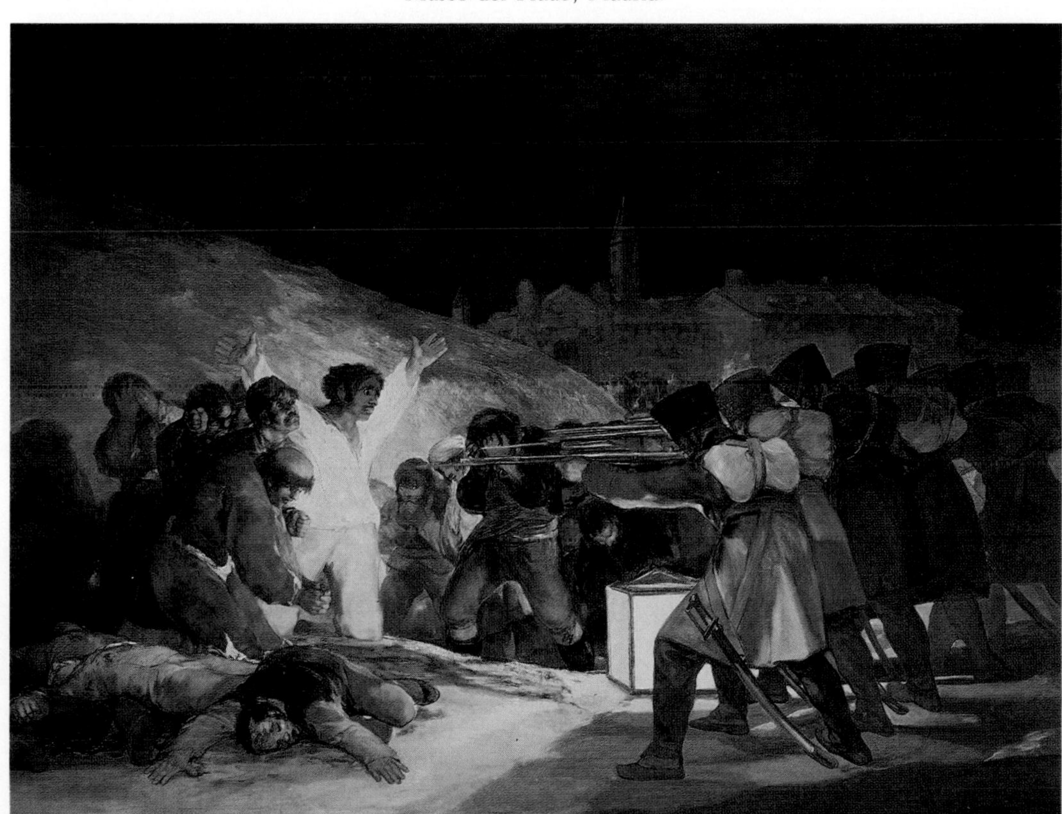

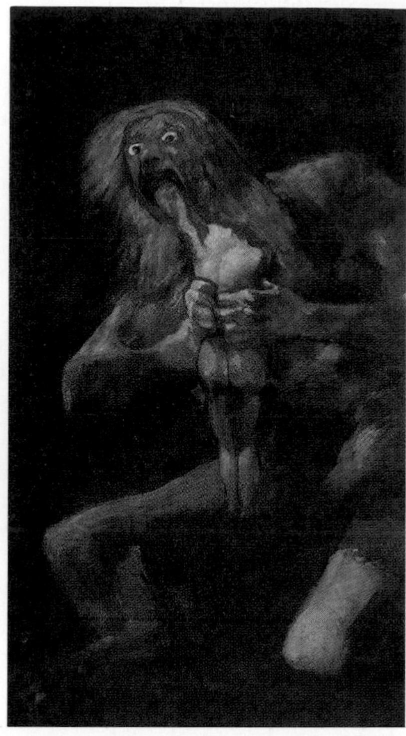

21-27 FRANCISCO GOYA, *Saturn Devouring His Children,* 1819–1823. Detail of a detached fresco on canvas, full size approx. 57″ × 32″. Museo del Prado, Madrid.

become an anonymous, murderous wall, while the victims are portrayed as separate individuals, each facing the moment of death in his own way. The intense psychological reality is modern in its stress on the experience of the individual as one among many (quite different from the more traditional, carefully choreographed Baroque staging in Callot's *Miseries of War* [FIG. 19-59]), and foreshadows Picasso's twentieth-century masterpiece on a related theme, *Guernica* (FIG. 22-83).

Toward the end of his life, the follies and brutalities he had witnessed and his own increasing infirmities, including deafness, combined to depress Goya's outlook further, as evidenced in his so-called Black Paintings, done for the walls of his own home. In ominous midnight colors, he created whole populations of subhuman monsters who worship the devil and swarm in nightmares. *Saturn Devouring His Children* (FIG. **21-27**) was one product of this pessimistic and misanthropic style. Saturn (Time) glares in lunatic frenzy while devouring part of a small body clutched in his hands. The forms are torn and jagged, the colors raw. Here, Goya's tragic vision returns to the haunted interior world of *The Sleep of Reason.* This appalling late work is not only a savage expression of man's inhumanity to man, but a recognition of the desperate conditions of life itself. Life is in time, and time devours all.

Similar to Goya's *Third of May* in its depiction of harsh social reality is *Rue Transnonain* (FIG. **21-28**), a print by the French lithographer and painter HONORÉ DAUMIER (1808–1879). At the time of this work, Daumier had been known primarily for the satirical lithographs he contributed to the liberal French Republican journal, *Caricature.* In these works, he lampooned the foibles and misbehavior of politicians, lawyers, and middle-class gentry. Daumier, however, was also in close touch with the acute political and social unrest in Paris at that time, unrest brought about by

21-28 HONORÉ DAUMIER, *Rue Transnonain,* 1834. Lithograph, approx. 12″ × 17½″. Philadelphia Museum of Art.

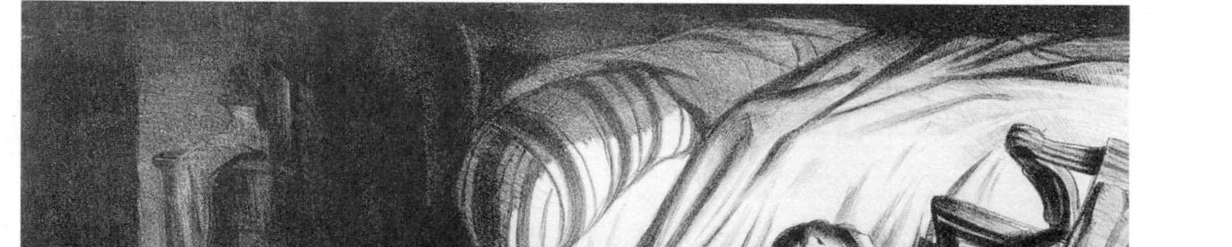

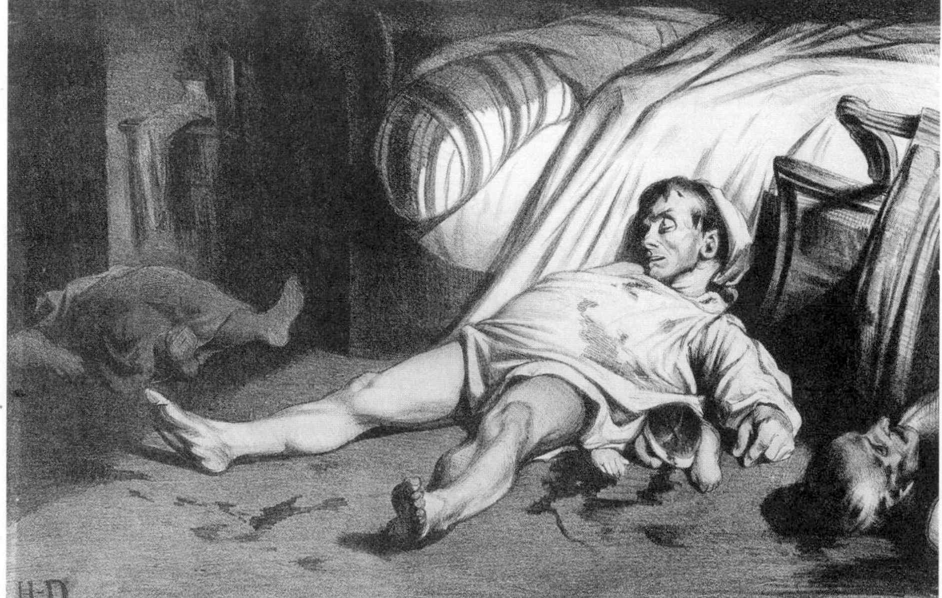

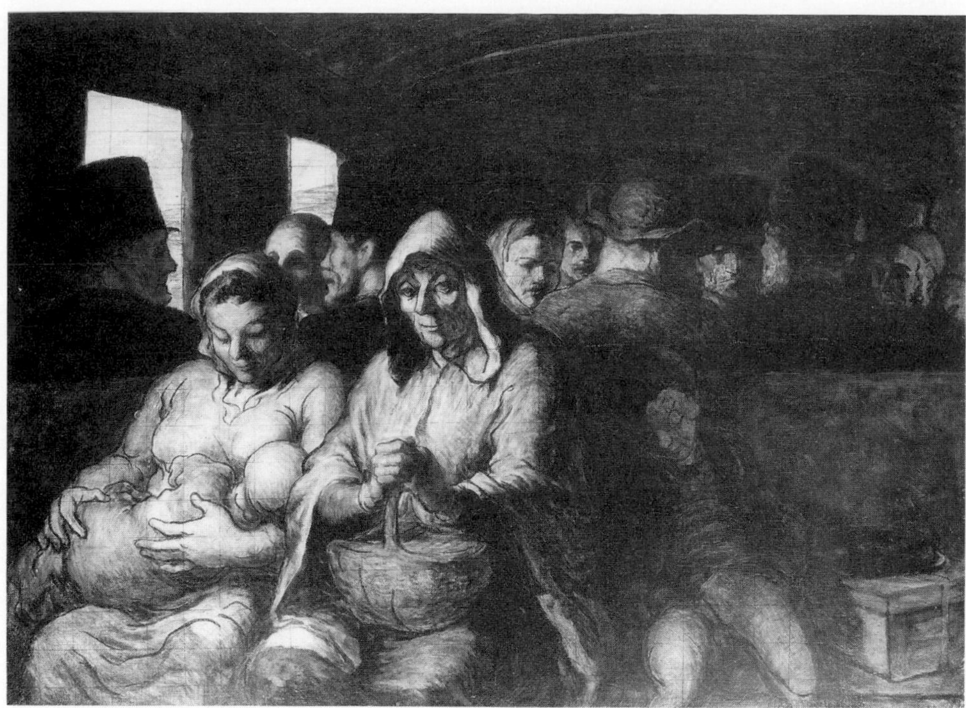

21-29 HONORÉ DAUMIER, *The Third-Class Carriage,* c. 1862. $25\frac{3}{4}'' \times 35\frac{1}{2}''$. The Metropolitan Museum of Art, New York (Havemeyer Collection, bequest of Mrs. H. O. Havemeyer, 1929).

the rapid development of an urban industrial society. As might be expected, the sharpness of his political criticism (in any form) often put him in conflict with the government. The title *Rue Transnonain* identified the incident being portrayed to Daumier's contemporaries; it was an event that occurred after a civil guard, part of a government force trying to repress a worker demonstration, was killed by a sniper. Because the fatal shot had come from a workers' housing block, the remaining guards immediately stormed the building and massacred all of its inhabitants. With the power of Goya, Daumier created a view of the atrocity from a sharp, realistic angle of vision. We see not the dramatic moment of execution, but the terrible, quiet aftermath. The broken, scattered forms, lying in the midst of violent disorder, are reported as if newly found. Daumier used every available device of his skill to make the situation real. The harsh facts speak for themselves; the artist did not have to interpret them for us. The print's significance lies in its *factualness.* What we find here is an example of an increasing artistic bias toward using fact as subject, if not yet always with the optical realization of fact as method. Daumier's manner is rough and spontaneous; the way it carries expressive exaggeration is part of its remarkable force. Daumier is true to life in content, but his style is uniquely personal.

Daumier brought the same concerns to the paintings he did, especially after 1848. His unfinished *The Third-Class Carriage* (FIG. **21-29**) gives us a glimpse into the rude railway compartment of the 1860s. The inhabitants are poor and can afford only third-class tickets. The disinherited masses of nineteenth-century industrialism were Daumier's indignant concern, and he made them his subject over and over again. He shows them to us in the unposed attitudes and unplanned arrangements of the millions thronging the modern city—anonymous, insignificant, dumbly patient with a lot they cannot change. Daumier saw people as they ordinarily appeared, their faces vague, impersonal, blank—unprepared for any observer. He tried to achieve the real by isolating a random collection of the unrehearsed details of human existence from the continuum of ordinary life, a vision that paralleled the spontaneity and candor of scenes being captured by the end of the century with the modern snapshot camera.

The realization of "fact" in both content and method was the goal of JOHN CONSTABLE (1776–1837), Turner's great contemporary, in the depiction of the English landscape. Constable's landscapes—for the most part placid, untroubled views of the English (Suffolk) countryside—are careful studies of nature rendered in the local colors of woodland, meadow pond and stream, hill and sky, interspersed with the architecture of mill, cottage, and country church. Constable portrayed these, his favorite subjects, as lighted by a mild sun or shadowed briefly by a changing cloud, bathed in an atmosphere fresh with dew or rain, moved by soft winds. He did not depict heroic

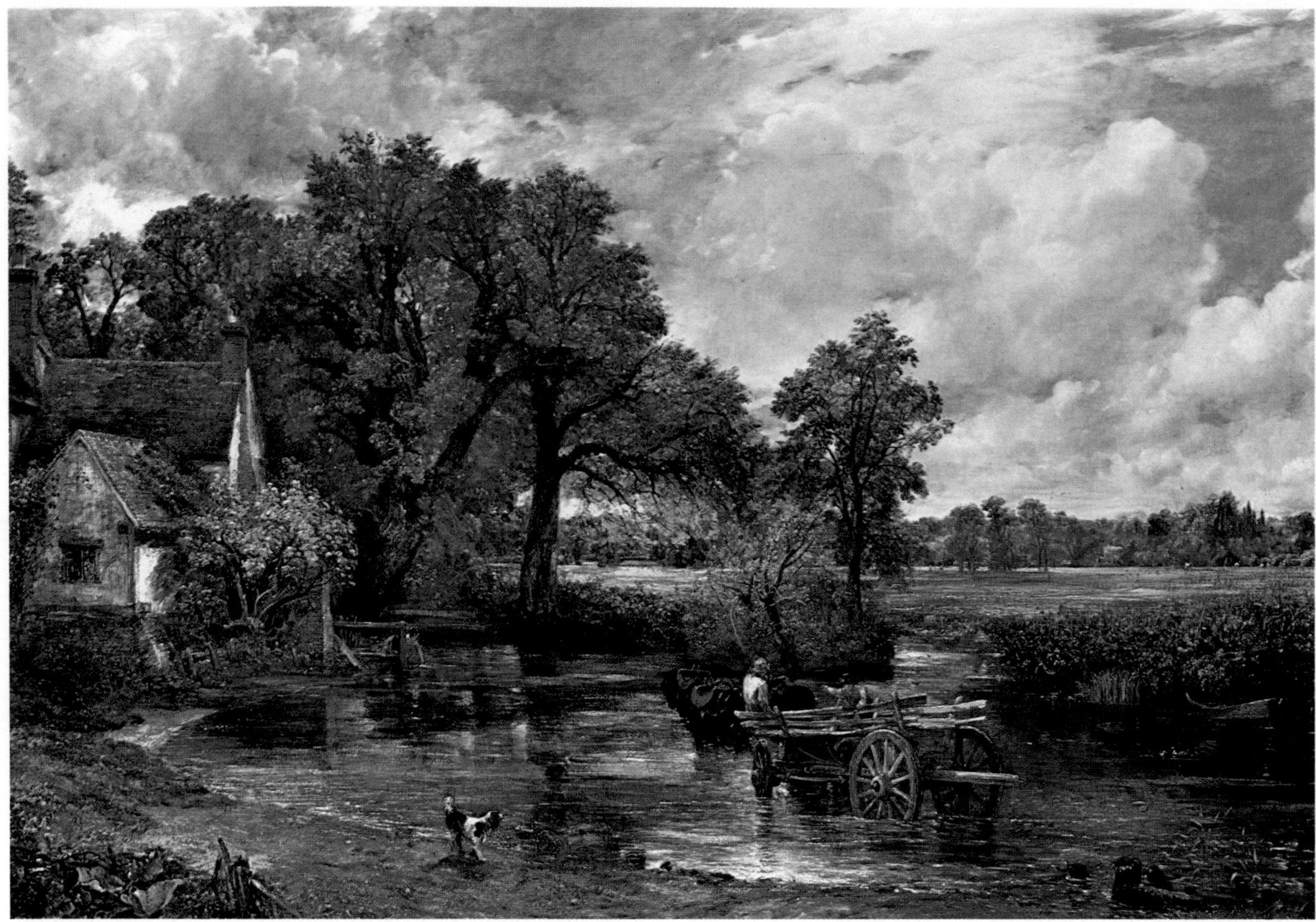

21-30 JOHN CONSTABLE, *The Haywain*, 1821. 4′ 3″ × 6′ 2″. National Gallery, London.

action, nor has the landscape been constructed to stage it. In *The Haywain* (FIG. **21-30**), which was a great success at the Paris Salon of 1824, a farmer in a cart fords a stream. Living nature includes him as it does the dog, the cottage, the stream, the copse, the distant park, the scudding clouds. Constable portrayed the oneness with nature sought by the Romantic poets; man is not the observer, but a participant in the landscape's being. The image is not a dream vision. The artist has insisted on the reality of the landscape as given to the eye and rendered with the brush: "I hope to show that our profession as painters is *scientific* as well as *poetic;* that imagination never did, and never can, produce works that are to stand by comparison with *realities*" (emphasis added). Constable made countless studies from nature for each of his canvases, which produced the convincing sense of reality in his works that was praised by his contemporaries. In his quest for the reality of landscape, Constable studied it like a meteorologist (which he was by avocation). His special gift was for capturing the texture given to landscape by atmosphere (the climate and the weather, which delicately veil what is seen) and for revealing that atmosphere as the key to representing the ceaseless process of nature, which changes constantly through the hours of the day, and through shifts of weather and season. Constable's use of tiny dabs of local color, stippled with white, created a sparkling shimmer of light and hue across the surface of the canvas—the vibration itself suggestive of movement and process. In speaking of the qualities he intended in his pictures, Constable mentioned "light—dews—breezes—bloom—and freshness, not one of which . . . has yet been perfected on the canvas of any painter in the world." These are the qualities that we sense in the fleeting states of changing nature—the qualities that startled the young Delacroix when he saw *The Haywain* in the Paris Salon. Constable's certainty that the painting of nature partook of science was his challenge and his bequest to the Impressionists.

Echoing the scientific thrust found in Constable and exemplifying the entire century's exploding interest in the recording and cataloguing of known and newly discovered natural realms is the work of JOHN JAMES AUDUBON (1785–1851), who devoted almost the whole of his career to naturalist paintings of the birds and animals of North America. Born of Creole and French parentage in what is now Haiti, Audubon studied painting in France (for a short while as a pupil of David) before coming to the United States in 1806. He began his American career as a portrait painter but soon turned his attention to works that would be collected and shown in a book entitled *The Birds of North America,* which was published in four volumes between 1827 and 1838. The paintings reproduced in this great work as hand-colored aquatints were not achieved without struggle. The artist collected specimens from the wild and brought them back to his studio, where he created paintings in a mixture of watercolor and pastel. *Gyrfalcon* (FIG. **21-31**) illustrates well how Audubon used the clarity and purity of David's Neoclassical style to present the naturalistic details of a North American bird. The white silhouettes of the birds fill the page, artfully arranged to display the avian forms as they posture against a clear blue sky. Audubon creates a drama of the wild while detailing the birds' features. The male gyrfalcon swoops down toward his mate in a way that magnificently shows the feather display on his back and head, while the female responds by lifting her wings, thus showing her talons and the understructure of her body. Their habitat is identified by the cliff ledge on which she stands, an extension of the mountain range in the background to the right and high above the plains and hills at the lower left. The scientific accuracy of Audubon's work still is a standard resource, and his images, as works of art, are still praised for the eloquent strength of their rich, yet simple composition. Working in the tradition of scientific illustration practiced at least from the time of Leonardo da Vinci and seen more recently in the work of Albinus (FIG. 20-27), Audubon's concern with the "living" qualities of his subjects carried an echo of Romanticism very different from the unmodulated scientific objectivity of his predecessors.

21-31 JOHN JAMES AUDUBON, *Gyrfalcon* from *The Birds of North America,* 1827–1838. Watercolor on paper, $25\frac{1}{2}'' \times 38\frac{1}{4}''$. The New-York Historical Society, New York.

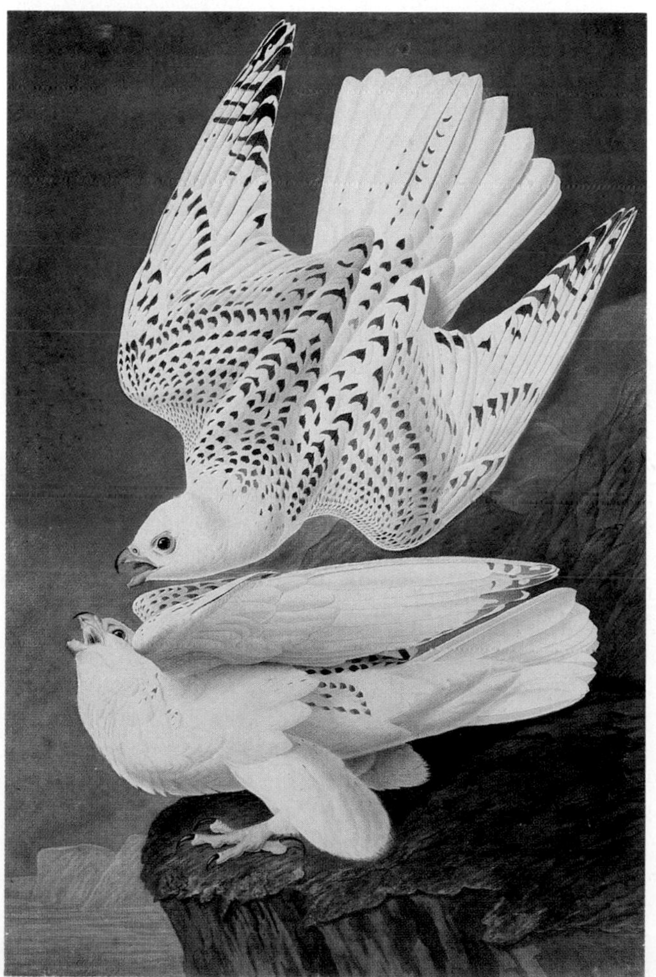

The Beginnings of Photography

"Reality," "truth," "fact"—that elusive quality sought by artists throughout time with painstaking effort in the traditional media of paint, crayon, and pen-and-ink—could be captured readily and with breathtaking accuracy in the new mechanical medium of photography. Artists themselves were instrumental in the development of this new technology. As early as the seventeenth century, as we saw with Vermeer (FIG. 19-54), artists had used an optical device called the camera obscura (literally, dark room) to help them render the details of their subjects more accurately. These instruments were darkened chambers (some virtually portable closets) with optical lenses fitted into a hole in one wall through which light entered to project an inverted image of a subject onto the chamber's opposite wall. The artist could trace the main details from this image for later reworking and refinement. In 1807, the invention of the *camera lucida* (lighted room) replaced the enclosed chamber with an arrangement in which a small prism lens, hung on a stand, projected the image of the object at which it had been "aimed" downward onto a sheet of paper. Artists using these two devices found this preliminary stage of the artistic process long and arduous, no matter how accurate the resulting work. All yearned for a better way of capturing the image of a subject directly. Two very different scientific inventions that accomplished this were announced, almost simultaneously, in France and England in 1839.

The first new discovery was the development of the *daguerreotype* process, named for LOUIS JACQUES MANDÉ DAGUERRE (1787–1851), one of its two inventors. Daguerre had trained as an architect before becoming a set painter and designer in the theater. This

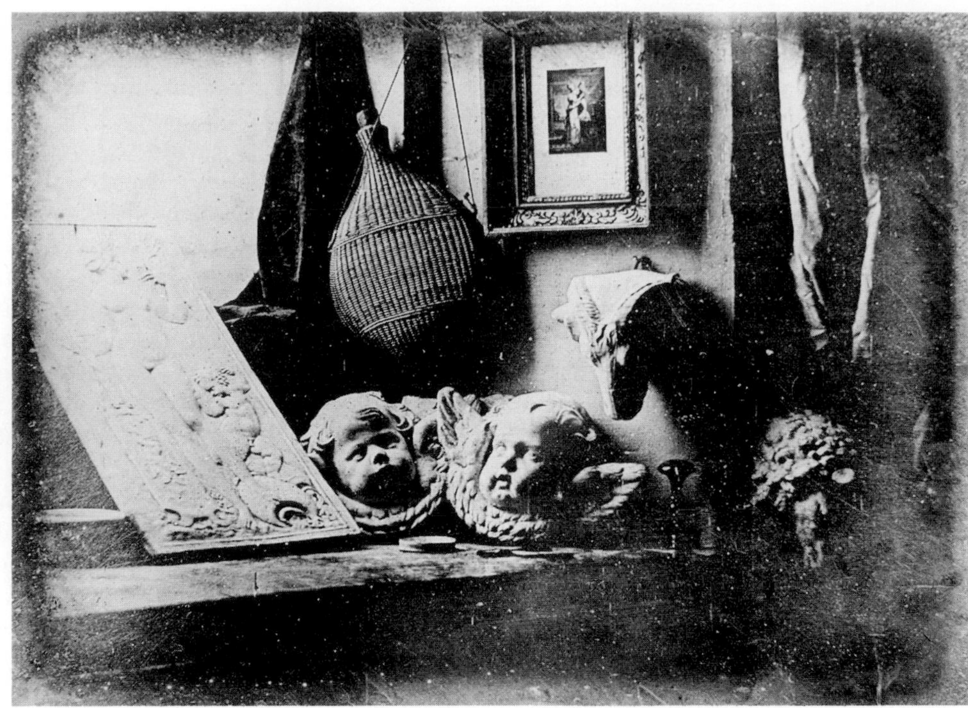

21-32 Louis Jacques Mandé Daguerre, *Still Life in Studio,* 1837. Daguerreotype. © Collection Société Française de Photographie, Paris.

background led him to open (with a friend) a popular entertainment called the Diorama, in which audiences witnessed performances of "living paintings" created by changing the lighting effects on a "sandwich" composed of a painted backdrop and several layers of painted, translucent front curtains. Daguerre used a camera obscura to make studies for the paintings for the Diorama, but he wanted to find a more efficient and effective procedure. Through a mutual acquaintance, he was introduced to Joseph Nicéphore Nièpce who, in 1826, had successfully made a permanent picture of the cityscape outside his upper-story window by exposing, in a camera obscura, a metal plate covered with a light-sensitive coating. Although the eight-hour exposure time needed to record Nièpce's subject hampered the process, Daguerre's excitement over its possibilities led to a partnership between the two men to pursue its development. Nièpce died in 1833, but Daguerre continued to work on his own. His contributions to the process consist of the discovery of latent development (in which the image is brought out through chemical solutions, considerably shortening the length of time needed for exposure) and the discovery of a better way to "fix" the image (again chemically) by stopping the action of light on the photographic plate, which otherwise would continue to darken until the image could no longer be discerned.

The French government presented the new daguerreotype process at the Academy of Science in Paris on January 7, 1839, with the understanding that the details of the process would be made available to all interested parties without charge (although the inventor received a large annuity in appreciation). Soon, people all over the world were taking pictures with the daguerreotype "camera" (a name shortened from camera obscura) in a process almost immediately christened "photography," from the Greek *photos* (light) and *graphos* (writing). From the start, painters were intrigued with the possibilities of the process as a new art medium. Paul Delaroche, a leading painter of the day, wrote in an official report to the French Government:

> Daguerre's process completely satisfies all the demands of art, carrying certain essential principles of art to such perfection that it must become a subject of observation and study even to the most accomplished painters. The pictures obtained by this method are as remarkable for the perfection of the details as for the richness and harmony of the general effect. Nature is reproduced in them not only with truth, but also with art.*

Each daguerreotype is a *unique* work, possessing amazing detail and finely graduated tones from black to white. Both qualities are evident in *Still Life in Studio* (FIG. **21-32**), which is one of the first success-

*Letter from Delaroche to François Arago, in Helmut Gernsheim, *Creative Photography* (New York: Bonanza Books, 1962), p. 24.

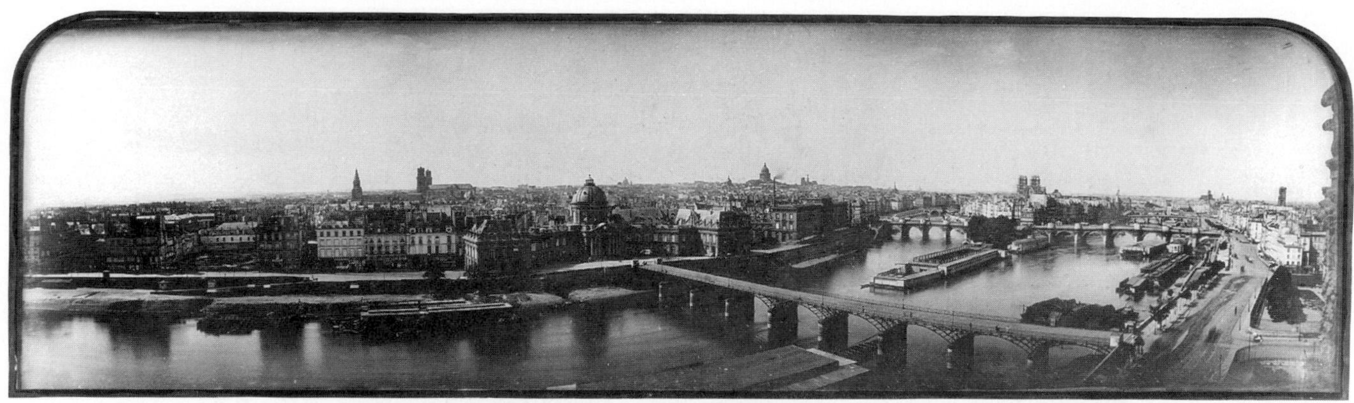

21-33 FRIEDERICH VON MARTENS, *Panorama of Paris,* c. 1844–1845. Panoramic daguerreotype, approx. $4\frac{1}{4}'' \times 14\frac{7}{8}''$. International Museum of Photography at George Eastman House, Rochester, New York.

ful plates Daguerre produced after perfecting his method. The process captured every detail—the subtle shapes, the varied textures, the diverse tones of light and shadow—in Daguerre's carefully constructed tableau. The three-dimensional forms of the sculptures, the basket, and the bits of cloth spring into high relief and are convincingly *there* within the image. The composition of this work was clearly inspired by seventeenth-century Dutch still lifes such as those of Willem Kalf (FIG. 19-55). Like Kalf, Daguerre arranged his objects to reveal clearly their textures and shapes. Unlike a painter, however, Daguerre could not alter anything within his arrangement to effect a stronger image. However, he could suggest a symbolic meaning within his array of objects. Like the peeled fruits and half-filled glasses of wine in Kalf's painting, Daguerre's sculptural and architectural fragments and the framed print of an embrace suggest that even art is *vanitas* and will not endure forever.*

The use of the daguerreotype spread quickly, with later photographic inventors and enthusiasts rapidly devising a host of improved cameras and techniques to extend the range of the new medium. Among these advancements was the swiveling panorama camera, for which photographers used special elongated and curved daguerreotype plates to make extreme wide-angle photographs in direct imitation of the panoramic view that had inspired Cole (FIG. 21-24), among others. The first photographer to master the special technical requirements of the panoramic daguerreotype was FRIEDERICH VON MARTENS (1809–1875). In his *Panorama of Paris* (FIG. **21-33**), Von Martens recorded the entire sweep of vision possible from the vantage point of the position of the camera, in this instance one of the pavilions of the Louvre overlooking the Seine. The angle is too wide for our eyes to encompass the view in a single look. Instead, the image must be scanned; as the eye moves across the plate, the viewer has a sense of traveling along and into the space of the image in a way not possible with a composition that can be absorbed with one glance. The luxurious expanse given to the viewer in photographs like *Panorama of Paris* suggests a vastness of the world akin to that in the Romantic landscape, but panoramic daguerreotype views also were intended as documents of the dramatic urban development occurring during the middle of the nineteenth century.

In the United States, where the first daguerreotype was taken within two months of Daguerre's presentation in Paris, two particularly avid and resourceful advocates of the new medium were JOSIAH JOHNSON HAWES (1808–1901), a painter, and ALBERT SANDS SOUTHWORTH (1811–1894), a pharmacist and teacher. Together, they ran a daguerreotype studio in Boston that specialized in portraiture, now popular due to the shortened exposure time required for the process (although it was still long enough to require a head brace to help the subject remain motionless while the photograph was being taken). The partners also, however, took their equipment outside of the studio to record places and events of particular interest to them. One such image is *Early Operation under Ether, Massachusetts General Hospital* (FIG. **21-34**). This daguerreotype was taken from the vantage point of the gallery of a hospital operating room, putting the viewer in the position of a medical student looking down on a lecture-demonstration of the type common in medical education midway through the nineteenth century. An image of historic record, this early daguerreotype gives the viewer a glimpse into the whole of Western medical practice. The focus of attention in *Early Operation* is the white-draped figure of the patient, who is surrounded by a circle of darkly clad doctors. The details of the figures and the furnishings and equipment of the room are recorded

*Evidently Daguerre was well satisfied with the artistic merit of *Still Life in Studio,* because he presented it to the curator of the Louvre, who accepted it for the state collections.

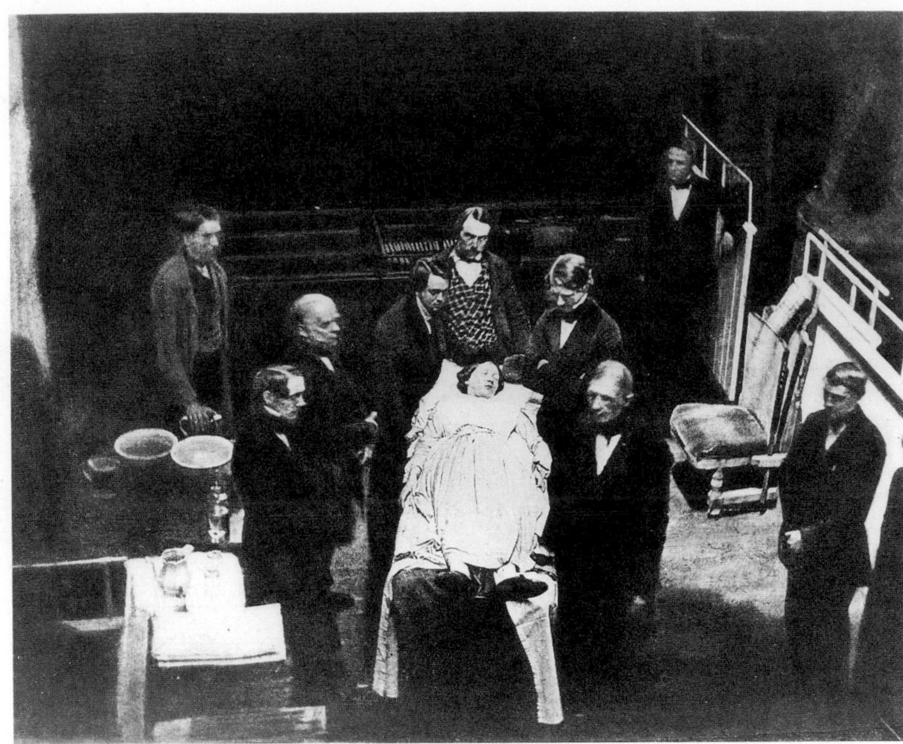

21-34 Josiah Johnson Hawes and Albert Sands Southworth, *Early Operation under Ether, Massachusetts General Hospital*, c. 1847. Daguerreotype. Massachusetts General Hospital, Boston.

clearly, but the slight blurring of several of the figures betrays motion during the exposure. The concentration of the action in the center of the work creates an image reminiscent of the vignette composition favored by the Romantics, while the elevated viewpoint flattens the spatial perspective and emphasizes the relationship of the figures in ways that will be of immense interest to the Impressionists, especially Degas.

The daguerreotype reigned supreme in photography until the 1850s, but the second major photographic invention—the ancestor of the modern negative-print system—was announced less than three weeks after Daguerre's method was unveiled in Paris, and eventually replaced it. On January 31, 1839, William Henry Fox Talbot (1800–1877) presented a paper on his "photogenic drawings" to the Royal Institution in London. A scientist and student of the classics who dabbled in painting, Talbot had for several years been experimenting with ways to capture the images of the camera obscura and camera lucida directly onto paper by using chemical coatings (emulsions) similar to those used to coat the daguerreotype's metal plates. As early as 1835, Talbot made "negative" images by placing objects on sensitized paper and exposing the arrangement to light, creating a design in which white silhouettes recorded the places where opaque or translucent objects had blocked light from darkening the emulsion on the paper. An example of the resulting images—said by Talbot to be "photogenic drawings" created with the "pencil of nature"—is the eerily attractive *Botanical Specimen* (FIG. **21-35**). The leaves and stem of the specimen emerge vividly from the dark ground as pale and mid-grey silhouettes. Talbot added no Romantic trappings, yet the evocative qualities of his negative image create a mysterious beauty in this composition that evokes the Romantic appreciation for nature. Photogenic drawings also were valued by scientists as records of the shape and structure of objects in the natural world. However, the process was limited both by the size of the subjects it could record and by the fact that its images incorporated the texture of the paper on which they were recorded, producing a slightly blurred effect very different from the crisp detail and wide range of tones available with the daguerreotype.

In his efforts to improve on his early work, Talbot soon discovered that if he let light shine through a negative image onto another sheet of sensitized paper, the result was a positive image of the original subject. Because the negative image was separate from the positive image (unlike the daguerreotype, in which both were contained on a single plate), many copies could be made from a single paper negative. This finding, combined with Talbot's work in latent development as it applied to paper-based photography and his incorporation of the "hypo" fixing solution (discovered by his friend, the physicist Sir John Herschel), which allowed the making of a more permanent image, led to the photographic process Talbot named the *calotype,* a term he derived from the Greek term *kalos,* meaning beautiful. Although the calotype image still retained a grainy and shadowy effect due to the texture of the papers used, its widespread adoption was precluded primarily by the stiff licensing and equipment fees charged for many years after Talbot patented his new process in 1841. As a result of both the look and cost of the calotype, many photographers elected to stay with the daguerreotype until photographic technology could overcome these problems.

21-35 WILLIAM HENRY FOX TALBOT, *Botanical Specimen,* 1839. Photogenic drawing. Royal Photographic Society, Bath, England.

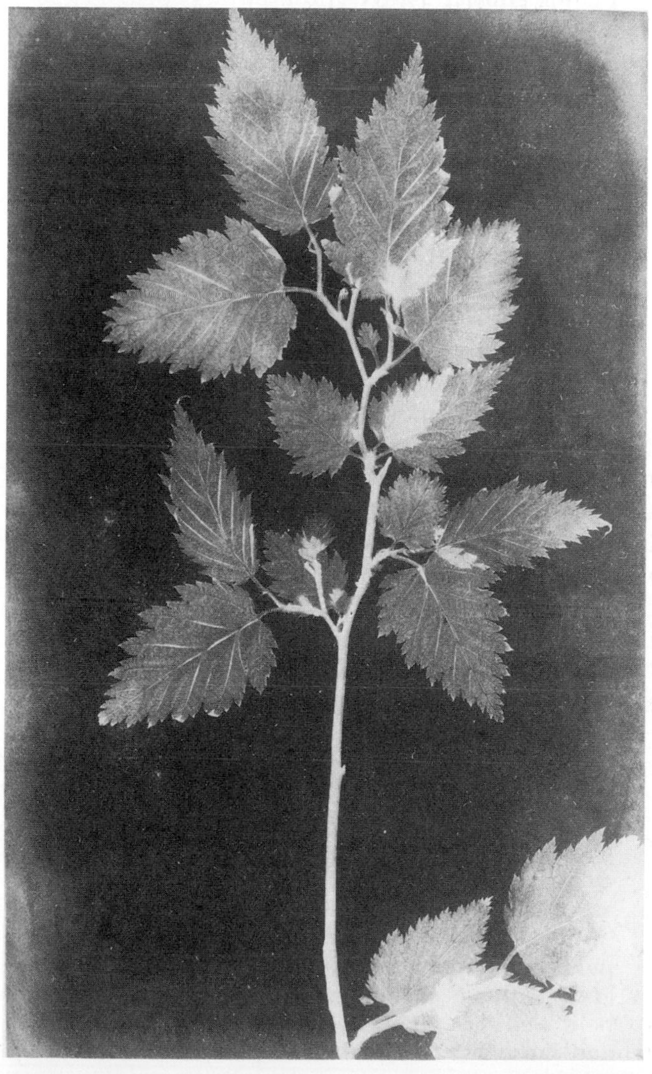

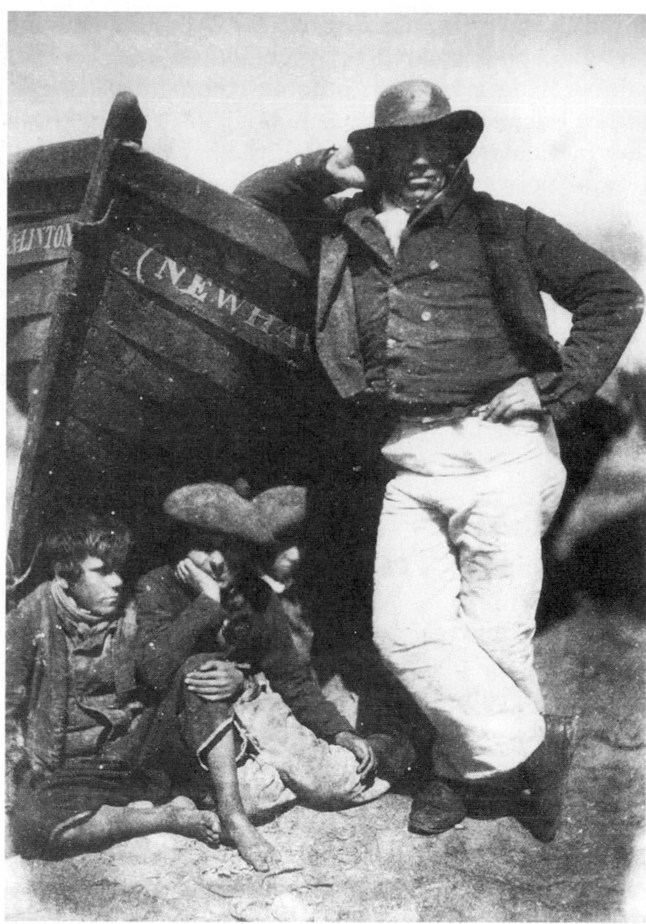

21-36 DAVID OCTAVIUS HILL and ROBERT ADAMSON, *Sandy Linton and His Boat and Bairns,* 1843–1847. Calotype. National Portrait Gallery, London.

Two Scotsmen, DAVID OCTAVIUS HILL (1802–1870) and ROBERT ADAMSON (1821–1848) were enthusiastic proponents of the calotype process, however, and they embraced Talbot's process to capture a wide variety of Scottish and English scenes. Hill, a well-known British painter, first contacted Adamson, who had been making calotypes since 1842, seeking help in the production of photographic studies for a monumental painting of a historic moment in the history of the Church of Scotland. Hill was to pose and arrange the subjects, while Adamson was responsible for the calotypes. This collaboration was the beginning of a partnership in which the two men extended their subject matter to encompass the calotyping of Romantic scenery and costume dramas, the major cities and monuments of Scotland, and straight genre scenes depicting the daily life of fisherfolk along the Scottish sea coast. *Sandy Linton and His Boat and Bairns* (FIG. **21-36**) is an example of the latter classification. Linton, the fisherman, dominates the composition as he leans against his boat, slanting into the frame of the picture from the left. The lively shapes of the three children (*bairn* is Scottish for child) animate the archlike space created between Linton and his boat and provide a kind of footnote commentary on the life of their father. The scene is given to us without any particular statement about the fisherman's situation or personality. No allusion is made to anything outside the immediacy of this particular, commonplace experience, although the slight diffuseness of the calotype image might invite such symbolic insights. In the end, the scene is but a frozen moment in the life of an actual person of the 1840s, captured with all the detail and fidelity to fact that this particular photographic process could produce.

REALISM IN THE SECOND HALF OF THE CENTURY

We already have seen realism in the first half of the century, particularly in the art of Constable, and we have seen realistic images mechanically produced by the camera. Actually, realism, in different degrees of focus, has been an ingredient in Western art for centuries, from Van Eyck to Velázquez and Vermeer and beyond. The nineteenth-century kind of realism can be described technically and iconographically. Technically, realism deals with the replication of an optical field achieved by matching its color tones on a flat surface, whether or not the subject matter has or could have been seen by the artist. Iconographically, nineteenth-century Realism can be described as the subject matter of everyday, contemporary life as seen or seeable by the artist, whether recorded photographically or by other modes of visual report. The quarrel between Realism and Romanticism at mid-century was primarily over subject matter. Realists disapproved of traditional and fictional subjects on the grounds that they were not real and visible and were not of the present world. These artists argued that only the things of one's own times, the things one can see, are "real." The Realist vision and method resulted in a *modern* style—one, by definition, cut off from the past.

The Realist position in art and literature was strengthened by the scientific and technological achievements of the nineteenth century. Proponents of scientific positivism asserted that only scientifically verified fact was "real" and that the scientific method was the only legitimate means of gaining knowledge; all other means—religion, revelation, intuition, imagination—produced only fictions and illusions. Writing in 1892, Karl Pearson insisted confidently that "science claims for its heritage the whole domain to which the word knowledge can be legitimately applied. . . . It refuses to admit any coheirs to its possession." Modern science was indeed the most prestigious of all nineteenth-century intellectual enterprises; its authority rose from its triumphs. Its rigorous practicality and its search for the facts necessarily served as an example to artists searching for a modern truth and a modern style free from fable and fantasy. Realism stood for what the eye could see in the modern world—for actuality in all subject matter and verisimilitude in all images. Works of imagination based on subjects from myth and history were believed false.

Numerous Realist painters (foremost among them, Gustave Courbet and Édouard Manet) recorded the life of their times in factual images of it, yet their styles had little in common. At the same time, many artists embodied imaginative subject matter in strikingly realistic forms. Indeed, a dialogue between Realism and Romanticism went on throughout the century, and, although technical Realism seemed predominant during the latter half of the century, Romantic subject matter and arbitrary formal experiment persisted, and by the end of the century, appeared to carry the day for pure artistic subjectivity.

The realism of Manet, which became the realism of the Impressionists, reveals the striking paradox in Realism. To capture the entire optical field spread before them, artists must paint it just as they see it. To record this instantaneous impression, however, painters must work swiftly in a sketchlike execution that blurs the visual field as it increasingly emphasizes the brush stroke and the blot of color. The wholeness of the field disintegrates into a plurality of color functions. Scientists would say that these artists are not painting the world, but only individual sensations of it. As those sensations belong to each artist's private world, the Realist artists found that the external reality they sought so avidly was *really* determined by their own inescapable subjectivity.

Courbet and the Theme of Realism

From fragmentary observations like the following, made by Jean Désiré Gustave Courbet (1819–1877), we get some general idea of Realism as the Realists and their friendly critics understood it.

> To be able to translate the customs, ideas, and appearances of my time as I see them—in a word, to create a living art—this has been my aim. . . . The art of painting can consist only in the representation of objects visible and tangible to the painter . . . , [who must apply] his personal faculties to the ideas and the things of the period in which he lives. . . . I hold also that painting is an essentially *concrete* art, and can consist only of the representation of things

> both *real* and *existing*. . . . An *abstract* object, invisible or nonexistent, does not belong to the domain of painting. . . . Show me an angel, and I'll paint one.*

Courbet has long been regarded as the father of the Realist movement in nineteenth-century art; certainly, he used the term "realism" in exhibiting his own works, even though he shunned labels. "The title of Realist," he insisted, "was thrust upon me, just as the title of Romantic was imposed upon the men of 1830. Titles have never given a true idea of things." In and since Courbet's time, confusion about what Realism *is* has been widespread. Writing in 1857, Champfleury, one of the first critics to recognize and appreciate Courbet's work, declared: "I will not define Realism. . . . I do not know where it comes from, where it goes, what it is. . . . The name horrifies me by its pedantic ending; . . . there is enough confusion already about that famous word." Confusion, or at least disagreement, about Realism still exists among historians of nineteenth- and, for that matter, twentieth-century art. Yet from Courbet's own brief statements, we gather that he wished to be only of his own time and to paint only what it made visible to him. Born into a wealthy family in the primarily rural area of Franche-Comté, Courbet became an anticlerical painter who took as his subjects the working-class people and ordinary landscapes around him. Although his early career was distinguished by self-portraits displaying a wildly Romantic mood, in most of his works he made a sharp break with the Tradition; all mythological, religious, and purely imaginative subjects were ruled out as not visible to the modern eye. The critic Jules Antoine Castagnary, writing in 1863, said of Courbet: "[His] great claim is to represent what he sees. It is, in fact, one of his favorite axioms that everything that does not appear upon the retina is outside the domain of painting." At this time, critics looking for an expressly modern art could find their hero in Courbet.

A man of powerful personality, Courbet was cut out to be the truculent champion of the Realist cause, defying both public taste and the art juries that rejected two of his major works for the Paris International Exhibition in 1855 on the grounds that his subjects and figures were too coarsely materialistic (so much so as to be plainly "socialistic") and too large. Plain people of the kind Courbet shows us in his work were considered by the public to be unsuitable for artistic representation and were linked in the middle-class mind with the dangerous, newly defined working class, which was finding outspoken champions in men like Marx, Engels, Proudhon, Balzac, Flaubert, Zola, and Dickens. Rejected by the exhibition jury, Courbet set up his own gallery outside the grounds, calling it the Pavilion of Realism. Courbet's pavilion and his utterances amounted to the manifestoes of the new movement. Although he maintained that he founded no school and was of no school, he did, as the name of his pavilion suggests, accept the term "realism" as descriptive of his art. With the unplanned collaboration of Millet, Daumier, and other artists, Courbet challenged the whole iconographic stock of the Tradition and called public attention to what Baudelaire termed the "heroism of modern life," which Courbet felt should replace all the heroism of traditional subject matter. For the public, it was a contest between the painters of the "ugly" (Courbet) and the painters of the "beautiful" (those who opposed Courbet), as the public understood those qualities.

Representative of Courbet's work is *Burial at Ornans* (FIG. **21-37**), which depicts a funeral in a bleak, provincial landscape, attended by obscure persons "of no importance," the type of people presented by Balzac and Flaubert in their novels. While an officious clergyman reads the Office of the Dead, those in attendance cluster around the excavated gravesite, their faces registering all degrees of response to the situation. Although the painting has the monumental scale of a traditional history painting, contemporary critics were horrified not only by the ordinariness of the subject matter, but also by the starkly antiheroic composition. Arranged in a wavering line extending across the broad width of the canvas, the figures are portrayed in groups—the somberly clad women at the back right, a semicircle of similarly clad men by the open grave, and assorted churchmen at the left. The observer's attention, however, is wholly on the wall of figures, seen at eye-level, that blocks any view into deep space. The faces of the figures are portraits; some of the models were friends of Courbet. Behind and above the figures are bands of overcast sky and barren cliffs. The dark pit of the grave opens into the viewer's space in the center foreground. Despite the unposed look of the figures (which in conjunction with the cut-off figures at the edges of the canvas, may owe something to Courbet's interest in photography), the artist controlled the composition in a masterful way by his sparing use of bright color. Patches of white carry the eye across the bank of figures. The strong red of the clerics' cassocks appears in the caps and skirts of the acolytes to the left; the red is then countered by its complement in the green-blue stockings of the mourner whose hand is extended toward the grave. The long, narrow rectangle of the canvas has something of the panoramic effect embraced by Cole and Martens; the viewer's eye cannot take in the

*In Robert Goldwater and Marco Treves, eds., *Artists on Art*, 3rd ed. (New York: Pantheon, 1958), pp. 295–97.

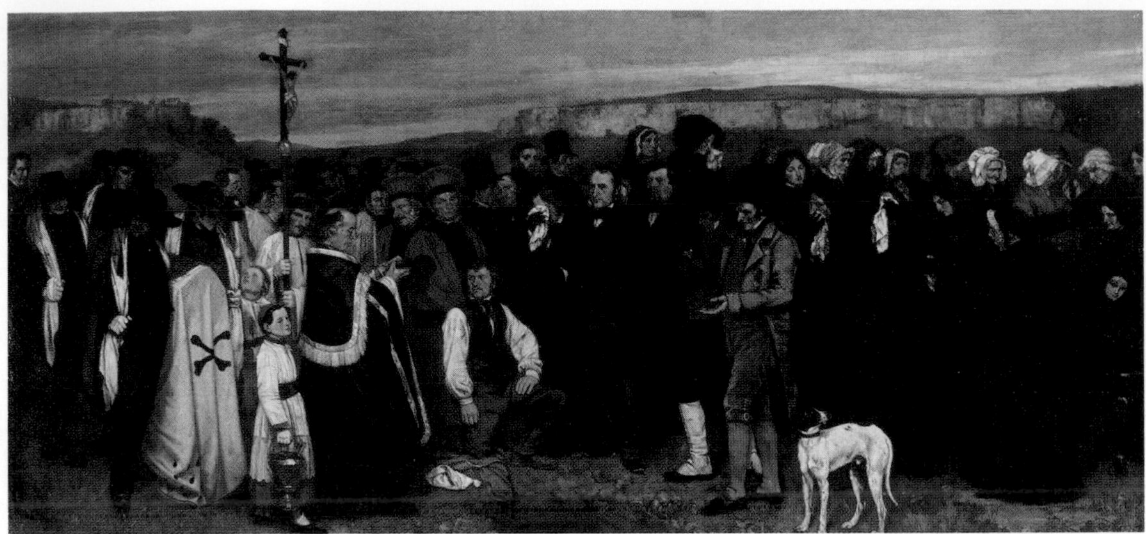

21-37 JEAN DÉSIRÉ GUSTAVE COURBET, *Burial at Ornans,* 1849. Approx. 10′ × 22′. Louvre, Paris.

whole with one glance but must scan across the composition from group to group. The heroic, the sublime, and the terrible are not found here—only the drab facts of undramatized life and death. In 1857, Champfleury wrote of *Burial at Ornans,* ". . . it represents a small-town funeral and yet reproduces the funerals of *all* small towns." Unlike the superhuman or subhuman actors on the grand stage of the Romantic canvas, this Realist work moves according to the ordinary rhythms of contemporary life.

Beyond his new subject matter, Courbet's intentionally simple and direct methods of expression in composition and technique seemed to many of his more traditional contemporaries to be unbearably crude, and he was called a primitive. Although his bold, somber palette was essentially traditional, Courbet often used the palette knife, with which he could quickly place and unify large daubs of paint, producing a roughly wrought surface. His example inspired the young men who worked with him (and later Impressionists like Claude Monet and Auguste Renoir), but the public accused him of carelessness and critics wrote of his "brutalities."

Although often embattled with critics over the spirit and form of Realism, Courbet had secure official backing from the late 1850s onward, and, in his later years, painted with greater intention to please the public. Indeed, the mode of these later pictures recalls traditional methods, with dark underpainting, heavy chiaroscuro, and subject matter familiar in the popular Salon. This conservatism disappointed younger artists who had come to rely strongly on Courbet's vigorous style and technique, as well as on his courageous individualism. Most of the Impressionists had associated and exhibited with him in their early years, but Courbet failed to catch the spirit of the new style that was emerging in their work. Despite this, neither the Impressionists, nor history itself, could deny the impetus Courbet's art had given the movement toward a modern style based on observations of the modern environment.

Where Courbet favored heavy paint, a dark palette, and a style in which he simplified details into planes of color, JEAN BAPTISTE CAMILLE COROT (1796–1875) achieved a cooler Realist style. In Corot's *The Harbor of La Rochelle* (FIG. **21-38**), we can see his interest in the full tonal spread—the careful arrangement of dark and light values—which the new medium of photography was achieving automatically. Corot's method was to be as faithful as possible to the scale of light to dark. His procedure was interesting. He wrote in his notebooks:

> The first two things to study are form and values. For me, these are the bases of what is serious in art. Color and finish put charm into one's work. In preparing a study or a picture, it seems to me very important to begin by an indication of the darkest values . . . and continue in order to the lightest value. From the darkest to the lightest I would establish twenty shades.

In Corot's *Harbor,* we can appreciate these careful gradations of tone. The forms in the work are thoughtfully placed, and the general ordering of them recalls the landscape tradition of Nicolas Poussin (FIG. 19-61). Indeed, Corot employed such a firm definition of the forms and such gradation of the halftones that he was said to "Ingres-ize" the landscape. Both Constable and Corot point toward the Impressionists, but in different ways. Constable foreshadows their work in his brilliant freshness of color and

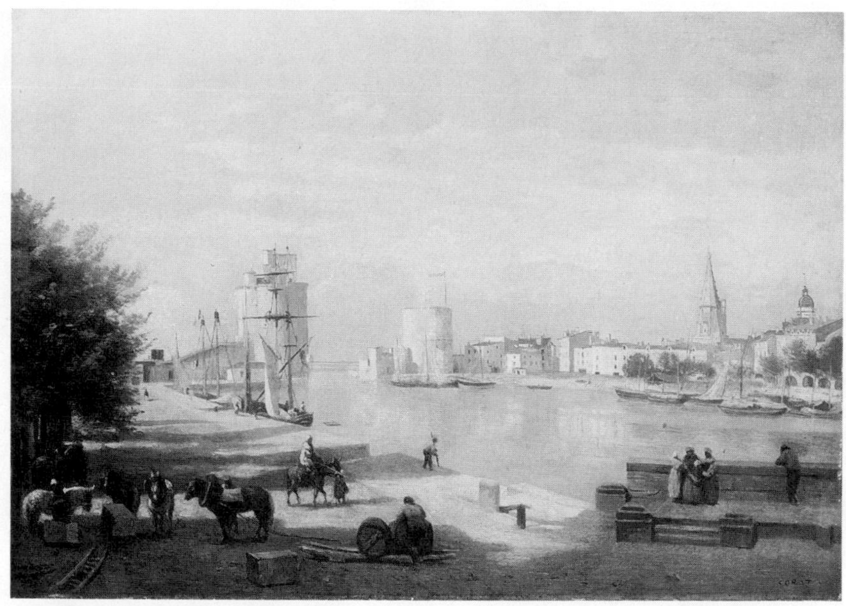

21-38 JEAN BAPTISTE CAMILLE COROT, *The Harbor of La Rochelle,* 1851. Approx. 20″ × 28″. Yale University Art Gallery, New Haven, Connecticut (bequest of Stephen Carlton Clark, B.A., 1903).

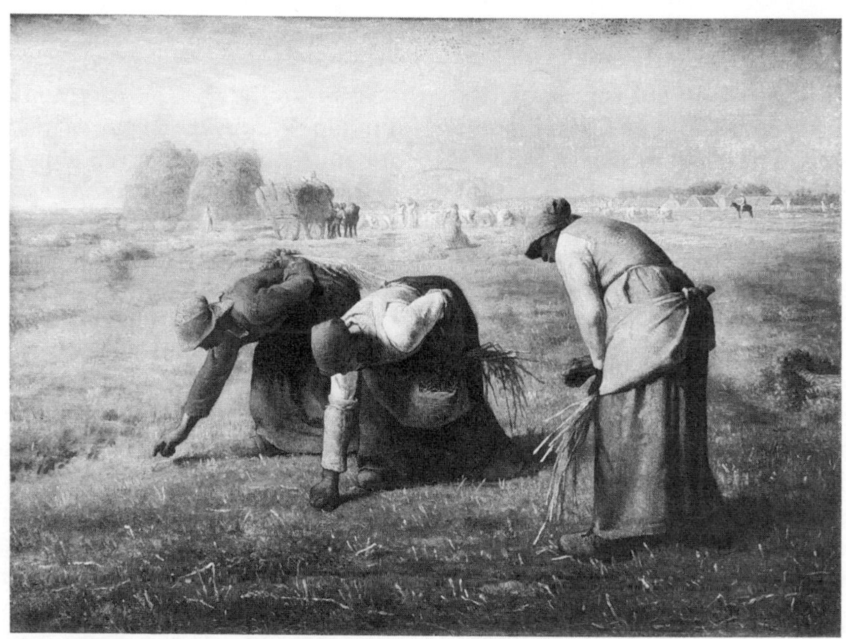

21-39 JEAN FRANÇOIS MILLET, *The Gleaners,* 1857. Approx. 33″ × 44″. Louvre, Paris.

divided brush stroke, while Corot prefigures their concerns for the rendering of outdoor light and atmosphere in terms of values.

Corot painted in close association with members of the "Barbizon school," a group of landscape and figure painters who settled near the village of Barbizon in the forest of Fontainebleau. The objective, carefully realistic landscapes of many of the painters of the Barbizon school, like Théodore Rousseau, Charles François Daubigny, and Narcisse Virgile Diaz, will powerfully influence the Impressionists and Post-Impressionists. However, the work of one of the chief Barbizon painters, JEAN FRANÇOIS MILLET (1814–1875), exemplified a different Realist intent. Of peasant stock himself, Millet took the humble country folk of France as his subjects. In *The Gleaners* (FIG. **21-39**), done in 1857, he characteristically posed three toiling female peasants as monumental figures

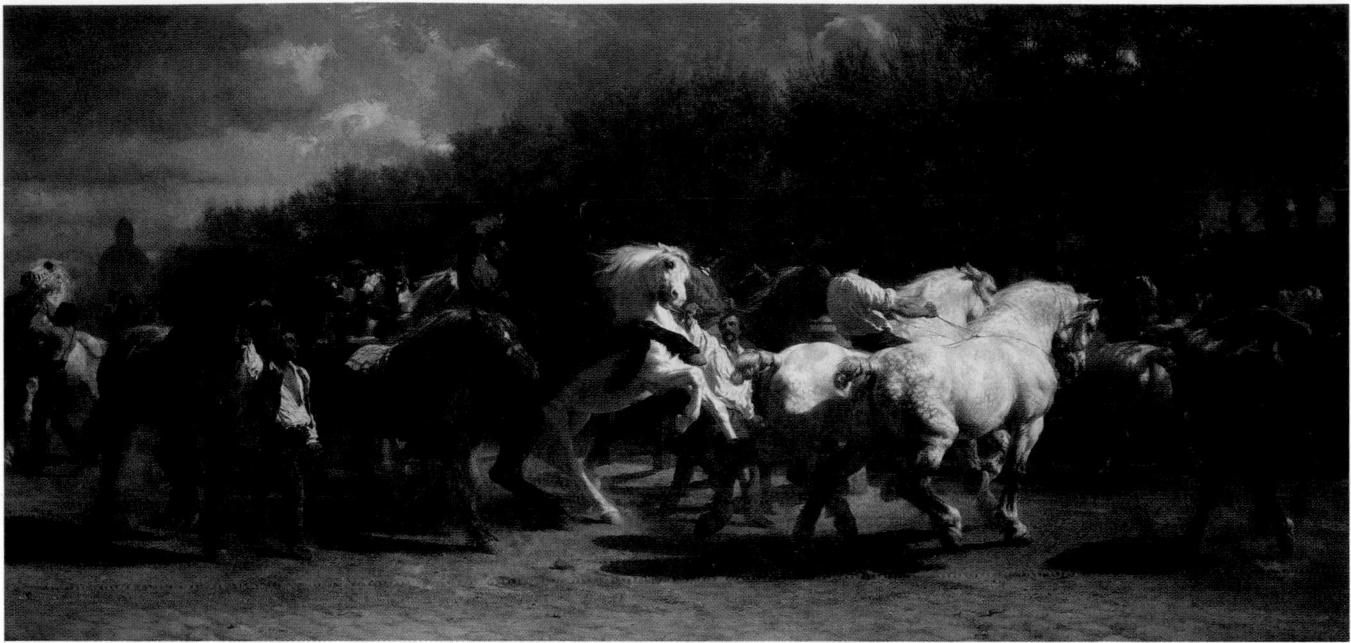

21-40 Rosa Bonheur, *The Horse Fair,* 1853. 8′ ¼″ × 16′ 7½″. The Metropolitan Museum of Art, New York (gift of Cornelius Vanderbilt, 1887).

in the foreground of a harvested field that stretches back to a rim of haystacks, cottages, trees, and distant workers near the horizon. The quiet design of Millet's painting shares the careful arrangement and calm mood of Corot's *Harbor,* but Millet's emphasis was on the figures; everything in the composition accents his scrupulous truth of detail and contributes to the dignity he gave to even the simplest rural tasks. The solemn grandeur with which Millet invested the poor caused him to be identified with a kind of socialism that was prevalent at the time he was painting. Actually, this socialist movement was a late echo of Enlightenment and Romantic intuition, held by such men as Jean Jacques Rousseau and Wordsworth, which found a touch of nobility in the humblest lives.

Courbet, Corot, and Millet depicted quiet moments in everyday life. Many French Realist artists, however, Rosa Bonheur (1822–1899) among them, chose more naturally dramatic subjects for their work. Trained as an artist by her father, Bonheur founded her career on his belief that, as a woman and an artist, she had a special role to play in creating a new and perfect society. In her work, she combined a naturalist's knowledge of equine anatomy and motion with an honest love and admiration for the brute strength of wild and domestic animals. Driven by a Realist passion for accuracy in her painting, she observed the anatomy of living horses at the great Parisian horse fair, where the animals were shown and traded, and also spent long hours studying the anatomy of carcasses in the Paris slaughterhouses. For her best-known work, *The Horse Fair* (FIG. **21-40**), she adopted a panoramic composition similar to that in Courbet's *Burial at Ornans,* painted a few years earlier. In contrast to the still figures in *Burial,* Bonheur filled her broad canvas with the sturdy farm animals and their grooms seen on parade at the annual Parisian horse sale. Some horses, not quite broken, rear up; others plod or trot, guided on foot or ridden by their keepers. The uneven line of the march, the thunderous pounding, and the seemingly overwhelming power of the Percherons were clearly based on close observations from life, even though Bonheur acknowledged some inspiration from the Classical model of the Parthenon frieze (FIG. 5-49). The dramatic lighting, loose brushwork, and roiling sky also reveal her admiration of the style of Géricault. Bonheur's depiction of Realist drama in *The Horse Fair* captivated viewers, who eagerly bought engraved reproductions of the work, making it one of the most well known paintings of the century.

Variations of Form in Realism

Although French artists took the lead in promoting Realism, lending especially strong support to the idea that Realism should be the depiction of the realities of modern life, Realism was not exclusively French. Often influenced by the appearance of photography and almost always inspired by the optical truth of the physical world, Realism appeared in all countries in a variety of forms and was taken for granted by the end of the century.

In the United States, a dedicated appetite for showing the realities of the human condition made THOMAS EAKINS (1844–1916) a master Realist portrait and genre painter. Eakins studied both painting and medical anatomy in Philadelphia before undertaking further study under Jean-Léon Gérôme (FIG. 21-60). Despite three years of study with Gérôme in Paris, Eakins turned out to have little of the Romantic in him. Instead, he was resolutely a Realist; his ambition was to paint things as he saw them rather than as the public might wish them to be portrayed. This attitude was very much in tune with nineteenth-century American taste, which was said to combine an admiration for accurate depiction with a hunger for truth. These twin attributes are reflected in Ralph Waldo Emerson's observation that "Our American character is marked by a more than average delight in accurate perception," and in Henry David Thoreau's declaration: "Let us not underrate the value of a fact. It will one day flower in a truth."

Eakins's early masterpiece, *The Gross Clinic* (FIG. **21-41**), was rejected for its too-brutal Realism by the art jury for the exhibition in Philadelphia that celebrated the centennial of American independence. The work represents the renowned surgeon Dr. Samuel Gross in the operating amphitheater of the Jefferson Medical College in Philadelphia, where the painting now hangs. The surgeon is accompanied by colleagues, all of whom have been identified, and by the patient's mother, who covers her face. Dr. Gross, with bloody fingers and scalpel, lectures on his procedure. The painting is indeed an unsparing description of a contemporary event, with a good deal more reality than many viewers could endure: "It is a picture," said one critic, "that even strong men find difficult to look at long, if they can look at it at all." True to the program of "scenes from modern life," Eakins put the surgeon in the context of his business, as Southworth and Hawes had done in their daguerreotype of a similar setting (FIG. 21-34). Each image records a particular event at a particular time.

Like Constable before him, Eakins believed that knowledge—and where relevant, *scientific* knowledge—was a prerequisite to his art. As a scientist (in his anatomical studies), Eakins preferred a slow, deliberate method of careful invention based on his observations of the perspective, the anatomy, and the actual details of his subject. His concern for anatomical correctness led him to investigate the human form and the human form in motion, both with regular photographic apparatus and with a special camera devised by the French kinesiologist (scholar of motion) Étienne-Jules Marey. Eakins's later collaboration with Eadweard Muybridge in the photographic study of animal and human action of all types drew favorable attention in France, especially from Degas, and anticipated the motion picture.

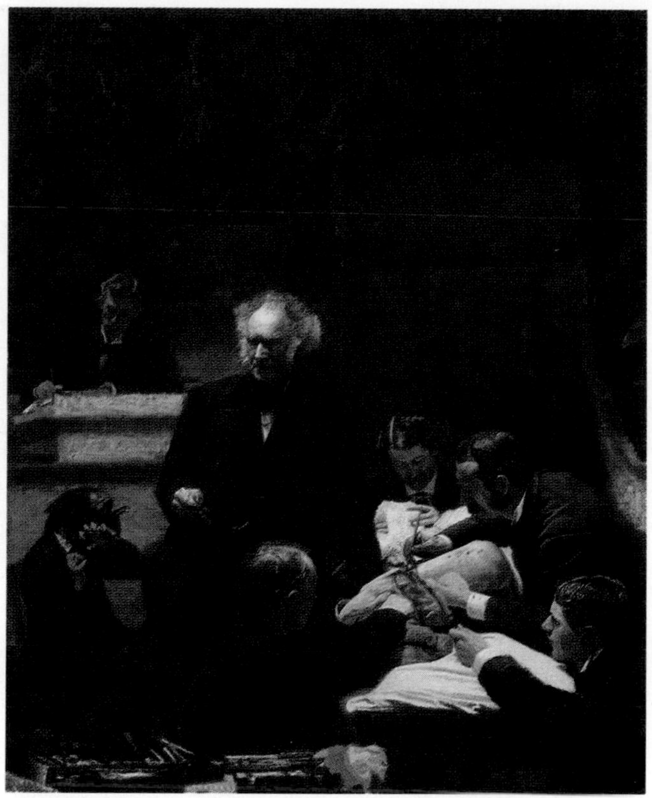

21-41 THOMAS EAKINS, *The Gross Clinic*, 1875. 8′ × 6′ 6″. Jefferson Medical College, Philadelphia.

The Realist photographer and scientist EADWEARD MUYBRIDGE (1830–1904) came to the United States from England in the 1850s and settled in San Francisco, where he established a prominent international reputation for his photographs of the western United States. (His large-plate landscape images of the Yosemite region won him a gold medal at the Vienna Exposition of 1873.) In 1872, the governor of California, Leland Stanford, sought Muybridge's assistance in settling a bet about whether, at any point in a stride, all four feet of a horse galloping at top speed are off the ground. Through his photography, Muybridge was able to prove that they were. This experience was the beginning of Muybridge's photographic studies of the successive stages in human and animal motion—detail too quick for the human eye to capture. These investigations culminated in 1885 at the University of Pennsylvania with a series of multiple-camera motion studies that recorded separate photographs of each progressive moment in a single action.

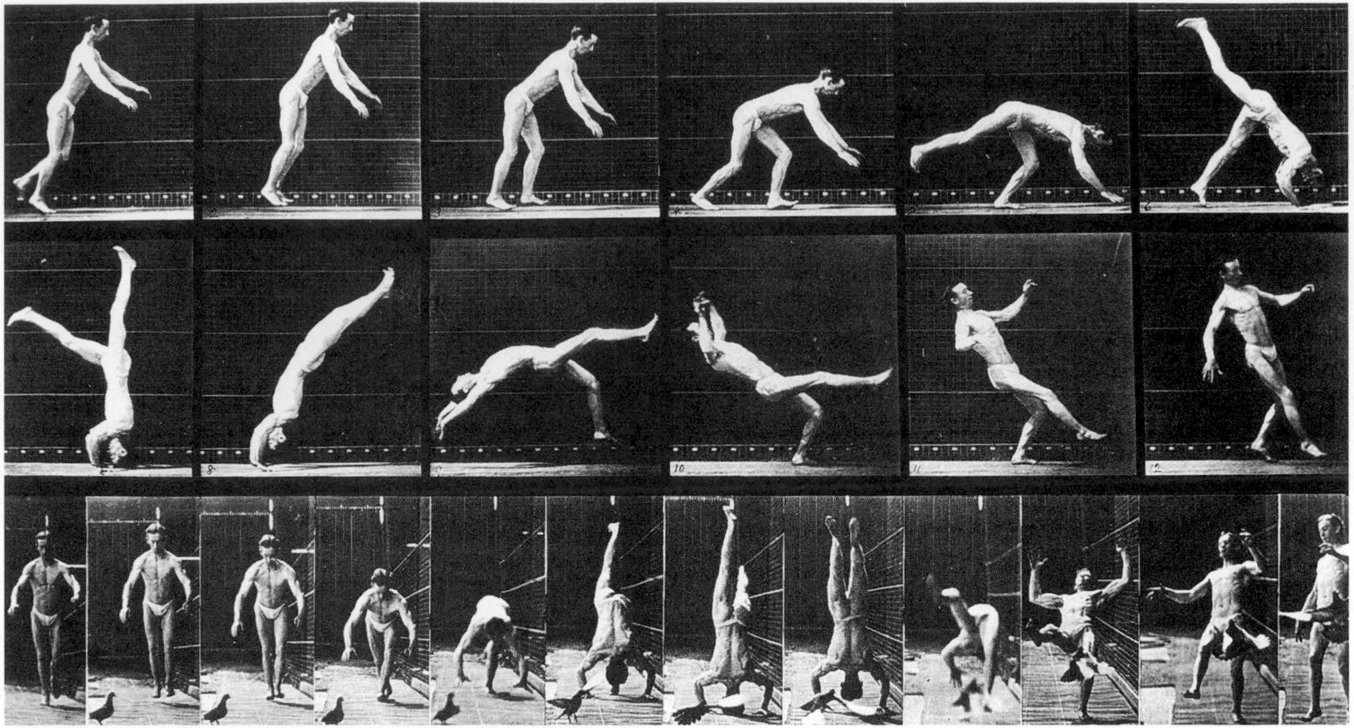

21-42 Eadweard Muybridge, *Hand-spring, a flying pigeon interfering, June 26, 1885,* Plate 365 of *Animal Locomotion,* 1887. Print from original master negative. International Museum of Photography at George Eastman House, Rochester, New York.

The results of this research were widely publicized in Muybridge's book *Animal Locomotion* (1887). *Hand-spring, a flying pigeon interfering* (fig. **21-42**) is a typical plate (No. 365) from the book. Taken with two batteries of cameras placed at right angles to one another, this photograph combines the side and front views of the successive instants in an athletic stunt. At the top is the series of twelve images shot from the side view, split into two rows to match in width the twelve narrower front views that are spread across the bottom. With our Western habit of reading type in books, we begin at the upper left and scan along the top two rows to reconstruct the hand-spring, perhaps wondering as we do so where the pigeon mentioned in the title comes in. The drama is revealed at the bottom, where we see the strolling pigeon startled into flight as the hand-spring unfolds, almost upsetting the athlete in the process. Muybridge's motion photographs earned him a place in the history of science as well as art. His sequential studies of motion, along with those of Eakins and Marey, influenced many other artists, including their contemporary, the painter and sculptor Edgar Degas, and twentieth-century artists like Marcel Duchamp.

Muybridge presented his work to scientists and general audiences by means of a device called the *zoopraxiscope,* which he invented to project his sequences of images (mounted on special glass plates) onto a screen. The effect was so lifelike that one viewer said it "threw upon the screen apparently the living, moving animals. Nothing was wanting but the clatter of hoofs upon the turf."* The illusion of motion here was created by a physical fact of human eyesight called "persistence of vision," which, stated simply, means that whatever the eye sees is held in the brain for a fraction of a second after the eye stops seeing it, causing a rapid succession of different images to merge one into the next and producing the illusion of continuous change.† This illusion lies at the heart of the "realism" of all cinema.

The expatriate American artist John Singer Sargent (1856–1925) was a younger contemporary of Eakins and Muybridge. In contrast to Eakins's carefully rendered details, Sargent developed a looser, more dashing Realist portrait style. Sargent studied art in Paris before settling in London, where he was

**Scientific American,* May 1880, cited in Kenneth MacGowan, *Behind the Screen* (New York: A Dell Book, Delta Publishing Co., 1965), p. 49.

†News of Muybridge's zoopraxiscope spread rapidly. One interested person was the inventor Thomas Alva Edison, who had just perfected the phonograph and wanted to add sound to Muybridge's moving images. Edison and his assistant, William Kennedy Laurie Dickson, eventually developed a true motion-picture camera (patented in 1891) that used strips of photographic film newly invented by George Eastman. Innovations such as these helped lay the foundations of the art of cinema.

renowned as a cultivated and cosmopolitan gentleman, and as a facile and fashionable painter of portraits. His fluent brushing of paint in thin films and his effortless achievement of quick and lively illusion were learned from his study of Velázquez, whose masterpiece, *Las Meninas* (FIG. 19-38), may have influenced Sargent's family portrait, *The Daughters of Edward Darley Boit* (FIG. **21-43**). The four girls (the children of one of Sargent's close friends) are grouped casually within a hall and small drawing room in their Paris home. The informal, eccentric arrangement of their slight figures suggests how much at ease they are within this familiar space and with objects like the monumental Japanese vases, the red screen, and the fringed rug, whose scale subtly emphasizes the diminutive stature of the children. Sargent must have known the Boit daughters well and liked them. Relaxed and trustful, they gave the artist an opportunity to record a gradation of young innocence in which he sensitively captured the naïve, wondering openness of the little girl in the foreground, the grave artlessness of the ten-year-old child, and the slightly self-conscious poise of the adolescents. From the positioning of the figures and the continuity of the space of hall and drawing room (conveyed by the lighting), we sense how spontaneously they function within this setting. They seem to be attending momentarily to an adult who has asked them to interrupt their activity and "look this way." Here is a most effective embodiment of the Realist belief that the business of the artist is to record the modern being in modern context. Through devices like the cut-off vase and rug, we see the beginnings of the way in which Realist painters increasingly will move into the space of their works, regulating the distance of the artist's (and viewer's) standpoint from the objects represented, so that the action and environment in the painting seem one with those outside it.

21-43 JOHN SINGER SARGENT, *The Daughters of Edward Darley Boit*, 1882. 7′ 3″ × 7′ 3″. Museum of Fine Arts, Boston (gift of Mary Boit, Florence D. Boit, Jane H. Boit, and Julia O. Boit, in memory of their father).

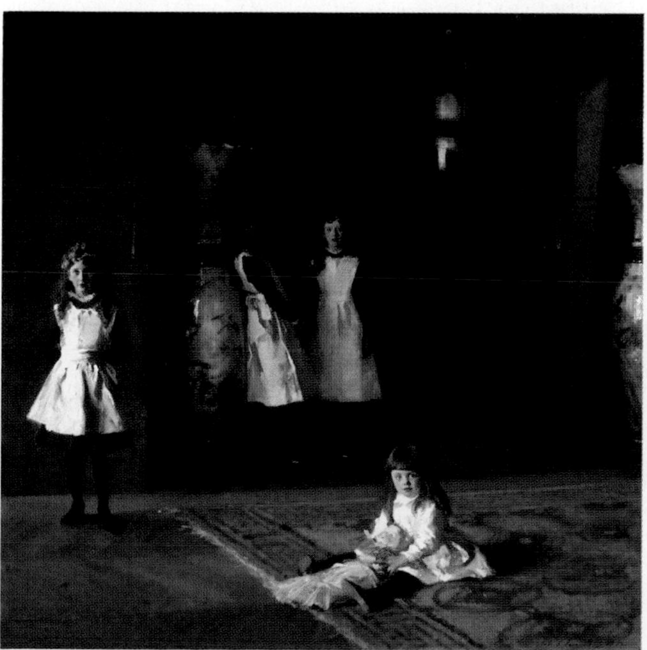

As Realism spread throughout the world, Realist artists expanded and diversified their subject matter to embrace all classes and levels of society, all types of people and environments: the urban and rural working class, the denizens of the big city, the burghers of the small town, the leisure class at its resorts, the rustics of the provinces. Added to the social sympathies we found in Daumier, Courbet, and Millet were motives of an anthropological kind, reflecting interest in national and regional characteristics, folk customs and culture, and the quaintness and picturesqueness of local color. WILHELM LEIBL (1844–1900), perhaps the most important German Realist painter in the later nineteenth century, is a master of the quaint and picturesque detail of country life. Influenced by Courbet, but lacking his breadth and depth, Leibl exemplified the Realist credo. His masterpiece, *Three Women in a Village Church* (FIG. **21-44**), is the record of a sacred moment—the moment of prayer—in the life of three country women of different generations. Dressed in rustic costume, their Sunday best, they pursue their devotions unselfconsciously, their prayer books held in big hands roughened by work. Their manners and their dress proclaim them innocent of the affectations and refinements of the metropolis, which they probably have never seen. Leibl chose to show their natural virtues: simplicity, honesty, steadfastness, patience. He could subscribe, doubtless, to the words of a poet from another country and another time: "Far from the madding crowd's ignoble strife / . . . / they kept the noiseless tenor of their way."* Leibl himself wrote in a letter: "Here in the open country and among those who live close to nature, one can paint naturally." For three years, he worked from his peasant models in the little church, often under impossible conditions of lighting and temperature. The light in *Three Women* is hard and neutral, without cast shadows and with only the slightest modeling. The focus is sharp, the forms and space flattening out into pattern. We are aware of the documentary power of the photograph-like approach. Yet, for all its objectivity, the picture is a moving expression of the artist's intelligent sympathy for his subjects, a reading of character without a trace of sentimentality, rare for a subject like this.

*Thomas Gray, *Elegy Written in a Country Churchyard.*

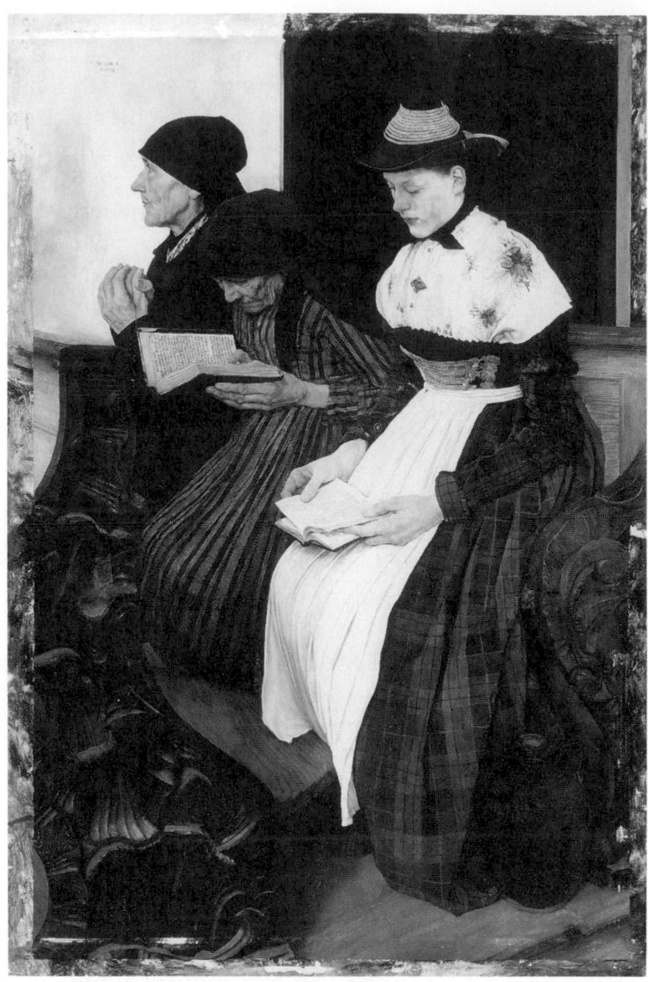

21-44 Wilhelm Leibl, *Three Women in a Village Church,* 1878–1881. Approx. 29″ × 25″. Kunsthalle, Hamburg.

Unlike the literature of nineteenth-century Russia, which has received a great deal of attention, nineteenth-century Russian art has been little known outside the Soviet Union. The Realist impulse was prized in Russia, and the painting *A Religious Procession in the Kursk District* (fig. **21-45**), by Ilya Repin (1844–1930), is a Realist work of extraordinary power. Simultaneously drama and document, this work makes us witness to a dense throng of people traveling along a road past us. They move in measured procession behind a shrine carried on the shoulders of monks, and beneath religious banners held proudly on high. Priests, peasants, burghers, students, soldiers, police, provincial officials, and bureaucrats all join in this homage to a saint on his feast day. Alongside the procession straggle beggars and cripples, perhaps hoping for a healing miracle. It is a multitude that, in itself, characterizes the society of "Holy Russia" before the revolutions of the twentieth century. The throng tramps along a country road, raising clouds of dust in the heat of noon as it crosses a featureless Russian landscape where trees recently have been hacked down. Closer inspection reveals two files of mounted riders—some in uniform, some priestly in appearance—coming slowly forward through the crowd. Their way is being cleared by men who savagely ply whips and cudgels to open a path. In the left foreground, a boy on a crutch has just been struck heavily with a staff wielded by the priest behind him. We can read in the crowded details of Repin's *Procession* the sullen poverty and misery of the people; the dogged, almost primitive religion; the

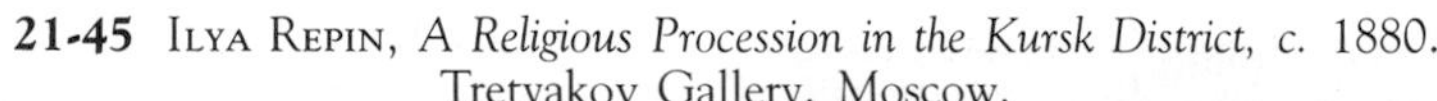

21-45 Ilya Repin, *A Religious Procession in the Kursk District,* c. 1880. Tretyakov Gallery, Moscow.

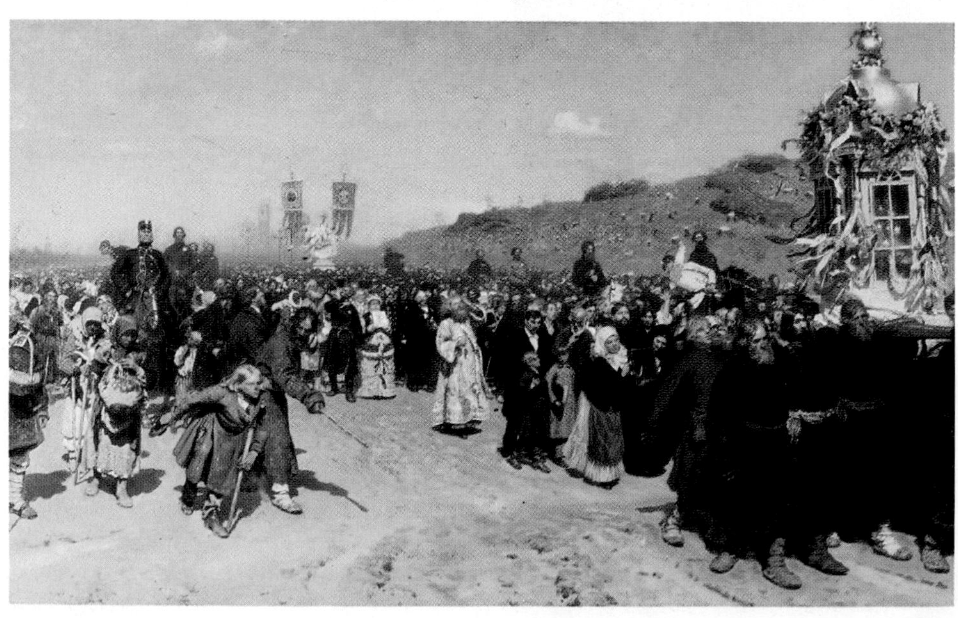

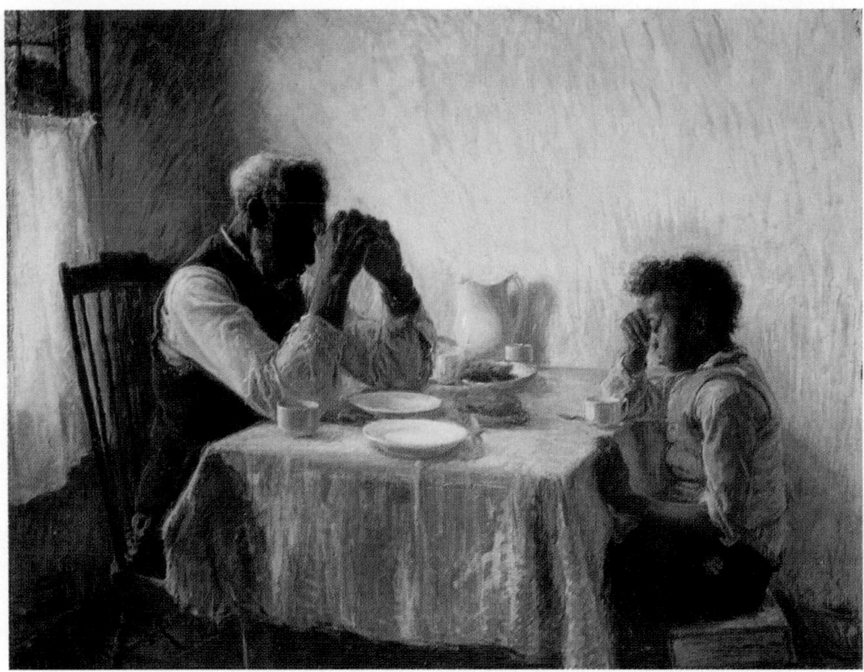

21-46 Henry Ossawa Tanner, *The Thankful Poor,* 1894. 49″ × 35½″. Private collection of William and Camille Cosby.

officious arrogance; and the pitiless harshness of the old Russian scene. These elements are much as they have been described in the novels of Dostoevsky (*Procession* and *The Brothers Karamazov* are contemporaneous works). One need suspect no interinfluence; painter and novelist are simply confronting the same realities.

Repin's painting expanded the program of Realism formulated in his time. It was a scene taken directly from modern life, at a particular place and time, objectively recorded with little of the artist's comment, unless it be a touch of sad irony or protest. The artist reconstructed the scene using his acute visual memory. He may have used sketches but certainly portrayed the event close to the way he saw it, in a manner similar to Eakins's method. The space is fluent and is assumed to continue, along with the action, beyond the frame. The light is out-of-doors, rather than of the studio, and the color, with its myriad modulations and accents, is suited to the time of day and the local color of landscape and costume.

Repin's crowd scene is unusual for Realist painting, which more often emphasized the dignity of individuals. Typical of the Realist painter's desire to depict the lives of ordinary people is the early work of the American artist Henry Ossawa Tanner (1859–1937). Tanner studied art with Eakins before moving to Paris, where he combined Eakins's belief in careful study from nature and reverence for the light and mood in Rembrandt's portraiture with a desire to portray with dignity the life of the ordinary people among whom he had been raised as the son of an African-American minister in Pennsylvania. The mood of quiet devotion in *The Thankful Poor* (fig. **21-46**) is as intense as that in Leibl's *Three Women in a Village Church* (fig. 21-44), but Tanner's lighting is softer (more Rembrandtesque) and his style incorporates a selective focus different from, but linked to the Realism of Millet (fig. 21-39) and to photography. In Tanner's painting, the grandfather, grandchild, and main objects in the room are painted with the greatest detail, while everything else dissolves into loose strokes of color and light that owe something to Impressionism but here remain more tied to the surfaces of things. Expressive lighting reinforces the reverent spirit of the painting, with deep shadows intensifying the devout concentration of the man and golden light pouring in the window to illuminate the quiet expression of thanksgiving on the younger face. The deep sense of sanctity that is expressed here in terms of everyday experience became increasingly important for Tanner. Within a few years of completing *The Thankful Poor,* he was painting only biblical subjects, seen in his imagination but still grounded in direct study from nature and the love of Rembrandt that had inspired him from his days as an art student in Philadelphia.

A very different mood fills *The Fox Hunt* (fig. **21-47**) by Tanner's contemporary, Winslow Homer (1836–1910), a leading American painter. Homer began his career making newspaper illustrations of daily life and went on to become famous for his paintings of

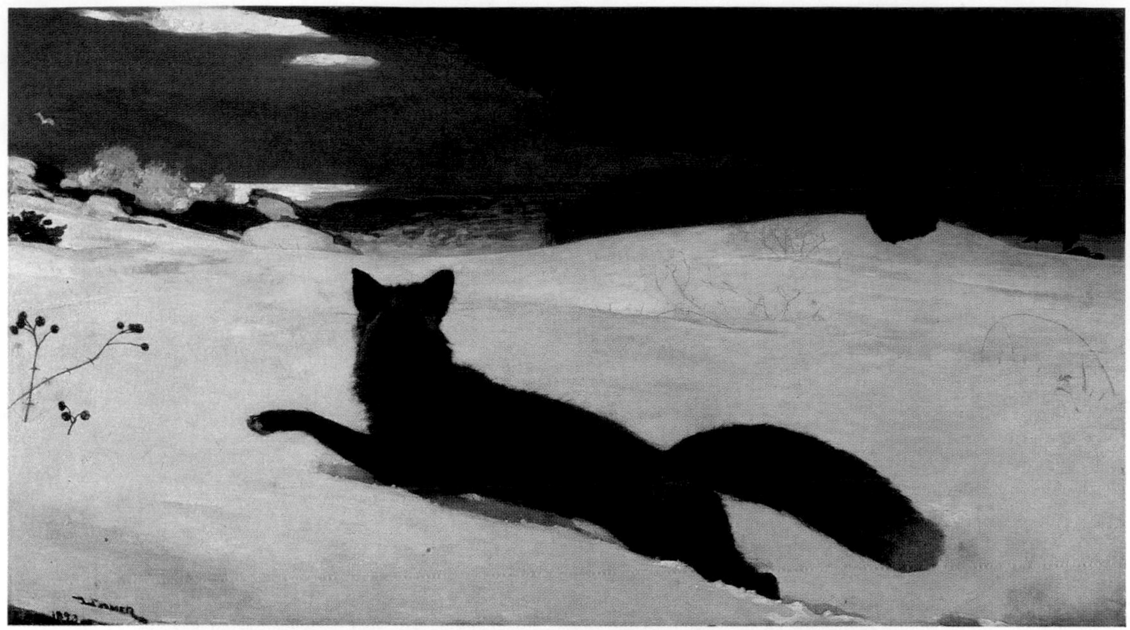

21-47 Winslow Homer, *The Fox Hunt,* 1893. 38" × $68\frac{1}{2}$". The Pennsylvania Academy of the Fine Arts, Philadelphia (Joseph E. Temple Fund).

unspoiled nature—especially the turbulent sea—and of individual human beings caught up in the natural world. *Fox Hunt* is rare among his works, both for its subject and for its composition. A fox, bogged down in heavy winter snow, is attacked by crows made fierce by starvation. The fox is trapped and its fate is certain. The figure of the fox is silhouetted against the flat white of the snowy ground; above, the dark shapes of the crows fill the sky, overshadowing and overwhelming the fox. Homer's method is objective and simple, conveying with Realist directness the mood of struggle and death in nature. Form and color convey the grim mood of the scene in reinforcement of what the images literally depict. The artist is "present" but powerless to intervene. In any event, this is a fact of nature. The color areas are sharp-edged and icy cold, except for the faintly warm tonality of the fox's coat and the spangle of red berries against the snow. The broad, short rectangle of the composition presents a low, panoramic view similar to that in Courbet's *Burial at Ornans* or Bonheur's *Horse Fair,* but Homer has filled most of his picture with the field of white snow, which pushes the action of fox and crows so close to the foreground (and the space of the viewer) that parts of the bodies of the leading attackers are cut off by the frame. This spacing emphasizes the double irony of the title: in the uneasy world of man and nature, where a fox is often hunted by mounted human beings for sport, it is now hunted by hungry crows in a morbid reversal of the process of nature that usually finds the fox hunting birds for food. In this work, Homer expressed with Realist intensity the impersonal, cruel competition of natural species asserted as a rule of life in the Darwinian-Spencerian theory of the survival of the fittest.

PHOTOGRAPHY

The Realist approach to art affected all media. Even in photography, a medium that could so effortlessly record the details of a subject, photographic artists sought to explore the new medium thoroughly and struggled to achieve its fullest expression. They often took their lead from painting, trying to combine the wonder of photographic details recorded directly from nature with the kind of control over composition and mood achieved by Realist painters.

The French photographer Gustave Le Gray (1820–1862), like his contemporary Rosa Bonheur, sought to portray the drama, as well as the reality, of everyday scenes. Having trained as a painter before becoming a photographer, Le Gray brought his painterly eye to his photographs of still lifes, cityscapes, and landscapes. He is best known, however, for seascapes topped with awe-inspiring, cloud-filled skies. The mood of *Seascape and Rough Waves* (fig. **21-48**) was inspired by Constable's landscape paintings, which Le Gray admired, and also recalls the Baroque glimpse of the infinite universe found in paintings by Van Ruisdael, like *View of Haarlem from the Dunes at Overveen* (fig. 19-56). The stirring play of light through the

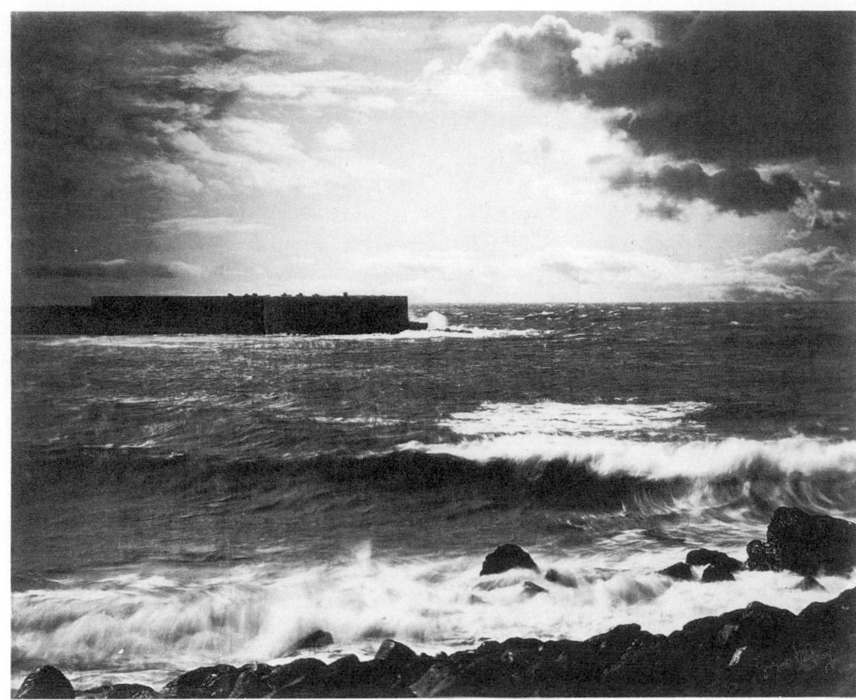

21-48 GUSTAVE LE GRAY, *Seascape and Rough Waves,* 1856. Albumen print, $13\frac{1}{2}'' \times 16\frac{1}{2}''$. The J. Paul Getty Museum, Malibu.

heavens and across the water and beach in *Seascape* was not as easy to record as it might look today. Struggling to overcome the blank, lackluster skies caused by the limited exposure range of the calotype process he used, Le Gray devised a method of making a single print by combining a waxed-paper negative (which captured nuances of light and shadow better than a plain paper negative) of the terrestrial regions with a separate negative of the sky. Viewers were enthralled by the way these photographs captured the spectacular effects of backlit clouds and sun-speckled sea, and Le Gray's work won wide acclaim from both art critics and members of the public.

Perhaps the person most determined to prove that photographers could exercise as much expressive control over their medium as painters could over theirs was the British photographer HENRY PEACH ROBINSON (1830–1901), who brought to his work with the camera his experience as a painter and printmaker. Although Robinson earned his living as a portrait photographer almost from the moment he opened his studio in 1852, he felt that his most serious works were his "art photographs," of which he made at least one each year. He planned these photographs with great care,

> to set forth the laws which govern—as far as laws can be applied to a subject which depends in some measure on taste and feeling—the arrangement of a picture, so that it shall have the greatest amount of pictorial effect, and to illustrate by examples those broad principles without regard to which imitation, however minute or however faithful, is not picturesque, and does not rise to the dignity of art.*

To accomplish all of this with camera equipment required dedication and skill. For each of his art photographs, Robinson began with a pencil sketch of the final work. For complex compositions, he made a composite print from many negatives; for simpler arrangements, he posed models in a specially constructed theatrical setting in his studio. The scene in *Women and Children in the Country* (FIG. **21-49**) was inspired by genre paintings of middle-class people in contemporary dress enjoying themselves on an outing in the country (a subject that would shortly become a favorite with the Impressionists). For this print, Robinson posed each of the three groups of figures separately to fit the design in his preliminary sketch, and he may have taken a separate negative of the background trees as well. From his individual prints, he cut out the desired details, pasted them on a study sketch (FIG. **21-50**), and rephotographed the whole for a final presentation print. To many of his contemporaries, Robinson proved that a photographer could be just as inventive as a painter; as one

*In Beaumont Newhall, *The History of Photography* (New York: The Museum of Modern Art, 1982), p. 76.

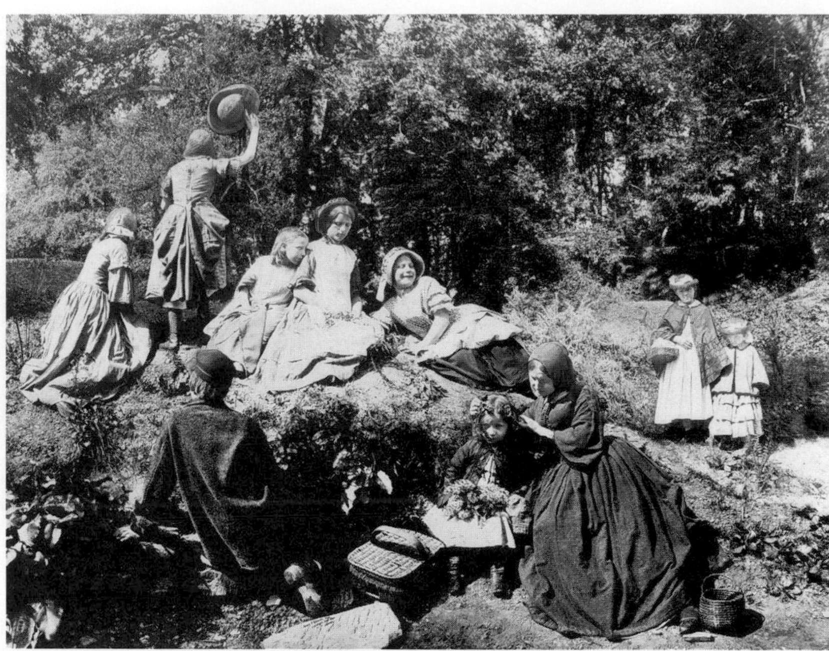

21-49 Henry Peach Robinson, *Women and Children in the Country,* 1860. Gelatin silver print. International Museum of Photography at George Eastman House, Rochester, New York.

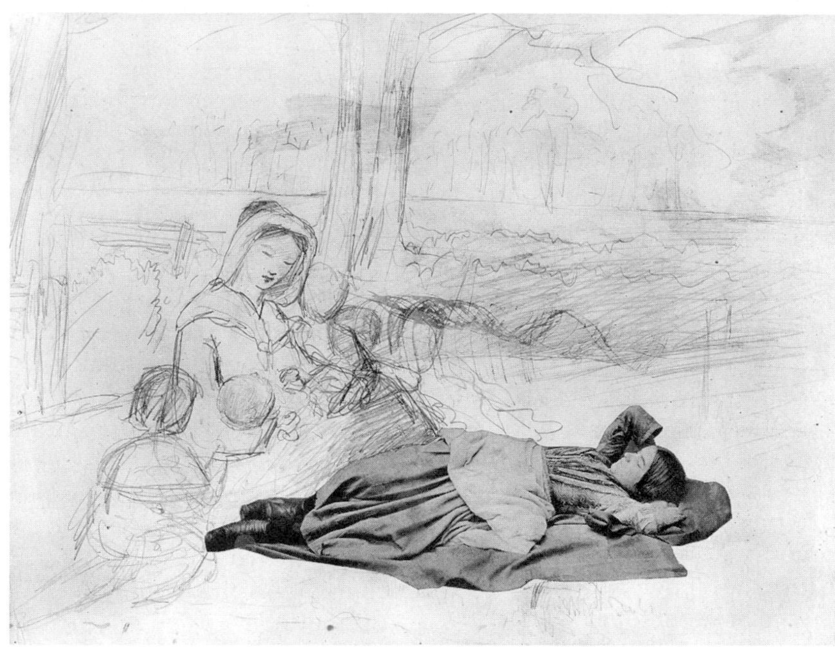

21-50 Henry Peach Robinson, study for a composite picture, 1860. Sketch of a woman and children with a gelatin silver print insert. Gernsheim Collection, Harry Ransom Humanities Research Center, The University of Texas at Austin.

critic said of him: "The photographer artist does no more than the Royal Academician does; he makes each figure an individual study, and he groups those separate 'negatives' together to form a complete positive picture."*

**Art Journal* review, in Aaron Scharf, *Art and Photography* (Baltimore: Penguin, 1968), p. 109.

Another Englishman, Dr. Peter Henry Emerson (1856–1936), took a somewhat different approach to establishing photography as a Realist art medium. Influenced by his early study of medicine and science, Emerson equated photography with science and argued that true photographic art represented only what the human eye saw, an idea he based on

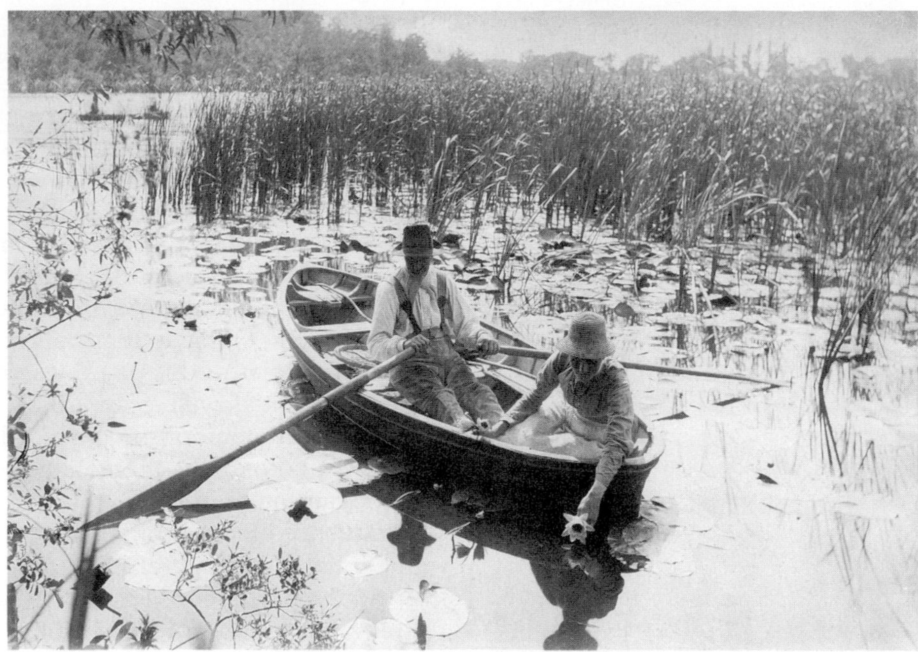

21-51 DR. PETER HENRY EMERSON, *Gathering Water Lillies* from the album *Life and Landscape of the Norfolk Broads*, 1886. Platinum print, $7\frac{3}{4}'' \times 11\frac{1}{2}''$. Collection, The Museum of Modern Art, New York (given anonymously).

Hermann von Helmholtz's *Handbook of Physiological Optics*. Emerson published his theories in a widely influential treatise, *Naturalistic Photography for Students of the Art* (1889), and illustrated them in photographs, like those in *Life and Landscape of the Norfolk Broads* (1886), which depicted the life of working people in the marshy lands of eastern England. Both the subject matter and composition of *Gathering Water Lilies* (FIG. **21-51**) were patterned after the peasant paintings by Millet, which Emerson greatly admired. In Emerson's image, as in Millet's *Gleaners*, our gaze is drawn to the workers and their task, both by their placement in the center foreground of an open landscape and by the graduated or differential focus, which shows everything in the foreground clearly while everything else is less distinct. Emerson believed that this differential focus mimicked the way the human eye actually sees and that photographers should imitate it carefully:

> A picture . . . should be made just *as sharp as the eye sees it and no sharper*, for it must be remembered that the eye does not see things as sharply as the photographic lens. . . . The chief point of interest should be slightly—very slightly—out of focus, while all things out of the plane of the principal object . . . should also be slightly out of focus, not to the extent of producing destruction of structure or fuzziness, but sufficiently to keep them back and in place.*

*In Vicki Goldberg, *Photography in Print* (New York: A Touchstone Book, Simon & Schuster, 1981), p. 194.

Emerson's ideas about selective focus influenced the work of the so-called Pictorialist photographers at the end of the nineteenth century, but their style was based on an overall soft focus that so horrified Emerson that he eventually repudiated his early ideas about photographic art in favor of the belief that photography could never be anything but a tool for science.

As might be expected, the Realist impulse inspired a widespread interest in portraiture, which had been a high art form in painting and sculpture throughout the ages for those who could afford it. Now photography made portraits available to ordinary men and women. Photographic portraits were not only less expensive, but they required much less of the sitter's time and were readily available (especially after the invention of the negative photographic processes) through the host of portrait studios that had sprung up everywhere. Portraiture was an important economic component in the work of most photographers, as we have seen with Daguerre, Southworth and Hawes, and Hill and Adamson, but the greatest of the early portrait photographers was undoubtedly the Frenchman Gaspard Félix Tournachon (1820–1910), who adopted the name NADAR for his professional career as novelist, journalist, enthusiastic balloonist, and caricaturist. Photographic studies for his caricatures, which followed the tradition of Daumier's most satiric lithographs (not illustrated), led Nadar to open a portrait studio. So talented was he at capturing the essence of his subjects that the most

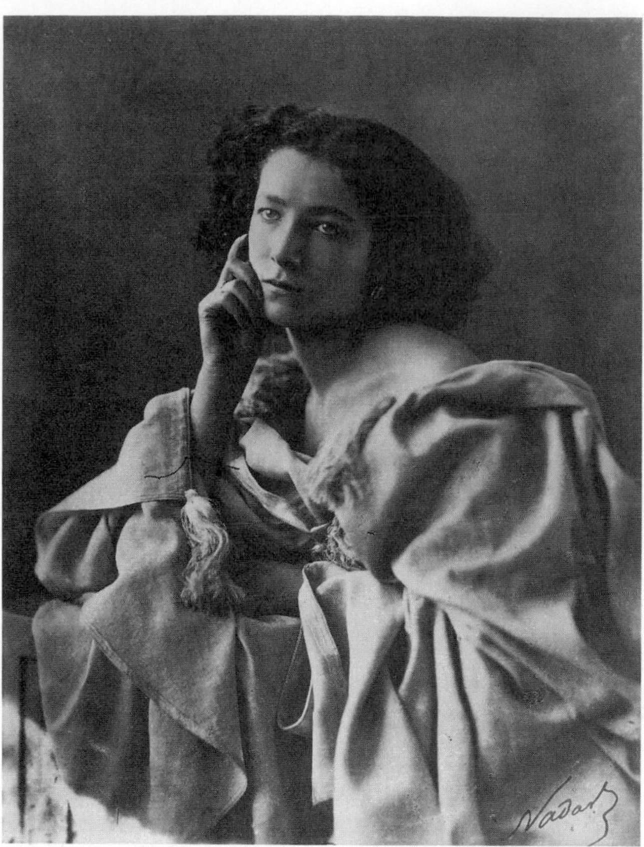

21-52 NADAR (Gaspard Félix Tournachon), *Sarah Bernhardt*, 1859. Woodburytype. Bibliothèque Nationale, Paris.

important people in France, including Daumier, Courbet, and Manet, flocked to his studio to have their portraits made. Nadar said he sought in his work "that instant of understanding that puts you in touch with the model—helps you sum him up, guides you to his habits, his ideas, and character and enables you to produce . . . a really convincing and sympathetic likeness, an intimate portrait."* Nadar's skill in the genre can be seen in *Sarah Bernhardt* (FIG. **21-52**), one of a series of portraits he did of this famous actress. In this photograph, the actress appears with remarkable presence; even in half-length, her gestures and her expression create a revealing mood that seems to tell us much about her. Perhaps Bernhardt responded to Nadar's famous gift for putting his clients at ease by assuming the pose that best expressed her personality. The rich range of tones in Nadar's images was made possible by new photographic materials. The glass negative and albumen printing paper could record finer detail and a wider range of light and shadow than Talbot's calotype process, and the Woodburytype process produced grainless, permanent, nonsilver positive prints. In *Sarah Bernhardt*, as in all his portraits, Nadar used lighting and composition to place the emphasis on the face; the effect may remind us of both Rembrandt's *Self-Portrait* (FIG. 19-51) and Ingres's *Granet* (FIG. 21-15). Unlike these painters, however, Nadar had to capture everything within his composition at the time he exposed his negative, and it was this direct impression from nature that amazed his contemporaries and continues to fascinate us today. The veracity of Nadar's portraits was recognized by Ingres, who sent some clients to have their photographic portraits taken as studies for his paintings. While Nadar had a scientific bent as well as an artistic one—he took the first aerial photographs (from a balloon) and some of the first photographs illuminated with flash powder (in the catacombs of Paris)—it was as a portraitist that he influenced most strongly the painters and photographers who came after him.

*In Naomi Rosenblum, *A World History of Photography* (New York: Abbeville Press, 1984), p. 69.

Nadar's portraits of celebrities were made for the sitter and perhaps a few friends. Soon, however, in response to a growing desire on the part of the public for copies of photographs of celebrities, several methods for creating mass-produced prints were invented. One such product—the *carte de visite* (visiting card) photograph—was invented in Paris in 1854 by ANDRÉ-ADOLPHE-EUGÈNE DISDÉRI (1819–1889). Disdéri used a camera with four lenses and a special sliding plate-holder that allowed him to take eight or ten separate photographs on a single negative, with the sitter either holding one pose for all images or changing poses between exposures. A print of the whole negative could then be cut into individual pictures. The individual pictures were mounted on a card the size of the standard calling card, although few of these prints were probably ever used for calling cards. Instead, as each could be sold separately and inexpensively, a craze for collecting carte de visite images of famous people swept Europe and the United States. *Princess Buonaparte-Gabrielli* (FIG. **21-53**) is an example of an uncut sheet of carte de visite photographs. The princess assumed five different poses, which present an intriguing sequence suggestive of her daily activities. Clues to her personality are evoked by her dress, her body language, and the props around her. Political leaders immediately saw the value of carte de visite photographs in building and reinforcing their public personae; Abraham Lincoln credited a carte de visite portrait taken of him by the American photographer Matthew Brady with having helped him win his first term of office as president of the United States. The low cost of carte de visite portraits and their slice-of-life quality made them the darling of the masses as well. Disdéri's work here can be seen as a Realistic portrait of aristo-

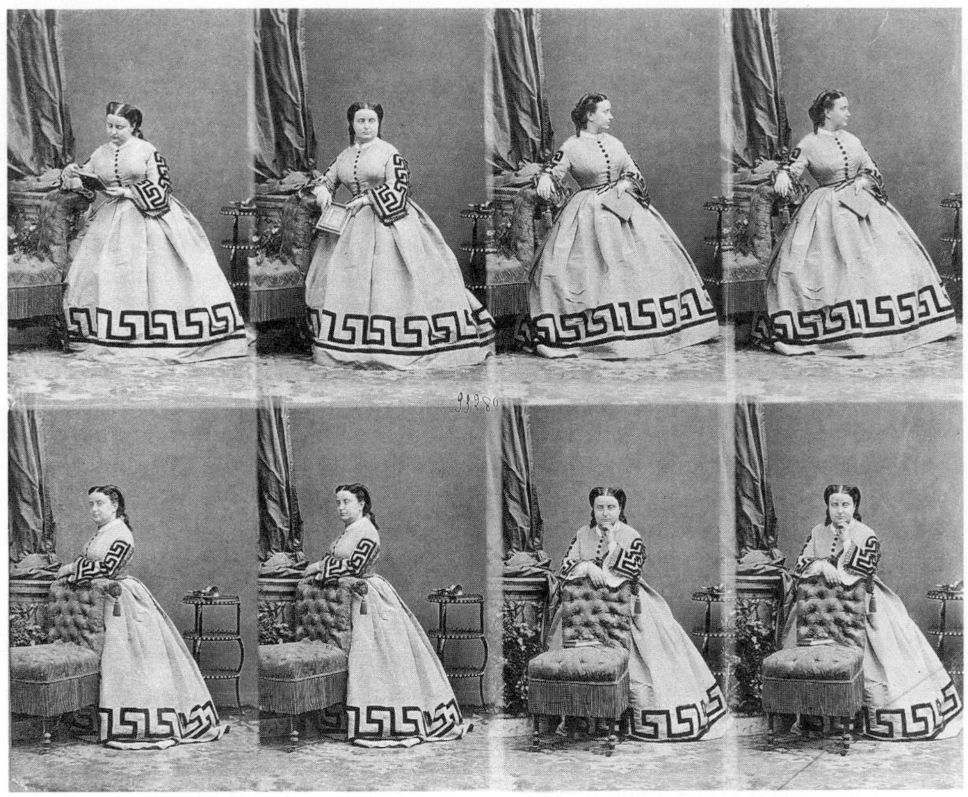

21-53 ANDRÉ-ADOLPHE-EUGÈNE DISDÉRI, *Princess Buonaparte-Gabrielli,* uncut sheet of carte de visite portraits, *c.* 1862. Albumen print, $7\frac{7}{16}'' \times 9\frac{5}{16}''$. Gernsheim Collection, Harry Ransom Humanities Research Center, The University of Texas at Austin.

cratic life; however, the carefully posed series of shots in works like *Princess Buonaparte-Gabrielli* is very different from the literal motion sequences that would be captured within a few years by Eadweard Muybridge (FIG. 21-42).

SCULPTURE

The three-dimensional art of sculpture was not readily adaptable to the optical realism favored by many painters and the public. Sculpture, by its very nature, occupies the same physical space as the viewer—it is palpably very much *there.* As art, traditionally, it has turned toward emphasizing a sense of its permanence as an enduring form. The timeless ideal, not the evanescent real, best suits it.

In the work of the French artist AUGUSTE RODIN (1840–1917), however, Realism found its sculptural counterpart and regained the artistic preeminence it had lost to the pictorial media in the nineteenth century. Primarily a Realist by impulse, Rodin ably assimilated and managed the century's other concurrent esthetic styles—Romanticism, Impressionism, and Symbolism, generating in the process a unique personal style that anticipated twentieth-century Expressionism. Avoiding the stilted formulas of the Academy, Rodin looked carefully, as would Carpeaux (FIG. 21-63), at the sculpture of Michelangelo and Pierre Puget (FIG. 19-72), learning from them to appreciate the unique possibilities of the human body for emotional expression. Rodin wanted to express the "existential situation of modern man, his inability to communicate, his despair." His goal, as he put it, was "to render inner feelings through muscular movement." He achieved this aim by joining his profound knowledge of anatomy and movement with special attention to the body's surfaces, saying, "The sculptor must learn to reproduce the surface, which means all that vibrates on the surface, soul, love, passion, life. . . . Sculpture is thus the art of hollows and mounds, not of smoothness, or even polished planes." Primarily a modeler of pliable material rather than a carver of hard wood or stone, Rodin worked his surfaces with fingers sensitive to the subtlest variations of plane, catching the fugitive play of living motion as it changed fluidly under light, a kind of "expressionist realism." Like Muybridge and Eakins, Rodin was fascinated by the human body in motion. Often in his studio, he would have a model move around in front of him, while he modeled sketches with coils of clay. *Walking Man* (FIG. **21-54**)

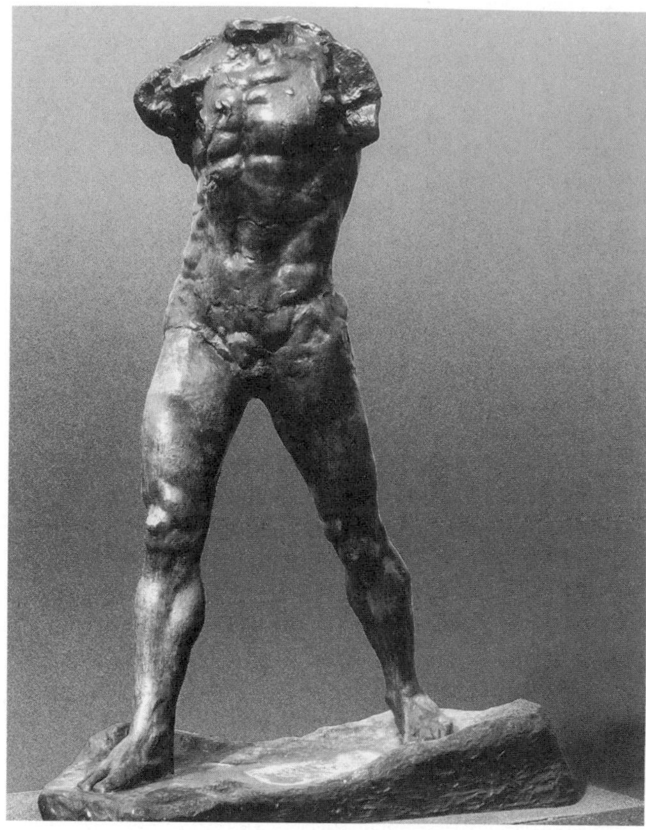

21-54 AUGUSTE RODIN, *Walking Man,* 1905. Bronze, $83\frac{3}{4}''$ high. Hirshhorn Museum and Sculpture Garden, Smithsonian Institution, Washington, D.C. (gift of Joseph H. Hirshhorn, 1966).

was the first major sculpture in which he captured the sense of a body in motion. Headless and armless, the figure is caught in mid-stride at the moment when weight is transferred across the pelvis from the back leg to the front. As with many of his other early works, Rodin executed *Walking Man* with such careful attention to details of muscle, bone, and tendon, that it is filled with forceful reality, despite the sketchy modeling of the torso. Rodin conceived this figure as a study for his sculpture of *St. John the Baptist Preaching,* part of the process by which he built his conception of how the human body would express the symbolism of the larger theme. Similarly, he made many nude and draped studies for each of the figures in the life-size group *Burghers of Calais* (FIG. **21-55**). This monument was commissioned to commemorate a heroic episode in the Hundred Years' War, in which, during the English siege of Calais in 1347, six of the city's leading citizens agreed to offer their lives in return for the English king's promise to lift the siege and spare the rest of the populace. Each of the individual figures is a convincing study of despair, resignation, or quiet defiance. The psychic effects were achieved through the choreographic placement of the members of the group and through the manipulation of a few simplified planes in each figure, so that the rugged surfaces catch and disperse the light. Rodin designed the monument without the traditional high base in the hope that modern-day citizens of Calais

21-55 AUGUSTE RODIN, *Burghers of Calais,* 1886. Bronze, $6'\ 10\frac{1}{2}''$ high, 7′ 11″ long, 6′ 6″ deep. Hirshhorn Museum and Sculpture Garden, Smithsonian Institution, Washington, D.C. (gift of Joseph H. Hirshhorn, 1966).

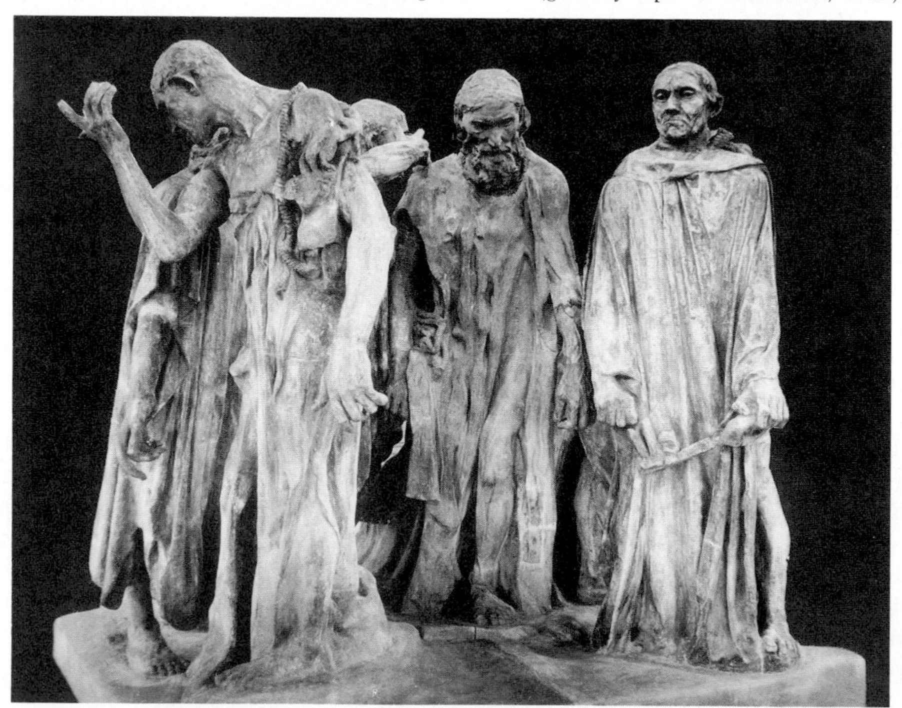

would be inspired by the sculptured representations of their ancestors standing in the city center and preparing eternally to set off on their sacrificial journey. The government commissioners found the Realism of Rodin's vision so offensive, however, that they banished the monument to an out-of-the-way site and modified the impact of the work by placing it high on an isolating pedestal.

Many of Rodin's projects were left unfinished or were deliberate fragments. Seeing the esthetic and expressive virtue of these works, modern viewers and modern sculptors have developed a taste for the way in which the sketch, the half-completed, the fragment, and the vignette lifted out of context, all have the power of suggestion and understatement. Rodin's *Balzac* (FIG. **21-56**) carries out the method on a heroic scale. The facial features are not clearly delineated but only suggested by indefinite surfaces that catch light and dark in deft blurs and smudges, producing a sketchlike effect. Contours melt away; volumes are not permitted to assert themselves. The great novelist, who surveyed mankind in his *La Comédie Humaine (The Human Comedy)*, draws himself up to a towering height. Wrapped in a dressing gown that seems like an enormous cloak, he again surveys the littleness of man from the lofty standpoint of immortality. Characteristically, although we feel the power of Rodin's art, we cannot quite describe exactly which traits make us feel it. His methods, grounded in Realism, achieved an overwhelmingly moving effect through daring emphasis and distortion.

21-56 AUGUSTE RODIN, *Balzac,* 1892–1897. Plaster, approx. 9′ 10″ high. Musée Rodin, Paris.

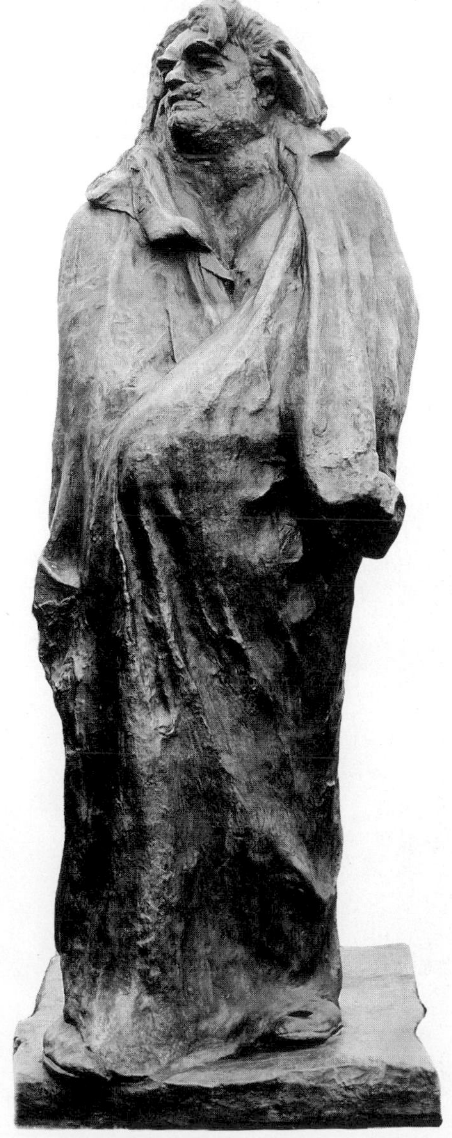

Romantic Responses to Realism

Realism stood for what the eye could see—for actuality in all subject matter and verisimilitude in all images. Reflecting the Realist credo of art, philosopher Friedrich Nietzsche wrote, "We do not demand beautiful, illusory lies from it. . . . Brutal positivism reigns, recognizing facts without becoming excited." Like the positivists of science, the Realists believed in the supremacy of cold fact and made it the basis of esthetic truth and personal honesty. Some artists who subscribed to the Realist view, however, found Realist doctrine arbitrary and too restrictive of that play of artistic imagination long honored in the Tradition. While using Realist techniques scrupulous to truth and detail, these artists gave full play to their imaginative faculties in idea and content in order to render their subject Romantically.

PAINTING

In England, JOHN EVERETT MILLAIS (1829–1896) was among a group of artists who refused to be limited to the contemporary scenes portrayed by the strict Realist. These artists chose instead to represent fictional, historical, and fanciful subjects, but to do so using the techniques of Realism. So painstakingly careful in his study of visual facts closely observed from nature that Baudelaire called him "the poet of meticulous detail," Millais was a founder of the so-called Pre-Raphaelite Brotherhood. This group of artists, organized in 1848, wished to create fresh and sincere art, free from what they considered to be the tired and artificial manner propagated by the successors of Raphael in the academies. Millais's method is seen to advantage in his *Ophelia* (FIG. **21-57**), which he exhibited in the Universal Exposition in Paris in 1855, where Courbet set up his Pavilion of Realism. The subject, from Shakespeare's *Hamlet,* is the drowning of Ophelia, who, in her madness, is unaware of her plight:

> Her clothes spread wide,
> And mermaid-like awhile they bore her up;
> Which time she chanted snatches of old tunes.
> IV.vii.176–78

Attempting to make the pathos of the scene visible, Millais became a faithful and feeling witness of its every detail, reconstructing it with a circumstantial stagecraft worthy of the original poetry. While Millais's technique is Realistic, the orthodox Realist would complain that the subject is not—that it is playacting. Yet it is unlikely that an impartial observer of the painting, familiar with *Hamlet,* would object that, as the subject is not of the artist's time and place, it is, of necessity, deficient in truth. It is certainly not deficient in truth to appearance. It may be that this conflict between the seen (in everyday experience) and the seeable (in plausible reconstructions of fictitious or past events) is resolved in modern cinema. The kind of picture drama we have in *Ophelia,* which brings the fictive action of a nonpictorial medium before our eyes with all optical fidelity, anticipates the dramatic motion picture in which fictions and facts are presented to the eye as equally real. Nineteenth-century Realists might have objected that the picture-drama was not painting, but stage production, and could only be judged as such.

A younger member of the Pre-Raphaelite Brotherhood, EDWARD BURNE-JONES (1833–1898) was one of the many painters during this period who did not accept Realism in terms of either subject or technique. A friend and protégé of John Ruskin and an associate of William Morris and Dante Gabriel Rossetti (who, as we shall see in our discussion of Manet, slurred the work of the Realists), Burne-Jones agreed with their distaste for the materialism and ugliness of the contemporary, industrializing world and shared their appreciation for the spirituality and idealism (as well as the art and craftsmanship) of past times, especially the Middle Ages and the Early Renaissance. Like Millais, Burne-Jones drew his subjects from literature, but he chose to depict them in a soft, languid style much influenced by Sandro Botticelli (FIG. 16-60). Burne-Jones's *King Cophetua and the Beggar Maid* (FIG. **21-58**) illustrates a poem of the same name, written by Alfred Tennyson in 1842, which itself was a

21-57 JOHN EVERETT MILLAIS, *Ophelia,* 1852. 30″ × 44″. Tate Gallery, London.

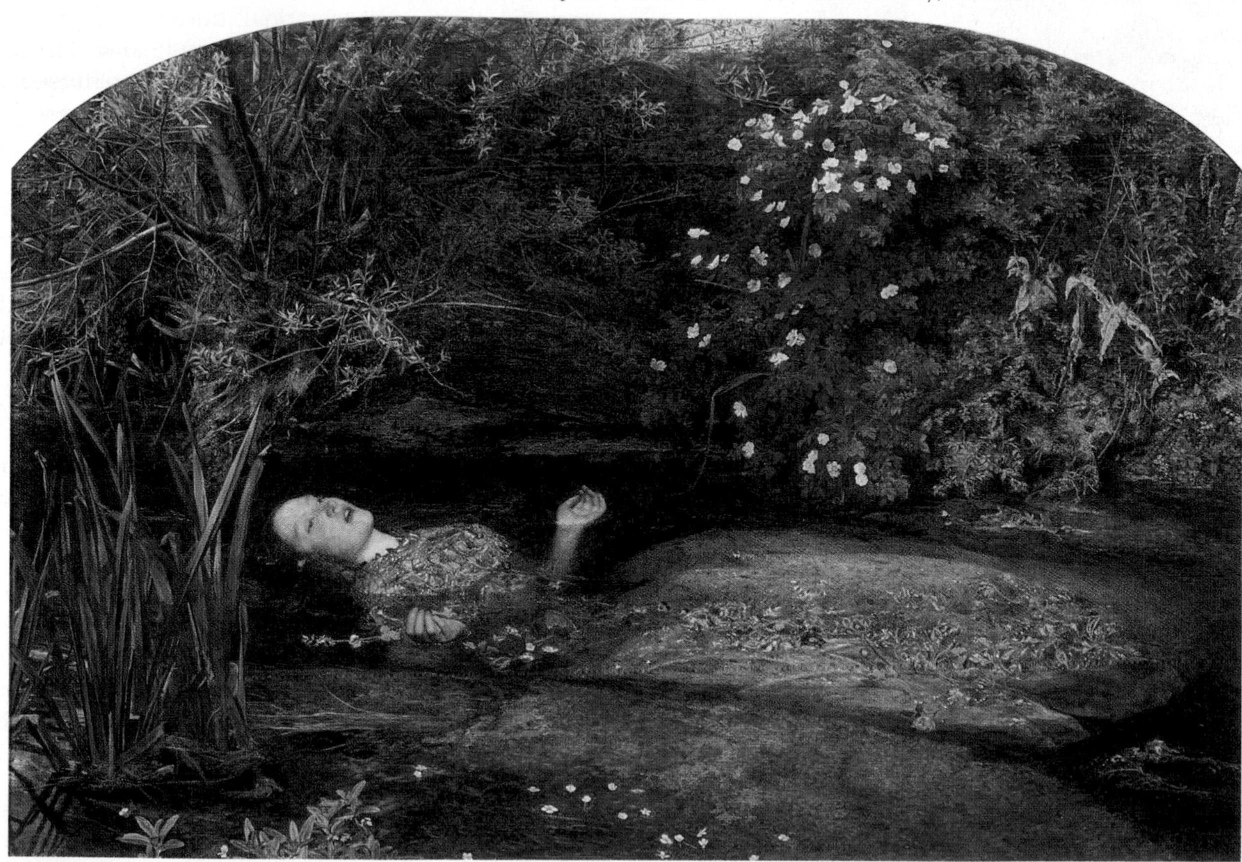

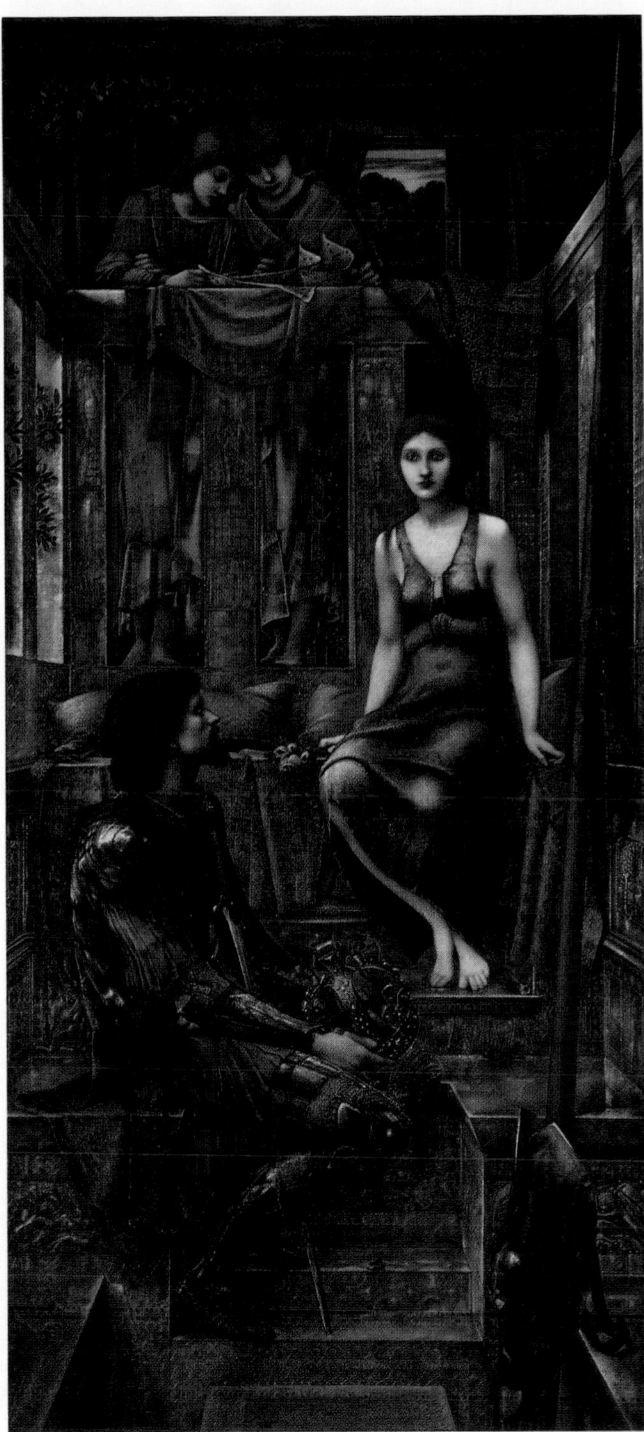

21-58 EDWARD BURNE-JONES, *King Cophetua and the Beggar Maid,* 1884. Approx. 9′ 7″ × 4′ 5″. Tate Gallery, London.

modern reworking of an ancient and popular ballad. The situation is given in the last lines:

> So sweet a face, such angel grace
> In all that land had never been.
> Cophetua sware a royal oath:
> "This beggar maid shall be my queen!"

The king, in grave reverie, contemplates the maiden, who sits serenely above him, like some pedestaled perfection oblivious to mortal presence. Although Burne-Jones insisted that he wanted the maid to resemble a beggar, she does not. Like the atmosphere, she belongs to the world of trance and dream, in which images arise from some lost age of beauty and innocence. The composition, planar and still, recalls the mural tableau of the Renaissance, the suspended action of stained glass and tapestry. Burne-Jones's dreamy, decorative manner was perfectly suited to the somewhat precious, estheticizing taste of the later nineteenth century. How far we are here from Realism, as well as the great diversity of style at the time, can be appreciated if we compare Burne-Jones's beggar maid with Manet's barmaid (FIG. 21-67), especially if we consider that the two paintings were completed only two years apart.

In the painting of ADOLPHE WILLIAM BOUGUEREAU (1825–1905), Realism was blended with a different kind of fantasy. Bouguereau depicted Classical, mythological subjects with a dynamic Rococo exuberance of composition, and an optical Realism that achieved a startling illusionism, as in his *Nymphs and Satyr* (FIG. **21-59**), where the playful and ideally beautiful nymphs strike graceful poses, yet seem based as closely on nature as are the details of their leafy surroundings. The painter even created the figure of his mythical beast-man by combining Realist depictions of a goat's hind quarters and horns and a horse's ears and tail with the upper body of a man. A painting like this presses the question of whether the subjects of myth, fancy, and fiction could be painted with the techniques of Realism without evoking incredulity and, perhaps, a sense of absurdity in the observer. For the Classicist, Bouguereau's *Nymphs and Satyr* would fail to fulfill a longing "for nothing more than the moment in which conception and representation will flow together." The Realist would find the picture false due to the incongruence of its form and content and the unrealistic nature of its subject. The obvious conflict of conception and representation in many of Bouguereau's pictures, as well as in those of other recognized artists of the time, did not displease the public. Bouguereau was immensely popular, enjoying the favor of state patronage throughout his career. His reputation has fluctuated violently; the moderns of his century damned him as the very archetype of the official painter, but critics of our own day acknowledge his love of beauty and his undeniable painterly skills, if not always his esthetic wisdom and taste.

The French painter JEAN-LÉON GÉRÔME (1824–1904) specialized in Romantic historical subjects rendered

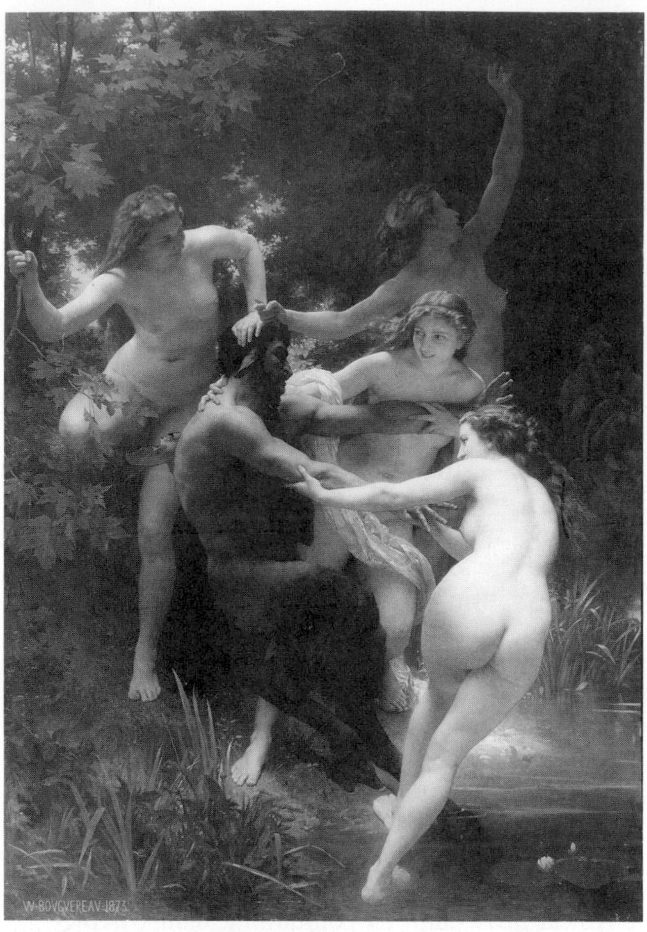

21-59 ADOLPHE WILLIAM BOUGUEREAU, *Nymphs and Satyr,* 1873. Approx. 8′ 6″ high. Clark Institute, Williamstown, Massachusetts.

with almost photographic detail. In his painting *Pollice Verso* (*Thumbs Down!*, FIG. **21-60**), the inherited formulas of the Tradition have been almost entirely transformed. The time and place specifications are as exact as they can be. Although we do not know the day, month, and year of the event portrayed, nor the names of the principals involved, we recognize it for what it is and where it is happening; we can even guess the time of day. Gladiatorial combats were part of the Roman imperial games held regularly in great arenas or amphitheaters like the one pictured—the Colosseum in Rome (FIG. 6-47). The incident represented here must have happened countless times, and its very ordinariness makes it dramatic and factual. A triumphant gladiator bestrides his fallen opponent and looks toward the box where the vestal virgins are seated. The fallen man gestures for mercy. The vestals deny his appeal by turning their thumbs down; he will be killed on the spot. Gérôme authenticates the scene to the last detail: the vestals, the emperor's party (in the box fronted with columns and trophies), the streaks of light (clue to the time of day) thrown on the tapestried barrier walls by chinks in the great awnings overhead, the texture of the bloodstained sand, and, conspicuously, the fantastic garb of the gladiators, their splendid helmets replicating originals found at Pompeii. The scenic illusion is produced by a smooth continuum of tone that runs through the whole scale of values. Gérôme is scrupulously faithful to optical fact. Evidence of brush strokes is suppressed in an exquisitely finished,

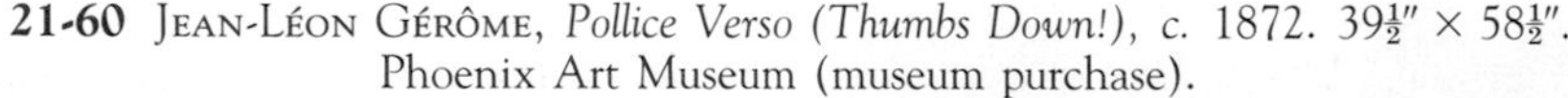

21-60 JEAN-LÉON GÉRÔME, *Pollice Verso (Thumbs Down!),* c. 1872. $39\frac{1}{2}'' \times 58\frac{1}{2}''$. Phoenix Art Museum (museum purchase).

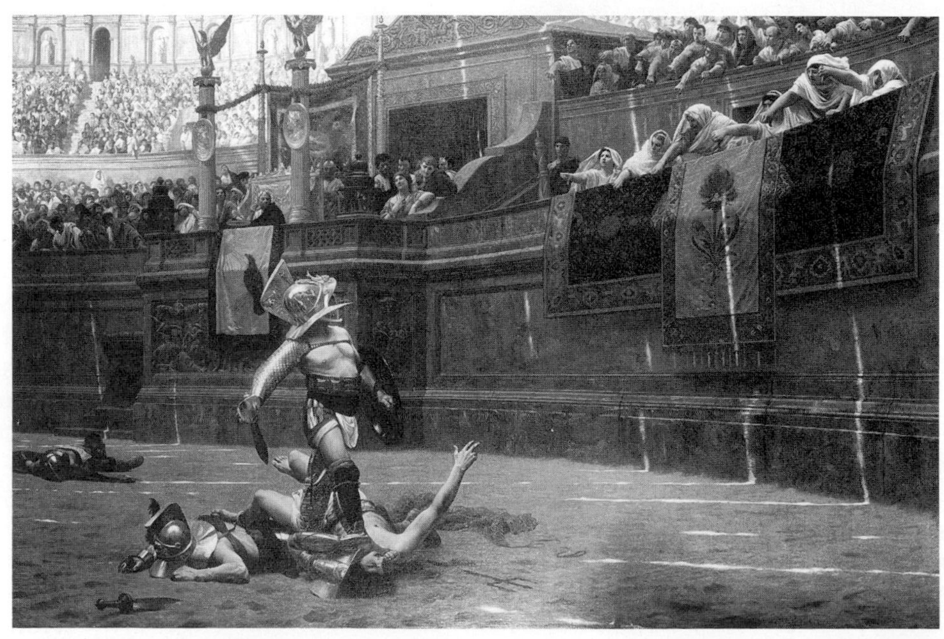

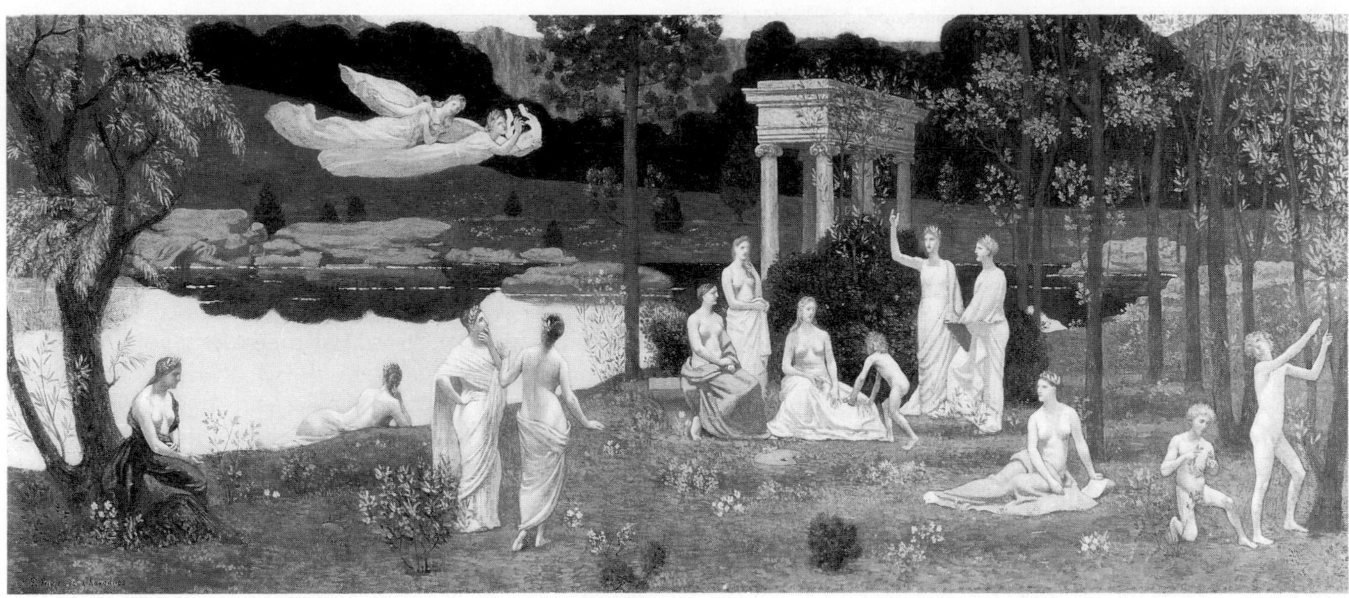

21-61 Pierre Puvis de Chavannes, *The Sacred Grove,* 1884. 2′ 11½″ × 6′ 10″. (Potter Palmer Collection) © The Art Institute of Chicago. All rights reserved.

glassy surface. The effect is photographic; the brush stroke is intended to be invisible. In this way, the artist reduced to the barest minimum any evidence of his own imagination or feeling, or even of the agent of that feeling, his "hand." Like a director in the theater, he expects to be judged on his interpretation, which is manifest in the characterizations he elicits, in the species of action, scene design, and authenticity of detail. Gérôme makes use of an off-centered, dynamic placement for his figures to make the viewers of the work spectators at a *real* event, which we witness from *within* the framed space of the action. The curving wall sweeps toward us, and we can feel that our own vantage point is continuous with that of the vestal virgins.

Much of the reputation of the popular, "official," "academic" art of the nineteenth century, which won the admiration of the public and the support of the government at the time, has since suffered both decline and resurgence in acceptance. Some painters, touched lightly or heavily by Realism, borrowed from it or compromised with it but remained independent of its principal dogma—that the artist must see and represent modern life in a modern way. A turning away from both Realism and the modern world that called for it can be seen in the work of Pierre Puvis de Chavannes (1824–1898). Puvis sought to adapt Classical mood and form to his own esthetic ends, an art that was ornamental and reflective, and removed from the noisy world of Realism. In *The Sacred Grove* (fig. **21-61**), he deployed statuesque figures in a tranquil landscape with a Classical shrine. Their motion has been suspended in timeless poses, their contours are simple and sharp, their modeling as shallow as bas-relief. Primarily a mural painter, Puvis was obedient to the requirements of the wall surface, neutralizing and restraining color, and banishing pictorial illusionism with its perspective and tone matching. The calm, almost bland atmosphere suggests some consecrated place, where all movements and gestures, undisturbed by the busyness of life, have a perpetual, ritual significance. The stillness and simplicity of the forms, the linear patterns created by their rhythmic contours, and the suggestion of their symbolic import amount to a kind of program of anti-Realism that impressed younger painters like Paul Gauguin and the Symbolists, who saw in Puvis the prophet of a new style that would replace Realism. Puvis had a double reputation: he was accepted by the Academy and the government for his Classicism, and he was revered by the avant-garde for his vindication of imagination and his artistic independence from the world of materialism and the machine. He asked a question significant for artists of his time and later: What will become of artists in the face of the invasion of engineers and mechanics?

PHOTOGRAPHY AND SCULPTURE

Many late nineteenth-century photographers, like the painters we have just studied, wanted to use their medium to depict fictional, historical, or religious subjects. These photographers often arranged symbolic scenes in suggestive settings, with figures dressed in costumes appropriate to the selected theme, and shot the photographs in soft light with slightly fuzzy focus to create a "pictorial" mood reminiscent of a painting by Rembrandt, Gainsborough, or another admired old master.

One of the leading practitioners of the Pictorial style in photography was the American GERTRUDE KÄSEBIER (1852–1934). Käsebier took up photography in 1897 after raising a family and working as a portrait painter. She soon became famous for photographs with symbolic themes, such as *Blessed Art Thou Among Women* (FIG. **21-62**). The title repeats the phrase used in the New Testament by the angel Gabriel to announce to the Virgin Mary that she will be the mother of Jesus. In the context of Käsebier's photograph, the words suggest a parallel between the biblical "Mother of God" and the modern mother in the image, who both protects and sends forth her daughter. The white setting and the mother's pale gown shimmer in soft focus behind the serious figure of the girl, who is dressed in darker tones and captured with sharper focus. Here, as in her other works, Käsebier was influenced by Peter Henry Emerson's ideas about naturalism in photography, but deliberately ignored his teachings about differential focus in favor of achieving an "expressive" effect by blurring the entire image slightly. In *Blessed Art Thou,* the whole scene is invested with an aura of otherworldly peace by the soft focus, the appearance of the centered figures, the vertical framing doors, and the relationship between the frontally posed girl and her gracefully bending mother. As one contemporary critic wrote: "The manner in which modern dress was handled, subordinated, and made to play its proper part in the composition . . . evidenced great artistic feeling."* *Blessed Art Thou* is a superb example of Käsebier's moving ability to invest scenes from everyday life with a sense of their connection to the realm of the spirit and the divine.

21-62 GERTRUDE KÄSEBIER, *Blessed Art Thou Among Women,* c. 1900. Platinum print on Japanese paper, $9\frac{3}{8}'' \times 5\frac{1}{2}''$. Collection, The Museum of Modern Art, New York (gift of Mrs. Hermine M. Turner).

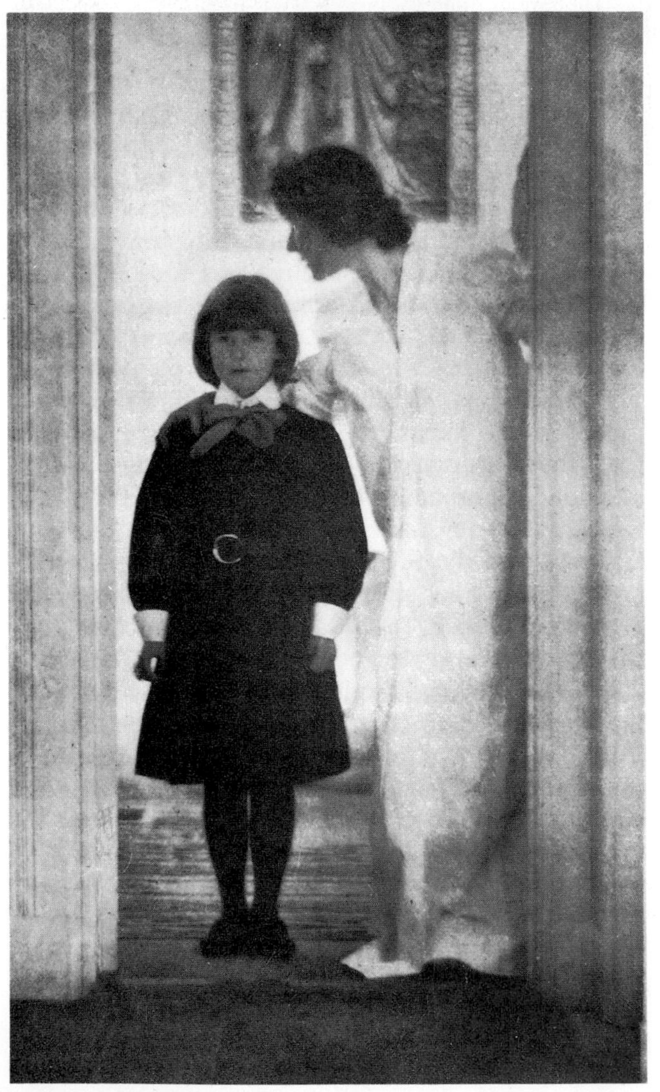

In sculpture, JEAN BAPTISTE CARPEAUX (1827–1875) combined his Realist intention with a love of Baroque and Antique sculpture and of the work of Michelangelo. Carpeaux's group *Ugolino and His Children* (FIG. **21-63**) is based on a passage from Dante's *Inferno* (XXXIII, 58–75) and shows Count Ugolino with his four sons shut up in a tower to starve to death. In Hell, Ugolino relates to Dante how, in a moment of extreme despair,

> I bit both hands for grief. And
> they, thinking I did it for hunger,
> suddenly rose up and said, "Father" . . .

and offered him their own flesh as food. The powerful forms—twisted, intertwined, and densely concentrated—suggest the self-devouring torment of frustration and despair that wracks the unfortunate Ugolino. A careful student of the male figures of Michelangelo, Carpeaux also said that he had the *Laocoön* group (FIG. 5-79) in mind. Certainly the storm and stress of the *Ugolino* recalls the Hellenistic "baroque" of that group and others, like the battling gods and giants on the frieze of the Pergamon altar

*Joseph T. Keiley, "Mrs. Käsebier's Prints," *Camera Notes* (July, 1899), in Robert A. Sobieszak, *Masterpieces of Photography from the George Eastman House Collection* (Rochester, NY: International Museum of Photography, 1985), p. 214.

(FIG. 5-78). Regardless of such influences, the sense of vivid reality about the anatomy of the *Ugolino* figures shows Carpeaux's interest in study from life.

AUGUSTUS SAINT-GAUDENS (1848–1907), an American sculptor trained in France, used realism effectively in a number of his portraits, where realism was highly appropriate. For the design of a memorial monument of Mrs. Henry Adams, wife of the historian (FIG. **21-64**), Saint-Gaudens chose a Classical mode of representation, which he modified freely. Of course, he had no need to specify a particular character; he wanted to represent a generality outside of time and place. The resultant statue is that of a woman of majestic bearing sitting in mourning, her classically beautiful face partly shadowed by a sepulchral drapery that voluminously enfolds her body. The immobility of her form, set in an attitude of eternal vigilance, is only slightly stirred by a natural, yet mysterious and exquisite gesture. Saint-Gaudens's masterpiece is a work worthy of the grave stelae of Classical Athens (FIG. 5-56).

21-63 JEAN BAPTISTE CARPEAUX, *Ugolino and His Children*, 1865–1867. Marble, 6′ 5″ high. The Metropolitan Museum of Art, New York (Josephine Bay Paul and C. Michael Paul Foundation and the Charles Ulrick and Josephine Bay Foundation gifts, 1967).

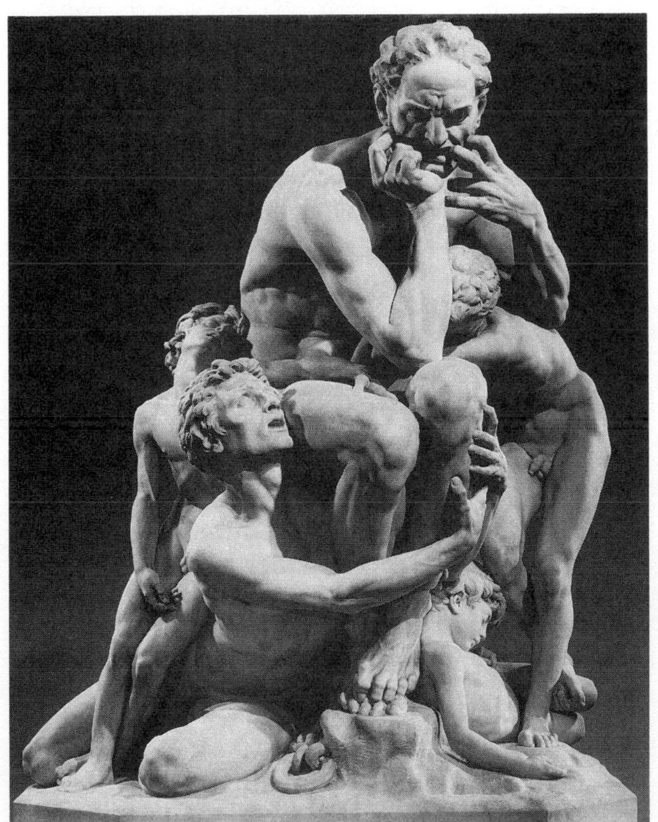

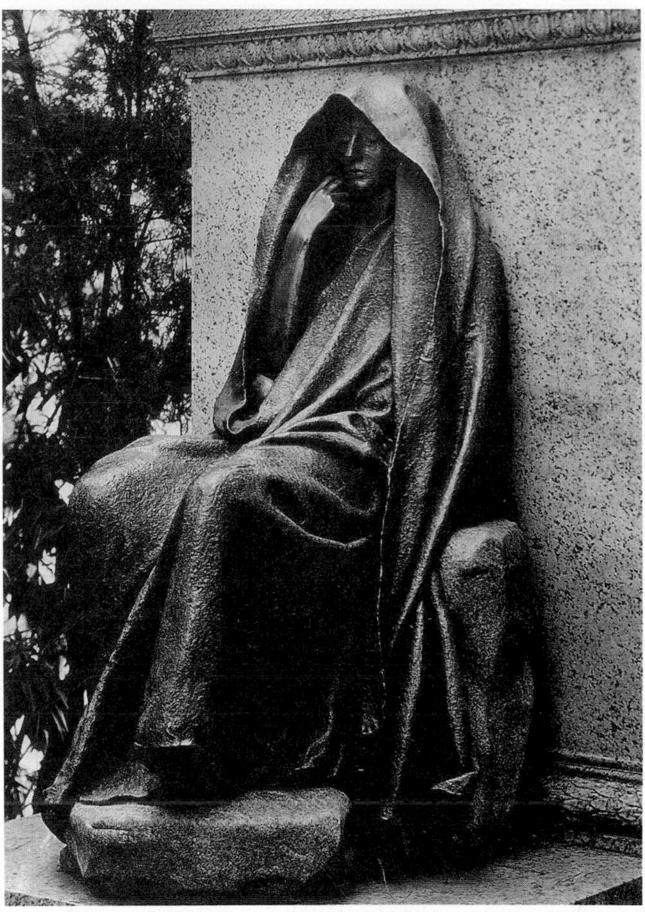

21-64 AUGUSTUS SAINT-GAUDENS, Adams Memorial, 1891. Bronze, 70″ high. Rock Creek Cemetery, Washington, D.C.

Manet and Impressionism

The Realism of Courbet and his followers had hardly established one kind of Realism before a different version, leading away from Courbet, took its place. In the fall of 1864, the English painter Dante Gabriel Rosetti wrote home describing French Realism as he had seen it in visits to the studios of Courbet and Manet: "There is a man named Manet . . . whose pictures are for the most part mere scrawls, and who seems to be one of the lights of the Realist school. Courbet, the head of it, is not much better." This somewhat priggish dismissal of Courbet and Manet linked the two artists as Realists, yet overlooked the differences between them. Courbet, himself, said of Manet's work in 1867: "I myself shouldn't like to meet this young man. . . . I should be obliged to tell him I don't understand anything about his paintings, and I don't want to be disagreeable to him." It was with ÉDOUARD MANET (1832–1883), however, that the course of modern painting shifted into a new phase, one that, in addition to accurately

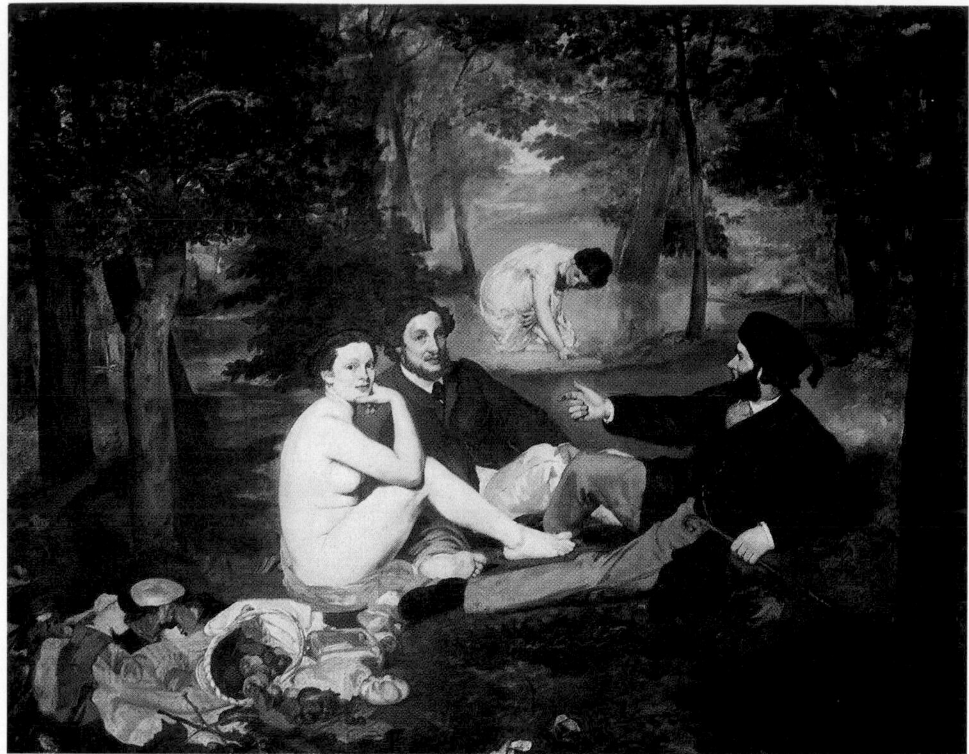

21-65 Édouard Manet, *Le Déjeuner sur l'herbe,* 1863. Approx. 7′ × 8′ 10″. Musée d'Orsay, Paris.

recording the appearance of the physical world, had as its aim the authentic representation of the color and light that reveal that world to the eye. In his work, Manet, the Realist, became the point of departure for the later Impressionist transformation of the great tradition in painting that had begun with Giotto.

Although the term *Impressionism* was first used in 1874 by a journalist ridiculing a landscape by Monet called *Impression—Sunrise,* the battle over the merits of Impressionist painting began eleven years earlier with Manet's *Le Déjeuner sur l'herbe (Luncheon on the Grass,* FIG. **21-65**). In 1863, Manet exhibited this then controversial painting at the Salon des Refusés (Salon of the Rejected) in Paris. As the name suggests, the exhibit consisted of a large number of works rejected by the jury for the major Academy Salon that year. The Academy Salons were government-subsidized arbiters of French art—"warehouses," as Zola called them—where the artists of France annually exhibited thousands of canvases. Prizes or recognition at the Salon could ensure professional success; refusal or rejection often led to neglect or failure. The Salon, at least until the 1880s, was the field of intense professional competition among artists and the battleground of "modern" versus "traditional." Ironically, it was a public seeking the avant-garde at the Salon des Refusés that was shocked by Manet's *Le Déjeuner sur l'herbe,* originally titled simply *The Bath.*

Manet may have been "a child of the century," as Zola called him in praise of his daring modernity, but he did not care to isolate himself as such. Instead, he wished to shine in the Salon with works (preferably figure paintings) as strong as the masterpieces of the Tradition. In *Le Déjeuner,* Manet does not attempt to revive "great painting," but tries to speak in a new voice and with an authority equal to that of his celebrated predecessors. The source of the work is proper enough; it takes as its theme the pastoral paradise familiar in paintings from Giorgione to Watteau. We know that at first Manet had Giorgione's (and Titian's?) *Pastoral Symphony* (FIG. 17-59) in mind as the source for *Le Déjeuner*, but for the actual composition, he used an engraving by Marcantonio Raimondi, a pupil of Raphael. Manet also may have been mindful of Baudelaire's observation (made as early as 1845) that "we are surrounded by the heroism of modern life, [but there is as yet no painter] who will know how to tear out of life its epic side and make us see, with color or drawing, how grand we are in our neckties and varnished boots!"

Nothing about the foreground figures in *Le Déjeuner* is very heroic. In fact, the foreground figures were all based on living, identifiable people. The seated nude was Victorine Meurand (Manet's favorite model at the time) and the gentlemen were his brother Eugène (with cane) and the sculptor Ferdinand Leenhof. The two men wear fashionable Parisian attire of the 1860s, and the foreground nude is not only a distressingly un-idealized figure type, but she seems disturbingly unabashed and at ease, looking directly at the viewer without shame or flirtatiousness.

This outraged the public—the pastoral brought up to date in a manner that seemed merely to represent the promiscuous in a Parisian park. One hostile critic, no doubt voicing public opinion, said:

> A commonplace woman of the demimonde, as naked as can be, shamelessly lolls between two dandies dressed to the teeth. These latter look like schoolboys on a holiday, perpetrating an outrage to play the man. . . . This is a young man's practical joke—a shameful, open sore.*

Manet's work would have been accepted had he shown men and women as nymphs and satyrs in Classical dress or undress, as did his contemporary, Bouguereau (FIG. 21-59). In *Le Déjeuner,* Manet raised the veils of allusion and reverie, and bluntly confronted the public with reality.

The public and the critics disliked Manet's subject matter only slightly less than the method he used to present his figures. The landscape and the background pool, in which the second woman bathes, are rendered in soft focus and broadly painted compared to the clear forms of the harshly lit trio of figures in the foreground and the pile of discarded female attire and picnic foods at the lower left.† The lighting displays the strong contrasts between darks and highlighted areas found in many contemporaneous photographs. In the main figures, the middle values, so carefully observed and recorded by Corot, and even Courbet, are blotted out; in a "crowding of the lights" and a compensating "crowding of the darks," many values are summed up in one or two lights or darks. The effect is both to flatten the form and to give it a hard, snapping presence, similar to that in early photographs. A detail (FIG. **21-66**) shows Manet's broadly painted tones, a method which he learned primarily from Velázquez and Frans Hals. The paint directly reports what is given to the eye, without any presuppositions of form, structure, or contour. Form, here, no longer a matter of line, is only a function of paint and light. Manet himself declared that the chief actor in the painting is the light. The public and the critics, guardians of public taste, knew nothing of this. They saw only a crude sketch without the customary "finish."

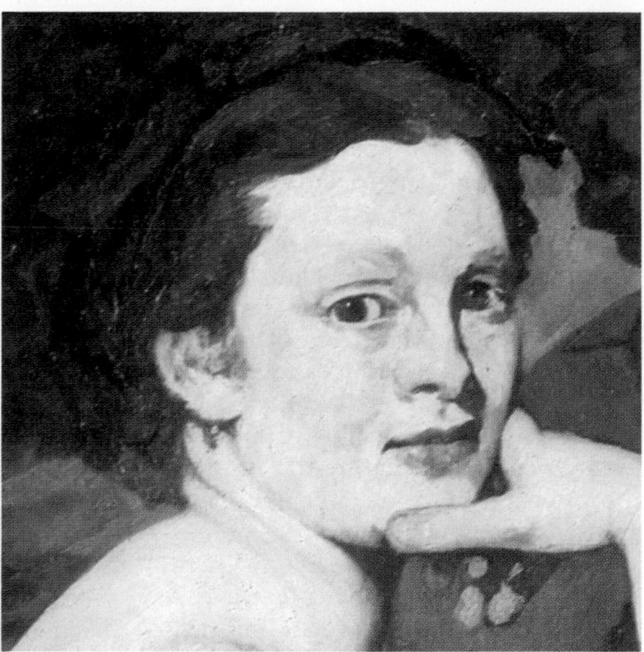

21-66 Detail of *Le Déjeuner sur l'herbe* (FIG. 21-65).

Manet's masterpiece, *A Bar at the Folies-Bergère* (FIG. **21-67**), was painted in 1882, after the artist had become associated with the Impressionists. This work shows both an impersonality toward the subject and Manet's fascination with the effects of light spilling from the gas globes onto the figures and the objects around them. In this study of artificial light (both direct light and that reflected in the mirrored background), the artist tells us little about the barmaid‡ and less about her customers, but much about the optical experience of this momentary pattern of light, in which the barmaid is only another *motif*—another still life amid the bottles on the counter. The painting tells no story, and has no moral, no plot, and no stage direction; it is simply an optical event, an arrested moment, in which lighted shapes of one kind or another participate. One is reminded of the novels of Manet's friend, Émile Zola, especially of *Nana,* whose heroine is nothing but a meaningless human consequence of the intersecting of social forces that create and destroy her. The barmaid in Manet's painting is primarily a compositional device—automatic and nonpersonal.

*In G. H. Hamilton, *Manet and His Critics* (New Haven, CT: Yale University Press, 1954), p. 45.

†An interesting comparison can be drawn between the foreground and background in Manet's *Le Déjeuner* and the lighting and focus in Robinson's *Women and Children in the Country* (FIG. 21-49).

‡Or is it *barmaids?* A lively debate currently rages about whether Manet has depicted two different girls or just one girl and her reflection.

The *Folies-Bergère* illustrates another quality that first made its appearance in *Le Déjeuner sur l'herbe* and was to loom with increasing importance in the works of later painters. Although the effect was perhaps unplanned, Manet's painting made a radical break with the Tradition by redefining the function of the picture surface. Ever since the Renaissance, the picture had been conceived as a "window" through which the viewer looked at an illusory space developed behind it. By minimizing the effects of modeling and perspective, Manet forced the viewer to look at the painted surface and to recognize it once more as a flat plane covered with patches of pigment. This "revolution of the color patch," combined with Manet's cool, objective approach, pointed painting in the direction of abstraction, with its indifference to subject matter and its emphasis on optical sensations and the problems of organizing them into form. In most nonobjective twentieth-century work, not only the subject matter, but even its supposed visual manifestation in the external world, will disappear.

Throughout his entire career, Manet suffered the hostility of the critics as surrogates of the public. This attitude wounded him deeply. He never understood their animosity and continued to seek their approval, but the doses of the real that he administered in his art were too harsh. His contemporary, the philosopher and historian Ernest Renan, expressed the real moral threat some of the public feared from the new realism in art:

> It is possible, then, that the ruin of idealistic beliefs is destined to follow the destruction of supernatural beliefs, and that a real abasement of human morality dates from *the day it saw the reality of things* [emphasis added].*

After the mid-1860s, Impressionist painters such as Monet, Pissarro, Renoir, and Degas followed Manet's lead in depicting scenes of contemporary middle-class Parisian life and landscape. Their desire for a more modern expression led them to prize the immediacy of visual impression and persuaded the landscapists, especially Monet, to work out of doors. From this custom of painting directly from nature came the spontaneous representation of atmosphere and climate so characteristic of Impressionist painting. The rejection of idealistic interpretation and literary anecdote was paralleled by an intense scrutiny of

*In J. C. Sloane, *French Painting Between the Past and the Present* (Princeton, NJ: Princeton University Press, 1951), p. 57.

21-67 ÉDOUARD MANET, *A Bar at the Folies-Bergère*, 1882. Approx. 37″ × 51″. The Courtauld Institute Galleries, London.

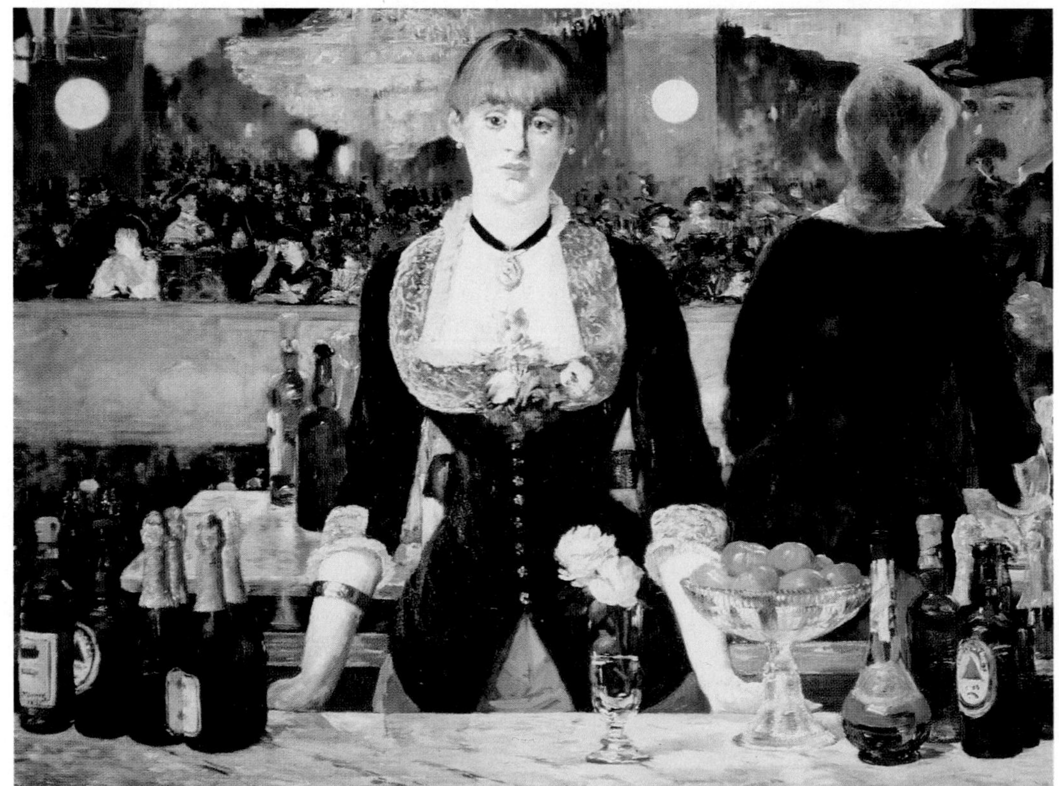

color and light. Scientific studies of light and the invention of chemical pigments increased artistic sensitivity to the multiplicity of colors in nature and gave artists new colors with which to work.* Most of the eight cooperative Impressionist exhibitions held between 1874 and 1886 irritated the public. However, Impressionist technique was actually less radical than it seemed at the time; in certain respects, these artists were simply developing the color theories of Leonardo and the actual practice of Rubens, Delacroix, Constable, and Turner.

The Impressionists sought to create the illusion of forms bathed in light and atmosphere. This goal required an intensive study of outdoor light as the source of our experience of color, which revealed the important truth that local color—the actual color of an object—is usually modified by the quality of the light in which it is seen, by reflections from other objects, and by the effects produced by juxtaposed colors. Shadows do not appear grey or black, as many earlier painters had thought, but seem to be composed of colors modified by reflections or other conditions. (One earlier artist, Jan Vermeer, evidently observed this.) In painting, if complementary colors are used side by side over large enough areas, they intensify each other, unlike the effect of small quantities of mixed pigments, which blend into neutral tones. Furthermore, the juxtaposition of colors on a canvas for the eye to fuse at a distance produces a more intense hue than the mixing of the same colors on the palette. Although it is not strictly true that the Impressionists used only primary hues, juxtaposing them to create secondary colors (blue and yellow, for example, to produce green), they did achieve remarkably brilliant effects with their characteristically short, choppy brush strokes, which so accurately caught the vibrating quality of light. The fact that the surfaces of their canvases look unintelligible at close range and their forms and objects appear only when the eye fuses the strokes at a certain distance accounts for much of the early adverse criticism leveled at their work, such as the conjecture that the Impressionists fired their paint at the canvas with pistols.

Of the Impressionists, CLAUDE MONET (1840–1926), whose *Impression—Sunrise* was mentioned earlier, carried the color method furthest. Monet called color his "day-long obsession, joy and torment." When he looked at scenes such as those found in his *Cliff at Étretat* (FIG. **21-68**), painted at a favorite location on

*Special luminance was achieved by using new colors like viridian green and cobalt violet (both invented in 1859) and cerulean blue (invented in 1860). These pigments, applied with newly available flat-bound brushes, often were placed on canvases covered with a base of white pigment (white ground), rather than with the brown or green tones favored by earlier artists.

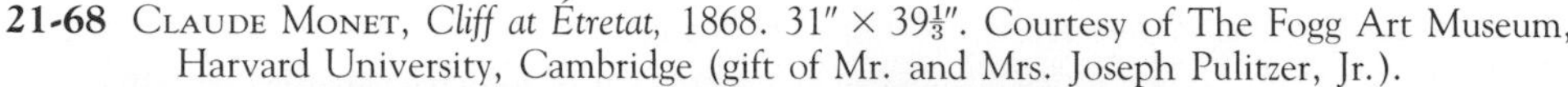

21-68 CLAUDE MONET, *Cliff at Étretat,* 1868. 31″ × 39⅓″. Courtesy of The Fogg Art Museum, Harvard University, Cambridge (gift of Mr. and Mrs. Joseph Pulitzer, Jr.).

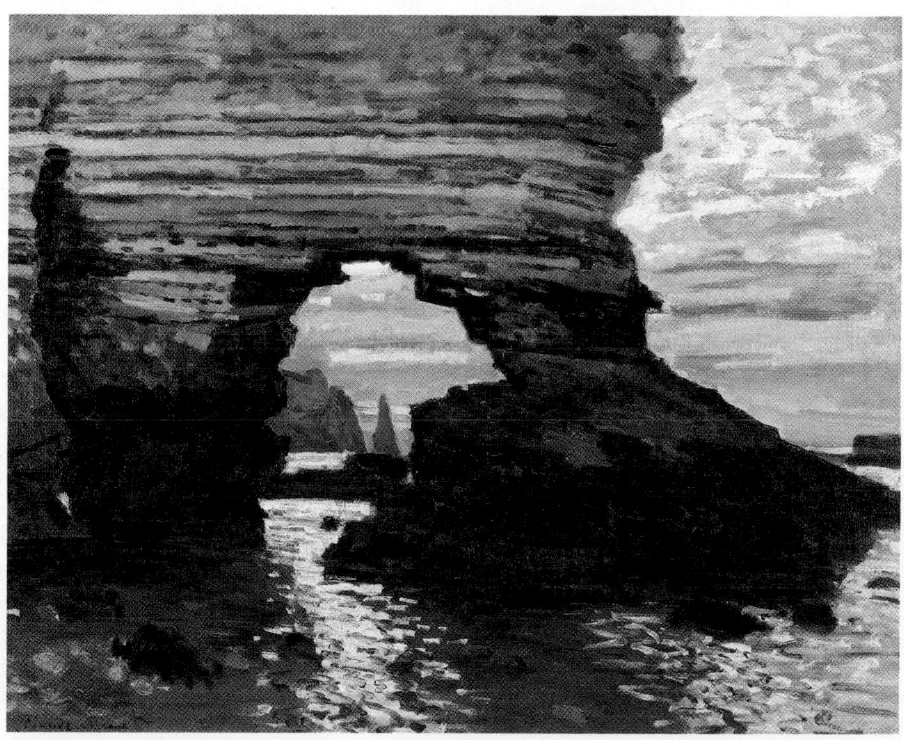

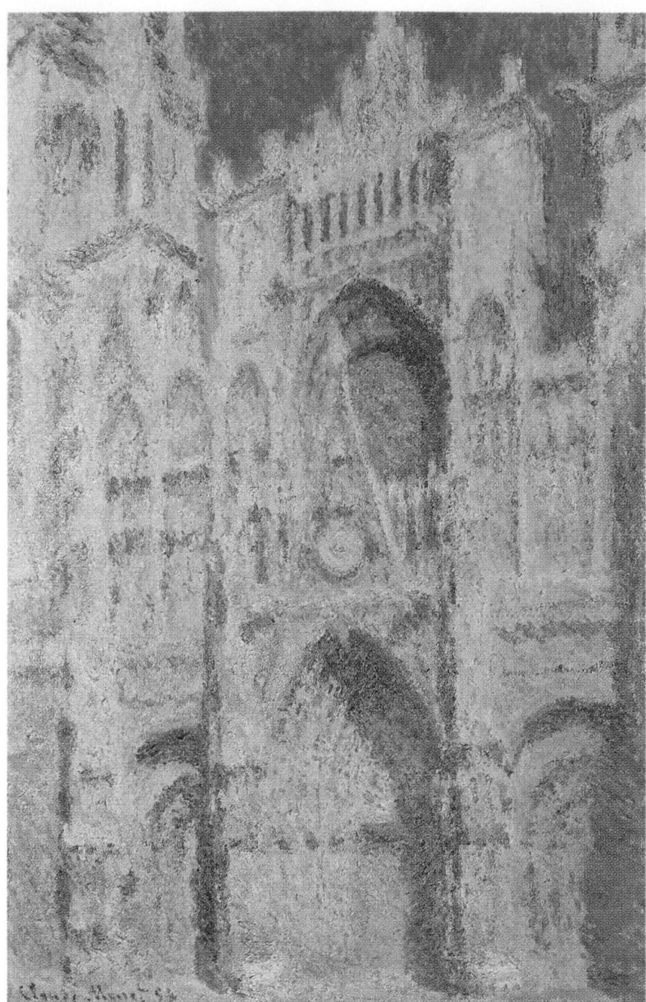

21-69 Claude Monet, *Rouen Cathedral* (façade), 1894. Approx. 39″ × 26″. The Metropolitan Museum of Art, New York (Theodore M. Davis Collection, bequest of Theodore M. Davis, 1915).

the coast near Le Havre, he responded to lighting and atmospheric conditions in terms of color, which he applied to the canvas with thick, dabbing strokes that caused the surface of the painting to shimmer. In *Étretat,* color is dominated by the glow of the sun low on the horizon, which bounces off the clouds in the sky and streams across the rippling water to reflect back up onto the side of the rock arch that faces us. The rock face is a symphony of greys, browns, and golds, and our eyes feel bathed in colored light that seems to emanate from the painting itself. Lila Cabot Perry, a student of Monet's late in his career, gave this description of his approach:

> I remember his once saying to me: "When you go out to paint, try to forget what objects you have before you—a tree, a house, a field, or whatever. Merely think, here is a little square of blue, here an oblong of pink, here a streak of yellow, and paint it just as it looks to you, the exact color and shape, until it gives your own naïve impression of the scene before you." He said he wished he had been born blind and then had suddenly gained his sight so that he could have begun to paint in this way without knowing what the objects were that he saw before him.*

Monet's contribution was especially evident in several series of paintings of the same subject. He painted sixteen views of Waterloo Bridge in London and some forty views of Rouen Cathedral (FIG. **21-69** and Introduction FIG. 5). In each canvas in the latter series, the cathedral was observed from the same point of view but at different times of the day or under various climatic conditions. Monet, with a scientific precision, created an unparalleled and unexcelled record of the passing of time as seen in the movement of light over identical forms. Later critics accused Monet and his companions of destroying form and order for the sake of fleeting atmospheric effects, but we may feel that light is properly the "form" of Monet's finest paintings, rather than accept the narrower definition that recognizes "formal" properties only in firm, geometric shapes. The Impressionist artists ignored much that was prized by the Realists—the world of Corot's "values," of graduated tones of lights and darks; rather, the Impressionists recorded their own sensations of color, and the outlines and solidities of the world as interpreted by common sense melt away.

The Impressionist emphasis on the prime reality of sensation in the process of apprehending nature or the world had its parallel in the work of contemporaneous scientists, philosophers of science, and psychologists who asserted that reality is sensation and that knowledge could be based only on the analysis of our sensations. Indeed, the Austrian physicist Ernst Mach held that the sole reality is sensation and all the laws and principles of physics are only a kind of shorthand referring to complex linkages of the data of sense. Modern experimental psychology began its history with measurements of sense experience before turning a large portion of its attention, in the early twentieth century, toward studying how emotion, past experience, and memory affect perceptual activity. Artists who shared the belief that a single, accepted model of unchanging optical truth no longer existed—just as a standard way of seeing could not be mandated—considered "nature," in the broadest sense of whatever the world reveals, to be the source of all sensation. In *The Place du Théâtre Français* (FIG. **21-70**), Camille Pissarro (1830–1903) records a panorama of blurred, dark accents against a light ground that represents clearly the artist's visual sensations of a crowded Paris square, viewed from several stories

*In Linda Nochlin, *Impressionism and Post-Impressionism 1874–1904* (Englewood Cliffs, NJ: Prentice-Hall, 1966), p. 35.

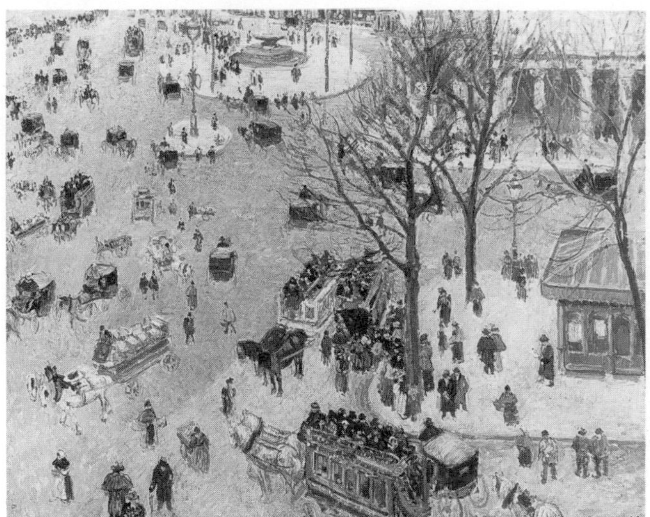

21-70 Camille Pissarro, *Place du Théâtre Français,* 1895. Approx. 28$\frac{1}{2}$″ × 36$\frac{1}{2}$″. Los Angeles County Museum of Art (the Mr. and Mrs. George Gard De Sylva Collection).

above street level. Like Monet, Pissarro sought to depict the fugitive effects of light at a particular moment, but the moment in Pissarro's *Place du Théâtre,* unlike those in Monet's work, is not so much one of light itself as of the life of the street, achieved through a deliberate casualness in the arrangement of his figures that is related to that in early photographs of street scenes. When Pissarro wrote in a letter to his son Lucien, "we have to approach nature sincerely, with our own modern sensibilities," he spoke of the Impressionist belief that what was real in nature was the light and color stimuli it revealed to the analytic eye of the modern painter.

Like many of his fellow Impressionists, Pissarro sometimes used the amazing "reality" of photography to supplement work directly from a model. Although he may not have known this particular example, the effect of Pissarro's *Place du Théâtre* is remarkably similar to that in the stereo photograph* *The Pont Neuf, Paris* (FIG. **21-71**) by Hippolyte Jouvin (active mid-1800s). In this stereograph, we look from the upper story of a building along the roadway of the "New Bridge," which stretches diagonally from lower left to upper right. Hurrying pedestrian figures become dark silhouettes, and the scene moves from sharp focus in the foreground to soft focus in the distance. These qualities, plus the arbitrary cutting off of figures at the edge of the frame and the curious flattening spatial effect caused by the high viewpoint, were of special interest to Pissarro and the other Impressionists.

Although the Impressionist artists were linked by what we might call "color sensationism" and fugitive effects of light and motion, each had very much an individualistic manner. Auguste Renoir (1841–1919),

*Stereo photographs were made with special twin-lensed cameras and viewed with special apparatus to recreate the illusion of seeing the world with two eyes (in three dimensions). Jouvin specialized in views of Paris and like many other stereographers, chose subjects or view points that exaggerated the dramatic effects of deep space.

21-71 Hippolyte Jouvin, *The Pont Neuf, Paris,* c. 1860–1865. Albumen stereograph. Collection, The Museum of Modern Art, New York.

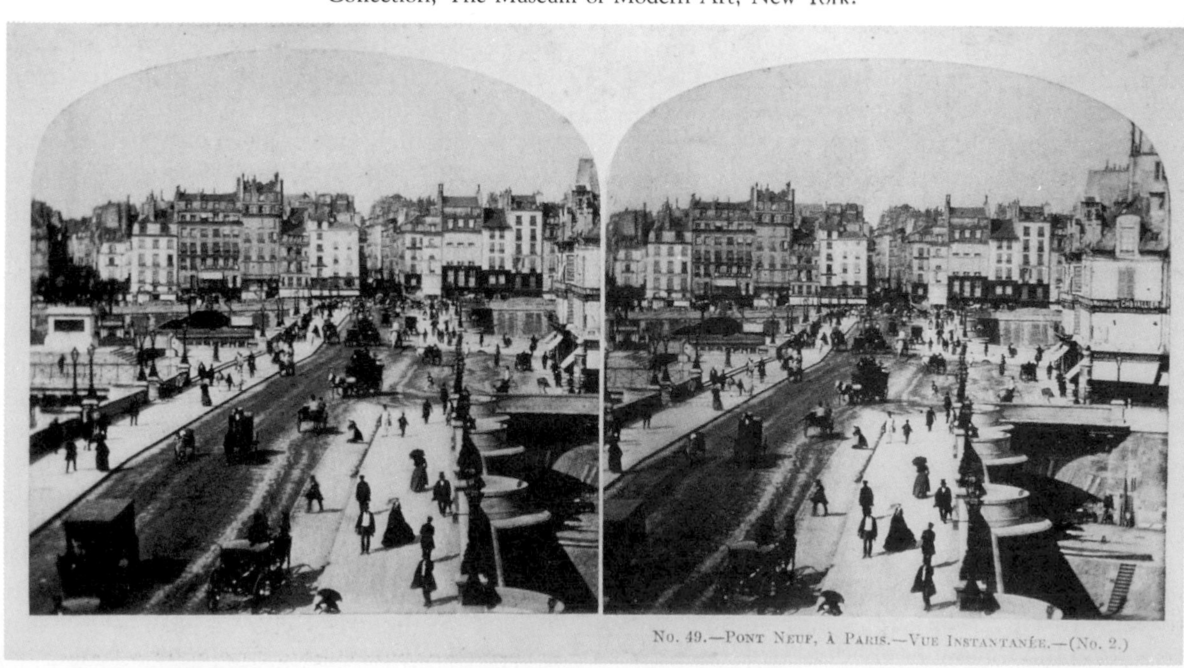

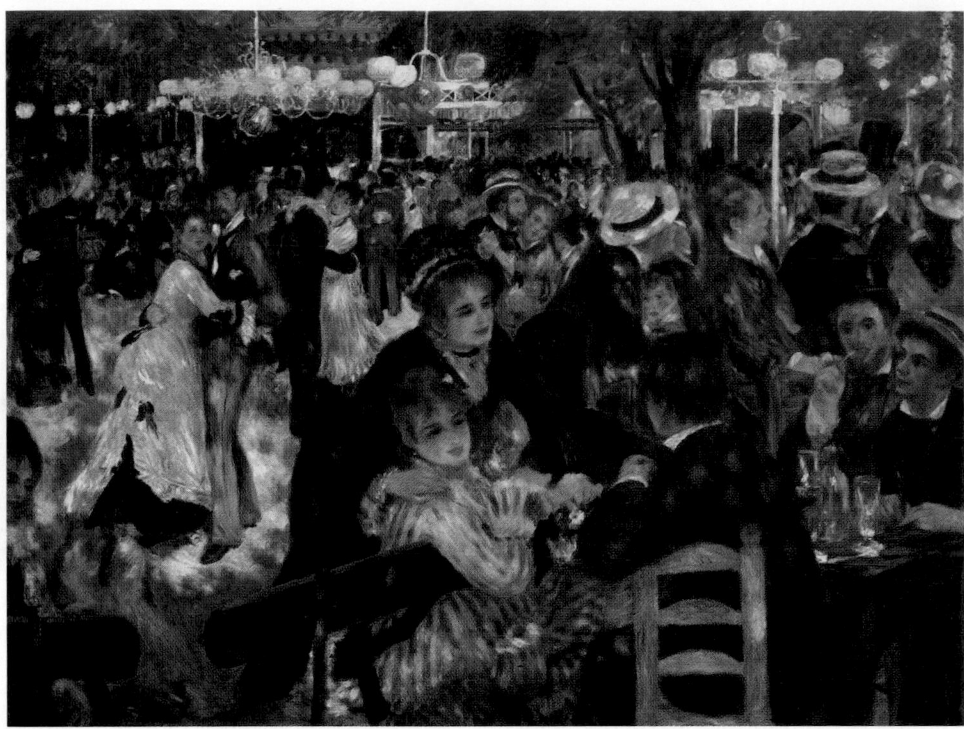

21-72 AUGUSTE RENOIR, *Le Moulin de la Galette,* 1876. Approx. 51″ × 68″. Louvre, Paris.

for example, was a specialist in the human figure, a sympathetic admirer of what was beautiful in the body and what was pleasurable in the simple round of human life. The bright gaiety of his *Le Moulin de la Galette* (FIG. **21-72**), where a Sunday throng enjoys a popular Paris dance hall, is characteristic of his celebration of vivacious charm. Some people crowd the tables and chatter, while others dance energetically. The whole scene is dappled by sunlight and shade, artfully blurred into the figures themselves to produce just that effect of floating and fleeting light so cultivated by the Impressionists. The casual, unposed placement of the figures, and the suggested continuity of space, spreading in all directions and only accidentally limited by the frame, introduce us, as observers, into the very scene. We are not, as with the Tradition, observing a performance on a stage set; rather, we ourselves are part of the action. Renoir's subjects are quite unconscious of the presence of an observer; they do not pose but merely go about the business of the moment. As Classical art sought to express universal and timeless qualities, so Impressionism attempted to depict just the opposite—the incidental, momentary, and passing aspects of reality.

EDGAR DEGAS (1834–1917) is usually included in any discussion of Impressionism. Although actively sympathetic with the Impressionists, he stood somewhat apart from them, an independent talent of great power. More than any of his contemporaries, Degas studied the infinite variety of particular movements and, even more, the kinesthetic qualities of bodies in motion—especially race horses, bathers, laundresses, milliners, and ballet dancers. Ballerinas in arrested movements—split-second poses cut from the sequence of their dance—were one of his favorite subjects. In *Ballet Rehearsal (Adagio)* (FIG. **21-73**), Degas used several devices to bring the observer into the pictorial space: the frame cuts off the spiral stair, the windows in the background, and the group of figures in the right foreground; the figures are uncentered and "accidental" in arrangement; the rapid diagonals of the wall bases and floorboards carry us into and along the directional lines of the dancers; and, as is customary in Degas's ballet pictures, a large, off-center, empty space creates the illusion of a continuous floor that connects us with the pictured figures. By seeming to stand on the same surface with them, we are drawn into their space. The often arbitrarily cutoff figures in this and other works by Degas reveal his fascination with photography. He not only studied the photography of others, but he used the camera consistently himself to make preliminary studies for his own works, particularly with figures in interiors. The cunning spatial projection in *Ballet Rehearsal* derived not only from careful observation and the artist's interest in photography, but was also undoubtedly inspired by eighteenth-century Japanese

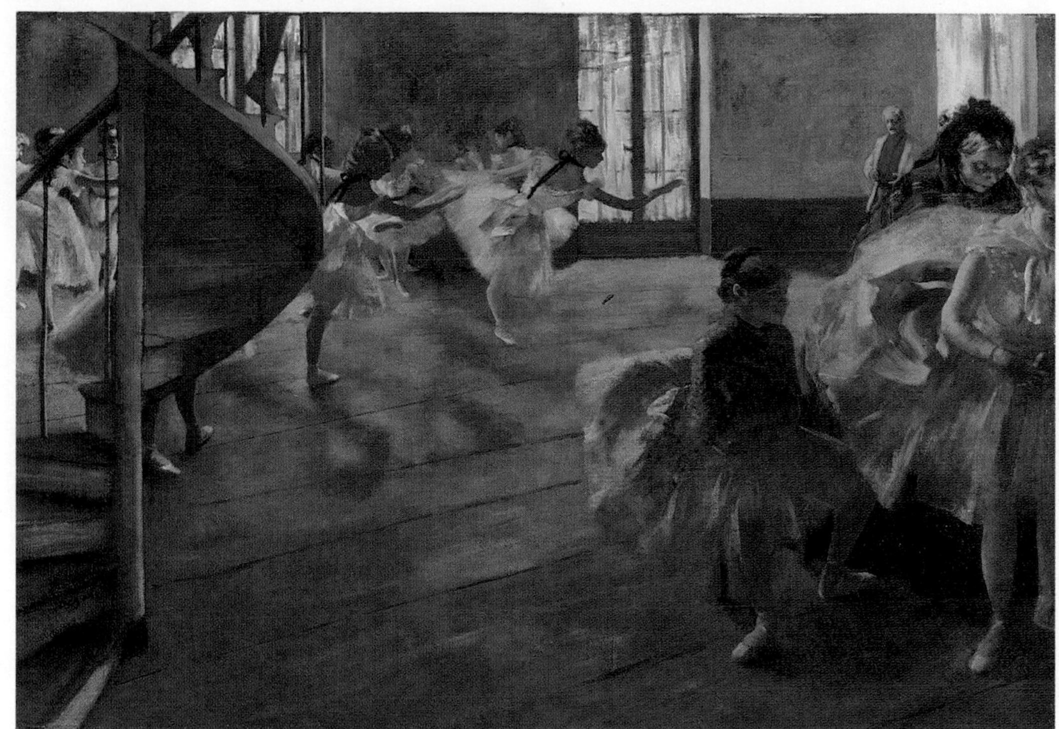

21-73 Edgar Degas, *Ballet Rehearsal (Adagio)*, 1876. 23″ × 33″. Glasgow Art Galleries and Museum (Burrell Collection).

woodblock prints (FIG. **21-74**), in which diverging lines not only organize the flat shapes of the figures but function as lines directing the viewer's attention into the picture space. The Impressionists, familiar with these prints as early as the 1860s, greatly admired their spatial organization, the familiar and intimate themes, and the flat, unmodeled color areas, and drew much instruction from them. These popular Japanese prints, "discovered" by European artists in the mid-nineteenth century, were the first definitive non-European influence on European pictorial design. Earlier borrowings from China, India, and Arabia had been superficial.

21-74 Suzuki Harunobu, *The Evening Glow of the Andon*, 1765. $11\frac{1}{4}'' \times 8\frac{1}{2}''$. (Clarence Buckingham Collection)

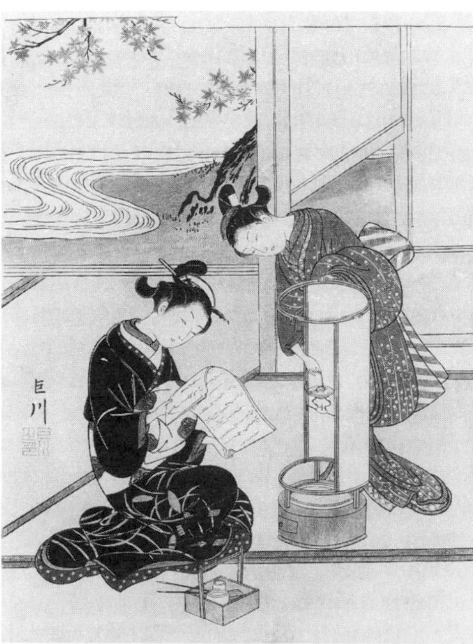

Viscount Lepic and His Daughters (FIG. **21-75**), painted by Degas in 1873, summarizes what the artist had learned from photography, from his own painstaking research, and from what his generation in general absorbed from the Japanese print: the clear, flat pattern; the unusual point of view; the informal glimpse of contemporary life. Whatever his subject, Degas saw it in terms of clear line and pattern, observed from a new and unexpected angle. In the divergent movements of the father and his small daughters, of the man entering the picture at the left, and of the horse and carriage passing across the background, we have a vivid pictorial account of a moment in time at a particular position in space, much as Monet, in his own way, defined such space and time in landscape painting. In another instant, this picture would disappear, for each of the figures would move in a different direction, and the group would dissolve. Here again, Degas made clever use of the empty space of the street to integrate the viewer into the

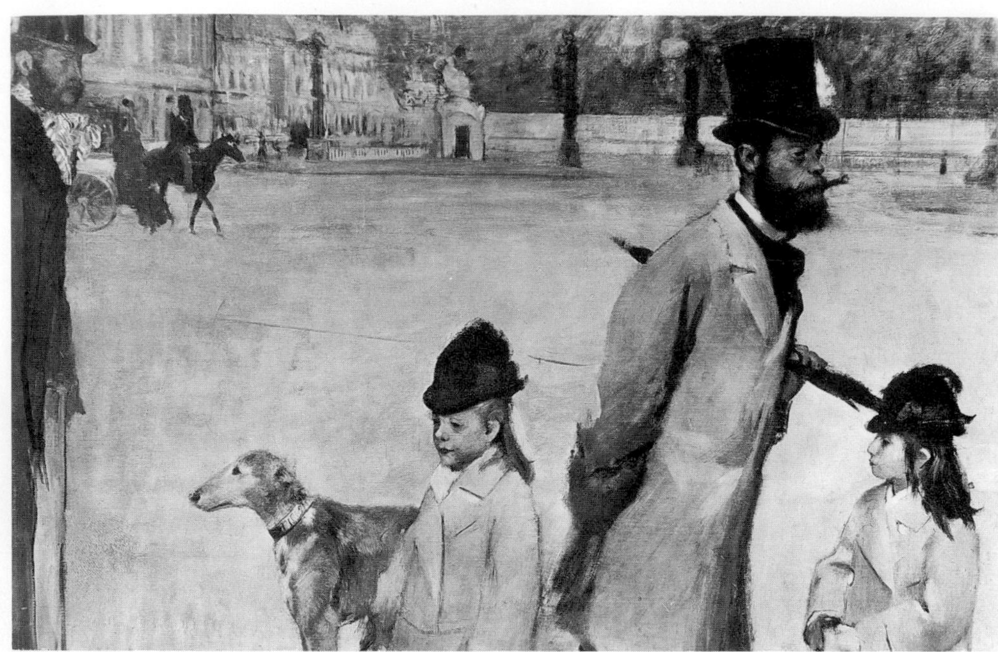

21-75 EDGAR DEGAS, *Viscount Lepic and His Daughters,* 1873. Approx. 32″ × 47″. Location unknown.

21-76 EDGAR DEGAS, *The Morning Bath,* c. 1883. Pastel on paper, 27¾″ × 17″. (Potter Palmer Collection) photograph © 1990, The Art Institute of Chicago. All rights reserved.

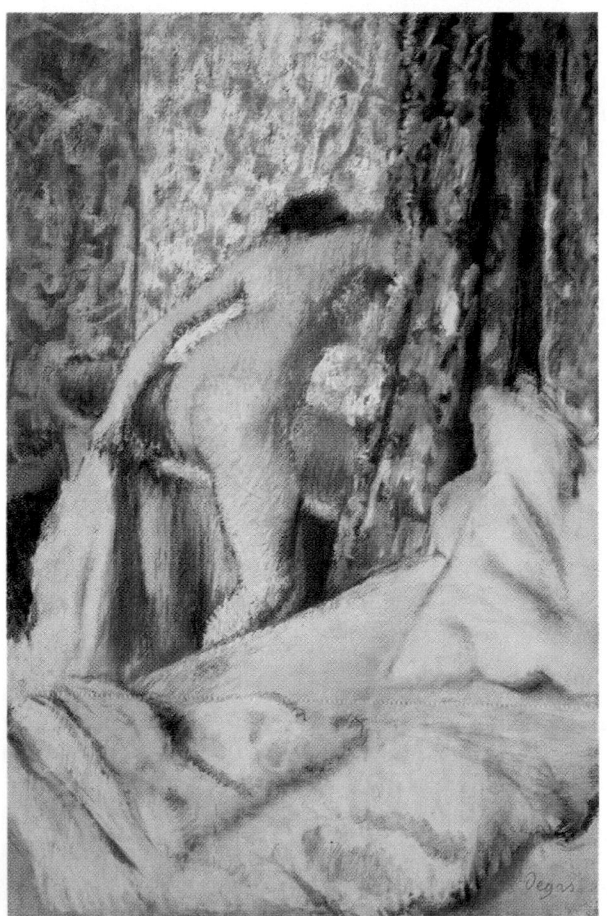

space containing the figures. Actually, the painter seems to have taken into account the range of the sweep of our glance—everything that we would see in a single split-second inspection; indeed, the picture resembles a snapshot made with a hastily aimed camera.

When Degas was a very young man and about to enter into a career as a painter, he met Ingres, whose work he greatly admired and who advised him to "draw lines, . . . many lines, from memory or from nature; it is this way that you will become a good painter." Degas, faithful to the old linearist's advice, became a superb master of line, so much so that his identification as an Impressionist, in the sense that Monet, Pissarro, and Renoir are Impressionists, seems a mistake to many critics. Certainly, Degas's designs do not cling to the surface of the canvas, as do Manet's and Monet's; they are developed in depth and take the viewer well behind the picture plane. We are always aware of the elastic strength of his firmly drawn contours. However, Degas did specialize in studies of figures in rapid and informal movement, recording the quick impression of arrested motion, and he did use the spectral color—the fresh, divided hues of the Impressionist—especially when he worked in his favorite medium, pastel. These dry sticks of powdered pigment cannot be "muddied" by mixing them on a palette, so they produce, almost automatically, those fresh and bright colors so favored by the Impressionists. All of these qualities are seen in *The Morning Bath* (FIG. **21-76**), which is like Renoir's treatment of the same subject (not illustrated) in its informality and intimacy but unlike Renoir's work in its indifference to either formal or physical beauty. Degas's concern was with the unplanned realism of the purely accidental attitude of the human figure, seen in an awkward yet natural enough moment. The broken volume of the nude body twists across "Japanese" angles, flat planes, and patterns. The informality and spontaneity of the pose again suggest snapshot photography, but photographic materials available at the time (including those of the motion picture, then just in its infancy) could not capture the range of light and the verity of motion that Degas sought to depict above all else.

In the Salon of 1874, Degas admired a painting by a young American artist, MARY CASSATT (1845–1926), the daughter of a Philadelphia banker. "There," he remarked, "is a person who feels as I do." Cassatt was befriended and influenced by Degas and exhibited regularly with the Impressionists. She had trained as a painter before moving to Europe to study masterworks in France and Italy. Her choice of subject matter was limited by the facts that, as a woman, she could not easily frequent the cafés with her male artist friends, and that she was responsible for the care of her aging parents, who had moved to Paris to join her. Because of these restrictions, Cassatt's subjects were principally women and children, whom she presented with an inimitable conjunction of objectivity and genuine sentiment. Works like *The Bath* (FIG. **21-77**) show the tender relationship between a mother and child. The mother's torso shelters the child against the diagonal slope of her lap. Color binds mother, child, and wash basin into one central form that is pushed against the flattened space of the darker-hued rug, wallpaper, and bureau by placement of the remarkably solid jug at the lower right. Cassatt's style in this work owed much to the compositional devices of Degas and of Japanese prints, but the painting's design has an originality and strength all its own.

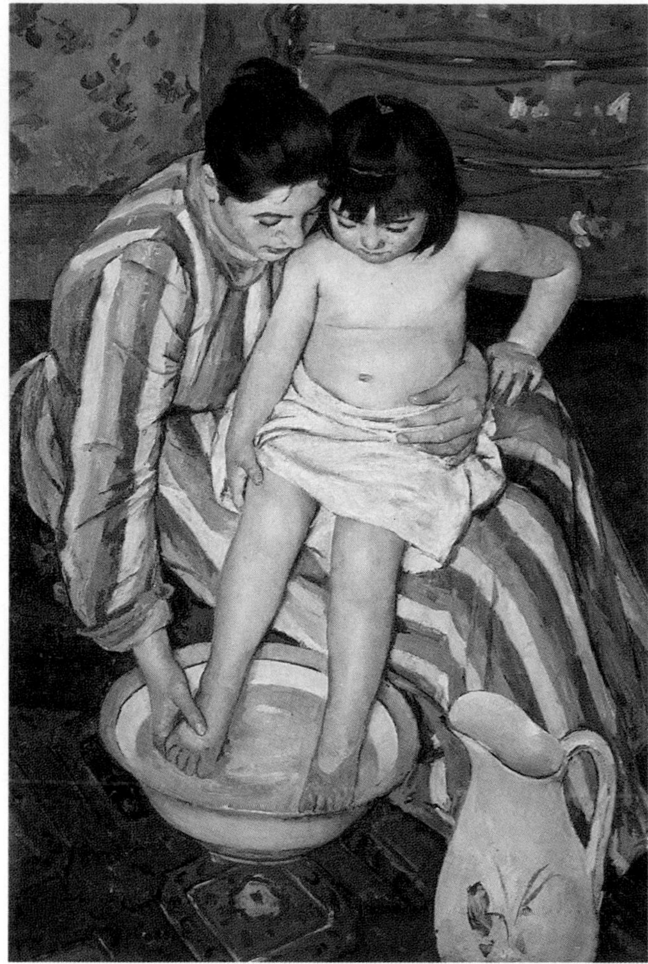

21-77 MARY CASSATT, *The Bath*, c. 1892. 39″ × 26″. Photograph © 1990, The Art Institute of Chicago.

JAMES ABBOTT MCNEILL WHISTLER (1834–1903) was an American expatriate artist, who worked on the Continent before settling finally in London. In Paris, he knew many of the Impressionists, and his art is an interesting mixture of some of their concerns and his own. He shared their interests in the subject matter of contemporary life and the sensations produced on the eye by color. To these influences he added his own interest in creating visual harmonies paralleling those achieved in music:

> Nature contains the elements, in color and form, of all pictures, as the keyboard contains the notes of all music. But the artist is born to pick, and choose, and group with science, these elements, that the result may be beautiful—as the musician gathers his notes, and forms his chords, until he brings forth from chaos glorious harmony.*

To underscore his artistic intentions, Whistler began calling his paintings "arrangements" or "nocturnes." *Nocturne in Blue and Gold (Old Battersea Bridge*, FIG. **21-78**) is a daring composition in which evening light simplifies shapes into hazy silhouettes. We are so close to the bridge that all we see is the thick T-shape made by a single buttress-support, the silhouette of a lone boat near its base, a band of distant shore, and the cropped section of the bridge roadway high overhead. Blue tones fill the canvas, relieved only by touches of yellow and red, indicating shore lights and the effects of the setting sun on the heavy clouds in the sky. The artist was clearly more interested in creating an elegantly simple color harmony for this spare arrangement of shapes than he was in giving details of the actual scene. In works like *Nocturne*, Whistler has taken the "impression" of what our eye sees in

*In Harold Spencer, *American Art: Readings from the Colonial Era to the Present* (New York: Scribners, 1980), pp. 154–55.

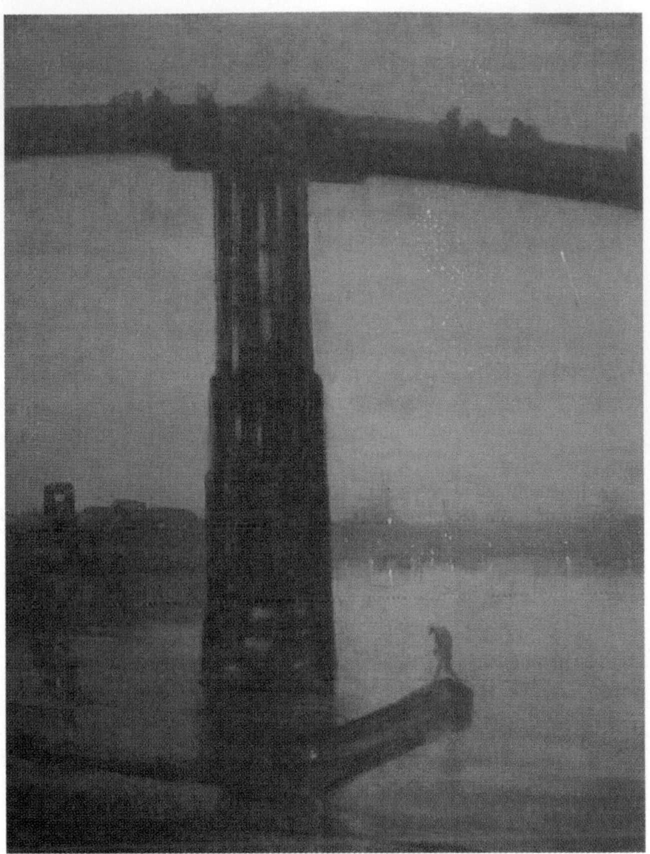

21-78 James Abbott McNeill Whistler, *Nocturne in Blue and Gold (Old Battersea Bridge),* 1877. $23\frac{3}{4}'' \times 18\frac{3}{8}''$. Tate Gallery, London.

nature further than any of the Impressionists. His emphasis was on creating a harmonious arrangement of shapes and colors on the rectangle of his canvas, an approach that will interest many twentieth-century artists from Matisse (fig. 22-5) to Pollock (fig. 23-1).

Such works angered many viewers. The British critic John Ruskin accused Whistler of "flinging a pot of paint in the public's face" with his style. In reply, Whistler sued Ruskin for libel. During the trial, Whistler defended his artistic methods by describing his approach in *Nocturne:*

> *I did not intend it to be a "correct" portrait of the bridge.* It is only a moonlight scene and the pier in the center of the picture may not be like the piers at Battersea Bridge as you know them in broad daylight. *As to what the picture represents, that depends upon who looks at it. To some persons it may represent all that is intended: to others it may represent nothing* [emphasis added].*

Although Whistler won the case, his victory had sadly ironic consequences for him. The judge in the case, showing where his sympathies—and perhaps those of the public—were, awarded the artist only one farthing (less than a penny) in damages and required him to pay all of the court costs, which ruined him financially. He continued to produce etchings and portraits for two decades after his bankruptcy.

The Impressionists' interest in representing form as the eye sees it revealed by light might seem an impossible approach for sculpture, but the Italian sculptor Medardo Rosso (1858–1928) was determined to try. The motivation that inspired him to create works like *Conversation in the Garden* (fig. **21-79**) was not quite the same, however, as that driving the Impressionists. Instead, Rosso was attempting to overcome what the poet and critic Charles Baudelaire had described as the deficiencies of sculpture in relation to painting. Baudelaire's basic charge was that a painter could control the viewer's response to a work, because a painting has only one point of view, but the sculptor has difficulty forcing viewers to see a work from any single angle, "for the spectator who moves around the figure can choose a hundred different points of view, . . . and it often happens that a chance trick of the light, an effect of the lamp, may discover a beauty which is not at all the one the artist had in mind." A Rosso sculpture, like *Conversation,* makes sense only from a viewpoint along one side—the front. Forms are simplified here to what one might see in a glance at a scene: no particulars of detail, but a faithful representation of the gestures and body language that hold the meaning of an interchange between people seen at a distance. The subject in *Conversation* is a casual incident from upper-middle-class life. Rosso has included himself as the portly figure standing at the left. In the middle, a lively lady (wearing a hat to shield her delicate skin from the sun) turns to address him. Rosso made the second seated figure, to the far right, an unimportant participant in the scene by modeling the shape in such general terms that the figure does not come "into focus." Light is important to the viewing of Rosso's sculpture, for it animates the work, increasing the illusion that we glimpse but one instant in an ongoing event. However, lighting cannot alter Rosso's intended expression of this moment in a conversation between a man and a woman in a garden. Like the Impressionist painters, Rosso viewed the world as a constantly changing place. But unlike the Impressionists' careful attention to recording the look of a place at a particular moment, and unlike Muybridge's analysis of successive moments (fig. 21-42), Rosso portrayed both an emotional response and the effect of light and shadow patterns on forms glimpsed at a particular instant in time.

*In McCoubrey, *American Art 1700–1960,* p. 184.

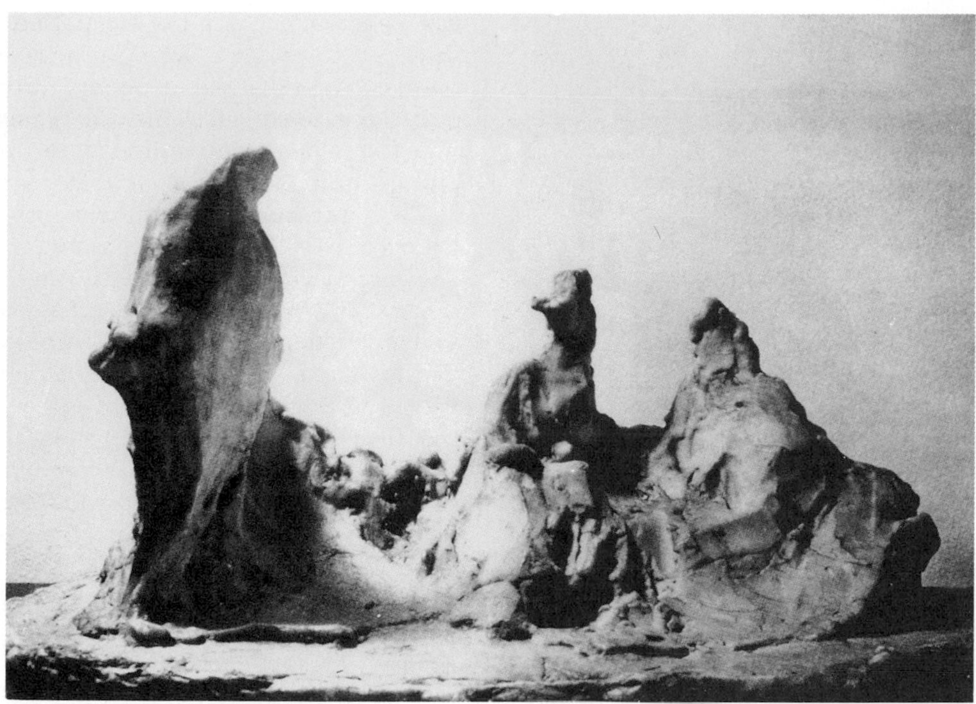

21-79 MEDARDO ROSSO, *Conversation in the Garden,* 1893. Wax over plaster, 17" high. Collection of Dr. Gianni Mattioli, Milan.

Post-Impressionism

By 1886, the Impressionists were accepted as serious artists by most critics and by a large segment of the public. Just at the time when their gay and colorful studies of contemporary life no longer seemed crude and unfinished, however, some of the painters themselves and a group of younger followers came to feel that too many of the traditional elements of picture making were being neglected in the search for momentary sensations of light and color. In a conversation with the influential art dealer Ambroise Vollard in about 1883, Renoir commented: "I had wrung Impressionism dry, and I finally came to the conclusion that I knew neither how to paint nor how to draw. In a word, Impressionism was a blind alley, as far as I was concerned." By the 1880s, a much more systematic examination of the properties of three-dimensional space, the expressive qualities of line, pattern, and color, and the symbolic character of subject matter was being undertaken by four artists in particular: Georges Seurat, Paul Cézanne, Vincent van Gogh, and Paul Gauguin. Because their art diverged so markedly from earlier Impressionism (although each of these painters at first accepted Impressionist methods and never rejected the new and brighter palette), these four artists and others sharing their views have come to be known as the Post-Impressionists, a classification that simply signifies their chronological position in nineteenth-century French painting.

At the eighth and last Impressionist exhibition in 1886, GEORGES SEURAT (1859–1891) showed his *Sunday Afternoon on the Island of La Grande Jatte* (FIG. **21-80**), which set forth the Impressionist interest in holiday themes and the analysis of light in a new and monumental synthesis that seemed strangely rigid and remote. Seurat's system of painting in small dots that stand in relation to each other was based on the color theories of Delacroix and the color scientists Hermann von Helmholtz and Michel Chevreul.* Seurat's system was a difficult procedure, as disciplined and painstaking as the Impressionist method had been spontaneous and exuberant. Seurat also developed a theory of expressive composition in which emotions were conveyed by the deliberate orchestration of the action of color and the emotional use of lines in a composition. For example, "gaiety of tone" would be created by using warm, luminous

*The method, called *divisionism* by Seurat, was often confused with *pointillism,* in which dots of color were distributed systematically on a white ground that remained partially exposed and hence visually functional. In one respect—the breaking of mass into discrete particles (and color into dots of the component colors)—Seurat's *La Grande Jatte* may be said to have been the forerunner of the modern techniques of photoengraving and color reproduction.

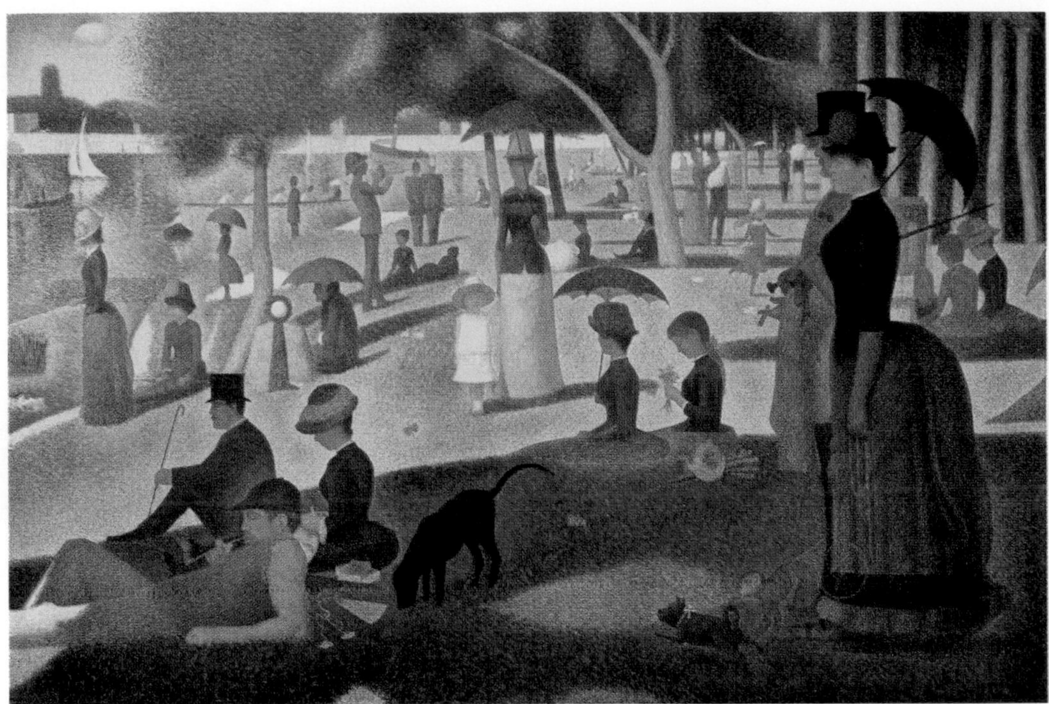

21-80 Georges Seurat, *Sunday Afternoon on the Island of La Grande Jatte,* 1884–1886. Approx. 6′ 9″ × 10′. (Helen Birch Bartlett Memorial Collection) photograph

colors and placing the most active lines and shapes in the composition above the perspective horizon line.

Seurat was less concerned with the recording of his immediate color sensations than he was with their careful and systematic organization into a new kind of pictorial order. The free and fluent play of color in his work was disciplined into a calculated arrangement by prior rules of design accepted and imposed by the artist. The apparent formlessness of Impressionism has hardened into severe regularity. The pattern in *La Grande Jatte* is based on the verticals of the figures and trees, the horizontals in the shadows and the distant embankment, and the diagonals in the shadows and shoreline, each of which contributes to the pictorial effect. At the same time, by the use of meticulously calculated values, the painter has carved out a deep rectangular space. In creating both flat pattern and suggested spatial depth, Seurat played on repeated motifs: the profile of the female form, the parasol, and the cylindrical forms of the figures, each placed in space so as to set up a rhythmic movement in depth as well as from side to side. The picture is filled with sunshine, but not broken into transient patches of color. Light, air, people, and landscape are fixed in an abstract design in which line, color, value, and shape cohere in precise and tightly controlled organization.

Seurat's art is a severely intellectual art, of which he himself said, "They see poetry in what I have done. No, I apply my method, and that is all there is to it." His work reveals something of the scientific attitude we have found manifesting itself throughout nineteenth-century painting and also recalls Renaissance geometric formalism; Seurat's stately stage space, with its perspective and careful placement of figures, is descended from the art of Paolo Uccello and Piero della Francesca and, like theirs, moves us by its serene monumentality. Seurat, in *La Grande Jatte,* turned traditional pictorial stage space into pattern by applying a color formula based on the belief that our optical experience of space can only be a function of color, which makes space a fairly unimportant variable. In the tradition of Giotto and Raphael, the reality was space, with color something added, but now with Seurat (and, as we shall see, with Cézanne), color is the reality and spaces and solids are merely illusion. Having found the formula of color relationships, the artist need no longer rely on the dubious evidence of his impressions. Paul Signac, Seurat's collaborator in the design of the "neo-impressionist" method, described their discovery:

> By the elimination of all muddy mixtures, by the exclusive use of the optical mixture of pure colors, by a

> methodical divisionism and a strict observation of the scientific theory of colors, the Neo-Impressionist ensures a maximum of luminosity, of color intensity, and of harmony—a result that has never yet been obtained.*

Indeed, although some of the brilliance of Seurat's pigments has faded with time, the effect of his system in *La Grande Jatte* remains powerfully moving today.

Like Seurat, PAUL CÉZANNE (1839–1906) turned from Impressionism to the development of a newer style. Although a lifelong admirer of Delacroix, Cézanne allied himself, early in his career, with the Impressionists, especially Pissarro, and at first accepted their theories of color and their faith in subjects chosen from everyday life. Yet his own studies of the old masters in the Louvre persuaded him that Impressionism lacked form and structure. He said: "I want to make of Impressionism something solid and lasting like the art in the museums."

The basis of Cézanne's art was his unique way of studying nature in works like *La Montagne Sainte-Victoire* (FIG. 21-81). His aim was not truth in appearance, especially not photographic truth, nor was it the "truth" of Impressionism, but rather a lasting *structure* behind the formless and fleeting screens of color the eye takes in. If all we see is color, then color gives us every clue about structure, and color must fulfill the structural purposes of traditional perspective and light and shade; color alone must give depth and distance, shape and solidity. Rather than employ the random approach of the Impressionists when he was face to face with nature, Cézanne attempted to bring an intellectual order into his presentation of the colors that comprised it by constantly and painfully checking his painting against the part of the actual scene—he called it the "motif"—that he was studying at the moment. When he said, "We must do Poussin over again, this time according to nature," he apparently meant that Poussin's effects of distance, depth, structure, and solidity must be achieved not by perspective and chiaroscuro but entirely in terms of the color patterns provided by an optical analysis of nature.

To apply his methods to the painting of landscapes was one of Cézanne's greatest challenges. The problems of representation were complicated by the need to select from the multiplicity of disorganized natural forms those that seemed most significant and to order them into pictorial structures with cohesive unity. Just as landscape had been the principal mode of Impressionist theory and experiment, so it became the subject for Cézanne's most complete transformation of Impressionism. His method was to use his intense powers of visual concentration to observe the motif and its colors, sustaining the process of minute inspection through days, months, and even years. He resembled the contemporary scientist who proves his hypothesis with repeated tests. With special care, Cézanne explored the properties of line, plane, and color, and their interrelationships: the effect of every kind of linear direction, the capacity of planes to create the sensation of depth, the intrinsic qualities of color, and the power of colors to modify the direction and depth of lines and planes. Through the recession of cool colors and the advance of warm ones, he controlled volume and depth. Having observed that saturation (or the highest intensity of a color) produced the greatest effect of fullness of form, he painted objects chiefly in one hue—apples, for example, in green—achieving convincing solidity by the control of color intensity alone, in place of the traditional method of modeling in light and dark.

La Montagne Sainte-Victoire (FIG. **21-81**), which was done in about 1886, is one of many views that Cézanne painted of this mountain near his home in Aix-en-Provence. In it, we can see how the transitory effects of changing atmospheric conditions, effects that occupied Monet, have been replaced by a more concentrated, lengthier analysis of the colors in large, lighted spaces. The main space stretches out behind and beyond the plane of the canvas (emphasized by the pattern of the pine tree in the foreground) and is made up of numerous small elements, such as roads, fields, houses, and the aqueduct at the far right, each seen from a slightly different point of view. Above this shifting, receding perspective rises the largest mass of all, the mountain, with an effect—achieved by stressing background and foreground contours equally—of being simultaneously near and far away. This portrayal is close to the actual experience a person observing such a view might have if the forms of the landscape are apprehended piecemeal so that the relative proportions of objects vary, rather than being fixed by a strict one- or two-point perspective, such as that normally found in a photograph. Cézanne immobilized the shifting colors of Impressionism into an array of clearly defined planes that compose the objects and spaces in his scene. Describing his method in a letter to a fellow painter, he wrote:

> Treat nature by the cylinder, the sphere, the cone, everything in proper perspective so that each side of an object or a plane is directed towards a central point. Lines parallel to the horizon give breadth, that is a section of nature. . . . Lines perpendicular to this

*In Goldwater and Treves, eds., *Artists on Art*, p. 378.

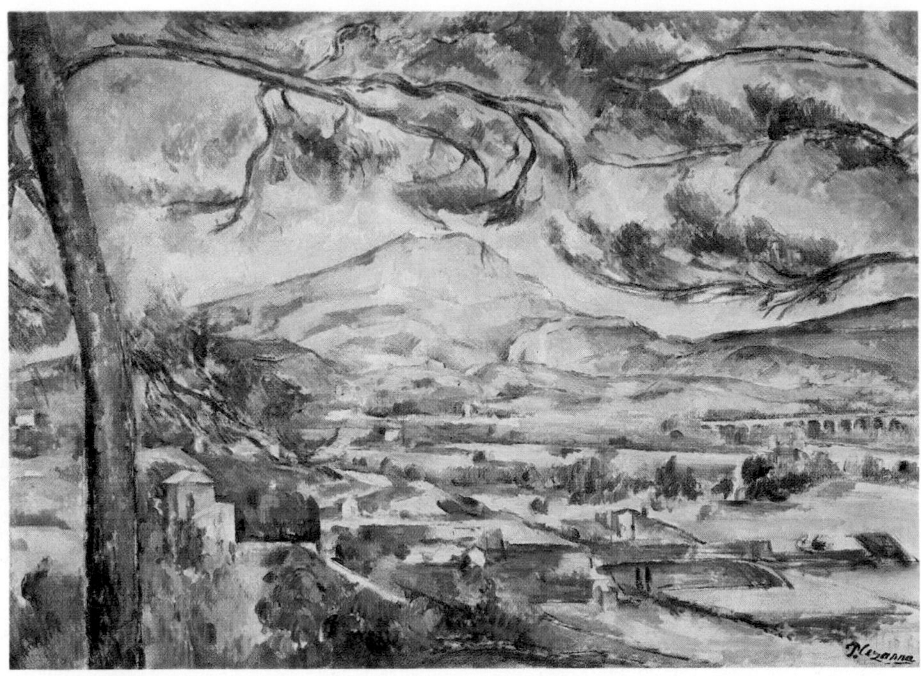

21-81 PAUL CÉZANNE, *La Montagne Sainte-Victoire*, c. 1886–1888. Approx. 26″ × 35½″. The Courtauld Institute Galleries, London.

horizon give depth. But nature for us men is more depth than surface, whence the need of introducing into our light vibrations, represented by reds and yellows, a sufficient amount of blue to give the impression of air.*

*Letter from Cézanne to Émile Bernard, April 15, 1904, in Herschel Chipp, *Theories of Modern Art* (Berkeley, CA: University of California Press, 1968), p. 19.

In his *Still Life with Peppermint Bottle* (FIG. **21-82**), painted in 1890, the individual forms have lost something of their private character as bottles and fruit and approach the condition of cylinders and spheres. The still life was another good vehicle for Cézanne's experiments, as a limited number of selected objects could be arranged by the artist to provide a well-

21-82 PAUL CÉZANNE, *Still Life with Peppermint Bottle*, c. 1894. Approx. 26″ × 32⅜″. National Gallery of Art, Washington, D.C. (Chester Dale Collection).

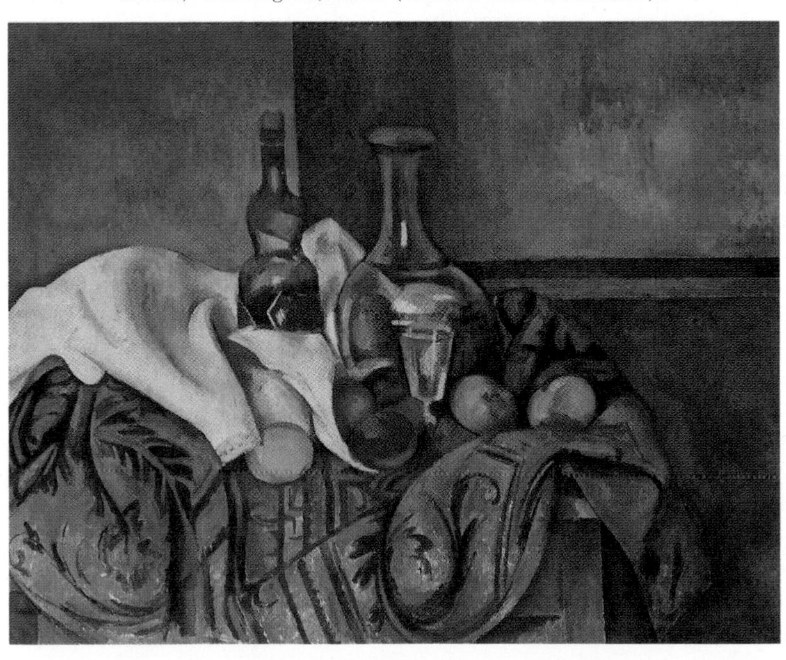

ordered point of departure. A sharp clarity of planes and of their edges set forth the objects as if they had been sculptured. Even the highlights of the glassware are as sharply defined as the solids. The floating color of the Impressionists has been arrested, held, and analyzed into interlocking planes. Cézanne created here what might be called, paradoxically, an architecture of color.

The *Boy in a Red Vest* (FIG. **21-83**) shows Cézanne's application of his method to the human figure. Here, the breaking up of the pictorial space, the volumes of the figure, and the drapery into emphatic planes is so advanced that the planes almost begin to take over the picture surface. The geometric character of the color areas pushes to the fore, and we at once become aware of the egglike shape of the head and the flexible, almost metallic shapes of the prominent planes of the body and drapery. The disproportionately long left arm is obvious, for the distortions and rearrangement of natural forms that may go unnoticed in landscape and still-life paintings are immediately apparent in the human figure and often disturbing to the viewer. Still, we may be sure that Cézanne's distortions—and they occur in most of his figure paintings—were not accidental. What Cézanne did, in effect, was to rearrange the parts of his figure, shortening and lengthening them in such a way as to make the pattern of their representation in two dimensions conform to the proportions of his picture surface. Like the Impressionists, Cézanne de-emphasized subject matter. Although the depicted object was primarily a light-reflecting surface to the Impressionists, however, to Cézanne it became a secondary aid in the organization of the picture plane. By reducing the importance of subject matter, Cézanne automatically enhanced the value of the picture he was making, which has its own independent existence and must be judged entirely in terms of its own inherent pictorial qualities. In Cézanne's works, the simplification of shapes and their sense of sculptural relief and weight give a peculiar look of stable calm and dignity that is reminiscent of the art of the fifteenth-century Renaissance and has led modern critics to find in Cézanne some vestige of that ancient Mediterranean sense of monumental and unchanging simplicity of form that produced Classical art.

Unlike Seurat and Cézanne, who, in different ways, sought, by almost scientific investigation, new rules for the ordering of the experience of color, VINCENT VAN GOGH (1853–1890) exploited new colors and distorted forms to express his emotions as he confronted nature. The son of a Dutch Protestant pastor, Van Gogh believed that he had a religious calling and did missionary work in the slums of London and in the mining districts of Belgium. Repeated failures exhausted his body and brought him close to despair. Only after he turned to painting did he find a means of communicating his experience of the sun-illuminated world in landscapes, which he represented pictorially in terms of his favorite color, yellow. His insistence on the expressive values of color led him to develop a corresponding expressiveness in his application of the paint. The thickness, shape, and direction of his brush strokes create a tactile counterpart to his intense color schemes. He moved the brush vehemently back and forth or at right angles, giving a textile-like effect, or squeezed dots or streaks onto the canvas from his paint tube. This bold, almost slapdash attack might have led to disaster had it not been controlled by sensibility.

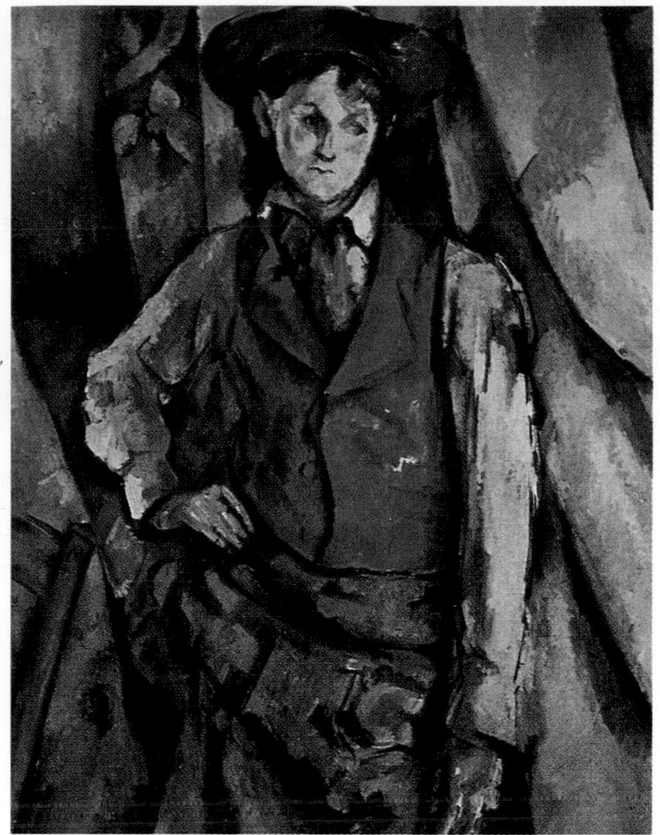

21-83 PAUL CÉZANNE, *Boy in a Red Vest,* 1893–1895. $35\frac{1}{4}'' \times 28\frac{1}{2}''$. National Gallery of Art, Washington, D.C. (collection of Mr. and Mrs. Paul Mellon).

A rich source of Van Gogh's thought on his art is left in the letters he wrote to his brother, Theo. In one of these, this minister's son who had once wanted to be a pastor wrote: "In life and in painting too I can easily do without God, but I cannot—I who suffer—do without something that is bigger than I, that is my life: the power to create." For Van Gogh, the power to create involved the expressive use of color. As he

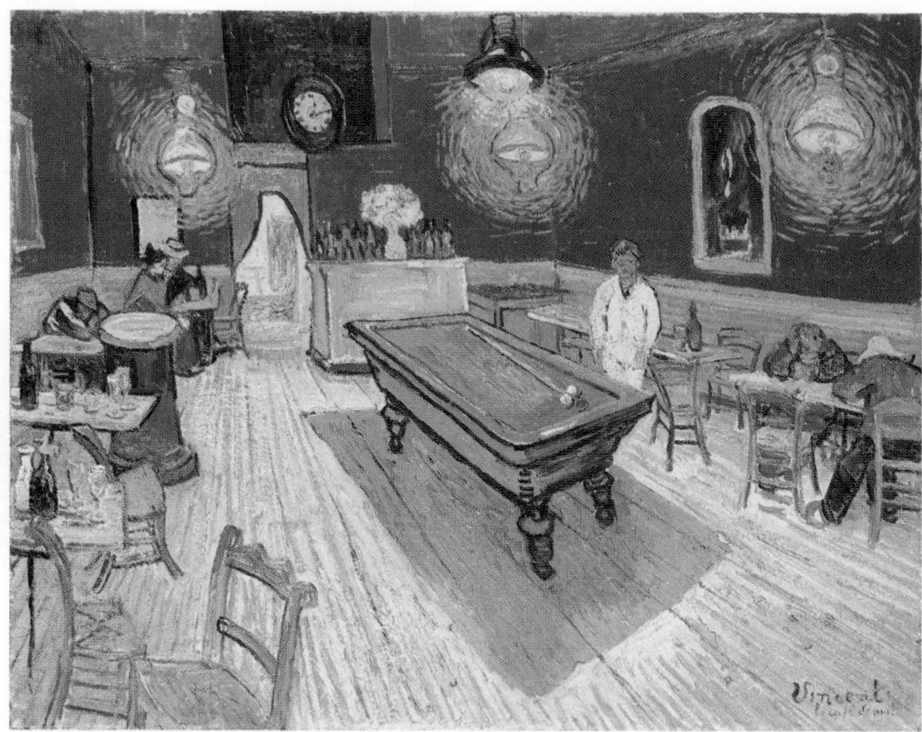

21-84 VINCENT VAN GOGH, *The Night Café*, 1888. Approx. 28½″ × 36″. Yale University Art Gallery, New Haven, Connecticut (bequest of Stephen Carlton Clark, B.A., 1903).

wrote to Theo: "Instead of trying to reproduce exactly what I have before my eyes, I use color more arbitrarily so as to express myself forcibly." In another letter, he explained that the color in one of his paintings was "not locally true from the point of view of the stereoscopic Realist, but color to suggest any emotion of an ardent temperament." This particular comment sounds like Delacroix, and indeed Van Gogh wrote: "And I should not be surprised if the Impressionists soon find fault with my way of working, for it has been fertilized by the ideas of Delacroix rather than by theirs," by which he seemed to mean that he took his color method from Delacroix directly rather than from the Impressionists.

The Night Café (FIG. **21-84**), as Van Gogh described it, was meant to convey an oppressive atmosphere of evil, through every possible distortion of color. The scene, a café interior in a dreary provincial town, is supposed to be felt, not simply observed. Van Gogh described it in a letter to Theo:

> I have tried to express the terrible passions of humanity by means of red and green.
>
> The room is blood red and dark yellow with a green billiard table in the middle; there are four citron-yellow lamps with a glow of orange and green. Everywhere there is a clash and contrast of the most disparate reds and greens in the figures of little sleeping hooligans, in the empty, dreary room, in violet and blue. The blood-red and the yellow-green of the billiard table, for instance, contrast with the soft, tender Louis XV green of the counter, on which there is a pink nosegay. The white coat of the landlord, awake in a corner of that furnace, turns citron-yellow, or pale luminous green.*

The proprietor, the pale demon who rules over the place, rises like a specter from the edge of the billiard table, which is depicted in a steeply tilted perspective that suggests the spinning, vertiginous world of nausea.

Even more illustrative of Van Gogh's "expressionist" method is *The Starry Night* (FIG. **21-85**), which was painted in 1889, the year before the artist's death. In this work, the artist did not represent the sky as we see it when we look up on a clear dark night—filled with twinkling pinpoints of light against a deep curtain of blue. Rather, he felt the vastness of the universe, filled with whirling and exploding stars and galaxies of stars, beneath which the earth and men's habitations huddle in anticipation of cosmic disaster. Mysteriously, a great cypress is in the process of

***Van Gogh: A Self-portrait, Letters Revealing His Life As a Painter*, selected by W. H. Auden (New York: Dutton, 1963), p. 320.

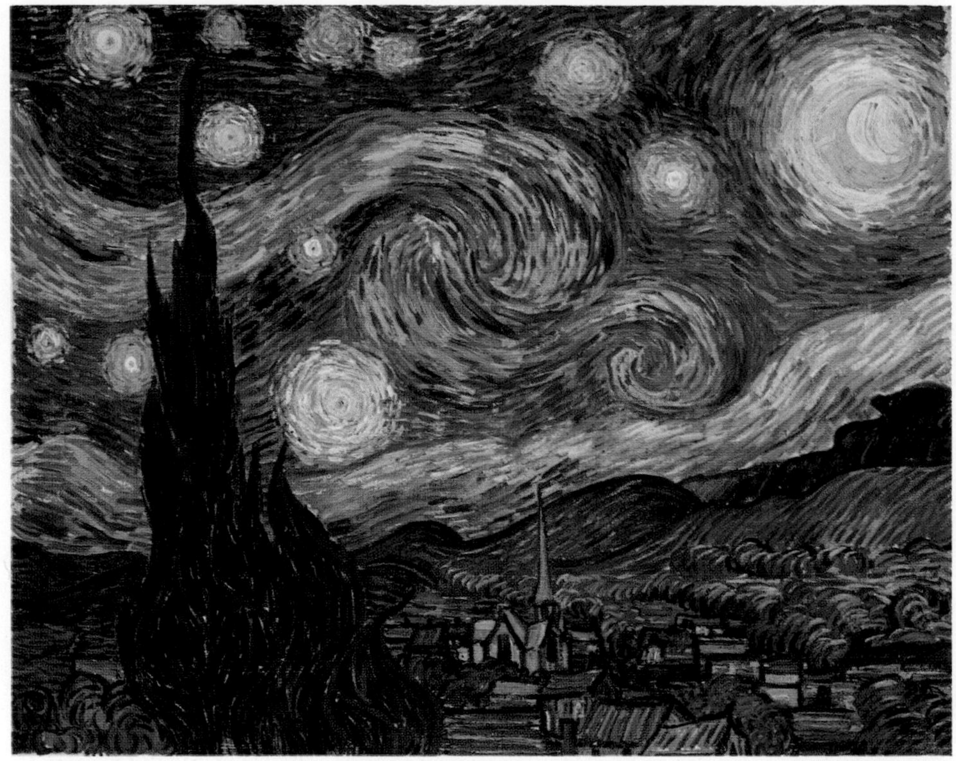

21-85 VINCENT VAN GOGH, *The Starry Night,* 1889. Approx. 29″ × 36¼″. Collection, The Museum of Modern Art, New York (acquired through the Lillie P. Bliss Bequest).

rapid growth far above the earth's surface and into the combustion of the sky. The artist did not seek or analyze the harmony of nature here. Instead, he transformed it by projecting on it a vision that was entirely his own. This painting, more than any of his others, seems to carry the meaning of a particularly poignant passage from a letter to his brother:

> Is the whole of life visible to us, or isn't it rather that this side of death we see only one hemisphere?
>
> Painters—to take them alone—dead and buried, speak to the next generation or to several succeeding generations through their work.
>
> Is that all, or is there more to come? Perhaps death is not the hardest thing in a painter's life.
>
> For my own part, I declare I know nothing whatever about it, but looking at the stars always makes me dream, as simply as I dream over the black dots representing towns and villages on a map. Why, I ask myself, shouldn't the shining dots of the sky be as accessible as the black dots on the map of France? Just as we take the train to get to Tarascon or Rouen, we take death to reach a star.*

Like Van Gogh, PAUL GAUGUIN (1848–1903) rejected objective representation in favor of subjective expression. Gauguin wrote disparagingly of Impressionism:

> The Impressionists study color exclusively, but without freedom, always shackled by the need of probability. For them the ideal landscape, created from many different entities, does not exist. Their edifice rests upon no solid base and ignores the nature of the sensations perceived by means of color. They heed only the eye and neglect the mysterious centers of thought, so falling into merely scientific reasoning.†

Gauguin used color in new and unexpected combinations, but his art was very different from Van Gogh's. It was no less tormented, perhaps, but more learned in its combination of rare and exotic elements and more broadly decorative. Gauguin had painted as an amateur, but after taking lessons with Pissarro, he resigned from his prosperous brokerage business in 1883 to devote his time entirely to painting. Although his work did not sell and he and his family were reduced to poverty, he did not abandon his art, for he felt that, despite ridicule and neglect, he was called to be a great artist. In his search for provocative subjects, as well as for an economical place to live, he stayed for some time in small villages in Brittany and

*Ibid. p. 299

†In Goldwater and Treves, eds., *Artists on Art,* p. 373.

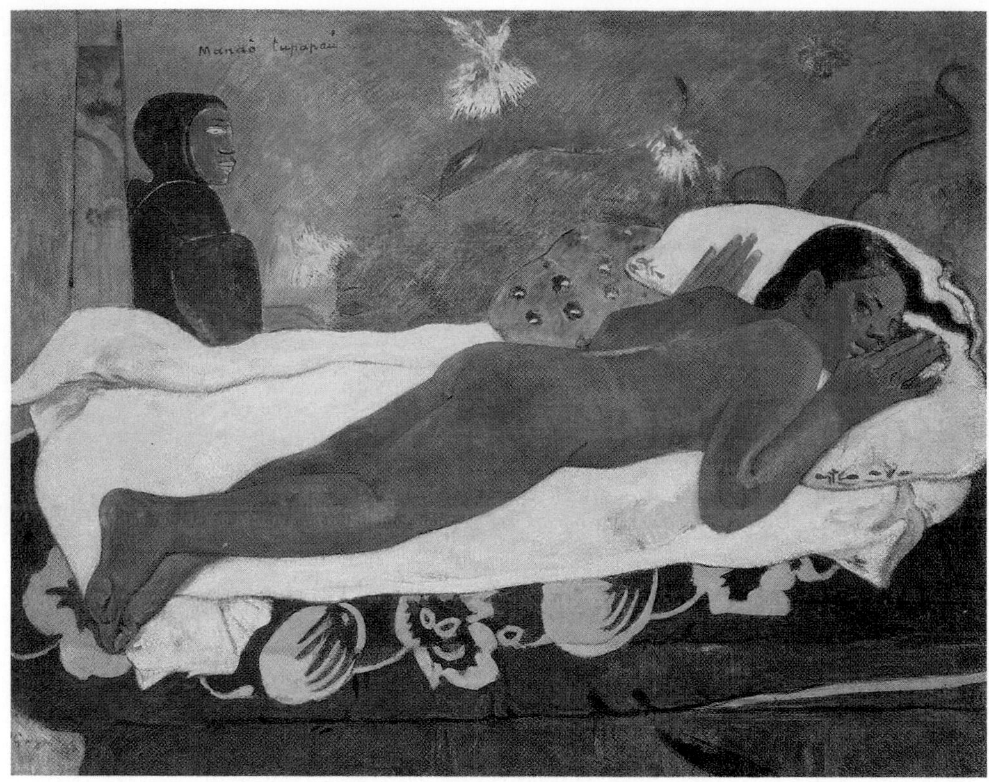

21-86 PAUL GAUGUIN, *Spirit of the Dead Watching*, 1892. Oil on burlap mounted on canvas, $28\frac{1}{2}'' \times 36\frac{3}{8}''$. Albright-Knox Art Gallery, Buffalo (A. Conger Goodyear Collection, 1965).

visited the tropics (Martinique). Thus, even before he settled in Tahiti in 1891, tropical color and subjects drawn from primitive life had entered his art. In his attitude toward color, Gauguin broke with the Impressionist studies of minutely contrasted hues because he believed that color above all must be expressive and that the power of the artist to determine the colors in a painting is an important part of creativity: "Art is an abstraction; derive this abstraction from nature while dreaming before it, but think more of creating than of the actual result. The only way to rise towards God is by doing as our divine Master does, create." The influence of Gauguin's art and ideas was felt especially by members of the younger generation, such as Parisian artist Maurice Denis, who wrote in *Definition of Neo-Traditionalism* in 1890:

> Gauguin freed us from all the restraints which the idea of copying nature had placed upon us. For instance, if it was permissible to use vermilion in painting a tree which seemed reddish . . . why not stress even to the point of deformation the curve of a beautiful shoulder or conventionalize the symmetry of a bough?

Gauguin's art, too, can be understood as a complex mixture of Eastern and Western elements, of themes common to the great masters of the European Renaissance treated in a manner based on his study of earlier arts and of non-European cultures. In Tahiti and the Marquesas, where he spent the last ten years of his life, Gauguin expressed his love of primitive life and brilliant color in a series of magnificent, decorative canvases. The design was often based, although indirectly, on native motifs, and the color owed its peculiar harmonies of lilac, pink, and lemon to the tropical flora of the islands. Nevertheless, the mood of such works is that of a sophisticated, modern man interpreting an ancient and innocent way of life already threatened by European colonization. Although the figure and setting in *Spirit of the Dead Watching* (FIG. **21-86**) are Tahitian, the theme of a reclining nude with a watching figure as a matching or balancing element belongs to the Renaissance and later periods. The simplified linear pattern and broad areas of flat color recall Byzantine enamels and Medieval stained glass, which Gauguin admired, and the slight distortion of the flattened forms is not unlike similar effects in Egyptian sculpture. Romantic art began with the admiration of "exotic" lands (and peoples) peripheral to Europe; with Gauguin, a kind of adaptation of non-European artistic styles was ini-

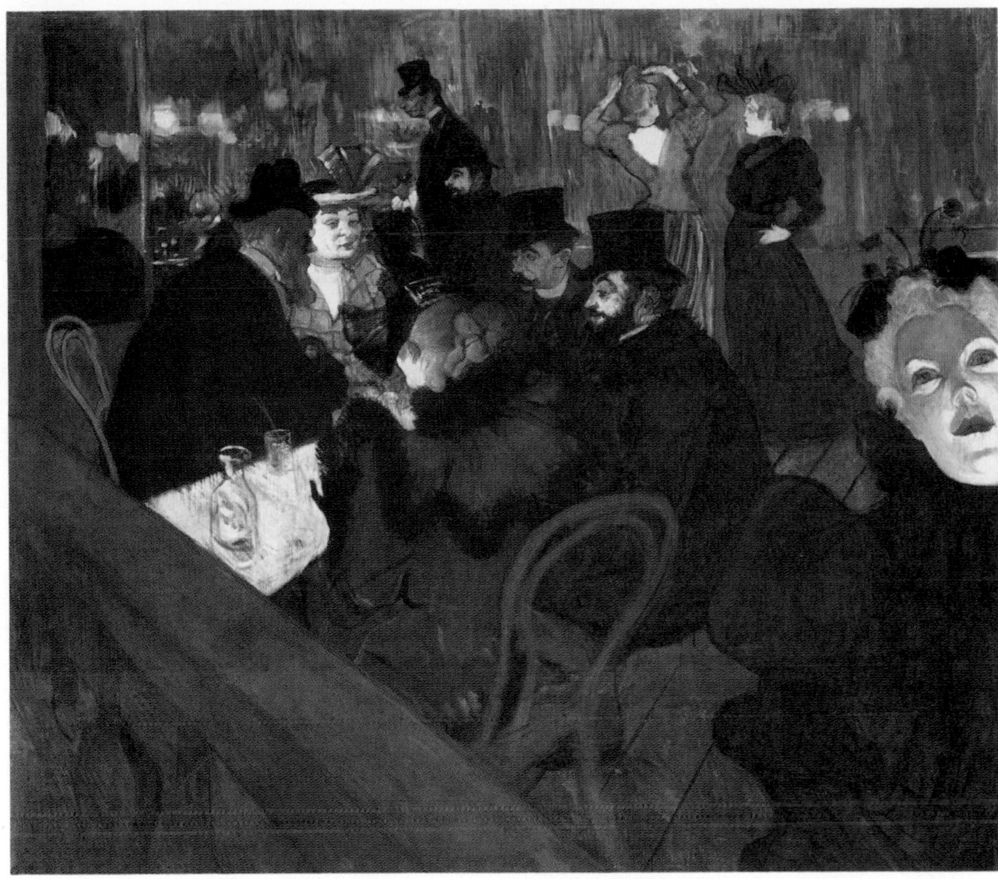

21-87 HENRI DE TOULOUSE-LAUTREC, *At the Moulin Rouge,* 1892–1895. Approx. 48″ × 55″. (Helen Birch Bartlett Memorial Collection) photograph

tiated. He represented a new rebelliousness, not just against the artistic tradition, but against the whole of European civilization. According to Gauguin, "civilization is what makes you sick." The search for vitality in new peoples and new life styles, launched in the eighteenth century, now quickened, prefiguring the twentieth-century interest in drawing artistic inspiration from Japan, from the Pacific islands, and from much of the non-European world.

A dissatisfaction with civilization, an anxious awareness of the psychic strains it imposed, and a perception of the banality and degradation it can bring with it colored the mood of many artists toward the end of the century and during the years before World War I. This period is the *fin de siècle* (end of the century), when art and literature languished in a kind of malaise compounded of despondency, boredom, morbidity, and hypersensitivity to the esthetic. In a switch from recording the contemporary scene, with all its variety and human interest, as the Impressionists had done, painters influenced by Gauguin and Van Gogh often interpreted it in bitter commentary communicated in harsh distortion of both form and color. In the work of HENRI DE TOULOUSE-LAUTREC (1864–1901), who deeply admired Degas, the older master's cool scrutiny of modern life was transformed into grim satire and mordant caricature. Toulouse-Lautrec's art was, to a degree, the expression of his life. Self-exiled by his odd stature and crippled legs from the high society that his ancient, aristocratic name would have entitled him to enter, he became a denizen of the night world of Paris, consorting with a tawdry population of entertainers, prostitutes, and other social outcasts. His natural environment became the din and nocturnal colors of cheap music halls, cafés, and bordellos. In his *At the Moulin Rouge* (FIG. **21-87**), the influence of Degas, of the Japanese print, and of photography can be seen in the oblique and asymmetrical composition, the spatial diagonals, and the strong patterns of line to which Toulouse-Lautrec added dissonant color. But each element, although closely studied in actual life and already familiar to us in the work of the older Impressionists, has been so emphasized or exaggerated that the tone is new. Compare, for instance, the mood of this painting with the relaxed and casual atmosphere of

Renoir's *Le Moulin de la Galette* (FIG. 21-72). Toulouse-Lautrec's scene is night life, with its glaring, artificial light, brassy music, and assortment of corrupt, cruel, and masklike faces. (He included himself in the background: the tiny man with the derby accompanying the very tall man, his cousin.) Such distortions by simplification of the figures and faces anticipated the later Expressionism, when artists would become ever more arbitrary in altering what they saw to increase the impact of their images on the observer.

LATE CENTURY ROMANTICISM: VISIONARY ART

We could argue that what seemed to be antagonistic movements—Realism, Impressionism, and Post-Impressionism—were only so many permutations of Romanticism, changing its earlier iconography, but always putting artistic autonomy at the center of the argument, no matter the subject or the technique. Nature, as given to the eye, was transformed by the artist's emotion and sensation until, by the end of the century, its representation came to be completely subjectivized, to the point that the artist did not *imitate* nature but *created* it by free interpretations of it. The optical world as given was rejected in favor of a world of fantasy, of forms conjured up and produced by the artist's free imagination, with or without reference to things conventionally seen. Technique and ideas were individual to each of these artists; color, line, and shape, separated from conformity to the optical image, might be used as symbols of personal emotions in response to the world. No requirement was recognized other than expressing reality in accord with the spirit and intuition. Deliberately choosing now to stand outside of conventional meanings and conventional images, such artists spoke like prophets, in signs and symbols. In the words of the critic Konrad Fiedler, writing in 1876:

> The artist is called upon to create another world beside and above the real one. . . . Artistic activity begins when man finds himself face to face with the visible world as with something immensely enigmatical. . . . What art creates is the world, made by and for the artistic consciousness. . . . It is not the artist who has need of nature; nature much more has need of the artist. . . . By comprehending and manifesting nature in a certain sense, the artist does not comprehend and manifest anything which could exist apart from his activity. . . . Only through artistic activity does man comprehend the visible world.*

*In Linda Nochlin, *Realism and Tradition in Art* (Englewood Cliffs, NJ: Prentice-Hall, 1966), pp. 168–76.

Thus the artist became not an imitator of nature, but an arbitrary interpreter of it, trusting absolutely to a personal vision. Romanticism, in fostering this view of the artist, presided over the proliferation of individual styles, which, within the broad realm of their variation, can be thought of as Romantic in intention, method, and effect.

In the late nineteenth century, many of the artists following this path adopted an approach to subject matter and form that associated them with a general European movement called *Symbolism*. The term had application to both art and literature, which, as critics in both fields noted, were in especially close relation at this time. A manifesto of literary Symbolism appeared in Paris in 1886, and, in 1891, the critic Albert Aurier applied the term to the painting of Gauguin and Van Gogh. Symbolists disdained the "mere fact" of Realism as trivial and asserted that fact must be transformed into a symbol of the inner experience of that fact. Fact was thus nothing in itself; mentally transformed, it was the utterance of a sensitized temperament responding in its own way to the world. In Symbolism, the subjectivity of Romanticism became radical; it would continue to be so in much of the art of the twentieth century. The task of Symbolist visual and verbal artists was not to *see* things but to see *through* them to a significance and reality far deeper than what is given in superficial appearance. In this function, as the poet Arthur Rimbaud insisted, the artist became a being of extraordinary insight. (One group of Symbolist painters, influenced by Gauguin, called itself *Nabis*, the Hebrew word for prophet.) Rimbaud, whose poems had great influence on the artistic community, went so far as to say, in his *Lettre du Voyant*, that to achieve the seer's insight, the artist must become deranged—in effect, systematically unhinging and confusing the everyday faculties of sense and of reason, which served only to blur artistic vision. The objects given us in our commonsense world must be converted by the artist's mystical vision into symbols of a reality beyond that world, and, ultimately, a reality from within the individual.

The extreme subjectivism of the Symbolists led them to cultivate all the resources of fantasy and imagination, no matter how recondite and occult. Moreover, it led them to urge the exclusiveness, even the elitism, of the artist against the vulgar materialism and conventional mores of industrial and middle-class society. Above all, by their philosophy of *estheticism*, the Symbolists wished to purge literature and art of anything utilitarian, to cultivate an exquisite esthetic sensitivity, and to make the slogan "art for art's sake" into a doctrine and a way of life. As early as 1856, Théophile Gautier wrote: "We believe in the autonomy of art; art for us is not the means but the end; any artist who has in view anything but the beautiful is not an artist in our eyes." Walter Pater, an English scholar and esthete, advanced the same point of view in 1868 in the conclusion to his work *The Renaissance:*

> Our one chance lies in expanding that interval [of our life], in getting as many pulsations as possible into the given time. Great passions may give us this quickened sense of life. . . . Of such wisdom, the poetic passion, the desire of beauty, the love of art for its own sake has most. For art comes to you proposing frankly to give nothing but the highest quality to your moments as they pass.

The subject matter of the Symbolists, determined by this worshipfulness toward art and exaggerated esthetic sensation, became increasingly esoteric and exotic, weird, mysterious, visionary, dreamlike, fantastic. (Perhaps not coincidentally, contemporary with the Symbolists, Sigmund Freud, the founder of psychoanalysis, began the new century and the age of psychiatry with his *Interpretation of Dreams,* an introduction to the concept and the world of unconscious experience.)

Elements of Symbolism appeared in the works of both Gauguin and Van Gogh, but their art differed from mainstream Symbolism in their insistence on showing unseen powers as linked to the surface of physical reality, instead of attempting to depict an alternate, wholly interior life. The artists who participated in the actual Symbolist movement were less important than the writers, but two great French artists—Gustave Moreau and Odilon Redon—had a strong influence on the movement, and a number of other painters followed the Symbolist-related path of imagination, fantasy, and inner vision in their works. Prominent figures in this group were the Frenchman Henri Rousseau, the Belgian James Ensor, the Norwegian Edvard Munch, and the American Albert Ryder. All of these artists were visionaries who anticipated the strong twentieth-century interest in creating art that expressed psychological truth.

GUSTAVE MOREAU (1826–1898) sought a form to suit the content of his fantasies that would incorporate reference to the facts of the optical world when he needed them. An influential teacher, Moreau expanded his natural love of sensuous design to embrace gorgeous color, intricate line, and richly detailed shape. He preferred subjects inspired by dreaming solitude and as remote as possible from the everyday world—subjects that could be submerged in all the glittering splendor that imagination could envision and painterly ingenuity could supply. *Jupiter and Semele* (FIG. **21-88**) is one of Moreau's rare finished works. The mortal girl Semele, one of Jupiter's loves, begged the god to appear to her in all his majesty, a sight so powerful that she dies from it. The theme is presented within an operalike setting of towering, opulent architecture. (Moreau was a lover of the music of Wagner and, like that great composer, dreamed of a grand synthesis of the arts.) The painter depicted the royal hall of Olympus as shimmering in iridescent color, with tabernacles filled with the glowing and flashing shapes that enclose the figure of Jupiter like an encrustation of gems. In this painting, the color of Delacroix is harmonized with the exotic hues of Medieval enamels, Indian miniatures, Byzantine mosaics, and the designs of exotic wares then influencing modern artists. Semele, in the lap of Jupiter, is overwhelmed by the apparition of the god, who is crowned with a halo of thunderbolts. Her

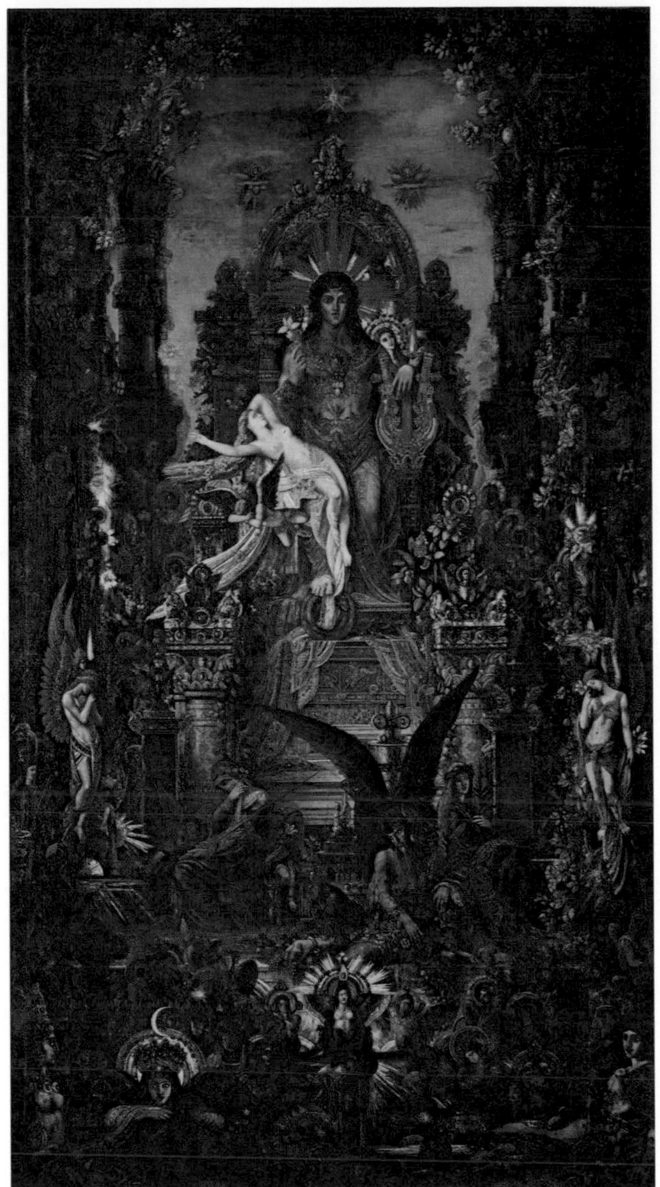

21-88 GUSTAVE MOREAU, *Jupiter and Semele,* c. 1875. Approx. 7′ × 3′ 4″. Musée Gustave Moreau, Paris.

languorous swoon and the suspended motion of all the entranced figures show the "beautiful inertia" that Moreau said he wished to render with all "necessary richness." His cherishing of the enigmas of fable, myth, vision, and dream caused Manet to remark of him: "I have a lively sympathy for him, but he is taking a bad road. . . . He takes us back to the incomprehensible, while we wish that everything be understood."

The sharp difference of artistic intention expressed in this comment is even more striking in any comparison of the work of Odilon Redon (1840–1916) and of Monet, who were born in the same year. Redon used the Impressionist palette and stippling brush stroke for a very different purpose. Like Moreau, Redon was a visionary. He had been aware of an intense inner world from childhood and later wrote of "imaginary things" that haunted him. In *The Cyclops* (FIG. **21-89**), Redon did not record a fleeting impression of a one-eyed giant in love; rather, he projected a figment of the imagination as if it were seeable, coloring it whimsically with a rich profusion of fresh, saturated hues that were in harmony with the mood he felt fitted the subject. The fetal head of the shy, simpering Polyphemus, with its huge, loving eye, rises balloonlike above the sleeping Galatea. The image born of the dreaming world and the color analyzed and disassociated from the waking world come together here at the will of the artist. As Redon himself observed: "My originality consists in bringing to life, in a human way, improbable beings and making them live according to the laws of probability, by putting—as far as possible—the logic of the visible at the service of the invisible." To evoke his world of fantasy, Redon developed a broadly brushed and suggestive style very different from the careful naturalism in Bouguereau's mythical scenes, a new style that generated rich visionary images on which the imagination of the viewer could project additional details.

21-89 Odilon Redon, *The Cyclops,* 1898. 25″ × 20″. State Museum Kröller-Müller, Otterlo, The Netherlands.

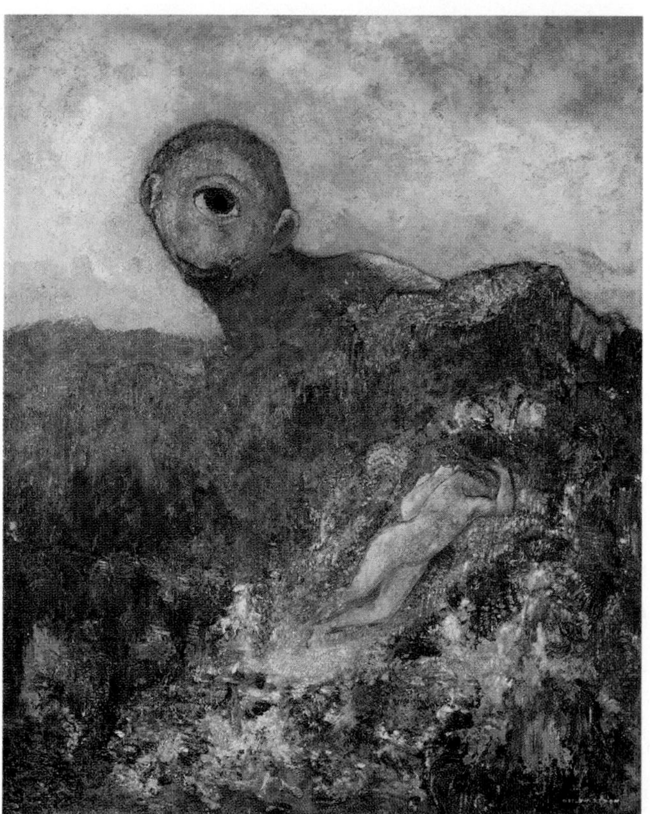

The imagination of the French artist Henri Rousseau (1844–1910) engaged a different but equally powerful world of personal fantasy. Gauguin had journeyed to the South Seas in search of primitive innocence; Rousseau was a "primitive" without leaving Paris—an untrained amateur painter who held a post as a customs collector (hence, his sobriquet, *le douanier*). Rousseau produced an art of dream and fantasy in a style that had its own sophistication and made its own departure from the artistic currency of the fin de siècle. His apparent visual, conceptual, and technical naïveté was compensated by a natural talent for design and an imagination teeming with exotic images of mysterious, tropical landscapes. In perhaps his best-known work, *The Sleeping Gypsy* (FIG. **21-90**), a desert world, silent and secret, dreams beneath a pale, perfectly round moon. In the foreground, a lion that resembles a stuffed but somehow menacing animal doll sniffs at the gypsy. A critical encounter impends, one that is not possible for most of us in the waking world but is all too common when our vulnerable, subconscious selves are menaced in uneasy sleep. Rousseau mirrored the landscape of the subconscious, and we may regard him as the forerunner of the Surrealists in the twentieth century, who will attempt to represent the ambiguity and contradiction of waking and dreaming experiences taken together.

As Goya proved earlier, a fantastic and horrifying image of human decadence and depravity may be revealed when imagination turns a critical eye toward society. The Belgian painter James Ensor (1860–1949) created a spectral and macabre visionary world in his paintings and filled it with grotesques, masked skeletons, and hanged men populating sideshows, carnivals, and city streets. His best-known work, which was severely criticized for blasphemy, is *Christ's Entry into Brussels in 1889* (FIG. **21-91**). In spirit, it recalls the demonizing, moralizing pictures of Hieronymus Bosch (FIG. 18-19) and Pieter Bruegel (FIG. 18-46) that

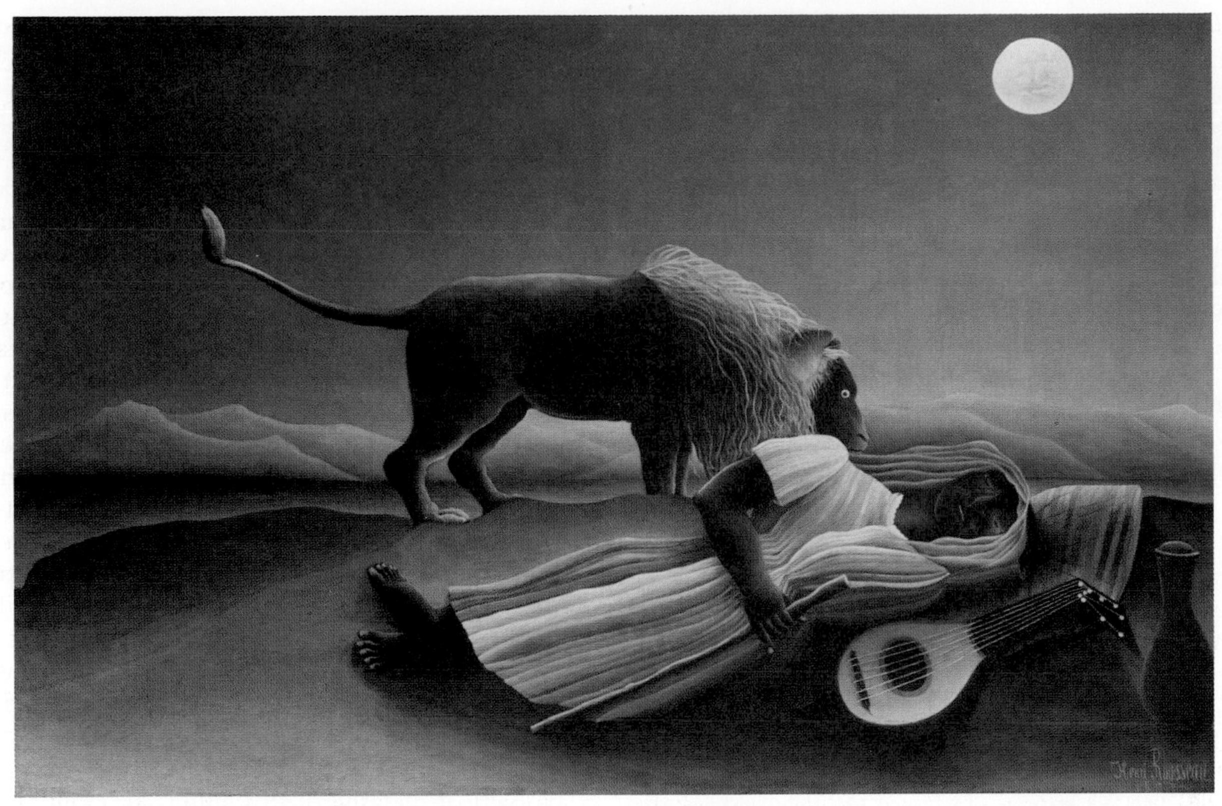

21-90 Henri Rousseau, *The Sleeping Gypsy,* 1897. 4′ 3″ × 6′ 7″. Collection, The Museum of Modern Art, New York (gift of Mrs. Simon Guggenheim).

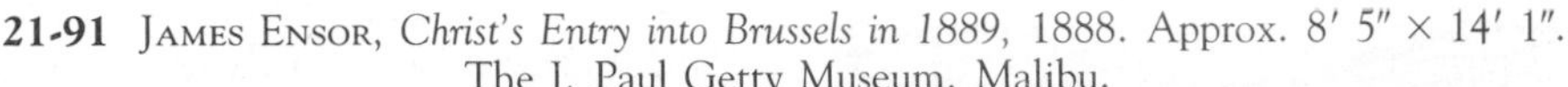

21-91 James Ensor, *Christ's Entry into Brussels in 1889,* 1888. Approx. 8′ 5″ × 14′ 1″. The J. Paul Getty Museum, Malibu.

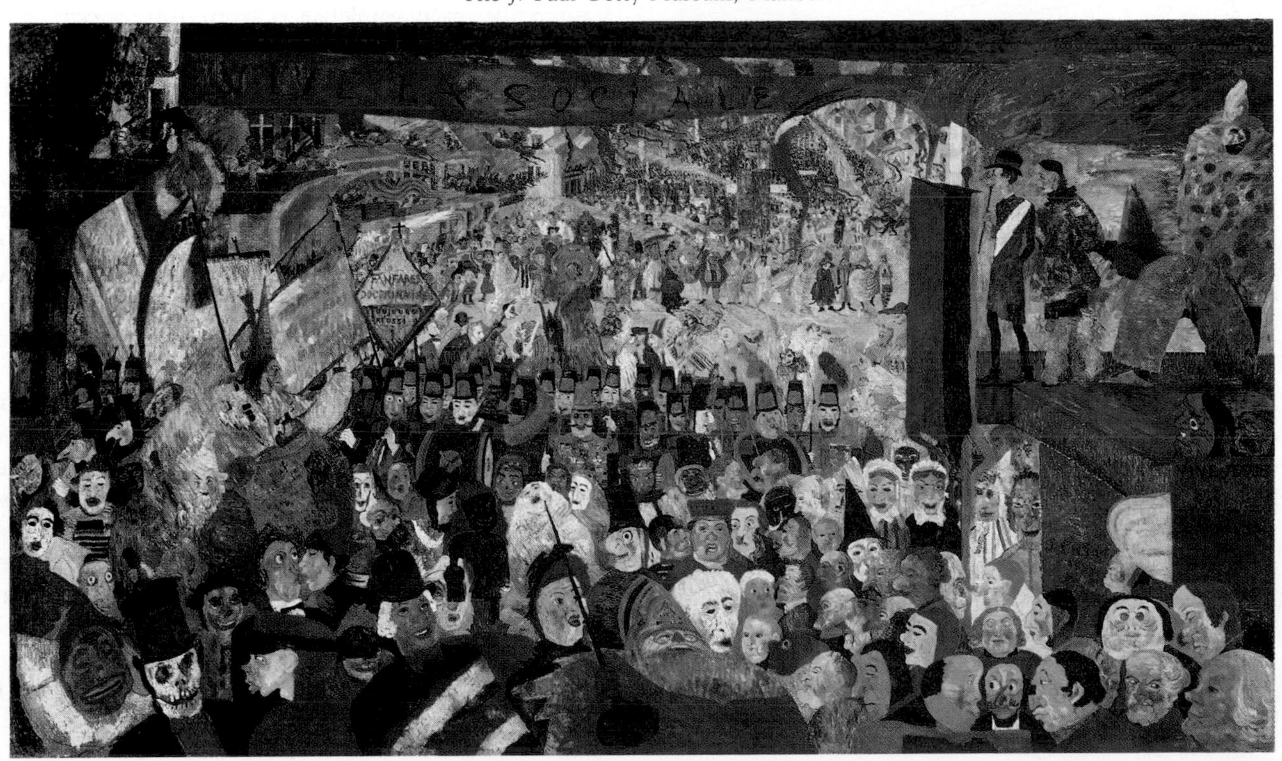

represent Christ surrounded by false and ugly creatures utterly unworthy of his mission. In Ensor's work, however, the human creatures are masked "hollow men" who have no real substance or genuine identity; they are only "images," a theme often sounded in criticism of modern civilization. Ensor's color is hard, strident, and spotted—a tonal cacophony that matches the sound of his repulsive crowd.

Linked in spirit to Ensor was the Norwegian painter and graphic artist EDVARD MUNCH (1863–1944), another moralizing critic of modern man. Munch felt deeply the pain of human life. His Romantic belief that humans were powerless before the great natural forces of death and love became the theme of most of his art. Specific ideas came to him spontaneously.

> I painted picture after picture after the impressions that my eye took in at moments of emotion—painted lines and colors that showed themselves on my inner eye. . . . I painted only the memories without adding anything—without details I could no longer see. . . . By painting colors and lines and shapes that I had seen in an emotional mood I wanted to make the emotional mood ring out again as happens on a gramophone.*

21-92 EDVARD MUNCH, *The Scream,* 1895. Lithograph, 20″ × 15$\frac{3}{16}$″. (Clarence Buckingham Collection) photograph © 1990, The Art Institute of Chicago. All rights reserved.

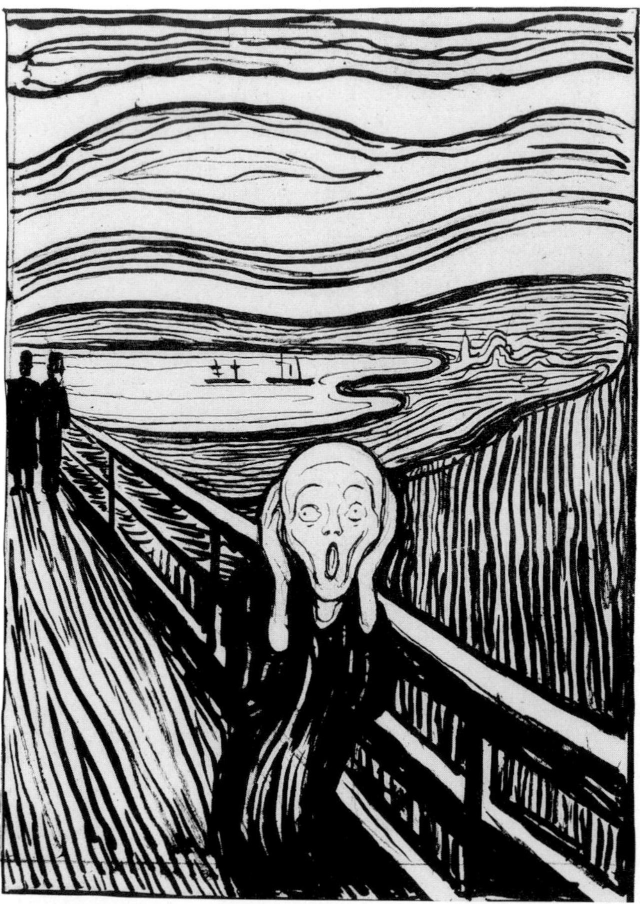

Often the same composition was repeated as an oil painting and as a woodcut or lithograph. Munch's genius for creating a stark design in black and white made the latter especially effective, as is evident in the lithograph version of *The Scream* (FIG. **21-92**). Here and in much of his other work, Munch created a disturbing vision of neurotic panic breaking forth in a dreadful but silent scream—the scream heard within the mind cracking under prolonged anxiety. Like his friend, the dramatist August Strindberg, Munch presented almost unbearable pictures of the tensions and psychic anguish that besiege human beings and the ultimate loneliness that, according to the modern philosophy of existentialism, is the inescapable lot of humanity. Influenced by Gauguin's use of strong patterns and color as well as his use of the print medium, Munch transmitted these influences through his own work to the German Expressionists of the early twentieth century.

The art of the American painter ALBERT PINKHAM RYDER (1847–1917) is filled with personal visions, most of which are based on literary or religious themes. It is the very essence of Romantic inwardness and is witness to the persistence of Romanticism and its seemingly endless variety of utterance. A recluse, shut away by choice from the world, Ryder found a depthless reservoir of subject in his own imagination, from which arose images uniquely private yet often universal. The power of Ryder's interior world was as strong as that of Munch, Redon, or Rousseau. Although he studied drawing at the American Academy of Design and made several trips abroad, Ryder's improvisational style was deeply rooted in his highly creative spirit. As he commented: "It is the first vision that counts. The artist has only to remain true to his dream, and it will possess his work in such a manner that it will resemble the work of no other man—for no two visions are alike. . . . Imitation is not inspiration, and inspiration only can give birth to a work of art."† Inspiration guided his *Death on a Pale Horse* (*The Racetrack,* FIG. **21-93**). The scythe-bearing specter speeds on its ceaseless round through a dead landscape that supports only the withered stalk of a tree. In the foreground, a malignant serpent

*In Johan H. Langaard and Reidar Revold, *Edvard Munch: Masterpieces from the Artist's Collection in the Munch Museum in Oslo* (New York: McGraw-Hill, 1964), p. 53.

†In McCoubrey, *American Art 1700–1960,* p. 187.

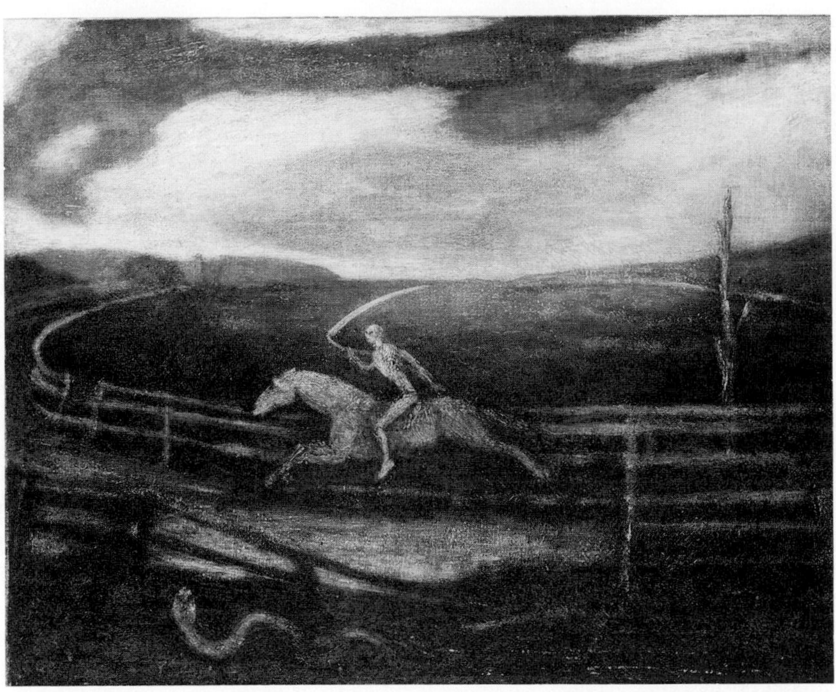

21-93 Albert Pinkham Ryder, *Death on a Pale Horse (The Racetrack)*, c. 1910. Approx. 28¼″ × 35¼″. The Cleveland Museum of Art (purchase from the J. H. Wade Fund).

with glowing eyes undulates. No one remains on earth but Death and the snake, the symbol of primordial evil. The utter simplicity of the conception and the execution require none but the barest reference to things outside the mind. Blank zones of dark and sombre light are traced through by the faint streaks of the fence rails, which remain undisturbed by the passage of the phosphorescent wraith. Ryder's indifference to the material world unfortunately extended to his material medium and technique. He painted in thick layers with badly prepared or unstable pigments, and many of his works have suffered serious deterioration.

ARCHITECTURE IN THE LATE NINETEENTH CENTURY: THE BEGINNINGS OF A NEW STYLE

The epoch-making developments in architecture that paralleled mid-century Realism in the other arts were rational, pragmatic, and functional. Toward the end of the nineteenth century, architects gradually abandoned sentimental and Romantic designs from the historical past and turned to a presentation of the honest expression of a building's purpose. Since the eighteenth century, bridges had been built of cast iron (FIG. 20-26), and most other utility architecture—factories, warehouses, dockyard structures, mills, and the like—had long been built simply and without historical ornament. Iron, along with other materials of the Industrial Revolution, permitted engineering advancements in the construction of larger, stronger, and more fire-resistant structures. The tensile strength of iron (and especially of steel, available after 1860) permitted architects to create new designs involving vast enclosed spaces, as in the great train sheds of railroad stations and in exposition halls.

The Bibliothèque Ste. Geneviève (1843–1850), built by Henri Labrouste (1801–1875), shows an interesting adjustment of the revived Romantic style—in this case, Renaissance—to a Realistic interior, the skeletal elements of which are cast iron (FIG. **21-94**). The row of arched windows in the façade recalls the flank of Alberti's San Francesco at Rimini (FIG. 16-41), yet the division of its stories distinguishes the levels of its interior—the lower, reserved for stack space and the upper, for the reading rooms. The latter consist essentially of two tunnel-vaulted halls, roofed in terracotta, and separated by a row of slender cast-iron columns on concrete pedestals. The columns, recognizably Corinthian, support the iron roof arches, which are pierced with intricate vine-scroll ornament out of the Renaissance architectural vocabulary. One could scarcely find a better example of how the forms of traditional masonry architecture are esthetically transformed by the peculiarities of the new structural material. Nor could one find a better example of how

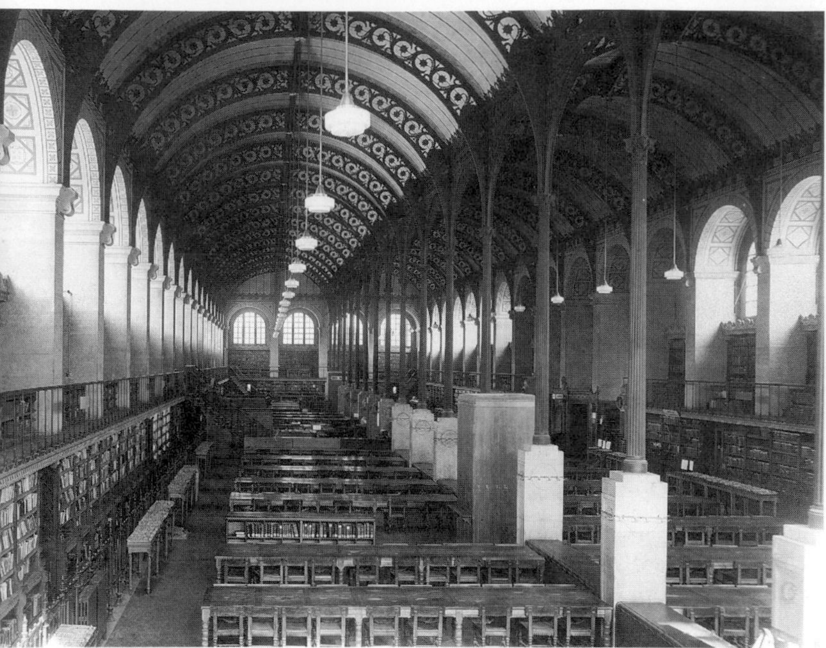

21-94 Henri Labrouste, reading room of the Bibliothèque Ste. Geneviève, Paris, 1843–1850.

reluctant the nineteenth-century architect was to surrender traditional forms, even when fully aware of new possibilities for design and construction. Architects would scoff at "engineers' architecture" for many years to come, and continue to clothe their steel and concrete structures in the Romantic "drapery" of a historical style.

Completely "undraped" construction first became popular in the conservatories (greenhouses) of English country estates. Joseph Paxton (1801–1865) built several such structures for his patron, the Duke of Devonshire; in the largest—300 feet long—he used an experimental system of glass-and-metal roof construction. Encouraged by the success of this system, Paxton submitted a winning glass-and-iron building plan to the design competition for the hall that was to house the Great Exhibition of 1851, which was organized to gather "Works of Industry of All Nations" together in London. Paxton's exhibition building, the Crystal Palace (fig. **21-95**) was built with prefabricated parts, which allowed the vast structure to be erected in the then unheard-of time of six months, and dismantled at the closing of the exhibition to avoid permanent obstruction of the park.* The plan borrowed much from ancient Roman and Christian basilicas, with a central, flat-roofed "nave" and a barrel-vaulted crossing "transept," which allowed ample interior space to contain displays of huge machines, as well as to accommodate such decorative touches as large working fountains and giant trees.

The iron structural supports used by Labrouste and Paxton were steps on the way to the twentieth-century skyscraper. The elegant metal skeleton structures of the French engineer-architect Alexandre Gustave Eiffel (1832–1923) constituted an equally important contribution. A native of Burgundy, Eiffel trained in Paris before beginning a distinguished career designing exhibition halls, bridges, and the inte-

*The public admired the building so much that when it was dismantled, it was re-erected at a new location on the outskirts of London, where it remained until it was destroyed by fire in 1936.

21-95 Joseph Paxton, Crystal Palace, London, 1850–1851. Iron and glass. (Contemporary print.)

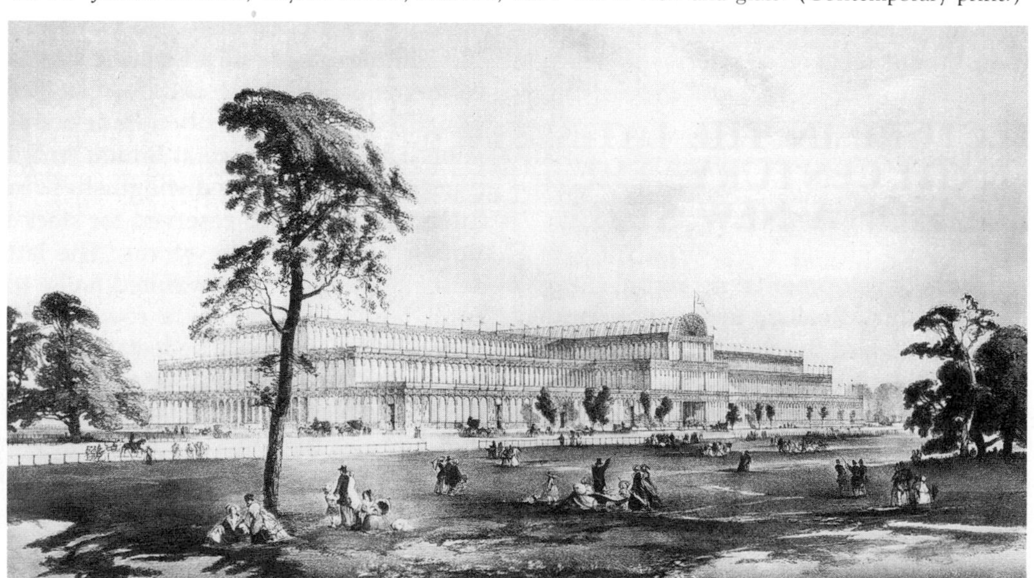

rior armature for France's anniversary gift to the United States—Bartholdi's Statue of Liberty. Eiffel's best-known work, the Eiffel Tower (FIG. **21-96**), was designed for a great exhibition in Paris in 1889. Originally seen as a symbol of modern Paris, and still considered as a symbol of nineteenth-century civilization, the elegant metal tower thrusts its needle shaft 984 feet above the city, making it at the time of its construction (and for some time to come) the world's highest structure. The tower's well-known configuration rests on four giant supports, connected by gracefully arching open-frame skirts that provide a pleasing mask for the heavy horizontal girders needed to strengthen the legs. Visitors can take two elevators to the top, or they can use the internal staircase. Architectural historian Siegfried Giedion described the sense of the tower well when he wrote:

> The airiness one experiences when at the top of the tower makes it the terrestrial sister of the aeroplane. . . . To a previously unknown extent, outer and inner space are interpenetrating. This effect can only be experienced in descending the spiral stairs from the top, when the soaring lines of the structure intersect with the trees, houses, churches, and the serpentine windings of the Seine. The interpenetration of continuously changing viewpoints creates, in the eyes of the moving spectator, a glimpse into four-dimensional experience.*

This interpenetration of inner and outer space would become a hallmark of twentieth-century art and architecture. At the time of their construction, however, Eiffel's metal skeleton structures and the iron skeletal frames designed by Labrouste and Paxton jolted some in the architectural profession into a realization that the new materials and new processes might contain the germ of a completely new style, a radically innovative approach to architectural design, something that picturesque, historical romanticism had failed to produce.

The desire for greater speed and economy in building, as well as for a reduction in fire hazards, encouraged the use of cast and wrought iron for many building programs, especially commercial ones. Designers in both England and the United States enthusiastically developed cast-iron architecture until a series of disastrous fires in the early 1870s in New York, Boston, and Chicago demonstrated that cast iron by itself was far from impervious to fire. This discovery led to the practice of encasing the metal in masonry, combining the strength of the first material with the fire-resistance of the second.

*Siegfried Giedion, *Space, Time, and Architecture* (Cambridge, MA: Harvard University Press, 1965), p. 282.

In cities, convenience required that buildings be closely grouped, and increased property values forced architects literally to raise the roof. Even an attic could command high rentals if the building were provided with one of the new elevators, used for the first time in the Equitable Building in New York (1868–1871). Metal could support such tall structures, and the American skyscraper was born. It was with rare exceptions, however, as in the work of Louis Sullivan (FIGS. 21-98 and 21-99), that this innovative type of building was treated successfully and produced distinguished architecture.

Sullivan's predecessor, HENRY HOBSON RICHARDSON (1838–1886), frequently used heavy round arches and massive masonry walls, and because he was particularly fond of the Romanesque architecture of the Auvergne in France, his work was sometimes thought of as a Romanesque revival. This designation does not do credit to the originality and quality of most of the buildings Richardson designed during the brief eighteen years of his practice. Although Trinity Church in Boston and his smaller public libraries, residences, railroad stations, and courthouses in

21-96 ALEXANDRE GUSTAVE EIFFEL, Eiffel Tower, Paris, 1889. Wrought iron, 984′ high.

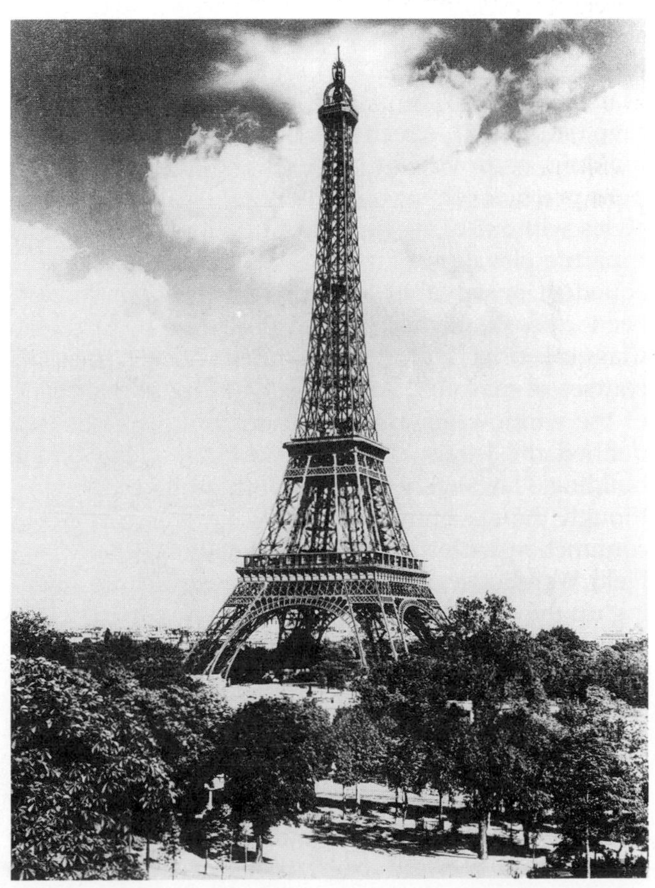

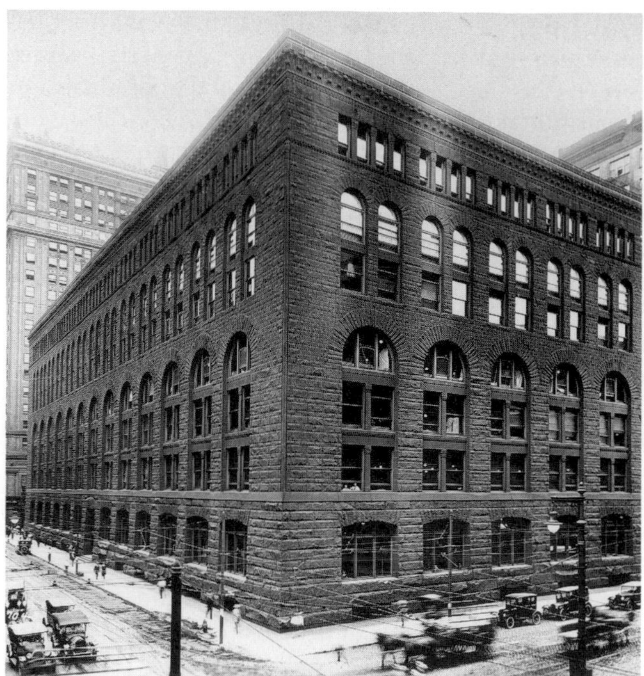

21-97 Henry Hobson Richardson, Marshall Field Warehouse, Chicago, 1885–1887.

New England and elsewhere best demonstrate his vivid imagination and the solidity (the sense of enclosure and permanence) so characteristic of his style, his most important and influential building was the Marshall Field Warehouse (now demolished) in Chicago (FIG. **21-97**), which was begun in 1885. This vast building, occupying a city block and designed for the most practical of purposes (storage) recalled historical styles without being at all in imitation of them. The tripartite elevation of a Renaissance palace or of the aqueduct near Nîmes, France (FIG. 6-42), may have been close to Richardson's mind, but he used no Classical ornament, made much of the massive courses of masonry, and, in the strong horizontality of the windowsills and the interrupted courses that defined the levels, stressed the long sweep of the building's lines, as well as its ponderous weight. Although the structural frame still lay behind and in conjunction with the masonry screen of the Marshall Field Warehouse, the great glazed arcades, in opening up the walls of a large-scale building, pointed the way to the modern, total penetration of the wall and the transformation of it into a mere screen or curtain that serves both to echo the underlying structural grid and to protect it from the weather.

Louis Sullivan (1856–1924), who has been called the first truly modern architect, recognized Richardson's architectural innovations early in his career and worked forward from them in designing his "tall buildings," especially the Guaranty (Prudential) Building in Buffalo, New York (FIG. **21-98**), built between 1894 and 1895. Here, the subdivision of the interior is expressed on the exterior, as is the skeletal (as opposed to the bearing-wall) nature of the supporting structure, with nothing more substantial than windows occupying most of the space between the terra-cotta-clad vertical members. In Sullivan's designs, one can be sure of an equivalence of interior and exterior design, not at all the case in Richardson's warehouse (FIG. 21-97) or in Labrouste's library (FIG. 21-94). Yet something of old habits of thought hung on; the Guaranty Building has a base and a cornice, even though the base is penetrated in such a way as to suggest the later free supports of twentieth-century architecture.

The form of the building, then, was beginning to express its function, and Sullivan's famous dictum that "form follows function," long the slogan of early twentieth-century architects, found its illustration here. Sullivan did not mean by this slogan that a functional building is automatically beautiful, nor did he advocate a rigid and doctrinaire correspondence between exterior and interior design. Rather, he espoused a free and flexible relationship—one that his

21-98 Louis Sullivan, Guaranty (Prudential) Building, Buffalo, New York, 1894–1895.

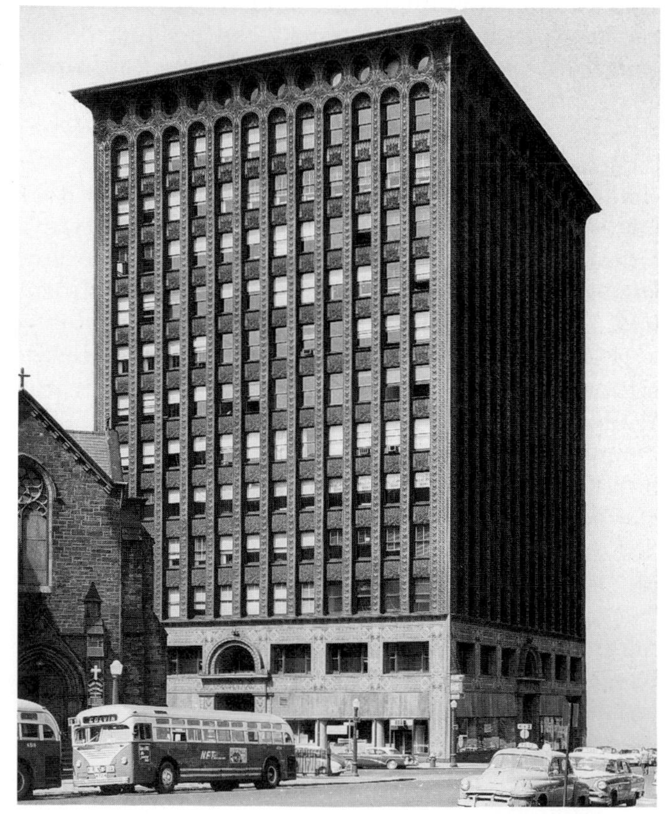

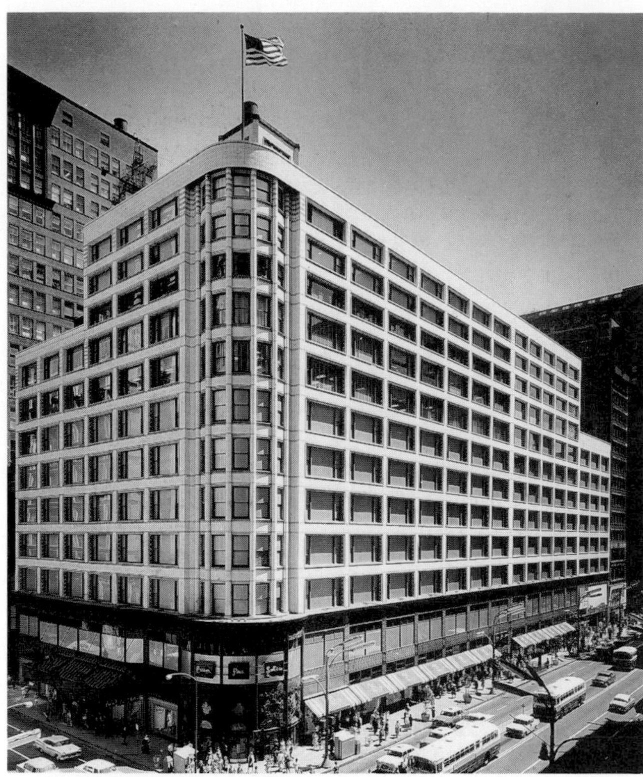

21-99 LOUIS SULLIVAN, Carson, Pirie, Scott Building, Chicago, 1899–1904.

great pupil, Frank Lloyd Wright, would later describe as similar to that between the bones and tissue of the hand.

Sullivan took a further step in the unification of exterior and interior design in his Carson, Pirie, Scott Building in Chicago, Illinois (FIG. **21-99**), built between 1899 and 1904. A department store, this building required broad, open, well-illuminated display spaces. The structural steel skeleton, being minimal, permitted the singular achievement of this goal. The relation of spaces and solids here is so logical that nothing in the way of facing had to be added, and the skeleton is clearly revealed in the exterior. The decklike stories, faced in white ceramic slabs, seem to sweep freely around the building and show several irregularities (notably the stressed bays of the corner entrance) that help the design to break out of the cubical formula of Sullivan's older buildings. The lower two levels of the Carson, Pirie, Scott Building are given over to an ornament in cast iron (of Sullivan's invention) made of wildly fantastic motifs that bear little resemblance to anything traditional architecture could show. In the general search for a new style at the end of the century, Sullivan was a leader. He gave as much attention to finding new directions in architectural ornament as in architecture itself. In this respect, he was an important figure in the movement called Art Nouveau, whose adherents sought an end to all traditional ornamental styles—indeed, to the whole preoccupation with historical style that had been postponing the true advent of a modern method of representing form in the arts.

By the end of the nineteenth century, the Western artist's vision of reality had changed. Throughout the century, a plurality of styles had opened new ways of seeing and expressed new understandings about visual and mental reality. Changes in architectural technique altered the possibilities for the look and shape of cities. In painting, attitudes stemming from the rise of experimental science stimulated the artist's interest in the distinction between what is seen and how it is seen, and encouraged a taste for experiment with the tools of the artist's trade—new pigments and new theories of light and color. At the same time, the invention of photography affected the pictorial mode and the artist's manner of expression. As the century progressed, sculptors and painters replaced the thematic material of Romanticism with scenes from the modern public world and a growing interest in human society and group behavior. Realism was a major impetus in art during much of the second half of the century, with the artist's method, like the scientific scholar's, being descriptive. In the latter part of the century, this approach was gradually replaced, on one hand, by formal analysis and expression, in which painters discovered that the canvas was not a transparent window opening onto the optical world of nature, but a tangible surface on which pigments could be arranged in a variety of ways. On the other hand, artists returned to valuing above all the role of imagination and fantasy in the creation of art. In the early twentieth century, Pablo Picasso clearly stated this separation between natural appearance and either formal or visionary art: "Nature and art, being two different things, cannot be the same thing. Through art we express our conception of what nature is not."

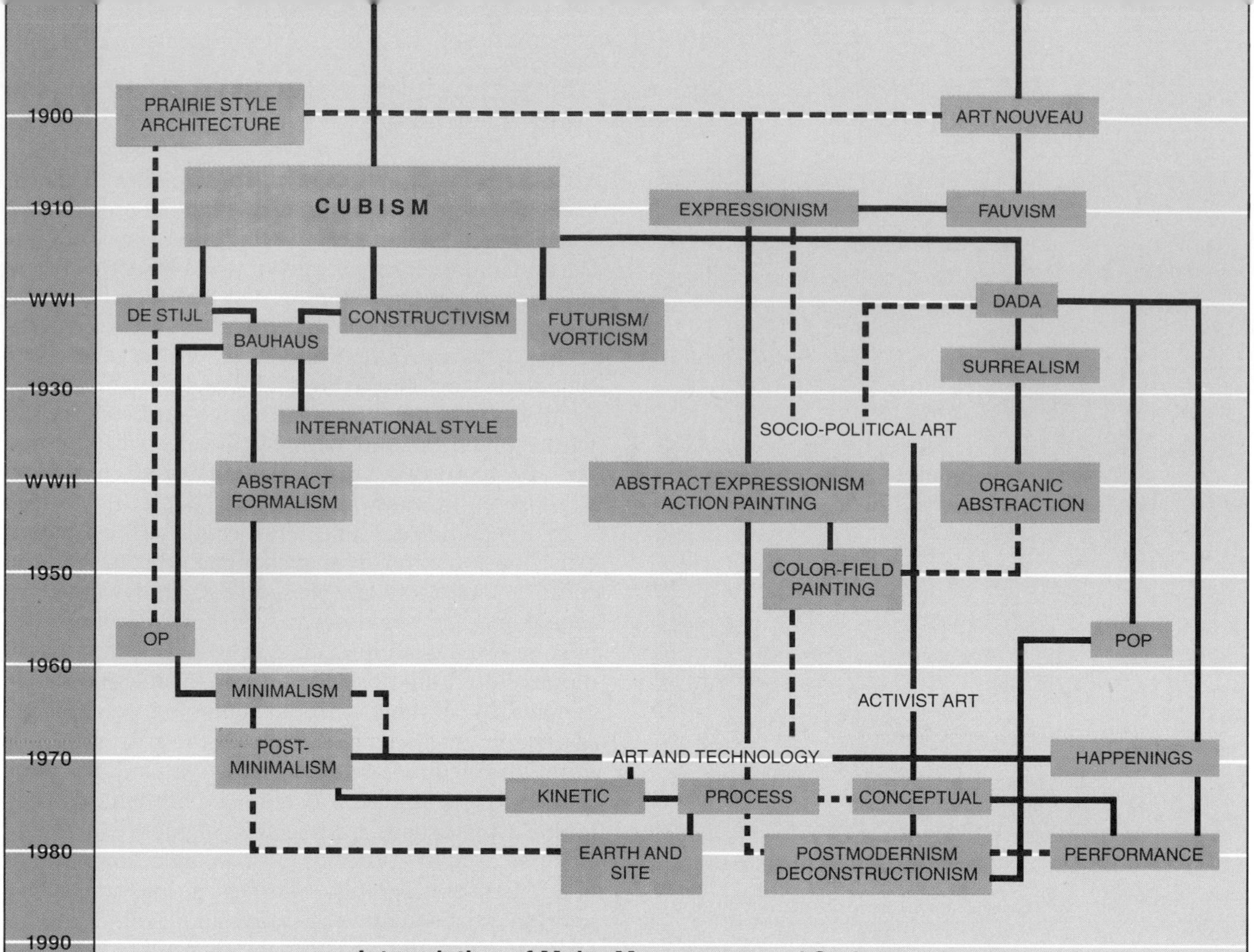

1900
PRAIRIE STYLE ARCHITECTURE
ART NOUVEAU

1910
CUBISM
EXPRESSIONISM
FAUVISM

WWI
DE STIJL
BAUHAUS
CONSTRUCTIVISM
FUTURISM/ VORTICISM
DADA
SURREALISM

1930
INTERNATIONAL STYLE
SOCIO-POLITICAL ART

WWII
ABSTRACT FORMALISM
ABSTRACT EXPRESSIONISM ACTION PAINTING
ORGANIC ABSTRACTION

1950
COLOR-FIELD PAINTING
OP
POP

1960
MINIMALISM
ACTIVIST ART

1970
POST-MINIMALISM
ART AND TECHNOLOGY
HAPPENINGS
KINETIC
PROCESS
CONCEPTUAL

1980
EARTH AND SITE
POSTMODERNISM DECONSTRUCTIONISM
PERFORMANCE

1990

Interrelation of Major Movements and Styles in the Art of the Twentieth Century

Solid black lines indicate direct influence; dashed lines, indirect

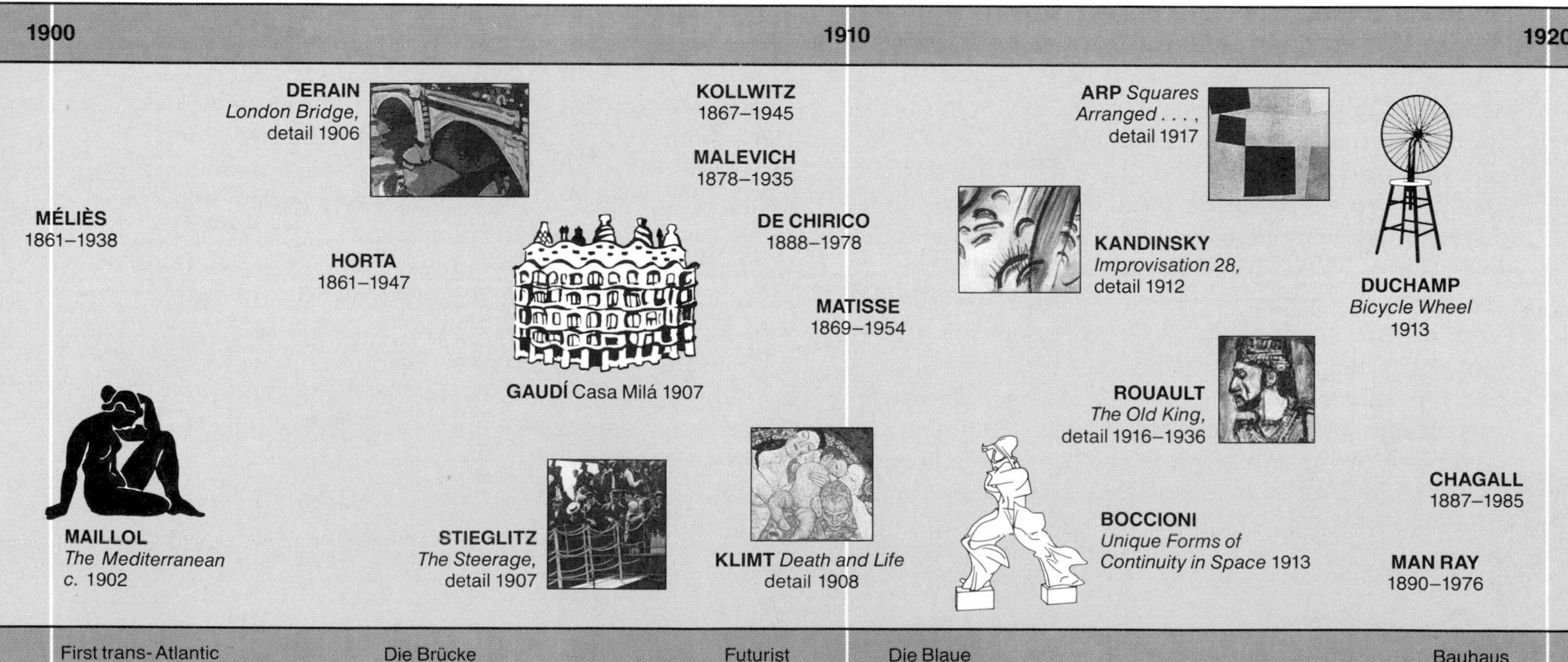

First trans-Atlantic radio signal 1901

Freud 1856–1939 *The Interpretation of Dreams*

Wright Brothers' first flight 1903

Die Brücke

Einstein 1879–1955 Theory of Relativity

Futurist Manifesto 1909

Queen Victoria's reign ends 1901

Die Blaue Reiter 1911

Jung 1875–1961

World War I 1914–1918

Russian Revolution 1917

Bauhaus founded 1919

Realistic Manifesto 1920

22
THE EARLY TWENTIETH CENTURY

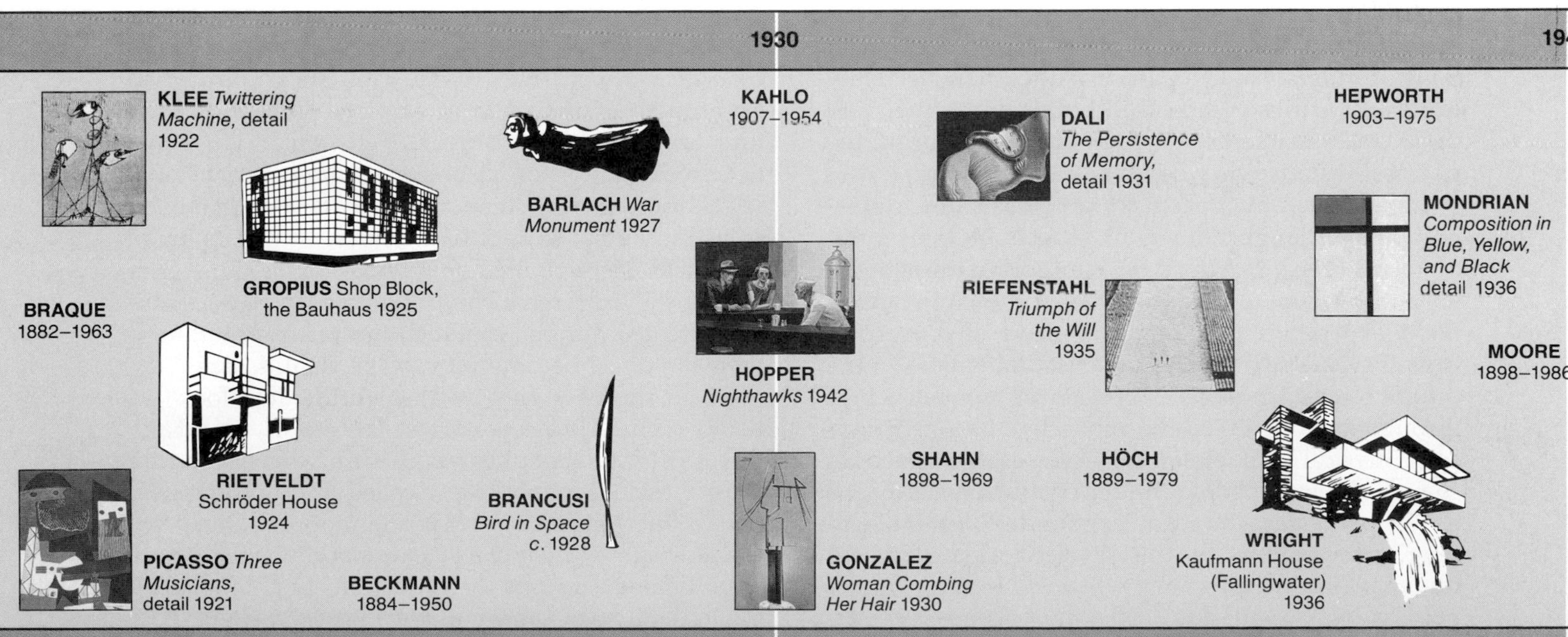

THE EARLY TWENTIETH CENTURY was a time of accelerated social change and intellectual ferment. World War I engulfed a generation of young men, twisted national economies, and extinguished the gracious, upper-class way of life that had dominated European society since the late nineteenth century. Peace brought new problems: disease, hunger, labor unrest, and bank failures led to the monetary speculation and raucous life-style of the 1920s that culminated in the stock market crash of 1929 and the Great Depression. Continuing social instability also generated the hunger for strong new government that saw both the birth of Soviet Russia (1917) and the rise of Adolf Hitler (1933).

The turmoil in the general social condition was accompanied by changes in the details of daily life. By now, the Industrial Revolution had changed work patterns to provide people with more leisure time, and new inventions helped individuals to shape this time to their own liking. Public libraries, public museums, and public recreation facilities spread. Movies, invented independently in the 1890s by Thomas Alva Edison in the United States and by the brothers Pierre and Auguste Lumière in France, developed rapidly, and by the early twentieth century had become the favorite public entertainment. Radio also gained widespread popularity and, with newsreels, began to change the way in which people received and perceived the news. New magazines flourished and were soon transformed by the rise of photojournalism, which created a new appetite for information communicated through a combination of words and images. The automobile replaced the horse and buggy for personal trips. Buses added new flexibility to travel for those who could not or did not wish to drive, and commercial air travel began to shrink the physical distance between cities and nations.

The early twentieth century also was a time of revolutionary thought about all aspects of the world. Sigmund Freud described the concepts of the ego, the id, and the superego, and revealed the power childhood experience and sexuality exert on our adult lives. Psychiatrist Carl Jung focused attention on the intuitive interconnection between all human beings through what he called the "collective unconscious." The physical and biological sciences continued to change the way people thought about physical reality. In particular, the ideas expounded at the beginning of the century by the physicist Albert Einstein underlay the reasons why "seeing" was no longer necessarily grounds for "believing." The world perceived by the five physical senses was now understood not to be exactly what it seemed. Einstein's theory of relativity described how the "reality" of any thing (as determined by that thing's ability to be measured) must be considered relative to the position both of the object being observed and of the person observing it, a relationship illustrated by the way in which the physical attributes and behavior of objects in a landscape appear markedly different to a passenger in a moving train and to a pedestrian on a hill near the train tracks. To know reality, all things must be understood in relationship to everything else, because every object is located on a point in a space-time continuum filled with electrical fields in which all motion is relative to systems themselves in motion. The universe is composed of *space* and *time*, and Einstein showed that there could be no stable "center" in this expanding, four-dimensional universe—no absolute standpoint that could certify our measurements of space and time, because perceptions change as a function of the location in time and space of the observer.

We have already seen how events in the late eighteenth and early nineteenth century began to shake people's faith in the moral certainties of Western society. Amid the increased pressures of the early twentieth century, many artists turned away from the certainties of art based on the Renaissance ideal, with its method of mathematical perspective. In its place, painters and sculptors increasingly drew inspiration from art not in the Western Renaissance tradition—work from the Western Middle Ages and, outside Europe, from Asia, Africa, Oceania, and pre-Columbian Central and South America. In painting, artists' desires to reveal their creative activities intensified, with special emphasis being placed on the process by which a work was made. Painters continued to experiment as they had in the late nineteenth century, conducting a "dialogue" between an illusionistic representation of a subject in three-dimensional space and the clear creation of a pattern of shapes in paint on the flat surface of a canvas. Sculptors made the marks of chisel, modeling finger, or welding torch part of the expressive content of their pieces. Architects created designs in which the inner structure of their buildings became part of the final design.

Given the new view of the world, the "look" of reality seemed problematic to many artists, as did any direct copy of its appearance. Hungarian-American artist László Moholy-Nagy called for nothing less than a "new vision . . . vision in motion" to express the new age: "*Vision in motion* is simultaneous grasp. Simultaneous grasp is . . . seeing, feeling, and thinking in relationship and not as a series of isolated phenomena. . . . *Vision in motion* is a synonym for simultaneity and space-time; a means to comprehend the new dimension."* Painters, sculptors, and architects invented new patterns to reflect their understanding of this new reality. The use of materials like glass, plastics, and industrial metal generated new techniques of construction, which in turn allowed a new interplay of solid mass with carefully created space-void shapes. Much of the new art was abstract or nonobjective. Although many people use the words *abstract* and *nonobjective* interchangeably to refer to art that is not based on the external, visible world, in the realm of art, the subject of an abstract work has been "abstracted" from natural appearance, and vestiges of figures or objects still may be detected in it. A nonobjective work, on the other hand, has no discernible reference to the external appearance of the physical world.†

The twentieth century is part of the modern era, and this era has included artists working in many styles and approaches. Yet the term *Modernism* is used by most scholars only to refer to the artistic styles that call attention to the processes of making art. Often these styles include the use of modern materials and technology to express the activity of the artist as creator and to depict the essence of the modern model of reality revealed by science. According to this view, Modernism in *painting* is the exploration of the way in which that medium is basically a design made on a flat surface, while Modernist *sculpture* stresses, above all, the arrangement of shapes in three-dimensional space. The critic Clement Greenberg summarized Modernism as "art [used] to call attention to art."

The Modernist formalist approach led from the nature-based paintings of the Impressionists and Post-Impressionists, through the more purely formal works of the Fauves and Cubists, to fulfillment in the second half of the century in the nonobjective Color-Field paintings of artists like Mark Rothko (FIG. 23-14). Early in the century, before the outbreak of World War I, Paris remained the major art center, and her most exciting artists were engaged in the formalist approach, basing their forms on abstractions from things in the visible world. However, spurred by the dislocations of the war, two other approaches—grounded in the ideas of the Enlightenment and its nineteenth-century aftermath—gained in importance: art with psychological and conceptual concerns and art with social and political concerns.

Art with psychological and conceptual concerns carried into the twentieth century the interest in depicting the inner world of fantasy, dream, and feeling explored earlier by artists like Stubbs, Blake, Van Gogh, Rousseau, and Munch. The new psychological and conceptual approach was based on an increasing self-consciousness about the way in which the understanding and perception of all things seen are affected by everything in each viewer's mind and heart. The ideas underlying this approach were eloquently stated by the theorist and critic Hermann Bahr in 1920. Bahr made special reference to painting, but the concepts are applicable to the other arts as well:

> The history of painting is nothing but the history of vision—or seeing. . . . A man views the world according to his attitude towards it. All the history of painting is therefore in a sense also a history of philosophy, especially of unwritten philosophy. . . . Seeing consists of two activities, an outer and an inner one. . . . As soon as a man realizes that his seeing is always the result of some external influence, as well as of his own inner influence, it depends on whether he trusts the outer world more—or himself. . . .—or a third choice is possible, that of halting on the boundary line between the two.‡

Artists following the psychological and conceptual approach early in the century produced works in all modes—figurative, abstract, and nonobjective, with artists of nonobjective works seeing their compositions, as critic Sheldon Cheney has noted, as symbols for universal qualities invisible to the eye:

> Form is revelation . . . not merely of a plastic organism, but *through* the plastic of something that might be termed universal or cosmic truth, and, commonly, of human emotion. . . . The Expressionist's business then, in creating the plastic synthesis, is to reveal through it the ultimate hidden principle, the all-relating harmony, the sense of cosmic unity. . . . The picture with a vitality of its own sort, determined physically by the nature of its materials and means—flat field, spatial sense, voluminous organization, dynamic colors—is in itself a universe in little, yet exhibiting the laws of original creation, and the rhythm and poise of celestial movement.§

*László Moholy-Nagy, *Vision in Motion* (1946, Chicago: Paul Theobald, 1969), pp. 10–12.

†Determining whether a work of art is abstract or nonobjective has become more complicated as science extends our knowledge about material nature. Many artists have been attracted by new forms revealed through the microscope, the telescope, and even the naked eye taken to a new vantage point above the earth or under the sea. The mass media have made all such images part of everyone's visual experience; the images have become part of the references brought to the viewing of any artwork. It is now almost impossible for an artist to design a piece that will not seem a close visual echo of objects seen somewhere in our everyday world.

‡In Francis Frascina and Charles Harrison, eds., *Modern Art and Modernism: A Critical Anthology* (New York: Harper & Row, 1982), pp. 165–66.

§In Frascina and Harrison, eds., *Modern Art and Modernism,* pp. 171, 173. Cheney used the term *expressionism* broadly; in art history the term is more usually assigned to specific groups of artists, as we shall see.

The third approach—art with social and political concerns—attracted artists with diverse styles and goals. Adhering in varying ways to the Enlightenment belief that art could help to educate human beings and change society, these artists also represented the increasing popularity of political and sociological ideas about modern civilization. Some of these artists, especially architects, believed they could help to design better communities. Others wanted to turn attention once again to the beauty and variety of the world around them. Many sought to reinvigorate the role of the artist within society by speaking to and about ordinary people rather than the moneyed classes. A major crystallizer of ideas for those supporting this approach was the theorist Walter Benjamin, who espoused the attitude that viewers bear an important responsibility with regard to understanding the social role of any work of art and the ways in which art is produced in the modern industrial age: "Rather than asking, what is the *attitude* of a work to the relations of production of its time, I should like to ask, what is its *position* in them?"* Artist and viewer alike were to be aware of the whole sociopolitical context of the art work and of its place within that context. Toward the end of the century, these considerations would, in themselves, become the foundation of a new approach termed "Postmodernism" by critics.

Although it is possible to distinguish these three approaches within Modernism, they quite naturally overlap one another somewhat. All artists have some interest in the formal qualities of their work, but those who followed the formalist approach made this interest the major theme. Similarly, most artists want their work to touch the emotions and mind of the viewer, but this was the *main* motive underlying the art of those who followed the psychological and conceptual approach. Finally, many artists working within the psychological and conceptual approach addressed some of the concerns with the conditions of the society around them held by the artists who followed the approach of art with social and political concerns, but only the adherents of the social and political approach made that content the central focus of their work. Whatever the artist's approach, two common themes ran through Modernism in the early years of this century. First, artists desired above all to express in their art something of what it was to be alive in the modern world. And second, early twentieth-century Modernist art contained a heightened sense of the personal vision of the artist and of the way materials could be used to create works that expressed that vision.†

*Ibid., pp. 213–15.

ART WITH FORMALIST CONCERNS

Artists with formalist concerns occupied center stage in the Paris art world early in this century. They shared a strong interest in what Clement Greenberg has described as "stressing . . . the ineluctable flatness of the support" and abandoning "the representation of the kind of space that recognizable, three-dimensional objects can inhabit."‡ First to develop the new formalist style were Art Nouveau and Fauve artists, whose works were inspired in part by the sinuous forms in the Post-Impressionist work of Van Gogh and Gauguin. Drawing on intuition and a joy in nature's flowing patterns, as well as on past art, these artists created colorful arrangements of flowing, flat shapes intended to be expressive in and of themselves. Balancing the free-flowing compositions of Art Nouveau and the Fauves were Cubist works created by artists attempting to add a twentieth-century notion of space-time to Cézanne's conceptual analysis of nature in terms of color planes.

Art Nouveau and Fauvism: Patterns of Delight

Art Nouveau was a movement whose proponents tried to synthesize all the arts, in a determined attempt to create art based on natural forms that could be mass-produced by the technologies of the industrial age.§ The Art Nouveau style emerged at the end of the nineteenth century and adapted twining plant forms to the needs of architecture, painting, sculpture, and all of the decorative arts. Its foliate patterns, rendered in cast iron, had adorned the ground floor of Louis Sullivan's Carson, Pirie, Scott building in Chicago (FIG. 21-99). The mature style, however, was first seen in houses designed in Brussels in the 1890s

†Despite the rejection of Renaissance conventions of representation of space, the Modernist artist could be said to follow what John Lane has called the Renaissance "concept of the artist as hero, as . . . a unique individual striving to bring new consciousness to birth." (Lane, *The Living Tree* [Hartland, Devon: Green Books, 1988], p. 33.)

‡In Frascina and Harrison, eds., *Modern Art and Modernism,* p. 6.

§The international style of Art Nouveau took its name from a shop in Paris dealing with "*L'Art Nouveau*" (new art) and was known by that name in France, Belgium, Holland, England, and the United States. In other places, it had other names: *Jugendstil* in Austria and Germany (after the magazine *Der Jugend,* youth), *Modernismo* in Spain, and *Floreale* or *Liberty* in Italy.

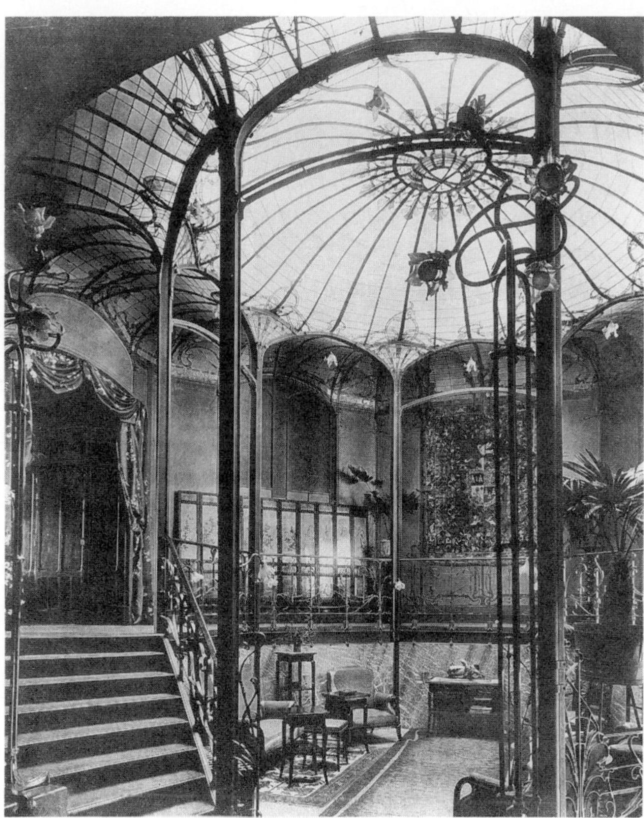

22-1 Victor Horta, staircase in the Hotel van Eetvelde, Brussels, Belgium, 1895.

by Victor Horta (1861–1947). The staircase in the Hotel van Eetvelde (fig. **22-1**), which Horta built in Brussels in 1895, is a good example of his Art Nouveau work. Every detail functions as part of a living whole. Furniture, drapery folds, veining in the lavish stone panelings, and the patterning of the door moldings join with real plants to provide graceful counterpoints for the metallic tendrils that curl around the railings and posts, the delicate metal tracery that fills the glass dome, and the floral and leaf motifs that spread across the fabric panels of the screen (left background).

A number of influences can be identified in Art Nouveau; they range from the rich, foliated, two-dimensional ornament and craftsman's respect for materials of the "Arts and Crafts" movement in late nineteenth-century England to the free, sinuous, whiplash curve of designs in Japanese prints. Art Nouveau also borrowed from the expressively patterned styles of Vincent van Gogh (fig. 21-85), Paul Gauguin (fig. 21-86), and their Post-Impressionist and Symbolist contemporaries.

In all Art Nouveau pictorial art, Renaissance perspective space was rejected in favor of motifs that emphasized the plane of the composition. The work of the Viennese artist Gustav Klimt (1862–1918) graced the walls of many Art Nouveau interiors. His masterly blend of rich patterning with modeled flesh can be seen in the painting *Death and Life* (fig. **22-2**). A visit in 1903 to the great Byzantine mosaics in Ravenna (fig. 7-36) added new richness to the artist's natural gifts for creating densely textured, two-dimensional designs that expressed his feeling for sensual fantasies. *Death and Life* is a modern representation of a vanitas picture. As in Hans Holbein's *The French Ambassadors* (fig. 18-41), Klimt's Death appears in the midst of Life. The figure of Death looms against a dim, featureless void, wrapped in a mantle of somber blues and greens sprinkled with chiromantic symbols and black crosses of varying sizes. He leans eagerly toward the teeming river of slumbering Life. Bright colors stud the surfaces that enwrap the voluptuously somnolent figures in the Life group, in which intertwined images of infancy, youth, maturity, and old age celebrate life bound up with love. Outlined shapes are modeled only to the extent needed to show the softness of flesh, the firmness of sinew, and the stark hardness of bone.

Art Nouveau achieved its most personal expression in the work of the Spanish architect Antoni Gaudí (1852–1926). Before becoming an architect, Gaudí had trained as an ironworker. Like many young artists of his time, he longed to create a style that was both modern and appropriate to his country. Taking inspiration from Moorish-Spanish architecture and from the simple architecture of his native Catalonia, Gaudí developed a personal esthetic in which he conceived a building as a whole and molded it almost as a sculptor might shape a figure from clay. Although work on his designs proceeded slowly under the guidance of his intuition and imagination, Gaudí was a master who invented many new structural techniques that facilitated the actual construction of his visions. His apartment house, Casa Milá (fig. **22-3**), is a wondrously free-form mass wrapped around a street corner. Lacy iron railings enliven the swelling curves of the cut-stone façade, while dormer windows peep from the undulating tiled roof, which is capped by fantastically writhing chimneys that poke energetically into the air above. The rough surfaces of the stone walls suggest naturally worn rock. The entrance portals look like eroded sea caves, but their design also may reflect something of the excitement that swept Spain following the 1879 discovery of Paleolithic paintings in a cave at Altamira. Gaudí felt that each of his buildings was a symbolically living thing, and the passionate naturalism of his Casa Milá is the spiritual kin of early twentieth-century Expressionist painting and sculpture.

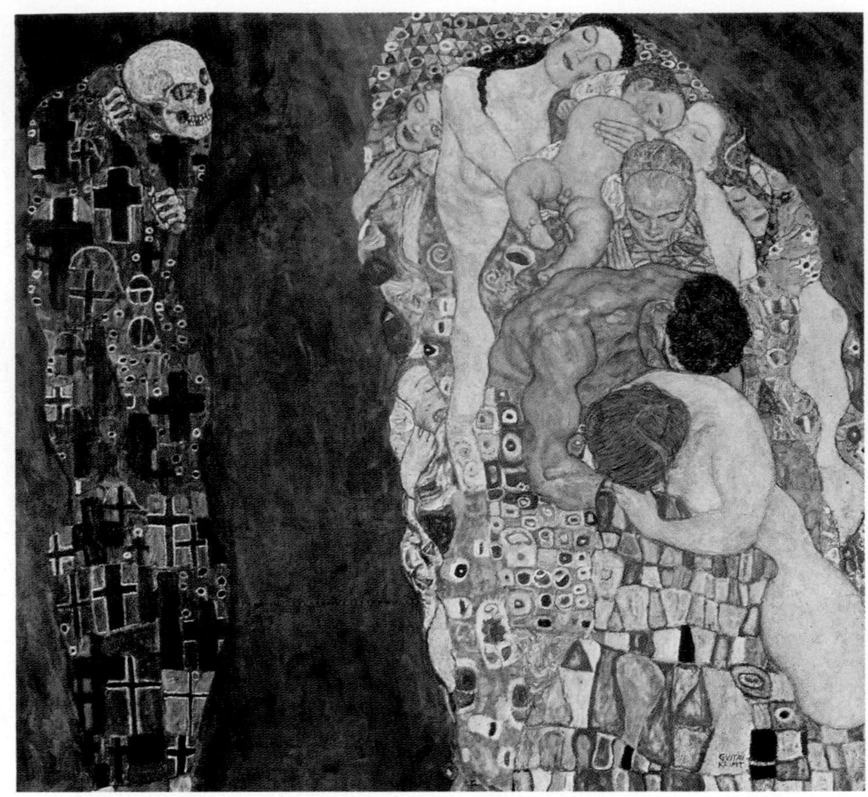

22-2 Gustav Klimt, *Death and Life,* 1908 and 1911. 5′ 10″ × 6′ 6″. Collection of Marietta Preleuthner, Salzburg.

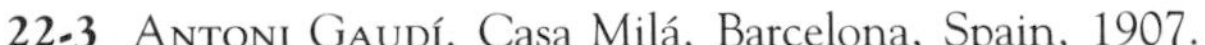

22-3 Antoni Gaudí, Casa Milá, Barcelona, Spain, 1907.

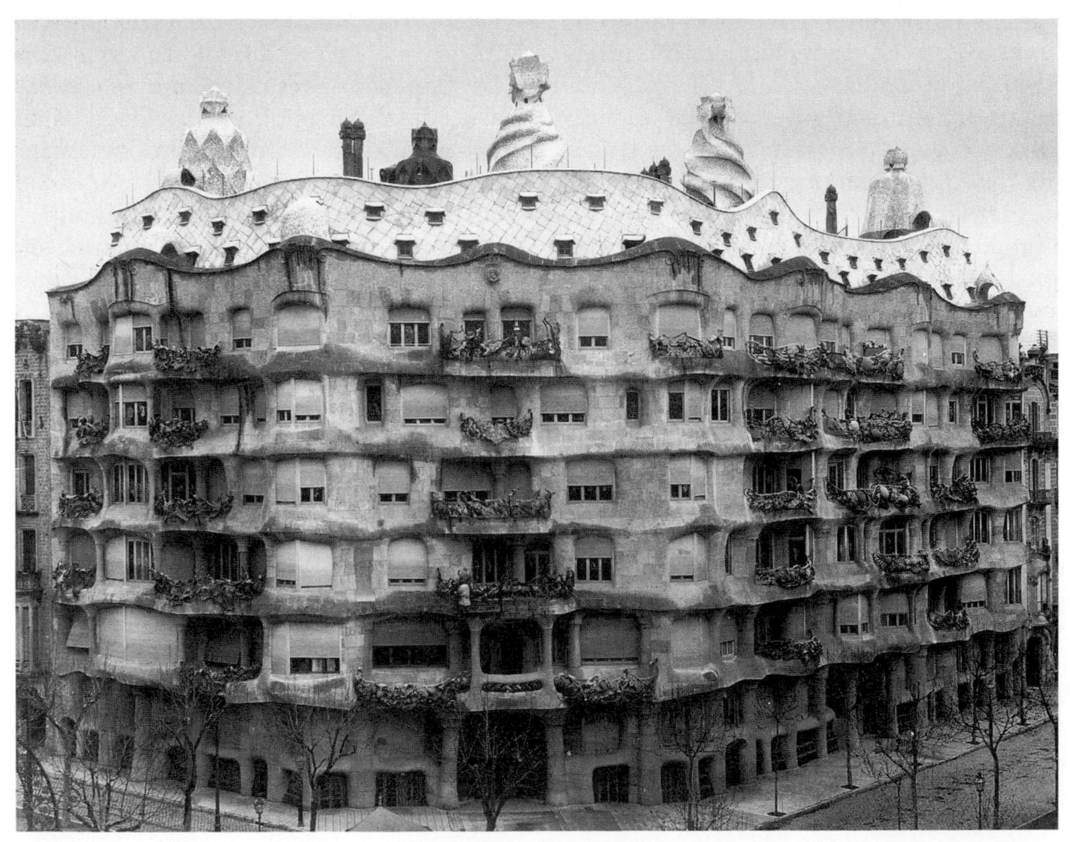

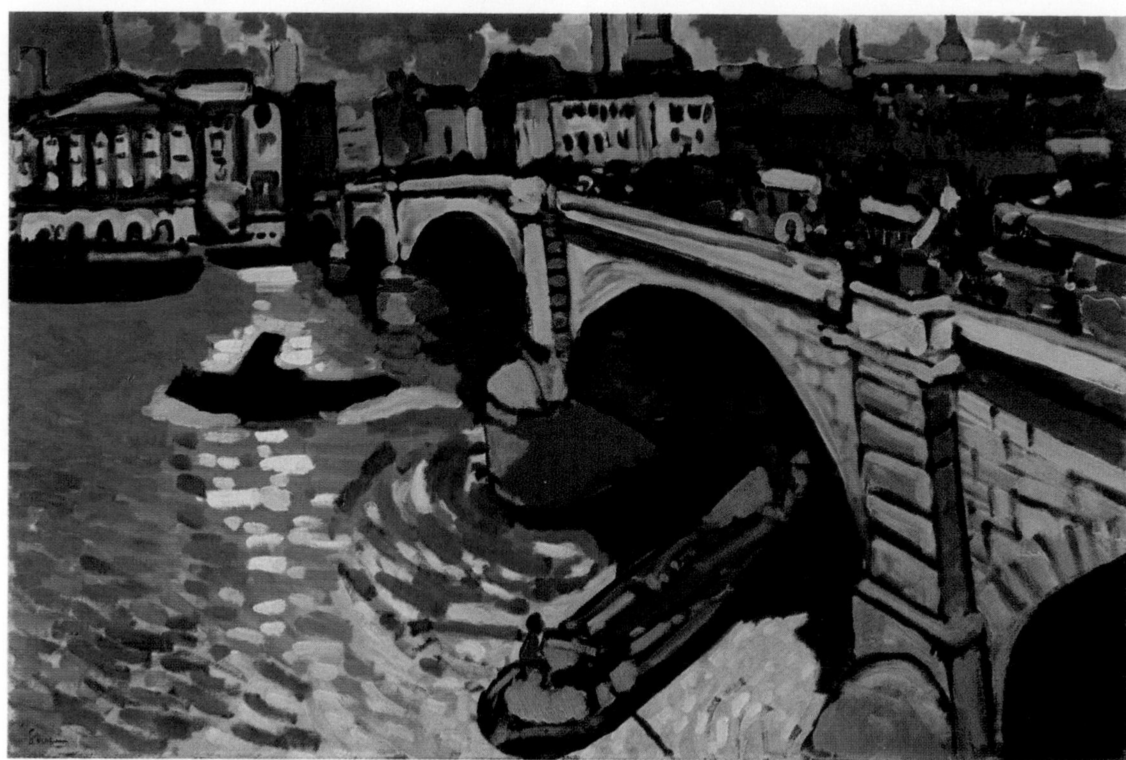

22-4 ANDRÉ DERAIN, *London Bridge*, 1906. Approx. 26″ × 39″. Collection, The Museum of Modern Art, New York (gift of Mr. and Mrs. Charles Zadok).

In 1905, the first signs of a specifically twentieth-century movement in painting appeared in Paris. In that year, at the third Salon d'Automne, a group of younger painters under the leadership of Henri Matisse exhibited canvases so simplified in design and so shockingly brilliant in color that a startled critic described the artists as *fauves* (wild beasts). The "Fauves" were totally independent of the French Academy and the "official" Salon, and their works were heavily influenced by the art of non-European cultures. They were among the first twentieth-century artists to be inspired by non-Western art. In African fetishes, in Polynesian decorative wood carvings, and in the sculptures and textiles of the ancient cultures of Central and South America, Fauve artists saw unexpected shapes and colors that suggested new ways of communicating emotion. These discoveries led them individually into paths of free invention and away from the traditions of the Renaissance. The Fauves produced portraits, landscapes, still lifes, and nudes of great spontaneity and verve, with rich surface textures, lively linear patterns, and boldly clashing primary colors. They were also inspired by the works of Van Gogh and Gauguin (shown in retrospective exhibitions in Paris in 1901 and 1903), but the Fauves went further than any earlier artist by bringing color to a new intensity with startling discords of vermilion and emerald green, cerulean blue and vivid orange held together by sweeping brush strokes and bold patterns. Typical of their vibrant vision is *London Bridge* (FIG. **22-4**) by ANDRÉ DERAIN (1880–1954). In this work, Derain rejected the harmonies of Impressionism, so expressive of atmospheric and light conditions, in favor of a distorted perspective emphasized by the contrast of the non-naturalistic colors—clashing yellows, blues, greens, reds, and oranges—against the black accents of the arches. Derain, like the other Fauves, believed that an artist's goal should be to make the strongest possible presentation of his emotional reaction to a subject by using bold color and strong linear patterns. In Fauve works, color no longer described the local tones of an object; instead, it created the expressive content of the picture, foreshadowing later nonobjective works whose entire content was the interaction of color and form.

The Fauve group was never an official organization of painters, and it lasted only a short time. Within five years, most of the artists had modified their violent colors and found their own, more personal styles. The artist who remained most faithful to Fauve principles, while transforming them through his extraordinary sensitivity for color, was HENRI MATISSE (1869–1954). Throughout his long life, Matisse's gifts for combining colors in unexpected ways and for inventing new combinations never flagged. He had trained as a lawyer, was employed as

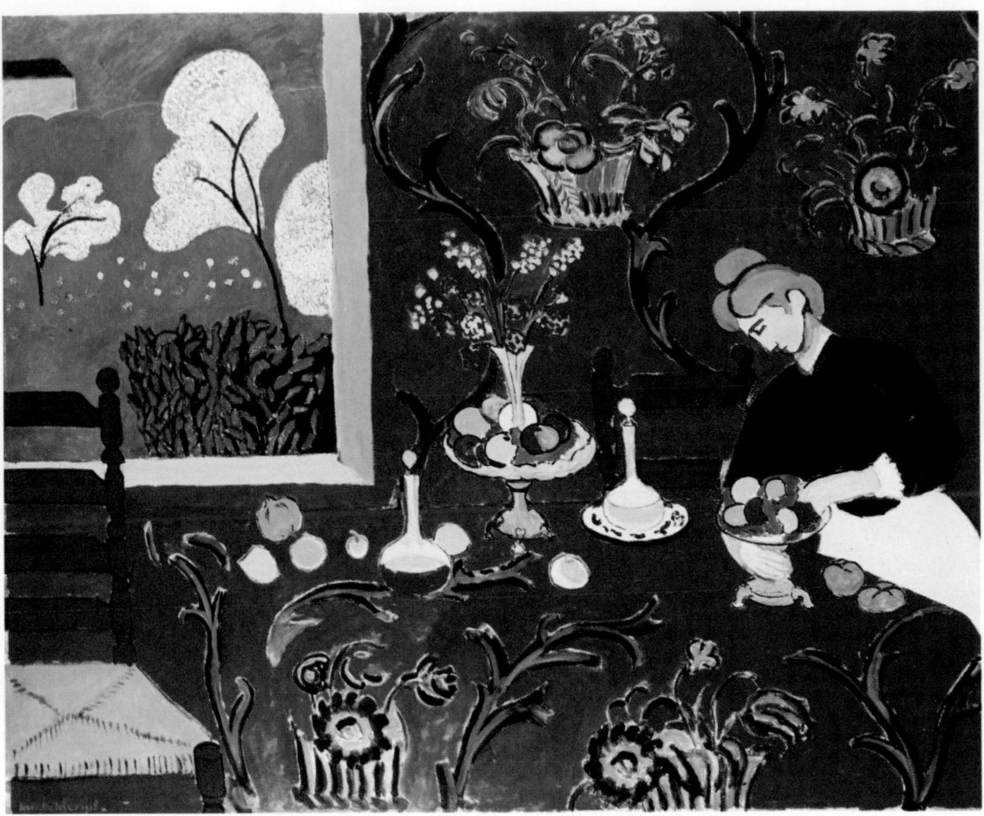

22-5 HENRI MATISSE, *Red Room (Harmony in Red)*, 1908–1909. Approx. 5′ 11″ × 8′ 1″. State Hermitage Museum, Leningrad.

a designer for tapestry and textiles, and began painting as a pupil of Gustave Moreau (FIG. 21-88), working his way through a variety of earlier styles before beginning to follow Cézanne's idea that light could not be reproduced in painting, but must be represented there by color. *Red Room (Harmony in Red)* (FIG. **22-5**) shows Matisse's mature style, one in which bold Fauve color is controlled by wonderful curving lines, partly inspired by the artist's strong interest in works as diverse as those of Duccio (FIG. 15-7) and Ingres (FIG. 21-14), as well as Japanese prints (FIG. 21-74), and Near Eastern textiles, pottery, and paintings (FIG. 7-85). The composition is a festive, lyrical arrangement of simplified interlocking shapes. The space of the room is suggested by the perspective view of the chair seat and the window's frame, but it is simultaneously transformed into a flat pattern of colored shapes and the patterned red-pink fields shared by the tablecloth and the wall paper. The work is a harmonious whole. Even the figure of the woman at the right is constructed from the same kind of forms as the other objects in the painting. Matisse himself said that his procedure was one of continuous adjustment—color to color, shape to shape, and color to shape—until he had achieved exactly the right "feel" and the painting was completed.

Composition for Matisse involved drawing on every element of color, shape, and arrangement to create a harmonious unity; he sought to soothe the mind and emotions of viewers in the midst of a demanding and often troubling world.

> The whole arrangement of my picture is expressive. The place occupied by figures or objects, the empty spaces around them, the proportions, everything plays a part. Composition is the art of arranging in a decorative manner the various elements at the painter's disposal for the expression of his feelings. . . . A work of art must be harmonious in its entirety; for superfluous details would, in the mind of the beholder, encroach upon the essential elements. . . . What interests me most is neither still life nor landscape but the human figure. It is through it that I best succeed in expressing the nearly religious feeling that I have towards life. . . . What I dream of is an art of balance, or purity and serenity devoid of troubling or depressing subject matter, an art which might be for every mental worker, be he businessman or writer, like an appeasing influence, like a mental soother, something like a good armchair in which to rest from physical fatigue.*

*In Herschel B. Chipp, ed., *Theories of Modern Art* (Berkeley: University of California Press, 1973), pp. 132, 135.

Matisse's way of allowing his paintings to "emerge" out of deep, even unconscious feelings, and of letting his artistic sensitivity and instinct be his guides, was a common practice among many other modern artists as well.

Cubism

A more analytical variant of the formalist approach in early twentieth-century art was found in Cubism—a style inspired partly by the desire to express the space-time qualities of reality newly revealed by scientists like Einstein. Cubism was developed jointly, between 1908 and 1913, by the Spanish artist PABLO PICASSO (1881–1973) and the French painter GEORGES BRAQUE (1882–1963), both through their continuing exchange of ideas and in their separate works. The new style received its name after Matisse described some of Braque's 1908 works to a critic as having been painted *"avec des petits cubes"* (with little cubes). The originality of Cubism lay in its discovery of a new kind of pictorial space to replace the kind that had been developing in Western art since the time of Giotto. Adopting Cézanne's suggestion that artists use the simple forms of cylinders, spheres, and cones to represent nature in art, the Cubists then expanded on his idea that each object could be depicted from a shifting point of view, as if seen from several markedly different angles at once. The central concepts of Cubism were beautifully summarized in 1913 by the French writer and theorist Guillaume Apollinaire:

> Authentic Cubism [is] the art of depicting new wholes with formal elements borrowed not from the reality of vision, but from that of conception. This tendency leads to a poetic kind of painting which stands outside the world of observation; for, even in a simple cubism, the geometrical surfaces of an object must be opened out in order to give a complete representation of it. . . . Everyone must agree that a chair, from whichever side it is viewed, never ceases to have four legs, a seat and back, and that if it is robbed of one of these elements, it is robbed of an important part.*

Picasso and Braque created two different and distinct variations of the basic style—Analytic Cubism and Synthetic Cubism, each of which was widely influential on later art.

ANALYTIC CUBISM

The first Cubist style developed by Picasso and Braque was "Analytic Cubism." Since the kind of total view described by Apollinaire could not be achieved by the traditional method of drawing or painting a model from one position, these artists began to *analyze* the forms of their subjects from every possible vantage point and to combine the various views into one pictorial whole.

The first steps toward this new style were taken by Picasso in a large painting, *Les Demoiselles d'Avignon* (FIG. **22-6**), which broke decisively with the art of the past. Picasso was a precocious student who had mastered all aspects of late nineteenth-century Realist technique by the time he entered the Barcelona Academy of Fine Art in the late 1890s. His prodigious talent led him to experiment with a wide range of visual expression, first in Spain and then in Paris, where he settled in 1904. Throughout his career, Picasso remained a traditional artist in the way he made careful studies in preparation for each major work. He was characteristic of the modern age, however, in his constant experimentation, in his sudden shifts from one kind of painting to another, and in his startling innovations in painting, graphic art, and sculpture. Inspired by Michelangelo, Rodin, and El Greco, Picasso explored the ways in which the human body could express emotion. By the time he settled permanently in Paris, his work had evolved from the sober Realism of Spanish painting, through a brightening of color in an Impressionistic manner (for a time, influenced by the early works of Toulouse-Lautrec), and into the so-called Blue Period (1901–1905), in which he used primarily blue colors to depict worn, pathetic, alienated figures in the pessimistic mood of the end of the nineteenth century.

By 1906, Picasso was searching restlessly for new ways to depict form. He found clues in African sculpture, in the sculpture of ancient Iberia, and in the late paintings of Cézanne. The three sources come together in *Les Demoiselles d'Avignon* (FIG. 22-6), which opened the way for a radically new method of representing form in space. Picasso began the work as a symbolic picture to be titled *Philosophical Bordello*, in which male clients intermingled with women in the "receiving" room of a brothel. By the time the artist began the final canvas, he had eliminated the male figures and simplified the details of the room to a suggestion of drapery and a schematic foreground still life; Picasso had become wholly absorbed in the problem of finding a new way to represent the five female figures in their interior space.† Instead of representing the figures as continuous volumes, Picasso fractured their shapes and interwove them with the equally jagged planes that represent drapery and

*In Edward Fry, ed., *Cubism* (London: Thames & Hudson, 1966), pp. 112–13, 116.

†The artist did keep a sly reference to the original subject in his final title—"Avignon" was the name of a well-known street in Barcelona's red-light district.

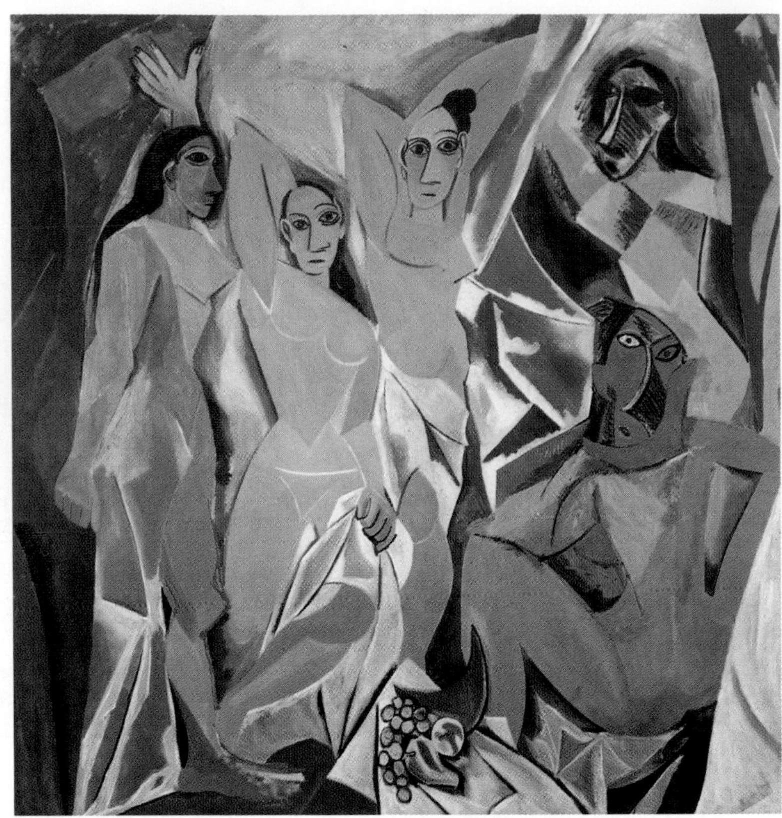

22-6 Pablo Picasso, *Les Demoiselles d'Avignon,* Paris (begun May, reworked July 1907). 8′ × 7′ 8″. Collection, The Museum of Modern Art, New York (acquired through the Lillie P. Bliss Bequest).

empty space. The treatment of form and space used by Cézanne is pushed here to a new tension between the representation of three-dimensional space and a statement of painting as a two-dimensional design lying flat on the surface of a stretched canvas. The radical nature of *Les Demoiselles* is extended even further by the disjunctive styles of the heads of the figures and by the pose of the figure at the bottom right. The calm, ideal features of the three ladies at the left were inspired by the sculpture of ancient Iberia, which Picasso saw during summer visits to Spain. The energetic, violently striated features of the two heads to the right came late in the making of the work and grew directly out of the artist's increasing fascination with the power of African sculpture. As if in response to the energy of these two new heads, Picasso also revised their bodies, breaking them into more ambiguous planes that suggest a combination of views, as if the figures are being seen from more than one place in space. The woman seated at the lower right shows these multiple views most clearly, seeming to present the viewer simultaneously with a three-quarter back view from the left, another from the right, and a front view of the head that adds the suggestion that we see the figure frontally as well. Gone is the traditional concept of an orderly, constructed, unified pictorial space that mirrors the world. In its place are the rudimentary beginnings of a new representation of the world as a dynamic interplay of time and space.

For many years, Picasso showed this extraordinary painting only to other painters. One of the first to see it was Braque, a Fauve painter, who was so agitated and challenged by it that he began reinventing his own painting style in response. One of Braque's paintings, *The Portuguese* (FIG. **22-7**), is a striking example of Analytic Cubism. The subject is derived from the artist's memories of a Portuguese musician seen years earlier in a bar in Marseilles. In this painting, all of Braque's energy has been concentrated on dissecting the form and placing it in dynamic interaction with the space around it; color is reduced to a monochrome of brown tones. The process of analysis has been carried so far that the viewer must work diligently to discover clues to the subject. The construction of large, intersecting planes suggests the forms of a man and a guitar. Smaller shapes interpenetrate and hover in the large planes. Light and dark passages suggest both chiaroscuro modeling and transparent planes that allow us to see through from

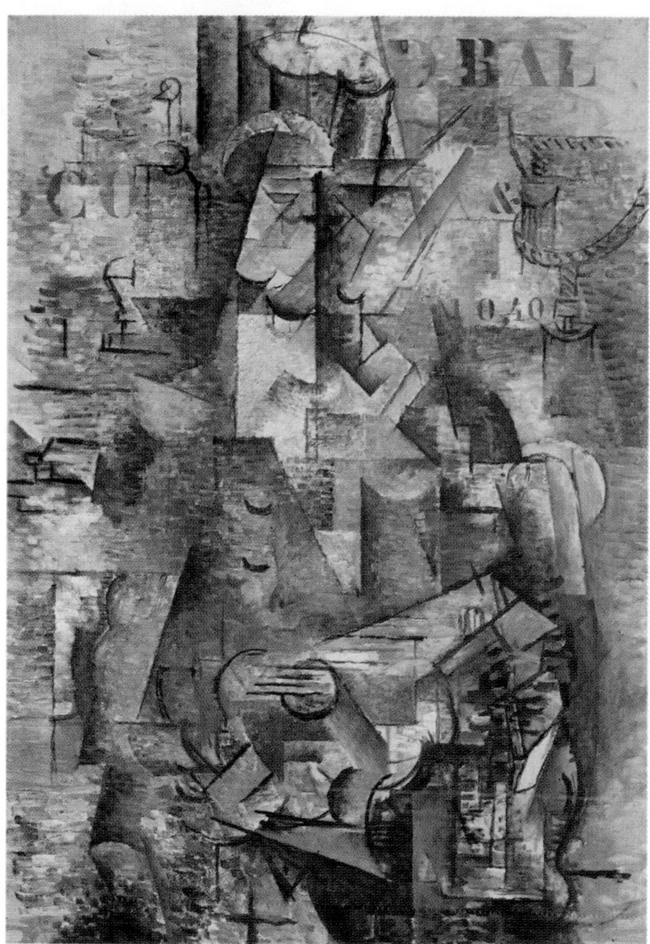

22-7 GEORGES BRAQUE, *The Portuguese,* 1911. $46\frac{1}{8}'' \times 32''$. Kunstmuseum, Basel, Switzerland (Emanuel Hoffmann-Stiftung).

one level to another. As we look, solid forms emerge only to be cancelled almost immediately by a different reading of the subject. The stenciled letters and numbers add to the painting's complexity. Letters and numbers are flat shapes; on the page of a book they exist outside of three-dimensional space, but as shapes in a Cubist painting like *The Portuguese,* they allow the painter to play with our perception of two- and three-dimensional space. The letters and numbers lie flat on the painted canvas surface, yet because the shading and shapes of the image seem to flow behind and underneath them, they are pushed forward into our space. Occasionally, they may seem to be attached to the surface of some object within the painting, but the combination of multiple views of each object causes such a perception to slide away in the next instant.

Analytic Cubism did not just open new ways of representing form on two-dimensional surfaces; it also inspired new approaches to sculpture. Picasso tested the possibilities of Cubism in sculpture throughout the years he and Braque were developing the style, but one of the most successful sculptors to adapt the spatial feeling of Analytic Cubist painting into three dimensions was JACQUES LIPCHITZ (1891–1973). Lipchitz was born in Lithuania but resided for many years in France and the United States. His ideas for many of his sculptures were worked out in clay before being transferred into bronze or into stone. *Bather* (FIG. **22-8**) is typical of his Cubist style. The continuous form in this work is broken down into cubic volumes and planes. As with Cubist painting, there is no single point of view, no continuity or simultaneity of image contour. Lipchitz was part of the "second generation" of Cubists, artists who invested

22-8 JACQUES LIPCHITZ, *Bather,* 1917. Bronze, $34\frac{3}{4}'' \times 13\frac{1}{4}'' \times 13''$. The Nelson-Atkins Museum of Art, Kansas City, Missouri (gift of the Friends of Art F70-12).

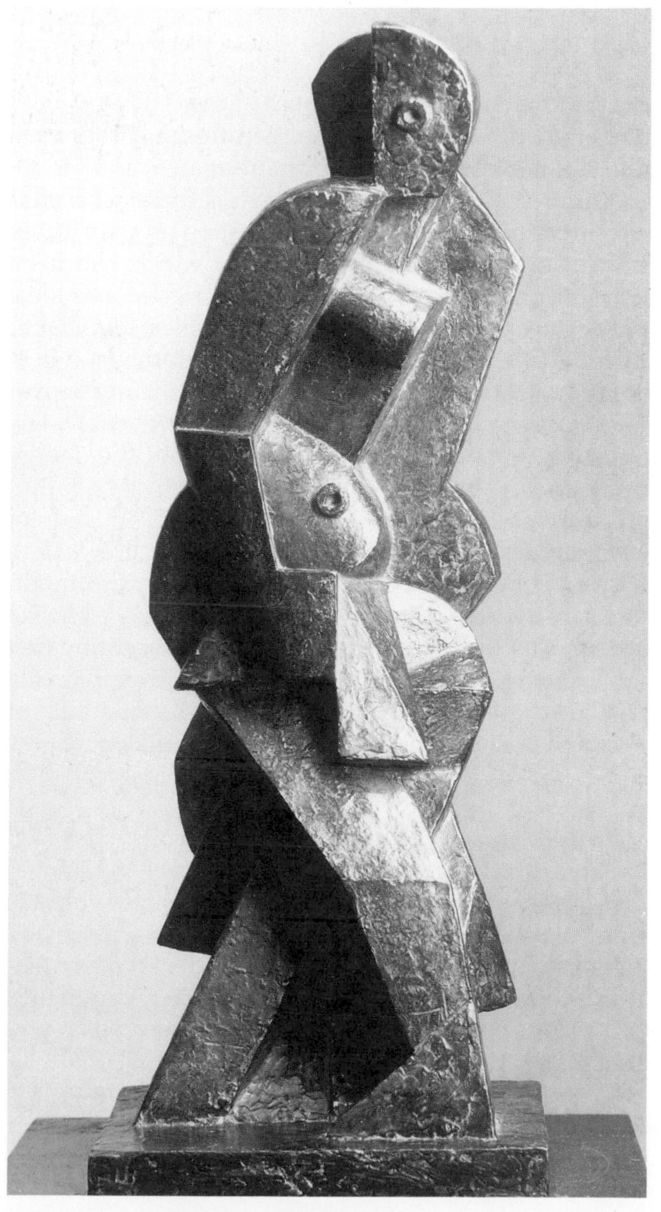

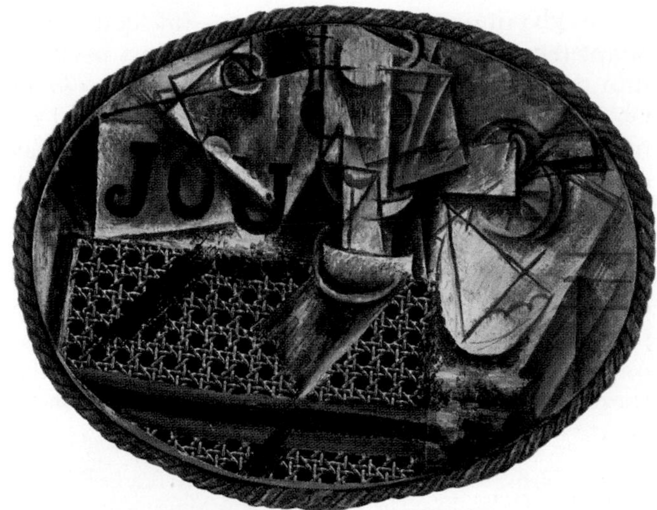

22-9 PABLO PICASSO, *Still Life with Chair-Caning,* 1911–1912. Oil and pasted paper simulating chair-caning on canvas. $10\frac{5}{8}'' \times 13\frac{3}{4}''$. Musée Picasso, Paris.

the innovations of Braque and Picasso with theory and a more consistent technical approach. Proportion and mathematics were important analytical tools for these artists. Like many of them, Lipchitz based a considerable number of his sculptures on the system of measure called the *Golden Mean,* which had been used in antiquity to suggest the perfection of ideal proportion and order.* Lipchitz combined this Classical mathematical formula with a modern energy to create what he called "the sense of twisting movement, of the figure spiraling around its axis." The spiraling movement in *Bather* recalls both the energy of El Greco's painted figures (FIG. 18-59), which Lipchitz much admired, and the twisting tension of Mannerist works like Giovanni da Bologna's *Rape of the Sabines* (FIG. 17-46). Yet these qualities are modified by the way in which the cubic shapes of *Bather* seem to slip and slide before our eyes, presenting first one view of the body parts and then another; Lipchitz has fully invested this figure with the qualities of space-time so important to the Cubist vision.

SYNTHETIC CUBISM

In 1912, Cubism entered a new phase during which the style no longer relied on a decipherable relation to the visible world. In this new phase, called Synthetic Cubism, paintings and drawings were constructed from objects and shapes cut from paper or other materials to represent parts of a subject. The work marking the point of departure for this new style was Picasso's *Still Life with Chair-Caning* (FIG. **22-9**), a painting done on a piece of oil cloth imprinted with the pattern of a cane chair seat and framed with a piece of rope. This work provided the means with which to play visual games with variations of illusion and reality. The photographically replicated chair-caning seems so "real" that one expects any brushstrokes laid upon it to be broken by the holes. The painted passages seem to hover magically in the air in front of the cane seat, lending the painted objects a visual tangibility that suggests relief sculpture more than painting. The visual play is extended in the way in which the letter *U* escapes from the space of the accompanying *J* and *O,* yet is partially covered by a painted cylindrical shape that pushes across its left side. The letters *JOU* appear in many Cubist paintings; these letters formed part of the masthead of the daily newspapers *(journals)* that were often found among the objects represented. Picasso and Braque especially delighted in the punning references to *Jouer* and *Jeu*—the French words for "to play" and "game."

22-10 GEORGES BRAQUE, *Fruit Dish and Cards,* 1913. Oil, pencil, and charcoal on canvas, $31\frac{7}{8}'' \times 23\frac{5}{8}''$. Collection Musée Nationale d'Art Moderne, Centre Georges Pompidou, Paris (gift of Paul Rosenberg).

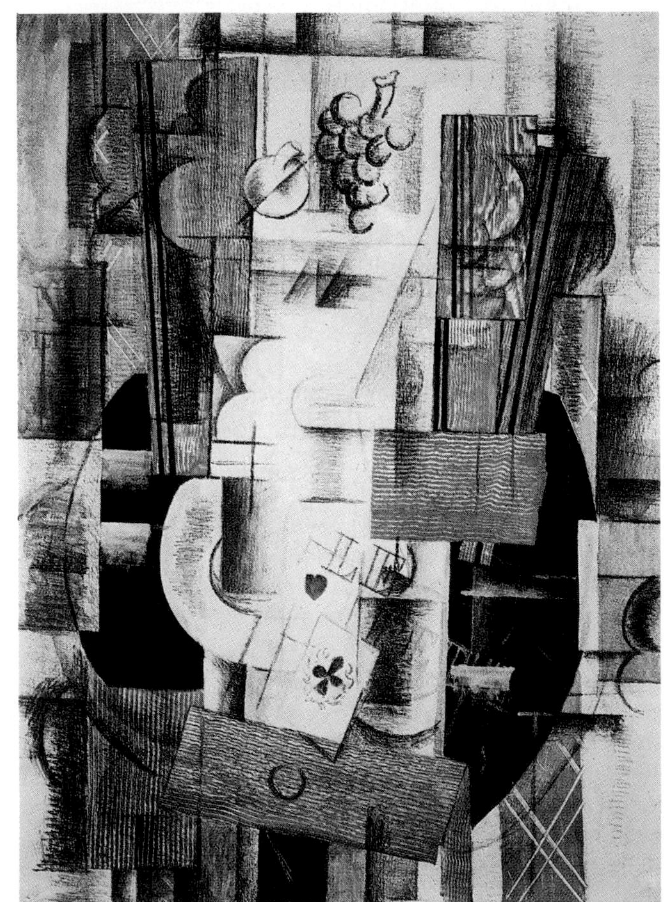

*The *Golden Mean* (also known as the Golden Rule or section) is a system of measuring in which units used to construct designs are subdivided into two parts in such a way that the longer subdivision is related to the length of the whole unit in the same proportion as the shorter subdivision is related to the longer subdivision.

After *Still Life with Chair-Caning,* both Picasso and Braque continued to explore the new medium introduced in that work. The wonderful new possibilities offered by *collage* (from the French word meaning "to stick") can also be seen in Braque's *Fruit Dish and Cards* (FIG. **22-10**), done in a variant of collage called *papier collé* (stuck paper), in which assorted paper shapes are glued to a drawing or painting. Charcoal and pencil lines and shadows provide us with clues to the Cubistic multiple views of table, dishes, playing cards, and fruit. Roughly rectangular strips of wood-grained, grey, and black paper run vertically up the composition, overlapping each other to create a layering of unmistakably flat planes that both echo the space suggested by the lines and establish the flatness of the surface of the work. All shapes in the image seem to oscillate between pushing forward and dropping back in space. Shading seems to carve space into the flat planes in some places and to turn them into transparent surfaces in others. The bottom edge of the ace of clubs seems to extend forward over a strip of wood-grained paper, while its top corner appears to slip behind a filmy plane. The viewer is always aware that this is a work of art created by an artist and that each observer must enter the visual game to decipher all levels of representation. Braque is no longer analyzing the three-dimensional qualities of the physical world; here, objects and space alike are constructed or *synthesized* from the materials used to make the work. Picasso stated his views on Cubism at this point in its development: "Not only did we try to displace reality; reality was no longer in the object. . . . In the *papier collé* . . . we didn't any longer want to fool the eye; we wanted to fool the mind. . . . If a piece of newspaper can be a bottle, that gives us something to think about in connection with both newspapers and bottles, too."* Cubism's papier collé was essentially a formalist activity. Like all collage, the technique was modern in its medium—mass-produced materials never before found in "high" art—and modern in the way the "message" of the art became the imagery and nature of these everyday materials.

The use of found materials in collages allowed Braque and Picasso to reintroduce color into their work. By the 1920s, both were going their separate ways as artists, and Picasso had developed a very colorful version of Synthetic Cubism into a highly personal painting style that mimicked the look of the earlier pasted works. In paintings like *Three Musicians* (FIG. **22-11**), Picasso constructed figures from simple

*In François Gilot and Carlton Lake, *Life with Picasso* (New York: McGraw Hill, 1964), p. 77.

22-11 PABLO PICASSO, *Three Musicians,* Fontainebleau, summer 1921. Approx. 6′ 7″ × 7′ 3¾″. Collection, The Museum of Modern Art, New York (gift of Mrs. Simon Guggenheim).

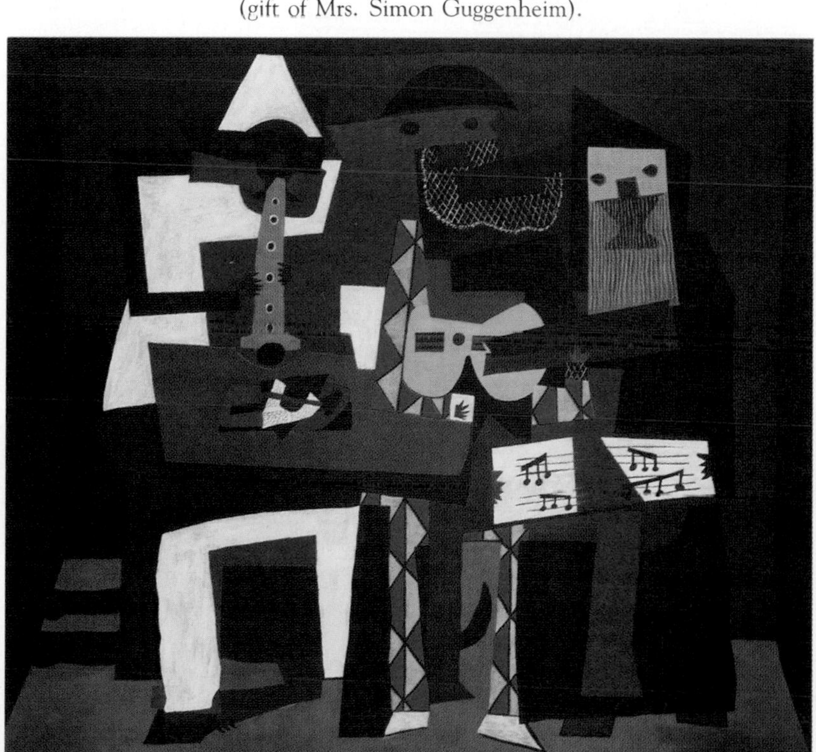

flat shapes that interlock and interpenetrate in a composition that whimsically combines a Modernist statement of the flat plane of the canvas with traditional modes of representation. The floor and walls of the room in which this lively musical trio performs suggest Renaissance perspective gone only a little awry, while the table, with an unlikely still life in its middle, is presented in reverse perspective. A jumble of flat shapes materializes into the figures of Pierrot on clarinet, Harlequin on guitar, and a mysterious masked monk as vocalist. Miraculously, the flat, syncopated shapes give each musician a different personality and simultaneously suggest the sprightly tune they are performing. Careful inspection reveals an alert dog sprawled behind the troupe, apparently beating its tail vigorously in time to the music.

Synthetic Cubism influenced many American artists. Two American painters created especially personal versions of the style. STUART DAVIS (1894–1964) tried to create what he believed was a modern American art style by combining the flat shapes of Synthetic Cubism with his own sense of jazz rhythms and his perception of the dynamism of the modern, urban industrial scene. Davis's long professional career began with the inclusion of some of his works in the Armory Show in New York City in 1913, an exhibition that introduced modern art to the general public in the United States. By the 1920s, Davis was investigating Synthetic Cubism. To master the style, he made repeated drawings, collages, and paintings of a single still life, gradually simplifying the shapes of its objects into compositions of flat, colored forms. As he described the process, he "brought drawings of different places and things into a single focus. The necessity to select and define the spatial limits of these separate drawings, in relation to the unity of the whole picture, developed an objective attitude toward size and shape."* Davis used his new style in paintings of street scenes in Manhattan and Paris. *House and Street* (FIG. **22-12**) is a simple combination of two views of New York City—one, a detail of a building façade seen head-on and the second, a more distant view of a city street presented as if seen through a window placed at an angle to the picture surface. All details are constructed from flat, colored shapes that interlock more than they overlap. Although the play of angular and rectilinear forms and flat, hard colors does not toy as obviously with our perception of two and three dimensions as do the Synthetic Cubist works of Braque or Picasso, the details in Davis's work create an intriguing ambiguity of figure and ground in which "forward" and "backward" alternate as convincingly as in the European examples. In addition to being a double scene, the whole visual field in *House and Street* sets up a lively vibration of colors and shapes.

*In Chipp, ed., *Theories of Modern Art*, p. 526.

22-12 STUART DAVIS, *House and Street*, 1931. 26" × 42¼".
Collection of Whitney Museum of American Art, New York (purchase).

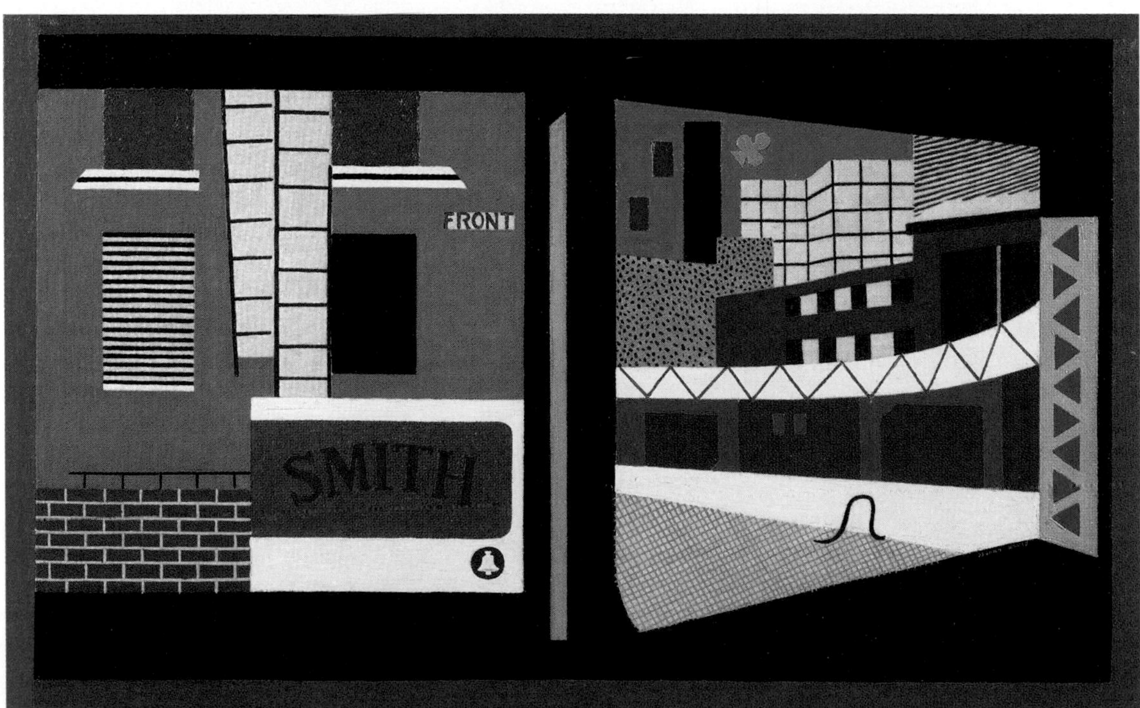

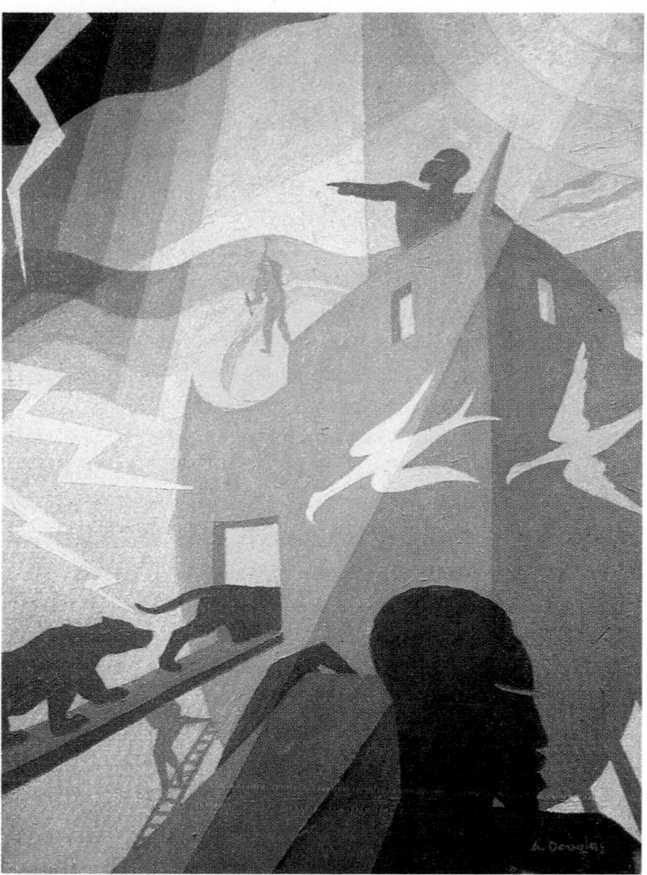

22-13 AARON DOUGLAS, *Noah's Ark,* c. 1927. Oil on masonite, 48″ × 36″. Afro-American Collection of Art, The Carl Van Vechten Gallery of Fine Arts, Fisk University, Nashville.

The personal Synthetic Cubism of the American painter AARON DOUGLAS (1898–1979) was filled with more symbolism and emotion than anything Davis painted. Douglas used the style to represent symbolically the historical and cultural memories of African-Americans. Born in Kansas, he studied in Nebraska and Paris before settling in New York City, where he became part of the flowering of art and literature in the 1920s known as the Harlem Renaissance. Encouraged by the German artist Winold Reiss to create an art that would express the cultural history of his race, Douglas incorporated motifs from African sculpture into compositions painted in a version of Synthetic Cubism that stressed angular, transparent planes. *Noah's Ark* (FIG. **22-13**) was one of seven paintings based on a book of poems by James Weldon Johnson called *God's Trombones: Seven Negro Sermons in Verse.* Rather than combining different viewpoints in space, Douglas used the flat planes of Synthetic Cubism to evoke a sense of mystical space and miraculous happenings. In *Noah's Ark,* lightning strikes and rays of light crisscross the area in which pairs of animals enter the ark, while men load supplies in preparation for departure across the heaving seas. Deep space is suggested by the difference in scale between the huge human head and shoulders of the worker in the foreground and the tiny person at work on the distant rear deck of the ship. At the same time, the unmodulated color shapes of the composition create a pattern on the surface of the masonite panel that cancels any illusion of three-dimensional depth. Here, Douglas used the formal language of Cubism to express a powerful religious vision, bending the style toward the second Modernist approach, that of art with psychological and conceptual concerns.

DERIVATIVES OF CUBISM

Early in the development of Cubism, a group of Italian artists adapted some of the style's analytic tricks to depict the emotional dynamism of modern life. The members of this group called themselves "Futurists," and their movement was inaugurated in 1909 with a manifesto written by the poet Filippo Marinetti, who called for a new art of "violence, energy, and boldness" that would proclaim the wonders of the machine age—an age "enriched by a new beauty; the beauty of speed." The Futurists believed that only a drastic overturning of traditional culture and art could accomplish this, and many of them followed Marinetti in saying that war was the most effective means to this end. In principle, the Futurist artist attempted to present aspects of modern, mechanized society in moments of violently energetic movement. In the words of a leading Futurist painter and sculptor, UMBERTO BOCCIONI (1882–1916), the Futurists proposed "to destroy the cult of the past . . . to despise utterly every form of imitation . . . to extol every form of originality . . . to sweep from the field of art all motifs and subjects that have already been exploited . . . to render and glorify the life of today, unceasingly and violently transformed by victorious science."* In practice, Futurist artists adopted the Cubist analysis of space, but by repetition of forms, they tried to impart movement to the static quality of Cubist works. Scientific discoveries about movement and time obsessed the Futurists. Boccioni's *Futurist Painting, Technical Manifesto* (1910) rings with a recognition of universal process:

> The gesture which we would reproduce on canvas shall no longer be a fixed *moment* in universal dynamism. It shall simply be the dynamic sensation itself. . . . The figure in front of us never is still, but ceaselessly appears and disappears. Owing to the persistence of images on the retina, objects in motion are multiplied and distorted, following one another

*In Robert Goldwater and Marco Treves, eds., *Artists on Art,* 3rd ed. (New York: Pantheon, 1964), p. 435.

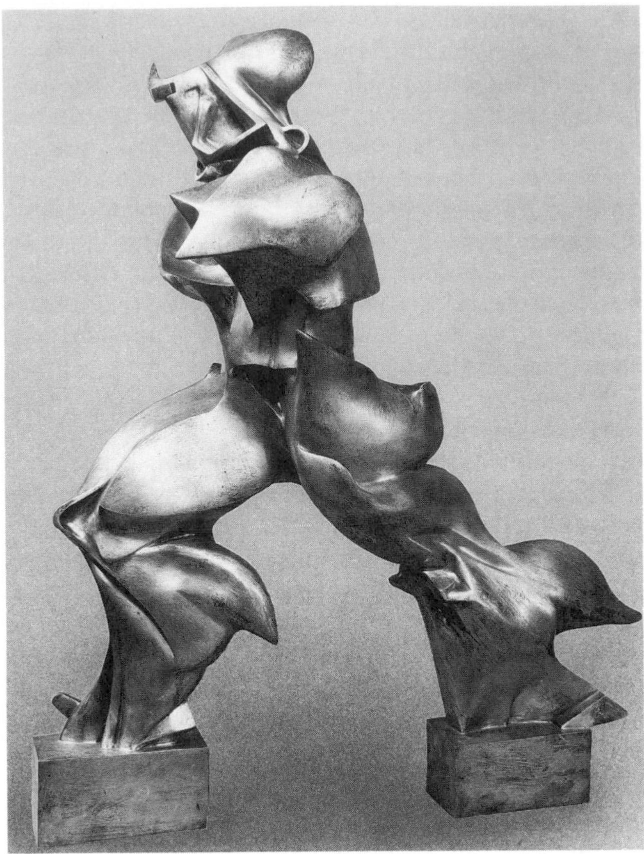

22-14 UMBERTO BOCCIONI, *Unique Forms of Continuity in Space*, 1913 (cast 1931). Bronze, approx. $43\frac{1}{3}$" high. Collection, The Museum of Modern Art, New York, (acquired through the Lillie P. Bliss Bequest).

> like waves through space. Thus, a galloping horse has not four legs; it has twenty, and their movements are triangular.

Boccioni began his art career as a commercial artist who painted seriously in his spare time. He began making Futurist sculpture in 1912. By 1913, he had pushed his forms so far toward abstraction that the title of his *Unique Forms of Continuity in Space* (FIG. **22-14**) calls attention to the formal and spatial effects of the work, ignoring the fact that its source was a striding human figure. The "figure" here has been so expanded, interrupted, or broken in plane and contour that it disappears, as it were, behind the blur of its movement; only the blur remains. Although Boccioni's sculpture bears a curious resemblance to the ancient *Nike of Samothrace* (FIG. 5-75), a brief comparison reveals how far apart these two visions of a figure moving through space really are.

The influences of Cubism and Futurism merged in the Vorticist movement in England, which was led by the British painter and writer Wyndham Lewis and the American expatriate poet Ezra Pound, who gave the style its name. Vorticism shared Futurism's interest in machine forms and in the dynamism of modern life, but the Vorticists did not join in the Futurists' admiration for the cleansing power of war. Among the most interesting Vorticist works were photographs (immediately called "vortographs" by Pound) produced in London by the American artist ALVIN LANGDON COBURN (1882–1966). From his boyhood on, Coburn was interested in pushing photography into new realms. Initially a successful pictorialist photographer, he experimented with photographs of New York and London taken from the upper floors of tall buildings before turning to multiple-exposure abstract work under the inspiration of Vorticist ideas about the dynamic space-time qualities of the modern industrial world. Many of Coburn's vortographs are pure abstractions, which he created by making multiple exposures of crystals and wood fragments, placed inside a triangle whose sides were composed of strip mirrors, which transformed his subjects into strange geometric patterns. Perhaps Coburn's best-known work is his vortograph portrait of the poet Ezra Pound (FIG. **22-15**). This work achieves its effect of the poet moving through space and time with a succession of exposures made on a

22-15 ALVIN LANGDON COBURN, *Ezra Pound Vortograph*, 1916. Gelatin silver print. International Museum of Photography at George Eastman House, Rochester, New York.

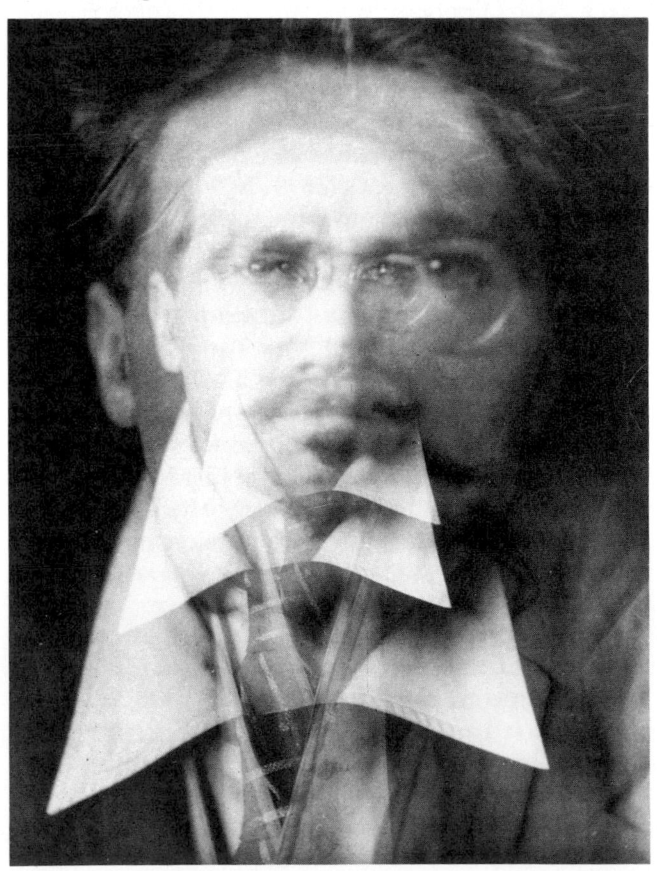

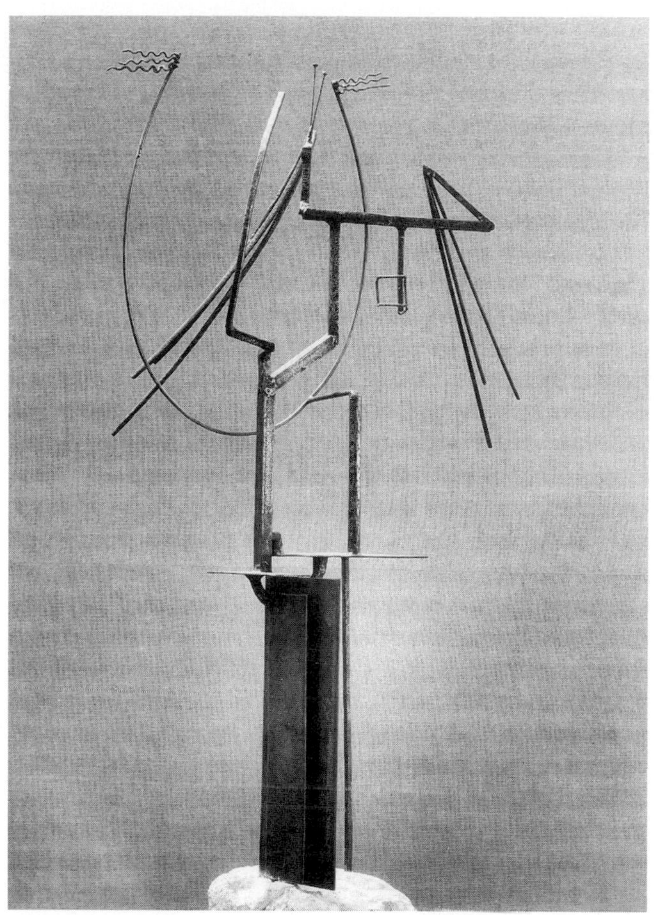

22-16 Julio Gonzalez, *Woman Combing Her Hair*, c. 1930–1933. Iron, 57″ high. Moderna Museet, Stockholm.

single negative as the artist moved closer to the poet. Like Boccioni's sculptured figure, Pound's head and clothing appear to dissolve into the space around them, and the poet's physical presence flickers eloquently in a metaphoric space-time. The multiple outlines of the figure, however, also suggest the layered edges in a Cubist painting, here given a particular expressive resonance by their position one within the other.

One artist who based his sculptural style on the ambiguity of edges in Cubist works was the Spanish sculptor Julio Gonzalez (1876–1942). A friend of Picasso, Gonzalez was especially interested in the artistic possibilities of new materials and new methods borrowed from industrial technology and from traditional metalworking, in which he had begun his career. Welding compositions from bronze rods and wrought-iron shapes, he created works that seem like three-dimensional drawings in space. His small *Woman Combing Her Hair* (fig. **22-16**) resembles a translation into metal lines and planes of the shapes of a section in Picasso's *Three Musicians*. As in Picasso's painting, the human figure here is freely reinterpreted as a series of bold curves and lines. Nature is symbolized, not represented in a traditional way. The viewer must work hard to transform the visual clues in this work into hair, nose, eyes, and other body parts. In the fluent openwork of this sculptured space, the solids function only as contours, boundaries, or dividing planes. The solidity of mass has dropped away, leaving a few traces of form in a space that science had shown to be filled with invisible atoms in ceaseless motion. As in all Cubist works, the head and features of Gonzalez's figure seem to be seen from many views at once. As in all Modernist works, the viewer is very aware of the processes by which this work was made. The free linear composition and antigravity qualities of works like *Woman Combing Her Hair* were explored further by later artists, like David Smith (fig. 23-6), as part of their reinvestigation of the basic nature of sculptural form.

ART WITH PSYCHOLOGICAL AND CONCEPTUAL CONCERNS

Many early twentieth-century artists strove to reintroduce into visual art the conceptual part of art they believed had been lost in the turn toward formalism. Despite this goal, their works were not dry and cerebral; like the Romanticists before them, most of these early twentieth-century artists worked not with the logic of reason, but with the dictates of their intuition and imagination. Their work can be classified as art with psychological and conceptual concerns. Some of these artists worked with figurative or abstract themes; some used completely nonobjective forms. All wanted to express something of the intellect and emotions, which they believed alone could help people perceive the true meaning in life. Many of them also thought of themselves as seers with special insight into the significance of the internal realm. One of them, the Swiss-German artist Paul Klee, described the power of their approach:

> In the highest sense, an ultimate mystery lies behind the ambiguity which the light of the intellect fails miserably to penetrate. Yet one can to a certain extent speak reasonably of the salutary effect which art exerts through fantasy and symbols. Fantasy, kindled by instinct-born excitements, creates illusory conditions which can rouse or stimulate us more than familiar, natural, or supernatural ones. Symbols reassure the mind that we need not depend exclusively upon mundane experience.*

Of special importance for the conceptual side of this approach in art were the work and ideas of the

*In Margaret Miller, ed., *Paul Klee* (New York: Museum of Modern Art, 1946), p. 13.

French artist Marcel Duchamp, an immensely influential figure for later artists. In his painting, sculpture, and a category of objects he invented called the "readymade," Duchamp emphasized the way in which the meaning of any work is determined not only by the intent of the artist, but also by the inherent qualities of the material used and by the mind and emotions of the viewer. Duchamp's kind of conceptual art prepared the way for the art of the late twentieth century (Postmodernist art), which self-consciously distinguishes itself from Modernist formalist art by analyzing the operation of all art styles and the place of art in culture.

Expressionism: Bold and Dark Visions

Although antecedents to Expressionist art before the twentieth century were found in the works of artists as diverse as Stubbs (FIG. 20-46) and Van Gogh (FIG. 21-84), the term *Expressionism* probably first was applied to works of art in France to describe the paintings of the Fauves. Indeed, Derain and Matisse each spoke about "expression" in their art, communicating their delight in patterns based on nature and presented as eloquent arrangements of colors, tones, and shapes. Soon, however, the term was adopted to identify the works of other artists, especially in Germany, who developed expressive styles that described the stress-filled conditions of modern life. Precursors for this darker German Expressionism include the works of Matthias Grünewald (FIG. 18-33), Caspar David Friedrich (FIG. 21-22), and Edvard Munch (FIG. 21-92). Several books published early in the twentieth century contributed to the esthetic bases of German Expressionism as well. These included the writings of Alois Riegl, who perceived art history as the spiritual history of humanity; Wilhelm Worringer, who believed that all art was basically subjective and that intuition was the most important quality in creativity; and Henri Bergson, who wrote about the "life force" underlying and countering the material world and known to us through intuition. These thinkers elaborated on nineteenth-century ideas of art as something lying beyond either the imitation of nature's shifting physical appearance or the expression of literary themes. For them, art was produced by an "inner necessity" in the artist springing from the unique insights and perceptions of that one individual. Building on this concept, many of the more anguished Expressionists also sought to incorporate in their work qualities of an ecstatic awareness of the cosmos and of man's links with it.

In France, one painter dealt with the darker vein of Expressionism in colors that revealed his early links to the Fauves. Throughout his career, GEORGES ROUAULT (1871–1958) treated themes of grave social and religious import. A member of a family of craftsmen, Rouault was apprenticed to a stained-glass maker before entering the studio of Gustave Moreau, where he met Henri Matisse. Rouault's themes reflected his deeply devout and moralistic Roman Catholic view of the evils of modern society. His grim studies of broken prostitutes, corrupt judges, and sad clowns, and his suite of anguished antiwar prints (*Miserere et Guerre*) express the existential misery of human beings in modern urban society. His religious pictures often show the suffering of Christ as the "man of sorrows" (owing much to Grünewald). More ambiguous subjects, like *The Old King* (FIG. **22-17**), share the same solemn, melancholy mood. The style of this painting has something of the simplified design and expressive color of the Fauves, but the forms of the king are contained within strong black lines that isolate the layered colors like the lead banding in Medieval stained glass, which Rouault knew and

22-17 GEORGES ROUAULT, *The Old King*, 1916–1936. $30\frac{1}{4}'' \times 21\frac{1}{4}''$. The Carnegie Museum of Art, Pittsburgh (Patrons' Art Fund, 1940).

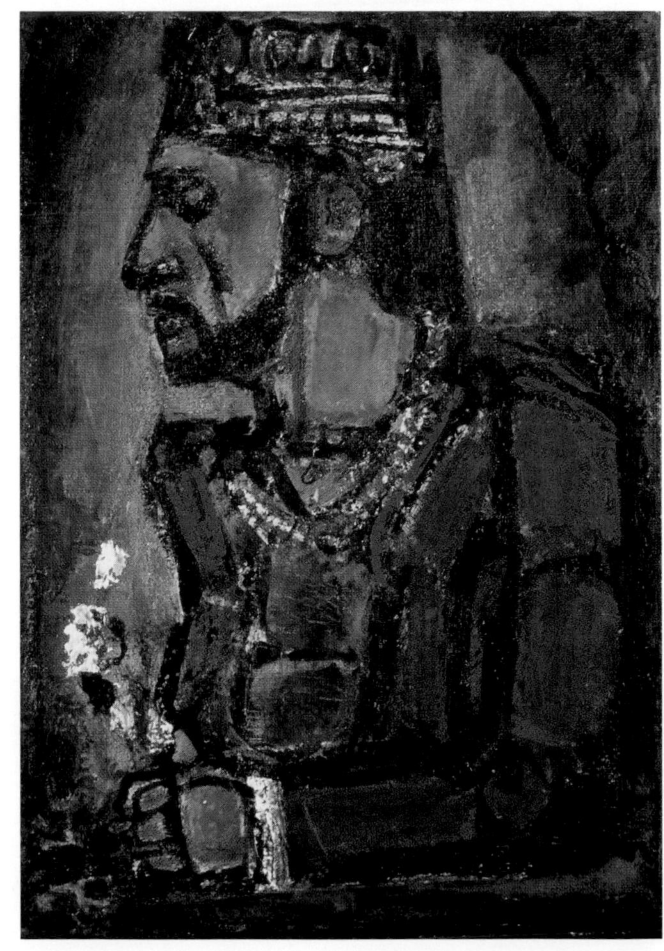

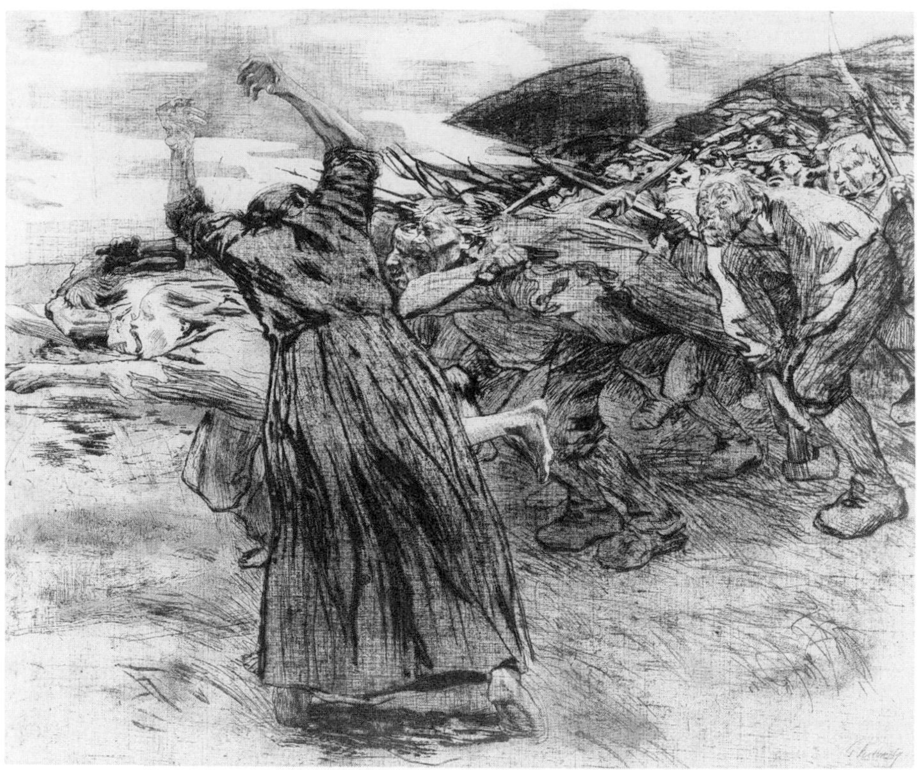

22-18 Käthe Kollwitz, *The Outbreak*, 1903. Plate No. 5 from *The Peasants' War*. Library of Congress, Washington D.C.

admired from his days as an apprentice. Dressed in a robe and crown reminiscent of the costumes in traditional paintings of Bible scenes, Rouault's king has the Semitic features of an Old Testament ruler. In contrast to the portraits of rulers we have seen so far, however, Rouault has focused on the vulnerability and human frailty of his monarch. The old king sits before us, imprisoned between the narrow arms of his throne, mysteriously clutching a spray of flowers, like a strange scepter, in his left hand.

In Germany, Expressionist qualities appeared in the work of Käthe Kollwitz (1867–1945) as early as the final years of the nineteenth century. Kollwitz poignantly expressed pity for the poor in moving prints. The daughter of parents with strong socialist beliefs and the wife of a doctor who shared this outlook, she had a life-long empathy with workers and the poor. She wanted to share her insight about the lives of these people with a wide audience and chose to do most of her art in print form so that more people could afford to purchase the images. Her first cycle of prints, completed in 1897, was inspired by a play written by Gerhart Hauptmann about a revolt of German weavers. Her next major group, *The Peasants' War,* contained seven prints that depicted different moments in a rebellion of German peasants in the sixteenth century. Kollwitz identified strongly with Black Anna, a woman who had led the laborers into battle against their oppressors. The first print completed in the series was *The Outbreak* (FIG. **22-18**), which shows Black Anna inciting her followers to action. Kollwitz combined the techniques of etching, aquatint, and *soft ground** to emphasize the figure of Black Anna, whose back is to the viewer as she leans to the left and raises her hands, signaling to the massed wedge of her followers to advance. The passion of the moment is conveyed in the expressions on the faces of the few individuals we can distinguish in the crowd and in the tense, forward-thrusting figure of Black Anna herself, which leads us into the picture and the onrushing fight for freedom.

The first group of artists to follow Expressionist ideas gathered in Dresden in 1905, under the leadership of Ernst Kirchner (1880–1938). The group's members thought of themselves as preparing the way for a more perfect age by forming a bridge from the old age to the new—a concept that gave them their

*Soft ground is an etching technique in which the artist obtains textures by pressing textured materials onto a soft gelatin-like coating spread over the printing plate. The coating remains soft and elastic enough that any textured material or object pushed into the soft ground surface leaves an imprint of its texture, the deepest parts of which fully or partially expose the metal to the acid when the plate is etched.

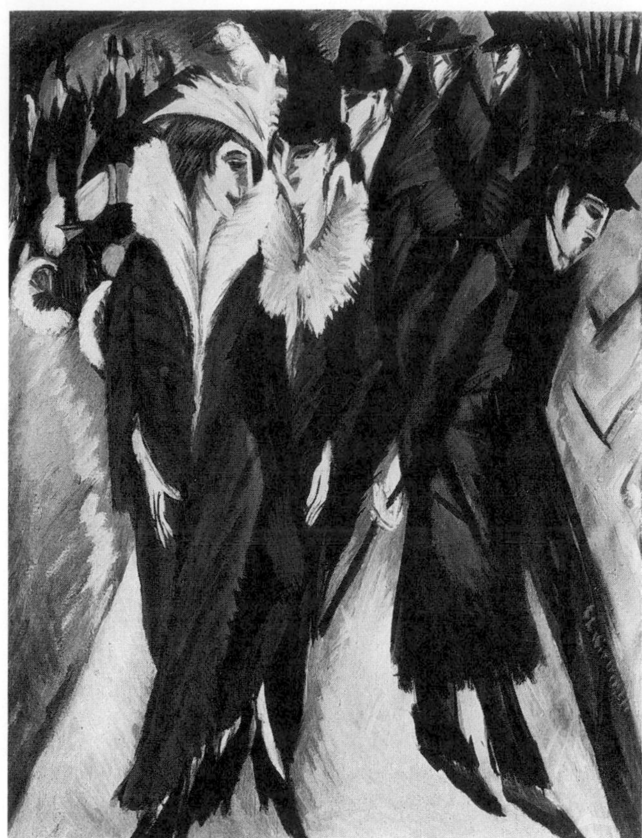

22-19 Ernst Kirchner, *Street, Berlin,* 1913. $47\frac{1}{2}'' \times 35\frac{7}{8}''$. Collection, The Museum of Modern Art, New York (purchase).

name: "the Bridge" (*Die Brücke*). Kirchner's early studies in architecture, painting, and the graphic arts had instilled in him a deep admiration for German Medieval art, which stirred the group to model themselves on their ideas of medieval craft guilds by living together and practicing all the arts equally. Kirchner described their lofty goals in a ringing statement: "With a profound belief in growth, a belief in a new generation of creators and appreciators, we summon the entire younger generation—and as the youth which carries within it the future, we wish to provide ourselves with a sphere of activity opposed to the entrenched and established tendencies. Everyone belongs to us who portrays his creative impulses honestly and directly."* Borrowing ideas from Van Gogh, Munch, the Fauves, and the art of Africa and Oceania, the Bridge artists created landscapes, cityscapes, genre scenes, portraits, and still lifes in which harsh colors, aggressively brushed paint, and distorted form expressed their feelings about the injustices of society or their belief in a healthful union of human beings and nature. After only a few years, many of the group, including Kirchner, moved to Berlin, where the tensions preceding World War I divided them further. By 1913, the last vestiges of the group dissolved and each of them was working independently.

In Berlin, Kirchner retained some of the Bridge group's energy and interest in social injustice in paintings like *Street, Berlin* (FIG. **22-19**), where steep perspective, jaggedly angular forms, acrid colors, and haunted people suggest the brittleness and fragility of life in the German metropolis as Europe moved closer to war. Kirchner's later painted and sculptured figures continued to show his interest in Medieval German woodcuts and in the fiercely emotive qualities of African and Oceanic art, which he and the members of the Bridge group had discussed in their magazine, *Die Brücke*.

As one might expect, the psychological interests and highly charged emotions of the Expressionist art of the Bridge group were well-suited to the new medium of cinema, especially in the early days of the "silent screen," before technology added synchronized sound. Silent films had already established themselves as the most democratic and the most magical of art forms, appealing to people of all ages and classes, who flocked to sit in darkened movie theaters and imagine themselves as part of the scenes unfolding on the screen before them. In German films like *The Cabinet of Dr. Caligari* (FIG. **22-20**), the Expressionist visual devices of the Bridge group were used to evoke a haunted world of psychological distress and turmoil. This movie tells a horror story about a traveling carnival hypnotist (Dr. Caligari) who controls César, a somnambulist (sleep walker), and sends him out to murder any citizen along the carnival's route who displeases Caligari; in the film, César murders a city official in a small medieval German town. The story of *Caligari* was intended by the original authors, the Czech Hans Janowitz and the Austrian Carl Mayer, as an attack on unjust authority. The film's director, Robert Wiene (1881–1938), assigned three painters—Hermann Warm, Walter Röhrig, and Walter Reimann—to design sets. The three designers read the script and realized that the film needed something other than ordinary sets. Reimann, "whose painting in those days had Expressionist tendencies," according to Warm, suggested that they utilize Expressionist devices in designing the film's sets. The sets they created for *Caligari* used the steep perspective and angular, distorted planes found in Expressionist paintings like Kirchner's *Street, Berlin.* The hallucinatory effect of this setting suggested perfectly the haunted memories of the hero, transformed by Wiene in the final film into a

*In Bernard S. Myers, *The German Expressionists: A Generation in Revolt* (New York: Praeger, *c.* 1956), pp. 111–12.

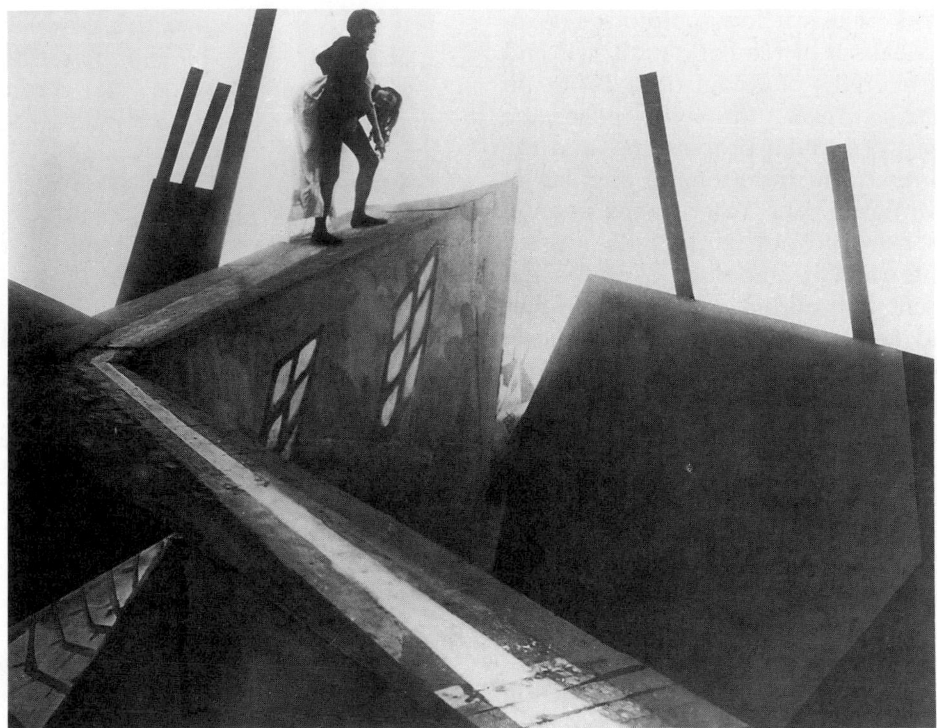

22-20 Hermann Warm, Walter Röhrig, and Walter Reimann, set for the film *The Cabinet of Dr. Caligari,* Robert Wiene, director, 1919.

mental patient recounting an imagined adventure. The emotive force of the Expressionist forms was heightened by creating strong highlights and deep dramatic shadows in the black-and-white movie, and by tinting whole sequences of the release prints eerie green, cold blue, or pale brown. *The Cabinet of Dr. Caligari* inaugurated the German Expressionist film, and its style affected horror films and psychological dramas in Europe and the United States throughout the 1920s and 1930s. As the French director René Clair said in 1922: "Caligari comes and affirms that the only interesting truth is the subjective. . . . We have to admit that reshaped nature is at least as expressive as 'natural' nature."*

In *Caligari,* German Expressionist distortions similar to those in the works of Kirchner and the Bridge group were used to symbolize an individual human psyche gone awry. A very different German Expressionist style was created by the sculptor Wilhelm Lehmbruck (1881–1919) to denote a different vision of the modern human condition. Lehmbruck studied sculpture, painting, and the graphic arts in Dusseldorf before moving (in 1910) to Paris, where he developed the style of his *Standing Youth* (fig. **22-21**). His sculpture combines the expressive qualities he much

*In Léon Barsacq, *Caligari's Cabinet and Other Grand Illusions: A History of Film Design* (New York: New American Library, 1978), pp. 27–30.

22-21 Wilhelm Lehmbruck, *Standing Youth,* 1913. Cast stone, approx. 7′8″ high, base dimensions 36″ × 26¾″. Collection, The Museum of Modern Art, New York (gift of Abby Aldrich Rockefeller).

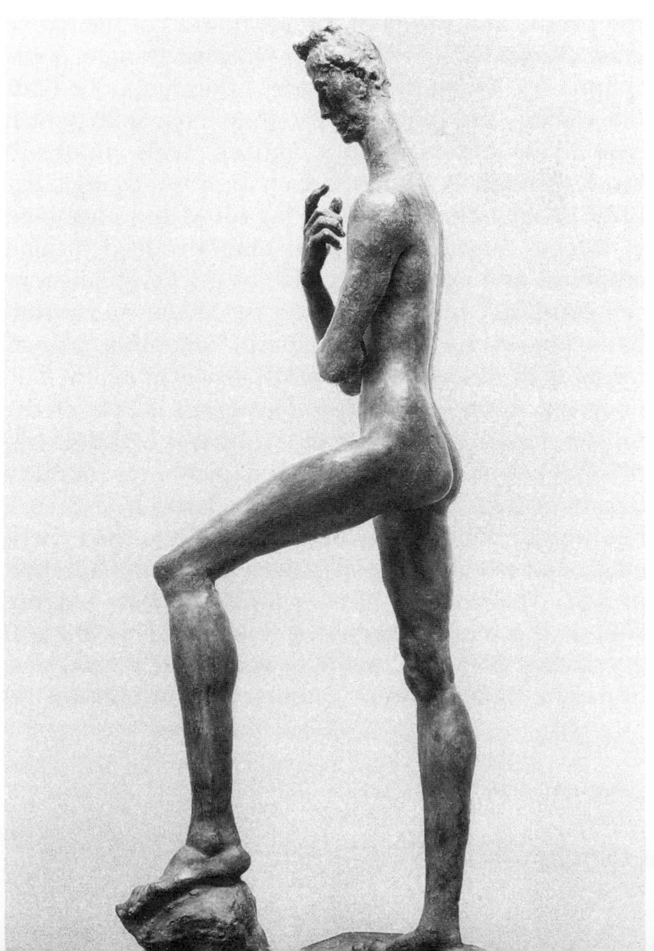

admired in the work of two fellow sculptors, reflecting the Classical idealism of Maillol (FIG. 22-44) and the psychological energies of Rodin (FIG. 21-56). In Lehmbruck's *Standing Youth*, the tense pose, the poignant elongation of human proportions, and the rippling hair all impart an undertone of anguish to the rather Classical figure. The *Youth* stands in quiet introspection, his head bowed in thought and his right hand raised toward his shoulder, as if in silent debate with himself. Lehmbruck's figure communicates by pose and gesture alone; it has no specific historical or symbolic significance. Its extreme proportions may recall Medieval (FIG. 9-37) and even Mannerist (FIG. 17-41) attenuation, but its distortions announce a new freedom in the interpretation of the human figure. Lehmbruck wrote that "sculpture is the essence of things, the essence of nature, that which is eternally human." For him, as for Rodin, the human figure could express every human condition and emotion. The introspection of *Standing Youth* reflects the bittersweet yearnings of an individual. *Seated Youth*, which we saw in the Introduction (FIG. 1), carries a broader symbolism, having been designed in grieving memory as a monument to all who gave their lives in World War I.

A work more mystical in its expression is the *War Monument* (FIG. **22-22**) by the German sculptor ERNST BARLACH (1870–1938), created for the cathedral in his hometown. As the son of a country doctor in northern Germany, Barlach found natural symbolism in the people and forms of the rural areas of his native land: "Country life lends the smallest thing a noble shape. . . . My mother tongue is the human body or the milieu, the object, through which or in which man lives, suffers, enjoys himself, feels, thinks."* Working often in wood, Barlach sculptured single figures, usually dressed in flowing robes and portrayed in strong, simple poses that embody deep human emotions and experiences such as grief, vigilance, or self-comfort. Much influenced by Medieval carving, Barlach's works combine sharp, smoothly planed forms with intense action and keen expression. The hovering figure of his *War Monument* is one of the most poignant memorials of World War I. Unlike traditional war memorials, which depict heroic military figures, often engaged in battle, Barlach creates a hauntingly symbolic figure that speaks to the experience of all who have been caught in the conflagration of war. The floating human form suggests a dying soul at the moment when it is about to awaken to everlasting life—the theme of death and transfiguration. The rigid economy of surfaces concentrates attention on the superb head (FIG. **22-23**). The spiritual anguish evoked by the disaster of war and the release from that anguish through the hope of salvation have rarely been expressed as movingly as they are in *War Monument*.

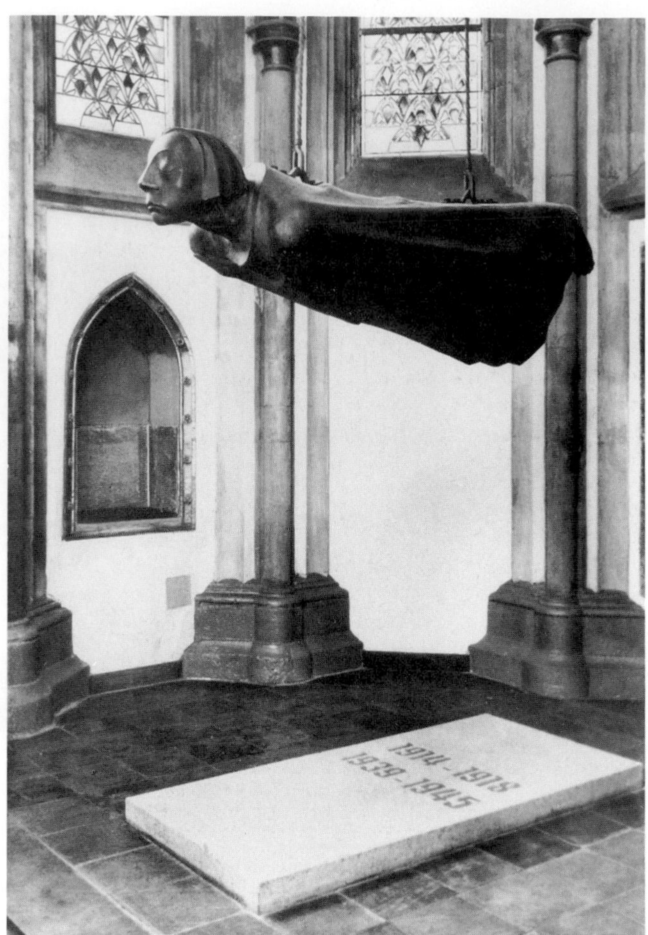

22-22 ERNST BARLACH, *War Monument*, Güstrow Cathedral, 1927. Bronze. Schildergasse Antoniterkirche, Cologne.

The brutality of life in post-war Europe and hope for a mythic escape from the despair and disillusionment of the period became the central themes in the works of MAX BECKMANN (1884–1950). Beckmann's early work was linked to a development of German Expressionism in the 1920s called New Objectivity (*Neue Sachlichkeit*), a movement whose members tried to build a new reality to replace the one that had been shattered by the disasters of the war. Beckmann filled his paintings with figures and objects stripped to a basic, almost sculptural simplicity. Their solidity, he said, provided a bulwark against the echoing void of space, which yawned threateningly everywhere. By the 1930s, Beckmann had evolved a more personal Expressionist style. He spoke of using a "transcendental realism" that would link "the real love for the things outside of us and the deep secrets of events

*In Carl Dietrich Carls, *Ernst Barlach* (London: Pall Mall Press, 1969), pp. 8, 9.

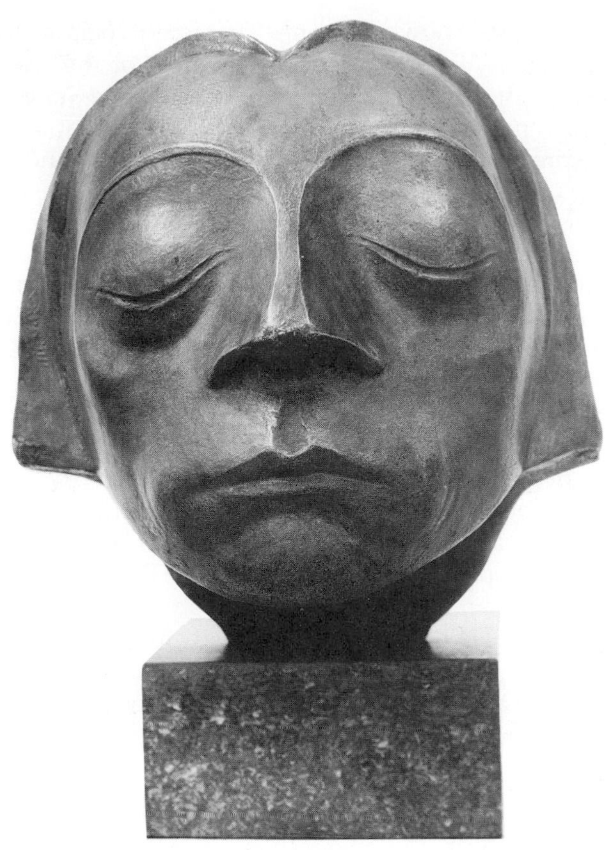

22-23 Ernst Barlach, *Head,* study for fig. 22-22, separately cast. Bronze, approx. 13½" high. Collection, The Museum of Modern Art, New York (gift of Edward M. M. Warburg).

within us." His was a world that mixed physical reality and the realm of the spirit:

> What I want to show in my work is the idea which hides itself behind so-called reality. I am seeking for the bridge which leads from the visible to the invisible, like the famous cabalist who once said: "if you wish to get hold of the invisible you must penetrate as deeply as possible into the visible." . . . What helps me most in this task is the penetration of space. Height, width, and depth are the three phenomena which I must transfer into one plane to form the abstract surface of the picture, and thus to protect myself from the infinity of space. . . . When spiritual, metaphysical, material, or immaterial events come into my life, I can only fix them by way of painting. It is not the subject which matters but the translation of the subject into the abstraction of the surface by means of painting. Therefore I hardly need to abstract things, for each object is unreal enough already, so unreal that I can only make it real by means of painting.*

Beckmann's art was elicited by some of the darkest moments of the twentieth century, when the rise of Nazi tyranny threatened European civilization. While his message was bitter, its reference was not specific to one time or place but concerned human cruelty and suffering in general. Works like *Departure* (**FIG. 22-24**) hauntingly show both Beckmann's primary

*In Myers, *The German Expressionists,* p. 307.

22-24 Max Beckmann, *Departure,* 1932–1933. Triptych, center panel 7' ¾" × 3' ⅜", side panels each 7' ¾" × 3' 3¼". Collection, The Museum of Modern Art, New York (given anonymously by exchange).

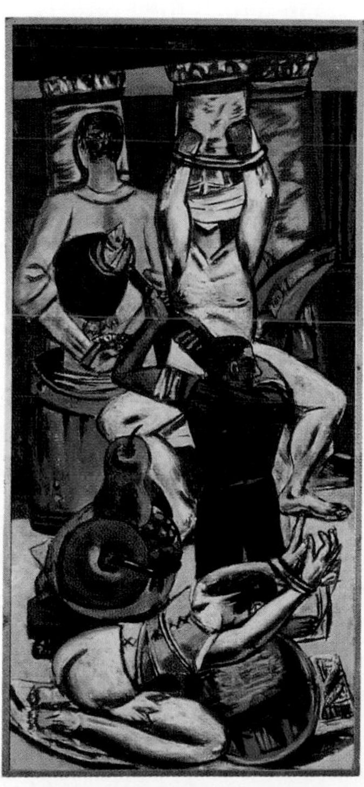

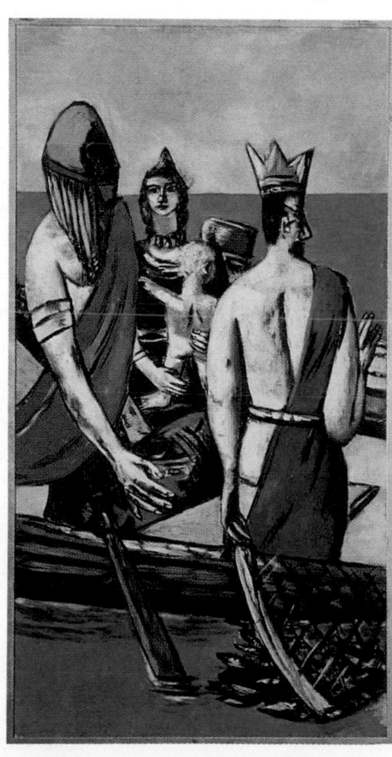

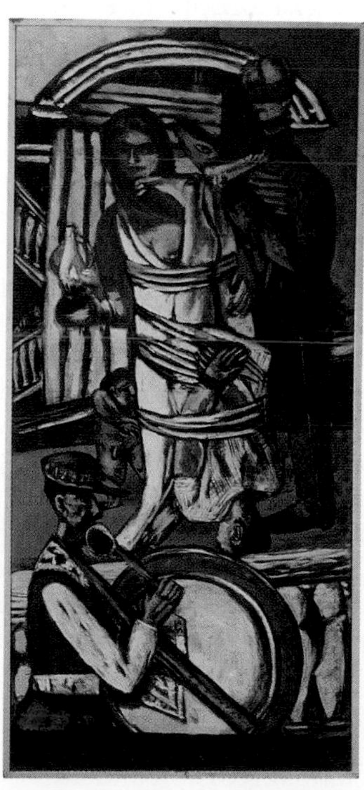

themes and the powerful tension he created between objects and space in his paintings. He used the three panels of *Departure* in the same way a filmmaker might use *jump cuts* to move between scenes that lack clear transitions. The side panels in the painting show bondage and torture. On the left, victims are mutilated by their tormenter; on the right, captive figures are helplessly bound together in a mysterious rite overseen by a blindfolded attendant, while a laconic figure passes by in the foreground, beating a bass drum. These side panels are claustrophobic; the space is crammed with figures, walls, curtains, balustrades, and other objects. The central panel is more tranquil, with a still sea, empty sky, and mysterious boat carrying the richly symbolic figures of a fisher-king, a hooded oarsman, and a queenly woman hugging a child close to her. The meaning may allude to Beckmann's own flight from Nazi Germany after his work (along with that of most of the German Expressionists and other avant-garde German artists) had been condemned and banned by Hitler as "degenerate." However, the power of *Departure* lies not so much in any moving personal references as in its expression of universals in the human condition.

Dada and the Surreal

The dark visions of the Expressionists were one kind of response to the disintegration of society in the early twentieth century. Other artists followed a different path, traveling into the worlds of anti-logic and psychologically provocative dreams, hoping by these means to shake people loose from habits of traditional thought, which were now seen as part of a decadent past that had produced a great war, widespread suffering, and the destruction of the human spirit. These artists were engaged in what they saw as a battle to help people relearn how to operate as whole and natural beings, with integrated bodies, psyches, and minds. Two major groups of these artists, the Dadaists and the Surrealists, developed at the end of the second decade of the century.

The Dadaists undertook the project of reform by way of protest, turning the conventions of art upside down and presenting performances, publications, and exhibitions filled with content intended to shock viewers by its outrageous lack of conventional meaning. Dadaists attained their artistic goals by using a variety of improvisational methods designed to disrupt reason and engage the full resources of intuition in the making of art. Among these processes were the use of nontraditional techniques (like making rubbings of wood textures) and the playful use of commonplace materials never before used in high art. The exuberant aggression and anti-esthetic activity of the Dadaists, however, only sustained their sharp spirit for a short time; after that, most of the Dada group's practitioners were absorbed into the Surrealist movement and its determined exploration of ways to express in art the world of dreams and the unconscious. The Surrealists borrowed many of the improvisational techniques of the Dadaists, believing these to be important methods for engaging the elements of fantasy and activating the unconscious forces that lie deep within every human being. But the Surrealists also drew inspiration from the great masters of fantastic art in the past (such as Bosch and Redon) and from a select group of individuals in the early twentieth century who were seen as powerful precursors for the Surrealist enterprise.

The Dada movement began independently in both New York and Zurich during the years of World War I and soon spread throughout Europe. It was more a mind-set than a single identifiable style; wherever it arose, its artists were committed to questioning everything about traditional artistic expression, in large part as an attempt to jolt the bourgeois art audience out of the complacent behavior and beliefs that had led to the madness of World War I. Much Dada work was intentionally ephemeral. Yet it had important consequences for later art—reinforcing a tendency toward a spontaneous, intuitive expression of the whimsical, fantastic, humorous, sardonic, and absurd. A whole new realm of artistic possibility opened, in which the remnants of the optical world, shattered by scientific and compositional analysis, emerged to play expressive new roles determined by the different contexts in which they now were found. The artist's free imagination drew on materials lying deep within human consciousness, and the artistic act of expression became the proclamation of new realities that were no less real because they were psychic. Dada work paralleled the psychoanalytic views of Sigmund Freud, Carl Jung, and others, and Dada artists believed that art was a powerfully practical means of self-revelation and catharsis, and that the images that arose out of the subconscious mind had a truth of their own, independent of the world of conventional vision. The attitude of the European Dadaists was summed up by Hans Richter, a Dada filmmaker:

> Possessed, as we were, of the ability to entrust ourselves to "chance," to our conscious as well as our unconscious minds, we became a sort of public secret society. . . . We laughed at everything. . . . But laughter was only the *expression* of our new discoveries, not their essence and not their purpose. Pandemonium, destruction, anarchy, anti-everything—why should we hold it in check? What of the pandemonium, destruction, anarchy, anti-everything of the

World War? How could Dada have been anything but destructive, aggressive, insolent, on principle and with gusto?*

Perhaps the most influential of all the Dadaists, and somewhat independent from them, was MARCEL DUCHAMP (1887–1968), the central artist of New York Dada and an active figure in Paris at the end of the Dada movement. Raised as a member of an artistic Parisian family (an older brother was a painter and a younger brother, a sculptor), Duchamp made an early reputation for expressive paintings before becoming fascinated simultaneously with the world of ideas (including a topsy-turvy pseudophysics called "pataphysics") and that of machines and their representation in the language of mechanical drawing. Soon he was producing paintings in which figures were rendered as mechanized forms. In 1913, he exhibited his first readymade sculptures, mass-produced objects selected by the artist and sometimes "rectified" by modification of their substance or combination with another object. *Bicycle Wheel* (FIG. **22-25**) was Duchamp's first readymade and initiated his interest in exploring the optical effects of motion in art. In *Bicycle Wheel,* he combined two ordinary mass-produced objects and displaced them from their expected, everyday locations by mounting a single bicycle wheel atop the seat of an ordinary wooden kitchen stool. Such works, he insisted, were created free from any consideration of either good or bad taste, qualities shaped by a society that he and other Dada artists found esthetically bankrupt. In place of "taste," Duchamp gave ideas. As he wrote in a "defense" published in 1917, after the exhibition committee for an unjuried show failed to exhibit his readymade *Fountain* (a detached urinal, set on its side and signed visibly with a witty pseudonym derived from the Mott plumbing manufactory's name and that of the short half of the *Mutt and Jeff* comic-strip team): "Whether Mr. Mutt with his own hands made the fountain or not has no importance. He *chose* it. He took an ordinary article of life, placed it so that its useful significance disappeared under the new title and point of view—created a new thought for that object."† Among the ideas in *Bicycle Wheel* are those connected with optical illusion and with motion (separated from usefulness). Spinning the wheel introduces the viewer to the visual illusions of strobing spokes, which seem to rotate forward or backward, or even to disappear completely into a shimmering blur, depending on the speed of rotation. Duchamp's interest in motion first appeared early in his career in diagrammatic paintings, partially inspired by the multiple-exposure, motion-study photographs of the French nineteenth-century kinesiologist Édouard Marey. Duchamp explored this interest in paintings, cinema, and various experiments in optical illusion throughout the rest of his career.

*Hans Richter, *Dada: Art and Anti-Art* (London: Thames & Hudson, 1961), pp. 64–65.

†In Arturo Schwarz, *The Complete Works of Marcel Duchamp* (London: Thames & Hudson, 1965), p. 466.

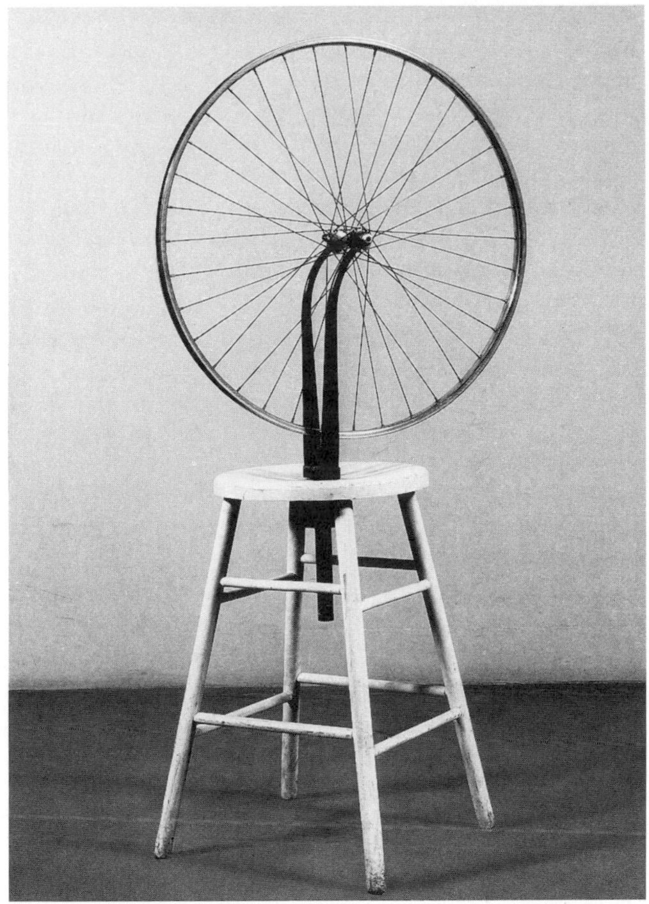

22-25 MARCEL DUCHAMP, *Bicycle Wheel,* 1951 (third version after lost original of 1913). Metal wheel mounted on painted wooden stool, 50½" high, 25½" wide; stool, 23¾" high. Collection, The Museum of Modern Art, New York (gift of the Sidney and Harriet Janis Collection).

Many of Duchamp's ideas appeared in a large, two-panel painting on glass, *The Bride Stripped Bare by Her Bachelors, Even* (FIG. **22-26**), whose complex iconography he began developing as early as 1912. Intrigued by the suggestion of space with four and more dimensions in the work of mathematician Edward Abbey, Duchamp chose to paint on glass because he felt the shapes he created there in rigorous Renaissance perspective would appear to float free of their support, suggesting "the projection of a four-dimensional shape in a three-dimensional world." Unlike traditional diptychs, the two panels in this painting are placed one above the other. Each plate of

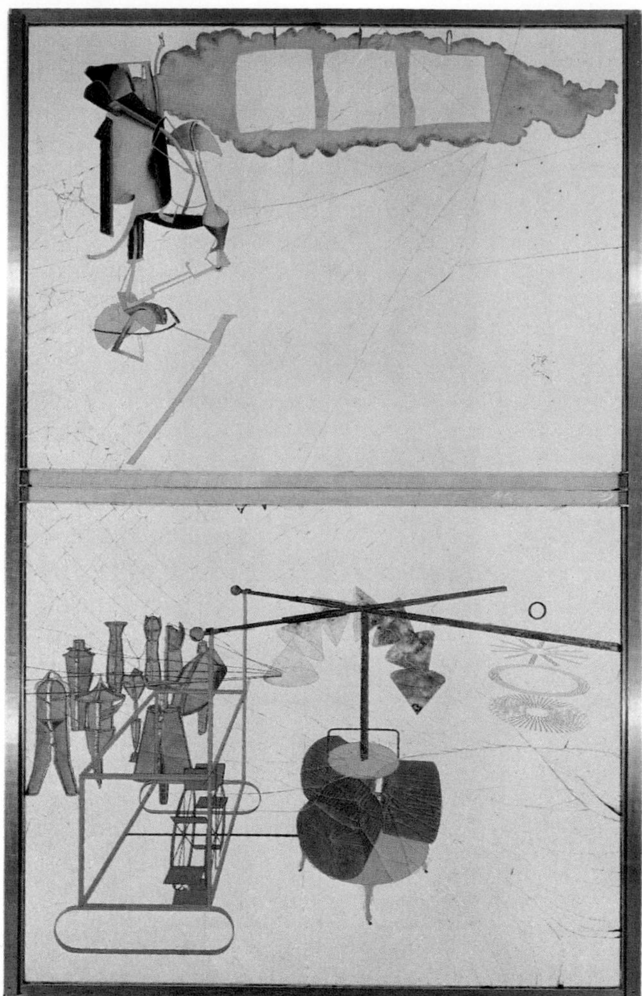

22-26 MARCEL DUCHAMP, *The Bride Stripped Bare by Her Bachelors, Even (The Large Glass)*, 1915–1923. Oil, lead wire, foil, dust and varnish on glass, 8′ 11″ × 5′ 7″. The Philadelphia Museum of Art (bequest of Katherine S. Dreier).

glass represents a separate realm. The artist's fascination with machines led him to invent a symbolism based on mechanical forms. The upper plate of glass contains the region of the bride, whose mechanized form is seen at the far left. Next to her is a cloud shape—the "Milky Way"—designated by Duchamp as the place of "blossoming." The bottom plate of glass contains the realm of the bachelors, represented at the left in a circle of nine "malic molds," whose shapes were based on the silhouettes of uniformed Frenchmen—among them a policeman, a bellboy, and a messenger. An admirer of the wacky machines devised by the American cartoonist Rube Goldberg, Duchamp here imagined an elaborate setup by which the bachelors could attempt to disrobe the bride. At the same time, however, the artist also introduced elements that would forever prevent that desired consummation. Duchamp made careful studies for each section of the composition, but he also employed methods of chance to determine many details. For example, the shapes of the "draft pistons" within the area of blossoming at the top were determined by having Duchamp's friend, the American artist Man Ray, take three photographs of a meter-square piece of dotted net fabric as it blew in the breeze coming through an open window. The three different contours determined the shapes of the three "openings" in the cloud, and the double meaning for "draft" (work and breeze) is a good example of the verbal puns Duchamp loved to include in his work. He found the operation of chance so intriguing that he even employed it in some of the innovative techniques with which he applied color to the glass. The most unusual of these probably occurred in the series of multiple cones (or "sieves") in the lower half, which were created by allowing dust to accumulate on the surface of the glass for several weeks and then using varnish to fix the dust in place, creating a translucent, mottled, warm brown hue within these shapes.*

According to Duchamp (and the generations of artists after him who were profoundly influenced by his art and especially by his attitude), life and art were matters of chance and choice freed from the conventions of society and tradition. Within his approach to art and life, each act was individual and unique: every person's choice of found objects would be different, each person's throw of dice would be at a different instant and probably would yield a different number. This philosophy of utter freedom for the artist is fundamental to the history of art in the twentieth century. In addition, the viewer of a Duchamp work must decipher the meaning of the work in a way that makes the experience an intellectual exercise that yields different and continually shifting "meanings" for each individual. All of these factors cause Duchamp's influence to continue to be as strong for much Postmodernist art late in the twentieth century as it was for much of Modernism.

Duchamp spent much of World War I in New York, inspiring a group of American artists and collectors with his radical rethinking of the role of the artist and of the nature of art. By 1916, another group of young

*Although Duchamp worked on painting the glass panels intermittently between 1915 and 1925, he had not added all planned details when the work was returned damaged to his studio after an exhibition. Regarding the pattern of diagonal cracks with some satisfaction, he declared the piece "incompleted" and did no further work on it. We know his intentions from voluminous notes he made for the painting (nicknamed "The Large Glass"), which he published in facsimile in two special "boxes," and we know the planned look of the final composition from a diagrammatic etching the artist made late in his career.

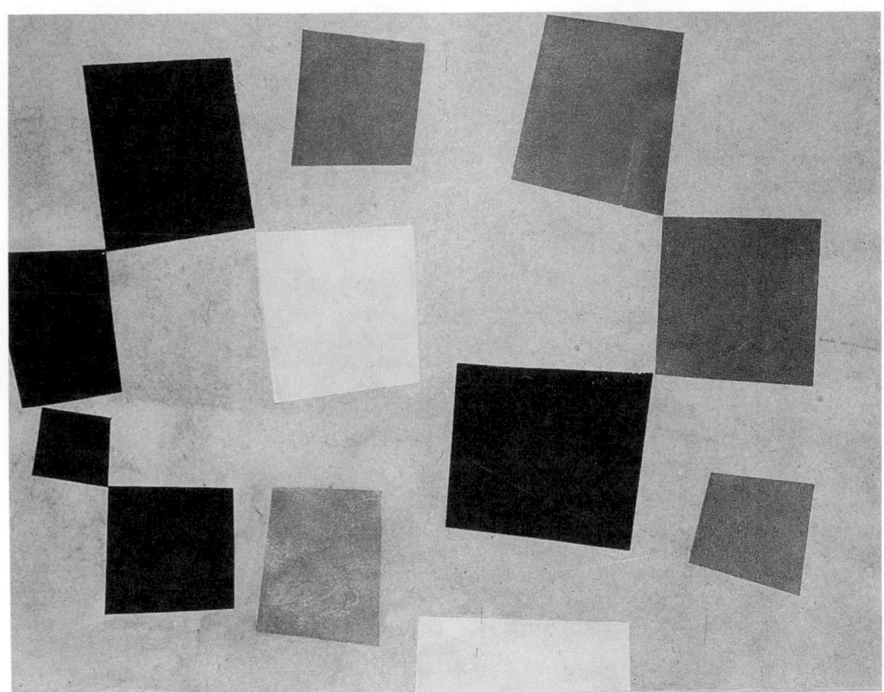

22-27 JEAN ARP, *Squares Arranged According to the Laws of Chance,* 1917. Cut-and-pasted papers, ink, and bronze paint, 13⅛" × 10¼". Collection, The Museum of Modern Art, New York (gift of Philip Johnson).

European artists had gathered in neutral Zurich, filled with a similar but more boisterous reaction against the norms of the society of their day. Collectively (and idealistically), this European group set out to use their art as a weapon to shock viewers into self-awareness and to stimulate action that would change civilization into something better. They called their anti-art "Dada" (a name made up of nonsense syllables) and themselves "Dadaists." They challenged people in their gathering place, the Cabaret Voltaire, through aggressive performances based on provocative insults, nonsense speeches, and a variety of outlandish pranks or *gestes,* which they described as "cerebral revolver shots." As one of the Zurich group, Hans Richter, later wrote: "Dada invited, or rather defied, the world to misunderstand it, and fostered every kind of confusion. . . . Dada has reaped the harvest of confusion that it sowed. However the confusion was only a façade. Our provocations, demonstrations, and defiances were only a means of arousing the bourgeoisie to rage and through rage to shame-faced self-awareness."* Like Duchamp, the Zurich Dadaists sought ways to stop relying on the operation of reason, which they saw as conditioned by upbringing and education. Many of their methods involved either "automatism" or the operations of chance.

*Richter, *Dada: Art and Anti-Art,* p. 9.

Automatism was the process of yielding oneself to instinctive actions after establishing a set of conditions (such as size of paper and medium), within which a work would be carried out. One of the Zurich Dadaists, JEAN (HANS) ARP (1887–1966), specialized in automatic drawings made in a two-step process that he began by letting his pencil wander over a sheet of paper with as little intellectual control as possible. Then he scrutinized the patterns made for shapes that seemed to have significance to him and filled those contours with ink to create a final design. Arp also was a leader in the use of chance in the making of art. Tiring of the look of some Cubist-related collages he was making at the time, he took sheets of paper, tore them into roughly shaped squares, haphazardly dropped them to a sheet of paper on the floor, and glued them into the arrangement that resulted. *Squares Arranged According to the Laws of Chance* (FIG. **22-27**) is such an art work; the rectilinearity of the shapes guaranteed a somewhat regular design, but chance had introduced an imbalance that seemed to Arp to restore to his work a special mysterious vitality that he wanted to preserve. The operations of "chance" were for the Dadaists a crucial part of this kind of improvisation. As Richter stated: "For us chance was the 'unconscious mind' that Freud had discovered in 1900. . . . Adoption of chance had another purpose, a secret one. This was to restore to the work of art its primeval magic power and to find a way back to the immediacy it had lost through contact with . . . classicism."*

From Zurich, Dada spread throughout much of Western Europe, arriving as early as 1917 in Berlin, where it soon took on an activist political edge, partially in response to the economic, social, and political chaos in that city in the years at the end of and immediately after World War I. The Berlin Dadaists developed to a new intensity a technique used earlier in popular art postcards. Pasting parts from many pictures together into one image, the Berliners christened their version of the technique *photomontage.* Unlike Cubist collage, the parts of a Dada collage were made almost entirely of "found" details, usually combined into deliberately anti-logical compositions. The collage technique allowed Dada artists in Berlin to make the realm of the machine their own. One of the technique's originators was HANNAH HÖCH (1889–1979), who wrote: "Our whole purpose was to integrate objects from the world of machines and industry in the world of art. . . . In an imaginative composition, we used to bring together elements borrowed from books, newspapers, posters, or leaflets, in an arrangement that no machine could yet compose."† *Cut With The Kitchen Knife* (FIG. **22-28**) illustrates Höch's approach to the chaotic, kaleidoscopic effect of much of the Berlin Dada work made in this medium. Her title makes ironic reference to the pretensions of the social scene during the Weimar period immediately following World War I. Words and images from clearly disparate sources are tumbled together in an energetic composition in which one section or another claims our attention fleetingly as our eyes dart to and fro. The difference in scale between large heads and tiny figures evokes the sense of moving backward and forward in space. Details embedded within the densely packed lower left and upper right sections merge into strange dreamlike visions that seem to combine moments across time, much as a series of quick cuts between different scenes does in a movie, suggesting the kind of cinematic montage that Sergei Eisenstein began creating in the early 1920s (see page 1020). In a different way, the collaged details within the largest head at the upper left suggest a psychological condition. The effect is disconcerting and confusing—Höch's version of the Dada attempt to shock viewers out of complacent reliance on familiar ways of seeing and into a new and active engagement with the image. Höch's friend and fellow Dadaist, Raoul Hausmann, defined their work as "a new dimension: the 'alienation' of photography." He maintained that "the Dadaists . . . were the first

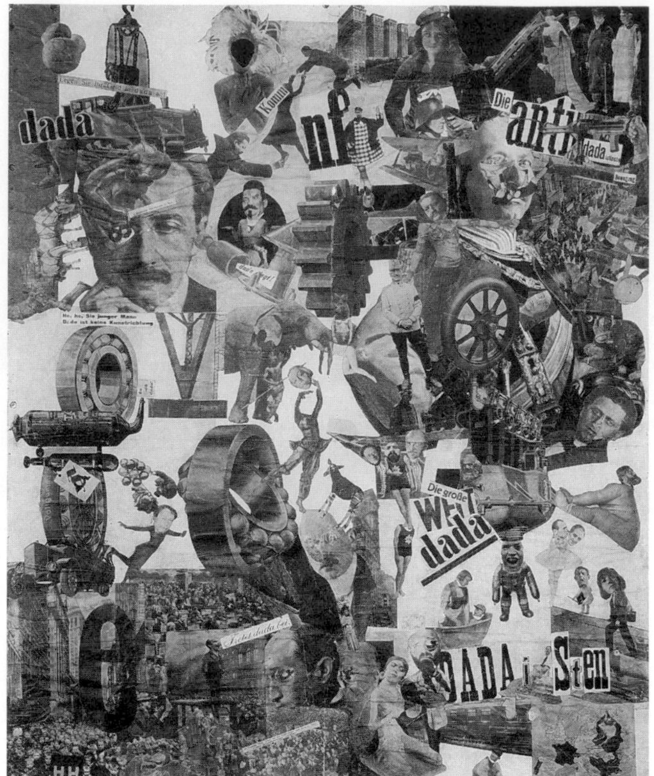

22-28 HANNAH HÖCH, *Schnitt mit dem Küchenmesser Dada durch die erste Weimarer Bierbauchkulturepoche Deutchlands (Cut With The Kitchen Knife Through The Last Weimar Beer Belly Cultural Epoch),* 1919. Staatliche Museen Preussbischer Kulturbesitz, Nationalgalerie, Berlin.

to use photography to create, from often totally disparate spatial and material elements, a new unity in which was revealed a visually and conceptually *new* image of the chaos of an age of war and revolution."‡

The technique of creating a composition by pasting together pieces of paper had been used in private and popular arts long before the twentieth century. In the early decades of this century, the process was named "collage" by the Cubists (see page 963). Collage lent itself well to the Dada desire to use chance in the creation of art and anti-art, but not all Dada collage was as savagely aggressive as that of the Berlin photomontagists. The Hanover Dada artist KURT SCHWITTERS (1887–1948) followed a gentler muse. Inspired by Cubist collage, but working in a nonobjective way, Schwitters found visual poetry in the cast-off junk of modern society and scavenged in trash bins for materials, which he pasted and nailed together into designs like *Merz 19* (FIG. **22-29**). He borrowed the term *merz* from a word fragment in one of his collages (part of *kommerz,* "commerce"). His compositions are nonobjective, yet they still resonate with the "meaning" of the fragmented found objects

*Ibid., p. 57.

†In Chipp, ed., *Theories of Modern Art,* p. 396.

‡In Richter, *Dada: Art and Anti-Art,* p. 116.

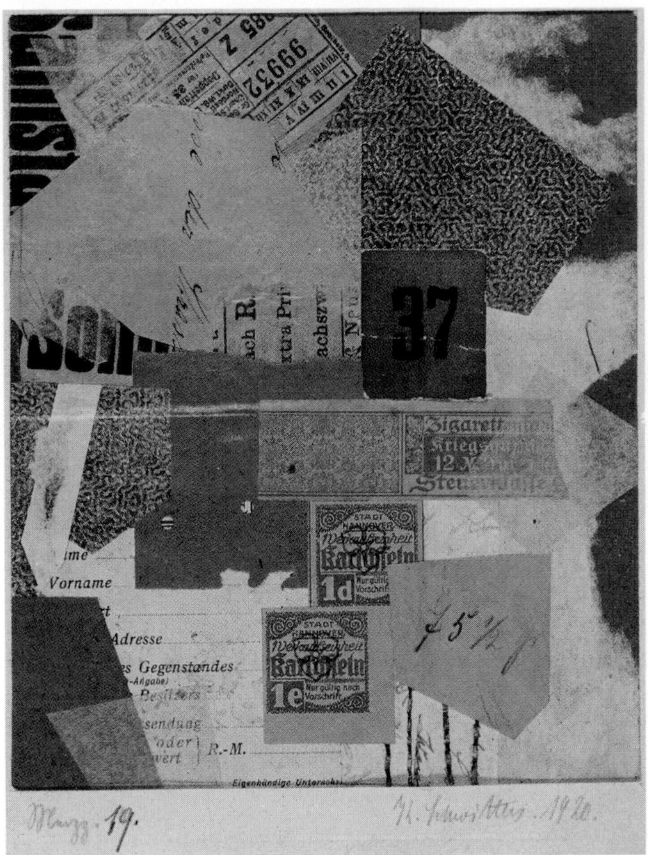

22-29 KURT SCHWITTERS, *Merz 19,* 1920. Paper collage, approx. $7\frac{1}{4}'' \times 5\frac{7}{8}''$. Yale University Art Gallery, New Haven, Connecticut (collection, Société Anonyme).

they contain. Like the readymades of Duchamp and the photomontage cutouts of Höch, the recycled elements of Schwitter's collages are invested with new meanings through their new uses and locations.

The American artist MAN RAY (1890–1976), who worked closely with Duchamp during the teens and twenties, incorporated readymades into many of his paintings, sculptures, movies, and photographs. Trained as an architectural draftsman and engineer, Man Ray earned his living as a graphic designer and portrait photographer, and brought to his personal work an interest in mass-produced objects and technology and a committed dedication to exploring the psychological realm through which we perceive the exterior world. Like Höch and Schwitters, Man Ray used chance and the dislocation of ordinary things from their everyday settings to surprise his viewers into new awareness. His displacement of found objects was particularly mysterious in works like *Rayograph* (FIG. **22-30**), made with a variant of the photogenic-drawing technique invented by Talbot (FIG. 21-35), and renamed by Man Ray after himself.* In the darkroom, Man Ray assembled a collection of objects on a sheet of photosensitive paper and then exposed the composition to light. He created a range of grey and white tones by turning off the light, removing some of the objects, and re-exposing the composition to light. The ghostly white silhouettes of the shapes lend each object an eerie presence, transforming them into participants in a strange, chaotic performance in which they appear to float freely against and within a void of darkened space. The improvisational Dada method here produces an evocative abstract fantasy that prophesies Man Ray's later practice of Surrealism.

The Dadaists were not alone in trying to subvert traditional art forms in the early years of the twentieth century. They found a kindred spirit in the work of the Greco-Italian painter GIORGIO DE CHIRICO (1888–1978), whose emphatically ambiguous works also make him a precursor of Surrealism. De Chirico's paintings of cityscapes and shop windows were part of a movement called Metaphysical Painting. As the son of a railroad engineer, his childhood was flavored by the continual arrival and departure of his father's trains. Returning to Italy after study in Munich, De Chirico found inspiration in the writings of Friedrich Nietzsche, who saw hidden reality revealed through

*Most other twentieth-century artists who practiced this technique called the works made in this way *photograms*.

22-30 MAN RAY, *Rayograph,* 1923. Camera-less image on light-sensitive paper. Collection, The Museum of Modern Art, New York.

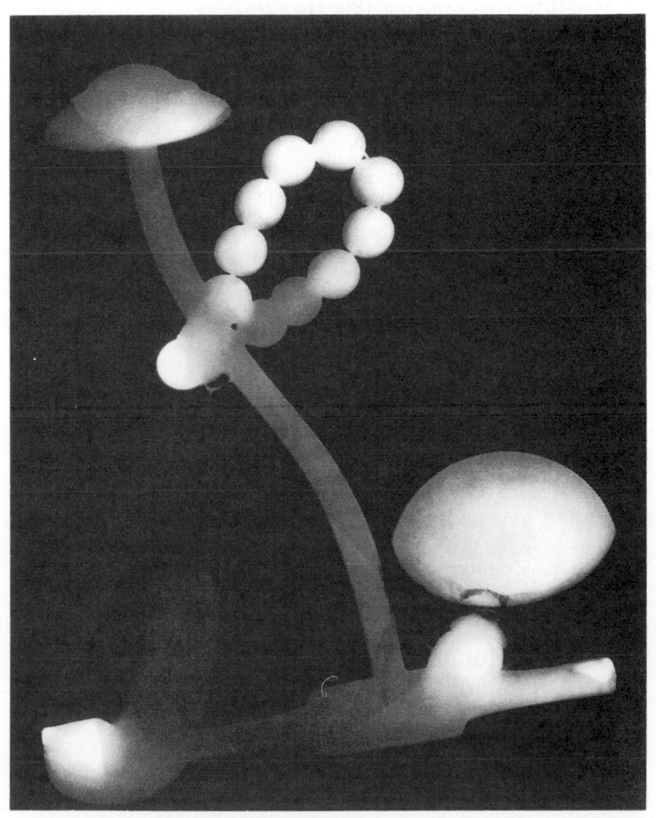

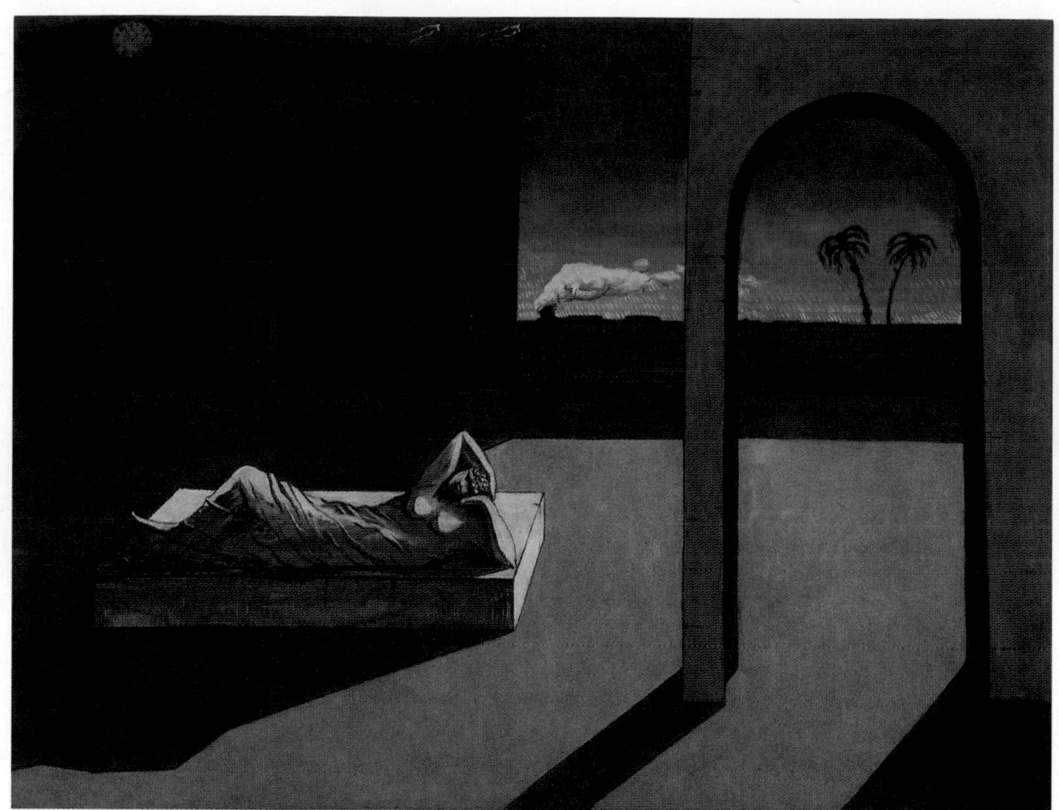

22-31 Giorgio de Chirico, *The Soothsayer's Recompense,* 1913. $53\frac{3}{8}'' \times 71''$. Philadelphia Museum of Art (The Louise and Walter Arensberg Collection).

strange juxtapositions, like those seen on late autumn afternoons in the city of Turin, when its vast open squares and silent public monuments were transformed by the long shadows of the setting sun into "the most metaphysical of Italian towns." De Chirico translated this vision into paint in works like *The Soothsayer's Recompense* (FIG. **22-31**), where the squares and palaces of Roman and Renaissance Italy are visualized in a mood of intense and mysterious melancholy. A strangely displaced reality is evoked by the clock, the distant train, the blank sky, the tilted perspective, the blank façade broken by a yawning arcade, and the empty piazza with its mysteriously alive sculpture and slanting shadows. This image is a perfect illustration of the world of Metaphysical Painting (*pittura metafisica*), which De Chirico described:

> In the construction of cities, in the architectural forms of houses, in squares and gardens and public walks, in gateways and railway stations . . . are contained the initial foundations of a great metaphysical aesthetic. . . . We who know the signs of the metaphysical alphabet are aware of the joy and the solitude enclosed by a portico, the corner of a street, or even in a room, on the surface of a table, between the sides of a box. The limits of these signs constitute for us a sort of moral and aesthetic code of representation, and more than this, with clairvoyance we construct in painting a new metaphysical psychology of objects.*

De Chirico's paintings were reproduced in periodicals almost as soon as he completed them, and his works quickly influenced artists outside Italy, including both the Dadaists and Surrealists. The disjunctive reality in his work intrigued the Dadaists, while the eerie mood and visionary quality of paintings like *The Soothsayer's Recompense* excited and influenced those Surrealist artists who sought to portray the world of dreams.

The Surrealists found similar hallucinatory magic in the strangely disconcerting photographs of Paris and its environs made by the French artist Jean Eugène Auguste Atget (1856–1927). Atget earned a precarious living as a photographer, having set for himself the goal of recording on film everything in Paris or its suburbs that was artistic or "picturesque." He was especially eager to photograph buildings slated for demolition to make way for more modern structures. Each day he set out early in the morning with a large view camera to capture subjects before

*In Massimo Carrá, Ewald Rathke, Caroline Tisdall, and Patrick Waldberg, *Metaphysical Art* (New York: Praeger, 1971), p. 90.

many people were in the streets. Even his most straightforward shot of a Paris street or a corner of the garden at Versailles often had an aura of mysterious life. His gift for seeing strangeness in the everyday, however, was most clearly expressed in pictures of shop windows, like that of *Avenue des Gobelins* (FIG. **22-32**). In such pictures, the everyday banality of ordinary objects is transformed into a dreamlike reality. The viewer is transported into an unusual world where store mannequins seem to be participating in some strange ritual and objects merge with the fuzzy reflections of distant buildings and trees. Atget's almost metaphysical photographs of Parisian shop windows, buildings, and gardens were known only to a few Parisian artists until the 1920s, when they were discovered by Man Ray and soon after praised by the Surrealists as the work of a genuine kindred spirit who believed in the world of dreams as strongly as they did themselves.

The Surrealists' interest in the world of dreams led them also to admire the work of the early twentieth-century French filmmaker GEORGES MÉLIÈS (1861–1938). The world of the cinema is, in many ways, by nature, a world of dreams in which viewers participate only if they mentally leave their seats in a darkened hall to experience the "reality" on the screen. Interested in drawing, theater, and the miraculous from earliest childhood, Méliès's first career as an adult was as a magician in a theater that he owned. Seeing the earliest films shown in Paris in 1895, he decided to employ films to create wonderful new illusions, using persistence of vision and the successive frames of film as units in a time-collage. In films, as in dreams, objects could appear and disappear in the flash of an eye, and one thing could change quickly into another. Fantasy sequences filled his movies. *A Trip to the Moon* (FIG. **22-33**) was inspired by the science-fiction stories of Jules Verne and H. G. Wells. This film begins plausibly enough with the launching of a rocket to the moon. From that point on, however, the filmmaker gave his imagination full play, and his space travelers find the alien lunar environment populated with hybrid creatures and other strange things that behave in enchantingly nonlogical ways. In his pioneering work on Surrealist cinema, Ado Kyrou credited Méliès with having achieved in his films "the perfect mixture of reality dreamed and dreams made real."* Méliès's filmic imaginings provided the base on which full Surrealist cinema was built.

22-32 JEAN EUGÈNE AUGUSTE ATGET, *Avenue des Gobelins*, Paris, 1925. Albumen silver print, $8\frac{1}{4}'' \times 9\frac{9}{16}''$. Collection, The Museum of Modern Art, New York (Abbott-Levy Collection. Partial gift of Shirley C. Burden).

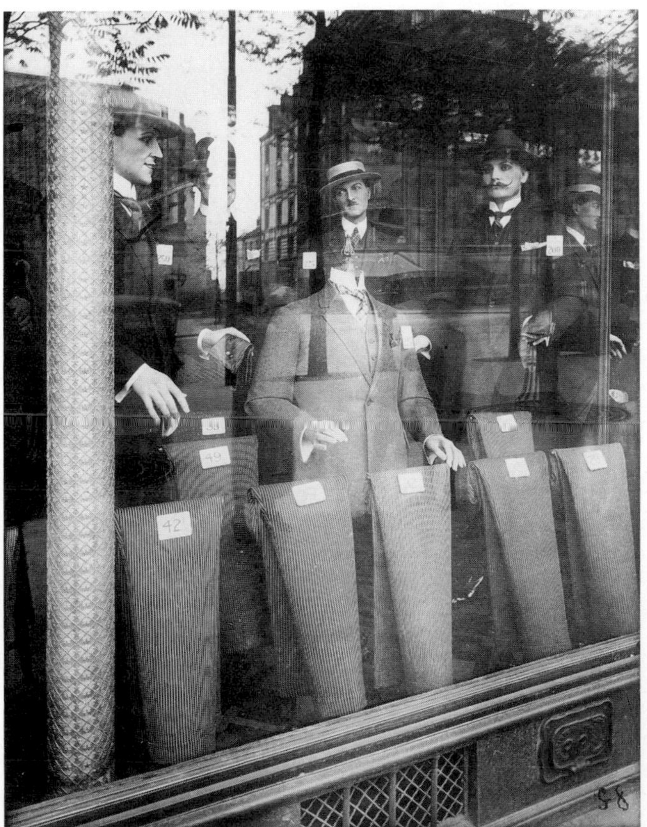

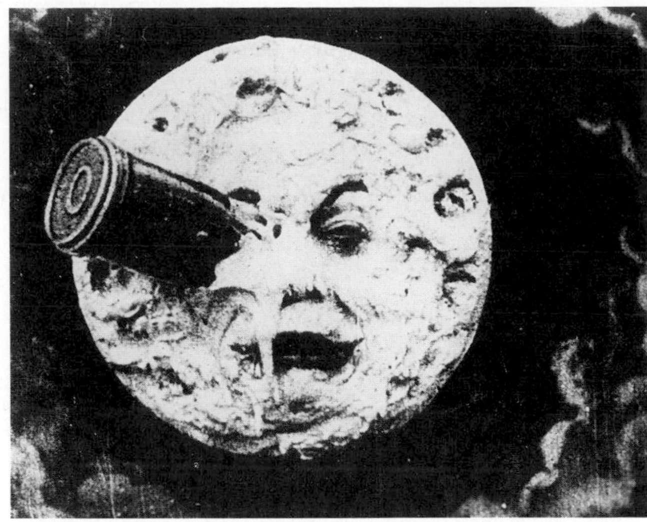

22-33 GEORGES MÉLIÈS, film still from *A Trip to the Moon*, 1902.

By 1924, much of the spirit of Dada had faded, and the energies of many of its adherents were turned toward the new movement of Surrealism. The Surrealists were determined to explore the inner world of the psyche, the realm of fantasy and the unconscious. Inspired in part by the ideas of the psychoanalysts Carl Jung and Sigmund Freud, the Surrealists were especially interested in the nature of dreams. They

*Ado Kyrou, *Le surréalisme au cinéma* (Paris: Le Terrain Vague, 1963), p. 66.

viewed dreams as occurring at the level at which all human consciousness connects and as constituting the arena in which people could move beyond the constricting forces of their environment to re-engage with the deeper selves that society had long suppressed. In 1924, these Surrealist beliefs were presented in the form of a dictionary definition of Surrealism formulated by one of its leading thinkers, the young Parisian writer André Breton:

> Pure psychic automatism, by which one intends to express verbally, in writing, or by any other method, the real functioning of the mind. Dictation by thought, in the absence of any control exercised by reason, and beyond any aesthetic or moral preoccupation. . . . Surrealism is based on the belief in the superior reality of certain forms of association heretofore neglected, in the omnipotence of dreams, in the undirected play of thought. . . . I believe in the future resolution of the states of dream and reality, in appearance so contradictory, in a sort of absolute reality, or surreality.*

Thus, the dominant motivation of Surrealist art was to bring the aspects of outer and inner "reality" together into a single position, in much the same way that seemingly unrelated fragments of life combine in the vivid world of dreams. The projection in visible form of this new conception required new techniques of pictorial construction. The Surrealists adapted some Dadaist devices and invented new techniques like automatic writing and various types of planned "accidents" not so much to reveal a world without meaning as to provoke reactions closely related to subconscious experience.

Originally a Dada activist in Cologne, MAX ERNST (1891–1976) became one of the early adherents of the Surrealist circle surrounding André Breton. As a child living in a small community near Cologne, Germany, Ernst had found his existence to be fantastic and filled with marvels. In autobiographical notes, written mostly in the third person, he said of his birth: "Max Ernst had his first contact with the world of sense on the 2nd April 1891 at 9:45 A.M., when he emerged from the egg which his mother had laid in an eagle's nest and which the bird had incubated for seven years." Early success as an Expressionist was swept away by Ernst's service in the German army during World War I; in his own words:

> Max Ernst died on 1st August 1914. He returned to life on 11th November 1918, a young man who wanted to become a magician and find the central myth of his age. From time to time he consulted the eagle which had guarded the egg of his prenatal existence. The bird's advice can be detected in his work."†

Beginning in 1918, as a Dadaist in Cologne, Ernst explored every means to achieve the sense of the psychic in his art. Like other Dadaists, he set out to incorporate chance and found objects into his works. Using a process called *frottage,* he created some works by combining the patterns achieved by rubbing a crayon or another medium across a sheet of paper that was placed over a surface with a strong and evocative texture pattern. In other works, he joined fragments of images he had cut from old books, magazines, and prints to form one hallucinatory collage.

Ernst soon began making paintings that shared the mysterious dreamlike effect of his collages. In the early 1920s, his works brought him into contact with Breton, who instantly recognized Ernst's affinity with the Surrealist group. Many of the creative bases of Surrealism (the chance association of things and events, the dislocation of images and meanings, the scrambling of conventional contexts, the exploration of the subconscious, and the radical freedom of artistic choice) are manifest in Ernst's *Two Children Are Threatened by a Nightingale* (FIG. **22-34**). In this work,

*In William S. Rubin, *Dada, Surrealism, and Their Heritage* (New York: Museum of Modern Art, 1968), p. 64.

†Richter, *Dada: Art and Anti-Art,* pp. 155, 159.

22-34 MAX ERNST, *Two Children Are Threatened by a Nightingale,* 1924. Oil on wood with wood construction, $27\frac{1}{2}''$ high, $22\frac{1}{2}''$ wide, $4\frac{1}{2}''$ deep. Collection, The Museum of Modern Art, New York (purchase).

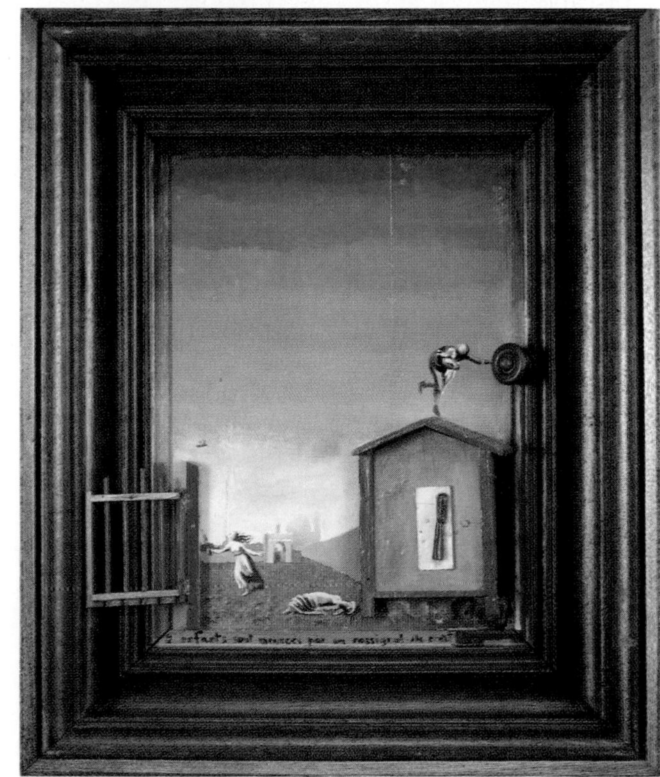

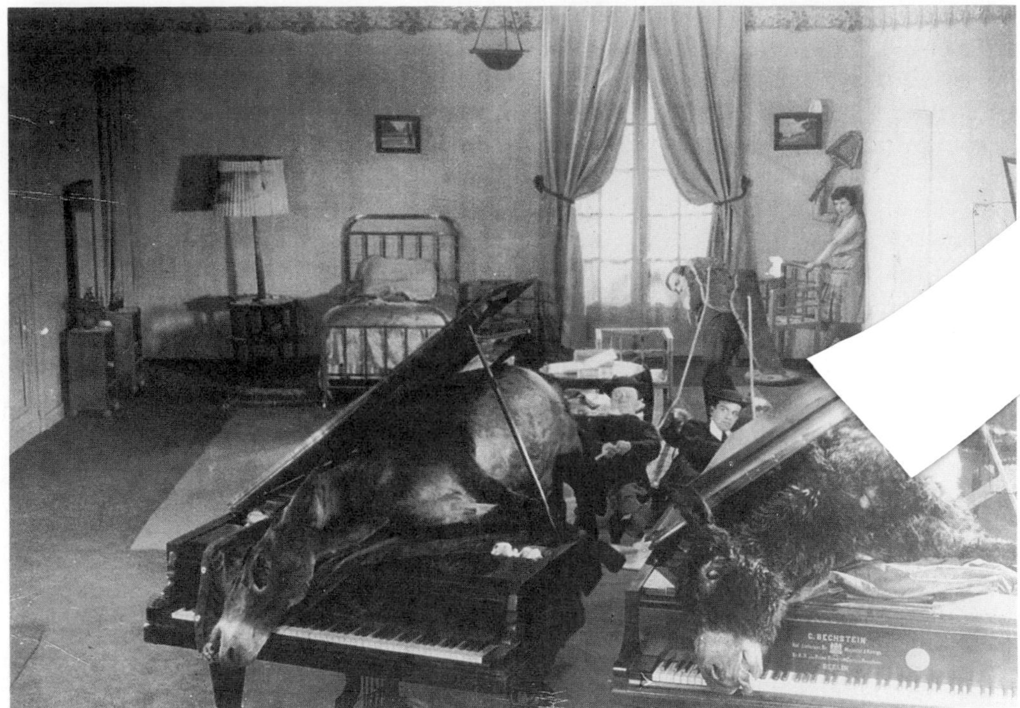

22-35 SALVADOR DALI and LUIS BUÑUEL, film still from *Un Chien Andalou*, 1929.

Ernst displayed a private dream, which challenged the post-Renaissance idea that a painting should resemble a window looking into a "real" scene that is rendered illusionistically three-dimensional through the use of mathematical perspective. In this work, the landscape, the distant city, and the tiny flying bird are traditionally painted; the artist followed all of the established rules of aerial and linear perspective. The three sketchily rendered figures, however, clearly belong to a world of dreams, and the literally three-dimensional miniature gate, the odd button-knob, and the strange, closed building "violate" the space of the bulky frame. Additional dislocation occurs in the traditional museum identification label, which has been displaced into a cutaway part of the frame. Handwritten, it announces the title of the work (taken from a poem written by Ernst before this work was painted), adding another note of irrational mystery. Like the title of many Surrealist works, that of *Two Children* is ambiguous and has an uneasy relation to what the spectator sees. The viewer must struggle to decipher connections between image and words. When Surrealists (and Dadaists and Metaphysical artists before them) used such titles, they intended for the seeming contradiction between title and picture to act like a "blow to the mind," knocking the spectator off balance, with all expectations challenged. Much of the impact of Surrealist works like this begins with the viewer's sudden awareness of the incongruous and the absurd in what is pictured.

Surrealist fantasy found some of its most haunting expression in cinema, and one of the most powerful Surrealist films is *Un Chien Andalou* (*An Andalusian Dog*, FIG. **22-35**), made in 1929 by the Spanish painter SALVADOR DALI (1904–1989) and the filmmaker LUIS BUÑUEL (1900–1983). The pair deliberately set out to write a movie script that would have no trace of rational order or expected meaning. From the initial shocking scene, in which sight is cancelled by the slicing of an eyeball, through the illogical succession of psychologically suggestive episodes that follow, the viewer is displaced from one dreamlike moment to the next. In one of the most memorable segments, a man seeks a weapon to attack a woman. Looking behind him, his eyes light up triumphantly as he bends to pick up a rope. He starts forward and almost topples backward from the weight of the burden at the other end of the rope. He gathers all his energy, leans against the dragging load, and slowly moves forward again. The camera shifts and the viewer sees (in the words of the script): "a cork, then a melon, two Brothers from a parochial school, and last two magnificent grand pianos. The pianos are filled with the rotting corpses of donkeys whose hooves, tails, rumps, and excrement overflow. When one of the pianos passes the camera we see a big donkey head resting on the keyboard."* This jumble of things have

*In J. H. Matthews, *Surrealism and Film* (Ann Arbor: The University of Michigan Press, 1971), p. 87.

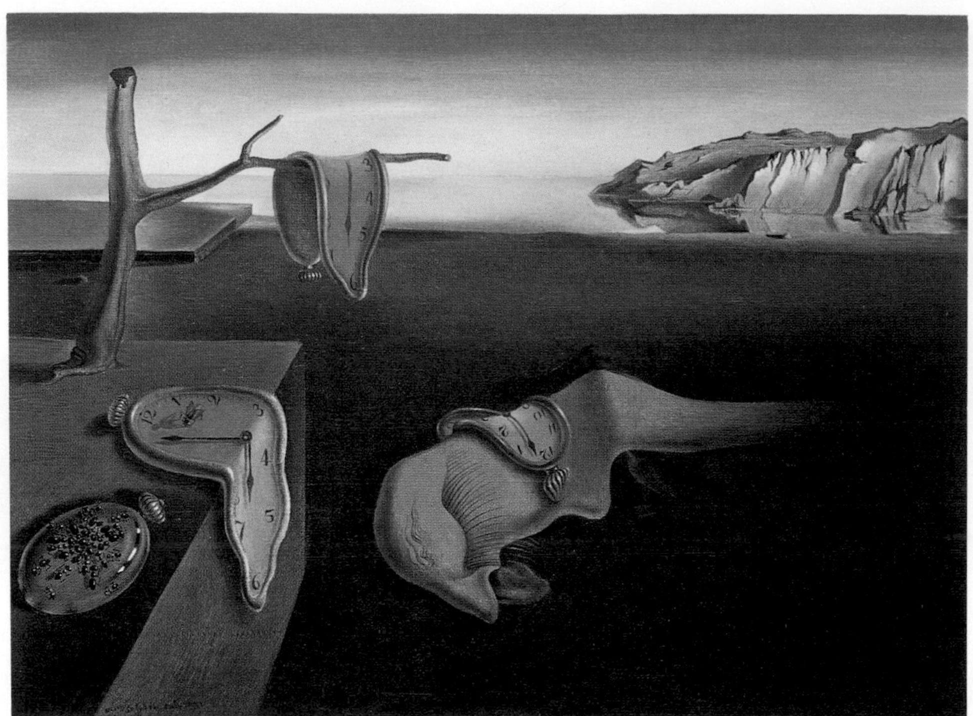

22-36 SALVADOR DALI, *The Persistence of Memory*, 1931. $9\frac{1}{2}'' \times 13''$. Collection, The Museum of Modern Art, New York (given anonymously).

no clear connection, no simple symbolism. Instead, their appearance and their behavior are the result of a pure Surrealist creative process, as Buñuel clearly stated in his "Notes on the Making of *Un Chien Andalou*":

> In *Un Chien Andalou*, . . . The plot is the result of a *conscious* psychic automatism, and, to that extent, it does not attempt to recount a dream, although it profits by a mechanism analogous to that of dreams. . . . Its aim is to provoke in the spectator instinctive reactions of attraction and of repulsion . . . . *nothing*, in the film, *symbolizes anything*. The only method of investigation of the symbols would be, perhaps, psychoanalysis.*

To critique the madness of modern society, Buñuel used Surrealist devices in his later films. Dali, already an established Surrealist painter, continued steadily to explore his own psyche and dreams in his paintings, sculptures, jewelry, and designs for furniture and movies. Dali also probed a deeply erotic dimension through his work, studying the writings of Freud and Richard von Krafft-Ebing and inventing what he called the "paranoiac-critical method" to assist his creative process. As he described it, his aim in painting was "to materialize the images of concrete irrationality with the most imperialist fury of precision . . . in order that the world of imagination and of concrete irrationality may be as objectively evident . . . as that of the exterior world of phenomenal reality."† All of these aspects of Dali's style can be seen in what is perhaps his most familiar work, *The Persistence of Memory* (FIG. **22-36**). Here, he creates a haunting allegory of empty space in which time is at an end. The barren landscape, without horizon, drifts to infinity, lit by some eerie, never-setting sun. An amorphous creature sleeps in the foreground; it is based on a figure in the *Paradise* section of *The Garden of Earthly Delights* by Hieronymus Bosch (FIG. 18-20), which Dali had studied in the Prado Museum in Madrid. Dali has draped his creature with a limp pocket watch. Another watch hangs from the branch of a dead tree that springs surprisingly from a blocky, architectonic form. A third watch hangs half over the edge of the rectangular form, beside a small timepiece resting dial-down on the block's surface. Ants swarm mysteriously over the small watch, while a fly walks along the face of its large neighbor, almost as if this assembly of watches were decaying, organic life—soft and viscous. Dali rendered every detail of this dreamscape with precise control, striving to make the world of his paintings as convincingly real as the most meticulously rendered landscape based on an actual scene from nature. Dali based his exacting,

*In "Art in Cinema," symposium held at the San Francisco Museum of Art (reprinted, New York: Arno Press, 1968), pp. 29–30.

†In Rubin, *Dada, Surrealism, and Their Heritage,* p. 111.

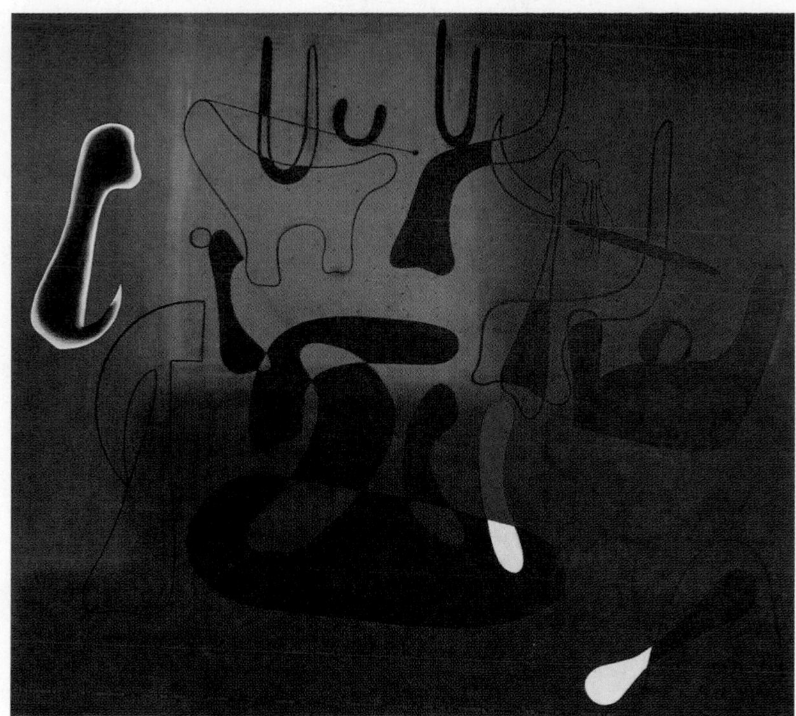

22-37 JOAN MIRÓ, *Painting,* 1933. Approx. 5′ 8½″ × 6′ 5¼″. Collection, The Museum of Modern Art, New York (Loula D. Lasker Bequest by exchange).

miniaturelike technique on careful studies of earlier art, especially that of Dutch and Spanish masters of the seventeenth century like Velázquez (FIG. 19-38), but Dali's subject matter is closer to the psychological world of Stubbs (FIG. 20-46), Fuseli (FIG. 20-47), Blake (FIG. 20-48), and Munch (FIG. 21-92).

Like the Dadaists, the Surrealists used many methods to free their creative process from reliance on the kind of conscious control they believed had been too much shaped by society. Dali used his paranoiac-critical approach to encourage the free play of association as he worked. Other Surrealists used automatism and various types of planned "accidents" to provoke reactions closely related to subconscious experience. The Spanish artist JOAN MIRÓ (1893–1983) was a master of this approach. From the beginning, his work contained an element of fantasy and hallucination. Introduced to the use of chance in the creation of art by Surrealist poets in Paris, the young Spaniard devised a new painting method that allowed him to create works like *Painting* (FIG. **22-37**). Miró began this painting by making a scattered collage composition with assembled fragments cut from a catalogue for machinery. The shapes in the collage became motifs that the artist freely reshaped to create biomorphic black silhouettes—solid or in outline, with dramatic accents of white and vermilion—that suggest, in the painting, a host of amoeba-like organisms floating in an immaterial background space filled with soft reds, blues, and greens. Miró described the creative process he used as switching back and forth between unconscious and conscious image making: "Rather than setting out to paint something, I begin painting and as I paint the picture begins to assert itself, or suggest itself under my brush. The form becomes a sign for a woman or a bird as I work. . . . The first stage is free, unconscious. . . . The second stage is carefully calculated."* Even the artist could not always explain the meanings of pictures like *Painting*. They are, in the truest sense, spontaneous and intuitive expressions of the little-understood, submerged, unconscious part of life.

JEAN (HANS) ARP adapted the automatism from his Dadaist period (see page 977) to initiate the design of biomorphic free forms in Surrealist sculptures like *Human Concretion* (FIG. **22-38**). Arp's French and German first names reflect the fact that he was born in Alsace-Lorraine, a region annexed to Germany in 1871 and returned to France in 1919. The absurdity of this political situation may have helped to color Arp's early poetry and his eager participation in the Dada and Surrealist movements. Interested at first in expressing his sense of the metaphysical qualities in everyday objects, the forms in his Surrealist works instead represent the natural processes that generate

*In William S. Rubin, *Miró in the Collection of The Museum of Modern Art* (New York: The Museum of Modern Art, 1973), p. 32.

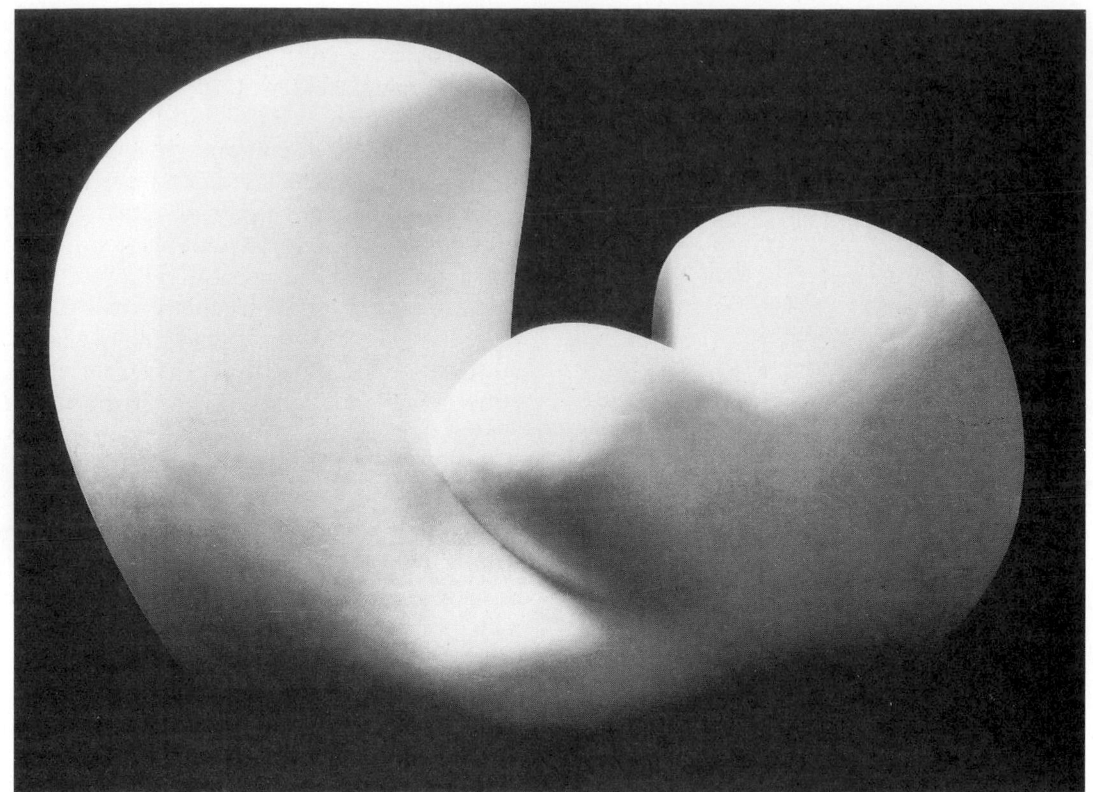

22-38 Jean Arp, *Human Concretion,* 1935. Original plaster, $19\frac{1}{2}'' \times 25\frac{1}{2}''$. Collection, The Museum of Modern Art, New York (gift of the Advisory Committee).

the shapes of the physical world. Borrowing a term from geology, Arp called many of his Surrealist sculptures "concretions": "Concretion signifies the natural process of condensation, hardening, coagulating, thickening, growing together. . . . Concretion designates solidification. . . . Concretion is something that has grown."* *Human Concretion* was designed so that it could be placed in a number of positions. The way in which its forms twist and push forward in many directions creates the effect that the piece is still in the process of growing toward its final state. Arp's definition and the title of this piece all reflect his deep belief that the whole earth is alive and that all living things share in the same vital forces. The biomorphic organicism of *Human Concretion* links Arp's Surrealism with the abstract forms created by Henry Moore (fig. 22-46) in England.

Surrealism began in Europe, but its ideas spread rapidly to artists in other countries. In the United States, Joseph Cornell (1903–1972) was inspired by the Surrealist collages of Max Ernst to fill open boxes with evocative groups of found images and objects arranged in compositions like *Soap Bubble Set* (fig. **22-39**). Cornell received a classical secondary-school

*In Herbert Read, *The Art of Jean Arp* (New York: Harry N. Abrams, 1968), p. 93.

22-39 Joseph Cornell, *Soap Bubble Set,* 1936. Glass case with inserts, $15\frac{3}{4}'' \times 14\frac{1}{4}'' \times 5\frac{3}{8}''$. Wadsworth Atheneum, Hartford, Connecticut (gift of Henry and Walter Keney).

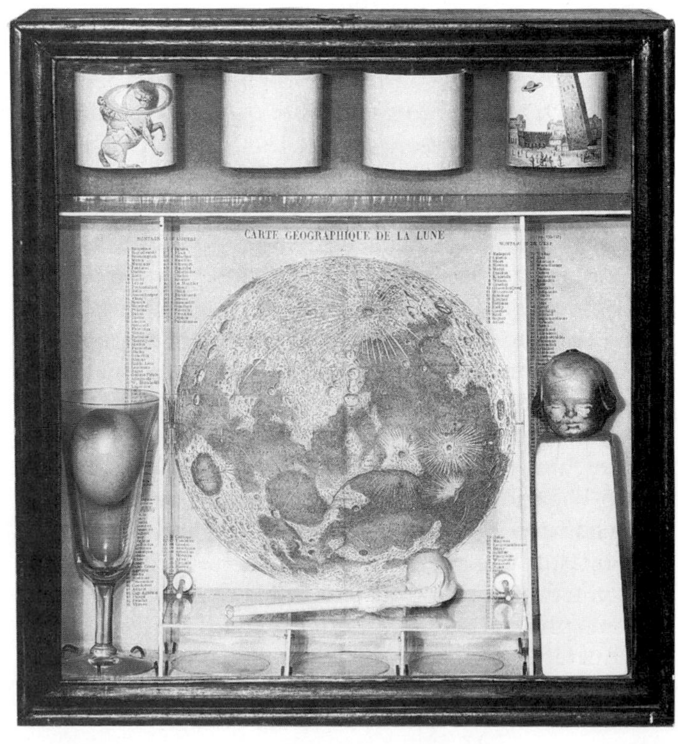

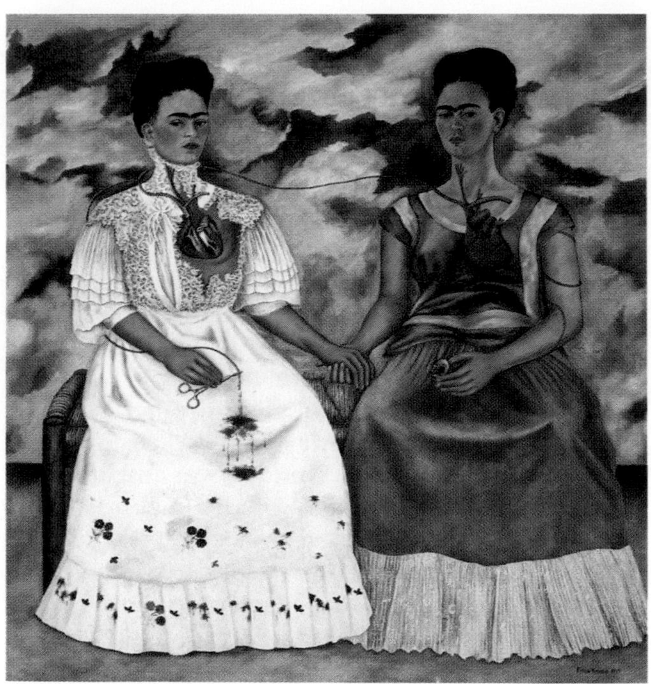

22-40 FRIDA KAHLO, *The Two Fridas,* 1939. 67″ × 67″. Collection of the Museo de Arte Moderno, Mexico City.

education but no formal art training. Working in New York as a salesman, he scoured the city for objects and printed images that carried for him reminiscences of astronomy, nature, and the nineteenth-century literature, opera, and ballet that he loved. Often he pursued a theme through variations in a series of different boxes. His compositions allude to many things but express no specific meaning. The juxtaposition of unlikely objects forces each viewer to invent connections and meanings for the assembly. The Surrealists recognized at once that Cornell shared their interest in the beauty that occurs in the "chance encounter" of unrelated things in an unexpected setting. In *Soap Bubble Set,* the doll's head can be seen as a reference to the artist himself; the clay pipes recall those used by the early Dutch settlers of New York City; the large cork floats (some adorned with decals of zodiacal signs) speak of the sea; the star maps suggest the heavens, and the goblets and the marbles allude, among other things, to drinking and to children's games. The composition of many of Cornell's boxes reveals his fascination with the cinema. The viewer takes in one section, then abruptly shifts attention to another, rather like experiencing a jump cut from one scene to a completely unexpected successor in Surrealist films like *Un Chien Andalou.*

Perhaps the most autobiographical of all artists connected with Surrealism was the Mexican painter FRIDA KAHLO (1907–1954), who used the details of her own life as powerful symbols for the psychological pain of human existence. Kahlo began painting seriously as a young student, during convalescence from a tragic accident that left her in constant pain. Her life became a heroic and tumultuous battle for survival against illness and stormy personal relationships. *The Two Fridas* (FIG. **22-40**) is typical of Kahlo's long series of unflinching self-portraits. The twin figures sit side by side on a low bench in a barren landscape under a stormy sky. One figure wears a simple Mexican costume, while the other is dressed in what might be an elaborate wedding dress. The figures suggest different sides of the artist's personality, inextricably linked by the clasped hands and by the thin artery that stretches between them, joining their exposed hearts and culminating on one side in surgical forceps and on the other in the hallucinatory mushroom. The French Surrealist André Breton found Kahlo to be a natural Surrealist. He recognized that her deeply personal double self-portrait touches sensual and psychological memories in each of us.

The Search for Eternal Forms

One strong impulse in psychological and conceptual Modernism early in the twentieth century was the desire of artists to find and use expressive forms to embody eternal qualities. Working figuratively or abstractly, artists striving to achieve this aim believed that true reality lay hidden behind the surface of the visible world, and they devised a range of symbols to represent the patterns of that innermost essence. These artists were interested above all in expressing the human spiritual dimension. Paul Klee articulated the goal of this group as art derived from "the source of it all." He went on to say that "what springs from this source—whatever it may be called, dream, idea or fantasy—must be taken seriously only if it unites with the proper creative means to form a work of art. . . . For not only do they, to some extent, add more spirit to the seen, but they also make secret visions visible."* Each of these artists developed an individual style to represent a sense of eternal form, and all believed that the universal reality expressed in their works would be perceived by every viewer.

ABSTRACT FIGURATION

Many artists before the twentieth century considered figurative art to be the most powerful means of representing universal ideals. In the first half of the twentieth century, however, such expression assumed a heightened psychological and conceptual dimension as artists adopted expressionistic devices

*In Robert L. Herbert, ed., *Modern Artists on Art* (Englewood Cliffs, NJ: Prentice-Hall, 1964), p. 89.

of bold color and simplified or exaggerated forms to invest their work with emotional power. Directing their works at the hearts of their viewers, each of these artists sought to give visual form to the eternal mysteries of life and death. To do so, they worked with symbols derived from those familiar to a wide population.

A dynamic use of symbol and fantasy was employed by the Russian artist MARC CHAGALL (1887–1985) to create works filled with the extremes of visionary joy and despair. Chagall studied and worked in Paris and Berlin, and incorporated into his work elements of Expressionism, Cubism, and Fauvism. However, he never forgot his early years in an obscure Russian village, and themes from his childhood returned as if in dreams and memories. Some, gay and fanciful, suggest the simpler pleasures of folk life; others, somber and even tragic, recall the trials and persecutions of the Jewish people. Through all of his work runs a sense of the deep religious experience that was an inextricable part of his early life. In *The Falling Angel* (FIG. **22-41**), Chagall combined his themes to symbolize the suffering of all ordinary people as Europe slid toward and into World War II. A flaming female angel plummets across a moonlit night sky, one wing stretched upward and the other pointing toward the earth. A mother and child, floating over a slumbering village, mingle with the earthside wing. To the right is a Crucifix. To the left, a bearded peasant holds a Torah scroll. Above him, a workman tumbles through the air. From a central position at the bottom of the composition, a strange yellow beast looks directly at the viewer. This enigmatic creature is placed beside a mysteriously floating violin. A lighted candle recalls the sacred light in both Christian and Jewish ritual. The terror of wars and pogroms is suggested by the pitiful little figure trudging along the path leading from the village, while resignation and hope are expressed in other symbols. The work is a moving portrayal of the artist's feeling that faith is important in a world of war and brutality. Clearly, Chagall was a highly individual artist who intuitively used diverse avant-garde styles to help him transform the personal themes of his Jewish childhood into symbols that suggest universal human experience.

Perhaps the most inventive artist using abstract figuration to express the world of the spirit was the Swiss-German painter PAUL KLEE (1879–1940). The son of a professional musician and an accomplished violinist in his own right, Klee thought of painting as similar to music in its expressiveness and in its ability

22-41 MARC CHAGALL, *The Falling Angel,* 1923, 1933, 1947. Kunstmuseum, Basel, Switzerland (Emanuel Hoffmann-Stiftung).

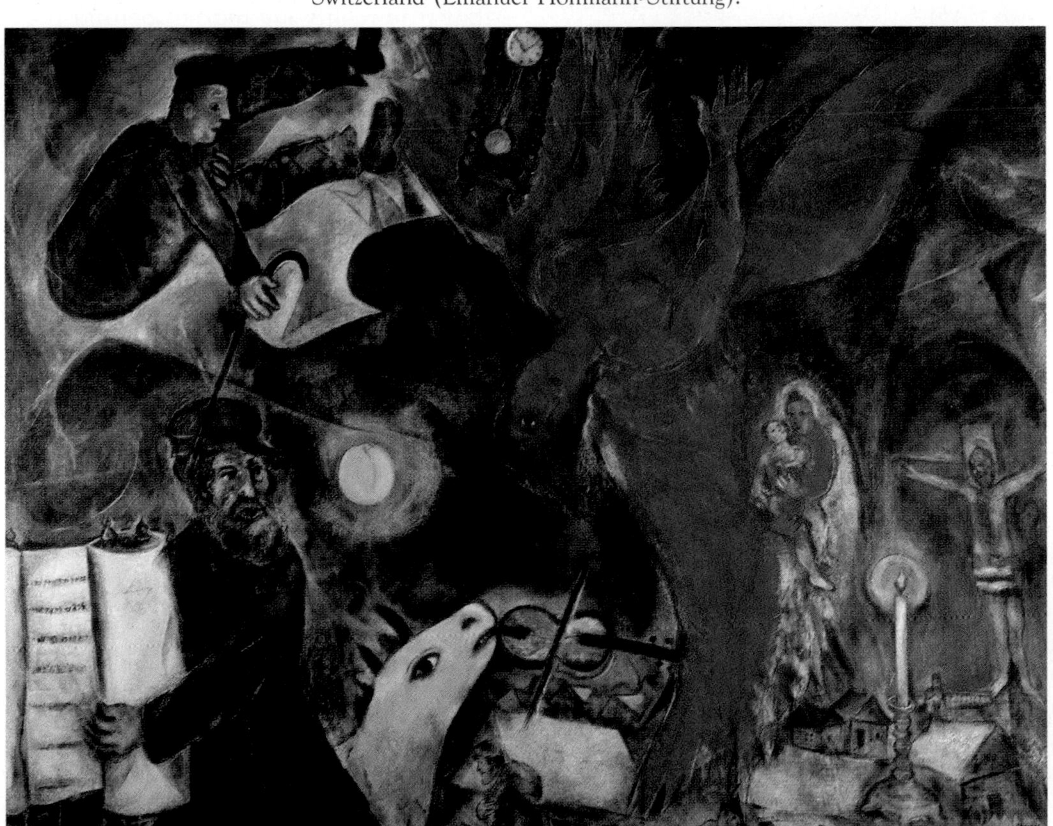

to touch the spirit of its viewers through a studied use of color, form, and line:

> Art does not reproduce the visible; rather it makes visible. . . . The formal elements of graphic art are dot, line, plane, and space—the last three charged with energy of various kinds. . . . Formerly we used to represent things visible on earth, things we either liked to look at or would have liked to see. Today we reveal the reality that is behind visible things. . . . By including the concepts of good and evil, a moral sphere is created. . . . Art is a simile of the Creation.*

To penetrate the reality that is behind visible things, Klee studied nature avidly, taking special interest in analyzing processes of growth and change. He coded these studies in diagrammatic form in notebooks, and the knowledge he gained in this way became so much a part of his consciousness that it influenced the "psychic improvisation" he used to create his art.

Klee's works, like *Twittering Machine* (FIG. **22-42**), are small and intimate in scale. A viewer must draw near to decipher the delicately rendered forms and enter this mysterious dream world. The ancient world of nature and the modern world of machines are joined in this picture, where four diagrammatic birds appear to be forced into twittering action by the turning of a crank-driven mechanism. We customarily associate birds with life and machines with man's ability to control nature. (Indeed, a 1921 drawing by Klee called *Concert on a Twig* shows these four birds with their double-curved perch clearly attached to a tree.) In *Twittering Machine,* however, Klee has linked the birds inextricably to the machine, creating an ironic vision of existence in the modern age. Each bird responds in such an individual way that we may see all of them as metaphors for ourselves—beings trapped by the operation of the industrial society we created. Some observers see an even darker meaning in *Twittering Machine:* the individual birds are said to represent the four temperaments of the medieval and Renaissance periods, while their loony appearance also features avian shapes capable of luring real birds into a trap in the rectangular trough at the bottom of the image. Perhaps no other artist of the twentieth century matches the subtlety of Klee as he adroitly plays with sense, creating an artistic device of ambiguity and understatement that draws each viewer into finding a unique or markedly individualistic interpretation of the work.

Klee shared the widespread modern apprehension concerning the rationalism behind a technological civilization that could be as destructive as it was constructive. As do some psychologists, he sought clues to man's deeper nature in primitive shapes and symbols. Like the psychologist Carl Jung, Klee seems to have accepted the existence of a collective unconscious that reveals itself in archaic signs and patterns and that is everywhere evident in the art of primitive peoples. Toward the end of his life, Klee suffered from a debilitating and painful illness. Its effects heightened his depression over the worsening of world conditions. *Death and Fire* (FIG. **22-43**) expresses the dark mood of his last years in the style of an ideogram—a simple, picturelike sign filled with implicit meaning. A stick figure moves left toward three vertical bars. A white death's-head, heavily outlined, dominates the work and seems to rise toward a glowing sun. The features of the skull may also be letters, perhaps *tod* (the German word for death). The pale green, harmonized with the chords of red, may suggest the element of water reconciled with fire in the ever-changing alternation of life and death. The eerie color, the primitive starkness of the images, and the mysterious arrangement convey an almost religious sense of awe, as if one were in the presence of a totem having magical powers. Enigmatic as the subject is, we feel its sources, as definitely as those of Chagall, in the human religious experience.

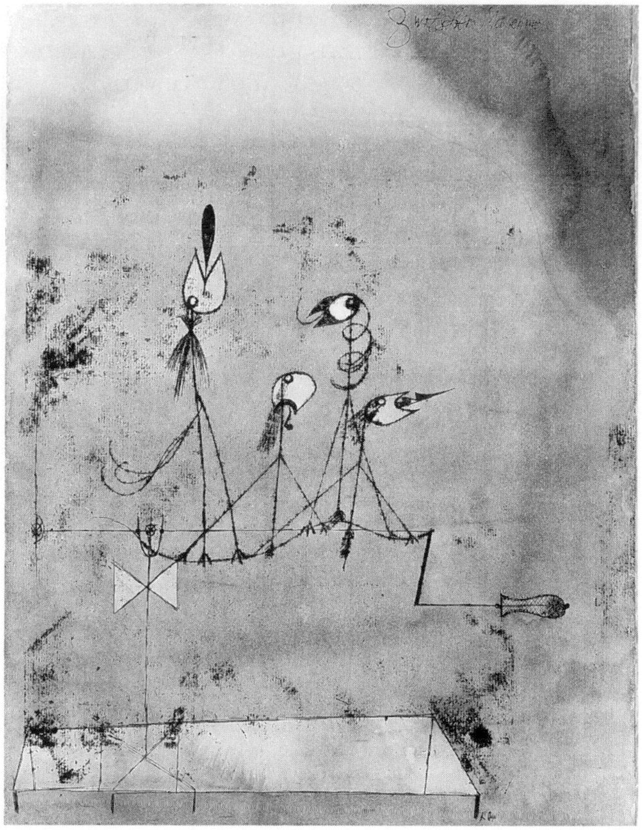

22-42 PAUL KLEE, *Twittering Machine,* 1922. Watercolor and pen and ink, approx. $16\frac{1}{4}'' \times 12''$. Collection, The Museum of Modern Art, New York (purchase).

*In Chipp, ed., *Theories of Modern Art,* pp. 182–85.

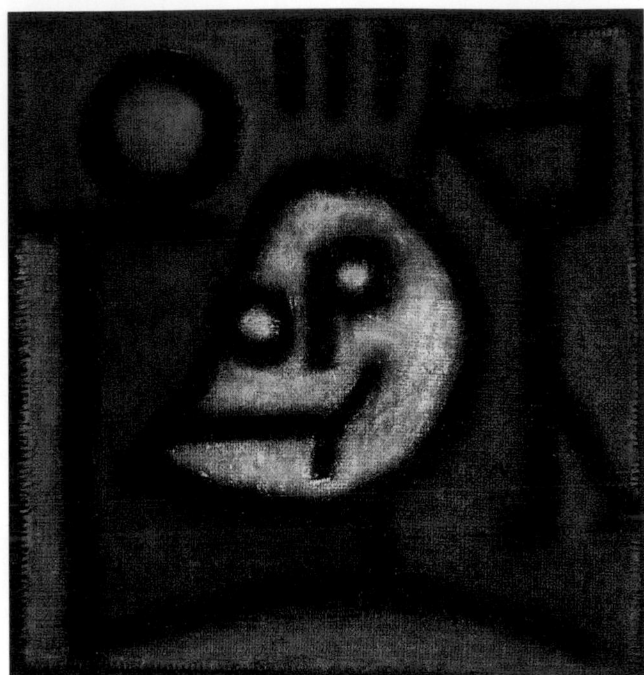

22-43 PAUL KLEE, *Death and Fire,* 1940. Oil drawing in black paste on jute burlap, mounted on stretched jute. Approx. 18″ × 17$\frac{5}{16}$″. Paul Klee Foundation, Kuntsmuseum, Berne, Switzerland. Copyright 1990 by Cosmopress, Genf.

The physicality of sculpture presented particular problems for artists determined to create eternal forms in real space. One of the earliest sculptural visions of universal form was that of the French artist ARISTIDE MAILLOL (1861–1944). In the opening years of the century, he created a new version of the Classical human nude to express his concept of ideal beauty. Maillol began his career as a painter, executing broadly decorative designs in the manner of Gauguin, and was also known as a graphic artist through his Art Nouveau woodcut book illustrations. About 1900, Maillol turned to sculpture. He developed a serene style of massive planes and volumes to express a Classical sense of an ideal that lies beyond the endlessly changing surfaces of the visible physical world. As he put it: "The particular does not interest me; I find meaning only in a general idea. . . . For my taste, sculpture should have as little movement as possible. . . . When a movement is excessive it is frozen: it no longer represents life."* One of Maillol's first and most important sculptural works, the seated figure *The Mediterranean* (FIG. **22-44**), was conceived as an organization of volumes based on an ideal simplification of the human female nude. This figure has weight and solidity, and the light flows evenly and quietly over the largely unbroken surfaces of the smoothly modeled masses. The pose resembles several Tahitian figures by Gauguin, whose art Maillol greatly admired, but the figure's tranquil monumentality and dignity also recall the Early Classical sculpture of ancient Greece. Unlike these earlier works, however, this figure was meant to have no meaning beyond the wonder of its beautifully composed shapes. (The title *The Mediterranean* was added later.) It is an abstract design that ponders the delight of the ideal female form.

*In Goldwater and Treves, eds., *Artists on Art,* pp. 406–408.

The Romanian sculptor CONSTANTIN BRANCUSI (1876–1957) created eternal shapes by uncovering the essential shapes hidden at the core of the things we see in the world. Brancusi worked his way to Paris where he at first used a style inspired by that of Rodin. Soon, however, he was searching for ways to express an inner reality lying beyond the surface of the physical world. Inspired by the teachings of an eleventh-century Tibetan monk (Milarepa) concerning the universality of all life, Brancusi developed his own creative philosophy:

> There is an aim in all things, to reach it we must detach ourselves from ourselves. . . . It is not making things that is difficult but putting ourselves in condition to make them. . . . Simplicity is not an end in art, but we arrive at simplicity in spite of ourselves as we approach the real sense of things. . . . They are fools who call my work abstract. What they think to be abstract is the most realistic, because what is real is not the outer form, but the idea, the essence of things."†

†In Carola Giedion-Welcker, *Contemporary Sculpture* (London: Faber & Faber, 1960), p. 126.

22-44 ARISTIDE MAILLOL, *The Mediterranean,* c. 1902–1905. Bronze, approx. 41″ high, base 45″ × 24$\frac{3}{4}$″. Collection, The Museum of Modern Art, New York (gift of Stephen C. Clark).

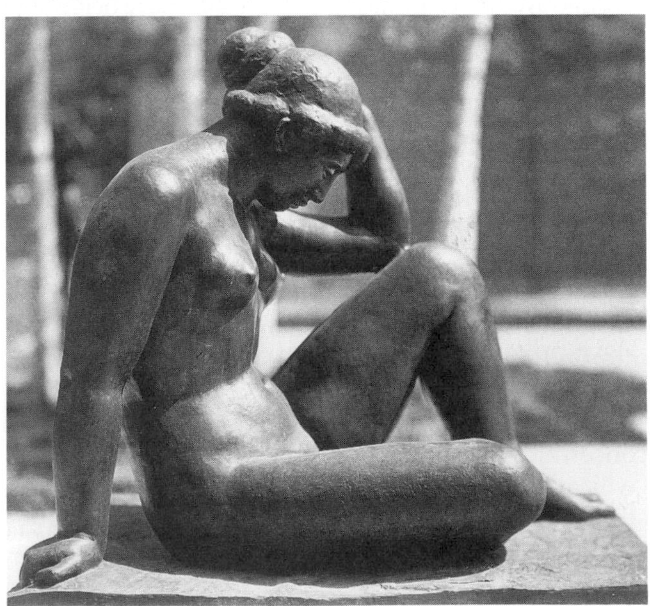

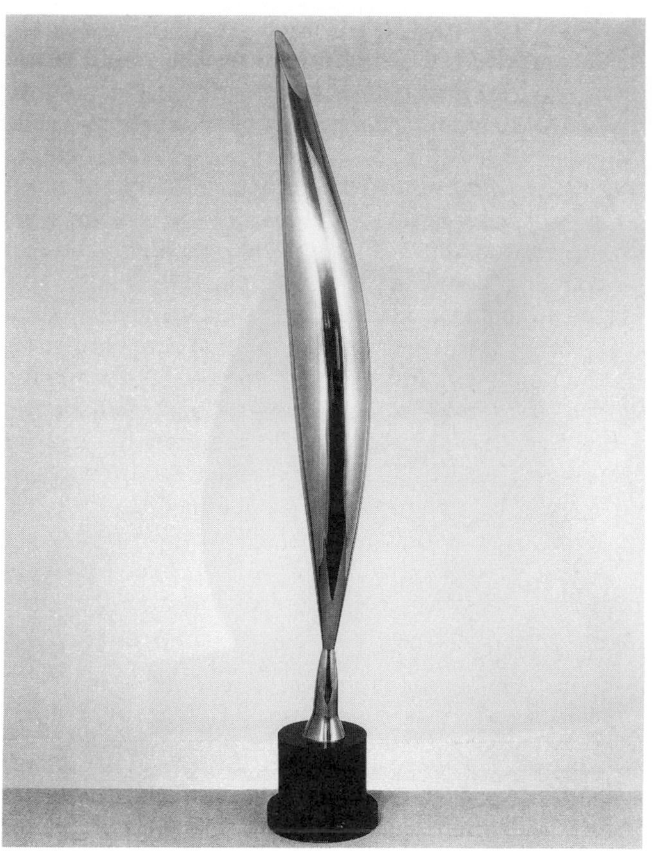

22-45 CONSTANTIN BRANCUSI, *Bird in Space,* 1928(?). Bronze, unique cast, approx. 54″ high. Collection, The Museum of Modern Art, New York (given anonymously).

Works like *Bird in Space* (FIG. **22-45**) were created at the end of a long process in which Brancusi began with a sculpture closer in detail to the shape of something in the world—in this case, a bird standing at rest with its wings folded at its sides. Gradually, he simplified the bird's shape until its feet and body merged, the final form suggesting that it is about to leave the ground to soar in free flight through the heavens.* Brancusi envisioned many of his works, including this one, enlarged to monumental scale. The subtitle for this work was *Project of bird which, when enlarged, will fill the sky,* and the sculptor spoke of the work's ability on that scale to fill viewers with comfort and peace. The polished bronze was intended to catch and reflect light. Brancusi always paid special attention to the intrinsic qualities in the materials he used. He made sculptures in wood, in marble, in stone, and in bronze. In each, he tried to create forms that respected and worked with the nature of the material itself. His stone pieces and some of his wood pieces are smooth and highly polished, allowing the patterns of the natural grain to become part of the work's meaning and expressiveness. Sometimes his wood pieces are roughly hewn, revealing the action of the chisel and adz in creating forms that in these cases seem related to those made by prehistoric people thousands of years ago. Whatever the form or subject, Brancusi said to his viewers: "Don't look for obscure formulas or mysteries. I am giving you pure joy. Look at the sculptures until you see them. Those nearest to God have seen them."†

The English sculptor HENRY MOORE (1898–1986) shared Brancusi's profound love of nature and knowledge of natural forms and materials. Moore maintained that every "material has its own individual qualities" and that these qualities could play a role in the creative process: "It is only when the sculptor works direct, where there is an active relationship with his material, that the material can take its part in the shaping of an idea." Moore combined this insight with memories of the shapes of the hilly Yorkshire countryside he had known as a boy to express the ways in which the shapes of landscape and the human figure echo one another in a marvelous unity of form: "The human figure is what interests me most deeply, but I have found principles of form and rhythm from the study of natural objects." One great recurring theme in Moore's work was the reclining female figure, whose simplified and massive forms were originally inspired by a tiny photograph of a Chacmool figure from pre-Columbian Mexico.‡ Although one can recognize a human figure in most of Moore's works, the artist pushed always toward an abstract symbolism that would express a universal truth beyond the physical world. He summarized his feelings about abstract figurative form in two passages from essays written in the 1930s: "Because a work does not aim at reproducing natural appearances, it is not, therefore, an escape from life—but may be a penetration into reality. . . . My sculpture is becoming less representational, less an outward visual copy . . . , but only because I believe that in this way I can present the human psychological content of my work with the greatest directness and intensity."§ *Reclining Figure* (FIG. **22-46**) is a wonderful example of Moore's handling of his particular abstract symbolism. The massive shapes of the figure suggest

*Many people have noted a resemblance between Brancusi's *Bird in Space* and the appearance of the streamlined *moderne* style being developed by industrial designers during the 1930s. The resemblance is fortuitous, but not surprising, as both artist and designers each based their concept on a careful study of birds in flight.

†In Carola Giedion-Welcker, *Constantin Brancusi* (New York: George Braziller, 1959), p. 219.

‡Chacmool figures are thought perhaps to represent a god or a worshiper bearing an offering. Usually carved in stone, each figure characteristically reclines on its back with the knees bent and its torso bent upright, head turning abruptly toward one side.

§In Herbert, ed., *Modern Artists on Art,* pp. 140–41, 145–46.

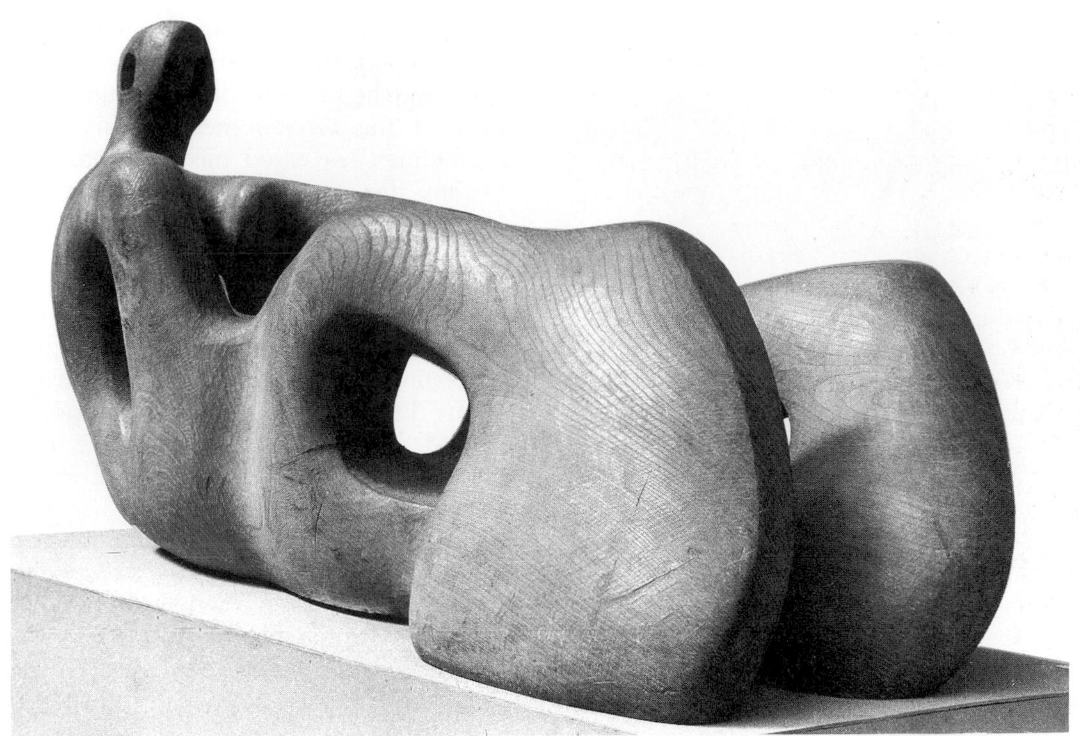

22-46 HENRY MOORE, *Reclining Figure,* 1939. Elmwood, 37″ × 6′ 7″ × 30″. © Detroit Institute of the Arts (gift of the Dexter M. Ferry, Jr., Trustee Corporation).

the biomorphic forms of Surrealism, but Moore's recumbent woman is also a powerful earth mother, whose undulant forms and hollows suggest nurturing human energy and at the same time evoke the contours of Yorkshire hills and the wind-polished surfaces of weathered wood and stone. Allusions in Moore's work to landscape and to biomorphic Surrealist forms are heightened by the interplay of mass and void, which the sculptor based on the intriguing qualities of cavities in nature: "The hole connects one side to the other, making it immediately more three-dimensional. . . . The mystery of the hole—the mysterious fascination of caves in hillsides and cliffs." The contours and openings of *Reclining Figure* follow the grain of the wood. Above all, *Reclining Figure* is filled with a tightly coiled, dynamic energy that seems to radiate from its innermost core outward through the breasts, the jutting knees, and the upthrust head.

ABSTRACT FORMALISM

For some artists, eternal qualities could only be expressed in forms so pure in their abstraction from any reference to the natural world that they appear completely nonobjective. Most of these artists wrote articulately about the actual symbolism in their individual styles. Most also believed that they were inventing a universal art language that could be understood by all peoples. These artists followed the beliefs of Wilhelm Worringer, who had written in 1908 about the way in which such forms stand above the particularities of the world:

> The simple line and its development in purely geometrical regularity was bound to offer the greatest possibility of happiness to the man disquieted by the obscurity and entanglement of phenomena. For here the last trace of connection with, and dependence on, life has been effaced, here the highest absolute form, the purest abstraction has been achieved; here is law, here is necessity, while everywhere else the caprice of the organic prevails.*

The artists who based their work on abstract symbolic forms believed such compositions would help viewers to perceive the profound truth that the artists had captured. The critic Sheldon Cheney summarized this position in his 1934 essay "Abstraction and Mysticism":

> At the present stage of comprehension—retarded by education—few people but an increasing group are sensitive to absolute abstraction, which they may or may not consider a sort of mystic revelation of harmonious cosmic order; and a larger group turn to partially objective painting in which the abstract skeleton or core is richly dominant. They will detect the qual-

*In Frascina and Harrison, eds., *Modern Art and Modernism,* p. 163.

> ity in greater purity as understanding and sensitivity grow; perhaps the individual will march on till he commonly demands abstraction washed of the last remnants of objectivity.*

To the artists who followed this approach, abstract symbolism was the only true art. Although the vast majority of artists working in this style produced spare and precise compositions, the Russian painter WASSILY KANDINSKY (1866–1944) is a notable exception to that general trend. Kandinsky adapted the energetic, intuitive approach of German Expressionism to create dynamic abstract representations of emotional and mystical themes. He embarked on a painting career in Munich in 1896 after an early law career in Russia. Travel introduced him to avant-garde art and took him outside Europe on a trip to Tunis. In 1911, with the painters Franz Marc, Ernst Macke, and Paul Klee (long before he developed his mature style), Kandinsky formed a new Expressionist group, the Blue Rider (*Die Blaue Reiter*). The members of the Blue Rider group had no common style, but they did share the belief that an artist should use the language of color and form to create works that speak directly from the heart of the creator to the souls of viewers. Believing that rational, post-Renaissance tradition was useless in the creation of such expressive works, the Blue Rider artists looked outside the artistic mainstream of the West (as had the Bridge group) to find inspiration in the art of German and Russian peasants, the ancient world, the Middle Ages, Africa, and Oceania. The artists of the Blue Rider group also admired the art of pre-Columbian Latin America and of Arabia, and showed a special appreciation for the art of children and the mentally ill. Blue Rider artists felt that the art produced by these cultures and groups contained a straightforward expressive power lacking in the Salon art of the time.

As the leading theorist of the group, Kandinsky formulated their ideas in written form both for their publications and for his own book, *Concerning the Spiritual in Art,* which was written in 1911 and published in 1912. As the title suggests, Kandinsky believed that great art contains the spiritual power of inner harmony, expressed through eternal shapes that speak through the sense of sight to the viewer's deepest intuitive link with the source of all being:

> Generally speaking, color is a power that directly influences the soul. Color is the keyboard, the eyes are the hammers, the soul is the piano with many strings. The artist is the hand which plays, touching one key or another, to cause vibrations in the soul. . . . The inner need is the basis of small and great problems in painting. We are seeking today for the road which is to lead us away from the outer to the inner basis. The spirit, like the body, can be strengthened and developed by frequent exercises. . . . A work of art is born of the artist in a mysterious and secret way. From him it gains life and being. Nor is its existence casual and inconsequent; it has a definite and purposeful strength, alike in its material and spiritual life. It exists and has power to create spiritual atmosphere; and from this internal standpoint alone can one judge whether it is a good work of art or a bad one.†

Kandinsky wrote about how each kind of shape, each color value, each pattern of line, had certain symbolic and psychological effects, and about how the artist could compose with them as the musical composer uses tone and harmony. His research into the emotional and expressive properties of color, line, and shape soon led him in his own work to the point at which subject matter and even representational elements were highly abstracted or eliminated altogether. Like Klee, Kandinsky saw strong parallels between expression in the visual arts and music.‡ A fine cellist and pianist, he yearned for an art that would speak as directly to the hearts of viewers as music communicated to its listeners. He gave his works titles used for musical pieces—Improvisations, Etudes, Compositions. His Compositions were characterized by carefully ordered arrangements of shapes, while his Improvisations, like *Improvisation 28* (FIG. **22-47**), were the result of a freer, more spontaneous approach to the canvas. Kandinsky's beliefs about the importance of the unconscious in artistic creation harmonized with Freud's conclusions concerning the subconscious and with Arthur Rimbaud's claim that the true artist is a visionary.

Kandinsky's countryman, the Russian KASIMIR MALEVICH (1878–1935) also studied art in Germany early in his career, but he then returned to Russia, where he developed an abstract formalist style to convey his belief that the supreme reality in the world is pure feeling, which rests in no object and thus calls for new, nonobjective forms in art—shapes not related to objects in the visible world. Malevich had studied painting, sculpture, and architecture, and had worked his way through most of the avant-garde styles of his youth before deciding that none was suited to the expression of the subject he found most important—"pure feeling." He christened his new artistic approach "Suprematism" and said of it: "Under Suprematism I understand the supremacy of pure feeling in creative art. To the Suprematist, the

*Ibid., p. 173.

†Wassily Kandinsky, *Concerning the Spiritual in Art,* trans. M. T. H. Sadler (New York: Dover, 1977), pp. 25, 35–36, 53.

‡Kandinsky also attempted to create a special kind of theatrical performance that would contain a synthesis of all the arts.

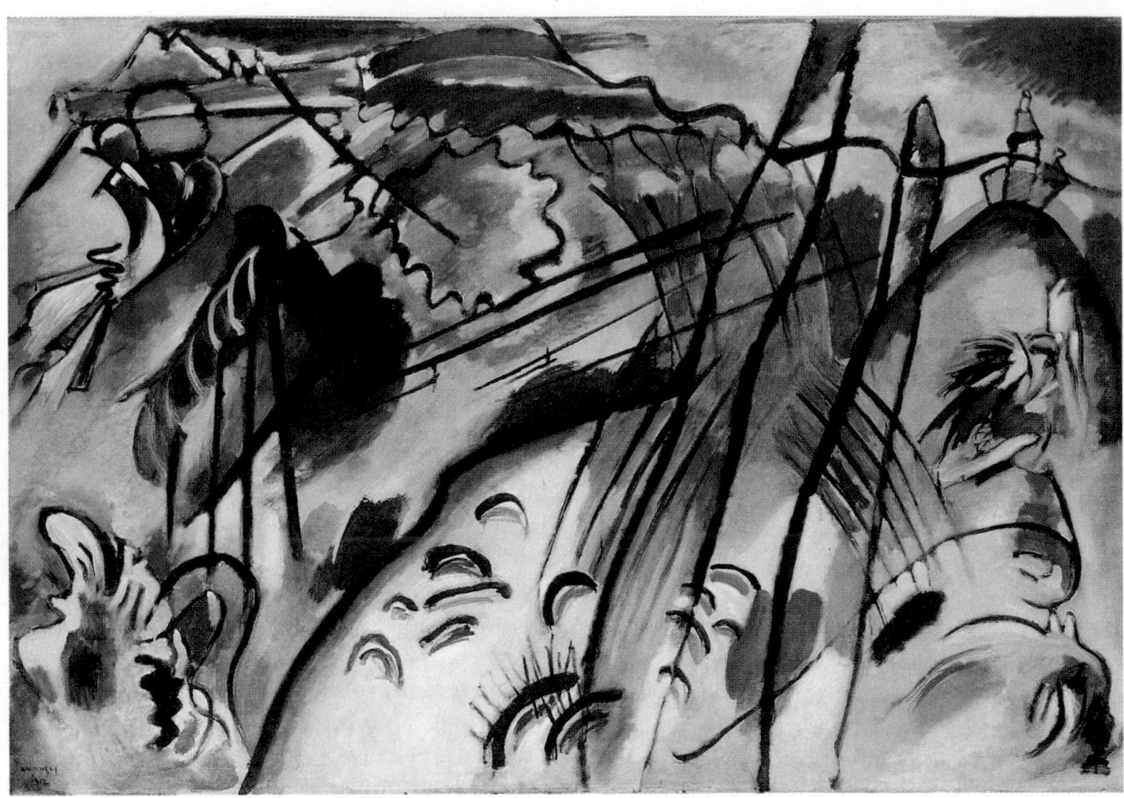

22-47 Wassily Kandinsky, *Improvisation 28* (second version), 1912. Approx. 44″ × 63¾″. Solomon R. Guggenheim Museum, New York.

visual phenomena of the objective world are, in themselves, meaningless; the significant thing is feeling, as such, quite apart from the environment in which it is called forth. . . . The Suprematist does not observe and does not touch—he feels."* The basic form of his new Suprematist nonobjective art was the square. Combined with its relatives, the straight line and the rectangle, the square soon filled paintings like *Suprematist Composition: Aeroplane Flying* (FIG. **22-48**), in which the brightly colored shapes float against and within a white space and are placed in dynamic relationship to one another. Malevich believed that his new art would be easily understood by all peoples, because it required no special education to comprehend its symbols. It used the pure language of form and color that everyone could understand intuitively. Having formulated his artistic approach, Malevich welcomed the Russian Revolution as a political act that would wipe out past traditions and begin to build a new culture in which his art could play a major role. In actuality, after a short period in which avant-garde art was in the vanguard of the new regime, the political leaders of post-Revolution Russia decided that the new society needed a more "practical" art that would teach citizens about their

*In Chipp, ed., *Theories of Modern Art,* pp. 341, 345.

22-48 Kasimir Malevich, *Suprematist Composition: Aeroplane Flying,* 1915 (dated 1914). 22⅞″ × 19″. Collection, The Museum of Modern Art, New York (purchase).

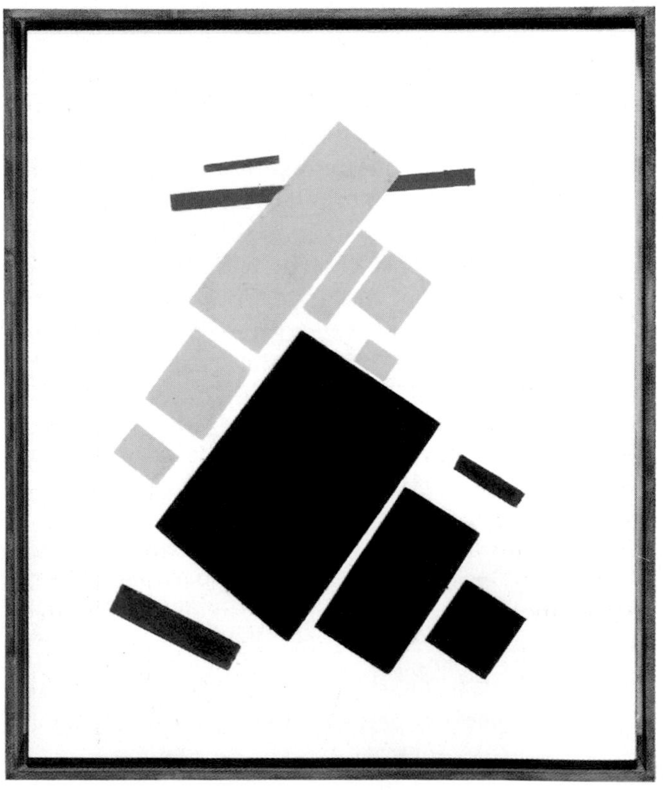

new government or produce goods that would help make their lives better. Malevich was horrified; to him, true art was forever divorced from such practical connections with life: "Every social idea, however great and important it may be, stems from the sensation of hunger; every art work, regardless of how small and insignificant it may seem, originates in pictorial or plastic feeling. It is high time for us to realize that the problems of art lie far apart from those of the stomach or the intellect."* Disappointed and unappreciated in his own country, Malevich eventually stopped painting and turned his attention to other things, such as mathematical theory.

Like Malevich, the Russian sculptor NAUM GABO (1890–1977) wanted to create a new art to express a new reality, and like Malevich, Gabo believed that such art would spring from sources separate from the everyday world. For Gabo, the new reality was the space-time world described by early twentieth-century advances in science. As he wrote in *Realistic Manifesto,* published with his brother Anton Pevsner in 1920: "Space and time are the only forms on which life is built and hence art must be constructed." Later he explained: "We are realists, bound to earthly matters. . . . The shapes we are creating are not abstract, they are absolute. They are released from any already existent thing in nature and their content lies in themselves. . . . It is impossible to comprehend the content of an absolute shape by reason alone. Our emotions are the real manifestation of this content."† According to Gabo, he called himself a "Constructivist" partly because he built his sculptures up piece by piece in space, instead of carving or modeling them in the traditional way. This method freed the Constructivists to work with "volume of mass and volume of space" as "two different materials" in creating compositions filled with the "kinetic rhythms" by which humans perceive "real time." The name *Constructivism* may have originally come from the title *Construction,* which had been used by the Russian artist Vladimir Tatlin for some relief sculptures he made in 1913–1914. Tatlin shared some ideas and goals with Gabo, but soon after the Revolution, Tatlin joined a variant of Constructivism—Productivist Constructivism—that was devoted to using artists' talents in practical ways for the good of society (see page 1019). Like Malevich, Gabo believed that pure art was apart from life, and he and Tatlin parted company. Although Gabo experimented briefly with real motion in his work, most of his sculptures relied on the relationship of mass and space to suggest the nature of space-time. To indicate the volumes of mass and space more clearly in his sculpture, Gabo used some of the new synthetic plastic materials, including celluloid, nylon, and lucite, to create constructions in which space seems to flow through as well as around the transparent materials. In works like *Column* (FIG. **22-49**), the depth through the sculpture is visible, because the circular mass of the column has been opened up so that the viewer can experience the volume of space it occupies. Two transparent planes extend through its diameter, crossing at right angles at the center of the implied cylindrical column shape. The opaque colored planes at the base and the inclined open ring set up counter rhythms to the crossed upright planes, establishing the sense of dynamic kinetic movement that Gabo always sought to express as an essential part of true reality.

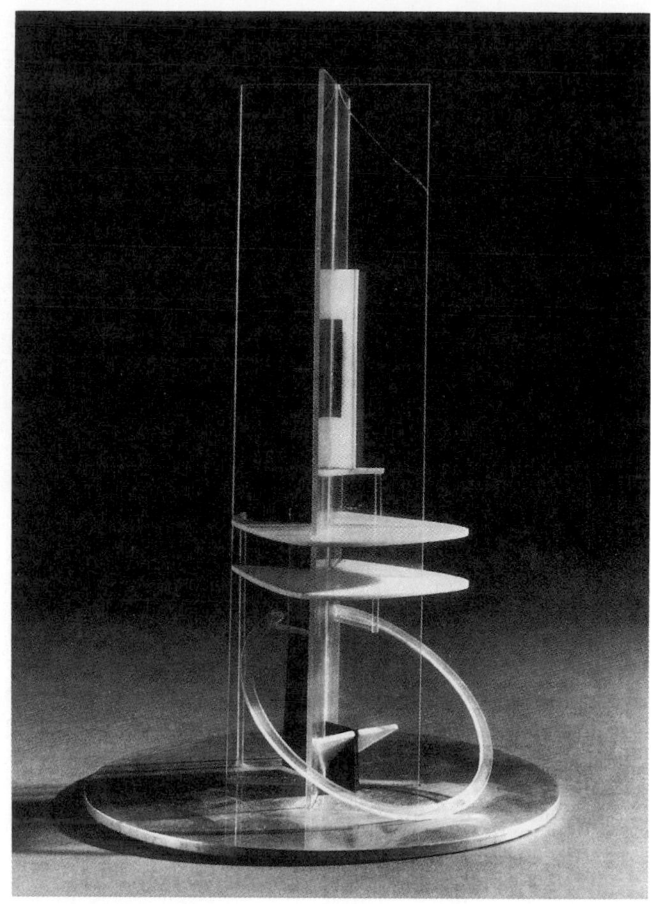

22-49 NAUM GABO, *Column,* 1922–1923. Perspex, on aluminum base, approx. $11\frac{1}{8}$" high. Family collection.

Malevich desired to express "pure feeling" in his paintings, and Gabo sought to convey in his sculpture the reality of the newly revealed world of space and time. The Dutch artist PIET MONDRIAN (1872–1944) went even further in representing hidden realities than any of these other artists by creating a style that he believed reflected the underlying eternal structure of existence. Inspired by the work of Van

*In Herbert, ed., *Modern Artists on Art,* pp. 140–41, 145–46.

†In Chipp, ed., *Theories of Modern Art,* pp. 341, 345.

Gogh, Mondrian began in an expressionist style. He was keenly interested in conveying mystical and spiritual ideas in his art. Study in Paris, just before World War I, introduced him to modes of abstraction in avant-garde modern art such as Cubism. However, as his attraction to contemporary theological writings (especially the teachings of Theosophy) grew, Mondrian sought to purge his art of every overt reference to individual objects in the external world. He turned toward a conception of nonobjective or pictorial design—"pure plastic art"—that he believed expressed universal reality. He stated his credo with great eloquence in 1914:

> What first captivated us does not captivate us afterwards (like toys). If one has loved the surface of things for a long time, later on one will look for something more. . . . The interior of things shows through the surface; thus as we look at the surface the inner image is formed in our soul. It is this inner image that should be represented. For the natural surface of things is beautiful, but the imitation of it is without life. . . . Art is higher than reality and has no direct relation to reality. Between the physical sphere and the ethereal sphere there is a frontier where our senses stop functioning. . . . The spiritual penetrates the real . . . but for our senses these are two different things. To approach the spiritual in art, one will make as little use as possible of reality, because reality is opposed to the spiritual. We find ourselves in the presence of an abstract art. Art should be above reality, otherwise it would have no value for man.*

Caught by the outbreak of hostilities while on a visit to Holland, Mondrian remained there during the war, developing his theories for what he called "Neo-Plasticism"—the new Pure Plastic Art. He believed that all great art has polar but coexistent goals: the attempt to create "universal beauty" and the desire for "esthetic expression of oneself." The first goal is objective in nature, while the second is subjective, existing within the mind and heart of the individual. To create such a universal expression, an artist must discover and work with laws of perfect equilibrium that lie beyond the disharmonies and unhappiness that occur daily, because life in the world cannot achieve this balance. To express his vision of the true balance that lies beyond the physical world, Mondrian eventually limited his formal vocabulary to the three primary colors (red, blue, and yellow), the three primary values (black, white, and grey), and the two primary directions (horizontal and vertical). Basing his ideas on a combination of teachings, he concluded that primary colors and values were the purest colors and therefore were the perfect tools to help an artist construct a harmonious artistic composition. Similarly, to Mondrian, horizontal and vertical elements were the most basically contrasted directions. They innately symbolized, among other things, the opposites of masculine and feminine, repose and upright attention, earth and the immaterial stretch of the sun's rays descending from the heavens. When vertical and horizontal elements were joined to form a right angle, they attained perfect balance. Shapes made from right angles were therefore the elemental harmonious forms. When such shapes were colored in the primary hues and set within an asymmetrical composition of horizontal and vertical black lines on a white ground, they represented the perfectly balanced asymmetry of perfect universal harmony.†

In *Composition in Blue, Yellow, and Black* (FIG. **22-50**), Mondrian used the elements of his Neoplastic style very sparingly, adjusting the design so that every portion of the composition engages in a dynamic play of color and form. The power of the colors and lines to hold the viewer's attention is subtly equivalent to the attraction exercised by the much larger blank areas. The proportions of each of these areas are cunningly varied to avoid a mechanical uniformity of the general equilibrium. The whole painting resonates with the kind of calm eternal order we saw earlier in ideal Classical works like Raphael's *School of Athens* (FIG. 17-16) and Poussin's *Burial of Phocion* (FIG. 19-61).

BARBARA HEPWORTH (1903–1975) developed her own kind of essential sculptural form, combining pristine shape with a sense of organic vitality. The rugged landscape of Yorkshire, in the north of England, helped to shape her sculptural vision; she had vivid childhood memories of driving there with her father. Reflecting on these drives years later, she wrote: "the sensation of moving physically over the contours of fulnesses and concavities, through hollows and over peaks—feeling, touching, seeing, through mind and hand and eye . . . has never left me. I, the sculptor, am the landscape. I am the form and I am the hollow, the thrust and the contour." This feeling led her ever deeper into a search for

*In Michel Seuphor, *Piet Mondrian: Life and Work* (New York: Harry N. Abrams, 1956), p. 177.

†In Herbert, ed., *Modern Artists on Art*, pp. 115–30. The meanings Mondrian attached to each of these elements were influenced by philosophical ideas that seemed to him true, especially those contained in the writings of Madame Blavatsky and Krishnamurti in *Theosophy*, and those expounded by the Dutch mathematician Dr. Schoomaekers in *The New Image of the World* and *The Principles of Plastic Mathematics* (1915 and 1916). For a time in the teens and early 1920s, Mondrian was associated with a group in Holland called *De Stijl* (see page 1004), whose members adhered to a modern version of the Enlightenment belief that art could help create a perfect environment and a more fully evolved human being. Mondrian, however, soon concentrated on his ideas for pure painting and left the practical applications of the theories to others in the group.

22-50 PIET MONDRIAN, *Composition in Blue, Yellow, and Black,* 1936. Approx. 17″ × 13″. Kunstmuseum, Basel, Switzerland (Emanuel Hoffmann-Stiftung).

forms that would express her sense both of the landscape and of the person who is in and observes it:

> The forms which have had special meaning for me since childhood have been the standing form (which is the translation of my feeling towards the human being standing in landscape); the two forms (which is the tender relationship of one living thing beside another); and the closed form, such as the oval, spherical or pierced form (sometimes incorporating colour) which translates for me the association and meaning of gesture in the landscape. . . . In all these shapes the translation of what one feels about man and nature must be conveyed by the sculptor in terms of mass, inner tension, and rhythm, scale in relation to our human size, and the quality of surface which speaks through our hands and eyes.*

Three Forms (FIG. **22-51**) was the first in a series of pieces that Hepworth began soon after she became the mother of triplets in 1934, an experience that apparently stimulated her to explore the relationships in size, shape, and position in space between three elements arranged on a thin base. In this piece, a small ovoid form nestles next to a tall, rounded, upright shape at one end of the base. A petite sphere rests on the corner of the base farthest from them. The artist has gathered here all the forms that had special meaning for her—the standing form, the two forms, and the closed form. The mysteriously irregular shapes and impeccably smooth surfaces of the units in this piece suggest both organic life and the perfection of things made by human hands and tools. Like those in all of her mature works, the shapes in Hepworth's *Three Forms* are contained and classical, expressing a sense of the timelessness of eternity.

The American sculptor ALEXANDER CALDER (1898–1976) used abstract organic forms and a sound knowledge of engineering techniques in a new kind of sculpture that used actual motion to express the innate dynamism of reality. Both the artist's father and grandfather were sculptors, but Calder initially studied to be a mechanical engineer. He was fascinated all his life by motion, and much of his sculpture explored that quality and its relationship to three-dimensional form. As a young artist in Paris in the late 1920s, Calder invented a circus full of miniature performers that were activated by the artist into realistic analogues of the motion of their counterparts in life. After a visit to Mondrian's studio in the early 1930s, Calder was filled with a desire to set the brightly colored rectangular shapes in the Dutch painter's compositions into motion. Intrigued by early motorized and hand-cranked examples of Calder's moving, abstract pieces, Marcel Duchamp named them "mobiles." Calder's engineering skills

22-51 BARBARA HEPWORTH, *Three Forms,* 1935. Marble. Tate Gallery, London.

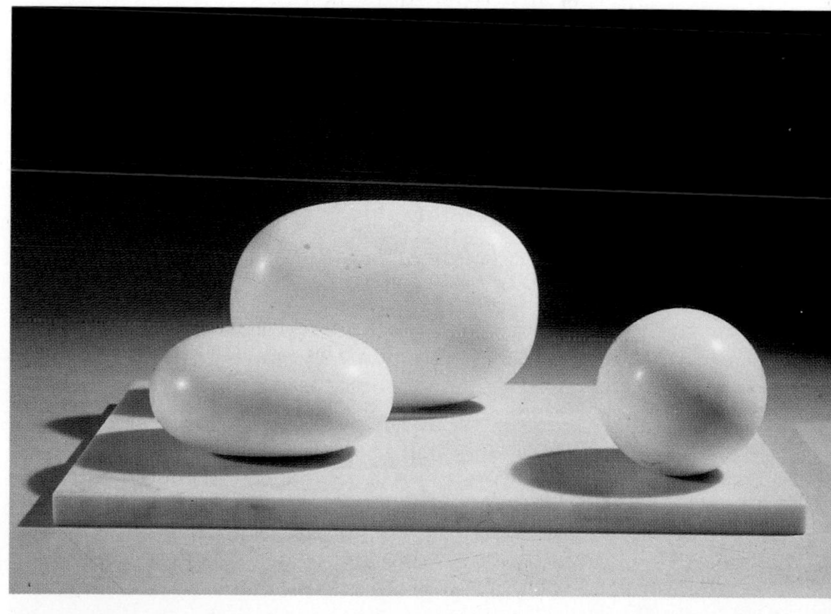

*Barbara Hepworth, *A Pictorial Autobiography* (London: The Tate Gallery, 1978), pp. 9, 53.

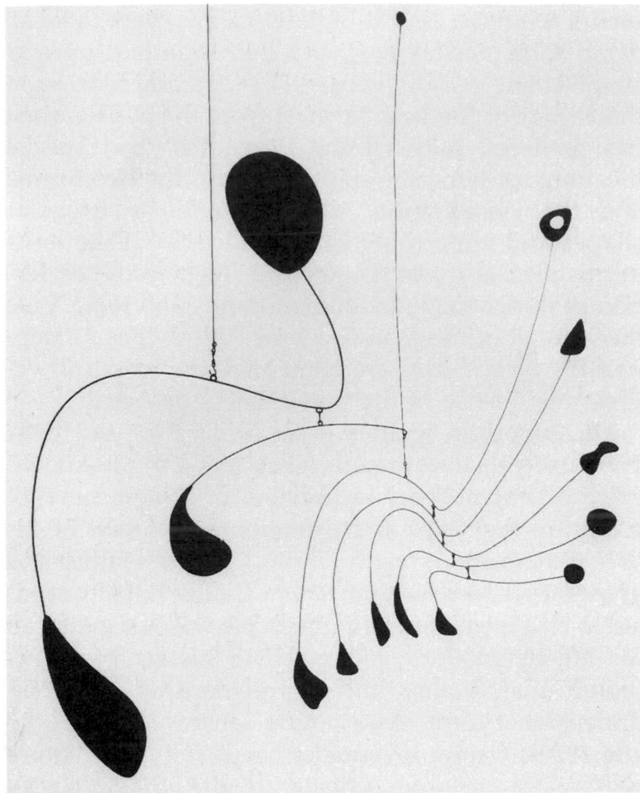

22-52 ALEXANDER CALDER, *Hanging Spider*, c. 1940. Painted sheet metal, wire, 51" high. Private collection.

soon helped him to fashion a series of balanced structures hanging from rods, wires, and colored biomorphic-shaped plates. *Hanging Spider* (FIG. **22-52**), like the other works in this series, was designed to perform in response to air currents and to suggest natural patterns like those of clouds, leaves, or waves blown by the wind. The initial inspiration for the mobiles may have come from the work of Mondrian, but the organic shapes in the mobiles resemble those in the Surrealist paintings of Miró (FIG. 22-37) and were actually generated by Calder's love of nature. The compositions of each of Calder's nonmechanized mobiles were carefully planned so that any air current would set the parts moving within a pattern to create a constantly shifting dance in space, an effect splendidly described by the sculptor's friend, the British painter Ben Nicholson:

> The first time I encountered a Calder was in Paris some years ago when I borrowed one and hung it from the center of the ceiling of a white room overlooking the Seine, and at night, with the river glistening outside, this mobile object turned slowly in the breeze in the light of an electric bulb hung near its center—a large black, six white, and one small scarlet, balls on their wires turned slowly in and out, around, above and below one another, with their shadows chasing, round the white walls in an exciting interchanging movement, suddenly hastening as they turned the corners and disappearing, as they crossed the windows, into the night—it was alive like the hum of the city, like the passing river, but it was not a work of art—imprisoned in a gold frame or stone-dead on a pedestal in one of our marble-pillared mausoleums. It was "alive" and that, after all, is not a bad qualification for a work of art.*

Traditionally, sculpture has been designed to stand still, sometimes with new views unfolding as the observer moves about a piece. Calder's work, as it moves, presents many unexpected transformations and relationships of line and shape. His sculptures, like those of the other artists who sought to work with abstract symbolism, present a vision of universal truth—in his case, a vision of the eternal rhythms of nature.

ART WITH SOCIAL AND POLITICAL CONCERNS

Many of the artists we have discussed in this chapter believed that their art expressed something important about society, but a stronger impetus toward putting their art directly at the service of society inspired artists creating art with social and political concerns. Unlike the abstract formalists, this group of artists emphatically believed that art should be embedded within life and society. Architects dreamed of creating buildings so beautifully designed, so well-suited to human needs, that their forms and spaces would help the people living in them and using them to attain their highest potential. Some artists believed their art could help people develop the special perception necessary to life in the modern world of space-time. Other artists, with more modest goals, revived the documentary impulse of Enlightenment scientific inquiry and applied it to recording the power of the visual world around them. Finally, yet another group of artists perpetuated the Enlightenment belief in the moral and educational benefits of art and used their work to highlight specific social and political subjects, with the goal of inspiring viewers toward conscious and responsible attitudes and actions in their communities.

Utopian Visions

Perhaps the most practically ambitious of the artists who based their work on social and political concerns were those who held the utopian belief that art

*In Michel Seuphor, *The Sculpture of This Century* (New York: George Braziller, 1960), p. 85.

should be used to provide well-designed environments in which people could function closer to their full potential. Some of these artists planned entire communities. Others conceived buildings and the furnishings that would go in them. Many believed that the artist must help to improve the design of every sort of manufactured and mass-produced good—from magazine ads to fountain pens. The American architect Buckminster Fuller even invented practical yet visionary structural systems that would protect the energy sources of the planet and assure the future comfort of its human inhabitants.

One of the most striking personalities in the development of early twentieth-century architecture was FRANK LLOYD WRIGHT (1867–1959). Born in Wisconsin, Wright trained as a civil engineer and worked for a local builder before moving to Chicago to join the firm headed by Louis Sullivan. Wright set out to create "architecture for democracy." Early influences were the volumetric shapes in a set of educational blocks designed by the German educator Friedrich Froebel (from Wright's childhood), the organic unity of a Japanese building he saw at the Columbian Exposition in Chicago in 1893, and a Jeffersonian belief in individualism and the common man. Always a believer in architecture as "natural" and "organic," Wright saw it in the service of free individuals who have the right to move within a "free" space, which he envisioned as a nonsymmetrical design that interacted spatially with its natural surroundings. He sought to develop an organic unity of planning, structure, materials, and site. He identified the principle of continuity as fundamental to the understanding of his view of organic unity: "Classic architecture was all fixation. . . . Now why not let walls, ceilings, floors become seen as component parts of each other, their surfaces flowing into each other? . . . You may see the appearance in the surface of your hand contrasted with the articulation of the bony structure itself. This ideal, profound in its architectural implications . . . I called . . . continuity."* Wright's ideas were not unique to architecture. The concepts of flux, of constant change, of evolution and progress are inherent in Wright's principle of continuity and also appeared in the work of Walt Whitman and in the writings of the greatly influential philosopher Henri Bergson, a contemporary of Wright, who stressed the reality of vitalism—living process—above any other.

Wright's vigorous originality was manifested early and, by 1900, he had arrived at a style entirely his own; in his work during the first decade of this century, his cross-axial plan and his fabric of continous roof planes and screens defined a new domestic architecture.† Although the skeleton frame made a significant appearance in the works of Sullivan and others, Wright attacked the concept in his studies of other systems. He rejected both posts and columns: "In my work, the idea of plasticity may now be seen as the element of continuity . . . the new reality that is space instead of matter." As for architectural interiors, he declared that he "came to realize that the reality of a building was not the container but the space within."

These elements and concepts are fully expressed in Wright's Robie House (FIG. 22-53), which was built

*In Edgar Kaufmann, ed., *American Architecture* (New York: Horizon, 1955), pp. 205, 208.

†Wright's designs for roof planes and screens were inspired by so-called shingle-plan resort houses designed in the late nineteenth century by H. H. Richardson.

22-53 FRANK LLOYD WRIGHT, Robie House, Chicago, 1907–1909.

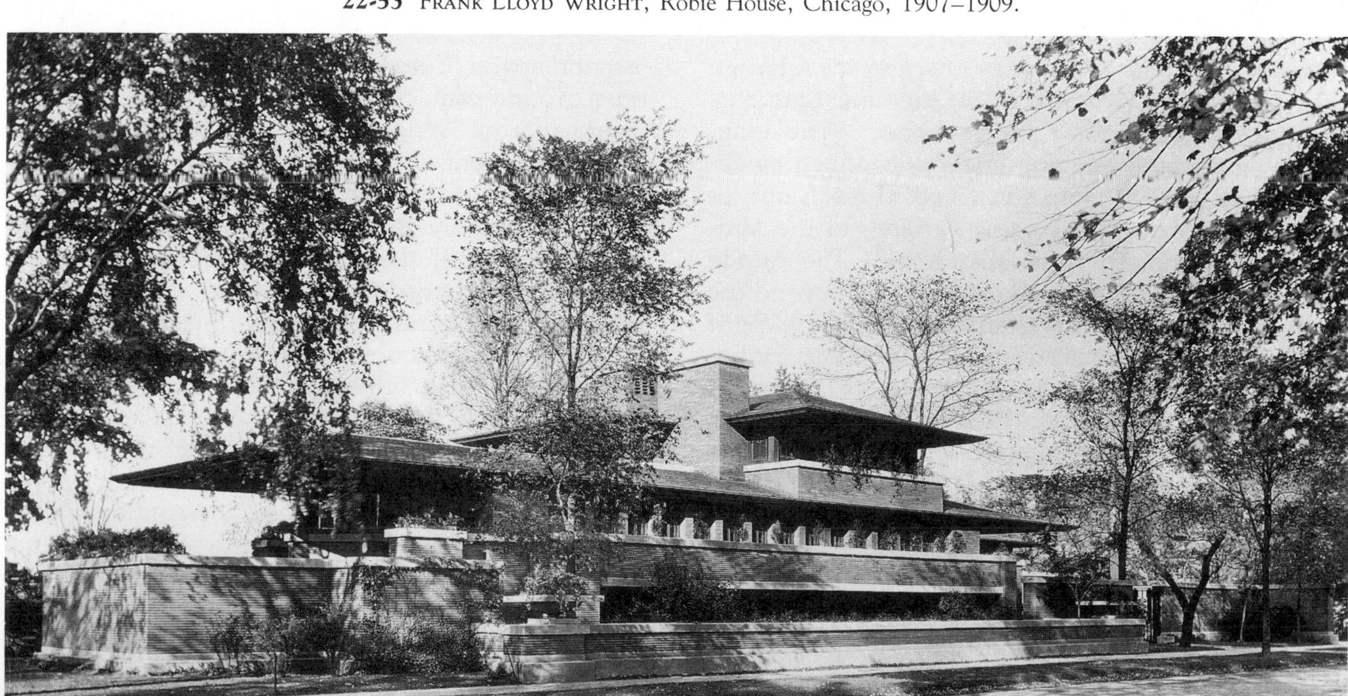

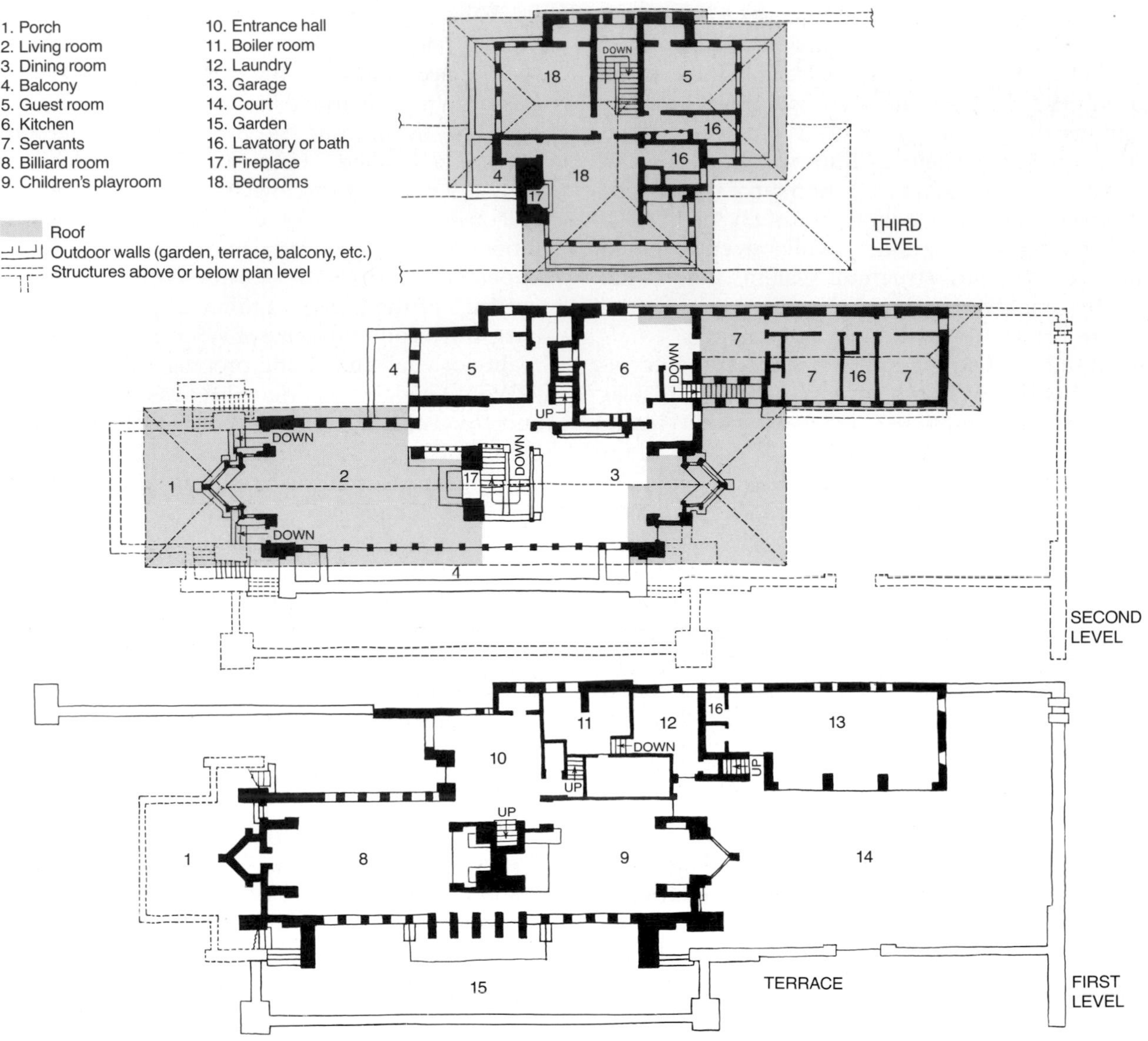

22-54 Frank Lloyd Wright, plan of the Robie House.

between 1907 and 1909. Like others in the Chicago area designed by Wright at about the same time, this building was called a "prairie house." The long, sweeping, ground-hugging lines, unconfined by abrupt limits of wall, were conceived to reach out toward and to express the great flatlands of the Midwest. All symmetry was abandoned. The façade disappeared, the roofs were extended far beyond the walls, and the entrance was all but concealed. Wright filled the "wandering" plan of the Robie House (FIG. **22-54**) with intricately articulated spaces (some, large and open; others, closed), grouped freely around a great central fireplace. (He felt strongly the age-old domestic significance of the hearth.) Enclosed patios, overhanging roofs, and strip windows were designed to provide unexpected light sources and glimpses of the outdoors as one moved through the interior space. These elements, together with the open ground plan, created a sense of space-in-motion inside and out. Wright's new and fundamental spatial arrangement of the interior was matched by his treatment of the exterior. Masses and voids were set in equilibrium; the flow of interior space determined the placement of the exterior walls. The "Cubist" aspect of the exterior, with its sharp, angular planes meeting at apparently odd angles, matches the complex play of interior solids that function not as inert, containing surfaces but as elements equivalent in role to the spaces in the design.

The Robie House is a good example of Wright's "naturalism" in the adjustment of building to site, although, in this particular case, the confines of the city lot constrained the building-to-site relationship more than did the sites of some of Wright's more

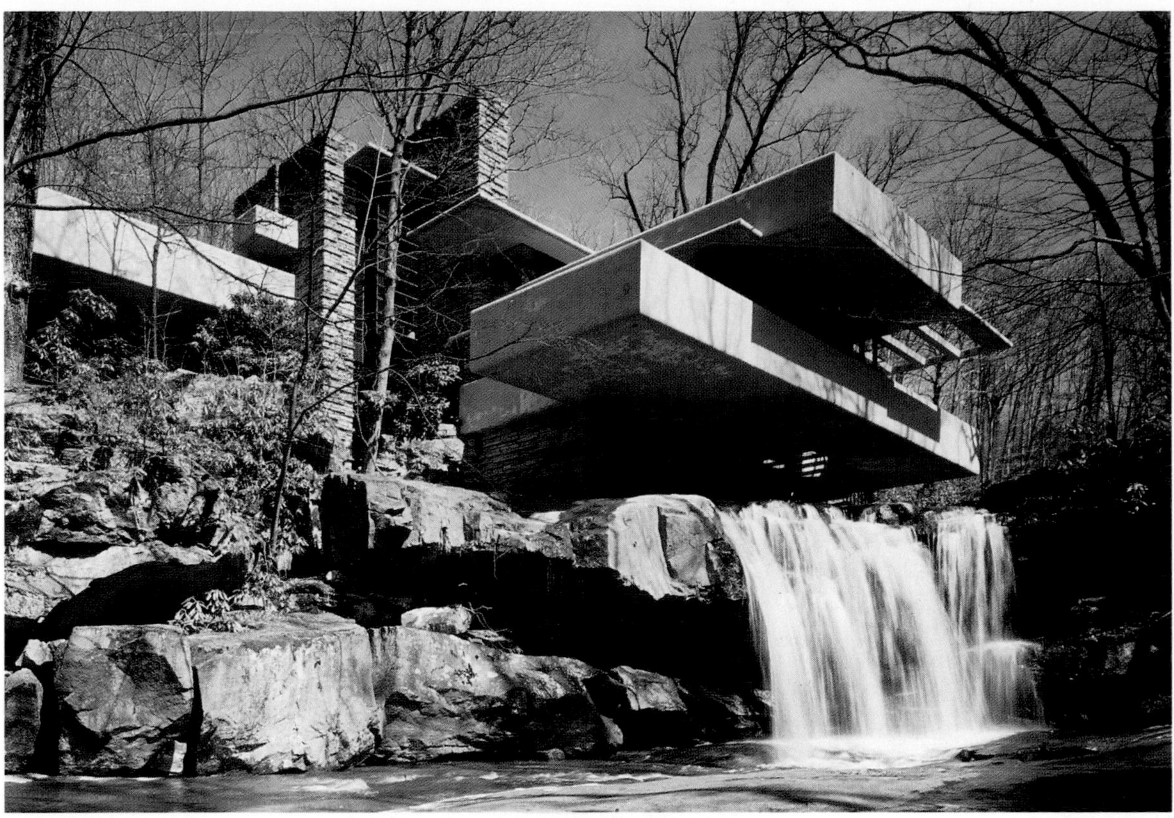

22-55 Frank Lloyd Wright, Kaufmann House (Fallingwater), Bear Run, Pennsylvania, 1936–1939.

expansive suburban and country homes. The Kaufmann House, nicknamed "Fallingwater" (FIG. **22-55**), which was designed as a weekend retreat at Bear Run near Pittsburgh, is a prime example of the latter. Perched on a rocky hillside over a small waterfall, this structure extends the blocky masses of the Robie House in all four directions. Its shapes are enlivened by the contrast in textures between concrete, painted metal, and natural stone in its walls, and by the way in which Wright used full-length strip windows to create a stunning interweaving of interior and exterior space. The implied message of Wright's new architecture was space, not mass—a space designed to fit the life of the patron, being enclosed and divided as required. Wright took special pains to meet the requirements of his clients, often designing all the accessories of the house himself (including, in at least one case, gowns for his client's wife!). In the late 1930s, he acted on a cherished dream to provide good architectural design for less well-to-do people by adapting the ideas of his prairie house to plans for smaller, less-expensive dwellings called "Usonian" houses.

The publication of Wright's plans brought him a measure of fame in Europe, especially in Holland and Germany. The issuance of a portfolio of his work in Berlin in 1910 and an exhibition of his designs the following year hastened the death of Art Nouveau and stimulated younger architects to adopt some of his ideas about open plans and the freedom they afforded clients. Some forty years before the end of his career, his work was already of revolutionary significance. Another great modern architect, Ludwig Mies van der Rohe, wrote in 1940 that "the dynamic impulse from [Wright's] work invigorated a whole generation. His influence was strongly felt even when it was not actually visible."*

Wright believed that people lived better when their houses allowed them easy contact with nature, and he designed his buildings accordingly. The Swiss architect Charles Édouard Jeanneret-Gris (1887–1965), called LE CORBUSIER, had a rather different idea about the ideal architectural setting for people. Trained as an architect in Paris and Berlin, Le Corbusier settled in Paris in 1917, where he became a painter, using his birth name, Jeanneret, for his work in this medium. With another artist, Amadée Ozenfant, Le Corbusier practiced painting in a style known as "Purism," in which he attempted to perfect Cubism by reducing it to patterns inspired by machine

*In Philip Johnson, *Mies van der Rohe,* rev. ed. (New York: Museum of Modern Art, 1954), pp. 200–201.

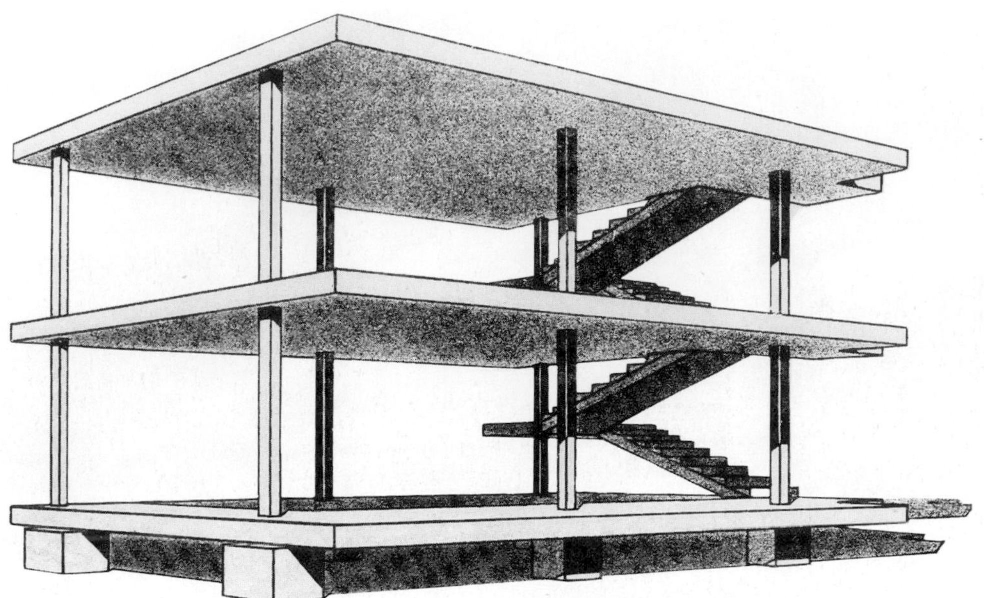

22-56 LE CORBUSIER, perspective drawing for Domino House project, Marseilles, France, 1914.

forms. However, Le Corbusier was best known as an influential architect and theorist on modern architecture. As such, he applied himself to the design of a "functional" living space, which he described as a "machine for living." The drawing for his Domino House project (FIG. **22-56**) shows the skeleton of his ideal dwelling. Every level can be used. Reinforced concrete slabs serve the double function of ceiling and floor, supported by thin steel posts (called *pilotis*) that rise freely inside the perimeter of the interior spaces of the structure. The whole structure is raised above ground on short blocks. The space underneath, as well as that on the roof, was utilized. As Le Corbusier later wrote: "The house is in the air, far from the soil; the garden spreads under the house; the garden is also on top of the house, on the roof." Exterior walls can be suspended from the projecting edges of the concrete slabs in this model, like free-hanging curtains. Because the skeleton is self-supporting, an architect using this plan has complete freedom to subdivide the interior, wherever desired, with light walls that bear no structural load. The scheme allowed the architect to provide for what Le Corbusier saw as the basic physical and psychosomatic needs of every human being—sun, space, and vegetation combined with controlled temperature, good ventilation, and insulation against harmful and undesired noise. He also believed that human scale must be the measure of dwelling design, because the house is the assertion of man within nature. The main principles of the Domino system had been anticipated about half a decade earlier in the designs of the German architects Walter Gropius and Peter Behrens (with whom Le Corbusier worked early in his career). However, Le Corbusier's drawing stated the ideas with such elegant simplicity that his image had enormous influence as the primary statement of the design concepts governing the structural principles used in many modern office buildings and skyscrapers, concepts practiced by so many architects (including Gropius and Mies van der Rohe) that the "look" was soon named the International Style.

Le Corbusier used the basic ideas of the Domino project in many single-family dwellings, the most elegant of which is the Villa Savoye (FIG. **22-57**), located at Poissy-sur-Seine, near Paris. The Villa Savoye is set conspicuously within its site, tending to dominate it, and has a broad view of the landscape. In this way, it resembles a Palladian villa and contrasts sharply with Frank Lloyd Wright's dwellings, which hug and adjust to the landscape, almost as if they were intended to be part of it and concealed by it. The Villa Savoye is a cube of lightly enclosed and deeply penetrated space. The ground floor (containing a three-car garage, some bedrooms, a bathroom, and some utility rooms) is only partially enclosed. Much of the house's interior is open space, with the main living floor and the roof garden area supported by the thin pilotis. Here one sees a parallel with Wright's open floor plans. The major living rooms in the Villa Savoye are on the second floor, wrapping around an open central court and lighted by strip windows that run along the membranelike exterior walls. From the second floor court, a ramp leads up to a flat roof-terrace and garden, protected by a curving windbreak along one side. The approach does not define an en-

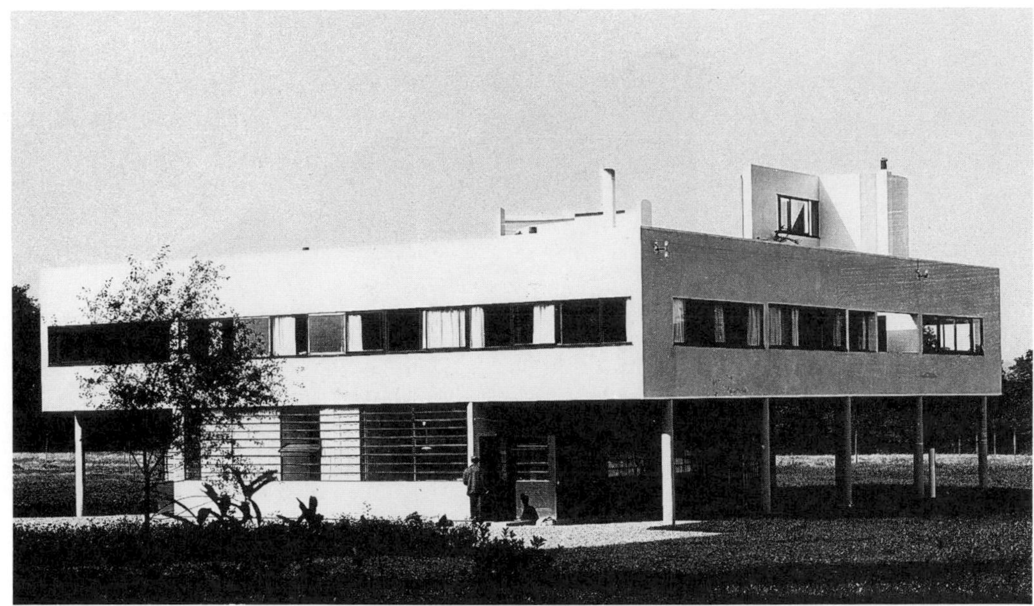

22-57 LE CORBUSIER, Villa Savoye, Poissy-sur-Seine, France, 1929.

trance; the building has no traditional façade. One must walk around and through the building to comprehend its layout. Spaces and masses interpenetrate so fluently that "inside" and "outside" space intermingle. The machine-planed smoothness of the surfaces, entirely without adornment, the slender "ribbons" of continuous windows, the buoyant lightness of the whole fabric—all present a total effect that is the reverse of the traditional country house (compare Andrea Palladio's Villa Rotunda and John Vanbrugh's Blenheim, FIGS. 17-51 and 20-1). Le Corbusier inverted the traditional design practice that placed light elements above and heavy ones below by refusing to enclose the ground story of the Villa Savoye with masonry walls, creating the effect that the "load" of the Villa Savoye's upper stories hovers lightly on the slender piloti supports. His use of color in this building—originally, dark-green base, cream walls, and rose-and-blue windscreen—was a deliberate analogy for that in the contemporary, machine-inspired Purist style of painting, in which he was actively engaged.

The Villa Savoye was a marvelous house for a single family, but Le Corbusier also dreamed of extending his ideas of the house as a "machine for living" to designs for efficient and humane cities. He believed that "great cities are the spiritual workshops in which the work of the world is done," and proposed to correct the deficiencies caused by poor traffic circulation, inadequate living "cells," and the lack of space for recreation and exercise in existing cities by replacing them with three types of new communities. Vertical cities would house workers and the business and service industries. Linear-industrial cities would run as belts along the routes between the vertical cities and would serve as centers for the people and processes involved in manufacturing. Finally, separate centers would be constructed for those people involved in intensive agricultural activity. Le Corbusier's cities would provide for human cultural needs in addition to serving every person's physical and psychosomatic comfort needs. The Domino project was a key part of Le Corbusier's thinking because the design was a module that could be repeated almost indefinitely, both horizontally and vertically. Its volumes could be manipulated and interlocked to provide interior spaces of different sizes and heights. It was not site-specific and could stand comfortably in any setting. Later in his career, Le Corbusier was able to design a few of his vertical cities, most notably the Unité d'Habitation in Marseilles (1945–1952). He also created the master plan for the entire city of Chandigarh, the capital city of the Punjab, India (1950–1957). He would end his career with a personal expressive style in the Chapel of Notre Dame du Haut at Ronchamp (FIGS. 23-9 and 23-10).

Le Corbusier wanted to create model cities in which each individual had dwelling spaces, work spaces, and recreation spaces suited to his or her needs. His approach was very different from that of Frank Lloyd Wright, who wanted to design houses that would bring their inhabitants into a close relationship with nature. In 1917, a group of young artists in Holland formed a new movement and began publishing a magazine; both movement and magazine were called *De Stijl* (the Style). The group was

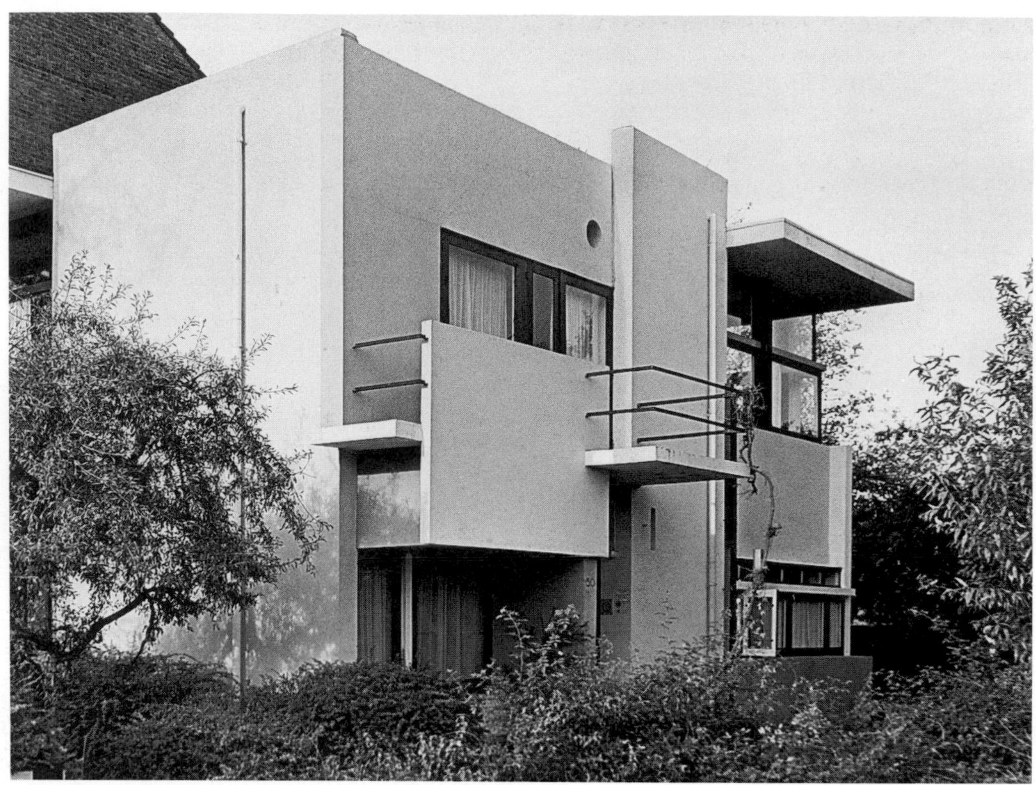

22-58 GERRIT RIETVELDT, Schröder House, Utrecht, Netherlands, 1924.

cofounded by Mondrian and the painter THEO VAN DOESBURG (1883–1931), and brought together some of the ideas expounded by Wright and Le Corbusier. Group members believed that a new age was being born in the wake of World War I—that it was a time of balance between individual and universal values, when the machine would bring a better life to all, and pure, open forms would assure ease of living: "There is an old and a new consciousness of the age. The old one is directed towards the individual. The new one is directed towards the universal."* The goal would be a total integration of art and life:

> We must realize that life and art are no longer separate domains. That is why the "idea" of "art" as an illusion separate from real life must disappear. The word "art" no longer means anything to us. In its place we demand the construction of our environment in accordance with creative laws based upon a fixed principle. These laws, following those of economics, mathematics, technique, sanitation . . . are leading to a new, plastic unit.†

Although Mondrian was associated with the De Stijl group early in his career, he embraced abstract formalism, leaving the practical application of these ideas to other artists, especially to architects and designers.

One of the masterpieces of De Stijl architecture is the Schröder House in Utrecht, Holland (FIG. **22-58**), built in 1924 by GERRIT RIETVELDT (1888–1964). Rietveldt came to the group as a cabinetmaker and made De Stijl furnishings throughout his career. His architecture carries the same spirit into a larger, integrated whole. Like Le Corbusier's Savoye House, the main living rooms of the Schröder House are on the second floor, with more private rooms on the ground floor. However, Rietveldt's house has an open plan and a relationship to nature more like the houses of Frank Lloyd Wright than those of Le Corbusier. The entire second floor is designed with sliding partitions that can be closed to define separate rooms or pushed back to create one open space broken into units only by the arrangement of the furniture. This shifting quality appears also on the outside, where railings, free-floating walls, and long rectangular windows give the effect of cubic units breaking up before our eyes. The Schröder House is the perfect expression of Van Doesburg's definition of De Stijl architecture:

> The new architecture is anti-cubic, *i.e.*, it does not strive to contain the different functional space cells in a single closed cube, but it throws the functional space (as well as canopy planes, balcony volumes, etc.) out from the centre of the cube, so that height,

*In Kenneth Frampton, *A Critical History of Modern Architecture* (London: Thames & Hudson, 1985), p. 142.

†Ibid., p. 147.

> width and depth plus time become a completely new plastic expression in open spaces. . . . The plastic architect . . . has to construct in the new field, time-space.*

The link between all the arts in De Stijl is clear in Rietveldt's design, where the rectangular planes, which seem to slide across each other on the façade of the Schröder House like movable panels, make this structure a kind of three-dimensional projection of the rigid but carefully proportioned flat planes in Mondrian's paintings.

The De Stijl group and Le Corbusier each dreamed of harnessing the machine to create whole environments. In reality, both actually built more private than public buildings. In Europe, German architects pioneered new industrial techniques for commercial and factory buildings, often under the inspiration of American silos, warehouses, and the early high-rise structures of Richardson and Sullivan (FIGS. 21-97 and 21-98). A particular vision of "total architecture" was developed by the German architect WALTER GROPIUS (1883–1969), who made this concept the foundation not only of his own work but also of the work of generations of pupils who came under his influence. Gropius's revolutionary ideas about the nature of architecture and architects developed during his early career in designs for objects and structures intended to serve large sections of the population: group farm dwellings, diesel locomotives, and model factories. In 1919 he had a chance to broaden his sphere of influence and to gain additional exposure for his ideas when he became the director of an art school in Weimar, East Germany. Founded in 1906 as the Weimar School of Arts and Crafts, with an educational program that emphasized craftsmanship, free creativity, and experimentation, under Gropius the school was renamed Das Staatliche Bauhaus (roughly translated as "State School of Building") and its mission was transformed to fit his ideas about the training of the modern architect:

> The complete Building is the final aim of the visual arts. . . . The objective of all creative effort in the visual arts is to give form to space. . . . But what is space, how can it be understood and given form? . . . True creative work can be done only by the man whose knowledge and mastery of the physical laws of statics, dynamics, optics, acoustics, equip him to give life and shape to his inner vision. In a work of art, the laws of the physical world, the intellectual world and the world of the spirit function and are expressed simultaneously. . . . We want to create a clear, organic architecture, whose inner logic will be radiant and naked, unencumbered by lying façades and trickeries; we want an architecture adapted to our world of machines, radios and fast motor cars, an architecture whose function is clearly recognizable in the relation of its forms. . . . A new esthetic of the Horizontal is beginning to develop which endeavors to counteract the effect of gravity. At the same time the symmetrical relationship of parts of the building and their orientation toward a central axis is being replaced by a new conception of equilibrium which transmutes this dead symmetry of similar parts into an asymmetrical but rhythmical balance.†

Gropius reorganized the various departments of the original Weimar school and redesigned its curriculum to stress the search for solutions to contemporary problems in such areas as housing, urban planning, and high-quality, utilitarian mass production—all vital needs in impoverished post–World War I Germany. Under the guidance of teachers like Kandinsky, Klee, and László Moholy-Nagy, the Bauhaus offered courses not only in architecture, but also in music, drama, painting, typography, and most crafts. In design, the study of handicraft was considered the natural way for artists to master the qualities of materials and form so that they could design well for mass production. In these respects, and in the minimizing of philosophy and other "verbal" disciplines, the Bauhaus was the earliest working example of much contemporary design education. Gropius worked actively to make the Bauhaus into a "consulting center for industry and the trades." By the time he designed new quarters for the school in 1925, in preparation for its move to a new location in Dessau, East Germany, a new generation of teachers had been trained as artists-craftsmen-industrial designers, and Bauhaus students and faculty were designing buildings, stained-glass windows, furniture, lighting, fabrics, pottery, metal objects of every kind, advertising, books, and commercial displays—all for mass production. Gropius's design for the Bauhaus buildings included a glass-walled workshop (FIG. **22-59**), a block of studio-bedrooms for students, and a building for technical instruction. Linking these three main blocks were other units, such as the administrative offices, which were located on the bridge that spans the road in our illustration. Gropius also designed houses nearby for himself and six major Bauhaus teachers. Planned as a series of units, each with its own specific function, the Bauhaus design is the direct expression, in glass, steel, and thin concrete veneer, of the technical program it housed. The forms are clear, cubic shapes—the epitome of classicizing purity. The workshop block is a cage of glass that extends beyond

*In Hans L. Jaffé, *De Stijl* (New York: Harry N. Abrams, n.d.), pp. 185–88.

†In Herbert Bayer, Walter Gropius, Ise Gropius, et al., *Bauhaus: 1919–1928* (Boston: Branford, 1959), *passim*.

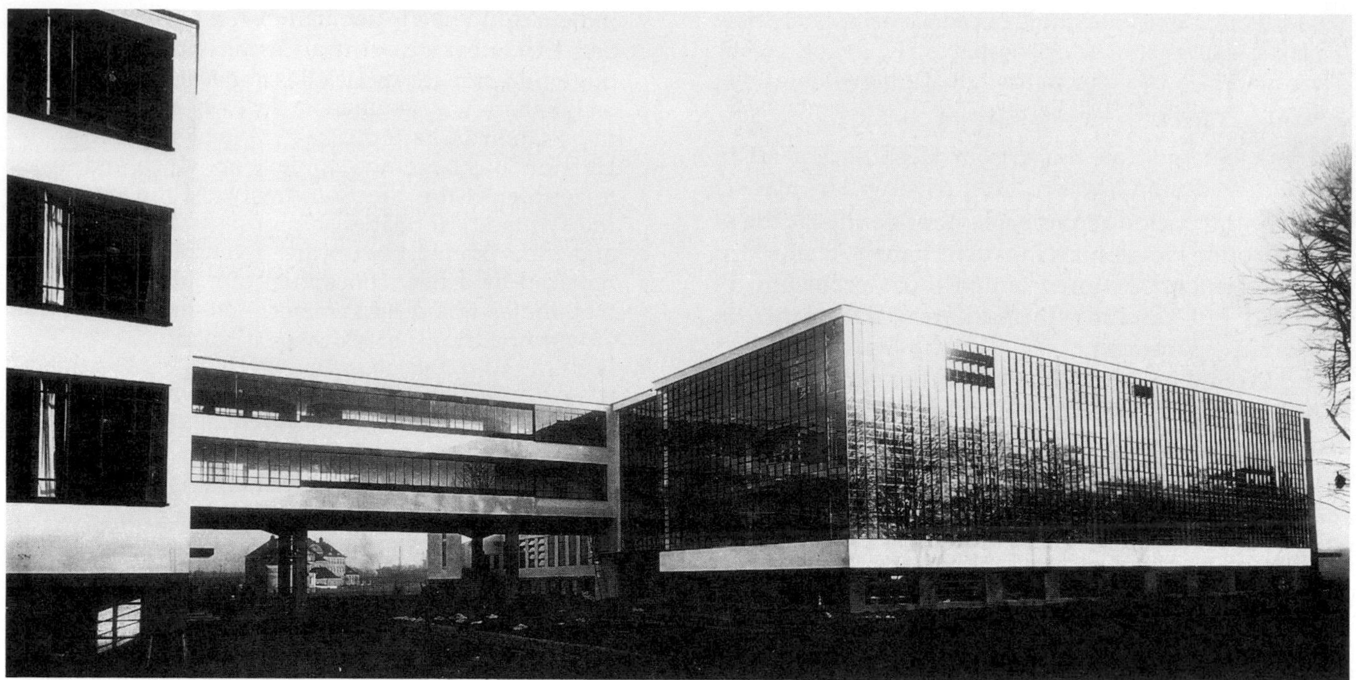

22-59 WALTER GROPIUS, shop block, the Bauhaus, Dessau, Germany, 1925–1926.

and encloses its steel supports in a way that echoes Le Corbusier's Domino project (FIG. 22-56). The transparent block makes an equilibrium of inner and outer space. The whole fulfilled Gropius's original dream for the kind of architecture that should be created by the Bauhaus. Bauhaus style spread rapidly as its students and faculty fled the rise of Nazi power, firmly establishing the principles of the International Style throughout much of the industrialized world during the next three decades.* The buildings themselves were abandoned for many years but are now in use again as an art school.

One of the most important ex-Bauhaus teachers to carry its style abroad was the Hungarian-American LÁSZLÓ MOHOLY-NAGY (1895–1946), who taught at the Bauhaus during Gropius's directorship and later extended the school's ideas of total architecture to embrace the concept of the total artist as an individual who puts personal talent at the service of humanity in any way possible. Born in Hungary, Moholy-Nagy studied law before experiences as a soldier during World War I made him realize he wanted to serve humanity as an artist. He moved from Hungary to Vienna and then Berlin before joining the faculty of the Bauhaus in 1923 to teach the "preliminary course" and to direct the metal workshop. Moholy-Nagy was a visionary who saw clearly the nature of the modern age and believed that society in this period was

> heading toward a kinetic, time-spatial existence; toward an awareness of the forces plus their relationships which define all life and of which we had no previous knowledge and for which we have as yet no exact terminology. . . . Space-time stands for many things: relativity of motion and its measurement, integration, simultaneous grasp of the inside and outside, revelation of the structure instead of the façade. It also stands for a new vision concerning materials, energies, tensions, and their social implications.†

Moholy-Nagy believed that artists should create works to help ordinary people develop this "*vision in motion* . . . seeing, feeling, and thinking in relationship and not as a series of isolated phenomena." Such art would capture the ways our space-time perceptions have been expanded as our eyes, ears, and senses of balance and equilibrium increasingly have functioned from within speeding cars, trains, and planes, and through x-ray cameras, telescopes, and microscopes. For himself, Moholy-Nagy experimented with light and color in painting, sculpture, prints, photograms, photography, experimental cinema, typography, advertisements, stage sets, and special effects for movies. Photography was an especially important medium for expressing his ideas. The bird's-eye view that he took from the top of the Radio

*The ideals of the Bauhaus were taken to the United States when its artists were forced to emigrate to escape the effects of Nazi power. Gropius headed the architecture program at Harvard University. In Chicago, Moholy-Nagy founded the New Bauhaus (later the Institute of Design) and Mies van der Rohe shaped the architecture department at Illinois Institute of Technology.

†László Moholy-Nagy, *Vision in Motion* (Chicago: Paul Theobald, 1969), p. 268.

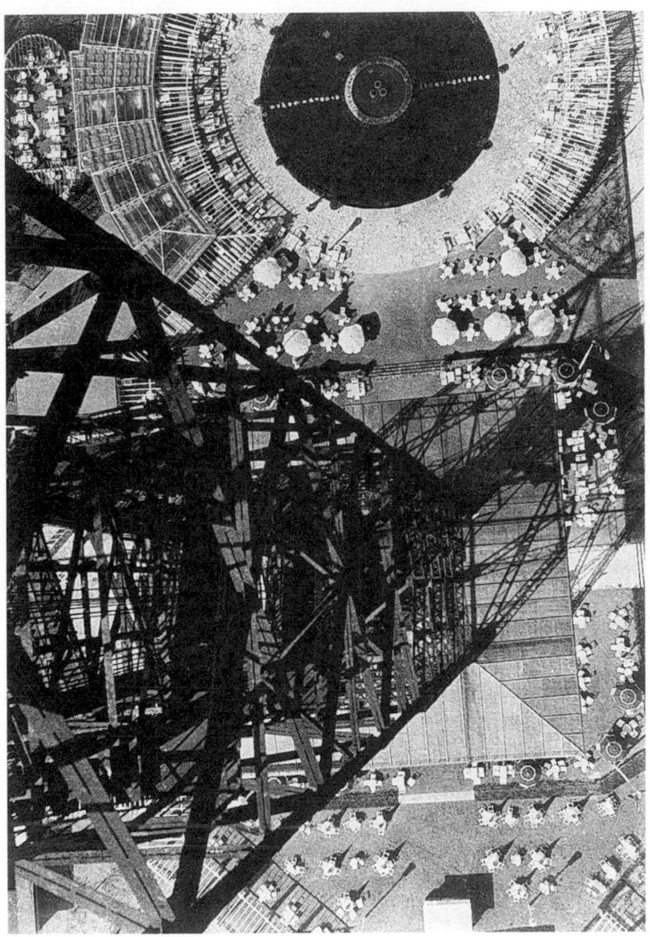

22-60 László Moholy-Nagy, *From the Radio Tower Berlin,* 1928. Gelatin silver print. Photograph © 1990, The Art Institute of Chicago. All rights reserved.

Tower in Berlin (FIG. **22-60**) is an exercise in his "new vision" of "seeing, feeling and thinking in relationship and not as a series of isolated phenomena." The abrupt shift from normal, eye-level viewing reveals new patterns of reality, unexpected formal associations, and an enchantingly different way of looking at the world.

When Walter Gropius resigned as head of the Bauhaus in 1930, Ludwig Mies van der Rohe (1886–1969) became its director, moving it to Berlin before political pressures forced it to close in 1933. Mies van der Rohe, who taught at the Bauhaus for a time before assuming the directorship, combined his father's and mother's surnames for his own professional name. In his architecture and furniture, he made such a clear and elegant statement of the International Style that his work had enormous influence on modern architecture. Taking as his motto "less is more" and calling his architecture "skin and bones," his esthetic was already fully formed in the model for a glass skyscraper office building he conceived in 1921 (FIG. **22-61**). Working with glass provided him with new freedom and many new possibilities: "I discovered by working with glass models that the important thing is the play of reflections and not the effect of light and shadow as in ordinary buildings. . . . At first glance the curved outline . . . seems arbitrary. These curves, however, were determined by three factors: sufficient illumination of the interior, the massing of the building viewed from the street, and lastly, the play of reflections."* In the glass model, three irregularly shaped towers flow outward from a central court designed to hold a lobby, a porter's room, and a community center. Two cylindrical entrance shafts rise at the ends of the court, each containing elevators, stairways, and toilets. The perimeter walls are wholly transparent, revealing the regular horizontal patterning of the cantilevered floor planes and their thin, vertical supporting elements. The weblike delicacy of the lines of the glass model, its radiance, and the illusion of movement created by reflection and by light changes seen through it prefigure many of the glass skyscrapers of major cities

*In A. James Speyer with Frederick Koeper, *Mies van der Rohe* (Chicago: The Art Institute of Chicago, 1968), p. 16.

22-61 Ludwig Mies van der Rohe, model for a glass skyscraper, 1920–1921. Present location of model unknown.

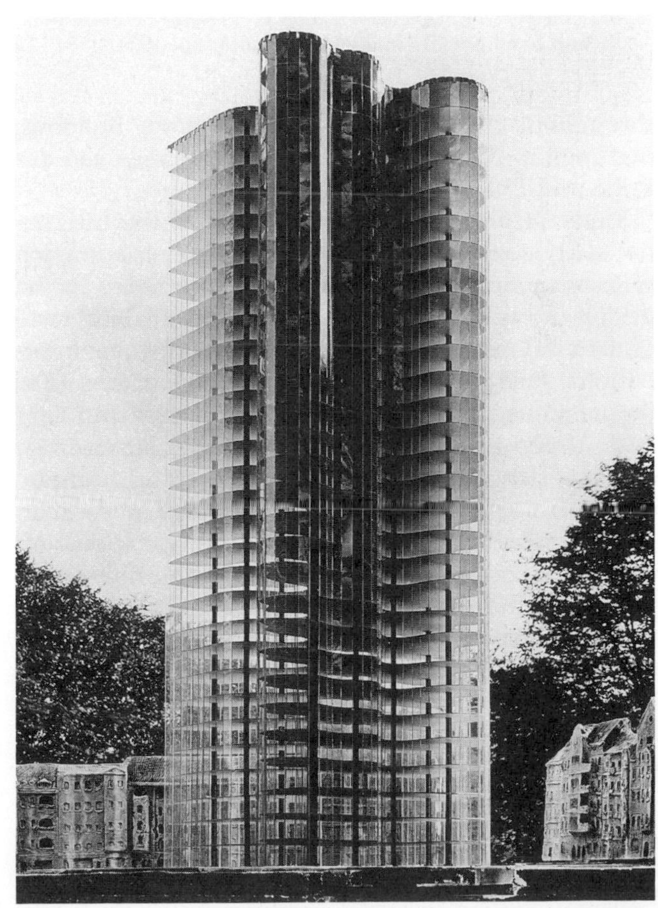

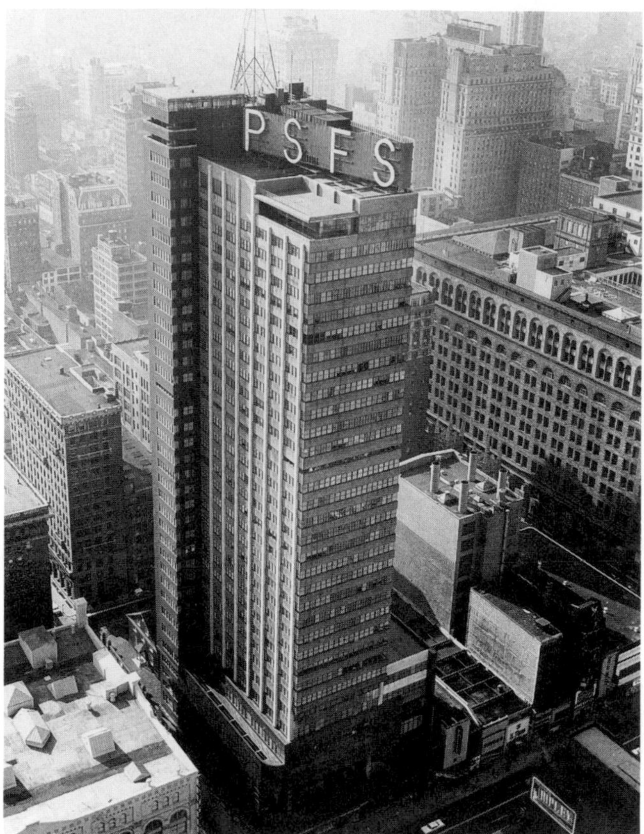

22-62 George Howe and William E. Lescaze, Philadelphia Savings Fund Society Building, Philadelphia, 1931–1932.

throughout the world, like the Seagram Building, designed in New York in the 1950s by Mies van der Rohe and Philip Johnson (fig. 23-17).

Many of the architects who adopted the International Style were wholly traditional in their approach to their métier—that is, they were specialists in the design of buildings according to the prevailing taste of their day. In America, something of the new International manner began to appear in the early 1930s. In the Philadelphia Savings Fund Society Building (fig. **22-62**), designed by George Howe (1886–1955) and William E. Lescaze (1896–1969), for example, the horizontal banding, ribbon windows, and clean, geometric planes of the International Style appear on the soaring scale of the American urban office building. This kind of assembly of cubic volumes was so quickly accepted as the perfect expression of urban corporate business that its look transformed the skylines of most modern cities. Unfortunately, although the International Style swept across the world, well-designed structures in this mode were never the norm; such buildings required more money to construct and more effort to maintain than less radical International Style buildings, many of whose designers stressed only the cubic volumes and basic patterns of steel-girder high-rise construction and demonstrated little gift for creating with the powerful geometric simplicity of the style's greatest monuments.

In the United States, one architect in particular, Buckminster Fuller (1895–1983), shared with Le Corbusier and the Bauhaus a belief that technology could be used to help people create a better world. Fuller studied for two years at Harvard University and served as a naval officer in World War I. Thereafter, he was self-educated through a number of jobs in business and industry. In 1927, Fuller set out "to rethink everything I knew" and decided, as had eighteenth-century Enlightenment thinkers before him, that he "must commit . . . to reforming the environment and not man; being absolutely confident that if you give man the right environment he will behave favorably." Fuller was acutely aware that stores of resources and energy on our planet are limited and that only a careful use of them would provide indefinitely for all of the earth's population.

One of the first designs Fuller conceived to conserve resources was that of the Multiple-Deck 4-D [four-dimensional] House (fig. **22-63**). (The 4-D concept was renamed "Dymaxion" in 1929 by combining two of Fuller's favorite words, *dynamic* and *maximum.*) Of the 4-D House, he wrote: "I was thinking then of housing as shelters that could be mass-produced and delivered as finished dwellings to any place its owner wanted it to be; this ten-deck building was designed to be so light and so strong that it could have been carried by the *Graf Zeppelin,* which was then being built, and was perfectly flyable economically to the North Pole where it could be anchored."* Like Le Corbusier's vertical city, Fuller's 4-D House was planned to be self-contained, with utilities, elevators, stores, and recreation and sports facilities, in addition to living spaces. However, Fuller's concept was a radical structural and conceptual departure from the traditional architectural practice of selecting a site and then carefully preparing it to receive its new structure. Fuller planned that a zeppelin carrying one of his prefabricated 4-D houses would hover over a site, anchor itself, drop a small bomb that would create a hole for the foundation, and lower the dwelling tower into the hole, where it would be held upright by temporary wire supports fastened to the airship, while cement was poured around the foot of the mast and allowed to harden. The self-contained utilities, installed in the mast at the factory, could then be activated and the building would be ready for occupancy. Fuller took the design of the functioning details of his buildings seriously, and he filed patents for such innovations as waterless toilets; water-

*R. Buckminster Fuller with Robert Snyder, *Buckminster Fuller: An Autobiographical Monologue Scenario* (New York: St. Martin's Press, 1980), *passim.*

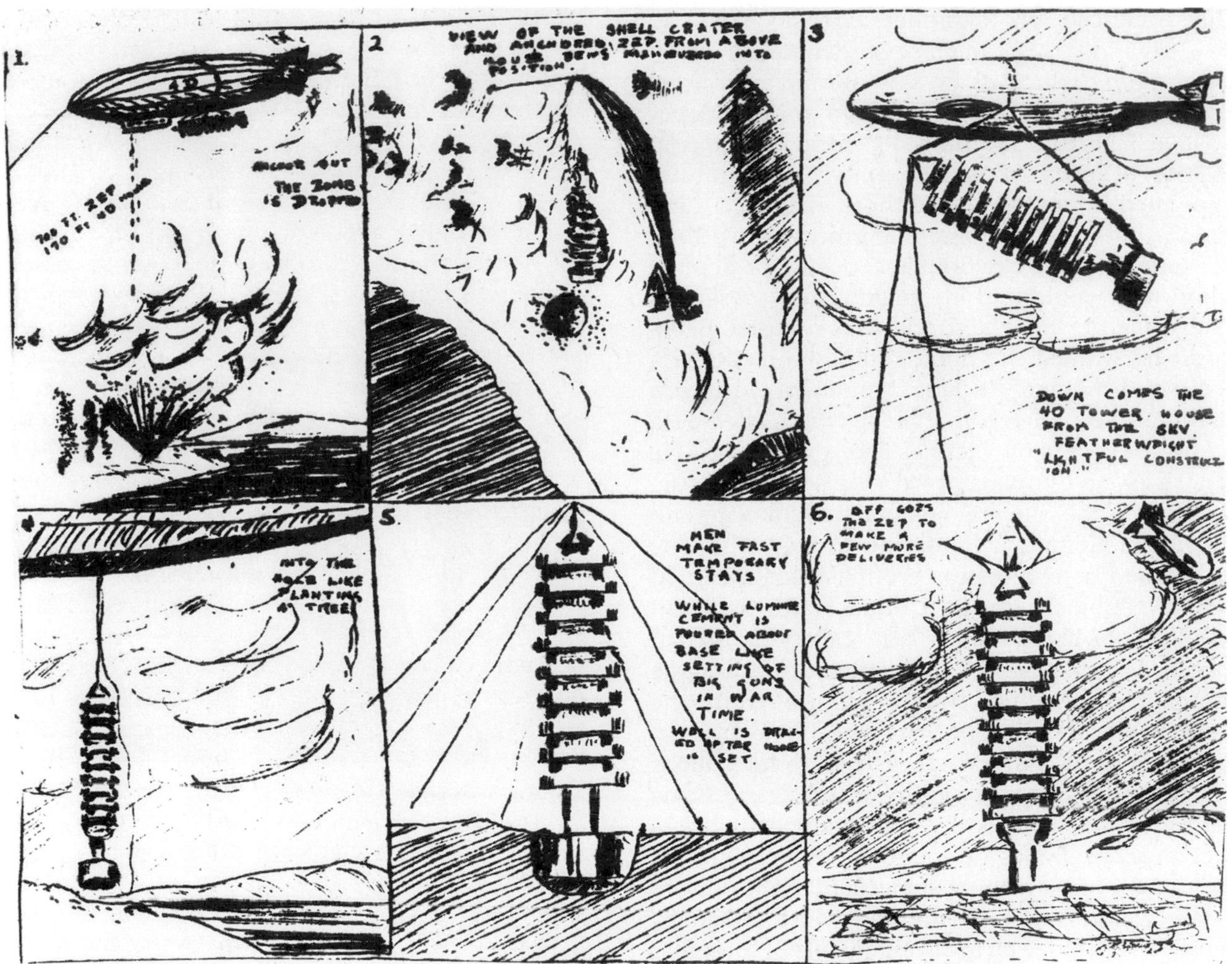

22-63 Buckminster Fuller, Multiple-Deck 4-D House, 1960. © 1980 Estate of Buckminster Fuller. Courtesy, the Buckminster Fuller Institute, Los Angeles.

conservative, intensive-spray showers; transparent but rapidly darkening vacuum-glass material to be used in place of window walls; a system for maintaining a dust-free environment through air that is cleaned, heated, and circulated in the central mast; and revolving storage wheels filled with different kinds of compartments to store every type of household good in a very compact space. Fuller's architecture did not lead to a movement like the International Style, perhaps because his emphasis was always on use and function rather than on beautiful form. Although he obtained funding to build only a few of these early structures, the effects of his work are to be found all around us in manufactured versions of many of the inventions he designed for his 4-D and Dymaxion systems. In addition, the geodesic dome, which Fuller invented in the early 1950s, won widespread adoption for use in structures ranging in scale from private homes to giant pavilions at international expositions. Fuller's planned projects and executed designs were among the most utopian of the works connected with the artists who followed a dream of building a more perfect world.

The Power of the Visual World

Many artists whose work was motivated by social or political concerns used their art to inspire a more ideal future or to criticize conditions in the present, but one group used art primarily to document and affirm the world around them. For this group, capturing the appearance of the visible world was an important impetus. Photography, from its beginning, had excelled in the documentary recording of physical reality, and many of the artists in this group were photographers, although some painters also sought to capture the qualities of the natural or urban scene. Photographers and painters alike wanted to heighten viewer awareness of the environment around them, sensitizing them to both the beauty and the variety of nature and the industrial/urban setting.

The American photographer ALFRED STIEGLITZ (1864–1946) took his camera everywhere he went, photographing whatever he saw around him, from the bustling streets of New York City to cloudscapes in upstate New York and the faces of friends and relatives. He believed in making only "straight, unmanipulated" photographs—those exposed and printed using basic photographic processes, without resort to techniques like double-exposure or double-printing that would add information not present in the subject at the time the shutter was released. Stieglitz said he wanted the photographs he made with this direct technique "to hold a moment, to record something so completely that those who see it would relive an equivalent of what has been expressed." He began a lifelong campaign to win a place for photography among the fine arts while a student of photochemistry in Germany. Returning to New York, he founded the Photo-Secession group, which mounted traveling exhibitions in the United States and sent loan collections abroad, and "291" gallery (located at 291 Fifth Avenue), where he exhibited avant-garde photography, painting, and sculpture from the United States and Europe. (Indeed, the works of many avant-garde European artists were introduced to a United States audience as the result of exhibitions at "291".) In his own works, Stieglitz specialized in photographs of scenes he found around him in his environment. He saw these subjects in terms of form and the "colors" of his black-and-white materials, being attracted above all to arrangements of form that stirred his deepest emotions. His esthetic approach crystallized during the making of one of his best-known works, *The Steerage* (FIG. **22-64**), taken during a voyage to Europe with his wife and daughter in 1907. Traveling first-class, Stieglitz rapidly grew bored with the company of the well-to-do passengers in the first-class section of the ship and walked as far forward on that level as he could, being brought up short by the rail around the opening onto the lower deck reserved for "steerage" passengers (those with the cheapest tickets). Later, he described what happened next:

> The scene fascinated me: A round hat; the funnel leaning left, the stairway leaning right; the white drawbridge, its railings made of chain; white suspenders crossed on the back of a man below; circular iron machinery; a mast that cut into the sky, completing a triangle. I stood spellbound. I saw shapes related to one another—a picture of shapes, and underlying it, a new vision that held me: simple people; the feeling of ship, ocean, sky; a sense of release that I was away from the mob called rich. Rembrandt came into my mind and I wondered would he have felt as I did . . . I had only one plate holder with one unexposed plate. Could I catch what I saw and felt? I released the shutter. If I had captured what I wanted, the photograph would go far beyond any of my previous prints. It would be a picture based on related shapes and deepest human feeling—a step in my own evolution, a spontaneous discovery.*

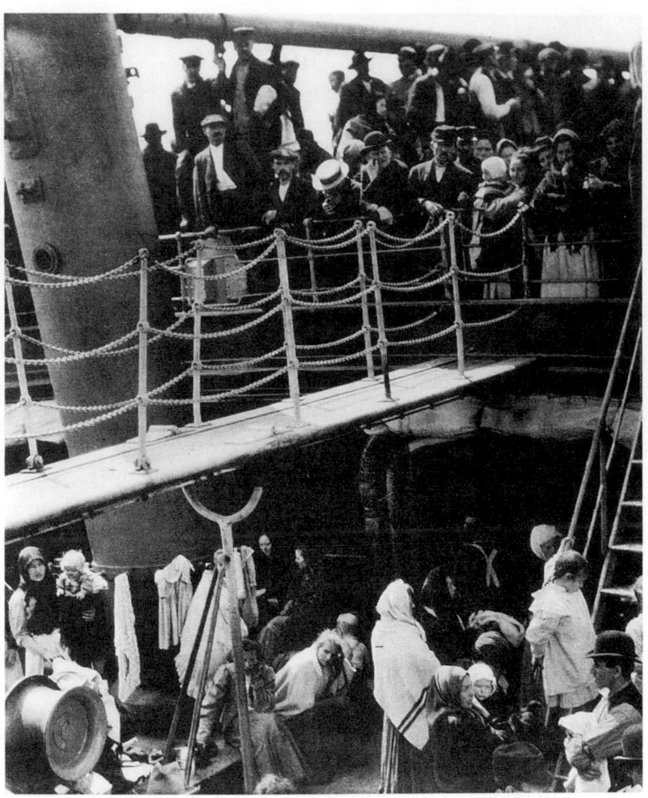

22-64 ALFRED STIEGLITZ, *The Steerage*, 1907 (print 1915). Photogravure (on tissue), $12\frac{3}{8}'' \times 10\frac{1}{8}''$. Courtesy Amon Carter Museum, Ft. Worth.

The finished print fulfilled Stieglitz's vision so well that it shaped his future photographic work, and its haunting mixture of found patterns and human activity has continued to stir the emotions of viewers to this day.

The American painter GEORGIA O'KEEFFE (1887–1986) was especially inspired by light and by the patterns of nature, stripping her subjects to their purest forms and colors to heighten their expressive power. Born in rural Wisconsin, O'Keeffe worked as a commercial artist and an art teacher as she developed a personal style that incorporated the ideas of the art theorist Arthur Wesley Dow and his follower, the artist-theorist-teacher Alon Bement, both of whom stressed "the idea of filling a space in a beautiful

*In Dorothy Norman, *Alfred Stieglitz: An American Seer* (Middleton, NY: Aperture, 1973), pp. 9–10, 161.

way," especially a space created with the simple flat shapes characteristic of Japanese paintings and prints. The look of things in the world inspired O'Keeffe's paintings of flowers, landscape, objects, and sun in Texas and New Mexico (the spiritual home in which she lived much of each year), and scenes in upstate New York and Manhattan, where she made her home part of the year with her husband, Alfred Stieglitz, until his death. In all her works, O'Keeffe reduced the incredible details of her subject to a symphony of basic colors, shapes, textures, and vital rhythms. Her style is fully realized in the watercolor *Light Coming on the Plains II* (FIG. **22-65**), where a few strokes of paint on dampened paper evoke the sun rising above the horizon in the vast, flat land of the Southwest. Light was a recurrent theme in O'Keeffe's work and in *Light Coming on the Plains II,* the miracle of light filling the world is rendered in a composition so simple that its abstraction becomes a serenely organic counterpart to Kandinsky's explosive nonobjective works or Mondrian's rectilinear absolutes.

22-65 GEORGIA O'KEEFFE, *Light Coming on the Plains II,* 1917. Watercolor, $11\frac{7}{8}'' \times 8\frac{7}{8}''$. Amon Carter Museum, Ft. Worth. Reproduced with permission of the Georgia O'Keeffe Estate.

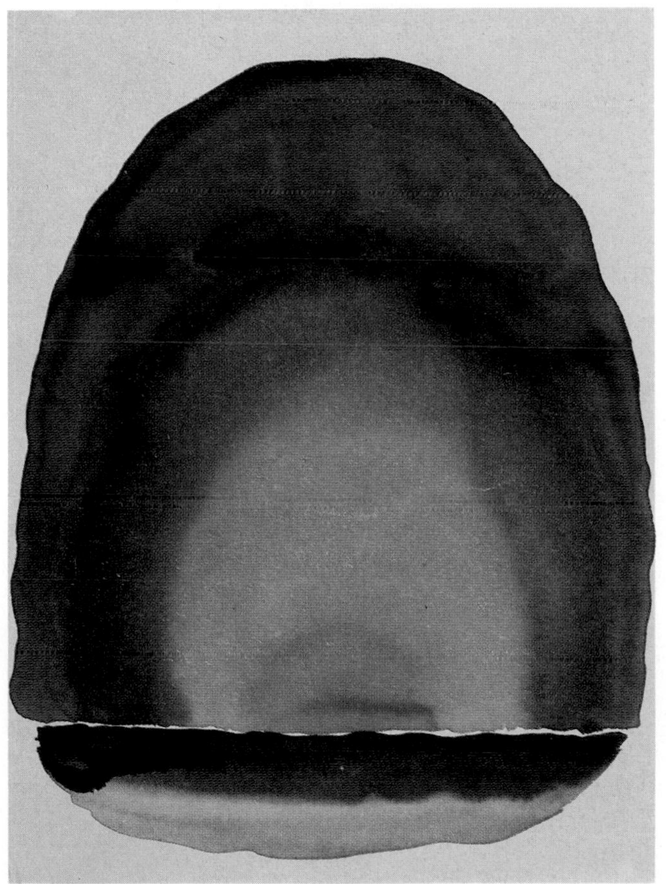

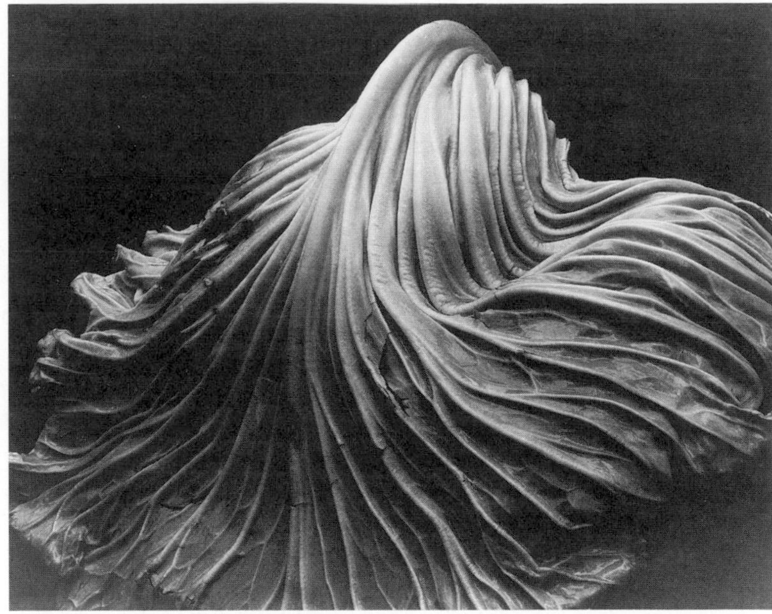

22-66 EDWARD WESTON, *Cabbage Leaf,* 1931. Gelatin silver print, $7\frac{9}{16}'' \times 9\frac{7}{16}''$. Collection, The Museum of Modern Art, New York (gift of T. J. Maloney). © 1981 Arizona Board of Regents, Center for Creative Photography, Tucson.

In addition to her landscapes and cityscapes, O'Keeffe was well-known for her close-up paintings of flowers, a vision that links her to the American photographer EDWARD WESTON (1886–1958), who also found beauty in the appearance of the natural world. Raised in Chicago, Weston began taking photographs with a simple camera as a boy and extended his technical knowledge working in professional photo studios. The settings in California and Mexico helped him to develop a style that captured the beauty he found in organic forms. Moving close and filling his picture with a subject like that in *Cabbage Leaf* (FIG. **22-66**), Weston detached the common vegetable from its everyday place in garden and kitchen and transformed it into a wonderfully sensual visual pattern. He set for himself the goal of recording *life,* of rendering the essence and substance of the thing he was photographing "whether it be polished steel or palpitating flesh." Weston termed himself "a realist, but not a literalist," saying, "To me good composition is simply the strongest way to put over my emotional reaction. I do not consciously compose. I make my negative entirely under the effect of my emotion in response to a given subject."* Weston's vision was so sensitive that even a humble leaf of cabbage is transfigured into a sensual, poetic vision of

*In Ben Maddow, *Edward Weston* (Boston: Aperture, 1963), pp. 55, 56.

rippled texture and undulant curves. Like Stieglitz, Weston believed that the photographer must see all elements of the finished picture in the camera before exposing the negative. He felt the artist must be carefully attuned to the qualities in a subject that touch the emotions and must seek a composition that expresses these in the clearest way. In Weston's case, he moved his camera carefully until the elements of his subject made a composition on the ground-glass focusing screen that conveyed to him the powerful complex of feelings that had initially attracted him to that particular subject in the first place.

The drama of the natural wilderness as a contrast to the urban scene was the primary subject of the American photographer ANSEL ADAMS (1902–1984). Born in San Francisco, Adams was a professional pianist before the vistas of Yosemite Valley inspired him to switch to photography as a profession. Trudging into the wilderness with the kind of large-plate view camera used by many nineteenth-century American photographers to capture western landscape, Adams set out to record the natural grandeur of scenery that moved him. He found his vision on a trip into Yosemite in 1927 during the making of *Monolith, the Face of Half Dome, Yosemite Valley, California* (FIG. **22-67**). He set up his tripod at the location from which he had the most dramatic view of the cliff face, arranged the camera, and covered the lens with a yellow filter, which would darken the sky somewhat in the final black-and-white print. Later he vividly described the process of recording the image:

> I began to think about how the print was to appear, and if it would transmute any of the feeling of the monumental shape before me in terms of its expressive-emotional quality. I began to see in my mind's eye the finished print I desired; the brooding cliff with a dark sky and the sharp rendition of distant, snowy Tenaya Peak. I realized that only a deep red filter would give me anything approaching the effect I felt emotionally.*

The change of filter created the dramatic contrasts that express so powerfully Adams's emotional response to this dazzling part of the landscape in Yosemite National Park. The rough, sheer-rock face of the cliff rises dramatically against the darkened sky. Every detail across its broad surface is in sharp focus, which is a tribute to Adams's skill in using the smallest possible aperture for his lens. Like Stieglitz, Adams believed that the photographer must master the techniques of the medium so thoroughly that they can be used almost instinctively at the moment a subject appears before the camera's lens. Adams called this kind of preparation "visualization." "A photograph," he said, "is not an accident—it is a concept. It exists at, or before, the moment of exposure of the negative." Every aspect of photo technology must be so perfectly mastered that the photographer and his equipment are one when the negative is exposed. Head and heart, technique and art must balance perfectly to achieve Adams's ultimate goal: "To photograph truthfully and effectively is to see beneath the surfaces and record the qualities of nature and humanity which live or are latent in all things."† During his long career, the most powerful images Adams "visualized" were those that captured the breathtaking grandeur of America's mountain wilderness—scenes such as *Monolith*.

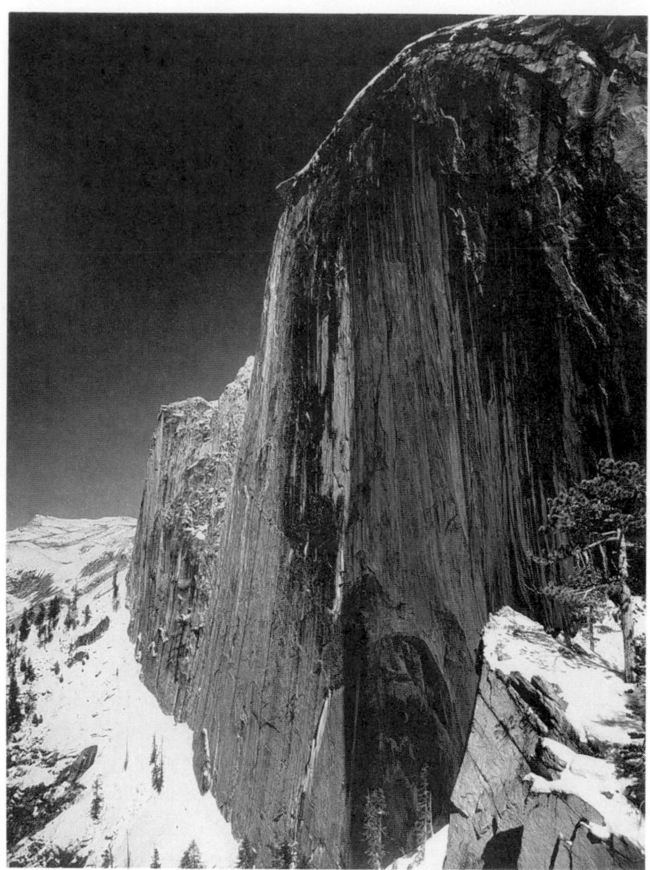

22-67 ANSEL ADAMS, *Monolith, the Face of Half Dome, Yosemite Valley, California*, c. 1927. Gelatin silver print. Courtesy of the Trustees of the Ansel Adams Publishing Rights Trust.

The American artist CHARLES SHEELER (1883–1965) was inspired more by the precise geometry of the new industrial and architectural shapes than by landscape. Trained as a traditional painter, Sheeler be-

*Ansel Adams with Mary Street Alinder, *Ansel Adams: An Autobiography* (Boston: Little, Brown, 1985), p. 76.

†In Nathan Lyons, ed., *Photographers on Photography* (Englewood Cliffs, NJ: Prentice-Hall, 1966), pp. 30, 31.

came interested in the forms of the man-made environment after he began supporting himself as a commercial photographer in 1912. His photographs of details of Shaker buildings and Chartres Cathedral, of the streets and buildings of Manhattan, and of a Ford automobile plant in Detroit captured the pure geometric compositions that caught his eye. In 1929 he was commissioned by a German steamship company to do a series of photographs of the *S.S. Majestic* for a publicity brochure. One image (FIG. **22-68**), which shows a detail of the ship's upper deck and ventilation system, intrigued Sheeler so much that he used it as the "blueprint" for a painting he called *Upper Deck* (FIG. **22-69**). In the painting, Sheeler has eliminated every trace of his painter's hand, the better to render the sleek forms. He simplified details in the photograph, eliminating rivets and rust and modifying the shadow patterns into a symphony of tawny and rosy whites. This painting was special for Sheeler; it signaled the attainment of an artistic goal: "This is what I have been getting ready for. I had come to feel that a picture could have incorporated in it the structural design implied in abstraction and be presented in a wholly realistic manner."* Inspired by

*In Carol Troyen and Erica E. Hirshler, *Charles Sheeler: Paintings and Drawings* (Boston: Museum of Fine Arts, 1987), p. 116.

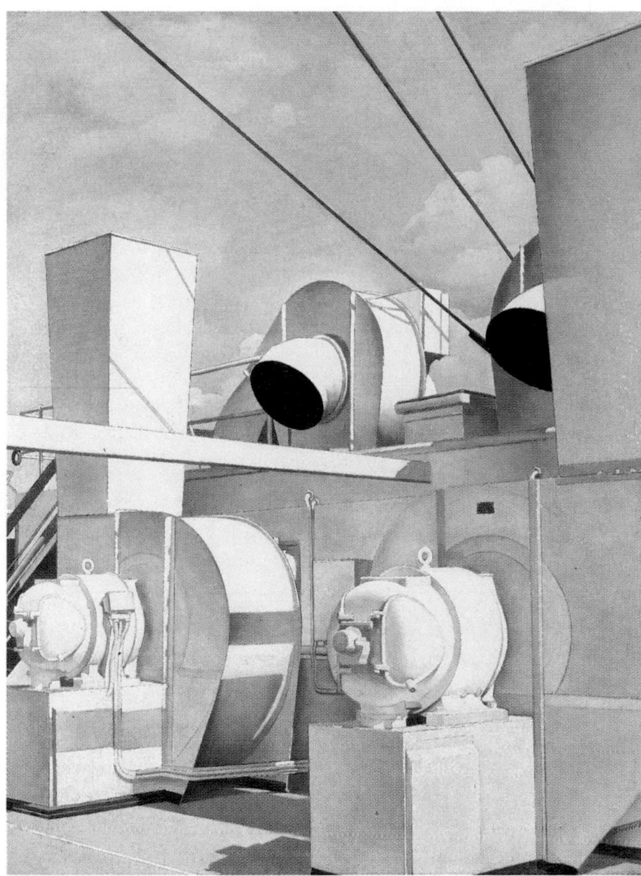

22-69 CHARLES SHEELER, *Upper Deck*, 1929. 29⅛″ × 22⅛″. Courtesy of the Fogg Art Museum, Harvard University, Cambridge, Massachusetts (Louise E. Bettens Fund).

22-68 CHARLES SHEELER, *The Upper Deck*, c. 1928. Vintage silver print, 8″ × 10″. Collection, Gilman Paper Company.

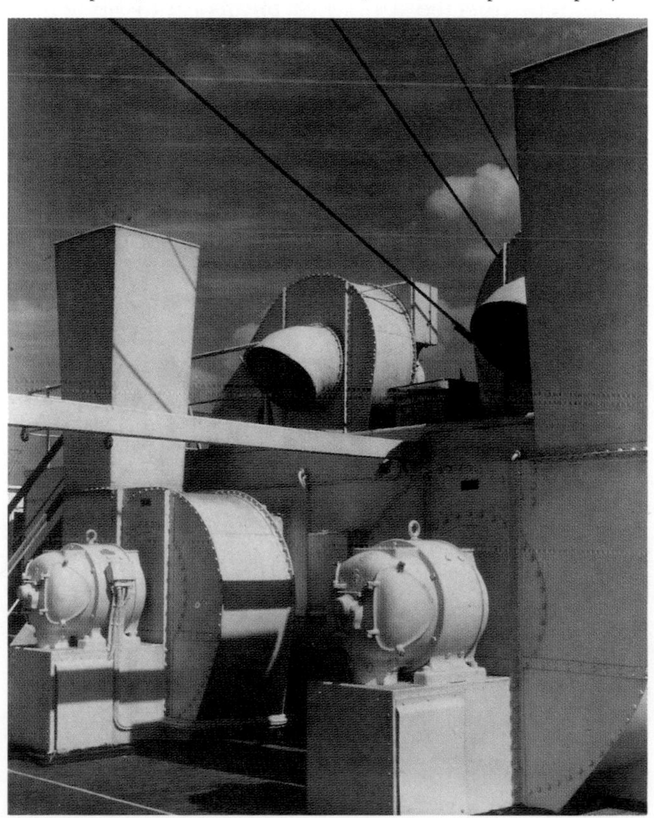

the power of this work, Sheeler continued to use photographs as studies for his paintings of the shapes of man-made environments, emptied of human beings and symbolic of the beauty of the new world of perfect and precise machine forms. The clarity of the scenes he painted and the precise manner of his style linked Sheeler to a group of American artists whom the critics called the Precisionists because of their loving depiction of the new industrial environment.

The American painter EDWARD HOPPER (1882–1967) took as his subject the awesome loneliness and echoing isolation of modern life in the United States. Trained as a commercial artist, Hopper studied painting and printmaking in New York and Paris before returning to the United States and concentrating on scenes of contemporary city and country life in which the buildings, streets, and landscapes he chose to paint are curiously muted, still, and filled with empty spaces. Motion is stopped and time is suspended, as if the artist has recorded the major details of a poignant personal memory. From the darkened streets outside a restaurant in *Nighthawks* (FIG. **22-70**), we glimpse the lighted interior through huge plate-glass

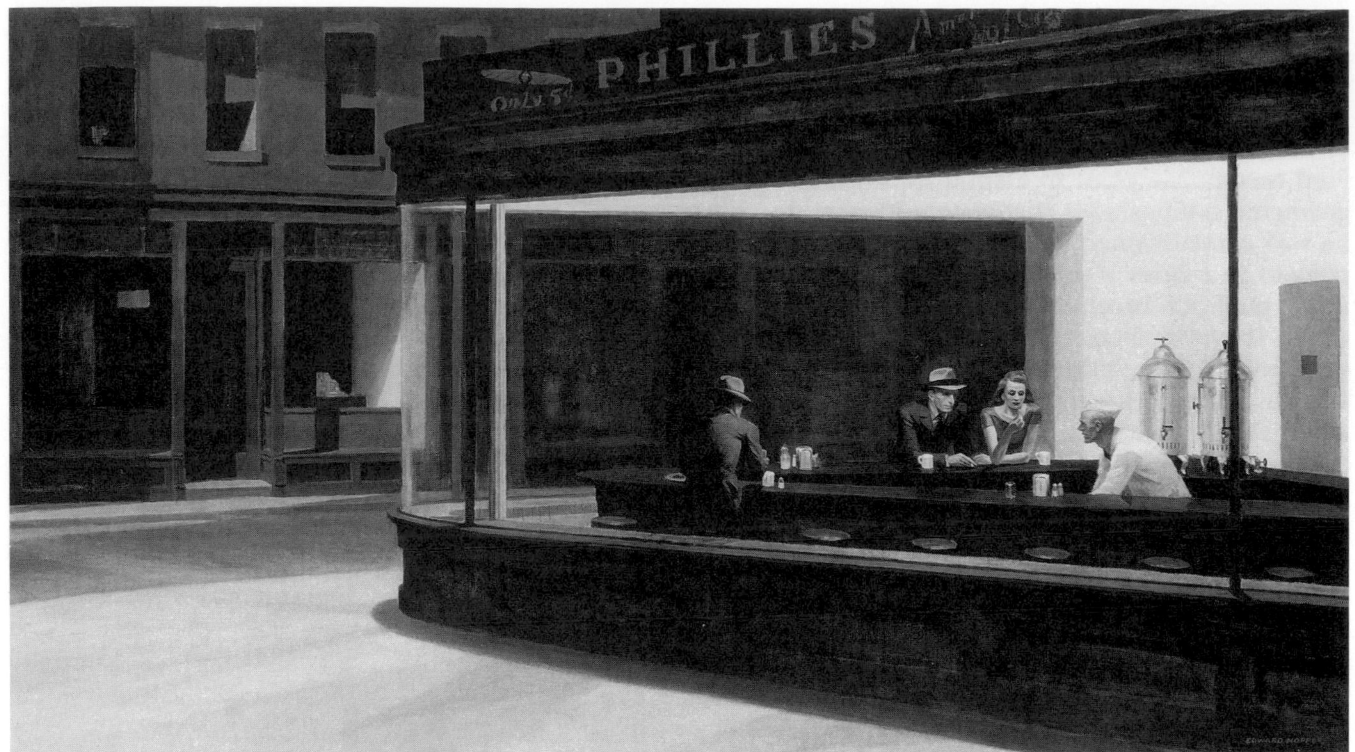

22-70 EDWARD HOPPER, *Nighthawks,* 1942. 30″ × 56$\frac{11}{16}$″. Friends of American Art Collection. Photograph © 1990, The Art Institute of Chicago. All rights reserved.

windows, which lend the inner space the paradoxical sense of being both a safe refuge and a vulnerable place for the three customers and the counterman. The interplay between small figures and empty space recalls the compositions of Poussin, but the seeming indifference of Hopper's characters to each other and the echoing spaces that surround them evoke the unmitigated loneliness of modern humans—a very different expression from the stately interplay of humans and environment in Poussin's *The Burial of Phocion* (FIG. 19-61). Hopper invested works like *Nighthawks* with the straightforward mode of representation valued by Americans, creating a kind of realist vision that recalls that of nineteenth-century artists like Whistler, Homer, and Sargent.

Photographer JAMES VAN DER ZEE (1886–1983) used his camera to capture scenes from the everyday lives of middle-class and well-to-do society in the Harlem section of Manhattan during the 1920s and early 1930s. A native of Massachusetts who settled in New York, Van Der Zee worked as an amateur photographer and professional musician before turning full-time to the compilation of a photographic record of the life and people of Harlem. Beginning in the teens, he took hundreds of straight portraits and documentary photographs of events in Harlem that form a fantastic visual record of aspects of urban life often invisible to those outside that neighborhood. He sometimes injected a note of fantasy into his works by adding imaginary painted backgrounds and ghostly double-exposure images that suggested a future or spiritual reality, producing pictures that combine a record of the physical appearance of his sitters with symbols representing their hopes and dreams. *Future Expectations* (FIG. **22-71**), created in about 1915, belongs in the last group. In this image, a young bridal couple sits before a painted backdrop showing the kind of gracious fireplace and living room they hope one day to own. At their feet sits the daughter they dream will become part of their future family. The soft light sets the mood, yet the crisp focus records every nuance of lace trim, shiny shoes, bouquet, and rug. The couple is posed with the child in an off-center pyramidal arrangement suggestive of earlier paintings of the Holy Family. Here, Van Der Zee stressed the beauty and harmony of the shapes and surfaces in his subject, capturing and sharing with the viewer his appreciation and reverence for the subtle patterns of the everyday life he saw around him and the rich emotions on which it was based. Like the other documentary realists, he touches our minds and imaginations through his intense vision of things in the visual world and our emotional response to them.

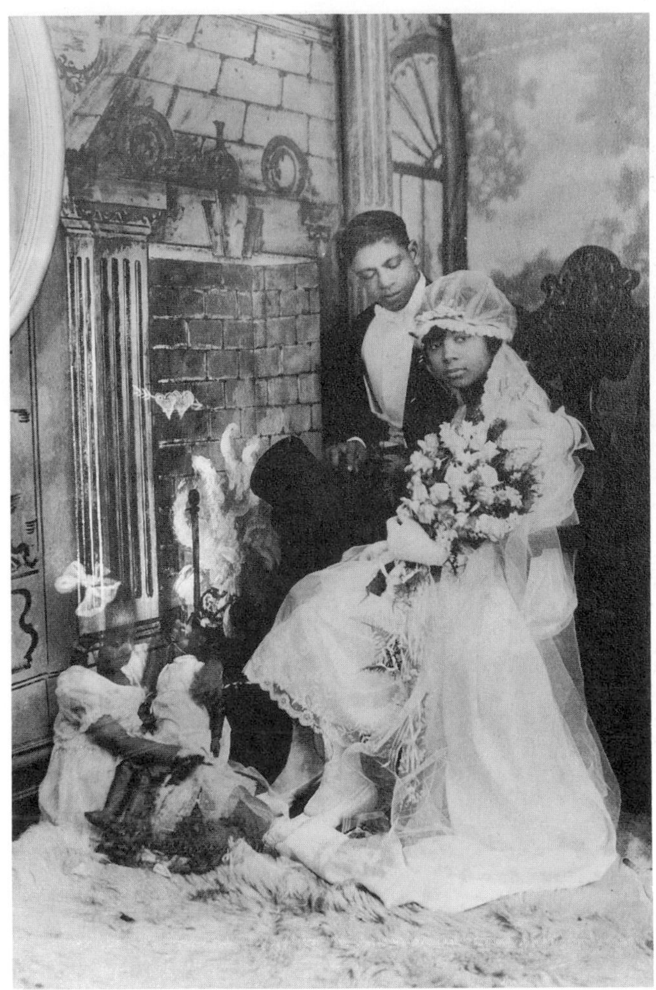

22-71 James Van Der Zee, *Future Expectations,* c. 1915. Gelatin silver print.

Activism and Art

Of all of the artists working with social and political concerns in the early part of the twentieth century, the most diverse were those individuals who believed that art must serve society by inspiring its citizens to moral and ethical behavior. This aim was to be achieved as a result of artists revealing social faults or developing pride for membership in a particular class or segment of the populace. Artists of all media bent their art to this task. Photographers sought to move viewers with the accuracy of the images of society their cameras could capture. Filmmakers used all the visual and narrative power of their medium to affect and inform their audience. Painters distilled onto canvases and walls the distressing subjects that had affected them most deeply, and one Soviet sculptor-architect even envisioned a monumental and dynamic skyscraper with parts that would provide an ongoing education to his countrymen.

The American photographer Lewis Wickes Hine (1874–1940) had great sympathy with workers and the poor. A native of Wisconsin, he studied briefly at the University of Chicago before moving to New York City to teach nature study and geography. He began taking photographs to aid in his teaching, but in 1904 he started making pictures of immigrants as they arrived in the United States and struggled to establish lives in their new land. He next became interested in the grim world of children who worked long hours in industries and businesses. Hine maintained that such practices stunted the development of children, who should be allowed to grow healthily into productive adults to assure a strong future for the country. In 1908 Hine was hired by the National Child Labor Committee to photograph child labor, and he traveled widely, photographing children at work in large and small businesses. *Breaker Boys* (fig. **22-72**) shows a group of grimy youngsters, prized by mine owners because their small size allowed them to work in small spaces. These children went to work at very young ages to help their impoverished families, and many died or were severely injured before they reached adulthood. The dim light in the location where Hine took *Breaker Boys* required the use of magnesium powder flash to illuminate the scene. The squalidness of the workplace and the helplessness of the boys is emphasized in the photograph by the quiet way the youngsters cluster together to face the camera. Like Kollwitz (fig. 22-18), Hine knew the power of images to stir people who knew nothing

22-72 Lewis Wickes Hine, *Breaker Boys,* South Pittston, Pennsylvania, January 1911. Gelatin silver print. International Museum of Photography at George Eastman House, Rochester, New York.

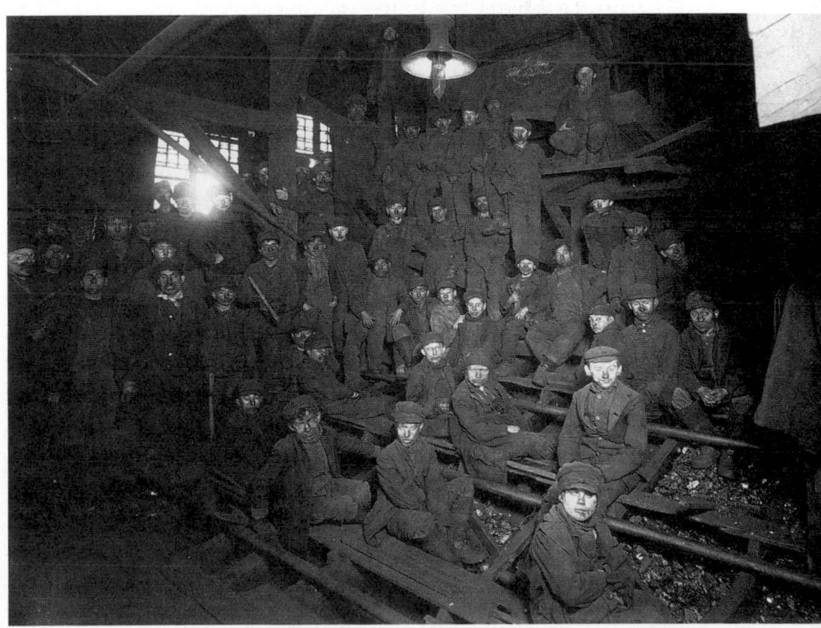

about workers and poverty. Photographs like *Breaker Boys* were remarkably effective in helping educate people about the conditions of child labor. Groups of these images were published in newspapers and magazines, and the incontrovertible testimony they provided gave such strong substantiation for the reports of the National Child Labor Committee to the U.S. Congress in the years before World War I that new laws were enacted governing child labor.

Emotional content of a much less dramatic kind was the goal of the German photographer AUGUST SANDER (1876–1964), who undertook to assemble a vast photo portrait of "man in the twentieth century"—all classes, all occupations, all ages. Sander labored as a miner and was an itinerant photographer before he went to work taking portraits in studios in Linz, Austria, and Cologne. In about 1915, he began photographing the farmers, tradesmen, and landowners of the area near Cologne, where he had been born. In an approach very much like that of the eighteenth-century Encyclopedists, he thought of his project as a way of cataloguing all human types: "These people [in a restricted area of Westerwald], whose way of life I had known from my youth, appealed to me because of their closeness to nature. . . . Thus the beginning was made and all the types discovered were classed under archetype, with all the characteristic common human qualities noted."* Believing that the only way to uncover true archetypes was to make "natural portraits that show the subjects in an environment corresponding to their own individuality," Sander encouraged each of his subjects to face the camera in a pose comfortable to them. The model for *Lackarbeiter (Varnisher,* FIG. **22-73**) stands with quiet dignity and a self-conscious smile, holding the can of his trade in one hand. The vast, dark rectangle of the open door behind him isolates his figure almost as though it were part of a sculptural relief. The spareness of the composition and the potent sense of individual presence in works like this made Sander's work an inspiration to later photographers, including Robert Frank (FIG. 23-67). However, Sander's images were less satisfying to the Nazi government, who found the selection of his work published in his books *Face of Our Time* and *German Land, German People* so contradictory to their ideas about the "master race" that they confiscated all copies of the books and many of Sander's negatives as well. He managed to hide some of his archives, and the negatives and prints that survive give us a vivid glimpse into the vast human panorama he recorded with his camera.

*In John von Hartz, *August Sander* (Millerton, NY: Aperture, 1977), p. 7.

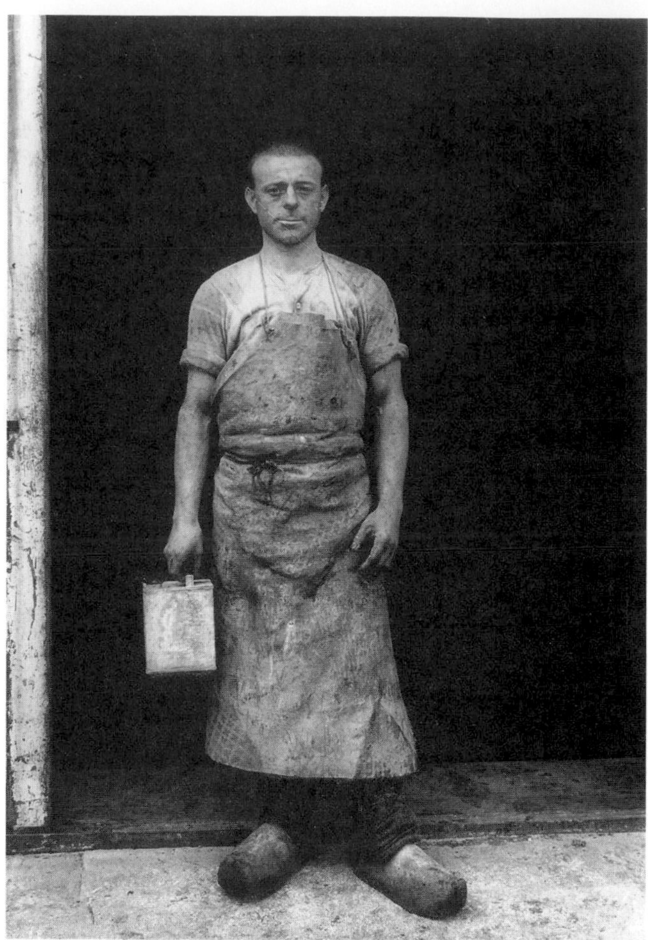

22-73 AUGUST SANDER, *Lackarbeiter (Varnisher)*, 1932. Vintage silver print, 8⅞″ × 6⅛″. The University of Michigan Museum of Art, Ann Arbor.

It was Sander's intention to reveal universal human archetypes in self-posed portraits of individuals. The French photographer HENRI CARTIER-BRESSON (b. 1908) wanted to reveal the depth of human drama by recording significant instants of action and interaction. He was interested in the specially revealing times—the "decisive moments"—when all that had happened before and all that will happen in future were suggested by the action in front of the lens. Cartier-Bresson began as a painter, before becoming a serious photographer and cinematographer. His inspiration in photography came not only from the work of artists like Atget, but also from early movies, like Sergei Eisenstein's *Potemkin* (FIG. 22-77). Cartier-Bresson worked mostly with a lightweight, small-format Leica camera that allowed him great flexibility in moving around a subject and permitted him to take many pictures in rapid succession before having to reload with fresh film. "Above all," he said, "I craved to seize the whole essence, in the confines of one single photograph, of some situation that was in the process of unrolling itself before my eyes." His photographs of "situations" like that shown in *Seville, Spain* (FIG. **22-74**) sent him to many countries to record what he saw there for news magazines and newspapers throughout the nations of Europe and the United States. To get his picture, Cartier-Bresson knew how to become almost invisible. In *Seville, Spain*, the boys go on with their activity and, although they seem to acknowledge the photographer's presence, they do not apparently alter their behavior for his camera. The exuberance of the childhood game and the energetic participation of the youngster on crutches contrast tellingly with the rubble-filled street and the odd, blasted hole through which we view the scene. This image touches our hearts with its evocation of the resilience of the human spirit. Cartier-Bresson's work found a wide audience in magazines like *Harper's Bazaar*, *Vu*, and *Life Magazine*. He became a professional photojournalist, making picture stories to show readers events and lives far removed from their own. On assignments to cover a specific subject, Cartier-Bresson did not always find a single, decisive moment that revealed the human drama unfolding before him; therefore, he mastered the art of the photo story—a series of photographs that, taken together, captured the human experience at the core of the event being pictured. *Seville, Spain* was part of a photo story Cartier-Bresson did on Spain during 1933–1934, just before that country erupted into civil war between the fascist troops of General Francisco Franco and the irregular forces that opposed him. The whole series shows the gathering tensions as well as the threads of life going on in the midst of crisis. On that assignment, and throughout the rest of his career, Cartier-Bresson tried to express his sense of the aggregate human nature that binds all people together.

The American photographer DOROTHEA LANGE (1895–1965) shared with Cartier-Bresson a desire to reveal the connectedness of all human experience, and like him, she worked for most of her life on assignment taking pictures for publication in books, newspapers, and magazines. Her best-known photographs, however, like those of Hine, were made for a branch of the United States government to show Americans the plight of the poor—in Lange's case the dire situation of the rural poor who had been displaced by the Great Depression of the 1930s. Lange trained to be a teacher and studied photography in New York City before moving west and opening a portrait studio in San Francisco where she gained some fame with soft-focus, Pictorialist images. The effects of the deepening Depression outside her studio window drew her out to photograph the people whose lives had been thrown into disarray. Hired in 1935 as the photographer for a sociological study of migrant agricultural workers in California, Lange went to work the following year for the Resettlement

22-74 HENRI CARTIER-BRESSON, *Seville, Spain*, 1933. Gelatin silver print.

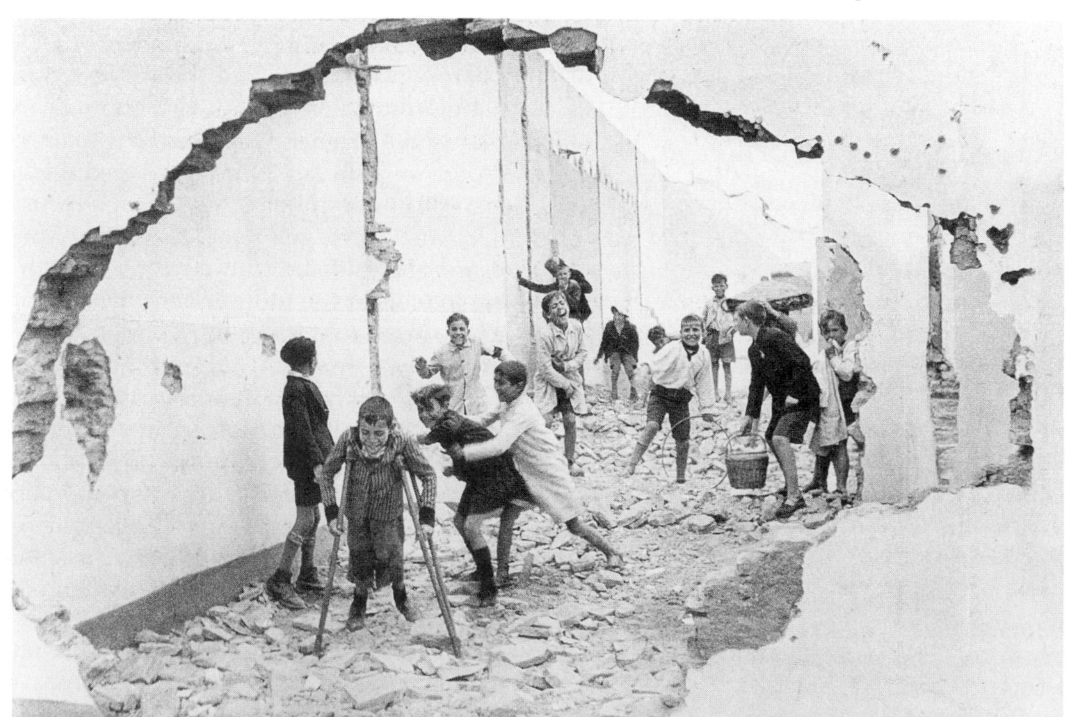

Administration (RA), later the Farm Securities Administration (FSA), which had been established to oversee emergency programs designed to aid farm families caught in the Depression and to provide information to the public about both the government programs and the plight of the people such programs were intended to serve.* At the end of an assignment to document the lives of migratory pea pickers in California, Lange stopped at a camp in Nipomo and found the migrant workers there starving; the crops had frozen in the fields. Among the pictures she made on this occasion was one of the best-known photographs ever taken, *Migrant Mother, Nipomo Valley* (FIG. **22-75**). Generations of viewers have now been moved by the mixture of strength and worry in the raised hand and careworn face of a young mother, who holds a baby on her lap and is flanked by two older children, who cling to her trustfully while turning their faces away from the camera. Lange has described how she was able to get the picture:

> [I] saw and approached the hungry and desperate mother, as if drawn by a magnet. I do not remember how I explained my presence or my camera to her, but I remember she asked me no questions. I made five exposures, working closer and closer from the same direction. . . . There she sat in that lean-to tent with her children huddled around her, and seemed to know that my pictures might help her, and so she helped me.†

Social historian William Stott has identified different types of documentary images common in the United States in the 1930s. They include the "objective documentary," which is an emotionally neutral record of a subject; the "human documentary," which attempts to stir viewers' emotions about the conditions portrayed; and the "social documentary," which not only attempts to arouse emotions but chooses as its subjects those things that enlightened action could change.‡ Lange specialized in the human documentary, but many of her images, like *Migrant Mother,* functioned as powerful social documentary images as well. Together, Lange and her migrant mother sensed that a photograph of the desperate situation could move people to help. Having already won the right (unique among RA and FSA photographers) to develop and proof her own negatives, Lange immediately took the Nipomo story and her first prints to a San Francisco newspaper; within days food was rushed to Nipomo to feed the hungry workers. Throughout her career, Lange focused her attention on individual people. During the Depression years, she said she wanted above all "to get my camera to register the things about these people that were more important than how poor they were—their pride, their strength, their spirit."

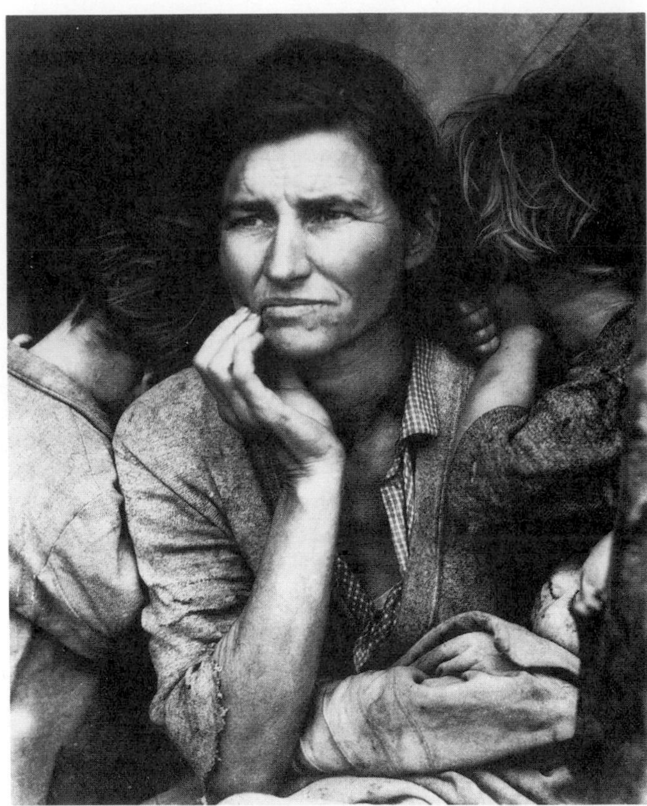

22-75 DOROTHEA LANGE, *Migrant Mother, Nipomo Valley,* 1936. Gelatin silver print. Courtesy of the Dorothea Lange Collection. © The City of Oakland, The Oakland Museum, 1991.

Following the revolution in 1917, the Soviet Union was the home of a new art movement whose members were activist counterparts of the Bauhaus utopian dream of an artist-craftsperson-engineer who would devote every talent to designing a better environment for human beings. The Russians called their movement "Productivism"; it developed as an arm of the Constructivist movement and one of its most gifted leaders was VLADIMIR TATLIN (1885–1953), a painter and sculptor who had been a sailor before

*The RA/FSA was one of a number of relief programs established in the 1930s that were developed to utilize the special talents of artists. Among the most important programs were those of the Treasury Relief Art Project (TRAP), established in 1934 to commission art for federal buildings and the Works Progress Administration (WPA), founded in 1935 to relieve all unemployment, including that of artists. Under the wing of the WPA were the varied activities of the Federal Art Project (FAP), which paid artists, writers, and theater people a regular wage in exchange for work in their fields.

†In Milton Meltzer, *Dorothea Lange: A Photographer's Life* (New York: Farrar, Strauss, Giroux, 1978), pp. 133, 220.

‡William Stott, *Documentary Expression and Thirties America* (New York: Oxford University Press, 1973), pp. 5–45.

turning to art. Influenced by the formal analysis of Cubism, the dynamism of Futurism, and the rhythmic compositions of flat, curved planes in traditional Russian icon paintings (FIG. 7-59), Tatlin turned to abstract relief constructions and models for stage sets after a brief period as a Cubo-Futurist painter. He experimented with every kind of material—glass, iron, sheet metal, wood, plaster—to lay the basis for what he called the "Culture of Materials." The Revolution in October 1917 was the signal to Tatlin and other avant-garde artists in Russia that the hated old order was ending, and they determined to play a full role in the creation of a new world, one that would fully use the power of industrialization for the benefit of all the people. Initially, like Malevich and Gabo, Tatlin believed that abstract art was ideal for the new society, free as such art was from any symbolism from the past. For a few years, all Russian avant-garde artists worked together, designing public festivals and demonstrations, presenting plays and exhibitions designed to help educate the public about their new government and the possibilities for their future. The Russian Futurist-Constructivist poet Vladimir Mayakovskii proclaimed their new goal: "We do not need a dead mausoleum of art where dead works are worshiped, but a living factory of the human spirit—in the streets, in the tramways, in the factories, workshops, and workers' homes." Art schools like the College of Painting, Sculpture, and Architecture in Moscow were reorganized and combined with craft schools to form new educational programs—the one in Moscow was renamed the Higher Technical-Artistic Studios (*Vkhutemas*). Tatlin, Malevich, and Gabo's brother, sculptor Anton Pevsner, had studios there, and Gabo (a frequent visitor) described the school's activities:

> [It is] both a school and a free academy where not only the current teaching of special professions was carried out (. . . Painting, Sculpture, Architecture, Ceramics, Metalwork and Woodwork, Textile, and Typography) but general discussions were held and seminars conducted amongst the students on diverse problems where the public could participate, and artists not officially on the faculty could speak and give lessons. . . . During these seminars . . . many ideological questions between opposing artists in our abstract group were thrashed out.*

As Gabo's statement indicates, a split was developing between members of the avant-garde. On one side were Malevich, Gabo, Kandinsky, and all the other artists who believed that art was an expression of man's spiritual nature. On the other side were the "Productivist Constructivists"—Tatlin and other artists who felt the artist must be both creator and technician and must direct art toward the creation of useful products for the new society. The position of the Productivist Constructivists was connected to that of a group called "Proletkult" (The Organization for Proletarian Culture), which had been founded in 1906, but became free to follow its primary doctrine ("Art is a social product, conditioned by the social environment") only after the 1917 revolution. Tatlin enthusiastically abandoned abstract art for functional art by designing such things as an efficient stove and a "functional" set of worker's clothing; for a time, he even worked in a metallurgical factory near Petrograd (now Leningrad).

Tatlin's most famous work is his design for a *Monument to the Third International* (FIG. **22-76**), commissioned early in 1919 to honor the Revolution. His

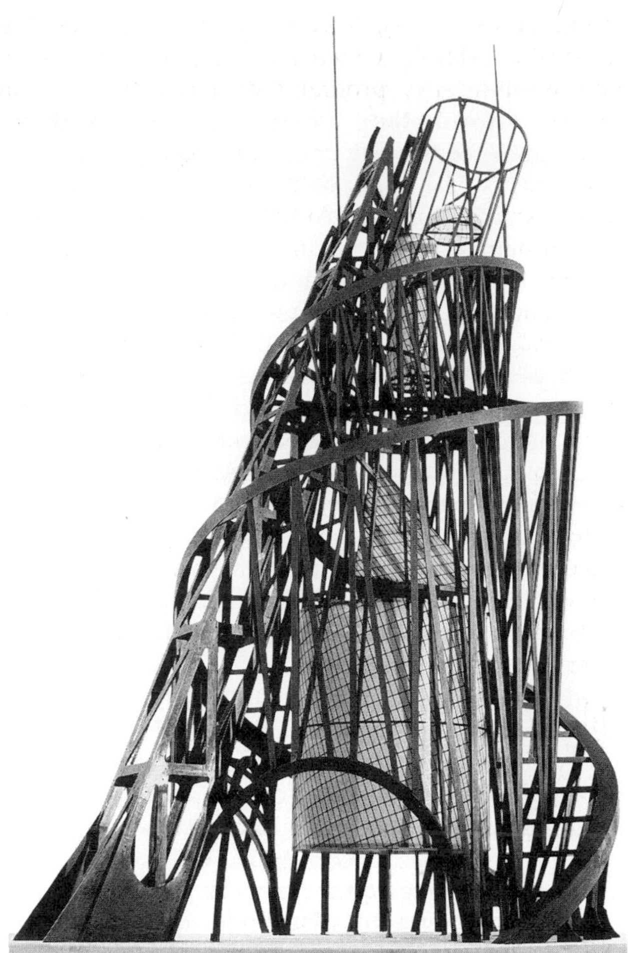

22-76 VLADIMIR TATLIN, *Monument to the Third International*, 1919–1920. Model in wood, iron, and glass. Re-created in 1968 for exhibition at the Moderna Museet, Stockholm.

*In Camilla Gray, *The Russian Experiment in Art 1863–1922* (New York: Harry N. Abrams, 1970), pp. 232–33.

concept was for a huge glass and iron symbol-building that would have been twice as high as the Empire State Building. On its proposed site in the center of Moscow, it would have served as a propaganda* and news center for the Soviet people. Within a dynamically tilted spiral cage, three geometrically shaped chambers were to rotate around a central axis, each chamber housing facilities for a different type of governmental activity and rotating at a different speed. At the bottom, a huge, glass cylindrical structure, meant to house lectures and meetings, was to revolve once a year. The next highest chamber was to be a cone-shaped structure assigned to administrative functions and rotating once a month. At the top, a cubic information center would revolve daily, issuing news bulletins and proclamations via the most modern means of communication, including an open air news screen (illuminated at night) and a special instrument designed to project words on the clouds on any overcast day. Tatlin envisioned the whole complex as a dynamic communications center, perfectly suited to the exhilarating pace of the new age. Due to the desperate economic situation in Russia during these years, Tatlin's ambitious design was never realized as a building; it existed only in models in metal and wood, which were exhibited on various official occasions before disappearing. The only record of the model that survives today is to be found in a few drawings, photographs, and recent reconstructions.

The early Russian filmmaker Sergei M. Eisenstein (1898–1948) developed a whole theory of film to create movies that depicted the revolutionary history of his country. Before the Revolution, films in Russia were produced primarily by foreigners, most of whom left the country when the tsar was overthrown. The Soviets saw cinema as a perfect medium for communication and education, and they established schools to train Russians in the art of film production. The Russian directors Dziga Vertov and Lev Kuleshov began trying to formulate methods that would allow film to be used as a precise visual language. Eisenstein was a student engineer at the time of the Revolution. He worked as a propaganda poster artist and in the Proletkult Theater before being commissioned to make several films tracing the rise of the Communist Party. Like the other avant-garde artists connected with the Revolution, Eisenstein wanted to create a new art, in his case one free from the narrative formulas of "bourgeois" film. In *Strike!* (1924), he combined shots in a kind of conceptual cinematic collage, called "montage," to draw viewers emotionally into the story. In a cinematic montage, an image of a pistol firing might be followed by a picture of a teeming crowd in a great square; the next image would be that of a statue falling to create an emotional image of a political uprising. Eisenstein perfected his montage technique in *Battleship Potemkin,* made in 1925 to celebrate the anniversary of a failed 1905 rebellion against the tsarist government. This film is divided to depict both an uprising of the seamen on the battleship *Potemkin* in Odessa Harbor and the struggles of ordinary citizens against armed troops in the city. The most masterful part of the film is the "Odessa Steps Sequence" (FIG. **22-77**), which shows the mass killing of citizens by soldiers relentlessly descending a long flight of steps. The scenes that make up the steps sequence were filmed with several cameras simultaneously—one running along a long track placed the length of the steps and another strapped to the waist of an acrobatic cameraman. Shots from different cameras and different moments in the scene were edited to catapult the viewer into the midst of the confusion and horror of the event.

In Germany, the filmmaker Leni Riefenstahl (b. 1902) created documentary movies to arouse patriotic emotion in support of the new Nazi leader, Adolf Hitler. Once a successful actress, Riefenstahl attracted Hitler's attention with a film she directed in 1932. The mystical visual style and story of that film, *Blue Light (Blaue Licht),* seemed to him eminently adaptable to propaganda expressing his dreams for the future of German society. Hitler commissioned Riefenstahl to create a documentary film about the Nazi Party Congress in Nürnberg in 1934. The result was *Triumph of the Will* (FIG. **22-78**). Hitler chose the title himself, and with his help, all of the details of the Congress—marches, meetings, rallies, speeches, activities in the camp of the Youth Corps, and the placement of banners, flowers, and onlookers throughout the city—were carefully planned in advance to serve Riefenstahl's cinematic needs. During the actual filming, she worked with 120 assistants and a host of cameras, shooting from multiple viewpoints, including a specially built track that ran for several blocks along the second story of the buildings adjacent to the main procession route. Riefenstahl spent eight months editing the film. In the final product Hitler is shown as a beloved messiah, descending from the clouds at the picture's beginning to preside benevolently over the increasingly demonstrative outpourings of mass devotion to him that culminate in an impassioned speech he makes to his followers about the future glory that will come to Germany under his leadership. A film with such a clearly propagandistic

*The word propaganda comes from the Latin *propaganda fides,* and the term was originally used to designate activities designed to spread and reinforce the teachings of the Roman Catholic church. Propaganda, then, means anything designed to persuade an audience to follow a particular set of beliefs.

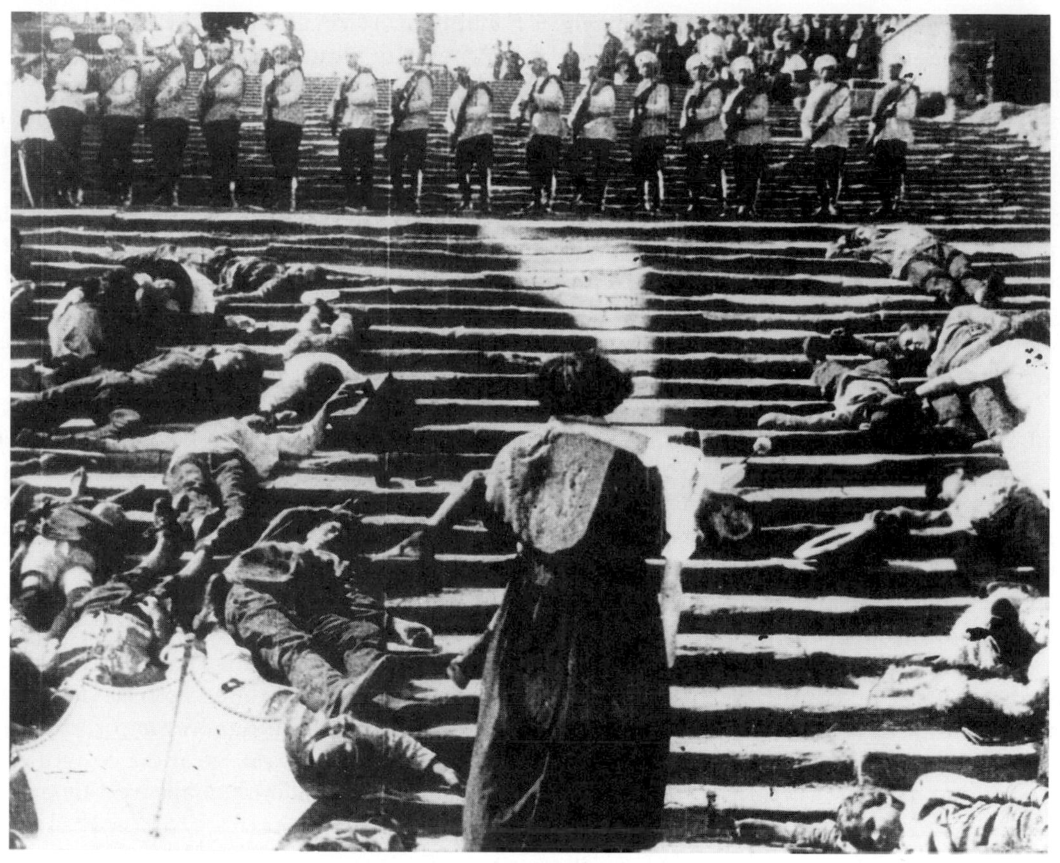

22-77 Sergei M. Eisenstein, film still from *Battleship Potemkin:* "Odessa Steps Sequence," 1925.

22-78 Leni Riefenstahl, film still from *Triumph of the Will,* 1935.

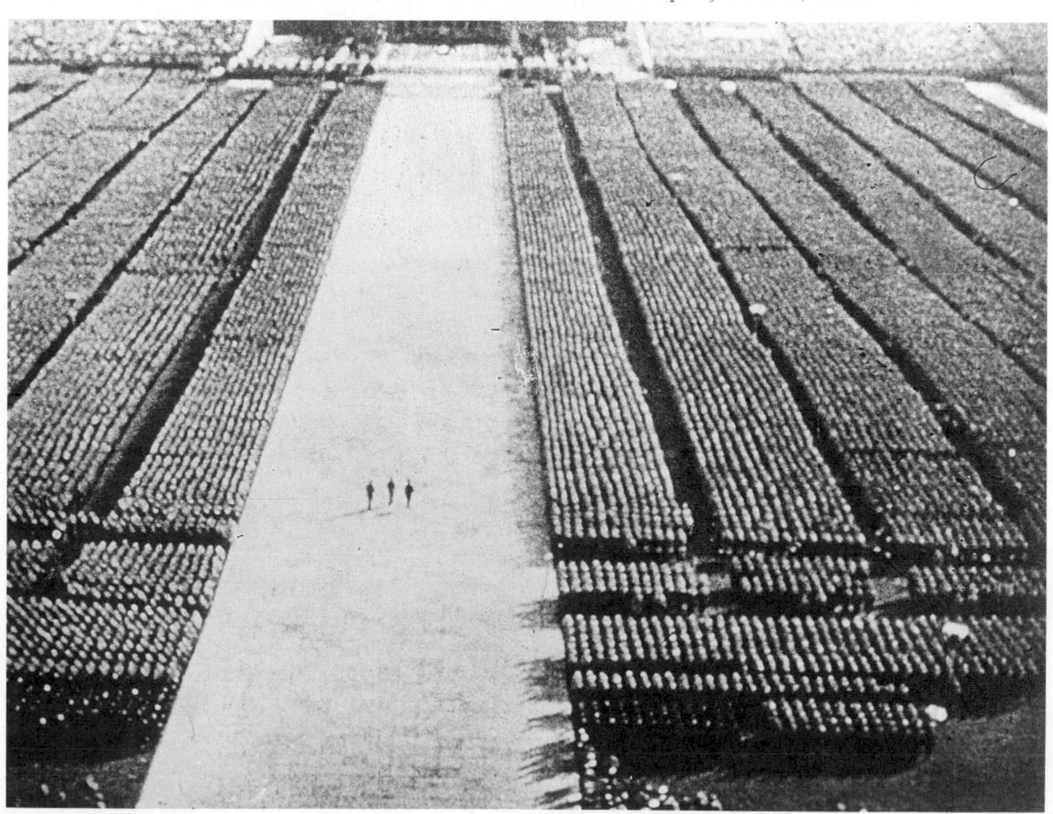

goal might have been trite or dull, but Riefenstahl managed to turn the characters and events of the Nürnberg Congress into abstract and symbolic visual patterns. She played these patterns against one another on many levels. In a tour-de-force of rhythmic editing, she achieved the highest degree of emotional and esthetic impact by juxtaposing close-ups and distant views, aerial and low-angle shots, and intercuts between people and the flag-bedecked monuments and buildings of the seemingly welcoming town. Riefenstahl shared Eisenstein's ability to use montage to create a convincing emotional environment for the viewers of her film, but the patterns she created are less dislocating than those in *Potemkin.* As she later boasted, she staged nothing; everything in the film happened as part of an historical event that took place in front of her. But this was history planned with the greatest care to have maximum effect and shaped to make each scene compound the effect of the one before, making an unforgettable impact on viewers. Indeed, *Triumph of the Will* was so effective that it was banned in several countries, including the United States, Canada, and Great Britain.

Riefenstahl's documentary showed masses of people behaving with mechanical precision, united in the happy service of their political leader. The British-American filmmaker CHARLIE CHAPLIN (1889–1977) created the character of the Little Tramp, a good-natured, poor, and bewildered Everyman who never quite fit into the society around him. Chaplin's empathy with the poor stemmed from the poverty he himself experienced as a boy in England. He developed the great abilities that shaped the character of the Little Tramp working as a comic and mime in vaudeville. The humor surrounding the hapless adventures of the plucky and perennially impoverished "Charlot" won the hearts of viewers around the world. After 1918, this success allowed Chaplin to write, direct, produce, star in, and distribute his feature films himself. Increasingly, he made films that showed people trapped by the monolithic qualities of modern industrialized society. In 1936 he made *Modern Times* (FIG. **22-79**), the last film in which the Little Tramp appeared, "to say something about the way life is being standardized and channelized and men turned into machines." In this film, hapless Charlie is a factory worker who tangles with the machines he is supposed to be operating. In one of the great comic sequences in the movie, he and a co-worker are trapped on a moving belt and swallowed by a large machine,

22-79 CHARLIE CHAPLIN, film still from *Modern Times,* 1936.

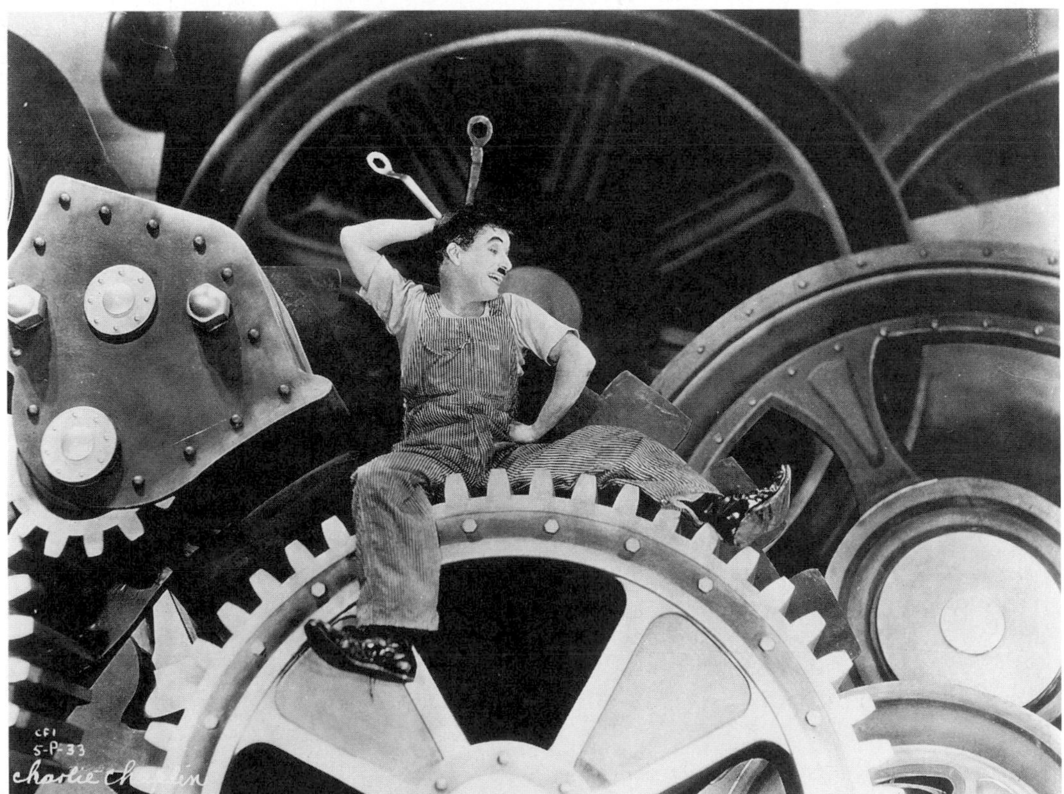

reappearing from time to time among its gears, wheels, and drive belts. Chaplin's satirical picture of modern industry in the midst of the Depression won frowns from many business magnates, who dismissed it as Communist propaganda, but the film tickled the funny bones of many viewers, who seemed to find in it a perfect expression of the feelings Chaplin put into the mouth of a character in his next film, *The Great Dictator*: "We think too much and feel too little. More than machinery, we need humanity."*

Eisenstein, Riefenstahl, and Chaplin each used the realistic recording power of the camera to transform the objects and people in their films into symbols for the ideas they wanted to express in their art. The American painter BEN SHAHN (1898–1969) used photographs as a point of departure for semi-abstract figures he felt would express the emotions and facts of social injustice that were his main subject throughout his career. Shahn came to the United States from Lithuania in 1906 and trained as a lithographer before broadening the media in which he worked to include easel painting, photography, and murals. In France in 1929, he found his life's direction in art: "If I am to be a painter, I must show the world how it looks through my eyes." He focused on the lives of ordinary people and the injustices often done to them by the structure of an impersonal society. In the early 1930s, he completed a cycle of twenty-three paintings and prints inspired by the trial and execution of the two Italian anarchists Nicola Sacco and Bartolommeo Vanzetti, whom many people considered to have been unjustly convicted of killing two men in a holdup in 1920. Shahn felt he had found in this story a subject the equal of any in Western art history: "Suddenly I realized . . . I was living through another crucifixion." Basing many of the works in this cycle on newspaper photographs of the events, Shahn devised a style that adapted his knowledge of Synthetic Cubism and his training in commercial art to an emotionally expressive use of flat, intense color in figural compositions filled with sharp, dry, angular forms. The major work in the series was called simply *The Passion of Sacco and Vanzetti* (FIG. **22-80**). This tall, narrow painting compresses time as well as space in a symbolic representation of the trial and its aftermath. The two executed men lie in coffins at the bottom of the composition. Presiding over them are the three members of the commission chaired by Harvard University president A. Laurence Lowell, who declared the original trial fair and cleared the way for the executions to take place. Behind, on the wall of a schematized government building, is the framed portrait of Judge Webster Thayer, who pronounced the initial sentence. The grey pallor of the dead men, the stylized mask-faces of the mock-pious mourning commissioners, and the sanctimonious, distant judge all contribute to the mood of anguished commentary that makes this image one of Shahn's most powerful works.

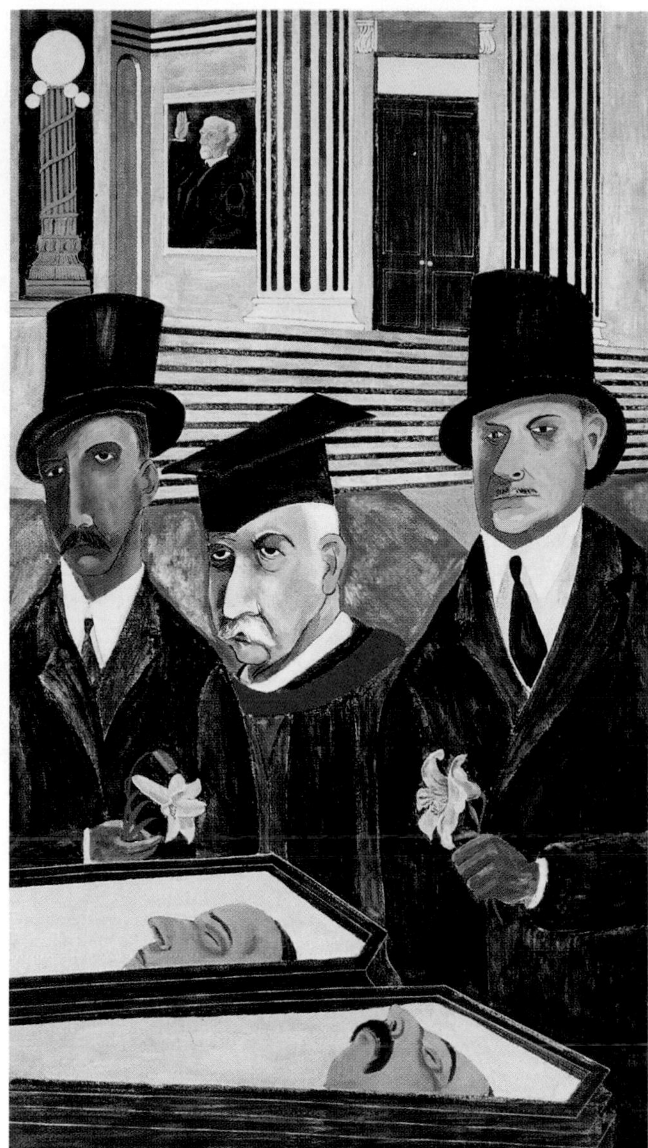

22-80 BEN SHAHN, *The Passion of Sacco and Vanzetti*, 1931–1932. Tempera on canvas, $84\frac{1}{2}'' \times 48''$. Collection of Whitney Museum of American Art, New York (gift of Edith and Milton Lowenthal in memory of Juliana Force).

Like Shahn, the American artist JACOB LAWRENCE (b. 1917) found his subjects in modern history, but unlike Shahn, Lawrence concentrated on the culture

*In Gene D. Phillips, *The Movie Makers: Artists in an Industry* (Chicago: Nelson-Hall, 1973), pp. 25–42

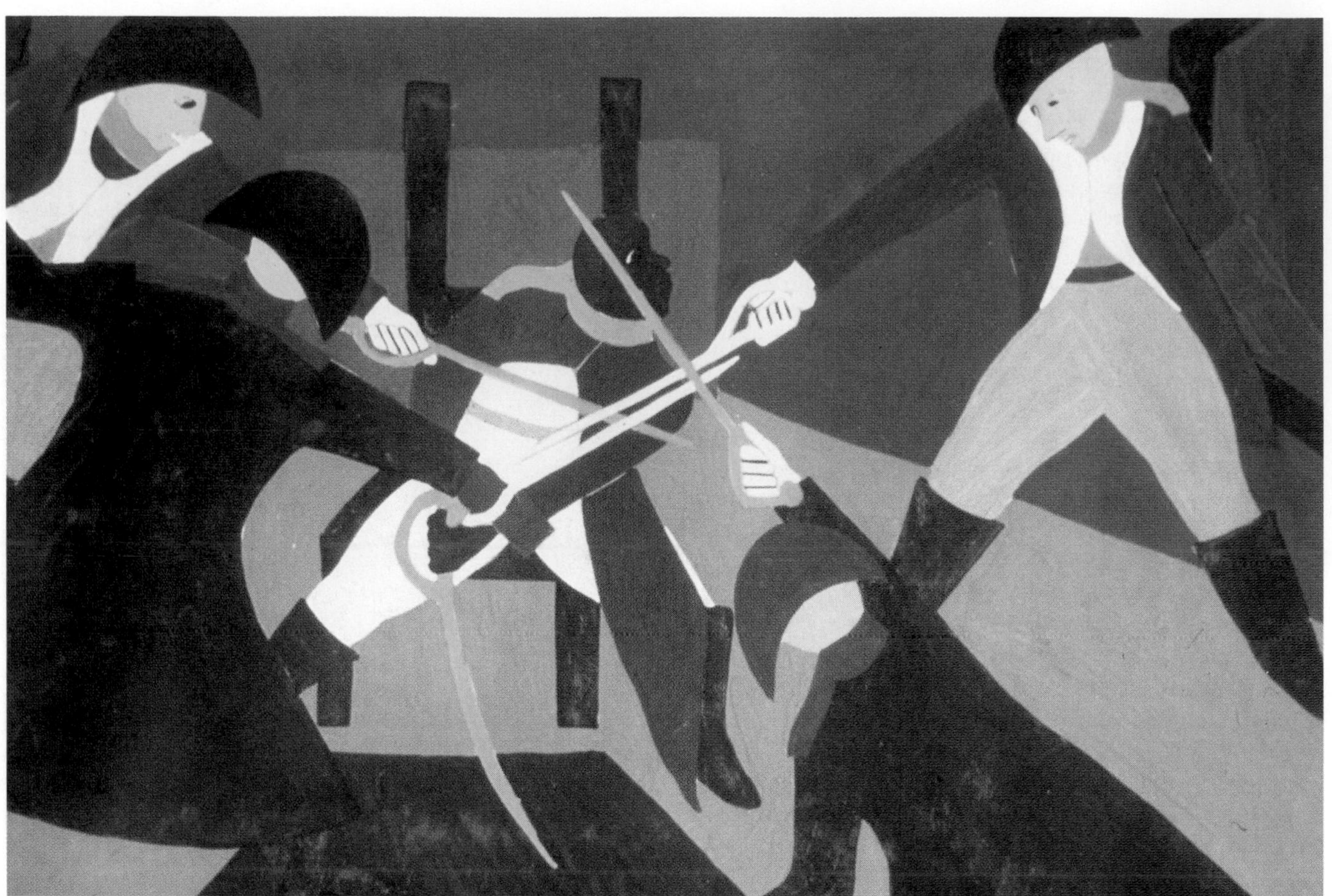

22-81 Jacob Lawrence, *No. 36: During the truce Toussaint is deceived and arrested by LeClerc. LeClerc led Toussaint to believe that he was sincere, believing that when Toussaint was out of the way, the Blacks would surrender*, from *l'Ouverture Series*, Plate 8, 1937–1938. Tempera on paper, 11″ × 19″. The Amistad Research Center's Aaron Douglas Collection, New Orleans.

and history of African-Americans. Lawrence moved to Harlem in 1927 at about the age of ten. There, he studied art and came under the spell of the African art and African-American history he found in lectures and exhibitions, and in the special programs sponsored by the 125th Street Public Library, which had outstanding collections of African-American art and archival data. Inspired by the politically committed art of Goya (FIG. 21-26), Daumier (FIG. 21-28), and Orozco (FIG. 22-82), Lawrence found his subjects in the everyday life of Harlem and the history of his people. He interpreted his themes in rhythmic arrangements of bold, flat, strongly colored shapes, using a style that drew equally from his interest in the push-pull effects of Cubist space and his memories of the patterns made by the colored scatter rugs that had brightened the floors of his childhood homes. His first historical subject was a series of forty-one paintings showing key incidents from the life of Toussaint L'Ouverture, a slave who led a revolution in the late eighteenth and early nineteenth century, winning independence from French rule for Haiti and establishing the first black Western republic. *No. 36: During the truce Toussaint is deceived and arrested by LeClerc. LeClerc led Toussaint to believe that he was sincere, believing that when Toussaint was out of the way, the Blacks would surrender* (FIG. **22-81**) is typical of Lawrence's masterful compositions and the way in which he added long narrative titles to make the series a kind of history text for younger viewers. Everything is arranged to draw the viewer's attention to the figure of Toussaint, who is held prisoner by his captors in the center of the picture space behind a wall of crisscrossed swords. The steep perspective of the walls of the room and the foreground rug, the thrusting figures of the captors, and the outspread legs of the hero dramatically draw the viewer into empathy with Toussaint's heroic defiance of foreign authority in the face of overwhelming odds. Like every other subject Lawrence painted during his long career, he believed this story had important things to teach viewers: "I didn't do it just as a historical thing, but because I

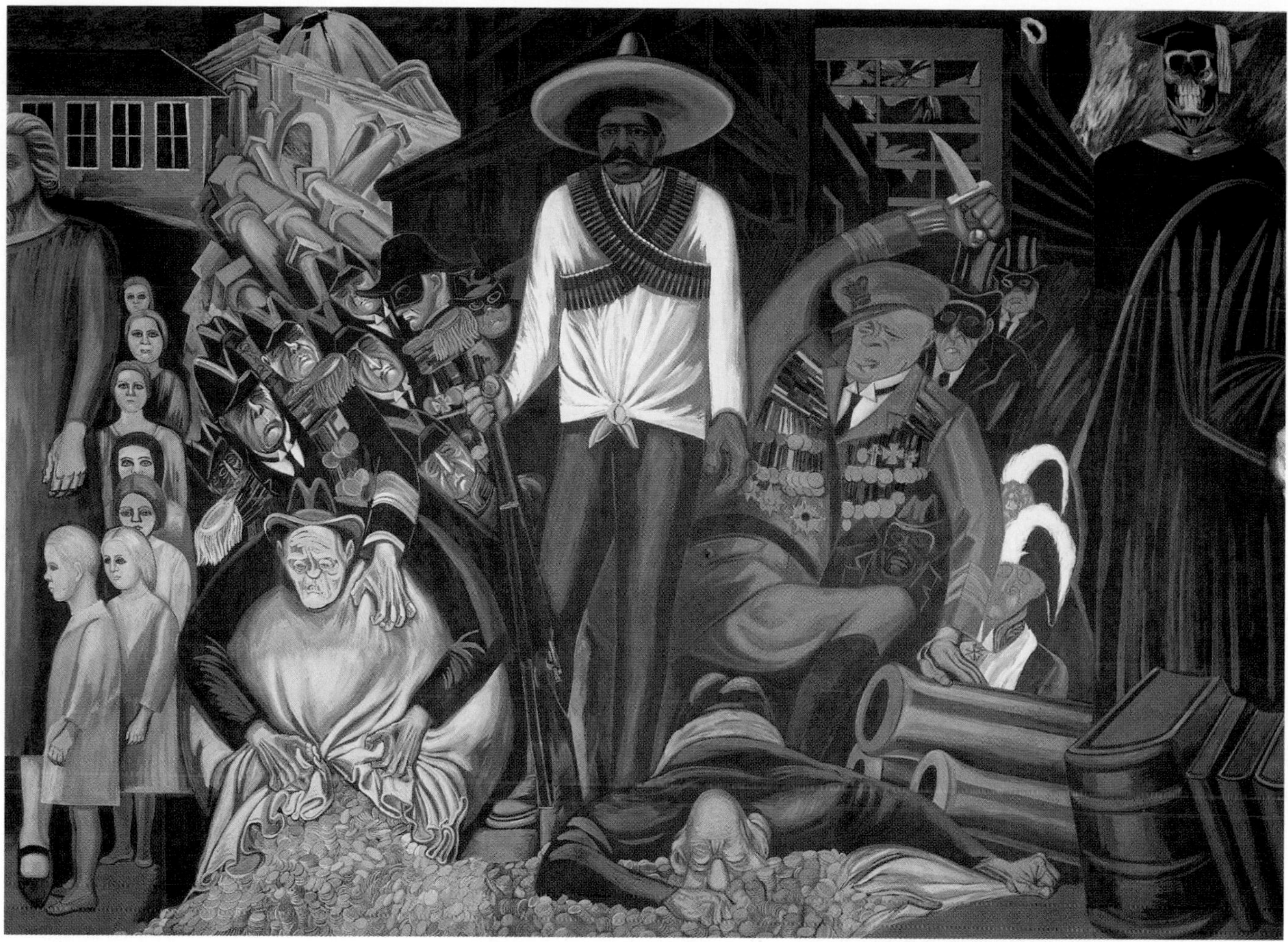

22-82 José Clemente Orozco, *Epic of American Civilization: Hispano-America*, c. 1932–1934. Fresco. Baker Memorial Library, Dartmouth College, Hanover, New Hampshire.

believe these things tie up with the Negro today. We don't have a physical slavery, but an economic slavery. If these people, who were so much worse off than the people today, could conquer their slavery, we certainly can do the same thing."*

Lawrence found inspiration for his early art in the example of José Clemente Orozco (1883–1949), one of a group of Mexican artists determined to base their art on the indigenous history and culture that existed in Mexico before the arrival of Europeans. The movement formed by these artists was part of the idealistic rethinking of society that took place during the political turmoil of the period of the Mexican Revolution between 1910 and the 1920s. Among the projects undertaken by these politically motivated artists were vast mural cycles placed in public buildings to dramatize and validate the history of Mexico's native peoples. Orozco worked on one of the first major cycles, painted in 1922 on the walls of the National Training School in Mexico City. He carried the ideas of this mural revolution to the United States, completing many commissions for wall paintings between 1927 and 1934. From 1932 to 1934, he worked on one of his finest mural cycles in the Baker Library at Dartmouth College, partly in honor of its superb collection of books in Spanish. The choice of subject was left up to him. What he depicted, in fourteen large panels and ten smaller ones, was a panoramic and symbolic history of ancient and modern Mexico, from the early mythic days of the feathered-serpent god, Quetzalcóatl, to a contemporary and bitterly satiric vision of modern education. The imagery in our detail, *Epic of American Civilization: Hispano-America* (FIG. **22-82**), revolves around the monumental figure of a heroic Mexican peasant armed to participate in the Mexican Revolution. Looming on either side of him are

*In Ellen Harkins Wheat, *Jacob Lawrence: American Painter* (Seattle: University of Washington Press, 1986), p. 40.

mounds crammed with symbolic figures of his oppressors—bankers, government soldiers, officials, gangsters, and the rich. Money-grubbers pour hoards of gold at the feet of the incorruptible *peón,* cannon threaten him, and a bemedaled general raises a dagger to stab him in the back. Orozco's training as an architect gave him a sense of the framed wall surface, which he easily commanded, projecting his quickly grasped figures onto the solid mural plane in monumental scale. In addition, Orozco's early training as a maker of political prints and as a newspaper artist had taught him the rhetorical strength of graphic brevity and simplicity, which he used here to assure that his allegory was easy to read. His special merging of the effects of the graphic and mural media give his work an originality and force rarely seen in mural painting after the Renaissance and Baroque periods.

Modern artists who have sought to stir the emotions of viewers about specific incidents of human injustice have found it difficult to record or symbolize enough information in a single image to accomplish their purpose. Paintings like David's *Death of Marat* (FIG. 20-41), Géricault's *Raft of the Medusa* (FIG. 21-12), Goya's *Third of May, 1808* (FIG. 21-26), and Daumier's *Rue Transnonain* (FIG. 21-28) are rare. The greatest twentieth-century painting inspired by outrage directed toward brutal human behavior is *Guernica* (FIG. **22-83**), created by Pablo Picasso in 1937 in response to the saturation bombing of an ancient Basque city by German forces acting for Francisco Franco during the Spanish Civil War. Throughout his career, Picasso had never been content to work for long in any one style. While still painting Synthetic Cubist pictures, he also made "Ingres-like" drawings and painted figure subjects in a broadly Realistic manner often influenced by Antique sculpture. He often moved back and forth between creating works with symbolic significance, like those of his Blue Period, and works in which he explored esthetic problems of style, like *Les Demoiselles d'Avignon* (FIG. 22-6) and *Three Musicians* (FIG. 22-11). In the latter work, he had also bent Synthetic Cubism to express irony and whimsy. In the late 1920s and early 1930s, Picasso's Cubism took on a Surrealistic quality; the forms became more biomorphic and the interweaving of planes began to suggest the qualities of a dreamy metamorphosis from one state of being to another. As Franco's forces assumed power in Spain, Picasso began using motifs from bullfighting and mythology to symbolize the struggles in his homeland. His political commitment, his feelings, and his role as an artist were painfully united in a new and powerful way: "Painting is not done to decorate apartments. It is an instrument of war for attack and defence against the enemy."

In January 1937, the Spanish Republican government in exile in Paris asked Picasso to do a work for their pavilion at the Paris International Exposition to be held that summer. He agreed but had done nothing when he received word that the Basque capital, Guernica, had been almost totally destroyed in an air

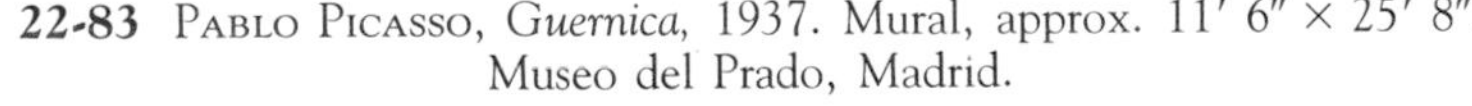

22-83 PABLO PICASSO, *Guernica,* 1937. Mural, approx. 11′ 6″ × 25′ 8″. Museo del Prado, Madrid.

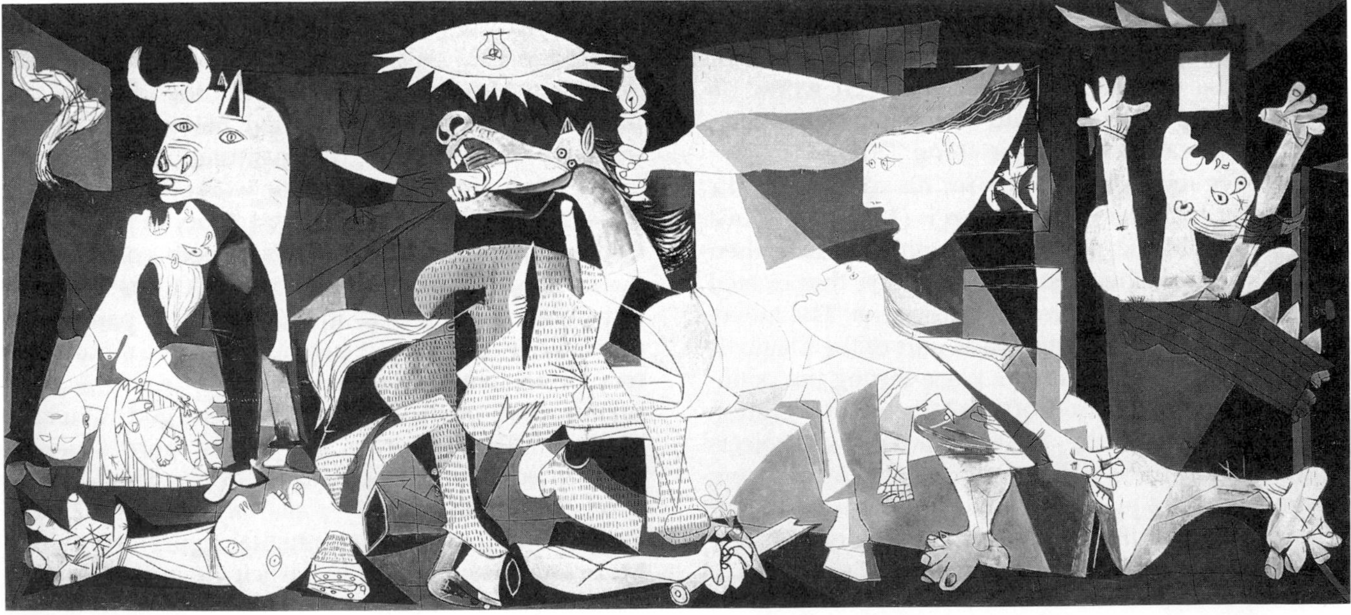

raid on April 26 by German planes acting on behalf of General Franco. The event jolted Picasso into action; by the end of June, the mural-sized canvas of *Guernica* was complete. Picasso used a fluid, expressive Synthetic Cubist style to organize his figures into a three-part composition with a triangular middle and two flanking rectangular wings. Forms bend and stretch in response to the emotional stress of the characters. Borrowed from the picador's mount in the bullfight, the horribly wounded dying horse at the center stands for all innocent victims, while (according to the artist) the bull represents "brutality and darkness." A slain soldier stretches awkwardly across the ground at the lower left, in front of a shrieking woman who holds her dead child in helpless agony. A searching head balloons from an upper window, accompanied by an eerily elongated arm holding an oil lamp. A woman falls in flames from a building, while, beneath, another woman attempts to run in fright; her suddenly swollen and weighted legs and feet refuse to move. The black, white, and grey colors, the patterns of light and dark, and the action of the figures lead the viewer's eyes relentlessly back to the upthrust head of the central victim-horse and to its open mouth, exposed teeth, and agonizedly pointed tongue—the unforgettable emblem of helpless terror and suffering.

Within his own career, Picasso embodied most of the strands of Modernism that blossomed in the first half of the twentieth century. His earliest works were expressionistic; then he became one of the leaders in creating art with formalist concerns. He never followed a utopian dream nor sought to express eternal forms, but in *Guernica,* he joined a large number of his contemporaries who believed that art is the most effective means of exploring psychological truth, criticizing social evil, and affirming the preeminent worth of individual human beings.

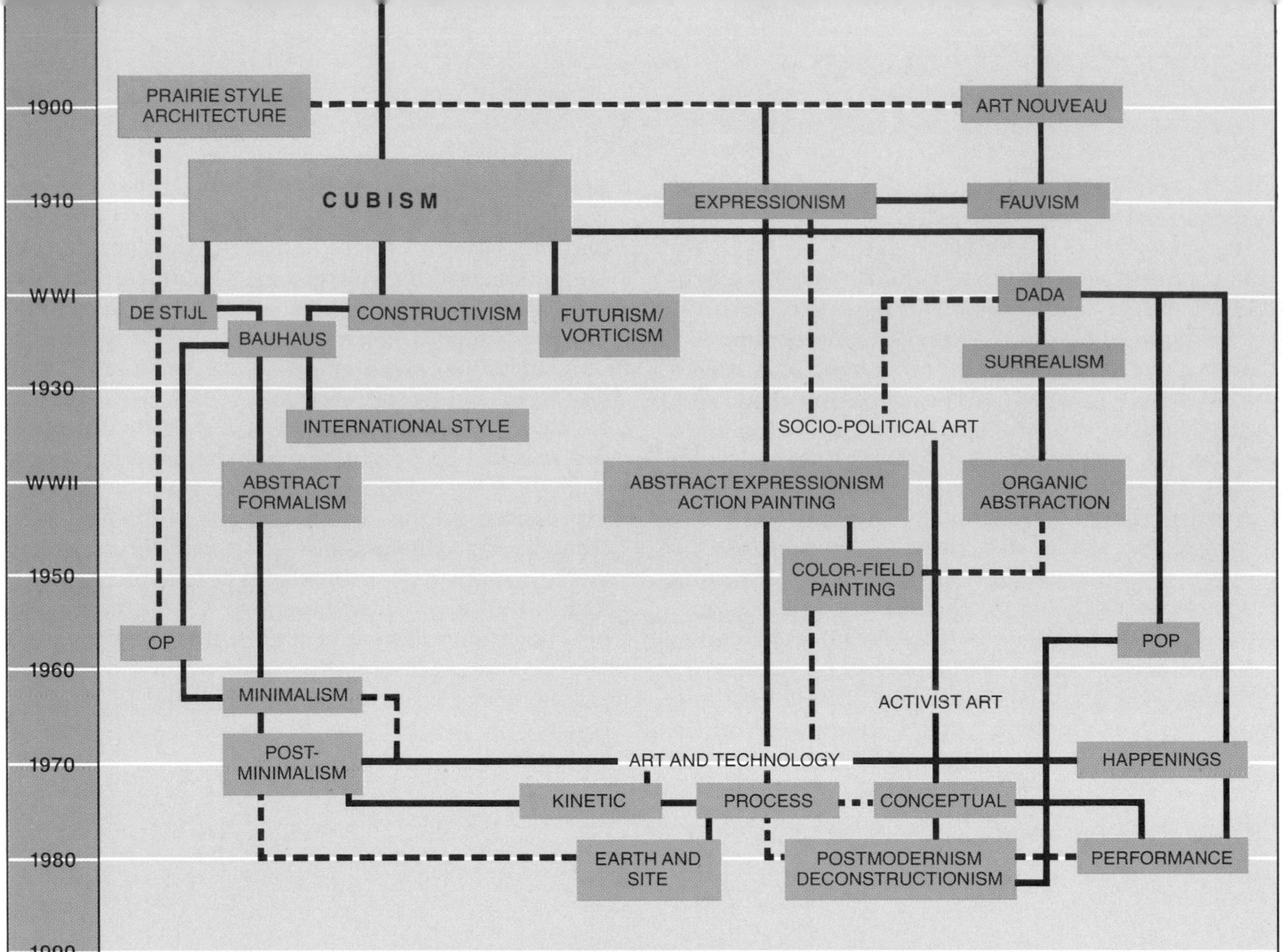

1900
1910
WWI
1930
WWII
1950
1960
1970
1980
1990

PRAIRIE STYLE ARCHITECTURE
ART NOUVEAU
CUBISM
EXPRESSIONISM
FAUVISM
DE STIJL
BAUHAUS
CONSTRUCTIVISM
FUTURISM/ VORTICISM
DADA
SURREALISM
INTERNATIONAL STYLE
SOCIO-POLITICAL ART
ABSTRACT FORMALISM
ABSTRACT EXPRESSIONISM ACTION PAINTING
ORGANIC ABSTRACTION
COLOR-FIELD PAINTING
OP
POP
MINIMALISM
ACTIVIST ART
POST-MINIMALISM
ART AND TECHNOLOGY
HAPPENINGS
KINETIC
PROCESS
CONCEPTUAL
EARTH AND SITE
POSTMODERNISM DECONSTRUCTIONISM
PERFORMANCE

Interrelation of Major Movements and Styles in the Art of the Twentieth Century

Solid black lines indicate direct influence; dashed lines, indirect

1940 **1950** **1960**

POLLOCK *Lucifer* 1947

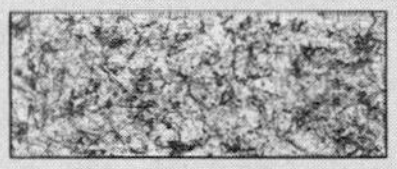

ARCHULETA *b.* 1910

DIEBENKORN *b.* 1922

FRANKENTHALER *b.* 1928

CAMPUS *b.* 1937

ROTHKO 1903–1970

BACON *Study . . . of Pope Innocent X* 1953

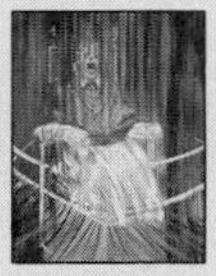

RAUSCHENBERG *b.* 1925

DE KOONING *b.* 1904

DE SICA *Bicycle Thieves* 1948

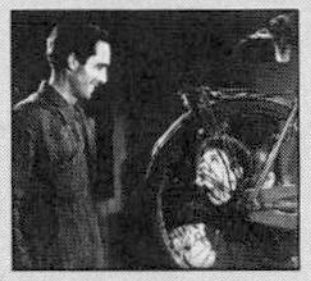

NEWMAN 1905–1970

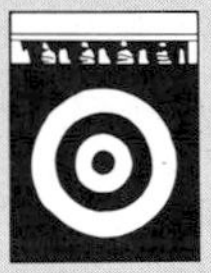

JOHNS *Target with Four Faces* 1955

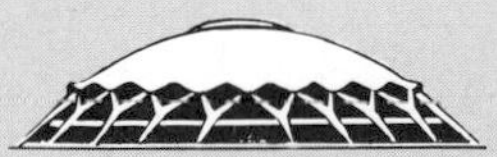

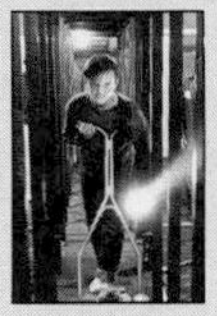

KAPROW *A Spring Happening* 1961

BOURGEOIS *b.* 1911

NEVELSON 1899–1988

CHRISTO *b.* 1935

VASARELY *b.* 1908

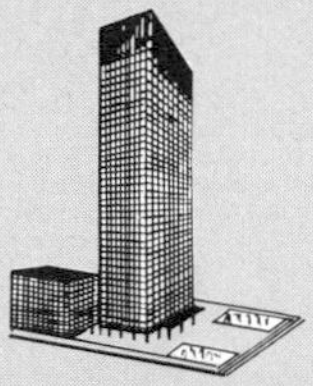

MIES VAN DER ROHE and **JOHNSON** Seagram Building 1956–1958

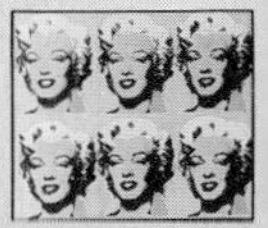

JUDD *b.* 1928

DE STAEL 1914–1955

GIACOMETTI *City Square (La Place)* 1948

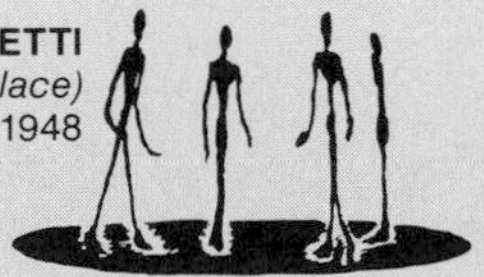

NERI *b.* 1930

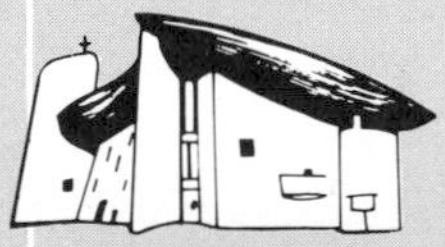

LE CORBUSIER Notre Dame du Haut 1950–1955

NERVI Palazzetto dello Sport 1958

WARHOL *Marily[n] Diptych*, detail 19[…]

Commercial television begins

United Nations organized 1945

Transistor invented 1948

Republic of India begun *c.* 1949

Korean Conflict 1950–1953

Sputnik I launched 1957

First manned space flight 1961

Atomic bomb devastates Hiroshima and Nagasaki 1945

People's Republic of China established 1949

Computer chip invented 1959

John F. Kennedy assassinated 1963

Jean-Paul Sartre 1905–1980

State of Israel created 1948

Lasers invented 1960

23

THE CONTEMPORARY WORLD

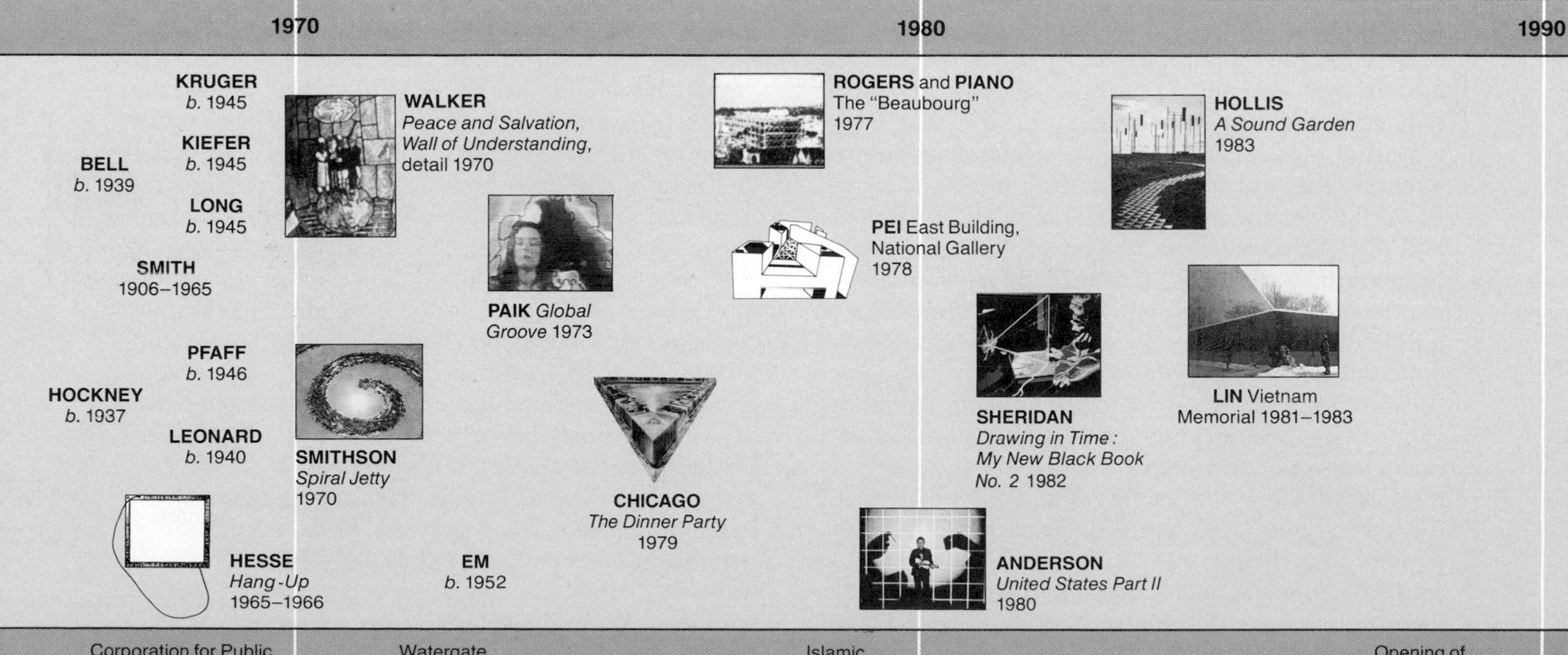

The contemporary world was ushered in by the dark period of World War II, which affected more of the globe's population than any earlier military conflict and left in its wake a twin legacy. On the one hand, the military activity of the war years spawned new technologies that changed the way humans worked, played, and thought; on the other hand, however, the war's conflagration posed the persistent threat of nuclear annihilation. A growing recognition of widespread human suffering and a haunting fear among many that life had no meaning or value contributed further to a global climate of dislocation.

Politically, the postwar world balanced between the powers of capitalism and communism. Western culture was split between those nations in Western Europe allied with the United States and those in Eastern Europe linked with the Soviet Union. In Asia, the communist leadership of Mao Tse-tung in postwar China initiated decades of change and political contests in surrounding countries, including Korea and Vietnam. One-time colonies in Asia and Africa won their independence from European control; some, like Zaire (formerly Congo), took new names to celebrate their changed status. The increased self-awareness that accompanied independence in these nations sometimes resulted in armed conflict like that which split Moslem Pakistan off from Hindu India. Religious and political conflict also erupted in South America and the Near East. More recently, the uneasy equilibrium between capitalism and communism, between Islamic and non-Islamic countries, and between established and emerging nations has been increasingly threatened by global population growth, widespread famine, disease, poverty, and an endangered natural environment.

During these same years, new technology shaped scientific theories about the nature of the universe. Powerful instruments like microscopes, telescopes, and nuclear accelerators helped generate new areas of thought. In the field of particle physics, researchers taught that everything in nature is composed of infinitely tiny particles in constant motion, whose apparent behavior is affected by the expectations of the observers who attempt to study them. Advances in medicine brought new control over physical and mental disease, and helped to develop social awareness about the needs of the sick, the handicapped, the very young, and the aged. Space exploration expanded knowledge of the universe, while affordable air travel allowed increasing numbers of people to visit cultures very different from their own and learn more about life on our planet. The widespread availability of technological innovations changed details of daily life in developed countries in ways that affected perceptions of society. The increased availability of innovations like refrigeration, electric lighting, central heating, and air-conditioning provided a hitherto unknown degree of control over time and weather and helped to create more leisure time.

Many of the activities people chose to fill their leisure time were connected with absorbing and using information acquired, processed, and shared through the new technologies. Television displaced radio and cinema as the most common transmitter of data, sending vivid images into homes around the globe. The mass marketing of long-playing records, paperback books, special-interest magazines, and personal equipment like cameras, videotape recorders, and computers allowed each individual to create and manipulate personal stores of information. The widespread transmission of information in most industrial countries contributed to a new awareness of the multiple traditions and values that existed in the world and helped to focus attention on the fragile interconnectedness of all sectors of what Buckminster Fuller called "this spaceship earth." Increasingly, people spoke of "truths" and "beauties" rather than *the* truth or a single universal beauty; truth and beauty were recognized to exist in many forms, each valid in its particular place and time. Amid this questioning of values, some people found traditional religion too much caught up in past habits to provide help in the chaotic conditions of the new age, and were attracted to new spiritual paths. In the stressful years of the late 1940s and the 1950s, many individuals (especially in the United States) turned to Zen Buddhism and to existentialism, which shared an emphasis on the importance of living wholly in each moment—"the eternal now." In the 1960s, 1970s, and 1980s, the search for spiritual values often was linked to social commitment, producing action for a cause or belief and resulting in antiwar and antinuclear demonstrations and "movements" like feminism, environmentalism, and black power.

Without the kind of shared beliefs and values common to art of the past, artists became increasingly conscious of their responsibility for the content and role of their art. As the critic Michael Kirby wrote about art in the contemporary period: "The key word in aesthetic theory is not *beauty* as has been suggested by traditional aesthetics, but *significance*. . . . The creation of art depends upon the artist's personal attempt to achieve what he feels to be significant."* Significant form and content in art were strongly affected by artists' abilities to view a variety of works, both directly, in the rapidly growing number of gal-

*In Richard Kostelanetz, ed., *Esthetics Contemporary* (Buffalo, NY: Prometheus Books, 1978), p. 43.

leries and museums, and secondhand, in the burgeoning array of art magazines, films, and television programs that brought to life André Malraux's "museum without walls."

Artists responded to the vast changes in the world around them with a wide array of new styles, yet continued to work within the three major approaches discussed in the last chapter—art with formalist concerns, art with psychological and conceptual concerns, and art with social and political concerns. Many artists found continued inspiration in non-art sources like archeology, anthropology, science, and technology. New works of art were often offered for sale through a centralized commercial system located primarily in major metropolises. Many works were treated as "commodities" in an art "market" in which artists functioned almost as piecework employees of ambitious and commercially minded galleries. An increasing number of artists rebelled by working outside this system, showing their art in cooperative galleries or deliberately creating works with no obvious commercial value.

Artists with formalist concerns struggling to express feeling in abstract art were influenced by the ideas of art theorist-critic Suzanne Langer, who wrote in her widely read book *Feeling and Form: A Theory of Art* (1953): "Vital organization is the frame of all feeling, because feeling exists only in living organisms; and the logic of all symbols that can express feeling is the logic of organic processes. The most characteristic principle of vital activity is rhythm."

Some artists with formalist concerns and some artists with psychological and conceptual concerns turned again to the idea of the artist as a seer who could restore to art the power of magic and mystery they believed had been lost in the industrial age. The theorist José Argüelles proposed that these artists operated by developing a kind of rigorous and antihistorical "internal technology," which allowed them to act with their whole creative beings to uncover and communicate visions of inner truth: "What separates the art of most modern Western visionaries from the kind of integral achievement that characterizes the archaic, however, is an intense inner discipline—the development of an internal technology. . . . Slowly and often painfully uncovering an authentically open and destructured vision of the world, the internal technologist appears in his or her role as *a healer, one who makes whole.*"*

Significant rhythm and form were of primary importance to artists with formalist interests, but these qualities did not satisfy those with psychological and conceptual concerns who wanted to reflect both the pain and the majesty of existence in this troubled period. Many of these artists used the human body expressionistically to carry their vision. Others explored the world or nature conceptually, borrowing images and objects and juxtaposing them in ways that stimulated the viewer's imagination, sharing something of the attitude described by the sculptor and theorist Allan Kaprow in 1966: "At present, any avant-garde is primarily a philosophical quest and a finding of truths, rather than purely an esthetic activity."†

By the late 1970s, many believed that traditional Modernist concerns had been overturned by a Postmodernist era of which the critic Craig Owens wrote: "Postmodernism is usually treated . . . as a crisis of cultural authority, specifically of the authority vested in Western European culture and its institutions."‡ While Modernist art embraced new technology as helpful to the evolution of human society, Postmodernist art distrusted both progress and objective truth as concepts tied too completely to Western culture's view of history. All cultures were seen as equally valid, making our own assume a role of "distance" or "otherness"—just one among many of interest and worth. Postmodernist art often appropriated artistic styles and concepts in an attempt to make the viewer reexamine all "traditional" ideas and experiences.

Most artists with social and political concerns in the contemporary post-1940 period used their art to help change the perceptions and even the behavior of viewers. As the feminist Performance artists Leslie Labowitz and Suzanne Lacy wrote in 1979: "All images are political in that they portray a set of values and attitudes about how the world is or could be. . . . Whether contending with or agreeing with the flow of media images, the artist in the technological society must be cognizant as never before of the way in which his or her visual product hits its audience."§ While many artists with social and political concerns used their art to call attention to the darker side of contemporary experience, a separate group tried instead to restore to humanity a sense of connectedness with nature and the continuum of human history.

The varied strands of continuing Modernist and Postmodernist visions have made the period from 1940 to the present one of the richest and most complex in the history of art. Nevertheless, it is important to recognize the impossibility of doing historical justice to contemporary works, especially when many of

*Ibid., pp. 174, 176.

†In Kostelanetz, ed., *Esthetics Contemporary*, p. 31.

‡In Howard Risatti, ed., *Postmodern Perspectives* (Englewood Cliffs, NJ: Prentice-Hall, 1990), p. 186.

§In Richard Hertz, ed., *Theories of Contemporary Art* (Englewood Cliffs, NJ: Prentice-Hall, 1985), p. 177.

the men and women who created them are still living. The selection and presentation of certain contemporary monuments may suggest that a judgment of their superiority has already been made by history. This is not the case; historical judgment moves slowly, and identification of the masterpieces of the current epoch has scarcely begun. The fact that all of this work stands so close to us means that in this chapter, more than in any other, artists are discussed as significant representatives of the major approaches taken during the contemporary period.

ART WITH FORMALIST CONCERNS

Sometime during World War II, the center of the Western art world shifted from Europe to the United States. Émigré artists arrived and their influence merged with native American traditions to create new ideas and styles, the most important of which were formalist. The art of the moment was abstract, but its expressions took many paths. The style that first drew the eyes of the world toward America was a vigorous, freewheeling mode called New York Abstract Expressionism, Action Painting, or Gestural Abstraction. The biomorphic shapes of certain buildings and sculptures and the vast canvases of Color-Field painting, activated by subtle modulations of hue and an ambiguous sense of figure-ground, were somewhat quieter in appearance, but equally linked to the intuitive methods of Surrealism. Like the Surrealists, Abstract Expressionists, Organic and Formalist Abstractionists, and Color-Field painters favored methods that bypassed the rational mind by emphasizing feeling, emotion, and the unconscious. Equally idealistic in inspiration, but different from abstraction based on feeling and allusion, was a structured kind of abstraction that carried further the precise formalist investigations of Suprematism, Constructivism, and Neo-Plasticism. Like its predecessors, the art produced by this formalist approach was based less on the operation of intuition and process than on the exercise of reasoned control and measured design as reflections of eternal order.

Abstract Expressionism

Abstract Expressionism was the first major new abstract style developed in the United States after the influx of refugee artists from Europe in the years just before World War II. The movement was centered in New York City but rapidly spread throughout the Western world. In part as a response to the chaos of the time in which they lived, Abstract Expressionist artists turned, as had the Dadaists before them, against the use of reason. They tried to broaden their artistic processes to express what Carl Jung called the "collective unconscious" by adopting the methods of Surrealist improvisation and using their creative minds as open channels through which the forces of the unconscious could make themselves visible. The Abstract Expressionists saw themselves as leaders in the quest to find the path to the future. The New York artists viewed their art as a weapon in the struggle to maintain their humanity in the midst of the world's increasing insanity. To create, they turned inward. Their works had a look of rough spontaneity and exhibited a refreshing energy; their content was intended to be grasped intuitively by each viewer, in a state free from structured thinking. Abstract Expressionist artists believed their work could help to counter the forces of dislocation by reawakening in people a sense of interconnectedness with all living things. As the painter Robert Motherwell eloquently wrote:

> The emergence of abstract art is a sign that there are still men of feeling in the world. . . . From their perspective, it is the social world that tends to appear irrational and absurd. . . . Nothing as drastic as abstract art could have come into existence save as the consequence of a most profound, relentless, unquenchable need. The need is for felt experience—intense, immediate, direct, subtle, unified, warm, vivid, rhythmic. If a painting does not make a human contact, it is nothing. But the audience is also responsible. Through pictures our passions touch. Pictures are vehicles of passion, of all kinds and orders, not pretty luxuries like sports cars. In our society, the capacity to give and receive passion is limited. For this reason, the act of painting is a deep human necessity, not the production of a hand-made commodity.*

JACKSON POLLOCK (1912–1956) is the artist most often associated with the Abstract Expressionist or Gestural Abstractionist approach, and the power of his works influenced artists throughout the world. Pollock brought to his paintings his memories of the vast open spaces of the southwestern United States, where he grew up, and of the sand painting techniques of the Native American medicine men he had seen there. After a brief period as a Socialist Realist, Pollock transformed his interest in the dynamic rhythms of Rubens (FIG. 19-40), Ryder (FIG. 21-93), and Orozco (FIG. 22-82) into a free, abstract style that had him working with his whole body in dynamic

*In Frank O'Hara, *Robert Motherwell* (New York: Museum of Modern Art, 1965), pp. 45, 50.

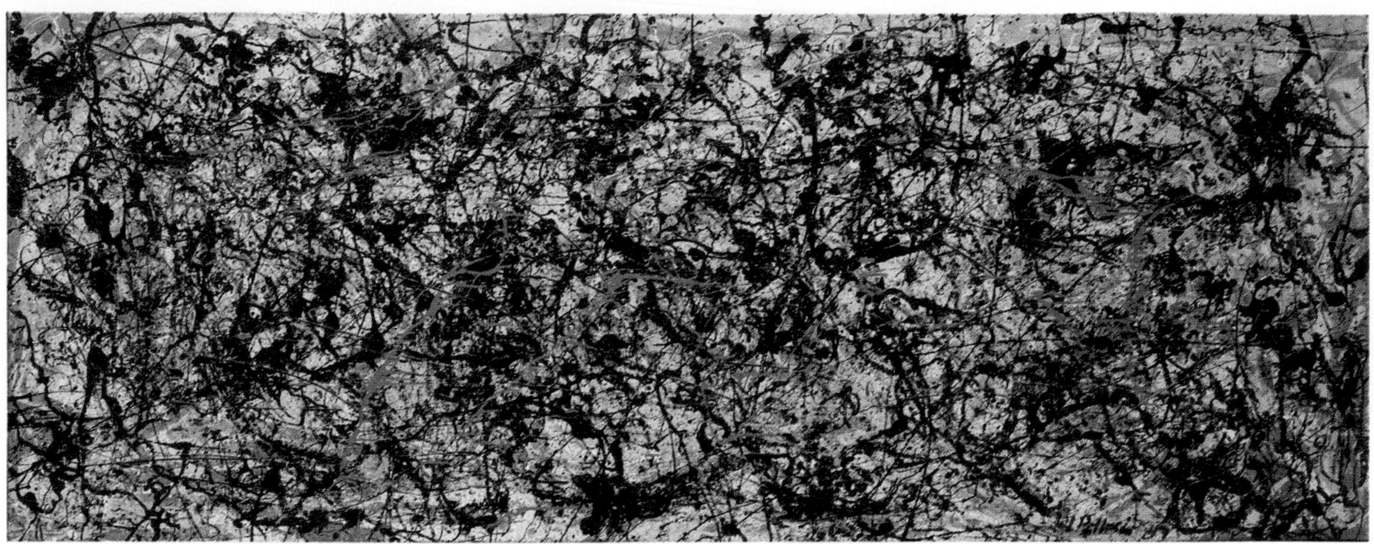

23-1 JACKSON POLLOCK, *Lucifer*, 1947. Oil, aluminum paint, and enamel on canvas, approx. 3′ 5″ × 8′ 9″. Collection of Mr. and Mrs. Harry W. Anderson.

swirling gestures as he poured or flung paint onto the surface of his canvases. As a rationale for his method, Pollock commented that "new needs need new techniques. . . . The modern painter cannot express this age . . . in the old forms of the Renaissance or of any other past culture."*

For a work like *Lucifer* (FIG. **23-1**), Pollock unrolled a large section of canvas directly onto the floor of his studio and dripped and splattered paint on it while moving energetically along its edge or across it. On the floor, he felt more comfortable: "I feel nearer, more a part of the painting, since this way I can walk around it, work from the four sides and internally be *in* the painting." Like Miró, Pollock alternated between periods of spontaneous improvisation and periods of careful scrutiny of his developing composition. However, his methods also had roots in Kandinsky's automatic and spontaneous nonobjectivity (FIG. 22-47),† and even in the improvisation used by jazz musicians admired at the time by most of the New York Abstract Expressionists. The random fall and scatter of the paint in *Lucifer* emphasizes the liquid nature of the medium itself, but the gestures of the artist have turned the paint into loose skeins of color that loop back and forth across the canvas, thickening in some places and falling in almost straight lines in others. No easily identifiable shapes help the viewer to establish the familiar depth of a normal figure-ground relationship; instead, the rhythmic layers of line spread out laterally across the canvas and seem to extend far beyond its edges. As he worked, Pollock looked not out (as from a viewpoint) but *down,* seeing his "landscape" unfold. When the works were exhibited, this "plane of action" on which they were created was transformed into a "plane of confrontation" on a vertical wall, lending the compositions a sense of floating, gravityless space. The overall pattern of interweaving lines may suggest the patterns of motion and energy found in micro- and macro-photographs of the basic structures of the physical world, but the artist intended no direct reference to nature. Instead, the painting becomes almost a record of Pollock's actions in making it. Indeed, in works like *Lucifer,* the sense of the process of painting is stronger than the awareness of the painted surface itself.

Gestural Abstract Expressionism had many possible methods of approach. In the work of FRANZ KLINE (1910–1962), it was a vehicle of very personal psychic revelation, possibly as mysterious to the artist as to the observer. Kline trained in Boston and London before settling in New York City. His early work was expressive and realistic, but gradually he concentrated on abstract form. He used a special opaque projector to enlarge designs onto a wall as a means of achieving simplification and abstraction in his paintings. His mature works include many large black-and-white canvases, like *Painting* (FIG. **23-2**), which are filled with ragged bars and stripes of black that play against white slablike areas as sharp-edged as broken planes of glass. These configurations suggest Chinese characters boldly brushed and greatly magnified, a kind of ideogram of the artist's psychic state. As

*In Francis V. O'Conner, *Jackson Pollock* (New York: Museum of Modern Art, 1967), pp. 40, 79.

†The label "abstract expressionism" was attached to Kandinsky's art as early as 1919. A large retrospective exhibition of the Russian artist's works in 1945 at the Museum of Non-Objective Painting (now the Solomon H. Guggenheim Museum) in New York City impressed many young artists, including Pollock.

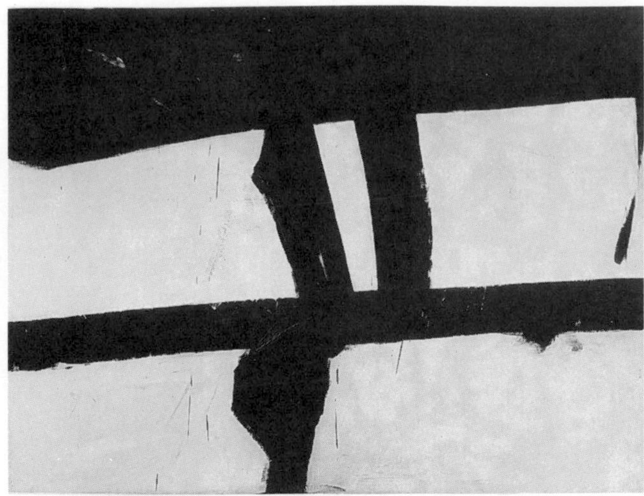

23-2 Franz Kline, *Painting*, 1952, 1955–1956. Approx. 6′ 5″ × 8′ 4″. Present location unknown.

hieratic and quasi-magical shapes, the forms can be interpreted as the observer pleases; as purely nonobjective forms in a wide variety of arrangements, they are expressive in their blunt esthetic force and bold, free execution.

The Dutch-born painter Willem de Kooning (b. 1904) has used the techniques of New York Action Painting to make both abstract works and the energetic images of massive women for which he is best known. De Kooning embraced Gestural Abstract Expressionism after an early career in commercial art and as a figure and portrait painter, experience that gave him a special command of fluid line and subtle color. His series of huge women, like *Woman I* (fig. **23-3**), was inspired in part by female models on advertising billboards, but the forms also suggest fertility figures and a satiric inversion of the traditional image of Venus, goddess of love. In *Woman I,* the figure is defined with manic excitement, apparently slashed out at full speed with a brush held at arm's length. Shapes and colors play through, over, and across one another with no definable order. The brazen and baleful mask of the face mixes a toothpaste smile (inspired by an ad for Camel cigarettes) with the grimace of a death's head. The effect is one of simultaneous delineation and defacement, of construction and cancellation—a conflict between sketch and finished picture. As with other Action Painting, the image seems to be eternally coming into being before the eyes of the viewer, but the tension between flat design and lines in space, between image and process, is heightened by the recognizable figure whose violent power demands recognition. It is for such qualities that De Kooning has been called an "artist who makes ambiguity a hypothesis on which to build."*

The spontaneity and visible processes of New York Abstract Expressionism were used elsewhere for figurative images expressed in juicy, thick shapes of color and paint. One important group of artists, the Bay Area Figurative Painters, worked in this way during the 1950s and 1960s in the area around San Francisco. One of the best known of this group was Richard Diebenkorn (b. 1922), whose admiration for the work of Hopper, Sheeler, O'Keeffe, and Matisse helped inspire him to change in the mid-1950s from an early Abstract Expressionist style to the creation of broadly brushed paintings of figures in spacious settings. *Man and Woman in a Large Room* (fig. **23-4**) is typical of the way Diebenkorn expressed the clear light and spreading space of California through a careful arrangement of simplified forms. Shapes pile atop one another, light and dark hues alternate, steep perspective lines push back into space at one instant and the next lie flat as a pattern of sumptu-

*Thomas B. Hess, *Willem de Kooning* (New York: Museum of Modern Art, 1968), p. 25.

23-3 Willem de Kooning, *Woman I*, 1950–1952. Approx. 6′ 4″ × 4′ 10″. Collection, The Museum of Modern Art, New York (purchase).

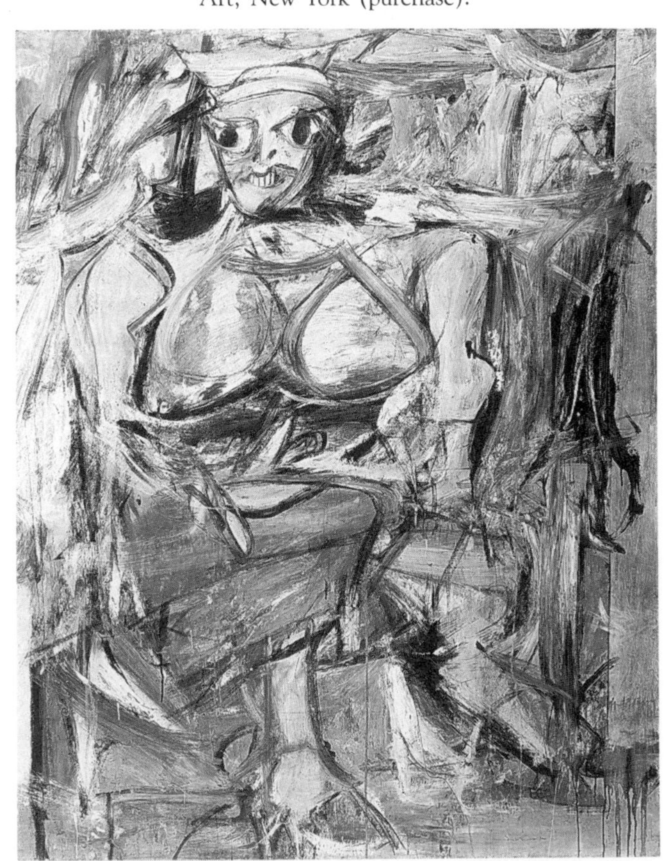

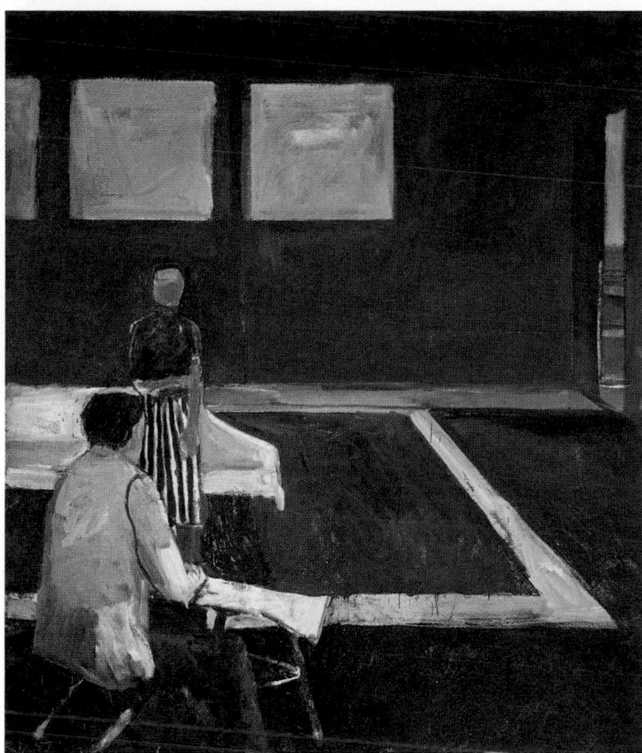

23-4 Richard Diebenkorn, *Man and Woman in a Large Room,* 1957. 5′ 11⅛″ × 5′ 2½″. Hirshhorn Museum and Sculpture Garden, Smithsonian Institution, Washington, D.C. (gift of the Joseph H. Hirshhorn Foundation, 1966).

ously colored blocks of paint. Still, the viewer does not forget that this play of forms also describes two figures pushed to one side of a vast, almost empty room whose curtainless windows reveal roughly clouded sky and whose door mysteriously opens directly onto the sea. As with De Kooning's paintings of women, Diebenkorn's paintings of figures in settings balance between existence as powerful abstract compositions and depictions of scenes with emotional resonance. The artist clearly recognized the importance of the emotional component: "A figure exerts a continuing and unspecified influence on a painting as the canvas develops. The represented forms are loaded with psychological feeling. It can't ever just be *painting*."* The psychological feeling in Diebenkorn's work during the late 1950s and early 1960s suggests the loneliness and isolation of contemporary human existence, but the rich patterns of abstract composition interested the California artist so much that by the late 1960s, he had abandoned direct references to the visible world and had returned to the creation of paintings filled with stately, nonobjective shapes.

Like Diebenkorn, the Russian-French painter Nicolas de Stael (1914–1955) created figurative works in the 1950s with the direct painterliness of the Abstract Expressionist mode, but De Stael's compositions are further removed than Diebenkorn's from a sense of palpable physical forms and are imbued instead with a static, timeless mood, somewhat like a Classicism based on style rather than subject. De Stael's early nomadic life took him from his native Russia to Poland, Belgium, Morocco, and Algeria. He settled in Paris in the late 1930s. Like Matisse, De Stael used figures, objects, and their settings as the source for harmonious arrangements of colors and shapes. *Musicians* (FIG. **23-5**) is typical of his work, presenting an image in which mosaiclike color shapes resolve themselves into a group of performing music makers. Simpler in composition and less involved with the character of each figure than Picasso's *Three Musicians* (FIG. 22-11), De Stael's *Musicians* focuses

23-5 Nicolas de Stael, *Musicians,* 1953. 5′ 6⅞″ × 3′ 9″. © The Phillips Collection, Washington, D.C.

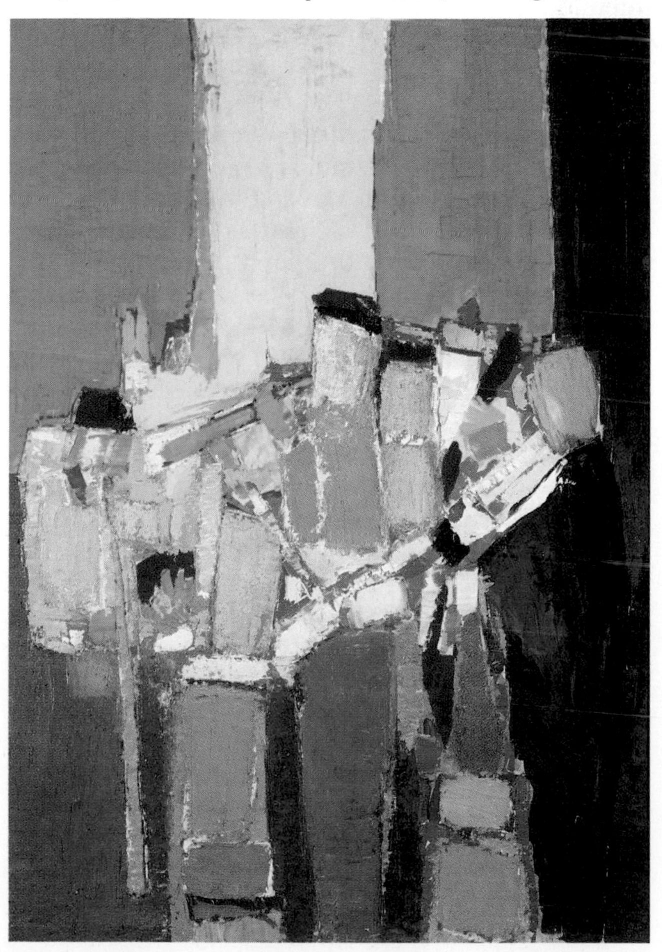

*In Robert T. Buck, Jr., Linda L. Cathcart, Gerald Nordland, and Maurice Tuchman, *Richard Diebenkorn; Paintings and Drawings, 1943–1980* (Buffalo, NY: Albright-Knox Art Gallery, 1980), p. 31.

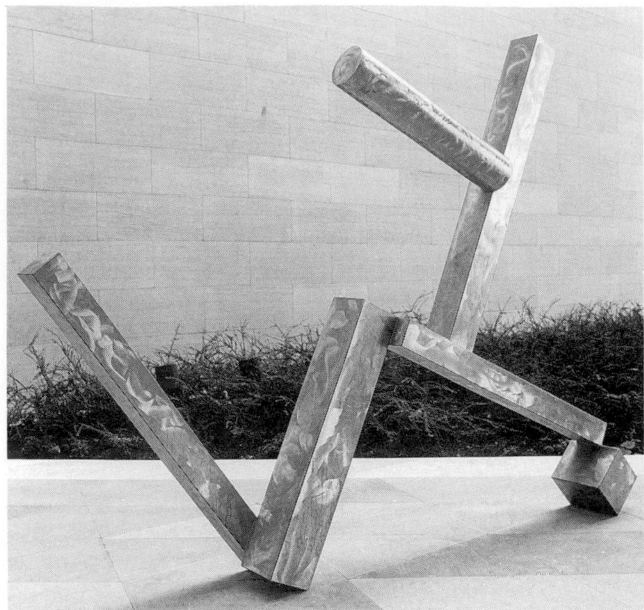

23-6 David Smith, *CUBI XXVI*, 1965. Steel, approx. 10′ × 12½′ × 2¼′. National Gallery of Art, Washington, D.C. (Ailsa Mellon Bruce Fund, 1978).

attention instead on the process of painting, and the viewer is most aware of the way that light, color, and space fill the canvas in a serenely orchestrated manner.

Only a handful of sculptors were associated with Gestural Abstract Expressionism, and they translated its forms into a kind of drawing in space. The most influential of these artists was David Smith (1906–1965), whose mastery of spatial composition was widely admired by younger artists. Smith began as a painter, which helps explain his fascination with line and the way it can create a sense of shape and space. His early sculptures were done in a linear, open style influenced by the work of Julio Gonzalez (fig. 22-16). In his later work, Smith used the metal-fabrication techniques he had learned earlier as a factory worker in Indiana: "The equipment I use, my supply of material comes from factory study, and duplicates as nearly as possible the production equipment used in making a locomotive." Sculptures like *Cubi XXVI* (fig. **23-6**) are monumental constructions in stainless steel in which Smith arranged solid, geometric masses in remarkable equilibriums of strength and buoyancy. Smith was at ease in the age of the machine: "What associations the metal possesses are those of this century: power, structure, movement, progress, suspension, destruction, brutality." His welded compositions were tough enough to allow the remarkably free balancing in space that is characteristic of his last style. Here, as in all Smith's work, the viewer has a sharp awareness of the linear outlines of the planes that make up the composition and help to create and reinforce the rhythms of the piece, including the kinesthetic sense of motion created by a strong axis and the thrusting of elements at angles against and away from that axis. Like much of the work of the other New York Abstract Expressionists, Smith's work addresses the viewer's sense of gesture in space; his sculptures always seem poised on the edge of moving between one position in space and another.

Organic and Color-Field Abstraction

Very different in approach from the improvisation and spontaneity of Abstract Expressionism were the architecture, sculpture, and painting in which suggestive organic forms and evocative fields of color hinted at myth, ritual, and the themes of psychology—especially Freud's ideas of sexuality and Jung's ideas concerning universal archetypes. The links with universal imagery were extremely important to artists working in these modes. Even architects with long careers behind them, like Frank Lloyd Wright and Le Corbusier, invested many of their buildings during the post-1940 period with powerful organic sculptural qualities.

The long, incredibly productive career of Frank Lloyd Wright ended with his design for the Solomon R. Guggenheim Museum (figs. **23-7** and **23-8**), which was built in New York City between 1943 and 1959. Here, using reinforced concrete almost as a sculptor might use resilient clay, Wright designed a structure inspired by the spiral of a snail's shell. Wright had introduced curves and circles into some of his plans in the 1930s, and as the architectural historian Peter Blake noted: "The spiral was the next logical step; it is the circle brought into the third and fourth dimensions."* Inside the building, the shape of the shell expands toward the top, and a winding interior ramp spirals to connect the gallery bays, which are illuminated by a strip of skylight embedded in the museum's outer wall. Visitors can stroll up the ramp or be brought by elevator to the top of the building and proceed down the gently inclined walkway, viewing the works of art displayed along the way. Thick walls and the solid organic shape give the building the sense of turning in on itself, with the long viewing area opening onto a 90-foot central well of space that seems a sheltered environment secure from the bustling city outside.

*Peter Blake, *Frank Lloyd Wright* (Harmondsworth, Middlesex: Penguin Books, 1960), p. 115.

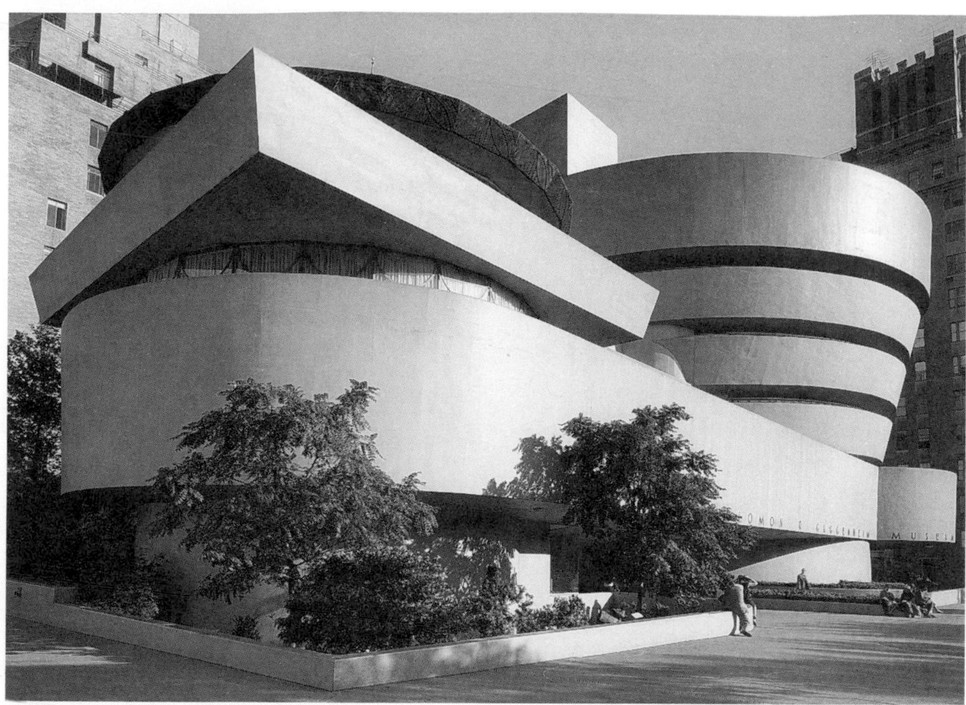

23-7 FRANK LLOYD WRIGHT, Solomon R. Guggenheim Museum, New York, 1943–1959 (exterior view from the north).

23-8 FRANK LLOYD WRIGHT, interior of the Solomon R. Guggenheim Museum.

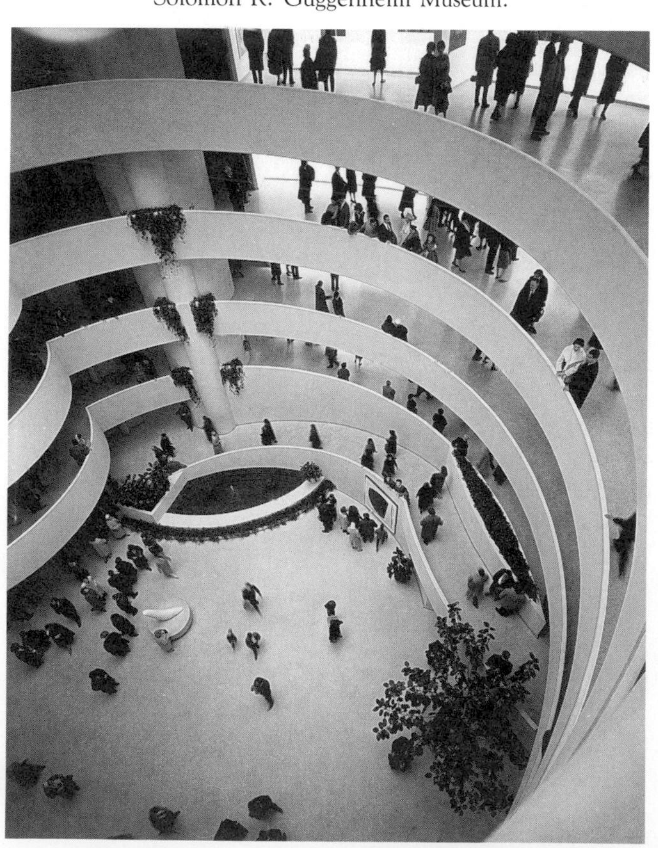

The startling forms of LE CORBUSIER's Notre Dame du Haut (FIG. **23-9**), completed in 1955 at Ronchamp, France, challenge the viewer in their fusion of architecture and sculpture in a single expression. This small chapel on a pilgrimage site in the Vosges Mountains was designed to replace a building destroyed in World War II. The monumental impression of Notre Dame du Haut seen from afar is somewhat deceptive. Although one massive exterior wall contains a pulpit facing a spacious outdoor area for large-scale, open-air services on special holy days, the interior holds at most two hundred people. The intimate scale, stark, heavy walls, and mysterious illumination (jewel tones cast from the deeply recessed stained-glass windows) give this space (FIG. **23-10**) an aura reminiscent of a sacred cave or a medieval monastery. The structure of Notre Dame du Haut may look free-form to a lay person, but it is actually based, like the medieval cathedral, on an underlying mathematical system. The fabric was formed from a frame of steel and metal mesh, which was sprayed with concrete and painted white, except for two interior private chapel niches with colored walls, and the roof, which was left unpainted to darken naturally with the passage of time. The quality of mystery in the interior space is intensified by the way the roof is elevated above the walls on a series of nearly invisible blocks, which has the effect of making the roof appear to float freely

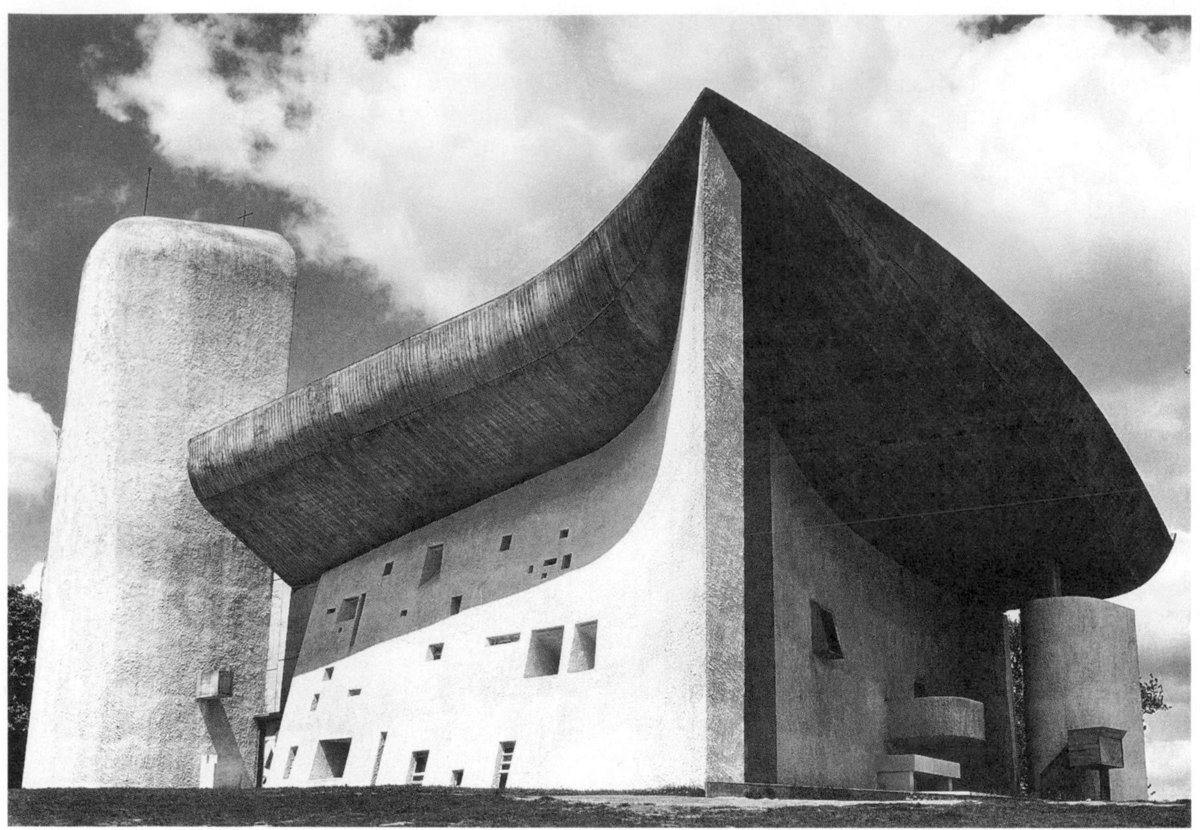

23-9 Le Corbusier, Notre Dame du Haut, Ronchamp, France, 1950–1955.

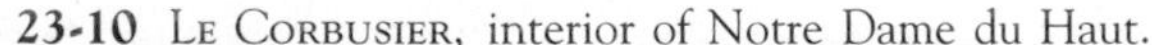

23-10 Le Corbusier, interior of Notre Dame du Haut.

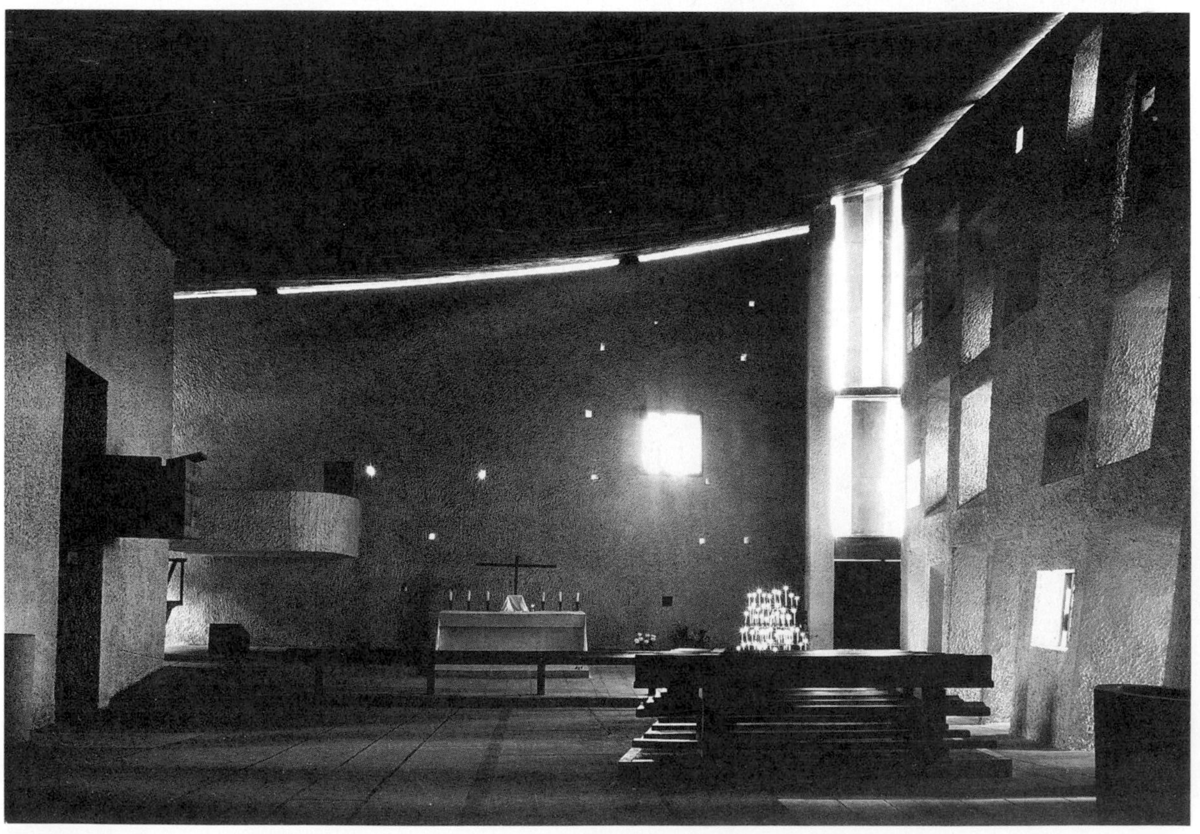

above the sanctuary. Le Corbusier's preliminary sketches for the building indicate that he linked the design with the shape of praying hands, the wings of a dove (representing both peace and the Holy Spirit), and the prow of a ship (reminding us that the Latin word used for the main gathering place in Christian churches is *nave*—"ship"). The artist envisioned that in these powerful sculptural solids and voids, human beings could find new values—new interpretations of their sacred beliefs and of their natural environment.

While Wright worked with inspiration from nature and Le Corbusier with the shared symbols and traditions of religion, LOUISE NEVELSON (1899–1988) created sculpture that combined a sense of the architectural fragment with the power of Dada and Surrealist found objects to express her personal sense of the underlying meanings of life. Multiplicity of meaning was important to Nevelson. She sought "the in-between place . . . the dawns and the dusks" where one could sense the transition between one state of being and another. Born in Russia, Nevelson moved as a child with her family to Maine, where she began her training in music, dance, theater, painting, and the graphic arts. By the late 1950s, she was making assemblages of found wooden objects and forms, enclosing smaller sculptural compositions in boxes of varied sizes, and joining the boxes to one another to form "walls," which she then painted in a single hue—usually black, white, or gold. The monochromatic color scheme unifies the diverse parts of pieces like *Tropical Garden II* (FIG. **23-11**) and also creates a mysterious field of shapes and shadows. The structures suggest magical environments that resemble the treasured secret hideaways dimly remembered from childhood. Yet, the boxy frames and the precision of the manufactured found objects create a rough geometrical structure over which the viewer's eye roams freely, lingering on some details before moving on. The parts of a Nevelson sculpture and their interrelation recall the *Merz* constructions of Kurt Schwitters (FIG. 22-29). The effect is also rather like viewing the side wall of an apartment building from a moving elevated train or looking down on a city from the air.

If Nevelson's works recall the allusive qualities of a nailed-together Dada work by Schwitters, the sculpture of the French-American artist LOUISE BOURGEOIS (b. 1911) is heir to the evocative biomorphic Surrealist shapes of Jean Arp. Bourgeois studied mathematics and art in Paris before moving to New York, where her early paintings and prints focus on the theme of the female body as a building. In her sculpture, her subject has been "groups of objects relating to each other . . . the drama of one among many." *Cumul I*

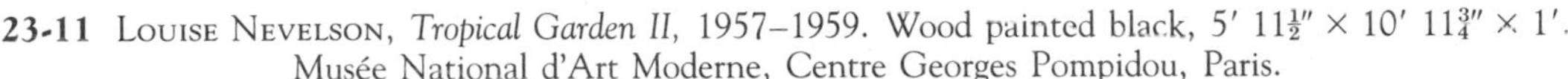

23-11 LOUISE NEVELSON, *Tropical Garden II*, 1957–1959. Wood painted black, 5′ $11\frac{1}{2}$″ × 10′ $11\frac{3}{4}$″ × 1′. Musée National d'Art Moderne, Centre Georges Pompidou, Paris.

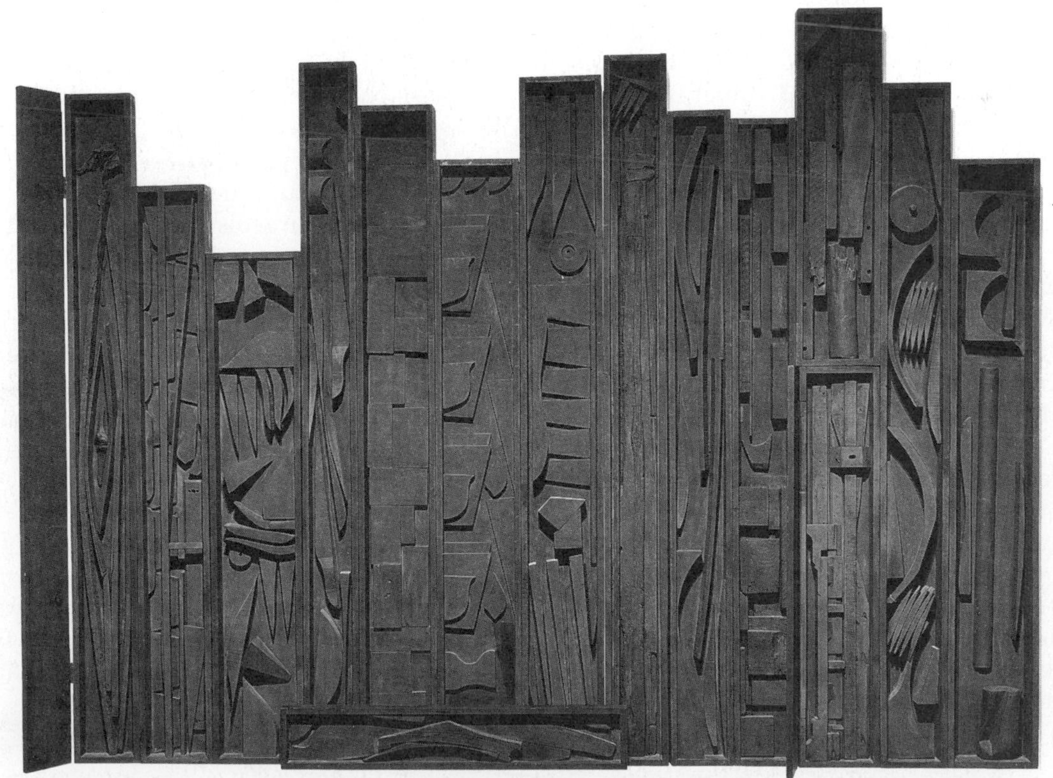

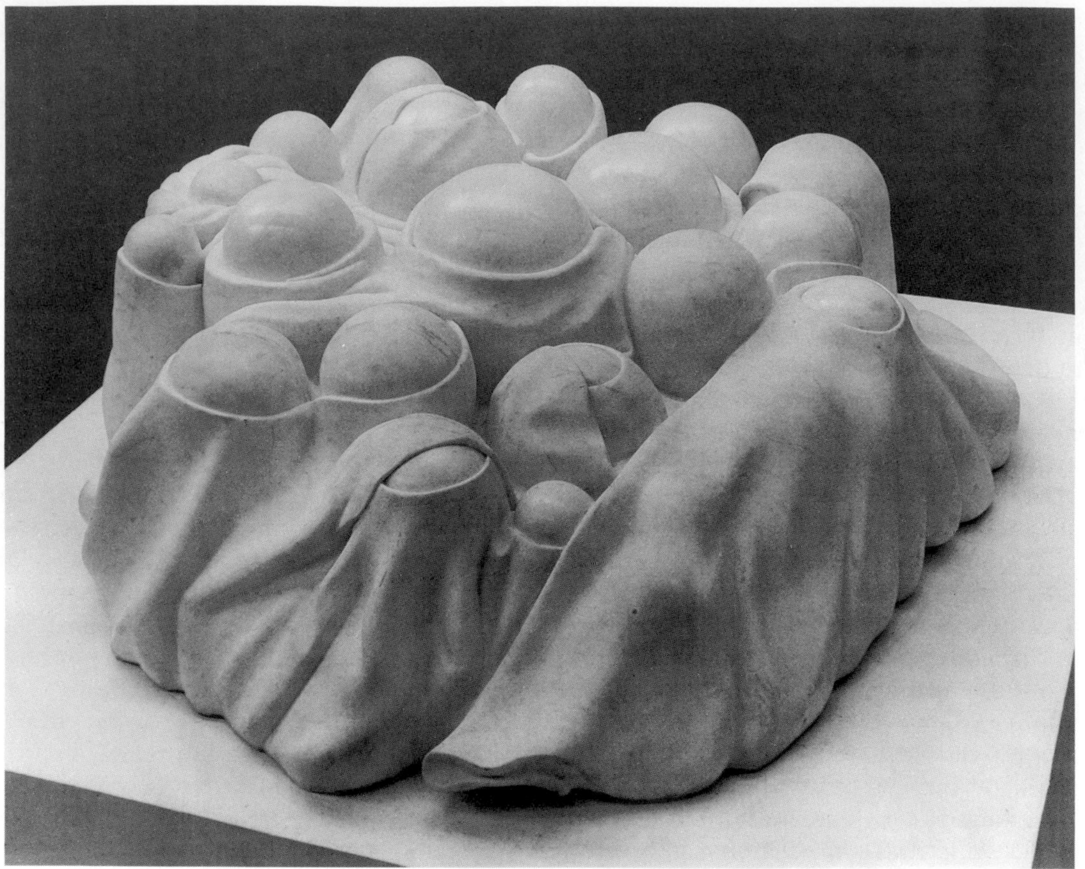

23-12 LOUISE BOURGEOIS, *Cumul I,* 1969. Marble, $22\frac{3}{8}''$ × 50″ × 48″. Musée National d'Art Moderne, Centre Georges Pompidou, Paris.

(FIG. **23-12**) is a collection of round-headed units huddled within a collective cloak dotted with holes, through which the tops of the individual units protrude. The units differ in size, and their position within the group lends a distinctive personality to each. Although the shapes remain abstract, the reference to human figures is strong. Bourgeois uses a wide variety of materials in her works, including wood, plaster, latex, and plastics, in addition to alabaster, marble, and bronze. She exploits the qualities of the material to suit the expressiveness of the piece. In *Cumul I,* the fact that marble can take either a high gloss or a matte finish increases the sensuous distinction between the group of swelling forms and the soft folds that swaddle them. Like Hepworth (FIG. 22-51), Bourgeois connects her sculpture with the multiple relationships of the body to landscape: "[My pieces] are anthropomorphic and they are landscape also, since our body could be considered from a topographical point of view, as a land with mounds and valleys and caves and holes." However, Bourgeois's pieces are more personal and more openly sexual than those of the English sculptor. *Cumul I* represents perfectly the allusions Bourgeois seeks: "There has always been sexual suggestiveness in my work. Sometimes I am totally concerned with female shapes—characters of breasts like clouds—but often I merge the imagery—phallic breasts, male and female, active and passive."*

Nevelson's sculptures suggest whole environments, while Bourgeois likes to work with groupings that suggest communities. Painters with similarly expansive vision expressed a sense of limitless space by covering canvases with fields of color. Critics termed these artists "Color-Field painters." Among the earliest artists working in this way were Barnett Newman and Mark Rothko, who each explored a quieter esthetic than that followed by their contemporary associates, the New York Abstract Expressionists.

In the works of BARNETT NEWMAN (1905–1970), such "fields" of color suggest space of an almost purely perceptual kind. Newman's early works were organic abstractions inspired by his study of biology and his fascination with Native American art. Soon,

*In Deborah Wye, *Louise Bourgeois* (New York: Museum of Modern Art, 1982), pp. 22, 25, 27.

23-13 BARNETT NEWMAN, *Vir Heroicus Sublimis*, 1950–1951. 7′ 11$\frac{3}{8}$″ × 17′ 9$\frac{1}{4}$″. Collection, The Museum of Modern Art, New York (gift of Mr. and Mrs. Ben Heller).

however, he simplified his compositions so that each canvas is filled with a single, modulated color split by narrow bands the artist called "zips," which run from one edge of the painting to the other. As the artist explained it, "The streak was always going through an atmosphere; I kept trying to create a world *around* it." Newman had a special feeling for scale, proportion, and the absolute quality of each particular hue, and he used these elements in large paintings to express his feelings about the tragic condition of modern life and the human struggle to survive. He said, "The artist's problem is the idea complex that makes contact with mystery—of life, of men, of nature, of the hard black chaos that is death, or the greyer, softer chaos that is tragedy." The title of his huge painting *Vir Heroicus Sublimis* (FIG. **23-13**) suggests the epic nature of these themes. Newman used the vast color field as a way to engage even the peripheral vision of his viewers, to create a particular sense of sublime and infinite space.

The best known of the Color-Field painters is probably MARK ROTHKO (1903–1970), who, like Newman, used the Color-Field approach to represent the sublime. Rothko was born in Russia but grew up in the United States and studied liberal arts before becoming a painter. His early paintings were figurative works, but he soon came to believe that references to anything specific in the physical world conflicted with the sublime idea of the universal, supernatural "spirit of myth," which he saw as the core of meaning in art. In a statement co-written with Newman and another artist, Rothko articulated his beliefs about art: "We favor the simple expression of complex thought. We are for the large shape because it has the impact of the unequivocal. We wish to reassert the picture plane. . . . We assert that . . . only that subject matter is valid which is tragic and timeless. That is why we profess spiritual kinship with primitive and archaic art."* Rothko gradually reduced his compositions to two or three large rectangles composed of layers of color with hazily brushed contours, spreading almost to the edges of the canvas. Subtle tonal variations in his works transcend the essentially monochromatic effect and create a mysterious sense of forms or images hovering in an ambiguously defined space. Works like *Four Darks in Red* (FIG. **23-14**) are perceived at once as a whole. Their still, shimmering veils of color encourage a calm and contemplative mood in the viewer, and to maximize this effect, Rothko preferred that they be exhibited either in isolation or with other paintings by him.

Newman stretched one color to fill a vast canvas field and Rothko created radiant clouds of color that seem to float within the rectangular shape of his canvases; in the works of both artists, the paint lies on the surface of the canvas. The American painter HELEN FRANKENTHALER (b. 1928) was one of the first artists to explore the effects of drenching the fabric of the canvas with fluid paint. This technique, called *soak-stain*, was inspired by a series of paintings Pollock made in the early 1950s by pouring thinned black paint onto raw canvas—bare fabric that had not been treated with the traditional protective coating of glue

*In Diane Waldman, *Mark Rothko, 1903–1970: A Retrospective* (New York: Solomon R. Guggenheim Museum, 1978), p. 39.

23-14 MARK ROTHKO, *Four Darks in Red,* 1958. 102″ × 116″. Collection of the Whitney Museum of American Art (gift of the Friends of the Whitney Museum of American Art, Mr. and Mrs. Eugene M. Schwartz, Mrs. Samuel A. Seaver, Charles Simon, and purchase).

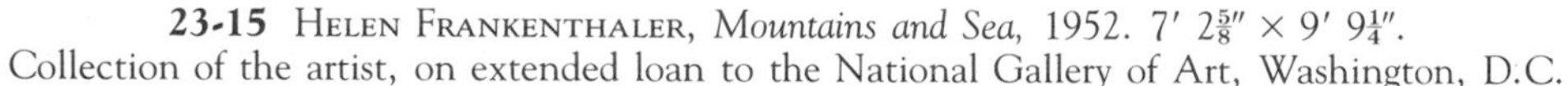

23-15 HELEN FRANKENTHALER, *Mountains and Sea,* 1952. 7′ $2\frac{5}{8}$″ × 9′ $9\frac{1}{4}$″. Collection of the artist, on extended loan to the National Gallery of Art, Washington, D.C.

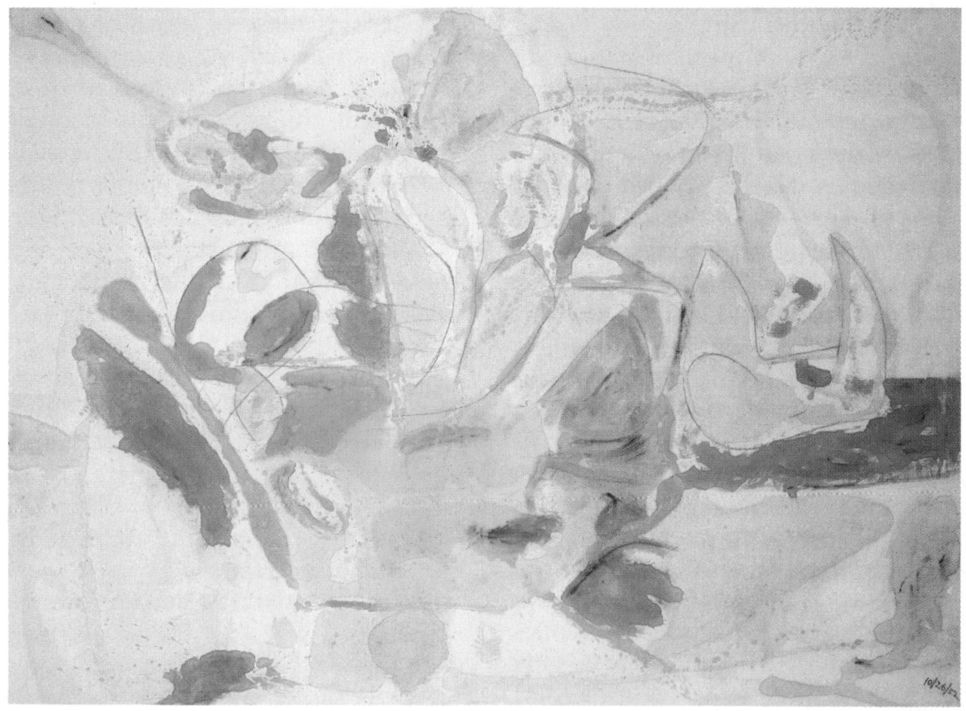

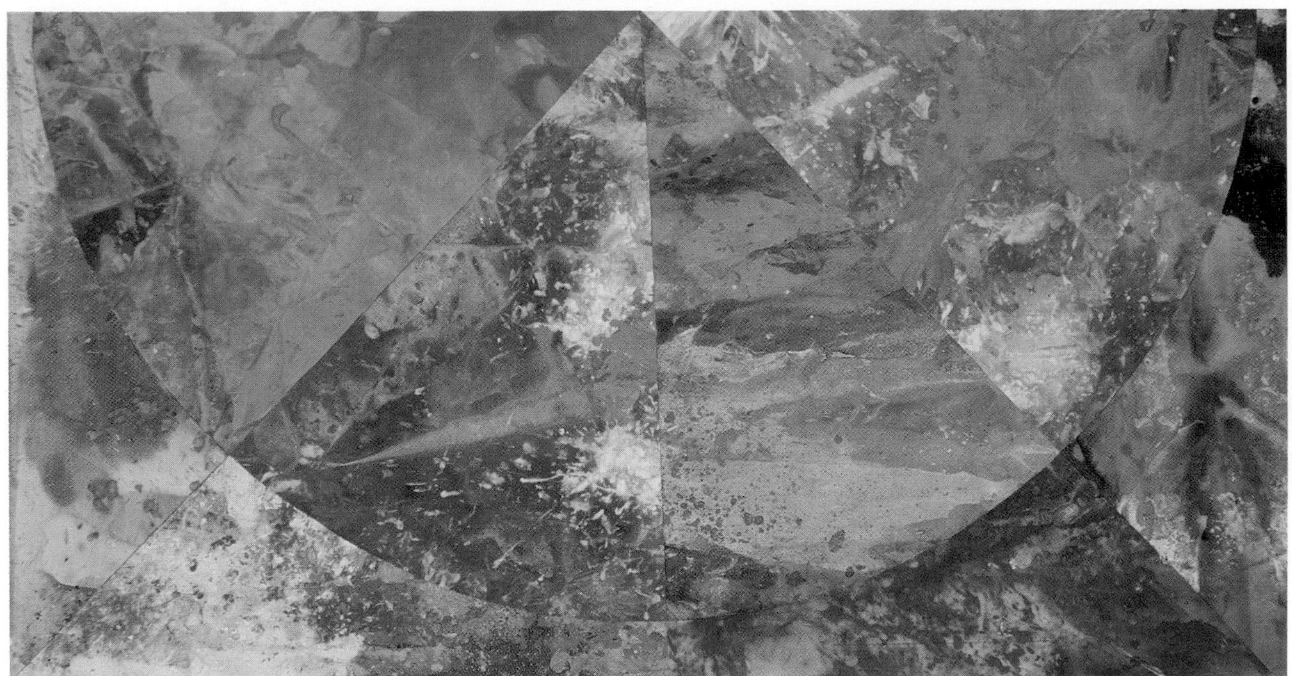

23-16 SAM GILLIAM, *Darted Again,* 1974–1975. Acrylic on canvas, 51″ × 96″. Collection of the Joseph Caleb Community Center, Miami. Courtesy of the Fendrick Gallery, New York.

sizing nor covered with the traditional layer of colored or white primer paint. Frankenthaler's early work was influenced by the spatial complexity of Cubism and the free expressive abstraction of Kandinsky; these influences helped her to understand the implications for her personal style when she saw pictures of Pollock painting one of his works on raw canvas. Inspired by his method, she created *Mountains and Sea* (FIG. **23-15**), whose forms were suggested by her memories of a summer doing watercolor studies of landscapes in Nova Scotia. For this seminal painting, Frankenthaler thinned her oil paint and choreographed the flow of liquid shapes over huge areas of raw canvas laid on her studio floor. However, she ignored Pollock's swinging lines in favor of fluid, flowing shapes, and she replaced Pollock's black-and-white color scheme with elegantly varied hues. In the 1960s, Frankenthaler began using water-soluble acrylic paint, which gave her a greater range of color and allowed a different degree of control over the creation of her shapes. The medium now soaked into the canvas support and dried without forming any of the "halo" silhouettes that occurred with the oil-based paints she used for her early soak-stain works. The method made her works look spontaneous, almost as if they had been conceived in the inspiration of a single moment. This quality is prized by the artist, but as she admits, it is not achieved without some effort, however masked that effort may seem to be in the final work:

> A really good picture looks as if it's happened at once. It's an immediate image. For my own work, when a picture looks labored and overworked, and you can read in it—well, she did this and then she did that, and then she did that—there is something in it that has not got to do with beautiful art to me. And I usually throw those out, though I think very often it takes ten of those over-labored efforts to produce one really beautiful wrist motion that is synchronized with your head and heart, and you have it, and therefore it looks as if it were born in a minute.*

Since the early 1960s, African-American painter SAM GILLIAM (b. 1933) has expanded Frankenthaler's soak-stain method by exploiting the soft spreading flow of one hue into the next and by incorporating patterns made by creasing and pressing wet canvas surfaces to create rich, multicolored works. Gilliam was introduced to the soak-stain technique in Washington in 1962, after a more traditional painting career in Mississippi and Kentucky. Influenced in part by the Impressionists, Gilliam made the soak-stain approach his own by folding his canvases at various stages during the process of applying the paint. By 1968, he was designing his works to hang unframed, as pieces of stiff cloth, either pinned against the wall or standing free in space. In works like *Darted Again* (FIG. **23-16**), Gilliam collaged together pieces cut from different stained canvases to create finished works in

*In Barbara Rose, *Frankenthaler* (New York: Harry N. Abrams, 1975), p. 85.

which the free, amorphous stain shapes play against and with the crisp edges of the cut-out geometric fragments. The sources of this work stretch far beyond the New York and Washington art communities, as Gilliam has invested his Modernist soak-stain process with an individual energy partially based on the bold colors and patterns of tie-dye and other methods used in African and American folk art.

Formalist Abstraction

The art of abstract allusion was countered with formalist precision by artists who believed that pure form and crisp mathematical shapes were the most relevant means to express the new technological age. The majority of these artists favored the clarity of straight sides and simple shapes as eloquent representatives of scientific and man-made structures. Some architects working in this mode continued the simple block forms of the International Style. Others built fantastical structures based on curved mathematical planes or played prismatic triangular shapes against one another to create magical interior spaces. Painters and sculptors stripped their formalist abstract compositions to basic shapes and colors or pursued an opposite strategy by creating complex and lively arrangements of geometrical patterns that dazzled the eyes of their viewers.

The purest shape created in post–World War II architecture undoubtedly is the rectilinear glass and bronze tower in Manhattan (FIG. **23-17**) designed for the Seagram Company by MIES VAN DER ROHE and PHILIP JOHNSON (b. 1906). By the time this structure was built (1956–1958), the concrete, steel, and glass towers of the International Style, which had been pioneered in the works of Louis Sullivan (FIG. 21-98) and in Mies van der Rohe's own models for glass skyscrapers (FIG. 22-61), had become a familiar sight in cities all over the world. Appealing in its structural logic and clarity, the style, although often vulgarized, was easily emulated and quickly became the norm for postwar, commercial high-rise buildings. The Seagram Building still stands as a perfect statement of the best aspects of the International Style. The architects deliberately designed the building as a thin shaft, leaving the front quarter of the structure's midtown site as an open pedestrian plaza. The tower appears to rise from the pavement on stilts; even the recessed lobby is surrounded by glass walls. The bronze metal and the grey glass windows give the building a richness found in few of its neighbors. Every detail, inside and out, was carefully planned to create an elegant whole; even the interior and exterior lighting were planned to make the edifice an effective sight by day or by night.

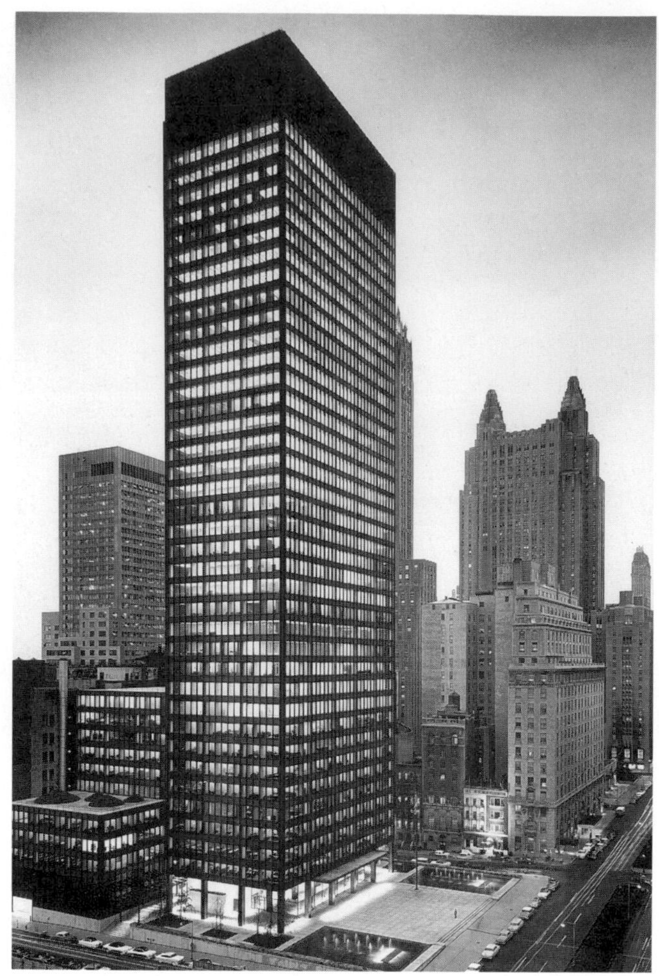

23-17 LUDWIG MIES VAN DER ROHE and PHILIP JOHNSON, Seagram Building, New York, 1956–1958.

In stark contrast to the simple, blocky form of the Seagram Building are the fanciful mathematical curves in the works of the engineer-architects Pier Luigi Nervi and Frei Otto. Like the designers of Coalbrookdale bridge (FIG. 20-26) and the Eiffel Tower (FIG. 21-96), Nervi and Otto created beautiful structures by combining mathematical form and modern construction materials. PIER LUIGI NERVI (1891–1978) used the remarkable tensile strength of prestressed concrete to cover huge spaces with designs of dazzling geometric beauty. His method and materials made it possible to omit the spare, steel supporting columns of the International Style. In 1958, he used prefabricated concrete units to create the spectacular Y-shaped flying buttresses that support the scallop-edged, circular dome over his Palazzetto dello Sport in Rome (FIG. **23-18**). (In an effect much like that of the buttresses in Gothic cathedrals [FIGS. 10-10 and 10-20], the buttresses here carry the lateral thrust of the vaults to the ground.) Nervi's style had a grace and crispness of detail that belong to a new vision of

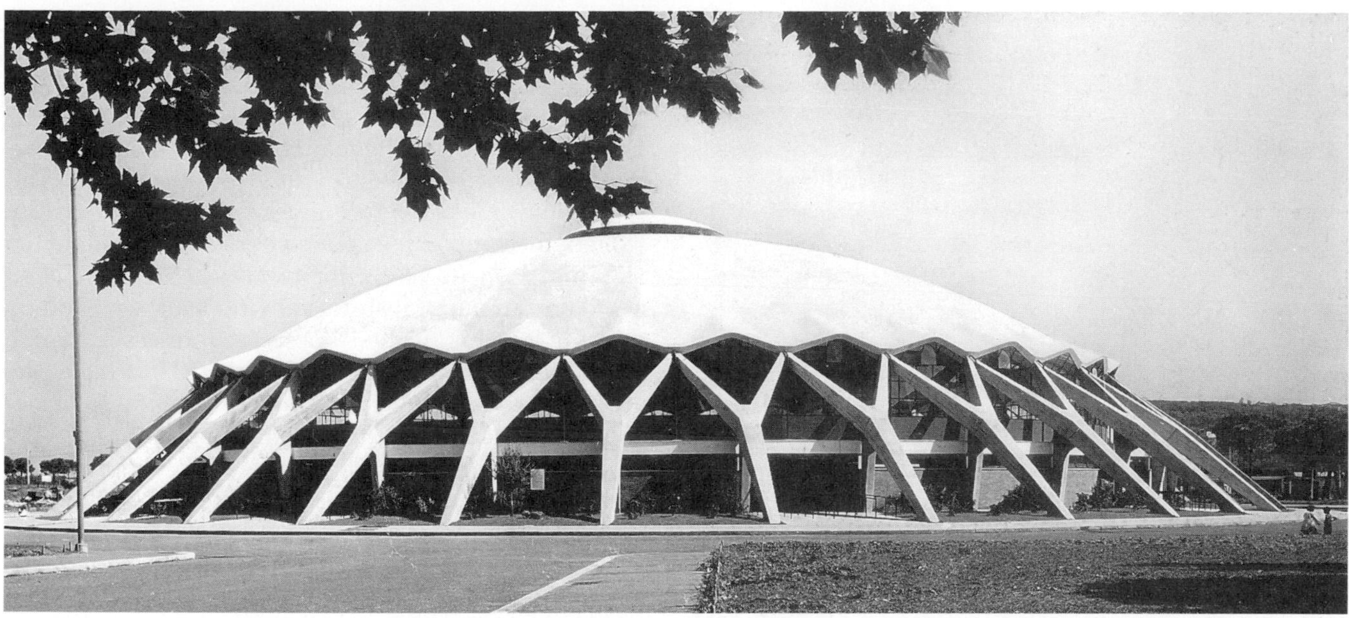

23-18 Pier Luigi Nervi, Palazzetto dello Sport, Rome, 1958.

architectural form, a vision that is organic rather than mechanical.

Frei Otto (b. 1925) has combined different traditions in the mathematical designs of the temporary pavilions he created for events at the 1972 Olympic Games in Munich (fig. **23-19**). Here, the gossamer plastic membrane suspended from his system of upright poles and support wires created an airy, transparent, tentlike enclosure that provided a vast area of enveloped space without the interruption of interior supports. In such works, Otto exploited the tensile strength of steel to create a structural system based on *tension,* the engineering principle used in suspension bridges. He combined this structural system

23-19 Frei Otto, model for the roof of the Olympic Stadium, Munich, 1971–1972.

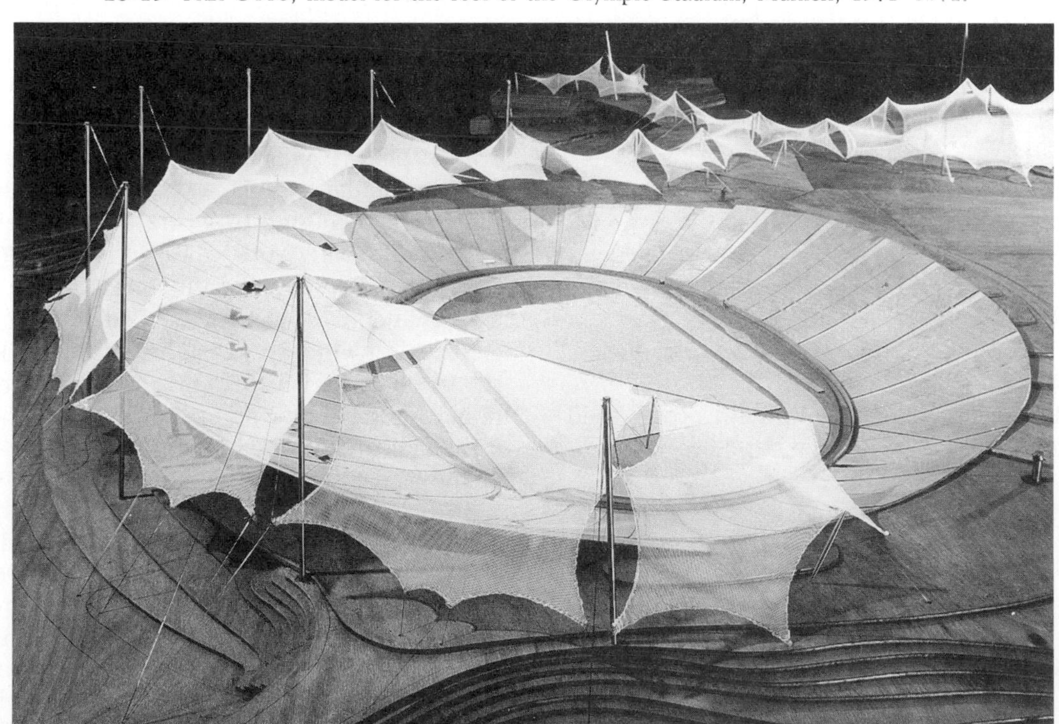

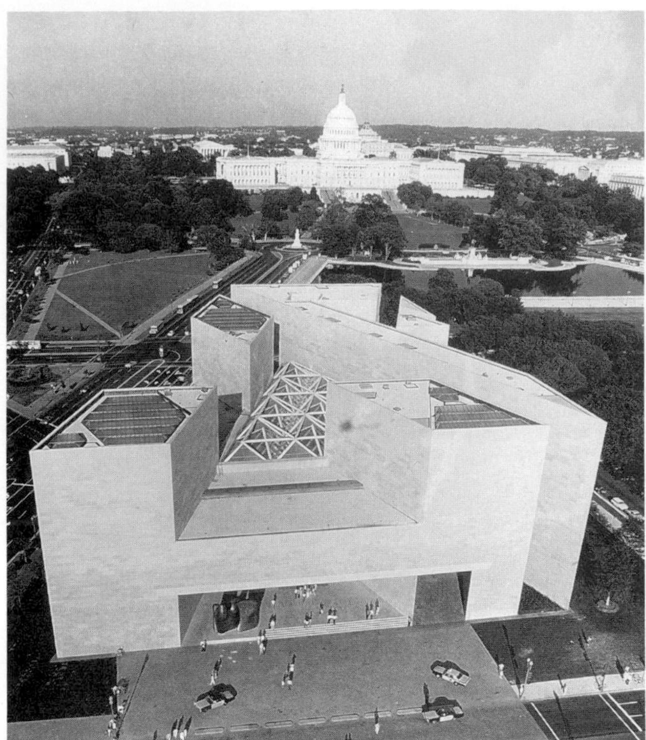

23-20 I. M. Pei, East Building of the National Gallery, Washington, D.C., 1978 (*above*); site plan of the East Building (*below*).

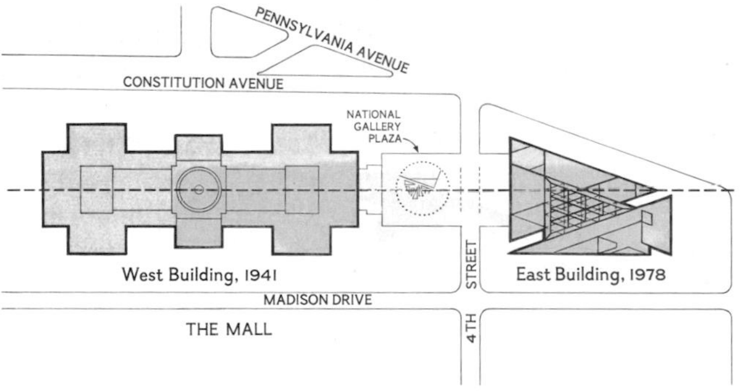

with the fabric walls and pole supports used in the homes of nomadic peoples and in the enclosed booths and showplaces of traveling fairs and circuses. By comparison, Nervi's Palazzetto seems massive and dense. For all his experiments with prestressed concrete, Nervi still conceived of structure in traditional terms of *compression,* the basic principle underlying all the architecture we have studied to this point, from the Egyptians onward. Otto, on the other hand, used his mathematical system to work with traditions of impermanent buildings and utilitarian structures in order to provide a festive, almost spontaneous look for his special-occasion works.

I. M. (Ieoh Ming) Pei (b. 1917), an American architect born in China, combined pristine geometric shapes to create versatile spaces suited to the dynamic pace of activities in a modern art museum in his award-winning design for the East Building of the National Gallery in Washington, D.C. (fig. **23-20**). An irregular, trapezoidal site had been set aside in 1937 for the expansion of the main building—a handsome, domed, Neoclassical structure of the Jeffersonian type, built in 1941. The new East Building was designed to complement the older West Building by aligning with its axis (the two structures are connected by an underground, moving walkway) and by wearing a facing of the same pink Tennessee marble that adorns the older structure. In Pei's design, the awkward building site became a virtue made of necessity, somewhat as the Campidoglio (fig. 17-29) had in the hands of Michelangelo. Pei ingeniously maximized his use of the difficult site by bisecting the trapezoid into a large isosceles triangle and a smaller right triangle. The larger triangle, with its diamond-shaped towers, provides exhibition space; the smaller, with its dramatic wedge shape (the walls meet in a sharp nineteen-degree angle), provides space for art-historical research. The two are unified by a vast, faceted skylight 80 feet above a spacious courtyard six levels high. The great central courtyard was designed both as an internal reception "piazza" and as the large public area necessary to accommodate crowds of people for the special events that are a part of the museum's role in the Washington social scene. The glass tetrahedra of the skylight (fig. **23-21**), with their complex tracery of frames, seem to change, multiply, and create shapes as one moves. The experience of fluid space and transformation of form is intensified by the Alexander Calder mobile that hangs majestically above the courtyard. Bridges, escalators, and stairways casually connect the central space with numerous irregularly shaped and randomly placed galleries, which range in size from those intimate enough to show very small pictures to those ample enough to accommodate the largest canvases of the New York school. The whole structure is a marvel of coherence and order and a triumph of craftsmanship down to the least detail; the last is creditable to the donor, who stipulated that no expense be spared in bringing the building to perfection. This collaboration of patron and architect is reminiscent of that of the Medici and the artistic geniuses of the Renaissance.

The dynamism of Otto's pavilion and Pei's museum was created through mathematical shape and line. In painting, Victor Vasarely (b. 1908) achieves two-dimensional visual energy by controlling color and the placement of mathematical shapes. After studying medicine and then art in Hungary, Vasarely arrived in Paris in 1938 to work in advertising. As an admirer of De Stijl, the Bauhaus, Constructivism, and the influential theories about optical illusions that can

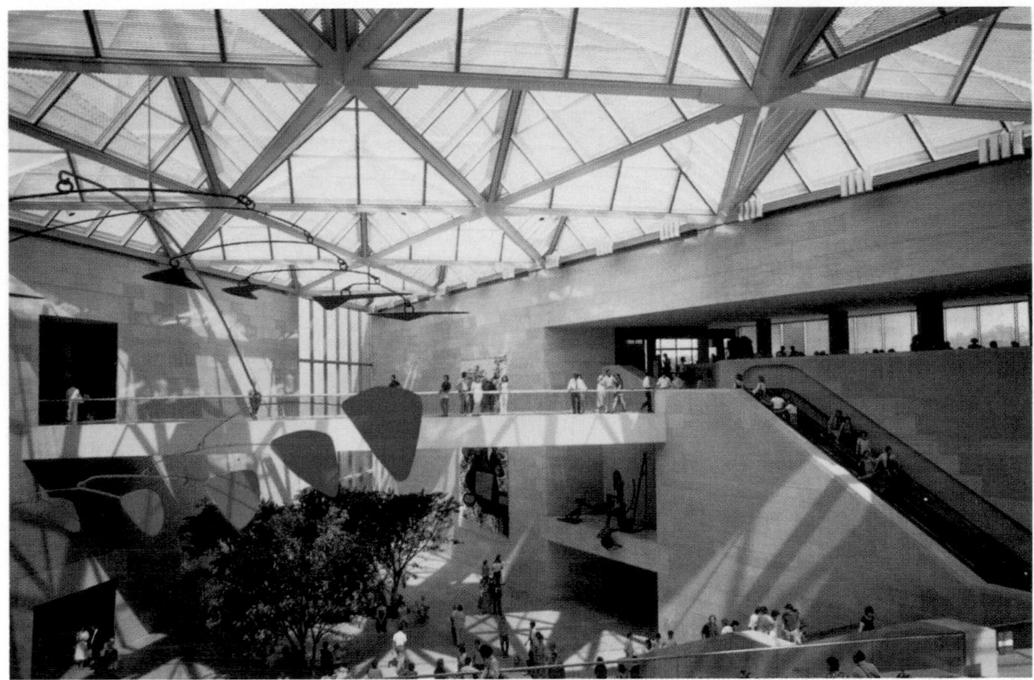

23-21 I. M. PEI, interior of the East Building of the National Gallery. (Mobile shown in the foreground by ALEXANDER CALDER.)

be created with color developed by the chemist and philosopher Wilhelm Ostwald, Vasarely was interested in optical and structural effects, especially the three-dimensional illusions produced by introducing mathematical perspective into patterns of stripes or checkerboards. Paintings like *Orion* (FIG. **23-22**) attract the eye with their regular order and bright colored shapes. A longer look reveals that the rows of flat squares filled with circles and ellipses do not lie flat on the surface of the canvas. Instead, the eye reads one square in relation to the next so that the darkening or lightening of the ground, any shifts from warm to cool hues, and all changes in the size or shape of the central form create illusions of movement in space as the eye travels along a row of squares. In the 1950s and 1960s, especially, Vasarely dreamed of filling whole cities with buildings whose walls would vibrate with his patterns, echoing in pure abstraction the dynamism of modern urban life. His works were sometimes connected with the so-called Op Art of the 1960s, and his theories inspired a number of younger artists in Paris to form the Groupe de Recherche d'Art Visuel (Research Group for Visual Art) to explore similar ideas.

A very different mode of formalist abstraction from Vasarely's visual complexity were paintings so cleanly brushed, so unrevealing of the process by which they were made, that they were called "Post-Painterly Abstraction" by the critic Clement Greenberg. ELLSWORTH KELLY (b. 1923) is one of the best-known artists working in this way, which aims at a radical simplicity and purity of shape and color related to works by Malevich (FIG. 22-48) and Mondrian (FIG. 22-50). Unlike the earlier artists, however, the Post-Painterly Abstractionists do not intend their compositions to symbolize anything beyond the

23-22 VICTOR VASARELY, *Orion*, 1956. Paper on paper mounted on wood, 6′ 10½″ × 6′ 6¾″. Hirshhorn Museum and Sculpture Garden, Smithsonian Institution, Washington D.C. (gift of Joseph H. Hirshhorn, 1966).

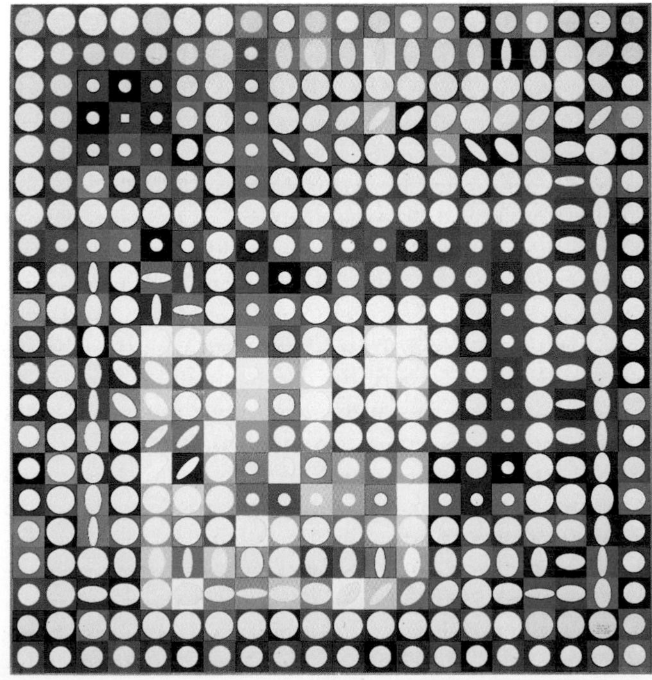

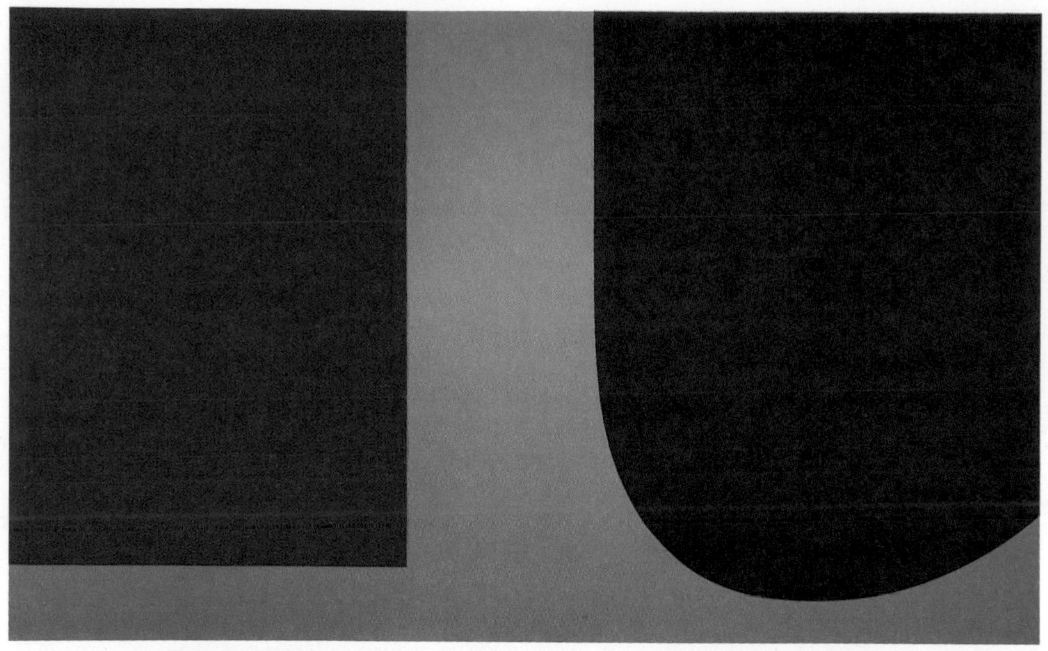

23-23 Ellsworth Kelly, *Red, Blue, Green,* 1963. Approx. 7′ × 11′ 4″. San Diego Museum of Contemporary Art, La Jolla.

patterns of color and shape that can be seen by the eye. They delight in the optical effects of color against color and shape against shape, on huge canvases that fill entire walls and the entire field of a viewer's vision. Kelly studied art before serving in the camouflage unit of the U.S. Army Corps of Engineers during World War II. Intrigued by the fact that camouflage patterns are able to misdirect the eye, he began exploring parts of the visual world that generally go unnoticed—the patterns made by the shadow of a railing falling along a flight of steps, or by a series of window blinds pulled to individual heights by the inhabitants of a row of apartments. He treated such details as found images, removing them from their context and reducing them to their basic forms. He also experimented with using chance to determine the color sequence in grid paintings. Finally, he enlarged the shapes in his paintings so that just a few hard edges defined one shape against a "ground" of a different color that could itself be read as a form. The scale of Kelly's *Red, Blue, Green* (FIG. **23-23**)—7 feet high by 12 feet long—makes it a kind of hard-edge Color-Field painting, within which the three hues, shaped by the contours of their areas, act with and against each other. Indeed, Kelly's work, and that of other artists working with a similar clear, crisp Abstract Formalism was called "Hard-Edge Abstraction" by some critics.

The paintings of Post-Painterly Abstraction have no reference to the world outside of their compositions. Critics dubbed sculptures that similarly banished all reference beyond themselves "Minimal art" or "primary structures," because of the extreme reduction of their shapes and textures. By its very nature, sculpture is less illusionistic than painting. All elements of a sculptural composition are more literally a part of our physical space than are the details of most paintings. This powerful sense of the physical presence of sculpture caused many minimalist sculptors to speak of their pieces as "presences." One of the most rigorous practitioners of the Minimalist approach in sculpture is Donald Judd (b. 1928). To his sculpture, Judd brings his study of art history and his experience as a painter and critic. He aspired to create sculpture so unified in effect that even if a piece had more than one part, the parts would be seen as a whole rather than in relation to one another. To Judd and the other Minimalists, this unity is the basic and true statement of form in space; anything else is a distortion. Against all two-dimensional space that invites illusionistic figuration, including even Mondrian's paintings (FIG. 22-50), the Minimalist sculptors insist that only the spatial wholeness of the third dimension in the simple reductive shapes of solid geometry contains the truth of art. In the untitled work illustrated here (FIG. **23-24**), Judd aligned eight identical, brightly machined stainless-steel cubes in the center of a gallery floor. Even though this grouping includes a series of distinct box forms, no single shape stands out. The only real difference among the cubes is one of placement within the group. The cubes' identical repetitiveness creates, for

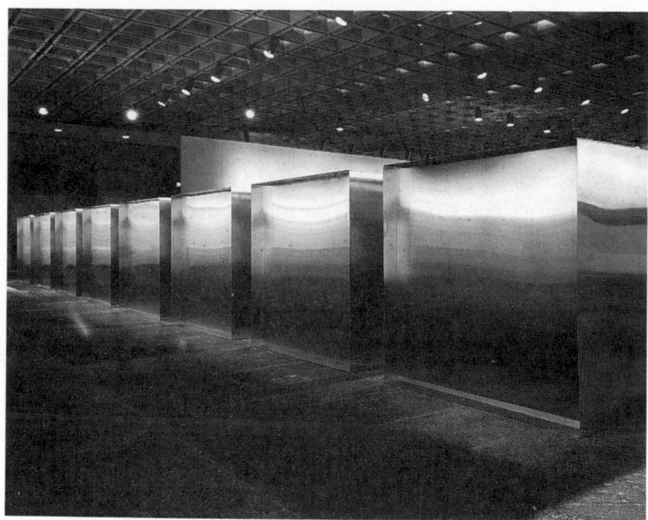

23-24 DONALD JUDD, untitled, 1968. Stainless steel, each box is 4′ sq. Collection of Miles Fiterman, Minneapolis.

Judd, the sense of wholeness he sought. As in Post-Painterly Abstract painting, little trace of the artist can be seen in this work; the surfaces of the cubes exhibit, in their superhuman precision and exactitude, the depersonalized technological order that produced them. Although none of Judd's structures is intended to carry an allusion to anything outside itself, he is as interested as Kelly in making us aware of how we see form in space. The scale of the whole work is huge, but the modules of each box are comprehensible in terms of human size. This characteristic can help us to sharpen our ability to perceive three-dimensional forms because the identical units serve as visual markers for measuring an area of wall space and the section of air before it. Our viewing of form in space, however, is also complicated by the playful way in which these clear, Minimal shapes appear to dissolve as their polished sides reflect their neighbors and the environment around them.

By the end of the 1960s, some Minimal artists tired of Minimal art's restrictive, reductive forms and reintroduced a sense of visible process in their work. EVA HESSE (1936–1970), a Minimalist in the early part of her career, was a leading figure in this approach, called Post-Minimalism by the critics. Using nontraditional sculptural materials like fiberglass, cord, and latex, Hesse created sculpture in which the pure forms of Minimal art appear to crumple, sag, and warp under the pressures of atmospheric force and gravity. Born a Jew in Hitler's Germany, Hesse was hidden as a child with a Christian family when her parents and elder sister had to flee the Nazis, and only was reunited with them in the early 1940s, just before her parents divorced. This complex set of extraordinary circumstances helped to give her a lasting sense that the central qualities of modern life are strangeness and absurdity. Struggling to express these qualities in her art, she created informal sculptural arrangements in which units often hung from the ceiling, leaned against the walls, or spilled out along the floor. She said she wanted her pieces to be "non art, non connotive, non anthropomorphic, non geometric, no nothing, everything, but of another kind, vision, sort." Amazingly, *Hang-Up* (FIG. **23-25**) fulfills these requirements. The piece looks like a carefully made, empty frame sprouting a strange feeler that extends out into the viewer's space. Hesse wrote that in this work, for the first time, her "idea of absurdity or extreme feeling came through." In her words, "[*Hang-Up*] has a kind of depth I don't always achieve and that is the kind of depth or soul or absurdity of life or meaning or feeling or intellect that I want to get."* Absurd and nontraditional the piece certainly is, but it also possesses a disquieting and touching presence, suggesting the fragility and grandeur of life amidst the pressures of the modern age.

*In Linda Shearer, *Eva Hesse: A Memorial Exhibition* (New York: Solomon R. Guggenheim Museum, 1972), unpaginated.

23-25 EVA HESSE, *Hang-Up*, 1965–1966. Acrylic on cloth over wood and steel, 6′ × 7′ × 6′ 6″. The Art Institute of Chicago (gift of Arthur Keating and Mr. and Mrs. Edward Morris by exchange).

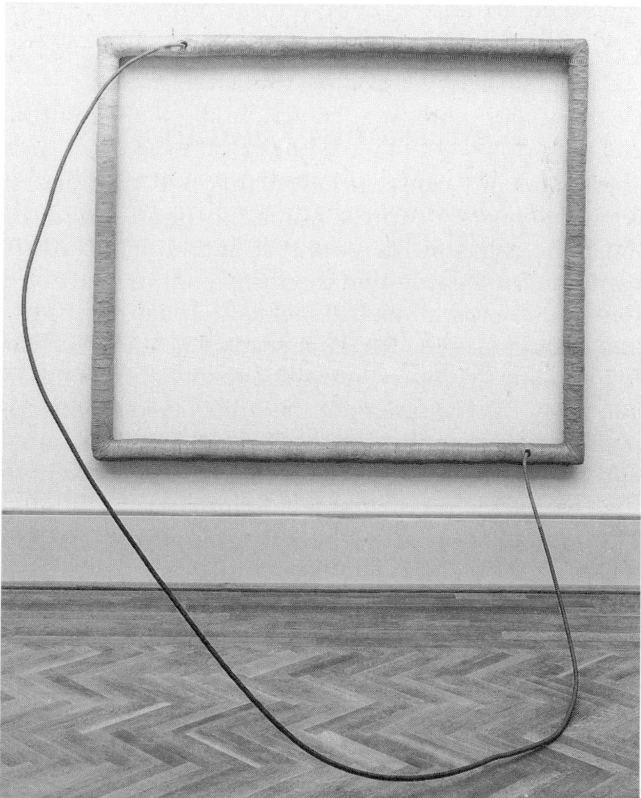

ART WITH PSYCHOLOGICAL AND CONCEPTUAL CONCERNS

During the second half of the twentieth century, most art could be classified as displaying some element of psychological or conceptual concerns; most artists wanted to touch the emotions of viewers as an antidote to the numbing trauma of World War II. The desire to touch the emotions of viewers underlay the improvisational methods of Abstract Expressionism, the allusive symbolism of Organic Abstraction, and the intimations of sublime space in Color-Field painting. Artists with political concerns also attempted to use the content of their work to address the feelings and psyches of viewers. But for a number of other artists, psychological and conceptual concerns affected both the content and the mode of expression in their work. Some of this latter group of artists used the human figure or images of the human environment symbolically to express the experience and conditions of human life in what often has been perceived as the dark and savage present. Others used figurative art in their exploration of the expressive possibilities of new technological media, while a different group concentrated on exploring the mechanisms of artistic expression conceptually, focusing the viewer's attention on how each medium communicates ideas. Finally, beginning in the 1970s, other groups—Postmodernists and Deconstructionists—examined art and its communicative powers by appropriating and analyzing historic and cultural styles.

Expressionist Figuration

Just as many artists believed that only abstract art could adequately express human feelings and ideals amid the chaos of the post-1940 world, other artists continued to believe that the things of the real world remain the most powerful means to touch the hearts and minds of viewers. This second group of artists felt that any art representing the reality of the human condition could not ignore the links between the appearance of the physical world and the perceptual and psychological responses of artists and viewers to that world. Some of these individuals concentrated on the human figure. Others invented new forms of narrative to suit the conditions of modern life. Still others experimented with art that makes viewers more aware of their relationship to the physical environment. All tried to put viewers back in touch with their deepest human feelings of connectedness to each other and to the planet on which we live. For large numbers of artists, the human body remained the most potent subject by which to accomplish this goal in art. The majority of these artists expressed, through distorted anatomy, the modern struggle for survival in an increasingly chaotic world, but some represented this distortion with humor, and even in the most troubled times, a few managed to use a calm, ideal style that stated their continued belief in beauty and the eternal qualities of the human spirit.

Among the most successful of the rare artists who used the human figure as a symbol of hope and beauty during this period is the Italian sculptor GIACOMO MANZÙ (b. 1908). Manzù's sculptures combine something of the humanism of Maillol (FIG. 22-44) with the simple expressiveness of Barlach (FIG. 22-22). Although Manzù is not a practicing Catholic, his sculptures of cardinals, serene female nudes, and relief panels on religious subjects all express his belief in the unquenchable and enduring nature of the human spirit, which survives even the brutalizing effects of the modern age. Works like *Cardinal* (FIG. **23-26**) combine the artist's love for Antique sculpture

23-26 GIACOMO MANZÙ, *Cardinal*, 1949–1951. Bronze, 44" high. Museum Ludwig, Cologne.

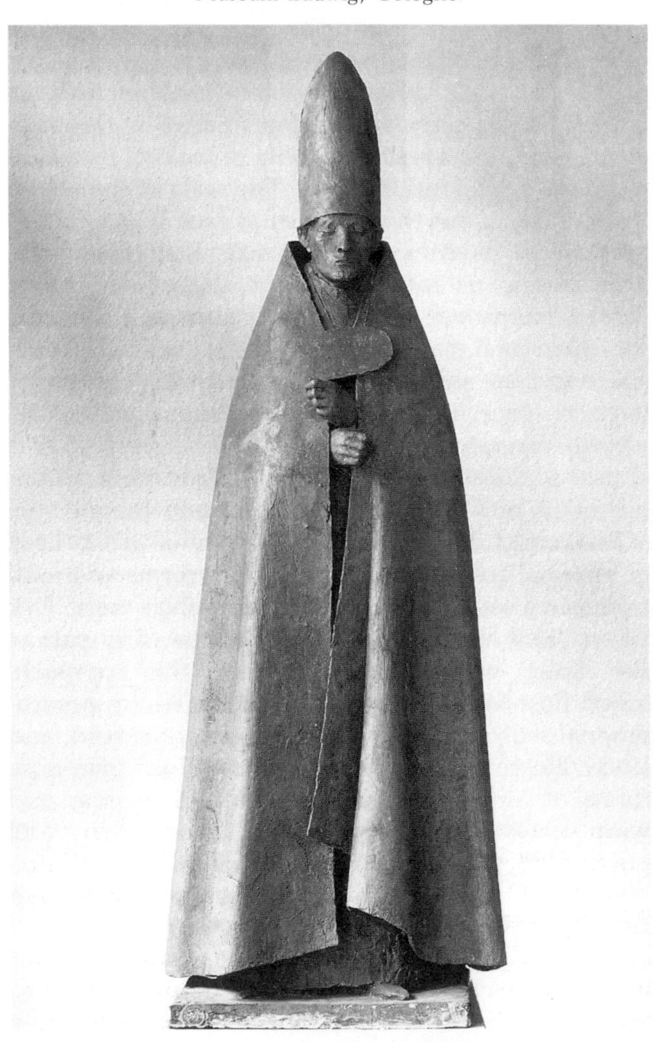

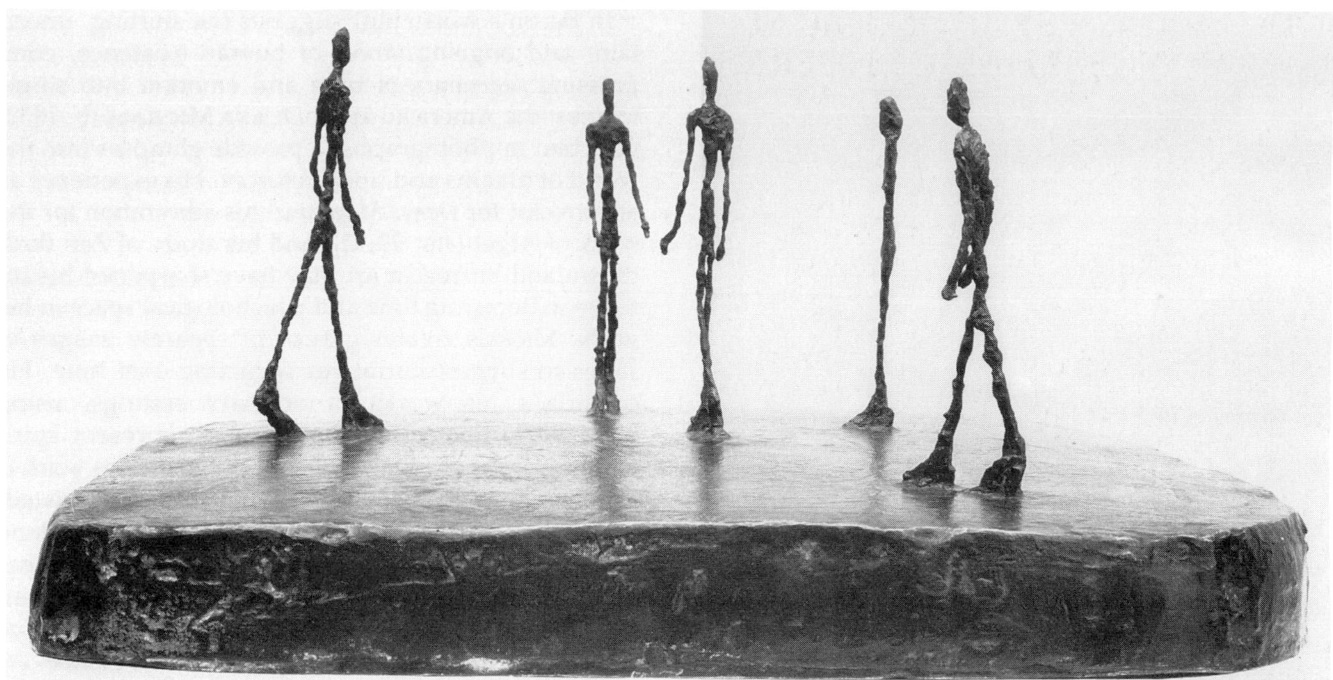

23-27 ALBERTO GIACOMETTI, *City Square (La Place)*, 1948. Bronze, $8\frac{1}{2}'' \times 25\frac{3}{8}'' \times 17\frac{1}{4}''$. Collection, The Museum of Modern Art, New York (purchase).

and for the works of Donatello (FIGS. 16-6 and 16-12) with his admiration for the sculpture of Rodin (FIG. 21-55) and Rosso (FIG. 21-79). *Cardinal* is one of Manzù's many freestanding sculptures of clerics in which the strong, simple, elegant shapes of the cardinal's robes and ecclesiastical headgear and the still, frontal stance create a mood of protection and security. The sense of enduring calm is humanized by delicately modeled irregularities in the surface, creating a potent statement of faith in the basic strength and goodness of the human spirit.

Much more common to figurative sculpture in the postwar period than Manzù's hopeful works was the use of expressive distortion to suggest the anguish and torment of the human spirit. One of the earliest artists to adopt this approach was the Swiss sculptor ALBERTO GIACOMETTI (1901–1966), who, in the 1940s, turned from his earlier Cubist and Surrealist work to the roughly modeled, emaciated figures for which he is best known. Giacometti found that his sculptured figures seemed most real when they represented a human form at the distance from which one would be able to recognize an approaching person as an acquaintance. To achieve this effect, Giacometti covered basic wire figures with rough blobs of clay or plaster to create the impression of individual faces and body features. Seen from afar, the figures seem full of specific details, but these do not materialize as one moves closer. In sculptures like *City Square (La Place,* FIG. **23-27**), Giacometti's pencil-thin, elongated figures stride abstractedly through endless space; they never meet. At certain angles, the forms are so attenuated that they almost disappear, just as in the human condition, people often fade noiselessly out of sight. Such figures suggest to many viewers the modern experiences of bewilderment, loss, and alienation—the increased sense of strangeness and loneliness felt by people in contemporary urban society. Giacometti denied that this was his theme; he insisted that he was merely trying to render the effect of great space as it presses around a figure and nothing more. He was apparently unwilling to recognize the way in which such a representation might echo the modern individual's awareness of the distance in physical and psychic space that separates one human being from another. If we compare Giacometti's figures with those in Rodin's *Burghers of Calais* (FIG. 21-55), we can readily appreciate the changes wrought during the first half of the twentieth century in the interpretation of the human form in art.

Some artists, like Giacometti, may have discounted a psychological reading of their works, but the existential anguish that permeates the work of the British artist FRANCIS BACON (b. 1909) has been a conscious part of his expression throughout his career. The human struggle against the bestial forces in society and human nature is visible in many of Bacon's paintings. Drawing inspiration from sources as varied as Muybridge's photographs of wrestlers and the image of the screaming face of a wounded nurse in

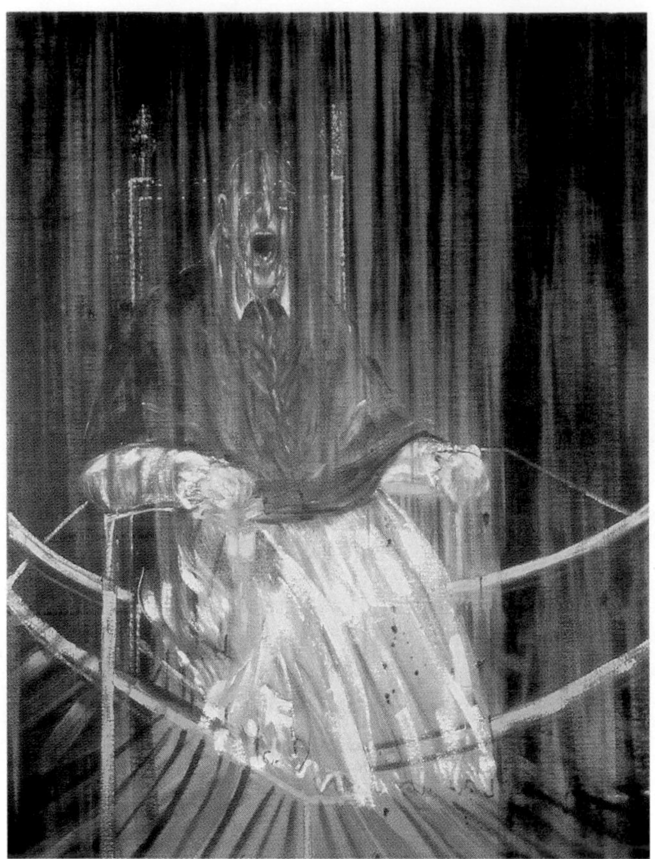

23-28 Francis Bacon, *Study after Velásquez's Portrait of Pope Innocent X,* 1953. 5′ ¼″ × 3′ 8⅞″. Des Moines Art Center (Nathan Emory Coffin Collection, purchased with funds from the Coffin Fine Arts Trust).

Eisenstein's film *Battleship Potemkin,* Bacon has invented a setting and situation in which human figures are perpetually being stretched *in extremis.* In *Study after Velásquez's Portrait of Pope Innocent X* (FIG. **23-28**), the individual who once posed self-confidently for the seventeenth-century Spanish painter has been transplanted into a twentieth-century space-cage and suffers unbearably from unseen horrors. His mouth is wrenched open in an agonized scream, at once more personal and more terrifying than that of Munch's screaming man (FIG. 21-92). The figure merges with the dark rays of the miasma surrounding it, imprisoned as if bound in an electric chair, and wracked by suffering so severe that it is almost unbearable to look at the image. The comfort, security, and promise of Manzù's *Cardinal* have vanished here. For Bacon, existence is fraught with change and the sense that reality is eternally elusive. His style is crafted to express this: "I would like my pictures to look as if a human being had passed between them, like a snail, leaving a trail of human presence and memory trace of past events, as the snail leaves its slime."

In Bacon's work, blur suggests the shifting, uncertain, and ongoing stress of human existence, compressing segments of time and emotion into single images; the American artist Duane Michals (b. 1932) uses blur in photographs to provide glimpses into the world of dreams and unseen forces. His experience as art director for *Dance Magazine,* his admiration for the work of Atget (FIG. 22-32), and his study of Zen Buddhism and Surrealist art may have sharpened his interest in depicting time and psychological space in his work. Michals creates groups of separate images in series to suggest narratives occurring over time. He constructs his works in ordinary settings, using blurred or superimposed images to represent spiritual or ghostly presences. Typical of his series work is *Death Comes to the Old Lady* (FIG. **23-29**), which visualizes its metaphysical subject in the most mundane terms. An old woman sits in a nondescript room near a doorway leading into a room behind. An old man approaches from the back room and passes in front of the woman without acknowledging her presence. As he departs, she rises to follow and her form dissolves into a blur of motion. Here, death is a familiar contemporary and companion. The quality of the moment is expressed with the casual literalness and grainy soft-focus of an ordinary snapshot. Nothing in this vision of death echoes the heroism or pathos seen in West (FIG. 20-32), David (FIG. 20-41), or Goya (FIG. 21-26); instead, Michals depicts the kind of peaceful death we all might wish for.

The stoic, everyday toughness of the human spirit is the subject of figurative works by the Polish fiber artist Magdalena Abakanowicz (b. 1930). A leader in the recent exploration in sculpture of the expressive powers of weaving techniques, Abakanowicz gained fame with experimental, freestanding pieces in both abstract and figurative modes. For Abakanowicz, fiber materials are deeply symbolic: "I see fiber as the basic element constructing the organic world on our planet, as the greatest mystery of our environment. It is from fiber that all living organisms are built—the tissues of plants and ourselves. . . . Fabric is our covering and our attire. Made with our hands, it is a record of our souls."* To all of her work, the artist brings the experiences of her early life as a member of an aristocratic family disturbed by the dislocations of World War II and its aftermath. Initially attracted to weaving as a medium that would adapt well to being used in the small space she had available for a studio, Abakanowicz gradually developed huge abstract hangings, called *Abakans,* which suggest organic spaces as well as giant pieces of clothing.

*In Mary Jane Jacob, *Magdalena Abakanowicz* (New York: Abbeville, 1982), p. 94.

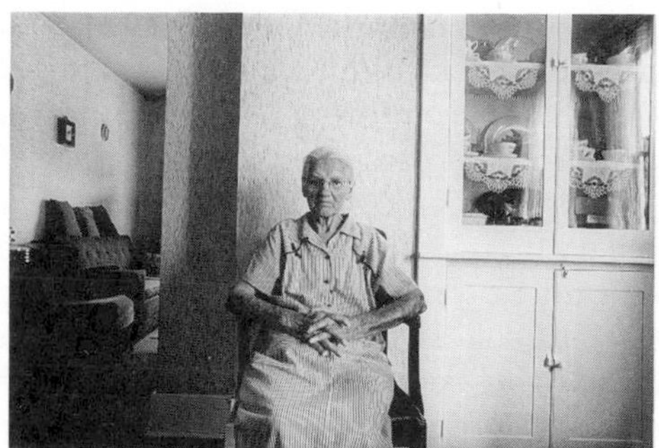

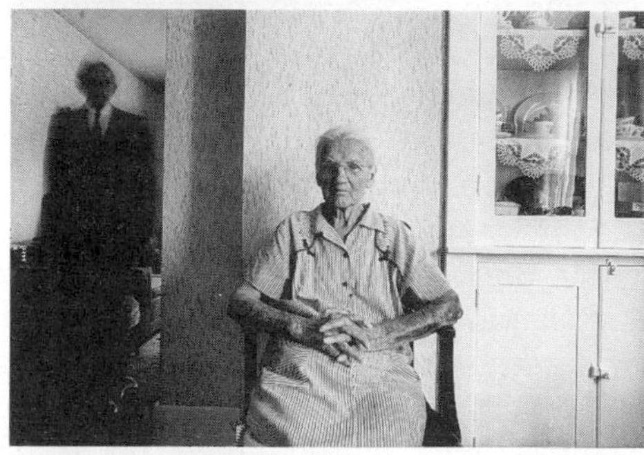

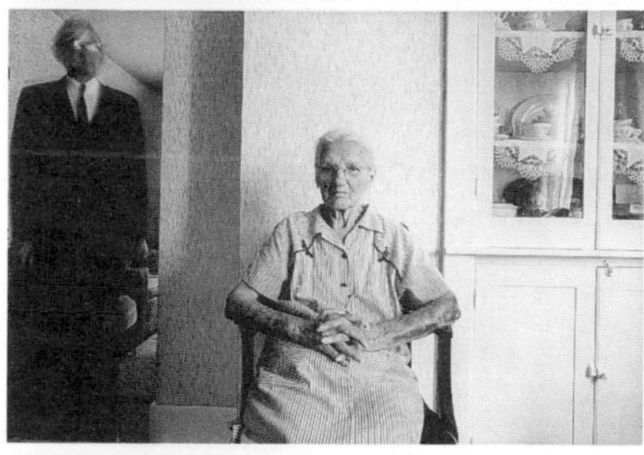

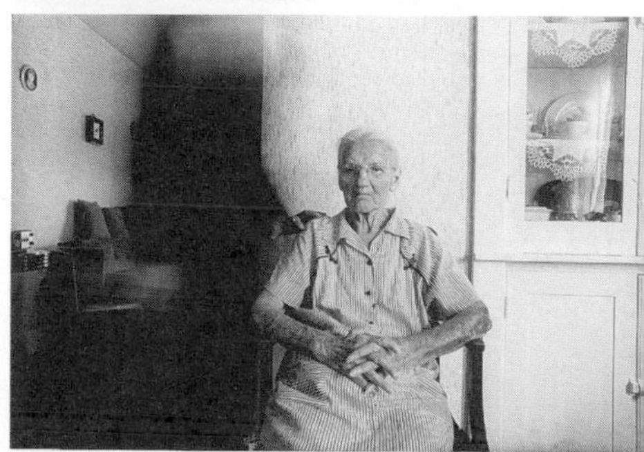

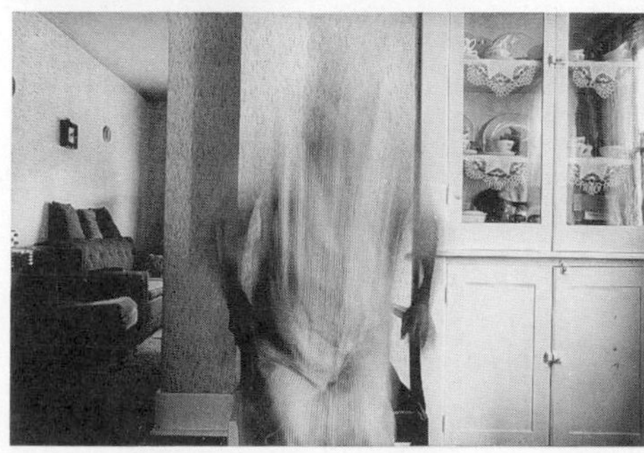

23-29 DUANE MICHALS, *Death Comes to the Old Lady*, 1969. Gelatin silver prints. Collection, The Museum of Modern Art, New York (The Parkinson Fund).

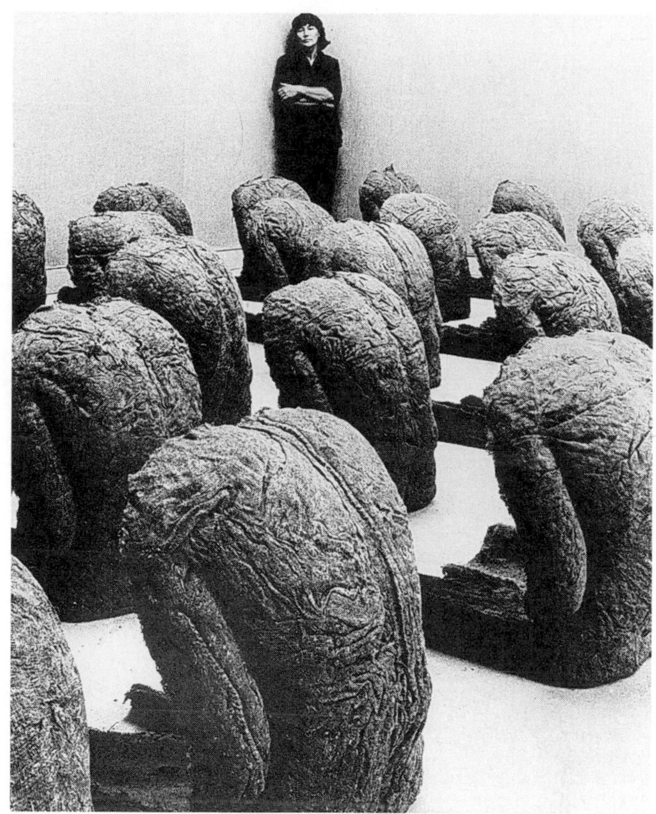

23-30 MAGDALENA ABAKANOWICZ, artist with *Backs*, at the Musée d'Art Moderne de la Ville de Paris, 1982.

She returned to a smaller scale with works based on human forms—*Heads, Seated Figures,* and *Backs*—multiplying each type for exhibition in groups as symbols for the individual in society, lost in the crowd yet retaining some distinctiveness. This impression is especially powerful in an installation of *Backs* (FIG. **23-30**), each piece of which was made by pressing layers of natural organic fibers into a plaster mold depicting the slumping shoulders, back, and arms of a figure of indeterminate sex, which rests legless directly on the floor. The repeated pose of the figures in *Backs* suggests meditation, submission, and anticipation. Although made from a single mold, the figures achieve a touching sense of individuality by means of the slightly different posture each assumed as the material dried and as a result of the different pattern of fiber texture imprinted on each.

Abakanowicz's *Backs* have a rough, primitive look, yet they clearly are the work of a highly trained artist. Their rough quality reminds us, however, that many twentieth-century painters and sculptors admire the powerful, direct vision of artists who create without traditional academic training in art. Recent decades have seen a widespread appreciation for the expressive qualities of works like *Baboon* (FIG. **23-31**), by the self-taught Mexican-American sculptor FELIPE

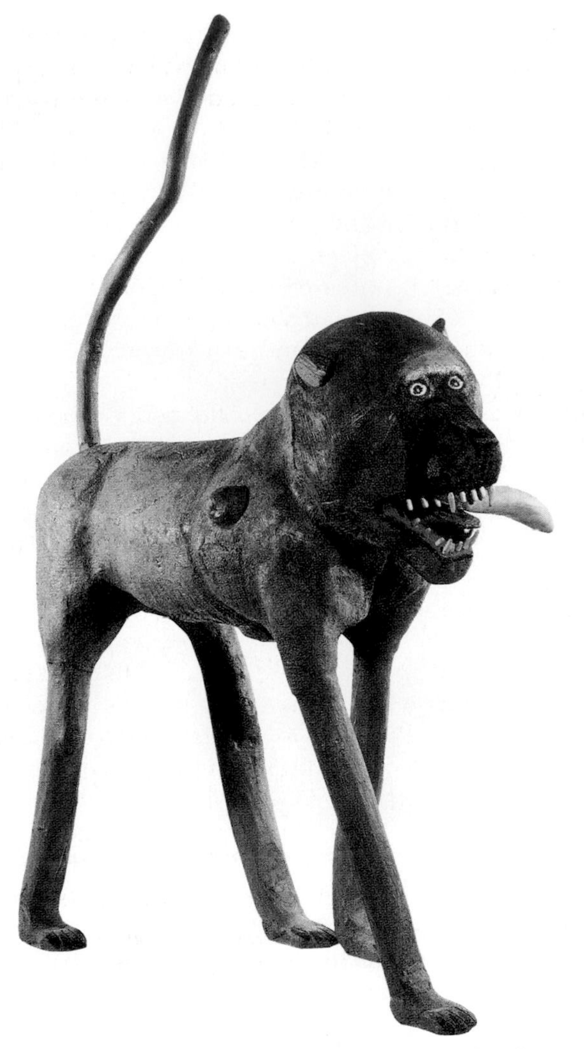

23-31 Felipe Archuleta, *Baboon,* 1978. Carved and painted wood, glue, and sawdust, 3′ 10½″ × 3′ 6½″ × 13″. Herbert Wade Hemphill, Jr., Collection.

Archuleta (b. 1910). Coming late to sculpture, after working as a day laborer and carpenter, Archuleta specializes in imaginative, visionary representations of animal personalities. His figures owe much to a Spanish-American tradition of simple, painted wooden folk sculptures of holy figures called *santos,* but *Baboon* is the product of an authentic original vision. Its stiff alertness seems as closely related to the magical presence of figures and animals in paintings by the self-taught French painter Henri Rousseau (fig. 21-90) as to local American versions of sacred Spanish imagery. Like all of Archuleta's work, *Baboon* has a jaunty vitality and a somewhat off-beat spirit that make it speak strongly as a metaphor for the powerful life of nature, which we must not ignore in our fascination with the technological age.

The primal forces suggested in the works of Abakanowicz and Archuleta are given new expression in the mixed-media works of the Mexican-American artist Manuel Neri (b. 1930), who combines Expressionism and Classicism in sculptured and painted representations of female nudes. Trained as an Expressionist ceramist, Neri began making rough-textured improvisational sculpture with plaster and found objects, often splashing the surface of his figures with vivid strokes of paint. More recently, Neri has found a different vision in which painted compositions related to Gestural Abstract Expressionism form the background for nude bronze figures, which combine almost Classical proportions with rough modeling of some details. Typical of this work is *Mujer Pegada Series No. 2* (fig. **23-32**), with its expressive interplay between multiple possible meanings of the words in the title and the complex visual dialogue that occurs between the bronze relief woman taking shape at the left, the ghostly figure silhouetted in thick paint in the center, and the swirling painted shapes in the surrounding space. Further tension between painting and sculpture springs from the fact that the figure stands on a ledge projecting from the painted back plane, which, on close inspection, turns out to be bronze rather than the canvas intimated by its appearance. Neri used expressive techniques here that recall those used by Van Gogh (fig. 21-84), Rouault (fig. 22-17), De Kooning (fig. 23-3), and Bacon (fig. 23-28), but Neri's work

23-32 Manuel Neri, *Mujer Pegada Series No. 2,* 1985–1986. Bronze with enamel paint, 5′ 10″ × 4′ 8½″ × 11¼″. Laila and Thurston Twigg-Smith, Honolulu.

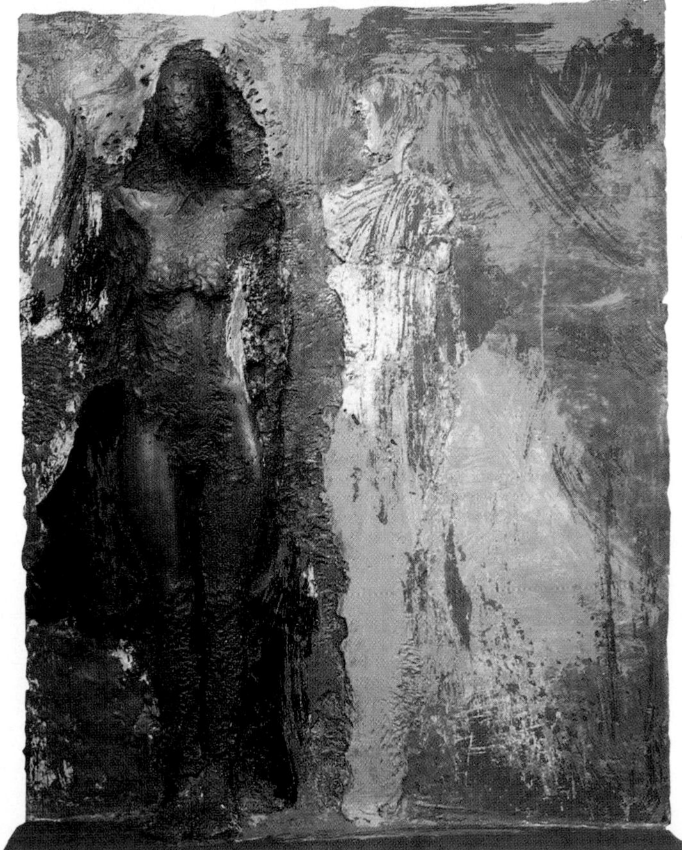

does not carry the anguished undertones of these earlier artists. Instead, *Mujer Pegada Series No. 2* evokes the total mental and emotional experiences of a woman in today's world. The way in which the painted and sculptured forms seem to slip between one state and another reinforces the resonating sense of shifting thoughts and feelings.

If Neri's Expressionism conveys the universal human experience we first saw in the *Venus of Willendorf* (FIG. 1-13) in a modern psychological guise, the recent paintings of American artist LEON GOLUB (b. 1923) depict the psychological effects of experiencing the world at second hand, through the news media. Golub's early subjects developed from symbolic pictures of seers and kings to paintings of heroic, damaged, Everyman figures. In the 1960s, Golub painted mythic battles between crudely rendered groups of naked giants inspired by ancient Hellenistic reliefs. The work for which he is best known, however, deals with the violent events of our own time—the implied narratives we have learned to read in news photos of anonymous characters participating in the brutalities of street violence, terrorism, and torture. Paintings in Golub's *Assassins* and *Mercenaries* series suggest not specific stories, but a condition of being. As the artist has said: "Through media we are under constant, invasive bombardment of images—from all over—and we often have to take evasive action to avoid discomforting recognitions. . . . The work [of art] should have an edge, veering between what is visually and cognitively acceptable and what might stretch these limits as we encounter or try to visualize the real products of the uses of power."* *Mercenaries (IV)* (FIG. **23-33**) is a huge canvas that represents a mysterious tableau in which three mercenaries (tough, free-lance, military professionals willing to fight for any political cause) cluster at the far right of the canvas, in the process of reacting with tense physical gestures to something being said by one of the two other mercenaries standing at the far left. The dark uniforms and skin tones of the four black fighters flatten their figures and make them stand out against the searing, flat red background, which seems to push their forms forward toward the picture plane and becomes an echoing void in the space between the two groups. The menacing figures loom over the viewer. Golub has painted them as if our eyes are level with their knees, placing the men so close to the front that their feet are cut off by the painting's lower edge and we are trapped with them in the painting's compressed space. Our gaze is drawn repeatedly to the scarred, light tones of the white leader's skin and to the weapons, modeled with shadow and gleaming highlights, which contrast with the harshly scraped, flattened surfaces of the figures. The feeling of peril confronts the viewer mercilessly; we become one with all the victims who have been caught by the political battles of our age.

*In Richard Marshall and Robert Mapplethorpe, *50 New York Artists* (San Francisco: Chronicle Books, 1986), pp. 48–49.

23-33 LEON GOLUB, *Mercenaries (IV)*, 1980. Figures life size. Courtesy Susan Caldwell Gallery/Barbara Gladstone Gallery.

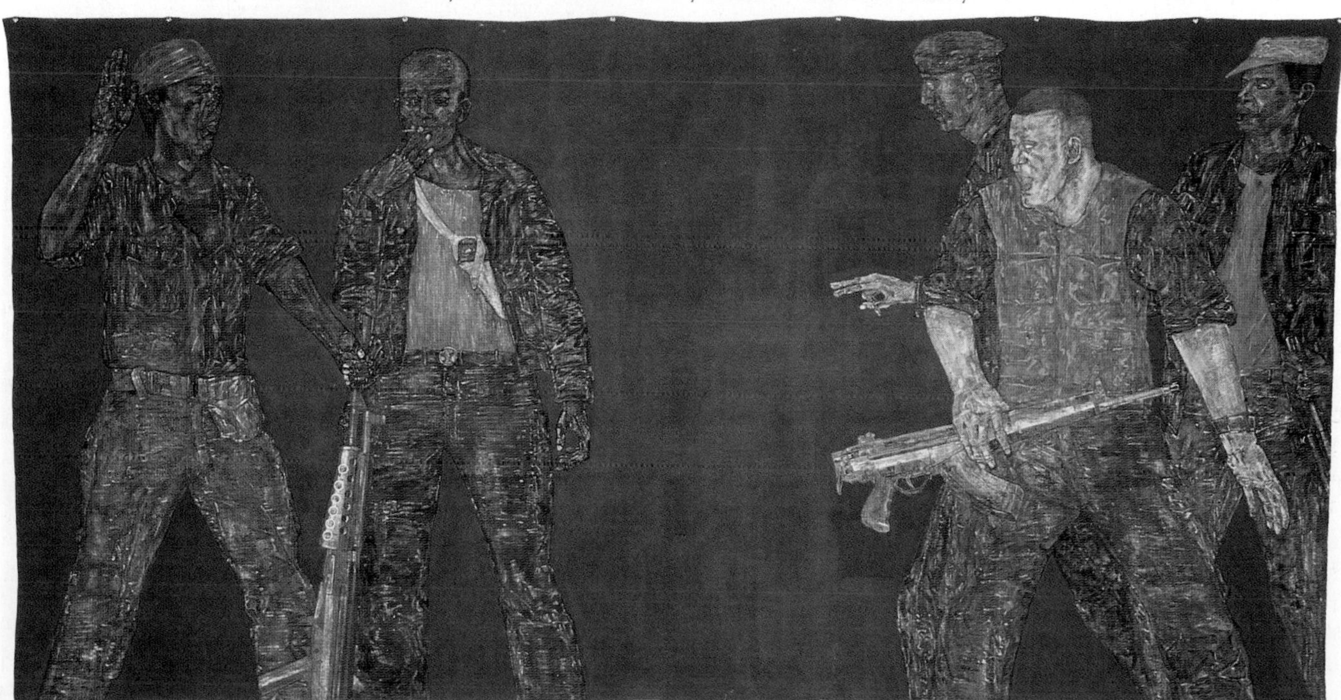

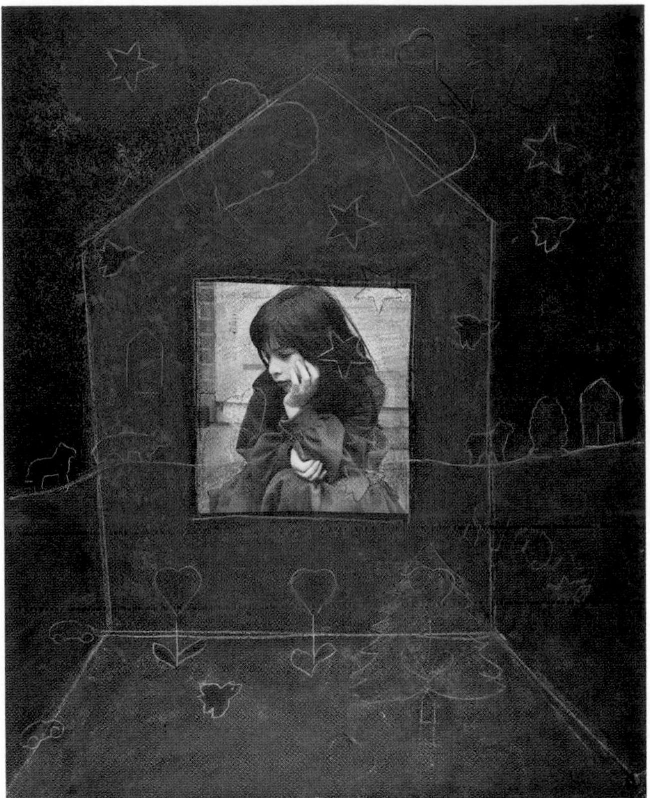

23-34 JOANNE LEONARD, *Julia and the Window of Vulnerability*, 1983. Photograph with chalk pastel, 20″ × 16″. Collection of Rene di Rosa, Napa, California. Courtesy of Jeremy Stone Gallery, San Francisco.

Like Golub, JOANNE LEONARD (b. 1940) has been haunted by the fragility of human life in the present day. She explores this theme, however, in the light of her personal experience. Convinced from childhood that "photography should say something about people's lives," Leonard studied social sciences and used her camera to document the social environment around her, especially that of her own life and of other women she knew. Gradually she began to add details on the surfaces of her black-and-white photographs, using collage techniques and oil crayons to depict the effects of the interior, psychological world upon the exterior, physical one. Her *Dreams and Nightmares* series deals with the painful disintegration of a marriage. The *Dream Kitchens* series inserted painted, housewifely fantasies of outdoor scenes into the back walls of photographed kitchen counters and stoves. The works in the series *Julia and the Window of Vulnerability* (FIG. **23-34**) are concerned with Leonard's fears for the future of the earth and for her young daughter, Julia. The pensive photograph of the girl is framed in a sketchily drawn window-house suspended in a dark sky. The image becomes an illustration of a narrative told in the mind of each viewer, based on that individual's personal experiences of risk, hope, and fear.

Leonard's work approaches the fate of humankind through the life of the individual. The German artist ANSELM KIEFER (b. 1945) tackled the same theme with a personal iconography that refers to his country's mythic past, its more troubled twentieth-century history, and the vital participation of human beings in all of that history. Kiefer noted that he paints in layers: "Each layer shines through and so I work according to a kind of 'inverted archeological' principle." In later works, the layers may be tangible (crusted with paint and materials like straw and wood), as well as mental. Kiefer's earlier paintings, like *Vater, Sohn, Heiliger Geist (Father, Son, Holy Ghost,* FIG. **23-35**), are large and relatively thinly painted, but they contain multiple strands of the symbols and themes important to him. In *Vater, Sohn, Heiliger Geist,* three

23-35 ANSELM KIEFER, *Vater, Sohn, Heiliger Geist (Father, Son, Holy Ghost)*, 1973. Oil, charcoal, synthetic resin on burlap, 9′ 6″ × 6′ 2¼″. Collection of Jeanette and Martijn Sanders.

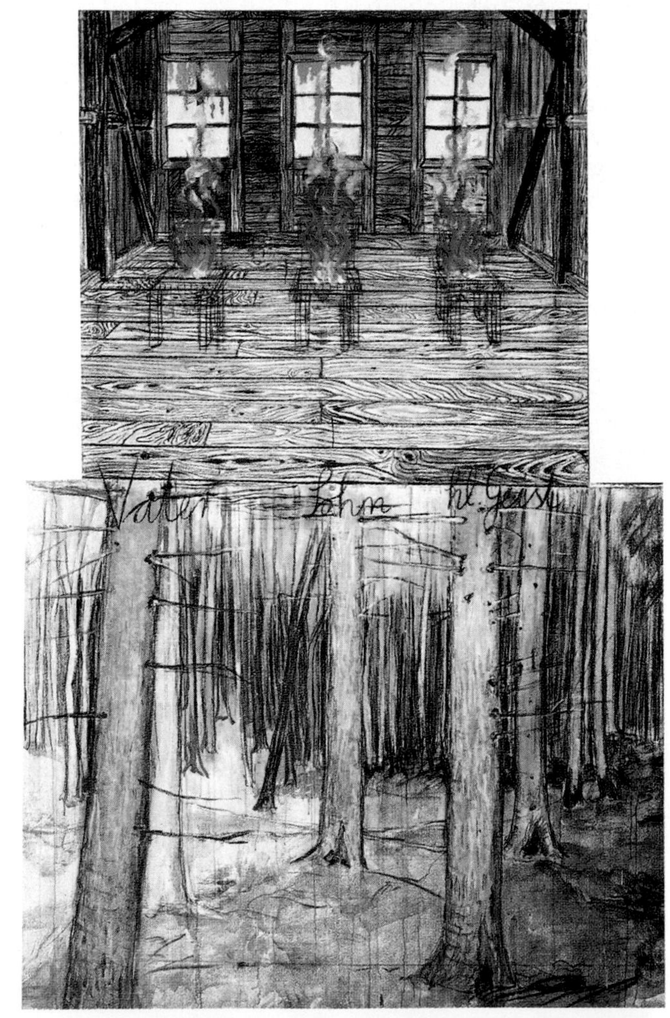

sketchy chairs sit in a bare, wood-paneled room patterned after the attic studio in an old schoolhouse used by Kiefer at the time this work was painted. Hovering within each seat is a briskly burning flame. Below the scene in the room is a second, slightly larger canvas, containing a view through densely packed rows of almost dead tree trunks that stand in a deserted forest. Steep perspective and carefully rendered wood grain transform the attic room into a vast hall. Rough, handwritten words—*"Vater, Sohn, hl.* [for *heiliger*] *Geist"*—scrawled across the top of the forest scene identify the three chairs/flames as members of the traditional Christian Trinity: "Father, Son, Holy Ghost." The forest scene, the bare room, the flames, and the words all call up associations in the viewer's mind. Memory joins with the viewing of the canvas in the present to create layers of experience for the observer. The jump between the canvases, the sketchy forms, and the unevenly brushed paint surfaces all heighten the feeling of flux related to Kiefer's belief that humans function at full power only when connected with the ongoing processes of history: "History for me is like the burning of coal, it is like a material. History is a warehouse of energy." The energy is produced, like that created when flammable materials burn, by an "exchange of materials."* In this painting, the wooden walls, chairs, and trees are all potential sources of energy for the spirit flames that govern the future.

Pop Art

Although the turmoil of World War II was responsible for the mood of desperation and suffering that inspired much expressive figurative art, the war's aftermath brought a vast increase in the production and availability of consumer goods, especially in the United States, with a concurrent rise in billboard, magazine, and newspaper advertising to entice the public to buy brand items "guaranteed" to provide a "good life." In England, Europe, and the United States, artists soon were using the images, artifacts, and style of American advertising as emblems of the sumptuous, materialistic side of modern life. For artists living under the conditions of postwar austerity outside the United States, the images spoke of a life of almost unimagined richness and surfeit. In England, the critic Lawrence Alloway invented the term "Pop Art" to describe the interest in the artifacts of popular culture, and the term was soon applied to art that adopted the look and the techniques of advertising, industrial design, Hollywood movies, and illustrations in pulp literature. A group of young artists, architects, and writers joined Alloway to form the Independent Group at the Institute of Contemporary Art in London. This group's members sought to initiate fresh thinking in art, in part by sharing their fascination with the symbol and content of American advertising, comic books, and popular movies. In America, artists used Pop images to give art the immediacy of life. Some Pop artists mixed mass-media images with gestural painting and found objects, some rendered advertising images with commercial art techniques, and some used Pop motifs to pose questions about the nature of verbal and visual symbols. By the early 1960s, Pop Art was an important force in England, New York, California, and Europe, especially France and Italy. Its success with the public was due in large part to its use of easily recognizable images, an iconography of commerce and culture as widely known in the modern world as earlier symbols tied to religion and government had been in premodern society.

Discussions at the Independent Group in London probed the role and meaning of symbols from mass culture and the advertising media. In 1956, a group member, RICHARD HAMILTON (b. 1922), made a small collage, *Just What Is It That Makes Today's Homes So Different, So Appealing?* (FIG. **23-36**), that symbolized many of the attitudes of British Pop Art. Trained as

*In Peter Winter, "Whipping Boy with Clipped Wings," and "Interview at Diesel Strasse," *Art International* (Spring 1988), pp. 64, 70.

23-36 RICHARD HAMILTON, *Just What Is It That Makes Today's Homes So Different, So Appealing?*, 1956. Collage, $10\frac{1}{4}'' \times 9\frac{3}{4}''$. Kunsthalle Tübingen, Germany.

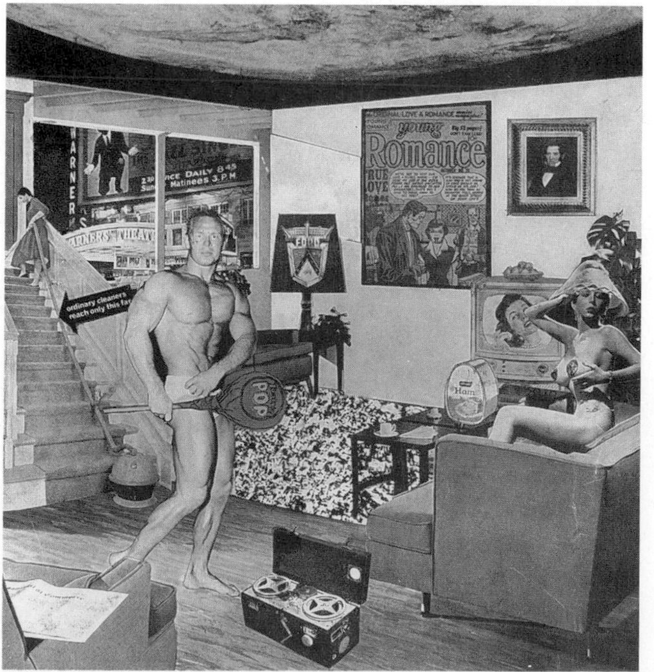

an engineering draftsman, exhibition designer, and painter, Hamilton was very interested in the way advertising shapes our attitudes. Long intrigued by the ideas of Duchamp, Hamilton has consistently combined elements of popular art and fine art, seeing both as belonging to the whole world of visual communication. *Just What Is It* was created for the poster and catalogue of one section of an exhibition entitled *This Is Tomorrow*—an environment/installation filled with images from Hollywood cinema, science fiction, the mass media, and one reproduction of a Van Gogh painting to represent popular fine art works. The fantasy interior in Hamilton's collage reflects the values of modern consumer culture through figures and objects cut from glossy magazines by Hamilton's wife, Terry, and his friend, the artist Magda Crodell McHale, who followed a list of themes he gave them. *Just What Is It* reconstructs the found images into a new whole, wittily transforming an Abstract Expressionist painting into a rug, and turning a comic book cover and an automobile logo into paintings on the wall. Much has been written about the possible deep meaning of this piece, and few would deny the work's sardonic effect, whether or not the artist intended to make a pointed comment. Although *Just What Is It* has none of the dialogue between lushly illusionistic painting and popular iconography found in much of Hamilton's other work, the way in which this collage suggests the contents of a mass mind stimulates wide-ranging speculation by viewers about society's values, and this kind of intellectual toying with mass-media meaning and imagery typifies British and European Pop Art.

Hamilton's contemporary in the Independent Group, EDUARDO PAOLOZZI (b. 1924), has used images from mass media in a different, but equally analytical way. As a student in London and Paris, Paolozzi expanded his childhood fascination with American movies, comic books, and pulp fiction to include interest in the works of Picasso, Dada, Surrealism, non-Western culture, and the natural and physical sciences. He invested the products of mass media and mass production with a mythic dimension, seeing them almost as the sacred objects of our age. The artist used these ideas in both sculpture and screenprints. In his sculpture, by the mid-1950s, Paolozzi had devised a process for making evocative bronze figures from forms built by assembling sheets of wax into which he had pressed the shapes of multitudes of throw-away, mass-produced objects. Each object in these works had many associations for Paolozzi, and he presumed that viewers would add interpretations of their own. In the 1960s, Paolozzi's graphic work drew on the huge store of mass-media images he had collected since his student days. Using

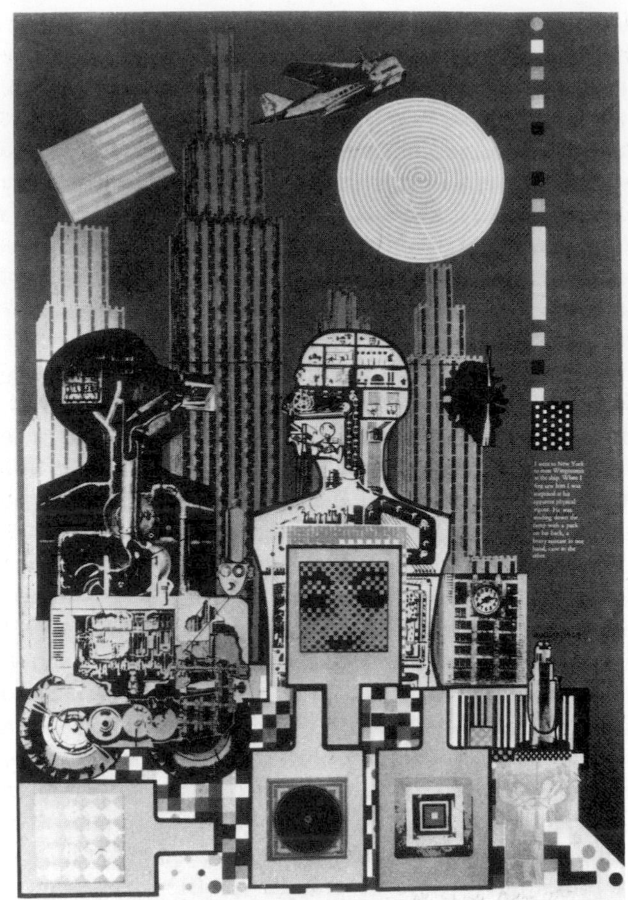

23-37 EDUARDO PAOLOZZI, *Wittgenstein in New York*, from *As Is When* (series of 12 prints, edition of 65), 1965. Screenprint, 22″ × 32″. Published by Editions Alecto and printed by Kelpra Studio. Collection of the artist.

photoscreen (a medium newly annexed by fine artists from commercial art) he incorporated these images into prints. Photoscreen employs photo processes to create stencil screens from graphic images, which in turn become part of a complex printing process that can involve an almost infinite number of colors. Typical of Paolozzi's work in this medium is *Wittgenstein in New York* (from the portfolio *As Is When*, FIG. **23-37**), based on collages of images and patterns appropriated from the mass media and commercial products. Both the print's title and the text included along its borders were taken from the writings of the Austrian philosopher Ludwig Wittgenstein, whose ideas on language theory intrigued Paolozzi. Wittgenstein had actually spent some time in New York, but Paolozzi's print is not an illustration of that journey. Instead, the image is a fantasy montage of the metropolis seen by an outsider as an assemblage of symbols. The American flag, a prop-driven airplane, and a dynamic spiral float above skyscraper silhouettes. An assemblage of rectangular forms suggests a printed circuit board composed of signs representing the way a city dweller perceives life—television, machinery, traffic signals, signboards, road markers, and two cut-away heads that reveal how we process information and feed our bodies (the latter has an ironic twist, as the mannequin here is ingesting a headache remedy). Hamilton's images in *Just What Is It* had a scale that allowed him to combine them into a seemingly coherent interior space. In *Wittgenstein in New York,* Paolozzi poured out a dazzling cornucopia of symbols that represent physical and mental space and past and present time, leaving each viewer to decode the images individually out of personal experience.

Pop Art reached maturity later in the United States than in England. ROBERT RAUSCHENBERG (b. 1925) was called a "father of Pop" because he began using mass-media images in his work in the mid-1950s. For him, as an admirer of the ideas of the composer John Cage, such images were important bits of the world that could be used in an attempt to narrow the gap between art and life. Cage was a charismatic and widely influential teacher, who encouraged his students to link their art directly with life. He brought to his music composition an interest in the thoughts of Duchamp and in Eastern philosophy. In his own work, Cage used methods like chance and indeterminancy to avoid the closed structures that marked traditional music and, in his view, separated it from the unpredictable and multilayered qualities of daily existence. For example, the score for one of Cage's piano compositions instructs the performer to appear, sit down at the piano, raise the keyboard cover to mark the beginning of the piece, remain motionless at the instrument for "four minutes and twenty-two seconds" (during which time all ambient sounds "become" the music), and then close the keyboard cover, rise, and bow to signal the end of the work. Rauschenberg set out to create works that would be as open and indeterminate as Cage's pieces, and he began by making "combine paintings," in which the parts coexisted equally and simultaneously. In the 1950s, such works contained an array of art reproductions, magazine and newspaper clippings, and segments painted in an Abstract Expressionist style. In the early 1960s, Rauschenberg adopted the commercial medium of photoscreen, first in black and white and then in color, and began filling entire canvases with appropriated news images and anonymous photographs of city scenes. *Estate* (FIG. **23-38**) is typical of his color photoscreen paintings. A jumble of images sprawls across the canvas. Familiar sights, like traffic signs, the Statue of Liberty, and a view of the Sistine Chapel in Rome showing the *Last Judgment* by Michelangelo (FIG. 17-35), are intermixed with abstract painted shapes, and "anonymous" pictures of city buildings, human legs, a clock face, a mysterious group of objects, and a "palette" of color patches containing the tonal values and the colors red, blue, and yellow—the basic vocabulary of painting. Some of the images tilt or turn sideways; each overlays or is invaded by part of its neighbor. The compositional confusion may resemble that in a Dada collage, but the parts of Rauschenberg's combine paintings retain their individuality more than those in a Schwitters piece (FIG. 22-29), yet they lack the psychic collision of details in Berlin Dada works (FIG. 22-28). The eye scans a Rauschenberg canvas much as it might survey the environment on a walk through the city. As John Cage perceptively noted: "There is no more subject in a *combine* [by Rauschenberg] than there is in a page from a newspaper. Each thing that is there is a subject. It is a situation involving multiplicity."* Individually, Rauschenberg's works resist

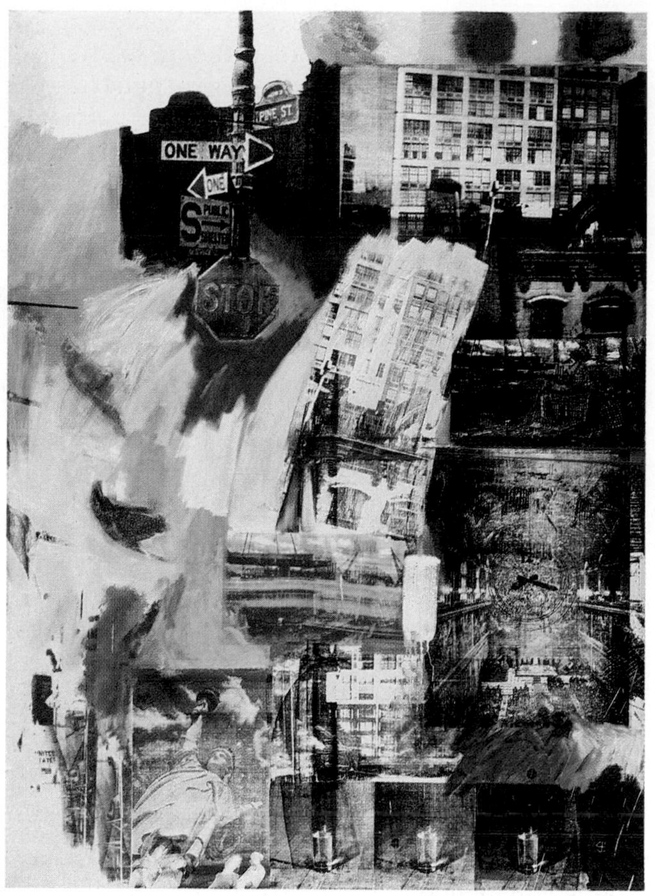

23-38 ROBERT RAUSCHENBERG, *Estate,* 1963. Oil and printer's ink, 8′ × 5′ 10″. Philadelphia Museum of Art (given by the Friends of the Philadelphia Museum of Art).

*John Cage, *Silence* (Middletown, CT: Wesleyan University Press, 1961), p. 101.

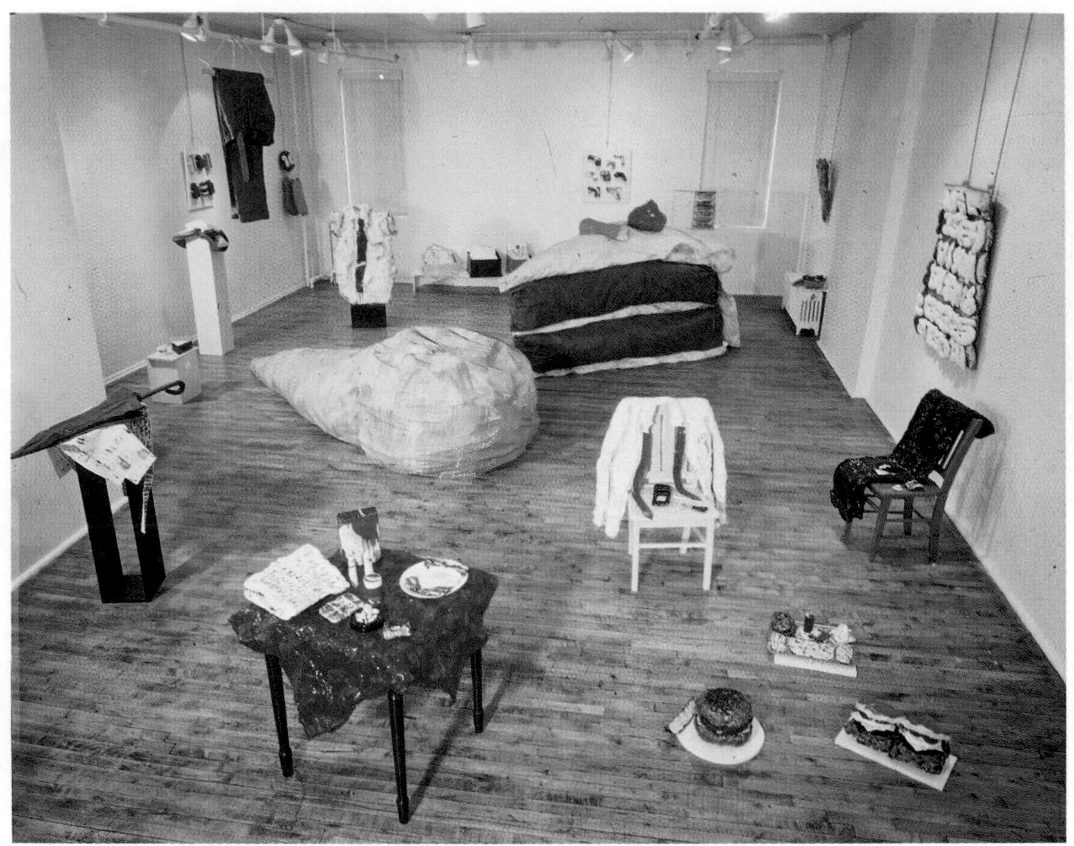

23-39 Claes Oldenburg, one-man show at the Green Gallery, New York (including pieces from *The Store* and the first large-scale "soft" sculptures), fall 1962.

precise memorization. Collectively, they represent the experience of day-to-day life in modern cities.

Like Rauschenberg, the sculptor Claes Oldenburg (b. 1929) sometimes has been associated by critics with New York Pop Art because his works contain objects from everyday modern life. As with Rauschenberg, this association is imperfect, but for different reasons. In his work, Oldenburg plays with scale and texture to invest ordinary objects with something of the threat and mystery of Bacon's figures, while adding a playful twist that renders them ironic rather than darkly existential. The son of a Swedish diplomat, Oldenburg grew up in Chicago. After settling in lower Manhattan in the 1950s, Oldenburg began using found materials, plaster, and commercial paint to make sculptures and drawings of the objects he saw in the streets and shopfronts around him. He spoke about wanting to lead his viewers "deeper into things," saying, "I am for an art that takes its form from the lines of life, that twists and extends impossibly and accumulates and spits and drips and is as sweet and stupid as life itself."

In the early 1960s, Oldenburg was briefly involved in Happenings—performances whose creators were trying to suggest the dynamic and confusing qualities of everyday life.* For a Happening in 1962, Oldenburg fabricated some huge objects to use as props. He discovered that the increased scale transformed his inanimate subjects into "characters" that seemed capable of leading independent lives. The anthropomorphic quality of Oldenburg's chosen objects was heightened further when he created giant items out of sewn and stuffed cloth. Thus re-made in limp and softened shapes, ordinary things, like kitchen appliances and pieces of food, exhibited "personalities" as individual as those of people. This quality was most apparent when the artist exhibited groups of such objects in exhibitions like his one-man show at Manhattan's Green Gallery in 1962 (FIG. **23-39**). In 1965, Oldenburg presented the first of his "monument" proposals: single objects were to be enlarged to huge scale and installed at specific sites where their appearance would spark laughter and create a certain uneasiness on the part of viewers. For example, Oldenburg suggested that a giant teddy bear (not illustrated) be placed at the northern end of Central Park in New York City. He said the bear would be comfort-

*For a more complete discussion of Happenings and their place in contemporary art, see discussion on page 1070.

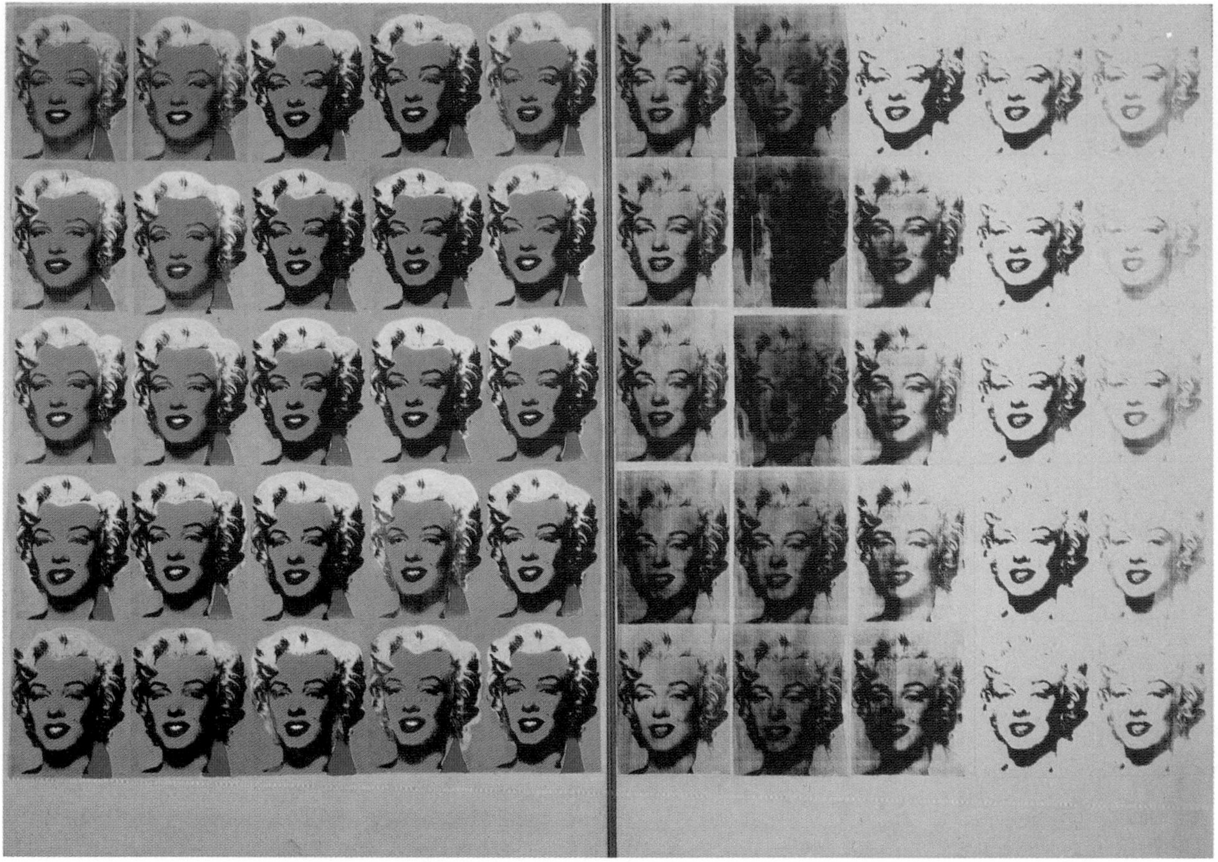

23-40 ANDY WARHOL, *Marilyn Diptych,* 1962. Oil, acrylic, and silkscreen enamel on canvas. Tate Gallery, London.

ing as it rose over the skyline, but it would also seem helplessly handless as it looked from Harlem toward more affluent neighborhoods downtown. Although the artist suggested such serious meanings for his "monuments," he tried always to make his pieces so allusive that their full significance could never be pinned down.

The quintessential New York Pop artist was undoubtedly ANDY WARHOL (1925–1987). Like Rauschenberg, whom he greatly admired, Warhol found his subjects in mass media, but mostly in commercial design, mass advertising, and news photos of ordinary people rather than in images of fine art, famous events, or anonymous buildings. After producing a few works in which he carefully mimicked the look of commercial printing, Warhol began using photoscreen to create paintings of subjects like Campbell's Soup can labels, sheets of stamps, ads for dance lessons and other self-improvement courses, and news photos of disasters, wanted criminals, and famous people. An early career as a commercial artist and illustrator may have helped interest Warhol in the expressive force of the harsh colors and simplified shapes to be found in labels and publicity photos, which he used to powerful effect in his celebrity series. The initial work in the celebrity series was inspired by the suicide of Marilyn Monroe in 1962. *Marilyn Diptych* (FIG. **23-40**) contains fifty reproductions of a well-known publicity photo of the actress, twenty-five in a color panel and twenty-five in a black-and-white panel. For the color side, Warhol simplified the areas of Monroe's hair and face into stark color patches that suggest both a mask and the high-key look of a publicity poster. The images on the black-and-white side have been screened unevenly, with one row almost obliterated by smeared paint and another so faintly imprinted as to create a ghostly effect. Although it is hard not to try to read symbolic meaning into such manipulation, Warhol denied any such intention. Yet the artist remained fascinated all of his life with the idea of fame, especially its fragility and the way in which those in its limelight can suffer from a double life of public glamour and private sorrow. Warhol predicted that the age of mass media would enable everyone to become famous for fifteen minutes at some time in the future, and he became a renowned public figure himself, as did some of those who worked with him in his studio, the Factory.

Paralleling Warhol's use of the impersonality of mass-media techniques to heighten the effect of his

23-41 EDWARD RUSCHA, *Noise, Pencil, Broken Pencil, Cheap Western,* 1963. 5′ 11¼″ × 5′ 7″. Virginia Museum of Fine Arts, Richmond (gift of Sydney and Frances Lewis).

work, California artist EDWARD RUSCHA (b. 1937) has utilized the impersonality of hand-painted billboard advertising to provide an almost philosophical consideration of the arbitrariness and mystery of painted and printed representation. *Noise, Pencil, Broken Pencil, Cheap Western* (FIG. **23-41**) illustrates Ruscha's approach. At the extreme edges of this composition, the artist placed four things: a real pulp western magazine, two illusionistically painted pencils, and letters spelling the word *noise.* The title is a literal list of the painting's contents, but the artist also is playing with levels of representation and "reality" in the work. The main field of the canvas is a dark blue, which reads as infinite space. Against it float the pulp magazine and the two painted pencils. Part of each pencil disappears beyond the edge of the canvas, and the broken one can be seen either as in the process of breaking (with chips flying from the fracture) or as lying on a solid plane amid the flakes of its ruin. The word *noise* is similarly equivocal. Letters of the alphabet, as the Cubists knew, usually emphasize the flatness of the surface, but modern graphic design often energizes them into dynamic, three-dimensional shapes. Here, the word blares forth as a series of bright red letters against the face of a white, three-dimensional block drawn in steep perspective. Like Warhol's work, Ruscha's paintings exemplify American Pop Art; he takes as subjects the thematic clichés and appearance of advertising and popular culture and in so doing reshapes the way in which viewers see the commercially oriented aspects of the world around them.

Art and Technology

Many Pop artists adopted the technology of the mass media as an integral part of their content, but they did not exploit those techniques for new expressions. That kind of exploration was left to artists who were determined to work with technologies originally developed for the military during World War II. New materials and the world of electronic apparatus and media were eagerly explored by artists as means of expressing the qualities of space-time and "vision in motion" with renewed energy. Some of the resultant work was abstract, some of it was figurative, but all of it had content that resonated with psychological or conceptual concerns.

SCULPTURE

In sculpture, advances in technology provided the means for representing the effects of change in a new kind of kinetic art. One of the most engaging of the sculptors of kinetic works is JEAN TINGUELY (b. 1925), who creates machines that are as cranky and unpredictable as human beings. Trained as a painter in his native Switzerland, Tinguely turned to motion sculpture as the result of his growing belief that "the only stable thing is movement." In the 1950s, he made a series of *metamatic* machines, programmed electronically to act with an antimechanical unpredictability when viewers inserted felt-tipped marking pens into a pincer and pressed a button to initiate motion of the pen across a small sheet of paper clipped to an "easel." Different colored markers could be used in succession, and the viewer could stop and start the device to achieve some degree of control over the final image; the results of these operations were a series of small works that resembled Abstract Expressionist paintings. In 1960, Tinguely expanded the scale of his work with a piece designed to "perform" and then destroy itself in a large area of the courtyard at the Museum of Modern Art in New York City. *Homage to New York* (FIG. **23-42**) was created with the aid of engineer Billy Klüver, who helped Tinguely scrounge wheels and other objects from a dump near Manhattan.* The completed structure, painted white to show up against the dark night sky, included a player piano modified into a metamatic painting ma-

*Klüver was later involved with Robert Rauschenberg and others in the establishment of EAT (Experiments in Art and Technology), a group of artists and engineers, mostly from the New York area, who fostered interactions between art and technology in the 1960s and early 1970s.

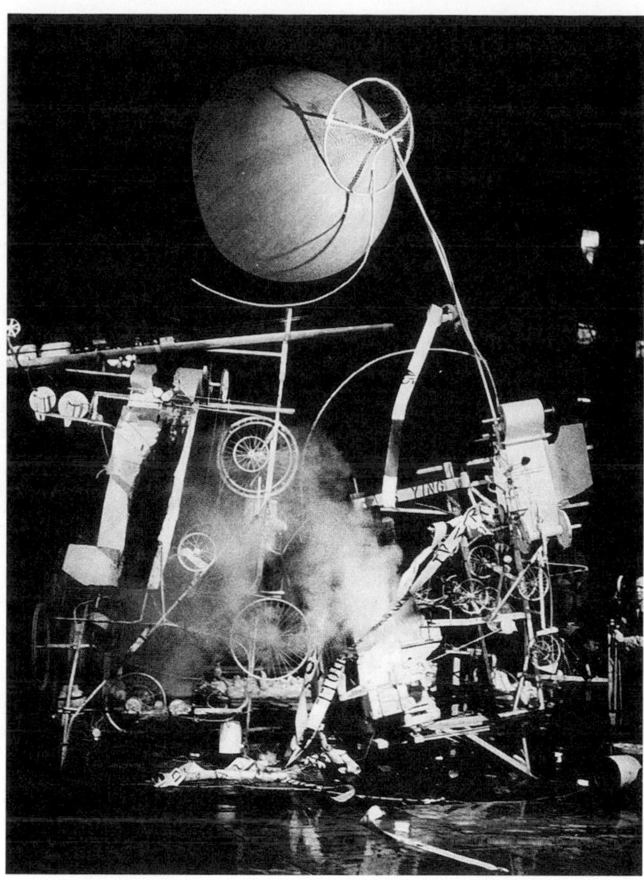

23-42 Jean Tinguely, *Homage to New York*, 1960, just prior to its self-destruction in the garden of The Museum of Modern Art, New York.

chine, a weather balloon that inflated during the performance, vials of colored smoke, and a host of gears, pulleys, wheels, and other found machine parts. Like Tinguely's other kinetic sculptures, *Homage to New York* shared something of the satiric, Dadaist spirit of Duchamp (FIG. 22-25) and the droll import of Klee's *Twittering Machine* (FIG. 22-42). But the wacky behavior of *Homage to New York* was deliberately more playful and more endearing. Having been given a "freedom" of eccentric behavior unprecedented in the mechanical world, Tinguely's creations often seem to behave with the whimsical individuality of human actors.

The messy unpredictability of Tinguely's kinetic sculpture offers one interpretation of life in space-time. Nicolas Schöffer (b. 1912) took a more controlled and ordered approach to expressing this theme, creating geometric constructions with parts that actually move in response to electronic stimuli from light, sound, and movement in their environment. A native of Hungary, Schöffer moved to Paris in 1936, bringing with him an admiration for the ideas about dynamic space-time art formulated by Moholy-Nagy and Naum Gabo. After World War II, Schöffer began making what he called *spatiodynamic* towers, which are constructed of slender frames hung with metal or plastic planes designed to catch and reflect light in ever-changing patterns that mirror the ceaseless permutations going on in the physical world. Soon Schöffer set the parts of such towers in motion using motors programmed by the kind of electronic cells used in early computers. He called these works CYSP, for "cybernetic spatiodynamic," because they drew on research in cybernetics—the study of the operation of communication and control processes in biological, mechanical, and electronic systems, first pioneered during World War II. Some of Schöffer's CYSPs were designed to "perform" interactively with dancers in response to motion or changes in sound, color, or intensity of light. By the late 1950s, his works had become elaborate constructions with multiple shafts bearing discs and blades of steel on which he projected beams of colored light. He envisioned some of these enlarged into huge spatiodynamic towers that would operate high in the skylines of modern cities. In 1962, for a festival at Liège, Belgium, Schöffer constructed *The Spatiodynamic Tower* (FIG. **23-43**), 171 feet tall, next to the city's Congress Palace, and added a special installation behind the building's enormous glass wall, which faced the Meuse River.

23-43 Nicolas Schöffer, *The Spatiodynamic Tower*, Liège, Belgium, 1961. Sound-equipped and cybernetic, 170′ $7\frac{1}{4}$″ high.

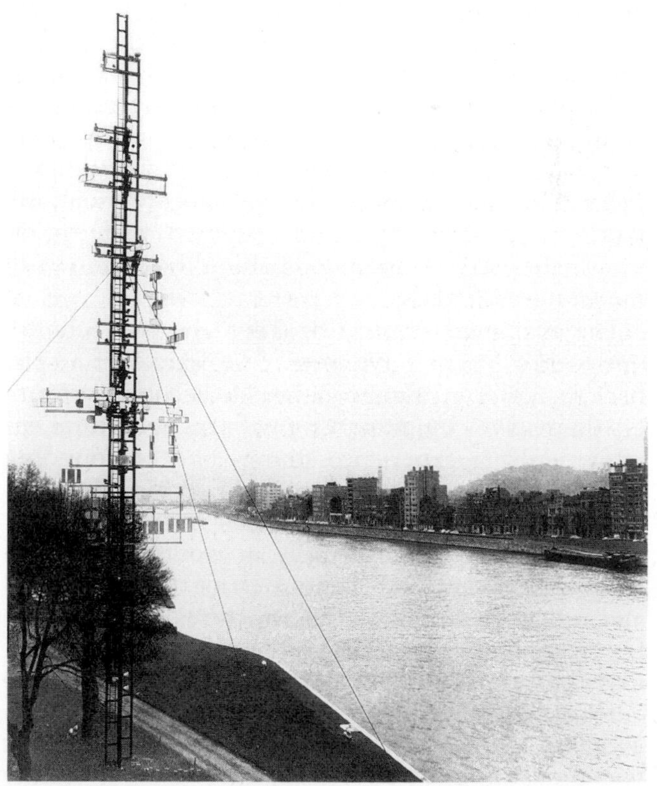

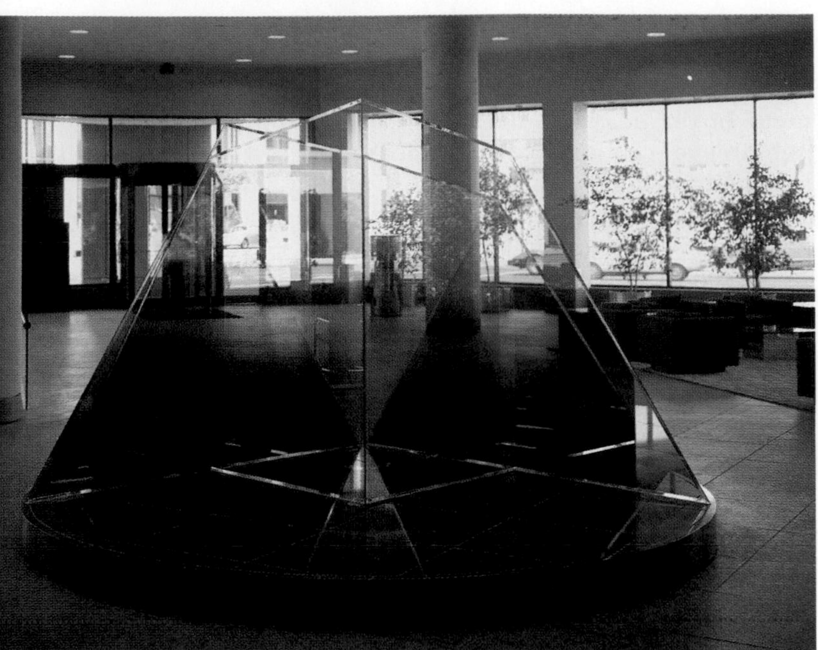

23-44 LARRY BELL, *Homage to Griffin,* 1980. Vaporized metal on glass, 9′ 6″ high × 14′ wide. Valley Bank of Nevada Fine Arts Collection, Reno, Nevada.

Sixty-four mirrored panels on thirty-three turning axes in the tower shifted position in response to signals from a huge electronic brain inside the Congress Palace, which collected data from wind, light, temperature, moisture, and noise sensors mounted on the tower and combined the resultant information with programs for varied motion sequences. The spectacle was accompanied by five aural collages of electronically manipulated music and city noise. At night, 120 multicolored spotlights played over the tower's mirrored blades, and, on holidays, the electronic brain also operated banks of seventy projectors that played slides of abstract colored patterns on translucent screens mounted behind the windows of the Congress Palace.

The machines created by Tinguely and Schöffer "perform" for their viewers. The works of LARRY BELL (b. 1939) encourage viewers to become performers themselves by interacting with his sculptural environments to experience strange and confounding shifts in the perception of space. From his early days as a sculptor in Los Angeles, Bell has played with perceptual illusion, especially in works made with glass and coated with various transparent, opaque, and reflective surfaces. The structures of works like *Homage to Griffin* (FIG. **23-44**) are made of freestanding glass panels, coated by the artist to obtain different amounts of reflection, refraction, or opacity. Set up in a gallery, the sculptural forms dissolve as a viewer walks past and around them, one moment able to look through the glass plates into the space beyond, and the next seeing one's reflection fade into nothingness in a nonreflective area. Viewers are easily enticed into playful engagement with these pieces to discover the wonderful ways in which their visual properties continually alter one's perception of the space they inhabit. Advanced technology enables Bell to craft the surfaces of his abstract shapes in ways that use reflection and blocked vision to transform the site of one of his pieces into a magical wonderland where visual expectations are continually overturned, and the viewer comes to a new understanding of how one perceives actual forms in space.

COMPUTER GRAPHICS AND HOLOGRAPHY

While some new technologies were revolutionizing the way artists could work with sculptural space, other technologies, especially those of computer graphics and holography, were transforming the ways in which artists could create and manipulate illusionistic three-dimensional forms. Computer graphics and holography both use light for the making of images, and, like photography, both media can incorporate specially recorded camera images. However, these two media differ in that only computer graphics allows the artist to work with wholly invented forms, as a painter can.

The medium of computer graphics was developed during the 1960s and 1970s and opened up new possibilities for both abstract and figurative art. Computer graphics operates by means of electronic programs that divide the surface of the cathode-ray tube (CRT) of the computer monitor into a grid of tiny boxes called "picture elements" (pixels), which can be individually addressed electronically to create a design, much as knitting or weaving patterns use a gridded matrix as a guide for making a design in fabric. Once created, parts of a computer-graphic design can be changed quickly through the operation of an electronic program, allowing the artist to revise or duplicate shapes in the design and to manipulate at will the color, texture, size, number, and position of any desired detail. A computer-graphic picture is displayed in luminous color on the cathode-ray tube; the effect suggests a view into a vast world that exists inside the tube.

One of the best known of the artists working in this electronic painting mode is DAVID EM (b. 1952), who uses what he terms *computer imaging* to fashion fantastic imaginary landscapes that have an eerily believable existence within the "window" of the computer monitor. As artist-in-residence at the California Institute of Technology's Jet Propulsion Laboratory, Em has created brilliantly colored scenes of alien worlds using the laboratory's advanced computer graphic

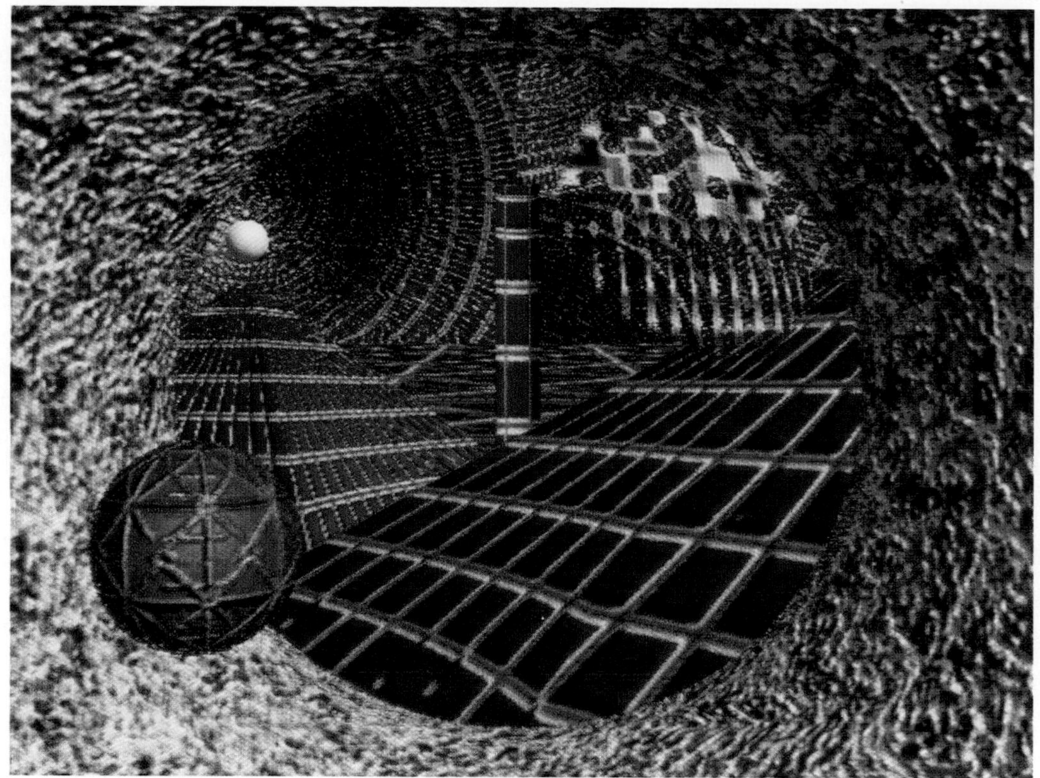

23-45 DAVID EM, *Nora,* 1979. Computer-generated color photograph, 17″ × 23″. Private collection. © David Em/represented by Spieckerman Associates, San Francisco.

equipment. He also had access to software programs developed to create computer-graphic simulations of NASA missions in outer space. Creating images with the computer allows Em great flexibility in manipulating simple geometric shapes—shrinking or enlarging them, stretching or reversing them, repeating them, adding texture to their surfaces, and creating the illusion of light and shadow. In images like *Nora* (FIG. **23-45**), Em created futuristic geometric versions of Surrealistic dreamscapes in which the forms seem familiar and strange at the same time. The illusion of space in these works is immensely vivid and seductive. It almost seems as if one could wander through the tubelike foreground "frame" and up the inclined foreground plane or hop aboard the hovering globe at the lower left for a journey through the strange patterns and textures of this mysterious labyrinthine setting.

SONIA LANDY SHERIDAN (b. 1925) is one of the most inventive artists to combine, in a single computer-graphic work, images made by an electronic camera and those drawn by hand. Sheridan finds the computer-graphic medium to be a powerful means of providing psychological and conceptual insights into the human experience. From her days studying French and art in grade school, Sheridan has been fascinated with the ways in which both verbal and visual languages work. Although she trained as a painter and printmaker, she holds a strong belief (like Moholy-Nagy) that art and science belong together. In the mid-1960s, her interests led her to initiate a series of collaborations with research scientists to explore artistic uses for technological media. She brought this approach to the Generative Systems Program, which she founded at the School of the Art Institute of Chicago in 1970 to help students investigate the artistic potential of technological tools. Sheridan's personal work includes art created with diffraction gratings,* a variety of copy machines, early FAX machines, and computer graphics. *Drawing in Time: My New Black Book No. 2* (FIG. **23-46**) is one of the works done with Easel, the versatile computer-graphic program designed by one of Sheridan's ex-students, John Dunn, to run on a computer. On this small desktop system, as on the more complex system used by Em, the artist has immense control over manipulation of color, size, shape, and texture. Sheridan can mix hand-drawn shapes with those captured by a video camera, or use each kind of image alone.

*Diffraction gratings, used mainly in scientific experimentation, are sheets of glass, plastic, or metal that are inscribed with grids whose lines diffract any light directed at the gridded surface and break this light up into its color spectra so that the rays may be accurately measured.

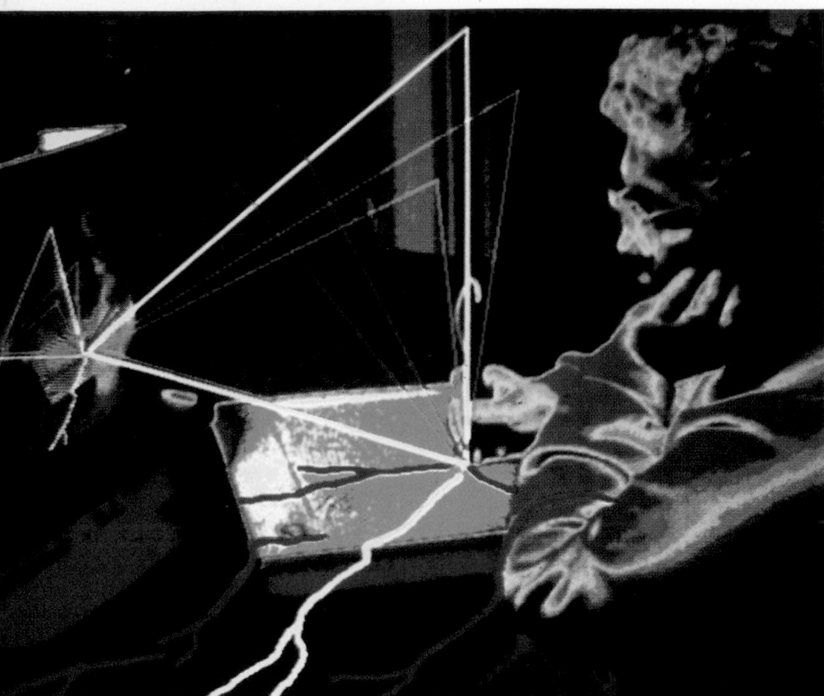

23-46 Sonia Landy Sheridan, *Drawing in Time: My New Black Book No. 2*, 1982. Easel (John Dunn Software), Cromemco Z-2D hardware, $5\frac{1}{4}''$ computer disc and in multiple dimensions as photographs. Artist's collection.

Although not as powerful overall as the mainframe computer program used by Em, Easel is immensely easier to use, and Sheridan can work in the intimacy of her home studio, which gives a different flavor to the content of her work. She created *Drawing in Time: My New Black Book No. 2* with a combination of techniques, giving instructions to the computer through the instrument's keyboard or by moving a special pencil-shaped electronic stylus over a flat, electronic "graphic tablet." She began by adding color (a process called *colorizing*) to a black-and-white image of herself working at the computer, which she had made with a video camera. She then modified the video image by adding bright-hued lines that connect her electronic pad and stylus with the picture she is creating on the computer screen. Process and content act on each other in this work—the image is both an illustration of the computer-graphic process and a personal representation of Sheridan's creative process. In addition, the drawn lines provide an intriguing variation on the Modernist tension between two- and three-dimensional space by simultaneously seeming to exist in the three-dimensional world of the camera image and to float near the surface of the monitor, in front of the artist's figure. The title *Drawing in Time: My New Black Book* refers both to the way layered computer-graphic images suggest multiple moments in time and to Sheridan's sketchbooks (often with black covers), which the artist has always used as a visual-verbal journal in an attempt to understand the relationship between the artist's hand and mind. Like Moholy-Nagy, Sheridan has found that technological tools, drawing, and painting each give her particular insights into the nature of art and of the world.

Holography, from the Greek words *holos* (whole or entire) and *graphos* (to write or inscribe), differs from any other medium by providing the viewer with a real, three-dimensional *image* (a virtual image) that duplicates in light alone the surface appearance of a subject. Although modern holographic techniques differ, basically all holographic images are recorded with a special beam of light, called a *laser*, which is split so that one part of the light illuminates the subject and is reflected toward the holographic film, while the other part of the light is directed away from the subject and bounced off a mirror to travel separately through space until it meets the beam from the subject just in front of the holographic film plate. The interaction (interference pattern) of the two beams of light records a virtual image of the entire half of the subject facing the film on the film plate, and this image can be re-created in the air by passing light through or into the holograph. Moving in front of a holographic plate allows one to look over and around the sides of the holographed subject, but if one tries to touch objects in a holographic image, the hand passes right through the shapes. The mesmerizing effect of holograms owes something to the observation made during the Renaissance by Leonardo da Vinci that "it is by its surface that the body of any visible thing is represented." The surface of an object is what holography encodes so faithfully on the holographic plate. Early holographic subjects had to be small, immobile, and nonbiological; today's holographer can create human portraits with a "pulsed-laser" that freezes living subjects in short bursts of light and opens the way to investing holograms with an entirely new psychological intensity.

The British artist Margaret Benyon (b. 1940) is one of the most interesting artists currently experimenting with holographed portraits. Working in high-tech labs with scientist partners, Benyon has investigated many of the parameters of the relationship between perceptions of physical and holographic reality. Her *Tigirl* (FIG. **23-47**) is a double exposure made from a hologram of a painting of a tiger and a pulsed-laser holographic self-portrait made from life. The flat space of the painted tiger mask interweaves with, and contradicts, the stripes laid across the three-dimensional contours of the artist's face created by holographic "fringe patterns" formed in the image when Benyon moved during the expo-

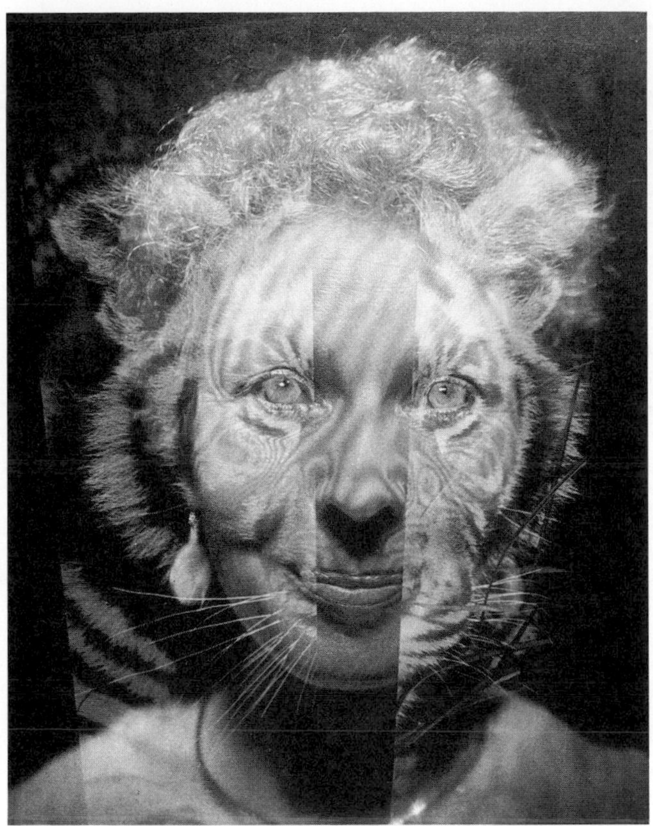

23-47 Margaret Benyon, *Tigirl,* 1985. Glass plate reflection hologram and reproduction, $11\frac{3}{4}'' \times 15\frac{3}{4}''$. Collection of the artist.

sure. Benyon is not the first artist to merge the faces of a female human being and a feline, but holography has added a powerful new intensity to this combination of human and animal energy. A holographic double exposure presents an impossible dilemma to the viewer's eyes and brain, because two apparently solid objects are seen occupying exactly the same volume of space. From one angle, the viewer of *Tigirl* can see only the girl; from another, only the tiger is visible. No photograph can capture the startling effect of the view from the front, in which the three-dimensional woman's head coexists in the same space occupied by the painted cat face. The three-dimensional complexity of Benyon's holographic rendering makes it operate with exceptional power on both the physical and the metaphysical levels.

VIDEO ART

Initially, the medium of video was available only in commercial television studios and only occasionally accessible to artists. With the invention of relatively inexpensive portable video recording equipment and electronic devices that allowed the manipulation of the recorded video material, artists began to explore in earnest the particularly expressive possibilities of this new medium. In its basic form, video technology uses a special motion-picture camera to capture images from the world and to translate them into electronic data that can be displayed on a video monitor or television screen. Video pictures resemble photographs in the amount of detail they contain, but like computer-graphic pictures, a video image is displayed as a series of points of light on a grid, giving the impression of soft focus. A viewer looking at television or video art is not aware of the surface of the monitor; instead, fulfilling the Renaissance ideal, we concentrate on the image and look through the glass surface, as through a window, into the "space" beyond. Video images combine the realism of photography with the sense that the subjects are moving in "real time" in a deep space "inside" the monitor.

Peter Campus (b. 1937) has utilized all the qualities of the basic medium of video with immense imagination to tantalize viewers with his real-time recordings of "impossible" events. A native New Yorker who studied psychology and filmmaking before working in commercial television, Campus brings to his video art his keen interest in the relativity of human perception and a comprehensive knowledge of film traditions and video techniques. He has produced video environments, in which the viewer interacts with video cameras, and videotapes that confound the viewer's perception of space and reality. One of the most intriguing of the videotape pieces is *Three Transitions,* three short works that each document an impossible physical transition taking place in real time as we watch. The first transition (FIG. **23-48**) begins with the artist standing against a plain white background wearing a simple jacket, white shirt, and dark trousers. His head turns slightly to one side while he performs, to check the live action shown on a video monitor. The action begins as Campus gestures toward the background plane with one arm. Without warning, a startling vertical slit opens down the middle of his back. A few seconds later, the rip has been extended so that when he bends down and thrusts his head forward, the top of his skull appears in the middle of his back, and he then proceeds to literally step through himself. This transition is made possible by carefully positioning two video cameras facing each other on opposite sides of a white sheet, but the psychological disorientation of seeing such an impossible physical feat take place before our eyes resonates so strongly that our imagination and reason struggle to adjust our notions of perception to fit these "facts."

The medium of video is new enough that most viewers know little about its techniques. Commercial television has taught us that video, like cinema and

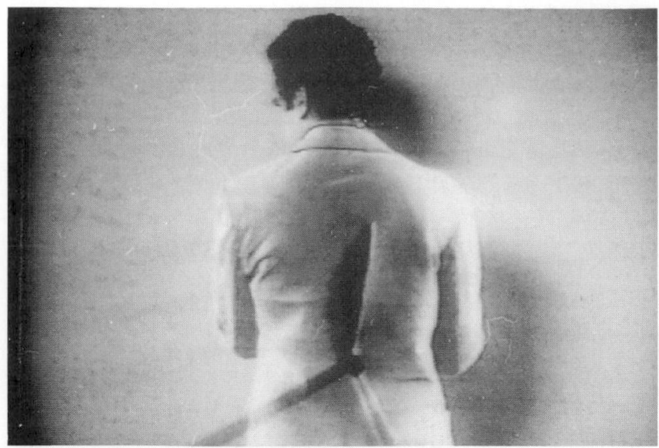

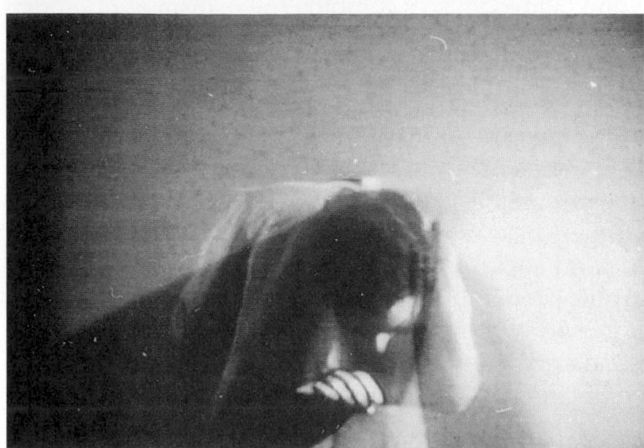

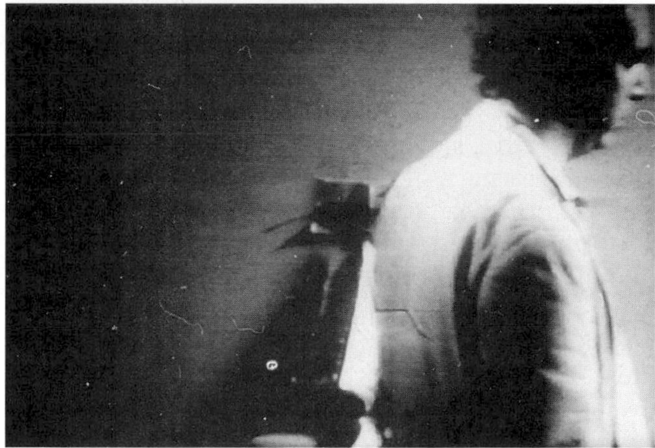

23-48 Peter Campus, *Three Transitions*, c. 1971. Videotape stills.

photography, can be said to have two expressive sides: one connected with straight recording and the other produced by manipulations like montage or double exposure. In cinema and in photography, straight recording represents direct, real-time seeing, while montage or double-exposure techniques combine images made at different moments in time. Real-time seeing in movies can occur in fictional as well as in documentary films; conventions have been developed in each ("invisible" editing and "logical" shifts in camera position, for example) to compress the experience of real-time into viewing packages of acceptable length (the one-minute news story about an event stretching over hours or the two-hour feature film that spans days or decades). Eisenstein's psychological jump cuts (FIG. 22-77) and the fantasy montages of Méliès (FIG. 22-33) clearly signal their nonnatural character.

When video introduced the possibility of doing such manipulation in real-time, artists like the Korean-born, New York–based videographer Nam June Paik (b. 1932) were eager to work with the medium. Inspired by the ideas of American composer John Cage after studying music performance, art history, and Eastern philosophy in Korea and Japan, Paik worked with electronic music in Germany in the late 1950s before turning to performances using modified television sets. In 1965, relocated to New York City, Paik acquired the first inexpensive video recorder sold in Manhattan (the Sony Porta-Pak) and immediately recorded everything he saw out the window of his taxi on the return trip to his studio downtown. Stints as artist-in-residence at television stations WGBH in Boston and WNET in New York allowed Paik to experiment with the most advanced broadcast video technology, and a grant permitted him to collaborate with the gifted Japanese engineer-inventor Shuya Abe in the development of a video synthesizer—a special instrument that allows the artist to manipulate and change the electronic video information in various ways, causing images or parts of images to stretch, shrink, change color, or break up. Using the synthesizer, the artist also could layer images, inset one image into another, or merge images from various cameras with those from videotape recorders to make a single, visual, kaleidoscopic "time-collage." This kind of compositional freedom allowed Paik to combine his interests in the ideas of Cage, painting, music, Eastern philosophy, global politics for survival, humanized technology, and cybernetics.

Paik's best-known video work, *Global Groove* (FIG. **23-49**), combines in quick succession fragmented sequences of female tap dancers, poet Allen Ginsberg reading his work, a performance of a Paik musical composition in which cellist Charlotte Moorman uses a man's back as her instrument, Pepsi commercials from Japanese television, Korean drummers, and a shot of the Living Theater group performing a controversial piece called *Paradise Now*. Commissioned originally to be broadcast over United Nations satellite, the cascade of imagery in *Global Groove* was intended to give viewers a glimpse of the rich worldwide television menu Paik had predicted would be ours in the future. Paik called his videotape works "physical

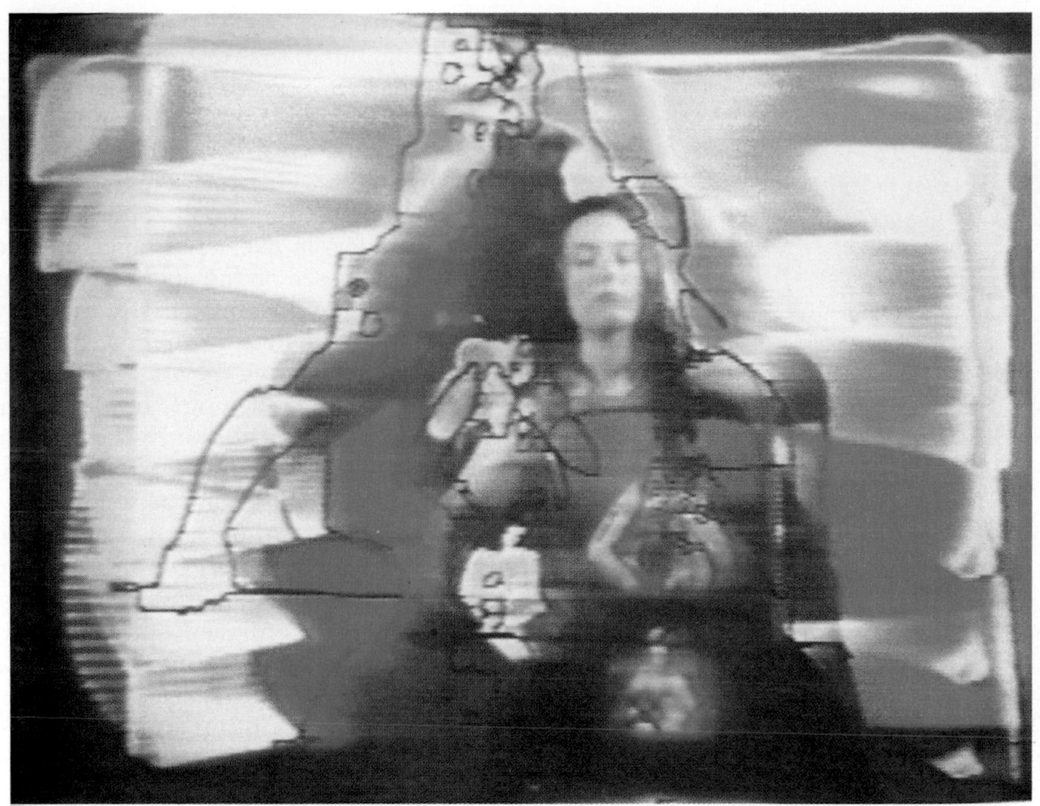

23-49 Nam June Paik, *Global Groove*, 1973. Videotape still.

music" and said that his musical background made him able to understand time better than video artists trained in painting or sculpture. As critic Jonathan Price reported, Paik considered the effect on the viewer of his kind of video narrative to be similar to both the style of writing in James Joyce's *Finnegan's Wake* and to "a classical Taoist way of meditation; by becoming aware of everything going on in the present, you discover eternity right now."* James Joyce developed his writing style to express the layering of thought, feeling, and experience of the exterior physical world made apparent to us through the work of psychologists and physical scientists. Nam June Paik used the methods of new technology to extend this kind of composition into the visual world.

Conceptual Art

As the twentieth century progresses, artists and those who write about art have become increasingly interested in thinking about the way art communicates. Conceptual art self-consciously examines these matters, addressing the intellect through the visual sense. In conceptual art, the ideas generate the works. Some conceptual artists have examined the means of representation in painting, sculpture, and cinema; others have created art that operates almost like philosophical propositions. Conceptual work sometimes is a simple epigrammatic text that generates an image in the mind; at other times, it becomes a complex visual display of the relationship between ideas and visual appearance.

One of the earliest and most provocative contemporary artists working conceptually is the American Jasper Johns (b. 1930), who was keenly interested in the complex processes involved in perceiving simple symbols. In the mid-1950s, Johns began including generic symbols, like the American flag and targets, in his work. These objects interested him because they were common things, often seen but seldom examined with careful attention.† Viewers cannot ignore the presence of one of Johns's painted targets; such images fill the entire canvas and are rendered with the unmistakable texture of a hand-applied art medium—in this case, encaustic. As a representation of a target, a Johns target has no reference beyond the design and the fact that it represents a target. Such a

*Jonathan Price, *Video Visions: A Medium Discovers Itself* (New York: New American Library, 1977), pp. 128–29.

†The inclusion of such commonplace subjects in his works caused some American critics in the early 1960s to link Johns with Pop Art. His subsequent work, however, has clearly reinforced the understanding of his art as concerned with issues and methods of representation very different from the ideas, techniques, and subjects of Pop Art.

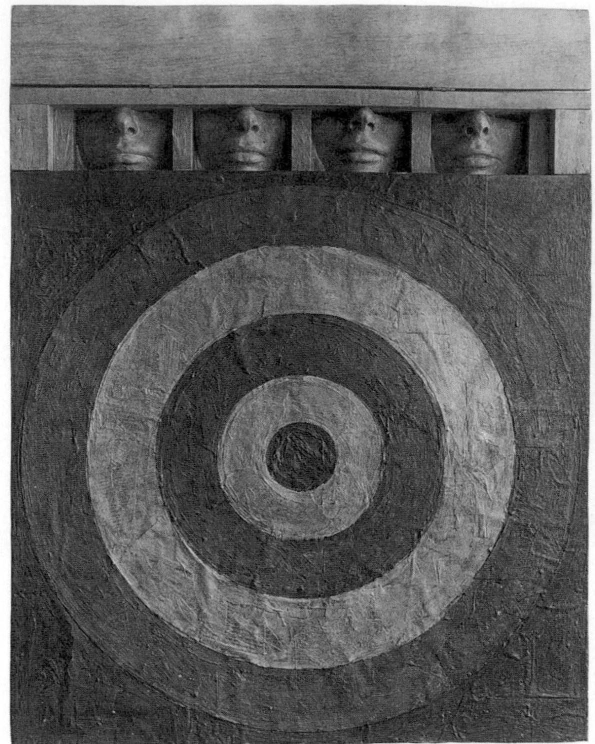

23-50 JASPER JOHNS, *Target with Four Faces,* 1955. Assemblage of encaustic and collage on canvas with objects, 26″ × 26″, surmounted by four tinted plaster faces in wood box with hinged front, overall dimensions with box open, 33$\frac{5}{8}$″ × 26″ × 3″. Collection, The Museum of Modern Art, New York (gift of Mr. and Mrs. Robert C. Scull).

painted target remains the replica of a target, but it also has become an art object, with no clear significance, because it cannot be used as a target and remain a painting. The puzzle of the relationship between the painting and its design was set down by Johns as a formula: "*A* = *B*. *A* is *B*. *A* represents *B*." In *Target with Four Faces* (FIG. **23-50**), the artist has complicated the situation by adding, above the flat painted target, four boxes (with a single hinged lid), each containing a cast of the lower portion of a human face. These casts are not portraits. They seem to be the same face, although slight differences between them are evident (they were cast at four distinct but successive moments). Like the target, the faces represent only themselves. They are seen or not seen, depending on whether their lid is raised or lowered. When they are visible, they simply *are.* In the faces, as with the target, Johns has picked a part of life—nose and mouth—that we generally see but do not examine; it is the eyes that usually capture our attention in the human face. In Johns's work, such simple, appropriated things acquire a haunting "presence" that forces us to wrestle with the relationship between the thing and its representation. As the artist himself said: "Meaning is determined by the use of the thing, the way an audience uses a painting once it is put in public."

ALLAN KAPROW (b. 1927) extended Johns's concern with the "use" of art by its audience to sculpture and performance, trying to represent more fully the impermanent, shifting qualities of modern life. Using fragile materials like newspaper and compositional techniques based on the operation of chance, Kaprow constructed temporary environments whose parts viewers were invited to change. He also was instrumental in developing the art form for which he is best known—the "Happening." Influenced heavily by his knowledge of art history, his study of music composition with John Cage, and a belief that Jackson Pollock's actions in making a painting were more important than the painting itself, Kaprow's Happenings were loosely structured performances presented in varied public indoor and outdoor sites. Generally, they combined ordinary and pseudo-ritualistic actions. Kaprow's first Happening took place in 1958 at the Reuben Gallery in New York City, and the art form soon spread throughout the United States, Europe, and Japan. Happenings occurred in lofts and studios, in department stores, in auditoriums, on college campuses, and on private estates. Usually Happenings lacked specific plots, but they always contained a collage of actions that suggested a narrative or ritual reflecting the contemporary human condition. Their mood often recalled that of Dada and Futurist performances or events, but rather than taking the role of onlookers, as had the viewers of the earlier works, the audience at a Happening participated fully in the action.

Kaprow's *A Spring Happening* (FIG. **23-51**), held at the Reuben Gallery in 1961, is a good example of the

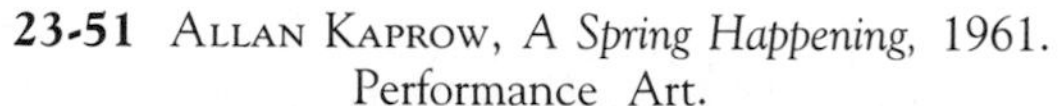

23-51 ALLAN KAPROW, *A Spring Happening,* 1961. Performance Art.

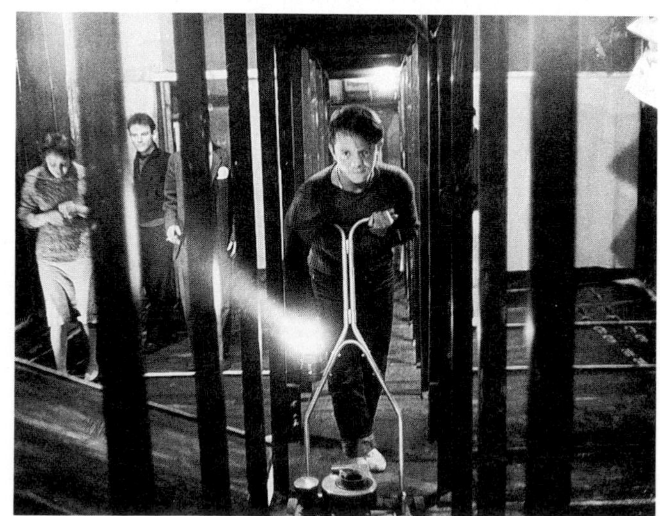

form. At the advertised time, the audience was ushered into a dark, narrow "tunnel," which had rectangular peepholes at regular intervals along its sides. In the moments that followed, lights went on and off, and figures executed mysterious actions outside the tunnel on both sides. Threatening noises poured from loudspeakers or occurred as objects were beaten, thrown, or rattled on all sides of the tunnel, and the structure vibrated. Finally, a power motor was pushed through the tunnel, crowding the spectators toward one end, where they were met by powerful blasts of air from a huge floor fan. Just at the moment when they felt completely trapped, the tunnel's plywood walls fell outward and the crowd escaped to the sides. Most Happenings shared with *Spring Happening* the qualities of unexpectedness, improvised ritual, aggression, discomfort, surprise, variety, quick changes, and wonder. Their spontaneous and homemade flavor made them particularly appropriate symbolic dramas for reflecting on the human condition during a period of rapid social change. Many of them, like *A Spring Happening*, mimicked in some way the distressing pressures of modern life, and some of them, especially those created by Europeans, contained specific political references. Happenings also encouraged viewers to think anew about the nature of sculptural representation.

While painters and sculptors were experimenting during the late 1950s and early 1960s with the expressive qualities of their media, some filmmakers were similarly exploring the expressive mechanisms of cinema and the way these acted on the minds of viewers. Taking the lead in this activity was JEAN-LUC GODARD (b. 1930), who believed that a movie should continually call attention to itself as it "plays" on the screen. Godard was part of a group of French "New Wave" (*La Nouvelle Vague*) film directors who developed distinctive, individual cinema styles in the 1950s and 1960s based on their deep knowledge of traditional big studio classic films. New Wave cinema characteristically attempted to subvert the expectations of viewers by substituting for the carefully designed, clearly photographed, and logically constructed plots of the big studios, a menu of ambiguity, surprise, fuzzy and shaky camera work, and abrupt changes in space, time, and mood. Godard's first feature-length film, *Breathless* (*À bout de souffle*, FIG. **23-52**), is typical of the New Wave mode, and, like many New Wave works, it is also both an homage to American "B" gangster films and a self-conscious analysis and parody of their style. *Breathless* was loosely constructed around a minimal story—an amoral young crook drifts through a series of actions involving his mistress, car theft, a joy ride in the country, the killing of a cop, and his eventual betrayal (by his mistress) to the police. The methods Godard employed, however, violated the invisible and sequential editing used in traditional commercial films. The viewer experiences everything in Godard's work in fragments that flow past in a seemingly uncoordinated way, much as we remember actual past experiences. Yet the viewer of a Godard film is never allowed to forget that he or she is watching a film. Godard worked hard to ensure that the viewer remains aware at all times of filmmaking processes at work. Scenes were shot with shaky hand-held cameras (rather than with steady, tripod-mounted equipment), on real (not designed) locations, with available light (instead of carefully controlled studio illumination). Sound was taped on-site with portable machines synchronized with the cameras (to capture all ambient sounds as they happened), rather than with separate, more easily manipulated sound tapes that could be mixed with other sounds and even partially re-recorded later in the studio. Finally, Godard never allowed his audiences to become totally immersed in the illusion of a story comfortably unfolding in traditional filmic time and space. Instead, he disrupted narrative flow by arbitrarily omitting chunks from the middle of long continuous shots to produce jump cuts that dislocated any sense of progressive action. Jump cuts were not new in themselves. Méliès had

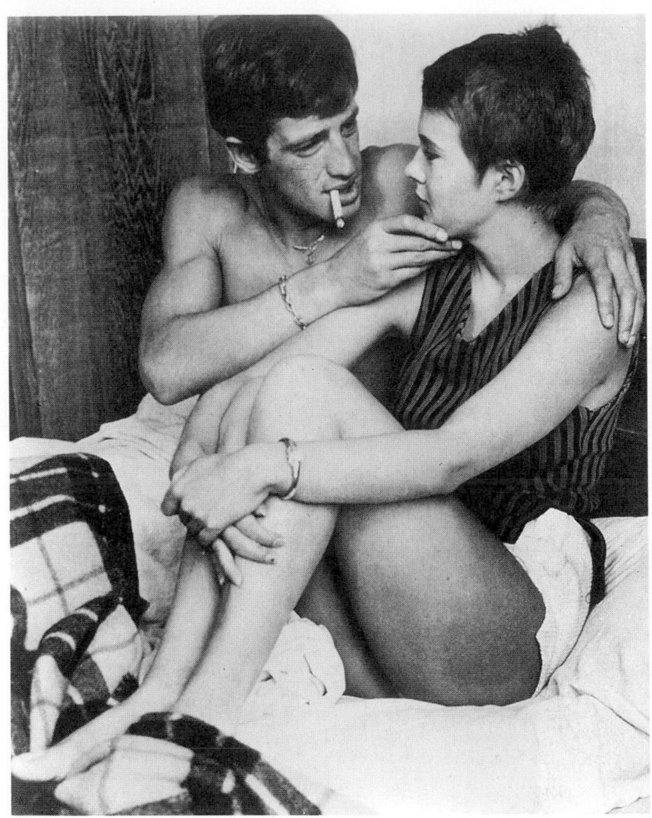

23-52 JEAN-LUC GODARD, film still from *Breathless* (*À bout de souffle*), 1959.

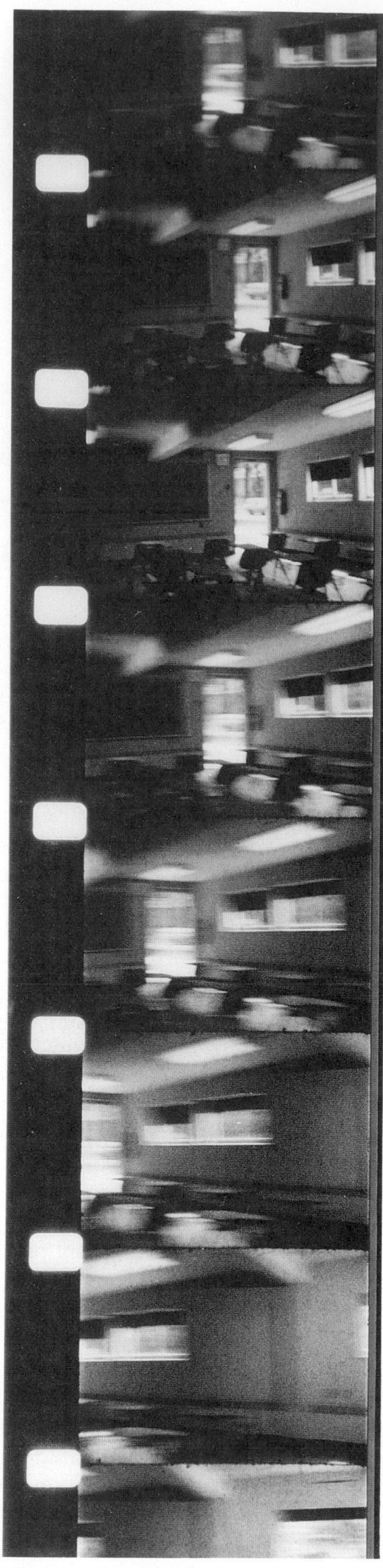

23-53 Michael Snow, ⟷, 1969. Section of film.

(FIG. 22-33) had used them to produce fantasy, and Eisenstein (FIG. 22-77) had utilized montage to express mental and emotional states. But Godard's editing underscores unmistakably the nature of motion-picture images unfolding as a reel of film passes through a projector.

The Canadian artist and musician Michael Snow (b. 1929) narrows his investigation of the film medium to make his central subject the motion of the camera and the effects of this motion on the recorded film and the viewer's perception. ⟷ (FIG. **23-53**) is based on the real-time, back-and-forth pans of a camera mounted, at the height of a standing person's eyes, on a tripod in a closed space in which its back-and-forth sweep includes a view into a classroom. The space of the pan is 180 degrees from left to right. A click sound marks the end of each swing and the beginning of the return arc. At the film's start, the left-and-right movement is slow, and the viewer becomes familiar with the physical facts of the scene. Gradually, the camera swings back and forth more rapidly, and as the camera passes, it catches people who have entered the space, only to disappear again before the camera returns to that spot on its next circuit. The viewing experience rapidly becomes shaped by memory of what has been seen, anticipation of seeing that same material again, and the memories of different "states" of parts of the scene being scanned. As the film progresses, the speed of the pan increases until what is seen is a smear of color and shape as the lens sweeps along its route because of the way that the cinema camera records and the way that we perceive the sequence of recorded images projected at a steady rate onto a screen. Snow clearly described the effect of the film and the way it both calls attention to itself and to the process of viewing it:

> If properly orchestrated, it [the circular sweep pan motion] can do some powerful physical-psychic things. . . . If you become completely involved in the reality of these circular movements it's *you* who is spinning surrounded with everything, or conversely, you are a stationary centre and it's all revolving around you. But on the screen it's the centre which is never seen, which is mysterious. . . . The film has a time of its own which overrides the time of the things photographed.*

In much the same way that Snow devises a shooting system to isolate certain aspects of cinema recording and viewing, the American artist Mel Bochner (b. 1940) uses ideas from mathematical set theory to generate sculptures, paintings, and drawings that illustrate the operation of units in a set of numbers.

*In Dennis Wheeler, ed., *Form and Structure in Recent Film* (Vancouver, BC: Vancouver Art Gallery, 1972), unpaginated.

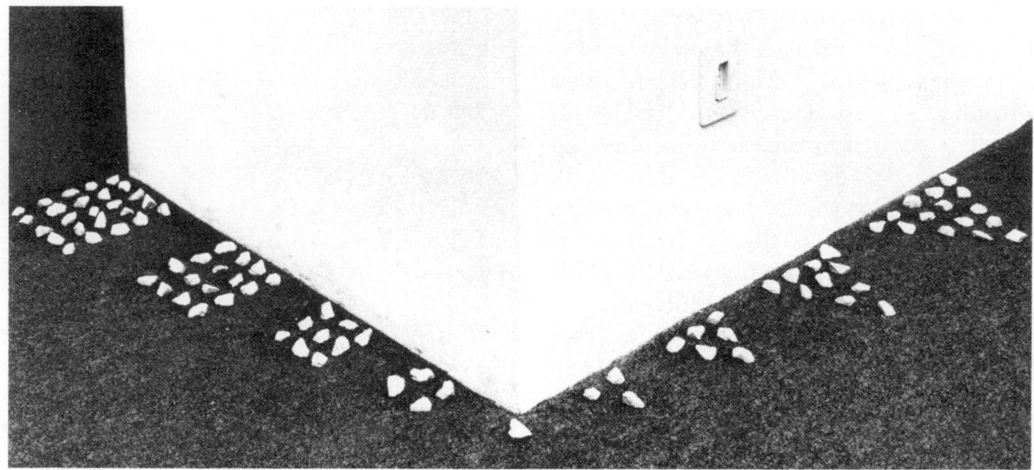

23-54 MEL BOCHNER, *Triangular and Square Numbers,* 1972. Installation of pebbles on floor, approx. 36″ on a side, 72″ overall. Galleria Marilena Bonomo, Bari, Italy.

The appearance of each of Bochner's works is determined by the system that is its subject; in that way each work is self-generating. Sculptures like *Triangular and Square Numbers* (FIG. **23-54**), from the series *The Theory of Sculpture: Counting,* were constructed in gallery spaces with simple materials like pebbles arranged temporarily for each showing. The counting system at work in *Triangular and Square Numbers,* as indicated in the title, is related to the series of numbers necessary to generate the square shapes on one side and the triangular shapes on the other. The mystery of the ways in which these geometric shapes have "grown" along the walls is balanced by the viewer's delight in uncovering the nature of the relationship between the numbers of pebbles in the triangles and the squares: the single corner stone together with the three stones in the first triangle equal the four stones in the first square; the three stones in the first triangle plus the six stones in the second triangle equal the nine stones in the second square, and so forth.

One of the most philosophical of the painters to take a conceptual approach with a realist style is New York artist SYLVIA PLIMACK MANGOLD (b. 1938), who uses illusionistically painted subjects to challenge viewers with concepts about the nature of realism in art. In the art world of the 1960s, where little acclaim was accorded illusionistic painting, Mangold devised an approach that turned realistically rendered subjects into dramatic geometric designs. Forced to paint at home by her duties as wife and mother, Mangold became interested in the visual possibilities of her studio floor and made a series of painstaking paintings of floorboards, whose space was confounded by reflections in mirrors resting on the floor's surface. Later works have explored more fully the ways in which representation can fool the eye. *Two Exact Rules on Dark and Light Floor* (FIG. **23-55**) is a meticulously rendered painting of a section of black-and-white tiled floor, seen from above in subtle perspective, sloping away from us. This illusion is cancelled wittily and abruptly by what appear to be two identical metal "Exact Rule" yardstick fragments fastened to the surface of the canvas. These rulers suggest the precise measuring tools used to create the straight perspective lines in the painting; at the same time, they appear to lie outside the illusionistic painted space, on our side of the painted canvas surface. However, the realization that the top one is actually

23-55 SYLVIA PLIMACK MANGOLD, *Two Exact Rules on Dark and Light Floor,* 1975. Acrylic on canvas, 24″ × 30″.

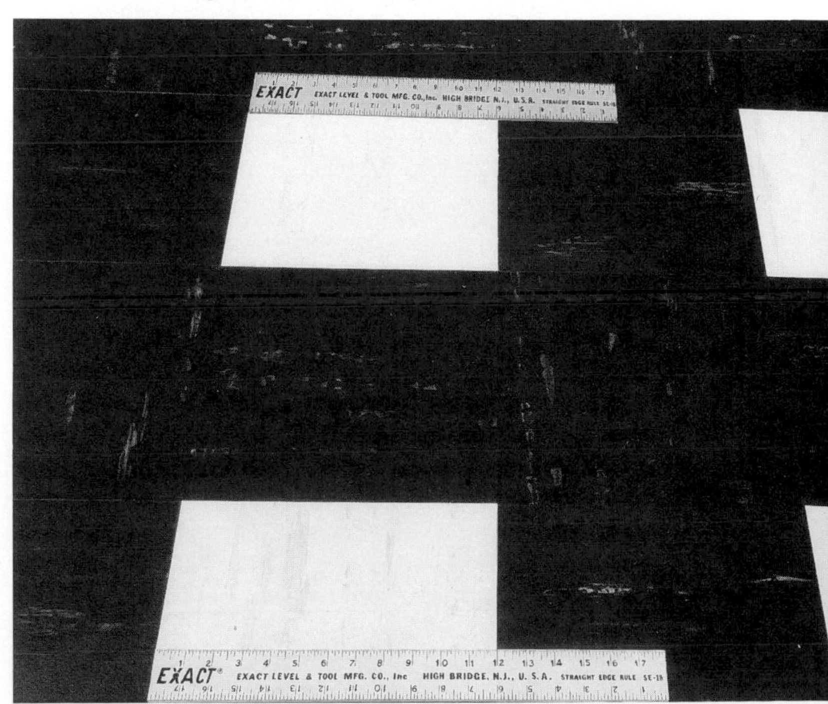

smaller in scale than the bottom one, making it seem to rest further back in space, reveals that each ruler is in fact a painted replica of a ruler. Mangold has toyed here with contradictory visual cues and the paradoxes they establish about the relationship between illusion and reality.

A conceptual approach to realist painting of a different sort is found in the work of the American artist NEIL WELLIVER (b. 1929), whose lushly painted landscapes let viewers ponder the magical ability of paint strokes to be both art medium and an analogue for details from the physical world. For works like *Deep Pool* (FIG. **23-56**), Welliver appropriated some of the qualities of nineteenth-century Impressionist and Realist painting and reworked them for his own needs. Yet the presence of the thick paint in *Deep Pool* maintains a shimmering life of its own, both as a pattern lying flat on the surface of the canvas and as an element calling attention to the artistic processes that create the illusion of a world seen through the canvas. The rural, wooded scene in *Deep Pool* has been simplified into an X-shaped pattern composed of the lighted sky, the water reflections, and the stony ledges. Where Courbet and Monet painted to reveal nature more clearly, Welliver's patiently rendered translation of his subject and the overall patterning of his even-handed strokes focus the viewer's attention as much on the process of painting as on the ostensible subjects of water, rocks, trees, light, and shadow.

The dialogue between painted illusion and the materials of art is even more intense in the mixed-media pieces created by American artist JUDY PFAFF (b. 1946). Works like *Rock/Paper/Scissors* (FIG. **23-57**) have the quality of an exploded Abstract Expressionist painting that has taken over a whole interior space. The title refers to a children's game that is played with hand-symbols for "rock," "paper," and "scissors," in which each symbol is able to "conquer" one of the others; chance alone creates a tied score between the players.* Pfaff's *Rock/Paper/Scissors*, thus, might be considered a metaphor for the Cold War or for the complex social maneuvering of modern urban life. The exuberant, overall clutter of Pfaff's installation counteracts such a reading, however, by evoking such subjects as the sights of a New Year's Eve party or of a giant kaleidoscope. Yet, above all, the forms in *Rock/Paper/Scissors*, as in all of Pfaff's installation works, remain resolutely nonobjective. The main "subject" of *Rock/Paper/Scissors* (like that in a painting

23-56 NEIL WELLIVER, *Deep Pool*, 1983. 8′ × 8′. The Collection of Exxon Corporation, Courtesy Marlborough Gallery, New York.

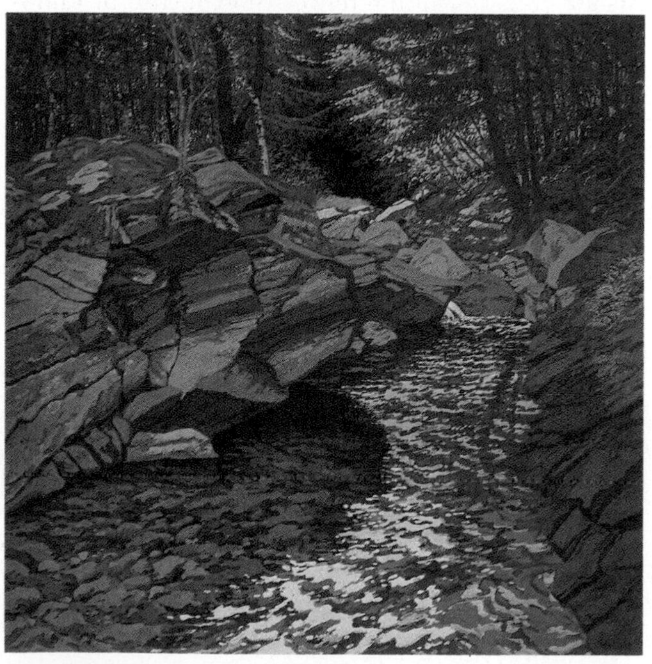

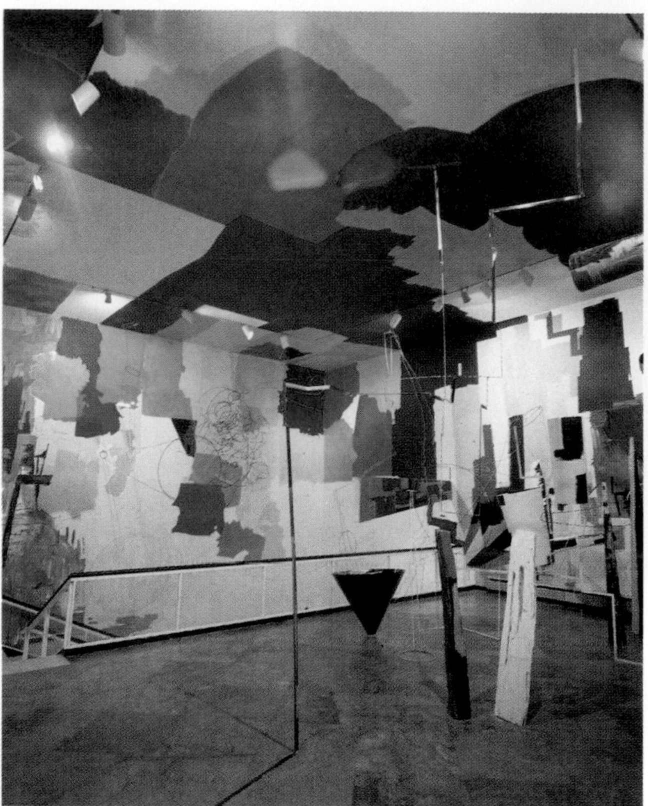

23-57 JUDY PFAFF, *Rock/Paper/Scissors*, September 24, 1982–January 9, 1983. Mixed media installation. Albright-Knox Art Gallery, Buffalo, New York.

*In unison, the players raise and lower their right hands rapidly three times; on the third "throw" each player forms their hands into one of three symbols—fist for "stone," flat-out for "paper," or with the first two fingers spread apart for "scissors." In the game, every symbol can conquer; every symbol also can be conquered, because paper covers rock, rock breaks scissors, and scissors cut paper. For each round of throwing, the player with the dominant hand-symbol wins. If all players form the same hand-symbol, the round is a tie.

by Pollock) is the variety and impact of the materials, shapes, and colors, a brilliant reflection of Pfaff's stated interest "in opening up the language of sculpture as far and as wide as I can, . . . in trying to include all the things that are permissible in painting but absent in sculpture." Installations like *Rock/Paper/Scissors* are planned to activate a certain space temporarily and to vanish at the end of the special occasion or exhibition that gave them birth. Even the works that Pfaff creates for specific museum collections occupy so much space that they are designed to be taken down and stored when the space is needed for other exhibitions. Each time a Pfaff work is in place, however, it provides the viewer with an exuberant and festive sight, like a modern-day descendent of a Matisse painting expanded to a scale that can enfold the viewer in its joyous midst.

Concepts about the relationship between representation and perception, especially the comprehension of space, underlie the photographic collages of DAVID HOCKNEY (b. 1937). Trained as a painter and printmaker in his native England, Hockney was briefly associated with a group of young British artists at the Royal College of Art in London who constituted the second generation of British Pop Art.* But he soon developed a distinctive style of his own, which evolved rapidly after he moved to Los Angeles in 1963, attracted by the extraordinary light, space, and culture there. His first photographs were personal snapshots. Then he used the camera to make studies for paintings. Eager to explore ways of extending the space in his photographs, he began scanning subjects with a Polaroid camera, assembling the series of prints he had made of different parts of a scene into one picture. He capitalized on his realization that "the most important thing that we feel and see—space—the camera cannot even record," noting that the camera "is good for recording surfaces." Hockney's technique of capturing the surface of every object within the space of his subject by moving the camera from side to side and top to bottom across that space creates an effective "map" of his subject that not only documents the position and appearance of the objects in the space but also includes all evidence of shifts in location or stance by the subject during the time it took the artist to complete his scanning of the scene. The figures in his scenes often move between exposures, so the final collages are records of several points in time, as well as several positions in space, and these works reflect the path of eye movement scanning the entire site. Feeling constrained by the grids created by the white borders of the Polaroid prints, Hockney acquired a 35mm camera and began making photomontages (called *joiners*) that reflected his increased interest in the kind of nonperspective space found in Chinese and Japanese scroll paintings. *The Grand Canyon Looking North, September 1982* (FIG. **23-58**) is a fan-shaped sweep of vision across that natural monument. The image cannot be taken in without moving the eyes; viewers must scan the details much as they would the actual canyon. Sometimes Hockney's prints join almost invisibly; sometimes differences in exposure or jumps

*Hockney did include a few subjects from popular culture in his early work (such as a box of Ty-Phoo tea) and was quickly included by British and American critics among the large group of artists collected under the title of Pop Art. However, throughout his career, Hockney's approach in all media has been so distinctive and original that he really belongs to no particular movement or style.

23-58 DAVID HOCKNEY, *The Grand Canyon Looking North, September 1982.* Photographic collage, 3′ 9″ × 8′ 3½″. © David Hockney, 1982.

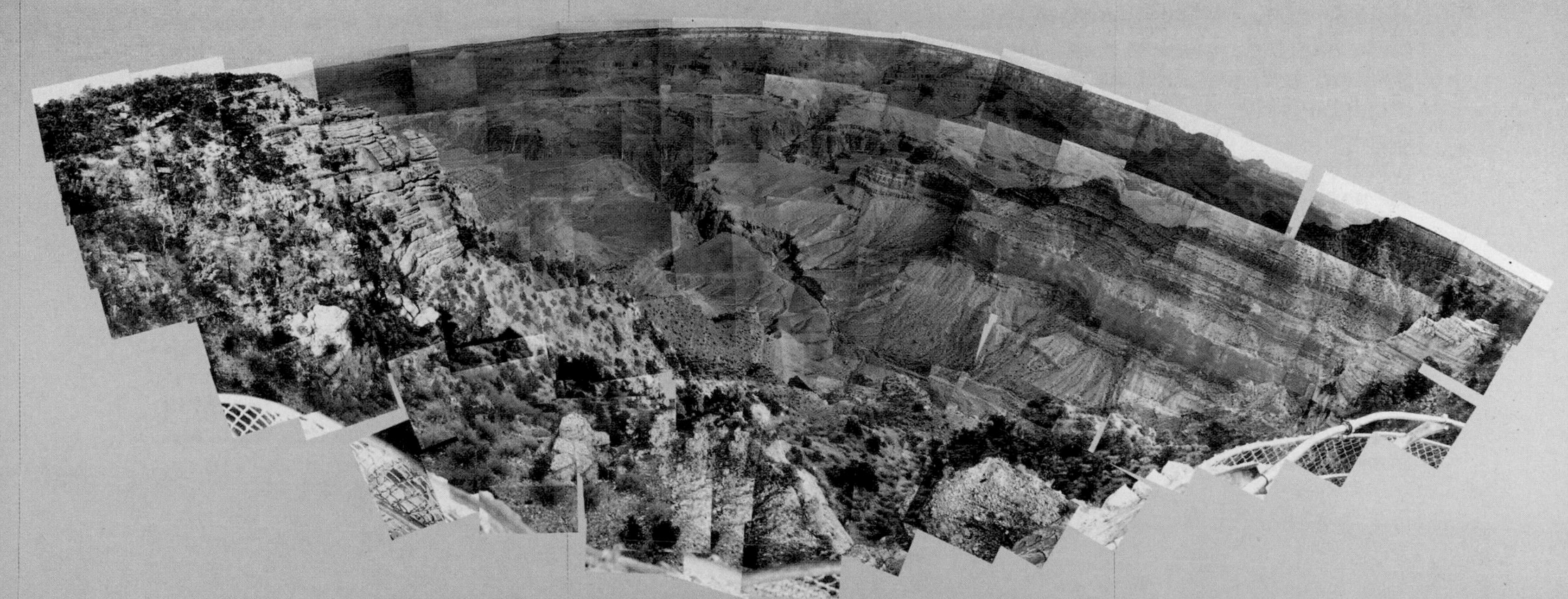

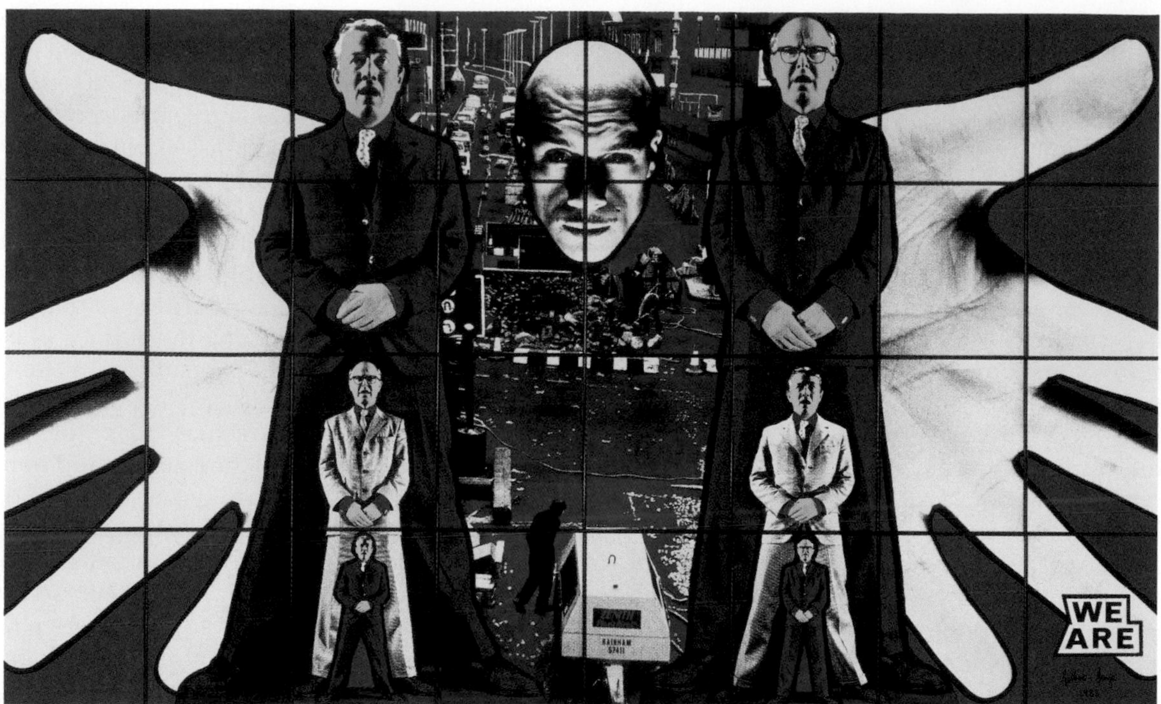

23-59 Gilbert and George, *We Are,* 1985. 7′ 10⅞″ × 6′ 7⅛″.

in detail emphasize the modular nature of the picture. Nevertheless, the artist manages in works like *The Grand Canyon* to emphasize the process of making the work at the same time that he makes us conscious of the motion that is a part of our natural process of observing the world around us.

Perhaps the boldest of all conceptual art is that produced by the British team of Gilbert and George (Gilbert, b. 1943 in Italy, and George, b. 1942 in England), who question every aspect of traditional art and assert that they are "living sculpture" and that their entire "proper English lives" together contribute to their art. Adopting the respectable, middle-class "uniform" of conservatively cut suits, shirts, and ties, Gilbert and George have given varied forms to the ongoing artwork of their lives together through postcard collages, stylized performances, autobiographical books, drawings, and, most recently, giant "sculpture" pieces in which collages of hand-colored photographs use a personal iconography to express the pair's response to their life in London's working-class East End and to their experiences with religion, sex, and the vision of the volatile connections between youthful vigor and the life of the urban poor in contemporary England. *We Are* (fig. **23-59**) is typical of their large-scale photo-sculptures, with the sculptors themselves standing frontally, in identical poses a short distance from one another, their legs spread apart and their hands clasped. Their forms are lit from each side, throwing a band of shadow down the middle of their faces. George wears glasses; Gilbert does not. The figures repeat three times, one pair above the other in increasing size with Gilbert and George changing sides at each stage. Each set fits neatly between the spread legs of the next largest to form two hieratic human columns that frame the central "window," in which we see a confused scene of road repair and an enigmatic disembodied head, lit from the bottom to create eerie highlights and shadows. Sprouting from the figure-columns like wings are a pair of giant hands with palms facing us and fingers spread wide. The clear, formal arrangement, the bold transparent colors, and the stiff black outlines and grid lines suggest devotional stained-glass windows, but the images convey a sense of ritual bestowed upon the whole messy range of everyday life, echoing the simple declarative words of the title—"We are."

Postmodernism and Deconstructionism

In response to the increasing loss of belief in the validity of traditional Eurocentric ideas about art, style, and society, conceptual art took a new turn in the late 1970s. Artists attempted to give fair consideration to art and values from all world cultures. Adopting the posture of analysis, they borrowed tools of theory and assessment from other fields (especially anthropology, sociology, political science, and psychology) and appropriated styles from older art and other cultures to create works that questioned every aspect of art-making, the operation of the art market, and the relationship between meaning in art and the society in which it was made.

In architecture, a variety of past and current styles were combined without the traditional attempts to make them cohere as a whole. This new eclecticism has swept aside the International Style and replaced it with elements borrowed from both "low" and "high" art. One of the most influential architects to use elements from vernacular (nonprofessional, popular) architecture in his designs is the American Robert Venturi (b. 1925). Venturi called for the incorporation into "high architecture" of varied "honky-tonk elements" from structures like Las Vegas casinos and the eateries, gas stations, and stores of commercial "strips" leading into and out of all big American cities. Seeing such structures as expressions of popular fantasy, Venturi has produced "collage" architectural works that reflect his ideas. At Vail, Colorado, he and his associates built a four-story vacation lodge (fig. **23-60**) whose exterior suggests a rustic mountain cabin, with some of the flavor of a chalet. Setting the building into a steep slope, Venturi reversed the traditional distribution pattern for the rooms in a dwelling. The private rooms here are on the two lower floors, while the public rooms occupy the two upper stories, taking advantage of the higher view. The fourth floor dramatically caps the design, in all its "complexity and contradiction," with a vaulted parlor, luminous with outdoor light from the lunette dormers and the sheen of cedar. The material throughout is wood (cedar siding and shingles, oak stairs, maple counters), all scrupulously handcrafted. The massive, peaked roof, pulled tightly down onto the exterior walls, contrasts with the large, lunette-shaped dormers. The free proportions, the asymmetries, and the almost random placement of features suggest an architectural montage based on inspiration from both "high" and "low" sources—Palladio, Art Nouveau, the "romantic" Finnish Internationalist architect Alvar Aalto, and Le Corbusier—that are widely separated in time and tone. Venturi's building is an expression of a self-conscious manner that deliberately looks away from any single tradition and forcefully sets itself against the rigorous consistency of the International Style.

23-60 Robert Venturi and Associates, Brant-Johnson house, Vail, Colorado, 1977.

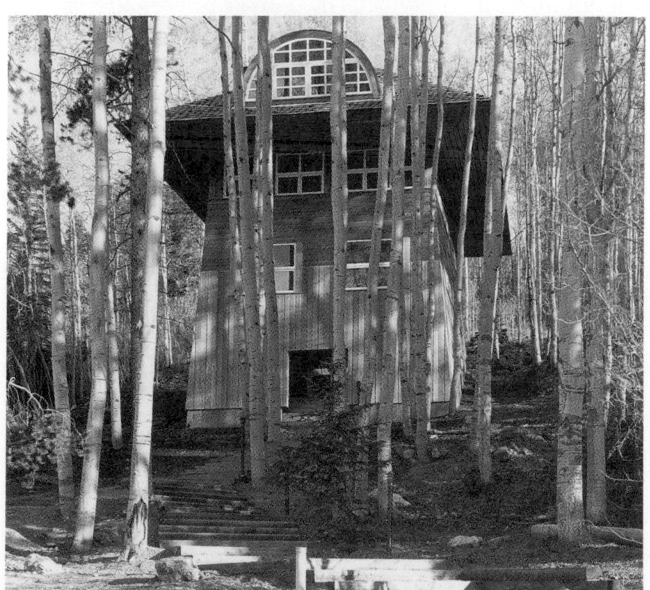

In Paris, the short-lived partnership of British architect Richard Rogers (b. 1933) and Italian architect Renzo Piano (b. 1937) resulted in the use of motifs and techniques from ordinary industrial buildings in the design for the Georges Pompidou National Center of Art and Culture, known popularly as the "Beaubourg" (fig. **23-61**). The anatomy of this six-level building, which opened in 1977, is fully exposed, rather like an updated version of the Crystal Palace (fig. 21-95). However, in the case of the Pompidou Center, the structure's "metabolism" is also visible. Pipes, ducts, tubes, and corridors are coded in color according to function (red for the movement of people; green, for water; blue, for air conditioning; yellow, for electricity), much as in a sophisticated factory. Critics who deplore the Beaubourg's vernacular qualities have pointed out that its exposed entrails require excessive maintenance to protect them from the elements and disparagingly refer to the complex as a "cultural supermarket." Nevertheless, the building has been popular with people since it opened. The flexible interior spaces and the colorful "archigraphic" revelation of the structural body provide a festive environment for the great crowds that flow through the building, enjoying its art galleries, industrial design center, library, science and music centers, conference rooms, research and archival facilities, movie theaters, rest areas, and restaurant (which looks down and through the building to the terraces outside). The sloping plaza in front of the main entrance has become part of the local scene. This "square" is filled with peddlers, street performers, Parisians, and tourists at almost all hours of the day and night. The kind of secular activity that once took place in the open spaces in front of cathedral entrances interestingly has shifted here to a center for culture and popular entertainment—perhaps the things shared now by the largest number of people. As a former director of the museum, K. G. Pontus-Hultén said: "If the hallowed, cult-like calm of the

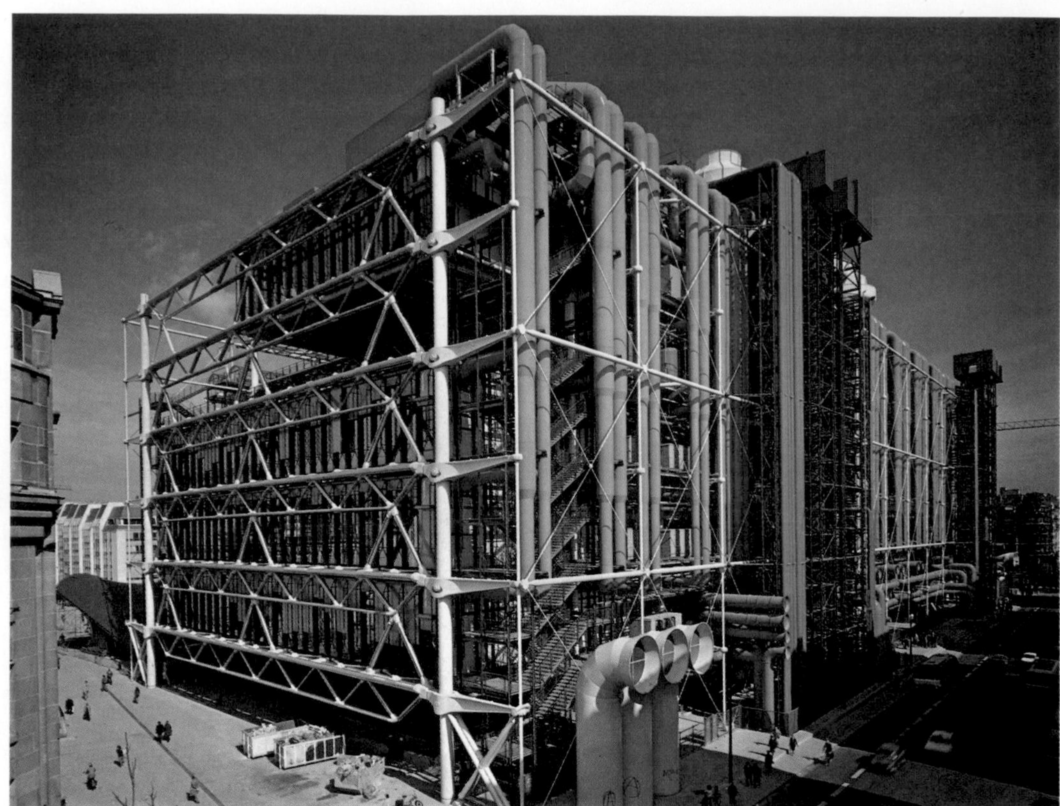

23-61 Richard Rogers and Renzo Piano, Georges Pompidou National Center of Art and Culture (the "Beaubourg"), Paris, 1977.

traditional museum has been lost, so much the better. . . . We are moving toward a society where art will play a great role, which is why this museum is open to disciplines that were once excluded by museums and which is why it is open to the largest possible public."*

The American architect John Portman (b. 1924) combined the look of the giant interior spaces of ancient Rome with the sleek luxurious appointments of modern corporate skyscrapers to invent a popular new kind of public building—a tower block built around a spacious central atrium. Such designs are part of the shifting focus in technological societies that is moving architects and their businessmen patrons away from a concentration on the efficiency of buildings and toward a special concern for the "humanization" of interior space to benefit the occupants. Portman's Peach Tree Plaza, Atlanta (fig. **23-62**) is a sumptuous example of the style initiated by the architect in his earlier design for the Atlanta Hyatt Regency Hotel to address what he saw as a diminishing supply of crucial public space in modern buildings: "Our approach has been to try to open things up and to let buildings breathe. . . . Within an

*K. G. Pontus-Hultén, *Architectural Record* (February 1978), p. 103.

23-62 John Portman, Peach Tree Plaza, Atlanta.

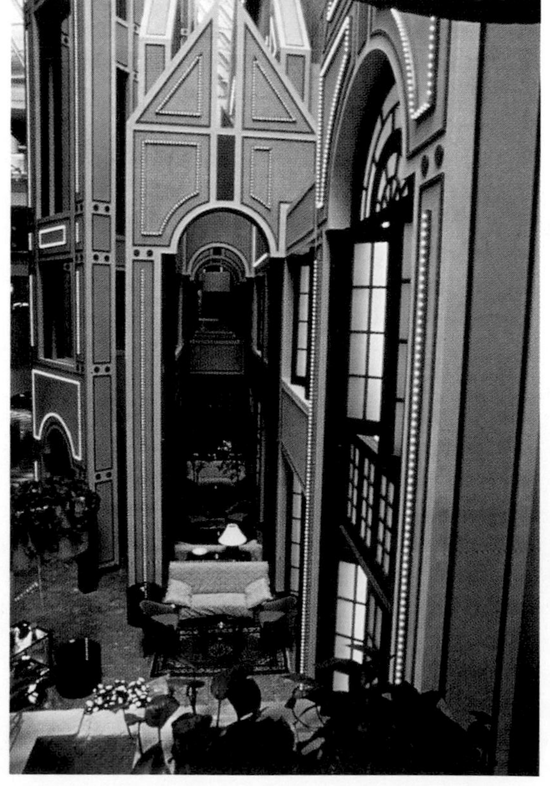

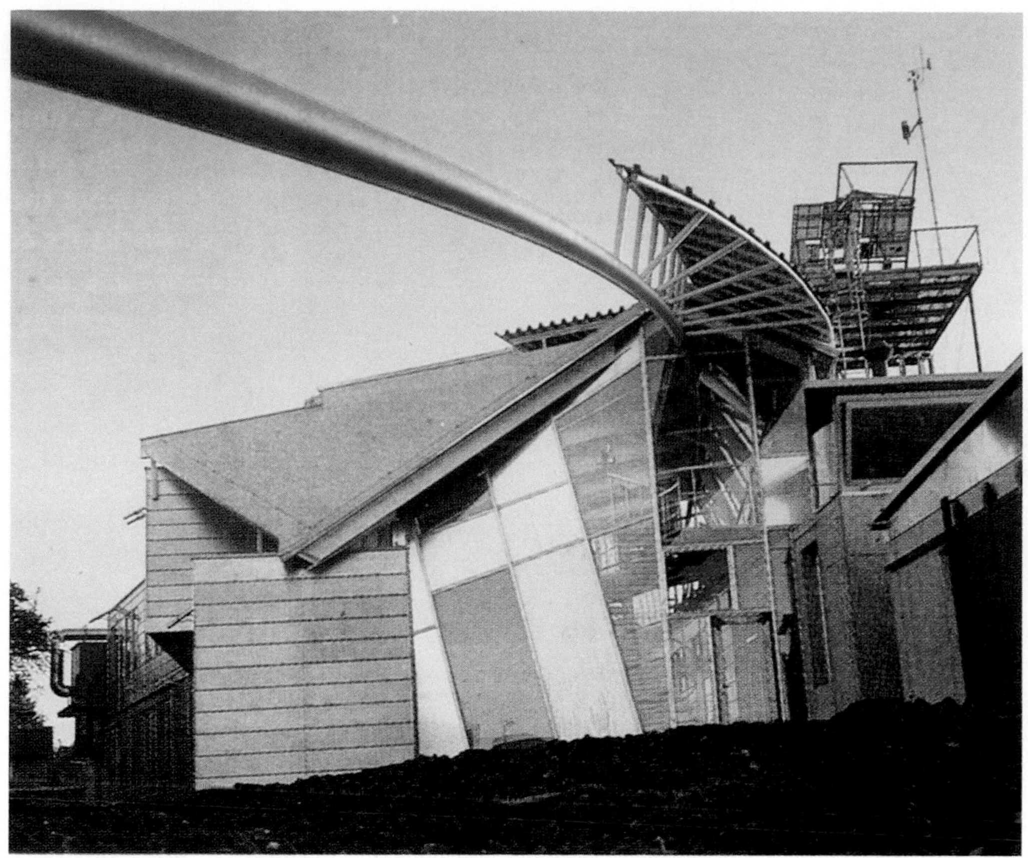

23-63 GÜNTER BEHNISCH, Hysolar Institute Building, University of Stuttgart, 1987.

urban setting, off the heavily trafficked area, we wanted to create the feeling of a resort."* Portman uses glass-sided elevator towers and corridors opening onto the atrium to allow all inhabitants of his hotels and shopping centers to feel part of the festive atmosphere created by the elegant details of carefully placed sculpture, kiosks, plants, and activity areas. The psychological effect is directed at the pleasure of the people using the space.

In the 1980s, a very different architectural approach from that of Postmodernism appeared in the work and writings of "Deconstructionist" architects who create works that challenge every aspect of accepted thought about the nature of building design and significance. Deconstructionism was originally developed as a mode of analytical thinking by the French philosopher Jacques Derrida to accommodate the present understanding of the universe as a constantly shifting state of being. Deconstructionists feel that the meaning assigned to any word or thing is always arbitrary—tied to cultural and social conditions that change constantly. Artists and architects inspired by Deconstructionism want to create works that confound all traditional expectations about architectural qualities. GÜNTER BEHNISCH (b. 1922) borrows nothing from the past for the design of his buildings. The walls of structures like his Hysolar Institute Building at the University of Stuttgart (FIG. **23-63**) no longer seem to enclose space; the arrangement of the parts appears as elusive as the space in one of Bell's sculptural environments (FIG. 23-44). The shapes of the Hysolar Institute's roof, walls, and windows seem to explode, avoiding any suggestion of clear, stable masses. There is not even a pastiche of vernacular or familiar forms appropriated from popular culture or earlier styles. Instead, Behnisch is aggressively playing with the whole concept of architecture and our relationship to it. The meaning of the building is dislocated by the building itself, and the viewer/inhabitant cannot avoid thinking about the nature of architecture and of building.

Typical of Postmodernism in painting is the work of MARK TANSEY (b. 1949), who took as his subject the role of mass media in the art world. Drawing fully on the resources of photographic reproductions, especially those in newspapers and magazines, and adopting the sepias and grey-greens of rotogravure pictures in the Sunday newspaper supplements early in the century, Tansey's works assemble unlikely

*In Barbara Lee Diamonstein, *American Architecture Now* (New York: Rizzoli, 1980), p. 213.

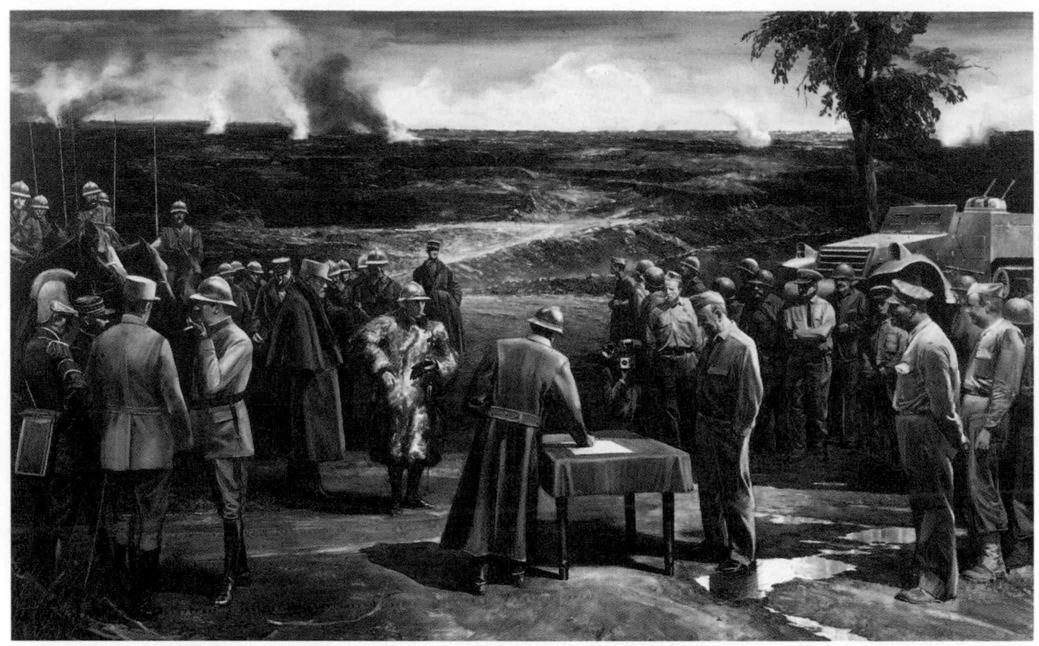

23-64 MARK TANSEY, *Triumph of the New York School,* 1984. 6′ 2″ × 10′.
Collection of the Whitney Museum of American Art (promised gift of Robert M. Kaye).

gatherings of references to art world persons, things, times, places, and events. These are paintings for insiders who know the history of art and the people who have made it. *Triumph of the New York School* (FIG. **23-64**) depicts, as an allegory, the historical shift of the artistic fulcrum from Paris to New York after 1945. The passing of power is dramatized here as a surrender of the French army (on the left), clad in the uniforms of World War I, to the American army (on the right), dressed in the garb of a World War II fighting unit, replete with motorized armor. The landscape is populated with recognizable portraits of the main artists and critics involved. Among the French are Pablo Picasso, Henri Matisse, the French poet and critic Guillaume Apollinaire, and the Surrealist poet and theoretician André Breton. Among the Americans are key figures of the New York school: Jackson Pollock, the painter Robert Motherwell, and the critics Clement Greenberg and Harold Rosenberg. The elegant dandyism of the French troops and the firm ground on which they stand are metaphors for the Abstract Formalism that continued to flourish in Paris. The slouchiness of the GIs and the puddles beneath their feet represent the drip and splatter techniques of Action Painting and the workingman's esthetic affected by many Abstract Expressionists in the style of their daily life. The composition of this modern "surrender" echoes that of a well-known masterpiece by Velázquez, *The Surrender of Breda* (*The Lances*), but that source is cancelled by the twentieth-century uniforms and the modern armor. The kneeling news photographer symbolizes the vast amount of attention paid to all events in the art world today and also lends a note of "authenticity" to this allegory of a formalized single gathering as a metaphor for a transfer of power that occurred in a much more general manner.

Tansey's *Triumph of the New York School* can be considered the picture of an event staged to express an idea; as a "performance," it falls within the tradition of Performance Art practiced by the Zurich Dadaists, some of the Surrealists, and various other modern and contemporary artists. Postmodernist sculpture and Performance Art have found their most striking expression in the recent works of LAURIE ANDERSON (b. 1947), who has borrowed styles from all kinds of popular performing arts, from cabaret through rock music to cinema and television. Her high-energy and high-tech art incorporates the power of master storytelling into a style built on the modern audience's ability to absorb fast-paced, multilayered visual and oral fragments. Anderson trained initially as a sculptor and supported herself by teaching art history, illustrating children's books, and writing art criticism, before turning full-time to Performance Art. With a strong interest in the potency of words and in the symbols of visual communication, Anderson studied both the hand gestures (*mudras*) of Indian culture and the sign language of the deaf. As her style evolved toward her tour de force performance works, she mastered all kinds of technological media, including electronic musical instruments, photo projection,

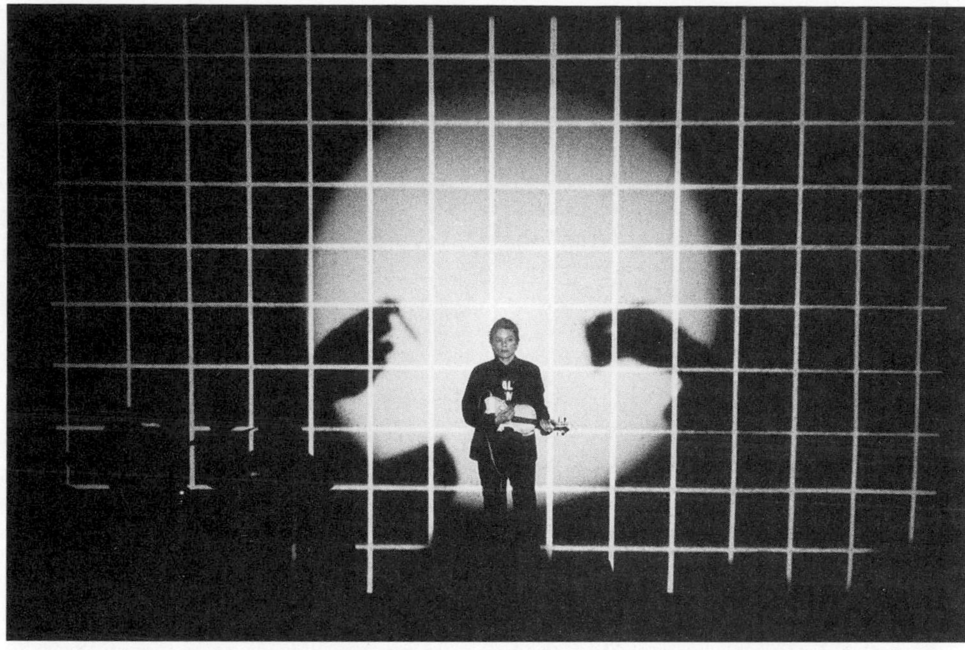

23-65 LAURIE ANDERSON, *United States Part II,* presented by the Kitchen at the Orpheum Theater, New York, 1980. Performance Art.

manipulated video, and devices that altered the timber of her voice. Along the way, she has invented special instruments (many of which are variations on her ever-present violin) that incorporate tape players with which she accompanies herself in multilayered ways. Her four-part piece *United States* was part grand opera, part multimedia avant-garde performance, and part popular art-rock concert. Each section had a motif—Transportation, Politics, Money, Love. *United States Part II* (FIG. **23-65**), the Politics section, used recurrent Anderson visual themes like the grid, magnified shadow hands, and the artist herself (dressed in a black jacket and pants and using a white violin) in a performance that included a dense collage of sounds, projected words, and spoken narrative to suggest ideas connected with the political realities in today's world. Performed first in the Orpheum Theater in New York City, rather than in the alternative spaces used by Happenings and other avant-garde Performance Art pieces, *United States II* appealed to an audience that crossed the lines between fans of popular music and the elite art audience. Anderson's piece was influenced by Philip Glass's Minimalist opera *Einstein on the Beach,* the element of shock in Dada performance, the quality of dislocating dream in Dali's and Buñuel's *Un Chien Andalou* (FIG. 22-35), and the high-technology fantasy of some Bauhaus theater. (An early Anderson piece re-created one of the most well-known Bauhaus works, *Sharkey's Day* by Oskar Schlemmer.) But *United States* also made hypnotic use of the clichés of ordinary speech, autobiographical memories, and invented fragments of allegory and ritual. Anderson's costume was deliberately androgynous; her "vocoder" transformed her voice into eight variations ranging from that of a young girl to that of an impersonal male authority figure. To the audience, seeing *United States* was like existing in a combination of past and present, fact and fantasy, the most personal reminiscences and mass-media messages. At any moment, many things happened simultaneously, not in layers as in Paik's *Global Groove* or Kaprow's *Spring Happening,* but as a collection of clear parts, each claiming attention, while Anderson was always at the center as "ringmaster," star performer, and teller of fables about modern life.

ART WITH SOCIAL AND POLITICAL CONCERNS

The increased interest in art of all cultures and times in the contemporary period led many artists to a new awareness of the power of art's role and to a belief that the artist has a responsibility to wield this power with great care. Understanding that all art is shaped to some extent by the beliefs of the artist and the culture in which it is made, some artists with political and social concerns, working in a variety of media, used their art self-consciously to share perceptions about inequities in the lives of the poor, the elderly, blacks, and women, or the effect on life of the operations of big business, government, and the military. Less strident in tone than the admonitory voice of these activist artists was the art of another group—Earth and Site artists—whose works were aimed at helping human beings return to a sense of oneness with nature and other human beings. This group created works, usually outdoors, that involved the viewer imaginatively or literally in interaction with the pieces.

Activist Art

Even in the troubled period since World War II, certain artists have retained a faith that art can teach, modify behavior, and help motivate people to create a more fully human world. The works of some of these artists give voice and visibility to parts of society hitherto less valued by the mainstream. The works of others deal with the effects of political forces. All of these artists bring to their work a contemporary version of the Enlightenment belief that art has the power and obligation to change hearts, minds, and society.

Cinema remains one of the most powerful mediums for vivid presentation of the lives of others. In Italy, Neo-Realists like Vittorio de Sica (1902–1974) created a new form of feature film, applying a documentary style to stories based on the everyday life of poor people in postwar Italy. In the 1940s, De Sica abandoned a career as a popular matinee idol and director of comedies to work with the screenwriter and theoretician Cesare Zavattini (b. 1902) on a new kind of Italian film that abandoned artificial, contrived plots and the "falseness" of professional acting for stories based on the authentic problems of the urban poor in postwar Italy. These movies were filmed on location with performances by people who were not professional actors. *Bicycle Thieves* or *The Bicycle Thief* (*Ladri di biciclette*, FIG. **23-66**) was the second film by De Sica and Zavattini and a Neo-Realist masterpiece. In a time when unemployment in Italy was over 20 percent, the movie tells the story of an out-of-work family man in Rome who gets a job posting bills but must pawn the family's sheets to buy the bicycle he needs to do the work. Almost immediately, the bicycle is stolen, and the film follows the fruitless search for the stolen vehicle undertaken by the man and his small son. Toward the end of the movie, desperation drives the man to attempt to steal a bicycle himself, but he is caught in the act. Despite the filmmakers' dedication to realism, as many details of the film as possible were planned in advance. To put his actors at ease and to get them ready for their parts, De Sica spent a lot of time with them before shooting started. No part of the film's action was left to chance. Even the theft of the workingman's bicycle was timed so the thief could escape through green traffic lights while six hidden cameras recorded the sequence. *The Bicycle Thief* touched audiences as being more authentic and true to life than anything they had seen before. Even today the film touches audiences with its poignant depiction of the relationship between a father and his son and its vision of individual human isolation and helplessness in a brutal, impersonal urban environment.

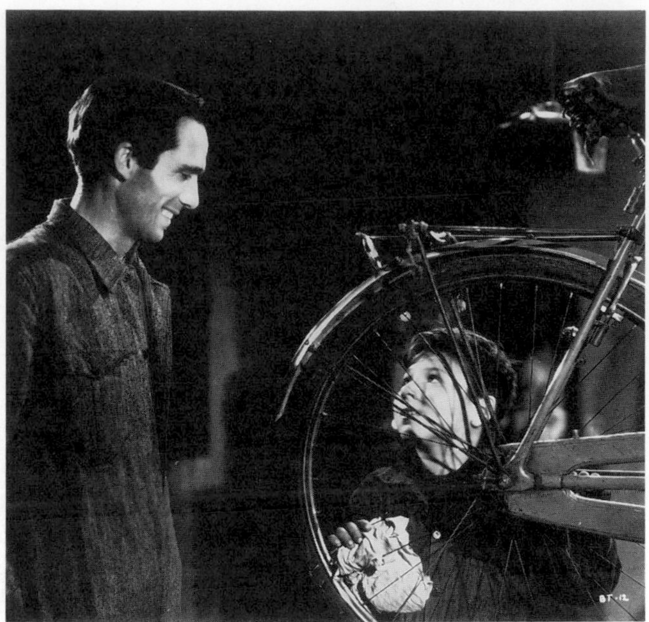

23-66 Vittorio de Sica, film still from *Bicycle Thieves*, 1948.

A somewhat similar vision of the life of ordinary people in America was captured in photographs taken on a cross-continental trip in 1955–1956 by the Swiss-born American artist Robert Frank (b. 1924). Working with a lightweight 35mm camera and an unerring eye for the pervasive and uneasy edginess of much of modern life, Frank took over thirty-eight thousand photographs on his journey. The eighty-three he selected for publication in his book *The Americans*, among them *Trolley, New Orleans* (FIG. **23-67**), provide sometimes uncomfortable glimpses into everyday life in America. An occasional locale was depicted emptied of its human inhabitants, but even when groups of people were present, as on the New Orleans trolley car, Frank captured the sense of alienated loneliness in the most ordinary activity. These images have an informal, almost haphazard style very different from that of Cartier-Bresson's "decisive moments" (FIG. 22-74), yet each of Frank's pictures contains a slice of life. Taken as a whole in the book, they present a loose narrative about life in America, paralleling the 1950s spirit of the book *On the Road* by the "beat" poet-writer Jack Kerouac, who also wrote the introduction for the English language edition of *The Americans*.

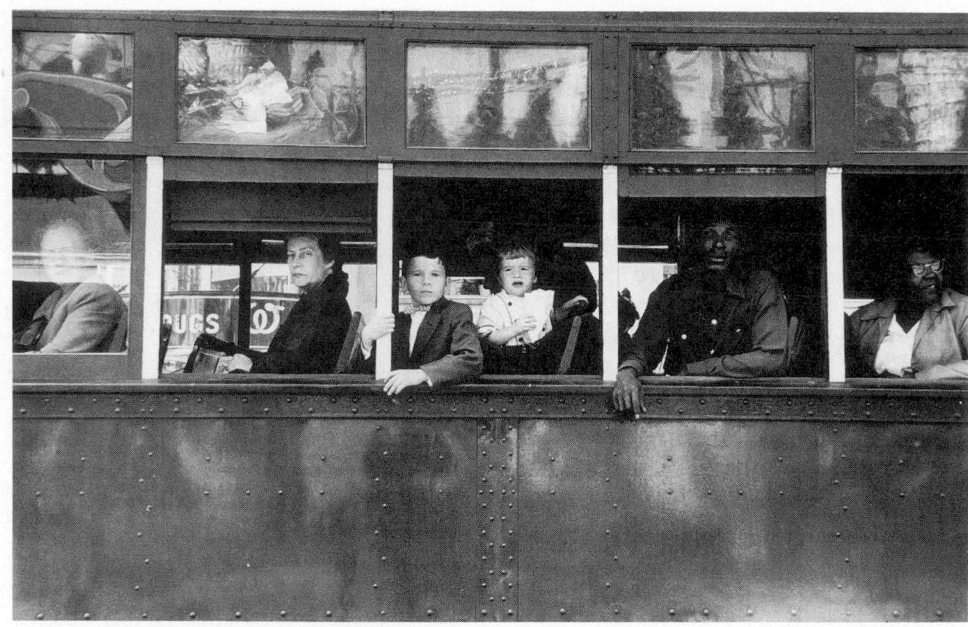

23-67 ROBERT FRANK, *Trolley, New Orleans,* 1955–1956. Gelatin silver print, 9″ × 13″. © Robert Frank, courtesy Pace/MacGill Gallery, New York.

More accusatory in tone than Frank's photographs were the "tableaus" created by the American sculptor EDWARD KIENHOLZ (b. 1927) to express the empathy and distress he felt at witnessing the pathos and dignity in the lives of ordinary people. Pieces like *The Wait* (FIG. **23-68**) dramatically confronted gallery visitors with uncomfortable scenes from the lives of people living on the fringes of society. *The Wait* shows an old woman sitting alone in a room filled with mementos of her earlier life. For this work, as for all his tableaus, Kienholz haunted junk shops and rummage sales to assemble the actual objects he used here to create the room—the woman's clothing, her sampler, the sewing basket, the framed family photographs, the wallpaper, the furniture, and the taxidermist-stuffed cat. The emotional effect of the tableau is intensified by the fact that the emaciation of old age is suggested by the large animal bones that serve as the woman's arms and legs, and by the distressing fact that close examination reveals her head to be an animal's skull within a bell jar that bears on its front surface a portrait taken of her on her wedding day.

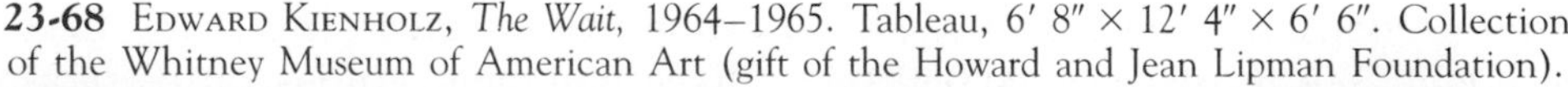

23-68 EDWARD KIENHOLZ, *The Wait,* 1964–1965. Tableau, 6′ 8″ × 12′ 4″ × 6′ 6″. Collection of the Whitney Museum of American Art (gift of the Howard and Jean Lipman Foundation).

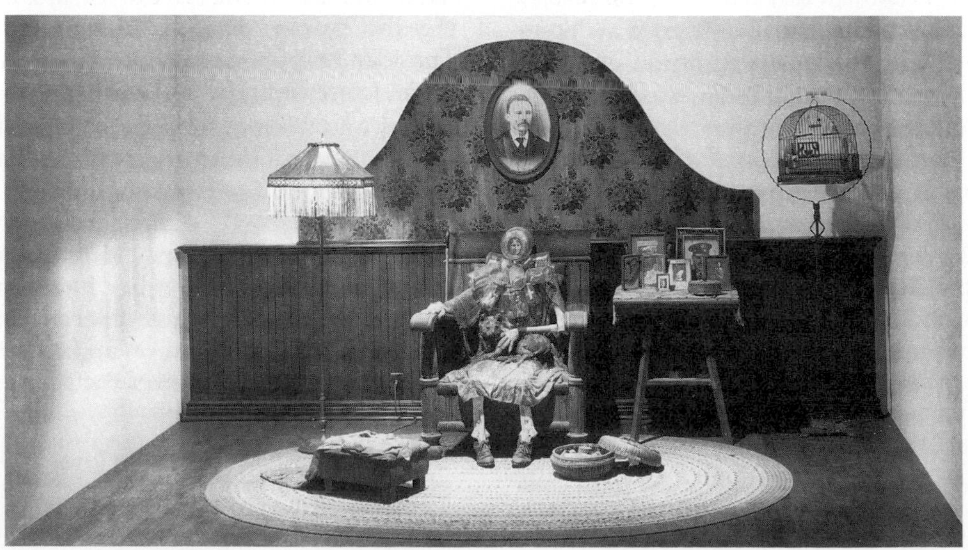

The way in which real objects blend with the layers of their possible meanings gives Kienholz's tableau the immediacy of the present moment combined with the resonance of remembered dreams or nightmares. The combined objects act to distill within this fragment of a room a situation familiar to us all, but one that we usually try to ignore, as the artist himself has noted: "The ongoing theme of my work is probably death—and how it is not used as energy by society. It's hidden and repressed, it's not talked about . . . but it's the motivation that we call upon to be successful. It's the fear of death that pushes everyone along. Immortality and fame versus ordinary, mortal, human, clay selves."* It is this resonance that makes the narrative in Kienholz's tableaus so powerfully moving and so unforgettable.

Racial injustice has been the central theme of the mural paintings of artist WILLIAM WALKER (b. 1927), who was one of the first Americans to emulate the political and cultural murals painted in the 1920s and 1930s by Orozco (FIG. 22-82) and other Mexican artists. Stimulated by the black power movement, the new mural movement began in 1967, when Walker and a group of other African-American artists filled one wall of a deserted two-story Chicago building with a montage painting (called the *Wall of Respect*) on the theme of the accomplishments of black leaders in all fields, aiming the content of the work toward the people who lived in the surrounding neighborhood. A painted label on the *Wall of Respect* read: "This Wall was created to Honor our Black Heroes, and to Beautify our Community." Unfortunately, much of the mural disappeared in urban renewal a short time after its completion, although some panels were rescued and installed at a new location at Malcolm X College in Chicago. The idea of a new "art for the people," however, inspired a public mural movement that spread throughout the United States, Europe, and Central and South America. Whether painted on the walls by teams of untrained workers from the neighborhood under the direction of a professional artist, or created by a single artist with the backing of local citizens, these murals were intended to instill pride in local people about their culture and heritage. Walker's *Peace and Salvation, Wall of Understanding* (FIG. **23-69**) recalls the visual chaos of a Dada montage (FIG. 22-28), with abrupt jumps in scale, space, and subject. However, the images in Walker's work have none of the ambiguity of a Dada piece. Gun battles between local gangs and between residents and white policemen are depicted on the wall, as are marchers for peace (at the bottom) and a multiracial group standing on a globe of the world within the sleeve of a black arm and hand (at the top). Walker used his art to further understanding between individuals. In 1971, he wrote: "People are now realizing that public art is essential because it is relevant to each of them. Art is a universal language, destroying the barriers that stand so firm before man."† The idea of public mural art has been picked up in other communities by African-Americans, Asian-Americans, Latinos, and other groups who feel such art can help to affirm their cultural heritage.

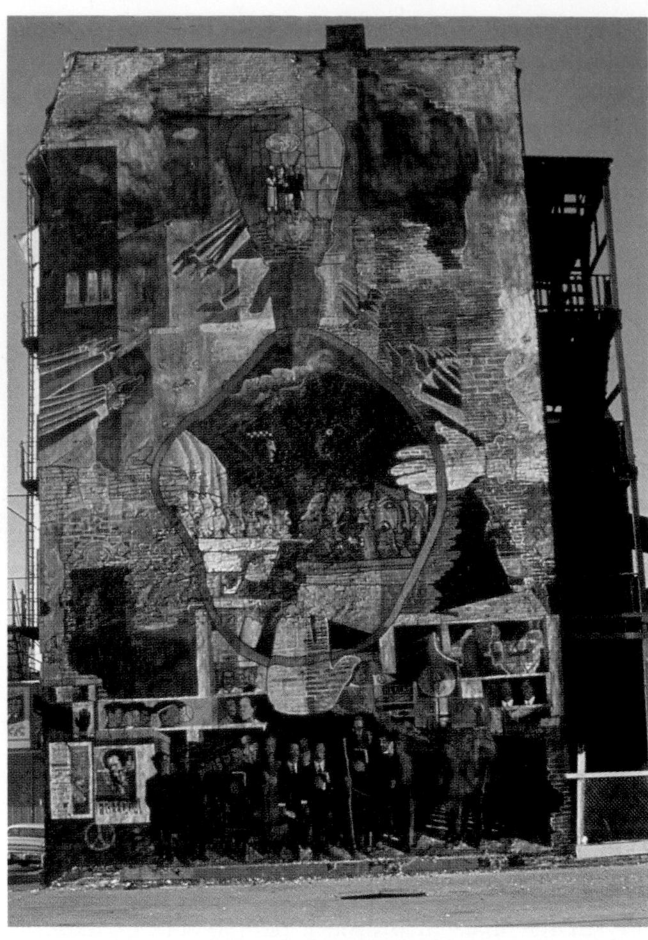

23-69 WILLIAM WALKER, *Peace and Salvation, Wall of Understanding,* 1970. Wall mural on four-story building at Locust and Orleans Streets, Chicago.

"Private" art also has been affected by the new social consciousness. American artist BETTYE SAAR (b. 1926) creates personal works that draw on imagery and symbols from her heritage as an African-American and as a woman. Her pieces are small, and many of them are based on an intuitive personal iconography. Hers is an art of the found object, initially

*In Ruth Askey, "Ed Kienholz—Still a Humorist and Social Commentator," *Artweek* (May 14, 1977), p. 1.

†In Eva Cockcroft, John Weber, and James Cockcroft, *Toward a People's Art: The Contemporary Mural Movement* (New York: E. P. Dutton, 1977), p. 71.

inspired by the boxes of Joseph Cornell (FIG. 22-39). Saar continually scours junk stalls, antique markets, and jumble sales for objects that hold meaning for her. Her assemblages combine objects whose significance she recognizes instantly with other items whose attraction for her is more deeply hidden. The assassination of African-American leader Dr. Martin Luther King, Jr. in 1968 inspired Saar to create several series of assemblages dealing with the stereotypes developed by white society to characterize African-Americans. These assemblages were expressions of Saar's anger at the injustices continually faced by African-Americans. Into the works the artist built dolls, artifacts, news stories on lynchings, and historical newspaper notices offering African-Americans for sale that featured poignant phrases like "four children sold separately." One of her earliest series on this theme is *The Liberation of Aunt Jemima,* in which Saar presents the image of the faithful, smiling black woman—but with a savage twist: the introduction of rebellion in her daily household routine. In our 1972 example (FIG. **23-70**), *Aunt Jemima* is a stereotypically plump, grinning black doll-woman, dressed in a polka-dotted dress, kerchief, and turban. The wall behind her is papered with rows of the familiar beaming face from the label of the pancake mix, and the doll's apron has been replaced by a found illustration of a smiling black servant holding a white child. Flanking this image, the doll figure holds a broom in one hand and a rifle in the other. The work is an unforgettable icon, intended to raise viewer consciousness about the history and destructive power of such stereotypes in American society.

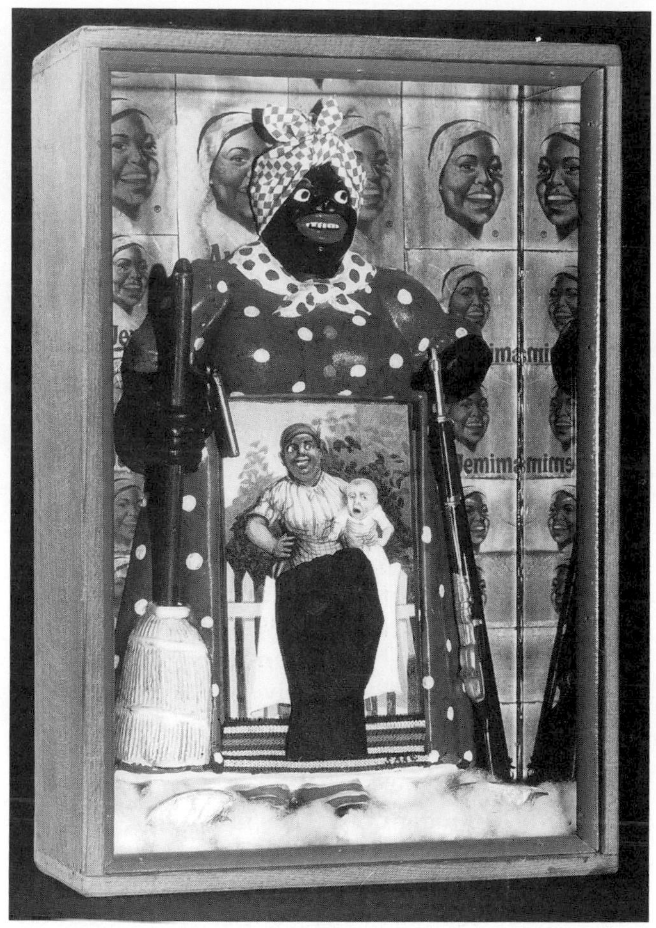

23-70 BETTYE SAAR, *The Liberation of Aunt Jemima,* 1972. Mixed media, $11\frac{3}{4}'' \times 8'' \times 2\frac{3}{4}''$. University Art Museum, University of California at Berkeley (purchased with the aid of funds from the National Endowment for the Arts and selected by the Committee for the Acquisition of Afro-American Art).

In the 1970s, the feminist movement focused the attention of women on their history and their place in society. In art, the feminist movement was given shape by two women—Judy Chicago and Miriam Schapiro—under the auspices of the Feminist Art Program, which they founded at the California Institute of the Arts in Valencia, California. As part of this program, teachers and students joined to create projects like *Womanhouse,* for which they completely converted an abandoned house in Los Angeles in 1972 into a suite of "environments," each based on a different aspect of women's lives and fantasies.

23-71 JUDY CHICAGO, *The Dinner Party,* 1979. Multimedia, 48′ × 48′ × 48′ installed. © Judy Chicago, 1979.

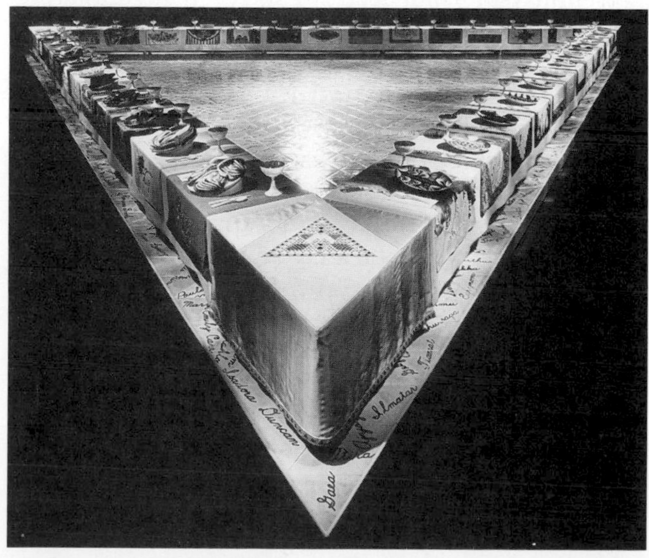

In her own work, JUDY CHICAGO (born Judy Cohen in 1939) wanted to educate viewers about women's role in history and the fine arts. Inspired early in her career by the work of Hepworth (FIG. 22-51), O'Keeffe (FIG. 22-65), and Nevelson (FIG. 23-11), Chicago developed a personal painting style that consciously included abstract floral vaginal images. In the early 1970s, Chicago became interested in the expressive possibilities of china painting, and she began planning an ambitious piece, *The Dinner Party* (FIG. **23-71**),

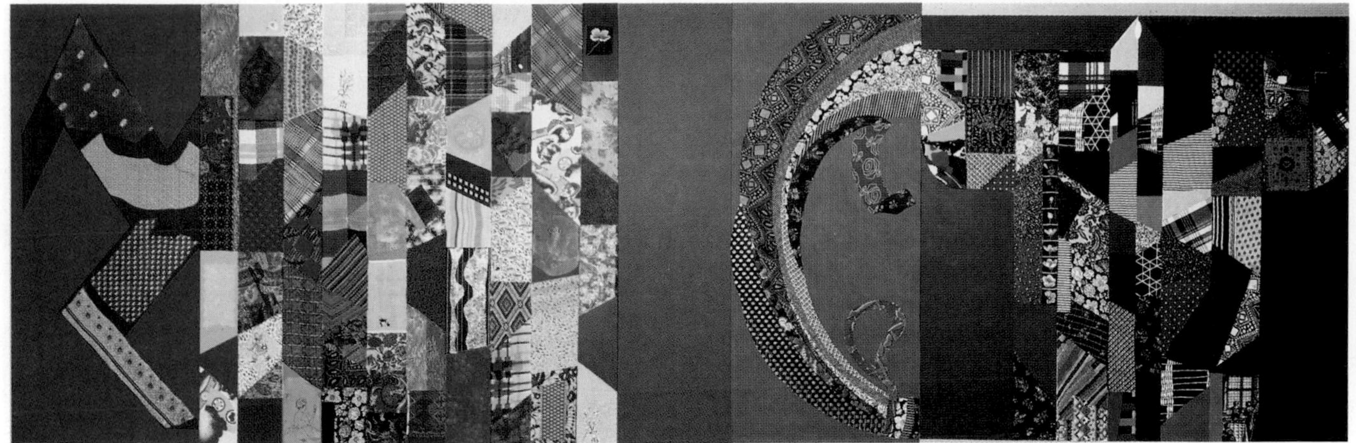

23-72 MIRIAM SCHAPIRO, *Anatomy of a Kimono* (section), 1976. Fabric and acrylic on canvas, 6′ 8″ × 11′ 11″. Collection of Bruno Bishofberger, Zurich.

which used "crafts" techniques traditionally practiced by women (china painting and stitchery) to depict the roles played by women throughout history. The work was originally conceived as a feminist "Last Supper" attended by thirteen women (the "honored guests"), in a selection embodying both the positive and negative meanings associated with the number thirteen (the number of persons present at the Christian Last Supper and the number of witches in a coven). Research uncovered so many worthy women that Chicago expanded the number of guests threefold to thirty-nine and placed them around a triangular table 48 feet long on a side that symbolizes both the traditional sign for woman and for the "Goddess." The piece's assembly was carried out by a team of workers under Chicago's supervision and to her designs. The *Dinner Party* table rests on a white tile floor inscribed with the names of 999 additional "women of achievement" to signify that the accomplishments of the thirty-nine honored guests rest on a foundation laid by other women. Among the "invited" women at the table are Georgia O'Keeffe, the Egyptian Pharaoh Hatshepsut, the British writer Virginia Woolf, the Native American guide Sacajawea, and the American suffragist Susan B. Anthony. Each guest was given a place setting with identical eating utensils and goblet. All of the guests also have an individual, oversized, porcelain plate bearing a stylized butterfly design and a long place mat or table runner filled with symbols that reflect significant facts about their lives. The plates range from simple concave shapes with china-painted designs to dishes from which sculptured three-dimensional designs almost seem to be trying to fly away. Each table runner is worked with a combination of traditional needlework techniques, including needlepoint, embroidery, crochet, French knots, and appliqué. The rigorous arrangement of *The Dinner Party* and its sacramental qualities draw visitors in and let them experience the importance of forgotten details in the history of women.*

Pursuing a somewhat different path than that undertaken by Chicago, MIRIAM SCHAPIRO (b. 1923) tries in her work to rouse her viewers to a new appreciation of the beauty in humble materials and techniques used by women artists/craftspersons throughout history. Schapiro was in the midst of a thriving career as a Hard-Edge Abstract Formalist painter when she moved to California, co-founded the Feminist Art Program, and became fascinated with the hidden metaphors for womanhood she now saw in her Abstract Formalist paintings. Intrigued by the materials she had used to create a doll's house for her part in *Womanhouse,* Schapiro began to make huge sewn collages (called *femmages*), which she assembled from fabrics, quilts, buttons, sequins, lace trim, and rickrack collected at antique shows and fairs. *Anatomy of a Kimono* (FIG. **23-72**) is one of a series of monumental femmages based on the patterns of Japanese kimonos, fans, and robes. This vast composition repeats the kimono shape in a sumptuous array of fabric fragments. Schapiro is not alone in finding magic in pattern, and her femmages were part of a movement in the 1970s called "Pattern and Decoration Painting," because its members were dedicated to making decorative pattern the content of their works. However, Schapiro's femmages are not solely formalist abstractions, as are many other Pattern and Decoration works; instead, her materials carry references to the whole history of women's crafts and needlework,

*Judy Chicago formed the nonprofit Through the Flower Corporation to take charge of sending *The Dinner Party* on tour to many locations around the United States, of storing it at tour's end, and of publishing a book containing the biographical details of the women included in the piece.

and call attention to the often complex abstract compositions in handwork hitherto considered beyond the arena of fine art. Viewing her works encourages observers to rethink traditional ideas about media, subject matter, and the artistic energies of women.

Creating a broader social awareness, often with a feminist twist, is the goal of the American artist BARBARA KRUGER (b. 1945), whose best-known subject has been the manipulation of attitudes by modern mass media. Kruger's serious art career began with fiber sculpture inspired by the works of Abakanowicz (FIG. 23-30), but she soon began creating pieces that drew on her early training and work as a graphic designer for the magazine *Mademoiselle*. Mature works, like *Untitled* (*Your Gaze Hits the Side of My Face*, FIG. **23-73**), play with media layout techniques used in the mass media to sell consumer goods. But Kruger's huge word-and-photograph collages (often 4 by 6 feet in size) express the cultural attitudes embedded in commercial advertising. In *Untitled* (*Your Gaze Hits the Side of My Face*), she has targeted feminist concerns by overlaying a ready-made photograph of the head of a classically beautiful female sculpture with a vertical row of text composed of seven words selected by the artist. The words are isolated into bold, black-and-white rectangles. They cannot be taken in with a single glance. Reading them is a staccato exercise, with an overlaid cumulative quality that delays understanding and intensifies the meaning (rather like reading one of the old Burma Shave series of roadside signs from a speeding car). The message in Kruger's piece reflects the interest of contemporary feminist theorists in the way that much of Western art has been constructed to present female beauty for the enjoyment of a "male gaze." Although many of Kruger's pieces deal with feminist concerns, she also has tackled attitudes of political and economic power. One of her best-known works in this mode calls attention ironically to the marketplace economy of the modern art world. A detail of the eyes, nose, and mouth of a Howdy-Doody puppet is overlaid with three bands of words: "when I hear the word," "culture," "I take out my checkbook." As in each of Kruger's works, viewers here can read multiple meanings into the image, drawing on their own experience, but her art forces nearly everyone into some consideration of how our attitudes are molded by the bombardment of mass media that surrounds us daily.

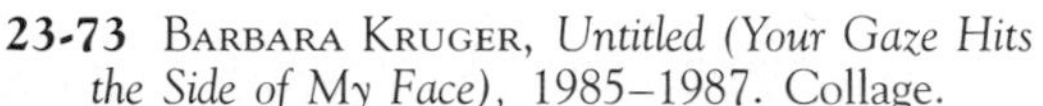

23-73 BARBARA KRUGER, *Untitled (Your Gaze Hits the Side of My Face)*, 1985–1987. Collage.

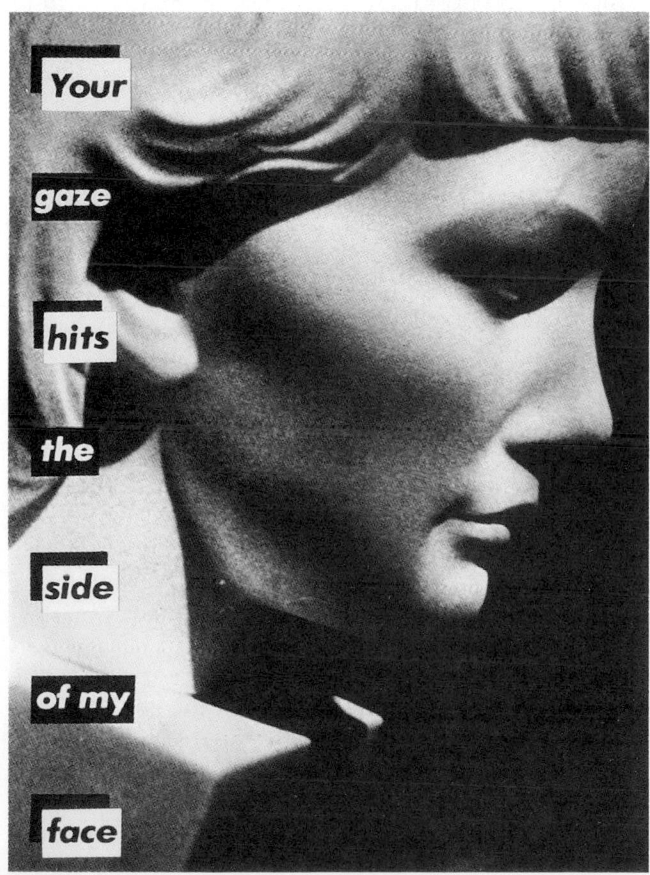

The social and political concerns of the German artist JOSEPH BEUYS (1921–1986) were directed at the whole condition of modern human beings, especially those in Western developed nations. Beuys strongly believed that the spiritual nature of humans is expressed through creativity and ability, in vigorous opposition to the negative forces of what he called "the principle of Auschwitz." After narrowly escaping death as a Nazi pilot shot down in a remote part of the Crimea, Beuys dedicated himself to working for the future of humanity. First, he studied natural science but left that field to take up sculpture. He wanted to make a new kind of sculptural object that would include "Thinking Forms: how we mould our thoughts . . . Spoken Forms: how we shape our thoughts into words . . . [and] Social Sculpture: how we mould and shape the world in which we live." Believing that all art belongs to the same sphere of human activity, no matter what medium the creator uses, Beuys accepted sculptors, musicians, and writers into his classes at the Düsseldorf Art Academy. Beuys's objects and installations seem to be connected with mysterious rites. Charismatic in person, he also created one-person performances in which his stylized actions evoked a sense of mystery, profound human meaning, and sacred ritual. *Iphigenia/Titus Andronicus* (FIG. **23-74**) was developed from an invitation to create modern performances of two historic theatrical masterpieces—Goethe's *Iphigenia* and Shakespeare's *Titus Andronicus*. Beuys contrived a

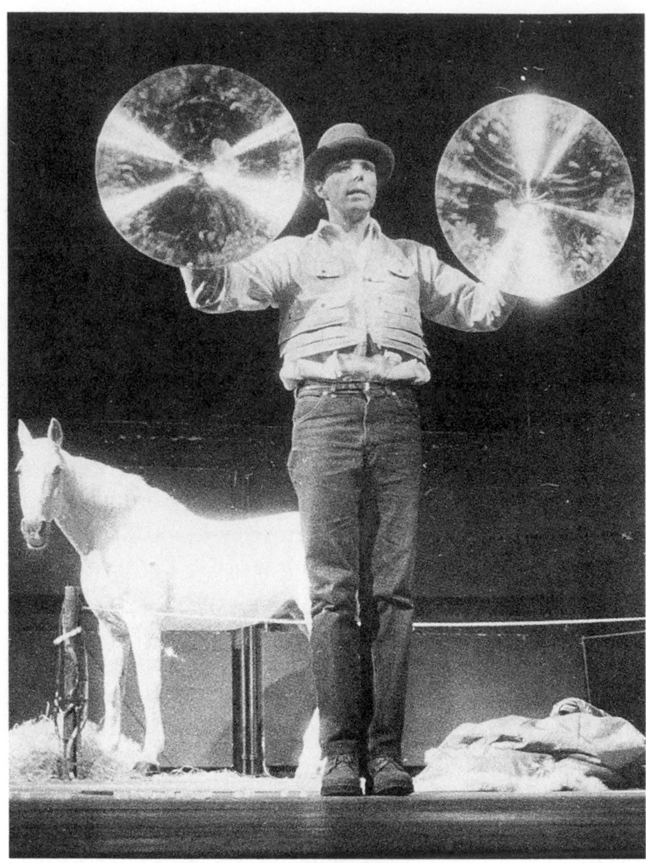

23-74 JOSEPH BEUYS, *Iphigenia/Titus Andronicus,* 1969. Performance Art.

divided setting, incorporating a spotlighted, tethered white horse standing on a metal plate that resounded every time the horse moved. In this dual setting, the artist read from each play and performed mysterious actions using objects positioned near a microphone, including a pair of cymbals, which he clashed when necessary to quiet boisterous behavior in the audience. In such performances, Beuys considered himself as a shaman carrying out actions to help "revolutionize human thought," so that each human being could become a truly free and creative person. As was fitting for the actions of a shaman, most of Beuys's performances were not public events, but were witnessed only by small audiences. Through the effect on the viewers, and even more, through the efficacy of the acts themselves, the artist believed that the world could be changed.

More direct in trying to sensitize large numbers of viewers to the consequences of actions by government, big business, and the military are the "countermonuments" created by the expatriate Polish artist KRZYSZTOF WODICZKO (b. 1943). Wodiczko has used special, powerful projectors to throw carefully selected slide images onto public buildings and memorial monuments, creating large-scale montages that carry political meanings. He has chosen structures and monuments with the clearest historic and official meanings within the society—churches, museums, office buildings, housing projects, and sculptures honoring military heroes. The images he has projected most often are those of human body parts, creating the same kind of metaphor that led Le Corbusier to think of Notre Dame du Haut (FIG. 23-9) as a pair of praying hands. Although Wodiczko moved to Canada in 1977 and, since 1983, has divided his time between Toronto and New York City, he has created counter-monuments all over the world. In Australia, his projection of naked arms transformed the Gallery of New South Wales into a structure that both welcomed visitors and reminded them of the authoritarian power that governed the selection of the works of art inside. Anti-apartheid ideas inspired the artist's projection of a swastika onto the pediment of the South African embassy in London; his negative attitudes toward big business spurred his projected image of two hands—one with keys and one with a roll of money—onto the walls of a low-income hous-

23-75 KRZYSZTOF WODICZKO, *Projection on the Martin Luther Kirche,* Kassel, Germany, 1987. Projected images on building created for Documenta 8. Courtesy Hal Bromm Gallery, New York.

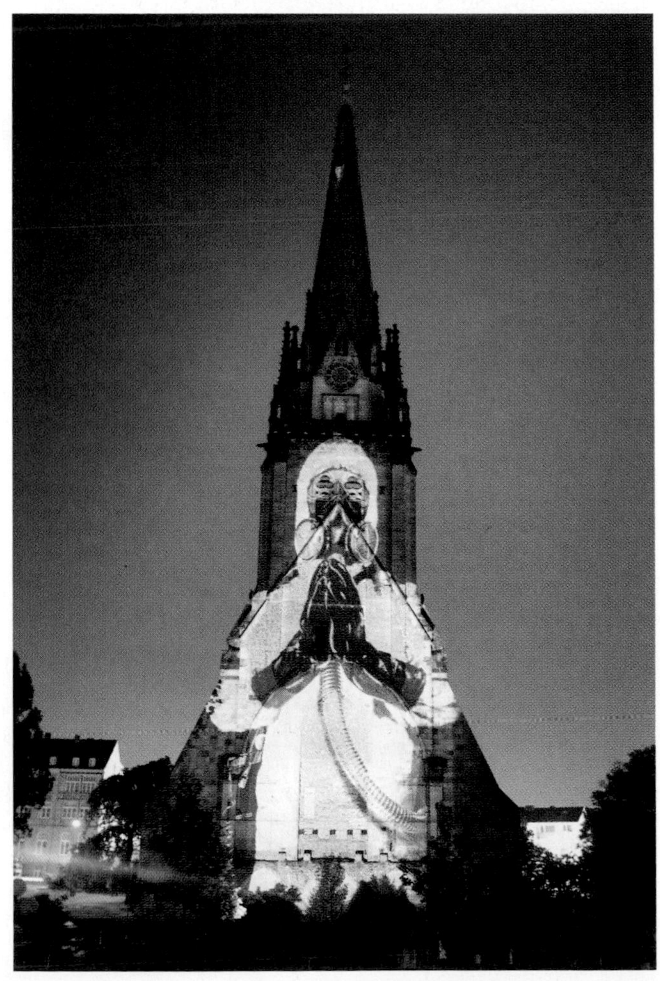

ing project in Chicago; and government ineptness sparked his proposal to project the image of a wheelchair-bound homeless person onto a statue of George Washington to call attention to the increasing plight of people without permanent housing. Industrial pollution was the target of Wodiczko's 1987 projection of a figure in a protective suit and gloves onto the façade of the Martin Luther Church (*Kirche*) in Kassel, West Germany (FIG. **23-75**). Like his other works, this gigantic montage created an unforgettable symbol with its strong suggestion of the powerlessness and sanctimoniousness of individual piety and organized religion in the face of industrial and political authority. In works like this, Wodiczko undercut the official symbolism in public buildings with ideas about their true function in society.

Earth and Site Art

As we have seen, artists have responded to the pressures of life in the contemporary world with a variety of styles and diverse content. Perhaps the most lyrical art produced during the period is that designed to sensitize viewers to the special and wonderful qualities of the natural and urban environments around us. Working variously in remote locations or on sites in the midst of human habitation, the artists creating this art come the closest of any in the contemporary world to expressing hope for the future of humanity and our world. Depending on the individual artist's approach, their work has been called Earth Art, Environmental Art, or Site Art.

A leading member of this group was ROBERT SMITHSON (1938–1973), who used industrial construction equipment to manipulate vast quantities of earth and rock on isolated sites in order to express his ideas about the meaning for our lives of natural systems, geological time, and entropy (the amount of disorder in a closed system, which increases as the system loses energy and enters decay). Beginning with early works based on the structure and behavior of crystals, Smithson moved to a series of *Site/Nonsite* pieces. In these, he transported materials from specific distant locations to museum settings and displayed the collected material (with accompanying topographical maps and photographs) in constructed metal bins, establishing a dialogue for the viewer between the original site and the museum location. He then did a series of temporary on-location pieces in which he modified the landscape physically (through processes such as pouring asphalt down a rock face) or visually (through placement of mirrored plates throughout the space). In seeking to do a more permanent Site piece, Smithson was attracted to a site on the Great Salt Lake in Utah. He built *Spiral Jetty* (FIG. **23-76**), a vast coil of earth and stone that symbolized the reality of time, on a monumental scale, so that it extended out into the lake. The idea grew from Smithson's first impression of the location: "As I looked at the site, it reverberated out to the horizons only to suggest an

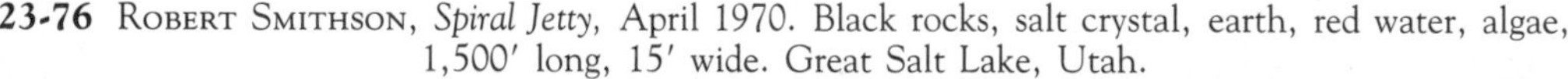
23-76 ROBERT SMITHSON, *Spiral Jetty*, April 1970. Black rocks, salt crystal, earth, red water, algae, 1,500′ long, 15′ wide. Great Salt Lake, Utah.

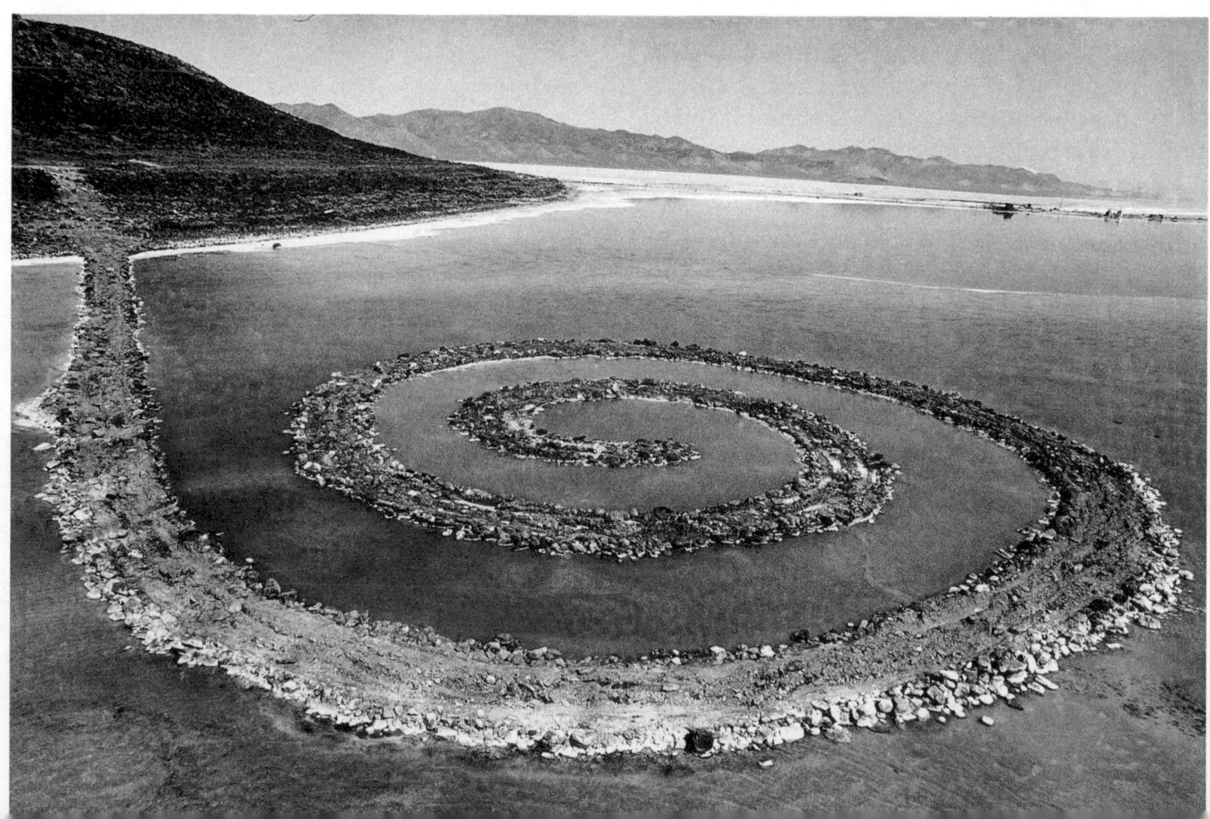

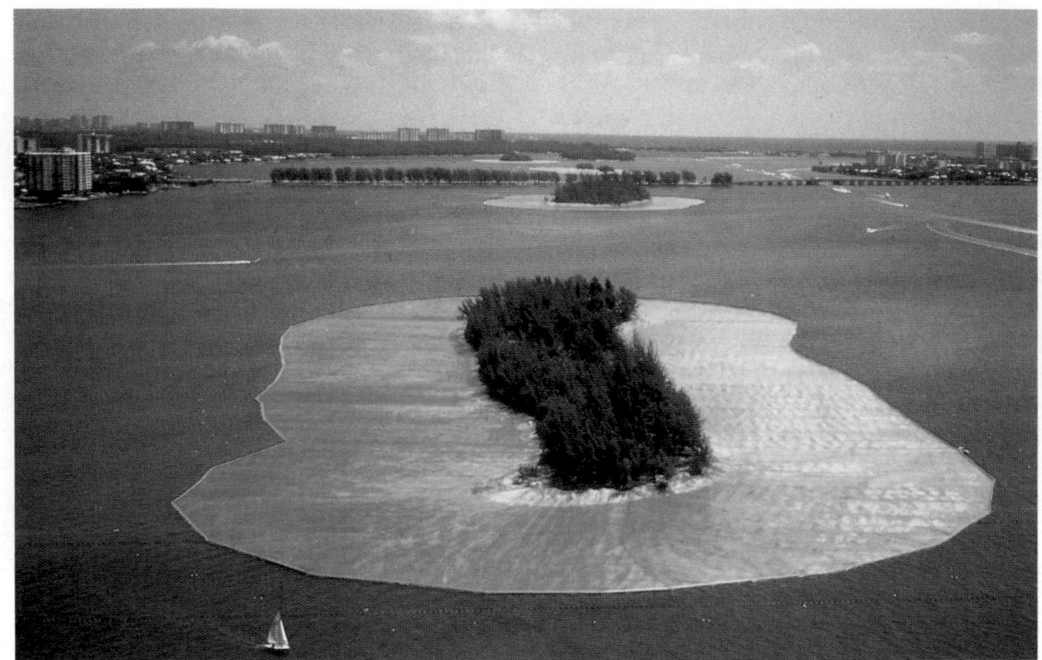

23-77 CHRISTO, *Surrounded Islands,* Biscayne Bay, Greater Miami, Florida, 1980–1983. Pink woven polypropylene fabric, $6\frac{1}{2}$ million sq. ft.

immobile cyclone while flickering light made the entire landscape appear to quake. A dormant earthquake spread into the fluttering stillness, into a spinning sensation without movement. The site was a rotary that enclosed itself in an immense roundness. From that gyrating space emerged the possibility of the *Spiral Jetty.*"* Smithson tried in this piece for an indissoluble unity of art and nature, much like the suspension of the boundaries between "self" and "nonself" that he hoped to instill in his viewers. As was the case with many other Earth Art works, *Spiral Jetty*'s location made it difficult for viewers to see in person. People know of such works mostly through photographs, and artists working in this mode have become increasingly self-conscious about how they document their work visually. Smithson not only recorded *Spiral Jetty* in photographs, but he filmed its construction in a movie that describes the forms and life of the whole site, including its relative inaccessibility. The photographs and the film have become increasingly important because shifts in the water level of the Great Salt Lake have placed *Spiral Jetty* underwater for several years.

CHRISTO (born Christo Javacheff in 1935) intensifies the viewer's awareness of the space and features of natural and urban sites by modifying parts of them with cloth. His pieces also incorporate the relationship between human social/political action, art, and the environment. Study of art in his native Bulgaria and in Vienna was followed by a period in Paris, where Christo began to encase objects in clumsy wrappings, in this way appropriating bits of the real world into the mysterious world of the unopened package whose contents can be dimly seen in silhouette under the wrap. Settling in New York City in 1964, Christo made storefronts like strange stage sets surrounded with windows wrapped in paper and cloth, and constructed ambitious temporary installations in which he wrapped sections or even entire buildings. Turning his attention to the environment, he created giant "air packages" in Minneapolis and Germany. Then he dealt with the land itself, carrying out projects like wrapping over 1 million square feet of Australian coast and hanging a vast curtain across a canyon at Rifle Gap, Colorado. The land pieces required years of preparation, research, and scores of meetings with local authorities and interested groups of local citizens. Christo has always considered that his Site pieces include the lobbying activity and the visual documentation that goes into them as well as the actual short-lived physical pieces themselves. *Surrounded Islands* (FIG. **23-77**), created in Biscayne Bay in Miami, Florida, for only two weeks in May of 1983, is typical of his Site work. For this project, eleven small man-made islands in the bay were surrounded with specially fabricated pink polypropyl-

*In Nancy Holt, ed., *The Writings of Robert Smithson* (New York: New York University Press, 1975), p. 111. Smithson was tragically killed in 1973, when the airplane in which he was surveying a site for a new Earth sculpture crashed near Amarillo, Texas.

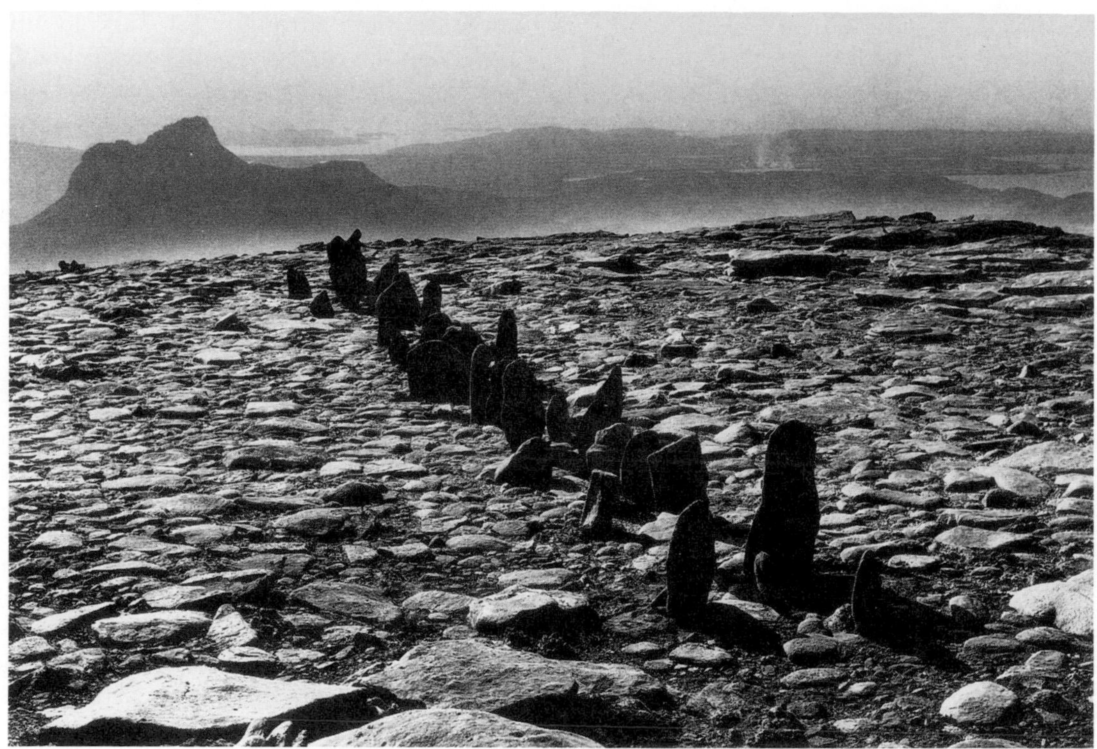

23-78 RICHARD LONG, *A Line in Scotland,* 1981. Photograph of constructed earthworks, Cul Mór, Scotland. Photograph in collection of Philip and Psiche Hughes.

ene fabric, following two years of preparation to gain the required permissions, assemble the necessary troop of ordinary and professional workers, and raise the $3.2 million cost of the project (which was accomplished entirely through the sale of preliminary drawings, collages, and models of the piece made by Christo). Huge crowds watched as Christo's crews stripped accumulated trash from the islands (to assure maximum contrast between their dark colors, the pink of the cloth, and the blue of the bay), anchored the huge cloth "cocoons" in the island vegetation, and then unfolded the fabric to form magical "skirts" around each tiny bit of land. Because each of his Site pieces has the quality of spectacle, some critics have compared Christo's works to Happenings, but the artist disagrees: "All Happenings are make-believe situations. Everything in my work is strongly literal. If three hundred people are used, it is not because we want three hundred people to play roles, but because we have work for them. When we go to work, there is a tense feeling, not a relaxed, joyous feeling as in a Kaprow Happening. . . . My work may look very theatrical, but it is a very professional activity."* Despite its short actual life, *Surrounded Islands* lives on in the host of stunning photographs and books that document the piece.

The British artist RICHARD LONG (b. 1945) takes as his theme the experience of walking through remote wilderness areas. Attracted to climbing, camping, and other outdoor activities as a boy, he began working with natural materials, like sand, while studying sculpture in London and Bristol. The walking pieces for which he is best known are each actually carried out by Long, before being shared with viewers through photographs, annotated maps, panels of text, and arrangements of materials gathered along his route and placed in circles, lines, or spirals on the floors or walls of art galleries. The photograph *A Line in Scotland* (FIG. **23-78**) documents a walk by Long through the Scottish Highlands, during which he erected a line of stones atop a rocky promontory and photographed them so that the tiny backlit monoliths recall their larger brothers at Neolithic ritual sites of standing stones like Stonehenge (FIG. 1-15). Few viewers are insensitive to the aura of awesome mystery in Long's work; through pieces like *A Line in Scotland,* modern city-bound individuals touch the wellspring of human history in the midst of the contemporary world.

Like Long, the American sculptor DOUGLAS HOLLIS (b. 1948) has a strong empathy for natural forces.

*In David Bourbon, *Christo* (New York: Harry N. Abrams, 1972), p. 25.

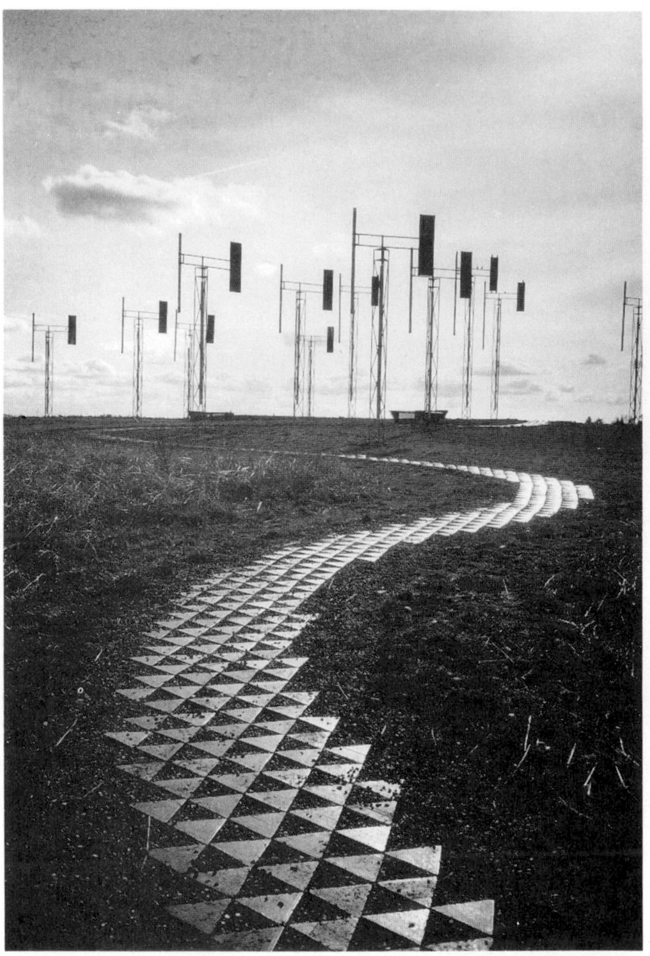

23-79 Douglas Hollis, *A Sound Garden,* National Oceanic and Atmospheric Administration, Seattle, 1983. Wind-organ towers 23′ high.

Hollis has selected accessible sites and designed works intended to re-awaken the sensory perception of visitors to natural processes, especially those of wind. Born in Michigan, Hollis spent many boyhood summers with a Native American family on a reservation in Oklahoma, and this experience left him with a vision of humans as an integral part of nature. This view has guided much of his art, including Site pieces like *A Sound Garden* (FIG. **23-79**), commissioned by the National Oceanic and Atmospheric Administration (NOAA) as one of five art works for their Northwest Center on Lake Washington near Seattle. Hollis selected the hilltop site overlooking the lake for his *Sound Garden* because he felt a strong empathy with the place. He wanted to create an ongoing "conversation" with the wind—a sound environment that could help people become more attuned to themselves and to nature. Hollis developed his techniques for sound sculpture in earlier kite pieces, wind harps, and wind organs at sites as varied as the roof of San Francisco's Exploratorium and the Niagara River gorge running through Art Park in upstate New York. The eleven sound units of *A Sound Garden* have upper sections that respond, much like weather vanes, to the action of wind blowing across Lake Washington. Tuned wind-organ pipes embedded in their structures "play" chords as the wind blows across their tops (rather in the manner children use to coax sounds from pop bottles). Hollis designed a special path leading to this piece. The triangular brick paver units used in the path were specially made in different clay mixtures to create different sonic rings as people followed this route to the sculpture site. In contrast to Smithson's and Christo's pieces, which can be well appreciated through photographs and films, Hollis's works are best experienced on-location by individuals. The visitor to *A Sound Garden* enters a mysterious world in which the physical forms become one with the action and sound of the wind accompanied by sonorous tones created by these giant musical instruments.

One of the most dramatic pieces of political art created in the twentieth century actually shares more qualities with Earth and Site art than with Activist art. The Vietnam Memorial (FIG. **23-80**), designed by Maya Ying Lin (b. 1960) while a Yale undergraduate student in architecture, does not preach, castigate, or offer inflated praise. Instead, the extraordinary simplicity of Lin's monument touches the hearts of those who visit it in ways that, in the few years since its erection in 1983, have helped to heal the divisions caused in the United States by the prolonged "police action" in Southeast Asia. Located on the Mall in Washington, D.C., the Vietnam Memorial consists of a long wall constructed of seventy slabs of highly polished granite. The wall bends in the middle to form two triangular wings that widen as they descend into the earth from a shallow height at the outer corners toward a depth of over 10 feet at their joint. Carved into the face of the wall are the names of all of the Americans who died in the Vietnam conflict, listed chronologically in the order of their deaths. The slabs are numbered and directories containing alphabetical lists of the names are placed at the entrances to the site, so visitors can find the memorial location of a loved one. Like Judy Chicago (FIG. 23-71), Lin understands the resonant power of a name to signify a person. Those who lost relatives and friends visit the wall to linger over a particular name, making paper rubbings of it and leaving photographs, mementos, and flowers at its base as tributes. But all who come are filled with the enormity of the loss as the columns of names unroll as one walks along the adjacent path. Unlike the usual monument, the names carved here do not vanish into the comfort of a list ordered by rank or alphabetical placement. Each life lost in Viet-

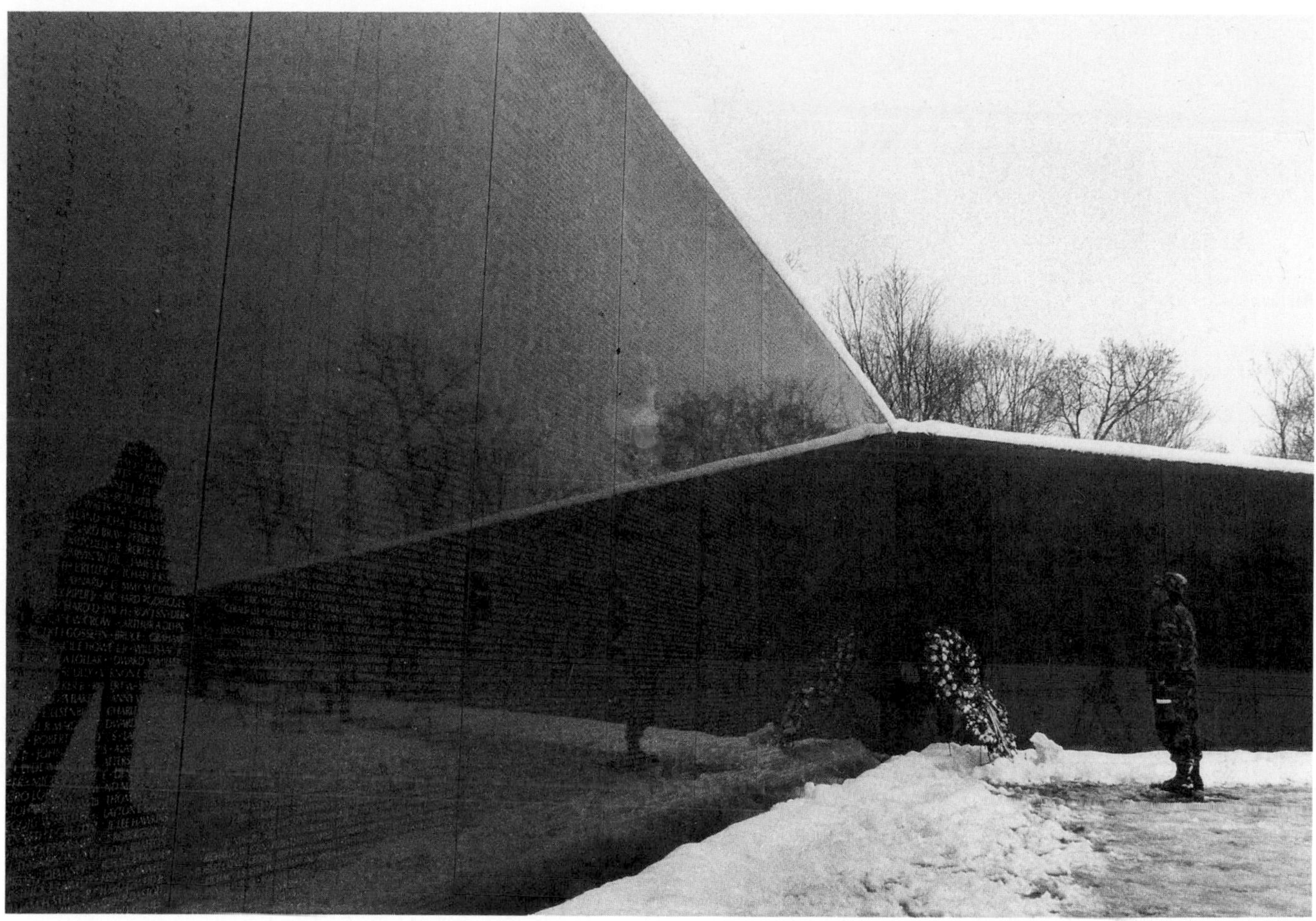

23-80 Maya Ying Lin, Vietnam Memorial, Washington, D.C., 1981–1983. Marble, each wing 246′ long.

nam has equal importance, equal value. Furthermore, as visitors move along the wall, its highly polished surface acts as a mirror, joining viewers with those who died. Rare is the visitor to this monument who is not drawn into silent meditation on the immeasurable cost of human life lost in the Vietnam conflict. The power of the wall to heal has been so great that replicas of the panels have been made and sent on tour throughout the country; at each stop this traveling monument attracts crowds who come to make connections with the silent rows of names.*

*When Lin's winning design was first announced, one group of Vietnam veterans felt that it was not a suitable memorial for their lost comrades. They lobbied successfully for an additional monument of three naturalistically modeled bronze fighting men, representing the branches of military service that were most active in the conflict. These figures stand on the Mall in a nearby grove of trees and look toward Lin's memorial. More recently, the nurses who served in Vietnam won the addition of a fourth figure, representing the women who lost their lives. Curiously, these figures draw fewer visitors than the wall, perhaps because they are more in the tradition of monuments to be looked at, whereas Lin's memorial invites its visitors to engage in active participation with its information and its symbolism.

EPILOGUE

Almost every aspect of life has changed during the modern era. Art has assumed an astonishing variety of guises during this period to express the richness and diversity of these changes and the insights they have provided about the visual world and the inner realms of ideas, emotions, and unseen powers. Art has been used to sensitize viewers to color and form, to the inequities of society, to the possibilities for self-fulfillment, and to the wonders of science and nature. As we near the end of the twentieth century, the diversity of artistic expression has widened to include the esthetic approaches to cultures outside the Western and Asian traditions. As artists travel more widely than ever before, and as the mass media acquaint all of us with a wider range of artistic styles, we may be moving toward a period in which a truly international world art will develop, one more all-encompassing than anything that has gone before. Should this come to pass, it may provide spiritual and esthetic experiences of incalculable worth for the whole human race.

PRONUNCIATION GUIDE*

Artist's Name	Phonetic Pronunciation
Aalto, Alvar	AHL-toe, AHL-vore
Abakanowicz, Magdalena	Ah-bah-KAHN-oh-veetz, Mahg-dah-LAY-nah
Agesander	Ag-uh-SAN-dur
Alberti, Leon Battista	All-BEAR-tee, Lay-OWN Bah-TEE-stah
Albinus, Bernard Siegfried	ALL-bee-noose, BAYRN-hart SEEG-freed
Altdorfer, Albrecht	AHLT-dore-fur, AHL-bresht
Andokides Painter	Ahn-DOH-kee-days
Andrea del Castagno	Ahn-DRAY-ah dayl Cah-STAN-yo
Andrea del Sarto	Ahn-DRAY-ah dayl SAAR-toe
Angelico, Fra	On-JAY-lee-coe, Frah
Anguissola, Sofonisba	On gwee-SO-lah, So-fone-EE-spah
Anthemius of Tralles	Ahn-THAY-mee-us of TRAH-layss
Antonello da Messina	Ahn-TOHN-ay-lo dah May-SEE-nah
Antonio da Sangallo the Younger	*See* Sangallo, Antonio da, the Younger
Apollodorus	Ah-poe-low-DOE-russ
Apollonius	Ah-poe-LOW-nee-oose
Aqa Mirak	Ah-KAH MEE-rahk
Archuleta, Felipe	Are-chu-LAY-tah, Fay-LEE-pay
Arnolfo di Cambio	Are-NAWL-foe dee KAHM-bee-oh
Arp, Jean	Arp, Jaw(n)
Asam, Cosmas Damian	Ah-SAHM, KOZ-mahs DAY-mee-en
Asam, Egid Quirin	Ah-SAHM, A-gheed KEER-in
Atget, Jean Eugène Auguste	Aht-JAY, Jaw(n) uh-JEN oh-GOOST
Athenodoros	Ahth-an-ah-DOHR-us
Barlach, Ernst	BAR-lock, Airnst
Bartolommeo, Michelozzo di	*See* Michelozzo di Bartolommeo
Barye, Antoine Louis	Bah-REE(yuh), On-TWAHN Loo-EE
Beckmann, Max	BAYK-mahn, Mox
Behnisch, Günter	BAYHN-ish, GOON-tare
Bellini, Giovanni	Bay-LEE-nee, Joe-VAH-nee
Berlinghieri, Bonaventura	Bare-leen-ghee-AY-ree, Bone-ah-vane-TOO-rah
Bernini, Gianlorenzo	Bare-NEE-nee, Jon-loe-REN-zoh
Bertoldo di Giovanni	Bear-TOLL-doh dee Joe-VAH-nee
Beuys, Joseph	Boyss, YO-zef
Bihzad	Bee-ZAHD
Boccioni, Umberto	Bo-chee-OH-nee, Oom-BEAR-toe
Bochner, Mel	BOKE-ner
Bodmer, Karl	BODE-mare
Boethos	Bo-AY-toss
Boffrand, Germain	Bohff-RAH(n), Jayr-MEH(n)
Bologna, Giovanni da	*See* Giovanni da Bologna
Bonheur, Rosa	Bone-UR, ROE-zah
Borromini, Francesco	Bore-oh-MEE-nee, Frahn-CHAY-skoe
Bosch, Hieronymus	Bosh, He-air-ON-ee-moose
Botticelli, Sandro	Bo-tee-CHAY-lee, SAHN-droh
Boucher, François	Booh-SHAY, Frahn-swah
Bouguereau, Adolphe William	Boo-gher-OH, Ah-DOHLF VEAL-yam
Bourgeois, Louise	Bor-JWAH
Bouts, Dirk	Boats, Durk
Bramante	Brah-MAHN-tay
Brancusi, Constantin	Braun-COOSH, Cone-stahn-TEEN
Braque, Georges	Brahk, Joerj
Broederlam, Melchior	Broo-dare-lam, Male-key-ORE
Bronzino	Brone-ZEE-noh
Bruegel, Pieter, the Elder	BREW-gull, PEE-ter
Brunelleschi, Filippo	Broo-nay-LAY-skay, Fee-LEE-poh
Brygos Painter	BRIG-ohs
Buffalmacco, Buonamico	Boo-fall-MA-coe, Bone-ah-MEE-coe
Buñuel, Luis	Boon-WHALE, Lou-EESS
Buson, Yosa	Boo-SONE, YO-sah
Callot, Jacques	Kah-LOW, Jock
Cambio, Arnolfo di	*See* Arnolfo di Cambio
Campin, Robert	Kah(n)-PEH(n), Roe-BEAR
Canaletto, Antonio	Kahn-ah-LAY-toe, On-TONE-ee-oh
Canova, Antonio	Kah-NO-vah, On-TOE-nee-oh
Caradosso, Christoforo Foppa	Car-ah-DOE-so, Kree-STOW-fore-oh FO-pah
Caravaggio	Kah-rah-VAH-gee-oh
Carpeaux, Jean Baptiste	Car-POH, Jaw(n) Bahp-TEESTE
Carracci, Agostino	Car-RAH-chee, Ah-gust-EENO
Carracci, Annibale	Car-RAH-chee, on-NEE-ball-ay
Carracci, Lodovico	Car-RAH-chee, Loo-doe-VEE-ko
Carriera, Rosalba	Car-ree-AY-rah, Roe-SAHL-bah
Cartier-Bresson, Henri	Car-tee-AY-Bress-OH(n), On-REE
Cassatt, Mary	Kah-SAHT
Castagno, Andrea del	*See* Andrea del Castagno
Cavallini, Pietro	Kah-vah-LEAN-ee, Pee-AY-troh
Cellini, Benvenuto	Chay-LEE-nee, Ben-ven-OO-to
Cézanne, Paul	Say-ZAH(n), Pole
Chagall, Marc	Shah-GALL, Mark
Chardin, Jean Baptiste Siméon	Shahr-DAH(n), Jaw(n) Bahp-TEEST See-may-OH(n)
Chelles, Jean de	SHELL, Jaw(n) duh
Ch'i Pai-shih	Chee By-shur
Chirico, Giorgio de	Key-REE-coe, JOR-gee-oh day
Christo	KREE-stoh
Christus, Petrus	KREES-tuhs, PAY-tross
Cimabue, Giovanni	Cheem-ah-BOO-ay, Joe-VAH-ee
Clodion	Kloh-dee-OH(n)
Clouet, Jean	Cloo-AY, Jaw(n)
Corot, Jean Baptiste Camille	Kore-OH, Jaw(n) Bahp-TEEST Kah-MEAL
Correggio	Core-AY-gee-oh
Courbet, Gustave	KOOR-bay, Goo-STAVH
Cranach, Lucas, the Elder	KRAH-nahk, LOO-cus
Cuvilliés, François de	Koo-vee-YAY(s), Frahn-swah duh

*Compiled by Cara-lin Getty, University of South Carolina at Sumter, and Mikle Ledgerwood, Rhodes College.

Artist's Name	Phonetic Pronunciation
Daguerre, Louis Jacques Mandé	Dah-GHAIR, Loo-EE Jock Mahn-DAY
Dali, Salvador	Dah-LEE, Sahl-vah-DORE
Daumier, Honoré	DOH-mee-ay, Oh-nor-AY
David, Jacques Louis	Dah-VEED, Jock Loo-EE
De Chelles, Jean	*See* Chelles, Jean de
De Chirico, Giorgio	*See* Chirico, Giorgio de
Degas, Edgar	Day-GAH, Aid-GAR
De Kooning, Willem	Deh KOON-eeng, VIL-em
Delacroix, Eugène	Duh-lah-KRAWH, Uh-JEN
De La Tour, Georges	*See* La Tour, Georges de
Della Francesca, Piero	*See* Piero della Francesca
Della Porta, Giacomo	*See* Giacomo della Porta
Della Quercia, Jacopo	*See* Jacopo della Quercia
Della Robbia, Luca	*See* Robbia, Luca della
Derain, André	Dare-EH(n), On-DRAY
De Sica, Vittorio	Day SEE-kah, Vee-TORE-ee-oh
Desiderio da Settignano	Day-see-DAY-ree-oh dah Say-teen-YAWN-oh
De Stael, Nicolas	*See* Stael, Nicolas de
Diebenkorn, Richard	DEEB-in-corn
Disdéri, André-Adolphe-Eugène	Deez-DAY-ree, On-DRAY Ah-DOLF Uh-JEN
Domenichino	Do-mane-ee-KEY-no
Domenico Veneziano	Doh-MEH-nee-coh Vay-nee-zee-AH-no
Donatello	Done-ah-TAY-loh
Duccio	DOOCH-ee-oh
Duchamp, Marcel	Dyu-SHAH(n), Mahr-SELL
Dürer, Albrecht	DYURE-ur, ALL-brekt
Durieu, Eugène	DURE-ree-UH, Uh-JEN
Eakins, Thomas	AY-kinz
Eiffel, Alexandre Gustave	Eh-FELL, AHL-ex-ahn-druh Goo-STAVH
Eisenstein, Sergei	EYE-zen-stine, SAYR-gay
El Greco	Ale GRAY-koe
Ergotimos	Ehr-GOH-tee-mohs
Ernst, Max	Airnst, Mox
Euphronios	U-FROHN-ee-ohs
Euthymides	U-THEEM-ee-days
Exekias	Ek-ZEE-kee-ahs
Eyck, Hubert van	IKE, HUE-beart fahn
Eyck, Jan van	IKE, Yawn fahn
Fabriano, Gentile da	*See* Gentile da Fabriano
Falconet, Étienne-Maurice	FAHL-cone-AY, Ay-tee-EN-Moe-REESE
Fan K'uan	Fahn Kwahn
Fiorentino, Rosso	*See* Rosso Fiorentino
Fossati, Chevalier	Foh-SAH-tee, Shev-AH-lee-ay
Fouquet, Jean	Foo-KAY, Jaw(n)
Fra Filippo Lippi	Frah Fay-LEE-poh LEE-pee
Fragonard, Jean Honoré	Frah-goh-NAHR, Jaw(n) Oh-no-RAY
Frankenthaler, Helen	FRANK-in-tall-ur
Friedrich, Caspar David	FREED-reek, KOSS-par DAH-vid
Fuseli, Henry	Foo-SAY-lee
Gabo, Naum	GAH-boh, Nowm
Gaddi, Taddeo	Gah-DEE, Tah-DAY-oh
Gainsborough, Thomas	GAINZ-burr-oh
Garnier, J. L. Charles	Gahr-nee-AY, Shahrl
Gaudí, Antoni	Gow-DEE, On-TONE-ee
Gauguin, Paul	Go-GEH(n), Pole
Gentile da Fabriano	Jayn-TEE-lay dah Fah-bree-AH-no
Gentileschi, Artemisia	Jane-teel-ESS-key, Are-tay-MEESE-ee-ah
Gentileschi, Orazio	Jane-teel-ESS-key, oh-RAH-tsee-oh
Géricault, Théodore	Jay-ree-KOE, Tay-oh-DORE
Gérôme, Jean-Léon	Jay-ROME, Jaw(n) Lay-OH(n)
Ghiberti, Lorenzo	Ghee-BEAR-tee, Lo-REN-tsoh
Ghirlandaio, Domenico	Gear-lon-DIE-oh, Doh-MANE-ee-coe
Giacometti, Alberto	Jah-coe-MAY-tee, All-BEAR-toe
Giacomo da Vignola	*See* Vignola, Giacomo da
Giacomo della Porta	*See* Porta, Giacomo della
Giorgione	Gee-ore-gee-OH-nay
Giotto	Gee-OH-toh
Giovanni, Bertoldo di	*See* Bertoldo di Giovanni
Giovanni da Bologna	Joe-VAH-nee dah Bo-LOAN-ya
Girardon, François	Gee-rahr-DOH(n), Frahn-SWAH
Girodet-Trioson, Anne Louis	Jee-roh-DAY-Tre-oh-SOH(n), On Loo-EE
Gislebertus	Geez-lay-BARE-tuss
Giuliano da Sangallo	*See* Sangallo, Giuliano da
Godard, Jean-Luc	Go-DAHR, Jaw(n)-LUKE
Goes, Hugo van der	Guhs, HYOU-go fahn dare
Gogh, Vincent van	Vahn Go (Dutch Fahn-hohk)
Golub, Leon	Go-LUBE, Lee-on
Gonzalez, Julio	Goan-ZAH-lay(z), HOO-Lee-oh
Gossaert, Jan	GO-sayrt, Yawn
Goujon, Jean	Goo-JOE(n), Jaw(n)
Goya, Francisco	GOE-yah, Frahn-SEESE-coe
Greenough, Horatio	GREEN-oh, Hore-AY-shee-oh
Greuze, Jean Baptiste	Gruhz, Jaw(n) Bahp-TEEST
Gropius, Walter	GROW-pee-oohss, VAHL-ter
Gros, Antoine Jean	Groh, On-TWAHN Jaw(n)
Grünewald, Matthias	GROO-nuh-vahld, Mah-TEE-ahss
Guarini, Guarino	Gwah-REE-nee, Gwah-REE-noh
Hals, Frans	Halls, Frahnz
Han Kan	Hahn Gahn
Hardouin-Mansart, Jules	Are-DWEH(n)-Mahn-SAHR, Jool
Harunobu, Suzuki	Har-roon-NO-boo, Su-zoo-kee
Hasegawa Tohaku	Hah-saw-GAH-wah Toe-HAH-coo
Hawes, Josiah Johnson	Hawz, Joe-SIGH-uh
Herrera, Juan de	Hay-RAH-rah, Hwahn day
Hippodamos	Ee-POH-deh-muss
Höch, Hannah	Hoke, HAHN-ah
Holbein, Hans, the Younger	HOLE-bine, Hahnz
Hon-Ami Koetsu	Hone-AH-mee Coe-ET-sue
Honnecourt, Villard de	UN-uh-coor, Vee-YA(r) duh
Honthorst, Gerard van	HAUNT-horst, HAY-ralt fahn
Horta, Victor	Ore-TAH, Veek-TORE
Houdon, Jean Antoine	Oo-DOH(n), Jaw(n) On-TWAHN
Hsu Pei-hung	Shoo Bay-hong
Huang Kung-wang	Hwahn Gong-wang
Hugo van der Goes	*See* Goes, Hugo van der
Iktinos	Eek-TEE-nohs
Il Guercino	Eel Gwair-CHEE-no
Imhotep	Im-HOH-tep
Ingres, Jean Auguste Dominique	AING(ruh), Jaw(n) Oh-GOOST Doh-mee-NEEK
Isidorus of Miletus	Ee-see-DOE-russ of My-LEE-tuss
Jacopo da Pontormo	*See* Pontormo, Jacopo da
Jacopo della Quercia	JAH-coe-poe DAY-lah KWAIR-chee-ah
Jones, Inigo	IN-ago
Jouvin, Hippolyte	Jew-VAN, Ee-poh-LEET
Juvara, Filippo	Jew-VAH-rah, Fee-LEE-poh
Kahlo, Frida	KAH-low, FREE-duh
Kalf, Willem	Kahlf, VIL-em
Kallikrates	Kal-EE-krah-tees
Kandinsky, Wassily	Kahn-DEEN-skee, VAH-see-lee

Artist's Name	Phonetic Pronunciation
Kaprow, Allan	CAP-roe
Käsebier, Gertrude	KAY-zuh-beer, Gayr-TRUE-duh
Katsushika Hokusai	Kaht-su-SHEE-kah Hok-oo-SIGH
Kauffmann, Angelica	KOWF-mahn, Anne-JAY-lee-kah
Kiefer, Anselm	KEY-fer, On-selm
Kienholz, Edward	KEEN-holtz
Kirchner, Ernst	KEERCH-nair, Airnst
Kiyotada	Key-oh-TAH-dah
Klee, Paul	Clay, Pole
Kleitias	KLAY-tee-ahs
Klimt, Gustav	Kleemt, GOO-stahv
Kline, Franz	Kline, Frahnz
Koça	COE-suh
Kollwitz, Käthe	COLE-vits, KATE-eh
Ku K'ai-chih	Goo Kai-jur(n)
Labrouste, Henri	La-BROOSTE, On-REE
La Tour, Georges de	Lah Tour, Jorg duh
Le Brun, Charles	Luh Bruh(n), Sharl
Le Corbusier	Luh Core-BOO-see-AY
Le Gray, Gustave	Luh Gray, Goo-STAHV
Lehmbruck, Wilhelm	LAME-broook, VEEL-helm
Leibl, Wilhelm	LIE-bul, VEEL-helm
Le Nain, Louis	Luh Neh(n), Loo-EE
Le Nôtre, André	Luh NOH(treh), On-DRAY
Lescaze, William	Lez-KAHZ
Lescot, Pierre	Luh-SKOH, Pee-AIR
Le Vau, Louis	Luh Voh, Loo-EE
Liang K'ai	Lee-ong Kai
Limbourg, Hennequin	Lem(h)-BOOR, En-nee-KIN
Limbourg, Herman	Lem(h)-BOOR, Air-MAHN
Limbourg, Pol	Lem(h)-BOOR, Pole
Lin, Maya Ying	Leen, MY-yah Yeen
Lipchitz, Jacques	Leep-SHITZ, Jock
Lippi, Fra Filippo	*See* Fra Filippo Lippi
Lochner, Stephan	LOHK-ner, STAY-fahn
Longhena, Baldassare	Loan-GAY-nah, Ball-dah-SARE-ay
Lorenzetti, Ambrogio	Low-ren-ZET-ee, Ahm-BROH-gee-oh
Lorenzetti, Pietro	Low-ren-ZET-ee, Pee-AY-troh
Lorrain, Claude	Loh-REHN, Clodh
Luca Signorelli	*See* Signorelli, Luca
Luzarches, Robert de	Lose-AHRSH, ROH-bear duh
Lysippos	Lee-SEE-poess
Ma Yuan	Ma You-an
Mabuse	Mah-BYOUZ
Machuca, Pedro	Ma-CHEW-kah, PAY-droh
Maderno, Carlo	Mah-DARE-no, CAR-low
Maillol, Aristide	MY-yole, Are-ee-STEED
Malevich, Kasimir	MAH-lay-veech, Kah-zee-MEER
Manet, Édouard	Mah-NAY, Aid-ooh-AHR
Mansart, François	Mahn-SAR, Frahn-swah
Mantegna, Andrea	Mahn-TANE-yah, Ahn-DRAY-ah
Manzù, Giacomo	Mahn-ZOO, Gee-AH-kah-moe
Martens, Friedrich von	MAHR-tenz, FREED-rick fahn
Martini, Simone	Mar-TEE-nee, See-MOAN-ay
Masaccio	Ma-SAH-chee-oh
Masolino da Panicale	Mah-so-LEE-no dah Pah-nee-KAH-lee
Matisse, Henri	Ma-TEES, On-REE
Méliès, Georges	May-lee-AYSS, Jee-orge
Memling, Hans	Maym-LEENG, Hahnz
Messina, Antonello da	*See* Antonello da Messina
Metsys, Quentin	Met-seese, KWEN-tin
Michelangelo	Mee-kell-AHN-jay-low
Michelozzo di Bartolommeo	Mee-kell-OH-tsoe dee Bar-toe-low-MAY-oh
Mies van der Rohe, Ludwig	Meese fahn dare ROE(huh), LOOD-vig
Millais, John	Mee-lay
Millet, Jean François	Mee-LAY, Jaw(n) Frahn-swah
Mirak, Aqa	*See* Aqa Mirak
Miró, Joan	Mee-ROE, Joe-ON
Mnesikles	Mee-NES-see-klayz
Moholy-Nagy, László	Moe-HOE-lee-NAH-ghee, LAHZ-low
Mondrian, Piet	Moan-dree-ON, Pate
Monet, Claude	Moan-AY, Klohd
Moreau, Gustave	More-OH, Goo-STAHV
Munch, Edvard	Moonk, ED-vahrd
Mungarawai	Mung-ar-AH-wah
Muybridge, Eadweard	MY-bridge, Ed-WARD
Nadar	Nah-DAHR
Nanni di Banco	Nah-nee dee BANH-coe
Neri, Manuel	NAY-ree, Mahn-WHALE
Nervi, Pier Luigi	NAIR-vee, PEE-ayr Loo-EE-gee
Neumann, Balthasar	NOY-mahn, Ball-tar-ZAHR
Nièpce, Joseph Nicéphore	KNEE-eps, KNEE-say-for
Niobid Painter	Nee-OH-bid
Novius Plautius	NOH-vee-oohss PLOW-tee-oohss
Ogata Korin	Oh-GAH-tah Coe-REEN
Okyo, Maruyama	OAK-yo, Mah-roo-YAH-mah
Oldenburg, Claes	OLD-in-burg, Klayss
Olowe of Ise	O-lah-WAY of EE-see
Orozco, José Clemente	Oh-ROZ-coe, Hoe-ZAY Clay-MEN-tay
Otto, Frei	OH-toe, FRAY-ee
Pacher, Michael	Pock-er, MOEK-aisle
Paik, Nam June	Pike, NAHM Joon
Palladio, Andrea	Pa-LA-dee-oh, Ahn-DRAY-ah
Pannini, Giovanni	Pah-NEE-nee, Joe-VAH-nee
Paolozzi, Eduardo	Pow-LOH-zee, Aid-WAHR-do
Parmigianino	Par-mee-gee-ah-NEE-noh
Patinir, Joachim	PAHT(ee)-neer, Yo-AH-keem
Pei, Ieoh Ming	Pay, Yueh Ming
Perrault, Claude	Pay-RO, Clohd
Perugino	Pay-roo-GEE-no
Pfaff, Judy	P(uh)faff
Phiale Painter	Fee-AH-lay
Phidias	FHEE-dee-ahs
Piano, Renzo	Pee-AH-no, REN-tzoh
Picasso, Pablo	Pee-KaH-so, PA-bloh
Piero della Francesca	Pee-AY-roh DAY-lah Frahn-CHEE-skah
Pilon, Germain	Pee-LOH(n), Jer-MEH(n)
Piranesi, Giovanni Battista	Pee-rah-NAY-see, Joe-VAH-nee Bah-TEE-stah
Pisano, Andrea	Pee-SAHN-no, Ahn-DRAY-ah
Pisano, Giovanni	Pee-SAHN-no, Joe-VAHN-ee
Pisano, Nicola	Pee-SAHN-oh, NEE-koh-la
Pissarro, Camille	Pee-ZAHR-oh, Kah-MEAL
Pollaiuolo, Antonio	Poh-lie-oo-OH-loh, Ahn-TOE-nee-oh
Pollock, Jackson	PAUL-ock
Polydoros	Poh-lee-DOH-rahs
Polygnotos	Pol-og NO-tus
Polykleitos	Poh-lee-KLY-tohss
Pontormo, Jacopo da	Pone-TORE-mo, JAH-coe-poe dah
Porta, Giacomo della	PORE-tah, JAH-coe-moe DAY-lah
Poussin, Nicolas	Poo-SEH(n), NEE-koe-lah
Pozzo, Fra Andrea	POE-tzo, Frah On-DRAY-ah
Praxiteles	Prax-EE-tell-ees
Primaticcio, Francesco	Pree-mah-TEE-chee-oh, Frahn-CHAY-skoh
Pucelle, Jean	Pyou-CELL, Jaw(n)

Artist's Name	Phonetic Pronunciation
Puget, Pierre	Pyou-JAY, Pee-AIR
Pugin, A. W. N.	PYU-gin
Puvis de Chavannes, Pierre	Pyou-VEE duh Shah-VAHN, Pee-AIR
Quarton, Enguerrand	Kvar-TON(n), In-gher-OH(n)
Raphael	RAH-fah-el
Rauschenberg, Robert	ROWSH-en-burg ("ow" as in "now")
Redon, Odilon	Ruh-DOH(n), Oh-dee-LOH(n)
Reimann, Walter	RYE-mahn, VAHL-tare
Rembrandt van Rijn	Rem-BRAN(DT) fahn RINE
Reni, Guido	RAY-nee, GWEE-doe
Renoir, Auguste	Ruh-NWAHR, Oh-GOOSTE
Repin, Ilya	RYE-pin, EEL-yah
Ribera, José de	Ree-BAY-rah, Ho-SAY day
Richter, Hans	RICK-tur, HAHNZ
Riefenstahl, Leni	REE-fen-stall, LAY-nee
Riemenschneider, Tilman	REE-MEN-schnigh-dare, TEEL-mahn
Rietveldt, Gerrit	REET-felld, GARE-it
Rigaud, Hyacinthe	Ree-GOH, Ee-ah-SEH(n)t
Robbia, Luca della	ROBE-ee-ah, LOO-kah DAY-lah
Rodin, Auguste	Roe-DEH(n), Oh-GOOSTE
Rogier van der Weyden	*See* Weyden, Rogier van der
Röhrig, Walter	ROAR-igg, VAHL-tare
Romano, Giulio	Ro-MA-no, JEW-lee-oh
Rosa, Salvator	ROE-sah, Sal-vah-TORE
Rossellino, Antonio	Ro-say-LEE-no, Ahn-TOE-nee-oh
Rossellino, Bernardo	Ro-say-LEE-no, Bear-NAHR-do
Rosso Fiorentino	ROH-so Fee-ore-in-TEE-no
Rosso, Medardo	Roh-soe, May-DAHR-do
Rouault, Georges	Roo-OH, JEE-orge
Rousseau, Henri	Roo-SO, On-REE
Rublëv, Andrei	Roob-LEY-ayv, Ahn-DRAY-ee
Rude, François	Rood, Frahn-swah
Ruisdael, Jacob van	ROIS-dahl, YA-kobe fahn
Runge, Philipp Otto	ROON-guh, Fee-LEEP O-toe
Ruscha, Edward	ROO-shah
Saar, Bettye	Sahr, Bet-ee
Saint-Gaudens, Augustus	Saint-GAW-dens
Sangallo, Antonio da, the Younger	Sahn-GALL-oh, Ahn-TONE-ee-oh dah
Sangallo, Giuliano da	Sahn-GALL-oh, Jew-lee-AH-no dah
Sansovino, Andrea	Sahn-so-VEE-no, On-DRAY-ah
Sansovino, Jacopo	Sahn-so-VEE-no, YAH-coe-poe
Sarto, Andrea del	*See* Andrea del Sarto
Schöffer, Nicolas	SHOFF-er, Neck-oh-LAH
Schongauer, Martin	SHONE-gow-er, MAR-teen ("ow" as in "now")
Schwitters, Kurt	SHVIT-ers, Koort
Scopas	SKOH-pahs
Senmut	Sen-MOO(m)
Sesshu	SESS-you
Settignano, Desiderio da	*See* Desiderio da Settignano
Seurat, Georges	Suh-RAH, JEE-orge
Severus	Sev-AIR-oose
Shen Chou	Sun Joe
Signorelli, Luca	Seen-yore-ALE-ee, LOO-kah
Sinan the Great	SEE-nahn
Sluter, Claus	SLOO-ter, Klows

Artist's Name	Phonetic Pronunciation
Soufflot, Jacques-Germain	Soo-FLOH, Jock-Jayr-MEH(n)
Southworth, Albert Sands	SUHTH-uhrth
Spranger, Bartholomeus	SPRAHN-gurr, Bar-toe-low-MAY-us
Stael, Nicolas de	STAH-ell, Neck-oh-LAH duh
Stieglitz, Alfred	STEEG-litz, ALL-fred
Stoss, Veit	Shtohss, Fite
Takayoshi	Tah-kah-YO-shee
Tao-chi	Dao-jee
Tatlin, Vladimir	Taht-LEEN, Vlah-DEE-meer
Tawaraya Sotatsu	Tah-WAH-rah-yah So-TAHT-sue
Theotokopoulos, Domenikos	Tay-oh-toe-KOE-poe-lohss, Doe-MANE-ee-kos
Tiepolo, Giambattista	Tee-EH-poh-loe, Jahm-bah-TEESE-tah
Tinguely, Jean	Tehng-LEE, Jaw(n)
Tintoretto	Teen-toe-RAY-toe
Titian	TEE-shun
Toba Sojo	TOE-bah SO-jue
Toledo, Juan Bautista de	Toe-LAY-doe, Wahn Bough-TEE-stah day
Tori Busshi	TOE-ree BOO-shee
Toulouse-Lautrec, Henri de	TOO-looze-Low-TREK, On-REE duh
Tournachon, Gaspard Félix	Toor-nah-SHOH(n), Gah-SPAHR Fay-LEEKS
Traini, Francesco	Trah-EE-nee, Frahn-CHEE-skoh
Tung Ch'i-ch'ang	Dung Chee-chang
Uccello, Paolo	Oo-CHAY-loh, Pah-OH-loh
Vanbrugh, John	Van-BROO
Van der Rohe	*See* Mies van der Rohe, Ludwig
Van Der Zee, James	VAHN Dayr Zee
Van Dyck, Anthony	Fahn Dike
Van Honthorst, Gerard	*See* Honthorst, Gerard van
Vasarely, Victor	Vah-SAR-uh-lee, VEEK-tore
Vecelli, Tiziano	Vay-CHAY-lee, Tee-tsee-AH-no
Velázquez, Diego	Vay-LAHSS-kayss, Dee-AY-go
Veneziano, Domenico	*See* Domenico Veneziano
Venturi, Robert	Ven-TOO-ree
Vermeer, Jan	Fare-MEER, Yawn
Veronese	Vay-roe-NAY-say
Verrocchio, Andrea del	Vay-RO-kee-oh, Ahn-DRAY-ah dayl
Vigée-Lebrun, Élisabeth Louise	Vee-JAY-Luh-BROH(n), Ay-leez-ah-BET Loo-EEZ
Vignola, Giacomo da	Veen-YO-lah, JAH-koe-moe dah
Vignon, Pierre	Veen-YOHN, Pee-AYR
Vitruvius	Vee-TROO-vee-oose
Warhol, Andy	WAR-hall
Warm, Hermann	Vahrm, HAIR-mahn
Watteau, Antoine	Wah-TOH, On-TWAHN
Welliver, Neil	WELL-ih-vur
Wen Cheng-ming	Wone Jung-ming
Weyden, Rogier van der	VAY-den, ROE-jeer fahn dare
Wiligelmus	Vee-lee-GHELL-moose
Witz, Conrad	Vits
Wodiczko, Krzysztof	Voh-DYAY-skoh, KREE-stofe
Wu Chen	Woo Jun
Zavattini, Cesare	ZAH-vah-tee-nee, Chay-sah-ruh
Zurbarán, Francisco de	Thoor-bah-RAHN, Frahn-SEE-skoy day

GLOSSARY

Italicized terms in definitions are defined elsewhere in the Glossary.

abacus (AB-a-kus) The uppermost portion of the *capital* of a *column,* usually a thin slab.

abstract In painting and sculpture, emphasizing a derived, essential character that has only a stylized or symbolic visual reference to objects in nature.

academy A place of study, derived from the name of the grove where Plato held his philosophical seminars. Giorgio Vasari founded the first academy of fine arts, properly speaking, with his *Accademia di Disegno* in Florence in 1563.

acroterium or **acroterion** (ak-roh-TEE-ri-um) In Classical buildings, a figure or ornament usually at the apex of the *pediment.*

acrylic A painting medium that uses *pigment* in a synthetic base (made with acrylic thermal-plastic resins).

addorsed Set back-to-back, especially as in heraldic design.

adobe (a-DOE-bee) The clay used to make a kind of sun-dried brick of the same name; a building made of such brick.

aerial perspective See *perspective.*

agora (AG-o-ra) An open square or space used for public meetings or business in ancient Greek cities.

aisle The portion of a church flanking the *nave* and separated from it by a row of *columns* or *piers.*

alabaster A variety of gypsum or calcite of dense, fine texture, usually white, but also red, yellow, grey, and sometimes banded.

alla prima (A-la PREE-ma) A painting technique in which pigments are laid on in one application, with little or no drawing or underpainting.

altarpiece A panel, painted or sculptured, situated above and behind an altar. See also *retable.*

ambulatory A covered walkway, outdoors (as in a *cloister*) or indoors; especially the passageway around the *apse* and the *choir* of a church.

amphora (AM-fo-ra) A two-handled, egg-shaped jar used for general storage purposes.

anamorphic image An image that must be viewed by some special means (such as a mirror) to be recognized.

apadana (ap-a-DAN-a) The great audience hall in ancient Persian palaces.

apse A recess, usually singular and semicircular, in the wall of a Roman *basilica* or at the east end of a Christian church.

arabesque Literally, "Arabian-like." A flowing, intricate pattern derived from stylized organic motifs, usually floral, often arranged in symmetrical *palmette* designs; generally, an Islamic decorative motif.

arcade A series of *arches* supported by *piers* or *columns.*

arcading An uninterrupted series of *arches.*

arch A curved structural member that spans an opening and is generally composed of wedge-shaped blocks (*voussoirs*) that transmit the downward pressure laterally. A **diaphragm arch** is a transverse, wall-bearing arch that divides a *vault* or a ceiling into compartments, providing a kind of firebreak. See also *thrust.*

architectonic Having structural or architectural qualities, usually as elements of a nonarchitectural object.

architrave (ARK-i-trayv) The *lintel* or lowest division of the *entablature;* sometimes called the *epistyle.*

archivolt (ARK-i-volt) One of a series of concentric *moldings* on a Romanesque or a Gothic arch.

arcuated (AR-kew-ate-id) Of *arch–column* construction.

armature In sculpture, a skeleton-like framework to support material being modeled.

aspara In India, a nymph of the sky or air; in Chinese Buddhism, a heavenly maiden.

assemblage A three-dimensional composition made of various materials such as *found objects,* paper, wood, and cloth. See also *collage.*

atlantid A male figure that functions as a supporting *column.* See also *caryatid.*

atmospheric perspective See *perspective.*

atrium (AY-tree-um) The court of a Roman house that is near the entrance and partly open to the sky. Also, the open, colonnaded court in front of and attached to a Christian *basilica.*

automatism Process of yielding oneself to instinctive actions after establishing a set of conditions (such as size of paper or medium) within which a work is to be carried out.

avant-garde (a-vahn-GARD) Artists whose work is in the most advanced stylistic expression.

avatar (AH-vah-tar) In Hinduism, an incarnation of a god.

axial plan See *plan.*

axis An imaginary line or lines about which a work, a group of works, or a part of a work is visually or structurally organized, often symmetrically.

baldacchino (bal-da-KEE-no) A canopy on columns, frequently built over an altar.

barrel vault See *vault.*

bas (bah) **relief** See *relief.*

basilica (ba-SIL-i-kah) In Roman architecture, a public building for assemblies (especially tribunals), that is rectangular in plan with an entrance on a long side. In Christian architecture, an early church somewhat resembling the Roman basilica, usually entered from one end and with an *apse* at the other, creating an *axial plan.*

batter To slope inward, often almost imperceptibly, or such an inward slope of a wall.

bay A subdivision of the interior space of a building. In Romanesque and Gothic churches, the transverse *arches* and *piers* of the *arcade* divide the building into bays.

beehive tomb A beehive-shaped type of subterranean tomb constructed as a *corbeled vault* and found at pre-Archaic Greek sites.

belvedere (bell-vuh-DARE-eh) An open, roofed story built to provide a scenic view.

ben-ben A pyramidal stone; a *fetish* of the Egyptian god Re.

benizuri-e (BEN-i-ZUR-i-ee) A two-color method of Japanese printing in pink and green that produces strong color vibration.

bevel See *chamfer.*

bhakti (buh-HOCK-tee) In Hinduism, the devout, selfless direction of all tasks and activities of life to the service of one god; the adoration of a personalized deity.

black-figure technique In early Greek pottery, the silhouetting of dark figures against a light background of natural, reddish clay.

blind arcade (wall arcade) An *arcade* having no actual openings, applied as decoration to a wall surface.

Bodhisattva (bo-dee-SOT-va) In Buddhism, a being who is a potential Buddha.

bottega (but-TAY-ga) A shop; the studio-shop of an Italian artist.

bouleuterion (boo-loo-TEE-ri-on) In ancient Greece, an assembly hall or council chamber.

broken pediment A *pediment* in which the *cornice* is discontinuous at the apex or the base.

bucrania (pl.) In classical architecture, an ornament, usually in the friezes, having the shape of an ox skull.

Buddha The supreme enlightened being of Buddhism; an embodiment of divine wisdom and virtue. **Buddhist** *(adj.)*

burin (BYOOR-in) A pointed steel tool for *engraving* or *incising.*

buttress An exterior masonry structure that opposes the lateral thrust of an *arch* or a *vault.* A **pier buttress** is a solid mass of masonry; a **flying buttress** consists typically of an inclined member carried on an arch or a series of arches and a solid buttress to which it transmits lateral *thrust.*

calidarium The hot-bath section of a Roman bathing establishment.

calligraphy Handwriting or penmanship, especially elegant or "beautiful" writing as a decorative art.

calotype Photographic process in which a positive image is made by shining light throught a negative image onto a sheet of sensitized paper.
camera lucida A device in which a small lens projects the image of an object downward onto a sheet of paper. Literally, "lighted room."
camera obscura An ancestor of the modern camera in which a tiny pinhole, acting as a lens, projects an image on a screen, the wall of a room, or the ground-glass wall of a box; used by artists in the seventeenth, eighteenth, and early nineteenth centuries as an aid in drawing from nature. Literally, "dark room."
campanile (kam-pa-NEEL-eh) A bell tower, usually freestanding.
capital The upper member of a *column,* serving as a transition from the *shaft* to the *lintel.*
Caravaggisti (kara-va-GEE-stee) Artists influenced by Caravaggio's dramatically contrasting dark–light effects; painters of "night pictures" in the "dark manner" (*tenebroso*).
cardo The north–south road in Etruscan and Roman towns, intersecting the *decumanus* at right angles.
carte de visite (KART duh VEE-zeet) Separate photographs made on a single negative and mounted on a card the size of the standard calling card; in the nineteenth century, an inexpensive means of creating mass-produced prints.
cartoon In painting, a full-size drawing from which a painting is made. Before the modern era, cartoons were customarily worked out in complete detail; the design was then transferred to the working surface by coating the back with chalk and going over the lines with a *stylus,* or by pricking the lines and "pouncing" charcoal dust through the resulting holes.
cartouche (kar-TOOSH) A scroll-like design or medallion, purely decorative or containing an inscription or heraldic device. In ancient Egypt, an oval device containing such elements as *hieroglyphic* names of Egyptian kings.
caryatid (KAR-ee-AT-id) A female figure that functions as a supporting *column.* See also *atlantid.*
casting In sculpture, process of duplicating a modeled or fabricated original in which a mold is used to make a cast in plaster, metal, polyester, or other hard-setting material.
castrum A Roman military encampment.
cella (SEL-a) An enclosed chamber (Greek, *naos*); the essential feature of a Classical temple, in which the cult statue usually stood.
centering A wooden framework to support an *arch* or a *vault* during its construction.
central plan See *plan.*
ceramics The art of making objects such as pottery out of clay; also, the objects themselves.
chaitya (CHIGHT-yuh) An Indian shrine, especially a Buddhist assembly hall having a votive *stupa* at one end.
chalice A cup or goblet, especially that used in the sacraments of the Christian Church.
chamfer The surface formed by cutting off a corner of a board or post; a *bevel.*
chandi A Javanese temple.
chatra See *parasol.*
chevet (sheh-VAY) The eastern end of a Gothic church, including *choir, ambulatory,* and radiating chapels.
chevron A zigzag or V-shaped motif of decoration.
chiaroscuro (kee-AR-o-SKOOR-o) In drawing or painting, the treatment and use of light and dark, especially the gradations of light that produce the effect of *modeling.*
chiton (KITE-on) A Greek tunic, the essential (and often only) garment of both men and women, the other being the *himation* or *mantle;* a kind of cape.
choir The space reserved for the clergy in the church, usually east of the *transept* but, in some instances, extending into the *nave.*
ciborium (sih-BOR-ee-um) A canopy, often freestanding and supported by four columns, erected over an altar; also, a covered cup used in the sacraments of the Christian Church. See *baldacchino.*
cinematic montage Motion-picture effects produced by superimposing separate, unrelated images or showing them in rapid sequence.
cinquecento (cheenk-way-CHAIN-toh) The sixteenth century in Italian art. Literally, the "1500s."
cire perdue (seer pair-DEW) The **lost-wax process.** A bronze-casting method in which a figure is modeled in wax and covered with clay; the whole is fired, melting away the wax and hardening the clay, which then becomes a mold for molten metal.
clerestory (KLEER-sto-ry) The *fenestrated* part of a building that rises above the roofs of the other parts.
cloison (klwa-ZOHN) Literally, a partition. A cell made of metal wire or a narrow metal strip that is soldered edge-up to a metal base to hold enamel or other decorative materials.
cloisonné (klwa-zoh-NAY) A process of enameling employing *cloisons.*
cloister A court, usually with covered walks or *ambulatories* along its sides.
closed form A *form,* especially in painting, with a contour that is not broken or blurred.
cluster pier See *compound pier.*
codex Separate pages of *vellum* or *parchment* bound together at one side and having a cover; the predecessor of the modern book. In Mesoamerica, a painted and inscribed book on long sheets of fig-bark paper or deerskin coated with plaster and folded into accordionlike pleats.
coffer A sunken panel in a *soffit,* a *vault,* or a ceiling; often ornamental.
collage (kul-LAHZH) A composition made by combining on a flat surface various materials such as newspaper, wallpaper, printed text and illustrations, photographs, and cloth. See also *photomontage.*
colonnade A series or row of *columns,* usually spanned by *lintels.*
colonnette A small *column.*
color See *hue, saturation,* and *value.*
column A vertical, weight-carrying architectural member, circular in cross section and consisting of a base (sometimes omitted), a *shaft,* and a *capital.*
complementary after-image The image (in a *complementary color*) that is retained briefly by the eye after the stimulus is removed.
complementary colors Those pairs of colors, such as red and green, that together embrace the entire spectrum. The complement of one of the three *primary colors* is a mixture of the other two. In pigments, they produce a neutral grey when mixed in the right proportions.
compluvium An opening in the center of the roof of a Roman *atrium* to admit light.
compound or **cluster pier** A *pier* composed of a group or cluster of members, especially characteristic of Gothic architecture.
computer graphics Medium developed during the 1960s and 1970s that uses computer programs and electronic light to make designs and images on the surface of a computer or television screen.
concretion In the work of Jean Arp, Surrealistic sculptural form characterized by twisting and growing effects.
connoisseur (kon-nuh-SER) An expert on works of art and the individual styles of artists.
contour A visible border of a *mass* in space; a *line* that creates the illusion of *mass* and *volume* in space.
contrapposto (kon-tra-POH-stoh) The disposition of the human figure in which one part is turned in opposition to another part (usually hips and legs one way, shoulders and chest another), creating a counter-positioning of the body about its central *axis.* Sometimes called **weight shift** because the weight of the body tends to be thrown to one foot, creating tension on one side and relaxation on the other.
cool color Blue, green, or blue-violet. Psychologically, cool colors are calming, unemphatic, depressive; optically, they generally appear to recede. See also *warm color.*
corbel (KOR-bel) A projecting wall member used as a support for some element in the superstructure. Also, courses of stone or brick in which each course projects beyond the one beneath it. Two such structures, meeting at the topmost course, create an *arch.*
cornice The projecting, crowning member of the *entablature;* also, any crowning projection.
cramp (or **clamp**) A device, usually metal, to hold together blocks of stone of the same course. See also *dowel.*
crenelated (KREN-el-ate-id) Notched or

indented, usually with respect to tops of walls, as in battlements.

crocket A projecting, foliate ornament of a *capital, pinnacle, gable, buttress,* or spire.

Cro-Magnon (kro-MAG-non) Of or pertaining to the *homo sapiens* whose remains, dating from the Aurignacian period, were found in the Cro-Magnon caves in Dordogne, France.

cromlech (KROM-lek) A circle of *monoliths.*

crossing The space in a cruciform church formed by the intersection of the *nave* and the *transept.*

crossing square The area in a church that is formed by the intersection (crossing) of a *nave* and a *transept* of equal width.

crown The topmost part of an *arch,* including the *keystone;* also, an open *finial* of a tower.

cruciform (KROO-suh-form) Cross-shaped.

crypt A *vaulted* space under part of a building, wholly or partly underground; in Medieval churches, normally the portion under an *apse* or a *chevet.*

cubiculum A small room constructed in the wall of an Early Christian catacomb to serve as a mortuary chapel.

cuneiform (kyoo-NEE-ih-form) Literally, "wedge-shaped." A system of writing used in ancient Mesopotamia, the characters of which were wedge-shaped.

Cyclopean (sike-lo-PEE-an) Gigantic; vast and rough; massive. **Cyclopean architecture** is a method of stone construction using large, irregular blocks without mortar.

daguerreotype (dah-GAIR-oh-type) A photograph made by an early method on a plate of chemically treated metal; developed by Louis J. M. Daguerre.

decumanus (dek-yoo-MAN-us) The east–west road in an Etruscan or Roman town, intersecting the *cardo* at right angles.

differential focus Photographic technique in which everything in the foreground shows clearly while everything else is less distinct.

diffraction gratings Sheets of glass, plastic, or metal inscribed with grids whose lines or dots diffract any light directed at the gridded surface and break this light up into its color spectra so that the rays may be measured accurately.

diptych (DIP-tik) A two-paneled painting or *altarpiece;* also, an ancient Roman and Early Christian two-hinged writing tablet, or two ivory memorial panels.

di sotto in sù (dee SUH-toe in soo) A technique of representing perspective in ceiling painting. Literally, "from below upwards."

divisionism System of painting in small color dots that stand in relation to each other based on certain color theories. See *pointillism.*

dolmen (DOHL-men) Several large stones (*megaliths*) capped with a covering slab, erected in prehistoric times.

dome A hemispheric *vault;* theoretically, an *arch* rotated on its vertical *axis.*

double-exposure techniques Photographic techniques that combine images made at different moments in time. See *straight photography.*

dowel In ancient architecture, a wooden or metal pin placed between stones of different courses to prevent shifting. See also *cramp.*

dromos The passage to a *beehive tomb.*

drum The circular wall that supports a *dome;* also, one of the cylindrical stones of which a non-monolithic *shaft* of a *column* is made.

dry point An engraving in which the design, instead of being cut into the plate with a *burin,* is scratched into the surface with a hard steel "pencil." The process is quicker and more spontaneous than standard engraving and lends itself to the creation of painterly effects. Its disadvantage is the fact that the plate wears out very quickly. See also *engraving, etching, intaglio.*

duecento (doo-ay-CHAIN-toh) The thirteenth century in Italian art. Literally, the "1200s."

earth colors Pigments, such as yellow ochre and umber, that are obtained by mining; usually compounds of metals.

echinus (eh-KY-nus) In architecture, the convex element of a *capital* directly below the *abacus.*

eclecticism (eh-KLEK-ti-sism) The practice of selecting from various sources, sometimes to form a new system or style.

écorché (ay-kor-SHAY) A figure painted or sculptured to show the muscles of the body without skin.

elevation In drawing and architecture, a geometric projection of a building on a plane perpendicular to the horizon; a vertical projection.

embrasure A *splayed* opening in a wall that enframes a doorway or a window.

emulsion Chemical coatings used to transfer photographic images directly onto metal plates (for the daguerreotype), paper, fabric, or other surfaces.

enamel A vitreous, colored paste that solidifies when fired. See also *champlevé, cloisonné.*

encaustic A method of painting with colored, molten wax in which the wax is fused with the surface by the application of heat.

engaged column A columnlike, nonfunctional form projecting from a wall and articulating it visually. See also *pilaster.*

engobe (en-GOHB) A slip of finely sifted clay used by Greek potters; applied to a pot, it would form a black *glaze* in firing.

engraving The process of *incising* a design in hard material, often a metal plate (usually copper); also, the print or impression made from such a plate. See also *dry point, etching, intaglio.*

entablature The part of a building above the *capitals* of *columns* and below the roof or the upper story.

entasis (EN-tah-sis) An almost imperceptible convex tapering (an apparent swelling) in the *shaft* of a *column.*

epistyle See *architrave.*

esthetic The distinctive vocabulary and theory of a given *style.*

esthetics Theories about the nature of art and artistic expression.

etching A kind of *engraving* in which the design is *incised* in a layer of wax or varnish on a metal plate. The parts of the plate left exposed are then **etched** (slightly eaten away) by the acid in which the plate is immersed after incising. See also *dry point, engraving, intaglio.*

extrados (eks-TRAH-dohs) The upper or outer surface of an *arch.* See *intrados.*

façade Usually, the front of a building; also, the other sides when they are emphasized architecturally.

faïence (feye-AHNCE) Earthenware or pottery, especially with highly colored design (from Faenza, Italy, a site of manufacture for such ware).

fan vault See *vault.*

fenestration The arrangement of the windows of a building.

ferroconcrete See *reinforced concrete.*

fête galante (fet ga-LAHNT) An elegant and graceful celebration; often represented in the works of Antoine Watteau and other Rococo painters.

fetish An object believed to possess magical powers, especially one capable of bringing to fruition its owner's plans; sometimes regarded as the abode of a supernatural power or spirit.

fibula A decorative pin, usually used to fasten garments.

figure-ground In two-dimensional works of art, the visual unity, yet separability, of a form and its background.

filigree A delicate, lacelike, intertwined, ornamental work or design.

fin de siècle (fan duh SEE-akl) Characteristic of the progressive ideas and customs of the last years of the nineteenth century.

finial A knoblike ornament (usually with a foliate design) in which a vertical member, such as a *pinnacle,* terminates.

flamboyant Flamelike, flaming; applied to aspects of Late Gothic style, especially architectural tracery.

flute or **fluting** Vertical channeling, roughly semicircular in cross section and used principally on *columns* and *pilasters.*

flying buttress See *buttress.*

foreshortening The use of *perspective* to represent in art the apparent visual contraction of an object that extends back in space at an angle to the perpendicular plane of sight.

form In its widest sense, total structure; a synthesis of all the visible elements of that structure and of the manner in which they are united to create its distinctive character. The *form* of a work is what enables us to apprehend it. See also *closed form* and *open form.*

formalism Strict adherence to, or dependence on, stylized shapes and methods of composition.

forum The public square or marketplace of an ancient Roman city.

found images (or **materials** or **objects**) Images, materials, or objects as found in the everyday environment that are appropriated into works of art.

fresco Painting on plaster, either dry **(dry fresco** or **fresco secco)** or wet **(wet** or **true fresco).** In the latter method, the pigments are mixed with water and become chemically bound to the plaster. Also, a painting executed in either method.

fret or **meander** An ornament, usually in bands but also covering broad surfaces, consisting of interlocking geometric motifs.

frieze (freez) The part of the *entablature* between the *architrave* and the *cornice;* also, any sculptured or ornamented band in a building, on furniture, etc.

frigidarium The cold-bath section of a Roman bathing establishment.

frottage A process that combines patterns achieved by rubbing a crayon or other medium across a sheet of paper placed over a surface with a strong and evocative texture pattern.

full round Sculpture in full and completely rounded form (not in *relief*).

gable See *pediment.*

gallery The second story of an *ambulatory* or *aisle.*

garbha griha The *cella* or inner sanctum of the Hindu temple.

gargoyle In architecture, a waterspout (usually carved), often in the form of a *grotesque.*

genre (ZHAHN-reh) A style or category of art; also, a kind of painting realistically depicting scenes from everyday life.

gesso (JESS-oh) Plaster mixed with a binding material and used for *reliefs* and as a *ground* for painting.

glaze A vitreous coating applied to pottery to seal the surface and as decoration; it may be colored, transparent, or opaque, and glossy or *matte.* In oil painting, a thin, transparent, or semitransparent layer put over a color to alter it slightly.

glory See *nimbus.*

Golden Mean or **Golden Section** A proportional relation obtained by dividing a line so that the shorter part is to the longer part as the longer part is to the whole. The *esthetic* appeal of these proportions has led artists of varying periods and cultures to employ them in determining basic dimensions.

gopuram (GO-poor-am) The massive, ornamented entrance structure of South Indian temples.

graphic arts Visual arts that are linear in character, such as drawing and *engraving;* also, generally, visual arts that involve impression (printing and printmaking).

graver A cutting tool used by engravers and sculptors.

Greek cross A cross in which all the arms are the same length.

grisaille (greez-EYE) A monochrome painting done mainly in neutral greys to simulate sculpture.

groin The edge formed by the intersection of two *vaults.*

groin vault See *vault.*

grotesque In art, a kind of ornament used in antiquity—and sometimes called (imprecisely) *arabesque*—consisting of representations of medallions, sphinxes, foliage, and imaginary creatures.

ground A coating applied to a canvas or some other surface to prepare that surface for painting; also, background.

guilloche (gee-USH) An ornament consisting of interlaced, curving bands.

hallenkirche (HOLL-en-keer-sheh) A hall church. In this variety of Gothic church, especially popular in Germany, the *aisles* are as high as the *nave.*

haniwa Sculptured pottery tubes, modeled in human, animal, or other forms, and placed around early (archaic) Japanese burial mounds.

Happenings Loosely structured performances initiated in the 1960s, whose creators were trying to suggest the dynamic and confusing qualities of everyday life; most shared qualities of unexpectedness, variety, and wonder.

harmika A square enclosure on top of the *dome* of a *stupa* from which the *yasti* arises.

hatching A technique used in drawing, engraving, etc., in which fine lines are cut or drawn close together to achieve an effect of shading.

haunch The part of an *arch* (roughly midway between the *springing* and the *crown*) at which the lateral *thrust* is strongest.

herringbone perspective See *perspective.*

hieratic (higher-AT-tic) The priestly supernaturalism disparaging matter and material values that prevailed throughout the Christian Middle Ages, especially in Orthodox Byzantium.

hieroglyphic (high-roh-GLIF-ic) A system of writing using symbols or pictures; also, one of the symbols.

himation (him-MAT-ee-on) A Greek *mantle* worn by men and women over the tunic and draped in various ways.

historiated Ornamented with representations, such as plants, animals, or human figures, that have a narrative—as distinct from a purely decorative—function. Historiated initial letters were a popular form of manuscript decoration in the Middle Ages.

holography Medium that reconstructs in light alone the surface appearance of the subject, providing a real, three-dimensional image; recorded with the light of a laser.

horror vacui (VACK-ui) Literally, "fear of empty space"; crowded design.

hue The name of a color. *Pigment* colors combine differently than colors of light. The *primary colors* (in pigment: blue, red, and yellow; in light: blue, red, and green) together with the *secondary colors* (in pigment: green, orange, and violet; in light: cyan, magenta, and yellow) form the chief colors of the spectrum. See also *complementary colors, cool color, saturation, value, warm color.*

hydria (HIGH-dree-a) An ancient Greek three-handled water jar.

hypostyle hall A hall with a roof supported by columns; applied to the colonnaded hall of the Egyptian *pylon* temple.

icon (EYE-con) A portrait or image; especially in the Greek church, a panel with a painting of sacred personages that are objects of veneration. In the visual arts, a painting, a piece of sculpture, or even a building regarded as an object of veneration.

iconography (eye-con-OG-ra-fee) The analytic study of the symbolic, often religious, meaning of objects, persons, or events depicted in works of art.

iconostasis (eye-con-OS-ta-sis) In eastern Christian churches, a screen or a partition, with doors and many *tiers* of *icons,* that separates the sanctuary from the main body of the church.

idealization The representation of things according to a preconception of ideal *form* or type; a kind of *esthetic* distortion to produce idealized forms. See also *realism.*

ideogram A simple, picturelike sign filled with implicit meaning.

illumination Decoration with drawings (usually in gold, silver, and bright colors), especially of the initial letters of a manuscript.

imagines (i-MAJ-i-nees; *sing.* **imago**) In ancient Rome, wax portraits of ancestors.

imam (eye-MAHM) One who leads worshipers in prayer in Moslem services.

impasto (im-PAH-stoh) A style of painting in which the pigment is applied thickly or in heavy lumps, as in many of Rembrandt's paintings.

impluvium A depression in the floor of a Roman *atrium* to collect rainwater.

impost block A stone with the shape of a truncated, inverted pyramid, placed between a *capital* and the *arch* that springs from it.

incising Cutting into a surface with a sharp instrument; also, a method of decoration, especially on metal and pottery.

incrustation A style of wall decoration in Pompeii and Herculaneum in which the wall was divided into bright, polychrome panels of solid colors with occasional, schematically rendered textural contrasts.

in situ (SI-too) In place; in original position.

insula A multistoried Roman apartment block.

intaglio (in-TAL-yoh) A category of graphic technique in which the design is *incised,* so that the impression made is in *relief.* Used especially on gems, seals, and dies for coins, but also in the kinds of printing or printmaking in which the ink-bearing surface is depressed. Also, an object so decorated. See also *dry point, engraving, etching.*

intarsia (in-TAHR-sya) Inlay work, primarily in wood and sometimes in mother-of-pearl, marble, etc.
intercolumniation The space or the system of spacing between *columns* in a *colonnade*.
intrados (in-TRAH-dohs) The underside of an *arch* or a *vault*. See *extrados*.
isocephaly (eye-soh-SEF-ah-lee) The arrangement of figures so that the heads are at the same height.

jataka (JAH-tah-kah) Tales of the lives of the Buddha.
jump cuts Cinema technique used to disrupt narrative flow by arbitrarily omitting chunks from the middle of long continuous shots to dislocate any sense of progressive action.

ka (kah) In ancient Egypt, immortal human substance; the concept approximates the Western idea of the soul.
kagle A rough, highly abstracted African (Dan) mask.
kakemono (KAH-keh-moh-noh) A Japanese hanging or scroll.
karma (KAR-muh) In Buddhist and Hindu belief, the ethical consequences of a person's life, which determine his or her fate.
keystone The central, uppermost *voussoir* in an *arch*.
khutbah (KOOT-bah) In Moslem worship, a sermon and a declaration of allegiance to a community leader.
kiln A large stove or oven in which pottery is fired.
kinesiologist Scholar of motion who often uses photographs to study the discrete phases of a particular movement.
kore (KOR-ay) Greek for "girl."
kouros (COOR-aus) Greek for "young man."
krater/crater (KRAY-ter) An ancient Greek wide-mouthed bowl for mixing wine and water.
kuang (gwahng) A Chinese covered libation vessel.
kylix/cylix (KYE-liks) An ancient Greek drinking cup, shallow and having two handles and a stem.

lacquer A resinous spirit varnish, such as shellac; often colored.
lantern In architecture, a small, often decorative structure with openings for lighting that crowns a *dome, turret,* or roof.
lapis lazuli (LA-pis LA-zyoo-lye) A rich, ultramarine, semiprecious stone used for carving and as a source of *pigment*.
Latin cross A cross in which the vertical member is longer than the horizontal member.
lectionary A list, often illustrated, of **lections,** selections from the Scriptures that are read in church services.
lierne (lee-ERN) A short *rib* that runs from one main rib of a *vault* to another.
line The mark made by a moving point, which has psychological impact according to its direction and weight. In art, a line defines space and may create a silhouette or define a *contour,* creating the illusion of *mass* and *volume*.
linear perspective See *perspective*.
lintel A beam of any material used to span an opening.
lithography In graphic arts, a printmaking process in which the printing surface is a polished stone or a special metal or plastic plate on which the design is drawn with a greasy material. Greasy ink, applied to the moistened surface, is repelled by all surfaces except the lines of the drawing. The process permits linear and tonal *values* of great range and subtlety.
local color In painting, the actual *color* of an object.
loggia (LUH-jee-uh) A gallery that has an open *arcade* or a *colonnade* on one or both sides.
lost-wax process See *cire perdue*.
lotiform In the form of a lotus petal.
lunette A semicircular opening (with the flat side down) in a wall over a door, a niche, or a window.
luster A thin *glaze* (usually metallic) sometimes used on pottery to produce a rich, often iridescent color. Used particularly in Persian pottery and in *majolica*.

machicolation (mah-CHIK-oh-lay-shun) An opening in the floor of an overhanging gallery through which the defenders of a castle dropped stones and boiling liquids on attackers.
madrasah (muh-DRAH-suh) A combined Moslem school and *mosque*.
magazine A room or building designed for storage.
majolica (ma-JO-lik-ah) A kind of Italian Renaissance pottery coated with a whitish tin-compound enamel, brilliantly painted and often *lustered*.
makimono (MAH-kee-MOH-noh) A Japanese horizontal scroll.
malanggan (mah-LOHNG-gahn) Intricately carved Melanesian ceremonial masks.
mandala (MAN-duh-luh) In Hinduism and Buddhism, a magical, geometric symbol of the cosmos.
mandapa (man-DOP-ah) A Hindu assembly hall, part of a temple.
mandorla An almond-shaped *nimbus,* or *glory,* surrounding the figure of Christ.
maniera greca (man-YERA GRE-ka) A formal Byzantine style that dominated Italian painting in the twelfth and thirteenth centuries; characterized by shallow space and linear flatness.
mantle A sleeveless, protective outer garment or cloak. See *himation*.
mass The effect and degree of bulk, density, and weight of matter in space. As opposed to plane and area, mass is three-dimensional.
mastaba (MAH-sta-bah) A bench-shaped ancient Egyptian tomb.
matte (mat) In painting, pottery, and photography, a dull finish.
mbari Ceremonial houses filled with clay sculptures and paintings, honoring community deities of the Ibo tribe in Africa.
meander See *fret*.
medium The substance or agency in which an artist works; also, in painting, the vehicle (usually liquid) that carries the *pigment*.
megalith Literally, "great stone"; a large, roughly hewn stone used in the construction of monumental, prehistoric structures. **megalithic** (*adj.*) See also *cromlech, dolmen, menhir*.
megaron (MEH-ga-ron) A rectangular hall, fronted by an open, two-columned porch, traditional in Greece since Mycenaean times.
menhir (MEN-heer) A prehistoric *monolith,* uncut or roughly cut, standing singly or with others in rows or circles.
metamatic In the work of Jean Tinguely, machines programmed electronically to act with antimechanical unpredictability.
métier (MAY-tee-yay) One's area of expertise.
metope (MET-a-pee) The space between *triglyphs* in a Doric *frieze*.
mihrab (MEE-rahb) In the wall of a *mosque,* the niche that indicates the direction of Mecca.
minbar (MEEN-bar) The pulpit found near the *qiblah* wall in a *mosque*.
miniature A small picture illustrating a manuscript; also, any small portrait, often on ivory or *porcelain*.
modeling The shaping or fashioning of three-dimensional forms in a soft material, such as clay; also, the gradations of light and shade reflected from the surfaces of matter in space, or the illusion of such gradations produced by alterations of *value* in a drawing, painting, or print.
module (MOD-yool) A basic unit of which the dimensions of the major parts of a work are multiples. The principle is used in sculpture and other art forms, but it is most often employed in architecture, where the module may be the dimensions of an important part of a building, such as a *column,* or simply some commonly accepted unit of measurement (the centimeter or the inch, or, as with Le Corbusier, the average dimensions of the human figure).
molding In architecture, a continuous, narrow surface (projecting or recessed, plain or ornamented) designed to break up a surface, to accent, or to decorate.
monochrome A painting, drawing, or print in one color; also, the technique of making such an artwork.
monolith A column that is all in one piece (not built up); a large, single block or piece of stone used in *megalithic* structures.
monumental In art criticism, any work of art of grandeur and simplicity, regardless of its size.
mortice See *tenon*.
mosaic Patterns or pictures made by embedding small pieces of stone or glass (*tesserae*) in cement on surfaces such as walls and floors; also, the technique of making such works.
mosque A Moslem place of worship.
mudra (muh-DRAH) A stylized gesture of mystical significance, usually in representations of Hindu deities.

mullion A vertical member that divides a window or that separates one window from another.

mural A wall painting; a *fresco* is a type of mural medium and technique.

naos See *cella.*

narthex A porch or vestibule of a church, generally colonnaded or arcaded and preceding the *nave.*

Naturalism The doctrine that art should adhere as closely as possible to the appearance of the natural world. Naturalism, with varying degrees of fidelity to appearance, recurs in the history of Western art.

nave The part of a church between the chief entrance and the *choir,* demarcated from *aisles* by *piers* or *columns.*

necking A groove at the bottom of the Greek Doric *capital* between the *echinus* and the *flutes* that masks the junction of *capital* and *shaft.*

necropolis (neh-KROP-o-lis) A large burial area; literally, a city of the dead.

New Wave cinema (La Nouvelle Vague) Cinema style developed in the 1950s and 1960s that characteristically attempted to subvert viewer expectations by using ambiguity, surprize, fuzzy camera work, and abrupt changes in space, time, and mood.

niello (nee-EL-o) Inlay in a metal of an alloy of sulfur and such metals as gold or silver. Also, a work made by this process, or the alloy itself.

nimbus A halo, aureole, or **glory** appearing around the head of a holy figure to signify divinity.

nirvana (neer-VAH-nah) In Buddhism and Hinduism, a blissful state brought about by absorption of the individual soul or consciousness into the supreme spirit.

nonobjective Having no discernible reference to the external appearance of the physical world.

objet d'art (objay-DAR) A relatively small object (such as a figurine or vase) of artistic value.

obverse On coins or medals, the side that bears the principal type or inscription. See also *reverse.*

oculus A round, central opening or "eye" in a *dome.*

odalisque (OH-dah-lisk) A female slave or concubine; a favorite subject of such artists as Ingres and Matisse.

oenochoe (eh-NUK-oh-ee) An ancient Greek wine pitcher.

oeuvre (UH-vreh) The whole of an artist's output; literally, the artist's "work."

ogee (OH-jee) A *molding* having in profile a double or S-shaped curve. Also, an *arch,* each side of which has this *form.*

ogive The diagonal *rib* of a Gothic *vault;* a pointed, or Gothic, *arch.* **ogival** (*adj.*)

oil color/paint *Pigment* ground with oil.

open form A *mass* penetrated or treated in such a way that space acts as its environment rather than as its limit. See also *closed form.*

order In Classical architecture, a style represented by a characteristic design of the *column* and its *entablature.* See also *superimposed order.*

orthogonal A line imagined to be behind and perpendicular to the *picture plane;* the *orthogonals* in a painting appear to recede toward a *vanishing point* on the horizon.

pagoda A Buddhist tower with a multiplicity of winged eaves; derived from the Indian *stupa.*

palestra A Roman exercise room.

palette (PAL-it) A thin board with a thumb hole at one end on which an artist lays and mixes colors; any surface so used. Also, the colors or kinds of colors characteristically used by an artist.

palmette (pal-MET) A conventional, decorative ornament of ancient origin composed of radiating petals springing from a cuplike base.

panorama Originally, a specially designed building that housed colossal, circular murals. Also, any broad, spectacular vista.

Pantheon (PAN-thee-on) All the gods of a people, or a temple dedicated to all such gods; especially, the Pantheon in Rome (although it is not certain that this was its function).

papier collé (PAH-pee-yay CAHL-lay) Variety of collage in which paper shapes are combined into one work of art; literally, "stuck paper."

papyrus (pah-PIE-rus) A plant native to Egypt and adjacent lands used to make a paperlike writing material; also, the material or any writing on it.

parasol An umbrella atop a Chinese *pagoda;* a vestige of the **chatra** on an Indian *stupa.*

parchment Lambskin prepared as a surface for writing or painting.

passage grave A burial chamber entered through a long, tunnel-like passage.

pastel Finely ground *pigments* compressed into chalklike sticks. Also, work done in this *medium,* or exhibiting its characteristic paleness.

pastiche (pas-TEESH) An artistic hodgepodge that imitates or ridicules another artist's style.

patina (pa-TEEN-a) The colored, oxidized layer, often green, that forms on bronze and copper; also, the creation of a colored surface on metal sculpture by the application of an acid solution.

pediment (PED-i-ment) In Classical architecture, the triangular space (**gable**) at the end of a building, formed by the ends of the sloping roof and the *cornice;* also, an ornamental feature having this shape.

pendentive (pen-DEN-tiv) A concave, triangular piece of masonry (a triangular section of a hemisphere), four of which provide the transition from a square area to the circular base of a covering *dome.* Although they appear to be hanging (**pendent**) from the dome, they in fact support it.

peripteral (per-IP-ter-al) A style of building in which the main structure is surrounded by a *colonnade.*

peristyle (PAIR-i-stile) A *colonnade* surrounding a building or a court.

persistence of vision Retention in the brain for a fraction of a second of whatever the eye has seen; causes a rapid succession of images to merge one into the next, producing the illusion of continuous change and motion in media such as cinema.

perspective A formula for projecting an illusion of the three-dimensional world onto a two-dimensional surface. In **linear perspective,** the most common type, all parallel lines or lines of projection seem to converge on one, two, or three points located with reference to the eye level of the viewer (the horizon line of the picture), known as *vanishing points,* and associated objects are rendered smaller the further from the viewer they are intended to seem. **Atmospheric** or **aerial perspective** creates the illusion of distance by the greater diminution of *color* intensity, the shift in color toward an almost neutral blue, and the blurring of *contours* as the intended distance between eye and object increases. In **herringbone perspective,** the lines of projection converge not on a vanishing point, but on a vertical *axis* at the center of the picture, as in Roman paintings.

photogram An assemblage of objects on photosensitive paper exposed to light to yield an image of ghostly silhouettes floating in a void of darkened space.

photomontage (MOHN-tahzh) A composition made by fitting together pictures or parts of pictures, especially photographs. See also *collage.*

photoscreen Technique employing photo processes to create stencil screens from graphic images, which then become part of complex printing or painting processes.

pi (bee) The Chinese symbol of Heaven; a jade disk.

piano nobile (PEEA-no NO-bee-lay) The principal story, usually the second, in Renaissance buildings.

pictograph A picture, usually stylized, that represents an idea; also, writing using such means. See also *hieroglyphic.*

picture plane The surface of a picture.

pier A vertical, unattached masonry support.

Pietà (pee-ay-TA) A work of art depicting the Virgin mourning over the body of Christ.

pigment Finely powdered coloring matter mixed or ground with various vehicles to form paint, crayon, etc.

pilaster (pil-LAS-ter) A flat, rectangular, vertical member projecting from a wall of which it forms a part. It usually has a base and a *capital* and is often *fluted.*

pillar Usually a weight-carrying member, such as a *pier* or a *column;* sometimes an isolated, freestanding structure used for commemorative purposes.

pilotis (pee-LOW-teez; *sing.* **piloti**) Thin steel or reinforced concrete posts used by architects in the early twentieth century to support concrete roof and floor slabs, avoiding the need for load-bearing walls.

pinnacle A tower, primarily ornamental, that also functions in Gothic architecture to give additional weight to a *buttress* or a *pier.* See also *finial.*

pithos (PITH-oss; *pl.* **pithoi**) A large, clay storage vessel frequently set into the earth and therefore possessing no flat base.

plan The horizontal arrangement of the parts of a building, or a drawing or a diagram showing such an arrangement as a horizontal *section.* In **axial plan,** the parts of a building are organized longitudinally, or along a given *axis;* in a **central plan,** the parts radiate from a central point.

plasticity In art, the three-dimensionality of an object. **plastic** (*adj.*)

plinth The lowest member of a base; also, a block serving as a base for a statue.

pointillism The method of painting of some French Post-Impressionists in which a white ground is covered with tiny dots of color, which, when viewed at a distance, blend together to produce a luminous effect. See *divisionism.*

polychrome Done in several colors.

polyptych (POL-ip-tik) An *altarpiece* made up of more than three sections.

porcelain Translucent, impervious, resonant *pottery* made in a base of **kaolin,** a fine white clay; sometimes any pottery that is translucent, whether or not it is made of kaolin.

porphyry (POUR-feary) An Egyptian rock containing large crystals of feldspar in a purplish groundmass; used in ancient architecture and sculpture.

portico A porch with a roof supported by *columns;* an entrance porch.

post-and-lintel system A *trabeated* system of construction in which two posts support a *lintel.*

potsherds Broken pottery, discarded by earlier civilizations, that settles into firmly stratified mounds over time and provides archeological chronologies.

pottery Objects (usually vessels) made of clay and hardened by firing.

Poussinistes (Poo-sehn-EESTS) Adherents to the doctrine that form, rather than color, was the most important element in painting. See *Rubénistes.*

predella The narrow ledge on which an *altarpiece* rests on an altar.

primary colors In *pigment,* the *hues* red, yellow, and blue. From these three colors, with the addition of white or black, it is theoretically possible to mix the full range of colors in the spectrum. In light, the hues red, blue, and green, which can be combined in varying amounts to produce the full range of colors in the spectrum. Combining the three primary colors of light in equal proportions produces pure white light. The primary colors of either pigment or light cannot be produced by mixing other colors together.

program The architect's formulation of a design problem with respect to considerations of site, function, materials, and aims of the client; also, in painting and sculpture, the conceptual basis of a work.

pronaos (pro-NAY-os) The space in front of the *cella* or *naos* of a Greek temple.

propylaeum (prah-pi-LAY-um; *pl.* **propylaea**) A gateway building leading to an open court preceding a Greek or Roman temple.

proscenium (pro-SEEN-i-um) The stage of an ancient Greek or Roman theater.

prostyle A style of Greek temple in which the *columns* stand in front of the *naos* and extend its full width.

provenance Origin; source.

psalter A book containing the Psalms of the Bible.

putto (*pl.* **putti**) A young child, a favorite subject in Italian painting and sculpture.

pylon (PIE-lon) The *monumental* entrance of an Egyptian temple.

qiblah (KEEB-lah) The direction (toward Mecca) in which Moslems face in prayer. (Often *kibla.*)

quadro riportato (kwahd-roh ree-por-TAH-toh) The simulation of a wall painting for a ceiling design in which painted scenes are arranged in panels resembling frames on the surface of a shallow, curved *vault.*

quatrefoil (KAT-re-foyl) An architectural ornament having four lobes or **foils.** See also *trefoil.*

quattrocento (KWAT-tro-CHAIN-toh) The fifteenth century in Italian art. Literally, the "1400s."

quoin (koin) A large, sometimes *rusticated,* usually slightly projecting stone (or stones) that often form the corners of the exterior walls of masonry buildings.

raking cornice The *cornice* on the sloping sides of a *pediment.*

Ramayana A Sanskrit epic telling of Rama, an incarnation of the Hindu god Vishnu.

rathas Small, freestanding Hindu temples, perhaps sculptured as architectural models.

rayograph In the work of Man Ray, a *photogram.*

rayonnant The "radiant" style in thirteenth-century architecture that is associated with the royal Paris court of Louis IX.

readymades Manufactured objects, sometimes altered or joined with other objects and displayed as works of art to stimulate thought.

realism The representation of things according to their appearance in visible nature (without *idealization*). In the nineteenth century, an approach that supported the representation of the subject matter of everyday life in a realistic mode. Iconographically, nineteenth-century Realism is the subject matter of everyday life as seen by the artist.

red-figure technique In later Greek pottery, the silhouetting of red figures against a black background; the reverse of the *black-figure technique.*

reinforced concrete (ferroconcrete) Concrete with increased tensile strength produced by iron or steel mesh or bars embedded in it.

relief In sculpture, figures projecting from a background of which they are part. The degree of relief is designated high, low (**bas**), sunken (hollow), or *intaglio.* In the last, the backgrounds are not cut back and the points in highest relief are level with the original surface of the material being carved. See also *repoussé; stiacciata.*

reliquary A small receptacle for a sacred relic, usually of a richly decorated, precious material.

repoussé (ruh-poo-SAY) Formed in *relief* by beating a metal plate from the back, leaving the impression on the face. The metal is hammered into a hollow mold of wood or some other pliable material and finished with a *graver.* See also *relief.*

reserve column In Egyptian rock-cut and Etruscan domed tombs, a *column* that is hewn from the living rock and serves no supporting function.

respond An engaged *column, pilaster,* or similar structure that either projects from a *compound pier* or some other supporting device or is bonded to a wall and carries one end of an *arch,* often at the end of an *arcade.* A **nave arcade,** for example, may have nine *pillars* and two responds.

retable (ruh-TAY-bl) An architectural screen or wall above and behind an altar, usually containing painting, sculpture, carving, or other decorations. See also *altarpiece.*

reverse On coins or medals, the side opposite the *obverse.*

rhyton (RIGHT-on) An ancient Greek ceremonial drinking vessel with a base usually in the form of the head of an animal, a woman, or a mythological creature.

rib A relatively slender, molded masonry *arch* that projects from a surface. In Gothic architecture, the *ribs* form the framework of the *vaulting.*

ribbed vault See *vault.*

ridgepole The horizontal beam at the ridge of a roof, to which the upper ends of the rafters attach.

rinceau (ran-SO) An ornamental design composed of undulating foliate vine motifs.

rocaille (row-cah-EEE) Literally, "pebble." Refers to small stone and shell motifs in some eighteenth-century ornamentation.

Romanitas (Roh-MAN-ee-tahs) The religion of the Holy Roman Empire; its ritual and practice was based on imperial dominion.

rose or **wheel window** The large, circular window with *tracery* and stained glass frequently used in the *façades* of Gothic churches.

rotulus A long manuscript scroll used by the Egyptians, Greeks, and Romans; predecessor of the *codex.*

Rubénistes (Rue-bay-NEESTS) Adherents to a doctrine proclaiming the supremacy of color, rather than form, as the proper guide for the artist. See *Poussinistes.*

rusticate To give a rustic appearance by roughening the surfaces and *beveling* the edges of stone blocks to emphasize the joints between them. A technique popular during the Renaissance, especially for stone courses at the ground-floor level.

sacra conversazione (SAH-krah cone-ver-sotz-ee-OHN-ee) In Italian, literally "holy conversation"; a grouping of the Madonna, Child, and saints in the same spatial setting, so that they appear to be conversing with one another.

sacral-idyllic scene A landscape depicting country life and idealized nature.

Salon (sah-LON) The government-sponsored exhibition of works by living artists held in Paris, first biennially and (since the mid-eighteenth century) annually.

salon In the eighteenth and early nineteenth centuries, a social assembly, in a private dwelling, of leaders in art and public affairs.

samsara (som-SAH-rah) In Hindu belief, the rebirth of the soul into a succession of lives.

santos (SAHN-toes) Simple, painted, wooden folk sculptures of holy figures found throughout Latin America and the Southwest.

sarcophagus (sar-KOF-a-gus) A stone coffin.

saturation The purity of a *hue*; the higher the *saturation*, the purer the hue. *Value* and saturation are not constantly related. For example, high-saturation yellow tends to have a high value, but high-saturation violet tends to have a low value.

satyr (SAT-er) In Greek mythology, a kind of demi-god or deity; a follower of Dionysos; wanton and lascivious and often represented with goatlike ears and legs and a short tail.

scale The dimensions of the parts or the totality of a building or an object in relation to its use or function. In architectural *plans*, the relation of the actual size of a structure to its representative size.

scriptorium A Medieval writing room in which scrolls were also housed.

sculpture in the round Freestanding figures, carved or modeled in three dimensions.

secondary colors The colors (in pigment: green, orange, and purple; in light: cyan, magenta, and yellow) that result from mixture of pairs of *primary colors.*

section In architecture, a diagram or representation of a part of a structure or building along an imaginary plane that passes through it vertically.

seicento (say-CHAIN-toh) The seventeenth century in Italian art. Literally, the "1600s."

serdab A small, concealed chamber in an Egyptian tomb for the statue of the deceased.

severe style An early, pre-Classical, transitional style of mid-fifth-century Greek statuary that is formal but not rigid in pose and emphasizes the principle of weight distribution; a liberation from the Archaic limitations of frontal rigidity found in Egyptian portrait statues.

sfumato (sfoo-MA-toh) A smokelike haziness that subtly softens outlines in painting; term is particularly applied to the painting of Leonardo and Correggio.

sgraffito (zgra-FEE-toh) Decoration produced by scratching through a surface layer of plaster, *glazing*, etc., to reveal a different colored *ground;* also, pottery or other ware so decorated.

shaft The part of a *column* between the *capital* and the base.

shaft grave A grave in the form of a deep pit, the actual burial spot being at the base of the shaft or in a niche at the base.

shaman (SHAH-mon) A priest or medicine man who can influence good and evil spirits; **shamanism** is the religion of some American Indians and Eskimos.

shinto Indigenous faith of the Japanese people.

shoji (SHOW-jee) A translucent rice-paper-covered sliding screen that serves as a room divider in traditional Japanese houses.

sikhara (SHIH-ka-rah) In Hindu temples of Vishnu, the tower above the shrine.

silver point A drawing technique involving the use of a silver-tipped "pencil" on a paper with a white *matte* coating; also, the delicate drawings so made.

sinopia or **sinopie** Reddish-brown earth color; also, the *cartoon* or underpainting for a *fresco.*

sistrum An instrument of metal rods loosely held in a metal frame, which jingle when shaken. Peculiarly Egyptian, it was used especially in the worship of Isis and is still used in Nubia.

sizing Traditional protective coat of glue applied to canvas.

slip Potter's clay dispersed in a liquid and used for *casting,* decoration, and to attach parts of clay vessels, such as handles.

smalto The colored glass or enamel used in *mosaics.*

socle (SOH-kel) A molded projection at the bottom of a wall or a *pier*, or beneath a pedestal or a *column* base.

soffit The underside of an architectural member such as an *arch, lintel, cornice,* or stairway. See also *intrados.*

soft focus A term used especially in photography to refer to an image made when the lens is thrown slightly out of sharp focus so that the contours of any object appear moderately soft and blurred.

space-time A concise way of referring to the understanding of the universe as an entity composed of inextricably interwoven space and time; a conception based especially on the theories of Albert Einstein. In this view of the universe, anything that happens to alter the condition of space also affects the condition of time, and vice versa.

spandrel The roughly triangular space enclosed by the curves of adjacent *arches* and a horizontal member connecting their vertexes; also, the space enclosed by the curve of an *arch* and an enclosing right angle.

splay A large *bevel* or *chamfer.*

splayed opening An opening (as in a wall) that is cut away diagonally so that the outer edges are farther apart than the inner edges. See also *embrasure.*

springing The lowest stone of an *arch,* resting on the *impost block.*

square schematism A church *plan* in which the *crossing square* is used as the *module* for all parts of the design.

squinch An architectural device used to make a transition from a square to a polygonal or circular base for a *dome.* It may be composed of *lintels, corbels,* or *arches.*

stave A wedge-shaped timber; vertically placed staves embellish the architectural features of a building.

stele (STEE-lee) A carved stone slab or *pillar* used especially by the ancient Greeks as grave or site markers and for similar purposes. Also found in Maya area of Mesoamerica to commemorate historical events.

stiacciata or **sciacciata** (stee-ah-CHAH-tah) A kind of very low relief, originated by Donatello, that incorporates much of the illusionism of painting into carving, which in places is hardly more than a scratching of the surface.

still life A painting representing inanimate objects, such as flowers, fruit, or household articles.

stoa (STOH-a) In ancient Greek architecture, an open building with a roof supported by a row of *columns* parallel to the back wall.

straight photography Photography that represents direct, "real-time" seeing as opposed to the combination of images made at different moments in time. See *double-exposure techniques* and *photomontage.*

stringcourse A horizontal *molding* or band in masonry, ornamental but usually reflecting interior structure.

stucco Fine plaster or cement used as a coating for walls or for decoration.

stupa (STOO-puh) A large, mound-shaped Buddhist shrine.

style A manner of treatment or execution of works of art that is characteristic of a civilization, a people, or an individual; also, a special and superior quality in a work of art.

stylobate (STY-loh-bate) The upper step of the base of a Greek temple, which forms a platform for the *columns.*

stylus A needlelike tool used in *engraving* and *incising.*

superimposed orders *Orders* of architecture that are placed one above another in an *arcaded* or *colonnaded* building, usually in the following sequence: **Doric** (the first story), **Ionic**, and **Corinthian**. Superimposed orders are found in Greek *stoas* and were used widely by Roman and Renaissance builders.

sutra (SOO-truh) In Buddhism, an account of a sermon by or a dialogue involving the *Buddha.*

swag A kind of decoration for walls, furniture, etc., done in *relief* and resembling garlands and gathered drapery, that was particularly popular in the eighteenth century.

symmetry *Esthetic* balance that is usually achieved by disposing *forms* about a real or an imaginary *axis* so that those on one side more-or-less correspond with those on the other. The correspondence may be in terms of shape, *color*, texture, etc.

tablinum A room behind the *atrium* in a Roman house in which family archives and statues were kept.
tectiforms Shapes resembling man-made structures found painted on the walls of Paleolithic caves.
tell In Near Eastern archeology, a hill or a mound, usually an ancient site of habitation.
tempera A technique of painting using *pigment* mixed with egg yolk, glue, or casein; also, the *medium* itself.
Tenebrists (TEN-i-brists) A group of seventeenth-century European painters who used violent contrasts of light and dark.
tenebroso Painting in the "dark manner"; a technique of the *Caravaggisti*.
tenon A projection on the end of a piece of wood that is inserted into a corresponding hole (**mortice**) in another piece of wood to form a joint.
tepidarium The warm-bath section of a Roman bathing establishment.
terra cotta Hard-baked clay, used for sculpture and as a building material, that may be *glazed* or painted.
tesserae (TESS-er-ee) Small, shaped pieces of glass or stone used in making *mosaics*.
tholos (THOH-los) A circular structure, generally in Classical Greek style; also an ancient, circular tomb.
thrust The outward force exerted by an *arch* or a *vault* that must be counterbalanced by *buttresses*.
tier A series of architectural rows, layers, or ranks arranged above or behind one another.
tondo A circular painting or *relief* sculpture.
torano (TOR-uh-nuh) Gateway in the stone fence around a *stupa*, located at the cardinal points of the compass.
torus A convex *molding* or part of a molding, usually the lowest in the base of a *column*.
totem An animal or object and its representation or image, considered to be a symbol of a given family or clan.
trabeated (TRAY-bee-ate-id) Of *post-and-lintel* construction. Literally, "beamed" construction.
tracery Branching, ornamental stonework, generally in a window, where it supports the glass; particularly characteristic of Gothic architecture.
transept The part of a *cruciform* church with an *axis* that crosses the main axis at right angles.
trecento (tray-CHAIN-toh) The fourteenth century in Italian art. Literally, the "1300s."
trefoil An architectural ornament having three lobes or *foils*. See also *quatrefoil*.
triforium In a Gothic cathedral, the blind, *arcaded* gallery below the *clerestory*.
triglyph A projecting, grooved member of a Doric *frieze* that alternates with *metopes*.
trilithon A pair of *monoliths* topped with a *lintel;* found in *megalithic* structures.
triptych (TRIP-tik) A three-paneled painting or *altarpiece*.
trompe l'oeil (trohmp-LOY) A form of illusionistic painting that attempts to represent an object as if it exists in three dimensions at the surface of the painting; literally, "eye-fooling."
trumeau (troo-MOH) A *pillar* in the center of a Romanesque or Gothic portal.
turret A small, often ornamental tower projecting from a building, usually at a corner.
tympanum The space enclosed by a *lintel* and an *arch* over a doorway; also, the recessed face of a *pediment*.

ukiyo-e (OO-kee-oh-ee) A style of Japanese *genre* painting ("pictures of the floating world") that influenced nineteenth-century Western art.
urna The whorl of hair, represented as a dot, between the brows of a Hindu diety.
ushnisha (ush-NISH-uh) Stylized protuberance of the *Buddha*'s forehead, emblematic of his superhuman consciousness.

value The amount of light reflected by a *hue;* the greater the amount of light, the higher the value. See also *saturation*.
vanishing point In *linear perspective*, that point on the horizon toward which parallel lines appear to converge and at which they seem to vanish.
vanitas (VAHN-ee-tahs) Painting subject, often a still life, in sixteenth and seventeenth centuries, meant to encourage the viewer to meditate on death as the inevitable end of all human life.
vault A masonry roof or ceiling constructed on the *arch* principle. A **barrel** or **tunnel vault,** semicylindrical in cross section, is in effect a deep arch or an uninterrupted series of arches, one behind the other, over an oblong space. In a **cross-barrel vault,** the main barrel (tunnel) vault is intersected at right angles with other barrel (tunnel) vaults at regular intervals. A **quadrant vault** is a half-barrel (tunnel) vault. A **sexpartite vault** is a rib vault with six panels. A **fan vault** is a development of *lierne* vaulting characteristic of English Perpendicular Gothic, in which radiating *ribs* form a fan-like pattern. A **groin** or **cross vault** is formed at the point at which two *barrel (tunnel) vaults* intersect at right angles. In a **ribbed vault,** there is a framework of ribs or arches under the intersections of the vaulting sections.
veduta (veh-DUE-tah) Type of naturalistic landscape and cityscape painting popular in eighteenth-century Venice. Literally, "view" painting.
vellum Calfskin prepared as a surface for writing or painting.
vernacular architecture Nonprofessional, popular architecture.
video synthesizer Special instrument that allows video artists to manipulate and change electronic video information, causing images to stretch, shrink, change color or break up, and to layer, inset, or merge with other images.
vignette Originally, a decorative element of vine leaves and tendrils in the page margins of Gothic manuscripts; later, a decorative design with no distinct borders to separate it from the text of a book page.
vihara (vee-HAH-rah) A Buddhist monastery, often cut into a hill.
vimana (vih-MAH-nuh) In Hindu and Buddhist temples, the pyramidal tower above the shrine (composed of the *garbha griha* and the *sikhara*).
volume See *mass*.
volute A spiral, scroll-like form characteristic of the Greek Ionic *capital*.
voussoir (voo-SWAHR) A wedge-shaped block used in the construction of a true *arch*. The central voussoir, which sets the arch, is the *keystone*.

warm color Red, orange, or yellow. Psychologically, warm colors tend to be exciting, emphatic, and affirmative; optically, they generally seem to advance or to project. See also *cool color*.
wash In *watercolor* painting especially, a thin, transparent film of color.
watercolor A painting technique using *pigment* (usually prepared with gum) mixed with water and applied to an absorbent surface; also, the *medium* itself. The painting is transparent, with the white of the paper furnishing the lights.
weight shift See *contrapposto*.
westwork A multistoried *mass*, including the *façade* and usually surmounted by towers, at the western end of a Medieval church, principally in Germany.
woodcut A wooden block on the surface of which those parts not intended to print are cut away to a slight depth, leaving the design raised; also, the printed impression made with such a block.

yaksha (YAK-shah) A divinity in the Hindu and Buddhist pantheon. (*f.* **yakshi**)
Yamato-e (yah-MAH-toh-ee) A purely Japanese style of sophisticated and depersonalized painting created for the Fujiwara nobility.
yasti (YAHS-tee) The mast surmounting the *dome* of a *stupa*.
yu A covered Chinese libation vessel.

Zen A Buddhist sect and its doctrine, emphasizing enlightenment through intuition and introspection rather than the study of scripture. In Chinese, *Ch'an*.
ziggurat (ZIG-oor-at) A roughly pyramidal structure, built in ancient Mesopotamia, consisting of stages; each succeeding stage is stepped back from the one beneath.
zoomorphism The representation of gods in the form or with the attributes of animals; the use of animal forms in art or symbolism.
zoopraxiscope (zoe-oh-PRAX-is-cope) Device invented by Eadweard Muybridge, which he developed to project sequences of images (mounted on special glass plates) onto a screen in rapid succession, creating the illusion of motion pictures. See *perspective of vision*.

BIBLIOGRAPHY

This supplementary list of books is intended to be comprehensive enough to satisfy the reading interests of the unspecialized student and general reader, as well as those of more advanced readers who wish to become acquainted with fields other than their own. The books listed range from works that are valuable primarily for their reproductions to scholarly surveys of schools and periods. No entries for periodical articles appear, but a few of the periodicals that publish art-historical scholarship in English are noted.

SELECT PERIODICALS

Archaeology
The Art Bulletin
Art History
The Art Journal
The Burlington Magazine
Journal of the Society of Architectural Historians
Journal of the Warburg and Courtauld Institutes

REFERENCE BOOKS

Arntzen, Etta, and Rainwater, Robert. *Guide to the Literature of Art History*. Chicago: American Library Association/Art Book Company, 1980. (Later edition available.)

Bator, Paul M. *The International Trade in Art*. Chicago: University of Chicago Press, 1983. (Later edition available.)

Bindman, David, ed. *The Thames & Hudson Encyclopedia of British Art*. London: Thames & Hudson, 1985. (Later editions available.)

Broude, Norma, and Garrard, Mary D., eds. *Feminism and Art History: Questioning the Litany*. New York: Harper & Row, 1982.

Chilvers, Ian, and Osborne, Harold, eds. *The Oxford Dictionary of Art*. New York: Oxford University Press, 1988.

Christe, Yves, et al. *Art of the Christian World, 200–1500: A Handbook of Styles and Forms*. New York: Rizzoli, 1982.

Encyclopedia of World Art. 15 vols. New York: Publisher's Guild, 1959–1968. Supplementary vols. 16, 1983; 17, 1987.

Feilden, Bernard B. *The Conservation of Historic Buildings*. London: Butterworth Scientific Books, 1982.

Fielding, Mantle. *Dictionary of American Painters, Sculptors, and Engravers*. 2nd rev. and enl. ed. Poughkeepsie, NY: Apollo, 1986.

Fleming, John; Honour, Hugh; and Pevsner, Nikolaus. *Penguin Dictionary of Architecture*. Baltimore: Penguin, 1980.

Fletcher, Sir Banister. *A History of Architecture*. 18th rev. ed. New York: Scribner, 1975.

Giedion, Siegfried. *The Beginnings of Architecture: The Eternal Present, a Contribution on Constancy and Change*. Princeton: Princeton University Press, 1981.

———. *Space, Time and Architecture: The Growth of a New Tradition*. 5th ed., rev. and enl. Cambridge: Harvard University Press, 1982.

Gombrich, Ernst Hans Josef. *Art and Illusion*. 5th ed. London: Phaidon, 1977.

Haggar, Reginald G. *A Dictionary of Art Terms: Architecture, Sculpture, Painting, and the Graphic Arts*. Poole, England: New Orchard Editions, 1984.

Hall, James. *Dictionary of Subjects and Symbols in Art*. 2nd rev. ed. London: J. Murray, 1977. (Later edition available.)

Harris, A. S., and Nochlin, L. *Women Artists: 1550–1950*. Los Angeles: County Museum of Art; New York: Knopf, 1976. (Later edition available.)

Hauser, Arnold. *The Sociology of Art*. Chicago: University of Chicago Press, 1982.

Hind, Arthur M. *A History of Engraving and Etching from the Fifteenth Century to the Year 1914*. 3rd rev. ed. New York: Dover, 1963.

Holt, Elizabeth G., ed. *A Documentary History of Art*. 2nd ed. 2 vols. Princeton: Princeton University Press, 1981.

Huyghe, René, ed. *Larousse Encyclopedia of Byzantine and Medieval Art*. New York: Prometheus Press, 1963; Excalibur Books, 1981.

———. *Larousse Encyclopedia of Renaissance and Baroque Art*. New York: Prometheus Press, 1964; Hamlyn/American (paperbound), 1976.

James, John, et al. *The Traveler's Key to Medieval France: A Guide to the Sacred Architecture of Medieval France*. New York: Knopf, 1986.

Janson, H. W., ed. *Sources and Documents in the History of Art Series*. Englewood Cliffs, NJ: Prentice-Hall, 1966.

Kostof, Spiro. *A History of Architecture: Settings and Rituals*. Oxford: Oxford University Press, 1985.

Kronenberger, Louis. *Atlantic Brief Lives: A Biographical Companion to the Arts*. Boston: Little, Brown, 1971.

Lucie-Smith, Edward. *The Thames & Hudson Dictionary of Art Terms*. London: Thames & Hudson, 1984.

Murray, Peter, and Murray, Linda. *A Dictionary of Art and Artists*. New York: Penguin, 1976; (paperbound) 1984.

Myers, Bernard Samuel, ed. *Encyclopedia of Painting: Painters and Painting of the World from Prehistoric Times to the Present Day*. 4th rev. ed. New York: Crown, 1979.

———. *Encyclopedia of World Art*, Suppl. vol. 16. Palatine, IL: McGraw-Hill/The Publishers Guild, 1983. (Later edition available.)

Myers, Bernard S., and Myers, Shirley D., eds. *Dictionary of 20th-Century Art*. New York: McGraw-Hill, 1974.

Osborne, Harold, ed. *The Oxford Companion to 20th Century Art*. New York: Oxford University Press, 1981.

Pevsner, Nikolaus. *A History of Building Types*. 1979. Reprint. London: Thames & Hudson (paperbound), 1987.

———. *An Outline of European Architecture*. 8th rev. ed. Baltimore: Penguin, 1974.

Pierson, William H., Jr., and Davidson, Martha, eds. *Arts of the United States, A Pictorial Survey*. 1960. Reprint. Athens: University of Georgia Press, 1975.

Placzek, A. K., ed. *Macmillan Encyclopedia of Architects*. 4 vols. New York: Macmillan/Free Press, 1982.

Podro, Michael. *The Critical Historians of Art*. New Haven: Yale University Press, 1982.

Quick, John. *Artists' and Illustrators' Encyclopedia*. 2nd ed. New York: McGraw-Hill, 1977.

Read, Herbert, and Stangos, Nikos, eds. *The Thames & Hudson Dictionary of Art and Artists*. Rev. ed. London: Thames & Hudson, 1988.

Redig de Campos, D., ed. *Art Treasures of the Vatican*. New York: Park Lane, 1974.

Rubenstein, Charlotte Streifer. *American Women Artists from Early Indian Times to the Present*. Boston: G. K. Hall/Avon Books, 1982.

Schiller, Gertrud. *Iconography of Christian Art*. 2 vols. Greenwich, CT: New York Graphic Society, 1971.

Smith, G. E. Kidder. *The Architecture of the United States: An Illustrated Guide to Buildings Open to the Public*. 3 vols. Garden City, NY: Doubleday/Anchor, 1981.

Stierlin, Henri. *Encyclopedia of World Architecture 1978*. 1978. Reprint. New York: Van Nostrand, Reinhold, 1983.

Stratton, Arthur. *The Orders of Architecture: Greek, Roman and Renaissance*. London: Studio, 1986.

Trachtenberg, Marvin, and Hyman, Isabelle. *Architecture, from Prehistory to Post-Modernism*. New York: Abrams, 1986.

Tufts, Eleanor. *American Women Artists, Past and Present, A Selected Bibliographic Guide*. New York: Garland Publishers, 1984.

———. *Our Hidden Heritage, Five Centuries of Women Artists*. London: Paddington Press, 1974.

Waterhouse, Ellis. *The Dictionary of British 18th Century Painters in Oils and Crayons*. Woodbridge, England: Antique Collectors' Club, 1981.

Wittkower, Rudolf. *Sculpture Processes and Principles*. New York: Harper & Row, 1977.

Wölfflin, Heinrich. *The Sense of Form in Art*. New York: Chelsea, 1958.

Young, William, ed. *A Dictionary of American Artists, Sculptors, and Engravers*. Cambridge, MA: W. Young, 1968.

CHAPTER 1 THE BIRTH OF ART

Bandi, Hans-Georg; Breuil, Henri; et al. *The Art of the Stone Age: Forty Thousand Years of Rock Art*. 2nd ed. London: Methuen, 1970.

Bataille, Georges. *Lascaux: Prehistoric Painting or the Birth of Art*. Lausanne: Skira, 1980.

Breuil, Henri. *Four Hundred Centuries of Cave Art*. New York: Hacker, 1979. Reprint.

Graziosi, Paolo. *Paleolithic Art*. New York: McGraw-Hill, 1960.

Hawkes, Jacquetta. *The Atlas of Early Man*. New York: St. Martin's Press, 1976.

Kubba, Shamil A. A. *Mesopotamian Architecture and Town-planning: From the Mesolithic to the End of the Proto-historic Period*. Oxford: B. A. R., 1987.

Leroi-Gourhan, Andre. *The Dawn of European Art: An Introduction to Paleolithic Cave Painting*. Cambridge: Cambridge University Press, 1982.

———. *Treasures of Prehistoric Art*. New York: Abrams, 1967.

Lewin, Roger. *In the Age of Mankind: A Smithsonian Book of Human Evolution*. Washington DC: Smithsonian Institution Books, 1988.

Megaw, J. V. S. *The Art of the European Iron Age*. New York: Harper & Row, 1970.

Pfeiffer, John E. *The Creative Explosion: An Inquiry into the Origins of Art and Religion*. New York: Harper & Row, 1982.

Powell, T. G. E. *Prehistoric Art*. New York: Praeger, 1966.

Renfrew, Colin, ed. *British Prehistory: A New Outline*. London: Noyes Press, 1975.

Sandars, Nancy K. *Prehistoric Art in Europe*. 2nd ed. New York: Penguin, 1985.

Sieveking, Ann. *The Cave Artists*. London: Thames & Hudson, 1979.

Trump, David H. *The Prehistory of the Mediterranean*. New Haven: Yale University Press, 1980. (Later edition available.)

Wainwright, Geoffrey. *The Henge Monuments: Ceremony and Society in Prehistoric Britain*. London: Thames & Hudson, 1990.

Windels, Fernand. *The Lascaux Cave Paintings*. New York: Viking, 1950.

CHAPTER 2 THE ANCIENT NEAR EAST

Amiet, Pierre. *Art of the Ancient Near East*. New York: Abrams, 1980.

Amiet, Pierre, et al. *Art in the Ancient World: A Handbook of Styles and Forms*. New York: Rizzoli, 1981.

Culican, William. *The Medes and Persians*. London: Thames & Hudson, 1965; New York: Praeger, 1965.

Frankfort, Henri. *The Art and Architecture of the Ancient Orient*. Baltimore: Penguin, 1971. (Later edition available.)

Ghirshman, Roman. *Iran from Earliest Times to the Islamic Conquest*. New York: Penguin, 1978.

Groenewegen-Frankfort, H. A. *Arrest and Movement: An Essay on Space and Time in Representational Art of the Ancient Near East*. Cambridge, MA: Belknap Press, 1987.

Hinz, Walther. *The Lost World of Elam*. New York: New York University Press, 1973.

Kenyon, Kathleen M. *Digging Up Jericho*. New York: Praeger, 1974.

Kramer, Samuel N. *The Sumerians: Their History, Culture, and Character*. Chicago: University of Chicago Press, 1963. (Later edition available.)

Leick, Gwendolyn. *A Dictionary of Ancient Near Eastern Architecture*. New York: Routledge, 1988.

Lloyd, Seton. *The Archaeology of Mesopotamia: From the Old Stone Age to the Persian Conquest*. London: Thames & Hudson, 1978. (Later edition available.)

———. *The Art of the Ancient Near East*. New York: Praeger, 1969.

Lloyd, Seton, and Muller, Hans Wolfgang. *Ancient Architecture: Mesopotamia, Egypt, Crete*. New York: Electa/Rizzoli, 1986.

Mellaart, James. *Çatal Hüyük: A Neolithic Town in Anatolia*. New York: McGraw-Hill, 1967.

———. *The Earliest Civilizations of the Near East*. New York: McGraw-Hill, 1965.

———. *The Neolithic of the Near East.* New York: Scribner, 1975.
Oppenheim, A. Leo. *Ancient Mesopotamia.* Rev. ed. Chicago: University of Chicago Press, 1977.
Paris, Pierre. *Manual of Ancient Sculpture.* Rev. and enl. ed. New Rochelle, NY: Caratzas, 1984.
Parrot, André. *The Arts of Assyria.* New York: Golden Press, 1961.
———. *Sumer: The Dawn of Art.* New York: Golden Press, 1961.
Porada, Edith, and Dyson, R. H. *The Art of Ancient Iran: Pre-Islamic Cultures.* Rev. ed. New York: Greystone Press, 1969.
Wolf, Walther. *The Origins of Western Art: Egypt, Mesopotamia, the Aegean.* New York: Universe Books, 1989.
Woolley, Charles L. *The Art of the Middle East, Including Persia, Mesopotamia and Palestine.* New York: Crown, 1961.
———. *The Development of Sumerian Art.* Westport, CT: Greenwood Press, 1981.

CHAPTER 3 THE ART OF EGYPT

Aldred, Cyril. *The Development of Ancient Egyptian Art from 3200 to 1315 B.C.* 3 vols. London: Academy Edition, 1973.
Badawy, Alexander. *A History of Egyptian Architecture.* 3 vols. Berkeley: University of California Press, 1973.
Baines, John, and Malek, Jaromir. *Atlas of Ancient Egypt.* New York: Facts on File, 1980.
Emery, Walter B. *Archaic Egypt.* Baltimore: Penguin, 1972. (Later edition available.)
Gardiner, Sir Alan Henderson. *Egypt of the Pharaohs.* London: Oxford University Press, 1978.
Lange, Kurt, with Hirmer, Max. *Egypt: Architecture, Sculpture and Painting in Three Thousand Years.* 4th ed. London: Phaidon, 1968.
Lurker, Manfred. *The Gods and Symbols of Ancient Egypt: An Illustrated Dictionary.* New York: Thames & Hudson, 1980. (Later edition available.)
Mahdy, Christine, ed. *The World of the Pharaohs: A Complete Guide to Ancient Egypt.* London: Thames & Hudson, 1990.
Mekhitarian, Arpag. *Egyptian Painting.* New York: Skira, 1978.
Mendelsohn, Kurt. *The Riddle of the Pyramids.* New York: Thames & Hudson, 1986.
Robins, Gay. *Egyptian Painting and Relief.* Aylesbury, England: Shire Publications, 1986.
Romer, John. *Valley of the Kings.* New York: William Morrow, 1981.
Schafer, Heinrich. *Principles of Egyptian Art.* Rev. reprint. Oxford: Aris and Phillips, 1986.
Smith, E. Baldwin. *Egyptian Architecture as Cultural Expression.* Watkins Glen, NY: American Life Foundation, 1968.
Smith, William Stevenson, and Simpson, W. *The Art and Architecture of Ancient Egypt.* Rev. ed. New York: Viking, 1981.
Woldering, Irmgard. *Gods, Men and Pharaohs: The Glory of Egyptian Art.* New York: Abrams, 1967.

CHAPTER 4 THE AEGEAN: CYCLADIC, MINOAN, AND MYCENAEAN ART

Chadwick, John. *The Mycenaean World.* New York: Cambridge University Press, 1976.
Cottrell, Arthur. *The Minoan World.* New York: Scribner, 1980.
Demargne, Pierre. *Aegean Art: The Origins of Greek Art.* London: Thames & Hudson, 1964.
Doumas, Christos. *Thera, Pompeii of the Ancient Aegean: Excavations at Akrotiri, 1967–1979.* New York: Thames & Hudson, 1983.
Evans, Sir Arthur John. *The Palace of Minos.* 4 vols. 1921–1935. Reprint. New York: Biblo & Tannen, 1964.
Graham, James W. *The Palaces of Crete.* Princeton: Princeton University Press, 1969. (Later edition available.)
Higgins, Reynold Alleyne. *Minoan and Mycenaean Art.* Rev. ed. New York: Oxford University Press, 1981.
Marinatos, Spyridon, with Hirmer, Max. *Crete and Mycenae.* London: Thames & Hudson, 1960.
Matz, Friedrich. *The Art of Crete and Early Greece.* New York: Crown, 1965.
Palmer, Leonard R. *Mycenaeans and Minoans.* 2nd rev. ed. 1963. Reprint. Westport, CT: Greenwood Press, 1980.
Pendlebury, John. *The Archeology of Crete.* London: Methuen, 1967.
Schliemann, Heinrich. *Ilios: The City and the Country of the Trojans.* 1881. Reprint. New York: B. Blom, 1968. (Other reprints available.)
———. *Mycenae.* 1880. Reprint. New York: Arno Press, 1976.
———. *Tiryns.* 1885. Reprint. New York: Arno Press, 1976.
Vermeule, Emily. *Greece in the Bronze Age.* Chicago: University of Chicago Press, 1972.
Wace, Alan. *Mycenae, an Archeological History and Guide.* New York: Biblo & Tannen, 1964.
Warren, Peter. *The Aegean Civilizations.* London: Elsevier-Phaidon, 1975.
Willetts, R. F. *The Civilization of Ancient Crete.* Berkeley: University of California Press, 1978.

CHAPTER 5 THE ART OF GREECE

Arias, Paolo. *A History of One Thousand Years of Greek Vase Painting.* New York: Abrams, 1962. (Later edition available.)
Ashmole, Bernard. *Architect and Sculptor in Classical Greece.* New York: New York University Press, 1972.
Beazley, John D. *Attic Red-Figure Vase-Painters.* 3 vols. 1963. Reprint. New York: Hacker, 1984.
———. *The Development of the Attic Black-Figure.* Rev. ed. Berkeley: University of California Press, 1986.
Beazley, John D., and Ashmole, Bernard. *Greek Sculpture and Painting to the End of the Hellenistic Period.* Cambridge: Cambridge University Press, 1966.
Berve, Helmut. *Greek Temples, Theatres, and Shrines.* New York: Abrams, 1963.
Bieber, Margarete. *Sculpture of the Hellenistic Age.* 1961. Reprint. New York: Hacker, 1980.
Blumel, Carl. *Greek Sculptors at Work.* London: Phaidon, 1969.
Boardman, John. *Greek Art.* Rev. ed. New York: Thames & Hudson, 1987.
———. *Greek Sculpture: The Classical Period: A Handbook.* London: Thames & Hudson, 1987.
Branigan, Keith, and Vickers, Michael. *Hellas, the Civilizations of Ancient Greece.* New York: McGraw-Hill, 1980.
Brilliant, Richard. *Arts of the Ancient Greeks.* New York: McGraw-Hill, 1973.
Buschor, Ernst. *Greek Vase Painting.* New York: Hacker, 1978.
———. *On the Meaning of Greek Statues.* Amherst: University of Massachusetts Press, 1980.
Carpenter, Rhys. *Greek Sculpture: A Critical Review.* Chicago: University of Chicago Press, 1960.
Charbonneaux, Jean. *Archaic Greek Art.* New York: Braziller, 1971.
Charbonneaux, Jean; Martin, Roland; and Villard, François. *Hellenistic Art.* New York: Braziller, 1973.
Chitham, Robert. *Classical Orders of Architecture.* New York: Rizzoli, 1985.
Cook, Robert M. *Greek Art: Its Development, Character and Influence.* Harmondsworth, England: Penguin, 1976.
Coulton, J. J. *Ancient Greek Architects at Work.* Ithaca, NY: Cornell University Press, 1977. (Later edition available.)
Dinsmoor, W. B. *The Architecture of Ancient Greece.* 3rd ed. New York: Norton, 1975.
Hampe, Roland, and Simon, Erika. *The Birth of Greek Art.* New York: Oxford University Press, 1981.
Havelock, Christine Mitchell. *Hellenistic Art: The Art of the Classical World.* 2nd rev. ed. New York: Norton, 1981.
Lawrence, Arnold W. *Greek Architecture.* 2nd ed. Baltimore: Penguin, 1967. (Later edition available.)
Lullies, Reinhard, and Hirmer, Max. *Greek Sculpture.* Rev. ed. New York: Abrams, 1960.
Martin, Roland. *Greek Architecture: Architecture of Crete, Greece, and the Greek World.* New York: Electa/Rizzoli, 1988.
Onians, John. *Art and Thought in the Hellenistic Age: The Greek World View, 350–50 B.C.* London: Thames & Hudson, 1979.
Papaioannou, Kostas. *The Art of Greece.* New York: Abrams, 1989.
Pfuhl, Ernst. *Masterpieces of Greek Drawing and Painting.* 2nd ed. Chicago: Argonaut, 1967.
Pollitt, Jerome J. *The Ancient View of Greek Art.* New Haven: Yale University Press, 1974.
———. *Art and Experience in Classical Greece.* Cambridge: Cambridge University Press, 1972.
———. *Art in the Hellenistic Age.* Cambridge: Cambridge University Press, 1986.
———. *The Art of Greece 1400–31 B.C.* Englewood Cliffs, NJ: Prentice-Hall, 1965.
Richter, Gisela M. *Attic Red-Figure Vases: A Survey.* New Haven: Yale University Press, 1958.
———. *A Handbook of Greek Art.* 9th ed. Oxford: Phaidon, 1987.
———. *The Portraits of the Greeks.* Rev. ed. Ithaca, NY: Cornell University Press, 1984.
———. *The Sculpture and Sculptors of the Greeks.* 4th ed. New Haven: Yale University Press, 1970.
Ridgway, Brunilde Sismondo. *Fifth Century Styles in Greek Sculpture.* Princeton: Princeton University Press, 1981.
———. *The Severe Style in Greek Sculpture.* Princeton: Princeton University Press, 1970.
Robertson, Donald S. *Greek and Roman Architecture.* 2nd ed. Cambridge: Cambridge University Press, 1969.
Robertson, Martin. *Greek Painting.* New York: Rizzoli, 1979.
———. *A History of Greek Art.* 2 vols. Cambridge: Cambridge University Press, 1976.
———. *A Shorter History of Greek Art.* Cambridge: Cambridge University Press, 1981.
Scranton, Robert L. *Greek Architecture.* New York: Braziller, 1962.
Scully, Vincent. *The Earth, the Temple, and the Gods: Greek Sacred Architecture.* Rev. ed. New Haven: Yale University Press, 1979.
Stewart, Andrew. *Greek Sculpture.* 2 vols. New Haven: Yale University Press, 1990.
Swindler, Mary H. *Ancient Painting from the Earliest Times to the Period of Christian Art.* 1929. Reprint. New Haven: Yale University Press, 1929.
Travlos, John. *Pictorial Dictionary of Ancient Athens.* 1971. Reprint. New York: Hacker, 1980.
Vermeule, Cornelius C. *The Art of the Greek World, Prehistoric through Pericles.* Boston, MA: Department of Classical Art, Museum of Fine Arts, 1982.
———. *Greek and Roman Sculpture in America: Masterpieces in Public Collections.* Berkeley: University of California Press, 1981.
———. *Greek Art, Socrates to Sulla.* Boston, MA: Department of Classical Art, Museum of Fine Arts, 1980.

CHAPTER 6 ETRUSCAN AND ROMAN ART

Andreae, Bernard. *The Art of Rome.* New York: Abrams, 1977.
Bianchi Bandinelli, Ranuccio. *Rome, the Late Empire.* New York: Braziller, 1971.
Boethius, Axel. *The Golden House of Nero.* Ann Arbor: University of Michigan Press, 1960.
Brilliant, Richard. *Roman Art, from the Republic to Constantine.* New York: Praeger, 1974.
———. *Visual Narratives: Storytelling in Etruscan and Roman Art.* Ithaca, NY: Cornell University Press, 1984.
Brown, Frank Edward. *Roman Architecture.* New York: Braziller, 1961.
Buchthal, Hugo. *Art of the Mediterranean World, A.D. 100 to 1400.* Art History Series 5. Washington, DC: Decatur House Press, 1983.
Goldscheider, Ludwig. *Roman Portraits.* London: Phaidon, 1940.
Hanfmann, George. *Roman Art.* Greenwich, CT: New York Graphic Society, 1964.
Kraus, Theodor. *Pompeii and Herculaneum: The Living Cities of the Dead.* New York: Abrams, 1975.
Leach, Eleanor Winsor. *The Rhetoric of Space: Literary and Artistic Representations of Landscape in Republican and Augustan Rome.* Princeton: Princeton University Press, 1988.
L'Orange, Hans Peter. *The Roman Empire: Art Forms and Civic Life.* New York: Rizzoli, 1985.
MacDonald, William L. *The Architecture of the Roman Empire.* Rev. ed. New Haven: Yale University Press, 1982.
McKay, Alexander G. *Houses, Villas, and Palaces in the Roman World.* Ithaca, NY: Cornell University Press, 1975.
Maiuri, Amedeo. *Pompeii.* 14th ed. Rome: Istituto Poligrafico dello Stato, 1970.
———. *Roman Painting.* Geneva: Skira, 1953.

Mansuelli, Guido. *The Art of Etruria and Early Rome.* New York: Crown, 1965.
Nash, Ernest. *Pictorial Dictionary of Ancient Rome.* 2 vols. New York: Hacker, 1981.
Pollitt, Jerome J. *The Art of Rome, 753 B.C.–A.D. 337.* Englewood Cliffs, NJ: Prentice-Hall, 1966.
Richardson, Emeline. *The Etruscans: Their Art and Civilization.* Chicago: University of Chicago Press, 1976.
Rivoira, Giovanni. *Roman Architecture and Its Principles of Construction Under the Empire.* New York: Hacker, 1972.
Robertson, Donald S. *Greek and Roman Architecture.* 2nd ed. Cambridge: Cambridge University Press, 1969.
Sprenger, Maja, and Bartoloni, Gilda. *The Etruscans: Their History, Art, and Architecture.* New York: Abrams, 1983.
Strong, Donald, and Ling, Roger. *Roman Art.* 2nd rev. ed. New York: Penguin, 1988.
Vermeule, Cornelius C. *Roman Art: Early Republic to Late Empire.* Boston: Museum of Fine Arts, Department of Classical Art, 1979.
Vickers, Michael. *The Roman World.* Oxford: Elsevier-Phaidon, 1977.
Ward-Perkins, John B. *Roman Architecture.* New York: Electa/Rizzoli, 1988.
———. *Roman Imperial Architecture.* 2nd integrated ed. New York: Penguin, 1981.
Ward-Perkins, John, and Boethius, Axel. *Etruscan and Roman Architecture.* Harmondsworth, England: Penguin, 1970.
Zanker, Paul. *The Power of Images in the Age of Augustus.* Ann Arbor: University of Michigan Press, 1988.

CHAPTER 7 EARLY CHRISTIAN, BYZANTINE, AND ISLAMIC ART

Arnold, Thomas W. *Painting in Islam.* New York: Dover, 1965.
Aslanapa, Oktay. *Turkish Art and Architecture.* London: Faber & Faber, 1971.
Atil, Esin. *Renaissance of Islam: Art of the Mamluks.* Washington, DC: Smithsonian Institution Press, 1981.
Beach, Milo Cleveland. *Early Mughal Painting.* Cambridge: Harvard University Press, 1987.
Beckwith, John. *The Art of Constantinople: An Introduction to Byzantine Art (330–1453).* New York: Phaidon, 1968.
———. *Early Christian and Byzantine Art.* New York: Penguin, 1979. (Later edition available.)
Chatzidakis, Manolis. *Byzantine and Early Medieval Painting.* New York: Viking, 1965.
Crespi, Gabriele. *The Arabs in Europe.* New York: Rizzoli, 1986.
Creswell, K. A. C. *A Short Account of Early Muslim Architecture.* Rev. and enl. ed. Aldershot, England: Scolar, 1989.
Dalton, Ormonde M. *Byzantine Art and Archaeology.* New York: Dover, 1961.
Demus, Otto. *Byzantine Art and the West.* New York: New York University Press, 1970.
———. *The Mosaic Decoration of San Marco, Venice.* Chicago: University of Chicago Press, 1988.
Du Bourguet, Pierre. *Early Christian Art.* New York: William Morrow, 1971.
Ettinghausen, Richard. *Arab Painting.* Geneva: Skira, 1977.
———. *From Byzantium to Sasanian Iran and the Islamic World.* Leiden: Brill, 1972.
Ettinghausen, Richard, and Grabar, Oleg. *The Art and Architecture of Islam, 650–1250.* New York: Viking Penguin, 1987. (Later edition available.)
Golombek, Lisa, and Wilber, Donald. *The Timurid Architecture of Iran and Turan.* 2 vols. Princeton: Princeton University Press, 1988.
Goodwin, Godfrey. *A History of Ottoman Architecture.* New York: Thames & Hudson, 1987.
Gough, Michael. *The Origins of Christian Art.* New York: Praeger, 1973.
Grabar, André. *The Beginnings of Christian Art, 200–395.* London: Thames & Hudson, 1967.
———. *Byzantine Painting.* Geneva: Skira, 1953.
———. *Christian Iconography.* Princeton: Princeton University Press, 1980.
———. *The Golden Age of Justinian: From the Death of Theodosius to the Rise of Islam.* New York: Odyssey Press, 1967.
Grabar, André, and Chatzidakis, Manolis. *Greek Mosaics of the Byzantine Period.* New York: New American Library, 1964.
Grabar, Oleg. *The Formation of Islamic Art.* Rev. and enl. ed. New Haven: Yale University Press, 1987.
Grover, Satish. *The Architecture of India: Islamic (727–1707).* New Delhi: Vikas, 1981.
Grunebaum, Gustave von. *Classical Islam: A History, 600–1258.* Chicago: Aldine, 1970.
Hamilton, George H. *The Art and Architecture of Russia.* 2nd ed. New York: Viking, 1975. (Later edition available.)
Hamilton, John A. *Byzantine Architecture and Decoration.* 1933. Freeport, NY: Books for Libraries/Arno Press, 1972.
Hoag, John D. *Islamic Architecture.* New York: Abrams, 1977; Rizzoli (paperbound), 1987.
Hutter, Irmgard. *Early Christian and Byzantine Art.* London: Herbert Press, 1988.
Huyghe, René, ed. *Larousse Encyclopedia of Byzantine and Medieval Art.* See **Reference Books**.
Kitzinger, Ernst. *Byzantine Art in the Making.* Cambridge: Harvard University Press, 1977.
———. *Early Medieval Art with Illustrations from the British Museum Collection.* Rev. ed. Bloomington: Indiana University Press, 1983.
Krautheimer, Richard, and Curcic, Slobodan. *Early Christian and Byzantine Architecture.* 4th rev. ed. New York: Penguin, 1986.
Kühnel, Ernst. *Islamic Art and Architecture.* London: Bell, 1966.
Lane, Arthur. *Early Islamic Pottery, Mesopotamia, Egypt and Persia.* New York: Faber & Faber, 1965.
Levey, Michael. *The World of Ottoman Art.* New York: Scribner, 1975.
Lewis, Bernard, ed. *Islam and the Arab World.* New York: Knopf, 1976.
Lowrie, Walter S. *Art in the Early Church.* New York: Norton, 1969.
MacDonald, William L. *Early Christian and Byzantine Architecture.* New York: Braziller, 1962. (Later edition available.)
Maguire, Henry. *Art and Eloquence in Byzantium.* Princeton: Princeton University Press, 1981.
Mango, Cyril. *Byzantine Architecture.* New York: Electa/Rizzoli, 1985.
———. *Byzantium and Its Image: History and Culture of the Byzantine Empire and Its Heritage.* London: Variorum Reprints, 1984.
Meyer, Peter. *Byzantine Mosaics: Torcello, Venice, Monreale, Palermo.* London: Batsford, 1952.
Milburn, Robert L. P. *Early Christian Art and Architecture.* Berkeley: University of California Press, 1988.
Perkins, Ann Louise. *The Art of Dura-Europos.* Oxford: Clarendon Press, 1973.
Pope, Arthur, and Ackerman, Phyllis. *A Survey of Persian Art from Prehistoric Times to the Present.* London: Oxford University Press, 1977.
Rice, David T. *The Appreciation of Byzantine Art.* London: Oxford University Press, 1972.
———. *The Art of Byzantium.* New York: Abrams, 1959.
———. *Byzantine Art.* London: Variorum Reprints, 1973.
———. *Islamic Art.* London: Thames & Hudson, 1975.
Schiller, Gertrud. *Iconography of Christian Art.* See **Reference Books.**
Schimmel, Annemarie. *Islam in India and Pakistan.* Leiden: Brill, 1982.
Smith, Earl Baldwin. *Architectural Symbolism of Imperial Rome and the Middle Ages.* Princeton: Princeton University Press, 1956.
———. *The Dome, a Study in the History of Ideas.* Princeton: Princeton University Press, 1971.
Snyder, James. *Medieval Art: Painting, Sculpture, and Architecture, 4th–14th Century.* New York: Abrams, 1989.
Swift, Emerson H. *Hagia Sophia.* New York: Columbia University Press, 1980.
Volbach, Wolfgang. *Early Christian Mosaics, from the Fourth to the Seventh Centuries.* New York: Oxford University Press, 1946.
Volbach, Wolfgang, and Hirmer, Max. *Early Christian Art.* New York: Abrams, 1962.
Von Simson, Otto G. *Sacred Fortress: Byzantine Art and Statecraft in Ravenna.* Chicago: University of Chicago Press, 1976. (Later edition available.)
Walter, Christopher. *Art and Ritual of the Byzantine Church.* London: Variorum, 1982.
Weitzmann, Kurt. *Ancient Book Illumination.* Cambridge: Harvard University Press, 1959.
———. *Art in the Medieval West and Its Contacts with Byzantium.* London: Variorum, 1982.
———. *Illustrations in Roll and Codex.* Princeton: Princeton University Press, 1970.
Weitzmann, Kurt, et al. *The Icon.* New York: Knopf, 1982.

CHAPTER 8 EARLY MEDIEVAL ART

Arnold, Bruce. *Irish Art: A Concise History.* Rev. ed. London: Thames & Hudson, 1989.
Beckwith, John. *Early Medieval Art: Carolingian, Ottonian, Romanesque.* New York: Oxford University Press, 1974.
Calkins, Robert G. *Illuminated Books of the Middle Ages.* Ithaca, NY: Cornell University Press, 1983.
Conant, Kenneth. *Carolingian and Romanesque Architecture 800–1200.* 2nd integrated rev. ed. Harmondsworth, England: Penguin, 1978. (Later edition available.)
Dodwell, C. R. *Anglo-Saxon Art: A New Perspective.* Ithaca, NY: Cornell University Press, 1982. (Later edition available.)
Finlay, Ian. *Celtic Art: An Introduction.* London: Faber & Faber, 1973.
Goldschmidt, Adolf. *German Illumination.* New York: Hacker, 1970.
Grabar, André, and Nordenfalk, Carl. *Early Medieval Painting from the Fourth to the Eleventh Century.* New York: Skira, 1967.
Harbison, Peter, et al. *Irish Art and Architecture from Prehistory to the Present.* London: Thames & Hudson, 1978.
Henderson, George. *Early Medieval Art.* Pelican Style and Civilization Series. New York: Penguin, 1972.
Henry, Françoise. *Irish Art During the Viking Invasions, 900–1020.* Ithaca, NY: Cornell University Press, 1970.
———. *Irish Art in the Early Christian Period, to 800.* Rev. ed. London: Methuen, 1965.
Hinks, Roger P. *Carolingian Art.* Ann Arbor: University of Michigan Press, 1974.
Klindt-Jensen, Ole, and Wilson, David M. *Viking Art.* 2nd ed. Minneapolis: University of Minnesota Press, 1980.
Laszlo, Gyula. *The Art of the Migration Period.* London: Allen Lane, 1974.
Leeds, Edward T. *Early Anglo-Saxon Art and Archaeology.* Westport, CT: Greenwood Press, 1970. (Later reprint available.)
Lucas, A. T. *Treasures of Ireland: Irish Pagan and Early Christian Art.* New York: Viking, 1973.
Megaw, Ruth, and Megaw, John V. *Celtic Art: From Its Beginning to the Book of Kells.* London: Thames & Hudson, 1989.
Mütherich, Florentine, and Gaehde, J. E. *Carolingian Painting.* New York: Braziller, 1976. (Later edition available.)
Nordenfalk, Carl. *Celtic and Anglo-Saxon Painting: Book Illumination in the British Isles 600–800.* New York: Braziller, 1977.
Porter, Arthur K. *The Crosses and Culture of Ireland.* New York: Benjamin Blom, 1971.
Simons, Gerald. *Barbarian Europe.* New York: Time-Life Books, 1979.
Stokstad, Marilyn. *Medieval Art.* New York: Harper & Row, 1986.
Taylor, Harold M., and Taylor, Joan. *Anglo-Saxon Architecture.* 2 vols. Cambridge: Cambridge University Press, 1980. (Later volume available.)
Wilson, David M., ed. *The Northern World: The History and Heritage of Northern Europe A.D. 400–1100.* New York: Abrams, 1980.
Zarnecki, George. *Art of the Medieval World.* New York: Abrams, 1975. (Later edition available.)

CHAPTER 9 ROMANESQUE ART

Clapham, Alfred W. *English Romanesque Architecture After the Conquest.* Oxford: Clarendon Press, 1964.
———. *Romanesque Architecture in Western Europe.* Oxford: Clarendon Press, 1959.
Conant, Kenneth John. *Carolingian and Romanesque Architecture, 800–1200.* 2nd integrated rev. ed. New York: Penguin, 1979.
Crichton, George H. *Romanesque Sculpture in Italy.* London: Routledge & Paul, 1954.
Decker, Heinrich. *Romanesque Art in Italy.* New York: Abrams, 1959.
Demus, Otto. *Romanesque Mural Painting.* New York: Abrams, 1970.
Deschamps, Paul. *French Sculpture of the Romanesque Period—Eleventh and Twelfth Centuries.* 1930. Reprint. New York: Hacker, 1972.

Dodwell, C. R. *Painting in Europe 800–1200*. Harmondsworth, England: Penguin, 1971.

Duby, Georges. *History of Medieval Art, 980–1440*. New York: Skira/Rizzoli, 1986.

Evans, Joan. *Art in Medieval France 987–1498*. Oxford: Clarendon Press, 1969.

Focillon, Henri. *The Art of the West in the Middle Ages*. Vol. 1. 2nd ed. London: Phaidon, 1969; Ithaca, NY: Cornell University Press (paperbound), 1980. (Later volume available.)

Gantner, Joseph; Pobé, Marcel; and Roubier, Jean. *Romanesque Art in France*. London: Thames & Hudson, 1956.

Gibbs-Smith, Charles H. *The Bayeux Tapestry*. London: Phaidon, 1973.

Grabar, André, and Nordenfalk, Carl. *Romanesque Painting*. New York: Skira, 1958.

Hearn, Millard F. *Romanesque Sculpture in the Eleventh and Twelfth Centuries*. Ithaca, NY: Cornell University Press/Phaidon, 1981.

Holt, Elizabeth Gilmore, ed. *A Documentary History of Art, I: The Middle Ages*. Princeton: Princeton University Press, 1981.

Kubach, Hans E. *Romanesque Architecture*. New York: Abrams, 1975. (Later edition available.)

Kuenstler, Gustav, ed. *Romanesque Art in Europe*. New York: Norton, 1973.

Leisinger, Hermann. *Romanesque Bronzes: Church Portals in Mediaeval Europe*. New York: Praeger, 1957.

Male, Emile. *Art and Artists of the Middle Ages*. Redding Ridge, CT: Black Swan Books, 1986.

Michel, Paul H. *Romanesque Wall Paintings in France*. Paris: Editions Chêne, 1949.

Morey, Charles R. *Medieval Art*. New York: Norton, 1970.

Porter, Arthur K. *Medieval Architecture*. 2 vols. 1909. Reprint. New York: Hacker, 1969.

———. *Romanesque Sculpture of the Pilgrimage Roads*. 1923. Reprint. New York: Hacker, 1969.

Rickert, Margaret. *Painting in Britain: The Middle Ages*. 2nd ed. Harmondsworth, England: Penguin, 1965.

Rivoira, Giovanni. *Lombardic Architecture: Its Origin, Development, and Derivatives*. 1933. Reprint. New York: Hacker, 1975.

Saalman, Howard. *Medieval Architecture: European Architecture 600–1200*. New York: Braziller, 1962.

Schapiro, Meyer. *Romanesque Art: Selected Papers*. London: Chatto & Windus, 1977; New York: Braziller, 1976.

Stoddard, Whitney. *Art and Architecture in Medieval France*. New York: Harper & Row, 1972.

Stone, Lawrence. *Sculpture in Britain in the Middle Ages*. Baltimore: Penguin, 1972.

Swarzenski, Hanns. *Monuments of Romanesque Art*. Chicago: University of Chicago Press, 1974.

Webb, Geoffrey F. *Architecture in Britain: The Middle Ages*. Harmondsworth, England: Penguin, 1965.

Zarnecki, George. *Romanesque Art*. New York: Universe Books, 1971.

———. *Studies in Romanesque Sculpture*. London: Dorian Press, 1979.

CHAPTER 10 GOTHIC ART

Adams, Henry B. *Mont-Saint-Michel and Chartres*. New York: Doubleday/Anchor, 1959. (Later reprint available.)

Arnold, Hugh. *Stained Glass of the Middle Ages in England and France*. London: A. & C. Black, 1956.

Arslan, Edoardo. *Gothic Architecture in Venice*. London: Phaidon, 1971.

Aubert, Marcel. *The Art of the High Gothic Era*. New York: Crown, 1965.

———. *Gothic Cathedrals of France and Their Treasures*. London: N. Kay, 1959.

Bony, Jean. *The English Decorated Style*. Ithaca, NY: Cornell University Press, 1979.

———. *French Gothic Architecture of the XII and XIII Centuries*. Berkeley: University of California Press, 1983.

Branner, Robert. *Chartres Cathedral*. New York: Norton, 1969.

———. *Gothic Architecture*. New York: Braziller, 1961.

Duby, George. *The Age of the Cathedrals*. Chicago: University of Chicago Press, 1981.

Dupont, Jacques, and Gnudi, Cesare. *Gothic Painting*. New York: Rizzoli, 1979.

Evans, Joan. *Art in Medieval France 987–1498*. Oxford: Clarendon Press, 1969.

———. *The Flowering of the Middle Ages*. London: Thames & Hudson, 1985.

Fitchen, John. *The Construction of Gothic Cathedrals: A Study of Medieval Vault Erection*. Chicago: University of Chicago Press, 1977; Phoenix Books, 1981.

Focillon, Henri. *The Art of the West in the Middle Ages*. Vol. 2. Ithaca, NY: Cornell University Press, 1980.

Foster, Richard. *Discovering English Churches*. New York: Oxford University Press, 1982.

Frankl, Paul. *Gothic Architecture*. Baltimore: Penguin, 1963.

———. *The Gothic Literary Sources and Interpretations*. Princeton: Princeton University Press, 1960.

Grodecki, Louis. *Gothic Architecture*. New York: Electa/Rizzoli, 1985.

Harvey, John H. *The Gothic World*. New York: Harper & Row, 1969.

Huizinga, Johan. *The Waning of the Middle Ages*. 1924. Reprint. New York: St. Martin's Press, 1988.

Jantzen, Hans. *High Gothic: The Classic Cathedrals of Chartres, Reims, and Amiens*. Princeton: Princeton University Press, 1984.

Johnson, James. *The Radiance of Chartres*. New York: Random House, 1965.

Johnson, Paul. *British Cathedrals*. New York: William Morrow, 1980.

Katzenellenbogen, Adolf. *The Sculptural Programs of Chartres Cathedral*. Baltimore: Johns Hopkins Press, 1959.

Male, Emile. *The Gothic Image: Religious Art in the Twelfth Century*. Rev. ed. Princeton: Princeton University Press, 1978.

———. *Religious Art in France: The 13th Century—A Study of Medieval Iconography and Its Sources*. Princeton: Princeton University Press, 1984.

———. *Religious Art in France: The Late Middle Ages—A Study of Medieval Iconography and Its Sources*. Princeton: Princeton University Press, 1986. (Later editions available.)

Mark, Robert. *Experiments in Gothic Structure*. Cambridge: MIT Press, 1982.

Martindale, Andrew. *Gothic Art*. London: Thames & Hudson, 1967. (Later edition available.)

———. *The Rise of the Artist in the Middle Ages and Early Renaissance*. New York: McGraw-Hill, 1972.

Panofsky, Erwin. *Abbot Suger on the Abbey Church of St. Denis and Its Art Treasures*. 2nd ed. Princeton: Princeton University Press, 1979.

———. *Gothic Architecture and Scholasticism*. New York: Meridian Books, 1963.

Pevsner, Nikolaus. *The Buildings of England*. 46 vols. Harmondsworth, England: Penguin, 1951–1974.

Robb, David M. *The Art of the Illuminated Manuscript*. Cranbury, NJ: A. S. Barnes, 1973. (Later edition available.)

Sauerlander, Willibald, and Hirmer, Max. *Gothic Sculpture in France 1140–1270*. New York: Abrams, 1973.

Sheridan, Ronald, and Ross, Anne. *Gargoyles and Grotesques: Paganism in the Medieval Church*. Boston: New York Graphic Society, 1975.

Stoddard, Whitney. *Monastery and Cathedral in Medieval France*. Middletown, CT: Wesleyan University Press, 1966. (Later editions available.)

Swaan, Wim. *The Late Middle Ages: Art and Architecture from 1350 to the Advent of the Renaissance*. Ithaca, NY: Cornell University Press, 1977.

Thompson, Daniel. *The Materials and Techniques of Medieval Painting*. New York: Dover, 1956.

Von Simson, Otto Georg. *The Gothic Cathedral: Origins of Gothic Architecture and the Medieval Concept of Order*. 3rd enl. ed. Princeton: Princeton University Press, 1988.

Zarnecki, George. *Art of the Medieval World*. New York: Abrams, 1975

CHAPTER 11 THE ART OF INDIA

Acharya, Prasanna Kumar. *An Encyclopedia of Hindu Architecture*. 2nd ed. New Delhi: Oriental Books Reprint Corporation, 1979.

Archer, William G. *Indian Miniatures*. Greenwich, CT: New York Graphic Society, 1960.

———. *Indian Paintings from the Punjab Hills*. 2 vols. London: Sotheby Parke Bernet, 1973.

Asher, Frederick M. *The Art of Eastern India, 300–800*. Minneapolis: University of Minnesota Press, 1980.

Bachhofer, Ludwig. *Early Indian Sculpture*. 1929. Reprint. New York: Hacker, 1972. (Later edition available.)

Balasubrahmanyam, S. R. *Early Chola Art—Part I*. New York: Asia Publishing House, 1966.

———. *Early Chola Temples: Parantakat to Rajaraja I, A.D. 907–985*. Bombay: Orient Longman, 1971.

Barrett, Douglas E. *Early Chola Bronzes*. Bombay: Bhulabhai Memorial Institute, 1965.

Barrett, Douglas E., and Gray, Basil. *Painting of India*. Geneva: Skira, 1963.

Basham, Arthur L. *The Wonder That Was India*. 3rd rev. ed. Paris: Arthaud, 1976.

Bhattacharji, Sukumari. *The Indian Theogony, a Comparative Study of Indian Mythology*. London: Cambridge University Press, 1970. (Later edition available.)

Coomaraswamy, Ananda K. *History of Indian and Indonesian Art*. New Delhi: Munshiram Manaharlal, 1972. (Later edition available.)

———. *Yaksas*. New Delhi: Munshiram Manaharlal, 1971.

Craven, Roy C. *Indian Art: A Concise History*. London: Thames & Hudson, 1985.

Dehejia, Vidya. *Early Buddhist Rock Temples*. Ithaca, NY: Cornell University Press, 1972.

Ghosh, Amalananda. *Ajanta Murals*. New Delhi: Archaeological Survey of India, 1967.

Ghosh, Sankar Prosad. *Hindu Religious Art and Architecture*. Delhi: D. K. Publications, 1982.

Gopinatha Rao, T. A. *Elements of Hindu Iconography*. 2nd ed. 4 vols. New York: Paragon, 1968.

Gray, Basil, ed. *The Arts of India*. Ithaca, NY: Cornell University Press/Phaidon, 1981.

Groslier, Bernard P., and Arthaud, Jacques. *The Arts and Civilization of Angkor*. New York: Praeger, 1957.

Grover, Satish. *The Architecture of India: Buddhist and Hindu*. Sahibabad, Distt. Ghaziabad: Vikas, 1980.

Harle, James C. *The Art and Architecture of the Indian Subcontinent*. New York: Penguin, 1986. (Later edition available.)

———. *Gupta Sculpture: Indian Sculpture of the Fourth to the Sixth Centuries*. Oxford: Clarendon Press, 1974.

Head, Raymond. *The Indian Style*. Boston: Allen and Unwin, 1986.

Huntington, Susan L, and Huntington, John C. *The Art of Ancient India: Buddhist, Hindu, Jain*. New York: Weatherhill, 1985.

Khosa, Sunil. *Art History of Kashmir and Ladakh, Medieval Period*. New Delhi: Sagar, 1984.

Kramrisch, Stella. *The Art of India through the Ages*. 3rd ed. London: Phaidon, 1965. (Later editions available.)

———. *The Hindu Temple*. 2 vols. Delhi: Motilal Banarsidass, 1976. (Later reprint available.)

———. *Indian Sculpture*. The Heritage of India Series. London: Oxford University Press, 1933.

Krishna, Deva. *Temples of North India*. New Delhi: National Book Trust, 1969.

Krishna Murthy, C. *Saiva Art and Architecture in South India*. New Delhi: Sundeep Prakashan, 1985.

Lee, Sherman E. *Ancient Cambodian Sculpture*. New York: Intercultural Arts Press, 1970.

Manwani, S. N. *Evolution of Art and Architecture in Central India: With Special Reference to the Kalachuris of Ratanpur*. Delhi: Agam Kala Prakashan, 1988.

Meister, Michael W. *Encyclopedia of Indian Temple Architecture*. Philadelphia: University of Pennsylvania Press, 1983.

Munsterberg, Hugo. *Art of India and Southeast Asia*. New York: Abrams, 1970.

Rawson, Philip. *The Art of Southeast Asia*. New York: Praeger, 1967.

Rosenfield, John. *Dynastic Arts of the Kushan*. Berkeley: University of California Press, 1967.

Rowland, Benjamin. *The Art and Architecture of India: Buddhist, Hindu, Jain*. Harmondsworth, England: Penguin, 1977.

Sivaramamurti, C. *South Indian Bronzes*. New Delhi: Lalit Kala Akademi, 1963.

———. *South Indian Paintings*. New Delhi: National Museum, 1968.

Srinivasan, K. R. *Temples of South India*. New Delhi: National Book Trust, 1972.

Stutley, Margaret. *An Illustrated Dictionary of*

Hindu Iconography. Boston: Routledge and Keegan Paul, 1985.
Welch, Stuart Cary. *India: Art and Culture, 1300–1900*. New York: Metropolitan Museum of Art/Holt, Rinehart & Winston, 1985.
Williams, Joanna Gottfried. *The Art of Gupta India: Empire and Province*. Princeton: Princeton University Press, 1982.
Zimmer, Heinrich, and Campbell, Joseph, eds. *The Art of Indian Asia; Its Mythology and Transformations*. Bollingen Series 39. 2 vols. Princeton: Princeton University Press, 1983.

CHAPTER 12 THE ART OF CHINA

Bush, Susan, and Murck, Christian, eds. *Theories of the Arts in China*. Princeton: Princeton University Press, 1983.
Cahill, James. *Chinese Painting*. New ed. Geneva: Skira, 1977; New York: Rizzoli, 1977.
Davidson, J. Leroy. *The Lotus Sutra in Chinese Art: A Study in Buddhist Art to the Year 1880*. New Haven: Yale University Press, 1954.
Gray, Basil, and Vincent, John B. *Buddhist Cave Paintings at Tun-Huang*. Chicago: University of Chicago Press, 1959.
Honey, William B. *The Ceramic Art of China and Other Countries of the Far East*. New York: Beechhurst Press, 1954.
Hutt, Julia. *Understanding Far Eastern Art: A Complete Guide to the Arts of China, Japan, and Korea*. New York: Dutton, 1987.
Lee, Sherman E. *Chinese Landscape Painting*. 2nd ed. Cleveland: Cleveland Museum of Art, 1962. (Later edition available.)
———. *Past, Present, East and West*. New York: Braziller, 1983.
Loehr, Max. *The Great Painters of China*. New York: Harper & Row, 1980.
———. *Ritual Vessels of Bronze Age China*. New York: Asia Society, 1968.
Mizuno, Seiichi. *Bronzes and Jades of Ancient China*. Tokyo: Nihon Keizai, 1959.
Mizuno, Seiichi, and Nagahiro, Toshio. *A Study of the Buddhist Cave Temples at Lung-Men, Honan*. Tokyo: Zanho Press, 1941.
Munsterberg, Hugo. *Dictionary of Chinese and Japanese Art*. New York: Hacker, 1981.
———. *Symbolism in Ancient Chinese Art*. New York: Hacker, 1986.
Rudolph, Richard. *Han Tomb Art of West China*. Berkeley: University of California Press, 1951.
Sickman, Lawrence C., and Soper, Alexander. *The Art and Architecture of China*. Baltimore: Penguin, 1956. (Later edition available.)
Siren, Oswald. *Chinese Painting: Leading Masters and Principles*. New York: Hacker, 1973.
———. *Chinese Sculpture from the Fifth to the Fourteenth Centuries*. 4 vols. 1925. Reprint. New York: Hacker, 1970.
———. *A History of Later Chinese Painting*. 1938. Reprint. London: Medici Society, 1978.
Sullivan, Michael. *The Arts of China*. 3rd ed. Berkeley: University of California Press, 1984.
———. *The Birth of Landscape Painting in China*. Berkeley: University of California Press, 1962.
———. *A Short History of Chinese Art*. Berkeley: University of California Press, 1970.
Sullivan, Michael, and Darbois, Dominique. *The Cave Temples of Maichishan*. London: Faber & Faber, 1969.
Thorp, Robert L. *Son of Heaven: Imperial Arts of China*. Seattle: Son of Heaven Press, 1988.
Van Oort, H. A. *The Iconography of Chinese Buddhism in Traditional China*. Leiden: Brill, 1986.
Watson, William. *The Art of Dynastic China*. New York: Abrams, 1981. (Later edition available.)
Weber, Charles D. *Chinese Pictorial Bronze Vessels of the Late Chou Period*. Ascona, Switz: Artibus Asiae, 1968.
Willetts, William. *Foundations of Chinese Art*. New York: McGraw-Hill, 1965.

CHAPTER 13 THE ART OF JAPAN

Akiyama, Terukazu. *Japanese Painting*. Geneva: Skira; New York: Rizzoli, 1977.
Cahill, James F. *Scholar Painters of Japan: The Nanga School*. New York: Arno Press, 1976. (Later edition available.)
Drexler, Arthur. *The Architecture of Japan*. New York: Arno Press, 1966.
Eliseef, Danielle, and Eliseef, Vadime. *The Art of Japan*. New York: Abrams, 1985.
Fontein, Jan, and Hickman, M. C., eds. *Zen Painting and Calligraphy*. Greenwich, CT: New York Graphic Society, 1970.
Kanda, Christine Guth. *Shinzo: Hachiman Imagery and Its Development*. Cambridge: Harvard University Press, 1985.
Kidder, J. Edward. *Early Japanese Art*. London: Thames & Hudson, 1969.
———. *Japanese Temples: Sculpture, Painting, and Architecture*. Tokyo: Bijutsu Shuppansha, 1964.
Lee, Sherman E. *A History of Far Eastern Art*. London: Thames & Hudson, 1975. (Later edition available.)
———. *Japanese Decorative Style*. New York: Harper & Row, 1972.
Paine, Robert Treat, and Soper, Alexander. *The Art and Architecture of Japan*. 3rd rev. ed. Harmondsworth, England: Penguin, 1981.
Rosenfield, John M. *Japanese Art of the Heian Period, 749–1185*. New York: Asia Society, 1967.
Rosenfield, John M., and Shimada, Shujiro. *Traditions of Japanese Art*. Cambridge: Fogg Art Museum, Harvard University, 1970.
Soper, Alexander. *The Evolution of Buddhist Architecture in Japan*. 1942. Reprint. New York: Hacker, 1978.
Stanley-Smith, Joan. *Japanese Art*. New York: Thames & Hudson, 1984.
Stern, Harold P. *Master Prints of Japan: Ukiyo-e Hanga*. New York: Abrams, 1969.
Sugiyama, Jiro. *Classic Buddhist Sculpture: The Tempyo Period*. New York: Kodansha/Harper & Row, 1982.

CHAPTER 14 THE NATIVE ARTS OF THE AMERICAS, AFRICA, AND THE SOUTH PACIFIC

Pre-Columbian Art of the Americas

Anderson, Richard L. *Art in Small-Scale Societies*. 2nd ed. Englewood Cliffs, NJ: Prentice-Hall, 1989.
Anton, Ferdinand, et al. *Primitive Art: Pre-Columbian, North American Indian, African, Oceanic*. New York: Abrams, 1979.
Bennett, Wendell C. *Ancient Arts of the Andes*. New York: Museum of Modern Art/Arno Press, 1966.
Bernal, Ignacio. *The Olmec World*. Berkeley: University of California Press, 1977.
Coe, Michael D. *The Maya*. London: Thames & Hudson, 1980. (Later edition available.)
———. *Mexico*. 3rd ed. New York: Thames & Hudson, 1984. (Later edition available.)
Coe, Michael D., and Diehl, R. A. *In the Land of the Olmec*. 2 vols. Austin: University of Texas Press, 1980.
Coe, William R. *Tikal: A Handbook of the Ancient Maya Ruins*. 3rd ed. Philadelphia: University Museum, University of Pennsylvania, 1970. (Later edition available.)
Emmerich, André. *Sweat of the Sun and Tears of the Moon: Gold and Silver in Pre-Columbian Art*. New York: Hacker, 1977.
Franch, José Alcina. *Pre-Columbian Art*. New York: Abrams, 1983.
Grider, Terence. *Origins of Pre-Columbian Art*. Austin: University of Texas Press, 1982.
Heyden, Doris, and Gendrop, Paul. *Pre-Columbian Architecture of Mesoamerica*. New York: Abrams, 1975.
Kubler, George. *The Art and Architecture of Ancient America: The Mexican, Maya, and Andean Peoples*. 2nd ed. Harmondsworth, England: Penguin, 1975. (Later edition available.)
Lapiner, Alan C. *Pre-Columbian Art of South America*. New York: Abrams, 1976.
Lehmann, Walter, with Doering, Heinrich. *The Art of Old Peru*. New York: Hacker, 1975.
Los Angeles County Museum of Art. *Sculpture of Ancient West Mexico: Nayarit*. Los Angeles: Los Angeles County Museum of Art, 1970.
Mason, John Alden. *The Ancient Civilizations of Peru*. Rev. ed. Harmondsworth, England: Penguin, 1975. (Later edition available.)
Miller, Mary Ellen. *The Art of Mesoamerica: From Olmec to Aztec*. New York: Thames & Hudson, 1986.
Morley, Sylvanus G. *The Ancient Maya*. 3rd rev. ed. Stanford: Stanford University Press, 1973. (Later edition available.)
Paddock, John, ed. *Ancient Oaxaca: Discoveries in Mexican Archeology and History*. Stanford: Stanford University Press, 1970.
Pasztory, Esther. *Aztec Art*. New York: Abrams, 1983.
Peterson, Frederick. *Ancient Mexico*. New York: Capricorn Books, 1962.
Pettersen, Carmen L. *The Maya of Guatemala: Their Life and Dress*. Guatemala City: University of Washington Press, 1976. (Later edition available.)
Proskouriakoff, Tatiana Avenirovna. *A Study of Classic Maya Sculpture*. Washington, DC: Carnegie Institute of Washington, 1950.
Robertson, Donald. *Pre-Columbian Architecture*. New York: Braziller, 1963.
Robertson, Merle G.; Rands, Robert L.; and Graham, John A. *Maya Sculpture from the Southern Lowlands*. Berkeley: Lederer, Street & Zeus, 1972.
Rowe, John H. *Chavín Art: An Inquiry into Its Form and Meaning*. New York: Museum of Primitive Art, 1962.
Sabloff, Jeremy A. *The Cities of Ancient Mexico*. New York: Thames & Hudson, 1989.
Schele, Linda, and Miller, Mary Ellen. *The Blood of Kings: Dynasty and Ritual in Maya Art*. New York: Braziller, 1986.
Steward, Julian H. *Handbook of the South American Indians*. 7 vols. New York: Cooper Square Publishers, 1963.
Stierlin, Henri. *Art of the Aztecs and Its Origins*. New York: Rizzoli, 1982.
———. *Art of the Incas and Its Origins*. New York: Rizzoli, 1984.
Thompson, J. E. S. *Maya History and Religion*. Norman: University of Oklahoma Press, 1972. (Later edition available.)
Wauchope, Robert, ed. *Handbook of Middle American Indians*. 16 vols. Austin: University of Texas Press, 1964–1976.
Weaver, Muriel Porter. *The Aztecs, Maya, and their Predecessors: The Archaeology of Mesoamerica*. 2nd ed. New York: Academic Press, 1981.

North America

Boas, Franz. *Primitive Art*. 1927. Reprint. Magnolia, MA: Peter Smith, 1962.
Broder, Patricia Janis. *American Indian Painting and Sculpture*. New York: Abbeville Press, 1981.
Collins, Henry, et al. *The Far North: Two Thousand Years of American Eskimo and Indian Art*. Bloomington: Indiana University Press in association with the National Gallery of Art, Washington, DC, 1977.
Corbin, George A. *Native Arts of North America, Africa, and the South Pacific: An Introduction*. New York: Harper & Row, 1988.
Curtis, Edward S. *The North American Indian*. 30 vols. Cambridge: Cambridge University Press, 1907–1930. (Later reprint available.)
Dockstader, Frederick. *Indian Art in America: The Arts and Crafts of the North American Indian*. Greenwich, CT: New York Graphic Society, 1961.
———. *Indian Art of the Americas*. New York: Museum of the American Indian, Heye Foundation, 1973.
Ewers, John C. *Plains Indian Painting*. Stanford: Stanford University Press, 1939. (Later reprint available.)
Feder, Norman. *Two Hundred Years of North American Art*. New York: Praeger, 1972.
Feest, Christian F. *Native Arts of North America*. New York: Oxford University Press, 1980. (Later edition available.)
Grant, Campbell. *Rock Art of the American Indian*. 1967. Reprint. New York: Promontory Press, 1974. (Later edition available.)
Gunther, Erna. *Art in the Life of the Northwest Coast Indians*. Portland, OR: Portland Art Museum, 1966.
Kopper, Philip. *The Smithsonian Book of North American Indians*. Washington, DC: Smithsonian Institution Books, 1986.
Murdock, George P., and O'Leary, Timothy. *Ethnographic Bibliography of North America*. 4th ed. New Haven: Human Relations Area Files Press, 1972.
Ray, Dorothy J. *Artists of the Tundra and the Sea*. Seattle: University of Washington Press, 1961. (Later edition available.)

Ritchie, Carson I. A. *The Eskimo and His Art.* New York: St. Martin's Press, 1976.
Snow, Dean. *The Archaeology of North America/American Indians.* New York: Thames & Hudson, 1980. (Later edition available.)
Whiteford, Andrew H. *North American Indian Arts.* New York: Golden Press, 1973.

Africa

Allison, Philip. *African Stone Sculpture.* New York: Praeger, 1968.
Bascom, William R. *African Art in Cultural Perspective: An Introduction.* New York: Norton, 1973.
Ben-Amos, Paula. *The Art of Benin.* New York: Thames & Hudson, 1980.
Brentjes, Burchard. *African Rock Art.* London: Dent, 1967.
Cornet, Joseph. *Art of Africa: Treasures from the Congo.* London: Phaidon, 1971.
D'Azevedo, Warren L., ed. *The Traditional Artist in African Societies.* Bloomington: Indiana University Press, 1973. (Later edition available.)
Delange, Jacqueline. *Art and Peoples of Black Africa.* New York: Dutton, 1974.
Elisofon, Eliot, and Fagg, William. *The Sculpture of Africa.* New York: Hacker, 1978.
Eyo, Ekpo, and Willett, Frank. *Treasures of Ancient Nigeria.* New York: Knopf, 1980.
Fagg, William B. *Nigerian Images: The Splendor of African Sculpture.* New York: Praeger, 1963.
Forman, Werner. *Benin Art.* London: Hamlyn, 1960.
Fraser, Douglas F., and Cole, H. M., eds. *African Art and Leadership.* Madison: University of Wisconsin Press, 1972.
Gaskin, L. J. P. *A Bibliography of African Art.* London: International African Institute, 1965.
Gillon, Werner. *A Short History of African Art.* New York: Facts on File, 1984. (Later edition available.)
Laude, Jean. *The Arts of Black Africa.* Berkeley: University of California Press, 1973.
Lieris, Michel, and Delange, Jacqueline. *African Art.* New York: Golden Press, 1968.
Thompson, Robert F. *Black Gods and Kings: Yoruba Art at U.C.L.A.* Bloomington: Indiana University Press, 1976.
———. *Flash of the Spirit: African and Afro-American Art and Philosophy.* New York: Random House, 1983.
Trowell, Kathleen M. *Classical African Sculpture.* London: Faber & Faber, 1970.
Walker Art Center. *Art of the Congo.* Minneapolis: Walker Art Center, 1967.
Wassing, René S. *African Art: Its Background and Traditions.* New York: Abrams, 1968. (Later edition available.)
Willett, Frank. *African Art: An Introduction.* New York: Thames & Hudson, 1985.
———. *Life in the History of West African Sculpture.* New York: McGraw-Hill, 1967.

Oceania

Barrow, Terence. *An Illustrated Guide to Maori Art.* Honolulu: University of Hawaii Press, 1984.
Barrow, Tui T. *Art and Life in Polynesia.* Rutland, VT: Charles E. Tuttle, 1973.
———. *Maori Wood Sculpture of New Zealand.* Rutland, VT: Charles E. Tuttle, 1970.
Batterberry, Michael, and Ruskin, Ariane. *Primitive Art.* New York: McGraw-Hill, 1973.
Bernot, Ronald M. *Australian Aboriginal Art.* New York: Macmillan, 1964.
Buck, Peter H. *Arts and Crafts of Hawaii.* Honolulu: Bishop Museum Press, 1964.
Dodd, Edward H. *Polynesian Art.* New York: Dodd, Mead, 1967.
Firth, Raymond. *Art and Life in New Guinea.* 1936. Reprint. New York: AMS Press, 1977.
Fraser, Douglas. *Primitive Art.* London: Thames & Hudson, 1962.
Guiart, Jean. *Arts of the South Pacific.* New York: Golden Press, 1963.
Kooijman, S. *The Art of Lake Sentani.* New York: Museum of Primitive Art, 1959.
Linton, Ralph, and Wingert, Paul. *Arts of the South Seas.* 1946. Reprint. New York: Arno Press, 1972.
Newton, Douglas. *Art Styles of the Papuan Gulf.* New York: Museum of Primitive Art, 1961.
Rockefeller, Michael C. *The Asmat of New Guinea: The Journal of Michael Clark Rockefeller.* Greenwich, CT: New York Graphic Society, 1967.
Schmitz, Carl A. *Oceanic Art; Myth, Man and Image in the South Seas.* New York: Abrams, 1971.
Stubbs, Dacre. *Prehistoric Art of Australia.* New York: Scribner, 1975.
Taylor, Clyde R. H. *A Pacific Bibliography: Printed Matter Relating to the Native People of Polynesia, Melanesia, and Micronesia.* 2nd ed. Oxford: Clarendon Press, 1965.
Wingert, Paul. *Primitive Art: Its Traditions and Styles.* Cleveland: World Publishing, 1970.

CHAPTER 15 THE "PROTO-RENAISSANCE" IN ITALY

Andrés, Glenn, et al. *The Art of Florence.* 2 vols. New York: Abbeville Press, 1988.
Antal, Frederick. *Florentine Painting and Its Social Background.* London: Keegan Paul, 1948.
Cole, Bruce. *Sienese Painting: From Its Origins to the Fifteenth Century.* Bloomington: Indiana University Press, 1985. (Later edition available.)
Fremantle, Richard. *Florentine Gothic Painters from Giotto to Masaccio: A Guide to Painting in and near Florence.* London: Secker & Warburg, 1975.
Hills, Paul. *The Light of Early Italian Painting.* New Haven: Yale University Press, 1987.
Meiss, Millard. *Painting in Florence and Siena after the Black Death.* New York: Harper & Row, 1973. (Later edition available.)
Panofsky, Erwin. *Renaissance and Renascences in Western Art.* New York: Harper & Row, 1969. (Later edition available.)
Pope-Hennessy, John. *Introduction to Italian Sculpture.* 3rd. ed. 3 vols. New York: Phaidon, 1986.
———. *Italian Gothic Sculpture.* 3rd ed. Oxford: Phaidon, 1986.
Schevill, Ferdinand. *The Medici.* New York: Harper & Row, 1960.
Smart, Alastair. *The Dawn of Italian Painting.* Ithaca, NY: Cornell University Press, 1978.
Stubblebine, James, ed. *Giotto: The Arena Chapel Frescoes.* New York: Norton, 1969.
———. *Assisi and the Rise of Vernacular Art.* New York: Harper & Row, 1985.
Van Marle, Raimond. *The Development of the Italian Schools of Painting.* 19 vols. 1923–1938. Reprint. New York: Hacker, 1970.
Venturi, Lionello, and Skira-Venturi, Rosabianca. *Italian Painting: The Creators of the Renaissance.* 3 vols. Geneva: Skira, 1950–1952.
White, John. *Art and Architecture in Italy 1250–1400.* 2nd integrated ed. New York: Viking Penguin, 1987. (Later edition available.)

CHAPTER 16 FIFTEENTH-CENTURY ITALIAN ART

Baxandall, Michael. *Painting and Experience in Fifteenth Century Italy. A Primer in the Social History of Pictorial Style.* 2nd ed. New York: Oxford University Press, 1988.
Berenson, Bernard. *The Italian Painters of the Renaissance.* Ithaca, NY: Phaidon/Cornell University Press, 1980.
———. *Italian Pictures of the Renaissance.* Ithaca, NY: Phaidon/Cornell University Press, 1980.
Bober, Phyllis Pray, and Rubinstein, Ruth. *Renaissance Artists and Antique Sculpture: A Handbook of Sources.* Oxford: Oxford University Press, 1986.
Borsook, Eve. *The Mural Painters of Tuscany.* New York: Oxford University Press, 1981.
Burckhardt, Jacob. *The Architecture of the Italian Renaissance.* Rev. ed. London: Secker & Warburg, 1985. (Later edition available.)
———. *The Civilization of the Renaissance in Italy.* 4th ed. 1867. Reprint. London: Phaidon, 1960.
Chastel, André. *The Age of Humanism.* New York: McGraw-Hill, 1964.
———. *A Chronicle of Italian Renaissance Painting.* Ithaca, NY: Cornell University Press, 1984.
———. *Studios and Styles of the Italian Renaissance.* New York: Braziller, 1971.
Cole, Bruce. *Masaccio and the Art of Early Renaissance Florence.* Bloomington: Indiana University Press, 1980.
Decker, Heinrich. *The Renaissance in Italy: Architecture, Sculpture, Frescoes.* New York: Viking, 1969.
De Wald, Ernest T. *Italian Painting, 1200–1600.* New York: Holt, Rinehart & Winston, 1961.
Earls, Irene. *Renaissance Art: A Topical Dictionary.* New York: Greenwood Press, 1987.
Edgerton, Samuel Y., Jr. *The Renaissance Rediscovery of Linear Perspective.* New York: Harper & Row, 1976.
Ferguson, Wallace K., et al. *The Renaissance.* New York: Henry Holt, 1940.
Gadol, Joan. *Leon Battista Alberti: Universal Man of the Early Renaissance.* Chicago: University of Chicago Press, 1969.
Gilbert, Creighton. *History of Renaissance Art throughout Europe.* New York: Abrams, 1973.
———. *Italian Art 1400–1500: Sources and Documents.* Englewood Cliffs, NJ: Prentice-Hall, 1970.
Godfrey, F. M. *Early Venetian Painters, 1415–1495.* London: Tiranti, 1954.
Gombrich, E. H. *Norm and Form: Studies in the Art of the Renaissance.* 4th ed. Oxford: Phaidon, 1985.
Hale, John R. *Italian Renaissance Painting from Masaccio to Titian.* New York: Dutton, 1977.
Hartt, Frederick. *History of Italian Renaissance Art: Painting, Sculpture, Architecture.* 3rd ed. Englewood Cliffs, NJ: Prentice-Hall, 1987.
Helton, Tinsley, ed. *The Renaissance: A Reconsideration of the Theories and Interpretations of the Age.* Madison: University of Wisconsin Press, 1964.
Heydenreich, Ludwig H., and Lotz, Wolfgang. *Architecture in Italy 1400–1600.* Harmondsworth, England: Penguin, 1974.
Holt, Elizabeth B. *A Documentary History of Art.* 2nd ed. Vol. 1. Garden City, NY: Doubleday, 1957.
Huyghe, René. *Larousse Encyclopedia of Renaissance and Baroque Art.* See **Reference Books.**
Janson, Horst W. *The Sculpture of Donatello.* 2 vols. Princeton: Princeton University Press, 1957. (Later edition available.)
Krautheimer, Richard, and Krautheimer-Hess, Trude. *Lorenzo Ghiberti.* Princeton: Princeton University Press, 1956. (Later edition available.)
Lieberman, Ralph. *Renaissance Architecture in Venice.* New York: Abbeville Press, 1982.
Lowry, Bates. *Renaissance Architecture.* New York: Braziller, 1962.
McAndrew, John. *Venetian Architecture of the Early Renaissance.* Cambridge: MIT Press, 1980.
Meiss, Millard. *The Painter's Choice, Problems in the Interpretation of Renaissance Art.* New York: Harper & Row, 1976. (Later edition available.)
Murray, Peter. *The Architecture of the Italian Renaissance.* Rev. ed. New York: Schocken, 1986.
———. *Renaissance Architecture.* New York: Electa/Rizzoli (paperbound), 1985.
Murray, Peter, and Murray, Linda. *The Art of the Renaissance.* London: Thames & Hudson, 1981. (Later edition available.)
Panofsky, Erwin. *Renaissance and Renascences in Western Art.* New York: Harper & Row, 1969. (Later edition available.)
Pater, Walter. *The Renaissance: Studies in Art and Poetry.* Edited by D. L. Hill. Berkeley: University of California Press, 1980.
Pope-Hennessy, John. *An Introduction to Italian Sculpture.* 3rd ed. 3 vols. New York: Phaidon, 1986.
———. *Sienese Quattrocento Painting.* New York: Oxford University Press, 1947.
Schevill, Ferdinand. *The Medici.* New York: Harper & Row, 1960.
Seymour, Charles. *Sculpture in Italy, 1400–1500.* Baltimore: Penguin, 1966.
Symonds, John Addington. *The Renaissance in Italy.* 7 vols. 1875–1886. Reprint. New York: Modern Library, 1935. (Other reprints available.)
Van Marle, Raimond. *The Development of the Italian Schools of Painting.* 19 vols. 1923–1938. Reprint. New York: Hacker, 1970.
Vasari, Giorgio. *The Lives of the Most Eminent Painters, Sculptors, and Architects, 1550–1568.* 3 vols. New York: Abrams, 1979.
Werkmeister, William H., ed.; Ferguson, Wallace, et al. *Facets of the Renaissance.* New York: Harper & Row, 1963.
White, John. *The Birth and Rebirth of Pictorial Space.* 3rd ed. Boston: Faber & Faber, 1987.
Wilde, Johannes. *Venetian Art from Bellini to Titian.* Oxford: Clarendon Press, 1981.
Wittkower, Rudolf. *Architectural Principles in the Age of Humanism.* 4th ed. London: Academy, 1988.

CHAPTER 17 SIXTEENTH-CENTURY ITALIAN ART

Ackerman, James S. *The Architecture of Michelangelo.* Rev. ed. Chicago: University of Chicago Press, 1986.
———. *Palladio.* New York: Penguin, 1978.

Bialostocki, Jan. *The Art of the Renaissance in Eastern Europe.* Ithaca, NY: Cornell University Press, 1976.
Blunt, Anthony. *Artistic Theory in Italy, 1450–1600.* London: Oxford University Press, 1975.
Briganti, Giuliano. *Italian Mannerism.* London: Thames & Hudson, 1962.
Castiglione, Baldassare. *Book of the Courtier.* 1528. Reprint. New York: National Alumni, 1907.
Cellini, Benvenuto. *Autobiography.* Reprint. New York: Grolier, 1969. (Other reprints available.)
Freedberg, Sydney J. *Painting in Italy, 1500–1600.* 2nd ed. New York: Penguin, 1983.
———. *Painting of the High Renaissance in Rome and Florence.* Rev. ed. New York: Hacker, 1985.
Friedlaender, Walter. *Mannerism and Anti-Mannerism in Italian Painting.* New York: Schocken, 1965.
Holt, Elizabeth Gilmore, ed. *A Documentary History of Art.* Vol. 2, *Michelangelo and the Mannerists.* Rev. ed. Princeton: Princeton University Press, 1982.
Levey, Michael. *High Renaissance.* Harmondsworth, England: Penguin, 1975.
Murray, Linda. *The High Renaissance and Mannerism.* New York: Oxford University Press, 1977.
Partner, Peter. *Renaissance Rome, 1500–1559: A Portrait of a Society.* Berkeley: University of California Press, 1977.
Perlingieri, Ilya Sandra. "Lady in Waiting." *Art & Antiques,* April 1988, page 67.
Pietrangeli, Carlo, et al. *The Sistine Chapel: The Art, the History, and the Restoration.* New York: Harmony Books, 1986.
Pope-Hennessy, John. *Cellini.* London: Macmillan, 1985.
———. *Italian High Renaissance and Baroque Sculpture.* 3rd ed. 3 vols. Oxford: Phaidon, 1986.
Shearman, John K. G. *Mannerism.* Baltimore: Penguin, 1978.
Venturi, Lionello. *The Sixteenth Century: From Leonardo to El Greco.* New York: Skira, 1956.
Von Einem, Herbert. *Michelangelo.* London: Methuen, 1976.
Wölfflin, Heinrich. *The Art of the Italian Renaissance.* New York: Schocken, 1963.
———. *Classic Art: An Introduction to the Italian Renaissance.* 4th ed. Oxford: Phaidon, 1980.
Würtenberger, Franzsepp. *Mannerism: The European Style of the Sixteenth Century.* New York: Holt, Rinehart & Winston, 1963.

CHAPTER 18 THE RENAISSANCE OUTSIDE OF ITALY

Benesch, Otto. *Art of the Renaissance in Northern Europe.* Rev. ed. London: Phaidon, 1965.
———. *German Painting from Dürer to Holbein.* Geneva: Skira, 1966.
Blunt, Anthony. *Art and Architecture in France 1500–1700.* 4th ed. Baltimore: Penguin, 1982.
Chatelet, Albert. *Early Dutch Painting.* New York: Rizzoli, 1981. (Later edition available.)
Cuttler, Charles P. *Northern Painting from Pucelle to Bruegel.* New York: Holt, Rinehart & Winston, 1968.
Evans, Joan. *Monastic Architecture in France from the Renaissance to the Revolution.* New York: Hacker, 1980.
Friedlander, Max J. *Early Netherlandish Painting.* 14 vols. New York: Praeger/Phaidon, 1967–1976.
———. *From Van Eyck to Bruegel.* 3rd ed. Ithaca, NY: Cornell University Press, 1981.
Fuchs, Rudolph H. *Dutch Painting.* London: Thames & Hudson, 1978.
Hind, Arthur M. *History of Engraving and Etching from the Fifteenth Century to the Year 1914.* 3rd rev. ed. New York: Dover, 1963.
———. *An Introduction to a History of Woodcut.* New York: Dover, 1963.
Hitchcock, Henry-Russell. *German Renaissance Architecture.* Princeton: Princeton University Press. 1981.
Huizinga, Johan. *The Waning of the Middle Ages.* 1924. Reprint. New York: St. Martin's Press, 1988.
Kaufmann, Thomas DaCosta. *The School of Prague.* Chicago: University of Chicago Press, 1988.
Meiss, Millard. *French Painting in the Time of Jean de Berry.* New York: Braziller, 1974.
Panofsky, Erwin. *Early Netherlandish Painting.* Cambridge: Harvard University Press, 1953.
———. *The Life and Art of Albrecht Dürer.* 4th ed. Princeton: Princeton University Press, 1971.
Prevenier, Walter, and Blockmans, Wim. *The Burgundian Netherlands.* Cambridge: Cambridge University Press, 1986.
Snyder, James. *Northern Renaissance Art.* New York: Abrams, 1985.
Waterhouse, Ellis. *The Dictionary of 16th and 17th Century British Painters.* Woodbridge, England. Antique Collectors' Club, 1988.
Wolfthal, Diane. *The Beginnings of Netherlandish Canvas Painting, 1400–1530.* New York: Cambridge University Press, 1989.

CHAPTER 19 BAROQUE ART

Alpers, Svetlana. *The Art of Describing: Dutch Art in the Seventeenth Century.* Chicago: University of Chicago Press, 1983. (Later edition available.)
Bazin, Germain. *Baroque and Rococo Art.* New York: Praeger, 1974.
Blunt, Anthony, ed. *Baroque and Rococo: Architecture and Decoration.* Cambridge: Harper & Row, 1982.
Brown, Jonathon. *Velázquez: Painter and Courtier.* New Haven: Yale University Press, 1986.
Fokker, Timon H. *Roman Baroque Art: The History of a Style.* London: Oxford University Press, 1938.
Freedberg, Sydney J. *Circa 1600: A Revolution of Style in Italian Painting.* Cambridge: Harvard University Press, 1983. (Later edition available.)
Gerson, Horst, and ter Kuile, E. H. *Art and Architecture in Belgium 1600–1800.* Baltimore: Penguin, 1960. (Later edition available.)
Haak, Bob. *The Golden Age: Dutch Painters of the Seventeenth Century.* London: Thames & Hudson, 1984.
Held, Julius, and Posner, Donald. *17th and 18th Century Art.* New York: Abrams, 1974.
Hempel, Eberhard. *Baroque Art and Architecture in Central Europe.* Baltimore: Penguin, 1965. (Later edition available.)
Hibbard, Howard. *Bernini.* Harmondsworth, England: Penguin, 1976.
———. *Caravaggio.* New York: Thames & Hudson, 1983.
———. *Carlo Maderno and Roman Architecture, 1580–1630.* London: Zwemmer, 1971.
Hinks, Roger P. *Michelangelo Merisi da Caravaggio.* London: Faber & Faber, 1953.
Howard, Deborah. *The Architectural History of Venice.* London: B. T. Batsford, 1981.
Huyghe, René, ed. *Larousse Encyclopedia of Renaissance and Baroque Art.* See **Reference Books.**
Kahr, Madlyn Millner. *Dutch Painting in the Seventeenth Century.* New York: Harper & Row, 1978.
———. *Velázquez: The Art of Painting.* New York: Harper & Row, 1976.
Kitson, Michael. *The Age of Baroque.* London: Hamlyn, 1976.
Lees-Milne, James. *Baroque in Italy.* New York: Macmillan, 1960.
Martin, John R. *Baroque.* New York: Harper & Row, 1977.
Millon, Henry A. *Baroque and Rococo Architecture.* New York: Braziller, 1965.
Nicolson, Benedict. *The International Caravaggesque Movement.* Oxford: Phaidon, 1979.
Norberg-Schulz, Christian. *Baroque Architecture.* New York: Rizzoli, 1985. (Later edition available.)
———. *Late Baroque and Rococo Architecture.* New York: Electa/Rizzoli, 1985.
Pope-Hennessy, Sir John. *The Study and Criticism of Italian Sculpture.* New York: Metropolitan Museum, 1981.
Portoghesi, Paolo. *The Rome of Borromini.* London: Phaidon, 1972.
Powell, Nicolas. *From Baroque to Rococo: An Introduction to Austrian and German Architecture from 1580 to 1790.* London: Faber & Faber, 1959.
Rosenberg, Jakob; Slive, Seymour; and ter Kuile, E. H. *Dutch Art and Architecture, 1600–1800.* Baltimore: Penguin, 1979.
Spear, Richard E. *Caravaggio and His Followers.* New York: Harper & Row, 1975.
Stechow, Wolfgang. *Dutch Landscape Painting of the 17th Century.* Oxford: Phaidon, 1981.
Summerson, Sir John. *Architecture in Britain: 1530–1830.* 7th rev. and enl. ed. Baltimore: Penguin, 1983.
Tapie, Victor-Lucien. *The Age of Grandeur: Baroque Art and Architecture.* New York: Praeger, 1966.
Varriano, John. *Italian Baroque and Rococo Architecture.* New York: Oxford University Press, 1986.
Waterhouse, Ellis Kirkham. *Baroque Painting in Rome.* London: Phaidon, 1976.
———. *Italian Baroque Painting.* 2nd ed. London: Phaidon, 1969.
———. *Painting in Britain, 1530–1790.* 4th ed. New York: Penguin, 1978. (Later edition available.)
White, Christopher. *Peter Paul Rubens: Man and Artist.* New Haven: Yale University Press, 1987.
Wittkower, Rudolf. *Gian Lorenzo Bernini: The Sculptor of the Roman Baroque.* 3rd rev. ed. Oxford: Phaidon, 1981.
Wölfflin, Heinrich. *Principles of Art History: The Problem of the Development of Style in Later Art.* 7th ed. New York: Dover, 1950.
———. *Renaissance and Baroque.* London: Collins, 1984.
Wright, Christopher. *The French Painters of the 17th Century.* New York: New York Graphic Society, 1986.

CHAPTER 20 THE EIGHTEENTH CENTURY: ROCOCO AND THE BIRTH OF THE MODERN WORLD

Arnason, H. H. *The Sculptures of Houdon.* New York: Oxford University Press, 1975.
Bacou, Roseline. *Piranesi: Etchings and Drawings.* Boston: New York Graphic Society, 1975.
Blunt, Anthony. *Art and Architecture in France, 1500–1700.* 2nd ed. Harmondsworth, England: Penguin, 1970.
Braham, Allan. *The Architecture of the French Enlightenment.* Berkeley: University of California Press, 1980.
Burchard, John, and Bush-Brown, Albert. *The Architecture of America: A Social and Cultural History.* Boston: Little, Brown/The American Institute of Architects, 1965.
Chatelet, Albert, and Thuillier, Jacques. *French Painting from Le Nain to Fragonard.* Geneva: Skira, 1964.
Cobban, Alfred, ed. *The Eighteenth Century: Europe in the Age of the Enlightenment.* New York: McGraw-Hill, 1969.
Conisbee, Philip. *Painting in Eighteenth-Century France.* Ithaca, NY: Phaidon/Cornell University Press, 1981.
Crow, Thomas E. *Painters and Public Life in Eighteenth-Century Paris.* New Haven: Yale University Press, 1985.
Hayes, John T. *Gainsborough: Paintings and Drawings.* London: Phaidon, 1975.
Herrmann, Luke. *British Landscape Painting of the Eighteenth Century.* New York: Oxford University Press, 1974.
Hitchcock, Henry Russell. *Rococo Architecture in Southern Germany.* London: Phaidon, 1968.
Holt, Elizabeth Gilmore, ed. *From the Classicists to the Impressionists: A Documentary History of Art and Architecture in the Nineteenth Century.* Garden City, NY: Anchor Books/Doubleday, 1966.
Irwin, David. *English Neoclassical Art.* London: Faber & Faber, 1966.
Kalnein, Wend Graf, and Levey, Michael. *Art and Architecture of the Eighteenth Century in France.* New York: Viking/Pelican, 1973.
Kimball, Sidney F. *The Creation of the Rococo.* New York: W. W. Norton, 1964.
Levey, Michael. *Painting in Eighteenth-Century Venice.* Ithaca, NY: Phaidon/Cornell University Press, 1980.
———. *Rococo to Revolution: Major Trends in Eighteenth-Century Painting.* London: Thames & Hudson, 1966.
Millon, Henry A. *Baroque and Rococo Architecture.* New York: George Braziller, 1961, 1965.
Norberg-Schulz, Christian. *Late Baroque and Rococo Architecture.* New York: Harry N. Abrams, 1974.
Pierson, William. *American Buildings and Their Architects: Vol. 1, The Colonial and Neo-Classical Style.* Garden City, NY: Doubleday, 1970.
Pignatti, Terisio. *The Age of Rococo.* New York: Hamlyn, 1969.
Pevsner, Nikolaus. *An Outline of European Architecture.* 6th ed. Baltimore, MD: Penguin Books, 1960.
Powell, Nicolas. *From Baroque to Rococo: An Introduction to Austrian and German Architecture from 1580 to 1790.* London: Faber & Faber, 1959.
Raine, Kathleen. *William Blake.* New York: Oxford University Press, 1970.

Rosenblum, Robert. *Transformations in Late Eighteenth Century Art*. Princeton, NJ: Princeton University Press, 1970.
Waterhouse, Ellis K. *Painting in Britain, 1530–1790*. 4th ed. New York: Penguin, 1978.
Whinney, Margaret Dickens. *English Art, 1625–1714*. Oxford, England: Clarendon Press, 1957.
———. *Sculpture in Britain, 1530–1830*. Baltimore, MD: Penguin, 1964.
Whinney, Margaret D., and Millar, Oliver. *English Sculpture, 1720–1830*. London: H. M. Stationery Office, 1971.
Wittkower, Rudolf. *Art and Architecture in Italy, 1600–1750*. New York: Penguin, 1980.

CHAPTER 21 THE NINETEENTH CENTURY: PLURALISM OF STYLE

Aslin, Elizabeth. *The Aesthetic Movement: Prelude to Art Nouveau*. New York: Frederick A. Praeger, 1969.
Baudelaire, Charles; Mayne, Jonathan, tr. *The Mirror of Art, Critical Studies*. Garden City, NY: Doubleday & Co., 1956.
Barr, Margaret Scolari. *Medardo Rosso*. New York: The Museum of Modern Art, 1963.
Bisanz, R. M. *German Romanticism and Philipp Otto Runge*. De Kalb: Northern Illinois University Press, 1970.
Boime, Albert. *The Academy and French Painting in the 19th Century*. London: Phaidon, 1971.
Bonnat, Jean. *Degas: His Life and Work*. New York: Tudor Publishing Company, 1965.
Borsch-Supan, H. *Caspar David Friedrich*. New York: George Braziller, 1974.
Brion, Marcel. *Art of the Romantic Era: Romanticism, Classicism, Realism*. New York: Frederick A. Praeger, 1966.
Broun, Elizabeth. *Albert Pinkham Ryder*. Washington, DC: National Museum of American Art/Smithsonian Institutions, 1989.
Clark, Kenneth. *The Gothic Revival: An Essay in the History of Taste*. New York: Humanities Press, 1970.
Clay, Jean. *Romanticism*. New York: Phaidon, 1981.
Courthion, Pierre. *Romanticism*. Geneva: Skira, 1961.
Delacroix, Eugène; Pach, Walter, tr. *The Journal of Eugène Delacroix*. New York: Grove Press, 1937, 1948.
Dixon, Roger, and Muthesius, Stefen. *Victorian Architecture*. London: Thames & Hudson, 1978.
Dorra, Henri. *The American Muse*. London: Thames & Hudson, 1961.
Eitner, Lorenz. *Neo-Classicism and Romanticism 1750–1850: Sources and Documents on the History of Art*. 2 vols. Englewood Cliffs, NJ: Prentice-Hall, 1970.
Elsen, Albert. *Rodin*. New York: Museum of Modern Art, 1963.
Friedlaender, Walter. *From David to Delacroix*. New York: Schocken Books, 1968.
Fusco, Peter, and Janson, H. W. *The Romantics to Rodin: French 19th-Century Sculpture from American Collections*. Los Angeles: Los Angeles County Art Museum/New York: George Braziller, 1980.
Hamilton, George Heard. *Manet and His Critics*. New Haven, CT: Yale University Press, 1954.
Hanson, Anne Coffin. *Manet and the Modern Tradition*. New Haven, CT: Yale University Press, 1977.
Harker, Margaret F. *Henry Peach Robinson: Master of Photographic Art, 1830–1901*. Oxford, England: Basil Blackwell, 1988.
Hawley, Henry. *Neo-Classicism: Style and Motif*. Cleveland: Cleveland Museum of Art, 1964.
Hilton, Timothy. *The Pre-Raphaelites*. New York: Oxford University Press, 1970.
Holt, Elizabeth B. *From the Classicists to the Impressionists: Art and Architecture in the Nineteenth Century*. Garden City, NY: Doubleday/Anchor, 1966.
Honour, Hugh. *Neo-Classicism*. New York: Harper & Row, 1979.
———. *Romanticism*. New York: Harper & Row, 1979.
Janson, Horst W. *19th-Century Sculpture*. New York: Harry N. Abrams, 1985.
Leymarie, Jean. *French Painting in the Nineteenth Century*. Geneva: Skira, 1962.
Macaulay, James. *The Gothic Revival, 1745–1845*. Glasgow, Scotland: Blackie, 1975.
Middleton, Robin, ed. *The Beaux-Arts and Nineteenth-Century French Architecture*. Cambridge, MA: MIT Press, 1982.
Miller, Lillian B. *Patrons and Patriotism: The Encouragement of the Fine Arts in the United States, 1790–1860*. Chicago: The University of Chicago Press, 1966.
Newhall, Nancy. *P. H. Emerson*. New York: An Aperture Monograph, 1975.
Newton, Eric. *The Romantic Rebellion* New York: Schocken Books, 1964.
Nochlin, Linda. *Gustave Courbet: A Study of Style and Society*. New York: Garland, 1976.
———. *Impressionism and Post-Impressionism, 1874–1904: Sources and Documents*. Englewood Cliffs, NJ: Prentice-Hall, 1966.
———. *Realism and Tradition in Art: Sources and Documents*. Englewood Cliffs, NJ: Prentice-Hall, 1966.
Novak, Barbara. *American Painting of the Nineteenth Century*. New York: Frederick A. Praeger, 1969.
Novotny, Fritz. *Painting and Sculpture in Europe: 1780–1880*. 2nd ed. Harmondsworth, England: Penguin, 1978.
Pelles, Geraldine. *Art, Artists and Society: Origins of a Modern Dilemma: Painting in England and France, 1750–1850*. Englewood Cliffs, NJ: Prentice-Hall, 1963.
Pevsner, Nikolaus. *Pioneers of Modern Design*. Harmondsworth, England: Penguin, 1964.
Poole, Phoebe. *Impressionism*. London: Thames & Hudson, 1967.
Rewald, John. *The History of Impressionism*. New York: Museum of Modern Art, 1973.
———. *Post-Impressionism: From Van Gogh to Gauguin*. New York: Museum of Modern Art, 1956.
Rewald, John; Ashton, Dore; and Joachim, Harold. *Odilon Redon, Gustave Moreau, Rodolphe Bresdin*. New York: Museum of Modern Art, 1962.
Roberts, Keith. *The Impressionists and Post-Impressionists*. New York: E. P. Dutton, 1977.
Rosen, Charles, and Zerner, Henri. *Romanticism and Realism: The Mythology of Nineteenth-Century Art*. London: Faber and Faber, 1984.
Rosenblum, Robert, and Janson, Horst W. *19th Century Art*. New York: Harry N. Abrams, 1984.
Russell, John. *Seurat*. New York: Frederick A. Praeger, 1965.
Sambrook, James, ed. *Pre-Raphaelitism: A Collection of Critical Essays*. Chicago: University of Chicago Press, 1974.
Sloane, Joseph C. *French Painting Between the Past and the Present: Artists, Critics, and Traditions from 1848 to 1870*. Princeton, NJ: Princeton University Press, 1973.
Sullivan, Louis. *The Autobiography of an Idea*. New York: Dover Publications, 1956.
Van Gogh: A Self Portrait: Letters Revealing His Life as a Painter. Selected by W. H. Auden. New York: E. P. Dutton, 1963.
Vaughan, William. *German Romantic Painting*. New Haven, CT: Yale University Press, 1980.
Weisberg, Gabriel P. *The Realist Tradition: French Painting and Drawing, 1830–1900*. Cleveland: Cleveland Museum/Indiana University Press, 1980.
Wood, Christopher. *The Pre-Raphaelites*. New York: Viking Press, 1981.

CHAPTER 22 THE EARLY TWENTIETH CENTURY

Ades, Dawn. *Dali and Surrealism*. New York: Harper & Row, 1982.
Adams, Ansel with Alinder, Mary Street. *Ansel Adams: An Autobiography*. Boston: Little, Brown & Co., 1985.
Anderson, Troels. *Malevich*. Amsterdam, Netherlands: Stedelijk Museum, 1970.
Apollinaire, Guillaume. *The Cubist Painters: Aesthetic Meditations, 1913*. New York: Wittenborn, 1970.
Barr, Alfred H., Jr. *Cubism and Abstract Art*. New York: Museum of Modern Art, 1936.
———. *Picasso: Fifty Years of His Art*. New York: Museum of Modern Art, 1946.
Barsacq, Lon. *Caligari's Cabinet and Other Grand Illusions: A History of Film Design*. New York: New American Library, 1978.
Bayer, Herbert; Gropius, Walter; Gropius, Ise, eds. *Bauhaus 1919–1928*. Boston: Charles T. Branford Co., 1959.
Benevolo, Leonardo. *History of Modern Architecture*. 2 vols. Cambridge, MA. MIT Press, 1977.
Blake, Peter. *Frank Lloyd Wright*. Harmondsworth, Middlesex: Penguin Books, 1960.
———. *The Master Builder*. New York: W. W. Norton, 1976.
Boesinger, Willy, ed. *Le Corbusier*. New York: Frederick A. Praeger, 1972.
Breton, André. *Surrealism and Painting*. New York: Harper & Row, 1972.
Campbell, Mary Schmidt; Driskell, David C.; Levering, David Lewis; and Ryan, Deborah Willis. *Harlem Renaissance: Art of Black America*. New York: The Studio Museum, Harlem/Harry N. Abrams, 1987.
Carls, Carl Dietrich. *Ernst Barlach*. London: Pall Mall Press, 1969.
Carrá, Massimo; Rathke, Ewald; Tisdall, Caroline; and Waldberg, Patrick. *Metaphysical Art*. New York: Frederick A. Praeger, 1971.
Carter, Peter. *Mies van der Rohe at Work*. London: Pall Mall Press, 1974.
Cassou, Jean. *Chagall*. New York: Frederick A. Praeger, 1965.
Cassou, Jean, and Pevsner, Nikolaus. *Gateway to the Twentieth Century*. New York: McGraw-Hill, 1962.
Dupin, Jacques. *Alberto Giacometti*. Paris: Maeght Éditeur, 1963.
Duthuit, Georges. *The Fauvist Painters*. New York: Wittenborn, Schultz, 1950.
Edwards, Ehrlig. *Painted Walls of Mexico*. Austin, TX: University of Texas Press, 1966.
Eisner, Lotte. *The Haunted Screen*. Berkeley: The University of California Press, 1965.
Elderfield, John. *Kurt Schwitters*. New York: Museum of Modern Art/Thames & Hudson, 1985.
———. *The "Wild Beasts": Fauvism and Its Affinities*. New York: The Museum of Modern Art/Oxford University Press, 1976.
Elsen, Albert. *Origins of Modern Sculpture*. New York: George Braziller, 1974.
Frampton, Kenneth. *A Critical History of Modern Architecture*. London: Thames & Hudson, 1985.
Friedman, Mildred, ed. *De Stijl: 1917–1931, Visions of Utopia*. Minneapolis: Walker Art Center/New York: Abbeville Press, 1982.
Fry, Edward, ed. *Cubism*. London: Thames & Hudson, 1966.
Fuller, R. Buckminster, and Marks, Robert. *The Dymaxion World of Buckminster Fuller*. Garden City, NY: Anchor Press/Doubleday, 1960.
Geist, Sidney. *Constantin Brancusi, 1876–1957: A Retrospective Exhibition*. New York: Solomon R. Guggenheim Museum/Philadelphia: Philadelphia Museum of Art/Chicago: Chicago Art Institute, 1969.
George, Waldemar, and Vierny, Dina. *Maillol*. London: Cory, Adams, and Mackay, 1965.
Giannetti, Louis D. *Understanding Movies*. 2nd ed. Englewood Cliffs, NJ: Prentice-Hall, 1976.
Giedion-Welcker, Carola. *Constantin Brancusi*. New York: George Braziller, 1959.
Gilot, François, and Lake, Carlton. *Life with Picasso*. New York: McGraw-Hill, 1964.
Golding, John. *Cubism: A History and an Analysis, 1907–1914*. rev. ed. Boston: Boston Book & Art Shop, 1968.
Gowing, Lawrence. *Matisse*. New York: Oxford University Press, 1979.
Gray, Camilla. *The Russian Experiment in Art: 1863–1922*. New York: Harry N. Abrams, 1970.
Gray, Christopher. *Cubist Aesthetic Theories*. Baltimore: Johns Hopkins University Press 1953.
Grohmann, Will. *Kandinsky: Life and Work*. New York: Harry N. Abrams, 1958.
Gropius, Walter. *Scope of Total Architecture*. New York: Collier Books, 1962.
Herrera, Hayden. *Frida: A Biography of Frida Kahlo*. New York: Harper & Row, 1983.
Hepworth, Barbara. *A Pictorial Autobiography*. London: The Tate Gallery, 1978.
Hof, August. *Wilhelm Lehmbruck*. London: Pall Mall Press, 1969.
Jaffé, Hans L. *De Stijl*. New York: Harry N. Abrams, 1971.
James, Philip. *Henry Moore on Sculpture*. New York: Viking Press, 1971.
Janis, Sidney. *Abstract and Surrealist Art in America*. 1944. reprint. New York: Arno Press, 1969.

Jean, Marcel; Taylor, Simon Watson, tr. *The History of Surrealist Painting*. New York: Grove Press, 1960.

Kahnweiler, Daniel H. *The Rise of Cubism*. New York: Wittenborn, Schultz, 1949.

Kandinsky, Wassily; Sadler, M. T. H., tr. *Concerning the Spiritual in Art*. New York: Dover Publications, 1977.

Kyrou, Ado. *Le Surréalisme au cinéma*. Paris: Le Terrain Vague, 1963.

Langaard, Johan H., and Revold, Reidar. *Edvard Munch: Masterpieces from the Artist's Collection in the Munch Museum in Oslo*. New York: McGraw-Hill, 1964.

Le Corbusier. *The City of Tomorrow*, Cambridge, MA: MIT Press, 1971.

Levin, Gail. *Edward Hopper: The Art and the Artist*. New York: Whitney Museum of American Art/Norton, 1980.

Leyda, Jay. *Kino, A History of the Russian and Soviet Film: A Study of the Development of Russian Cinema from 1896 to the Present*. New York: Collier Books, 1973.

Lodder, Christina. *Russian Constructivism*. New Haven, CT: Yale University Press, 1983.

Maddow, Ben. *Edward Weston*. Boston: Aperture, New York Graphic Society, 1963.

Martin, Marianne W. *Futurist Art and Theory*. Oxford, England: Clarendon Press, 1968.

Martinell, César. *Gaudí: His Life, His Theories, His Work*. Cambridge, MA: MIT Press, 1975.

Mashek, Joseph, ed. *Marcel Duchamp in Perspective*. Englewood Cliffs, NJ: Prentice-Hall, 1975.

Mast, Gerald, and Cohen, Marshall, eds. *Film Theory and Criticism: Introductory Readings*. 2nd ed. New York: Oxford University Press, 1979.

Matthews, J. H. *Surrealism and Film*. Ann Arbor: The University of Michigan Press, 1971.

Meltzer, Milton. *Dorothea Lange: A Photographer's Life*. New York: Farrar, Strauss, Giroux, 1978.

Miller, Margaret, ed. *Paul Klee*. New York: Museum of Modern Art, 1946.

Moholy-Nagy, László. *Vision in Motion*. Chicago: Paul Theobald and Company, 1969, first published in 1946.

Mondrian, Pieter Cornelius. *Plastic Art and Pure Plastic Art*. 3rd ed. New York: Wittenborn, Schultz, 1952.

Morse, John D., ed. *Ben Shahn*. London: Secker & Warburg, 1972.

Motherwell, Robert, ed. *The Dada Painters and Poets*. New York: Wittenborn, Schultz, 1951.

Myers, Bernard S. *The German Expressionists: A Generation in Revolt*. New York: Frederick A. Praeger, 1956.

Norman, Dorothy. *Alfred Stieglitz: An American Seer*. Middleton, NY: Aperture, 1973.

O'Keeffe, Georgia. *Georgia O'Keeffe*. New York: Penguin, 1977.

Overy, Paul. *De Stijl*. London: Studio Vista, 1969.

Passuth, Krisztina. *Moholy-Nagy*. New York: Thames & Hudson, 1985.

Raymond, Marcel. *From Baudelaire to Surrealism*. London: Methuen, 1970.

Read, Herbert. *The Art of Jean Arp*. New York: Harry N. Abrams, 1968.

———, ed. *Surrealism*. New York: Frederick A. Praeger, 1971.

Richter, Hans. *Dada: Art and Anti-Art*. London: Thames & Hudson, 1961.

Rosenblum, Robert. *Cubism and Twentieth-Century Art*. New York: Harry N. Abrams, 1976.

Rubin, William S. *Dada and Surrealist Art*. New York: Harry N. Abrams, 1968.

———. *Dada, Surrealism and Their Heritage*. New York: Museum of Modern Art, 1968.

———. *Miró in the Collection of The Museum of Modern Art*. New York: Museum of Modern Art, 1973.

Rubin, William S., ed. *Pablo Picasso: A Retrospective*. New York: Museum of Modern Art/Boston: New York Graphic Society, 1980.

———. *"Primitivism" in 20th-Century Art: Affinity of the Tribal and the Modern*. 2 vols. New York: Museum of Modern Art, 1984.

Russell, John. *Max Ernst: Life and Work*. New York: Harry N. Abrams, 1967.

Schiff, Gert, ed. *Picasso in Perspective*. Englewood Cliffs, NJ: Prentice-Hall, 1976.

Schneede, Uwe M. *Surrealism*. New York: Harry N. Abrams, 1974.

Schwarz, Arturo. *The Complete Works of Marcel Duchamp*. London: Thames & Hudson, 1965.

———. *Man Ray: The Rigors of Imagination*. New York: Rizzoli, 1977.

Selz, Peter. *German Expressionist Painting*. 1957. reprint. Berkeley: University of California Press, 1974.

Selz, Peter, and Dubuffet, Jean. *The Work of Jean Dubuffet*. New York: Museum of Modern Art, 1962.

Seuphor, Michel. *Piet Mondrian: Life and Work*. New York: Harry N. Abrams, 1956.

Shattuck, Roger; Béhar, Henri; Hoog, Mitchell; Lauchner, Carolyn; and Rubin, William. *Henri Rousseau*. New York: Museum of Modern Art, 1985.

Snyder, Robert. *Buckminster Fuller: An Autobiographical Monologue Scenario*. New York: St. Martin's Press, 1980.

Soby, James Thrall. *Georges Rouault: Paintings and Prints*. New York: Museum of Modern Art/Simon and Schuster, 1947.

Sotriffer, Kristian. *Expressionism and Fauvism*. New York: McGraw-Hill, 1972.

Speyer, James A. with Koeper, Frederick. *Mies van der Rohe*. Chicago: Art Institute of Chicago, 1968.

Stephenson, Robert C., tr. *Orozco: An Autobiography*. Austin, TX: University of Texas Press, 1962.

Stott, William. *Documentary Expression and Thirties America*. New York: Oxford University Press, 1973.

Taylor, Joshua C. *Futurism*. New York: Museum of Modern Art, 1961.

Troyen, Carol, and Hirshler, Erica E. *Charles Sheeler: Paintings and Drawings*. Boston: Museum of Fine Arts, 1987.

Tucker, William. *Early Modern Sculpture*. New York: Oxford University Press, 1974.

Vogt, Paul. *Expressionism: German Painting, 1905–1920*. New York: Harry N. Abrams, 1980.

Von Hartz, John. *August Sander*. Millerton, NY: Aperture, 1977.

Waldman, Diane. *Joseph Cornell*. New York: George Braziller, 1977.

Wright, Frank Lloyd; Kaufmann, Edgar, ed. *American Architecture*. New York: Horizon, 1955.

Wheat, Ellen Harkins. *Jacob Lawrence: American Painter*. Seattle: University of Washington Press, 1986.

CHAPTER 23 THE CONTEMPORARY WORLD

Albright, Thomas. *Art in the San Francisco Bay Area: 1945–1980*. Berkeley: University of California Press, 1985.

Alloway, Lawrence. *American Pop Art*. New York: Whitney Museum of American Art/Macmillan Publishing Co., 1974.

———. *Robert Rauschenberg*. Washington, DC: National Collection of Fine Arts/ Smithsonian Institutions, 1976.

———. *Topics in American Art Since 1945*. New York: W. W. Norton, 1975.

Amaya, Mario. *Pop Art and After*. New York: Viking Press, 1972.

Armes, Roy. *Patterns of Realism: A Study of Italian Neo-Realist Cinema*. New York: A. S. Barnes and Company, 1971.

Battcock, Gregory, ed. *Minimal Art: A Critical Anthology*. New York: Studio Vista, 1969.

———. *The New Art: A Critical Anthology*. New York: E. P. Dutton, 1973.

———. *New Artists Video: A Critical Anthology*. New York: E. P. Dutton, 1978.

———. *Super Realism: A Critical Anthology*. New York: E. P. Dutton, 1975.

Battcock, Gregory, and Nickas, Robert, eds. *The Art of Performance: A Critical Anthology*. New York: E. P. Dutton, 1984.

Beardsley, Richard. *Earthworks and Beyond: Contemporary Art in the Landscape*. New York: Abbeville Press, 1984.

Beardsley, John, and Livingston, Jane. *Hispanic Art in the United States: Thirty Contemporary Painters and Sculptors*. Houston: Museum of Fine Arts/New York: Abbeville Press, 1987.

Benthall, Jeremy. *Science and Technology in Art Today*. New York: Frederick A. Praeger, 1972.

Bourdon, David. *Christo*. New York: Harry N. Abrams, 1972.

Brion, Marcel; Hunter, Sam; et al. *Art Since 1945*. New York: Harry N. Abrams, 1958.

Buck, Robert T., Jr.; Cathcart, Linda L.; Nordland, Gerald; and Tuchman, Maurice. *Richard Diebenkorn: Paintings and Drawings, 1943–1980*. Buffalo, NY: Albright-Knox Art Gallery, 1980.

Carmean, E. A., Jr.; Rathbone, Elizabeth; and Hess, Thomas B. *American Art at Mid-Century: The Subjects of the Artists*. Washington, DC: The National Gallery of Art, 1978.

Cassou, Jean; Hultèn-Pontus, K. G.; and Hunter, Sam, with statement by Schöffer, Nicolas. *Two Kinetic Sculptors: Nicolas Schöffer and Jean Tinguely*. New York: Jewish Museum/October House, 1965.

Chicago, Judy. *The Dinner Party: A Symbol of Our Heritage*. Garden City, NY: Anchor Press/Doubleday, 1979.

Cockcroft, Eva; Weber, John; and Cockcroft, James. *Toward a People's Art*. New York: E. P. Dutton, 1977.

Crichton, Michael. *Jasper Johns*. New York: Whitney Museum of American Art/Harry N. Abrams, 1977.

Cummings, Paul. *Dictionary of Contemporary American Artists*. 3rd ed. New York: St. Martin's Press, 1977.

Davies, Hugh, and Yard, Sally. *Francis Bacon*. New York: Abbeville Press, 1986.

Deken, Joseph. *Computer Images: State of the Art*. New York: Stewart, Tabori, and Chang Publishers, 1983.

Diamondstein, Barbaralee. *American Architecture Now*. New York: Rizzoli, 1980.

Diehl, Gaston, and Hennessey, Eileen B. *Vasarely*. New York: Crown Publishers, 1972.

Gilbert and George, and Ratcliff, Carter. *Gilbert and George: The Complete Pictures, 1971–1985*. London: Thames & Hudson, 1986.

Glaeser, Ludwig. *The Work of Frei Otto*. New York: Museum of Modern Art, 1972.

Goodman, Cynthia. *Digital Visions: Computers and Art*. New York: Harry N. Abrams, 1987.

Goodyear, Frank H., Jr. *Contemporary American Realism Since 1960*. Boston: New York Graphic Society, 1981.

Gordon, John. *Louise Nevelson*. New York: Whitney Museum of American Art, 1967.

Gough, Harry F. *The Vital Gesture: Franz Kline*. Cincinnati: Cincinnati Art Museum/New York: Abbeville Press, 1985.

Graham, Peter. *The New Wave*. Garden City, NY: Doubleday, 1968.

Gray, Cleve, ed. *David Smith on David Smith: Sculpture and Writings*. London: Thames & Hudson, 1968.

Hamilton, Richard. *Collected Words 1953–1982*. London: Thames & Hudson, 1982.

Hertz, Richard, ed. *Theories of Contemporary Art*. Englewood Cliffs, NJ: Prentice-Hall, 1985.

Hess, Thomas B. *Barnett Newman*. New York: Walker and Company, 1969.

———. *Willem de Kooning*. New York: Museum of Modern Art, 1968.

Jacob, Mary Jane. *Magdalena Abakanowicz*. New York: Abbeville Press, 1982.

Jacobus, John. *Twentieth-Century Architecture: The Middle Years, 1940–1964*. New York: Frederick A. Praeger, 1966.

Jencks, Charles. *Architecture 2000: Prediction and Methods*. New York: Frederick A. Praeger, 1971.

Joyce, Paul. *Hockney on Photography: Conversations with Paul Joyce*. New York: Harmony Books, 1988.

Kaprow, Allan. *Assemblage, Environments, and Happenings*. New York: Harry N. Abrams, 1966.

Kepes, Georgy. *Arts of the Environment*. New York: George Braziller, 1970.

Kirby, Michael. *Happenings*. New York: E. P. Dutton, 1966.

Kostelanetz, Richard, ed. *Esthetics Contemporary*. Buffalo, NY: Prometheus Books, 1978.

Lippard, Lucy R. *Eva Hesse*. New York: New York University Press, 1976.

———, ed. *Pop Art*. New York: Frederick A. Praeger, 1966.

———, ed. *Six Years: The Dematerialization of the Art Object from 1966 to 1972*. New York: Frederick A. Praeger, 1973.

Livingstone, Marco. *David Hockney*. London: Thames & Hudson, 1981.

Lovejoy, Margot. *Postmodern Currents: Art and Artists in the Age of the Electronic Media*. Ann Arbor, MI: UMI Research Press, 1989.

Lucie-Smith, Edward. *Movements Since 1945*. new rev. ed. New York: Thames & Hudson, 1984.

McShine, Kynaston. *Andy Warhol: A Retrospective*. New York: Museum of Modern Art, 1989.

———. *An International Survey of Recent Painting and Sculpture*. New York: Museum of Modern Art, 1984.

Meyer, Ursula. *Conceptual Art*. New York: E. P. Dutton, 1972.

Monaco, James. *The New Wave: Truffaut, Godard, Chabrol, Rohmer, Rivette*. New York: Oxford University Press, 1976.

Nervi, Pier Luigi. *Aesthetics and Technology in Building*. Cambridge, MA: Harvard University Press, 1965.

Norris, Christopher, and Benjamin, Andres. *What Is Deconstruction?* New York: St. Martin's Press, 1988.

O'Connor, Francis V. *Jackson Pollock*. New York: Museum of Modern Art, 1967.

O'Hara, Frank. *Robert Motherwell*. New York: Museum of Modern Art, 1965.

Price, Jonathan. *Video Visions: A Medium Discovers Itself*. New York: New American Library, 1977.

Reichardt, Jasia, ed. *Cybernetics, Art & Ideas*. Greenwich, CT: New York Graphics Society, 1971.

Risatti, Howard, ed. *Postmodern Perspectives*. Englewood Cliffs, NJ: Prentice-Hall, 1990.

Robbins, Corinne. *The Pluralist Era: American Art, 1968–1981*. New York: Harper & Row, 1984.

Robbins, David, ed. *The Independent Group: Postwar Britain and the Aesthetics of Plenty*. Cambridge, MA: MIT Press, 1990.

Rose, Barbara. *Claes Oldenburg*. New York: Museum of Modern Art, 1970.

———. *Frankenthaler*. New York: Harry N. Abrams, 1975.

Rosenberg, Harold. *The Tradition of the New*. New York: Horizon Press, 1959.

Russell, John. *Francis Bacon*. London: Thames & Hudson, 1971.

Russell, John, and Gablik, Suzi. *Pop Art Redefined*. New York: Frederick A. Praeger, 1969.

Sandler, Irving. *The Triumph of American Painting: A History of Abstract Expressionism*. New York: Frederick A. Praeger, 1970.

Schneider, Ira, and Korot, Beryl. *Video Art: An Anthology*. New York: Harcourt Brace Jovanovich, 1976.

Schwarz, Paul Waldo. *The Hand and Eye of the Sculptor*. New York: Frederick A. Praeger, 1969.

Sitney, P. Adams. *Visionary Film: The American Avant-Garde*. New York: Oxford University Press, 1974.

Smagula, Howard. *Currents: Contemporary Directions in the Visual Arts*. 2nd ed. Englewood Cliffs, NJ: Prentice-Hall, 1989.

Smith, Patrick S. *Andy Warhol's Art and Films*. Ann Arbor, MI: UMI Research Press, 1986.

Smithson, Robert; Holt, Nancy, ed. *The Writings of Robert Smithson*. New York: New York University Press, 1975.

Solomon, Alan. *Jasper Johns*. New York: The Jewish Museum, 1964.

Sonfist, Alan, ed. *Art in the Landscape: A Critical Anthology of Environmental Art*. New York: E. P. Dutton, 1983.

Stangos, Nikos. *Concepts of Modern Art*. 2nd ed. New York: Harper & Row, 1985.

Tisdall, Carolyn. *Joseph Beuys*. New York: Solomon R. Guggenheim Museum, 1979.

Tomkins, Calvin. *The Scene Reports on Post-Modern Art*. New York: Viking Press, 1976.

Tuchman, Maurice. *American Sculpture of the Sixties*. Los Angeles: Los Angeles County Museum of Art, 1967.

Venturi, Robert; Scott-Brown, Denise; and Isehour, Steven. *Learning from Las Vegas*. Cambridge, MA: MIT Press, 1972.

Waldman, Diane. *Mark Rothko, 1903–1970: A Retrospective*. New York: Solomon R. Guggenheim Museum, 1978.

Wallis, Brian, ed. *Art After Modernism: Rethinking Representation*. New York: New Museum of Contemporary Art in association with David R. Godine, 1984.

Wheeler, Dennis, ed. *Form and Structure in Recent Film*. Vancouver, BC: Vancouver Art Gallery, 1972.

Wye, Deborah. *Louise Bourgeois*. New York: Museum of Modern Art, 1982.

Youngblood, Gene. *Expanded Cinema*. New York: E. P. Dutton, 1970.

Books Spanning the Eighteenth, Nineteenth, and Twentieth Centuries

Ades, Dawn. *Art in Latin America: The Modern Era, 1820–1980*. London: The Hayward Gallery, 1989.

Antreasian, Garo, and Adams, Clinton. *The Tamarind Book of Lithography: Art and Techniques*. Los Angeles: Tamarind Workshop and New York: Harry N. Abrams, 1971.

Armstrong, John; Craven, Wayne; and Feder, Norma, et al. *200 Years of American Sculpture*. New York: Whitney Museum of American Art/Boston: David R. Godine, 1976.

Battcock, Gregory. *Minimal Art: A Critical Anthology*. New York: Studio Vista, 1969.

Brown, Milton; Hunter, Sam; and Jacobus, John. *American Art: Painting, Sculpture, Architecture, Decorative Arts, Photography*. New York: Harry N. Abrams, 1979.

Canaday, John. *Mainstreams of Modern Art*. New York: Holt, Rinehart & Winston, 1959.

Chipp, Herschel. *Theories of Modern Art*. Berkeley: University of California Press, 1968.

Coke, Van Deren. *The Painter and the Photograph From Delacroix to Warhol*. rev. and enl. ed. Albuquerque: University of New Mexico Press, 1972.

Collins, Peter. *Changing Ideals in Modern Architecture, 1750–1950*. London: Faber & Faber, 1971.

Condit, Carl W. *The Rise of the Skyscraper: Portrait of the Times and Career of Influential Architects*. Chicago: University of Chicago Press, 1952.

Driskell, David C. *Two Centuries of Black American Art*. Los Angeles: Los Angeles County Museum of Art/New York: Alfred A. Knopf, 1976.

Elsen, Albert. *Origins of Modern Sculpture*. New York: George Braziller, 1974.

Fine, Sylvia Honig. *Women and Art: A History of Women Painters and Sculptors from the Renaissance to the 20th Century*. Montclair, NJ: Alanheld and Schram, 1978.

Flexner, James Thomas. *America's Old Masters*. New York: McGraw-Hill, 1982.

Freund, Gisele. *Photography and Society*. Boston: David R. Godine, 1980.

Gernsheim, Helmut. *Creative Photography*. New York: Bonanza Books, 1962.

Giedion, Siegfried. *Mechanization Takes Command: A Contribution to Anonymous History*. New York: Norton, 1948.

———. *Space, Time and Architecture: The Growth of a New Tradition*. 4th ed. Cambridge, MA: Harvard University Press, 1965.

Giedion-Welcker, Carola. *Contemporary Sculpture: An Evolution in Volume and Space*. London: Faber & Faber, 1960.

Goldberg, Vicki. *Photography in Print*. New York: A Touchstone Book, Simon and Schuster, 1981.

Goldwater, Robert, and Treves, Marco, eds. *Artists on Art*. 3rd ed. New York: Pantheon, 1958.

Greenough, Sarah; Snyder, Joel; Travis, David; and Westerbeck, Colin. *On the Art of Fixing a Shadow: One Hundred and Fifty Years of Photography*. Washington, DC: The National Gallery of Art/Chicago: The Art Institute of Chicago, 1989.

Hamilton, George Heard. *Nineteenth- and Twentieth-Century Art*. Englewood Cliffs, NJ: Prentice-Hall, 1972.

Hammacher, A. M. *The Evolution of Modern Sculpture: Tradition and Innovation*. New York: Harry N. Abrams, 1969.

Hitchcock, Henry-Russell. *Architecture: Nineteenth and Twentieth Centuries*. 4th ed. Baltimore: Penguin, 1977.

Hopkins, H. J. *A Span of Bridges*. Newton Abbot, Devon, England: David & Charles, 1970.

Hunter, Sam. *Modern French Painting, 1855–1956*. New York: Dell, 1966.

Irving, Donald J. *Sculpture: Material and Process*. New York: Van Nostrand Reinhold Company, 1970.

Kaufmann, Edgar, Jr., ed. *The Rise of an American Architecture*. New York: Metropolitan Museum of Art/Frederick A. Praeger Publishers, 1970.

Klingender, Francis Donald and Elton, Arthur ed. and rev. *Art and the Industrial Revolution*. London: Evelyn, Adams and MacKay, 1968.

Licht, Fred. *Sculpture, Nineteenth and Twentieth Centuries*. Greenwich, CT: New York Graphic Society, 1967.

Loyer, Francois. *Architecture of the Industrial Age*. New York: Rizzoli, 1983.

Lyons, Nathan, ed. *Photographers on Photography*. Englewood Cliffs, NJ: Prentice-Hall, 1966.

McCoubrey, John W. *American Art, 1700–1960: Sources and Documents*. Englewood Cliffs, NJ: Prentice-Hall, 1965.

Mason, Jerry, ed. *International Center of Photography Encyclopedia of Photography*. New York: Crown Publishers, 1984.

Newhall, Beaumont. *The History of Photography*. New York: The Museum of Modern Art, 1982.

Pehnt, Wolfgang. *Encyclopedia of Modern Architecture*. New York: Harry N. Abrams, 1964.

Peterdi, Gabor. *Printmaking: Methods Old and New*. New York: Macmillan Company, 1961.

Pevsner, Nikolaus. *An Outline of European Architecture*. 6th ed. Baltimore: Penguin, 1960.

Phillipe, Robert. *Political Graphics: Art as a Weapon*. New York: Abbeville Press, 1980.

Pierson, William. *American Buildings and Their Architects: Technology and the Picturesque*. vol. 2. Garden City, NY: Doubleday, 1978.

Risebero, Bill. *Modern Architecture and Design: An Alternative History*. Cambridge: MIT Press, 1983.

Rosenblum, Naomi. *A World History of Photography*. New York: Abbeville Press, 1984.

Rosenblum, Robert. *Modern Painting and the Northern Romantic Tradition: Friedrich to Rothko*. New York: Harper & Row, 1975.

Ross, John, and Romano, Clare. *The Complete Printmaker*. New York: The Free Press, 1972.

Ross, Stephen David, ed. *Art and Its Significance: An Anthology of Aesthetic Theory*. Albany, NY: SUNY Press, 1987.

Sachs, Paul, Jr. *Modern Prints and Drawings: A Guide to a Better Understanding of Modern Draughtsmanship*. New York: Alfred A. Knopf, 1954.

Schapiro, Meyer. *Modern Art: 19th and 20th Centuries*. New York: George Braziller, 1980.

Scharf, Aaron. *Art and Photography*. Baltimore, MD: Penguin Books, 1974.

Scully, Vincent. *American Architecture and Urbanism*. New York: Frederick A. Praeger, 1969.

Selz, Peter; Michelson, Annette, tr. *Modern Sculpture: Origins and Evolution*. London: Heinemann, 1963.

Seuphor, Michel. *The Sculpture of this Century*. New York: George Braziller, 1960.

Shikes, Ralph E. *The Indignant Eye: The Artist as Social Critic, from the Renaissance to Picasso*. Boston: Banion Press, 1969.

Slatkin, Wendy. *Women Artists in History: From Antiquity to the 20th Century*. 2nd ed. Englewood Cliffs, NJ: Prentice-Hall, 1985.

Spencer, Harold. *American Art: Readings from the Colonial Era to the Present*. New York: Charles Scribner's Sons, 1980.

Summerson, Sir John. *Architecture in Britain: 1530–1830*. 7th rev. and enl. ed. Baltimore: Penguin, 1983.

Sypher, Wylie. *Rococo to Cubism in Art and Literature*. New York: Random House, 1960.

Szarkowski, John. *Photography Until Now*. New York: Museum of Modern Art, 1989.

Weaver, Mike. *The Art of Photography: 1839–1989*. New Haven, CT: Yale University Press, 1989.

Whiffen, Marcus, and Koeper, Frederick. *American Architecture, 1607–1976*. Cambridge: MIT Press, 1983.

Wilmerding, John. *American Art*. Harmondsworth, England: Penguin, 1976.

———. *The Genius of American Painting*. London: Weidenfeld & Nicolson, 1973.

Wilson, Simon. *Holbein to Hockney: A History of British Art*. London: The Tate Gallery & The Bodley Head, 1979.

Books Spanning the Whole of the Twentieth Century

Ades, Dawn. *Photomontage*. Rev. and enl. ed. London: Thames & Hudson, 1976.

Andersen, Wayne. *American Sculpture in Process: 1930–1970*. Boston: New York Graphic Society, 1975.

Andrew, J. Dudley. *The Major Film Theories: An Introduction*. New York: Oxford University Press, 1976.

Arnason, H. H. *History of Modern Art: Painting, Sculpture, Architecture*. 3rd rev. and enl. ed. Englewood Cliffs, NJ: Prentice-Hall 1988.

Ashton, Dore. *Twentieth-Century Artists on Art*. New York: Pantheon Books, 1985.

Banham, Reyner. *Guide to Modern Architecture*. Princeton, NJ: D. Van Nostrand, 1962.

Barsam, Richard Meran. *Nonfiction Film: A Critical History*. New York: E. P. Dutton, 1973.

Burnham, Jack. *Beyond Modern Sculpture. The Effects of Science and Technology on the Sculpture of This Century*. New York: George Braziller, 1968.
Castelman, Riva. *Prints of the 20th Century: A History*. New York: Oxford University Press, 1985.
Compton, Susan, ed. *British Art in the 20th Century*. London: Royal Academy of Arts/Berlin: Prestel Verlag, 1986.
Cook, David A. *A History of Narrative Film*. New York: Norton, 1981.
Curtis, David. *Experimental Cinema: A Fifty-Year Evolution*. New York: Dell, 1971.
Davis, Douglas. *Art and the Future: A History/Prophecy of the Collaboration Between Scientists, Technology and the Arts*. New York: Frederick A. Praeger, 1973.
Diehl, Gaston. *The Moderns: A Treasury of Painting Throughout the World*. Milan: Uffizi, 1961.
Frascina, Francis, and Harrison, Charles, eds. *Modern Art and Modernism: A Critical Anthology*. New York: Harper & Row, 1982.
Goldberg, Rosalee. *Performance: Live Art, 1909 to the Present*. New York: Harry N. Abrams, 1979.
Haftmann, Werner. *Painting in the Twentieth Century*. New York: Frederick A. Praeger, 1960.
Hamlin, Talbot F., ed. *Forms and Functions of Twentieth-Century Architecture*. 4 vols. New York: Columbia University Press, 1952.
Hatje, Gerd, ed. *Encyclopedia of Modern Architecture*. London: Thames & Hudson, 1963.
Herbert, Robert L., ed. *Modern Artists on Art*. Englewood Cliffs, NJ: Prentice-Hall, 1964.
Hertz, Richard, and Klein, Norman M., eds. *Twentieth-Century Art Theory: Urbanism, Politics, and Mass Culture*. Englewood Cliffs, NJ: Prentice-Hall, 1990.
Hunter, Sam, and Jacobus, John. *Modern Art: Painting, Sculpture, and Architecture*. New York: Harry N. Abrams, 1985.
Hunter, Sam. *Modern American Painting and Sculpture*. New York: Dell, 1959.
Jencks, Charles. *Modern Movements in Architecture*. Garden City, NY: Anchor Press/ Doubleday, 1973.
Joachimides, Christos. M.; Rosenthal, Norma; and Schmied, Wieland, eds. *German Art in the 20th Century: Painting and Sculpture, 1905–1985*. Munich: Prestel-Verlag, 1985.
Kraus, Rosalind E. *Passages in Modern Sculpture*. Cambridge, MA: MIT Press, 1981.
Lynton, Norbert. *The Story of Modern Art*. 2nd ed. Englewood Cliffs, NJ: Prentice-Hall, 1989.
MacGowan, Kenneth. *Behind the Screen*. New York: A Dell Book, Delta Publishing Co., 1965.
Monaco, James. *How to Read a Film: The Art, Technology, Language, History, and Theory of Film and Media*. New York: Oxford University Press, 1977.
Phaidon Dictionary of Twentieth-Century Art. Oxford: Phaidon Press, 1973.
Phillips, Gene D. *The Movie Makers: Artists in an Industry*. Chicago: Nelson-Hall Company, 1973.
Pontus-Hultén, K. G. *The Machine as Seen at the End of the Mechanical Age*. New York: Museum of Modern Art, 1968.
Popper, Frank, et. al. *Electra: Electricity and Electronics in the Art of the 20th Century*. Paris: Musée d'art moderne de Paris, 1983.
———.; Benn, Stephen, tr. *Origins and Development of Kinetic Art*. Greenwich, CT: New York Graphic Society, 1968.
Raynal, Maurice. *History of Modern Painting*. 3 vols. Geneva: Skira, 1949–1950.
Read, Herbert. *Concise History of Modern Painting*. 3rd ed. New York: Frederick A. Praeger, 1975.
———. *A Concise History of Modern Sculpture*. rev. and enl. ed. New York: Frederick A. Praeger, 1964.
Rickey, George. *Constructivism: Origins and Evolution*. New York: George Braziller, 1967.
Ritchie, Andrew Carnduff, ed. *German Art of the Twentieth Century*. New York: Museum of Modern Art, 1957.
———. *Sculpture of the Twentieth Century*. New York: The Museum of Modern Art, n.d.
Rose, Barbara. *American Art Since 1900*. rev. ed. New York: Frederick A. Praeger, 1975.
Russell, John. *The Meanings of Modern Art*. New York: Museum of Modern Art/Thames & Hudson, 1981.
Scully, Vincent. *American Architecture and Urbanism*. New York: Frederick A. Praeger, 1969.
———. *Modern Architecture*. rev. ed. New York: George Braziller, 1974.
Sloane, J. C. *French Painting Between the Past and the Present*. Princeton, NJ: Princeton University Press, 1951.
Spalding, Francis. *British Art Since 1900*. London: Thames & Hudson, 1986.
Tomkins, Calvin. *The Bride and the Bachelors, Five Masters of the Avant-Garde*. New York: Viking Press, 1968.
Tuchman, Maurice, and Freeman, Judi, eds. *The Spiritual in Art: Abstract Painting, 1890–1985*. Los Angeles: Los Angeles County Art Museum/New York: Abbeville Press, 1986.
Wescher, Herta; Wolf, Robert E., tr. *Collage*. New York: Harry N. Abrams, 1968.
Whittick, Arnold. *European Architecture in the Twentieth Century*. Aylesbury, England: Leonard Hill Books, 1974.

PICTURE CREDITS

The authors and publisher are grateful to the proprietors and custodians of various works of art for photographs of these works and permission to reproduce them in this book. Sources not included in the captions are listed below.

KEY TO ABBREVIATIONS

ACL	Copyright A.C.L., Brussels
AMNH	American Museum of Natural History, New York
AL	Fratelli Alinari
AR	Art Resource
Bulloz	J. E. Bulloz, Paris
C.M.N.	Cliché des Musées Nationaux, Paris
Fototeca	Fototeca Unione at the American Academy, Rome
Gab	Gabinetto Fotografico Nazionale, Rome
Gir	Giraudon
Harding	Robert Harding Picture Library, London
Hinz	Colorphoto Hans Hinz
Hir	Hirmer Fotoarchiv, Munich
Mansell	The Mansell Collection, London
Mar	Bildarchiv Foto Marburg
MAS	Ampliaciones y Reproducciones MAS, Barcelona
NYPL	New York Public Library
OI	Courtesy of the Oriental Institute of the University of Chicago
PRI	Photo Researchers, Inc., New York
R.M.N.	Photo, Reunion des Musées Nationaux
Scala	Scala Fine Art Publishers

Note: All references in the following credits are to figure numbers unless otherwise indicated.

Introduction Opening illustration: Ken Hedges; AL/AR: 4, 9, 10; Hir: 12; Photo courtesy Soichi Sunami/The Museum of Modern Art.

Part I Opening illustration: Adam Woolfitt/Susan Griggs Agency; page 24: Metropolitan Museum of Art (Egyptian Expedition).

Chapter 1 Courtesy Department of Library Services/AMNH: 9, 10, 13; Arch. Phot. Paris/S.P.A.D.E.M.: 7, 8, 11; Hinz: 1, 4; Hunting Aerofilms, Ltd.: 15; Photo Láborie, Bergerac, France: 5; MAS: 14; Edwin Smith. 16, Jean Vertut: 6, 12 (Coll. Begouen).

Chapter 2 AL/AR: 43; British School of Archaeology in Jerusalem: 1, 2; C.M.N.: 25, 37, 40; Hir: 13, 15, 27, 30, 34; Mansell: 31, 32; Arlette Mellaart: 6, 7, 8; James Mellaart: 5; OI: 16, 17, 21, 38, 41, 42; The University Museum/University of Pennsylvania: 19, 20; R.M.N.: 24, 26; Scala/AR: 22; Staatliche Museen zu Berlin: 10.

Chapter 3 Photo by Bruno Balestrini by courtesy of Elemond, Milano: 9; Bettmann Archive: 26; Bildarchiv Preussischer Kulturbesitz, Berlin: 39; © Lee Boltin: 41; C.M.N.: 44; Egyptian Antiquities Organization: 24, 46; Egyptian Museum, Cairo: 1; Harding: 13, 30, 42, 43; Hir: 2, 3, 14, 15, 16, 17, 18, 19, 25, 33, 38; Mar/AR: 27; Metropolitan Museum of Art (Egyptian Expedition): 22, 36; OI: 23; George Gerster/PRI: 10; Geoffrey Clifford/Wheeler Pictures: 6, 20, 29.

Chapter 4 AR: 13; © "Cahiers d'Art": 1, 2, 3; Conway Library/Courtauld Institute of Art, London: 25; Alison Frantz: 23; Gir/AR: 20; Hir: 4, 5, 7, 8, 9, 12, 15, 16, 17, 18, 19, 22, 26, 27, 28, 29; Scala/AR: 14; TAP Service: 10, 11.

Chapter 5 AL/AR: 14, 26, 58, 62, 64, 66, 76, 86; Anderson/AR: 63; AR: 6; C.M.N.: 9, 60; Deutsches Archäologisches Institut, Rome: 12; Alison Frantz: 39, 40, 41, 51, 52; Gir/AR: 2; Harding: 55; Walter Hege: 45; Hinz: 10; Hir: 8, 11, 17, 18, 19, 22, 29, 32, 33, 37, 38, 44, 46, 47, 48, 49, 50, 53, 56, 57, 65, 75, 82, 87; Herschell Levit: 24; Barbara Malter/Instituto Centrali per il Catalogo e la Documentazione: 84; Mar/AR: 69, 70; Caecilia H. Moessner, Munich: 5, 7; J. Powell, Rome: 59; Frederick Ayer III/PRI: 71; Scala/AR: 34, 35, 36, 61, 79; Dr. Franz Stoedtner: 28; TAP Service: 4, 16, 68, 74, 95.

Chapter 6 AL/AR: 6, 10, 11, 17, 25, 35, 41, 64, 66, 67, 68, 70, 71, 80, 94, 96, 97; Anderson/AR: 38, 56, 65, 74; Photo by Bruno Balestrini by courtesy of Electa Editrice, Milano: 55; C.M.N.: 46; Deutsches Archäologisches Institut, Rome: 14, 73, 75, 93, 95; Walter Drayer: 2, 9, 12; Fototeca: 15 (Frank E. Brown), 16, 18, 19, 20, 21, 43, 50, 52, 59, 61, 63; Gab: 3, 76; Madeline Grimoldi Archive: 39, 98; HBJ Collection: 33, 36, 42; Hir: 4, 8; The Israel Museum, Jerusalem: 90; G. E. Kidder-Smith: 91; Photo KLM: 48; Amedeo Maiuri, *Roman Painting*, Editions d'Art Albert Skira: 26; Mar/AR: 82; Monumenti Musei e Gallerie Pontificia: 31; Rapho/PRI: 77; Leonard von Matt/PRI: 69; Rheinisches Landesmuseum, Trier: 85, 86; Charles Rotkin/PRI: 47; Scala/AR: 5, 23, 28, 29, 30, 32, 34, 37, 88, 89; Gunter Heil/ZEFA: 84.

Chapter 7 AL/AR: 35, 62; Anderson/AR: 17, 22, 25, 66; Benedettine di Priscilla, Rome: 2; Byzantine Visual Resources, © 1989 and 1990, Dumbarton Oaks, Washington, D.C.: 41, 56; Enrico Ferorelli © 1989: 55; Sostegni/Fotocielo: 47; Alison Frantz: 43, 46; Gir/AR: 23; HBJ Collection: 5, 13, 50, 51, 69; Photo André Held: 10, 19, 57; Hir: 7, 16, 18, 20, 21, 24, 29, 32, 34, 40; Hunting Aerofilms, Ltd.: 64; State of Israel/Department of Antiquities and Museums, Jerusalem: 73; A. F. Kersting: 82; G. E. Kidder-Smith: 77; Angelo Longo Editore, Ravenna: 26, 27, 36, 37; MAS: 67, 68, 76; NYPL: 52; Novosti from Sovfoto: 60; Pontifica Commissione Centrale per l'Arte Sacra in Italia: 3; J. Powell, Rome: 53, 54, 74; Scala/AR: 9, 11, 12, 28, 30, 31, 38, 49; TASS/Sovfoto: 59; Staatliche Museen zu Berlin: 71; Russell A. Thompson/Taurus Photos: 79; Tourism Counselor's Office/Turkish Embassy, Washington, D.C.: 80; Weitzman/Princeton University: 39; Linares/Yale University Photo Collection: 75.

Part II Opening illustration: Scala/AR; page 316: Hunting Aerofilms, Ltd.

Chapter 8 ©Lee Boltin: 1; Bridgeman Art Library/AR: 2-b; Dr. Harold Busch: 20; HBJ Collection: 16, 24, 26, 27; Hir: 21; Mar/AR: 28; Copyright University Museum of National Antiquities, Oslo, Norway/Photo by Erik Irgens Johnsen: 5; NYPL: 10, 14; R.M.N.: 2-a; © Mick Sharp, Photographer: 11; Photo Zodiaque: 6.

Chapter 9 AL/AR: 10, 11, 12, 19, 27; © Arch. Phot. Paris/S.P.A.D.E.M.: 1, 29, 30; Bulloz: 28, 32, 34; Jean Dieuziade: 3, 24; Sergio Sostegni/Fotocielo: 18; Gir/AR: 35, 38, 39; HBJ Collection: 9, 33; Hir: 8; Evelyn Hofer: 20; A. F. Kersting: 16; Jean Roubier: 5, 13, 22, 26, 31; Scala/AR: 21; SEF/AR: 37; W. S. Stoddard: 14; Tapisserie de Bayeux, avec autorisation speciale de la Ville de Bayeux: 36; The Master and Fellows of Trinity College, Cambridge: 42.

Chapter 10 AL/AR: 62, 63; Anderson/AR: 60; Dr. Harold Busch/AR: 49, 52; F. Damm/Stadt Köln: 57; D.P.I., Inc.: 58; Electa Editrice: 18; Gir/AR: 32, 34, 36, 39; HBJ Collection: 1, 3, 35; Hir: 8, 10, 12, 13, 23, 25; Hunting Aerofilms, Ltd.: 16, 30; Mar/AR: 31, 33, 51, 53, 55; National Monuments Record, London: 41, 44, 45, 46; George Holton/PRI: 64; Rapho/PRI: 40; Rheinisches Bildarchiv, Cologne: 56; Jean Roubier: 9, 15; H. Rogier-Viollet: 14, 28; Scala/AR: 27, 29, 61; Helga Schmidt-Glassner: 54; Edwin Smith: 47; W. S. Stoddard: 20; Superstock International: 42; Clarence Ward, Photographic Archives, National Gallery of Art, Washington, D.C.: 7, 22, 26, 48.

Part III Opening illustration, National Film Board of Canada: page 422.

Chapter 11 Archaeological Survey of India, Government of India: 1, 2, 3, 4, 6, 9, 11, 12, 14, 15, 17; Borromeo/AR: 5, 21; Asian Art Photographic Distribution, Department of the History of Art, University of Michigan: 16; Barnaby's Picture Library: 19, 20; Photograph by Ananda Coomaraswamy, Courtesy Fine Arts Library, Harvard University: 7; Photograph by Edgar Oscar Parker, courtesy of the Visual Collections, Fine Arts Library, Harvard University: 13; J. Leroy Davidson: 27; Eliot Elisofon, LIFE Magazine © Time Inc.: 28; Courtesy of the Fogg Art Museum, Harvard University, Cambridge, Mass.: 13; HBJ Collection: 22, 25; Marie J. Mattson: 32; R. Rowan/PRI: 30; © Allan Eaton/Sheridan Photo Library: 26; Superstock International: 33; I. Job Thomas: 23.

Chapter 12 Harry N. Abrams, Inc.: 4; Chavannes: 6; Courtesy of the Cultural Relics Bureau, Beijing and the Metropolitan Museum of Art, New York: 5; Editions d'Art, Paris: 30; HBJ Collection: 9, 13; Harding: 7, 23; © Joan Lebold Cohen: 32; © Marc Riboud/Magnum: 31; NYPL: 14; R.M.N.: 10, 26; Audrey R. Topping: 28.

Chapter 13 From *A History of Far Eastern Art* by Sherman E. Lee, Harry N. Abrams, Inc.: 7, 9, 26, 27; Photograph courtesy of the International Society for Educational Information, Inc.: 19, 25; Japan National Tourist Organization: 30; National Commission for Protection of Cultural Properties, Tokyo: 3, 10, 12; Sakamoto Photo Research Lab: 4, 8; Shashinka Photo: 15, 16, 17, 21, 22, 23; © 1981, Shogakukan Publishing Co. Ltd., Tokyo: 2, 5, 6, 11.

Chapter 14 © Albert Moldvay/AR: 1; Archive of Hispanic Culture, Library of Congress: 22-b; Tom Bahti: 34; © Lee Boltin: 5, 13; by Bill Ballenberg © 1988 National Geographic Society: 19; Chicago Natural History Museum: 22-a; From H. S. and C. B. Cosgrove, *The Swarts Ruin: A Typical Mimbres Site in Southwestern New Mexico*, Peabody Museum Papers, Vol. 15 No. 1. Reprinted with permission.: 31; Herbert M. Cole: 51; Todd Disotel: 73; David Gebhard, The Art Galleries, University of California, Santa Barbara: 30; Abraham Guillen: 24-b; E. Hadingham: 21; Dr. Norman Hammond, Boston University: 7; David Hiser/Photographers Aspen: 15; © Susan Holtz: 32; Peter Horner: 64; Dr. George Kennedy, University of California, Los Angeles: 65; © Justin Kerr: 8, 9, 10; Rene Millon, 1973: 4; Courtesy of the Native Land Foundation, Hampton, CT: 24; National Commission for Museums and Monuments, Lagos: 43, 44, 45; Peabody Museum, Harvard University, Cambridge: 11; John Running: 33; Photo Jerry Thompson: 58; From Karl von Steiner, *Die Marquesaner und ihre Kunst I:* 62; Frank Willett: 48; ZEFA: 14; © Neville Presho/ZEFA: 23.

Part IV Opening illustration: Scala/AR; page 555: AR.

Chapter 15 AL/AR: 2, 3, 4, 5, 8, 14, 15, 17; Anderson/AR: 16, 22; Dmitri Kessel/LIFE Magazine © Time Inc.: 12; Scala/AR: 1, 6, 7, 9, 10, 11, 13, 18, 19, 20, 21.

Chapter 16 AL/AR: 4, 5, 6, 9, 13, 14, 17, 20, 22, 42, 45, 47, 48, 49, 52, 54, 57, 63; Anderson/AR: 12, 18, 25, 38, 41, 53; Brogi/AR: 3, 24; Gir/AR: 7; HBJ Collection: 1, 2, 39, 44; Hinz: 58; Mar/AR: 11, 15, 66; Nimatallah/AR: 36; Scala/AR: 8, 10, 26, 28, 30, 31, 32, 33, 34, 35, 37, 51, 60, 61, 62, 64, 65; Copyright 1990 Antonio Quattrone: 27; Gerhard Reinhold, Leipzig-Mölkau: 67.

Chapter 17 Harry N. Abrams, Inc.: 50; Alinari/AR: 3, 9, 11, 27, 28, 45, 46, 47; Anderson/AR: 31, 37; AR: 49, 55; Artothek: 64; British Architectural Library, RIBA, London: 10; Fototeca: 30, 33; HBJ Collection: 13, 20; Phyllis Dearborn Massar: 51, 53, 54; NYPL: 34; Nimatallah/AR: 14; © Nippon Television Corporation: 26; R.M.N.: 4, 18, 21, 22, 59, 63; Rotkin/P.F.I.: 29; Scala/AR: 1, 15, 16, 17, 19, 23, 24, 25, 35, 36, 39, 40, 41, 56, 57, 60, 61, 62, 65, 66, 67, 68; Edwin Smith: 48; Vanni/AR: 6.

Chapter 18 ACL: 6, 7, 18, 19; Alinari/AR: 53; Anderson/AR: 45; ©Arch. Phot. Paris/S.P.A.D.E.M.: 1, 24, 49; Artothek: 31, 40; Bildarchiv Preussischer Kulturbesitz: 38; Bulloz: 52; Giraudon/AR: 4, 34, 51; Hinz: 22; HBJ Collection: 23, 27, 50; Kavaler/AR: 43; MAS: 12, 20, 21, 54, 55, 56, 57, 58, 59; R.M.N.: 1, 24, 48, 49; Photo Verlag Gundermam, Würzburg: 28; Rheinisches Bildarchiv: 25; Scala/AR: 16, 17, 33, 34.

Chapter 19 ACL: 39; Alinari/AR: 10, 13, 14, 25, 26, 49, 72; Anderson/AR: 5, 16, 36; © Arch. Phot. Paris/S.P.A.D.E.M.: 48, 71, 73; Artothek: 40, 41; Avery Architectural and Fine Arts Library, Columbia University, New York: 1; British Stationery Office: 74; © 1966, Henri Dauman. All rights reserved.: 68; Gab: 21; HBJ Collection: 19, 22, 67, 69; Hunter Aerofilms, London: 65; A. F. Kersting: 4, 64; G. E. Kidder-Smith: 18, 20; NYPL: 66; Novosti/Sovfoto: 50; MAS: 34, 38; R.M.N.: 28, 42, 44, 48, 57, 58, 60, 61, 71, 73; H. Roger-Viollet: 70; Rotkin/P.F.I.: 3; Scala/AR: 7, 8, 9, 12, 24, 27, 29, 31, 33, 45; Helga Schmidt-Glassner: 63.

Chapter 20 ACL: 41; Alinari/AR: 14, 24; AR: 5; © Arch. Photo. Paris/S.P.A.D.E.M.: 3, 29; Photo British Museum: 31; British Stationery Office: 2; HBJ Collection: 12, 15, 25; Hir: 18; Hunting Aerofilms: 38; A. F. Kersting: 16, 33, 36; Reproduced from the Collections of the Library of Congress: 43; NYPL: 11; Printing Services Collection (#NPS-2645), Special Collections Department, University Archives, University of Virginia Library: 44; R.M.N.: 4, 6, 29, 40; Rapho/PRI: 1; Royal Commission on the Historical Monuments of England: 26; Scala/AR: 13, 20; Tate Gallery/AR: 46; Virginia State Library: 42.

Part V Opening illustration: Courtesy Jeremy Stone Gallery, San Francisco.

Chapter 21 Alinari/AR: 2, 7; Wayne Andrews: 98; © Arch. Phot. Paris: 1, 8 (Moreau); Photograph © 1990 The Art Institute of Chicago. All rights reserved: 76, 80, 87, 92; Copyright 1990 ARS N.Y./A.D.A.G.P.: 91; Copyright 1990 ARS N.Y./S.P.A.D.E.M.: 54, 55, 56; Bulloz: 6, 15; Richard Cheek/The Preservation Society of Newport County: 9; Chicago Architectural Photography Co.: 97; French Government Tourist Office: 96; Gernsheim Collection, Harry Ransom Humanities Research Center, The University of Texas at Austin: 50, 53; Gir/AR: 12, 39; Hedrich-Blessing, Chicago: 99; HBJ Collection: 75, 95; A. F. Kersting: 5; Library of Congress: 64; MAS: 25, 26, 27; Mar/AR: 94; Massachusetts General Hospital, News and Public Affairs, Boston: 34; Novosti/Sovfoto: 45; Brownlie/PRI: 4; R.M.N.: 10, 11, 13, 14, 16, 18, 19, 37, 72, 88; The Royal Photographic Society, Bath, England: 35; Scala/AR: 65, 66; Staatliche Museen zu Berlin: 22; Tate Gallery/AR: 57, 58, 78.

Chapter 22 Jörg P. Anders, Berlin: 28; George Roos/AR: 5; Copyright 1990 ARS N.Y./A.D.A.G.P.: 4, 7, 10, 16, 17, 25, 26, 30, 37, 45, 47, 52; Copyright 1990 ARS N.Y./Cosmopress: 38, 42, 43; Copyright 1990 ARS N.Y./S.P.A.D.E.M.: 6, 9, 11, 56, 57, 83; Copyright 1990 ARS N.Y./S.P.A.D.E.M./A.D.A.G.P.: 34; Henri Cartier-Bresson/Magnum Photos, Inc.: 74; Courtesy of the Center for Creative Photography, University of Arizona: 67; Chicago Architectural Photography Co.: 53; Photo by Geoffrey Clements, New York: 12; Courtesy of the Trustees of Dartmouth College, Hanover, N.H.: 82; Copyright 1990 DEMART PRO ARTE/ARS N.Y.: 36; For more information concerning Buckminster Fuller, please contact the Buckminster Fuller Institute, 1743 South La Cienega Blvd, Los Angeles, CA 90035.: 63; © Hans Hammarskiold: 76; HBJ Collection: 22, 58; Photo by David Heald: 47; Lucien Hervé: 56, 57; Hinz: 7, 41, 50; William Lescaze and Associates: 62; Library of Congress: 18; The Museum of Modern Art, New York: 1, 59, 61; The Museum of Modern Art/Film Stills Archive: 20, 33, 35, 77, 78, 79; MAS: 3, 83; R.M.N.: 9; Photo by Sandak, Inc.: 80; Ezra Stoller © Esto: 55; Copyright 1990 SUCCESSION H. MATISSE/ARS N.Y.: 5; Tate Gallery/AR: 51; Courtesy Donna Van Der Zee: 71.

Chapter 23 Courtesy of Brooke Alexander, New York: 55; Photograph © 1990 The Art Institute of Chicago. All rights reserved: 25; Copyright 1990 ARS N.Y./A.D.A.G.P.: 5, 27; Copyright 1990 ARS N.Y./S.P.A.D.E.M.: 9, 10, 22; Photo © Margaret Benyon: 47; Mel Bochner: 54; Rudolph Burckhardt: 24, 39; © Christo 1983/photo by Wolfgang Volz: 77; Photo by Geoffrey Clements: 64; Paula Court: 65; Electronic Arts Intermix: 48, 49; Esto Photography: 21; Lee Fatherree: 1; Through the Flower Corporation: 71; David Gahr: 42; © Gianfranco Gorgoni, New York: 76; Solomon R. Guggenheim Museum, New York/Photo by Robert E. Mates: 7, 8; HBJ Collection: 2; Douglas Hollis: 79; Institut für Leichte Flachentragwerke, Stuttgart: 19; G. E. Kidder-Smith: 10; Photo courtesy Barbara Kruger: 73; Photo courtesy Richard Long: 78; Robert McElroy: 51; Middendorf Gallery, New York: 16; The Museum of Modern Art/Film Stills Archive: 52, 66; Courtesy National Gallery of Canada/Experimental Film Office and Michael Snow: 53; © 1990 Dolores Neuman: 80; Copyright 1990 Pollock-Krasner Foundation/ARS N.Y.: 1; Michel Proulx, *Architectural Record:* 61; George Holton/PRI: 9; Rapho/PRI: 43; Rheinische Bildarchiv, Cologne: 26; Copyright 1990 Kate Rothko-Prize and Christopher Rothko/ARS N.Y.: 24; Oscar Savio: 18; Photo by Steven Sloman: 14; Courtesy Holly Solomon Gallery, New York: 57; Courtesy Sonnabend Gallery, New York: 59; Artur Starewicz, Warsaw: 30; Bernice Steinbaum Gallery, New York: 72; Ezra Stoller © Esto: 17; James A. Sugar, © National Geographic Society: 20; Tate Gallery/AR: 40; Venturi and Rauch: 60; Virginia Museum of Fine Arts: 41; © William Walker, 1970/Photo courtesy J. P. Weber: 69; Copyright 1990 The Estate and Foundation of Andy Warhol/ARS N.Y.: 40; Courtesy Westin Hotels: 62.

Illustration Credits

FIGS. 1-2, 1-3 From "The Archeology of Lascaux Cave," by Arlette Leroi-Gourhan. Copyright © 1982 by *Scientific American.* All rights reserved.

FIGS. 2-3, 2-4 From Arlette Mellaart.

FIG. 2-11 From E. S. Piggott, Ed., *The Dawn of Civilization,* London: Thames and Hudson, 1961, p. 70.

FIG. 2-12 From H. Frankfort, *The Art and Architecture of the Ancient Orient,* Harmondsworth and Baltimore: Penquin, 1970, p. 69.

FIG. 2-28 From © 1975 The Royal Institute of British Architects and the University of London, by permission of the Athlone Press.

FIG. 2-29 From *Sir Bannister Fletcher's A History of Architecture,* 19th ed. Ed. John Musgrove, 1987. Plan H, p. 76. The Royal Institute of British Architects and the University of London.

FIG. 3-4 Adapted from the "Later Canon" of Egyptian Art, figure 1 in Erwin Panofsky, *Meaning in the Visual Arts.* Copyright © 1955 by Erwin Panofsky. Used by permission of Doubleday and Company, Inc.

FIG. 3-7 From K. Lange and M. Hirmer, *Ägypten, Architectur, Plastik, und Malerei in drei Jahrtausenden,* Munich, 1957. Used by permission of Phaidon Press and Hirmer Fotoarchiv.

FIG. 3-8 From J. P. Lauer, La Pyramide à degrés: L'Architecture, 3 vols., Cairo, 1936–1939.

FIGS. 3-21, 3-31, 5-27, 6-24, 6-49, 6-57a, 6-60, 7-48, 10-59 From Sir Bannister Fletcher, *A History of Architecture on the Comparative Method,* 17th ed., rev. by R. A. Cordingly, 1961. Used by permission of the Athlone Press of the University of London and the British Architectural Library, Royal Institute of British Architects, London.

FIGS. 4-6, 7-1, 7-8 From Hirmer Fotoarchiv.

FIGS. 5-23, 16-40 From Marvin Trachtenberg and Isabelle Hyman, *Architecture From Prehistory to Post-Modernism/The Western Tradition,* Englewood Cliffs, NJ: Prentice Hall, 1986, p. 86, p. 293. Used by permission.

FIG. 5-54 From *Sir Bannister Fletcher's A History of Architecture,* 19th ed. Ed. John Musgrove, 1987. B&C elevations, p. 117. The Royal Institute of British Architects and the University of London.

FIGS. 5-89, 5-90, 5-92 From Richard Brilliant, *Arts of the Ancient Greeks,* 1973. Adapted by permission of McGraw-Hill Book Co.

FIG. 5-93 From J. Charbonneaux, et al., *Hellenistic Art 330–50 B.C.,* 1973. Adapted by permission of George Braziller, Inc.

FIG. 6-51 From *The Architecture of the Roman Empire, I, Introductory Study,* rev. ed. William L. MacDonald, New Haven and London: Yale University Press, 1982, Fig. 75.

FIG. 6-53 From *A Concise History of Western Architecture* by Robert Furneaux Jordan, © 1969 by Harcourt Brace Jovanovich, Inc. Reproduced by permission of the publisher.

FIG. 6-54 From J. B. Ward-Perkins, *Roman Architecture.* Adapted by permission of Electa Editrice, Milan.

FIG. 6-81 From Deutsches Archäologisches Institut, Rome.

FIG. 6-83 From Fiske Kimball, M. Arch, and G. H. Edgell, *A History of Architecture,* 1918. Used by permission of Harper & Row, Inc., publishers.

FIG. 6-87 After George M. A. Hanfamann, *Roman Art: A Survey of the Art of Imperial Rome.* A New York Graphic Society Book. By permission of Little, Brown and Co.

FIGS. 7-6, 9-4, 9-17 From Kenneth J. Conant, *Early Medieval Church Architecture.* Used by permission of The John Hopkins Press.

FIGS. 7-63, 7-70 From K. A. C. Creswell, *Early Muslim Architecture.* Adapted by permission of Clarendon Press/Oxford University Press.

FIG. 7-65 From G. Marçais, *L'Architecture Musulmane d'Occident.* By permission of Arts et Metiers Graphiques, Paris.

FIG. 7-72 Staatliche Museen zu Berlin.

FIG. 7-81 Plan drawn by Christopher Woodward.

FIG. 7-83 From "Sinan" by D. Kuban from *Macmillan Encyclopedia of Architects,* Adolf K. Placzek, Editor-in-Chief, Vol. 4 p. 68, © 1982 by the Free Press, a division of Macmillan, Inc.

FIGS. 9-2, 16-16 From H. Stierlin, *Die Architektur der Welt,* Vol 1, p. 147, p. 188, © 1977 Hirmer Verlag, Munich.

FIGS. 10-4, 10-5, 10-6 From Ernst Gall, Gotische Kathedralen, 1925. Used by permission of Klinkhardt & Biermann, publishers.

FIG. 10-19 Used by permission of Umschau Verlag, Frankfort.

FIG. 11-8 From Benjamin Rowland, *The Art and Architecture of India,* 1953, Penquin Books.

FIG. 11-29 From Madeleine Giteau, *The Civilization of Angkor.* Adapted by permission of Rizzoli International Publications.

FIG. 12-29 From William Watson, *Art of Dynastic China,* 1981. Used by permission of Harry N. Abrams, Inc.

FIG. 14-22 From "The Serpent Mound of Adams County, Ohio" by Charles C. Willoughby from *Art and Archaeology,* IV, 6, © 1916. Reproduced by permission of the Archaeological Institute of America.

FIG. 16-43 From Nikolaus Pevsner, *An Outline of European Architecture,* 6th ed., 1960, Penguin Books, Ltd., © Nikolaus Pevsner, 1943, 1960, 1963.

FIG. 19-23 Christian Norberg-Schulz, *Baroque Architecture,* 1971. Used by permission of Harry N. Abrams, Inc.

INDEX

Page numbers in italics indicate illustrations.

A

F

G

H

I

J

K

L

N

O

P

Q

R

S

T

W

Y

Z

3
E 4
F 5
G 6
H 7
I 8
J 9